Forgotten Books

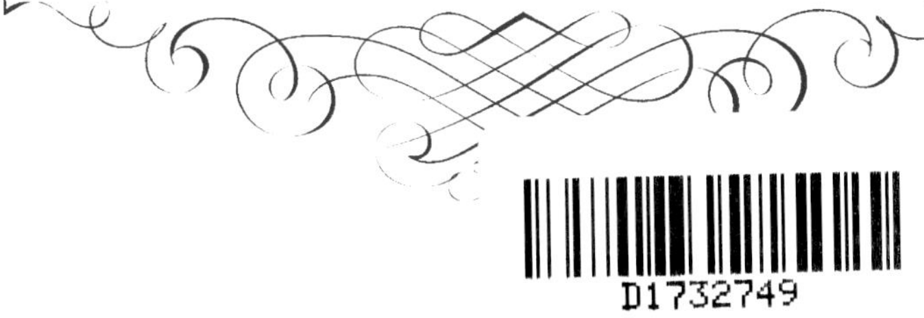

ISBN 978-0-282-34926-4
PIBN 10848595

A LEXICON

ABRIDGED FROM

LIDDELL & SCOTT'S GREEK-ENGLISH LEXICON

THE TWENTY-FOURTH EDITION

CAREFULLY REVISED THROUGHOUT

WITH AN APPENDIX OF PROPER AND GEOGRAPHICAL NAMES PREPARED BY GEORGE RICKER BERRY, PH. D., PROFESSOR OF SEMITIC LANGUAGES IN COLGATE UNIVERSITY, AND EDITOR OF THE NEW GREEK-ENGLISH NEW TESTAMENT LEXICON

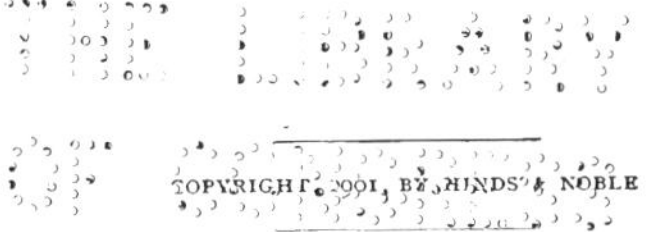

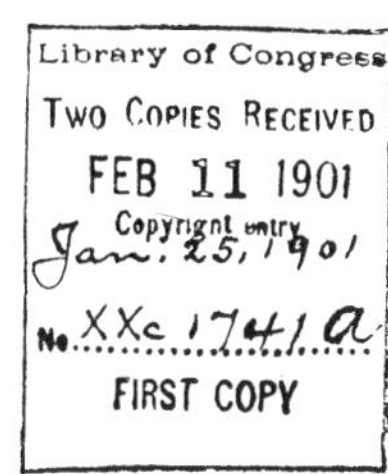

NEW YORK
ECONOMY BOOK HOUSE

HINDS & NOBLE, Sole Agents
4-5-6-12-13-14 COOPER INSTITUTE NEW YORK CITY
Schoolbooks of all publishers at one store

WHITE'S LATIN-ENGLISH DICTIONARY

FOR THE USE OF STUDENTS IN ACADEMIES, HIGH SCHOOLS AND COLLEGES.

NEW EDITION—HALF LEATHER—650 PAGES.

IN the treatment of the words in this Dictionary the principles upon which the larger Dictionary of White and Riddle is based are uniformly followed as fully as circumstances allow or require. The course which has been pursued may be thus described. Immediately after the assigned origin of each word the literal interpretation is given between parentheses; and that English rendering of which such interpretation holds good in a pre-eminent degree is placed first in order, and regarded as the proper or primary meaning. When the source of a word is not discoverable, the fact is stated, and the ordinary interpretation is accepted and assigned the first place. When figurative and metonymical powers exist, either separately or conjointly, these are given, when they fall within the necessarily restricted scope of the work. A brief reference is usually made to some author; invariably so, indeed, when a quotation is deemed desirable or needful. Peculiar or unusual grammatical constructions are noticed. In the case of adjectives and adverbs, the comparative and superlative degrees are mentioned when they are known to exist; and whenever either one or the other or both are omitted, it is to be considered that no authority is to be found for their use. Proper names are included in the body of the work, and will be found in their alphabetical order; added to which their meaning is stated, whenever their origin is clearly traceable or may be reasonably conjectured; such meaning being printed in Roman type in the case of Latinized Greek names, and in Italic type in the case of pure Latin names. French derivatives from such Latin words as are comprised in this Dictionary are, moreover, mentioned.

In one respect, however, this book differs from the parent work, and, indeed, from any other Dictionary that has yet appeared. This peculiarity consists in the mode of printing each leading word so as to exhibit its process of formation, and thus show the reason for the etymological meaning assigned to it.

ECONOMY BOOK HOUSE, Publishers.

ADVERTISEMENT.

E Abridgment of Liddell and Scott's Greek-English Lexicon is in-
d chiefly for use in Schools. It has been reduced to its present
ass by the omission

I. Of passages cited as Authorities, except where examples seemed necessary to explain more clearly the usage of a word,

II. Of discussions upon the Derivation of words;

III. Of words used only by authors not read in Schools, or of the particular meanings of words not in general use, such as medical or scientific terms. But words used by Theocritus, the writers of the Anthology, Lucian, and Plutarch in his Lives, have been retained; and especial care has been taken to explain all words contained in the New Testament.

ords are printed in Capitals, when they are radical forms, or when no
m nearer the original Root is known to exist. The Derivation, when it
certain, is placed before the English explanation: when this is not the
se, some notice will be found at the end of the word.

Many additional tenses and cases, mostly Homeric or Doric, have been
serted to give a clue to the simple word, when there seemed to be any
ifficulty or irregularity in the formation. All tenses and forms of words in
ie Gospels that presented any difficulty have been inserted in their place.

The quantity of doubtful syllables has been marked, except in such tenses
f Verbs, cases of Nouns, and words, as are regularly derived. In such forms
ie quantity ought to be known to young students from grammatical rules.

For the sake of clearness, the parts of which compound words are made
p have been marked by placing a hyphen between them, as, ἀπο-βάλλω,
φ-ίημι, ἄ-βατος, ἔφ-οδος. But when a word is compounded of two parts, one
which is already a compound, this latter compound is left undivided, and
iust be sought in its own place, as φιλο-κισσοφόρος. And a word imme-
iately derived from a compound is left undivided, so that the elements of
ie derivation must be sought under the word from which it is derived, as
ie elements of φιλομουσέω under φιλό-μουσος. In Verbs compounded of a
reposition and a simple Verb, and whenever the component parts remain
naltered by the composition, mere division has been considered sufficient
mark the formation.

The present Edition has been completely revised and has also been
onsiderably enlarged—chiefly by the addition of a number of irregular
enses of Verbs.

OXFORD, *October*, 1871.

For convenience, the following Abbreviations have been used :—

= means *equal* or *equivalent to*
absol. = absolute, absolutely
acc. = accusative: acc. to = according to
Act. = active voice
act. = active signification
Adj. = adjective
Adv. = adverb
Aeol. = Aeolic, in the Aeolic dialect
aor. = aorist tense
Att. = Attic, in Attic Greek
c. = cum (with)
c. acc. cognato = with cognate accusative, i. e. with a Subst. which has the same or a similar signification with the Verb
c. gen. pers. = cum genitivo personae
cf. = confer (compare)
collat. = collateral
Com. = Comic, in Comic Greek
Compar. or Comp. = comparative
Conjunct. = conjunction
contr. = contracted, contraction
cp. = compare
dat. = dative
Dep. = Deponent Verb, i. e. a Verb of Middle or Passive forms with Active sense
deriv. = derived, derivation
dissyll. = dissyllable
Dor. = in Doric Greek
e. g. = exempli gratia
Ep. = in Epic Greek
esp. = especially
etc. = et cetera
f. or fut. = future tense
fem. = feminine
fin. = ad finem or fine
freq. = frequent, frequently
gen. or genit. = genitive
Hom. = Homer
i. e. = id est
imperat. or imper. = imperative mood
imperf. or impf. = imperfect tense
impers. = impersonal
indic. = indicative mood
inf. = infinitive mood
intr. or intrans. = intransitive
Ion. = Ionic, in the Ionic dialect
irreg. = irregular
Lat. = Latin
lengthd. = lengthened
masc. = masculine
Med. = medial or middle voice
med. = medial or middle signification
metaph. = metaphorically
metri grat. = metri gratia (for the sake of the metre)
n. pr. = nomen proprium (proper name)
N. T. = New Testament
negat. = negativum (negative)
neut. = neuter
nom. = nominative
opp. to = opposed to
opt. or optat. = optative mood
orig. = originally
part. = participle
Pass. = passive voice
pass. = passive signification
pecul. = peculiar
perf. or pf. = perfect tense
pl. or plur. = plural
plqpf. = plusquamperfectum (pluperfect)
poët. = poetically
Prep. = preposition
pres. = present tense
priv. or privat. = privativum
q. v. = quod vide
qq. v. quae vide
radic. = radical
regul. = regular, regularly
shortd. = shortened
signf. = signification
sing. = singular
sq. = sequens (the following word)
sub. = subaudi, subaudito
subj. = subjunctive mood
Subst. = Substantive
syll. = syllable
Trag. = Tragic, in Tragic Greek
trans. = transitive
trisyll. = trisyllable
usu. = usually
v. = vide
verb. Adj. = verbal adjective
voc. = voce, vocem
vocat. = vocative

A

A, **α**, **ἄλφα**, **τό**, indecl., first letter of the Gr alphabet. As numeral α′ = εἷς, and πρῶτος. but ͵α = 1000.

In Ion. Greek ᾱ becomes η, as σοφία, σοφίη. In Dor. Greek ᾱ is used instead of η, as, ἁδύς for ἡδύς: but the verbal term. ᾶτο is changed into ῆτο, as ἐκνυζᾶτο into ἐκνυζῆτο

α, as prefix in compos.: I. α privativum, *not*, as σοφός wise, ἄ-σοφος *un*wise. II. α copulativum, *together*, as in ἀ-τάλαντος, ἀ-κόλουθος III. α intensivum, *very much*, as in ἀ-τενής, ἀ-σπερχές, though this is very rare. IV. α euphonicum, affecting the sound only, not the sense, as ἀ-βληχρός for βληχρός, ἀ-σπαίρω for σπαίρω, ἀ-στεροπή for στεροπή.

ἆ, **ἆ** or **ἀᾶ**, exclamations used to express strong emotion, like our *ah!*

ἅ, **ἅ**, to express laughter, like our *ha ha*

ἁ, Dor. for artic ἡ. 2. **ἅ**, Dor. for relat. pron. ἥ. 3. **ᾇ**, Dor. for ᾗ, dat. of ὅς.

ἀ-άᾰτος, ον, (α privat., ἀάω) *not to be hurt, inviolable*, of the Styx, by which the gods swore:—but ἄεθλος ἀ-άατος a *dangerous* or *difficult* task.

ἀ-ᾱγής, ές, (α privat., ἄγνυμι) *unbroken, not to be broken, hard, strong.*

ἄ-απτος, ον, (α privat., ἅπτομαι) *not to be touched: invincible.*

ἄασα, **ἀασάμην**, **ἀάσθην**, v. ἈΑ′Ω.

ἀ-άσχετος, ον, lengthd. poët. for ἄ-σχετος.

ἄᾰτος, contr. **ἆτος**, ον, (α privat., ἄω, ἆσαι *to satiate*) *insatiate*, ἆτος πολέμοιο *insatiate of* battle.

ἈΑ′Ω, old Ep. Verb, used chiefly in aor. 1 act. **ἄᾰσα** contr. ἆσα, med. ἀᾰσάμην, contr. ἀσάμην, and pass. ἀάσθην: the pres. occurs only in 3 sing. of Med., ἀᾶται—all in Hom.:—*to hurt, damage*, esp. *to hurt mentally, mislead, infatuate:* so too in Med., Ἄτη ἣ πάντας ἀᾶται Il. But the Med. and Pass. usu. have an intr. sense, *to go astray, to be infatuated* or *bewildered, to go wrong, err, sin, do foolishly.* [Hom. has ἄᾰσας, ἄᾰσεν, ἆασαν: so too ἀᾰσάμην, but ἀάσᾰτο.]

ἀάω, = ἄω, *to satisfy*, whence 3 sing. ἄαται.

ἄβα, Dor. for ἥβη.

ἀβᾰκέω, (ἀβακής) *to be speechless.*

ἀβᾰκής, ές, (α privat., βάζω) *speechless.*

ἀ-βάκχευτος, ον, (α privat., βακχεύω) *without Bacchic frenzy, uninspired, joyless.*

ἀ-βάπτιστος, ον, (α privat., βαπτίζω) *not to be dipped, that will not sink*, Lat *immersabilis.* II. *unbaptized.*

ἀ-βᾰρής, ές, (α privat., βάρος) *not heavy: not burdensome.*

ἀ-βᾰσάνιστος, ον, (α privat., βασανίζω) *not examined by torture, unquestioned.* Adv. -τως, *without question* or *trial*

ἀ-βᾰσίλευτος, ον, (α privat., βασιλεύω) *not ruled by a king.* [ῐ]

ἀ-βάσκαντος, ον, (α privat., βασκαίνω) *unenvied.* Adv. -τως, *without envy*

ἄ-βᾰτος, ον, also η, ον, (α privat., βαίνω) *untrodden inaccessible:* of a river, *not fordable:* of holy places, *not to be trodden, inviolate:* hence *pure, chaste.*

ἀ-βέβαιος, ον, (α privat, βέβαιος) *unsteady, wavering, fickle.*

ἀ-βέβηλος, ον, (α privat., βέβηλος) *not profane, inviolable.*

ἀβελτερία, ἡ, *stupidity:* from

ἀ-βέλτερος, ον, (α privat., βέλτερος) *good-for-nothing, silly, stupid.*

ἀ-βίαστος, ον, (α privat., βιάζομαι) *unforced.*

ἄ-βιος, ον, (α privat., βίος) *not to be lived* or *survived, intolerable, insupportable;* βίος ἄβιος. II. *without subsistence, poor.*

ἀ-βίοτος, ον, (α privat., βίοτος) = ἄβιος.

ἀ-βίωτος, ον, (α privat., βιόω) = ἄβιος.

ἀβλάβεια, ἡ, *freedom from harm: security:* from

ἀ-βλᾰβής, ές, (α privat., βλάβη) *without harm:* I. pass. *unharmed, unhurt.* II. act. *harmless, innocent: preventing harm:*—Adv. -βῶς, Ep. -βέως, *without harming, without infringement.*

ἀ-βλάβια, ἡ, poët. for ἀ-βλάβεια.

ἀ-βλής, ῆτος, ὁ, ἡ, (α privat., βάλλω) *not thrown* or *shot*, of an arrow.

ἄ-βλητος, ον, (α privat., βάλλω) *not hit* by a dart or arrow.

ἀ-βληχής, ές, (α privat., βληχή) *without bleatings.*

ἀ-βληχρός, ά, όν, (α euphon., βληχρός) *weak, feeble, defenceless*:—of death, *easy, light.*

ἀβληχρώδης, ες, = ἄβληχρος.

ἀ-βοᾱτί, Dor. for ἀ-βοητί.

ἀ-βόᾱτος, ον, Dor. for ἀ-βόητος.

ἀ-βοήθητος, ον, (α privat., βοηθέω) *helpless.*

ἀ-βοητί, Dor. -ᾱτί, Adv. (α privat., βοάω) *uncalled, without summons.*

ἀ-βόητος, Dor. -ᾱτος, ον, (α privat., βοάω) *uncalled.* II. *unmourned.*

ἀβολέω, = ἀντιβολέω, *to meet.*

ἀ-βόσκητος, ον, (α privat., βόσκω) *ungrazed.*

ἀ-βουκόλητος, ον, (α privat., βουκολέω) *untended, unheeded.*

ἀ-βουλέω, ήσω, = οὐ βούλομαι, *to be unwilling.*

ἀ-βούλητος, ον, (α privat., βούλομαι) *unwilling, involuntary.* Adv. -τως.

ἀ-βουλία, ἡ, *ill counsel, thoughtlessness*: from

ἄ-βουλος, ον, (α privat., βουλή) *inconsiderate, ill-advised*:—Adv. -ως, superl. ἀβουλότατα.

ἀ-βούτης, ου, ὁ, (α privat., βοῦς) *without oxen*: hence *poor.*

ἄ-βρεκτος, ον, (α privat., βρέχω) *unwetted.*

ἀ-βρῑθής, ές, (α privat., βρίθω) *without weight.*

ἀβρο-βάτης, ου, ὁ, (ἀβρός, βαίνω) *softly* or *delicately stepping.* [βᾰ]

ἀβρό-γοος, ον, (ἀβρός, γόος) *womanishly wailing.*

ἀβρο-δίαιτος, ον, (ἀβρός, δίαιτα) *living delicately* or *effeminately*: τὸ ἀβροδίαιτον *effeminacy.*

ἀβρο-κόμης, ου, ὁ, (ἀβρός, κόμη) *with delicate, luxuriant hair* or *leaves.*

ἀ-βρόμιος, ον, (α privat., Βρόμιος) *without Bacchus.*

ἄ-βρομος, ον, (α copul., βρόμος) *noisy, boisterous.*

ἀβρο-πέδῑλος, ον, (ἀβρός, πέδιλον) *soft-sandalled.*

ἀβρό-πλουτος, ον, (ἀβρός, πλοῦτος) *richly luxuriant.*

ʽΑΒΡΟ'Σ, ά, όν, also ός, όν, *delicate, pretty, dainty, soft, luxurious.* (Akin to ἥβη.)

ἀβροσύνη, ἡ, = ἀβρότης.

ἀβροτάζω, f. άξω, *to miss*, c. gen.—Ep. word formed from **ἀμβροτεῖν**, q. v.

ἀβρότης, ητος, ἡ, (ἀβρός) *delicacy, luxuriousness.*

ἄβροτος, ον, also η, ον, (α privat., βροτός) like ἄμβροτος, ἀμβρόσιος, *immortal, divine, holy.*

ἀβρο-φυής, ές, (ἀβρός, φύω) *tender of nature.*

ἀβρο-χαίτης, ου, ὁ, (ἀβρός, χαίτη) = ἀβρο-κόμης.

ἀβρο-χίτων, ωνος, ὁ, ἡ, (ἀβρός, χιτών) *softly clad*: *with soft coverings.* [ῐ]

ἄ-βροχος, ον, (α privat., βρέχω) *unwetted, waterless.* Adv. -χως.

ἀβρύνω, f. ὕνω: aor. 1. ἥβρῡνα: (ἀβρός):—*to make delicate, treat delicately*:—Pass. *to live delicately, wax wanton, give oneself* airs; ἀβρύνεσθαί τινι *to pride oneself on* a thing.

ἀ-βρώς, ῶτος, ὁ, ἡ, = ἄ-βρωτος.

ἄ-βρωτος, ον, (α privat., βιβρώσκω) *not having eaten.* II. pass. *not to be eaten, uneatable.*

ἄ-βυσσος, ον, (α privat., βύσσος) *bottomless, unfathomed*: generally, *unfathomable, enormous.* II. as Subst. ἡ ἄβυσσος, *the abyss, bottomless pit.*

ἀγάασθαι, ἀγάασθε, v. sub ἄγαμαι.

ἀγαγεῖν, redupl. aor. 2 inf. of ἄγω: **ἄγαγον**, Ep. for ἤγαγον, aor. 2 ind.

ἀγάγωμι, Ep. for ἀγάγω, aor. 2 subj. of ἄγω.

ἀγάζομαι, poët. form of ἄγαμαι, *to admire.*

ἀγαθο-ειδής, ές, (ἀγαθός, εἶδος) *seeming good.*

ἀγαθοεργέω, contr. -ουργέω, *to do good*; and

ἀγαθοεργία, contr. -ουργία, ἡ, *a good* or *noble deed*: *good service.* From

ἀγαθο-εργός, contr. -ουργός, όν, (ἀγαθός, ἔργον) *doing good*: οἱ Ἀγαθοεργοί, at Sparta, the five oldest knights, who went on missions for the state.

ἀγαθοποιέω, = ἀγαθο-εργέω; and

ἀγαθοποιία, ἡ, = ἀγαθο-εργία. From

ἀγαθο-ποιός, όν, (ἀγαθός, ποιέω) = ἀγαθο-εργός.

ʼΑΓΑ-ΘΟ'Σ, ή, όν, *good in its kind*, opp. to κακός, *bad*: 1. in Homer usu. of heroes, *brave, noble*: later in moral sense, *good, virtuous.* 2. of things, etc., *good in their kind*; neut. τὰ ἀγαθά *the goods of fortune, wealth*, also *good fare, dainties*; τὸ ἀγαθόν, Lat. *summum bonum.*—There are no regular forms of comparison. The Comp. in use are βελτίων, also ἀμείνων, κρείσσων, λωΐων (λῴων): Ep. βέλτερος, λωΐτερος, also φέρτερος. Sup. βέλτιστος, ἄριστος, κράτιστος, λώϊστος (λῷστος): Ep. βέλτατος, φέρτατος, φέριστος. The Adv. in common use is εὖ, *well.*

ἀγαθουργέω, contr. form of ἀγαθοεργέω.

ἀγαθύνω, (ἀγαθός) *to make good, exalt.* II. *to do good*:—Pass. *to be of good cheer.*

ἀγαθωσύνη, ἡ, (ἀγαθός) *goodness, kindness.*

ἀγαίομαι, (ἄγη) collat. form of ἄγαμαι, **ἀγάομαι**, only in bad sense, *to be angry at*: *to envy.*

ἀγα-κλεής, ές, (ἄγαν, κλέος) *very glorious, famous, renowned*: gen. ἀγακλῆος; shortd. poët. forms, acc. sing. ἀγακλεᾶ, pl. ἀγακλεᾶς, dat. sing. ἀγακλεῖ.

ἀγα-κλειτός, ή, όν, = ἀγακλεής.

ἀγα-κλῡτός, όν, (ἄγαν, κλυτός) like ἀγακλεής, Lat. *inclytus.*

ἀγα-κτῐμένη, (ἄγαν, κτίζω) a poët. fem. = εὐκτιμένη, *well-built* or *placed.*

ἀ-γάλακτος, ον, (α privat., γάλα) *without milk, giving none.* II. *getting none, weaned*, Lat. *lacte depulsus.*

ἀγαλλίᾱσις, εως, ἡ, *exceeding great joy.* From

ἀγαλλιάω, aor. ἠγαλλίᾱσα: also as Dep. **ἀγαλλιάομαι**, f. άσομαι [ᾱ], strengthd. for ἀγάλλομαι:—*to rejoice exceedingly.*

ʼΑΓΑΛΛΙ'Σ, ίδος, ἡ, a plant, *the iris* or *flag.*

ʼΑΓΑ'ΛΛΩ, f. ἀγᾰλῶ: aor. ἤγηλα, inf. ἀγῆλαι: = ἀγλαὸν ποιῶ, *to make glorious, glorify, honour*, esp. *a god*: also *to deck, adorn*:—mostly in Pass. ἀγάλλομαι, *to glory, delight, exult in* a thing, c. dat. Hence

ἄγαλμα, ατος, τό, *that wherein one delights, a glory, delight, ornament*: *a pleasing gift*, esp. for the gods: hence, 2. *a statue* in honour of a god; *the image* of a god as an object of worship. 3. *any statue* or *image.*

ἀγαλματο-ποιός, *οῦ, ὁ,* (ἄγαλμα, ποιέω) *a maker of statues, a statuary, sculptor.*

ἌΓΑΜΑΙ, 2 pl. ἄγασθε Ep. ἀγάασθε, inf. ἄγασθαι Ep. ἀγάασθαι: impf. ἠγάμην, Ep. 2 pl. ἠγᾱσθε: fut. ἀγάσομαι [ᾰ] Ep. ἀγάσσομαι: the aor. 1 mostly in Pass. form ἠγάσθην, but also Med. ἠγασάμην (even in Att.), Ep. ἠγασσάμην, ἀγασσάμην: Dep.: I. *to wonder:* more freq. *to wonder at* or *admire* a person or thing, τινά, but also τινί, Lat. *admirari.* II. in bad sense, *to envy, be angry at,* τί, τινί, περί τινος.—Homer uses in this sense only aor. 1 ἠγασάμην, and as pres. ἀγάομαι or ἀγαίομαι.

ἀγαμία, *ἡ, celibacy.* From

ἄ-γᾰμος, *ον,* (α privat., γάμος) *unmarried, unwedded, single,* Lat. *coelebs:*—Tragic phrase, γάμος ἄ-γαμος *a marriage that is no marriage, a fatal marriage.*

ἌΓΑΝ, Adv. *very, much, very much:* the word generally is only Dor. and Att., λίην being its equiv. in Ep. and Ion. II. *too, too much,* Lat. *nimis,* as in the proverb μηδὲν ἄγαν, Lat. *ne quid nimis, not too much* of any thing. [ᾰγᾱν, but later sometimes ᾰγᾰν.]

ἀγανᾰκτέω, f. ήσω, (ἄγαν) *to feel irritation:*—*to be vexed, displeased,* or *angry at* a thing. Hence

ἀγᾰνάκτησις, *εως, ἡ, irritation, vexation.*

ἀγᾰνακτητικός, *ή, όν,* (ἀγανακτέω) *irritable.*

ἀγᾰνακτητός, *ή, όν,* verb. Adj. of ἀγανακτέω, *irritating, vexatious.*

ἀγᾰνακτικός, *ή, όν, irritable,* = ἀγανακτητικός. Adv. -κῶς.

ἀγᾰνῇσι, poët. for ἀγαναῖς, dat. plur. fem. of ἀγανός.

ἀγάν-νῐφος, *ον,* (ἄγαν, νίφω) *much snowed upon, snow-capt,* Ὄλυμπος.

ἀγᾱνόρειος, *α, ον,* Dor. for ἀγηνόρειος.

ἀ-γᾰνός, *ή, όν,* (α copul., γάνος, γάνυμαι) *mild, gentle, kindly:* esp. of the arrows of Artemis, to which sudden death was ascribed. Only poët.

ἀγᾰνοφροσύνη, *ἡ, gentleness, kindliness.* From

ἀγᾰνό-φρων, *ον,* gen. ονος, (ἀγανός, φρήν) *kindly disposed: benign.*

ἀγανῶπις, *ιδος, ἡ,* (ἀγανός, ὤψ) *mild-eyed.*

ἀγ-άνωρ, *ορος, ὁ, ἡ,* Dor. for ἀγ-ήνωρ.

ἀγάομαι, Ep. form of ἄγαμαι, only found in part. ἀγώμενος, in act. sense *admiring.*

ἀγαπάζω, f. άσω, see ἀγαπάω.

ἀγαπᾱτός, *όν,* Dor. for ἀγαπητός.

ἀγαπάω, f. ήσω: aor. ἠγάπησα, Ep. ἀγάπησα: pf. ἠγάπηκα: (ἄγαμαι, ἀγάζομαι):—of persons, *to welcome, entertain,* in which sense ἀγαπάζω and Dep. ἀγαπάζομαι are used by Homer:—also *to take leave of:*—generally, *to be fond of, to love dearly.* II. of things, *to be well pleased, to be contented at* or *with a thing:* c. inf. *to be wont to do,* like φιλέω. [ᾰγᾰ] Hence

ἀγαπεῦντες, Ion. for ἀγαπῶντες, pres. part. pl.

ἀγάπη, *ἡ,* (ἀγαπάω) *brotherly love: charity.* [ᾰγᾰ]

ἀγάπημα, *τό,* (ἀγαπάω) *an object of love,* Lat. *deliciae.*

ἀγαπ-ήνωρ, *ορος, ὁ,* (ἀγαπάω, ἀνήρ) = ἠνορέην ἀγαπῶν, *loving manliness, manly.*

ἀγάπησις, *εως, ἡ,* (ἀγαπάω) *the feeling of love, affection.*

ἀγᾰπητέος, *ον,* verb. Adj. of ἀγαπάω, *to be loved, acquiesced in.*

ἀγᾰπητικός, *ή, όν,* (ἀγαπάω) *disposed to love, affectionate.* Adv. -κῶς.

ἀγᾰπητός, *ή, όν,* verb. Adj. of ἀγαπάω, *beloved, dearly beloved: worthy of love.* 2. *to be acquiesced in,* as the least evil. II. Adv. ἀγαπητῶς, *cheerfully, contentedly;* ἀγαπητῶς ἔχειν *to be contented,* like ἀγαπᾶν. 2. in Att. prose, *so as only just to content one,* i. e. *only just, scarcely* = μόλις.

ἀγάρ-ροος, *ον,* contr. ἀγάρ-ρους, *ουν,* (ἄγαν, ῥέω) *strong* or *swift-flowing.*

ἄγασθαι, pres. inf. of ἄγαμαι.

ἀγασθείς, aor. 1 pass. part. of ἄγαμαι.

ἄγασμα, *τό,* (ἄγαμαι) *that which is admired, a wonder, marvel.*

ἀγάσομαι [ᾰ], poët. ἀγάσσομαι, fut. of ἄγαμαι.

ἀγάσσατο, poët. for ἠγάσατο, 3 sing. aor. 1 of ἄγαμαι.

ἀγά-στονος, *ον,* (ἄγαν, στένω) *much groaning, howling,* of the waves, *loud-wailing.*

ἀγαστός, *ή, όν,* (ἄγαμαι) *admirable.* Adv. -τῶς.

ἀγᾰτός, *ή, όν,* poët. for ἀγαστός, as θαυματός for θαυμαστός.

ἀγαυός, *ή, όν,* (ἄγαμαι) *illustrious, noble.*

ἀγαυρός, *ά, όν,* akin to ἀγαυός, *stately, proud:* sup. Adv. ἀγαυρότατα.

ἀγά-φθεγκτος, *ον,* (ἄγαν, φθέγγομαι) *loud-sounding.*

ἀγγᾰρεύω, f. σω, (ἄγγαρος) *to despatch a courier* or *messenger: to press* one *to serve as a courier.*

ἀγγαρήϊος, *ὁ,* Ion. form = ἄγγαρος:—τὸ ἀγγαρήϊον *the business of an* ἄγγαρος.

ἄγγᾰρος, *ὁ,* Persian word, *a mounted courier,* such as were kept ready at regular stages throughout Persia for carrying the royal despatches.

ἀγγεῖον, Ion. **-ήϊον,** *τό,* (ἄγγος) *a vessel, pail: a reservoir.*

ἀγγελία, Ion. -ίη, *ἡ,* (ἄγγελος) *a message, tidings, news,* ἀγγελίη ἐμή *a message* concerning me; ἀγγελίης ἐλθεῖν to come *on account of a message.* 2. *a proclamation: a command, order.*

ἀγγελια-φόρος, Ion. **ἀγγελιη-φόρος,** *ὁ,* (ἀγγελία, φέρω) *a messenger.*

ἀγγελιώτης, *ου, ὁ,* (ἀγγελία) *a messenger.*

ἀγγέλλω: f. ἀγγελῶ, Ep. ἀγγελέω: aor. 1 ἤγγειλα: pf. ἤγγελκα, pass. ἤγγελμαι: aor. 1 pass. ἠγγέλθην: (ἄγω):—*to bear a message, bring tidings* or *news, to proclaim, report, tell:*—Med. *to announce oneself:*—Pass. *to be reported of.* Hence

ἄγγελμα, *τό, a message, tidings, news.*

ἄγγελος, ὁ, ἡ, (ἀγγέλλω) *a messenger, envoy.* II. *a messenger from God, an angel.*

ἀγγήϊον, τό, Ion. for ἀγγεῖον.

ἌΓΓΟΣ, εος, τό, *a vessel* of any kind, *a jar, pan, pail: a chest, box.*

ἄγδην, Adv. (ἄγω) *by carrying.*

ἄγε, ἄγετε, properly Imperat. of ἄγω, used as Adv. like φέρε, *come! come on! well!* Lat. *age!*

ἀγείρω: aor. 1 ἤγειρα: pf. ἀγήγερκα: (ἄγω):—*to bring together gather together, collect.* II. Pass. **ἀγείρομαι**: aor. 1 ἠγέρθην, Ep. 3 pl. ἤγερθεν: pf. ἀγήγερμαι, Ep. 3 pl. ἀγηγέραται: Ep. 3 pl. plqpf. ἀγηγέρατο:—*to come together, assemble:* in which sense we also have an Ep. aor. 2 med. ἀγέρεσθαι, ἀγέροντο, partic. syncop. ἀγρόμενος, η, ον, *assembled, gathered together.*

ἀ-γείτων, ον, gen. ονος, (α privat., γείτων) *without neighbour: solitary, desolate.*

ἀγελᾱδόν, Dor. for ἀγεληδόν.

ἀγελάζομαι, Pass. (ἀγέλη) *to live in herds, to be gregarious.*

ἀγελαῖος, α, ον, (ἀγέλη) *belonging to a herd, feeding at large.* II. *in herds* or *shoals, gregarious.* 2. *of the herd* or *multitude, common.*

ἀγελάρχης, ου, ὁ, (ἀγέλη, ἄρχω) *the leader of a company.*

ἀ-γελαστί, Adv. (α privat., γελάω) *without laughter.*

ἀ-γέλαστος, ον, (α privat., γελάω) *not laughing, grave, sullen.* II. *not to be laughed at, not trifling.*

ἀγελεία, ἡ, (ἄγω, λεία) epith. of Athena, = ληῖτις, λείαν ἄγουσα, *she that drives off the spoil.*

ἀγέλη, ἡ, (ἄγω) *a herd* of oxen or kine, Lat. *armentum, grex*:—later any *herd* or *company.*

ἀγεληδόν, Adv. (ἀγέλη) *in herds* or *companies.* Also ἀγεληδά.

ἀγέληθεν, Adv. (ἀγέλη) *from a herd.*

ἀγέληφι, Ep. dat. of ἀγέλη.

ἁγεμόνευμα, ἁγεμονεύω, ἁγεμών, Dor. for ἡγεμ-.

ἄγεν, Dor. and Ep. for ἐάγησαν, 3 pl. aor. 2 pass. from ἄγνυμι: [ᾰ] 2. Ep. 3 sing. for ἦγεν, impf. from ἄγω *to lead.*

ἀ-γενεαλόγητος, ον, (α privat., γενεαλογέω) *without pedigree, of unknown descent.*

ἀγένεια, ἡ, (ἀγένης) *low birth: meanness.*

ἀ-γένειος, ον, (α privat., γένειον) *beardless, boyish.*

ἀ-γενής, ές, (α privat., γένος) *unborn, uncreated:* but usu. II. *of no family,* i. e. *low-born,* opp. to ἀγαθός.

ἀ-γένητος, ον, (α privat., γενέσθαι) *unborn, uncreated.* II. *not having happened,* Lat. *infectus:* hence *false, groundless.*

ἀ-γεννής, ές, = ἀγενής II. Adv. -νῶς.

ἀ-γέννητος, ον, (α privat., γεννάω) *unbegotten, unborn: without origin.* II. like ἀγενής II, *low-born, mean.*

ἁγέομαι, Dor. for ἡγέομαι.

ἀ-γέραστος, ον, (α privat., γέρας) *without a gift of honour, unrecompensed, unrewarded.*

ἀγέρεσθαι, Ep. aor. 2 med. inf. of ἀγείρω.

ἄγερθεν, Ep. for ἠγέρθησαν, 3 pl. aor. 1 pass. of ἀγείρω.

ἀγέροντο, 3 pl. Ep. aor. 2 med. of ἀγείρω.

ἀγέροχος, ον, = ἀγέρωχος.

ἄγερσις, εως, ἡ, (ἀγείρω) *a gathering, mustering.*

ἀγέρωχος, ον, in good sense, *brave, high-minded, lordly:* in bad sense, *overweening, haughty, fierce.* Adv. -χως. (Deriv. uncertain.)

ἄγεσκον, Ion. impf. of ἄγω.

ἀγέ-στρᾰτος, ὁ, ἡ, (ἄγω, στρατός) *leading the host*

ἁγέτης, ὁ, Dor. for ἡγέτης.

ἄ-γευστος, ον, (α privat., γεύομαι) *not tasting: without taste of,* c. gen.

ἄγη [ᾰ] ἡ, (ἄγαμαι) in good sense, *wonder, awe, reverence.* 2. in bad sense, *envy, hatred, spite:* of the gods, *jealousy.*

ἀγή [ᾱ], ἡ, (ἄγνυμι) *a fragment, piece, splinter.*

ἄγη, Ep. for ἐάγη, 3 sing. Ep. aor. 2 pass. of ἄγνυμι, *to break.*

ἀγηγέραται, ἀγηγέρατο, Ep. 3 pl. pf. and plqpf. pass. of ἀγείρω.

ἀγήγερκα, -ερμαι, pf. act. and pass. of ἀγείρω.

ἀγῆλαι, aor. 1 inf. of ἀγάλλω.

ἀγ-ηλατέω, ήσω, (ᾶγος, ἐλαύνω) *to drive away pollution* or *a polluted person,* Lat. *piaculum exigere:* cf. ἀνδρ-ηλατέω.

ἄγημα, τό, (ἄγω) Lat. *agmen, a body* or *division of an army, a corps,* esp. of the Lacedaemonians.

ἀγ-ηνόρειος, Dor. ἀγᾱνόρ-, α, ον, = ἀγήνωρ.

ἀγ-ηνορία, ἡ, *manliness, manhood, courage.*

ἀγ-ήνωρ, Dor. ἀγ-άνωρ, ορος, ὁ, ἡ, (ἄγαν, ἀνήρ) *manly, heroic:* also *headstrong, haughty:* and sometimes *stately, splendid.*

ἀγήοχα, pf. act. of ἄγω *to lead.*

ἀ-γήραντος, ον, = sq.

ἀ-γήρᾰος, ον, (α privat., γῆρας) *free from old age, not growing old:* generally, *undying, undecaying.* Contr. **ἀγήρως**, ων: acc. sing. ἀγήρων or ἀγήρω: nom. dual. ἀγήρω, nom. and acc. plur. ἀγήρῳς.

ἀ-γήρᾰτος, ον, = ἀγήραος.

ἀ-γήρως, ων, contr. for ἀγήραος.

ἁγησί-χορος, ον, (ἁγέομαι Dor. for ἡγέομαι, χορός) *leading the chorus* or *dance.*

ἁγητήρ, ῆρος, Dor. for ἡγητήρ. [ᾱ]

ἀγητός, ή, όν, (ἄγαμαι) *admirable, wondrous.* [ᾰ]

ἁγιάζω, (ἅγιος) *to hallow, consecrate.*

ἁγιασθήτω, 3 sing. aor. 1 pass. imper. of ἁγιάζω.

ἁγίασμα, ατος, τό, (ἁγιάζω) *that which is hallowed, a holy place, sanctuary.*

ἁγιασμός, οῦ, ὁ, (ἁγιάζω) *consecration, sanctification.*

ἁγιαστήριον, τό, = ἁγίασμα.

ἁγίζω, f. Att. ιῶ, (ἅγιος) *to hallow, make sacred,* Lat. *dedicare.*

ἀγῑνέω, f. ησω: Ep. pres. inf. ἀγινέμεναι: impf. ἠγίνεον, Ion. ἀγίνεσκον: lengthd. Ion. form of ἄγω, *to carry, bring*:—Med. *to have brought one.* II. *to bear fruit.*

ἁγιό-γρἄφος, *ον*, (ἅγιος, γράφω) *written by inspiration*: τὰ ἁγιό-γρἄφα (sub. βιβλία), *the Psalms and other books of the Old Testament* as distinguished from the Law and the Prophets.

ἅγιος, *α*, *ον*, (ἅγος) *devoted to the gods*, Lat. *sacer*, *sacred, holy*: of persons, *pious, pure*: as Subst., ἅγιον, τό, *a sanctuary.* II. sometimes like Lat. *sacer*, *accursed.*—In old Att. ἁγνός is used instead. [ᾰγ]

ἁγιότης, *ητος*, ἡ, (ἅγιος) *sanctity, holiness.*

ἁγιστεία, ἡ, mostly in pl. *holy rites, the service of the temple* or *sanctuary.* From

ἁγιστεύω, f. *εύσω*, (ἁγίζω) *to perform sacred rites*: hence *to be pious, live piously.*

ἁγιωσύνη, ἡ, (ἅγιος) = ἁγιότης.

ἀγκ-, poët. abbrev. for ἀνακ- in compds. of the prep. ἀνά with words beginning with κ, e. g. ἀγκεῖσθαι for ἀνα-κεῖσθαι.

ἀγκάζομαι, f. *άσομαι*: Dep.: (ἄγκας, ἄγκη):—*to take* or *lift up in the arms.*

ἄγκᾰθεν, Adv. for ἀγκάς, *on the arm*, i.e. resting on it, Lat. *cubito presso*: also *in the arms.*

ἀγ-κᾰλέω, poët. for ἀνα-καλέω.

ἀγκάλη, ἡ, (ἀγκή) *the bent arm*, mostly in plur. II. metaph. *anything closely enfolding*, as *the arms* of the sea, etc. [κᾰ]

ἀγκαλίζομαι, f. Att. *ιοῦμαι*: aor. 1 ἠγκαλισάμην: pf. ἠγκάλισμαι: Dep.: (ἀγκάλη): = ἀγκάζομαι, *to take in the arms.*

ἀγκᾰλίς, *ίδος*, ἡ, in plur. = ἀγκάλαι, *arms.* II. *a bundle*, Lat. *manipulus.*

ἀγκάλισμα, τό, (ἀγκαλίζομαι) *that which is embraced.*

ἄγκᾰλος, ὁ, (ἀγκάλη) *an armful*: *a bundle.*

ἀγκάς, Adv. (ἀγκή) *into* or *in the arms.*

ἄγ-κειμαι, poët. for ἀνά-κειμαι.

ἌΓΚΗ, ἡ, = ἄγκος or ἀγκάλη, *an arm.*

ἀγ-κηρύσσω, poët. for ἀνα-κηρύσσω.

ἀγκιστρεία, ἡ, (ἄγκιστρον) *angling.*

ἀγκιστρευτικός, ἡ, όν, (ἄγκιστρον) *of* or *for angling*: τὸ ἀγκιστρευτικόν, *angling.*

ἀγκίστριον, τό, Dim. of ἄγκιστρον, *a small hook.*

ἀγκιστρό-δετος, *ον*, (ἄγκιστρον, δέω) *with a hook bound to it*, of a fishing-rod.

ἀγκιστρο-ειδής, *ές*, (ἄγκιστρον, εἶδος) *hook-shaped.*

ἄγκιστρον, τό, (akin to ἄγκος, ἀγκύλος) *a fish-hook.*

ἀγ-κλίνω and **ἄγ-κλιμα**, τό, poët. for ἀνα-κλίνω, ἀνά-κλιμα.

ἀγκοίνη, ἡ, (ἀγκών) poët. for ἀγκάλη, used only in plur. *the bent arms.* II. metaph. *anything closely enfolding*; cf. ἀγκάλη.

ἀγ-κομίζω, poët. for ἀνα-κομίζω.

ἀγ-κονίω, for ἀνα-κονίω, *to hasten.*

ἌΓΚΟΣ, *εος*, τό, *a bend* or *hollow*, esp. of the arm: hence *a mountain-glen, dell, valley.*

ἀγ-κρεμάσας, poët. for ἀνακρεμάσας, aor. 1 part. of ἀνακρεμάννυμι.

ἄγ-κρῐσις, poët. for ἀνά-κρισις.

ἀγ-κρούομαι, poët. for ἀνα-κρύομαι.

ἀγκύλη [ῠ], ἡ, like ἀγκάλη, *the bend of the arm.* II. *a loop* in a cord: esp. *the thong of a javelin*, by which it was hurled, Lat. *amentum*: also *the javelin* itself. 2. *any thong* or *string*, e. g. *the leash* of a hound, *a bow-string.*

ἀγκῠλητός, ἡ, όν, verb. Adj. of ἀγκυλέομαι, *thrown from the bent arm*:—as Subst., τὸ ἀγκυλητόν, *a javelin.*

ἀγκύλιον, τό, Dim. of ἀγκύλη, *a small dart* or *javelin.* II. τὰ ἀγκύλια used to translate the Lat. *ancilia.*

ἀγκυλο-γλώχιν, *ῖνος*, ὁ, (ἄγκυλος, γλωχίς) *with hooked spurs*, of a fighting cock.

ἀγκῠλ-όδους, *οντος*, ὁ, ἡ, (ἀγκύλος, ὀδούς) *crook-toothed, barbed*, of weapons.

ἀγκῠλο-μήτης, *ου*, ὁ, ἡ, (ἀγκύλος, μῆτις) *crooked of counsel, wily.*

ἀγκῠλό-πους, *πουν*, (ἄγκυλος, πούς) *with curved* feet, δίφρος ἀγκ. the Roman *sella curulis.*

ἀγκύλος, *η*, *ον*, (ἄγκος, Lat. *uncus*) *crooked, curved*, of a bow: of the eagle's beak, *hooked.* [ῠ]

ἀγκῠλό-τοξος, *ον*, (ἀγκύλος, τόξον) *with curved bow.*

ἀγκῠλο-χείλης, *ου*, ὁ, (ἀγκύλος, χεῖλος) *with hooked beak.*

ἀγκῠλο-χήλης, *ου*, ὁ, (ἀγκύλος, χήλη) *with crooked claws.*

ἀγκῠλόω, f. *ώσω*: pass. pf. ἠγκύλωμαι: (ἀγκύλος): *to make crooked* or *hooked.* Hence

ἀγκῠλωτός, ἡ, όν, of javelins, *furnished with a thong, thonged.*

ἄγκῡρᾰ, (ἄγκος, ἀγκών) ἡ, Lat. *ancŏra*, *an anchor*, so called from its shape, first in Pind.; for in Homer we read only of εὐναί, i. e. *stones used as anchors.*

ἀγκῡρίζω, f. Att. ιῶ: aor. 1 ἠγκύρῐσα: (ἄγκυρα):—*to hook, catch as with a fish-hook.*

ἀγκύριον, τό, Dim. of ἄγκυρα, *a small anchor.*

ἀγκῡρ-ουχία, ἡ, (ἄγκυρα, ἔχω) *a holding by the anchor*; ἐν ἀγκυρουχίαις when safe at anchor.

ἈΓΚΩ'Ν, *ῶνος*, ὁ, like ἀγκάλη, *the bend* or *hollow of the arm, the bent arm, the elbow*: hence II. *any bend*, as *the angle* of a wall, *the bend* of a river, *a bay* or *creek* of the sea; also *the curved horns* of the lyre. Hence

ἀγκωνίσκος, ὁ, Dim. of ἀγκών.

ἀγλᾰ-έθειρος, *ον*, (ἀγλαός, ἔθειρα) *bright-haired.*

ἀγλαιεῖσθαι, fut. med. inf. of ἀγλαΐζω, with pass. sense.

ἀγλᾰΐα, ἡ, (ἀγλαός) *splendour, beauty, brightness*: hence as opp. to what is useful, *pomp, show, vanity*, and in plur. *vanities*: also *festive joy, triumph*, and in plur. *festivities.*

ἀγλᾰΐζω, f. Att. ιῶ: aor. 1 ἠγλάϊσα: (ἀγλαός):—*to make splendid, adorn*: also *to give as an ornament*:—Pass. *to be adorned with* a thing, *be proud of it*, *delight in* it. Hence

ἀγλάϊσμα, τό, *an ornament*; cf. ἄγαλμα.

ἀγλᾰό-γυιος, ον, (ἀγλαός, γυῖον) *with beautiful limbs.*

ἀγλᾰό-δενδρος, ον, (ἀγλαός, δένδρον) *with beautiful trees.*

ἀγλᾰό-δωρος, ον, (ἀγλαός, δῶρον) *bestowing splendid gifts.*

ἀγλᾰό-θρονος, ον, (ἀγλαός, θρόνος) *with splendid throne.*

ἀγλᾰο-καρπος, ον, (ἀγλαός, καρπός) *bearing* or *bestowing goodly fruit.*

ἀγλᾰό-κουρος, ον, (ἀγλαός, κοῦρος) *rich in fair youths.*

ἀγλᾰό-κωμος, ον, (ἀγλαός, κῶμος) *gracing the feast.*

'ΑΓΛΑ'Ο'Σ, ή, όν, also ός, όν, *splendid, stately, beautiful, brilliant, bright:* of men, *famous, noble:* c. dat. *famous for* a thing. Adv. -ῶς. (Akin to αἴγλη, ἀγάλλομαι.)

ἀγλᾰο-τρῐαίνης, ου, ὁ, acc. -ᾰν, (ἀγλαός, τρίαινα) *the god of the bright trident.*

ἀγλᾰ-ώψ, ῶπος, ὁ, ἡ, (ἀγλαός, ὤψ) *bright-eyed:* generally, *flashing.*

ἀ-γλευκής, ές, (α privat., γλεῦκος) *not sweet: sour, harsh.*

'ΑΓΛΙΣ, ἄγλῑθος, only used in plur. ἄγλῑθες, *a head of garlic,* which is made up of several cloves.

ἀ-γλῠκής, ές, = ἀ-γλευκής.

ἀγλωσσία, Att. **ἀγλωττία**, ἡ, *dumbness.* From

ἄ-γλωσσος, Att. **ἄ-γλωττος**, ον, (α privat., γλῶσσα) *without tongue: silent, dumb,* Lat. *elinguis.* II. *speaking a strange tongue,* = βάρβαρος.

ἄγμα, τό, (ἄγνυμι) *a fragment.*

ἀγμός, ὁ, (ἄγνυμι) *a breakage, fracture* of a bone. II. *a broken cliff, precipice.*

ἄ-γναμπτος, ον, (α privat., γνάμπτω) *unbending.*

ἄ-γναπτος, ον, = sq. II. also *not cleansed.*

ἄ-γνᾰφος, ον, (α privat., γνάπτω) of cloth, *not carded,* i. e. *new.*

ἁγνεία, ἡ, (ἁγνεύω) *purity, chastity.*

ἅγνευμα, τό, (ἁγνεύω) *chastity.*

ἁγνεύω, f. εύσω, (ἁγνός) *to observe scrupulously, make a point of conscience of,* c. inf.:—also simply, *to be pure* or *chaste:* c. gen. *to keep oneself pure from.*

ἁγνίζω, f. Att. ἰῶ: aor. 1 ἥγνισα: (ἁγνός):—*to make pure, purify, cleanse,* Lat. *lustrare.* II. *to offer, burn as a sacrifice.*

ἄγνιος, α, ον, (ἄγνος) *made of withy* or *agnus castus.*

ἅγνισμα, τό, (ἁγνίζω) *a means of purification, atonement.*

ἁγνισμός, ὁ, (ἁγνίζω) *purification, expiation.*

ἁγνίτης, ου, ὁ, (ἁγνίζω) *a purifier.* [ῑ]

ἀγνοέω, Ep. **ἀγνοιέω**: f. ήσω: aor. 1 ἠγνόησα, Ep. ἀγνοίησα, Ion. and Ep. 3 sing. ἀγνώσασκε: pf. ἠγνόηκα:—Pass., aor. 1 ἠγνοήθην: pf. ἠγνόημαι: (as if from *ἄ-γνοος = ἄ-νοος):—*not to perceive* or *know, to be ignorant,* Lat. *ignorare:* in Homer mostly, οὐκ ἀγνοίησεν *he perceived* or *knew well:*—Pass. *not to be known.* II. absol. *to mistake, be wrong;* hence in part. ἀγνοῶν, *by mistake.* Hence

ἀγνόημα, τό, *a fault of ignorance, oversight;* and

ἀγνοητικός, ή, όν, *apt to err from ignorance.*

ἄγνοιᾰ, ἡ (ἀγνοέω) *want of perception, ignorance.* II. = ἀγνόημα, *a fault of ignorance.* [poët. sometimes ἀγνοίᾱ: cf. ἄνοια.]

ἀγνοιέω, poët., esp. Ep., form for ἀγνοέω.

ἀγνοίησι, Od. 24. 218, 3 sing. aor. 1 opt. of ἀγνοέω: but if written ἀγνοιῇσι, it is 3 sing. pres. subj.

ἀγνοούντως, Adv., pres. act. part. of ἀγνοέω, *ignorantly.*

ἁγνό-ρῡτος, ον, (ἁγνός, ῥέω) *pure-flowing.*

ἁγνός, ή, όν, *pure, chaste, unsullied: holy, sacred.* II. c. gen. *pure from* a thing. Adv -νῶς. (Akin to ἅζω, ἅγιος, ἄγος.)

'ΑΓΝΟΣ, ἡ, Att. ὁ, = λύγος, a tall tree like the willow, *the agnus castus.*

ἁγνότης, ητος, ἡ, (ἁγνός) *purity, chastity.*

'ΑΓΝΥ'ΜΙ, 3 dual ἄγνῠτον: fut. ἄξω: aor. 1 ἔαξα, Ep. ἦξα, imperat. ἆξον, inf. ἆξαι, part. ἄξας: aor. 2 pass. ἐάγην [ᾰ˘, v. sub fin.]: pf. ἔᾱγα, Ion. ἔηγα:—*to break, snap, crush, shiver,* Lat. *frango*:—Pass. with pf. act. ἔᾱγα, *to be broken, to snap, shiver in pieces:* of sound, *to spread around:* of a river, *to flow in a broken,* i. e. *winding course.* [ᾱ in pf. ἔᾱγα, Ion. ἔηγα: but in aor. 2 pass. ἐάγην, ᾰ in Hom., ᾱ long in Att.; v. κατάγνυμι.]

ἀγνωμονέω, f. ήσω, (ἀγνώμων) *to act without judgment, act ignorantly* or *unfairly.*

ἀγνωμόνως, Adv. of ἀγνώμων, *senselessly.*

ἀγνωμοσύνη, ἡ, *want of sense* or *judgment:* I. *senselessness, ignorance.* II. *senseless pride, arrogance.* III. *unfairness, unkindness,* Lat. *iniquitas:* in plur. *misunderstandings.* From

ἀ-γνώμων, ον, ονος, (α privat., γνώμη) *wanting sense* or *judgment: senseless, thoughtless, headstrong.* II. *unfeeling, unkind: unjust.*

ἀ-γνώς, ῶτος, ὁ, ἡ, (α privat., γνῶναι) pass. *unknown: obscure.* 2. *obscure, ignoble.* II. act. *not knowing, ignorant of* a thing.

ἁγνῶς, Adv. of ἁγνός.

ἀγνωσία, ἡ, (ἀγνώς) *a not knowing, ignorance.* II. *a being unknown, obscurity.*

ἀγνώσσασκε or **ἀγνώσασκε**, Ion. and Ep. for ἠγνόησε, 3 sing. aor. 1 of ἀγνοέω.

ἀγνώσσω, pres. formed from foreg. = ἀγνοέω.

ἄ-γνωστος or **ἄ-γνωτος**, ον, (α privat., γιγνώσκω) *unknown,* ἄγνωστος γλῶσσα an *unknown* tongue: *unheard of, forgotten.* 2. *not to be known.* II. act. *not knowing, ignorant of,* τινός.

ἀγξηρᾶναι, aor. 1 inf. of ἀναξηραίνω.

ἀγονία, ἡ, *unfruitfulness.* From

ἄ-γονος, ον, (α privat., γονή) pass. *unborn.* II. act. *not producing, unfruitful, barren:* c. gen. *not productive of, destitute of;* τόκος ἄγονος, *fruitless* travail, when the mother dies before the child is born. 2. *left childless.*

ἄ-γοος, ον, (α privat., γόος) *unmourned.*

ἀγορά, ᾶς, Ep. and Ion. **ἀγορή**, ῆς, ἡ, (ἀγείρω) *any*

assembly, esp. *an Assembly of the People*, opp. to the Council (βουλή). II. *the place of Assembly*, used not only for public debating, elections, and trials, but also for buying and selling, and all kinds of business, Lat. *forum*:—especially, the *market-place*. III. *a speech made in the forum, speaking, gift of speaking*, Lat. *concio*. IV. *things sold in the forum*, esp. *provisions*, Lat. *annona*; ἀγορὰν παρέχειν, to hold *a market*. V. as a mark of time, ἀγορὰ πλήθουσα, or ἀγορῆς πληθώρη, *the forenoon*, when the market-place was full: opp. to ἀγορῆς διάλυσις, *the time just after noon*: when they went home from market.

ἀγοράασθε, Ep. for ἀγορᾶσθε, 2 pl. pres. ind. of ἀγοράομαι. [ᾱγορᾰασθε]

ἀγοράζω, f. άσω: aor. ἠγόρασα: pf. ἠγόρακα:—Pass., aor. ἠγοράσθην: pf. ἠγόρασμαι: (ἀγορά):—*to be in the market-place, to attend it*: hence 2. *to do business there, buy* or *sell*: Med. *to buy for oneself*. 3. of idle people, *to haunt the market-place, lounge there*, cf. sq.

ἀγοραῖος, ον, *in, of*, or *belonging to the market-place*, an epith. of several gods. II. *frequenting the market-place*:—οἱ ἀγοραῖοι (with or without ἄνθρωποι): 1. *hucksters, petty traffickers, retail-dealers*. 2. *idlers* or *loungers*, like Lat. *subrostrani*, and so generally *the common sort*:—hence the word is used of things, *low, mean, vulgar*. III. generally, *proper to the assembly, suited to forensic speaking, business-like*: ἀγοραῖος (sc. ἡμέρα), ἡ, *a court-day*.

ἀγορᾰνομικός, ή, όν, *of* or *for the* ἀγορανόμος or *his office*, Lat. *Aedilicius*.

ἀγορᾰνόμιον, τό, *the court of the* ἀγορανόμος.

ἀγορᾰ-νόμος, ὁ, (ἀγορά, νέμω) *a clerk of the market*, who regulated the buying and selling there, like the Rom. *Aedilis*.

ἀγοράομαι, Ep. aor. 1 ἀγορησάμην: Dep.: (ἀγορά):—*to meet in the Assembly, sit in debate*: also *to speak in the Assembly*, Lat. *concionari*.

ἀγοράσδω, Dor. for ἀγοράζω.

ἀγόρᾰσις, εως, ἡ, (ἀγοράζω) *buying, purchase*.

ἀγόρασμα, τό, (ἀγοράζω) *that which is bought* or *sold*: in plur. *wares, merchandise*.

ἀγοραστής, οῦ, ὁ, (ἀγοράζω) *the slave who had to buy* provisions, *the purveyor*, Lat. *obsonator*.

ἀγοραστικός, ή, όν, (ἀγοράζω) *of* or *for trafficking* or *trade*: ἡ ἀγοραστική (sub. τέχνη) *commerce, trade*.

ἀγορεύω, impf. ἠγόρευον, Ep. ἀγόρευον: fut. -εύσω: aor. ἠγόρευσα, Ep. ἀγ-: pf. ἠγόρευκα: Med., aor. ἠγορευσάμην: Pass., aor. ἠγορεύθην: pf. ἠγόρευμαι: (but in Att. the fut. in use is ἐρῶ, pf. εἴρηκα, aor. εἶπον): (ἀγορά):—*to speak in the Assembly, to counsel*:—generally *to speak*; κακὸν or κακῶς ἀγορεύειν τινά *to speak* ill *of* one. 2. *to proclaim, declare*: Med. *to get* a thing *proclaimed*.

ἀγορή, Ep. and Ion. for ἀγορά. Hence

ἀγορῆθεν, Adv. *from the Assembly* or *market*; and

ἀγορήνδε, Adv. *to the Assembly* or *market*.

ἀγορήσατο, Ep. for ἠγορήσατο, 3 sing. aor. 1 med. of ἀγοράομαι.

ἀγορητής, οῦ, ὁ, (ἀγοράομαι) *a speaker, orator*.

ἀγορητύς, ύος, ἡ, (ἀγοράομαι) *the gift* or *power of speaking, eloquence*.

ἄγορος, ὁ, poët. for ἀγορά.

ἄγος or ἀγος, εος, τό, (ἅζομαι) *any matter of religious awe*: hence 1. *pollution, guilt*, Lat. *piaculum*: also *the curse which follows it*. 2. *the person* or *thing accursed, an abomination*. 3. *an expiatory sacrifice*.

ἀγός, οῦ, ὁ, (ἄγω) *a leader, chief*.

ἀγοστός, ὁ, *the flat of the hand*. II. *the bent arm*, like ἀγκών, ἀγκοίνη. (Akin to ἀγκών, ἄγνυμι.) [ᾰ]

***ΑΓΡΑ**, Ion. ἄγρη, ἡ, *a catching, hunting*; ἄγραν ἐφέπειν to follow *the chase*:—also, *a way of catching*. II. *that which is taken in hunting, the booty, prey*:—of birds or beasts, *game*; of fish, *a draught* or *haul*.

ἀγραμματία, ἡ, *want of learning*: from

ἀ-γράμμᾰτος, ον, (α privat., γράμμα) *without learning* (γράμματα), *unlettered*, Lat. *illiteratus*, esp. *unable to read* or *write*. II. = ἄγραφος, *unwritten*.

ἄ-γραπτος, ον, (α privat., γράφω) *unwritten*; ἄγρ. νόμιμα the *unwritten* moral law: cf. ἄγραφος.

ἀγραυλέω, f. ήσω, *to be an* ἄγραυλος, *to dwell in the fields*, of shepherds.

ἄγρ-αυλος, ον, (ἀγρός, αὐλή) *dwelling in the fields*, of shepherds:—of things, *rural, rustic*.

ἄ-γρᾰφος, ον, = ἄγραπτος, *unwritten*; ἄγραφοι νόμοι, *unwritten laws*, which are 1. the laws of nature, moral law. 2. laws of custom. II. *not registered in a written list*.

ἄγρει, ἀγρεῖτε, 2 sing. and plur. imperat. of ἀγρέω: in Homer as Adv. just like ἄγε, ἄγετε, *come! come on! quick!*

ἀγρεῖος, α, ον, (ἀγρός) *of the country, rural, rustic*: also, *clownish, boorish*, like ἄγροικος. Hence

ἀγρειοσύνη, ἡ, *clownishness*: *the life of a clown* or *boor*.

***ΑΓΡΕΙΦΝΑ**, ης, ἡ, *a harrow, rake*.

ἀγρέμιος, ον, (ἄγρα) *taken in hunting*.

ἀγρεσία, ἡ, = ἄγρα, *spoil taken in the chase*.

ἄγρευμα, τό, (ἀγρεύω) *that which is taken in the chase, booty, spoil*. II. *a net, toil*.

ἀγρεύς, έως, ὁ, (ἀγρεύω) *a hunter*.

ἀγρευτήρ, ῆρος, ὁ, = ἀγρευτής.

ἀγρευτής, οῦ, ὁ, *a hunter*, like ἀγρεύς. II. as Adj. *used in hunting* or *fishing*; ἀγρ. κύνες, *hounds*; ἀγρ. κάλαμος *a fishing*-rod.

ἀγρευτικός, ή, όν, *fit for, skilled in hunting*. From

ἀγρεύω, f. εύσω, (ἄγρα) *to hunt, take by hunting, catch*: metaph. *to hunt after, pursue eagerly*.

ἀγρέω, Aeol. form of ἀγρεύω, *to hunt after, pursue eagerly*:—see ἄγρει, ἀγρεῖτε.

ἄγρη, ἡ, Ion. for ἄγρα.

ἀγριαίνω, f. ᾰνῶ: aor. ἠγρίᾱνα: (ἄγριος):—I. intrans.

to be savage, provoked, angry. 2. causal, *to make angry, provoke.*

ἀγρι-έλαιος, ον, (ἄγριος, ἐλαία) *of a wild olive:* as Subst. ἀγριέλαιος, ἡ, *a wild olive, oleaster.*

ἀγριο-δαίτης, ου, ὁ, (ἄγριος, δαίνυμαι) *eating wild fruits,* like βαλανηφάγος.

ἀγριο-ποιός, όν, (ἄγριος, ποιέω) *making wild:* of a poet, *writing wildly.*

ἄγριος, α, ον, also ος, ον, (ἀγρός) *living in the fields, living wild:* hence I. of animals, opp. to τιθασός, *wild, savage,* Lat. *ferus;* σῦς ἄγριος a *wild* boar. 2. of trees, opp. to ἥμερος, *wild.* 3. of countries, *wild, uncultivated, unreclaimed.* II. of men and animals, 1. in moral sense, *wild, savage, fierce,* Lat. *ferus, ferox.* 2. in Att. also opp. to ἀστεῖος, (as Lat. *rusticus* to *urbanus*) *boorish, rude.* 3. also of any violent passion, *wild, vehement, furious.* III. Adv. -ίως, also neut. pl. ἄγρια, *wildly, fiercely.* Hence

ἀγριότης, ητος, ἡ, *wildness, fierceness,* Lat. *feritas.*

ἀγριό-φωνος, ον, (ἄγριος, φωνή) *with a rough voice,* like βαρβαρό-φωνος.

ἀγριόω, f. ώσω: aor. ἠγρίωσα:—Pass., aor. ἠγριώθην: pf. ἠγρίωμαι: (ἄγριος):—*to make wild* or *savage.* II. mostly in Pass. *to grow wild,* and in pf. ἠγρίωμαι, *to be wild,* of plants, etc.:—of men, *to be savage* or *fierce,* Lat. *efferari.*

ἀγρίφη, ἡ, = ἀγρεῖφνα. [ῐ]

ἀγρι-ώδης, ες, (ἄγριος, εἶδος) *of a wild nature.*

ἀγρι-ωπός, όν, (ἄγριος, ὤψ) *wild-looking.*

ἀγρο-βότης, ου, ὁ, (ἄγρος, βόσκω) *feeding in the field, dwelling in the country.*

ἀγρο-γείτων, ονος, ὁ, (ἀγρός, γείτων) *a country neighbour,* opp. to ἀστυγείτων.

ἀγρο-δότης, ου, ὁ, (ἄγρα, δίδωμι) *a giver of booty.*

ἀγρόθεν, Adv. of ἀγρός, *from the country.*

ἀγροικία, ἡ, (ἄγροικος) *boorishness, coarseness.* II. *country life, the country:* pl. *country houses.*

ἀγροικίζομαι, f. Att. -ιοῦμαι, Dep. *to be boorish.* From

ἄγρ-οικος, ον, (ἀγρός, οἰκέω) *living in the country, rustic:* hence 2. of men, *boorish, rude:* opp. to ἀστεῖος. 3. of fruits, *grown in the country, common,* opp. to γενναῖος: but also 4. of land, *rough, uncultivated,* like ἄγριος. Hence

ἀγροίκως, Adv. *like a clown, rudely.*

ἀγροιώτης, ου, ὁ, poët. for ἀγρότης, *a countryman, clown.* II. as Adj. *rustic.*

ἀγρό-κομος, ὁ, (ἄγρος, κομέω) *a land-steward.*

ἀγρόμενος, η, ον, part. Ep. aor. 2 med. of ἀγείρω, *assembled.*

ἀγρόνδε, Adv. of ἀγρός, *to the country.*

ἀγρό-νομος, ον, and in Anth. η, ον, (ἀγρός, νέμομαι) *hunting the country, rural:* also = ἄγριος, *wild.*

'ΑΓΡΟ'Σ, οῦ, ὁ, Lat. *AGER, a field, land:* also *the country,* as opp. to the town.

ἀγρότερος, α, ον, (ἀγρός) poët. for ἄγριος, *wild,* of plants:—of men, *rustic.* II. (ἄγρα) *fond of the chase:* hence ἡ ἀγροτέρα, *the huntress.*

ἀγροτήρ, ῆρος, ὁ, = ἀγρότης, *a countryman:* fem. ἀγρότειρα, as Adj. *rustic.*

ἀγρότης, ου, ὁ, fem. **ἀγρότις**, ιδος, (ἀγρός) *a countryman, countrywoman.* 2. as Adj. *living in the country, rural, rustic.*

ἀγρο-φύλαξ, ἄκος, ὁ, (ἀγρός, φύλαξ) *a watcher of the country.*

ἀγρυπνέω, f. ήσω, (ἄγρυπνος) *to be wakeful, lie awake:* ἀγρυπνεῖν τινι or εἴς τι, *to be watchful for* or *intent upon* a thing, Lat. *invigilare rei.* Hence

ἀγρυπνία, ἡ, *sleeplessness, waking, watching.*

ἄγρ-υπνος, ον, (ἀγρέω, ὕπνος) = ἄυπνος, *sleepless, wakeful.*

ἀγρώσσω, = ἀγρεύω, *to catch.*

ἀγρώστης, ου, ὁ, (ἀγρός) = ἀγρότης, *a countryman.* II. (ἄγρα) *a hunter:* fem. **ἀγρῶστις**, ιδος, ἡ, *a huntress.*

ἄγρωστις, ιος and εως, ἡ, *a grass* that mules feed on.

ἀγρώτης, ου, ὁ, = ἀγρότης, *a countryman:*—as Adj. *of the field, wild.*

ἀγυιά, ἡ, (ἄγω) *a way* or *road:* in towns, *a street, a public place;* in plur. *a city, town.* [ἄγυιᾰ] Hence

ἀγυιάτης, ου, ὁ, = 'Αγυιεύς: voc. 'Αγυιᾶτα. [ἄγυιᾰ]

ἀγυιᾶτις, ιδος, ἡ, fem. of foreg. *a neighbour.* II. as Adj. 'Αγυιάτιδες θεραπεῖαι, the worship *of Apollo Agyieus.*

'Αγυιεύς, έως, ὁ, (ἀγυιά) name of Apollo *as guardian of the streets and public places.*

ἀγυμνᾰσία, ἡ, *want of exercise* or *training.* From

ἀ-γύμναστος, ον, (α privat., γυμνάζω) *without exercise, untrained;* ἀγύμναστός τινος *unpractised in* a thing, also εἴς or πρός τι. 2. *unharassed, undisturbed.* II. Adv., ἀγυμνάστως ἔχειν to be *unpractised.*

ἄγῠρις, ιος, ἡ, Aeol. form of ἀγορά, *a gathering, crowd, assembly.* [ᾰ]

ἀγυρμός, οῦ, ὁ, (ἀγείρω) *a collection.*

ἀγυρτάζω, (ἀγύρτης) *to collect by begging.* [ᾰ]

ἀγύρτης, ου, ὁ, (ἀγείρω) properly *a gatherer, collector:* hence *a beggar, vagabond, mountebank, cheat.* Hence

ἀγυρτικός, ή, όν, *like a mountebank.*

ἀγύρτρια, ἡ, fem. of ἀγυρτήρ.

ἀγχέ-μαχος, ον, (ἄγχι, μάχομαι) *fighting hand to hand;* ἀγχ. ὅπλα, arms *for close fight.*

"ΑΓΧΙ, Adv. of place, = ἐγγύς, *near, nigh at hand, close by,* c. gen.:—Comp. ἄγχιον and ἆσσον: Sup. ἄγχιστα, ἀγχοτάτω. Cf. ἀγχοῦ, ἄγχιστος. [ῐ]

ἀγχί-ἁλος, ον, also η, ον, (ἄγχι, ἅλς) *near the sea,* of cities: but of islands, *near the sea on all sides, sea-girt,* like ἀμφί-αλος.

ἀγχι-βᾰθής, ές, (ἄγχι, βαθύς) *deep close to shore.*

ἀγχι-γείτων, ον, gen. ονος, (ἄγχι, γείτων) *near, neighbouring.*

ἀγχί-γυος, ον, (ἄγχι, γύα) *of a neighbouring land.*

ἀγχί-θεος, ον, (ἄγχι, θεός) *near the gods,* i. e. *like gods* or *dwelling with the gods.*

ἀγχί-θῠρος, *ον*, (ἄγχι, θύρα) *near the door, neighbouring.* [ῐ]

ἀγχι-μᾰχητής, οῦ, ὁ, = ἀγχέμαχος.

ἀγχί-μολος, *ον*, (ἄγχι, μολεῖν) *coming near:* always in neut. as Adv. ἀγχίμολον ἐλθεῖν or στῆναι to come or stand *near;* ἐξ ἀγχιμόλοιο from *nigh* at *hand.*

ἀγχι-νεφής, *ές*, (ἄγχι, νέφος) *near the clouds.*

ἀγχι-νοία, ἡ, (ἄγχι, νοέω) *a ready wit, shrewdness,* Lat. *sagacitas.*

ἀγχί-νοος, *ον*, contr. **ἀγχί-νους**, *ουν*, (ἄγχι, νοῦς) *ready of mind, shrewd,* Lat. *sagax.*

ἄγχιον, Comp. Adv. of ἄγχι, *nearer.*

ἀγχί-πλοος, *ον*, contr. **ἀγχί-πλους**, *ουν*, (ἄγχι, πλοῦς) *near by sea;* ἀγχ. πόρος *a short* voyage.

ἀγχί-πολις, poët. **ἀγχί-πτολις**, εως, ὁ, ἡ, (ἄγχι, πόλις) *near the city, dwelling in the land.*

ἀγχί-πορος, *ον*, (ἄγχι, πορεύομαι) *passing near;* κόλακες ἀγχίποροι flatterers *at one's elbow.*

ἀγχί-πτολις, poët. for ἀγχί-πολις.

ἄγχιστα, v. ἄγχιστος.

ἀγχιστεία, ἡ, (ἀγχιστεύω) *nearness of kin.* II. *rights of kin, right of inheritance.*

ἀγχιστεῖα, τά, = ἀγχιστεία.

ἀγχιστεύς, έως, ὁ, (ἄγχιστα) *the next of kin: the heir at law.*

ἀγχιστεύω, f. εύσω, (ἄγχιστος) *to be near to* one, c. dat.: esp. *to be next of kin, to be heir at law.*

ἀγχιστήρ, ῆρος, ὁ, poët. for ἀγχιστεύς, ἀγχιστὴρ τοῦ πάθους *immediate author* of the suffering.

ἀγχιστῖνος, *η*, *ον*, poët. lengthd. form of ἄγχιστος, *close-packed, in a heap.*

ἄγχιστος, *ον*, Sup. Adj. (ἄγχι) *next* or *nearest:* ἄγχιστος γένει *nearest* of kin: neut. ἄγχιστον, or ἄγχιστα, as Sup. Adv. *most nearly*, ἄγχιστα ἔοικας *most nearly* like; οἱ ἄγχιστα *the next of kin:* freq. c. gen. as ἄγχιστά τινος, *nearest to* him. II. of time, *last,* Lat. *proximus.*

ἀγχί-στροφος, *ον*, (ἄγχι, στρέφω) *turning near, quick-wheeling*, of a bird. 2. *quick-changing, changeable, sudden:* neut. pl. ἀγχίστροφα as Adv. *suddenly.*

ἀγχι-τέρμων, *ον*, gen. *ονος*, (ἄγχι, τέρμα) *near the borders, neighbouring.*

ἀγχί-τοκος, *ον*, (ἄγχι, τόκος) *near the birth.*

ἀγχόθεν, Adv. (ἀγχοῦ) *from nigh at hand.*

ἀγχόθι, Adv. = ἀγχοῦ, *nigh at hand.* c. gen.

ἀγχόνη, ἡ, (ἄγχω) *throttling, strangling, hanging:* κρεῖσσον ἀγχόνης worse than *hanging;* ἀγχόνης πέλας as bad as *hanging;* ἀγχόνη καὶ λύπη *anguish* and grief. 2. *a rope for hanging, halter.*

ἀγχόνιος, *α*, *ον*, (ἀγχόνη) *fit for strangling* or *hanging.*

ἀγ-χορεύω, poët. for ἀνα-χορεύω.

ἀγχότατος, *η*, *ον*, Sup. Adj. (ἄγχι) *nearest, next:* mostly as Adv. ἀγχοτάτω, like ἄγχιστα, c. gen.; οἱ ἀγχοτάτω προσήκοντες the *nearest* of kin.

ἀγχότερος, *α*, *ον*, Comp. Adj. (ἄγχι) *nearer.*

'ΑΓΧΟΥ = ἄγχι, *near, nigh at hand.* absol., or c. gen., also c. dat., cf. ἄγχι.

"ΑΓΧΩ, impf. ἦγχον: f. ἄγξω: aor. ἦγξα:—Lat. *ANGO, to press tight,* esp. the throat: *to strangle, throttle, hang.*

ἀγχ-ώμᾰλος, *ον*, (ἄγχι, ὁμαλός) *nearly equal;* ἀγχώμαλος μάχη a *doubtful* battle. Adv. ἀγχωμάλως, also ἀγχώμαλα, *doubtfully,* Lat. *aequo Marte.*

"ΑΓΩ, Lat. *AGO:* impf. ἦγον, Ep. ἄγον, Ion. ἄγεσκον: fut. ἄξω: aor. 2 ἤγαγον, inf. ἀγαγεῖν; less freq. aor. 1 ἦξα, inf. ἄξαι Ep. ἀξέμεν or ἀξέμεναι: pf. ἦχα, redupl. ἀγήοχα.—Med., fut. ἄξομαι: aor. 1 ἠξάμην, aor. 2 ἠγαγόμην.—Pass., fut. ἀχθήσομαι, but also fut. med. ἄξομαι, with pass. signf.: aor. 1 pass. ἤχθην: pf. ἦγμαι: verb. Adj. ἀκτέον:—Lat. *AGO:* I. Act. *to lead, lead away,* of persons, φέρειν being used of things; ἄγειν καὶ φέρειν *to carry off the spoil of a land,* both cattle and movables, like Lat. *agere et ferre:* ἄγειν εἰς δίκην or δικαστήριον, or ἄγειν ἐπὶ τοὺς δικαστάς, *to carry* before a court of justice, Lat. *rapere in jus.* 2. *to lead on, lead towards;* ἄγεν θανάτοιο τέλοσδε *led on* to death; c. inf., ἄγει θανεῖν it *leads* to death: hence *to lead,* as a general; *to guide,* as the gods, etc. 3. *to bring up, train, educate,* καλῶς or κακῶς ἠχθῆναι. 4. *to draw out* in length; τεῖχος ἄγειν, Lat. *murum ducere, to build* a wall. 5. like Lat. *agere, to hold, celebrate,* ἑορτήν, etc.. also *to hold, keep, observe,* εἰρήνην, σπονδάς, etc.: ἄγειν βίον, Lat. *agere vitam, to lead* a life, live. 6. like Lat. *ducere, to hold, consider;* ἐν τιμῇ ἄγει or ἄγεσθαι, *to hold* in honour, etc. 7. like ἕλκειν, *to weigh* so much, e. g. ἄγειν μνᾶν, τριακοσίους δαρεικούς, etc., *to weigh* a mina, 300 darics, etc. II. Med. ἄγομαι, *to lead away for oneself, carry off,* as χρυσόν τε καὶ ἄργυρον οἴκαδ' ἄγεσθαι. 2. ἄγεσθαι γυναῖκα, Lat. *uxorem ducere, to take to oneself* a wife; absol. ἄγεσθαι, *to marry;* but also of the father, *to choose* a wife *for his son.* 3. διὰ στόμα ἄγεσθαι μῦθον *to let pass* through the mouth, i. e. to utter. 4. ἄγεσθαί τι ἐς χεῖρας, *to take* a thing into *one's* hands.

ἀγωγαῖος, *ον*, (ἀγωγή) *fit for leading by,* of a dog's collar or leash.

ἀγωγεύς, έως, ὁ, (ἄγω *to lead*) *a leader, one that draws* or *drags.* II. *that by which one leads, a rein, leash.*

ἀγωγή, ἡ, (ἄγω) *a leading away, a carrying away* or *off:* also in intrans. sense, *a going away.* 2. *a bringing to* or *in, bringing before an assembly.* 3. *a leading towards* a point, *guiding: the leading* of an army, *guiding* a state. 4. *a training, educating:* and intrans. *conduct, mode of life.*

ἀγώγῐμος, *ον*, (ἄγω) *easy to be carried.* τὰ ἀγώγιμα, *things portable, a cargo of wares.* II. *that may be carried away:* of persons, *outlawed,* or *delivered into bondage.* III. *easily led, complaisant.*

ἀγώγιον, τό, (ἄγω) *the load of a wagon.*

ἀγωγός, όν, (ἄγω) *leading, guiding:* as Subst., ἀγωγός, ὁ, *a guide;* ἀγωγοί *an escort.* II. *leading towards.* III. *drawing to oneself, eliciting,* c. gen.: *attractive,* τὸ ἀγωγόν, *attractiveness.*

'ΑΓΩ'Ν, ῶνος, ὁ, *an assembly,* like ἀγορά: esp. *an assembly met to see games.* 2. *a place of assembly: a place of contest, the arena* or *stadium.* II. *the assembly* of the Greeks *at their great national games,* as, ἀγὼν 'Ολυμπιάς, ἀγὼν 'Ολυμπικός, etc.: hence the *contest for a prize* at their games. 2. generally, *any struggle* or *contest,* ἀγὼν περὶ τῆς ψυχῆς. 3. *a battle.* 4. *an action at law, trial.* 5. metaph., ἐστὶν ἀγὼν λόγων, μάχης, etc., now is *the time for* speaking, fighting, etc.

ἀγων-άρχης, ου, ὁ, (ἀγών, ἄρχω) *a president* or *judge of a contest.*

ἀγωνία, ἡ, *a struggle for victory.* 2. *gymnastic exercise, wrestling.* 3. of the mind, *agony, anguish.*

ἀγωνιάω: impf. ἠγωνίων: f. άσω [ᾱ]: aor. 1 ἠγωνίᾱσα: pf. ἠγωνίᾱκα:—*to be engaged in a contest, to compete,* like ἀγωνίζομαι. III. *to strive eagerly,* to be *anxious* about a thing.

ἀγωνίδαται, v. ἀγωνίζομαι.

ἀγωνίζομαι, fut. ίσομαι, Att. ἰοῦμαι, aor. 1 ἠγωνισάμην:—for the pass. forms see signf. II. 2: (ἀγών): —*to contend for a prize,* esp. in the public games; ἀγωνίζεσθαι στάδιον *to contend* in the foot-race; ἀγ. περί τινος to contend for a prize; ἀγ. τινι or πρός τινα *to contend with* one. 2. *to fight.* 3. *to contend for the prize on the stage, act.* II. *to contend against in a law-suit;* ἀγ. δίκην, γραφήν, *to fight* a cause *to the last;* ἀγ. φόνον *to fight against* a charge of murder. 2. in Pass. *to be won by a hard contest,* but rarely save in pf., e. g. πολλοὶ ἀγῶνες ἀγωνίδᾰται (Ion. for ἠγωνισμένοι εἰσί), many battles *have been fought;* so also in aor. 1 ἠγωνίσθην.

ἀγώνιος, ον, (ἀγών) *presiding over the contest* or *the games,* as an epithet of the gods:—σχολὴ ἀγώνιος cessation *from combat.* [ᾰ]

ἀγώνισις, ἡ, (ἀγωνίζομαι) *a contending for a prize.*

ἀγώνισμα, τό, (ἀγωνίζομαι) *a contest for a prize,* generally, *a contest:* in plur. *achievements, exploits* II. *an object to strive for; the prize of contest, distinction.* III. *that with which one contends, an essay, declamation.*

ἀγωνισμός, ὁ, (ἀγωνίζομαι) *rivalry.*

ἀγωνιστέον, verb. Adj. of ἀγωνίζομαι, *one must contend.*

ἀγωνιστής, οῦ, ὁ, (ἀγωνίζομαι) *a combatant, rival,* esp. at the games: *an advocate:* also *an actor;* hence πρωτ-αγωνιστής, δευτερ-αγωνιστής, etc. 2. *a champion.*

ἀγωνιστικός, ή, όν, (ἀγωνίζομαι) *fit for contesting* or *striving:* also *fitted for winning:*—ἡ ἀγωνιστική (sub. τέχνη) the art *of winning* or *prevailing.* Adv. -κῶς, ἀγωνιστικῶς ἔχειν to be *disposed for combat.*

ἀγωνοθετέω, f. ήσω, *to be a judge* or *director of the games:* generally, *to direct, promote, judge, decide.* From

ἀγωνο-θέτης, ου, ὁ, (ἀγών, τίθημι) *a president in the games: a judge.*

ἀδαγμός, ὁ, Ion. for ὀδαγμός, *an itching, sting.*

ἀδᾰημονία or **ἀδαημοσύνη**, ἡ, *ignorance, unskilfulness in* doing. From

ἀ-δᾰήμων, ον, (α privat., δαῆναι) *unknowing, ignorant of,* c. gen. μάχης ἀδαήμων: but, ἀδ. κακῶν *beyond the knowledge,* i. e. *reach* of ill.

ἀδᾰής, ές, (α privat., δαῆναι) = foreg. *unknowing, ignorant of,* c. gen. also c. inf. *unknowing how to..*

ἀ-δάητος, ον, (α privat., δαῆναι) *unknown.*

ἀ-δάϊος, ον, (α privat., δάϊος) Dor. for ἀδήϊος.

ἄ-δαιτος, ον, (α privat., δαίνυμαι) *not to be eaten, unlawful to eat.*

ἄ-δακρῠς, υ, gen. υος, (α privat., δάκρυ) = ἀδάκρυτος I. II. = ἀδάκρυτος II.

ἀ-δακρῡτί, Adv. *without tears.* From

ἀ-δάκρῡτος, ον, (α privat., δακρύω) *without tears:* hence I. act. *not weeping, tearless.* II. pass. *unwept.*

ἀ-δᾱλής, ές, Dor. for ἀ-δήλητος.

ἀδαμάντινος, ον, (ἀδάμας) *adamantine, of steel:* hence, *hard as adamant, stubborn.* Adv. -νως.

ἀδᾰμαντό-δετος, ον, (ἀδάμας, δέω) *iron-bound.*

ἀ-δάμας, αντος, ὁ, (α privat., δαμάω) *unconquerable:* hence I. as Subst. *adamant,* i. e. the hardest metal, prob. *steel:* also *the diamond.* II. as Adj. *inexorable.*

ἀ-δάμαστος, ον, (α privat., δαμάζω) properly of horses, *unbroken, untamable:*—metaph. *inexorable.*

ἀ-δάμᾰτος, ον, Trag. form of foreg.: also of females, *unwedded.* [ἀδᾰ-: but also ᾱδ- as in ᾱ-θάνατος.]

ἀ-δάπᾰνος, ον, (α privat., δᾰπάνη) *without expense, costing nothing.* Adv. -νως.

ἄ-δασμος, ον, *tribute-free.*

ἄ-δαστος, ον, (α privat., δάσασθαι aor. 1 of δατέομαι) *undivided.*

ἀδδεές, Ep. vocat. of ἀδεής.

ἀδδηκότες, poët. for ἀδηκότες, pf. part. of ἀδέω.

ἄδδην, poët. for ἄδην.

ἀδδήσειε, aor. 1 opt. of ἀδέω.

ἀδδη-φαγέω, etc., v. sub ἀδηφ–.

ἅδε, 3 sing. Ep. aor. 2 of ἁνδάνω. [ᾰ]

ἀδέα, Dor. poët. for ἡδεῖα, fem. of ἡδύς: also as Dor. acc. masc. and fem.

ἀ-δεής, Ep. ἀ-δειής, ές, Ep. voc. ἀδδεές, (α privat., δέος) *fearless, shameless.* 2. *fearless, secure:* τὸ ἀδεές, *security:*—Adv. ἀδεῶς, *without fear* or *scruple, confidently, abundantly.* II. *causing no fear, not formidable.*

ἄδεια, ἡ, (ἀδεής) *freedom from fear, safety, security;* ἄδειαν διδόναι, παρέχειν, etc., to grant *an am-*

nesty; ἐν ἀδείῃ εἶναι to feel *secure;* μετ' ἀδείας with a *promise of security.*

ἀ-δειής, ές, Ep. for ἀ-δεής.

ἀ-δείμαντος, ον, (α privat., δειμαίνω) *undaunted:* c. gen. *without fear for* a person. Adv. -τως.

ἀδεῖν, aor. 2 inf. of ἀνδάνω.

ἄ-δειπνος, ον, (α privat., δεῖπνον) *without food, unfed.*

ἀ-δέκαστος, ον, (α privat., δεκάζω) *unbribed.* Adv. -τως.

ἀ-δεκάτευτος, ον, (α privat., δεκᾰτεύω) *not tithed.*

ἄ-δεκτος, ον, (α privat., δέχομαι) *not received* or *believed.* II. act. *not receiving, not capable of,* τινός.

ἀδελφεα, ἡ, Dor. for ἀδελφή.

ἀδελφεή, ἡ, Ion. for ἀδελφή.

ἀδελφειός, ὁ, Ep. for ἀδελφός.

ἀδελφεο-κτόνος, ον, Ion. for ἀδελφο-κτόνος.

ἀδελφεός, ὁ, Ep. and Ion. for ἀδελφός.

ἀδελφή, ἡ, fem. of ἀδελφός, *a sister.*

ἀδελφιδέος, ου, contr. **ἀδελφιδοῦς,** οῦ, ὁ, (ἀδελφός) *a brother's* or *sister's son, a nephew.*

ἀδελφιδῆ, ἡ, Att. contr. for ἀδελφιδέη, (ἀδελφός) *a brother's* or *sister's daughter, a niece.*

ἀδελφίδιον, τό, Dim. of ἀδελφός, *a little brother.*

ἀδελφίζω, fut. Att. ιῶ, (ἀδελφός) *to adopt as brother.*

ἀδελφικός, ή, όν, *brotherly.* Adv. -κῶς.

ἀδελφο-κτόνος, Ion. **ἀδελφεο-κτόνος,** ον, (ἀδελφός, κτείνω) *murdering a brother* or *sister.*

ἀδελφός, (α copul., δελφύς): I. as Subst. ἀδελφός, Ion. -φεός, Ep. -φειός, ὁ, *a brother;* in pl. ἀδελφοί *brothers and sisters.* II. as Adj. ἀδελφός, ή, όν, *brotherly* or *sisterly:* hence like Lat. *geminus, in pairs, twin,* also *twin to* a thing, *just like it.* Hence

ἀδελφότης, ητος, ἡ, *brotherhood, brotherly kindness.* 2. *a family of brothers, a brotherhood.*

ἄ-δενδρος, ον, (α privat., δένδρον) *without trees.*

ἀ-δέξιος, ον, (α privat., δεξιός) *awkward.*

ἀ-δερκής, ές, (α privat., δέρκομαι) *unseen, invisible.*

ἄ-δερκτος, ον, (α privat., δέρκομαι) *not seeing, sightless,* ὄμματα. Adv. -τως, *without looking.*

ἄ-δεσμος, ον, (α privat., δεσμός) *unfettered, unbound;* ἄδεσμος φυλακή, Lat. *libera custodia,* of prisoners suffered to be at large *on parole.*

ἀ-δέσποτος, ον, (α privat., δεσπότης) *without a master:*—of writings, *anonymous.*

ἄ-δετος, ον, (α privat., δέω) *unbound: free.*

ἀ-δευκής, ές, (α privat., δεῦκος) *not sweet, sour, bitter,* Lat. *acerbus.*

ἀ-δέψητος, ον, (α privat., δεψέω) *untanned.*

***ἉΔΕ΄Ω,** *to please,* obsol. pres., whence ἀνδάνω has its fut., aor. 2, and pf.: v. ἀνδάνω.

***ἈΔΕ΄Ω,** *to be sated,* obsol. pres., whence come aor. 1 opt. ἀδδήσειε or ἀδήσειε, *may he be sated;* and pf. part. ἀδδηκότες or ἀδηκότες, *sated.* Cf. ἄω, *satio.*

ἀ-δήϊος, contr. **ἀ-δῇος,** Dor. **ἀ-δάϊος,** ον, (α privat., δήϊος) *unassailed.*

ἄ-δηκτος, ον, (α privat., δάκνω) *not gnawed* or *worm-eaten: not carped at.*

ἀδηλέω, (ἄδηλος) *to be at a loss about* a thing.

ἀ-δήλητος, ον, (α privat., δηλέομαι) *unhurt.*

ἀδηλία, (ἄδηλος) *uncertainty.*

ἄ-δηλος, ον, *unknown, ignoble.* II. *unknown, unseen, secret;* ἄδηλόν ἐστιν εἰ.., or ὅτι.., it is uncertain whether ... Adv. -λως, *secretly:* Sup. ἀδηλότατα.

ἀδηλότης, ητος, ἡ, (ἄδηλος) *uncertainty.*

ἀδημονέω, f. ήσω, *to be in great distress* or *anguish* at a thing.. (Deriv. uncertain.)

ἀδημονία, ἡ, *great distress* or *anguish.*

ἄδην, Ep. **ἄδδην,** Att. **ἄδην,** Adv. (*ἀδέω) Lat. *SATIS, enough, abundantly;* ἔδμεναι ἄδδην to eat *their fill,* of horses; ἄδην πολέμοιο *enough* of war; ἄδην ἔχειν τινός to have *enough of* a thing.

ἄ-δηρις, εως, ὁ, ἡ, (α privat., δῆρις) *without strife.*

ἀ-δήρῑτος, ον, (α privat., δηρίομαι) *without strife* or *battle, uncontested.* II. *unconquerable.*

ἀδήσειε, aor. 1 opt. of ἀδέω.

ἀδήσω, fut. of ἀνδάνω.

ᾅδης or **ᾍδης,** ου, ὁ, Att., but also **Ἀΐδης** [⏑ ⏑ –], αο and εω:—*Hades,* the god of the lower world, Lat. *Pluto:* εἰν and εἰς Ἀΐδαο, Attic ἐν and ἐς ᾍδου (with or without δόμος), in or into the house of *Hades.* II. later, *the grave, death.*

ἀδη-φάγος, ον, (ἄδην, φᾰγεῖν) *eating to excess, devouring, gluttonous.*

ἀ-δήωτος, ον, (α privat., δηόω) *not wasted.*

ἀ-διάβᾰτος, ον, (α privat., διαβαίνω) *not to be crossed, impassable.*

ἀ-διάκρῐτος, ον, (α privat., διακρίνω) *undistinguishable: unintelligible.* 2. *undecided.*

ἀ-διάλειπτος, ον, (α privat., διαλείπω) *unintermitting, unceasing.* Adv. -ως.

ἀ-διάλλακτος, ον, (α privat., διαλλάσσω) *irreconcilable, allowing no reconciliation.* Adv., ἀδιαλλάκτως ἔχειν to be *irreconcilable.*

ἀ-διάλῠτος, ον, (α privat., διαλύω) *undissolved: indissoluble.* 2. *irreconcilable.* Adv., ἀδιαλύτως ἔχειν to be *irreconcilable.*

ἀ-διανόητος, ον, (α privat., διανοέομαι) *incomprehensible.* II. act. *not understanding, silly.*

ἀ-δίαντος, ον, also η, ον, (α privat., διαίνω) *unwetted:*—**ἀδίαντον,** τό, a plant, *maiden's hair.*

ἀ-διάπαυστος, ον, (α privat., διαπαύω) *not to be stilled, incessant, violent.*

ἀ-διά-πτωτος, ον, (α privat., διαπίπτω) *not liable to error, infallible.* Adv. -τως.

ἀ-διάσπαστος, ον, (α privat., διασπάω) *not torn asunder, unbroken.* Adv. -τως.

ἀ-διάτρεπτος, ον, (α privat., διατρέπω) *immovable, headstrong.* Adv. -τως. Hence

ἀδιατρεψία, ἡ, *immovableness, obstinacy.*

ἀ-διάφθαρτος, ον, (α privat., διαφθείρω) *incorruptible.*

ἀδιαφθορία, ἡ, *freedom from corruption.* From

ἀ-διάφθορος, ον, (α privat., διαφθείρω) *incorrupt, incorruptible.* II. *imperishable.*

ἀ-διάφορος, ον, (α privat., διαφέρω) *not different: indifferent.*

ἀ-δίδακτος, ον, (α privat., διδάσκω) of persons, *untaught, unlearned, rude.* II. of things, *not learnt:* also, *learnt without teaching.*

ἀ-διεξέργαστος, ον, (α privat., διεξεργάζομαι) *not to be wrought out* or *finished.*

ἀ-διέξοδος, ον, (α privat., διέξοδος) *without outlet.* II. act. *unable to get out.*

ἀ-διέργαστος, ον, (α privat., διεργάζομαι) *not worked out, unfinished.*

ἀ-διερεύνητος, ον, (α priv., διερευνάω) *unexamined.*

ἀ-διήγητος, ον, (α privat., διηγέομαι) *indescribable.*

ἀ-δίκαστος, ον, (α privat., δικάζω) *without judgment given, undecided.*

ἀδικειμένος, Boeot. for ἠδικημένος, part. perf. pass. of ἀδικέω.

ἀδῐκέω: impf. ἠδίκεον, Ion. εῦν: f. ήσω: aor. 1 ἠδίκησα: pf. ἠδίκηκα: Pass., with fut. med. ἀδικήσομαι: pf. ἠδίκημαι: (ἄδικος):—*to do wrong.* II. trans. c. acc. pers. *to do* one *wrong, to wrong, injure:* c. dupl. acc., ἀδ. τινά τι *to wrong* one *in* a thing:—Pass. *to be wronged* or *injured.*

ἀδίκημα, τό, (ἀδικέω) *a wrong done, a wrong, injury,* Lat. *injuria:* c. gen., ἀδ. τινος *a wrong done to* one.

ἀδῐκητέον, verb. Adj. of ἀδικέω, *one ought to do wrong.*

ἀδῐκία, ἡ, (ἀδικέω) *a wrong, offence,* = ἀδίκημα. II. *injustice.*

ἀδίκιον, τό, = ἀδίκημα, *an act of wrong.*

ἄ-δῐκος, ον, (α privat., δίκη) of persons and things, *doing wrong, unrighteous, unjust;* ἄδικος εἴς τι *unjust in* a thing, περί τινα *in respect to* a person: ἄδικος λόγος a plea *of injustice;* ἀδίκων χειρῶν ἄρξαι to begin *lawless* acts of violence; ἄδικος πλοῦτος *unrighteous* gain. II. *wrong, improper, ill-matched,* as horses. III. ἄδικος ἡμέρα, i. e. ἄνευ δικῶν, a day *on which the courts were shut,* Lat. *dies nefastus.* Hence

ἀδίκως, Adv. *without right* or *reason.*

ἀδῐνός, ή, όν, (ἄδην) *close, thick:* hence 1. *crowded* or *thronged, close-packed.* 2. *vehement, loud,* esp. of sounds:—more freq. as Adv. ἀδινῶς, also neut. ἀδινόν and ἀδινά, *vehemently, loudly;* Comp. ἀδινώτερον. [ᾰ]

ἀ-διοίκητος, ον, (α privat., διοικέω) *unarranged.*

ἀ-διόρθωτος, ον, (α privat., διορθόω) *not corrected: incorrigible.*

ἀ-δίστακτος, ον, (α privat., διστάζω) *without doubting.* Adv. -τως.

ἄ-διψος, ον, (α privat., δίψα) *without thirst, not thirsty.*

ἀ-δμής, ῆτος, ὁ, ἡ, = ἄδμητος.

ἀδμῆτις, ιδος, acc. ἀδμῆτιν, fem. of ἀδμής.

ἄ-δμητος, η, ον, (α privat., δαμάω) poët. for ἀδάματος, *untamed:* of cattle, *unbroken, wild;* of maidens, *unmarried.*

ᾁδο-βάτης, ου, ὁ, (ᾅδης, βαίνω) *one who has gone to Hades.* [βᾰ]

ἅδιον, Dor. for ἥδιον, neut. Comp. of ἡδύς.

ἅδοι, 3 sing. aor. 2 opt. of ἁνδάνω.

ἀ-δόκητος, ον, (α privat., δοκέω) *unexpected.* II *inglorious.* Adv. -τως, also neut. ἀδόκητα as Adv. *unexpectedly;* so also, ἀπὸ τοῦ ἀδοκήτου.

ἀ-δοκίμαστος, ον, (α privat., δοκιμάζω) *untried, unproved.* [ῐ]

ἀ-δόκῐμος, ον, (α privat., δόκιμος) *unproved, spurious, base, mean.* II. *rejected as spurious, reprobate.*

ἀδολεσχέω, fut. ήσω, *to talk idly, to prate.* [ᾱ] From

ἀδο-λέσχης, ου, ὁ, also **ἀδό-λεσχος**, ον, (ἄδος, λέσχη) *a prating fellow.* II. in good sense, *a keen, subtle reasoner.* [ᾱ] Hence

ἀδολεσχία, ἡ, *prating, frivolity.* II. *keenness, subtlety.* [ᾱ] Hence

ἀδολεσχικός, ή, όν, *disposed to prate, frivolous.* [ᾱ]

ἄ-δολος, ον, *guileless, artless:* in Att. esp. of treaties, *without dishonest intent.* II. of liquids, *unmixed, pure.* Adv. -λως, *without fraud.*

ἄδον, Ep. for ἕαδον, aor. 2 of ἁνδάνω.

ᾆδον, impf. of ᾄδω.

ἀ-δόνητος, ον, (α privat., δονέω) *not shaken.*

ἀδονίς, ίδος, ἡ, poët. for ἀηδονίς. [ᾱ]

ἀ-δόξαστος, ον, (α privat., δοξάζω) *unexpected.* II. *not matter of opinion,* i. e. *certain.*

ἀδοξέω, f. ήσω, (ἄδοξος) *to be of no reputation, stand in ill repute.* II. trans. *to hold in no esteem.* Hence

ἀδοξία, ἡ, *ill repute, dishonour.*

ἄ-δοξος, ον, (α privat., δόξα) *disreputable, disgraceful.* 2. *obscure, ignoble.*

ἍΔΟΣ, εος, τό, *satiety, loathing.*

ἆδος, εος, τό, Dor. for ἦδος, *joy.*

ἄ-δοτος, ον, (α privat., δίδωμι) *without gifts.*

ἄ-δουλος, ον, (α privat., δοῦλος) *without slaves, unattended, deserted.*

ἀ-δούλωτος, ον, (α privat., δουλόω) *unenslaved.*

ἀ-δούπητος, ον, (α privat., δουπέω) *noiseless.*

ἀδράνεια, Ep. **ἀδρανίη**, ἡ, *inactivity.* From

ἀ-δρᾰνής or **ἀ-δρᾰνέης**, ές, (α privat., δραίνω) *inactive, listless, feeble.*

Ἀδράστεια, Ion. **Ἀδρήστεια**, ἡ, a name of Nemesis, from an altar erected to her by Adrastus: later as Adj., epith. of Νέμεσις, *not to be escaped,* as if from διδράσκω, cf. sq.

ἄ-δραστος, Ion. **ἄ-δρηστος**, ον, (α privat., διδράσκω) *not running away, not inclined to run away.*

ἄ-δρεπτος, ον, (α privat., δρέπω) *unplucked.*

ἄ-δρηστος, ον, Ion. for ἄ-δραστος.

Ἀδρίας, ου, Ion. **Ἀδρίης**, εω, ὁ, *the Adriatic Sea.* Hence

'Αδριατικός and **'Αδριηνός**, ή, όν, *of the Adriatic.*
ἄ-δρῖμυς, υ, (α privat., δριμύς) *not tart* or *pungent.*
'ΑΔΡΟ'Σ, ά, όν, properly *stout, thick*:—hence *full-grown, ripe: well-grown: stout, large, fat:* generally, *strong, great* in any way. Hence
ἁδροσύνη, ἡ, = sq.
ἁδροτής, ῆτος, ἡ, (ἁδρός) *stoutness: ripeness, fulness,* esp. of the body. II. *abundance.*
ἁδρόομαι, Pass. (ἁδρός) *to grow ripe: to come to one's strength.*
ἁδρύνω, (ἁδρός) *to make ripe*:—Pass. *to grow ripe.*
ἁδύ-γλωσσος, -επής, -μελής, Dor. for ἡδύ–.
ἀ-δῠνᾰμία, ἡ, (α privat., δύναμις) *want of strength, weakness: poverty.*
ἀ-δυνᾰσία, ἡ, = ἀδυναμία.
ἀδῠνᾰτέω, f. ήσω, (ἀδύνατος) *to want strength, power,* or *ability.* Hence
ἀδῠνᾰτία, ἡ, = ἀδυναμία.
ἀ-δύνᾰτος, ον, *unable to do* a thing, c. inf. 2. absol. *without strength, powerless, weakly:* of things, *disabled*:—*τὸ ἀδύνατον want of strength.* II. Pass. *unable to be done, impossible: τὸ ἀδ. impossibility.* III. Adv. -τως, *without power, feebly.* [ῠ]
ἁδύς, έα, ύ, Dor. for ἡδύς.
ἄ-δῠτος, ον, (α privat., δύω) *not to be entered*:—hence as Subst. ἄδυτον, τό, *the innermost sanctuary* or *shrine,* Lat. *adytum:* also ἄδυτος, ὁ.
ᾄδω, Att. contr. for ἀείδω, q. v.
ἀδών, όνος, ἡ, Dor. for ἀηδών, *the nightingale.* [ᾰ]
'Αδώνια, τά, *the mourning for Adonis.*
'Αδωνιάζω, *to keep the Adonia.* Hence
'Αδωνιασμός, οῦ, ὁ, *the mourning for Adonis.*
'Άδωνις, ιδος, ὁ, *Adonis.* 2. 'Αδώνιδος κῆποι, pots for sowing quick-growing herbs in. [ᾰ]
ἀ-δώρητος, ον, (α privat., δωρέομαι) = ἄ-δωρος.
ἀ-δωροδόκητος, ον, (α privat., δωροδοκέω) = sq. Adv. -τως.
ἀ-δωροδόκος, ον, *unbribed, incorruptible.*
ἄ-δωρος, ον, (α privat., δῶρον) *without gifts, taking no gifts, unbribed*:—ἄδωρα δῶρα gifts *that are no gifts.* II. *giving no gifts, fruitless.*
ἀ-δώτης, ου, ὁ, (α privat., δίδωμι) *one who gives nothing.*
ἀέ, Dor. for ἀεί. [ᾰ]
ἄ-εδνος, ον, (α privat., ἕδνα) *undowered.*
ἀεθλεύω, Ep. and Ion. for ἀθλεύω.
ἀεθλέω, Ep. and Ion. for ἀθλέω: Ion. impf. ἀέθλεον.
ἀεθλητής, Ep. and Ion. for ἀθλητής.
ἀέθλιον, τό, Ep. and Ion. for ἆθλον: properly neut. from
ἀέθλιος, ον, also α, ον, (ἄεθλον) *running for the prize;* ἀέθλιος ἵππος a *race*-horse; ἀέθλιον μῆλον the apple *of discord.*
ἄεθλον, τό, Ep. and Ion. for ἆθλον.
ἄεθλος, ὁ, Ep. and Ion. for ἆθλος.
ἀεθλο-φόρος, ον, Ep. and Ion. for ἀθλο-φόρος.
ἀεί, Adv. *ever, always, for ever:* δεῦρ' ἀεί ever up to this time; also εἰς ἀεί or εἰσαεί. With the Artic. ὁ ἀεὶ κρατῶν the ruler *for the time being,* who*ever* is ruler; ὁ ἀεὶ βασιλεύς the *reigning* king. Besides ἀεί the Ion. and poet. forms αἰεί and αἰέν are very common: in Dor. also αἰές, ἀές, and ἀέ.
ἀεί-βολος, ον, (ἀεί, βάλλω) *continually thrown.*
ἀει-γενέτης, poët. **αἰει-γενέτης**, ου, ὁ, (ἀεί, γενέσθαι) epith. of the gods in Homer, like αἰὲν ἐόντες, *ever existing, immortal.*
ἀει-γενής, ές, Att. for ἀει-γενέτης.
ἄειδε, Ep. 3 imperf. or 2 imperat. of ἀείδω.
ἀ-είδελος, ον, (α privat., *εἴδω) *unseen, dark.*
ἀ-ειδής, ές, (α privat., *εἴδω) *unseen, without bodily form.* II. (α privat., εἰδέναι) *unknown, obscure*
ἀει-δίνητος, ον, (ἀεί, δινέω) *ever revolving.* [ῑ]
'ΑΕΙ'ΔΩ, Att. contr. ᾄδω: impf. ἤειδον, Ep. ἄειδον, Att. ᾖδον: fut. ἀείσομαι, Att. ᾄσομαι, Dor. ἀσεῦμαι; rarely ἀείσω, Att. ᾄσω, Dor. ᾀσῶ: aor. 1 ἤεισα, Ep. ἄεισα, Att. ᾖσα:—Pass., aor. 1 ᾔσθην: pf. ᾖσμαι:—*to sing:* hence of all kinds of voices, *to crow, twitter, croak,* etc.—also of other sounds, of the bow-string *to twang,* of the wind *to whistle,* of a stone *to ring.* II. trans.:—1. c. acc. rei, *to sing, chaunt, descant on.* 2. c. acc. pers. *to sing, praise.* 3. Pass. *to resound with song.*
ἀεί-ζωος, ον, Att. contr. **ἀεί-ζως**, ων, (ἀεί, ζωή) *everliving, everlasting.*
ἀει-θαλής, ές, (ἀεί, θάλος) *ever-green.*
ἀ-εικείη or **–ίη** [ῑ], Att. contr. **αἰκία** [ῑ], ἡ, *unseemly treatment, an outrage, insult, affront.*
ἀ-εικέλιος, α, ον, also ος, ον, poët. form for sq.: contr. αἰκέλιος. Adv. -ίως.
ἀ-εικής, ές, Att. contr. **αἰκής**, ές, (α privat., εἶκος) *unseemly, pitiful, mean, shameful.* Neut. ἀεικές as Adv. *in unseemly manner.*
ἀ-εικίη, ἡ, = ἀεικείη.
ἀεικίζω, Att. contr. **αἰκίζω**, fut. Att. -ιῶ: aor. 1 ἠείκισα, Ep. ἀείκισσα:—Ep. aor. pass. inf. ἀεικισθῆναι: (ἀεικής):—*to treat unseemly, insult, abuse.*
ἀει-κίνητος, ον, (ἀεί, κινέω) *ever moving, in perpetual motion.* [ῑ]
ἀεικισθήμεναι, aor. 1 pass. inf. of ἀεικίζω.
ἀείκισσα, ἀεικισσάμην, Ep. aor. 1 act. and med. of ἀεικίζω.
ἀεικιῶ, Att. fut. of ἀεικίζω.
ἀεικῶς, Ion. **ἀεικέως**, Adv. of ἀεικής, *shamefully.*
ἀεί-λᾰλος, ον, (ἀεί, λαλέω) *ever-babbling.*
ἀειλογία, ἡ, as Att. law-term, τὴν ἀειλογίαν παρέχειν, προτείνεσθαι to court *continual inquiry.* From
ἀει-λόγος, ον, (ἀεί, λέγω) *always talking.*
ἀεί-μνηστος, ον, also η, ον, (ἀεί, μιμνήσκομαι) *had in everlasting remembrance: ever-memorable, everlasting.* Adv. -τως.
ἀεί-ναος, ον, contr. **ἀεί-νως**, ων, (ἀεί, νάω) = ἀέναος, *ever-flowing.*
ἀεί-νηστις, ιος, ὁ, ἡ, *ever-fasting.*
ἀεί-πλᾰνος, ον, (ἀεί, πλανάομαι) *ever-wandering.*
ἄειρα, Ep. for ἤειρα, aor. 1 of ἀείρω.
ἀεῖραι, aor. 1 inf. of ἀείρω.

ἀεί-ροος, ον, contr. ἀεί-ρους, ουν, = sq.

ἀεί-ρῠτος, ον, (ἀεί, ῥέω) *ever-flowing*.

'ΑΕΙ'ΡΩ, Att. **αἴρω**: fut. ἀρῶ [ᾱ], contr. from ἀερῶ: aor. 1 act. ἤειρα, Ep. ἄειρα.—Med., fut. ἀροῦμαι [ᾱ], contr. from ἀεροῦμαι: aor. 1 ἠειράμην.—Pass., aor. 1 ἠέρθην, Ep. ἀέρθην: pf. ἤερμαι: Ep. 3 sing. plqpf. ἄωρτο: for the Att. forms, v. αἴρω:—*to lift, heave, raise up*, hence *to bear, carry*: *to carry off* as plunder: but also, *to hand, offer*:—Med. *to lift up for oneself*, i. e. *bear off, win, take for oneself*:—Pass. *to be hung up, to hang*; μάχαιρα παρὰ ξίφεος κουλεὸν ἄωρτο the dagger *hung* beside the sword sheath. 2. *to raise* or *stir up*; ἀείρασθαι τὰ ἱστία *to hoist* sail: Pass. *to raise up, arise*.

ἄεισα, Ep. aor. 1 of ἀείδω.

ἀεῖσαι, part. nom. pl. fem. of ἄημι.

ἄεισμα, τό, poët. and Ion. for ᾆσμα, as ἀείδω for ᾄδω.

ἄεισι, 3 pl. of ἄημι.

ἀείσομαι, fut. of ἀείδω.

ἀει-φᾰνής, ές, (ἀεί, φανῆναι) *ever-shining* or *appearing*.

ἀεί-φρουρος, ον, (ἀεί, φρουρά) *ever-watched* or *ever-watching, ever-wakeful*.

ἀει-φῠγία, ἡ, (ἀεί, φυγή) *exile for life*.

ἀει-χρόνιος, ον, (ἀεί, χρόνος) *everlasting*.

ἀεκαζόμενος, η, ον, (ἀέκων) *unwilling, resisting*; πόλλ' ἀεκαζόμενος, Virgil's *multa reluctans*.

ἀ-εκήλιος, ον, for ἀεικέλιος.

ἀέκητι or **ἀεκητί**, (ἀέκων) Ep. Adv. *against the will*, often in Homer c. gen.; σεῦ ἀέκητι, Lat. *te invito*; θεῶν ἀέκητι, Lat. *Diis non propitiis*.

ἀ-εκούσιος, ον, also α, ον, Att. contr. **ἀκούσιος**, ον, (α privat., **ἑκούσιος**) *against the will, forced, involuntary*.

ἀ-έκων, Att. contr. **ἄκων** [ᾱ], ουσα, ον, (α privat., ἑκών) *against the will, unwilling*: *without design* or *purpose*.

ἀέλιος, Dor. for ἠέλιος, ἥλιος.

ἄελλα, Ep. **ἀέλλη**, ης, ἡ, (ἄω, ἄημι) *a stormy wind, a whirlwind*. 2. metaph. of any *whirling motion*. [ᾰε]

ἀελλαῖος, α, ον, (ἄελλα) *stormy, swift as the storm*.

ἀελλάς, άδος, ἡ, = ἀελλαῖος.

ἀελλής, ές, (ἄελλα) *eddying*.

ἀελλο-μάχος, ον, (ἄελλα, μάχομαι) *struggling with the storm*. [ᾰ]

ἀελλό-πος, Homeric form of sq.

ἀελλό-πους, ὁ, ἡ, πουν, τό, gen. **ποδος**, (ἄελλα, πούς) *storm-footed, swift as the storm*, only found in Ep. form **ἀελλό-πος**, like ἀρτί-πος, πουλύ-πος, etc.: dat. pl. ἀελλοπόδεσσιν.

ἀελπτέω, (ἄελπτος) *to be without hope, to despair*.

ἀ-ελπτής, ές, (α privat., ἔλπομαι) *unhoped for, unexpected*.

ἀελπτία, ἡ, *an unlooked for event*: ἐξ ἀελπτίης, Lat. *ex insperato, unexpectedly*. 2. *despair*. From

ἄ-ελπτος, ον, (α privat., ἔλπομαι) *unlooked for, unexpected*: *to be despaired of*: ἄελπτα, neut. pl. as Adv. *unexpectedly*. II. act. *hopeless, desperate*.

ἀελπτῶς, Adv. of ἀελπτής, *unexpectedly*.

ἀέ-νᾰος, ον, also Ep. **ἀεί-ναος**, contr. **ἀεί-νως**, ων, (ἀεί, νάω) *ever-flowing*: generally, *everlasting, never-failing*. Adv. -άως.

ἀε-νάων, ουσα, ον, = ἀέναος.

ἀέντες, part. pl. of ἄημι.

ἀεξί-γυιος, ον, (ἀέξω, γυῖον) *strengthening the limbs*.

ἀεξί-νοος, ον, contr. **ἀεξί-νους**, ουν, (ἀέξω, νόος) *strengthening the mind*.

ἀεξί-φυλλος, ον, (ἀέξω, φύλλον) *making leaves grow, leafy*.

ἀεξί-φῠτος, ον, (ἀέξω, φυτόν) *making plants grow*.

'ΑΕ'ΞΩ, Ion. and poët. for ΑΥ'ΞΩ, αὐξάνω, Lat. *AUGEO*: used by the old poets only in pres. and impf.: later poets have a fut. ἀεξήσω, aor. 1 ἠέξησα; fut. med. ἀεξήσομαι, pf. pass. ἠέξημαι:—*to make to grow, increase, foster, strengthen*: *to heighten, multiply*:—Pass. and Med. *to increase, wax great*: *prosper*.

ἀεργείη or -ίη [ῑ], Ion. for ἀεργία.

ἀ-εργής, ές, = ἀεργός.

ἀεργία, Ion. -ίη [ῑ], ἡ, *a not working, idleness*. [ῑ] 2. of a field, *a lying fallow* or *waste*. From

ἀ-εργός, contr. **ἀργός**, όν, (α privat., *ἔργω) *not working, idle*. Adv. -γῶς.

ἀέρδην, contr. **ἄρδην**, Adv. (ἀείρω) *lifting up*.

ἀερθείς, aor. 1 pass. part. of ἀείρω.

ἄερθεν, Dor. and Ep. for ἠέρθησαν, 3 pl. aor. 1 pass. of ἀείρω: **ἀέρθη**, 3 sing. of same tense.

ἀέριος, ον, also α, ον, Ion. **ἠέριος**, η, ον, (ἀήρ, ἦρ, ἦρι) *in mist*, or *thick air*: *cloudy*. II. *in the air, high in air*.

ἄ-ερκτος, ον, (α privat., ἔργω) *unfenced, open*.

ἀεροβᾰτέω, f. ήσω, *to tread in air, walk the air*. From

ἀερο-βάτης, ου, ὁ, (ἀήρ, βαίνω) *one who treads in air*.

ἀερο-δῑνής, Ion. **ἠερο-δινής**, ές, (ἀήρ, δινέω) *wheeling in air*.

ἀερο-δόνητος, ον, (ἀήρ, δονέω) *tossed in mid air, soaring*.

ἀεροδρομέω, f. ήσω, *to traverse air*. From

ἀερο-δρόμος, ον, *traversing air*.

ἀερο-ειδής, ές, (ἀήρ, εἶδος) *like the sky* or *air, misty*: see ἠεροειδής.

ἀερο-κόραξ, ᾰκος, ὁ, *an air-raven*.

ἀερο-κώνωψ, ωπος, ὁ, *an air-gnat*.

ἀερο-μᾰχία, ἡ, (ἀήρ, μάχη) *a battle in the air*.

ἀερο-μετρέω, f. ήσω, (ἀήρ, μετρέω) *to measure the air*: *to lose oneself in vague speculation*.

ἀερο-νηχής, ές, (ἀήρ, νήχομαι) *floating in air*, of the clouds.

ἀέρρω, Aeol. for ἀείρω.

ἀερσι-κάρηνος, ον, (ἀείρω, κάρηνον) *carrying the head high*. [κᾰ]

ἀερσι-πότης, ου, ὁ, and **ἀερσι-πότητος**, ον, (ἀείρω, ποτάομαι) *hovering on high*.

ἀερσί-πους, ὁ, ἡ, πουν, τό, gen. ποδος, (ἀείρω, πούς) *lifting up the feet, brisk-trotting.*

ἀερτάζω, poët. form of ἀείρω, *to lift up:* impf. ἠέρταζον.

ἀερτάω, = ἀερτάζω :—aor. 1 ἠέρτησα : pf. pass. ἠέρτημαι.

ἀές, Dor. for ἀεί. [ᾰ]

ἄεσα, 1 pl. ἀέσαμεν and ἄσαμεν, 3 pl. ἄεσαν, inf. ἀέσαι, aor. 1 prob. from an obsol. root ἀέω, = εὕδω, *to sleep:* no other tenses in use. Akin to ἄημι, ἰαύω, ἀωτέω.

ἀεσιφροσύνη, ἡ, *silliness, folly,* in plur. ἀεσιφροσύναι. From

ἀεσί-φρων, ον, gen. ονος, (ἀάω, φρήν) *injured in mind: witless, silly, infatuated.* [ᾰ]

'ΑΕΤΟ'Σ or **αἰετός**, also poët. **αἰητός**, οῦ, ὁ, *an eagle,* Lat. *aquila.* II. *an eagle as a standard.* [ᾱ]

ἀετ-ώδης, ες, (ἀετός, εἶδος) *eagle-like.* [ᾱ]

***'ΑΕ'Ω**, *to sleep,* v. ἄεσα.

"ΑΖΑ, ἡ, properly *dryness, heat:* also *mould,* (v. sub ἄζω.)

ἀζᾰλέος, α, ον, (ἄζω) pass. *dry, parched:* hence *harsh, cruel.* II. act. *parching, scorching.*

ἀζάνω, (ἄζω) *to dry* or *parch up.*

ἀζηλία, ἡ, *freedom from jealousy: simplicity.* From

ἄ-ζηλος, ον, like ἀζήλωτος, *unenviable, miserable: inconsiderable, mean.*

ἀ-ζήλωτος, ον, (α privat., ζηλόω) *not to be envied.*

ἀ-ζήμιος, ον, (α privat., ζημία) *without loss, scot-free: not deserving punishment:*—Adv. –ίως, *with impunity.* 2. *not amounting to punishment, harmless.*

ἄζηται, 3 sing. pass. subj. of ἄζω.

ἀ-ζήτητος, ον, (α privat., ζητέω) *unexamined.*

ἀζηχής, ές, *unceasing, excessive:* more freq. as Adv. ἀζηχές, *unceasingly, beyond measure.* II. *hard, rough.* (Deriv. uncertain.)

ἄ-ζῠγος, ον, = ἄ-ζυξ, *ill-matched: unmarried.*

ἄ-ζῡμος, ον, (α privat., ζύμη) *unleavened:* τὰ ἄζυμα, *the feast of unleavened bread.*

ἄ-ζυξ, ῠγος, ὁ, ἡ, (α privat., ζῠγῆναι) *unyoked, unpaired: unmarried, unwedded.*

"ΑΖΩ, *to dry, dry up, parch:*—Pass. *to be parched up, pine away* through grief.

"ΑΖΩ, mostly used as Dep. **ἅζομαι**, and only in pres. and impf.: *to stand in awe of, dread* the gods or one's parents: also followed by inf. *to be afraid of doing;* or μή . ., *to fear lest:*—absol. *to be awe-struck.*—Cf. σέβω.

ἄ-ζωστος, ον, (α privat., ζώννυμι) *ungirt* from hurry: generally, *not girded.*

ἄη, 3 sing. impf. of ἄημι.

ἀ-ηδής, ές, (α privat., ἦδος) *unpleasant, annoying:* of persons, *unfriendly, morose.* Hence

ἀηδία, ἡ, (ἀηδής) *a being displeased, disgust, dislike.* II. *unpleasantness, odiousness.*

ἀηδονιδεύς, έως, Ep. gen. ῆος, ἡ, *a young nightingale.*

ἀηδόνιος, ον, (ἀηδών) *of* or *belonging to a nightingale.*

ἀηδονίς, ίδος, ἡ, = ἀηδών, *a nightingale.*

ἀηδώ, οῦς, ἡ, = ἀηδών, *a nightingale.*

ἀηδών, ἡ, Att. ὁ, gen. ἀηδόνος or ἀηδοῦς, (ἀείδω) *a nightingale;* properly *the songstress.*

ἀηδῶς, Adv. of ἀηδής, ἀηδῶς ἔχειν *to be unfriendly.*

ἀήθεια, Ion. **ἀηθίη** [ῑ], ἡ, (ἀήθης) *unaccustomedness, novelty, the being unaccustomed* to a thing: ἀήθ. τινός *inexperience* of a thing.

ἀηθέσσω, poët. for ἀηθέω, *to be unaccustomed to a* thing, c. gen.: impf. ἀήθεσσον.

ἀ-ήθης, ες, (α privat., ἦθος) *unwonted, unusual, strange:*—Adv. -θως. 2. *unused to* a thing, c. gen. II. *without* ἦθος or *character.*

ἀηθίη, ἡ, = ἀήθεια, q. v.

ἀηθίζομαι, Dep. (ἀήθης) *to be unaccustomed.*

ἀήθως, Adv. of ἀήθης, *unexpectedly.*

ἄημα, τό, (ἄημι) *a blast, wind.*

ἀήμεναι, Ep. for ἀῆναι, inf. of ἄημι.

"ΑΗΜΙ, 3 sing. ἄησι, 3 dual ἄητον (not ἄετον), 3 pl. ἄεισι; imper. 3 sing. ἀήτω; inf. ἀῆναι, Ep. ἀήμεναι; part. ἀείς: Ep. 3 sing. impf. ἄη, 3 pl. ἄεσαν:—Pass. ἄημαι, part. ἀήμενος: Ep. 3 sing. impf. ἄητο:—*to breathe hard, blow,* of the wind: the pass. forms sometimes mean *to be beaten by the wind,* but more often *to toss* or *wave about as if in the wind;* hence *to be spread abroad.*

ἀῆναι, inf. of ἄημι.

ἀήρ, ἀέρος, ἡ, Att. ὁ, Ion. and Ep. **ἀήρ** or **ἠήρ**, ἠέρος, ἡ:—in Hom. and Hes. *the lower air, the atmosphere* or *thick air* that surrounds the earth, opp. to αἰθήρ *the pure upper air,* v. esp. Il. 14. 288: hence *misty darkness, mist, gloom:* but later generally *air.* (From *ἄω, ἄημι.) [ᾱ]

ἄησις, εως, ἡ, (ἄημι) = ἄημα, *a blowing.* [ᾰ]

ἀ-ήσσητος, Att. **ἀ-ήττητος**, ον, (α privat., ἡσσάομαι) *unconquered, not beaten: unconquerable.*

ἀήσῠλος, for αἴσυλος, *wicked.*

ἀήσῠρος, ον, (*ἄω, ἄημι) *light as air: little.*

ἀήτη, ἡ, = ἀήτης.

ἀήτης, ου, ὁ, (ἄω, ἄημι) *a blast, gale, wind.*

ἄητο, Ep. 3 sing. impf. pass. of ἄημι.

ἄητον, 3 dual pres. of ἄημι.

ἄητος, ον, an old word, only in Il. 21. 395, prob. from ἄημι, hence orig. *stormy,* and so *violent, terrible;* cp. αἴητος.

ἀήτω, 3 sing. imperat. of ἄημι.

ἀ-θάλασσος, Att. **-ττος**, ον, (α privat., θάλασσα) *without sea, inland.*

ἀ-θᾰλάσσωτος, Att. **-ττωτος**, ον, (α privat., θαλασσόω) *never having been at sea.*

ἀ-θαλής, ές, (α privat., θάλος) *not verdant.*

ἀ-θαλπής, ές, (α privat., θάλπος) *without warmth.*

ἀ-θαμβής, ές, (α privat., θάμβος) *fearless.*

ἀθᾰνᾰσία, ἡ, (ἀθάνατος) *immortality.*

ἀθᾰνᾰτίζω, (ἀθάνατος) *to make immortal:*—Pass. *to become* or *be immortal,* II. *to hold oneself immortal.*

ἀ-θάνατος, ον, also η, ον, *not subject to death, undying, immortal*, opp. to θνητός and βροτός:—hence ἀθάνατοι, οἱ, *the Immortals*, of the Gods, also of a body of troops *that is kept at a certain number*: of things, *everlasting*.

ἄ-θαπτος, ον, (α privat., θάπτω) *unburied*. II. *unworthy of burial*.

ἀθάρη, also **ἀθήρη**, ἡ, *groats* or *meal, porridge made of it*. [ἄθᾰ-]

ἀ-θαρσής, ές, (α privat., θάρσος) *discouraged*.

ἀ-θαύμαστος, ον, (α privat., θαυμάζω) *not wondering at* anything. Adv. -τως. II. *not admired*.

ἀ-θέᾱτος, ον, (α privat., θεάομαι) *unseen, invisible: secret*. II. act. *not seeing, blind to*.

ἀθεεί, Adv. (ἄθεος) *without the aid of God*.

ἀ-θείαστος, ον, (α privat., θειάζω) *uninspired*.

ἄ-θελκτος, ον, (α privat., θέλγω) *implacable*.

ἄ-θεμις, ιτος, ὁ, ἡ, *lawless*.

ἀ-θεμίστιος, **ἀ-θέμιστος**, and **ἀ-θέμῑτος**, ον, (α privat., θέμις) *lawless, without law* or *government, godless*, Lat. *nefarius*. Adv. -τως.

ἄ-θεος, ον, *without God, denying the gods*: generally, *godless, ungodly*. II. *abandoned by the gods*. Hence.

ἀ-θεότης, ητος, ἡ, *godlessness, ungodliness*.

ἀθερᾰπευσία, ἡ, *want of attendance* or *care*: c. gen. *neglect of* a thing. From

ἀ-θεράπευτος, ον, (α privat., θερᾰπεύω) *not attended to, neglected*. II. *unhealed, incurable*.

ἀ-θερίζω: Ep. aor. 1 ἀθέριξα or -ισσα: (α privat., θέρω = θεραπεύω) :—*to slight, make light of*, Lat. *nihil curare*, c. acc.

ἀ-θέρμαντος, ον, (α privat., θερμαίνω) *unheated; not excited by passion*.

ἄ-θερμος, ον, *without warmth*.

ἀθεσία, ἡ, (ἄθετος) *unsteadiness, fickleness*.

ἄ-θεσμος, ον, *lawless*.

ἀ-θέσφᾰτος, ον, *impossible even for gods to tell, inexpressible*: hence *marvellously great, enormous*.

ἀ-θετέω, f. ήσω, (ἄθετος) *to set aside, disregard*.

ἀθέτησις, εως, ἡ, (ἀθετέω) *abolition, rejection*.

ἄ-θετος, ον, (α privat., τίθημι) *not placed, set aside, useless*:—Adv. ἀθετῶς = ἀθέσμως, *lawlessly*.

ἀθέως, Adv. of ἄθεος, *in a godless manner*.

ἄ-θηλος, ον, (α privat., θηλή) *unsuckled, weaned*.

ἀ-θήλυντος, ον, (α privat., θηλύνω) *not made womanish: masculine*.

Ἀθηνᾶ, ᾶς, ἡ, contr. from Ἀθηνάα or Ἀθηναία, Ion. Ἀθήνη, Ἀθηναίη, Dor. Ἀθάνα, Ἀθαναία, Aeol. Ἀθηνάα, *Athena*, Lat. *Minerva*, the tutelary goddess of Athens.

Ἀθήναζε, Adv. *to* or *towards Athens*. From

Ἀθῆναι, ῶν, αἱ, *the city of Athens*, used in pl. like Θῆβαι, Μυκῆναι, because it consisted of several parts.

Ἀθηναῖον, τό, (Ἀθηνᾶ) *the temple of Athena*.

Ἀθηναῖος, α, ον, (Ἀθηνᾶ) *Athenian, of* or *from Athens*.

Ἀθήνηθεν or **-θε**, Adv. *from Athens*.

Ἀθήνησι, Adv. *at Athens*.

ἀθηνιάω, *to long to be at Athens*.

Ἀθήνοθεν, Adv. *from Athens*.

ἈΘΗ΄Ρ, έρος, ὁ, *the beard* or *spike* of an ear of corn, *an ear of corn* itself, Lat. *spica*. II. *the point* or *barb* of a weapon. [ᾰ]

ἀ-θήρᾱτος, ον, (α privat., θηράω) *not to be caught*.

ἀ-θήρευτος, ον, (α privat., θηρεύω) *not hunted*.

ἀθηρη-λοιγός, ὁ, (ἀθήρ, λοιγός) *consumer of ears of corn*, of a winnowing fan: cf. ἀθηρό-βρωτος.

ἀθηρό-βρωτος, ον, (ἀθήρ, βιβρώσκω) *devouring ears of corn*: ἀθηρόβρωτον ὄργανον *a winnowing fan*.

ἄ-θηρος, ον, (α privat., θήρ) *without wild beasts* or *game*.

ἀ-θησαύριστος, ον, (α privat., θησαυρίζω) *not fit for hoarding up*.

ἀ-θῐγής, ές, (α privat., θιγεῖν) = ἄθικτος.

ἄ-θικτος, ον, (α privat., θιγγάνω) *untouched*: c. gen. *untouched by* a thing; κερδῶν ἄθικτος *untainted* by money; also c. dat. νόσοις ἄθικτος. 2. *not to be touched, holy, sacred*. II. act. *not touching*.

ἀθλεύω, contr. from Ep. ἀεθλεύω: fut. εύσω: (ἆθλος): —*to contend for a prize, combat, wrestle*. 2. *to struggle, endure, suffer*.

ἀθλέω, f. ήσω: aor. 1 ἤθλησα: pf. ἤθληκα: (ἆθλος): —*to contend for a prize*. 2. *to endure, suffer*. II. *to be an athlete*.

ἄθλημα, τό, (ἀθλέω) *a contest, struggle*. II. *an implement of labour*.

ἄθλησις, εως, ἡ, (ἀθλέω) *a contesting: a struggle, hard trial*.

ἀθλητήρ, ῆρος, ὁ, older form of ἀθλητής.

ἀθλητής, contr. from ἀεθλητής, οῦ, ὁ, (ἀθλέω) *a combatant, champion: a prize-fighter*, Lat. *athleta*. II. generally *one practised* or *skilled in* a thing, *master of* a thing, c. gen.

ἄθλιος, α, ον, also ος, ον, contr. from ἀέθλιος, (ἄεθλον, ἆθλον) *subject to the toils of conflict*: hence generally, *wretched*, Lat. *miser*. Hence

ἀθλιότης, ητος, ἡ, *suffering wretchedness*.

ἀθλο-θετήρ, ῆρος, ὁ, (ἆθλον, τίθημι) = ἀθλοθέτης.

ἀθλο-θέτης, ου, ὁ, (ἆθλον, τίθημι) *one who awards the prize, the judge* in the games, also βραβεύς.

ἎΘΛΟΝ, τό, contr. from Ep. ἄεθλον, *the prize of contest*, generally *a gift, present: a reward, recompence*. II. in plur. also = ἆθλος, *a contest, combat*.

ἎΘΛΟΣ, ὁ, contr. from Ep. ἄεθλος, *a contest* either in war or sport, esp. *contest for a prize: a conflict trouble*.

ἀθλοσύνη, ἡ, = ἆθλος.

ἀθλο-φόρος, ον, (ἆθλον, φέρω) *bearing away the prize, victorious*, of horses.

ἄ-θολος, ον, (α privat., θολός) *not muddy, clear*.

ἀ-θόλωτος, ον, (α privat., θολόω) *not muddied, untroubled*.

ἀ-θορύβητος, ον, (α privat., θορυβέω) *undisturbed*.

ἀ-θόρῠβος, ον, (α privat., θόρυβος) *without uproar, undisturbed, tranquil*. Adv. -βως.

ἄ-θραυστος, *ον*, (α privat., *θραύω*) *unbroken.*

'ΑΘΡΕ'Ω, Att. **ἀθρέω**: f. *ήσω*: aor. 2 *ἤθρησα*:—*to look closely at, gaze at, observe.* 2. later, of the mind, *to consider, think on, ponder*:—esp. in pres. and aor. 1 imperat. *ἄθρει, ἄθρησον, see, look, consider.*

ἀθρητέον, verb. Adj. of *ἀθρέω*, *one must consider.*

ἀθροίζω or **ἁθροίζω**: f. *σω*: aor. 1 *ἤθροισα*:—Pass., aor. 1 *ἠθροίσθην*: pf. *ἤθροισμαι*: (*ἀθρόος*):—*to gather together, collect*, esp. *to levy* forces; *πνεῦμα ἀθροίζειν to collect* one's breath:—Pass. *to be gathered* or *crowded together*: of armies, *to muster*: *φόβος ἤθροισται* fear *has gathered*, i. e. *has arisen.*

ἄθροισις, *εως*, *ἡ*, (*ἀθροίζω*) *a gathering, levying.*

ἄθροισμα, *τό*, (*ἀθροίζω*) *that which is gathered, a gathering, collection.*

ἀθροιστέον, verb. Adj. of *ἀθροίζω*, *one must collect.*

ἀθρόος, *α*, *ον*, old Att. **ἄθρους**, *ουν*: Comp. *ἀθροώτερος*, later *ἀθρούστερος*: (*ἅμα, θρόος*) *assembled in crowds, collected together*: *ἄθροοι* in crowds. II. *all at once, once for all*; *τὸ ἀθρόον the whole body, the mass*: *collective*; *ἀθρόα πάντ' ἀπέτισεν* he paid the penalty of all at once:—Adv. *ἀθρόον* and *ἀθρόως*, *at once, suddenly.* III. *immense, vast*: also *continuous, incessant.*

ἄ-θρυπτος, *ον*, (α privat., *θρύπτω*) *unbroken, imperishable.* II. *not enervated.*

ἀθῡμέω, f. *ήσω*, (*ἄθυμος*) *to be disheartened, to despond at* or *for* a thing.

ἀθῡμητέον, verb. Adj. of *ἀθυμέω*, *one must lose heart.*

ἀθῡμία, *ἡ*, (*ἄθυμος*) *want of heart, faintheartedness, despondency.*

ἄ-θῡμος, *ον*, *without heart* or *spirit, spiritless, fainthearted.* Adv., *ἀθύμως ἔχειν* to be *despondent.*

ἄθυρμα, *τό*, (*ἀθύρω*) *a plaything* or *toy*: *a delight.*

ἀθυρμάτιον, *τό*, Dim. of foreg., *a little toy, a pet.*

ἀθῠρό-γλωττος, *ον*, (*ἄθυρος, γλῶττα*) *unable to keep one's tongue within doors*: *a babbler, chatterer.*

ἄ-θῠρος, *ον*, (α privat., *θύρα*) *without a door.*

ἀθῠρό-στομος, *ον*, (*ἄθυρος, στόμα*) = *ἀθυρόγλωττος*, *babbling*, of Echo.

ἄ-θυρσος, *ον*, (α privat., *θύρσος*) *without thyrsus.*

'ΑΘΥ'ΡΩ, *to play, amuse oneself.* II. c. acc. *to play at* a thing, *do it in play.* [ᾰθῡ]

ἀ-θύρωτος, *ον*, (α privat., *θῠρόω*) *not closed by a door.*

ἄ-θῡτος, *ον*, (α privat., *θύω*) *not offered, not to be offered, not accepted in sacrifice*: generally, *unhallowed.* II. act. *without sacrificing.*

ἀ-θῷος, *ον*, (α privat., *θωή*) *unpunished, scot-free.* 2. c. gen. *free from the penalty of*, *ἄθῳος πληγῶν.* II. act. *harmless.*

ἀ-θώπευτος, *ον*, (α privat., *θωπεύω*) *without flattery*: hence, *rough, rude.*

ἀ-θωράκιστος, *ον*, (α privat., *θωρᾱκίζω*) *without breastplate.*

῎Αθως, *ω*, Ep. **'Αθόως**, *οῶ*, *ὁ*, *Mount Athos.*

αἰ, Conj., Ep. and Dor. for *εἰ*, *if.*

αἴ, Exclam. of strong desire, *O that! would that!* Lat. *utinam*, in Hom. always *αἰ γάρ.* See *αἴθε.*

ΑΙ'Α, *ἡ*, gen. *αἴης*, poët. for *γαῖα, γῆ*, *earth, land.*

αἴαγμα, *τό*, *a wailing cry, lament.* From

αἰάζω, f. *ξω*, *to cry αἰαῖ* or *ah! to wail*, and c. acc. *to bewail.*

αἰαῖ, Exclam. *alas!* Lat. *vae.*

αἰακτός, *ή*, *όν*, verb. Adj. of *αἰάζω*, *lamentable.*

αἰᾱνής, Ion. **αἰηνής**, *ές*, prob. from *αἰεί*, and so properly, *everlasting, never-ending*: hence *wearisome, irksome*: then generally, *dismal, horrible.*

Αἰαντίδης, *ου*, *ὁ*, (*Αἴας*, gen. *-αντος*) *son of Ajax.* II. at Athens, *a citizen of the tribe Αἰαντίς*, named after the Hero.

αἰᾱνῶς, Adv. (*αἰανής*) *for ever.*

Αἴας, *αντος*, *ὁ*, Ep. voc. *Αἶαν*, *Ajax.*

αἰβοί, *faugh!* exclam. of disgust or astonishment.

αἴγ-αγρος, *ὁ*, (*αἴξ, ἄγρος*) *a wild goat.*

Αἰγαῖος, *ον*, *Aegaean*: *Αἰγαῖον πέλαγος the Aegaean* sea, also called **Αἰγαίων**, *ωνος*, *ὁ*.

αἰγᾰνέη, *ἡ*, (*αἴξ*) *a hunting-spear, javelin.*

αἴγειος, *α* Ion. *η*, *ον*, (*αἴξ*) lengthd. for *αἴγεος*, *of a goat* or *goats*, Lat. *caprinus*: as Subst. *αἰγείη* (sub. *δορά*), *ἡ*, *a goat's skin.*

ΑΙ'ΓΕΙΡΟΣ, *ἡ*, *the black poplar*, Lat. *pōpulus*: cf. **λεύκη**.

αἰγ-ελάτης, *ου*, *ὁ*, (*αἴξ, ἐλαύνω*) *a goatherd.* [ᾰ]

αἴγεος, **α**, *ον*, = *αἴγειος.*

αἰγῐᾰλίτης, *ου*, *ὁ*, fem. *ῖτις*, *ιδος*, *on the shore.* From

αἰγῐᾰλός, *ὁ*, (*ἀΐσσω, ἅλς*) *the sea-shore, beach, strand.*

αἰγί-βοσις, *εως*, *ἡ*, (*αἴξ, βόσκω*) *a goat-pasture.*

αἰγῐ-βότης, *ου*, *ὁ*, (*αἴξ, βοτής*) *feeding goats.*

αἰγί-βοτος, *ον*, (*αἴξ, βόσκω*) *browsed by goats.*

αἰγί-θαλλος, *ἡ*, a bird, *the tit*, Lat. *parus.*

αἰγί-κνημος, *ον*, (*αἴξ, κνήμη*) *goat-shanked.*

αἰγῐ-κορεῖς, *έων*, *οἱ*, (*αἴξ, κορέννυμι*) *feeders of goats, goatherds.*

αἰγί-λιψ, *ῐπος*, *ὁ*, *ἡ*, (*αἴξ. λιπεῖν*) properly, *deserted even by goats*: hence *steep, sheer.* [γῐ]

αἴγῐλος, *ἡ*, (*αἴξ*) *an herb of which goats are fond.*

αἰγῐ-νόμος, *ον*, (*αἴξ, νέμω*) *browsed by goats.* 2. as Subst., *αἰγονόμος*, *ὁ*, *a goatherd.*

αἰγί-οχος, *ον*, (*αἰγίς, ἔχω*) *aegis-bearing.*

αἰγῐ-πόδης, *ου*, *ὁ*, (*αἴξ, πούς*) *goat-footed.*

αἰγί-πους, *ὁ*, *ἡ*, *πουν*, *τό*, gen. *ποδος*, = *αἰγιπόδης.*

αἰγί-πῡρος, *ὁ*, (*αἴξ*) a plant with a red flower, of which *goats* were fond.

αἰγίς, *ίδος*, *ἡ*, *the aegis*, or shield of Jupiter, described in Il. 5. 738; (from *ἀΐσσω*, *to rush* or *move violently*): hence 2. later *a rushing storm, hurricane*, terrible as the shaken aegis. II. from *αἴξ*, *a goat-skin coat.*

αἰγίσκος, *ὁ*, Dim. of *αἴξ*, *a little goat.*

αἰγλάεις, Dor. for *αἰγλήεις.*

αἰγλᾶς, *ᾶντος*, contr. for *αἰγλάεις.*

ΑΙ'ΓΛΗ, *ἡ*, *the light of the sun, daylight*: *any bright light, glitter, lustre, gleam*, of metal. 2. metaph. *splendour, glory.* Hence

αἰγλήεις, εσσα, εν, *beaming, radiant.*

αἰγλο-φᾰνής, ές, (αἴγλη, φανῆναι) *beaming: brilliant, lustrous.*

αἰγο-βοσκός, όν, (αἴξ, βόσκω) *tending goats:* as Subst. *a goatherd.*

αἰγό-κερως, ων, gen. ω, also **αἰγοκέρως**, ωτος, ὁ, (αἴξ, κέρας) *goat-horned.* II. as Subst., αἰγόκερως, ὁ, *Capricorn* in the Zodiac.

αἰγο-νόμος, ὁ, = αἰγινόμος, *a goatherd.*

αἰγ-όνυξ, ῠχος, ὁ, ἡ, (αἴξ, ὄνυξ) = αἰγῶνυξ.

αἰγο-πόδης, ὁ, = αἰγιπόδης.

αἰγο-πρόσωπος, ον, (αἴξ, πρόσωπον) *goat-faced.*

αἰγο-τρῐχέω, f. ήσω, (αἴξ, θρίξ) *to have goat's hair.*

αἰγῠπιός, ὁ, (γύψ) *a vulture*, Lat. *vultur.*

Αἰγυπτιάζω, f. άσω, *to speak Egyptian.*

Αἰγυπτιστί, Adv. *in the Egyptian tongue.* II. *like an Egyptian, craftily.*

Αἰγυπτο-γενής, ές, (Αἴγυπτος, γένος) *of Egyptian race.*

Αἴγυπτος, ὁ, *the river Nile.* II. Αἴγυπτος, ἡ, *Egypt:* as Adv., Αἰγυπτόνδε, *to Egypt.*

αἰγ-ῶνυξ, ῠχος, ὁ, ἡ, (αἴξ, ὄνυξ) *goat-hoofed.*

Ἀΐδας, Dor. for Ἀΐδης, Ἅιδης.

αἰδεῖο, Ep. for αἴδεο, αἴδου, pres. imperat. of αἰδέομαι.

ΑἸΔΕ΄ΟΜΑΙ: fut. αἰδέσομαι, Ep. -έσσομαι: aor. 1 ᾐδεσάμην, Ep. imperat. αἴδεσσαι; also in pass. form ᾐδέσθην, Ep. 3 pl. αἴδεσθεν: Dep.:—*to feel shame, be ashamed* or *fear:* also *to respect, reverence* a person:—c. inf. *to be ashamed* or *afraid* to do a thing. 2. as Att. law-term, *to feel pity for*, hence *to pardon*, esp. in aor. 1 αἰδέσασθαι.

αἴδεσθεν, for αἰδέσθησαν, 3 pl. aor. 1 of αἰδέομαι.

αἰδέσθητι, aor. 1 imper. of αἰδέομαι.

αἰδέσιμος, ον, (αἰδέομαι) *venerable.*

αἴδεσις, εως, ἡ, (αἰδέομαι) *reverence, compassion.*

αἰδέσσομαι, Ep. fut. of αἰδέομαι.

ἀ-ΐδηλος, ον, (α privat., ἰδεῖν) *making unseen:* hence *annihilating, destroying.* II. pass. *unseen, unknown, obscure.*

αἰδήμων, ον, gen. ονος, (αἰδέομαι) *bashful, modest:* Sup. αἰδημονέστερος. Adv. -μόνως.

ἀ-ϊδής, ές, (α privat., ἰδεῖν) *unseen: destroyed.*

Ἀΐδης, εω, ὁ, Att. Ἅιδης or ᾅδης, ου, (ἀϊδής) *Hades*, the god of the world below, Lat. *Pluto.*

ἀΐδιος, ον, (ἀεί) *everlasting*, for ἀείδιος.

ἀ-ϊδνός, ή, όν, (α privat., ἰδεῖν) poët. for ἀ-ϊδής, *unseen, hidden, dark.*

αἰδοιέστερος, -έστατος, Comp. and Sup. of αἰδοῖος.

αἰδοῖον, τό, mostly in plur. τὰ **αἰδοῖα**, *the genitals, pudenda:* properly neut. from

αἰδοῖος, α, ον: Comp. αἰδοιότερος and -έστερος, Sup. -έστατος: (αἰδέομαι) *regarded with awe* or *reverence, august, venerable:* of women, *deserving respect, tender:* of things, *valuable, excellent.* II. act. *bashful, modest.* 2. *reverent.*

αἰδοίως, Adv. of αἰδοῖος, *reverently.*

ΑἼΔΟΜΑΙ, impf. αἰδόμην, Ep. for αἰδέομαι, ᾐδεόμην.

Ἄϊδος, **Ἄϊδι**, Ep. gen. and dat. of Ἀΐδης, from an obsol. nom. **Ἄϊς**: Ἄϊδόσδε, and εἰς Ἄϊδόσδε, *to the dwelling of Hades:* εἰν Ἄϊδος (sc. οἴκῳ), Att. ἐν ᾅδου, *in Hades.* [ᾰϊδ-, but ᾱ sometimes.]

αἰδό-φρων, ον, gen. ονος, (αἰδώς, φρήν) *feeling respect in mind, compassionate.*

ἀ-ϊδρείη or -ίη [ῐ], ἡ, Ep. and Ion. word (ἄϊδρις) *want of knowledge, ignorance:* Ep. dat. pl. ἀϊδρείῃσι.

ἄ-ϊδρις, ι, gen. ιος and εος, (α privat., ἴδρις) *unknowing, ignorant.*

ἀϊδρο-δίκης, ου, Dor. **-δίκας**, α, ὁ, (ἄϊδρις, δίκη) *unknowing of right* or *law, lawless, savage.* [δῐ]

ἀ-ΐδρῡτος, ον, = ἀν-ίδρυτος, *unsettled, unsteady*

Ἀϊδωνεύς, ὁ, lengthd. Ep. form of Ἀΐδης.

ΑἸΔΩ΄Σ, όος, contr. οῦς, ἡ, *sense of shame, bashfulness, modesty: a sense of shame* or *honour*, αἰδῶ θέσθ' ἐνὶ θυμῷ: *regard for others, respect, reverence.* II. *that which causes shame* or *respect*, and so 1. *a shame, scandal;* αἰδώς, Ἀργεῖοι *shame*, ye Argives! 2. = τὰ αἰδοῖα. 3. *dignity, majesty.*

αἰεί, Ion. and poët. for ἀεί.

αἰει-γενέτης, ὁ, poët. for ἀει-γενέτης, *ever existing.* (For compds. of αἰεί here omitted, v. sub ἀεί-.)

αἰέλ-ουρος, ὁ, ἡ, Ion. for αἴλουρος.

αἰέν, = αἰεί.

αἰέν-υπνος, ον, (αἰέν, ὕπνος) *lulling in eternal sleep.*

αἰές, Dor. for ἀεί, αἰεί.

αἰετός, ὁ, lengthd. form of ἀετός, *an eagle.*

αἰζήϊος, lengthd. form of αἰζηός.

αἰζηός, ὁ, *an active, vigorous, lusty person: a man.* (Deriv. uncertain.)

αἴητος, like ἄητος, *terrible, mighty.*

αἰητός, ὁ, Dor. of ἀετός, αἰετός, *an eagle.*

αἰθάλη, ἡ, (αἴθω) = αἴθαλος, *soot.* [θᾰ]

αἰθᾰλίων, ωνος, (αἴθαλος) *swarthy, dusky.*

αἰθᾰλόεις, όεσσα, όεν, contr. **αἰθαλοῦς**, οῦσσα, οῦν, (αἴθαλος) *smoky, sooty, black.* II. *burning, blazing.*

ΑἼΘΑΛΟΣ, ὁ, like λιγνύς, *a smoky flame*, the *thick smoke* of fire, *soot.* [θᾰ] Hence

αἰθᾰλόω, f. ώσω, *to burn to soot* or *ashes:*—Pass. *to lie in ashes.*

αἶθε, Dor. and Ep. for εἴθε, *O that! would that!* Lat. *utinam*, αἴθ' ὄφελες *O that* thou hadst.., c. inf.

αἰθερ-εμβᾰτέω, (αἰθήρ, ἐμβατέω) *to walk in ether.*

αἰθέριος, α, ον or ος, ον, (αἰθήρ) *of* or *belonging to the ether* or *upper air*, as opp. to ἠέριος, and so 1. *high in air, on high.* 2. *ethereal, heavenly.*

αἰθερο-βᾰτέω, (αἰθήρ, βατέω) = αἰθερεμβατέω, *to walk in ether.*

αἰθεροδρομέω, *to skim the ether.* From

αἰθερο-δρόμος, ον, (αἰθήρ, δραμεῖν) *skimming the ether.*

αἰθήρ, έρος, in Homer always ἡ, in Att. prose always ὁ, in Pindar and Att. Poets common: (αἴθω):

μόρροια, ἡ, *a discharge of blood.*
μόρ-ροος, ον, (αἷμα, ῥέω) *streaming with blood.*
μόρ-ρῦτος, poët. **αἱμό-ρῦτος**, ον, (αἷμα, ῥέω) *od-streaming.*
ΓΜΟΣ, ὁ, *a thorn.*
μο-στᾰγής, ές, = αἱματο-σταγής.
μο-φόρυκτος, ον, (αἷμα, φορύσσω) *defiled with od.*
μόω, = αἱματόω.
ιμύλιος, ον, (αἱμύλος) *flattering, winning, wily.* [ῡ]
αἱμῠλο-μήτης, ου, ὁ, (αἱμύλος, μῆτις) *of winning iles.*
ΑΙΜΥ΄ΛΟΣ, η, ον, also **ος, ον**, *flattering, winning, heedling, wily.* [ῡ]
αἵμων, ονος, ὁ, = δαίμων, δαήμων, *knowing, skilul.* II. (αἷμα) *bloody.*
αἱμ-ωπός, όν, = αἱματωπός, *bloody to behold.*
αἰν-ᾰρέτης, ου, ὁ, (αἰνός, ἀρετή) *terribly brave.*
Αἰνείας, ου, ὁ, *Aeneas*, Ep. gen. Αἰνείᾱο or Αἰνείω.
αἴνεσις, εως, ἡ, (αἰνέω) *a praising, praise.*
αἰνετός, ή, όν, verb. Adj. *praised, praiseworthy.* From
αἰνέω: impf. ᾔνεον, contr. ᾔνουν, Ion. αἴνεον: fut. -ήσω, Att. -έσω: aor. 1 ᾔνησα, Att. ᾔνεσα, Ion. αἴνεσα: pf. Att. ᾔνεκα:—Mid., aor. ᾐνεσάμην:—Pass., aor. 1 ᾐνέθην: pf. ᾔνημαι:—properly *to tell* or *speak of* (cf. αἶνος); but usu. *to speak in praise of, praise, approve*, c. acc., Lat. *laudare.* 2. *to allow, recommend.* 3. like ἀγαπάω, *to be content with, acquiesce in.* 4. *to decline courteously*, like Lat. *laudare.* II. *to promise* or *vow.*
ΑΙ΄ΝΗ, ἡ, = αἶνος, *praise, fame.*
αἴνημι, Aeol. for αἰνέω.
αἰνῇσι, Ion. for αἰναῖς, dat. pl. of αἰνός.
αἰνητός, ή, όν, poët. for αἰνετός.
αἴνιγμα, ατος, τό, (αἰνίσσομαι) *a dark saying, riddle*: oft. in plur. διὰ or ἐξ αἰνιγμάτων *in riddles*, darkly; also ἐν αἰνίγμασιν.
αἰνιγματ-ώδης, ες, (αἴνιγμα, εἶδος) *riddling, dark.*
αἰνιγμός, ὁ, (αἰνίσσομαι) *a speaking in riddles*: mostly in plur. like αἴνιγμα.
αἰνίζομαι, Dep. = αἰνέω.
αἰνικτήριος, ον, (αἰνίσσομαι) *riddling.* Adv. -ίως, *riddlingly.*
αἰνικτός, ή, όν, *expressed in riddles, riddling*: from
αἰνίσσομαι, Att. **αἰνίττομαι**, f. ίξομαι: aor. 1 ᾐνιξάμην: Dep.: (αἶνος):—*to speak darkly* or *in riddles, to hint* a thing, *give to understand.* II. in pass. sense, aor. 1 pass. ᾐνίχθην, pf. ᾔνιγμαι, *to be spoken riddlingly.*
αἰνο-βίας, Ion. **αἰνο-βίης**, ου, ὁ, (αἰνός, βία) *fearfully strong.*
αἰνό-γᾰμος, ον, (αἰνός, γαμέω) *fatally wedded.*
αἰνόθεν, Adv. of αἰνός,—ἐξ αἰνοῦ, in the phrase αἰνόθεν αἰνῶς, *from horror to horror, very horribly.*
αἰνό-θρυπτος, ον, (αἰνός, θρύπτομαι) *dreadfu enervated.*
... **λαμπής**, ές, (αἰ... ...λάμπω) *horrid-gleaming*
... (α... ...ος) *fatally wedded*

αἰνο-λέων, οντος, ὁ, (αἰνός, λέων) *a dreadful lion.*
αἰνό-λῐνος, ον, (αἰνός, λίνον) *of fearful destiny*, in allusion to the *thread* of life.
αἰνό-λῠκος, ὁ, (αἰνός, λύκος) *a horrible wolf.*
αἰνό-μορος, ον, (αἰνός, μόρος) *doomed to a sad end*
αἰνο-πᾰθής, ές, (αἰνός, παθεῖν) *suffering dire ills.*
Αἰνό-παρις, ὁ, (αἰνός, Πάρις) *terrible Paris*: cp Δύσπαρις.
αἰνο-πᾰτήρ, έρος, ὁ, (αἰνός, πατήρ) *unhappy fat*
ΑΙ΄ΝΟΣ, ὁ, *a tale, story*, elsewh. μῦθος; αἰνεῖν αἶνον to tell *a tale*: *a fable*, like Aesop's: generally, *a saying, proverb.* II. later, *that which is said to one's praise, praise.*
ΑΙΝΟ΄Σ, ή, όν, Ep. word = δεινός, *dread, dire*: of persons, *dread, terrible*, esp. of Zeus:—neut. pl. αἰνά as Adv. *terribly*; Sup. αἰνότατον, *most terribly.*
αἰνο-τόκεια, ἡ, as fem. Adj. (αἰνός, τόκος) *unhappy in giving birth, unhappy in being a mother.*
αἰνο-τύραννος, ὁ, (αἰνός, τύραννος) *dreadful tyrant.*
ΑΙ΄ΝΥΜΑΙ, defect. Dep. used only in pres., & impf. without augm., like αἴρω, ἄρνυμαι, *to take, to hold of*, c. gen.: also *to enjoy, feed on.*
αἰνῶς, Adv. of αἰνός, *terribly*, i. e. *very much, exceedingly*; αἰνῶς πικρός *terribly* bitter.
αἴξ, αἰγός, ὁ, ἡ, dat. pl. **αἴγεσιν**, (ἀΐσσω) *a goat*; αἲξ ἀγρία or ἄγριος, *the chamois*; **αἲξ ἴξαλος** ἀγρία, *the ibex.*
ἀΐξασκε, Ep. 3 sing. aor. of ἀΐσσω.
ἀΐξω, fut. of ἀΐσσω.
ΑΙΟ΄ΛΛΩ, *to shift rapidly to and fro*:—Pass. *to change in colour* or *hue*; ὄμφακες αἰόλλονται the grapes *begin to turn*, Lat. *variegantur.*
αἰολο-βρόντης, ου, ὁ, (αἰόλος, βροντή) *wielder of forked lightning.*
αἰολο-θώρηξ, ηκος, ὁ, (αἰόλος, θώρηξ) *with gleaming breastplate.*
αἰολό-μητις, ιος, ὁ, ἡ, (αἰόλος, μῆτις) *full of various wiles.*
αἰολο-μίτρης, ου, ὁ (αἰόλος, μίτρα) *with gleaming belt* (for it was plated with metal); cf. αἰολοθώρηξ. II. *with variegated turban.*
αἰολό-πωλος, ον, (αἰόλος, πῶλος) *with quick-moving steeds.*
ΑΙΟ΄ΛΟΣ, η, ον, *quick-moving, rapid*: of worm *wriggling*: as epith. of armour, *easily-wielded, manageable.* II. *changeful of hue, gleaming, glancing*; αἰόλη νύξ *spangled* night; αἰ... flesh *discoloured* from disease. III *changeful, shifting, varied.*
As prop. n., pr... god of the win...
αἰολό-στ...
ing, riddli...
αἰ...
s

—*ether, the upper, purer air*, opp. to ἀήρ (*the lower air* or *atmosphere*) :—hence *the clear sky* or *heaven*, as the abode of the gods. Cp. ἀήρ.

Αἰθιοπῆας, irregular pl. acc. of Αἰθίοψ.

Αἰθί-οψ, *οπος*, ὁ, fem. **Αἰθιοπίς**, *ίδος*, (αἴθω, ὄψ) *an Ethiop, negro*, properly *Burnt-face*.

αἶθος, *τό*, and ὁ, (αἴθω) *burning heat, fire*.

αἰθός, *ή, όν*, (αἴθω) *burnt* :—*fire-coloured, fiery*.

αἴθουσα (sc. *στοά*), ἡ, (αἴθω) *the corridor* or *vestibule* of a house; mostly looking East or South, to catch the sun,—whence the name.

αἴθ-οψ, *οπος*, (αἰθός, ὄψ) *fiery-looking*, of metal, *flashing*; of wine, *sparkling*. II. metaph. *fiery, hot, keen*.

αἴθρη, later **αἴθρα**, ἡ, (αἰθήρ) *clear sky, fair weather*, Lat. *sudum*.

αἰθρη-γενέτης, *ου*, ὁ, = *αἰθρηγενής*.

αἰθρη-γενής, *ές*, (αἴθρη, γενέσθαι) *born from ether*.

αἰθρία, ἡ, = *αἴθρη* : used absol. in gen. *αἰθρίας* (sub. ..ης), *in fine weather*, Lat. *per purum*. II. *the* ..*n sky*.

..ἰθριάζω or –*ιάω*, *to be clear*, of the sky.

..ἰθριο-κοιτέω, f. *ήσω*, (αἰθρία, κοίτη) *to sleep in the* ..*en air*.

αἴθριος, *ον*, (αἴθρη) *clear, bright, fair*. II. *in the open air* : hence *cold, chill*.

αἶθρος, ὁ, = *αἴθρη* : esp. *the clear chill air* of morn.

ΑΙ'ΘΥΙΑ, ἡ, *a sea-gull* or *diver*, Lat. *mergus*.

αἰθυκτήρ, *ῆρος*, ὁ, (αἰθύσσω) *one that darts rapidly*.

αἰθύσσω, f. *ύξω* (αἴθω) *to put in rapid motion; to kindle* :—Pass. *to move rapidly, quiver*.

ΑΙ'ΘΩ, only found in pres. and impf. *ῇθον*, *to light up, kindle* :—Pass. *to burn*. 2. rarely intr. *to burn* or *blaze*.

αἴθων, *ωνος*, ὁ, (αἴθω) properly *fiery, burning*. II. of metal, *flashing, glittering*. III. of animals, *fiery, fierce*; or perh. of their colour, *yellow, tawny*, like Lat. *fulvus, rufus*.

αἶκα, conj., Dor. for *εἴ κε*, *ἐάν*, with subj. *if haply*.

ΑΙΓΚΑ'ΛΛΩ, f. *αἰκᾰλῶ*, properly of a dog, *to wag the tail fawningly* : *to wheedle, fondle*.

αἴκε, αἴκεν, Conj., Ep. and Dor. for *ἐάν*.

αἰκεία, ἡ, = *αἰκία*, q. v.

αἰκέλιος, *ον*, = *ἀεικέλιος*.

ἀΐκή, ἡ, (ἀΐσσω) *rapid motion, a rush*, Lat. *im-* .. [ῑ]

.. poet. for *ἀεικής*, contr. **αἰκής**, *unseemly*. ..*nseemly fashion*.

..he Ion. *ἀεικείη*, *injurious* ..*ffront* : oft. also in

affront, out- .. : m..tly as

ἄ-ϊκτος, *ον*, (α privat., *ἱκνέομαι*) *unapproachabl*

αἴ-λῐνος, ὁ, *a mournful dirge*, (from *αἴ*, *Λίνος me for Linus!*) 2. also Adj. *ος, ον*, *plain mournful*.

αἴλ-ουρος or **αἰέλ-ουρος**, *ον*, ὁ, ἡ, (αἰόλος, οὐρ. *cat*, so called from the *wavy motion of the tail*.

ΑΙ'ΜΑ, *ατος, τό*, *blood* : in plur. *streams of bl*.. —also *bloodshed*; *εἴργασται μητρῷον αἷμα* a mot.. *blood* has been shed; *αἷμα πράττειν* to shed *bl*.. *ἐφ' αἵματι φεύγειν* to be banished for *homicide*. like Lat. *sanguis, blood-relationship, kin*.

αἱμᾰ-κορίαι or **αἱμα-κουρίαι**, *ῶν, αἱ*, (αἷμα, κορ.. *νυμι*) *offerings of blood*, made upon the grave appease the manes.

αἱμακτός, *ή, όν*, verb. Adj. of **αἱμάσσω**, *stained wi*.. *blood, bloody*.

αἱμᾰλέος, *α, ον*, (αἷμα) *bloody, blood-red*.

αἱμάς, *άδος*, ἡ, (αἷμα) *a gush* or *stream of blood*.

αἱμᾰσία, ἡ, *a wall of dry stones*, Lat. *maceria* : a.. *fence*. (Deriv. uncertain.)

αἱμᾰσι-ώδης, *ες*, (αἱμασία, εἶδος) *like a fence* .. *hedge*.

αἱμάσσω, Att. **αἱμάττω** : f. *άξω* : aor. 1 *ᾕμαξ*.. (αἷμα) :—*to make bloody, stain with blood* : hence *to wound, draw blood, slay* :—Pass. *to welter in blood, be slain*.

αἱμᾰτ-εκχῠσία, ἡ, (αἷμα, ἐκχέω) *shedding of blood*

αἱμᾰτηρός, *ά, όν*, (αἷμα) *bloody, blood-stained, murderous*. II. *consisting of blood*.

αἱμᾰτη-φόρος, *ον*, (αἷμα, φέρω) *bringing b'oo*.. *murderous*.

αἱμᾰτόεις, *εσσα, εν*, (αἷμα) *bloody, covered wit*.. *blood*. 2. *blood-red*, or *consisting of blood*. 3 *bloody, murderous*.

αἱμᾰτο-λοιχός, *όν*, (αἷμα, λείχω) *licking blood*; ἔρα.. *αἱμ.* thirst *for blood*.

αἱμᾰτο-πώτης, *ου*, ὁ, (αἷμα, πίνω) *a blood-drinker blood-sucker*.

αἱμᾰτορ-ρόφος, *ον*, (αἷμα, ῥοφέω) *blood-drinking*.

αἱμᾰτόρ-ρῠτος, *ον*, (αἷμα, ῥέω) *blood-streaming*.

αἱμᾰτο-στᾰγής, *ές*, (αἷμα, στάζω) *blood-dripping*.

αἱμᾰτό-φυρτος, *ον*, (αἷμα, φύρω) *blood-stained*.

αἱμᾰτο-χάρμης, *ου*, ὁ, (αἷμα, χαίρω) *delighting in blood*.

αἱμᾰτόω, f. *ώσω* : aor. 1 *ᾑμάτωσα* :—Pass., pf. *ᾑμάτωμαι* : (αἷμα) *to make bloody*.

αἱμᾰτ-ώδης, *ες*, (αἷμα, εἶδος) *looking like blood, blood-red*.

αἱμᾰτ-ωπός, *όν*, and **αἱματ-ώψ**, *ῶπος*, ὁ, ἡ, (αἷμα, ὤψ) *bloody to behold*.

αἵμνιον, *τό*, (αἷμα) *a basin for blood*.

αἱμο-βᾰφής, *ές*, (αἷμα, βάπτω) *bathed in blood*.

αἱμο-βόρος, *ον*, (αἷμα, βορά) *greedy for blood*.

αἱμό-διψος, *ον*, (αἷμα, δίψα) *bloodthirsty*.

αἱμορ-ρᾰγής, *ές*, (αἷμα, ῥαγῆναι) *bleeding violently*.

αἱμόρ-ραντος, *ον*, (αἷμα, ῥαίνω) *blood-sprinkled*.

αἱμορροέω, f. *ήσω*, (α.. ..ροος) *to lose blood* ..*ave a discharge of* .. ..ence

αἰπήεις, εσσα, εν, poët. for *αἰπεινός*.

αἰπολέω, f. ήσω, (αἰπόλος) *to be a goatherd*:—Pass. *feed, browse*.

αἰπολικός, ή, όν, (αἰπόλος) *of* or *for goatherds*.

αἰπόλιον, τό, (αἰπόλος) *a herd of goats*. II. *a* *oat-pasture*.

αἰ-πόλος, for αἰγο-πόλος, ὁ, (αἴξ, πολέω) *a goatherd*.

ΑΙ'ΠΟΣ, εος, τό, *a height, a steep*; πρὸς αἶπος p-*hill*.

ΑΙΠΟ'Σ, ή, όν, Ep. for *αἰπύς, high, lofty*, of cities: *ιπὰ ῥέεθρα rapid* torrent

αἰπῠ-μήτης, ου, ὁ, (αἰπύς, μῆτις) *with high thoughts*.

αἰπύ-νωτος, ον, (αἰπύς, νῶτος) *high-backed, on a igh ridge*. [ῠ]

ΑΙΠΥ'Σ, εῖα, ύ, *high and steep*, of cities on steep ocks; *βρόχος αἰπύς* a noose *hanging straight own*. 2. *headlong; αἰπὺς ὄλεθρος sheer, utter* estruction; *αἰπὺς χόλος towering* wrath. 3. meaph. *hard, difficult; αἰπύ οἱ ἐσσεῖται* it will be *hard vork* for him.

αἱρέσιμος, ον, (αἱρέω) *that can be taken*.

αἵρεσις, εως, (αἱρέω) *a taking, conquering*, esp. of town. II. (αἱρέομαι) *a taking for oneself, hoosing, choice; αἵρεσιν διδόναι* to give *choice; αἵρειν λαμβάνειν* to have *choice* given one. 2. *choice* r *election* of magistrates. III. *a choice, plan, urpose*. 2. *a sect* or *school* of philosophy. 3. *heresy*.

αἱρετέον, verb. Adj. of *αἱρέω, one must take* or *hoose*. II. **αἱρετέος**, α, ον, *desirable*.

αἱρετίζω, f. ίσω, (αἱρέω) *to choose*. II. *to belong o a sect*.

αἱρετικός, ή, όν, (αἱρέω) *able to choose*. 2. *hereical*.

αἱρετός, ή, όν, verb. Adj. of *αἱρέω, that may be aken* or *conquered*. II. (αἱρέομαι) *to be chosen, referable, desirable*. 2. *chosen, elected*.

ΑΙ'ΡΕ'Ω: impf. ᾕρεον, Ion. αἵρεον: fut. αἱρήσω: f. ᾕρηκα, Ion. ἀραίρηκα: Ion. plqpf. ἀραιρήκεα.—Ied., fut. αἱρήσομαι: aor. 1 ᾑρησάμην.—Pass., fut. ἱρεθήσομαι, also ᾑρήσομαι: aor. 1 ᾑρέθην: pf. ᾕρηαι: plqpf. ᾑρήμην.—Also from the root *ἝΛΩ, aor. εἷλον, Ion. 3 sing. ἕλεσκε, inf. ἑλεῖν: fut. med. λοῦμαι; aor. 2 εἱλόμην; Ep. 3 sing. γέντο, for λετο: rarely aor. 1 εἱλάμην.

Act. *to take with the hand, grasp, seize*. 2. *to ke away*. II. *to get into one's power, conquer, erpower, seize: to kill*. 2. *to catch, take: to n, seduce*. 3. generally, *to win, gain*. 4. as t. law-term, *to convict* a person of a thing. 5. ὁ γος αἱρεῖ, Lat. *ratio evincit*, reason *proves*. III. *grasp with the mind, take in, understand*.

Med. *αἱρέομαι, to take for oneself*. II. *to take oneself, choose*: hence *to take in preference, prefer* thing to another: also *μᾶλλον αἱρεῖσθαι to choose* preference, Lat. *potius malle*. 2. *to choose by* , *elect* to an office.

-ϊρος, ὁ, Ἶρος Ἄ-ϊρος, Irus *unhappy Irus*.

ΑΙ'ΡΩ, Att. for **ἀείρω**: f. ἀρῶ [ᾰ]: aor. ἦρα, imperat. ἆρον, inf. ἆραι: pf. ἦρκα.—Med., impf. ᾑρόμην: fut. ἀροῦμαι [ᾰ]: aor. 1 ἠράμην: aor. ἠρ Ep. ἀρόμην: Pass., fut. ἀρθήσομαι: aor. 1 ἤρ pf. ἦρμαι.

Act. *to raise, raise* or *lift up, to carry*; α πόδα to walk; *αἴρ. σημεῖον to hoist* a signal; *ναῦς to get* ships *under way*: hence 2. in *to get under way, start, set out; αἴρειν ταῖς νι* to set sail; *αἴρειν τῷ στρατῷ* to march:—Pass *mount up, ascend*. II. *to raise, exalt; αἴρ θυμόν to raise* one's courage, etc. 2. *to raise words, extol, exaggerate*, Lat. *tollere*:—Pass. *to ris to a height, increase*. III. *to lift and take away, to take away, put an end to*: later *to kill*.

Med. *to lift, raise for oneself*: hence *to carry off, win, gain*. II. *to take upon oneself, undergo, bear*. 2. *to undertake, begin*. III. of sound, *αἴρεσθαι φωνήν to lift up* one's voice.

ΑΙ'ΣΑ, ἡ, as pr. n., like Μοῖρα, *the goddess of fate*, Lat. *Parca*. II. as appellat. *the fatal decree* of a god; *Διὸς αἶσα the fate decreed* by Jove. 2. *one's appointed lot, fate, destiny, κακῇ αἴσῃ* by ill *luck*:—*one's share* or *lot in* a thing; *ληΐδος αἶσα one's share* of booty. 3. *one's due* or *right; κατ' αἶσαν*, like *κατὰ μοῖραν, fittingly, rightly*.

αἰσθάνομαι, impf. ᾐσθανόμην: fut. αἰσθήσομαι: aor. 2 ᾐσθόμην, later aor. 1 ᾐσθησάμην: Dep.: (ἀΐω, ἀίσθω):—*to perceive* or *apprehend by the senses*, and therefore sometimes *to feel*, sometimes *to see*, sometimes *to hear* or *learn*. Often followed by acc.; but also c. gen. *to be sensible of, to take notice of* a thing. Hence

αἴσθημα, ατος, τό, *the thing perceived: perception* or *sense of* a thing.

αἴσθησις, εως, ἡ, (αἰσθάνομαι) *perception by the senses*, esp. by feeling, but also by seeing, hearing, etc., *a sensation, sense* of a thing; *αἴσθησιν ἔχειν to have perception of* a thing; *αἴσθησιν παρέχειν* to give *the means of perception*. II. in plur. *the senses*. III. like *αἴσθημα, a perception*: in hunting, *the scent*.

αἰσθητήριον, τό, (αἰσθάνομαι) *an organ of sense*.

αἰσθητής, οῦ, ὁ, (αἰσθάνομαι) *one who perceives*.

αἰσθητικός, ή, όν, (αἰσθάνομαι) *of* or *capable of perception, perceptive*. 2. pass. *perceptible*.

αἰσθητός, ή, όν, verb. Adj. of *αἰσθάνομαι, perceived by the senses, sensible*.

ἀΐσθω, (*ἄω, ἄημι) *to breathe forth*, Lat. *expiro; θυμὸν ἄϊσθε he was giving up* the ghost, *was expiring*.

αἰσιμία, *happiness*. From

αἴσιμος, ον, also η, ον, (αἶσα) Lat. *fatalis, appointed by fate, fated, destined; αἴσιμον ἦμαρ* the *fated* day, i. e. the day *of death*. II. *agreeable to fate, meet, right; αἴσιμα εἰδώς* knowing *what is right and proper*.

αἴσιος, ον, also α, ον, (αἶσα) *bodi*-- *happy: opportu*--.

ἄ-ϊσος, ον, (α privat., ἴσος) = ἄν-ισος, unlike, unequal.

ΑΙ'ΣΣΩ, Att. ᾄσσω or ᾄττω: impf. ἤϊσσον, Att. ᾖσσον, Ion. ἀΐσσεσκον: fut. ἀΐξω, Att. ᾄξω: aor. ἤϊξα, Att. ᾖξα, Ion. ἀΐξασκον.—Med., aor. 1 ἠϊξάμην. Pass., aor. ἠΐχθην, Ion. ἀΐχθην:—to move with a shooting motion, to shoot, dart, glance, Lat. ..., ..ipetu ferri; so also in aor. 1 med. ἀΐξασθαι, in aor. 1 pass. ἀϊχθῆναι. 2. later, to be eager ...r. II. trans. to move a thing quickly. [ᾱ in Homer: in Trag. ᾰ when trisyll.]

ἄ-ϊστος, Att. ἄιστος, ον, (α privat., ἰδεῖν) unseen, unknown, not to be seen and heard: hence vanished, destroyed: see ἀΐδηλος. II. act. not seeing or knowing, ignorant of, c. gen.

ἀϊστόω, Att. αἰστόω: f. ώσω: aor. 1 ἠΐστωσα, Att. ᾔστωσα.—Pass., aor. 1 ἠϊστώθην, Ion. ἀϊστώθην: (ἄϊστος):—to make unseen, to destroy: to slay, kill.

ἀΐστωρ, ορος, ὁ, ἡ, (ἀ-ἵστωρ) unknowing, inexperienced.

ἀϊστώσειαν, 3 pl. aor. 1 opt. of ἀϊστόω.

αἴσυλος, ον, opp. to αἴσιμος, unseemly, evil, impious. (Deriv. uncertain.)

αἰσυμνάω, f. ήσω, (αἶσα) to give each his due or portion of a thing, hence to be ruler over, c. gen. Hence

αἰσυμνήτης, ου, ὁ, a regulator of games, chosen by the people, a judge or umpire. II. a ruler, king, esp. one chosen by the people: a president, manager.

αἰσχίων, ον, gen. ονος, and αἴσχιστος, η, ον, Comp. and Sup. of αἰσχρός, formed from αἶσχος.

ΑΙ'ΣΧΟΣ, εος, τό, shame, disgrace. II. ugliness or deformity.

αἰσχρήμων, ον, gen. ονος, (αἶσχος) shameful.

αἰσχροκέρδεια, ἡ, sordid love of gain. From

αἰσχρο-κερδής, ές, (αἰσχρός, κέρδος) sordidly greedy of gain, covetous. Adv. -δῶς.

αἰσχρολογία, ἡ, foul language, abuse. From

αἰσχρο-λόγος, ον, (αἰσχρός, λέγω) foul-mouthed, abusive.

αἰσχρό-μητις, ιος, ὁ, ἡ, (αἰσχρός, μῆτις) forming base designs.

αἰσχρο-ποιός, όν, (αἰσχρός, ποιέω) acting shamefully.

αἰσχρός, ά, όν, also ός, όν, (αἶσχος) in Homer causing shame, disgracing; αἰσχρὰ ἔπεα abusive words. II. opp. to καλός: 1. ugly, ill-favoured. 2. in moral sense, shameful, disgraceful, base, infamous; τὸ καλὸν καὶ τὸ αἰσχρόν, Lat. honestum et turpe, virtue and vice.—Instead of the regul. Comp. and Sup. αἰσχρότερος, αἰσχρότατος, the forms αἰσχίων, αἴσχιστος are used. Hence

αἰσχρότης, ητος, ἡ, ugliness. 2. shame, infamy.

αἰσχρουργία, ἡ, contr. for αἰσχροεργία, (αἰσχρός, ἔργον) lewd conduct.

... of αἰσχρός, shamefully.

... of αἰσχύνω.

αἰσχύνη, ἡ, (αἶσχος) shame done one, disgrace, dishonour. II. shame for an ill deed, Lat. pudor, generally, shame, the sense of shame. [ῡ]

αἰσχυντέον, verb. Adj. of αἰσχύνομαι, one must be ashamed.

αἰσχυντηλός, ή, όν, (αἰσχύνομαι) bashful, modest.

αἰσχυντήρ, ῆρος, ὁ, (αἰσχύνω) a dishonourer, seducer.

αἰσχυντηρός, ά, όν, = αἰσχυντηλός, bashful.

αἰσχύνω: f. ὑνῶ, Ion. ὑνέω: aor. 1 ᾔσχῡνα: pf. ᾔσχυγκα.—Pass., fut. med. in pass. sense, αἰσχῠνοῦμαι; also αἰσχυνθήσομαι: aor. ᾐσχύνθην: pf. ᾔσχυμμαι: (αἶσχος):—to make ugly, disfigure, mar. to disgrace, dishonour, tarnish, γένος αἰσχύνειν. II. Pass. to be ashamed, feel shame: but more freq. to be ashamed at a thing, c. acc. rei: also c. acc. pers. to feel shame before one: c. part. to be ashamed at doing a thing: but c. inf. to be ashamed to do a thing.

ΑΙ'ΤΕ'Ω: impf. ᾔτεον, Ion. αἴτεον: fut. αἰτήσω: aor. 1 ᾔτησα; pf. ᾔτηκα:—to ask, beg, usu. c. acc. rei, to ask, crave, demand something; ὁδὸν αἰτεῖν to beg leave to depart: c. acc. pers. to ask a person; αἰτεῖν τινά τι to ask a person for a thing; c. inf. to ask one to do:—Med. to ask for oneself, for one's own use or purpose, to claim, Lat. vindicare sibi:—Pass. to be asked a thing begged of one.

αἴτημα, ατος, τό, (αἰτέω) that which is asked, a request, demand.

αἴτημι, Aeol. for αἰτέω.

ἀΐτης, ου, Dor. ἀΐτας, α or εω, ὁ, a favourite.

αἴτησις, εως, ἡ, (αἰτέω) a request, demand.

αἰτητέον, verb. Adj. of αἰτέω, one must ask.

αἰτητός, ή, όν, verb. Adj. of αἰτέω, asked for, begged.

ΑΙ'ΤΙ'Α, ἡ, a cause, origin, ground, occasion; αἰτίαν παρέχειν to give occasion. II. the occasion of something bad, a charge, accusation, blame, fault, Lat. crimen: remonstrance, expostulation with a friend; αἰτίαν ἔχειν, Lat. crimen habere, to be accused; αἰτίαν ὑπέχειν to lie under a charge; ἐν αἰτίᾳ ἔχειν to hold guilty; τὴν αἰτίαν ἐπιφέρειν τινί to impute the fault to one, ἀπολύειν τινὰ τῆς αἰτίας to acquit of guilt.

αἰτιάασθαι, Ep. pres. inf. of αἰτιάομαι.

αἰτιάζομαι, Pass. (αἰτία) to be charged or accused.

αἰτίᾱμα, ατος, τό, a charge, guilt imputed. From

αἰτιάομαι, f. άσομαι [ᾱ]: aor. 1 ᾐτιᾱσάμην, Ion. αἰτιησάμην: (αἰτία): I. as Dep. to give as the cause or occasion: esp. of a fault: to charge, accuse, blame; αἰτιᾶσθαί τινά τινος to accuse of a thing. as Pass. in fut. αἰτιᾱθήσομαι, aor. 1 ᾐτιάθην, pf. ᾐτίαμαι:—to be accused. Hence

αἰτίᾱσις, εως, ἡ, a complaint, accusation.

αἰτιᾱτέον, verb. Adj. of αἰτιάομαι, one must accuse.

αἰτίζω, (αἰτέω) to ask or beg for a thing, c. acc. rei: c. acc. pers. to beg, solicit.

αἴτιον, τό, neut. of αἴτιος, = αἰτία, a cause.

αἴτιος, α, ον, more rarely ος, ον, *causing, occasioning;* hence *chargeable with* a thing: but mostly in bad sense, *causing ill, blamable, guilty:*—ὁ αἴτιος, *the party to be blamed, the culprit,* Lat. *reus:*—τὸ αἴτιον *the cause of* a thing.

αἰτιόωνται, Ep. 3 pl. pres. indic. of αἰτιάομαι.

αἰτιόῳο, αἰτιόῳτο, Ep. 2 and 3 sing. pres. opt. of αἰτιάομαι.

αἰτίσσα, Ep. aor. 1 of αἰτίζω.

Αἰτναῖος, α, ον, *of* or *belonging to Etna:* of a horse, *Etnean, Sicilian;* or *big as Etna, enormous.*

ΑΙΓΦΝΗΣ, Adv. = ἄφνω, ἄφνως, *on a sudden.* Hence

αἰφνίδιος, ον, *unforeseen, sudden, quick.* Adv. -δίως, also -διον, *suddenly.*

ἀϊχθῆναι, aor. 1 pass. inf. of ἀΐσσω.

ἀϊχθήτην, 3 dual aor. 1 pass. of ἀΐσσω.

αἰχμάζω, f. άσω: aor. 1 ᾔχμασα: (αἰχμή):—*to throw the spear, to fight with the spear.* II. *to arm with the spear.*

αἰχμᾰλωσία, ἡ, (αἰχμάλωτος) *captivity.* II. *a body of captives.*

αἰχμᾰλωτεύω, f. εύσω, (αἰχμάλωτος) *to make prisoner of war.*

αἰχμᾰλωτίζω, f. ίσω, = αἰχμαλωτεύω:—also Dep. **αἰχμᾰλωτίζομαι** in same sense: fut. ίσομαι: aor. 1 ᾐχμαλωτισάμην: pf. ᾐχμαλώτισμαι.

αἰχμᾰλωτικός, ή, όν, (αἰχμάλωτος) *befitting a prisoner.*

αἰχμᾰλωτίς, ίδος, ἡ, *a captive woman.* From

αἰχμ-άλωτος, ον, (αἰχμή, ἁλωτός) *taken by the spear* or *in war;* οἱ αἰχμάλωτοι *prisoners of war;* τὰ αἰχμάλωτα *booty.*

αἰχμή, ἡ, (ἀΐσσω) *the point of a spear,* Lat. *cuspis.* II. *a spear:* also *a staff* or *a sceptre.* 2. as collective noun *a body of spearmen,* as ἀσπίς a body of shielded men. 3. *war, battle.* 4. also, *warlike spirit, mettle.*

αἰχμήεις, εσσα, εν, (αἰχμή) *armed with the spear.*

αἰχμητά, ὁ, Ep. for αἰχμητής.

αἰχμητής οῦ, ὁ, (αἰχμή) *a spearman, warrior.* II. Adj. *warlike, brave.* Fem. **αἰχμῆτις**, ιδος.

αἰχμο-φόρος, ον, (αἰχμή, φέρω) *bearing a spear.*

ΑΙ'ΨΑ, Adv. *quickly, with speed, on a sudden.*

αἰψηρο-κέλευθος, ον, (αἰψηρός, κέλευθος) *swift-speeding.*

αἰψηρός, ά, όν, (αἶψα) *quick, speedy, sudden.*

ΑΙ'Ω, used only in pres. and impf. ἄϊον, *to perceive, become aware of,* esp. *to hear:* but also *to see, observe, know,* c. gen. and also c. acc. [α long or short, acc. to the metre.]

ΑΙ'Ω [ᾰ¯], used only in impf. ἄϊον [ᾱ], = ἄημι, *to breathe.* 2. = ἀΐσθω, *to breathe out, expire;* φίλον ἄϊον ἦτορ *I breathed out* my life.

ἀϊών, όνος, ἡ, Dor. for ἠϊών. [ᾱῐ]

ΑΙΏΝ, ῶνος, ὁ, also ἡ, sometimes with shortened acc. αἰῶ:—the Lat. *AEVUM, a space* or *period of time, a lifetime, life.* 2. of longer periods, *an age, generation, period.* 3. *an infinitely long space of time, eternity.* II. *one's age* or *time of life.*

αἰώνιος, ον, also α, ον, *lasting, eternal.*

αἰώρα, ἡ, (ἀείρω) *a machine for suspending* bodies: *a chariot* on springs. II. *a hovering in air, oscillation.*

αἰωρέω, f. ήσω, (ἀείρω) *to lift and hang up, let hang:* and so *to wave,* or *set waving.* II. more freq. in Pass. **αἰωρέομαι**, aor. 1 ᾐωρήθην, *to hang, to vibrate, to wave* or *float* in air, *hover* or *flit about.* 2. metaph. *to be in suspense,* Lat. *suspensus esse:* but αἰωρεῖσθαι ἔν τινι *to depend upon* a person, Lat. *pendere ab aliquo;* αἰωρεῖσθαι ὑπὲρ μεγάλων to play for a high stake. Hence

αἰώρημα, ατος, τό, *that which is hung up: a hanging cord* or *halter.* II. *a being hung up, hovering: a hanging.*

αἰώρητος, ον, verb. Adj. of αἰωρέω, *hovering.*

ἀκᾶ, (ἀκή 2), Adv. = ἀκήν, *softly, gently.*

Ἀκαδήμειᾰ, ἡ, also written Ἀκαδημία [ῑ], a gymnasium in the suburbs of Athens, where Plato taught: hence the Platonic school were called *Academics.*

ἀκαθαρσία, ἡ, (ἀκάθαρτος) *uncleanness.*

ἀκαθάρτης, ητος, ἡ, = foreg.

ἀ-κάθαρτος, ον, (α privat., καθαίρω) *uncleaned, impure: unclean: unpurified.* Adv. -τως.

ἀκαιρέομαι, f. ήσομαι, (ἄκαιρος) *to be without opportunity,* or *occasion.*

ἀκαιρία, ἡ, (ἄκαιρος) *an unseasonable time: want of opportunity, unseasonableness.* II. *importunity.*

ἄ-καιρος, ον, *not in season, unseasonable, ill-timed;* ἐς ἄκαιρα πονεῖν, Lat. *operam perdere:*—Adv. -ρως. II. of persons, *importunate,* Lat. *molestus: ill-suited* to do a thing, c. inf.

ἀ-κάκης, ου, ὁ, poët. for ἄκακος, *guileless.*

ἀκάκητα, Ep. for ἀκακήτης, = ἄκακος, *benignant, gracious.*

ἀκᾰκία, ἡ, *guilelessness.* From

ἄ-κᾰκος, ον, *without evil, unknowing of ill, guileless:* esp. *without malice.* Adv. -κως.

ἀκᾰλανθίς, ίδος, ἡ, *the goldfinch.*

ἀκᾰλαρ-ρείτης, ου, ὁ, (ἀκαλός, ῥέω) *soft-flowing.*

ἈΚΑΛΗ'ΦΗ, ἡ, *a nettle,* Lat. *urtica: the sting as of a nettle.* [ᾰκᾰ]

ἀ-καλλής, ές, gen. έος, (α privat., κάλλος) *without charms.*

ἀ-καλλιέρητος, ον, (α privat., καλλιερέω) *not accepted in sacrifice, ill-omened.*

ἀ-καλλώπιστος, ον, (α privat., καλλωπίζω) *unadorned.*

ἀ-κάλυπτος, ον, (α privat., καλύπτω) *uncovered.*

ἀ-κᾰλῠφής, ές, = ἀκάλυπτος.

ἀκᾰμαντο-λόγχης, ου, ὁ, (ἀκάμας, λόγχη) *unwearied with the spear.*

ἀκᾰμαντο-μάχης, ου, ὁ, (ἀκάμας, μάχη) *unwearied in fight.*

ἀκᾰμαντό-πους, ὁ, ἡ, πουν, τό, gen. ποδος, (ἀκάμας, πούς) *untiring of foot.*

ἀκᾰμαντο-χάρμας, ὁ, (ἀκάμας, χάρμη) *unwearied in fight.*

ἀ-κάμας, αντος, ὁ, (α privat., καμεῖν) *untiring, unresting.* [κᾰ]

ἀ-κάμᾰτος, ον, also η, ον, (α privat., κάματος) *without sense of toil,* hence *untiring, unresting:* —neut. ἀκάματα as Adv. *untiringly.*

ἄ-καμπτος, ον, (α privat., κάμπτω) *unbent, stiff:—from which none can return.* II. *unbending, inexorable.*

ἄκανθα, ης, ἡ, (ἀκή) *a thorn, prickle:* hence I. *a prickly plant, thistle:* a[illegible] *tree.* 2. *the back-bone* or *spine* o[illegible] 3. metaph. *thorny* or *difficult* [illegible]

ἀκάνθῐνος, η, [illegible] *of thorns.* II. *of the thorn-tree* [illegible]

ἀκανθίς, ίδος, [illegible] a small bird, *the goldfinch* or *linnet,* Lat. [illegible] II. as fem. Adj. *prickly.*

[illegible], ὁ, fem. -βάτις, ιδος, ἡ, (ἄκανθα, [illegible] *thorns.*

[illegible], ον, (ἄκανθα 3, λέγω) *picking out* [illegible]*ons, wrangling.*

[illegible]ΘΟΣ, ἡ, Lat. *acanthus, bear's breech,* a [illegible] used in Corinthian capitals.

[illegible]-ώδης, [illegible] gen. εος, (ἄκανθα, εἶδος) *full of thorns,* [illegible]

ἀ-κά[illegible]ς, ον, (α privat., καπνίζω) *unsmoked.*

ἄ-καπνος, ον, (α privat., καπνός) *without smoke, not smoking, making no smoke.*

ἀ-κάρδιος, ον, (α privat., καρδία) *wanting the heart:* metaph. *heartless,* Lat. *excors.*

ἀ-κάρηνος, ον, (α privat., κάρηνον) *headless.*

ἀ-κᾰρής, ές, (α privat., κάρῆναι) properly of hair, *too short to be cut:* generally, *short, small, tiny:* mostly of time, ἀκαρές *a moment,* ἐν ἀκαρεῖ χρόνου *in a moment* of time; ἀκαρῆ διαλιπὼν (sc. χρόνον) having waited *a moment;* οὐδ' ἀκαρῆ not *a bit:*—but also of things, ἀκαρές *a morsel.*

ἀ-καριαῖος, α, ον, (ἀκαρής) *momentary, brief.*

ἀκαρπία, ἡ, (ἄκαρπος) *unfruitfulness.*

ἀ-κάρπιστος, ον, (α privat., καρπίζω) = ἀκάρπωτος, *where nothing is to be reaped, unfruitful,* of the sea.

ἄ-καρπος, ον, *without fruit, barren.* II. act. *making barren, blasting.* Adv. -πως.

ἀ-κάρπωτος, ον, (α privat., καρπόω) *not made fruitful, without fruit, fruitless:* of an oracle, *unfulfilled.*

ἀκασκᾶ, (ἀκή 2) Adv. *gently.* Hence

ἀκασκαῖος, α, ον, *gentle, delicate.*

ἀ-κατάβλητος, ον, (α privat., καταβάλλω) *not to be overthrown, irrefragable.*

ἀ-κατάγνωστος, ον, (α privat., καταγιγνώσκω) *not to be condemned, blameless.*

ἀ-κατακάλυπτος, ον, (α privat., κατακαλύπτω) *uncovered.*

ἀ-κατάκρῐτος, ον, (α privat., κατακρίνω) *uncondemned.*

ἀ-κατάληκτος, ον, (α privat., καταλήγω) *without end:* of verses, *acatalectic.*

ἀ-κατάληπτος, ον, (α privat., καταλαμβάνω) *not to be conquered.* II. *incomprehensible.*

ἀ-κατάλλακτος, ον, (α privat., καταλλάσσω) *irreconcilable.* Adv. -τως.

ἀ-κατάλῠτος, ον, (α privat., καταλύω) *indissoluble.*

ἀ-καταμάχητος, ον, (α privat., καταμάχομαι) *not to be subdued, unconquerable.*

ἀ-κατανόητος, ον, (α privat., κατανοέω) *inconceivable.*

ἀ-κατάπαυστος, ον, (α privat., καταπαύω) *not to be set at rest, incessant: unable to cease from* a thing.

ἀκαταστᾰσία, ἡ, *a state of disorder, anarchy, confusion.* From

ἀ-κατάστᾰτος, ον, (α privat., καθίστημι) *unstable, unsettled: unsteady, fickle:* — Adv., ἀκαταστάτως ἔχειν to be *unstable.*

ἀ-κατάσχετος, ον, (α privat., κατέχω) *not to be checked, unruly.* Adv. -τως.

ἀ-καταφρόνητος, ον, (α privat., καταφρονέω) *not to be despised, important,* Lat. *haud spernendus.*

ἀκάτιον, τό, Dim. of ἄκατος, *a light boat,* esp. of pirates, Lat. *actuaria.* II. *a small sail.*

ἌΚΑΤΟΣ, ἡ, *a light vessel,* Lat. *actuaria:* esp. *a transport-vessel:* generally, *a ship.* [ᾰκᾰ]

ἄ-καυστος, ον, (α privat., καίω) *unburnt.*

ἀκαχείατο or -ήατο, Ep. for ἠκάχηντο, 3 pl. plqpf. pass. of ἀχέω.

ἀκαχήσω, redupl. fut. of ἀχέω.

ἀκάχησα, Ep. for ἠκάχησα, redupl. aor. 1 of ἀχέω.

ἀκαχῆσθαι, ἀκαχήμενος, Ep. for ἠκαχῆσθαι, ἠκαχημένος, inf. and part. of ἠκάχημαι, redupl. pf. pass. of ἀχέω,

ἀκάχηται, redupl. aor. 2 med. subj. of ἀχέω,

ἀκᾰχίζω, redupl. from ἀχέω. *to trouble:*—Pass. *to be troubled.*

ἀκαχμένος, η, ον, (ἀκή) *pointed, sharpened,* a part. pf. pass., as if from *ἄκω *to sharpen,* but with no verb in use.

ἀκάχοιτο, redupl. aor. 2 med. opt. of ἀχέω.

ἀκάχοντο, Ep. for ἠκάχοντο, redupl. aor. 2 med. of ἀχέω.

ἀκειόμενος, Ep. part. pres. pass. of ἀκέομαι.

ἀκειρε-κόμας, ου, ὁ, = ἀκερσεκόμης.

ἀ-κέλευστος, ον, (α privat., κελεύω) *unbidden.*

ἀ-κέντητος, ον, (α privat., κεντέω) *ungoaded, needing no spur.*

ἄ-κεντρος, ον, (α privat., κέντρον) *stingless.*

ἀκέομαι: Ep. impf. ἀκειόμην: f. ἀκέσομαι, Ep. ἀκέσσομαι, Att. ἀκοῦμαι: aor. 1 ἠκεσάμην, Ep. imper. ἄκεσσαι: Dep.: (ἄκος):—*to heal, cure.* 2. *to stanch, quench,* δίψαν. 3. generally, *to amend, repair, make good: to mend* or *darn* clothes.

ἀ-κέραιος, ον, (α privat., κεράννυμι) *unmixed, pure: pure in blood: guileless,* Lat. *integer.* II. u[illegible] *harmed*, *unravaged*, of countries. generally, *unimpaired*, *untouched*, *inviolate*: *fresh*, *active*.

ἀ-κέραστος, *ον*, (α privat., *κεράννυμι*) *unmixed*, *pure from* a thing.

ἀ-κέρᾱτος, *ον*, (α privat., *κέρας*) *without horns*.

ἀ-κεραύνωτος, *ον*, (α privat., *κεραυνόω*) *not struck by lightning*.

ἀκέρδεια, ἡ, (*ἀκερδής*) *want of gain*, *loss*. From

ἀ-κερδής, *ές*, (α privat., *κέρδος*) *without gain*, *bringing loss*. Adv. -*δῶς*, *gratis*.

ἀκέρκιστος, *ον*, (α privat., *κερκίζω*) *unwoven*.

ἀ-κερσε-κόμης, *ου*, ὁ, (α privat., *κείρω*, *κόμη*) *with unshorn hair*, epith. of Apollo: also *ever-young*, for the Greek youths wore their hair long, till they reached manhood.

ἄ-κερως, *ων*, gen. *ω*, and **ἀ-κέρωτος**, *ον*, = *ἀκέρατος*.

ἀκέσασθε, aor 1 imperat. of *ἀκέομαι*.

ἀκεσί-νοσος, Ep. **ἀκεσσί-**, *ον*, (*ἀκέομαι*, *νόσος*) *healing disease*.

ἄκεσις, *εως*, ἡ, (*ἀκέομαι*) *a healing*, *cure*, *remedy*.

ἄκεσμα, *τό*, (*ἀκέομαι*) *a remedy*, *cure*.

ἀκέσομαι, fut. of *ἀκέομαι*.

ἀκεσσ-, for words so beginning, v. sub *ἀκεσ-*.

ἀκεστήρ, *ῆρος*, ὁ, (*ἀκέομαι*) *a healer*, *restorer*, *physician*; *ἀκεστὴρ χαλινός* the rein *that tames the steed*.

ἀκεστής, *οῦ*, ὁ, = *ἀκεστήρ*: *a mender* of torn clothes.

ἀκεστορία, ἡ, (*ἀκέστωρ*) *the healing art*.

ἀκεστός, *ή*, *όν*, (*ἀκέομαι*) *curable*: *easy to be cheered* or *revived*.

ἄκεστρα, ἡ, (*ἀκέομαι*) *a darning-needle*.

ἀκέστρια, ἡ, fem. of *ἀκεστής*, *a sempstress*.

ἄκεστρον, *τό*, (*ἀκέομαι*) *a remedy*.

ἀκεστύς, *ύος*, ἡ, Ion. for *ἄκεσις*.

ἀκέστωρ, *ορος*, ὁ, (*ἀκέομαι*) *a healer*, *saviour*.

ἀκεσ-φόρος, *ον*, (*ἄκος*, *φέρω*) *bringing a cure*, *healing*.

ἀκεσ-ώδῠνος, *ον*, (*ἀκέομαι*, *ὀδύνη*) *allaying pain*.

ἀ-κέφᾰλος, *ον*, (α privat., *κεφαλή*) *without a head*: *without beginning*.

ἀκέων, **ἀκέουσα**, (*ἀκήν*) in form a participle, used by Hom. as an Adv. *stilly*, *softly*, *silently*: mostly in sing. nom. even with a plur. verb, as *ἀκέων δαίνυσθε* feast ye *in silence*:—the dual *ἀκέοντε* occurs once, the plur. form never. Although fem. *ἀκέουσα* is found, yet *ἀκέων* stands also with the fem., as *Ἀθηναίη ἀκέων ἦν*.

ἈΚΗ´, ἡ, a Subst. said to have 3 senses: 1. *a point*, *edge*, (whence *ἀκίς*, *ἀκωχή*, *ἀκμή*, *αἰχμή*, *ἀκόνη*, *ἄκρος*, and Lat. *acies*, *acuo*). 2. *silence*, (whence *ἀκήν*, *ἀκέων*, *ἀκᾶ*, *ἄκασκα*). 3. *healing*, (whence *ἀκέομαι*).

ἀ-κήδεστος, *ον*, (α privat., *κηδέω*) *uncared for*, *unheeded*: *without funeral rites*, *unburied*. Hence

ἀκηδέστως, Adv. of *ἀκήδεστος*, but in act. sense, *without heed for any one*, *remorselessly*.

ἀκηδέω, f. *ήσω*: aor. 1 *ἠκήδησα*, Ep. *ἀκήδεσα*:—*to neglect*, *slight*, c. gen. From

ἀ-κηδής, *ές*, (α privat., *κῆδος*) pass. *uncared for*: *unburied*. II. act. *without care* or *sorrow*, Lat. *securus*. 2. *heedless*, *careless*.

ἀκήκοα, pf. med. of *ἀκούω*.

ἀ-κήλητος, *ον*, (α privat., *κηλέω*) *to be won by no charms*, *not to be charmed* or *won over*, *inexorable*, *unassuageable*.

ἄκημα, *τό*, = *ἄκεσμα*, *a cure*, *remedy*.

ἀκήν, properly acc. of *ἀκή* 2, but used only as Adv. *stilly*, *softly*, *silently*.

ἀ-κηράσιος, *ον*, (α privat., *κεράννυμι*) *unmixed*, *pure*: hence *untouched*, Lat. *integer*: generally, *pure*, *fresh*.

ἀ-κήρᾰτος, *ον*, (α privat., *κεράννυμι*) *unmixed*, *pure*, *clear*: of persons, *incorrupt*, *undefiled*, *upright*:—c. gen. *pure from*, *free from taint of* . . II. *unimpaired*, *in full vigour*, *fresh*, *unbroken*.

ἀ-κήριος, *ον*, (α privat., *κήρ*) *unharmed by the fates*, *uninjured*. II. act. *unharming*, *harmless*.

ἀ-κήριος, *ον*, (α privat., *κῆρ*) *without heart* or *soul*, *lifeless*. II. *without heart* or *courage*, *heartless*, *spiritless*, Lat. *vecors*.

ἀκηρότατος, Ep. for *ἀκηρατώτατος*, Sup. of *ἀκήρατος*.

ἀκηρυκτεί and **ἀκηρυκτί**, Adv. *without proclamation*: esp. *without a flag of truce*: From

ἀ-κήρυκτος, *ον*, (α privat., *κηρύσσω*) *unannounced*: *unproclaimed*; *ἀκήρυκτος πόλεμος* a war *without announcement*, *sudden*, or, one *in which no herald was admitted*, *implacable*. 2. *inglorious*, *unknown*. 3. *unheard of*, *sending no tidings*. Hence

ἀκηρύκτως, Adv. = *ἀκηρυκτί*.

ἀ-κήρωτος, *ον*, (α privat., *κηρόω*) *not covered with wax*, *unwaxed*.

ἀκηχέδαται or **ἀκηχέαται**, Ep. for *ἠκήχηνται*, 3 pl. redupl. pf. pass. of *ἀχέω*.

ἀκηχέμενος, Ep. for *ἀκαχημένος*, part. of redupl. pf. pass. of *ἀχέω*.

ἀ-κίβδηλος, *ον*, (α privat., *κίβδηλος*) *unadulterate*, *unalloyed*, *pure*: also *guileless*, *honest*.

ἀκιδνός, *η*, *ον*, *weak*, *feeble*, *faint*, in Homer only in Comp. *ἀκιδνότερος*. (Deriv. uncertain.)

ἀ-κίθᾰρις, *ι*, gen. *ιος*, (α privat., *κιθάρα*) *without the harp*.

ἄκῑκυς, *υος*, ὁ, ἡ, (α privat., *κῖκυς*) *powerless*, *feeble*.

ἀκῑνάκης, *ου*, or *εος*, ὁ, Lat. *acinăces*, a Persian word, *a short sword*.

ἀ-κίνδῡνος, *ον*, *without danger*. hence *shunning danger*, *cowardly*. Adv. -*νως*.

ἀ-κίνητος, *ον*, rarely *η*, *ον*, (α privat., *κινέω*) *unmoved*, *motionless*: hence *idle*, *sluggish*. 2. *unaltered*, *settled*, *steady*. II. *immovable*, *hard to move*. 2. *not to be stirred* or *touched*, *inviolable*, like Lat. *non movendus*: *not to be divulged*. [ῑ]

ἄ-κῑος, *ον*, (α privat., *κίς*) *without worms*, *not worm-eaten*, *sound*: Sup. *ἀκιώτατος*.

ἀκῐρός, *όν*, = *ἀκιδνός*.

ἀκίς, *ίδος*, ἡ, (*ἀκή*, Lat. *acies*) *a point*, *barb*, *a pointed instrument*: metaph. *a sting*; *πόθων ἀκίδες the stings* of desires. [ᾰ]

ἀ-κίχητος, *ον*, (α privat., κιχάνω) *not to be reached, unattainable*: of persons, *not to be reached by prayer, inexorable.*

ἀκκίζομαι, Dep. (ἀκκώ) *to pretend indifference to* a thing, *to affect coyness*: generally, *to dissemble.*

ἀκκώ, *ἡ*, *a bugbear*: acc. to others *a vain woman.*

ἀκλάρωτος, Dor. for ἀκλήρωτος.

ἄ-κλαστος, *ον*, (α privat., κλάω) *unbroken.*

ἄ-κλαυστος or **ἄ-κλαυτος**, *ον*, (α privat., κλαίω) pass. *unwept*: *without lamentation.* II. act. *unweeping, tearless.*

ἀ-κλεής, *ές*, gen. *έος*: acc. ἀκλεᾶ, Ion. ἀκλεῆ, poët. ἀκλέα: (α privat., κλέος):—*without fame, inglorious, ignoble*: neut. ἀκλεές as Adv. *ingloriously.*

ἀ-κλεία, *ἡ*, (ἀ-κλεής) *ingloriousness.*

ἀ-κλειής, *ές*, Ep. for ἀκλεής: Ep. Adv. ἀκλειῶς.

ἄ-κλειστος, *ον*, Ion. **ἀ-κλήϊστος**, Att. contr. **ἄ-κληστος**, (ἀ privat., κλείω): *not shut, not bolted* or *fastened.*

ἀκλεῶς, Adv. of ἀκλεής, *ingloriously.*

ἀ-κληής, *ές*, poët. for ἀκλεής.

ἀκλήϊστος, Ion. for ἄκλειστος.

ἄ-κληρος, *ον*, *without lot* or *portion, poor, needy.* 2. *without lot* or *share in* a thing, c. gen. II. *unallotted, without an owner.*

ἀ-κλήρωτος, *ον*, (α privat., κληρόω) *without lot* or *portion in* a thing, c. gen.

ἄκληστος, *ον*, Att. for ἄκλειστος.

ἄ-κλητος, *ον*, (α privat., καλέω) *uncalled, unbidden.*

ἀ-κλινής, *ές*, (α privat., κλῐνῆναι) *bending to neither side*: *unswerving, stedfast.*

ἄ-κλυστος, *ον*, also *η, ον*, (α privat., κλύζω) *unwashed by waves.*

ἀκμάζω, f. άσω, (ἀκμή) *to be in full bloom, be at the prime* or *perfection*: hence *to flourish, abound in* a thing, ἀκμάζειν πλούτῳ, etc.: c. inf. *to be strong enough* to do; but impers. ἀκμάζει, c. inf., *it is high time* to do.

ἀκμαῖος, *α, ον*, (ἀκμή) *in full bloom, at the prime, blooming, vigorous*; ἀκμαῖος φύσιν *in the prime of strength.* II. *in time, in season*, Lat. *opportunus.*

ἀκμή, *ἡ*, (ἀκή, Lat. *acies*) *a point, edge*; proverb ἐπὶ ξυροῦ ἀκμῆς on the rasor's *edge*, i. e. at the critical moment; ἀμφιδέξιοι ἀκμαί *the fingers* of both hands, like ποδῶν ἀκμαί. 2. *the highest point* of anything, *the bloom, flower, prime*, esp. of man's age, ἀκμὴ ἥβης, Lat. *flos aetatis*; ἀκμὴ θέρους *mid*-summer:—generally, *strength, vigour.* 3. like καιρός, *the time*, i. e. *the best, most fitting time*; ἀκμὴ [ἐστι], c. inf., 'tis *high time* to do; ἐπ' ἀκμῆς εἶναι, c. inf., to be on *the point of* doing.

ἀκμήν, properly acc. of ἀκμή, but used as Adv. *in a moment, directly*: *even now, still*, like ἔτι.

ἀκμηνός, *ἡ, όν*, (ἀκμή) *full-grown, in full vigour.*

ἄκμηνος, *ον*, *fasting from food.* (Deriv. uncertain.)

ἀ-κμής, *ῆτος, ὁ, ἡ*, (α privat., κάμνω) = ἀκάμας, *untiring, fresh.*

ἄ-κμητος, *ον*, (α privat., κάμνω) *unwearied, untiring.*

ἀκμό-θετον, *τό*, (ἄκμων, τίθημι) *the anvil-block.*

ἌΚΜΩΝ, *ονος, ὁ*, *an anvil*, Lat. *incus.*

ἄ-κνισσος or rather **ἄ-κνῖσος**, *ον*, (α privat., κνῖσα) *without fat*, esp. *without the fat of sacrifice.*

ἀκοή, Ep. **ἀκουή**, *ἡ*, (ἀκούω) *hearing*: I. *the sense of hearing*: *the ear*; esp. in plur., ἀκοαῖς δέχεσθαι to hear, etc. II. *a hearing, listening to*; ἀκοῆς ἄξιος worth *hearing.* III. *the thing heard, a report, saying, fame*; ἀκοῇ εἰδέναι τι to know a thing by *hearsay.*

ἀ-κοίμητος, *ον*, (α privat., κοιμάομαι) *sleepless.*

ἀ-κοινώνητος, *ον*, (α privat., κοινωνέω) *not shared in common.* II. act. *not sharing in, not partaking of*: hence *unsocial.*

ἀ-κοίτης, *ου, ὁ*, (α = ἅμα, κοίτη) *a bedfellow, spouse, husband*: fem. **ἄ-κοιτις**, *ιος, ἡ*, *a wife.*

ἀ-κολάκευτος, *ον*, (α privat., κολακεύω) *not flattered, not won by flattery.*

ἀκολασία, *ἡ*, (ἀκόλαστος) *licentiousness, intemperance*: *excess, extravagance*: opp. to σωφροσύνη.

ἀκολασταίνω, (ἀκόλαστος) *to be licentious, debauched, intemperate*: *to live a riotous life.*

ἀ-κόλαστος, *ον*, (α privat., κολάζω) Lat. *non castigatus, unchastened, undisciplined, unbridled*: also *uneducated.* 2. *intemperate*, opp. to σώφρων. Hence

ἀκολάστως, Adv. *intemperately*: Comp., ἀκολαστοτέρως ἔχειν πρός τι to be *too intemperate* in a thing.

ἄ-κολος, *ου, ὁ*, (α privat., κόλον) *a bit, morsel.*

ἀκολουθέω, f. ήσω, (ἀκόλουθος) *to follow, go after* or *with.* II. metaph. *to follow* or *obey* one *in* a thing. Hence

ἀκολούθησις, *εως, ἡ*, *a following, sequence.*

ἀκολουθητέον, verb. Adj. of ἀκολουθέω, *one must follow.*

ἀκολουθία, *ἡ*, (ἀκολουθέω) *a following, attendance, train.* II. *agreement* or *conformity with.*

ἀ-κόλουθος, *ον*, (α copul., κέλευθος) *following, attending on*:—as Subst. **ἀκόλουθος**, *ὁ*, *a follower, attendant*; οἱ ἀκόλουθοι *the camp followers.* II. *following after*; *agreeing with, suitable to, like*, c. gen.; but also c. dat. Adv *-θως*, *in accordance with*, c. dat.

ἀ-κόλυμβος, *ον*, *unable to swim.*

ἀ-κομιστία, Ep. *-ίη* [ῐ], *ἡ*, *want of tending.* From

ἀ-κόμιστος, *ον*, (α privat., κομίζω) *untended.*

ἄ-κομος, *ον*, (α privat., κόμη) *without hair, bald*: of trees, *leafless.*

ἀ-κόμπαστος, *ον*, (α privat., κομπάζω) *unboastful.*

ἄ-κομπος, *ον*, *without boast, unboasting.*

ἄ-κομψος, *ον*, *unadorned, simple, plain*, Lat. *simplex.* II. *rude in speech.*

ἀκονάω, f. ήσω, (ἀκονή) *to sharpen, whet.*

ἀ-κόνδυλος, *ον*, (α privat., κονδύλη) *without blows.*

ἀκονή, *ἡ*, (ἀκή) *a whetstone, hone*, Lat. *cos.*

ἀ-κονιτί, Adv. of ἀκόνιτος, (α privat., κονίω) *without the dust of the arena*, hence *without combat, toil* or *effort*, Lat. *sine pulvere.*

ἀκόνῑτον, τό, a poisonous plant, *aconite, monkshood.*

ἄκοντι, later form for ἀέκοντι.

ἀκοντίζω, f. ίσω, Att. ιῶ: aor. 1 ἠκόντισα, Ep. ἀκόντισα: (ἄκων):—*to hurl a javelin:* also *to throw, fling, dart: to dart at*, c. gen. pers.: later c. acc. pers. *to hit* or *strike with a javelin, to wound;* and Pass. *to be so hit* or *wounded.* 2. *to shoot forth rays*, of the moon. II. intrans. *to dart* or *pierce.*

ἀκόντιον, τό, Dim. of ἄκων, *a dart, javelin.*

ἀκόντῐσις, ἡ, (ἀκοντίζω) *the throwing a javelin.*

ἀκόντισμα, τό, (ἀκοντίζω) *that which is darted, a javelin;* ἐντὸς ἀκοντίσματος within *a dart's throw.*

ἀκοντιστήρ, ῆρος, ὁ, and **ἀκοντιστής**, οῦ, ὁ, (ἀκοντίζω) *a darter, hurler of javelins.*

ἀκοντιστικός, ή, όν, (ἀκοντίζω) *skilled in throwing the dart.*

ἀκοντιστύς, ύος, ἡ, Ion. for ἀκόντισις, *the game of the dart, a contest at throwing the dart.*

ἀκοντο-δόκος, ον, (ἄκων, δέχομαι) *watching the dart*, i. e. *shunning it.*

ἄ-κοπος, ον, *without weariness:* I. pass. *unwearied, untiring.* II. act. *not wearying, easy.* 2. *removing weariness, refreshing.*

ἀκορέστατος, *most shameless*, a Sup. either from ἀ-κορής = ἀκόρεστος; or shortened for ἀκορεστότατος, Sup. of ἀκόρεστος, like μέσσατος, νέατος.

ἀ-κόρεστος, ον, (α privat., κορέννυμι) *insatiate, unceasing:* c. gen. *insatiate of, unsated with.* II. act. *not satiating: not disgusting.*

ἀ-κόρετος, ον, = ἀκόρεστος.

ἀ-κόρητος, ον, (α privat., κορέννυμι) *insatiate:* c. gen. *unsated with*, [illegible] πολέμου, ἀπειλῶν. 2. (α privat., κορέω) *unswept, untrimmed.*

ἄ-κορος, ον, = ἀκόρητος, *insatiate:* metaph. *ceaseless*, Lat. *improbus.*

ἌΚΟΣ, εος, τό, *a cure, relief, remedy, help, resource for* or *against* a thing, c. gen.: ἄκος τέμνειν to prepare *a remedy.*

ἀκοσμέω, f. ήσω, (ἄκοσμος) *to be disorderly, unruly: to be out of order, to offend.*

ἀ-κόσμητος, ον, (α privat., κοσμέω) *unarranged, disorderly.* 2. *unadorned, unfurnished.*

ἀκοσμία, ἡ, *disorder: extravagance: unruliness, offence.* From

ἄ-κοσμος, ον, *without order, disorderly:* in moral sense, *unruly, rebellious:*—Adv. -μως, *without order.* II. κόσμος ἄκοσμος a world *that is no world*, like γάμος ἄγαμος, etc.

ἀκοστάω or **ἀκοστέω**, only used in aor. 1 part. ἀκοστήσας, *well-fed, over-fed.* From

ἈΚΟΣΤΗ', ἡ, *barley.*

ἀκουάζομαι, Dep., like ἀκούω, *to hearken to*, c. gen. II. *to be called, bidden;* δαιτὸς ἀκουάζεσθον *ye are bidden* to the feast, like καλεῖσθαι, Lat. *vocari.*

ἀκουή, ἡ, Ep. for ἀκοή, *hearing;* πατρὸς ἀκουή *tidings* of his father:—*a sound.*

ἄ-κουρος, ον, (α privat., κοῦρος) *childless, without male heir.* II. (α privat., κουρά) *unshorn.*

ἀκούσειαν, Aeol. form of ἀκούσαιεν, 3 pl. aor. 1 opt. of ἀκούω.

ἀκουσείω, Desiderat. of ἀκούω, *to wish to hear.*

ἀκουσί-θεος, ον, (ἀκούω, θεός) *heard of God.*

ἀκούσιμος, η, ον, (ἀκούω) *audible.*

ἀκούσιος, ον, Att. contr. for ἀεκούσιος, *unwilling, under constraint:*—Adv. -ίως, *unwillingly*, or *in an unwelcome manner;* Sup. ἀκουσιώτατα, *most unwillingly.*

ἄκουσμα, τό, (ἀκούω) *a thing heard, a sound, strain.* 2. *a rumour, report, tale.* [ᾰ] Hence

ἀκουσμάτιον, τό, *a little tale.*

ἀκουστέον, also **ἀκουστέα**, verb. Adj. of ἀκούω, *one must hear* or *hearken to*, c. gen.

ἀκουστής, οῦ, ὁ, (ἀκούω) *a hearer, listener.*

ἀκουστός, ή, όν, verb. Adj. of ἀκούω, *heard, audible: that should be heard.*

ἈΚΟΥ'Ω, f. ἀκούσομαι: aor. 1 ἤκουσα: pf. Att. ἀκήκοα, Dor. ἄκουκα: plqpf. ἀκηκόειν, Att. ἀκηκόη:—Pass., fut. ἀκουσθήσομαι: aor. 1 ἠκούσθην: pf. ἤκουσμαι:—*to hear*, used both with gen. and acc. 2. absol. *to hear, give ear;* ἀκούετε λεῴ *hear, O people.* II. *to listen* or *give ear to*, mostly c. gen.; more rarely c. dat., hence *to obey.* III. *to hear oneself called, be called, pass for;* with an Adj. or Subst., ἀκούειν κακός, Lat. *malus audire;* or with an Adv. εὖ, κακῶς ἀκούειν, Lat. *bene, male audire.*

ἄκρα, Ion. **ἄκρη**, ἡ, (properly fem. of ἄκρος) *the end, point*, esp. *the highest point, the top of the hill, peak, headland: a citadel*, Lat. *arx:*—κατ' ἄκρης πέρθειν, Att. κατ' ἄκρας, to destroy *from top to bottom*, i. e. *utterly*, Lat. *funditus evertere.*

ἀκράαντος, ον, = ἄκραντος, *without result, unfulfilled, fruitless*, Lat. *irritus.*

ἀ-κρᾰγής, ές, (α privat., κραγεῖν) *not barking.*

ἀκραῆ, contr. form of ἀκραέα, acc. masc. of ἀκραής.

ἀκρ-ᾱής, ές, (ἄκρος, ἄημι) of certain winds, *blowing strongly, fresh-blowing.*

ἀκραιφνής, ές, contr. from ἀκεραιο-φανής, (ἀκέραιος, φανῆναι) *unmixed, pure, sheer:* hence II. *unharmed*, Lat. *integer:* c. gen. *untouched by* a thing.

ἄ-κραντος, ον, (α privat., κραίνω) *unaccomplished, unfulfilled, fruitless, idle.* II. *endless.*

ἀκρᾰσία, ἡ, (ἀκρατής) *the character of an ἀκρατής, incontinence*, Lat. *impotentia*, opp. to ἐγκράτεια.

ἀ-κράτεια, ἡ, earlier form of foreg. [ᾰ]

ἀκρᾱτέστερος, irreg. Comp. of ἄκρᾱτος.

ἀ-κρᾰτής, ές, (α privat., κράτος) *powerless: not having power* or *command over* a thing; ἀκρατὴς ὀργῆς, Lat. *impotens irae:* esp. in a moral sense, *without power* or *command over oneself, incontinent*, Lat. *impotens sui.*

ἀ-κρᾱτίζομαι, fut. Att. [illegible]οῦμαι, Dep. *to drink pure wine* (ἄκρατος, *merum*). II. *to breakfast*, because this meal consisted of *bread dipped in wine.* Hence

ἀκράτιστος, ον, *having breakfasted.* [κρᾱ]

ἀκρᾱτοποσία, Ion. -ίη, ἡ, *a drinking of unmixed wine.* From

ἀκρᾱτο-πότης, ου, Ion. **ἀκρητο-πότης**, εω, ὁ, (ἄκρᾱτος, πίνω) *a drinker of unmixed wine.*

ἄ-κρᾱτος, Ion. **ἄ-κρητος**, ον: Comp. and Sup. ἀκρᾱτέστερος, -έστατος: (α privat., κεράννυμι):—*unmixed, pure, sheer, unadulterate:* esp. of wine, ἄκρατος (sub. οἶνος), ὁ, *wine without water, sheer* wine, Lat. *merum;* metaph., ἄκρατος νοῦς *pure* intellect. 2. *untempered, unrestrained, excessive: intemperate, violent.*

ἀ-κράτωρ, ορος, ὁ, = ἀ-κρατής, *without control.* [κρᾰ]

ἀκρᾰτῶς, Adv. of ἀκρατής, *without control;* ἀκρατῶς ἔχειν *to be incontinent.*

ἀκρᾱχολέω, f. ήσω, *to be passionate.* From

ἀκρά-χολος, Ion. ἀκρή-χολος, ον, (ἄκρος, χόλος) *quick* or *sudden to anger, passionate;* κύων ἀκράχολος an *ill-tempered* dog. [κρᾱ]

ἀκρέμων, ονος, ὁ, (ἄκρος) *the end of a branch* or *bough, a small branch, spray, twig.*

ἀκρ-έσπερος, ον, (ἄκρος, ἑσπέρα) *at the beginning of evening, at eventide.*

ἀκρ-ήβης, ες, and **ἄκρ-ηβος**, ον, (ἄκρος, ἥβη) *in earliest youth, very young.*

ἄ-κρητος, ον, Ion. for ἄκρατος, *unmixed, pure.*

ἀκρη-χολία, ἀκρή-χολος, Ion. for ἀκραχολία, etc.

ἄκριας, acc. pl. of ἄκρις.

ἀκρίβεια, ἡ, *exactness, accuracy, precision: perfection.* II. *strictness, severity: parsimony, frugality.* From

ἀκρῑβής, ές, *exact, accurate, precise, perfect* in its kind; of thoughts, *clear, definite, precise.* II. of persons, *exact, strict, scrupulous:*—also *frugal, stingy.* (Deriv. uncertain.)

ἀκρῑβολογέομαι, Dep. (ἀκριβολόγος) *to be exact, accurate,* or *precise in language:* c. acc. rei, *to weigh accurately.* Hence

ἀκρῑβολογία, ἡ, *precision of language.*

ἀκρῑβο-λόγος, ον, (ἀκριβής, λόγος) *exact in language.*

ἀκρῑβόω, f. ώσω, (ἀκριβής) *to make exact* or *accurate: to arrange precisely:* but commonly, *to examine* or *understand thoroughly: to express accurately:*—Pass. *to be made exact* or *perfect.*

ἀκριβῶς, Adv. of ἀκριβής, *exactly, accurately, precisely.* II. *sparingly;* ἀκριβῶς καὶ μόλις, Lat. *vix et ne vix quidem.*

ἀκρῐδο-θήκη, ἡ, (ἀκρίς, τίθημι) *a locust-cage.*

ἄκρις, ιος, ἡ, Ion. for ἄκρα, *a hill-top, peak;* mostly in pl., ἄκριες ἠνεμόεσσαι the windy *mountain-tops.*

'ΑΚΡΙ'Σ, ίδος, ἡ, *a locust,* Lat. *gryllus.*

ἀκρῐσία, ἡ, (ἄκριτος) *want of distinctness and order, confusion.* II. *want of judgment.*

ἀκρῐτό-δακρυς, υ, gen. υος, (ἄκριτος, δάκρυ) *shedding floods of tears.*

ἀκρῐτό-μῡθος, ον, (ἄκριτος, μῦθος) *talking recklessly.* II. *hard to interpret.*

ἄ-κρῐτος, ον, (α privat., κρίνω) *unarranged, confused, disorderly: countless.* 2. *lasting, unceasing:* of mountains, *continuous.* II. *undecided, doubtful.* 2. *unjudged, untried,* of persons and things; ἄκριτόν τινα κτείνειν, to put to death *without trial,* Lat. *indicta causa:*—also *not subject to trial.* III. act. *not giving judgment.* 2. *not exercising judgment, undistinguishing.*

ἀκρῐτό-φυλλος, ον, (ἄκριτος, φύλλον) *of blended foliage.*

ἀκρῐτό-φυρτος, ον, (ἄκριτος, φύρω) *undistinguishably mixed.*

ἀκροάζομαι, Dep. = ἀκροάομαι.

ἀκρόᾱμα, τό, (ἀκροάομαι) Lat. *acroāma, anything heard with pleasure, anything read, recited, played* or *sung: a play* or *musical piece.*

'ΑΚΡΟΑ'ΟΜΑΙ: impf. ἠκροώμην: fut. ἀσομαι [ᾱ]: aor. 1 ἠκροᾱσάμην: pf. ἠκρόᾱμαι: Dep.:—*to hearken* or *listen to,* esp. *to hear* or *attend lectures;* ὁ ἀκροώμενος *a hearer, student.* II. *to obey.*

ἀκρόᾱσις, εως, ἡ, (ἀκροάομαι) *a hearkening* or *listening to.* 2. *obedience.*

ἀκροᾱτέον, verb. Adj. of ἀκροάομαι, *one must listen to.*

ἀκροᾱτήριον, τό, (ἀκροάομαι) *a place of audience: lecture-room.* II. *an audience.*

ἀκροᾱτής, οῦ, ὁ, (ἀκροάομαι) *a hearer: a pupil.*

ἀκροᾱτικός, ή, όν, (ἀκροάομαι) *proper for hearing* or *attending lectures;* μισθὸς ἀκροατικός, Lat *honorarium, a pupil's fee.*

ἀκρο-βᾰτέω, (ἄκρος, βαίνω) *to walk on tiptoe* or *erect.*

ἀκρο-βᾰφής, (ἄκρος, βᾰφῆναι) *wetted at the end.* II. *tinged at the point,* or *slightly.*

ἀκρο-βελής, ές, (ἄκρος, βέλος) *with a point at the end.*

ἀκροβολέω, (ἀκροβόλος) *to be a slinger, to skirmish.*

ἀκροβολίζομαι, (ἀκροβολέω) Dep. *to throw* or *strike from afar: to skirmish.* Hence

ἀκροβόλῐσις, εως, ἡ, *a skirmishing.*

ἀκροβολισμός, οῦ, ὁ, = ἀκροβόλισις.

ἀκροβολιστής, οῦ, ὁ, = ἀκροβόλος.

ἀκρο-βόλος, ὁ, (ἄκρος, βαλεῖν) as Subst. *one that throws from afar, a slinger, skirmisher:* but II. as Adj. proparox. ἀκρό-βολος, ον, *struck from afar.*

ἀκροβυστία, ἡ, (ἀκρόβυστος) *uncircumcision.*

ἀκρό-βυστος, ον, (ἄκρος, βύω) *uncircumcised.*

ἀκρο-γωνιαῖος, ον, (ἄκρος, γωνία) *at the extreme angle;* ἀκρ. λίθος the *corner foundation*-stone.

ἀκρό-δετος, ον, (ἄκρος, δέω) *bound at the end* or *top.*

ἀκρόδρυα, τά, (ἄκρος, δρῦς) *fruit-trees.* II. *fruits,* esp. *hard-shelled* fruits.

ἀκρο-έλικτος, ον, (ἄκρος, ἑλίσσω) *twisted at the end.*

ἀκρο-θῐγής, ές, (ἄκρος, θιγεῖν) *touching on the surface* or *lightly.*

ἀκρό-θῑνα, τά, v. ἀκρο-θίνιον.

ἀκροθῑνιάζομαι, Dep. (ἀκροθίνιον) *to take of the best, pick out for oneself.*

ἀκρο-θίνιον, τό, (ἄκρος, θίς) mostly in plur. ἀκροθίνια, also ἀκρόθινα, properly, *the top of the heap, the* *best* or *choice parts*: hence *the first-fruits of the field, of booty*, etc., like ἀπαρχαί:—properly a neut. Adj. from ἀκροθίνιος, whence θύη ἀκροθίνια offerings *of first-fruits*. [θῐ]

ἀκρο-κελαινιάω, (ἄκρος, κελαινός) only used in Ep. part. ἀκροκελαινιόων, *growing black on the surface*.

ἀκρο-κνέφαιος, ον, and **ἀκρο-κνεφής**, ές, (ἄκρος, κνέφας) *at the beginning* or *end of night, in twilight*.

ἀκρό-κομος, ον, (ἄκρος, κόμη) *with hair on the crown*. II. *with leaves at the top*.

ἀκρο-κόρινθος, ὁ, *the citadel of Corinth*.

ἀκρο-κῡματόω, f. ώσω, (ἄκρος, κῦμα) *to float on the topmost waves*.

ἀκρό-λῐθος, ον, (ἄκρος, λίθος) *with the extremities of stone*, epith. of statues of wood with marble head, hands, and feet.

ἀκρο-λίνιον, τό, (ἄκρος, λίνον) *the edge of a net*.

ἀκρο-λογέω, (ἄκρος, λέγω) *to gather at top*.

ἀκρολοφίτης, [ῑ], ου, ὁ, (ἄκρος, λόφος) *a mountaineer*.

ἀκρό-λοφος, ὁ, (ἄκρος, λόφος) *a mountain ridge*.

ἀκρο-λῠτέω, (ἄκρος, λύω) *to untie only at the end*.

ἀκρο-μᾰνής, ές, (ἄκρος, μᾰνῆναι) *at the height of madness, raving mad*.

ἀκρο-μόλιβδος, ον, (ἄκρος, μόλιβδος) *leaded at the edge*, epith. of a net.

ἄκρον, ου, τό, neut. of ἄκρος, *the highest* or *topmost point*: I. *a mountain-top, peak*. II. metaph. *the highest pitch, the height* of a thing. III. pl. ἄκρα, of persons, *the chiefs*.

ἀκρ-ονῠχί, Adv. (ἄκρος, ὄνυξ) *with the edge of the nail*.

ἀκρ-όνῠχος, ον, (ἄκρος, ὄνυξ) = ἀκρώνυχος.

ἀκρό-νῠχος, ον, (ἄκρος, νύξ) *at nightfall, at even*.

ἀκρο-πενθής, ές, (ἄκρος, πένθος) *exceeding sad*.

ἀκρο-ποδητί, Adv. (ἄκρος, πούς) *on tiptoe, stealthily*.

ἀκρό-πολις, εως, ἡ, (ἄκρος, πόλις) *the upper* or *higher city*, hence *the citadel, castle*: in Att. esp. the Acropolis of Athens, which served as the treasury. II. metaph. *a tower of defence*. 2. *the highest point*.

ἀκρο-πόλος, ον, (ἄκρος, πολέω) *high-ranging*: generally, *high*.

ἀκρο-πόρος, ον, (ἄκρος, πείρω) *boring through, piercing with the point*.

ἀκρό-πτερον, τό, (ἄκρος, πτερόν) *the tip of the wing*.

ἀκρό-πτολις, ἡ, poët. for ἀκρόπολις.

ἄκρος, α, ον, (ἀκή) *at the end*, i.e. either *outermost*, Lat. *extremus*, or *at the top*, Lat. *summus*; ἄκρα χείρ, ἄκροι πόδες, etc., the *end* of the hand or feet, etc.; πόλις ἄκρη = ἀκρόπολις, the citadel; ὕδωρ ἄκρον the *surface* of the water; so also, ἐπ' ἄκροις (sc. δακτύλοις) *on tiptoe*; οὐκ ἀπ' ἄκρας φρενός not from *the surface of* the heart, i. e. from the inmost heart; ἄκροισι λαίφους κρασπέδοις with the *outermost* edges of the sail, with a close-reefed sail. II. of Time, ἄκρα ἑσπέρα *the end of* evening, night-fall. III. of Degree, *the highest* in its kind, *first, exceeding, good, excellent*; ἄκροι Δαναῶν, ποιητῶν *the first* among the Greeks, the poets; ψυχὴν οὐκ ἄκρος not *strong* of mind. IV. neut. ἄκρον and ἄκρα, as Adv. *very, exceedingly, highly*: v. ἄκρως.

ἀκρο-σίδηρος, ον, (ἄκρος, σίδηρος) *pointed* or *shod with iron*.

ἀκρό-σοφος, ον, (ἄκρος, σοφός) *high in wisdom*.

ἀκρο-στόλιον, τό, (ἄκρος, στολή) *the gunwale* of a ship.

ἀκρο-σφᾰλής, ές, (ἄκρος, σφᾰλῆναι) *apt to stumble*.

ἀκροτάτη, fem. Sup. of ἄκρος.

ἀκρο-τελεύτιον, τό, (ἄκρος, τελευτή) *the fag-end* of anything, esp. of a verse.

ἀκρότης, ητος, ἡ, (ἄκρος) *a summit, height*.

ἀκροτομέω, *to lop off* or *shave the surface*. From

ἀκρό-τομος, ον, (ἄκρος, τεμεῖν) *cut off at the edge*.

ἀκρ-ουχέω, (ἄκρον, ἔχω) *to inhabit the heights*.

ἀκρο-φύσιον, τό, (ἄκρος, φύσα) *the snout* or *pipe of a pair of bellows*.

ἀκρο-χᾰνής, ές, (ἄκρος, χᾰνεῖν) *wide-yawning*.

ἀκρο-χειρίζομαι, Dep. (ἄκρος, χείρ) *to struggle at arm's length*, of a kind of wrestling, in which they *grasped one another's hands*, without clasping the body.

ἄ-κρυπτος, ον, (α privat., κρύπτω) *unhidden*.

ἀ-κρύσταλλος, ον, *without ice, unfrozen*.

ἀκρ-ωλένιον, τό, (ἄκρος, ὠλένη) *the point of the elbow*.

ἀκρ-ωνῠχία, ἡ, (ἄκρος, ὄνυξ) *the tip of the nail*: hence *any extremity, the ridge of a mountain*.

ἀκρ-ώνῠχος, ον, (ἄκρος, ὄνυξ) *with nails, claws, hoofs*.

ἀκρ-ώρεια, ἡ, (ἄκρος, ὄρος) *a mountain-ridge*.

ἄκρως, regul. Adv. of ἄκρος, *very, exceedingly*.

ἀκρωτηριάζω, f. σω: aor. 1 ἠκρωτηρίασα: pf. pass. ἠκρωτηρίασμαι:—*to cut off the extremities*, esp. *the hands and feet, to mutilate*. From

ἀκρωτήριον, τό, (ἄκρος) *any topmost* or *prominent part*; ἀκρ. οὔρεος a mountain-*peak*; ἀκρ. νηός a ship's *beak*, Lat. *rostra*. 1. in plur. *the extremities of the body, hands and feet*. 2. in sing. *a promontory*.

ἀκταινόω, = ἀκταίνω.

ἀκταίνω, seems to be a strengthd. form of ἄγω, *to put in motion*, or, if intr., *to move rapidly*.

ἀκταῖος, α, ον, (ἀκτή) *on the shore* or *coast*. II. Ἀκταία (sc. γῆ) ἡ, *Coast-land*, an old name of Attica, also Ἀκτή.

ἈΚΤΕ´Α, ἡ, *the elder-tree*, Lat. *sambucus*.

ἀ-κτέᾰνος, ον, (α privat., κτέανον) *without property*.

ἀ-κτένιστος, ον, (α privat., κτενίζω) *uncombed, unkempt*.

ἀκτέον, verb. Adj. of ἄγω, *one must lead*: εἰρήνην ἀκτέον *one must keep* peace. II. intr. *one must go* or *march*.

ἀ-κτερέϊστος or **ἀ-κτέριστος**, ον, (α privat., κτερείζω or κτερίζω) *without funeral-rites*.

ἀκτή, ἡ, (ἄγνυμι) *the place where the waves break*, i. e. *the beach, sea-shore, strand*; in plur., ἀκταὶ προβλῆτες jutting *cliffs*. 2. *a tract by the sea*. II.

generally, *any raised place* or *edge*, like the sea-coast, Lat. *ora*.

ἀκτή, ἡ, (ἄγνυμι) properly fem. of ἀκτός (*broken, bruised*), *bruised corn*, Lat. *mola*: *groats, meal, bread made of it*.

ἀ-κτήμων, ον, gen. ονος, (α privat., κτῆμα) *without property*, c. gen., ἀκτήμων χρυσοῖο *poor* in gold.

ἄ-κτητος, ον, (α privat., κτάομαι) *not worth getting*.

ἀκτίνεσσιν, Ep. for ἀκτῖσιν, dat. pl. of ἀκτίς.

ἀκτῑνηδόν, (ἀκτίς) Adv. *like a ray*.

ἄκτιος, ον, (ἀκτή) *of* or *inhabiting the sea-shore*.

ἀκτίς, ῖνος, ἡ, *a ray, beam*, esp. of the sun; μέσσα ἀκτίς midday: also *the flash* of fire and lightning: metaph. *brightness, splendour*. II. like Lat. *radius, the spoke* of a wheel.

ἀκτίτης, ου, ὁ, (ἀκτή) *a dweller on the coast*. [ῑ]

ἄ-κτῐτος, ον, (α privat., κτίζω) *uncultivated*.

ἄκτωρ, ορος, ὁ, (ἄγω) *a leader, chief*.

ἀ-κῠβέρνητος, ον, (α privat., κυβερνάω) *without pilot, not steered*.

ἌΚΥ῎ΛΟΣ, ἡ, *an esculent acorn*, fruit of the *ilex*.

ἀ-κύμαντος, ον, (α privat., κῡμαίνω) *not washed by the waves, waveless, calm*.

ἄ-κῡμος, ον, = ἀκύμαντος: metaph. *calm, serene*.

ἀ-κύμων, ον, gen. ονος, (α privat., κῦμα) = ἀκύμαντος. [ῡ]

ἀ-κύμων, ον, gen. ονος, (α privat., κυέω) *without fruit* or *offspring, barren*. [ῡ]

ἄ-κῡρος, ον, (α privat., κῦρος) *without authority*. I. of laws, sentences, etc., *no longer in force, cancelled, annulled, set aside*; ἄκυρος γίγνεσθαι, εἶναι to have no force, be set aside. II. of persons, *having no right* or *power*, c. gen. Hence

ἀκῡρόω, f. ώσω, *to cancel, set aside*.

ἀ-κύρωτος, ον, verb. Adj. *unratified*.

ἀ-κωδώνιστος, ον, (α privat., κωδωνίζω) *untried, unexamined*.

ἀκωκή, ἡ, (ἀκή) *a point, edge*, Lat. *acies*.

ἀ-κώλῡτος, ον, (α privat., κωλύω) *unhindered*. Adv. -τως, *without hindrance*.

ἀ-κωμῴδητος, ον, (α privat., κωμῳδέω) *not made the subject of comedy*: generally, *not ridiculed*.

ἄκων, οντος, ὁ, (ἀκή) *a javelin, dart*, smaller and lighter than ἔγχος.

ἄκων, ἄκουσα, ἆκον, gen. -οντος, Att. contr. for ἀέκων, *against one's will, perforce*. II. = ἀκούσιος, *involuntary*. [ᾱ]

ἄ-κωπος, ον, (α privat., κώπη) *without oars*.

ἀλαβαστο-θήκη, ἡ, (ἀλάβαστος, θήκη) *a case for alabaster ornaments*.

ἀλάβαστος, ὁ, ἀλαβαστίτης, ὁ, ἀλαβάστιον, τό, Att. for ἀλάβαστρος.

ἀλάβαστρον, τό, and ἀλάβαστρος, ὁ, also ἡ, a calcareous spar, *alabaster*. II. *that which is wrought* or *made of it, a casket* or *case of alabaster*.

ἅλαδε, Adv. (ἅλς) *to* or *into the sea*: in Homer also εἰς ἅλαδε.

ἀλά-δρομος, ον, ὁ, by some derived from ἄλλομαι, δρόμος, *the bounding race*; by others from ἅλς, δρόμος, *a race over the sea*.

ἀλαζονεία, ἡ, (ἀλαζών) *the character of a braggart, vain-boasting, imposture*.

ἀλαζόνευμα, τό, *an imposture*. From

ἀλαζονεύομαι, f. εύσομαι, Dep. *to swagger, use false pretensions*. From

ἀλαζών, όνος, ὁ, ἡ, (ἄλη) *a wanderer about the country, vagabond*:—hence, *a false pretender, an impostor*. II. as Adj. *making false pretences, swaggering, braggart*, Lat. *gloriosus*:—Sup. ἀλαζονέστατος or -ίστατος.

ἀλάθεια, ἀλαθής, Dor. for ἀλήθεια, ἀληθής.

ἀλᾱθείς, Dor. aor. 1 pass. part. of ἀλάομαι.

ἀλαίνω, = ἀλάομαι, *to wander about*.

ἀλακάτα, ἡ, Dor. for ἠλακάτη.

ἀλᾰλά, Dor. for ἀλαλή.

ἀλᾰλᾰγή, ἡ, (ἀλαλάζω) *a shouting*.

ἀλᾰλαγμός, ὁ, = ἀλαλαγή.

ἀλᾰλάζω: f. άξομαι: aor. 1 ἠλάλαξα, poët. ἀλάλαξα: (ἀλαλή):—*to raise the war-cry*: generally, *to shout aloud* in sign of joy; νίκην ἀλαλάζειν to *shout* the *shout* of victory.

ἀλᾰλή, Dor. ἀλᾰλά, ἡ, *alala! a loud cry*: the *battle-shout, war-cry*.

ἀλάλημαι, a pf. form of ἀλάομαι, but only used in pres. sense, *to wander* or *roam about*, like a beggar.

ἀ-λάλητος, ον, (α privat., λαλέω) *unspeakable*.

ἀλᾰλητός, οῦ, ὁ, (ἀλαλή) *the war-cry, shout of victory*: also *a cry of woe, wailing*.

ἀλαλκεῖν, aor. 2 inf. of ἀλέξω.

ἀλαλκέμεναι, -έμεν, Ep. aor. 2 inf. of ἀλέξω.

Ἀλαλκο-μενηΐς, ΐδος, ἡ, (ἀλαλκεῖν, μένος) *the guardian goddess*, name of Minerva.

ἄ-λᾰλος, ον, (α privat., λάλος) *speechless, dumb*.

ἀλᾰλύκτημαι, a pf. form as if from ἀλυκτέω (ἀλύω), but like ἀλάλημαι only used in pres. sense, *to wander about in anguish*: *to wander in mind from grief*.

ἀ-λάμπετος, ον, (α privat., λάμπω) *without light; darksome*.

ἀ-λαμπής, ές, = ἀλάμπετος; ἀλαμπὴς ἡλίου *without the light of* the sun.

ἀλάομαι, impf. ἠλώμην: aor. 1 ἠλήθην, Ep. ἀλήθην: pf. ἀλάλημαι: Dep.: (ἄλη):—*to wander, stray*, or *roam about*: sometimes c. acc., ἀλᾶσθαι γῆν *to wander through* or *over* the land: also *to wander from home, be banished*. II. metaph. *to wander in mind, be distraught*.

ἀλᾰός, όν, *not seeing, blind*; ἀλαοί, as opp. to δεδορκότες, *the dead*; ἀλαὸν ἕλκος ὀμμάτων a wound that brings blindness. II. *dark, obscure*.

ἀλᾰο-σκοπίη, ἡ, (ἀλαός, σκοπέω) *a blind*, i. e. *useless, careless watch*.

ἀλᾰόω, f. ώσω: aor. 1 inf. ἀλαῶσαι: (ἀλαός):—*to make blind*.

ἀλᾰπαδνός, ή, όν, (ἀλαπάζω) *easily mastered, weakened*: *powerless, feeble*.

ἀ-λᾰπάζω, Ep. impf. ἀλάπαζον: f. ἀλαπάξω: Ep.

aor. ἀλάπαξα: (α euphon., λαπάζω):—*to empty, drain, make poor*: esp. *to drain of power* and *strength, overcome, slay.*

ἅλας, ἅτος, τό, = ἅλς, *salt.*

ἀλαστέω, (ἄλαστος) *to be wrathful, bear hate.*

ἀλάστορος, ον, (ἀλάστωρ) *under the influence of an avenger.*

ἄ-λαστος, ον, (α privat., λανθάνομαι) *not to be forgotten, insufferable, unceasing*: *abominable, accursed.* Hence

ἀ-λάστωρ, ορος, ὁ, (α privat., λανθάνομαι) *he who forgets not, the Avenging Deity*, Lat. *Deus Vindex*, with or without δαίμων: then, generally, *an avenger, persecutor, tormentor*; βουκόλων ἀλάστωρ the herdsmen's *plague.* II. pass. *one who suffers from divine vengeance*: *a sinner, evil-doer, accursed and polluted man.*

ἀλάτας, ὁ, Dor. for ἀλήτης.

ἀλᾶτεία, ἡ, Dor. for ἀλητεία.

ἀλᾶτο, 3 sing. Ep. impf. of ἀλάομαι.

ἀλαωτύς, ύος, ἡ, (ἀλαόω) *a making blind, blinding.*

ἀλγεινός, ή, όν, (ἄλγος) *giving pain, painful, grievous*:—Adv. -νῶς. II. act. *feeling pain, suffering.* For Comp. and Sup., v. ἀλγίων.

ἀλγεσί-δωρος, ον, (ἄλγος, δῶρον) *bringing pain.*

ἀλγέω, f. ήσω: aor. 1 ἤλγησα: (ἄλγος):—*to feel bodily pain, suffer pain*: *to be sick.* II. metaph. *to feel pain of mind, to grieve, be troubled* or *distressed*: *to suffer pain at* or *about* a thing.

ἀλγηδών, όνος, ἡ, (ἀλγέω) *a sense of pain, pain, grief*, of body or mind.

ἄλγημα, ατος, τό, (ἀλγέω) *pain felt* or *caused.*

ἄλγησις, εως, ἡ, (ἀλγέω) *sense of pain.*

ἀλγινόεις, εσσα, εν, (ἄλγος) *painful, grievous.*

ἀλγίων, ον, gen. ονος, and **ἄλγιστος**, η, ον, irreg. Comp. and Sup. of ἀλγεινός, formed from Subst. ἄλγος (as καλλίων, κάλλιστος from κάλλος). [ῐ Ep., but ῑ Att.]

ἌΛΓΟΣ, εος, τό, *pain*, Lat. *dolor*, whether of body or mind; *pain, sorrow, grief, distress.* II. later, *anything that causes pain.* Hence

ἀλγύνω, f. ὑνῶ: aor. 1 ἤλγῦνα.—Pass. with f. med. ἀλγυνοῦμαι: aor. 1 ἠλγύνθην:—*to pain, grieve, distress*:—Pass. *to feel pain, be grieved* or *distressed at* a thing.

ἀλδαίνω: aor. 2 ἤλδᾰνον:—*to make to grow, nourish, strengthen*; ἤλδανε μέλεα she *filled out* his limbs: *to increase, multiply.* Only poët. (From *ἄλω, Lat. *alo.*)

ἀλδήσκω, *to grow, wax, thrive.* II. trans. = ἀλδαίνω. (From Root 'ΑΛ-, as in Lat. *alĕre.*)

ἀλέα, Ion. ἀλέη, ἡ, (ἄλη, ἀλεύω) *an avoiding, escaping*: c. gen. *flight from* a thing, *shelter from* it.

'ΑΛΕ'Α, Ion. ἀλέη, ἡ, = εἵλη, *heat* or *warmth*, of the sun, or of fire. Hence

ἀλεαίνω, *to warm, make warm, sun*: intr. *to grow warm, be warm.*

ἀλέασθαι, ἀλέασθε, Ep. aor. 1 inf. and imper. pl. of ἀλέομαι.

ἀλεγεινός, ή, όν, (ἀλέγω) cf. ἀλγεινός) *painful, grievous, troublesome*: c. inf., ἵπποι ἀλεγεινοὶ δαμήμεναι horses *hard* to break.

ἀλεγίζω, only used in pres. and Ep. impf. ἀλέγιζον: (ἀλέγω):—*to trouble oneself about* a thing, *to care for, mind, heed*, c. gen. rei.

ἀλεγύνω, chiefly used in pres. and impf.: (ἀλέγω):—in Odyssey with δαῖτα and δαῖτας, *to care for* a meal: generally afterwards *to prepare a meal for guests.*

ἀ-λέγω, (α copul., λέγω) only used in pres. *to trouble oneself, have a care, mind, heed*; mostly with the negat., οὐκ ἀλέγειν *to have no care, heed not*; rarely without negat., Λιταὶ ἀλέγουσι κιοῦσαι *they are heedful* in their course; also c. acc. vel gen. *to care for* a person or thing.—Pass., ἀλέγεσθαι ἔν τισι, *to be regarded* or *counted among.*

ἀλεεινός, ή, όν, (ἀλέα, ἄλω) *hot, warm.*

ἀλεείνω, only used in pres. and impf. = ἀλέομαι, ἀλεύομαι, (ἀλέα, ἄλη) *to shun, avoid.*

ἀλέη, ἡ, Ion. for ἀλέα.

ἄλειαρ, ἄτος, τό, (ἀλέω) *wheaten flour.*

ἄλειμμα, ατος, τό, (ἀλείφω) *anything used to anoint with, an unguent, fat, oil.*

ἀλείπτης, ου, ὁ, (ἀλείφω) *an anointer*: *a trainer, master*, properly in the wrestling-school.

ἀλείς, εῖσα, έν, aor. 2 pass. part. of εἴλω.

ἄ-λεισον, τό, (α privat., λεῖος) *an embossed cup*, generally = δέπας.

ἀλείτης, ου, ὁ, (ἄλη) *one who leads* or *goes astray, a sinner.*

ἄλειφα, τό, = ἄλειφαρ.

ἄλειφαρ, ἄτος, τό, (ἀλείφω) *unguent, oil*, used in funeral sacrifices. II. generally, *anything for smearing with, pitch, resin.*

'ΑΛΕΙ'ΦΩ, f. ψω: aor. 1 ἤλειψα, Ep. ἄλ-: pf. ἀλήλῐφα:—Pass., aor. 1 ἠλείφθην, also aor. 2 ἠλίφην [ῐ]: pf. ἀλήλιμμαι:—*to anoint with oil, oil* the skin: Homer joins ἀλεῖψαι or ἀλείψασθαι λίπ' ἐλαίῳ *to anoint* with oil (see λίπα); esp. of anointing for gymnastic exercises; οἱ ἀλειφόμενοι *the athletes.* II. like ἐπ-αλείφω, *to anoint, besmear*; οὔατα ἀλεῖψαι *to stop up* the ears. Hence

ἄλειψις, εως, ἡ, *an anointing, dyeing.*

ἀλεκτορίσκος, ὁ, Dim. of ἀλέκτωρ, *a cockerel.*

ἀλεκτορίς, ίδος, ἡ, (ἀλέκτωρ) *a hen.*

ἀλεκτοριδεύς, έως, ὁ, (ἀλέκτωρ) *a chicken.*

ἀλεκτορο-φωνία, ἡ, (ἀλέκτωρ, φωνή) *the crowing of a cock*: *cock-crow.*

ἄ-λεκτρος, ον, (α privat., λέκτρον) *unwedded*; ἄλεκτρα γάμων ἁμιλλήματα an *unlawful* contest of marriage: ἄλεκτρα is also used Adv. *without marriage.*

ἀλεκτρύαινα, ἡ, *a hen*, comic fem. of ἀλεκτρύων, by analogy of λέαινα to λέων.

ἀλεκτρῠών, όνος, ὁ, ἡ, (ἀλέκτωρ) *a cock* or *hen.*

'ΑΛΕ'ΚΤΩΡ, ορος, ὁ, *a cock*, Lat. *gallus.*

'ΑΛΕ'ΚΩ, less common form for ἀλέξω, *to ward off, avert*, τινί τι.

ἀλέματος, Dor. for ἠλέματος.

ἄλεν, Dor. and Ep. for ἐάλησαν, 3 pl. aor. 2 pass. of εἴλω :—but **ἀλέν**, aor. 2 part. neut., v. ἀλείς.

ἀλέξ-ανδρος, ον, (ἀλέξω, ἀνήρ) *defending men.* II. *the usual name of Paris* in the Iliad.

ἀλεξ-άνεμος, ον, (ἀλέξω, ἄνεμος) *keeping off the wind.*

ἀλέξασθαι, aor. 1 med. inf. of ἀλέξω.

ἀλεξέμεναι, -έμεν, Ep. inf. of ἀλέξω.

ἀλεξήσειε, 3 sing. aor. 1 opt. of ἀλέξω.

ἀλέξημα, τό, (ἀλέξω) *a defence, guard, help.*

ἀλέξησις, εως, ἡ, (ἀλέξω) *a keeping off, resistance.*

ἀλεξήσω, fut. of ἀλέξω.

ἀλεξήτειρα, ἡ, fem. of ἀλεξητήρ.

ἀλεξητήρ, ῆρος, ὁ, (ἀλέξω) *one who keeps off, a helper, guardian; ἀλεξητὴρ μάχης one who keeps* the *fight off* the rest, a champion. Hence

ἀλεξητήριος, α, ον, *able to keep off, defend* or *help*, esp. as epith. of the gods, like Lat. *Averrunci.* II. ἀλεξητήριον (sub. φάρμακον), τό, *a remedy, protection.*

ἀλεξήτωρ, ορος, ὁ, = ἀλεξητήρ.

ἀλεξι-άρη, ἡ, (ἀλέξω, ἀρά) *she that keeps off a curse;* or (from ἀλέξω, Ἄρης) *she that guards from death and ruin.* [ᾰρ]

ἀλεξι-βέλεμνος, ον, (ἀλέξω, βέλεμνον) *keeping off arrows* or *darts.*

ἀλεξί-κᾰκος, ον, (ἀλέξω, κακόν) *keeping off evil.*

ἀλεξίμ-βροτος, ον, (ἀλέξω, βροτός) *protecting mortals.*

ἀλεξί-μορος, ον, (ἀλέξω, μόρος) *warding off death.*

ἀλεξι-φάρμακον, τό, *a means of keeping off poison, an antidote.*

ἈΛΕ'ΞΩ :—the tenses are formed partly from ἀλεξέω, partly from ἀλέκω :—fut. ἀλεξήσω; 3 sing. aor. 1 act. opt. ἀλεξήσειε; fut. med. ἀλεξήσομαι :—but also fut. ἀλέξω; aor. 1 ἤλεξα; fut. med. ἀλέξομαι; aor. 1 ἠλεξάμην :—also an Ep. aor. 2 without augm. (as if from *ἄλκω) ἄλαλκον, inf. ἀλαλκεῖν, -έμεναι, -έμεν, part. ἀλαλκών; whence again is formed a fut. ἀλαλκήσω :—*to ward* or *keep off, turn away* or *aside*, hence *to defend, assist, aid* :—Construct., c. dat. pers. et acc. rei separately, as, ἀλέξειν τινί *to help* one; Ζεὺς τόγ' ἀλεξήσειε *may Jove avert* this; but most freq. together, as, ἀλέξειν Δαναοῖς κακὸν ἦμαρ *to avert* the day of evil from the Danai; cf. ἄλαλκε :—Med., ἀλέξεσθαί τινα *to keep* another *off from oneself, defend oneself against* him, Lat. *defendere*: also absol. *to defend oneself.* II. in Med. also, *to requite, repay, recompense.*

ἀλέομαι, contr. **ἀλεῦμαι**, also **ἀλεύομαι**: 3 sing. opt. ἀλέοιτο: part. ἀλεύμενος: but chiefly used by Homer in 3 sing. aor. 1 ἠλεύατο or ἀλεύατο; imper. ἄλευαι, ἀλέασθε; subj. ἀλέηται or ἀλεύεται; opt. ἀλέαιτο; inf. ἀλέασθαι, ἀλεύασθαι; part. ἀλευάμενος: Dep.: (ἀλεύω) :—*to avoid, shun*, usu. c. acc. rei, ἀλ. βέλος, θάνατον, rarely c. acc. pers.: also c. inf. *to avoid* doing, *omit to* do: absol. *to escape, flee, avoid*: *to neglect*: cf. ἀλεῦ.

ἄλεσσαν, Ep. for ἤλεσαν, 3 plur. aor. 1 of ἀλέω.

ἄλεται, Ep. for ἄληται, 3 sing. aor 2 subj. of ἅλλομαι, *to leap.*

ἀλέτης, ου, ὁ, (ἀλέω) *a grinder; ἀλέτης ὄνος* a mill-stone.

ἀλετός, ὁ, (ἀλέω) *a grinding.*

ἀλετρεύω, f. εύσω, longer form of ἀλέω, *to grind.* [ᾰ]

ἀλε-τρίβᾰνος, ὁ, (ἀλέω, τρίβω) *that which grinds* or *pounds, a pestle.*

ἀλετρίς, ίδος, ἡ, (ἀλέω) *a female slave who grinds corn*, Lat. *molitrix.* [ᾰ]

ἀλεῦ or **ἄλευ**, prob. shortened for ἀλέου, imper. of ἀλέομαι, *avoid! cease!*

ἀλευάμην, aor. 1 of ἀλέομαι.

ἄλευρον, τό, (ἀλέω) *wheaten flour, fine meal*, mostly in plur. ἄλευρα, distinguished from ἄλφιτα (*barley-meal*).

ἀλεύω, f. ἀλεύσω, aor. 1 ἤλευσα, used as Act. to ἀλέομαι or ἀλεύομαι (v. ἀλέομαι) :—*to remove, keep far away.*

ἈΛΕ'Ω : impf. ἤλουν: fut. ἀλέσω: aor. 1 ἤλεσα, Ep. ἄλεσσα: pf. ἀλήλεκα, pass. ἀλήλεσμαι or ἀλήλεμαι :—*to grind, bruise, pound*, Lat. *molĕre.*

ἀλεωρή, Att. **ἀλεωρά**, ἡ, (ἀλέομαι) *an avoiding, shunning, escaping.* 2. *a means of escape from, a defence against* a person or thing, δηίων ἀνδρῶν ἀλεωρή :—absol. *help, succour.*

ἌΛΗ, ἡ, (ἀλάομαι) *ceaseless wandering* or *roaming.* 2. metaph. *a wandering of mind, distraction, madness*, Lat. *error mentis.*

ἀλήθειᾰ, poët. **ἀληθείᾱ**, ἡ, (ἀληθής) *truth.* II. *the character of one who speaks truth, frankness, sincerity.*

ἀληθέστερον, **-έστατα**, Comp. and Sup. of ἀληθῶς.

ἀληθεύω, f. εύσω, (ἀληθής) of persons, *to speak truth, to be truthful*: of things, *to be true*: of divinations, in Pass. *to come true, be fulfilled* :—ἀλήθευσον πάντα *speak truth* in all things.

ἀ-ληθής, ές, (α privat., λήθω) *without reserve* :—of persons, *true, sincere; truthful, frank, honest*: of things, *real, actual.* 2. neut. as Adv. with ironical signf.; proparox. ἄληθες; *itane? indeed? in sooth?* but τὸ ἀληθές, *in very truth, really and truly*, Lat. *revera.*

ἀληθίζομαι, Dep. = ἀληθεύω.

ἀληθῐνός, ή, όν, (ἀληθής) *agreeable to truth* :—of persons, *truthful, honest*: of things, *real, actual, genuine.* Adv. -νῶς.

ἀληθό-μαντις, εως, ὁ, ἡ, (ἀληθής, μάντις) *prophet of truth.*

ἀληθοσύνη, ἡ, poët. for ἀλήθεια.

ἀλήθω, fut. ήσω, = ἀλέω, *to grind.*

ἀληθῶς, Ion. -έως, Adv. of ἀληθής, *really, truly*; also ὡς ἀληθῶς :—Comp. ἀληθέστερον, *more truly*; Sup. ἀληθέστατα, *most truly.*

Ἀλήϊον πεδίον, τό, (ἄλη) *land of wandering*, in Lycia or Cilicia.

ἀ-λήϊος, ον, (α privat., λήϊον) *without corn-land, poor.*

ἄ-ληκτος, Ep. **ἄλληκτος**, ον, (α privat., λήγω) *unceasing, incessant*; ἄλληκτος θυμὸς *implacable* anger; ἄλληκτος χόλου *abating not from* wrath.

ἀλήλεκα, ἀλήλεσμαι or **–εμαι,** Att. pf. act. and pass. of ἀλέω, *to grind.*

ἀλήλῐφα, ἀλήλιμμαι, Att. pf. act. and pass. of ἀλείφω.

ἄλημα, τό, (ἀλέω) properly *that which is ground, fine flour:* metaph. *a wily knave.*

ἀλήμεναι, Ep. for ἀλῆναι, aor. 2 pass. inf. of εἴλω.

ἀλήμων, *ονος,* ὁ, ἡ, (ἀλάομαι) *a wanderer, rover.*

ἀλῆναι, aor. 2 pass. inf. of εἴλω.

ἄ-ληπτος, *ον,* (α privat., λαμβάνω) *not to be laid hold of, hard to catch:* Comp. ἀληπτότερος, *less amenable.* 2. *incomprehensible.*

'ΑΛΗ'Σ or **ἀλής,** *ές,* Ep. and Ion. Adj. = Att. ἀθρόος, *thronged, in a mass,* Lat. *confertus.* [ᾱ]

ἄληται, 3 sing. aor. 2 med. subj. of ἅλλομαι.

ἀλητεία, Dor. **ἀλᾱτεία,** ἡ, *a wandering, roaming.* From

ἀλητεύω, f. εύσω, (ἀλήτης) *to be a wanderer, live a vagrant life.*

ἀλητός, ὁ, (ἀλέω) *a grinding* in the mill.

ἀλήτης, *ου,* ὁ, (ἀλάομαι) *a wanderer, stroller, rover, vagabond.* 2. as Adj. *vagrant, roving.*

'ΑΛΘΟΜΑΙ, Ep. impf. ἀλθόμην: fut. ἀλθήσομαι: —*to become whole* or *sound;* ἄλθετο χείρ.

ἁλία, Ion. **ἁλίη,** ἡ, (ἀλής) *an assembly, gathering* of the people, Dor. and Ion. word for the Attic ἐκκλησία.

ἁλιά, ἡ, (ἅλς) *a salt-cellar.*

ἁλιάδαι, ῶν, οἱ, (ἅλς) *seamen.*

ἁλῐ-άετος, poët. **ἁλιαίετος,** ὁ, (ἅλς, ἀετός) *the sea-eagle, osprey.*

ἁλι-ᾱής, *ές,* (ἅλς, ἄημι) *blowing on the sea, blowing sea-ward.*

ἁλι-ανθής, *ές,* (ἅλς, ἄνθος) *sea-blooming,* i.e. *purple.*

ἀ-λίαστος, *ον,* (α privat., λιάζομαι) *unyielding, unabating:* neut. ἀλίαστον as Adv., *incessantly.*

ἁλί-βᾰτος, *ον,* Dor. for ἠλίβατος.

ἁλί-βρεκτος, *ον,* (ἅλς, βρέχω) *washed by the sea.*

ἀλίγκιος, *α, ον, resembling, like.* (Deriv. uncertain.) [ᾰ]

ἁλί-δονος, *ον,* (ἅλς, δονέω) *sea-tossed.*

ἁλι-ερκής, *ές,* (ἅλς, ἕρκος) *sea-girt, surrounded by the sea.*

ἁλιεύς, gen. έως, Ion. ῆος, ὁ, (ἅλς, ἅλιος) *one who has to do with the sea,* and so I. *a fisher.* II. *a seaman, sailor:* with another Subst. ἐρέτας ἁλιῆας rowers *on the sea.*

ἁλιευτικός, ή, όν, (ἁλιεύω) *of* or *for fishing.*

ἁλιεύω, f. σω, (ἁλιεύς) *to be a fisher, to fish.*

ἁλίζω, f. ίσω: aor. ἥλῐσα:—Pass., aor. 1 ἡλίσθην: pf. ἥλισμαι, Ion. ἅλισμαι: (ἁλής) :—*to gather together, assemble:*—Pass. *to assemble, meet together.* [ᾱ]

ἁλίζω, f. ίσω, (ἅλς) *to salt.* [ᾰ]

ἁλί-ζωνος, *ον,* (ἅλς, ζώνη) *sea-girt.*

ἁλίη, ἡ, Ion. for ἁλία.

ἁλι-ήρης, *ες,* (ἅλς, ἐρέσσω) *sweeping the sea.*

ἁλιήτωρ, *ορος,* ὁ, poët. for ἁλιεύς.

ἁλίῃσι, Ep. dat. plur. of ἁλίη.

ἀλίθιος, Dor. for ἠλίθιος.

ἄ-λῐθος, *ον, without stones, not stony.*

ἁλικία, ἡ, Dor. for ἡλικία.

ἁλί-κλυστος, *ον,* (ἅλς, κλύζω) *sea-beaten.*

ἁλί-κμητος, *ον,* (ἅλς, κάμνω) *wearied by the sea.*

ἁλίκος, *α, ον,* Dor. for ἡλίκος.

ἁλί-κτῠπος, *ον,* (ἅλς, κτυπέω) *sounding in the sea, sea-beaten,* of ships. II. act. *roaring over the sea,* of waves.

ἁλῐ-κύμων, *ον,* gen. *ονος,* (ἅλς, κῦμα) *surrounded by waves.* [ῡ]

ἁλι-μέδων, *οντος,* ὁ, (ἅλς, μέδων) *lord of the sea.*

ἀ-λίμενος, *ον,* (α privat., λιμήν) *without harbour,* Lat. *importuosus:* generally, *giving no shelter, inhospitable.* Hence

ἀ-λῐμενότης, ἡ, *the being without harbours.*

ἁλῐ-μῡρήεις, εσσα, εν, (ἅλς, μύρω) *flowing into the sea,* of rivers.

ἀλίνδω, aor. 1 ἤλῑσα, inf. ἀλῖσαι: pf. ἤλῑκα:—*to make* a horse *roll:*—Pass. **ἀλινδέομαι** or **ἁλίνδομαι,** *to roll* like a horse; also *to wander up and down, roam about.* Hence

ἀλινδήθρα, ἡ, *a place for horses to roll in,* Lat. *volutabrum.*

ἁλῐ-νήκτειρα, ἡ, fem. noun, as if from ἁλι-νηκτήρ (ἅλς, νήχω) *swimming in the sea.*

ἁλῐ-νηχής, *ές,* (ἅλς, νήχομαι) *swimming in the sea.*

ἅλῐνος, *η, ον,* (ἅλς) *made of* or *from salt.*

ἄ-λῐνος, *ον,* (α privat., λίνον) *without a net, without hunting toils.*

ἆλιξ, Dor. for ἧλιξ.

ἁλί-ξαντος, *ον,* (ἅλς, ξαίνω) *worn by the sea.*

ἅλιος, ὁ, Dor. for ἥλιος, *the sun.* [ᾱ]

ἅλιος, *α, ον,* also *ος, ον,* (ἅλς) *of, from,* or *belonging to the sea,* Lat. *marinus.* [ᾰ]

ἅλιος, *α, ον,* = μάταιος, *fruitless, unprofitable, idle, erring:* also in neut. as Adv. *in vain.* [ᾰ] (Deriv. uncertain.)

ἁλιο-τρεφής, *ές,* (ἅλιος, τρέφω) *sea-nurtured.*

ἁλιόω, f. ώσω: aor. 1 ἡλίωσα, Ep. ἁλίωσα: (ἅλιος II) :—*to make fruitless, disappoint.*

ἀ-λῑπᾰρής, *ές, not fit for a suppliant.*

ἁλίπεδον, τό, (ἅλς, πεδίον) *a plain by the sea, a sand tract,* esp. one near the Piraeeus.

ἁλί-πλαγκτος, *ον,* (ἅλς, πλάζω) *roaming in* or *by the sea.*

ἁλίπλακτος, Dor. for ἁλίπληκτος.

ἁλι-πλᾰνής, *ές,* (ἅλς, πλάνη) *sea-wandering, wandering over the sea.* Hence

ἁλιπλᾰνία, ἡ, *a wandering over the sea, wandering voyage.*

ἁλί-πληκτος, Dor. **-πλακτος,** *ον,* (ἅλς, πλήσσω) *sea-beaten, lashed by the sea.*

ἁλί-πλοος, *ον,* contr. **ἁλί-πλους,** *ουν,* (ἅλς, πλέω) *merged in the sea, covered with water.*

ἁλι-πόρος, *ον,* (ἅλς, πείρω) *ploughing the sea.*

ἁλι-πόρφῠρος, *ον,* (ἅλς, πορφύρα) *of sea-purple, of deep purple dye.*

ἁλιρ-ρᾰγής, ές, (ἅλς, ῥᾰγῆναι) *breaking the waves, against which the tide breaks.*

ἁλίρ-ραντος, ον, (ἅλς, ῥαίνω) *sea-surging.*

ἁλίρ-ρηκτος, ον, = ἁλιρραγής.

ἁλιρ-ρόθιος, ον, also η, ον, (ἅλς, ῥόθος) *roaring with waves, sea-beaten.*

ἁλίρ-ροθος, ον, = ἁλιρρόθιος.

ἁλίρ-ρῠτος, ον, (ἅλς, ῥέω) *washed by the sea.*

ἍΛΙΣ, Adv. (ἁλής) *in heaps, crowds, swarms, in abundance, enough*, Lat. *satis:* also c. gen., ἅλις ἀργύρου silver *enough*, Lat. *sat argenti;* ἅλις ἔχω τινός I have *enough* of a thing: rarely *just enough*, = μετρίως.

ἁλῖσαι, aor. 1 inf. of ἁλίνδω.

ἉΛΙΣΓΕ'Ω, f. ήσω, *to pollute.* Hence

ἁλίσγημα, ατος, τό, *a pollution.*

ἁλίσκομαι, a defect. Pass., the Act. of which is supplied by αἱρέω: impf. ἡλισκόμην: fut. ἁλώσομαι: aor. 2 syncop. ἥλων, Att. also ἑάλων [ᾱ]; subj. ἁλῶ, Ep. ἁλώω; opt. ἁλοίην, Ep. ἁλῴην; inf. ἁλῶναι [ᾰ]; part. ἁλούς: pf. ἥλωκα, Att. also ἑάλωκα [ᾰ]: plqpf. ἡλώκειν:—*to be taken, conquered, fall into the enemy's hand.* 2. *to be caught, seized.* 3. *to be taken* or *caught* in hunting: also absol. *to be overpowered.* 4. rarely in good sense, *to be won, achieved.* II. *to be caught* or *detected* in a thing: as Att. law-term, *to be convicted*, and so *condemned*, c. gen. criminis; ἁλῶναι κλοπῆς *to be convicted* of theft.

ἁλι-στέφᾰνος, ον, = sq.

ἁλι-στεφής, ές, (ἅλς, στέφω) *sea-girt.*

ἁλί-στονος, ον, (ἅλς, στένω) *sea-resounding.*

ἁλιστός, ή, όν, (ἁλίζω) *salted, pickled.*

ἁλί-στρεπτος, ον, (ἅλς, στρέφω) *whirled* or *rolled to and fro in the sea, sea-tossed.*

ἀλῐταίνω, f. ἀλιτήσω: aor. 2 ἤλιτον, inf. ἀλιτεῖν: later also aor. 1 ἠλίτησα.—Med., aor. 2 ἠλιτόμην, 3 pl. Ep. ἀλίτοντο, inf. ἀλιτέσθαι: see ἀλιτήμενος: (ἄλη):—*to sin* or *offend against, to transgress, err.*

ἀ-λῐτάνευτος, ον, (α privat., λιτανεύω) *not to be moved by prayer.*

ἀλῐτεῖν, aor. 2 inf. of ἀλιταίνω.

ἁλι-τενής, ές, (ἅλς, τείνω) *stretching along the sea*, and so *level, flat.*

ἁλῐ-τέρμων, ον, gen. ονος, (ἅλς, τέρμα) *bounded by the sea, bordering on it.*

ἀλίτημα, ατος, τό, (ἀλῐτεῖν) *a sin, offence.*

ἀλῐτήμενος, a part. med. of ἀλιταίνω, with accent and signf. of pres., sinning, as if formed from ἀλίτημι. Compare τιθήμενος, Ep. for τιθέμενος.

ἀλῐτ-ήμερος, ον, (ἀλιτεῖν, ἡμέρα) *missing the right day* or *right time:* hence *untimely born.*

ἀλῐτήμων, ον, gen. ονος, (ἀλιτεῖν) *sinful, wicked.*

ἀλῐτήριος, ον, (ἀλιτεῖν) *sinful, laden with guilt:* ἀλιτήριός τινος *sinning against* him.

ἀλίτοντο, Ep. 3 pl. aor. 2 med. of ἀλῐταίνω.

ἀλῐτό-ξενος, ον, (ἀλιτεῖν, ξένος) *sinning against a guest.*

ἀλῐτο-φροσύνη, ἡ, (ἀλιτεῖν, φρήν) *a wicked mind.*

ἀλιτραίνω, = ἀλιταίνω.

ἀλιτρία, ἡ, (ἀλιτρός) *sinfulness, wickedness, mischief.*

ἀλιτρό-νοος, ον, (ἀλιτρός, νόος) *wicked-minded.*

ἀλιτρός, όν, syncop. for ἀλιτηρός, (ἀλιτεῖν) *sinful, sinning:* as Subst., ἀλιτρός, ὁ, *a sinner, a knave.*

ἁλί-τρῡτος, ον, also η, ον, (ἅλς, τρύω) *sea-beaten, sea-worn.*

ἁλί-τῠπος, ον, (ἅλς, τύπτω) *sea-beaten, sea-tossed:* as Subst., ἁλίτυπος, ὁ, *a seaman.*

ἁλί-τῡρος, ὁ, (ἅλς, τυρός) *a salt cheese.*

ἁλίως, Adv. of ἅλιος, *in vain.*

ἀλῐφῆναι, aor. 2 pass. inf. of ἀλείφω.

ἁλιφθορία, ἡ, *shipwreck.* From

ἁλι-φθόρος, ον, (ἅλς, φθείρω) *destroying on the sea:* as Subst. **ἁλιφθόρος**, ὁ, *a pirate.*

ἀλκαῖος, α, ον, (ἀλκή) *strong, mighty.*

ἄλκᾰρ, τό, only used in nom. and acc., (ἀλκή) *a safeguard, bulwark, defence.*

ἀλκᾶς, ᾶντος, ὁ, ἡ, Dor. contr. from ἀλκάεις, = ἀλκήεις.

ἀλκή, ἡ, (ἀλαλκεῖν) *bodily strength, force, prowess, power, might:* in plur. ἀλκαί, *feats of strength.* II. *spirit, courage.* III. *a safeguard, defence;* and so *help, succour.* IV. *battle, fight.*

ἀλκήεις, εσσα: Dor. **ἀλκάεις** contr. **ἀλκᾶς**, gen. ἀλκᾶντος: (ἀλκή) *valiant, mighty.*

ἀλκί, heterocl. Ep. dat. of ἀλκή, formed as if from ἄλξ.

ἀλκί-μαχος, ον, (ἀλκή, μάχομαι) *bravely-fighting.*

ἄλκῐμος, ον, also η, ον, (ἀλκή) *strong, stout, brave.*

ἀλκί-φρων, ον, gen. ονος, (ἀλκή, φρήν) *stout-hearted.*

ἀλκτήρ, ῆρος, ὁ, (ἀλαλκεῖν) *one who wards off, a protector.*

ἀλκῠονίδες, αἱ, with or without ἡμέραι, (ἀλκύων) *halcyon days, the 14 winter days during which the halcyon builds its nest, supposed to be quite calm.*

'ΑΛΚΥ˘Ω'Ν, όνος, ἡ, *the kingfisher, halcyon.*

'ΑΛΛΑ', Conjunct., neut. pl. of ἄλλος, but with a change of accent:—*in another way, otherwise:* I. to oppose single clauses, *but*, Lat. *autem.* II. to oppose whole sentences, *but, yet*, Lat. *at:*—it may even be used with imperat., to encourage, persuade, etc., like Lat. *tandem;* ἀλλ' ἴθι, ἀλλ' ἄγε, *well* come, come *now.* III. joined with other Particles: 1. ἀλλ' οὖν, *but then, however.* 2. ἀλλὰ γάρ, Lat. *enimvero, but really, certainly.*

ἀλλᾰγή, ἡ, (ἀλλάσσω) *a change: exchange, barter.*

ἄλλαγμα, ατος, τό, *that which is given* or *taken in exchange, the price* of a thing.

ἀλλαντοπωλέω, *to sell sausages.* From

ἀλλαντο-πώλης, ου, ὁ, (ἀλλᾶς, πωλέω) *a sausage-seller.*

ἀλλάξαι, ἀλλάξασθαι, aor. 1 act. and med. inf. of ἀλλάσσω.

ἄλλαξις, εως, ἡ, (ἀλλάσσω) *a changing, interchange.*

'ΑΛΛΑ͂Σ, ᾶντος, ὁ, *a sausage.*

ἀλλάσσω, Att. -ττω, f. άξω: aor. 1 ἤλλαξα: pf. ἤλλαχα:—Pass., fut. 1 ἀλλαχθήσομαι, fut. 2 ἀλλαγήσομαι: aor. 1 ἠλλάχθην, aor. 2 ἠλλάγην: pf. ἤλλαγμαι: (ἄλλος):—*to make other than it is, to change, alter.* II. *to give in exchange, to requite, repay.* 2. *to change,* and so *leave, quit.* III. *to take in exchange, exchange,* τί τινος or ἀντί τινος one thing *for* another. 2. *to go to,* c. acc. loci, like Lat. *mutare.* IV. Med. *to change* or *alter one's own,* but oftener *to exchange for oneself, exchange, interchange:* hence *to barter, traffic:*—and so, either 1. *to buy,* or 2. *to sell.*

ἀλλᾰχῆ, Adv. (ἄλλος) *elsewhere, in another place,* Lat. *alibi;* ἄλλοτε ἀλλαχῆ at one time *in one place,* at another *in another.*

ἀλλαχόθεν, Adv. (ἄλλος) *from another place: by another way.*

ἀλλᾰχόθι, Adv. (ἄλλος) *elsewhere, somewhere else.*

ἀλλαχόσε, Adv *elsewhither, to another place.*

ἀλλᾰχοῦ, Adv. *elsewhere, somewhere else,* Lat. *alibi.*

ἄλλεγον, ἀλλέξαι, Ep. for ἀνέλεγον, ἀναλέξαι, v. ἀναλέγω.

ἄλλῃ, Adv. properly dat. fem. of ἄλλος, I. Adv. of Place: 1. *in another place, elsewhere,* Lat. *alibi.* 2. *to another place, elsewhither,* Lat. *aliorsum.* II. Adv. of Manner, *in another way, somehow else, otherwise,* Lat. *alias.*

ἀλλ' ἤ, i. e. ἄλλο ἤ, *except.*

ἀλλ-ηγορέω, (ἄλλος, ἀγορεύω) *to speak* so as *to imply other than what is said, to express* or *to interpret allegorically.*

ἄλ-ληκτος, ον, poët. for ἄ-ληκτος.

ἀλληλοφᾰγία, ἡ, *an eating one another.* From

ἀλληλο-φάγος, ον, (ἀλλήλων, φᾰγεῖν) *eating one another.*

ἀλληλοφθορία, ἡ, *mutual destruction.* From

ἀλληλο-φθόρος, ον, (ἀλλήλων, φθείρω) *destroying one another.*

ἀλληλοφονία, ἡ, *mutual slaughter.* From

ἀλληλο-φόνος, ον, (ἀλλήλων, *φένω) *murdering one another.*

ἀλλήλων, a gen. plur. which has no nom.: dat. ἀλλήλοις, αις, οις: acc. ἀλλήλους, ας, α: (ἄλλος):—*of one another, to one another, one another.* Hence

ἀλλήλως, Adv. *reciprocally, mutually.*

ἄλ-λιστος, ον, poët. for ἄ-λιστος, (α privat., λίσσομαι) *inexorable.*

ἀλ-λιτάνευτος, ον, poët. for ἀ-λιτάνευτος, (α privat., λιτανεύω) *inexorable.*

ἀλλο-γενής, ές, (ἄλλος, γένος) *of another race: a foreigner.*

ἀλλό-γλωσσος, ον, (ἄλλος, γλῶσσα) *of a strange tongue, foreign.*

ἀλλο-γνοέω, Ion. aor. 1 part. ἀλλογνώσας, (ἄλλος, νοέω) *to take one person* or *thing for another, to mistake.*

ἀλλό-γνωτος, ον, (ἄλλος, γιγνώσκω) *mistaken for another* person or thing, *unknown.*

ἀλλο-δᾰπός, ή, όν, *strange, foreign, belonging to another, people* or *land:* ἀλλοδαπῇ (sc. γῇ) *in a strange land.* (Deriv. of -δαπος uncertain.)

ἀλλοδοξέω, f. ήσω, (ἀλλόδοξος) *to mistake one* thing *for another.* Hence

ἀλλοδοξία, ἡ, *a mistaking one* thing for *another.*

ἀλλό-δοξος, ον, (ἄλλος, δόξα) *holding another opinion.*

ἀλλο-ειδής, ές, (ἄλλος, εἶδος) *of different form, looking differently.*

ἄλλοθ', Ep. elision for ἄλλοθι.

ἄλλοθεν, Adv. (ἄλλος) *from another place,* Lat. *aliunde.*

ἄλλοθι, Adv. (ἄλλος) *elsewhere, in another place,* Lat. *alibi.* II. *in another way, in another case, otherwise,* Lat. *alias.*

ἀλλό-θροος, ον, contr. -θρους, ουν, (ἄλλος, θρόος) *speaking another tongue, strange, foreign.*

ἀλλοῖος, α, ον, (ἄλλος) *of another sort* or *kind, different, other:*—Comp. ἀλλοιότερος, *different.*

ἀλλοιόω, f. ώσω: aor. 1 ἠλλοίωσα:—Pass., pf. ἠλλοίωμαι: (ἀλλοῖος):—*to make different, to change, alter:*—Pass. *to become different, be changed:* esp. *to be changed for the worse.*

ἀλλοίως, Adv. of ἀλλοῖος, *otherwise.*

ἄλλοκα, Aeol. for ἄλλοτε.

ἀλλόκοτος, ον, (ἄλλος) *of unusual kind, strange, monstrous:* also *utterly changed.* Adv. -τως.

ἍΛΛΟΜΑΙ, Lat. *SAL-IO:* fut. ἁλοῦμαι: aor. 1 ἡλάμην, inf. ἅλασθαι: aor. 2 ἡλόμην; Ep. syncop. 2 and 3 sing. (without aspirate) ἆλσο, ἆλτο; 3 subj. ἅληται, Ep. ἅλεται; inf. ἁλέσθαι; part. ἁλόμενος, Ep. ἅλμενος: Dep.:—*to spring, leap, bound.*

ἀλλο-πρόσ-αλλος, ὁ, i. e. ἄλλοτε πρὸς ἄλλον, *one who inclines first to one side then to the other, uncertain.*

ἌΛΛΟΣ, η, ο, Lat. *ALIUS, another, other:* 1. ἄλλος τις, or τὶς ἄλλος, *any other, some other:* εἴ τις ἄλλος, Lat. *si quis alius,* whoever *else.* 2. ἄλλος is often joined with other of its own cases or adverbs derived from it; as ἄλλος ἄλλο λέγει *one man* says *one thing, one another.* 3. joined with the Art., ὁ ἄλλος, *the other, the rest;* in plur. οἱ ἄλλοι, *all the others, the rest, all besides,* Lat. *ceteri;* τὰ ἄλλα, Lat. *cetera, reliqua,* in Att. often used as Adv. *for the rest, besides:* οἵ τε ἄλλοι καί.. *all others and especially..:* so also ἄλλως τε καί.., both *otherwise* and.., i. e. *especially.* 4. ἄλλος is used with numerals, when it means *yet, still, further,* etc.; πέμπτος ποταμὸς ἄλλος, *yet* a fifth river. II. more rarely like ἀλλοῖος, *of other sort, different:* hence 1. *other than what is common, strange, foreign.* 2. *other than what is, untrue, unreal.*

ἄλλοσε, Adv. (ἄλλος) *to another place, elsewhither, to foreign lands,* Lat. *aliorsum.*

ἄλλοτε, Adv. (ἄλλος, ὅτε) *at another time, at other times;* ἄλλοτε.., ἄλλοτε.., *at one time, at another.*

ἄλλο τι; Adv. (ἄλλος, τίς) *anything else?* Lat. *numquid aliud?* when followed by ἤ, the sentence is elliptic, e. g. ἄλλο τι ἢ πεινήσονται; i. e. ἄλλο τι πείσονται, ἢ πεινήσονται; will they feel *aught else* but hunger, i. e. how shall they escape hunger? but ἤ is sometimes omitted.

ἀλλοτριάζω, (ἀλλότριος) *to be estranged.*

ἀλλοτριο-επίσκοπος, ον, (ἀλλότριος, ἐπίσκοπος) *a busy-body in other men's matters.*

ἀλλοτριο-πρᾱγέω, (ἀλλότριος, πράσσω) *to meddle with other people's business.* Hence

ἀλλοτριοπρᾱγία, ἡ, *meddlesomeness.*

ἀλλότριος, α, ον, (ἄλλος) *of* or *belonging to another*, Lat. *alienus*, opp. to ἴδιος; ἀλλοτρίων χαρίσασθαι to be bountiful *of what is another's*; ἀλλοτρίοις γναθμοῖς γελᾶν to laugh with a face *unlike one's own*, Horace's *ridere malis alienis.* II. *foreign*, Lat. *peregrinus*: hence *strange, alien*: also *estranged, hostile.*

ἀλλοτριότης, ητος, ἡ, (ἀλλότριος) *estrangement.*

ἀλλοτριό-χρως, χρωτος, ὁ, ἡ, (ἀλλότριος, χρώς) *of divers colours.*

ἀλλοτριόω, f. ώσω, *to make strange, estrange, make hostile* or *ill-disposed*:—Pass. *to become estranged, be made an enemy.* II. *to bring into another's hands*:—Pass. *to fall into strangers' hands.* Hence

ἀλλοτρίως, Adv. of ἀλλότριος, *strangely*; ἀλλοτρίως ἔχειν to be *estranged.*

ἀλλοτρίωσις, εως, ἡ, *estrangement.*

ἄλλου, Adv. *elsewhere, in another place*, Lat. *alibi.*

ἄλ-λοφος, ον, Ep. for ἄ-λοφος.

ἀλλο-φρονέω, f. ήσω, (ἄλλος, φρονέω) *to be of another mind*: *to give no heed* to a thing. II. *to think otherwise* than as one should, *to think wrongly.* 2. *to be absent* or *unheeding*: also *to be senseless, lose one's wits.*

ἀλλό-φῦλος, ον, (ἄλλος, φυλή) *of another tribe, foreign, strange.*

ἀλλό-χροος, ον, contr. -**χρους**, ουν, (ἄλλος, χρόα) *of another colour, changeful of hue.*

ἀλλό-χρως, ωτος, ὁ, ἡ, = ἀλλόχροος, *foreign.*

ἄλλῠδις, Adv. (ἄλλος) = ἄλλοσε, *elsewhither*: Hom. has it only with ἄλλος, e. g. ἄλλυδις ἄλλος one *hither* another *thither.*

ἀλλύεσκε, **ἀλλύουσα** [ῠ], Ep. for ἀνέλυε, ἀναλύουσα: see ἀναλύω.

ἄλλως, Adv. of ἄλλος, *in another way* or *manner, otherwise*; ἄλλως πως *in* some *other way*; ἄλλως τε καί.. both *otherwise* and.., i. e. *especially, above all.* II. *otherwise than..*, *differently*: hence in good sense, *better* 2. *otherwise than as should be*: *heedlessly, without purpose*: *without reason*: also *in vain*: *for nothing*, like προῖκα, Lat. *gratis*: hence = μόνον, *only, merely.*

ἅλμα, τό, (ἅλλομαι) *a spring, leap, bound.*

ἅλμη, ἡ, (ἅλς) *sea-water that has dried*: also *the sea.* 2. *salt-water, brine.* II. *saltness.*

ἁλμήεις, εσσα, εν, (ἅλμη) *salt, briny.*

ἁλμῠρός, ά, όν, (ἅλμη) *salt, briny.* 2. metaph. *bitter, distasteful*, like Lat. *amarus.*

'ΑΛΟΑ'Ω, poët. ἀλοιάω: 3 sing. Ep. impf. ἀλοία: fut. ἀλοήσω: aor. 1 ἠλόησα, Ep. ἠλοίησα:—Pass., aor. 1 ἠλοήθην: pf. ἠλόημαι:—*to thresh, thresh out*: *to cudgel.*

ἄ-λοβος, ον, *with a lobe wanting*, of the livers of victims.

ἀλογέω, f. ήσω, (ἄλογος) *to pay no regard to* a thing, *take no heed of it*, Lat. *rationem rei non habere.* 2. *to be out of one's senses.* Hence

ἀλογία, ἡ, *want of regard* or *esteem, contempt.* II. *want of reason, senselessness, folly.*

ἀ-λόγιστος, ον, (α privat., λογίζομαι) *unreasoning, thoughtless, silly.* II. *not to be reckoned.* 2. *not to be heeded, vile.*

ἄ-λογος, ον, I. *without speech, speechless.* 2. *unspoken*, i. e. *unutterable*, Lat. *infandus* II. *without reason, irrational.* 2. *not according to reason*: *contrary to reason, absurd.* 3. *not reckoned upon, unexpected.*

'ΑΛΟ'Η, ἡ, *the aloe*, a plant.

ἀλοητός, ὁ, (ἀλοάω) *thresbing* or *threshing-time*

ἁλόθεν, Adv. (ἅλς) *from* or *out of the sea.*

ἀλοία, 3 sing. Ep. impf. of ἀλοιάω.

ἀλοιάω, poët. for ἀλοάω.

ἁλοίην, aor. 2 opt. of ἁλίσκομαι.

ἀ-λοιδόρητος, ον, (α privat., λοιδορέω) *unreviled*: *not to be reviled.*

ἀ-λοίδορος, ον, *not reviling.*

ἀλοιφή, ἡ, (ἀλείφω) *anything for smearing*: *hog's lard, grease*: also *anointing-oil, unguent*: generally, *ointment, varnish, paint.*

ἀλοκίζω, f. σω, (ἄλοξ) *to trace furrows, to write, draw.*

ἁλόντε [ᾰ], dual aor. 2 part. of ἁλίσκομαι.

'ΑΛΟΞ, οκος, ἡ, a poët. form of αὖλαξ, never used in nom. sing., *a furrow* ploughed in a field: *ploughed land, corn-land.* 2. in the skin, *a gash, wound.*

'Αλοσ-ύδνη, ἡ, (ἅλς, ὕδνης) *the sea-born*: *child of the sea*, a name of Amphitritè and of Thetis.

ἁλό-τριψ, ῐβος, ὁ, (ἅλς, τρίβω) *a pestle for pounding salt.*

ἁλ-ουργής, see ἁλουργός.

ἁλ-ουργίς, ίδος, ἡ, (ἁλουργός) *a purple robe.*

ἁλ-ουργός, όν, and **ἁλ-ουργής**, ές, (ἅλς, *ἔργω) *purple-wrought*, i. e. *dyed with sea-purple, of a genuine purple*: in pl., τὰ ἁλουργῆ *purple robes.*

ἁλούς, **ἁλοῦσα**, aor. 2 part. of ἁλίσκομαι. [ᾰ]

ἀλουσία, ἡ, *want of the bath.* From

ἄ-λουτος, (α privat., λούω) *unwashen.*

ἄ-λοφος, Ep. **ἄλ-λοφος**, ον, *without a crest.*

ἄ-λοχος, ου, ἡ, (α copul., λέχος) *the partner of one's bed, a wife.*

ἀλόω, Ep. for ἀλάου, pres. imperat. of ἀλάομαι.

ἄλπνιστος, η, ον, Sup. of obsol. **ἄλπνος**, *sweetest, loveliest.*

'ΑΛΣ, ἁλός, ὁ, Lat. *SAL*, Engl. *SALT*: in sing. *a grain* or *lump of salt*; in plur. *salt* as prepared for use.

'ΑΛΣ, ἁλός, ἡ, *the sea.*

ἄλσο, **ἄλτο**, Ep. 2 and 3 sing. aor. 2 of ἅλλομαι.

'ΑΛΣΟΣ, εος, τό, *a place grown with trees and grass, a grove*, esp. *a sacred grove*: also *a glade.*

ἀλσ-ώδης, ες, (ἄλσος, εἶδος) *like a grove, woodland.*

ἁλτῐκός, ή, όν, (ἅλλομαι) *good at leaping, nimble.*

ἁλῠκός, ή, όν, (ἅλς) *salt.*

ἀλυκτάζω, f. άσω, (ἀλύω) *to be in trouble or dis-*

tress: also pf. pass. ἀλαλύκτημαι, as if from a pres. ἀλυκτέω,

ἀλυκτο-πέδη, ἡ, (ἄλυκτος II, πέδη) *an indissoluble bond* or *fetter.*

ἄλυκτος, ον, (ἀλύω) *troubled.* II. (α privat., λύω) = ἄλυτος, *indissoluble.*

ἀλύξαι, aor. I inf. of αλύσκω.

ἄλυξις, εως, ἡ, (ἀλύσκω) *an escaping, avoiding.*

ἀ-λύπητος, ον, (α privat., λυπέω) *not pained* or *grieved.* II. act. *not paining* or *distressing.*

ἄ-λῡπος, ον, (α privat., λύπη) *without pain* or *grief, unpained.* II. act. *not paining, causing no pain* or *grief, harmless.*

ἄ-λῠρος, ον, (α privat., λύρα) *without the lyre, unaccompanied by it:* hence *mournful.*

ἄλυσις, εως, ἡ, *a chain, bond.* (Deriv. uncertain.)

ἀ-λῡσῐτελής, ές, *useless, unprofitable:* hence *hurtful.* Adv. -λῶς.

ἀλυσκάζω, strengthd. for ἀλύσκω, used only in pres. and impf.

ἀλυσκάνω, lengthd. form of ἀλύσκω.

ἀλύσκω: fut. ἀλύξω and ἀλύξομαι: aor. I ἤλυξα, Ep. ἄλυξα: (ἀλέω):—*to flee from, shun, avoid, forsake.*

ἀλύσσω, f. ύξω, (ἀλύω) *to be uneasy, have no rest.*

ἄ-λῠτος, ον, (α privat., λύω) *not to be loosed* or *broken, indissoluble: continuous, ceaseless.*

ἄ-λυχνος, ον, *without lamp* or *light.*

ἈΛΥ'Ω, Att. **ἀλύω**, used only in pres. and impf.: (ἄλη, ἀλάομαι):—*to wander,* of the mind, *to be ill at ease, be troubled, distraught: to be at a loss,* like ἀπορέω: more rarely *to be beside oneself for joy.* [ῠ in Hom., ῡ in Att.]

ἈΛΦΑ'ΝΩ; aor. 2 ἦλφον, 3 sing. opt. ἄλφοι:—*to bring in, yield: to get, acquire:* metaph. φθόνον ἀλφάνειν *to incur* envy.

ἀλφεῖν, aor. 2 inf. of ἀλφάνω.

ἀλφεσί-βοιος, α, ον, (ἀλφεῖν, βοῦς) *bringing in oxen:* hence of maidens whose parents receive many oxen as presents from their suitors, *much-courted.*

ἀλφηστής, οῦ, ὁ, (ἀλφεῖν) always in phrase ἄνδρες ἀλφησταί, *gain-seeking, enterprizing, industrious men,* esp. applied to *trading, sea-faring* people.

ἀλφῐτ-ᾰμοιβός, ὁ, (ἄλφιτον, ἀμείβω) *a dealer in barley-meal.*

ἌΛΦΙΤΟΝ [ῐ], τό, *peeled* or *pearl-barley,* Lat. *polenta:* sing. only in phrase ἀλφίτου ἀκτή, *barley-meal:* elsewhere in plur. ἄλφιτα, *barley-groats,* and *the cakes* or *porridge made of it.* 2. metaph. *one's daily bread,* one's *substance:* πατρῷα ἄλφιτα one's patrimony.

ἀλφῐτοποιία, ἡ, *a preparing of barley-meal.* From

ἀλφιτο-ποιός, ὁ, (ποιέω) *a preparer of barley-meal.*

ἀλφῐτο-σῑτέω, f. ήσω, (ἄλφιτον, σιτέω) *to eat, live on barley-meal,* or *bread made of it.*

ἄλφοι, 3 sing. aor. 2 opt. of ἀλφάνω.

ἅλω, acc. of ἅλως.

ἁλῶ, aor. 2 subj. of ἁλίσκομαι. [ᾰ]

ἀλωεινός, ή, όν, (ἅλως) *used on a threshing-floor.*

ἀλωεύς, έως, Ep. ῆος, ὁ, (ἀλωή) *a thresher, vine-dresser.*

ἀλωή, Dor. **ἀλωά**, poët. for Att. ἅλως: I. *a threshing-floor.* II. *any levelled plot of ground, a garden, orchard, vineyard,* etc.

ἁλώῃ, Ep. for ἁλῷ, 3 sing. aor. 2 subj. of **ἁλίσκομαι.** II. **ἁλῴη**, Ep. for ἁλοίη, 3 sing. aor. 2 opt. of same verb.

ἀλωΐτης, ου, ὁ, (ἀλωή) *a husbandman, gardener.* [ᾰ]

ἁλωμέναι, Ep. for ἁλῶναι, aor. 2 inf. of **ἁλίσκομαι.** [ᾰ]

ἀλώμενος, η, ον, part. of ἀλάομαι.

ἅλων, ωνος, ἡ, = ἅλως.

ἁλῶναι, aor. 2 inf. of ἁλίσκομαι. [ᾰ]

ἀλωπεκῆ, ἡ, Att. contr. from Ion. **ἀλωπεκέη** (sub. δορά): (ἀλώπηξ) *a foxskin.*

ἀλωπεκίας, ου, ὁ, (ἀλώπηξ) *branded with a fox.*

ἀλωπεκιδεύς, έως, ὁ, (ἀλώπηξ) *a fox's cub.*

ἀλωπεκίζω, f. ίσω, (ἀλώπηξ) *to play the fox,* Lat. *vulpinari.*

ἀλωπέκιον, τό, Dim. of ἀλώπηξ, *a little fox.*

ἀλωπεκίς, ίδος, ἡ, (ἀλώπηξ) *a mongrel between fox and dog.* II. *a fox-skin cap.*

ἈΛΩ'ΠΗΞ, εκος, ἡ, *a fox,* Lat. *vulpes:* metaph. of men.

ἍΛΩΣ, ω, ἡ: gen. ἅλω or ἅλωος: acc. ἅλω, **ἅλων** or ἅλωα: pl. n. ἅλω:—*a threshing-floor.* II. *the disk* of the sun or moon.

ἁλώσῐμος, ον, (ἁλῶναι) *easy to take, catch, win,* or *conquer.* 2. of the mind, *easy to apprehend.* II. (ἅλωσις) *of* or *belonging to capture* or *conquest.*

ἅλωσις, εως, ἡ, (ἁλῶναι) *a taking, capture, conquest* II. as law-term, *detection, conviction.*

ἁλώσομαι, fut. of ἁλίσκομαι.

ἁλωτός, ή, όν, verb. Adj. of ἁλῶναι, *to be taken, caught* or *conquered: to be acquired.*

ἁλώω, Ep. for ἁλῶ, aor. 2 subj. of **ἁλίσκομαι.**

ἀμ, for ἀνά:—but **ἀμ**, for ἅμα.

ἍΜΑ, I. Adv. *at once,* Lat. *simul.* II. Prep. c. dat. *at the same time with, together with.*

ἁμᾶ, Dor. for ἅμα.

Ἀμαζών, όνος, ἡ, mostly in plur. *the Amazons:* also Ἀμαζονίδες.

ἀμᾰθαίνω, (ἀμαθής) *to be ignorant, stupid.*

ἀ-μᾰθής, ές, (α privat., μαθεῖν) *untaught, unlearned, stupid, dull:* also *coarse, rude:* also *without knowledge of* a thing. II. pass. *not learnt, unknown.* Hence

ἀμᾰθία, ἡ, *want of knowledge, ignorance.*

ἀμᾱθόεις, οεσσα, οεν, contr. ἀμαθοῦς, οῦσσα, οῦν, (ἄμαθος) = Ep. ἠμαθόεις, *sandy.*

ἌΜΑΘΟΣ, ἡ, (ἄμμος) *sand, a sandy soil;* see ψάμμος. [ᾰμᾰ-]

ἀμᾰθύνω, (ἄμαθος) *to level with the sand, utterly destroy.*

ἀμαθῶς, Adv. of ἀμαθής, *ignorantly;* ἀμαθῶς ἔχειν to be *ignorant.*

ἀ-μαιμάκετος, η, ον, lengthd. form of ἄμαχος, *irresistible, huge, enormous.*

ἀμαλδύνω, poët. for ἀμαλύνω, (ἀμαλός) properly *to*

soften: hence *to crush, destroy, ruin.* 2. metaph. *to hide, disguise.*

ἀ-μάλθακτος, ον, (α privat., μαλθάσσω) *unsoftened.*

ἄμαλλα, ἡ, (ἀμάω) *a bundle of ears of corn, sheaf.*

ἀμαλλο-δετήρ, ῆρος, and **ἀμαλλο-δετής**, οῦ, ὁ, (ἄμαλλα, δέω) *a binder of sheaves.*

ἀμᾰλός, Att. **ἁμαλός**, ή, όν, = ἁπαλός, *soft, light,* Lat. *tener.* 2. *weak, feeble.*

ἄμαξα, Att. **ἅμαξα**, ἡ, (ἄγω) *a carriage, a wagon* or *wain.* 2. *the carriage of the plough,* Lat. *currus.* 3. *Charles' wain* in the heavens, *the great bear.* 4. *a carriage-road.* Hence

ἁμαξεύομαι, Pass. *to be traversed by wagons, to have wagon-roads through it.*

ἁμαξεύς, έως, ὁ, (ἅμαξα) *a wagoner.*

ἁμαξ-ήλᾰτος, ον, (ἅμαξα, ἐλαύνω) *traversed by wagons.*

ἁμαξ-ήρης, ες, (ἅμαξα, *ἄρω, Root of ἀραρίσκω) *attached* or *belonging to a wagon* or *carriage.*

ἁμαξιαῖος, α, ον, (ἅμαξα) *fit for a wagon: large enough to load a wagon,* of stones.

ἁμαξίς, ίδος, ἡ, Dim. of ἅμαξα, *a little wagon,* Lat. *plostellum: a go-cart.*

ἁμαξίτης, ου, ὁ, (ἅμαξα) *of* or *belonging to a wagon.* [ῑ]

ἁμαξ-ῐτός, όν, (ἅμαξα, εἶμι) *traversed by wagons:* as Subst. ἁμαξιτός (sub. ὁδός), ἡ, *a high-road for wagons.*

ἁμαξο-πληθής, ές, (ἅμαξα, πλῆθος) *large enough to fill a wagon.*

ἁμαξ-ουργός, όν, (ἅμαξα, *ἔργω) *making wagons* or *carriages.*

ἆμαρ, ατος, τό, Dor. for ἦμαρ.

'ΑΜΑ'ΡΑ, ἡ, *a trench, conduit, water-course.* [ᾰμᾰρᾱ]

ἀμαράντῐνος, η, ον, = ἀμάραντος.

ἀ-μάραντος, ον, (α privat., μαραίνω) *unfading.*

'ΑΜΑΡΤΑ'ΝΩ; fut. ἁμαρτήσομαι, later -ήσω: aor. 1 ἡμάρτησα: aor. 2 ἥμαρτον, inf. ἁμαρτεῖν, Ep. by metath. (with β inserted) ἤμβροτον: pf. ἡμάρτηκα: Pass., aor. 1 ἡμαρτήθην: pf. ἡμάρτημαι:—*to miss, miss the mark,* c. gen.: hence 2. generally, *to fail of doing, fail of one's purpose, go wrong: to be deprived of* a thing, *lose* it. II. *to fail, do wrong, err, sin.*

ἅμαρτον, Ep. aor. 2 of ἁμαρτάνω.

ἁμαρτεῖν, aor. 2 inf. of ἁμαρτάνω.

ἁμαρτῆ, or **ἁμαρτῇ**, Adv. (ἅμα) *together, at the same time, at once.* [ᾰμ-]

ἁμαρτήσομαι, fut. of ἁμαρτάνω.

ἁμάρτημα, τό, (ἁμαρτεῖν) *a failure, error, sin.*

ἁμαρτητικός, ή, όν, (ἁμαρτεῖν) *prone to fail* or *err.*

ἁμαρτία, ἡ, (ἁμαρτεῖν) *a failure, error, sin.*

ἁμαρτί-νοος, ον, (ἁμαρτεῖν, νόος) *erring in mind, distraught.*

ἀμάρτιον, τό, = ἁμάρτημα.

ἁμαρτο-επής, ές, (ἁμαρτεῖν, ἔπος) *failing in words, speaking at random* or *idly.*

ἀ-μαρτύρητος, ον, (α privat., μαρτῠρέω) *without witness.*

ἀ-μάρτῠρος, ον, (α privat., μάρτυς) *without witness, unattested.*

ἁμαρτωλή, ἡ, = ἁμαρτία.

ἁμαρτωλός, όν, (ἁμαρτάνω) *sinful, hardened in sin.*

ἀμᾰρυγή, ἡ, = μαρμαρυγή, *a sparkling, twinkling, glancing,* of objects in motion. [ῠ, but in Ep. ῡ.]

ἀμάρυγμα, τό, *a sparkle, twinkle, quick motion.* From

'ΑΜΑΡΥ'ΣΣΩ, only used in pres. and impf. *to sparkle, twinkle, glance.*

ἁμᾶς, Dor. for ἡμᾶς.

ἁμα-τροχάω, only used in Ep. part. ἁματροχόων, (ἅμα, τρέχω) *to run together, run along with.* Hence

ἁματροχιά, ἡ, *a running together* or *clashing of wheels.*

ἀμαυρός, ά, όν, *dark, dim, faint, obscure.* 2. *having no light:* hence *blind, sightless, dusky, gloomy.* II. metaph. *dim, uncertain.* 2. *obscure, unknown.* (Deriv. uncertain.) Hence

ἀμαυρόω, f. ώσω: aor. 1 ἠμαύρωσα: pf. ἠμαύρωκα: —*to make dark* or *dim:*—mostly in Pass. *to become dark* or *dim; also to come to nothing.* II. metaph. *to eclipse: to weaken, impair.*

ἀμαχεί, Adv. of ἄμαχος, *without resistance.*

ἀ-μάχετος, ον, poët. for ἀμάχητος.

ἀμᾰχητί, Adv. of ἀμάχητος, *without fighting.*

ἀ-μάχητος, ον, (α privat., μάχομαι) *not to be fought with, unconquerable.* II. *never having fought.*

ἀμᾰχί, Adv. of ἄμαχος, = ἀμαχεί.

ἄ-μᾰχος, ον, (α privat., μάχη) *without battle,* and so I. *with whom no one fights, unconquered: unconquerable,* of persons: of places, *impregnable.* II. act. *not having fought.* 2. *disinclined to fight.*

'ΑΜΑ'Ω: contr. impf. ἤμων: f. ἀμήσω: aor. 1 ἤμησα:—Pass., aor. 1 ἠμήθην: pf. ἤμημαι:—*to reap, to mow:* also *to gather* in, as a reaper does corn, *to collect.* [generally, ᾱ Ep.: ᾰ Att.]

ἀμβ-, for ἀναβ-, at the beginning of words.

ἀμβαίη, Ep. for ἀναβαίη, 3 sing. aor. 2 opt. of ἀναβαίνω.

ἀμβαλλώμεθα, Ion. and Ep. for ἀναβαλλ-.

ἄμβᾰσις, ἡ, poët. for ἀνά-βασις.

ἀμβλίσκω and **ἀμβλόω**: f. ἀμβλώσω: aor. 1 ἤμβλωσα: pf. ἤμβλωκα: (ἀμβλός):—*to have an abortion, miscarry.*

ἀμβλύνω [ῡ], υνῶ: aor. 1 ἤμβλῡνα:—Pass., fut. ἀμβλυνθήσομαι: aor. 1 ἠμβλύνθην: pf. ἤμβλυμμαι: (ἀμβλύς):—*to blunt, dull, take the edge off,* Lat. *hebetare:*—Pass. *to become blunt* or *dull, lose the edge.*

'ΑΜΒΛΥ'Σ, εῖα, ύ, *blunt, dulled, with the edge* or *point taken off,* Lat. *hebes:* metaph. *dull, faint, feeble:* of persons, *spiritless, sluggish.* Hence

ἀμβλύτης [ῠ], ητος, ἡ, *dulness: sluggishness.*

ἀμβλύ-ωπος, ον, = ἀμβλωπός.

ἀμβλυώσσω, Att. -ττω, (ἀμβλύς) *to be dim-sighted* or *blind.*

ἀμβλ-ωπός, όν, and **ἀμβλ-ώψ**, ῶπος, ὁ, ἡ, (ἀμβλύς, ὤψ) *dim-looking, dark, obscure.*

ἀμ-βολάδην, Adv., poët. for ἀνα-βολάδην, (ἀναβάλλω) *bubbling up.* II. (ἀναβολή) *like a prelude.*

ἀμ-βολάς, for **ἀνα-βολάς**, άδος, ἡ, (ἀναβάλλω) γῆ ἀμβολάς earth *thrown up*.

ἀμβολι-εργός, όν, (ἀναβάλλω, ἔργον) poët. for ἀναβολ., *putting off work, lazy*.

ἀμβροσία, Ion. -ίη, ἡ, (properly fem. of ἀμβρόσιος) *ambrosia, the food of the gods*.

ἀμ-βρόσιος, α, ον, lengthd. form of ἄμ-βροτος, *immortal, divine, of divine nature*. II. of things belonging to the gods, *ambrosial, divinely fair*.

ἀμβροτεῖν, Ep. for ἁμαρτεῖν, aor. 2 inf. of ἁμαρτάνω.

ἄμ-βροτος, ον, (α privat., βροτός) *immortal, divine*.

ἀμβώσας, Ion. for ἀναβοήσας, aor. 1 part. of ἀναβοάω.

ἀμέ or **ἀμέ**, Dor. for ἡμᾶς.

ἀ-μέγαρτος, ον, (α privat., μεγαίρω) *unenvied, unenviable, unhappy*: as a reproach, *wretched, miserable*: also *horrible*.

ἀμεθύστινος, η, ον, *of amethyst*. From

ἀ-μέθυστος, ον, (α privat., μεθύω) *not drunken*. II. as Subst. ἀμέθυστος, ἡ, or ἀμέθυστον, τό, *a remedy against drunkenness*: 1. *a kind of herb*. 2. the precious stone, *amethyst*.

'**ΑΜΕΙ'ΒΩ**, Ep. impf. ἄμειβον: fut. ἀμείψω: aor. 1 ἤμειψα: I. Act. *to change, exchange*; χάλκεα χρυσείων τεύχεα ἀμείβειν *to exchange* golden arms *for* brasen: esp. of place, *to change it*, and so *to pass, cross*: like Lat. *muto*, either *to quit* a place, or *to go to* it. II. intrans. in part. ἐν ἀμείβοντι = ἀμοιβαδίς, *in exchange*: ἀμείβοντες οἱ, *rafters* that *cross* each other. III. Med. *to change one with another, do in turn* or *alternately*. 2. *to answer, reply to*. 3. *to repay, requite, avenge*. 4. like Act. *to change*, esp. of place, *to pass* either *out* or *in*: metaph. *to surpass*.

ἀ-μείδητος, ον, (α privat., μειδάω) *not smiling, gloomy*.

ἀ-μείλικτος, ον, (α privat., μειλίσσω) *unsoothed*: *harsh, cruel*.

ἀ-μείλιχος, ον, = foreg. *harsh, severe*: *relentless, unassuaged*.

ἀμείνων, ον, gen. ονος, irreg. Comp. of ἀγαθός, *better*: of persons, *abler, stronger, braver*.

'**ΑΜΕΙ'ΡΩ**, = ἀμέρδω.

ἀμειψάμενος, ἀμείψασθαι, aor. 1 med. of ἀμείβω.

ἄμειψις, εως, ἡ, (ἀμείβω) *exchange*: *succession*.

'**ΑΜΕ'ΛΓΩ**, f. ξω, *to MILK*, Lat. *MULGERE*. II. *to press* or *squeeze out*: metaph. *to drain, exhaust*. III. *to sip, drink*.

ἀμέλει, imperat. of ἀμελέω, *never mind*. Hence as Adv. *by all means, of course*.

ἀμέλεια, ἡ, (ἀμελής) *heedlessness, indifference*.

ἀμελετησία, ἡ, *want of practice* or *attention*. From

ἀ-μελέτητος, ον, (α privat., μελετάω) *unpractised, unprepared*.

ἀμελέω, f. ήσω: aor. 1 ἠμέλησα, Ep. ἀμ-: pf. ἠμέληκα: (ἀμελής):—*to be careless, heedless, negligent*. 2. *to neglect, have no care for, slight*. 3. *to overlook*, and so *to let, suffer*. 4. *to neglect to do*:—Pass. *to be neglected, slighted, overlooked*.

ἀ-μελής, ές, (α privat., μέλει) *careless, heedless, negligent*. II. pass. *uncared for, unheeded*.

ἀμελητέον, verb. Adj. of ἀμελέω, *one must neglect*.

ἀμέλητος, ον, (ἀμελέω) like ἀμελής, *not cared for*: *unworthy of care*.

ἀμελία, ἡ, poët. for ἀμέλεια, *heedlessness*.

ἀ-μέλλητος, ον, (α privat., μέλλω) *not delayed*: *not to be delayed*.

ἄμελξις, εως, ἡ, (ἀμέλγω) *a milking*.

ἀμελῶς, Adv. of ἀμελής, *carelessly*: ἀμελῶς ἔχειν to be *careless*.

ἄ-μεμπτος, ον, (α privat., μέμφομαι) *not to be blamed, blameless*: of things, *perfect*:—Adv. -τως, *so as to merit no blame*. II. act. *not blaming, find ing no fault, well content*.

ἀ-μεμφής, ές, = ἄμεμπτος II.

ἀμεμφία, ἡ, (ἀμεμφής) *blamelessness, freedom from blame*.

ἄμεναι, for ἀέμεναι, Ep. inf. of ἄω, *to satisfy*.

ἀ-μενηνός, όν, (α privat., μένος) *faint, feeble*: *weakly* or *sickly*. Hence

ἀ-μενηνόω, Ep. aor. 1 ἀμενήνωσα, *to make weak deaden the force of*.

ἀμέρα, Dor. for ἡμέρα.

'**ΑΜΕ'ΡΓΩ**, f. ξω, *to pluck* or *pull*, Lat. *decerpere*.

ἀμέρδω, f. σω: aor. 1 ἤμερσα, Ep. ἄμ-: aor. 1 pass. ἠμέρθην: (prob. from α privat., μέρος):—*to deprive of one's share, bereave one of*:—Pass. *to be bereft of* a thing, *lose it*.

ἀ-μέριμνος, ον, (α privat., μέριμνα) *free from care, unconcerned*. II. pass. *uncared for, unheeded*. III. *driving away care*.

ἀμέριος, Dor. for ἡμέριος.

ἀ-μέριστος, ον, (α privat., μερίζω) *undivided*.

ἀμερό-κοιτος, Dor. for ἡμερό-κοιτος.

ἅμερος, Dor. for ἥμερος.

ἄμερσε, **ἀμέρσαι**, 3 sing. and inf. aor. 1 of ἀμέρδω.

ἀμές or **ἀμές**, Dor. for ἡμεῖς.

ἀ-μετάθετος, ον, (α privat., μετατίθημι) *unchangeable*: τὸ ἀμετάθετον, *unchangeableness*.

ἀ-μετακίνητος, ον, (α privat., μετακινέω) *immovable*.

ἀ-μετάκλαστος, ον, (α privat., μετακλάω) *not to be broken*: *unalterable*.

ἀ-μεταμέλητος, ον, (α privat., μεταμέλει) *unrepented of*. II. act. *not repenting, unchanging*.

ἀ-μετανόητος, ον, (α privat., μετανοέω) = *unrepented of*. II. act. *unrepentant*.

ἀ-μετάπειστος, ον, (α privat., μεταπείθω) *unpersuadable*.

ἀ-μετάπτωτος, ον, (α privat., μεταπίπτω) *unchangeable*

ἀ-μετάστατος, ον, (α privat., μεθίστημι) *unalterable*.

ἀ-μεταστρεπτεί, Adv. (α privat., μεταστρέφω) *without turning about*.

ἀ-μετάστροφος, ον, (α privat., μεταστρέφω) *unalterable*.

ἀ-μετάτρεπτος, ον, (α privat., μετατρέπω) *unalterable*.

ἀμέτερος, Dor. for **ἡμέτερος**.

ἀ-μέτρητος, ον, (α privat., μετρέω) *immeasurable, immense*, Lat. *immensus: unnumbered, exhaustless.*

ἀμετρό-βιος, ον, (ἄμετρος, βίος) *of an immeasurable life.*

ἀμετρο-επής, ές, (ἄμετρος, ἔπος) *immoderate in words, unbridled of tongue.*

ἀμετρο-πότης, ου, ὁ, (ἄμετρος, πότης) *drinking to excess.*

ἄ-μετρος, ον, (α privat., μέτρον) *without measure, immense, boundless, incessant.* 2. *immoderate.*

ἀ-μέτρως, Adv. of ἄμετρος, *infinitely.*

ἀμευσί-πορος, ον, (ἀμεύων πόρος) = τρίοδος, Lat. *trivium, where three paths cross.*

ἀμεύω, Aeol. for ἀμείβω: aor. 1 med. inf. ἀμεύσασθαι:—*to surpass, excel, conquer.*

ἈΜΗ, ἡ, *a shovel* or *mattock.* 2. *a water-bucket, pail*, Lat. *hama.* 3. *a barrow, rake.*

ἀμῆ, Att. **ἁμῆ**, Adv., properly for ἀμῇ, dat. fem. of ἀμός = τὶς, *in a certain way:* ἀμηγέπη, *in some way, somehow* or *other.* [ᾰ]

ἀμήν, Hebr. Adv. *verily, of a truth: so be it:* also as a Subst. τὸ ἀμήν, *certainty.*

ἀ-μήνῑτος, ον, (α privat., μηνίω) *not wrathful.*

ἈΜΗΣ, ητος, ὁ, a kind of *milk cake.*

ἀμησάμενος, aor. 1 med. part. of ἀμάω.

ἀμητήρ, ῆρος, ὁ, (ἀμάω) *a reaper:* metaph. *one who cuts down, a destroyer.* [ᾱ]

ἄμητος, ὁ, (ἀμάω) *a reaping, harvesting:* also *harvest, harvest-time.* II. *a harvest* or *crop.*

ἀ-μήτωρ, *ορος*, ὁ, ἡ, (α privat., μήτηρ) *without mother, motherless.* II. *unlike a mother.*

ἀμηχᾰνέω: impf. ἠμηχάνουν: fut. ήσω: (ἀμήχανος):—*to be at a loss* or *in want.* Hence

ἀμηχᾰνία, Ion. -ίη, ἡ, *want of means, helplessness, distress.* II. *hardship, trouble.*

ἀ-μήχᾰνος, ον, (α privat., μηχανή) *without means* or *resource, helpless.* II. more freq. in pass. sense, *impracticable, irresistible:* also *inexplicable.*

ἀμηχανόωσι, **ἀμηχανόων**, Ep. 3 pl. and part. pres., as if from ἀμηχανάω.

ἀ-μίαντος, ον, (α privat., μιαίνω) *undefiled, pure.*

ἀμί-θεος, Dor. for ἡμί-θεος.

ἄ-μικτος, ον, (α privat., μίγνυμι) *unmixed, pure.* II. *not mingling with others, unsociable, savage.* III. *not to be mingled, irreconcilable:*—Adv. ἀμίκτως, Sup. ἀμικτότατα.

ἍΜΙΛΛΑ, ης, ἡ, *a contest for superiority, rivalry;* generally, *a struggle, conflict.* [ᾰ] Hence

ἁμιλλάομαι, fut. ήσομαι: aor. 1 med. ἡμιλλησάμην and pass. ἡμιλλήθην: pf. ἡμίλλημαι: Dep.:—*to compete, vie,* or *contend with* one, Lat. *aemulari.* II. generally, *to strive, struggle, exert oneself.* Hence

ἁμιλλητέον, verb. Adj. *one must compete.*

ἅμιλλημα, τό, (ἁμιλλάομαι) *a contest, conflict.*

ἁμιλλητήρ, ῆρος, (ἁμιλλάομαι) *a competitor, rival.*

ἀμιμητό-βιος, ον, (ἀμίμητος, βίος) *inimitable in one's life.*

ἀ-μίμητος, ον, (α privat., μιμέομαι) *inimitable.*

ἀμιξία, Ion. -ίη, ἡ, (ἄμικτος) *a being unmixed, purity.* 2. *want of intercourse, unsociableness.*

ἄμ-ιππος, ον, (ἅμα, ἵππος) *along with horses*, i. e. *fleet as a horse.* 2. ἄμιπποι, οἱ, *infantry mixed with cavalry.*

ἈΜΙ'Σ, ίδος, *a chamber-pot.*

ἀμῑσής, ές, (α privat., μῖσος) *without hatred, not hateful:* Comp. ἀμισέστερος.

ἀμισθί, Adv. of ἄμισθος, *without reward.*

ἄ-μισθος, ον, (α privat., μισθός) *without pay* or *reward.*

ἀ-μίσθωτος, ον, (α privat., μισθόω) *not let out on hire, not leased.*

ἀ-μῑτρο-χίτωνες, οἱ, (α privat., μίτρα, χιτών) *wearing no girdle with their coat of mail.*

ἀ-μιχθᾰλόεις, εσσα, εν, lengthd. form of ἄμικτος, *inaccessible, inhospitable.*

ἀμμ-, poët. for ἀναμ-. For words omitted under ἀμμ-, see under ἀναμ-.

ἅμμα, ατος, τό, (ἅπτω) *anything tied* or *made to tie:* 1. *a knot.* 2. *a noose, halter.* 3. *a cord, band.*

ἄμμε, Aeol. and Ep. for ἡμᾶς.

ἀμ-μένω, poët. for ἀνα-μένω.

ἄμμες, Aeol. and Ep. for ἡμεῖς.

ἀμ-μέσον, poët. for ἀνὰ μέσον.

ἀμμέων, Aeol. for ἡμῶν.

ἄμμι, Aeol. and Ep. for ἡμῖν.

ἄμ-μῐγα, Adv. poët. for ἀνά-μιγα.

ἀμμίξας, Ep. aor. 1 part. of ἀναμίγνυμι.

ἀμμνάσει, **ἀμμνάσειεν**, Dor. for ἀναμνήσει, ἀναμνήσειεν, fut. and aor. 1 of ἀναμιμνήσκω.

ἀμμο-δύτης, ου, ὁ, (ἄμμος, δύω) *sand-burrower*, a kind of snake.

ἀμμορία, Ion. -ίη, ἡ, (ἄμμορος) *ill fortune.*

ἄμμορος, ον, poët. for ἄ-μορος, *without lot* or *share in* a thing: absol. *unfortunate, unhappy.*

ἍΜΜΟΣ or **ἄμμος**, ἡ, *sand:* also *a sandy place, race-course.* See ψάμμος.

ἀμμό-τροφος, ον, (ἄμμος, τρέφω) *growing in sand.*

ἀμμ-ώδης, ες, (ἄμμος, εἶδος) *sandy.*

Ἀμμωνιάς, άδος, or **Ἀμμωνίς**, ίδος, ἡ, (Ἄμμων) *of* or *belonging to Jupiter Ammon*, i. e. *African.*

ἀμνάμων [ᾱ], Dor. for ἀμνήμων.

ἀμναστέω, **ἄμναστος**, Dor. for ἀμνηστ-.

ἀμνεῖος, α, ον, (ἀμνός) *of a lamb.*

ἀμνή, ἡ, fem. of ἀμνός, *a ewe-lamb.*

ἀ-μνημόνευτος, ον, (α privat., μνημονεύω) *unmentioned, unheeded.*

ἀμνημονέω, f. ήσω: aor. 1 ἠμνημόνησα:—*to be* ἀμνήμων, *be unmindful: to make no mention of, pass over.*

ἀμνημοσύνη, ἡ, *forgetfulness.* From

ἀ-μνήμων, ον, gen. ονος, (α privat., μνήμη) *unmindful, forgetful.* 2. pass. *forgotten, not mentioned.*

ἀ-μνήστευτος, ἡ, (α privat., μνηστεύω) *unwooed, not sought in marriage.*

ἀμνηστέω, (ἄμνηστος) *to be unmindful, to forget:* —Pass. *to be forgotten.*
ἀμνήσω, poët. fut. of ἀναμιμνήσκω.
ἀμνηστία, ἡ, *forgetfulness: an amnesty.* From
ἄ-μνηστος, ον, (α privat., μνάομαι) *forgotten, no longer remembered.*
ἀμνίον, τό, *a bowl in which the blood of victims was caught.* (Deriv. uncertain.)
ἀμνίς, ίδος, ἡ, = ἀμνή.
ἀμνο-κῶν, οῦντος, ὁ, (ἀμνός, κοέω) *sheep-minded,* i. e. *simple.*
'ΑΜΝΟ'Σ, ὁ and ἡ, *a lamb:* declined ἀρνός, ἀρνί, ἄρνα, ἄρνες, etc., as if from a nom. *ἄρς.
ἀμνο-φόρος, should be μαννο-φόρος.
ἀμογητί, Adv. *without toil* or *effort.* From
ἀ-μόγητος, ον, (α privat., μογέω) *without toil, unwearied, untiring.*
ἀμόθεν, Att. ἁμόθεν, Adv. (ἀμός) *from some place* or *other.*
ἀμόθι or **ἀμοθεί**, Adv. (ἀμός) *somewhere.*
ἀμοῖ, Adv. (ἀμός) *somewhither.*
ἀμοιβάδιος, α, ον, = ἀμοιβαῖος.
ἀμοιβᾰδίς, Adv. (ἀμοιβή) *by turns,* Lat. *alternatim.*
ἀμοιβαῖος, ον, also η, or α, ον, (ἀμοιβή) *interchanging, alternate:* of verses, *amoebaean, answering one another.* II. *giving like for like, retributive:*— Adv. -ως, *in requital.*
ἀμοιβάς, άδος, ἡ, pecul. fem. of ἀμοιβαῖος; χλαῖνα ἀμοιβάς a cloak *for a change.*
ἀμοιβή, ἡ, (ἀμείβω) *a recompence, return:* hence *repayment, atonement: revenge.* 2. *an answer.* II. *change, exchange, barter.*
ἀμοιβηδίς, Adv. (ἀμοιβή) *alternately.*
ἀμοιβός, ὁ, (ἀμείβω) *a successor, follower.* II. as Adj. *in requital* or *in exchange for.*
ἀμοιρέω, *to have no share in* a thing. From
ἄ-μοιρος, ον, (α privat., μοῖρα) *without share in* a thing, *bereft of* it. II. absol. *unfortunate.*
ἀμολγαῖος, α, ον, (ἀμέλγω) *of milk, made with milk.*
ἀμολγεύς, έως, ὁ, (ἀμέλγω) *a milk-pail,* Lat. *mulctra.*
ἀμολγός, ὁ, (ἀμέλγω) *the milking time,* i. e. *morning* and *evening twilight; the four hours either before daybreak* or *after sunset,* and so generally *night-time.*
ἄ-μομφος, ον, (α privat., μομφή) *blameless.*
ἀμορβός, οῦ, ὁ, *a follower, attendant.*
ἀμόργῐνος, ον, *made of fine flax.* From
ἀμοργίς, ίδος, ἡ, *fine flax from* the isle *of Amorgos.*
ἄ-μορος, ον, (α privat., μόρος) *without share of, destitute of.* II. absol. *unlucky, wretched.*
ἀμορφία, ἡ, *ill shape, deformity.* From
ἄ-μορφος, ον, (α privat., μορφή) *shapeless, misshapen, unshapely, unseemly:* Comp. ἀμορφέστερος.
ἀμός or **ἀμός**, ή, όν, Aeol. and Ep. for ἡμός, ἡμέτερος.
ἀμός, in Att. Poets for ἐμός.
ἀμός, Att. ἁμός, an old form for εἷς, and so = τὶς, but only used in the Adv. forms ἀμῇ, ἀμόθεν, ἀμοῦ, ἀμῶς.
ἆμος, Dor. for ἦμος, *as, when.*

ἄμοτος, ον, *insatiate, ravening, savage:* neut. ἄμοτον, as Adv. *insatiably, incessantly.* (Deriv. uncertain).
ἀμοῦ, Att. ἁμοῦ, Adv. of ἀμός, *somewhere.*
ἀμουσία, ἡ, *want of harmony: rudeness, grossness, boorishness.* From
ἄ-μουσος, ον, (α privat., Μοῦσα) *without the Muses, without taste for the arts, unpolished, rude, boorish:* of things, *coarse, vulgar, gross.*
ἀμοχθεί, Adv. of ἄμοχθος, *without toil* or *trouble.*
ἀ-μόχθητος, ον, (α privat., μοχθέω) = sq. Adv. -τως.
ἄ-μοχθος, ον, (α privat., μόχθος) *without toil* or *trouble.* II. *not weary.*
ἀμπ-, poët. abbrev. for ἀναπ-, under which will be found many words beginning with ἀμπ-.
ἀμ-πεδίον, **ἀμ-πεδιήρεις**, **ἀμ-πέλαγος**, should be written ἀμ πεδίον, i. e. ἀνὰ πεδίον, etc.
ἀμπείραντες, Ep. aor. 1 part. of ἀναπείρω.
ἀμ-πέλαγος, for ἀνὰ πέλαγος.
ἀμπελεών, ῶνος, ὁ, poët. for ἀμπελών, *a vineyard.*
ἀμπέλῐνος, ον, also η, ον, (ἄμπελος) *of the vine.*
ἀμπέλιον, τό, Dim. of ἄμπελος.
ἀμπελίς, ίδος, ἡ, = foreg., *a vine-plant.* II. a kind of bird.
ἀμπελόεις, εσσα, εν, (ἄμπελος) *rich in vines, vine-clad.*
ἀμπελο-εργός, όν, = contr. ἀμπελουργός, q. v.
ἀμπελο-μιξία, ἡ, (ἄμπελος, μίξις) *an intermixture of vines.*
"ΑΜΠΕΛΟΣ, ἡ, *a vine,* Lat. *vitis.*
ἀμπελουργέω, *to dress* or *prune vines.* From
ἀμπελ-ουργός, ὁ, (ἄμπελος, ἔργον) *a vinedresser.*
ἀμπελο-φύτωρ, ορος, ὁ, (ἄμπελος, φύω) *producer of the vine,* a name of Bacchus.
ἀμπελών, ῶνος, ὁ, (ἄμπελος) *a vineyard.*
ἀμ-πεπαλών, Ep. for ἀναπεπαλών, redupl. aor. 2 part. of ἀναπάλλω.
ἀμπερές, Adv. only found in compd. δι-αμπερές, resolved, as, διὰ δ' ἀμπερές, for διαμπερὲς δέ.
ἀμπετάσον, ἀμπετάσας, poet. aor. 1 imper. and part. of ἀναπετάννυμι.
ἀμπεχόνη, ἡ, (ἀμπέχω) *a fine upper garment.*
ἀμπ-έχω and **ἀμπ-ίσχω**: Ep. impf. ἄμπεχον: fut. ἀμφέξω: aor. 2 ἤμπισχον, inf. ἀμπισχεῖν, part. ἀμπισχών:—Med. ἀμπέχομαι and ἀμπίσχομαι: impf. ἠμπειχόμην: fut. ἀμφέξομαι: aor. 2 ἠμπεσχόμην, part. ἀμπισχόμενος: (ἀμφί, ἔχω):—*to surround, cover,* Lat. *cingere.* II. *to put round* or *over,* Lat. *circumdare.* See **ἀμπισχνέομαι.**
ἀμπήδησε, for ἀνεπήδησε.
ἀμ-πίπλημι, for ἀνα-πίμπλημι.
ἀμπισχεῖν, aor. 2 inf. of ἀμπ-έχω.
ἀμπισχνέομαι, = ἀμπέχομαι, *to put on,* **Lat. *circum-induor.***
ἀμπίσχω, v. sub ἀμπέχω.
ἀμπλακεῖν, aor. 2 inf. of ἀμπλακίσκω.
ἀμπλάκημα, ατος, τό, (ἀμπλακεῖν) *an error, offence.*
ἀμπλάκητος, ον, (ἀμπλακεῖν) *sinful, loaded with guilt.*

ἀμπλακία, ἡ, = ἀμπλάκημα.

ἀμπλάκιον, τό, = ἀμπλάκημα.

ἀμπλακίσκω, fut. ἀμπλακήσω: pf. ἠμπλάκηκα: aor. 2 ἤμπλακον:—Pass., pf. ἠμπλάκημαι:—like ἁμαρτάνω, *to miss, fail, fall short of*, c. gen.

ἀμ-πνευμα, ἀμπνεῦσαι, etc., poët. for ἀναπν—.

ἄμπνῠε, 3 sing. Ep. aor. 2 imper. of ἀναπνέω.

ἀμπνύνθην, Ep. aor. 1 pass. of ἀναπνέω.

ἄμπνῡτο, 3 sing. Ep. aor. 2 pass. of ἀμπνέω.

ἀμ-πόνον, for ἀνὰ πόνον.

ἀμπτάμενος, ἀμπταίην, v. ἀναπέτομαι.

ἀμπυκάζω: aor. 1 pass. ἠμπυκάσθην: (ἄμπυξ):—*to bind the hair with a band*: generally, *to bind, wreathe*.

ἀμπυκτήρ, ῆρος, ὁ, = (ἄμπυξ) *a band, fillet*: also *a horse's bridle*. Hence

ἀμπυκτήριος, α, ον, *of a horse's bridle* or *frontlet*.

ἄμπυξ, ῠκος, ὁ or ἡ, (ἀμπέχω) *a band* or *fillet* for binding the hair, *a head-band, snood*. II. *the head-band of horses*: also *a bridle*. III. *anything rounded, a wheel*

ἄμπωτις, ἡ, gen. εως Ion. ιος, shortened from ἀνάπωτις (ἀναπίνω), *a being drunk up*: of the sea, *the ebb-tide*.

ἀμυγδαλέα, contr. -αλῆ, ἡ, *the almond-tree*.

'ΑΜΥΓΔΑ'ΛΗ, ἡ, *an almond*. [δᾰ] Hence

ἀμυγδάλῐνος, η, ον, *of almonds*.

ἄμυγμα, ατος, τό, (ἀμύσσω) *a tearing, rending*: *a scar*.

ἀμυγμός, ὁ, (ἀμύσσω) *a tearing, mangling*.

ἄμῠδις, Adv. = ἅμα, of Time, *together, at the same time*: oftener of Place, *together*.

'ΑΜΥΔΡΟ'Σ, ά, όν, akin to ἀμαυρός, *dark, dim, faint, indistinct*. Adv. -δρῶς: also neut. ἀμυδρόν as Adv.

ἀ-μύητος, ον, (α privat., μυέω) *uninitiated, profane*.

ἀ-μύθητος, ον, (α privat., μυθέομαι) *not to be told, inexpressible*.

ἀ-μύκητος, ον, (α privat., μῡκάομαι) *without lowing* or *bellowing*: of places, *where no herds low*.

'Αμυκλαΐζω, *to speak in the dialect of Amyclae* (a Laconian city).

ἄ-μῠλος, ὁ, (α privat., μύλη) *a cake of fine meal*, so called from the meal not being ground at a common mill.

ἀ-μύμων, ον, gen. ονος, (α privat., μῶμος) *blameless, excellent*. [ᾰμῡ]

ἀμύνᾰθε, ἀμυνᾰθεῖν, 3 sing. and inf. poët. aor. 2 of ἀμύνω.

ἀμυνᾰθοῦ, 2 sing. poët. aor. 2 med. of ἀμύνω.

ἀμῦναι, ἀμύνασθαι, aor. 1 act. and med. inf. of ἀμύνω.

'Αμυνίας, ου, ὁ, masc. pr. n. used as Adj. (ἀμύνω) *on its guard*.

ἄμυνον, aor. 1 imper. of ἀμύνω.

ἀμυντέον, verb. Adj. of ἀμύνω, *one must assist*; so too **ἀμυντέα**. II. *one must repel*.

ἀμυντήρ, ῆρος, ὁ, (ἀμύνω) *a defender*.

ἀμυντήριος, ον, (ἀμύνω) *fit for defending, defensive*; ἀμυντήρια ὅπλα *defensive* armour. II. ἀμυντήριον, τό, as Subst. *a means of defence*.

ἀμυντικός, ή, όν, (ἀμύνω) *able to defend* or *avenge*.

ἀμύντωρ, ορος, ὁ, = ἀμυντήρ, *a helper*: *an avenger*.

'ΑΜΥ'ΝΩ [ῡ], Ep. impf. ἄμυνον: fut. ἀμῠνῶ, Ion. ἀμῠνέω: aor. 1 ἤμῡνα, Ep. ἄμῡνα: poët. aor. 2 ἠμύνᾰθον:—*to keep off, ward off*, Lat. *defendo*: *to defend, fight for, aid*: rarely *to requite, repay*. II. Med. *to keep* or *ward off from oneself, to defend oneself*. *to avenge oneself on* another, *requite, repay, punish*.

ἄμυξις, εως, ἡ, (ἀμύσσω) *a tearing, scratching*.

'ΑΜΥ'ΣΣΩ, Att. -ττω: Ep. impf. ἄμυσσον: fut. ἀμύξω: aor. 1 ἤμυξα:—*to tear, scratch, wound*: *to tear in pieces*. II. metaph., θυμὸν ἀμύξεις χωόμενος thou wilt *lacerate* thy heart with rage. [ᾰ]

ἀ-μυστί, Adv. (α privat., μύω) properly *without closing the mouth*, i. e. *at one draught*. Hence

ἀμυστίζω, f. σω: pf. ἠμύστικα: *to drink deep, tipple*. From

ἄ-μυστις, ιος and ιδος, ἡ, *a long draught* of drink. II. *a large cup*, used by the Thracians.

ἀμυχή, ἡ, = ἄμυξις.

ἀμφ—, old and poët. abbrev. for ἀναφ—; cf. ἀμπ—.

ἀμφ-ᾰγᾰπάζω, only used in pres. and impf. (ἀμφί, ἀγαπάζω) *to embrace with love, treat kindly, greet warmly*.

ἀμφ-ᾰγᾰπάω, = ἀμφαγαπάζω.

ἀμφ-ᾰγείρω, Ep. aor. 2 med. ἀμφαγερόμην: (ἀμφί, ἀγείρω):—*to collect around*:—Med. *to gather around*.

ἀμφ-ᾰγερέθομαι and **-αγέρομαι**, poët. for **-αγείρομαι**.

ἀμφάδην, Adv. = ἄμφαδον.

ἀμφάδιος, α, ον, (ἄμφᾰδος) *public, known*: **ἀμφαδίην** as Adv. *publicly, openly*, Lat. *palam*.

ἀμφᾰδόν, Adv. *publicly, openly, without disguise*. From

ἄμ-φᾰδος, η, ον, (ἀνα-φαίνω) *public, notorious*.

ἀμ-φαίνω, poët. for ἀνα-φαίνω.

ἀμφ-ᾱΐσσομαι, Pass. (ἀμφί, ἀΐσσω) *to rush on from all sides, flutter* or *float around*.

ἀμφᾱκής, Dor. for ἀμφηκής.

ἀμ-φανδόν, Adv. poët. for ἀνα-φανδόν.

ἀμφᾰνέειν, poët. for ἀναφανεῖν, fut. inf. of ἀναφαίνω.

ἀμφ-ᾰρᾰβέω, f. ήσω, (ἀμφί, ἀραβέω) *to rattle* or *ring about*.

ἀμφ-αραβίζω, only used in pres. and impf., = ἀμφαραβέω.

ἀμ-φᾰσίη, ἡ, poët. for ἀ-φασία (with μ inserted) *speechlessness* from fear, amazement, or rage.

ἀμφᾰφάασθαι, Ep. for ἀμφαφᾶσθαι, pres. med. inf of ἀμφαφάω.

ἀμφ-ᾰφάω, and Med. **ἀμφ-αφάομαι**, (ἀμφί, ἀφάω) *to touch all round, feel on all sides*: *to fondle*: *to handle*

ἀμφᾰόων, -όωσα, Ep. for ἀμφαφῶν, ῶσα, pres. part of ἀμφαφάω.

ἀμφαόωντο, 3 pl. Ep. impf. med. of ἀμφαφάω

ἀμφέθετο, aor. 2 med. of ἀμφιτίθημι.

ἀμφ-ελικτός, όν, poët. for ἀμφιελ—, *coiled round*.

ἀμφ-ελίσσω, Att. -ττω, f. ίξω, poët. for **ἀμφιελίσσω**, *to wrap, fold*, or *twine round*.

ἀμφ-έπω, poët. for ἀμφι-έπω.

ἀμφ-ερέφω, f. ψω, (ἀμφί, ἐρέφω) *to cover around.*

ἀμφ-έρχομαι, aor. 2 ἀμφήλυθον or ἀμφῆλθον: Dep.: (ἀμφί, ἔρχομαι):—*to come round one, surround.*

ἀμ-φέρω, poët. for ἀναφέρω.

ἀμφεστᾶσι for ἀμφεστήκᾱσι, 3 pl. pf. of ἀμφίστημι.

ἀμ-φεύγω, poët. for ἀναφεύγω.

ἀμφέσταν, Ep. 3 pl. aor. 2 of ἀμφίστημι.

ἀμφέχᾰνον, aor. 2 of ἀμφιχαίνω.

ἀμφεχύθην [ῠ], aor. 1 pass. of ἀμφιχέω.

ἀμφέχῠτο, 3 sing. Ep. aor. 2 pass. of ἀμφιχέω.

ἀμφ-ήκης, ες, (ἀμφί, ἀκή) *two-edged, double-biting:* of lightning, *forked.* II. metaph. *that will cut both ways, false* or *ambiguous.*

ἀμφήλῠθε, 3 sing. aor. 2 of ἀμφέρχομαι.

ἀμφ-ηρεφής, ές, (ἀμφί, ἐρέφω) *covered all round, close-covered.*

ἀμφ-ήρης, ες, (ἀμφί, ἐρέσσω) *having oars on both sides.* 2. (*ἄρω) *fitted* or *joined on all sides, well-fitted.* Hence

ἀμφ-ηρικός, ή, όν, *worked by sculls,* of a boat.

ἀμφ-ήριστος, ον, (ἀμφί, ἐρίζω) *contested on both sides, disputed.* 2. *equal in the contest.*

'ΑΜΦΙ', Praep. c. gen., dat., et acc.:—Radic. signf. *on both sides, around.* I. c. GEN. *about, for, for the sake of* a thing:—*about, concerning* a thing, *of it.* 2. rarely of Place, *about, around.* II. c. DAT. 1. of Place, *about, around, round about:* —*at, by, near, with.* 2. not of Place, *about, for, on account of, for the sake of: regarding, concerning.* 3. by *means* of. III. c. ACC., of Place, *about, around, on, at: near about:*—mostly with motion implied. IV. WITHOUT CASE, as Adv. *about, around, round about, on all sides.* V. IN COMPOS. *about, on all sides, on both sides.*

ἀμφί-ἄλος, ον, (ἀμφί, ἅλς) *sea-girt,* esp. *having the sea on both sides, between two seas,* Lat. *bimaris.*

ἀμφ-ιάχω, (ἀμφί, ἰάχω) *to sound on all sides: to fly about shrieking,* in irreg. pf. part. ἀμφῐαχυῖα, υῖα.

ἀμφι-βαίνω, f. -βήσομαι: pf. -βέβηκα:—*to go about* or *around.* 2. *to bestride:* hence *to guard, protect.* II. *to surround, encompass, wrap round.*

ἀμφι-βάλλω, f. -βᾰλῶ: pf. -βέβληκα: Med., Ion. fut. -βαλεῦμαι: aor. 2 inf. -βαλέσθαι:—*to throw* or *put round,* esp. of clothes, etc., *to put* them *on* a person, Lat. *circumdare:*—Med. *to put on oneself, put on,* Lat. *accingi.* 2 esp. *to throw* one's arms *round, embrace:* also *to grasp.* 3. *to surround, encompass:* but also *to strike on all sides.* II. intr. *to go to another place;* so also in Med

ἀμφιβάς, aor. 2 part. of ἀμφι-βαίνω.

ἀμφιβᾰσία, ἡ, v. ἀμφισβασία.

ἀμφίβᾰσις, εως, ἡ, (ἀμφιβαίνω) *a going round, encompassing.*

ἀμφίβλημα, ατος, τό, (ἀμφιβάλλω) *something thrown round, an enclosure.* II. *a garment.*

ἀμφίβληστρον, τό, (ἀμφιβάλλω) *anything thrown round:* 1. *a large fishing-net.* 2. *a garment.* 3. *a fetter, bond.*

ἀμφίβλητος, ον, (ἀμφιβάλλω) *put* or *thrown round.*

ἀμφι-βόητος, ον, (ἀμφί, βοάω) *noised abroad, far-famed.*

ἀμφιβολία, ἡ, *the state of being attacked on both sides.* II. *uncertainty, doubt.* From

ἀμφίβολος, ον, (ἀμφιβάλλω) *thrown round:* hence τὸ ἀμφίβολον *a garment.* II. *struck, attacked on both* or *all sides.* 2. act. *striking with both ends, double-pointed.* III. *ambiguous, doubtful.*

ἀμφί-βουλος, ον, (ἀμφί, βουλή) *double-minded, doubting.*

ἀμφί-βροτος, η, ον, also ος, ον, (ἀμφί, βροτός) *covering the whole man,* of a large shield.

ἀμφί-βροχος, ον, (ἀμφί, βρέχω) *thoroughly soaked.*

ἀμφι-βώμιος, ον, (ἀμφί, βωμός) *round the altar.*

ἀμφι-γηθέω, *to rejoice around* or *exceedingly.*

ἀμφι-γνοέω, impf. ἠμφεγνόουν: f. ἀμφιγνοήσω: aor. 1 ἠμφεγνόησα:—Pass., aor. 1 part. ἀμφιγνοηθείς: (ἀμφί, γνοέω Aeol. for νοέω):—*to be doubtful about* a thing, *not to know* or *understand* it:—Pass. *to be unknown.*

ἀμφι-γόητος, ον, (ἀμφί, γοάω) *bewailed all round.*

'Αμφι-γυήεις, ὁ, (ἀμφί, γυιός) *he that halts in both feet, the lame one,* name of Vulcan.

ἀμφί-γυος, ον, (ἀμφί, γυῖον) properly *having limbs on both sides:*—in Homer of a spear, *double-pointed:* in Sophocles of men, *well-practised.*

ἀμφι-δαίω, *to light up around:*—intrans. in pf. ἀμφι-δέδηα, plqpf. -δεδήειν, *to burn around.*

ἀμφι-δάκνω, f. δήξομαι, *to bite all round.*

ἀμφι-δάκρῡτος, ον, (ἀμφί, δακρύω) *causing tears on all sides:* *all mournful.*

ἀμφι-δᾰσυς, εια, υ, (ἀμφί, δασύς) *fringed all round.*

ἀμφι-δέαι, αἱ, (ἀμφί, δέω) *anything that is bound around, bracelets, anklets.*

ἀμφιδέδηα, -δεδήειν, pf. and plqpf. of ἀμφιδαίω.

ἀμφι-δέξιος, ον, *with two right hands, very dextrous.* Lat. *ambidexter.* 2. *ambiguous,* Lat. *anceps: two-edged.* 3. sometimes simply like ἀμφότερος; ἀμφιδέξιοι ἀκμαί *both* hands.

ἀμφι-δέρκομαι, pf. -δέδορκα, Dep. *to look round about one.*

ἀμφί-δετος, ον, (ἀμφί, δέω) *bound all round.*

ἀμφι-δήρῑτος, ον, (ἀμφί, δηρίομαι) *disputed, doubtful.*

ἀμφι-διαίνω, *to water around.*

ἀμφι-δῑνέω, f. ήσω, *to wind* or *roll* a thing *all round:* hence in pf. pass. ἀμφιδεδίνημαι, *to be fitted close.*

ἀμφι-δοκεύω, f. εύσω, *to lie in wait for.*

ἀμφι-δονέω, f. ήσω, *to whirl round, agitate violently.*

ἀμφιδοξέω, *to be doubtful:*—Pass. *to be disputed.* From

ἀμφί-δοξος, ον, (ἀμφί, δόξα) *of double sense, doubtful.*

ἀμφί-δορος, ον, (ἀμφί, δέρω) *skinned all round, quite flayed.*

ἀμφί-δοχμος, ον, (ἀμφί, δοχμή) *as large as can be grasped.*

ἀμφί-δρομος, ον, (ἀμφί, δραμεῖν) *running round: encompassing.*

ἀμφί-δρυπτος, ον, = ἀμφίδρυφος.

ἀμφι-δρυφής, ές, (ἀμφί, δρῠφῆναι) *tearing both cheeks.*

ἀμφί-δρυφος, ον, (ἀμφί, δρῠφῆναι) *torn on both sides.*

ἀμφί-δυμος, ον, (ἀμφί, δύομαι) *approachable on both sides.*

ἀμφι-δύω, f. δύσω [ῡ], *to put round* or *on*:—Med. *to put on oneself.*

ἀμφιελικτός, όν, (ἀμφιελίσσω) *turned round and round, circling, revolving.*

ἀμφιέλισσα, fem. Adj. *rowed on both sides:* or *swaying to and fro, rocking.* From

ἀμφι-ελίσσω, f. ίξω, *to wind round.*

ἀμφι-έννυμι and **ἀμφι-εννύω**: fut. ἀμφιέσω, Att. ἀμφιῶ: aor. 1 ἠμφίεσα, Ep. ἀμφίεσα:—Pass., aor. 1 ἠμφιέσθην: pf. ἠμφίεσμαι, poët. ἀμφιεῖμαι:—*to put round, to put garments on* a person, Lat. *induere*:—Pass. *to be clothed in, to wear*, esp. in pf. II. Med. ἀμφιέννυμαι: aor. 1 ἠμφιεσάμην, 3 pl. ἀμφιέσσαντο, imperat. ἀμφιέσασθε:—*to put on oneself, dress oneself in.*

ἀμφι-έπω, poët. also **ἀμφ-έπω**: aor. 2 ἀμφίεπον and ἄμφεπον: (ἀμφί, ἕπω):—*to go about, encompass.* II. *to be busy about, take care of: to do honour to:* esp. *to tend, protect.* III. Med. *to follow and crowd round.*

ἀμφίεσαν, ἀμφιέσαντο, Ep. 3 pl. aor. 1 of ἀμφιέννυμι.

ἀμφ-ιζάνω, (ἀμφί, ἱζάνω) *to sit around* or *on a* thing, *settle upon* it, as dust does. [ᾰ]

ἀμφί-ζευκτος, ον, (ἀμφί, ζεύγνυμι) *joined from both sides.*

ἀμφι-θάλασσος, Att. **-ττος**, ον, (ἀμφί, θάλασσα) *sea-girt: near the sea.*

ἀμφιθᾰλής, ές, *blooming on both sides:* hence *flourishing, rich.* From

ἀμφι-θάλλω, pf. ἀμφιτέθηλα, *to bloom all round, to be in full bloom.*

ἀμφι-θάλπω, f. ψω, *to warm on all sides, warm thoroughly.*

ἀμφι-θέᾱτρον, τό, (ἀμφί, θέατρον) *a double theatre, amphitheatre.*

ἀμφίθετος, ον, (ἀμφιτίθημι) of a cup, *that will stand on both ends*, or *with handles on both sides.*

ἀμφι-θέω, f. θεύσομαι, *to run round about.*

ἀμφι-θηγής, ές, = sq.

ἀμφί-θηκτος, ον, (ἀμφί, θήγω) *sharpened on both sides, two-edged.*

ἀμφί-θρεπτος, ον, (ἀμφί, τρέφω) *clotted around, congealed*, of blood.

ἀμφί-θῠρος, ον, (ἀμφί, θύρα) *with a door* or *opening on both sides:* as Subst. ἀμφίθυρον, τό, *a hall.*

ἀμφι-κᾰλύπτω, f. ψω, *to cover all round, enfold, shroud.* II. *to put* a thing *round as a veil* or *shelter, to envelope in.*

ἀμφι-κεάζω; Ep. aor. 1 part. ἀμφικεάσσας; —*to cleave asunder.*

ἀμφί-κειμαι, used as Pass. of ἀμφιτίθημι, *to lie close upon: to lean on.*

ἀμφι-κείρω, f. κερῶ, *to shear* or *clip all round.*

ἀμφικέφαλος, Ep. **-κέφαλλος**, ον, (ἀμφί, κεφαλή) *double-headed.*

ἀμφι-κίων, ον, gen. ονος, (ἀμφί, κίων) *with pillars all round.* [κῐ]

ἀμφί-κλαστος, ον, (ἀμφί, κλάω) *broken all round.*

ἀμφί-κλυστος, ον, (ἀμφί, κλύζω) *flooded around.*

ἀμφι-κομέω, f. ήσω, *to tend on all sides* or *carefully.*

ἀμφί-κομος, ον, (ἀμφί, κόμη) *with hair all round, thick-haired:* of trees, *thick-leafed.*

ἀμφίκρᾱνος, ον, (ἀμφί, κάρα) = ἀμφικέφαλος.

ἀμφι-κρέμᾰμαι, Pass. declined like δύναμαι: (ἀμφί, κρεμάννυμι):—*to hover* or *flutter round.* Hence

ἀμφι-κρεμής, ές, *hanging round one: hanging round the shoulder.*

ἀμφίκρημνος, ον, (ἀμφί, κρημνός) *with cliffs all round.*

ἀμφίκρηνος, ον, Ion. for ἀμφίκρᾱνος, *surrounding the head.*

ἀμφι-κτίονες, ων, οἱ, (ἀμφί, κτίζω) *they that dwell round* or *near.* Hence

Ἀμφι-κτύονες, ων, οἱ, *the Amphictyons*, a Council composed of deputies chosen by all the states of Greece. II. *the presidents of the Pythian games.* Hence

Ἀμφικτυονία, ἡ, *the Amphictyonic League* or *Council.*

Ἀμφικτυονικός, ή, όν, *of* or *for the Amphictyons* or *their League.*

Ἀμφικτυονίς, ίδος, ἡ, fem. of Ἀμφικτυονικός: I. (sub. πόλις), a city or state *in the Amphictyonic League.* II. *a name of Artemis at Anthēla, the meeting-place of the Amphictyonic Council.*

ἀμφι-κῠλίνδω, f. -κυλίσω [ῐ], *to roll about* or *upon.*

ἀμφι-κύπελλος, ον, (ἀμφί, κύπελλον) in Homer always with δέπας, *a double cup:* cf. ἀμφίθετος. [ῠ]

ἀμφί-λᾰλος, ον, (ἀμφί, λάλος) *chattering everywhere.*

ἀμφι-λᾰφής, ές, (ἀμφί, λᾰβεῖν) *far-spreading:* hence generally *wide, large, vast:* also *excessive, violent.*

ἀμφι-λᾰχαίνω, *to dig* or *hoe round.*

ἀμφι-λέγω, f. ξω, *to speak on both sides, dispute.* Hence

ἀμφίλεκτος, ον, *discussed on all hands, doubtful.* II. act. *disputing, captious.*

ἀμφιλογία, ἡ, *dispute, doubt.* From

ἀμφί-λογος, ον, (ἀμφί, λέγω) *disputed, questionable, doubtful.* II. act. *disputatious, contentious.*

ἀμφί-λοφος, ον, (ἀμφί, λόφος) *encompassing the neck.*

ἀμφι-λύκη νύξ, ἡ, (ἀμφί, λύκη, Lat. *lux*) *the morning-twilight, gray of morning.* [ῠ]

***ἀμφι-μάομαι**, (ἀμφί, μάω) pres. of Ep. aor. 1 ἀμφιμασάμην, *to wipe* or *rub all round.*

ἀμφι-μάσχᾰλος, ον, (ἀμφί, μασχάλη) *covering both shoulders, two-sleeved.*

ἀμφι-μάτορες, Dor. for ἀμφι-μήτορες.

ἀμφιμάχητος, ον, *contended for, contested on both hands.* [ᾰ] From

ἀμφι-μάχομαι, f. -μαχοῦμαι: Dep.:—*to fight round*: 1. *to attack*. 2. *to fight for*. [ᾰ]

ἀμφι-μέλᾱς, αινα, ᾰν, *black all round*, *wrapt in darkness*.

ἀμφιμέμῡκε, 3 sing. pf. act. of ἀμφι-μυκάομαι.

ἀμφι-μερίζομαι, Pass. *to be completely parted*.

ἀμφι-μήτορες, οἱ, αἱ, (ἀμφί, μήτηρ) *brothers* or *sisters by different mothers*.

ἀμφι-μῡκάομαι, pf. act. μέμῡκα: Dep.:—*to low* or *bellow around*, properly of cattle; δάπεδον ἀμφιμέμῡκε the floor *echoed all around*.

ἀμφι-νεικής, ές, (ἀμφί, νεῖκος) *made an object of contest*, *eagerly wooed*.

ἀμφι-νείκητος, ον, (ἀμφί, νεικέω) = ἀμφίνεικος.

ἀμφι-νέμομαι, Med. *to dwell round about*, *inhabit*.

ἀμφι-νοέω, f. ήσω, *to think both ways*, *doubt*.

ἀμφι-ξέω, f. έσω, *to smooth* or *polish all round*.

ἀμφίξοος, ον, contr. **ἀμφίξους**, ουν, (ἀμφιξέω) *polishing all round*.

ἀμφί-παλτος, ον, (ἀμφί, πάλλω) *reëchoing*.

ἀμφι-πᾰτάσσω, f. ξω, *to strike on* or *from all sides*.

ἀμφί-πεδος, ον, (ἀμφί, πέδον) *surrounded by a plain*.

ἀμφι-πέλομαι, Dep. *to be all round*, *hover around*.

ἀμφι-πένομαι, Dep. *to be busied about*, *take care of*, *pay heed to*.

ἀμφι-περικτίονες, ων, *the dwellers round about*.

ἀμφι-περιπλέγδην, Adv. (ἀμφί, περιπλέκω) *twined round about*.

ἀμφι-περιστέφω, *to put round as a crown*.

ἀμφι-περιστρωφάω, *to keep turning round about* or *in every direction*.

ἀμφι-περιτρύζω, *to chirp* or *twitter all round*.

ἀμφι-περι-φθινύθω, (ἀμφί, περί, φθίνω) *to decay* or *die all around*. [ῠ]

ἀμφιπεσών, οῦσα, όν, aor. 2 part. of ἀμφιπίπτω.

ἀμφι-πιάζω, f. άξω, *to press all round*.

ἀμφι-πίπτω, f. πεσοῦμαι, *to fall around*, *embrace eagerly*.

ἀμφι-πίτνω, = ἀμφι-πίπτω.

ἀμφί-πλεκτος, ον, (ἀμφί, πλέκω) *twisted on both sides*, *intertwining*.

ἀμφί-πληκτος, ον, (ἀμφί, πλήσσω) *beating* or *dashing on all sides*.

ἀμφι-πλήξ, ῆγος, ὁ, ἡ, (ἀμφί, πλήσσω) *striking with both sides*, *double-biting*.

ἀμφιπολεύω, (ἀμφίπολος) *to be an attendant*: *be busied about*, *take charge of*: of slaves, *to serve*, *to minister to*.

ἀμφιπολέω, = ἀμφιπολεύω.

ἀμφί-πολις, poët. **ἀμφί-πτολις**, ὁ, ἡ, (ἀμφί, πόλις) *around a city*, *pressing a city on all sides*. 2. as fem. Subst. *a city between two seas* or *rivers*.

ἀμφί-πολος, ον, (ἀμφί, πέλω) properly *being about*, *busied about*: generally as fem. Subst. *a handmaid*, *waiting-woman*: as masc. *an attendant*, *follower*. II. as Adj. *much frequented*.

ἀμφι-πονέομαι, Dep. with aor. 1 pass. ἀμφεπονήθην: (ἀμφί, πονέω):—*to bestow labour about*, *attend to*, *provide for*.

ἀμφι-ποτάομαι, Dep. *to fly* or *flutter around*.

ἀμφι-πρόσωπος, ον, (ἀμφί, πρόσωπον) *double-faced*, Lat. *bifrons*.

ἀμφι-πτύσσω, f. ξω, *to clasp around*. Hence

ἀμφιπτῠχή, ἡ, *a clasping round*, *embrace*.

ἀμφί-πῠλος, ον, (ἀμφί, πύλη) *with two entrances*.

ἀμφί-πῠρος, ον, (ἀμφί, πῦρ) *surrounded by fire*; *with fire all round*.

ἀμφί-ρῠτος, η, ον, poët. for **ἀμφίρ-ρυτος**, ον, (ἀμφί, ῥέω) *flowed around*, *sea-girt*.

'ΑΜΦΙ'Σ, as Adv. 1. *on* or *at both sides*: hence 2. *apart*, *asunder*; γαῖαν καὶ οὐρανὸν ἀμφὶς ἔχειν to keep heaven and earth *asunder*. 3. generally, *around*, *round about*. II. more rarely as Prep. c. gen. *around*: *apart from*, *far from*. 2. rarely c. dat. like ἀμφί, *round about*. 3. c. acc. *about*, *around*, when it always follows its case.

ἀμφι-σαλεύομαι, Pass. *to toss about*, like a ship at sea.

ἀμφίσ-βαινα, ης, ἡ, (ἀμφίς, βαίνω) a kind of serpent, *that can go both ways*, *forward* or *backward*.

ἀμφισ-βᾰσίη, ἡ, Ion. for ἀμφισ-βήτησις.

ἀμφισ-βητέω: impf. ἠμφισβήτουν, or with double augm. ἠμφεσβήτουν: so, aor. 1 ἠμφισβήτησα or ἠμφεσβήτησα:—Pass., fut. med. in pass. sense ἀμφισβητήσομαι:—aor. 1 ἠμφισβητήθην or ἠμφεσβ–: (ἀμφίς, βῆναι aor. 2 of βαίνω):—*to stand apart*, and so *to dispute*, *differ*, *argue*:—Pass. *to be the subject of dispute*. Hence

ἀμφισβήτημα, ατος, τό, *a point in dispute*. And

ἀμφισβητήσῐμος, ον, *debatable*, *doubtful*.

ἀμφισβήτησις, εως, ἡ, (ἀμφισβητέω) *a dispute*, *controversy*, *ground* or *occasion of dispute* or *debate*.

ἀμφισβήτητος, ον, *disputed*, *debatable*.

ἀμφ-ίστᾰμαι, v. ἀμφίστημι.

ἀμφι-στέλλω, *to fold about* another:—Med. *to fold round oneself*, *deck oneself in*.

ἀμφι-στεφᾰνόομαι, Pass. (ἀμφί, στέφανος) *to stand round like a crown*.

ἀμφι-στεφής, ές, (ἀμφί, στέφω) *placed round like a crown*.

ἀμφ-ίστημι, *to place round*:—Pass. ἀμφίσταμαι, with the intr. act. tenses, aor. 2 ἀμφέστην, pf. ἀμφέστηκα:—*to stand around*.

ἀμφί-στομος, ον, (ἀμφί, στόμα) *with double mouth* or *opening*: *double*.

ἀμφι-στρᾰτάομαι, 3 pl. Ep. impf. ἀμφεστρατόωντο: Dep. (ἀμφί, στρατός):—*to beleaguer*, *besiege*.

ἀμφι-στρεφής, ές, (ἀμφί, στρέφω) *twisting round*, *turning all ways*.

ἀμφιτᾰθείς, aor. 1 pass. part. of ἀμφιτείνω.

ἀμφι-τάμνω, Ion. for ἀμφι-τέμνω.

ἀμφι-τᾰνύω, = ἀμφι-τείνω.

ἀμφι-τᾰράσσω, *to trouble all round*.

ἀμφιτεθείς, aor. 1 pass. part. of ἀμφιτίθημι.

ἀμφι-τείνω, *to stretch out and throw round*.

ἀμφι-τειχής, ές, (ἀμφί, τεῖχος) *encompassing the walls.*

ἀμφι-τέμνω, Ion. –τάμνω, *to cut off all round, to intercept.*

ἀμφι-τίθημι, imperat. –τίθει : f. θήσω : aor. 1 ἔθηκα : aor. 2 ἀμφέθην : aor. 1 pass. ἀμφετέθην :—*to put round, to put on :* Med. *to put on oneself.*

ἀμφι-τῐνάσσω, f. άξω, *to shake around.*

ἀμφι-τιττῠβίζω, *to twitter around.*

ἀμφι-τόμος, ον, (ἀμφί, ταμεῖν) *cutting on both sides, two-edged.*

ἀμφί-τορνος, ον, (ἀμφί, τορνόω) *well-rounded.*

ἀμφι-τρέμω, *to tremble all over.*

ἀμφι-τρέχω, *to run round, surround.*

ἀμφι-τρής, ῆτος, ὁ, ἡ, = ἀμφίτρητος.

ἀμφί-τρητος, ον, (ἀμφί, *τράω Root of τετραίνω) *bored through, with double entrance.*

ἀμφι-τρομέω, f. ήσω, (ἀμφί, τρέμω) *to tremble for.*

ἀμφι-φᾰείνω, (ἀμφί, φάω) *to shine around.*

ἀμφί-φᾰλος, ον, *with* φάλοι *all round ;* see φάλος.

ἀμφι-φᾰνής, ές, (ἀμφί, φᾰνῆναι) *visible all round.*

ἀμφι-φοβέομαι, Pass. (ἀμφί, φοβέω) *to fear* or *tremble all round.*

ἀμφι-φορεύς, gen. έως Ep. ῆος, ὁ, (ἀμφί, φέρω) *a large jar* or *pitcher with two handles.*

ἀμφι-φράζομαι, Med. *to consider on all sides.*

ἀμφι-χαίνω, aor. 2 ἀμφ-έχᾰνον :—*to yawn round, threaten to swallow : to yawn wide.*

ἀμφι-χέω, f. –χέω : aor. 1 ἀμφέχεα :—Pass. aor. 1 ἀμφεχύθην [ῠ] : Ep. 3 sing. aor. 2 pass. ἀμφέχῠτο : pf. –κέχυμαι :—*to pour* or *shed around :*—Pass. *to be poured around : to embrace.*

ἀμφι-χορεύω, f. σω, *to dance around.*

ἀμφί-χρῡσος, ον, (ἀμφί, χρυσός) *gilded all over.*

ἀμφιχῠθείς, aor. 1 pass. part. of ἀμφι-χέω.

ἀμφίχῠτος, ον, (ἀμφιχέω) *poured around, heaped up around.*

ἀμφί-χωλος, ον, *lame in both feet.*

ἄμφ-οδον, τό, (ἀμφί, ὁδός) *part of a town with streets round it, a quarter of a town,* Lat. *vicus.*

ἄμφ-οδος, ἡ, (ἀμφί, ὁδός) *a road round, a street.*

ἀμ-φορεύς, έως, ὁ, shortened form of ἀμφι-φορεύς, *a jar,* also *a cinerary urn :* as liquid measure, = $1\frac{1}{2}$ Roman *amphorae,* or nearly 9 gallons.

ἀμφοτέρῃ, as Adv. (ἀμφότερος) *in both ways,* Lat. *utrinque.*

ἀμφότερος, α, ον, (ἄμφω) Lat. *uterque, both : κατ'* ἀμφότερα *on both sides,* Lat. *utrinque ;* ἐπ' ἀμφότερα towards *both sides.* Hence

ἀμφοτέρωθεν, Adv. *from* or *on both sides,* Lat. *ex utraque parte : from both ends.*

ἀμφοτέρωθι, Adv. *on both sides.*

ἀμφοτέρως, Adv. *in both ways.* And

ἀμφοτέρωσε, Adv. *to* or *on both sides.*

ἀμφ-ουδίς, Adv. (ἀμφίς, οὖδας) *from the ground.*

ἀμφράσσαιτο, poët. for ἀναφράσσαιτο, 3 sing. aor. 1 opt. of ἀναφράζομαι.

ἀμ-φύω, poët. ἀναφύω.

'ΑΜΦΩ, τώ, τά, τώ, also οἱ, αἱ, τά, Gen. and Dat. ἀμφοῖν, *both of two,* Lat. *AMBO :* (same Root as ἀμφί.)

ἀμφώβολος, ὁ, (ἀμφί, ὀβολός) *a double spit.*

ἀμφ-ώης, ες, (ἀμφί, οὖς) *two-eared, two-handled.*

ἄμφ-ωτις, ιδος, ἡ, (ἀμφί, οὖς) *a two-handled pail.*

ἄμφ-ωτος, ον, = foreg., *two-eared, two-handled.*

ἀμῷεν, for ἀμάοιεν, 3 pl. pres. opt. of ἀμάω.

ἀ-μώμητος, ον, (α privat., μωμέομαι) *unblamed, blameless.* Adv. –τως, *blamelessly.*

ἄμωμον, τό, *amomum,* an Indian spice.

ἄ-μωμος, ον, (α privat., μῶμος) *without blame, blameless.*

ἀμῶς, Att. **ἁμῶς**, Adv. from the absol. ἀμός = τὶς, esp. in compd. ἀμωσ-γέ-πως, *in a certain manner.*

'ΑΝ, a conditional particle, used like the Ep. and Lyr. particle κε, κεν.

A. WITH INDICAT. ἄν makes an assertion, instead of being positive, dependent on circumstances : hence ἄν cannot be joined with *pres.* or *perf.,* because that which *is,* or *has been,* cannot be made so dependent. I. WITH INDIC. :—with fut. (only in Ep. poets) ἄν expresses that which *certainly will happen, if something else happens first :*—with imperf. ἄν expresses the frequent repetition of an act under certain circumstances, *what would always happen ;* ἔλεγεν ἄν he *would* say (whenever he had an opportunity) ; κλαίεσκεν ἄν he *would* keep on weeping :—with aorists ἄν expresses *what would have happened* on a *particular occasion ;* εἶπεν ἄν *he would have said.* II. WITH OPTAT. it turns the *wish,* which the mood expresses when alone, into *a conditional assertion.* III. WITH SUBJUNCT. ἄν belongs rather to the particle on which the verb depends, than to the verb itself. IV. WITH INFINIT. ἄν is used in cases where the indic. or optat. would be joined with it.—ἄν never begins a sentence, and *regularly* follows the word whose signf. it limits, as εἶχον ἄν : but when words dependent on the verb precede it in the sentence, ἄν may follow any of them, because, in sense, they follow the verb, as πρόφασιν ἂν εἶχον = εἶχον ἂν πρόφασιν.

ἄν, Conj. = ἐάν, with subjunctive. [ᾱ]

ἄν or **ἀν**, shortd. Ep. form of ἀνά. [ᾰ]

ἄν, shortened from ἄνα, for ἀνέστη (like ἔνι for ἔνεστι), *he stood up, arose.*

ἀν–, sometimes for α privat. before a vowel.

'ΑΝΑ', Prep. c. gen., dat. et acc., used also in forms ἀν–, ἀγ–, ἀμ– : in general signf. opp. to κατά. I. C. GEN. *on board ;* ἀνὰ νηός *on board* ship. II. C. DAT. *on, upon.* III. C. ACC. the common usage, implying *motion upwards,* 1. of Place, *up :—throughout.* 2. of Time, *throughout.* 3. in numbers, *up to.* 4. taken *distributively,* e. g. ἀνὰ πᾶσαν ἡμέραν day *by* day : for ἀνὰ κράτος, v. sub κράτος. IV. as Adv. *thereon, thereupon : throughout, all over.* V. IN COMPOS. *up to, towards, up,* opp. to κατά : hence with a sense of *strengthening.* Also *back, backwards* = Lat. *re–, retro–.* [ᾰνᾰ]

, for ἀνάστηθι, *up! arise!*

, vocat. of ἄναξ, *king*, only addressed to gods.

βᾶ, Att. for **ἀνάβηθι**, aor. 2 imperat. of ἀναβαίνω.

βάδην, Adv. (ἀναβαίνω) *going up, mounting: up on high, aloft;* opp. to **κατα-βάδην**. [βᾰ]

βαθμός, ὁ, (ἀναβαίνω) *a means of going up, a of steps, stair.*

-βάθρα, ἡ, (ἀνά, βάθρον) *a ladder.*

α-βαίνω, f. -βήσομαι: aor. 2 **ἀνέβην**; also aor. 1 . ἀνεβησάμην, Ep. 3 sing. ἀνεβήσετο: pf. ἀναηκα: I. intrans. *to go up, mount, to go on -board, put to sea.* II. in aor. 1 ἀνέβησα, sal, *to make to go up, make to go on board ship, e to mount:*—Pass., aor. 1 part. ἀναβαθείς, *moun-:* so also pf. part. ἀναβεβαμένος.

α-βακχεύω, f. σω, (ἀνά, Βάκχος) *to rouse to Bac- frenzy.* 2. intr. *to break into Bacchic frenzy.*

α-βακχιόω, = ἀναβακχεύω.

α-βάλλω, f. -βᾰλῶ: pf. -βέβληκα:—*to throw* or *up.* II. *to put back, put off:*—Med. *to lift up* 's voice, *to make a prelude, begin to sing.* III. *ut off, delay;* in Act. and Med. IV. in Med. *hrow one's cloak around* one.

-βαπτίζω, f. σω, *to dip repeatedly.*

αβάς, ᾶσα, άν, aor. 2 part. of ἀναβαίνω.

άβᾰσις, εως, ἡ, (ἀναβαίνω) *a going up, mount-.* 2. *an expedition up from the* coast, esp. into tral Asia, like that of the younger Cyrus. 3. *rising* of a river. II. *a way up, the ascent* of nountain, etc.

ναβάτης, poët. **ἀμβάτης**, ου, ὁ, (ἀναβαίνω) *one o is mounted, a horseman.* [ᾰ]

ναβᾰτικός, ή, όν, (ἀναβαίνω) *skilled in mounting.*

ναβᾰτός, poët. **ἀμβατός**, όν, (ἀνα-βαίνω) *that may mounted* or *scaled, easy to be scaled.*

ναβέβηκα, pf. of ἀναβαίνω.

ναβέβρῠχεν, pf. of an obsol. ἀναβρύζω, *to boil* or *bble up.*

νάβηθι, ἀναβῆναι, aor. 2 imper. and inf. of ἀναβαίνω.

να-βῐβάζω: fut. med. βιβάσομαι, Att. βιβῶμαι: r. 1 ἀνεβίβᾰσα, med. -ασάμην:—Causal of ἀναίνω, *to make go up:* 1. *to mount* one on horse- ck. 2. *to draw* a ship *up.* 3. in Med. *to put board ship.* 4. *to bring up* to the bar of a court justice. Hence

ναβῐβαστέον, verb. Adj. *one must set on.*

να-βιόω: f. ἀναβιώσομαι: aor. 2 ἀνεβίων, inf. αβιῶναι, rarely aor. 1 ἀνεβίωσα: (ἀνά, βίος):—*to me to life again, return* to life.

ναβίωσις, εως, ἡ, (ἀναβιόω) *recovery of life.*

ναβιώσκομαι, aor. 1 ἐνεβιωσάμην, Dep. *to bring ck to life.*

να-βλαστάνω, f. βλαστήσω: aor. 2 ἀνέβλαστον: *to* [illegible] or *grow up again.*

νάβλεμμα, ατος, τό, *a look cast upwards.* From

να-βλέπω, f. ψω, *to look up.* 2. *to look back on*, Lat. *respicere.* II. *to see again, recover e's sight.* Hence

ἀνάβλεψις, εως, ἡ, (ἀναβλέπω) *a seeing again, recovery of sight.*

ἀναβλήδην, poët. shortd. **ἀμβλήδην**, Adv. (ἀναβάλλομαι) *boiling up:*—*with sudden bursts.*

ἀνάβλησις, εως, ἡ, (ἀναβάλλω) *a putting off, delay.*

ἀνα-βλύζω, f. ύσω: aor. 1 ἀνέβλυσα:—*to gush forth;* ἀναβλύζειν ἔλαιον *to gush out with* oil.

ἀνα-βλώσκω, aor. 2 ἀνέμολον, *to go up* or *back.*

ἀνα-βοάω, fut. ήσομαι: aor. 1 ἀνεβόησα, Ion. inf. ἀμβῶσαι (for ἀναβοῆσαι):—*to cry* or *shout aloud, utter a loud cry: to cry out* something. II. *to call on.*

ἀναβολάδην, poët. **ἀμβ-**, Adv. (ἀναβολή) *bubbling up.* II. *as a prelude* or *beginning of song.*

ἀναβολάς, shortd. **ἀμβολάς**, άδος, ἡ, (ἀναβάλλω) *thrown up*, of earth.

ἀνα-βολή, poët. **ἀμβολή**, ἡ, (ἀναβάλλω) *that which is thrown up, a mound of earth.* 2. *that which is thrown around one, a cloak.* II. *a lifting up* of the voice, *a prelude.* 2. *a putting off, delaying.*

ἀναβολία, poët. **ἀμβ-**, ἡ, (ἀναβολή) *delay.*

ἀνα-βράσσω, Att. **-ττω**: Pass., aor. 1 ἀνεβράσθην: —*to make foam* or *boil up, to boil.* Hence.

ἀνά-βραστος, ον, *boiled.*

***ανα-βράχω**, only found in 3 sing. aor. 2 ἀνέβρᾰχεν, q. v.

***ἀνα-βρόχω**, aor. 1 ἀνέβροξα, opt. ἀναβρόξεια, pf. ἀναβέβροχα, *to swallow again, gulp down:* also aor. 2 pass. part. ἀνα-βροχείς, εῖσα, έν, *swallowed back, swallowed down again.* Cf. καταβρόχω.

ἀνα-βρυάζω, aor. 1 -εβρύαξα, *to shout aloud for joy.*

ἀνα-βρῡχάομαι, Dep. *to roar aloud.*

ἀναβῶσαι, Ion. for ἀναβοῆσαι, aor. 1 inf. of ἀναβοάω.

ἀνά-γαιον, τό, = ἀνώ-γαιον.

ἀν-αγγέλλω, for the tenses see ἀγγέλλω:—*to carry back tidings of* a thing, *report*, Lat. *renunciare.*

ἀνα-γελάω, f. άσομαι [ᾰ]: aor. 1 -εγέλᾰσα: *to laugh aloud.*

ἀνα-γεννάω, f. ήσω, *to beget anew, regenerate.*

ἀν-ᾱγέομαι, Dor. for ἀν-ηγέομαι.

ἀνα-γεύω, f. σω: aor. 1 ἀνέγευσα: *to give to taste.*

ἀνα-γιγνώσκω, later **ἀναγῑνώσκω**: f. ἀναγνώσομαι, aor. 2 ἀνέγνων: ἀνέγνωκα:—*to know accurately.* 2. *to know again, recognise, own*, Lat. *agnoscere.* 3. *to distinguish, discern:* hence *to read.* II. in Ion. Greek the aor. 1 ἀνέγνωσα is used in causal sense *to persuade;* and aor. 1 pass. ἀνεγνώσθην, pf. ἀνέγνωσμαι, *to be persuaded.*

ἀναγκάζω, f. άσω: pf. ἠνάγκᾰκα: (ἀνάγκη):—*to force, compel: to constrain*, esp. by argument: also *to force by torture*, and so *to harass, annoy.* 2. *to prove of necessity, to demonstrate.* 3. with double acc. *to force* a person *to do* a thing.

ἀναγκαίη, ἡ, Ep. and Ion. for ἀνάγκη.

ἀναγκαῖος, α, ον, also ος, ον, (ἀνάγκη) *of* or *with force:* I. Act. *constraining, forcing, pressing:* ἦμαρ ἀναγκαῖον the day *of constraint*, i. e. *slavery.* 2.

forcible, convincing. 3. of things, *requiring to be done.* II. pass. *forced:* hence *painful.* 2. *necessary:* τὰ ἀναγκαῖα, *necessaries:* also *absolutely necessary, barely sufficient.* 3. *connected by necessary* or *natural ties:* as Subst., ἀναγκαῖοι, οἱ, Lat. *necessarii, relations.*

ἀναγκαίως, Adv. of ἀναγκαῖος, *of necessity, perforce;* ἀναγκαίως ἔχει it is *necessary:* Sup. ἀναγκαιότατα.

ἀναγκαστέον, verb. Adj. of ἀναγκάζω, *one must compel.*

ἀναγκαστικός, ή, όν, (ἀναγκάζω) *compulsory.*

ἀναγκαστός, ή, όν, verb. Adj. of ἀναγκάζω, *forced, constrained.*

'ΑΝΑΓΚΗ, Ion. and Ep. **ἀναγκαίη**, ἡ, Lat. *necessitas, force, constraint, necessity:* often in dat. ἀνάγκῃ as Adv. *perforce, of necessity,* also *forcibly, by force.* 2. *necessity, natural want* or *desire,* such as hunger. 3. *actual force, violence:* hence *bodily pain, suffering.* II. like Lat. *necessitudo, the tie of kin, relationship.*

ἀνα-γνάμπτω, f. ψω: Pass., aor. 1 ἀνεγνάμφθην:—*to bend back* or *round.* 2. *to undo, loose.*

ἀναγνοίην, ἀναγνῶναι, aor. 2 opt. and inf. of ἀναγιγνώσκω.

ἄν-αγνος, ον, (α privat., ἁγνός) *impure, unchaste,* generally *unholy, guilty.*

ἀνα-γνωρίζω: f. ίσω, Att. ιῶ: *to know again, recognise.* Hence

ἀναγνώρἴσις, εως, ἡ, *recognition.*

ἀνάγνωσις, εως, ἡ, (ἀναγνῶναι) *a knowing again, recognition, owning.* II. *reading.*

ἀνάγνωσμα, ματος, τό, (ἀναγνῶναι) aor. 2 of ἀναγιγνώσκω) *a passage read aloud.*

ἀναγόρευσις, εως, ἡ, *a crying aloud, proclamation.* From

ἀν-ᾰγορεύω: the Att. fut. is ἀνερῶ, aor. 2 ἀνεῖπον:—*to cry aloud, proclaim publicly:*—Pass. *to be proclaimed: to be generally called* or *surnamed.*

ἀνάγραπτος, ον, (ἀναγράφω) *written up* or *out, registered.*

ἀναγρᾰφεύς, έως, ὁ, (ἀναγραφω) *a notary, secretary.*

ἀναγρᾰφή, ἡ, *a writing out: that which is written out, a public record.* From

ἀνα-γράφω, f. ψω: aor. 1 ἀνέγραψα:—*to write up,* generally *to enter in a public register* or *record.* II. *to describe.* [γρᾰ]

ἀνα-γρύζω, strengthd. for γρύζω *to mutter.*

ἀν-άγω, f. ἀνάξω: aor. 2 ἀνήγᾰγον: (ἀνά, ἄγω): I. *to lead up* from a lower place to a higher, but in Homer = ἄγω, *to conduct, carry.* 2. ἀνάγειν ναῦν *to put* a ship *out to sea;* and then ἀνάγειν or ἀνάγεσθαι, absol. in same sense. 3. *to lead up* into the interior of a country. 4. *to lead up, raise up, conduct,* hence *to celebrate.* 5. *to bring up, educate.* II. *to bring back*: *to refer* III. intrans. (sub. ἑαυτόν) *to withdraw, retreat.*

ἀναγωγεύς, έως, ὁ, (ἀνάγω) properly *one that leads up:* hence *anything by which one leads, a rein, thong,* etc.

ἀναγωγή, ἡ, (ἀνάγω) *a leading up: a putting to sea.* 2. *a leading back, referring.*

ἀν-άγωγος, ον, (α privat., ἀγωγή) *without guidance* or *education, ill-bred:* of horses and dogs, *unbroken.*

ἀν-ᾰγώνιστος, ον, (α privat., ἀγωνίζομαι) *without contest, never having contended for a prize.*

ἀνα-δαίω, *to divide anew:* generally *to divide* or *apportion* a conquered land.

ἀνα-δαίω, poët. **ἀν-δαίω**, = ἀνακαίω, *to light up.*

ἀνα-δάσασθαι, aor. 1 med. inf. of ἀναδατέομαι.

ἀναδασμός, ὁ, (ἀναδάσασθαι) *a re-distribution:* generally *a distribution, division.*

ἀνάδαστος, ον, (ἀναδάσασθαι) *divided anew, redistributed:* generally, *distributed.*

ἀνα-δατέομαι, f. -δάσομαι: aor. 1 ἀνεδασάμην:—*to divide again, re-distribute.*

ἀναδέδρομα, pf. 2 of ἀνατρέχω.

ἀνάδειγμα, ματος, τό, *a means of shewing forth: a mouth-piece used by criers.*

ἀνα-δείκνῡμι and **ἀνα-δεικνύω**: fut. -δείξω, Ion. -δέξω:—*to lift up and shew, shew forth.* II. *to make public, declare.* Hence

ἀνάδειξις, εως, ἡ, *a shewing forth, display: a proclaiming, election.*

ἀνα-δέκομαι, Ion. for ἀνα-δέχομαι.

ἀν-άδελφος, ον, (α privat., ἀδελφός) *without brother* or *sister.*

ἀνάδεμα, poët. **ἄνδεμα**, ατος, τό, (ἀναδέω) *a head-band.*

ἀνα-δέξαι, Ion. for ἀναδεῖξαι, aor. 1 inf. of ἀναδείκνυμι.

ἀνα-δέρκομαι, aor. 2 ἀν-έδρακον:—*to look up, to open the eyes again.*

ἀνα-δέρω, f. δερῶ: *to draw off the skin,* esp. *to strip off* the scar of a wound, Lat. *refricare ulcus:* hence *to rip up old sores.*

ἀνάδεσις, εως, ἡ, (ἀναδέω) *a binding on.*

ἀναδέσμη, ἡ, and **ἀνάδεσμος**, ὁ, (ἀναδέω) *a band* or *fillet for women's hair, a headband.*

ἀνάδετος, ον, (ἀναδέω) *binding up.*

ἀνα-δεύω, *to dye, imbue.*

ἀνα-δέχομαι, fut. med. -δέξομαι: aor. ἀνεδεξάμην:—but Ep. aor. 2 pass. ἀνεδέγμην: pf. ἀναδέδεγμαι: Dep.:—*to take up, receive:* also *to take back.* II. *to take upon oneself, submit to.* 2. *to undertake, promise to* do; also *to be surety to one.*

ἀνα-δέω, poët, **ἀν-δέω**: f. -δήσω: aor. 1 -έδησα: pf. pass. δέδεμαι:—*to bind up, bind round;* ἀναδεῖν τινα εὐαγγέλια *to crown* one for one's good news. II. ἀναδῆσαι ἑαυτοὺς ἔς τινα *to trace up* one's family to a founder. III. Med. *to fasten with a rope to oneself;* ἀναδούμενος ἕλκειν (sc. ναῦς), *to take* a ship *in tow.*

ἀνάδημα, poët. **ἄνδημα**, ατος. τό, (ἀναδέω) *a head-band.*

ἀνα-διδάσκω, f. άξω, *to teach over again: to teach*

otherwise or *better*, Lat. *dedocere:* also simply = διδάσκω, *to teach:*—Pass. *to learn better.* II. *to expound, interpret.*

ἀνα-δίδωμι, poët. **ἀνδίδωμι**: f. -δώσω:—*to give up: to give forth*, esp. of the earth, *to yield.* 2. intr. of springs, fire, etc., *to burst forth.* II. *to give round, distribute:* also *to give back, restore.*

ἀνά-δῐκος, ον, (ἀνά, δίκη) *tried over again.*

ἀνα-διπλόω, f. ώσω, (ἀνά, διπλοῦς) *to make double.*

ἀνάδοτος, ον, (ἀναδίδωμι) *given up* or *to be given up.*

ἀνάδου, for ἀνάδοσο, aor. 2 imper. of ἀναδίδωμι.

ἀναδοῦναι, ἀναδούς, οῦσα, aor. 2 inf. and part. of ἀναδίδωμι.

ἀναδοῦνται, ἀναδούμενος, 3 pl. and part. pres. med. of ἀναδέω.

ἀναδοχή, ἡ, (ἀναδέχομαι) *a taking up, acceptance:* ἀναδοχὴ πόνων *the undertaking* of labours.

ἀναδραμεῖν, aor. 2 inf. of ἀνατρέχω.

ἀναδράμομαι, poët. for -οῦμαι, fut. of ἀνατρέχω.

ἀναδῦναι, aor. 2 inf. of ἀναδύομαι.

ἀνα-δύνω, *to come to the top of the water.*

ἀνα-δύομαι, f. δύσομαι: Dep. with aor. 2 act. ἀνέδῡν, pf. ἀναδέδῡκα: (ἀνά, δύω):—*to come up, rise*, esp. from the sea: but absol. of the sun, *to rise*, of springs, *to gush forth.* 2. *to draw back, retire:*—c. acc. *to shun:* c. inf. *to delay to* do, *avoid* doing.

ἀναδῶν, Att. pres. part. of ἀναδέω.

ἀν-άεδνος, ἡ, (α privat., ἕδνον) *without presents from the bridegroom, without bridal gifts.*

ἀναεῖραι, aor. 1 inf. of ἀναείρω.

ἀν-αείρω, (ἀνά, ἀείρω) *to lift* or *raise up.*

ἀν-άελπτος, ον, (α privat., ἔλπομαι) *unhoped, unlooked for.*

ἀν-αερτάω, lengthd. for ἀν-αείρω.

ἀνα-ζάω, inf. ἀναζῆν: f. ζήσω: *to return to life.*

ἀνα-ζεύγνυμι and -ύω, f. ζεύξω, *to yoke* or *harness again:* hence *to prepare to go away again*, esp. with an army, *to break up, move off:* and so of ships, νῆας ἀν. *to set sail again.* 2. intr. (sub. στρατόν, etc.) *to march off.* Hence

ἀνάζευξις, εως, ἡ, *a marching away.*

ἀνα-ζέω, f. ζέσω, *to boil* or *bubble up.*

ἀνα-ζητέω, *to search into, examine*, Lat. *anquirere: to search out, discover.* Hence

ἀναζήτησις, εως, ἡ, *investigation.*

ἀνα-ζωγρέω, *to recal to life.*

ἀνα-ζώννυμι, f. ζώσω, *to gird up.*

ἀνα-ζωπῠρέω, *to light up again:*—Pass. *to gain fresh life.*

ἀνα-θάλπω, *to warm again.*

ἀνα-θαρσέω, Att. -θαρρέω, *to regain one's courage.*

ἀνα-θαρσύνω, Att. -θαρρύνω, *to fill with fresh courage.* II. intr. = ἀναθαρσέω.

ἀνα-θεῖναι, ἀνα-θείς, aor. 2 inf. and part. of ἀνατίθημι.

ἀνάθεμα, ατος, τό, (ἀνατίθημι) *anything devoted* or *accursed.* Hence

ἀνα-θεμᾰτίζω, *to make accursed, to bind by a curse.*

ἀνα-θερμαίνω, *to warm* or *heat again.*

ἀναθετέον, verb. Adj. of ἀνατίθημι, *one must refer: one must defer.*

ἀνα-θέω, f. -θεύσομαι and -θευσοῦμαι, *to run up* or *back, return.*

ἀνα-θεωρέω, *to look at* or *observe carefully; to view* or *observe again.*

ἀνα-θηλέω, like ἀνα-θάλλω, (ἀνά, θῆλυς) *to grow green, bloom*, or *sprout afresh.*

ἀνάθημα, ατος, τό, (ἀνατίθημι) *that which is set up*, esp. as *a votive offering:* in Homer only used of a *delight* or *ornament.* Cf. ἄγαλμα.

ἀνα-θλίβω, f. ψω, *to press hard.*

ἀναθορεῖν, aor. 2 inf. of ἀναθρώσκω.

ἀνα-θορυβέω, f. ήσω, *to shout in applause.*

ἀνάθρεμμα, ατος, τό, (ἀνατρέφω) *a nursling.*

ἀν-αθρέω, (ἀνά, ἀθρέω) *to look up at: observe closely.*

ἀνα-θρώσκω, poët. and Ion. ἀνθρώσκω: fut. ἀναθοροῦμαι: aor. ἀνέθορον, inf. ἀναθορεῖν:—*to spring up, bound up, rebound: to spring upon.*

ἀναίδειᾰ, Ep. and Ion. **ἀναιδείη**, ἡ, (ἀναιδής) *shamelessness, assurance, effrontery.*

ἀναιδεύομαι, Dep. (ἀναιδής) *to behave impudently.*

ἀν-αιδής, ές, (α privat., αἰδέομαι) *shameless, unabashed, reckless:* the stone of Sisyphus is called λᾶας ἀναιδής, *reckless, ruthless.*

ἀν-αιθύσσω, *to fan* the flame.

ἀν-αίθω, (ἀνά, αἴθω) *to set on fire, to inflame.*

ἀν-αιμακτί, Adv. of sq., *without bloodshed.*

ἀν-αίμακτος, ον, (α privat., αἱμάσσω) *bloodless, unstained with blood*, Lat. *incruentus.*

ἀν-αίμᾰτος, ον, = ἄναιμος.

ἄν-αιμος, ον, and **ἀν-αίμων**, ον, gen. ονος, (α privat., αἷμα) *without blood, bloodless.*

ἀν-αιμωτί, Adv. like ἀν-αιμακτί. [τῑ]

ἀναίνομαι: impf. ἠναινόμην, Ep. ἀναινόμην: fut. ἀνᾰνοῦμαι (not in use): aor. 1 ἠνηνάμην, inf. ἀνήνασθαι, subj. ἀνήνηται: Dep.:—*to refuse, reject, spurn:* c. inf. *refuse to* do: hence *to excuse oneself from* a thing, *renounce, disown: to repent, be ashamed of* doing a thing. (Deriv. uncertain.)

ἀναΐξας, aor. 1 part. of ἀναΐσσω.

ἀναιρεθῆναι, aor. 1 pass. inf. of ἀναιρέω.

ἀναίρεσις, εως, ἡ, *a taking up* of dead bodies: *burial.* 2. *a taking upon* oneself, *an undertaking.* II. *a destroying, destruction.* From

ἀν-αιρέω: f. ήσω: pf. ἀνῄρηκα, pass. ἀνῄρημαι: (v. αἱρέω):—*to take up*, Lat. *tollere*, and so I. *to bear away, carry off*, esp. of prizes: simply, *to take up, lift.* II. *to take away, destroy:* of laws and customs, *to abolish.* III. *to appoint, ordain*, esp. of an oracle's answer; but absol. *to answer, give a response.*

Med. *to take up for oneself:* hence *to gain, win, receive: exact.* 2. *to take up* dead bodies *for burial.* 3. *to take up* newborn children. Lat. *tollere, suscipere liberos.* 4. *to conceive.* 5. *to take up* money at interest. II. *to take upon oneself, undertake.* III. *to take back to oneself, cancel.*

ἀν-αίρω, f. *ἀνᾰρῶ*, *to raise up.*

ἀναισθησία, ἡ, *want of perception, insensibility.* From

ἀν-αίσθητος, *ον*, (α privat., *αἰσθέσθαι* aor. 2 of *αἰσθαίνομαι*) *unfeeling, without feeling.* 2. *without common sense, senseless.* II. pass. *unfelt.*

ἀν-αισῐμόω: impf. *ἀναισίμουν*: aor. 1 *ἀναισίμωσα*:—Pass., aor. 1 *ἀναισιμώθην*: pf. *ἀναισίμωμαι*: (α priv., *αἴσιμος*,—the simple *αἰσιμόω* being never used):—an Ion. Verb, = Att. *ἀναλίσκω*, *to use up, use*; of time, *to spend*; of food, *to consume.* Hence

ἀναισίμωμα, *ατος*, *τό*, *that which is used up*, = Att. *δαπάνη*, *expenditure, outlay.*

ἀν-αΐσσω, Att. **ἀν-ᾴσσω**, **ἀν-ᾴττω** (*ἀνά*, *ἀΐσσω*):—*to start up, rise up quickly, spring* or *burst forth*: c. acc. *to leap upon.* [*ανᾱ-*]

ἀναισχυντέω, (*ἀναίσχυντος*) *to be shameless, behave impudently.*

ἀναισχυντία, ἡ, *shamelessness.* From

ἀν-αίσχυντος, *ον*, (α privat., *αἰσχύνη*) *shameless, impudent*: of things, *abominable, detestable.*

ἀν-αίτητος, *η*, *ον*, (α privat., *αἰτέω*) *unasked.*

ἀν-αίτιος, *ον*, (α privat., *αἰτία*) *without cause, groundless.* II. of persons, *guiltless, not chargeable, not to blame.*

ἀνα-καθαίρω, *to clear thoroughly*:—Pass. *to become quite clear.*

ἀνα-καθίζω, *to set up* or *upright*:—Med. *to sit up.* II. intr. *to sit down again.*

ἀνα-καινίζω, f. *ίσω*, Att. *ιῶ*, *to renew.*

ἀνα-καινουργέω, *to restore anew.*

ἀνα-καινόω, (*ἀνά*, *καινός*) *to renew, restore.* Hence

ἀνακαίνωσις, *εως*, ἡ, *renewal, restoration.*

ἀνακαῖον, *τό*, *a prison.*

ἀνα-καίω, aor. 1 *ἀνέκαυσα*, *to kindle, light up*:—Med. *to light oneself* a fire: metaph. *to fire, rouse, encourage*: in Pass. *to burn* with anger.

ἀνα-κᾰλέω, poët. **ἀγ-καλέω**: fut. *έσω*:—*to call up*, esp. *the dead.* II. *to call upon* or *call again and again*, and so *to invoke* the gods. 2. *to summon.* 3. *to call* by a name. III. *to call back, recal*, esp. *from* exile.

ἀνα-κᾰλύπτω, f. *ψω*, *to uncover, unveil.* II. intr. *to unveil.*

ἀνα-κάμπτω, f. *ψω*, *to bend upwards* or *back* 2. intrans. (sub. *ἑαυτόν*) *to bend back, return.*

ἀν-άκανθος, *ον*, (α privat., *ἄκανθα*) *without thorns* or *bones*: *without a spine.*

ἀνα-κάπτω, f. *ψω*, *to snap up, swallow, gulp down.*

ἀνακέαται, Ion. for *ἀνάκεινται*, 3 pl. of

ἀνα-κειμαι, poët. **ἄγ-κειμαι**: f. *-κείσομαι*:—used as Pass. of *ἀνατίθημι*, *to be laid up*, as a votive offering; and so, *to be dedicated*; also, *to be set up*, as a statue. II *to be referred to, depend upon.*

᾿Ανάκειον, *τό*, *the temple of Castor and Pollux.* From

῎Ανακες, *οἱ*, old form of *ἄνακτες*, *the Kings*, i. e. Castor and Pollux.

ἀνα-κέκλομαι, poët. for *ἀνα-καλέω*, *to call out.*

ἀνα-κέλᾰδος, *ὁ*, (*ἀνά*, *κέλομαι*) *a loud shout.*

ἀνα-κέομαι, Ion. for *ἀνά-κειμαι.*

ἀνα-κεράννῡμι and **-ύω**: f. *κεράσω* [*ᾰ*]:—*to mix again*: generally, *to mix up, mix well.*

ἀνα-κεφᾰλαιόω, f. *ώσω*, (*ἀνά*, *κεφαλή*) *to comprehend in a summary, sum up.*

ἀνα-κηκίω, *to spout up, gush forth*: also, *to throb violently.* [*ῐ* Ep.]

ἀνα-κηρύσσω, Att. **-ττω**, f. *ύξω*, *to publish, to proclaim*, esp. *to proclaim as conqueror*: *to offer by voice of herald*: and so *to put up to auction*, which was done by proclamation of the *κήρυξ.*

ἀνα-κινδῡνεύω, f. *σω*, *to rush into danger again, to run a fresh risk.*

ἀνα-κῑνέω, *to move upwards, to sway to and fro.* 2. *to rouse, awaken*, Lat. *suscitare.* Hence

ἀνακίνησις, *εως*, ἡ, *a swinging to and fro.* 2. *excitement, emotion.* [*κῑ*]

ἀνα-κίρνᾰμαι, Dep. = *ἀνα-κεράννυμι.*

ἀνα-κλάζω, f. *-κλάγξω*: aor. 2 *ἀνέκλᾰγον*:—*to cry aloud, scream out*: of a dog, *to bark, bay.*

ἀνα-κλαίω, f. *-κλαύσομαι*, *to weep aloud, burst into tears*, also *to weep for, to bewail.*

ἀνα-κλάω, f. *-κλάσω* [*ᾰ*]: aor. 1 *ἀνέκλᾰσα*:—*to break upwards* or *back, to break in pieces.*

ἀνάκλησις, *εως*, ἡ, (*ἀνακαλέω*) *a calling on, invocation*: *a summoning.* II. *a recalling*, esp. from banishment.

ἀνακλιθήσομαι, fut. pass. of *ἀνακλίνω.*

ἀνακλινθείς, later **ἀνακλιθείς**, poët. aor. 1 pass. of

ἀνα-κλίνω, poët. **ἀγ-κλίνω** [*ῑ*]: fut. *-κλῐνῶ*: aor. 1 *ἀνέκλῑνα*:—*to make to lie back, to lean* one thing *against* another: Pass. *to lie, sink* or *lean back.* II. *to push* or *put back* a trap-door, and so *to open* it.

ἀνάκλῐτος, *η*, *ον*, (*ἀνακλίνω*) *leaning back.*

ἀνα-κογχῠλιάζω, f. *σω*, (*ἀνά*, *κόγχη*) *to open and counterfeit a seal.*

ἀνα-κοινόω, f. *ώσω*, *to communicate* or *impart* something to another: *to communicate with* another, *consult* him.—Med. with pf. pass. *-κεκοίνωμαι*, *to communicate* what *is one's own* to another: *to impart.*

ἀνα-κοιρᾰνέω, *to rule in* or *over.*

ἀνα-κολπάζω, f. *σω*, (*ἀνά*, *κόλπος*) *to gird up into a fold* (Lat. *sinus*): absol. *to gird oneself up.*

ἀνακομῐδή, ἡ, *recovery of* a thing or *from* an illness. From

ἀνα-κομίζω, poët. **ἀγ-κομίζω**: f. *-ίσω* Att. *-ιῶ*: aor. 1 *ἀνεκόμισα*:—*to carry up*: esp. *to carry up* or *against stream*: Pass. *to go up.* II. *to bring back, recover*:—Med. with pf. pass. *to bring back with one*: *to recover one's own*: *to bring to pass again*:—Pass. *to go back.*

ἀν-ακοντίζω, f. *ίσω*, *to dart* or *fling up.* II. intr. *to shoot up*, as blood from a wound.

ἀνακοπή, ἡ, *a beating back*: *a recoil.* From

ἀνα-κόπτω, f. *ψω*, *to beat, force* or *drive back*:—Pass. *to stop short.*

ἀνα-κουφίζω, f. *ίσω*, Att. *ιῶ*, *to lift* or *raise up*:—Pass. *to be lifted up, lightened in spirits.* **Hence**

ἀν-κούφῐσις, εως, ἡ, *a lifting up, lightening: relief* from a thing.

ἀνα-κράζω, f. άξομαι. aor. 2 ἀνέκρᾰγον:—*to cry out, lift up the voice.*

ἀνα-κρᾱθείς, aor. 1 pass. part. of ἀνακεράννυμι.

ἀνάκρᾱσις, εως, ἡ, (ἀνακεράννυμι) *a mixing up.*

ἀνα-κρέκομαι, Dep. *to begin to play:* of a bird, *to tune* its *voice.*

ἀνα-κρεμάννυμι, poët. **ἀγ-κρεμ-**: f. -κρεμάσω: aor. 1 ἀνεκρέμασα:—*to hang up upon* a thing:—Pass. *to be hanging up:* metaph. *to be in suspense,* Lat. *suspensus esse.*

ἀνα-κρίνω [ῑ]: (for the tenses, v. κρίνω): *to examine well, search out.* II. *to examine beforehand:*—Med., ἀνακρίνεσθαι πρὸς ἑαυτούς, *to question* one *with another.* Hence

ἀνάκρῐσις, poët. **ἄγκρισις**, εως, ἡ, *an examination, inquiry.*

ἀνα-κροτέω, f. ήσω, *to lift up and strike together:* absol. *to clap with uplifted hands, applaud vehemently.*

ἀνάκρουσις, εως, ἡ, (ἀνακρούω) *a pushing back, checking,* esp. *pushing* a ship *back, backing water.*

ἀνακρουστέον, verb. Adj. of ἀνακρούω, *one must check.*

ἀνα-κρούω, f. σω, *to thrust back, check:*—in Med. of a ship, ἀνακρούεσθαι ἐπὶ πρύμνην *to put her back* sternwards, by backing water. 2. Med. also in music, *to strike the strings, make a prelude,* like ἀναβάλλεσθαι.

ἀνα-κτάομαι, f. -κτήσομαι: pf. ἀνέκτημαι: Dep.:—*to regain for oneself, recover, retrieve.* II. *to win* a person *over, gain his favour.*

ἀνάκτεσι, Ep. for ἄναξι, dat. pl. of ἄναξ.

ἀνακτόριος, α, ον, (ἀνάκτωρ) *belonging to a lord* or *king, royal:* ἀνακτόριον, τό, = sq. *a temple.*

ἀνάκτορον, τό, (ἀνάκτωρ) *a king's dwelling, palace:* also *a temple.*

ἀνάκτωρ, ορος, ὁ, (ἀνάσσω) *a lord, king.*

ἀνα-κυκάω, f. ήσω, *to stir up* and *mix: to confuse.*

ἀνα-κυκλέω, *to turn round again:*—Pass. *to revolve, come round again.* Hence

ἀνακύκλησις, εως, ἡ, *a coming round again, a circuit, revolution.*

ἀνα-κυμβᾰλιάζω, (ἀνά, κύμβαλον) *to rattle like* κύμβαλα: δίφροι ἀνεκυμβαλίαζον the chariots *were overturned with a rattling noise,* like that of cymbals.

ἀνα-κύπτω, fut. -κύψω and -κύψομαι: aor. 1 ἀνέκυψα: pf. ἀνακέκῡφα:—*to lift up the head:* esp. *to come up out of the water:* hence *to rise out of difficulties, to recover, emerge.*

ἀνα-κωκύω, f. ύσω, *to wail aloud.* [ῡ]

ἀνᾰκῶς, Adv. = ἐπιμελῶς, *carefully,* ἀνακῶς ἔχειν τινός *to look well* to a thing. (From ἄνακος, Adj. of ἄναξ, *a manager.*)

ἀνακωχεύω, f. σω, *to hold back, stay,* esp. of ships, *to keep them riding at anchor:* but ἀν. τὸν τόνον τῶν ὅπλων *to keep up* the tension of the ropes, *keep taught.* 2. intr. (sub. ἑαυτόν) *to keep still.* From

ἀνακωχή, ἡ, incorrect form of ἀνοκωχή.

ἀναλαβεῖν, aor. 2 inf. of ἀναλαμβάνω.

ἀνα-λάζομαι, Dep. *to take again.*

ἀν-ᾰλᾰλάζω, aor. 1 ἀνηλάλαξα: *to raise a war-cry: to cry aloud.*

ἀνα-λαμβάνω, f. -λήψομαι: aor. 2 ἀνέλᾰβον: pf. ἀνείληφα:—*to take up, take into one's hands:* generally, *to take with one.* 2. *to take into one's service, to adopt.* 3. like Lat. *recipere, to take upon one:* esp. in Med. *to undertake,* ἀναλαβέσθαι πόλεμον. 4. *to take up again, resume,* ἀναλαβεῖν λόγον. II. *to take back, regain, retrieve, repair.* III. *to pull short up,* of a horse. IV. *to gain quite over, attach to oneself.*

ἀνα-λάμπω, f. λάμψω, *to flame up, take fire.*

ἀναλγησία, ἡ, *insensibility, want of feeling.* From

ἀν-άλγητος, ον, (α privat., ἀλγέω) *without pain:* I. of persons, *unfeeling, hard-hearted, ruthless:*—Adv. -τως, *unfeelingly.* II. of things, 1. *not painful.* 2. *very painful, cruel.*

ἀν-αλδής, ές, (α priv., ἀλδεῖν) *not thriving, feeble.*

ἀνα-λέγω: Ep. impf. ἄλλεγον: fut. ἀναλέξω: aor. 1 ἀνέλεξα, Ep. inf. ἀλλέξαι:—*to pick up, gather up:*—Med. *to pick up for oneself.* 2. *to recount.* II. *to read aloud.*

ἀνα-λείχω, f. ξω, *to lick up.*

ἀνάληψις, εως, ἡ, (ἀναλαμβάνω) *a taking up: a taking again, a means of regaining: a repairing, making amends.* II. *a being taken up: the Ascension.*

ἀν-αλθής, ές, (α privat., ἄλθομαι) *not healing.*

ἀνάλῐπος, ον, Dor. for ἀνήλιπος, *barefoot.*

ἀν-ᾱλίσκω: f. ἀνᾱλώσω: aor. 1 ἀνήλωσα or ἀνάλωσα: pf. ἀνήλωκα or ἀνάλωκα:—Pass., fut. ἀνᾱλωθήσομαι: aor. 1 ἀνηλώθην or ἀνᾱλώθην: pf. ἀνήλωμαι or ἀνᾱλωμαι: the pres. ἀν-ᾱλόω, impf. ἀνάλουν are rare:—*to use up, spend,* esp. in a bad sense, *to squander:*—metaph., ἀν. ὕπνον *to use to the full,* i.e. *enjoy,* sleep. II. of persons, *to kill, destroy.*

ἀνάλκεια, ἡ, *want of strength.* From

ἄν-αλκις, ιδος, ὁ, ἡ, acc. -ιδα or -ιν, (α priv., ἀλκή) *without strength, impotent, unwarlike.*

ἀν-άλλομαι, Dep. *to leap up.*

ἄν-αλμος, ον, (α privat., ἅλμη) *not salted.*

ἀνα-λογία, ἡ, (ἀνά, λόγος) *proportion, analogy.*

ἀνα-λογίζομαι, Dep. *to count up: sum up: to think over, calculate, consider.* Hence

ἀναλογισμός, ὁ, *a counting up, calculation, reasoning with oneself:* also *a course of reasoning.*

ἄν-αλος, ον, (α privat., ἅλς) *not salt, without salt.*

ἀν-ᾱλόω, a rare form of ἀν-αλίσκω.

ἄν-αλτος, ον, (α privat., ἄλθομαι) *not to be filled, insatiate,* Lat. *inexplebilis.*

ἀνάλῠσις, εως, ἡ, (ἀναλύω) *a loosing, releasing: dissolution, death.*

ἀνα-λύω, Ion. and Ep. ἀλ-λύω: f. -λύσω [ῡ]: pf. -λέλῠκα, pass. -λέλῠμαι:—*to unloose, undo again:* also *to set free.* II. *to do away, get rid of: to stop, put an end to.* III. intr. (sub. ἵππον, ναῦν, etc.) *to loose for departure,* and so *to depart, return.*

ἀνάλωκα, -ωμαι, pf. act. and pass. of *ἀνᾱλίσκω.*

ἀνάλωμα, *ατος, τό*, (*ἀνᾱλόω*) *that which is used* or *spent: expense, cost, outlay:* in plur. *expenses.*

ἀνάλωσα, ἀνᾱλῶσαι, aor. 1 of *ἀναλίσκω.*

ἀνάλωσις, *εως, ἡ*, (*ἀναλόω*) *expenditure.* [ᾰνᾱ]

ἀν-άλωτος, *ον*, (*a* privat., *ἁλῶναι*) *not taken, not to be taken, impregnable.*

ἀνα-μαιμάω, *to rage through* or *throughout.*

ἀνα-μανθάνω, f. *-μᾰθήσομαι*, *to learn again* or *anew, learn differently: to inquire closely.*

ἀν-ᾰμάξευτος, *ον*, (*a* privat., *ἁμαξεύω*) *impassable for wagons.*

ἀν-ᾰμάρτητος, *ον*, (*a* privat., *ἁμαρτεῖν*) *without missing* or *failing, unfailing:* in a moral sense, *faultless.* Adv. *-τως, without fail.*

ἀνα-μᾰσάομαι, Dep. *to chew over again*, Lat. *ruminari.*

ἀνα-μάσσω, Att. **-ττω**: f. *-μάξω*: aor. 1 *ἀνέμαξα*:—*to wipe up, wipe off; ἔργον, ὃ σῇ κεφαλῇ ἀναμάξεις* a deed which thou wilt *wipe off on thine own* head, (as if it were a stain). II. Med. *to knead one's bread.*

ἀνα-μάχομαι, f. *-μαχοῦμαι*, sometimes *-μαχέσομαι* or *-ήσομαι*: Dep. :—*to renew the fight, to retrieve a defeat.*

ἀν-άμβᾰτος, *ον*, poët. for *ἀν-ανάβατος*, (*a* privat., *ἀναβαίνω*) of a horse, *not to be mounted, unmanageable.*

ἀνα-μέλπω, f. *ψω*, *to begin to sing.*

ἀνα-μένω, poët. **ἀμμένω**: f. *-μενῶ*: aor. 1 *ἀνέμεινα*:—*to wait for, await:* absol. *to wait, stay.* 2. *to await, endure.* 3. *to put off, delay.*

ἀνά-μεσος, *ον*, *in the middle.*

ἀνά-μεστος, *ον*, *filled full.* Hence

ἀναμεστόω, f. *ώσω*, *to fill up, fill full.*

ἀνα-μετρέω, f. *ήσω*, *to measure back* or *over again, to remeasure the same road* one came by: generally, *to do* or *say over again, repeat.* II. *to measure out* Hence

ἀναμέτρησις, *εως, ἡ, a measuring out, admeasurement.*

ἀνά-μῐγα, poet **ἄμμῐγα**, also **ἀνά-μιγδα**, Adv. *promiscuously.*

ἀνα-μίγνῡμι and **-ύω**, f. *-μίξω*: aor. 1 *ἀνέμιξα*, *to mix up together, to mingle.* II. Med. *to have social intercourse, join company.*

ἀνα-μιμνήσκω: f. *ἀναμνήσω*, poët. *ἀμμνήσω*: aor. 1 *ἀνέμνησα*:—*to remind* one *of* a thing: c. inf. *to remind* one to do: also *to recal to memory, make mention of*:—Pass. *to remember.*

ἀνα-μίμνω, poët. for *ἀνα-μένω.*

ἀνα-μίξ, (*ἀναμίγνυμι*) Adv. *mixed up, pell-mell.*

ἀνάμιξις, *εως, ἡ*, (*ἀναμίγνυμι*) *social intercourse.*

ἀνα-μίσγω, poët. and Ion. for *ἀναμίγνυμι.*

ἀναμνησθείς, part. aor. 1 pass. of *ἀναμιμνήσκω.*

ἀνά-μνησις, *εως, ἡ*, (*ἀναμιμνήσκω*) *a calling to mind, recollection.*

ἀνα-μολεῖν, inf. aor. 2 of *ἀναβλώσκω.*

ἀνα-μορμύρω, *to roar loudly, foam up*, of the sea. [ῡ]

ἀνα-μοχλεύω, (*ἀνά, μοχλός*) *to lift with a lever: to force open.*

ἀν-αμπλάκητος, *ον*, (*a* privat., *ἀμπλάκητος*) *unerring, without wandering.*

ἀνα-μυχθίζομαι, Dep. *to groan deeply.*

ἀν-αμφίλογος, *ον*, (*a* privat., *ἀμφίλογος*) *undisputed, undoubted.*

ἀν-αμφισβήτητος, *ον*, (*a* privat., *ἀμφισβήτητος*) *undisputed, indisputable, about which there is no dispute.* II. act. *without dispute* or *controversy.*

ἀνανδρία, *ἡ*, *unmanliness, cowardice.* From

ἄν-ανδρος, *ον*, (*a* privat., *ἀνήρ*), I = *ἄνευ ἀνδρός, without a husband: without men, desolate.* II. *unmanly, cowardly, unworthy of a man.*

ἀν-ανδρόω, f. *ώσω*, *to deprive of a husband.* Hence

ἀνάνδρωτος, *ον*, *widowed.*

ἀνα-νεάζω, f. *άσω*, (*ἀνά, νέος*) *to make young again*

ἀνα-νέμω, poët. **ἀννέμω**, *to divide* or *distribute anew.* II. Med. *to count up, recount: to rehearse.*

ἀνα-νέομαι, poët. **ἀννέομαι**, Dep. *to mount up, rise.*

ἀνα-νεόομαι, f. *ώσομαι*: aor. 1 *ἀνενεωσάμην*, poet inf. *ἀννεώσασθαι*: Dep. :—*to renew, revive.*

ἀνα-νεύω, f. *σω*, properly *to throw the head back* in token of denial: hence *to deny, refuse.*

ἀνανέωσις, *εως, ἡ*, (*ἀνανεόομαι*) *a renewal, revival.*

ἀνα-νήφω, f. *ψω*, *to become sober again, come to one's senses.* 2. trans. *to make sober again.*

ἄν-αντα, Adv. of *ἀν-άντης*, *uphill*, opp. to *κάταντα.*

ἀν-ανταγώνιστος, *ον*, (*a* privat., *ἀνταγωνίζομαι*) *without a rival, without a struggle: undisputed.*

ἀν-άντης, *ες*, (*ἀνά, ἀντάω*) *up-hill, steep*, opp. to *κατάντης*: hence like Lat. *arduus, difficult.*

ἀν-αντίρρητος, *ον*, (*a* privat., *ἀντερῶ*) *not to be gainsaid.* Adv. *-ως, without contradiction.*

ἌΝΑΞ, *ἄνακτος, ὁ*: Ep. dat. pl. *ἀνάκτεσι*: *a lord, king*, applied to all the gods, esp. to Apollo. II. *any earthly lord, prince, chief, king:* also of the *sons* or *kinsmen of kings*, and generally, the *chief persons of a state.* 2. so too *the master of the house*, Lat. *herus.* 3. generally, *one who is lord* or *master* over anything, as *κώπης ἄνακτες*: cf. *χειρ-ῶναξ.*

ἀνα-ξαίνω, *to rub* or *irritate afresh.*

ἀνάξασθαι, aor. 1 med. inf. of *ἀνάσσω.*

ἀνα-ξηραίνω, f. *ᾰνῶ*: aor. 1 *-εξήρᾱνα*, poët. inf. *ἀγξηρᾶναι*:—*to dry up.*

ἀν-άξιος, *ον*, also *α, ον*, (*a* privat., *ἄξιος*) *unworthy, not deemed worthy*, c. gen.: absol. *worthless.* 2. *undeserving of evil.*

ἀναξι-φόρμιγξ, *ιγγος, ὁ, ἡ*, (*ἀνάσσω, φόρμιγξ*) *lord of the lyre.*

ἀναξίως, Adv. of *ἀνάξιος*, *unworthily.*

ἀνα-ξῡνόω, (*ἀνά, ξυνός*) = *ἀνα-κοινόω.*

ἀναξυρίδες, *ίδων, αἱ*, *the trowsers* worn by eastern nations. (Persian word.)

ἀνα-ξύω, f. *ύσω* [ῡ]: aor. pass. *ἀνεξύσθην*:—*to scrape off.*

ἀνάξω, fut. of *ἀνάσσω.*

ἀν-αοίγω, f. *ξω*, poët. for *ἀν-οίγω.*

ἀνα-παιδεύω, *to educate afresh.*

ἀνάπαιστος, *ον*, (*ἀναπαίω*) *struck back, rebounding:*

as Subst. ἀνάπαιστος (sub. πούς), ὁ, *an anapaest*, i. e. a dactyl *reversed.*

ἀνα-παίω, f. σω, *to strike again* or *back.*

ἀνά-πᾰλιν, Adv. *back again.* II. *over again.* III. *reversely.*

ἀνα-πάλλω, poët. **ἀμπάλλω**: fut. ἀναπᾰλῶ: aor. 1 **ἀνέπηλα**: Ep. aor. 2 part. ἀμπεπαλών:—*to swing to and fro, to put in motion*:—Pass. with Ep. aor. 2 ἀν-έπαλτο, *to dart* or *spring up.*

ἀνα-πάσσω, f. άσω, *to scatter upon.*

ἀνάπαυλα, ης, ἡ, (ἀναπαύω) *rest, repose, ease* from a thing: of watches, κατ' ἀναπαύλας διῃρῆσθαι to be divided *into reliefs.* II. *a resting-place.*

ἀνάπαυσις, poët. **ἄμπαυσις**, εως, ἡ, (ἀναπαύω) *rest, repose, ease: rest from* a thing, *cessation.*

ἀναπαυστήριος, Ion. **ἀμπ-**, ον, (ἀναπαύω) *belonging to resting* or *rest*:—as Subst. **ἀναπαυστήριον** or **ἀναπαυτήριον**, τό, *a resting-place: the time* or *hour of rest:* also (sub. σημεῖον), the sound of trumpet *for all to go to rest.*

ἀνα-παύω, Ion. **ἀμπαύω**, (for the tenses, v. παύω): —*to make cease, stop from* a thing: later *to give rest* or *relieve from* a thing II. Med. *to cease, leave off, desist from* a thing: absol. *to take one's rest, sleep:* also *to die.* 2. *to stop, halt, rest.* 3. *to regain strength.*

ἀνα-πείθω, f. πείσω: aor. 1 ἀνέπεισα:—*to bring over to another opinion, to persuade against one's will:* also in bad sense, *to seduce, mislead.*

ἀνα-πειράομαι, f. ήσομαι, Dep. *to try* or *attempt again, to make trial of.* II. as a military and naval term, *to exercise, practise.*

ἀνα-πείρω, f. -περῶ: aor. 1 ἀνέπειρα, Ep. part. ἀμπείρας: Pass., aor. 2 ἀνεπάρην [ᾰ]: pf. ἀναπέπαρμαι, poët. ἀμπέπαρμαι:—*to pierce through, spit.*

ἀναπειστήριος, α, ον, (ἀναπείθω) *persuasive.*

ἀνα-πεμπάζω and **-άζομαι**, *to count over again.*

ἀναπέμπω, poët. **ἀμπέμπω**, f. ψω, (for the tenses, v. πέμπω):—*to send up* or *forth*:—Med. *to send up from oneself.* II. *to send back.*

ἀναπεπτᾰμένος, pf. pass. part. of ἀναπετάννυμι.

ἀναπεσεῖν, **ἀναπεσών**, aor. 2 inf. and part. of ἀναπίπτω.

ἀνα-πετάννῡμι and **ἀνα-πεταννύω**, also **ἀνα-πετάω**: fut. -πετάσω, Att. -πετῶ: aor. 1 ἀνεπέτασα, poët. imper. and part. ἀμπέτασον, ἀμπετάσας:—*to spread out* or *open, expand, unfold, unfurl*:—pf. pass. part. ἀναπεπτᾰμένος, η, ον, *outspread, open.*

ἀνα-πέτομαι, f. πτήσομαι: aor. 2 ἀνεπτόμην or ἀνεπτάμην, poët. part. ἀμπτάμενος; and in act. form ἀνέπτην, poët. opt. ἀμπταίην: (v. πέτομαι):—*to fly up, fly up and away.*

ἀναπέφηνα, pf. of ἀναφαίνω.

ἀνα-πήγνυμι or -ύω, *to transfix, spit.*

ἀνα-πηδάω, poët. **ἀμπηδάω**: f. ήσομαι: (v. πηδάω): —*to leap, spring up* or *forth, start up;* ἀν. ἐπ' ἔργον *to jump up* to work: of springs, *to gush forth.* II. *to spring back.*

ἀνά-πηρος, ον, (ἀνά, πηρός) *maimed, crippled, halt.*

ἀνα-πῑδύω, f. ύσω, *to make to spring up.*

ἀνα-πίμπλημι, f. -πλήσω: aor. 1 ἀνέπλησα:—*to fill up*, Lat. *explere*:—*to fulfil, accomplish.* II. *to fill up, appease.* III. *to fill full of* a thing, esp. with the notion of defiling: whence in Pass. *to be infected.*

ἀνα-πίπτω, f. -πεσοῦμαι: aor. 2 ἀνέπεσον: pf. ἀναπέπτωκα:—*to fall back.* 2. *to fall back, give ground:* hence *to slacken, lose heart*, Lat. *concidere animo.*

ἀνα-πίτνημι, poët. for ἀνα-πετάννυμι.

ἀνα-πλάσσω, Att. **-πλάττω**, f. -πλάσω [ᾰ]: aor. 1 ἀνέπλᾰσα:—*to form anew, remodel, recast*, generally, *to mould, shape.*

ἀνα-πλέκω, f. ξω, *to braid up, entwine, wreath.*

ἀνα-πλέω, f. -πλεύσομαι or -πλευσοῦμαι: aor. 1 ἀνέπλευσα: Ion. pres. **ἀνα-πλώω**:—*to sail upwards, to sail up stream:* also *to put out to sea.* II. *to sail the same way back again, sail back:* of fish, *to swim back.*

ἀνά-πλεως, ων, gen. ω: also fem. ἀναπλέα:—Ion. and Att. for ἀνάπλεος: (ἀνά, πλέως = πλέος):—*filled up, quite full of* a thing. II. *defiled* or *infected with* a thing.

ἀνα-πληρόω, f. ώσω, *to fill up, fill full.* II. *to fill up again*:—Pass. *to return to one's full size*, of the sun after an eclipse.

ἀναπλῆσαι, **ἀναπλήσας**, aor. 1 inf. and part. of ἀναπίμπλημι.

ἀνάπλοος, contr. **ἀνάπλους**, ὁ, (ἀναπλέω) *a sailing upwards*, esp. *up stream:* also *a putting out* to sea.

ἀν-απλόω, f. ώσω, *to unfold, open.*

ἀνα-πλώω, Ion. for ἀναπλέω.

ἀνα-πνείω, Ion. **ἀμπνείω**, Ep. for ἀναπνέω.

ἀναπνεύσειε, 3 sing. aor. 1 opt. of ἀναπνέω.

ἀνάπνευσις, εως, ἡ, (ἀναπνέω) *a breathing again: respite, rest* from a thing. II. *a drawing breath.*

ἀνάπνευστος, ον, poët. for ἄπνευστος, *without drawing breath, breathless.*

ἀνα-πνέω, f. πνεύσομαι: aor. 1 ἀνέπνευσα:—*to breathe again, have a respite, rest oneself from* a thing: (for the forms ἄμπνυε, ἄμπνῡτο, ἀμπνύνθη v. sub vocc.) II. *to draw breath, breathe*, Lat. *respiro.* III. *to breathe forth, send forth.*

ἀναπνοή, poët. **ἀμπνοή**, ἡ, (ἀναπνέω) *recovery of breath, rest.* II. *a drawing breath*, Lat. *respiratio.*

ἀνάπνυε, poët. pres. imperat. of ἀναπνέω.

ἀν-απόδεικτος, ον, *undemonstrated, indemonstrable.*

ἀνα-ποδίζω: f. ίσω, Att. ιῶ: aor. 1 ἀνεπόδισα: (ἀνά, πούς):—*to make to step back, call back and question;* ἀναποδίζειν ἑαυτόν *to correct* oneself. II. intrans. *to step back.*

ἀν-άποινος, ον, (α privat., ἄποινα) *without ransom* or *reward:* neut. ἀνάποινον, Adv. *without recompense.*

ἀνα-πολέω, poët. **ἀμπολέω**, properly *to turn up* the ground *again, plough up:* hence *to go over again, to repeat, reconsider.*

ἀν-απολόγητος, ον, (ἀ privat., ἀπολογέομαι) *indefensible, inexcusable.* 2. act. *unable to defend* oneself, *without excuse.*

ἀναπομπή, ἡ, (ἀναπέμπω) *a sending up; θησαυρῶν ἀν. a digging up* of treasures.

ἀναπομπός, ὁ, (ἀναπέμπω) *one that sends up* or *back.*

ἀν-απόνιπτος, ον, (ἀ privat., ἀπονίζω) *unwashen.*

ἀνα-ποτάομαι, Dep. = ἀναπέτομαι.

ἀνα-πράσσω, Att. -ττω, fut. -πράξω, *to exact, levy; ἀν. ὑπόσχεσιν to exact the fulfilment of* a promise.

ἀνα-πρήθω, f. σω, properly *to set on fire, light up: δάκρυ' ἀναπρήσας letting* tears *burst forth.*

ἀνα-πτερόω, f. ώσω: aor. 1 ἀν-επτέρωσα: pf. -επτέρωκα:—*to furnish with wings* or *to raise the wings* for flight: generally, *to raise, set up.* 2. of the mind, *to set on the wing, excite vehemently:*—Pass. *to be on the wing, be in a state of excitement.* II. *to furnish with new wings:*—Pass. *to get new wings.*

ἀναπτῆναι, ἀναπτάσθαι, ἀναπτέσθαι, inf. of ἀνέπτην, ἀνεπτάμην, ἀνεπτόμην, aor. 2 of ἀναπέτομαι.

ἀνα-πτύσσω, fut. ύξω:—Pass., aor. 1 ἀνεπτύχθην, aor. 2 ἀνεπτύγην [ῠ]: (v. πτύσσω):—*to unfold, undo,* esp. of rolls of books; and so, like Lat. *evolvere, to unrol for reading:* hence *to unfold, bring to light,* Lat. *explicare.* II. as military term, **τὴν** φάλαγγα ἀναπτύσσειν *to fold back* the phalanx, i. e. deepen it by wheeling men from either flank into rear; but, τὸ κέρας ἀναπτύσσειν *to open out* the wing, i. e. extend the front, Lat. *explicare.* Hence

ἀναπτυχή, ἡ, *an opening, unfolding: an expanse.*

ἀνα-πτύω, f. ύσω [ῡ], *to spit up* or *out:* absol. *to sputter.*

ἀν-άπτω, f. ψω: aor. 1 ἀνῆψα:—*to hang up to, fasten on* or *to* a thing; ἀγάλματα ἀνάπτειν, = ἀνατιθέναι, *to hang up* votive gifts; μῶμον ἀνάπτειν *to fasten* disgrace upon one:—Med. *to fasten for oneself; ἀνάπτεσθαι* ναῦν *to fasten* a ship *to oneself and tow* it *away:*—Pass. *to be fastened* or *fasten oneself on, cling to.* II. *to light up, light, kindle:* metaph. *to inflame.*

ἀνα-πυνθάνομαι, f. -πεύσομαι: aor. 2 ἀνεπυθόμην: Dep.:—*to search out, inquire into:* also *to learn by inquiry* Hence

ἀνάπυστος, ον, *searched out, ascertained, notorious.*

ἀνάπωτις, shortened **ἄμπωτις**, gen. εως Ion. ιος, ἡ, (ἀναπίνω) *a being drunk up:* of the sea, *the ebb-tide, returning* of the waters.

ἀναρ-, in compds. of ἀνά with words beginning with ῥ the ῥ is usually doubled, as in ἀναρ-ραίζω, etc., though in poets and Ion. Greek it is sometimes single.

ἀναραιρηκώς, Ion. for ἀνῃρηκώς, pf. part. of ἀναιρέω.

ἀν-άργυρος, ον, (ἀ privat., ἄργυρος) *without silver: without money.*

ἄν-αρθρος, ον, (ἀ privat., ἄρθρον) *without joints: disjointed, nerveless.* 2. of sounds, *inarticulate.*

ἀν-αριθμέω, f. ήσομαι, *to count up, enumerate.*

ἀν-αρίθμητος, ον, (ἀ privat., ἀρίθμητος) = sq.

ἀν-άριθμος, ον, (ἀ privat., ἀριθμός) *without number, countless: without bounds in* a thing: c. gen. *taking no account of* a thing.

ἄν-αρκτος, ον, (ἀ privat., ἄρχω) *not governed* or *subject: not submitting to be governed.*

ἀναρμοστία, ἡ, *unsuitableness: discord.* From

ἀν-άρμοστος, ον, (ἀ privat., ἁρμόζω) *unfit, incongruous:* of sound, *inharmonious:* of persons, *absurd.* 2. *unfitted, unprepared.*

ἀναρπαγή, ἡ, *recapture.* From

ἀν-αρπάζω: fut. άξω, Att. άσω or άσομαι [ᾰ]: aor. 1 ἀνήρπασα:—*to tear up, snatch up.* II. *to hurry along, to carry off, to drag by force,* esp. before a magistrate, Lat. *rapere in jus.* III. *to take by storm,* and so *to plunder,* generally, *to treat with violence.* Hence

ἀναρπαστός, όν, also ή, όν, *torn away, carried off,* esp. into Persia, *treated with violence.*

ἀναρ-ρέω, f. -ρεύσομαι, (ἀνά, ῥέω) *to flow back* or *to the source.*

ἀναρ-ρήγνῡμι or -ύω: f. -ρήξω: aor. 1 ἀνέρρηξα:—*to break up, break through* or *open.* II. *to make break forth; ἀναρρῆξαι ἔπη,* like Lat. *rumpere voces:*—Pass. *to burst forth.* III. intr., like Pass. *to burst forth.*

ἀναρ-ρηθῆναι, aor. 1 pass. of aor. 2 act. ἀνειπεῖν.

ἀναρρήξας, aor. 1 part. of ἀναρρήγνυμι.

ἀναρ-ρίπτω or έω: f. -ρίψω: aor. 1 ἀνέρριψα:—*to throw up; ἀναρριπτεῖν* ἅλα πηδῷ *to throw up* the sea with the oar. II. ἀναρρίπτειν κίνδυνον *to run the hazard of* a thing, *run a risk:* also without κίνδυνον, εἰς ἅπαν τὸ ὑπάρχον ἀναρρίπτειν *to throw for* one's all, stake one's all.

ἀν-αρρῐχάομαι, impf. ἀνερριχώμην: fut. ἀναρρῑχήσομαι: aor. 1 ἀνερρῑχησάμην: Dep.:—*to clamber up with the hands and feet, to scramble up.*

ἀνάρροια, ἡ, (ἀναρρέω) *a flowing back, reflux, ebb.*

ἀναρ-ροιβδέω, *to swallow back, gulp down again.*

ἀνάρ-ρῠσις, εως, ἡ, (ἀνά, ῥύω = ἐρύω) *a snatching away, rescuing.* 2. *the second day of the festival* Ἀπατούρια.

ἀναρ-ρώννῡμι and -ύω, fut. -ρώσω: aor. 1 ἀνέρρωσα:—*to strengthen again:*—Pass. *to regain strength* or *spirit.*

ἀν-άρσιος, ον, also α, ον, (ἀ privat., ἄρσιος) *not fitting together:* hence *hostile, unpropitious, implacable* of things, *untoward, strange, monstrous.*

ἀν-αρτάω, f. ήσω: aor. ἀνήρτησα:—*to hang up* on *upon, to attach to, make dependent upon.*—Med. with pf. pass. ἀνήρτημαι, *to attach to oneself:* also *to subdue:*—Pass. also with pf. ἀνήρτημαι, *to be dependent upon; ὅτῳ* πάντα εἰς ἑαυτὸν ἀνήρτηται who has everything *dependent on* himself; but ἀνήρτητα c. inf. *to be prepared* to do.

ἀν-άρτιος, ον, (ἀ privat., ἄρτιος) *uneven, odd;* cf. ἄρτιος.

ἀν-αρχαΐζω, f. σω, *to make old again.*

ἀναρχία, ἡ, *the state of a people without government anarchy.* From

-αρχος, *ον*, (α privat., ἀρχή) *without head* or . 2. *without beginning*.

α-σειράζω, f. άσω, (ἀνά, σειρα) *to pull back with in*, *draw aside*.

α-σείω, poët. **ἀνασσείω**, f. σείσω, *to shake up* or : *to swing to and fro, move up and down*.

ασεσυρμένος, part. pf. pass. of ἀνασύρω.

α-σεύω, *to move upwards* :—Pass. with Ep. aor. 2 σσύμην, 3 sing. **ἀνέσσῦτο**, *to spring up* or *forth*.

α-σκάπτω, f. ψω, *to dig up*.

α-σκέπτομαι, see **ἀνα-σκοπέω**.

α-σκευάζω, f. άσω : pf. ἀνεσκεύακα :—Pass., aor. 1 σκευάσθην : pf. **ἀνεσκευάσμαι** :—opp. to κατα-νάζω, *to pack up the baggage* (τὰ σκεύη), Lat. *a colligere* : hence of an army, in Med., *to break* their quarters, *march away*. 2. *to disfur-b*, *dismantle* a place : Med. *to dismantle one's* use. 3. *to waste, ravage*. 4. in Pass. *to bankrupt* ; ἀνεσκευάσμεθα *we are undone*.

ν-άσκητος, *ον*, (α privat., ἀσκέω) *unpractised, un-rcised*.

να-σκολοπίζω, f. ίσω, *to fix on a pole* or *stake*, *pale* :—fut. med. inf. ἀνασκολοπιεῖσθαι occurs in ss. sense.

να-σκοπέω, fut. -σκέψομαι : aor. ἀνεσκεψάμην :— *look at, view attentively, inquire into*.

να-σπαράσσω, f. ξω, *to tear up*.

νάσπαστος, *ον*, *dragged up*, esp. *from one's untry up into central Asia*. 2. of a door, *drawn ck*, i. e. *opened*. From

ἀνα-σπάω, poët. **ἀνσπάω** : f. -σπάσω [ᾰ] : aor. 1 έσπᾰσα :—*to draw* or *pull up* : *to draw* a ship . 2. *to draw* or *suck up* : *to draw back*. II. ς ὀφρῦς ἀνασπᾶν *to draw up* the eyebrows, and so it on an important air ; λόγους ἀνασπᾶν *to utter asful* words.

ἄνασσα, ἡ, fem. of ἄναξ, *a queen, lady, mistress*.

ἀν-άσσῡτος, Dor. for ἀν-ήσσητος.

ἀνασσείασκε or **-εσκε**, Ion. for ἀνέσειε, 3 sing. ipf. of ἀνασείω.

ἀνάσσω, impf. ἤνασσον, Ep. **ἄνασσον** : fut. ἀνάξω : or. 1 ἤναξα, Ep. ἄναξα : (ἄναξ) :—*to be lord* or *aster, to rule, reign over* :—Med., τρὶς ἀνάξασθαι ἐνεα ἀνδρῶν *to have reigned* for three generations :— ss. *to be ruled*.

ἀν-ᾴσσω, Att. for **ἀναΐσσω**.

ἀνάστα, for ἀνάστηθι, aor. 2 imperat. of ἀνίστημι.

ἀναστᾰδόν, Adv. (ἀνίστημι) *upright*.

ἀναστάς, ἀναστῆναι, aor. 2 part. and inf. of ἀνίστημι.

ἀνάστᾰσις, gen. **εως** Ion. ιος, ἡ : I. causal νίστημι) *a making to stand up, awakening*. 2. *making to rise and leave their place, removal* : usu. bad sense, *laying waste, destruction*. 3. *a re-ilding*. II. pass. (ἀνίσταμαι) *a standing* or *sing up*, esp. in token of respect : ἀνάστασις ἐξ νου *an awakening* : *the Resurrection*.

ἀναστᾰτήρ, ῆρος, ὁ, (ἀνίστημι) *a destroyer*.

ἀναστάτης, *ου*, *ὁ*, = ἀναστατήρ.

ἀνάστᾰτος, *ον*, (ἀνίσταμαι) *made to rise up and depart, driven from one's house and home* : hence *laid waste, ravaged*. Hence

ἀναστᾰτόω, f. ώσω, *to ruin, put in confusion*.

ἀνα-σταυρόω, f. ώσω, *to impale* or *crucify*, like ἀνα-σκολοπίζω. II. *to crucify afresh*.

ἀνα-στέλλω, f. -στελῶ (for the tenses, v. **στέλλω**) : —*to send up, raise* :—Med. *to gird up* one's clothes. 2. *to keep back, check* :—Pass. *to go back, retire*. 3. seemingly intr. (sub. **ἑαυτόν**), *to withdraw*.

ἀνα-στενάζω, f. άξω, = ἀναστένω.

ἀνα-στενᾰχίζω, = ἀναστένω.

ἀνα-στενάχω, *to groan aloud over, bewail aloud*. [ᾰχ]

ἀνα-στένω, *to groan aloud*. 2. *to bewail aloud*.

ἀνα-στέφω, f. ψω, *to crown, wreath* :—Pass., pf. ἀνέστεμμαι κάρα *I have* my head *wreathed*.

ἀνα-στηρίζω, f. ξω, *to fix on a firm base*.

ἀναστησείω, Desiderative from ἀναστήσω (fut. of ἀνίστημι), *I desire to set up*.

ἀναστήσομαι,-στήσω, fut. med. and act. of ἀνίστημι.

ἀναστολή, ἡ, (ἀναστέλλω) *a putting back*.

ἀνα-στομόω, f. ώσω, *to furnish with a mouth* ; ἀνα-στομοῦν τάφρον *to open, clear out* a trench.

ἀνα-στρέφω, f. ψω : pf. ἀνέστραμμαι :—*to turn up-side down, to turn up by digging*. II. *to turn back, around* or *about* ; ἀναστρέφειν πάλιν *to repeat* : *to rally*. 2. intr. (sub. ἑαυτόν), *to turn back, re-turn*. III. Pass. with fut. med. -στρέψομαι, *to turn oneself about* in a place, *tarry there*, like Lat. *versari* ; γαῖαν ἀναστρέφομαι *to go and dwell* in a land. 2. *to be busied in* a thing. 3. *to re-volve*. 4. of soldiers, *to rally*. Hence

ἀναστροφή, ἡ, *a turning back* or *about, a return* : *a turning about* in battle, whether to flee or rally. 2. *a turning about in* a place, *dwelling in* a place ; hence *the place where one tarries, an abode*.

ἀνα-στρωφάω, poët. for ἀνα-στρέφω, *to turn every way*.

ἀνα-σύρω [ῡ], f. -σῠρῶ : aor. 1 ἀνέσῡρα :—*to draw* or *pull up* : in Med. *to pull up one's clothes*.

ἀνα-σφάλλω, f. -σφᾰλῶ : aor. 1 ἀνέσφηλα :—*to re-cover from a fall, recover*.

ἀνασχεθέειν, contr. **ἀνασχεθεῖν**, inf. of ἀνέσχεθον, poët. aor. 2 of ἀνέχω.

ἀνασχεῖν, ἀνασχέσθαι, aor. 2 act. and med. inf. of ἀνέχω.

ἀνασχετός, poët. **ἀνσχετός**, *όν*, (ἀνέχομαι) *to be undergone* or *suffered, tolerable*.

ἀνασχεῖν, ἀνασχών, aor. 2 inf. and part. of **ἀνέχω**.

ἀνα-σχίζω, f. ίσω, *to split up, rip up*.

ἀνα-σώζω, f. -σώσω : aor. 1 ἀνέσωσα :—*to recover what is lost* :—Med. *to regain for oneself*. 2. *to bring back, restore* :—Pass. *to return safe*. 3. *to keep in mind*.

ἀνα-τᾰράσσω, Att. **-ττω** : fut. -ταράξω : *to stir up and trouble* : hence *to excite, rouse to phrensy* : pf. pass. part. **ἀνατεταραγμένος**, *in confusion*.

ἀνα-τάσσω, Att. **-ττω**: f. -τάξω: *to set in order again*:—Med. *to go regularly through again.*

ἀνατέθραμμαι, pf. pass. of ἀνατρέφω.

ἀνᾱτεί or **ἀνατί**, Adv. of ἄνατος, *with impunity.*

ἀνα-τείνω, poët. **ἀντείνω**: f. -τενῶ: aor. 1 ἀνέτεινα:—*to stretch up* or *forth*; χεῖρα ἀνατείνειν *to lift up* the hand in adjurations; μάχαιραν ἀνατεταμένος *having his sword stretched forth.* II. intrans. *to reach up.* III. *to stretch* or *spread out*, as a line of battle.

ἀνα-τειχίζω: fut. ίσω, Att. ιῶ: *to rebuild* or *repair new walls.* Hence

ἀνατειχισμός, ὁ, *building of new walls.*

ἀνα-τέλλω, poët. **ἀν-τέλλω**: f. -τελῶ: aor. 1 ἀνέτειλα:—*to make* or *let rise up*, Lat. *submitto*: hence *to bring forth, bring to light.* II. intr. (sub. ἑαυτόν), *to rise up, come to light, rise*, esp. of the sun and moon: of the *rising* or *source* of a river: φλὸξ ἀνατελλομένη a flame *blazing forth*: *to grow.*

ἀνα-τέμνω, f. τεμῶ: (for the tenses, v. τέμνω):—*to cut up, cut open*: *to cut off.*

ἀνᾱτί, Adv.=ἀνατεί.

ἀνα-τίθημι, f. ἀναθήσω: (for the tenses, v. τίθημι):—*to lay on* as a burden; but also *to attribute* or *ascribe* in token of honour: *to entrust.* II. *to set up as a votive gift, dedicate*: hence *the votive gift* was ἀνάθημα. III. *to put back, remove*: c. gen. *to remove from*; προσθεῖσα κἀναθεῖσα τοῦ γε κατθανεῖν adding to or *taking away from* the necessity of death IV. Med. *to take upon oneself, undergo.* 2. *to place differently, rearrange*: in Att. *to retract one's opinion.*

ἀνα-τῑμάω, f. ήσω, *to raise in price.*

ἀνα-τῑνάσσω, f. ξω, *to sway to and fro, brandish.*

ἀνατλάς, part. of sq.

ἀνα-τλῆναι, inf. of aor. 2 ἀν-έτλην, with no pres. ἀνά-τλημι in use (ἀνατολμάω being used instead): fut. -τλήσομαι:—*to bear, suffer, sustain.*

ἀνατολή, poët. **ἀντολή**, ἡ, (ἀνατέλλω) *a rising*, esp. of the sun and moon; *the East.*

ἀνα-τολμάω, f. ήσω, *to regain courage.*

ἄν-ᾱτος, ον, (α privat., ἄτη) *without harm, unpunished.* II. act. *not harming, harmless.*

ἀνα-τρέπω, poët. **ἀντρέπω**: f. -τρέψω: aor. 1 ἀνέτρεψα:—*to turn up* or *over, upset.* 2. *to overthrow*, Lat. *evertere.* 3. Pass. with fut. med. -τρέψομαι, *to be cast down, disheartened.*

ἀνα-τρέφω, fut. -θρέψω: aor. 1 ἀνέθρεψα:—*to bring up, nourish, educate.*

ἀνα-τρέχω, fut. ἀναθρέξομαι and ἀναδραμοῦμαι: aor. 2 ἀνέδρᾰμον:—*to run back.* 2. *to start up.* 3. *to go straight up*; ἀναδέδρομε πέτρη (pf. with pres. sense) the rock *runs sheer up.* 4. *to run up, shoot up*, of plants: thence of cities.

ἀνά-τρησις, εως, ἡ, (ἀνά, τετραίνω) *a boring through.*

ἀνα-τρίβω, f. ψω, *to rub well, rub clean.* II. *to rub in pieces*: Pass. *to be worn away.* [ῑ]

ἀνατροπή, ἡ, (ἀνατρέπω) *an overturning, upset.*

ἀνα-τυρβάζω, f. άσω, *to stir up and confound.*

ἀν-αύγητος, ον, (α privat., αὐγή) *rayless.*

ἀν-αύδητος, Dor. **-ᾱτος**, ον, (α privat., αὐδάω) *unutterable*, Lat. *infandus.* 2. *speechless.*

ἄν-αυδος, ον, (α privat., αὐδή) *speechless, voiceless*: *preventing speech.* II. *unutterable.*

ἄν-αυλος, ον, (α privat., αὐλός) *without the music of the flute*: hence *joyless, sad.*

***ἄ-ναυς**, gen. ἄνᾱος, ὁ, ἡ, (α privat., ναῦς) *without ships*; νᾶες ἄναες ships *that are ships no more*, Lat. *naves nenaves.*

ἀνα-φαίνω, poët. **ἀμφαίνω**, f. -φᾰνῶ: aor. 1 ἀνέφηνα, or -έφᾱνα:—*to make shine*: *to bring to light, shew forth*: *to proclaim.* II. Pass. with fut. med. ἀναφᾰνήσομαι, pf. act. ἀναπέφηνα, *to be shewn forth, appear plainly*: also *to reappear*: *to be seen* or *shewn to be*, hence *to be accounted.*

ἀναφάνας, aor. 1 part. of ἀναφαίνω, *having made to appear, having come in sight of.* [φᾱ]

ἀναφανδά, Adv. (ἀναφαίνω) *visibly, openly.*

ἀναφανδόν, Adv.=foreg.

ἀναφᾰνείς, aor. 2 part. pass. of ἀναφαίνω.

ἀνα-φέρω, poët. **ἀμφέρω**: f. ἀνοίσω: aor. 1 ἀνήνεγκα, Ion. ἀνήνεικα, also ἄνῳσα:—*to bring* or *carry up*, esp. into central Asia:—Pass. *to rise up*:—Med. *to carry up for oneself* or *what is one's own*: ἀνενείκασθαι, absol. *to heave a deep sigh.* 2. *to lift up, praise.* 3. *to uphold, take upon one.* II. intr. *to rise*, as the stars. III. *to bring* or *carry back*: 1. *to bring back* tidings. 2. *to bring back from exile.* 3. *to throw back upon* another, *refer* something *to* him: absol. *to refer to* a person, *consult* him. 4. *to bring back to oneself, restore*: intrans. and in Pass. *to refresh oneself, recover.*

ἀνα-φεύγω, f. -φεύξομαι, *to flee back, escape.*

ἀναφῆναι, aor. 1 inf. of ἀναφαίνω.

ἀν-ᾰφής, ές, (α privat., ἁφή) *untouched, not to be touched.*

ἀνα-φθέγγομαι, Dep. *to call out aloud.*

ἀνα-φθείρομαι, Pass. *to be undone, perish utterly.*

ἀνα-φλέγω, f. ξω, *to light up, rekindle*: hence *to inflame.*

ἀνα-φλογίζω, f. σω,=ἀναφλέγω.

ἀνα-φλύω, *to bubble up* like boiling water.

ἀνα-φοβέω, f. ήσω, *to frighten away.*

ἀναφορά, ᾶς, ἡ, (ἀναφέρω) *a carrying up, raising.* 2. intr. *a rising.* II. *a carrying back*: 1. *a referring, a reference.* 2. *a giving way, respite, remission.* 3. intr. *a going back*: *a means of recovery.*

ἀνα-φορέω,=ἀναφέρω.

ἀνάφορον, τό, (ἀναφέρω) *anything to carry with*; *a yoke* or *beam for carrying.*

ἀνα-φράζομαι, f. άσομαι, Med. *to observe again, recognise.*

ἀν-αφρόδιτος, ον, (α privat., Ἀφροδίτη) *without the favour of Venus*: *without beauty.*

ἀνα-φρονέω, f. ήσω, *to come back to one's senses, come to oneself*

ἀναφῠγή, ἡ, (ἀναφεύγω) *a fleeing back, escape. release from.* II. *a retreat.*

ἀνα-φύρω [ῡ], pf. pass. -πέφυρμαι, *to mix up, confound, defile.*

ἀνα-φῡσάω, f. ησω, *to breathe up* or *forth*:—Pass. *to be puffed up* or *arrogant.*

ἀνα-φῡσιάω, *to blow* or *spout up*, like a dolphin.

ἀνα-φύω, f. ύσω, *to make to grow up, to produce.* Med. with aor. 2 act. ἀνέφυν, pf. ἀναπέφυκα, *to grow up: to grow again.*

ἀνα-φωνέω, f. ήσω, *to call aloud, proclaim.* Hence

ἀναφώνημα, ατος, τό, *a proclamation.*

ἀνα-χάζω, f. άσω, *to make give way, drive back*:—mostly used as Dep. **ἀνα-χάζομαι**, f. άσομαι, Ep. aor. 1 ἀνεχασσάμην, *to draw back, retire.*

ἀνα-χαίνω, aor. 2 ἀνέχᾰνον, pf. ἀνακέχηνα:—*to open the mouth wide, gape wide.*

ἀνα-χαιτίζω, f. ίσω, (ἀνά, χαίτη) of a horse, *to throw the mane back, rear up*:—c. acc. *to rear up and throw* the rider; hence *to overthrow, upset.*

ἀνα-χάσκω, = ἀναχαίνω.

ἀνα-χέω, f. χεῶ, *to pour over.*

ἀνα-χνοαίνομαι, (ἀνά, χνόος) Pass. *to get the first down* on the chin.

ἀνα-χορεύω, f. σω, *to begin a choral dance*:—intr. *to dance on high.*

ἀνάχῠσις, εως, ἡ, (ἀναχέω) *a pouring over, spending: excess.*

ἀνα-χώννῡμι, f. χώσω, *to heap up.*

ἀνα-χωρέω, f. ήσω, *to go back, retire, retreat, withdraw.* II. *to come back, revert to the right owner.* Hence

ἀναχώρησις, εως, Ion. ιος, ἡ, *a going back, retiring, retreating.* 2. *a means* or *place of retreat*, Lat. *recessus.*

ἀνα-χωρίζω, f. ίσω, Att. ιῶ, *to make to go back* or *retire.*

ἀνα-ψηφίζω: fut. ίσω, Att. ῐῶ: (ἀνά, ψῆφος) *to put to the vote again.* Hence

ἀναψήφῐσις, εως, ἡ, *a putting to the vote again.*

ἀνάψυξις, εως, ἡ, (ἀναψύχω) *a cooling, refreshing.*

ἀναψῠχή, ἡ, *a cooling, refreshing.* II. *recovery from* a thing: *rest.* From

ἀνα-ψύχω, fut. ψύξω:—Pass., aor. 1 ἀνεψύχθην: aor. 2 ἀνεψύχην [ῠ]: (ἀνά, ψῦχος):—*to revive by fresh air, to cool, refresh*: generally, *to cheer*: ναῦς ἀναψύχειν *to overhaul* the ships, *make* them *sound again*:—Med. *to breathe fresh air again, revive.* [ῡ]

ἀν-δαίω, poët. for ἀνα-δαίω.

ἁνδάνω: impf. ἥνδανον, Ep. ἑήνδανον, Ion. ἑάνδανον: fut. ἁδήσω: aor. 2 ἕᾰδον, Ep. εὔᾰδον and ἅδον [ᾰ]: pf. ἅδηκα, also ἕᾱδα, Dor. ἕᾱδα: (the Root is ʽΑΔ-, which appears in aor. 2 and fut.):—*to please, delight*, like ἥδομαι: in Homer and Herodotus always c. dat. pers. ἁνδάνει μοι: impers., ἁνδάνει μοι ποιεῖν, like Lat. *placet.*

ἄν-δεμα, poët. for ἀνά-δεμα.

ἄνδηρον, τό, mostly in plur. ἄνδηρα, quasi ἄνθηρα, τά, *a raised border, flower-bed: any earth dug* or *thrown up.*

ἀνδησάμενος, poët. part. aor. 1 of ἀναδέω.

ἄν-δῐχα, Adv. (ἀνά, δίχα) *asunder, in twain.*

ἀνδρ-αγαθέω, f. ήσω, (ἀνήρ, ἀγαθός) *to be* or *behave like a brave man.* Hence

ἀνδρᾰγᾰθία, ἡ, *the character of a brave good man, bravery, manly virtue.* Hence

ἀνδρᾰγᾰθίζομαι: f. ίσομαι, Att. ῐοῦμαι: Dep.:—*to act bravely, honestly, play the honest man.*

ἀνδρ-άγρια, ων, τά, (ἀνήρ, ἄγρα) *the spoils of a slain enemy.*

ἀνδρᾰκάς, Adv. (ἀνήρ) *man by man*, like κατ' ἄνδρας, Lat. *viritim*: generally, *separately, apart.*

ἀνδραπόδεσσι, heterocl. dat. of ἀνδράποδον, for ἀνδραπόδοις, as if from ἀνδράπους.

ἀνδραποδίζομαι, Dep. = ἀνδραποδίζω.

ἀνδρᾰποδίζω: fut. ίσω, Att. ιῶ: aor. 1 ἠνδραπόδισα:—Pass., fut. ἀνδραποδισθήσομαι, but also med. ἀνδραποδιοῦμαι: aor. 1 ἠνδραποδίσθην: pf. ἠνδραπόδισμαι: (ἀνδράποδον):—*to reduce to slavery*, esp. *to sell freemen into slavery*, (and so worse than δουλόω,) Lat. *vendere sub corona*:—Pass. *to be sold into slavery.*

ἀνδρᾰπόδῐσις, εως, ἡ, and **ἀνδρᾰποδισμός**, ὁ, (ἀνδραποδίζομαι) *a selling a freeman into slavery, enslaving: kidnapping.*

ἀνδρᾰποδιστής, οῦ, ὁ, (ἀνδραποδίζομαι) *a slave-dealer, one who kidnaps men to sell them.*

ἀνδράποδον, *a slave*, esp. one made in war and sold: Homer uses it in dat. ἀνδραπόδεσσι as if from ἀνδράπους. (Deriv. uncertain.)

ἀνδρᾰποδ-ώδης, ες, (ἀνδράποδον, εἶδος) *slavish, servile*, Lat. *servilis*, opp. to ἐλεύθερος.

ἀνδράριον, τό, Dim. of ἀνήρ, *a manikin.* [ᾰρ]

ἀνδράσι, dat. plur. of ἀνήρ.

ἀνδρ-αχθής, ές, (ἀνήρ, ἄχθος) *loading a man, as much as a man can carry.*

ἀνδρεία, Ion. -ηΐη, ἡ, (ἀνήρ) *manliness, manly spirit, courage*, Lat. *virtus, fortitudo.*

ἀνδρ-είκελον, τό, (ἀνήρ, εἴκελος) *an image of a man, a statue.* II. *a flesh-coloured paint.*

ἀνδρεῖος, α, ον, Ion. **ἀνδρήϊος**, η, ον, (ἀνήρ) *of* or *belonging to a man, manly, masculine*: neut. τὸ ἀνδρεῖον, *manliness.* II. τὰ ἀνδρεῖα, the public meals of the Cretans, also the older name for the Spartan φειδίτια. Hence

ἀνδρειότης, ητος, ἡ, = ἀνδρεία.

ἀνδρει-φόντης, ου, ὁ, (ἀνήρ, *φένω) *man-slaying.*

ἀνδρειών, ῶνος, ὁ, poët. for ἀνδρεών: see ἀνδρών.

ἄνδρεσσι, Ep. for ἀνδράσι, dat. plur. of ἀνήρ.

ἀνδρεύμενος, Ion. for ἀνδρούμενος, pres. pass. part of ἀνδρόω.

ἀνδρεύομαι, Dep. = ἀνδρίζομαι.

ἀνδρεών, ῶνος, ὁ, Ion. for ἀνδρών.

ἀνδρηΐη, Ion. for ἀνδρεία.

ἀνδρήϊος, η, ον, Ion. for ἀνδρεῖος.

ἀνδρηλᾰτέω, f. ήσω, *to banish from home.* From

ἀνδρ-ηλάτης, ου, ὁ, (ἀνήρ, ἐλαύνω) *he that drives one from his home, the avenger of blood* in cases of murder. [ᾰ]

ἀνδρία, late form of ἀνδρεία.

ἀνδριαντοποιέω, (ἀνδριαντοποιός) *to be a statuary.* Hence

ἀνδριαντοποιΐα, ἡ, *statuary, sculpture.*

ἀνδριαντο-ποιός, οῦ, ὁ, (ἀνδριάς, ποιέω) *a statue-maker, statuary, sculptor.*

ἀνδριάς, άντος, ὁ, (ἀνήρ) *the image of a man, a statue.*

ἀνδρίζω, f. ίσω, (ἀνήρ) *to make a man of*:—Pass. *to become a man, to think and act like a man.*

ἀνδρικός, ή, όν, (ἀνήρ) *of* or *for a man, masculine, manly*: also of things, *strong, stout*:—Adv. ἀνδρικῶς, *like a man*; Sup. ἀνδρικώτατα. II. *composed of men.*

ἀνδρίον, τό, Dim. of ἀνήρ, *a manikin.*

ἀνδριστέον, verb. Adj. of ἀνδρίζω, *one must play the man.*

ἀνδριστί, Adv. *after the manner of men.*

ἀνδρο-βρώς, ῶτος, ὁ, ἡ, (ἀνήρ, βιβρώσκω) *man-eating, cannibal.*

ἀνδρο-γόνος, ον, (ἀνήρ, γενέσθαι) *begetting men.*

ἀνδρό-γῠνος, ον, (ἀνήρ, γυνή) *a man-woman, hermaphrodite*:—*a weak effeminate person.* II. as Adj., of baths, *used both by men and women.*

ἀνδρο-δάϊκτος, ον, (ἀνήρ, δαΐζω) *man-slaying, murderous.*

ἀνδρο-δάμας, αντος, ὁ, ἡ, (ἀνήρ, δαμάω) *man-taming*: *man-slaying.* [ᾰ]

ἀνδρο-δόκος, ον, (ἀνήρ, δέχομαι) *receiving men.*

ἀνδρο-θέα, ἡ, (ἀνήρ, θεά) *the man-goddess*, i. e. Minerva.

ἀνδρόθεν, Adv. (ἀνήρ) *from a man, from men.*

ἀνδρο-κμής, ῆτος, ὁ, ἡ, (ἀνήρ, κάμνω) *man-wearying*:—*man-slaying, murderous.*

ἀνδρό-κμητος, ον, (ἀνήρ, κάμνω) *wrought by men's hands.*

ἀνδρο-κτᾰσία, ἡ, (ἀνήρ, κτείνω) *slaughter of men.*

ἀνδροκτονέω, f. ήσω, (ἀνδροκτόνος) *to slay men.* Hence

ἀνδροκτονία, ἡ, = ἀνδροκτασία.

ἀνδρο-κτόνος, ον, (ἀνήρ, κτείνω) *man-slaying.*

ἀνδρ-ολέτειρα, ἡ, (ἀνήρ, ὄλλυμι) *a murderess.*

ἀνδρο-μάχος, η, ον, (ἀνήρ, μάχομαι) *fighting with men*: hence the prop. n. *Andromaché.* [ᾰ]

ἀνδρόμεος, α, ον, (ἀνήρ) *of man* or *men, human.*

ἀνδρο-μήκης, ες, (ἀνήρ, μῆκος) *of a man's height.*

ἀνδρό-παις, ὁ, (ἀνήρ, παῖς) *a youth near manhood.*

ἀνδρο-πλήθεια, ἡ, (ἀνήρ, πλῆθος) *a multitude of men.*

ἀνδρό-σῑνις, ιδος, ἡ, (ἀνήρ, σίνομαι) *hurtful to men.*

ἀνδρό-σφιγξ, ὁ, (ἀνήρ, Σφίγξ) *a man-sphinx.*

ἀνδρότης, ητος, ἡ, = ἀνδρεία, *manhood.*

ἀνδρο-τῠχής, ές, (ἀνήρ, τυχεῖν) *getting a man* or *husband*, ἀνδρ. βίοτος *wedded* life.

ἀνδροφᾰγέω, f. ήσω, *to eat men.* From

ἀνδρο-φάγος, ον, (ἀνήρ, φᾰγεῖν) *eating men*: οἱ Ἀνδροφάγοι, *Cannibals*, mentioned in Herodotus.

ἀνδρο-φθόρος, ον, (ἀνήρ, φθείρω) *man-destroying.* II. pass. ἀνδρόφθορος, ον: hence αἷμα ἀνδρόφθορον the blood *of slain men.*

ἀνδρο-φόνος, ον, (ἀνήρ, *φένω) *man-slaying*: fem. ἡ ἀνδροφόνος, *murderess of her husband.*

ἀνδρο-φόντης, ου, ὁ, = ἀνδρει-φόντης, *a man-slayer, homicide.*

ἀνδρόω, f. ώσω, (ἀνήρ) *to rear up to manhood*:—Pass. *to become a man, reach manhood.*

ἀνδρ-ώδης, ες, (ἀνήρ, εἶδος) *like a man, manly.* Adv. -δως: Sup. ἀνδρωδέστατα.

ἀνδρωθείς, aor. 1 pass. part. of ἀνδρόω.

ἀνδρών, Ion. **ἀνδρέων**, ῶνος, ὁ, (ἀνήρ) *a man's apartment.*

ἀνδρωνῖτις, ιδος, ἡ, = ἀνδρών.

ἀν-δύεται, poët. for ἀναδύεται.

ἄνδωκε, poët. for ἀνέδωκε, aor. 1 of ἀναδίδωμι.

ἀν-έβην, aor. 2 of ἀναβαίνω.

ἀν-εβήσετο, Ep. 3 sing. aor. 1 med. of ἀναβαίνω.

ἀνεβιωσάμην, aor. 1 of ἀναβιώσκομαι.

ἀν-έβραχε, 3 sing. aor. 2 with no pres. in use, of armour, *to clash, ring loudly*; of doors, *to creak* or *grate loudly.*

ἀνέβωσε, Ion. for ἀνεβόησε, aor. 1 of ἀναβοάω.

ἀν-έγγυος, ον, (α privat., ἐγγύη) *not vouched for*: *unwedded.*

ἀν-εγείρω, f. -εγερῶ: aor. 1 ἀνέγειρα;—*to wake up, rouse*, esp. from sleep; metaph. *to rouse, encourage*:—Pass. *to be awaked, wake up.* Hence

ἀνεγέρμων, ον, gen. ονος, *waked up, wakeful.*

ἀν-έγκλητος, ον, (α privat., ἐγκαλέω) *not accused*: *without reproach.*

ἀνέγναμψα, **ἀνεγνάμφθην**, aor. 1 act. and pass. of ἀναγνάμπτω.

ἀνέγνωκα, **ἀνέγνων**, pf. and aor. 2 of ἀναγιγνώσκω.

ἀνεδέγμεθα, 1 pl. Ep. aor. 2 pass. of ἀναδέχομαι.

ἀνέδειξα, aor. 1 of ἀναδείκνυμι.

ἀν-έδην, Adv. (ἀνίημι) *let loose, without restraint*: *carelessly.* II. *without more ado, simply.*

ἀνέδρακεν, 3 sing. aor. 2 of ἀναδέρκομαι.

ἀνέδραμον, irreg. aor. 2 of ἀνατρέχω.

ἀνεδύσετο, Ep. 3 sing. aor. 1 of ἀναδύομαι.

ἀνεέργω, impf. ἀνέεργον, old Ep. form of ἀνέργω, ἀνείργω.

ἀνέζησα, aor. 1 of ἀναζάω.

ἀν-εθέλητος, ον, (α privat., ἐθέλω) *unwished for*. *melancholy.*

ἀν-έθην, aor. 1 pass. of ἀνίημι. 2. aor. 2 act. o ἀνατίθημι.

ἀνείην, opt. aor. 2 act. of ἀνίημι.

ἀν-ειλείθυια, ἡ, (α privat., Εἰλείθυια) *without the ai of Eileithyia.*

ἀν-ειλέω, f. ήσω, (v. εἴλω) *to wind up* or *roll together*—Pass. *to crowd* or *throng together.*

ἀνείληφα, **ἀνείλημμαι**, pf. act. and pass. of ἀναλαμβάνω.

ἀνεῖλον, -όμην, aor. 2 act. and med. of *ἀναιρέω*.

ἀνειμένως, Adv. of *ἀνειμένος*, pf. pass. part. of *ἀνίημι*, *let loose, carelessly : without restraint.*

ἄν-ειμι, (*ἀνά, εἶμι ibo*) *to go up: to sail out to sea:* but also *to go up inland.* II. *to approach*, as a suppliant. III. *to go back, go home, return.*

ἀν-είμων, *ον*, gen. *ονος*, (*α* privat., *εἶμα*) *without clothing, unclad.*

ἀν-ειπεῖν, (*ἀνά, εἰπεῖν*) aor. 2 with no pres. in use: aor. 1 pass. *ἀνεῤῥήθην* (as if from *ἀναρ-ρέω*): pf. *ἀνείρημαι* (from *ἀν-ερέω*) :—*to say aloud, proclaim, give notice.*

ἀν-είργω, f. *ξω*, *to keep back, ward off*, in poët. impf. *ἀνέεργον*.

ἀνείρημαι, pf. pass., v. *ἀνειπεῖν*.

ἀν-είρομαι, Ep. and Ion. **ἀνέρομαι**, (*ἀνά, εἴρομαι, ἔρομαι*) :—*to inquire of, inquire about.*

ἀν-ειρύω, f. *ύσω* [ῠ], poët. and Ion. for *ἀν-ερύω*, *to draw back.*

ἀν-είρω, (for the tenses, **v.** *εἴρω*) *to fasten on* or *to: to wreathe together.*

ἀνείς, part. aor. 2 of *ἀνίημι*.

ἀν-έκᾰθεν, (*ἄνω, ἑκάς*) Adv. of Place, *from above:* cf. *ἄγκαθεν*. II. of Time, *from the first.*

ἀν-εκάς, Adv. (*ἄνω, ἑκάς*) *upwards, on high*, Lat. *sursum.*

ἀν-έκβᾰτος, *ον*, (*α* privat., *ἐκβαίνω*) *without outlet.*

ἀν-εκδιήγητος, *ον*, (*α* privat., *ἐκδιηγέομαι*) *indescribable, extraordinary.*

ἀν-έκδρομος, *ον*, (*α* privat., *ἐκδραμεῖν*) *without escape, inevitable.*

ἀν-εκλάλητος, *ον*, (*α* privat., *ἐκλαλέω*) *unspeakable.*

ἀν-έκλειπτος, *ον*, (*α* privat., *ἐκλείπω*) *unfailing.*

ἀνεκλίθην [ῐ], aor. 1 pass. of *ἀνακλίνω*.

ἀνέκλῑνα, aor. 1 act. of *ἀνακλίνω*.

ἀν-εκπίμπλημι, fut. *-εκπλήσω*, *to fill up* or *again.*

ἀν-έκπληκτος, *ον*, (*α* privat., *ἐκπλήσσω*) *undaunted:* *τὸ ἀνέκπληκτον dauntlessness.*

ἀνέκρᾰγον, aor. 2 of *ἀνακράζω*.

ἀν-εκτέος, *ον*, verb. Adj. of *ἀνέχομαι*, *to be borne.*

ἀνεκτός, *όν*, later *ή, όν*, (*ἀνέχομαι*) *bearable, tolerable* :—Adv. **ἀνεκτῶς**, *so as to be borne.*

ἀν-έκφραστος, *ον*, (*α* privat., *ἐκφράζω*) *unutterable, indescribable.*

ἀν-έλεγκτος, *ον*, (*α* privat., *ἐλέγχω*) *safe from being questioned: not to be refuted, unrefuted.*

ἀν-ελεήμων, *ονος, ὁ, ἡ*, (*α* privat., *ἐλεήμων*) *unmerciful.*

ἀνελεῖν, ἀνελέσθαι, aor. 2 act. and med. inf. of *ἀναιρέω*.

ἀν-έλεος, *ον*, (*α* privat., *ἔλεος*) *unmerciful.*

ἀνελευθερία, *ἡ*, (*ἀνελεύθερος*) *illiberality.*

ἀνελευθεριότης, *ητος, ἡ*, = *ἀνελευθερία*. From

ἀν-ελεύθερος, *ον*, *illiberal, slavish*, Lat. *illiberalis:* in money matters, *niggardly.*

ἀνελήφθην, aor. 1 pass. of *ἀναλαμβάνω*.

ἀν-ελίσσω, Att. *-ττω*, f. *ξω*, *to unroll*, like Lat. *evolvere*, of books in rolls, and so *read and explain.* 2. metaph. *ἀνελίσσειν βίον to pass* one's life.

ἀν-έλκω: f. *ἀνέλξω*, but in Att. *ἀνελκύσω* [ῠ], with aor. 1 *ἀνείλκῠσα*, pf. pass. *ἀνείλκυσμαι* (as if from *ἀν-ελκύω*) :—*to draw up, to hold up:* esp. *to draw up* a bow *to its full stretch: ἀνελκύσαι ναῦς to haul up* ships *high and dry: to drag to light, to drag into open court:*—Med. *to draw to oneself; ἀνέλκεσθαι τρίχας to tear one's own* hair. II. *to draw back.*

ἄν-ελπις, *ιδος, ὁ, ἡ*, (*α* privat., *ἐλπίς*) *without hope.*

ἀν-έλπιστος, *ον*, (*α* privat., *ἐλπίζω*) *unhoped for, unlooked for.* II. act. of persons, *having no hope, hopeless.* 2. of things, *leaving no hope, hopeless.* III. Adv. *-τως*, *hopelessly; ἀνελπίστως ἔχειν* to be *in despair.*

ἀν-έμβᾰτος, *ον*, (*α* privat., *ἐμβαίνω*) *inaccessible.* II. act. *not going to* or *into.*

ἀ-νεμέσητος, *ον*, (*α* privat., *νεμεσάω*) *free from blame, without offence.*

ἀ-νέμητος, *ον*, (*α* privat., *νέμω*) *not distributed.* II. *having no share.*

ἀνεμιαῖος, *α, ον*, (*ἄνεμος*) *full of wind, windy.*

ἀνεμίζομαι, (*ἄνεμος*) Pass. *to be driven with the wind.*

ἀνεμο-δρόμος, *ον*, (*ἄνεμος, δραμεῖν*) *swift as the wind.*

ἀνεμνήσθην, aor. 1 pass. of *ἀναμιμνήσκω*.

ἀνεμόεις, *εσσα, εν*, (*ἄνεμος*) *windy, exposed to the wind: like wind, swift as wind, airy.* [ᾱ]

ἌΝΕΜΟΣ, *ὁ*, *a wind*, Lat. *ventus; θύελλα ἀνέμοιο a whirlwind; ἄνεμος κατὰ Βορέαν ἑστηκώς the wind* being in the north. Homer and Hesiod mention four winds, Boreas, Eurus, Notus (in Hes. Argestes), and Zephyrus: Aristotle gives twelve, which served as points of the compass. [ᾰ]

ἀνεμο-σκεπής, *ές*, (*ἄνεμος, σκέπη*) *sheltering from the wind.*

ἀνεμο-τρεφής, *ές*, (*ἄνεμος, τρέφω*) *fed by the wind*, of a wave; *ἔγχος ἀνεμοτρεφές* a spear from a tree *made tough by the wind.*

ἀνεμόω, f. *ώσω*: pf. pass. *ἠνέμωμαι*: (*ἄνεμος*) :—*to expose to the wind:*—Pass. of a wave, *to be raised by the wind.*

ἀν-εμποδίστος, *ον*, (*α* privat., *ἐμποδίζω*) *unhindered.*

ἀνεμ-ώκης, *ες*, (*ἄνεμος, ὠκύς*) *swift as the wind.*

ἀνεμώλιος, *ον*, (*ἄνεμος*) *windy*, i. e. *vain, fruitless.*

ἀνεμώνη, *ἡ*, (*ἄνεμος*) *the wind-flower, anemoné.*

ἀν-ενδεής, *ές*, *not in want.*

ἀν-ένδεκτος, *ον*, (*α* privat., *ἐνδέχομαι*) *inadmissible.*

ἀνένεικα, poët. for *ἀνήνεικα*, aor. 1 act. of *ἀναφέρω*: **ἀνενείκατο**, aor. 1 med, *ἀνενειχθείς* aor. 1 pass. part.

ἀνενήνοθε, see *ἐνήνοθε*.

ἀνέντες, aor. 2 part. pl. of *ἀν-ίημι*.

ἀν-εξάλειπτος, *ον*, (*α* privat, *ἐξαλείφω*) *indelible.*

ἀν-εξέλεγκτος, *ον*, (*α* privat., *ἐξελέγχω*) *not put to the proof, not convicted* or *refuted: impossible to be refuted: irreproachable.*

ἀν-εξερεύνητος, *ον*, (*α* privat., *ἐξερευνάω*) *not to be searched out, unsearchable.*

ἀν-εξέταστος, *ον*, (*α* privat., *ἐξετάζω*) *not searched out, not inquired into.* II. *βίος ἀνεξέταστος a* life *without inquiry.*

ἀν-εξεύρετος, *ον*, (α privat., ἐξευρίσκω) *not to be found out.*

ἀνεξί-κακος, *ον*, (ἀνέχω, κακόν) *enduring evil : forbearing.*

ἀν-εξιχνίαστος, *ον*, (α privat., ἐξιχνιάζω) *not to be traced out.*

ἀν-έξοδος, *ον*, (α privat., ἐξοδός) *with no outlet, without return*, Lat. *irremeabilis.*

ἄνεοι or **ἀνεοί**, v. sub ἄνεως.

ἀνέονται, see ἀνέωνται.

ἀν-έορτος, *ον*, (α privat., ἑορτή) *without festival ;* ἀνέορτος ἱερῶν *without share in festal* rites.

ἀν-επαίσχυντος, *ον*, (α privat., ἐπαισχύνομαι) *having no cause for shame.*

ἀν-έπαλτο, Ep. for ἀν-επάλετο, 3 sing. aor. 2 med. from ἀναπάλλω with pass. sense, *he was thrown up, rushed up.*

ἀνέπαυσα, aor. 1 of ἀναπαύω.

ἀν-επαχθής, *ές*, (α privat., ἐπαχθής) *not burdensome, without offence.* Adv., ἀνεπαχθῶς φέρειν *not to take ill.*

ἀνέπεσον, aor. 2 of ἀνα-πίπτω.

ἀν-επιβούλευτος, *ον*, (α privat., ἐπιβουλεύω) *without plots :* act. *not plotting.* 2. *not plotted against.*

ἀν-επίδικος, *ον*, (α privat., ἐπίδικος) *undisputed :* of an heiress, *about whose marriage there is no dispute.*

ἀν-επιδόκητος, *ον*, (α privat., ἐπιδοκέω) *unexpected, unforeseen.*

ἀνεπιείκεια, ἡ, *unfairness.* From

ἀν-επιεικής, *ές*, (α privat., ἐπιεικής) *unreasonable, unfair :* Adv. -κῶς.

ἀν-επίκλητος, *ον*, (α privat., ἐπικαλέω) *unblamed.* Adv. -τως, *without censure.*

ἀν-επίληπτος, *ον*, (α privat., ἐπιλαμβάνομαι) *not to be laid hold of* or *attacked : blameless.* Adv. -τως.

ἀν-επίξεστος, *ον*, (α privat., ἐπιξέω) *not polished over, not finished off.*

ἀν-επίπληκτος, *ον*, (α privat., ἐπιπλήσσω) *not to be reproved : faultless :* but in bad sense, *incorrigible.*

ἀν-επίρρεκτος, *ον*, (α privat., ἐπιρρέζω) *not used for sacrifices.*

ἀν-επίσκεπτος, *ον*, (α privat., ἐπισκέπτομαι) *not examining, inattentive.* II. pass. *not considered.*

ἀνεπιστημοσύνη, ἡ, *ignorance, inexperience : want of skill* or *science.* From

ἀν-επιστήμων, *ον*, gen. *ονος*, (α privat., ἐπιστήμων) *unknowing, unskilful : unscientific :* c. inf. *not knowing how* to do a thing. Adv. -μόνως.

ἀν-επίτακτος, *ον*, (α privat., ἐπιτάσσω) *not commanded, subject to no one.* Adv. -τως.

ἀν-επιτήδειος, *ον*, Ion. **ἀν-επιτήδεος**, *η, ον*, (α privat., ἐπιτήδειος) *unfit, inconvenient, not suitable : prejudicial, hurtful.* 2. of persons, *ill-disposed, unfriendly.*

ἀν-επιτίμητος, *ον*, (α privat., ἐπιτιμάω) *not to be censured.*

ἀν-επίφθονος, *ον*, (α privat., ἐπίφθονος *without envy* or *reproach : not invidious.* Adv. -νως.

ἀνέπνευσα, aor. 1 of ἀναπνέω.

ἀνεπτάμην, **ἀνέπτην**, aor. 2 med. and act. of ἀνίπτᾰμαι ; cf. ἀναπέτομαι.

ἀν-εράομαι, aor 1 ἀνηράσθην, Dep. (ἀνά, ἐράω) *to love again.*

ἀν-έραστος, *ον*, (α privat., ἐράω) *not worthy of love.* II. act. *not loving.*

ἄν-εργος, *ον*, (α privat., ἔργον) *not done ;* ἔργα ἄνεργα, Lat. *facta infecta.*

ἀν-έργω, old form of ἀν-είργω.

ἀν-ερεθίζω, f. ίσω, *to provoke again.*

***ἀν-ερείπομαι**, (ἀνά, ἐρείπω) Dep., only used by Homer in 3 pl. aor. 1 ἀνηρείψαντο : *to snatch up and carry off.*

ἀν-ερευνάω, f. ήσω, *to search out.*

ἀν-ερεύνητος, *ον*, (α privat., ἐρευνάω) *not searched out : not to be searched out.*

ἀν-έρομαι, Ep. **ἀνείρομαι** : aor. ἀνηρόμην : Dep. : (ἀνά, ἐρέομαι) : *to question, ask.*

ἀν-έρπω, aor. 1 ἀνείρπῠσα (as if from ἀνερπύζω) :— *to creep up.*

ἀν-έρρω : aor. 1 ἀνήρρησα :—*to come* or *go away*, with notion of *bad luck :* ἄνερρε, *away with you*, Lat. *abi in malam rem.*

ἀν-ερυθριάω, f. άσω [ᾱ] : *to begin to blush.*

ἀν-ερύω, Ion. **ἀν-ειρύω** : f. ύσω [ῠ] : *to draw up.*

ἀν-έρχομαι, fut. ἀνελεύσομαι : aor. 2 ἀνήλῠθον or ἀνῆλθον : pf. ἀνελήλυθα :—*to go up*, of trees, *to grow up :* of the sun, *to rise :* of fire, *to blaze up.* II. *to go* or *come back, return : recur to* a thing. 2. εἴς τινα ἀνέρχεσθαι *to be referred to* or *made dependent upon* one.

ἀν-ερωτάω, f. ήσω, *to ask again* or *repeatedly.*

ἀνέσαιμι, Ep. aor. 1 opt. of ἀνίημι.

ἄνεσαν, 3 pl. aor. 2 of ἀνίημι.

ἀνέσαντες, part. of ἀνεῖσα, aor. 1 of ἀνίζω.

ἀνέσει, Ep. for ἀνήσει, 3 sing. fut. of ἀνίημι.

ἄνεσις, *εως*, Ion. *ιος*, ἡ, (ἀνίημι) *a relaxing*, as of the strings of a lyre, *relaxation : listlessness :* ἄνεσις κακῶν *an abating* of evils. 2. *a letting loose*, esp. of the passions, *licence.*

ἀνέσσῠτο, 3 sing. aor. 2 pass. of ἀνασεύω.

ἀνέστην, aor. 2 of ἀνίστημι.

ἀν-έστιος, *ον*, (α privat., ἑστία) *without hearth* or *home.*

ἀνέσχεθε, **ἀνεσχέθομεν**, poët. lengthd. for ἀνέσχε, ἀνέσχομεν, aor. 2 of ἀν-έχω.

ἀν-ετάζω, f. σω, *to search thoroughly.*

ἀνέτειλε, 3 sing. aor. 1 of ἀνα-τέλλω.

ἀνέτλην, aor. 2 of *ἀνάτλημι.

ἄν-ετος, *ον*, (ἀνίημι) *relaxed, slack ;* properly of a bow. 2. *set free from labour, ranging freely.*

ἀνετράφην [ᾰ], aor. 2 pass. of ἀνατρέφω.

ἄνευ, Prep. with gen. *without ;* ἄνευ θεῶν, Lat. *sine Diis, without* divine aid ; ἄνευ τοῦ κραίνοντος, Lat. *injussu regis.* 2. *away from, far from.* 3. in prose, *except, besides.*

ἀν-ευάζω, *to honour with cries of evae !*

ἄνευθε, before a vowel **ἄνευθεν**, (ἄνευ): I. Prep. with gen. *without.* 2. *apart from, far from.* II. Adv. *far away, distant: out of the way.*

ἀν-εύθετος, ον, (α privat., εὔθετος) *not well placed, inconvenient.*

ἀν-εύθῡνος, ον, (α privat., εὐθύνη) *not having to render an account, irresponsible:* hence *guiltless.*

ἄν-ευκτος, ον, (α privat., εὔχομαι) *not wished for.* II. act. *not wishing* or *praying for.*

ἀνευρεῖν, aor. 2 inf. of ἀνευρίσκω.

ἀνεύρεσις, εως, ἡ, (ἀνευρίσκω) *a finding out.*

ἀν-εύρετος, ον, (α privat., εὑρίσκω) *not found out, not to be found out.*

ἀν-ευρίσκω, f. ἀνευρήσω: aor. 2 ἀνεῦρον: un-Att. aor. I med. ἀνευράμην: aor. I pass. ἀνευρέθην:—*to find out, discover*:—Pass. *to be found out* or *discovered to be.*

ἀν-ευφημέω, f. ήσω, *to cry out*, εὐφήμει, εὐφημεῖτε: *to shout aloud with joy.*

ἀν-εύχομαι, Dep. *to recall a prayer.*

ἀ-νέφελος, Ep. ἀννέφελος, ον, (α privat., νεφέλη) *cloudless: unveiled.*

ἀν-εχέγγῠος, ον, (α privat., ἐχέγγυος) *unwarranted.*

ἀν-έχησι, v. sub sq.

ἀν-έχω, impf. ἀνεῖχον: also ἀ· ίσχω, ἀνίσχον: f. ἀνέξω, also ἀνασχήσω: aor. 2 ἀνέσχον, poet. ἀνέσχεθον: pf. ἀνέσχηκα:—Pass., aor. I ἀνεσχέθην: pf. ἀνέσχημαι:—a 3 sing. pres. ind. ἀνέχησι also occurs, as if from ἀνέχημι: (ἀνά, ἔχω):—*to hold up, lift up* one's hands in prayer or in battle: *to hold up and shew* to one; ἀνέχειν φάος, *to hold up* a light; esp. in phrase ἄνεχε, πάρεχε φῶς, or simply ἄνεχε, πάρεχε, *hold up and shew* the light to lead the nuptial procession, *make ready, go on.* 2. *to exalt, extol.* 3. of land, ἀνέχειν τὴν ἄκρην *to put forth* a headland. 4. *to uphold, support: to continue* to do; c. part., στέρξας ἀνέχει *continues* to love: of the nightingale, ἀνέχειν κισσόν *to keep constant to* the ivy. II. *to hold in, keep in;* Ζεὺς ἀνέχων, opp. to ὕων, *holding up, stopping* the rain. III. intrans. *to rise up, rise*, esp. in form ἀνίσχω, of the sun: of events, *to happen:* c. gen. *to rise from, recover from.* 2. *to come forth, project:* esp. of a headland, *to jut out* into the sea. 3. *to hold on, keep doing.*

B. Med. **ἀν-έχομαι**: f. ἀνέξομαι or ἀνασχήσομαι: Att. impf. and aor. 2 c. dupl. augm. ἠνειχόμην, ἠνεσχόμην:—properly *to hold oneself up*, and so *to hold up against* a thing, *endure, allow, hold out, last:* so in part., ἀνεχόμενοι φέρουσι they bear *with patience.* 2. ἀνέχεσθαι ξείνους *to allow the presence* of guests, and so *to receive* them. II. *to hold up what is one's own;* ἀνέχεσθαι χεῖρας *to hold up* one's hands *to fight.* III. rarely, *to hold on by one another.*

ἀνεψία, ἡ, fem. of ἀνέψιος, *a female cousin.*

ἀνεψιαδοῦς, οῦ, ὁ, *a first-cousin's son.* From

ἈΝΕΨΙΟ'Σ, ὁ, *a first cousin, a cousin.* Hence

ἀνεψιότης, ητος, ἡ, *cousinship.*

ἀνέψυχθεν, Ep. 3 pl. aor. I pass. of ἀνα-ψύχω.

ἄνεῳ or **ἄνεω**, see ἄνεως.

ἀνέῳγα, Att. pf. of ἀνοίγω, part. ἀνεῳγώς, always intr.

ἀνέῳγον, impf. of ἀνοίγω.

ἀνέῳξα, aor. I of ἀνοίγω.

ἀνέωνται (not ἀνέονται), for ἀνεῖνται, 3 pl. perf. pass. of ἀνίημι (as if from ἀν-εύω), *they have been given up* or *devoted.*

ἄνεως, gen. ω, ὁ, ἡ, Att. form. of an obsol. Adj. ἄναυος, ἄναος (α privat., αὔω *to cry*), *without a voice, mute:* ἄνεῳ nom. plur.

ἀνεῴχθην, aor. I pass. of ἀνοίγω.

ἄνη, ἡ, (ἄνω) *fulfilment.*

ἀν-ηβάω, f. ήσω, *to grow young again*, Lat. *repuerascere.* Hence

ἀνηβητήριος, α, ον, *making young again.*

ἄν-ηβος, ον, (α privat., ἥβη) *not arrived at man's estate.*

ἀνήγαγον, aor. 2 of ἀνάγω.

ἀν-ηγεμόνευτος, ον, (α privat., ἡγεμονεύω) *without a leader.*

ἀν-ηγέομαι, f. ήσομαι, Dep. *to tell as in a narrative, relate.*

ἀν-ήδυντος, ον, (α privat., ἡδύνω) *not sweetened* or *seasoned.*

ἀνήῃ, Ep. for ἀνῇ, 3 sing. aor. 2 subj. of ἀνίημι.

ἀνήθῐνος, η, ον, (ἄνηθον) *made of dill.*

ἌΝΗΘΟΝ, τό, *dill, anise*, Lat. *anethum:* also ἄννηθον; Ion. ἄννησον or ἄνησον: poët. ἄννητον or ἄνητον.

ἀνῆϊξα, aor. I of ἀναΐσσω.

ἀνήϊον, Ep. for ἀνῄειν, impf. of ἄνειμι.

ἀνῆκα, aor. I of ἀν-ίημι.

ἀν-ήκεστος, ον, (α privat., ἀκέομαι) *not to be healed, incurable:* ἀνήκεστα ποιεῖν τινα to do one *irremediable* hurt: ἀνήκεστα πάσχειν to suffer the same. II. act. *damaging beyond remedy, deadly:*—Adv., ἀνηκέστως διατιθέναι to treat *with shocking cruelty.*

ἀν-ήκοος, ον, (α privat., ἀκοή) *without hearing: never having heard* a thing, *ignorant of* it. 2. *not willing to hear, disobedient.*

ἀνηκουστέω, f. ήσω, *to be unwilling to hear, to be disobedient.* From

ἀν-ήκουστος, ον, (α privat., ἀκούω) *unheard of.* II. act. *unwilling to hear, disobedient.*

ἀν-ήκω, f. ξω, (ἀνά, ἥκω) *to reach up to.* 2. *to have come up to* a point, ἐς τὰ μέγιστα ἀνήκειν: *to refer* or *pertain to* a person or thing.

ἀνηλάλαζον, **ἀνηλάλαξα**, impf. and aor. I of ἀναλαλάζω.

ἀνήλατο, 3 sing. aor. I of ἀνάλλομαι.

ἀν-ήλῐκος, ον, (α privat., ἧλιξ) *not yet arrived at man's estate.*

ἀν-ήλιος, ον, (α privat., ἥλιος) *sunless, gloomy.*

ἀνήλῐπος, Dor. **ἀνάλιπος**, ον, (α privat., ἦλιψ a kind of shoe) *unshod, barefoot.*

ἀνήλῠσις, εως, ἡ, (ἀνέρχομαι) *a going up.* 2. *a coming back*

ἀνήλωσα, aor. 1 of ἀναλίσκω.

ἀν-ήμελκτος, ον, (α privat., ἀμέλγω) *unmilked.*

ἀν-ήμερος, ον, (α privat., ἥμερος) *not tame, wild, savage:* of plants, *wild.*

ἀνήνασθαι, aor. 1 inf. of ἀναίνομαι, of which tense ἀνήνᾰτο is 3 sing. ind., ἀνήνηται 3 sing. subj.

ἀνηνεμία, ἡ, *a calm.* From

ἀν-ήνεμος, ον, (α privat., ἄνεμος) *without wind, calm;* ἀνήνεμος χειμώνων for ἄνευ ἀνέμου χειμώνων, *without the blast* of storms.

ἀνήνοθε, Ep. pf. 2 intr., with pres, signf.: Homer has it twice, αἷμα ἀνήνοθεν ἐξ ὠτειλῆς blood *gushed from forth* the wound; κνίση ἀνήνοθεν steam *mounted up*. (Formed as if from a Verb *ἀνέθω.)

ἀν-ήνυστος and **ἀν-ήνῠτος**, ον, (α privat., ἀνύω) *not to be accomplished, endless, aimless.*

ἀν-ήνωρ, ορος, ὁ, (α privat., ἀνήρ) *unmanly, dastardly,* like ἄνανδρος.

ἀνῆπται, 3 sing. pf. pass. of ἀνάπτω.

ἀν-ηπύω, f. σω, *to cry aloud.*

ἈΝΗ΄Ρ, ὁ, gen. ἀνδρός, dat. ἀνδρί, acc. ἄνδρα, voc. ἄνερ: plur. ἄνδρες, –δρῶν, –δράσι, –δρας. Ep. also gen. ἀνέρος, etc., dat. pl. ἄνδρεσσι:—*a man,* as opp. to *woman,* Lat. *vir* (not *homo*). II. *a man,* as opp. to God, πατὴρ ἀνδρῶν τε θεῶν τε. III. *a man,* as opp. to a youth. IV. *a man,* emphatically, *a man indeed,* opp. to ἄνθρωπος; πολλοὶ μὲν ἄνθρωποι, ὀλίγοι δὲ ἄνδρες. V. *a husband;* αἰγῶν ἀνήρ, Virgil's *vir gregis.*

ἀνήρ, Att. crasis for ὁ ἀνήρ.

ἀνηρέθην, aor. 1 pass. of ἀναιρέω.

ἀν-ήριθμος, ον, poët. for ἀν-άριθμος.

ἀνηρόμην, aor. 2 of ἀνέρομαι.

ἀν-ήροτος, ον, (α privat., ἀρόω) *unploughed.*

ἀνήρτησα, **ἀνήρτημαι**, aor. 1 act. and pf. pass. of ἀν-αρτάω.

ἄνησον or **ἄννητον**, τό, Ion. for ἄνηθον.

ἀν-ήσσητος, Att. **ἀ-ήττητος**, ον, (α privat., ἡσσάω) *unconquered, unconquerable.*

ἀνήτῑνος, η, ον, Dor. for ἀνήθινος.

ἄνητον or **ἄννητον**, τό, Dor. and Aeol. for ἄνηθον.

ἀν-ήττητος, ον, Att. for ἀν-ήσσητος.

ἀν-ήφαιστος, ον, (α privat., Ἥφαιστος) *without real fire;* πῦρ ἀνήφαιστον, i.e. the fire of discord.

ἀνήφθην, aor. 1 pass. of ἀνάπτω.

ἀνήφθω, 3 sing. pf. pass. imperat. of ἀνάπτω.

ἀνήχθην, aor. 1 pass. of ἀνάγω.

ἀνῆψα, aor. 1 of ἀνάπτω.

ἀνθ-αιρέομαι, f. ήσομαι: Dep.: (ἀντί, αἱρέω):—*to choose* one thing *instead of* another: *to prefer, choose instead.* II. *to dispute, lay claim to.*

ἀνθ-ᾰλίσκομαι, f. –αλώσομαι, Pass. *to be caught* or *killed in turn.*

ἀνθᾰμιλλάομαι, f. ήσομαι, Dep. *to vie with* another, *be rivals: to race* one another. From

ἀνθ-άμιλλος, ον, (ἀντί, ἅμιλλα) *rivalling.*

ἀνθ-άπτομαι, Ion. ἀντ-άπτομαι, f. ψομαι: Dep.:—*to lay bold of, meddle with, engage in.* 2. *to lay bold of, seize, attack.* II. *to lay bold of in return.*

ἄνθειον, τό, (ἄνθος) *a blossom.*

ἀνθ-εκτέον, verb. Adj. of ἀντέχω, *one must hold to, cleave to:* so also plur. **ἀνθεκτέα**.

ἀνθ-έλκω, f. ξω, *to draw* or *pull against.*

ἄνθεμα, ατος, τό, prët. for ἀνάθεμα or ἀνάθημα.

ἀνθέμιον, τό, = ἄνθος: ἀνθέμιον ἐστιγμένος tattooed *with flowers.*

ἀνθεμίς, ίδος, ἡ, = ἄνθος.

ἀνθεμόεις, εσσα, εν, also εις in fem., *flowery, flowered:* of works in metal, *embossed with flowers.* From

ἄνθεμον, τό, (ἀνθέω) = ἄνθος, *a flower.*

ἀνθεμό-ρῠτος, ον, (ἄνθεμον, ῥέω) *flowing from flowers.*

ἀνθεμ-ουργός, όν, (ἄνθεμον, *ἔργω) *working in flowers.*

ἀνθεμ-ώδης, ες, contr. for ἀνθεμο-ειδής, (ἄνθεμον, εἶδος) *flowery, blooming.*

ἀνθέξομαι, fut. med. of ἀντέχω.

ἄνθεο, Ep. for ἀνάθου, aor. 2 med. imperat. of ἀνατίθημι.

ἀνθερεών, ῶνος, ὁ, (ἀνθέω) *the chin,* Lat. *mentum.*

ἀνθερίκη, ἡ, and ἀνθέρικος, ὁ, = ἀνθέριξ, *a stalk.*

ἀνθέριξ, ικος, ὁ, (ἀθήρ) *the beard* of an ear of corn, *the ear.* 2. *a stalk.*

ἄνθεσαν, Ep. for ἀνέθεσαν, 3 plur. aor. 2 of ἀνατίθημι.

ἀνθ-εστιάω, *to feast in return.*

Ἀνθεστήρια. ων, τά, *the Feast of Flowers,* the three days' festival of Bacchus at Athens, in the month Anthesterion.

Ἀνθεστηριών, ῶνος, ὁ, the month *Anthesterion,* eighth of the Attic year, answering to the end of February and beginning of March.

Ἀνθεσφόρια, ων, τά, *the Anthesphoria,* a festival in honour of Proserpine, who was carried off while *gathering flowers.* From

ἀνθεσ-φόρος, ον, (ἄνθος, φέρω) *bearing flowers.*

ἄνθετο, Ep. for ἀνέθετο, 3 sing. aor. 2 med. of ἀνατίθημι.

ἀνθέω, f. ήσω, *to bloom, blossom:* metaph. of the sea, ἀνθεῖν νεκροῖς *to be overspread* with corpses: of colours, *to be bright:* metaph. *to bloom, flourish,* ἀνθεῖν ἀνδράσι *to abound* in men: *to be at the height,* as a disease.

ἄνθη, ἡ, = ἄνθος, *a blossom.*

ἀνθηρός, ά, όν, (ἀνθέω) *flowering, blooming:* hence *fresh, young:*—metaph. *in full force,* in *perfection.* 2. *bright-coloured.* 3. of style, *florid.*

ἀνθ-ησσάομαι, pf. ἀνθήσσημαι: Pass.:—*to be beaten in turn, give way in turn.*

ἀνθη-φόρος, ον, = ἀνθεσφόρος, *flower-bringing.*

ἀνθίζω, f. ίσω, (ἄνθος) *to strew with flowers: to deck as with flowers;* and so, *to dye with colours:*—Pass. *to bloom: to be dyed;* part. pf. ἠνθισμένος, metaph. of one whose hair is *sprinkled with white.*

ἄνθινος, η, ον, (ἄνθος) *of flowers, blooming, fresh.*

ἀνθ-ιππάζομαι, f. άσομαι: Dep. *to ride against.* Hence

ἀνθιππᾰσία, ἡ, *a sham-fight of horse.*

ἀνθ-ιππεύω, = ἀνθιππάζομαι.

ἀνθ-ίστημι, (ἀντί, ἵστημι). I. Causal in pres. and impf., in fut. ἀναστήσω and aor. 1 ἀνέστησα, *to set against*, esp. in battle: *to set over against*: *to compare*, Lat. *componere*. II. intrans. in Med. or Pass. ἀνθίσταμαι, also in pf. act. ἀνθέστηκα, aor. 2 ἀντέστην, *to stand against, withstand, oppose.*

ἀνθοβολέω, f. ήσω, *to bestrew with flowers*:—Pass. *to have flowers showered* upon one. From

ἀνθό-βολος, ον, (ἄνθος, βάλλω) *garlanded with flowers.*

ἀνθο-δίαιτος, ον, (ἄνθος, δίαιτα) *living on flowers.*

ἀνθο-δόκος, ον, (ἄνθος, δέχομαι) *receiving flowers.*

ἀνθοκομέω, f. ήσω, *to produce flowers.* From

ἀνθο-κόμος, ον, (ἄνθος, κομέω) *bearing flowers.*

ἀνθο-κρόκος, ον, (ἄνθος, κρέκω) *woven* or *worked with flowers, partly-coloured.*

ἀνθολογέω, f. ήσω, (ἀνθολόγος) *to gather flowers.* Hence

ἀνθολογία, ἡ, *a flower-gathering*: Ἀνθολογίαι were collections of small Greek poems, which one editor made up (as it were) into a *nosegay.*

ἀνθο-λόγος, ον, (ἄνθος, λέγω) *gathering flowers.*

ἀνθ-ομολογέομαι, Dep. (ἀντί, ὁμολογέομαι):—*to make a mutual agreement* or *compact.* 2. *to confess* or *give thanks in turn.*

ἀνθονομέω, *to feed on flowers.* From

ἀνθο-νόμος, ον, (ἄνθος, νέμομαι) *feeding on flowers.*

ἀνθ-οπλίζω, f. ίσω, *to arm against*:—Pass. and Med. *to be armed, arm oneself against.*

ἄνθορε, poët. for ἀνέθορε, 3 sing. aor. 2 of ἀναθρώσκω.

ἀνθ-ορμέω, f. ήσω, *to lie at anchor, be moored opposite one another.*

ἌΝΘΟΣ, εος, τό, *that which buds, a young bud* or *sprout; a flower; the bloom of a flower*: also of things, *the froth* or *scum on water*: ἄνθος οἴνου, Lat. *flos vini, the crust* on old wines. II. metaph. *the bloom* or *flower* of a thing, ἥβης ἄνθος *the bloom* of youth: generally, *grace, pride, honour*: also *the height* of anything, bad as well as good. 2. *brightness of colour, brilliancy*, as of gold.

ἀνθ-οσμίας, ου, ὁ, (ἀντί, ὀσμή) *redolent of flowers*: generally, *sweet-scented*, as epithet of wine.

ἀνθοσύνη, ἡ, (ἄνθος) *a flowering, bloom.*

ἀνθοφορέω, f. ήσω, (ἀνθοφόρος) *to bear flowers.*

ἀνθοφορία, τά, = Ἀνθεσφόρια. From

ἀνθο-φόρος, ον, (ἄνθος, φέρω) *bearing flowers, flowery: blooming.*

ἀνθο-φυής, ές, (ἄνθος, φυή) *of the nature of flowers, bright-coloured.*

ἀνθρᾰκεύς, έως, ὁ, (ἄνθραξ) *a charcoal-burner.* Hence

ἀνθρᾰκεύω, f. σω, *to be a charcoal-burner*: *to burn to a cinder.*

ἀνθρᾰκιά, ᾶς, Ep. **ἀνθρακιή**, ῆς, ἡ, (ἄνθραξ) *a heap of coal* or *charcoal, hot coals.* 2. *blackness as of coals.*

ἀνθρᾰκόομαι, pf. ἠνθράκωμαι: Pass.: (ἄνθραξ):—*to be burnt to cinders.*

ἌΝΘΡΑΞ, ᾶκος, ὁ, *coal* or *charcoal*, mostly in plur.

ἀνθρηδών, όνος, ἡ, *a wasp* or *hornet.*

ἈΝΘΡΗ´ΝΗ, ἡ, *a wild bee*: *a bee* or *wasp.* Hence

ἀνθρήνιον, τό, *the honeycomb of a wild bee*: *a wasps' nest.*

ἀνθρωπ-άρεσκος, ου, ὁ, (ἄνθρωπος, ἀρέσκω) *a man-pleaser.*

ἀνθρωπάριον, τό, Dim. of ἄνθρωπος, *a manikin.*

ἀνθρωπέη, contr. **ἀνθρωπῆ** (sub. δορά), ἡ, *a man's skin.*

ἀνθρώπειος, α, ον, Ion. **ἀνθρωπήϊος**, η, ον, (ἄνθρωπος) *of* or *belonging to man, befitting man's nature, human*: Adv. -ως, *by human means, in all human probability.*

ἀνθρωπήϊος, η, ον, Ion. for ἀνθρώπειος.

ἀνθρωπίζω, f. ίσω, (ἄνθρωπος) *to behave like a man*: Pass. *to become man.*

ἀνθρωπῐκός, ή, όν, *of* or *for a man, human.*

ἀνθρώπῐνος, η, ον, (ἄνθρωπος) *of, from* or *belonging to man, human*; πᾶν τὸ ἀνθρώπινον all *mankind*; τὰ ἀνθρώπινα *the fortunes of man.*—Adv., ἀνθρωπίνως ἁμαρτάνειν to commit *human*, i.e. venial, errors.

ἀνθρώπιον, τό, Dim. of ἄνθρωπος.

ἀνθρωπίσκος, ὁ, Dim. of ἄνθρωπος, *a little man, manikin*, Lat. *homuncio.*

ἀνθρωπο-δαίμων, ονος, ὁ, ἡ, (ἄνθρωπος, δαίμων) *a man-god*, i.e. *a deified man, hero.*

ἀνθρωπο-ειδής, ές, (ἄνθρωπος, εἶδος) *in the shape of a man.*

ἀνθρωπο-κτόνος, ον, (ἄνθρωπος, κτείνω) *murdering men, homicidal.* II. proparox. ἀνθρωπό-κτονος, *murdered by men; βορὰ ἀνθρ.* a feeding *on slaughtered men.*

ἀνθρωποποιΐα, ἡ, *a making of man.* From

ἀνθρωπο-ποιός, όν, (ἄνθρωπος, ποιέω) *making man.*

ἌΝΘΡΩΠΟΣ, ὁ, *man*, Lat. *homo* (not *vir*): plur. οἱ ἄνθρωποι, *men in general, mankind*; so, μάλιστα ἢ ἥκιστα ἀνθρώπων most or least *of all men.* Like ἀνήρ, it is joined to another Subst., as ἄνθρωπος ὁδίτης a wayfaring *man.* As opp. to ἀνήρ, it expresses contempt, as Lat. *homo* opp. to *vir*: used in addressing slaves, ὦ ἄνθρωπε. The fem. ἄνθρωπος, ἡ, (like *homo* fem. in Lat.) *a woman.*

ἅνθρωπος, Att. crasis for ὁ ἄνθρωπος.

ἀνθρωπο-σφᾰγέω, f. ήσω, (ἄνθρωπος, σφάττω) *to slay* or *sacrifice men.*

ἀνθρωποφᾰγέω, f. ήσω, (ἀνθρωποφάγος) *to eat men* or *man's flesh.* Hence

ἀνθρωποφαγία, ἡ, *an eating of men.*

ἀνθρωπο-φάγος, ον, (ἄνθρωπος, φᾰγεῖν) *eating men, cannibal.*

ἀνθρωπο-φυής, ές, (ἄνθρωπος, φυή) *of man's nature.*

ἀν-θρώσκω, poët. and Ion. for ἀνα-θρώσκω.

ἀνθ-υβρίζω, f. ίσω, *to abuse one another, abuse in turn.*

ἀνθ-υπάγω, *to bring to trial* or *indict in turn.*

ἀνθῠπᾰτεύω, f. σω, *to be proconsul.* And

ἀνθυπατικός, ή, όν, *proconsular.* From

ἀνθ-ύπᾰτος, ὁ, *a proconsul*, for ἀντὶ ὑπάτου, Lat. *pro consule.*

ἀνθ-ῠπείκω, f. ξω, (ἀντί, ὑπείκω) *to yield in turn.* Hence

ἀνθύπειξις, εως, ἡ, *a mutual yielding.*

ἀνθ-υποκρίνομαι, fut. -κρῐνοῦμαι: Dep.: (ἀντί, ὑποκρίνομαι) :—*to dissemble* or *make pretences instead*, or *in answer.* [ῑν]

ἀνθ-υπόμνυμι, f. -ομόσω, (ἀντί, ὑπόμνυμι) *to make a counter-affidavit.*

ἀνθ-υποπτεύω, (ἀντί, ὑποπτεύω) *to suspect mutually.*

ἀνθ-υπουργέω, (ἀντί, ὑπουργέω) *to return a kindness.* Hence

ἀνθυπούργημα, ατος, τό, *a kindness done in return.*

ἀνθ-υφαιρέω, (ἀντί, ὑφαιρέω) *to take away in return.*

ἀνθ-υφίσταμαι, fut. -υποστήσομαι: aor. 2 -υπέστην, (ἀντί, ὑφίστημι) :—*to place oneself under* a thing *in* another's *stead, to take on oneself, undertake for* another.

ἀνθώπλισμαι, pf. pass. of ἀνθοπλίζω.

'ΑΝΙ'Α, Ion. ἀνίη, ἡ, *grief, sorrow, distress, trouble:* Homer uses it act. of a person, δαιτὸς ἀνίη *the annoyance* of our feast. [ᾱνῑη in Hom., later ἀνῐα or sometimes ἀνῑα.] Hence

ἀνιάζω, aor. 1 ἠνίᾱσα, *to grieve, distress.* II. intr. *to be grieved* or *distressed, feel grief, sorrow.* [ῑ]

ἀν-ῐάομαι, fut. ᾰσομαι [ᾱ], Dep. *to cure again, restore.*

ἀνῑαρός, ά, όν, Ion. and Ep ἀνιηρός, ή, όν, (ἀνιάω) *grievous, distressing:* irreg. Comp. ἀνῑηρέστερος. II. *grieved, distressed.* Adv. -ρῶς. [In Homer ἀνῑηρός, later also ἀνῐ-.]

ἀν-ίᾱτος, ον, (α privat., ἰάομαι) *incurable:* of men, *incorrigible.*

ἀνιάω, fut. ᾱσω [ᾱ], Ion. ήσω: aor. 1 ἠνίᾱσα, Dor. ἀνίασα: pf. ἠνίᾱκα :—Pass. with fut. med. ἀνιᾱσομαι: aor. 1 ἠνιάθην: pf. ἠνίᾱμαι: (ἀνία) :—*to grieve, distress* :—Pass. *to be grieved*, etc.; ἀνιᾶσθαι τοῦτο *to be vexed at* this :—Homer has Ion. aor. 1 pass. part. ἀνιηθείς, as Adj. *a joyless, melancholy man.* [ῑ in Homer always, later also ῐ.]

ἀνιδεῖν, aor. 2 inf. of a pres. *ἀν-είδω, *to look up.*

ἀν-ίδρῡτος, ον, (α privat., ἱδρύω) *unsettled, restless:* esp *having no fixed home, vagabond.*

ἀν-ῑδρωτί, Adv. of ἀνίδρωτος, *without sweat:* hence *lazily, slowly.*

ἀν-ίδρωτος, ον, (α privat., ἱδρόω) *not thrown into a sweat, not exerting oneself.*

ἀνίεις, ἀνίει, 2 and 3 sing. impf. of ἀνίημι.

ἀνιεῖς, 2 sing. pres. of ἀνίημι.

ἀνίεμαι, Pass. and Med. of ἀνίημι.

ἀνιέναι, pres. inf. of ἀν-ίημι, *to send up.* 2. pres. inf. of ἄν-ειμι (εἶμι *ibo*) *to go up.*

ἀν-ίερος, ον, (α privat., ἱερός) *unholy, impious.* [ῐ]

ἀνίεσκε, Ion. impf. of ἀνίημι.

ἀν-ίζω, aor. 1 ἀνεῖσα, (ἀνά, ἵζω) *to set up.*

ἀνιηθείς, Ion. for ἀνιᾱθείς, aor. 1 pass. part. of ἀνιάω.

ἀν-ίημι, impf. ἀνίην; also 2 sing. pres. ἀνιεῖς, 2 and 3 sing. impf. ἀνίεις, ει; Ion. 3 sing. ἀνίεσκε (as if from ἀνιέω): fut. ἀνήσω, also ἀνέσω: aor. 1 ἀνῆκα, Ion. ἀνέηκα, Ep. also ἄνεσα: aor. 2 not used in sing. ind., but in Ep. subj. ἀνήῃ for ἀνῇ, opt. ἀνείη, inf. ἀνεῖναι, part. ἀνέντες :—Pass. ἀνίεμαι: aor. 1 ἀνέθην: pf. ἀνεῖμαι: (ἀνά, ἵημι) :—*to send up* or *forth, make spring up, produce*, as the earth: esp. *to send up* from the nether world. II. *to send back.* III. *to let go.* 2. ἀνιέναι τινὶ *to let loose* against one, *set upon* him, like Lat. *immittere alicui:* hence generally, *to set on.* 3. *to let alone, let* :—Med. ἀνίεμαι, *to loosen, undo* :—Pass. *to be let go, go free;* part. pf. pass. ἀνειμένος *going free, left to one's will and pleasure;* ἀνειμένος εἴς τι *wholly engaged in* a thing: hence IV. like Lat. *remittere, to relax*, properly of a bow, *to unstring:* hence *to neglect, give over, remit* :—Pass. *to be slack* or *unstrung.* V. intrans. in Act. *to relax, be remiss*, Lat. *remisse agere.*

ἀνιηρός, ή, όν, Ion. for ἀνιαρός.

ἀνίκα, Dor. for ἡνίκα. [ῐ]

ἀν-ῐκᾰνος, ον, (α privat., ἱκανος) *insufficient.*

ἀν-ῐκέτευτος, ον, (α privat., ἱκετεύω) *not entreated:* act. *not entreating.*

ἀ-νίκητος, ον, (α privat., νῑκάω) *unconquered, unconquerable.*

ἀν-ίλεως, ων, gen. ω, Att. for ἀν-ίλαος, (α privat., ἵλεως) *unmerciful.* [ῐ]

ἀν-ῑμάω, f. ήσομαι: (ἀνά, ἱμάς) :—*to draw up* water by leather straps: generally *to draw* or *haul up* :—Pass. *to get up, mount up;* so also intr. (sub. ἑαυτόν), *to mount up.*

ἄνῑος, ον, (ἀνία) = ἀνιαρός.

ἀν-ίουλος, ον, (α privat., ἴουλος) *beardless.*

ἀν-ιππεύω, f. σω, *to ride on high.*

ἄν-ιππος, ον, (α privat., ἵππος) *without a horse, not serving on horseback:* of countries, *unsuited for horses.*

ἀν-ίπτᾰμαι, Dep., = ἀνα-πέτομαι.

ἀνιπτό-πους, ὁ, ἡ, πουν, τό, gen. ποδος, (ἄνιπτος, πούς) *with unwashen feet.*

ἄ-νιπτος, ον, (α privat., νίζω) *unwashen.* 2. *not to be washed out.*

ἄνις, Boeot. for ἄνευ, also Megarean.

ἄν-ισος, ον, also η, ον, (α privat., ἴσος) *unequal, uneven:* metaph. *unfair.* [ῑ Ep., ῐ Att.] Hence

ἀνισόω, f. ώσω, *to make equal, equalise* :—Med. and Pass. *to be equal* in a thing.

ἀνίστα and **ἀνίστη**, for ἀνίστηθι, imperat. of ἀνίστημι.

ἀν-ιστάνω, later form for sq.

ἀν-ίστημι, (ἀνά, ἵστημι): I. Causal in pres. and impf., in fut. ἀναστήσω and aor. 1 ἀνέστησα, *to make to stand up, raise up, set up: to raise from sleep*, Lat. *excito*, and *from the dead:* later, *to set up, build:* also *to build up again.* 2. *to rouse to action: to stir up to rebellion.* 3. *to make* people *rise to leave their homes: transplant them;* though in Pass., and intr. tenses, it usu. means *to be unpeopled, laid waste;* χώρα ἀνεστηκυῖα a *wasted* land: also *to make* suppliants *rise and leave sanctuary.* 4. *to raise men for war.* II. in aor. 1 med. also trans., ἀναστήσασθαι πόλιν *to raise* a city *for oneself.* III.

intrans. in Pass. *ἀνίσταμαι*, with aor. 2 act. *ἀνέστην*, pf. *ἀνέστηκα* and plqpf. *-εστήκειν*, *to stand up, rise: to start up* for action, *ἀν. τινί to rise up* against one: *to rise from one's seat* as a mark of respect: *to rise from sleep: to rise from the dead: to rise from* an illness: *to rise to go, set out.*

ἀν-ιστορέω, f. *ήσω*, *to make inquiry, ask.*

ἀν-ίστω, for *ἀνίστασο*, imperat. of *ἀν-ίσταμαι.*

ἀν-ίσχω = *ἀν-έχω*, *to raise, lift up.* 2. intr., *ἀνίσχει ἥλιος* the sun *rises.*

ἀνίσως, Adv. of *ἄνῖσος*, *unequally.*

ἀνίσωσις, εως, ἡ, (*ἀνισόω*) *an equalising.*

ἀν-ιχνεύω, f. *σω*, *to trace back*, of a hound.

ἀνιῷατο, Ion. for *ἀνιάοιντο*, 3 pl. opt. of *ἀνιάομαι.*

ἀν-νείμῃ, poët. aor. 1 subj. of *ἀνανέμω.*

ἀννεῖται, poët. for *ἀνανεῖται*, 3 sing. of *ἀνανέομαι.*

ἀννέφελος, Ep. for *ἀνέφελος.*

ἀννεώσασθαι, poët. inf. aor. 1 of *ἀνανεόομαι.*

ἀν-ξηραίνω, poët. for *ἀνα-ξηραίνω.*

ἀν-οδηγέω, f. *ήσω*, (*ἀνά, ὁδηγέω*) *to guide back.*

ἄν-οδος, ον, (α privat., *ὁδός*) *having no road, impassable.*

ἄν-οδος, ἡ, (*ἀνά, ὁδός*) *a way up:* esp. into central Asia. II. *a way back.*

ἀν-οδύρομαι, Dep. *to set up a wailing.* [ῡ]

ἀ-νοήμων, ον, gen. ονος, (α privat., *νοέω*) *senseless.*

ἀ-νόητος, ον, (α privat., *νοέω*) *not thought on, not to be thought on.* II. act. *not understanding, foolish: unreasonable*, Lat. *amens*

ἄνοια, Ep. **ἀνοίη**, ἡ, (*ἄνοος*) *want of understanding, folly.*

ἀν-οίγνῡμι and **ἀν-οίγω**, Ep. **ἀνα-οίγω**: f. *ἀνοίξω*: with double augm., impf. *ἀνέῳγον*, Ion. *ἀναοίγεσκον*: aor. 1 *ἀνέῳξα*, Att. *ἤνοιξα*, Ion. *ἄνοιξα* or *ἄνῳξα*; pf. 1 *ἀνέῳχα*, pf. 2 *ἀνέῳγα*:—Pass. *ἀνοίγνῠμαι*: fut. *ἀνοιχθήσομαι*, fut. 2 *ἀνοιγήσομαι*, fut. 3 *ἀνεῴξομαι*: aor. 1 *ἀνεῴχθην*, inf. *ἀνοιχθῆναι*: (*ἀνά, οἴγω*): 1. *to open, undo.* 2. metaph. *to lay open, disclose.* 3. as nautical term, absol., *to get into the open sea*:—Pass. *to be open.*

ἀν-οίγω, f. *ξω*, v. foreg.

ἀν-οιδαίνω, (*ἀνά, οἰδαίνω*): fut. *ἀνοιδήσω*: pf. *ἀνῴδηκα*:—*to swell up: to swell with passion.*

ἀν-οικίζω, fut. *ίσω*, Att. *ιῶ*, *to rebuild.* II. *to make* a person *change his dwelling, to remove* him *from his abode*:—Pass. and Med. *to migrate.* 2. *ἀνοικίζειν πόλιν to dispeople* a city. III. in Pass. *to be built up the country, away from the coast.*

ἀν-οικοδομέω, f. *ήσω*, (*ἀνά, οἰκοδομέω*) *to build up.* II. *to rebuild.* III. *to wall up.*

ἄν-οικος, ον, (α privat., *οἶκος*) *houseless, homeless.*

ἀν-οικτέον, verb. Adj. of *ἀν-οίγω*, *one must open.*

ἀν-οικτίρμων, ονος, (α privat., *οἰκτίρμων*) *unpitying, merciless.*

ἀν-οίκτιστος, ον, (α privat., *οἰκτίζω*) *unpitied.*

ἀνοικτός, ή, όν, (*ἀνοίγνυμι*) *opened.*

ἄν-οικτος, ον, (α privat., *οἶκτος*) *pitiless, ruthless.*

ἀν-οιμώζω, fut. *ώξομαι*, *to wail aloud.*

ἀν-οιμωκτί, Adv. of *ἀνοιμωκτός*, *without wailing*: also *without need to wail*, i. e. *with impunity.* [ῑ]

ἀν-οίμωκτος, ον, (α privat., *οἰμώζω*) *unmourned.*

ἀνοῖξαι, aor. 1 inf. of *ἀνοίγνυμι.*

ἄνοιξις, εως, ἡ, (*ἀνοίγνυμι*) *an opening.*

ἀνοιστέον, verb. Adj. of *ἀναφέρω*, *one must report.*

ἀνοιστός, Ion. **ἀνώϊστος**, ή, όν, (*ἀναφέρω*) *reported, referred for decision.*

ἀν-οιστρέω, f. *ήσω*, (*ἀνά, οἶστρος*) *to goad to madness.*

ἀνοίσω, fut. of *ἀναφέρω.*

ἄνοιτο, 3 sing. pres. pass. opt. of *ἄνω.*

ἀνοιχθῶσιν, 3 pl. aor. 1 pass. subj. of *ἀνοίγνυμι.*

ἀνοκωχή, ἡ, (*ἀν-όκωχα* pf. of *ἀν-έχω*) *a cessation of arms, armistice.* II. *a hindrance.*

ἀνολβία, ἡ, *the state of an ἄνολβος, misery.*

ἀν-όλβιος, ον, = *ἄνολβος.*

ἄν-ολβος, ον, (α privat., *ὄλβος*) *unblest, wretched.*

ἀν-όλεθρος, ον, (α privat., *ὄλεθρος*) *not ruined.*

ἀνολκή, ἡ, (*ἀνέλκω*) *a drawing up.*

ἀν-ολολύζω, *ύξω*, (*ἀνά, ὀλολύζω*) *to cry aloud, to shout with joy.* 2. *to wail* or *bewail loudly.* II. Causal, *to make one shout.*

ἀν-ολοφύρομαι, Dep. (*ἀνά, ὀλοφύρομαι*) *to break into loud wailing.* [ῡ]

ἄν-ομβρος, ον, (α privat., *ὄμβρος*) *without rain.*

ἀνομέω, f. *ήσω*, (*ἄνομος*) *to act lawlessly.*

ἀνομία, Ion. **ἀνομίη**, ἡ, (*ἄνομος*) *lawlessness.*

ἀν-ομίλητος, ον, (α privat., *ὁμῑλέω*) *having no intercourse with others, unsociable.*

ἀν-όμμᾰτος, ον, (α privat., *ὄμμα*) *without eyes.*

ἀν-όμοιος, ον, also α, ον, (α privat., *ὅμοιος*) *unlike.*

ἀνομοιότης, τητος, ἡ, (*ἀνόμοιος*) *unlikeness.*

ἀνομοιόω, (*ἀνόμοιος*) *to make unlike*: Pass. *to be so.*

ἀνομοίωσις, εως, ἡ, *a making unlike: unlikeness.*

ἀν-ομολογέομαι, f. *ήσομαι*: pf. *ἀνῳμολόγημαι*: Dep.: (*ἀνά, ὁμολογέω*):—*to agree upon* a thing.

ἀνομολογούμενος, η, ον, (α privat., *ὁμολογέω*) *not agreeing, inconsistent: not admitted, not granted.*

ἄ-νομος, ον, (α privat., *νόμος*) *without law, lawless, impious.* Adv. *-μως*, *without law.* II. (*νόμος* II) *unmusical.*

ἀν-όνητος, Dor. **ἀν-όνᾱτος**, ον, (α privat., *ὀνίνημι*) *unprofitable, useless*: neut. pl. *ἀνόνητα*, as Adv., *unprofitably, in vain.*

ἄ-νοος, ον, contr. **ἄνους**, ουν, (α privat., *νόος*) *without understanding, foolish.*

ἀνοπαῖα, Adv., either (from α privat., *ὄψομαι*, fut. of *ὁράω*), *unnoticed*; or (from *ἄνω*) *upwards, up in the air.*

ἄν-οπλος, ον, (α privat., *ὅπλον*) *without the large shield* which distinguished the hoplite, *not heavy-armed*: generally, *unarmed.*

ἄν-οπτος, ον, (α privat., *ὄψομαι*) *unseen.*

ἀν-όρᾱτος, ον, also **ἀ-όρατος**, (α privat., *ὁράω*) = foreg.

ἀν-όργᾰνος, ον, (α privat., *ὄργανον*) *without instruments.*

ἀν-οργίαστος, ον, (α privat., *ὀργιάζω*) *attended by no orgies.* II. *in whose honour no orgies are held.*

ἀνορέα, Ion. ἠνορέη, ἡ, (ἀνήρ) manhood, courage. [ᾰ]

ἀνόρεος, α, ον, (ἀνήρ) manly, courageous, like ἀνδρεῖος. [ᾰ]

ἀν-ορθόω, f. ώσω: with double augm., impf., ἠνώρθουν, aor. 1 ἠνώρθωσα:—to set upright again, restore: to set straight again, set right.

ἄν-ορμος, ον, (α privat., ὅρμος) without harbour, inhospitable.

ἀν-ορούω, f. ούσω: aor. 1 ἀνόρουσα:—to start up, leap up: to mount swiftly.

ἀν-όροφος, ον, (α privat., ὄροφος) roofless.

ἀν-ορταλίζω, f. ίσω, (ἀνά, ὀρταλίζω) to flap the wings and crow, to strut.

ἀν-ορύσσω, Att. -ττω: fut. ξω: (ἀνά, ὀρύσσω):—to dig up what has been buried; ἀν. τάφον to break open a grave.

ἀν-ορχέομαι, f. ήσομαι, Dep. to jump up and dance about.

ἀν-όσιος, ον, or α, ον, (α privat., ὅσιος) unholy, wicked, Lat. profanus: ἀνόσιος νέκυς a corpse with all the rites unpaid. Hence

ἀνοσιότης, ητος, ἡ, unholiness.

ἄ-νοσος, Ion. ἄ-νουσος, ον, (α privat., νόσος) without sickness, healthy, sound: of things, free from all defect, healthy; ἄνοσος κακῶν untouched by ill.

ἀν-όστεος, ον, (α privat., ὀστέον) without bones.

ἀ-νόστῐμος, ον, (α privat., νόστιμος) not returning. II. not to be retraced.

ἄ-νοστος, ον, (α privat., νόστος) without return.

ἀν-οτοτύζω, (ἀνά, ὀτοτοῖ) to break out into wailing.

ἀν-ούᾰτος, ον, (α privat., οὖς) without ear: without handle.

ἄ-νους, contr. for ἄ-νοος.

ἄ-νουσος, ον, Ion. for ἄ-νοσος.

ἀν-ούτᾰτος, ον, (α privat., οὐτάω) unwounded.

ἀν-ουτητί, Adv of foreg., without wound. [ῑ]

ἀνοχή, ἡ, (ἀνέχω) a holding back, stopping, esp. of hostilities, an armistice. II. (ἀνέχομαι) long-suffering, forbearance.

ἀν-οχμάζω, f. άσω, to hold up, lift up.

ἄνστα, Ep. shortd. imperat for ἀνάστα, ἀνάστηθι.

ἀνστάς, ἀνστήμεναι, Ep. for ἀναστάς, ἀναστῆναι: aor. 2 part. and inf. of ἀνίστημι.

ἀνστήσω, Ep. for ἀναστήσω, fut. of ἀνίστημι.

ἀνστήτην, Ep. for ἀνεστήτην, 3 dual aor. 2 of ἀνίστημι.

ἀνστρέψειαν, for ἀναστρέψειαν.

ἀνσχεθέειν, ἄνσχεο, Ep. for ἀνασχεθεῖν, ἀνάσχου, aor. 2 inf. act. and imper. med. of ἀνέχω.

ἀν-σχετός, Ep. for ἀνα-σχετός.

ἄντα, (ἀντί, ἄντην) Adv. over against, face to face, Lat. coram. II. as Prep. c. gen., over against; ἄντα παρειάων before the cheeks, of a veil: confronted with: most freq. in hostile sense, against, ἄντα Διὸς πολεμίζειν.

ἀντ-ᾰγοράζω, f. άσω, to buy in return.

ἀντ-ᾰγορεύω, f. σω, to speak against, reply: to contradict.

ἀντ-ᾰγωνίζομαι, f. ίσομαι, Att. ιοῦμαι: Dep.:—to struggle against, vie with, esp. in war: to dispute with: as Pass. to be set against. Hence

ἀντᾰγωνιστής, οῦ, ὁ, an adversary, rival.

ἀντ-αδικέω, f. ήσω, to wrong or injure in return.

ἀντ-αείρω, = ἀντ-αίρω:—Med., ἀνταείρεσθαι χεῖράς τινι to raise one's hands against one.

ἄντ-αθλος, ον, (ἀντί, ἆθλος) struggling against, rivalling.

ἀντ-αιδέομαι, f. έσομαι, Med. to respect one another.

ἀνταῖος, α, ον, (ἄντα) set over against, right opposite: ἀνταία (sub. πληγή), a wound in front. 2. hostile. II. besought with prayers; τὰ ἀνταῖα θεῶν prayers to the gods.

ἀντ-αίρω, f. ἀντᾰρῶ: aor. 1 ἀντῆρα:—to raise against. II. seemingly intr. (sub. χεῖρας), to resist, withstand.

ἀντ-αιτέω, f. ήσω, to demand in return.

'ΑΝΤΑΚΑΙΟΣ, ὁ, a sort of sturgeon.

ἀντ-ᾰκούω, f. ούσομαι, to hear in turn: to listen in return.

ἀντ-ακροάομαι, f. άσομαι, Dep. = ἀντακούω.

ἀντ-ᾰλᾰλάζω, f. άξω, to return a shout.

ἀντάλλαγμα, ατος, τό, that which is given or taken in exchange, an exchange. From

ἀντ-αλλάσσω, Att. -ττω, fut. ξω: aor. 1 -ήλλαξα:—to give or take in exchange:—Med. to take one thing in exchange for another.

ἀντ-ᾰμείβομαι, f. ψομαι, Med. to give or take in exchange, to exchange. 2. to give punishment in exchange for ill-conduct, to requite, punish. 3. to give words in exchange, answer. Hence

ἀντάμειψις, εως, ἡ, an exchanging.

ἀντ-ᾰμύνομαι, Med. to defend oneself against another, resist. 2. to requite.

ἀντ-αναβῐβάζω, to make go up in turn.

ἀντ-ανάγω, f. ξω, to lead up against, esp. to put out to sea against: generally to attack. 2. to bring up instead.

ἀντ-ανᾱλίσκω, f. -ανᾱλώσω, to destroy in return.

ἀντ-αναμένω, to wait instead.

ἀντ-αναπίμπλημι, to fill in turn or in opposition.

ἀντ-αναπλέκω, f. ξω, to plait in rivalry with.

ἀντ-αναπληρόω, f. ώσω, to put in as a complement.

ἀντ-άνειμι, (ἀντί, ἀνά, εἶμι ibo) to go up against.

ἀντ-ανίστημι, I. Causal. in pres. and impf., fut. and aor. 1, to set up against or instead of. II. intr. in Pass., with aor. 2 and pf. act., to rise up against.

ἀντ-άξιος, α, ον, worth just as much as, equivalent to. Hence

ἀνταξιόω, f. ώσω, to demand as an equivalent or in turn.

ἀντ-απαιτέω, f. ήσω, to demand in return.

ἀντ-απαμείβομαι, Med. to obey in turn.

ἀντ-απερύκω, to keep off in turn.

ἀντ-αποδείκνυμι, f. -δείξω, to prove in return or answer.

ἀντ-αποδίδωμι, f. -δώσω: aor. 1 ἀνταπέδωκα:—*to give back, repay.* II. *to render*, i. e. *make*, so and so. III. intr. *to answer, correspond with.* IV. *to deliver in turn: to explain in turn.* Hence

ἀνταπόδομα, ατος, τό, *requital, recompense.* And

ἀνταπόδοσις, εως, ἡ, *a giving back in turn, repayment: reward.*

ἀνταποδοῦναι, aor. 2 inf. of ἀνταποδίδωμι.

ἀντ-αποκρίνομαι, Med. *to answer again.*

ἀντ-αποκτείνω, f. -κτενῶ, *to kill in return.*

ἀντ-απολαμβάνω, f. -λήψομαι, *to receive in return.*

ἀντ-απόλλῡμι, *to destroy in return*:—Pass. and Med., with perf. 2 act. -όλωλα, *to perish in turn.*

ἀντ-αποτίνω, f. -τίσω, *to r quite.*

ἀντ-αποφαίνω, f. -φανῶ, *to shew on the other hand.*

ἀντ-άπτομαι, Ion. for ἀνθ-άπτομαι.

ἀντ-αρκέω, f. έσω, *to hold out against: to hold out.*

ἀντ-ασπάζομαι, f. άσομαι: Dep.:—*to greet in turn: to receive kindly.*

ἀνταυγέω, f. ήσω, *to reflect light, to reflect.* From

ἀντ-αυγής, ές, (ἀντί, αὐγή) *reflecting light.*

ἀντ-αυδάω, f. ήσω, *to speak against, answer.*

ἀντάω, Ion. ἀντέω, f. ήσω: aor. 1 -ήντησα: (ἄντα, ἀντί):—of persons, *to come opposite to, meet face to face:* also ἀντῆσαι μάχης, δαιτός, etc., *to meet with, take part in, partake of.*

ἀντεβόλησα, aor. 1 of ἀντιβολέω.

ἀντ-εγκαλέω, f. έσω, *to accuse in turn.*

ἀντ-εικάζω, f. άσομαι: aor. 1 -ήκασα:—*to compare in return.*

ἀν-τείνω, poët. for ἀνα-τείνω.

ἀντ-εῖπον, aor. 2 without any pres. in use, *to speak against* or *in answer, gainsay.* Cf. ἀντ-ερῶ.

ἀντ-είρομαι, Ion. for ἀντ-έρομαι.

ἀντ-εισάγω, f. ξω, *to introduce instead, substitute.*

ἀντ-εισφέρω, f. -εισοίσω, *to pay* or *contribute for another*: cf. εἰσφορά. II. *to substitute* one thing *for* another.

ἀντ-εκκλέπτω, f. ψω, *to steal away in return.*

ἀντ-εκκόπτω, f. ψω, *to knock out in return.*

ἀντ-εκπέμπω, f. ψω, *to send out in return.*

ἀντ-εκπλέω, f. -πλεύσομαι, *to sail out against.*

ἀντ-εκτείνω, f. -εκτενῶ, *to stretch out against:* hence *to compare* one *with* another.

ἀντ-εκτρέχω, f. -εκδρᾰμοῦμαι, *to sally out against.*

ἀντελαβόμην, aor. 2 med. of ἀντιλαμβάνω.

ἀντέλλοισα, Dor. for ἀντέλλουσα, part. fem. of ἀνατέλλω.

ἀντέλλω, poët. for ἀνα-τέλλω.

ἀντ-ελπίζω, fut. ίσω, Att. ιῶ, *to hope instead.*

ἀντ-εμβάλλω, f. -εμβᾰλῶ, intr. *to make an inroad in turn.*

ἀντ-εμβῐβάζω, f. άσω, *to put on board instead.*

ἀντεμπᾰγῇ, 3 sing. aor. 2 pass. subj. of sq.

ἀντ-εμπήγνυμι, f. -εμπήξω, *to stick right in.*

ἀντ-εμπίπρημι, f. -εμπρήσω, *to set on fire in return.*

ἀντ-ενδίδωμι, f. -ενδώσω, *to give way in turn.*

ἀντ-εξάγω, f. άξω, *to export instead.*

ἀντ-εξαιτέω, f. ήσω, *to demand in return.*

ἀντ-έξειμι, (εἶμι *ibo*) *to march out against.*

ἀντ-εξέρχομαι, Dep. = ἀντέξειμι.

ἀντ-εξετάζω, f. σω, *to try one by the standard of another*:—Med. *to measure oneself against another.*

ἀντ-εξιππεύω, f. σω, *to ride out against.*

ἀντεξόρμησις, εως, ἡ, (ἀντί, ἐξορμάω) *a sailing out against.*

ἀντ-επάγω, f. ξω, *to lead* or (intr.) *to advance against.*

ἀντ-επαινέω, f. έσω, *to praise in return.*

ἀντ-επανάγομαι, Med. *to put to sea against.*

ἀντ-έπειμι, *to rush upon, attack.*

ἀντ-επεξάγω, f. ξω, *to lead* or *march out against.*

ἀντ-επέξειμι, (εἶμι *ibo*) *to march out against.*

ἀντ-επεξελαύνω, f. Att. -εξελῶ, *to march out against.*

ἀντ-επεξέρχομαι, Dep. = ἀντεπέξειμι.

ἀντ-επιβουλεύω, f. σω, *to form counter-designs.*

ἀντ-επιδείκνυμι, f. δείξω, *to shew forth in turn.*

ἀντ-επιθῡμέω, f. ήσω, *to desire in turn*:—Pass., ἀντεπιθυμεῖσθαί τινος *to have* a thing *desired* from one.

ἀντ-επικουρέω, f. ήσω, *to help in return.*

ἀντ-επιμελέομαι, fut. med. ήσομαι: aor. 1 pass. -επεμελήθην: Dep.:—*to give heed in turn.*

ἀντ-επιστρᾰτεύω, f. σω, *to take the field against.*

ἀντ-επιτάσσω, f. ξω, *to enjoin in turn.*

ἀντ-επιτειχίζομαι, f. med. ίσομαι, Att. ιοῦμαι: pf. pass. -τετείχισμαι: Dep.:—*to build forts against in retaliation.*

ἀντ-επιτίθημι, fut. θήσω, *to entrust in answer.*

ἀντ-ερᾰνίζω, f. ίσω, (ἀντί, ἔρανος) *to contribute one's share in turn*:—Pass. *to be repaid.*

ἀντεραστής, οῦ, ὁ, *a rival in love.* From

ἀντ-εράω, *to love in return: to rival in love.*

ἀντ-ερείδω, f. σω, *to set firmly against, to plant firm.* II. intr. *to set oneself steadfastly against.* Hence

ἀντέρεισις, εως, ἡ, *obstinate resistance.*

ἀντ-έρομαι, Ion. -είρομαι: aor. 2 -ηρόμην: Dep.: *to ask in turn.*

ἀντ-ερύομαι, Dep. *to make equal in weight with:* hence, *to value equally with.* [ῠ]

ἀντ-ερῶ, fut. without any pres. in use: pf. ἀντείρηκα: (cf. ἀντεῖπον):—*to speak against, gainsay*:—fut. pass., οὐδὲν ἀντειρήσεται no *denial shall be given.*

ἀντ-έρως, ωτος, ὁ, *return-love, love-for-love.*

ἀντ-ερωτάω, f. ήσω, *to ask in turn.*

ἀντ-έστην, aor. 2 ind. of ἀνθίστημι.

ἀντ-ευεργετέω, f. ήσω, *to return a kindness.*

ἀντ-ευνοέω, f. ήσω, *to wish well in return.*

ἀντ-έχω or **ἀντ-ίσχω**, f. ἀνθέξω: (ἀντί, ἔχω or ἴσχω):—*to hold against;* χεῖρα κρατὸς ἀντέχειν *to hold* one's hand so as to shade one's eyes. II. intrans. *to hold out against, withstand:* absol. *to hold out:* hence *to suffice, be enough.* III. Med. *to hold out against* something: later, with gen. only, *to hold on by, hold to, cleave to.*

ἀντ-ήλιος, ον, (ἀντί, ἥλιος) *opposite the sun:* i. e.

looking east, eastern; δαίμονες ἀντήλιοι, statues of gods *facing the sun.* II. *like the sun.*

ἀντέω, Ion. for ἀντάω.

ἄντην, Adv. (ἀντί) *against, face to face.* 2. *fase to face, openly, before all.* 3. ἄντην ἔρχεσθαι to go *straight forward;* ἄντην βάλλεσθαι to be struck *in front.*

ἀντ-ήνωρ, *opos*, ὁ, ἡ. (ἀντί, ἀνήρ) *instead of a man.*

ἀντ-ηρέτης, *ου*, ὁ, (ἀντί, ἐρέτης) *one who rows against* another: generally, *a rival.*

ἀντ-ήρης, *ες*, (ἀντί) *set over against, opposite;* πληγαὶ στέρνων ἀντήρεις blows *aimed straight* at the breast.

ἀντηρίς, *ίδος*, ἡ, (ἀντερείδω) *a prop: a beam to support* the outer timbers of a ship's bow, in case of a shock.

ἀντήσειε, 3 sing. aor. 1 opt. of ἀντάω.

ἀντ-ηχέω, Dor. -ᾱχέω, f. ήσω, *to re-echo.*

'ANTI', Prep. with gen.: orig. sense *over against:* I. of Place, *opposite, before.* II. to denote worth, value, *put for, for,* Lat. *pro, instar;* ἀντὶ πολλῶν λαῶν ἐστι, he is *worth* many people: hence 1. *in return for.* 2. *for the sake of.* 3. *instead of, for.* 3. to mark comparison; ἓν ἀνθ' ἑνὸς one *set against* the other, *compared with* it. 5. with verbs of entreaty, like πρὸς with gen., *by,* Lat. *per.*

In Compos. it signifies 1. *over against,* as in ἀντί-πορος. 2. *in opposition to,* as in ἀντι-πολεμέω. 3. *one against another, mutually,* as in ἀντι-δεξιόομαι. 4. *in return,* as in ἀντι-βοηθέω. 5. *instead,* as in ἀντ-ήνωρ. 6. *equal to, like,* as in ἀντί-θεος. 7. *corresponding,* as in ἀντί-μορφος.

ἀντία, Adv. = ἄντην, properly neut. pl. of ἀντίος.

ἀντιάαν, Ep. pres. inf. of ἀντιάω.

ἀντιάασθε, -θαι, Ep. 2 pl. ind. and inf. Med. of ἀντιάω.

ἀντιάζω, f. άσω, Dor. άξω: aor. 1 ἠντίασα: (ἀντί):—*to come* or *go towards, meet,* as friend or foe. 2. of things, *to meet with, obtain.* II. *to approach with prayer, entreat.*

ἀντι-άνειρᾰ, ἡ, fem. Adj. (ἀντί, ἀνήρ) *a match for men, as good as man,* of the Amazons.

ἀντιάω, f. άσω: Ep. pres. ἀντιόω, 3 pl. imperat. ἀντιοώντων, part. ἀντιόων, όωσα, όωντες, inf. ἀντιάαν, med. ἀντιάασθαι: (ἀντί, ἀντίος):—*to meet,* as friend or foe: *to match, measure oneself with:* rarely in sense of *coming to aid.* 2. of things, *to go to meet, go in quest of,* c. gen. rei: of an arrow, *to hit:* of the gods, *to come to meet* an offering, i.e. *accept graciously of* it: so, generally, *to partake of* a thing. II. c. dat. *to meet with, light upon.* II. c. acc. *to arrange, prepare,* λέχος ἀντιόωσα.

ἀντι-βαίνω, f. -βήσομαι: aor. 2 ἀντέβην:—*to withstand, resist: to stand in the gap;* ἀντιβὰς ἐλᾶν to pull *stoutly against* the oar, *going well back.*

ἀντι-βάλλω, f. -βᾰλῶ, *to throw against* or *in turn.*

ἀντίβᾰσις, *εως*, ἡ, (ἀντιβαίνω) *resistance.*

ἀντι-βιάζομαι, f. σομαι, Dep. *to retort violence.*

ἀντιβίην, Adv. *against, with force to force.* Properly acc. fem. from

ἀντί-βιος, *α, ον,* also *ος, ον,* (ἀντί, βία) *opposing force to force;* ἀντιβίοις ἐπέεσσι with *wrangling* words: neut. ἀντίβιον, as Adv. = ἀντιβίην.

ἀντι-βλέπω, f. ψω, *to look straight at, look in the face.*

ἀντίβλεψις, *εως*, ἡ, *a looking in the face.*

ἀντι-βοηθέω, f. ήσω, *to help in turn* or *mutually.*

ἀντιβολέω, f. ήσω: aor. with double augm. ἠντεβόλησα, Ep. ἀντεβ-: (ἀντιβάλλω):—*to meet by chance, hit upon,* esp. in battle. II. *to meet with, partake of,* c. gen. rei. III. *to meet as a suppliant, entreat,* c. acc. pers. Hence

ἀντιβόλησις, *εως*, ἡ, and **ἀντιβολία**, ἡ, *an entreaty, prayer.*

ἀντι-γέγωνα, perf. with pres. sense, *to return a cry.*

ἀντι-γενεαλογέω, f. ήσω, *to rival in pedigree.*

ἀντιγνωμονέω, *to be of a different opinion.* From

ἀντι-γνώμων, *ον*, gen. *ονος*, (ἀντί, γνώμη) *of a different opinion.*

ἀντιγρᾰφεύς, *έως*, ὁ, (ἀντιγράφω) *one who keeps a counter-reckoning, a check-clerk.*

ἀντιγρᾰφή, ἡ, (ἀντιγράφω) *a reply in writing.* II. as law-term, properly *the answer* put in *by the defendant;* but also of the plaintiff, *an indictment.*

ἀντίγρᾰφος, *ον*, *copied:* hence as Subst. ἀντίγραφα, τά, *copies.* From

ἀντι-γράφω, f. ψω, *to write against* or *in answer, write back:*—Med., with pf. pass. ἀντιγέγραμμαι, *to put in as a plea, to plead against:* cf. ἀντιγραφή.

ἀντι-δάκνω, f. -δήξομαι: pf. pass. -δέδηγμαι:—*to bite at* or *in turn.*

ἀντι-δεξιόομαι, Med. *to give one another the right hand, to greet in return.*

ἀντι-δέρκομαι, Dep. = ἀντιβλέπω.

ἀντι-δέχομαι, f. ξομαι, Dep. *to receive in return.*

ἀντι-δημαγωγέω, f. ήσω, *to rival as a demagogue.*

ἀντι-διαβαίνω, f. βήσομαι, *to cross in turn.*

ἀντι-διατίθημι, f. -θήσω, *to dispose* or *arrange in turn:*—Med. *to set oneself against others, offer resistance.*

ἀντι-δῐδάσκᾰλος, ὁ, mostly in plur. of *poets who bring rival plays on the stage:* cf. sq.

ἀντι-δῐδάσκω, f. -δῐδάξω, *to teach in turn or against;* of dramatic poets, *to bring rival plays on the stage.*

ἀντι-δίδωμι, f. -δώσω, *to give in return, repay.* II. as law-term, *to offer to change fortunes with one:* cf. ἀντίδοσις.

ἀντι-διέξειμι, (εἶμι *ibo*) *to go through again.*

ἀντιδῐκέω, f. ήσω: the augm. is prefixed to the prep., impf. ἠντιδίκουν, aor. 1 ἠντιδίκησα, or with double augm., ἠντεδίκουν, ἠντεδίκησα:—*to be a defendant,* or generally, *party in a suit.* From

ἀντί-δῐκος, *ον*, (ἀντί, δίκη) *an opponent in a suit,* properly *the defendant,* but also *the plaintiff:* οἱ ἀντίδικοι *the two parties in a suit.*

ἀντι-δοκέω, f. -δοκήσω or -δόξω, *to be of a contrary opinion.*

ἀντί-δορος, ον, (ἀντί, δορά) *clothed with something instead of a skin.*

ἀντίδοσις, εως, ἡ, (ἀντιδίδωμι) *a giving in return, an exchange: repayment.* 2. at Athens, *a form, by which a citizen charged with a public charge might call upon any other citizen*, whom he thought richer than himself, *either to exchange properties*, or *submit to the charge himself.*

ἀντίδοτος, ον, (ἀντιδίδωμι) *given as a remedy against* poison: as Subst. **ἀντίδοτον**, τό, *an antidote.*

ἀντι-δουλεύω, f. σω, *to be as a slave* to another, *to be no better than a slave.*

ἀντί-δουλος, ον, *instead of a slave, no better than a slave.*

ἀντί-δουπος, ον, *resounding.*

ἀντι-δράω, f. άσω, *to do in return, retaliate, requite.*

ἀντι-δωρέομαι, f. ήσομαι, Dep. *to present in return with* a thing.

ἀντι-ζητέω, f. ήσω, *to seek in return.*

ἀντι-ζωγρέω, f. ήσω, *to save alive in turn.*

ἀντι-θάπτω, f. ψω, *to bury opposite.*

ἀντί-θεος, η, ον, *godlike, equal to the gods.*

ἀντι-θεραπεύω, f. σω, *to take care of in return.*

ἀντίθεσις, εως, ἡ, (ἀντιτίθημι) *opposition, antithesis.*

ἀντι-θέω, f. θεύσομαι, *to run against: to run a race with.*

ἀντί-θυρος, ον, (ἀντί, θύρα) *opposite the door:* as Subst. **ἀντίθυρον**, τό, *the inner part of the house opposite the door.*

ἀντι-καθέζομαι, fut. -καθεδοῦμαι: aor. 2 -καθεζόμην: Med.:—*to sit over against.*

ἀντι-καθεύδω, f. ευδήσω, *to sleep opposite to.*

ἀντι-κάθημαι, Ion. **-κάτημαι**, Dep. = ἀντικαθέζομαι.

ἀντι-καθίζω, *to set opposite*:—Med. = ἀντικαθέζομαι, *to sit opposite.*

ἀντι-καθίστημι, Ion. **ἀντι-κατίστημι**: f. -καταστήσω: I. Causal in pres., impf., fut. and aor. 1, *to lay down* or *establish instead: to set against, oppose: to set up again.* II. intr. in Pass., with aor. 2 act. ἀντέστην and pf. ἀνθέστηκα, *to be put in another's place, to succeed, supersede.* 2. *to resist.*

ἀντι-κακουργέω, *to injure in turn.*

ἀντι-καλέω, f. έσω, *to call* or *invite in turn.*

ἀντι-καταθνήσκω, aor. 2 -έθανον, *to die in turn.*

ἀντι-καταλλάσσω, Att. **-ττω**, f. ξω, *to exchange* one thing *for* another.

ἀντι-κάτημαι, **ἀντι-κατίζομαι**, **ἀντι-κατίστημι**, Ion. for ἀντι-καθ-.

ἀντί-κειμαι, f. -κείσομαι, used as Pass. of ἀντιτίθημι, *to lie opposite to.*

ἀντι-κελεύω, f. σω, *to command in turn.*

ἀντί-κεντρος, ον, (ἀντί, κέντρον) *sharp as a goad.*

ἀντι-κηδεύω, f. σω, *to take care of instead.*

ἀντι-κηρύσσω, f. ύξω, *to proclaim in answer to.*

ἀντι-κλάζω, f. -κλάγξω, *to sound in answer*:—*to sound by striking against*, τινί.

ἀντι-κνήμιον, τό, (ἀντί, κνήμη) *the shin, leg.*

ἀντι-κολακεύω, f. σω, *to flatter in turn.*

ἀντι-κομίζω, f. ίσω Att. ιῶ, *to bring back in reply.*

ἀντι-κόπτω, f. ψω, intr. *to resist, oppose.*

ἀντι-κορύσσομαι, Dep. *to take arms against.*

ἀντι-κρατέω, f. ήσω, *to hold instead.*

ἀντίκρουσις, εως, ἡ, *a striking against:* hence, *a hindrance, sudden check.* From

ἀντι-κρούω, f. σω, *to strike* or *push back, stop, hinder.* 2. intr. *to be a hindrance, stand in the way.*

ἀντικρύ and **ἄντικρυς**, Adverbs, (ἀντί, ἄντην) have generally distinct meanings: I. ἀντικρύ, *over against, right opposite.* 2. in Hom. also = ἀντικρύς, *straight on, outright, entirely.* II. **ἄντικρυς** (never in Homer), *straight, right.* 2. *outright, thoroughly, without disguise* or *reserve* 3. of Time, *straightway.*

ἀντι-κτόνος, ον, (ἀντί, κτείνω) *killing in return.*

ἀντι-κτυπέω, f. ήσω, *to clash against, re-echo.*

ἀντι-κύρω [ῡ], f. κύρσω, *to hit upon something, meet.*

ἀντι-κωμῳδέω, f. ήσω, *to ridicule in turn.*

ἀντιλαβή, ἡ, (ἀντιλαμβάνω) *a handle*, Lat. *ansa.*

ἀντι-λαγχάνω, fut. -λήξομαι: pf. ἀντείληχα:—*to draw lots for, obtain in turn.*

ἀντι-λάζομαι and -λάζυμαι, Dep. *to receive in turn.* 2. *to hold fast by: to take a share of.*

ἀντι-λακτίζω, ίσω, *to kick against.*

ἀντι-λαμβάνω, f. -λήψομαι: pf. ἀντείληφα: aor. 2 ἀντέλαβον:—*to receive instead of* or *in turn.* II. Med. c. gen., *to lay hold of:* hence, 1. *to take part with, assist.* 2. *to lay claim to.* 3. *to take part in* a thing. 4. *to take hold of for the purpose of finding fault.* 5. *to captivate, charm.* 6. *to grasp with the mind, apprehend.*

ἀντι-λάμπω, f. ψω, *to light up in turn.* II. intr. *to reflect light.*

ἀντι-λέγω, f. λέξω, *to speak against, gainsay.* Hence

ἀντιλεκτέον, verb. Adj. *one must gainsay;* and

ἀντίλεκτος, ον, *questionable, to be disputed.*

ἀντι-λέων, οντος, ὁ, (ἀντί, λέων) *lion-like.*

ἀντι-ληπτέον, verb. Adj. of ἀντιλαμβάνομαι, *one must assist* or *take part in.* II. *one must check.*

ἀντίληψις, εως, ἡ, (ἀντιλαμβάνω) *a receiving in turn.* II. (from Med.) *a laying hold of, seizure:* hence *a claim to* a thing. 2. *a hold, support: help, succour.* 3. *an attacking, attack, objection.*

ἀντιλογέω, f. ήσω, = ἀντιλέγω.

ἀντιλογία, ἡ, (ἀντιλέγω) *controversy, discussion*, Lat. *disceptatio:* generally, *opposition, resistance.*

ἀντι-λογίζομαι, Dep. *to calculate on the other hand.*

ἀντιλογικός, ή, όν, (ἀντιλέγω) *given to contradiction, disputatious.*

ἀντίλογος, ον, (ἀντιλέγω) *contradictory.*

ἀντι-λοιδορέω, f. ήσω, *to rail at* or *abuse in turn.*

ἀντίλυρος, ον, (ἀντί, λύρα) *in harmony with the lyre.*

ἀντίλυτρον, ου, τό, (ἀντί, λύτρον) *a ransom.*

ἀντι-μαίνομαι, f. -μανήσομαι, Pass. *to rave against.*

ἀντι-μανθάνω, f. -μαθήσομαι, *to learn instead.*

ἀντι-μάχομαι, f. -μαχήσομαι, Dep. *to fight against.*

ἀντι-μεθέλκω, *to drag to the opposite side.*

ἀντι-μεθίστημι, fut. -στήσω: I. Causal in pres. and impf., fut. and aor. 1, *to remove from one side to the other: to revolutionise.* II. intr. in Pass., with aor. 2 act. -μετέστην, pf. -μεθέστηκα, *to pass over to the other side, give way.*

ἀντι-μελίζω, *to rival in music.*

ἀντι-μέλλω, f. -μελλήσω *to wait and watch against.*

ἀντι-μέμφομαι, f. ψομαι, Dep. *to blame in turn, retort upon.*

ἀντι-μερίζομαι, Dep. *to impart in turn.*

ἀντι-μετρέω, f. ήσω, *to measure out in turn.*

ἀντι-μέτωπος, ον, (ἀντί, μέτωπον) *front to front, face to face.*

ἀντι-μηχᾰνάομαι, Dep. *to contrive* or *scheme against: to counteract.*

ἀντι-μίμησις, εως, ἡ, *close imitation, aping.* [μῐ]

ἀντί-μῑμος, ον, (ἀντί, μιμέομαι) *closely imitating, aping: modelled after.*

ἀντι-μῑσέω, f. ήσω, *to hate in return.*

ἀντιμισθία, ἡ, *a reward, requital.* From

ἀντί-μισθος, ον, *for* or *instead of a reward.*

ἀντι-μοιρία, ας, ἡ, (ἀντί, μοῖρα) *a compensation.*

ἀντί-μολπος, ον, (ἀντί, μολπή) *sounding against, differing in sound from:* ἀντίμολπον ἄκος ὕπνου *song*, sleep's *substitute.*

ἀντι-ναυπηγέω, f. ήσω, *to build ships against, fit out a navy against.*

ἀντι-νῑκάω, f. ήσω, *to conquer in turn.*

ἀντιξοέω, f. ήσω, *to set oneself against.* From

ἀντί-ξοος, ον, Ion. ἀντί-ξους, ουν, (ἀντί, ξέω) properly *scraped against;* hence *opposed to, hostile:* τὸ ἀντίξοον *opposition.*

ἀντίον, Adv. of ἀντίος; see ἀντίος.

ἀντίον, τό, (ἀντί) *a part of the loom.*

ἀντιόομαι, fut. med. ώσομαι: aor. 1 pass. ἠντιώθην: Dep.:—*to meet* in battle, *to resist, oppose.*

ἀντίος, α, ον, (ἀντί) *set against*, and so, I. *over against, opposite:* c. gen. *meeting, confronting.* II. *opposite, contrary.* III. as Adv., ἀντία and ἀντίον, like ἄντην and ἄντα, *opposite: against, straight at.* 2. *against one's will.*

ἀντι-οχεύομαι, Pass. *to drive against.*

ἀντιο-στᾰτέω, poët. for ἀνθίσταμαι, *to oppose.*

ἀντιόω, ἀντιόων, -όωσα, **ἀντιοώντων**, see ἀντιάω.

ἀντι-πᾰθής, ές, (ἀντί, πᾰθεῖν) *in return for suffering.* II. *of opposite feelings* or *passions.*

ἀντι-παίζω, *to play one with another.*

ἀντί-παις, παιδος, ὁ, ἡ, *like a child, no better than a child.*

ἀντίπᾰλος, ον, (ἀντί, πάλη) properly *wrestling against:* hence *antagonist, rival: matched against each other, nearly balanced: corresponding to.* II. *fighting against* the enemy. III. as Subst., ἀντίπαλος, ὁ, *a rival, adversary.* 2. *a champion.*

ἀντι-παραβάλλω, f. βαλῶ, *to hold side by side, compare closely.*

ἀντι-παραγγέλλω, f. ελῶ, *to countermand, to order in turn.* II. *to compete for a public office.*

ἀντι-παράγω, f. ξω, *to lead on against.* II. intr. *to advance against* or *parallel with.*

ἀντι-παραθέω, f. θεύσομαι, *to run past against: to outflank.*

ἀντι-παρακᾰλέω, f. έσω, *to summon in turn* or *contrariwise.*

ἀντι-παρακελεύομαι, Dep. *to exhort in turn* or *to the contrary.*

ἀντι-παραλῡπέω, f. ήσω, *to annoy in turn.*

ἀντι-παραπλέω, f. πλεύσομαι, *to sail along on the other side.*

ἀντι-παρασκευάζομαι, f. άσομαι: Dep. *to prepare oneself in turn: to arm on both sides.* Hence

ἀντι-παρασκευή, ἡ, *hostile preparation.*

ἀντι-παρατάσσω, Att. -ττω, f. ξω:—*to draw out against*, in order of battle:—Pass. *to stand in array against.*

ἀντι-παρατίθημι, *to set side by side against, compare closely.*

ἀντι-πάρειμι, (εἶμι *ibo*) *to march parallel to.*

ἀντι-παρέρχομαι, = ἀντιπάρειμι.

ἀντι-παρέχω, *to supply in turn.*

ἀντι-πάσχω, f. -πείσομαι: pf. -πέπονθα:—*to suffer* or *endure in turn:* τὸ ἀντιπεπονθός, neut. part. pf., *retaliation.*

ἀντι-παταγέω, f. ήσω, *to clatter against.*

ἀντι-πέμπω, f. ψω, *to send back an answer: to send in return.* II. *to send against.* III. *to send instead.*

ἀντι-πέραιος, α, ον, *lying over against*, esp. *beyond sea.* From

ἀντι-περαίνω, f. περανῶ, *to pierce through in turn.*

ἀντι-πέρᾱν, Ion. -πέρην, Adv. = ἀντιπέρας: also as Adj. in phrase Ἀσίαδ' ἀντιπέρην τε, Asia and *the opposite coast.*

ἀντι-πέρᾱς or -πέρα, Adv. *over against, on the other side of, opposite.* Hence

ἀντι-πέρηθεν, Adv. *from the opposite side.*

ἀντι-πέρην, Ion. for ἀντιπέραν.

ἀντι-περιλαμβάνω, f. -λήψομαι, *to embrace in turn.*

ἀντι-περιχωρέω, *to go round in turn* or *against.*

ἀντί-πετρος, ον, (ἀντί, πέτρα) *hard as stone, rocky.*

ἀντί-πηξ, ηγος, ἡ, (ἀντί, πήγνυμι) *a chest, ark.*

ἀντι-πίπτω, f. -πεσοῦμαι, *to fall against.* 2. *to strive against, resist.*

ἀντι-πλέω, f. -πλεύσομαι, *to sail against.*

ἀντι-πλήξ, ῆγος, ὁ, ἡ, (ἀντί, πλήσσω) *beaten by the storm.*

ἀντι-πληρόω, f. ώσω, *to man* ships *against* 2. *to fill up by new members.*

ἀντι-πνέω, f. πνεύσομαι, *to blow against.* Hence

ἀντίπνοος, ον, contr. **ἀντίπνους**, ουν, *blowing against, caused by adverse winds.*

ἀντι-ποθέω, f. ήσω, *to long for in turn.*

ἀντι-ποιέω, f. ήσω, *to do in return*, opp. to ἀντιἴσχω. II. Med. *to lay claim to: to contend with one for* a thing.

ἀντί-ποινος, ον, (ἀντί, ποινή) *in requital:* as Subst. ἀντίποινα, τά, = ἄποινα, *requital, retribution.*

ἀντι-πολεμέω, f. ήσω, *to wage war against one.*

ἀντι-πολέμιος, ον, = ἀντιπόλεμος.

ἀντι-πόλεμος, ον, *warring against:* οἱ ἀντιπόλεμοι *enemies.*

ἀντι-πολιορκέω, f. ήσω, *to besiege in turn.*

ἀντι-πορεύομαι, Pass., with f. med. -εύσομαι: aor. I pass. ἀντεπορεύθην:—*to advance against: march to meet* another.

ἀντι-πορθέω, f. ήσω, *to lay waste in return.*

ἀντί-πορθμος, ον, *on the opposite side of the straits.*

ἀντί-πορος, ον, *on the opposite coast, over against.*

ἀντι-πράσσω, Att. -ττω, Ion. -πρήσσω: fut. ξω: *to act against, oppose.*

ἀντι-πρεσβεύομαι, Med. *to send counter-ambassadors.*

ἀντι-πρήσσω, Ion. for ἀντι-πράσσω.

ἀντι-πρόειμι, (εἶμι ibo) *to come forward against.*

ἀντί-προικα, Adv. *for next to nothing, cheap.*

ἀντι-προκαλέομαι, Med. *to challenge in return.*

ἀντι-προσᾰμάομαι, Med. *to heap in turn.*

ἀντι-πρόσειμι, (εἶμι ibo) *to go against.*

ἀντι-προσεῖπον, aor. 2 without pres. in use, *to address in turn:* aor. pass. ἀντιπροσερρήθην.

ἀντι-προσκαλέομαι, Med. *to summon in turn.*

ἀντι-προσφέρω, f. προσοίσω, *to bring in turn.*

ἀντι-πρόσωπος, ον, (ἀντί, πρόσωπον) *with the face towards, face to face.*

ἀντι-προτείνω, f. -τενῶ, *to hold out in turn.*

ἀντί-πρῳρος, ον, (ἀντί, πρῷρα) *with the prow towards, prow to prow:* hence *fronting, face to face.*

ἀντί-πῠλος, ον, (ἀντί, πύλη) *opposite the gate.*

ἀντί-πυργος, ον, *like a tower.*

ἀντι-πυργόω, f. ώσω, *to build a tower over against:* ἀντ. πόλιν *to build up* a city *as a rival.*

ἀντιρ-ρέπω, f. ψω, *to counterpoise.* Hence

ἀντίρροπος, ον, *counterpoising.*

ἀντι-σηκόω, f. ώσω, *to weigh against, to compensate.* 2. intr. *to be equal in weight, to counterpoise;* δὶς ἀντισηκῶσαι ῥοπῇ to weigh twice as heavy. Hence

ἀντισήκωσις, εως Ion. ιος, ἡ, *a restoring the balance:* hence, *compensation, retribution.*

ἀντι-σιωπάω, f. ήσομαι, *to be silent in turn.*

ἀντι-σκευάζομαι, f. άσομαι, Dep. (ἀντί, σκευάζω) *to arrange in turn.*

ἀντ-ῐσόομαι, Pass. (ἀντί, ἰσόω) *to stand against* one *on equal terms.*

ἀντισπασμός, ὁ, (ἀντισπάω) *a convulsion.*

ἀντίσπαστος, ον, *drawn in the contrary direction:* hence *spasmodic, convulsive.* II. as Subst. ἀντίσπαστος, ὁ, *an antispastus,* a foot made up of an iambus and trochee, as Ἀλέξανδρος. From

ἀντι-σπάω, f. άσω [ᾰ], *to draw the contrary way, drag back.*

ἀντί-σταθμος, ον, (ἀντί, στάθμη) *balancing: equivalent to.*

ἀντι-στᾰσιάζω, f. άσω, *to form a party against.*

ἀντίστᾰσις, εως, ἡ, (ἀνθίσταμαι) *an opposite faction.*

ἀντι-στᾰσιώτης, ου, ὁ, *one of the opposite faction.*

ἀντιστᾰτέω, f. ήσω, *to stand against, resist:* esp. *to be a political opponent.* From

ἀντι-στάτης, ου, ὁ, (ἀνθίσταμαι) *an adversary.* [ᾰ]

ἀντ-ίστημι, Ion. for ἀνθίστημι.

ἀντιστοιχέω, f. ήσω, *to stand opposite in rows: to be ranged opposite.* From

ἀντί-στοιχος, ον, *ranged opposite in rows: standing over against.*

ἀντι-στρᾰτεύομαι, Dep. (ἀντί, στρατεύω) *to take the field, make war against.*

ἀντι-στρᾰτηγος, ὁ, *a rival general, the enemy's general:*—also the Rom. *Propraetor* or *Proconsul.*

ἀντι-στρᾰτοπεδεύω, and Med. -στρατοπεδεύομαι, (ἀντί, στρατόπεδον) *to encamp over against.*

ἀντι-στρέφω, f. ψω: pf. ἀντέστροφα:—*to turn to the other side: to retort.* II. intr. (sub. ἑαυτόν, etc.), *to turn about, face about.*

ἀντιστροφή, ἡ, (ἀντιστρέφω) *a turning back* or *about.* II. in the dance of the chorus, *the antistrophé* or *returning of the Chorus,* answering to a previous στροφή, except that they now danced from left to right instead of from right to left.

ἀντίστροφος, ον, (ἀντιστρέφω) *set over against:* τὸ ἀντίστροφον *the opposite* of a thing, or its *counterpart.* Adv. -φως, *contrariwise to.*

ἀντι-συναντάω, f. ήσω, *to meet face to face.*

ἀντι-σφαιρίζω, f. ίσω Att. ιῶ: (ἀντί, σφαῖρα):—*to play at ball against.*

ἀντισχεῖν, aor. 2 inf. of ἀντέχω.

ἀντίσχεσθε, 2 pl. aor. 2 med. imperat. of ἀντέχω.

ἀντ-ισχῡρίζω, fut. ίσω Att. ιῶ, *to strengthen against:* Med. *to maintain stoutly a contrary opinion.*

ἀντ-ίσχω, collat. form of ἀντέχω.

ἀντι-ταλαντεύω, f. εύσω, = ἀντισηκόω.

ἀντι-τᾰμεῖν, aor. 2 inf. of ἀντιτέμνω.

ἀντίταξις, εως, ἡ, *a setting in array against* another, *an opposite line of battle.* II. *opposition.* From

ἀντι-τάσσω, Att. -τάττω, fut. τάξω, *to range in battle against* another:—Pass. *to be ranged against.*

ἀντι-τείνω, f. -τενῶ, *to offer in return, repay.* II. intr. and Med. *to strive against, counteract, resist.*

ἀντι-τειχίζω, *to build a fort against.* Hence

ἀντιτείχισμα, ατος, τό, *a counter-fortification.*

ἀντι-τέμνω, f. -τεμῶ: aor. 2 ἀντέταμον:—*to cut against,* i. e. *provide a remedy* or *antidote.*

ἀντι-τεχνάομαι, Dep. *to form a counter-plan.*

ἀντιτέχνησις, εως, ἡ, *counter-manœuvring.*

ἀντί-τεχνος, ον, (ἀντί, τέχνη) *rivalling in an art* or *craft.*

ἀντι-τίθημι, f. -θήσω, *to set one against* the other, *compare, oppose:*—Pass. *to be compared* or *matched* one *against* another. II. *to place in return: give* one thing *for* another.

ἀντι-τῑμάω, f. ήσω, *to do honour to in return*:—Med. as law-term, *to fix a counter-estimate of damages*. Hence

ἀντιτίμησις, εως, ἡ, as Att. law-term, *a counter-estimate* of the penalty made by the defendant *in answer to the τίμησις* of the plaintiff.

ἀντι-τῑμωρέω, f. ήσω, *to punish in return*:—Med. *to revenge oneself on in turn*.

ἀντι-τίνω, f. τίσω, *to pay* or *suffer punishment for* a thing. II. Med. *to exact* or *inflict it* in turn.

ἀντι-τολμάω, f. ήσω, *to dare to stand against* another.

ἀντί-τολμος, ον, (αντί, τόλμα) *daring against, over-bold*.

ἀντίτομος, ον, (ἀντιτᾰμεῖν) *cut as a remedy for*: as Subst. ἀντίτομον, τό, *a remedy, antidote*.

ἀντίτονος, ον, (ἀντιτείνω) *stretched contrariwise, well-strung*.

ἀντι-τοξεύω, f. σω, *to shoot arrows in turn*.

ἀντι-τορέω, f. ήσω, *to bore right through*.

ἄντῐτος, ον, for ἀνά-τιτος, (ἀνατίνω) *requited, revenged; ἄντιτα ἔργα* works *of revenge*.

ἀντι-τρέφω, *to maintain in turn*.

ἀντι-τυγχάνω, f. -τεύξομαι: aor. 2 -έτῠχον:—*to meet with in return*.

ἀντί-τῠπος, ον, (ἀντί, τυπῆναι) *struck back, echoed; τύπος ἀντίτυπος* blow *against blow*:—*answering to, correspondent*:—as Subst., ἀντίτυπον, τό, *an antitype, exact representation*. II. act. *striking back*: hence *resisting: stubborn, obstinate: adverse; ἀντίτυπος Διός the adversary* of Jupiter.

ἀντι-τύπτω, f. ψω, *to beat in turn*.

ἀντιφερίζω, (ἀντιφέρω) *to set oneself against, match oneself with*: *to fight for a prize with*.

ἀντί-φερνος, ον, (ἀντί, φερνή) *instead of a dower*.

ἀντι-φέρω, f. ἀνοίσω, *to set against*:—Med. and Pass. ἀντιφέρομαι, *to set oneself against*.

ἀντι-φεύγω, f. -φεύξομαι, *to flee in turn*.

ἀντι-φθέγγομαι, f. -φθέγξομαι, *to return a sound, re-echo*. II. *to contradict*. Hence

ἀντίφθογγος, ον, *echoing, imitating*.

ἀντι-φιλέω, f. ήσω, *to love* or *kiss in turn*.

ἀντι-φιλονεικέω, *to strive zealously against*.

ἀντι-φιλοτιμέομαι, Pass. *to be moved by jealousy against*.

ἀντι-φιλοφρονέομαι, Dep. *to receive kindly in turn*.

ἀντι-φλέγω, f. ξω, *to light up so as to meet*.

ἀντί-φονος, ον, *in return for slaughter*. II. θάνατοι ἀντίφονοι deaths *by mutual slaughter*.

ἀντι-φορτίζομαι, f. ίσομαι, Dep. (ἀντί, φόρτος) *to import in exchange for exports*.

ἀντι-φράσσω, Att. -ττω, fut. ξω, *to block up*.

ἀντι-φῠλᾰκή, ἡ, *a watching against* one.

ἀντι-φύλᾰξ, ακος, ὁ, *a watch posted to observe* another. [ῠ]

ἀντι-φῠλάσσω, Att. -ττω, f. ξω, *to watch in turn*:—Med. *to be on one's guard against*.

ἀντιφωνέω, f. ήσω, *to sound in answer, reply*. From

ἀντί-φωνος, ον, (ἀντί, φωνή) *returning a sound, responsive to*. 2. *disagreeing with*.

ἀντι-χαίρω, *to rejoice in turn*.

ἀντι-χᾰρίζομαι, fut. ίσομαι Att. ἰοῦμαι, Dep. *to shew kindness to in turn*.

ἀντι-χειροτονέω, f. ήσω, *to vote against*.

ἀντιχορηγέω, *to be a rival choregus*. From

ἀντι-χορηγος, ὁ, *a rival choregus*.

ἀντι-χράω, aor. 1 ἀντέχρησα, *to be sufficient*.

ἀντί-χριστος, ὁ, *antichrist*.

ἀντι-ψάλλω, f. -ψᾰλῶ, *to play a stringed instrument in accompaniment*. Hence

ἀντίψαλμος, ον, *responsive*.

ἀντί-ψηφος, ον, *voting against*.

ἀντί-ψῡχος, ον, (ἀντί, ψυχή) *instead of life, given for life*.

ἀντλέω, f. ήσω, (ἄντλος) properly, *to bale out bilge-water, bale the ship*: generally, *to draw water*. II. metaph. *to drain, use to the last, exhaust*, of resources: of toil, etc., *to drain*, i. e. *bear to the last*, like Lat. *exantlare, exhaurire*: but also *to squander*.

ἄντλημα, ατος, τό, (ἀντλέω) *a vessel to draw water with*.

ἀντλία, ἡ, (ἄντλος) *the hold* of a ship. II. *bilge-water, filth*.

ἀντλίον, τό, (ἄντλος) *a bucket*.

ἌΝΤΛΟΣ, ὁ, *the hold* of a ship where the bilge-water settles, Lat. *sentīna*. II. the *bilge-water* itself; ἄντλον δέχεσθαι to let in *water*, leak; ἄντλον εἴργειν Lat. *sentinam exhaurire*, to pump it out:—poët. *the sea, sea-water*.

ἀντ-οικτείρω, *to pity in return*.

ἀντ-οικτίζω, f. σω, = ἀντοικτείρω.

ἀντολή, ἡ, poët. contr. for ἀνατολή.

ἄντομαι, Dep. only used in pres. and impf.: (ἄντα, ἀντί):—*to meet* or *light upon*. II. = ἀντιάζω, *to approach with prayers, entreat*.

ἀντ-όμνυμι, fut. -ομόσω and -ομοῦμαι: aor. 1 ἀντώμοσα:—*to swear in turn*. II. as Att. law-term, *to swear in answer*, take an ἀντωμοσία.

ἀντ-ονομάζω, f άσω, *to call by a new name*. II. *to speak in tropes*.

ἀντ-ορύσσω, f. ύξω, *to dig against, dig a countermine*.

ἀντ-οφείλω, f. -οφειλήσω, *to owe* one *a good turn*.

ἀντ-οφθαλμέω, f. ήσω, (ἀντί, ὀφθαλμός) *to look in the face, withstand, bear up against*.

ἀν-τρέπω, poët. for ἀνα-τρέπω.

ἀντριάς, άδος, ἡ, (ἄντρον) *of* or *belonging to a cave*. Νύμφαι ἀντριάδες *grot*-Nymphs.

ἄντροθε, Adv. *from a cave*. From

ἌΝΤΡΟΝ, τό, Lat. *antrum, a cave, grot, cavern*.

ἌΝΤΥΞ, ῠγος, ἡ, properly *any rounded* body, and so in Homer, 1. *the rim of the round* shield. 2. *the rail round the front of the chariot*, sometimes made double: it rose in front to a point, on which the reins might be hung:—after Hom., in plur., *the chariot itself*. 3. *the frame of the lyre*. 4. *the orbit* of the planets.

ἀντ-υποκρίνομαι, ἀντ-υπουργέω, Ion. for *ἀνθ-υπ–*.

ἀντ-ῳδός, *όν*, (*ἀντί, ἀοιδός*) *singing in answer to, responsive.*

ἀντ-ωμοσία, *ἡ*, (*ἀντ-όμνυμι*) *an oath taken by one against another:* and so as Att. law-term, *the oath taken on the one side by the plaintiff, on the other by the defendant.*

ἀντ-ωνέομαι, Dep. *to buy instead: to bid against.*

ἀντ-ωπός, *όν*, (*ἀντί, ὤψ*) *looking straight at, facing, fronting, straight opposite.*

ἀντ-ωφελέω, f. *ήσω*, *to benefit in turn:*—Pass. *to derive benefit in turn.*

ἀν-ύβριστος, *ον*, (α privat., *ὑβρίζω*) *not insulted.* II. *not insolent, decorous.*

ἀνυδρία, *ἡ*, *want of water, drought.* From

ἄν-υδρος, *ον*, (α privat., *ὕδωρ*) *wanting water:* *ἡ ἄνυδρος* (sub. *γῆ*), or *τὸ ἄνυδρον* (sub. *χωρίον*), *the region without water.*

ἀν-υμέναιος, *ον*, (α privat., *ὑμεναῖος*) *without the nuptial song, unwedded.*

ἄνυμες, Dor. for *ἤνυμεν*, 1 pl. impf. of *ἄνυμι*.

ἄνυμι, = *ἀνύω*:—Pass. *ἄνυμαι*, impf. *ἤνυτο ἔργον* the work *was finished.*

ἀν-υμνέω, f. *ήσω*, (*ἀνά, ὑμνέω*) *to praise in song.*

ἀ-νύμφευτος, *ον*, (α privat., *νυμφεύω*) *unwedded;* *ἀνύμφευτον γονὴν ἔχειν* to be born of an ill marriage.

ἄ-νυμφος, *ον*, (α privat., *νύμφη*) *not bridal, unwedded;* *ἄνυμφα γάμων ἁμιλλήματα unhallowed* embraces. II. *without bride* or *mistress.*

ἀν-υπέρβλητος, *ον*, (α privat., *ὑπερβάλλω*) *not to be surpassed* or *outdone.*

ἀν-υπεύθυνος, *ον*, (α privat., *ὑπεύθυνος*) *not liable to account, irresponsible, absolute.*

ἀν-υποδεσία, *ἡ*, **ἀνυποδετέω, ἀνυπόδετος**, *ον*, are later forms of *ἀνυποδησία, -δητέω, -δητος.*

ἀνυποδησία, *ἡ*, *a going barefoot.* From

ἀνυποδητέω, f. *ήσω*, *to go barefoot.* From

ἀν-υπόδητος, *ον*, (α privat., *ὑποδέω*) *unshod, barefoot:* also *with old shoes, ill-shod.*

ἀν-υπόδικος, *ον*, (α privat., *ὑπόδικος*) *not liable to action.*

ἀν-υπόκριτος, *ον*, (α privat., *ὑποκρίνομαι*) *undisguised, without dissimulation.*

ἀν-υπονόητος, *ον*, (α privat., *ὑπονοέω*) *unsuspected: unexpected.* II. act. *unsuspecting.*

ἀν-ύποπτος, *ον*, (α privat., *ὕποπτος*) *without suspicion*, i. e. 1. pass. *unsuspected.* 2. act. *unsuspecting.*

ἀν-υπόστατος, *ον*, (α privat., *ὑφίστημι*) *not to be withstood, irresistible.* II. *without foundation.*

ἀν-υπότακτος, *ον*, (α privat., *ὑποτάσσω*) *not made subject, unruly.*

ἀνύσειε, 3 sing. aor. 1 opt. of *ἀνύω*.

ἀνυσι-εργός, *όν*, (*ἀνύω, ἔργον*) *industrious.*

ἀνύσιμος, *ον*, (*ἀνύω*) *efficacious, effectual.*

ἄνυσις, *εως*, *ἡ*, (*ἀνύω*) *accomplishment, end.*

ἄνυσσα, Ep. for *ἤνυσα*, aor. 1 of *ἀνύω*.

ἀνυστός, *όν*, (*ἀνύω*) *to be accomplished, possible;* *σιγῇ ὡς ἀνυστόν* as silently as *possible.*

ἀνυτικός, *ή, όν*, = *ἀνύσιμος*,

ἄνυτο, Dor. for *ἤνυτο*, 3 sing. impf. pass. of *ἄνυμι*.

ἀνύτω or **ἁνύτω** [ῠ], Att. form of *ἀνύω*, only used in pres. and impf.

ἀν-υφαίνω, (*ἀνά, ὑφαίνω*) *to weave anew.*

ἀν-υψόω, f. *ώσω*, *to raise up on high.*

ἀνύω, Att. **ἀνύτω** or better **ἁνύτω** [ῠ], poët. **ἄνυμι**: f. *ἀνύσω* [ῠ]: aor. 1 *ἤνυσα*, Ep. *ἄνυσσα*: pf. *ἤνυκα*:—Pass., aor. 1 *ἠνύσθην*: pf. *ἤνυσμαι*: (*ἄνω*):—*to accomplish, complete*, Lat. *conficere;* *οὐδὲν ἤνυε he did* no *good:*—Med. *to accomplish for one's own advantage:*—Pass. *to be finished*, and of persons, *to grow up.* 2. *to make an end of, destroy.* 3. *to come to the end of a journey*, absol.; *ἀνύτειν εἰς* .., for *ἀνύτειν ὁδὸν εἰς*.., *to make one's way* to a place; also, *ἀνύτειν θάλαμον* for *ἀνύτειν εἰς θάλαμον*, *to arrive at* the chamber. 4. *to attain to, get, procure.* II. with a Partic., *οὐκ ἀνύω φθονέουσα I gain* nothing by grudging: in Att. like *φθάνω*, in the sense of doing a thing *speedily;* *ἄνυε πράττων make haste* about it; but more freq. *ἀνύσας*, with imperat., *make haste and*.., as *ἀνύσας ἄνοιγε make haste and* open, etc.: also *ἄνυε* alone, *make haste! dispatch!* III. less freq. with inf., *στρατὸς ἤνυσε περᾶν* the army *succeeded* in crossing.

ἌΝΩ, impf. *ἦνον*, *to accomplish, finish:*—Pass. *to come to an end, be finished;* esp. of a period of time, *νὺξ ἄνεται* the night *draws to its end;* *ἔτος ἀνόμενον* the *waning* year. [ᾱ]

ἄνω, Adv. (*ἀνά*) *up, upwards*, Lat. *sursum*, c. gen., *αἰθέρος ἄνω up to* ether: absol. *above, on high*, Lat. *supra.* 2. of the quarters of the heaven, *northwards*, opp. to *κάτω*, *southwards.* 3. of countries, *inland, up from the coast.* 4. of time, *formerly;* *εἰς τὸ ἄνω reckoning upwards;* *οἱ ἄνω θεοί* the gods *above*, Lat. *superi;* *οἱ ἄνω the living*, opp. to *οἱ κάτω the dead;* *ἄνω καὶ κάτω up and down, topsy-turvy*, also *up and down, to and fro, always in the same place.* II. as Prep. with gen. *above.* III. Comp. *ἀνωτέρω higher up:* as Prep., *ἀνωτέρω Σαμοῦ beyond* Samos: Sup. *ἀνωτάτω*, *highest up.*

ἀνῶ, aor. 2 subj. of *ἀνίημι*. [ᾰ]

ἄνωγα, old Ep. pf. with pres. sense, *to command, bid, order*, Lat. *jubeo:* also *to advise, urge* one to do. From *ἄνωγα* we have 1 plur. ind. *ἄνωγμεν;* imperat. *ἄνωγε* and *ἄνωχθι*, 3 sing. *ἀνωγέτω* and *ἀνώχθω*, 2 pl. *ἀνώγετε* and *ἄνωχθε;* inf. *ἀνωγέμεν:* plqpf. *ἠνώγειν*, without augm. *ἀνώγειν*, Ion. *ἠνώγεα*. There is also a 3 sing. pres. *ἀνώγει* (as if from *ἀνώγω*); whence we have an impf. *ἄνωγον*, fut. *ἀνώξω*, aor. 1 *ἤνωξα*.

ἀνώ-γαιον, *τό*, (*ἄνω, γαῖα*) properly *anything above ground: a raised building, the upper floor of a house:* used as *a dining-room*, like Lat. *coenaculum.*

ἀνῷγεν, Ep. for *ἀνέῳγεν*, 3 sing. impf. of *ἀνοίγνυμι:* but **ἄνωγεν** 3 sing. of *ἄνωγα*.

ἀνώ-γεων, ω, τό, and **ἀνώ-γεως**, ω, ὁ, ἡ, = ἀνώγαιον.

ἄνωγμεν, Ep. 1 plur. ind. of ἄνωγα.

ἀνώγω, see ἄνωγα.

ἀν-ώδῠνος, ον, (α privat., ὀδύνη) *free from pain.* II. act. *allaying pain.*

ἄνωθεν, Dor. **ἄνωθα**, Adv.* (ἄνω) of place, *from above, from heaven.* 2. *above, on high*, and so οἱ ἄνωθεν, *the living*, opp. to οἱ κάτω: c. gen., ἄνωθε γῆς *above* ground. II. of time, *from the beginning.*

ἀν-ωθέω, fut. -ωθήσω and -ώσω:—*to push up* or *forth*, of a ship, *to shove off; ἀνώσαντες πλέον* (sc. τὴν ναῦν) *they pushed off* and sailed:—Med. *to put away from oneself.*

ἀνωϊστί, Adv. of sq., *unlooked for.* [τῑ]

ἀν-ώϊστος, ον, (α privat., οἴομαι) *unlooked for, unforeseen.* II. Ion. for ἀν-οιστός, (ἀναφέρω) *referred, submitted to* a person.

ἀν-ώλεθρος, ον, (α privat., ὄλεθρος) *indestructible.*

ἀν-ώμαλος, ον, (α privat., ὁμαλός) *uneven, unequal, irregular:* τὸ ἀν. *unevenness* of ground.

ἀν-ωμοτί, Adv. of ἀνώμοτος, *without oath.*

ἀν-ώμοτος, ον, (α privat., ὄμνυμι) *unsworn, not bound by oath.* II. *not sworn to.*

ἀν-ωνόμαστος, ον, (α privat., ὀνομάζω) *not to be named, indescribable.*

ἀν-ωνῠμεί and **ἀνωνυμί**, Adv. of ἀνώνυμος.

ἀν-ώνῠμος, ον, (α privat., ὄνυμα Aeol. for ὄνομα) *without name, anonymous.* II. *nameless, inglorious.*

ἀνῶξαι, aor. 1 inf. of ἀνώγω: see ἄνωγα.

ἀνώξω, fut. of ἀνώγω: see ἄνωγα.

ἀνωρία, ἡ, *untimeliness; ἀνωρία τοῦ ἔτους the bad season* of the year, i. e. winter. From

ἄν-ωρος, ον, (α privat., ὥρα) like ἄ-ωρος, *untimely, unripe*, Lat. *immaturus.*

ἀν-ωρύομαι, Dep. (ἀνά, ὠρύομαι) *to howl aloud.*

ἀνῷσαι, Ion. for ἀνοῖσαι = Att. ἀνενέγκαι, aor. 1 act. inf. of ἀναφέρω.

ἀνώσας, ασα, αν, aor. 1 part. of ἀνωθέω.

ἀνώτατος, η, ον, Sup. formed from ἄνω, *topmost.*

ἀνωτάτω, Sup. Adv. of ἄνω, *highest up, at top.*

ἀνωτερικός, ή, όν, (ἀνωτέρω) *upper* or *higher.*

ἀνώτερον, Comp. Adv. (ἄνω) *higher up: above.*

ἀνωτέρω, Comp. Adv. of ἄνω, *higher up, above.*

ἀν-ωφελής, ές, (α privat., ὠφελέω) *useless:* also *hurtful*, like Lat. *inutilis.*

ἀν-ωφέλητος, ον, (α privat., ὠφελέω) *fruitless, unprofitable.* 2. *worthless.*

ἄνωχθι, **ἀνώχθω**, 2 and 3 sing. Ep. pf. imperat. of ἄνωγα: **ἄνωχθε**, 2 plur. of same.

ἄξαι, aor. 1 inf. of ἄγνυμι, *to break;* **ἄξαντο**, 3 pl. med.

ἄξασθε, aor. 1 imperat. med. of ἄγω, *to lead.*

Ἄ-ξεινος, ον, Ion. for ἄξενος, II. **Ἄξεινος** (sc. πόντος), ὁ, *The Axine* or *Inhospitable*, a name altered (for the omen's sake) to Εὔξεινος, *the Euxine.*

ἀξέμεναι, **ἀξέμεν**, Ep. for ἄξειν, fut. inf. act. of ἄγω.

ἄ-ξενος, Ion. **ἄ-ξεινος**, ον, (α privat., ξένος) *inhospitable: uninhabitable.*

ἄ-ξεστος, ον, (α privat., ξέω) *unhewn, unwrought.*

ἄξῃ, aor. 1 subj. of ἄγνυμι.

ἀξία, ἡ, properly fem. of ἄξιος, *the worth* or *value* of a thing: of persons, *worth, rank:* generally, a man's *due* or *deserts;* κατ' ἀξίαν according *to his desert*, ὑπέρ or παρ' ἀξίαν contrary *to his desert.*

ἀξι-άγαστος, ον, (ἄξιος, ἄγαμαι) *worth admiring, admirable.* [ἄγ]

ἀξι-άκουστος, ον, (ἄξιος, ἀκούω) *worth hearing.*

ἀξι-ακρόᾱτος, ον, (ἄξιος, ἀκροάομαι) *worth listening to.*

ἀξι-αφήγητος, Ion. **ἀξιαπήγ-**, ον, (ἄξιος, ἀφηγέομαι) *worth telling.*

ἀξι-έπαινος, ον, (ἄξιος ἐπαινέω) *praiseworthy.*

ἀξι-έραστος, ον, (ἄξιος, ἔραμαι) *worthy of love.*

ἀξίνη, ἡ, (ἄγνυμι) *an axe*, esp. for hewing wood: *a battle-axe.* [ῑ]

ἀξιο-βίωτος, ον, (ἄξιος, βιόω) *worth living for.*

ἀξιο-εργός, όν, (ἄξιος, ἔργον) *capable of work.*

ἀξιο-θαύμαστος, ον, (ἄξιος, θαυμάζω) *worthy of wonder, marvellous.*

ἀξιο-θέᾱτος, Ion. **-ητος**, ον, (ἄξιος, θεάομαι) *worth seeing.*

ἀξιό-θρηνος, ον, (ἄξιος, θρῆνος) *worthy of lamentation.*

ἀξιό-κτητος, ον, (ἄξιος, κτάομαι) *worth getting.*

ἀξιό-λογος, ον, (ἄξιος, λόγος) *worthy of mention, remarkable.* Adv. **-γως.**

ἀξιο-μᾰκάριστος, ον, (ἄξιος, μακαρίζω) *worthy to be deemed happy.*

ἀξιό-μᾰχος, ον, (ἄξιος, μάχομαι) *a match for in battle: fit to give battle.*

ἀξιο-μῑσής, ές, (ἄξιος, μῖσος) *worthy of hatred, hateful.*

ἀξιο-μνημόνευτος, ον, (ἄξιος, μνημονεύω) *worthy of mention.*

ἀξιό-νῑκος, ον, (ἄξιος, νίκη) *worthy of victory.*

ἀξιο-πενθής, ές, (ἄξιος, πένθος) *worthy of lamentation, lamentable.*

ἀξιό-πιστος, ον, (ἄξιος, πιστός) *trustworthy.*

ἀξιο-πρεπής, ές, (ἄξιος, πρέπω) *becoming, goodly.*

ἀξι-όρᾱτος, ον, (ἄξιος, ὁράω) *worth seeing.*

ἄξιος, α, ον, (ἄγω IV, *to weigh*) *of like value, worth as much as*, c. gen.; βοὸς ἄξιος *worth* an ox; πολλοῦ ἄξιον *worth* much: also c. inf., ἄξιος θανεῖν *worthy* of death, 2. absol. *worthy, goodly:* in Homer the word gives the notion of *high price:* in Att. it has also an exactly opp. sense, *not overpriced, cheap.* II. *worthy, estimable:* hence *befitting, deserving;* ἄξιός εἰμι I *deserve* to be, as ἄξιός εἰμι οἰκτείρεσθαι I *deserve* to be pitied.

ἀξιό-σκεπτος, ον, (ἄξιος, σκέπτομαι) *without considering.*

ἀξιο-σπούδαστος, ον, (ἄξιος, σπουδάζω) *worthy of zealous endeavours.*

ἀξιο-στράτηγος, ον, (ἄξιος, στρατηγός) *worthy of being general, worthy of a great general.*

ἀξιο-τέκμαρτος, ον, (ἄξιος, τεκμαίρω) *worthy of being brought in evidence, credible.*

ἀξιο-φίλητος, ον, (ἄξιος, φιλέω) *worth loving.*

ἀξιό-χρεος, ον, Ion. for sq.

ἀξιό-χρεως, εων, gen. ω: Ion. **ἀξιό-χρεος**, ον, neut. pl. ἀξιόχρεα: (ἄξιος, χρέος) *worthy of a thing*, and so *worth considering, considerable, remarkable.* 2. *serviceable, sufficient.* II. with inf. *able, sufficient to* do. III. like ἄξιος, with gen., *worthy* of a thing.

ἀξιόω, f. ώσω: pf. ἠξίωκα:—Pass., fut. ἀξιωθήσομαι, but also in med. form ἀξιώσομαι: pf. ἠξίωμαι: (ἄξιος):—*to think* or *deem worthy* of a thing: of things, *to value at* a certain rate: also absol. *to esteem, honour.* II. but mostly with inf. *to think* one *worthy* to do or be: hence 1. of others, *to think fit, expect, require*, Lat. *postulare;* ἀξιῶ κομίζεσθαι I *think* I *have a right to* receive: absol. *to make a claim.* 2. of oneself, *to think fit to do* or *be;* ἀξιῶ θανεῖν I *consent* to die; ἀξιῶ πράσσειν I *dare, determine* to do: esp. *to design, condescend* to do: so in Med., ἀξιοῦσθαι μέλειν *to deign* to care for. 3. *to think, suppose; to lay down, maintain.* Hence

ἀξίωμα, ατος, τό, *that of which one is thought worthy*, and so, *esteem, reputation, rank*, Lat. *dignitas.* II. *that which is thought fit, a decision, a purpose.* 2. in philosophy, *a self-evident proposition, an axiom.*

ἀξίως, Adv. of ἄξιος, *worthily, as becomes.*

ἀξίωσις, εως, Ion. ιος, ἡ, (ἀξιόω) *a being thought worthy: estimation, reputation, character.* II. (from Med.) *a thinking oneself worthy, a demand, claim.* III. *a thinking fit, an opinion, maxim.*

ἄξομαι, fut. med. (with pass sense) of ἄγω.

ἀξόνιος, α, ον, (ἄξων) *belonging to the axle.*

ἄξος, ὁ, Cretan word for ἀγμός.

ἀ-ξυγκρότητος, ον, for ἀσυγκ., (α privat., συγκροτέω) *not welded together by the hammer:* of rowers, *not rowing in time.*

ἀξῠλία, ἡ, (ἄξυλος) *want of wood.*

ἄ-ξῠλος, ον, (α privat., ξύλον) *unfelled, unthinned*, hence *thickly wooded.* II. *without wood, ill-wooded.*

ἀ-ξυμ-, ἀ-ξυν-, v. ἀσυμ-, ἀσυν-.

ἀ-ξύστᾰτος, ον, v. ἀσύστ-.

ἄξων, ονος, ὁ, (ἄγω) *an axle*, Lat. *axis:* also the whole *wheel:* also, *the* supposed *axis of the heavens, the pole.* II. οἱ ἄξονες, *the wooden tablets of the laws* in Athens, *made to turn upon an axis.*

ἄοζος, ὁ, *an attendant, minister*, esp. belonging to a temple. (Deriv. uncertain.)

ἀοιδή, contr. ᾠδή, ἡ, (ἀείδω) *song, a singing:* also the *subject of song:* hence *a legend, tale.*

ἀοιδιάω, poët. for ἀείδω.

ἀοίδῐμος, ον, (ἀείδω) *sung of, famous in song:* in bad sense, *notorious.*

ἀοιδο-θέτης, ου, ὁ, (ἀοιδή, τίθημι) *a lyric poet.*

ἀοιδο-πόλος, ὁ, (ἀοιδή, πολέω) *one busied with song, a poet.*

ἀοιδός, ὁ, (ἀείδω) *a singer, minstrel, bard*, Lat. *vates:* fem. *a songstress*, of the Sphinx. II. as Adj. ἀοιδός, όν, *tuneful, musical.*

ἀοιδο-τόκος, ον, *inspiring song.*

ἀ-οίκητος, ον, (α privat., οἰκέω) *uninhabited: houseless, without a home*

ἄ-οικος, ον, (α privat., οἶκος) *houseless, without home* or *country.*

ἄ-οινος, ον, (α privat., οἶνος) *without wine: not worshipped with oblations of wine:* of men, *drinking no wine, sober:* of a place, *having none.*

ἀοῖος, α, ον, Aeol. and Dor. for ἠοῖος.

ἄ-οκνος, ον, (α privat., ὄκνος) *without fear* or *hesitation, untiring, restless.* Adv. -νως.

ἀολλέα, ἀολλέας, acc. sing. and plur. of ἀολλής.

ἀολλήδην, Adv. of ἀολλής, *in a body, together.*

ἀολλής, ές, (α copul., εἴλλω) *all together, in throngs, shoals* or *crowds.* Hence

ἀολλίζω, f. ίσω, *to gather together:*—Pass. *to come together, assemble.*

ἄ-οπλος, ον, (α privat., ὅπλον) *without armour, unarmed.*

ἄορ and **ἄορ**, ἄορος, τό, (ἀείρω) *a sword*, properly *a hanger:* later, *any weapon.*

ἄορᾱς, acc. pl. for ἄορα, from ἄορ, τό, *a sword.*

ἀ-όρᾱτος, ον, (α privat., ὁράω) *unseen, invisible.*

ἀ-όριστος, ον, (α privat., ὁρίζω) *without boundaries: indefinite, indeterminate.* II. ὁ ἀόριστος (sub. χρόνος), *the aorist tense.*

ἄ-ορνος, ον, (α privat., ὄρνις) *without birds.*

ἀορτή, ἡ, (ἀείρω) *a knapsack.* II. *the aorta* or *great artery.*

ἀορτήρ, ῆρος, ὁ, (ἀείρω) *a strap over the shoulder to hang* anything to, *a belt, a sword-belt;* but also *a knapsack-strap.*

ἄορτο, Ion. for ἤορτο, 3 sing. plqpf. pass. of ἀείρω; cf. ἄωρτο.

ἀοσσέω, f. ήσω, (ἄοζος) *to help, aid.* Hence

ἀοσσητήρ, ῆρος, ὁ, *a helper, aider.*

ἄ-ουτος, ον, (α privat., οὐτάω) *not wounded, unhurt.*

ἀπαγγεῖλαι, ἀπαγγείλας, aor. 1 inf. and part. of ἀπαγγέλλω.

ἀπαγγελία, ἡ, *a report given in: a narrative, recital.* From

ἀπ-αγγέλλω, f. -ελῶ, Ion. -ελέω: aor. 1 -ήγγειλα:—Pass., aor. 1 -ηγγέλθην, aor. 2 -ηγγέλην: pf. -ήγγελμαι:—*to bring tidings, report, announce: to relate, tell:*—Med., πάλιν ἀπαγγέλλεσθαι *to bring* back *tidings.* Hence

ἀπαγγελτήρ, ῆρος, ὁ, *a messenger.*

ἄπ-αγε, Adv. *away! be gone!* Lat. *apage!* properly imperat. of ἀπάγω (sub. σεαυτόν).

ἀ-πᾱγής, ές, (α privat., παγῆναι) *not firmly fixed: of loose texture.*

ἀπ-ᾱγῐνέω, Ion. for ἀπ-άγω, esp. of paying tribute.

ἀπ-αγλαΐζω, f. ίσω Att. ιῶ, *to deprive of ornament.*

ἀπ-ᾰγορεύω, f. σω (the Att. fut. is ἀπερῶ, pf. ἀπείρηκα, aor. ἀπεῖπον):—*to forbid:* absol. *to dissuade.* II. intr. *to bid farewell to, to renounce*, c. dat.; c. part. *to give up* doing: also *to grow weary of*, 2. *to* *fail, sink, give way;* also of things, τὰ ἀπαγορεύοντα *things worn out.*

ἀπ-αγριόομαι, Pass. (ἀπό, ἄγριος) *to become wild* or *savage.*

ἀπ-αγχονίζω, f. ίσω Att. ιῶ, = ἀπάγχω.

ἀπ-άγχω, f. -άγξω, *to strangle, throttle:*—Med. *to hang oneself; to be ready to choke.*

ἀπ-άγω, f. άξω: (for the tenses, v. ἄγω):—*to lead away, carry off:*—Med. *to take away for oneself.* II. *to take home.* III. *to return what one owes, pay.* IV. as Att. law-term, *to bring before a magistrate and accuse.* 2. *to lead away to death.* V. *to lead away, perplex: to divert* from a thing. VI. as if intr. (sub. ἑαυτόν), *to make off, go away,* esp. in imperat. ἄπαγε, q. v. Hence

ἀπᾰγωγή, ἡ, *a leading* or *dragging away.* II. *a taking home.* III. *payment* of tribute. IV. as Att. law-term, *a bringing before the magistrate.*

ἀπᾰδεῖν, -έειν, Ion. for ἀφαδ-, aor. 2 inf. of ἀφανδάνω.

ἀπ-ᾴδω, f. -ᾴσομαι, *to sing out of tune:* metaph. *to dissent from: to wander away from.*

ἀπ-αείρομαι, Pass. *to depart from.*

ἀπ-αθανατίζω, *to aim at immortality.*

ἀπάθεια, ἡ, *insensibility to suffering, apathy.* From

ἀ-πᾰθής, ές, (α privat., πάθος) *without suffering, not suffering: insensible, apathetic.* 2. *unwilling to suffer, impatient of.* 3. *not having suffered, unharmed.*

ἀπαθῶς, Adv. of ἀπαθής, *without passion.*

ἀπαί, poët. for ἀπό.

ἀπαιδευσία, ὁ, *want of education, ignorance: coarseness.* II. *want of control over* a thing. From

ἀ-παίδευτος, ον, (α privat., παιδεύω) *uneducated, ignorant, boorish.* Adv. ἀπαιδεύτως ἔχειν to be *boorish.*

ἀπαιδία, ἡ, (ἄπαις) *childlessness.*

ἀπ-αιθριάζω f. άσω, (ἀπό, αἰθρία) *to drive away* [clouds], *and make fair weather.*

ἀπ-αίνῠμαι, Ep. **ἀπο-αίνυμαι,** Dep. (ἀπό, αἴνυμαι): —*to take away, withdraw: pluck off.*

ἀπαίνῠτο, 3 sing. impf. of foreg.

ἀπαιολάω, *to cheat: to perplex, confound.* From

ἀπ-αιόλη, ἡ, (ἀπό, αἰόλος) *cheating, duping, any means of cheating.*

ἀπαιόλημα, ατος, τό, *a knavish trick.*

ἀπαιρεθέω, Ion. for ἀφαιρεθῶ, aor. 1 subj. pass. of ἀφαιρέω.

ἀπ-αιρέω, Ion. for ἀφ-αιρέω.

ἀπ-αίρω, Ep. lengthd. **ἀπ-αείρω:** Ion. impf. ἀπαίρεσκον: fut. ἀπᾰρῶ: aor. 1 ἀπῆρα: pf. ἀπῆρκα:—*to lift off:* hence *to carry, take away.* II. *to lead away* an army or fleet; hence, as if intr. *to sail away, march away:* generally, *to set out, depart:* also c. gen., ἀπαίρειν χθονὸς *to depart from* the land.

ἄ-παις, ἄπαιδος, ὁ, ἡ, (α privat., παῖς) *childless:* c. gen., ἄπαις ἔρσενος γόνου *without* male *heirs.*

ἀπ-αΐσσω, Att. **-ᾴσσω,** f. ξω: Att. aor. 1 ἀπῇξε —*to rush down:* generally, *to dart away.*

ἀπ-αιτέω, f. ήσω, *to demand back,* or simply *to d mand of* one:—Pass. *to have* a thing *demanded one.* Hence

ἀπαίτησις, εως, ἡ, *a demanding back, demand.*

ἀπ-αιτίζω, f. ίσω, = **ἀπαιτέω,** *to demand back.*

ἀπ-αιωρέω, f. ήσω, *to make to hang down, suspenc* —Pass., with fut. med. -ήσομαι, *to hang down fro hover about.*

ἀπ-ακρῑβόομαι, pf. ἀπηκρίβωμαι: Pass. (ἀπό, ἀκρ βής):—*to be finished off, carefully finished:* pf. pas part. ἀπηκρῑβωμένος, *highly wrought* or *finished.*

ἀ-πάλαιστος, ον, (α privat., πᾰλαίω) *not thrown wrestling:* generally, *unconquerable.*

ἀ-πάλαιστρος, ον, (α privat., πᾰλαίστρα) *not traine in the palaestra, awkward.* II. *not customary c the palaestra.*

ἀπάλαλκε, ἀπᾰλαλκοι, 3 sing. aor. 2 ind. and op of ἀπαλέξω, but formed by redupl. from *ἀπάλκω:— Ep. inf. ἀπαλαλκέμεν.

ἀ-πάλαμνος, ον, = ἀπάλαμος, *helpless, silly.* I *unmanageable, lawless.*

ἀ-πάλᾰμος, ον, (α privat., πᾰλάμη) *without hand* or *without the use of them: helpless, lazy.* I *which cannot be helped, unmanageable.*

ἀπ-ᾰλάομαι, Pass. *to go astray, wander.*

ἀπ-αλγέω, f. ήσω, (ἀπό, ἀλγέω) *to be without sens of pain, to be past feeling.*

ἀπ-ᾰλείφω, f. ψω: pf. ἀπ-αλήλῐφα:—*to wipe o expunge,* esp. from a register.

ἀπ-ᾰλέξω, fut. -αλεξήσω: aor. 1 opt. ἀπαλεξήσαιμ Ep. aor. 2 ἀπάλαλκον, see ἀπάλαλκε: (ἀπό, ἀλέξω *to ward off* from another, c. acc. rei et gen. pers ἀπαλέξειν βέλος τινός *to ward off* a dart *from* a ma also c. acc. pers. et gen. rei, *to keep* one *from,* as ἀ τινὰ κακότητος *to keep* a man *from evil:*—Med. *defend oneself against.*

ἀπ-ᾰληθεύω, f. σω, *to speak the whole truth.*

ἀπ-αλθέομαι, f. -ήσομαι: Dep. (ἀπό, ἀλθέω) *to be thoroughly.*

ἀπαλθήσεσθον, 3 dual. fut. ind. of ἀπαλθέομαι.

ἀπαλλᾰγή, ἡ, (ἀπαλλάσσω) *deliverance, relea riddance from* a thing. II. *a removal, a vorce.* III. (from Pass.) *a going away, escap departure.*

ἀπ-αλλαξείω, Desiderat. of ἀπαλλάσσομαι, *to wi to be rid of.*

ἀπαλλάξις, εως, ἡ, = ἀπαλλαγή.

ἀπ-αλλάσσω, Att. **-ττω:** f. ξω: aor. 1 -ήλλαξ pf. -ήλλᾰχα:—*to set free, release, rid of* a thing. *to put away from, remove from:* also *to get of.* II. intrans. *to get off free, escape,* esp. w an Adv., e. g. εὖ, κακῶς ἀπαλλάσσειν: *to go aw depart.*

Pass., with fut. and aor. 1 med., ἀπαλλάξομαι, ηλλαξάμην; but also fut. pass. ἀπαλλαχθήσομ aor. 1 ἀπηλλάχθην or aor. 2 ἀπηλλάγην: pf. ἀπ λαγμαι:—*to be set free, released from* a thing, *get rid of* it. 2. *to get off*, usu. with some Adj. or Adv., e. g. καλῶς, ἀζήμιος ἀπαλλαχθῆναι *to get off* well, without injury, etc., like the intrans. Act.: hence alone, *to be let off, acquitted.* II. *to remove, depart from, go away*, hence *to depart* from life, *to be deceased; ἐκ παίδων ἀπαλλαχθῆναι* like Lat. *e pueris excedere, to come forth* from a boyish state, to become a man: *to be far removed from.* 2. *to leave off from, give over, cease.*

ἀπ-αλλοτριόω, f. ώσω: pf. -ηλλοτρίωκα: (ἀπό, ἀλλότριος):—*to estrange.*

ἀπ-ἄλοάω, poët. -αλοιάω, f. ήσω, properly *to thresh out:* hence *to bruise, crush.*

ἀπᾰλό-θριξ, τρῐχος, ὁ, ἡ, (ἀπαλός, θρίξ) *with soft hair.*

ʽΑΠΑ´ΛΟ´Σ, ή, όν, *soft, tender:* metaph. *soft, gentle: delicate.* Hence

ἀπᾰλότης, ητος, ἡ, *softness, tenderness.*

ἀπᾰλο-τρεφής, ές, (ἀπαλός, τρέφω) *well fed, plump.*

ἀπαλό-φρων, ον, (ἀπαλός, φρήν) *soft-hearted.*

ἀπᾰλά-χροος, ον, contr. -χρους, χρουν, (ἀπαλός, χρόος) *soft-skinned:* also with heterocl. gen., ἀπαλόχροος, dat. -χροΐ, etc.

ἀπαλύνω, f. ῠνῶ, (ἀπαλός) *to soften.*

ἀπ-αμαλδύνω, *to destroy utterly.*

ἀπ-αμάω, f. ήσω, *to cut off.*

ἀπ-αμβλύνω, f. ῠνῶ:—Pass., pf. ἀπήμβλυμμαι. *To blunt, dull the edge of* a thing: Pass. *to be blunted, lose its edge.*

ἀπαμβροτεῖν, inf. aor. 2 of ἀφαμαρτάνω.

ἀπ-ᾰμείβομαι, f. -αμείψομαι: aor. 1 -ημείφθην: Dep.: (ἀπό, ἀμείβω):—*to reply to, answer.*

ἀπ-αμείρω, *to deprive of share in* a thing: Pass. *to be bereft.*

ἀπ-αμελέω, f. ήσω, *to neglect utterly.*

ἀπαμμένος, η, ον, Ion. for ἀφημμένος, pf. pass. part. of ἀφάπτω.

ἀπ-αμπλακίσκω, f. ήσω: aor. 2 ἀπήμπλακον, inf. ἀπαμπλακεῖν: = ἀφαμαρτάνω.

ἀπ-ᾰμύνω, fut. ῠνῶ, *to keep off, ward off, to repulse:* —Med. *to keep off from oneself, to drive back, repel.* 2. *to defend oneself.*

ἀπ-ᾰναίνομαι: aor. 1 ἀπηνηνάμην: Dep.: *to refuse* or *reject utterly.*

ἀπ-αναισχυντέω, f. ήσω, *to be utterly shameless: to be shameless enough to do* or *say.*

ἀπ-ανᾱλίσκω, fut. -ανᾱλώσω: pf. -ανάλωκα:—*to utterly consume* or *expend.*

ἀπανάστᾰσις, εως, ἡ, (ἀπανίσταμαι) *a removing from* one place *to* another.

ἀπ-ανδρόομαι, pf. ἀπήνδρωμαι: Pass.: (ἀπό, ἀνδρός gen. of ἀνήρ):—*to become a man.*

ἀπ-άνευθε and -θεν, strengthd. for ἄνευθε, Adv. *afar off, far away.* II. as Prep. with gen. *far away from: aloof from:* but also *out from.*

ἀπ-ανήνασθαι, aor. 1 med. inf. of ἀπαναίνομαι.

ἀπ-ανθέω, f. ήσω: pf. ἀπήνθηκα:—*to leave off blooming, fade, wither.* Hence

ἀπάνθησις, εως, ἡ, *a fading, withering.*

ἀπ-ανθίζω, f. ίσω, (ἀπό, ἄνθος) *to pluck off flowers:* metaph., ματαίαν γλῶσσαν ἀπανθίζειν *to cull the flowers of* idle talk, i. e. talk as boldly as they please.

ἀπ-ανθρᾰκίζω, f. ίσω Att. ιῶ, *to broil on the coals, roast.* Hence

ἀπ-ανθρακίς, ίδος, ἡ, (ἀπό, ἄνθραξ) *a small fish for broiling.* II. *a cake baked on coals.*

ἀπ-ανθρακόω, f. ώσω, *to burn to a cinder.*

ἀπανθρωπία, ἡ, *inhumanity.* From

ἀπ-άνθρωπος, ον, *far from man, inhuman, savage.* II. *unsocial:* of countries, *uninhabited.*

ἀπ-ανίστημι, fut. -αναστήσω: I. Causal in pres. and impf., fut. and aor. 1, *to make rise up and depart, take* or *send away.* II. Pass. ἀπανίσταμαι, with intr. aor. 2 act. -έστην, pf. -έστηκα, *to arise and go away: leave one's country, emigrate.*

ἀπαντᾰχόθι, Adv. = ἀπανταχοῦ.

ἀπαντᾰχοῦ, Adv. (ἅπας) *everywhere.*

ἀπ-αντάω: Att. impf. ἀπήντων: f. ἀπαντήσομαι: aor. 1 ἀπήντησα: pf. ἀπήντηκα:—*to come* or *go to meet, encounter*, whether as friend or foe: hence *to resist.* 2. *to meet with, light* or *fall upon.* 3. of things, *to happen, come upon* one: also *to turn out well, prosper.* 4. *to go* or *come to, arrive* or *be present* at: also *to have recourse* to a thing.

ἁπάντῃ, Adv. (ἅπας) *everywhere.* II. *every-way.*

ἀπ-άντη, Dor. 3 sing. impf. of ἀπαντάω.

ἀπάντησις, εως, ἡ, (ἀπαντάω) *a meeting, encountering.*

ἀπ-αντῐκρύ, Adv. (ἀπό, ἀντῐκρύ) *right opposite.*

ἀπ-αντίον, Adv. (ἀπό, ἀντίον) *right opposite.*

ἀπ-αντλέω, f. ήσω, *to draw off* like water from a ship's hold: hence *to lighten, lessen.*

ἀπ-άντομαι, = ἀπ-αντάω.

ἀπ-ανύω, f. ύσω [ῠ], *to accomplish* or *finish entirely:* ἀπανύειν [sub. ὁδόν] *to finish* a journey.

ʼΑΠΑΞ, Adv. *once, once only, once for all*, Lat. *semel.* II. without any notion of number, after ἐπεί, ὡς, etc., like Lat. *ut semel;* ὡς ἅπαξ ἤρξατο when *once* he began.

ἅπαξ-ἅπᾱς, ᾱσα, ᾰν, mostly in plur. *all at once, all together:* in sing. *every one.*

ἅπαξ-ἁπλῶς, Adv. *in general, upon the whole.*

ἀπ-αξία, ἡ, (ἀπό, ἄξιος) *unworthiness.*

ἀπ-άξιος, ον, (ἀπό, ἄξιος) = ἀνάξιος, *unworthy of.*

ἀπ-αξιόω, f. ώσω, *to deem unworthy of one: to disclaim as unworthy, disown*, Lat. *dedignari.*

ἀπάορος, ον, Dor. for ἀπήορος.

ἄ-παππος, ον, (α privat., πάππος) *with no grandfather* or *ancestors.*

ἀπ-άπτω, Ion. for ἀφ-άπτω.

ἀ-παράβᾰτος, ον, (α privat., παραβαίνω) *not transgressed.* II. act. *not passing over to* another; *not passing away, unchangeable.*

ἀπ-ᾰραιρημένος, Ion. pf. pass. part. of ἀφ-αιρέω.

ἀ-παραίτητος, ον, (α privat., παραιτέω) *not to be turned away by prayers: not to be begged off, in-*

evitable. II. of persons, *not to be entreated, inexorable:* Adv. -τως, *inexorably.*

ἀ-παρακάλυπτος, ον, (α privat., παρακαλύπτω) *uncovered:* Adv. -τως, *undisguisedly.* [κᾰ]

ἀ-παράκλητος, ον, (α privat., παρακαλέω) *unsummoned, without being called upon.*

ἀ-παράλλακτος, ον, (α privat., παραλλάσσω) *unchangeable.*

ἀ-παραλόγιστος, ον, (α privat., παραλογίζομαι) *not to be deceived.*

ἀ-παραμύθητος, ον, (α privat., παραμυθέομαι) *not to be persuaded:* hence *incorrigible:* also *inconsolable.* II. *not to be entreated, inexorable.* [ῡ]

ἀ-παράμῡθος, ον, = ἀπαραμύθητος, *inexorable: unbending, stubborn, savage.* [Aesch. ᾱπᾰρᾰ-, like ᾱθάνατος.]

ἀπᾶραι, aor. 1 inf. of ἀπαίρω.

ἀπάραξα, Ep. aor. 1 of ἀπαράσσω.

ἀ-παρασκεύαστος, ον, (α privat., παρασκευάζω) = sq.

ἀ-παράσκευος, ον, (α privat., παρασκευή) *without preparation, unprepared.*

ἀπ-ᾰράσσω, Att. **-ττω,** fut. ξω: aor. 1 ἀπήραξα:—*to strike off: to sweep off,* Lat. *decutere.*

ἄπ-αργμα, ατος, τό, (ἀπάρχομαι) = ἀπαρχή.

ἀπ-ᾰρέσκω, f. -αρέσω, *to displease, be disagreeable to.* 2. Med. with pass. sense, οὐ νεμεσητὸν βασιλῆα ἄνδρα ἀπαρέσσασθαι one must not take it ill that a king *should be displeased.* Hence

ἀπᾰρέσσασθαι, Ep. aor. 1 med. inf. of ἀπαρέσκω.

ἀ-παρθένευτος, ον, (α privat., παρθενεύω) *unmaidenly, unfitting a maiden:* in neut. pl. as Adv.

ἀ-πάρθενος, ον, (α privat., παρθένος) *no more a maid;* νύμφην ἄνυμφον παρθένον τ' ἀπάρθενον 'virgin wife and widow'd maid.'

ἀπ-ᾰριθμέω, f. ήσω, *to count over: to reckon up.* II. *to reckon* or *pay back.* Hence

ἀπᾰρίθμησις, εως, ἡ, *a counting over.*

ἀπ-αρκέω, f. έσω, *to suffice, be sufficient.* II. intr. *to be contented, acquiesce.*

ἀπ-αρνέομαι, fut. med. ήσομαι: aor. 1 pass. ἀπηρνήθην: Dep.:—*to deny utterly, deny:*—fut. ἀπαρνηθήσεται in pass. sense, *it shall be denied.*

ἄπ-αρνος, ον, (ἀπό, ἀρνέομαι) *denying utterly;* ἄπαρνός ἐστι μὴ νοσέειν *he denies* that he is sick; c. gen., ἄπαρνος οὐδενὸς καθίστατο she *denied* nothing. II. pass. *denied, refused.*

ἀπ-αρτάω, f. ήσω: Pass., pf. -ήρτημαι:—properly, *to hang from: to hang, strangle.* II. *to take away and hang up:*—Pass. *to be in suspense.* III. *to remove, part:* then, seemingly intr. (sub. ἑαυτόν), *to remove oneself, go away.*

ἀπ-αρτί, (ἀπό, ἄρτιος) Adv. *completely:* in numbers, *exactly, just.* II. *just the reverse, quite the contrary.* III. of time, = ἀπὸ ἀρτί, for ἀπὸ τοῦ νῦν, *from now, from this time:*—*just now, even now.*

ἀπ-αρτίζω, f. ίσω Att. ιῶ, *to get ready, complete:*—Pass. *to be completed, exactly made up.*

ἀπ-αρτῐ-λογία, ἡ, (ἀπό, ἄρτιος, λόγος) *a round, full, even number* or *sum.*

ἀπαρτισμός, ὁ, (ἀπαρτίζω) *completion.*

ἀπ-ᾰρυστέον, verb. Adj. *one must draw off.* From

ἀπ-ᾰρύω, f. ύσω [ῠ], *to draw off, skim off.*

ἀπ-αρχή, ἡ, mostly used in plur. **ἀπαρχαί,** *the beginning of a sacrifice, the first part of offerings,* of the hair cut from the forehead. 2. *the firstlings* for sacrifice, *first-fruits.* From

ἀπ-άρχομαι, f. ξομαι, Dep. *to make a beginning,* esp. in sacrifice; τρίχας ἀπάρχεσθαι *to begin the sacrifice with* the hair, i. e. by cutting off the hair from the forehead and throwing it into the fire. II. c. gen. *to cut off part* of a thing *to offer it: to offer part of.* 2. *to offer the firstlings* or *first-fruits of* a thing: absol. *to begin a sacrifice.*

ἀπ-άρχω, f. ξω, *to lead the way.*

ἅ-πᾱς, ἅπᾱσα, ἅπαν, (ἅμα, πᾶς) strengthd. for πᾶς, *quite all, all together:* ἐν ἅπασι and εἰς ἅπαντα, *entirely:*—in Att. also like πᾶς in the sense of *every one,* Lat. *unusquisque.*

ἀπ-ασπαίρω, *to struggle convulsively.*

ἀπαστία, ἡ, *a fasting, fast.* From

ἄ-παστος, ον, (α privat., πάομαι) *not having tasted.*

ἀπ-ασχολέομαι, Dep. *to have no leisure.*

ἀπᾰτάω, f. ήσω: aor. 1 ἠπάτησα, Ep. ἀπ-: pf. ἠπάτηκα: (ἀπάτη):—*to cheat, trick, outwit, beguile:* like Lat. *fallere tempus, to beguile* the time:—Pass. *to be deceived, mistaken.*

ἀπ-άτερθε and **-θεν,** Adv. (ἀπό, ἄτερθε) *far apart, aloof, all alone.* II. Prep. with gen. *far from, away from.*

ἀπᾰτέω, Ion. for ἀπαταω.

ἀπᾰτεών, ῶνος, ὁ, *a cheat, rogue.* From

'ΑΠΑ'ΤΗ, ἡ, *cheating, trickery, fraud, guile, deceit:* in a less bad sense, *cunning, craft: a stratagem* in war. Hence

ἀπᾰτήλιος, ον, *deceitful, wily.*

ἀπᾰτηλός, ή, όν, = ἀπατήλιος.

ἀπάτημα, ατος, τό, (ἀπατάω) *a deceit.*

ἀπατητικός, ή, όν, (ἀπατάω) *fallacious.*

ἀ-πάτητος, ον, (α privat., πᾰτέω) *untrodden.*

ἀπ-ατῑμάζω, f. άσω, = ἀπατιμάω.

ἀπ-ατῑμάω, f. ήσω, strengthd. for ἀτιμάω, *to dishonour greatly.*

'Απατούρια, ων, τά, *the Apaturia,* a festival at Athens in the month Pyanepsion, lasting three days, during which the Athenians had their grown up sons enrolled among the citizens. (Prob. derived from πατήρ or φρατρία, with a euphon.)

ἀ-πάτωρ, ορος, ὁ, ἡ (α privat., πᾰτήρ) *fatherless, orphan: disowned by the father.*

ἀπ-αυγάζω, f. σω, *to beam with light.* Hence

ἀπαύγασμα, ατος, τό, *a reflection.*

ἀπ-αυδάω, f. ήσω, *to tell* or *bid plainly,* Lat. *edicere,* c. inf. II. *to forbid,* foll. by μή and inf., ἀπαυδῶ τινα μὴ ποιεῖν *I forbid* his doing. III. *to decline, renounce.* IV. *to deny.* V. intr. *to be wanting* rds; ἀπαυδᾶν φίλῳ, *to fail* a friend: also *to faint*, *ink*; ἀπαυδᾶν κόπῳ *to faint* with toil.

ἀπ-αυθᾱδίζομαι, f. ίσομαι: Dep. *to speak* or *act* *oldly*, *speak out*.

ἀπ-αυθημερίζω, f. ίσω, Att. ιῶ, (ἀπό, αὐθήμερος) *o do* a thing *on the same day*, *to go and return on* *same day*.

ἀπ-αυράω, only found in impf. with aor. sense, πηύρων, ἀπηύρᾱς, ἀπηύρᾱ, to which must be added he aor. 1 part. act. and med., ἀπούρας, ἀπουράμενος: (αὐράω the simple is not found):—*to take away* *rom*, *wrest from*, *rob of*, τινά τι. II. *to receive* *good* or *ill*, *to enjoy* or *suffer*: (but wherever this sense occurs, ἀπηύρα, etc., should be altered into ἐπαυρεῖ, etc.)

ἄ-παυστος, ον, (α privat., παύω) *not to be stopped* or *assuaged*: *never-ending*. II. c. gen. *never ceasing from*.

ἀπ-αύτῐκα, Adv. *forthwith*, *on the spot*.

ἀπ-αυτομολέω, f. ήσω, *to go of one's own accord*, *desert*.

ἀπᾰφίσκω, fut. ἀπαφήσω: aor. 2 ἤπαφον, part. ἀπαφών: aor. 2 med. opt. ἀπάφοιτο in act. sense:—like ἀπατάω *to cheat*, *beguile*.

ἀπ-άχθομαι, Dep. *to be hateful* or *grievous*: *to become disliked*, *incur odium*.

ἀπέβαλον, aor. 2 of ἀποβάλλω.

ἀπέβην, **ἀπέβησα**, aor. 2 and 1 of ἀποβαίνω.

ἀπέβλῐσα, aor. 1 of ἀποβλίττω.

ἀπεδᾰνός, όν, Dor. for ἠπεδανός.

ἀ-πέδῐλος, ον, (α privat., πέδῑλον) *unshod*, *barefoot*.

ἄ-πεδος, ον, (α copul., πέδον) *even*, *level*, *flat*.

ἀπεδρύφθην, aor. 1 pass. of ἀποδρύπτω.

ἀπ-έδω, see ἀπ-εσθίω.

ἀπέῃσιν, Ep. for ἀπῇ, 3 sing. pres. subj. of ἄπειμι (εἰμί *sum*).

ἀπ-έειπε, Ep. 3 sing. indic. of ἀπεῖπον.

ἀπέεργε, 3 sing. imperf. of ἀποέργω.

ἀπέθανον, aor. 2 of ἀποθνήσκω.

ἀπ-εῖδον, inf. ἀπῐδεῖν, aor. 2 without pres. in use, serving as aor. to ἀφοράω:—*to look away from other things at*, and so simply *to look at*.

ἀπείθεια, ἡ, (ἀπειθής) *disobedience*.

ἀπειθέω, f. ήσω, (ἀπειθής) *to refuse compliance*, *to be disobedient*

ἀπ-είθη, **ἀπ-είθησαν**, Ion. for ἀφ-είθη, ἀφ-είθησαν, 3 sing. and plur. aor. 1 pass. of ἀφίημι.

ἀ-πειθής, ές, (α privat., πείθομαι) *disobedient*: of ships, *unmanageable*. II. (πείθω) act. *not persuading*.

ἀπ-εικάζω, f. άσω, *to copy*, *represent*, *express by a comparison*: hence *to compare with*, *liken to*. II. ὡς ἀπεικάσαι, *to conjecture*, *ut licet conjicere*.

ἀπ-εικονίζω, (ἀπό, εἰκών) *to represent* or *portray in a statue*.

ἀπεικότως, **ἀπ-εικώς**, see ἀπεοικώς.

ἀπειλείω, Ep. for ἀπειλέω, *to threaten*.

ἀπ-ειλέω, f. ήσω, (ἀπό, εἱλέω) *to press hard*: Pass., ἀπειληθεὶς ἐς ἀπορίην, ἐς ἀναγκαίην *driven* into great straits.

ἀπειλέω, f. ήσω, (ἀπειλή) *to threaten*, Lat. *minari*: c. inf. *to threaten to* do. II. *to make boastful threats*: *to boast*, *brag*, Lat. *gloriari*. III. *to assure*, *promise*, *vow*:—Pass. *to be terrified by threats*.

ἀπειλή, ἡ, mostly in plur. ἀπειλαί, *threats*; also *boasts*, *braggart words*: in sing *a threatening*. (Deriv. uncertain.) [ᾰ]

ἀπ-ειληθείς, aor. 1 pass. part. of ἀπ-ειλέω (ἀπό, εἱλέω).

ἀπείλημα, ατος, τό, = ἀπειλή.

ἀπ-ειλημένος, pf. part. pass. of ἀπ-ειλέω (ἀπό, εἱλέω).

ἀπ-είλημμαι, perf. pass. of ἀπολαμβάνω.

ἀπειλήτην, Ep. for ἠπειλείτην, 3 dual impf of ἀπειλέω (ἀπειλή).

ἀπειλητήρ, ῆρος, ὁ, (ἀπειλέω) *a threatener*, *boaster*. Hence

ἀπειλητήριος, α, ον, *threatening*, *menacing*.

ἀπειλητής, οῦ, ὁ, = ἀπειλητήρ.

ἀπειλητικός, ή, όν, = ἀπειλητήριος.

ἀπείληφα, perf. act. of ἀπολαμβάνω.

ἄπ-ειμι, fut. ἀπέσομαι, (ἀπό, εἰμί *sum*) *to be away from*: absol. *to be away* or *absent*: of things, *to be wanting*. Hom. mostly uses impf. ἀπῆν, Ep. ἀπέην, 3 pl. ἄπεσαν, and Ep. fut. ἀπέσσομαι.

ἄπ-ειμι, (ἀπό, εἶμι *ibo*) *to go away*, *depart*: the pres. mostly as fut. *I will go*: imperat. ἄπιθι, part. ἀπιών.

ἀπειπέμεν, = ἀπειπεῖν, v. sq.

ἀπ-εῖπον: inf ἀπειπεῖν, Ep. ἀποειπεῖν: also aor. 1 ἄπειπα, med. ἀπειπάμην: fut. ἀπερῶ, pf. ἀπείρηκα: the pres. being supplied by ἀπόφημι, ἀπαγορεύω:—*to speak*, *say*, or *tell out*, *tell plainly*. II. *to forbid*, foll. by μή with inf.; ἀπεῖπον αὐτὸν μὴ ποιεῖν *I forbade* him to do: τὸ ἀπειρημένον, *a forbidden* thing. III. *to renounce*, *disown*, *give up*; ἀπείπασθαι τὸν υἱόν *to disown* his son; ἀπειπεῖν ὄψιν *to avert* a vision *by offerings*. IV. *to deny*, *refuse*. V. intrans. *to give up*, *be worn out*, *fail*: c. dat. pers. *to fail* or *be wanting to* one: ἀπειρηκέναι φίλοις *to fail* one's friends; but, ἀπειρηκέναι χρήμασι to be bankrupt:—c. part., ἀπ. καθήμενος *to be tired of* sitting.

ἀ-πείραντος, ον, (α privat., πέρας) *endless*, *boundless*.

ἀ-πείραστος, ον, (α privat., πειράζω) *inexperienced*.

ἀ-πείρᾱτος, ον, (α privat., πειράομαι) Dor. for ἀπείρητος, *untried*.

ἀπ-είργαθον, Ep. 3 sing. **ἀπο-έργαθε**, inf. **ἀπ-εργαθεῖν**, poët. aor. 2 of ἀπείργω.

ἀπ-είργω, in Herodotus mostly **ἀπ-έργω**, Ep. also ἀπο-έργω: f. ξω: aor. 1 ἀπεῖρξα: poët. aor. 2 ἀπείργαθον, Ep. ἀποέργαθον: Pass., pf. ἀπείργμαι, Ep. ἀπέργμαι:—*to keep away* or *shut out from*: *part from*: *to keep* or *hinder from*, *to keep back*: of a river, ἀπεργμένος, *shut out from* its old course. II. *to part*, *divide*, and so *to bound*, of seas and rivers, etc. III. *to shut up*, *confine*.

ἀ-πειρέσιος, α, ον, and ος, ον, lengthd. form for ἄπειρος. II. *boundless*, *endless*, *countless*.

ἀπ-είρηκα, inf. *ἀπειρηκέναι*, perf. of *ἀπεῖπον*.

ἀπ-είρημαι, perf. pass. of *ἀπεῖπον*.

ἀ-πείρητος, *ον*, also *η*, *ον*, (α privat., *πειράομαι*) *without trial*, and so I. act. *without making trial of*, or absol. *making no attempt:* also *without experience of*, *inexperienced* or *unskilled* in a thing. II. pass. *untried*, *unattempted*.

ἀπειρία, *ἡ*, (*ἄπειρος* I, *πεῖρα*) opp. to *ἐμπειρία*, *want of skill*, *inexperience*. II. (*ἄπειρος* II, *πέρας*) *infinity*.

ἀ-πείρῐτος, *ον*, Ep. for *ἀπειρέσιος*.

ἀπειρό-δακρυς, *υ*, gen. *υος*, (*ἄπειρος*, **δάκρυ**) *weeping to excess*.

ἀπειρό-δροσος, *ον*, (*ἄπειρος*, *δρόσος*) *unbedewed*.

ἀπειρό-κᾰκος, *ον*, (*ἄπειρος*, *κακός*) *inexperienced in ill:* *τὸ ἀπειρόκακον* *simplicity*. II. *unused to evil*.

ἀπειροκᾰλία, *ἡ*, *ignorance of the beautiful*, *want of taste:* in plur. *vulgarities*. From

ἀπειρό-κᾰλος, *ον*, (*ἄπειρος*, *καλός*) *without taste*, *coarse*, *vulgar*. Adv. -*λως*.

ἀπειρο-λεχής, *ές*, (*ἄπειρος*, *λέχος*) *unmarried*.

ἀπειρο-μάχης, *ου*, Dor. **-μάχας**, *α*, *ὁ* (*ἄπειρος*, *μάχη*) *untried in battle*. [ᾰ]

ἄ-πειρος, *ον*, I. (α privat., *πεῖρα*, *πειράομαι*) *without trial* or *experience of* a thing, *unused* to it: *ignorant of:* hence absol. *inexperienced*, *ignorant*. II. (α privat., *πεῖρας*, *πέρας*) like *ἀπειρέσιος*, *boundless*, *endless*, *countless*. 2. of garments, etc., *endless*, i. e. *without end* or *outlet*.

ἀ-πειροσύνη, *ἡ*, = *ἀπειρία*, *inexperience*.

ἀπειρό-τοκος, *ον*, (*ἄπειρος*, *τόκος*) *without experience of childbirth*, *not having yet brought forth*.

ἀ-πείρων, *ον*, gen. *ονος*, (α privat., *πεῖραρ*, Ep. for *πέρας*) = *ἄπειρος* II, *boundless*, *endless*, *countless*. II. (α privat, *πεῖρα*) = *ἄπειρος* I, *inexperienced*.

ἀπ-είς, Ion. for *ἀφ-είς*, aor. 2 part. of *ἀφ-ίημι*.

ἀπ-έκ, Prep. with gen. *away out of*.

ἀπ-εκδέχομαι, f. *δέξομαι*, Dep. *to expect*.

ἀπ-εκδύνω or **-δύω**, f. *δύσω* [ῡ], *to strip* clothes *off from* another. II. Med. **ἀπεκδύομαι**, fut. -*δύσομαι* [ῡ]: aor. 2 act. *ἀπεξέδῡν*, perf. *ἀπεκδέδῡκα*:—*to strip oneself; to put off one's* clothes. Hence

ἀπέκδῠσις. *εως*, *ἡ*, *a putting off* the clothes.

ἀπέκιξε. a Dor. aor. I (as if from **ἀπο-κίχω*) = *ἀπέβαλε*, *be lost*.

ἀπ-εκλανθάνομαι, Med. *to forget entirely:*—Ep. aor. 2 med. imperat. **ἀπεκλελάθεσθε** **θάμβεος** *forget entirely* your surprise.

ἀπεκλελάθεσθε, v. foreg.

ἀπ-εκρέμᾰσα, aor. I of *ἀποκρεμάννυμι*.

ἀπ-έκτᾰνον, aor. 2 of *ἀποκτείνω*.

ἀπ-έκτᾰτο, pf. pass. plqpf. of *ἀποκτείνω*.

ἀ-πέκτητος, *ον*, (α privat., *πεκτέω*) *uncombed*, *unkempt*.

ἀπ-ελαύνω: fut. *ἀπελάσω*, Att. *ἀπελῶ*: pf. *ἀπελήλακα*:—Pass., aor. I *ἀπηλάθην* [ᾰ]: pf. *ἀπελήλασμαι* and -*ᾰμαι*:—also *ἀπέλα* as imperat. of simple pres. **ἀπελάω**: Dor. aor. 2 *ἀπήλαον*:—*to drive away*, *expel*. II. *ἀπελαύνειν στρατόν*, *to lead away* an army: hence as if intr. *to march*, *go away:* also (sub. *ἵππον*), *to ride away:*—Pass. *to be driven away:* hence *to be excluded from* a thing: generally *to be far from*.

ἀπ-ελάω, = *ἀπελαύνω*.

ἀπέλεγμα, *τό*, and **ἀπελεγμός**, *ὁ*, *ill repute*. From

ἀπ-ελέγχω, f. *έγξω*, *to refute thoroughly*.

ἀ-πέλεθρος, *ον*, (α privat., *πέλεθρον*) *immeasurable:* neut. as Adv. *immeasurably far*.

ἀπέλειψα, aor. I of *ἀπολείβω*, not of *ἀπολείπω*.

ἀπελέσθαι, **ἀπελόμενος**, Ion. for *ἀφελ-*, aor. 2 med. inf. and part. of *ἀφαιρέω*.

ἀπελευθερία, *ἡ*, (*ἀπελεύθερος*) *the enfranchisement of a slave*.

ἀπελευθερικός, *ή*, *όν*, *in the condition of a freedman*. From

ἀπ-ελεύθερος, *ὁ*, *an emancipated slave*, *a freedman*, Lat. *libertus*, *libertinus*. Hence

ἀπ-ελευθερόω, f. *ώσω*, *to set free*, *emancipate*.

ἀπελήλᾰκα, pf. of *ἀπελαύνω*.

ἀπελήλῠθα, perf. of *ἀπέρχομαι*.

ἀπελθεῖν, aor. 2 act. inf. of *ἀπέρχομαι*.

ἀπ-έλκω, Ion. for *ἀφ-έλκω*.

ἀπελλάζω, Laconian for *ἐκκλησιάζω*.

ἀπ-ελπίζω, fut. *ίσω* Att. *ιῶ*, *to drive to despair*. 2. = *ἐλπίζειν ἀπό τινος* *to hope from one*.

ἀπέλου, 3 sing. old Att. impf. of **ἀπολούω** (formed from *ἀπολόω*).

ἀπ-εμέω, f. *έσω*, *to spit up*, *throw out*.

ἀπεμνήσαντο, 3 plur. aor. I med. of *ἀπομιμνήσκω*.

ἀπεμόρξατο, 3 sing. aor. I med. of *ἀπομόργνυμι*.

ἀπ-εμπολάω, f. *ήσω*, *to dispose of by sale* or *barter*. 2. *to buy and sell*, *betray*.

ἀπ-έναντι, Adv. (*ἀπό*, *ἔναντι*) *over against*, *opposite*, c. gen.: also

ἀπ-εναντίον, Adv. = *ἀπέναντι*.

ἀπ-ενᾰρίζω, f. *ίξω*, *to despoil one of his arms*.

ἀπενάσσατο, 3 sing. Ep. aor. I med. of *ἀποναίω*.

ἀπενέγκασθαι, aor. I med. inf. of *ἀποφέρω*.

ἀπένεικα, Ep. for *ἀπήνεικα* or *ἀπήνεγκα*, aor. I of *ἀπο-φέρω*: aor. I pass. inf. *ἀπενειχθῆναι*.

ἀπ-ενέπω, v. *ἀπ-εννέπω*.

ἀ-πενθής, *ές*, (α privat., *πένθος*) *free from grief*.

ἀ-πένθητος, *ον*, (α privat., *πενθέω*) *not subject to grief*.

ἀπ-ενιαυτέω, f. *ήσω*, or **ἀπ-ενιαυτίζω**, f. *ίσω*, (*ἀπό*, *ἐνιαυτός*) *to go into banishment for a year*.

ἀπ-εννέπω, *to forbid*; *ἀπεννέπω σε μὴ ποιεῖν* *I forbid* thee to do. II. *to order away from;* *ἀπεννέπειν τινὰ θαλάμων*.

ἀπ-έξ, v. *ἀπέκ*.

ἀπεοικώς, Att. **ἀπεικώς**, *υῖα*, *ός*, perf. part. of *ἀπέοικα*, *unreasonable*, *unfair*. Adv. *ἀπεικότως*.

ἀ-πέπειρος, *ον*, (α privat., *πέπειρος*) *not ripe*.

ἀπεπλάγχθην, aor. I pass. of *ἀποπλάζω*.

ἀπέπλευσα, aor. I of *ἀποπλέω*.

ἄ-πεπλος, *ον*, (α privat., *πέπλος*) *without the πέπλος* or *robe*, *clad in the tunic only*.

ἀπ-έπλω, shortd. for ἀπ-έπλωσε, which is Ion. for ἀπ-έπλευσε, 3 sing. aor. 1 act. of ἀποπλέω.

ἀπέπνευσα, aor. 1 of ἀπο πνέω.

ἀπεπτάμην, aor. 2 of ἀποπέτομαι.

ἄ-πεπτος, ον, (α privat., πέσσω, f. πέψω) *uncooked, undigested.*

ἅπερ, neut. pl. of ὅσπερ, q. v. In Att. oft. used as Adv. = ὥσπερ, *as, so as.*

ἀ-πέραντος, ον, (α privat., περαίνω) *boundless, infinite, endless.*

ἀπ-εργάζομαι, f. άσομαι: pf. ἀπείργασμαι used both in act. and pass. sense: Dep.:—*to work off, finish off;* pf. part. ἀπειργασμένος, *completely finished:* of a painter, *to fill up with colour, to represent perfectly:* generally *to form, create.* 2. *to finish a contract.* Hence

ἀπεργᾰσία, ἡ, *a finishing off, completing: a creating, causing.*

ἀπ-έργω, Ion. for ἀπείργω.

ἀπ-έρδω, f. ξω, *to bring to an end, finish.*

ἀπερ-εί, Adv. = ὡσπερεί, from ἅπερ.

ἀπ-ερείδω, *to fix firmly:*—Med., fut. ἀπερείσομαι, aor. ἀπερεισάμην, but pf. pass. ἀπερήρεισμαι:—*to fix oneself fast* upon, i. e. *to support oneself upon* a thing: *to dwell* or *insist upon,* also *to settle in* a particular part: absol. *to lean* or *bend away.*

ἀπερείσιος, ον, poët., = ἀπειρέσιος: in phrase ἀπερείσια ἄποινα, a *countless* ransom.

ἀπ-ερημόω, f. ώσω, *to make utterly desolate.*

ἀ-περιλάλητος, ον, (α privat., περιλαλέω) *not to be outdone in talking.* [ᾰ]

ἀ-περίληπτος, ον, (α privat., περιλαμβάνω) *uncircumscribed.*

ἀ-περιμέριμνος, ον, (α privat., περί, μέριμνα) *careless.* Adv. -νως, *careles-ly.*

ἀ-περίοπτος, ον, (α privat., περιόψομαι) *unregarding, reckless of.*

ἀ-περίσκεπτος, ον, (α privat., περισκέπτομαι) *inconsiderate, thoughtless, heedless.* Adv. -τως.

ἀ-περίσπαστος, ον, (α privat., περισπάω) *undistracted.* Adv. -τως, *without distraction.*

ἀ-πέρισσος, Att. -ττος, ον, (α privat., περισσός) *without superfluity, simple.*

ἀ-περίστᾰτος, ον, (α privat., περιΐσταμαι) *defenceless.*

ἀ-περίτμητος, ον, (α privat., περιτέμνω) *uncircumcised.*

ἀ-περίτροπος, ον, (α privat., περιτρέπω) *not returning:* also *not heeding.*

ἀπερρήθην, aor. 1 pass. of ἀπερῶ.

ἀπερρίγᾱσι, 3 plur. perf. 2 of ἀπορριγέω, [ῑ]

ἀπ-έρρω, *to be gone quite away:* imperat. ἄπερρε, *away, begone,* Lat. *abi in malam rem.*

ἀπ-ερυθριάω, fut. άσω [ᾱ], *to put away blushes, be past blushing.*

ἀπ-ερύκω, f. ξω, (ἀπό, ἐρύκω) *to keep off, scare away:*—Med. *to abstain, desist.* [ῡ]

ἀπ-ερύω, f. ύσω [ῠ], *to tear off from.*

ἀπ-έρχομαι, fut. -ελεύσομαι: aor. 2 -ήλῠθον, -ῆλθον: pf. -ελήλυθα:—*to go away, depart from;* ἀπέρχεσθαι εἰς.., *to go from* one place *to* another.

ἀπ-ερῶ, Ion. ἀπερέω, fut. without pres. in use: pf. ἀπείρηκα: fut. med. ἀπεροῦμαι: aor. 1 pass. ἀπερρήθην: (see ἀπεῖπον):—*to speak plainly out.* II. *to forbid;* ἀπερῶ σε μὴ πράττειν *I forbid* thee to do. III. *to renounce, disown.* IV. *to deny, refuse.* V. intr. *to give up, sink, fail:* see in ἀπεῖπον.

ἀπερωεύς, έως, ὁ, *one who thwarts.* From

ἀπ-ερωέω, f. ήσω, *to withdraw from.*

ἀπ-ερωή, ἡ, *a drawing back.* II. *a hindrance.*

ἀπερωήσειας, 2 sing. aor. 1 opt. of ἀπερωέω.

ἀπ-έρωτος, ον, (ἀπό, ἔρως) *unloving.*

ἄπες, Ion. for ἄφες, aor. 2 imperat. of ἀφίημι.

ἀπ-εσθίω, f. ἀπέδομαι: pf. ἀπεδήδοκα: aor. 1 pass. ἀπηδέσθην: *to eat* or *gnaw off: to eat up.*

ἀπ-εσκέδασα, aor. 1 of ἀποσκεδάννυμι.

ἀπ-εσσεῖται, for ἀπέσεται, 3 sing. fut. of ἄπειμι.

ἀπ-έσσουα, Lacon. for ἀπεσσύη, aor. 2 pass. of ἀποσεύω, *he is gone,* i. e. *is dead.*

ἀπ-εσσύμην, Ep. aor. 2 pass. of ἀποσεύω.

ἀπ-έστην, aor. 2 of ἀφίστημι.

ἀπεστράφατο, Ion. 3 pl. pf. pass. of ἀποστρέφω.

ἀπ-εστώ, οῦς, ἡ, (ἄπειμι *abibo*) Ion. noun, *a being away, absence:* see εὐεστώ

ἀ-πέτηλος, ον, (α privat., πέτηλον) *leafless.*

ἀπέτρᾰπον, aor. 2 of ἀποτρέπω.

ἀ-πευθής, ές, (α privat., πυνθάνομαι) *not inquired into, unknown,* Lat. *ignotus.* II act. *not inquiring, ignorant,* Lat. *ignarus.*

ἀπ-ευθύνω [ῡ], f. ὑνῶ, *to make straight again: to set up again:* metaph. *to restore: to guide, rule;* χέρας δεσμοῖς ἀπευθύνειν *to guide* the arms with chains, i. e. bind them.

ἀπευκτός, όν, (ἀπεύχομαι) *to be deprecated, abominable.*

ἀπ-ευνάζω, f. άσω, *to lull to sleep.*

ἀπεύχετος, ον, = ἀπευκτός. From

ἀπ-εύχομαι, f. ξομαι, Dep. *to wish* a thing *away, to wish that it may not happen,* Lat. *deprecari.*

ἀπ-έφθῐθον, Ep. aor. 2 of ἀποφθίνω.

ἀπέφθῐτο, 3 sing. Ep. aor. 2 pass. of ἀποφθίνω.

ἄπ-εφθος, ον, for ἄφεφθος, (ἀφ-έψω) *boiled down, refined;* ἄπ. χρυσός *refined* gold, Lat. *aurum recoctum.*

ἀπ-εχθαίρω, f. -ᾰρῶ: aor. 1 ἀπήχθηρα:—*to hate utterly.* II. *to make utterly hateful.*

ἀπ-εχθάνομαι, f. -εχθήσομαι: aor. 2 ἀπηχθόμην, inf. ἀπεχθέσθαι: pf. ἀπήχθημαι: Pass.:—*to be hated: to incur hatred* or *odium,* also *to be roused to hatred;* οὔτε τί μοι πᾶς δῆμος ἀπεχθόμενος χαλεπαίνει nor does all the people being *roused to hate against* me distress me. II. Dep. in causal sense, *to cause hatred;* λόγοι ἀπεχθανόμενοι words *that cause hatred:* c. dat. pers. *to be* or *become hateful to* one.

ἀπέχθεια, ἡ, (ἀπεχθής) *enmity, hatred;* in plur. *enmities;* δι' ἀπεχθείας τινὶ ἐλθεῖν to be hated by him, like δι' ὀργῆς ἐλθεῖν, etc.

ἀπέχθημα, *ατος*, **τό**, (ἀπεχθάνομαι) *that which is hated, the object of hate.*

ἀπ-εχθής, *ές*, (ἀπό, ἔχθος) *hateful, hostile.*

ἀπ-έχθομαι, like *ἀπ-εχθάνομαι*: Pass.: (ἀπό, ἔχθος):—*to be hated* or *hateful.*

ἀπεχθῶς. Adv. of *ἀπεχθής*; *ἀπ. ἔχειν* to be *at enmity.*

ἀπ-έχω, f. *ἀφέξω* and *ἀποσχήσω*: aor. 2 *ἀπέσχον*:—*to hold off, keep off, away from: to part*:—Med., *ἀπέχεσθαι χεῖράς τινος to hold one's* hands *off* him: but *ἀπέχεσθαι* absol. *to hold oneself off* a thing, *abstain* or *desist from,* II. intrans. *to be away* or *far from*, c. gen. loci; *τῆς πόλεως οὐ πολλὴν ὁδὸν ἀπέχει it is* not *far distant* from the city: also like Med. *to abstain from* a thing. III. *to have in full; ἀπέχειν μισθόν to have a full* reward.

ἀπ-έψω, Ion. for *ἀφ-έψω.*

ἀπέωσα, aor. 1 of *ἀπωθέω.*

ἀπ-ηγέομαι, ἀπ-ήγημα, ἀπ-ήγησις, Ion. for *ἀφ-ηγ-.*

ἀπ-ηθέω, f. *ήσω*, *to strain off, filter.*

ἀπηλάθην, aor. 1 pass. of *ἀπελαύνω.*

ἀπ-ηλεγέως, Adv. formed as if from **ἀπηλεγής, ές*, (ἀπό, ἀλέγω) *without caring for anything; μῦθον ἀπηλεγέως ἀποειπεῖν* to speak out *reckless of consequences, bluntly.*

ἀπῆλθον, aor. 2 of *ἀπέρχομαι.*

ἀπ-ηλιαστής, *οῦ, ὁ*, (ἀπό, Ἡλιαία) *one who keeps away from the* Ἡλιαία, i. e. *an enemy to law*, with allusion to *ἥλιος*, *not fond of basking in the sun.*

ἀπ-ῆλιξ, Ion. for *ἀφ-ῆλιξ.*

ἀπ-ηλιώτης (sub. *ἄνεμος*), *ου, ὁ*, (ἀπό, ἥλιος) *the east wind*, Lat. *subsolanus.*

ἀ-πήμαντος, *ον*, (α privat., *πημαίνω*) *unharmed, without misery.*

ἀπ-ήμβροτον, Ep. for *ἀφ-ήμαρτον*, aor. 2 of *ἀφαμαρτάνω.*

ἀπ-ῆμεν, 1 pl. impf. of *ἄπειμι* (*εἰμί, sum*).

ἀπημοσύνη, *ἡ*, (*ἀπήμων*) *freedom from harm, safety.*

ἀπημπόλα, 3 sing. impf. of *ἀπεμπολάω.*

ἀ-πήμων, *ον*, gen. *ονος*, (α privat., *πῆμα*) *unharmed, unhurt: without sorrow* or *suffering.* II. act. *doing no harm, safe, kindly*: of the gods, *propitious.*

ἀπήνεια, *ἡ*, (*ἀπηνής*) *harshness, roughness.*

ἀπήνη, *ἡ*, *a four-wheeled wagon*: later, *any carriage, a car, chariot.* II. like *ζεῦγος, a yoke, pair, couple.* (Deriv. unknown.)

ἀπηνήναντο, 3 pl. aor. 1 med. of *ἀπαναίνομαι.*

ἀπ-ηνής, *ές*, *harsh, rough.* See *προσ-ηνής.*

ἀπῆνθον, Dor. for *ἀπῆλθον*, aor. 2 of *ἀπέρχομαι.*

ἀπ-ήορος, Dor. and Att. **ἀπ-άορος**, Ep. **ἀπ-ήωρος**, *ον*, (ἀπό, ἀείρω) *hovering on high*, Lat. *suspensus.*

ἄ-πηρος, *ον*, (α privat., *πήρα*) *without a scrip.* II. (α privat., *πηρός*) *unmaimed.*

ἀπηύρων, **ρα**, 1 and 3 sing. impf. of *ἀπαυράω.*

ἀπ-ηχής, *ές*, (ἀπό, ἦχος) *discordant, noisy.*

ἀπήχθετο, 3 sing. aor. 2 med. of *ἀπεχθάνομαι.*

ἀπ-ήωρος, Ep. for *ἀπήορος.*

ἀπία γῆ, v. *ἄπιος.*

ἀπ-ιάλλω, Dor. or Lacon. for *ἀποπέμπω.*

ἀπ-ίημι, Ion. for *ἀφίημι.*

ἀ-πίθανος, *ον*, *not winning belief, incredible, unlikely.* II. *not persuasive.* [ῐ]

ἀπιθέω, Ep. aor. 1 *ἀπίθησα*, poët. for **ἀπειθέω**. From

ἀ-πιθής, *ές*, poët. for *ἀ-πειθής.*

ἀπιθυντήρ, *ῆρος, ὁ*, *a restorer.* From

ἀπ-ιθύνω, = *ἀπ-ευθύνω.*

ἀπ-ικνέομαι, ἀπ-ικόμην, Ion. for *ἀφικ-.*

ἀ-πινύσσω, (α privat., *πινυτός*) *to be without one's wits, to be senseless.*

ἄπιξις, Ion. for *ἄφιξις.*

ἄπιον, *τό*, (*ἄπιος*) *a pear*, Lat. *pirum.*

ἌΠΙΟΣ, *ἡ*, *a pear-tree*, Lat. *pirus.*

ἄπιος, *η, ον*, (ἀπό) *far away, far off, far,* **ἐξ ἀπίης** *γαίης* Hom. II. **Ἄπιος**, *α, ον*, *Apian*, i. e. *Peloponnesian*, said to be so called from Apis, a king of Argos, hence Ἀπία γῆ, or Ἀπία alone, *the Peloponnese*: also Ἀπίς, *ίδος, ἡ.* [The former sense has ᾰ, the latter ᾱ.]

ἀπ-ιπόω, f. *ώσω*, *to squeeze out.*

ἀπ-ισόω, f. *ώσω*, *to make equal* or *even.*

ἀπιστέω, f. *ήσω*: pf. *ἠπίστηκα*: (*ἄπιστος*):—*to disbelieve, distrust*: absol. *to be unbelieving* or *distrustful*:—Pass., with fut. med. *ἀπιστήσομαι*, *to be distrusted.* II. = *ἀπειθέω*, *to disobey.*

ἀπ-ίστημι, Ion. for *ἀφ-ίστημι.*

ἀπιστία, Ion. **-ίη**, *ἡ*, (*ἀπιστέω*) *disbelief, distrust*; *πολλὰς ἀπιστίας ἔχει* the thing admits of many *doubts.* II. *want of faith, unbelief: faithlessness.*

ἄ-πιστος, *ον*, (α privat., *πιστός*): I. pass. *not to be trusted*, and so, 1. of persons, *faithless.* 2. of things, *not credible, beyond belief.* II. act. *not believing* or *trusting, mistrustful.* 2. *not obeying.*

ἀπιστοσύνη, = *ἀπιστία.*

ἀπίστως, Adv. of *ἄπιστος*: I. act. *suspiciously.* II. pass. *beyond belief, incredibly.*

ἀπ-ισχυρίζομαι, f. *ίσομαι* Att. *ιοῦμαι*: Dep.:—*to oppose* or *resist stoutly.*

ἀπ-ίσχω, poët. for *ἀπέχω*, *to keep far away.*

ἀπ-ιτέον, verb. Adj. of *ἄπειμι*, *one must go away.*

ἀπλακέω, ἀπλακία, etc., see *ἀμπλακέω*, etc.

ἀ-πλανής, *ές*, (α privat., *πλανάομαι*) *not wandering: fixed.*

ἄ-πλαστος, *ον*, (α privat., *πλάσσω*) *not moulded*: hence *genuine, sincere.* II. (α privat., *πελάζω*) shortened for *ἀπελάστος*, *unapproachable, terrible.*

ἄ-πλατος, Ion. **ἄ-πλητος**, *ον*, (α privat., *πελάω*, poët. for *πελάζω*) shortened for **ἀπέλατος**, *unapproachable, terrible.*

ἄ-πλεκτος, *ον*, (α privat., *πλέκω*) *unplaited.*

ἄ-πλετος, *ον*, collat. form of *ἄπλατος* or of **ἄπληστος**, only used in the sense of *immense, extraordinary.*

ἄ-πλευστος, *ον*, (α privat., *πλεύσομαι* fut. of *πλέω*) *not navigable, not navigated.*

ἄ-πληκτος, *ον*, (α privat., *πλήσσω*) *unstricken*: of a horse, *needing no whip* or *spur.*

ἀπληστία, ἡ, *insatiate desire.* From

ἄ-πληστος, ον, (α privat., πίμπλημι) *not to be filled, satiate:* c. gen., ἄπλ. αἵματος *insatiate of* blood.

ἄπλοια, Ion. **ἀπλοΐη**, ἡ, (ἄπλους) *difficulty of sailing*, from stress of weather.

ἀπλοΐζομαι, Dep. (ἁπλόος) *to deal openly* or *frankly.*

ἁπλοΐς, ΐδος, ἡ, (ἁπλόος) *a single garment.*

ἁπλόος, όη, όον, contr. **ἁπλοῦς**, ῆ, οῦν, Lat. *simplex, onefold*, (opp. to διπλόος, Lat. *duplex, twofold*), *single.* II. *single-minded, simple*, and that either (in good sense) *frank, open, sincere;* or (in bad sense) *silly.* III. *simple*, opp. to *compound:* hence, *absolute, sheer.* (Derived from ἅμα, *all in one way*, as is Lat. *simplex* from *simul.*)

ἄ-πλοος, ον, contr. **ἄ-πλους**, ουν, (α privat., πλέω) *not sailing:* 1. of ships, *unfit for sea, not seaworthy.* 2. of men, *never having been at sea.* II. pass., of the sea, *closed to navigation.*

ἁπλός, ή, όν, poët. for ἁπλόος, ἁπλοῦς.

ἁπλότης, ητος, ἡ, (ἁπλόος) like Lat. *simplicitas, simplicity, plainness, frankness.*

ἁπλοῦς, ῆ, οῦν, contr. for ἁπλόος.

ἄ-πλους, ουν, contr. for ἄ-πλοος.

ἄ-πλουτος, ον, (α privat., πλοῦτος) *without riches.*

ἁπλῶς, Adv. of ἁπλοῦς, Lat. *simpliciter, simply, plainly: absolutely.* II. *in a word*, Lat. *denique.*

ἄ-πνευστος, ον, (α privat., πνεύσομαι fut. of πνέω) *without breath, breathless:* hence *lifeless.*

ἄ-πνοος, ον, contr. **ἄ-πνους**, ουν, (α privat., πνέω) *without wind, calm.* II. *without breath, lifeless*

᾿ΑΠΟ´, Prep. with Gen. only, = Lat. *AB, ABS*, whether place, time, or any object be denoted: I. of Place, implying motion *from, away from:* also *down from.* 2. without motion implied, *far from, at a distance from.* II. later of Time, *from, after, since;* ἀπὸ δείπνου γενέσθαι to have done supper. III. of Origin of all kinds, as, 1. of *descent, birth;* οὐκ ἀπὸ δρυὸς οὐδ' ἀπὸ πέτρης not *sprung from* oak or rock; ἀπὸ Σπάρτης *of* Sparta *by birth.* 2. of the *means* or *instrument;* ἀπὸ βιοῖο πέφνεν with arrow *from* his bow. 3. *of the cause* or *occasion;* ἀπὸ δικαιοσύνης *by reason of.* 4. *of* the *material* of which a thing is made; ἀπὸ ξύλου πεποιημένα made *of* wood.

As Adverb, without case, *far away:* but almost always with verbs *in tmesi.*

In Compos., 1. *from, asunder*, as in ἀποτέμνω: and hence *away from*, as in ἀποβαίνω. 2. *ceasing from*, as in ἀπαλγέω: and hence, *finishing, completing*, as in ἀπεργάζομαι. 3. *back again*, as in ἀποδίδωμι. 4. *by way of abuse*, as in ἀποκαλέω. 5. *almost* = α *priv.*, as in ἀπαυδάω, ἀπαγορεύω: also with Adjectives, as in ἀπόσιτος.

ἄπο, anastroph. for ἀπό, when it follows its noun.

ἀπο-αίνῦμαι, poët. for ἀπ-αίνυμαι, *to take away.*

ἀπο-αιρέομαι, poët. for ἀφ-αιρέομαι.

ἀπόβα, Att. for ἀπόβηθι, aor. 2 imperat. for ἀποβαίνω.

ἀποβάθρα, ἡ, *steps* or *a ladder for descending from* a ship, *the gangway.* From

ἀπο-βαίνω, f. βήσομαι: Ep. 3 sing. aor. 1 ἀπεβήσετο: aor. 2 ἀπέβην: pf. ἀποβέβηκα:—*to step off, dismount, alight* or *disembark from.* 2. *to go away, depart.* II. of events, *to issue* or *result from:* absol. *to turn out, end* or *issue* in a certain way, Lat. *evenire;* τὸ ἀπόβαινον *the issue, event;* τὰ ἀποβαίνοντα, τὰ ἀποβάντα *the results;* τὰ ἀποβησόμενα *the probable results:* also ἀποβαίνειν alone, *to turn out well, succeed.* 2. also of persons and things, with an Adj., *to turn out, prove* or *be* so and so, Lat. *evadere;* ἀποβαίνειν κοινοί *to prove* impartial. 3. of conditions, etc.; ἀποβαίνειν εἴς τι *to come at last to, end in.*

B. Causal, only in aor. 1 ἀπέβησα, *to make to dismount, disembark, land.*

ἀπο-βάλλω, f. -βαλῶ: aor. 2 ἀπέβᾰλον: pf. ἀποβέβληκα:—*to throw off from:* c. acc. only, *to throw away.* 2. *to throw away, reject:* also *to throw away, sell too cheap.* 3. *to lose.*

ἀπο-βάπτω, f. ψω, *to dip entirely.*

ἀποβάς, βᾶσα, βάν, aor. 2 part. of ἀπο-βαίνω.

ἀπόβᾰσις, εως, ἡ, (ἀποβαίνω) *a stepping off, dismounting: a disembarking, landing:* also *a landing-place.*

ἀποβῆναι, aor. 2 inf. of ἀποβαίνω.

ἀπο-βιάζομαι, f. άσομαι, Dep. *to force away:* aor. 1 pass. ἀποβιασθῆναι in pass. sense, *to be forced* away.

ἀπο-βῐβάζω: f. βιβάσω Att. -βῐβῶ:—Causal of ἀποβαίνω, *to make to get off*, esp. from a ship, *to disembark, set on land.*

ἀπο-βιβρώσκω, aor. 1 pass. ἀπεβρώθην:—*to eat off.*

ἀπο-βλάπτω, f. ψω, *to ruin utterly:*—aor. 1 pass. ἀποβλαφθῆναι, *to be robbed of.*

ἀπο-βλαστάνω, f. -βλαστήσω: aor. 2 ἀπέβλαστον: —*to shoot forth from, spring from.*

ἀπόβλεπτος, ον, *looked at, gazed on by all*, hence *admired.* From

ἀπο-βλέπω, f. ψω, *to look away from* all other objects *at* one, *to look steadfastly at, gaze at* or *upon.*

ἀπόβλητος, ον, (ἀποβάλλω) *to be thrown away* as worthless.

ἀπο-βλίσσω, Att. -ττω, f. ίσω; aor. 1 ἀπέβλῐσα:—*to cut out the comb from* the hive, *take the honey:* metaph. *to steal.*

ἀπο-βλύζω, f. σω, *to spirt out;* ἀποβλύζειν οἶνον *to spirt* or *slobber out* some wine.

ἀποβολή, ῆς, ἡ, (ἀποβάλλω) *a throwing away, losing, loss.*

ἀποβολιμαῖος, ον, (ἀποβάλλω) *apt to throw away.* II. pass. *apt to be thrown aside.*

ἀπο-βόσκομαι, Dep. *to eat up.*

ἀπο-βουκολέω, f. ήσω, *to let cattle stray:* hence *to make to lose.* 2. *to soothe, beguile.*

ἀπο-βρίζω, f. ξω, *to sleep without waking, go sound asleep.*

ἀπο-βρύχω, *to bite off from.*

ἀπο-βώμιος, *ον*, (ἀπό, βωμός) *far from an altar, godless.*

ἀπό-γαιος or **ἀπό-γειος**, *ον*, (ἀπό, γῆ) *from land, coming off land.*

ἀπο-γεισόω, *to make jut out like a coping* or *cornice.*

ἀπο-γεύω, f. *σω*, *to make* another *taste of* a thing :—Med. *to taste of* it *oneself.*

ἀπο-γεφῡρόω, f. *ώσω*, *to furnish with a bridge* or *with dykes.*

ἀπο-γηράσκω, f. *άσομαι*, *to grow old*

ἀπο-γίγνομαι, late Att. **-γίνομαι** : fut. *-γενήσομαι* : aor. 2 *ἀπεγενόμην* : pf. *ἀπογεγένημαι* :—*to be away from, have no part in.* II. absol. *to be taken away*, and so *to depart life, die* : *οἱ ἀπογενόμενοι the dead.*

ἀπο-γιγνώσκω, late Att. **-γῑνώσκω** : fut. *-γνώσομαι* : aor. 2 *ἀπέγνων* : pf. *ἀπέγνωκα* :—*to depart from a judgment, give up an intention* of doing, c. gen. : *to resolve not.* 2. *to despair.* II. c. acc. *to give up* as useless. III. as law-term, *to refuse to receive an accusation* : hence *to acquit.*

ἀπόγνοια, *ἡ*, (ἀπογιγνώσκω) *despair.*

ἀπόγονος, *ον*, (ἀπογίγνομαι) *descended* or *sprung from* : in plur. *descendants.*

ἀπογρᾰφή, *ἡ*, (ἀπογράφω) *a copy of an indictment* (γραφή) : *a deposition.* II. *a list, register*, esp. of property alleged to belong to the state, but held by a private person.

ἀπο-γράφω, f. *ψω*, *to write out, copy*, esp. *to enter in a list, register* :—Med. *to have* a thing *registered* by others, or *to register for one's own use.* II. Att. law-term, 1. *ἀπογράφειν τινά to give in a copy of the charge* against a person : esp. *to give in a list* of property alleged to belong to the state, but held by a private person. 2. *ἀπογράφειν τὰ ὑπάρχοντα to give in such a list* of property.

ἀπο-γυιόω, *to deprive* one *of the use of his limbs, to enfeeble, unnerve.*

ἀπο-γυμνάζω, f. *άσω*, *to bring into hard exercise, to ply hard.*

ἀπο-γυμνόω, f. *ώσω*, *to strip quite bare* : esp. *to strip of arms, disarm* :—Pass. *to be stript bare* :—Med. *to strip oneself.*

ἀπο-δάκνω, f. *-δήξομαι*, *to bite off a piece of*, c. gen. : absol. *to bite.*

ἀπο-δακρύω, f. *ύσω* [ῡ], *to weep much* ; c. acc. *to weep much for, lament.*

ἀποδάσμιος, *ον*, *parted off* or *from.* From

ἀποδασμός, *ὁ*, *a division, part of a whole.* From

ἀπο-δατέομαι : f. *-δάσομαι* [ᾰ], Ep. *-δάσσομαι* : aor. 1 *ἀπεδασάμην*, Ep. inf. *ἀποδάσσασθαι* :—*to portion out, apportion* II. *to part off, separate.*

ἀπο-δεῖ, Ion. **ἀπο-δέει**, impers. of *ἀποδέω.*

ἀπο-δειδίσσομαι, Dep. *to frighten away.*

ἀπο-δείκνυμι and **-ύω** : f. *-δείξω* Ion. *-δέξω* :—Pass., aor. 1 *ἀπεδείχθην* : pf. *ἀποδέδειγμαι*, Ion. *-δέδεγμαι* : I. *to point out, shew forth, make known* : hence, 1. *bring forward, shew, produce, publish* as a law. 2. *to appoint* or *assign* ; *χῶρος ἀποδεδεγμένος an appointed* place. 3. *to shew by argument, prove.* II. *to shew forth* a person or thing *as* so and so, hence, 1. *to appoint, name, create.* 2. *to make, render.* 3. *to represent as.* 4. *to prove that* a thing is. 5. c. inf. *to ordain* a thing to be : —Med. *to shew forth* something of one's own ; *ἀποδείξασθαι γνώμην to deliver* one's opinion ; *ἀποδείξασθαι ἀρετάς to display* high qualities.

ἀπο-δειλιάω, f. *άσω* [ᾱ], *to be a coward, shrink from danger.*

ἀπόδειξις, Ion. **-δέξις**, **εως**, *ἡ*, (ἀποδείκνυμι) *a shewing forth* : hence 1. *a setting forth, delivery, publication.* 2. *a shewing, proof, demonstration.* II. (from Med.) *a display, achievement, performance.*

ἀπο-δειπνίδιος, *ον*, (ἀπό, δεῖπνον) *without supper.*

ἀπο-δειροτομέω, f. *ήσω*, *to cut off by the neck, behead.*

ἀπο-δείρω, Ion. for *ἀπο-δέρω.*

ἀπο-δεκᾰτόω, f. *ώσω*, *to pay tithe of.* II. *to take tithe from, τινά.*

ἀπο-δέκομαι, Ion. for *ἀπο-δέχομαι.*

ἀποδεκτέον, verb. Adj. of *ἀποδέχομαι*, *one must receive* or *accept.*

ἀποδεκτήρ, *ῆρος*, *ὁ*, (ἀποδέχομαι) *a taker from, receiver.*

ἀποδεκτός, *όν*, (ἀποδέχομαι) *acceptable.*

ἀποδέξασθαι, aor. 1 inf. of *ἀποδέχομαι.* 2. Ion for *ἀποδείξασθαι*, aor. 1 inf. of *ἀποδείκνυμι.*

ἀπόδεξις, **εως**, *ἡ*, Ion. for *ἀπόδειξις.*

ἀπόδερμα, *ατος*, *τό*, (ἀποδέρω) *a hide stripped off.*

ἀπο-δέρω, Ion. **-δείρω** : f. *-δερῶ* : aor. 1 *ἀπέδειρα* :—*to flay* or *skin completely* ; *ἀποδέρειν τὴν κεφαλήν to scalp.* II. *to fetch the skin off one's back by flogging.*

ἀποδεχθείς, Ion. aor. 1 part. pass. of *ἀποδείκνυμι.*

ἀπο-δέχομαι, Ion. **-δέκομαι** : f. *-δέξομαι* : aor. *ἀπεδεξάμην* : pf. *-δέδεγμαι* : Dep. :—*to accept in full, accept gladly, be content with.* 2. *to accept as a proof* : *to admit, allow, approve.* 3. *to accept* as a teacher, *follow* : *ἀπ. τινός to receive from* another, *agree with* him. 4. *to take* or *understand* in a certain sense. II. *to receive back, recover.*

ἀπο-δέω, f. *-δήσω*, *to bind fast.*

ἀπο-δέω, Ion. fut. *-δεήσω* :—*to be wanting, to lack* : —impers. *ἀπο-δεῖ*, *there lacks.*

ἀποδημέω, f. *ήσω*, (ἀπόδημος) *to be away from home, to go abroad*, *ἀποδημεῖν εἰς Θετταλίαν to go and live* in Thessaly. Hence

ἀποδημητής, *οῦ*, *ὁ* ; *one who is abroad.*

ἀποδημία, *ἡ*, *a being from home, a going* or *being abroad.* From

ἀπό-δημος, *ον*, *away from home, abroad.*

ἀπο-διαιτάω, f. *ήσω*, *to decide for* a person *in an arbitration.*

ἀπο-δῐδάσκω, f. *διδάξω*, *to teach not* to do, Lat. *dedocere.*

ἀπο-διδράσκω, Ion. -διδρήσκω: f. -δράσομαι, Ion. -δρήσομαι: aor. 2 ἀπέδρην, part. ἀποδράς:—*to run away* or *off, flee from*, esp. *by stealth*. 2. in prose also c. acc., *to flee, shun*.

ἀπο-δίδωμι, f. -δώσω: aor. 1 ἀπέδωκα:—*to give back, restore*: esp. *to give back what is due*. 2. *to render, yield*, of land. 3. *to grant, allow*. 4. *to render* or *make* so and so. 5. *to deliver over, give up*, e. g. as a slave; also *to deliver* a letter, Lat. *reddere*. II. intr., εἰ τὸ ὅμοιον ἀποδιδοῖ ἐς αὔξησιν [sc. ἡ Αἴγυπτος], where it seems to be = ἐπιδίδωμι:—Med. *to give away of one's own, sell*; also *to let out for hire*.

ἀπο-δικάζω, f. άσω, *to acquit*, opp. to καταδικάζω.

ἀποδικεῖν, inf. of ἀπέδικον, poët. aor. 2 without pres. in use, *to throw off*: *to throw down*.

ἀπο-δικέω, f. ήσω, (ἀπό, δίκη) *to defend oneself on trial*.

ἀπο-δινέω, f. ήσω, *to turn* or *whirl violently about*.

ἀπο-δίομαι, Dep. (ἀπό, δίω) poët. for ἀποδιώκω.

ἀπο-διορίζω, f. ίσω, *to mark off, distinguish*.

ἀπο-διώκω, fut. διώξομαι, *to chase away*.

ἀπο-δοκεῖ, impers., (ἀπό, δοκέω) mostly with μή and inf., ἀπέδοξέ σφι μὴ πράττειν *it seemed good* to them *not* to do: absol., ὥς σφι ἀπέδοξε when *they resolved* . . .

ἀπο-δοκιμάζω, f. άσω, *to reject on proof* or *trial*, generally, *to reject*. Hence

ἀποδοκιμαστέον, verb. Adj. *one must reject*.

ἀποδόσμος, ον, (ἀποδίδωμι) *meet to be restored*.

ἄπ-οδος, Ion. for ἄφ-οδος.

ἀπόδοσις, εως, ἡ, (ἀποδίδωμι) *a giving back, restitution, return*: *repayment, payment*.

ἀποδοτέον, verb. Adj. of ἀποδίδωμι, *one must give back, refer*.

ἀποδοῦναι, aor. 2 inf. of ἀποδίδωμι.

ἀποδοχή, ἡ, (ἀποδέχομαι) *a receiving back*, opp. to ἀπόδοσις: *reception*. II. *praise, approbation*.

ἀπο-δοχμόω, f. ώσω, *to bend backwards* or *sideways*.

ἀποδραθεῖν, aor. 2 inf. of ἀποδαρθάνω.

ἀποδράς, aor. 2 part. of ἀποδιδράσκω.

ἀπόδρασις, Ion. ἀπόδρησις, εως, ἡ, (ἀποδιδράσκω) *a running away, escape*.

ἀπο-δρέπτομαι, Dep. = ἀποδρέπω.

ἀπο-δρέπω, f. ψω, *to pluck off*:—Med. *to gather for oneself*.

ἀποδρῆναι, Ion. for -δρᾶναι, aor. 2 inf. of ἀποδιδράσκω.

ἀπο-δρύπτω, f. ψω: aor. 1 ἀπέδρυψα: aor. 2 ἀπέδρυφον: aor. 1 pass. ἀπεδρύφθην:—*to scrape off, to graze by a slight wound*.

ἀποδρύφοι, 3 sing. aor. 2 opt. of ἀποδρύπτω.

ἀπο-δύνω, *to pull* or *strip off*; v. ἀποδύω. [ῡ]

ἀπ-οδύρομαι [ῡ], f. -οδυροῦμαι, *to lament bitterly*.

ἀποδύς, aor. 2 part. of ἀποδύω.

ἀποδυτήριον, τό, *an undressing room*. From

ἀπο-δύω, I. trans. in fut. ἀποδύσω, aor. 1 ἀπέδυσα, *to strip off* the arms from the slain; c. acc. pers. *to strip* another *of* his arms, etc. II. intrans. in Med., with aor. 2 act. ἀπέδυν (formed as if from ἀπόδυμι), and pf. ἀποδέδυκα:—*to strip oneself, undress*: ἀποδύεσθαι πρός τι *to strip for* a thing, *to strip and get ready for*. 2. metaph. *to put away*.

ἀπο-είκω, f. ξω, *to withdraw from*.

ἀπό-ειπον, ες, ε, Ep. for ἀπεῖπον, aor. 2 without pres. in use.

ἀπο-έργαθε, 3 sing. poët. aor. 2 of ἀπέργω, ἀπείργω, *to keep far away, keep off from*.

ἀποέργω, poët. for ἀπέργω, ἀπείργω: partic. ἀποεργμένη for ἀπεργομένη.

ἀπό-ερσε, an old Ep. aor. 1 only found in 3 pers., *to hurry* or *sweep away*, of running water; subj. ἀποέρσῃ, opt. ἀποέρσειε. (Deriv. uncertain.)

ἀπο-ζάω, f. ζήσω, *to live off*; ὅσον ἀποζῆν enough *to live off*.

ἀπο-ζεύγνῡμι and -ύω, f. -ζεύξω:—*to unyoke, part*: —Pass. *to be parted from*, τινός: absol., δεῦρ' ἀπεζύγην πόδας on foot *did I start and come* hither.

ἀπο-ζέω, f. -ζέσω, *to boil off, throw off by fermenting*.

ἀπ-όζω, fut. -οζήσω, *to smell of* something. II. impers., ἀπόζει τῆς Ἀραβίης *there comes a scent* from Arabia.

ἀπο-θάλλω, f. -θαλῶ, *to leave off blooming*.

ἀποθᾰνεῖν, aor. 2. inf. of ἀποθνήσκω.

ἀποθᾰνοῦμαι, fut. of ἀποθνήσκω.

ἀπο-θαρρέω and **ἀπο-θαρσέω**, f. ήσω, *to take courage, have full confidence*.

ἀπο-θαυμάζω, Ion. **ἀπο-θωμάζω**, f. άσω, *to wonder at* a thing: absol. *to wonder much*.

ἀπο-θείομαι, Ep. for ἀποθέωμαι, ἀποθῶμαι, aor. 2 med. subj. of ἀποτίθημι.

ἀπο-θειόω, f. ώσω, poët. for ἀποθεόω.

ἄποθεν, Adv. (ἀπό) *from afar*. II. *afar off*.

ἀπό-θεος, ον, *far from the gods*: hence *godless*.

ἀπο-θεόω, f. ώσω, *to deify*.

ἀπο-θερίζω, fut. ίσω Att. ιῶ, *to cut off like ears of corn*.

ἀποθέσθαι, aor. 2 med. inf. of ἀποτίθημι.

ἀπόθεσις, εως, ἡ, (ἀποτίθημι) *a putting off* or *away*: —*a putting away, laying up in store*:—*exposure*.

ἀπόθεστος, ον, (ἀποτίθημι) *despised, abhorred*.

ἀποθεταί, ῶν, αἱ, *a place* in Lacedæmon, *into which all misshapen children were thrown* on birth. From

ἀπόθετος, ον, (ἀποτίθημι) *laid by*; hence *hidden, mysterious, reserved*.

ἀπο-θέω, f. -θεύσομαι, *to run off* or *away*.

ἀποθήκη, ἡ, (ἀποτίθημι) *any place wherein to lay up* a thing, *a granary*: *a magazine, storehouse*. II. *anything laid by* or *stored up*; ἀποθήκην ποιεῖσθαι εἴς τινα to lay up *a store* of favour with another.

ἀπο-θησαυρίζω, f. ίσω, *to treasure* or *hoard up*.

ἀπο-θλίβω, f. ψω, *to press hard, crowd upon*. [ῑ]

ἀπο-θνήσκω, f. -θᾰνοῦμαι: aor. 2 ἀπέθανον:—*to die off, to die*, serving as Pass. to ἀποκτείνω.

ἀπο-θορεῖν, aor. 2 inf. of ἀποθρώσκω.

ἀπο-θρασύνομαι [ῡ], f. ὺνοῦμαι, *to be very bold*.

ἀπο-θραύω, f. σω, *to break off* or *from*:—Pass., ἀποθραύεσθαι τῆς εὐκλείας *to be broken off from*, i.e. *lose all*, one's fair fame.

ἀπο-θρῑάζω, f. σω, (ἀπό, θρῖον) properly, *to cut off fig-leaves*: generally, *to cut off, curtail*.

ἀπο-θρύπτω, f. ψω, *to crush in pieces*: Pass. *to be broken in spirit, enervated*.

ἀπο-θρώσκω, f. -θοροῦμαι: aor. 2 ἀπέθορον:—*to spring* or *leap off from*. II. *to leap up from, rise from*: absol. *to rise sheer up*, of steep rocks.

ἀπο-θύμιος, ον, (ἀπό, θυμός) *not according to one's mind, unpleasant, hateful*.

ἀπο-θύω, f. ύσω, *to offer up*.

ἀ-ποίητος, ον, (α privat., ποιέω) *not done, undone: not to be done*.

ἀποικέω, f. ήσω, (ἄποικος) *to go away from home, to settle in a foreign country, emigrate*. II. *to dwell afar off*, generally, *to live far away*: ἡ Κόρινθος ἐξ ἐμοῦ μακρὰν ἀπῳκεῖτο Corinth *was inhabited* far away *from* me, i. e. I settled far from Corinth. III. c. acc., = ἀποικίζω, *to colonise*. Hence

ἀποικία, ἡ, *a settling away from home, a colony, settlement*.

ἀπ-οικίζω, f. ίσω Att. ιῶ: Pass., aor. 1 ἀπῳκίσθην: pf. -ῴκισμαι:—*to send away from home, transplant*: generally, *to send* or *carry away*:—Pass. *to be settled in a far land: to emigrate*. II. *to colonise* a place.

ἀποικίς, ίδος, ἡ, fem. of ἄποικος:—ἡ ἀποικίς (sc. πόλις) *a colony*.

ἀπ-οικοδομέω, f. ήσω, *to cut off by building, to wall off, wall up*.

ἄπ-οικος, ον, (ἀπό, οἶκος) *away from home, abroad*: hence as Subst., 1. of persons, *a settler, colonist*. 2. of cities, ἄποικος (sub. πόλις), ἡ, *a colony*.

ἀπ-οικτίζομαι, fut. -ίσομαι Att. -ιοῦμαι: Dep.:—*to complain loudly*.

ἀ-ποίμαντος, ον, (α privat., ποιμαίνω) *unfed, untended*.

ἀπ-οιμώζω, fut. -οιμώξομαι, *to bewail loudly*.

ἄποινα, ων, τά, only used in plur., (α copul., ποινή) *a ransom* or *price paid*, either for life or liberty. II. generally, *compensation, repayment: reward*. Hence

ἀποινάω, f. ήσω, *to demand a ransom* or *price*:—Med. *to hold to ransom*.

ἀποινό-δῐκος, ον, (ἄποινα, δίκη) *exacting the penalty: atoning*.

ἀπ-οϊστεύω, f. εύσω, *to kill with arrows*.

ἀποίσω, fut. of ἀποφέρω: cf. φέρω.

ἀπ-οίχομαι, fut. -οιχήσομαι: pf. -ῴχημαι: Dep.:—*to be gone away, to be far from*: absol. *to be gone, to have departed*: hence *to be dead and gone*. II. more rarely, *to go away, withdraw from*.

ἀπο-καθαίρω, fut. -ᾰρῶ, *to clear off, cleanse*:—Pass. *to be removed by cleansing*. Hence

ἀποκάθαρσις, εως, ἡ, *a lustration, expiation: a purging off*.

ἀπο-κάθημαι, Ion. **-κάτημαι**, Pass. *to sit apart*.

ἀπο-καθίζω, fut. ίσω, *to set down*:—Med. *to sit down*.

ἀπο-καθιστάνω and **ἀπο-καθίστημι**, fut. -καταστήσω: I. Causal in pres. and impf., fut. and aor. 1, *to reëstablish, restore*. II. intr. in Pass., with aor. 2 and pf. act., *to be restored*.

ἀπο-καίνῠμαι, Pass. *to surpass, excel*

ἀπο-καίρῐος, ον, = ἄκαιρος.

ἀπο-καίω, fut. -καύσω, *to burn off*: also of intense cold, *to freeze off*.

ἀπο-κᾰλέω, f. έσω: (for the tenses, v. καλέω):—*to call back, recal* from exile. 2. *to call away*. II. *to call* by *a name*, esp. by way of abuse. III. *to warn off*.

ἀποκᾰλύπτω, f. ψω, *to disclose, uncover*:—Med. *to reveal oneself*. Hence

ἀποκάλυψις, εως, ἡ, *revelation*.

ἀπο-κάμνω, f. κᾰμοῦμαι: (for the tenses, v. κάμνω):—*to grow quite weary, to flag utterly*: c. inf. *to cease* to do. II. c. acc., ἀποκάμνειν πόνον *to flinch from* toil.

ἀπο-κάμπτω, f. ψω, intr. *to bend off, turn aside*. 2. trans. *to turn aside from, shun*. Hence

ἀπόκαμψις, εως, ἡ, *a turning off the road*.

ἀπο-κᾰπύω, Ep. aor. 1 -εκάπυσσα: (ἀπό, κάπτω):—*to breathe out*; ἀποκαπύειν ψυχήν *to give up* the ghost.

ἀπο-κᾰρᾱδοκέω, *to expect earnestly*. Hence

ἀποκᾰρᾱδοκία, ἡ, *earnest expectation*.

ἀπο-καρτερέω, f. ήσω, *to kill oneself by fasting*.

ἀπο-καταλλάσσω, Att. -ττω, *to reconcile again*.

ἀποκατάστᾰσις, εως, ἡ, (ἀποκαθίστημι) *a complete restoration, reëstablishment*.

ἀπο-κάτημαι, Ion. for ἀπο-κάθημαι.

ἀποκαυλίζω, f. ίσω Att. ιῶ (ἀπό, καυλός) *to break short off*.

ἀπόκαυσις, εως, ἡ, (ἀποκαίω) *a burning off*.

ἀπό-κειμαι, fut. -κείσομαι: used as Pass. of ἀποτίθημι, *to be put away, be laid up in store*: hence *to be kept in secret, be in reserve*:—impers., ἀπόκειταί τινι *it is in store* for one.

ἀπο-κείρω: fut. -κερῶ Ep. -κέρσω: pf. -κέκαρκα, pass. -κέκαρμαι:—*to shear* or *cut off*: generally, *to cut in pieces, cut through*:—metaph. *to cut off*.

ἀπο-κερδαίνω, fut. -κερδήσω and -κερδᾰνῶ:—*to have benefit* or *enjoyment from* or *of* a thing.

ἀπο-κερματίζω, *to change into small coin, dissipate*.

ἀπο-κεφᾰλίζω, fut. ίσω Att. ιῶ, (ἀπό, κεφαλή) *to behead*.

ἀπο-κηδεύω, f. σω, *to cease to mourn for*.

ἀπο-κηδέω, fut. ήσω, = ἀκηδέω, *to put away care, be careless*.

ἀπο-κηρύσσω, Att. -ττω, fut. ξω:—*to proclaim publicly*, esp. *to offer for public sale*. II. *to renounce publicly, disinherit* a son: also *to declare outlawed*. III. *to forbid by proclamation*.

ἀποκινδύνευσις, εως, ἡ, *the making a venturous attempt*. [ῡ] From

ἀποκινδῡνεύω, f. σω, *to make a bold stroke, make a*

venture:—Pass., with paullo p. fut. ἀποκεκινδυνεύσομαι, *to be put to the uttermost hazard.*

ἀπό-κῖνος, ὁ, (ἀπό, κινέω) *a comic dance*: ἀπόκινον εὑρέ find *some way of dancing off, escaping.*

ἀπο-κλάζω, f. -κλάγξω, *to ring* or *shout forth.*

ἀπ-οκλάζω, f. άσω, (ἀπό, ὀκλάζω) *to bend one's knees*, and so *to rest*, like κάμπτειν γόνυ.

ἀπο-κλαίω, Att. **ἀποκλάω** [ᾱω]: fut. -κλαύσομαι:—*to weep aloud*: c. acc. *to bewail much, mourn deeply for.* II. *to cease to wail.*

ἀποκλᾳξῶ, ἀποκλᾷξον, Dor. fut. and aor. 1 imperat. of ἀποκλείω.

ἀπό-κλᾱρος, Dor. for ἀπό-κληρος.

ἀπο-κλάω, f. άσω [ᾰ], *to break off.*

ἀπο-κλάω, Att. for ἀπο-κλαίω. [ᾱ]

ἀπόκλεισις or **ἀπόκλησις**, εως, ἡ, (ἀποκλείω) *a shutting off* or *out.*

ἀπόκλειστος, ον, *shut off, enclosed.* From

ἀπο-κλείω, f. κλείσω: Ion. **-κληΐω**, f. -κληΐσω: Att. **-κλῄω**, f. -κλῄσω: Dor. fut. -κλᾳξω:—*to shut off from* or *out of.* 2. *to cut off* or *hinder from* a thing:—Pass. *to be cut off* or *hindered from.* II. c. acc. only, *to shut up, close*: *to cut off, prevent, hinder.*

ἀπο-κλέπτω, f. ψω, *to steal away.*

ἀπο-κληΐω, f. -κληΐξω, Ion. for ἀποκλείω, f. -κλείσω.

ἀπό-κληρος, Dor. **ἀπό-κλᾱρος**, ον, *away from* (i. e. *without*) *lot* or *share of* a thing.

ἀπο-κληρόω, f. ώσω, *to choose by lot from among* a number, *to elect by lot.*

ἀποκλινθείς, later **ἀποκλῐθείς**, aor. 1 pass. part. of ἀποκλίνω.

ἀπο-κλίνω [ῑ]: fut. -κλῐνῶ: aor. 1 ἀπέκλῑνα: pf. -κέκλῐκα, pass. -κέκλῐμαι:—*to turn off* or *aside*: *to turn back.* II. intr. *to turn aside*: metaph. *to turn off to something worse, fall away, decline.* Hence

ἀπόκλῐσις, εως, ἡ, *a turning away*: of the sun, *sinking.*

ἀπο-κλύζω, fut. ύσω [ῠ], *to wash away, avert by purifications.*

ἀπο-κναίω, Att. **-κνάω**: f. -κνήσω: (for the tenses, v. κνάω):—*to scrape* or *rub off*; ἀποκνῆν τινα *to wear* one *out, weary to death*:—Med. *to wear away, diminish.*

ἀπ-οκνέω, f. ήσω, *to shrink from, hesitate about* a thing, c. acc.: absol. *to shrink back, hesitate.* Hence

ἀπόκνησις, εως, ἡ, *a shrinking from.*

ἀπο-κνίζω, f. ίσω, *to nip off.* Hence

ἀπόκνισμα, τό, *that which is nipt off, a little bit.*

ἀπο-κοιμάομαι, Pass. with f. med. -κοιμήσομαι, *to sleep away from home.* 2. *to get a little sleep.*

ἀποκοιτέω, f. ήσω, *to sleep away from* one's post. From

ἀπό-κοιτος, ον, (ἀπό, κοῖτος) *sleeping away from.*

ἀπο-κολυμβάω, f. ήσω, *to dive and swim away.*

ἀπο-κομῐδή, ἡ, *a carrying away.* II. (from Med.) *a getting away* or *back.* From

ἀπο-κομίζω, fut. ίσω Att. ῐῶ, *to carry* or *conduct away*:—Med. *to carry off with one*:—Pass. *to take oneself off, get away.*

ἀπόκομμα, ατος, τό, (ἀποκόπτω) *a piece cut* or *knocked off, a splinter, chip, shred.*

ἀπο-κομπάζω, f. άσω, *to break with a snap.*

ἀποκοπή, ἡ, (ἀποκόπτω) *a cutting* or *knocking off*: ἀποκοπὴ χρεῶν = Lat. *tabulae novae, a cancelling* of all debts.

ἀπο-κόπτω, f. ψω, *to cut off, hew off, knock off.* II. *to beat off from* a place. III. Med. *to smite the breast in mourning*, hence, *to mourn for.*

ἀπο-κορῠφόω, f. ώσω, *to sum up briefly.*

ἀπο-κοσμέω, f. ήσω, *to clear away*, so *as to restore order.*

ἀπο-κοτταβίζω, f. ίσω Att. ιῶ, *to dash out the last drops of wine*, as in playing at the cottabus.

ἀπο-κουφίζω, fut. ίσω Att. ῐῶ, *to relieve* or *set free from.*

ἀπο-κράδιος, ον, (ἀπό, κράδη) *plucked from the fig-tree.*

ἀπο-κρᾱνίζω, f. ίσω, *to strike from the head.*

ἀπο-κρᾰτέω, f. ήσω, *to overcome, surpass.*

ἀπο-κρεμάννυμι f. -κρεμάσω [ᾰ], Att. -κρεμῶ: (for the tenses, v. κρεμάννυμι):—*to let* a thing *hang down, let hang.* II. *to hang up.*

ἀπό-κρημνος, ον, *precipitous, craggy.*

ἀπόκρῐμα, ατος, τό, (ἀποκρίνω) *a judicial sentence, sentence of death.*

ἀπο-κρινθείς, ἀποκρῐθείς, aor. 1 pass. part. of sq.

ἀπο-κρίνω [ῑ], fut. -κρῐνῶ: Pass., aor. 1 ἀπεκρίθην [ῐ]: pf. -κέκρῐμαι:—*to part, separate, distinguish*:—Pass. *to be parted* or *separated* one *from* another; ἀποκεκρίσθαι εἰς ἓν ὄνομα *to be separated and brought* under one name. II. *to choose out, choose.* III. Med. *to give answer* or *reply to* a question: esp. *to answer charges*; ἀποκρίνεσθαί τι *to give* an *answer*: so also in aor. 1 pass. ἀπεκρίθην. Hence

ἀπόκρῐσις, εως, ἡ, *a separating.* II. (from Med.), *an answer.*

ἀποκρῐτέον, verb. Adj. of ἀποκρίνω, *one must separate.* II. (from Med.) *one must answer.*

ἀπό-κροτος, ον, *beaten* or *trodden hard*, esp. of earth.

ἀπο-κρούω, f. σω, *to beat off from* a place, c. gen.:—Med. *to beat off from oneself, beat off*:—Pass. *to be beaten* or *knocked off*; κοτυλίσκιον τὸ χεῖλος ἀποκεκρουμένον a cup *with its* rim *knocked off.*

ἀποκρύπτασκε, 3 sing. Ion. impf. of ἀποκρύπτω.

ἀπο-κρύπτω, f. ψω, *to hide from, keep hidden from*: ἀποκρύπτειν τινί τι, or c. dupl. acc., ἀπ. τινά τι, like Lat. *celare aliquem aliquid, to hide* or *keep back from* one. 2. *to hide close*: *to obscure.* II. *to lose from sight*; ἀποκρύπτειν γῆν *to lose sight of land*, as in Virgil, *Phaeacum abscondimus arces.* Hence

ἀπόκρῠφος, ον, *hidden*; ἐν ἀποκρύφῳ *in secret.* II. *obscure, hard to understand.*

ἀπο-κτάμεν, -κτάμεναι, Ep. for -κτᾰνεῖν, aor. 2 inf. of ἀποκτείνω.

ἀποκτάμενος, Ep. aor. 2 pass. part. of ἀποκτείνω.

ἀπο-κτείνω, f. -κτενῶ: aor. 1 ἀπέκτεινα: aor. 2 ἀπέκτᾰνον, poët. ἀπέκτᾰν, ας, α; Ep. also in pass. form *ἀπεκτάμην*: perf. *ἀπέκτονα*, more rarely *ἀπεκτόνηκα*, *ἀπέκτἄκα*. and *ἀπέκταγκα*:—*to kill, slay*: of judges, *to condemn to death*; of the executioner, *to put to death*: metaph., like *ἀποκνάειν*, *to weary to death*, Lat. *enecare*.

ἀποκτέννω, later form of *ἀποκτείνω*.

ἀπο-κῠέω, f. *ήσω*, *to bear young, bring forth*.

ἀπο-κυλίνδω, f. *κυλίσω* [ῑ], *to roll away*.

ἀπο-κύπτω, f. *ψω*: pf. *-κεκῡφα*: *to stoop away from*.

ἀπο-κωκύω, f. *ύσω* [ῡ], *to mourn loudly over*.

ἀποκώλῡσις, *εως*, *ἡ*, *a hindrance*. From

ἀπο-κωλύω, f. *ύσω* [ῡ], *to hinder* or *prevent from* a thing: c. inf., *to prevent from* doing: absol. *to keep off*.

ἀπολᾰβών. **-λαβόμενος**, aor. 2 part. act. and med. of *ἀπολαμβάνω*.

ἀπο-λαγχάνω, f. *-λήξομαι*: aor. 2 *ἀπέλᾰχον*:—*to obtain a portion of* a thing *by lot*: *ἀπολαχεῖν μέρος τινός*: generally, *to obtain*.

ἀπο-λάζῠμαι, Dep., poët. for *ἀπο-λαμβάνω*.

ἀπο-λακτίζω, f. *ίσω* Att. *ιῶ*, *to kick off* or *away*, *shake off*: generally, *to spurn*. Hence

ἀπολακτισμός, *ὁ*, *a kicking away*.

ἀπολᾰλέω, f. *ήσω*, *to chatter much*.

ἀπο-λαμβάνω, fut. *-λήψομαι*, in Herodotus *-λάμψομαι*: pf. *ἀπείληφα*, pass. *ἀπείλημμαι*: for the aorist, we have in act. only aor. 2 *ἀπέλᾰβον*, in pass. only aor. 1 *ἀπελήφθην* Ion. *ἀπελάμφθην*. *To take* or *receive from* another: absol. *to receive what is one's due*. 2. *to carry off*. 3. *to hear* or *learn*, like Lat. *accipio*. II. *to take back, regain, recover*. 2. *to have* a thing *rendered to one*. III. *to take apart* or *aside*. IV. *to cut off* as by a wall: *to stop, arrest*, Lat *deprehendere*, esp. of contrary winds.

ἀπο-λαμπρύνω, *to make famous*:—Pass. *to become* so.

ἀπο-λάμπω, f. *ψω*, *to shine forth, to reflect light, to flash*; *αἰχμῆς ἀπέλαμπε* (sc. *φῶς*) light *beamed from* the spear-head.

ἀπο-λάπτω, f. *ψω*, *to lap up* like a dog.

ἀπόλαυσις, *εως*. *ἡ*, (*ἀπολαύω*) *enjoyment*: c. gen. *enjoyment* or *advantage derived from* a thing.

ἀπολαυστικός. *ή*, *όν*, *of* or *for enjoyment*. From

ἀπο-λαύω, f. *ἀπολαύσομαι*: impf. *ἀπέλαυον*. aor. 1 *ἀπέλαυσα*, sometimes written *ἀπήλαυον*, *ἀπήλαυσα*:—*to take of* a thing, *enjoy*: also *to get* something *from* or *by* another, e. g. *ἀγαθὸν ἀπολαύειν τινός*. 2. ironical, *to come finely off, profit*, whence also in bad sense, *to get harm* or *loss by* a thing. (The simple *λαύω* is obsolete. No doubt the Root is *λαυ-*, i. e. *λαϝ-*, *λαβ-*, which is also the Root of *λαμβάνω*.)

ἀπολᾰχεῖν, aor. 2 inf. of *ἀπολαγχάνω*.

ἀπο-λέγω, f. *ξω*: pf. pass. *ἀπολέλεγμαι* or *ἀπείλεγμαι*:—*to pick out from among, choose*:—Med. *to pick out for oneself*:—Pass., *ἀπολελεγμένοι picked* men.

ἀπο-λείβω, f. *ψω*: aor. 1 *ἀπέλειψα*:—*to let drop off, pour a libation*:—Pass. *to drop* or *run down from*.

ἀπο-λείπω, f. *ψω*: aor. 2 *ἀπέλῐπον*:—*to leave over* or *behind*. II. *to leave behind one*, i. e. *lose*. 2. *to leave behind*, as in the race, *to distance, to surpass*. III. *to leave utterly, forsake, abandon*: of things, *to leave alone. leave undone*. IV. intrans. *to be wanting, to be away* or *absent*: of rivers, *to fail, sink*. 2. *to be wanting of* or *in* a thing; *ἀπὸ τεσσέρων πηχέων ἀπολείπων τρεῖς δακτύλους wanting* three fingers *of* four cubits. 3. with part. *to leave off* doing. 4. *to depart from*. V. Pass. *to be left behind, inferior to*. 2. *to be parted from, be absent from*. c. gen.; *πολὺ τῆς ἀληθηίης ἀπολελειμμένοι* being far *distant from* the truth: *to be deprived of*. 3. *to be wanting in* a thing, also c. gen.

ἀπο-λείχω, f. *ξω*, *to lick off, lick up*.

ἀπόλειψις, *εως*, *ἡ*, (*ἀπολείπω*) *a leaving behind, forsaking*. II. intr. *a failing, deficiency*.

ἀπόλεκτος, *ον*, (*ἀπολέγω*) *chosen out, picked*.

ἀπολέλῠμαι, pf. pass. of *ἀπολύω*.

ἀ-πόλεμος, poët. **ἀπτόλεμος**, *ον*, *unwarlike, unfit for war*: *peaceful*. II. *not to be warred on, invincible*. III. *πόλεμος ἀπόλεμος* a war *that is no war*, i. e. a hopeless struggle.

ἀπο-λέπω, f. *ψω*, *to peel off, take off the skin*: pf. part. pass. *ἀπολελεμμένος*.

ἀπολέσθαι, aor. 2 med. inf. of *ἀπόλλυμι*.

ἀπολέσκετο, Ep. for *ἀπώλετο*, 3 sing. aor. 2 med. of *ἀπόλλυμι*.

ἀπο-λήγω, poët. **ἀπολλήγω**, f. *ξω*, *to leave off* or *desist from* a thing: c. part. *to cease* doing.

ἀπο-ληρέω, f. *ήσω*, *to chatter at random*.

ἀπόληψις, *εως*, *ἡ*, (*ἀπολαμβάνω*) *a taking from*: *taking back, recovery*. II. *an intercepting, cutting off*.

ἀπο-λιβάζω, f. *ξω*, *to drop off*.

ἀπο-λῐγαίνω, *to make a great din, talk loud*.

ἀπο-λιμπάνω, Ion. for *ἀπο-λείπω*.

ἄ-πολις, neut. *ι*: gen. *ιδος*, also *εως*, Ion. *ιος*: dat. *ἀπόλι*:—*one without city, state*, or *country, an outlaw*. II. *πόλις ἄπολις* a city *that is no city, a* ruined city.

ἀπ-ολισθάνω, f. *-ολισθήσω*: aor. 1 *-ωλίσθησα*: aor. 2 *-ώλισθον*:—*to slip off* or *away from*.

ἀπο-λῐταργίζω, f. *ίσω* Att. *ιῶ*, *to slip off, pack off*.

ἀπο-λιχμάομαι, f. *ήσομαι*, Dep. = *ἀπολείχω*, *to lick off*.

ἀπολλήγω, Ep. for *ἀπολήγω*.

ἀπ-όλλῡμι or **ἀπ-ολλύω**: impf. *ἀπώλλυν* or *ἀπώλλυον*: fut. *ἀπολέσω*, *ἀπολέσσω*, Att. *ἀπολῶ*, Ion. *ἀπολέω*: aor. 1 *ἀπώλεσα*, Ep. *ἀπόλεσσα*; pf. *ἀπώλεκα*, Att. *ἀπολώλεκα*:—*to destroy utterly, kill, slay*: o things, *to demolish, to lay waste*. II. *to lose utterly*.

Med. *ἀπόλλῠμαι*: f. *ἀπολοῦμαι*, Ion. *ἀπολέομαι*: aor. 2 *ἀπωλόμην*: perf. *ἀπόλωλα*: plqpf. *ἀπολώλειν* or *ἀπωλώλειν*:—*to perish, die*: also simply *to fall into ruin, to be undone*. II. *to be lost, fall away, fail*. III. *to be wretched* or *miserable*.

'Απόλλων, *ωνος*, *ὁ*: acc. *ωνα* or *ω*: voc. **Ἄπολλον**:—*Apollo*, son of Jupiter and Latona.

'Απολλώνειον and **'Απολλώνιον**, τό, *a temple of Apollo.*

ἀπο-λογέομαι, fut. ήσομαι: aor. 1 med. ἀπελογησάμην, pass. ἀπελογήθην: pf. ἀπολελόγημαι: Dep.: (ἀπό, λόγος):—*to speak in defence:* also *to speak in defence* of a fact. 2. ἀπολογεῖσθαί τι, *to defend oneself against* a charge. 3. ἀπολογεῖσθαι δίκην θανάτου *to speak against* sentence of death being passed. Hence

ἀπολόγημα, ατος, τό, *a plea alleged in defence.*

ἀπολογία, ἡ, (ἀπολογέομαι) *a speech in defence, defence.*

ἀπο-λογίζομαι: f. ίσομαι Att. ἴοῦμαι: aor. 1 -ελογισάμην: pf. -λελόγισμαι: Dep.:—*to reckon up, give in an account,* Lat. *rationes reddere.* II. *to give a full account of, recount fully.* 2. *to calculate* or *consider well.* Hence

ἀπολογισμός, ὁ, *a giving an account, a statement of facts* or *reasons.*

ἀπό-λογος, ὁ, *a story, tale;* ἀπόλογος 'Αλκίνου proverb. of long stories, from that told by Ulysses to Alcinöus in Od. 9–12. II. *a fable,* like those of Aesop, *an apologue.*

ἀπολοίατο, Ion. for ἀπόλοιντο, 3 plur. aor. 2 opt. med. of ἀπόλλυμι.

ἀπ-ολολύζω, f. ξω, *to utter a loud cry.*

ἀπολόμενος, aor. 2 med. part. of ἀπόλλυμι.

ἀπολοῦμαι, fut. med. of ἀπόλλυμι.

ἀπόλουσις, εως, ἡ, *a washing off, ablution.* From

ἀπο-λούω, f. λούσω, *to wash off:*—Med., ἅλμην ὤμοιν ἀπολούσομαι *I will wash* the brine *from off my* shoulders. II. c. acc. pers. *to wash clean.*

ἀπ-ολοφύρομαι, f. -ῠροῦμαι, *to bewail loudly.* 2. *to cease from wailing.*

ἀπο-λῡμαίνομαι, f. -μᾰνοῦμαι: Dep. (ἀπό, λῦμα):—*to cleanse oneself by bathing.*

ἀπολῡμαντήρ, ῆρος, ὁ, (ἀπό, λυμαίνομαι) *a destroyer, waster.*

ἀπολύσῐμος, ον, (ἀπολύω) *deserving acquittal.*

ἀπόλῠσις, εως, ἡ, (ἀπολύω) *release, deliverance:* c. gen., κατὰ τὴν ἀπόλυσιν τοῦ θανάτου as far as *acquittal from* a capital charge went.

ἀπολῠτικός, ή, όν, (ἀπολύω) *disposed to acquit.* Adv., ἀπολυτικῶς ἔχειν to be *disposed to acquit.*

ἀπο-λῠτρόω, f. ώσω, *to release on payment of ransom:*—Med. *to redeem for money.* Hence

ἀπολύτρωσις, εως, ἡ, *a releasing, redemption.*

ἀπο-λύω, f. -λύσω [ῡ]: aor. 1 ἀπέλῡσα: pf. ἀπολέλῠκα:—*to loose from: to set free* or *release from;* ἀπολύειν αἰτίης *to acquit* of a charge: absol. *to acquit.* 2. in Il. always = ἀπολυτρόω, *to release* a prisoner *for ransom;* and in Med. *to ransom* him, χρυσοῦ *for* gold. 3. *to disband* an army: *to discharge* a debt. II. Med. *to release for oneself, redeem.* 2. ἀπολύεσθαι διαβολάς, etc., *to do away with* calumnies *against one,* like Lat. *diluere:* hence absol. *to defend oneself.* 3. *to get free, depart.* III. Pass. *to be released, let free from.* 2. *to get clear: to depart, go away.*

ἀπο-λωβάομαι, f. ήσομαι, Dep. *to insult grossly:* aor. 1 ἀπελωβήθην in pass. sense, *to be insulted.*

ἀπόλωλα, pf. med. of ἀπόλλυμι.

ἀπο-λωτίζω, f. ίσω, (ἀπό, λωτός) = ἀπανθίζω, *to pluck off flowers:* hence generally, *to pluck off.*

ἀπομαγδᾰλία, ἡ, (ἀπομάσσω) *the crumb* or *inside of the loaf,* on which the Greeks wiped their hands at dinner, and then threw it to the dogs.

ἀπο-μαίνομαι, fut. -μᾰνήσομαι: pf. ἀπομέμηνα: Dep. *to rave till one is satisfied: to rage violently.*

ἀπο-μανθάνω, f. -μᾰθήσομαι, *to unlearn,* Lat. *dediscere.*

ἀπο-μαντεύομαι, f. σομαι, Dep. *to announce as a prophet:* hence *to divine, presage.*

ἀπο-μᾰραίνομαι, Pass. *to dry up, wither away: to die away,* of a tranquil death.

ἀπο-μαρτῠρομαι, Dep. *to confirm by witnesses, maintain stoutly.* [ῡ]

ἀπο-μάσσω, Att. -ττω, fut. ξω, *to wipe off, to wipe clean:*—Med. *to wipe one's hands.* 2. *to sweep off* or *level* corn *with a strickle;* κενεὰν ἀπομάξαι (sc. χοίνικα) to lose one's labour. II. *to make an impression of:*—Med. *to stamp* or *impress* something *on oneself, copy from* another.

ἀπο-μαστῑγόω, f. ώσω, *to scourge severely.*

ἀπο-ματαΐζω, f. ίσω, (ἀπό, μάταιος) *to behave idly* or *unseemly.*

ἀπο-μάχομαι, f. -μαχέσομαι, contr. -μαχοῦμαι:—*to fight from,* as from a fort; τείχεα ἱκανὰ ἀπομάχεσθαι strong enough *to fight from.* II. ἀπομάχεσθαί τι *to fight off* a thing, *decline* it. III. ἀπομάχεσθαί τινα *to drive off in battle.* IV. *to finish a battle, fight it out.*

ἀπό-μᾰχος, ον, (ἀπό, μάχη) *not fighting: unfit for service.*

ἀπο-μείρομαι, f. -μεροῦμαι, Dep. *to distribute.* 2. Pass. *to be parted from* another.

ἀπο-μερίζω, f. ίσω Att. ιῶ, *to give a share of, distribute.* II. *to distinguish from* a number.

ἀπο-μερμηρίζω, fut. ίσω and ίξω, *to slumber and forget one's cares.*

ἀπο-μεστόω, f. ώσω, *to fill to the brim.*

ἀπο-μετρέω, f. ήσω, *to mete out, distribute.*

ἀπο-μηκύνω [ῡ], f. ῠνῶ, *to prolong, draw out.*

ἀπο-μηνίω, f. ίσω [ῑ], *to be very wroth.*

ἀπο-μῑμέομαι, f. ήσομαι, Dep. *to copy after, to represent faithfully.*

ἀπο-μιμνήσκομαι, Pass., with fut. med. -μνήσομαι, aor. 1 ἀπεμνησάμην: pf. ἀπομέμνημαι:—*to recollect, remember.*

ἀπό-μισθος, ον, like ἄμισθος, *without pay: defrauded of pay.* II. *paid off,* i. e. *past service,* Lat. *emeritus.*

ἀπο-μισθόω, f. ώσω, *to let out for hire, let:* c. inf., ἀπομισθοῦν ποιεῖν τι *to contract for the doing* of a thing, Lat. *locare aliquid faciendum.*

ἀπο-μνάομαι, Ion. for *ἀπο-μιμνήσκομαι.*

ἀπομνημόνευμα, *τό*, mostly in plur. *a narrative of sayings and doings, memoirs*, Lat. *Memorabilia*, as those of Socrates by Xenophon. From

ἀπο-μνημονεύω, f. *σω*, *to remind.* II. *to relate from memory, recount:* hence *to remember, bear in mind.* 2. *ἀπομνημονεύειν τινί τι to bear something in mind against* another, *owe* him *a grudge.*

ἀπο-μνησικᾰκέω, f. *ήσω*, *to bear a grudge against.*

ἀπ-όμνῡμι or **ἀπομνύω**: 3 sing. impf. *ἀπώμνυ*: fut. *ἀπομοῦμαι*: (v. *ὄμνυμι*:)— *to take an oath against doing* a thing, *swear that one will not do.* 2. *to swear one has not done: to deny with an oath, disclaim upon oath.* II. strengthd. for *ὄμνυμι*, *to take a solemn oath.*

ἀπο-μονόω. f. *ώσω*, *to leave quite alone:*—Pass. *to be excluded from* a thing.

ἀπο-μόργνῡμι or **ἀπ-ομόργνυμι**, also **ἀπομοργνύω**: Ep. 3 sing. impf. *ἀπομόργνυ*:—Med., Ep. aor. 1 *ἀπομορξάμην*:—Pass., aor. 1 part. *ἀπομορχθείς*: (*ἀπό, μόργνυμι* or *ὀμόργνυμι*):—*to wipe off* or *away from: to wipe clean:*—Med., *ἀπομόρξασθαι παρειάς to wipe one's* cheeks; *ἀπομόρξασθαι δάκρυ to wipe away one's* tears.

ἀπομόρξατο, 3 sing. Ep. aor. 1 med. of foreg.

ἀπομόσαι, aor. 1 inf. of *ἀπόμνυμι.*

ἀπό-μουσος, *ον*, like *ἄμουσος*, (*ἀπό*, **Μοῦσα**) *away from the Muses, coarse, rude.* Adv., *ἀπομούσως γράφεσθαι* to be painted *in unfavourable colours.*

ἀπο-μῡθέομαι, f. *ήσομαι*, Dep. *to dissuade.*

ἀπο-μῡκάομαι, f. *ήσομαι*, Dep. *to bellow loud.*

ἀπο-μυκτέον. verb. Adj. of *ἀπομύσσομαι*, *one must wipe one's mouth.*

ἀπο-μύσσω, Att. **-ττω**, f. *ξω*, *to wipe* a person's *nose:* hence *to sharpen* his *wits;* comp. Horace's *vir emunctae naris:*—Med. *to blow one's nose.*

ἀπόναιο, 2 sing. aor. 2 opt. med. of *ἀπονίνημι*: and **ἀποναίατο**, 3 pl., for *ἀπόναιντο.*

***ἀπο-νάω**, obsol. pres., whence aor. 1 act. *ἀπένᾰσα*, Ep. *ἀπένασσα*: (*ἀπό, νάω*):—*to remove* one to another place: also *to send back:*—Med., in 3 sing. aor. 1 *ἀπενάσατο*, Ep. *ἀπενάσσατο*, *to remove oneself to* another place, *depart:* but also *to send away:*—aor. 1 pass. *ἀπονασθῆναι*, *to be taken away, depart from* a place.

ἀπο-νέμω, fut. *-νεμῶ* and later *-νεμήσω*: aor. 1 *ἀπένειμα*:—*to portion out, distribute, assign severally: to impart:*—Med. *to assign to oneself, take.* 2. *to feed on* or *off.* II. *to part off, separate.*

ἀπονενοημένως, Adv. pf. pass. part. of *ἀπονοέομαι*, *desperately.*

ἀπο-νέομαι, Dep. *to go away, to go back, return*, Ep. word, used only in pres. and impf. [ᾱ Ep.]

ἀπονέστερος, **-τατος**, Comp. and Sup. of *ἄπονος.*

ἀπο-νεύω, f. *σω*, *to bend away from* other objects towards one, hence *to incline towards;* cf. *ἀποβλέπω.* II. *to refuse by shaking the head*, Lat. *abnuere.*

ἀπο-νέω, f. *νήσω*, *to unload:*—Med. *to throw off a load from.*

ἀπονήμενος, aor. 2 med. part. of *ἀπονίνημι.*

ἀπονητί, Adv. of *ἀπόνητος*, *without fatigue.*

ἀπ-όνητο, Ion. for *ἀπ-ώνητο*, 3 sing. aor. 2 med. of *ἀπονίνημι.*

ἀ-πόνητος, *ον*, (α privat., *πονέω*) *not worked* or *wrought.* II. *without trouble, easy:* Sup. *ἀπονητότατα with least trouble.* 2. *without sufferings.*

ἀπονία, *ἡ*, (*ἄπονος*) *freedom from toil, laziness.*

ἀπο-νίζω, f. *-νίψω* (as if from *ἀπο-νίπτω*, which is a late form):—*to wash off:* Med. *to wash off from oneself.* 2. *to wash clean:* Med. *to wash oneself clean.*

ἀπ-ονίνημι, f. *-ονήσω*, *to give enjoyment.* II. mostly in Med., **ἀπ-ονίνᾰμαι**: fut. *-ονήσομαι*: aor. 2 *ἀπωνήμην*, Ep. without augm. *ἀπονήμην*, 2 opt. *ἀπόναιο*, part. *ἀπονήμενος*:—*to have the use* or *enjoyment of* a thing; *τῶνδ' ἀπόναιο mayest thou have joy of* these things.

ἀπό-νιπτρον, *τό*, *water for washing the hands*, etc.: from

ἀπο-νίπτω, see *ἀπονίζω.*

ἀπο-νοέομαι, fut. *-ήσομαι*: pf. *ἀπονενόημαι*: Dep. *to be out of one's mind, to have lost all sense.* 1. of fear, *to be desperate; ἄνθρωποι ἀπονενοημένοι*, Lat. *perditi, desperate* men. 2. of shame, *ὁ ἀπονενοημένος an abandoned fellow.* Hence

ἀπόνοια, *ἡ*, *loss of all sense, folly, madness:* esp. *desperation.*

ἄ-πονος, *ον*, c. irreg. Comp. and Sup. *ἀπονέστερος*, *-έστατος*, *without toil* or *trouble, untroubled: gentle, easy.* 2. of persons, *not toiling, lazy.* 3. of things, pass. *done without trouble, easy.*

ἀπο-νοστέω, f. *ήσω*, *to return home.* Hence

ἀπονόστησις, *εως*, *ἡ*, *a return home.*

ἀπο-νόσφι, before a vowel **-φιν**, (*ἀπό, νόσφι*) Adv. *far apart* or *aloof.* II. as Prep. with gen. *far away from*, mostly following its case.

ἀπο-νοσφίζω, f. *ίσω* Att. *ιῶ*, *to put asunder, keep aloof from: to bereave* or *rob of:*—Pass. *to be robbed of*, c. acc. II. with acc. only, *to flee from, shun.*

ἀπ-ονῠχίζω: f. *ίσω* Att. *ῐῶ*: Pass., aor. *ἀπωνυχίσθην*: pf. *ἀπωνύχισμαι*: (*ἀπό, ὀνυχίζω*):—*to pare the nails.* II. *to tear with the nails.* III. *to try* or *examine by the nail; ἀκριβῶς ἀπωνυχισμένος* Horace's *ad unguem factus*, closely *tried by the nail.*

ἀπο-νωτίζω, f. *ίσω* Att. *ιῶ*, *to make turn* his *back and flee:*—Med. *to turn the back and flee.*

ἀπό-ξενος, *ον*, like *ἄξενος*, *inhospitable.* 2. *ἀπόξενος γῆς far from* a country.

ἀπο-ξενόω, f. *ώσω*, *to drive from house and home* generally, *to estrange* or *banish from:*—Pass. *to live away from home, be banished, migrate.*

ἀπο-ξέω, f. *-ξέσω*, *to shave off: cut off.*

ἀπο-ξηραίνω, f. *ᾰνῶ*, *to dry up, drain off* a river:—Pass. *to be dried up, to become dry;* hence Ion. part. pf. *ἀποξηρασμένος.*

ἀπ-οξύνω [ῡ], f. ὑνῶ, *to bring to a point, make taper.*
ἀπο-ξῠράω, Ion. -έω, f. ήσω, *to shave clean.*
ἀπο-ξύρω, = ἀποξυράω:—Med. *to be clean shaved.* [ῠ]
ἀποξύω, f. ύσω [ῡ], *to shave* or *scrape off:* hence *to strip off* like skin.
ἀπο-παπταίνω: f. -παπτᾰνῶ, Ion. -έω: aor. 1 part. ἀποπαπτήνας:—*to look about one*, as if to flee.
ἀποπᾰτέω, f. ήσω or ήσομαι, *to retire from the way.* From
ἀπό-πᾰτος, ὁ or ἡ, *a going out of the way:* εἰς ἀπόπατον to ease himself.
ἀπόπαυσις, εως, ἡ, (ἀποπαύω) *a stopping, binderance.* II. (from Med.) *a ceasing, end.*
ἀπο-παύω, f. σω, *to stop* or *binder* one *from* a thing: c. inf. *to binder* from doing: c acc. only, *to stop.* II. Med. *to leave off* or *cease from* a thing.
ἀπό-πειρα, ἡ, (ἀπό, πεῖρα) *a trial, venture.*
ἀπο-πειράζω, f. άσω [ᾰ], rarer form of sq.
ἀπο-πειράομαι, with fut. med. άσομαι [ᾱ]: aor. 1 pass. ἀπεπειράθην, Ion. -ήθην: Dep.:—*to make trial, essay*, or *proof of* a person or thing. Rare in Act., ἀποπειρᾶσαι τοῦ Πειραέως (aor. 1 inf.) *to make an attempt on* the Peiræeus.
ἀπο-πελεκάω, f. ήσω, *to hew off with an axe.*
ἀπο-πέμπω, f. ψω, *to send off* or *away, to dismiss;* also in bad sense, *to drive off.* 2. *to escort:* of things, *to give back:*—Med. *to remove from oneself, get rid of:* of a wife, *to divorce* her. Hence
ἀπόπεμψις, εως, ἡ, *a sending away: a dismissal, divorcing.*
ἀπο-περάω, f. άσω Ion. ήσω, (ἀπό, περάω) *to carry over.*
ἀπο-πέρδομαι: fut. -παρδήσομαι: Dep. with aor. 2 act. -έπαρδον:—*to break wind*, Lat. *pedo.*
ἀποπέσῃσι, Ep. 3 sing. aor. 2 subj. of ἀποπίπτω.
ἀπο-πέτομαι, fut. πτήσομαι: aor. 2 ἀπεπτάμην, part. ἀποπτάμενος, and act. ἀπέπτην:—*to fly off* or *away.*
ἀπο-πήγνυμι, f. -πήξω, *to make to freeze* or *curdle:* —Pass., fut. -πᾰγήσομαι, of men, *to be frozen:* of blood, *to curdle.*
ἀπο-πηδάω, f. ήσω and ήσομαι, *to leap off from: to turn away from.*
ἀπό-πίμπλημι and -πιμπλάω, poët. also -πίπλημι, -πιπλάω: fut. -πλήσω: aor. 1 ἀπέπλησα:—*to fill up, fill to the brim: to fill up a number.* II. *to satisfy, fulfil: to appease*, Lat. *explere.*
ἀπο-πίνω [ῐ], fut. πίομαι, *to drink up, drink off.*
ἀπο-πίπτω, f. -πεσοῦμαι: aor. 2 ἀπέπεσον:—*to fall off from.*
ἀποπλαγχθείς, aor. 1 pass. part. of ἀποπλάζω.
ἀπο-πλάζω, fut. -πλάγξω, *to lead astray, lead away from:*—Pass. *to go astray, be driven off:* Homer uses only aor. 1 pass. ἀπεπλάγχθην, *to stray from, be deprived off;* τρυφάλεια ἀποπλαγχθεῖσα a helm *struck off.*
ἀπο-πλανάω, f. ήσω, *to lead astray:*—Med. *to go astray.*
ἀπο-πλάσσομαι, f. -πλάσομαι [ᾰ], *to copy.*
ἀπο-πλέω, Ep. -πλείω, Ion. -πλώω: f. -πλεύσομαι or -πλευσοῦμαι: aor. 1 ἀπέπλευσα:—*to sail away, sail off: to sail back.*
ἀπόπληκτος, ον, (ἀποπλήσσω) *stricken* or *disabled by a stroke*, 1. in mind, *dumb, astounded.* 2. in body, *crippled, paralysed.* Hence
ἀποπληξία, ἡ, *a stroke of apoplexy.*
ἀπο-πληρόω, f. ώσω, *to fill quite full, satisfy*, Lat. *explere.* II. *to fulfil.*
ἀπο-πλήσσω, Att. -ττω: fut. -ξω:—Pass., aor. 1 -επλήχθην: aor. 2 -επλήγην: pf. -πέπληγμαι:—*to strike to earth, disable in body* or *mind:*—Pass. *to lose one's senses, become dizzy, be struck by apoplexy.*
ἀπο-πλίσσομαι, Att. -ττομαι, fut. ξομαι, Dep. *to trip off.*
ἀπόπλοος, contr. **ἀπόπλους**, ὁ, (ἀποπλέω) *a sailing away: an outward-bound voyage.*
ἀπο-πλύνω [ῡ], f. ὑνῶ, *to wash off* or *away:* Ion. impf. ἀποπλύνεσκον.
ἀπο-πλώω, Ion. for ἀπο-πλέω.
ἀπο-πνέω, Ep. -πνείω: f. -πνεύσομαι: aor. 1 ἀπέπνευσα:—*to breathe forth;* θυμὸν or ψυχὴν ἀποπνεῖν *to give up the ghost*, Lat. *expirare animam.* 2. *to blow from* a particular quarter. 3. *to breathe* or *smell of* a thing.
ἀπο-πνίγω, f. -πνίξω or -πνίξομαι, *to choke, throttle:* —Pass., f. -πνιγήσομαι: aor. 2 -επνίγην [ῐ]: pf. -πέπνιγμαι:—*to be choked: to be drowned: to be choked with rage.*
ἀπο-πολεμέω, f. ήσω, *to fight off* or *from.*
ἀπό-πολις, poët. **ἀπό-πτολις**, ι, gen. ιδος and εως, *far from the city, banished.*
ἀποπομπή, ἡ, (ἀποπέμπω) *a sending away, getting rid of.*
ἀπο-πονέω, f. ήσω, *to finish a work: stop working.*
ἀπο-πορεύομαι, Pass. with fut. med. -εύσομαι, aor. 1 pass. ἀπεπορεύθην:—*to depart, go away.*
ἀπο-πραΰνω, f. ὑνῶ, *to soften down.*
ἀπο-πρίασθαι, aor. 2 inf. of ἀπ-ωνέομαι, with no pres. ἀπο-πρίαμαι in use.
ἀπο-πρίζω, f. ίσω [ῐ], = ἀποπρίω, *to saw off.*
ἀπο-πρίω, f. ίσω, *to saw through, file off.* [ῑ]
ἀπο-πρό, Adv. *far away, afar off.* 2. as Prep. with gen. *far from, away from.*
ἀπο-προαιρέω, *to take away from before:* aor. 2 part., σίτου ἀποπροελών *having taken some of* the bread.
ἀποπροέηκα, Ion. aor. 1 of ἀποπροΐημι.
ἀποπροελών, aor. 2 part. of ἀποπροαιρέω.
ἀπόπροθε, before a vowel -θεν, Adv. (ἀπο-πρό) *from afar: far off, far away.*
ἀπόπροθι. Adv. (ἀποπρό) *far off, far away.*
ἀποπροϊείς, part. pres. of
ἀπο-προΐημι, f. -προήσω: Ep. aor. 1 -προέηκα:—*to throw away.* 2. *to shoot forth.* 3. *to let fall.*
ἀπο-προνοσφίζω, fut. ίσω Att. ιῶ, *to remove afar off, carry far away.*
ἀπο-προτέμνω, f. -τεμῶ: aor. 2 -έταμον:—*to cut off from;* νώτου ἀποπροταμών *having cut off a slice from* the chine.

ἀπο-προφεύγω, f. -φεύξομαι, *to flee far away.*

ἀποπτάμενος, η, ον, aor. 2 part. of ἀποπέτομαι, as if from ἀφίπταμαι.

ἀποπτῆναι, aor. 2 inf. of ἀποπέτομαι, as if from ἀφίπτημι.

ἀπό-πτολις, poët. for ἀπόπολις.

ἄποπτος, ον, (ἀπόψομαι, fut. of ἀφοράω) *seen* or *to be seen from* a place. 2. *seen at a distance*, hence *far away from*; ἐξ ἀπόπτου *from afar*, opp. to ἐγγύθεν: hence II. *dimly seen.*

ἀπόπτυστος, ον, *spit out; loathed, detested.* From

ἀπο-πτύω, f. ύσω [ῡ], *to spit out* or *up*; of the sea, ἀποπτύει ἁλὸς ἄχνην *vomits forth* its foam: hence *to loathe, spurn*, Lat. *respuere.*

ἀπο-πυνθάνομαι, f. -πεύσομαι: Dep. *to inquire* or *ask of.*

ἀπ-οράω and **ἀπ-ορέω**, Ion. for ἀφοράω.

ἀπο-ρέπω, f. ψω, *to slink away.*

ἀπορέω, f. ήσω, (ἄπορος) *to be without resource, to be at a loss, not know what to do, be in doubt*, mostly followed by a Conjunction, ἀπορεῖν ὅπως διαβήσεται *to be at a loss* how he shall cross: c. inf. *to be at a loss how* to do: οὐκ ἀπορεῖν *to have no doubt.* II. Pass. *to be made matter of question*: also *to be left unprovided for.* 2. c. gen. rei, *to be at a loss for, in want of*, e. g. τροφῆς. 3. but, ἀπορεῖν τινι *to be at a loss because of, by means* of something. Hence

ἀπόρημα, ατος, τό, *a matter of doubt, disputed point.*

ἀπορητικός, ή, όν, (ἀπορέω) *inclined to doubt.*

ἀ-πόρθητος, ον, also η, ον, (α privat., πορθέω) *not sacked* or *taken.*

ἀπ-ορθόω, f. ώσω, *to make straight again, restore, guide aright.* Hence

ἀπόρθωσις, εως, ἡ, *a setting upright, restoring.*

ἀπορία, ἡ, (ἄπορος) of places, *difficulty of passing*: of things, *difficulty, straits*: of questions, *a difficulty.* II. of persons, *difficulty of dealing with* or *finding out.* 2. *want of means* or *resource, embarrassment, hesitation.* 3. ἀπορία τινός *want of* a thing: absol. *need, poverty.*

ἀπ-όρνῦμαι, (ἀπό, ὄρνυμι) Pass. *to start from* a place.

ἄ-πορος, ον, *without passage*, and so of places, *impassable, trackless*: of things, *hard to see one's way through, impracticable*: τὰ ἄπορα *difficulties, straits*, ἐν ἀπόροις εἶναι to be in *great straits.* 2. *hard to get, scarce.* II. of persons, *hard to deal with, unmanageable, impracticable*: c. inf., ἄπορος προσφέρεσθαι *impossible* to deal with. 2. *without means* or *resource*, and so *at a loss, not knowing what to do.* 3. *poor, needy.*

ἀπ-ορούω, f. σω, *to leap off, dart away.*

ἀπορρ-, ρ is doubled in Att. in all compds. after ἀπό, but in Ion. it remains single.

ἀπορ-ρᾱθῡμέω, f. ήσω, *to neglect from carelessness*: *to leave off in despair.*

ἀπορ-ραίνω, f. -ρᾰνῶ, *to spirt* or *shed about.*

ἀπορ-ραίω, f. σω, *to bereave of*; ἦτορ ἀπορραίειν τινά *to deprive* one of life.

ἀπορραντήριον, τό, (ἀπορραίνω) *a vessel for holy water.*

ἀπορ-ράπτω, f. ψω, *to sew up again.*

ἀπορ-ραψῳδέω, f. ήσω, *to utter like a ῥαψῳδός, to speak in fragments of Epic poetry.*

ἀπορ-ρέω, f. -ρεύσομαι or -ρῠήσομαι: aor. 2 pass. ἀπερρύην:—*to flow away from, run off from*: absol. *to stream forth*, of blood. 2. *to fall off*, as fruit, etc. 3. *to melt away.*

ἀπορ-ρήγνῡμι or **ἀπορ-ρηγνύω**: f. -ρήξω:—*to break off, snap asunder*:—Pass., aor. 2 ἀπερράγην [ᾰ], *to be broken off* or *severed.*

ἀπορρηθέν and **ἀπορρηθῆναι**, aor. 1 pass. part. and inf. of ἀπερῶ.

ἀπόρρησις, εως, ἡ, (ἀπ-ερῶ) *a prohibition.* 2. *a refusal: renunciation.*

ἀπόρρητος, ον, (ἀπ-ερῶ) *forbidden*; τὰ ἀπόρρητα *forbidden exports.* II. *not to be spoken, that should not be spoken*; ἀπόρρητον, τό, *a state-secret*: hence *mystical, sacred*, ἀπόρρητον ποιεῖσθαι to keep *secret.* 2. τὰ ἀπόρρητα *things unfit to be spoken.*

ἀπορ-ρῑγέω, f. ήσω: pf. ἀπέρρῑγα:—*to shrink shivering from* a thing, *shrink from doing* it.

ἀπορ-ρίπτω, poët. **ἀπορίπτω**, later also **ἀπορριπτέω**: fut. ἀπορρίψω: aor. 1 ἀπέρριψα:—*to throw away, throw aside*: *to throw off* a garment. II. *to cast forth*, e. g. from one's country: *to reject, renounce.* III. *to shoot forth bold* words, εἴς τινα at one.

ἀπορροή and **ἀπόρροια**, ἡ, (ἀπορρέω) *a flowing off, stream.* II. *an emanation, efflux.*

ἀπορ-ροιβδέω, f. ήσω, *to shriek forth.*

ἀπορροφάω or -έω, f. ήσω, *to gulp down, swallow a part of.*

ἀπόρρῠτος, ον, = ἀπόρροος, *flowing from*; ἀπόρρυτα σταθμά stables *with drains.*

ἀπορ-ρυήσομαι, fut. of ἀπορ-ρέω.

ἀπορ-ρυῆναι, aor. 2 pass., with act. sense, of ἀπορρέω.

ἀπορρώξ, ῶγος, ὁ, ἡ, (ἀπορρήγνυμι) *broken off, abrupt, steep.* II. as Subst. fem. *a piece broken off* or *divided from* anything; Στυγὸς ὕδατος ἀπορρώξ *an off-stream* of the Styx.

ἀπ-ορφανίζομαι, f. ίσομαι, Pass. *to be taken away like an orphan from, to be torn away from.*

ἀπ-ορχέομαι, f. ήσομαι, Dep. *to dance* a thing *away*, i. e. *lose by dancing.*

ἄπος, εος, τό, = κάματος, *weariness.*

ἀπο-σᾰλεύω, f. εύσω, *to lie to in the open sea* (*in the offing*:—metaph. *to keep aloof from.*

ἀπο-σᾰφέω, f. ήσω, (ἀπό, σαφής) *to make clear.*

ἀπο-σβέννῡμι or -**σβεννύω**: f. -σβέσω:—*to extinguish, quench*: *to destroy, blot out*:—Pass. with fut. med. -σβήσομαι; intr. aor. 2 act. ἀπέσβην, pf. act. ἀπέσβηκα: *to go out, vanish, die.*

ἀπο-σείω, f. σω, *to shake off*:—Med. *to shake off from oneself*; of a horse, *to throw* his rider.

ἀπο-σεμνύνω, *to extol pompously*:—Pass., with f. med. ἀποσεμνῠνοῦμαι, *to give oneself airs.*

ἀπο-σεύω, *to chase away*:—Pass. *to dart away*, aor. ἀπεσσύθην [ῡ]; 3 sing. Ep. aor. 2 pass. ἀπέσσυτο.

ἀπο-σημαίνω, f. ἄνῶ, *to announce by signs, to give notice: to give a sign, to confirm* or *prove by a sign.* II. ἀποσημαίνειν εἴς τινα *to allude to him.* III. Med. *to seal up as confiscated, to confiscate*: of persons, *to proscribe.*

ἀπο-σήπω, f. ψω, *to make rotten, spoil utterly*:—Pass., fut. -σᾰπήσομαι, aor. 2 ἀπεσάπην [ᾰ]; with intr. pf. act. ἀποσέσηπα: *to rot off, lose by mortification.*

ἀπο-σῑμόω, f. ώσω, *to make flat-nosed*:—Pass. *to be so.* II. ἀποσιμοῦν τὰς ναῦς *to turn the line* of sailing *aside, make a movement sidewards*, so as to avoid the direct shock.

ἀπ-οσιόομαι, Ion. for ἀφ-οσιόομαι.

ἀπο-σῑωπάω, f. ήσομαι, *to be silent after* speaking, *be quite silent* II. trans. *to keep secret.* Hence

ἀποσῑώπησις, εως, ἡ, *a becoming silent.* 2. *a rhetorical figure, when the sentence is broken off*, as Virg. Ecl. 3. 8, Aen. 1. 139.

ἀπο-σκάπτω, f. ψω, *to cut off* or *intercept by trenches.*

ἀπο-σκεδάννῡμι: f. -σκεδάσω [ᾰ] contr. -σκεδῶ:—*to scatter abroad*:—Pass. *to be scattered, straggle away.*

ἀποσκέψομαι, fut. of ἀποσκοπέω.

ἀπο-σκευάζω, f. άσω, *to pack and carry away*:—Med. *to pack one's baggage, prepare for a journey.*

ἀποσκηνέω, f. ήσω, *to encamp apart from.* From

ἀπό-σκηνος, ον, (ἀπό, σκηνή) *living and messing alone*, opp. to σύσσιτος.

ἀπο-σκήπτω, f. ψω, *to prop one* thing *upon* another, *to dash* one thing *upon* or *against* another; esp. of the gods, ἀποσκήπτειν βέλεα ἔς τι *to hurl down* thunderbolts *upon* or *at* a thing. II. intr. *to burst* or *break forth*, like thunder; ἀποσκήπτειν ἐς φλαῦρον *to come to* a sorry *ending, end in* nothing.

ἀπο-σκιάζω, f. σω, *to cast a shadow.* Hence

ἀποσκίασμα, ατος, τό, *a shade, shadow: an adumbration.*

ἀπο-σκίδνᾰμαι, Pass., = ἀποσκεδάννυμαι, *to be scattered.*

ἀπο-σκλῆναι, aor. 2 inf. as if from ἀπό-σκλημι (see σκέλλω) *to be dried up, withered.*

ἀπο-σκοπέω, f. -σκέψομαι, *to look away from* other objects *at* one, and so *to look steadily at, gaze at*, πρός τινα or τι: c. acc. *to look to, regard.*

ἀπο-σκόπιος, ον, (ἀπό, σκοπός) *away from the mark.*

ἀπο-σκυδμαίνω, *to be enraged with*

ἀπο-σκῠθίζω, f. ίσω Att. ιῶ, *to strip off the scalp* like the Scythians, *to scalp*: metaph. *to shave bare.*

ἀπο-σκῡλεύω, f. σω, *to plunder and carry off.*

ἀπο-σκώπτω, f. ψομαι, *to banter, rally.*

ἀπο-σμύττω, f. ξω, *to deceive*:—aor. 2 pass. part. ἀποσμυγέντες, *being deceived.*

ἀπο-σοβέω, f. ήσω, *to scare away*, as one does birds. II. intr. *to be off in a hurry*, in phrase **οὐκ ἀποσοβήσεις; be off!**

ἀπο-σπᾰράσσω, Att. -ττω, f. ξω, *to tear off.*

ἀπόσπασμα, ατος, τό, *that which is torn off, a shred.* From

ἀπο-σπάω, f. -σπάσω [ᾰ], *to tear* or *drag away, sever* or *part from*; ἀποσπᾶν πύλας *to tear off* the gates; ἀπ. τὸ στρατόπεδον *to draw off* the army:—Pass. *to be dragged away from*: of an army, *to be separated* or *broken.*

ἀπο-σπένδω, f. -σπείσω, *to pour out wine as a drink-offering* at sacrifices, Lat. *libare.*

ἀπο-σπεύδω, f. -σπεύσω, *to be eager in preventing, to dissuade earnestly.*

ἀπο-σποδέω, f. ήσω, *to rub off, knock off.*

ἀποσ-σεύω, poët. for ἀπο-σεύω.

ἀπόστᾰ, for ἀπόστηθι, aor. 2 imperat. of ἀφίστημι.

ἀπο-στᾰδόν, Adv. (ἀφίστημι) *standing afar, far off.*

ἀπο-στάζω, f. ξω, *to let fall drop by drop.* II. intr. *to fall in drops*; μανίας δεινὸν ἀποστάζει μένος the fury of madness is *trickling, is ebbing away.*

ἀποστάς, ἀποστῆναι, aor. 2 act. part. and inf. of ἀφίστημι.

ἀποστᾰσία, ἡ, (ἀφίσταμαι) later form for ἀπόστασις, *defection, revolt, apostasy.*

ἀποστάσιον, το, (ἀφίσταμαι) *a divorce*; ἀποστᾰσίου βιβλίον, τό, a writing or bill *of divorce.* The nom. is not found in good authors.

ἀπόστᾰσις, εως, ἡ, (ἀφίσταμαι) *a standing away from*, and so 1. *a defection, revolt.* 2. *departure* or *removal from.* 3. *distance, interval.*

ἀποστᾰτέον, verb. Adj. of ἀφίσταμαι, *one must recede from.*

ἀποστᾰτέω, f. ήσω, *to stand off* or *aloof from*: *to differ from*: *to fall off* or *revolt from.* II. absol. *to stand aloof, be absent.* From

ἀποστατής, οῦ, ὁ, (ἀφίσταμαι) *a runaway, deserter, rebel.* Hence

ἀποστατικός, ή, όν, *rebellious*: Adv., ἀποστατικῶς ἔχειν *to be rebelliously inclined.*

ἀπο-σταυρόω, f. ώσω, *to fence off with pales.*

ἀπο-στεγάζω, f. άσω, *to uncover, unroof.*

ἀπο-στέγω, f. ξω, *to shelter from*:—*to shelter, keep safe.* II. *to keep off* water, and generally *to keep off*, as, ὄχλον πύργος ἀποστέγει.

ἀπο-στεινόω, poët. for ἀπο-στενόω.

ἀπο-στείχω, f. ξω: aor. 2 ἀπέστῐχον:—*to go away*, esp. *to go back.*

ἀπο-στέλλω, f. -στελῶ: aor. 1 ἀπέστειλα: pf. -έσταλκα:—Pass., aor. 2 ἀπεστάλην [ᾰ]: pf. -έσταλμαι:—*to send away from*: absol. *to send away, banish.* II. *to send off, dispatch*, on some service. III. *to drive back*:—Pass. *to be sent off*: also, *to go away.* IV. intr. *to go back.*

ἀπο-στενόω, poët. **-στεινόω**: f. ώσω: *to straiten*: ἀπεστείνωντο 3 pl. plqpf. pass.

ἀπο-στέργω, f. ξω, *to love no more*:—*to deprecate.*

ἀπο-στερέω, fut. ήσω, *to rob, bereave*, or *defraud* one of a thing: c. acc. rei only, *to take away, withhold*:—Pass. with fut. pass. and med. -στερηθήσομαι and *-στερήσομαι*, pf. *ἀπεστέρημαι*:—*to be robbed* or *in want of*. II. impers., *ἀποστερεῖ με* there *fails me, I lack*. Hence

ἀποστέρησις, *εως, ἡ*, *a robbery: deprivation.*

ἀποστερητής, *οῦ, ὁ*, (*ἀποστερέω*) *a robber, cheat*: fem. **ἀποστερητίς** or **-τρίς**, *ίδος, ἡ*, as Adj. = *ἀποστερητική*.

ἀποστερητικός, *ή, όν*, (*ἀποστερέω*) *able to rob* or *deprive; γνώμη ἀποστερητικὴ τόκου* a device for *cheating* one of his interest.

ἀποστερητρίς, *ίδος, ἡ*, v. sub. *ἀποστερητής*.

ἀπο-στερίσκω, = *ἀποστερέω*.

ἀπο-στηρίζω, f. *ξω*, *to fix firmly.*

ἀπο-στιλβόω, f. *ώσω*, *to make to shine.*

ἀπο-στίλβω, f. *ψω*, *to be bright with.*

ἀπο-στλεγγίζω, f. *ίσω* Att. *ιῶ*, *to scrape with a strigil*:—Med. *to scrape off* sweat *from oneself*; pf. pass. part. *ἀπεστλεγγισμένοι*, *scraped clean*, Lat. *lauti.*

ἀποστολεύς, *έως, ὁ*, (*ἀποστέλλω*) *one who equips a fleet.*

ἀποστολή, *ἡ*, (*ἀποστέλλω*) *a sending off, a mission: a dispatching.* II. (from Pass.) *an expedition.* III. *the office of an apostle, apostleship.*

ἀπόστολος, *ὁ*, (*ἀποστέλλω*) *a messenger, ambassador.* 2. *an apostle.* II. = *στόλος*, *a naval expedition.*

ἀπο-στοματίζω, f. *ίσω* Att. *ιῶ*, = *ἀπὸ* **στόματος** *εἰπεῖν*, *to speak from memory* or *off-hand.* II. *to put questions to*, so as to require an *immediate* answer.

ἀπ-οστρᾰκίζω, f. *ίσω* Att. *ιῶ*, *to banish by* ostracism.

ἀπο-στρᾰτοπεδεύω, or Dep. **ἀποστρατοπεδεύομαι**, *to encamp away from*: *ἀποστρατοπεδεύεσθαι* **πόρσω** *to encamp* at a distance.

ἀποστραφῶ, *ῇς, ῇ*, aor. 2 pass. subj. of

ἀπο-στρέφω, f. *ψω*: 3 sing. Ion. aor. 1 *ἀποστρέψασκε*:—Pass., aor. 2 *ἀπεστράφην*: pf. *ἀπέστραμμαι*. *To turn back*, either *to turn to flight*, or *to turn back from* flight; *πόδας καὶ χεῖρας ἀποστρέφειν*, *to twist back* the hands and feet so as to bind them. 2. *to turn away* or *aside*: hence *to dissuade from* a thing. II. intr. (sub. *ἑαυτόν*, etc.), *to turn oneself, turn back*:—Pass., with fut. med. *-στρέψομαι*, *to be turned back; ἀπεστράφθαι τοὺς ἐμβόλους*, of ships, *to have* their beaks *bent back.* III. *to turn oneself from* or *away, abhor*, Lat. *aversari*, c. acc.; *μή. μ' ἀποστραφῇς do* not *turn away from* me, like Lat. *avertor; ἀπεστραμμένοι λόγοι hostile* words. 2. *to get away, escape.* 3. *to turn and flee.* Hence

ἀποστροφή, *ἡ*, *a turning away, averting.* II. (from Pass.) *a turning oneself.* 2. *an escape*, or *a place of refuge from* a thing, *resource; ἀπ. κακῶν a refuge from* evil; *ὕδατος ἀποστροφή a resource against the want* of water, *a means of getting* it.

ἀπό-στροφος, *ον*, (*ἀποστρέφω*) *turned away, averted.*

ἀπο-στῠγέω, f. *-στύξω*: aor. 1 *-εστύγησα* and *-έστυξα*: aor. 2 *-έστῠγον*; perf. *-εστύγηκα*:—*to hate utterly, loathe.*

ἀπο-στῠφελίζω, f. *ξω*, *to chase away by force.*

ἀπο-σῡκάζω, f. *άσω*, (*ἀπό, σῦκον*) *to squeeze figs*, to try whether they are ripe: metaph. of informers.

ἀπο-σῡλάω, f. *ήσω*, *to strip off spoils from* a person: *to rob* or *defraud* one *of* a thing.

ἀπο-συνάγωγος, *ον*, (*ἀπό, συναγωγή*) *put out of the synagogue.*

ἀπο-σῡρίζω, f. *ξω*, *to whistle aloud* for want of thought.

ἀπο-σύρω [ῡ], f. *-σῠρῶ*, *to strip off, tear away: lay bare.*

ἀπο-σφάζω Att. **-σφάττω**, f. *ξω*: (for the tenses, v. *σφάζω*):—*to cut the throat; ἀποσφάζειν τινὰ ἐς* ἄγγος, so that the blood runs into a pail: generally, *to slay*:—Med. *to kill oneself.*

ἀπο-σφᾰκελίζω, f. *ίσω*, *to have one's limbs mortified: to die of mortification.*

ἀπο-σφάλλω, f. *-σφᾰλῶ*: aor. 1 *-έσφηλα*:—*to lead astray, drive baffled away; ἀποσφάλλειν τινὰ* **πόνου** *to make one miss* the fruits of toil: Pass., esp. in aor. 2 *ἀπεσφάλην* [ᾰ], *to be cheated of* a thing, *miss* it.

ἀπο-σφάττω, = *ἀποσφάζω*.

ἀποσφήλειε, ἀποσφήλωσιν, aor. 1 opt. and subj. of *ἀποσφάλλω*.

ἀπο-σφρᾱγίζω, Ion. **σφρηγ-**, f. *ίσω* Att. *ιῶ*: *to seal up, shut up.*

ἀπ-οσφραίνω, f. *-οσφρήσω*, *to make to smell.*

ἀπο-σχᾰλιδόω, f. *ώσω*, *to prop nets on poles.* Hence

ἀποσχᾰλίδωμα, *ατος, τό*, *a forked piece of wood for propping hunting-nets.*

ἀποσχήσω, fut. of *ἀπέχω*.

ἀπο-σχεῖν, -σχεσθαι, aor. 2 act. and med. inf. of *ἀπέχω*.

ἀπο-σχίζω, f. *ίσω*: aor. 1 pass. *ἀπεσχίσθην*:—*to split* or *cleave off.* 2. *to sever, part*, or *detach from*: esp. in Pass., of a river *being parted from* the main stream, a tribe *detached from* its parent stock, etc.

ἀπο-σώζω, f. *-σώσω*, *to save, restore again: ἀπ. οἴκαδε to bring safe* home:—Pass., *ἀποσωθῆναι ἐς* .. *to get safe* to a place, *to get off safe.*

ἀποτακτός, *όν*, (*ἀποτάσσω*) *set apart for a special use, specially appointed.*

ἀπο-τάμνω, Ion. for *ἀπο-τέμνω*.

ἀπο-τάσσω, Att. **-ττω**, f. *ξω*, *to set apart* or *assign specially; ἀπετέτακτο πρὸς τὸ δεξιόν he had been stationed* on the right. II. Med., *ἀποτάσσομαί τινι to bid adieu to* a person or thing.

ἀποταυρόομαι, Pass. *to act like a bull; δέργματα ἀποταυροῦσθαι to cast fierce* glances on.

ἀπο-ταφρεύω, f. *σω*, *to fence with a ditch, intrench.*

ἀποτέθνασαν, Ep. 3 pl. plqpf. of *ἀποθνήσκω*, *they were dead.*

ἀποτεθνειώς, for *ἀποτεθνεώς, ἀποτεθνηκώς*, Ion. pf. part. of *ἀποθνήσκω*.

ἀπο-τείνω, fut. *-τενῶ*: (for the tenses, v. *τείνω*):—*to stretch out, to lengthen*: c. part., *to continue* doing:—Med. *to exert oneself.* 2. intr., like Lat. *contendere, to hasten onwards.*

ro-τειχίζω, f. ίσω Att. ιῶ, to wall off, 1. so as ortify. 2. so as to blockade. Hence

ποτείχῐσις, εως, ἡ, the walling of a town, blocking. And

ποτείχισμα, τό, walls built to blockade, lines of ckade.

ποτελευτάω, f. ήσω, to bring quite to an end. 2. 1. to come to an end, cease, εἴς τι in a thing.

πο-τελέω, f. -τελέσω Att. τελῶ: pf. -τετέλεκα: Pass., aor. 1 -ετελέσθην: pf. -τετέλεσμαι. To ing quite to an end: pf. pass. part. ἀποτετελεσμένος, perfect. 2. to fulfil an obligation. 3. nerally to accomplish, perform, do. 4. to render make of a certain kind; τὴν πόλιν ἀποτελεῖν εὐδαίμονα to make the state quite happy.

πο-τέμνω, Ion. and Ep. -τάμνω: fut. -τεμῶ: aor. ἀπέτᾰμον: pf. ἀποτέτμηκα:—to cut off; ἀποτέμνειν τινός to cut off part of a thing. 2. to separate cut off from:—Med. to cut off for oneself, esp. with ew of appropriating.

πο-τήκω, f. ξω, to make to melt away:—Pass., esp. aor. 2 ἀπετάκην [ᾰ], to melt away.

πο-τηλοῦ, Adv. far away.

-ποτίβᾰτος, ον, Dor. and poët. for ἀ-πρόσβατος.

πο-τίθημι, f. -θήσω, to put away: to stow away:—Med. to put from oneself, put off; lay aside. 2. to ut by for oneself, stow away. 3. ἀποτίθεσθαι εἰς ὖθις to put aside for another time.

ἀπο-τίλλω, f. -τῐλῶ: aor. 1 -ἔτῑλα: to pluck out. Hence

ἀπότιλμα, ατος, τό, that which is plucked, a shred.

ἀπο-τῑμάω, f. ήσω, not to honour, to slight. II. to value, fix a price by valuation; διμνέως ἀποτιμησάμενοι having fixed their price at two minae: Hence III. as Att. law-term, Act. to mortgage property according to valuation:—Med. to lend on mortgage:—Pass. of the property, to be pledged or mortgaged. Hence

ἀποτίμημα, τό, a sum settled by valuation.

ἀπό-τῑμος, ον, (ἀπό, τιμή) = ἄτιμος, dishonoured.

ἀπο-τινάσσω, Att. -ττω, fut. ξω, to shake off.

ἀπο-τίνῠμαι, Dep., poët. for ἀπο-τίνομαι.

ἀπο-τίνω, f. -τίσω [ῑ], to pay back, repay what is owing:—Med. ἀποτίνομαι, f. -τίσομαι, to get paid one, exact; ἀποτίσασθαί τινα to avenge oneself on another: absol. to take vengeance.

ἀπο-τμήγω, f. ξω, Ep. for ἀπο-τέμνω, to cut off from; κλιτῦς ἀπ. to cut up or plough the hills.

ἀποτμήξειε, 3 sing. aor. 1 opt. of ἀποτμήγω.

ἄ-ποτμος, ον, unhappy, ill-starred.

ἀπο-τολμάω, f. ήσω, to make a bold venture. II. absol. to be fearless, bold.

ἀποτομή, ἡ, (ἀποτέμνω) a cutting off.

ἀποτομία, ἡ, steepness, severity. From

ἀπότομος, ον, (ἀποτέμνω) cut off, abrupt, precipitous. 2. metaph. harsh, rough:—Adv. -μως, sharply.

ἀπο-τοξεύω, f. σω, to shoot off arrows: to aim at a thing.

ἄ-ποτος, ον, (α privat., ποτός) not drunk, not drinkable. II. act. never drinking: without drink.

ἀποτρᾰγεῖν, aor. 2 inf. of ἀποτρώγω.

ἀπο-τρέπω, f. ψω, to turn away from a thing; and so to hinder or dissuade from. 2. c. acc. only, to turn away or back: to avert evil. 3. also to turn away from others at one, hence to aim at. II. Med. and Pass. to turn from a thing, to desist from. 2. to turn away. 3. to turn one's face away, like Lat. aversari.

ἀπο-τρέχω; fut. -θρέξομαι, also -δραμοῦμαι: aor. 2 ἀπέδρᾰμον (from obsol. δρέμω):—to run off or away.

ἀπο-τρίβω [ῑ], f. ψω, to rub or scour clean; ἀποτρίβειν ἵππον to rub down a horse. II. to rub off:—Med. to rub off from oneself, get rid of.

ἀποτρόπαιος, ον, turning away, averting, esp. of the gods that avert ill, Lat. Dii averrunci. II. pass. that ought to be averted, ill-omened. From

ἀποτροπή, ἡ, (ἀποτρέπω) a turning away, averting. 2. a turning off of water. II. a hindering. III. (from Med.) a desertion of one's party.

ἀπότροπος, ον, (ἀποτρέπω) turned away, banished. 2. from which one turns away. II. act. turning away, averting.

ἀπό-τροφος, ον, (ἀπό, τροφή) reared away from one's parents.

ἀπ-οτρύνω, f. -οτρῠνῶ, to excite.

ἀπο-τρύω, f. ύσω [ῡ], to rub away, and so lose. II. to vex, harass; so in Med., ἀποτρύεσθαι γῆν to vex the earth.

ἀπο-τρώγω, f. -τρώξομαι: aor. 2 ἀπέτρᾰγον:—to bite or nibble off.

ἀπο-τρωπάω, poët. Frequent. of ἀποτρέπω.

ἀπο-τυγχάνω, f. -τεύξομαι, to fail in hitting, miss, lose. II. absol. to be unlucky, fail: to miss the truth, be wrong.

ἀπο-τυμπανίζω, f. ίσω Att. ιῶ, to beat or cudgel severely.

ἀπο-τύπτω, f. ψω, to cease beating:—Med. to cease beating oneself in sign of mourning.

ἀπούρας, Ep. aor. 1 act. part. of ἀπαυράω, to take away: part. aor. 1 med. ἀπουράμενος in pass. sense occurs in Hesiod.

ἀπ-ουρίζω, f. ίσω, Ion. for ἀφ-ορίζω, to mark off the boundaries; ἄλλοι γάρ οἱ ἀπουρίσσουσιν ἀρούρας, others will mark off, i. e. lessen, the boundaries of his fields: others read ἀπουρήσουσι, as if from *ἀπουράω = ἀπαυράω, will take them away.

ἄπ-ουρος, ον, (ἀπό, οὖρος Ion. for ὅρος) far from the boundaries; ἄπουρος πάτρας far away from one's fatherland.

ἄ-πους, ὁ, ἡ, ἄπουν, τό, gen. ἄποδος, without foot or feet: without the use of one's feet: slow of foot.

ἀπουσία, ἡ, (ἄπειναι) a being away, absence. II. deficiency, want.

ἀποφᾰγεῖν, aor. 2 inf. of ἀπεσθίω, to eat up.

ἀπο-φαιδρύνω [ῡ], f. ὑνῶ, to make quite bright.

ἀπο-φαίνω, f. -φᾰνῶ: aor. 1 ἀπέφηνα:—to show

forth, display: to shew by word, declare. 2. *to shew by reasoning, shew, prove.* II. like ἀποδείκνυμι *to shew*, and so *to make* or *render*:—Med. *to shew forth something of one's own, to make a display of oneself*: ἀποφαίνεσθαι γνώμην *to declare* one's opinion: Pass. *to be shewn* or *declared.* III. *to appear, come to light*

ἀπόφᾰσις, εως, ἡ, (ἀπόφημι) *a denial, negation.*

ἀπόφᾰσις, εως, ἡ, (ἀποφαίνω) = ἀπόφανσις, *a sentence, decision.*

ἀπο-φάσκω, = ἀπόφημι, *to deny.*

ἀπο-φᾰτικός, ή, όν, (ἀπόφημι) *denying, negative.*

ἀπο-φέρβομαι, Dep. *to feed off* or *on.*

ἀπο-φέρω, f. ἀποίσω: aor. ἀπήνεγκα, Ion. ἀπένεικα: (v. φέρω):—*to carry off* or *away.* II. *to carry* or *bring back*. hence 2. *to report.* 3. *to pay back, return*: generally, *to pay what is due.* III. *to deliver in, give in* an accusation, etc. IV. intr. in imperat., like ἄπαγε, ἀπόφερε, *begone*:—Med. *to take for oneself, gain, obtain.*

ἀποφεύγω, f. -φεύξομαι: aor. 2 ἀπέφῠγον:—*to flee from, escape.* II. as law-term; ἀποφεύγειν τοὺς διώκοντας *to make good one's defence*: absol. *to be acquitted*, opp. to ἁλίσκομαι. Hence

ἀποφευκτικός, ή, όν, *ready for escaping*; τὰ ἀποφευκτικά *means of escape.* And

ἀπόφευξις, εως, ἡ, *an escaping, getting off.*

ἀπό-φημι, f. -φήσω, *to speak out, declare plainly.* 2. *to say no, to deny*: also *to refuse.*

ἀπο-φθέγγομαι, f. -φθέγξομαι, Dep. *to speak one's opinion plainly.* Hence

ἀπόφθεγκτος, ον, = ἄφθεγκτος.

ἀπόφθεγμα, ατος, τό, (ἀποφθέγγομαι) *a thing uttered*: esp. *a sententious answer, a terse saying, an apophthegm.*

ἀπο-φθείρω, f. -φθερῶ: pf. ἀπέφθαρκα:—*to destroy utterly, ruin*:—Pass., with fut. med. ἀποφθεροῦμαι, *to be lost, perish*, οὐκ εἰς κόρακας ἀποφθερεῖ μου; *wilt* not *be gone* with a murrain? Lat. *abi in malam rem.*

ἀπο-φθῐνύθω [ῠ], *to perish.* II. trans., ἀποφθινύθειν θυμόν *to lose* one's life.

ἀπο-φθίνω: Ep. aor. 2 act. ἀπέφθῐθον: also as in Ep. aor. 2 pass. ἀπεφθίμην [ῐ], part. ἀποφθίμενος:—*to perish utterly, to die away.* II. Causal. in fut. ἀποφθίσω, aor. ἀπέφθῐσα, *to make to perish, to destroy.*

ἀποφθίσθω, 3 sing. Ep. aor. 2 pass. imperat. of foreg.

ἀποφθορά, ἡ, (ἀποφθείρω) *utter destruction.*

ἀπο-φλαυρίζω, f. ίσω Dor. ίξω, *to treat very slightingly, make no account of.*

ἀπο-φλοιόω, f. ώσω, (ἀπό, φλοιός) *to strip off the rind.*

ἀπο-φοιτάω, f. ήσω, *to go quite away*: esp. of scholars, *to leave their masters.*

ἀπό-φονος, ον, *murderous.*

ἀποφορά, ἡ, (ἀποφέρω) *a carrying away.* II. *a bringing what is due, paying*: also *that which is paid, tax, tribute.*

ἀπο-φορτίζομαι, f. ίσομαι, Dep. *to unload oneself, to unlade.*

ἀπο-φράγνῡμι and -ύω, fut -φράξω, *to fence off, block up.* Hence

ἀπόφραξις, εως, ἡ, *a fencing off, blocking up.*

ἀπο-φράς, άδος, ἡ, (ἀπό, φράζω) properly *not to be spoken of*, like Lat. *nefandus, unlucky, ominous* ἀποφράδες ἡμέραι, Lat. *dies nefasti*, days on which no assembly or court was held, opp to καθαραὶ ἡμέραι.

ἀπο-φράσσω Att. -ττω, = ἀποφράγνυμι.

ἀπο-φυάς, άδος, ἡ, (ἀπό, φύομαι) *an offshoot.*

ἀποφῠγή, ἡ, (ἀποφεύγω) *an escape, flight, place of refuge.*

ἀπό-φυξις, v. sub ἀπόφευξις

ἀπο-φύομαι, Pass., with aor. 2 act ἀπέφυν and perf ἀποπέφῡκα, *to grow out like a shoot.*

ἀπ-οφώλιος, ον, (ἀπό, ὄφελος?) *empty, vain, idle*, Lat. *irritus.*

ἀπο-χάζομαι, f. -χάσομαι, Dep *to withdraw from*

ἀποχᾰλασμός, ὁ, *a slackening.* From

ἀπο-χᾰλάω, f. άσω [ᾰ], *to slack* or *loose away*, as one pays out a rope.

ἀπο-χᾰλῑνόω, f. ώσω, *to unbridle.*

ἀπο-χαλκεύω, f. σω, *to forge of brass*

ἀπο-χαλκίζω, f. σω, *to strip of brass.*

ἀπο-χειρο-βίωτος, ον, (ἀπό, χείρ, βιόω) *living by one's hands*, i. e. *by manual labour*

ἀπο-χειροτονέω, f. ήσω, *to vote a charge away from* one, *acquit him.* II. of persons, *to reject, to supersede, depose.* 2 of things, *to reject, vote against to abrogate, annul.* Hence

ἀποχειροτόνησις, εως, ἡ, *rejection by show of hands*

ἀπ-οχετεύω, f. σω, *to draw off water by a canal.*

ἀπο-χέω, f. -χεῶ: aor. 1 ἀπέχεα. Pass., aor. 1 ἀπεχύθην [ῠ]: pf ἀποκέχῠμαι —*to pour out, spill, shed*

ἀπο-χραίνω, *to soften off the colour, shade off*

ἀπο-χράω, Ion. -χρέω, inf ἀποχρῆν Ion -χρᾶν: impf. ἀπέχρην: fut ἀποχρήσω aor. 1 ἀπέχρησα:—*to suffice, be sufficient, be enough*, ἑκατὸν νέες ἀποχρῶσι. 2. with dat, ποταμὸς οὐκ ἀπέχρησε τῇ στρατιῇ *was not enough* for the army with infin., ἀποχρᾷ μοι ποιεῖν *'tis sufficient* for me to do; also 3 sing. impf. med. ἀπεχρέετο = ἀπέχρη. 3 Pass *to be contented with* a thing; ἀποχρεωμένων τούτοις τῶν Μυσῶν the Mysians being *satisfied therewith.* II. Med. *to use to the full.* 2 *to abuse, misuse*, Lat *abuti.*

ἀπο-χρέομαι, -χρέω, Ion. for ἀποχράομαι, χράω

ἀπό-χρη, impers., v. ἀποχράω.

ἀπο-χρήματος, ον, (ἀπό, χρῆμα) *not to be paid in money.*

ἀπόχρησις, εως, ἡ, (ἀποχράομαι) *a using to the full, misuse*: *a getting rid of.*

ἀποχρώντως, Adv. pres. part. of ἀποχράω, ἀπόχρη, *enough, sufficiently.*

ἀποχῠθείς, aor. 1 pass. part. of ἀποχέω.

ἀπο-χωλόω, (ἀπό, χωλός) *to make quite lame.*

ἀπο-χώννυμι, f. -χώσω, *to dam up, bank up* the mouth of a river, etc.

ἀπο-χωρέω, f. ήσω or ήσομαι, *to go from* or *away from*, c. gen. 2. absol. *to go away, depart: to retreat*. 3. ἀποχωρεῖν ἐκ.., *to withdraw from* a thing, i. e. *give* it *up*. II. *to pass off*, esp. of the humours of the body. Hence

ἀποχώρησις, εως, ἡ, *a going away* or *off*, *retreat: a place* or *means of safety*.

ἀπο-χωρίζω, f. ίσω Att. ιῶ, *to part* or *separate from: to set apart*.

ἀπο-ψάω, inf. ἀποψῆν: impf. ἀπέψην: aor. 1 ἀπέψησα:—*to wipe off*. 2. *to wipe clean*:—Med. *to wipe off from oneself*. 3. *to wipe one's nose*.

ἀπο-ψηφίζομαι, fut. ίσόυμαι Att. ιοῦμαι, Dep.: I. c. acc. pers. *to vote* an office *away from* one, *to reject* him:—aor. 1 ἀπεψηφίσθην and pf. ἀπεψήφισμαι are sometimes used in pass. sense, *to be rejected*. II. c. acc. rei, ἀπ. γραφήν *to vote against receiving* the indictment; ἀπ. νόμον *to reject* the law; αἰτίαν ἀποψηφίζομαί τινος *to vote a charge away from* one, *acquit*: absol. *to vote an acquittal*. III. ἀποψηφίζεσθαι μὴ ποιεῖν *to vote against* doing. Hence

ἀποψήφισις, εως, ἡ, *an acquittal*.

ἀπο-ψιλόω, f. ώσω, *to strip of hair, make bald*: generally, *to strip bare, bereave* of a thing.

ἄποψις, εως, ἡ, (ἀπόψομαι, fut. of ἀφοράω) *a looking from, a view, prospect*.

ἀπ-όψομαι, fut. from an obsol. pres. ἀπ-όπτομαι, used as fut. of ἀφοράω.

ἀπο-ψύχω [ῡ], f. ξω: pf. pass. ἀπέψυγμαι: (ἀπό, ψυχή):—*to leave off breathing, to faint, swoon*. 2. acc., ἀποψύχειν ψυχήν *to breathe out* life: absol. *to expire, die*. II. (ἀπό, ψῦχος) *to cool, refresh*:—Pass. *to be refreshed, recover, revive*: Med., ἱδρῶτα ἀπεψύχοντο *they got* the sweat *dried off*. III. impers. ἀποψύχει, *it grows cool, the air cools*.

ἀπ-πέμψει, Ep. contr. for ἀποπέμψει.

ἀπραγμόνως, Adv. of ἀπράγμων, *easily*.

ἀπραγμοσύνη, ἡ, *freedom from business, public affairs* and *law-suits: love of ease*, Lat. *otium*. 2. *easiness, supineness*. From

ἀπράγμων, ον, gen. ονος, (α privat., πρᾶγμα) *without business, free from business, state-affairs* or *law-suits* (πράγματα); τόπος ἀπράγμων, a place *free from law and strife*. 2. of things, *not troublesome* or *painful*. II. pass. *got* or *to be got without pains*.

ἀπρακτέω, f. ήσω. *to do nothing, to be idle*. 2. *to gain nothing*. From

ἄ-πρακτος, Ion. **ἄ-πρηκτος**, ον: I. act. *doing* or *effecting nothing, unprofitable, idle*; ἄπρακτος νέεσθαι to depart *without success*, Lat. *re infecta*:—Adv. -τως, *unsuccessfully*. II. pass. *against which nothing can be done, unmanageable, incurable*. 2. *not to be done, impossible*. 3. μαντικῆς ἄπρακτος ὑμῖν, *unassailed* by your divining arts. Hence

ἀπραξία, ἡ, *inaction: ill-success*. II. *a being at a loss, embarrassment, helplessness*.

ἄ-πρᾱτος, ον, (α privat., πέπρᾱται, 3 sing. pf. pass. of πιπράσκω) *unsold, unsaleable*.

ἀ-πρεπής, ές, (α privat., πρέπω) *unseemly, unbecoming*.

ἀπρεπία, ἡ, poët. for ἀπρέπεια.

ἄ-πρηκτος, Ion. for ἄπρακτος.

ἀ-πράϋντος, Ion. ἀπρήϋντος, ον, (α privat., πρᾱΰνω) *implacable*.

ἀπρῐάτην, Adv. *without price* or *ransom*. [ᾰτ] From

ἀ-πρίᾰτος, η, ον, (α privat., πρίαμαι) *unbought*.

ἄ-πριγδα, prob. = ἀπρίξ.

ἀπρικτό-πληκτος, ον, (ἀπρίξ, πλήσσω) *struck unceasingly*.

ἀ-πρίξ, Adv. (α copul., πριω) properly *with closed teeth*, like ὀδάξ, Lat. *mordicus*: metaph. *importunately, ceaselessly*.

ἀ-πρόβουλος, ον, *without previous design, unpremeditated*. Adv. -λως, *rashly, thoughtlessly*.

ἀ-πρόθῡμος, ον, *not ready, disinclined, backward*.

ἀ-προϊδής, ές, (α privat., προϊδεῖν) *unforeseen*.

ἀ-προμήθητος, ον, *unforeseen*.

ἀ-προνοήτως, Adv. of ἀπρονόητος, (α privat., προνοέω) *without foresight* or *forethought, heedlessly*.

ἀ-πρόξενος, ον, *without a* πρόξενος.

ἀ-πρόοπτος, ον, *unforeseen*.

ἀ-πρόσβᾰτος, Dor. **ἀποτίβατος**, ον, *inaccessible*: of disease, *not to be healed*.

ἀ-προσδόκητος, ον, *unexpected, unlooked for*:—Adv. -τως. II. act. *not expecting*.

ἀ-προσήγορος, ον, (α privat., προσήγορος) *not to be spoken to, stern, savage*. II. act. *not accosting, not greeting*.

ἀ-πρόσικτος, ον, (α privat., προσικνέομαι) *not to be reached* or *won*.

ἀ-πρόσῑτος, ον, (α privat., πρόσ-ειμι) *unapproachable*.

ἀ-πρόσκεπτος, ον, (α privat., προσκέψομαι, fut. of προσκοπέω) *unforeseen, not thought of beforehand*.

ἀ-πρόσκλητος, ον, (α privat., προσκαλέω) *not summoned to attend a trial*.

ἀ-πρόσκοπος, ον, (α privat., προσκόπτω) *not striking against, not stumbling, void of offence*.

ἀ-πρόσμᾰχος, ον, (α privat., προσμάχομαι) *irresistible*.

ἀ-πρόσμικτος, ον, (α privat. προσμίγνυμι) *holding no intercourse* or *commerce with* others.

ἀ-πρόσοιστος, ον, (α privat., προσοίσω fut. of προσφέρω) *not to be withstood, irresistible*.

ἀ-προσόμῑλος, ον, *unsociable*

ἀ-προστᾰσίου γραφή, ἡ, (α privat., προστάτης) *an indictment laid against a* μέτοικος at Athens, *for not having chosen a* προστάτης or *patron* from among the citizens. The nom. **ἀπροστάσιον**, τό, is not used.

ἀ-πρόσφορος, ον, (α privat., προσφέρω) *unsuitable, inconvenient, dangerous*

ἀ-προσωπο-λήπτως, (α privat., πρόσωπον, λαμβάνω) Adv. *without respect of persons*

ἀ-προτίμαστος, ον, Dor. for ἀ-πρόσμαστος, (α privat., προσμάσσω) *untouched, undefiled*.

ἀ-προφάσιστος, ον, (α privat., προφασίζομαι) *offer-*

ing no excuse, ready. Adv. -τως, *without evasion, honestly.*

ἀ-πρόσφᾰτος, *ον*, (α privat., πρόφημι) *unforetold.*

ἀ-προφύλακτος, *ον*, (α privat., προφυλάσσομαι) *not guarded against, unforeseen.*

ἄ-πταιστος, *ον*, (α privat., πταίω) *not stumbling;* ἀπταιστότερον παρέχειν τὸν ἵππον to make the horse *less apt to stumble.*

ἄ-πτερος, *ον*, (α privat., πτερόν) *without wings, unwinged:* in Homer, τῇ δ' ἄπτερος ἔπλετο μῦθος the speech was to her *without wings*, i. e. *flew not away again*, sank into her mind; ἄπτερα πωτήματα *wingless* flight; of arrows, *unfeathered;* of young birds, etc., *unfledged, callow;* ἄπτερος φάτις *an unfledged*, i. e. *unconfirmed*, report.

ἀ-πτήν, gen. ἀπτῆνος, ὁ, ἡ: dat. pl. ἀπτῆσι: (α privat., πτηνός) *unfledged, callow*, of young birds: *unwinged.*

ἀ-πτο-επής, ές, (α privat., πτοέω, ἔπος) *undaunted in speech.*

ἀ-πτόλεμος, *ον*, poët. for ἀπόλεμος.

ἁπτός, ή, όν, (ἅπτω) *touched, handled: to be touched, subject to the sense of touch.*

ἍΠΤΩ, f. ἅψω: aor. 1 ἧψα:—Pass., aor. 1 ἥφθην, Ep. ἑάφθην: pf. ἧμμαι, Ion. ἅμμαι. *To fasten, fasten to* or *on, fix upon* a thing; ἐπὶ δ' ἀσπὶς ἑάφθη his shield *was fastened*, i. e. *clung closely*, to him:—more freq. as Med., ἅπτομαι, fut. ἅψομαι: aor. 1 ἡψάμην:—*to fasten oneself to*, hence *to cling to, hang on by, grasp;* ἅψασθαι γούνων *to cling to one's* knees: later, *to engage in, undertake, begin.* 2. *to fasten upon, attack.* 3. *to touch, affect.* 4. *to grasp with the senses, apprehend, perceive.* 5. *to reach, overtake: to gain.* II. *to kindle, set on fire:*—Pass. *to take fire: to be set on fire.*

ἀ-πτώς, ῶτος, ὁ, ἡ, (α privat., πίπτω) *not falling* or *failing, unfailing.*

ἀ-πύλωτος, *ον*, (α privat., πυλόω) *not closed by a gate.*

ἄ-πυργος, *ον*, *without tower and wall, unfortified.*

ἀ-πύργωτος, *ον*, (α privat., πυργόω) *not girt with towers.*

ἄ-πῦρος, *ον*, (α privat., πῦρ) *without fire*, in Homer only of tripods, *that have not yet been on the fire*, i. e. *new;* ἄπυρος οἶκος *a cold, cheerless* house; χρυσὸς ἄπυρος *unrefined*, opp. to ἄπεφθος; ἱερὰ ἄπυρα sacrifices *in which no fire was used*, but also *not offered by fire*, and so like = ἄθυτα, *unoffered:* ἄπ. ἄρδις a sting *not forged by fire*, i. e. of the gadfly. Adv. -ρως.

ἀ-πύρωτος, *ον*, (α privat., πυρόω) *not yet exposed to fire.*

ἄ-πυστος, *ον*, (α privat., πυνθάνομαι) *of which nothing has been learnt, unknown.* II. act. *having learnt nothing, ignorant:* c. gen. *ignorant of.*

ἀπύτης, ὁ, Dor. for ἠπύτης. [ᾱπῠ-]

ἀπύω, Dor. for ἠπύω.

ἈΠΦΥ͂Σ or **ἀπφῦς**, gen. ύος, ὁ, a term of endearment used by children to their father, *papa*, Hebr. *Abba.*

ἀπ-ῳδός, όν, (ἀπό, ᾠδή) *discordant, out of tune.*

ἄπωθεν, Adv. = ἄποθεν, *from afar.*

ἀπ-ωθέω, f. -ωθήσω and -ώσω: aor. 1 ἀπέωσα or ἄπωσα:—*to thrust off, drive away:* of the wind, *to beat off, beat from* one's course: later, *to drive away from the land, banish.* 2. *to repel, drive back.* 3. in Med. *to reject, disdain.* Hence

ἀπώθητος, *ον*, *thrust* or *driven away, rejected.*

ἀπώλεια, ἡ, (ἀπόλλυμι) *destruction: loss: waste.*

ἀπώλεσα, aor. 1 of ἀπόλλυμι.

ἀπωλόμην, aor. 2 med., in pass. sense, of ἀπόλλυμι.

ἀ-πώμαστος, *ον*, (α privat., πῶμα) *without a lid.*

ἀπώμοσα, aor. 1 of ἀπόμνυμι.

ἀπωμοσία, ἡ, (ἀπόμνυμι) *a denial upon oath*, as Att. law-term, opp. to ἐξωμοσία.

ἀπώμοτος, *ον*, (ἀπόμνυμι) *forsworn, abjured, declared impossible with an oath*, Lat. *abjurandus;* βροτοῖσιν οὐδὲν ἔστ' ἀπώμοτον mortals should never make a vow against anything. II. act. *under oath not to do a thing.*

ἀπῶσαι, aor. 1 inf. of ἀπωθέω.

ἀπωσάμην, -σασθαι, aor. 1 med. ind. and inf. of ἀπωθέω.

ἀπωσι-κύματος, *ον*, (ἀπωθέω, κῦμα) *repelling waves.*

ἄπωσις, εως, ἡ, (ἀπωθέω) *a thrusting* or *driving away.*

ἀπωστός, ή, όν, (ἀπωθέω) *thrust* or *driven away from.* II. *that can be driven away.*

ἀπώτερος, α, *ον*, Comp. Adj. (ἀπό) *further off:*—Sup. **ἀπώτατος**, η, *ον*, *furthest off.*

ἀπωτέρω, Comp. Adv. of ἀπώτερος: **ἀπωτάτω**, Sup. Adv. of ἀπώτατος.

ἄρ, Ep. before a consonant for ἄρα.

ἎΡΑ, Ep. ῥά (which is enclitic), and before a consonant ἄρ: I. EPIC USAGE 1. *then, straightway;* ὣς φάτο, βῆ δ' ἄρ' ὄνειρος thus he spake and *then* the dream proceeded:—*then, next in order,* οἱ δ' ἄρ' Ἀθήνας εἶχον. 2. *explanation* of a thing going before; φῆ ῥ' ἀέκητι θεῶν φυγέειν *for* he said that he would flee: with relat. Pron. ἄρα makes it more precise; ἐκ δ' ἔθορε κλῆρος, ὃν ἄρ' ἤθελον αὐτοί *just* the one, the *very* one, which they wished. II. ATTIC USAGE:—here it always is like οὖν, *then, therefore, so then;* κάλλιστον ἄρα ἡ ἀρετή *therefore you must allow* virtue is best; μάτην ἄρ', ὡς ἔοικεν, ἥκομεν *so it seems then* we are come in vain:—in *questions,* τίς ἄρα ῥύσεται; *who then* is there to save?—Ἄρα cannot begin a sentence.

ἆρᾰ, interrog. particle, a stronger form of ἄρα, usually expecting a negat. answer, Lat. *num?* 2. if an affirmative answer is expected, ἆρα οὐ is used, = Lat. *nonne?* 3. ἆρα is also used in exclamations; ὀδυνηρὸς ἆρ' ὁ πλοῦτος! *grievous then* is wealth!—In prose ἆρα always stands first in the sentence.

ἈΡΆ, Ion. **ἈΡΉ**, ἡ, *a prayer:* in Homer mostly *a prayer for evil, a curse,* hence *the effect of the curse, mischief, ruin.* II. Ἀρά personified is the goddess of destruction and revenge, Lat. *Dira.*

ἀρᾰβέω, f. ήσω, *to rattle, ring, clang,* always of armour. From

Ἄ́ΡΑΒΟΣ, ὁ, *a rattling; ἄραβος ὀδόντων gnashing* or *grinding* of teeth.

ἄραγμα, ατος, τό, and **ἀραγμός**, ὁ, (ἀράσσω) *a clashing, rattling; ἄραγμος στέρνων beating* of the breast in grief, Lat. *planctus*.

ἆραι, aor. 1 inf. of *αἴρω*.

ἈΡΑΙΟ'Σ, Att. **ἀραιός**, ά, όν, also ός, όν, *thin, narrow, weak, slight*.

ἀραῖος, α, ον, also ος, ον, (ἀρά) *prayed to* or *entreated; Ζεὺς ἀραῖος*, = ἱκέσιος. 2. *prayed against, accursed*. II. act. *cursing, bringing mischief upon*. [ᾰ]

ἀραίρηκα, *ἀραιρηκώς, ἀραιρημένος, ἀραίρητο*, Ion. redupl. for *ᾕρηκα, ᾑρηκώς, ᾑρημένος, ᾕρητο*, pf. and plpqf. redupl. forms from *αἱρέω*.

ἀράμενος, aor. 1 med. part. of *αἴρω*.

ἀράομαι: f. *ἀσομαι* [ᾱ], Ion. *ήσομαι*: pf. *ἤρᾱμαι* only found in compos.: Dep.: (ἀρά) :—*to pray to* a god. 2. *to pray* or *vow that* a thing may happen, c. inf. 3. *to pray* something for one, sometimes in good sense, but mostly in bad, *to imprecate upon* one; esp. with cognate acc., *ἀρὰς* **ἀρᾶσθαί** *τινι to imprecate* curses upon one.

ἀρᾱρε, Dor. for *ἄρηρε*, 3 sing. pf. med. of *ἀραρίσκω* in intr. sense, *it is fixed, decreed*: but, II. *ἄρᾰρε*, Ep. for *ἤρᾰρε*, aor. 2 in trans. sense, *appeased, satisfied*.

ἀρᾰρεῖν, aor. 2 inf. of *ἀραρίσκω*.

ἀραρίσκω, redupl. pres. from the Root **ἄρω*: I. trans. in pres. and impf., in f. *ἀρῶ* Ion. *ἄρσω*: aor. 1 **ἦρσα** Ion. *ἄρσα*: aor. 2 *ἤρᾰρον* Ep. *ἄρᾰρον* :—*to join, fasten, fit together: fit* or *furnish with* a thing. II. intr. in Pass. and Med., in perf. *ἄρηρα* Att. *ἄρᾱρα*, Ep. part. fem. **ἀρᾰρυῖα**: plqpf. *ἠράρειν* [ᾰ]: also pf. pass. part. *ἀρηρεμένος*, and Ep. aor. 2 pass. part. *ἄρ*-**μενος**:—*to be joined closely together: to be fitted closely, fit well: to be fixed: to be fitting, meet*, or *suitable*.

ἄρᾰρον, Ep. aor. 2 of *ἀραρίσκω*: part. *ἀρᾰρών*.

ἀρᾱρώς, *ἀρᾱρυῖα* Ep. *ἀρᾰρυῖα*, *ἀρᾱρός*, perf. part. of *ἀραρίσκω, fitted, fitting* :—Adv. *-ότως*.

ἀράσσω, Att. **-ττω**: f. *ἀράξω* Dor. *-αξῶ*: aor. *ἤραξα* Ep. *ἄραξα* :—Pass., aor. 1 *ἠράχθην*: (α euphon., *ῥάσσω*) :—*to strike hard, dash in pieces*, with collat. notion of *rattling, clanging*, as of horses; *πύλας* **ἀράσσειν** *to knock furiously at* the gates; metaph., *ἀράσσειν ὀνείδεσι to strike with reproaches* :—Pass. *to dash one against other with a noise, to clash, rattle*. [ᾰ]

ἀρᾱτός Ion. **ἀρητός**, ή, όν, (ἀράομαι) *prayed for*. 2. *accursed, unblest*.

ἀράχνειος, α, ον, *of* or *belonging to a spider*. From

ἈΡΑ'ΧΝΗ, ἡ, = ἀράχνης. II. *a spider's web, cobweb*, Lat. *aranea*.

ἈΡΑ'ΧΝΗΣ, ὁ, *a spider*, Lat. *araneus*. Hence

ἀράχνιον, τό, *a spider's web, cobweb*.

Ἄραψ, αβος, ὁ, *an Arab*: also **Ἄραβος**, ου, ὁ.

ἈΡΒΥ'ΛΗ, ἡ, *a strong shoe*, coming up to the ankle, used by hunters, travellers, etc., *a half-boot*. [ῠ]

ἀρβυλίς, ίδος, ἡ, = ἀρβύλη.

ἀργᾱείς, Dor. for *ἀργηείς*.

ἀργᾰλέος, α, ον, (ἄλγος, as if **ἀλγαλέος**) *hard, painful, grievous*, Lat. *gravis*: also of persons, *troublesome*.

ἀργᾶς, contr. for *ἀργαείς*.

Ἀργει-φόντης, ου, ὁ, for Ἀργο-φονευτής, (Ἄργος, φονεύω) *slayer of Argus*.

ἀργέλοφοι, ων, οἱ, *the feet of a sheepskin*: generally, *offal, refuse*. (Deriv. uncertain.)

ἀργεννός, ή, όν, Aeol. and Dor. for *ἀργός, white*, mostly of sheep.

ἀργεστής, οῦ, ὁ, (ἀργός) *white*. II. paroxytone, *ἀργέστης*, ου, ὁ, epith. of the South wind, *clearing, brightening*, like Horace's *Notus albus, detergens nubila caelo*. 2. later, from being the epithet of Ζέφυρος, it was *the north-west wind*, the Athenian *σκίρων*.

ἀργέτι, ἀργέτα, poët. dat. and acc. for *ἀργῆτι, ἀργῆτα*, from *ἀργής, white*.

ἀργέω, f. *ήσω*, (ἀργός = ἀεργός) *to be idle, do nothing*: of a field, *to lie fallow*. II. trans. *to leave* a thing *undone*:—Pass. *to be left undone: to be fruitless*.

ἀργηείς Dor. **ἀργᾱείς**, εσσα, εν, contr. **ἀργᾶς**, gen. *ἀργᾶντος*, = *ἀργής*.

ἀργής, ῆτος, ὁ, ἡ, also with poët. dat. and acc. *ἀργέτι, ἀργέτα*: (ἀργός) :—*white, bright, vivid*.

ἀργηστής, οῦ, ὁ, = *ἀργής, white, glancing*.

ἀργία, ἡ, = *ἀεργία*, (ἀργός = ἀεργός) *idleness, laziness*: in good sense, *leisure*.

ἀργι-κέραυνος, ον, (ἀργής, κεραυνός) *with white, vivid lightning*.

ἄργιλλος or **ἄργῖλος**, ἡ, (ἀργός) *white clay, potter's earth*, Lat. *argilla*.

ἀργιλλ-ώδης or **ἀργῖλ-ώδης**, ες, (ἄργιλλος, εἶδος) *like clay, clayey*.

ἀργῐνόεις, εσσα, εν, = *ἀργός, white, shining*.

ἀργι-όδους, *όδοντος*, ὁ, ἡ, (ἀργός, ὀδούς) *white-toothed, white-tusked*.

ἀργί-πους, ὁ, ἡ, **-πουν**, **τό**, gen. **ποδος**, (ἀργός, πούς) *swift-footed* or *white-footed*.

ἄργμα, τό, (ἄρχω) only used in plur. *ἄργματα* = *ἀπαρχαί, the firstlings* at a sacrifice.

Ἀργολίζω, f. *ίσω, to take the part of Argos*. From

Ἀργολίς, *ίδος*, ἡ, *Argolis*, a district in Peloponnesus. 2. as Adj. ὁ, ἡ, *of Argolis, Argolic*.

Ἄργος, εος, τό, name of several Greek cities, of which that in the Peloponnesus is best known: in Homer it is also put for the district Argolis, or even for the whole Peloponnesus.

ἈΡΓΟ'Σ, ή, όν, *shining, bright, glistening*; *πόδας ἀργοί* as epith. of dogs, *swift-footed*, because *rapid motion* is accompanied by *a kind of flickering light*.

ἀργός, όν, contr. from *ἀεργός*, (α privat., ἔργον) *not working*, esp. *not working the ground*: hence *doing nothing, idle, lazy*: c. gen. rei, *idle at* a thing, *free from* it, *ἀργὸς πόνων*: of land, *lying fallow*. II. pass. *not done*, Lat. *infectus*; *unattempted*.

ἀργυρ-άγχη, ἡ, (ἄργυρος, ἄγχω) *silver-quinsy*, which Demosthenes was said to have, when he held back from appearing in public on the plea of quinsy, though really (it was alleged) because he was bribed.

ἀργῠρ-ἀμοιβός, ὁ, (ἄργυρος, ἀμείβω) *a money-changer*.

ἀργῠρεῖον, τό, *a silver-mine*. Properly neut. from

ἀργύρειος or **ἀργῠρεῖος**, ον, = ἀργύρεος, ἀργυρεῖα μέταλλα *silver*-mines.

ἀργύρεος or **ἀργῠρέος**, α, ον, contr. **ἀργῠροῦς**, ᾶ, οῦν, (ἄργυρος) *silver*, *of silver*.

ἀργῠρ-ήλᾰτος, ον, (ἄργυρος, ἐλαύνω) *wrought of silver*.

ἀργῠρίδιον, τό, Dim. of ἀργύριον.

ἀργύριον, τό, (ἄργῠρος) *a piece of silver*: hence '*silver*,' i. e. *money*, *cash*.

ἀργῠρίς, ίδος, ἡ, (ἄργυρος) *a silver vessel*.

ἀργῠρίτης [ῑ], fem. **ἀργυρῖτις**, ιδος, ἡ, (ἄργυρος) *of* or *belonging to silver*: as Subst. (sub. γῆ), *silver-ore*.

ἀργῠρο-δίνης, ου, ὁ, (ἄργυρος, δίνη) *running in silver eddies*, epith. of rivers. [ῑ]

ἀργῠρο-ειδής, ές, (ἄργυρος, εἶδος) *like silver*.

ἀργῠρό-ηλος, ον, (ἄργυρος, ἧλος) *silver-studded*.

ἀργῠρο-κόπος, ὁ, (ἄργυρος, κόπτω) *a worker in silver*, *silversmith*.

ἀργῠρολογέω, (ἀργυρολόγος) *to levy money*: c. acc. *to lay* a country *under contribution*. Hence

ἀργῠρολογία, ἡ, *a levying of money*.

ἀργῠρο-λόγος, ον, (ἄργυρος, λέγω) *levying money*.

ἀργῠρό-πεζα, ἡ, (ἄργυρος, πέζα) *silver-footed*: also **ἀργυρό-πεζος**, ον.

ἀργυρο-ποιός, ὁ, (ἄργυρος, ποιέω) *a worker in silver*.

ἀργῠρό-πους, ὁ, ἡ, –πουν, τό, gen. ποδος, (ἄργυρος, πούς) *with silver feet*.

ἀργῠρορ-ρύτης, ου, ὁ, (ἄργυρος, ῥέω) *silver-flowing*. [ρῠ]

ἄργ-ῠρος, ὁ, (ἀργός, *white*) like Lat. *arg-entum*, *the white metal*, i. e. *silver*, first in Homer. 2. *silver-money*, *money*.

ἀργῠρό-τοξος, ον, (ἄργυρος, τόξον) *with silver bow*, epith. of Apollo.

ἀργυρο-φεγγής, ές, (ἄργυρος, φέγγος) *silver-shining*.

ἀργῠρόω, f. ώσω, (ἄργυρος) *to turn into silver*. 2. *to reward with silver*:—Pass. *to be so rewarded*.

ἀργῠρ-ώδης, ες, = ἀργυροειδής. 2. *rich in silver*.

ἀργύρωμα, ματος, τό, (ἀργυρόω) *silver-plate*.

ἀργῠρ-ώνητος, ον, (ἄργυρος, ὠνέομαι) *bought with silver*.

ἀργύφεος, α, ον, (ἄργυρος) *silver-white*. [ῠ]

ἄργῠφος, ον, = ἀργύφεος, epith. of sheep.

Ἀργώ, όος, contr. οῦς, ὁ, (ἀργός, *swift*) *the Argo* or ship in which Jason sailed to Colchis.

ἀρδεύω, f. σω, = ἄρδω, *to water*, Lat. *irrigare*.

ἄρδην, Adv. contr. for ἀέρδην, (αἴρω) *lifted up*, *raised on high*. II. *utterly*, Lat. *penitus*.

ἌΡΔΙΣ, εως, ἡ, *the point of* anything, *an arrow-head*: *a sting*.

ἀρδμός, ὁ, *a watering*: *a watering-place*. From

ἌΡΔΩ, f. ἄρσω: aor. 1 ἦρσα:—*to water* cattle, *give them to drink*:—Pass. *to drink*. 2. of rivers, *to water* land, Lat. *irrigare*. II. metaph. *to refresh*, *foster*.

Ἀρέθουσα, ἡ, name of several fountains, perhaps for **Ἄρδουσα**, *waterer*: the most famous was at Syracuse.

ἀρειά, Ion. **ἀρειή**, ἡ, (ἀρά) *cursing*, *threatening language*.

Ἄρειος, ον also α, ον, Ion. **Ἀρήϊος**, η, ον, (Ἄρης) *warlike*, *martial*, Lat. *Mavortius*: Comp. Ἀρειότερος, α, ον, = ἀρείων.

Ἄρειος πάγος, ὁ, *hill of Ares*, *Mars' Hill*, over against the Acropolis at Athens on the west side. Here was held the highest judicial court, called by the same name: *capital* crimes came specially under its jurisdiction.

ἀρειότερος, α, ον, = ἀρείων.

Ἀρεί-τολμος, ον, (Ἄρης, τόλμα) *full of martial boldness*.

Ἀρεί-φᾰτος, Ep. **Ἀρηΐφατος**, ον, (Ἄρης, πέφαται 3 sing pf. pass. of *φένω) *slain by Ares*, i. e. *slain in war*. 2. later generally = Ἄρειος, *martial*.

ἀρείων, ὁ, ἡ, –ον, τό, gen. ονος, *better*, *stronger*, *braver*: it serves as Comp. of ἀγαθός. (On the deriv., see Ἄρης.)

ἄ-ρεκτος, ον, poët. for ἄρρεκτος, *undone*.

ἀρέομαι, Ion. for ἀράομαι.

ἀρέσαι, **ἀρέσασθαι**, aor. 1 inf. act. and med. of ἀρέσκω.

ἀρεσάσθω Ep. **ἀρεσσάσθω**, 3 sing. aor. 1 med. imperat. of ἀρέσκω.

ἀρέσθαι, aor. 2 med. inf. of αἴρω.

ἀρεσκεία, ἡ, (ἀρέσκω) *a desire to please*, *complaisance*: in bad sense, *obsequiousness*, *flattery*.

ἀρεσκόντως, Adv. pres. part. of ἀρέσκω, *agreeably*.

ἄρεσκος, η, ον, *desirous to please*, *complaisant*: in bad sense, *obsequious*, *flattering*. From

ἀρέσκω: fut. ἀρέσω: aor. 1 ἤρεσα, inf. ἀρέσαι: pf. ἀρήρεκα:—Med., fut. ἀρέσομαι Ep. ἀρέσσομαι: aor. 1 ἠρεσάμην, Ep. part. ἀρεσσάμενος:—Pass., aor. 1 ἠρέσθην: (*ἄρω, ἄρσω):—*to make good*, *make it up*, ταῦτα δ' ἀρεσσόμεθα this will we *make up among* ourselves; ἂψ ἀρέσαι *to make amends*: c. acc. pers. *to conciliate*, *propitiate*, αὐτὸν ἀρεσσάσθω ἐπέεσσιν; c. gen. rei, ἀρέσαντο φρένας αἵματος *they sated* their heart with blood:—Pass. *to be contented*, *acquiesce*. II. c. dat. pers., *to be pleasing to*, *gratify*, *please*, *flatter*, ταῦτα ἀρέσκοι μοι; ἀρέσκειν τρόποις τινός *to conform* to his ways:—impers., ἤρεσέ σφι ταῦτα ποιεῖν *it pleased* them to do so.

ἀρεστός, ή, όν, verb. Adj. of ἀρέσκω, *pleasing*, *grateful*: *acceptable*, *approved*. Adv. –τῶς.

ἀρετάω, f. ήσω, (ἀρετή) *to be fit* or *proper*, *to thrive*, *prosper*.

ἀρετή, ἡ, *goodness*, *excellence*, of any kind; but in Homer, like Lat. *virtus* (from *vir*), *manhood*, *prowess*, *valour*: also *manly beauty*, *dignity*, etc. 2. in Prose, of the *virtues* of land, fountains, etc. 3. *excellence* *in art* or *workmanship, skill.* II. in moral sense, *goodness, virtue:*—also *character for virtue, reputation, merit.* (For deriv. see Ἄρης.)

ἀρή, ἡ, Ion. and Hom. for ἀρά.

ἄρηαι, Ep. for ἄρῃ, 2 sing. aor. 2 med. subj. of αἴρω.

ἀρηγοσύνη, ἡ, = ἄρηξις.

ἈΡΗΓΩ, f. ξω, *to help, aid, succour in war,* c. dat. 2. absol. *to be of use, be fit; σιγᾶν ἀρήγει it is meet* to be silent. II. c. acc. rei, *to ward off, prevent,* ἀρήγειν ἅλωσιν: also, ἀρήγειν τινί τι *to ward off from* one, *to avert* the capture, as φόνον τέκνοις ἀρήγειν. (Same Root as ἀρκέω, Lat. *arceo.*)

ἀρηγών, όνος, ὁ, ἡ, *a helper, aid.*

Ἀρηΐ-θοος, ον, (Ἄρης, θοός) *swift as Ares, swift in war.*

Ἀρηϊ-κτάμενος, η, ον, (Ἄρης, κτείνω) *slain by Ares* or *in war.*

Ἀρήϊος, η, ον, Ion. for Ἄρειος.

Ἀρηΐ-φᾰτος, ον, Ion. for Ἀρεί-φατος.

Ἀρηΐ-φῐλος, ὁ, ἡ, also η, ον, (Ἄρης, φίλος) *dear to Ares.*

ἀρήμεναι, an Ion. infin., prob. for ἀρᾶν, *to pray,* an act. form of ἀρᾶσθαι (from ἀράομαι).

ἀρημένος, η, ον, *distressed, harassed,* = βεβλαμμένος. (Origin uncertain.)

ἄρηξις, εως, ἡ, (ἀρήγω) *help, succour.* II. c. gen. rei, *help against* a thing, *means of averting* it.

ἄρηρα, pf. med. of ἀραρίσκω: plqpf. ἀρήρειν.

ἀρηρεμένος, pf. pass. part. of ἀραρίσκω.

ἀρήροκα, ἀρήρομαι, pf. act. and pass. of ἀρόω.

ἀρηρομένος, pf. part. pass. of ἀρόω.

ἌΡΗΣ, ὁ: gen. Ἄρεος or Ἄρεως (never Ἄρους): dat. Ἄρεϊ, Att. contr. Ἄρει, poët. Ἄρῃ: acc. Ἄρη, also Ἄρην and Ἄρεα: voc. Ἄρες: Ion. and Ep. declension Ἄρηος, ηϊ, ηα. *Ares,* Lat. *Mars,* son of Jupiter and Juno, the god of war and destruction, the spirit of strife, plague, famine. Hence often used to denote *war, slaughter, murder,* etc. (Akin to ἄρρην, ἄρσην, as the Lat. *Mars* to *mas.* From the same Root come ἀρετή, ἀρι-, ἀρείων, ἄριστος, the first notion of *goodness* being that of *manhood, bravery in war:* cf. Lat. *virtus.*)

ἀρητήρ, ῆρος, ὁ: fem. ἀρήτειρα, (ἀράομαι) properly *one that prays:* hence *a priest, priestess.* [ᾰ]

ἀρητός, Ion. for ἀρατός.

ἀρθείς, aor. 1 pass. part. of αἴρω.

ἄρθεν, Aeol. for ἤρθησαν, 3 pl. aor. 1 pass. of αἴρω.

ἀρθμέω, f. ήσω, (ἀρθμός) *to be joined together.*

ἄρθμιος, α, ον, *joined, united: at peace with* another: —as Subst. ἄρθμια, ων, τά, *peaceful relations, concord.*

ἀρθμός, ὁ, (ἀραρίσκω) *a bond, league: friendship.*

ἄρθρον, τό, (ἀραρίσκω) *a joint,* esp. *the socket of the joint:* in plur. *the limbs;* often joined with some other word, as ἄρθρα ποδοῖν *the* ankles; ἄρθρα τῶν κύκλων the eyes; ἄρθρα στόματος the mouth. Hence

ἀρθρόω, f. ώσω, *to fasten by joints: to articulate, utter distinctly:* also *to nerve, strengthen.*

ἀρθρ-ώδης, ες, (ἄρθρον, εἶδος) *well-jointed.*

ἈΡΙ-, insep. Prefix, like ἐρι-, strengthening the notion conveyed by its compd.: of same root with ἄρης, ἀρείων, ἄριστος.

ἀρι-γνώς, ῶτος, ὁ, ἡ, = ἀρίγνωτος.

ἀρί-γνωτος, η, ον, also ος, ον, *easy to be known, well-known:* in bad sense, *notorious, infamous.*

ἀρί-δακρυς, υ, gen. υος, (ἀρι-, δάκρυ) *much weeping, very tearful.*

ἀρί-δᾱλος, Dor. for ἀρίδηλος.

ἀρι-δείκετος, ον, (ἀρι-, δείκνυμι) *much shewn:* hence *famous:* Homer also uses it as a Sup., ἀριδείκετος ἀνδρῶν *most renowned* of men.

ἀρί-δηλος, ον, *very clear* or *conspicuous, far-seen,* of mountains: *manifest, much known.*

ἀρί-ζηλος, ον, also η, ον, Ep. form of ἀρίδηλος, *very conspicuous* or *manifest.* Adv. -λως.

ἀρι-ζήλωτος, ον, *very enviable.*

ἀρίθματος, ον, Dor. for ἀρίθμητος.

ἀριθμεῦντι, Dor. for ἀριθμοῦσι, 3 pl. of ἀριθμέω.

ἀριθμέω, f. ήσω, (ἀριθμός) *to number, count, reckon up: to count out.* 2. *to reckon, count.*

ἀριθμηθήμεναι, Ep. for ἀριθμηθῆναι, aor. 1 pass. inf. of ἀριθμέω.

ἀρίθμημα, ατος, τό, (ἀριθμέω) *a number.*

ἀρίθμησις, εως, ἡ, *a counting* or *reckoning up.*

ἀριθμητικός, ή, όν, *of* or *for numbering* or *reckoning, skilled therein:* ἡ -κή (sc. τέχνη), *arithmetic.* Adv. -κῶς, *arithmetically.*

ἀριθμητός, ή, όν, *easily numbered, few in number:* οὐκ ἀριθμητός, *not counted, held of no account,* Lat. *nullo in numero habitus.*

ἀριθμός, ὁ, *number, a number,* Lat. *numerus.* 2. *amount, size,* etc.; πολὺς ἀριθμὸς χρόνου. 3. *number,* as a mark of worth, rank, etc.; μετ' ἀνδρῶν ἵζεσθαι ἀριθμῷ to sit *in rank* among men; οὐκ ἐν ἀριθμῷ εἶναι, like Lat. *nullo esse in numero,* to be in no *account.* 4. *mere number, quantity,* opp. to *quality* or *worth;* λόγων ἀριθμός *a mere set* of words; so of men, οὐκ ἀριθμὸς ἄλλως not *a mere lot,* like Horace's *nos numerus sumus.* II. *a numbering, counting;* ἀριθμὸν ποιεῖσθαι τῆς στρατιῆς to hold *a muster* of the army. 2. *numeration.*

ἄ-ρῑν, = ἄρρις.

Ἄριος, α, ον, old word for Μηδικός, *Median.*

ἀρι-πρεπής, ές, (ἀρι-, πρέπω) *very stately* or *showy, very splendid.*

ἄ-ρῑς, = ἄρρις.

ἀρί-σημος, ον, (ἀρι-, σῆμα) *very remarkable: very plain* or *manifest.*

ἀριστ-αθλος, ον, (ἄριστος, ἆθλον) *victorious in the contest.*

ἀριστ-αρχος, ον, (ἄριστος, ἀρχός) *best-ruling.*

ἀρι-στάφῠλος, ον, (ἀρι-, σταφυλή) *rich in grapes.*

ἀριστάω, f. ήσω: pf. ἠρίστηκα, syncop. 1 pl. ἠρίσταμεν, syncop. inf. ἠριστάναι: (ἄριστον):—*to take the morning meal,* Lat. *prandere:* generally, *to take any meal,* cf. ἄριστον.

ἀριστεία, ἡ, (ἀριστεύω) *the feats of the hero that*

won the meed of valour (τὰ ἀριστεῖα), *any great, heroic action.* Single books of the Iliad were so called, in which the deeds of some one hero are described, e. g. Book 5 is Διομήδους ἀριστεία.

ἀριστεῖα, τά, always in plur., (ἀριστεύω) *the prize of the bravest, meed of valour.*

ἀριστερός, ά, όν, *left, on the left*; ἐπ' ἀριστερᾶ towards *the left*; ἐξ ἀριστερῶν on *the left.* 2. ἡ ἀριστερά (with or without χείρ), *the left hand.* 3. metaph. *boding ill, ominous*, because to a Greek augur, looking northward, the unlucky signs came *from the left.* 4. of men, *left-handed, clumsy*, like French *gauche.* (Deriv. uncertain.)

ἀριστεύς, έως, ὁ, (ἄριστος) *the best man*: in Homer mostly in plur. ἀριστῆες, Lat. *optimates, the noblest chiefs, princes.*

ἀριστεύω: 3 sing. Ion. impf. ἀριστεύεσκε: f. εύσω (ἄριστος):—*to be the best* or *bravest*; Τρώων ἀριστεύεσκε *he was the best of the Trojans*; ἀριστεύειν τι *to be best in* a thing; c. inf., ἀριστεύεσκε μάχεσθαι *he was best* at fighting.

ἀριστήϊον, Ion. for ἀριστεῖον.

ἀριστίζω, f. ίσω, (ἄριστον) *to give one breakfast*:—Med. *to breakfast.*

ἀριστίνδην, Adv. (ἄριστος) *according to rank* or *merit.*

ἀριστο-κρατία, ἡ, (ἄριστος, κρατεῖν) *the rule of the best-born* or *nobles, an aristocracy.* Hence

ἀριστοκρατικός, ή, όν, *aristocratical.*

ἀριστό-μαντις, εως, ὁ, ἡ, (ἄριστος, μάντις) *best of prophets.*

ἀριστο-μάχος, ον, (ἄριστος, μάχη) *fighting best.*

ἌΡΙΣΤΟΝ, τό, *a morning meal, breakfast*, taken at sunrise: later, *the midday meal*, the Roman *prandium.*

ἀριστό-νοος, ον, (ἄριστος, νόος) *of the best disposition.*

ἀριστο-ποιέω, f. ήσω, (ἄριστον, ποιέω) *to prepare breakfast*; τὰ ἀριστοποιούμενα things *prepared for breakfast*:—Med. *to get one's breakfast.*

ἄριστος, η, ον, *best* in its kind, used as Sup. to ἀγαθός: of persons, *best*, i. e. *bravest* or *noblest*: c. inf., ἄριστοι μάχεσθαι *best* to fight; ἄριστος ἀπατᾶσθαι *best, easiest* to cheat:—In Att. *best*, i. e. *most excellent*: neut. pl. ἄριστα as Adv., *best, most excellently*: contr. with article, ὤριστος Hom., ἄριστος, Att., ὤριστος Dor. (On deriv., see Ἄρης.)

ἀριστοτόκεια, ἡ, poët. fem. of

ἀριστο-τόκος, ον, (ἄριστος, τεκεῖν) *bearing the best children.*

ἀριστό-χειρ, ειρος, ὁ, ἡ, (ἄριστος, χείρ) *with the best hand*; ἀγὼν ἀριστόχειρ a contest *won by the stoutest hand.*

ἀριστ-ωδῖν, ῖνος, ὁ, ἡ, (ἄριστος, ὠδίς) *bearing the best children.*

ἀρι-σφᾰλής, ές, (ἀρι—, σφᾰλεῖν) *very slippery* or *treacherous.*

ἀρι-φρᾰδής, ές, (ἀρι—, φράζομαι) *easily known, very manifest*: *clearly visible.* Adv. ἀριφραδέως, *very plainly.*

ἄρκειος, α, ον, = ἄρκτειος, *of a bear.*

ἀρκεόντως, Att. contr. ἀρκούντως, Adv. pres. part. of ἀρκέω, *enough*; ἀρκούντως ἔχει it is *enough.*

ἄρκεσις, εως, ἡ, (ἀρκέω) *help, aid, service.*

ἀρκετός, ή, όν, (ἀρκέω) *sufficient.* Adv. -τῶς.

ἀρκεῦν, Ion. for ἀρκοῦν, pres. part. neut. of

ἈΡΚΕ'Ω, f. έσω: aor. 1 ἤρκεσα:—pf. pass. ἤρκεσμαι:—Lat. ARCEO, *to ward off, keep off*: c. dat. only, *to assist, aid.* II. *to be of use, avail, be strong enough*, mostly c. inf.: also c. dat. *to suffice, satisfy*: absol. *to be enough, be strong enough.* 2. impers., ἀρκεῖ μοι *it is enough for me, I am well content*; ἀρκεῖν δοκεῖ it seems *enough*, seems *good.* III. Pass. *to be satisfied, contented with* a thing. (The Root is the same as that of ἀρήγω.)

ἄρκιος, α, ον, also ος, ον, *safe, sure*; νῦν ἄρκιον ἢ ἀπολέσθαι ἠὲ σαωθῆναι now *it is safe* that we perish or be saved: ἄρκιος μισθός a *sure* reward. II. *enough, sufficient.*

ἀρκούντως, contr. for ἀρκεόντως.

ἄρκτειος, α, ον, (ἄρκτος) *of a bear.*

ἀρκτέον, verb. Adj. of ἄρχομαι, *one must begin.* II. (from ἄρχω) *one must govern.* 2. in pass. sense, *one must be ruled*, i. e. *one must obey.*

ἌΡΚΤΟΣ, ὁ and ἡ, *a bear.* 2. Ἄρκτος, ἡ, *the great bear* or *Charles' wain*, elsewhere ἅμαξα: hence *the north pole*, or generally, *the North.*

Ἀρκτ-οῦρος, ὁ, (ἄρκτος, οὖρος) *Arcturus* or *Bear-guard*, a bright star close behind the Bear, also called Boötes. II. *the time of his rising, the middle of September.*

Ἀρκτο-φύλαξ, ακος, ὁ, (ἄρκτος, φύλαξ) = Ἀρκτοῦρος, *Arctophylax, the bear-keeper.*

ἌΡΚΥΣ, Att. ἄρκυς, υος, ἡ, *a net, hunter's net*, Lat. *cassis*; ἄρκυες ξίφους *the toils*, i. e. *perils*, of the sword.

ἀρκυ-στᾰσία, ἡ, or

ἀρκυ-στάσιον, τό, (ἄρκυς, ἵστημι) *a line of nets.*

ἀρκύ-στᾰτος, η, ον, or ος, ον, (ἄρκυς, ἵστημι) *surrounded with nets*; ἀρκυστάτη πημονή death *amid the toils*: ἀρκύστατον, τό, *a net* or *place beset with nets.*

ἀρκυ-ωρός, ὁ, (ἄρκυς, οὖρος) *a watcher of nets.*

ἅρμα, ατος, τό, (same Root as ἁρμός, ἁρμόζω) *a chariot, war-chariot, car.* 2. *chariot and horses, the yoked chariot*: also *the horses.*

ἁρμαλία, ἡ, (ἁρμόζω) *sustenance allotted, food.*

ἁρμ-άμαξα, ης, ἡ, (ἅρμα, ἅμαξα) *an eastern carriage* with a cover, esp. for women and children.

ἁρμάτειος, α, ον, (ἅρμα) *of* or *belonging to a chariot*: esp. of music, whether of a mournful or martial cast.

ἁρμᾰτεύω, f. σω, (ἅρμα) *to drive a chariot, go therein.*

ἁρμᾰτηλᾰσία, ἡ, *chariot-driving.* From

ἁρμᾰτηλᾰτέω, f. ήσω, *to drive a chariot.* From

ἁρμᾰτ-ηλάτης, ου, ὁ, (ἅρμα, ἐλαύνω) *a driver of chariots, charioteer.*

ἁρμᾰτό-κτῠπος, ον, (ἅρμα, κτυπέω) *rattling with chariots.*

ἁρμᾰτο-πηγός, όν, (ἅρμα, πήγνυμι) *making chariots;* ἁρματόπηγος, ὁ, *a wheelwright, chariot-maker.*

ἁρμᾰτο-τροφέω, f. ήσω, (ἅρμα, τρέφω) *to keep chariot horses*, esp. for racing. Hence

ἁρμᾰτοτροφία, ἡ, *a keeping of chariot horses.*

ἁρμᾰτο-τροχιά Ion. -ιή, ἡ, (ἅρμα, τροχός) *the course of a chariot, wheel-track.*

ἁρμᾰτωλία, ἡ, = ἁρματηλασία.

ἄρμενα, τά, *the tackle* or *rigging* of a ship: any *tools* or *implements*, like ὅπλα. (From same Root as ἁρμός, ἁρμόζω.)

ἄρμενος, η, ον, Ep. aor. 2 pass. part. of ἀραρίσκω.

ἁρμόδιος, α, ον, also ος, ον, (ἁρμόζω) *fitting together:* hence *well-fitting, agreeable.*

ἁρμόζω, Att. **ἁρμόττω**, Dor. **ἁρμόσδω**: f. ἁρμόσω: aor. 1 ἥρμοσα: pf. ἥρμοκα:—Pass., aor. 1 ἡρμόσθην: pf. ἥρμοσμαι: (ἁρμός, ἄρω):—*to fit together, join*, esp. of *joiner's* work:—Med. *to join for oneself, put together: to prepare, make ready.* 2. of marriage, *to give in marriage:*—Med. *to marry, take to wife:*—Pass. *to be married to.* 3. *to bind fast.* 4. *to set in order, arrange, govern.* II. intrans. *to fit, fit well: to be adapted, fit for.* III. impers., ἁρμόζει *it is fitting*, Lat. *decet*, c. inf.; σιγᾶν ἂν ἁρμόζοι.

ἁρμοῖ, Adv., = ἄρτι, *just, newly, lately.* (Properly an old dat. of ἁρμός.)

ἁρμο-λογέω, f. ήσω, (ἁρμός, λέγω) *to join together.*

ἁρμονία, ἡ, (ἁρμόζω) *a fitting together: a joint.* II. *a union* between persons, *covenant.* III. *an ordinance, decree;* hence *fate.* IV. as a term in music, *harmony, concord.* 2. in Rhet. *the intonation* of the voice. 3. generally, *harmony, agreement*, etc.; δύστροπος γυναικῶν ἁρμονία woman's perverse *temper.*

ἁρμονικός, ή, όν, (ἁρμόζω) *skilled in music:* τὰ ἁρμονικά *the theory of music.*

ἁρμός, ὁ, (ἁ for ἅμα, ἄρω) *a joining, a joint;* ἁρμὸς χώματος λιθοσπαδὴς *a joint* or *opening* in the tomb made by tearing away the stones.

ἁρμόσδω, Dor. for ἁρμόζω.

ἅρμοσμα, ατος, τό, (ἁρμόζω) *joined work.*

ἁρμοστήρ, ῆρος, ὁ, = sq.: poët., also ἁρμόστωρ, *a commander.*

ἁρμοστής, οῦ, ὁ, (ἁρμόζω) *one who arranges* or *governs, a governor:* esp. *a harmost, the governor* of the Greek islands and towns in Asia Minor sent out by the Lacedaemonians during their supremacy: also *the governor of a dependent colony.*

ἁρμόττω, Att. for ἁρμόζω, q. v.

ἄρνα, acc. with no nom. in use, dual ἄρνε, plur. ἄρνες, etc.; v. sub ἀρνός.

ἀρνᾰκίς, ίδος, ἡ, (ἀρνός) *a sheep's skin.*

ἄρνειος, α, ον, (ἀρνός) *of a lamb* or *sheep;* ἄρνειος φόνος slaughtered sheep.

ἀρνειός, ὁ, (ἀρνός) *a young ram;* but as Adj., ἀρνειὸς ὄϊς *a male* sheep.

ἀρνεο-θοίνης, ου, ὁ, (ἀρνός, θοινάω) *feasting on sheep.*

'ΑΡΝΕ'ΟΜΑΙ, fut. ήσομαι: aor. 1 pass. ἠρνήθην, but also aor. med. 1 ἠρνησάμην: Dep.:—opp. to εἰπεῖν, *to deny:* opp. to δοῦναι, *to refuse:* absol. *to say no, decline:* c. inf. *to refuse to* do.

ἀρνευτήρ, ῆρος, ὁ, (ἀρνεύω) *a tumbler:* also *a diver.*

ἀρνεύω, f. σω, (ἀρνός) *to frisk like a lamb, tumble.*

ἀρνήσιμος, η, ον, (ἀρνέομαι) *to be denied.*

ἄρνησις, εως, ἡ, (ἄρνησις) *denial.*

ἀρνίον, τό, Dim. of ἀρνός, *a young lamb, lambkin.*

'ΑΡΝΟ'Σ, τοῦ, τῆς, gen. of an obsol. nom. *ἄρς, the nom. in use being ἀμνός: dat. ἀρνί, acc. ἄρνα; du. ἄρνε; pl. ἄρνες, gen. ἀρνῶν, dat. ἀρνάσι (Ep. ἄρνεσσι), acc. ἄρνας:—*a lamb*, Lat. *agnus, agna:* also *a sheep.*

ἄρνῠμαι, defect. Dep., used only in pres. and impf., lengthd. form of αἴρομαι, *to receive for oneself, gain, earn, carry off* as *a prize.*

ἀρξεῦμαι, Dor. for ἄρξομαι, fut. of ἄρχομαι.

ἀρόμην, Ep. aor. 2 med. of αἴρω.

ἆρον, -άτω, aor. 1 imperat. of αἴρω.

ἀρόσιμος, ον, (ἀρόω) *arable, fruitful:* metaph. *fit for engendering* children.

ἄροσις, εως, ἡ, (ἀρόω) *a ploughing, tillage.* II. *arable land, corn-land*, Lat. *arvum.*

ἀροτήρ, ῆρος, ὁ, (ἀρόω) *a ploughman, husbandman;* βοῦς ἀροτήρ a steer *for ploughing.* II. metaph. *a father.*

ἀρότης, ου, ὁ, = ἀροτήρ, *a ploughman;* Πιερίδων ἀρόται labourers of the Muses, i. e. poets.

ἄροτος, ὁ, (ἀρόω) *tillage, ploughing, husbandry;* ζῆν ἀπ' ἀρότου to live *by husbandry.* 2. *the crop, fruit of the field:* also *a field.* II. *the season of tillage, seed-time.*

ἀροτραῖος, α, ον, (ἄροτρον) *of corn-land.*

ἀροτρεύς, έως, ὁ, = ἀροτήρ. Hence

ἀροτρεύω, f. σω, = ἀρόω, *to plough.*

ἀροτρήτης, ου, ὁ, *of* or *for the plough.*

ἀροτριάω, f. άσω [ā], = ἀρόω, *to plough.*

ἀροτρο-δίαυλος, ὁ, (ἄροτρον, δίαυλος) *one who ploughs to and fro*, like a runner in the δίαυλος.

ἀροτρο-πόνος, ον, (ἄροτρον, πόνος) *labouring at the plough.*

ἀροτρο-φορέω, f. ήσω, (ἄροτρον, φέρω) *to draw the plough.*

ἄροτρον, τό, (ἀρόω) *a plough*, Lat. *aratrum.*

ἀροῦμαι [ā], fut. med. of ἀείρω: but ἀροῦμαι (ᾰ) of αἴρω.

ἄρουρα, ἡ, (ἀρόω) *tilled* or *arable land, seed-land, corn-land*, Lat. *arvum:* also generally, *soil, land;* πατρὶς ἄρουρα father-*land:*—metaph. of a woman as *giving birth to* children. Hence

ἀρουραῖος, α, ον, *belonging to corn-land, rustic;* μῦς ἀρουραῖος a *field*-mouse.

ἀρούριον, τό, Dim. of ἄρουρα.

ἀρουρό-πονος, ον, (ἄρουρα, πόνος) *working in the field.*

'ΑΡΟ'Ω: f. όσω, poët. -όσσω: aor. 1 ἤροσα: pf.

ἀρήροκα:—Pass., aor. 1 ἠρόθην pf. ἀρήρομαι:—*to plough, till*, Lat. *arare*. II. *to sow*, ἀροῦν εἰς κῆπους. 2. metaph. of the husband, *to beget:* Pass. of the child, *to be begotten*.

ἀρόωσι, Ep. for ἀροῦσι, 3 pl. pres. of ἀρόω.

ἁρπᾰγή, ἡ, (ἁρπάζω) *seizure, robbery, rape*. II. *the thing seized, booty, plunder*. III. *rapacity*.

ἁρπάγη, ἡ, (ἁρπάζω) *a hook* for drawing up a bucket. 2. *a rake*, Lat. *harpăgo*.

ἅρπαγμα, ματος, τό, (ἁρπάζω) *that which is seized, booty, plunder*.

ἁρπαγμός, ὁ, (ἁρπάζω) *robbery*. 2. *anything that is seized, plunder*.

ʽΑΡΠΑ'ΖΩ: fut. ἁρπάξω, Att. ἁρπάσω or ἁρπάσομαι: aor. 1 ἥρπαξα, Att. ἥρπασα: pf. ἥρπᾰκα:—Pass., aor. 1 ἡρπάχθην or ἡρπάσθην: aor. 2 ἡρπάγην [ᾰ]: pf. ἥρπαγμαι or ἥρπασμαι:—*to ravish away, to carry off;* in part., ἁρπάξας φέρειν, Lat. *raptim ferre*. 2. *to grasp hastily, snatch up:* also *to grasp* with the mind, *apprehend*. 3. *to seize and overpower*. II. *to plunder*. Hence

ἁρπακτήρ, ὁ, *a robber*.—Fem. **ἁρπάκτειρα**.

ἁρπακτός, ή, όν, (ἁρπάζω) *seized in haste*.

ἁρπᾰλέος, α, ον, and ος, ον, (ἁρπάζω) *grasping, greedy:* also *attractive, pleasant*. Adv. -έως, *eagerly*. Hence

ἁρπαλίζω, f. ίσω, *to catch at, seize upon, receive*.

ἅρπαξ, αγος, ὁ, ἡ, (ἁρπάζω) *robbing, rapacious*, Lat. *rapax*. II. as Subst. ἅρπαξ, ὁ, *a robber, plunderer*. 2. ἅρπαξ, ἡ, *robbery, rapine*.

ἁρπεδόνη, ἡ, (ἁρπάζω) *a rope, cord*, for snaring game: *the twist* or *thread* of which cloth is made: also *a bow-string*.

ἅρπη, ἡ, (ἁρπάζω) *a bird of prey*, a kind of falcon. II. *a sickle: a scimetar*.

ἅρπυιαι, αἱ, (ἁρπάζω) *the snatchers*, i. e. *whirlwinds*. In later mythology they appear as winged monsters *who snatched away* food from table.

'ΑΡΡΑ'ΒΩ'Ν, ῶνος, ὁ, *earnest-money, caution-money: a pledge, earnest*, Lat. *arrhăbo, arrha*.

ἄρ-ρᾰφος, ον, (α privat., ῥαφῆναι) *unsewed, without seam* or *suture*.

ἄρ-ρεκτος, poët. **ἄ-ρεκτος**, ον, (α privat., ῥέζω) *undone: unfinished*.

ἀρρενικός, ή, όν, (ἀρρήν) *masculine, male*.

ἀρρενό-παις, παιδος, ὁ, ἡ, (ἄρρην, παῖς) *of male children*. 2. *with a boy*.

ἀρρέν-ωπος, ον, (ἀρρήν, ὤψ) *masculine-looking, masculine*.

ἄρ-ρηκτος, ον, (α privat., ῥήγνυμι) *unbroken, not to be broken* or *wounded:* metaph. *untiring*. Adv. τως.

'ΑΡΡΗΝ, ὁ, ἡ, ἄρρεν, τό, gen. ενος: old Att. ἄρσην: Ion. ἔρσην:—*male*, opp. to θῆλυς: hence *masculine, manly, strong:* as Subst. ἄρρην, ὁ, *the male*.

ἀρρηνής, ές, (ἄρρην) *fierce, savage*.

ἄρ-ρητος, ον, also η, ον, (α privat., ῥηθῆναι) *unsaid*, Lat. *indictus: not divulged, untaught*. II. *not to be told, secret, mysterious;* διδακτά τ' ἄρρητά τε things that may be published and *must not be told*. 2. *that cannot be told, horrible, shocking*, Lat. *nefandus*, ἄρρητ' ἀρρήτων things *most horrible*. 3. *shameful to be spoken;* ῥητὰ καὶ ἄρρητα, Lat. *dicenda tacenda*.

ἀρρηφορέω, f. ήσω, (ἀρρηφόρος) *to carry the peplos of Pallas*. Hence

ἀρρηφορία, ἡ, *the procession with the peplos* in honour of Pallas.

ἀρρη-φόροι, αἱ, (ἄρρητα, φέρω) at Athens, *two maidens who carried the peplos and other holy things* (ἄρρητα) of Pallas in the Scirophoria.

ἀρ-ρίγητος, ον, (α privat., ῥιγέω) *not shivering* from cold or fear.

ἄρ-ριζος, ον, (α privat., ῥίζα) *not rooted*.

ἄρ-ρῑς, ῖνος, ὁ, ἡ, (α privat., ῥίς) *without nose, without smell*.

'ΑΡΡΙΧΟΣ, ὁ, Att. ἡ, *a basket*. [ῐ]

ἄρ-ρυθμος, ον, (α privat., ῥυθμός) *without rhythm* or *proportion: in undue measure, unsuitable, not fitting* Adv. -μως, *out of time*.

ἀρ-ρυτίδωτος, ον, (α privat., ῥυτίς) *unwrinkled*.

ἀρ-ρώξ, ῶγος, ὁ, ἡ, (α privat., ῥώξ) *without cleft, unbroken*.

ἀρρωστέω, f. ήσω, (ἄρρωστος) *to be weak* or *sickly*. Hence

ἀρρώστημα, ματος, τό, *a sickness*.

ἀρρωστία, ἡ, (ἀρρωστέω) *weakness, sickness, ill health;* ἀρρωστία τοῦ στρατεύειν *inability* to serve *from ill health*.

ἄρ-ρωστος, ον, (α privat., ῥώννυμι) *weak, sickly:* hence *languid, remiss*.

ἄρσαι, **ἄρσον**, **ἄρσαντες**, and **ἀρσάμενος**, aor. 1 act. and med. of ἀραρίσκω.

ἄρσε, Ep. for ἦρσε, 3 sing. aor. 1 of ἀραρίσκω.

ἀρσενικός, ή, όν, = ἀρρενικός.

ἀρσενο-κοίτης, ου, ὁ, (ἀρσήν, κοίτη) *one guilty of unnatural offences*.

'ΑΡΣΗΝ, εν, Ion. and Att. for later ἄρρην

ἄρσιος, ον, (ἄρω) *fitting, agreeing, friendly*.

ἀρσί-πους, ὁ, ἡ, πουν, τό, gen. ποδος, contr. for ἀερσίπους (αἴρω, πούς) *lifting the feet*.

ἄρσις, εως, ἡ, (αἴρω) *a raising* or *lifting*. II. in prosody, *the rise of the voice on the first syllable, arsis, ictus*, opp. to θέσις the letting it sink

ἄρσω, Ion. for ἀρῶ, fut. of ἀραρίσκω.

ἀρτάβη, ἡ, a Persian measure, *artaba*, = 1 medimnus + 2 choenices.

ἀρτᾰμέω, f. ήσω, *to cut in pieces, cut up*. From

'ΑΡΤΑ'ΜΟΣ, ὁ, *a butcher, cook*.

ἀρτάνη [ᾰ], ἡ, (ἀρτάω) *that by which something is hung up, a rope, halter*

ἀρτάω, Ion. **ἀρτέω**: f. ήσω: pf. ἤρτηκα:—Pass., aor. 1 ἠρτήθην: pf. ἤρτημαι, Ion. 3 pl. ἀρτέαται: (same Root as ἀραρίσκω):—*to fasten to, hang* one thing *upon* another:—Pass. *to be hung upon, hang upon*, ἔκ τινος: hence *to depend upon*, Lat. *pendere ab aliquo*. II. Pass. *to be fitted, prepared, made ready*.

ἀρτέαται, Ion. for ἤρτηνται or ἠρτημένοι εἰσί, 3 pl. f. pass. of ἀρτάω.

ἀρτεμής, ές, (ἄρτιος) *safe and sound.* Hence

ἀρτεμία, ἡ, *safety, soundness.*

ἌΡΤΕΜΙΣ, gen. ιδος, acc. ιν or ιδα, ἡ, *Artemis,* the Roman *Diana,* goddess of the chace, daughter of Zeus and Leto, sister of Apollo. In Homer women who die suddenly and without pain are said to be slain by her ἀγανὰ βέλεα, as men by those of Apollo. Hence

Ἀρτεμίσιον, τό, *a temple of Artemis.*

Ἀρτεμίσιος, ὁ, a Spartan month, answering to part of Att. Elaphebolion.

ἀρτέμων, ονος, ὁ, (ἀρτάω) *the foresail;* or *top-sail, suppărum.*

ἀρτέω, Ion. for ἀρτάω.

ἄρτημα, τό, (ἀρτάω) *that which hangs down, a hanging ornament, pendant.*

ἀρτηρία, ἡ, (ἀείρω) *the windpipe* or *trachea.*

ἌΡΤΙ, Adv. *just, exactly: just now, even now: straightway, forthwith:* but also of something *just past,* opp. to πάλαι. II. in compos. it mostly denotes what has *just* happened.

ἀρτιάζω, f. άσω, (ἄρτιος) *to play at odd and even,* Lat. *par impar ludere.* II. *to count.*

ἀρτιάκις, Adv. (ἄρτιος) *an even number of times.*

ἀρτι-βρεχής, ές, (ἄρτι, βρέχω) *just steeped.*

ἀρτί-γᾰμος, ον, (ἄρτι, γάμος) *just married.*

ἀρτι-γένειος, ον, (ἄρτι, γένειον) *with the beard just growing.*

ἀρτι-γέννητος, ον, *new-born.*

ἀρτι-γλῠφής, ές, (ἄρτι, γλύφω) *newly carved.*

ἀρτί-γονος, ον, *just born.*

ἀρτι-δᾱής, ές, (ἄρτι, δαῆναι) *just taught.*

ἀρτί-δακρυς, υ, (ἄρτι, δάκρυ) *just weeping, ready to weep.*

ἀρτί-δορος, ον, (ἄρτι, δέρω) *just stript off.*

ἀρτίεπεια, ἡ, pecul. fem. of

ἀρτι-επής, ές, (ἄρτιος, ἔπος) *ready of speech, glib.*

ἀρτι-ζῠγία, ἡ, (ἄρτι, ζυγός) *a late union;* ἀνδρῶν ἀρτιζυγία newly-married husbands.

ἀρτίζω, f. ίσω, (ἄρτιος) *to get ready, perform.*

ἀρτι-θᾰλής, ές, (ἄρτι, θάλλειν) *just blooming.*

ἀρτι-θᾰνής, ές, (ἄρτι, θανεῖν) *just dead.*

ἀρτί-κολλος, ον, (ἄρτι, κολλάω) *close-glued, clinging close to.* II. metaph. *fitting well together;* εἰς ἀρτίκολλον *in the nick of time, opportunely.*

ἀρτι-κόμης, ου, ὁ, (ἄρτι, κομάω) *just having got hair or leaves.*

ἀρτι-λόγος, ον, (ἄρτι, λέγω) *speaking readily.*

ἀρτι-λόχευτος, ον, (ἄρτι, λοχεύω) *just born.*

ἀρτι-μᾰθής, ές, (ἄρτι, μαθεῖν) *having just learnt.*

ἄρτιος, α, ον, (ἀραρίσκω, ἄρτι) *complete, perfect of its kind, exactly fitted;* ἄρτια βάζειν to speak *to the purpose;* ἄρτια ᾔδη thought *things fitting* or *agreeable.* 2. *active, quick, ready,* c. inf. II. of numbers, *even,* opp. to περισσός, *odd.*

ἀρτι-πᾰγής, ές, (ἄρτι, παγῆναι aor. 2 pass. of πήγνυμι) *just put together, just made:*—of cheese, *just coagulated,* Lat. *recens coactus.*

ἀρτί-πλουτος, ον, *newly gotten,* epith. of money.

ἄρτι-πος, Ep. for ἀρτί-πους.

ἀρτί-πους, ὁ, ἡ, πουν, τό, gen. ποδος, (ἄρτιος, πούς) *sound* or *swift of foot,* opp. to χωλός. II. *coming just in time.*

ἄρτῐσις, εως, ἡ, (ἀρτίζω) *a preparing, adorning.*

ἀρτί-σκαπτος, ον, (ἄρτι, σκάπτω) *just dug.*

ἀρτί-στομος, ον, (ἄρτι, στόμα) *speaking readily.*

ἀρτί-τοκος, ον, (ἄρτι, τεκεῖν) *just born.* 2. paroxyt. ἀρτιτόκος, ον, act. *having just given birth.*

ἀρτι-φᾰνής, ές, (ἄρτι, φανῆναι) *just become visible.*

ἀρτί-φρων, ον, gen. ονος, (ἄρτιος, φρήν) *sound of mind, intelligent.*

ἀρτι-φυής, ές, and **ἀρτίφῠτος**, ον, (ἄρτι, φύω) *just born, just made.*

ἀρτι-χᾰνής, ές, (ἄρτι, χανεῖν) *just yawning* or *opening.*

ἀρτί-χνους, ουν, (ἄρτι, χνόος contr. χνοῦς) *with the down just growing.*

ἀρτί-χριστος, ον, (ἄρτι, χρίω) *just smeared over, ready spread.*

ἀρτίως, Adv. of ἄρτιος, like ἄρτι, *just, exactly.*

ἀρτο-κόπος, ον, (ἄρτος, κόπτω) *working at bread, baking bread:* as Subst. *a baker.*

ἀρτο-λάγῡνος, ον, (ἄρτος, λάγυνος) *with bread and bottle in it,* epith. of a wallet.

ἀρτο-ποιός, όν, (ἄρτος, ποιέω) *making bread:* as Subst. *a baker.*

ἀρτο-πώλης, ου, ὁ, (ἄρτος, πωλέομαι) *a dealer in bread: baker.* Hence

ἀρτοπώλιον, τό, *a baker's shop.*

ἀρτο-πῶλις, ιδος, ἡ, fem. of ἀρτοπώλης, *a bread-woman.*

ἌΡΤΟΣ, ὁ, *a loaf,* esp. *of wheat,* for barley-bread is μάζα: when it means *bread* it is commonly in plur.

ἀρτο-σῑτέω, f. ήσω, (ἄρτος, σιτέομαι) *to eat wheaten bread,* opp. to ἀλφιτοσιτέω to eat barley-bread.

ἀρτοφᾰγέω, *to eat bread.* From

ἀρτο-φάγος, ου, ὁ, (ἄρτος, φαγεῖν) *bread-eater.*

ἄρτῡμα, τό, (ἀρτύνω) *seasoning, spice.*

ἀρτύνας, ὁ, (ἀρτύνω) *a magistrate* at Argos and Epidaurus, like ἁρμοστής.

ἀρτύνω [ῡ]: fut. ἀρτῠνῶ, Ep. ἀρτῠνέω: aor. 1 ἤρτῡνα: aor. 1 pass. ἠρτύνθην:—also **ἀρτύω**: fut. ἀρτύσω [ῡ]: aor. 1 ἤρτῡσα: pf. ἤρτῡκα, pass. ἤρτῡμαι: (same Root as ἀραρίσκω.) *To arrange, manage, contrive:* in bad sense, *to scheme,* hence δόλον ἀρτύνειν, Lat. *insidias struere, to contrive a trick:* generally, *to prepare, make ready:*—Med. *to prepare, make ready.*

ἀρύβαλλος, ὁ, (ἀρύω) *a pail for drawing water, bucket,* larger than the ἀρύταινα·

ἀρυσάμενος, aor. 1 med. part. of ἀρύω.

ἀρύσσω, Ion. for ἀρύω.

ἀρυστήρ, ῆρος, ὁ, = ἀρυτήρ.

ἀρύστῐχος, ὁ, Dim. of ἀρυτήρ, *a small ladle.*

ἀρύταινα, ης, ἡ, = ἀρυτήρ, *a ladle:* cf. ἀρύβαλλος.

ἀρῡτήρ, ῆρος, ὁ, (ἀρύω) *a vessel for taking up liquids, ladle, cup.*

ἀρυτήσῐμος, ον, (ἀρύω) *fit to drink.*

'ΑΡΥ'Ω, Att. **ἀρύτω** [ῠ]: f. ύσω [ῠ]: aor. 1 ἤρῠσα:—Pass., aor. 1 ἠρύθην [ῠ] or ἠρύσθην: cf. ἀνύω, ἀνύτω. Lat. *HAUR-IRE, to draw water* for another: Med. *to draw for oneself:* c. gen., ἀρύτεσθαι Νείλου ὑδάτων *to draw from* the waters of the Nile:—metaph. *to win, gain.*

ἀρχ-άγγελος, ὁ, (ἀρχός, ἄγγελος) *an archangel.*

ἀρχαϊκός, ή, όν, (ἀρχαῖος) *old-fashioned, antiquated.*

ἀρχαιό-γονος, ον, (ἀρχαῖος, γονή) *of ancient race.*

ἀρχαιολογέω, f. ήσω, *to discuss antiquities* or *things out of date.* From

ἀρχαιο-λόγος, ον, (ἀρχαῖος, λέγω) *one who writes ancient history.*

ἀρχαιο-μελη-σῑδωνο-φρῡνῐχ-ήρᾰτος, ον, (ἀρχαῖος, μέλος, Σιδώνιος, Φρύνιχος, ἐρατός) μέλη ἀρχ. *dear old* songs *from Phrynichus' Phoenissae.*

ἀρχαῖον, (sub. δάνειον), τό, properly neut. of ἀρχαῖος, *the original sum, the principal*, Lat. *sors.*

ἀρχαιό-πλουτος, ον, (ἀρχαῖος, πλοῦτος) *rich from olden time.*

ἀρχαιο-πρεπής, ές, (ἀρχαῖος, πρέπω) *distinguished of old, time-honoured.*

ἀρχαῖος, α, ον, (ἀρχή I) *from the beginning, ancient:* in good sense, *time-honoured;* but in bad sense, like ἀρχαϊκός, *antiquated, gone by:* also *simple, silly.* 2. *ancient, former.*

ἀρχαιό-τροπος, ον, (ἀρχαῖος, τρόπος) *old-fashioned.*

ἀρχ-αιρεσία, ἡ, (ἀρχή, αἵρεσις) *an election of magistrates*, Lat *Comitia.* Hence

ἀρχαιρεσιάζω, f. σω, *to hold the Comitia:* also *to canvass for election.*

ἀρχαίως, Adv. of ἀρχαῖος, *anciently.* 2. *in antiquated style.*

ἀρχε-, insep. Prefix from ἄρχω, with idea of excellence or superiority.

ἀρχεῖον, Ion. **ἀρχήϊον**, τό, properly neut. of an Adj. ἀρχεῖος, α, ον: (ἀρχή):—*a public building*, such as *a town-hall, senate-house, residence of the chief magistrates*, Lat. *Curia.*

ἀρχέ-κᾰκος, ον, (ἀρχε-, κακός) *beginner of ill.*

ἀρχέ-λᾱος, ον, Att. **ἀρχέ-λεως**, ων, (ἀρχε-, λαός) *leading the people, a chief*, contr. **ἀρχέ-λᾱς.**

ἀρχέμεναι, Ep. inf. of ἄρχω.

ἀρχέ-πλουτος, ον, (ἀρχε-, πλοῦτος) *enjoying ancient wealth*

ἀρχέτας, ὁ, Dor. for ἀρχέτης, (ἄρχω) *a leader, prince* II as Adj., ἀρχέτας θρόνος *a princely* throne

ἀρχέ-τυπον, τό, (ἀρχε-, τύπος) *an archetype, pattern, model.*

ἀρχεύω, f. σω, (ἄρχω) *to command, lead.*

ἀρχέ-χορος, ον, (ἀρχε-, χορός) *leading the chorus* or *dance.*

'ΑΡΧΗ', ἡ, *a beginning, first cause, origin;* κατ' ἀρχάς *in the beginning, at first;* ἐξ ἀρχῆς from *the first;* absol., ἀρχήν *at first;* οὐκ ἀρχήν not *at first*, i.e. never *at all*, not *at all*, like Lat. *omnino non.* 2. *a first principle, element.* 3. in plur., = **ἀπαρχαι**, *firstlings.* 4. *the corner of a sheet.* II. *supreme power, sovereignty, dominion*, Διὸς ἀρχή; c. gen. rei, ἀρχὴ τῆς 'Ασίας *power over* Asia:—also *an empire.* 2. in Att. prose, *a magistracy, office* in the government: they were mostly obtained in two ways, χειροτονηταί by election, κληρωταί by lot.

ἀρχη-γενής, ές, (ἄρχω, γενέσθαι) *causing the first beginning of* a thing.

ἀρχηγετεύω, f. σω, *to be a leader* or *ruler;* and

ἀρχηγετέω, f. ήσω, *to make a beginning.* From

ἀρχ-ηγέτης, ου, ὁ: fem. **ἀρχηγέτις**, ιδος, but dat. ἀρχηγέτι: Dor. **ἀρχᾱγέτης**: (ἀρχή, ἡγέομαι) *a leader: the founder* of a city or family. II. *a first leader, prince, chief.*

ἀρχ-ηγός, Dor. **ἀρχ-ᾱγός**, όν, (ἀρχή, ἡγέομαι) *beginning, originating.* II. as Subst. like ἀρχηγέτης, *a leader, founder*, Lat. *auctor; a first father.* 2. *a prince, chief.*

ἀρχῆθεν, Adv. (ἀρχή) *from the beginning.*

ἀρχήϊον, τό, Ion. for ἀρχεῖον.

ἀρχήν, Adv., v. ἀρχή I.

'ΑΡΧΙ-, insep. Prefix from ἄρχω, like **ἀρχε-.**

ἀρχίδιον, τό, Dim. of ἀρχή, *a little office.*

ἀρχιερατικός, ή, όν, (ἀρχιερεύς) *belonging to the Chief Priest.*

ἀρχ-ιερεύς, έως, ὁ: Ion. nom. **ἀρχιερέως**, εω; also **ἀρχιρεύς**, whence acc. pl. ἀρχιρέας: (ἄρχω, ἱερεύς) *a chief priest, high priest.*

ἀρχ-ιερωσύνη, ἡ, (ἀρχι-, ἱερωσύνη) *the chief priesthood.*

ἀρχι-θάλασσος, ον, (ἀρχι-, θάλασσα) *ruling the sea.*

ἀρχιθεωρέω, f. ήσω, *to be* ἀρχιθέωρος. From

ἀρχι-θέωρος, ὁ, (ἀρχι-, θεωρός) *the chief of a* θεωρία or *sacred embassy.*

ἀρχί-κλωψ, ωπος, ὁ, *a chief of robbers.*

ἀρχικός, ή, όν, (ἀρχή) *royal.* 2. *fit for rule: skilled in government.*

ἀρχι-κυβερνήτης, ου, ὁ, *a chief pilot.*

ἀρχί-μιμος, ὁ, *a chief comedian*

ἀρχι-οινόχοος, ὁ, *a chief cupbearer.*

ἀρχι-πειρατής, οῦ, ὁ, *a chief of pirates.*

ἀρχι-ποίμην, gen. ενος, ὁ, (ἀρχι-, ποιμήν) *a chie[f] shepherd.*

ἀρχ-ιρεύς, ὁ, Ion. for ἀρχιερεύς.

ἀρχι-συνάγωγος ὁ, (ἀρχι-, συναγωγή) *the ruler [o]f a synagogue.*

ἀρχιτεκτονέω, f. ήσω, *to be a chief builder* or *architect: to construct, contrive*, Lat. *struere.* From

ἀρχι-τέκτων, ονος, ὁ, *a master-builder, director [o]*

orks, architect, engineer: generally, an author, con-iver.

ʼρχι-τελώνης, ου, ὁ, a chief collector of taxes. chief blican.

ρχι-τρίκλῖνος, ὁ, the president of a banquet or clinium, so called because the guests reclined on uches placed along three sides of the table.

ρχός, ὁ, a leader, chief, commander. From

ΑΡΧΩ, f. ἄρξω: aor. 1 ἦρξα: pf. ἦρχα:—more mmonly in Med. ἄρχομαι: fut. ἄρξομαι: aor. 1 ξάμην: pf. ἦργμαι:—Pass., fut. ἀρχθήσομαι: aor. 1 χθην. I. of Time, to begin: c. gen. to make beginning of a thing, ἄρχειν πολέμοιο: with inf. or irt., ἄρχεσθαι οἰκοδομεῖν to begin to build; ἡ ψυχὴ ›χεται ἀπολείπουσα the soul begins to sink. 2. begin from or with; ἄρχεσθαι Διός, to begin from ove, Lat. a Jove principium. 3. c. gen. rei et at. pers., ἄρχειν θεοῖς δαιτός to make preparations or a banquet to the gods:—Med. also in a religious ense, like ἀπάρχεσθαι, ἄρχεσθαι μελέων to begin a acrifice with the limbs. 4. c. acc., ἄρχειν ὁδόν ινι, to shew him the way:—imperat., ἄρχε begin!—art. ἀρχόμενος, at first. II. of Place and Sta-ion, mostly c. gen. to rule, be leader of:—more arely c. dat., ἀνδράσιν ἄρχειν:—c. acc. cognato, ἄρ-ειν ἀρχήν to hold an office. 2. Pass. to be ruled r governed: οἱ ἀρχόμενοι, subjects.

ἄρχων, οντος, ὁ, (properly part. of ἄρχω) a ruler, captain, chief, king. 2. οἱ Ἄρχοντες, the chief magistrates at Athens, nine in number, the first being called emphatically ὁ Ἄρχων or Ἄρχων ἐπώνυμος, the second ὁ Βασιλεύς, the third ὁ Πολέμαρχος, the remaining six οἱ Θεσμοθέται.

*ἌΡΩ, a form assumed as the Root of ἀραρίσκω.

ἀρῶ [ᾱ], fut. of ἀείρω: but ἀρῶ [ᾰ], of αἴρω.

ἀρωγή, ἡ, (ἀρήγω) help, succour, protection; ἀρωγὴ νόσου help against disease.

ἀρωγο-ναύτης, ου, ὁ, (ἀρωγός. ναύτης) helper of sailors.

ἀρωγός, όν, (ἀρήγω) helping, aiding, propitious; c. gen. useful in a thing. II. as Subst. ἀρωγός, ὁ, a helper, defender, an advocate before a tribunal.

ἌΡΩΜΑ, τό, any seasoning, spice.

ἄρωμα, τό, (ἀρόω) corn-land, Lat. arvum.

ἀρώμεναι, Ep. for ἀροῦν, contr. from ἀροέμεναι, pres. inf. of ἀρόω.

ἀρωραῖος, Dor. for ἀρουραῖος.

ἇς, ἅς or ἄς, Aeol. and Dor. for ἕως, till, until.

ἇς, Dor. gen. for ἧς, from ὅς, ἥ, ὅ.

ἆσαι, contr. for ἀάσαι, aor. 1 inf. of ἀάω, to hurt.

ἆσαι, aor. 1 inf. of ἄω, to satiate.

ᾆσαι, contr. for ἀεῖσαι, aor. 1 inf. of ἀείδω.

ἄσαιμι, aor. 1 opt. of ἄω, to satiate.

ἄ-σακτος, ον, (α privat., σακτός) not trodden down.

ἀ-σᾰλᾰμίνιος, ον, (α privat., Σάλαμις) not having been at Salamis, no true seaman. [μῑ]

ἀ-σάλευτος, ον, (α privat., σαλευτός) unshaken, calm.

ἄσαμεν, 1 plur. aor. 2 of ἄω, to sleep.

ἀσάμινθος, ἡ, a bathing-tub. (Deriv. uncertain.)

Ἀσάνᾱ, Ἀσᾶναι, Ἀσᾱναῖος, Lacon. for Ἀθήνη, Ἀθῆναι, Ἀθηναῖος.

ἀ-σάνδᾰλος, ον, (α priv., σάνδαλον) without sandals.

ἄ-σαντος, ον, (α privat., σαίνω) not to be flattered, harsh, morose.

ἄ-σαρκος, ον, (α privat., σάρξ) without flesh, lean.

ἄσατο, contr. for ἀάσατο, 3 sing. aor. 1 med. of ἀάω, to hurt.

ἄσασθαι, aor. 1 med inf. of ἄω, to satiate.

ἀσάφεια, ἡ, indistinctness. From

ἀ-σᾰφής, ές, (α privat., σαφής) indistinct, dim, faint, uncertain, obscure. Adv. -φῶς, indistinctly.

ἀσάω, f. ήσω, (ἄση) to surfeit, cloy, satiate:—Pass.

ἀσάομαι, with aor. 1 pass. ἀσήθην, and med. ἀσά-μην, to feel loathing or nausea, to be disgusted or vexed at a thing.

ἄ-σβεστος, ον, also η, ον, (α privat., σβεστός) un-quenched, not to be quenched: endless, cease-less. II. as Subst., ἄσβεστος (sub. τίτανος); ἡ, unslaked lime. 2. asbestus, a mineral which resists the action of fire.

ἌΣΒΟΛΟΣ, ἡ, rarely ὁ, also ἀσβόλη, ἡ, soot.

ἆσε, for ἄασε, 3 sing. aor. 1 of ἀάω, to hurt.

ἀσέβεια, ἡ, (ἀσεβής) impiety, profaneness.

ἀσεβέω, f. ήσω, (ἀσεβής) to act profanely or impi-ously, sin against the gods. Hence

ἀσέβημα, ατος, τό, an impious act, a sin.

ἀ-σεβής, ές, (α privat., σέβω) ungodly, unholy, profane.

ἄσειν, fut. inf. of ἄω, to satiate. [ᾱ]

ἀ-σείρωτος, ον, (α privat., σειρόω) not drawing by a trace (but by the yoke), of the two middle horses in a team of four abreast, the outer two being called σειραφόροι.

ἀ-σέλαστος, ον, (α privat., σέλας) not lighted.

ἀσελγαίνω, f. ἄνῶ: pf. pass. ἠσέλγημαι: (ἀσελ-γής):—to behave licentiously.

ἀσέλγεια, ἡ, (ἀσελγής) licentiousness.

ἀ-σελγής, ές, (α privat., θέλγω) licentious, brutal. Adv. -ῶς, extravagantly.

ἀ-σέληνος, ον, (α privat., σελήνη) without moon.

ἀσεπτέω, = ἀσεβέω, to act impiously. From

ἄ-σεπτος, ον, (α privat., σέβω) not to be reverenced, unholy.

ἄσεσθε, 2 pl. fut. med. of ἄω, to satiate.

ᾀσεῦμαι, Dor. for ἀείσομαι, Att. ᾄσομαι, fut. of ἀείδω.

ἄση, ἡ, (ἄω, to satiate) surfeit, loathing, disgust. 2. generally, anguish, distress.

ἀσηθῇς, ἀσηθῆναι, aor. 1 pass. subj. and inf. of ἀσάω.

ἀ-σήμαντος, ον, (α privat., σημαίνω) without leader, untended. II. unsealed, unmarked.

ἄ-σημος, ον, (α privat., σῆμα) without sign or mark; ἄσημος χρυσός uncoined gold; ἄσημα ὅπλα arms with-out device. II. of sacrifices, etc., giving no sign, obscure. III. indistinct, unseen, unheard: of sounds, inarticulate. 2. of persons and places, un-known, obscure, ignoble.

ἀ-σήμων, *ον*, gen. *ονος*, = *ἄσημος*.

ἀσθένεια, ἡ, (ἀσθενής) *want of strength, weakness, sickliness*. 2. *a disease*.

ἀσθενέω, f. ήσω, (ἀσθενής) *to be weak, feeble, sickly*.

ἀσθένημα, ατος, τό, (ἀσθενέω) *an infirmity*.

ἀ-σθενής, ές, (α privat., σθένος) *without strength, weak: feeble, sickly*. 2. of property, *poor; οἱ ἀσθενέστεροι the weaker sort*, i. e. *the poor*. 3. *insignificant:* so of streams, *small*.

ἀ-σθενόω, f. ώσω, (ἀσθενής) *to weaken*.

ἀσθενῶς, Adv. of ἀσθενής, *weakly, feebly, slightly*.

ἆσθμα, ατος, τό, (ἄω, *to blow*) *hard-drawn breath, panting, gasping from toil*. II. *a breath, breathing*.

ἀσθμαίνω, (ἆσθμα) *to breathe hard, gasp for breath*.

Ἀσι-άρχης, ου, ὁ, (Ἀσία, ἄρχω) *an Asiarch*, the highest religious official under the Romans in the province of Asia.

Ἀσιάς, άδος, ἡ, (Ἀσία) fem. Adj. *Asiatic: ἡ Ἀσίας* (with or without *κιθάρα*), the lyre as improved by Cepion of Lesbos.

Ἀσιατο-γενής, ές, (Ἀσία, γένος) *of Asiatic descent*.

ἀ-σίδηρος, ον, (α privat., σίδηρος) *not of iron*. 2. *without sword*.

ἀ-σῖνής, ές, (α privat., σίνομαι) of persons, *unhurt, unharmed:* of things, *undamaged*. II. act. *not harming, doing no harm: innocent*. 2. *protecting from harm*. Hence

ἀ-σῖνῶς, Adv. *innocently:* Sup. ἀσινέστατα.

ἄσιος, α, ον, (ἄσις) *slimy, miry*.

ἌΣΙΣ, εως, ἡ, *slime, mud*.

ἀσῖτέω, f. ήσω, (ἄσιτος) *to go without food, to fast*.

ἀσῖτία, ἡ, *want of food, fasting*. From

ἄ-σῖτος, ον, (α privat., σῖτος) *without eating, fasting*.

ἀσκάλαβος or **ἀσκᾰλᾰβώτης**, ὁ, a kind of *lizard*.

ἄ-σκᾰλος, ον, (α privat., σκάλλω) *unhoed, undug*.

ἀσκάντης, ου, ὁ, *a mean bed*. II. *a bier*.

ἀ-σκαρδαμυκτεί and **-κτί**, Adv. of ἀσκαρδάμυκτος, *without winking, without unchanged look*.

ἀ-σκαρδάμυκτος, ον, (α privat., σκαρδαμύσσω) *not blinking, with steady impudent look*. II. of time, *in a twinkling*.

ἀ-σκελής, ές, (α euphon., σκέλλω) *dried up, withered*. 2. neut. ἀσκελές, as Adv., also ἀσκελέως, *obstinately, stubbornly*.

ἀ-σκέπαρνος, ον, (α privat., σκέπαρνον) *unhewn*.

ἄ-σκεπτος, ον, (α privat., σκέψομαι fut. of σκοπέω) *inconsiderate:*—Adv. -τως, *inconsiderately*. II. *unconsidered, unobserved*.

ἀ-σκευής, ές, = ἄσκευος.

ἄ-σκευος, ον, (α privat., σκευή) *unfurnished:* c. gen. *unfurnished with* . ., ἄσκευος ἀσπίδων τε καὶ στρατοῦ.

ἈΣΚΕ'Ω, f. ήσω: pf. ἤσκηκα, pass. ἤσκημαι:—*to work curiously, fashion, dress out, adorn:* also, 2. *to honour* a divinity, Lat. *colere*. II. in Att. and prose, *to practise, exercise*, Lat. *exercere;* said either of the person, as, ἀσκεῖν τὸ σῶμα *to exercise* the body; or of the thing, as, ἀσκεῖν τέχνην *to practise* an art. 2. c. inf., ἀσκῶ τοιαύτη μένειν I *practise* or *endeavour* to remain such. 3. absol. *to practise, train*.

ἀσκηθής, ές, *unhurt, unharmed: unscathed*. (Deriv. uncertain.)

ἄσκημα, ατος, τό, (ἀσκέω) *an exercise*.

ἄ-σκηνος, ον, (α privat., σκηνή) *without tents*.

ἄσκησις, εως, ἡ, (ἀσκέω) *exercise, training; ἄσκησίς τινος practice of* or *in* a thing. II. *a trade, profession*, Lat. *ars*.

ἀσκητέος, α, ον, verb. Adj. of ἀσκέω, *to be practised*.

ἀσκητής, οῦ, ὁ, (ἀσκέω) *one who practises any art* or *trade*, opp. to ἰδιώτης: *an athlete*. Hence

ἀσκητικός, ή, όν, *industrious: athletic*.

ἀσκητός, ή, όν, (ἀσκέω) *curiously wrought*. 2. *exercised in* a thing. 3. *to be acquired by practice*, as opp. to διδακτός.

ἄ-σκιος, α, ον, (α privat., σκιά) *without shade*.

ἀ-σκίπων, ονος, ὁ, ἡ, (α privat., σκίπων) *without a staff*. [ῐ]

Ἀσκληπιεῖον, τό, *the temple of Aesculapius*. From

Ἀσκληπιός, ὁ, *Asclepios*, Lat. *Aesculapius*, in Homer a Thessalian prince, famous as a physician: later, son of Apollo and Coronis, tutelary god of medicine.

ἄ-σκοπος, ον, (α privat., σκοπέω) *not seeing: imprudent: unregardful of*, τινός. II. pass. *unseen*. 2. *not to be seen, obscure: incredible*.

ἈΣΚΟ'Σ, ὁ, *a leathern bag, a wineskin*. 2. generally, *an animal's hide:*—proverb., ἀσκὸν δέρειν τινά *to flay* one *alive;* ἀσκὸς δεδάρθαι *to be flayed alive*

ἀσκώλια, τά, (ἀσκός) the second day of the rural Dionysia, on which they danced upon *wine-skins*. Hence

Ἀσκωλιάζω, f. σω, *to dance as at the Ascolia*.

ἄσκωμα, ατος, τό, (ἀσκός) *the leather padding* of the hole which served for the row-lock, put there to make the oar work easily.

ᾆσμα, τό, (ᾄδω) *a song, lay*.

ᾀσμᾰτο-κάμπτης, ου, ὁ, (ᾆσμα, κάμπτης) *twister of song*.

ἄσμενος, η, ον, as if for ἡσμένος, perf. pass. part. of ἥδομαι: *well-pleased, glad:* often in dat., ἀσμένῳ μοι ἂν εἴη it would be to me *well-pleased*, glad should I be of it:—Comp. ἀσμενώτερος, -έστερος and -αίτερος. Adv. -νως, *gladly, readily*.

ᾄσομαι, contr. for ἀείσομαι, fut. of ἀείδω, *to sing*.

ἄ-σοφος, ον, (α privat., σοφός) *unwise, foolish*.

ἈΣΠΑ'ΖΟΜΑΙ, fut. άσομαι: Dep.:—*to welcome kindly, bid welcome, greet*, Lat. *salutare:* also *to greet on taking leave*. 2. *to embrace, kiss, caress*. 3. *to cling fondly to, cleave to*, as a disciple to his master. 4. ἀσπάζεσθαι ὅτι . . *to be glad* that . .

ἀ-σπαίρω, Ion. impf. ἀσπαίρεσκον, (α euphon., σπαίρω) *to pant, gasp, struggle convulsively*.

ἀσπάλαθος, ὁ, *a sweet-scented shrub*.

ἀσπάραγος, Att. **ἀσφάραγος**, ὁ, *asparagus*.

ἄ-σπαρτος, ον, (α privat., σπείρω) of land, *unsown, untilled:* of plants, *not sown, growing wild*.

πάσιος, *α*, *ον*, also *ος*, *ον*, (ἀσπάζομαι) *welcome*, *-pleasing*. II. *well-pleased*, *glad*. Hence

πασίως, Adv. *readily*, *gladly*.

πασμα, *ατος*, *τό*, (ἀσπάζομαι) *a welcome*, *greet-*: in plur. *embraces*.

σπασμός, ὁ, (ἀσπάζομαι) *an embrace*: *affection*.

σπαστός, ή, όν, = ἀσπάσιος, *welcome*.

-σπειστος, *ον*, (α privat., σπένδομαι) *to be appeased no libations*, *implacable*.

-σπερμος, *ον*, (α privat., σπέρμα) *without seed*, i.e. *thout posterity*.

-σπερχές, Adv., (α euphon., σπέρχω) *hastily*, *hotly*, *ceasingly*.

-σπετος, *ον*, (α privat., εἰπεῖν) *unspeakable*, *unut-able*, *unspeakably great*: neut. ἄσπετον as Adv., *speakably*:—but, φωνὴ ἄσπετος an *indistinct* ice.

ισπῐδ-αποβλής, ῆτος, ὁ, (ἀσπίς, ἀποβάλλω) *one at throws away his shield*, *a runaway*, *coward*.

ισπῐδη-στρόφος, *ον*, (ἀσπίς, στρέφω) *wielding a ield*.

ισπιδη-φόρος, *ον*, (ἀσπίς, φέρω) *shield-bearing*: as bst. *a shield-bearer*, *warrior*.

ισπιδιώτης, ὁ, (ἀσπίς) *shield-bearing*, *a warrior*.

ισπιδ-οῦχος, ὁ, (ἀσπίς, ἔχω) *a shield-bearer*.

ἀσπιδοπηγεῖον, *τό*, *an armourer's shop*. From

ἀσπιδο-πηγός, ὁ, (ἀσπίς, πήγνυμι) *a shield-maker*.

ἀσπιδο-φέρμων, *ον*, gen. *ονος*, (ἀσπίς, φέρβω) *liv-g by the shield*, *a warrior*.

ἄ-σπῐλος, ὁ, ἡ, (α privat., σπίλος) *without stain*, *potless*, *pure*.

'ΑΣΠΙ'Σ, *ίδος*, ἡ, *a round shield*, Lat. *clipeus*, made f bull's hide, overlaid with metal plates, with a boss ὀμφαλός) in the middle, and fringed with tassels θύσανοι): the long oblong shield was ὅπλον, Lat. *scutum*. 2. in common language used for *a body f men-at-arms* (ὁπλῖται), ὀκτακισχιλίη ἀσπίς 8000 *heavy-armed* men; ἐπ' ἀσπίδας πέντε καὶ εἴκοσι τάξασθαι to draw men up twenty-five deep; ἐπ' ἀσπίδα, ἀφ' ἀσπίδα *on* or *to the left*, *right shoulders forward*, ecause the shield was held with the left hand, opp ο ἐπὶ δόρυ. II. *an asp*, *a kind of snake*.

ἀσπιστήρ, ῆρος, ὁ, and **ἀσπιστής**, οῦ, ὁ, (ἀσπίς) *ne armed with a shield*, *a warrior*: also **ἀσπίστωρ**, s Adj., κλόνοι ἀσπίστορες din *of shielded warriors*.

ἄ-σπλαγχνος, *ον*, (α privat., σπλάγχνα) *without owels*: metaph. *heartless* or *merciless*.

ἀσπονδεί, Adv. *implacably*. From

ἄ-σπονδος, *ον*, (α privat., σπονδή) *without drink-ffering*, *to whom no drink-offering is poured*. II. *without regular truce* (which was ratified by σπονδαί): τὸ ἄσπονδον *a keeping out of treaty* or *covenant* with others. III. *admitting of no truce*, *implacable*; ἄσπονδος ἀρά a *deadly* curse.

ἀ-σπούδαστος, *ον*, (α privat., σπουδάζω) *not zeal-usly pursued*. II. *not worth zeal*, *mischievous*.

ἀ-σπουδεί and **ἀ-σπουδί**, Adv. (α privat., σπουδή) *without zeal*: *without a struggle*, *ignobly*.

ἄσσα, Att. **ἄττα**, Ion. for ἅτινα, neut. pl. of ὅστις, *which*, *whichsoever*, *what*, *whatever*.

ἀσσα, Att. **ἀττα**, Ion. for τινά, *something*, *some*.

ἀσσάριον, *τό*, Dim. of Lat. *as*, *a farthing*.

ἆσσον, Adv., Comp. of ἄγχι, *nearer*: sometimes c. gen., ἆσσον ἐμεῖο *nearer to* me:—also Adv. ἀσσοτέρω, whence was formed the Comp. Adj. **ἀσσότερος**, Sup. ἀσσότατος, Adv. ἀσσοτάτω.

ᾄσσω, Att. contr. for ἀΐσσω.

ἀ-σταθής, *ές*, (α privat., ἵσταμαι) *unsteady*, *unstable*.

ἀ-στάθμητος, *ον*, (α privat., σταθμάομαι) *unsteady*, *unstable*: of things, *uncertain*.

ἄ-στακτος, *ον*, (α privat., στάζω) *not trickling*, i.e. *gushing in streams*:—Adv. **ἀστακτί**, *in floods*.

ἀ-στᾰσίαστος, *ον*, (α privat., στασιάζω) *without party-spirit*, *quiet*. Adv. *-τως*.

ἀστᾰτέω, f. ήσω, *to be unstable*: *be a wanderer*. From

ἄ-στᾰτος, *ον*, (α privat., ἵσταμαι) *not steadfast*, *uncertain*, *unstable*.

ἀσταφῐδῖτις, ῐδος, ἡ, fem. Adj. *consisting of raisins*. [δῐ] From

ἀ-στᾰφίς, *ίδος*, ἡ, (α euphon., σταφίς) *a raisin*.

ἀσταχύεσσιν, dat. pl. of

ἄ-στᾰχυς, *υος*, ὁ, (α euphon., σταχυς) *an ear of corn*.

ἀ-στέγαστος, *ον*, (α privat., στεγάζω) *uncovered*, of a ship, *undecked*; διὰ τὸ ἀστέγαστον from their *having no shelter*.

ἀστεΐζομαι, Dep. *to be witty*. From

ἀστεῖος, *ον*, also *α*, *ον*, (ἄστυ) *of the town*; then, like Lat. *urbanus*, *courteous*, *polite*, *witty*, *elegant*, *neat*, *pretty*; opp. to ἄγροικος.

ἄ-στειπτος, *ον*, (α privat., στείβω) *untrodden*.

ἀ-στεμφής, *ές*, (α privat., στέμβω) *unmoved*, *unshaken*: Adv., ἀστεμφέως ἔχειν τινά to hold one *fast*. 2. of persons, *inexorable*.

ἀ-στένακτος, *ον*, (α privat., στενάζω) *without sigh* or *groan*: *without need for groans*.

ᾀστέον, verb. Adj. of ᾄδω, *one must sing*.

ἄ-στεπτος, *ον*, (α privat., στέφω) *uncrowned*: hence, *unhonoured*.

ἀστεργ-άνωρ, *ορος*, ὁ, ἡ, (ἀστεργής, ἀνήρ) *without love of man*, *hating wedlock*. [γᾱ]

ἀ-στεργής, *ές*, (α privat., στέργω) *without love*, *unkind*, *hateful*.

ἀστερο-ειδής, *ές*, (ἀστήρ, εἶδος) *starry*.

ἀστερόεις, *εσσα*, *εν*, (ἀστήρ) *starry*: *sparkling*, *glittering*.

ἀστεροπή, ἡ, poët. for ἀστραπή, *lightning*. Hence

ἀστεροπητής, οῦ, ὁ, *the lightener*.

ἀστερ-ωπός, όν, (ἀστήρ, ὤψ) *starry*: *star-like*, *bright*.

ἀ-στέφᾰνος, *ον*, (α privat., στέφανος) *without crown*, *ungarlanded*.

ἀ-στεφάνωτος, *ον*, (α privat., στεφανόω) *not crowned*

ἀστή, ἡ, fem. of ἀστός, *a female citizen*.

ἄ-στηλος, *ον*, (α privat., στήλη) *without tombstone*

'ΑΣΤΗ'Ρ, ὁ, gen. *έρος*: dat. pl. ἄστρασι, Lat. ASTRUM, *a star*. **2.** *any luminous body*, *a meteor*.

ἀ-στήρικτος, *ον*, (α privat., *στηρίζω*) *not firmly fixed, unsettled, unstable.*

ἀ-στῐβής, *ές*, (α privat., *στείβω*) *not to be trodden, holy.* 2. *untrodden, solitary.*

ἀστικός, *ή*, *όν*, (*ἄστυ*) *of a city* or *town*, opp. to country; *τὰ ἀστικὰ Διονύσια*, like *τὰ κατ' ἄστυ*, the Dionysia *celebrated in the city;* cf. sub *Διονύσια* II: also *native*, opp. to *ξενικός* foreign. II. = *ἀστεῖος*, *neat, pretty.*

ἄ-στικτος, *ον*, (α privat., *στίζω*) *not branded, not marked with spots.*

ἀ-στλέγγιστος, *ον*, (α privat., *στλεγγίζω*) *not scraped with the strigil, unclean, dirty.*

ἄ-στολος, *ον*, (α privat., *στολή*) *without the stole.*

ἄ-στομος, *ον*, (α privat., *στόμα*) *speechless.* II. of horses, *hard-mouthed, unmanageable.* III. of dogs, *bad-mouthed, unable to bite.* IV. of a sword, *without edge.*

ἀστό-ξενος, *ὁ*, *ἡ*, (*ἄστυ*, *ξένος*) *the public guest of a city.*

ἄ-στοργος, *ον*, (α privat., *στέργω*) *without natural affection, heartless, barbarous.*

ἀστός, *ὁ*, (*ἄστυ*) *a townsman, citizen, fellow-citizen*, opp. to *ξένος*.

ἀστοχέω, f. *ήσω*, *to miss the mark: to fail.* From

ἄ-στοχος, *ον*, (α privat., *στόχος*) *missing the mark, aiming badly: aimless, absurd.*

ἀ-στράβη, *ἡ*, *a pack-saddle, an easy saddle.* From

ἀ-στρᾰβής, *ές*, (α privat., *στραφῆναι*) *untwisted, straight.*

ἀστραγάλη, *ἡ*, Ion. for *ἀστράγαλος* III.

ἀστράγᾰλος, *ὁ*, *one of the vertebrae* of the neck. II. *the ankle bone*, Lat. *talus.* III. mostly in plur. *ἀστράγαλοι*, *οἱ*, *dice*, which at first were made of the ankle-bones, Lat. *tali:* hence *the game of dice.* They had only 4 flat sides, whereas the *κύβοι* had 6: they played with 4; the best throw was when all came different, *Ἀφροδίτη*, Lat. *jactus Veneris;* the worst, when all came alike, *κύων*, Lat. *canis.*

ἈΣΤΡΑΠΗ', *ἡ*, *a flash of lightning, lightning.* [ᾰπ]

ἀστρᾰπηφορέω, f. *ήσω*, *to carry lightnings.* From

ἀστρᾰπη-φόρος, *ον*, (*ἀστραπή*, *φέρω*) *lightning-bearing, flashing.*

ἀστράπτω, f. *ψω*, (*ἀστραπή*) *to lighten:* impers., *ἀστράπτει it lightens:* trans. *to flash forth.* II. intr. *to flash* or *glance like lightning.*

ἄστρᾰσι, dat. pl. of *ἀστήρ*.

ἀ-στρᾰτεία, *ἡ*, (α privat., *στρατεύω*) *exemption from service.* 2. *a shunning of service*, which at Athens was a heavy offence; *φεύγειν γραφὴν ἀστρατείας* to be indicted for it; *ἀστρατείας ἁλῶναι* to be convicted of it.

ἀ-στράτευτος, *ον*, (α privat., *στρᾰτεύω*) *exempt from service.* 2. *never having served.*

ἄ-στρεπτος, *ον*, (α privat., *στρέφω*) *not to be bent:* of persons, *unbending.*

ἀστρο-γείτων, *ον*, gen. *ονος*, (*ἄστρον*, *γείτων*) *near the stars.*

ἀστρολογία, *ἡ*, *astrology.* From

ἀστρο-λόγος, *ὁ*, (*ἄστρον*, *λέγω*) *an astronomer:* later, *an astrologer.*

ἌΣΤΡΟΝ, *τό*, Lat. *ASTRUM*, *a star, constellation.*

ἀστρονομέω, f. *ήσω*, and **ἀστρονομίζω**, f. *ίσω*; *to be an astronomer, study astronomy:* and

ἀστρονομία, *ἡ*, *astronomy.* From

ἀστρο-νόμος, *ον*, (*ἄστρον*, *νέμω*) *classing the stars:* as Subst., *ἀστρονόμος*, *ὁ*, *an astronomer.*

ἄ-στροφος, *ον*, (α privat., *στρέφω*) *without turning round*, Lat. *irretortus;* *ἄστροφος ἐλθεῖν* to go *without turning the back.*

ἀστρῷος, *α*, *ον*, (*ἄστρον*) *of the stars, starry.*

ἀστρ-ωπός, *όν*, = *ἀστερωπός*.

ἄ-στρωτος, *ον*, (α privat., *στρώννυμι*) *without bed* or *bedding: unsmoothed, rugged.*

ἌΣΤΥ, *τό*: gen. *εος*, contr. *ους*, also *εως*:—*a city, town:* the Athenians called their own city *Ἄστυ*, as the Romans called theirs *Urbs;* though *ἄστυ* also denoted *the Upper Town*, as opp. to *Peiraeus.*

ἀστῠ-άναξ, *ακτος*, *ὁ*, (*ἄστυ*, *ἄναξ*) *lord of the city.*

ἀστῠ-βοώτης, *ου*, *ὁ*, (*ἄστυ*, *βοάω*) *crying through the city*, epith. of a herald.

ἀστῠ-γείτων, *ον*, gen. *ονος*, (*ἄστυ*, *γείτων*) *near* or *bordering on a city:* as Subst. *a neighbour.*

ἄστῠδε, Adv. (*ἄστυ*) *into, to*, or *towards the city.*

ἀστυκός, *ή*, *όν*, = *ἀστικός*.

ἄ-στῡλος, *ον*, (α priv., *στῦλος*) *without pillar* or *prop.*

ἀστύ-νῑκος, (*ἄστυ*, *νίκη*) *victorious.*

ἀστῠνομέω, *to be an ἀστυνόμος.* From

ἀστῠ-νόμος, *ὁ*, (*ἄστυ*, *νέμω*) *a magistrate* at Athens, who *had the care of the police, streets, and public buildings:* they were ten in number, five for the City and five for the Peiraeus. II. as Adj. *protecting cities:* also *public, social;* *ὀργαὶ ἀστυνόμοι* the feelings *of social life.*

ἀστῠ-όχος, *ον*, (*ἄστυ*, *ἔχω*) *keeping the city.*

ἀ-στῠφέλικτος, *ον*, (α privat., *στυφελίζω*) *unshaken.*

ἀ-στύφελος, *ον*, (α privat., *στυφελός*) *not rocky.*

ἀ-συγγνώμων, *ον*, (α privat., *συγγνώμων*) *without forgiveness, relentless, merciless.*

ἀ-συγκέραστος, *ον*, (α privat., *συγκέραστος*) *not to be mixed.*

ἀ-συγκόμιστος, *ον*, (α privat., *συγκομίστος*) *not gathered together, unreaped.*

ἀ-σύγκρῐτος, *ον*, (α privat., *σύγκριτος*) *not to be mixed, unsocial.*

ἀ-συγκρότητος, *ον*, see *ἀξυγκρότητος*.

ἀ-σῡκοφάντητος, *ον*, (α privat., *συκοφαντέω*) *not calumniated.*

ἀσυλαῖος, *α*, *ον*, (*ἄ-σῡλον*) *of an asylum.*

ἀ-σύλητος, *ον*, (α privat., *συλάω*) *inviolable.*

ἀσῡλία, *ἡ*, (*ἄσυλος*) *inviolability, security*, esp. of a suppliant.

ἀ-συλλόγιστος, *ον*, (α privat., *συλλογίζομαι*) *unable to reason:*—Adv., *ἀσυλλογίστως ἔχειν* to be *unable to reason.*

ἄ-σῡλος, *ον*, (α privat., *σύλη*) *free from plunder.*

unbarmed, inviolate: also c. gen., γάμων ἄσυλος *safe from* marriage.

ἀ-σύμβᾰτος, *ον*, (α privat., συμβαίνω) *not coming to terms: incompatible.* Adv. –τως.

ἀ-σύμβλητος, *ον*, (α privat., συμβάλλω) *not to be guessed, unintelligible.*

ἀ-σύμβολος, *ον*, (α privat., σύμβολον) *without paying one's contribution* or *subscription.*

ἀ-σύμμετρος, *ον*, (α privat., σύμμετρος) *incommensurate.* II. *disproportionate, unequal.*

ἀ-συμπαθής, *ές*, (α privat., συμπαθής) *without sympathy.*

ἀ-σύμφορος, *ον*, (α privat., συμφέρω) *inexpedient, useless: prejudicial*, like Lat. *inutilis.* Adv. –ρως.

ἀ-σύμφωνος, *ον*, (α privat., σύμφωνος) *not accordant.*

ἀ-σύνδετος, *ον*, (α privat., συνδέω) *unconnected.*

ἀσυνεσία, ἡ, (ἀσύνετος) *want of understanding* or *apprehension, stupidity.*

ἀ-σύνετος, Att. **ἀ-ξύνετος**, *ον*, (α privat., συνετός) *void of understanding, stupid.* II. *unintelligible.* Adv. –τως. [ῠ]

ἀ-σῠνήμων, Att. **ἀ-ξυνήμων**, *ον*, gen. *ονος*, (α privat., συνίημι) *without understanding.*

ἀ-σύνθετος, Att. **ἀ-ξύνθετος**, *ον*, (α privat., συντίθεμαι, cf. συνθήκη) *bound by no treaties, faithless.* Adv. –τως.

ἀ-σύντακτος, Att. **ἀ-ξύντακτος**, *ον*, (α privat., συντάσσω) *not arranged together*, esp. of soldiers, *not in battle-order:* hence *disorderly.* II. *unsocial.* III. *ill-proportioned.* IV. *not assessed, free from taxes.*

ἀ-σύντονος, *ον*, (α privat., συντείνω) *not strained, slack.* Adv. –νως, *lazily*, Sup. –ώτατα.

ἀ-συσκεύαστος, *ον*, (α privat., συσκευάζω) *not well arranged, not convenient.*

ἀ-σύστᾰτος, Att. **ἀξύστατος**, *ον*, (α privat., συνίσταμαι) *not holding together:* metaph. *irregular, uneven, uncouth, rugged.*

ἀσύφηλος, *ον*, *vile, dishonoured:* also *dishonouring, reproachful.* (Deriv. unknown.)

ἀσυχία, ἀσύχιμος, ἄσυχος, Dor. for ἡσυχ–.

ἀ-σφάδαστος, *ον*, (α privat., σφαδάζω) *without convulsion* or *struggle.*

ἄ-σφακτος, *ον*, (α privat., σφάττω) *unslaughtered.*

ἀσφάλεια, ὁ, (ἀσφαλής) *firmness, stability.* 2. *assurance from danger, security, personal safety:* also *a safe conduct.* 3. *certainty, surety.*

ἀσφᾰλεῖος, *ον*, of Neptune, *the Securer.* From

ἀ-σφᾰλής, *ές*, (α privat., σφᾰλεῖν aor. 2 inf. of σφάλλω) *firm, fast, steadfast.* 2. of persons, *unfailing, sure, trusty:* of things, *sure, certain.* 3. *safe, secure;* ἐν ἀσφαλεῖ or ἐξ ἀσφαλοῦς, in *safety;* τὸ ἀσφαλές *safety.* Hence

ἀσφᾰλίζω, f. ίσω Att. ιῶ, *to secure, guarantee.*

ἀσφαλισθῆναι, aor. 1 pass. inf. of ἀσφαλίζω.

ἀσφαλτίτης, *ου*, ὁ, fem. **-ῖτις**, ἡ, *of asphalt, bituminous:* λίμνη Ἀσφαλτῖτις, Lat. *Lacus Asphaltites*, the Dead Sea. [ῑ] From

ἄσφαλτος, *ου*, ἡ, *asphalt* or *bitumen*, forming in lumps on the surface of water near Babylon, where it was used as mortar. (Foreign word.)

ἀσφᾰλῶς, Ion. -έως, Adv. of ἀσφαλής, *firmly, securely:* Comp. ἀσφαλέστερον, Sup. -έστατα.

ἀ-σφᾰρᾰγέω, (α euphon., σφαραγέω) *to ring, resound.*

ἀσφάρᾰγος, ὁ, (α euphon., σφάραγος) *the throat, gullet.*

ἄσφι, ἄσφε, Aeol. for σφί, σφέ.

ἀσφόδελος, ὁ, *asphodel*, a plant like the lily. II. as Adj., ἀσφοδελὸς λειμών *the asphodel* meadow, which the shades of heroes haunted. (Deriv. unknown.)

ἀσχᾰλάω, only used in pres.: Ep. 3 sing. ἀσχαλάᾳ, 3 plur. ἀσχαλόωσι, inf. ἀσχαλάαν, part. ἀσχαλόων:—another form is ἀσχάλλω. *To be vexed, grieved*, c. part., ἀσχαλάαν μένων *to be vexed at* waiting; ἀσχαλᾶν τινι *to be vexed at* a thing; c. acc., ἀσχάλλειν θάνατον *to feel a horror of* death. (Deriv. uncertain.)

ἄ-σχετος, *ον*, (α privat., σχεῖν, aor. 2 inf. of ἔχω) *not to be checked* or *restrained, irrepressible.*

ἀσχημονέω, *to behave unseemly, act indecorously;* and

ἀσχημοσύνη, ἡ, *deformity, indecency.* From

ἀ-σχήμων, *ον*, gen. *ονος*, (α privat., σχῆμα) *shapeless: unseemly, shameful.* Adv. ἀσχημόνως.

ἀσχολία, ἡ, *occupation, industry, business.* II. *want of leisure: a hindrance from* other things; ἀσχολίαν παρέχειν τινί to be a hindrance to one. From

ἄ-σχολος, *ον*, (α privat., σχολή) *without leisure, busy, industrious.* Adv. -λως.

ἀσχολόων, ἀσχολόωσι, Ep. pres. part. and 3 plur. of ἀσχαλάω.

ἀ-σώμᾰτος, *ον*, (α privat., σῶμα) *without body, incorporeal.*

ἀσωτία, ἡ, *prodigality, dissoluteness.* From

ἄ-σωτος, *ον*, (α privat., σώζω) *not to be saved: abandoned, profligate*, Lat. *perditus.* Adv. -τως, *dissolutely.*

ἀτακτέω, f. ήσω, *to be undisciplined* or *disorderly.* 2. generally, *to lead a disorderly life.* From

ἄ-τακτος, *ον*, (α privat., τάσσω) *out of order, not in order of battle, not at one's post.* 2. *undisciplined, disorderly, irregular, lawless.* Adv. -τως.

ἀ-τᾰλαίπωρος, *ον*, (α privat., ταλαίπωρος) *not toiling patiently, careless, indifferent.*

ἀ-τάλαντος, *ον*, (α copul., τάλαντον) *equal in weight, equivalent* or *equal to.*

ἀτᾰλά-φρων, *ον*, gen. *ονος*, (ἀταλός, φρήν) *tender-minded.*

ἀτάλλω, only used in pres. (ἀταλός) *to gambol, sport about.* II. trans. *to bring up a child, rear, foster:*—Pass. *to grow up, wax.*

ἀτᾰλός, ή, όν, (akin to ἁπαλός) *tender, delicate.*

ἀταλό-ψῡχος, *ον*, (ἀταλός, ψυχή) *soft-hearted.*

ἀταξία, ἡ, (ἄτακτος) *a want of discipline.* 2. *disorder, confusion, licentiousness.*

'ΑΤΑΡ, Ep. αὐτάρ, Conjunct. *but, yet*, Lat. *at*, to

introduce an objection; ἀτάρ που ἔφης *still* thou didst say: it often stands for δέ after μέν.

ἀ-τάρακτος, ον, (α privat., τᾰράσσω) *without confusion, cool, steady.* Hence

ἀταραξία, ἡ, *freedom from passion, calmness.*

ἀ-ταρβής, ές, (α privat., τάρβος) *fearless;* ἀταρβὴς τῆς θέας *having no fear about* the sight.

ἀ-τάρβητος, ον, (α privat., ταρβέω) *undaunted.*

ἀταρπῑτός, ἡ, Ion. for ἀτραπιτός.

ἀταρπός, ἡ, Ion. for ἀτραπός.

ἀταρτηρός, όν, Ep. for ἀτηρός, *mischievous, baneful.*

ἀτασθᾰλία, ἡ, (ἀτάσθαλος) *blind folly, presumptuous sin, recklessness.*

ἀτασθάλλω, *to act presumptuously.* From

ἀτάσθᾰλος, ον, (ἀτάω, ἀτέω) *presumptuous, reckless.*

ἀ-ταύρωτος, ον, also η, ον, (α privat., ταῦρος) *unwedded, virgin, pure.*

ἄ-τᾰφος, ον, (α privat., τᾰφῆναι) *unburied.*

ἀτάω, f. ήσω, (ἄτη) *to hurt, harm:* Pass. *to suffer, be in distress.*

ἅτε, acc. plur. neut. of ὅστε, used as Adverb, like ἅπερ, *just as, as if, so as.* II. only in Prose, *inasmuch as, seeing that,* Lat. *quippe, utpote.*

ἄ-τεγκτος, ον, (α privat., τέγγω) *unwetted, not softened: hard-hearted, relentless.*

ἀ-τειρής, ές, (α privat., τείρω) *not to be worn away: untiring, unwearied:* also *stubborn, unbending: wearisome.*

ἀ-τείχιστος, ον, (α privat., τειχίζω) *without walls and towers, unfortified.* II. *not walled in, not blockaded.*

ἀ-τέκμαρτος, ον, (α privat., τεκμαίρομαι) *not to be guessed, obscure, vague, dark:* of men, *uncertain.* Adv., ἀτεκμάρτως ἔχειν to be *in the dark.*

ἀτεκνία, ἡ, *childlessness.* From

ἄ-τεκνος, ον, (α privat., τέκνον) *childless.*

ἀτέλεια, ἡ, (ἀτελής) at Athens, *exemption from public burdens* (τέλη), Lat. *immunitas.*

ἀ-τέλεστος, ον, (α privat., τελέω) *without end* or *effect: unfinished:*—neut. pl. ἀτέλεστα, as Adv., *in vain.* II. *uninitiated in.*

ἀ-τελεύτητος, ον, (α privat., τελευτάω) *not coming to an end, unaccomplished.* II. *endless, impracticable.*

ἀ-τέλευτος, ον, (α privat., τελευτή) *endless.*

ἀ-τελής, ές, (α privat., τέλος) *without end, unaccomplished.* 2. *ineffectual,* Lat. *irritus.* 3. *imperfect, unripe,* II. act. *not bringing to an end, not accomplishing* a thing. III. at Athens, *free from public burdens* (τέλη), *exempt,* Lat. *immunis.* IV. *uninitiated in* a thing, τινός.

ἀτελίη, ἡ, Ion. for ἀτέλεια.

ἀτέμβω, only used in pres. *to bring to harm, to maltreat, confound:*—Pass. *to be bereft of* a thing; ἀτεμβονται νεότητος they are *deprived of,* i. e. past, youth. (Deriv. uncertain.) [ᾰ]

ἀ-τενής, ές, (α copul., τείνω) *strained tight:* hence *intent, intense: excessive.* 2. *straight, direct: straightforward.* 3. *unbending, stubborn.* II. Adv. ἀτενῶς, or ἀτενές, *exceedingly.* Hence

ἀτενίζω, f. ίσω, *to look at intently, gaze at.*

ἌΤΕΡ, Prep. with. gen. *without, except, besides.* II. *aloof, apart, away from.*

ἀ-τέραμνος, ον, (α privat., τέραμνος) *unsoftened, unfeeling, inexorable.*

ἀ-τεράμων [ᾰ], ον, gen. ονος, Att. for ἀτέραμνος.

ἄτερθε, before a vowel ἄτερθεν, = ἄτερ.

ἀ-τέρμων, ον, gen. ονος, (α privat., τέρμα) *without bounds: having no outlet, inextricable.*

ἅτερος [ᾰ], ον, Dor. for ἕτερος, ον 2. ἅτερος [ᾱ], Att. contr. for ὁ ἕτερος, gen. θατέρου, dat. θᾰτέρῳ, θατέρᾳ etc., or with mark of *crasis,* θἀτέρου, etc.

ἀ-τερπής, ές, (α privat., τέρπω) *unpleasing, joyless, sad.* II. *not enjoying* a thing, τινός.

ἄ-τερπος, ον, = ἀτερπής.

ἀ-τευχής, ές, and **ἀ-τεύχητος**, ον, (α privat., τεῦχος) *unarmed.*

ἄ-τεχνος, ον, or **ἀ-τεχνής**, ές, (α privat., τέχνη) *without art, unskilled, rude:* of things, *inartificial.* II. *without art* or *cunning, simple.*

ἀ-τεχνῶς, Adv. of ἀτεχνής, and **ἀ-τέχνως**, of ἄτεχνος, *without art* or *skill, rudely.* II. *really, absolutely, utterly,* Lat. *plané, prorsus,* in which sense it is mostly written ἀτεχνῶς; as ἀτεχνῶς ξένως ἔχω I am an *utter* stranger.

ἀτέω, only in part. ἀτέων, *fool-hardy, reckless.* From

ἄτη, ἡ, (ἀάω) *distraction, folly, delusion: judicial blindness* sent by the gods. 2. *ruin, mischief:* of persons, *a bane, pest.* 3. Ἄτη personified, *the goddess of mischief:* the Λιταί come slowly after her, undoing the evil she has worked, v. Il. 9. 500. [ᾱ]

ἄ-τηκτος, ον, (α privat., τήκω) *unmelted.*

ἀτημελέω, f. ήσω, *to be careless.* From

ἀ-τημελής, ές (α privat., τημελής) *careless.*

ἀτημέλητος, ον, (ἀτημελέω) *unheeded, uncared for.* 2. *baffled, disappointed.* II. act. *taking no heed:* Adv., ἀτημελήτως ἔχειν τινός to take *no heed of* a thing.

ἀτηρός, ά, όν, (ἄτη) *deluded, driven to ruin.* II. *baneful, ruinous.* Add. -ρῶς. [ᾱ]

Ἀτθίς, ίδος, ἡ, *Attic;* cf. Ἀττικός. II. as Subst. (sub. γῆ), *Attica.* 2. (sub. γλῶττα), *the Attic dialect.*

ἀ-τίετος, ον, (α privat., τίω) *unhonoured.* II. act. *not honouring.*

ἀ-τίζω, f. ίσω, (α privat., τίζω = τίω) *not to honour:* absol. in part., ἀτίζων *unheeding:* but c. acc. *to slight, treat lightly.*

ἀ-τιθάσευτος, ον, (α privat., τιθασεύω) *untamed, not to be tamed, wild.*

ἀτῑμ-ἄγέλης, ου, ὁ, (ἀτιμάω, ἀγέλη) *despising* or *forsaking the herd, feeding alone.*

ἀ-τῑμάζω, f. άσω: aor. 1 ἠτίμᾰσα: pf. ἠτίμᾰκα:—Pass., aor. 1 ἠτῑμάσθην: pf. ἠτίμασμαι: (α privat., τιμάω). *To esteem lightly, dishonour, slight:*—Pass.

to suffer dishonour or *insult.* II. = ἀτιμόω in legal sense, *to deprive of civil rights.*

ἀτῑμαστέος, α, ον, verb. Adj. of ἀτιμάζω, *to be despised.* 2. ἀτιμαστέον, *one must dishonour.*

ἀτῑμαστήρ, ῆρος, ὁ, (ἀτιμάζω) *a dishonourer.*

ἀτίμαστος, ον, (ἀτῑμάζω) *dishonoured, despised.*

ἀ-τῑμάω, f. ήσω: aor. 1 ἠτίμησα: pf. ἠτίμηκα:—Pass., aor. 1 ἠτιμήθην: (α privat., τιμάω):—*to insult, slight, dishonour.* Hence

ἀτίμητος, ον, *unhonoured, despised.* II. in legal sense, *not estimated;* δίκη ἀτίμητος a cause *in which the penalty is not assessed in court,* but fixed by law.

ἀτῑμία, ἡ, (ἄτιμος) *dishonour, disgrace.* 2. at Athens, *the loss of civil rights,* Lat. *deminutio capitis.*

ἄ-τῑμος, ον, (α privat., τιμή I) *unhonoured, dishonoured:* c. gen. *without the honour of.* 2. at Athens, of a citizen *deprived of his privileges* either totally or in part, Lat. *capite deminutus,* opp. to ἐπίτιμος: cf. ἀτιμία. II. (τιμή II) *without price* or *value.* 2. *unrevenged, unpunished.* Hence

ἀτῑμόω, f. ώσω, *to dishonour:*—Pass. *to suffer dishonour.* 2. in legal sense, *to punish with loss of civil privileges* (ἀτιμία), Lat. *aerarium facere.*

ἀτίμων, Ep. impf. of ἀτιμάω.

ἀ-τῑμωρητεί, and **ἀ-τῑμωρητί,** Adv. of

ἀ-τῑμώρητος, ον, (α privat., τιμωρέομαι) *unavenged, unpunished.* 2. *unprotected.*

ἀτίμως, Adv. of ἄτιμος, *disgracefully.*

ἀ-τίμωσις, εως, ἡ, (ἀτιμόω) *a dishonouring.* [τῐ]

ἀτῐτάλλω, aor. 1 Ion. ἀτίτηλα: (ἀταλός):—*to rear, foster, tend:* generally, *to cherish.*

ἄ-τῐτος, ον, also η, ον, (α privat., τίω) *unhonoured, dishonoured.* 2. *unavenged.* II. *unpaid.*

ἀ-τίω, (α privat., τίω) *not to honour, not to revenge.* [ῐ]

Ἀτλᾱ-γενής, ές, (Ἄτλας, γένος) *sprung from Atlas.*

Ἀτλαντίς, ίδος, ἡ, *daughter of Atlas.* From

Ἄ-τλας, αντος, ὁ, (α euphon., τλῆναι) *Atlas,* one of the older gods, who bears up the pillars of heaven: also one of the Titans. 2. the pillar of heaven, *Mount Atlas* in West Africa.

ἀτλητέω, *to be unable to bear, be impatient.* From

ἄ-τλητος, Dor. **ἄ-τλᾱτος,** ον, (α privat., τλῆναι) *not to be borne, insufferable.* II. *not to be dared.*

ἀτμή, ἡ, = ἀτμός, *smoke, heat.*

ἄ-τμητος, ον, (α privat., τέμνω) *uncut:* of a country, *unravaged, not laid waste.* 2. of mines, *unopened.*

ἀτμίζω, f. ίσω, (ἀτμός) *to smoke:* of water, *to steam.*

ἀτμίς, ίδος, ἡ, (ἄω, ἄημι) *steam, vapour.* [ῐ]

ἀτμός, ὁ, (ἄω, ἄημι) *smoke,* Lat. *vapor.*

ἄ-τοιχος, ον, (α privat., τοῖχος) *unwalled.*

ἄ-τοκος, ον, (α privat., τεκεῖν) *never having had a child.* II. *without interest,* of borrowed money.

ἀ-τόλμητος, ον, (α privat., τολμάω) *not to be dared:* also *not to be endured, insufferable.*

ἀτολμία, ἡ, *want of daring, cowardice.* From

ἄ-τολμος, ον, (α privat., τόλμα) *wanting courage, cowardly.* 2. *not overdaring, retiring.*

ἄ-τομος, ον, (α privat., τομή) *uncut: unmown.* II. *not able to be cut, indivisible;* ἐν ἀτόμῳ *in a moment of time.*

ἄ-τονος, ον, (α privat., τείνω) *not stretched, slack, languid,* Lat. *remissus.* II. (τόνος) *without accent.*

ἄ-τοξος, ον, (α privat., τόξον) *without bow* or *arrow.*

ἀτοπία, ἡ, *strangeness, oddness, absurdity: unusual nature: unnatural conduct.* From

ἄ-τοπος, ον, (α privat., τόπος) *out of place, out of the way, strange, marvellous, odd.* 2. *absurd,* Lat. *ineptus.* 3. *unnatural, disgusting.* Hence

ἀτόπως. Adv. *absurdly.*

ἆτος, ον, contr. for ἄατος, *insatiate,* c. gen.

ἄτρακτος, ὁ, and ἡ, *a spindle.* II. also *an arrow,* cf. ἠλακάτη. (Deriv. uncertain.)

ἀ-τρᾰπῐτός, Ep. **ἀτάρπιτος,** ἡ, *a path.*

ἀ-τρᾰπός, Ep. **ἀ-ταρπός,** ἡ, (α euphon., τρέπω) *a path that does not turn, a path, way, road.*

ἀτρέκεια, ἡ, *reality, strict truth, accuracy.* II. *justice, uprightness.* From

ἈΤΡΕΚΉΣ, ές, *real, true, exact.* II. *strict, just, upright.*

ἀ-τρέμᾰ, and before a vowel **ἀ-τρέμᾰς,** Adv., (α privat., τρέμω) *without trembling.* 2. *quietly, calmly, gently.*

ἀ-τρεμαῖος, α, ον, poët. for ἀτρεμής, *calm, gentle;* ἀτρεμαία βοά a whisper.

ἀτρεμέω, *not to tremble* or *move, to keep still* or *quiet.* From

ἀ-τρεμής, ές, (α privat., τρέμω) *not trembling, unmoved, calm:* Adv. **ἀτρεμί,** *quietly.*

ἀτρεμία, ἡ, (ἀτρεμής) *a keeping still: calmness.*

ἀτρεμίζω, f. ίσω Att. ιῶ, (ἀτρεμής) *to keep quiet:* οὐκ ἀτρεμίζειν *to be restless* or *unquiet.*

ἄ-τρεπτος, ον, (α privat., τρέπω) *unmoved, indifferent.*

ἄ-τρεστος, ον, (α privat., τρέω) *not trembling, fearless.*

ἀ-τρίακτος, ον, (α privat., τριάζω) *unconquered.*

ἀ-τρίβαστος, ον, (α privat., τρίβω) *not accustomed.*

ἀ-τρῐβής, ές, (α privat., τρῐβεῖν) *not rubbed:* of places, *not traversed, pathless:* of roads, *not used.* 2. of clothes, *not much worn, new,* Lat. *integer.*

ἄτριον, τό, Dor. for ἤτριον.

ἄ-τριπτος, ον, (α privat., τρίβω) *not worn hard by work.* 2. of corn, *not threshed.* 3. ἄτριπτοι ἄκανθαι thorns *on which one cannot tread* or *walk.*

ἀ-τρόμητος, ον, (α privat., τρομέω) *fearless, dauntless.*

ἄ-τρομος, ον, (α privat., τρέμω) *fearless, dauntless,* Lat. *intrepidus.*

ἀτροπία, ἡ, *obstinacy.* From

ἄ-τροπος, ον, (α privat., τρέπω) *not turning, unchangeable.* 2. of persons, *inflexible:* ἡ Ἄτροπος, name of one of the Μοῖραι or Parcae.

ἀτροφέω, f. ήσω, *to pine away.* From

ἄ-τροφος, *ον*, (α privat., *τρέφω*) *taking no food: pining away, ill of an atrophy.*

ἀ-τρύγετος, *ον*, also *η*, *ον*, (α privat., *τρῠγάω*) *unfruitful, barren:* generally, *waste, desert.*

ἀ-τρῠγής, *ές*, (α privat., *τρύγη*) *not gathered.*

ἀ-τρύμων, *ον*, gen. *ονος*, = *ἄτρυτος*, c. gen., *ἀτρύμων κακῶν not worn out* by ills. [ῡ]

ἄ-τρῡτος, *ον*, (α privat., *τρύω*) *not worn down, unabating:* of a road, *wearisome.*

Ἀ-τρῡτώνη, *the Unwearied.* (Lengthd. form from *ἀτρύτη*, as *Ἀϊδωνεύς* from *Αἴδης*.)

ἄ-τρωτος, *ον*, (α privat., *τιτρώσκω*) *unwounded.*

ἄττα, Att. for *τινά*, **ἅττα** for *ἅτινα*, v *ἄσσα*, *ἅσσα*.

ἌΤΤΑ, a salutation used to elders, *father;* cf. *ἄππα*, *ἄπφα*, *πάππα*, [τᾰ]

ἀττᾰγᾶς, ᾶ, ὁ, Lat. *attagen*, prob *the godwit.*

ἀτταταῖ, *a cry of pain* or *grief:* sometimes prolonged, *ἀταττατᾶι*, etc.: also used ironically.

ἀττέλαβος, Ion. **ἀττέλεβος**, ὁ, *a kind of locust* without wings.

Ἀττικίζω, f. *ίσω* Att. *ιῶ*, (*Ἀττικός*) *to side with the Athenians, Atticize:* later, *to live like an Athenian*, esp. *to speak Attic.* Hence

Ἀττικισμός, ὁ, *a siding with Athens, attachment to her.* II. *an Attic expression, Atticism.*

Ἀττικίων, Dim. of *Ἀττικός*, *a little Athenian.*

Ἀττικός, *ή*, *όν*, (*ἀκτή*) *Attic, Athenian:* ἡ *Ἀττική* (sub. *γῆ*) = *Ἀτθίς*, *Attica.*

Ἀττικωνικός, *ή*. *όν*, a comic alteration of *Ἀττικός*, imitated from the form of *Λακωνικός*.

ἆττον, Att. for *ἆσσον*, *nearer.*

ᾄττω, Att. for *ᾄσσω*, *ἀΐσσω*, q. v.

ἀτύζομαι, aor. 1 part. *ἀτυχθείς*: Pass.: (*ἀτάω*):—*to be distraught* from fear, *amazed, bewildered; ἀτυζόμενος πεδίοιο flying wildly* over the plain: also *distraught* with grief: c. acc. *to be amazed at* a thing. II. rarely in Act. *ἀτύζω*, f. *ύξω*, *to strike with terror.*

ἀ-τῠράννευτος, *ον*, (α privat., *τυραννεύω*) *not ruled by tyrants, free from tyrants.*

ἄ-τῡφος, *ον*, (α privat., *τύφω*) *not puffed up.*

ἀτῠχέω, f. *ήσω*, (*ἀτυχής*) *to be unlucky* or *unfortunate, fail, miscarry:* c. gen *to fail in getting* or *gaining* a thing. 2 *ἀτυχεῖν πρός τινα to fail with* another, i. e. fail in one's request. Hence

ἀτύχημα, *ατος*, *τό*, *a misfortune, mishap.*

ἀ-τῠχής, *ές*, (α privat., *τυχεῖν*) *luckless, unfortunate, unsuccessful.* Adv. -*χῶς*

ἀτῠχία, *ή*, (*ἀτυχέω*) *ill luck, bad fortune.* II. *a miscarriage, mishap*

ΑΥ̓, Adv. of Place, *back, backwards*, Lat. *retro.* II. of Time, *again, anew, afresh, once more*, Lat. *denuo.* III. *further, moreover, besides*, Lat. *porro.* 2. *on the other hand, in turn*, Lat. *vicissim*.

αὐαίνω, impf. *αὔαινον*: f. *αὐᾰνῶ*: aor. 1 pass. *αὐάνθην*: (*αὔω*):—*to dry.* 2. *to wither* or *parch up; βίον αὐαίνειν to waste* life *away:* fut. med. *αὐανοῦμαι* in pass. sense, *I shall wither away.*

αὐᾰλέος, α, *ον*, (*αὖος*) *dry, parched, withered:* of hair, *rough, squalid:* of eyes, *sleepless.*

Αὔασις, *ή*, = *Ὄασις*, the name of the fertile islets in the Libyan deserts.

αὐάτα, Aeol. for *ἄτη*, *calamity, mischief;* to be pronounced *ἄϝᾰτᾱ*.

αὐγάζω, f. *άσω*: aor. 1 *ηὔγασα*: (*αὐγή*):—*to see distinctly, discern, behold:* so also in Med. II. intr. *to shine.*

ΑΥ̓ΓΗ', *ή*, *a bright light*, esp. of the sun, and so in plur. *the rays, beams* of the sun; *ὑπ' αὐγὰς ἠελίοιο* under *the light* of the sun, i. e. still alive. *αὐγὰς λεύσσειν* to behold *the light*, i. e. to be alive; *κλύζειν πρὸς αὐγάς* to rise surging towards heaven. 2. *any light*, esp. of the eyes; *ὀμμάτων αὐγαί* and *αὐγαί* alone, like Lat. *lumina, the eyes.* 3. *any gleam* on the surface of bright objects, *sheen.*

αὐδάζομαι, f. *άξομαι*: aor. 1 *ηὐδαξάμην*: Dep.: (*αὐδή*):—*to cry out, speak.*

αὐδάω, impf. *ηὔδων*: f. *ήσω* Att. *ᾱσω*: aor. 1 *ηὔδησα*, Ion. 3 sing. *αὐδήσασκε*: pf. *ηὔδηκα*:—also **αὐδάομαι**, as Dep.:—*to talk, speak:* c. acc. rei, *to speak, say* a thing: of oracles, *to utter, proclaim.* 2. *to speak, to address.* 3. c. inf. *to tell, bid, order* to do. 4. *to call by name; αὐδῶμαι παῖς Ἀχιλλέως I am called* Achilles' son. 5. like *λέγειν*, Lat. *dicere, to mean.* From

ΑΥ̓ΔΗ', *ή*, *the human voice, a voice, tone:* metaph. *any other sound*, e. g. *the twang* of the bowstring. 2. *a report, account.* Hence

αὐδήεις, *εσσα*, *εν*, *speaking with human voice.*

αὐ-ερύω (i. e. *αὖ ἐρύω*), aor. 1 *αὐέρῠσα*:—*to draw back: to draw* the bow: in a sacrifice, *to draw back* the victim's head, so as to cut its throat.

αὐθάδεια, poët. **αὐθᾱδία**, *ή*, *self-will, wilfulness, stubbornness, presumption.* From

αὐθ-άδης [ᾱ], *ες*, (*αὐτός*, *ἥδομαι*) *self-willed, wilful, stubborn, headstrong:* also *unfeeling.* Adv. -*δῶς*.

αὐθ-ᾱδία, *ή*, poët. for *αὐθάδεια*.

αὐθᾱδίζομαι, f. *ίσομαι*: (*αὐθάδης*): Dep.:—*to be self-willed* or *stubborn.*

αὐθᾱδικός, *ή*, *όν*, (*αὐθάδης*) *disposed to be self-willed.*

αὐθάδισμα, *ατος*, *τό*, (*αὐθάδης*) *an act of self-will, wilfulness.*

αὐθᾱδό-στομος, *ον*, (*αὐθάδης*, *στόμα*) *wilful* or *proud of speech.*

αὐθ-αίμων, *ον*, gen. *ονος*, (*αὐτός*, *αἷμα*) *of the same blood:* as Subst. *a brother* or *sister, near kinsman.*

αὐθ-αίρετος, *ον*, (*αὐτός*, *αἱρέω*) *self-chosen, self-elected.* II. *taken upon oneself, self-incurred: voluntary, optional.* Adv. -*τως*.

αὐθεντέω, f. *ήσω*, *to have power over.* From

αὐθ-έντης, *ου*, ὁ, contr. for *αὐτοέντης*, (*αὐτός*, *ἔντεα*) *an actual murderer:* esp. of murders *done by those of the same family:* also *a self-murderer, suicide.* 2. *an absolute master* or *ruler.* II. as Adj., *αὐθέντης φόνος* death *by murder.*

αὐθ-ήμερος, *ον*, (*αὐτός*, *ἡμέρα*) *made* or *happening* on the very day: Adv. αὐθημερόν Ion. αὐτημερόν, on the very day.

αὖθι, Adv. shortd. for αὐτόθι, of Place, on the spot, here, there: of Time, forthwith, straightway.

αὐθι-γενής, Ion. αὐτιγ-, ές, (αὖθι, γενέσθαι) born on the spot, born in the country, native, Lat. indigĕna: of rivers, rising in the country; αὐθιγενὲς ὕδωρ spring water. 2. genuine, sincere.

αὖθις, Ion. αὖτις, Adv., a lengthd. form of αὖ: I. of Place, back, back again. II. of Time, again, afresh, anew: also hereafter. III. moreover, besides, in turn, on the other hand.

αὐθ-όμαιμος, (αὐτός, ὅμαιμος) akin, of the selfsame blood.

αὐ-ΐαχος, ον, (α copul., ἰαχή) shouting together or in common, of the Trojans marching to battle.

αὖλαξ, ἄκος, ἡ, = ἄλοξ, a furrow: also ὦλαξ, for which Homer used ὦλξ. (Deriv. uncertain.)

αὔλειος, α, ον, sometimes also ος, ον, (αὐλή) of or belonging to the αὐλή or court; ἐπ' αὐλείῃσι θύρῃσι at the door of the court, i. e. at the outer door, house-door.

αὐλέω, f. ήσω, (αὐλός) to play on the flute:—Pass., of tunes, to be played on the flute; αὐλεῖται πᾶν μέλαθρον the whole house is filled with music:—Med. to get oneself played to, hear music.

αὐλή, ἡ, (*ἄω, ἄημι) in Homer the open court before the house, the court-yard, surrounded with outbuildings, the altar of Ζεὺς Ἑρκεῖος being in the middle; it had two doors, one the house-door (cf. αὔλειος), and one leading through the αἴθουσα into the πρόδομος. II. after Hom., the αὐλή was the court or quadrangle, round which the house was built, having a corridor (περιστύλιον) all round, from which were doors leading into the men's apartments; opposite the house door (cf. αὔλειος) was the (μέσαυλος or μέταυλος), leading into the women's part of the house. III. generally, any court or hall. IV. any dwelling, abode, chamber.

αὔλημα, ατος, τό, (αὐλέω) a piece of music for the flute.

αὐλησεῦντι, Dor. for αὐλήσουσι, 3 pl. fut. of αὐλέω.

αὐλητήρ, ῆρος, ὁ, and **αὐλητής**, οῦ, ὁ, (αὐλέω) a flute-player. Hence

αὐλητικός, ή, όν, of or for a flute-player; ἡ αὐλητική (sub. τέχνη), his art.

αὐλητρίς, ίδος, ἡ, fem. of αὐλητήρ, a flute-girl.

αὐλιάς, άδος, ἡ, (αὐλή) protecting cattle-folds, name of a Nymph.

αὐλίζομαι: fut. med. αὐλίσομαι: aor. 1 ηὐλισάμην: aor. 1 pass. ηὐλίσθην: pf. ηὔλισμαι: Dep.: (αὐλή):—to lie in the αὐλή or court-yard, to lie out at night: generally, to take up one's abode, lodge, live: as a military term, to encamp, bivouac.

αὔλιον, τό, (αὐλη) any country house, a cottage: a fold. II. a chamber, cave.

αὔλιος, α, ον, (αὐλή) of or belonging to cattle-folds, rustic.

αὖλις, ιδος, ἡ, (αὐλίζομαι) a stall, fold, tent, esp. for passing the night in; αὖλιν θέσθαι to pitch one's tent.

αὐλίσκος, ὁ, Dim. of αὐλός, a small reed, a pipe.

αὐλιστρίς, ίδος, ἡ, (αὐλίζομαι) a female inmate in a house.

αὐλο-δόκη, ἡ, (αὐλός, δέχομαι) a flute-case.

αὐλο-θετέω, (αὐλός, τίθημι) to make flutes or pipes.

αὐλο-ποιός, ὁ, (αὐλός, ποιέω) a flute-maker.

αὐλός, ὁ, (*αὔω, to blow) any wind-instrument, a flute, made of reed, wood, bone, ivory, or metal; αὐλοὶ ἀνδρήϊοι καὶ γυναικήϊοι, prob. like Lat. tibia dextra et sinistra, i. e. bass and treble; αὐλὸς Ἐνυαλίου the pipe of Mars, i. e. a trumpet. 2. any tube, pipe, groove, socket.

αὐλών, ῶνος, ὁ, poët. also ἡ, (αὐλός) a hollow way, defile, ravine: a canal, aqueduct: a channel, strait: αὐλῶνες πόντιοι the sea-straits, i. e. the Archipelago.

αὐλ-ῶπις, ιδος, ἡ, (αὐλός, ὤψ) epith. of a helmet, with a tube (αὐλός) to hold the plume (λόφος).

ΑΥ'ΞΑ'ΝΩ or **ΑΥ'ΞΩ**, poët. ἀέξω: f. αὐξήσω: aor. 1 ηὔξησα: pf. ηὔξηκα:—Lat. AUGEO, to make grow, increase: to promote to honour, exalt, extol. II. Pass., with fut. med. αὐξήσομαι and pass. αὐξηθήσομαι: aor. 1 ηὐξήθην: pf. ηὔξημαι:—to grow, wax, increase: of a child, to grow up: of the wind, to rise; ηὐξανόμην ἀκούων I grew taller as I heard. III. intrans. in Act. to grow, wax. Hence

αὔξη, ἡ, growth, increase.

αὐξηθείς, aor. 1 pass. part. of αὐξάνω.

Αὐξησία, ἡ, (αὔξω) the goddess of growth.

αὔξησις, εως, ἡ, (αὔξω) growth, increase.

αὔξῐμος, ον, (αὔξω) promoting growth.

αὐξο-σέληνον, τό, (αὐξάνω, σελήνη) the new moon.

αὐξώ, οῦς, ἡ, (αὐξάνω) the goddess of growth, called to witness in an Athenian citizen's oath.

αὔξω, v. sub αὐξάνω.

αὐονή, ἡ, (αὖος) dryness, withering.

αὖος, η, ον, (αὔω) dry, dried, of fruit; αὖον ἀϋτεῖν to ring dry and harsh, of metal. 2. withered, parched. 3. drained dry, exhausted.

ἀϋπνία, ἡ, sleeplessness. From

ἄϋ-πνος, ον, (α privat., ὕπνος) sleepless, wakeful; ὕπνος ἄϋπνος a sleep that is no sleep.

αὔρα, Ion. αὔρη, ἡ, (*ἄω, ἄημι) air in motion, a breeze, esp. the fresh air of morning, Lat. aura.

αὔριον, (from αὐώς, Aeol. for ἠώς) Adv. to-morrow; ἐς αὔριον on the morrow, next morning or till morning: ἡ αὔριον (sub. ἡμέρα), the morrow; also, ἡ ἐς αὔριον ἡμέρα, ὁ αὔριον χρόνος.

ἀῦσαι, aor. 1 inf. of αὔω to shout.

αὔσιος, Dor. for τηΰσιος.

αὐσταλέος, poët. **ἀϋσταλέος**, α, ον, (αὖος) sunburnt, shrivelled, parched, Lat. siccus.

αὐστηρός, ά, όν, (*ἄω, αὔω, ἄζω) making the tongue dry and rough; rough, bitter. 2. metaph. like Lat. austerus, stern, harsh, austere. Hence

αὐστηρότης, ητος, ἡ, roughness, rough flavour. 2. metaph. harshness, sternness, austerity.

αὐτ-άγγελος, ον, (αὐτός, ἀγγέλλω) *carrying one's own message: bringing news of what one has seen.*

αὐτ-άγρετος, ον, (αὐτός, ἀγρέω) *self-chosen, left to one's choice.* II. act. *choosing for oneself.*

αὐτ-άδελφος, ον, (αὐτός, ἀδελφός) *related as brother* or *sister: one's own brother* or *sister.*

αὔτ-ανδρος, ον, (αὐτός, ἀνήρ) *with the men themselves, men and all.*

αὐτ-ανέψιος, α, (αὐτός, ἀνεψιός) *an own cousin, cousin-german.*

αὐτάρ, Conjunct., Ep. for ἀτάρ, *but, yet, however, still, besides, moreover.* Like ἀτάρ it always begins a proposition.

αὐτάρκεια, ἡ, (αὐτάρκης) *sufficiency in oneself, independence.*

αὐτ-άρκης, ες, (αὐτός, ἀρκέω) *sufficient in oneself, independent* of others; πόλις αὐτάρκης a country *that supplies itself, that wants no imports*; c. inf., αὐτάρκης ἀναγκάζειν *fully able* to compel.

αὖτε, Adv., I. of Time, *again, over again.* II. to mark Sequence, *again, furthermore,* like Lat. *autem.* 2. *however, on the contrary.*

αὐτ-έκμαγμα, ατος, τό, (αὐτός, ἐκμάσσομαι) *an exact impression, true portrait.*

αὐτ-εξούσιος, ον, (αὐτός, ἐξουσία) *in one's own power*: τὸ αὐτεξούσιον *free power.*

αὐτ-επάγγελτος, ον, (αὐτός, ἐπαγγέλλομαι) *offering of oneself, of oneself, freely,* Lat. *sponte.*

αὐτ-επώνυμος, ον, (αὐτός, ἐπώνυμος) *of the same surname.*

αὐτ-ερέτης, ου, ὁ, (αὐτός, ἐρέτης) *rower and soldier at once.*

ἀυτέω, Ep. impf. ἀΰτευν, only used in pres. and impf., *to cry, shout*: also in Act., *to call.* [ῡ] From

ἀϋτή, ἡ, (αὔω) *a shout, call,* esp. *a battle-shout, war-cry,* hence also *the battle itself.* [ῡ]

αὐτ-ήκοος, ον, (αὐτός, ἀκούω) *one who has himself heard, an ear-witness.*

αὐτ-ῆμαρ, Adv., = αὐθημέρον, *on the selfsame day.*

αὐτι-γενής, ές, Ion. for αὐθιγενής.

αὐτίκα [ῐ], Adv. (αὐτός) *forthwith, straightway, immediately*; αὐτίκα καὶ μετέπειτα *now* and hereafter: *presently, directly,* Lat. *mox.* II. *for example, just to give an example*; αὐτίκα γὰρ ἄρχει διὰ τίν' ὁ Ζεύς; *for example,* by what means does Zeus rule the gods?

αὖτις, Ion. and Dor. for αὖθις.

ἀϋτμή, (*ἄω, αὔω, *to blow*) *breath: the blast* of a bellows. II. *a scent, odour.*

ἀϋτμήν, μένος, ὁ, = ἀϋτμή.

αὐτο-βοεί, Adv. (αὐτός, βοή) *by a mere shout*; αὐτοβοεὶ ἑλεῖν to take *without resistance.*

αὐτό-βουλος, ον, (αὐτός, βουλή) *self-willed.*

αὐτο-γέννητος, ον, (αὐτός, γεννάω):—κοιμήματα μητρὸς αὐτ. a mother's intercourse *with her own child.*

αὐτογνωμονέω, f. ήσω, *to act of one's own will* or *judgment* From

αὐτο-γνώμων, ον, gen. ονος, (αὐτός, γνώμη) *acting of one's own will* or *judgment.* Adv. –μόνως.

αὐτό-γνωτος, ον, (αὐτός, γιγνώσκω) *self-resolved, self-chosen.*

αὐτό-γυος, ον, (αὐτός, γύης):—ἄροτρον αὐτόγυον a plough *in which the* γύης *is of one piece with the* ἔλυμα and ἱστοβοεύς.

αὐτο-δαής, ές, (αὐτός, δαῆναι) *unpremeditated.*

αὐτο-δάϊκτος, ον, (αὐτός, δαΐζω) *self-slain* or *mutually slain.*

αὐτ-οδάξ, Adv. (αὐτός, ὀδάξ) *with clenched teeth*: hence *stubborn.*

αὐτό-δεκα, (αὐτός, δέκα) *just ten.*

αὐτό-δηλος, ον, (αὐτός, δῆλος) *self-evident.*

αὐτο-δίδακτος, ον, (αὐτός, διδάσκω) *self-taught.*

αὐτό-δικος, ον, (αὐτός, δίκη) *with one's own law-courts: conducting one's own suits at home.*

αὐτόδιον, Adv. (αὐτός) *straightway.*

αὐτο-έλικτος, ον, (αὐτός, ἑλίσσω) *curling naturally.*

αὐτο-έντης, ου, ὁ, = αὐθέντης, *a murderer.*

αὐτο-ετής, ές, (αὐτός, ἔτος) *in* or *of the same year*: Adv. αὐτόετες, *in the same year, within the year.*

αὐτο-θελεί, Adv. of αὐτοθελής, *voluntarily.*

αὐτο-θελής, ές, (αὐτός, θέλω) *of one's own will, voluntary.*

αὐτόθεν, Adv. (αὐτοῦ) of Place, *from the very spot where one is, from hence, from thence,* Lat. *illinc.* II. of Time, *on the spot, at once,* Lat. *illico.*

αὐτόθι, Adv. for αὐτοῦ, *on the very spot, there.*

αὐτο-κασίγνητος, ὁ, and –τη, ἡ, (αὐτός, κασίγνητος) *an own brother* or *sister.*

αὐτο-κατάκριτος, ον, (αὐτός, κατακρίνω) *self-condemned.*

αὐτο-κέλευθος, ον, (αὐτός, κέλευθος) *going one's own way.*

αὐτο-κέλευστος, ον, (αὐτός, κελεύω) *self-bidden, of one's own accord.*

αὐτο-κελής, ές, (αὐτός, κέλομαι) = foreg.

αὐτό-κλητος, ον, (αὐτός, καλέω) *self-called,* i. e. *uncalled, unbidden.*

αὐτό-κομος, ον, (αὐτός, κόμη) *with natural hair, shaggy.* II. *hair and all.*

αὐτο-κρατής, ές, (αὐτός, κράτος) *ruling by oneself, having full power, absolute*: τὸ αὐτοκρατὲς *free will.*

αὐτο-κράτωρ, ορος, ὁ, ἡ, (αὐτός, κρατέω) *one's own master*: 1. of persons or states, *free and independent,* Lat. *sui juris.* 2. of ambassadors, etc., *possessing full powers.* 3. of rulers, *absolute: peremptory.*

αὐτό-κτιτος, ον, (αὐτός, κτίζω) *self-produced, made by nature.*

αὐτοκτονέω, *to slay themselves* or *one another.* From

αὐτο-κτόνος, ον, (αὐτός, κτείνω) *self-slaying.* II. *slaying one another*; θάνατος αὐτοκτόνος *mutual* death *by each other's hand.*

αὐτο-κυβερνήτης, ου, ὁ, (αὐτός, κυβερνάω) *one who steers himself.*

αὐτό-κωπος, ον, (αὐτός, κώπη) *together with the*

handle; βέλη αὐτόκωπα weapons *with a handle*, i. e. swords.

αὐτο-μᾰθής, ές, (αὐτός, μαθεῖν) *self-taught*, τινός in a thing.

αὐτό-μαρτῠς, ῠος, ὁ, ἡ, (αὐτός, μάρτυς) *oneself the witness*, i. e. *an eyewitness*.

αὐτομᾰτίζω, f. ίσω, *to act of one's own will, to act of oneself*, and so *to act unadvisedly*. From

αὐτό-μᾰτος, η, ον, also ος, ον, (αὐτός, μέμαα, pf. of *μάω) *acting of one's own will, of oneself, unbidden;* esp. *self-moving; τὰ αὐτόματα self-moving machines, automatons.* 2. of plants, *growing of themselves, spontaneous.* 3. of events, *happening of themselves: without cause, accidental; ἀπὸ τοῦ αὐτομάτου, naturally* or *by chance.* Adv. -τως, Lat. *ultro, sponte sua.*

αὐτομολέω, f. ήσω, (αὐτόμολος) *to desert.* Hence

αὐτομόλησις, εως, ἡ, and **αὐτομολία**, ἡ, *desertion.*

αὐτό-μολος, ον, (αὐτός, μολεῖν) *going of oneself:* as Subst. *a deserter.*

αὐτονομέομαι, Dep. (αὐτόνομος) *to live by one's own laws, be independent.*

αὐτονομία, ἡ, *independence.* From

αὐτό-νομος, ον, (αὐτός, νέμω) *living by one's own laws: independent.* II. (νέμομαι) *feeding at will.*

αὐτο-νῠχί, Adv. (αὐτός, νύξ) *that very night.*

αὐτό-ξῠλος, ον, (αὐτός, ξύλον) *of mere wood.*

αὐτό-παις, παιδος, ὁ, ἡ, (αὐτός, παῖς) *an own child, son* or *daughter.*

αὐτο-πήμων, ον, gen. ονος, (αὐτός, πῆμα) *for one's own woes.*

αὐτο-ποιός, όν, (αὐτός, ποιέω) *self-produced.*

αὐτό-πολις, εως, ὁ, (αὐτός, πόλις) *self-administered, independent.* Hence

αὐτοπολίτης, ου, ὁ, *a citizen of a free state.* [ῑ]

αὐτο-πόνητος, ον, (αὐτός, πονέω) *self-wrought, natural.*

αὐτό-πρεμνος, ον, (αὐτός, πρέμνον) *together with the root, root and all; αὐτόπρεμνος ὄλλυσθαι* to perish *root and branch.*

αὐτο-πρόσωπος, ον, (αὐτός, πρόσωπον) *in one's own person.*

αὐτ-όπτης, ου, ὁ, (αὐτός, ὄψομαι, fut. of ὁράω) *seeing oneself, an eyewitness.*

αὐτο-πώλης, ου, ὁ, (αὐτός, πωλέω) *selling one's own goods.*

αὐτόρ-ριζος, poët. **αὐτόριζος**, ον, (αὐτός, ῥίζα) *self-rooted.* II. *with the roots, roots and all.*

αὐτόρ-ρῠτος, poët. **αὐτό-ρυτος**, ον, (αὐτός, ῥέω) *self-flowing.*

ΑΥ'ΤΟ'Σ, **αὐτή**, **αὐτό**, Pron. of 3rd pers., *self*, Lat. *ipse:* in oblique cases often for the person. Pron., *him, her, it:* with artic. ὁ αὐτός, ἡ αὐτή, τὸ αὐτό, *the same.*

I. *self, myself, thyself:* 1. *oneself*, i. e. the part properly called *self*, as the *soul*, opp. to the *body;* or *oneself*, as opp. to *others*, e. g. the king to his subjects: hence it is used emphatically for *a master*, as in the Pythag. phrase Αὐτὸς ἔφα, Lat. *Ipse dixit.* 2. *of oneself, of one's own accord.* 3. *by oneself, alone,* = μόνος; αὐτοί ἐσμεν we are *by ourselves.* 4. in dat. with a Subst., *together with; ἀνόρουσεν αὐτῇ σὺν φόρμιγγι* he sprang up *lyre in hand:* but mostly without σύν, ἵππους αὐτοῖσιν ὄχεσφιν horses, chariot *and all;* this use is freq. in Att., αὐτοῖσι συμμάχοισι allies *and all; αὐτοῖς τοῖς ἵπποις* horses *and all.* 5. added to ordinal numbers, e. g. πέμπτος αὐτός *himself* the fifth, i. e. *himself* with four others, αὐτός being the chief person. 6. also joined with the personal Pron., ἐγὼ αὐτός, σὲ αὐτόν, etc., always *divisim* in Homer: sometimes the personal Pron. is omitted, as, αὐτὸν ἐλέησον, for ἐμὲ αὐτόν: again αὐτός is joined with the reflexive ἑαυτοῦ, αὑτοῦ, etc., to give greater force, as αὐτὸς καθ' αὑτοῦ. II. Comp. αὐτότερος, *more himself;* and Sup. αὐτότατος, Lat. *ipsissimus, his very self.*

II. *He, she, it*, Lat. *ille*, for the simple Pron. of third person, *only in oblique cases*, and never at the beginning of a sentence. On the difference between the oblique cases αὐτοῦ, αὐτῷ, αὐτόν, and the reflex. Pron. αὑτοῦ, αὑτῷ, αὑτόν, v. sub ἑαυτοῦ.

III. with Article, ὁ αὐτός, ἡ αὐτή, τὸ αὐτό, Att. contr. αὑτός, αὑτή, ταὐτό and ταὐτόν; gen. ταὐτοῦ, etc.; Ion. ὡὐτός, τωὐτό:—*the same*, Lat. *idem.* It freq. takes a dat., like ὅμοιος, etc., ὁ αὐτὸς τῷ λίθῳ *the same as* the stone; τὸ αὐτὸ πράσσειν or πάσχειν τινί to fare *the same as* one: also in phrases κατὰ ταὐτό, ὑπὸ ταὐτό, *at, about the same time*, Lat. *sub idem tempus:* εἰς ταὐτό, ἐν ταὐτῷ, ἐκ τοῦ αὐτοῦ, *to, in, from the same place.*

IV. in Compos., 1. *of itself*, i. e. *natural, native*, as in αὐτόκτιτος. 2. *of mere, of nothing but*, as in αὐτόξυλος. 3. *of oneself*, as in αὐτοδίδακτος. 4. *the very, the ideal*, as in αὐτοάγαθον, αὐτοάνθρωπος, etc. 5. *just, exactly*, as in αὐτόδεκα. 6. rarely, with reflex. sense of αὑτοῦ and ἀλλήλων, as αὐθέντης, αὐτοκτονέω. 7. *together with*, as in αὐτότοκος young *and all.* 8. *alone, by oneself*, as in αὐτόσκηνος.

αὐτόσε, Adv. (αὐτοῦ) *to the very place*, Lat. *illuc.*

αὐτο-σίδηρος, ον, (αὐτός, σίδηρος) *of sheer iron.*

αὐτόσ-σῠτος, ον, (αὐτός, σεύομαι) *self-moved.*

αὐτο-στᾰδία, ἡ, (αὐτός, ἵσταμαι) *a stand-up fight, close fight.*

αὐτό-στολος, ον, (αὐτός, στέλλομαι) *self-sent, going of oneself.*

αὐτό-στονος, ον, (αὐτός, στένω) *sighing for* or *by oneself.*

αὐτο-σφᾰγής, ές, (αὐτός, σφαγῆναι) *slain by oneself* or *by kinsmen.*

αὐτο-σχεδά, Adv. = αὐτοσχεδόν.

αὐτοσχεδιάζω, f. άσω, (αὐτοσχέδιος) *to act* or *speak off-hand:* hence in bad sense, *to act* or *speak unadvisedly: to judge superficially.* 2. in good sense, *to devise a plan off-hand.* Hence

αὐτοσχεδίασμα, ατος, τό, *work done off-hand, an impromptu:* and

αὐτοσχεδιαστής, οῦ, ὁ, *one who acts* or *speaks off-hand: a novice*, Lat. *tiro*.

αὐτο-σχέδιος, α, ον, also ος, ον, (αὐτός, σχέδιος) *hand to hand*:—as fem. Subst. **αὐτοσχεδίη**, (sc. μάχη) ἡ, *a close fight, fray*; acc. αὐτοσχεδίην as Adv. *close at hand*. II. *off-hand, on the spur of the moment*.

αὐτο-σχεδόν, Adv. (αὐτός, σχεδόν) *near at hand, hand to hand*, Lat. *cominus*.

αὐτότατος, see αὐτός II.

αὐτο-τέλεστος, ον, (αὐτός, τελέω) *self-accomplished*.

αὐτο-τελής, ές, (αὐτός, τέλος) *complete in itself, sufficient*:—Adv. αὐτοτελῶς, *absolutely, arbitrarily*. II. *taxing oneself*.

αὐτότερος, see αὐτός II.

αὐτο-τόκος, ον, (αὐτός, τοκος) *young and all*.

αὐτο-τράγικος, ον, (αὐτός, τραγικός) *arrant tragic*.

αὐτο-τροπήσας, aor. 1 part. as if from αὐτοτροπάω, (αὐτός, τρέπω) *to turn straightway*.

αὐτοῦ, Adv., properly gen. neut. of αὐτός, *at the very place, there, here, on the spot*, Lat. *illico*.

αὑτοῦ, Att. contr. for ἑαυτοῦ.

αὐτουργία, ἡ, *a working with one's own hand*; αὐτουργία φόνου self-inflicted murder. From

αὐτ-ουργός, όν, (αὐτός, ἔργον) *self-working*. 2. as Subst., *one who tills his own land, a husbandman, farmer*. II. pass. *self-wrought, extemporary*.

αὐτόφι, αὐτόφιν, Ep. gen. and dat. sing. and plur. of αὐτός: ἐπ' αὐτόφι or παρ' αὐτόφι *on the very spot*; ἀπ' αὐτόφι from *the very spot*.

αὐτό-φλοιος, ον, (αὐτός, φλοιός) *bark and all*.

αὐτο-φόνος, ον, (αὐτός, *φένω) *self-murdering, murdering one's own kin*.

αὐτο-φόντης, ου, ὁ, (αὐτός, *φένω) *a murderer*.

αὐτό-φορτος, ον, (αὐτός, φόρτος) *bearing one's own baggage*.

αὐτο-φυής, ές, (αὐτός, φύω) *self-growing, self-existent*. 2. *of home growth* or *production*. 3. *natural*, opp. to *artificial*; αὐτοφυεῖς λόφοι hills *in their natural state*, not quarried or mined. Hence

αὐτοφυῶς, Adv. *naturally*.

αὐτό-φυτος, ον, (αὐτός, φύω) *self-caused*.

αὐτό-φωρος, ον, (αὐτός, φώρ) *caught in the act of theft*; ἐπ' αὐτοφώρῳ λαμβάνειν to catch *in the act*; ἐπ' αὐτοφώρῳ ἁλῶναι to be caught *in the very act*.

αὐτό-χειρ, ρος, ὁ, ἡ, (αὐτός, χείρ) *working with one's own hand*: c. gen. *the very maker* or *worker of* a thing. II. absol. *one who kills himself* or *one of his kin: a murderer, homicide*. 3. as Adj. *murderous*. Hence

αὐτοχειρί, Adv. *with one's own hand*.

αὐτοχειρία, ἡ, (αὐτόχειρ) *a doing with one's own hands*; Lat. αὐτοχειρίᾳ *with one's own hand*.

αὐτό-χθονος, ον, (αὐτός, χθών) *country and all*.

αὐτό-χθων, ον, gen. ονος, (αὐτός, χθών) *of the land itself*, Lat. *terrigena*: αὐτόχθονες, οἱ, like Lat. *Aborigines, Indigenae, of the original race, not settlers*.

αὐτο-χόλωτος, ον, (αὐτός, χολόω) *angry at oneself*.

αὐτο-χόωνος, ον, lengthd. for αὐτοχόανος, (αὐτός, χοάνη) *rudely cast, shapeless*, of a quoit.

αὐτό-χρημα, Adv. (αὐτός, χρῆμα) *indeed, really: at once, plainly*.

αὔτως, Adv. of αὐτός with Aeol. accent, *even so, just so, as it is*; γυμνὸν ἐόντα, αὔτως, being unarmed, *just as I am*. 2. *just so, no better*; often joined with other words implying contempt; νήπιος αὔτως a *mere* child. II. *just as before, as it was*; λευκὸν ἔτ' αὔτως still white *as when new*.

αὐχενίζω, f. ίσω Att. ιῶ, (αὐχήν) *to cut the throat of, behead*.

αὐχένιος, α, ον, (αὐχήν) *belonging to the neck*; αὐχένιοι τένοντες *the* sinews *of the neck*.

αὐχέω, f. ήσω: aor. 1 ηὔχησα:—like καυχάομαι, *to boast, pride oneself*: c. inf. *to boast that*: generally, *to protest, declare*. From

ΑΥ'ΧΗ', ἡ, *boasting, pride*.

αὔχημα, ατος, τό, (αὐχέω) *a thing boasted of, the pride, boast*. II. *a boast*: also = αὐχή, *boasting*.

ΑΥ'ΧΗ'Ν, ένος, ὁ, *the neck, throat*: metaph. *a narrow passage, a neck of land, isthmus*; also *a narrow sea, strait*: *the narrow bed* of a river: *a defile*.

αὔχησις, εως, ἡ, (αὐχέω) *boasting, exultation*.

αὐχμέω, f. ήσω, (αὐχμός) *to be squalid*, Lat. *squalēre*.

αὐχμήεις, εσσα, εν, = αὐχμηρός.

αὐχμηρός, ά, όν, (αὐχμέω) *dry, parched, dusty, squalid*, Lat. *squalidus*. 2. *impoverished, needy*.

αὐχμός, ὁ, (ἄω, αὔω, αὖος) *drought*: *dearth*.

αὐχμ-ώδης, ες, (αὐχμός, εἶδος) *looking dry and dusty*; τὸ αὐχμῶδες *drought*.

ΑΥ"Ω, Att. **αὕω**, *to dry, wither*: also *to singe, set on fire*.

ΑΥ'Ω, f. ἀΰσω: aor. ἤϋσα:—*to shout out, shout, call aloud*: also of things, *to sound, echo*: c. acc. pers. *to call upon*.

αὔως, ἡ, Aeol. for ἀώς, ἠώς, *morning*.

ἀφ-αγνίζω, f. ίσω Att. ιῶ, *to purify*:—Med. *to devote oneself with purifying offerings*.

ἀφ-αιρέω: f. ήσω: pf. ἀφῄρηκα: Pass., aor. 1 ἀφῃρέθην: pf. ἀφῄρημαι:—from the Root 'ΕΛ- we have aor. 2 ἀφεῖλον, fut. med. ἀφελοῦμαι: (ἀπό, αἱρέω). *To take from, take away from another*; c. dupl. acc., ἀφαιρεῖν τινά τι *to rob of* a thing; ἀφαιρεῖν τινος *to take from* a thing, hence *to diminish*: *to let off, pardon*. II. Med. more freq. than Act., *to take away for oneself, bear off*: ἀφαιρεῖσθαί τινά τι *to bereave, deprive, rob of* a thing, always with the notion of *taking for oneself*. 2. followed by μή and inf., *to prevent, hinder from* doing. III. Pass. *to be robbed* or *deprived* of a thing.

ἄφαιστος, Dor. for Ἥφαιστο.

ἀφ-άλλομαι, f. ἀφαλοῦμαι: aor. 1 ἀφηλάμην: Dep.: (ἀπό, ἅλλομαι):—*to spring off* or *down from*: *to jump off*.

ἄ-φαλος, ον, *without the* φάλος or *metal boss* in which the plume was fixed.

ἀφ-αμαρτάνω, f. -αμαρτήσομαι: aor. 2 ἀφήμαρτον,

Ep. by metath. ἀπήμβροτον: (ἀπό, ἁμαρτάνω):—*to miss one's aim, fail in gaining.*

ἀφάμαρτε, Ep. 3 aor. 2 of foreg.

ἀφαμαρτο-επής, ές, (ἀφαμαρτεῖν, ἔπος) *missing the point, talking at random.*

ἀφ-ανδάνω, f. -αδήσω: Ion. aor. 2 inf. ἀπᾰδέειν: (ἀπό, ἀνδάνω):—*to displease, fail to please.*

ἀ-φάνεια, ἡ, *darkness, obscurity.* II. *disappearance, utter destruction.* From

ἀ-φᾰνής, ές, (α privat., φανῆναι) *unseen, invisible: inscrutable.* 2. *vanished: hidden, secret:* hence *unknown:* **τὸ ἀφανές** *uncertainty.* 3. ἀφανὴς οὐσία *personal* property, *which can be secreted,* opp. to φανερά, *real,* as land. Hence

ἀφᾰνίζω, f. ίσω Att. ιῶ: pf. ἠφάνικα:—*to make unseen, hide, suppress: to make away with.* 2. *to rase* to the ground, *erase* writing: *to obliterate* footsteps, etc. 3. *to secrete, steal, embezzle.* 4. *to darken, obscure, tarnish: to efface.* II. Pass. *to disappear and be heard of no more, vanish:* esp. of persons lost at sea. 2. *to keep out of public, live retired.* Hence

ἀφάνισις, εως, ἡ, *a making away with.* II. *a vanishing, disappearance.*

ἀφανισμός, ὁ, = ἀφάνισις.

ἄ-φαντος, ον, (α privat., φαίνομαι) *invisible, forgotten: obscure, secret.* 2. *unlooked for.*

ἀφ-άπτω, fut. ψω: pf. pass. ἀφῆμμαι: (ἀπό, ἅπτω): —*to fasten from* or *upon;* ἀφ. ἅμματα *to tie* knots *on a string:*—Pass. *to be hung on, hang on;* ἀπαμμένος Ion. pass. pf. part. for ἀφημμένος.

ἄφᾰρ, Adv., I. *straightway, forthwith: at once, quickly.* II. *thereupon, then, after that.* III. *continuously, without intermission.*

ἄ-φαρκτος, ον, old Att. for ἄφρακτος.

ἀφ-αρπάζω: f. άξω, Att. άσω or rather άσομαι:—Pass., aor. 1 -ηρπάσθην: pf. -ήρπασμαι:—*to tear off* or *from: to snatch away: to snatch eagerly.*

ἀφάρτερος, α, ον, Comp. Adj. of ἄφαρ, *hastier.*

ἀ-φᾱσία, ἡ, (ἄφατος) *speechlessness.*

ἀφάσσω, f. ἀφάσω: aor. 1 ἤφασα, imperat. ἄφασον: (ἅπτω, ἀφάω):—*to take hold of, handle, feel, touch.*

ἄ-φᾰτος, ον, (α privat., φατός) *not named, nameless: that should not be named* or *uttered;* ἄφατα χρήματα *untold* sums; ἄφατον ὡς.. there's *no saying* how. 2. *unutterable: huge, monstrous.*

ἀφ-αυαίνω, fut. pass. αὐανθήσομαι, = ἀφαύω.

ἀφαυρός, ά, όν, *weak, feeble.* (Deriv. uncertain.)

ἀφ-αύω, (ἀπό, αὔω) *to dry up, parch,* Lat. *torrere:* —Pass. *to become parched, to pine away.*

ἀφάω or **ἀφάω,** (ἅπτω, ἀφή) *to handle, feel.*

ἀ-φεγγής, ές, (α privat., φέγγος) *without light, dark:* metaph. *ill-starred.* 2. *dim, faint.*

ἀφ-εδρών, ῶνος, ὁ, (ἀπό, ἕδρα) *the draught: a privy.*

ἀφέῃ, Ep. for ἀφῇ, 3 sing. aor. 2 subj. of ἀφίημι.

ἀφέηκα, Ep. for ἀφῆκα, aor. 1 of ἀφίημι.

ἀφεθήσομαι, fut. pass. of ἀφίημι.

ἀφειδέστερον, Comp., **ἀφειδέστατα,** Sup., of Adv. ἀφειδῶς.

ἀφειδέω, f. ήσω, *to be unsparing* or *lavish of;* ἀφειδεῖν πόνου *to be careless of,* i. e. *to neglect, avoid* toil: absol., ἀφειδήσαντες *recklessly.* From

ἀ-φειδής, ές, (α privat., φείδομαι) *unsparing, lavish: bountiful.* 2. *unsparing, cruel, harsh.* Hence

ἀφειδία, ἡ, *profuseness.* 2. *harshness, severity.*

ἀφειδῶς, Ion. -έως, Adv. of ἀφειδής, *lavishly.*

ἀφείη, 3 sing. aor. 2 opt. of ἀφίημι.

ἀφεῖλον, -όμην, aor. 2 act. and med. of ἀφαιρέω.

ἀφεῖμαι, pf. pass. of ἀφίημι.

ἀφεῖμεν, 1 pl. aor. 2 of ἀφίημι.

ἀφείς, εἶσα, aor. 2 part. of ἀφίημι.

ἀφεκτέον, verb. Adj. of ἀπέχω, *one must abstain.*

ἀφέλεια, ἡ, (ἀφελής) *simplicity, plainness.* From

ἀφελεῖν, ἀφελέσθαι, aor. 2 act. and med. inf. of ἀφαιρέω.

ἀ-φελής, ές, (α privat., φελλεύς) *without a stone, level, smooth.* II. metaph. of persons, *simple, plain.*

ἀφ-έλκω, f. έλξω: but the usu. fut. is ἀφελκύσω [ῠ], aor. 1 ἀφείλκῠσα (as if from ἀφελκύω):—*to drag away, draw back: to draw aside.* 2. *to drink up.*

ἀφελότης, ητος, ἡ, (ἀφελής) *smoothness, evenness:* hence *simplicity, sincerity.*

ἀφελών, aor. 2 part. of ἀφαιρέω.

ἀφελῶς, Adv. of ἀφελής, *rudely, coarsely.*

ἄφενος, τό, *wealth, abundance.*

ἄφ-ερκτος, ον, (ἀπείργω) *shut out from.*

ἀφ-έρπω, f. ψω: but aor. 1 ἀφείρπῠσα (as if from ἀφερπύζω):—*to creep off, steal away.*

ἄ-φερτος, ον, (α privat., φέρω) *insufferable.*

ἄφες, 2 imperat. aor. 2 of ἀφίημι.

Ἀφέσιος, ὁ, (ἀφίημι) *the Releaser,* epith. of Zeus.

ἄφεσις, εως, ἡ, (ἀφίημι) *a letting go, setting free: a quittance, discharge: remission, forgiveness: a starting* of horses in a race, *the starting-post* itself.

ἀφεσταίη, shortened for ἀφέστηκοι, 3 sing. pf. opt. of ἀφίστημι.

ἀφετός, όν, (ἀφίημι) *let loose, freely ranging,* esp. of sacred flocks that *were free from work:* hence *dedicated to some god.*

ἄ-φευκτος, ον, = ἄφυκτος, q. v.

ἀφ-εύω, aor. 1 ἄφευσα (without augm.): pf. pass. ἤφευμαι:—*to singe off.* 2. *to toast, roast.*

ἀφ-έψω, Ion. ἀπέψω: fut. ἀφεψήσω:—*to boil off, boil down.* II. *to boil free of all dross, to refine, purify: to boil young again.*

ἀφέωκα, Dor. for ἀφεῖκα, pf. act., and **ἀφέωνται,** Dor. for ἀφεῖνται, 3 plur., pf. pass. of ἀφίημι.

ἀφή, ἡ, (ἅπτω) *a fastening, joint:* 2. *a lighting, kindling.* II. (ἅπτομαι) *a touching, handling: the sense of touch.*

ἀφ-ηγέομαι, f. -ηγήσομαι, *to lead away, lead off:* generally, *to lead the way, go first.* II. *to tell, relate, explain.* III. the perf. ἀφήγημαι is used in pass. sense. Hence

ἀφήγημα Ion. **ἀπήγημα, ατος, τό,** *a tale, narrative:* and

ἀφήγησις Ion. **ἀπήγησις,** εως, ἡ, *a telling, narrating;* ἄξιον ἀπηγήσιος worth *the telling.*

ἀφῆκα, aor. 1 of ἀφίημι.

ἀφ-ῆλιξ, Ion. **ἀπ-ῆλιξ, ικος,** ὁ, ἡ, *beyond youth, elderly:* mostly used in Comp. and Sup. ἀφηλικέστερος, -έστατος.

ἄφ-ημαι, Pass. *to sit apart.*

ἀφῄρηκα, pf. of ἀφαιρέω.

ἀφ-ήτωρ, ορος, ὁ, (ἀφίημι) *the archer.*

ἀφθαρσία, ἡ, *incorruption, immortality.* From

ἄ-φθαρτος, ον, (α privat., φθείρω) *uncorrupted, incorruptible.*

ἄ-φθεγκτος, ον, (α privat., φθέγγομαι) *speechless: not to be spoken of;* ἐν ἀφθέγκτῳ νάπει in a grove *where none may speak.*

ἄφθη, Ion. and Dor. for ἥφθη, 3 sing. aor. 1 pass. of ἅπτω.

ἄ-φθῐτος, ον, later also η, ον, (α privat., φθίνω) *undestroyed, undecaying, imperishable.*

ἄ-φθογγος, ον, (α privat., φθέγγομαι) *voiceless.*

ἀφθονέστερος, -έστατος, Irreg. Comp. and Sup. of ἄφθονος.

ἀ-φθόνητος, ον, (α privat., φθονέω) *unenvied.*

ἀφθονία, ἡ, *freedom from envy, readiness:* more often of things, *plenty, abundance.* From

ἄ-φθονος, ον, act. *free from envy: ungrudging, bounteous.* II. pass. *not grudged, bounteously given, plentiful.* 2. = ἀνεπίφθονος, *unenvied, provoking no envy.* III. Adv. -νως, ἀφθόνως ἔχειν τινός to have *enough* of a thing.

ἀφθορία, ἡ, *incorruption, purity.* From

ἄ-φθορος, ον, (α privat., φθείρω) *uncorrupt, chaste.*

ἀφ-ιδρύω, f. ύσω [ῡ]:—Pass., aor. 1 -ύθην [ῡ] or -ύνθην: pf. ἀφίδρῡμαι:—*to place elsewhere, to remove.*

ἀφ-ιερόω, f. ώσω: pf. pass. ἀφιέρωμαι:—*to purify, hallow.*

ἀφ-ίημι: impf. (as if from ἀφιέω) ἠφίουν, 3 sing. ἠφίει Ep. ἀφίει, 3 pl. ἠφίουν, ἠφίεσαν: fut. ἀφήσω: aor. 1 ἀφῆκα: pf. ἀφεῖκα Dor. ἀφέωκα:—Pass., fut. ἀφεθήσομαι: aor. 1 ἀφείθην: pf. ἀφεῖμαι, Dor. 3 pl. ἀφέωνται with pres. sense:—*to send forth, discharge,* Lat. *emittere,* esp. of missiles: in prose, *to send forth on an expedition, send out.* II. *to send away, let go,* Lat. *dimittere:* hence *to throw away.* 2. *to let go, set free,* esp. from an accusation, etc.: *to remit:* absol., ἀφιέναι τινά *to acquit.* 3. *to dissolve, disband, break up,* of an army: so also of the council at Athens. 4. *to put away, divorce.* 5. ἀφιέναι πλοῖον εἰς . . *to loose* ship for a place. III. *to give up:* hence *to leave off, let alone; to let pass, neglect.* IV. *to let, suffer, permit* to do or to be done. V. seemingly intr. (sub. στρατόν, ναῦς, etc.), *to break up, march, sail.*

B. Med. *to send forth from oneself, to send forth.* 2. *to loose oneself from:* freq. in Att., c. gen. only, ἀφοῦ τέκνων *let go* the children.

ἀφ-ῑκάνω, = ἀφικνέομαι, *to arrive at.*

ἀφικέσθαι, aor. 2 med. inf. of ἀφικνέομαι.

ἀφίκεο, Dor. for ἀφίκου, 2 sing. aor. 2 of sq.

ἀφ-ικνέομαι, f. ἀφίξομαι: aor. ἀφῑκόμην: pf. pass. ἀφῖγμαι: Dep.:—*to arrive at, to come to, to reach:* ἀφικέσθαι ἐπί or εἰς πάντα to try every means; ἀφικέσθαι ἐς τὸ ἔσχατον κακοῦ *to come* into extremest misery; διὰ μάχης, δι' ἔχθρας ἀφικέσθαι τινί *to come* to battle, or into enmity with one. II. *to come back, return.*

ἀφικόμενος, aor. 2 part. of ἀφικνέομαι.

ἀ-φιλ-άγαθος, ον, (α privat., φίλος, ἀγαθός) *unfriendly to good men.*

ἀ-φῐλ-άργῠρος, ον, (α privat., φίλος, ἄργυρος) *not loving money, not avaricious, not covetous.*

ἀ-φίλητος, ον, (α privat., φιλέω) *unloved.*

ἀφῐλοδοξία, ἡ, *want of ambition.* From

ἀ-φῐλόδοξος, ον, (α privat., φίλος, δόξα) *not ambitious.*

ἄ-φῐλος, ον, of persons, *friendless.* 2. of persons and things, *unfriendly, disagreeable, hateful:*—Adv. -λως.

ἄφιξις, Ion. **ἄπιξις,** εως, ἡ, (ἀφικνέομαι) *an arrival.* II. *a going home again, departure.*

ἀφιππεύω, f. εύσω, (ἄφιππος) *to ride off, away,* or *back.*

ἀφιππία, ἡ, *bad riding.* From

ἄφιππος, ον, *unsuited for riding* or *for cavalry.* II. *riding badly.*

ἀφ-ίστημι, impf. ἀφίστην: f. ἀποστήσω: aor. 1 ἀπέστησα and aor. 1 med. ἀπεστησάμην;—in which tenses it is causal:—*to put away, remove, separate:* hence *to hinder, frustrate:* but mostly, *to make revolt.* 2. *to weigh out;* μὴ χρεῖος ἀποστήσωνται lest they *weigh out,* i. e. *pay in full* the debt. II. intr. in Pass., with aor. 2 act. ἀπέστην: perf. ἀφέστηκα: plqpf. ἀφεστήκειν: and fut. med. ἀποστήσομαι:—*to stand off, away,* or *aloof from;* ἀποστῆναι πραγμάτων, etc., *to withdraw from* business; ἀποστῆναι ἀπό τινος *to revolt from,* and freq. absol. *to revolt;* also c. inf., ἀποστῆναι ἐρωτῆσαι *to give over* asking. 2. absol. *to stand aloof, keep off.*

ἀφῖχθαι, pf. inf. of ἀφικνέομαι.

ἄφλαστον, τό, Lat. *aplustre, the curved stern of a ship* with its ornaments (Deriv. uncertain.)

ἀφλοισμός, ὁ, *a foaming* or *gnashing of teeth.* (Prob. like φλοῖσβος, formed from the sound.)

ἀφνειός, όν, also ή, όν, (ἄφενος) *rich, wealthy:* also *rich in* a thing, c. gen.

ἀφνεός, ά, όν, collat. form of ἀφνειός.

ΆΦΝΩ, Adv. *unawares, of a sudden:* also ἄφνως.

ἀ-φόβητος, ον, (α privat., φοβέομαι) *fearless, without fear of,* c. gen.

ἄ-φοβος, ον, (α privat., φόβος) *fearless.* 2. *causing no fear, not to be feared.*

ἀφοβό-σπλαγχνος, ον, (ἄφοβος, σπλάγχνον) *fearless of heart, stout-hearted.*

ἀφόβως, Adv. of ἄφοβος, *without fear, securely.*

ἄφ-οδος, ἡ, (ἀπό, ὁδός) *a going away, departure:* also *a going back.* II. = ἀπόπατος.

ἀ-φοίβαντος, ον, (α privat., φοιβαίνω) *uncleansed.*

ομοιόω, f. *ώσω*, *to liken, make like.* II. *to are.* III. *to portray, copy.*

οπλίζω, f. *ίσω*, *to disarm, strip of arms*:—Med., λίζεσθαι ἔντεα *to put off one's* armour.

οράω, impf. ἀφεώρων: pf. ἀφεύρακα: with bor- d fut. ἀπόψομαι (as if from ἀπ-όπτομαι), and 2 ἀπεῖδον (as if from ἀπ-είδω):—*to look away* all others at one, and so *to look at*, Lat. *respi-* :—*to see clearly, have in full view.* II. *to from* a place. III. rarely, *to look away, the back turned.*

όρητος, *ον*, (α privat., φορητός) *unbearable, in- able.*

ορία, ἡ, (ἄφορος) *a not bearing, dearth* of a g. II. *barrenness.*

οριεῖ, 3 sing. fut. act. or 2 sing. fut. med. of

-ορίζω, f. *ίσω* Att. *ιῶ*: aor. ἀφώρισα: pf. pass. ρισμαι:—*to mark off by boundaries: to part off, rmine, define*:—Med. *to mark off for oneself, opriate.* II. *to set apart, ordain:* also *to t, banish.*

-ορμάω, f. ήσω, *to make to start from* a place. II. *to start from* a place, *set off*: so in Pass. *to go), start, depart.*

-ορμή, ἡ, (ἀπό, ὁρμή) *a starting-place, means of ting, base of operations*: hence also *a place to e to, a place of safety.* 2. *a starting-point, the sion* or *pretext of* a thing. 3. *means, re- rces*: esp. *the means* or *sinews of war*, as money, ps, etc.: *capital*, Lat. *fundus.* II. *a making tart, undertaking.*

φορμηθεῖεν, 3 pl. aor. 1 pass. opt. of ἀφορμάω.

φ-ορμίζομαι, Med. *to unmoor* ships *from barbour.*

-φόρμικτος, *ον*, (α privat., φορμίζω) *without the lyre.*

φ-ορμος, *ον*, (ἀπό, ὅρμος) *without barbour in* a ce.

-φορος, *ον*, (α privat., φέρω) *not bearing, barren.*

-φόρυκτος, *ον*, (α privat., φορύσσω) *undefiled, un- ined.*

φ-οσιόω, fut. *ώσω*, (ἀπό, ὅσιος) *to purify* or *liberate m guilt*:—Med. *to purify oneself from sins of ligence*; ἀφοσιοῦσθαι τῷ θεῷ *to make expiatory rings* to the god. II. Med. also *to acquit self of service due*; ἀφοσιοῦσθαι ἐξόρκωσιν *to dis- rge oneself of the obligation* of an oath.

φοῦ, aor. 2 imper. med. of ἀφίημι.

φόωντα, Ep. for ἀφῶντα, pres. act. part. acc. of ίω.

φρᾰδέω, f. *ήσω*, *to act without sense.* From

-φρᾰδής, *ές*, (α privat., φράζομαι) *thoughtless, silly*: the dead, *senseless.* Adv. ἀφραδέως, *foolishly, sense- ly.* Hence

φρᾰδία, ἡ, *folly, thoughtlessness, silliness.*

-φράδμων, *ον*, gen. *ονος*, = ἀφραδής, *thoughtless.*

φραίνω, (ἄ-φρων) *to be silly.*

-φρακτος, old Att. **ἄ-φαρκτος**, *ον*, (α privat., ίσσω) *unfenced, unguarded.* II. *off one's guard.*

-φράσμων, *ον*, gen. *ονος*, = ἀφράδμων.

ἄ-φραστος, *ον*, (α privat., φράζω) *unutterable, strange.* 2. *untold, numberless.* II. (α privat., φράζομαι) *not thought of, unseen, unexpected.* Hence

ἀφράστως, Adv. *unexpectedly.*

ἀφρέω, f. *ήσω*, (ἀφρός) *to foam*: c. acc. *to cover with foam.*

ἀφρη-λόγος, *ον*, (ἀφρός, λέγω) *gathering froth, skimming.*

ἀφρηστής, *οῦ*, ὁ, (ἀφρέω) *the foaming one.*

ἀφρήτωρ, *ορος*, ὁ, Ion. for ἀφράτωρ, (α privat., φράτρα) *without brotherhood, bound by no social tie.*

ἀφρίζω, f. *ίσω*, = ἀφρέω, *to foam.*

ἀφριόεις, *εσσα*, *εν*, (ἀφρός) *foaming.*

ἀφρογένεια, ἡ, *the foam-born.* From

ἀφρο-γενής, *ές*, (ἀφρός, γενέσθαι) *foam-born.*

Ἀφροδισιάς, *άδος*, fem. Adj. *sacred to Venus.*

Ἀφροδίσιος, *α*, *ον*, also *ος*, *ον*, *belonging to Venus.* II. Ἀφροδίσιον, τό, *the temple of Venus*: Ἀφροδίσια, τά, *her festival.* From

Ἀφροδίτη [ῑ], ἡ, (ἀφρός) *Aphrodité*, Lat. *Venus*, the goddess of love and beauty, born from the *sea-foam.* II. as appellat. *love, desire*:—also *beauty.*

ἀφρονέστερος, **-έστατος**, Comp. and Sup. of ἄφρων.

ἀφρονέω, f. *ήσω*, (ἄφρων) *to be silly, to act foolishly.*

ἀφροντιστέω, f. *ήσω*, *to be heedless: to have no care* of a thing. From

ἀ-φρόντιστος, *ον*, (α privat., φροντίζω) *thoughtless, heedless*:—so in Adv., ἀφροντίστως ἔχειν to be *thoughtless.* II. pass. *unthought of, unexpected.*

ἀ-φρόνως, Adv. of ἄφρων, *foolishly.*

ἈΦΡΟ΄Σ, ὁ, *foam, froth.*

ἀφροσύνη, ἡ, (ἄφρων) *folly, thoughtlessness.*

ἄ-φρουρος, *ον*, (α privat., φρουρά) *unwatched.*

ἀφρο-φυής, *ές*, (ἀφρός, φύω) *froth-producing, milky.*

ἄ-φρων, *ον*, gen. *ονος*, (α privat., φρήν) *senseless, witless, foolish, crazed, silly*, Lat. *amens, demens.* Comp. and Sup., ἀφρονέστερος, -έστατος.

ἀφ-υδραίνω, (ἀπό, ὑδραίνω) *to wash clean*: Med. *to wash oneself, bathe.*

ἀφύη, ἡ, *a* sort of *anchovy* or *sardine.*

ἀ-φυής, *ές*, (α privat., φυή) *without natural talent, dull*: *naturally unfit* for a thing. II. in good sense, *simple.*

ἄ-φυκτος, *ον*, (α privat., φυκτός) *not to be shunned, inevitable*: of arrows, *unerring.* 2. act. *unable to escape.*

ἀφῠλακτέω, f. *ήσω*, *to be off one's guard*: c. gen. *to be careless about, neglect.* From

ἀ-φύλακτος, *ον*, (α privat., φυλάσσω) *unguarded.* II. of persons, *unguarded, unheeding*; ἀφυλακτόν τινα λαμβάνειν to catch one *off his guard.* Adv. -τως. Hence

ἀφῠλαξία, ἡ, *want of vigilance, unguardedness.*

ἀφ-υλίζω, f. *ίσω*, (ἀπό, ὑλίζω) *to strain off.*

ἄ-φυλλος, *ον*, (α privat., φύλλον) *leafless*, of dry wood; ἄφυλλον στόμα speech *not seconded by the suppliant's olive-branch.*

ἀφύξειν, fut. inf. of ἀφύσσω.

ἀφ-υπνίζω, f. ίσω, (ἀπό, ὕπνος) *to wake from sleep.*

ἀφ-υπνόω, f. ώσω: aor. 1 ἀφύπνωσα: (ἀπό, ὑπνόω): —*to wake or rouse from sleep.* II. *to fall asleep.*

ἀφυσγετός, ὁ, (ἀφύσσω) *the mud and dirt* which a stream carries with it, *rubbish.*

ἈΦΥ'ΣΣΩ, fut. ἀφύξω Dor. -ξῶ: aor. 1 ἤφῠσα Ep. ἄφυσσα: aor. 1 med. ἠφῠσάμην Ep. ἀφυσσάμην: —*to draw* liquids; πίθων ἠφύσσετο οἶνος wine *was drawn from* the casks:—Med. *to draw for oneself, to drink, quaff.* 2. *to pour in a heap, to pile up,* πλοῦτον ἀφύξειν:—Med., φύλλα ἠφυσάμην *I heaped me up a pile* of leaves.

ἀ-φύτευτος, ον, (α privat., φυτεύω) *not planted.*

ἀφυῶς, Adv. of ἀφυής: ἀφυῶς ἔχειν to have no *natural talent.*

ἀ-φώνητος, ον, (α privat., φωνέω) *unspeakable, unutterable.* II. *voiceless, speechless.*

ἀφωνία, ἡ, *speechlessness.* From

ἄ-φωνος, ον, (α privat., φωνή) *voiceless, speechless, dumb: inarticulate.* Adv. -νως.

ἀχά [ᾱ], Dor. for ἠχή.

Ἀχαία, Ion. **Ἀχαιΐη**, ἡ, (ἄχος) epith. of Demeter in Attica.

ἀχαΐνης, ὁ, (ἀκίς) *with single points to his horns,* epith. of a young stag: also **ἀχαΐνη**, ἡ, *a deer.*

Ἀχαιΐς, Att. **Ἀχαΐς**, ΐδος, ἡ, *the Achaian land,* with or without γαῖα. 2. (sub. γυνή) *an Achaian woman:* so also **Ἀχαιϊάς**, άδος, ἡ.

Ἀχαιός, ά, όν, *Achaian,* Lat. *Achivus.* II. as Subst., 1. Ἀχαιοί, οἱ, *the Achaians,* in Homer *the Greeks* generally. 2. Ἀχαία, ἡ, *Achaia,* in Peloponnesus.

ἀ-χάλῖνος, ον, (α privat., χαλινός) *unbridled.*

ἀ-χᾰλίνωτος, ον, (α privat., χαλινόω) *unbridled.*

ἀ-χάλκεος, ον, (α privat., χαλκοῦς) *without a farthing.* Hence

ἀχαλκέω, *to be without a farthing.*

ἀ-χάλκευτος, ον, (α privat., χαλκεύω) *not forged of metal.*

ἄ-χαλκος, ον, *without brass,* esp. *without brasen arms;* ἄχαλκος ἀσπίδων = ἄνευ ἀσπίδων χαλκῶν.

ἀ-χάλκωτος, ον, (α privat., χαλκόω) = ἀχάλκευτος.

ἀχάνη [ᾰχᾱ-], ἡ, *a Persian measure,* = 45 μέδιμνοι.

ἀ-χᾰνής, ές, (α privat., χανεῖν) *not opening the mouth.* II. (α euphon.) *yawning, vast.*

ἀ-χᾰράκωτος, ον, (α privat., χαρακόω) *not palisaded.*

ἄ-χᾰρις, ὁ, ἡ, ἄχαρι, τό, gen. ιτος, (α privat., χάρις) *without grace or charms, unpleasant, wretched.* II. *ungracious, thankless,* Lat. *ingratus.*

ἀχᾰριστέω, f. ήσω, (ἀχάριστος) *to be ungrateful.*

ἀχαριστία, ἡ, *ingratitude, ungraciousness.*

ἀ-χάριστος, Ion. and poët. **ἀ-χάριτος**, ον, (α privat., χαρίζομαι) *unpleasing: without grace.* II. *ungracious: ungrateful, thankless.* 2. pass. *unthanked:* Adv., οὐκ ἀχαρίστως ἔχειν τινί *thanks are not wanting* to him. 3. *with an ill will:* hence in Adv., ἀχαρίστως ἕπεσθαι to follow *with a bad grace.*

ἀχεδών, όνος, Dor. for ἠχεδών.

ἀ-χείμαντος, ον, (α privat., χειμαίνω) *not vexed with storms.*

ἄ-χειρ, ρος, ὁ, ἡ, (α privat., χείρ) *without hands: without dexterity, awkward.*

ἀ-χειρής, ές, *without hands.*

ἀ-χειροποίητος, ον, *not made by hands.*

ἄ-χειρος, ον, = ἄχειρ: τὰ ἄχειρα *the hinder parts of the body.*

ἀ-χείρωτος, ον, (α privat., χειρόω) *not trained by the hand.* II. *unconquered.*

Ἀχελῷος, poët. **Ἀχελώϊος**, ὁ, *Achelōus,* name of several rivers; the best known ran through Aetolia and Acarnania. II. as appellat. *any running water,* as in Virgil, *Acheloïa pocula.*

ἈΧΕΡΔΟΣ, ἡ, more rarely ὁ, *a wild prickly shrub,* used for hedges: *the wild pear.*

Ἀχερόντιος and **Ἀχερούσιος**, α, ον, *of* or *belonging to Acheron:* fem. -ιάς, άδος.

ἀχερωΐς, ΐδος, *the white poplar,* supposed to have been brought by Hercules from the banks of *Acheron.*

Ἀχέρων, *οντος*, ὁ, *Acheron,* a river in Hades. (Derived from ἄχος, as Κωκυτ is from κωκύω.)

ἀχέτας, ου, ὁ, Dor. for ἠχέτης, (ἀχέω) *sounding:* esp. *the male cicada,* from its *chirping.*

ἀχεύω, (ἄχος) *to mourn, be sad,* τινός for one.

ἀχέω, (ἄχος) *to mourn, be sad,* only used in part., κῆρ ἀχέων *sorrowing* in heart. II. from the same Root ἈΧ-, came 1. Ep. redupl. aor. 2 ἤκᾰχον, in causal sense, *to make to grieve, vex, distress:* so also redupl. fut. ἀκαχήσω, aor. 1 ἀκάχησα (as if from ἀχέω). 2. Med. and Pass. *to grieve,* subj. ἀκάχηται, opt. ἀκάχοιτο, impf. 3 pl. ἀκάχοντο:— pf. pass., ἀκάχημαι, Ep. 3 pl. ἀκηχέδαται or ἀκηχέαται (for ἀκήχηνται); 3 pl. pf. ἀκαχείατο (for ἀκήχηντο); inf. ἀκάχησθαι; part. ἀκαχήμενος, Ep. also ἀκηχέμενος.

ἀχέω [ᾱ], Dor. and poët. form for ἠχέω.

ἄχημα, Dor. for ἤχημα.

ἈΧΗ'Ν, ένος, ὁ, ἡ, *poor, needy.* [ᾱ] Hence

ἀχηνία, ἡ, *need, want;* ὀμμάτων ἀχηνία the eyes' *blank gaze.*

ἀχθεινός, ή, όν, (ἄχθος) *burdensome, oppressive.* Adv. -νῶς, *unwillingly,* Lat. *aegre, moleste.*

ἀχθείς, aor. 1 pass. part. of ἄγω.

ἀχθηδών, όνος, ἡ, (ἄχθομαι) *grief, annoyance.*

ἀχθήσομαι, fut. pass. of ἄγω.

ἄχθομαι, Pass. with fut. med. ἀχθέσομαι and pass. ἀχθεσθήσομαι: aor. 1 ἠχθέσθην: pf. ἤχθημαι: (ἄχθος):—*to be burdened, loaded:—to be weighed down, discontented, vexed, disgusted.*

ἌΧΘΟΣ, εος, τό, *a weight, burden, load;* ἄχθος ἀρούρης *a dead weight* on earth. II. *a load of grief: sorrow, grief, distress.*

ἀχθοφορέω, f. ήσω, *to bear burdens, to bear as a burden.* From

ἀχθο-φόρος, ον, (ἄχθος, φέρω) *bearing burdens.*

Ἀχίλλειος, α, ον, *of* or *belonging to Achilles:*

'Αχίλλειαι μᾶζαι, ***cakes of fine*** barley-meal, *dainty food.* From

'Αχιλλεύς, έως, Ep. ῆος, ὁ: Ep. also **'Αχιλεύς**: *Achilles.* son of Peleus and Thetis, chief of the Myrmidons, hero of the Iliad.

ἀ-χίτων, *ον.* gen. *ωνος. without tunic, thinly clad.*

ἀχλαινία, ἡ, *want of a cloak:* generally, *want of clothing* From

ἄ-χλαινος, *ον*, (α privat., χλαῖνα) *without cloak.*

ἄ-χλοος. *ον*, contr. **ἄ-χλους**, *ουν*, (α privat., χλόα) *without herbage.*

ἀχλῠόεις, *εσσα, εν*, (ἀχλύς) *murky, gloomy.*

'ΑΧΛΥ'Σ, ύος, ἡ, *a mist, gloom, darkness*, Lat. *caligo:* in Homer also *the mist which comes over the eyes* of the dying or swooning: metaph. *trouble.* Hence

ἀχλύω, f. ύσω [ῡ]: aor. 1 ἤχλῡσα: *to be* or *grow dark.*

ἌΧΝΗ, Dor. **ἄχνα**, ἡ, *anything that comes off the surface* of a thing, as of liquids, *foam, froth*; ἄχνη οὐρανία *the dew* of heaven; δακρύων ἄχνη *dewy* tears. II. of solids, *chaff: the down* on fruit. III. ἄχνην in acc. as Adv., *a morsel, a little bit.*

ἄχνῠμαι, Dep. only used in pres. and impf.: (ἄχος): *to trouble oneself, grieve.*

ἄ-χολος, *ον*, (α privat., χολή) *lacking gall:* metaph. *meek, gentle.* II. *allaying bile* or *anger.*

ἄχομαι, Dep. (ἄχος) *to mourn, bewail oneself.*

ἀ-χόρευτος, *ον*, (α privat., χορεύω) like ἄχορος, *not attended with the dance, joyless, wretched.*

ἄ-χορος, *ον, without the dance: mournful, sad.*

ἌΧΟΣ, εος, τό, *an* ACHE, *pain, distress*, in Homer only of the mind.

ἀ-χραής, ές, =ἄχραντος.

ἄ-χραντος, *ον*, (α privat., χραίνω) *undefiled.*

ἀχράς, άδος, ἡ, a kind of *wild pear.*

ἀ-χρεῖος, *ον*, rarely **α**, *ον*, Ion. **ἀ-χρήϊος**, (α privat., χρεία) *useless, unprofitable, unserviceable* in war. II. neut. ἀχρεῖον as Adv., ἀχρεῖον ἰδών giving *a helpless* look, looking *foolish;* ἀχρεῖον γελᾶν to laugh *without use* or *cause*, make a *forced* laugh; ἀχρεῖον κλάζειν to bark *without cause*, of dogs. Hence

ἀχρειόω, f. *ώσω, to make useless, disable.*

ἀ-χρήϊος, *ον*, Ion. for ἀχρεῖος.

ἀχρημᾰτία, ἡ, *want of money.* From

ἀ-χρήμᾰτος, *ον*, (α privat., χρῆμα) *without money* or *means:* οἱ ἀχρήματοι *the poor.*

ἀχρημοσύνη, ἡ, *want of money.* From

ἀ-χρήμων, *ον*, gen. *ονος*, (α privat., χρῆμα)=ἀχρήματος, *poor, needy.* [ᾰ]

ἀχρηστία, ἡ, *uselessness, unfitness.* From

ἄ-χρηστος, *ον*, (α privat., χρηστός) *useless, unprofitable, unserviceable;* ἄχρηστος ἔς τι *unfit for* a thing:—*without effect*, Lat. *irritus.* II. *unkind, cruel.* III. act. *making no use of*, c. dat.

ἄχρι, and before a vowel **ἄχρις**, (ἄκρος) Prep. with gen. *until*, Lat. *usque ad;* ἄχρι μάλα κνέφαος *until* deep in the night:—*as far as*, ἄχρι τῆς καρδίας. II. Conj. *until, to the time that*, Lat. *donec:* so also ἄχρι οὗ. III. Adv. of manner, *to the uttermost, utterly*, Lat. *penitus.*

ἀ-χρώμᾰτος, *ον*, (α privat., χρ[illegible]) *without colour.*

ἄ-χρωστος, *ον*, (α privat., χρώζω) [illegible]*coloured: untouched.*

ἀχῠρῖτις, ιδος, (ἄχυρον) fem. Adj. *of chaff.*

ἀχυρμία, ἡ, (ἄχυρον) *a heap of chaff.*

ἀχῠρο-δόκη, ἡ, (ἄχυρον, δέχομαι) *a chaff-holder.*

ἌΧΥ˘ΡΟΝ, τό, mostly in plur. *chaff, bran, husks.*

ἀχῠρό-τριψ, τρῐβος, ὁ, (ἄχυρον, τρίβω) *threshing out the husks.*

ἀχώ, ἡ, Dor. for ἠχώ.

ἀ-χώριστος, *ον*, (α privat., χωριστός) *not parted.* II. (α privat., χῶρος) *without a place assigned one.*

ἌΨ, Adv. of Place, *backwards, back, away from, away.* 2. of actions, *again, over again.*

ἁψάμενος, aor. 1 med. part. of ἅπτομαι.

ἄ-ψαυστος, *ον*, (α privat., ψαύω) *untouched.* II. act. *without touching.*

ἀ-ψεγής, ές, (α privat., ψέγω) *unblamed, blameless.*

ἄ-ψεκτος, *ον*, =ἀψεγής.

ἀψεύδεια, ἡ, *truthfulness;* and

ἀψευδέω, f. *ήσω, not to lie, to speak truth.* From

ἀ-ψευδής, ές, (α privat., ψεῦδος) *without falsehood, truthful:* of things, *genuine, pure.* Hence

ἀψευδῶς, Ion. -έως, Adv. *really and truly.*

ἄ-ψευστος, *ον*, (α privat., ψεύδομαι) *unfeigned.*

ἄ-ψηκτος, *ον*, (α privat., ψήχω) *not rubbed off.*

ἀ-ψήφιστος, *ον*, (α privat., ψηφίζομαι) *not having voted.*

ἁψῑδόομαι, f. ἡψίδωμαι: Pass.: (ἁψίς):—*to be tied in a circle* or *curve.*

ἁψί-κορος, *ον*, (ἅπτομαι, κόρος) *satisfied with touching, fastidious, dainty.*

ἁψῐμᾰχία, ἡ, *a skirmishing.* From

ἁψί-μᾰχος, *ον*, (ἅπτομαι, μάχη) *skirmishing.*

ἀψί[illegible]ον, τό, Lat. *absinthium, wormwood.* From

ἌΨΙΝΘΟΣ, ἡ, *wormwood.*

ἁψίς, Ion. ἀψίς, ῖδος, ἡ, (ἅπτω) *a juncture: a loop, knot;* ἁψῖδες λίνου *the meshes of* a net. 2. *the felloe* or *felly* of a wheel, *the wheel* itself; κύκλος ἁψῖδος the potter's *wheel.* 3. *an arch* or *vault.*

ἁψῖσι, dat. pl. of ἁψίς.

ἀψόρ-ροος, *ον*, contr. **ἀψόρρους**, *ουν*, (ἄψ, ῥέω) *back-flowing, flowing back into itself.*

ἄψορ-ρος, *ον*, shortd. form of foreg. *moving backwards, going back:*—neut. **ἄψορρον** as Adv., *backward, back again.*

ἅψος, εος, τό, (ἅπτω) *a juncture: a joint.*

ἀ-ψόφητος, *ον*, (α privat., ψοφέω) *without noise;* c. gen., ἀψόφητος κωκυμάτων *without cry* of wailing.

ἄ-ψοφος, *ον*, (α privat., ψόφος)=ἀψόφητος.

ἄ-ψυκτος, *ον*, (α privat., ψύχω) *uncooled, warm.*

ἀψῡχία, ἡ, *cowardice.* From

ἄ-ψῡχος, *ον*, (α privat., ψυχή) *lifeless.* II. *spiritless, fainthearted.*

*ἌΩ, root of ἄημι, *to blow;* cf. ἄζω, αὔω.

**ΑΩ, root of ἰαύω, ἀωτέω, *to sleep:* aor. 1 ἄεσα, Ep. ἄεσσα, contr. ἆσα.

**ΑΩ, *to hurt*, contr. from ἀάω, q. v.

**ΑΩ, *to satiate*, inf. ἄμεναι [ᾱ], contr. for ἀέμεναι, Ep. for ἄειν: aor. 1 ἆσα: verb. Adj. ἀτός [ᾰ]; but with α privat., ἄατος [ᾰᾰ], contr. ἆτος.

ἀῶθεν, Adv. Dor. for ἠῶθεν.

ᾀών, ᾀόνος, ἡ, Dor. for ἠϊών.

ἀ-ωρί, Adv. of ἄωρος, *at an untimely hour.*

ἀ-ωρία, ἡ, (ἄωρος) *untimely fate* or *death, an unseasonable time:* in acc. as Adv., ἀωρίαν ἥκειν to have come *too late.* [ᾰ]

ἀ-ώριος, ον, = ἄωρος.

ἀωρό-νυκτος, ον, (ἄωρος, νύξ) *at midnight*, Lat. *intempesta nocte.*

ἄ-ωρος, ον, (α privat., ὥρα) *untimely, unseasonable*, χειμών, θάνατος. II. *before the time, unripe.* III. *misshapen, ugly.* [ᾰ]

ἄωρτο, Ep. plqpf. pass. of ἀείρω.

Ἀώς, ἡ, Dor. for Ἠώς, Ἕως. Hence

Ἀωσ-φόρος, ὁ, = Ἑωσφόρος, *the bringer of light, the morning-star*, Lat. *Lucifer*

ἀωτέω, f. ήσω, (ἄω) *to sleep soundly.* From

ἄωτον, τό, and **ἄωτος**, ὁ, *the best* or *choicest of its kind, the flower* of the whole; in Homer of the *finest wool*, οἰὸς ἄωτον; also of the *finest linen*, λίνοιο λεπτὸν ἄωτον.

B

B, β, βῆτα, indecl., second letter of the Greek alphabet: hence as a numeral, β′ = δύο and δεύτερος, but ,β = 2000.

The Aeol. and Dor. used it as the simple aspirate before ρ, as βρόδον βράκος, for ῥόδον ῥάκος. It was often inserted between μλ and μρ to give a fuller sound, as in μεσημβρία, γαμβρός, cf. ἄμβροτος.

The change of β into other consonants was chiefly owing to the different pronunciations of the several dialects: I. into π, e. g. βατεῖν for πατεῖν. II. Arcad., into ζ, as ζέρεθρον for βέρεθρον, βάραθρον. III. into γ, as γλήχων for βλήχων.

βᾶ, shortd. form of βασιλεῦ, *O King!*

βαβάζω, redupl. for βάζω, *to chatter.*

βαβαί, βαβαιάξ, Lat. *papae*, exclamation of surprise, *bless me! dear me!*

βάβαξ, ὁ, *a chatterer.*

βαβύκα, ἡ, Lacon. for γεφύρα, *a bridge.*

βάγμα, ατος, τό, (βάζω) *a speech.*

βάδην, Adv. (βαίνω) *step by step, pacing*, Lat. *pedetentim*, opp. to quick running. II. *marching on foot*, opp. to riding. III. *gradually*, Lat. *gradatim.*

βᾰδίζω: fut. Att. ιοῦμαι, later ιῶ: aor. 1 ἐβάδισα: pf. βεβάδικα: (βάδος, βαίνω):—*to go on foot, to walk: to go slowly, pace:* generally, *to go.* Hence

βάδῐσις, εως, ἡ, *a walking, going.*

βᾰδιστέον, verb. Adj. of βαδίζω, *one must go.*

βᾰδιστής, οῦ, ὁ, (βαδίζω) *one that goes on foot, a walker, goer;* ταχὺς βαδιστής a quick *goer.*

βᾰδιστικός, ή, όν, (βαδίζω) *good at walking.*

βάδος, ὁ, (βαίνω) *a walk.*

BA'ΖΩ, f. βάξω, *to speak, say:* 3 sing. pf. pass., ἔπος βέβακται a word *has been spoken.*

βᾰθέα, Ion. for βαθεῖα, fem. of βαθύς.

βᾰθέως, Adv. of βαθύς, *deeply.*

βάθιστος, η, ον, Sup. of βαθύς.

βαθμίς, ίδος and ῖδος, ἡ, *a step.* From

βαθμός, ὁ, (βαίνω) *a step, stair.* II. metaph *a step, degree, rank*, Lat. *gradus.*

βάθος, εος, τό, (βαθύς) *depth* or *height*, Lat. *altitudo;* ἐπὶ βάθος *in file*, of soldiers.

βαθρεία, ἡ, = βάθρον.

βάθρον, τό, (βαίνω) *that on which one stands, a base, pedestal: foundation.* 2. *a step* or *set of steps, the round of a ladder:* in plur. *ladders.* 3. *a threshold:* metaph. *an edge, verge.* 4. *a bench, seat.*

βαθυ-αγκής, ές, (βαθύς, ἄγκος) *with deep vales.*

βαθύ-βουλος, ον, (βαθύς, βουλή) *deep-counselling.*

βαθύ-γειος, Ion. βαθύγεος, ον, Att. **βαθύγεως**, ων, (βαθύς, γῆ) *with deep soil, fruitful.*

βαθυ-γήρως, ων, (βαθύς, γῆρας) *in great old age, decrepit.*

βαθύ-γλυπτος, ον, (βαθύς, γλύπτω) *deep-carved.*

βαθυ-δῑνήεις, εσσα, εν, (βαθύς, δινάω) *deep-eddying.*

βαθυ-δίνης, ου, ὁ, (βαθύς, δίνη) *deep-eddying.* [ῑ]

βαθύ-δοξος, ον, (βαθύς, δόξα) *far-famed.*

βαθύ-ζωνος, ον, (βαθύς, ζώνη) *deep-girded*, i. e. not under the breast, but over the hips, so that the gown fell over the girdle in full folds; esp. of the Ionian dress: cf. βαθύκολπος.

βαθύ-θριξ, τρῐχος, ὁ, ἡ, (βαθύς, θρίξ) *with thick hair:* of sheep, *with thick wool.*

βαθυ-καμπής, ές, (βαθύς, κάμπτω) *strongly curved.*

βαθυ-κήτης, ες, (βαθύς, κῆτος) *very deep.*

βαθυ-κλέης, ες, (βαθύς, κλέος) *far-famed.*

βαθύ-κολπος, ον, (βαθύς, κόλπος) *deep-bosomed*, with *the dress in deep, full folds*, like βαθύζωνος. 2. *with swelling breasts.* II. of the earth, *with deep valleys.*

βαθύ-κρημνος, ον, (βαθύς, κρημνός) *with high cliffs.*

βαθυ-κρύσταλλος, ον, *with thick ice.*

βαθυ-κτέᾰνος, ον, (βαθύς, κτέανον) *with great possessions*, esp. of flocks and herds.

βαθύ-λειμος, ον, and **βαθυ-λείμων**, ον, gen. ονος, (βαθύς, λειμών) *with rich meadows.*

βαθυ-λήῑος, ον, (βαθύς, λήϊον) *with deep, thick crops.*

βαθύ-μαλλος, ον, (βαθύς, μαλλός) *thick-fleeced.*

βαθυ-μήτης, ου, ὁ, also **βαθυμῆτα**, (βαθύς, μῆτις) *deep-counselling.*

βαθύ-νοος, ον, contr. **βαθύ-νους**, ουν, (βαθύς, νόος) *profoundly wise.*

βαθύνω [ῠ], fut. βαθῠνῶ: pf. βεβάθυγκα: (βαθύς): —*to deepen, hollow out, excavate;* βαθύνειν τὴν φάλαγγα *to deepen* the phalanx by increasing the number of ranks.

βαθύ-ξῠλος, ον, (βαθύς, ξύλον) *with thick wood.*

βαθύ-πεδος, ον, (βαθύς, πέδον) *forming a deep vale.*

βαθύ-πελμος, ον, (βαθύς, πέλμα) *thick-soled.*

βαθύ-πλουτος, ον, (βαθύς, πλ ῦτος) *exceeding rich.*

βαθυ-πόλεμος, ον, (βαθύς, πόλεμος) *plunged in war.*

βαθυρ-ρείτης, ου, ὁ, (ῥέω) = βαθύρροος.

βαθύρ-ρηνος, ον, (βαθύς, ῥήν) *with thick wool.*

βαθύρ-ριζος, ον, (βαθύς, ῥίζα) *deep-rooted.*

βαθύρ-ροος, ον, contr. **βαθύρ-ρους**, ουν, (βαθύς, ῥέω) *deep-flowing, with deep, full stream.*

ΒΑ˘ΘΥ'Σ, βαθεῖα, Ion. βαθέᾰ, βαθύ: Comp. βαθύτερος, poët. βαθίων, Dor. βάσσων: Sup. βαθύτατος, poët. βάθιστος. *Deep* or *high*, Lat. *altus*. 2. *deep, thick, luxuriant*, as of the hair and beard: generally, *large, abundant:* of the voice, *deep:* of thought, *deep:*—then in various senses, of time, age, etc.; βαθὺς ὄρθρος *morning-prime;* βαθὺ γῆρας *great* old age; βαθεῖα φάλαγξ a column *deep in file.*

βαθυ-σκᾰφής, ές, (βαθύς, σκάπτω) *deep-dug.*

βαθύ-σκῐος, ον, (βαθύς, σκιά) *deep-shaded.*

βαθύ-σπορος, ον, (βαθύς, σπείρω) *deep-sown, fruitful.*

βαθύ-στερνος, ον, (βαθύς, στέρνον) *deep-chested;* βαθύστερνος αἶα *deep-bosomed* earth.

βαθύ-στολμος, ον, (βαθύς, στολμός) *with deep, full robes.*

βαθύ-στρωτος, ον, (βαθύς, στρώννυμι) *deep-covered, well-covered*, of a bed.

βαθύ-σχοινος, ον, (βαθύς, σχοῖνος) *deep grown with rushes.*

βαθύ-φρων, ον, gen. ονος. (βαθύς, φρήν) *deep-counselling.*

βαθύ-φυλλος, ον, (βαθύς, φύλλον) *thick-leafed.*

βαθυ-χαίτης, ου, ὁ, also **βαθυχαιτήεις**, ήεσσα, ῆεν, (βαθύς, χαίτη) *with deep thick hair, with thick mane.*

βαθύ-χθων, ον, gen. ονος, (βᾰθύς, χθών) *of deep soil, fertile.*

βαίην, ης, η, aor. 2 opt. of βαίνω.

ΒΑΙ'ΝΩ, formed from the Root *βάω: fut. βήσομαι, Ep. βέομαι and βείομαι, Dor. βᾱσεῦμαι:—pf. βέβηκα, Ep. 3 pl. βεβάασι, βεβᾶσι; inf. βεβάμεν; part. βεβᾰώς, βεβᾰυῖα, contr. βεβώς, βεβῶσα, βεβώς:—aor. 2 ἔβην, Ep. 3 sing. βῆ, Ep. 3 dual βάτην [ᾰ]; imperat. βῆθι, in compds. βα (as κατάβα); subj. βῶ, Ep. βείω, Ep. 3 sing. βήῃ; opt. βαίην; inf. βῆναι, Ep. βήμεναι; part. βάς, βᾶσα, βάν.—Med., Ep. 3 sing. aor. 1 ἐβήσετο, for ἐβήσατο:—Pass., aor. 1 ἐβάθην [ᾰ] in compds. as συνεβάθην: pf. βέβᾰμαι in compds. as παραβέβαμαι. *To go, walk, step.* 2. Ep. with inf., βῆ δ' ἴμεν, βὰν δ' ἰέναι he, they *set out* to go; βῆ δὲ θέειν he *started* to run. 3. βαίνειν μετά τι *to go* after a thing; βαίνειν ἐπ' ἐλπίδος, etc., *to proceed* upon hope, i. e. *to feel* hope, etc. 4. the pf. βέβηκα chiefly has the sense of *being in a place, being settled;* εὖ βεβηκέναι *to stand* fast; οἱ ἐν τέλει βεβῶτες they *who are* in office. 5. of lifeless things, ἐννέα ἐνιαυτοὶ βεβάα σι nine years *have come and gone.* 6. *to mount*, β. δίφρον; of animals, *to cover;* ἵπποι βαινόμεναι *brood* mares. 7. with cognate acc., βαίνειν κέλευθον *to go* a path; βαίνειν πόδα *to advance* the foot: also later c. acc., αἶνον ἔβα κόρος disgust *comes after* praise; χρέος ἔβα με debts *came on* me.

II. Causal. in fut. act. βήσω: aor. 1 ἔβησα (answering to pres. βιβάζω):—*to make to go;* φῶτας βῆσεν ἀφ' ἵππων *he made* the men *dismount* from the chariot.

βάϊον, τό, (βάϊς) *a palm-branch.*

ΒΑΙΟ'Σ, ά, όν, *little, slight, short, small, humble;* ἐχώρει βαιός he was travelling with *small* escort; ἀπὸ βαιῆς (sub. ἡλικίας) from *childhood;* βαιόν, as Adv. *a little.*

ΒΑ'ΙΣ, ἡ, *a palm-branch.*

ΒΑΙ'ΤΗ, ἡ, *a peasant's coat of skins.*

βακέλας, ὁ, *a priest of Cybelé.*

Βᾰκίζω, f. ίσω, (Βακις) *to prophesy like Bacis.*

βάκκᾰρις, ιδος or εως, ἡ, *baccar*, an aromatic plant.

βακτηρία, ἡ, = βάκτρον.

βακτήριον, τό, = βάκτρον.

βάκτρευμα, ατος, τό, *a staff, support.* From

βακτρεύω, f. σω, *to lean on a staff.* From

βάκτρον, τό, (*βάω, βιβάζω) Lat. *baculus, a staff.*

βακτρο-προσαίτης, ου, ὁ, (βάκτρον, προσαίτης) *one who begs leaning on a staff.*

Βακχάω, (Βάκχος) *to rave with Bacchic frenzy.*

Βακχέ-βακχον ᾆσαι, *to raise the strain* Βάκχε, Βάκχε, *to invoke Bacchus.*

Βακχεία, ἡ, (Βάκχος) *Bacchic revelry.*

Βακχεῖον, τό, *the temple of Bacchus.* II. = Βακχεία, ἡ.

Βάκχειος, α, ον, (Βάκχος) *Bacchic, belonging to Bacchus* or *his rites: like a priest of Bacchus, inspired, frenzied.*

Βάκχευμα, ατος, τό, (Βακχεύω) *Bacchic revelry.*

Βακχεύς, έως, ὁ, = Βάκχος. Hence

Βακχεύσῐμος, ον, *Bacchanalian, frenzied.*

Βάκχευσις, εως, ἡ, (Βακχεύω) *Bacchic revelry.*

Βακχεύω, f. εύσω, (Βάκχος) *to keep the feast of Bacchus.* 2. *to speak* or *act like one frantic*, Lat. *bacchari.* II. causal, *to inspire with frenzy.*

Βάκχη, ἡ, (**Βάκχος**) *a Bacchanté.* II. *any inspired* or *frenzied woman.*

Βακχιάζω, = Βακχεύω.

Βάκχιος, α, ον, and **Βακχικός**, ή, όν, = Βάκχειος, *Bacchanalian:* generally, *inspired, raving.* II. as Subst., ὁ **Βάκχιος** (sub. θεός), *the Bacchic god*, i. e. *Bacchus.*

βακχίς, ίδος, ἡ, = Βάκχη.

Βακχιώτης, ου, ὁ, (Βάκχιος) *a Bacchanalian.*

ΒΑ'ΚΧΟΣ, ὁ, *Bacchus*, the planter of the vine, god of wine and inspiration, and particularly of dramatic poetry. The same word with **Ἴακχος**, and so from ἰάχω. II. *a Bacchanal:* generally, *any one inspired* or *frantic with passion.*

βᾰλᾰν-άγρα, ἡ, (βάλανος, (ἄγρα) *a hook to pull out the* βάλανος or *bolt-pin, a key.*

βᾰλᾰνεῖον, τό, Lat. *balneum, a bath, bathing-room.*

ΒΑ˘ΛΑ˘ΝΕΥ΄Σ, έως, ὁ, *the bath-man*, Lat. *balneātor.* Hence

βᾰλᾰνεύω, f. σω, *to wait upon* a person *at the bath:* generally, *to serve, wait upon.*

βᾰλᾰνη-φάγος, ον, (βάλανος, φαγεῖν) *acorn-eating.*

βᾰλᾰνη-φόρος, ον, (βάλανος, φέρω) *bearing acorns* or *dates.*

βᾰλᾰνίζω, (βάλανος) *to shake acorns from a tree.*

βᾰλάνισσα, ἡ, fem. of βαλανεύς.

ΒΑ΄ΛΑ˘ΝΟΣ, ἡ, *an acorn:* also of other fruit, esp. *the date;* Διὸς βάλανος *the sweet chestnut.* II. *an iron peg*, Lat. *pessulus*, passed through the bar into a hole in the doorpost behind it, and taken out with a hook (βαλανάγρα) when the door was to be opened, *a bolt-pin.* Hence

βᾰλᾰνόω, f. ώσω, *to bar the door with a bolt-pin, to close up.*

βαλαντιη-τόμος, ὁ, (βαλάντιον, τεμεῖν) *a cutpurse.*

ΒΑΛΑ΄ΝΤΙΟΝ, τό, *a bag, pouch, purse.*

βαλαντιοτομέω, *to cut purses.*

ΒΑΛΒΙ΄Σ, ῖδος, ἡ, mostly in pl. βαλβῖδες, Lat. *carcĕres, the post of the race-course, whence the racers started and to which they returned*, both in running and driving: *any starting point.* II. *any point to be gained, the battlement of a wall:—an end, term.*

βάλε, for ἔβαλε, 3 sing. aor. 2 of βάλλω.

βᾰλήν, also **βαλλήν**, ῆνος, ὁ, *a king*, akin to Hebr. *Bel* or *Baal, Lord.*

βᾰλιός, ά, όν, (βάλλω) *spotted, dappled.*

βαλλάντιον, τό, = βαλάντιον.

βαλλήναδε βλέπειν, a play on the words βάλλω and the Attic deme Παλλήνη.

ΒΑ΄ΛΛΩ; fut. βᾱλῶ, Ion. βᾰλέω, rarely βαλλήσω:—aor. 2 ἔβᾰλον, Ion. inf. βαλέων:—perf. βέβληκα: plqpf. ἐβεβλήκειν, Ep. βεβλήκειν.—Med., Ion. impf. βαλλέσκετο: fut. βαλοῦμαι:—aor. 2 ἐβᾰλόμην, Ion. imperat. βᾰλεῦ.—Pass., fut. βληθήσομαι, fut. 3 βεβλήσομαι: aor. 1 ἐβλήθην; 3 sing. Ep. aor. 2 ἔβλητο, subj. βλήεται, opt. 2 sing. βλεῖο, inf. βλῆσθαι, part. βλήμενος:—pf. βέβλημαι, Ion. 3 pl. βεβλήαται: plqpf. ἐβεβλήμην. I. Act. *to throw, cast, hurl at*, properly of a missile as opp. to striking, *to hit with a dart:* metaph. of sound, *to strike*, κτύπος οὔατα βάλλει:—of ships, *to dash, strike:* also *to push: to let fall:* and of tears, *to shed:—*also *to put on* or *over*, κύκλα ἀμφὶ ὀχέεσσι βάλε. 2. intr. *to fall, tumble*, ποταμὸς εἰς ἅλα βάλλων. II. Med. *to weigh with oneself, ponder, deliberate.* 2. *to throw around oneself;* ξίφος ἀμφ' ὤμοις βάλλεσθαι *to throw* over *one's* shoulder. 3. *to lay a foundation*, βάλλεσθαι ἄστυ *to found* a city.

βαλοῖσαι, Dor. for βαλοῦσαι, aor. 2 part. nom. pl. fem. of βάλλω.

βᾱλός, οῦ, ὁ, Dor. for βηλός.

βαλῶ, fut. ind. and aor. 2 subj. of βάλλω.

βᾶμα, τό, Dor. for βῆμα.

βαμβαίνω, *to chatter with the teeth: to stammer.* (Formed from the sound.)

βᾶμες, Dor. for βῶμεν, 1 pl. aor. 2 subj. of βαίνω.

βάμμα, ατος, τό, (βάπτω) *that in which a thing is dipped, dye:* see βάπτω

βάν, Ep. for ἔβαν, ἔβησαν, 3 pl. aor. 2 of βαίνω.

βᾰναυσία, ἡ, (βάναυσος) *handicraft, the life and habits of a mechanic*, hence *vulgarity, bad taste.* Hence

βᾰναυσικός, ή, όν, *of* or *for mechanics:* τέχνη βαναυσική a *mechanical* trade, Lat. *ars sellularia.*

βάν-αυσος, ον, (for βαύναυσος, from βαῦνος, αὔω) *working by* or *with fire:* hence generally *a mechanic:* metaph. *low, vulgar, illiberal.*

βαναυσ-ουργία, ἡ, (βάναυσος, *ἔργω) *handicraft.*

βάξις, εως, ἡ, (βάζω) *a saying, report, announcement*, esp. of an oracle; ἁλώσιμος βάξις *the telling* or *tidings* of the capture.

βαπτίζω, fut. Att. βαπτιῶ, (βάπτω) *to dip repeatedly, dip under:—*Med. *to bathe.* II. *to baptize.* Hence

βάπτισμα, ατος, τό, *that which is dipped.* II. = βαπτισμός.

βαπτισμός, ὁ, *a dipping in water: baptism.*

βαπτιστής, οῦ, ὁ, *one that dips, a dyer.* II. *a baptizer:* ὁ Βαπτιστής, *the Baptist.*

βαπτός, ή, όν, *dipped, dyed: bright-coloured.* II. *drawn like water.* From

ΒΑ΄ΠΤΩ, fut. βάψω.—Pass., aor. ἐβάφθην, aor. 2 ἐβάφην [ᾰ]: pf. βέβαμμαι. I. transit. *to dip, dip under*, Lat. *immergere.* 2. *to dye, colour, steep:* proverb., βάπτειν τινὰ βάμμα Σαρδιανικόν *to steep* one in Sardian dye, give him a bloody coxcomb. 3. *to fill by dipping in, draw.* II. intrans. *to dip, sink;* ναῦς ἔβαψεν the ship *sank.*

βάραθρον Ion. **βέρεθρον**, τό, (akin to βάθρον, βόθρος) *a gulf, cleft, pit:* at Athens a cleft behind the Acropolis, into which criminals were thrown, = Spartan κεάδαι: hence, II. metaph. *ruin, perdition.*

βαρβᾰρίζω, f. ίσω Att. ιῶ, (βάρβαρος) *to behave* or *speak like a barbarian, speak a foreign tongue: to ape foreigners.* II. *to hold with barbarians*, esp. *the Persians;* cf. Μηδίζω.

Βαρβᾰρικός, ή, όν, *barbaric, foreign, like a foreigner*, opp. to Ἑλληνικός. Adv. -κῶς, *in a foreign tongue*, i. e. *Persian.* From

ΒΑ΄ΡΒΑ˘ΡΟΣ, ον, *barbarous*, i. e. *not Greek, foreign:* as Subst., βάρβαροι, οἱ, *all that were not Greeks*, or *that did not speak Greek.* Plato divides mankind into Barbarians and Hellenes, as the Hebrews gave the name of Gentiles to all but themselves. II. from the Augustan age, the term was applied by the Romans to all nations except themselves and the Greeks: but the Greeks still affected to look upon the Romans as Barbarians.

βαρβᾰρό-φωνος, ον, (βάρβαρος, φωνή) *speaking a strange* or *foreign tongue.*

βαρβᾰρόω, f. ώσω, (βάρβαρος) *to make barbarous*

or *foreign*: Pass. *to become barbarous*: *to be inarticulate.*

BA'PBITON, *τό*, and **βάρβῖτος**, *ὁ* or *ἡ*, *a musical instrument of many strings*, like the lyre: used also for *the lyre itself.*

βάρδιστος, *η*, *ον*, by poët. metath. for *βράδιστος*, Sup. of *βραδύς*: so Comp. *βαρδύτερος* for *βραδύτερος*.

βᾰρέω, (*βάρος*) intr. in Ep. pf. part. *βεβαρηώς*, *weighed down*, *overcome*, *οἴνῳ βεβαρηότες*.

βᾰρέως, Adv. of *βαρύς*, *heavily*, *grievously*; *βαρέως φέρειν* Lat. *aegrè ferre*, *to take* a thing *ill*; *βαρέως ἀκούειν* to hear *with disgust.*

βᾶρις, *ιδος*, Ion. *ιος*, *ἡ*, Ion. plur. *βάρῖς*, *αἱ*, *an Egyptian boat*, *a sort of raft*: generally, *a canoe*, *boat*, Lat. *ratis.*

BA'POΣ, *εος*, *τό*, *weight*, *burden*, *pressure*: hence *grief*, *misery*: also *a quantity*, *excess.*

βαρυ-αλγής, *ές*, (*βαρύς*, *ἄλγος*) *grievously suffering.* 2. *very grievous.*

βᾰρῠ-άλγητος, *ον*, (*βαρύς*, *ἀλγέω*) *very grievous.*

βαρυ-ᾱχής *ές*, (*βαρύς*, *ἄχος*) *groaning heavily.*

βαρυ-ᾱχής, *ές*, Dor. for *βαρυηχής*.

βαρυ-βρεμέτης, *ου*, *ὁ*, and *-ετήρ*, *ῆρος*, *ὁ*, fem. **-έτειρα**, *ἡ*, (*βαρύς*, *βρέμω*) *loud-thundering.*

βαρυ-βρομήτης, *ου*, *ὁ*, (*βαρύς*, *βρομέω*) *loud-roaring.*

βαρύ-βρομος, *ον*, (*βαρύς*, *βρέμω*) *loud-roaring.*

βαρυ-βρώς, *ῶτος*, *ὁ*, *ἡ*, (*βαρύς*, *βιβρώσκω*) *greedily eating*: *gnawing*, *corroding.*

βαρύ-γδουπος, *ον*, (*βαρύς*, *δοῦπος*) *heavy-sounding*, *loud-roaring*, *thundering.*

βαρυ-γούνατος and **βαρύ-γουνος**, *ον*, (*βαρύς*, *γόνυ*) *with heavy knees*, *loitering*, *lazy.*

βαρύ-γυιος, *ον*, (*βαρύς*, *γυῖον*) *weighing down the limbs.*

βαρυδαιμονέω, f. *ήσω*, (*βαρυδαίμων*) *to be possessed by an evil genius*: generally, *to be unlucky.* Hence

βαρυδαιμονία, *ἡ*, *a heavy fate*, *ill luck.*

βαρυ-δαίμων, *ον*, gen. *ονος*, (*βαρύς*, *δαίμων*) *pressed by a heavy fate*, *unlucky.*

βαρύ-δακρυς, *υ*, (*βαρύς*, *δάκρυ*) *weeping grievously.*

βαρύ-δῐκος, *ον*, (*βαρύς*, *δίκη*) *taking heavy vengeance.*

βαρυ-δότειρα, *ἡ*, (*βαρύς*, *δοτήρ*) *giver of ill gifts.*

βαρύ-δουπος, *ον*, = *βαρύγδουπος*.

βαρύ-ζηλος, *ον*, (*βαρύς*, *ζῆλος*) *exceedingly jealous.*

βαρυ-ηχής, *ές*, (*βαρύς*, *ἦχος*) *heavy-sounding.*

βαρυθῡμία, *ἡ*, *sullenness.* From

βαρύ-θῡμος, *ον*, (*βαρύς*, *θυμός*) *heavy in spirit*: *indignant*, *sullen.*

βαρύθω, (*βαρύς*) *to be weighed down*: *to be heavy*, *dull*, *sluggish.* [ῠ]

βαρύ-κομπος, *ον*, (*βαρύς*, *κομπέω*) *loud-roaring.*

βαρύ-κοτος, *ον*, (*βαρύς*, *κοτέω*) *grievous in wrath.*

βαρύ-κτῠπος, *ον*, (*βαρύς*, *κτυπέω*) *heavy-sounding*, *loud-thundering.*

βαρυ-λαῖλαψ, *απος*, *ὁ*, *ἡ*, (*βαρύς*, *λαῖλαψ*) *loud-storming.*

βαρύ-λογος, *ον*, (*βαρύς*, *λόγος*) *vexatious of speech*; *βαρύλογα ἔχθεα* hate vented in *bitter words.*

βαρυ-μήνιος, *ον*, and **βαρύμηνις**, *ι*, gen. *ιος*, (*βαρύς*, *μῆνις*) *exceeding wrathful.*

βαρύ-μισθος, *ον*, (*βαρύς*, *μισθός*) *exacting heavy sums.*

βαρύ-μοχθος, *ον*, (*βαρύς*, *μόχθος*) *very toilsome* or *painful.*

βάρυνθεν, Ep. and Aeol. for *ἐβαρύνθησαν*, 3 pl. aor 1 pass. of *βαρύνω*.

βαρύνω [ῡ], f. *ῠνῶ*, (*βαρύς*) *to load heavily*, *to burden*: *to torment*:—Pass. *to be weary*, *oppressed*; *βαρύνεσθαι χεῖρα to be maimed* in hand:—metaph. *to be vexed*, *annoyed*, Lat. *gravari.*

βαρυ-όπης, *ου*, *ὁ*, (*βαρύς*, *ὄψ*) *loud-voiced.*

βαρυ-όργητος, *ον*, (*βαρύς*, *ὀργή*) *exceeding angry.*

βαρυ-πάλᾰμος, *ον*, (*βαρύς*, *παλάμη*) *heavy-handed.*

βαρυ-πενθής, *ές*, (*βαρύς*, *πένθος*) *causing grievous woe.*

βαρυ-πένθητος, *ον*, (*βαρύς*, *πενθέω*) *mourning heavily.*

βαρυ-πεσής, *ές*, (*βαρύς*, *πεσεῖν*) *heavy-falling.*

βαρύ-ποτμος, *ον*, (*βαρύς*, *πότμος*) *with heavy fate*, *ill-fated*, *ill-starred.*

βαρύ-πους, *ὁ*, *ἡ*, *πουν*, *τό*, gen. *ποδος*, (*βαρύς*, *πούς*) *heavy-footed*: *heavy at the end.*

BAPY'Σ, *εῖα*, *ύ*: Comp. *βαρύτερος*, Sup. *βαρύτατος*: *heavy*, Lat. *gravis*: *burdensome*, *grievous*, *oppressive*: of persons, *troublesome.* 2. in good sense, *weighty*, *impressive.* II. of soldiers, *heavy-armed.* III. of sound, *strong*: *deep*, *bass*, opp. to *ὀξύς*.

βαρυ-σίδηρος, *ον*, (*βαρύς*, *σίδηρος*) *heavy with iron.*

βαρύ-σταθμος, *ον*, (*βαρύς*, *σταθμός*) *weighing heavy.*

βαρυ-στενάχων, *ουσα*, *ον*, (*βαρύς*, *στενάχω*) *sobbing heavily.*

βαρύ-στονος, *ον*, (*βαρύς*, *στένω*) *groaning heavily.*

βαρυ-σύμφορος, *ον*, (*βαρύς*, *συμφορά*) *weighed down by ill luck.*

βαρυ-σφάρᾰγος, *ον*, (*βαρύς*, *σφάραγος*) *loud thundering.*

βαρύτης, *ητος*, *ἡ*, (*βαρύς*) *weight*, *heaviness*: *importunity*: *harshness*, *oppression*; *gravity* of manners. [ῠ]

βαρύ-τῑμος, *ον*, (*βαρύς*, *τιμή*) *of great worth*: *venerable*, *costly.*

βαρύ-τλητος, *ον*, (*βαρύς*, *τλῆναι* aor. 2 of **τλάω*) *heavy to bear.*

βαρύ-φθογγος, *ον*, (*βαρύς*, *φθογγή*) *heavy-sounding*, *loud-roaring.*

βαρύ-φρων, *φρονος*, *ὁ*, *ἡ*, (*βαρύς*, *φρήν*) *weighty of mind* or *purpose.*

βαρύ-χειλος, *ον*, (*βαρύς*, *χεῖλος*) *thick-lipped.*

βαρύ-χορδος, *ον*, (*βαρύς*, *χορδή*) *deep-toned.*

βαρύ-ψῡχος, *ον*, (*βαρύς*, *ψυχή*) *heavy of soul*, *mean-spirited*, *dejected.*

βάς, **βᾶσα**, **βάν**, aor. 2 part. of *βαίνω*.

βασανίζω, f. *ίσω* Att. *ιῶ*, *to rub upon the touchstone* (*βάσανος*): *to try the genuineness of* a thing, *test*, *make proof of*: *to convict*: *to put to the torture.*

βᾰσᾰνισμός, *ὁ*, (*βασανίζω*) *torturing*, *torture.*

βασανιστής, οῦ, ὁ, pecul. fem. **βασανίστρια**, ἡ, (βασανίζω):—*an examiner, questioner, torturer.*

ΒΑ'ΣΑ'ΝΟΣ, ἡ, *the touch-stone*, Lat. *lapis Lydius*, by which gold was proved, see παρατρίβω. II. metaph. *a test to try whether a thing be genuine* or *not.* III. *inquiry*, esp. *by torture, the question.* 2. *torture, anguish, disease.*

βασεῦμαι, βασεῦνται, Dor. for βήσομαι, βήσονται, fut. of βαίνω.

βᾰσίλειᾰ, ἡ, (βασιλεύς) *a queen, princess, lady of royal blood.*

βᾰσιλείᾱ, ἡ, (βασιλεύω) *a kingdom, dominion: hereditary monarchy*, opp. to τυραννίς.

βᾰσίλειον, τό, mostly in plur., *a palace:* also *the royal treasury* or *tent.* Strictly neut. from

βᾰσίλειος, ον, and α, ον, Ion. **βασιλήϊος**, η, ον, *kingly, royal.* From

ΒΑ'ΣΙΛΕΥ'Σ, έως Ion. ῆος, ὁ. acc. βασιλέα, contr. βασιλῆ: pl., nom. βασιλεῖς, old Att. -ῆς, Ion. -ῆες:—*a king, prince*, of gods and men:—hence are formed the Comp. βασιλεύτερος, α, ον, *more kingly;* Sup. βασιλεύτατος, η, ον, *most kingly.* II. *the second of the nine Archons* at Athens was called βασιλεύς: he had charge of the public worship, and the conduct of criminal processes. III. after the Persian war the king of Persia was called βασιλεύς (without the Art.), or ὁ μέγας βασιλεύς. Hence

βᾰσιλεύω, f. σω, *to be king, to rule:* in aor. 1 βασιλεῦσαι, *to be made king.* II. c. dat. *to rule over a people:*—Pass. *to be governed by a king, to be under a king.*

βᾰσιλητη, ἡ, Ion. for βασιλείᾱ.

βᾰσιλήϊος, η, ον, Ion. for βασίλειος.

βᾰσιλητς, ΐδος, ἡ, pecul. fem. of βασίλειος, *royal.*

βασιλίζω, f. σω, (βασιλεύς) *to be of the king's party.*

βᾰσιλικός, ή, όν, like βασίλειος, *royal, of a king.* 2. *of* or *for a king, princely* II. as Subst., βασιλικός, ὁ, *a courtier, nobleman.*

βασιλῖναῦ, barbaric form of βασίλιννα, βασίλισσα.

βασίλιννα and **βασίλισσα**, ἡ, = βασίλειᾰ, *a queen.*

βᾰσιλίς, ίδος, η, = βασίλειᾰ, *a queen, princess.* 2. as Adj. = βασιλητς, *royal.*

βάσιμος, ον, (βαίνω) *passable: accessible.*

βάσις, εως, ἡ, (βαίνω) *a stepping: a step, walk.* II. *that whereon one steps, ground: a pedestal.*

βασκαίνω, fut. ᾰνῶ: aor. 1 ἐβάσκηνα: aor. 1 pass. ἐβασκάνθην: (βάσκω):—*to use ill words of* another, esp. *to slander, disparage.* II. *to use ill words to* another, *bewitch* by spells or by means of an evil eye, Lat. *fascinare.*

βασκᾰνία, ἡ, (βάσκανος) *slander, envy, malice.*

βάσκᾰνος, ον, (βασκαίνω) *slanderous, envious, malignant.* 2. *a sorcerer.*

βασκάς, άδος, ἡ, a kind of *duck.*

βάσκε, imperat. of an obsol. verb βάσκω, another form of βαίνω, as χάσκω of χαίνω; βάσκ' ἴθι, *speed thee! away!* βάσκετε *away!*

βασμός, Ion. for βαθμός.

βᾶσσα, Dor. for βῆσσα.

βασσάρα, ἡ, = ἀλώπηξ, *a fox.* (Of Thracian origin.)

βασσάριον, τό, Dim. of βασσάρα.

βάσσων, ον, gen. ονος, Dor. comparat. of βαθύς.

βάσταγμα, ατος, τό, *that which is borne, a burden.* II. *that which bears, a staff.* From

ΒΑΣΤΑ'ΖΩ, f. άσω: aor. 1 ἐβάστασα, later ἐβάσταξα: aor. 1 pass. ἐβαστάχθην:—*to lift, lift up, raise:* metaph. *to extol, exalt.* II. *to bear, support, hold upright: to bear in mind, consider.* III. *to carry off.* IV. *to handle, touch.* Hence

βαστακτός, ή, όν, verb. Adj., *to be borne.*

βατᾰλος, ὁ, *a lisper.*

βᾰτέω, f. ήσω, (βαίνω) *to mount, cover*, of animals.

βάτην, Ep. for ἐβήτην, 3 dual aor. 2 of βαίνω.

βᾰτηρίς, ίδος, ἡ, (βατέω) fem. Adj. *for mounting.*

βατία, ἡ, = βάτος, *a bush, thicket.*

βατιδο-σκόπος, ον, (βάτις, σκοπέω) *looking after roaches* or *skaits, greedy for them.*

βᾰτίς, ίδος, ἡ, (βάτος) *the prickly roach* or *the skait.*

βᾰτο-δρόπος, ον, (βάτος, δρέπω) *pulling thorns off* or *up.*

ΒΑ'ΤΟΣ, ἡ, *a bramble* or *any prickly bush.*

βάτος, ὁ, the Hebrew solid measure *bath.*

βᾰτός, ή, όν, (βαίνω) *passable.*

βατράχειος, ον, (βάτραχος) *of* or *belonging to a frog:* βατράχειον (sub. χρῶμα), *frog-colour, pale green.*

βατρᾰχίς, ῖδος, and ίδος, ἡ, *a frog-green coat.* From

ΒΑ'ΤΡΑΧΟΣ, ὁ, *a frog*, Lat. *rana.* 2. *the frog of a horse's hoof.* [ᾰ]

βατταρίζω, fut. Att. ιῶ, (Βάττος) *to stammer.*

βαττο-λογέω, = βατταρίζω, (Βάττος, λόγος) *to babble, use vain repetitions.*

Βάττος, ὁ, *Stammerer*, name of a king of Cyrenė. (Formed from the sound.)

βαΰζω, Dor. **βαΰσδω**: fut. βαΰξω:—*to cry* βαῦ, βαῦ, *to bark:* hence *to wail, mutter: to reproach.* II. transit. *to cry aloud for.*

βαυκάλις, ιδος, ἡ, *a wine-cooler.*

βαῦνος or **βαυνός**, ὁ, (αὔω) *a furnace, forge.*

βαΰσδω, Dor. for βαΰζω.

βᾰφή, ἡ, (βάπτω) *a dipping*, as of red-hot iron in cold water. II. *a dipping* of cloth *in dye, dyeing:* also *the dye itself.*

βᾰφῆναι, aor. 2 inf. pass. of βάπτω.

βάψις, εως, ἡ, (βάπτω) *a dipping, dyeing.*

ΒΔΕ'ΛΛΑ˘, ἡ, *a leech*, Lat. *hirūdo.*

βδέλυγμα, τό, (βδελύσσω) *an abomination*, esp. of idols.

βδελυκτός, ή, όν, (βδελύσσω) *disgusting, abominable.*

βδελύκ-τροπος, ον, (βδελυκτός, τρόπος) = foreg.

ΒΔΕΛΥ'ΡΟ'Σ, ά, όν, *abominable, disgusting.* Hence

βδελύσσω, Att. -ττω: fut. ξω: *to cause to stink, make loathsome.* II. mostly used as Dep. βδελύττομαι, with fut. med. and pass. βδελύξομαι, βδελυχθήσομαι, aor. 1 med. and pass. ἐβδελυξάμην, ἐβδελύχθην:—*to feel disgust at, to detest, have a* *horror of.* But all these forms, as well as perf. ἐβδέλυγμαι occur in pass. sense, *to be abominated.*

ΒΔΕ´Ω, f. βδέσω, *to break wind: to stink.*

βδύλλω, = βδέω: c. acc. *to be afraid of.*

βεβάᾱσι, Ep. 3 pl. pf. of βαίνω.

βέβαιος, α, ον, also ος, ον, (βαίνω) *firm, steady: steadfast, trusty, sure, safe:* τὸ βέβαιον *certainty.* Hence

βεβαιότης, ητος, ἡ, *firmness, steadfastness, safety.*

βεβαιόω, f. ώσω, *to make firm, establish:*—Med. *to establish for oneself, to confirm, secure.*

βεβαίως, Adv. of βέβαιος, *steadfastly, firmly.*

βεβαίωσις, εως, ἡ, *a making fast* or *sure, establishing.*

βεβάμεν, βεβάναι, Ep. syncop. forms of βεβηκέναι, inf. of βαίνω. [ᾰ]

βέβαμμαι, pf. pass. of βάπτω.

βεβᾰρηώς, *weighed down*, Ep. pf. part. of βαρέω.

βέβᾰσαν, Ep. 3 pl. plqpf. of βαίνω.

βεβᾶσι, Att. contr. from βεβάασι, Ep. 3 pl. pf. of βαίνω.

βεβᾰώς, βεβᾰυῖα, Ep. for βεβηκώς, pf. part. of βαίνω.

βέβηκα, pf. of βαίνω.

βεβήκειν, Ion. for ἐβεβήκειν, plqpf. of βαίνω.

βέβηλος, ον, (βαίνω, βηλός) *allowable to tread, permitted to human use*, like Lat. *profanus*, opp. to *sacred.* II. of men, *unhallowed, profane, unholy.* Hence

βεβηλόω, f. ώσω, *to profane, to pollute.*

βεβίασμαι, pf. pass. of βιάζω.

βεβίηκα, pf. of βιάω.

βεβλάστηκα, pf. of βλαστάνω.

βέβλᾰφα, βεβλάμμαι, pf. act. and pass. of βλάπτω.

βεβλάψομαι, fut. 3 pass. of βλάπτω.

βέβλεφα, βέβλεμμαι, pf. act. and pass. of βλέπω.

βέβληαι, 2 sing. pf. pass. of βάλλω.

βεβλήαται, βεβλήατο, Ion. 3 plur. pf. and plqpf. pass. of βάλλω.

βέβληκα, βέβλημαι, pf. act. and pass. of βάλλω.

βεβλήκειν, βεβλήμην, Ep. plqpf. act. and pass. of βάλλω.

βέβληται, βέβλητο, 3 sing. pf. and plqpf. pass. of βάλλω.

βέβλῐκα, pf. of βλίττω.

βεβολήατο, 3 plur. plqpf. pass., and **βεβολημένος**, pf. pass. part., of βολέω for βάλλω.

βεβούλημαι, pf. of βούλομαι.

βεβούλευκα, βεβούλευμαι, pf. act. and pass. of βουλεύω.

βέβρασμαι, pf. pass. of βράσσω.

βέβρῑθα, pf. of βρίθω.

βεβροτωμένος, pf. part. pass. of βροτόω.

βέβρῡχε, v. βρυχάομαι.

βεβρώθω, poët. form. of βιβρώσκω, *to eat up.*

βέβρωκα, βέβρωμαι, pf. act. and pass. of βιβρώσκω.

βεβρώς, syncop. for βεβρωκώς, pf. part. of βιβρώσκω.

βεβρώσομαι, fut. 3 pass. of βιβρώσκω.

βέβυσμαι, pf. pass. of βύζω.

βεβώς, βεβῶσα, Att. contr. of βεβαώς, Ep. pf. part. of βαίνω.

βέῃ, 2 sing. of βέομαι, Ep. fut. of βαίνω.

βείομαι, Ep. for βήσομαι, fut. of βαίνω, *I will walk* or *live.*

βείω, Ep. for βῶ, aor. 2 subj. of βαίνω.

βεκκε-σέληνος, ον, (βεκύς, σελήνη) *old-fashioned, out of date, dotard: simple, silly.*

βεκός, τό, *bread:* said to be a Phrygian word.

βέλεμνον, τό, poët. for βέλος, *a dart, javelin.*

βελόνη, ἡ, (βέλος) *an arrow-head: point of a spear: a needle.*

βελονο-πώλης, ου, ὁ, (βελόνη, πωλέομαι) *a needle-seller.*

βέλος, εος, τό, (βάλλω) like Lat. *jaculum* (from *jacio*), *anything thrown, a bolt, arrow, dart.* 2. metaph., ἀγανὰ βέλεα of Apollo and Artemis are used of sudden, easy *death;* δύσομβρα βέλη *the arrows* of the storm; ὀμμάτων βέλος *glances* shot from the eye.

βέλτερος, α, ον, = βελτίων, poët. Comp. of ἀγαθός, *better.* Hence also a rare Sup. **βέλτατος**, η, ον.

βέλτιστος, η, ον, Sup. of ἀγαθός, *best.*

βελτίων, ον, gen. ονος, Comp of ἀγαθός, *better.*

βεμβῑκιάω, (βέμβιξ) *to spin like a top.*

βεμβῑκίζω, f. ίσω, (βέμβιξ) *to spin as one does a top, to set a going.*

ΒΕ´ΜΒΙΞ, ῑκος, ἡ, Lat. *turbo, a top.*

βενδίδειον, τό, *the temple of Bendis*, (a name of Diana).

ΒΕ´ΝΘΟΣ, εος, τό, (poët. for βάθος, as πένθος for πάθος) *the depth* of the sea, Lat. *fundus;* βένθοσδε *to the bottom;* βένθεα ὕλης the *depths* of the wood.

βέντιστος, α, ον, Dor. for βέλτιστος.

βέομαι, Ep. for βήσομαι, fut. of βαίνω.

βέρεθρον, τό, Ep. and Ion. for βάραθρον.

βερέσχεθος, ὁ, *a booby.*

βῆ, poët. for ἔβη, 3 sing. aor. 2 of βαίνω.

βῆθι, βῆναι, aor. 2 imperat. and inf. of βαίνω.

βηλός, ὁ, (βαίνω) *the threshold*, Lat. *limen.*

βῆμα, ατος, τό, (βαίνω) *a pace, step, footstep: a place to set foot on.* II. *a raised step: a tribune* to speak from, esp. in the Pnyx at Athens, Lat. *rostra, suggestum* or *-us.*

βῆμεν, Ep. for ἔβημεν, 1 plur. aor. 2 of βαίνω.

βήμεναι, Ep. for βῆναι, aor. 2 inf. of βαίνω.

βῆν, Ep. for ἔβην, aor. 2 of βαίνω.

βῆναι, aor. 2 inf. of βαίνω.

βήξ, βηχός, ἡ, or ὁ, (βήσσω) *a cough*, Lat. *tussis.*

βήρυλλος, ἡ, *a jewel of sea-green colour, beryl.*

βῆσα, Ep. for ἔβησα, aor. 1 act of βαίνω.

βήσεο, Ep. for βῆσαι, aor. 1 med. imperat. of βαίνω.

βήσετο, Ep. for ἐβήσατο, sing. aor. 1 med. of βαίνω.

βήσομαι, fut. of βαίνω.

βῆσσα, Dor. **βᾶσσα**, ἡ, (βαίνω) Lat. *saltus, a wooded valley* or *glen;* οὔρεος ἐν βήσσῃσι in the mountain *glens.* Hence

βησσήεις, εσσα, εν, *woody.*

ΒΗ´ΣΣΩ, Att. **βήττω**, f. βήξω: aor. 1 ἔβηξα:—*to cough.*

βήτ-αρμων, ονος, ὁ, (βαίνω, ἁρμός) *a dancer.*

βήτην, poët. for ἐβήτην, 3 dual aor. 2 of βαίνω.

ΒΙ΄Α, Ion. **βίη**, ἡ, *bodily strength, force, might*, Lat. *vis*: often periphr. with a gen. of the person, βίη Ἡρακλῆος *the strong* Hercules. II. *force, an act of violence*; βίᾳ τινός *against* one's *will*. [ῐ] Hence

βῐάζω, f. άσω. *to force, constrain*: Pass., aor. 1 ἐβιάσθην: pf. βεβίασμαι:—*to have violence done one, to suffer violence*; βιάζομαι τάδε *I am wronged* herein. II. Dep., with aor. 1 med. ἐβιασάμην, and (sometimes) pf. pass. βεβίασμαι:—*to force* a man, *constrain, overpower*; βιάζεσθαι αὑτόν *to do* oneself *violence*: *to carry by force* or *assault*: absol. *to use force, force one's way*.

βῐαιο-μάχας, α, ὁ, (βίαιος, μάχη) *fighting violently*.

βίαιος, α, ον, also ος, ον, (βία) *forcible, violent*: *acting with violence*; πρὸς τὸ βίαιον by *force*. 2. pass. *forced*: *compulsory*. Hence

βῐαιότης, ητος, ἡ, *violence*.

βιαίως, Adv. of βίαιος, *by force, perforce*.

βῐ-αρκής, ές, (βίος, ἀρκέω) *supplying the necessaries of life*.

βῐαστής, οῦ, ὁ, (βιάζω) *one who uses force, a violent man*.

βῐατής, οῦ, ὁ, = βιαστής.

βῐάω: perf. βεβίηκα:—older Ep. form of βιάζω, *to force, constrain*:—Med., βιάομαι, f. ήσομαι, *to force, treat with violence*: also *to overreach, defraud*, νῶϊ μισθὸν βιήσατο he *cheated* us of our pay:—Pass., aor. 1 ἐβιήθην, *to be constrained* or *overpowered*.

βῐβάζω, f. άσω Att. βιβῶ, Causal of βαίνω, *to make to go up, lift up, exalt*.

βῐβάς, ᾶσα, άν, part. pres. formed as if from a verb βίβημι, = βαίνω.

βῐβάσθων, ουσα, ον, part. pres. of a verb βιβάσθω, = βαίνω, *to stride*; μακρὰ βιβάσθων long-*striding*.

βῐβάω, poët. collat. form of βαίνω, *to stride*; πέλωρα βιβᾶν *to take* huge *strides*; part. βιβῶν, βιβῶσα.

βιβλάριον, τό, Dim. of βίβλος, *a little book* or *scroll*:—so also **βιβλαρίδιον**, τό.

Βίβλινος οἶνος, ὁ, *Biblian wine*, from Biblis, a hill in Thrace.

βιβλιοθήκη, ἡ, (βιβλίον, θήκη) *a book-case*: *library*.

βιβλίον, τό, Dim. of βίβλος, *a paper, scroll*.

βιβλιο-πώλης, ου, ὁ, (βιβλίον, πωλέω) *a bookseller*.

ΒΙ΄ΒΛΟΣ, ἡ, *the inner bark of the papyrus*. II. *the paper made of this bark*: hence *a paper, book*.

ΒΙΒΡΩ΄ΣΚΩ, fut. βρώσομαι: aor. 1 ἔβρωσα: aor. 2 ἔβρων: perf. βέβρωκα, part. βεβρωκώς, by syncop. βεβρώς.—Pass., fut. βρωθήσομαι: fut. 3 βεβρώσομαι: aor. 1 ἐβρώθην: pf. βέβρωμαι:—*to eat, gnaw, eat up, consume*: c. gen. *to eat of* a thing.

βιβῶ, Att. fut. of βιβάζω.

βιβῶν, contr. from βιβάων, part. of βιβάω.

βιήσατο, Ep. 3 sing. aor. 1 med. of βιάω.

ΒΙ΄ΚΟΣ, ὁ, *an earthen wine-vessel*.

ΒΙ΄ΝΕ΄Ω, *coïre*, of illicit intercourse, opp. to ὀπυίω.

βιο-δότης, ὁ, (βίος, δίδωμι) *the giver of life* or *food*.

βιό-δωρος, ον, (βίος, δῶρον) *life-giving, bounteous*.

βιο-δώτης, ὁ, poët. for βιοδότης.

βιο-θάλμιος, ον, (βίος, θάλλω) *lively, strong, hale*.

βιο-θρέμμων, ον, gen. ονος, (βίος, τρέφω) *supporting life*.

ΒΙ΄ΟΣ, ὁ, *life, the course of life*: *lifetime*. II. *manner* or *means of living*: one's *living, livelihood*.

ΒΙΟ΄Σ, ὁ, *a bow*.

βιο-στερής, ές, (βιός, στερέω) *robbing of life* or *means*. II. pass. *in want of means*.

βιοτεία, ἡ, (βιοτεύω) *a way of life, livelihood*.

βιοτεύω, f. σω, (βιόω) *to live, subsist*; βιοτεύειν ἀπό τινος, *to live by* a thing.

βιοτή, ἡ, Lat. *vita*, = βίοτος.

βιότης, ητος, ἡ, = βίοτος.

βιότιον, τό, Dim. of βίοτος, *a scant living*.

βίοτος, ὁ, (βιόω) *life*: *means of life*.

βιούς, aor. 2 part. of βιόω.

βιο-φειδής, ές, (βίος, φείδομαι) *stingy, sparing*.

βιόω: f. βιώσομαι, later βιώσω: aor. 1 ἐβίωσα:—aor. 2 ἐβίων (as if from a verb βίωμι); 3 sing. imperat. βιώτω; subj. βιῶ; opt. βιῴην; inf. βιῶναι; part. βιούς: (βίος, Lat. *vivo*):—*to live*, esp. *to live happily*:—Pass., βιοῦται *one lives*, Lat. *vivitur*.

βιόωνται, βιόωντο, Ep. 3 plur. pres. and imperf. med. of βιάω.

βιῷατο, for βιῷντο, 3 pl. pres. med. opt. of βιάω.

βιῴην, aor. 2 med. opt. of βιόω.

βιῶναι, inf. of βιόω.

βιώσιμος, ον, (βιόω) *to be lived, worth living, possible to live*.

βίωσις, εως, ἡ, (βιόω) *a living, manner of life*.

βιώσκομαι, Dep., causal of βιόω, *to quicken, make alive*: 2 sing. Ep. aor. 1 ἐβιώσαο.

βιωτικός, ή, όν, (βιόω) *fit for life, lively*. II. *of* or *pertaining to life*.

βιωτός, ή, όν, = (βιόω) *to be lived, worth living for*.

βιώτω, 3 sing. imperat. aor. 2 of βιόω.

βλάβεν, Ep. for ἐβλάβησαν, 3 pl. aor. 2 pass. of βλάπτω.

βλᾰβερός, ά, όν, (βλάπτω) *hurtful, noxious*.

βλάβη, ἡ, (βλάπτω) *hurt, harm, damage*: βλάβης δίκη an action *for damage done*.

βλᾰβῆναι, aor. 2 pass. inf. of βλάπτω.

βλαβήσομαι, fut. 2 of βλάπτω.

βλάβομαι, = βλάπτομαι, only in 3 sing. βλάβεται.

βλάβος, εος contr. ους, τό, = βλάβη, *hurt, damage*.

ΒΛΑΙΣΟ΄Σ, ή, όν, *having the legs bent inwards*: generally, *crooked*.

βλᾰκεία, ἡ, (βλακεύω) *slackness, sloth, stupidity*.

βλᾱκεύω, (βλάξ) *to be slack, lazy, indolent*.

βλᾱκικός, ή, όν, (βλάξ) *indolent, stupid*. Adv. -κῶς.

βλᾱκώδης, ες, (βλάξ, εἶδος) *lazy, sluggish*.

ΒΛΑ΄Ξ, βλᾱκός, ὁ, ἡ, (akin to μαλακός) *lazy, inactive, sluggish*. Irreg. Comp. βλᾱκίστερος or βλᾱκώτερος.

ΒΛΑ΄ΠΤΩ: fut. βλάψω: Ep. aor. 1 βλάψα: pf. βέβλᾰφα or ἔβλᾰφα.—Pass., fut. 2 βλᾰβήσομαι, fut. 3 βεβλάψομαι; fut. med. βλάψομαι, used as pass.: aor. 1 ἐβλάφθην, more usu. aor. 2 ἐβλάβην [ᾰ]: pf.

βέβλαμμαι:—*to hinder, weaken, stop*; c. gen. *to hinder from*; *βλαβέντα λοισθίων δρόμων arrested* in its last course; *βλαφθεὶς ἐν ὄζῳ caught* in the branches. 2. of the mind. *to blind, deceive, mislead*: 3. *to harm, damage, hurt, mar*.

βλαστάνω, fut. *βλαστήσω*: aor 2 *ἔβλαστον*; later aor. 1 *ἐβλάστησα*: pf. *βεβλάστηκα* or *ἐβλαστηκα*: (*βλαστέω*) :—*to bud, sprout*: generally, *to burst forth, grow*.

βλάστη, ἡ, = *βλαστός*, *a bud, sprout, leaf*. II. *increase, growth*.

βλάστημα, *ατος*, τό, and **βλάστημος**, ὁ, = *βλάστη*.

ΒΛΑΣΤΟ'Σ, ὁ, *a bud, shoot, sucker*, Lat. *germen*.

βλασφημέω, f. *ήσω*: pf. *βεβλασφήμηκα*: (*βλάσφημος*) :—*to drop profane words, speak profanely*. 2. *to speak ill* or *to the prejudice of one, to defame*: *to blaspheme*. Hence

βλασφημία, ἡ, *profane language*. 2. *evil-speaking, blasphemy*

βλάσφημος, *ον*, (*βλάξ*, *φήμη*) *speaking profanely*. 2. *evil-speaking, slanderous*.

ΒΛΑΥ'ΤΗ, ἡ, mostly in plur. *βλαῦται*. *ῶν*, *αἱ*, *a kind of slippers* or *sandals*, Lat. *soleae*.

βλαυτίον, τό, Dim. of *βλαύτη*.

βλαφθείς, aor. 1 pass. part. of *βλάπτω*.

βλαχά, Dor. for *βλαχή*.

βλάψα, Ep. for *ἔβλαψα*, aor. 1 of *βλάπτω*.

βλάψις, *εως*, ἡ, (*βλάπτω*) *a harming, hurting*.

βλαψί-φρων, *ον*, gen. *ονος*, (*βλάπτω*, *φρήν*) *maddening*. 2. *mad*: Adv. *βλαψιφρόνως*, *madly*.

βλεῖο, 2 sing. Ep. aor. 2 med. opt. of *βάλλω*.

βλεμεαίνω, (*βρέμω*) *to vaunt* or *be proud of* a thing; *σθένεϊ βλεμεαίνων exulting* in his strength.

βλέμμα, *ατος*, τό, (*βλέπω*) *a look, glance the eye*.

βλέποισα, Dor. for *βλέπουσα*.

βλέπος, τό, = *βλέμμα*, *a look*.

βλεπτέον, verb. Adj. of *βλέπω*, *one must look*.

βλεπτικός, ή, όν, (*βλέπω*) *of* or *for sight*.

βλεπτός, ή, όν, *seen, worth seeing*. From

ΒΛΕ'ΠΩ, f. *ψω*; aor. 1 *ἔβλεψα*: pf. *βέβλεφα*:—Pass., aor. 1 *ἐβλέφθην*: pf. *βέβλεμμαι*:—*to look, see*: *to look on, look at*: also c. acc., *Ἄρη*, *φόβον βλέπειν to look* fury, terror; in Comedy, *κάρδαμα*, *νᾶπυ βλέπειν to look* cress, mustard, i. e. *to have* a sour or bitter *look*. II. *to look in a particular direction, to turn towards*: esp. of aspects; *οἰκία πρὸς μεσημβρίαν βλέπουσα* a house *looking* towards the south. III. *to see the light*, with or without *φάος*, hence, *to live*. IV. *to look and long after a thing*, c. inf. 2. *to take care of, look to* or *to beware of* a thing.

βλεφᾰρίς, ίδος, ἡ, *an eyelash*. From

βλέφᾰρον, τό, (*βλέπω*) *an eyelid*. II. in plur. *the eyes*: *ἁμέρας βλέφαρον*, *eye* of day, i. e. the sun; *νυκτὸς βλέφαρον*, i. e. the moon.

βλήεται for *βλήηται*, *βλῆται*, Ep. aor. 2 pass. subj. of *βάλλω*.

βληθείς, aor. 1 pass. part. of *βάλλω*.

βληθήσομαι, fut. 3 pass. of *βάλλω*.

βλῆμα, *ατος*, τό, (*βάλλω*) *a throw, cast*. 2. *a shot, wound*. 3. *a coverlet*.

βλήμενος, *η*, *ον*, Ep. aor. 2 pass. part. of *βάλλω*.

βλῆναι, **βλῆσθαι**, aor. 2 inf. of *βάλλω*.

βλῆσθαι, Ep. aor. 2 pass. inf. of *βάλλω*.

βλήσομαι, Ep. fut. of *βάλλω*.

βλητέος, *α*, *ον*, verb. Adj. of *βάλλω*, *to be thrown*. 2. **βλητέον**, *one must throw*.

βλῆτο, 3 sing Ep. aor. 2 pass. of *βάλλω*.

βλητός, ή, όν, (*βάλλω*) *hurled, struck*.

βλῆτρον, τό, (*βάλλω*) *an iron nail*.

βληχάομαι, fut. *ήσομαι*: Dep.: (*βληχή*) :—*to bleat*, of sheep and goats.

ΒΛΗΧΗ', ἡ, *a bleating*: generally, *the wailing of children*, Lat. *vagitus*.

βληχρός, ά, όν, *weak, feeble, sluggish*: also with α euphon., *ἀβληχρός*. Adv. *-ρῶς*, *slightly*.

ΒΛΗ'ΧΩΝ, *ωνος*, ἡ: acc. *βλήχω*: Ion. **γλήχων**, Dor. **γλάκων** :—*pennyroyal*. Hence

βληχωνίας, *ου*, ὁ, *prepared with pennyroyal*.

ΒΛΙ'ΤΤΩ, Ion. **βλίσσω**: f. *βλίσω*: aor *ἔβλῐσα*:—*to cut out the comb of bees, to take the honey*. (From *μέλι* with *β* added, as *βλάξ* from *μαλακός*.)

ΒΛΟΣΥΡΟ'Σ, ά, όν, *grim, stern*: also *burly, manly, valiant*, or *coarse, rough*.

βλοσῠρ-ῶπις, *ιδος*, ἡ, (*βλοσυρός*, *ὤψ*) *grim-looking*.

ΒΛΥ'ΖΩ, f. *βλύσω* [ῠ] aor. 1 *ἔβλῠσα*, = *βλύω*. Hence

βλύσις, *εως*, ἡ, and **βλυσμός**, ο, *a bubbling up*.

βλύσσειε, poët. for *βλύσαι*, 3 sing. opt. aor. 1 of *βλύζω*.

ΒΛΥ'Ω, f. *βλύσω* [ῡ], *to bubble, spout*, or *gush forth*: hence *to be full, to be haughty*.

βλῶμαι, aor. 2 med. subj. of *βάλλω*.

βλωθρός, ά, όν, (*βλώσκω*) *shooting up, high growing*, of trees.

βλώσκω: (tenses formed from Root ΜΟ'ΛΩ), f. *μολοῦμαι*, aor. 2 *ἔμολον* (cf. *θρώσκω*, *θοροῦμαι*, *ἔθορον*): pf. *μέμβλωκα* (for *μεμόλωκα*):—*to come* or *go*.

βοάγριον, τό, *a shield of wild bull's hide*. From

βό-αγρος, ἡ, (*βοῦς*, *ἄγριος*) *a wild bull*.

βοα-θόος, Dor. for *βοηθόος*.

βόᾱμα, *ατος*, τό, (*βοάω*) *a shriek, cry*: *a loud strain*.

βοάτης, *ου*, ὁ, fem. **βοᾶτις**, *ιδος*, ἡ, (*βοάω*) *crying, screaming*. [ᾱ]

βό-αυλος, ὁ, **βό-αυλον**, τό, (*βοῦς*, *αὐλή*) *an ox-stall*.

βοάω, Ep. 3 sing. *βοάᾳ*, 3 pl. *βοόωσιν*, part. *βοόων*: f. *βοήσω*, Att. *βοήσομαι*, Ion. contr. *βώσω*, *βώσομαι*: aor. 1 *ἐβόησα*, Ion. *ἔβωσα*: pf. *βεβόηκα*:—Med., aor. 1 *ἐβοησάμην* Ion. *ἐβωσάμην*:—Pass., aor. 1 *ἐβοήθην* Ion. *ἐβώσθην*: pf. *βεβόημαι* Ion. *βέβωμαι*: (*βοή*) :—*to utter a cry* from joy or grief, *to shout*: of things, *to thunder, roar, howl*: *to echo*. II. trans., c. acc. pers. *to call to* one, *call on*: *to call to aid*. 2. *to demand in a loud voice*. 3. *to noise abroad, proclaim*.

βοεικός, ή, όν, (βοῦς) *of* or *for oxen; ζεύγη βοεικά* wagons *drawn by oxen.*

βόειος or **βόεος**, α, ον, (βοῦς) *of an ox* or *of oxen, of ox-hide:* ἡ βοεία or βοέα, contr. βοῆ, (sub. δορά), *an ox-hide, a shield of ox-hide.*

βοεύς, έως, ὁ, (βοῦς) *a thong* or *cord of ox-leather.*

βοῆ, ἡ, contr. from βοέη, v. βόειος.

ΒΟΗ', ἡ, *a cry, shout,* whether of joy or grief: *the battle-cry, the battle itself; βοὴν ἀγαθός,* good *at the battle-cry* or *in battle:* also of *the roar* of the sea. II. = *βοήθεια aid called for, succour.*

βοη-γενής, ές, (βοῦς, γενέσθαι) *born of an ox.*

βοηδρομέω, (βοηδρόμος) *to run on bearing a cry, haste to help, succour.*

Βοη-δρομιών, ῶνος, ὁ, *the third Attic month,* in which the Βοηδρόμια were celebrated, in memory of the conquest of the Amazons by Theseus; answering to the latter half of September and beginning of October.

βοη-δρόμος, ον, (βοή, δρόμος) *running to aid:* as Subst. *a helper.*

βοήθεια, ἡ, (βοηθός) *help, aid, rescue, support.* II. *an auxiliary force.*

βοηθέω, Ion. **βωθέω**, f. ήσω, (βοηθός) *to assist, succour, come to the rescue.* Hence

βοηθητέον, verb. Adj. *one must assist.*

βοηθητικός, ή, όν, (βοηθέω) *ready* or *able to help.*

βοη-θόος, ον, (βοή, θέω) *hasting to the battle-shout, warlike; βοήθοον ἅρμα* a chariot *hasting to the battle.*

βοηθός, όν, contr. from βοηθόος: as Subst., βοηθός, ὁ, *an assistant, auxiliary, ally.*

βοηλᾰσία, ἡ, *a driving of oxen, cattle-lifting, cattle-stealing.* II. *a place where oxen feed, a pasture.* From

βο-ηλάτης, ου, ὁ, fem. **βοηλάτις**, ιδος, ἡ, (βοῦς, ἐλαύνω) *one that drives away oxen, a cattle-stealer.* II. *a drover.*

βοη-νόμος, ον, = βουνόμος.

βόης, ου, ὁ, (βοάω) *a crier.*

βόησις, εως, Ion. **βοητύς**, ύος, ἡ, (βοάω) *a crying, shouting:* esp. *a cry for assistance.*

ΒΟ'ΘΡΟΣ, ὁ, *a pit* or *hole dug in the ground, a trench,* Lat. *puteus.*

βόθῡνος, ὁ, = βόθρος.

βοιδάριον, τό, Dim. of βοῦς.

βοίδιον, τό, Dim. of βοῦς, *a young cow* or *ox.*

Βοιωταρχέω, f. ήσω, *to be a Boeotarch.* From

Βοιωτ-άρχης, ου, ὁ, (Βοιωτός, ἄρχω) *a Boeotarch,* one of the chief magistrates of Boeotia. Hence

Βοιωτ-αρχία, ἡ, *the office of Boeotarch.*

Βοιωτία, ἡ, *Boeotia,* so called from its rich *cattle-pastures.* Hence

Βοιωτιάζω and **Βοιωτίζω**, *to be like a Boeotian: to be heavy, dull: to speak Boeotian.* II. *to side with the Boeotians.*

Βοιωτίδιον, τό, Dim. of **Βοιωτός**, *a little Boeotian.*

Βοιωτός, οῦ, ὁ, *a Boeotian.*

Βοιωτι-ουργής, ές, (Βοιωτία, ἔργον) *of Boeotian work.*

ΒΟΛΒΟ'Σ, ὁ, Lat. *BULBUS, a bulb, bulbous root.*

βολή, ἡ, (βάλλω) *a throw, stroke, the wound of a missile:*—metaph. *a glance:*—βολαὶ ἡλίου sun-*beams.*

βολίζω, f. σω, (βολίς) *to heave the lead, sound.*

βολίς, ίδος, ἡ, (βάλλω) *anything thrown, a missile: the sounding-lead.* II. *a cast of the dice.*

βολίτινος, η, ον, *of cow-dung.* From

βόλῐτον, **βόλῐτος**, (βόλος) *cow-dung.*

βόλλομαι and **βόλομαι**, Aeol. for βούλομαι.

βολο-κτυπία, ἡ, (βόλος, κτυπέω) *the rattling of the dice.*

βόλος, ὁ, (βάλλω) *a throw with a casting-net:* also *the thing caught; βόλος ἰχθύων a draught of fishes.* II. *a throw with dice.*

βομβ-αύλιος, ὁ, (βόμβος, αὐλός) *a bagpiper.*

βομβεῦντι, Aeol. for βομβοῦσι, 3 pl. of βομβέω.

βομβέω, f. ήσω, (βόμβος) *to make a humming noise, to sound deep* or *hollow: to hum, buzz.*

βομβήεις, εσσα, εν, (βομβέω) *buzzing, humming.*

βομβητής, οῦ, ὁ, (βομβέω) *a buzzer, hummer.*

ΒΟ'ΜΒΟΣ, ὁ, Lat. *BOMBUS, any deep hollow sound, humming, buzzing.* (Formed from the sound.)

βομβυλιός, οῦ, ὁ, and ἡ, (βόμβος) *a buzzing* or *humming insect, a humble bee.*

βόμβυξ, ῡκος, ὁ, *the silk-worm.*

βοο-θύτης, ου, ὁ, = βουθύτης.

βοο-κτᾰσία, ἡ, (βοῦς, κτείνω) *a slaying of oxen.*

βοο-νόμος, βοο-σφαγία, etc., = βου—.

βοο-σφᾰγία, ἡ, (βοῦς, σφάζω) *a slaying of oxen.*

βοόω, Ep. for βοάω.

ΒΟΡΑ', ἡ, *food, meat.*

βορβορό-θῡμος, ον, (βόρβορος, θυμός) *muddy-minded.*

ΒΟ'ΡΒΟΡΟΣ, ὁ, *slime, mud, mire,* Lat. *coenum.*

βορβορο-τάραξις, ὁ, (βόρβορος, ταράσσω) *a mud-stirrer, mud-lark.*

βορβορ-ώδης, ες, (βόρβορος, εἶδος) *miry, slimy.*

ΒΟΡΕ'ΑΣ, ου, ὁ; Ion. **Βορέης**, contr. **Βορῆς**, έω; Att. **Βορρᾶς**, ᾶ:—*the North wind:* more strictly, the wind from NNE., *Aquilo.* II. *the North, πρὸς βορῆν ἄνεμον* towards *the North; πρὸς βορέαν τινὸς northward* of a place.

Βορεάς, άδος, ἡ, Ion. **Βορειάς**, poët. **Βορεϊάς**, **Βορηΐς**, *a Boread, daughter of Boreas.* II. fem. Adj. *northern.*

Βόρειος, α, ον, also ος, ον, (Βορέας) *belonging to the North wind, northern.*

Βορεῶτις, ίδος, ἡ, = Βορεάς.

Βορήϊος, η, ον, Ion. for Βόρειος.

Βορηΐς, ΐδος, ἡ, = Βορεάς.

βορός, ά, όν, (βορά) *devouring, gluttonous.*

Βορραῖος, α, ον, or ος, ον, = Βόρειος.

Βορρᾶς, ᾶ, ὁ, Att. for Βορέας.

βόρυες, οἱ, unknown Libyan animals.

βόσις, εως, ἡ, (βόσκω) *food, fodder.*

βόσκε, Ep. 3 sing. impf. of βόσκω.

βοσκή or **βόσκη**, ἡ, (βόσκω) *food, fodder.*

βόσκημα, ατος, τό, (βόσκω) *that which is fed* or *fatted, cattle: a herd of cattle* or *sheep.* II *food.*

βοσκητέον, verb. Adj. of βόσκω, *one must feed.*

βοσκός, ὁ, *the feeder* or *herd of the cattle.* From
ΒΟ'ΣΚΩ: fut. *βοσκήσω*. as if from obsol. *βοσκέω*:—Act. of the herdsman, Lat. *pascere, to feed, drive to pasture. nourish, support, maintain*:—Pass., of cattle, Lat. *pasci, to feed, graze.*

Βοσπόριος, α. ον, *of the Bosphorus.*

βόσ-πορος, ὁ, (*βοῦς, πόρος*) *Bosphorus*, i. e. *ox-ford*, name of several straits, esp. the Thracian and Cimmerian.

βόστρυξ, ῠχος. ὁ = *βόστρῠχος*,

βοστρύχιον, τό, Dim. of *βόστρῠχος*.

ΒΟ'ΣΤΡΥΧΟΣ, ὁ, in plur. also *βόστρυχα, τά, a curl* or *lock of hair*: poët., *anything twisted* or *wreathed*. as *a flash of lightning, the tendril of a vine.*

βοτάμια, ων, τά, (*βόσκω*) *pastures.*

βοτάνη, ή, (*βόσκω*) *pasture. grass, fodder.*

βοτήρ, ῆρος, ὁ, (*βόσκω*) *a herdsman, herd; οἰωνῶν βοτήρ a watcher* of birds, *a soothsayer: κύων βοτήρ a herdsman's dog.*

βοτηρικός. ή, όν, (*βοτήρ*) *of* or *for a herdsman.*

βοτόν, τό, (*βόσκω*) *anything that is fed, a beast.*

βοτρῡδόν Adv. (*βότρυς*) *like a bunch of grapes, in clusters.*

βοτρυΐος, α, ον, (*βότρυς*) *of grapes.*

βοτρυό-δωρος, ον, (*βότρυς, δῶρον*) *grape-producing.*

βοτρυόεις, εσσα, εν, (*βότρυς*) *clustering.*

βοτρυό-παις. παιδος, ὁ, ή, (*βότρυς, παῖς*) *child of the grape*

βοτρυο-χαίτης. ου. ὁ, (*βότρυς, χαίτη*) *with clustering hair*; or *with grapes in one's hair.*

ΒΟ'ΤΡΥΣ, υος, ὁ, *a cluster* or *bunch of grapes.* Lat. *racemus* II. — *βότρυχος, βόστρυχος, a curl.*

βότρῠχος, ὁ, = *βόστρυχος.*

βότρυχ-ώδης. ες. (*βότρυχος, εἶδος*) *like curls, curly.*

βότρυ-ώδης. ες, (*βότρυς, εἶδος*) *like a cluster of grapes*

βου-. a form of *βοῦς* used in compos. to express something *monstrous*, e. g. *βού-παις, βου-φάγος*; as we say *horse-chestnut, horse-radish*, etc.

ΒΟΥ'ΒΑ'ΛΙΣ, ιος, ή, *an antelope.*

ΒΟΥ'ΒΑΛΟΣ, ὁ, Lat. *bubălus, a buffalo.*

βου-βότης. ου. ὁ, (*βοῦς, βόσκω*) *feeding cattle*: as Subst., *βουβότης*, ου, *a cowherd.*

βου-βότος, ον, (*βοῦς, βόσκομαι*) *grazed by cattle*

βού-βρωστις. εως. ή, (*βου-, βιβρώσκω*) *a ravenous unnatural appetite*: metaph. *grinding poverty* or *misery*

ΒΟΥΒΩ'Ν, ῶνος. ὁ, *the groin*, Lat. *inguen.* Hence

βουβωνιάω *to suffer from swollen groins.*

βου-γάϊος, ὁ, (*βου-, γαίω*) *a braggart, bully.* [ᾱ]

βου-δόρος, ον, (*βοῦς, δέρω*) *flaying oxen: galling* II. as Subst. *a knife for flaying.*

βου-θερής, ές, (*βοῦς. θέρω*) *giving summer pasture: summer-feeding.*

βου-θοίνης, ου, ὁ, (*βοῦς, θοινάω*) *beef-eater.*

βουθῠσία, ή, *a sacrifice of oxen.* From

βουθυτέω, *to slay, sacrifice oxen*: generally, *to sacrifice* or *slaughter.* From

βού-θῠτος, ον, (*βοῦς, θύω*) *of* or *belonging to sacrifices: sacrificial.*

βουκαῖος, ὁ, (*βοῦκος*) *one who ploughs with oxen.*

βού-κερως, ων, gen. *βούκερω*, acc. pl. *βούκερως*, (*βοῦς, κέρας*) *horned like an ox*:—for the accent see Wordsw. Gk. Gr. p. 140.

βου-κέφᾰλος, ον, (*κεφαλή*) *bull-headed*: epith. of horses, because *branded with a bull's head*: Maced. **βουκεφάλας**, gen. α, name of the horse of Alexander the Great.

βουκολέω, f. ήσω, (*βουκόλος*) *to tend cattle*:—Med. *to graze, range over the pasture.* II metaph. *to delude, beguile*: Med., *ἐλπίδι βουκολοῦμαι I feed myself* on hopes, *cheat myself* with them.

βουκολία, ή, (*βουκόλος*) *a herd of cattle.* II. *a byre, ox-stall.* Hence

βουκολιάζομαι, Dor. **βωκ-**, f. *άξομαι, to sing* or *write pastorals.* Hence

βουκολιαστής, οῦ, ὁ Dor. **βωκ-**, *a singer* or *maker of pastorals.*

βουκολικός, ή, όν, Dor. **βωκολικός**, ά, όν, (*βουκόλος*) *rustic, pastoral*: τὰ *βουκολικά* (sc. *ποιήματα*) *pastoral poetry.*

βουκόλιον, τό, *a herd of cattle.* From

βου-κόλος, Dor. **βω-κόλος**, ὁ, (*βοῦς*, and obsol. *κολέω* = Lat. *colo*) *a cowherd: herdsman.*

βοῦκος, Dor. **βῶκος**, ὁ, (*βοῦς*) = *βουκαῖος.*

βουλαῖος, α, ον, (*βουλή*) *of* or *in the Council.*

βουλ-άρχος, ὁ, (*βουλή, ἄρχω*) *the adviser of a plan*, Lat. *auctor consilii.*

βουλεία, ή, (*βουλεύω*) *the office of counsellor.*

βούλευμα, ατος, τό, (*βουλεύω*) *a decree of the Council*: generally, *a resolution, plan, design.*

βουλευμάτιον, τό, Dim. of *βούλευμα.*

βούλευσις, εως, ή, (*βουλεύω*) *deliberation.*

βουλευτέον, verb. Adj. of *βουλεύω*, *one must take counsel.*

βουλευτήρ, ῆρος, ὁ, = *βουλευτής.* Hence

βουλευτήριος, ον, *fit for counsel.* II. as Subst. *βουλευτήριον*, τό, *a Council-chamber, court-house.*

βουλευτής, οῦ, ὁ, (*βουλεύω*) *a councillor, one who sits in Council.* II. *a counsellor, adviser.* Hence

βουλευτικός, ή, όν, *of* or *for the Council* or *a Councillor*; *ὅρκος βουλευτικός* the oath *taken by the councillors.* 2. as Subst., *τὸ βουλευτικόν* in the Athenian theatre, the seats next the orchestra, *belonging to the Council of* 500. II. *of or for a counsellor, able to advise.*

βουλευτός, ή, όν, *devised, plotted.* From

βουλεύω, f. σω: pf. *βεβούλευκα*:—Med., fut. *-εύσομαι*: aor. 1 *ἐβουλευσάμην*:—Pass., aor. 1 *ἐβουλεύθην*: pf. *βεβούλευμαι*: but fut. med. is also used in pass. sense; and aor. 1 and pf. pass. in med. sense, (*βουλή*):—*to take counsel, consider*: in past tenses, *to have considered*, and so *to determine* or *resolve upon* a thing: Med. *to take counsel with oneself*, and so much like the Act.:—Pass. *to be determined* or *resolved on.* II. *to be a member of the Council: to give counsel.*

βουλή, ἡ, (βούλομαι) *will, determination*, Lat. *consilium*:—*a project, plan, intention*. 2. *counsel, advice*, whether taken or given. II. also like Lat. *concilium, the Council* or *Senate*, esp. that of the 500 at Athens.

βούληαι, Ep. for βούλῃ, 2 sing. subj. of βούλομαι.

βουλήεις, εσσα, εν, (βουλή) *of good counsel, sage.*

βουληθείς, part. aor. 1 of βούλομαι.

βούλημα, ατος, τό, (βούλομαι) *a will, purpose.*

βούλησις, εως, ἡ, (βούλομαι) *a willing: will, purpose.*

βουλήσομαι, fut. of βούλομαι.

βουλη-φόρος, ον, (βουλή, φέρω) *counselling, advising.*

βου-λῑμία, ἡ, (βου-, λιμός) *ravenous hunger.* Hence

βουλῑμιάω, f. άσω, *to suffer from ravenous hunger.*

βούλιος, ον, (βουλή) = βουλευτικός.

ΒΟΥ´ΛΟΜΑΙ: impf. ἐβουλόμην, Att. also ἠβουλόμην: fut. βουλήσομαι: aor. 1 ἐβουλήθην, Att. also ἠβουλήθην: pf. βεβούλημαι, in compos. also med. βέβουλα (προ): Dep.:—*to will, wish, be willing*: usu. c. inf., but also c. dat., Τρώεσσιν ἐβούλετο νίκην *be willed* victory to the Trojans, or in full, Τρώεσσιν ἐβούλετο κῦδος ὀρέξαι. Βούλει or βούλεσθε, with the subj. adds force to the demand, βούλει φράσω *would you have* me tell; ὁ βουλόμενος, Lat. *quivis*, the first that offers, *any one that likes*. II. *to have rather, choose, prefer*, mostly with ἤ, as, βούλομ' ἐγὼ λαὸν σόον ἔμμεναι, ἢ ἀπολέσθαι *I had rather* the host were saved than lost.

βουλό-μᾰχος, ον, (βούλομαι, μάχη) *strife-desiring.*

βουλύσιος, ον, *fit for unyoking the oxen*, [ῡ]. From

βου-λῡτός, ὁ, (βοῦς, λύω) *the time for unyoking oxen, evening*: in Homer only as Adv., βουλῡτόνδε *towards evening, at eventide.*

βου-μολγός, ὁ, (βοῦς, ἀμέλγω) *cow-milking.*

βουνίτης, ου, ὁ, (βουνός) *a dweller on hills.*

βου-νόμος, ον, (βοῦς, νέμω) *cattle-feeding.* II. **βού-νομος**, *grazed by cattle;* ἀγέλαι βούνομαι herds *of grazing oxen.*

ΒΟΥΝΟ´Σ, ὁ, *a hill, mound.*

βού-παις, παιδος, ὁ, (βου-, παῖς) *a big, lubberly boy.* 2. of bees, *born of the ox;* see Virg. Georg. 4. 281.

βού-παλις, εως, ὁ, ἡ, (βου-, πάλη) *hard-struggling.*

βου-πάμων, ον, gen. ονος, (βοῦς, πέπᾱμαι pf. of πάομαι) *rich in cattle.*

βού-πληκτρος, ον, (βοῦς, πλῆκτρον) *ox-goading.*

βου-πλήξ, ῆγος, ὁ, ἡ, (βοῦς, πλήσσω) *an ox-goad: an axe for felling an ox.*

βου-ποίμην, ενος, ὁ, (βοῦς, ποιμήν) *a herdsman.*

βου-πόρος, ον, (βοῦς, πείρω) *ox-piercing;* βουπόρος ὀβελός a spit *that would spit a whole ox.*

βού-πρῳρος, ον, (βοῦς, πρῷρα) *with the face of an ox.*

ΒΟΥ´Σ, ὁ or ἡ: gen. βοός, also poët. βοῦ: acc. βοῦν, Ep. βῶν, poët. also βόα:—plur., nom. βόες, rarely contr. βοῦς. gen. βοῶν, rarely contr. βῶν: dat βουσί, poët. βόεσσι, rarely βοσί:—*a bullock* or *cow. an ox;* in plur. *cattle.* II. βοῦς, ἡ, *a shield covered with ox-hide.* III. proverb., βοῦς ἐπὶ γλώσσῃ βέβηκε, βοῦς ἐπὶ γλώσσης ἐπιβαίνει, like ὗς ἐπὶ στόμα, of people who keep silence from some *weighty* reason, from the notion of a heavy body keeping down the tongue.

βοῦς, contr. from βόας, acc. pl. of foreg.

βού-σταθμον, τό, (βοῦς, σταθμός) *an ox-stall.*

βου-στάσις, εως, ἡ, = foreg.

βου-στροφηδόν, Adv. (βοῦς, στροφή) *turning like oxen in ploughing:* of the early Greek manner of writing, which went from left to right, and right to left alternately. So Solon's Laws were written.

βου-στρόφος, ον, (βοῦς, στρέφω) *ox-guiding*:—as Subst. *an ox-goad.*

βου-σφᾰγέω, (βοῦς, σφάζω) *to slaughter oxen.*

βούτᾰλις, ιος, ἡ, *a night bird.*

βούτης, ου, ὁ, (βοῦς) *a cow-herd, herdsman.*

βου-φάγος, ον, (βοῦς, φᾰγεῖν) *ox-eating.*

βουφονέω, f. ήσω, (βουφόνος) *to slaughter oxen.*

βουφονία (sub. ἱερά), τά, *a festival with sacrifices of oxen.* From

βου-φόνος, ον, (βοῦς, φόνος) *ox-sacrificing.* 2. *at which oxen are slain.*

βουφορβέω, f. ήσω, (βουφορβός) *to tend cattle.*

βουφόρβια, ων, τά, *a herd of oxen.* From

βου-φορβός, όν, (βοῦς, φέρβω) *ox-feeding*:—as Subst. **βουφορβός**, ὁ, *a herdsman.*

~~**βού-φορτος**, ον, (βου-, φόρτος) *with a great load.*~~

βου-χανδής, ές, (βοῦς, χανδάνω) *holding an ox.*

βού-χῑλος, ον, (βοῦς, χιλός) *rich in fodder.*

βοῶν, contr. part. of βοάω. 2. gen. pl. of βοῦς.

βο-ώνης, ου, ὁ, (βοῦς, ὠνέομαι) *one who buys oxen* for sacrifice.

βο-ῶπις, ιδος, ἡ, (βοῦς, ὤψ) *ox-eyed*, i. e. *with large, full eyes.*

βοωτέω, f. ήσω, *to plough.* From

βοώτης, ου, ὁ, (βοῦς) *a ploughman.* II. *Boötes*, a name of the constellation Arcturus.

βρᾰβεία, ἡ, (βραβεύω) *the office of judge* or *umpire, presidency of the games:* generally, *arbitration.*

βρᾰβεῖον, τό, (βραβεύω) *a prize in the games.*

ΒΡΑΒΕΥ´Σ, έως, ὁ: Att. acc. sing. βραβῆ, nom. plur. βραβῆς:—*the judge who assigned the prizes at the games:* generally, *a judge, arbitrator, umpire: a chief, leader.*

βρᾰβεύω, f. σω, (βραβεύς) *to be a judge* or *umpire: to arbitrate, direct, govern.*

βράβῦλον, τό, *a kind of plum* or *sloe.*

βράβῦλος, ἡ, the tree which bears βράβυλα.

ΒΡΑΓΧΟΣ, ὁ, *hoarseness, sore throat.* Hence

βραγχός, ή, όν, *hoarse.*

βραδέως, Adv. of βραδύς, *slowly.*

βρᾰδῐνός, ά, όν, Aeol. for ῥαδινός.

βραδίων [ῐ], **βράδιστος**, poët. Comp. and Sup. of βραδύς.

βράδος, εος, τό, (βραδύς) *slowness.*

βρᾰδύνω, f. ὑνῶ, (βραδύς) *to delay*:—Pass. *to be delayed.* II. intrans. *to be slow* about a thing:—Med. *to be slow, to loiter.*

βραδυ-πειθής, *ές*, (*βραδύς*, *πείθομαι*) *slow of persuasion, slow to believe.*

βραδυ-πλοέω, f. *ήσω*, (*βραδύς*, *πλέω*) *to sail slowly.*

βραδύ-πους, *ὁ*, *ἡ*, *πουν*, *τό*, gen. *ποδος*, (*βραδύς*, *πούς*) *slow of foot.*

ΒΡΑΔΥ'Σ, *εῖα*, *ύ*: Comp. *βραδύτερος* by poët. metath. *βαρδύτερος*, poët. also *βραδίων* [ῑ] and *βράσσων*: Sup. *βραδύτατος*, poët. *βράδιστος*, and by metath. *βάρδιστος*: *slow, heavy; βάρδιστοι θείειν slowest at* running.—metaph. *slow of understanding, slow.* II. of time, *late.*

βραδυ-σκελής, *ές*, (*βραδύς*, *σκέλος*) *slow of foot.*

βραδῠτής, *ῆτος*, *ἡ*, (*βραδύς*) *slowness: dullness.*

βράκος, *τό*, Aeol. for *ῥάκος*, *a rich female garment.*

βρασθείς, aor. 1 pass. part. of *βράζω*.

ΒΡΑ'ΣΣΩ, Att. **βράττω**: f. *βράσω* [ᾰ]: aor. 1 *ἔβρασα*:—Pass., aor. 1 *ἐβράσθην*: pf. *βέβρασμαι*:—*to shake violently, to throw up*, of the sea: *to winnow* or *sift* grain:—Pass. *to boil up.*

βράσσων, *ον*, gen. *ονος*, poët. Comp. of *βραδύς*.

βράχε, see *βράχω*.

βρᾰ ίς, *εῖσα*, *έν*, aor. 2 pass. part. of *βρέχω*.

βρᾰχέως, Adv. of *βραχύς*, *shortly.*

βρᾰχίων, *ονος*, *ὁ*, (*βραχύς*) *the arm*, Lat. *brachium.* [ῑ]

βρᾰχίων, *ον*, gen. *ονος*, [Ion. ῐ, Att. ῑ], **βράχιστος**, Comp. and Sup. of *βραχύς*.

βράχος, *εος*, *τό*, plur. *βράχεα*, contr. *βράχη*, (*βραχύς*) *shallow, stagnant pools*, Lat. *brevia et syrtes.*

βραχύ-βωλος, *ον*, (*βραχύς*, *βῶλος*) *with few clods*, *βραχύβωλος χέρσος a narrow* piece of land.

βρᾰχῠ-γνώμων, *ον*, gen. *ονος*, (*βραχύς*, *γνώμη*) *of small understanding.*

βραχύ-δρομος, *ον*, (*βραχύς*, *δρόμος*) *running a short way.*

βραχυλογία, *ἡ*, *brevity in speech.* From

βραχυ-λόγος, *ον*, (*βραχύς*, *λέγω*) *short in speech, of few words.*

βραχύνω, f. *ῠνῶ*, *to make short.* From

ΒΡΑ˘ΧΥ'Σ, *εῖα*, *ύ*: Comp. *βραχύτερος* and *βραχίων*: Sup. *βραχύτατος* and *βράχιστος*:—of Space and Time, *short;* of Number and Degree, *few, little: βραχύ, a little, a short time* or *distance; ἐπὶ βραχύ for a short distance; κατὰ βραχύ little by little; ἐν βραχεῖ shortly, briefly; διὰ βραχέων in few words*, Lat. *brevibus, paucis; διὰ βραχυτάτων* or *ἐν βραχυτάτοις*, Lat. *quam brevissime.*

βραχυ-σίδηρος, *ον*, (*βραχύς*, *σίδηρος*): *ἄκων βραχυσίδηρος*) *a dart with a short, small head.*

βραχυ-σκελής, *ές*, (*βραχύς*, *σκέλος*) *short-legged.*

βραχυ-σύμβολος, *ον*, (*βραχύς*, *σύμβολον*) *bringing a small contribution.*

βραχύ-τονος, *ον*, (*βραχύς*, *τείνω*) *reaching a short way.*

βραχυ-τράχηλος, *ον*, (*βραχύς*, *τράχηλος*) *short-necked.*

βραχύτης, *ητος*, *ἡ*, (*βραχύς*) *shortness: scantiness, deficiency.*

βραχυ-φεγγίτης, *ου*, *ὁ*, (*βραχύς*, *φέγγος*) *giving a short* or *scant light.* [ῑ]

βραχύ-φυλλος, *ον*, (*βραχύς*, *φύλλον*) *with few leaves.*

***ΒΡΑ˘ΧΩ**, only used in 3 sing. aor. 2 *ἔβραχε* or *βράχε*, *to rattle, clash, ring, roar.*

βρέγμα, *ατος*, *τό*, (*βρέχω*) *the top of the head*, Lat. *sinciput.*

βρεκεκεκέξ, sound to imitate *the croaking of frogs.*

ΒΡΕ'ΜΩ, only used in pres. and impf., the Lat. *FREMO*, *to roar*, of the wave or wind; *to clash*, of arms; *to roar, clamour*, of a crowd. Also in Med.

ΒΡΕ'ΝΘΟΣ, *ὁ*, *an unknown water-bird*, of stately bearing: hence II. *arrogance.* Hence

βρενθύομαι, Dep., only used in pres. and impf., *to be of a proud carriage, hold one's head high, swagger.*

βρέξις, *εως*, *ἡ*, (*βρέχω*) *a wetting.*

ΒΡΕ'ΤΑΣ, *τό*, gen. *βρέτεος*, nom. pl. *βρέτη*, *a wooden image of a god.*

ΒΡΕ'ΦΟΣ, *εος*, *τό*, *the child unborn*, Lat. *foetus*, = *ἔμβρυον.* II. *the new-born babe, whelp* or *cub.*

βρεχμός, *ὁ*, = *βρέγμα*.

ΒΡΕ'ΧΩ, f. *ξω*: aor. 1 *ἔβρεξα*:—Pass., aor. 1 *ἐβρέχθην*: aor. 2 *ἐβράχθην* [ᾰ]: pf. *βέβρεγμαι*:—*to wet on the surface, moisten, sprinkle*, opp. to *τέγγω*:—Pass. *to be wetted* or *drenched.* 2. impers. *βρέχει*, like *ὕει*, Lat. *pluit, it rains.*

ΒΡΙ–, [ῐ], insepar. intensive Prefix, whence come *βριάω*, *βριαρός*.

Βρῐάρεως, *ὁ*, *Strong*, a hundred-handed giant, so called by the gods, but by men Aegaeon. [In Ep., trisyll. Βρῐάρ'ως.]

βρῐᾰρός, *ά*, *όν*, Ion. **βριερός**, *ή*, *όν*, (*βριάω*) *strong.*

βρῐάω, (*βρι–*) *to strengthen, to make strong.* II. intr. *to be strong.*

ΒΡΙ'ΖΩ, fut. *ξω*, *to nod, slumber, sleep.*

βρῐ-ήπῠος, *ον*, (*βρι–*, *ἀπύω*) *loud shouting.*

βρῖθος, *εος*, *τό*, (*βρίθω*) *weight.*

βρῑθοσύνη, *ἡ*, (*βρῖθος*) *weight, heaviness.*

βρῑθύ-νοος, *ον*, (*βριθύς*, *νόος*) *grave-minded, thoughtful.*

βρῑθύς, *εῖα*, *ύ*, (*βρίθω*) *weighty, heavy.*

ΒΡΙ'ΘΩ, f. *βρίσω*, Ep. inf. *βρίσεμεν*: aor. 1 *ἔβρῑσα*: perf. *βέβρῑθα*:—*to be heavy, to be weighed down* or *heavy laden* with a thing:—Med., *μήκων καρπῷ βριθομένη* a poppy *laden* with fruit;—*ἔρις βεβρῖθυῖα*, Ep. for *βεβρῑθυῖα*, *weighty* strife. 2. of men, *to outweigh, prevail: to be superior in the fight, to be master.* II. trans. *to load, press.*

βρῑμάομαι and **βρῑμόομαι**, Dep. *to snort with anger, be wrathful, furious.* (Formed from the sound.)

βρῑσ-άρματος, *ον*, (*βρίθω*, *ἅρμα*) *loading the car.*

ΒΡΟΤΧΟΣ, *ὁ*, *the windpipe, trachea.*

βρομέω, = *βρέμω*, *to buzz, hum*, of gnats.

βρομιάζομαι, Dep. *to revel like Bacchus.* From

βρόμιος, *α*, *ον*, (*βρόμος*) *roaring, boisterous*:—hence *ὁ Βρόμιος*, *the boisterous god*, a name of Bacchus. 2. = *Βάκχειος*, *Bacchic.*

Βρομι-ώδης, *ες*, (*Βρόμος*, *εἶδος*) *Bacchic.*

βρόμος, *ὁ*, (*βρέμω*) Lat. *fremitus*, *any loud noise* or *roaring*, as of fire, etc.

βροντάω, f. ήσω, *to thunder*: βροντᾷ, impers., *it thunders*, Lat. *tonat*. From

ΒΡΟΝΤΗ', ἡ, *thunder*. II. *the state of one struck with thunder, astonishment*.

βρόντημα, ατος, τό, (βροντάω) *a thunder-clap*.

Βρόντης, ου, ὁ, (βροντή) *Thunderer*, name of one of the Cyclopes, who forged the bolts of Zeus.

βροντησι-κέραυνος, ον, (βροντάω, κεραυνός) *sending thunder and lightning*.

βροντ-ώδης, ες, (βροντή, εἶδος) *thundering*.

βρότειος, ον, also α, ον, Ep. **βρότεος**, η, ον, (βροτός) *mortal, human*.—So also **βροτήσιος**, α, ον.

βροτο-βάμων, ον, (βροτός, βῆμα) *trampling on men*. [ῑ]

βροτό-γηρυς, υ, gen. υος, (βροτός, γῆρυς) *with human voice*, of a parrot.

βροτόεις, εσσα, εν, (βροτός) *bloody, gory*.

βροτοκτονέω, f. ήσω, *to murder men*. From

βροτο-κτόνος, ον, (βροτός, κτείνω) *man-slaying*.

βροτο-λοιγός, όν, (βροτός, λοιγός) *bane of men*.

ΒΡΟΤΟ'Σ, ὁ, *a mortal, man*, opp. to ἀθάνατος or θεός: as Adj. *mortal*.

ΒΡΟ'ΤΟΣ, ὁ, *blood from a wound, gore*.

βροτο-σκόπος, ον, (βροτός, σκοπέω) *watching men*.

βροτο-στῠγής, ές, (βροτός, στυγέω) *man-hating*. II. pass. *hated by men*.

βροτο-φεγγής, ές, (βροτός, φέγγος) *giving light to men*.

βροτο-φθόρος, ον, (βροτός, φθείρω) *man-destroying*.

βροτόω, (βρότος) *to stain with gore*.

βροχετός, ὁ, (βρέχω) *a wetting, rain*.

βροχέως, Aeol. for βραχέως.

ΒΡΟ'ΧΘΟΣ, ὁ, *the throat*.

βροχίς, ἡ, (βρέχω) *an ink-horn*.

ΒΡΟ'ΧΟΣ, ὁ, *a noose* or *slip-knot, for hanging* or *strangling; a snare for birds; the mesh of a net*.

***ΒΡΟ'ΧΩ**, aor. 1 ἔβροξα, *to gulp down*: cp. ἀναβρύχω, καταβρύχω.

βρῠάζω, (βρύω) *to teem with plenty, overflow*.

βρύγδην, Adv. (βρύκω) *snarling* or *with clenched teeth*.

βρυγμός, ὁ, (βρύχω) *a snarling, biting: a grinding* or *gnashing of teeth*.

ΒΡΥ'ΚΩ, f. ξω: aor. 1 ἔβρυξα: *to bite, devour*. Cf. βρύχω. [ῡ]

ΒΡΥ'ΛΛΩ, = βρῦν εἰπεῖν, v. sq.

βρῦν, **βρῦν εἰπεῖν** to cry *for drink*.

βρύξ, only in acc. βρύχα, *the depth of the sea*.

βρῡχάομαι, fut. med. βρυχήσομαι, aor. 1 pass. ἐβρυχήθην: Ep. pf. βέβρῡχα (so μέμηκα, μέμυκα from μηκάομαι, μυκάομαι): Dep.: (βρύχω):—*to roar, howl, bellow*, Lat. *rugire*. Hence

βρύχημα, ατος, τό, *a roaring*: and

βρῡχητής, οῦ, ὁ, *a bellower, howler*.

βρύχιος, ον, also α, ον, (βρύξ) *from the depths of the sea*, βρυχία ἠχώ an echo *from the deep*. [ῠ]

ΒΡΥ'ΧΩ, fut. βρύξω: aor. 2 ἔβρῠχον:—Pass., aor. 1 ἐβρύχθην:—the same as βρύκω. [ῡ]

ΒΡΥ'Ω, mostly in pres. and impf.; rare in fut. βρύσω:—*to be full of* anything, *swell* or *teem with*. II. trans. *to cause to burst forth*.

βρῶμα, ατος, τό, (βιβρώσκω) *that which is eaten, food*.

βρωμάομαι, aor. 1 ἐβρωμησάμην: Dep.: (βρέμω):—*to bray like an ass*, Lat. *rudĕre*.

βρώμη, ἡ, (βιβρώσκω) βρῶμα, *food*.

βρώσῐμος, ον, (βρῶσις) *eatable, solid*.

βρῶσις, εως, ἡ, (βιβρώσκω) *meat*, opp. to πόσις (*drink*). II. *an eating into, corrosion, rust*.

βρωτήρ, ῆρος, ὁ, (βιβρώσκω) *an eater, devourer*.

βρωτός, ή, όν, verb. Adj. of βιβρώσκω, *eatable*:—βρωτόν, τό, = βρῶσις.

βρωτύς, ύος, ἡ, (βιβρώσκω) Ion. for βρῶσις.

βύβλινος, η, ον, (βύβλος) *made of byblus*.

ΒΥ'ΒΛΟΣ, ἡ, *the Egyptian papyrus*. II. *its coats* or *fibres*, of which were made ropes, paper, etc.: βύβλοι, αἱ, *leaves of byblus*; hence, *a book*: also in pl τὰ βίβλα. [ῠ]

βύζην, Adv. (βύω) *close-pressed, closely, thickly*.

βῡθίζω, f. ίσω, (βυθός) *to sink in the deep, immerse*.

βύθιος, α, ον, (βυθός) *in the deep, sunken, deep*. II. *of the deep*; βύθια (sub. ζῷα) *water-animals*. [ῠ]

βῡθίτης, ου, ὁ, **βυθῖτις**, ιδος, ἡ, = βύθιος.

ΒΥΘΟ'Σ, ὁ, *the depth, the deeps* of the sea.

βύκτης, ου, ὁ, (βύω) masc. Adj. *blustering*: Ep. gen. pl. βυκτάων.

βῡνέω, Att. for βύω.

ΒΥ'ΡΣΑ ἡ, *the skin stripped off, a hide*.

βυρσ-αίετος, ὁ, (βύρσα, αἰετός) *leather-eagle*, nickname of Cleon the tanner.

βυρσεύς, έως, ὁ, *a tanner*. From

βυρσεύω, f. σω, (βύρσα) *to dress hides, tan*.

βυρσίνη, ἡ, *a leathern thong*. [ῐ] Fem. from

βύρσινος, η, ον, (**βύρσα**) *made of skin* or *leather*.

βυρσοδεψέω, f. ήσω, *to dress hides, be a tanner*. From

βυρσο-δέψης, ου, ὁ, (βύρσα, δέψω) *a tanner*.

βυρσο-παφλᾰγών, όνος, ὁ, (βύρσα, Παφλαγών) *the leather-Paphlagonian*, nickname of Cleon.

βυρσο-πώλης, ου, ὁ, (βύρσα, πωλέω) *a leather-seller*.

βυρσο-τενής, ές, and **βυρσό-τονος**, ον, (βύρσα, τείνω) *with skin* or *leather stretched over*.

βύσσῐνος, η, ον, (βύσσος) *made of fine linen*.

βυσσο-δομεύω, (βυσσός, δομέω) *to build in the deeps*: hence *to meditate deeply*.

βυσσόθεν, Adv. (βυσσός) *from the bottom*.

βυσσο-μέτρης, ου, ὁ, (βυσσός, μετρέω) *measuring the deeps*.

βυσσός, ὁ, = βυθός, *the depth* or *bottom of the sea*.

ΒΥ'ΣΣΟΣ, ἡ, *fine flax: fine linen*.

βυσσό-φρων, ον, (βυσσός, φρήν) *deep-thinking*.

ΒΥ'Ω: f. βύσω [ῡ]: aor. 1 ἔβῡσα:—Pass., aor. 1 ἐβύσθην: pf. βέβυσμαι:—*to stuff full*; νήματος βεβυσμένος *stuffed full* of spun-work; σπογγίῳ βεβυσμένος *bunged up* with sponge.

βῶ, aor. 2 act. subj. of βαίνω.

βωθέω, Ion. contr. for βοηθέω.

βωκολιάσδω, -αστής, Dor. for βουκ–.
βωκόλος, βωκολικός, Dor. for βουκ–.
βῶκος, ὁ, Dor. for βοῦκος.
βωλάκιος, α, ον, (βῶλαξ) *forming clods, of rich loam.*
βῶλαξ, ἄκος, ἡ, = βῶλος, *a clod of earth.*
βώλιον, τό, Dim. of βῶλος, *a clod.*
ΒΩ'ΛΟΣ, ἡ, Lat. *GLEBA, a clod of earth: a piece of land, ground, soil:* generally, *a lump* or *mass of anything:* so even of the sun.
βωλο-τόμος, ον, (βῶλος, τεμεῖν) *clod-breaking.*
βώμιος, α, ον, also ος, ον, (βωμός) *on* or *at the altar.*
βωμίς, ίδος, ἡ, Dim. of βωμός: *a step.*
βωμολόχευμα, ατος, τό, *a ribald jest.* From
βωμολοχεύομαι, Dep. *to practise coarse buffoonery, indulge in ribald jests.* From
βωμο-λόχος, ον, (βωμός, λοχάω) *lurking about the altars, for the scraps that could be got there, a starveling, beggar:* hence *a low flatterer, ribald jester, buffoon.*
βωμός, ὁ, (βαίνω) *any raised place for standing on, a stand,* Lat. *suggestus: a raised place for sacrificing, an altar;* later also a *funeral mound, cairn,* Lat. *tumulus.*
βῶν, Ep. for βοῦν, acc. of βοῦς: also contr. gen. plur.
βώσας, contr. for βοήσας, aor. 1 part. of βοάω.
βῶσι, 3 plur. aor. 2 subj. of βαίνω.
βωστρέω, (βοάω) *to call on, to call to aid.*
βώτας, Dor. for βούτης.
βωτι-άνειρα, ἡ, (βόσκω, ἀνήρ) *man-feeding, nurse of heroes.* [ᾰ]
βώτωρ, ορος, ὁ, = βοτής, *a herdsman.*

Γ

Γ, γ, γάμμα, indecl., third letter in Gr. alphabet: as numeral γʹ, = *three, third:* but ͵γ = 3000.—Before the palatals γ κ χ and before ξ, γ is pronounced like *n* in *ng,* as ἄγγος ἄγκος ἄγχι ἄγξω.

For the *digamma,* v. sub σ.

Homer uses γ as an aspirate before some words, as αἶα γαῖα, δοῦπος γδοῦπος: so also in Att., before λ and ν, e.g. λήμη γλήμη, νέφος γνόφος.

In Dor. δ is sometimes put for γ, as δᾶ δνόφος for γῆ γνόφος: also γ for β, βλέφαρον γλέφαρον; but in Att., β for γ, γλήχων βλήχων; also for κ, γνάπτω κνάπτω: and for λ, γήϊον λήϊον.

γᾰ, Dor. for γε.
γᾶ, Dor. and Aeol. for γῆ, *earth.*
γαγγάμη, ἡ, or **γάγγᾰμον,** τό, *a small round net.*
γάγγραινα, ἡ, (γράω, γραίνω) *a gangrene, an eating sore ending in mortification.*
γάζα, ἡ, *the royal treasure: riches.* (Persian word.)
γαζο-φῠλάκιον, τό, (γάζα, φυλᾰκή) *a treasury,* Lat. *aerarium.*
γᾱθέω, Dor. for γηθέω.
γαῖα, ἡ, gen. γαίας, Ep. **γαίης** (but not γαίη in nom., except in late Poets), like **αἶα,** poët. for γῆ, *earth, ground, soil:* one's *country.*
γαιάοχος, ον, Dor. for γαιήοχος.
γαιηγενής, ές, poët. for γηγενής.
γαιήϊος, η, ον, (γαῖα) *sprung from Earth.*
γαιή-οχος, ον, (γαῖα, ἔχω) poët. for γηοῦχος, *earth-upholding, earth-surrounding,* epith. of Poseidon: of other gods, *protecting a country.*
γάϊος, ον, Dor. for γήϊος, *on land.*
ΓΑΙ'Ω, only used in partic., κύδεϊ γαίων *exulting in* his strength.
ΓΑ'ΛΑ, gen. γάλακτος, τό, *milk.* (Lat. *LAC* appears in gen. γά-λακ-τος).
γᾰλᾰθηνός, όν, (γάλα) *sucking, infant.*
γαλάκτῐνος, η, ον, *milky, milk-white.*
γᾰλακτο-πᾰγής, ές, (γάλα, παγῆναι) *like curdled milk.*
γαλακτο-πότης, ου, ὁ, (γάλα, πέ-ποται, 3 sing. pf. pass. of πίνω) *a milk-drinker.*
γαλάνα, γαλανός, Dor. for γαλήνη, γαληνός.
ΓΑΛΕΈΗ, έης, contr. **γᾰλῆ,** ῆς, ἡ, *the marten-cat* or *polecat,* Lat. *mustela.*
γαλερός, ά, όν, *cheerful.* Adv. -ρῶς.
γᾰλεώτης, ου, ὁ, (γαλέη) *a kind of spotted lizard.*
γᾰλῆ, ἡ, contr. for γαλέη.
γᾰληναῖος, α, ον, = γαληνός.
γᾰλήνεια, Dor. **γαλάνεια,** ἡ, = sq.
ΓΑ'ΛΗ'ΝΗ, ἡ, *stillness of wind and wave, calm,* γαλήνην ἐλαύνειν to sail through *the calm:* generally, *calm, tranquillity.* Hence
γαληνιάω, Ep. part. fem. γαληνιόωσα, *to be calm.*
γᾰληνός, όν, (γαλήνη) *calm, still, serene:* esp. of the sea, in neut. pl., γαληνά *a calm,* γαλήν' ὁρῶ I see *a calm.*
Γάλλος, ὁ, *a priest of Cybelé: a eunuch.*
γᾰλ-ουργέω, -ουργός, -ουχέω, -ουχία, = γαλακτ–.
ΓΑ'ΛΟΩΣ, ἡ, gen. γάλοω, nom. pl. γαλόῳ: Att. γάλως, gen. γάλω, *a sister-in-law:* the corresponding masc. is δαήρ. [ᾰ]
γᾶμαι, Dor. for γῆμαι, aor. 1 inf. of γαμέω.
γαμβρός, ὁ, (γαμέω) *any connexion by marriage,* Lat. *affinis:* 1. *a son-in-law.* 2. *a brother-in-law.* 3. *a father-in-law.* II. in Dor. and Aeol. *a bridegroom.*
γᾶμεν, Dor. for ἔγημεν, 3 sing. aor. 1 of γαμέω.
γᾰμετή, ἡ, fem. of γαμέτης, *a wife.*
γᾰμέτης, ου, Dor. gen. γαμέτᾱ, ὁ, *a husband, spouse:* and
γᾰμέτις, ιδος, ἡ, *a wife.* From
γᾰμέω: fut. γαμέω, Att. γαμῶ, later γαμήσω: fut. aor. 1 ἔγημα; later ἐγάμησα: pf. γεγάμηκα.—Med., fut. γαμέσομαι, Ep. 3 sing. γαμέσσεται, Att. γαμοῦμαι: aor. 1 ἐγημάμην.—Pass., aor 1 ἐγαμήθην, poët. part. γαμεθείς: pf. γεγάμημαι: (γάμος). *To marry, to take to wife,* Lat. *ducere;* ἐκ κακοῦ, ἐξ ἀγαθοῦ γῆμαι *to marry* of a good or bad stock. II. Med. *to give in marriage,* 1. of the woman, *to give herself in marriage, to wed,* Lat. *nubere.* 2.

of the parents, *to get their children married, betroth, to get a wife for the son* or *a husband for the daughter.* III. Pass. *to be wedded* or *taken to wife.*

γᾰμήλευμα, ατος, τό, = γάμος.

γαμήλιος, α, ον, (γαμέω) *bridal*, Lat. *nuptialis:* γαμηλία (sub. θυσία), ἡ, *a marriage-feast.*

Γαμηλιών, ῶνος, ὁ, *the seventh month of the Attic year*, from γαμέω, because it was the usual time for weddings: it answered to the end of January and beginning of February. See Ληναιών.

γᾰμίζω, f. ίσω, (γάμος) *to give in marriage.*

γᾰμικός, ή, όν, (γάμος) *bridal; τὰ γαμικά a wedding*, Lat. *nuptiae.* Adv. -κῶς, *as at a wedding.*

γᾰμίσκω, = γαμίζω.

γᾰμο-κλόπος, ον, (γάμος, κλέπτω) *adulterous:* as Subst. *an adulterer.*

γᾱ-μόρος, ὁ, Dor. for γημόρος.

ΓΑ'ΜΟΣ, ὁ, *a wedding, marriage:* also *wedlock, matrimony:* in pl. *a marriage-feast*, Lat. *nuptiae.*

γαμό-στολος, ον, (γάμος, στέλλω) *preparing marriage.*

γαμφηλαί, ῶν, αἱ, (γαμψός, γναμπτός) *the jaws* of a beast; *the beak* of a bird.

γαμψός, ή, όν, (κάμπτω) *bent, curved, crooked.*

γᾶν, Dor. for γῆν, γαῖαν.

γᾰνάω, (γάνος) *to shine, glitter, gleam: to look bright and fresh*, Lat. *nitere:* metaph. *to be cheerful.*

ΓΑ'ΝΟΣ, εος, τό, *brightness, sheen: beauty, a charm, delight.* [ᾰ] Hence

γᾰνόω, *to make bright* or *shining:* pf. pass. part. γεγανωμένος, *glad-looking, joyous*, Lat. *nitidus.*

γανόων, όωσα, Ep. part. of γανάω.

γάνῠμαι, Ep. fut. γανύσσομαι: Dep.: (γάνος):—*to brighten up, be delighted at* a thing. Hence

γάνυσμα, ατος, τό, = γάνος.

γά-πεδον, τό, Dor. for γήπεδον. [ᾱ]

γᾱ-πετής, **γᾱ-πόνος**, **γά-ποτος**, Dor. for γηπ-.

ΓΑ'Ρ, Conjunction, *for*, Lat. *enim*, and like it placed after the first word in a sentence. Its chief usages are I. *to introduce the reason:* when the reason precedes that of which it is the reason, it may be rendered by *since* or *as;* Ἀτρείδη, πολλοὶ γὰρ τεθνᾶσιν Ἀχαιοί, *since* many Achaeans are dead, etc.; so in parenthesis, as καί, ἦν γὰρ ὁ Μαραθὼν ἐπιτηδειότατον, etc., and, *since* Marathon was the fittest place, etc. II. to strengthen 1. *a question*, like Lat. *nam*, Engl. *why, what*, τίς γάρ σε ἧκεν *why* who hath sent thee? 2. *a wish*, κακῶς γὰρ ἐξόλοιο O that you might perish! in Homer usu. αἰ γάρ, Att. εἰ or εἴθε γάρ, Lat. *utinam, O that!* so also πῶς γάρ, *would that!*

γαργαίρω, f. ἀρῶ, (γόργᾰρα) *to swarm with.*

γαργᾰλίζω, Att. for γαγγαλίζω, (γάργαλος) *to tickle.* Hence

γαργαλισμός, οῦ, ὁ, *a tickling.*

ΓΑ'ΡΓΑΛΟΣ, ὁ, *a tickling, itching.* [ᾰ]

ΓΑ'ΡΓΑ'ΡΑ, τά, *heaps, lots, plenty.*

γᾱρύω, Dor. for γηρύω.

γαστήρ, gen. γαστέρος syncop. γαστρός, dat. plur. γαστράσι [ᾰ], ἡ:—*the paunch, belly*, Lat. *venter;* γαστὴρ ἀσπίδος *the hollow* of a shield. 2. *the womb*, ἐν γαστρὶ φέρειν or ἔχειν *to be with child.* 3. metaph. *appetite*, in a bad sense, *gluttony.* Hence

γάστρα, Ion. **γάστρη**, ἡ, *the belly of a jar*, etc.

γαστρίδιον, τό, Dim. of γαστήρ, γαστρίον.

γαστρίζω, f. ίσω, (γάστρις) *to fill one's belly.* II. *to hit on the belly*, a trick in boxing.

γαστρί-μαργος, ον, (γαστήρ, μάργος) *gluttonous.*

γαστρίον, τό, Dim. of γαστήρ.

γάστρις, ιος, ὁ, ἡ, (γαστήρ) *pot-bellied: a glutton.*

γαστρο-βᾰρής, ές, (γαστήρ, βαρύς) *heavy with child.*

γαστρο-φορέω, f. ήσω, (γαστήρ, φέρω) *to bear in the womb, be pregnant.*

γαστρ-ώδης, ες, (γαστήρ, εἶδος) *pot-bellied.*

γαυλικός, ή, όν, (γαῦλος) *of* or *for a merchant ship.*

γαυλιτικός, ή, όν, = γαυλικός.

ΓΑΥ̃ΛΟΣ, ὁ, *a milk-pail: a water-bucket: any round vessel*, e. g. *a bee-hive:* hence II. γαῦλος, ὁ, *a round built merchant-vessel, galley.*

γαυριάω, only used in pres. *to bear oneself proudly, pride oneself.* From

γαῦρος, ον, also α, ον, (γαίω) *exulting in* a thing: *haughty, disdainful: skittish.* Hence

γαυρόομαι, Pass. *to exult in* a thing: *to be haughty, disdainful.* Hence

γαύρωμα, ατος, τό, *a subject for boasting.*

ΓΕ, Dor. **γα**, enclitic Particle, Lat. *quidem, at least, at any rate;* ὅ γ' ἐνθάδε λεώς *at any rate* the people here: often attached to pronouns, ἔγωγε, σύγε, ὅγε. 2. *well then, then*, implying unwillingness, εἶμί γε *well*, I will go. 3. *and indeed, too;* καλῶς γε ποιῶν *and* quite *right* too! 4. to strengthen oaths, νὴ Δία .. γε, with a word between, to which γε usu. refers. II. *even;* ἦλθον Ἀμφιάρεώ γε πρὸς βίαν against *even* Amphiaraus' will.

γεά-οχος, ον, Dor. for γαιήοχος.

γέγᾰα, Ep. for γέγονα, perf. of γίγνομαι, *to have been born, to be, live:* pl. γέγᾰμεν, γεγάᾱτε, γεγάᾱσι: but γεγάμεν [ᾰ] inf., for γεγαένι, Dor. γεγάκειν [ᾰ]: part. γεγαώς, -άωσα, Att. contr. γεγώς, -ῶσα, like βεβαώς, βεβώς.

γέγᾱθα, Dor. for γέγηθα; pf. of γηθέω.

γεγάκειν, Dor. pf. inf. of γίγνομαι: see γέγαα.

γέγαμεν, **γεγάμεν**, see γέγαα.

γεγάμηκα, pf. of γαμέω.

γεγένημαι, pf. of γίγνομαι.

γέγευμαι, pf. pass. of γεύω.

γέγηθα, **γεγήθειν**, pf. and Ep. plqpf. of γηθέω.

γεγήρᾱκα, pf. of γηράσκω.

γέγλυμμαι, pf. pass. of γλύφω.

γεγόμφωμαι, pf. pass. of γομφόω.

γέγονα, pf. of γίγνομαι.

γέγραφα, **γέγραμμαι**, pf. act. and pass. of γράφω.

γεγράψομαι, fut. 3 pass. of γράφω.

γεγύμνακα, γεγύμνασμαι, pf. act. and pass. of *γυμνάζω.*

ΓΕΓΩΝΑ, perf. with pres. sense, part. *γεγωνώς,* plqpf. *ἐγεγώνειν* with impf. sense :—the other tenses are formed as if from pres. *γεγώνω* or *γεγωνέω,*—inf. *γεγωνεῖν,* Ep. *γεγωνέμεν*; impf. *ἐγεγώνευν* or *γεγώνευν* for *ἐγεγώνεον,* 3 sing. also *ἐγέγωνε*; aor. 1 inf. *γεγωνῆσαι* : verb. Adj. *γεγωνητέον.* *To call* or *cry so as to be heard, to call aloud; ὅσον τε γέγωνε βοήσας* as far as *he could make himself heard* by shouting: c. acc. rei, *to call out, proclaim aloud:* of things, *to sound, ring,* etc.

γεγωνητέον, verb. Adj. of *γεγωνέω, one must proclaim aloud.*

γεγωνίσκω, lengthd. pres. for *γέγωνα, to proclaim.*

γεγωνός, *όν,* Adj. from part. *γεγωνώς,* (like *ἀραρός, όν,* from *ἀραρώς*), *loud-spoken, loud-sounding.*

γεγώς, *ῶσα, ώς,* Att. part. pf. of *γίγνομαι,* for *γεγονώς, γεγαώς,* see *γάω.*

Γεέννα, *ἡ,* Heb. *Gehenna,* i. e. the valley of Hinnom, in which the corpses of the worst malefactors were burnt :—hence as a name for *hell-fire, hell.*

γεη-πόνος, etc., v. *γεωπ-.*

γει-ἄροτής, *οῦ, ὁ,* (*γῆ, ἀρόω*) *a plougher of earth.*

γεινάμενος, aor. 1 part. of *γείνομαι.*

γείνεαι, Ep. for *γείνηαι,* 2 sing. aor. 1 med. subj. of *γείνομαι.*

γείνομαι, Pass. *to be begotten, be born.* II. the aor. 1 *ἐγεινάμην, γείνασθαι* is always used in causal sense, = *γεννάω,* of the father, *to beget;* of the mother, *to bear, bring forth; οἱ γεινάμενοι the parents.*

γειο-μόρος, etc., = *γεωμόρος.*

γειο-φόρος, *ον,* (*γῆ, φέρω*) *earth-bearing.*

ΓΕΙΣΟΝ or **γεῖσσον,** *τό, anything projecting so as to shelter, the eaves of a roof, the cornice, coping: the hem of a garment.* (Of Carian origin.)

γειτνίασις, *εως, ἡ, neighbourhood: the neighbours.* From

γειτνιάω, (*γείτων*) *to be a neighbour, to border on.*

γειτονεύω and **γειτονέω,** = *γειτνιάω.*

γειτόσῠνος, *ον, neighbouring, near.* From

ΓΕΙΤΩΝ, *ονος, ὁ, ἡ, a neighbour.* III. as Adj. *neighbouring bordering:*—metaph. *akin to, like.*

γελαίσας, Aeol. for *γελάσας.*

γελάξας, Dor. for *γελάσας.*

γελᾱνής, *ές,* (*γελάω*) *laughing, cheerful.*

γελᾶντι, Dor. for *γελῶντι,* dat. part. of *γελάω.*

γελάοισα and **γελεῦσα,** Dor. for *γελάουσα.*

γελᾶσα, Dor. for *γελῶσα,* fem. nom. part. of *γελάω.*

γελασείω, Desiderat. of *γελάω, to like to laugh, to be ready to laugh.*

γέλασμα, *ατος, τό,* (*γελάω*) *a laugh; κυμάτων ἀνήριθμον γέλασμα* 'the many-twinkling *smile* of Ocean.'

γελαστής, *οῦ, ὁ,* (*γελάω*) *a laugher, sneerer.*

γελαστός, *ή, όν, laughable, laughed at.* From

ΓΕΛΑΩ, Ep. **γελόω,** Ep. part. pl. *γελόωντες, γελώοντες,* or *γελοίωντες*: Ep. impf. *γελοίων* or *-ωων*: fut. *γελάσομαι*: aor. 1 *ἐγέλᾰσα,* Ep. *ἐγέλασσα,* Dor. *ἐγέλαξα.*—Pass., aor. 1 *ἐγελάσθην*: pf. *γεγέλασμαι*: —*to laugh,* Lat. *rideo; ἐγέλασσε φίλον κῆρ* his heart *laughed* within him. II. *to laugh at, sneer at.*

ΓΕΛΓΙΣ, *ιδος, ἡ;* pl. *γέλγιδες* or *γέλγεις*: = *ἀγλίς, a head, clove of garlic,* Lat. *spica allii.*

γελοίῐος, Ep. for *γέλοιος.*

γέλοιος, *α, ον,* also *ος, ον,* (*γελάω*) *laughable, absurd.* II. *humorous, facetious: γέλοια jests.*

γελοίων, Ep. impf. of *γελάω.*

γελοίωντες, part. pres. of *γελοιάω.*

γελόω, γελόωντες, Ep. for *γελάω, γελάοντες.*

γελῶντι, Dor. for *γελῶσι.*

γελώοντες, poët. for *γελόωντες.*

γέλως, *ὁ*: gen. *ωτος* Att. *ω*: dat. *γέλωτι* Ep. *γέλῳ*: acc. *γέλωτα* Ep. *γέλω,* in Att. Poets *γέλων*: (*γελάω*): *laughter,* Lat. *risus; ἐπὶ γέλωτι* for *laughter's sake,* for *a joke.* II. *a subject of laughter,* Lat. *ludibrium; γέλωτα ποιεῖσθαί τι* to make *a joke* of it.

γελωτοποιΐα, *ἡ, buffoonery.* From

γελωτο-ποιός, *όν,* (*γέλως, ποιέω*) *exciting laughter:* as Subst., **γελωτοποιός,** *οῦ, ὁ, a jester.*

γελώων, Ep. impf., **γελώωντες,** Ep. part. of *γελάω.*

γεμίζω, f. *ίσω,* Att. *ιῶ,* (*γέμω*) *to fill, load* or *freight with* a thing :—Pass. *to be freighted.*

γέμος, *τό,* = *γόμος, a freight.* From

ΓΕΜΩ, used only in pres. and impf. *to be full of a* thing, *to be full.*

γενεά, *ᾶς,* Ion. **γενεή,** *ῆς, ἡ,* (**γένω*) *birth; ὁπλότερος γενεῇ* younger *by birth; ἐκ γενεῆς* from *birth.* II. *birth, race, descent; γενεῇ ὑπέρτερος* higher *by blood:* of horses, *breed.* III. *a generation,* Lat. *saeculum; δύω γενεαὶ μερόπων ἀνθρώπων.* IV. *offspring, descendants.*

γενεᾱλογέω, f. *ήσω,* (*γενεαλόγος*) *to trace a pedigree; γενεαλογεῖν τινα to trace* his *pedigree:*—Pass. *to derive one's pedigree.* Hence

γενεᾱλογία, *ἡ, a tracing one's descent, genealogy.* From

γενεᾱ-λόγος, *ὁ,* (*γενεά, λέγω*) *a genealogist.*

γενεή, *ῆς, ἡ,* Ion. for *γενεά*: Ep. dat. *γενεῆφι.*

γενέθλη, *ἡ, birth, origin, descent:* of horses, *breed.* 2. *birth-place; ἀργύρου γενέθλη a mine* of silver.

γενεθλίδιος, *ον,* = *γενέθλιος.*

γενέθλιος, *ον, belonging to one's birth,* Lat. *natalis; γενέθλιον ἦμαρ* one's *birth-day; τὰ γενέθλια a birthday feast; γενέθλιοι θεοί* the gods *of one's race; γενέθλιον αἷμα kindred* blood.

γίνεθλον, *τό,* = *γενέθλη, descent.* 2. *offspring.*

γενειάζω Dor. **-άσδω,** (*γένειον*) *to get a beard, come to man's estate.*

γενειάς, *άδος, ἡ,* (*γένειον*) *a beard.* 2 in plur. *the cheeks.*

γενειάσκω, = *γενειάζω, to get a beard.*

γενειάτης, Ion. **γενειήτης,** *ὁ*: fem. **γενειᾶτις** or **-εᾶτις,** *ιδος,* (*γενειάς*) *bearded.*

γενειάω, f. *ήσω,* = *γενειάζω, to get a beard.*

γένειον, τό, (γένυς) *the part covered by the beard, the lower part of the face, the chin.*

γένεο, Ep. for ἐγένου, 2 sing. aor. 2 of γίγνομαι.

γενέσθαι, aor. 2 inf. of γίγνομαι.

γενέσιος, ον, = γενέθλιος. II. τὰ γενέσια *a birth-day feast*:—also, *a day kept in memory of the dead.*

γένεσις, εως, ἡ, (*γένω) *an origin, source: birth, race, descent.*

γενέσκετο, Ion. for ἐγένετο, 3 sing. aor. 2 of γίγνομαι.

γενέτειρα, fem. of γενετήρ, (*γένω) *she that gives birth, a mother.* II. *she that is born, a daughter.*

γενετή, ἡ, = γενεή, *birth.*

γενετήρ, ῆρος, ὁ, = γενέτης.

γενέτης, ου, ὁ, (*γένω) *the begetter, a father, ancestor.* 2. *the begotten, son.* II. as Adj., = γενέθλιος.

γενετυλλίς, ίδος, ἡ, (*γένω) *goddess of one's birth hour.*

γενέτωρ, ορος, ὁ, = γενέτης, *a father.*

γένευ, Ion. for ἐγένου, 2 sing. aor. 2 of γίγνομαι.

γενηθήτω, 3 sing. aor. 1 pass. imperat. of γίγνομαι.

γενηΐς, ἡ: gen. γενηΐδος, contr. γενῇδος: = γενύς, *the edge of an axe: an axe, pickaxe, mattock.*

γένημα, ατος, τό, = γέννημα.

γέννᾰ, ἡ, poët. for γένος, *descent, offspring.*

γεννάδας [ᾰ], ου, ὁ, plur. γεννάδαι, (γέννα) *noble,* in mind or birth, Lat. *generosus.*

γενναιο-πρεπής, ές, (γενναῖος, πρέπω) *befitting a noble.* Adv. -πῶς.

γενναῖος, α, ον, also ος, ον, (γέννα) *suitable to one's birth* or *descent;* οὔ μοι γενναῖον it *fits* not *my high blood: noble* both in mind and blood, *high-born, high-minded:* of animals, *thorough-bred:* of things, *good of their kind:* but also, γενναία δύη *genuine, intense* misery. Hence

γενναιότης, ητος, ἡ, *nobility, nobleness of character:* of land, *fertility.*

γενναίως, Adv. of γενναῖος, *nobly:* Sup. γενναιότατα.

γεννάω, f. ήσω, (γέννα) *to beget,* of the father; *to bear, bring forth,* of the mother; οἱ γεννήσαντες *the parents.* II. *to generate, produce.* Hence

γέννημα, ατος, τό, *that which is produced, a child:* any *product.* II. *one's nature.* III. *a begetting.*

γέννησις, εως, ἡ, *a begetting, producing.*

γεννήτης, ου, ὁ, (γεννάω) *a parent,* Lat. *paterfamilias.*

γεννητός, ή, όν, (γεννάω) *begotten* or *born.*

γεννήτωρ, ορος, ὁ, = γενέτωρ.

γεννικός, ή, όν, = γενναῖος, *brave, spirited.* Adv. -ῶς.

γενοίατο, Ep. and Ion. for γένοιντο.

γενοίμαν, Dor. aor. 2 opt. of γίγνομαι.

γένος, εος, τό, (*γένω) *race, descent:* freq. in acc. absol. γένος, as ἐξ Ἰθάκης γένος εἰμί I am of Ithaca *by descent;* so in dat., γένει πολίτης a citizen *by birth.* II. *a descendant, a child,* as Virgil's *Divi genus.* III. *a race* in regard to number, *a nation.* 2. *a race* in regard to time, *an age, generation.* IV. *sex: gender.* V. *kind, genus,* opp. to εἶδος, *species.*

γέντο, *he grasped,* = ἔλαβεν, 3 sing. of an old Verb, only found in this form: prob. Aeol. for ἕλετο,—γ representing the digamma. II. contr. for ἐγένετο.

ΓΕ'ΝΥΣ, ἡ, gen. γένυος; dat. γένυι: plur., dat. γένυσι, Ep. γένυσσι; acc. γένυας, contr. γένῡς *The under jaw;* γένυες, *both jaws, the mouth:* hence also *the cheek, chin.* II. *the edge of an axe, a biting axe.*

***ΓΕ'ΝΩ**, obsol. pres., Root of γίγνομαι.

γέρα, Ep. contr. from γέρεα, pl. of γέρας.

γεραιός, ά, όν, (γέρων, γηραιός) *old: venerable.* Comp. γεραίτερος; οἱ γεραίτεροι, *the elders,* Lat. *senatores.* Sup. γεραίτατος

γεραιό-φλοιος, ον, (γεραιός, φλοιός) *with wrinkled skin.*

γεραίρω, f. γερᾰρῶ: aor. 1 ἐγέρημα, inf. γεράραι: aor. 2 ἐγέρᾰρον: (γέρας):—*to honour* or *reward with a gift:* generally, *to honour.*

γεραίτερος, -τατος, Comp. and Sup. of γεραιός.

ΓΕ'ΡΑ'ΝΟΣ, ἡ, Lat. *GRUS, a crane.*

γερᾰός, ή, όν, = γεραιός

γερᾰρός, ά, όν, (γεραίρω) *reverend, stately;* γεραροί *priests,* γεραραί *priestesses.*

ΓΕ'ΡΑΣ, αος, τό, nom. pl. γέρατα, Ion γέρεα, Ep. contr. γέρα:—*a gift of honour, prize,* generally, *a gift, honour;* metaph., γέρας θανόντων *the last honour* of the dead. II. *a privilege, prerogative.* Hence

γεράσμιος, ον, *honouring.* II. *honoured.*

Γεράστιος, *a Spartan month.*

γερασ-φόρος, ον, (γέρας, φέρω) *winning honour.*

γέρεα, Ion. nom. pl. of γέρας.

γεροντᾰγωγέω, f. ήσω, *to guide an old man.* From

γεροντ-ᾰγωγός, ὁ, (γέρων, ἄγω) *guiding an old man.*

γεροντία, ἡ, Lacon. for γερουσία.

γερόντιον, τό, Dim. of γέρων, *a little old man.*

γερουσία, ἡ, (γέρων) *a Council of Elders, Senate,* esp. at Sparta, where it consisted of 28. II. *an embassy.*

γερούσιος, α, ον, (γέρων) *belonging to the elders* or *chiefs;* οἶνος γερούσιος wine *reserved for them.*

γέρρον, τό, (εἴρω) Lat. *gerra, anything made of wicker-work,* esp. *an oblong shield,* such as the Persians wore. 2. *a wattled hut.*

γερρο-φόροι, οἱ, (γέρρον, φέρω) *troops that wore wicker shields:* v. foreg.

ΓΕ'ΡΩΝ, οντος, ὁ, *an old man,* Lat. *senex:* οἱ γέροντες *the Elders* or *Chiefs, who with the King formed the chief Council:* hence *the Senators,* like Lat. *Patres,* esp. at Sparta, where they were 28 in number. II. as Adj. γέρων, ον, but almost always with masc. Subst. as γέρων λόγος: γέρον σάκος however occurs in Homer.

γεῦμα, ατος, τό, (γεύω) *a taste of a thing.*

γεύσασθαι, aor. 1 med. inf. of γεύω.

ΓΕΥ'Ω, f. γεύσω: aor. 1 ἔγευσα:—*to give* one *a taste* of a thing. II. Med. γεύομαι, fut. γεύσομαι:

aor. 1 ἐγευσάμην: with pf. pass. γέγευμαι:—*to taste* or *eat* of a thing; 3 pl. plqpf. ἐγέγευντο, *they had tasted, eaten:* hence *to try, make proof, have experience of;* δουρὸς γεύσασθαι *to taste,* i. e. *feel,* the spear: *to enjoy.*

ΓΕ΄ΦΥ˘ΡΑ, ἡ, *a mound of earth to dam* or *bar* a stream, or *a bridge to cross* it, used by Hom. always in plur.:—in Hom. also, πολέμοιο γέφυραι *the lane between two lines of battle, the battle-field.* II. later in sing. *a bridge,* γέφυραν ζευγνύναι or γεφύρᾳ ζευγνύναι ποταμόν to build a bridge over a river, Lat. *ponte jungere fluvium.* Hence

γεφῡρόω, f. ώσω, *to make passable by a bridge, to bridge over;* γεφύρωσε ποταμόν [the tree] *made a bridge over* the river; γεφύρωσε κέλευθον *made a bridge*-way:—Pass., ἐγεφυρώθη ὁ πόρος the strait *had a bridge made* over it.

γεωγραφία, ἡ, *geography.* From

γεω-γράφος, ον, (γῆ, γράφω) *earth-describing:* as Subst., **γεωγράφος**, ου, ὁ, *a geographer.*

γεώ-λοφος, ὁ, (γῆ, λόφος) *a hill, billock:* also **γεώλοφον**, τό, and **γεωλοφία**, ἡ.

γεωμετρέω, f. ήσω, *to measure land, to measure.* From

γεω-μέτρης, ου, ὁ, (γῆ, μετρέω) *a land-measurer, geometer.* Hence

γεωμετρία, ἡ, *land-measuring, geometry:* and

γεωμετρικός, ή, όν, *of* or *for land-measuring, geometrical:* ἡ **γεωμετρική** (sub. τέχνη), *geometry:* γεωμετρικός, οῦ, ὁ, *a geometrician.* Adv. -κῶς.

γεωμορία, ἡ, *a division of lands: tillage.* From

γεω-μόρος, also **γη-μόρος**, **γα-μόρος**, and **γειο-μόρος**, ὁ, ἡ, (γῆ, μείρομαι) *a sharer in the division of lands, landholder:* οἱ γεωμόροι, *the landowners* or *nobles in a state,* Lat. *optimates.*

γεώ-πεδον or **γεω-πέδιον**, τό, Ion. for γήπεδον.

γεω-πείνης, ου, ὁ, (γῆ, πένομαι) *poor in land.*

γεωπόνος, ὁ, (γῆ, πονέω) *a tiller of the earth, husbandman.*

γεωργέω, f. ήσω, (γεωργός) *to be a farmer:* also *to till, cultivate:* metaph. *to work at, practise* a thing.

γεωργία, ἡ, (γεωργός) *agriculture, tillage.* II. in plur. *tilled lands.*

γεωργικός, ή, όν, (γεωργός) *of* or *for tillage, rustic.* II. *skilled in farming.*

γεώργιον, τό, *a field: cultivation: a crop.* From

γε-ωργός, όν, (γῆ, ἔργον) *tilling the ground:* as Subst., **γεωργός**, οῦ, ὁ, *a tiller of the earth, husbandman.*

γεωρῠχέω, f. ήσω, *to dig* or *trench the earth.* From

γε-ωρύχος, ον, (γῆ, ὀρύσσω) *trenching the earth.* [ῠ]

γεω-τόμος, ον, (γῆ, τεμεῖν) *cutting the ground: ploughing.*

ΓΗ^, ἡ, contr. for **γέα**, *earth, land;* γῆν καὶ ὕδωρ διδόναι to give *earth* and water as token of submission; κατὰ γῆν *on land,* by land, opp. to κατὰ θάλασσαν; also κατὰ γῆς, which means *beneath* the earth: ποῦ γῆς; Lat. *ubi terrarum? where on the earth?*

γη-γενής, ές, (γῆ, *γένω) *earthborn: indigenous.* II. as Subst., **γηγενής**, οῦ, ὁ, *a son of the Earth, a giant.*

γῆθεν, Adv. of **γῆ**, *out of* or *from the earth.*

γηθέω, f. ήσω: aor. ἐγήθησα, perf. γέγηθα, Dor. γέγᾱθα (used in pres. sense): plqpf. ἐγεγήθειν: (γαίω):—*to be delighted, to rejoice.*

γηθοσύνη, ἡ, (γηθέω) *joy, delight.*

γηθόσῠνος, η, ον, (γηθέω) *joyful, glad.*

ΓΗ΄ΘΥΟΝ, τό, Lat. *getbyum, a kind of leek.*

γήῐνος, ον, and **γήῐος**, ον, (γῆ) *of earth* or *clay.*

γηΐτης, contr. **γῄτης**, ου, ὁ, (γῆ) *a husbandman.*

γή-λοφος, ὁ, = γεώλοφος, *a hill.*

γῆμαι, **γήμας**, γήμασθαι, **γημάμενος**, aor. 1 inf. and part. act. and med. of γαμέω.

γη-μόρος, ὁ, = γεωμόρος.

γη-οχέω, (γῆ, ἔχω) *to possess land.*

γή-πεδον, τό, = γεώπεδον, (γῆ, πέδον) *a plot of ground.*

γη-πετής, ές, (γῆ, πεσεῖν) *falling to earth.*

γήπονος, ὁ, = γεώπονος.

γή-ποτος, Dor. **γάποτος**, ον, (γῆ, πέ-ποται 3 sing. pf. pass. of πίνω) *to be drunk up by Earth.*

γηραιός, ά, όν, (γῆρας) *old, aged.*

γηρᾰλέος and **γηράλιος**, α, ον, = γηραιός.

γηράναι, aor. 2 inf., or **γηρᾶναι**, aor. 1 inf., of γηράσκω.

γηράντεσσι, Ep. for γήρασι, dat. plur. of **γηράς**, part. aor. 2 of γηράσκω.

γηραός, ά, όν, poët. for γηραιός.

γηράς, aor. 2 part. of γηράσκω.

ΓΗ^ΡΑΣ, τό, gen. γήραος, Att. contr. γήρως: dat. γήραϊ, Att. contr. γήρᾳ: *old age,* Lat. *senectus.* Hence

γηράσκω or **γηράω**: fut. άσω Att. άσομαι [ᾱ]: aor. 1 ἐγήρᾱσα: aor. 2 ἐγήραν, inf. γηράναι [ᾰ], part. γηράς (as if from a verb in -μι): pf. γεγήρᾱκα:—*to grow aged, become old and infirm.* II. in aor. 1 ἐγήρᾱσα, Causal, *to bring to old age.*

γηροβοσκέω, f. ήσω, *to feed and cherish in old age:*—Pass. *to be cherished in old age.* From

γηρο-βοσκός, όν, (γῆρας, βόσκω) *cherishing in old age;* esp. of one's parents.

γηρο-κόμος, ον, (γῆρας, κομέω) *cherishing the old.*

γήρῡμα, ατος, τό, (γηρύω) *a voice, sound, tone.*

ΓΗ΄ΡΥΣ, υος, ἡ, *a voice: speech.* Hence

γηρύω, Dor. **γαρύω**; f. ύσω [ῡ]: aor. 1 ἐγήρῡσα:—Med., fut. -ύσομαι: aor. 1 ἐγηρυσάμην, but also in same sense pass. ἐγηρύθην [ῡ]:—*to utter, speak, say, sing, cry,* Lat. *garrire.*

γήρως, contr. for γήραος, gen. of **γῆρας**.

γήτειον, τό, Att. for γήθυον, *a leek.*

γήτης, ὁ, contr. for γηΐτης.

γη-τόμος, ον, (γῆ, τεμεῖν) *ploughing the earth.*

γιγαντ-ολέτης, ου, ὁ, (γίγας, ὄλλυμι) *giant-killer.*

γῐγαντο-φόνος, ον, (γίγας, *φένω) *giant-killing.*

ΓΙ΄ΓΑΡΤΟΝ, *a grape-stone.* [ῐ]

ΓΙ΄ΓΑΣ, αντος, voc. γίγαν, ὁ, (γῆ or γαῖα) mostly in plur. *the Giants,* a rebellious race, destroyed by the gods. In Hesiod, *the sons of Gaia* or *Earth,* whence the name = γηγενής.

γί-γνομαι, syncop. from **γι-γένομαι**, which is formed by redupl. from the Root ***ΓΕ΄ΝΩ**: from this root come fut. γενήσομαι: αοτ. 2 ἐγενόμην: perf. γεγένημαι and γέγονα: aor. I (in late authors) ἐγενήθην: for the Ep. pf. γέγᾰα, see γέγαα:—*to become, to happen: to be born: to be;* in perf. γέγονα *to be by birth,* or *to have become* so. 2. of events, *to occur, happen.* II. with Preps. or Advs. of motion, *to be at,* as ἐγίγνετο ἐς Λακεδαίμονα. 2. πάντα, παντοῖος, παντοδαπὸς γίγνεσθαι to take all shapes, turn every way; ἑαυτοῦ γενέσθαι *to be master of* oneself; ἐντὸς ἑαυτοῦ γενέσθαι *to recover* oneself. 3. τί γένωμαι; more rarely τίς γένωμαι; what *is to become of me?* 4. γίγνεσθαι δι' ὀργῆς, διὰ λόγων, periphras. for ὀργᾶν, λέγειν, etc. 5. c. gen. pretii, *to cost* so much, as, ὀβολοῦ γίγνεσθαι *to cost* an obol.

γι-γνώσκω, formed by redupl. from the root *ΓΝΟΈΩ, ΓΝΩ͂ΝΑΙ, Lat. *NOSCO:* fut. γνώσομαι: aor. 2 ἔγνων, imperat. γνῶθι, opt. γνοίην, inf. γνῶναι, part. γνούς: perf. ἔγνωκα, pass. ἔγνωσμαι: aor. I pass. ἐγνώσθην.

To perceive, gain knowledge of, mark, and so *to know,* of persons and things: *to be aware of, understand:* sometimes c. gen. instead of acc., *to know of..,* γνῶ χωομένου, *he knew that he was* angry: rarely also c. part., ἔγνων ἡττημένος *I perceived that I was* beaten. II. *to examine, to form an opinion, decide upon, determine, decree,* γνῶναι τὰ δίκαια.

γίνομαι, Ion. and in late Greek for γίγνομαι.

γῑνώσκω, Ion. and in late Greek for γιγνώσκω.

γλαγάω, (γλάγος) *to be milky, juicy.*

γλαγερός, ά, όν, (γλάγος) *full of milk, milky.*

γλαγόεις, εσσα, εν, (γλάγος) *full of milk, milky.*

γλᾰγο-πήξ, ῆγος, ὁ, ἡ, (γλάγος, πήγνυμι) *of* or *for curdling milk.*

ΓΛΑ'ΓΟΣ, εος, τό, poët. for γάλα, *milk.*

γλακτο-φάγος, ον, (γάλα, φᾰγεῖν) contr. for γαλακτοφάγος, *living on milk.*

ΓΛΑ'ΜΗ, ἡ, = λήμη, *humour in the eyes.*

γλάμων, ον, gen. ονος, (γλάμη) *blear-eyed.* [ᾰ]

γλαυκιάω, (γλαυκός) only found in Ep. part. γλαυκιόων, *glaring with the eyes.*

ΓΛΑΥΚΟ'Σ, ή, όν, Aeol. **γλαῦκος**, α, ον, *gleaming, glancing, bright-gleaming.* II. with notion of Colour, *pale-green, bluish-green, gray,* Lat. *glaucus,* of the olive, of the willow, and also of the vine. III. of the eye, *light blue* or *gray,* Lat. *caesius:* of persons, *blue-eyed.*

γλαυκό-χροος, ὁ, ἡ, acc. γλαυκόχροα, (γλαυκός, χρόος) *gray-coloured, gray.*

γλαυκ-ῶπις, ιδος, ἡ: acc. ιδα, but also ιν: (γλαυκός, ὤψ) epith. of Minerva, *with gleaming eyes.*

γλαυκ-ώψ, ῶπος, ὁ, ἡ, = γλαυκῶπις.

γλαύξ, Att. **γλαῦξ**, κός, ἡ, (γλαυκός) *the owl,* Lat. *noctua,* so called from its *glaring* eyes. Proverb., γλαῦκ' Ἀθήναζε, γλαῦκ' εἰς Ἀθήνας, like our 'carry coals to Newcastle:' Athenian coins were called γλαῦκες Λαυριωτικαί, *from the stamp of the owl* on them.

γλάφῠ, τό, (γλάφω) *a hollow, cavern.* [ᾰ]

γλαφυρία, ἡ, *smoothness, polish.* From

γλᾰφῠρός, ά, όν, (γλάφω) *hollow, hollowed:* hence γλ. λιμήν a *deep* harbour. II. *smoothed, polished,* of persons, *critical, exact.* Adv. -ρῶς, *smoothly, nicely, prettily.*

ΓΛΑ'ΦΩ, *to hew, carve:* of a lion, *to tear the ground* with his feet.

γλάχων [ᾱ], Dor. for γλήχων.

γλευκο-πότης, ου, ὁ, (γλεῦκος, πέ-ποται 3 sing. pf. pass. of πίνω) *drinker of new wine.*

γλεῦκος, εος, τό, (γλυκύς) Lat. *mustum, must, sweet new wine.*

γλέφαρον, τό, Dor. for βλέφαρον.

ΓΛΗ'ΝΗ, ἡ, *the pupil, eye-ball:* and, II. because figures are reflected small in the pupil, *a puppet,* esp. *a girl,* cf. κόρη, Lat. *pupilla:* as a taunt, ἔρρε κακὴ γλήνη away, *weak girl!*

ΓΛΗ'ΝΟΣ, τό, in plur. *things to stare at, wonders.*

ΓΛΗ'ΧΩΝ, ωνος, ἡ: acc. γλήχωνα, by apocop. γλήχω:—*pennyroyal,* Ion. for βλήχων.

γλισχρ-αντιλογ-εξεπίτριπτος, ον, comic word in Aristophanes, *a greedy pettifogging knave.* (γλίσχρος, ἀντιλογία, ἐξεπίτριπτος)

ΓΛΙ'ΣΧΡΟΣ, α, ον, *gluey, clammy, slippery.* II. metaph. *sticking close to, importunate.* 2. *close, greedy, stingy.* 3. of disputations, *quibbling, petty.*

γλίσχρων, ονος, ὁ, (γλίσχρος) *a niggard.*

γλισχρῶς, Adv. of γλισχρός, *importunately: scantily:* also *pettily.*

ΓΛΙ'ΧΟΜΑΙ [ῑ], Dep., only used in pres. and impf., *to strive after a* thing, *struggle for* it, c. gen. 2. γλίχεσθαι περί τινος *to be eager about* or *for* a thing.

ΓΛΟΙ'Α or **γλοιά**, ἡ, *glue.* Hence

γλοιός, ὁ, *anything sticky* or *clammy,* as *oil and dirt.* II. as Adj. γλοιός, ά, όν, *slippery, knavish.*

ΓΛΟΥΤΟ'Σ, ὁ, *the rump:* plur. *the buttocks.*

γλυκαίνομαι, Pass. *to become sweet.*

γλῠκερός, ά, όν, = γλυκύς, *sweet.*

γλυκερό-χρως, ωτος, ὁ, ἡ, (γλυκερός, χρῶς) *with sweet, fair skin.*

γλύκιος, α, ον, = γλυκύς. [ῠ]

γλῠκύ-δακρυς, υ, gen. υος, (γλυκύς, δάκρυ) *causing sweet tears.*

γλυκύ-δωρος, ον, (γλυκύς, δῶρον) *with sweet gifts.*

γλυκυ-ηχής, ές, (γλυκύς, ἠχέω) *sweet-sounding.*

γλυκυθυμία, ἡ, *benevolence.* From

γλυκύ-θῡμος, ον, (γλυκύς, θυμός) *sweet-minded.* II. act. *charming the mind, delightful.*

γλυκύ-μᾱλον, Aeol. and Dor. for γλυκύμηλον.

γλυκυ-μείλῐχος, ον, (γλυκύς, μείλιχος) *sweetly winning.*

γλυκύ-μᾱλον, τό, Dor. for γλυκύμηλον (γλυκύς μῆλον) *a sweet-apple.*

γλυκυμῡθέω, f. ήσω, *to speak sweetly.* From

γλυκύ-μῡθος, (γλυκύς, μῦθος) *sweet-speaking.*

γλυκύ-παις, αιδος, ὁ, ἡ, (γλυκύς, παῖς) *having a fair offspring.*

γλυκυ-πάρθενος, ἡ, (γλυκύς, παρθένος) *a sweet maid.*

γλυκύ-πικρος, ον, (γλυκύς, πικρός) *sweetly bitter.*

ΓΛΥΚΥ'Σ, εῖα, ύ, *sweet to the taste, sweet:* metaph. *sweet, delightful:* of men, *dear, kind.* Comp. and Sup. γλυκίων [ῑ], γλύκιστος: also γλυκύτερος, -τατος.

γλῠκύτης [κῠ], ητος, ἡ, (γλυκύς) *sweetness.*

γλυπτήρ, ῆρος, ὁ, and **γλύπτης**, ου, ὁ, (γλύφω) *a carver, a sculptor.*

γλυπτός, ή, όν, verb. Adj. of γλύφω, *fit for carving, carved.*

γλύφᾰνον, τό, (γλύφω) *a knife* or *chisel for carving.*

γλῠφίς, ίδος, ἡ, mostly in plur., γλυφίδες *the notch* of the arrow, which fits on the string: later, *the arrow* itself. II. = γλύφανον, *a knife.* From

ΓΛΥ'ΦΩ, f. ψω: aor. 1 ἔγλυψα:—Pass., aor. 1 ἐγλύφθην, aor. 2 ἐγλύφην [ῠ]: pf. γέγλυμμαι and ἔγλυμμαι: — *to hollow out:* esp. *to engrave* or *carve.* II. *to write on a tablet.*

ΓΛΩ'Ξ, ωχός, ἡ, *the beard of corn,* only in plur.

ΓΛΩ'ΣΣΑ, Att. **γλῶττα**, ης, ἡ, *the tongue,* Lat. *lingua;* ἀπὸ γλώσσης by *word of mouth;* οὐκ ἀπὸ γλώσσης not from another's *tongue,* not from *hearsay;* γλῶσσαν ἱέναι to let loose one's *tongue,* speak freely. II. *a tongue, language;* γλῶσσαν νομίζειν to use a *language* or *dialect.*

γλωσσαλγία, Att. γλωσσαργία, ἡ, *endless talking, wordiness.* From

γλώσσ-αλγος, Att. **γλώσσ-αργος**, ον, (γλῶσσα, ἄλγος) *talking till one's tongue aches, very talkative.*

γλωσσό-κομον, τό, (γλῶσσα, κομέω) properly *a case for the mouthpiece* of a flute: *a case* or *bag* for money.

γλῶττα, ἡ, Att. for γλῶσσα.

γλωττο-στροφέω, f. ήσω, (γλῶττα, στρέφω) *to ply the tongue.*

ΓΛΩΧΙ'Ν or **γλωχίς**, gen. ῖνος, ἡ, *any projecting point: the end of the yoke-strap.* 2. *the point* of an arrow: *the arrow* itself.

γναθμός, ὁ, *the jaw,* poët. form of γνάθος.

ΓΝΑ'ΘΟΣ, ἡ, *the jaw, mouth:* properly *the lower jaw.* II. like γένυς, *the point* or *edge* of a weapon. [ᾰ]

γναμπτός, ή, όν, *curved, bent: supple, pliant:* metaph. *bending, yielding.* From

ΓΝΑ'ΜΠΤΩ, f. ψω: aor. 1 ἔγναμψα:—*to crook, bend.*

γναπτός, ή, όν, (γνάπτω) *carded, fulled.*

ΓΝΑ'ΠΤΩ, **γνάπτωρ**: **γναφεῖον**, **-φεύς**, **-φευτικός**,**-φεύω**, **-φικός**: **γνάφος**. -ψις, v. sub κνάπτω, etc.

γνήσιος, α, ον, syncop. for γενέσιος, *belonging to the true race, legitimate,* opp. to νόθος: *genuine, true;* γνήσιαι γυναῖκες *lawful* wives, opp. to παλλακίδες; γνήσιοι Ἕλληνες *true* Greeks; φρονεῖν γνήσια to have a *noble* mind.

γνησίως, Adv. of γνήσιος, *lawfully, really, truly.*

γνοίην, ης, η, aor. 2 opt. of γιγνώσκω.

γνοῖμεν, Ep. for γνοίημεν, 1 pl. aor. 2 opt. of γιγνώσκω.

γνούς, aor. 2 part. of γιγνώσκω.

ΓΝΟ'ΦΟΣ, ὁ, = δνόφος, *darkness.*

γνοφ-ώδης, ες, (γνόφος, εἶδος) *darksome, dark.*

γνύξ, Adv. (γόνυ) *with bent knee;* γνὺξ ἐριπεῖν to fall *on the knee.*

γνῶ, Ion. for ἔγνω, 3 sing. aor. 2 of γιγνώσκω.

γνῶ, ῷς, ῷ, aor. 2 subj. of γιγνώσκω.

γνῶθι, γνώτω, aor. 2 imperat. of γιγνώσκω.

γνῶμα, ατος, τό, (γνῶναι) *that by which a thing is known, a mark, token,* like γνώμων. II. *judgment.*

γνώμεναι, Ep. for γνῶναι, aor. 2 inf. of γιγνώσκω.

γνώμη, ἡ, (γνῶναι) *a means of knowing, a mark, token.* II. *the mind, the judgment;* γνώμῃ τῇ ἀρίστῃ to the best of one's *judgment.* 2. *will, purpose;* ἀφ' ἑαυτοῦ γνώμης of his own *accord.* 3. *a judgment, opinion;* γνώμην ἀποφαίνεσθαι to deliver *an opinion;* also *a mistaken judgment, fancy,* γνῶμαι *the opinions* of wise men, *maxims.* 4. *a purpose, intention, resolution: a vote, decree.*

γνωμίδιον, τό, Dim. of γνώμη, *a fancy.*

γνωμο-λογία, ἡ, (γνώμη, λέγω) *a collection of maxims.*

γνωμονικός, ή, όν, (γνώμων) *fit to give judgment: experienced* or *skilled in* a thing. II. *of* or *for sun-dials.*

γνωμοσύνη, ἡ, (γνώμων) *prudence, judgment.*

γνωμοτῠπέω, *to coin maxims:* and

γνωμοτῠπικός, ή, όν, *clever at coining maxims.* From

γνωμο-τύπος, ον, (γνώμη, τύπτειν) *maxim-coining, sententious.*

γνώμων, ονος, ὁ, (γνῶναι) *one that knows, a judge, interpreter.* II. *the gnomon* or *index* of the sun-dial. III. οἱ γνώμονες *the teeth that mark* a horse's age. IV. a carpenter's *rule,* Lat. *norma:* hence *a rule* or *guide* of life.

γνῶν, Ep. for ἔγνων, aor. 2 of γιγνώσκω.

γνῶναι, aor. 2 inf. of γιγνώσκω.

γνώομεν, Ep. for γνῶμεν, 1 pl. aor. 2 subj. of γιγνώσκω.

γνωρίζω, f. ίσω Att. ιῶ: pf. ἐγνώρικα:—*to make known, declare.* 2. *to discover, detect: to acknowledge, recognise.* 3. *to be acquainted with.* From

γνώρῐμος, ον, rarely η, ον, (γνωτός) *well-known:* as Subst., γνώριμος, ὁ, *an acquaintance, a friend,* Lat. *familiaris.* II. οἱ γνώριμοι *the notables,* Lat. *optimates.*

γνωρίμως, Adv. of γνώριμος, *so as to be known, intelligibly, familiarly;* γνωρίμως ἔχειν τινί to be *on friendly terms* with him.

γνώρῐσις, εως, ἡ, (γνωρίζω) *acquaintance: knowledge.*

γνώρισμα, ατος, τό, (γνωρίζω) *that by which a thing is made known, a mark, token.*

γνωρισμός, οῦ, ὁ, (γνωρίζω) *a making known.*

γνωριστικός, ή, όν, (γνωρίζω) *capable of making known.*

γνῷς, 2 sing. aor. 2 subj. of γιγνώσκω.

γνωσθήσομαι, fut. pass. of γιγνώσκω.

γνῶσι, 3 pl. aor. 2 subj. of γιγνώσκω.

γνωσι-μᾰχέω, f. ήσω, (γνῶσις, μάχομαι) *to dispute*

one's own opinion, i. e. *to confess oneself in the wrong, change one's purpose, give way; γνωσιμαχεῖν μὴ εἶναι ὅμοιον to confess* that one is not equal.

γνῶσις, εως, ἡ, (γνῶναι) *a seeking to know: a judicial inquiry*, Lat. *cognitio*. II. *knowledge: wisdom*. 2. *acquaintance with* a person. 3. *a recognising*.

γνώσομαι, fut. of γιγνώσκω.

γνωστήρ, ῆρος, ὁ, (γιγνώσκω) *one that knows* or *warrants the truth of a thing*, Lat. *cognitor*.

γνώστης, ου, ὁ, = γνωστήρ.

γνωστός, ή, όν, collat. form of *γνωτός, known* · as Subst. *a friend*. II. *to be known*.

γνῶτε, 2 pl. aor. 2 imperat. of γιγνώσκω:—γνῶτον, γνώτην, 2 and 3 dual aor. 2 indic.

γνωτός, ή, όν, also ός, όν, (γνῶναι) *known, well-known*:—as Subst. *a friend, kinsman, brother; γνωτοί τε γνωταί τε brothers* and *sisters*.

γνώω, Ep. for γνῶ. aor. 2 subj. of γιγνώσκω.

γνώωσι, Ep. for γνῶσι, 3 pl. aor. 2 of γιγνώσκω.

γοάασκεν, Ion. for ἐγόα, 3 sing. impf. of γοάω.

γοάοιεν or **γοάῳεν**, 3 pl. opt. of γοάω.

γοάοντι, Dor. for γοάουσι, 3 pl. of γοάω.

ΓΟΑ'Ω, Ep. inf. γοήμεναι; Ep. part. γοόων, όωσα: Ep. impf. ἔγοον, also γοάασκον: fut. γοήσομαι, later γοήσω: aor. 1 ἐγόησα:—Pass., aor. 1 ἐγοήθην: (γόος): —*to wail, groan, weep*. II. c. acc. *to bewail, mourn, weep for*.

ΓΟΓΓΥ'ΖΩ, f. σω, *to mutter*, a word formed from the sound.

γογγύλη, ἡ, and **γογγυλίς**, ίδος, ἡ, (γογγύλος) *a turnip*.

γογγύλλω, *to round, round off*. From

ΓΟΓΓΥ'ΛΟΣ, η, ον, also **γογγύλιος**, α, ον, = στογγύλος, *round, spherical*. [ῠ]

γογγυσμός, ὁ, (γογγύζω) *a muttering*.

γογγυστής, οῦ, ὁ, (γογγύζω) *a mutterer*.

γοεδνός, ή, όν, = γοερός.

γοερός, ά, όν, (γοάω) *lamentable, mournful*: of persons, *lamenting, mourning*.

ΓΟ'Η, ἡ, = γόος, κατᾳείδοντες γόησι τῷ ἀνέμῳ charming the wind *with howls*.

γοήμεναι, Ep. for γοᾶν, pres. inf. of γοάω.

γοήμων, ον, gen. ονος, = γοερός.

γόης, ητος, ὁ: dat. pl. γόησι: (γοάω) *one who howls out enchantments: a wizard, sorcerer: a juggler cheat*.

γοήσομαι, fut. of γοάω.

γοητεία, ἡ, (γοητεύω) *sorcery, witchcraft*.

γοητεύω, f. σω, (γόης) *to spell-bind, bewitch*

γοήτης, ου, ὁ, (γοάω) *a wailer*.

γοῆτις, ιδος, ἡ, pecul. fem. of γόης, *a witch*.

γόμος, ὁ, (γέμω) *a ship's cargo, a freight, load*.

γομφιό-δουπος, ον, (γομφίοι, δοῦπος) *rattling against the teeth*.

γομφίος, ὁ, (γόμφος) *a grinder-tooth*, Lat. *molaris*, opp. to προσθίος. II. *the tooth of a key*.

γομφό-δετος, ον, (γόμφος, δέω) *nail-bound*.

γομφο-πᾰγής, ές, (γόμφος, παγῆναι) *nail-fastened*.

ΓΟ'ΜΦΟΣ, ὁ, *a large wedge-shaped bolt* or *nail*, for shipbuilding: *any bond* or *fastening*: in pl. γόμφοι, the *cross-ribs* of the Egyptian canoes. Hence

γομφόω, f. ώσω, *to fasten with bolts* or *nails; γεγόμφωται σκάφος* the ship's hull *is ready built*. Hence

γόμφωμα, ματος, τό, *framework*.

γομφωτήρ, ῆρος, ὁ, (γομφόω) *one that fastens with bolts* or *nails, a ship-builder*.

γονεύς, έως, ὁ, (*γένω) *a father, ancestor*: in pl. *the parents*.

γονή, ἡ, (*γένω) *that which is begotten, offspring, a race, family*. II. *the seed*. III. *generation, childbirth: the womb*. IV. *birth, descent*. V. *a generation*.

γόνιμος, ον, also η, ον, (γόνος) *productive, fruitful; ποιητὴς γόνιμος* a poet *of creative powers, of true genius*: hence *genuine, true*.

γόνος, ὁ or ἡ, (*γένω) *that which is begotten, a child, offspring*: also *the young* of animals, *the fruit* of plants, *the produce* of anything. II. *race, birth, descent*. III. *a begetting*.

ΓΟ'ΝΥ, τό, gen. γόνατος, dat. pl. γόνασι: Ion. γόνυ, γούνατος, etc.; Ep. γόνυ, γουνός, γουνί, pl. γοῦνα, γούνων, γούνεσσι:—cf. δόρυ:—Lat. *GENU*, *the knee; ἅψασθαι γούνων* to clasp *the knees* as a suppliant; ἄντεσθαι, λίσσεσθαί τινα πρὸς γονάτων to entreat one *by clasping his knees*; γόνυ κάμπτειν to bend *the knee*, i. e. *sit down, take rest*, but also to bend *the knee* in running, *to run; τιθέναι τὰ γόνατα to kneel* down; θεῶν ἐν γούνασι κεῖται it lies on *the knees* of the gods, i. e. depends on their will and pleasure:—metaph. from warriors stricken down, ἐς γόνυ βάλλειν, κλίνειν, ῥίπτειν, to throw *on the knee*. II. *the knee* or *joint* of grasses, such as the cane, Lat. *geniculum*.

γονύ-κροτος, ον, (γόνυ, κροτέω) *knock-kneed*.

γονυπετέω, *to fall on the knee: γονυπετεῖν τινι* or τινα *to fall down before* one. From

γονυ-πετής, ές, (γόνυ, πεσεῖν) *falling on the knee; ἕδρα γονυπετὴς* a *kneeling* posture.

γόον, Ep. for ἐγόαον, 3 pl. impf. of γοάω.

ΓΟ'ΟΣ, ὁ, *a weeping, wailing, groaning*.

γοόων, όωσα, Ep. part. of γοάω.

Γοργεῖος, Att. **Γόργειος**, α, ον, (**Γοργώ**) *of, belonging to the Gorgon*.

Γοργο-λόφας, ου, ὁ, (Γοργῶ, λόφος) *he of the Gorgon crest*: fem. **Γοργολόφα**, ης, ἡ.

Γοργόνειος, ον, = Γοργεῖος.

Γοργό-νωτος, ον, (Γοργώ, νῶτος) *with the Gorgon on its back*.

γοργόομαι, Pass. *to be spirited*, of a horse. From

ΓΟΡΓΟ'Σ, ή, όν, *terrible, fearful, fierce; γοργὸν βλέπειν to look* fierce; γοργὸς εἰσιδεῖν *fearful* to behold: of horses, *hot, spirited*.

Γοργο-φόνος, ον, (Γοργώ, *φένω) *Gorgon-killing*: fem. Γοργοφονή, a name of Minerva.

ΓΟ'ΡΓΥΡΑ, ἡ, *an underground dungeon*.

Γοργώ, όος, contr. οῦς, ἡ; later decl. **Γοργώ**, όνος,

and in pl. Γοργόνες: (γοργός) :—*the Gorgon*, a monster *of fearful aspect;* Hesiod names three Gorgons, Euryalé, Stheino, and Medusa, the last the most fearful: her snaky head was fixed on the aegis of Athena, and all who looked on it became stone.

γοργ-ῶπις, ιδος, ἡ, pecul. fem. of γοργώψ.

γοργ-ωπός, όν, (γοργός, ὤψ) *fierce-eyed, terrible.*

γοργ-ώψ, ῶπος, ὁ, ἡ, = γοργωπός.

γοῦν, Ion. γῶν, (γε οὖν) restrictive Particle, *at least then, at any rate: of a truth, in sooth*, freq. in answers.

γοῦνα, γούνων, Ep. plur. of γόνυ, also found in Trag.

γουνάζεο, Ep. imperat. of γουνάζομαι.

γουνάζομαι, f. σομαι: Dep.: (γόνυ):—*to fall down and clasp* another's *knees, to entreat, supplicate; ὑπέρ τινος* and τινός *in behalf of* another: but also γουνάζεσθαί τινος and πρός τινος to entreat *by* such and such things.

γούνατος, γούνατι, γούνατα, γούνασι, Ion. and poët. decl. of γόνυ.

γουνόομαι, Dep., = γουνάζομαι: Ep. impf. γουνούμην.

γουνο-πᾰγής, ές, (γόνυ, πήγνυμι) *cramping the knees.*

γουνο-πᾰχής, ές, (γουνός, poët. gen. of γόνυ, παχύς) *thick-kneed.*

γουνός, poët. gen. of γόνυ.

γουνός, ὁ, (γόνος, γονή) *corn-land, fruitful land*, Lat. *uber; γουνὸς ἀλωῆς* a *fruitful* vineyard.

γρᾶες and **γρῆες**, pl. n. from γραῦς and γρηῦς.

γρᾴδιον, τό, contr. for γραΐδιον.

γραῖα, Ep. **γραίη**, ἡ, special fem. of γραῖος, *an old woman.* II. as fem. Adj. *old*, γραῖαι δαίμονες, γραίᾳ χερί, etc.

γραΐδιον, τό, Dim. of γραΐς, γραῦς, *an old hag.*

γραιόομαι, Pass. *to become an old woman.* From

γραῖος, γραία, γραῖον, (syncop. for γεραιός) *old, aged, gray; γραίη σταφυλή*, Lat. *uva passa, raisins.*

γράμμα, ατος, τό, (γράφω) *that which is drawn* or *written, a written character, letter*, Lat. *litera:* in plur. *letters, the alphabet.* 2. *a note* in music. 3. *a drawing, picture.* II. in plur. also, like Lat. *literae, a letter; an inscription: state-papers, documents, records, accounts:* also *a book, treatise.* III. *letters, learning*, = μαθήματα.

γραμμᾰτεῖον, τό, (γράφω) *that on which one writes, tablets, a note-book.*

γραμματεύς, έως, ὁ, (γράφω) *a secretary, clerk*, Lat. *scriba.* Hence

γραμματεύω, *to be secretary.*

γραμματίζω, (γράμματα) *to teach rudiments.*

γραμματικός, ή, όν, (γράμματα) *knowing one's letters, grounded in the rudiments:* as Subst., γραμματικός, ὁ, *a grammarian.* Adv. -κῶς.

γραμματιστής, οῦ, ὁ, (γραμματίζω) *one who teaches the rudiments, a schoolmaster.* 2. = γραμματεύς.

γραμματο-κύφων, ωνος, ὁ, (γράμματα, κύπτω) *one who pores over musty records.*

γραμμή, ἡ, (γράφω) *a stroke in writing, a line: ἡ μακρὰ the long line* of condemnation, drawn on the tablet of the dicast. II. *the line across the course*, to mark the starting or winning place. III. *the middle line* on a draught-board called ἡ ἱερά; τὸν ἀπὸ γραμμῆς κινεῖν λίθον to move a man from *this line*, i. e. try one's last chance.

γρᾱο-σόβης, ου, ὁ, (γραῦς, σοβέω) *scaring old women.*

γραπτέος, α, ον, verb. Adj. of γράφω, *to be written:* **γραπτέον**, *one must write.*

γραπτήρ, ῆρος, ὁ, (γράφω) *a writer.*

γραπτός, ή, όν, verb. Adj. of γράφω, *painted: marked with letters: written.*

γραπτύς, ύος, ἡ, (γράφω) *a scratching, tearing.*

ΓΡΑΥ'Σ, γρᾱός, ἡ, nom. pl. γρᾶες, acc. γραῦς: Ion. decl. **γρηῦς**, γρηός; poët. also **γρηΰς**:—*a gray woman, old woman.* II. *scum*, as of boiled milk.

γρᾰφεύς, έως, ὁ, (γράφω) *a painter.* II. = γραμματεύς, *a clerk.*

γρᾰφή, ἡ, (γράφω) *representation by means of lines: drawing, painting; ὅσον γραφῇ* only *in a picture.* 2. *writing.* II. *a painting, a figure, shape.* III. (γράφομαι) as Att. law term, *an indictment for a public offence, prosecution*, opp. to δίκη a private action; ἀστρατείας γραφή *an indictment for* neglect of service.

γρᾰφικός, ή, όν, *able to draw* or *paint: ἡ γραφική* (sub. τέχνη) *the art of painting.* 2. *suited for writing.*

γρᾰφίς, ίδος, ἡ, (γράφω) *a style* for writing on waxen tablets. II. *embroidery.*

ΓΡΑ'ΦΩ, f. ψω: pf. γέγραφα, later γεγράφηκα:—Pass., fut. γραφήσομαι, fut. 3 γεγράψομαι: aor. 2 ἐγράφην, later aor. 1 ἐγράφθην: pf. γέγραμμαι:—*to GRAVE, scratch; σήματα γράψας ἐν πίνακι having scratched* marks or figures on tablets. II. *to draw lines with a pencil, to sketch, draw, paint.* III. *to write; γράφειν εἰς διφθέρας to write* on skins. 2. *to inscribe*, e. g. γράφειν εἰς στήλην: Pass. γράφεσθαί τι *to be inscribed with* a thing. 3. *to write down; γράφειν τινὰ αἴτιον to set him down* as the cause: *to register, enrol.* 4. *to write down* a law hereafter to be proposed, hence *to propose, move.*

B. Med. *to write for oneself* or *for one's own use, note down.* 2. as Att. law-term, γράφεσθαί τινα *to indict* one, τινός *for* some public offence; in full, δίκην or γραφὴν γράψασθαί τινα; also c. inf., γράφεσθαί τινα ἀδικεῖν *to indict* him for wrong-doing; absol., οἱ γραψάμενοι *the prosecutors;* but γράφεσθαί τι, *to denounce* a thing as unlawful:—Pass. *to be indicted.*

γρα-ώδης, ες, (γραῦς, εἶδος) *of* or *belonging to an old woman*, Lat. *anilis: silly, trifling.*

γρηγορέω, *to be awake, be watchful*, a late pres., formed from the pf. ἐγρήγορα.

γρηῦς, ἡ, Ion. for γραῦς, poët. also γρηΰς.

γριπεύς, έως, ὁ, (γρῖπος) *a fisherman:* whence fem. Adj., γριπηΐς τέχνη the art *of fishing.*

ΓΡΙ'ΠΟΣ, ὁ, *a fishing-net.*

γρίπων, ὁ, = γριπεύς, *a fisherman.* [ῑ]

ΓΡΙ'ΦΟΣ, ὁ, like γρῖπος, *a fishing-net* or *basket*, made *of rushes.* 2. *anything intricate, a dark saying, riddle.*

γρῑφώδης, ες, (γρῖφος, εἶδος) *riddling.*
ΓΡΟ'ΣΦΟΣ, ὁ, *a kind of javelin.*
ΓΡΥ', *a grunt*, like that of swine; οὐδὲ γρῦ ἀποκρίνασθαι not even to give *a grunt;* οὐδὲ γρῦ not even *a syllable*, not *a bit.* Hence
γρύζω, f. ξω or ξομαι: aor. 1 ἔγρυξα:—*to say* γρῦ, *grunt*, Lat. *grunnio:* hence *to grumble mumble. mutter.*
γρυλλίζω or **γρῡλίζω**, (γρύλλος or γρῦλος) *to grunt.*
γρύλλος or **γρῦλος**, ὁ, (γρῦ) *a pig, porker.*
γρῡπ-άετος, ὁ, (γρύψ, ἀετός) *a kind of griffin* or *dragon.*
ΓΡΥΠΟ'Σ, ή. όν, *curved*, esp. *hook-nosed, with an aquiline nose*, opp. to σιμός. Hence
γρῡπότης, ητος, ἡ, *hookedness* of the nose.
γρῡπόω, f. ώσω, (γρυπός) *to curve* or *bend.*
γρύψ, gen. γρῡπός, ὁ, (γρυπός) *a griffin, hippogriff.*
γρώνη, ἡ, *a cavern: a kneading trough.*
ΓΥ'Α, ἡ, *a piece of land, field.*
γύαια, τά, (γύα) *cables made fast to land.*
ΓΥ'ΑΛΟΝ, τό, *a hollow;* in Homer, θώρηξ γυάλοισιν ἀρηρώς the body-armour composed *of back-piece and breast-piece*, joined under the arms:—*any hollow:* πέτρας γύαλον a *cave, grot;* κρατῆρος γύαλον *the hollow* of a bowl:—in plur. *hollow ground, vales, a valley.*
ΓΥ'ΗΣ, ου, ὁ, *the curved piece of wood* in a plough, to which the share was fitted, *the tree*, Lat. *buris.* II. = γύα, *a field.*
γυι-αρκής, ές, (γυῖον, ἀρκέω) *strengthening the limbs.*
γυιο-βαρής, ές, (γυῖον, βάρος) *weighing down the limbs.*
γυι-οβόρος, ον, (γυῖον, βορά) *gnawing the limbs.*
γυιο-δάμας, ου, ὁ, (γυῖον, δαμάω) *limb-subduing*, i. e. *victorious.*
ΓΥΙ'ΟΝ, τό, always used by Hom. in plur., *the limbs*, Lat. *membra;* esp. *the lower limbs, the knees.*
γυιο-παγής, ές, (γυῖον, πήγνυμι) *stiffening the limbs.*
γυιο-πέδη, ἡ, (γυῖον, πέδη) *a fetter.*
ΓΥΙΟ'Σ, ά, όν, *lame.*
γυιο-τακής, ές, (γυῖον, τήκω) *wasting the limbs.*
γυιο-τόρος, ου, (γυῖον, τορέω) *piercing the limbs.*
γυιό-χαλκος, ον, (γυῖον, χαλκός) *of brasen limb.*
γυιόω, (γυιός) *to lame:*—Pass. *to be* or *become lame;* γυιωθείς aor. 1 part., *lamed.*
γῡλι-αύχην, ενος, ὁ, ἡ, (γύλιος, αὐχήν) *long-necked.*
ΓΥ'ΛΙΟΣ, ὁ, *a long-shaped wallet* or *knapsack.*
γυμνάζω, f. άσω: pf. γεγύμνακα: Pass., pf. γεγύμνασμαι: (γυμνός):—*to train naked, to train in gymnastic exercises, to train, exercise;* c. inf., γυμνάζειν τοὺς παῖδας ποιεῖν *to train* them *to* do a thing:—Pass. *to practise gymnastic exercises:* then, generally, *to practise* or *exercise oneself.*
γυμνάς, άδος, properly fem. of γυμνός. *naked.* II. *trained* or *exercised.*
γυμνασία, ἡ, (γυμνάζω) *exercise.*
γυμνᾰσιαρχέω or Med. -έομαι, *to be gymnasiarch.* Pass. *to be supplied with gymnasiarchs.* From
γυμνᾰσι-άρχης and **γυμνασί-αρχος**, ὁ. (γυμνάσιον. ἄρχω) *a gymnasiarch*, who superintended the palaestrae, and paid the training-masters: *a training-master* Hence
γυμνᾰσιαρχία, ἡ, *the office of gymnasiarch*
γυμνάσιον, τό, (γυμνάζω) *the place where exercises were practised, the gymnastic-school;* ἐκ θ' ἡμετέρου γυμνασίου from our *school.* II. in plur. *bodily exercises.* [ᾰ]
γυμναστέον, verb. Adj. of γυμνάζω, *one must practise.*
γυμναστής, οῦ, ὁ, (γυμνάζω *the trainer of the athletes.* Hence
γυμναστικός, ή, όν, *fond of athletic exercises:* ἡ γυμναστική (sub. τέχνη) *gymnastics.* Adv. -κῶς, *like an athlete.*
γυμνής, ῆτος, ὁ, (γυμνός) *a light-armed foot-soldier.*
γυμνητεύω, *to be light-armed: to go naked.* From
γυμνήτης, ου, ὁ, fem. γυμνῆτις, ιδος, ἡ = γυμνής.
γυμνητία, ἡ, (γυμνής) *the light-armed troops.*
γυμνητικός, ή, όν, (γυμνής) *for a light-armed soldier.*
γυμνικός, ή, όν, (γυμνός) *of* or *for gymnastic exercises;* γυμνικὸς ἀγών a *gymnastic* contest.
γυμν-ιτεύω, = γυμνητεύω.
γυμνο-παιδίαι, ἡ, (γυμνός, παιδία) mostly in plur., a yearly festival in honour of those who fell at Thyrea, *at which naked boys danced and went through gymnastic exercises.*
ΓΥΜΝΟ'Σ, ή, όν, *naked, unclad: unarmed, defenceless:* of things, γυμνὸν τόξον an *uncovered* bow, i. e. out of the case: c. gen. *stripped of* a thing, γυμνὸς ὅπλων:—γυμνός often meant *lightly clad*, i. e. *wearing the tunic* or *under garment only* (χιτών), without the cloak (ἱμάτιον): τὰ γυμνά *the exposed parts* of an army, *the flanks.* 2. also *bare, mere.* Hence
Γυμνο-σοφισταί, οἱ, (γυμνός, σοφιστής) *the naked philosophers of India.*
γυμνότης, ητος, ἡ, *nakedness.*
γυμνόω, f. ώσω, (γυμνός) *to strip naked* or *bare:* Pass., of warriors, *to be stript of arms, to be left defenceless;* of things, τεῖχος ἐγυμνώθη the wall *was left bare:* but also *to strip oneself naked, be naked;* ἐγυμνώθη ῥακέων *he stript himself of* his rags.
γύμνωσις, εως, ὁ, (γυμνόω) *a stripping naked.* II. *nakedness: the naked parts.*
γύναι, voc. of γυνή.
γυναικάριον, τό, Dim. of γυνή, *a weak, silly woman.*
γυναικεῖος, α, ον, also ος, ον, Ion. **γυναικήϊος**, ηΐη, ήϊον, (γυνή) *of* or *belonging to women, feminine*, Lat. *muliebris.* 2. as Subst., ἡ γυναικηΐη = γυναικών, *the women's part of the house.* II. *womanish, effeminate.*
γυναικίζω, f. ίσω Att. ιῶ, (γυνή) *to be womanish, play the woman.*

γυναικό-βουλος, ον, (γυναικός, βουλή) *devised by a woman.*

γυναικο-γήρυτος, ον, (γυνή, γηρύω) *proclaimed by women.*

γυναικό-θῡμος, ον, (γυναικός, θυμός) *of womanish mind.*

γυναικο-κρασία, ἡ, (γυνή, κρᾶσις) *a woman's temper.*

γυναικο-κήρυκτος, ον, (γυναικός, κηρύσσω) *proclaimed by women.*

γυναικομᾰνέω, *to be mad for women.* From

γυναικο-μᾰνής, ές, (γυναικός, μαίνομαι) *mad for women.*

γυναικό-μῑμος, ον, (γυναικός, μιμέομαι) *aping women, womanish.*

γυναικό-μορφος, ον, (γυναικός, μορφή) *in woman's shape.*

γυναικο-πληθής, ές, (γυναικός, πλῆθος) *full of women.*

γυναικό-ποινος, ον, (γυναικός, ποινή) *woman-avenging.*

γῠναικός, gen. of γυνή, whence derivatives are formed.

γυναικο-φίλης, ου, Dor. **-φίλας**, α, (γύνη, φιλέω) *loving women.*

γυναικό-φρων, ον, gen. ονος, (γυναικός, φρήν) *of womanish mind.*

γυναικό-φωνος, ον, (γυναικός, φωνή) *with woman's voice.*

γυναικών, ῶνος, ὁ, (γυναικός) *the women's part of the house*, opp. to ἀνδρών.

γυναι-μᾰνής, ές, = γυναικομανής, *mad for women.*

γύναιον, τό, Dim. of γυνή, *a little woman.*

γύναιος, α, ον, *of* or *belonging to a woman.* From

ΓΥΝΗ', ἡ, gen. γυναικός, acc. γυναῖκα, voc. γύναι; pl. γυναῖκες, γυναικῶν, etc., (as if from γύναιξ):—*a woman*, Lat. *femina*, opp. to man: vocat. γύναι, a term of respect, *mistress, lady*: Homer often joins it with a second Subst., γυνὴ ταμίη, δέσποινα, etc. II. *a wife, spouse.* III. *a mortal woman*, opp. to a goddess. IV. *the female, mate* of animals.

γύννις, ιδος, ὁ, (γυνή) *a womanish man, weakling.*

γῡπάριον, τό, Dim. of γύπη, *a nest, eyrie, cranny.*

γύπεσσιν, dat. pl. of γύψ.

γύπη, ἡ, (γύψ) *a vulture's nest*: generally, *a hole, cranny.* Hence

γῡπιάς, ἡ, fem. Adj. *vulture-haunted.*

γυρη-τόμος, ον, (γῦρος, τεμεῖν) *tracing a circle.*

ΓΥ'ΡΙΣ, εως, ἡ, *the finest meal*, Lat. *pollen.*

ΓΥΡΟ'Σ, ά, όν, *round*, Lat. *curvus*; γυρὸς ἐν ὤμοισι *round*-shouldered.

ΓΥ'ΡΟΣ, ὁ, *a ring, circle.*

ΓΥ'Ψ, γῡπός, ὁ, *a vulture*, Lat. *vultur.*

ΓΥ'ΨΟΣ, ἡ, *chalk.* 2. later, *gypsum.* Hence

γυψόω, f. ώσω, *to rub over with chalk.*

γῶν, Ion. for γοῦν, as ὦν for οὖν.

ΓΩΝΙ'Α, ἡ, *a corner, angle.* II. *a joiner's square.* Hence

γωνιασμός, ὁ, *a squaring the angles*; ἐπῶν γωνιασμός *nicely-fitted, well-finished verses.*

γωνι-ώδης, ες, (γωνία, εἶδος) *angular.*

ΓΩΡΥΤΟ'Σ, ὁ or ἡ, *a bow-case, quiver.*

Δ

Δ, δ, δέλτα, indecl., fourth letter of the Gr. alphabet: as numeral, δ' = τέσσαρες and τέταρτος, ͵δ = 4000.

Changes of δ in the dialects: I. Aeol. into β, as ὀβελός into ὀδελός. II. Dor. into γ, as γᾶ γνόφος into δᾶ δνόφος. III. Ion. into ζ, as Ζεύς, ζα- into Δεύς, δα-: while Dor. ζ changes into σδ, as μελίζω φράζομαι into μελίσδω φράσδομαι; sometimes into δδ, as γυμνάζομαι into γυμνάδδομαι. IV. into κ, as δαίω καίω. V. into λ, as δάκρυ lacryma, δασύς λάσιος. VI. into σ, as ὀδμή ὀσμή, also with another consonant added, as βάδος βασμός, ἔδω ἐσθίω. VII. sometimes δ is inserted to give a softer or fuller sound, as ἀνέρος ἀνδρός. VIII. at the beginning of some words δ is added or omitted, as in δείλη εἵλη, δή ἦ, διώκω ἰώκω.

δᾰ-, intensive prefix, = ζα-, as in δά-σκιος.

δᾶ, Dor. for γᾶ, γῆ, mostly in voc.: acc. δᾶν.

δᾶγμα, τό, Dor. for δῆγμα.

δᾰγύς, ῦδος, ἡ, *a waxen image*, used in magic rites, *a puppet.* (Thessal. word.) [ῠ]

δᾳδουχέω, f. ήσω, *to be a torch-bearer*, esp. in sacred processions. From

δᾳδ-οῦχος, ον, (δᾷς, ἔχω) *holding torches*: as Subst., δᾳδοῦχος, ἡ, *a torch-bearer* at the festival of Eleusinian Ceres, whose torch represented her as searching for her daughter Proserpine.

δᾳδοφορέω, f. ήσω, *to bear torches.* From

δᾳδο-φόρος, ον, (δᾷς, φέρω) *torch-bearing.*

δαείην, aor. 2 opt. of *δάω.

δαείς, aor. 2 part. of *δάω.

δᾰείω, Ep. for δαῶ, aor. 2 pass. subj. of *δάω.

δαήμεναι, Ep. for δαῆναι, aor 2 pass. inf. of *δάω.

δᾰήμων, ον, gen. ονος, (δαῆναι) *knowing, experienced in* a thing.

δαῆναι, aor. 2 pass. inf. of *δάω.

ΔΑΗ'Ρ, έρος, ὁ, voc. δᾶερ, *a husband's brother, brother-in-law*, answering to γάλως, ἡ, *a daughter-in-law.*

δαήσομαι, fut. of *δάω.

δάηται, 3 sing. aor. 2 med. subj. of δαίω (A).

δαί, (δή) used after interrogatives, expressing wonder or curiosity, τί δαί; what *then*? πῶς δαί; how *so*?

δαῖ, Ep. apocop. for δαΐδι, dat. of δαΐς. [ῐ]

δαιδάλεος, α, ον, also ος, ον, *cunningly* or *curiously wrought.* From

δαιδάλλω, used only in pres. act.; but pass. aor. 1 ἐδαιδάλθην, pf. δεδαίδαλμαι: (δαίδαλος):—*to work cunningly, work with curious art*: *to deck out, embellish.* Hence

δαίδαλμα, ατος, τό, *a work of art*

δαιδαλόεις, εσσα, εν, = δαιδάλεος.

δαιδαλο-εργός, όν, (δαίδαλος, ἔργον) *curiously working*.

ΔΑΙ'ΔΑ˘ΛΟΣ, η, ον, Adj. *cunningly* or *curiously wrought*; δαίδαλα πάντα all *cunning works*. II. as prop. n., Δαίδαλος, ὁ, *Daedalus*, i. e. *the cunning worker*, *the Artist*, of Cnossus in Crete, contemporary with Minos, mentioned by Homer as the maker of a χορός (q. v.) for Ariadné.

δαιδᾰλό-χειρ, ειρος, ὁ, ἡ, (δαίδαλος, χείρ) *cunning of hand*.

δαιδαλόω, = δαιδάλλω: poët. inf. fut. δαιδαλωσέμεν.

δαΐζω, f. ξω: aor. 1 ἐδάϊξα:—Pass., aor. 1 part. δαϊχθείς: pf. part. δεδαϊγμένος: (δαίω):—*to cleave asunder*, χιτῶνα περὶ στήθεσσι δαΐξαι; δεδαϊγμένος ἦτορ *pierced through* the heart:—also of doubts, ἐδαΐζετο θυμὸς ἐνὶ στήθεσσιν his soul *was divided* within him; δαϊζόμενος κατὰ θυμὸν διχθάδια *divided* in mind between two opinions. Hence

δᾰῒ-κτάμενος, η, ον, (δάϊς, κτείνω) or in two words δάϊ κτάμενος, *slain in battle*.

δαϊκτήρ, ῆρος, and **δαϊκτής**, οῦ, ὁ, (δαΐζω) only joined with masc. Subst. *heart-cleaving*.

δαιμονάω, (δαίμων) *to be subject to an avenging deity*; δαιμονᾷ δόμος κακοῖς the house *is plunged by the divinity* in woes. 2. c. acc., δαιμονᾶν ἄχη *to have* griefs *decreed one*. II. absol. *to be possessed by an evil spirit, be driven to madness*.

δαιμονίζομαι, Med. (δαίμων) *to have an allotted fate*. II. Pass., with aor. 1 part. δαιμονισθείς, *to be possessed by a devil*.

δαιμόνιον, τό, (properly neut. of δαιμόνιος) *the Deity, Divinity*, or *divine operation*, Lat. *numen*. II. the δαιμόνια were *an inferior race of divine beings, demons*, opp. to θεοί. 2. the name by which Socrates called his *genius*. 3. in N. T. *an evil spirit*.

δαιμόνιος, α, ον, also ος, ον: (δαίμων): I. used by Homer only in vocat. δαιμόνιε, in good sense, *noble sir*; but more freq. as a reproach, *unhappy man, wretch*: in Att. mostly ironical, *my fine fellow! my good sir!* II. *of things proceeding from the Deity* or *from Fate*; εἰ μή τι δαιμόνιον εἴη were it not *a divine intervention*; τὰ δαιμόνια *divine visitations*. III. of persons, *divine, godlike*.

δαιμονι-ώδης, ες, (δαιμόνιον, εἶδος) *devilish*.

δαιμονίως, Adv. of δαιμόνιος, *marvellously, strangely*.

δαίμων, ονος, ὁ, ἡ, (δαίω) *a god, goddess*. II. *the Deity*, Lat. *numen*: *fate, destiny, fortune*, good or bad; πρὸς δαίμονα against *fate*; σὺν δαίμονι with *the favour of the gods, non sine diis*; in Trag., *death*, like Lat. *sors*. III. *one's genius, one's lot* or *fortune*. IV. δαίμονες was a name given to *the souls of men of the golden age*, who formed the connecting link between gods and men: hence later, *departed souls*, Lat. *manes, lemures*. V. *an evil spirit, devil*.

δαίμων, ὁ, as Adj., = δαήμων, *skilled in* a thing.

δαίνῡ, Ep. for ἐδαίνυ, 3 sing. impf. of **δαίνυμι**.

δαίνυ', Ep. for ἐδαίνυο, 2 sing. impf. med. of **δαίνυμι**.

δαινύατο, for ἐδαίνυντο, 3 pl. impf. med. of δαίνυμι.

δαινύῃ, 2 sing. pres. med. subj. of δαίνυμι.

δαίνῡμι, also **δαινύω**: Ep. 3 sing. impf. δαίνυ: fut. δαίσω: aor. 1 ἔδαισα: (δαίς):—*to give a banquet* or *feast*; δαίνυ δαῖτα γέρουσι *he gave* a feast to the elders; δαινύειν τινά *to feast* a person. II. Med. δαίνῠμαι, fut. δαίσομαι: aor. 1 ἐδαισάμην:—*to have a feast given one, to feast*: also c. acc. δαῖτα, κρέα, etc., *to feast on, consume, eat*: *to eat, burn* like poison.

δαίνυο, Ep. for ἐδαίνυσο, 2 sing. impf. med. of δαίνυμι.

δαινῦτο, Ep. for δαινύοιτο, 3 sing. opt. med. of δαινύμι.

δάϊος, α, ον, also ος, ον: Ion. and Hom. **δήϊος**, η, ον: Att. contr. **δᾷος**: (δαίω, δάϊς):—*hostile, destructive*: as epith. of *fire, burning, consuming*: in pl. δάϊοι, *enemies*. 2. *unhappy, wretched*. II. (δαῆναι) *knowing, cunning*.

δαίρω, f. δαρῶ: aor. 1 inf. δῆραι, poët. for δέρω, δείρω, *to flay, cudgel*.

δαΐς (A), gen. δαΐδος, Att. contr. **δᾷς**, δᾳδος, ἡ, (δαίω A): *a fire-brand, pine-torch*, Lat. *taeda*:—*pinewood*, such as torches were made of. II. *war, battle*, ἡ, mostly in apocopate dat. δάϊ and acc. δάϊν.

δαίς (B) gen. δαιτός, ἡ, (δαίω B) *a meal, feast, banquet*, Lat. *DAPES* 2. *meat* or *food* itself.

δαίσασθαι, δαισάμενος, aor. 1 inf. and part. med. of δαίνυμι.

δαιταλεύς, έως, ὁ, (δαίνυμι) *a guest, banquetter*.

δαίτη, ἡ, poët. for δαίς, *a feast, banquet*.

δαίτηθεν, Adv. of δαίτη, *from a feast*

δαιτρεύω, f. σω, (δαιτρός) *to cut up* or *carve, to portion out, distribute*.

δαιτρόν, τό, (δαίω B) *one's portion*.

δαιτρός, ὁ, (δαίω B) *a carver, distributer*. Hence

δαιτροσύνη, ἡ, *the art of carving*: *a helping at table*.

δαιτῠμών, όνος, ὁ, (δαίς B) *an invited guest*. 2. in plur. *guests who bring each his own provisions*.

δαιτύς, ύος, ἡ, Ion. for δαίς, *a meal*.

δᾰῒ-φρων, ον, gen. ονος: (δάϊς, φρήν): *of warlike mind, eager for the fray, bold*. II. (δαῆναι) *of knowing mind, prudent, thoughtful*.

δαϊχθείς, aor. 1 part. of δαΐζω.

ΔΑΙ'Ω (A), = καίω, only used in pres. and impf., *to light up, kindle*; δαῖε οἱ ἐκ κόρυθος πῦρ, *she* (sc. Minerva) *made* fire *blaze* from his helm:—Pass., aor. 1 part. δαισθείς: pf. part. δεδαυμένος:—*to burn, blaze*: δαίεται ὄσσε the eyes *sparkle*: to this also belong pf. δέδηα, plqpf. ἐδεδήειν, poët. δεδήειν; πόλεμος δέδηε war *blazes forth*; ὄσσα δεδήει the report *spread like wild-fire*.

ΔΑΙ'Ω (B), *to divide, part out, distribute*; in Act. sense δαΐζω is used, but in Med. and Pass. δαίομαι; Med., κρέα δαιόμενος *distributing portions* of meat; Pass., δαίεται ἦτορ my heart *is divided*; Ep. 3 pl. δεδαίαται.—But ἔδαισα, ἐδαισάμην belong to δαίνυμι: δάσομαι ἐδασάμην, δέδασμαι to δατέομαι.

δᾰκέ-θῦμος, ον, = δηξίθυμος, *heart-eating.*
δάκε, Ep. for ἔδακε, 3 sing. aor. 2 of δάκνω.
δακεῖν, aor. 2 inf. of δάκνω.
δάκετον, τό, = δάκος, *a venomous animal.*
δακνάζω, poët. for δάκνω: Pass. *to be sore vexed.*
ΔΑ'ΚΝΩ, f. δήξομαι: pf. δέδηχα: aor. 2 ἔδᾰκον: Ep. inf. δακέειν:—Pass., aor. 1 ἐδήχθην: pf. δέδηγμαι: —*to bite*, esp. of dogs and gnats; στόμιον δάκνειν *to champ* the bit; δάκνειν ἑαυτόν *to bite one's lips* for fear of laughing. II. metaph. *to bite, sting, prick*:—Pass., καρδίαν δέδηγμαι *I was vexed* at heart.
δάκος, εος, τό, (δακεῖν) *an animal whose bite or sting is dangerous, any noxious animal.*
ΔΑ'ΚΡΥ, υος, τό, poët. for δάκρυον, *a tear*, Lat. *LACRYMA.* II. *a drop*, as of *gum.*
δακρύδιον, τό Dim. of δάκρυ.
δάκρῦμα, ατος, τό, (δακρύω) *that which is wept for, a subject for tears.* II. *a tear.*
δακρυο-γόνος, ον, (δακρύ, *γένω) *author of tears.*
δακρυόεις, εσσα, εν, (δάκρυον) *tearful;* of persons, *much weeping;* of things, *calling forth tears*:—δακρυόεν γελάσαι, as Adv., *to smile through one's tears.*
ΔΑ'ΚΡΥΟΝ, τό, = δάκρυ: Ep. gen. pl. δακρυόφι.
δακρυ-πλώω, (δάκρυ, πλέω) *to swim with tears.*
δακρυρροέω, f. ήσω, *to melt into tears.* From
δακρύρ-ροος, ον, (δάκρυ, ῥέω) *melting into tears.*
δάκρῦσα, Ep. aor. 1 of δακρύω.
δακρυσί-στακτος, ον, (δάκρυ, στάζω) *dropping with tears.*
δακρυσῶ, Dor. for δακρύσω.
δακρῦτός, ή, όν, verb. Adj. of δακρύω, *wept over, tearful.*
δακρυ-χᾰρής, ές, (δάκρυ, χαίρω) *rejoicing in tears.*
δακρυ-χέων, ουσα, ον, a participial Adj., (δάκρυ, χέω) *shedding tears, weeping.*
δακρύω [ῡ], fut. ύσω: aor. 1 ἐδάκρῡσα: pf. δεδάκρῡκα: (δάκρυ):—*to weep, shed tears*:—pf. pass. δεδάκρῡμαι, *to be tearful, be all in tears;* part. δεδακρυμένος, *all in tears*: c. acc. cognato, δακρύειν γόους *to utter tearful* groans. II. transit. *to weep for* a thing, *lament*:—Pass. *to be wept for.* III. δ. βλέφαρα *to flood* one's eyes *with tears.*
δακρυ-ώδης, ες, (δάκρυ, εἶδος) *like tears: tearful.*
δακτῠλήθρα, ἡ, (δάκτυλος) *a finger-sheath.*
δακτῠλίδιον, τό, Dim. of δάκτυλος, *a toe.*
δακτῠλικός, ή, όν, (δάκτυλος) *of* or *for the finger*, Lat. *digitalis;* αὐλὸς δακτυλικὸς a flute *played with the fingers.* II. of metre, *dactylic.*
δακτύλιος, ὁ, (δάκτυλος) *a ring, seal-ring.*
δακτῠλο-δεικτός, όν, (δάκτυλος, δείκνυμι) *pointed at with the finger*, as in Horace *digito monstrari.*
δακτῠλο-ειδής, ές, (δάκτυλος, εἶδος) *like a finger.*
δάκτῠλος, ὁ, plur. δάκτυλοι, poët. also δάκτυλα: (δείκνυμι):—*a finger*, Lat. *digitus;* ἐπὶ δακτύλων συμβάλλεσθαι to reckon *on the fingers.* 2. δάκτυλος τοῦ ποδός *a toe*, also without ποδός, like Lat. *digitus.* II. the shortest Greek measure of length, *a finger's breadth*, = about $\frac{7}{10}$ of an inch. III. a metrical foot, *dactyl*, — ᴗ ᴗ: e. g. ἄξιος.
δακτῠλό-τριπτος, ον, (δάκτυλος, τρίβω) *worn by the fingers.*
δᾰλέομαι, Dor. for δηλέομαι.
δᾰλίον, τό, Dim. of δαλός.
δᾱλός, ὁ, (δαίω) *a firebrand, piece of blazing wood.* II. *a burnt out torch*, of an old man. III. *a beacon-light.*
δᾰμάζω, later form of δαμάω: see δαμάω.
δᾰμαῖος, ὁ, (δαμάω) epith. of Neptune, *the Tamer.*
δᾰμάλη, ἡ, = δάμαλις.
δᾰμᾰλη-βοτος, ον, (δαμάλη, βόσκω) *fed on by young cattle.*
δαμαλη-φάγος, ον, (δαμάλη, φαγεῖν) *beef-eating*, epith. of Hercules.
δᾰμᾰλίζω, f. ίσω, poët. form of δαμάω, *to subdue.*
δάμᾰλις, εως, ἡ, (δαμάω) *a young cow, heifer, calf*, Lat. *juvenca.* II. like μόσχος, *a girl.*
δάμᾰλος, ὁ, (δαμάω) *a calf*, Lat. *vitulus.*
δάμαρ, αρτος, ἡ, (δαμάω) *a wife, spouse.*
δαμάσδω, Dor. for δαμάζω.
δᾰμασίμ-βροτος, ον, (δαμάω, βροτός) *man-subduing.*
δᾰμάσ-ιππος, ον, (δαμάω, ἵππος) *horse-taming.*
δάμᾰσις, εως, ἡ, (δαμάω) *a taming, subduing.*
δαμασί-φρων, ον, gen. ονος, (δαμάω, φρήν) *heart-subduing.*
δᾰμασί-φως, ωτος, ὁ, ἡ, (δαμάω, φώς) *man-subduing.*
δᾰμάτειρα, ἡ, fem. Subst. *a tamer.*
Δαμᾶτερ, Dor. vocat. from Δημήτηρ.
ΔΑΜΑ'Ω, Ep. 3 sing. δαμάᾳ, 3 pl. δαμόωσι: fut. δαμάσω [μᾰ], Ep. δαμάσσω: aor. 1 ἐδάμᾰσα Ep. ἐδάμασσα, δάμασσα: pf. δεδάμακα:—Pass., aor. 1 ἐδμήθην, part. δμηθείς; aor. 2 ἐδάμην, inf. δᾰμήμεναι, part. δαμείς: pf. δέδμημαι:—another aor. 1 part. δᾰμασθείς, pf. part. δεδαμασμένος are found, as if from δαμάζω. *To tame, to bring under the yoke, subdue, overpower.* II. of maidens, *to yoke in marriage, give to wife:* also *to force, lie with*, Lat. *subigere.* III. generally, *to subdue, conquer*, esp. in war:—Pass. *to be subject, to obey.* 2. *to slay, kill.*
δᾰμείην, aor. 2 opt. pass. of δαμάω.
δᾰμείω, Ep. for δαμῶ, aor. 2 pass. subj. of δαμάω: 2 and 3 pass. δαμήῃς, -ηῃ, Ep. for δαμῇς, δαμῇ: 2 pl. δαμείετε, for δαμῆτε.
δάμεν, Ep. for ἐδάμησαν, 3 pl. aor. 2 pass. of δαμάω.
δᾰμήμεναι, Ep. for δαμῆναι, aor. 2 pass. inf. of δαμάω.
δάμνα, Ep. for ἐδάμνα, 3 sing., impf. of δάμνημι.
δαμνᾷ, 3 sing. of δαμνάω, also 2 sing. pres. Med. of δάμνημι.
δαμνάω, = δαμάω, only in pres. and impf.
δάμνημι, = δαμάω:—Pass. and Med. δάμναμαι.
δᾶμος and **δᾱμόσιος**, α, ον, Dor. for δημ—.
δᾰμόωσι, Ep. 3 pl. of δαμάω.
δᾱμώματα, τά, (δᾶμος) *hymns sung in public.*
δᾶν, Dor. for δῆν, γῆν:—οὐ δᾶν, *No, by earth!*

ΔΑΝΑΟΙ', οἱ, *the Danaans*, subjects of Δάναος, king of Argos; in Homer for *the Greeks* generally: Δαναΐδαι, ῶν, οἱ, *the sons* or *descendants of Danaus*: Δαναΐδες, αἱ, his *daughters*. Hence a Comic Sup. **Δα-ναώτατος**, *oldest of the Danaans*. [Δᾰ]

δᾰνείζω, f. είσω: pf. δεδάνεικα, pass. δεδάνεισμαι: (δάνος):—*to put out money at usury, to lend*:—Pass., of the money, *to be lent*:—Med. *to have lent to one, to borrow*.

δάνειον, τό, (δάνος) *money lent* or *borrowed, a loan*.

δάνεισμα, ατος, τό, (δανείζω) = δάνειον.

δᾰνεισμός, ὁ, (δανείζω) *money-lending*.

δᾰνειστής, οῦ, ὁ, (δανείζω) *a money-lender, usurer*.

δανειστικός, ή, όν, (δανείζω) *disposed to lend*.

ΔΑ'ΝΟΣ, εος, τό, *a gift*. II. *money lent out at interest, a loan, debt*.

δᾱνός, ή, όν, (δαίω A) *burnt, dried, parched*.

δάος, εος, τό, (δαίω A) = δαλός, *a firebrand, torch*.

δᾰπᾰνάω, f. ήσω:—Pass., aor. 1 ἐδαπανήθην, pf. δε-δαπάνημαι, both used also in med. sense:—*to spend*; δαπανᾶν εἴς τι *to spend upon* a thing:—Med. *to spend of one's own*. II. Causal, δαπανᾶν τὴν πόλιν *to put* the state *to expense, exhaust* the state. From

ΔΑΠΑ'ΝΗ, ἡ, *cost, expense, expenditure*. II. *money spent*: also *money for spending*. III. *ex-pensiveness, extravagance*. [πᾰ]

δᾰπάνημα, ατος, τό, *money spent, expense*.

δᾰπᾰνηρός, ά, όν, (δαπάνη) of men, *extravagant*: of things, *expensive*. Adv. -ρῶς, *expensively*.

δάπανος, ον, = δαπανηρός, *extravagant*.

δά-πεδον, τό, (δα-, πέδον) *land, soil*: *the floor of a chamber*: in pl. *plains, flat country*.

ΔΑ'ΠΙΣ, ιδος, ἡ, = τάπης, *a carpet, rug*. [ᾰ]

δαπτέμεν, Ep. for δάπτειν, inf. of δάπτω.

ΔΑ'ΠΤΩ, f δάψω, *to devour*.

Δάρδᾰνος, ὁ, *Dardanus*, son of Jupiter, founder of Dardania or Troy. As Adj., Δάρδανος ἀνήρ *a Trojan*, mostly in plur. Δάρδανοι: **Δαρδάνιος**, α, ον, *Trojan*: **Δαρδανίς**, ίδος, ἡ, *a Trojan woman*: **Δαρ-δανία**, ἡ, *Troy*: **Δαρδανίδης**, ου, ὁ, *a son* or *descendant of Dardanus*: **Δαρδανίωνες**, οἱ, *sons of Dardanus*.

δαρδάπτω, lengthd. form of δάπτω, *to devour*.

δαρεικός or **δαρεικὸς στατήρ**, ὁ, a Persian gold coin, = 20 Attic drachmae: so that 5 = a mina, 300 = a talent. (Said to have been first coined by *Darius*, but prob. derived from Persian *darâ, a king*, cf. Δά-ρειος, like our *sovereign*.)

Δᾱρεῖος, ὁ, *Darius*, acc. to Herodotus = Gr. ἑρξείης, q. v.: a Greek form of Persian *darâ, a king*.

δᾰρήσομαι, fut. 2 pass. of δέρω.

ΔΑΡΘΑ'ΝΩ: aor. 2 ἔδαρθον, poët ἔδρᾰθον:—*to sleep* Lat. *DORMIO*. Cp. καταδαρθάνω.

δᾱρό-βιος, ον, = δηρόβιος.

δᾱρός, ά, όν, Dor. and Trag. for δηρός.

δᾰρῶ, fut. of δέρω.

δᾴς, gen. δᾳδός, ἡ, Att. contr. for δαΐς.

δάσασθαι, aor. 1 med. inf. of δατέομαι; Ion. 3 sing. indic. δᾰσάσκετο; 1 pl. opt. δασαίμεθα: δασεῖται is fut. Dor. Cf. πάσασθαι from πατέομαι.

δασέως, Adv. of δασύς; δασέως ἔχειν to be *hairy*.

δά-σκῐος, ον, (δα-, σκιά) *thick-shaded, dark*.

δάσμευσις, εως, ἡ, (δασμός) *a dividing, distributing*.

δασμολογέω, f. ήσω, *to exact as tribute*: c. dupl. acc., *to exact tribute from* a person. Hence

δασμολογία, ἡ, *collection of tribute*.

δασμο-λόγος, ὁ, (δασμός, λέγω) *a tax-collector*.

δασμός, ὁ, (δάσασθαι) *a division, sharing of spoil*: *distribution*. II. in Att. *an impost, tribute*.

δασμοφορέω, f. ήσω, *to pay tribute*:—Pass., δασμο-φορεῖταί τινι *tribute is paid* one. From

δασμο-φόρος, ον, (δασμός, φέρω) *paying tribute, tributary*.

δάσομαι, fut. of δατέομαι: cf. δάσασθαι.

δασ-πλής, ῆτος, ὁ, ἡ, and **δασ-πλῆτις**, ἡ, (δα-, πλήσσω) *horrid, frightful*.

δάσσασθαι, Ep. for δάσασθαι, q. v.

δασύ-θριξ, τρῐχος, ὁ, ἡ, (δασύς, θρίξ) *thick-haired*.

δασύ-κερκος, ον, (δασύς, κέρκος) *bushy-tailed*.

δασύ-κνημος, ον, and **δασυ-κνήμων**, ον, gen. ονος, (δασύς, κνήμη) *shaggy-legged*.

δασύ-μαλλος, ον, (δασύς, μαλλός) *thick-fleeced*.

δᾰσύνω [ῡ], f. ῠνῶ, (δασύς) *to make rough* or *hairy*: Pass. *to become rough* or *hairy*.

δασύ-πους, ποδος, ὁ, (δασύς, πούς) *hairy-foot*, i. e. a *hare* or *rabbit*.

δασυ-πώγων, ωνος, ὁ, ἡ, (δασύς, πώγων) *with shaggy beard*.

ΔΑΣΥ'Σ, εῖα, ύ, Ion. fem. δασέα, *thick with hair, hairy, rough*: *downy*, opp. to ψιλός: of places, *thick grown with bushes, bushy*; δασέα θρίδαξ a lettuce *with the leaves on*. II. like Lat. *densus, thick, crowded*.

δασύ-στερνος, ον, (δασύς, στέρνον) *shaggy-breasted*.

δασυ-χαίτης, ου, ὁ, (δασύς, χαίτη) *shaggy-haired*.

δᾰτέομαι, fut. δάσομαι: aor. 1 ἐδασάμην Ep. ἐδασ-σάμην: pf. δέδασμαι: (for the forms, cf. πατέομαι, ἐπασάμην): Dep.:—*to divide among themselves, to share in*: *to tear in pieces*; χθόνα ποσσὶ δατεῦντο *they measured* the ground with their feet. 2. *to cut in two*. 3. *to divide* or *distribute to others*.

δατεῦντο, Aeol. 3 pl. impf. of δατέομαι.

δᾰτήριος, α, ον, (δατέομαι) *distributing*; and

δᾰτητής, οῦ, ὁ, *a distributer*.

δαφναῖος, α, ον, *of* or *belonging to a laurel*. From

ΔΑ'ΦΝΗ, ἡ, *the laurel* or *bay*, sacred to Apollo.

δαφνηφορέω, f. ήσω, *to bear laurel-boughs*. From

δαφνη-φόρος, ον, (δάφνη, φέρω) *planted with laurels*. II. *bearing laurel-boughs*.

δαφνιᾰκός, ή, όν, (δάφνη) *belonging to a laurel*.

δαφνο-γηθής, ές, (δάφνη, γηθέω) *delighting in the laurel*.

δαφνό-κομος, ον, (δάφνη, κόμη) *laurel-crowned*.

δαφν-ώδης, ες, (δάφνη, εἶδος) *laurelled*.

δᾰ-φοινεός, όν, = δαφοινός; εἷμα δαφοινεὸν αἵματι a garment *red* with blood.

δᾰ-φοινός, όν, (δα-, φοινός) of wild beasts, *blood-red, tawny;* or perhaps *bloody, murderous.*

δαψίλεια, ἡ, *abundance, plenty.* From

δαψῐλής, ές, (δάπτω) *abundant, plentiful:* of persons, *liberal, profuse.* Adv. δαψιλῶς, *lavishly:* Sup. δαψιλέστατα.

***ΔΑ'Ω**, an old root meaning *to learn*, which sometimes takes a causal sense, *to teach:* I. Causal, *to teach:* only in redupl. aor. 2 act. δέδαε, *he taught*, like Lat. *doceo;* later also ἔδαον.—The pres. in this sense is διδάσκω. II. *to learn:* fut. δαήσομαι (ἐμεῦ δαήσεαι *thou wilt learn from* me): pf. δεδάηκα, part. δεδαηκώς, δεδαώς, also pass. δεδαημένος: aor. 2 ἐδάην, subj. δαῶ, Ep. δαείω, inf. δαῆναι, Ep. δαήμεναι, part. δαείς:—from δέδαα, is formed a pres. med. inf. δεδάασθαι, *to search out.*—The pres. in this sense is διδάσκομαι.

δαῶμεν, 1 pl. aor. 2 pass. subj. of *δάω.

ΔΕ', *but:* conjunctive Particle, with an *opposing* or *adversative* force. It answers to μέν, esp. in Prose, when it may be rendered by *while, on the other hand*, see μέν. 2. it often serves merely to pass from one thing to another, when it may be rendered, *and, further.* II. δέ properly stands second in the sentence, but it is also found third or fourth, when the preceding words are closely connected.

-δε, enclitic Particle: joined I. to names of Places in acc., to denote *motion towards*, as if it were an enclitic preposit.; οἶκόνδε home-*wards*, Οὔλυμπόνδε *to* Olympus, θύραζε (for θύρασδε) to the door; more rarely repeated with the possess. Pron., ὅνδε δόμονδε; and sometimes even after εἰς, as εἰς ἅλαδε: in Att. often added to the names of cities, Ἀθήναζε, Θήβαζε (for Ἀθήνασδε, Θήβασδε):—sometimes it denotes *purpose* only, μήτι φόβονδ' ἀγόρευε speak naught *tending to fear.* II. to the demonstr. Pron., to give it greater force, ὅδε, τοιόσδε, etc., such a man *as this*, Att. ὁδί, etc.

δεά, ἡ, Dor. for θεά, Lat. *dea.*

δέᾰτο, Ep. for ἐδέατο, 3 sing. impf. of an obsolete Verb δέαμαι, = δοκέω, *he seemed.*

δέγμενος, Ep. aor. 2 part. of δέχομαι.

δεδάασθαι, Ep. pres. med. inf. of *δάω.

δέδαε, 3 sing. aor. 2 act. of *δάω.

δεδάηκα, δεδάημαι, pf. act. and pass. of *δάω.

δεδαίαται, Ion. for δέδαινται, 3 pl. pf. pass. of δαίω B.

δεδαϊγμένος, pf. pass. part. of δαΐζω.

δεδαιδαλμένος, part. pf. pass. of δαιδάλλω.

δέδᾰκον, redupl. poët. aor. 2 of δάκνω.

δεδάκρῡκα, pf. of δακρύω.

δέδαργμαι, Att. for δέδραγμαι, pf. pass. of δράσσομαι.

δέδαρμαι, pf. pass. of δέρω.

δέδασμαι, pf. pass. of δατέομαι.

δεδαώς, pf. act. part. of *δάω.

δέδεγμαι, pf. of δέχομαι, (also Ion. pf. of δείκνυμι).

δεδέημαι, pf. pass. (in med. sense) of δέω, *to want.*

δεδείξομαι, paullo p. fut. of δέχομαι.

δεδειπνάναι, irreg. pf. inf. of δειπνέω.

δέδειχα, δέδειγμαι, pf. act. and pass. of δείκνυμι.

δέδεκα, δέδεμαι, pf. act. and pass. of δέω, *to bind.*

δέδεξο, imperat. pf., and **δεδέξομαι**, p. p. fut., of δέχομαι.

δέδετο, Ep. 3 sing plqpf. pass. of δέω, *to bind.*

δεδέχαται, Ion. for δεδεγμένοι εἰσί, 3 plur. pf. of δέχομαι.

δέδηγμαι, pf. pass. of δάκνω.

δέδηε, δεδήει, 3 sing. pf. and plqpf. of δαίω.

δεδήμευμαι, pf. pass. of δημεύω.

δεδήσομαι and **δεθήσομαι**, fut. pass. of δέω, *to bind.*

δέδηχα, pf. of δάκνω.

δέδια, poët. **δείδια**, pf., with pres. sense, of δείδω; imperat. δέδιθι; part. δεδιώς.

δεδιᾱκόνηκα, pf. of διακονέω.

δεδιδάχθαι, pf. pass. inf. of διδάσκω.

δεδιῄτηκα, pf. of διαιτάω.

δεδίσκομαι, = δειδίσκομαι.

δεδίττομαι, Att. for δειδίσσομαι.

δεδίωγμαι, pf. pass. of διώκω.

δεδμήατο, Ion. for ἐδέδμηντο, 3 pl. plqpf. pass. of δαμάω.

δέδμηκα, pf. of δέμω.

δέδμημαι, pf. pass. of δαμάω; also of δέμω.

δέδμητο, -ήατο, 3 sing. and pl. plqpf. of δαμάω.

δέδογμαι, pf. pass. of δοκέω.

δέδοικα, pf. with pres. sense of δείδω.

δεδοίκω, Dor. pres. formed from δέδοικα = δείδω.

δεδόκημαι, pf. pass. of δοκέω.

δεδοκημένος, Ep. pf. part. of δέχομαι, with sense of pres., *waiting for, lying in wait.*

δεδοκίμασμαι, pf. pass. of δοκιμάζω.

δέδομαι, pf. pass. of δίδωμι: poët. 3 pl. δέδονται.

δεδόνατο, Dor. for ἐδεδόνητο, 3 sing. plqpf. of δονέω.

δέδορκα, pf. of δέρκομαι, with sense of pres.

δέδουπα, pf. of δουπέω.

δεδραγμένος, pf. part. pass. of δράσσω.

δέδρᾱκα, pf. of διδράσκω, also of δράω.

δέδρᾱμαι, pf. pass. of δράω.

δεδράμηκα, pf. of τρέχω (formed from *δρᾰμέω).

δέδρομα, poët. pf. of τρέχω (formed from *δρέμω).

δεδυστύχηκα, pf. of δυστυχέω.

δέδωκα, pf. of δίδωμι.

δέελος, η, ον, resolved form of δῆλος.

δεηθῆτε, 2 pl. aor. 1 subj. of δέομαι.

δέημα, ατος, τό, (δέομαι) *a prayer, entreaty.*

δέησις, εως, ἡ, (δέομαι) *an entreating.*

δεήσομαι, fut. med. of δέω, *to want.*

ΔΕΓ; subj. δέῃ contr. δῇ; opt. δέοι; inf. δεῖν; part. δέον Att. δεῖν: imperf. ἔδει Ion. ἔδεε: fut. δεήσει: aor. 1 ἐδέησε. Impers. from δέω, *to bind:* I. c. acc. et inf., δεῖ τινα ποιῆσαι *it is binding on one* to do a thing, *one must, one ought*, Lat. *oportet, decet;* so, δεῖ τινα ὅπως ποιήσει. II. c. gen. *there is need of*, Lat. *opus est re;* πολλοῦ δεῖ *there wants much, far from it;* ὀλίγου δεῖ *there wants little, all but;* πλεῦνος δεῖ *it is still further from it:*—with the person added, δεῖ μοί τινος, Lat. *opus est mihi re.*

δεῖγμα, ατος, τό, (δείκνυμι) *a sample, proof, specimen*, Lat. *documentum*. 2. a place in the Peiræus, where merchants set out their wares for sale, as in an Eastern *bazaar*. Hence

δειγμᾰτίζω, f. σω, *to make a show of.*

δείδεκτο, 3 sing. plqpf. of δείκνυμι, in sense of impf., *to welcome*: **δειδέχαται**, for δεδεγμένοι εἰσί, 3 plur. perf.: **δειδέχατο**, 3 pl. plqpf.

δειδήμων, ον, gen. ονος, (δείδω) *cowardly.*

δείδια, ας, ε, like δέδια, pf. of δείδω with pres. signf., *I fear*; plur. δείδιμεν, δείδιτε; imperat. δείδιθι; inf. δειδίμεν; part. δειδιώς, dual δειδιότε: **δείδισαν**, 3 plur. plqpf.

δειδίσκομαι, Dep. (δείκνυμι) *to greet with outstretched hand, to welcome, bid hail*; δειδίσκετο δέπαϊ he *hailed* with the cup. 2. = δείκνυμι, *to shew.*

δειδίσσομαι, Att. **δεδίττομαι**: fut. ίξομαι: aor. 1 ἐδειδιξάμην: (δείδω):—Causal of δείδω, *to frighten, alarm.*

δείδοικα, Ep. for δέδοικα, q. v.

ΔΕΙ'ΔΩ, the pres. only used in first pers., *I fear*: fut. δείσομαι: aor. 1 ἔδεισα Ep. ἔδδεισα: pf. in pres. sense δέδοικα; also δέδια, Ep. δείδια (see δείδια): 3 pl. plqpf. ἐδείδισαν, Ep. δείδισαν: I. intr. *to be afraid, to fear*, mostly with μή.., like Lat. *vereor ne.., I fear it is..*; but, δείδω μὴ οὐ.., *vereor ne non.., vereor ut.., I fear it is not.* 2. c. inf. *to fear to do.* 3. δείδειν περί τινι *to be alarmed* or *anxious* about. 4. c. acc. *to be afraid of, to fear, stand in awe of.* 5. perf. part. τὸ δεδιός, *one's fearing, one's fear*, like δέος.

δειελιάω, f. ήσω: aor. 1 ἐδειελίησα: (δείελος):—*to wait till evening.*

δειελινός, ή, όν, = sq., *at evening.* From

δείελος, ον, (δείλη) *of* or *belonging to evening*; δείελον ἦμαρ *eventide*. II. as Subst., δείελος (sub. ὥρη), = δείλη, *evening.*

δεικανάασκε, 3 sing. Ep. impf. of δεικανάω.

δεικᾰνάω, = δείκνυμι, *to point out, shew.* II. Med. = δείκνυμαι, δέχομαι, *to salute, welcome, greet.*

δεικανόωντο, 3 pl. Ep. impf. med. of δεικανάω.

δείκελον and **δείκηλον**, τό, (δείκνυμι) *a representation, exhibition.*

δείκνυ, Ep. shortened form of δείκνυθι.

δεικνύμεν, -ύμεναι, Ep. for δεικνύναι. [ῠ]

ΔΕΙ'ΚΝΥΜΙ and **δεικνύω**, imperat. δείκνυ or δείκνυε: fut. δείξω Ion. δέξω: aor. 1 ἔδειξα Ion. ἔδεξα: pf. δέδειχα:—Pass., fut. δειχθήσομαι, and fut. 3 δεδείξομαι: aor. 1 ἐδείχθην Ion. ἐδέχθην: pf. δέδειγμαι; on the forms δειδέχαται, δείδεκτο, see below II:—*to shew, point out*, Lat. *monstro*; impers. δείξει, *time will shew*; δεικνύναι εἴς τινα *to point towards* a person. 2. *to bring to light, display*; θεὸς ἡμῖν δεῖξε τέρας the god *shewed* us a marvel:—Med. δείκνῠμαι, *to set before one.* 3. *to point out* by words, *to tell, explain, teach*: *to shew, prove*; ἔδειξαν ἕτοιμοι ὄντες *they shewed that* they were ready. 4. of accusers, *to inform against.* II. pres. part. **δεικνύμενος** = δεχόμενος, δεξιούμενος, *welcoming, greeting*: 3 pl. pf. δειδέχαται, 3 sing. and pl. plqpf. δείδεκτο, δειδέχατο, are used in the same sense; τοὺς μὲν κυπέλλοις δειδέχατο they *pledged them* with the cup; δειδέχατο μύθοισι they *greeted* them with words.

δεικτέος, α, ον, verb. Adj. of δείκνυμι, *to be shewn.* II. **δεικτέον** [ἐστί], impers., *one must shew.*

δείλαιος, α, ον, lengthd. form of δειλός, *fearful*: and so *wretched, sorry, paltry, miserable.*

δειλακρίων, ωνος, ὁ, properly, *a coward*, but mostly in addresses, *poor fellow!* From

δείλ-ακρος, α, ον, (δειλός, ἄκρος) *very pitiable.*

ΔΕΙ'ΛΗ (sub. ὥρα), ἡ, properly, *the time when the day is hottest*, i. e. *just after noon*; then generally, *afternoon*, ἔσσεται ἢ ἠὼς ἢ δείλη ἢ μέσον ἦμαρ; δείλη πρωΐα and δείλη ὀψία *early* and *late afternoon*; afterwards δείλη alone stood for *the later part of the afternoon, evening*; δείλης or δείλην, as Adv., *in the evening.*

δειλία, ἡ, (δειλός) *timidity, cowardice*; δειλίην ὀφλεῖν to be charged *with cowardice.*

δειλιάω, f. άσω, (δειλία) *to be afraid.*

δείλομαι, Dep. (δείλη) *to decline towards evening.*

δειλός, ή, όν, (δέος, δείδω) *cowardly, craven*: *vile, worthless.* II. *miserable, wretched, unhappy*, like Lat. *miser*. Adv. -λῶς.

δεῖμα, ατος, τό, (δείδω) *fear, affright.* II. *an object of fear, a terror, horror.* Hence

δειμαίνω, only used in pres. and impf., *to be afraid, to be alarmed*: c. acc. *to fear* a thing.

δειμᾰλέος, α, ον, (δεῖμα) *timid.* II. *horrible, fearful.*

δείμας, aor. 1 part. of δέμω.

δείματο, 3 sing. aor. 1 med. of δέμω.

δειμᾰτόεις, εσσα, εν, (δεῖμα) *frightened.*

δειμᾰτόω, f. ώσω, (δεῖμα) *to frighten.*

δείμομεν, Ep. 1 pl. aor. 1 subj. of δέμω.

δειμός, ὁ, (δέος) *fear, terror*, Lat. *timor.*

δεῖν, inf. of δέω. II. Att. for δέον, part. neut. of δεῖ, as πλεῖν for πλέον.

ΔΕΙ^ΝΑ, ὁ, ἡ, τό, gen. δεῖνος, dat. δεῖνι, acc. δεῖνα, *such an one, a certain one*, whom one cannot or will not name; also pl. δεῖν.

δεινο-θέτης, ου, ὁ, (δεινός, τίθημι) *a knave.*

δεινο-λογέομαι, f. ήσομαι, Dep. (δεινός, λέγω) *to complain loudly.*

δεινο-παθέω, f. ήσω, (δεινός, πάθος) *to complain loudly of suffering.*

δεινό-πους, ὁ, ἡ, πουν, τό, gen. ποδος, (δεινός, πούς) *terrible of foot.*

δεινός, ή, όν, (δέος): I. *terrible, fearful*, in milder sense, *awful*: later, τὸ δεινόν *danger, sufferings*; οὐδὲν δεινοί, μὴ ἀποστέωσιν no fear of their revolting; δεινὸν ποιεῖν or ποιεῖσθαι *to take ill*, Lat. *aegre ferre.* II. implying Force or Power, *mighty, powerful*, for good or ill. 2. *wondrous, marvellous, strange*; τὸ συγγενές τοι δεινόν the ties of kin *have strange power.* III. the sense of *powerful* *wondrous*, passed into that of *able, clever, skilful*, as in phrase δεινός τε καὶ σοφός; often c. inf., δεινὸς λέγειν *clever at* talking; also c. acc., δεινὸς τὴν τέχνην *skilful* in his art. Hence

δεῖνος, gen. of δεῖνα, ὁ, ἡ.

δεινότης, ητος, ἡ, *terribleness: harshness, sternness.* 2. *natural ability, cleverness.*

δεινόω, f. ώσω, (δεινός) *to make dreadful* or *formidable: to exaggerate, enhance.*

δειν-ωπός, όν, (δεινός, ὤψ) *terrible to behold.*

δεινῶς, Adv. of δεινός, *terribly: marvellously, exceedingly.*

δείνωσις, εως, ἡ, (δεινόω) *exaggeration.*

δείν-ωψ, ωπος, ὁ, ἡ, = δεινωπός.

δείξω, fut. of δείκνυμι.

δεῖος, τό, Ep. for δέος, *fear.*

δειπνεῦντες, Dor. for δειπνοῦντες.

δειπνέω, f. ήσω: pf. δεδείπνηκα, Att. pf. 2 δέδειπνα, inf. δεδειπνάναι: (δεῖπνον):—*to make a meal, dine;* in Att. always *to take the chief meal:* c. acc., δειπνεῖν ἄρτον *to make a meal on* bread. Hence

δειπνηστός or **δείπνηστος**, ὁ, *meal-time.*

δειπνητήριον, τό, (δειπνέω) *a supper-room.*

δειπνητής, οῦ, ὁ, *a supper guest.* Hence

δειπνητικός, ή, όν, *of* or *for dinner.* Adv. -κῶς, *like a clever cook.*

δειπνίζω, f. ίσω Att. ιῶ, (δεῖπνον) *to entertain at dinner.*

δειπνο-λόχος, η, ον, (δεῖπνον, λοχάω) *fishing for invitations to dinner, parasitic.*

δεῖπνον, τό, *a meal* or *meal-time*, sometimes = ἄριστον, *the early meal*, sometimes = δόρπον *the late one:* in Att. *the chief meal*, answering to our *dinner*, Lat. *coena;* ἀπὸ δείπνου straight from, i. e. just after, *dinner.* 2. generally *food, provender.*

δειπνοποιέω, *to prepare a meal:* Med. *to dine.* From

δειπνο-ποιός, όν, (δεῖπνον, ποιέω) *preparing dinner.*

δειράς, άδος, ἡ, (δειρή) *the ridge of a chain of hills*, like λόφος, Lat. *jugum.* II. = δειρή, *the neck.*

δείρας, aor. 1 part. of δέρω.

ΔΕΙΡΗ', Att. **δέρη**, ἡ, *the neck, throat.* II. = δειράς, *the ridge of a hill.*

δειρο-τομέω, f. ήσω, (δειρή, τέμνω) *to cut the throat* of a person, *behead him*, Lat. *jugulo.*

ΔΕΙ'ΡΩ, Ion. for δέρω.

δεισ-ήνωρ, ορος, ὁ, ἡ, (δείδω, ἀνήρ) *fearing man.*

δεισιδαιμονία, ἡ, *fear of the gods, religion.* 2. in bad sense, *superstition.* From

δεισι-δαίμων, ον, gen. ονος, (δείδω, δαίμων) *fearing the gods:* in good sense, *pious, religious.* 2. in bad sense, *superstitious, bigoted.*

ΔΕ'ΚΑ, οἱ, αἱ, τά, indecl., Lat. *DECEM*, our *TEN*, Germ. *ZEHN:* οἱ δέκα, *the Ten*, Lat. *Decemviri:* οἱ δέκα [ἔτη] ἀφ' ἥβης those who are *ten years* past 20, the age of military service.

δεκάδ-αρχος, ὁ, (δέκα, ἄρχω) *a commander of ten men*, Lat. *decurio.*

δεκά-βοιος, ον, (δέκα, βοῦς) *worth ten oxen.*

δεκαδεύς, έως, ὁ, (δέκα) *one of a decury* or *party of ten soldiers.*

δεκά-δυο, οἱ, αἱ, τά, = δυώδεκα, *twelve.*

δεκά-δωρος, ον, (δέκα, δῶρον II) *ten palms long* or *broad.*

δεκα-έτηρος, ον, (δέκα, ἔτος) *ten-yearly.*

δεκα-ετής, ές, (δέκα, ἔτος) *lasting ten years.*

δεκάζω, f. άσω, (δέκα) *to bribe, corrupt*, Lat. *decuriare.*

δεκάκις, Adv. (δέκα) *ten times: ten-fold.*

δεκά-κλῖνος, ον, (δέκα, κλῖναι) *holding ten dinner-couches.*

δεκα-κῡμία, ἡ, (δέκα, κῦμα) *the tenth wave*, Lat. *fluctus decumanus;* cf. τρικυμία.

δεκά-μηνος and **δεκα-μηνιαῖος**, ον, (δεκά, μήν) *ten months old.* 2. *in the tenth month.*

δεκά-μνους, ουν, (δεκά, μνᾶ) *worth ten minae.*

δεκ-άμφορος, ον, (δέκα, ἀμφορεύς) *holding ten* ἀμφορεῖς, i. e. about ninety gallons.

δεκά-παλαι, Adv. *a very long time ago.*

δεκά-πεντε, οἱ, αἱ, τά, *fifteen.*

δεκά-πηχυς, υ, (δέκα, πῆχυς) *ten cubits long.*

δεκα-πλάσιος, ον, (δέκα) *tenfold:* c. gen. *ten times greater than:* ἡ δεκαπλασία (sub. τιμή) as Subst. *ten times the amount.*

δεκά-πλεθρος, ον, (δέκα, πλέθρον) *enclosing ten plethra* (v. πλέθρον II.)

δεκάπλοος, ον, contr. -**πλους**, ουν, = δεκα-πλάσιος.

δεκά-πολις, ἡ, (δέκα, πόλις) *a district including ten cities, Decapolis.*

δεκά-πους, ὁ, ἡ, πουν, τό, gen. ποδος, *ten feet long.*

δεκ-άρχης, ου, ὁ, (δέκα, ἄρχω) *a decurion.* Hence

δεκ-αρχία, ἡ, *the government of the Ten.*

δεκάς, άδος, ἡ, (δέκα) *a body of ten men*, Lat. *decuria.* II. *the number ten.*

δεκά-σπορος, ον, (δέκα, σπείρω) *consisting of ten seed-times*, i. e. *ten years.*

δεκαταῖος, α, ον, (δέκατος) *on the tenth day.*

δεκα-τάλαντος, ον, (δέκα, τάλαντον) *weighing* or *worth ten talents: estimated at ten talents.*

δεκα-τέσσαρες, -ρα, *fourteen.*

δεκατευτήριον, τό, *the tenths-office, custom-house:* and

δεκατευτής, οῦ, ὁ, *a farmer of tenths, tithe-collector*, Lat. *decumanus.* From

δεκατεύω, f. σω, (δεκάτη) *to exact the tenths, to tithe, take tithe of* a person: *to take the tenth* of booty, esp. *as an offering to the gods:*—also *to exact the tenths as a tax on all imports.*

δεκατη-λόγος, ὁ, (δεκάτη, λέγω) = δεκατευτής.

δεκατό-σπορος, ον, (δέκατος, σπορά) *in the tenth generation.*

δέκᾰτος, η, ον, (δέκα) *tenth.* II. as Subst., δεκάτη (sub. μέρις), ἡ, *the tenth part, tithe.* 2. δεκάτη (sub. ἡμέρα), ἡ, *the tenth day:* at Athens, *the festival on the tenth day after birth*, when the child had a name given it; τὴν δεκάτην θύειν to give a feast *on the day of naming the child.*

δεκατόω, f. ώσω, (δέκατος) *to take tithe of* a person.

δεκά-φῦλος, ον, (δέκα, φυλή) *consisting of ten tribes.*

δεκά-χαλκον, τό, (δέκα, χαλκοῦς) *a coin worth ten* χαλκοῖ, Lat. *denarius.*

δεκά-χῖλοι, αι, α, (δέκα, χίλιοι) *ten thousand.*

δεκ-έτηρος, ον, = δεκέτης.

δεκ-έτης, ου, ὁ, (δέκα, ἔτος) *lasting ten years.* II. *ten years old.*

δεκ-έτις, ιδος, ἡ, pecul. fem. of δεκέτης.

δέκομαι, Ion. and Aeol. for δέχομαι.

δεκ-όργυιος, ον, (δεκά, ὀργυιά) *ten fathoms long.*

δεκτήρ, ῆρος, ὁ, = δέκτης.

δέκτης, ου, ὁ, (δέχομαι) *a receiver:* hence *a beggar.*

δέκτο, 3 sing. Ep. aor. 2 of δέχομαι.

δεκτός, ή, όν, verb. Adj. of δέχομαι, *received: to be received, acceptable,* Lat. *acceptus.*

δέκτρια, ἡ, poët. fem. of δεκτήρ, δέκτης.

δέκτωρ, ορος, poët. for δέκτης, δεκτήρ, *one who takes upon himself.*

δεκ-ώρῠγος, ον, more correct form of δεκόργυιος.

δελεάζω, f. άσω, (δέλεαρ) *to entice by a bait: to allure, entice, catch.* II. c. acc. cognato, νῶτον ὑὸς δελεάζειν *to put* the chine of a pig *as a bait.*

ΔΕ΄ΛΕΑΡ, ατος, τό, *a bait,* Lat. *esca.*

δελε-άρπαξ, αγος, ὁ, ἡ, (δέλεαρ, ἁρπάζω) *greedy of the bait, biting freely at it.*

δελέασμα, ατος, τό, = δέλεαρ.

ΔΕ΄ΛΤΑ, τό, indecl., v. sub Δ. 2. a name for *the islands formed at the mouths of large rivers,* esp. of the Nile. so called from their shape.

δελτίον, τό, Dim. of δέλτος.

δελτο-γράφος, ον, (δέλτος, γράφω) *writing on a tablet, registering, recording.*

δέλτος, ἡ, *a writing-tablet,* so called from the letter Δ, the old shape of tablets: metaph., δέλτοι φρενῶν *the tablets* of the heart. Hence

δελτόω, f. ώσω, *to note down on tablets, record.*

δελφάκιον, τό, *a sucking-pig,* Dim. of δέλφαξ.

δελφᾰκόομαι, Pass. *to grow up to pighood.* From

ΔΕ΄ΛΦΑΞ, ᾰκος, ὁ, *a young pig, porker.*

Δελφίνιος, ὁ, (Δελφοί) *Delphian,* epith. of Apollo.

δελφῖνο-φόρος, ον, (δελφίς, φέρω) *bearing dolphins;* κεραῖαι δ. beams *with pulleys to lower the* δελφίς.

ΔΕΛΦΙ΄Σ and **δελφίν**, ῖνος, ὁ, *the dolphin.* II. *a mass of iron* or *lead, shaped like a dolphin,* which was hung at the yard-arm, and then suddenly let down on the enemy's ships.

ΔΕΛΦΟΙ΄, ῶν, αἱ, *Delphi,* a famous oracle of Apollo in Phocis at the foot of Parnassus. II. **Δελφοί**, οἱ, *the inhabitants of Delphi, Delphians.*

ΔΕ΄ΜΑΣ, τό, used only in nom. and acc., *the body,* esp *of man:* properly *the living body,* σῶμα being the corpse; μικρὸς δέμας small *in stature.* II. as Adv., like δίκην, δέμας πυρὸς αἰθομένοιο *in form* or *fashion like* burning fire, Lat. *instar ignis.*

δέμνιον, τό, (δέμω) *a bed, bedding;* mostly in plur.

δεμνιο-τήρης, ες, (δέμνιον, τηρέω) *keeping one to one's bed;* μοῖρα δεμνιοτήρης *a lingering* fate.

ΔΕ΄ΜΩ; aor. 1 act. ἔδειμα, med. ἐδειμάμην: pf. δέδμηκα: pf. pass. δέδμημαι. *To build;* Med., **ἐδείματο** οἴκους *he built him* houses: generally, *to construct, make;* δέμειν ὁδόν Lat. *munire viam.*

δενδίλλω, *to give a glance at,* so as to make a sign.

δένδρεον, τό, Ion. for δένδρον, *a tree.* Hence

δενδρεών, ῶνος, ὁ, (δένδρον) *a grove.*

δενδρήεις, εσσα, εν, *woody.*

δενδριακός or –ικός, ή, όν, (δένδρον) *of a tree.*

δένδριον, τό, Dim. of δένδρον.

δενδρίτης, ου, ὁ, fem. **δενδρῖτις**, ιδος, *of* or *belonging to a tree.*

δενδρο-βᾰτέω, (δένδρον, βαίνω) *to climb trees.*

δενδρο-κόμης or **δενδρό-κομος**, ον, (δένδρον, κομή) *shaggy with wood.*

δενδρο-κοπέω, (δένδρον, κόπτω) = δενδροτομέω.

ΔΕ΄ΝΔΡΟΝ, τό, Ion. and Att. **δένδρος**, εος, τό, *a tree;* δένδρον ἐλάας *an olive-tree:* generally, δένδρα are *fruit-trees,* opp. to ὕλη, timber.

δενδροτομέω, f. ήσω, *to cut down the fruit-trees, to lay waste a country.* From

δενδρο-τόμος, ον, (δένδρον, τεμεῖν) *cutting down trees.*

δενδρο-φόρος, ον, (δένδρον, φέρω) *bearing trees.*

δενδρό-φῠτος, ον, (δένδρον, φύω) *planted with trees.*

δενδρ-ώδης, ες, (δένδρον, εἶδος) *tree-like;* **δενδρώδεις** Νύμφαι *wood*-nymphs.

δενδρῶτις, ιδος, ἡ, (δένδρον) *wooded.*

δεννάζω, f. άσω, *to abuse, revile.* From

ΔΕ΄ΝΝΟΣ, ὁ, *a reproach, disgrace.*

δέξαι, aor. 1 med. imper. of δέχομαι.

δεξαμενή, ἡ, (properly aor. 1 part. fem. of **δέχομαι**) *a receptacle* of water, *a reservoir, tank.*

δεξιά, Ion. –ιή, (fem. of δεξιός, sub. **χείρ**) *the right hand;* ἐκ δεξιᾶς on *the right hand;* **δεξιὰν διδόναι** to salute by offering *the right hand.*

δεξί-μηλος, ον, (δέχομαι, μῆλον) *receiving sheep, rich in sacrifices.*

δεξιό-γυιος, (δεξιός, γυῖον) *ready of limb, nimble.*

δεξιο-λάβος, ὁ, (δεξιός, λαβεῖν) *a spearman, guard.*

δεξιόομαι, f. ώσομαι: aor. 1 ἐδεξιωσάμην: Dep.:—*to offer the right hand, greet with the right hand.* From

ΔΕΞΙΟ΄Σ, ά, όν, Lat. *DEXTER:* I. *on the right hand* or *side;* ἐπὶ δεξιά to *the right.* II. *fortunate, boding good,* of the flight of birds and other omens. III. metaph. *dexterous, ready:* and of the mind, *shrewd, clever.*

δεξιό-σειρος, ὁ, (δεξιός, σειρά) *harnessed by traces on the right side,* of a horse, which was not put under the yoke, but attached *as a third* abreast with the regular pair.

δεξιότης, ητος, ἡ, (δεξιός) *dexterity, activity;* of mind, *cleverness.*

δεξιόφιν, Adv., old gen. of **δεξιός**; **ἐπὶ δεξιόφιν** *towards the right.*

δεξί-πῡρος, ον, (δέχομαι, πῦρ) *fire-receiving.*

δέξις, εως, ἡ, (δέχομαι) *reception.*

δεξιτερός, ά, όν, poët. form for **δεξιός**, *right, the right;* δεξιτερά, like δεξιά (sub. χείρ), *the right hand;* δεξιτερῆφι, old dat., *on the right band.*

δεξίωμα, ατος, τό, (δεξιόομαι) *a pledge of friendship.*

δεξι-ώνῠμος, ον, (δεξιός, ὄνομα) *lucky in name.*

δεξιῶς, Adv. of δέξιος, *dexterously:* Sup. δεξιώτατα.

δεξίωσις, εως, ἡ, (δεξιόομαι) *an offering of the right hand: greeting, salutation: canvassing.*

δέξο, 2 sing. Ep. aor. 2 imperat. of δέχομαι.

δέξομαι, fut. of δέχομαι.

δέξω, δέξομαι, Ion. for δείξω, δείξομαι, fut. act. and med. of δείκνυμι.

δέομαι, *to need, want, ask;* v. sub δέω (B).

δέον, οντος, τό, Att. **δεῖν**, part. neut. of the impers. δεῖ, *that which is binding, needful, right, proper;* μᾶλλον τοῦ δέοντος more *than needful;* ἐν δέοντι (sub. καιρῷ), *in good time,* Lat. *opportune;* εἰς τὸ δέον *for needful purposes.* II. used. absol. *it being needful;* οὐδὲν δέον *there being* no *need.*

δέον, Ion. for ἔδεον, impf. of δέω, *to bind.*

δεόντων, 3 pl. imperat. of δέω, *to bind.*

ΔΕ'ΟΣ, gen. δέους, τό: poët. **δεῖος**: *fear, alarm, affright.* II. *awe, reverence.* III. *a terror, means of inspiring fear.*

ΔΕ'ΠΑΣ, αος, τό: nom. pl. δέπᾰ; poët. dat. pl. δεπάεσσι and δέπασσι:—*a beaker, goblet, chalice.*

δερ-άγχη, ἡ, (δέρη, ἄγχω) *a collar.*

δερ-αγχής, ές, (δέρη, ἄγχω) *throttling.*

δέραιον, τό, (δέρη) *a necklace: a collar.*

δεραιο-πέδη, ἡ, (δέραιον, πέδη) *a collar.*

δέρας, ατος, τό, poët. for δέρμα, *skin, hide.*

δεράς, άδος, ἡ, = δειράς.

δέργμα, τό, (δέρκομαι) *a look, glance.*

δέρη, ἡ, Att. for δειρή, *the neck.*

δερκέσκετο, Ion. 3 sing. impf. of δέρκομαι.

δερκιάομαι, Dep., poët. for δέρκομαι, *to look.*

ΔΕ'ΡΚΟΜΑΙ, Dep.: fut. δέρξομαι: pf. with pres. sense δέδορκα: aor. 2 ἔδρᾰκον: also aor. 1 pass. ἐδέρχθην, aor. 2 ἐδράκην; and aor. 1 med. ἐδερξάμην, aor. 2 ἐδρακόμην:—*to look, see:* hence *to behold the light, to live.* 2. *to look on* or *at:* generally, *to perceive, be aware of.* II. of light, *to flash* or *gleam,* like the eye.

δέρμα, ατος, τό, (δέρω) *the skin, hide* of beasts, Lat. *pellis:* also of *skins prepared for bottles,* etc.: *the shell* of a tortoise. 2. generally, *one's skin,* Lat. *cutis.* Hence

δερμάτῐνος, η, ον, *of skin, leathern.*

δέρξατο, Ion. 3 sing. aor. 1 med. of δέρκομαι.

δέρον, Ep. for ἔδερον, impf. of δέρω.

δέρος, εος, τό, poët. for δέρμα, *skin, hide.*

δέρρις or **δέρις**, εως, ἡ, (δέρος, δέρμα) *a leathern covering.* II. in plur. *screens of skin,* hung to deaden the enemy's missiles, Lat. *cilicia.*

δέρτρον, τό, (δέρω) *the caul* or *membrane which contains the bowels,* Lat. *omentum;* δέρτρον ἔσω δύνοντες penetrating *even to the bowels.*

δερχθείς, part. aor. 1 of δέρκομαι; **δέρχθητι**, imperat., and **δερχθῆναι**, inf., of same tense.

ΔΕ'ΡΩ, Ion. **δείρω**: fut. δερῶ: aor. 1 ἔδειρα:—Pass., fut. 2 δᾰρήσομαι: aor 1 ἐδάρθην, aor. 2 ἐδάρην [ᾰ]: pf. δέδαρμαι:—*to skin, flay.* II. also *to cudgel, thrash.*

δέσμα, ατος, τό, (δέω) poët. for δεσμός, *a bond, fetter.* II. *a head-band.*

δεσμεύω, f. σω, (δεσμός) *to fetter, put in chains: to tie together,* as corn in the sheaf.

δεσμέω, f. ήσω, (δεσμός) = δεσμεύω.

δέσμη, ἡ, (δέω) *a bundle.*

δέσμιον, τό, = δεσμός.

δέσμιος, ον, also α, ον, (δεσμός) *binding:* hence *binding with a spell.* II. pass. *bound, captive.*

δεσμός, ὁ, pl. δεσμοί or δεσμά, (δέω) *a band, bond, fetter: a halter: a mooring cable: a door-latch.* 2. *bonds, imprisonment.*

δεσμο-φύλαξ, ᾰκος, ὁ, ἡ, (δεσμός, φύλαξ) *a gaoler.*

δεσμόω, = δεσμεύω, *to bind, fetter.* Hence

δέσμωμα, ατος, τό, *a fetter.*

δεσμωτήριον, τό, (δεσμόω) *a prison.*

δεσμώτης, ου, ὁ, (δεσμόω) *a prisoner.* 2. as Adj. *in chains, fettered:* fem. δεσμῶτις ιδος.

δεσπόζω, f. όσω, (δεσπότης) *to be lord and master of,* c. gen.: absol. *to gain the mastery.* II. *to make oneself master of* a thing; and so, *to comprehend.*

δέσποινα, ἡ, fem. of δεσπότης, *the mistress* or *lady of the house,* Lat. *hera:* often joined with the name of goddesses.

δεσπόσιος, ον, = δεσπόσυνος.

δεσποσύνη, ἡ, (δεσπότης) *absolute sway.*

δεσπόσῠνος, ον, (δεσπότης) *of* or *belonging to the master, arbitrary.* II. as Subst. = δεσπότης.

δεσποτέω, f. ήσω, = δεσπόζω:—Pass. *to be despotically ruled.*

ΔΕΣΠΟ'ΤΗΣ, ου, ὁ, voc. δέσποτᾰ: Dor. nom. δεσπότας: Ion. acc. sing. and pl. δεσπότεα, -εας, but prob. these are incorrect:—*a master,* properly of slaves: hence *a despot, absolute ruler,* whose subjects are slaves. II. generally, *an owner, master, lord.* Hence

δεσποτικός, ή, όν, *of* or *for a master.* 2. *fit to be a master: inclined to tyranny, despotic.*

δεσπότις, ιδος, ἡ, = δέσποινα.

δεσποτίσκος, ὁ, Dim. of δεσποτής, *little master.*

δετή (sub. λαμπάς), ἡ, *sticks bound up to make a fagot, a fagot.* Fem. of

δετός, ή, όν, verb. Adj. of δέω, *bound.*

δεύεσκον, Ion. impf. of δεύω, *to wet.*

δευήσεσθαι, fut. med. inf. of δεύω, *to want.*

δεῦμα, ατος, τό, (δεύω) *that which is wet, soaked;* δεύματα κρεῶν *boiled* flesh.

δευοίατο, poët. for δεύοιντο, 3 pl. pres. opt. of δεύω (B).

δεύομαι, v. δεύω (B).

δευρί, Att. strengthened form of δεῦρο.

ΔΕΥ'ΡΟ, Adv. of Place, *hither, come hither!* δεῦτε is used with plur. II. of Time, *until now, up to this time, hitherto;* δεῦρ' ἀεί continually *up to this time.*

Δεύς, Aeol. for Ζεύς.

δεύτᾰτος, η, ον, *the last*, Sup. of δεύτερος.

δεῦτε, Adv., p ur. of δεῦρο, *hither! Come hither!*

δευτερ-ᾰγωνιστής, οῦ, ὁ, (δεύτερος, ἀγωνιστής) *the actor who takes the second part*, cf. πρωταγωνιστής: metaph. *the second advocate in a court of law.*

δευτεραῖος, α, ον, (δεύτερος) *on the second day.*

δευτερεῖα (sub. ἆθλα), τά, (δεύτερος) *the second prize* in a contest: generally, *the second place* or *rank.*

δευτεριάζω, f. άσω, *to play the second part.*

δευτερό-πρωτον σάββατον, τό, *the first* sabbath *after the second* day of the feast of unleavened bread.

δεύτερος, α, ον, *the second*, Lat. *secundus:* as a Comp., ἐμεῖο δεύτεροι *after* my *time:* in neut. as Adv., δεύτερον αὖ, δεύτερον αὖτις, *secondly, next afterwards, a second time.* II. in point of Place, *second*, i. e. *inferior;* δεύτερος οὐδενός *second* to none: τὰ δεύτερα, = δευτερεῖα, *the second prize* or *place.* III. *the second of two;* δευτέρη αὐτή herself *with another.*

δευτερο-στάτης, ου, ὁ, (δεύτερος, ἵσταμαι) *one who stands in the second file of the Chorus.*

ΔΕΥ'Ω (A), Ion. impf. δεύεσκον: f. δεύσω: aor. 1 ἔδευσα:—Pass., pf. δέδευμαι:—*to wet, soak, steep;* Med., πτερὰ δεύεται ἅλμῃ *wets his* wings in the brine. II. *to fill with liquid, fill up.* III. *to make to flow, shed.*

ΔΕΥ'Ω (B), f. δευήσω, Aeol. and Ep. form for δέω, *to need, miss, want;* ἐδεύησεν δ' οἰήϊον ἄκρον ἱκέσθαι *he missed* reaching the top of the mast. II. more often as Dep. **δεύομαι**, f. δευήσομαι:—*to feel the want* or *loss of, to be at a loss for:* hence *to be wanting, deficient in;* ἄλλα πάντα δεύεαι Ἀργείων *thou art inferior to* them in all else.

ΔΕ'ΦΩ, f. δέψω, *to soften by working by the hand, to make supple, to tan hides.*

δεχ-άμματος, ον, (δέκα, ἅμμα) *with ten meshes.*

δέχαται, Ep. for δεδεγμένοι εἰσί 3 pl. pf. of δέχομαι.

δεχ-ήμερος, ον, (δέκα, ἡμέρα) *lasting ten days.* 2. *terminable at ten days' notice.*

δέχθαι, Ep. aor. 2 inf. of δέχομαι.

δεχθείς, aor. 1 part. of δέχομαι, in pass. sense.

δέχνῠμαι, poët. for δέχομαι.

ΔΕ'ΧΟΜΑΙ, Ion. and Aeol. **δέκομαι**: fut. δέξομαι and δεδέξομαι: aor. 1 ἐδέχθην (also used in pass. sense): pf. δέδεγμαι: plqpf. ἐδεδέγμην:—Ep. aor. 2 ἐδέγμην or δέγμην, 3 sing. δέκτο, 2 sing. imperat. δέξο; inf. δέχθαι; part. δέγμενος: Dep.: I. of things, *to take, accept:* esp. *to take well, receive kindly* or *graciously;* τὸν οἰωνὸν δέχεσθαι *to accept* or *hail* the omen: hence *to approve:* c. inf. *to take rather, to choose.* II. of persons, *to receive hospitably, entertain.* 2. *to receive as an enemy, to watch for: to await the onset.* 3. *to expect, wait for.* III. of events, *to succeed, come next*, Lat. *excipere.*

δεψέω, f. ήσω, Lat. *depso*, = δέφω, *to soften;* δεψήσας κηρὸν *having worked* wax *till it is soft.*

δέψω, = foreg.

ΔΕ'Ω (A); fut. δήσω: aor. 1 ἔδησα: pf. δέδεκα: plqpf. ἐδεδήκειν:—Pass., fut. δεθήσομαι, fut. 3 δεδήσομαι: aor. 1 ἐδέθην: pf. δέδεμαι: plqpf. ἐδεδέμην, Ep. 3 sing. δέδετο;—*to bind, tie, fasten, fetter:* absol. *to imprison.* 2. metaph. *to bind fast, enchain:* later, *to bind by spells, enchant.* 3. c. gen. *to let, prevent, hinder from* a thing. II. Med. *to bind* or *tie on oneself;* ποσσὶ δ' ὑπαὶ λιπαροῖσιν ἐδήσατο καλὰ πέδιλα *tied* them on *his* feet; but in plqpf. pass., περὶ κνήμῃσι κνημῖδας δέδετο *he had* greaves *bound* round his legs.

ΔΕ'Ω (B), fut. δεήσω: aor. 1 ἐδέησα, Ep. 3 sing. δῆσεν: pf. δεδέηκα:—*to want, lack, miss, stand in need of*, c. gen.; ὀλίγου δέω *I want* little, i. e. am near; πολλοῦ δέω *I want* much, i. e. am far from; ὀλίγου δέω δακρῦσαι *I want* little of tears; δυοῖν δέοντα τεσσαράκοντα forty *lacking* two, like Lat. *duodeviginti.* II. for δεῖ impers., and δέον, see the words. III. Dep. **δέομαι**: fut. δεήσομαι: aor. 1 ἐδεήθην: pf. δεδέημαι. *To stand in need of, want*, c. gen.: hence, *to long* or *strive after, wish, beg for:* c. dupl. gen. *to beg a thing* from a person. 2. absol. *to be in want* or *need*, mostly in part., as κάρτα δεόμενος.

ΔΗ', Particle, properly of Time, *now, already;* ὀκτὼ δὴ προέηκα .. ὀϊστούς *already* have I shot; πολλάκι δή, Lat. *jam saepe:* with imperat. and fut. *now, forthwith, directly.* II. marking Connection, *then;* in summing up numbers, γίγνονται δὴ οὗτοι χίλιοι these *then* make up a thousand; καὶ δή marks the thing meant to be emphatic, εἰς Αἴγυπτον ἀπίκετο .., καὶ δὴ καὶ ἐς Σάρδις, he reached Egypt, and *what is more* Sardis also; also to put a supposed case, καὶ δὴ δέδεγμαι well *suppose* I have accepted. III. belonging to the word which it follows, with Verbs, ἄγε δή, φέρε δή, *do but* come, *only* come; with a Sup., μέγιστος δή the *very* greatest. 2. in ironical sense, Lat. *scilicet;* εἰσήγαγε τὰς ἑταιρίδας δή he brought in the *pretended* courtesans. 3. with Pronouns, ἐμὲ δὴ ὧδε διαθεῖναι thus to use *a man like* me; σὺ δὴ .. ἐτόλμησας; you *of all persons.* 4. with other Particles, δή adds explicitness; ὡς δή, ἵνα δή, that [it may be] *exactly* so, *just* so; also ὡς δή, ἅτε δή, οἷα δή *in that, inasmuch as.*

δῃ-άλωτος, ον, contr. for δηϊάλωτος.

δῆγμα, ατος, τό, (δάκνω) *a bite, sting.*

δηγμός, ὁ, = δῆγμα.

δηθά, = δήν, Adv. *long, for a long time.*

δῆθε and **δῆθεν**, Adv. (δή) *perhaps: I suppose:* mostly iron., like Lat. *scilicet, to wit, forsooth:* with ὡς, *as if forsooth;* ὡς ἄγρην δῆθεν *pretending* it was game.

δηθύνω [ῡ], f. ὑνῶ, (δηθά) *to tarry, be long, delay.*

δηϊάασκον, Ep. impf. of δηϊόω.

δηϊ-άλωτος, ον, (δήϊος, ἁλῶναι) *taken by the enemy, captive.*

δήϊος, η, ον, Ep. for δάϊος, *hostile.* Hence

δηϊοτής, ῆτος, ἡ, *battle-strife, battle.*

δηϊόω, Att. **δῃῶ**, inf. δῃοῦν: part. **δῃῶν** Ep. **δηιόων**:

pf. ἐδηΐουν Att. ἐδῄουν Ion. ἐδῄευν Ep. δῄουν : ıt. δῃώσω: aor. ἐδηΐωσα, Att. ἐδῄωσα, part. δῃώσας: f. δεδῄωκα:—Med., Ep. 3 pl. impf. δηΐόωντο: aor. 1 δῃωσάμην:—Pass., aor. 1 ἐδῃώθην, part. δῃωθείς: f. δεδῄωμαι: (δήϊος):—*to treat as an enemy: to cut own, slay, rend, cleave.* II. *to waste* or *ravage* country.

δηκτήριος, *ον*, (δάκνω) *biting, torturing.*

δηκτικός, *ή, όν*, (δάκνω) *biting: pungent.*

δηλα-δή, Adv. (δῆλος, δή) *clearly, plainly, of course:* n answers, *yes plainly.*

δηλαίνω, collat. form of δηλέομαι.

ΔΗΛΕ'ΟΜΑΙ, fut. ήσομαι: pf. δεδήλημαι, inf. εδηλῆσθαι in pass. sense: Dep.:—*to hurt greatly,* o *a mischief to, destroy,* Lat. *delere:* absol. *to do uischief, be hurtful:* of things, καρπὸν δηλήσασθαι *waste* the fruit; ὅρκια δηλήσασθαι *to break* oaths. ence

δήλημα, *ατος, τό, mischief, ruin, bane.*

δηλήμων, *ον*, gen, *ονος*, *baneful:* as Subst., βροτῶν δηλήμων *destroyer* of men.

δήλησις, *εως, ἡ*, (δηλέομαι) *ruin, bane.*

δηλητήρ, *ῆρος, ὁ*, (δηλέομαι) *a destroyer.* Hence

δηλητήριος, *ον*, *baneful, destructive.*

Δήλια, *τό*, v. sub Δήλιος.

Δηλιάς, *άδος, ἡ*, (Δῆλος) *a Delian woman.*

Δήλιος, *α, ον*, (Δῆλος) *Delian:* τὰ Δήλια (sub. ἱερά), *the festival of Apollo at Delos.*

δηλον-ότι, Adv. for δῆλον ὅτι, = δηλαδή, *it is plain that, clearly, of course:* also *namely,* Lat. *videlicet.*

δηλο-ποιέω, f. ήσω, (δῆλος, ποιέω) *to make manifest.*

Δῆλος, *ὁ*, *Delos,* one of the Cyclades, birthplace of Apollo and Artemis: called also Ὀρτυγία. From

δῆλος, *η, ον*, also *ος, ον*; contr. from δέελος, *visible, clear.* 2. *manifest, evident, certain;* δῆλον as Adv. *clearly, plainly.* Hence

δηλόω, f. ώσω *to shew, make visible* or *clear: to point out, make known.* 2. *to prove: to declare, explain, set forth:* also *to signify.* 3. *to point out, order.* II. intrans. = δῆλός εἰμι, *to be clear* or *plain;* δηλοῖ ὅτι οὐκ Ὁμήρου τὰ Κύπρια, ἔπεά ἐστι *it is clear* that... Hence

δήλως, Adv. of δῆλος, *manifestly.*

δήλωσις, *εως, ἡ*, *a pointing out, explaining.* 2. *a direction, command.*

δημᾰγωγέω, f. ήσω, (δημαγωγός) *to be a popular leader* or *demagogue*

δημᾰγωγία, *ἡ*, *the conduct* or *character of a public leader:* and

δημᾰγωγικός, *ή, όν*, *fit for a popular leader.* From

δημ-ᾰγωγός, *ὁ*, (δῆμος, ἄγω) *a popular leader, a mob-leader, demagogue.*

δημᾱκίδιον, *τό*, a comic Dim. of δῆμος.

δημ-άρᾱτος, *ον*, (δῆμος, ἀράομαι) *prayed for by the people:* prop. n. of a king of Sparta.

δημαρχέω, f. ήσω, *to be demarch* or *tribune.* Hence

δημαρχία, *ἡ*, *the office of demarch, tribunate;* and

δημαρχικός, *ή, όν*, *tribunician.* From

δήμ-αρχος, *ὁ*, (δῆμος, ἄρχω) at Athens, *the president of a δῆμος,* who kept the registers, *a demarch:*—at Rome, *a tribune,* Lat. *tribunus plebis.*

δήμευσις, *εως, ἡ*, *confiscation.* From

δημεύω, f. σω, (δῆμος) *to declare public property: to confiscate* a citizen's goods, Lat. *publicare.* 2. generally, *to make public.*

δημηγορέω, f. ήσω, (δημηγόρος) *to be a public orator, to harangue the people,* Lat. *concionari.*

δημηγόρια, *ἡ*, *a deliberative speech: a speech in the public assembly;* and

δημηγορικός, *ή, όν*, *of public speaking, qualified for it.* From

δημ-ηγόρος, *ὁ*, (δῆμος, ἀγορεύω) *one who harangues the people, a public speaker,* Lat. *concionator.*

δημηλᾰσία, *ἡ*, *exile.* From

δημ-ήλᾰτος, *ον*, (δῆμος, ἐλαύνω) *publicly exiled.*

Δη-μήτηρ, *ἡ*: gen. τερος and τρος: acc. τερα or τρα, also Δημήτραν: (δῆ for γῆ, μήτηρ):—*Demeter,* Lat. *Ceres,* goddess of agriculture, mother of Proserpine.

δημίδιον, *το*, comic Dim. of δῆμος. [ῐδ]

δημίζω, f. ίσω, (δῆμος) *to affect the popular side, cheat the people.*

δημιό-πρᾱτα, *τά*, (δήμιος, πιπράσκω) *goods seized by public authority, confiscated goods.*

δήμιος, *ον*, Dor. **δάμιος**, *α, ον*: (δῆμος):—*belonging to the people;* δήμιοι αἰσυμνῆται judges *elected by the people:*—as Adv., δήμια πίνειν to drink *at the public cost.* 2. δήμιος, *ὁ*, as Subst., *the public executioner.*

δημιουργέω, f. ήσω, *to be a workman, to work;* and

δημιουργία, *ἡ*, *workmanship, work;* and

δημιουργικός, *ή, όν*, *of* or *for a workman.* Adv. -κῶς, *in a workmanlike fashion.* From

δημι-ουργός, poët. **δημιο-εργός**, *όν*: (δῆμος, ἔργον): *working for the people:* as Subst., δημιουργός, ὁ, *a workman, handicraftsman:* generally, *a maker, author:* metaph., ὄρθρος δημιοεργός morn *that calls man to work.* 2. *the Maker of the world.* II. name of *a magistrate.*

δημο-βόρος, *ον*, (δῆμος, βορά) *devourer of the people.*

δημο-γέρων, *οντος, ὁ*, (δῆμος, γέρων) *an elder of the people;* generally, *an elder, chief:* in plur., *the nobles, chiefs,* like Lat. *senatores.*

δημόθεν, Adv. (δῆμος) *at the public cost.* II. *by deme* or *birthplace.*

δημό-θροος, *ον*, contr. **-θρους**, *ουν* (δῆμος, θρέω) *uttered by the people.*

δημοκοπέω, f. ήσω, *to curry mob favour;* and

δημοκοπικός, *ή, όν*, *suited to a demagogue.* From

δημό-κοπος, *ὁ*, (δῆμος, κόπτω) *a demagogue.*

δημό-κραντος, *ον*, (δῆμος, κραίνω) *ratified by the people.*

δημο-κρᾰτέομαι, Pass. (δῆμος, κρατέω) *to have a democratical constitution, live in a democracy.* Hence

δημοκράτια, *ἡ*, *democracy, popular government.* Hence

δημοκρᾰτικός, ή, όν, *suited to a democracy.*

δημό-λευστος, ον, (δῆμος, λεύω) *stoned by the people; δημόλευστος φόνος* death *by public stoning.*

δημόομαι, Dep. (δῆμος) *to talk popularly, to jest.*

δημο-πίθηκος, ὁ, (δῆμος, πίθηκος) *a mob-monkey, charlatan.*

δημορ-ρῖφής, ές, (δῆμος, ῥίπτω) *hurled by the people.*

ΔΗ'ΜΟΣ, ὁ, *a country-district*, opp. to πόλις; ἐν δήμῳ Ἰθάκης; μάλα πίονα δῆμον, etc. II. *the commons, common people, plebeians*, Lat. *plebs*, δήμου ἀνήρ, opp. to βασιλεύς; also δῆμος ἐών being *a commoner.* III. in democratical states, esp. at Athens, *the commons, the people, the citizens*: hence 2. *a popular constitution, democracy.* IV. δῆμοι in Attica, *townships* or *hundreds*, Lat. *pagi*, subdivisions of the φῦλαι; in the time of Herodotus, 100 in number, 10 in each φυλή.

ΔΗΜΟ'Σ, ὁ, *fat.*

δημοσίᾳ, Adv. see δημόσιος.

δημοσιεύω, = δημεύω, *to confiscate.* II. intr. *to lead a public life*, opp. to ἰδιωτεύω *to belong to the state.* From

δημόσιος, α, ον, (δῆμος) *belonging to the people* or *state*, Lat. *publicus.* II. ὁ δημόσιος (sub. δοῦλος), *a public officer* or *servant* of mean rank, as *the public crier*, or *watchman.* III. as neut., δημόσιον, τό, *the state*, Lat. *respublica.* 2. *any public building: the public prison.* IV. Doric fem. ἡ δαμοσία (sub. σκηνή), *the tent of the Spartan kings.* 2. dat. δημοσίᾳ, Ion. -ίῃ, as Adv., *in public, at the public expense.* Hence

δημοσιόω, f. ώσω, = δημεύω, *to confiscate.*

δημο-τελής, ές, (δῆμος, τέλος) *at the public cost, public, national.*

δημότερος, α, ον, (δῆμος) *common, vulgar.*

δημότης, ου, ὁ, (δῆμος) *one of the people: a commoner, plebeian.* II. *a member of the same δῆμος, a fellow-citizen.*

δημοτικός, ή, όν, (δῆμος) *suiting the people, common: public.* II. *of the populace, one of them*, Lat. *plebeius.* III. *on the democratic side*, Lat. *popularis*: generally, *popular*:—Adv. -κῶς, *affably, kindly.* IV. at Athens, *of* or *belonging to a deme*, opp. to δημόσιος.

δημ-οῦχος, ον, (δῆμος, ἔχω) *protecting the people, tutelary*, of divinities: as Subst., δημοῦχοι γᾶς *guardians* of the land.

δημο-φάγος, ον, (δῆμος, φαγεῖν) = δημοβόρος.

δημο-χᾰριστής, οῦ, ὁ, (δῆμος, χαρίζομαι) *flatterer of the people.*

δημ-ώδης, ες, (δῆμος, εἶδος) *like the people, popular, common.*

δήν, Dor. **δάν**, (δή, ἤδη) Adv. Lat. *diu, long, for a long while, this long time: long ago.* Hence

δηναιός, Dor. **δαναιός**, ά, όν, *long-lived: aged, ancient.*

δηνάριον, τό, a Roman coin, not quite = Gr. δραχμή, being about 8½d.

ΔΗ'ΝΕΑ, τά, *counsels, plans, arts*: only in plur.

δηξί-θῡμος, ον, (δάκνω, θυμός) *heart-eating.*

δήξομαι, fut. of δάκνω.

δηοῦν, inf. of δηϊόω: but **δῄουν**, Ep. impf.

δή-ποθεν, indef. Adv. *from any quarter*, Lat. *undecunque; ὁπόθεν δήποθεν from some quarter or other.*

δή-ποτε, Dor. **δή-ποκα**, indef. Adv., often written δή ποτε, *at some time, once, once on a time*:—εἰ δήποτε, Lat. *si quando*:—τί δήποτε; Lat. *quidnam?*

δή-που, indef. Adv., often written δή που, *perhaps, it may be: doubtless, I suppose*, Lat. *scilicet, nimirum.* II. as interrog. implying an affirm. answer; τὴν αἰχμάλωτον κάτοισθα δήπου; you know the captive woman, *I presume?*

δή-πουθεν, indef. Adv., = δήπου.

δηριάομαι, Ep. 3 dual δηριάασθον, 3 pl. δηριόωντο, inf. δηριάασθαι: Dep.: (δῆρις):—*to contend, fight: to quarrel, wrangle.*

δηρινθήτην, v. sub sq.

ΔΗ'ΡΙΣ, ιος and εως, ἡ, *fight, battle, contest.*

δηρί-φᾰτος, ον, (δῆρις, φάω) *slain in fight.*

δηρίω, aor. 1 ἐδήρῖσα, = δηριάομαι:—Med. δηρίομαι, fut. δηρίσομαι [ῑ]: 3 pl. aor. 1 med. δηρίσαντο; also 3 dual aor. 1 pass. δηρινθήτην, as if from δηρίνομαι.

δηρό-βιος, Dor. **δαρόβιος**, ον, (δηρός, βίος) *longlived.*

δηρός, ά, όν, (δήν) *long, too long*:—in bad sense, neut. δηρόν as Adv., *all too long.*

δησάσκετο, Ep. for ἐδήσατο, 3 sing. aor. 1 med. of δέω.

δῆσε, Ep. for ἔδησε, 3 sing. aor. 1 of δέω, *to bind*: also Ep. for ἐδέησε, aor. 1 of δέω, *to want.*

δῆτα, Adv. (δή) *certainly, to be sure, of course*; in answers, *yes certainly; οὐ δῆτα, certainly not.* In questions, τί δῆτα; what *then?*

δηχθείς, δηχθῆναι, aor. 1 pass. part. and inf. of δάκνω.

δῃώσας, δηωθείς, aor. 1 part. act. and med. of δηϊόω.

ΔΗ'Ω, *I shall find*: pres. with fut. sense.

Δηώ, ἡ, gen. όος, contr. οῦς, = Δημήτηρ, Lat. *Ceres.*

δῃῶν, contr. for δηϊόων, pres. part. of δηϊόω.

Δηῷος, α, ον, (Δηώ) *sacred to Demeter (Ceres).*

δῃώσω, fut. of δηϊόω.

Δἰ, contr. for Διΐ, dat. of Ζεύς; v. *Δίς.

ΔΙΑ', poët. **διαί**, Prep. with gen. and acc.—Radic. sense, *right through.*

WITH GEN., I. of Place or Space, *through, out at*; δι' ἠέρος αἰθέρ' ἵκανεν *quite through* the lower air even to the ether; ἔκπρεπε καὶ διὰ πάντων he stood *out from among* them. 2. of Intervals of Space, διὰ πολλοῦ *at a* great *distance*; διὰ πέντε σταδίων *at a distance of* 5 stades; διὰ δέκα ἐπάλξεων *at intervals* of ten battlements, i. e. *at every* tenth battlement. II. of Time, *through, throughout, during*, and, of the past, *since*; διὰ χρόνου *after* some time. 2. of Successive Intervals; διὰ τρίτης ἡμέρης every third day; διὰ πέντε ἐτῶν every five years. III. *arising from, through, by means of.*

by, Lat. *per*; δι' ἀγγέλου λέγειν, etc.: hence of the Manner in which a thing is done, διὰ σπουδῆς *with* earnestness.

WITH ACC. of Place, *through, throughout*; διὰ δῶμα *throughout* the house. 2. of Time, *during, by*; διὰ νύκτα *by night*. II. *with a view to, on account, for the sake, by reason of*; διὰ πολλά *for* many reasons.

WITHOUT CASE, as Adv., *throughout*.

IN COMPOS., I. *all through, across*, as in δια-βαίνω. 2. *to the end*, as in δια-βιόω, δια-μάχομαι: hence simply to add strength, *throughly, completely*. II. *between, partly*, esp. in Adj., as διά-λευκος, etc. III. *one with* or *against another*, as δι-ᾴδω. IV. *one from another, asunder*, Lat. *dis-*, as in δια-λύω.

Δία, acc. of Ζεύς; v. nom. *Δίς.

δῖα, ἡ, *the godlike one*, fem. of δῖος; δῖα θεάων or γυναικῶν, *a goddess* among goddesses or women.

δια-βᾰδίζω, f. ίσω Att. ιῶ, *to go across*.

δια-βαίνω, f. -βήσομαι: aor. 2 -έβην, part. διαβάς: pf. -βέβηκα: I. intr. *to make a stride, stand with the legs apart*, and so *to stand firm*, of warriors. II. c. acc., *to step across, step over*: also absol., *to cross over*, like Lat. *trajicere*.

δια-βάλλω (for the tenses, v. βάλλω), *to throw over* or *across, carry over* or *across*: seemingly intr. (sub. ἑαυτόν, στρατόν, etc.) like Lat. *trajicere, to pass over, cross over*. II. *to accuse falsely, slander, calumniate*: *to accuse* a man to another. III. *to mislead, impose upon*.

διαβάς, aor. 2 part. of διαβαίνω.

διάβᾰσις, εως, ἡ, (διαβαίνω) *a crossing over, passage*. 2. *a means* or *place of crossing*.

διαβάσκω, Frequent. of διαβαίνω, *to strut about*.

δια-βαστάζω, f. άσω, *to weigh in the balance*.

δια-βᾰτέος, α, ον, verb. Adj. of διαβαίνω, *that must be crossed*.

διαβᾰτήριος, ον, (διαβαίνω) *with a view to a fortunate passage*: διαβατήρια (ἱερά), τά, *offerings for a happy passage*.

διαβᾰτός, ή, όν, verb. Adj. of διαβαίνω, *to be crossed* or *passed, fordable*.

δια-βεβαιόομαι, Dep. *to maintain strongly*.

διαβέβηκα, pf. of διαβαίνω.

διαβεβίωκα, pf. of διαβιόω.

διαβέβληκα, pf. of διαβάλλω.

διαβέβρωμαι, pf. pass. of διαβιβρώσκω.

διαβήμεναι, Ep. for διαβῆναι, aor. 2 inf. of διαβαίνω.

διαβήσομαι, fut. of διαβαίνω.

διαβήτης, ου, ὁ, (διαβαίνω) *a pair of compasses*.

δια-βιάζομαι, f. άσομαι, strengthd. for βιάζομαι.

δια-βῐβάζω: fut. -βιβάσω Att. -βιβῶ, Causal of διαβαίνω, *to carry across*.

δια-βιβρώσκω, f. -βρώσομαι: pf. pass. βέβρωμαι: —*to devour*.

δια-βῐόω, f. -ώσομαι: aor. 2 -εβίων, inf. -βιῶναι (as if from a pres. δια-βίωμι):—*to live through, pass*. 2. absol. c. part., μελετῶν διαβεβιωκέναι *to spend one's life* in practising.

δια-βλέπω, f. ψομαι, *to look through*: *to look straight before one*. 2. *to see clearly*.

διαβληθείς, aor. 1 pass. part. of διαβάλλω.

διαβοάω, f. ήσομαι, *to shout* or *cry out, proclaim, publish*:—Med. *to contend in shouting*.

διαβολή, ἡ, (διαβάλλω) *false accusation, slander, calumny*.

διαβολία, ἡ, = διαβολή.

διάβολος, ον, (διαβάλλω) *falsely accusing, slanderous, calumnious*:—as Subst., διάβολος, ὁ, *a slanderer*; esp. ὁ διάβολος, *the Slanderer, the Devil*. Adv. **διαβόλως**, *invidiously*.

διαβόρος, ον, (διαβιβρώσκω) *eating through*: c. acc., νόσος διαβόρος πόδα a sore *that eats through* my foot. II. διάβορος, ον, pass. *eaten through, consumed*.

δια-βουλεύομαι, Dep., *to deliberate well*.

δια-βρέχω, f. ξω, *to wet through*. Hence

διάβροχος, ον, *very wet, wet, moist*. 2. *soaked, steeped*; ναῦς διάβροχοι *soaked*, i. e. *rotten* ships.

διαβρώσομαι, fut. of διαβιβρώσκω.

δια-βῡνέω, δια-βύνω, δια-βύω, *to thrust through*:—Pass. *to be thrust* or *passed through*.

διαβῶ, ῇς, ῇ, aor. 2 subj. of διαβαίνω.

δια-γᾰληνίζω, f. ίσω, (διά, γαλήνη) *to make quite calm*.

δι-αγγέλλω, f. -ελῶ: aor. 1 διήγγειλα:—*to send as a message*: generally, *to give notice, notify, proclaim*: c. inf. *to order* to do:—Med. *to pass* the word of command *from man to man, inform one another*.

δι-άγγελος, ὁ, *a messenger between two*, Lat. *internuncius*: *a go-between, spy*.

διᾶγε, Dor. for διῆγε, 3 sing. impf. of διάγω.

διαγεγένημαι, pf. of διαγίγνομαι.

δια-γελάω, f. άσομαι [ᾰ], *to laugh at, mock*.

διαγενήσομαι, fut. of διαγίγνομαι.

διαγενόμενος, aor. 2 part. of sq.

δια-γίγνομαι, f. -γενήσομαι, pf. -γεγένημαι:—*to go through, pass*: absol. *to go through life, survive, live*. 2. *to be between, intervene, elapse*.

δια-γιγνώσκω: f. -γνώσομαι:—*to discern between two, to distinguish*, Lat. *dignoscere*. II. *to resolve finally, determine, vote to do* so and so. 2. as Athen. law-term, *to give judgment, decide*.

διαγίνομαι, Ion. and in late Greek for διαγίγνομαι.

διαγῑνώσκω, Ion. and in late Greek for διαγιγνώσκω.

δι-αγκῠλίζομαι, f. ίσομαι, Att. ιοῦμαι, Dep.: (διά, ἀγκύλη):—*to hold the javelin by its thong*; pf. pass. part. διηγκυλισμένος, *with the thong ready fastened, ready to throw* or *shoot*.

δι-αγκῠλόομαι, = διαγκυλίζομαι.

δια-γλάφω, f. ψω, aor. 1 διέγλαψα, *to hollow out*.

διά-γλυπτος, η, ον, (διά, γλύφω) *all carved*.

διαγνώμη, ἡ, *a final decree, resolution*. From

διαγνῶναι, aor. 2 inf. of διαγιγνώσκω.

δια-γνωρίζω, f. ίσω Att. ιῶ, *to inquire accurately*.

διάγνωσις, εως, ἡ, (διαγιγνώσκω) *a discerning between*

two, distinguishing, discrimination. II. *a resolving, deciding.*

διαγνώσομαι, fut. of διαγιγνώσκω.

δια-γογγύζω, f. σω, *to mutter, murmur.*

δι-ᾱγορεύω, (for the tenses, v. ἀγορεύω) *to speak plainly, declare.* II. *to speak of.*

διάγραμμα, ατος, τό, (διαγράφω) *that which is marked out by lines, a figure, form, plan : a geometrical figure, diagram.* 2. *a register.* 3. *an edict.*

διαγραφή, ἡ, (διαγράφω) *a marking out by lines : a diagram.*

δια-γράφω, f. ψω, *to mark out by lines, draw out.* II. *to cross out, strike off the list,* Lat. *circumscribere;* δ. δίκην *to strike* a cause *out of the list, cancel, quash* it: in Med., διαγράψασθαι δίκην *to cross one's own* cause *out, withdraw* it.

δια-γρηγορέω, f. ήσω, *to remain awake.*

δι-αγριαίνω, *to be much provoked.*

δι-αγρυπνέω, f. ήσω, *to lie wide awake.*

δι-άγχω, f. γξω, *to strangle to death.*

δι-άγω, f. άξω: aor. 2 διήγαγον :—*to carry over* or *across, take across.* II. of Time, *to pass, spend;* διάγει βίον, etc.: but often without βίον, *to live, pass* life, like Lat. *degere:* also *to delay, put off:* c. part. *to continue, go on* doing. III. *to make to continue, keep, support.* IV. *to entertain.* V. *to keep, celebrate.* Hence

διᾰγωγή, ἡ, *a carrying across.* II. *a passing of life, a course of life:* also *a way of passing time, amusement, pastime.*

δι-ᾰγωνίζομαι, Dep. *to contend* or *fight against.* II. *to struggle earnestly: to fight to the end.*

δια-δάπτω, f. ψω, *to tear asunder, rend.*

δια-δᾰτέομαι, fut. -δάσομαι: aor. 1 -εδασάμην (cf. δατέομαι) :—*to divide among themselves.* 2. *to distribute.*

διαδέδεγμαι, pf. of διαδέχομαι.

διαδέδρᾱκα, pf. of διαδιδράσκω.

δια-δείκνυμι, f. -δείξω, *to shew through:* hence *to make clear, shew :*—Pass. *to be shewn clearly,* διαδεικνύσθων ἐὼν πολέμιος *let him be declared* the king's enemy. II. sometimes intrans. in Ion. aor. 1 διέδεξε, *it was clear, manifest*

διαδέκτωρ, ορος, ὁ, (διαδέχομαι) as Adj. *inherited.*

δια-δέξιος, ον, (διά, δεξιός) *of right good omen.*

δια-δέρκομαι, aor. 2 ἔδρᾰκον: Dep. :—*to see* a thing *through* another; οὐδ' ἂν νῶϊ διαδράκοι he *would not see* us *through* it, sc. the cloud.

διάδετος, ον, (διαδέω) *bound fast;* χαλινοὶ διάδετοι γενύων ἱππείων *firm-bound through* the horse's mouth.

δια-δέχομαι, f. -δέξομαι: pf. -δέδεγμαι: Dep. :—*to receive one from another,* Lat. *excipere: to take up:* c. dat. pers. *to succeed to, relieve* on guard :—hence in pf. part. διαδεδεγμένοι, *in turns, by turns,* Lat. *vicissim.*

δια-δέω, f. δήσω, *to bind round, bind fast;* generally, *to bind on, fasten.*

δια-δηλέομαι, Dep. *to tear in pieces.*

διά-δηλος, ον, *manifest* or *distinguished among others.*

διάδημα, ατος, τό, (διαδέω) *a band* or ***fillet:*** esp. *the blue band worked with white* which went round the turban (τιάρα) of the Persian king: *a diadem.*

δια-διδράσκω, f. -δράσομαι (ᾱ): Ion. **διαδιδρήσκω,** -δρήσομαι: aor. 2 -έδραν: pf. -δέδρᾱκα :—*to run off, escape, get away.*

δια-δίδωμι, f. δώσω, *to give from hand to hand, pass on, give over,* Lat. *tradere.* 2. *to distribute, assign.* 3. *to spread about, publish.*

δια-δῐκάζω, f. άσω, *to give judgment in a case:* c. acc. rei, *to decide, rule :*—Med. *to go to law: to plead one's cause.*

δια-δῐκαιόω, f. ώσω, *to hold to be right.*

διαδικασία, ἡ, (διαδικάζω) *an action to settle disputed claims.*

δια-διφρεύω, f. σω, *to run a chariot-race.*

δια-δοκῐμάζω, f. άσω, *to test closely.*

διαδοθείς, aor. 2 part. pass. of διαδίδωμι.

δίαδος, ότω, aor. 2 imperat. of διαδίδωμι.

διάδοσις, εως, ἡ, (διαδίδωμι) *distribution.*

διαδοῦναι, aor. 2 inf. of διαδίδωμι.

διαδοχή, ἡ, (διαδέχομαι) *a succession;* ἐκ διαδοχῆς or κατὰ διαδοχήν *in turn.* 2. *a relief on guard.*

διάδοχος, ὁ, ἡ, (διαδέχομαι) *succeeding;* as Subst., διάδοχος, ὁ, *a successor:* ὕπνου φέγγος διάδοχον Sleep's *successor,* Light; διάδοχοι ἐφοίτων they went to work *in gangs or reliefs.*

διαδράκοι, 3 sing. aor. 2 opt. of διαδέρκομαι.

διαδρᾰμεῖν, aor. 2 inf. of διατρέχω.

διαδρᾶναι Ion. -δρῆναι, aor. 2 inf. of διαδιδράσκω.

δια-δραπετεύω Ion. **δια-δρηπ-,** *to escape entirely.*

διαδρᾱσι-πολῖται, οἱ, (διαδιδράσκω, πολίτης) *citizens who evade public duties.*

διαδράσομαι, Ion. -δρήσομαι, fut. of διαδιδράσκω.

δια-δρηστεύω, lengthd. Ion. form for διαδιδράσκω.

δια-δρομή, ἡ, (διαδραμεῖν) *a running through* a place. 2. *a passage through.*

διάδρομος, ον, (διαδραμεῖν) *running through* or *about, wandering: vagabond, stray.*

δια-δύνω or **-δύω;** also as Dep. **δια-δύομαι;** fut. δύσομαι: aor. 2 διέδυν :—*to pass through: slip away, get off, escape.*

διαδύς, aor. 2 part. of διαδύω, διαδύομαι.

δια-δύω, v. διαδύνω.

δι-ᾴδω, f. ᾴσομαι, v. διαείδω.

δια-δωρέομαι, Dep. *to distribute in presents.*

δι-άει, Ep. 3 sing. impf. of διάημι.

***δια-είδω:** f. -είσομαι: aor. 2 διεῖδον (q. v.):—*to shew forth, prove:* as Pass., ἀρετὴ διαείδεται courage *is discerned.*

δι-αείδω, Att. contr. διᾴδω: f. -αείσομαι contr. -ᾴσομαι :—*to sing for a prize.*

δια-ειμένος, pf. part. pass of διΐημι.

δια-ειπεῖν, δια-ειπέμεν, Ep. inf. of διεῖπον.

δια-ζάω, inf. διαζῆν: impf. διέζην: fut. διαζήσω:—*to live through, pass:* absol. *to live:* c. part. *to live by* doing so and so, διαζῶσι ποηφαγέοντες: διαζῆν ἀπό τινος *to live off* or *by* a thing.

δια-ζεύγνυμι, f. ζεύξω, *to disjoin.* Hence

διάζευξις, εως, ἡ, *a disjoining.*

διαζητέω, f. ήσω, *to search through: to seek out, invent.*

διαζυγία, ἡ, (διά, ζυγόν) = διάζευξις.

διάζωμα, ατος, τό, *that which is girt, the waist.* II. *that which girds, a girdle.* From

δια-ζώννῡμι or -ύω: fut. ζώσω:—*to gird round:* Med. *to gird oneself with* a belt, etc.

δια-ζώω, Ion. for δια-ζάω.

δι-άημι, Ep. 3 sing. impf. διάει *to blow* or *breathe through.*

δια-θεάομαι, f. άσομαι [ᾱ], Ion. ήσομαι: Dep.:—*to look through, look closely at, examine.*

δια-θειόω, f. ώσω, *to fumigate.*

διάθεσις, εως, ἡ, (διατίθημι) *a disposing in order, arrangement.* 2. = διαθήκη. II. (from Pass.) *a disposition, state, condition.*

διαθέτης, ου, ὁ, (διατίθημι) *one who disposes in order, a regulator, arranger.*

δια-θέω, f. -θεύσομαι, *to run about:* of reports, *to spread.*

διαθήκη, ἡ, (διατίθημι) *a disposition* of property by will; *a will and testament:* also *a covenant.*

δια-θορῠβέω, f. ήσω, *to confound utterly.*

δι-αθρέω, f. ήσω, *to look through, look closely into, examine closely.*

δια-θροέω, f. ήσω, *to spread a report, give out.*

δια-θρῡλέω or -θρυλλέω, f. ήσω, *to spread abroad:*—Pass. *to be the common talk, be commonly reported.* II. in Pass. also *to be talked deaf;* pf. part. διατεθρυλημένος.

δια-θρύπτω, f. ψω: aor. 2 pass. διετρύφην [ῠ]:—*to break in pieces, shiver.* II. metaph. *to weaken, enervate:*—Pass. *to be broken down, enervated: to live riotously:*—Med. *to be affected, give oneself airs.*

διαιθριάζω, f. άσω, *to be quite clear and fine.* From

δί-αιθρος, ον, (διά, αἴθρα) *quite clear and fine.*

δι-αιθύσσω, *to rush* or *dart to and fro.*

δί-αιμος, ον, (διά, αἷμα) *blood-stained.*

δῐαίνω, f. ᾰνῶ: aor. ἐδίηνα:—much like ἰαίνω, *to wet, moisten:*—Med., διαίνεσθαι ὄσσε to *wet one's* eyes: absol. *to weep.* II. *to weep for, bewail.*

διαίρεσις, εως, ἡ, *a dividing, division,* esp. of a class into its constituent parts: and

διαιρετός, η, ον, *divided: divisible:* hence *distinguishable.* II. *distributed.* From

δι-αιρέω, f. ήσω: aor. 2 διεῖλον:—Pass., aor. 1 διῃρέθην: pf. διῄρημαι:—*to divide, part* or *cleave in twain: to cut open, to tear away, pull down.* II. *to divide, distribute:*—Med. *to divide among themselves.* III. *to determine, put an end to: to define, interpret.*

δι-αίρω, f. -ᾰρῶ, *to raise up, lift up.* II. *to part asunder;* διαίρειν τὸ στόμα *to open* the mouth.

δι-αΐσσω, f. -αΐξω: Att. δι-ᾴσσω, -ᾴττω, fut. ᾴξω: aor. 1 διῇξα:—*to rush through* or *across:* of sound, *to shoot through the air.*

δι-ᾰϊστόω, f. ώσω, (διά, ἄϊστος) *to make an end of.*

ΔΙ'ΑΙΤΑ, ἡ, *life, a way of living, mode of life.* 2. *a place for living, a dwelling.* II. at Athens, *arbitration.* Hence

δῐαιτάω, f. ήσω: impf. ἐδιαίτων or διῄτων: aor. 1 ἐδιαίτησα or διῄτησα: pf. δεδιῄτηκα: plqpf. ἐδεδιῃτήκειν:—Pass., aor. 1 διῃτήθην: pf. δεδιῄτημαι:—*to maintain, support:*—Pass. *to lead a certain course of life, to live.* II. *to be arbiter* or *umpire:* generally, *to regulate, govern.* Hence

δῐαίτημα, ατος, τό, mostly in plur. *rules of life, a mode* or *course of life.*

δῐαιτητήριον, τό, (διαιτάω) *dwelling-rooms.*

δῐαιτητής, οῦ, ὁ, (διαιτάω II) *an arbitrator, umpire,* Lat. *arbiter.*

δια-κᾰθαίρω, f. -καθᾰρῶ, and **δια-καθαρίζω**, f. ιῶ, *to cleanse* or *purge thoroughly.*

διακαθαριεῖ, 3 sing. fut. of διακαθαρίζω.

δια-καθίζω, fut. -ιζήσω and -ῐῶ, *to make to sit apart, set apart.*

δια-καίω, f. -καύσω: pass. pf. διακέκαυμαι:—*to burn through, set on fire, heat to excess.*

δια-κανάσσω, aor. 1 διεκάναξα, of liquid, *to run gurgling through.* (Formed from the sound.)

δια-καρτερέω, f. ήσω, *to endure to the end, last out.*

δια-κατελέγχω, impf. med. διακατηλεγχόμην:—*to confute utterly.*

διάκαυμα, ατος, τό, (διακαίω) *burning heat.*

δια-καυνιάζω, (καυνός) *to determine by lot.*

δια-κεάζω, f. άσω, *to split asunder.*

διά-κειμαι, inf. -κεῖσθαι: fut. -κείσομαι:—used as Pass. of διατίθημι, *to be disposed* or *to be in a certain state:* *to be disposed* or *affected* in a certain manner; often with Adverbs, φιλικῶς διακεῖσθαι *to be* friendly *disposed;* ὑπόπτως διακεῖσθαι *to be* suspiciously *disposed;* κακῶς διακεῖσθαι *to be in a sorry plight,* etc. II. of things, *to be settled, fixed;* τὰ διακείμενα *certain terms.*

δια-κείρω: fut. -κερῶ and -κέρσω: pf. -κέκαρκα:—*to cut in pieces: to make null and void, frustrate: deprive of;* σκευάρια διακεκαρμένος *stripped of his* trappings. II. *to break through, transgress.*

διακέκναισμαι, pf. pass. of διακναίω.

διακέκρῐμαι, pf. pass. of διακρίνω.

δια-κελεύομαι, Dep. *to give orders to different persons, to exhort.* 2. *to encourage one another.* 3. *to admonish, inform.* Hence

διακελευσμός, ὁ, *an exhortation, cheering on.*

διά-κενος, ον, *quite empty, hollow.*

δια-κέομαι, Ion. for διάκειμαι.

δια-κερματίζω, f. ίσω Att. ιῶ, (διά, κέρμα) *to change into small coin.*

διακέρσαι, aor. 1 inf. of διακείρω.

δια-κηρῡκεύομαι, Dep. *to negotiate by herald.*

δια-κηρύσσω, f. ξω, *to proclaim by herald: to sell by auction.*

δια-κινδῡνεύω, f. σω, *to run all risks, make a despe-*

rate effort:—Pass. *to be hazarded; διακεκινδυνευμένος, η, ον, desperate.*

δια-κτνέω, f. ήσω, *to move throughout, throw into disorder.* II. *to sift thoroughly, scrutinise*, Lat. *excutere.* III. Pass. *to be put in motion, move.*

δια-κλάω, f. άσω [ᾰ]: aor. 1 διέκλᾰσα, Ep. part. διακλάσσας:—*to break in twain*:—διακεκλασμένος *enervated.*

δια-κλέπτω, f. ψω, *to carry off by stealth.* II. *to save by stealth*:—Med., with aor. 2 pass. διεκλάπην [ᾰ], *to steal away, get safe off.* III. *to keep back by stealth.*

δια-κληρόω, f. ώσω, *to assign by lot, allot.* 2. *to choose by lot*:—Med. *to cast lots.*

δια-κλίνω, *to turn away, retreat.* Hence

διάκλῐσις, εως, ἡ, *a turning away, retreat.*

δια-κλύζω, f. ύσω [ῠ], *to wash thoroughly, wash.*

δια-κναίω, f. -κναίσω:—Pass., fut. διακναισθήσομαι: pf. διακέκναισμαι:—*to scrape* or *grate to nothing: to wear away: to crush in pieces*:—Pass. *to be worn away, destroyed; τὸ χρῶμα διακεκναισμένος having lost all* his colour.

δια-κνίζω, f. σω, *to pull to pieces.*

δια-κοιρᾰνέω, *to rule through* or *over.*

διακομῐδή, ἡ, *a carrying over* or *across.* From

δια-κομίζω, (for the tenses, v. κομίζω) *to carry over* or *across*:—Med. *to carry over what is one's own*:—Pass. *to pass* or *cross over.*

διᾱκονέω, Ion. **διηκονέω**: f. ήσω: impf. ἐδιᾱκόνουν and διηκόνουν, aor. 1 ἐδιᾱκόνησα and διηκόνησα: pf. δεδιᾱκόνηκα:—Pass., aor. 1 ἐδιᾱκονήθην: pf. δεδιᾱκόνημαι: (διάκονος):—*to wait on, serve: to furnish, supply*:—Med. *to serve oneself.* Hence

διᾱκονία, ἡ, *service, business.* 2. *attendance on a duty, ministry.* 3. *the office of a deacon.*

διᾱκονικός, ή, όν, (διακονέω) *serviceable.*

διάκονος [ᾱ], Ion. **διήκονος**, ὁ, ἡ, *a servant, waiting-man: a messenger.* 2. *a minister of the church*, esp. *a deacon.* (Deriv. uncertain.)

δι-ᾰκοντίζω, f. ίσω, *to throw a javelin at*:—Med. *to contend with another at throwing the javelin.*

δια-κόπτω, f. ψω, *to cut in two, cut through: to break asunder, break through.* II. intr. *to break through, burst through.*

δια-κορέω and **-κορεύω**, (διά, κόρη) *to ravish.*

δια-κορκορῡγέω, f. ήσω, *to rumble through.*

διά-κορος, ον, (διά, κορέννυμι) *satiated, glutted.*

δι-ᾱκόσιοι, Ion. **διηκόσιοι**, αι, α, (δίς, ἑκατόν) *two hundred*, Lat. *ducenti*: in sing. with noun of multitude, ἵππος διακοσία *two hundred* horse.

δια-κοσμέω, f. ήσω, *to divide and arrange: to muster*:—Med. *to set all in order.*

διακοσμηθεῖμεν, Ep. for διακοσμηθείημεν, 1 pl. aor. 1 opt. of διακοσμέω.

δι-ᾰκούω, f. ούσομαι: pf. -ακήκοα:—*to hear through, hear out: to hear* from another.

δια-κράζω, f. ξω, *to cry aloud; to scream against another.*

δια-κρέκω, f. ξω, *to strike the strings of* the lyre.

δια-κρηνόω, Dor. -κρᾱνόω: f. ώσω: (διά, κρήνη): *to make to flow, pour forth.*

δι-ακρῑβόω, f. ώσω, (διά, ἀκριβής) *to inquire closely into, have an accurate knowledge of.*

διακρῐδόν, Adv. (διακρίνω) *separately: eminently, above all*, Lat. *eximié.*

διακρῐθήσομαι, fut. 1 pass. of διακρίνω.

διακριθῶ, aor. 1 pass. subj. of διακρίνω.

διακρίνειε, 3 sing. aor. 1 opt. of διακρίνω.

διακρινθείς, Ep. for διακρῐθείς, aor. 1 part. pass. of διακρίνω.

διακρινθήμεναι, Ep. for διακρῐθῆναι, aor. 1 inf. pass. of

δια-κρίνω, f. ῐνῶ: (for the tenses, v. κρίνω):—*to separate, divide: to part* combatants:—Pass. *to be parted* or *dissolved: to disperse.* 2. *to distinguish, tell one from another.* 3. *to settle, determine, decide* a dispute; διακρίνειν αἵρεσιν to make a choice:—Med. *to get* a dispute *decided*:—Pass. of persons, *to come to a decision*: but also of a thing, *to be decided.* II. *to make a distinction: set apart for holy purposes.* III. in Med. *to doubt, hesitate.* Hence

διάκρῐσις, εως, ἡ, *a separating, parting.* 2. *a deciding, judgment: the faculty of distinguishing.*

διακρῐτέον, verb. Adj. of διακρίνω, *one must decide.*

διάκρῐτος, ον, (διακρίνω) *distinguished: excellent.*

διακροτέω, f. ήσω, *to strike* or *break through.*

διάκρουσις, εως, ἡ, *a driving away, putting off.*

δια-κρούω, f. σω, *to try* or *prove by knocking.* II. Med. *to drive from oneself, to put off, get rid of, evade* or *elude by delays.*

διάκτορος, ου, or **διάκτωρ**, ορος, ὁ, (διάγω) *the Conductor, Guide;* epith. of Hermes.

δια-κυβάω, (κύβος) *to play at dice together.*

δια-κῠκάω, f. ήσω, *to mix together.*

δια-κύπτω, f. ψω, *to stoop* and *creep through: to peep through, pry into.*

διακωλῡτής, οῦ, ὁ, *a hinderer, obstructer.* From

δια-κωλύω, f. ύσω, *to hinder, check: to prevent.*

διακωχή, incorrect form of διοκωχή.

δια-λαγχάνω, f. -λήξομαι: aor. 2 διέλᾰχον:—*to divide* or *part by lot: to tear in pieces.*

διαλᾰθεῖν, aor. 2 inf. of διαλανθάνω.

δια-λᾱκέω, f. ήσω, *to crack asunder, burst.*

δια-λακτίζω, f. ίσω, *to kick away.*

δια-λᾰλέω, f. ήσω, *to talk over with.*

δια-λαμβάνω, f. λήψομαι: aor. 2 -έλᾰβον: pf. -είληφα; pass. -είλημμαι or διαλέλημμαι, Ion. -λέλαμμαι:—*to take* or *receive separately.* II. *to grasp with both hands, embrace*, Lat. *complecti*: as Gymnastic term, *to clasp round the waist.* 2. *to grasp with the mind, comprehend.* III. *to separate, divide*, Lat. *dirimere: to distinguish*: also *to interpret.* 2. *to cut off, intercept.* 3. *to distribute.*

δια-λάμπω, f. ψω, *to shine or flash through*: of the day, *to dawn.*

δια-λανθάνω, f. -λήσω: aor. 2 -έλᾰθον: pf. -λέληθα:—*to escape notice*: c. acc. pers. *to escape the notice of.*

διαλᾰχεῖν, aor. 2 inf. of διαλαγχάνω.

δι-αλγής, ές, (διά, ἄλγος) *giving great pain, grievous.* II. *suffering great pain.*

δια-λέγω, f. ξω, *to pick out, choose.* II. **διαλέγομαι**, Dep., with fut. med. -λέξομαι, also pass. -λεχθήσομαι: aor. 1 med. διελεξάμην, pass. διελέχθην: pf. -είλεγμαι:—*to converse, reason, talk with.* 2. absol. *to use a dialect* or *language.* 3. *to discourse, argue.*

δια-λείπω, f. ψω: aor. -έλῐπον: pf. -λέλοιπα, pass. -λέλειμμαι:—*to leave an interval:* plqpf. pass. διελέλειπτο impers. *a gap had been left.* 2. intrans. *to be placed at intervals; τὸ διαλεῖπον a gap.* II. *to leave off, cease:* c. part. *to leave off* doing. 2. of Time, *to intervene, elapse.*

δια-λείχω, f. ξω, *to lick clean.*

διαλεκτικός, ή, όν, (διαλέγομαι) *skilled in discourse* or *argument: ἡ διαλεκτική* (sub. τέχνη), *the art of debating* or *arguing.*

διάλεκτος, ή, (διαλέγω) *discourse, conversation: debate, argument.* II. *speech, language.* 2. *the language of a country*, technically *a dialect.*

διαλέληθα, pf. of διαλανθάνω.

διαλέλημμαι, pf. of διαλαμβάνω.

διαλέλῠκα, διαλέλῠμαι, pf. act. and pass. of διαλύω.

διαλελύμασμαι, pf. of διαλυμαίνομαι.

διάλεξις, εως, ή, = διάλεκτος I.

διαλέξομαι, fut. of διαλέγομαι.

διαλεπτο-λογέομαι, Dep. (διάλεπτος, λέγω) *to discourse subtly.*

διά-λεπτος, ον, (διά, λεπτός) *very small* or *narrow: very subtle.*

διά-λευκος, ον, *marked with white.*

διαλεχθῆναι, aor. 1 inf. of διαλέγομαι.

διαλήσω, fut. of διαλανθάνω.

διαλῐπεῖν, aor. 2 inf. of διαλείπω.

διαλλᾰγή, ή, (διαλλάσσω) *an interchange: a change from enmity to friendship, a reconciliation, treaty of peace:* usu. in plur.

διάλλαγμα, ατος, τό, (διαλλάσσω) *that which is put in the place of* another, *a changeling.*

διαλλακτήρ, ῆρος, ὁ, and **διαλλακτής**, οῦ, ὁ, (διαλλάσσω) *a mediator.*

δι-αλλάσσω, Att. -ττω: fut. ξω: pf. διήλλᾰχα:—*to give* or *take in exchange:* hence *to interchange, exchange.* 2. *to change from enmity to friendship, to reconcile* one to another. II. Pass., with fut. med. διαλλάξομαι: aor. 1 διηλλάχθην, also aor. 2 διηλλάγην [ᾰ]: pf. διήλλαγμαι:—*to be reconciled, become friends.* III. intr. *to differ from* one *in* a thing; so Pass., esp. in aor. 1 διαλλαχθῆναι, *to be different.*

δι-άλλομαι, f. -αλοῦμαι, Dep. *to leap over* or *across.*

δια-λογίζομαι, f. ίσομαι Att. ιοῦμαι: pf. -λελόγισμαι: Dep.:—*to settle accounts:* hence *to take full account of, consider fully.* II. *to converse, argue.* Hence

διαλογισμός, ὁ, *a settling of accounts.* II. *calculation, consideration, reasoning.* 2. *discourse, conversation.*

διάλογος, ὁ, (διαλέγομαι) *a conversation, dialogue.*

δια-λοιδορέομαι: aor. 1 pass. διελοιδορήθην: Dep.:—*to abuse, rail at.*

διαλῠθῆναι, aor. 1 inf. pass. of διαλύω.

δια-λῡμαίνομαι, aor. 1 διελῡμάνθην: pf. διαλελύμασμαι: Dep.:—*to maltreat shamefully.*

διάλῠσις, εως, ή, (διαλύω) *a loosing* one *from anything, parting: a breaking up, destroying.* II. *an ending, cessation: cessation of hostilities, peace.*

διαλυσί-φιλος, ον, (διαλύω, φίλος) *love-dissolving.*

δια-λῠτής, οῦ, ὁ, (διαλύω) *a breaker up, dissolver.*

διαλῠτός, ή, όν, (διαλύω) *dissolved: capable of dissolution.*

δια-λύω, f. ύσω [ῡ]: pf. -λέλῠκα: aor. 1 pass. -ελύθην [ῠ]: pf. -λέλῠμαι:—*to loose one from another, to part asunder: to break up, dismiss, disband.* 2. *to break off, put an end to.* 3. *to reconcile.* 4. διαλύειν διαβολήν *to do away with* false accusations: also *to pay off, discharge.* II. *to relax: to make supple and pliant.*

δι-αλφῐτόω, f. ώσω, (διά, ἄλφιτον) *to fill full of barley-meal.*

δια-λωβάομαι, pf. -**λελώβημαι** (in pass. sense), Dep. *to maltreat outrageously.*

δι-αμαθύνω, *to grind to powder, raze to the dust, utterly destroy.*

δια-μαντεύομαι, f. εύσομαι, *to decide by means of an oracle.*

δι-αμαρτάνω, f. ήσομαι: aor. 2 -ήμαρτον: pf. -ημάρτηκα. *To miss entirely, go quite astray from,* c. gen. 2. *to fail utterly of, fail of obtaining.* Hence

διαμαρτία, ή, *a total mistake: a wrong reckoning.*

δια-μαρτῠρέω, f. ήσω, as Att. law-term, *to use a* διαμαρτυρία (q. v.), *to call evidence for* or *against* an objection:—Pass., aor. 1 διεμαρτυρήθην, *to be affirmed on evidence.* Hence

διαμαρτῠρία, ή, *a calling evidence to support* or *refute an objection.*

διαμαρτύρομαι [ῠ], f. ῠροῦμαι, Dep. *to call solemnly to witness, to protest solemnly:* also *to abjure solemnly: to asseverate.* II. *to beg earnestly of, to conjure.*

δια-μάσσω Att. -ττω, fut. ξω, *to knead thoroughly, knead well up.*

δια-μάχομαι: fut. -μαχέσομαι, Att. -μαχοῦμαι, also μαχήσομαι: Dep.:—*to fight with, struggle against: to fight one with another.* 2. *to fight through, fight it out,* Lat. *depugnare.*

δι-αμάω, fut. ήσω: aor. 2 διήμησα (διά, ἀμάω):—*to mow* or *cut through.* 2. *to scrape* or *clear away;* so also in the Med.

δια-μεθίημι, *to leave quite off. to give up.*

δι-ᾰμείβω, f. ψω, *to exchange.* II. Med. *to change oneself from one place to another: to pass through* or *over.* 2. absol. *to change, alter.*

διαμεῖναι, aor. 1 inf. of διαμένω.

διάμειψις, εως, ἡ, (διαμείβω) *an exchange.*
δια-μελαίνω, f. ἄνῶ, *to make quite black.*
δια-μελειστί, Adv. (διά, μέλος) *limb by limb, piecemeal.*
διαμέλλησις, εως, ἡ, *a being always on the point* to do, *continual delay.* And
διαμελλητής, οῦ, ὁ, *one who continually delays.* From
δια-μέλλω, f. -μελλήσω, *to be always going* to do a thing: hence *to delay continually.*
διαμεμένηκα, pf. of διαμένω.
διαμέμνημαι, pf. of διαμιμνήσκομαι.
δια-μέμφομαι, Dep. *to blame exceedingly.*
δια-μένω, (for the tenses, v. μένω) *to remain by, continue with.* 2. *to be constant, persevere.* 3. *to continue, last, remain.*
δια-μερίζω, f. ίσω Att. ιῶ, *to divide:* metaph. *to cause dissension:*—Pass. *to disagree.* Hence
διαμερισμός, ὁ, *division: dissension.*
δια-μετρέω, f. ήσω, *to measure through, measure out* or *off: to measure out in portions:*—Med. *to have measured out to one, receive as one's share.* Hence
δια-μετρητός, ή, όν, *measured out* or *off.*
διάμετρον, τό, Lat. *dimensum, a portion measured out, a soldier's rations.* From
διά-μετρος, ἡ, (διά, μέτρον) *a diameter* or *diagonal line.* 2. *the rule for drawing the diameter.*
δια-μηχανάομαι, Dep. *to bring about, contrive.*
δι-αμιλλάομαι, f. ήσομαι: aor. 1 διημιλλήθην: Dep.:—*to contend furiously.*
δια-μιμνήσκομαι, f. μνήσομαι: pf. διαμέμνημαι: Pass.:—*to keep in memory.*
δια-μινύρομαι, Dep. *to sing plaintively.*
δια-μιστύλλω, f. ὕλῶ: aor. 1 -εμίστυλα:—*to cut up piecemeal.*
δια-μνημονεύω, f. σω, *to call to mind, remember:* hence *to record, mention.*
δια-μοιράω, (διά, μοῖρα) *to divide, rend asunder.* 2. Med. *to portion out.*
διάμπαξ, Adv. *right through.*
δι-αμπερές, (διά, ἀναπείρω) Adv. of Place, *through and through, right through:*—*all in a piece.* 2. of Time, *throughout, for ever.*
δια-μυδαλέος, α, ον, *drenching.*
δια-μυθολογέω, f. ήσω, *to tell by word of mouth, to speak, converse.*
δια-μυλλαίνω, f. ἄνῶ, (διά, μύλλω) *to make mouths* (in scorn or mockery).
δι-αμφίδιος, ον, (διά, ἀμφίς) *utterly different.*
δι-αμφισβητέω, f. ήσω, *to dispute, disagree.*
δια-ναυμαχέω, f. ήσω, *to maintain a long sea-fight.*
δι-άνδιχα, Adv. *two ways;* διάνδιχα μερμηρίζειν to halt *between two opinions.*
διανεῖμαι, aor. 1 inf. of διανέμω.
δι-ανεκής, ές, Dor. and Att. form of διηνεκής.
διανέμησις, εως, ἡ, *distribution.* From
δια-νέμω, f. -νεμῶ: aor. 1 διένειμα: pf. νενέμηκα: —*to distribute, divide into* portions:—Med. *to divide among themselves:*—Pass. *to spread abroad.* II. *to set in order, govern.*
δια-νέομαι, Pass. *to go through.*
διανέστην, **διανέστηκα**, aor. and 2 pf. of διανίστημι.
δια-νεύω, f. σω, *to nod, beckon to.*
δια-νέω, f. -νεύσομαι, *to swim across: swim through.*
δια-νήχομαι, Dep. = διανέω.
δια-νίζω, f. -νίψω, *to wash out, rinse.*
δια-νίσσομαι, Dep. *to go through.*
δι-ανίστημι, fut. διαναστήσω:—*to set up, make to stand.* II. Pass., with act. aor. 2 -έστην, pf. -έστηκα, *to stand aloof from, depart from.*
δια-νοέομαι, fut. -νοήσομαι: aor. 1 -ενοήθην: pf. -νενόημαι: Dep.:—*to think over, intend, purpose,* Lat. *meditari.* Hence
διανόημα, ατος, τό, *a thought, notion.*
διανοητικός, ή, όν, (διανοέομαι) *intellectual.*
διάνοιᾰ, also **διανοίᾱ**, ἡ, (διανοέομαι). I. *thought: the intellect, mind.* II. *a thought, intention: a notion, belief: the sense* or *meaning* of a thing.
δι-ανοίγω, f. ξω: *to open:* hence *to explain, expound.*
διανοίχθητι, aor. 1 imper. pass. of διανοίγω.
διανομεύς, έως, ὁ, (διανέμω) *a distributer.*
διανομή, ἡ, (διανέμω) *distribution.*
δι-ανταῖος, α, ον, *going right through;* ἡ διανταία (sc. πληγή) *a home-thrust:*—metaph. *unchanging, remorseless.*
δι-αντλέω, f. ήσω, *to drain out, exhaust:* metaph. *to drink to the dregs,* Lat. *exhaurire.*
δια-νυκτερεύω, f. σω, (διά, νύξ) *to pass the night.*
δι-ανύω or **δι-ανύτω** [ῠ]: f. ύσω [ῡ]:—*to bring quite to an end, finish;* ὁδὸν διανύτειν *to finish* a journey; so also διανύτειν, without ὁδόν.
δια-ξαίνω, f. ἄνῶ, *to tear in pieces.*
διαξεῖς, Dor. for διάξεις, 2 sing. fut. of διάγω.
δια-ξιφίζομαι, Dep. (δια, ξίφος) *to fight to the death.*
δια-παιδεύομαι, Pass. *to go through a course of education.*
δια-πᾰλαίω, f. σω, *to go on wrestling.*
δια-πάλη, ἡ, *a hard struggle.*
δια-πάλλω, f. -πᾰλῶ, *to distribute by lot.*
δια-πᾰλύνω, f. ὕνῶ, *to shiver, shatter.*
δια-παντός, Adv., = διὰ παντός, *throughout.*
δια-παπταίνω, *to look timidly round.*
δια-παρατρῐβή, ἡ, (διά, παρατρίβω) *an useless study: vain altercation.*
δια-παρθενεύω, f. σω, (διά, παρθένος) *to deflower.*
δια-πασσᾰλεύω, Att. -πατταλεύω: f. σω: (διά, πάσσαλος). *To stretch out by nailing,* e. g. of a hide *for tanning:* also *to fasten the extremities,* as in crucifixion.
δια-πάσσω, Att. -ττω: f. -πάσω:—*to sprinkle about.*
δια-παύω, f. σω, *to make to cease utterly:* Pass. *to cease to exist.*
δι-απειλέω, f. ήσω, *to threaten violently:*—also in Med.
δια-πεινάω, inf. -πεινῆν, *to hunger one against the other, to contend which is the most hungry.*

διά-πειρα, ἡ, *an experiment, trial.*

δια-πειράομαι: fut. άσομαι [ᾱ]: aor. 1 -επειράθην: pf. -πεπείραμαι: Dep.:—*to make trial* or *proof of* a thing: c. gen. *to have experience* of a thing.

δια-πείρω, f. -περῶ, *to drive through.*

δια-πέμπω, f. ψω, *to send about in different directions.* II. *to send over* or *across.*

διαπέπασμαι, pf. pass. of διαπάσσω.

διαπεπείρᾱμαι, pf. of διαπειράομαι.

διαπεπολεμήσομαι, fut. 3 of διαπολεμέω.

διαπέπυσμαι, pf. of διαπυνθάνομαι.

δια-περαίνω, fut. ᾰνῶ, *to bring to an end.*

δια-περαιόω, f. ώσω, *to take across, ferry over*:—Pass. *to be carried over, go across.* 2. *to draw entirely out of the sheath.*

διαπερᾶναι, aor. 1 inf. of διαπεραίνω.

δια-περάω, f. άσω [ᾱ]: *to go over* or *across, to pass: to pass through.*

δια-πέρθω, f. πέρσω: aor. 2 διέπρᾰθον, Ep. inf. διαπραθέειν: aor. 2 med. διεπράθετο, in pass. sense:—*to destroy utterly, to sack, waste.*

διαπέρσαι, aor. 1 inf. of διαπέρθω.

διαπεσεῖν, aor. 2 inf. of διαπίπτω.

διαπεσεῖσθαι, fut. inf. med. of διαπίπτω.

δια-πέτᾰμαι, = διαπέτομαι.

δια-πετάννυμι or -ύω: f. -πετάσω [ᾰ]:—*to open and spread out.*

δια-πέτομαι: fut. -πτήσομαι: aor. 2 -επτόμην or -επτάμην: Dep.:—*to fly through.* 2. *to fly away, vanish.*

διαπεύσομαι, fut. of διαπυνθάνομαι.

διαπεφοιβάσθαι, pf. inf. pass. of διαφοιβάζω.

διαπέφρᾰδα, pf. of διαφράζομαι.

δια-πήγνῡμι, f. -πήξω: aor. 1 med. διεπηξάμην:—*to fasten together.*

δια-πηδάω, f. ήσομαι, *to leap through* or *across.* II. intr. *to make a leap.*

δια-πῑαίνω, f. ᾰνῶ, (διά, πίων) *to make very fat.*

δια-πίμπλημι, f. -πλήσω (for the tenses, v. πίμπλημι), *to fill full of*: Pass. *to be quite full of.*

δια-πίνω, f. -πίομαι, *to drink against one another, challenge at drinking.* [ῐ]

δια-πίπτω, f. -πεσοῦμαι: (for the tenses, v. πίπτω):—*to fall through, fall off* or *away, escape: to fail utterly, go quite wrong, turn out ill.*

δια-πιστεύω, f. σω, *to entrust in confidence*:—Pass. *to have* a thing *entrusted* one.

δια-πλέκω, f. ξω, *to interweave, weave together.* II. *to weave asunder*, i. e. *unweave*; διαπλέκειν τὸν βίον *to end the web* or *tissue of* one's life.

διαπλεύσας, aor. 1 part. of

δια-πλέω, f. πλεύσομαι, *to sail through.*

δια-πληκτίζομαι, Dep. *to spar* or *skirmish with.*

δια-πλήσσω Att. -ττω, f. ξω, *to break in pieces, split, cleave.*

διάπλοος, contr. **πλους**, ὁ, (διαπλέω) as Adj. *sailing across, passing over.* II. as Subst., **διάπλους**, ὁ, *a voyage across, passage.* 2. *a channel.*

δι-απλόω, f. ώσω, (διά, ἁπλόος) *to unfold.*

δια-πνέω, Ep. -πνείω: f. πνεύσομαι: aor. 1 διέπνευσα:—*to blow through; refresh, revive.* II. *to breathe at intervals, revive.* III. Pass. *to evaporate.*

δια-ποικίλλω, f. ῐλῶ, *to variegate, adorn.*

διαπολεμέω, f. ήσω, *to carry the war through, end the war*, Lat. *debellare.* 2. *to carry on the war.* II. *to force from* another *by war.* Hence

δια-πολέμησις, εως, ἡ, *a finishing of the war.*

δια-πολῐορκέω, f. ήσω, *to besiege to the end, to blockade.*

δια-πομπεύω, f. σω, *to carry the procession to an end.* 2. *to carry all round.*

διαπομπή, ἡ, (διαπέμπω) *a sending backwards and forwards: negotiation.*

δια-πονέω, f. ήσω, *to work out with labour*, Lat. *elaborare: to practise*:—Pass. *to be administered*: also *to be troubled.* II. intr. *to work hard, toil.*

διά-πονος, ον, *having gone through many labours.*

δια-πόντιος, ον, (διά, πόντος) *beyond seas, foreign*, Lat. *transmarinus: going beyond seas.*

διαπόνως, Adv. of διάπονος, *laboriously.*

δια-πορεύω, f. σω, *to carry across.* II. Pass., with fut. med. -εύσομαι, aor. 1 pass. διεπορεύθην: *to go through, pass along.*

δι-απορέω, f. ήσω; and Dep. **διαπορέομαι**, aor. 1 διηπορήθην:—*to be quite at a loss.*

δια-πορθέω, f. ήσω, = διαπέρθω, *to ruin utterly.*

δια-πορθμεύω, f. σω, *to carry over* or *across: to carry a message;* διαπορθμεύειν ποταμόν, of ferry-boats, *to ply across* a river.

δια-πραγματεύομαι, Dep. *to treat of thoroughly.*

διαπρᾰθέειν, Ep. aor. 2 inf. of διαπέρθω.

δια-πράσσω, Att. -πράττω Ion. -πρήσσω: f. ξω: —*to accomplish*, Lat. *conficere: intr. to accomplish one's way across.* 2. *to bring about, effect*: Med., *to effect for oneself, gain one's point.* 3. *to make an end of, slay.*

διαπρεπής, ές, *eminent, conspicuous.* From

δια-πρέπω, *to be eminent, conspicuous*, or *distinguished above others.*

διαπρεπῶς, Adv. of διαπρεπής, *conspicuously*: Sup. διαπρεπέστατα.

δια-πρεσβεύομαι, Dep. *to send embassies to different places.*

δια-πρήσσω, Ion. for διαπράσσω.

δια-πρίω [ῑ]: fut. -πριοῦμαι: pf. pass. -πέπρισμαι: —*to saw through* or *in two: to cut to the heart;* διαπρίειν τοὺς ὀδόντας *to gnash* the teeth:—Med. *to gnash with the teeth.*

διαπρό, Adv. *thoroughly.*

δια-πρύσιος, α, ον, (διαπεράω) *going through, penetrating, piercing, thrilling*, of sounds: neut. διαπρύσιον, as Adv. *piercingly, thrillingly.* 2. *far-stretching;* πρὼν πεδίοιο διαπρύσιος τετυχηκώς a hill running *far into* the plain. 3. *manifest.*

διαπτάσθαι, aor. 2 inf. of διαπέταμαι.

δια-πτοέω, f. *ήσω*: Ep. aor. 1 *διεπτοίησα*:—*to scare away, startle: to strike with panic.*

δια-πτύσσω, f. *ξω*, *to unfold, disclose.*

δια-πτῠχή, ἡ, (*διά, πτυχή*) *a fold, folding leaf.*

δια-πτύω, f. *ύσω* [ῠ], *to spit upon, despise utterly.*

δια-πυκτεύω, f. *σω*, *to box* or *fight with.*

δια-πυνθάνομαι: f. *-πεύσομαι*: pf. *-πέπυσμαι*: aor. 2 *-επυθόμην*:—*to search out by questioning.*

διά-πῡρος, *ον*, (*διά, πῦρ*) *red-hot: hot, fiery.* Hence

διαπῡρόω, f. *ώσω*, *to set on fire.*

δια-πωλέω, f. *ήσω*, *to sell publicly.*

διᾶραι, aor. 1 inf. of *διαίρω.*

διαραίρημαι, Ion. for *διῄρημαι*, pf. pass. of *διαιρέω.*

δι-ᾰράσσω, Att. **-ττω**, f. *ξω*, *to break through, strike through.*

δι-άργεμος, *ον*, *flecked* or *spotted with white.*

δι-αρθρόω, f. *ώσω*, (*διά, ἄρθρον*) *to divide by joints, to articulate.* 2. *to complete in detail, describe distinctly*

δι-ᾰριθμέω, f. *ήσω*, *to reckon* or *count up:* also *to distinguish*, Lat. *enumerare.*

δι-αρκέω, f. *έσω*, *to have full strength: to endure, hold out, prevail.* II. *to nourish.* Hence

διαρκής, *ές*, *sufficient: lasting.* Adv. *-κῶς*, Sup. *-έστατα*, *in complete competence.*

δι-αρμόζω or **-ττω**, f. *σω*, *to distribute in various places, to dispose.*

διαρπᾰγή, ἡ, *plunder.* From

δι-αρπάζω, fut. *άσομαι*: (for the tenses, v. *ἁρπάζω*): —*to tear in pieces: to plunder*, Lat. *diripere: to carry off* as *plunder.*

διαρρᾰγῆναι, aor. 2 inf. pass. of *διαρρήγνυμι.*

διαρρᾰγήσομαι, fut. 2 pass. of *διαρρήγνυμι.*

διαρ-ραίνω, *to besprinkle*:—Pass. *to flow in various directions.*

διαρ-ραίω, f. *σω*: aor. 1 *διέρραισα*:—*to destroy utterly.*

διαρ-ρέω, f. *-ρεύσομαι*: aor. 2 pass. (in act. sense) *-ερρύην*: pf. *-ερρύηκα*:—*to flow through: to slip through:* absol. *to leak*:—pf. part. *διερρυηκώς*, *gaping.* II. *to fall away like water, waste away.*

διαρ-ρήγνῡμι, f. *-ρήξω* (for the tenses, v. *ῥήγνυμι*) *to break, rend in twain, cleave*:—Pass. *to burst.*

διαρρήδην, Adv. (*διερῶ, διαρρηθῆναι*) *expressly, distinctly.*

διαρρήξας, aor. 1 part. ot *διαρρήγνῡμι.*

διάρ-ριμμα, *ατος, τό*, *a casting about.* From

διαρρίπτασκεν, 3 sing. Ion. impf. of *διαρρίπτω.*

διαρ-ριπτέω, only used in pres. and impf., = *διαρρίπτω.* II. intr. *to throw oneself, plunge.*

διαρ-ρίπτω, poët. **διαρίπτω**, f. *ψω*, *to throw, fling, hurl, dart about.* Hence

διάρριψις, *εως*, ἡ, *a throwing about, scattering.*

διαρροή, ἡ, (*διαρρέω*) *a flowing through, a channel* or *pipe to flow through.*

διαρ-ροθέω, f. *ήσω*, *to roar* or *rustle through.*

διάρροια, ἡ, = *διαρροή*, *a flowing through:* esp. as Medical term, *diarrhoea.*

διαρ-ροιζέω, f. *ήσω*, *to whizz through.*

διαρρύδαν, Dor. for *-ύδην*, Adv. (*διαρρέω*) *melting away, vanishing.*

διαρρῠῆναι, aor. 2 inf. of *διαρρέω*,

διαρρυήσομαι, fut. of *διαρρέω.*

διαρρώξ, *ῶγος*, ὁ, ἡ, (*διαρρήγνυμι*) *rent asunder.*

δι-αρτᾰμέω, f. *ήσω*, *to cut in pieces.*

δι-αρτάω, f. *ήσω*, *to suspend and interrupt.*

δια-σαίνω, *to fawn upon.*

δια-σαίρω, pf. *-σέσηρα*, *to grin like a snarling dog.*

δια-σᾰλᾰκωνίζω, strengthd. for *σαλακωνίζω.*

διᾴσασθαι, aor. 1 inf. med. of *διᾴδω.*

δια-σᾰφέω, f. *ήσω*, (*διά, σαφής*) *to make quite manifest.*

δια-σᾰφηνίζω, f. *σω*, *to make quite manifest.*

δια-σείω, f. *σω*, *to shake violently:* intr., *διασείειν τῇ οὐρᾷ to keep wagging with* the tail. 2. *to confound.* II. *to harass, oppress.*

δια-σεύομαι: Ep. aor. 2 *διεσσύμην* [ῠ], 3 sing. *διέσσῠτο*: Pass.:—*to dart* or *rush through.*

δια-σημαίνω, f. *ᾰνῶ*, *to mark* or *point out: to make known, explain.*

διά-σημος, *ον*, (*διά, σῆμα*) *quite clear, distinct.*

Διάσια, *τά*, (*Διός*) *the feast of Jupiter* at Athens.

δια-σῑωπάω, f. *ήσομαι*, *to remain silent.* 2. trans. *to pass over in silence.*

δια-κανδῑκίζω, f. *σω*, (*διά, σκάνδιξ*) *to dose with wild chervil*, in allusion to Euripides.

δια-σκάπτω, f. *ψω*, *to dig through, make a breach in.*

δια-σκεδάννῡμι: f. *σκεδάσω* [ᾰ], Att. *σκεδῶ*: aor. 1 *-εσκέδᾰσα*:—*to scatter abroad: to dissipate: to disband.*

διασκεδάσειεν, 3 sing. aor. 1 opt. of foreg.

δια-σκευάζω, f. *άσω*, *to set in order*:—Pass. and Med. *to arm* or *equip oneself.*

διασκέψομαι, fut. of *διασκοπέω.*

δια-σκηνάω or **-έω**, f. *ήσω*; and **δια-σκηνόω**, f. *ώσω*: —*to take up different quarters: to retire each severally to his quarters.* 2. *to leave a* comrade's *tent.*

δια-σκίδνημι, for *διασκεδάννυμι*, *to disperse.*

δια-σκοπέω, in pres. and impf.: fut. *-σκέψομαι* (from root *σκέπτομαι*): pf. *-έσκεμμαι*:—*to look through, examine, consider.* II. *to look round one, keep watching.*

δια-σκοπιάομαι, Dep. (*διά, σκοπιά*):—*to look out from a watch-tower, to spy out.*

δια-σκορπίζω, f. *σω*, *to scatter abroad.*

δια-σκώπτω, f. *ώψω*, *to jest*:—Med. *to jest one with another, pass jokes to and fro.*

δια-σμάω, Ion. **-σμέω**: f. *ήσω*:—*to wipe out, to rinse, clean.*

δια-σμήχω, f. *ξω*, *to cleanse by rubbing.*

δια-σοφίζομαι, f. *ίσομαι*, Dep. *to act* or *speak like a sophist.*

διασπᾰρακτός, *ή, όν*, *torn to pieces.* From

δια-σπᾰράσσω Att. **-ττω**, fut. *ξω*, *to rend in sunder* or *in pieces.*

διασπᾰρῆναι, aor. 2 pass. inf. of *διασπείρω.*

δια-σπάω, f. *άσω* or more commonly *άσομαι*: (for

the tenses, v. *σπάω*): *to tear asunder, part*, Lat. *divellere: to break through, pull down:* of the laws, *to break through, transgress: to separate:*—Pass., of soldiers, *to be distributed in quarters*.

δια-σπείρω, f. *ερῶ*, *to sow, scatter* or *spread abroad: to squander*. II. *to separate*.

διασπορά, ἡ, (*διασπείρω*) *dispersion*.

δι-ᾴσσω, διᾴττω, Att. for *διαΐσσω*.

δια-σταθμάομαι, f. *ήσομαι*, Dep. *to order by rule, regulate*.

διαστάς, διαστῆναι, aor. 2 part. and inf. of *διΐστημι*.

διάστἄσις, εως, ἡ, (*διαστῆναι*) *a standing apart: distance, an interval* 2. *disagreement, dissension*.

δια-σταυρόω, f. *ώσω*, *to fortify with stakes* or *a palisade*.

δια-στείχω, aor. 2 **διέστῐχον**, *to go through* or *across: to continue*.

δια-στέλλω, f. *-στελῶ*, *to separate, to distinguish, determine*. II. *to command, give orders*.

διάστημα, ατος, τό, (*διαστῆναι*) *an interval*.

διαστήτην, Ep. for *διεστήτην*, 3 dual aor. 2 of *διΐστημι*.

δια-στίλβω, f. *ψω*, *to gleam* or *dawn through*.

δια-στοιβάζω, f. *άσω*, *to stuff in between*.

δια-στοιχίζομαι, f. *ίσομαι*, Dep. *to apportion regularly*.

διαστολή, ἡ, (*διαστέλλω*) *distinction, difference*.

δια-στρατηγέω, f. *ήσω*, *to serve as a general*.

δια-στρέφω, f. *ψω*: (for the tenses, v. *στρέφω*):—*to distort: to turn aside: to pervert:*—Pass. *to be distorted, to have one's eyes distorted: to squint*. Hence

διάστροφος, ον, *distorted:* metaph. *perverted*.

δια-σύρω, pf. *-σεσύρκα*, *to tear in pieces: to worry, disparage*.

δια-σφάζω Att. **-σφάττω**, f. *ξω*, *to cleave asunder, to slaughter*.

δια-σφαιρίζω, f. *ίσω* Att. *ιῶ*, *to throw about like a ball, to toss about*.

δια-σφάλλω, *to foil* or *overturn utterly*.

διασφάξ, άγος, ἡ, (*διασφάζω*) *any opening made by orce, a cleft, a rocky gorge*.

δια-σφενδονάω, f. *ήσω*, *to scatter from* or *as from a sling:*—Pass. *to fly in pieces*.

δια-σφηκόομαι, pf. *-εσφήκωμαι*, Pass. (*διά, σφήξ*) *to be compressed at the waist like a wasp*.

δια-σχίζω, f. *ίσω*, *to cleave asunder:*—Pass., aor. 1 *διεσχίσθην*, *to be cloven asunder, to be parted*.

διασχών, aor. 2 part. of *διέχω*.

δια-σώζω, f. *σώσω*: (for the tenses, v. *σώζω*):—*to keep safe through, bring one well through:* also *to keep in memory:*— Med. *to preserve to oneself:*—Pass. *to come safe through; διασώζεσθαι εἰς* .. or *πρός*.., *to come safe to* a place.

δια-σωπάομαι, f. *άσομαι* [ᾱ], Dor. for *διασιωπάω*.

δια-τᾱγεύω, f. *σω*, (*διά, τᾱγός*) *to arrange*.

διατᾰγή, ῆς, ἡ, (*διαταγῆναι*) *a disposition*.

διατᾰγῆναι, aor. 2 inf. pass. of *διατάσσω*.

διατάγμα, ατος, τό, (*διατάσσω*) *a commandment*.

δια-τάμνω, Ion. for *διατέμνω*.

διάταξις, εως, ἡ, (*διατάσσω*) *disposition, arrangement*; esp. *of troops in order of battle*.

δια-τᾰράσσω, Att. **-ττω**, f. *ξω*, *to throw into great confusion, confound*.

δια-τάσσω Att. **-ττω**: f. *ξω*:—Pass., aor. 1 *-ετάχθην*, aor. 2 *-ετάγην* [ᾰ]: pf. *-τέταγμαι*:—*to arrange: to set in order, draw up in order of battle:* also *to draw up separately*. 2. c. acc. et inf. *to appoint* one *to do* or *be:*—Med., aor. 1 part. in pass. sense *διαταξάμενοι posted in battle order:*—Pass. *to be in battle order*. II. in Med. also, *to order by will*.

διαταχθείς, aor. 1 pass. part. of *διατάσσω*.

διατέθρυμμαι, pf. pass. of *διαθρύπτω*.

δια-τείνω, f. *τενῶ*:—Pass., aor. 1 *-ετάθην* [ᾰ]: pf. *-τέτᾰμαι* (for the tenses, v. *τείνω*):—*to stretch out, stretch to the full:*—Med. *to strain oneself: to exert oneself, strive hard: to maintain stoutly*.

δια-τειχίζω, f. *ίσω*, Att. *ῐῶ*:—*to cut off and fortify by a wall: to draw a wall across: to divide as by a wall*. Hence

διατείχισμα, ατος, τό, *a place walled off*.

δια-τεκμαίρομαι, Dep. (*διά, τέκμαρ*) *to mark out*.

δια-τελευτάω, f. *ήσω*, *to bring to fulfilment*.

διατελέω, f. *έσω*, *to bring quite to an end: to fulfil: to continue* doing. From

δια-τελής, ές, (*διά, τέλος*) *incessant: permanent*.

δια-τέμνω, Ion. **τάμνω**: f. *τεμῶ*: (for the tenses, v. *τέμνω*):—*to cut through, cut in twain: to sever, part:*—Pass., *διατμηθῆναι λέπαδνα to be cut into* strips.

διατέτᾰχα, διατέταγμαι, pf. act. and pass. of *διατάσσω*,

δια-τετραίνω, f. *-τετρᾰνῶ*, Ion. *-τετρανέω* and *-τρήσω*:—*to bore through, make a hole in*.

δια-τήκω, f. *ξω* (v. *τήκω*), *to soften* or *melt by heat:*—Pass., with pf. *-τέτηκα*, *to melt entirely, thaw*.

δια-τηρέω, f. *ήσω*, *to watch closely*. II. (sub. *ἑαυτόν*), *to keep oneself from, abstain from*.

διατί; for **διά τι**, *wherefore?* Lat. *quamobrem?*

δια-τίθημι, f. *-θήσω*:—Pass., aor. 1 *διετέθην*: pf. *διατέθειμαι*:—*to place separately, arrange*. 2. *to dispose, manage: to treat:*—Pass. *to be disposed of, treated*. 3. *to set forth: to recite*. II. Med. *to set out for sale, dispose of*. 2. *to settle mutually; διατιθέναι διαθήκην τινί to make a covenant with* one: absol. *to make an agreement with, promise*.

δια-τῑμάω, f. *ήσω*, *to honour greatly*.

δια-τῐνάσσω, f. *ξω*, *to shake asunder, shake to pieces:* fut. med. *τινάξομαι* is used in pass. sense.

δια-τινθαλέος, α, ον, = *τινθαλέος*.

δια-τμήγω: aor. 1 *-έτμηξα*: aor. 2 *-έτμᾰγον*, pass. *-ετμάγην*, Ep. 3 pl. *διέτμαγεν*:—Ep. for *διατέμνω*, *to cut in twain, divide, sever; διέτμαγεν ἐν φιλότητι they parted* friends: absol. *they were scattered abroad*.

διατμῆξαι, aor. 1 inf. of *διατέμνω*.

δια-τοξεύω, f. *σω*, *to shoot through* or *across:*—Med. *to contend in shooting with*.

δια-τόρος, ον, act. *piercing:* of sound, *thrilling* II. διάτορος, ον, pass., *pierced.*

διατρᾰγεῖν, aor. 2 inf. of διατρώγω

δια-τρέπω, f. ψω, *to turn, divert, dissuade:*—Pass. with fut. med. –τρέψομαι, aor. 1 med. –ετραπόμην, aor. 2 pass. –ετράπην:—*to turn* or *be diverted from* a thing.

δια-τρέφω, f. θρέψω, *to maintain, support throughout.*

δια-τρέχω, f. –θρέξομαι: (for the tenses, v. τρέχω): —*to run through* or *over:* metaph. *to exhaust.* II. intr. *to run about,* Lat. *discurrere.*

δια-τρέω, f. έσω, *to run trembling about, flee all ways.*

διατρῐβή, ἡ, *a wearing away, a spending* of time. 2. *a pastime, amusement.* 3. *serious employment, study: a discussion, argument.* 4. *a way of life, living.* II. in bad sense, *a waste of time, loss of time, delay.* From

δια-τρίβω [ῑ]: f. ψω:—Pass., aor. 2 διετρίβην [ῐ]: pf. διατέτριμμαι:—*to rub between;* χερσὶ διατρίψας: —*to rub away, consume: to waste, destroy.* II. metaph. *to spend time, live.* 2. *to busy, employ oneself.* 3. *to waste time, delay.* III. *to put off by delay, thwart, hinder.* Hence

διατριπτικός, ή, όν, *dilatory.*

διά-τρῐχα, Adv. *in three ways.*

διά-τροπος, ον, *various in dispositions.*

διατροφή, ἡ, (διατρέφω) *sustenance, support.*

δια-τροχάζω, f. σω, of a horse, *to trot.*

δια-τρύγιος, ον, (διά, τρύγη) *planted with vines, ripening one after the other.*

διατρῠφείς, aor. 2 part. pass. of διαθρύπτω.

δια-τρώγω, f. –τρώξομαι: aor. 2 διέτρᾰγον:—*to nibble, gnaw through.*

δι-ᾴττω or **δι-άττω**, fut. διᾴξω, Att. for διαΐσσω.

δι-αυγάζω, f. σω, *to shine through, dawn.*

δι-αυγής, ές, (διά, αὐγή) *transparent, radiant.*

διαυλο-δρόμης, ου, ὁ, (δίαυλος, δρόμος) *a runner in the race.*

δί-αυλος, ὁ, (δίς, αὐλός) *a double pipe* or *channel:* in the race, *a double course,* where the runner ran to the furthest point of the στάδιον, turned round the post, and ran back by the other side: metaph., δίαυλοι κυμάτων ebb and flow, Lat. *fluctus reciproci.* II. *a strait.*

διαφᾰγεῖν, aor. 2 inf. of διεσθίω, *to bite through.*

διαφάδην [ᾰ], and **διαφάνδην**, Adv. *openly.* From

δια-φαίνω, f. –φᾰνῶ: (for the tenses, v. φαίνω):—*to shew through, make to shine through.* II. Pass., aor. 2 –εφάνην [ᾰ], *to be seen, appear through.* 2. *to glow, to be red-hot.* 3. metaph. *to be proved: to be conspicuous among* others. III. intr. in Act. *to dawn.* 2. *to be transparent.* Hence

διαφᾰνής, ές, *seen through, transparent.* 2. *glowing, red-hot.* II. metaph. *well-known, manifest: illustrious:*—Adv. –νῶς, *manifestly.*

δια-φαύσκω, Ion. **–φώσκω**: (διά, φάος):—*to shew light through, dawn.*

δια-φεγγής, ές, (διά, φέγγος) *transparent.*

διαφερόντως, Adv. pres. act. part. of διαφέρω, *differently from: especially, extremely.*

δια-φέρω:—fut. διοίσω and διοίσομαι, formed from *οἴω:—aor. 1 διήνεγκα, Ion. διήνεικα; aor. 2 διήνεγκον formed from *ἐνέγκω: (v. φέρω):—*to carry over* or *across.* 2. *to carry different ways: to tear asunder;* διαφέρειν τὴν ψῆφον *to give* their votes *a different way,* i. e. against one; but also *to determine by vote:* metaph. *to disperse* reports. 3. *to carry through, bring to perfection.* 4. *to bear through, endure, go through with.* 5. absol. *to continue, to live.* II. intr. *to differ, to be different from.* 2. impers., διαφέρει μοι *it makes a difference* to me, οὐ διαφέρει *it makes* no *difference;* τὰ διαφέροντα *points of difference.* 3. *to be different from* a man, *to surpass, excel* him. III. Pass. *to differ* or *be at variance with, quarrel with.*

δια-φεύγω, f. –φεύξομαι: aor. 2 –έφῠγον: pf. –πέφευγα: (v. φεύγω):—*to flee through, get away, escape.* Hence

διάφευξις, εως, ἡ, *an escaping, means of escape.*

δια-φημίζω, f. ίσω, *to make known, publish.*

δια-φθείρω: f. –φθερῶ Ep. –φθέρσω: pf. –έφθαρκα: —*to destroy utterly, kill:* generally, *to spoil, harm.* 2. *to lead astray, corrupt, ruin:* esp. *to bribe: to seduce.* II. Pass., fut. –φθαρήσομαι, also fut. med. –φθαροῦμαι, Ion. –φθερέομαι: aor. 2 –εφθάρην [ᾰ]: pf. –έφθαρμαι:—*to be destroyed, go to ruin, perish:* esp. *to be disabled:* διεφθαρμένος *corrupt.* III. the perf. διέφθορα is sometimes intr. *to be deranged, mad:* also *to be dead.* Hence

διαφθορά, ὁ, *destruction, ruin, death.* 2. in moral sense, *corruption, seduction.* 3. ἰχθύσιν διαφθορά *a prey* for fishes. Hence

διαφθορεύς, έως, ὁ, *a corrupter, seducer.*

δι-αφίημι, f. ήσω, *to dismiss, disband.*

δια-φοιβάζω, f. σω, *to drive mad:*—Pass. *to rave.*

δια-φοιτάω Ion. –έω, f. ήσω, *to wander abroad, run about: to get abroad.*

διαφορά, ἡ, (διαφέρω) *difference, distinction.* 2. *variance, disagreement.* II. *distinction excellence.* III. *advantage, profit.*

δια-φορέω, f. ήσω, *to drag about, spread abroad.* 2. *to carry off as plunder, to plunder:* also *to rend in pieces, destroy.* II. *to carry through* or *across.* Hence

διαφόρησις, εως, ἡ, *a plundering.*

διάφορος, ον, (διαφέρω) *different, unlike.* 2. *differing with* another: *at variance with.* II. *superior, excellent.* 2. *advantageous, profitable.* III. as Subst., διάφορον, τό, *difference: disagreement.*

διαφόρως, Adv. of διάφορος, *variously.* 2. *at variance.* 3. *excellently.*

διάφραγμα, ατος, τό, (διαφράσσω) *a partition-wall.* II. *the membrane which divides the lungs from the stomach, the midriff.*

δια-φράγνῡμι, = διαφράσσω.

δια-φράζω, *to tell clearly:* Ep. aor. 2 δι-επέφραδον.

δια-φράσσω, f. ξω, *to separate by a fence.*

δια-φρέω, f. -φρήσω, (διά, φρέω, which only occurs in compos., v. εἰσφρέω, ἐκφρέω) *:—to let through, let out.*

δια-φυγγάνω, = διαφεύγω.

διαφῠγή, ἡ, (διαφεύγω) *a means of escape.*

διαφῠή, ἡ, (διαφύω) *any natural partition*, as *the joints* in bodies: *a cleft, division*, as in nuts.

δια-φῠλάσσω, Att. -ττω, f. ξω, *to watch vigilantly, preserve: keep, maintain.*

δια-φῡσάω, f. ήσω, *to blow* or *breathe through.* II. *to blow away:* Pass. *to be scattered to the winds, vanish.*

δι-ἄφύσσω, f. ξω: aor. 1 διήφῠσα *:—to draw out, draw off.* II. *to tear up, rend.*

δια-φύω, f. φύσω, *to make to grow through.* II. Pass., with aor. 2 act. διέφῠν, pf. διαπέφῡκα *:—to intervene;* χρόνος διέφυ time *elapsed.*

δια-φωνέω, f. ήσω, *to sound discordantly, to disagree.*

δια-φώσκω, Ion. for διαφαύσκω.

δια-χάζω or **-χάζομαι**, *to draw back, withdraw.*

δια-χᾰλάω, f. άσω [ᾰ] *:—to loosen: to open, unbar.* II. *to make supple by exercise.*

δια-χάσκω, *to gape wide, yawn.*

διαχέαι, aor. 1 inf. of διαχέω.

δια-χειμάζω, f. άσω, *to pass the winter.*

δια-χειρίζω, f. ίσω Att. ιῶ, *to have in hand, conduct, manage.* Hence

διαχείρισις, εως, ἡ, *management, administration.*

δια-χειροτονέω, f. ήσω, *to choose between two* persons or things *by show of hands*, or *by open vote.* Hence

διαχειροτονία, ἡ, *a choice between two* persons or things.

δια-χέω, f. -χεῶ: aor. 1 -έχεα, Ep. -έχευα *:—to pour different ways: to pour out, dissolve:* of metals, *to soften, melt:* also *to disperse:* metaph. *to confound.* II. Pass. *to be poured from one vessel into another: to be melted: to fall to pieces:*—metaph. *to be relaxed.*

δια-χλευάζω, *to mock greatly.*

δια-χόω, old form for διαχώννυμι; in inf., διαχοῦν τὸ χῶμα *to complete* the mound.

δια-χράομαι: f. ήσομαι, with Dor. 3 sing. διαχρησεῖται *:—to use constantly:* also *to meet with, suffer under.* II. c. acc. pers. *to destroy, slay.*

δια-χρέομαι Ion. for foreg.: διαχρέωμαι, Ion. subj.

δια-χώννυμι, f. -χώσω, *to carry a mound across.*

δια-χωρέω, f. ήσω, *to go* or *pass through:* impers., κάτω διεχώρει αὐτοῖς they laboured under *diarrhoea.*

δια-χωρίζω, f. ίσω Att. ιῶ, *to separate.*

δια-ψαίρω, *to sweep away, blow away.*

δια-ψεύδω or **-ψεύδομαι**, *to deceive utterly.* II. διαψεύδομαι also as Pass., aor. 1 διεψεύσθην: pf. διέψευσμαι *:—to be deceived, mistaken.*

δια-ψηφίζομαι: f. ίσομαι Att. ιοῦμαι: Dep.:*—to vote with pebbles: decide by votes.* Hence

διαψήφισις, εως, ἡ, *a deciding by vote.*

δια-ψύχω, f. ξω, *to cool, refresh:* of ships, *to haul high and dry: to make water-tight.*

δί-βολος, ον, (δίς, βάλλω) *two-pointed.* [ῐ]

δί-γληνος, ον, (δίς, γλήνη) *with two eyeballs.*

δί-γλωσσος, Att. **-ττος**, ον, (δίς, γλῶσσα) *speaking two languages* Lat. *bilinguis:* as Subst., δίγλωσσος, ὁ, *an interpreter.* II. *double-tongued.*

δί-γονος, ον, (δίς, *γένω) *twice-born:—twin; double.*

δίδαγμα, ατος, τό, (διδάσκω) *a lesson.*

διδάκκη, Dor. for διδάσκει.

διδακτικός, ή, όν, (διδάσκω) *apt at teaching.*

δῐδακτός, ή, όν, (διδάσκω) of things, *taught: that can be taught: that ought to be taught.* II. of persons, *taught, instructed.*

δῐδάξω, fut. of διδάσκω.

δίδαξις, εως, ἡ, (διδάσκω) *teaching, instruction.*

δῐδασκᾰλεῖον, τό, (διδάσκω) *a teaching-place, school.*

δῐδασκᾰλία, ἡ, (διδάσκω) *teaching: education, training.* II. *the rehearsing of a drama;* cf. διδάσκω II.

δῐδασκᾰλικός, ή, όν, (διδάσκω) *fit for teaching, instructive.* Adv. -κῶς, *instructively.*

διδασκάλιον, τό, (διδάσκω) *a science, art.*

δῐδάσκᾰλος, ὁ and ἡ, (διδάσκω) *a teacher, master: a dramatic poet* was called διδάσκαλος, because he himself *taught the actors.*

διδασκεμέναι, -έμεν, Ep. inf. of διδάσκω.

δῐδασκῆσαι, poët. for διδάξαι, aor. 1 inf. of

δῐδάσκω: fut. διδάξω: aor. 1 ἐδίδαξα, poët. ἐδιδάσκησα (as if from διδασκέω): pf. δεδίδᾰχα: (redupl. causal form of *δάω) *:—to teach;* with double acc., ἱπποσύνας σε ἐδίδαξαν they *taught* thee riding:—Med. *to have* a person *taught;* also, *to teach oneself, learn:* Pass. *to be taught, to learn.* II. διδάσκειν is used of the scenic poets, *who taught the actors* their parts. Hence

διδαχή, ἡ, *teaching: doctrine.*

δίδημι, Ep. for δέω, *to bind, fetter:* 3 pl. pres. διδέᾶσι: 3 sing. imperf. δίδη, Ep. for ἐδίδη.

διδοῖς or **διδοῖσθα**, **διδοῖ**, Ion. 2 and 3 sing. pres. of δίδωμι, formed from *διδόω.

διδόμεν, **διδόμεναι**, **διδοῦναι**, Ep forms for διδόναι, inf. of δίδωμι.

δίδου, 2 sing. imperat. and Ep. 3 sing. impf. of δίδωμι, formed from *διδόω: **διδοῦν** inf.; **διδοῦσι** 3 plur.

διδράσκω: fut. δράσομαι [ᾱ]: pf. δέδρᾱκα: aor. 2 ἔδρᾱν, inf. δρᾶναι, part. δράς, imperat. δρᾶθι, subj. δρῶ, opt. δραίην: Ion. διδρήσκω, f. δρήσομαι, aor. 2 ἔδρην: (*δράω) *:—to run away, escape.*

δί-δραχμος, ον, (δίς, δράχμη) *of two drachms;* δίδραχμοι ὁπλῖται soldiers *with pay of two drachms a day.* II. δίδραχμον, τό, *a double drachm*, = *half a shekel*, paid annually to the treasury at Jerusalem.

δῐδῠμ-άνωρ, ορος, ὁ, ἡ, τό, (δίδυμος, ἀνήρ) *touching both the men.* [ᾱ]

διδυμᾱ-τόκος, ον, Dor. for διδυμητόκος, (δίδυμος, τεκεῖν) *bearing twins.*

δῐδῠμάων, ονος, ὁ, ἡ, (δίδυμος) *a twin-brother.* [ᾱ]

δίδυμνος, poët. for δίδυμος.

δῐδῠμο-γενής, ές, (δίδυμος, *γένω) *twin-born.*

δίδῠμος, η, ον, or ος, ον, (δίς) *double, twofold; δίδυμος κασίγνητος a twin*-brother; *δίδυμοι twins.*

διδῴην, = διδοίην, opt. of δίδωμι.

δίδωθι, Ep. for δίδοθι, imperat. of δίδωμι.

δίδωμι: fut. δώσω: aor. 1 ἔδωκα; aor. 2 ἔδων: pf. δέδωκα:—Med., aor. 2 ἐδόμην:—Pass., fut. δοθήσομαι: aor. 2 ἐδόθην: pf. δέδομαι: (*δόω):—*to give, give freely, present*:—in pres. and impf. *to offer.* 2. of the gods, *to grant*: so of the laws, *to permit* or *sanction.* 3. *to devote, offer to the gods: to give up, surrender*, in good or bad sense. 4. of parents, *to give* their daughter *to wife.* 5. διδόναι ἑαυτόν τινι *to put* oneself in his power. 6. διδόναι δίκην, v. sub δίκη. II. in vows, *to grant, allow, cause that*; δός με τίσασθαι *give* me to avenge myself. II. seemingly intr. *to give oneself up, devote oneself.*

διδῶν, part. of δίδωμι, formed from *διδόω.

διδώσω, Ep. for δώσω, fut. of δίδωμι.

δῖε, vocat. of δῖος, *godlike.*

δίε, poët. for ἔδιε, 3 sing. impf. of δίω.

διέβην, aor. 2 of διαβαίνω.

διεβίων, aor. 2 of διαβιόω.

διεβλήθην, aor. 1 pass. of διαβάλλω.

δι-εγγυάω, f. ήσω, *to give bail for*: Med. *to take bail for*:—Pass. *to be bailed, set free on his security.*

δι-εγείρω, *to arouse*: Ep. aor. 2 pass. διέγρετο, *be was aroused, awaked.*

διεγερθείς, aor. 1 pass. part. of διεγείρω.

διέγνων, aor. 2 of διαγιγνώσκω.

διεδασάμην, aor. 1 of διαδατέομαι.

διέδεξα, Ion. for διέδειξα, aor. 1 of διαδείκνυμι.

διεδηλησάμην, aor. 1 of διαδηλέομαι.

διεδίδοτο, 3 sing. impf. pass. of διαδίδωμι.

διεδόθην, aor. 1 pass. of διαδίδωμι.

διέδρᾰμον, aor. 2 of διατρέχω.

διέδραν, aor. 2 of διαδιδράσκω.

διέδυν, aor. 2 of διαδύω or διαδύομαι.

διέεργον, poët. impf. of διέργω, διείργω.

διέζην, impf. of διαζάω.

διέζωσα, aor. 1 of διαζώννυμι.

διέζωσμαι, pf. pass. of διαζώννυμι.

διεθείωσα, aor. 1 of διαθειόω.

διέθετο, 3 sing. aor. 2 med. of διατίθημι.

διεῖδον, inf. διϊδεῖν, aor. 2 of διοράω, which supplies the pres., *to look through, discern, distinguish.*

διείλεγμαι, pf. pass. of διαλέγομαι.

διειλημμένως, Adv. pf. pass. part. of διαλαμβάνω, *distinctly, precisely.*

διείληφα, pf. of διαλαμβάνω.

διεῖλον, aor. 2 of διαιρέω.

δί-ειμι, fut. διείσομαι: (διά, εἶμι *ibo*):—*to go about: to go away.* II. c. acc. *to pass* or *go through*: hence *to discuss* a subject.

δι-εῖπον. aor. 2 with no pres. in use (διαγορεύω being used instead); inf. διειπεῖν, poët. διαειπεῖν: fut. διερῶ: pf. διείρηκα: (διά, εἶπον):—*to tell at length, detail, explain.* II. *to speak one with another, converse.*

δι-είργω, f. ξω: Ep. and Ion. **διέργω**, Ep. also **διεέργω**:—*to keep asunder* or *apart: to keep off.* II. intr. *to lie between.*

διείρηκα, used as pt. of διειπεῖν, *to say clearly.*

δι-είρομαι, poët. for δι-έρομαι, *to question closely.*

δῐ-ειρύω, Ion. for δι-ερύω, *to draw across.*

δι-είρω: aor. 1 διεῖρσα: perf. διεῖρκα:—*to pass* or *draw* a thing *through.*

δι-ειρωνό-ξενος, ον, (διά, εἴρων, ξένος) *dissembling with one's guests.*

δι-έκ, before a vowel **δι-έξ**, Prep. *right through.*

διεκάναξα, aor. 1 of διακανάσσω.

διεκέκριτο, 3 sing. plqpf. pass. of διακρίνω.

διεκλάπην [ᾰ], aor. 2 pass. of διακλέπτω.

δι-εκπεραίνω, f. ᾰνῶ, *to bring quite to an end.*

δι-εκπεράω, f. ήσω and άσω, *to pass out through.* II. *to pass by, overlook.*

δι-εκπλέω, f. -πλεύσομαι: Ion. **-πλώω**, aor. 1 -έπλωσα:—*to sail out through: to sail out.* II. in naval tactics, *to break the enemy's line by sailing through it.* Hence

διέκπλοος, contr. **διέκπλους**, ὁ, *a sailing across* or *through.* 2. *a breaking the enemy's line* in a sea-fight.

δι-εκπλώω. Ion. for διεκπλέω.

δι-έκριθεν, Ep. for διεκρίθησαν, 3 pl. aor. 1 pass. of διακρίνω.

δι-έκροος, ὁ, (διά, ἐκρέω) *a channel through.*

διέλᾰθον, aor. 2 of διαλανθάνω.

διέλᾰσις, εως, ἡ, *a driving through.* II. *a charge* or *exercise of cavalry.* From

δι-ελαύνω· fut. διελάσω, Att. διελῶ: (for the tenses, v. ἐλαύνω):—*to drive through* or *across: to thrust through.* II. intr. *to drive* or *ride through.*

διελεῖν, aor. 2 inf. of διαιρέω.

διελέλειπτο, plqpf. pass. of διαλείπω.

διελέλοιπα, pf. of διαλείπω.

διελεξάμην, aor. 1 of διαλέγομαι.

διελεύσομαι, fut. of διέρχομαι.

διελέχθην, aor. 1 of διαλέγομαι.

διελθεῖν, Ep. **διελθέμεν**, aor 2 inf of διέρχομαι.

διέλῐπον, aor. 2 of διαλείπω.

δι-έλκω: fut. -ελκύσω [ῠ]: aor. 1 -είλκῠσα (v. ἕλκω):—*to tear asunder, pull open; διέλκειν τοὺς ὀφθαλμούς.* 2. *to pull through.* 3. *to keep on drinking.*

διελύθην [ῠ], aor. 1 pass. of διαλύω.

διελῡμάνθην, aor. 1 of διαλυμαίνομαι.

ΔΙ΄ΕΜΑΙ, Pass. (as if from *δίημι) *to speed, press on.*

διεμαρτύρω [ῡ], 2 sing. aor. 1 of διαμαρτύρομαι.

διέμεινα, aor. 1 of διαμένω.

δι-εμπολάω: fut. ήσω: pass. pf. διημπόλημαι:—*to make merchandise of, sell, dispose of*: hence *to betray.*

δι-ενέγκαι, Ion. **-ενεῖκαι**, aor. 1 inf of διαφέρω **διενεγχθῆναι**, aor. 1 inf. pass.

δι-ενθυμέομαι, Med. *to think within oneself.*

δι-ενιαυτίζω, f. ίσω, (διά, ἐνιαυτός) *to live out the year*

δίενται, 3 pl. of δίεμαι.

δι-εντέρευμα, ατος, τό, (διά, ἔντερον) *a looking through entrails*:—Comic word for *sharp-sightedness*.

δι-εξᾱΐσσω contr. -ᾴσσω Att. -ᾴττω: fut. ᾴξω: *to rush* or *spring forth*.

δι-έξειμι, (διά, ἔξειμι) *to go out through*: *to pass through*: hence *to count over*, *to number*.

δι-εξελαύνω· f. -ελάσω [ᾰ] Att. -ελῶ:—*to drive through*. II. intr. *to ride* or *march through* or *across*.

δι-εξελίσσω Att. -ττω, f. ξω, *to unroll*, *untie*.

δι-εξερέομαι, *to question closely*.

δι-εξερευνάω, f. ήσω, *to examine closely*.

δι-εξέρχομαι, f. -ελεύσομαι: aor. 2 -ῆλθον: pf. -ελήλῠθα: (cf. ἔρχομαι):—*to go out through*, *pass through*: *get to the end of*. 2. *to go through in order*. *to set forth*, *recount in full*. II. intr. *to be past*, *gone by*, of time.

δι-εξηγέομαι, strengthd. for ἐξηγέομαι.

δι-εξίημι, f. ήσω, *to let go through*, *give free passage*. II. intr. (sub. ἑαυτόν), of a river, *to empty itself*.

διεξίμεναι, Ep. inf. of διέξειμι.

δι-έξοδος, ἡ, *a way out through*, *a passage*, *outlet*: *the issue* or *event* of a thing: also *the sun's orbit*. II. *a full account*.

δι-εξυφαίνω, f. ᾰνῶ, *to finish the web*.

δι-εορτάζω, f. σω, *to keep the feast throughout*.

διεπέπαυντο, 3 pl. plqpf. of διαπαύω.

διεπειράθην [ᾱ], aor. 1 of διαπειράομαι.

διεπεραιώθην, aor. of διαπεραιόω.

διεπέρᾱσα, aor. 1 of διαπεράω.

διεπέφρᾰδον, Ep. aor. 2 of διαφράζω.

διέπλεξα, aor. 1 of διαπλέκω.

διέπλευσα, aor. 1 of διαπλέω.

διέπνευσα, aor. 1 of διαπνέω.

διεπορεύθην, aor. 1 of διαπορεύομαι.

διέπρᾰθον, -όμην, aor. 2 act. and med. of διαπέρθω.

διεπτάμην or -όμην, aor. 2 of διαπέταμαι.

διεπτοίησα, Ep. aor. 1 of διαπτοέω.

διέπτυξα, aor. 1 of διαπτύσσω.

διεπῠθόμην, aor. 2 of διαπυνθάνομαι.

δι-έπω, f. ψω, *to manage*, *order*, *arrange*.

δι-εργάζομαι: f. άσομαι; pf. -είργασμαι: plqpf. -ειργάσμην: Ion. -έργασμαι, -εργάσμην: aor. 1 pass. ειργάσθην: Dep.:—*to work at*, esp. of land, *to cultivate it*. II. *to destroy*, *ruin*, *kill*, Lat. *conficere*: also plqpf. in pass. sense, διέργαστο τὰ πράγματα, Lat. *actum erat de rebus*, the affairs *were ruined*.

δι-έργω, Ep. and Ion. for διείργω.

δι-ερείδω, f. σω, *to prop up*:—Med. *to lean upon*.

δι-ερέσσω: fut. διερέσω: aor. 1 διήρεσα, poët. διήρεσσα:—*to row about*, χερσὶ διερέσσειν to swim: *to swing about*.

δι-ερευνάω, f. ήσω, *to search through*, *examine closely*. Hence

διερευνητής, οῦ, ὁ, *a scout* or *vidette*.

διερμηνευτής, οῦ, ὁ, *an interpreter*. From

δι-ερμηνεύω, f. σω, *to interpret*, *expound*.

δι-έρομαι, Ep. for διείρομαι.

ΔΙΕΡΟ´Σ, ά, όν, *moist*, *fresh*, *juicy*: metaph. of men, *fresh*, *quick*, *active*: later, *wet*, *liquid*.

δι-έρπω, f. ψω, *to pass through*.

διέρρηξα, διέρρωγα, aor. 1 and pf. of διαρρήγνυμι.

διερρύηκα, διερρύην, pf. and aor. 2 of διαρρέω.

δι-έρχομαι: fut. -ελεύσομαι: aor. -ῆλθον: Dep.:—*to go through* or *across*, *pass through*. 2. *to come to the end*, *arrive at*. II. intr. *to pass*, of time: *to go abroad*, *prevail*, of a report. III. *to go through*, *narrate*.

διερῶ, used as fut. of διεῖπον.

δι-ερωτάω, f. ήσω, *to cross-question*, *to question continually*.

δίεσθαι, inf. of δίεμαι: also pres. inf. med. of δίω.

δι-εσθίω, fut. διέδομαι, *to eat through*.

διεσκέδασα, aor. 1 of διασκεδάννυμι.

διέσκεμμαι, pf. of διασκοπέω:—hence **δι-εσκεμμένως**, Adv. of the part., *prudently*, *considerately*.

διεσκόρπισμαι, pf. pass. of διασκορπίζω.

διεσπάρην [ᾰ], aor. 2 pass. of διασπείρω.

διέσπᾰσα, διεσπάσθην, aor. 1 act. and pass. of διασπάω.

διέσπασμαι, pf. pass. of διασπάω.

διέσπειρα, aor. 1 of διασπείρω.

διέσσῠτο· 3 sing. Ep. aor. 2 of διασεύομαι.

διεστειλάμην, aor. 1 med. of διαστέλλω.

δι-έστην, διέστηκα, aor. 2 and pf. of διΐστημι.

διέστῐχον, aor. 2 of διαστείχω.

διέστραμμαι, pf. pass. of διαστρέφω.

διεστράφην [ᾰ], aor. 2 pass. of διαστρέφω.

δι-εστώς, perf. part. of διΐστημι.

διεσφηκωμένος, pf. part. pass. of διασφηκόομαι.

διέσχε, 3 sing. aor. 2 of διέχω.

διέσχῐσα, διεσχίσθην, aor. 1 act. and pass. of σχίζω.

διέταξα, aor. 1 of διατάσσω.

διεταράχθην, aor. 1 pass. of διαταράσσω.

διετεθρύλητο, 3 sing. plqpf. pass. of διαθρῡλέω.

δι-ετής, ές, (δίς, ἔτος) *of two years*: *two years old*.

δι-ετήσιος, ον, (διά, ἔτος) *lasting through the year*.

δι-ετία, ἡ, (διετής) *the space of two years*.

διέτμᾰγεν, Ep. for διετμάγησαν, 3 pl. aor. 2 pass. of διατμήγω: **διέτμαγον**, aor. 2 act.

διέτμαξεν, Dor. for διέτμηξεν, aor. 1 of διατμήγω.

δι-ετρᾰπόμην, διετράπην, aor. 2 med. and pass. of διατρέπω

δι-ευκρῑνέω, f. ήσω, (διά, εὐκρινής) *to separate accurately*, *arrange carefully in order*.

δι-ευλᾰβέομαι, Dep. *to take good heed*, *beware of*.

δι-ευνάω, f. άσω, *to lay asleep*.

δι-ευτῠχέω, f. ήσω, (διά, εὐτυχής) *to continue prosperous*, *to prosper throughout*.

διεφάνην [ᾰ], aor. 2 pass. of διαφαίνω.

δι-εφθάρᾰτο, Ion. for διεφθαρμένοι ἦσαν, 3 pl. plqpf. of διαφθείρω.

διεφθάρην [ᾰ], aor. 2 of διαφθείρω.

δι-έφθορα, intrans. pf. of διαφθείρω.

διέφῠγον, aor. 2 of διαφεύγω.

δι-έχω, f. διέξω, *to keep apart*, *divide*. II.

intrans. *to go quite through*: *to stretch across, reach.* 2. *to stand apart, be distant*:—of time, *to intervene.*

ΔΙ'ΖΗΜΑΙ, Ep. 2 sing. δίζηαι: Dep.:—*to seek out*: *to seek after, try for* a thing. II. *to seek the meaning of.* III. c. inf. *to demand* or *require that.*

δίζομαι, = δίζημαι.

δί-ζυγος, ον, and **δίζυξ**, υγος, ὁ, ἡ, (δίς, ζυγόν) *doubly-yoked, double.*

ΔΙ'ΖΩ, Ep. impf. δίζον, *to be in doubt, at a loss.*

δί-ζωος, ον, (δίς, ζωή) *amphibious*: *living twice over.*

διηβολία, ἡ, Ion. for διαβολία.

διήγαγον, aor. 2 of διάγω.

διήγγειλα, aor. 1 of διαγγέλλω.

δι-ηγέομαι, Dep. *to describe* or *narrate in full.*

διήγησις, εως, ἡ, (διηγέομαι) *narration, the statement of the case.*

δι-ηέριος, ον, Ion. for διαέριος, *through the air.*

δι-ηθέω, f. ήσω, *to strain through, filter, sift.* 2. *to wash out, cleanse.* II. intrans., of the liquid, *to filter through, percolate.*

διηκονέω, διήκονος, Ion. for διακ–.

διηκόνουν, διηκόνησα, impf. and aor. 1 of διακονέω.

διηκόσιοι, αι, α, Ion. for διακόσιοι.

διηγκυλισμένος, pf. part. pass. of διαγκυλίζω.

διηγκυλωμένος, pf. part. pass. of διαγκυλόω.

δι-ήκω, f. ξω, *to go through, extend along* or *between.* II. *to pervade, fill*

διήλασα, aor. 1 of διελαύνω.

διῆλθον, aor. 2 of διέρχομαι.

δι-ηλιφής, ές, (διά, ἀλείφω) *smeared all over.*

διηλλάγην, διηλλάχθην, aor. 2 and 1 pass. of διαλλάσσω.

διήλλαχα, διήλλαγμαι, pf. act. and pass. of διαλλάσσω.

διημάρτηκα, διήμαρτον, pf. and aor. 2 of διαμαρτάνω.

δι-ημερεύω, f. σω, (διά, ἡμέρα) *to pass the whole day.*

διημιλλήθην, aor. 1 of διαμιλλάομαι.

διήνεγκα, aor. 1 of διαφέρω: whence

δι-ηνεκής, ές, *stretching evenly along, stretching the whole length, unbroken, uninterrupted.* Adv. διηνεκέως, Att. -κῶς, *from beginning to end*: *clearly, distinctly.*

δι-ήνεμος, ον, (διά, ἄνεμος) *wind-swept.*

διηνοίχθην, aor. 1 pass. of διανοίγω.

διήντλησα, aor. 1 of διαντλέω.

διήνυσα, διήνυκα, aor. 1 and pf. of διανύω.

διῇξα, aor. 1 of διαΐσσω: but **διῆξα** aor. 1 of διήκω.

διῇξα, aor. 1 of διάσσω, contr. for διαΐσσω.

διηπορήθην, aor. 1 pass. of διαπορέω.

δι-ηπόρουν, impf. of διαπορέω.

διῆρα, aor. 1 of διαίρω.

διήρεσα, aor. 1 of διερέσσω.

διηρέθην, aor. 1 pass. of διαιρέω.

διῄρημαι, pf. pass. of διαιρέω.

δι-ήρης, ες, (δίς, *ἄρω) *double*; **διῆρες** μέλαθρον, *an upper story, upper* chamber.

διήρθρουν, διήρθρωσα, impf. and aor. 1 διαρθρόω.

διῆρκα, pf. of διαίρω.

δίηται, 3 sing. pres. subj. med. of δίω.

διῄτησα, διῃτήθην, aor. 1 act. and pass. of διαιτάω.

διήφυσα, aor. 1 of διαφύσσω.

δι-θάλασσος Att. -ττος, ον, (δίς, θάλασσα) *between two seas, where two seas meet*, Lat. *bimăris.*

δί-θηκτος, ον, (δίς, θήγω) *twice-sharpened, two-edged.*

δί-θρονος, ον, (δίς, θρόνος) *two-throned.*

διθυραμβο-διδάσκαλος, ὁ, (διθύραμβος, διδάσκαλος) *the dithyrambic poet who taught his chorus.*

διθυραμβο-ποιός, ὁ, (διθύραμβος, ποιέω) *a dithyrambic poet.*

διθύραμβος, ὁ, *the dithyramb*, a kind of lyric poetry. II. epith. of Bacchus. (Deriv. unknown.)

δί-θυρσος, ον, (δίς, θύρσος) *with two thyrsi.*

Διΐ, dat. of Ζεύς; v. *Δίς.

διϊδεῖν, inf. of διεῖδον.

δι-ΐημι, fut. -ήσω: (for the tenses, v. ἵημι):—*to send through* or *across, let go through.* 2. *to thrust through.* II. *to dismiss, disband.* 2. *to dissolve, melt*; διέμενος aor. 2 part. med., in pass. sense, *being melted.*

δι-ϊθύνω, *to direct by steering straight.*

δι-ϊκνέομαι, fut. -ίξομαι; aor. 2 -ϊκόμην: Dep.:—*to go through*, in telling a story. II. *to reach.*

Διϊ-πετής, ές, (Διός, *πέτω, Root of πίπτω) *fallen from Zeus*, i. e. *from heaven*, epith. of streams *swollen by rain*: later, *heaven-sent, divine, holy, pure.*

Διϊ-πέτης, ες, (Διός, πέτομαι) *hovering in air.*

διϊστέον, verb. Adj. of διειδέναι, *one must inquire.*

δι-ΐστημι, f. διαστήσω: aor. 1 διέστησα:—*to set apart, divide, distract.* II. Pass., with aor. 2 act. -έστην, pf. -έστηκα, plqpf. -εστήκειν:—*to stand apart, to be divided*· hence 2. *to differ, be at variance, quarrel.* 3. *to part* after fighting. 4. *to stand at certain distances* or *intervals.* II. aor. 1 med. διεστησάμην is used trans., *to separate.*

δι-ϊσχυρίζομαι, Dep. *to lean upon, rely on.* II. *to affirm confidently.*

διῖχθαι, perf. inf. of διϊκνέομαι.

δικάζω: fut. δικάσω contr. δικῶ: aor. 1 ἐδίκασα:—Pass., f. δικασθήσομαι, f. 3 δεδικάσομαι: aor. 1 ἐδικάσθην: pf. δεδίκασμαι: (δίκη): 1. c. acc. rei, *to judge, adjudge*: *to decide, determine.* 2. c. dat. *to decide for* a person, *judge* his *cause.* 3. absol. *to be judge*: *to give judgment*: generally, *to come to a decision.* II. Med. *to plead, speak before the judges*: absol. *to go to law.* III. Pass. *to be brought before the judge, to be accused.*

δικαία, ἡ, poët. for δίκη.

δικαιεῦν, Ion. for δικαιοῦν, inf. of δικαιόω: **δικαιεῦσι**, Ion. for δικαιοῦσι, 3 pl. pres.

δικαιο-κρισία, ἡ, (δίκαιος, κρίνω) *just judgment.*

δικαιό-πολις, εως, ὁ, ἡ, (δίκαιος, πόλις) *just in public dealings.*

δίκαιος, α, ον, also ος, ον, (δίκη) *observant of right, righteous, just.* II. *equal, even: strict, exact.* III. *right, lawful, just.* 2. *fair, moderate.*—In phrase δίκαιός εἰμι, with the infin., *I am bound* to do, *I have a right* to do.

δικαιοσύνη, ἡ, *justice, righteousness.*

δικαιότης, ητος, ἡ, = δικαιοσύνη.

δικαιόω: fut. ώσω and ώσομαι:—Pass., aor. 1 ἐδικαιώθην: (δίκαιος):—*to make right: to think right: to consent:* also *to claim as one's right:* c. inf. *to desire* one to do. II. *to judge: to condemn: to punish.* III. *to make just, hold guiltless, justify.* Hence

δικαίωμα, ατος, τό, *an act of justice, the making good a wrong.* 2. *an acquittal, act of justification.* II. *a plea of right, just claim.*

δικαίως, Adv. of δίκαιος, *justly, rightly.*

δικαίωσις, εως, ἡ, *a setting right, doing justice to: punishment.* II. *a claim, demand of right.* III. *judgment, good pleasure.*

δικᾶν, contr. for δικάσειν, fut. inf. of δικάζω.

δικᾰνικός, ή, όν, (δίκη) *belonging to trials, judicial.* II. *skilled in law, lawyer-like.*

δι-κάρηνος, ον, (δίς, κάρηνον) *two-headed.*

δικασ-πόλος, ὁ, (δίκη, πολέω) *a law-giver, judge.*

δικαστηρίδιον, τό, Dim. of δικαστήριον, *a little court of justice.*

δικαστήριον, τό, (δικάζω) *a court of justice.*

δικαστής, οῦ, ὁ, (δικάζω) *a judge* or *juror.*

δικαστικός, ή, όν, (δικάζω) *of* or *for law* or *trials:* τὸ δικαστικόν *the juror's fee*, at first *one* obol, afterwards *three* obols. Adv. -κῶς.

ΔΙΚΕΙ͂Ν, inf. of ἔδικον, an aor. with no pres. in use, *to throw, hurl.*

δί-κελλα, ης, ἡ, (δίς, κέλλω) *a mattock* or *pickaxe with two teeth*, Lat. *bidens:* cp. μάκελλα.

δι-κέραιος, ον, (δίς, κεραία) *two-horned, two-pointed.*

δί-κερως, gen. ωτος or ω, ὁ, ἡ, neut. δίκερων (δίς, κέρας) *two-horned.*

ΔΙ´ΚΗ, ἡ, *right;* the orig. sense was *custom, usage, manner;* ἡ γὰρ δίκη ἐστὶ γερόντων for this is *the manner* of old men; acc. δίκην as Adv., *in the way of, after the manner of.* II. *order, law, right.* III. in plur. *judgments:* generally, *a sentence.* IV. *an action at law, law-suit:* properly, *a private suit* or *action*, opp. to γραφή (a public prosecution). 2. *a trial.* 3. the *satisfaction* or *penalty awarded by the judge;* δίκην or δίκας διδόναι to give *satisfaction* or *suffer punishment*, Lat. *poenas dare;* δίκας λαμβάνειν, = Lat. *sumere poenas*, to inflict *punishment;* δίκην φεύγειν to be the defendant *in the trial*, opp. to δίκην διώκειν to prosecute.

δικη-φόρος, ον, (δίκη, φέρω) *bringing justice, avenging:* as Subst., δικηφόρος, ὁ, *an avenger.*

δικίδιον, τό, Dim. of δίκη, *a little trial.*

δικλίς, ίδος, ἡ, (δίς, κλίνω) *double-folding*, of doors: as Subst., δικλίδες, αἱ, *folding-doors.*

δικο-λέκτης, ου, ὁ, (δίκη, λέγω) *a pleader.*

δικο-λόγος, ὁ, = δικολέκτης.

δικορ-ρᾰφέω, (δίκη, ῥάπτω) *to get up a law-suit.*

δι-κόρῠφος, ον, (δίς, κορυφή) *two-headed.*

δί-κρᾱνος, ον, (δίς, κρᾱνον) *two-headed, two-pointed*, as Subst., δίκρᾱνος, ὁ, *a pitchfork.*

δι-κρᾰτής, ές, (δίς, κράτος) *colleague in power, jointly-ruling: double-slaying.*

δί-κροτος, ον, (δίς, κροτέω) *double-beating: double-oared, with two banks of oars on a side.*

δικτῠβολέω, f. ήσω, *to cast the net.* From

δικτῠ-βόλος, ον, (δίκτυον, βάλλω) *casting nets:* as Subst., δικτυβόλος, ὁ, *a fisherman.*

δίκτυες, οἱ, unknown animals of Libya.

Δίκτῡνα or **Δίκτυννα**, ἡ, (δίκτυον) epith. of Artemis *the goddess of the chase.*

δικτυό-κλωστος, ον, (δίκτυον, κλώθω) *woven in meshes;* σπεῖραι δικτυόκλωστοι the *net's meshy* folds.

ΔΙ´ΚΤΥ˘ΟΝ, τό, *any net-work, a fishing-net: a hunting-net.* Hence

δικτυόομαι, Pass. *to be caught in a net.*

δικωπέω, f. ήσω, *to ply a pair of sculls:* generally, *to work double-handed;* and

δῐκωπία, ἡ, *a pair of sculls.* From

δί-κωπος, ον, (δίς, κώπη) *two-oared.*

διλογέω, f. ήσω, (διλόγος) *to say again, repeat.* Hence

διλογία, ἡ, *repetition.* From

δι-λόγος, ον, (δίς, λέγω) *saying twice, repeating.* II. *double-tongued, deceitful.*

δί-λογχος, ον, (δίς, λόγχη) *with two spears: double-pointed, twofold.*

δί-λοφος, ον, (δίς, λόφος) *with two crests.*

δι-μναῖος, α, ον, Att. **δι-μνέως**, ων, (δίς, μνᾶ) *of* or *worth two minae;* διμναίους ἀποτιμήσασθαι to value *at two minae.*

διμοιρία, ἡ, *a double share: double pay.* From

δί-μοιρος, ον, (δίς, μοῖρα) *divided between two;* as Subst., δίμοιρον, τό, *a half-drachma.*

δίνεον, Ep. impf. of δινέω.

δίνευμα, ατος, τό, *anything whirled round: a whirling, dancing.* From

δῑνεύω, f. εύσω, aor. 1 ἐδίνευσα; and **δῑνέω**, f. ήσω, aor. 1 ἐδίνησα: Ion. impf. δινεύεσκον:—Pass., aor. 1 ἐδινήθην, pf. δεδίνημαι: (δίνη):—*to make whirl* or *spin round: to drive round a circle.* II. intr. and Pass. *to whirl about* in the dance: generally, *to roam about.*

ΔΙ´ΝΗ, ἡ, *a whirling: a whirlpool, eddy: a whirlwind.* Hence

δῑνήεις, εσσα, εν, *whirling, eddying.* II. *rounded.*

δινηθῆναι, aor. 1 pass. inf. of δινέω.

δῑνητός, ή, όν, verb. Adj. of δινέω, *whirled round.*

ΔΙ˜ΝΟΣ, ὁ, like δίνη, *a whirl, eddy.* 2. also *the circular area where the oxen trod out the corn, a threshing-floor.* 3. *a large round goblet.*

δῑνόω, f. ώσω, *to turn with a lathe, to round.*

δίνω, (δῖνος) *to thresh out.*

δῖνωτός, ή, όν, (δινόω) *turned on the lathe, rounded: worked round.*

διξός, ή, όν, Ion. for διссός, *double.*

Διο- or **διο-** in compos. means *sprung from Jove* (Δίς, Διός) or from *the gods*, hence *excellent, god-like.*

δι-ό, Conjunct. contr. for δι' ὅ, *wherefore, on which account: therefore:* with enclit. added, **διόπερ**, Lat. *propter quod, propterea.*

Διό-βολος, *ον*, (Δίς, βάλλω) *hurled by Jove.*

Διο-γενέτωρ, *ορος*, ὁ, (Δίς, γενέτωρ) *giving birth to Jove.*

Διο-γενής, *ές*, (Δίς, *γένω) *Jove-born.*

Διό-γνητος, *ον*, contr. for Διογένητος, = Διογενής.

Διό-γονος, *ον*, = Διογενής.

δι-οδεύω, f. *σω*, *to travel through.*

δι-οδοιπορέω, (διά, ὁδοιπόρος) *to travel through.*

δί-οδος, ἡ, (διά, ὁδός) *a way through, thoroughfare, passage: the orbit* of a star. 2. *permission to pass, a pass-port, safe-conduct.*

Διόθεν, (Δίς) Adv. *sent from Jove.*

δι-οίγνυμι or **δι-οίγω**, f. *-οίξω*, *to open.*

δί-οιδα, pf. of διεῖδον, *to know the difference, distinguish, decide.*

δι-οικέω, f. *ήσω*: impf. διῴκουν: aor. 1 διῴκησα: pf. διῴκηκα:—Pass., aor. 1 διῳκήθην: pf. διῴκημαι, but also irreg. **δεδιῴκημαι**:—*to manage, direct: to conduct* the affairs of a state: *to treat* or *feed* in a certain way. II. *to inhabit distinct places*:—Med. *to live apart.* Hence

διοίκησις, *εως*, ἡ, *house-keeping: management, government.* II. *a government: a province, a diocese.*

δι-οικίζω: f. *ίσω* Att. *ιῶ*, *to make to live apart, to disperse*:—Pass. *to be scattered abroad.*

δι-οικοδομέω, f. *ήσω*, *to build across, wall off.*

διοιστέον, verb. Adj. of διαφέρω (f. διοίσω) *one must move round.*

δι-οϊστεύω, f. *σω*, *to shoot an arrow through.*

διοίσω and **διοίσομαι**, fut. of διαφέρω.

δίοιτο, 3 sing opt. med. of δίω.

δι-οιχνέω, f. *ήσω*, *to go through: to wander about.*

δι-οίχομαι: f. *-οιχήσομαι*: pf. *-οίχημαι*: Dep.:—*to be quite gone by:* of persons, *to be clean gone, to have perished.* II. *to be gone through, ended.*

διοκωχή, ἡ, (δι-όκωχα pf. of δι-έχω) *a cessation.*

δι-ολισθαίνω and **-άνω**, f. *-ολισθήσω*, *to slip through, slip away from.*

δι-όλλυμι: fut. *-ολέσω*, Att. *-ολῶ*: (for the tenses, v. ὄλλυμι):—*to destroy utterly, bring to naught: to put out of mind:* hence *to forget*, opp. to σώζω. II. Pass. and Med., with pf. διόλωλα: *to perish utterly.*

δι-όλου, for διά, ὅλου, Adv., *altogether.*

δι-ομαλίζω, f. *σω*, *to be always even-minded.*

Διομει-αλαζών, *όνος*, ὁ, (Διομεία, ἀλαζών) *the braggart of the deme Diomeia.*

δι-όμνῡμι, fut. *-ομοῦμαι*: aor. 1 med. *-ωμοσάμην*:—*to swear solemnly: to declare on oath.*

δι-ομολογέω, f. *ήσω*. *to make an agreement:* Pass. *to be agreed on:* Med. *to agree mutually to* a thing.

δῖον, acc. of δῖος: but **δίον** Ep. for ἔδιον, impf. of δίω.

Διονύσια (sub. ἱερά), τά, *the feast of* Διόνυσος or *Bacchus*, esp. at Athens: *four distinct feasts* in four consecutive months: viz. I. τὰ κατ' ἀγρούς or μικρά, in Poseideon (December). II. τὰ ἐν Λίμναις or Λήναια (in the Λίμναι, where the Λήναιον stood), in Gamelion (January). III. τὰ Ἀνθεστήρια, in Anthesterion (February). IV. τὰ μεγάλα, τὰ ἀστικά, τὰ κατ' ἄστυ, or simply τὰ Διονύσια, in Elaphebolion (March), the most famous of all. Hence

Διονῡσιᾰκός, ή, όν, *belonging to the Dionysia*, or *to Dionysos.*

Διόνῡσος, ὁ, and poët. **Διώνῡσος**, *Dionysos, Bacchus*; god of wine, vineyards, and dramatic poetry. (Deriv. uncertain.)

Διό-παις, *παιδος*, ὁ, (**Δίς**, παῖς) *son of Jove.*

δι-όπερ, v. sub διο-.

Διο-πετής, *ές*, = Διϊπετής.

διοπεύω, *to be in charge of a ship's cargo.* From

δίοπος, ὁ, (διέπω) *a director, ruler: a person in charge of a ship's cargo.*

δι-οπτεύω, f. *σω*, (διά, ὄψομαι) *to watch accurately, spy about: to gaze upon.*

δι-οπτήρ, *ῆρος*, ὁ, (διόψομαι) *a spy, scout.*

δι-όπτης, *ου*, ὁ, (διόψομαι) *a looker through.*

δι-οράω, fut. διόψομαι, *to see through, discern.*

δι-όργυιος, *ον*, (δίς, ὀργυιά) *two fathoms long.*

δι-ορθεύω, f. *σω*, *to judge rightly of.*

δι-ορθόω, f. *ώσω*, *to make straight: to set right: to make good, amend, correct, make amends for: to tell aright*:—so also in Med. Hence

διόρθωμα, *ατος*, τό, *a making straight, correction: amendment:* and

διόρθωσις, *εως*, ἡ, *a making straight, correcting, amending of a fault: reformation.*

δι-ορίζω, Ion. **-ουρίζω**: f. *ίσω*, Att. *ιῶ*:—*to divide by limits, separate.* 2. *to distinguish, determine, define: to ordain.* II. *to carry abroad, banish*, Lat. *ex-terminare.* III. intr. *to pass the boundaries*

δι-όρνῠμαι, Pass. *to hurry through.*

διορῠγῆναι, aor. 2 pass. inf. of διορύσσω.

διόρυγμα, *ατος*, τό, *a through-cut, a canal.* From

δι-ορύσσω, Att. **-ττω**: f. *ξω*: (for the tenses, v. ὀρύσσω): *to dig through:* metaph. *to undermine.*

δι-ορχέομαι, Dep. *to dance a match with* one.

Δῖος, δῖα, δῖον, (Δίς) *godlike, excellent, mighty*; joined with a genit., δῖα θεάων, δῖα γυναικῶν, with sup. force, *most divine* of goddesses, of women. 2. *noble, honest, trusty.* 3. *divine, marvellous.*

Διός, gen. of **Ζεύς**; v. ***Δίς**.

Διόσ-δοτος, *ον*, (Δίς, δίδωμι) *given by Jove, heaven-sent.*

Διο-σημία, ἡ, (Δίς, σῆμα) *a sign from Jove*, Lat. *ostentum: a portent.*

Διόσ κοροι, οἱ, Att. and poët. for **Διόσκουροι**: (Δίς, κόρος, κοῦρος): *sons of Jove*, esp. *the twins of Leda*,

Castor and Pollux. II. the constellation named from them *the Twins*, Lat. *Gemini*. The Dioscori were tutelary deities of sailors, cf. Hor. Carm. 1, 3, 2. Hence

Διοσ-κούρειον, τό, *the temple of the Dioscuri.*

δι-ότι, Conjunct. for διὰ τοῦτο ὅτι . . , *for the reason that, since*, Lat. *quocirca, quamobrem.* 2. indirect, *wherefore, for what reason.* 3. interrogat. *wherefore?* II. = ὅτι, *that.*

διο-τρεφής, ές, (Δίς, τρέφω) *cherished by Jove.*

δι-ουρίζω, Ion. for διορίζω.

δι-οχλέω, f. ήσω, *to annoy exceedingly.*

δι-όψομαι, fut. of διοράω, formed from *διόπτομαι.

δί-παις, παιδος, ὁ, ἡ, (δίς, παῖς) *with two children;* θρῆνος δίπαις a dirge *chanted by one's two children.*

δι-πάλαιστος, ον, (δίς, πᾰλαιστή) *two palms broad.*

δί-παλτος, ον, (δίς, πάλλω) *brandished with both hands;* δίπαλτα ξίφη *two-handed* swords.

δί-πηχυς, υ, (δίς, πῆχυς) *two cubits long, broad*, etc.

διπλάζω, (διπλάσιον) *to double:*—Pass. *to be doubled, to be made twofold.* II. intr., τὸ διπλάζον κακόν the *twofold* evil. Hence

δίπλαξ, ᾰκος, ἡ, *a double-folded mantle* or *cloak.* 2. δίπλακες are *ship-planks* (*which double* one over the other), and poët. for *ships*, like Lat. *trabes.* II. as Adj., *folded double.*

διπλασιάζω, f. άσω, *to double.* From

διπλάσιος, α, ον, Ion. **διπλήσιος**, η, ον, (δίς) *double, twice as much, as many*, etc.: τὸ διπλάσιον *as much again.* Adv. -ως, *doubly.* Hence

διπλᾰσιόω, *to double:*—Pass. *to become twofold.*

δί-πλεθρος, ον, (δίς, πλέθρον) *two* πλέθρα *long* or *broad.*

διπλῆ (sub. χλαῖνα), ἡ, *a cloak folded double.*

διπλῇ, Adv. *twice, twice over.*

διπλοΐζω, = διπλάζω.

διπλοΐς, ΐδος, ἡ, *a double cloak.* Hence

διπλόος, όη, όον, contr. **διπλοῦς**, ῆ, οῦν, *twofold, double.* 2. *doubled, bent double.* II. in plur., = ἄμφω or δύο, *both, two.* III. metaph. *double-minded, treacherous*, Lat. *duplex*, opp. to ἁπλοῦς. (From δισ-; see ἁπλόος.)

διπλός, ή, όν, = διπλόος: neut. Comp. διπλότερον as Adv. *twice as much.*

διπλόω, f. ώσω, (διπλόος) *to double, bend double.* II. *to repay twofold.*

δι-πόδης, ες, (δίς, πούς) *two feet long, broad*, etc.

Δῐ-πόλεια, τά, contr. of Διϊπόλια, (Δίς, πόλις) an ancient *festival of Jove* at Athens. Hence

Δῑπολι-ώδης, ες, (Διπόλεια, εἶδος) *like the feast of the Dipoleia*, i. e. *obsolete, out of date.*

δί-πολος, ον, (δίς, πολέω) *twice ploughed.*

δί-πορος, ον, (δίς, πόρος) *with two passages.*

δι-πότᾰμος, ον, (δίς, ποταμός) *lying between* or *on two rivers.*

δί-πους, ποδος, ὁ, ἡ, (δίς, πούς) *two-footed*, Lat. *bipes:*—as Subst., δίπους, ὁ, a Libyan kind of mouse, *the jerboa.* II. *two feet long, broad*, etc.

δι-πρόσωπος, ον, (δίς, πρόσωπον) *two-faced.*

δι-πτέρῠγος, ον, (δίς, πτέρυξ) *two-winged.*

δί-πτῠχος, ον, (δίς, πτυχή) *folded together, doubled;* δίπτυχον δελτίον, *a pair of* tablets. II. = δισσός, *twofold, two*, Lat. *geminus.*

δί-πῠλος, ον, (δίς, πύλη) *with two gates* or *entrances.*

δί-πῠρος, ον, (δίς, πῦρ) *with double lights.*

δίρ-ρῡμος, ον, (δίς, ῥυμός) *with two poles.*

δίς, (δύο) Adv. *twice, double.*

-δις, inseparable Suffix, like -δε, signifying motion to a place, as in ἄλλυδις, οἴκαδις, χαμάδις.

***ΔΙ'Σ**, an old nom., = Ζεύς, which appears in the oblique cases Διός, Διΐ contr. Δί, Δία, and the Lat. *Dis, Diespiter, Dijovis.*

δίσ-ᾱβος, ον, Dor. for δίσ-ηβος, *twice young.*

δίσ-ευνος, ον, (δίς, εὐνή) *with two wives.*

δισ-θᾰνής, ές, (δίς, θανεῖν) *twice dead.*

δισκεύω, f. σω, = δισκέω.

δισκέω, f. ήσω, (δίσκος) *to pitch the quoit:* generally, *to throw, toss.* Hence

δίσκημα, ατος, τό, *a thing thrown.* II. *the pitching of a quoit.*

δί-σκηπτρος, ον, (δίς, σκῆπτρον) *two-sceptred.*

δίσκος, ὁ, (δικεῖν) *a round plate, a quoit* of stone; later of metal or wood. II. *anything like a quoit: a trencher: a mirror.*

δίσκ-ουρα, τά, (δίσκος, οὖρον) *a quoit's cast.*

δισ-μύριοι, αι, α, *twenty thousand:* sing. δισμύριος, α, ον, with collective nouns, as, ἵππος δισμυρία 20,000 horse.

δισσ-άρχης, ου, ὁ, (δισσός, ἄρχω) *partners in sway, joint-ruling.*

δισσός Att. **διττός** Ion. **διξός**, ή, όν: (δίς): *twofold, double:* also *divided, disagreeing, doubtful.*

δισσῶς, Adv. of δισσός, *doubly.*

διστάζω, f. άσω, (δίς) *to doubt, be at a loss.*

δί-στῐχος, ον, (δίς, στίξ) *of two rows, lines*, or *verses:* as Subst., δίστῐχον, τό, *an elegiac couplet.*

δί-στολος, ον, (δίς, στέλλω) *in pairs, two together.*

δί-στομος, ον, (δίς, στόμα) *double-mouthed, with two entrances, double.* II. of a weapon, *two-edged.*

δι-σύλλᾰβος, ον, (δίς, συλλαβή) *of two syllables.*

δισ-χίλιοι [χῑ], αι, α, *two thousand:* also in sing., δισχίλιος, α, ον, with collective nouns, as, ἵππος δισχιλία 2000 horse.

δι-τάλαντος, ον, (δίς, τάλαντον) *worth* or *weighing two talents.*

δι-τόκος, ον, (δίς, τεκεῖν) *twin* or *twice bearing.*

διττός, etc., v. sub δισσ-.

δί-υγρος, ον, *thoroughly wet: melting.*

δι-ῡλίζω, (διά, ὕλη) *to strain* or *filter thoroughly: to strain off.*

δι-υπνίζω, f. ίσω Att. ιῶ, *to wake from sleep:* so also in Med.

διφάσιος, α, ον, *twofold, double*, Lat. *bifarius:* in Ion. used also for δύο.

ΔΙ'ΦΑ'Ω, Ion. -έω, *to dive after: seek after, hunt for.* Hence

δῑφήτωρ, ορος, ὁ, *a searcher after.*

διφθέρα, ἡ, (δέφω) *a prepared hide, leather*, and so opp. to δέρρεις which are *unworked hides.* II. *anything made of leather: a leathern garment* worn by peasants: *a leathern wallet.* Hence

διφθέρῐνος, η, ον, *of tanned leather.*

δι-φθερίς, ίδος, ἡ, = διφθέρα.

δί-φθογγος, ον, (δίς, φθέγγομαι) *with two sounds:* as Subst., δίφθογγος, ἡ, and δίφθογγον, τό, *a diphthong.*

δι-φόρος, ον, (δίς, φέρω) *bearing fruit twice in the year*, Lat. *biferus.*

δίφραξ, ἄκος, ἡ, poët. for δίφρος, *a seat, chair.*

διφρεία, ἡ, (διφρεύω) *chariot-driving.*

διφρ-ελάτειρα, ἡ, fem. of διφρηλάτης.

διφρευτής, οῦ, ὁ, *a charioteer.* From

διφρεύω, f. σω, (δίφρος) *to drive a chariot.*

διφρηλᾰσία, ἡ, *chariot-driving.* From

διφρηλᾰτέω, *to drive in a chariot.* From

διφρ-ηλάτης, ου, ὁ, (δίφρος, ἐλαύνω) *a charioteer.*

δίφριος, ον, (δίφρος) *of a chariot:* neut. pl. δίφρια as Adv., *at the chariot-wheels.*

διφρίσκος, ὁ, Dim. of δίφρος.

δί-φροντις, ιδος, ὁ, ἡ, (δίς, φροντίς) *of two minds, distraught in mind.*

δίφρος, ὁ, and later ἡ, (contr. of διφόρος, *bearing two*), in plur. οἱ δίφροι or τὰ δίφρα:—*the chariot-board*, on which *two* could stand; the *war-chariot: a travelling-chariot.* II. generally, *a seat, couch, stool.*

διφρ-ουλκέω, f. ήσω, (δίφρος, ἕλκω) *to draw a chariot.*

διφροφορέω, f. ήσω, *to carry a chair* or *litter:*—Pass. *to be carried* or *travel in one.* II. *to carry a camp-stool*, as the female μέτοικοι had to do for the Athenian women in processions. From

διφρο-φόρος, ον, (δίφρος, φέρω) *carrying a chair.*

δι-φυής, ές, (δίς, φυή) *of double nature* or *form:* generally, *twofold, double.*

δί-φυιος, ον, (δίς, φυή) *of two families.*

δίχᾰ, (δίς) I. Adv. *in two, asunder, apart.* 2. *at two, at variance: differently, oppositely.* II. Prep. with gen. *apart from, without: differently from, unlike:* like ἄνευ, *against the will of:* of Place, *away from.* 2. *except.* Hence

δῐχάζω, f. άσω, *to cleave asunder, disunite, make to disagree.*

δί-χαλκον, τό, *a double* χαλκοῦς, a copper coin.

δί-χᾱλος, Dor. for δί-χηλος.

διχῇ, Adv., = δίχα, *in two: in two ways.*

δί-χηλος, ον, (δίς, χηλή) *cloven-hoofed.* II. as Subst., δίχηλον, τό, *a forceps, pincers.*

διχήρης, ες, (δίχα) *divided.*

διχθά, Adv., poët. for δίχα, like τριχθά for τρίχα, *in twain.* Hence

διχθάδιος, α, ον, *double, divided.* [ᾰ]

δῐχθάς, άδος, ἡ. fem. of διχθάδιος.

δῐχό-βουλος, ον, (δίχα, βουλή) *adverse.*

δῐχο-γνωμονέω, (δίχα, γνώμη) *to differ in opinion.*

δῐχόθεν, (δίχα) Adv. *on* or *from both sides.*

δῐ-χοίνῑκος, ον, (δίς, χοῖνιξ) *holding* 2 χοίνικες, i. e. *nearly* 3 *pints.*

δι-χόλωτος, ον, (δίς, χολόομαι) *doubly enraged.*

διχό-μηνις, ιδος, ὁ, ἡ, = διχόμηνος.

διχό-μηνος, ον, (δίχα, μήν) *in the middle of the month, at* or *of the full moon.*

διχό-μῡθος, ον, (δίχα, μῦθος) *double-speaking.*

διχορ-ρᾰγής, ές, (δίχα, ῥαγῆναι) *broken in twain.*

διχόρ-ροπος, ον, (δίχα, ῥέπω) *wavering.* Adv. -πως, *doubtfully.*

διχοστᾰσία, ἡ, *a standing apart, quarrel, dispute: dissension.* II. *doubt.* From

διχο-στατέω, f. ήσω, (δίχα, στῆναι) *to stand apart, disagree.*

διχό-στομος, ον, (δίχα, στόμα) = δίστομος.

διχο-τομέω, f. ήσω, (δίχα, τέμνω) *to cut in two, cut asunder.*

διχοῦ, Adv., = δίχα.

δῐχό-φρων, ον, gen. ονος, (δίχα, φρήν) *apart in mind, at variance, discordant, disagreeing.*

διχῶς, Adv., like δίχα, *doubly, in two ways.*

ΔΙ'ΨΑ, ης, ἡ, *thirst.* Hence

διψᾰλέος, α, ον, *thirsty, dry;* and

διψάς, άδος, ἡ, fem. of δίψιος.

διψάω, ῇς, ῇ, inf. διψῆν: impf. ἐδίψηv, ης, η: fut. διψήσω: aor. 1 ἐδίψησα: pf. δεδίψηκα:—*to thirst:* of the ground, *to be dry, parched.* II. metaph. *to thirst after, long earnestly for.*

δίψιος, α, ον, (δίψα) *thirsty, athirst, dry, parched.*

δίψος, εος, τό, = δίψα, *thirst.*

δί-ψῡχος, ον, (δίς, ψυχή) *double-minded, wavering.*

ΔΙ'Ω, an Epic verb: in Act. always intr. *to run away, take to flight, flee: to be afraid.* II. in Med., subj. δίωμαι, δίηται, δίωνται, opt. δίοιτο, inf. δίεσθαι, mostly trans., *to frighten away, chase, put to flight: to drive: to hunt:* but 2. also, like δίω, *to be afraid.* [ῐ]

δίωγμα, ατος, τό, (διώκω) *a pursuit, pursuing, chase.* II. *that which is chased,* '*the chase.*'

δῐωγμός, ὁ, (διώκω) *the chase.* II. *persecution, harassing.*

δι-ώδῠνος, ον, (δία, ὀδύνη) *piercing with anguish.*

δι-ωθέω, fut. -ωθήσω and -ώσω: (for the tenses, v. ὠθέω):—*to push* or *tear away:* Med. *to push asunder for oneself, break through.* 2. *to thrust away:*—Med. *to push from oneself, push away: to repulse, drive back.* 3. *to reject: to refuse.*

δῐωκᾰθεῖν, poët. aor. 2 inf. of διώκω.

διωκέμεν, διωκέμεναι, for διώκειν, inf. of διώκω.

διῴκηκα, διῴκημαι, pf. act. and pass. of διοικέω.

διῴκησα, διῳκήθην, aor. 1 act. and pass. of διοικέω.

δῐωκτέος, α, ον, verb. Adj. of διώκω, *to be pursued, aimed at.*

διωκτήρ, ῆρος, ὁ, and **διώκτης**, ου, ὁ, *a pursuer.* From

δῐώκω, f. ξω or ξομαι: aor. 1 ἐδίωξα: poët. aor. 2 ἐδιώκαθον:—Pass., aor. 1 ἐδιώχθην: pf. δεδίωγμαι: (δίω): I. *to pursue, chase, hunt:* of persons, *to* *seek after, follow closely*:—Med. *to chase*. II. *to drive on drive away, chase away*: *to expel, to banish*: διώκειν ἅρμα *to drive* a chariot; hence seemingly intr. *to drive*; also *to speed, haste*. III. as law-term, *to prosecute, bring an action against*; ὁ διώκων *the prosecutor, plaintiff*, opp. to ὁ φεύγων *the defendant*.

δι-ωλένιος, ον, (διά, ὠλένη) *with outstretched arms*.

διώλεσα, aor. 1 of διόλλυμι.

διωμοσάμην, aor. 1 med. of διόμνυμι.

δι-ώμοτος, ον, (διόμνυμι) *on one's oath, bound by oath*.

Διώνη, ἡ, *Dioné*, mother of Venus (Jove being the father). II. *daughter of Dioné, Aphrodité*.

δι-ώνῠμος, ον, (δίς, ὄνυμα = ὄνομα) *with two names*: *named together*.

διωξι-κέλευθος, ον, (διώκω, κέλευθος) *urging on the way*.

δῐώξ-ιππος, ον, (διώκω, ἵππος) *horse-driving*.

δίωξις, εως, ἡ, (διώκω) *a chasing*: *chase, pursuit*. 2. as law-term, *prosecution*.

διώρισα, aor. 1 of διορίζω:—**διώρισμαι**, pf. pass.

διώρυγμαι, pf. pass. διορύσσω.

δι-ώρῠγος, ον, more correct form of διόργυιος.

διῶρυξ, ῠχος, ὁ, ἡ, (διορύσσω) *dug* or *cut through*: διῶρυξ (sub. γῆ) ἡ, *a trench, canal*; κρυπτὴ διῶρυξ *a* covered *passage*.

διῶσα, aor. 1 of διωθέω.

δμηθείς, aor. 1 pass. part. of δαμάω: **δμηθήτω**, 3 sing. imperat., *may he be prevailed upon*.

δμῆσις, εως, ἡ, (δαμάω) *a taming, breaking in*.

δμήτειρα, ἡ, *a tamer, subduer*; fem. of sq.

δμητήρ, ῆρος, ὁ, (δαμάω) *a tamer, breaker*.

δμῶε, dual nom. of δμώς.

δμωή, ἡ, (δαμάω) *a female slave taken in war*: generally, *any female slave*, Lat. *ancilla*.

δμώϊος, α, ον, (δμώς) *in servile condition*.

δμωΐς, ΐδος, ἡ, = δμωή.

δμώς, ωός, ὁ, (δαμάω) *a slave taken in war*: hence *any slave*.

δνοπᾰλίζω, f. ξω, *to swing* or *fling about*.

δνοφέρος, α, ον, *dark, dusky, murky*. From

ΔΝΟ'ΦΟΣ, ὁ, = κνέφας, *darkness, dusk, gloom*.

δοάσσατο, 3 sing. Ep. aor. 1 in impers. sense, = Att. ἔδοξε, *it seemed*: **δοάσσεται**, Ep. for –ηται, 3 sing. subj. = δόξῃ.

δόγμα, ατος, τό, (δοκέω) *that which one thinks true, an opinion*. 2. *a resolution, decree*. Hence

δογμᾰτίζω, f. ίσω Att. ιῶ, *to lay down a decree*:—Pass. *to submit to ordinances*.

δοθήσομαι, fut. pass. of δίδωμι.

ΔΟΘΙΗ'Ν, ῆνος, ὁ, *a small abscess, boil*.

δοιάζω, f. άσω, (δοιοί) *to consider two ways, hesitate between*:—Med. *to doubt, to imagine*.

δοιδῡκο-ποιός, ὁ, (δοῖδυξ, ποιέω) *a pestle-maker*.

ΔΟΙ'ΔΥΞ, ῡκος, ὁ, *a pestle*.

δοιή, ἡ, *doubt, perplexity*. From

δοίην, aor. 2 opt. of δίδωμι.

δοιοί, ά, = δύο, *two, both*: δοιά, Adv. *in two ways*.

δοιώ, = δοιοί, of which it is the dual, = δύο.

δοκεύω, f. εύσω, (δέχομαι) *to watch closely, to lie in wait for*.

ΔΟΚΕ'Ω; but many tenses are formed from pres. *δόκω: fut. δοκήσω and δόξω: aor. 1 ἐδόκησα and ἔδοξα: pf. δεδόκηκα:—Pass., aor. 1 ἐδοκήθην: pf. δεδόκημαι and δέδογμαι: I. *to think, suppose, expect, imagine*. II. intr. *to seem, appear*: esp. in 3 sing. δοκεῖ, ἔδοξε *it seems good, seemed good*: as Att. law-term, ἔδοξε τῇ βουλῇ, τῷ δήμῳ, *it was decreed* or *enacted by..*: but also in 1 pers., δοκῶ μοι, *I seem to myself, methinks*, Lat. *videor mihi*; ἔδοξά μοι *methought*. 2. *to appear to be something, to be of repute*; οἱ δοκοῦντες εἶναί τι *men who are held* to be of some account. 3. aor. 1 neut. part. δόξαν, used absol., and plqpf. δεδογμένον, *it having been resolved*, Lat. *quum statutum esset*; so δοκοῦν, *it being resolved*, Lat. *quum statueretur*.

δόκη, ἡ, = δοχή, (δοκέω) *a vision, fancy*.

δόκημα, τό, (δοκέω) *a vision, fancy*. 2. *an opinion, expectation*.

δόκησις, εως, ἡ, (δοκέω) *an opinion, belief*: *a conceit, fancy, suspicion*. II. *good report, credit*.

δοκησί-σοφος, ον, (δόκησις, σοφός) *wise in one's own conceit*.

δοκῐμάζω, f. άσω: aor. 1 ἐδοκίμασα:—Pass., aor. 1 ἐδοκιμάσθην: pf. δεδοκίμασμαι: (δόκιμος):—*to assay* metals: *to prove, test*: hence generally, *to prove, to examine*. II. *to approve, sanction*: *to hold as good, pure*, after trial. Hence

δοκῐμᾰσία, ἡ, *an assay, proving, examination*.

δοκῐμαστής, οῦ, ὁ, (δοκιμάζω) *an assayer, examiner*.

δοκῐμή, ἡ, *a proof, examination*: *approved character*, Lat. *probitas*: and

δοκίμιον, τό, *proof, trial*. From

δόκῐμος, ον, (δέχομαι) *tried, assayed, genuine*: of persons, *approved, esteemed*, Lat. *probus, probatus*: of things, *worthy, excellent*; also *notable, considerable*. Adv. –μως, *really, truly*.

δοκίς, ίδος, ἡ, Dim. of δοκός, *a stick*.

ΔΟΚΟ'Σ, ἡ, *a wooden beam* or *bar*: *a shaft*.

δοκώ, όος contr. οῦς, ἡ, = δόκησις, *an opinion*.

δολερός, ά, όν, (δόλος) *deceitful, treacherous*.

δολιό-μητις, ιδος, ὁ, ἡ, (δόλιος, μῆτις) *crafty-purposing*.

δολιό-πους, ὁ, ἡ, πουν, τό, gen. ποδος, (δόλιος, πούς) *of stealthy foot*.

δόλιος, α, ον, and ος, ον, (δόλος) *crafty, deceitful, treacherous, wily*.

δολιό-φρων, ὁ, ἡ, gen. ονος, (δόλιος, φρήν) *crafty of mind, wily*.

δολίχ-αυλος, ον, (δολιχός, αὐλός) *with long tube* or *socket*.

δολῐχ-αύχην, ενος, ὁ, ἡ, (δολιχός, αὐχήν) *long-necked*.

δολιχ-εγχής, ές, (δολιχός, ἔγχος) *with tall spear*.

δολιχ-ήρετμος, ον, (δολιχός, ἐρετμός) of a ship, *long-oared*: of persons, *using long oars*.

δολιόω, f. ώσω, (δόλιος) *to deal treacherously*.

δολιχο-γρᾰφία, ἡ, (δόλιχος, γράφω) *prolix writing*,

ΔΟΛΙΧΟ'Σ, ή, όν, *long*: of Time, *long, wearisome*. II. as Subst., δολιχός, ὁ, *the long course*, in racing, opp. to the course of the στάδιον.

δολιχό-σκιος, ον, (δολιχός, σκιά) *casting a long shadow*; or **δολιχ-όσκιος**, (δολιχός, ὄσχος) *with long shaft*.

δολόεις, εσσα, εν, (δόλος) *subtle, wily*. II. of things, *craftily contrived, artful*.

δολο-μήδης, ες, gen. εος, (δολός, μῆδος) *wily, crafty*.

δολο-μήτης, ου, ὁ, and **δολό-μητις**, ι, gen. ιος, (δόλος, μῆτις) *crafty-minded, wily*.

δολο-μήχανος, ον, (δόλος, μηχανή) *contriving wiles*.

δολό-μυθος, ον, (δόλος, μῦθος) *false-speaking*.

δολοπλοκία, ἡ, *subtlety, craft*. From

δολο-πλοκός, όν, (δόλος, πλέκω) *weaving wiles*.

δολο-ποιός, όν, (δόλος, ποιέω) *treacherous*.

δολορραφία, ἡ, *artful contrivance, subtlety*. From

δολόρ-ραφος, ον, (δόλος, ῥάπτω) *contriving wiles*.

δόλος, ὁ, (from ΔΕΛ–, the Root of δέλεαρ) properly *a bait* for fish: then *a piece of deceit, any cunning contrivance*: *craft, cunning, treachery*, Lat. *dolus*.

δολο-φόνος, ον, (δόλος, *φένω) *slaying by treachery*.

δολο-φραδής, ές, (δόλος, φράζω) *wily-minded*.

δολοφρονέων, ουσα, ον, (δολόφρων) *craft-devising*.

δολοφροσύνη, ἡ, *subtlety, wiliness*. From

δολό-φρων, ον, gen. ονος, (δόλος, φρήν) = δολοφραδής, *crafty-minded*.

δολόω, f. ώσω, (δόλος) *to beguile, ensnare*. II. *to counterfeit, adulterate, disguise*. Hence

δόλωμα, ατος, τό, *a trick, deceit*.

δόλων, ωνος, ὁ, (δόλος) *a small sail*. II. *a dagger*.

δολ-ῶπις, ιδος, ἡ, (δόλος, ὤψ) *artful-looking*.

δόλωσις, εως, ἡ, (δολόω) *a tricking, ensnaring*.

δόμα, ατος, τό, (δίδωμι) *a gift*.

δομαῖος, α, ον, (δέμω) *of* or *for building*.

δόμεναι, δόμεν, Ep. aor. 2 inf. of δίδωμι.

δόμονδε, Adv. *home, homeward*; ὅνδε δόμονδε *to* his own *house*. From

δόμος, ὁ, (δέμω) Lat. *domus, a house*: also *the household*. II. *a part of the house, chamber, room*. III. *anything that is built up*; διὰ τριήκοντα δόμων πλίνθου at every thirtieth *layer* of bricks.

δομο-σφαλής, ές, (δόμος, σφάλλω) *ruining the house*.

δονακεύομαι, Dep. (δόναξ) *to catch birds with reed and birdlime*.

δονακεύς, έως, ὁ, (δόναξ) *a thicket of reeds*.

δονακῖτις, ιδος, fem. Adj. (δόναξ) *of reed*.

δονακο-γλύφος, ον, (δόναξ, γλύφω) *reed-cutting*.

δονακόεις, εσσα, εν, (δόναξ) *abounding in reeds*; δόλος δονακόεις a reed covered with birdlime.

δονακο-τρόφος, ον, (δόναξ, τρέφω) *reed-producing*.

δονακό-χλοος, ον, contr. **-χλους**, ουν, (δόναξ, χλόα) *green with reeds*.

δόναξ Ion. **δοῦναξ** Dor. **δῶναξ**, ακος, ὁ, *a reed*, Lat. *calamus, arundo*. II. *anything made of reed*: *a dart, arrow*. 2. *a flute, shepherd's pipe*. 3. *a fishing-rod* or *limed reed* (see δονακόεις). 4. *the bridge of the lyre*. From

ΔΟΝΕ'Ω, f. ήσω, *to shake, stir*: *to excite, agitate*: *drive about*:—Pass., ἡ Ἀσίη ἐδονέετο Asia *was in commotion*. Hence

δόνημα, ατος, τό, *agitation, waving motion*; and

δονητός, ή, όν, verb. Adj. *shaken*.

δόντες, nom. pl. of δούς, aor. 2 part. of δίδωμι.

δόξα, ἡ, (δοκέω) *a notion, opinion*, Lat. *visum*: *expectation*. 2. *a sentiment, judgment*: esp. *a philosophic opinion*, Lat. *placitum*. 3. *mere opinion*, as opp. to knowledge. 4. *a fancy, vision*. II. *the opinion others have of one, one's reputation*, Lat. *existimatio*: *good report, credit, honour*. 2. *glory, splendour*. Hence

δοξάζω, f. άσω, *to hold an opinion, think, believe, judge*. II. *to glorify, extol*. Hence

δόξασμα, ατος, τό, *an opinion*: *a fancy*.

δοξοκοπία, ἡ, *love of popularity*. From

δοξο-κόπος, ον, (δόξα, κόπτω) *seeking popularity*.

δοξο-μανής, ές, (δόξα, μανῆναι) *mad after glory*. Hence

δοξομανία, ἡ, *mad love of glory*.

δοξο-ματαιό-σοφος, ὁ, (δόξα, ματαιός, σοφός) *a would-be philosopher*.

δοξο-σόφος, ον, (δόξα, σόφος) *wise in one's own conceit*.

δοξόω, f. ώσω, *to give one the character of being so and so*: Pass. *to have such a character*.

δόξω, fut. of δοκέω: **δόξαι**, aor. 1 inf.

δορά, ἡ, (δέρω) *a skin, hide*.

δόρατα, nom. pl., **δόρατι**, dat. sing., of δόρυ.

δοράτιον, τό, Dim. of δόρυ, *a small spear, dart*.

δορατο-πάχής, ές, (δόρυ, πάχος) *of a spear-shaft's thickness*.

δόρατος, gen. of δόρυ.

δορήϊος, α, ον, (δόρυ) *wooden*.

δορι-άλωτος, ον, (δόρυ, ἁλῶναι) *captive of the spear, taken in war*. [ἄ]

δορί-γαμβρος, ον, (δόρυ, γαμέω) *wooed by battle*.

δορι-θήρατος, ον, (δόρυ, θηράω) *taken by the spear*.

δορι-κανής, ές, (δόρυ, κανεῖν) *slain by the spear*.

δορι-κμής, ῆτος, ὁ, ἡ, (δόρυ, κάμνω) *slain by the spear*.

δορί-κρανος, ον, (δόρυ, κράνον) *spear-headed*.

δορί-κτητος, ον, (δόρυ, κτάομαι) *won by the spear*.

δορί-κτυπος, ον, (δόρυ, κτυπέω) *spear-clashing*.

δορί-ληπτος, ον, (δόρυ, λαμβάνω) *won by the spear*.

δορι-μανής, ές, (δόρυ, μανῆναι) *raging with the spear*.

δορί-μαργος, ον, (δόρυ, μάργος) *raging with the spear*.

δορι-μήστωρ, ορος, ὁ, (δόρυ, μήστωρ) *master of the spear*.

δορί-παλτος, ον, (δόρυ, πάλλω) *wielding the spear*; χεὶρ δορύπαλτος, i. e. the *right* hand.

δορι-πετής, ές, (δόρυ, *πέτω Root of πίπτω) *fallen by the spear*.

δορί-πληκτος, ον, (δόρυ, πλήσσω) *stricken by the spear*.

δορί-πονος, *ον*, (*δόρυ, πόνος*) *toiling with the spear, bearing the brunt of war.*

δορι-σθενής, *ές*, v. sub *δορυσθενής*.

δορι-στέφᾰνος, *ον*, (*δόρυ, στέφανος*) *crowned for bravery in war.*

δορι-τίνακτος, *ον*, (*δόρυ, τινάσσω*) *shaken by battle.*

δορί-τμητος, *ον*, (*δόρυ, τέμνω*) *pierced by the spear.*

δορί-τολμος, *ον*, (*δόρυ, τόλμα*) *bold in war.*

δορκᾰλίς, *ίδος, ἡ*, = *δορκάς*.

δορκάς, *άδος, ἡ*, (*δέδορκα*) *an antelope, gazelle*, so called from its large bright eyes.

δορός, *ὁ*, (*δέρω*) *a leathern bag* or *wallet.*

δορπέω, f. *ήσω*, (*δόρπον*) *to take supper.* Hence

δόρπηστος, *ὁ*, *supper-time, evening.*

Δορπία, *ἡ*, (*δόρπον*) *the first day of the feast Apaturia; τῆς δορτῆς τῇ δορπίᾳ* on the *eve* of the feast.

ΔΟ΄ΡΠΟΝ, *τό*, *the evening meal*, Lat. *coena*, *the chief meal* of the day, *dinner* or *supper.*

ΔΟ΄ΡΥ˘, *τό*: gen. *δόρᾰτος*, Ep. *δούρατος δουρός*, in Att. poets also *δορός*: dat. *δόρατι*, Ion. *δούρατι δουρί*, in Att. poets also *δόρει* or *δορί*.—Ion. dual *δοῦρε*.—Plur. nom. *δόρατα*, Ep. *δούρατα δοῦρα*, in Att. Poets also *δόρη*: gen. *δόρων*, Ep. *δούρων*: dat. *δόρασι*, Ep. *δούρασι δούρεσσι*. *The stem of a tree*, but only *when cut down: timber* for ships, *a beam, plank*, hence like Lat. *trabs*, *a ship.* II. *the wood* or *shaft of a spear*; hence *the spear itself: a hunting-spear*: since the spear was held *in the right hand*, *ἐπὶ δόρυ meant to the right hand*, opp. to *ἐπ' ἀσπίδα* to the left.

δορυ-άλωτος, false reading for *δοριάλωτος*.

δορυ-θαρσής, *ές*, (*δόρυ θαρσέω*) *daring in war.*

δορύ-ξενος, *ὁ, ἡ*, (*δόρυ, ξένος*) *a friend at the spear, an ally in war*: or *a friend made in war.*

δορυ-ξόος, *ον*, contr. **-ξοῦς**, *οῦν*, (*δόρυ, ξέω*) *spear-polishing*: as Subst., *δορυξόος*, *ὁ*, *a maker of spears*; also **δορυξός**, *ὁ*.

δορυ-πᾰγής, *ές*, (*δόρυ, παγῆναι*) *built of beams.*

δορύ-παλτος, **-πετής**, **-πληκτος**, v. *δορίπ-*.

δορυ-σθενής or **δορι-σθενής**, *ές*, (*δόρυ, σθένος*) *mighty with the spear.*

δορυσ-σόης, *ητος, ὁ*, masc. Adj., = *δορύσσοος*, *warlike.*

δορυσ-σόος, *ον*, contr. **δορυσ-σοῦς**, *οῦν*, poet. also **δορυ-σόος**, (*δόρυ, σεύω*) *brandishing the spear.*

δορυ-στέφᾰνος, **δορυ-τίνακτος**, v. *δορι-*.

δορυφορέω, f. *ήσω*, (*δορυφόρος*) *to attend as a body-guard: to keep guard over.* Hence

δορυφόρημα, *ματος, τό*, *a body-guard*; and

δορυφορία, *ἡ*, *a keeping guard over.*

δορυφορικός, *ή, όν*, (*δορυφορία*) *of* or *for the guard*; *τὸ δορυφορικόν the guard.*

δορυ-φόρος, *ον*, (*δόρυ, φέρω*) *spear-bearing*, Lat. *hastatus*; *οἱ δορυφόροι the body-guards* of kings, who were distinguished by carrying a spear.

δός, aor. 2 imperat. of *δίδωμι*.

δοσίδικος, *ον*, false reading for *δωσίδικος*.

δόσις, *εως, ἡ*, (*δίδωμι*) *a giving.* II. *a gift, present: a bequest.* III. *a portion: a dose.*

δόσκον, Ep. aor. 2 of *δίδωμι*.

δότειρα, *ἡ*, fem. of *δοτήρ*.

δοτέος, *α, ον*, verb. Adj. of *δίδωμι*, *to be given.* II. *δοτέον, one must give.*

δοτήρ, *ῆρος, ὁ*, (*δίδωμι*) *a giver, dispenser.*

δότης, *ου, ὁ*, = *δοτήρ*.

δουλ-ᾰγωγέω, f. *ήσω*, (*δοῦλος, ἄγω*) *to bring into slavery; δουλαγωγεῖν τὸ σῶμα to mortify* the body.

δουλάριον, *τό*, Dim. of *δοῦλος*.

δουλεία Ion. **δουληΐη**, *ἡ*, (*δουλεύω*) *servitude, slavery, bondage.* II. *the body of slaves, the bondmen, servile class.*

δούλειος, *α, ον*, or *ος, ον*, (*δοῦλος*) *slavish, servile.*

δούλευμα, *ατος, τό*, (*δουλεύω*) *a service.* II. *a slave*, Lat. *mancipium.*

δουλεύω, f. *σω*, (*δοῦλος*) *to be a slave*: generally, c. dat., *to be a slave to* another, *be subject to, to serve, obey*, Lat. *inservire alicui.*

δούλη, *ἡ*, fem. of *δοῦλος*.

δουληΐη, Ion. of *δουλεία*.

δουλία, *ἡ*, poët. for *δουλεία*.

δουλικός, *ή, όν*, = *δούλιος*. Adv. **-κῶς**, *like a slave.*

δούλιος, *α, ον*, (*δοῦλος*) *slavish, servile; δούλιον ἦμαρ* the day *of slavery*, i. e. a slave's lot or life.

δουλιχό-δειρος, Ion. for *δολιχόδειρος*, (*δολιχός, δειρή*) *long-necked.*

δουλιχόεις, *εσσα, εν*, Ion. for *δολιχόεις*, poët. for *δολιχός*.

δουλο-πρεπής, *ές*, (*δοῦλος, πρέπω*) *befitting a slave: low-minded, mean.*

ΔΟΥ˜ΛΟΣ, *ὁ*, *a slave, bondman*, properly *a born slave*, opp. to *ἀνδράποδον* (a slave taken in war). II. as Adj., *δοῦλος, η, ον*, *slavish, enslaved, subject*; Comp. *δουλότερος*, *more of a slave.*

δουλοσύνη, *ἡ*, (*δοῦλος*) *slavery, slavish work.*

δουλόσυνος, *ον*, (*δοῦλος*) *enslaved.*

δουλότερος, *α, ον*, Comp. of *δοῦλος*.

δουλόω, f. *ώσω*, (*δοῦλος*) *to make a slave of, enslave*:—Med. *to subject to oneself.* Hence

δούλωσις, *εως, ἡ*, *enslaving, subjugation.*

δοῦναι, aor. 2 inf. of *δίδωμι*.

δοῦναξ, **δουνακόεις**, Ion. for *δόναξ, δονακόεις*.

δουπέω, f. *ήσω*: Ep. aor. 1 *δούπησα*: pf. *δέδουπα*: (*δοῦπος*):—*to sound heavily*, of *the heavy fall of a corpse*: generally, *to fall in battle.*

δουπήτωρ, *ορος, ὁ*, (*δουπέω*) *a clatterer.*

ΔΟΥ˜ΠΟΣ, *ὁ*, *any dead, heavy sound; δοῦπος ἀκόντων the hurtling* of spears; *the sound* of soldiers marching; *the hum* of a multitude; *the din* of war; *the roar* of the sea.

δούρατα, syncop. **δοῦρα**, *τά*, Ep. plur. of *δόρυ*.

δουράτεος, *α, ον*, *of planks* or *beams.*

δουράτιον, Ion. for *δοράτιον*, *a dart.*

δούρειος, *α, ον*, = *δουράτεος*.

δούρεσσι, Ep. dat. pl. of *δόρυ*.

δουρ-ηνεκές, (*δόρυ, ἐνεγκεῖν*) Adv. *a spear's throw off* or *distant.*

δουρι-άλωτος, *ον*, Ion. for *δοριάλωτος*.

δουρι-κλειτός, *όν*, Ion. for *δορι-κλειτός*, (*δόρυ*, *κλειτός*) *famed for the spear*.

δουρι-κλῠτός, *ή*, *όν*, Ion. for *δορι-κλυτός*, (*δόρυ*, *κλυτός*) *famed for the spear*.

δουρι-κτητός, **δουρί-λήπτος**, **δουρι-μανής**, Ion. for *δορι-*.

δούριος, = *δούρειος*.

δουρί-πληκτος, *ον*, Ion. for *δορίπληκτος*.

δουρι-τῠπής, *ές*, (*δόρυ*, *τύπτω*) *wood-cutting*.

δουρο-δόκη, *ή*, (*δόρυ*, *δοχή*) *a stand for spears*.

δουρο-θήκη, *ή*, (*δόρυ*, *θήκη*) *a case for spears*.

δουρο-μᾰνής, *ές*, Ion. for *δοριμανής*.

δούς, aor. 2 part. of *δίδωμι*.

δοχεῖον, Ion. **δοχήϊον**, *τό*, (*δέχομαι*) *a holder*.

δοχή, *ή*, (*δέχομαι*) *reception*, *entertainment*. II. *a receptacle*.

δοχμή, *ή*, a measure of length, *a span*.

δόχμιος, *α*, *ον*, (*δοχμός*) *across*, *sideways*, *aslant*.

δοχμόλοφος, *ον*, (*δοχμός*, *λόφος*) *wearing one's plume aslant*, *with nodding plume*.

ΔΟΧΜΟ'Σ, *ή*, *όν*, *slanting*, *sideways*. Hence

δοχμόομαι, aor. 1 *ἐδοχμώθην*, Pass. *to turn sideways* or *aslant*.

δράγμα, *ατος*, *τό*, (*δράσσομαι*) *as much as one can grasp*, *a handful*, *truss*, *sheaf*, Lat. *manipulus*.

δραγματη-φόρος, *ον*, (*δράγμα*, *φέρω*) *carrying sheaves*.

δραγμεύω, f. *σω*, *to collect the corn into sheaves*.

δραγμός, *ὁ*, (*δράσσομαι*) *a taking hold of*, *handling*.

δρᾰθεῖν, aor. 2 inf. of *δαρθάνω*.

δρᾶθι, **δραίην**, aor. 2 imperat. and opt. of *διδράσκω*.

δραίνω, f. *δρᾰνῶ*, (*δράω*) *to be going to do*.

δράκαινα, *ης*, *ή*, fem. of *δράκων*, *a she-dragon*.

δρᾰκεῖν, aor. 2 inf. act. of *δέρκομαι*.

δρᾰκῆναι, aor. 2 inf. pass. of *δέρκομαι*.

δρᾰκόμενος, aor. 2 part. med. of *δέρκομαι*.

δράκον, Ion. for *ἔδρᾰκον*, aor. 2 of *δέρκομαι*.

δρακόντειος, *α*, *ον*, (*δράκων*) *of a dragon*.

δρακοντ-ολέτης, *ου*, *ὁ*, (*δράκων*, *ὄλλυμι*) *serpent-slayer*.

δρακοντό-μαλλος, *ον*, (*δράκων*, *μαλλός*) *with snaky locks*.

δρακοντ-ώδης, *ες*, (*δράκων*, *εἶδος*) *snake-like*.

δρᾰκών, aor. 2 part. act. of *δέρκομαι*.

δράκων, *οντος*, *ὁ*, (*δρακεῖν*) *a dragon*: later *a serpent*.

δρᾶμα, *ατος*, *τό*, (*δράω*) *a deed*, *act*, *acting*: *a business*, *duty*. 2. *an action represented on the stage*, *a drama*.

δρᾰμεῖν, aor. 2 inf. of *τρέχω*.

δράμημα, *ατος*, *τό*, (*δραμεῖν*) *a course*, *a race*.

δρᾰμοῦμαι, **δραμών**, fut. and aor. 2 part. of *τρέχω*.

δρᾶναι, aor. 2 inf. of *διδράσκω*.

δράξ, *δρᾰκός*, = *δράγμα*.

δρᾱπετεύω, f. *σω*, *to run away*, *flee*. From

δρᾱπέτης, *ου*, Ion. **δρηπέτης**, *εω*, *ὁ*, (*δρᾶναι*) *a runaway*: esp. *a runaway slave*. II. as Adj., *δραπέτης κλῆρος* a *fugitive* lot, i. e. a mouldering clod, *which fell in pieces so as never* to be drawn out of the urn.

δρᾱπετίδης, *ου*, *ὁ*, = *δραπέτης*.

δρᾱπέτις, *ιδος*, *ή*, fem. of *δραπέτης*.

δρᾱπετίσκος, *ὁ*, Dim. of *δραπέτης*.

δράς, *δρᾶσα*, aor. 2 part. of *δράω*.

δρᾱσείω, Desiderat. of *δράω*, *to have a mind to do*, *to be going to do*.

δρασθείς, aor. 1 part. pass. of *δράω*.

δράσῐμος, *ον*, (*δράω*) *active*; *τὸ δράσιμον action*.

δρασμός Ion. **δρησμός**, *ὁ*, (*δρᾶναι*) *a running away*, *flight*.

δράσομαι, fut. of *διδράσκω*. [ᾱ]

ΔΡΑ'ΣΣΟΜΑΙ Att. **δράττομαι**: fut. *δράξομαι*: aor. 1 *ἐδραξάμην*: pf. *δέδραγμαι* Att. *δέδαργμαι*: Dep.:—*to grasp with the hand*, *grasp a handful of*: *to lay hold of*:—c. acc. rei, *to take by handsful*.

δραστέος, *α*, *ον*, verb. Adj. of *δράω*, *to be done*. II. *δραστέον*, *one must do*.

δραστήριος, *ον*, *vigorous*, *active*, *efficacious*.

δράστης, *ου*, *ὁ*, (*δράω*) *a worker*: *servant*.

δραστικός, *ή*, *όν*, (*δράω*) *active*.

δρᾰτός, *ή*, *όν*, metath. for *δαρτός*, verb. Adj. of *δέρω*, *skinned*, *flayed*.

δραχμή, *ή*, (*δράσσομαι*) *a drachma*, a coin worth 6 obols, i. e. $9\frac{3}{4}$d, nearly = Roman *denarius*. II. an Attic weight, = about 66 *gr*. Avdp. (Properly *as much as one can hold in the hand*, cf. *δράγμα*.)

ΔΡΑ'Ω, f. *δράσω* [ᾱ]: aor. 1 *ἔδρᾱσα*: pf. *δέδρᾱκα*: —Pass., aor. 1 *ἐδράσθην*: pf. *δέδρᾱμαι*:—*to do*, *be doing*, *accomplish*:—c. dupl. acc., *εὖ* or *κακῶς δρᾶν τινα*, *to do* one good or ill.

δρεπάνη, *ή*, (*δρέπω*) *a sickle*, *reaping-hook*, *scythe* [ᾰ]

δρεπᾰνη-φόρος, *ον*, (*δρεπάνη*, *φέρω*) *bearing a scythe*; *ἅρμα δρεπανηφόρον a scythe-armed* car.

δρεπᾰνο-ειδής, *ές*, (*δρέπανον*, *εἶδος*) *sickle-shaped*.

δρέπᾰνον, *τό*, (*δρέπω*) = *δρεπάνη*, *a sickle*: *a curved scimitar*.

δρεπᾰν-ουργός, *ὁ*, (*δρέπανον*, **ἔργω*) *a sword-maker*.

δρέπτω, poët. for *δρέπω*, *to pluck*, *cull*.

ΔΡΕ'ΠΩ, f. *ψω*: aor. 1 *ἔδρεψα*: aor. 2 *ἔδρᾰπον*: —Med., Dor. fut. *δρεψεῦμαι*: aor. 1 *ἐδρεψάμην*:—Pass., aor. 1 *ἐδρέφθην*:—*to break off*, *pluck*: Med. *to pluck for oneself*, *cull*, *gather*: metaph. *to possess*, *enjoy*.

δρηπέτης, *εω*, *ὁ*, Ion. for *δραπέτης*.

δρησμοσύνη, *ή*, = *δρηστοσύνη*.

δρηστήρ, *ῆρος*, *ὁ*, (*διδράσκω*) Ion. for *δραστήρ*, *a run-away*.

δρηστήρ, *ῆρος*, *ὁ*, Ion. for *δραστήρ*, (*δράω*) *a labourer*, *worker*: fem. **δρήστειρα**.

δρηστής, *οῦ*, *ὁ*, Ion. for *δραστής*.

δρηστοσύνη, *ή*, Ion. for *δραστοσύνη*, (*δράω*) *service*.

δρῑμύλος, *ον*, Dim. of *δριμύς*, *sharp*, *piercing*. [ῠ]

ΔΡΙΜΥ'Σ, *εῖα*, *ύ*, *piercing*, *stinging*, *biting*, *pungent*. II. metaph. like Lat. *acer*, *sharp*, *keen*, *bitter*: *shrewd*. Adv. *-έως*. Hence

δριμύτης, *τητος*, *ή*, *sharpness*, *pungency*: *shrewdness*.

ΔΡΙ'ΟΣ, *τό*, plur. *δρία, τά*, (as if from *δρῖον*) *copsewood, thicket, brushwood.*

ΔΡΟΙ'ΤΗ, *ἡ*, *a bathing tub, a bath.*

δρομαῖος, *α, ον*, or *ος, ον*, (*δρόμος*) *running at full speed, swift, fleet.*

δρομάς, *άδος, ὁ*, (*δραμεῖν*) *running, whirling.*

δρομεύς, *έως*, (*δραμεῖν*) *a runner.*

δρόμημα, *ατος, τό*, = *δράμημα*.

δρόμος, *ὁ*, (*δραμεῖν*) *a course, race, running: flight: a fleeing, escape; ἡμέρης δρόμος* a day's *running*, i.e. the distance one can go in a day. 2. *the length of the stadium, a course; ἔξω δρόμου φέρεσθαι* to be carried out of *the course.* II. *a place for running, race-course: a public walk.*

δροσερός, *ά, όν*, (*δρόσος*) *dewy, watery.*

δροσίζω, f. *ίσω*, (*δρόσος*) *to bedew, besprinkle.*

δροσινός, *ή, όν*, (*δρόσος*) = *δροσερός*.

δροσόεις, *εσσα, εν*, poët. for *δροσερός*.

ΔΡΟ'ΣΟΣ, *ἡ*, Lat. *ROS*, *dew:* also *the time of dew, dew-fall.* 2. *pure water: tears.* 3. metaph. *anything tender, the young of animals.* Hence

δροσόω, *to bedew:* pf. pass. part. *δεδροσωμένος*, *dewy.*

δροσ-ώδης, *ες*, (*δρόσος, εἶδος*) *dew-like, dewy.*

Δρυάς, *άδος, ἡ*, (*δρῦς*) *a Dryad*, a wood-nymph whose life was bound up with that of her tree.

δρύϊνος [ῐ], *η, ον*, (*δρῦς*) *oaken; δρύϊνον πῦρ* a fire *of oak-wood; μέλι δρύϊνον* honey *from a hollow oak.*

δρυ-κολάπτης, *ου, ὁ*, = *δρυο-κολάπτης*.

δρῡμός, *ὁ*, pl. *δρῡμοί* and *δρῠμά*: (*δρῦς*): *an oak-coppice, a coppice, wood.* [ῡ, except in neut. pl.]

δρῡμών, *ῶνος, ἡ*, (*δρῦς*) *an oak-coppice.*

δρυο-γόνος, *ον*, (*δρῦς, *γένω*) *oak-grown.*

δρυο-κοίτης, *ου, ὁ*, (*δρῦς, κοίτη*) *couching on the oak*, epith. of the *τέττιξ*.

δρυο-κολάπτης, *ου, ὁ*, (*δρῦς, κολάπτω*) *the great woodpecker*, Lat. *picus major.*

δρυο-πᾰγής, *ές*, (*δρῦς, παγῆναι*) *built of oak.*

δρύ-οχοι, *οἱ*, or **δρύ-οχα**, *τά*, (*δρῦς, ἔχω*) *the oaken ribs* or *cross-timbers of a ship*, which hold her together; *δρυόχους τιθέναι δράματος* to lay *the keel* of a new play.

δρύοψ, *οπος, ὁ*, (*δρῦς, ὄψ*) a kind of *woodpecker.*

δρῠ-πεπής, *ές*, (*δρῦς, πέπτω*) *ripened on the tree, quite ripe: over-ripe, decayed;* or **δρυ-πετής**, *ές*, (*δρῦς, *πέτω* Root of *πίπτω*) *ready to fall from the tree.*

ΔΡΥ'ΠΠΑ˘, *ἡ*, *an over-ripe, mouldy olive.*

ΔΡΥ'ΠΤΩ, f. *ψω*: aor. 1 *ἔδρυψα* Ep. *δρύψα*:—Pass., aor. 1 *ἐδρύφθην*: pf. *δέδρυμμαι*:—*to tear, scratch, wound; δρύπτεσθαι παρειάν to tear one's* cheek; also absol.

ΔΡΥ^Σ, *ἡ*, gen. *δρυός*, acc. *δρῦν*: pl. nom. and acc. *δρύες, δρύας*, contr. *δρῦς*:—*the oak*, sacred to Zeus. II. *any timber tree; πίειρα δρῦς the* resinous *pine.* III. metaph. *an old tree*, i. e. *withered old man.*

δρῠ-τόμος, *ον*, (*δρῦς, τεμεῖν*) *felling timber.*

δρύφακτον, *τό*, and **δρύφακτος**, *ὁ*, (*δρῦς*) *a railed fence, railing, paling:* at Athens *the bar of the courts of law* or *the council-chamber.*

δρῠφῆναι, aor. 2 pass. inf. of *δρύπτω*.

δρύψα, Ep. aor. 1 of *δρύπτω*.

δρύψια, *τά*, (*δρύπτω*) *scraping, parings.*

δρώοιμι, Ep. for *δρῷμι*, lengthd. opt. of *δράω*.

δῦ, Ep. for *ἔδυ*, 3 sing. aor. 2 of *δύω*.

δυάκις, Adv. *twice*, = *δίς*.

δυάς, *άδος, ἡ*, (*δύο*) *the number two.*

δυάω, (*δύη*) *to plunge in misery.*

δυεῖν, later Att. for *δυοῖν*, gen. and dat. dual of *δύο*.

ΔΥ'Η, *ἡ*, *woe, misery, anguish: toil, pain: hard usage.* [ῠ]

δύην, (as if for *δυίην*), aor. 2 opt. of *δῦμι*.

δυηπᾰθίη, *ἡ*, *misery.* From

δυή-πᾰθος, *ον*, (*δύη, παθεῖν*) *suffering woe.*

δῦθι, aor. 2 imperat. of *δύω*.

δύϊος, *α, ον*, (*δύη*) *miserable.*

δύμεναι, **δῦμεν**, Ep. for *δῦναι*, aor. 2 inf. of *δύω*.

δῦμι, assumed as a collat. form of *δύω, δύνω*.

δῦναι, aor. 2 inf. of *δύω*.

δύνᾳ, Att. 2 sing. of *δύναμαι*.

ΔΥ'ΝΑΜΑΙ, in pres. and imperf. declined like *ἵσταμαι*, 2 sing. *δύνασαι*, Att. *δύνᾳ*, Ion. *δύνῃ δύνεαι*; 3 pl. *δύνανται* Ep. *δυνέαται*; subj. *δύνωμαι*, Ion. 2 sing. *δύνηαι*:—impf. *ἐδυνάμην*, 2 sing. *ἐδύνω*, 3 pl. *ἐδύναντο* Ion. *ἐδυνέατο*:—fut. *δυνήσομαι*: aor. 1 *ἐδυνησάμην* and *ἐδυνήθην* (or *ἐδυνάσθην* Ep. *δυνάσθην*):—pf. *δεδύνημαι*:—in Att. the double augment *ἠδυνάμην, ἠδυνήθην* is often used: Dep.: I. *to be able, capable, strong enough* to do, c. inf.: also c. acc., *δύνασθαι ἅπαντα to be able to do* all things, Lat. *omnia posse:* absol., *οἱ δυνάμενοι the powerful.* II. *to pass for, to be worth*, Lat. *valere; ὁ σίγλος δύναται ἑπτα ὀβόλους* the shekel *is worth* seven obols: *to avail: to signify, denote.*

δύνᾰμις, *ἡ*: gen. *εως* Ion. *ιος*: Ion. dat. *δύναμι*: (*δύναμαι*):—*strength, might, power, ability; κατὰ δύναμιν* to *the best of one's power*, Lat. *pro virili; παρὰ δύναμιν* or *ὑπὲρ δύναμιν* beyond *one's power.* 2. *a force for war, forces*, Lat. *copiae.* 3. *a quantity*, Lat. *vis*, e. g. *χρημάτων*. 4. *the force of a word*, etc., *meaning*, Lat. *vis.* 5. *a faculty, power:* hence *a faculty, art*, as Logic. 6. *worth, value*, as of money.

δῠνᾰμόω, f. *ώσω*, (*δύναμις*) *to strengthen.*

δυνάσθην, Ep. aor. 1 of *δύναμαι*.

δύνᾰσις, *εως, ἡ*, poët. for *δύναμις*.

δῠναστεία, *ἡ*, *power, lordship, sovereignty.* II. *an oligarchy.* From

δῠναστεύω, f. *σω*, *to hold power* or *lordship, be powerful: to be high in rank.* From

δῠνάστης, *ου, ὁ*, (*δύναμαι*) *a lord, master, ruler; οἱ δυνάσται the chief men*, Lat. *optimates.*

δυνάστωρ, *ορος, ὁ*, = *δυνάστης*.

δῠνᾰτέω, f. *ήσω*, (*δυνατός*) *to be powerful.*

δυνάτης, *ου, ὁ*, poët. for *δυνάστης*.

δῠνᾰτός, ή, όν, (δύναμαι) *strong, mighty: powerful, able.* II. of things, *possible.*

δυνατῶς, Adv. of δυνατός, *strongly, powerfully;* δυνατῶς ἔχει it is *possible.*

δῦνε, Ep. for ἔδυνε, 3 sing. impf. of δύνω.

δύνεαι, δύνῃ, Ion. 2 sing. of δύναμαι.

δυνέαται, Ion. 3 pl. of δύναμαι.

δύνηαι, Ep. 2 sing. pres. subj. of δύναμαι.

δυνήσομαι, fut. of δύναμαι.

δύντε, aor. 2 part. nom. dual of δύω.

δύνω, see δύω.

ΔΥ'Ο, Ep. **δύω**: gen. and dat. δυοῖν, in later Att. δυεῖν: plur. only in Ion. and late Att., gen. δυῶν, dat. δυσί Ion. δυοῖσι: sometimes indecl., e. g. τῶν δύο μοιράων:—Lat. *DUO*, our *TWO;* σὺν δύο *two together, by twos;* εἰς δύο *two and two.*

δυο-καί-δεκα, οἱ, αἱ, τά, *twelve*, Lat. *duo-decim.*

δυοκαιδεκά-μηνος, δυοκαιδεκάς, δυοκαιδέκατος, see δωδεκά-μηνος, δωδεκάς, etc.

δυόωσιν, Ep. for δυῶσιν, 3 pl. of δυάω.

δύρομαι, poët. for ὀδύρομαι.

δῠσ-, insepar. Prefix, opp. to εὖ, like our *un-* or *mis-* in *un-lucky, mis-chance,* always with a notion of *hard, bad, ill,* etc., destroying a word's good sense or increasing its bad sense.

δύς, δῦσα, δύν, aor. 2 part. of δύω.

δυσ-αγκόμιστος, δυσ-άγκριτος, poët. for δυσ-ανακ-.

δύσ-αγνος, ον, (δυσ-, ἁγνός) *unchaste, impure.*

δυσ-αγρέω, f. ήσω, *to have bad luck in fishing.*

δυσ-άδελφος, ον, *unhappy in one's brothers.*

δυσ-ᾱής, ές, (δυσ-, ἄημι) *ill-blowing, stormy, adverse;* δυσαήων Ep. gen. pl. for δυσαέων.

δυσ-άθλιος, α, ον, also ος, ον, *most miserable.*

δυσ-αιᾱνής, ές, *most direful, most horrible.*

δυσ-αίθριος, ον, (δυσ-, αἴθρα) *not clear, murky.*

δυσ-αίων, ωνος, ὁ, ἡ, *miserable in life, most miserable.*

δυσ-αλγής, ές, (δυσ-, ἄλγος) *very painful.*

δυσ-άλγητος, ον, (δυσ-, ἀλγέω) *unfeeling, hard-hearted.*

δυσ-άλιος, ον, Dor. for δυσ ήλιος. [ᾱ]

δυσ-άλωτος, ον, (δυσ-, ἁλῶναι) *hard to catch* or *conquer;* δυσάλωτος κακῶν *hard to be reached* by ills.

δυσ-άμβᾰτος, ον, by poët. syncop. for δυσ-ανάβατος.

δυσ-άμμορος, ον, *most miserable.*

δυσ-ανάβᾰτος, ον, *hard to mount.*

δυσ-ανακόμιστος, syncop. **δυσ-αγκόμιστος**, ον, (δυσ-, ἀνακομίζω) *hard to bring back* or *recall.*

δυσ-ανάκρῐτος, syncop. **δυσ-άγκρῐτος**, ον, (δυσ-, ἀνακρίνω) *hard to distinguish* or *examine.*

δυσ-ανασχετέω, f. ήσω, (δυσ-, ἀνασχετός) *to bear ill, to be unable to bear.*

δυσ-ανάτρεπτος, ον, (δυσ-, ἀνατρέπω) *hard to overthrow.*

δυσ-άνεκτος, ον, (δυσ-, ἀνέχω) *hard to bear.*

δυσ-άνεμος, ον, Dor. for δυσ-ήνεμος.

δυσ-αντίβλεπτος, ον, (δυσ-, ἀντιβλέπω) *hard to look in the face.*

δύσαντο, for ἐδύσ-, 3 pl. aor. 1 med. of δύω.

δυσ-άνωρ, ορος, ὁ, ἡ, (δυσ-, ἀνήρ) *with a bad husband.* [ᾱ]

δυσ-απάλλακτος, ον, (δυσ-, ἀπαλλάσσω) *hard to get rid of.*

δυσ-άπιστος, ον, *very disobedient.*

δυσ-απόκρῐτος, ον, (δυσ-, ἀποκρίνομαι) *hard to answer.*

δυσ-απότρεπτος, ον, (δυσ-, ἀποτρέπω) *hard to turn away, stubborn, refractory.*

δυσ-άρεστος, ον, (δυσ-, ἀρέσκω) *ill to please, implacable: peevish, morose.*

δυσ-ᾰριστο-τόκεια, ἡ, (δυσ-, ἄριστος, τοκος) *unhappy mother of the noblest son.*

δύσ-αρκτος, ον, (δυσ-, ἄρχω) *hard to govern.*

δυσαυλία, ἡ, *ill* or *hard lodging.* From

δύσ-αυλος, ον, (δυσ-, αὐλή) *ill for lodging.*

δύσ-αυλος, ον, (δυσ-, αὐλός) *ill-suited for the flute.*

δυσ-ᾱχής, ές, Dor. for δυσηχής.

δυσ-ᾰχής, ές, (δυσ-, ἄχος) *sorely painful.*

δυσ-βάστακτος, ον, (δυσ-, βαστάζω) *grievous to be borne.*

δύσ-βᾰτος, ον, (δυσ-, βαίνω) *hard to pass, impassable;* τὸ δύσβατον *difficult ground.* 2. *trodden painfully.*

δυσ-βάϋκτος, ον, (δυσ-, βαΰζω) *full of wailing.*

δυσ-βίοτος, ον, (δυσ-, βίοτος) *making life wretched.*

δυσβουλία, ἡ, *ill counsel, folly.* From

δύσ-βουλος, ον, (δυσ-, βουλή) *ill-advised.*

δύσ-βωλος, ον, (δυσ-, βῶλος) *of ill soil, unfruitful.*

δύσ-γᾰμος, ον, *ill-wedded.*

δυσ-γάργᾰλις, ι, (δυσ-, γαργαλίζω) *ticklish, skittish.*

δυσγένεια, ἡ, *low, mean birth.* From

δυσ-γενής, ές, (δυσ-, γένος) *low-born: low-minded.*

δύσ-γνοιᾰ, ἡ, (δυσ-, γνῶναι) *ignorance, perplexity.*

δυσγνωσία, ἡ, *difficulty of knowing.* From

δύσ-γνωστος, ον, (δυσ-, γνῶναι) *hard to know* or *recognise.*

δυσδαιμονία, ἡ, *misery: wretchedness.* From

δυσ-δαίμων, ον, gen. ονος, (δυσ-, δαίμων) *ill-fated.*

δυσ-δάκρῡτος, ον, (δυσ-, δακρύω) *much wept.* II. *much weeping.*

δύσ-δᾰμαρ, αρτος, ὁ, ἡ, *ill-wedded.*

δυσ-διάθετος, ον, (δυσ-, διατίθημι) *hard to settle.*

δύσ-εδρος, ον, (δυσ-, ἕδρα) *bringing ill luck to one's abode.*

δυσ-ειδής, ές, (δυσ-, εἶδος) *unshapely, deformed.*

δυσ-είμᾰτος, ον, (δυσ-, εἷμα) *meanly clad.*

δυσ-είσβολος, ον, (δυσ-, εἰσβάλλω) *hard to enter* or *invade:* Sup., -ώτατος, ον, *most inaccessible.*

δυσ-έκθῠτος, ον, (δυσ-, ἐκθύω) *hard to avert by sacrifice.*

δυσ-έκλῠτος, ον, (δυσ-, ἐκλύω) *hard to undo, inexplicable:*—Adv. -τως, *indissolubly.*

δυσ-εκπέρᾱτος, ον, (δυσ-, ἐκπεράω) *hard to pass from, hard to escape.*

δυσ-έκφυκτος, ον, (δυσ-, ἐκφεύγω) *hard to escape from.*

δυσ-ελένα, ἡ, *ill-starred Helen.*

δύσ-ελπις, ιδος, ὁ, ἡ, *with ill hope, desponding.*

δυσ-έλπιστος, ον, (δυσ-, ἐλπίζω) *unhoped for; ἐκ δυσελπίστων*, Lat. *ex insperato, unexpectedly.*

δυσ-έμβᾰτος, ον, (δυσ-, ἐμβαίνω) *hard to walk on, rugged: inaccessible.*

δυσ-έμβολος, ον, (δυσ-, ἐμβάλλω) *hard to invade.*

δυσ-εντερία, ἡ, and **δυσεντέριον**, τό, (δυσ-, ἔντερον) *a bowel complaint, dysentery.*

δυσ-έντευκτος, ον, (δυσ-, ἐντυγχάνω) *not affable.*

δυσ-εξαπάτητος, ον, (δυσ-, ἐξαπατάω) *hard to deceive.*

δυσ-έξαπτος, ον, (δυσ-, ἐξάπτω) *hard to unloose.*

δυσ-εξέλεγκτος, ον, (δυσ-, ἐξελέγχω) *hard to refute.*

δυσ-εξέλικτος, ον, (δυσ-, ἐξελίσσω) *hard to unfold* or *explain.*

δυσ-εξήνυστος, ον, (δυσ-, ἐξανύτω) *hard to make away with: indissoluble.*

δύσεο, aor. 1 med. imperat. of δύνω.

δυσ-επιβούλευτος, ον, (δυσ-, ἐπιβουλεύομαι) *hard to plot against* or *attack secretly.*

δυσ-έραστος, ον, (δυσ-, ἐράω) *unfavourable to love.*

δυσ-έρημος, ον, *very desolate.*

δύσ-ερις, ι, gen. ιδος, (δυσ-, ἔρις) *most contentious, very quarrelsome, peevish.*

δυσ-έριστος, ον, (δυσ-, ἐρίζω) *caused by evil strife.*

δυσ-ερμήνευτος, ον, (δυσ-, ἑρμηνεύω) *hard to explain.*

δύσ-ερως, ωτος, ὁ, ἡ, (δυσ-, ἔρως) *passionately loving, sick in love with*, Lat. *perditè amans.* II. *hardly loving, insensible to love.*

δύσετο, Ep. for δύσατο, 3 sing. aor. 1 med. of δύω.

δυσ-ευνήτωρ, ορος, ὁ, (δυσ-, εὐνή) *an ill bed-fellow.*

δυσ-εύρετος, ον, (δυσ-, εὑρίσκω) *hard to find out: hard to get: hard to get through, impervious.*

δύσ-ζηλος, ον, (δυσ-, ζῆλος) *exceeding jealous.*

δυσ-ζήτητος, ον, (δυσ-, ζητέω) *hard to seek out.*

δύσ-ζωος, ον, (δυσ-, ζωή) *most wretched.*

δυσ-ήκεστος, ον, (δυσ-, ἀκέομαι) *hard to cure.*

δυσ-ήκοος, ον, (δυσ-, ἀκούω) *hard of hearing.*

δυσ-ηλεγής, ές, (δυσ-, λέγω *to lay asleep*) of death, *stretching one on a hard bed: hard, painful, uneasy:* of men, *hard-hearted, unfeeling.*

δυσ-ήλιος, ον, *unlit by the sun, sunless, without the light of day.*

δυσ-ημερία, ἡ, (δυσ-, ἡμέρα) *an unlucky day.*

δυσ-ήνεμος, ον, (δυσ-, ἄνεμος) *with ill winds, stormy.*

δύσ-ηρις, ιδος, ὁ, ἡ, older form of δύσ-ερις, *very quarrelsome, contentious.*

δυσ-ηχής, ές, (δυσ-, ἠχέω) *ill-sounding: hateful to bear of, hateful.*

δυσ-θαλπής, ές, (δυσ-, θάλπος) *hard to warm: chilly.*

δυσθᾰνᾰτέω, f. ήσω, *to die a lingering death.* From

δυσ-θάνᾰτος, ον, *dying hard, struggling with death.* II. act. *bringing a painful death.*

δυσ-θᾰνής, ές, (δυσ-, θανεῖν) *having died a hard death.*

δυσ-θέᾱτος, ον, (δυσ-, θεάομαι) *ill to look on.*

δύσ-θεος, ον, *godless, ungodly.*

δυσ-θεράπευτος, ον, (δυσ-, θερᾰπεύω) *hard to cure.*

δυσ-θετέω, f. ήσω, (δυσ-, τίθημι) *to be in bad case:* Med. *to take* a thing *ill*, Lat. *aegrè ferre.*

δυσ-θνήσκω, = δυσθανατέω.

δυσ-θρήνητος, ον, (δυσ-, θρηνέω) *most mournful.*

δύσ-θροος, ον, (δυσ-, θρέω) *of harsh sound, grating.*

δυσθῡμαίνω, = δυσθυμέω.

δυσθῡμέω, f. ήσω, *to be down-hearted, despond:* Med. *to be melancholy, angry.* From

δύσ-θῡμος, ον, (δυσ-, θυμός) *down-hearted, dispirited, desponding, anxious.*

δυσ-ίατος, ον, (δυσ-, ἰάομαι) *hard to heal* or *cure.*

δῡσι-θάλασσος, ον, (δύω, θάλασσα) *dipped in the sea.*

δύσ-ιππος, ον, (δυσ-, ἵππος) *hard to ride in; τὰ δύσιππα ground unfit for cavalry.*

δύσις, εως, ἡ, (δύω) *a sinking* or *setting of the sun* or *stars; δύσις ἡλίου the west.*

δυσ-κάθαρτος, ον, (δυσ-, κᾰθαίρω) *hard to cleanse* or *expiate: hard to appease, inexorable.*

δυσ-κάθεκτος, ον, (δυσ-, κατέχω) *hard to hold in.*

δύσ-καπνος, ον, (δυσ-, καπνός) *very smoky.*

δυσ-κατάπαυστος, ον, (δυσ-, καταπαύω) *hard to check: restless.*

δυσ-κατάπρακτος, ον, (δυσ-, καταπράσσω) *hard to bring about, hard to effect.*

δυσ-κατάστᾰτος, ον, (δυσ-, καθίστημι) *hard to restore* or *reëstablish.*

δυσ-καταφρόνητος, ον, (δυσ-, καταφρονέω) *by no means to be despised.*

δυσ-κατέργαστος, ον, (δυσ-, κατεργάζομαι) = δυσκατάπρακτος.

δύσκε, Ion. for ἔδυ, 3 sing. aor. 2 of δύω.

δυσ-κέλᾰδος, ον, *shrill-screaming, grating: harsh.*

δυσ-κηδής, ές, (δυσ-, κῆδος) *full of care, painful.*

δύσ-κηλος, ον, (δυσ-, κηλέω) *past remedy.*

δυσ-κλεής, ές: acc. δυσκλεέα poët. δυσκλεᾶ: (δυσ-, κλέος) *injurious: infamous, shameful.* Hence

δύσκλεια, ἡ, *ingloriousness, dishonour: an ill name.*

δυσκλεῶς, Adv. of δυσκλεής, *ingloriously.*

δύσ-κληρος, ον, *unlucky.*

δυσκλής, poët. for δυσκλεής.

δυσκολαίνω, f. ᾰνῶ, (δύσκολος) *to be peevish, discontented, annoyed.*

δυσκολία, ἡ, (δύσκολος) *peevishness, discontent.*

δυσ-κόλλητος, ον, (δυσ-, κολλάω) *ill-cemented.*

δυσκολό-καμπτος, ον, (δύσκολος, κάμπτω) *hard to bend; δυσκολόκαμπτος καμπή an intricate* flourish in singing.

δυσκολό-κοιτος, ον, (δύσκολος, κοίτη) *making one's bed uneasy.*

δύσ-κολος, ον, (δυσ-, κόλον) *hard to satisfy with food: hard to please, fretful, peevish, discontented.* II. of things, *harassing: unpleasant.*

δύσ-κολπος, ον, *with ill-formed womb.*

δυσκόλως, Adv. of δύσκολος, *peevishly; δυσκόλως ἔχειν to be peevish.*

δυσκρᾱσία, ἡ, *bad temperament.* From

δύσ-κρᾱτος, ον, (δυσ-, κεράννυμι) *of bad temperament.*

δυσ-κόμιστος, ον, (δυσ-, κομίζω) *hard to be borne.*

δύσ-κρῐτος, ον, (δυσ-, κρίνω) *hard to discern: hard to determine, doubtful.* Adv. -τως, *doubtfully;* δυσκρίτως ἔχειν to be *in doubt.*

δυσ-κύμαντος, ον, (δυσ-, κυμαίνω) *of* or *from the stormy sea.*

δυσκωφέω, f. ήσω, *to be stone deaf.* From

δύσ-κωφος, ον, (δυσ-, κωφός) *stone deaf.*

δύσ-λεκτος, ον, (δυσ-, λέγω) *ill* or *hard to tell.*

δυσ-λόγιστος, ον, (δυσ-, λογίζομαι) *hard to reckon.* II. *misdirected, misguided.*

δυσ-λόφος, ον, (δυσ-, λόφος) *hard for the neck, hard to bear.* II. *impatient:* Adv. -φως, *impatiently.*

δύσ-λῠτος, ον, (δυσ-, λύω) *hard to loose, indissoluble.*

δυσμᾰθέω, f. ήσω, *to be slow at learning.* From

δυσ-μᾰθής, ές, (δυσ-, μαθεῖν) *hard to learn, difficult.* II. act. *slow at learning, dull:*—Adv. -θῶς, δυσμαθῶς ἔχειν to be *slow of learning.*

δυσ-μᾰχέω, f. ήσω, (δυσ-, μάχομαι) *to fight in vain; to fight an unholy fight with.* Hence

δυσμᾰχητέον, verb. Adj. *one must struggle hard.*

δύσ-μᾰχος, ον, (δυσ-, μάχομαι) *hard to fight with, unconquerable:* generally, *hard, difficult.*

δυσμεναίνω, (δυσμενής) *to bear ill-will.*

δυσμένεια, ἡ, (δυσμενής) *ill-will, enmity.*

δυσμενέων, *ill-affected, bearing ill-will, hostile:* masc. Adj. with particip. form. From

δυσ-μενής, ές, (δυσ-, μένος) *ill-affected, bearing ill-will, hostile;* δυσμενέες *enemies.*

δυσ-μεταχείριστος, ον, (δυσ-, μεταχειρίζω) *hard to take in hand* or *manage: hard to conquer.*

δυσμή Dor. **δυθμή**, ἡ, (δύω) = δύσις, *a sinking, setting,* esp. of the sun; mostly in pl., opp. to ἀνατολαί.

δύσ-μηνις, ι, gen. ιος, *savage, wrathful.*

δυσ-μήνῑτος, ον, (δυσ-, μηνίω) *visited by heavy wrath.*

δυσ-μήτηρ, ερος, ἡ, *a cruel mother, not a true mother.*

δυσμηχᾰνέω, f. ήσω, *to be at loss.* From

δυσ-μήχᾰνος, ον, (δυσ-, μηχανή) *quite at a loss.*

δύσ-μοιρος, ον, (δυσ-, μοῖρα) = δύσμορος.

δυσμορία, ἡ, *a hard fate.* From

δύσ-μορος, ον, *ill-fated, ill-starred.*

δυσμορφία, ἡ, *badness of form, ugliness.* From

δύσ-μορφος, ον, (δυσ-, μορφή) *misshapen, ugly.*

Δύσ-μουσος, ον, (δυσ-, Μοῦσα) *not favoured by the Muses, unmusical.*

δύσ-νιπτος, ον, (δυσ-, νίζω) *hard to wash out* or *off.*

δυσ-νόητος, ον, (δυσ-, νοέω) *hard to be understood.*

δυσνοέω, f. ήσω, (δύσνοος) *to be ill-affected.*

δύσνοια, ἡ, (δύσνοος) *dislike, ill-will.*

δυσνομία, ἡ, *lawlessness: a bad constitution, bad code of laws.* From

δύσ-νομος, ον, *lawless, unrighteous.*

δύσ-νοος, ον, contr. **-νους**, ουν, *ill-disposed, ill-affected, disaffected.*

δύσ-νοστος, ον, *not really a return.*

δυσ-νύμφευτος, ον, (δυσ-, νυμφεύω) *disagreeable to marry.*

δύσ-νυμφος, ον, (δυσ-, νυμφή) *ill-wedded.*

δυσ-ξύμβολος, ον, (δυσ-, ξύμβολον) *hard to deal with.*

δυσ-ξύνετος, ον, (δυσ-, ξυνίημι) *hard to understand, obscure, enigmatical.*

δυσοδμία, ἡ, = δυσοσμία. From

δύσ-οδμος, ον, = δύσοσμος.

δυσοδο-παίπᾰλος, ον, (δύσοδος, παιπάλη) *rugged and steep.*

δύσ-οδος, ον, *hard to pass, scarce passable.*

δυσ-οίζω, *to be sad, anxious:* Med. *to be afraid.* (From δυς, and οἴ *alas!*, as οἰμώζω from οἴμοι.)

δυσ-οίκητος, ον, (δυσ-, οἰκέω) *bad to dwell in.*

δύσ-οιμος, ον, (δυσ-, οἴμη) *with a bad path.*

δύσ-οιστος, ον, (δυσ-, οἴσω fut. of φέρω) *hard to bear, insufferable.*

δύσομαι, fut. med. of δύω.

δύσ-ομβρος, ον, *tempestuous.*

δυσ-όμῑλος, ον, *with an ill company, bringing evils in one's train.*

δυσ-όμμᾰτος, ον, (δυσ-, ὄμμα) *scarce-seeing.*

δυσ-όρᾱτος, ον, (δυσ-, ὁράω) *hard to see.*

δυσ-όργητος, ον, (δυσ-, ὀργάω) = δύσοργος.

δύσ-οργος, ον, (δυσ-, ὀργή) *quick to anger.*

δύσ-ορμος, ον, *with bad anchorage.* II. act. πνοαὶ δύσορμοι, gales *that keep ships at anchor.*

δύσ-ορνις, ῑθος, ὁ, ἡ, (δυσ-, ὄρνις) *boding ill.*

δυσ-όρφναιος, α, ον, (δυσ-, ὄρφνη) *dusky.*

δυσοσμία, ἡ, *an ill smell, rankness.* From

δύσ-οσμος, ον, (δυσ-, ὀσμή) *ill-smelling, stinking, rank.* II. *bad for scent.*

δυσ-ούριστος, ον, (δυσ-, οὐρίζω) *driven on by a too favourable wind, prospering unhappily.*

δυσπᾰθέω, f. ήσω, *to suffer a hard fate, be in affliction.* II. *to be impatient,* Lat. *aegrè ferre.* From

δυσ-παθής, ές, (δυσ-, πάθος) *impatient of suffering.* II. *hardly feeling, impassive.*

δυσ-πάλαιστος, ον, (δυσ-, πᾰλαίω) *hard to wrestle with, hard to conquer.*

δυσ-πάλᾰμος, ον, (δυσ-, πᾰλάμη) *hard to struggle with.* II. *hardly helping oneself, helpless:* Adv. -μως.

δυσ-πάλής, ές, (δυσ-, πάλη) *hard to wrestle with:* generally, *hard, difficult.*

δυσ-παράβλητος, ον, (δυσ-, παραβάλλω) *incomparable*

δυσ-παράβουλος, ον, (δυσ-, παρά, βουλή) *hard to persuade, stubborn.*

δυσ-παράθελκτος, ον, (δυσ-, παραθέλγω) *hard to soothe* or *assuage*

δυσ-παραίτητος, ον, (δυσ-, παραιτέομαι) *hard to move by prayer, inexorable.*

δυσ-πάρευνος, ον, (δυσ-, παρά, εὐνή) *ill-mated.*

δυσ-παμήγορος, ον, (δυσ–, παρηγορέω) *hard to console* or *appease.*

δυσ-πάρθενος, ἡ, *an unhappy maiden.*

Δύσ-πᾰρις, ιδος, ὁ, *ill-omened, ill-starred Paris:* cf. Αἰνόπαρις.

δυσ-πάρῐτος, ον, (δυσ–, πάρειμι *to pass by*) *hard to pass.*

δυσ-πειθής, ές, (δυσ–, πείθομαι) *hardly obeying, self-willed, stubborn: ill-trained.*

δύσ-πειστος, ον, (δυσ–, πείθω) *hard to persuade, stubborn, disobedient.* Adv., δυσπείστως ἔχειν to be *incredulous.*

δυσ-πέλαστος, ον, (δυσ–, πελάζω) *dangerous to come near.*

δύσ-πεμπτος, ον, (δυσ–, πέμπω) *hard to send away.*

δυσ-πέμφελος, ον, (δυσ–, πέμφιξ) of the sea. *rough and stormy:* metaph. *rude, discourteous.*

δυσ-πενθής, ές, (δυσ–, πένθος) *bringing sore affliction, grievous.*

δυσ-πέρᾱτος, ον, (δυσ–, περάω) *hard to pass through.*

δυσ-πετής, ές, (δυσ–, *πέτω Root of πίπτω) *falling out ill, grievous, difficult.* Adv. δυσπετῶς, Ion. –έως, *with difficulty.*

δυσ-πήμαντος, ον, (δυσ–, πημαίνω) *full of grievous evil.*

δυσ-πῑνής, ές, (δυσ–, πίνος) *squalid.*

δύσ-πλᾰνος, ον, (δυσ–, πλάνη) *wandering in misery.*

δυσ-πλοία, Ion. **–πλοΐη**, ἡ, *difficulty of sailing.* From

δύσ-πλοος, ον, (δυσ–, πλέω) *bad for sailing.*

δύσ-πλωτος, ον, = δύσπλοος.

δύσπνοια, ἡ, *difficulty of breathing.* From

δύσ-πνοος, ον, contr. **–πνους**, ουν, (δυσ–, πνέω) *scant of breath, breathless.* II. *unfit to breathe.* III. πνοαὶ δύσπνοοι *contrary* winds.

δυσ-πολέμητος, ον, (δυσ–, πολεμέω) *hard to war with.*

δυσ-πόλεμος, ον, *unlucky in war.*

δυσ-πολιόρκητος, ον, (δυσ–, πολιορκέω) *hard to take by siege.*

δυσ-πονής, ές, (δυσ–, πονέω) *toilsome.*

δυσ-πόνητος, ον, (δυσ–, πονέω) *hard-earned.* II. *bringing toil and trouble.*

δύσ-πονος, ον, *toilsome, wearisome.*

δυσ-πόρευτος, ον, (δυσ–, πορεύομαι) *hard to pass.*

δυσπορία, ἡ, *difficulty of passing.* From

δύσ-πορος, ον, *hard to pass, scarce passable.*

δύσ-ποτμος, ον, *unlucky, ill-starred.* Adv. δυσπότμως, *miserably.*

δύσ-ποτος, ον, (δυσ–, πότον) *hard to drink, unpalatable.*

δυσ-πρᾱγέω, f. ήσω, (δυσ–, πρᾶγος) *to fare ill.*

δυσ-πραξία, ἡ, (δυσ–, πράσσω) *ill success, ill luck.*

δύσ-πρᾱτος, ον, (δυσ–, πιπράσκω) *hard to sell.*

δυσ-πρεπής, ές, (δυσ–, πρέπω) *base, unseemly.*

δυσ-πρόσβᾰτος, ον, (δυσ–, προσβαίνω) *hard to approach, scarce accessible.*

δυσ-πρόσῑτος, ον, (δυσ–, πρόσειμι *to approach*) *hard to approach, difficult of access.*

δυσ-πρόσοδος, ον, *hard to get at.*

δυσ-πρόσοιστος, ον, (δυσ–, προσοίσω fut. of προσφέρω) *hard to deal* or *bear with, morose.*

δυσ-πρόσοπτος, ον, (δυσ–, προσόψομαι f. of προσοράω) *ill to look on: of ill aspect.*

δυσ-προσπέλαστος, ον, (δυσ–, προσπελάζω) *hard to approach.*

δυσ-πρόσωπος, ον, (δυσ–, πρόσωπον) *of ill aspect.*

δύσ-ρῑγος, ον, (δυσ–, ῥῖγος) *unable to bear cold.*

δυσσέβεια, ἡ, *impiety: a charge of impiety:* and

δυσσεβέω, f. ήσω, *to be impious: to act impiously.* From

δυσ-σεβής, ές, (δυσ–, σέβομαι) *ungodly, impious.*

δυσσεβία, poët. for δυσσέβεια.

δύσ-σοος, ον, (δυσ–, σώζω) *hard to save, ruined,* Lat. *perditus:* τὰ δύσσοα *the rogues.*

δυσ-τάλᾱς, αινα, ᾰν, *very wicked, most miserable.*

δύστᾱνος, ον, Dor. for δύστηνος.

δυσ-τέκμαρτος, ον, (δυσ–, τεκμαίρομαι) *hard to conjecture: dark and riddling.*

δύσ-τεκνος, ον, (δυσ–, τέκνον) *unhappy in one's children.*

δυσ-τερπής, ές, (δυσ–, τέρπω) *ill-pleasing, displeasing.*

δύστηνος, ον, *wretched, unhappy, unfortunate.* II. like Lat. *miser, wretched, profligate.* (Deriv. uncertain.)

δυσ-τλήμων, ον, gen. ονος, (δυσ–, τλήμων) *suffering evil, wretched.*

δύσ-τλητος, ον, (δυσ–, τλῆναι) *hard to endure.*

δυσ-τοκεύς, έως, ὁ, (δυσ–, τοκεύς) *an unhappy parent.*

δυστοκέω, f. ήσω, *to have a hard labour.* From

δύσ-τοκος, ον, (δυσ–, τεκεῖν) *bringing forth with pain.*

δυστομέω, f. ήσω, *to speak evil of.* From

δύ-στομος, ον, (δυσ–, στόμα) *evil-speaking.* II. of a horse, *hard-mouthed.*

δύ-στονος, ον, (δυσ–, στένω) *lamentable.*

δυσ-τόπαστος, ον, (δυσ–, τοπάζω) *hard to guess.*

δυ-στόχαστος, ον, (δυσ–, στοχάζομαι) *hard to hit upon.*

δυσ-τράπεζος, ον, (δυσ–, τράπεζα) *fed on horrid food.*

δυσ-τράπελος, ον, (δυσ–, τρέπω) *hard to turn: stubborn, unmanageable.* Adv. –λως, *awkwardly.*

δύσ-τροπος, ον, (δυσ–, τρέπω) *hard to turn* or *direct: stubborn, wayward.*

δυστῠχέω, f. ήσω: pf. δεδυστύχηκα: (δυστυχής):—*to be unlucky, unhappy:* of things, *to fail.* Hence

δυστύχημα, ατος, τό, *a mischance, a failure.*

δυσ-τῠχής, ές, (δυσ–, τύχη) *unlucky, unfortunate.* Adv. –χως. Hence

δυστῠχία, ἡ, *ill luck, ill fortune.*

δυσ-ὑποιστος, ον, (δυσ–, ὑποίσω fut. of ὑποφέρω) *hard to endure.*

δύσ-φᾱμος, Dor. for δύσφημος.

δύσ-φᾰτος, ον, (δυσ–, φημί) *hard to tell, unspeakable, horrible,* Lat. *infandus.*

δυσφημέω, f. ήσω, (δύσφημος) *to speak evil words:*

esp. *words of ill omen.* II. trans. *to speak ill of, blaspheme, slander.* Hence

δυσφημία, ἡ, *evil language*: esp. *words of ill omen, lamentations.*

δύσ-φημος, ον, (δυσ–, φήμη) *of ill omen, boding.* II. *slanderous*: *evil.*

δυσ-φιλής, ές, (δυσ–, φιλέω) *hateful.*

δυσφορέω, f. ήσω, (δύσφορος) *to bear ill, to be grieved*, Lat. *aegrè ferre*; *to be discontented.* Hence

δυσφόρητος, ον, *hard to bear.*

δυσ-φόρμιγξ, ιγγος, ὁ, ἡ, *ill suited to the lyre, mournful, melancholy.*

δύσ-φορος, ον, (δυσ–, φέρω) *hard to bear, oppressive, heavy*: *insufferable, grievous*:—Adv., δυσφόρως ἔχειν to be *intolerable.* II. (δυσ–, φέρομαι) *moving with difficulty, slow of motion.*

δυσφρόνως, Adv. of δύσφρων, *foolishly.*

δυσφροσύνη, ἡ, *anxiety, care.* From

δύσ-φρων, ον, gen. ονος, (δυσ–, φρήν) *heavy in heart, sorrowful.* II. *ill-disposed, hostile.* III. *senseless.*

δυσ-φύλακτος, ον, (δυσ–, φυλάσσω) *hard to watch* or *keep.* II. *hard to keep off.*

δυσ-χείμερος, ον, (δυσ–, χεῖμα) *very wintry, stormy.*

δυσ-χείρωμα, ατος, τό, (δυσ–, χειρόω) *a thing hard to subdue, a hard conquest.*

δυσ-χείρωτος, ον, (δυσ–, χειρόω) *hard to subdue.*

δυσχεραίνω, fut. ἀνῶ, *to bear with a bad grace*, Lat. *aegrè ferre*: *to be discontented, displeased.* II. *to make a thing hard, to make difficulties*; ῥήματα δυσχεράναντα (aor. I part.) *vexatious* words:—and

δυσχέρεια, ἡ, *difficulty.* II. *annoyance, trouble.* 2. of persons, *peevishness, ill-temper, moroseness.* From

δυσ-χερής, ές, (δυσ–, χείρ) *hard to manage.* II. *annoying, unpleasant, troublesome.* 2. of persons, *peevish, ill-tempered*:—Adv., δυσχερῶς ἔχειν to be *annoyed.*

δύσχῐμος, ον, (from δυσ–, as μελάγχιμος from μέλας) *troublesome, dangerous, fearful.*

δυσχλαινία, ἡ, *scanty, shabby clothing.* From

δύσ-χλαινος, ον, (δυσ–, χλαῖνα) *shabbily clad.*

δύσ-χορτος, ον, *ill-supplied with food.*

δύσ-χρηστος, ον, (δυσ–, χράομαι) *hard to use, inconvenient*: *intractable.*

δυσ-χωρία, ἡ, (δυσ–, χῶρος) *difficult ground.*

δυσ-ώδης, ες, (δυσ–, ὄζω) *ill-smelling.*

δυσ-ώδῖνος, ον, (δυσ–, ὠδίν) *causing grievous pangs.*

δυσωνέω, f. ήσω, *to beat down the price, cheapen.* From

δυσ-ώνης, ου, ὁ, (δυσ–, ὠνέομαι) *one who buys with difficulty, a hard customer.*

δυσ-ώνῠμος, ον, (δυσ–, ὄνομα) *bearing an ill name, bearing a name of ill omen*, such as Aïas.

δυσ-ωπέω, f. ήσω, (δυσ–, ὤψ) *to put a person out of countenance, to be importunate*:—Pass. *to be ashamed, shy, timid.*

δυσ-ωρέομαι, f. ήσομαι: Dep.: (δυσ–, ὦρος):—*to keep a troublesome, painful watch.*

δύσ-ωρος, ον, (δυσ–, ὥρα) *unseasonable.*

δῦτε, 2 pl. aor. 2 imperat. of δύω.

δύτης, ου, ὁ, (δύω) *a diver.*

δύω, Ion. for δύο, *two.*

ΔΥ´Ω or **δύνω**: fut. δύσω [ῡ]: aor. I act. ἔδῡσα:—Med., δύομαι: impf. ἐδυόμην: fut. δύσομαι [ῡ]: aor. I ἐδῡσάμην, with Ep. 2 and 3 sing. ἐδύσεο, ἐδύσετο, imperat. δύσεο, part. δυσόμενος used in pres. sense: with the Med. the aor. 2 and pf. act. agree in sense, aor. 2 ἔδῡν, υς, υ, dual ἐδύτην [ῡ], pl. ἔδῡμεν, ἔδῡτε, ἔδῡσαν Ep. ἔδυν; imperat. δῦθι, δῦτε, subj. δύω; opt. δυίην or δύην; inf. δῦναι, part. δύς: pf. δέδῡκα:

I. Causal in fut. and aor. I, δύσω, ἔδῡσα, *to put* clothes *on another.* II. intr. in all other tenses of Act., and in Med.: 1. of clothes, *to put* them *on oneself, put on*; metaph., εἰ μὴ σύ γε δύσεαι ἀλκήν if thou *wilt* not *put on* strength. 2. of places, *to enter, make one's way into*; δῦναι κόλπον θαλάσσης *to sink into* the lap of ocean; πόλεμον δῦναι and δύσασθαι *to plunge into* the fight; μνηστῆρας δύσασθαι *to go in among* the suitors. 3. *to come over* or *upon*; κάματος γυῖα δέδυκε weariness *came upon* his limbs; κρατερή ἑ λύσσα δέδυκε madness *came over* him. 4. absol. *to sink in*: *to dive*: *to set*, of the sun and stars.

δυώ-δεκα, οἱ, αἱ, τά, poët. for δώδεκα.

δυωδεκά-βοιος, ον, (δυώδεκα, βοῦς) *worth twelve beeves.*

δυωδεκά-δρομος, ον, (δυώδεκα, δρᾰμεῖν) *running twelve courses.*

δυωδεκά-μηνος, ος, (δυώδεκα, μήν) *twelve months old.*

δυωδεκά-μοιρος, ον, (δυώδεκα, μοῖρα) *divided into twelve parts.*

δυωδεκαταῖος, ον, *twelve days old.*

δυωδέκατος, ον, poët. for δωδέκατος.

δυωκαιεικοσί-μετρος, ον, (δύω καὶ εἴκοσι, μέτρον) *holding two-and-twenty measures.*

δυωκαιεικοσί-πηχυς, υ, (δύω καὶ εἴκοσι, πῆχυς) *twenty-two cubits long.*

δῶ, τό, Ep. apocopate form for δῶμα, only in nom. and acc. Also as plur. for δώματα.

δῶ, δῷς, δῷ, aor. 2 subj. of δίδωμι.

δώ-δεκα, οἱ, αἱ, τά, (δύο, δέκα) *twelve*, Lat. *duodecim.*

δωδεκά-γναμπτος, ον, (δώδεκα, γνάμπτω) *bent twelve times*; δωδεκάγναμπτον τέρμα the post *that has been doubled twelve times.*

δωδεκάδ-αρχος, ὁ, (δώδεκα, ἄρχω) *a leader of twelve.*

δωδεκά-δωρος, ον, (δώδεκα, δῶρον II) *twelve palms long.*

δωδεκ-άεθλος, ον, *conqueror in twelve contests.*

δωδεκα-ετής, ές, (δώδεκα, ἔτος) *of twelve years*:—but, **δωδεκαέτης**, ου, ὁ, *twelve years old.*

δωδεκάκις, Adv. (δώδεκα) *twelve times.*

δωδεκά-κρουνος, ον, *with twelve springs.*

δωδεκά-λῑνος, ον, (δώδεκα, λίνον) *of twelve threads.*

δωδεκά-μηνος, ον, (δώδεκα, μήν) *of twelve months.*

δωδεκα-μήχᾰνος, ον, (δώδεκα, μηχανή) *knowing twelve arts.*

δωδεκά-παις, -παιδος, ὁ, ἡ, *with twelve children.*

δωδεκά-πᾰλαι, Adv. *twelve times long ago*, i.e. *ever so long ago.*

δωδεκά-πηχυς, υ, *twelve cubits long.*

δωδεκά-πολις, ι, gen. ιος, *formed of twelve united states.*

δωδεκ-άρχης, ου, ὁ, = δωδέκ-αρχος.

δωδεκάς, άδος, ἡ, (δώδεκα) *the number twelve: a number of twelve, a dozen.*

δωδεκά-σκαλμος, ον, *twelve-oared.*

δωδεκά-σκῦτος, ον, *made of twelve different coloured pieces of leather.*

δωδεκαταῖος, α, ον, *on the twelfth day.* From

δωδέκατος, η, ον, (δώδεκα) *the twelfth.*

δωδεκά-φῦλος, ον, (δώδεκα, φυλή) *of twelve tribes: τὸ δωδεκάφυλον the twelve tribes* of Israel.

δωδεκ-έτης, ου, ὁ, (δώδεκα, ἔτος) *twelve years old;* fem. **δωδεκ-έτις**, ιδος, ἡ.

Δωδώνη, ἡ, *Dodona*, a town in Thesprotia, the seat of a very ancient oracle of Jupiter.

δώῃ, **δώῃσι**, Ep. 3 sing. aor. 2 subj. of δίδωμι.

δῴην, Ep. for δοίην, aor. 2 opt. of δίδωμι.

δῶκα, Ep. for ἔδωκα, aor. 1 of δίδωμι.

δῶλος, Dor. for δοῦλος.

δῶμα, ατος τό, (δέμω) *a house, dwelling.* II. *a part of the house, a chamber, room.* III. *a house, household.*

δωμάτιον, τό, Dim. of δῶμα.

δωματίτης, ου, ὁ: fem. -ῖτις, ιδος, ἡ: (δῶμα): *of, belonging to the house* or *household.*

δωματο-φθορέω, f. ήσω, (δῶμα, φθείρω) *to ruin house and home.*

δωματόω, f. ώσω, (δῶμα) *to house.*

δωμάω and **δωμάομαι**, Dep., (δέμω) *to build.*

δῶναξ, Dor. for δόναξ, δοῦναξ.

δώομεν, Ep. for δῶμεν, 1 pl. aor. 2 subj. of δίδωμι.

δωρεά, Ion. -εή, ἡ, *a gift, present*:—Acc. δωρεάν used as Adv., *as a free gift, freely*, Lat. *gratis*: hence *undeservedly, in vain.* From

δωρέω, f. ήσω: or **δωρέομαι**, Dep., f. ήσομαι:—*to give, present: to present one* with, Lat. *dono.* Hence

δώρημα, ατος, τό, *that which is given, a gift.*

δωρητός, ή, όν, (δωρέω) *open to gifts* or *presents, to be appeased by gifts.* II. *freely given.*

Δωριάζω, f. άσω, = Δωρίζω.

Δωριεύς, έως, ὁ, (Δῶρος) *a Dorian*: in plur. *the Dorians.*

Δωρίζω Dor. -ίσδω: f. ίσω: (Δῶρος):—*to imitate the Dorians.* 2. *to speak Doric Greek.* 3. *to dress like a Dorian girl.*

Δωρικός, ή, όν, and **Δώριος**, α, ον, (Δῶρος) *Doric, Dorian.*

Δωρίς, ίδος, ἡ, (Δῶρος) fem. Adj. *Dorian*: 1. (sub. γῆ) *the Dorian land*, i.e. *Peloponnesus.* 2. (sub. κοπίς) *a Dorian knife* used at sacrifices.

Δωρίσδεν, Dor. inf. of Δωρίζω.

Δωρίσδω, Dor. for Δωρίζω.

Δωριστί, (Δῶρος) Adv. *in Dorian fashion.*

δωροδοκέω, f. ήσω, (δωροδόκος) *to accept as a present, to take as a bribe*:—Pass. *to have a bribe given one*: c. acc. *to receive as a bribe.* Hence

δωροδόκημα, ατος, τό, *a bribe.*

δωροδοκητί, Adv. (δωροδοκέω) *in bribery fashion,* with allusion to the Dorians.

δωροδοκία, ἡ, (δωροδοκέω) *a taking of bribes, openness to bribery.*

δωρο-δόκος, ον, (δῶρον, δέχομαι) *taking presents* or *bribes.*

δωρο-δότης, ου, ὁ, (δῶρον, δίδωμι) *a giver of presents.*

δῶρον, τό, (δίδωμι) *a gift, present: a votive offering* to a god; δῶρα θεῶν *gifts* of or from the gods. II. *the breadth of the hand, the palm.*

δωρο-φάγος, ον, (δῶρον, φᾰγεῖν) *devouring gifts, greedy of presents.*

δωροφορέω, f. ήσω, *to bring presents* or *bribes.* From

δωρο-φόρος, ον, (δῶρον, φέρω) *bringing presents*: hence *tributary.*

δωρύττομαι, Dor. for δωρέομαι.

δώς, ἡ, Lat. *dos*, = δόσις, only in nom.

δωσείω, Desiderat. of δίδωμι, *to be ready to give.*

δωσέμεναι, -έμεν, Ep. fut. inf. of δίδωμι.

δῷσι, 3 pl. aor. 2 of δίδωμι.

δωσί-δῐκος, ον, (δίδωμι, δίκη) *giving oneself up to justice, abiding by a sentence.*

δώσω, fut. of δίδωμι.

δωσῶν, Dor. for δώσων, fut. act. part. of δίδωμι.

δωτήρ, ῆρος, ὁ, (δίδωμι) *a giver.*

δώτης, ου, ὁ, = δωτήρ.

δωτῑνάζω, f. άσω, *to receive presents.* From

δωτίνη, ἡ, (δίδωμι) *a gift, present*: acc. δωτίνην as Adv., *as a free gift, freely*, like δωρεάν. [ῐ]

δώτωρ, ορος, ὁ, = δωτήρ.

δώω, Ep. for δῶ, aor. 2 subj. of δίδωμι.

E

E, ε, called ἒ ψιλόν, the fifth letter of the Gr. alphabet: as numeral ε′ = πέντε and πέμπτος, ͵ε = 5000. When in the archonship of Euclides (B.C. 403) the Athenians adopted η from the Samian alphabet to represent long *e*, the Gramm. introduced the name of ἒ ψιλόν, ε *without the aspirate*, because E was one way of writing the rough breathing.

ἕ, *him-, her-,* or *it-self*, Lat. *se*, acc. sing. and plur. reflexive Pron. of 3rd pers., without nominat., and always enclitic. A rarer Ep. form is ἕε, never enclitic. II. without reflexive sense, for αὐτόν, αὐτήν, αὐτό, *him, her, it.* See οὗ, Lat. *sui.*

ἔᾱ, exclam. of wonder or displeasure: Lat. *vah!*

ἔᾱ, for εἴᾱ, 3 sing. impf. of ἐάω.

ἔᾰ, Ion. for ἦν, 1 sing. impf. of εἰμί *sum.*

ἐᾷ, lengthd. Ep. ἐάᾳ, 3 sing. pres. of ἐάω.

ἐάαν, lengthd. Ep. inf. of ἐάω.

ἔᾱγα, pf. of ἄγνυμι with pass. sense.

ἐάγην [ᾰ], aor. 2 pass. of ἄγνυμι.

ἕᾱδα, pf. of ἁνδάνω.

ἔᾰδον, aor. 2 of ἁνδάνω.

ἑάλη or **ἐάλη** [ᾰ], 3 sing. aor. 2 pass. of εἴλω.

ἑάλωκα [ᾰ], pf., **ἑάλων** [ᾱ], aor. 2 of ἁλίσκομαι.

ἐάν, Conj. (properly εἰ ἄν), *if haply, if so be that, in case that*, followed by Subjunctive, whereas εἰ is followed by Indic. and Optat.: Homer uses for it εἴ κε or αἴ κε: the Att. contract it into ἤν and ἄν. II. with Verbs of seeing and inquiring, it answers to Lat. *an, if, whether*; σκόπει ἐὰν ἱκανὸν ᾖ see *if* or *whether* it be enough. III. ἐὰν καί *even if, granting that*; ἐὰν μή *if not, except, unless*; ἐὰν ἄρα μή *if perhaps not*. IV. after relat. Pronouns and Particles ἐάν stands for ἄν; ὃς ἐάν *whosoever*; ὅπου ἐάν *wheresoever*; but only in very late writers.

ἑανόν, τό, v. sq.

ἑᾱνός, ή, όν, (ἕννυμι) used of all things *fit for putting on* or *wearing*; and so, generally, *fine, light*; ἑανὸς κασσίτερος tin *beat out thin* and *made fit for wear*. II. as Subst., **ἑᾰνόν** (sub. εἷμα or ἱμάτιον), τό, *a rich state-robe*.

ἐαξα for ἦξα, aor. 1 of ἄγνυμι.

ἜΑΡ, ἔᾰρος, τό; Ep. **εἶαρ**, εἴαρος; contr. **ἦρ**, ἦρος:—Lat. *VER, spring*; ἔαρος νέον ἱσταμένοιο in early *spring*; metaph. of *anything early* or *fresh, the prime* or *first bloom of* a thing; γενύων ἔαρ *the first down* on the chin.

ἐαρί-δρεπτος, ον, (ἔαρ, δρέπω) *plucked in spring*.

ἐαρίζω, f. ίσω Att. ιῶ, (ἔαρ) *to pass the spring*.

ἐᾰρῑνός Ep. **εἰαρινός** Att. **ἠρινός**, ή, όν: (ἔαρ): Lat. *vernus, of* or *belonging to spring*.

ἐαρο-τρεφής, ές, (ἔαρ, τρέφω) *spring-nurtured*.

ἔας, Ep. for ἦς, 2 sing. impf. of εἰμί *sum*.

ἔᾱσα, Ep. aor. 1 of ἐάω.

ἔᾱσι, Ep. for εἰσί, 3 plur. of εἰμί *sum*.

ἔασκον, Ion. for εἴων, impf. of ἐάω.

ἕᾰται, Ion. for ἦνται, 3 pl. of ἧμαι.

ἔατε, Ep. for ἦτε, 2 pl. impf. of εἰμί *sum*.

ἐᾱτέος, α, ον, verb. Adj. of ἐάω, *to be suffered: to be let alone*.

ἕᾰτο, Ion. for ἦντο, 3 pl. impf. of ἧμαι.

ἑ-αυτοῦ, ῆς, οῦ, pl. ἑαυτῶν, etc.; Ion. **ἑωυτοῦ**, etc.; Att. contr. **αὑτοῦ**, etc.: (ἕ, q.v., αὐτοῦ):—Reflexive Pron. of 3rd pers., *of himself, herself, itself*, etc., used in gen., dat., and acc. sing.

ἑάφθη, Ep. for ἥφθη, 3 sing. aor. 1 pass. of ἅπτω.

ἘΑ'Ω, contr. ἐῶ, Ep. εἰῶ: impf. εἴων, Ep. without augm. ἔων: fut. ἐάσω [ᾱ]: aor. 1 εἴᾱσα, Ep. ἔᾱσα: pf. εἴᾱκα:—Pass., f. med. in pass. sense, ἐάσομαι: pf. εἴᾱμαι. *To let, suffer, allow, permit*: with notion of carelessness, *to leave alone*. II. *to let go, let alone, let be: heed not*. 2. *to let alone, let be*; θεὸς τὸ μὲν δώσει, τὸ δ' ἐάσει he will give one thing, the other he will *let alone*, i. e. *not give*; ἐᾶν χαίρειν *to let alone*. III. Med., ἐᾶσθαί τινί τι *to give up* a thing to another.

ἐάων, Ep. for ἐήων, gen. pl. of ἐΰς.

ἔβαλον, aor. 2 of βάλλω.

ἔβᾰν, Ep. for ἔβησαν, 3 pl. aor. 2 of βαίνω.

ἐβάσκηνα, **ἐβασκάνθην**, aor. 1 act. and pass. of βασκαίνω.

ἐβάστασα, **ἐβάσταξα**, aor. 1 of βαστάζω.

ἐβάφθην, **ἐβάφην** [ᾰ], aor. 1 and 2 of βάπτω.

ἑβδομ-ᾱγέτης, ου, ὁ, (ἑβδόμη, ἄγω) epith. of Apollo, to whom the Spartans offered sacrifices *on the seventh of every month*.

ἑβδομαῖος, α, ον, (ἕβδομος) *on the seventh day*.

ἑβδομάς, άδος, ἡ, *a number of seven*.

ἑβδόματος, ον, (ἕβδομος) *the seventh*.

ἑβδομήκοντα, οἱ, αἱ, τά, (ἑπτά) indecl. *seventy*.

ἑβδομηκοντα-έξ, *seventy-six*.

ἕβδομος, η, ον, (ἑπτά) *the seventh*. II. ἡ ἑβδόμη (ἡμέρα), *the seventh day* of the month.

ἐβεβήκειν, plqpf. of βαίνω.

ἐβεβλήκειν, **ἐβεβλήμην**, plqpf. act. and pass. of βάλλω.

ἐβένινος, η, ον, *of ebony*. From

ἜΒΕΝΟΣ, ἡ, *the ebony-tree, ebony*.

ἔβην, aor. 2 of βαίνω.

ἔβηξα, aor. 1 of βήσσω.

ἔβησα, causal aor. 1 of βαίνω.

ἐβήσετο, Ep. for ἐβήσατο, aor. 1 med. of βαίνω.

ἐβιᾰσάμην, **ἐβιάσθην**, aor. 1 med. and pass. of βιάζω.

ἐβιήθην, aor. 1 pass. of βιάω.

ἐβίων, aor. 2 of βιόω.

ἐβιώσαο, 2 sing. aor. 1 of βιώσκομαι.

ἔβλᾰβεν, Aeol. and Ep. for ἐβλάβησαν, 3 pl. aor. 2 pass. of βλάπτω.

ἐβλάστηκα, pf. of βλαστάνω.

ἐβλάστησα, **ἔβλαστον**, aor. 1 and 2 of βλαστάνω.

ἔβλαφα, pf. of βλάπτω.

ἐβλέπην, aor. 2 pass. of βλέπω.

ἐβλέφθην, aor. 1 pass. of βλέπω.

ἐβλήμην, Ep. aor. 2 pass. of βάλλω.

ἔβλῐσα, aor. 1 of βλίσσω.

ἔβλῠσα, aor. 1 of βλύζω, but **ἔβλῡσα** of βλύω.

ἐβούλευσα, **ἐβουλεύθην**, aor. 1 act. and pass. of βουλεύω.

ἐβουλήθην, **ἐβουλόμην**, aor. 1 and impf. of βούλομαι.

ἙΒΡΑΙ͂ΟΣ, *a Hebrew*: **Ἑβραΐς**, ΐδος, fem. Adj. (sub. διάλεκτος), *the Hebrew* dialect. Hence

Ἑβραϊστί, Adv. *in the Hebrew tongue*.

ἔβρᾰσα, **ἐβράσθην**, aor. 1 act. and pass. of βράσσω.

ἔβρᾰχε, see βράχω.

ἐβράχην [ᾰ], aor. 2 pass. of βρέχω.

ἔβρεξα, **ἐβρέχθην**, aor. 1 act. and pass. of βρέχω.

ἔβριξα, aor. 1 of βρίζω.

ἔβρῑσα, aor. 1 of βρίθω.

ἔβρῠχον, aor. 2 of βρύχω [ῡ].

ἐβρώθην, aor. 1 act. and pass. of βιβρώσκω.

ἔβρων, aor. 2 of βιβρώσκω.

ἔβρωσα, **ἐβρώθην**, aor. 1 act. and pass. of βιβρώσκω.

ἔβῡσα, **ἐβύσθην**, aor. 1 act. and pass. of βύω.

ἔβωσα, contr. for ἐβόησα, aor. 1 of βοάω.

ἔγ-γαιος, α, ον, also **ἔγ-γειος**, ον, (ἐν, γῆ) *in* or *of the land, native.* II. of property, *in land, consisting of land.* III. *in* or *beneath the earth*, like χθόνιος.

ἐγ-γέγαα, Ep. pf. of ἐγγίγνομαι.

ἐγγέγλυμμαι, pf. pass. of ἐγγλύφω.

ἐγγέγραμμαι, pf. pass. of ἐγγράφω.

ἐγγεγύηκα, -ημαι, see ἐγγύαω.

ἐγ-γείνωνται, 3 pl. aor. 1 subj. of *ἐγγείνομαι in causal sense, *to engender* or *breed in.*

ἔγ-γειος, see ἔγγαιος.

ἐγγελάστης, ου, ὁ, *a mocker, scorner.* From

ἐγ-γελάω, f. άσομαι [ᾰ]: for the tenses, v. γελάω: —*to laugh at, mock at one:* absol. *to mock, jeer.*

ἐγ-γενής, ές, (ἐν, γένος) *in-born, native, innate, natural;* ἐγγενεῖς θεοί gods *of the race* or *country.* II. *born of the same race, kindred.*

ἐγ-γηράσκω, fut. άσομαι [ᾱ], *to grow old in* a place.

ἐγ-γίγνομαι, fut. -γενήσομαι: for the tenses, v. γίγνομαι: (ἐν, γίγνομαι): Dep.:—*to be produced in, grow in: to take place, happen, arise in,* or *among.* II. *to intervene, pass.* III. ἐγγίγνεται, *it is allowed,* like ἔξεστι.

ἐγγίζω, f. ίσω, (ἐγγύς) *to bring near* II. mostly intrans. *to draw nigh, be at hand.*

ἐγ-γίνομαι, Ion. and in later Gr. for ἐγγίγνομαι.

ἐγγίων, ον, Comp., and **ἔγγιστος**, η, ον, Sup. of ἐγγύς.

ἐγ-γλύσσω, (ἐν, γλυκύς) *to have a sweet taste.*

ἐγ-γλύφω, f. ψω, (ἐν, γλύφω) *to cut in, carve.*

ἐγ-γλωττο-τῠπέω, f. ήσω, (ἐν, γλῶσσα, τύπτω) *to strike out with the tongue, to be always talking of.*

ἔγ-γονος, ὁ, (ἐν, γόνος) *a grandson: descendant.*

ἐγ-γράφω, f. ψω: for the tenses, v. γράφω:—*to mark in* or *on: to paint* or *write on:* Med. and Pass. *to have written on;* ἐγγεγραμμένος τι *having* it *written on,* as in Virgil, *inscripti nomina.* II. *to enter in the public register, to set down:* also *to indict.*

ἐγ-γῠαλίζω, f. ξω: Ep. aor. 1 ἐγγυάλιξα: (ἐν, γύαλον):—*to put into one's hands, grant in full, give to* one's *charge.*

ἐγγυάω: impf. ἠγγύων: fut. ἐγγυήσω: aor. 1 ἠγγύησα: pf. ἠγγύηκα:—Pass., aor. 1 ἠγγυήθην: pf. ἠγγύημαι: (this Verb is often treated as a compd., and the forms given as ἐνεγύων, ἐνεγύησα, ἐγγεγύηκα: but it is derived from ἐγγύη, and these forms are erroneous):—*to hand over as a pledge, to plight, betroth: to engage, promise, answer:*—Med. *to pledge* or *plight oneself, to give a pledge:*—Pass. *to be plighted* or *betrothed: to accept as plighted husband* or *wife.*

ἐγ-γύη, ἡ, (ἐν, γυῖον or γύαλον) *a putting a pledge in one's hand:* hence generally, *surety, security, bail.*

ἐγγυητής, οῦ, ὁ, (ἐγγυάω) *one who gives bail* or *security, a surety.*

ἐγγυητός, ή, όν, (ἐγγυαω) *plighted, betrothed.*

ἐγγύθεν, Adv. (ἐγγύς) *from nigh at hand, hard by, near.* II. of Time, *nigh at hand.*

ἐγγύθι, (ἐγγύς) Adv. *hard by, near.* II. of Time, *nigh at hand.*

ἔγ-γῠος, ον, (ἐγγύη) *giving surety* or *bail.* II. as Subst., = ἐγγυητής, *a surety.*

ἘΓΓΥ'Σ, Adv. I. of Place, *near, nigh at hand,* absol. or c. gen. II. of Time, *nigh at hand.* III. of Numbers, *nearly.* IV. *coming near, like, akin to.* Comp. ἐγγίων, ον, and ἐγγύτερος, α, ον; Adv. ἐγγυτέρω, *nearer:*—Sup. ἐγγίστος and ἐγγύτατος; Adv. ἔγγιστα and ἐγγύτατα, *as near as possible:* see ἐγγίων.

ἐγ-γώνιος, ον, (ἐν, γῶνος) *angular, forming a right angle;* λίθοι ἐν τομῇ ἐγγώνιοι stones cut *square.*

ἐγδούπησα, Ep. for ἐδούπησα, aor. 1 of δουπέω.

ἐγέγωνε, 3 sing. impf. of γεγώνω: see γέγωνα.

ἐγεγώνειν, plqpf. of γέγωνα.

ἐγεγώνευν, impf. of γεγωνέω: see γέγωνα.

ἐγεινάμην, causal aor. 1 of γείνομαι, *to beget.*

ἐγεγόνει and **ἐγεγένητο**, 3 sing. plqpf. of γίγνομαι.

ἘΓΕΙ'ΡΩ, fut. ἐγερῶ: aor. ἤγειρα: pf. ἐγήγερκα:—Pass., aor. 1 ἠγέρθην Ep. 3 pl. ἔγερθεν: pf. ἐγήγερμαι:—for Ep. aor. 2 and pf. med., see ἔγρετο, ἐγρήγορα: I. Act. *to awaken, wake up, rouse, stir:*—metaph. *to rouse, stir up.* 2. *to raise* from the dead. 3. *to raise, erect* a building. II. Med. and Pass. *to wake, rise up* from sleep: in aor. *to keep watch: be awake.* 2. *to rouse oneself, be excited* by passion, etc.

ἐγέλασσα, ἐγέλαξα, Ep. and Dor. aor. 1 of γελάω.

ἔγεντο, syncop. for ἐγένετο, 3 sing. aor. 2 of γίγνομαι.

ἐγέρηρα, aor. 1 of γεραίρω.

ἐγερθείς, aor. 1 part. pass. of ἐγείρω.

ἐγερσί-γελως, ωτος, ὁ, ἡ, (ἐγείρω, γέλως) *laughter-stirring.*

ἐγερσι-θέᾱτρος, ον, (ἐγείρω, θέατρον) *exciting the spectators.*

ἐγερσι-μάχας, Dor. for -μάχης, ὁ: fem. ἐγερσιμάχη: (ἐγείρω, μάχη) *battle-stirring.*

ἐγέρσιμος, ον, (ἐγείρω) *waking, easily waked;* ἐγέρσιμος ὕπνος sleep *from which one wakes.*

ἔγερσις, εως, ἡ, (ἐγείρω) *a waking, exciting.*

ἐγερσι-φάης, ές, (ἐγείρω, φάος) *light-awakening.*

ἐγερτί, Adv. (ἐγείρω) *wakefully, busily.*

ἐγηγέρατο, Ion. for ἐγηγερμένοι ἦσαν, 3. pl. plqpf. pass. of ἐγείρω.

ἐγήγερκα, **ἐγήγερμαι**, pf. act. and pass. of ἐγείρω.

ἔγημα, aor. 1 of γαμέω.

ἐγήρα, 3 sing. aor. 2 of γηράσκω.

ἐγήρᾱσα, aor. 1 of γηράσκω.

ἐγήρῡσα, aor. 1 of γηρύω.

ἐγ-καθαρμόζω, f. όσω, *to fit in.*

ἐγ-καθέζομαι, f. -καθεδοῦμαι, Dep. *to sit* or *take one's seat in: to encamp in* a place.

ἐγκάθετος, ον, (ἐγκαθίημι) *suborned.*

ἐγ-καθηβάω, f. ήσω, *to pass one's youth in.*

ἐγ-κάθημαι, Dep. *to sit in* or *on, lie in ambush.*

ἐγ-καθιδρύω, f. ύσω [ῡ], *to set up in.*

ἐγ-καθίζω, f. ίσω Att. ιῶ, *to seat in* or *upon*. II. intr. *to sit in* or *upon*: *to take one's seat on*.
ἐγ-καθίημι, f. ήσω, *to let down into, send in*.
ἐγ-καθίστημι, f. -καταστήσω, *to place* or *set in*. II. Med. and Pass., with aor. 2 act. ἐγκατέστην; pf. ἐγκαθέστηκα; plqpf. ἐγκαθεστήκειν: *to be placed* or *established in*.
ἐγ-καθορμίζω, f. ίσω Att. ιῶ, *to bring into harbour*: Med. *to run into harbour*.
ἐγ-καθυβρίζω, f. ίσω Att. ιῶ, *to riot to excess in* a thing.
ἐγ-καίνια, τά, (ἐν, καινός) *a feast of renovation* or *dedication* Hence
ἐγκαινίζω, f. σω, *to renovate, dedicate, consecrate*.
ἐγ-καίω, f -καύσω, *to burn* or *heat in*. II. *to make a fire in*.
ἐγ-κᾰλέω, fut. ἐγκαλέσω: pf. ἐγκέκληκα:—*to call in*. II. *to summon for the purpose of accusing, to accuse, indict*; φόνον ἐγκαλεῖν τινι *to bring a charge* of murder *against* one: of actions, *to blame, censure*.
ἐγ-καλλωπίζομαι, Pass. *to pride oneself in* a thing. Hence
ἐγκαλλώπισμα, ατος, τό, *that of which one is proud*: *an ornament, decoration*.
ἐγκαλυμμός, ὁ, *a wrapping up*. From
ἐγ-κᾰλύπτω, f. ψω, *to veil in*: *to wrap up*:—Med. *to hide oneself*, esp. *one's face*: hence *to be ashamed*.
ἐγ-κάμπτω, f. ψω, *to bend in*.
ἐγ-κᾰνάσσω, f. ξω, *to pour gurgling in*; aor. 1 imperat. ἐγκάναξον. (Formed from the sound.)
ἐγ-κᾰνᾰχάομαι, Dep. (ἐν, καναχή) *to make a sound in* or *with* a thing.
ἐγ-κάπτω, f. ψω: pf. ἐγκέκᾰφα:—*to gulp in greedily, to snap up, bolt*.
ἔγ-καρπος, ον, *containing fruit*: *fruitful, prolific*.
ἐγ-κάρσιος, α, ον, *cross, transverse, oblique*.
ἐγ-καρτερέω, f. ήσω, *to persevere* or *persist in*. II. *to await steadfastly*. III. absol. *to hold out*.
ἔγκᾰτα, τα, (ἐν) *the entrails, bowels*: dat. ἔγκασι.
ἐγ-καταβαίνω, *to go down into*: *to put oneself in*.
ἐγ-καταγηράσκω: f. άσομαι [ᾰ]: *to grow old in*.
ἐγ-καταδέω, f. -δήσω, *to bind fast in, involve in*.
ἐγ-καταδύνω, *to creep down into*.
ἐγ-καταζεύγνυμι, f. -ζεύξω, *to associate with, adapt*.
ἐγκατάθοιτο, 3 aor. 2 med. opt. of ἐγκατατίθημι.
ἐγ-κατάκειμαι, Pass. *to lie in*: *to lie down*.
ἐγ-κατακλίνω, *to lay down* or *put to bed in* a place: —Pass. *to lie down* or *go to bed in*.
ἐγ-κατακοιμάομαι, Pass. with fut. med -ήσομαι, *to lie down and sleep in*.
ἐγ-κατακρούω, f. σω, *to beat in*; ἐγκατακρούειν χορείαν *to tread a measure* or *dance among*.
ἐγ-καταλαμβάνω, fut. -λήψομαι, *to catch in* a place: *to catch and hold fast, to bind* or *trammel*.
ἐγ-καταλέγω, f. ξω, *to lay in* or *build into* a wall. II. *to reckon among*: *to enlist soldiers*.
ἐγ-καταλείπω, f. ψω, *to leave behind*: *to forsake*:—Pass. *to be left behind in a race*.

ἐγκατάληψις, εως, ἡ, (ἐγκαταλαμβάνω) *a catching* and *holding fast*: *a being caught in* a place.
ἐγ-καταμίγνυμι, f. -μίξω, *to mix up in*.
ἐγ-καταπήγνυμι, f. -πήξω, *to thrust firmly into*: *to fix in*.
ἐγ-καταπίπτω, f. -πεσοῦμαι, *to fall in* or *upon*.
ἐγ-καταπλέκω, f. -πλέξω, *to interweave, entwine*.
ἐγ-καταρράπτω, f. ψω, *to sew in*.
ἐγ-κατασκήπτω, f. ψω, *to fall upon*: of epidemics, *to break out among*. II. trans. *to hurl down upon*.
ἐγ-κατασφάττω, f. ξω, *to slaughter in*.
ἐγ-κατατίθημι, f. -θήσω, *to put in* or *upon*:—Med., τελαμῶνα ἐῇ ἐγκάτθετο τέχνῃ *he included* the sword-belt *in his* art, i. e. *wrought* it *by his* art.
ἐγ-καταχέω, f. -χεῶ, *to pour in besides*.
ἐγκατελέγην, aor. 2 pass. of ἐγκαταλέγω.
ἐγκατέλῐπον, aor. 2 of ἐγκαταλείπω.
ἐγκατέπηξα, aor. 1 of ἐγκαταπήγνυμι.
ἐγκάτθεο, Ep. for ἐγκατάθου, 2 sing. imperat., and
ἐγκάτθετο, for ἐγκατέθετο, 3 sing. ind., aor. 2 med. of ἐγκατατίθημι.
ἐγ-κατιλλώπτω, f. ψω, *to scoff at*.
ἐγ-κατοικέω, f. ήσω, *to dwell in*.
ἐγ-κατοικοδομέω, f. ήσω, *to build on a spot*, also 2. *to build in, immure*.
ἔγ-κειμαι, Pass. with fut. med. -κείσομαι, *to lie in, to be wrapped in*. II. *to press upon, urge, importune, attack*: *to be vehement against*: *to press one hard*. 2. *to be devoted to*.
ἐγ-κείρω, only in pf. pass. part., ἐγκεκαρμένῳ κάρᾳ *with shorn head*.
ἐγκέκαυμαι, pf. pass. of ἐγκαίω.
ἐγκέκᾰφα, pf. of ἐγκάπτω.
ἐγκέκληκα, pf. of ἐγκαλέω
ἐγκέκλημαι, Att. pf. pass. of ἐγκλείω.
ἐγκέκλῐμαι, pf. pass. of ἐγκλίνω.
ἐγκέκτημαι, pf. of ἐγκτάομαι.
ἐγκεκύκλωμαι, pf. pass. of ἐγκυκλόω.
ἐγκέλευμα or -λευσμα, ατος, τό, (ἐγκελεύω) *an encouragement, cheer, huzzah*.
ἐγκέλευστος, ον, *urged on, bidden, ordered*. From
ἐγ-κελεύω, f. σω, *to urge on, cheer on*.
ἐγ-κεντρίζω, f. ίσω, *to goad on*. II. of plants, *to inoculate, ingraft*.
ἐγ-κεντρίς, ίδος, ἡ, (ἐν, κέντρον) *a sting*: *a spur*.
ἐγ-κεράννῡμι, fut. κεράσω [ᾰ]: (ἐν, κεράννῡμι): *to mix in, mix*: metaph. *to concoct, contrive*.
ἐγ-κερτομέω, f. ήσω, *to mock at*.
ἐγ-κέφᾰλος, ον, (ἐν, κεφαλή) *within the head*; ὁ ἐγκέφαλος (sub. μυελός), I. *the brain*. II. *the edible pith* of young palm-shoots.
ἐγκεχᾰλίνωμαι, pf. pass. of ἐγχαλῑνόω.
ἐγκέχοδα, pf. of ἐγχέζω.
ἐγκεχρημένος, pf. part. pass. of ἐγχράω.
ἐγκέχῠμαι, pf. pass. of ἐγχέω.
ἐγ-κῐθᾰρίζω, f. ίσω, *to play the harp among*.
ἐγ-κίρνημι, = ἐγκεράννυμι.

ἐγ-κλείω, f. σω, *to shut in, confine within.* II. *to shut to, shut fast.*

ἐγκληθείς, aor. 1 part. pass. of ἐγκαλέω.

ἐγ-κληΐω, Ion. for ἐγκλείω.

ἔγ-κλημα, ατος, τό, *an accusation, charge, complaint: a bill of indictment.*

ἐγκλήμων, μονος, ὁ, (ἐγκαλέω) *censorious.*

ἔγ-κληρος, ον, (ἐν, κλῆρος) *having a lot* or *share in an inheritance, an heir, heiress.*

ἐγ-κλῄω, Att. for ἐγκλείω: aor. 1 part. ἐγκλῄσας.

ἐγ-κλιδόν, Adv. (ἐγκλίνω) *leaning sideways, aslant.*

ἐγ-κλίνω, f. -κλῐνῶ: pf. -κέκλῐκα, pass. -κέκλῐμαι:—*to bend, incline to* or *towards*, Lat. *inclinare*:—Pass. *to lean over* or *on, weigh upon* one. II. intr. *to bend, incline.* 2. *to give way, flee*, Lat. *inclinari.*

ἐγ-κοιλαίνω, f. ᾰνῶ, *to hollow out, scoop out.*

ἔγ-κοιλος, ον, (ἐν, κοῖλος) *hollowed out, hollow.*

ἐγ-κοιμάομαι, Pass. with fut. med. ήσομαι, *to sleep in.*

ἐγ-κοιμίζω, f. ίσω, *to lull to sleep in* a place.

ἐγ-κοισῠρόω, f. ώσω, (ἐν, Κοισύρα) hence pf. part. pass. ἐγκεκοισυρωμένη, *as luxurious as Coesyra* (a female name in the Alcmæonid family).

ἐγ-κοιτάς, άδος, ἡ, (ἐν, κοίτη) *serving for a bed.*

ἐγ-κοληβάζω, f. σω, *to gulp down like a* κόλλαβος, *swallow.*

ἐγ-κονέω, f. ήσω, *to hasten, be quick and active.* Hence

ἐγ-κονητί, Adv. *in haste, diligently.*

ἐγ-κονίομαι, Med. (ἐν, κόνις) *to roll in the dust* or *sand, sprinkle sand over* oneself.

ἐγκοπή, ἡ, (ἐγκοπῆναι) *a hinderance.*

ἐγκοπῆναι, aor. 1 inf. pass. of ἐγκόπτω.

ἔγκοπος, ον, (ἐγκοπῆναι) *wearied.*

ἐγ-κόπτω, f. ψω, *to knock in:* metaph. *to hinder, weary.*

ἐγ-κορδῠλέω, f. ήσω, (ἐν, κορδύλη) *to wrap up in coverlets*: pf. part. pass. ἐγκεκορδυλημένος.

ἐγ-κοσμέω, f. ήσω, *to arrange in order*

ἐγκοτέω, f. έσω, *to be indignant at.* From

ἔγ-κοτος, ον, (ἐν, κότος) *bearing a grudge, spiteful, malicious.* II. ἔγκοτος is also found, like κότος, as Subst., *a grudge, hatred.*

ἐγ-κράζω, f. -κράξομαι: aor. 2 ἐνέκρᾰγον:—*to cry aloud at, to rate loudly.*

ἐγκράτεια, ἡ, *self-control*, Lat. *continentia*: and

ἐγκρᾰτεύομαι, Dep. *to exercise self-control.* From

ἐγ-κρᾰτής, ές, (ἐν, κράτος) *with a firm hold: stout, strong.* II. *having the mastery over, having possession of.* 2. *having control over oneself, self-disciplined*, Lat. *continens.* 3. in bad sense, *unyielding, stubborn.*

ἐγκρατῶς, Adv. of ἐγκρατής, *strongly, strictly: temperately.*

ἐγ-κρίνω, f. -κρῐνῶ, *to reckon in* or *among: to approve, admit, sanction.* II. *to reckon as.*

ἐγκροτέοισαι, Dor. for -έουσαι, fem. part. pl. of

ἐγ-κροτέω, f. ήσω, *to strike against*: of a dance, *to beat* or *keep time*:—Pass., πυγμαὶ ἐγκροτούμεναι fists *dashed one against the other.*

ἐγ-κρούω, f. σω, *to knock in: to strike against.* II. *to dance.*

ἐγ-κρύπτω, f. ψω, *to hide* or *conceal in.*

ἐγκρῠφιάζω, f. άσω, (ἐγκρύφιος) *to keep oneself hidden: to act underhand.*

ἐγκρυφιάς, άδος, ἡ, fem. Adj. *hidden* or *baked in the ashes*, of loaves. From

ἐγκρύφιος, ον, (ἐγκρύπτω) *hidden in.*

ἐγ-κτάομαι, Dep. with fut. ἐγκτήσομαι, pf. ἐγκέκτημαι, *to acquire possessions in a foreign country.* Hence

ἔγκτημα, ατος, τό, *property held in a foreign country.*

ἔγκτησις, εως, ἡ, (ἐγκτάομαι) *possession of property in a foreign country.*

ἐγ-κῠκάω, f. ήσω, *to mix up in.*

ἐγ-κύκλιος, ον, (ἐν, κύκλος) *circular, rounded.* II. *revolving in a circle, periodical, going round in succession*: hence *general, common.*

ἔγ-κυκλος, ον, (ἐν, κύκλος) *circular.*

ἐγ-κυκλόω, f. ώσω, (ἐν, κύκλος) *to move about in a circle*:—Pass. *to go round about*, and in trans. sense, *to surround, encircle.*

ἐγ-κύμων, ον, gen. ονος, (ἐν, κῦμα II) *pregnant.*

ἔγ-κῠος, ον, (ἐν, κύω) = ἐγκύμων.

ἐγ-κύπτω, f. ψω, *to stoop and peep in, to pry into.*

ἐγ-κύρω: impf. ἐνέκῡρον: fut. ἐγκύρσω: aor. 1 ἐνέκυρσα:—*to fall into* or *upon, light upon, meet with.*

ἐγκύρσαι, aor. 1 inf. of ἐγ-κύρω.

ἔγκῠτα, τά, Lacon. of ἔγκατα.

ἐγ-κωμιάζω, fut. άσω and άσομαι: pf. ἐγκεκωμίακα:—Pass., aor. 1 ἐνεκωμιάσθην: pf. ἐγκεκωμίασμαι:—(the augm. tenses are formed as if the Verb were a compd., and not derived directly from ἐγκώμιον):—*to praise, laud.*

ἐγκώμιον, τό, see ἐγκώμιος II. 2.

ἐγ-κώμιος, ον, (ἐν, κώμη) *at home, of the same village.* II. (ἐν, κῶμος) *belonging to a Bacchic festival* or *revel*: in which the victor was led home in procession. 2. as Subst. ἐγκώμιον (sub. ἔπος), τὸ, *a hymn in honour of the victor: a song of praise, panegyric.*

ἔγλυμμαι, pf. pass. of γλύφω.

ἔγνωκα, ἔγνωσμαι, pf. act. and pass. of γιγνώσκω.

ἔγνων, ως, ω, aor. 2 of γιγνώσκω.

ἐγνώσθην, aor. 1 pass. of γιγνώσκω.

ἐγ-ξέω, f. έσω, *to scrape.*

ἐγράφην [ᾰ], aor. 2 pass. of γράφω.

ἔγραψα, aor. 1 act. of γράφω.

ἐγρε-κύδοιμος, ον, (ἐγείρω, κύδοιμος) *strife-stirring.*

ἐγρε-μάχης, ου, ὁ, and **ἐγρέ-μᾰχος**, η, ον, (ἐγείρω, μάχη) *rousing the fight.*

ἐγρεσί-κωμος, ον, (ἐγείρω, κῶμος) *stirring up to revelry.*

ἔγρετο, 3 sing. Ep. aor. 2 med. of ἐγείρω; impera ἔγρεο; 3 sing. subj. ἔγρῃ; inf. ἐγρέσθαι.

ἐγρήγορα, *to be awake, watch*, intrans. pf. of ἐγείρω whence part. ἐγρηγορώς, 2 pl. imper. ἐγρήγορθε (Ep.

for ἐγρηγόρατε), inf. ἐγρηγόρθαι (Ep. for ἐγρηγορέναι):—plqpf. ἐγρηγόρη, 3 sing. ἐγρηγόρει. Homer uses the Ep. form ἐγρήγορθα in 3 pl. ἐγρηγόρθασι.

ἐγρηγορόων, Ep. part., as if from a pres. ἐγρηγοράω, formed from ἐγρήγορα, *watching, awake.*

ἐγρηγορτί, (ἐγρήγορα) Adv. *wakefully, awake.*

ἐγρήσσω, from ἐγρήγορα, *to be awake* or *watchful.*

ἔγροιτο, 3 sing. Ep. aor. 2 med. opt. of ἐγείρω.

ἐγρόμενος, Ep. aor. 2 med. part. of ἐγείρω.

ἐγ-χᾰλῑνόω, f. ώσω, *to put the bit in the mouth of, hold in check*:—Pass. *to have the bit in one's mouth.*

ἐγχανεῖται, 3 sing. fut. of ἐγ-χάσκω:—**ἐγχανῇ**, 3 sing. aor. 2 subj.

ἐγ-χᾰρίζομαι, f. ίσομαι, Dep. = χαρίζομαι.

ἐγ-χάσκω; (tenses formed from *ἐγ-χαίνω), fut. ἐγχᾰνοῦμαι: aor. 2 **ἐν-έχᾰνον**, inf. ἐγχανεῖν:—*to yawn* or *gape in one's face, to scoff at, jeer.*

ἐγ-χέζω, f. -χέσω also -χεσοῦμαι: pf. ἐγκέχοδα:—Lat. *incaco*: c. acc. *to be in a horrid fright at* one.

ἐγχειάων, Ep. gen. pl. of ἐγχείη.

ἐγχει-βρόμος, ον, (ἔγχος, βρέμω) *thundering with the spear.*

ἐγχείη, ἡ, (ἔγχος) *a spear, lance.*

ἐγχείῃ, Ep. for ἐγχέῃ, 3 sing. subj. of ἐγχέω.

ἐγχει-κέραυνος, ον, (ἔγχος, κεραυνός) *touching the thunderbolt.*

ἐγ-χειρέω, f. ήσω: aor. 1 ἐνεχείρησα: (ἐν, χείρ):—*to take in hand, undertake.* Hence

ἐγχείρημα, ατος, τό, *an undertaking*: and

ἐγχείρησις, εως, ἡ, *a taking in hand, an undertaking.*

ἐγχειρητέον, verb. Adj. of ἐγχείρεω, *one must undertake.*

ἐγχειρητής, οῦ, ὁ, (ἐγχειρέω) *one who takes in hand: an adventurer.*

ἐγχειρητικός, ή, όν, (ἐγχειρέω) *enterprising.*

ἐγ-χειρίδιος, ον, (ἐν, χείρ) *in the hand.* II. as Subst., ἐγχειρίδιον, τό, *a hand-knife, dagger.* 2. *a manual, hand-book.*

ἐγ-χειρίζω, f. ίσω Att. ιῶ, (ἐν, χείρ) *to put into one's hands, entrust* a thing to another:—Med. *to take in hand, take on oneself.*

ἐγ-χειρί-θετος, ον, (ἐν, χείρ, τίθημι) *put* or *delivered into one's hands.*

ἐγ-χείω, Ep. for ἐγχέω.

ἐγχέλειον, τό, Dim. of ἔγχελυς, *a little eel.*

ἐγχέλειος, ον, (ἔγχελυς) *of an eel.*

ἜΓΧΕΛΥΣ, υος, ἡ: pl. ἐγχέλυες, Att. ἐγχέλεις, εων:—*an eel*, Lat. *anguilla*:—proverb., ἐγχέλεις θηρᾶσθαι to be fond of fishing in troubled waters.

ἐγχεσί-μωρος, ον, *fighting with the spear.* (Deriv. uncertain.)

ἐγχέσ-πᾰλος, ον, (ἔγχος, πάλλω) *spear-brandishing.*

ἐγχεσ-φόρος, ον, (ἔγχος, φέρω) *spear-bearing.*

ἐγχεῦντα, Dor. for ἐγχέοντα, part. pr. of ἐγχέω.

ἐγ-χέω: f. -χεῶ: aor. 1 ἐνέχεα, Ep. ἐνέχευα: Pass., pf. ἐγκέχῠμαι:—*to pour in*:—Med. *to pour* or *flow in, be poured in.* II. *to fill by pouring in*; ἐγχέαι κρητῆρα *to fill the* bowl.

ἐγ-χθόνιος, ον, (ἐν, χθών) *in* or *of the country*, Lat. *indigena.*

ἜΓΧΟΣ, τό, *a spear, lance*, consisting of two parts, αἰχμή and δόρυ, *head* and *shaft.* II. generally, *a weapon, a sword, an arrow*:—metaph., φροντίδος ἔγχος *weapon* of thought.

ἔγχουσα, ἡ, = ἄγχουσα, q. v.

ἐγ-χραίνω, = sq.

ἐγ-χράω and **ἐγ-χραύω**, *to dash against*; ἐνέχραυεν ἐς τὸ πρόσωπον τὸ σκῆπτρον *he dashed* his staff in his face. The pf. pass. also occurs, ἔσαν πρός τινας καὶ ἄλλους ἐγκεχρημένοι (sc. πόλεμοι) there were wars *urged on* against others also.

ἐγ-χρέμπτομαι, Dep. *to expectorate.*

ἐγ-χρῄζω, *to want, have need*; τὰ ἐγχρῄζοντα *necessaries.*

ἐγ-χρίμπτω, f. ψω: aor. 1 ἐνέχριμψα part. ἐγχρίμψας:—Pass., aor. 1 ἐνεχρίμφθην part. ἐγχριμφθείς:—*to bring near to, to strike* or *dash against*; ἐγχρίμπτειν τὴν βάριν τῇ γῇ *to bring* the boat to land: absol. *to come to land*: hence *to approach*: also *to attack, press hard.* II. also intr. both in Act. and in Pass., *to fall upon, attack, pursue.*

ἐγ-χρίπτω, collat. form of ἐγχρίμπτω.

ἔγχριστος, ον, *applied as an unguent.* From

ἐγ-χρίω, *to rub in, to anoint.* II. like ἐγχρίμπτω, *to attack, assail.*

ἐγ-χρονίζω: f. ίσω Att. ιῶ: (ἐν, χρόνος):—*to be long about a thing, tarry, delay.*

ἐγ-χυτρίζω. f. σω, *to expose in a pan* or *pot.*

ἐγ-χωρέω, f. ήσω, *to give room* for doing a thing: *to make way for, yield: to concede, allow, admit.* 2. impers. ἐγχωρεῖ, *it is possible* or *permitted*; ἔτι ἐγχωρεῖ *there is* yet *time.*

ἐγ-χώριος, α, ον, also ος, ον, (ἐν, χώρα) *in* or *belonging to the country.*

ἔγ-χωρος, ον, = ἐγχώριος.

ἘΓΩ', Lat. *EGO*, Germ. *ICH*, our *I*: pers. Pron. of the first person, Ep. and Aeol. ἐγών before vowels:—strengthd. by compos. with enclit. γε, ἔγωγε, Lat. *equidem, I at least, for my part*; Dor. ἐγώγα and ἐγῶνγα: Boeot. ἰώνγα or ἰώγα:—gen. 'ΕΜΟΥ̃, enclit. ΜΟΥ, Lat. MEI, Ep. and Ion. ἐμέο, ἐμεῦ, μευ, Ep. also ἐμεῖο, ἐμέθεν, Aeol. and Dor. ἐμεῦς; Boeot. ἐμοῦς:—Dat. ἐμοί, enclit. μοί; Dor. ἐμίν:—Acc. ἐμέ, enclit. με. Dual, nom. and acc., ΝῺ, Ep. νῶϊ, Lat. *NOS*: gen. and dat. νῶν, Ep. νῶϊν. Plur., nom. ἡμεῖς, Dor. ἅμες, Aeol. ἄμμες:—gen. ἡμῶν, Ion. and Ep. ἡμέων, Ep. also ἡμείων, Dor. ἁμέων, Aeol. ἀμμέων:—dat. ἡμῖν, also ἧμιν or ἡμίν [ῐ], Dor. ἁμίν, ἄμμι, Aeol. ἀμμέσι:—acc., ἡμᾶς, Ion. ἡμέας, Ep. and Aeol. ἄμμε, Dor. ἁμέ.

ἔγωγα, Dor. for ἔγωγε.

ἐγᾦδα, Att. crasis for ἐγὼ οἶδα.

ἐγᾦμαι, Att. crasis for ἐγὼ οἶμαι.

ἐγών, **ἐγώνγα**, Dor. for ἐγώ, ἔγωγε.

ἐδάην, ης, η, aor. 2 of ΔΑΩ.

ἔδαισα, -άμην, aor. 1 act. and med. of δαίνυμι.

ἔδᾰκον, aor. 2 of δάκνω.
ἐδάμην [ᾰ], aor. 2 pass. of δαμάω.
ἐδᾰνός, ή, όν, (ἔδω) *eatable.*
ἑδᾰνός, ή, όν, (ἁδεῖν) *pleasant, grateful, agreeable* or *excellent.*
ἐδάρην [ᾰ], aor. 2 pass. of δείρω.
ἔδαρθον, aor. 2 of δαρθάνω.
ἔδαρκον, metath. for ἔδρᾰκον, aor. 2 of δέρκομαι.
ἐδασάμην, aor. 1 of δατέομαι.
ἐδᾰφίζω, f. ίσω Att. ιῶ, *to make level: to level with the earth.* From
ἔδᾰφος, εος, τό, *the bottom,* or *base* of anything: *the ground:* ἔδαφος νηός *the bottom* or *hold* of a ship: also *the ground-floor, pavement: level ground.* (From the same root as δάπ-εδον, τάπ-ης.)
ἔδδεισα, Ep. for ἔδεισα, aor. 1 of δείδω.
ἐδέγμην, Ep. aor. 2 of δέχομαι.
ἐδεδέατο, Ion. for ἐδέδεντο, 3 pl. plqpf. pass. of δέω.
ἐδεδέγμην, plqpf. of δέχομαι.
ἐδεδήκειν, plqpf. of δέω, *to bind.*
ἐδέδισαν, 3 pl. plqpf. of δείδω.
ἐδεδμήατο Ion. 3 plur., and **ἐδέδμητο** 3 sing., plqpf. pass. of δέμω.
ἐδεδοίκεσαν, 3 pl. plqpf. of δείδω.
ἐδεδόμην, plqpf. pass. of δίδωμι.
ἐδεδωκεῖν, plqpf. of δίδωμι.
ἐδεήθην, aor. 1 pass. (in med. sense) of δέω, *to want.*
ἐδέησα, aor. 1 of δέω, *to want.*
ἐδέθην, aor. 1 pass. of δέω, *to bind.*
ἐδείδῐμεν, -ῐσαν, Ep. 1 and 3 pl. plqpf. of δείδω.
ἔδειμα, aor. 1 of δέμω.
ἔδειξα, aor. 1 of δείκνυμι.
ἔδειρα, aor. 1 of δέρω.
ἔδεισα, aor. 1 of δείδω.
ἔδεκτο, Ep. 3 sing. sync. aor. 2 of δέχομαι.
ἐδέμεν, Ep. for ἔδειν, inf. of ἔδω.
ἔδεξα, -άμην, Ion. for ἔδειξα, -άμην, aor. 1 act. and med. of δείκνυμι; but **ἐδεξάμην** also aor. 1 of δέχομαι.
ἔδεσμα, ατος, τό, (ἔδω) *food, meat, a dish.*
ἐδεστής, οῦ, ὁ, (ἔδω) *an eater, devourer.*
ἐδεστός, ή, όν, (ἔδω) *to be eaten, eatable.* II. *eaten: consumed.*
ἐδεύησει, aor. 1 of δεύω, *to need.*
ἐδήδεσμαι, pf. pass. of ἐσθίω.
ἐδήδοκα. pf. act. of ἐσθίω.
ἐδήδοται, 3 sing. pf. pass. of ἔδω.
ἐδηδώς, pf. part. of ἔδω.
ἐδηΐουν, Att. ἐδῄουν, impf. of δηΐω.
ἔδησα, aor. 1 of δέω, *to bind:* also Ep. aor. 1 of δέω, *to want.*
ἐδητύς, ύος, ή, (ἔδω) *meat, food.* [ῠ]
ἐδήχθην, aor. 1 pass. of δάκνω.
ἐδιαίτησα, aor. 1 of διαιτάω.
ἐδῄωσα, ἐδῃώθην, aor. 1 act. and pass. of δηΐω.
ἐδίδαξα, poët. ἐδιδάσκησα, aor. 1 of διδάσκω.
ἐδίδουν, impf. of δίδωμι, formed from διδόω.
ἐδιζήμην, impf. of δίζημαι.
ἐδίηνα, aor. 1 of διαίνω.
ἔδικον, v. δικεῖν.
ἐδίνευσα, ἐδίνησα, aor. 1 of δινεύω, δινέω.
ἐδίψησα, aor. 1 of διψάω.
ἐδίωξα, ἐδιώχθην, aor. 1 act. and pass. of διώκω.
ἔδμεναι, Ep. pres. inf. of ἔδω.
ἐδμήθην, aor. 1 pass. of δαμάω.
ἑδνάομαι, Dep. = ἑδνόω. From
ἝΔΝΑ, Ep. ἔεδνα, τά, *nuptial gifts,* 1. *from the suitor to the bride.* 2. *from the suitor to the bride's father.* 3. *a portion* or *dowry,* given to the bride by her parents, also φέρνη or προίξ. 4. *wedding presents* to the wedded pair from their guests. Hence
ἑδνόω, f. ώσω, *to promise* or *betroth for presents.* Hence
ἑδνωτής Ep. ἐεδνωτής, οῦ, ὁ, *a betrother,* of a *father who portions a bride.*
ἐδόθην, aor. 1 pass. of δίδωμι.
ἐδοκεῦμες, Dor. for ἐδοκοῦμεν, 1 pl. impf. of δοκέω.
ἐδόκησα, aor. 1 of δοκέω.
ἐδοκίμασα, ἐδοκιμάσθην, aor. 1 act. and pass. of δοκιμάζω.
ἔδομαι, fut. of ἔδω and ἐσθίω.
ἔδομεν, ἔδοτε, ἔδοσαν (Dor. ἔδον), aor. 2 pl. of δίδωμι.
ἔδοντι, Dor. for ἔδουσι.
ἔδοξα, aor. 1 of δοκέω.
ἐδοξώθην, aor. 1 pass. of δοξόω.
ἕδος, εος, τό, (ἕζομαι) *a thing to sit on, a seat.* 2. *a seat, abode,* esp. of the gods. 3. *a foundation, base, the pedestal of a statue:* also *the statue* itself. II. *the act of sitting;* οὐχ ἕδος ἐστί 'tis no *time for sitting still.*
ἑδοῦμαι, fut. of ἕζομαι.
ἕδρα Ep. and Ion. ἕδρη, ή, (ἕζομαι) *any seat, a chair, bench,* etc. 2. *a seat, abode,* esp. of the gods, *a temple, altar.* 3. *a foundation, base.* II. *a sitting still, being idle* or *inactive, delay;* οὐκ ἕδρας ἀκμή it is not the season *for sitting still.* 2. *a sitting, session.* III. *the seat, fundament.*
ἔδρᾰθον, poët. for ἔδαρθον, aor. 2 of δαρθάνω.
ἑδραῖος, α, ον, (ἕδρα) *sitting, sedentary.* II. *steadfast, firm, constant.*
ἑδραιόω, f. ώσω, = ἑδριάω. Hence
ἑδραίωμα, ατος, τό, *a foundation, base.*
ἐδρακόμην, aor. 2 med. of δέρκομαι.
ἔδρᾰκον, ἐδράκην, aor. 2 act. and pass. of δέρκομαι.
ἔδρᾰμον, aor. 2 of τρέχω.
ἔδρᾱν, aor. 2 of διδράσκω.
ἕδρᾰνον, τό, (ἕδρα) *a seat, abode, dwelling*
ἔδρᾱσα, aor. 1 of δράω.
ἕδρη, Ep. and Ion. for ἕδρα.
ἔδρησα, Ion. for ἔδρᾱσα, aor. 1 of δράω.
ἑδριάομαι, Pass. (ἕδρα) *to sit:* Ep. inf. ἑδριάασθαι; Ep. 3 pl. impf. ἑδριόωντο.
ἑδρο-στρόφος, ὁ, (ἕδρα, στρέφω) *a wrestler who throws his adversary by a cross-buttock.*
ἔδρυψα, ἐδρύφθην, aor. 1 act. and pass. of δρύπτω.
ἔδῡν, 1 sing. aor. 2 of δύω; but also Ep. for ἔδυσαν, 3 pl. of same tense.

ἐδυνάσθην or -ήθην, aor. 1 of δύναμαι.

ἐδυνέατο, Ion. 3 pl. impf. of δύναμαι.

ἐδύσεο, -ετο, Ep. for ἐδύσω, -ατο, 2 and 3 sing. aor. 1 med. of δύω.

ἐδυστύχησα, aor. 1 of δυστυχέω.

ἜΔΩ, Ion. impf. ἔδεσκον: fut. ἔδομαι: pf. act. ἐδήδα, pass. ἐδήδομαι:—these are all Epic forms; for the Att. tenses, see ἐσθίω:—*to eat, devour:* metaph., οἶκον ἔδουσι *eat up*, i. e. *consume, waste*, house and home; θυμὸν ἔδοντες *eating* their heart, i. e. *wasting, consuming* their spirit. Hence

ἐδωδή, ἡ, *food meat, victuals* for men: *fodder* for cattle: *a bait* for fish. Hence

ἐδώδιμος, ον, *eatable:* τὰ ἐδώδιμα *provisions.*

ἔδωκα, aor. 1 of δίδωμι.

ἑδώλιον, τό, (ἕδος) *a seat, dwelling, abode.* II. in a ship, *the seat of the rowers, a rowing-bench*, Lat. *transtrum.*

ἕε, poët. for ἕ, *him*, acc. of οὗ.

ἔεδνα, ἐεδνόω, -ωτής, Ep. for ἕδνα, ἑδνόω, -ωτής.

ἐείδομαι, Ep. for εἴδομαι, Med. of εἴδω.

ἐεικοσά-βοιος, ἐείκοσι, ἐεικόσορος, ἐεικοστός, Ep. for εἰκ-.

ἐείλεον, Ep. for εἴλεον, impf. of εἰλέω.

ἔειπα, ας, ε, **ἔειπον**, ες, ε, Ep. for εἶπα, εἶπον.

ἔεις, Ep. for εἷς.

ἐείσαο, ἐείσατο, ἐεισάσθην, Ep. 2 and 3 sing., and 3 dual., aor. 1 of εἶμι *ibo.*

ἐείσατο, ἐεισάμενος, Ep. 3 sing. and part. aor. 1 of *εἴδω.

ἐέλδομαι, ἐέλδωρ, Ep. for ἔλδομαι, ἔλδωρ.

ἐέλμαι, ἐελμένος, pf. pass. ind. and part. of εἴλω.

ἐέλπομαι, Ep. for ἔλπομαι.

ἐέλσαι, Ep. for ἔλσαι, aor. 1 inf. of εἴλω.

ἐέργαθον, Ep. for εἴργαθον.

ἔεργε, ἐεργμένος, ἐέργνυμι, ἐέργω, Ep. for εἰργ-.

ἐερμένος, pf. part. pass. of εἴρω.

ἐέρση, ἐερσήεις, Ep. for ἑρσή, ἑρσήεις.

ἔερτο, Ep. 3 sing. plqpf. pass. of εἴρω.

ἐέρχατο, Ep. 3 pl. plqpf. pass. of εἴργω.

ἐέσσατο, Ep. 3 sing. aor. 1 med. of ἕννυμι.

ἐέσσατο, Ep. 3 sing. aor. 1 med. of ἵζω.

ἔεστο, Ep. 3 sing. plqpf. pass. of ἕννυμι.

ἐζευγμένος, pf. part. pass. of ζεύγνυμι.

ἔζευξα, ἐζεύχθην, aor. 1 act. and pass. of ζεύγνυμι.

ἝΖΟΜΑΙ, fut. ἑδοῦμαι: impf. and aor. 2 ἑζόμην: (the Root is ἙΔ-, see ἕδος):—*to seat oneself, sit;* ἐπὶ χθονὶ ἑζέσθην *they sank* to the earth.

ἐζύγην [ῠ], aor. 2 of ζεύγνυμι.

ἔζωσμαι, pf. pass. of ζώννυμι.

ἔῃ, Ion. for ᾖ, 3 sing. subj. of εἰμί *sum.*

ἑῇ, fem. of ἑός, *his.*

ἧκε, Ep. for ἧκε, 3 sing. aor. 1 of ἵημι.

ἔην, Ep. for ἦν, 3 sing. impf. of εἰμί *sum.*

ἑήνδᾰνε, Ep. for ἥνδανε, 3 sing. impf. of ἁνδάνω.

ἐῆος, gen. masc. of ἐΰς, *good, brave, noble.*

ἕης, Ep. for ἧς, gen. fem. of ὅς, ἥ, ὅ, *who, what:*—but ἑῆς gen. fem. of ἑός, *his.*

ἔησθα, Ep. for ἦς, 2 sing. impf. of εἰμί *sum.*

ἔῃσι, Ep. for ᾖ, 3 sing. subj. of εἰμί *sum.*

ἔθαλψα, ἐθάλφθην, aor. 1 act. and pass. of θάλπω.

ἔθᾰνον, aor. 2 of θνήσκω.

ἐθάς, άδος, ὁ, ἡ, (ἔθος) *accustomed, used.*

ἔθαψα, ἐθάφθην, aor. 1 act. and pass. of θάπτω.

ἐθεησάμην, Ion. aor. 1 of θεάομαι.

ἜΘΕΙΡΑ, ἡ, *hair;* in Homer, *a horse's mane*, or *the horsehair crest* on helmets: *a lion's mane.* Hence

ἐθειράζω, f. άσω, *to wear long hair.*

ἐθείρω, *to tend, take care of, till.* (Deriv. uncertain.)

ἐθελημός, όν, (ἐθέλω) *willing, voluntary.*

ἐθέλησθα, for ἐθέλῃς, Ep. 2 sing. subj. of ἐθέλω.

ἐθελητός, ή, όν, (ἐθέλω) *willed, voluntary.*

ἔθελξα, ἐθέλχθην, aor. 1 act. and pass. of θέλγω.

ἐθελο-, in compos., signifies *voluntarily* or *gladly.*

ἐθελό-δουλος, ον. *a willing slave.*

ἐθελο-θρησκεία, ἡ, (ἐθελο-, θρησκεύω) *will-worship, superstitious observance.*

ἐθελοκᾰκέω, f. ήσω, *to be slack in duty, play the coward purposely: to be beaten on purpose.* From

ἐθελό-κᾰκος, ον, *wilfully bad, neglectful of one's duty*, esp. in war, *cowardly.*

ἐθελοντηδόν, (ἐθέλω) Adv. *voluntarily.*

ἐθελοντήν, (ἐθέλω) Adv. *voluntarily.*

ἐθελοντήρ, ῆρος, ὁ, (ἐθέλω) *a volunteer.*

ἐθελοντής, οῦ, ὁ, (ἐθέλω) *a volunteer.*

ἐθελοντί, Adv. = ἐθελοντηδόν.

ἐθέλοντι, Dor. for ἐθέλουσι, 3 pl. of ἐθέλω.

ἐθελοπονία, ἡ, *love of work, diligence.* From

ἐθελό-πονος, ον, (ἐθελο-, πόνος) *willing to work.*

ἐθελο-πρόξενος, ον, (ἐθελο-, πρόξενος) *one who voluntarily charges himself with the office of πρόξενος* (q. v.) to a foreign state.

ἐθελ-ουργός, όν, (ἐθελο-, *ἔργω) *willing to work.*

ἐθελούσιος, α, ον, (ἐθέλω) *voluntarily.* II. of things, *optional.*

ἘΘΕΛΩ: impf. ἤθελον: fut. ἐθελήσω: aor. 1 ἠθέλησα; pf. ἠθέληκα:—like θέλω, *to will, be willing, wish, desire:* sometimes also merely as the sign of the fut., *will* or *shall.* 2. with a negat., almost like δύναμαι, *to be able, have the power;* as of a stream, οὐδ' ἔθελε προρέειν ἀλλ' ἴσχετο. 3. *to be wont* or *accustomed, to do* a thing *readily.* 4. *to mean, purport*, Lat. *volo;* often in phrases, such as, τί ἐθέλει τὸ τέρας; Lat. *quid sibi vult?* what *means*, what *purports* the prodigy?

ἔθεμεν, 1 pl. aor. 2 of τίθημι.

ἕθεν, Ep. and Att. poët. gen. for ἕο, οὗ, *of him, of her.*

ἔθεντο, 3 pl. aor. 2 med. of τίθημι.

ἐθέρμηνα, aor. 2 of θερμαίνω.

ἔθετε, ἔθεσαν, 2 and 3 pl. aor. 2 of τίθημι.

ἔθευ, Ion. for ἔθου, 2 sing. aor. 2 med. of τίθημι.

ἐθηεῖτο, ἐθηεύμεθα, ἐθηεῦντο, Ion. for ἐθεᾶτο, ἐθεώμεθα, ἐθεῶντο, 3 sing., 1 pl., 3 pl. of θεάομαι.

ἐθηεύμεσθα, Ion. 1 pl. of θεάομαι.

ἐθηήσαντο, Ion. for ἐθεάσαντο, 3 pl. aor. 1 med. of θεάομαι.

ἔθηκα, 1 sing. aor. 1 of *τίθημι.*

ἔθην, aor. 1 pass. of ἵημι: but **ἔθην,** aor. 2 act. of ·ἵθημι.

ἔθιγον, aor. 2 of θιγγάνω.

ἐθίζω, f. ίσω Att. ιῶ: aor. 1 εἴθισα: pf. εἴθικα:—Pass., aor. 1 εἰθίσθην: pf. εἴθισμαι: (ἔθος):—*to accustom, use:*—Pass. *to be accustomed* or *used to.* Hence

ἐθιστέον, verb. Adj. *one must accustom.*

ἔθλᾰσα, aor. 1 of θλάω.

ἔθλιψα, aor. 1 of θλίβω.

ἐθν-άρχης, ου, ὁ, (ἔθνος, ἄρχω) *a ruler of a nation: prefect: an ethnarch.*

ἐθνικός, ή, όν, *national.* II. *foreign: gentile:*—Adv. -κῶς, *like the Gentiles.* From

ἜΘΝΟΣ, εος, τό, *a company, body of men.* 2. *a race, tribe.* 3. *a nation, people; τὰ ἔθνη the nations, Gentiles,* i. e. all except Jews and Christians. 4. *a particular class* of men, *a caste.*

ἔθορον, aor. 2 of θρώσκω.

ἜΘΟΣ, εος, τό, *custom, usage, manners, habit.*

ἔθραυσα, aor. 1 of θραύω.

ἔθρεξα, aor. 1 of τρέχω.

ἐθρέφθην, aor. 1 pass. of τρέφω.

ἔθρεψα, aor. 1 of τρέφω.

ἐθρήνευν, Dor. for ἐθρήνουν, impf. of θρηνέω.

ἔθρισα, poët. for ἐθέρισα, aor. 1 of θερίζω.

ἜΘΩ, *to be accustomed, to be wont.* The Att. use the pf. εἴωθα Ion. ἔωθα as pres., and the plqpf. εἰώθειν Ion. ἐώθεα as impf.:—*to be wont* or *accustomed, to be in the habit:* part. εἰωθώς as Adj., *accustomed, customary, usual; τὸ εἰωθός one's custom.*

ΕΙ', a conditional Particle, Dor. and Ep. **αἰ**:—Lat. *SI, if:* with optat. or indic.:—see εἰ γάρ or αἰ γάρ, and εἴ-θε.

εἶ, Att. 2 sing. of εἶμι *ibo.*

εἶα, and trisyll. **ἔϊα,** Interj., Lat. *eia, on! up! away!* also *come on then! εἶα νυν, well now.*

εἴᾱ, 3 sing. impf. of ἐάω; also 2 sing. imperat. pres.

εἰάθην, εἴᾱμαι, aor. 1 and pf. pass. of ἐάω.

εἰᾰμενή, ἡ, *a river-side pasture, meadow.* (Deriv. uncertain.)

εἰ ἄν, Ep. and Ion. εἴ κε, contr. into ἐάν, ἤν, and ἄν.

εἰᾱνός, ή, όν, Ep. for ἑανός.

εἶαρ, εἰᾰρῑνός, Ep. for ἔαρ, ἐαρινός.

εἰαρό-μασθος, ον, (εἶαρ, μασθός) *with youthful breasts.*

εἴᾱς, 2 sing. impf. of ἐάω;—**εἴᾱσα,** aor. 1 of the same.

εἴασκον, Ion. for εἴων, impf. of ἐάω.

εἵᾰται, εἵᾰτο, Ep. for Ion. ἕαται, ἕατο, which is for ἧνται, ἧντο, 3 pl. pres. and impf. of ἧμαι.

εἵᾰτο, Ion. for εἶντο, 3 sing. plqpf. med. of ἕννυμι.

ΕΙ'ΒΩ, Ep. form of λείβω, *to drop, let fall in drops:*—Med. *to trickle* or *run down.*

εἰ γάρ, *for if;* and expressing a wish, *O if..! O that..! would that..!* Lat. *utinam!*

εἴ-γε, *if at least, if then,* Lat. *si-quidem.*

εἰ γοῦν, *if at any rate,* implying that the thing is unlikely.

εἰ δ' ἄγε, used in cheering, *on then, come on!* The phrase is elliptic, and would be in full, εἰ δ' ἐθέλεις, ἄγε.

εἰδάλιμος, η, ον, (εἶδος) *shapely, comely.* II. *like, looking like.*

εἶδαρ, ατος, τό, (ἔδω) *food, meat, victuals* for men: *fodder* for cattle: *a bait* for fish.

εἰδείην opt., and **εἰδέναι** inf. of οἶδα; v. *εἴδω B.

εἰ δὲ μή, elliptic for εἰ δὲ μὴ τοῦτό ἐστι, *if otherwise,* Lat. *sin aliter.*

εἰδέω, for εἰδῶ, subj. of οἶδα; v. *εἴδω B.

εἰ δή, *if now, seeing that,* expressing conviction: also in indirect questions, *whether now.*

εἰδήμων, ονος, ὁ, ἡ, (*εἴδω) *knowing* or *expert in* a thing.

εἰδησέμεν, Ep. for εἰδήσειν, fut. inf. of *εἴδω B.

εἰδήσω, fut. of *εἴδω.

εἴδομες, Dor. for εἴδομεν, 1 pl. aor. 2 of *εἴδω A.

εἶδον, aor. 2 of *εἴδω A.

εἶδος, εος, τό, (*εἴδω) *that which is seen, the form, shape, figure,* Lat. *species.* II. generally, *a form, sort, particular kind: a particular state* or *plan of action.* III. *species,* opp. to *genus.*

εἰδόσι, dat. pl. of εἰδώς, part. of οἶδα, v. *εἴδω B.

εἰδότα, acc. sing. of εἰδώς, part. of οἶδα, v. *εἴδω B.

εἰδότως, Adv. of εἰδώς, part. of οἶδα, *knowingly.*

εἰδυῖα, fem. nom. part. of οἶδα, v. *εἴδω B.

εἰδύλλιον, τό, Dim. of εἶδος, *a short, descriptive poem,* mostly *on pastoral subjects, an idyll.*

***ΕΙ'ΔΩ** (or more properly ϜΙ'ΔΩ, the Lat. *VIDEO*), *to see,* obsol. in pres. act., which is supplied by ὁράω: its meanings fall under two heads, one *to see,* the other *to know.*

A. *to see,* mostly in aor. 2 **εἶδον,** Ep. ἴδον, ἴδεσκον; subj. ἴδω, Ep. also ἴδωμι; inf. ἰδεῖν, Ep. also ἰδέειν; part. ἰδών. The same sense belongs also to aor. 2 med. εἰδόμην Ep. ἰδόμην; imperat. **ἰδοῦ**; subj. ἴδωμαι; inf. ἰδέσθαι. The aor. 2 imper. med. ἰδοῦ is mostly an exclamation, *see! lo! behold!* Lat. *ecce.* Ὁράω is used as pres., ἑώρᾱκα or ἑόρᾱκα, as pf., ὄψομαι as fut. II. in Ep. and Ion. we find Pass. and Med. εἴδομαι: aor. 1 εἰσάμην, Ep. also ἐεισάμην, αο, ατο, in pass. sense, *to be seen, appear, seem,* Lat. *videor; εἴδεται ἄστρα* the stars *are visible, appear:* hence, 2. *to have* or *take the appearance of* a thing: and c. dat. *to make oneself like; ἐείσατο φθογγὴν Πολίτῃ she made herself like* Polites in voice.

B. *to know:*—the pf. **οἶδα,** *I have seen,* is used as a pres. in the sense *I know,* (for what one *has seen, one knows*); so also plqpf. *I had seen,* in sense of impf. *I knew:*—indic. οἶδα, οἶσθα (poët. also οἶδας); 1 pl. ἴσμεν (Ep. and Dor. ἴδμεν), ἴστε, ἴσᾱσι:—imperat. ἴσθι, ἴστω:—subj. **εἰδῶ,** Ep. also ἰδέω;—opt. εἰδείην;—inf. **εἰδέναι,** Ep. ἴδμεναι and ἴδμεν:—part. **εἰδώς,** Ep. fem. **ἰδυῖα**:—impf., **ᾔδειν,** Ep. ᾔδεα, Att. ᾔδη; Ep. 2 sing. ἠείδης for **ᾔδης,** Att. ᾔδησθα; 3 sing., Ep. ἠείδη, Att. ᾔδη, ᾔδειν; plur., ᾔδειμεν, ᾔδειτε or ᾔδετε, ᾔδεισαν or ᾔδεσαν, Att. ᾖσμεν, ᾖστε, ᾖσαν (Ep. ἴσαν):—fut. εἴσομαι, more rarely and mostly Ep. εἰδήσω. *To know*; εὖ οἶδα *I know* well; εὖ ἴσθι *know well, be assured*; νοήματα, μήδεα οἶδε he *is knowing, skilled in* counsels; and so with Adjs., πεπνυμένα, φίλα, ἄρτια εἰδέναι, etc., *to be skilled in* prudent, fitting things, etc.; often in Part.; so also, εὖ εἰδώς well *skilled*. In this sense *to be skilled in*, the word also takes a genit. in Homer, τόξων εὖ εἰδώς *cunning with* the bow. Also with acc., χάριν εἰδέναι τινί *to acknowledge a debt to another, thank him*:—οἶδ' ὅτι, οἶσθ' ὅτι, *I know, you know it well*:—also, οἶσθ' ὅτι, οἶσθ' ὃ and οἶσθ' ὡς, followed by imperat., give a command without specifying what, as if this was known before; esp. in phrase, οἶσθ' ὃ δρᾶσον, for δρᾶσον, οἶσθ' ὅ, do, *thou knowest* what.

εἰδωλεῖον, τό, (εἴδωλον) *an idol's temple.*

εἰδωλό-θῠτος, ον, (εἴδωλον, θύω) *sacrificed to idols*; as Subst., τὸ εἰδωλόθυτον *meat offered to idols.*

εἰδωλολατρία, ἡ, *idolatry*. From

εἰδωλο-λάτρης, ου, ὁ, ἡ, (εἴδωλον, λάτρις) *an idol-worshipper, an idolater.*

εἴδωλον, τό, (εἶδος) *a shape, image, spectre, phantom*; βροτῶν εἴδωλα καμόντων *the phantoms* of dead men. II. *an image in the mind, idea: a vision, a fancy.* III. *an image, portrait*, esp. *of a god*: hence *an idol, false god.*

εἰδώς, part. of οἶδα, pf. of *εἴδω B.

εἶεν, Att. for εἴησαν, 3 pl. opt. of εἰμί *sum.*

εἶεν, Particle, *well, good, proceed*, Lat. *esto.*

εἴην, opt. of εἰμί *sum.*

εἵην, aor. 2 opt. of ἵημι.

εἶθαρ, Adv. (εὐθύς) *at once, forthwith.*

εἴ-θε, Dor. and Ep. αἴ-θε, Interj. *O that! would that!* Lat. *utinam!*

εἴθην, Ion. ἔθην, aor. 1 pass. of ἵημι.

εἰθίζω, f. ίσω, poët. for ἐθίζω,

εἴθισα, εἴθικα, aor. 1 and pf. of ἐθίζω.

εἶκα, Att. for ἔοικα.

εἷκα, pf. of ἵημι.

εἰκάζω, f. άσω: aor. 1 ᾔκασα Ion. εἴκασα:—Pass., aor. 1 ᾐκάσθην: pf. ᾔκασμαι Ion. εἴκασμαι: (εἰκός):—*to make like to, represent by a likeness*:—Pass. *to be like, resemble.* II. *to liken, compare: to infer from comparison, to conjecture, guess.*

εἰκᾰθον, poët. aor. 2 of εἴκω *to yield*; subj. εἰκάθω; inf. εἰκαθεῖν; part. εἰκαθών.

εἰκαῖος, α, ον, (εἰκῇ) *without purpose: random, hasty.* II. *common, worthless.*

εἰκάς, άδος, ἡ, (εἴκοσι) *the twentieth day of the month* (sub. ἡμέρα).

εἰκᾰσία, ἡ, (εἰκάζω) *a likeness, image: a conjecture.*

εἴκασμα, ατος, τό, (εἰκάζω) *a likeness.*

εἰκασμός, οῦ, ὁ, (εἰκάζω) *a conjecturing.*

εἰκαστής, οῦ, ὁ, (εἰκάζω) *one who conjectures, a guesser, diviner.*

εἰκαστός, ή, όν, (εἰκάζω) *to be compared, like.*

εἴκᾰτι, Dor. for εἴκοσι.

εἰκελ-όνειρος, ον, (εἴκελος, ὄνειρος) *dream-like.*

εἴκελος, η, ον, (εἰκός) *like, after the fashion of.*

εἰκελό-φωνος, ον, (εἴκελος, φωνή) *of like voice.*

εἰκέναι, Att. for ἐοικέναι, inf. of ἔοικα.

ΕἸΚΗ͂, Adv. *without plan* or *purpose, heedlessly, rashly, at random*, Lat. *temerè.*

εἰκονίζω, f. σω, (εἰκών) *to mould into form.* Hence

εἰκόνισμα, ματος, τό, *an image, copy.*

εἰκός Ion. **οἰκός**, ότος, τό, neut. part. of ἔοικα, Lat. *veri-simile, like truth, likely, probable, reasonable, fair equitable*; παρὰ τὸ εἰκός *unreasonable.*

εἰκοσά-βοιος, Ep. **ἐεικοσάβοιος**, ον, (εἴκοσι, βοῦς) *worth twenty oxen.*

εἰκοσα-ετής, ές, (εἴκοσι, ἔτος) *of twenty years.*

εἰκοσάκις, (εἴκοσι) Adv. *twenty times.*

εἰκοσά-μηνος, ον, (εἴκοσι, μήν) *twenty months old.*

ΕἼΚΟΣΙ before a vowel, **εἴκοσιν**, Ep. **ἐείκοσι**, Dor. **εἴκατι**, οἱ, αἱ, τά, indecl. *twenty*, Lat. *viginti.*

εἰκοσι-νήρῐτος, ον, *twenty-fold without dispute*; εἰκοσινήριτ' ἄποινα *a twenty-fold* ransom.

εἰκοσί-πηχυς, υ, (εἴκοσι, πῆχυς) *of twenty cubits.*

εἰκοσ-όργυιος, ον, (εἴκοσι, ὀργυιά) *of twenty fathoms.*

εἰκόσορος, poët. **ἐεικ-**, ον, (εἴκοσι) *with twenty oars.*

εἰκοστή, ἡ, see εἰκοστός II.

εἰκοστο-λόγος, ὁ, ἡ, (εἰκοστή, λέγω) *one who collects the tax of a twentieth, a tax* or *toll collector.*

εἰκοστός Ep. **ἐεικοστός**, ή, όν, *the twentieth.* II. **εἰκοστή**, ἡ, *a tax of a twentieth*, Lat. *vicesima.*

εἰκοσ-ώρῠγος, ον, (εἴκοσι, ὀργυία) *of twenty fathoms.*

εἰκότως, Adv. of εἰκός, *in all likelihood, probably, naturally: fairly, reasonably.*

ἔικτον, Ep. for ἐοίκατον, 3 dual of ἔοικα.

ἔικτο, ἐΐκτην, Ep. for ἐοίκει, ἐοικάτην, 3 sing. and 3 dual. plpqf.

***ΕἼΚΩ**, fut. εἴξω, *to be like*; 3 sing. impf. εἶκε, Att. ᾗκε, *it was like* or *likely, seemed good*:—but the pf. ἔοικα, plqpf. ἐῴκειν were used for the pres. and impf.; see ἔοικα.

ΕἼΚΩ, f. ξω: aor. 1 εἶξα: poët. aor. 2 εἴκᾰθον:—*to yield, give way to, draw back, retire.* 2. *to submit to, obey, follow*; ᾧ θυμῷ εἴξας *following* his own bent; πενίῃ εἴκων *urged* by poverty: hence *to yield to* another *in* a thing, *to be weaker* or *inferior.* II. trans. *to yield up, abandon, resign: to grant, allow.* III. impers. *it is allowable, possible.*

εἰκών, ἡ, gen. όνος, acc. όνα: Ion. gen. εἰκοῦς, acc. εἰκώ, acc. pl. εἰκούς: (*εἴκω, ἔοικα):—*a figure, image, likeness.* II. *a semblance, phantom, wraith.* 2. *a similé.*

εἰκώς, part. of ἔοικα, pf. of *εἴκω, *to be like.*

εἰλαδόν, Adv. (εἴλη) = ἰληδόν, *in a troop.*

εἰλᾰπῐνάζω, (εἰλαπίνη) only used in pres. *to feast in a large company, to be a boon-companion.* Hence

εἰλᾰπῐναστής, οῦ, ὁ, *a banqueter, boon-companion.*

εἰλᾰπίνη, ἡ, *a feast* or *banquet given by a single host*, opp. to ἔρανος. (Deriv. uncertain.)

εἶλαρ, αρος, τό, (εἴλω) *a covering: a protection, shelter*; εἶλαρ νηῶν τε καὶ αὐτῶν *a shelter for* ship and crew: but εἶλαρ κύματος *a defence against* the wave.

εἰλάτῐνος, η, ον, Ep. for ἐλάτινος, *of fir* or *pine.*

εἴλᾱχα, Dor. for **εἴληχα**, pf. of λαγχάνω.
εἴλεγμαι, for λέλεγμαι, pf. pass. of λέγω.
Εἰλείθυια, ἡ, *Ilithyia*, (from ἐληλυθυῖα, fem. part. pf. of ἔρχομαι) the goddess of child-birth, *who comes to aid* those who are in travail; the same as the Roman *Lucīna*, later made identical with Diana.
εἷλεν, **εἵλετο**, 3 sing. aor. 2 act. and med. of αἱρέω.
εἷλευ, Dor. for εἵλου, 2 sing. aor. 2 med. of αἱρέω.
εἰλεῦντο, Ep. 3 pl. imp. pass. of εἰλέω.
εἰλέω Att. εἱλέω, lengthd. form of εἴλω.
εἴλη, ἡ, = ἴλη, *a troop, company.*
εἵλη, ἡ, *the sun's warmth: warmth*; see ἕλη.
εἴληγμαι, pf. pass. of λαγχάνω.
εἰληδόν and **εἰληδά**, Adv. (εἴλη) = ἰληδόν, *in troops* or *companies.* II. (εἰλέω) *by coiling round.*
εἰλήλουθα, **εἰληλούθειν**, Ep. for ἐλήλυθα, ἐληλύθειν pf. and plqpf. of ἔρχομαι: **εἰλήλουθμεν**, Ep. for ἐληλύθαμεν, 1 plur. pf.
εἴλημμαι, pf. pass. of λαμβάνω.
εἴληφα, pf. of λαμβάνω.
εἴληχα, pf. of λαγχάνω.
εἰλικρίνεια, ἡ, *pureness: sincerity.* From
εἰλῐ-κρῑνής, (εἵλη, κρίνω) *examined by the sun's light, tested:* hence, 1. *unmixed: pure, uncorrupted*, Lat. *sincerus.* 2. *distinct, palpable, sheer.* 3. Adv. -νῶς, *of itself, absolutely.*
εἵλικτο, 3 sing. plqpf. of ἑλίσσω.
εἰλικτός, ή, όν, Ion. for ἑλικτός.
εἷλιξ, Ion. for ἕλιξ.
εἰλί-πους, ὁ, ἡ, -πουν, τό, gen. -ποδος: (εἴλω, πούς): *trailing the feet heavily in walking, with rolling walk*, epith. of oxen.
εἰλίσσω, poët. and Ion. for ἑλίσσω.
εἱλι-τενής, ές, epith. of the plant ἄγρωστις, (from ἕλος, τείνω), *stretching* or *spreading through marshes.*
εἰλίχᾰτο, Ion. 3 pl. plqpf. pass. of ἑλίσσω.
εἵλκῠσα, **εἱλκύσθην**, aor. 1 act. and pass. of ἕλκω.
εἵλκυσμαι, pf. pass. of ἕλκω.
εἷλον, **εἱλόμην**, aor. 2 act. and med. of αἱρέω.
εἴλοχα, Att. pf. of λέγω.
εἰλύᾰται, Ion. 3 pl. pf. pass. of εἰλύω.
εἴλῡμα, ατος, τό, (εἰλύω) *a cover, dress, clothing.*
εἰλῠός, ὁ, (εἰλύω) *a lurking-place, den.*
εἴλυτο, 3 sing. plqpf. pass. of εἰλύω.
εἰλῠφάζω, = εἰλύω, *to roll along.* II. intr. *to roll oneself along, whirl about.*
εἰλῠφάω, = εἰλυφάζω: Ep. part. εἰλυφόων.
ΕΙ'ΛΥ'Ω Att. **εἱλύω**: f. ύσω [ῡ]: pf. pass. εἴλῡμαι:—*to wrap round, enfold*:—Pass. *to be wrapt* or *covered*; esp. in pf. part., εἰλυμένος ψαμάθῳ *buried* in the sand. II. in Pass., also, *to wind, creep*, or *crawl along*
ΕΙ'ΛΩ, **εἴλλω**, or **ἴλλω**; also **εἰλέω** Att. εἱλέω:—from **εἴλω** are formed aor. 1 ἔλσα, inf. ἔλσαι Ep. ἐέλσαι; Pass., aor. 2 ἐάλην [ᾰ]; inf. ἁλῆναι Ep. ἀλήμεναι; part. ἁλείς, εῖσα, έν: Ep. pf. ἔελμαι:—from **εἰλέω** are formed impf. εἴλεον, Ep. 3 sing. ἐείλει; fut. εἰλήσω: aor. 1 εἴλησα: Pass., aor. 1 εἰλήθην: pf. εἴλημαι.—There are also Ep. impf. 3 sing ἐόλει, plqpf. ἐόλητο. I. Act. *to roll* or *twist tight up, to press hard* or *close: to force together: to coop up* or *shut up in* a place. 2. *to drive violently along, smite, strike*; νῆα κεραυνῷ ἔλσας *having struck* the ship with a thunderbolt. II. Pass. *to be rolled up together: to be shut* or *cooped up in* a place, *to throng together, assemble, crowd thickly together*; ἀλὲν ὕδωρ water *collected*: — also *to draw oneself together, crouch, cower*; Ἀχιλῆα ἀλεὶς μένεν *collecting himself* he waited the attack of Achilles. 2. *to go to and fro, go about*, Lat. *versari.* 3. *to turn* or *whirl round, revolve*, like εἱλίσσω, γῆ εἱλλομένη (or ἰλλομένη) the earth *turning on its axis.*
Εἵλως, ωτος, ὁ, and **Εἱλώτης**, ου, ὁ, fem. **Εἱλωτίς**, ίδος:—*a Helot*, i. e. *a serf* of the Spartans, employed in agriculture and other unwarlike labours. (From Ἕλος, a town of Laconia, whose inhabitants were enslaved.)
Εἱλωτεία, ἡ, *the condition of a Helot, slavery.* From
Εἱλωτεύω, f. σω, (εἱλώτης) *to be a Helot* or *serf.*
εἷμα, ατος, τό, (ἕννυμι) *a dress, garment, cloak*: later *clothing: an over-garment.* II. later also *a cover, carpet.*
εἷμαι, pf. pass. of ἕννυμι. II. pf. pass. of ἵημι. III. rarer form for ἧμαι, pf. pass. of ἕζω.
εἵμαρται, **εἵμαρτο**, 3 sing. pf. and plqpf. of μείρομαι.
εἰμέν, Ep. and Ion. for ἐσμέν, 1 pl. pres. of εἰμί *sum*: but **εἶμεν**, Dor. for εἶναι, inf. of εἰμί *sum.*
εἱμένος, part. pf. pass. of ἕννυμι.
εἰμές, Dor. for ἐσμέν, 1 pl. of εἰμί *sum*: but **εἶμες**, Dor. for εἶναι, inf. of εἰμί *sum.*
εἰμί, Aeol. ἐμμί (from Root ✱ἘΩ, *sum, esse*); εἶ Ep. εἶς, Ep. and Dor. ἐσσί; ἐστί Dor. ἐντί; plur., ἐσμέν Ep. and Ion. εἰμέν Dor. εἰμές; ἐστέ; εἰσί Ep. ἔᾱσι Dor. ἐντί:—Imper. ἴσθι, Ep. in med. form ἔσο, ἔσσο, ἔστω; plur. 3 ἔστωσαν Ep. ἔστων Att. ὄντων:—Subj. ὦ Ep. ἔω or εἴω:—Opt. εἴην Ep. ἔοιμι; plur. εἴημεν, εἴητε Ep. εἶμεν, εἶτε:—Infin. εἶναι Ep. ἔμμεναι, ἔμμεν, ἔμεναι, ἔμεν:—Part. ὤν Ep. ἐών, ἐοῦσα, etc.:—Imperf. ἦν (late Att. in med. form ἤμην), Ep. and Ion. ἔα, Ep. also ἦα, ἔον or ἔσκον, ες, ε, etc.; 2 sing. ἦσθα Ep. and ἔησθα; 3 sing. ἦ or ἦν Ep. ἦεν; 3 dual ἤτην or ἤστην; 3 pl. ἦσαν Ep. ἔσαν.—Fut. ἔσομαι, poët. ἔσσομαι, 3 sing. ἐσσεῖται from Dor. ἐσοῦμαι.—The whole of the pres. indic. may be enclitic, except the 2 sing. εἶ. The other persons are enclit., when εἰμί is not emphatic. But ἔστι is written ἔστι in cases of emphasis.
To be, Lat. *sum.* 2. as Verb Substant. *to be, to exist, be in existence*; οὐκέτ' ἔστι he *is* no more: esp. *to live*, οὐκ ἔσθ' οὗτος ἀνήρ, οὐδ' ἔσσεται *there lives* not the man, no nor *will live.* II. ἔστι, impers. with inf., *it is possible, lawful.* III. εἰμί with a gen. *expresses descent* or *extraction*; αἵματος εἰς ἀγαθοῖο *thou art of* good blood. 2. ἑαυτοῦ εἶναι *to be* one's own *master*, Lat. *sui juris esse.* 3. with the gen. put partitively; δήμου ἐστί *he belongs to* the people, *is one of* them. 4. also as in Lat., of the

duty or *property* of a thing; ἀνδρός ἐστι *it is the part of* a man; σωφροσύνης ἐστί *it is a mark of* temperance. IV. c. dat., ἔστι μοι, Lat. *est mihi, I have*; ἐμοὶ δέ κεν ἀσμένῳ εἴη, Lat. *esset mihi volenti.* V. τὰ ὄντα, *existing things*; τὰ ὄντα εἰρηκέναι to speak *the truth.* VI. ἔστιν ὅς, εἰσὶν οἵ, Lat. *est qui, sunt qui, some one, some, many*: ἔστιν or ἔσθ' ὅτε, Lat. *est quum, at times, sometimes*: ἔσθ' ὅπη or ὅπου, Lat. *est ubi, somewhere, somehow*: ἔστιν ὅπως *in some way.* VII. εἶναι often seems redundant, e.g. τὸ νῦν εἶναι, τὸ σήμερον εἶναι, τὸ σύμπαν εἶναι, for τὸ νῦν, etc.; esp. in phrase ἑκὼν εἶναι.

εἶμι (from Root *'ΙΩ, *eo*), εἶς Ep. εἶσθα, εἶσι, plur. ἴμεν, ἴτε, ἴασι or εἶσι:—imperat. ἴθι, ἴτω, pl. ἴμεν, ἴτε, ἴτωσαν Att. ἰόντων:—Subj. ἴω, ἴῃς Ep. ἴῃσθα, ἴῃ Ep. ἴῃσι:—Opt. ἴοιμι, ἰοίην, Ep. 3 sing. ἰείη or εἴη:—Inf. ἰέναι Ep. ἴμεναι, ἴμεν:—Part. ἰών:—Impf. ᾔειν Ep. and Ion. ᾔϊα, 3 sing. ᾔϊε contr. ᾖε; dual ᾔτην; plur., ᾔειμεν, ᾔειτε, ᾔεσαν, contr. ᾖμεν, ᾖτε, ᾖσαν, Ep. 3 pl. also ᾔϊσαν, ἴσαν, and 1 pl. ᾔομεν. In Att. the pres. has a fut. force, Lat. *IBO, I will go*: but in Ep. we have a fut. med. εἴσομαι, *to hasten*, with an aor. 1 med. εἰσάμην, 3 sing. εἴσατο, ἐείσατο, 3 dual ἐεισάσθην.

To go, Lat. *eo, ire*; ἰέναι τινὶ διὰ φιλίας, δι' ἔχθρας, διὰ πολέμου, etc., to live in friendship or enmity with any one; χροὸς εἴσατο *it went through* the skin; c. inf. fut., ἐεισάσθην συλήσειν *they went* to plunder. —It was used also of *going in a ship*, as, ἐπὶ νηὸς ἰέναι. 2. of birds, *to fly*, etc. 3. *of the motion of things*; πέλεκυς εἶσι διὰ δουρός the axe *goes, is driven* through the beam; ἔτος εἶσι the year *will pass* or *close*:—in Att., ἰέναι εἰς ταὐτόν *to come* together; ἰέναι εἰς λόγους *to come* to conference: Imperat. ἴθι δή *go* then, *well* then! *good!*

εἰν, poët. for ἐν, *in.*

εἰνᾰ-ετής, ές, (ἐννέα, ἔτος) *of nine years*: neut. εἰνά-ετες as Adv., *nine years long.*

εἰνᾰετίς, ίδος, fem. of εἰναετής, *nine years old.*

εἶναι, inf. of εἰμί *sum.* II. for ἰέναι, inf. of εἶμι *ibo.*

εἶναι, aor. 2 inf. of ἵημι, *to send.*

εἰνάκις, Adv., poët. for ἐννάκις, *nine times.*

εἰναχισ-χίλιοι, αι, *nine thousand.*

εἰνακόσιοι, αι, α, poët. and Ion. for ἐννακόσιοι.

εἰν-άλιος, η, ον, poët. for ἐνάλιος.

εἰνά-νῠχες, as Adv., (ἐννέα, νύξ) *nine nights long.*

εἰνάς, άδος, ἡ, poët. for ἐννέας II, *the ninth day.*

εἰνάτερες, αἱ, *brothers' wives, sisters-in-law.*

εἴνᾰτος, η, ον, poët. for ἔνατος, *the ninth.*

εἵνεκα, εἵνεκεν, Ion. and poët. for ἕνεκα, *on account, because of*, c. gen.

εἰνί, Ep. for the Prep. ἐν, *in.*

εἰν-όδιος, η, α, and ον, poët. for ἐνόδιος.

εἰνοσί-φυλλος, ον, (ἔνοσις, φύλλον) *with shaking foliage, quivering with leaves.*

εἶξα, aor. 2 of εἴκω, *to yield.*

εἴξασι, Att. for ἐοίκασι, 3 pl. pf. of *εἴκω, *to be like.*

εἴξασκε, 3 sing. Ion. aor. 1 of εἴκω, *to yield.*

εἷο, Ep. gen. for ἕο, οὗ, *of him, of her*; ἀπὸ εἷο from *himself.*

εἰοικυῖαι, Ep. part. nom. pl. fem. of ἔοικα.

εἷος, Ep. for ἕως, *until.*

εἶπα, aor. 1 for the common εἶπον, *I said*; see εἶπον.

εἰπέμεν, Dor. for εἰπεῖν.

εἴ-περ, *if at all events, if indeed.*

εἴπην, Dor. for εἰπεῖν, see εἶπον.

εἴ-ποθεν, Adv. *if from any place.*

εἴ-ποθι, Adv. *if, whether anywhere.*

εἶπον, *I spoke, I said*, aor. 2 from a pres. *εἴπω = *ἔπω imperat. εἰπέ, Ep. 2 pl. ἔσπετε; inf. εἰπεῖν Ep. εἰπέμεναι, –έμεν, Dor. εἴπην; part. εἰπών. There is also an aor. 1 εἶπα, used mostly in 2 sing. εἶπας, imperat. εἶπον, εἰπάτω, εἴπατον, εἴπατε: εἰπέ, like ἄγε, occurs also for εἴπετε before a plural. In Compos. a Med. form appears, as ἀπείπασθαι. The pres. is supplied by φημί, λέγω, or ἀγορεύω, the fut. and pf. by ἐρέω, ἐρῶ, εἴρηκα.

εἵποντο, 3 pl. impf. of ἕπομαι, *to follow.*

εἴ-ποτε, Adv. *if ever, if at all*, Lat. *si-quando.* II. indirect, *if* or *whether ever.*

εἴ που, Adv. *if anywhere*, Lat. *si-cubi.*

εἴ πως, Adv. *if at all, if by any means.*

εἰράνη, Dor. for εἰρήνη.

εἴργαθον, poët. aor. 2 of εἴργω.

εἰργασάμην, aor. 1 med. of ἐργάζομαι, used in act. sense: **εἰργάσθην**, aor. 1 pass. used in pass. sense.

εἴργασμαι, pf. of ἐργάζομαι, used in both act. and pass. sense.

εἰργμός, Att. **εἱργμός**, ὁ, (εἴργω) *a prison.*

εἰργμο-φύλαξ, ᾰκος, ὁ, (εἰργμός, φύλαξ) *a gaoler.*

εἴργνῡμι and –ύω, = εἴργω, *to shut in* or *up.*

ΕΙ'ΡΓΩ or εἵργω, Att. for the earlier form ἔργω.

εἰρέαται, Ion. for εἴρηνται, 3 pl. pf. pass. of ἐρέω.

εἶρερος, ὁ, (εἴρω) *bondage, slavery.*

εἰρεσία Ion. –ίη, ἡ, (ἐρέσσω) *a rowing.* 2. *any violent motion, throbbing.* II. *a complement* or *crew of rowers*, Lat. *remigium.*

εἰρεσιώνη, ἡ, (εἶρος) *a harvest-wreath* of olive or laurel *wound round with wool*, borne about by singing boys at the festivals of Πυανέψια and Θαργήλια, and afterwards hung up at the house-door. The song was likewise called Eiresioné.

εἰρέω, Ion. for ἐρέω, *to say.*

εἴρη, ἡ, (εἴρω) old word for ἀγορά, *a place of assembly.*

εἴρηκα, –ημαι, pf. act. and pass. of ἐρέω, ἐρῶ.

εἴρην or **ἴρην**, ενος, ὁ, (εἴρω or ἐρέω) a Laced. youth from his 18th year, when he was entitled *to speak* in the assembly and to lead an army; cf. Att. ἔφηβος.

εἰρηναῖος, α, ον, (εἰρήνη) *peaceful, in peace.*

εἰρηνεύω, f. σω, *to keep peace, live peaceably, be at peace.* II. trans. *to bring to peace, reconcile.* From

εἰρήνη, ἡ, *peace, time of peace*, Lat. *pax*; εἰρήνην ἄγειν to keep *peace*: metaph. *rest, repose.* (Deriv. uncertain.) Hence

εἰρηνικός, ή, όν, *of* or *for peace: peaceful, peaceable*:—Adv. -κῶς.
εἰρηνοποιέω, f. ήσω, *to make peace*. From
εἰρηνο-ποιός, όν, (εἰρήνη, ποιέω) *making peace*: as Subst., εἰρηνοποιός, ὁ, *a peace-maker*.
εἰρηνο-φύλαξ, ἄκος, ὁ, ἡ, (εἰρήνη, φύλαξ) *a guardian of peace*.
εἰρήσομαι, fut. 3 pass. of ἐρέω, ἐρῶ.
εἰρίνεος, η, ον, Ion. for ἐρίνεος, *woollen, of wool*. From
εἴριον, τό, (εἶρος) Ion. for ἔριον, *wool*.
εἰρκτέον, verb. Adj. of εἴργω, *one must prevent*.
εἰρκτή Ion. ἐρκτή, ἡ, (εἴργω) *an inclosure, prison*.
εἰρο-κόμος, ον, (εἶρος, κομέω) *dressing wool*.
εἴρομαι, Ion. for ἔρομαι, *to ask*: see εἴρω B.
εἰρο-πόκος, ον, (εἶρος, πόκος) *wool-fleeced, woolly*.
ΕἸΡΟΣ, τό, *wool*.
εἰρο-χαρής, ές, (εἶρος, χαρῆναι) *delighting in wool*.
εἴρπομες, Dor. for εἵρπομεν, 1 pl. impf. of ἕρπω.
εἰρύαται, Ion. 3 pl. pf. pass. of ἐρύομαι:—**εἰρύατο**, 3 pl. plqpf. (in sense of aor.)
εἴρυμαι, pf. pass. of ἐρύω.
εἰρύμεναι [ῠ], poët. for ἐρύειν, inf. of ἐρύω.
εἰρύσας [ῠ], Ion. aor. 1 part. of ἐρύω.
εἰρύσσαιτο, Ep. 3 sing. aor. 1 opt. of ἐρύω.
εἴρυτο, 3 sing. plqpf. pass. (with sense of aor. 2) of ἐρύω.
εἰρύω, εἰρύομαι, Ion. for ἐρύω, ἐρύομαι.
ΕἼΡΩ (A): aor. 1 εἶρα and ἔρσα: pf. pass. part. ἐρμένος, Ep. ἐερμένος:—Lat. *SERO, to tie, join, fasten together, string*; ἠλέκτροισιν ἐερμένος *set* with pieces of electron.
ΕἼΡΩ (B): *to say, speak, tell*; so also in Med. εἴρετο, εἴροντο:—but the Med. generally means *to cause* a thing *to be told one, to ask*; see ἐρῶ.
ΕἼΡΩΝ, ωνος, ὁ, *a dissembler, one who says less than he thinks* or *means*.
εἰρωνεία, ἡ, *dissimulation, an ignorance purposely affected* to provoke an antagonist, *irony*, used by Socrates against the Sophists. From
εἰρωνεύομαι, (εἴρων) Dep. *to dissemble*, esp. *to feign ignorance*.
εἰρωνικός, ή, όν, *befitting a dissembler*. Adv. -κῶς.
εἰρωτάω or **εἰρωτέω**, Ep. and Ion. for ἐρωτάω.
ΕἸΣ or **ἘΣ**, Prep. with acc. only. Radic. sense: *direction towards, motion to, in* or *into*. I. of place, the oldest and most freq. usage; but also of persons, *with all Verbs implying motion* or *direction*, and so *with Verbs of looking*, as, εἰς ὦπα ἰδέσθαι to look *in* the face: sometimes in Att. with the notion of *hostile direction*, Lat. *contra, adversus*, = πρός. 2. in pregnant usage, *joined with Verbs which express rest*, when a previous *motion* is implied, as, ἐς μέγαρον κατέθηκε he brought it *to* the house, and put it *there*: so, παρεῖναι εἰς τόπον to go *to* and be *at* a place: esp. in phrase, σώζεσθαι εἰς τόπον. 3. ellipt. c. gen., εἰς Ἀΐδαο [δόμον], Att. εἰς Ἅιδου, to the abode of Hades; ἐς Ἀθηναίης [ἱερόν] to the temple of Athena, ἐς Πριάμοιο [οἶκον] etc.; so in Prose, εἰς Δήμητρος to the temple of Ceres, etc.; as in Lat. *ad Apollinis, Castoris* (sub. *aedem*). II. of time, 1. *until*, ἐς ἠῶ, ἐς ἠέλιον καταδύντα, εἰς ὅτε *till* the time when.., *till* morn, *till* sunset; ἐς ὅ until; ἐς ἐμέ *up to* my time. 2. to determine a period, *for*, εἰς ἐνιαυτόν *for a* year, i.e. a whole year; ἐς θέρος, ἐς ὀπώρην *for* the summer, etc.; εἰς ἀεί *for* ever; εἰς ἡμᾶς *up to* our time; εἰς τρίτην ἡμέραν *to* the third day, i.e. in three days or *on* the third day. III. of an end or purpose, εἰπεῖν εἰς ἀγαθόν to speak *for* good, with a good object; ἐς πόλεμον θωρήξομαι I will arm me *for* war. IV. with numerals: ἐς μίαν (sc. βουλήν) βουλεύειν to resolve one way or unanimously; εἰς ἓν ἔρχεσθαι to agree together; with plurals, *up to*, εἰς μυρίους *as many as* ten thousand; εἰς δύο two deep; also of round numbers, *about, at most*. V. to express relation, ἐς ὅ *in regard to* which, i.e. *wherefore*: εἰς τί; *for* what? why? hence for Adv., ἐς τάχος for ταχέως.

Εἰς is sometimes parted from its acc. by several words, as, εἰς ἀμφοτέρω Διομήδεος ἅρματα βήτην. It is seldom put after its case. The notion is redoubled in εἰς ἅλαδε.

ΕἾΣ, μία, ἕν, gen. ἑνός, μιᾶς, ἑνός, Lat. *UNUS*, Engl. *ONE*: the fem. μία points to a second Root, which appears without the init. μ in the Ep. masc. ἴος, fem. ἴα: strengthd. εἷς οἶος, μία οἴα or οἴη, *a single one, one alone*: with Sup., εἷς ἄριστος: εἷς τις some *one*, Lat. *unus aliquis*: εἷς ἕκαστος each *one*, Lat. *unusquisque*: καθ' ἓν ἕκαστον each *singly*, piece by piece: εἷς ἀνήρ, Lat. *unus omnium*, *for one man*, πλείστας γυναῖκας εἷς ἀνὴρ ἐγήματο most *for one man*.
εἶς, Ep. 2 sing. pres. of εἰμί *sum*. II. 2 sing. pres. of εἶμι *ibo*.
εἵς, aor. 2 part. of ἵημι.
εἷσα, Causal aor. 1 of ἵζω, ἕζομαι, *to put, place, lay*; σκοπὸν εἷσε *he set* a spy; λόχον εἷσαν *they laid* an ambush: part. εἵσας, inf. ἕσαι, Ep. ἕσσαι. II. also fut. med. ἕσομαι Ep. ἕσσομαι: aor. 1 εἱσάμην: pf. pass. εἷμαι:—*to found, erect*, of building temples or setting up statues of deities. The other tenses are supplied from ἱδρύω.
εἰσ-αγαγών, aor. 2 part. of εἰσάγω.
εἰσαγγελεύς, έως, ὁ, (εἰσαγγέλλω) *one who announces, an usher*, an officer at the Persian court.
εἰσαγγελία, ἡ, *an accusation in the Athenian Council for some public offence: an information*. From
εἰσ-αγγέλλω, f. -ελῶ: for the tenses, v. ἀγγέλλω: I. —*to go in and announce* (the duty of an usher: see εἰσαγγελεύς): generally, *to announce, report*. II. *to accuse one of a state-offence*; see εἰσαγγελία.
εἰσ-ἀγείρω, f. -ερῶ: for the tenses, v. ἀγείρω:—*to gather into* a place.
εἰσ-άγω, f. ξω: aor. 2 -ήγαγον: pf. -αγήοχα:—*to lead in* or *into*; ἐσάγειν or ἐσάγεσθαι γυναῖκα *to lead* a wife *into one's house*. 2. *to import* foreign

wares; εἰσάγεσθαι καὶ ἐξάγεσθαι *to import* and export:—Med. *to admit* forces into a city: also *to introduce into* a league; *to introduce new* customs. II. as a political term, *to lay* or *bring before* an assembly; εἰσάγειν τι ἐς βουλήν, *to bring before* the Council. 2. as law-term, εἰσάγειν δίκην or γραφήν *to open the proceedings, state the case.*

εἰσἄεί, Adv. for εἰς ἀεί, *for ever.*

εἰσ-αείρομαι, Med. *to take to oneself.*

εἰσ-αθρέω, f. ήσω, *to look into, descry.*

εἰσ-αίρω, f. -ἄρῶ, *to lift* or *carry in.*

εἰσ-ᾱΐσσω, εἰσ-ᾴσσω, f. -ᾴξω, *to dart into.*

εἴσαιτο, 3 sing. aor. med. opt. of *εἴδω.

εἰσ-ἄκοντίζω, f. ίσω Att. ιῶ, *to hurl javelins at*: absol., *to dart* or *spout up*, of blood.

εἰσ-ἄκούω, f. σομαι: aor. 1 -ήκουσα: pf. -ακήκοα:—*to listen, hearken to*; and, simply, *to hear.* II. *to obey, comply with, give heed to.*

εἰσ-ακτέον, verb. Adj. of εἰσάγω, *one must bring in.*

εἰσ-άλλομαι, f. -αλοῦμαι: aor. 1 -ηλάμην: Ep. 3 sing. aor. 2 ἐσᾶλτο: Dep.:—*to leap* or *spring into*: also *to leap upon.*

εἰσ-ἄμείβω, f. ψω, *to pass into.*

εἰσάμην, Ep. aor. 1 med. of εἶμι *ibo.* II. Ep. aor. 1 med. of *εἴδω, *I see.*

εἰσάμην, aor. 1 med. of εἶσα, *I founded.*

εἰσ-αναβαίνω, aor. 2 -ανέβην, *to go up into.*

εἰσ-ἄναγκάζω, f. *to force into, constrain.*

εἰσ-ανάγω, f. ξω, *to lead up into.*

εἰσ-ανεῖδον, aor. 2 (see εἶδον): *to look up to.*

εἰσ-άνειμι, *to go up into.*

εἰσανιδών, part. of εἰσανεῖδον.

εἰσανιών, part. of εἰσάνειμι.

εἰσ-άντα, Adv. *straight into, into* or *in the face.*

εἰσάπαν, Adv. for εἰς ἅπαν, *altogether.*

εἰσάπαξ, Adv. for εἰς ἅπαξ, *at once.*

εἰσ-ἄράσσω Att. -ττω, fut. ξω, *to drive in upon.*

εἴσατο, εἴσατο, v. εἰσάμην, εἰσάμην.

εἰσ-ᾴττω, Att. for εἰσαΐσσω.

εἰσ-αυγάζω, f. σω, *to look at.*

εἰσαῦθις, Adv. for εἰς αὖθις, *hereafter.*

εἰσαύριον, Adv. for εἰς αὔριον, *on the morrow.*

εἰσ-αῦτις, Adv. Dor. and Ion. for εἰσαῦθις.

εἰσ-ἄφίημι, f. -αφήσω, *to send into*: *to let in.*

εἰσ-αφῐκάνω, = εἰσαφικνέομαι. [ᾱν]

εἰσαφῐκέσθαι, aor. 2 inf. of εἰσαφικνέομαι.

εἰσ-αφικνέομαι, f. ίξομαι, Dep. *to come* or *go into, to arrive at.*

εἰσ-βαίνω, f. -βήσομαι: aor. 2 -έβην: pf. -βέβηκα:—*to go into*: esp. *to go on board ship, embark.* 2. impers., εἰσβαίνει μοι *it comes into my head.* II. Causal in aor. 1 εἰσέβησα, *to make to go into, to put into*: see εἰσβιβάζω, which serves as pres. in this sense.

εἰσ-βάλλω, f. -βἄλῶ: pf. -βέβληκα, pass. -βέβλημαι:—*to throw into*:—Med. *to put on board one's ship.* II. (sub. ἑαυτόν or στρατιάν), *to throw oneself into, make an inroad* or *incursion into, invade*: also (sub. ναῦν) *to enter port*, Lat. *appellere.* 2. generally, *to go into*: of rivers, *to empty themselves into, fall into.* 3. also *to come to, fall into accidentally.*

εἴσβἄσις, εως, ἡ, (εἰσβαίνω) *an entrance, way of entering*: *embarkation.*

εἰσβἄτός, ή, όν, (εἰσβαίνω) *accessible.*

εἰσ-βῐάζομαι, f. άσομαι, Dep. *to force one's way into.*

εἰσ-βῐβάζω, f. -βιβάσω Att. -βιβῶ, Causal of εἰσβαίνω, *to make to go into, put into.*

εἰσ-βλέπω, f. ψω, *to look at, look upon.*

εἰσβολή, ἡ, (εἰσβάλλω II) *a throwing oneself into*: *an inroad, invasion, attack.* 2. *a way of entering, an entrance, pass*: in plur., also, *the mouth of a river.* 3. *an entering into a thing, a beginning.*

εἰσ-γράφω, f. ψω, *to write in, inscribe*:—Med. *to have oneself written down* or *inscribed*; εἰσγράφεσθαι ἐς τὰς σπονδάς *to have oneself written* or *received into* the league.

εἰσ-δέρκομαι, Dep., with aor. 2 act. εἰσέδρἄκον:—*to look at* or *upon, behold, observe.*

εἰσ-δέχομαι, Ion. ἐσ-δέκομαι: f. -δέξομαι: aor. 1 εἰσεδεξάμην and εἰσεδέχθην: Dep.:—*to take into, admit.*

εἰσ-δίδωμι, used intr., of rivers, *to flow into.*

εἰσδοχή, ἡ, (εἰσδέχομαι) *reception.*

εἰσδραμεῖν, aor. 2 inf. of εἰστρέχω.

εἰσδρομή, ἡ, (εἰσδραμεῖν) *an onslaught, assault.*

εἰσ-δύω or **εἰσ-δύνω**, and (in same sense) Med. **εἰσδύομαι**: f. -δύσομαι: aor. 2 -έδυν: pf. -δέδῡκα:—*to get into, slip into* or *in*; δεινόν τι ἐνέδυνε σφίσι a kind of fear *entered into* them; ἀκοντιστὺν ἐσδύσεαι *thou wilt enter into* a contest of archery.

εἶσε, see εἶσα.

εἰσέβην, aor. 2 of εἰσβαίνω: **εἰσέβησα**, causal aor. 1.

εἰσέγραψα, aor 1 of εἰσγράφω.

εἰσεδεξάμην, εἰσεδέχθην, aor. 1 of εἰσδέχομαι.

εἰσέδρἄκον, aor. 2 of εἰσδέρκομαι.

εἰσέδραμον, aor. 2 of εἰστρέχω.

εἰσ-έδῡν, aor. 2 of εἰσδύω.

εἰσ-εῖδον, aor. 2 (see εἶδον), *to look on* or *at.*

εἴσ-ειμι, inf. -ιέναι: impf. εἰσῄειν: (εἰς, εἶμι *ibo*):—*to go into, go in*; ὀφθαλμοὺς εἴσειμι *I will come into his sight*; ἀρχὴν εἰσιέναι *to enter on* an office. II. as law-term, *to come before the court.* III. metaph. *to come into one's mind.*

εἰσέκελσα, aor. 1 of εἰσκέλλω.

εἰσεκύλῖσα, aor. 1 of εἰσκῠλίνδω.

εἰσ-ελαύνω Ep. -ελάω: fut. -ελάσω [ἄ] Att. -ελῶ: for the tenses, v. ἐλαύνω:—*to drive into* or *in.* II. (sub. ἵππον or ναῦν) *to row into* a place, like Lat. *appellere.*

εἰσελθεῖν, aor. 2 inf. of εἰσέρχομαι.

εἰσ-έλκω: f. -έλξω: aor. 1 -είλκῠσα:—*to drag into.*

εἰσ-εμβαίνω, aor. 2 εἰσενέβην, *to go on board.*

εἰσενεγκεῖν, aor. 2 inf. of εἰσφέρω.

εἰσ-ενήνοχα, pf. of εἰσφέρω.

εἰσένθωμες, Dor. for εἰσέλθωμεν, 1 pl. aor. 2 subj. of εἰσέρχομαι.

εἰσενόησα, aor. 1 of εἰσνοέω.
εἰσέπαισα, aor. 1 of εἰσπαίω.
εἰσέπειτα, Adv. for εἰς ἔπειτα, *henceforward.*
εἰσέπτατο, 3 sing. aor. 2 of εἰσπέτομαι.
εἰσ-έργνῦμι or -ύω, *to shut up into, enclose in* a place.
εἰσερρύην, aor. 1 (in pass. form) of εἰσρέω.
εἰσ-έρρω, aor. 1 εἰσήρρησα: pf. εἰσήρρηκα:—*to go into, get in.*
εἰσ-ερύω, aor. 1 part. εἰσερύσας [ῠ], *to draw into.*
εἰσ-έρχομαι, fut. -ελεύσομαι: aor. 2 ἤλῠθον, -ῆλθον: Dep.:—*to go* or *come into, to enter,* Lat. *in-ire:* metaph. *to enter one's mind:* absol. of money, *to come in,* as πρόσοδοι εἰσῆλθον. II. as Att. law-term, of the accuser, *to come into court.*
εἰσ-έτι, Adv. *still yet.*
εἰσ-έχω, f. -έξω, intr. *to stretch into, reach.*
εἰσ-ηγέομαι, fut. ήσομαι, Dep. *to bring in, introduce, propound, bring forward.* II. εἰσηγεῖσθαί τινι *to represent to* any one, *instruct* him. Hence
εἰσήγημα, ματος, τό, *a proposition, motion:* and
εἰσήγησις, εως, ἡ, *a bringing in, proposing, bringing forward:* and
εἰσηγητέον, verb. Adj., *one must bring in:* and
εἰσηγητής, οῦ, ὁ, *one who brings in, a mover, proposer.*
εἰσ-ηθέω, f. ήσω, *to inject by a syringe.*
εἰσ-ήκω, f. -ήξω, *to be come in: to come in.*
εἰσ-ήλῠθον, εἰσῆλθον, aor. 2 of εἰσέρχομαι.
εἰσηλῠσία, ἡ, (εἰσήλυθον) *a coming in.*
εἰσήνεγκαι, aor. 1 of εἰσφέρω.
εἶσθα, Aeol. and Ep. for εἶς, εἶ, 2 sing. of εἶμι *ibo.*
εἷσθαι, pf. pass. inf. of ἵημι.
εἰσ-θέω, f. θεύσομαι, *to run into, run up to.*
εἰσ-θρώσκω, aor. -έθορον, *to leap into* or *in.*
εἰσί, εἰσίν, 3 pl. pres. of εἰμί *sum.*
εἶσι, εἶσιν, 3 sing. pres. of εἶμι *ibo.*
εἰσιδεῖν, Ep. **εἰσιδέειν,** aor. 2 inf. of εἰσεῖδον.
εἰσ-ιδρύω, f. σω: pf. pass. εἰσίδρῡμαι: (εἰς, ἱδρύω): *to build, found in* a place.
εἰσ-ίζομαι, Pass. (εἰς, ἵζω) *to be seated in, to sit down in.*
εἰσ-ίημι, f. -ήσω, *to send* or *put into:*—Med. *to betake oneself to;* also in act. sense, *to admit, let in.*
εἰσίθμη, ἡ, (εἴσ-ειμι) *an entrance.*
εἰσ-ικνέομαι, fut. -ίξομαι, Dep. *to go into.*
εἰσ-ίπταμαι, late form of εἰσπέτομαι.
εἰσ-καλαμάομαι, (εἰς, καλάμη) *to haul in with a fishing-rod.*
εἰσ-κᾰλέω, f. έσω, *to call in.*
εἰσ-καταβαίνω, f. -βήσομαι, aor. 2 εἰσκατέβην, *to go down into.*
εἰσ-κατατίθημι, f. -θήσω, *to put down into.*
εἴσ-κειμαι, as Pass. of εἰστίθημι, *to be put into, lie in: to be put on board ship.*
εἰσ-κέλλω, f. -κέλσω: aor. 1 -έκελσα:—*to push* or *thrust in:* (sub. ναῦν), *to put into shore, put to land.*
εἰσ-κηρύσσω Att. -ττω, f. ξω, *to call in by herald:* esp. *to call into the lists for combat.*
εἰσκομῐδή, ἡ, *a bringing in, importation.* From
εἰσ-κομίζω: fut. ίσω Att. ιῶ: *to bring into, import:*—Pass. *to get into* a place *for shelter.*
εἰσ-κυκλέω, f. ήσω, *to turn* or *wheel inwards* on the stage, so as *to withdraw from the eyes of the spectators,* v. ἐκκυκλέω:—metaph., δαίμων πράγματα εἰσκεκύκληκεν εἰς τὴν οἰκίαν some spirit *has brought* ill luck into the house.
εἰσ-κῠλίνδω, f. κυλίσω [ῑ]: *to roll into.*
εἴσκω: impf. ἤϊσκον: (ἶσος, ἔϊσος):—*to make like: to think like, liken:* metaph. *to compare:* and so *to guess, conjecture, believe.*
εἰσ-λεύσσω, *to look into.*
εἰσ-μαίομαι, aor. 1 εἰσεμασάμην, Ep. 3 sing. ἐσεμάσσατο Dor. -άξατο: Med.: (εἰς, μάσσω):—*to touch to the quick.* II. *to put in* the hand *to feel.*
εἰσ-νέομαι, Dep. *to go into.*
εἰσ-νέω, f. -νεύσομαι, *to swim into.*
εἰσ-νοέω, f. ήσω, *to perceive, remark.*
εἴσ-οδος, ἡ, (εἰς, ὁδός) *a way into, entry.* II. *a coming in, entrance,* esp. of the Chorus into the Orchestra: *a visit: a right of entrance.*
εἰσ-οικειόω, f. ώσω, (εἰς, οἰκεῖος) *to bring in as a friend:*—Pass. *to become friend to any one.*
εἰσ-οικέω, f. ήσω, *to dwell in, settle in.* Hence
εἰσοικήσις, εως, ἡ, *settlement: a dwelling.*
εἰσ-οικίζω, fut. ίσω Att. ιῶ, *to bring as a colonist into* a place:—Pass. *to settle oneself in* a place.
εἰσ-οικοδομέω, f. ήσω, *to build into.*
εἰσοιχνεῦσα, Aeol. for εἰσοιχνοῦσι, 3 pl. of
εἰσ-οιχνέω, f. ήσω, *to go into, enter.*
εἰσ-όκε or -εν Dor. **εἰσ-όκα,** (εἰς ὅ κε) *until such time as:*—so *long as.*
εἴσομαι, fut. of *εἴδω B: **εἴσεαι,** Ep. 2 sing. II. Ep. fut. of εἶμι *ibo.*
εἶσον, imperat. of εἶσα.
εἰσ-όπιν, (εἰς, ὄπις) Adv. *hereafter.*
εἰσ-οπίσω, Adv. *in time to come, hereafter.*
εἴσοπτος, ον, (εἰσόψομαι) *looked upon: to be seen, visible.*
εἰσοπτρίς, ίδος, ἡ, = εἴσοπτρον.
εἴσ-οπτρον, τό, (εἰσόψομαι) *a looking-glass, mirror.*
εἰσ-οράω, Ep. part. εἰσορόων, inf. med. εἰσοράασθαι: the fut. εἰσόψομαι and aor. 2 εἰσεῖδον are supplied from other Roots (see ὁράω):—*to look at* or *upon, view, behold:* also *to look on with admiration, revere, respect: to look at eagerly: to gaze upon steadily;* also of the gods, *to visit, punish, behold.*
εἰσ-ορμάω, f. ήσω, *to bring forcibly into:*—Pass. *to force one's way into.*
εἰσ-ορμίζω, fut. ίσω Att. ιῶ, *to bring into port:*—Pass., with aor. pass. and med., *to run into port.*
εἰσ-ορούω, f. σω, *to rush in.*
ἔϊσος, η, ον [ῐ], Ep. lengthd. form of ἶσος, *alike, equal,* used in these phrases: 1. δαὶς ἐΐση *the equal banquet,* i. e. *equally shared.* 2. νῆες ἐΐσαι the *equal* or *well-balanced* ships. 3. ἀσπὶς πάντοσ'

ἔΐση the all-even shield, i. e. *quite round.* 4. φρένες ἔνδον ἔΐσαι an *ever* mind, that is *well-balanced, calm*, Lat. *mens aequa*.

εἰσότε, for εἰς ὅτε, *until*.

εἰσ-οψις, εως, ἡ, *a looking upon: a spectacle*. From

εἰσόψομαι, fut. of εἰσοράω, formed from Root *εἰσόπτομαι.

εἰσ-παίω, aor. 1 εἰσέπαισα, *to burst* or *dash in*.

εἰσ-πέμπω, f. ψω, *to send in, bring in: to suborn*.

εἰσ-περάω, f. άσω [ᾱ] Ion. ήσω, *to pass over into*.

εἰσ-πηδάω, f. ήσω or ήσομαι, *to leap into, burst in*.

εἰσ-πέταμαι, f. -πτήσομαι: aor. 2 both in med. form εἰσεπτάμην and act. εἰσέπτην:—*to fly into*.

εἰσ-πίπτω, f. -πεσοῦμαι: aor. 2 -έπεσον: pf. -πέπτωκα:—*to fall* or *rush into: to be thrown into*. II. *to fall upon, attack*.

εἰσ-πίτνω, poët. form of εἰσπίπτω.

εἰσ-πλέω, f. -πλεύσομαι, *to sail into, enter*. Hence

εἴσπλοος, contr. **εἴσπλους**, ὁ, *a sailing in* of ships. II. *the entrance of a harbour*.

εἰσ-πνέω, f. -πνεύσομαι, *to breathe in, inhale*, Lat. *inspirare*. II. *to breathe upon*. Hence

εἰσπνήλας, ὁ, *one who inspires love, a lover*.

εἰσ-ποιέω, f. ήσω, *to put into the hands of, to give* (a son) *to be adopted by* another:—Pass. *to be adopted*. II. *to introduce*. Hence

εἰσποίητος, η, ον, *adopted*.

εἰσ-πορεύω, f. σω, *to lead into*:—Pass., with fut. med. -εύσομαι, *to go into, enter*.

εἴσπραξις, εως, ἡ, *exaction* or *collection* of taxes.

εἰσ-πράσσω Att. -ττω, f. ξω *to get in* or *collect taxes*:—Med. *to collect* or *exact for oneself*.

εἰσ-ρέω, f. -ρεύσομαι and -ρυήσομαι: aor. 2 -ερρύην:—*to stream into*.

εἰστήκειν, plqpf. intr. of ἵστημι.

εἰστίακα, **εἰστίασα**, pf. and aor. of ἑστιάω.

εἰσ-τίθημι, fut. -θήσω:—*to put into, place in*: also with or without ἐς ναῦν, *to put on board* ship:—Med., τέκνα ἐσθέσθαι (aor. 2 inf.) *to put* them *on board*.

εἰσ-τοξεύω, f. σω, *to shoot* or *dart into*.

εἰσ-τρέχω: fut. -δρᾰμοῦμαι: aor. 2 -έδρᾰμον (from *δρέμω). *To run in* or *into, to run upon*.

εἰσ-φέρω: fut. -οίσω (from *οἴω): aor. 1 -ήνεγκα and pf. -ενήνοχα (from *ἐνέγκω): cf. φέρω:—*to carry into: to bring in* or *upon*. II. *to bring in, contribute*: at Athens, *to pay tax on property*. III. *to introduce, bring forward, propose*. IV. Med. *to carry with one*: also like Act. *to introduce*. 2. *to import*. V. Pass. *to rush in*. 2. *to be imported*.

εἰσ-φοιτάω, f. ήσω, *to go continually to, to visit*.

εἰσφορά, ἡ, (εἰσφέρω) *a carrying into*. II. *a bringing in, contribution*: at Athens, *a property-tax*, raised to meet the exigencies of war.

εἰσ-φορέω, f. ήσω, = εἰσφέρω.

εἰσ-φρέω, fut. -φρήσω and -φρήσομαι: imperat. εἴσφρες: (εἰς, φρέω which only occurs in compos., v. διαφρέω, ἐκφρέω):—*to let in, admit*:—Med. *to bring*

εἰσ-χειρίζω, f. ίσω Att. ιῶ, *to put into one's hands, entrust*.

εἰσ-χέω, f. -χεῶ: aor. 1 -έχεα:—*to pour into*:—Pass., Ep. aor. 2 ἐσεχύμην [ῠ], *to stream in*.

εἴσω, more rarely ἔσω, Adv. (εἰς, ἐς) *into, within*, c. acc., δῦναι δόμον Ἄϊδος εἴσω: also c. gen., ἔσω βλεφάρων. II. *within, inside*.

εἰσ-ωθέω, fut. ωθήσω and ώσω, *to thrust into*:—Med. *to force oneself into, press in*.

εἰσ-ωπός, όν, (εἰς, ὤψ) *in face, in front of*; εἰσωποὶ ἐγένοντο νεῶν they came *in front of* the ships.

ΕἼΤΑ Ion. εἶτεν, Adv. of Time, *then, after, thereupon*, Lat. *deinde*. II. like Lat. *ita* and *itaque, and so then, and then*: also in ironical questions, Lat. *itane? itane vero? is it so? ay really? indeed?*

εἶται, 3 sing. pf. pass. of ἕννυμι.

εἴ-τε.., **εἴ-τε..**, Lat. *sive.., sive.., either.., or..; whether.., or..*; so that several cases are always put: in Homer the first εἴτε is sometimes answered by ἢ καί. The Trag. sometimes leave out the first εἴτε, or put εἰ instead.

εἶτε, for εἴητε, 2 pl. pres. opt. of εἰμί *sum*.

εἶτεν, Ion. for εἶτα, like ἔπειτεν for ἔπειτα.

εἰῶ, Ep. for ἐάω.

εἰω, Ep. for ἔω, ὦ, pres. subj. of εἰμί *sum*.

εἴωθα, pf. 2 (in pres. sense) of the Ep. verb ἔθω.

εἰώθειν, plqpf. (in impf. sense) of ἔθω.

εἰωθότως, Adv. of εἴωθα, *in the usual way*.

εἴων, impf. of ἐάω.

εἵως, Ep. for ἕως, *until*.

εἰῶσι, Ep. for ἐῶσι, 3 pl. of ἐάω.

ἘΚ, before a vowel ἐξ, Lat. *e, ex*, PREP. WITH GEN. Radic. sense, *from out of, away from*. I. OF PLACE, *out of, from forth*; ἐκ πάντων μάλιστα chief *from among* all, *of* all. 2. like ἔξω, *outside of, beyond*; ἐκ βελέων *out of* shot; ἐκ καπνοῦ *out of* the smoke. 3. with Verbs implying Rest, as, ἐκ πασσαλόφι κρέμασεν φόρμιγγα he hung his lyre *from*, i. e. *on*, the peg; ἀνάπτεσθαι ἔκ τινος to fasten *from*, i. e. *upon*, a thing. II. OF TIME, ἐξ οὗ *since, from the time when*, Lat. *ex quo*; ἐξ ἀρχῆς *from* the beginning; ἐκ θυσίας γενέσθαι to have *just finished* sacrifice; ἐξ εἰρήνης πολεμεῖν to go to war *out of*, i. e. *after*, peace. III. OF ORIGIN, ἔκ τινος γενέσθαι to be born or sprung *from* one; ἐξ ἐμοῦ γένος ἐσσί thou comest *of* me by blood. 2. of the materials of a thing, as πῶμα ἐκ ξύλου a cup *of* wood. 3. of Motive, Occasion, Means, ἐκ θεόφιν πολεμίζειν to war *at* the gods' *instance*; μήνιος ἐξ ὀλοῆς *because of* deadly wrath; ἐκ καύματος *in consequence of* the heat; ἐκ βίας ἄγειν = βίᾳ ἄγειν, to lead *by* force. 4. with a pass. Verb, ἐφίληθεν ἐκ Διός they were beloved *of* or *by* Zeus. 5. with a neut. Adj., as periphr. for Adv., ἐξ ἀγχιμόλου for ἀγχίμολον; ἐκ τοῦ ἐμφανοῦς and ἐξ ἐμφανοῦς for ἐμφανῶς, etc.

ἐκ is often separated from its Case by one or more words. It takes an accent if it is pecul. emphatic.

In Compos. ἐκ signifies *out, away, off*: also *utterly*.

ἑκά-εργος, ὁ, (ἑκάς, *ἔργω) epith. of Apollo, *working from afar, far-darting*, = ἑκηβόλος.

ἐκάην [ᾰ], aor. 2 pass. of *καίω*.

ἕκᾰθεν, Adv. (ἑκάς) *from afar :—far off, far away*.

ἐκάθηρα, aor. 1 of *καθαίρω*.

ἐκάλεσσα, Ep. aor. 1 of *κᾰλέω*.

ἕκᾱλος, Dor. for *ἕκηλος*.

ἐκάμμῠσα, for *κατέμυσα*, aor. 1 of *καταμύω*.

ἔκᾰμον, ἐκαμόμην, aor. 2 act. and med. of *κάμνω*.

ἐκαρτύναντο, 3 pl. aor. 1 med. of *καρτύνω*.

ἔκαρψα, aor. 1 of *κάρφω*.

ἑκάς Att. **ἕκας**, Adv. (ἐκ) *far, afar, far off*: c. gen. *far from, far away from*. II. of Time, *long after*.

ἑκαστάτω, Sup. of ἑκάς, *furthest off, furthest away*.

ἑκασταχόθεν, (ἕκαστος) Adv. *from every side*.

ἑκασταχόσε, (ἕκαστος) Adv. *to every side*.

ἑκασταχοῦ, (ἕκαστος) Adv. *everywhere*.

ἑκαστέρω, Comp. of ἑκάς, *further, further off*:— Sup. *ἑκαστάτω*.

ἑκάστοθι, Adv. *for each* or *every one*. From

ἝΚΑΣΤΟΣ, *η, ον, every, every one, each, each one*, Lat. *quisque*, opp. to a number: the sing. from its collective sense is freq. joined with a plur. Verb, *ἕκαστος ἐπίστασθε* ye know *each one of you*: *εἷς ἕκαστος*, Lat. *unusquisque, each one; πᾶς, ἕκαστος, one and all; οἱ καθ' ἕκαστον each one singly*, Lat. *singuli: καθ' ἑκάστην* [*ἡμέραν*] *every day, daily*. Hence

ἑκάστοτε, Adv. *each time, at all times*.

ἑκαστοτέρω, Adv. = *ἑκαστέρω*.

ἑκατέατο, Ion. for *ἐκάθηντο*, 3 pl. impf. of *κάθημαι*.

ἑκατεράκις, Adv. (*ἑκάτερος*) *at each time*.

ἑκάτερθε, before a vowel -**θεν**, Adv. for *ἑκατέρωθεν*, *from* or *on each side*, Lat. *utrinque*.

ἙΚΑ'ΤΕΡΟΣ, *α, ον, each of two, each singly*, Lat. *uterque*. Hence

ἑκατέρωθεν, Adv. *from each side*: and

ἑκατέρωθι, Adv. *on each side*: and

ἑκατέρωσε, Adv. *to each side, each way*.

Ἑκάτη [ᾰ], ἡ, (ἕκατος) *Hecaté*, daughter of Perses and Asteria, who had power from Zeus in heaven, earth, and sea. Later she was held to be the same as Artemis. *Ἑκάτης δεῖπνον*, or *Ἑκάταια, τά*, was an offering of purification made to her on the 30th of each month at three cross roads.

ἑκᾰτη-βελέτης, *ου, ὁ*, = *ἑκατηβόλος*.

ἑκᾰτη-βόλος, *ον*, (*ἑκάς, βάλλω*) *far-throwing, far-shooting, far-darting :—*as Subst. *the Far-darter*.

ἕκᾱτι, Att. and Dor. for *ἕκητι, on account of*.

ἑκατογ-κάρᾱνος, *ον*, (*ἑκατόν, κάρηνον*); and

ἑκατογ-κεφάλας, *ου, ὁ*, (*ἑκατόν, κεφαλή*); and

ἑκατόγ-κρανος, *ον*, (*ἑκατόν, κρᾶνον*) :—*hundred-headed*.

ἑκατόγ-χειρος, *ον*, (*ἑκατόν, χείρ*) *hundred-handed*.

ἑκατό-ζῠγος, *ον*, (*ἑκατόν, ζυγόν*) *with* 100 *benches for rowers*.

ἑκατομ-βαιών, *ῶνος, ὁ, the month Hecatombaeon*, the first of the Att. year, answering to the last half of July and first half of August. From

ἑκατόμ-βη, ἡ, (*ἑκατόν, βοῦς*) properly *an offering of a hundred oxen*: but commonly *a great public sacrifice*, not always of oxen, nor to the number of a hundred.

ἑκατόμ-βοιος, *ον*, (*ἑκατόν, βοῦς*) *of* or *worth a hundred oxen*.

ἑκατόμ-πεδος, *ον*, (*ἑκατόν, πούς*) 100 *feet long*.

ἑκατομ-πολίεθρος, *ον*, = *ἑκατόμπολις*.

ἑκατόμ-πολις, *ι*, gen. *εως*, (*ἑκατόν, πόλις*) *with a hundred cities*.

ἑκατόμ-πους, *ὁ, ἡ, πουν, τό*, gen. *ποδος*, (*ἑκατόν, πούς*) *hundred-footed*.

ἑκατόμ-πῠλος, *ον*, (*ἑκατόν, πύλη*) *hundred-gated*.

ἙΚΑΤΟ'Ν, *οἱ, αἱ, τά*, indecl. *a hundred*, Lat. *centum*.

ἑκατοντα-ετής, *ές*, (*ἑκατόν, ἔτος*) *of a hundred years, a hundred years old*.

ἑκατοντα-κάρηνος, Dor. -**κάρᾱνος**, *ον*, (*ἑκατόν, κάρηνον*) *hundred-headed*: cf *ἑκατόγκρανος*.

ἑκατον-τάλαντος, *ον*, (*ἑκατόν, τάλαντον*) *worth* 100 *talents*; *γραφὴ ἑκατοντάλαντος* an action where *damages* were *laid at that sum*.

ἑκατοντα-πλᾰσίων, *ον*, gen. *ονος*, (*ἑκατόν*) *a hundred-fold*, 100 *times as much* or *many*.

ἑκατοντά-πῠλος, *ον*, = *ἑκατόμπῠλος*.

ἑκατοντ-άρχης, *ου, ὁ*, (*ἑκατόν, ἄρχω*) *a leader of a hundred*, Lat. *centurio*.

ἑκατόντ-αρχος, *ὁ*, = *ἑκατοντάρχης*.

ἑκατοντάς, *άδος, ἡ*, (*ἑκατόν*) *the number one hundred*.

ἑκατοντ-όργυιος, *ον*, (*ἑκατόν, ὀργυιά*) *of* 100 *fathoms* :—poët., **ἑκατοντ-ορόγυιος, ον**.

ἕκᾰτος, *ὁ*, (*ἑκάς*) = *ἑκηβόλος*.

ἑκατό-στομος, *ον*, (*ἑκατόν, στόμα*) *hundred-mouthed*.

ἑκατοστός, *ή, όν*, (*ἑκατόν*) *the hundredth*, Lat. *centesimus*; *ἐφ' ἑκατοστά a hundred-fold*. II. *ἡ ἑκατοστή, the hundredth part*, a tax or duty at Athens.

ἑκατοστύς, *ύος, ὁ*, = *ἑκατοντάς*.

ἔκαυσα, aor. 1 of *καίω*.

ἐκ-βάζω, f. *ξω, to speak out, declare*.

ἐκ-βαίνω, f. *-βήσομαι*: aor. 2 *ἐξέβην*: pf. *ἐκβέβηκα* :—*to step out of, go* or *come out of*: *to step out of* a ship, *to disembark*. 2. *to go out of, depart from*. 3. metaph. *to come out* so and so, *to turn out*, Lat. *evadere*. 4. *to go out of due bounds, to digress*. II. in fut. act. *ἐκβήσω*, aor. 1 *ἐξέβησα*, Causal, *to make to step out of, put out of* a ship, etc.; cf. *ἐκβιβάζω*.

ἐκ-βακχεύω, f. *σω, to excite to Bacchic frenzy, to make frantic* :—Pass. and Med. *to be frenzied, rage*.

ἔκβαλε, aor. 2 imperat. of *ἐκβάλλω* :—also Ep. for *ἐξέβαλε*, 3 sing. ind.

ἐκ-βάλλω, f. *-βᾰλῶ*: aor. 2 *-έβᾰλον*; pf. *-βέβληκα*: —*to throw* or *cast out*: *to disembark, land*; but also *to carry out to sea*. 2. *πόλεως ἐκβάλλειν to cast out of* the country: and so *to drive out, banish*. II. *to strike out*, Lat. *excutere*; *δοῦρα ἐκβάλλειν to fell* trees, properly *to cut* them *out of* the forest. III. metaph., *ἔπος ἐκβάλλειν to let fall* or *drop* a word; so, *ἐκβάλλειν δάκρυα to drop* or *shed* tears. IV.

to throw away, depose, reject: to hiss off the stage, Lat. *explodere.* 3. *to break open.* V. *to send out, get rid of, lose.* VI. (sub. ἑαυτόν), of a river, *to empty* or *discharge itself.*

ἐκβαλεῖν, aor. 2 inf. of ἐκβάλλω.

ἐκβάς, aor. 2 part. of ἐκβαίνω.

ἔκβᾰσις, εως, ἡ, (ἐκβαίνω) *a going out of* a ship, *a landing.* II. *a way out, egress: an escape.*

ἐκ-βάω, Dor. for ἐκ-βαίνω.

ἐκ-βεβαιόω, f. ώσω, *to confirm.*

ἐκ-βῐάζω, *to force out: to wrest from.*

ἐκ-βῐβάζω, f. -βιβάσω Att. βιβῶ, Causal of ἐκβαίνω, *to make to step out of:* esp. *to put out of* a ship.

ἐκ-βιβρώσκω, fut. -βρώσω, pf. -βέβρωκα, *to devour.*

ἔκβλητος, ον, (ἐκβάλλω) *thrown out: rejected, despised, despicable.*

ἐκ-βλώσκω, aor. 2 ἐξ-έμολον, *to go* or *come out.*

ἐκ-βοάω, f. ήσομαι, *to call* or *cry out*

ἐκ-βοήθεια, ἡ, *a marching out to aid.* From

ἐκ-βοηθέω, f. ήσω, *to march out to aid: to make a sally.*

ἐκ-βολβίζω, f. ίσω Att. ιῶ, (ἐκ, βολβός) *to peel off from,* as the skin *off* an onion; ἐκβολβίζειν τινὰ τῶν κωδίων *to peel* one *of* his stolen skins.

ἐκβολή, ἡ, (ἐκβάλλω) *a throwing out, throwing overboard,* esp. of goods in a storm. II. *a casting out, banishment.* III. *a shooting forth;* ἐκβολὴ σίτου *the time* when the corn *shoots* or *comes into ear.* IV. *an outlet,* Lat. *exitus;* ἐκβολὴ ποταμοῦ *the mouth* of a river; ἐκβολαὶ ὄρους *a defile leading out* of a chain of mountains; ἐκβολὴ λόγου *a digression.* V. (from Pass.) *that which is cast out;* ἐκβολὴ δικέλλης *earth cast out* by a mattock; οὐρεία ἐκβολή *children exposed* on the mountains.

ἔκβολος, ον, (ἐκβάλλω) *cast out, exposed,* of a child: *abortive.* II. as Subst., ἔκβολος, ὁ, *a cape, promontory.* 2. ἔκβολα, τά, *cast off relics.*

ἐκ-βράσσω, f. -βράσω, *to throw out* or *up,* as froth: Pass. *to be cast up* or *thrown on shore,* of ships.

ἐκ-βροντάω, f. ήσω, *to strike out by lightning.*

ἐκ-βρῡχάομαι, Dep. *to bellow forth.*

ἔκ-βρωμα, ατος τό, (ἐκβιβρώσκω) *that which is eaten out;* ἔκβρωμα πρίονος *saw-dust.*

ἐκ-γᾰμίζω, f. ίσω Att. ιῶ, *to give away in marriage:*—Pass. *to be given in marriage, marry.*

ἐκ-γᾰμίσκομαι, Pass. *to be given in marriage.*

ἐκ-γαυρόομαι, (ἐκ, γαῦρος) Med. *to exult greatly in.*

ἐκ-γέγᾰα, poët. for ἐκγέγονα, pf. of ἐκγίγνομαι: 3 dual ἐκγεγάτην; inf. ἐκγεγάμεν [ᾰ]; part. ἐκγεγαώς, ἐκγεγαυῖα.

ἐκ-γελάω, f. άσομαι [ᾰ]: for the tenses, v. γελάω:—*to laugh out, laugh loud, burst out laughing:* metaph. of a liquid, *to gurgle out.*

ἐκ-γενής, ές, (ἐκ, γένος) *put out from one's family, without kith* or *kin.*

ἐκ-γίγνομαι, fut. -γενήσομαι: aor. 2 ἐξεγενόμην: pf. ἐκγέγονα, poët. ἐκγέγαα (q. v.): Dep.:—*to grow out of, spring from: to be descended from, born of.* II. *to have gone by;* χρόνου ἐκγεγονότος time *having gone by, elapsed.* 2. impers. ἐκγίγνεται, like ἔξεστι, *it is allowed, it is granted.*

ἔκγονος, ον, (ἐκγενέσθαι) *sprung, descended from* any one: as Subst., ἔκγονος, ὁ, *any descendant, son, grandson;* τὰ ἔκγονα *offspring, posterity.*

ἐκ-γράφω, f. ψω, *to write out, copy:*—Med. *to write out* or *copy for oneself.* II. *to strike out, expunge from* a list.

ἐκ-γίνομαι, Ion. and in late Gr. for ἐκγίγνομαι.

ἐκ-δακρύω, f. ύσω, *to burst into tears.* [ῡ]

ἐκ-δᾰπᾰνάω, f. ήσω, *to expend, consume, exhaust.*

ἐκ-δέδαρμαι, pf. pass. of ἐκδέρω.

ἐκδεδωρίευνται, 3 pl. Ion. plqpf. of ἐκδωριόομαι.

ἐκ-δεής, ές, (ἐκ, δεῖ) *defective.* Hence

ἔκδεια, ἡ, *a falling short, being in arrear.*

ἐκ-δείκνῡμι, f. -δείξω, aor. 1 ἐξέδειξα, *to shew forth, display.*

ἐκ-δέκομαι, Ion. for ἐκδέχομαι.

ἔκδεξις, εως, ὁ, (ἐκδέχομαι) *a taking from: succession.*

ἐκ-δέρκομαι, Dep. *to look out from.*

ἐκ-δέρω, Ion. -δείρω: f. -δερῶ:—*to skin, flay, strip off the skin:* hence *to cudgel soundly.*

ἔκ-δετος, ον, (ἐκδέω) *fastened to* or *upon.*

ἐκ-δέχομαι, Ion. -δέκομαι: f. -δέξομαι: aor. 1 ἐξεδεξάμην: Dep.:—*to take or receive from: to take up.* 2. ἐκδέχεσθαι τὴν ἀρχήν *to receive* the rule *from* another: absol. *to follow, succeed:* of countries, *to come next.* 3. *to wait for, expect,* Lat. *excipere.* . *to receive* at a feast.

ἐκ-δέω, f. -δήσω, *to bind from,* i. e. *to bind on* or *to:*—Med. *to bind a thing to oneself, hang it round one.*

ἔκ-δηλος, ον, *very manifest: conspicuous.*

ἐκ-δημέω, f. ήσω, (ἔκδημος) *to go abroad, travel: to be abroad,* or *on one's travels.* Hence

ἐκδημία, ἡ, *departure from home* or *from life.*

ἔκ-δημος, ον, (ἐκ, δῆμος) *from home, abroad.*

ἐκ-διαβαίνω, f. -βήσομαι: aor. 2 ἐκδιέβην:—*to go through out of, pass over.*

ἐκ-δῐαιτάομαι, Pass. (ἐκ, διαιτάω) *to depart from one's accustomed mode of life, change one's habits.*

ἐκδίδαγμα, τό, *prentice-work, a sampler.* From

ἐκ-δῐδάσκω, f. -διδάξω poët. -διδασκήσω:—*to teach thoroughly,* Lat. *edocere:*—Med. *to have another taught thoroughly:*—Pass. *to learn thoroughly.*

ἐκ-διδράσκω, Ion. -διδρήσκω: fut. -δράσομαι [ᾱ]: aor. 2 ἐξέδραν:—*to run away from, escape.*

ἐκ-δίδωμι, f. -δώσω: aor. 1 ἐξέδωκα: pf. ἐκδέδωκα: aor. 2 med. ἐξεδόμην:—*to give out, give up,* Lat. *reddere: to surrender.* 2. *to give out of one's house;* ἐκδιδόναι or ἐκδίδοσθαι θυγατέρα *to give away* one's daughter *in marriage.* 3. *to give out for money, farm out, let out for hire: to put out money to interest, lend out.* II. (sub. ἑαυτόν) *to issue forth from a place;* of a river, *to empty itself.*

ἐκ-διηγέομαι, Dep. *to tell to the end, recount in full.*

ἐκ-δῐκάζω, f. σω, *to decide by giving judgment,* of a judge. II. *to avenge.* Hence

ἐκδικαστής, οῦ, ὁ, *an avenger.*
ἐκδικέω, f. ήσω, (ἔκδικος) *to avenge, punish; ἐκδικεῖν τινα ἀπό τινος to avenge* one on another. Hence
ἐκδίκησις, εως, ἡ, *an avenging: vengeance.*
ἔκ-δῐκος, ον, (ἐκ, δίκη) *without law, lawless,* Lat. *exlex:* Adv. ἐκδίκως, *lawlessly.* II. *carrying out justice, avenging:* as Subst., ἔκδικος, ὁ, *an avenger.*
ἐκ-διφρεύω, f. σω, *to throw from the chariot.*
ἐκ-δῐώκω, f. ξομαι later ξω, *to drive away, banish.*
ἐκ-δονέω, f. ήσω, *to shake out, confound.*
ἔκδοσις, εως, ἡ, (ἐκδίδωμι) *a giving up, surrendering.* 2. *a giving in marriage.*
ἐκδώσομαι, fut. med. of ἐκδίδωμι.
ἐκδοτέον, verb. Adj. of ἐκδίδωμι, *one must give in marriage.*
ἔκδοτος, ον, (ἐκδίδωμι) *given up, betrayed.*
ἐκδοῦναι, aor. 1 inf. of ἐκδίδωμι.
ἐκδοχή, ἡ, (ἐκδέχομαι) *a receiving from another, succession.*
ἐκ-δρᾰκοντόομαι, Pass. (ἐκ, δράκων) *to become a serpent.*
ἐκδρᾰμεῖν, aor. 2 inf. of ἐκτρέχω.
ἐκδρομή, ἡ, (ἐκδραμεῖν) *a running out, sally, charge:* —also *a band of skirmishers.*
ἔκ-δρομος, ὁ, *one that sallies out, a skirmisher.*
ἔκδῠμα, ματος, τό, (ἐκδύω) *that which is put off,* a *skin, garment.*
ἐκδῦμεν, either Ep. for ἐκδῦναι, aor. 2 inf. of ἐκδύω, or for ἐκδύοιμεν 1 pl. opt.
ἐκ-δύνω, see ἐκδύω.
ἔκδῠσις, εως, ἡ, *a slipping out, escape.* From
ἐκ-δύω, f. -δύσω [ῡ]: aor. 1 ἐξέδῡσα: *to strip off from* another; ἐκδῦσαι αὐτὸν χιτῶνα *to strip* him *of* his tunic; ἐκδῦσαι αὐτόν *to strip* him. II. in pres. ἐκδύνω, with Med. ἐκδύομαι, aor. 2 act. ἐξέδυν, pf. ἐκδέδῠκα, *to put off.* 2. *to get out of, slip out of.* 3. metaph. *to get away from, escape.*
ἐκ-δωριόομαι, Pass. (ἐκ, Δώριος) *to become quite a Dorian.*
ἐκέασσα, Ep. for ἐκέασα, aor. 1 of κεάζω.
ἐκέατο, Ion. for ἔκειντο, 3 pl. impf. of κεῖμαι.
'ΕΚΕΙ͂, Adv. *at* or *in that place, there,* Lat. *illic.*
ἔκεια, Ep. aor. 1 of καίω.
ἐκεῖθεν, Adv. *from that place, thence,* Lat. *illinc;* c. gen., τοὐκεῖθεν ἄλσους *yon* side of the grove.
ἐκεῖθι, (ἐκεῖ) Adv. *at that place, there,* Lat. *illic:* Dor. τηνόθι.
ἐκεῖνος Ion. **κεῖνος**, η, ο, Aeol. **κῆνος**, Dor. **τῆνος**, Att. also strengthd. **ἐκεινοσί**: demonstr. Pron. (ἐκεῖ): —*that person* or *thing,* Lat. *ille, illa, illud:* when οὗτος and ἐκεῖνος refer to two things before mentioned, ἐκεῖνος, *ille,* refers to *the more remote,* οὗτος, *hic,* to *the nearer.* II. used also like *ille,* to denote well-known persons; κεῖνος μέγας θεός, *magnus ille Deus.* III. in Att., ἐκεῖνος precedes the Art. when it is emphatic, as, ἐκεῖνος ὁ ἀνήρ: and follows the Subst., when it is not emphatic, as ὁ ἀνὴρ ἐκεῖνος. IV. Adv. **ἐκείνως**, *in that way, in that case:* Ion. κείνως. V. the dat. fem. ἐκείνῃ is also used as Adv., 1. of Place, *there, at that place, on that road.* 2. of Manner, *in that manner.*
ἔκειρα, aor. 1 of κείρω.
ἐκεῖσε, Att. **κεῖσε**, Adv. (ἐκεῖ) *to that place, thither,* Lat. *illuc.*
ἐκέκαστο, 3 sing. plqpf. (in impf. sense) of καίνυμαι.
ἐκεκεύθει, 3 sing. plqpf. of κεύθω.
ἐκέκλετο, 3 sing. Ep. aor. 2 of κέλομαι.
ἐκέκλῐτο, 3 sing. plqpf. pass. of κλίνω.
ἐκεκοσμέατο, Ion. for ἐκεκόσμηντο, 3 pl. plqpf. pass. of κοσμέω.
ἐκέλευ, Dor. for ἐκέλου, 2 sing. impf. of κέλομαι.
ἔκελσα, aor. 1 of κέλλω.
ἔκερσα, Aeol. and Ep. aor. 1 of κείρω.
ἐκε-χειρία, ἡ, (ἔχω, χείρ) *a holding of hands, a cessation of hostilities, armistice.*
ἐκ-ζέω, f. -ζέσω, *to boil out* or *over:* c. gen., **εὐλέων** ἐξέζεσε she *ran over, swarmed* with worms.
ἐκ-ζητέω, f. ήσω, *to search out.*
ἐκ-ζωπῠρέω, f. ήσω, *to light up again, rekindle.*
ἔκηα, Ep. aor. 1 of καίω.
ἐκηβολία, ἡ, *a darting from afar, archery.* From
ἑκη-βόλος, ον, (ἑκάς, βάλλω) *far-darting, far-shooting,* epith. of Apollo in Iliad.
ἕκηλος, ον, collat. form of εὔκηλος, *at one's ease, quiet,* Lat. *securus.* II. metaph. of things, as of a field *lying at rest* or *fallow.*
'ΕΚΗΤΙ Att. ἕκᾱτι, Prep. with gen. *by means of, by virtue of, by the grace* or *help of.* II. later = ἕνεκα, *on account of, for the sake of.* 2. *as regards, as to,* Lat. *quod attinet ad.*
ἐκ-θάλπω, f. ψω, *to warm thoroughly.*
ἐκθαμβέω, f. ήσω, *to amaze, astonish:* Pass. *to be amazed, astonished.* From
ἔκ-θαμβος, ον, (ἐκ, θάμβος) *amazed, astounded.*
ἐκ-θαμνίζω, f. σω, (ἐκ, θάμνος) *to root out, extirpate.*
ἔκθᾰνον, Ep. for ἐξέθᾰνον, aor. 2 of ἐκθνήσκω.
ἐκ-θεάομαι, f. άσομαι, Ion. ήσομαι, Dep. *to see out, see to the end.*
ἐκ-θεᾱτρίζω, f. σω, (ἐκ, θέᾱτρον) *to make a spectacle of.*
ἐκ-θειάζω, f. σω, (ἐκ, θεῖον) *to deify.*
ἐκθέμεναι or **ἐκθέμεν**, Ep. for ἐκθεῖναι, aor. 2 inf. of ἐκτίθημι.
ἐκθείς, εῖσα, έν, aor. 2 part. of ἐκτίθημι.
ἐκ-θερίζω, f. ίσω Att. ιῶ, *to mow completely: to cut down.*
ἐκ-θερμαίνω, f. ᾰνῶ, (ἐκ, θερμός) *to warm* or *heat thoroughly.*
ἐκθέσθαι, aor. 2 med. inf. of ἐκτίθημι.
ἔκθεσις, εως, ἡ, (ἐκτίθημι) *a putting out, exposing.*
ἔκθετος, ον, (ἐκτίθημι) *put out, exposed.*
ἐκ-θέω, f. -θεύσομαι, *to run* or *sally out.*
ἐκ-θηράομαι, Dep. *to hunt out, catch.*
ἐκ-θηρεύω, f. σω, = ἐκθηράομαι.
ἐκ-θλίβω, f. ψω, *to press, squeeze out:* metaph. *to crush, oppress.*

ἐκ-θνήσκω, fut. -θᾰνοῦμαι: aor. ἐξέθᾰνον:—*to be dying, be at the last gasp; γέλω* or *γέλωτι ἐκθανεῖν to be nigh dead* with laughter.

ἐκ-θοινάομαι, f. ήσομαι, Dep. *to eat up, feast on.*

ἔκθορε, for ἐξέθορε, 3 sing. aor. 2 of ἐκθρώσκω.

ἐκ θρηνέω, f. ήσω, *to mourn out* or *aloud.*

ἐκ-θρώσκω, fut. -θοροῦμαι: aor. ἐξέθορον:—*to leap out of, leap forth from.*

ἐκ-θῡμιάω, f. άσω, *to burn as incense.*

ἔκ-θῡμος, ον, (ἐκ, θυμός) *very spirited, ardent, eager:* also *frantic*, like Lat. *amens.*

ἐκ-θύω, f. ύσω [ῡ]: for the tenses v. θύω:—*to offer up, sacrifice:* metaph. *to destroy utterly.* 2. Med. *to atone for, expiate by offerings:* of a god, *to propitiate, appease.*

ἐκίχεις [ῐ], 2 sing. impf. of κίχημι: of ἐτίθεις from τίθημι.

ἐκίχην [ῐ], impf. of κίχημι.

ἐκ-καγχάζω, f. σω, *to burst out into loud laughter.*

ἐκ-κᾰθαίρω, f. -καθᾰρῶ: aor. 1 ἐξεκάθηρα:—*to cleanse out, clear out: to clear away, get rid of.*

ἐκ-καθεύδω, f. -ευδήσω, *to sleep out, sleep away from one's quarters.*

ἑκ-καί-δεκα, οἱ, αἱ, τά, indecl. *sixteen.*

ἑκκαιδεκά-δωρος, ον, (ἑκκαίδεκα, δῶρον) *sixteen palms long.*

ἑκκαιδεκά-λῐνος, ον, (ἑκκαιδέκα, λίνον) *consisting of sixteen threads.*

ἑκκαιδέκατος, η, ον, (ἑκκαίδεκα) *sixteenth.*

ἑκκαιδεκ-έτης, ου, ὁ, (ἑκκαίδεκα, ἔτος) *sixteen years old:* fem. **-δεκέτις**, ιδος.

ἔκ-καιρος, ον, (ἐκ, καιρός) *out of date.*

ἐκ-καίω, Att. **ἐκκάω**: fut. -καύσω: aor. 1 ἐξέκεα:—*to burn out.* II. *to set on fire, kindle: inflame.*

ἐκ-κᾰκέω, f. ήσω, (ἐκ, κακός) *to be faint-hearted.*

ἐκ-καλᾰμάομαι, (ἐκ, καλάμη) Dep. *to pull out with a fishing-rod.*

ἐκ-κᾰλέω, f. έσω, *to call forth:*—Med. *to call out to oneself*, metaph. *to call forth, elicit, excite.*

ἐκ-κᾰλύπτω, f. ψω, *to uncover, reveal:*—Med. *to unveil oneself.*

ἐκ-κάμνω, f. -κᾰμοῦμαι: aor. 2 ἐξέκᾰμον:—*to be tired out:* c. acc. *to grow weary of* a thing.

ἐκ-καρπίζομαι, Med. (ἐκ, καρπός) *to yield as fruit.*

ἐκ-καρπόομαι, Med. (ἐκ, καρπόω) *to reap* or *enjoy the fruit of:* metaph. *to derive advantage from.*

ἐκ-κατεῖδον, aor. 2 of ἐξοράω, *to look down from.*

ἐκ-καυλίζω, f. σω, (ἐκ, καυλός) *to pull out the stalk:* metaph. *to destroy root and branch.*

ἐκ-καυχάομαι, f. ήσομαι, Dep. *to vaunt aloud.*

ἐκ-κάω, Att. for ἐκκαίω.

ἐκκέας, aor. 1 part. of ἐκκαίω.

ἔκ-κειμαι, used as Pass. of ἐκτίθημι, *to be cast out* or *exposed.* II. c. gen. *to fall from out of.*

ἐκκέκοφα, **ἐκκέκομμαι**, pf. act. and pass. of ἐκκόπτω.

ἐκκεκώφηκα, **ἐκκεκώφωμαι**, pf. act. and pass. of ἐκκωφέω, -όω.

ἐκ-κενόω, **-κεινόω**, f. ώσω, *to empty out, desolate.*

ἐκ-κεντέω, f. ήσω, *to prick out.* II. *to pierce, stab.*

ἐκ-κερᾰΐζω, f. σω, *to pillage: to cut off root and branch.*

ἐκκέχῠμαι, pf. pass. of ἐκχέω: whence

ἐκκεχῠμένως, Adv. *profusely, extravagantly.*

ἐκκέχωσμαι, pf. pass. of ἐκχώννυμι.

ἐκ-κηραίνω, f. ᾰνῶ, (ἐκ, κήρ) *to enfeeble, exhaust.*

ἐκ-κηρύσσω Att. **-ττω**: fut. ξω:—*to proclaim by a herald, declare publicly.* II. *to banish by public proclamation.*

ἐκ-κῑνέω, f. ήσω, *to move out: to put up, rouse.*

ἐκ-κλάζω, f. -κλάγξω, *to cry aloud.*

ἐκ-κλάω, f. -κλάσω [ᾰ], *to break off.*

ἐκ-κλείω Ion. **-κληΐω** Att. **-κλῄω**: Att. fut. ἐκκλῄσω:—*to shut out:* metaph. *to exclude* or *hinder from.*

ἐκ-κλέπτω, f. ψω, *to remove stealthily, purloin.*

ἐκ-κληΐω, Ion. for ἐκκλείω.

ἐκκλησία, ἡ, (ἔκκλητος) *an assembly of the citizens summoned by the crier, the legislative assembly:* at Athens, the *ordinary* assemblies were called κύριαι ἐκκλησίαι, four in each πρυτανεία: the *extraordinary* σύγκλητοι. II. *the Church.* Hence

ἐκκλησιάζω, f. σω: impf. ἠκκλησίαζον or ἐκκλησίαζον, but also ἐξεκλησίαζον (as if the Verb were a compd. and not derived from ἐκκλησία); so aor. 1 ἐξεκλησίασα:—*to hold an assembly, debate therein:* absol. *to debate.* II. *to sit in assembly.* III. *to summon to the assembly.*

ἐκκλῄσω, Att. fut. of ἐκκλείω.

ἔκκλητος, ον, (ἐκκαλέω) *called forth*, Lat. *evocatus: selected to arbitrate* on a point.

ἐκ-κλίνω, f. -κλῐνῶ, *to bend aside: to bend down*, of stakes. II. intr. *to turn away from:* absol. *to give ground, retire.* 2. *to decline* or *degenerate into.*

ἐκ-κναίω, f. σω, *to wear out:* metaph. *to tease to death*, like Lat. *enecare;* Dor. 3 pl. fut. ἐκναισεῦντι.

ἐκ-κνάω, f. ήσω, *to rub* or *cut deeply.*

ἐκ-κοβᾱλικεύομαι, Dep. (ἐκ, κόβαλα) *to cajole* or *cheat by juggling tricks.*

ἐκ-κοκκίζω, f. ίσω Att. ιῶ, (ἐκ, κόκκος) *to take out the kernel: to pull* anything *out of its place, dislocate;* ἐκκοκκίζειν σφυρόν *to put out* one's ancle; ἐκκοκκίζειν τὰς πόλεις *to empty* the cities.

ἐκ-κολάπτω, f. ψω, *to scrape out, erase, obliterate.*

ἐκ-κολυμβάω, f. ήσω, *to swim out of.*

ἐκκομῐδή, ἡ, *a carrying out* or *off.* From

ἐκ-κομίζω, f. ίσω Att. ῐῶ, *to carry out: to carry to a place of safety;* ἐκκομίζειν τινὰ ἐκ πρήγματος *to keep* one *out of* trouble. II. *to endure.*

ἐκ-κομπάζω, f. σω, *to utter vauntingly.*

ἐκ-κομψεύομαι, Dep. (ἐκ, κομψεύω) *to set forth in plausible terms.*

ἐκ-κόπτω, f. ψω: pf. -κέκοφα:—Pass., aor. 2 ἐξεκόπην: pf. ἐκκέκομμαι:—*to cut out, knock out:*—Pass., ἐξεκόπη τὠφθαλμώ *he had* his eyes *knocked out.* 2. *to cut down, fell: to cut off, destroy*, Lat. *exscindere.* 3. *to beat off from* a place, *repulse.*

ἐκ-κορέω, f. ήσω, *to sweep out: to sweep clean.*

ἐκ-κορίζω, (ἐκ, κόρις) *to clear of bugs.*

ἐκ-κορῠφόω, f. ώσω, *to sum up shortly.*

ἐκ-κρέμᾰμαι, Pass. *to hang upon, listen attentively to.*

ἐκ-κρεμάννῡμι, f. κρεμάσω [ᾰ]:—*to let hang from* or *by*:—Pass. *to hang from* or *upon, cling to.* Hence

ἐκκρεμής, ές, *hanging from* or *upon.*

ἐκ-κρήμναμαι, poët. Pass. of ἐκκρεμάννυμι.

ἐκ-κρίνω, f. ῐνῶ, *to choose* or *single out, select.* 2. *to expel, reject.* 3. *to separate, secrete.* Hence

ἔκκρῐτος, ον, *picked out, chosen*; ἔκκριτον as Adv., *above all, eminently.*

ἔκκρουσις, εως, ἡ, *a beating out, driving away*: and

ἔκκρουστος, ον, *beaten out*: of embossed work, *worked in relief.* From

ἐκ-κρούω, f. σω, *to beat* or *dash out.* 2. *to drive back, repulse: to hiss* an actor *off the stage*, Lat. *explodere.* 3. *to put off, adjourn.*

ἐκ-κῠβιστάω, f. ήσω, *to tumble headlong out of.*

ἐκ-κυέω, f. ήσω, *to bring forth.*

ἐκ-κυκλέω, f. ήσω, *to wheel out* by means of the ἐκκύκλημα (q. v.):—Pass. *to be brought to sight* by this means; ἀλλ' ἐκκυκλήθητι come, *wheel yourself out!* i. e. *shew yourself*; cf. εἰσκυκλέω. Hence

ἐκκύκλημα, ατος, τό, *a theatrical machine* which disclosed the interior of the house to the spectators: cf. εἰσκυκλέω.

ἐκ-κυλίνδω, f. -κυλῖσω: aor. 1 ἐξεκύλῖσα:—Pass., aor. 1 ἐξεκυλίσθην:—*to roll out* or *off*: Pass. *to be rolled* or *thrown out*; ἐξεκυλίσθη ἐκ δίφρου he *rolled headlong from* the chariot: also hence *to extricate oneself* or *escape from.*

ἐκ-κῡμαίνω, (ἐκ, κῦμα) *to undulate: to be uneven.*

ἐκκυνέω, (ἔκκυνος) of a hound, *to quest about.*

ἐκ-κῡνηγετέω, f. ήσω, *to hunt down.*

ἔκ-κῠνος, ον, (ἐκ, κύων) of a hound, *questing about, not keeping on one scent.*

ἐκ-κύπτω, f. ψω, *to peep out of: to get out.*

ἐκ-κωμάζω, f. σω, *to come forth in the festive procession: to rush madly out.*

ἐκ-κωφέω, f. ήσω, and **ἐκ-κωφόω**, f. ώσω, (ἐκ, κωφός) *to deafen, stun*:—metaph., ἐκκεκώφωται ξίφη the swords *grew blunt.*

ἔκλᾰγον, aor. 2 of κλάζω.

ἔκλαγξα, aor. 1 of κλάζω.

ἐκ-λαγχάνω, f. -λήξομαι: aor. 2 ἐξέλᾰχον:—*to obtain by lot* or *fate.*

ἐκλάθετο, Ep. 3 sing. aor. 2 med. of ἐκλανθάνω.

ἐκ-λακτίζω, f. ίσω Att. ῐῶ, *to kick out*: metaph. *to spurn at.*

ἐκ-λᾰλέω, f. ήσω, *to speak out, divulge.*

ἐκ-λαμβάνω, f. -λήψομαι: aor. 2 ἐξέλᾰβον: for the other tenses, v. λαμβάνω:—*to take* or *choose out.* II. *to receive, bear.* III. *to contract to do work*, opp. to ἐκδίδωμι (to let it out).

ἐκ-λάμπω, f. ψω: aor. 1 ἐξέλαμψα:—*to shine* or *flash forth.* II. trans. *to make to shine, light up, kindle.*

ἐκ-λανθάνω, aor. 2 ἐξέλᾰθον, *to escape notice utterly* II. **ἐκ-ληθάνω**, with aor. 1 ἐξέλησα Dor. -έλᾱσα, Ep. redupl. aor. 2 ἐκλέλαθον, Causal of ἐκλανθάνω, *to make quite forgetful of* a thing:—Med. ἐκλανθάνομαι, with Ep. redupl. aor. 2 ἐκλελαθέσθαι: pf. pass. ἐκλέλησμαι, *to forget utterly.*

ἐκλᾰπάζω, f. ξω, = ἐξαλαπάζω, *to cast out from.*

ἐκλάπην [ᾰ], aor. 2 pass. of κλέπτω.

ἔκλαυσα, aor. 1 of κλαίω.

ἐκ-λάπτω, f. ψομαι, *to lap up: to drink off.*

ἐκ-λέγω, f. ξω: for the tenses v. λέγω:—*to pick out, single out*:—Med. *to choose out for oneself, choose.* 2. in Med. also *to pick out, pull out one's* gray hairs. II. *to collect tribute.*

ἐκ-λείπω, f. ψω: aor. 2 ἐξέλῐπον: pf. ἐκλέλοιπα:—*to leave out, omit.* 2. *to forsake, abandon, quit.* 3. εἴ τις ἐξέλιπε τὸν ἀριθμόν if any one *left* the number *incomplete.* II. of the sun, *to be eclipsed*; in full, ἐκλείπειν τὴν ἐκ τοῦ οὐρανοῦ ἕδρην. III. intr. *to leave off, cease, stop.* Hence

ἔκλειψις, εως, ἡ, *a forsaking, quitting.* II. *a disappearance* of sun or moon, *an eclipse.*

ἐκλεκτός, ή, όν, (ἐκλέγω) *chosen out, selected*; οἱ ἐκλεκτοί *the elect.*

ἐκλελᾰθεῖν, **-έσθαι**, Ep. redupl. aor. 2 act. and med. of ἐκληθάνω.

ἐκλέλῠμαι, pf. pass. of ἐκλύω.

ἔκλεο, Ep. for ἐκλέεο, 2 sing. impf. of κλέω.

ἐκ-λέπω, f. ψω, *to free from the shell, to hatch.*

ἐκ-λήγω, f. ξω, *to cease entirely.*

ἐκ-ληθάνω, f. -λήσω, see ἐκλανθάνω II.

ἐκλήθην, aor. 1 pass. of καλέω.

ἔκλησις, εως, ἡ, (ἐκλανθάνομαι) *forgetfulness: forgetting and forgiving.*

ἐκ-λιμπάνω, poët. for ἐκλείπω.

ἐκλίνθημες, Dor. 1 pl. aor. 1 pass. of κλίνω.

ἐκ-λιπαίνω, f. ᾰνῶ, *to fatten*:—Pass. *to grow fat.*

ἐκλιπεῖν, aor. 2 inf. of ἐκλείπω.

ἐκλῐπής, ές, (ἐκλιπεῖν) *failing, deficient*: ἡλίου ἐκλιπές τι ἐγένετο = ἔκλειψις, there was *an eclipse* of the sun. II. *omitted.*

ἐκλογή, ἡ, (ἐκλέγω) *a picking out, choice, election: a levy of troops* or *taxes.* II. *a choice selection,* as of extracts from authors.

ἐκ-λογίζομαι, Dep. *to compute, reckon, calculate: to consider, reflect on.*

ἐκλόμην, aor. 2 of κέλομαι.

ἐκ-λούω, f. σω, *to wash out.*

ἐκ-λοχεύω, f. σω, *to bring forth*:—Pass. *to be born.*

ἐκλῠθῶ, aor. 1 subj. pass. of ἐκλύω.

ἔκλῠσις, εως, ἡ, (ἐκλύω) *a release, deliverance.*

ἐκλῠτήριος, (ἐκλύω) *able to release*; τὸ ἐκλυτήριον *a means of delivering, a release, an expiatory offering.*

ἔκλῠτος, ον, *let loose, discharged.* From

ἐκ-λύω, f. ύσω [ῡ]: for the tenses v. λύω—*to loose* or *set free from*; ἐκλύειν στόμα *to give a loose to* his tongue:—so also in Med. II. *to unloose, unstring* a bow: hence *to break up, put an end to*:—Pass. *to be faint, exhausted, despond.*

ἐκ-λωβάομαι, Dep. *to sustain grievous injuries.*

ἐκ-λωπίζω, f. σω, (ἐκ. λῶπος) *to lay bare.*

ἐκμαγεῖον, τό, (ἐκμαγῆναι) *the impression* of a seal, *a seal*; ἐκμαγεῖον πέτρης *a counterfeit* of rock,—said of a hardy fisherman.

ἐκμᾰγῆναι, aor. 2 pass. of ἐκμάσσω.

ἐκ-μαίνω, f. -μᾰνῶ: aor. 1 ἐξέμηνα:—*to drive mad* with any passion; πόθον ἐκμῆναι *to kindle passionate desire*:—Pass. with aor. 2 ἐξεμάνην: intr. pf. act. ἐκμέμηνα:—*to go mad with passion: to rave, be frantic.*

ἐκμακτρον, τό, (ἐκμάσσω) *an impress, image.*

ἐκ-μανθάνω, f. -μαθήσομαι: aor. 2 ἐξέμαθον: pf. ἐκμεμάθηκα:—*to learn thoroughly, to learn by heart*: in past tenses, *to have learnt thoroughly*, and so *to know full well, perceive* II. *to examine closely, search out.*

ἐκμᾰνῶ, aor. 2 subj. pass. of ἐκμαίνομαι.

ἐκμάξας, aor. 1 part. of ἐκμάσσω.

ἐκ-μαργόω, f. ώσω, (ἐκ, μάργος) *to drive raving mad*:—Pass. *to go raving mad.*

ἐκ-μαρτῠρέω, f. ήσω, *to bear witness to* a thing.

ἐκ-μάσσω Att. -ττω: fut. ξω: aor. 1 ἐξέμαξα: Pass., pf. ἐκμέμαγμαι:—*to wipe off*:—Med. *to wipe away one's tears* II. *to mould* or *model* in wax or plaster, *to take an impression of*: *to imprint* an image.

ἐκ-μαστεύω, f. σω, *to search out.*

ἐκ-μεθύσκω, *to make quite drunk.*

ἐκ-μείρομαι, Dep. *to have a chief share in* a thing; ἐξέμμορε, Ep. perf., used only in 3 pers. sing.

ἐκ-μελετάω, f. ήσω, *to train carefully*: *to practise diligently.*

ἐκμεμάθηκα, pf. of ἐκμανθάνω.

ἐκμέμηνα, pf. med. of ἐκμαίνω.

ἐκ-μετρέω, f. ήσω, *to measure out*:—Med. *to measure out for oneself*: *to take measure of.*

ἔκ-μετρος, ον, (ἐκ, μέτρον) *measureless, boundless*, Lat. *immensus.*

ἐκμῆναι, aor. 1 inf. of ἐκμαίνω.

ἔκ-μηνος, ον, (ἕξ, μήν) *of six months, half yearly*: as Subst., ἔκμηνος, ἡ, *a space of six months.*

ἐκ-μηρύομαι, Dep., of an army, *to defile out of.*

ἐκ-μῐαίνω, *to pollute.*

ἐκ-μῑμέομαι, Dep. *to imitate faithfully.*

ἐκ-μισθόω, f. ώσω, *to let out for hire*:—Med. *to hire.*

ἔκμολε, Ep. for ἐξέμολε, 3 sing aor. 2 of ἐκβλώσκω.

ἐκ-μουσόω, f. ώσω, (ἐκ, μοῦσα) *to teach fully*

ἐκ-μοχθέω, f. ήσω, *to work out with toil*, Lat. *elaborare*: *to win hardly* or *by great exertion, to achieve.*

ἐκ-μοχλεύω, f. σω, (ἐκ, μοχλός) *to heave with the lever, to force one's way.*

ἐκ-μυζάω, f. ήσω, *to suck out*

ἐκ-μυκτηρίζω, f. σω, (ἐκ, μυκτήρ) *to turn up one's nose at, mock* at.

ἐκ-νεάζω, f. σω, (ἐκ, νέος) *to grow young* or *fresh.*

ἐκ-νέμομαι, Med. *to feed off*, Lat. *depasci.* 2. *to go forth to feed, go forth.*

ἐκνενίκηκα, pf. of ἐκνῑκάω.

ἐκ-νευρίζω, f. σω, *to cut the sinews*:—Pass., pf. ἐκνενεύρισμαι, *to be unnerved.*

ἐκ-νεύω, f. σω: aor. 1 ἐξένευσα:—*to turn aside, turn away.* II. *to sink down.* III. *to give a nod* or *sign to do* a thing.

ἐκ-νέω, fut. -νεύσομαι: aor. 1 ἐξένευσα:—*to swim out* or *away, escape by swimming*: generally, *to escape.*

ἐκ-νήφω, f. ψω, *to sleep off a drunken fit, become sober again.*

ἐκ-νίζω, f. -νίψω (as if from ἐκνίπτω): aor. 1 ἐξένιψα: —*to wash out* or *away.*

ἐκ-νῑκάω, f. ήσω, *to conquer completely*: *to achieve by force.* II. intr. *to prevail, grow into use*; ἐπὶ τὸ μυθῶδες ἐκνενικηκέναι *to win its way to* the fabulous.

ἐκ-νόμιος, ον, (ἐκ, νόμος) *unusual, unwonted, strange.* Adv. -ίως, Sup. ἐκνομιώτατα.

ἔκ-νομος, ον, (ἐκ, νόμος) *unusual, unwonted, unlawful*:—Adv. -μως, *discordantly.*

ἐκ-νοστέω, f. ήσω, *to return from, to return.*

ἐκ-νοσφίζομαι, Dep. *to take for oneself.*

ἐκνυζῆτο, Dor. 3 sing. impf. of κνυζάομαι

ἐκόμισσα, Ep. aor. 1 of κομίζω.

ἑκοντί, Adv. (ἑκών) *freely, willingly.*

ἐκορέσσατο, Ep. 3 sing. aor. 1 med. of κορέννυμι.

ἑκούσιος, α, ον, (ἑκών) *of one's own free will, voluntary.* Adv. -ίως; also ἐξ ἑκουσίας or καθ' ἑκουσίαν.

ἐκπαγλέομαι, Pass. *to be astonished* or *amazed.* II. *to wonder at, admire exceedingly.* From

ἔκ-παγλος, ον, (metath. for ἔκ-πλᾰγος, from ἐκπλαγῆναι) *frightful, terrible, fearful.* Adv. ἐκπάγλως, also neut. ἔκπαγλον and ἔκπλαγα used as Adv., *terribly, fearfully, greatly.* II. *astonishing, wonderful.*

ἐκπαίδευμα, ατος, τό, *anything reared, a child.* From

ἐκ-παιδεύω, f. σω, *to bring up from a child*: *to educate*

ἐκ-παιφάσσω, *to rush furiously forth.*

ἐκ-παίω: f. -παιήσω: aor. 1 ἐξέπαισα:—*to strike out of* a thing, *disappoint.*

ἔκ-πᾰλαι, Adv. for ἐκ πάλαι, *of old, long ago.*

ἐκ-πάλλω, *to shake out*:—Pass. *to spirt out.*

ἔκπαλτο, Ep. for ἐξεπάλετο, 3 sing. Ep. aor. 2 pass. of ἐκπάλλω.

ἐκ-πᾰτάσσω, f. ξω, *to strike out of one's senses.*

ἐκ-πάτιος, α, ον, (ἐκ, πάτος) *out of the common path*· *excessive.*

ἐκ-παύω, f. σω, *to set quite at rest, put an end to*:—Med. *to take one's rest.*

ἐκ-πείθω, f. σω, *to persuade, over-persuade.*

ἐκ-πειράζω, f. άσω, *to tempt.*

ἐκ-πειράομαι, fut. -πειράσομαι [ᾱ]: aor. 1 ἐξεπειράθην [ᾱ]: Dep.:—*to make trial of, prove, tempt.* 2. *to inquire of another.*

ἐκ-πέλω, whence impers. ἐκπέλει, *it is allowed.*

ἐκ-πέμπω, fut. ψω: aor. 1 ἐξέπεμψα:—*to send out* or *forth from*: of things, *to export.* 2. *to call* or *fetch out, send for:* Pass. *to go forth, depart.* II. *to dismiss, drive away: to divorce.* Hence

ἔκπεμψις, εως, ἡ, *a sending out* or *forth.*

ἐκπεπέτασται, 3 sing. pf. pass. of ἐκπετάννυμι.

ἐκπέπληγμαι, pf. pass. of ἐκπλήσσω.

ἐκπεπόνημαι, pf. pass. of ἐκπονέω.

ἐκπεπόρθημαι, pf. pass. of ἐκπορθέω.

ἐκπεπόρθμευμαι, pf. pass. of ἐκπορθμεύω, both in med. and pass. sense.

ἐκπέποται, 3 sing. pf. pass. of ἐκπίνω.

ἐκπεπότāμαι, Dor. pf. of ἐκποτάομαι.

ἐκπεπταμένος, η, ον, pf. pass. part. of ἐκπετάννυμι, *expanded, open.* Adv. -νως, *extravagantly.*

ἐκπέπτωκα, pf. of ἐκπίπτω.

ἐκπεράᾳ, ἐκπερόωσιν, Ep. 3 sing. and pl. of ἐκπεράω.

ἐκ-περαίνω, f. ἄνῶ, *to bring to an end:*—Pass. *to be fulfilled.*

ἐκπέρāμα, ατος, τό, *a passing out.* From

ἐκ-περάω: f. άσω [ā] Ion. ήσω: Ion. aor. 1 ἐξεπέρησα:—*to pass through* or *over:* metaph., *to accomplish.*

ἐκ-περδῑκίζω, f. ίσω Att. ιῶ, (ἐκ, πέρδιξ) *to escape like a partridge, fly away.*

ἐκ-πέρθω, fut. -πέρσω, *to destroy utterly.*

ἐκ-περίειμι, *to go all round.*

ἐκπέρσαι, aor. 1 inf. of ἐκπέρθω.

ἔκπεσε, Ep. for ἐξέπεσε, 3 sing. aor. 2 of ἐκπίπτω: **ἐκπεσέειν**, for ἐκπεσεῖν, aor. 2 inf.

ἐκ-πέταμαι, f. -πτήσομαι: aor. 2 both in med. and act. forms ἐξεπτάμην and ἐξέπτην:—*to fly out, forth* or *away.*

ἐκ-πετάννῡμι, f. -πετάσω [ᾰ]: Ep. aor. 1 ἐξεπέτασσα:—*to spread out, unfurl, spread: to stretch out.*

ἐκπετήσιμος, ον, (ἐκπέταμαι) *ready to fly out of the nest:* metaph. of a girl, *marriageable.*

ἐκ-πέτομαι, aor. 2 -επτόμην, = ἐκπέταμαι.

ἐκ-πεύθομαι, Ep. for ἐκπυνθάνομαι.

ἐκπέφευγα, pf. of ἐκφεύγω.

ἐκπεφῠυῖαι, pf. part. pl. fem. nom. of ἐκφύω.

ἐκ-πηδάω, f. ήσομαι, *to leap out* or *forth:* esp. of a besieged force, *to sally forth.* 2. *to leap up.* Hence

ἐκπήδημα, ατος, τό, *a leap out* or *forth.*

ἐκ-πηνίζω, f. ίσω Att. ιῶ, (ἐκ, πήνιον) *to reel off, wind out:* fut. med., ἐκπηνιεῖσθαί τί τινος *to wind* something *out of* a man.

ἐκ-πῑδύομαι, Dep. (ἐκ, πιδύω) *to gush forth.*

ἐκ-πίμπλημι, f. -πλήσω: aor. 1 ἐξέπλησα, pass. ἐξεπλήσθην:—*to fill up, fill full of.* 2. *to satiate.* II. *to fulfil.* III. *to finish, complete.*

ἐκ-πίνω [ῐ]: f. -πίομαι; aor. 2 ἐξέπιον: for the other tenses, v. πίνω:—*to drink out* or *off, quaff, drain.* II. metaph. *to empty out, drain.*

ἐκ-πιπράσκω, *to sell off.*

ἐκ-πίπτω, f. -πεσοῦμαι: aor. ἐξέπεσον: pf. ἐκπέπτωκα:—*to fall out of* or *down from.* 2. *to fall from, be deprived of, lose,* Lat. *excidere.* 3. *to be driven out of one's country, be banished.* 4. *to be cast ashore, to be wrecked,* Lat. *ejici.* 5. of actors, *to be hissed off the stage,* Lat. *explodi.* 6. *to come out* or *forth, sally out: to get out of, escape: to depart from.* 7. *to issue, result in.*

ἐκ-πίτνω, poët. for ἐκπίπτω.

ἐκπλᾰγῆναι, aor. 2 inf. pass. of ἐκπλήσσω.

ἔκπλεθρος, ον, (ἕξ, πλέθρον) *six plethra long.*

ἔκ-πλεος, poët. **ἔκπλειος**, α, ον, Att. **ἔκπλεως**, ων: (ἐκ, πλέως) *quite full: complete, entire: abundant.*

ἐκ-πλέω, f. -πλεύσομαι: aor. 1 ἐξέπλευσα: Ion. **ἐκπλώω**, f. -πλώσω:—*to sail out, go out of port;* c. acc., ἐκπλεῖν τὰς ναῦς εἰς τὴν εὐρυχωρίαν *to outsail* the ships into the open sea.

ἔκ-πλεως, ων, Att. for ἔκπλεος.

ἐκπλήγην, Ep. aor. 2 pass. of ἐκπλήσσω.

ἐκ-πλήγνῡμι, = ἐκπλήσσω.

ἐκπληκτικός, ή, όν, (ἐκπλήσσω) *striking with terror, astounding.* Adv. -κῶς, *in amazement.*

ἔκπληξις, εως, ἡ, (ἐκπλήσσω) *panic fear, consternation;* ἔκπληξις κακῶν *terror caused by* misfortunes.

ἐκ-πληρόω, f. ώσω, *to fill quite up.* 2. of ships, *to man completely.* 3. *to fulfil.* II. ἐκπληροῦν λιμένα *to cross over* the harbour, Lat. *emetiri spatium.*

ἐκ-πλήσσω Att. -ττω: fut. ξω: aor. 1 ἐξέπληξα:—*to strike out of, drive away:*—*to frighten out of one's senses, scare, astound.* II. Pass., mostly in aor. 2 ἐξεπλάγην [ᾰ], Ep. 3 sing. and pl. ἐκπλήγη, ἔκπληγεν: later also aor. 1 ἐξεπλήχθην:—*to be panic-struck, amazed.*

ἔκπλοος contr. **ἔκπλους**, ὁ, (ἐκπλέω) *a sailing out, leaving port.*

ἐκ-πλύνω [ῡ], *to wash out.* Hence

ἔκπλῠτος, ον, *to be washed out.*

ἐκ-πλώω, Ion. for ἐκπλέω.

ἐκ-πνέω Ep. -πνείω, f. -πνεύσομαι or -οῦμαι: aor. 1 ἐξέπνευσα:—*to breathe out* or *forth.* 2. βίον ἐκπνεῖν *to breathe one's last, expire;* and so ἐκπνέω alone. II. intr., of the wind, *to blow out* or *outwards: to burst out.* Hence.

ἐκπνόη, ἡ, *a breathing out, expiring.*

ἐκ-ποδών, Adv. (ἐκ, ποδῶν) *out of the way;* ἐκποδὼν ἵστασθαι to stand *out of the way;* ἐκποδὼν χωρεῖν τινι to get *out of* his *way.* Opp. to ἐμποδὼν.

ἐκ-ποιέω, f. ήσω; aor. 1 ἐξεποίησα:—*to put out* a child, *give* him *in adoption,* II. Med. *to produce, bring forth.* III. *to make completely, finish off.* Hence

ἐκποίησις, εως, ἡ, *a putting forth, emission:* and

ἐκποίητος, η, ον, *put forth, given in adoption.*

ἐκ-ποκίζω, f. ίσω Att. ιῶ, *to pull out wool* or *hair.*

ἐκ-πολεμέω, f. ήσω, *to excite to war, make hostile.*

ἐκ-πολεμόω, f. ώσω, *to make hostile, involve in war:* Pass. *to become an enemy to.*

ἐκ-πολῐορκέω, f. ήσω, *to take by siege,* Lat. *expugnare.*

ἐκπομπή, ἡ, (ἐκπέμπω) *a sending out* or *forth*

ἐκ-πονέω, f. ήσω: aor. 1 ἐξεπόνησα:—*to work out, finish off, execute, bring to perfection,* Lat. *elaborare:*—Pass. *to be brought to perfection;* σῖτος ἐκπεπονημένος corn *prepared for use;* ἐκπεπονῆσθαι τὰ σώματα *to have* their bodies *in good training.* II. *to work hard for, to earn by labour.* III. *to prevail on by importunity.* IV. *to search out.* V. of food, *to digest by labour.*

ἐκ-πορεύω, f. σω, *to make to go out, fetch out:*—Med. and Pass., fut. -πορεύσομαι, aor. 1 ἐξεπορεύθην, *to go out* or *forth, to go away, march out.*

ἐκ-πορθέω, f. ήσω, = ἐκπέρθω, *to pillage:* metaph. *to undo.* II. *to carry off as plunder.* Hence

ἐκπορθήτωρ, ορος, ὁ, *a ravager, destroyer.*

ἐκ-πορθμεύω, f. σω, *to carry away by sea.*

ἐκ-πορίζω: f. ίσω Att. ιῶ; aor. 1 ἐξεπόρισα:—*to invent, contrive.* II. *to find means* for doing a thing, *to provide, furnish, supply:*—Med. *to provide for oneself, procure.*

ἐκ-πορνεύω, f. σω, *to be given to fornication.*

ἐκ-ποτάομαι, Ion. for ἐκ-πέτομαι: Dor. pf. ἐκπεπότᾱμαι: Dep.:—*to fly out* or *forth:* metaph. *to be lifted up* or *elated.*

ἐκ-πράσσω Att. **-ττω:** f. ξω: aor. 1 ἐξέπραξα:—*to do completely, bring about, achieve,* Lat. *efficere.* II. *to make an end of, kill,* Lat. *conficere.* III. *to exact* a fine: *to exact punishment for, to avenge.*

ἐκ-πρᾱΰνω, *to soothe, mollify.*

ἐκπρεπής, ές, (ἐκπρέπω) *distinguished out of all, pre-eminent.* II. (ἐκ, πρέπον) *unseemly, unbecoming.*

ἐκ-πρέπω, *to be pre-eminent in* a thing.

ἐκπρεπῶς, Adv. of ἐκπρεπής II, *unreasonably.*

ἐκ-πρήσσω, Ion. for ἐκπράσσω.

ἐκ-πρίω, f. -πριοῦμαι: aor. 2 ἐξέπριον:—*to saw out.*

ἐκ-προθῡμέομαι, f. ήσομαι: Dep. *to be very zealous.*

ἐκ-προΐημι, f. ήσω, *to pour forth.*

ἐκ-προκᾰλέομαι, f. έσομαι: Med. *to call forth to* or *for oneself;* Ep. aor. 1 part. ἐκπροκαλεσσάμενος.

ἐκπροκρῐθείς, aor. 1 pass. part. of

ἐκ-προκρίνω, f. -κρῐνῶ, *to select in preference.*

ἐκ-προλείπω, f. ψω, *to forsake;* aor. 2 part. ἐκπρολιπών.

ἐκ-προτῑμάω, f. ήσω, *to honour above all.*

ἐκ-προφεύγω, f. -φεύξομαι, *to escape from.*

ἐκ-προχέω, f. -χεῶ, *to pour forth.*

ἐκ-πτερύσσομαι, Dep. *to expand the wings.*

ἐκ-πτήσσω, f. ξω, *to scare away from.*

ἐκ-πτοέω, f. ήσω, = ἐκπτήσσω:—Pass. *to be scared.*

ἐκ-πτύω, f. ύσω or ύσομαι [ῠ]: aor. 1 ἐξέπτῠσα:—*to spit out: to spit in token of disgust.*

ἐκ-πυνθάνομαι, f. -πεύσομαι: aor. 2 ἐξεπῠθόμην: Dep.:—*to search out, make full inquiry about, hear of.*

ἐκ-πῠρόω, f. ώσω, *to burn to ashes, consume.* Hence

ἐκπύρωσις, εως, ἡ, *a conflagration.*

ἔκ-πυστος, ον, *heard of, discovered.*

ἔκπωμα, ατος, τό, (ἐκπίνω) *a drinking-cup.*

ἐκ-πωτάομαι, poët. for ἐκποτάομαι, ἐκπέτομαι.

ἐκράανθεν, Ep. for ἐκρανθήσαν, 3 pl. aor. 1 pass. of κραίνω.

ἐκ-ραβδίζω, f. σω, *to drive out with a rod.*

ἐκρᾰγῆναι, aor. 2 inf. pass. of ἐκρήγνυμι.

ἐκρᾰγήσομαι, fut. 2 pass. of ἐκρήγνυμι.

ἔκρᾰγον, aor. 2 of κράζω.

ἐκράθην [ᾱ], aor. 1 pass. of κεράννυμι.

ἐκραίαινον, Ep. impf. of κραίνω.

ἐκ-ραίνω, f. ᾰνῶ: aor. 1 ἐξέρρᾱνα:—*to scatter out from.*

ἐκρέμω, for ἐκρέμαο, 2 sing. impf. of κρέμαμαι.

ἐκ-ρέω, f. -ρεύσομαι: pf. ἐξερρύηκα: aor. 2 pass. (in act. sense) ἐξερρύην:—*to flow out* or *forth.* 2. of feathers, *to fall off.* 3. *to melt* or *fall away.* II. trans. *to shed, let fall.*

ἐκ-ρήγνυμι or **ἐκ-ρήσσω:** fut. -ρήξω: aor. 1 ἐξέρρηξα:—Pass., fut. 2 ἐκρᾰγήσομαι: aor. 2 ἐξερράγην:—*to break out, break off:*—Pass. *to snap asunder.* II. in Pass. also, *to break* or *burst out, to break forth.* III. also intr. in Act., *to break out* or *forth.*

ἐκ-ριζόω, f. ώσω, *to root out.*

ἐκρίθην, aor. 1 pass. of κρίνω.

ἐκ-ρίπτω, f. ψω: aor. 1 ἐξέρριψα:—*to throw out, cast forth.*

ἔκροος, contr. **ἔκρους,** ὁ, (ἐκρέω) *outflow, outfall.*

ἐκ-ροφέω, f. ήσω, *to gulp down.*

ἐκρύβην [ῡ], aor. 2 pass. of κρύπτω.

ἐκ-ρύομαι, f. -ρύσομαι, *to rescue, deliver.*

ἐκρύφθην, aor. 1 pass. of κρύπτω.

ἐκ-σᾰλάσσω, *to shake violently.*

ἐκ-σᾰόω, f. ώσω: aor. 1 ἐξεσάωσα:—Ep. for ἐκσώζω.

ἐκ-σείω, f. σω: aor. 1 ἐξέσεισα:—*to shake out.*

ἐκ-σεύομαι: pf. ἐξέσσῠμαι: plqpf. (in aor. sense) ἐξεσσύμην: Pass.: (ἐκ, σεύω):—*to rush forth from, flee away from.*

ἐκ-σημαίνω, f. ᾰνῶ, *to signify, denote.*

ἐκ-σιγάω, f. ήσομαι, *to put to utter silence.*

ἐκ-σκᾰλεύω, f. σω, *to rake out, pull away.*

ἐκ-σκεδάννῡμι, f. -σκεδάσω [ᾰ], *to scatter abroad.*

ἐκ-σκευάζω, f. σω, *to disfurnish.*

ἐκ-σμάω, inf. -σμῆν: impf. ἐξέσμων:—*to wipe out.*

ἐκ-σοβέω, f. ήσω: aor. 1 ἐξεσόβησα:—*to scare away.*

ἐκ-σπάω, f. άσω [ᾰ]: aor. 1 ἐξέσπᾰσα, Ep. part. med. ἐκσπασσάμενος:—*to draw out, pluck out.*

ἐκ-σπένδω, f. -σπείσω, *to pour out as a libation.*

ἐκ-σπεύδω, f. σω, *to hasten out.*

ἔκ-σπονδος, ον, (ἐκ, σπονδή) *out of the treaty, excluded from it.*

ἐκ-στάδιος, ον, (ἕξ, στάδιον) *six stades long.*

ἔκστᾰσις, εως, ἡ, (ἐξίστημι) *a being put out of its place:* of the mind, *distraction, astonishment:*—*a trance:* (hence Engl. *ecstasy*).

ἐκ-στέλλω, f. -στελῶ, aor. 1 ἐξέστειλα:—*to send out: to deck out.*

ἐκ-στέφω, f. ψω: aor. 1 ἐξέστεψα: pf. pass. ἐξέστεμμαι:—*to deck out with garlands.*

ἐκ-στρᾰτεία, ἡ, *a going out on service.* From

ἐκ-στρᾰτεύω, f. σω, *to march out: to take the field.*

ἐκ-στρᾰτοπεδεύομαι, f. εύσομαι: pf. ἐξεστρατοπέδευμαι: Dep.:—*to encamp outside.*

ἐκ-στρέφω, f. ψω: aor. 1 ἐξέστρεψα:—*to turn aside, overturn.* II. *to turn inside out:* metaph. *to change entirely: to pervert.*

ἐκ-συρίσσω Att. -ττω, f. ξω, *to whistle* or *hiss off the stage,* Lat. *explodere.*

ἐκ-σύρω [ῡ], *to drag out:* aor. 2 pass. ἐξεσύρην [ῠ].

ἐκ-σφρᾱγίζω, f. ίσω Att. ιῶ, *to seal up:*—Pass. *to be shut out from.*

ἐκ-σώζω, f. σω: aor. 1 ἐξέσωσα:—*to keep safe, preserve:*—Med. *to save oneself, save one's life:*—Pass., νῆσον ἐκσώζεσθαι *to seek for safety in* the island.

ἐκ-σωρεύω, f. σω, (ἐκ, σωρός) *to heap* or *pile up.*

ἔκτᾰ, Ep. 3 sing. aor. 2 of κτείνω.

ἐκτάδην [ᾰ], Adv. (ἐκτείνω) *outstretched.*

ἐκτάδιος, η, ον, (ἐκτείνω) *outspread.*

ἐκτᾰθείς, aor. 1 part. pass. of ἐκτείνω.

ἔκτᾰθεν, Ep. 3 pl. aor. 1 pass. of κτείνω.

ἐκτᾰθήσομαι, fut. 1 pass. of ἐκτείνω.

ἔκτᾰμε, Ep. for ἐξέταμε, 3 sing. aor. 2 of ἐκτέμνω.

ἔκταμεν, Ep. for ἐκτάνομεν, 1 pl. aor. 2 of κτείνω.

ἐκτάμην, Ep. aor. 2 med. (with pass. sense) of κτείνω.

ἐκ-τάμνω, Ion. for ἐκτέμνω.

ἔκτᾰν, Ep. 3 pl. aor. 2 of κτείνω.

ἔκτᾰνον, aor. 2 of κτείνω.

ἐκ-τᾰνύω, f. ύσω: aor. 1 ἐξετάνῠσα, Ep. -υσσα: aor. 1 pass. ἐξετανύσθην:—poët. for ἐκτείνω, *to stretch out in the dust, lay low:*—Pass, *to lie outstretched.*

ἐκ-τᾰράσσω Att. -ττω, f. ξω: aor. 1 ἐξετάραξα:—*to disquiet, confound, agitate.*

ἐκ-τάσσω Att. -ττω, f. ξω, *to draw* an army *out in order:*—Med., of an army, *to draw up in line.*

ἐκτέατο, Ion. 3 pl. plqpf. of κτάομαι.

ἐκ-τέθραμμαι, pf. pass. of ἐκτρέφω.

ἐκτεθείς, aor. 1 pass. part. of ἐκτίθημι.

ἐκ-τείνω, fut. -τενῶ: aor. 1 ἐξέτεινα: pf. ἐκτέτᾰκα:—Pass., aor. 1 ἐξετάθην: pf. ἐκτέτᾰμαι:—*to stretch out, to stretch along,* esp. of a corpse: hence, *to lay low:*—Pass. *to lie outstretched, lie along:* metaph. of the mind, *to be on the stretch, on the rack.* II. *to stretch out, extend, prolong.* III. *to strain to the uttermost.*

ἐκ-τειχίζω, f. ίσω Att. ιῶ, *to fortify completely: to build from the ground.*

ἐκ-τελευτάω, f. ήσω, *to bring quite to an end.*

ἐκ-τελέω: Ep. impf. ἐξετέλειον: f. -τελέσω, Ep. -τελέω:—fut. med. ἐκτελέεσθαι in pass. sense:—*to bring to an end, accomplish, achieve.*

ἐκ-τελής, ές, (ἐκ, τέλος) *brought to an end, perfect: ripe, mature.*

ἐκ-τέμνω Ion. -τάμνω: f. τεμῶ: aor. 2 ἐξέτᾰμον:—*to cut out from, cut out: to cut* trees *out of a wood, to cut down.* 2. *to hew out, hew into shape.* II. *to castrate.*

ἐκτένεια, ἡ, *earnestness, zeal.* From

ἐκτενής, ές, (ἐκτείνω) *stretched out:* metaph. *earnest, zealous, assiduous.* 2. *abundant.* Hence

ἐκτενῶς, Adv. *earnestly, zealously, assiduously:* Comp. ἐκτενέστερον *more earnestly.*

ἐκτέος, α, ον, verb. Adj. of ἔχω, *to be held.* II. neut. ἐκτέον, *one must have* or *hold.*

ἐκτέτηκα, intrans. pf. of ἐκτήκω.

ἐκτέτιλμαι, pf. pass. of ἐκτίλλω.

ἐκτεύς, έως, ὁ, (ἕκτος) *the sixth part* (*sextarius*) *of the μέδιμνος*, = 8 chœnixes.

ἐκ-τεχνάομαι, f. ήσομαι: aor. 1 ἐξετεχνησάμην: Dep.:—*to contrive, devise.*

ἐκ-τήκω, f. ξω: aor. 2 ἐξέτᾰκον:—*to make melt away:*—Pass., with intr. pf. act. ἐκτέτηκα, *to melt away.* II. Pass., also, *to slip from the mind,* opp. to ἐμμένειν.

ἔκτημαι, for κέκτημαι, pf. of κτάομαι.

ἐκτήσω, 2 sing. aor. 1 of κτάομαι.

ἐκ-τίθημι, f. -θήσω: *to set out, put outside:*—*to put out, expose.* II. *to set up, exhibit.*

ἐκ-τίκτω, f. -τέξω: aor. 2 ἐξέτεκον:—*to bring forth.*

ἐκ-τίλλω, f. -τῐλῶ: pf. pass. ἐκτέτιλμαι:—*to pluck* or *pull out:* Pass., κόμην ἐκτετιλμένος *having* one's hair *plucked out.*

ἐκ-τῑμάω, f. ήσω, *to honour highly.*

ἔκ-τῑμος, ον, (ἐκ, τιμή) *without honour.*

ἐκ-τῑνάσσω, f. ξω, *to shake out* or *off.*

ἐκ-τίνω, f. -τίσω: aor. 1 ἐξέτῑσα:—*to pay off, pay in full;* ἐκτῖσαι δίκην *to pay the full penalty.* II. Med. *to exact full payment for* a thing, *avenge: to take vengeance on.*

ἐκ-τιτρώσκω, f. -τρώσω: aor. 1 ἐξέτρωσα:—*to cause a miscarriage.* II. intr. *to miscarry.*

ἔκτοθεν, Adv. (ἐκτός) Ep. for ἔξωθεν, *from without,* c. gen.: *outside.*

ἔκτοθι, Adv. (ἐκτός) *out of, outside,* c. gen.

ἐκ-τολῠπεύω, f. σω, *to wind quite off, to bring to an end.*

ἐκτομεύς, έως, ὁ, (ἐκτέμνω) *one that cuts out:* fem. ἐκτομίς, ίδος.

ἐκτομή, ἡ, (ἐκτέμνω) *a cutting out: castration.* Hence

ἐκτομίας, ου, ὁ, *one castrated, a eunuch.*

ἐκ-τοξεύω, f. σω, *to shoot out, shoot away: to throw away.* 2. *to shoot from* a place, *shoot arrows.*

ἐκ-τόπιος, α, ον, also ος, ον, = ἔκτοπος.

ἔκ-τοπος, ον, (ἐκ, τόπος) *away from a place, distant:* hence *out of the way, foreign, strange.*

ἐκ-τορέω, f. ήσω, *to bore through, stab to death.*

ἕκτος, η, ον, (ἕξ) *the sixth.*

ἐκτός, Adv. (ἐκ) Lat. *extrinsecus*, opp. to ἐντός: I. of Place, *without, outside:* as Prep. with gen. *out of, far from: free from.* 2. *out of, beyond.* 3. *except.* II. of Time, *beyond, over.*

ἔκτοσε, (ἐκτός) Adv. *outwards.*

ἔκτοσθε, ἔκτοσθεν, (ἐκτός) Adv. *from without, without, outside: far from, apart from.*

ἐκ-τράπεζος, ον, (ἐκ, τράπεζα) *away from* or *banished from the table.*

ἐκ-τρᾰχηλίζω, f. ίσω Att. ιῶ, of a horse, *to throw*

the rider over its head: generally, *to throw off* or *down* :—Pass. *to break one's neck.*

ἐκ-τρᾱχύνω [ῡ], f. ὔνῶ, *to make rough.*

ἐκ-τρέπω, f. ψω, *to turn off* or *aside, divert* :—metaph., *to turn aside, dissuade* :—Pass. and Med. *to turn aside from, to avoid.*

ἐκ-τρέφω, f. -θρέψω: aor. 1 ἐξέθρεψα :—*to bring up from childhood, rear up* :—Med. *to rear up f. oneself.*

ἐκ-τρέχω, f. -θρέξομαι and -δρᾰμοῦμαι (from *δρέμω) :—*to run out* or *forth* : *to make a sally.* 2. *to run off* or *away.* 3. metaph. of anger, *to burst forth.*

ἐκ-τρίβω, f. ψω: aor. 1 ἐξέτριψα ;—Pass., fut. 2 ἐκτριβήσομαι : pf. ἐκτέτριμμαι :—*to rub out; πῦρ ἐκτρίβειν to produce fire by rubbing.* II. *to rub hard.* III. *to destroy by rubbing, destroy root and branch; βίον ἐκτρίβειν to bring* life *to a wretched end.*

ἐκτρίψαι, aor. 1 inf. of ἐκτρίβω.

ἐκτροπή, ἡ, (ἐκτρέπω) *a turning off* or *aside.* II. *a turning oneself from, avoidance* :—ἐκτροπὴ ὁδοῦ a *resting*-place ; ἐκτροπὴ λόγου *a digression.*

ἐκ-τρῡχόω, f. ώσω, *to wear out, exhaust.*

ἐκ-τρώγω, f. -τρώξομαι, *to eat up, devour.*

ἔκτρωμα, ατος, τό, (ἐκτιτρώσκω) *a child untimely born, an abortion.*

ἔκτῠπον, aor. 2 of κτυπέω.

ἔκ-τῠπος, ον, (ἐκ, τύπτω) *beaten out, wrought in relief.* Hence

ἐκ-τυπόω, f. ώσω, *to work in relief.*

ἐκ-τυφλόω, f. ώσω, *to make quite blind.* Hence

ἐκτύφλωσις, εως, ἡ, *a making quite blind.*

ἐκύει, 3 sing. impf. of κυέω.

ἑκῠρά, ἡ, *a step-mother*, Ep. word for πενθερά.

ἔκῠρον, aor. 2 of κυρέω.

ἑκῠρός, ὁ, *a step-father*, Ep. word for πενθερός. (Deriv. uncertain.)

ἔκῠσα, aor. 1 of κυνέω.

ἔκῡσα, aor. 1 of κύω.

ἐκ-φᾰγεῖν, *to eat up, devour:* only used in aor. 2, the pres. in use being ἐξεσθίω.

ἐκ-φαιδρύνω [ῡ], f. ὔνῶ, *to make quite clear.*

ἐκ-φαίνω, f. -φᾰνῶ : aor. 1 ἐξέφηνα :—*to shew forth, bring to light : to betray, make known ;* ἐκφαίνειν πόλεμον *to declare* war :—Pass. and Med., f. -φᾰνοῦμαι and -φᾰνήσομαι : aor. 1 ἐξεφάνθην, aor. 2 ἐξεφάνην [ᾰ] :—*to shine out* or *forth, to shew oneself, appear, come to light.* Hence

ἐκφᾰνής, ές, *shining forth, manifest.* Adv. -νῶς.

ἐκφάσθαι, pres. inf. med. of ἔκφημι.

ἔκφᾰσις, εως, ἡ, (ἔκφημι) *a declaration.*

ἔκφᾰτος, ον, (ἔκφημι) *beyond power of speech* :— Adv. ἐκφάτως, *expressly, plainly* ; or, *beyond words to express*, i. e. *impiously.*

ἐκ-φαυλίζω, f. ίσω Att. ιῶ, *to depreciate.*

ἐκφερέμεν, Ep. for ἐκφέρειν, inf. of ἐκφέρω.

ἐκ-φέρω, f. ἐξοίσω: aor. 1 and 2 ἐξήνεγκα, ἐξήνεγκον :—fut. med. ἐξοίσομαι in pass. sense :—*to carry out of: to carry out* a corpse for burial, Lat. *efferre* : also *to carry away : to carry off* as prize :—Pass. *to be carried out;* metaph. *to be carried away by passion.* 2. *to put out* of a ship. II. *to bring forth, to produce.* 2. *to accomplish, fulfil : bring about.* 3. *to bring out, put forward, to publish, proclaim : to tell abroad, betray.* 4. *to put forth, exert.* 5. ἐκφέρειν πόλεμον, Lat. *inferre bellum, to begin* war. 6. *to shew signs of, shew.* III. *to carry out* or *to the end.* IV. intr. (sub. ἑαυτόν) *to run out of* the course, of race-horses : also *to run away.* 2. *to come to an end.*

ἐκ-φεύγω, f. -φεύξομαι and -φευξοῦμαι : aor. 2 ἐξέφῠγον : pf. ἐκπέφευγα :—*to flee out* or *away, escape : to flee out of, escape from;* βέλος ἔκφυγε χειρός. 2. *to escape from danger ;* esp. *to be acquitted.*

ἔκ-φημι, *to speak out, speak :* aor. 2 inf. med. ἐκφάσθαι.

ἐκ-φθείρω, *to destroy utterly* : Pass. *to be undone ;* imper. ἐκφθείρου, *begone !* aor. 2 part. ἐκφθᾰρείς.

ἐκ-φθίνω, only used in Pass. *to perish utterly* ; 3 pl. pf., ἐξέφθινται *they have utterly perished* ; 3 sing. plqpf., ἐξέφθῐτο οἶνος νηῶν the wine *had* all *been consumed out of* the ships.

ἐκ-φιλέω, f. ήσω, *to love passionately.*

ἐκ-φλαυρίζω, f. ίσω Att. ιῶ, = ἐκφαυλίζω.

ἐκ-φλέγω, f. ξω : aor. 1 ἐξέφλεξα :—*to set on fire.*

ἐκ-φοβέω, f. ήσω, *to frighten out* or *away, affright :* —Pass. *to be affrighted.*

ἐκ-φοινίσσω, fut. ξω, *to make red* or *bloody.*

ἐκ-φοιτάω, Ion. -έω, fut. ήσω, *to go out* or *forth.*

ἐκφορά, ἡ, (ἐκ-φέρω) *a carrying out* of a corpse to burial. 2. *a blabbing, betrayal.* II. (from Pass.) of horses, *a running away.*

ἐκ-φορέω, = ἐκφέρω, *to carry out* a corpse for burial :—Med. *to take out with one :*—Pass. *to move forth.* II. *to carry quite out.* III. in Pass., *to be cast up on shore*, Lat. *ejici.*

ἐκφόριον, τό, (ἐκφέρω) *that which is brought forth, fruit, produce* ; also *rent, tithe.*

ἔκφορος, ον, (ἐκφέρω) *to be carried out, exportable.* II. *to be made known.*

ἐκ-φορτίζομαι, Pass., *to be sold like merchandise :* hence *to be betrayed.*

ἐκ-φράζω, f. άσω, *to tell in full.*

ἐκ-φρέω poët. **ἐκφρείω** : f. ήσομαι, also ήσω : (ἐκ, φρέω which only occurs in compos., v. δια-φρέω, ἐκ-φρέω) :—*to let out, bring out* :—Pass. *to go out.*

ἐκ-φροντίζω, f. ίσω Att. ιῶ, *to think out, devise, invent*, Lat. *excogitare.*

ἔκ-φρων, ον, gen. ονος, (ἐκ, φρήν) *out of one's mind, mad, senseless*, Lat. *amens :* also, *frenzied.*

ἐκ-φυγγάνω, = ἐκφεύγω.

ἔκφῠγε, Ep. for ἐξέφυγε, 3 sing. aor. 2 of ἐκφεύγω.

ἐκ-φῠλάσσω, f. ξω, *to watch carefully.*

ἐκφῦναι, aor. 2 inf. of ἐκφύω, formed from ἔκφυμι.

ἐκ-φῡσάω, f. ήσω, *to blow* or *breathe out :* metaph., ἐκφυσᾶν πόλεμον *to blow* up a war from a spark.

ἐκ-φύω, I. Causal in pres., in f. ἐκφύσω [ῡ]: aor. 1 ἐξέφῡσα:—*to beget, produce.* II. intr. in pf. ἐκπέφῡκα, aor. 2 ἐξέφυν, and in Med. ἐκφύομαι:—*to be produced* or *born from, grow from,* c. gen.: absol. λάλημα ἐκπεφυκός *a born* tattler.

ἐκ-φωνέω, f. ήσω, *to pronounce aloud.*

ἐκ-χαλάω, f. άσω [ᾰ], *to let go from.*

ἐκ-χαυνόω, f. ώσω, *to puff up, make vain.*

ἐκχεύατο, 3 sing. Ep. aor. 1 med. of ἐκχέω.

ἐκ-χέω, f. -χεῶ: aor. 1 ἐξέχεα, Ep. ἐξέχευα: pf. ἐκκέχῠκα:—*to pour out,* Lat. *effundo: to pour forth in vain, lavish, squander.* II. Pass., aor. 1 ἐξεχύθην [ῠ]: pf. ἐκκέχῠμαι: Ep. forms, 3 pl. plqpf. ἐξεκέχυντο, aor. 2 ἐξέχῠτο or ἔκχῠτο, part. ἐκχύμενος:—*to be poured out, to stream out* or *forth:* generally, *to spread out* or *abroad:—to give loose to passion,* Lat. *effundi in . . .*

ἐκ-χορεύω, f. σω, *to break out of the chorus.* II. **ἐκχορεύομαι,** as Dep., *to drive out of the chorus.*

ἐκ-χράω, Ion. -χρέω, like ἀποχράω:—*to suffice, be enough for:* only used as impers. ἐκχρήσει, ἐξέχρησε, *it will be, was enough* or *sufficient for.*

ἐκ-χράω, f. ήσω, *to declare as an oracle.*

ἐκ-χρηματίζομαι, Dep. *to squeeze money from, levy contributions on.*

ἐκχῠθείς, aor. 1 part. pass. of ἐκχέω.

ἐκχυθήσομαι, fut. ind. of ἐκχέω.

ἐκχύμενος [ῠ], Ep. aor. 2 part. pass. of ἐκχέω

ἔκχῠτο, 3 sing. Ep. aor. 2 pass. of ἐκχέω.

ἔκχῠτος, ον, (ἐκχέω) *poured out: unconfined, outspread,* Lat. *effusus:*—**ἔκχυτον,** τό, *drink.*

ἐκ-χώννῡμι, f. -χώσω: pf. pass ἐκκέχωσμαι:—*to raise by heaping up soil: to silt up,* of a river.

ἐκ-χωρέω, f. ήσω, *to go out and away, depart from.* 2. *to slip out of:* hence of a joint, *to be dislocated.* 3. *to give way: to give place to.*

ἐκ-ψύχω, f. ξω, *to give up the ghost,* Lat. *exspiro.*

ἙΚΩ´Ν, ἑκοῦσα, ἑκόν, *willing, voluntary, of free will.* II. often in phrase ἑκὼν εἶναι (where the inf. seems to be pleonastic), *willingly, purposely.*

ἐλάα, Att. for ἐλαία.

ἐλάαν, Ep. for ἐλᾶν, inf. of ἐλαύνω.

ἔλᾰβον, aor. 2 of λαμβάνω.

ἔλᾰθον, aor. 2 of λανθάνω.

ἘΛΑΙ´Α Att. **ἐλάα,** ἡ, *the olive-tree,* Lat. *olea, oliva:*—proverb., φέρεσθαι ἐκτὸς τῶν ἐλαῶν to run beyond *the olives,* which stood at the end of the Athenian racecourse, i. e. to go too far. II. *the fruit of the olive-tree, an olive.* Hence

ἐλαιήεις Att. -άεις, εσσα, εν, *of the olive-tree.*

ἐλᾱΐνεος, α, ον, and **ἐλᾱϊνός,** ή, όν, (ἐλαία) *of the olive-tree, of olive-wood.*

ἐλαιο-λόγος, ὁ, (ἐλαία, λέγω) *an olive-gatherer.*

ἔλαιον, τό, (ἐλαία) *olive-oil, oil,* Lat. *olivum.*

ἔλαιος, ὁ, (ἐλαία) *the wild-olive,* Lat. *oleaster.*

ἐλαιο-φόρος, ον, (ἐλαία, φέρω) *olive-bearing.*

ἐλαιο-φυής, ές, (ἐλαία, φύω) *olive-planted.*

ἐλαιό-φῠτος, ον, (ἐλαία, φύω) *olive-planted.*

ἐλᾱΐς, ΐδος, ἡ, = ἐλαία: Att. pl. ἐλᾱδες.

ἐλαιών, ῶνος, ὁ, (ἐλαία) *an olive-garden, olive-yard,* Lat. *olivētum:*—as prop. n., *the Mount of Olives, Olivet.*

ἐλάκηκα, ἔλᾰκον, ao. 1 and 2 of λάσκω.

ἐλάμφθην, Ion. for ἐλήφθην, aor. 1 pass. of λαμβάνω.

ἔλ-ανδρος, ον, (ἑλεῖν, ἀνήρ) *man-slaying.*

ἔλᾰσα, Ep. for ἤλασα, aor. 1 of ἐλαύνω:—**ἐλάσασκε,** Ion. and Ep. 3 sing.—**ἐλασαίατο,** Ion. and Ep. for ἐλάσαιντο, 3 plur. aor. 1 opt. med.

ἐλασᾶς, ὁ, *an unknown bird.*

ἐλᾰσείω, Desiderat. of ἐλαύνω, *to wish to drive.*

ἐλᾰσία, ἡ, (ἐλαύνω) *riding, driving.*

ἐλᾰσί-βροντος, ον, (ἐλαύνω, βροντή) *thunder-hurling.* II. *hurled like thunder.*

ἐλάσ-ιππος, ον, (ἐλαύνω, ἵππος) *horse-driving.*

ἔλᾰσις, εως, ἡ, (ἐλαύνω) *a driving, riding:* also *rowing.* 2. *a driving away, banishing.* 3. (sub. στρατοῦ), *a march, expedition;* (sub. ἵππου) *riding.*

ἔλασσα, Ep. for ἔλασα, ἤλασα, aor. 1 of ἐλαύνω.

ἐλασσόω, Att. -ττόω, f. ώσω: aor. 1 Att. ἠλάττωσα:—Pass., fut. ἐλασσωθήσομαι, but also f. med. ἐλασσώσομαι in pass. sense: aor. ἠλασσώθην:—*to make less, smaller,* or *worse: to lessen, damage:* hence *to detract from.* II. Pass. *to become smaller, diminish: to come short of, have too little of* a thing: c. gen. *to be inferior to.* From

ἐλάσσων Att. -ττων, ον, gen. ονος:—*smaller, less, fewer, worse;* ἔλασσον ἔχειν to have *the worse:* —neut. ἔλασσον as Adv., *in a less degree;* also reg. Adv. ἐλασσόνως:—Used as Comp. of μικρός, with Sup. ἐλάχιστος: the Posit. ἐλαχύς is found only in old Ep.

ἐλαστρέω, f. ήσω, Ep. and Ion. for ἐλαύνω, *to drive: to row:* also *to drive about.*

ἐλάσω, fut. of ἐλαύνω. [ᾰ]

ἐλᾰτέον, verb. Adj. of ἐλαύνω, *one must ride.*

ἘΛΑ´ΤΗ [ᾰ], *the pine* or *fir.* II. *an oar,* as being *made of pine-wood:* later also *the whole ship.*

ἐλᾰτήρ, ῆρος, ὁ, (ἐλαύνω) *a driver, a charioteer;* ἐλατὴρ βροντῆς *hurler* of thunder. II. *one that drives away.* III. *a broad, flat cake.* Hence

ἐλᾰτήριος, α, ον, *driving away.*

ἐλάτῐνος, η, ον, (ἐλάτη) *of the pine* or *fir: of pine* or *fir-wood.*

ἔλαττον, Att. neut. for ἔλασσον, as Adv., *less.*

ἐλαττονέω, f. ήσω, (ἐλάσσων) *to have less, have too little, be lacking.*

ἐλάττων, ἐλαττόω, ἐλάττωμα, Att. for ἐλασσ-.

ἘΛΑΥ´ΝΩ: fut. ἐλάσω [ᾰ], Ep. ἐλάσσω, Att. ἐλῶ, inf. ἐλᾶν, Ep. also ἐλόω:—aor. 1 act. ἤλᾰσα, Ep. ἔλᾰσα, ἔλασσα:—pf. ἐλήλᾰκα:—Med., aor. 1 ἠλασάμην, Ep. 2 sing. ἐλάσαιο, part. ἐλασσάμενος:—Pass., aor. ἠλάθην and ἠλάσθην: pf. ἐλήλαμαι and ἐλήλασμαι: plqpf. 3 sing. ἠλήλατο, Ep. ἐλήλατο:—v. ἐλάω:—*to drive, drive on, set in motion,* esp. of horses, chariots, ships. 2. seemingly intrans., *to ride, drive, sail, row;* ἐλαύνοντες *the rowers:*—in this sense it sometimes took a new acc., γαλήνην ἐλαύνειν *to sail on* a calm sea; πόντον ἐλάταις ἐλαύνειν *to urge* the sea with oars:—then really intrans., *to advance, proceed, push on, go on*; ἐς τοσοῦτον ἤλασαν *they proceeded* so far. 3. *to drive away, carry off*, Lat. *abigere*, properly of stolen cattle; but Att. also μύσος, μίασμα, ἄγος ἐλαύνειν *to drive away* pollution. 4. *to drive into narrow compass, press in battle*: Att. also, *to harass, trouble, annoy.* II. *to strike, to cut, wound by cut* or *thrust*; c. dupl. acc., ὦμον ἐλαύνειν τινά *to wound* him on the shoulder. 2 *to thrust, drive through*: Pass. *to go through.* III. *to beat out* metal, Lat. *ducere*; ἀσπίδα ἐλαύνειν *to make* a shield *of beaten metal.* 2. *to draw out, to draw*; ἐλαύνειν ὄρχον ἀμπελίδος *to draw* a line of vines, i. e. plant them in line: hence generally, *to plant, produce.* 3. κολῳὸν ἐλαύνειν *to prolong, keep up* the brawl.

ἐλάφειος, ον, (ἔλαφος) *of* or *belonging to deer.*

ἐλᾰφηβολία, ἡ, (ἐλαφηβόλος) *a shooting of deer.*

ἐλᾰφηβόλια (sub. ἱερά), τά, *a festival of Artemis.* Hence

ἐλᾰφηβολιών, ῶνος, ὁ, the ninth month of the Attic year, in which *the Elaphebolia* were held, answering to the last half of March and first half of April.

ἐλᾰφη-βόλος, ον, (ἔλαφος, βάλλω) *hitting* or *shooting deer*: as Subst. *a deer-hunter.*

ἐλᾰφο-κτόνος, ον, (ἔλαφος, κτείνω) *deer-killing.*

ἜΛΑ'ΦΟΣ, ὁ and ἡ, *a deer*; whether male, *a hart* or *stag*, or female, *a hind.*

ἐλᾰφοσ-σοῖη, ἡ, (ἔλαφος, σείω) *deer-hunting.*

ἐλαφρία, ἡ, *lightness*: *thoughtlessness.* From

ἘΛΑΦΡΟ'Σ, ά, όν, and ός, όν, *light in weight*, Lat. *LEVIS*: metaph. *light, not burdensome, easy*, ἐν ἐλαφρῷ ποιεῖσθαι to make *light of*:—Adv. ἐλαφρῶς, *lightly, easily.* II. *light in moving, nimble, swift, active*; οἱ ἐλαφροί *light troops*, Lat. *levis armatura.* III. metaph. *light-minded, thoughtless.*

ἐλάχιστος, η, ον, Sup. of ἐλάσσων, *fewest, smallest, least, worst*:—τὸ ἐλάχιστον, as Adv. *at the least*; so neut. pl. as Adv. ἐλάχιστα.—Hence comes a new Comp. ἐλαχιστότερος, *less than the least*; Sup. ἐλαχιστότατος, *the very least.*

ἔλᾰχον, aor. 2 of λαγχάνω.

ἐλᾰχυ-πτέρυξ, υγος, ὁ, ἡ, (ἐλαχύς, πτέρυξ) *short-winged*; of fishes, *short-finned.*

ἘΛΑΧΥ'Σ, εῖα, ύ, *small, short, little*: Ep. word, whence ἐλάσσων, ἐλάχιστος are formed.

ἐλάω, rare poët. pres. for ἐλαύνω; Ep. inf. ἐλάαν, impf. ἔλαον, ἔλων.

ἜΛΔΟΜΑΙ, ἐέλδομαι, Dep. *to wish, long*: *to wish for, strive after, covet, desire.* Hence

ἔλδωρ, ἐέλδωρ, τό, indecl. *a wish, longing, desire.*

ἕλε, Ep. for εἷλε, 3 sing. aor. 2 of αἱρέω.

ἐλεαίρω, poët. for ἐλεέω, *to take pity on.*

ἘΛΕΑ'Σ, ᾶντος, ὁ, *a kind of owl.*

ἐλεγεία, ἡ, = ἔλεγος, *an elegiac poem.*

ἐλεγεῖον, τό, (ἔλεγος) *a distich consisting of a hexameter and a pentameter, the metre of the elegy*:—in plur. = ἐλεγεία ἔλεγος.

ἐλεγεῖος, α, ον, (ἔλεγος) *of the elegy, elegiac.*

ἐλέγευ, Dor. for ἐλέγου, 2 sing. impf. pass. of λέγω

ἔλεγξις, εως, ἡ, (ἐλέγχω) *a refuting, reproving.*

ἔλεγος, ὁ, *a song of mourning, a lament*, at first without reference to metrical form, later always in alternate hexameters and pentameters.

ἐλεγχείη, ἡ, (ἐλέγχω) *a reproach, disgrace.*

ἐλεγχής, ές, (ἔλεγχος) *liable to reproach, shameful*, esp. *cowardly*:—irreg. Sup. ἐλέγχιστος.

ἔλεγχος, τό, (ἐλέγχω) *a reproach, disgrace, dishonour*; κάκ' ἐλέγχεα base *reproaches to your name.*

ἔλεγχος, ὁ, *a means of testing, a trial, test*, Lat. *argumentum*: *disproval, refutation.* II. *an examination, scrutiny.* From

ἘΛΕ'ΓΧΩ, fut. ξω: aor. 1 ἤλεγξα:—Pass., aor. 1 ἠλέγχθην: pf. ἐλήλεγμαι:—*to disgrace put to shame, dishonour.* II. *to convince, refute, confute*, Lat. *arguere*: of arguments, *to disprove*: also *to accuse, reprove, reproach.* 2. *to examine, question*: *to prove, attest.*

ἐλε-δεμνάς, ἡ, (*ἕλω, δέμνιον) *couch-destroying.*

ἑλέειν, Ep. for ἑλεῖν, aor. 2 inf. of αἱρέω.

ἐλεεινός, in Att. Poets. ἐλεινός, ἡ, όν, (ἔλεος) *pitiable, piteous*: *pitied*: generally, *wretched, miserable.*—Adv. ἐλεεινῶς, poët. ἐλεινῶς, *pitiably*: also neut. pl. ἐλεεινά as Adv.

ἐλεέω, f. ήσω, (ἔλεος) *to have pity on, shew mercy upon.*

ἐλεημοσύνη, ἡ, *pity, mercy*: *an alms.* From

ἐλεήμων, ον, gen. ονος, (ἐλεέω) *pitiful, merciful.*

ἐλεητύς, ύος, ἡ, Ion. for ἔλεος, *pity, mercy.*

Ἐλείθυια, ἡ, = Εἰλείθυια.

ἑλεῖν, aor. 2 inf. of αἱρέω.

ἐλεινός, Att. for ἐλεεινός.

ἑλειο-βάτης, ου, ὁ, (ἕλος, βαίνω) *marsh-dwelling.*

ἕλειος, ον, and α, ον, (ἕλος) *of* or *in the marsh.*

ἐλειψάμην, aor. 1 med. of λείβω.

ἔλεκτο, 3 sing. Ep. aor. 2 pass. of λέγομαι, *to lie.*

ἘΛΕΛΕΥ' or **ἐλελεῦ**, like ἀλαλά, *a loud cry.*

ἐλελήθεε, Ion. 3 sing. plqpf. of λανθάνω.

ἐλελίζω (A): f. ξω: Ep. aor. 1 ἐλέλιξα, pass. ἐλελίχθην: 3 sing. plqpf. pass. (in aor. sense) ἐλέλικτο:—Ep. lengthd. form of ἑλίσσω, *to whirl round.* II. of soldiers, *to wheel* them *round, rally* them. III. generally, *to make to tremble* or *quake*:—Pass. *to quake, tremble, quiver.* IV. in Pass. also *to wind* or *twist oneself along.*

ἐλελίζω (B): f. ξω: aor. 1 ἠλέλιξα:—*to cry* ἐλελεῦ, *to raise the battle-cry*: *to raise any loud cry.*

ἐλέλικτο, 3 sing. plqpf. pass. (in aor. sense) of ἐλελίζω (A).

ἐλελίχθη, Ep. 3 sing. aor. 1 pass. of ἐλελίζω (A).

ἐλελί-χθων, ον, ονος, (ἐλελίζω, χθών) *earth-shaking.*

ἐλελόγχειν, plqpf. of λαγχάνω.

ἑλένᾱς, ἡ, (ἑλεῖν, νᾶς Dor. for ναῦς) *ship-destroying*

ἑλεό-θρεπτος, ον, (ἕλος, τρέφω) *marsh-bred.*

ἐλεόν, Adv. like ἐλεεινόν, *piteously.*

ἘΛΕΌΣ, ὁ, and ἐλεόν, τό, *a kitchen-table, a dresser.*

ἜΛΕΟΣ, ου, ὁ, also ἔλεος, εους, τό, *pity, mercy, compassion.* II. *an object of compassion, a piteous thing.*

ἑλέπολις, poët. **ἑλέ-πτολις**, ι, gen. ιδος and εως: (ἑλεῖν, πόλις) *city-destroying*, of Helen.

ἑλέσθαι, aor. 2 med. inf. of αἱρέω.

ἑλετός, ή, όν, (ἑλεῖν) *that can be taken* or *caught.*

ἐλευθερία Ion. -ίη, ἡ, (ἐλεύθερος) *freedom, liberty: freedom from* a thing.

ἐλευθέριος, ον, (ἐλεύθερος) *dealing like a free man, free-spirited, frank*, Lat. *liberalis:* esp. *freely-giving, bountiful, liberal.* It bears the same relation to ἐλεύθερος as *liberalis* to *liber.* II. as epith. of Jove, *the Releaser, Deliverer.* Hence

ἐλευθεριότης, ητος, ἡ, *freedom of spirit, liberality.*

ἐλευθεριώς, Adv. of ἐλευθέριος: Comp. -ιώτερον, Sup. -ιώτατα.

ἐλευθερό-παις, παιδος, ὁ, *having free children.*

ἘΛΕΎΘΕΡΟΣ, α, ον, and Att. ος, ον, *free*, Lat. *LIBER;* ἐλεύθερον ἦμαρ the day *of freedom;* τὸ ἐλεύθερον *freedom.* 2. *free* or *freed from a thing.* 3. of things, *free for all to use, open to use.* II. like ἐλευθέριος, *fit for a freeman, free-spirited*, Lat. *liberalis.*

ἐλευθεροστομέω, f. ήσω, *to be free of speech.* From

ἐλευθερό-στομος, ον, (ἐλεύθερος, στόμα) *free-spoken.*

ἐλευθερ-ουργός, όν, (ἐλεύθερος, ἔργον) *bearing himself freely*, of a horse.

ἐλευθερόω, f. ώσω, (ἐλεύθερος) *to set free, deliver, release: to free from blame, acquit.* Hence

ἐλευθέρως, Adv. of ἐλεύθερος, *freely, with freedom.*

ἐλευθέρωσις, εως, ἡ, *a setting free.*

Ἐλευθώ, όος, contr. οῦς, ἡ, = Εἰλείθυια.

Ἐλευσίν or **Ἐλευσίς**, ῖνος, ἡ, *Eleusis*, an ancient city of Attica, sacred to Ceres and Prosperine:—Adv. **Ἐλευσινᾶδεν**, *to Eleusis;* **Ἐλευσινόθεν**, from *Eleusis.* Hence

Ἐλευσίνιος, α, ον, *of Eleusis.*

ἔλευσις, εως, ἡ, *a coming:* esp. *the Advent.* From

ἐλεύσομαι, fut. of ἔρχομαι: but in Att. εἶμι *ibo* was chiefly used.

ἐλεφαίρομαι, Dep. *to cheat with empty hopes:* hence generally, *to trick, overreach, destroy.*

ἐλεφαντίνεος, α, ον, and **ἐλεφάντινος**, η, ον, (ἐλέφας) *of ivory, ivory*, Lat. *eburneus.*

ἐλεφαντό-δετος, ον, (ἐλέφας, δέω) *inlaid with ivory.*

ἐλεφαντο-μαχία, ἡ, (ἐλεφας, μάχομαι) *a battle of elephants.*

ἘΛΈΦΑΣ, αντος, ὁ, *the elephant*, Lat. *elephas.* II. *the elephant's tusk, ivory*, Lat. *ebur.*

ἔλεψα, aor. 1 of λέπω.

ἕλη, ἡ, = εἵλη, ἀλέα, *the heat* or *light of the sun.*

ἕλῃ, 3 sing. act. or 2 sing. aor. 2 med. subj. of αἱρέω: and **ἑλῆαι**, Ion. for ἕλῃ, 2 sing. aor. 2 med. subj.

ἐλήλᾰκα, **ἐλήλᾰμαι**, pf. act. and pass. of ἐλαύνω.

ἐλήλᾰται, -το, 3 sing. pf. and plqpf. pass. of ἐλαύνω.

ἐλήλεγμαι, pf. pass. of ἐλέγχω.

ἐληλέδατο, for ἐλήλαντο, 3 pl. plqpf. of ἐλαύνω.

ἐλήλιγμαι, pf. pass. of ἑλίσσω.

ἐλήλῠθα, pf. of ἔρχομαι.

ἐλήφθην, aor. 1 pass. of λαμβάνω.

ἐλθέ, -έτω, aor. 2 imperat. of ἔρχομαι.

ἐλθεῖν, Ep. **ἐλθέμεν**, -έμεναι, aor. 2 inf. of ἔρχομαι.

ἑλίγδην, Adv. (ἑλίσσω) *whirling, spinning.*

ἕλιγμα, ματος, τό, (ἑλίσσω) *that which is rolled: a curl, ringlet.*

ἑλιγμός, ὁ, (ἑλίσσω) *a rolling, twisting, winding*, esp. of a winding passage.

ἑλικ-άμπυξ, υκος, ὁ, ἡ, (ἕλιξ, ἄμπυξ) *with a circlet round the hair.*

ἑλικο-βλέφᾰρος, ον, (ἕλιξ, βλέφαρον) *with quick-moving eyelids, quick-glancing.*

ἑλικό-δρομος, ον, (ἕλιξ, δραμεῖν) *twisting, winding.*

ἑλικτός, ή, όν, (ἑλίσσω) *rolled, wound, wreathed.*

Ἑλικών, ῶνος, ὁ, *Helicon*, a mountain in Bœotia the seat of the Muses.

Ἑλικώνιος, α, ον, *Heliconian, of Helicon.*

ἑλίκ-ωψ, ωπος, ὁ, ἡ, (ἕλιξ, ὤψ) *with rolling quick-glancing:* fem. ἑλικῶπις.

ἐλῑνύω or **ἐλινύω**, f. ύσω [ῡ]: aor. 1 ἐλίνῡσα.—Verb, *to rest, keep peace, enjoy leisure: to sleep. to be lazy.*

ἕλιξ, ῐκος, ὁ, ἡ, (ἑλίσσω) Adj. *rolled, twisted ing, spiral:* epith. of oxen, probably from their *crumpled horns.*

ἕλιξ poët. **εἷλιξ**, ῐκος, ἡ, (ἑλίσσω) *anything twisted* or *spiral: an armlet* or *ear-ring:*—*a whirl, eddy, whirlwind*, Lat. *vortex;* ἕλικες στεροπῆς, flashes of forked lightning:—*the tendril* of the vine or of ivy:—*the coil* of a serpent:—*a curl* or *lock of hair.*

ἑλιξό-κερως, ωτος, ὁ, ἡ, neut. ων, (ἑλίσσω, κέρας) *with crumpled horns.*

ἔλιπον, aor. 2 of λείπω.

ἑλισσέμεν, Ep. inf. of ἑλίσσω.

ἙΛΊΣΣΩ Att. -ττω, Ep. and Ion. **εἱλίσσω**: fut. ἑλίξω: aor. 1 εἵλιξα:—Pass. aor. 1 εἱλίχθην: pf. ἐλήλιγμαι: 3 sing. plqpf. εἵλικτο:—*to turn about, turn round and round, roll*, Lat. *VOLVO: to whirl, move rapidly;* πλάταν ἑλίσσειν *to ply the rapid* oar. 2. metaph. *to turn in one's mind, revolve.* 3. intrans. *to hurry, move quickly about.* II. Pass. and Med. *to turn quick round, face about, turn to bay:*—*to go to and fro, to be constantly engaged: to wind one's way: to spin round;* ὧραι ἑλισσόμεναι *the circling* hours.

ἑλί-τροχος, ον, (ἑλίσσω, τροχός) *whirling the wheel round.*

ἑλί-χρῡσος, ὁ, (ἑλίσσω, χρυσός) *helichryse*, a creeping plant *with yellow flowers.*

ἑλκαίνω, (ἕλκος) *to be sore from a wound.*

ἑλκεσί-πεπλος, ον, (ἕλκω, πέπλος) *trailing the robe, long-robed.*

ἑλκε-χίτων, ωνος, ὁ, (ἕλκω, χιτών) *trailing the tunic, with a long tunic.*

ἑλκέω, f. ήσω, strengthd. for ἕλκω, *to drag about, tear asunder:—to maltreat, treat rudely.* Hence

ἑλκηδόν, Adv. *by dragging, pulling:* and

ἑλκηθμός, ὁ, *a being carried off, rough usage.*

ἕλκημα, ατος, τό, (ἑλκέω) *that which is dragged away, a prey.*

ἑλκο-ποιός, όν, (ἕλκος, ποιέω) *making wounds, having power to wound.*

ἝΛΚΟΣ, εος, τό, *a wound:* later, *a sore, ulcer, abscess,* Lat. *ULCUS.* Hence

ἑλκόω, f. ώσω, *to wound sorely.*

ἑλκύδριον, τό, Dim. of ἕλκος, *a slight sore.*

ἑλκύσαι [ῠ], aor. 1 inf. of ἕλκω.

ἑλκυστάζω, Frequent. of ἕλκω, *to drag about.*

ἝΛΚΩ, f. ἕλξω: aor. 1 εἵλξα, poët. ἕλξα: but also (as if from *ἑλκύω) fut. ἑλκύσω [ῠ]: aor. 1 εἵλκῠσα: Pass., aor. 1 εἱλκύσθην: pf. εἵλκυσμαι, Ion. ἕλκυσμαι.

To draw, drag, Lat. *traho: to draw* ships *down* into the sea, Lat. *deducere naves: to drag* along a dead body: also *to tear:* metaph. *to carp at.* 2. *to draw* a bow: *to draw* a sword. 3. *to stretch, bend* sails. 4. *to draw* or *hold up* scales *to weigh* with. 5. *to pull* an oar. 6. *to drink in long draughts, quaff:* also, ἕλκειν κόρδακα *to dance* in *long* measured steps. 7. ἕλκειν βίοτον, *to drag out* a *weary* life. 8. *to draw to oneself, attract,* esp. of the magnet. 9. ἕλκειν σταθμόν, *to draw down* the balance, i. e. *to weigh* so *much;* absol. *to weigh* ἕλκει πλεῖον it *weighs* more. 10. ἑλκύσαι πλίνθους *to mould* bricks, Lat. *ducere lateres.* II. Med., ξίφος ἕλκεσθαι *to draw one's* sword. 2. *to draw to oneself, amass.*

ἑλκ-ώδης, ες, (ἕλκος, εἶδος) *like a wound, ulcerous.*

ἕλκωσις, εως, ἡ, (ἑλκόω) *ulceration.*

ἔλλᾰβον, Ep. for ἔλαβον, aor. 2 of λαμβάνω.

ἐλ-λαμπρύνομαι, Pass. (ἐν, λαμπρύνω) *to gain distinction in.*

ἐλ-λάμπω, f. ψω, (ἐν, λάμπω) *to shine in* or *upon:* —Med. *to be illustrious, gain glory in* a thing.

Ἑλλᾱνο-δίκαι, ῶν, οἱ, (Ἕλλην, δίκη) *the chief judges at the Olympic games.* II. at Sparta, *a court-martial to try disputes among the allied troops.*

Ἑλλάς, άδος, ἡ, (Ἕλλην) *Hellas a city of Thessaly,* said to have been *founded by Hellen.* II. *that part of Thessaly in which the Myrmidons dwelt,* also called Phthiotis. III. *Greece.*

Ἑλλάς, άδος, ὁ, ἡ, pecul. fem. of Ἑλληνικός.

ἔλλᾰχον, Ep. for ἔλαχον, aor. 2 of λαγχάνω.

ἐλλέβορος, ὁ, *hellebore,* Lat. *verātrum,* a plant used by the ancients as a cure for madness; πῖθ' ἐλλέβορον drink *hellebore,* i. e. you are mad.

ἐλλεδᾰνός, ὁ, (εἴλω) *a band to bind corn-sheaves: straw-rope.*

ἔλλειμμα, ματος, τό, *a short-coming: deficiency.* From

ἐλ-λείπω, f. ψω: aor. 2 ἐνέλῐπον: (ἐν, λείπω):—*to leave in, leave behind.* II. *to leave out, pass by, omit.* III. intrans. *to lack, stand in need of, be in want of,* c. gen.: also *to come short of, be inferior to:*—c. inf., *to fail of* doing. 2. absol. *to come short, fail: to fail in duty.* IV. in Med. or Pass. *to fail of: be inferior to.* Hence

ἔλλειψις, εως, ἡ, *a falling short, defect.*

ἔλ-λεσχος, ον, (ἐν, λέσχη) *of common talk.*

Ἕλλην, ηνος, ὁ, *Hellen,* son of Deucalion: his descendants were the Ἕλληνες, at first, *dwellers in the Thessalian Hellas;* later, the common name for *the Greeks,* opp. to βάρβαροι. 2. as opp. to a Jew, *a pagan, gentile.* II. as Adj., = Ἑλληνικός. Hence

Ἑλληνίζω, f. ίσω, *to imitate the Greeks: to speak Greek:*—Pass., Ἑλληνισθῆναι τὴν γλῶσσαν *to be made Greeks* in language.

Ἑλληνικός, ή, όν, (Ἕλλην) *Hellenic, Greek;* τὸ Ἑλληνικόν = οἱ Ἕλληνες, *the Greeks.* Adv. Ἑλληνικῶς, *in Greek fashion.*

Ἑλλήνιος, α, ον, = Ἑλληνικός.

Ἑλληνίς, ίδος, ἡ, (Ἕλλην) *a Grecian woman.* 2. opp. to a Jewess, *a heathen* or *gentile woman.*

Ἑλληνιστής, οῦ, ὁ, (Ἑλληνίζω) *an imitator of the Greeks: an Hellenist, a Greek-Jew.*

Ἑλληνιστί, (Ἑλληνίζω) Adv. *in Greek fashion:* Ἑλληνιστὶ ξυνιέναι to understand *Greek.*

Ἑλληνο-τᾰμίαι, ῶν, οἱ, (Ἕλλην, ταμίας) *the stewards of Greece,* i. e. *officers appointed by Athens to levy the contributions paid by the Greek states towards the Persian war.*

Ἑλλήσ-ποντος, ὁ, (Ἕλλη, πόντος) *the Hellespont* or *sea of Hellé;* now the *Dardanelles.*

ἐλλῐπεῖν, aor. 2 inf. of ἐλλείπω. Hence

ἐλλῐπής, ές, *wanting, defective.*

ἐλλῐσάμην, Ep. for ἐλισάμην, aor. 1 of λίσσομαι.

ἐλλῐτάνευον, Ep. for ἐλιτ–, impf. of λιτανεύω.

ἐλ-λόβιον, τό, (ἐν, λόβος) *an earring,* Lat. *inauris.*

ἐλ-λογέω, f. ήσω, (ἐν, λόγος) *to reckon in: to impute.*

ἐλ-λόγιμος, ον, (ἐν, λόγος) *whatever comes into account, worth reckoning, notable, famous.*

ἐλλοπιεύω, f. σω, (ἔλλοψ) *to fish.*

ἘΛΛΟ'Σ or ἐλλός, ὁ, *a young deer, fawn.*

ἘΛΛΟ'Σ, ἡ, όν, *mute,* epith. of fish.

ἐλλο-φόνος, ον, (ἐλλός, *φένω) *fawn-slaying.*

ἐλ-λοχίζω, f. ίσω, (ἐν, λόχος) *to lie in ambush.*

ἔλλοψ, οπος, (ἐλλός) *mute,* epith. of fish.

ἐλ-λύχνιον, τό, (ἐν, λύχνος) *a lamp-wick.*

ἕλξα, poët. for εἷλξα, aor. 1 of ἕλκω.

ἕλξις, εως, ἡ, (ἕλκω) *a drawing, dragging: attraction.* II. *a draught.*

ἑλοίμαν, Dor. for ἑλοίμην, aor. 2 opt. med. of αἱρέω.

ἕλοιμι, aor. 2 opt. act. of αἱρέω.

ἑλοῖσα, Dor. for ἑλοῦσα, aor. 2 part. of αἱρέω.

ἕλον, ἑλόμην, poët. for εἷλον, εἱλόμην, aor. 2 act. and med. of αἱρέω.

ἝΛΟΣ, εος, τό, *low ground by rivers, a marsh-meadow, marsh.*

ἐλοῦμεν, 1 pl. old Att. impf. of λούω.

ἑλοῦσα, aor. 2 part. fem. of αἱρέω.

ἐλοῦτο, 3 sing. Ion. and old Att. impf. med. of λούω.

ἐλόωσι, Ep. for ἐλάσουσι, 3 pl. fut. of ἐλαύνω.

ἐλπίζω, fut. ίσω Att. ιῶ, (ἔλπω): aor. 1 ἤλπισα:—Pass., aor. 1 ἠλπίσθην:—*to hope, expect:* also, in bad sense, *to fear:* c. acc. *to hope for, expect:* c. dat. *to hope in.*

'ΕΛΠΙ'Σ, ίδος, ἡ, *hope*, Lat. *spes:* later, *expectation* either of good or evil, *hope* or *fear.*

'ΕΛΠΩ, Causal, *to make to hope:*—Med. ἔλπομαι Ep. ἐέλπομαι: pf. ἔολπα (with pres. sense), plqpf. ἐώλπειν (with impf.):—*to hope, expect, think, believe;* and in bad sense, *to fear.*

ἐλπωρή, ἡ, Ep. form of ἐλπίς.

ἕλσαι, ἕλσας, aor. 1 inf. and part. of εἴλω.

ἐλύθην [ῠ], aor. 1 pass. of λύω.

ἔλῠμα, ατος, τό, (ἐλύω) *the stock of the plough*, on which the share was fixed, Lat. *dentāle.*

ἔλῠμος, ὁ, (ἐλύω) *a case, sheath, quiver.*

ἔλῠτρον, τό, *a cover, covering, case, sheath.* 2. *a place for holding water, a reservoir.* From

ἐλύω, (εἴλω):—*to roll round:* only used in Ep. aor. pass. ἐλύσθην, *to be rolled up, to roll* or *twist oneself close up.*

ἕλω, aor. 2 subj. of αἱρέω.

ἔλων, impf. of ἐλάω: but **ἑλών**, aor. 2 part. of αἱρέω.

ἕλωρ, τό, only used in nom. and acc., (ἑλεῖν) *booty, spoil, prey.* II. pl., Πατρόκλοιο ἕλωρα ἀποτίνειν to pay for leaving Patroclus *a prey to all dishonour.*

ἑλώριον, τό, = ἕλωρ.

ἔμᾰθον, aor. 2 of μανθάνω.

ἐμάνην [ᾰ], aor. 2 of μαίνομαι.

ἐμαρνάσθην, 3 dual impf. of μάρναμαι.

ἐμάρνατο, 3 sing. impf. of μάρναμαι.

ἐμ-αυτοῦ, ἐμ-αυτῆς, Ion. ἐμ-εωυτοῦ or ἐμ-ωυτοῦ, ῆς, (ἐμοῦ, αὐτοῦ): reflexive Pronoun of first person, *of myself*, Lat. *mei ipsius:* only used in gen., dat., and acc. sing., both masc. and fem.: in plur. separated, ἡμῶν αὐτῶν, etc.

ἔμβᾰ, for ἔμβηθι, aor. 2 imperat. of ἐμβαίνω.

ἐμβᾰδόν, Adv. (ἐμβαίνω) *on foot, by land.*

ἐμ-βαίνω, f. -βήσομαι: aor. 2 ἐνέβην: pf. ἐμβέβηκα, Ep. part. ἐμβεβᾱώς:—*to step in:*—*to step on, go on.* 2. *to step into, to go into, go on board, embark: to mount on: to be fixed upon.* 3. *to tread upon.* 4. *to enter upon, embark in* a thing. II. Causal in aor. 1 ἐνέβησα, *to make to enter, bring in* or *into:*—cf. ἐμβιβάζω.

ἐμ-βάλλω, f. -βᾰλῶ: pf. -βέβληκα: aor. 2 ἐν-έβᾰλον:—*to throw, lay, put in;* κώπαις ἐμβαλέειν (sub. χεῖρας) *to lay* oneself to the oar; also without κώπαις, *to lay to, pull hard.* 2. *to put into the mind* of another:—Med., ἐμβάλλεσθαί τι θυμῷ *to lay* a thing to heart. 3. ἐμβάλλειν εἴς τι *to throw* one *into* a thing, *involve in.* 4. *to throw at* another. II. intr. *to break, burst, rush in: to fall on, encounter, run against*, Lat. *illidi*, esp. of a ship *that falls on another with its beak:* cf. ἔμβολος.

ἔμβαμμα, ατος, τό, *sauce, soup.* From

ἐμ-βάπτω, f. ψω, *to dip in.*

ἐμβάς, άδος [ᾰ], ἡ, (ἐμβαίνω) *a kind of felt shoe*, used by the Bœotians; also by old men and poor people.

ἐμβάς, aor. 2 part. of ἐμβαίνω.

ἐμ-βᾰσιλεύω, f. σω, *to be king among* or *over.*

ἔμβᾰσις, εως, ἡ, (ἐμβαίνω) *a going in* or *upon: a going on board ship, embarking.* II. *that on which one goes;* ἔμβασις ποδὸς *a shoe*, like ἐμβάς. 2. *the sole, foot, hoof.*

ἐμ-βαστάζω, f. σω, *to bear on, carry.*

ἐμβᾰτεύω, f. εύσω, (ἐμβάτης) *to step in* or *on, stand on:* hence *to dwell in, frequent, haunt:* also *to protect, watch:* c. gen. *to set foot upon.* II. *to enter on possession of* property.

ἐμβᾰτέω, f. ήσω, (ἐμβάτης) = ἐμβατεύω.

ἐμβατήριος, ον, (ἐμβατεύω) *of* or *for marching:* ἐμβατήριον (sub. μέλος), τό, *a march-tune, march.*

ἐμβάτης, ου, ὁ, (ἐμβαίνω) *he that goes in* or *upon*, esp. *on board ship, a passenger.* II. *a kind of boot*, cf. ἐμβάς. [ᾰ]

ἐμβάφιος, ον, (ἐμβάπτω) *fit for dipping in* or *into:* τὸ ἐμβάφιον *a flat vessel.* [ᾰ]

ἐμβεβᾱώς, -υῖα, Ep. pf. part. of ἐμβαίνω: **ἐμβέβᾰσαν**, Ep. 3 pl. plqpf.

ἔμβη, Ep. 3 sing. aor. 2 of ἐμβαίνω: **ἔμβητον**, 2 dual: **ἐμβήῃ**, for ἐμβῇ, 3 sing. subj.

ἐμ-βῐβάζω: f. -βιβάσω Att. -βιβῶ:—Causal of ἐμβαίνω, *to make to step in* or *upon: to put on board ship: to lead* or *guide to.*

ἔμβλεμμα, ατος, τό, *a looking straight at.* From

ἐμ-βλέπω, f. ψω, *to look in the face, look at:* simply, *to look.*

ἐμ-βοάω, f. ήσομαι, *to call upon: to shout aloud.*

ἐμβολεύς, έως, ὁ, (ἐμβάλλω) *a dibble for putting in plants.*

ἐμβολή, ἡ, (ἐμβάλλω) *a throwing in.* II. intrans. *an inroad into an enemy's country, an invasion, foray.* 2. *the charge* made by one ship upon another, *an assault;* ἐμβολαὶ χαλκόστομοι *the shock* of brazen beaks. 3. *an entrance: pass.* III. *the head of a battering-ram.* Hence

ἐμβόλιμος, ον, (ἐμβάλλω) *thrown in, inserted;* μὴν ἐμβ. an *intercalary* month.

ἔμβολον, τό, (ἐμβάλλω) *anything running in;* ἔμβ. τῆς χώρης *a tongue* of land. 2. *a bolt, bar: a wedge: the beak* of a ship of war. 3. *a beam, architrave.*

ἔμβολος, ὁ, (ἐμβάλλω) *anything put in, a wedge.* 2. *the brasen beak* of ships of war.

ἔμβρᾰχυ, Adv. (ἐν, βραχύς) *in brief, shortly.*

ἐμ-βρέμομαι, Med. *to roar* or *bluster in.*

ἐμ-βρεφος, ον, (ἐν, βρέφος) *boy-like.*

ἐμ-βρῑθής, ές, (ἐν, βρῖθος) *heavy, weighty.* II. metaph. *grave, stately, dignified, important.* 2. in bad sense, *heavy, grievous, oppressive:* of persons, *violent, savage, fierce.* III. Adv. -θῶς, *firmly.*

ἐμ-βρίθω [ῑ], f. ίσω, *to weigh heavily upon.*

ἐμ-βρῑμάομαι, f. ήσομαι: Dep.:—*to snort with rage,*

of horses: of men, *to be sore vexed, be indignant*, Lat. *commoveri*: *to charge strictly, censure.*

ἐμ-βροντάω, f. ήσω, *to strike with lightning*: *to strike dumb.* Hence

ἐμβρόντητος, ον, *thunder-stricken, stupid.*

ἐμ-βροχή, ἡ, (ἐν, βρόχος) *a noose, halter.*

ἐμ-βρύ-οικος, ον, (ἐν, βρύον, οἰκέω) *dwelling in sea-weed.*

ἔμβρῠον, τό, (ἐν, βρύω) *the fruit of the womb before birth, the embryo*, Lat. *foetus.* 2. *a thing newly born*: *a lamb* or *kid.*

ἐμ-βύθιος, α, ον, or ος, ον, (ἐν, βυθός) *at the bottom.*

ἐμ-βύω, f. ύσω [ῡ], *to stuff in, stop up.*

ἐμέ, acc. of ἐγώ, enclit. με.

ἐμέγηρα, aor. 1 of μεγαίρω.

ἐμέθεν, old poët. gen. for ἐμοῦ.

ἐμεί, Dor. for ἐμέ, as τεί for τέ (σέ).

ἔμεινα, aor. 1 of μένω.

ἐμεῖο, ἐμέο, Ep. gen. of ἐγώ.

ἐμέλλησα, aor. 1 of μέλλω.

ἐμέμηκον, Ep. redupl. aor. 2 of μηκάομαι.

ἐμέμικτο, 3 sing. plqpf. pass. of μίγνῡμι.

ἐμεμνέᾰτο, Ion. 3 pl. plqpf. pass. of μιμνήσκω.

ἐμέν, poët. for ἐσμέν, 1 pl. of εἰμί *sum.*

ἔμεν, ἔμεναι, Ep. for εἶναι, inf. of εἰμί *sum.*

ἕμεν, ἕμεναι, Ep. for εἶναι, aor. 2 inf. of ἵημι.

ἕμενος, aor. part. med. of ἵημι.

ἐμετικός, ή, όν, *provoking sickness.* II. *one who uses emetics.* From

ἔμετος, ὁ, (ἐμέω) *sickness, vomiting.*

ἐμεῦ, Ep. for ἐμοῦ, enclit. μεῦ: Dor. ἐμεῦς.

ἘΜΕ'Ω, impf. ἤμουν: f. ἐμέσω Att. ἐμῶ and ἐμοῦμαι: aor. ἤμεσα Ep. ἔμεσσα: pf. ἐμήμεκα:—Lat. *VOMO, to vomit, throw up*: absol. *to be sick*; ἐμεῖν πτίλῳ *to make oneself sick* with a feather.

ἐμεωυτοῦ, Ion. for ἐμαυτοῦ.

ἐμήσατο, 3 sing. aor. 1 of μήδομαι.

ἐμίγην [ῐ], aor. 2 pass. of μίγνυμι.

ἔμικτο, 3 sing. Ep. aor. 2 pass. of μίγνυμι.

ἔμιξα, aor. 1 of μίγνυμι.

ἐμίχθην, aor. 1 pass. of μίγνυμι.

ἐμίν, poët. Dor. for ἐμοί, dat. of ἐγώ.

ἔμμᾰθον, Ep. for ἔμαθον, aor. 2 of μανθάνω.

ἐμ-μαίνομαι, Dep. *to be mad at.* Hence

ἐμμᾰνής, ές, *mad, frantic, raving.* Adv. -νῶς.

ἐμμᾰπέως, Adv. *forthwith, immediately, hastily.* (Deriv. uncertain.)

ἐμ-μάσσω, f. ξω, *to impress upon.*

ἐμ-μάχομαι, f. -μαχέσομαι, Dep. *to fight a battle in.*

ἐμ-μειδιάω, f. άσω [ᾱ], *to smile at.*

ἐμμέλεια, ἡ, (ἐμμελής) *a kind of dance, accompanied by music*: *the tune of this dance.*

ἐμ-μελετάω, f. ήσω, *to exercise in* a thing. Hence

ἐμμελέτημα, ματος, τό, *an exercise, practice.*

ἐμ-μελής, ές, (ἐν, μέλος) *in tune, well-timed, harmonious, melodious*: generally, *regular, agreeable*: *elegant, graceful*: *well-bred.* Adv. ἐμμελῶς, Ion. -λέως.

ἐμμεμᾰώς, υῖα, ός, *pressing eagerly on, eager, hasty, ardent*: pf. part. with no verb in use.

ἐμ-μέμονα, pf. with no pres. in use, *to be lost in passion.*

ἔμμεν, ἔμμεναι, Ep. inf. of εἰμί *sum.*

ἐμμενής, ές, *abiding in*: neut. ἐμμενές as Adv., *unceasingly.* Adv. ἐμμενῶς, Ep. and Ion. -έως. From

ἐμ-μένω, f. -μενῶ: aor. 1 ἐνέμεινα:—*to abide in*: *to abide by, stand by, cleave to*, Lat. *stare ab aliquo*: absol. *to continue.*

ἐμ-μετρέω, f. ήσω, *to measure in* or *by.*

ἔμ-μετρος, ον, (ἐν, μέτρον) *in measure, measured, moderate.* II. *in metre, metrical.*

ἔμ-μηνος, ον, (ἐν, μήν) *in a month, lasting a month.* II. *occurring every month, monthly.*

ἐμμί, Dor. for εἰμί *sum.*

ἐμ-μίγνυμι or -ύω, f. -μίξω, *to mix* or *mingle in.* II. intrans. *to encounter, meet.*

ἐμ-μίμνω, poët. for ἐμ-μένω.

ἔμ-μισθος, ον, (ἐν, μισθός) *in pay, in receipt of pay.*

ἔμμονος, ον, (ἐμμένω) *abiding in, steadfast.*

ἔμμορα, pf. 2 of μείρομαι.

ἔμ-μορος, ον, (ἐν, μείρομαι) *partaking in* or *of.* II. (ἐν, μόρος) *fortunate.*

ἔμ-μοτος, ον, (ἐν, μότος) *spread on lint.*

ἔμ-μοχθος, ον, (ἐν, μόχθος) *toilsome, painful.*

ἐμ-μυέω, f. ήσω, *to initiate at the mysteries in.*

ἔμνησα, aor. 1 of μιμνήσκω.

ἐμνήσθην, aor. 1 pass. (in med. sense) of μιμνήσκω.

ἐμνώοντο, Ep. for ἐμνῶντο, 3 pl. impf. of μνάομαι.

ἐμοί, dat. of ἐγώ.

ἔμολον, aor. 2 of βλώσκω.

ἐμός, ή, όν, possess. Adj. of first pers. from ἐγώ, ἐμοῦ, *mine*, Lat. *meus*; joined with gen. to strengthen the *possessive* notion ἐμὸν αὐτοῦ *mine* own; ἐμὴ ἀγγελίη a message *about me*; τὸ ἐμὸν *mine, my part*; also in plur., τὰ ἐμά, τἀμά:—τό γε ἐμόν, τὸ μὲν ἐμόν, *for my part, as far as concerns me.*

ἐμοῦμαι, fut. of ἐμέω.

ἐμοῦς, Dor. gen. of ἐγώ.

ἔμπᾰ, Adv., v. ἔμπας.

ἐμπᾰγείς, aor. 2 pass. part. of ἐμπήγνῡμι.

ἐμπάζομαι, Dep. used only in pres. *to busy oneself about, take heed of, care for.*

ἐμ-πᾰθής, ές, (ἐν, πάθος) *in a state of emotion, much affected.* Adv. ἐμπαθῶς, *passionately.*

ἐμπαιγμονή, ἡ, = ἐμπαιγμός.

ἐμπαιγμός, ὁ, *a jesting, mocking.* From

ἐμ-παίζω, f. -παίξομαι, *to mock*, Lat. *illudere*: *to trick, deceive.* II. *to sport in* or *on.* Hence

ἐμπαίκτης, ου, ὁ, *a mocker, deceiver.*

ἐμπαῖξαι, aor. 1 inf. of ἐμπαίζω.

ἐμπαιχθήσομαι, fut. pass. of ἐμπαίζω.

ἔμπαιος, ον, (B) = ἔμπειρος, *knowing, practised in*, c. gen. (Deriv. uncertain.)

ἔμπαιος, ον, (B) *bursting upon* one, *sudden.* From

ἐμ-παίω, f. -παίσω or -παιήσω, *to strike in, stamp.* II. intr. *to burst in upon.*

ἐμ-πακτόω, f. ώσω, *to close up, caulk.*

ἐμ-πᾰλάσσω, f. ξω, *to entangle in* or *together.*

ἔμ-πᾰλιν, poët. also **ἔμ-πᾰλι**, (ἐν, πάλιν) Adv. *backwards, back.* II. *contrary to,* c. gen. III. *in return.* IV. τὸ ἔμπαλιν, τὰ ἔμπαλιν, by crasis τοὔμπαλιν, τἄμπαλιν, *the contrary, the reverse.*

ἐμ-παρέχω, f. ξω, *to hand over, put in one's power.*

ἐμ-πᾶς, Ion. and Ep. **ἔμ-πης**, Adv. (properly ἐν πᾶσι) *altogether, at all events.* II. *on the whole, nevertheless, still.* III. joined with περ, *however much, ever so much.*

ἐμ-πάσσω Att. **-ττω**: fut. άσω [ᾰ]: aor. 1 ἐνέπᾰσα:—*to sprinkle in* or *on*: metaph. *to weave in, embroider.*

ἐμ-πᾰτέω, f. ήσω, *to tread in, walk into.*

ἐμπεδό-μοχθος, ον, (ἔμπεδος, μόχθος) *ever-painful.*

ἐμπεδ-ορκέω, f. ήσω, (ἔμπεδος, ὅρκος) *to abide by one's oath.*

ἔμ-πεδος, ον, (ἐν, πέδον) *in its place, steadfast, unshaken.* 2. of Time, *lasting, continual.* II. Advs. ἔμπεδον and ἔμπεδα, ἐμπέδως, *fast, of a surety, truly, certainly.*

ἐμπεδο-σθενής, ές, (ἔμπεδος, σθένος) *with force unshaken.*

ἐμπεδόω, f. ώσω, (ἔμπεδος) *to make firm, establish.*

ἐμπείραμος, ον, = ἐμπέραμος.

ἐμπειρία, ἡ, *experience: experience in* or *acquaintance with* a thing. From

ἔμ-πειρος, ον, (ἐν, πεῖρα) *experienced in, acquainted with, skilful at: proved good* by *experience*: τὸ ἐμπειρότερον *greater experience.* Adv., ἐμπείρως τινὸς ἔχειν to know a thing *by experience.*

ἐμπελᾰδόν, Adv. *near, hard by.* From

ἐμ-πελάζω, f. σω: aor. 1 ἐν πέλασα:—*to bring near* or *close to*:—also intrans. *to come near.* II. Pass. *to be brought near, approach.*

ἐμπέπηγα, pf. intr. of ἐμπήγνυμι.

ἐμπεπλησμένος, pf. part. pass. of ἐμπίπλημι.

ἐμπεπόδισμαι, pf. pass. of ἐμποδίζω.

ἐμπέπτωκα, pf. of ἐμπίπτω.

ἐμ-πέρᾰμος, ον, = ἔμπειρος, *acquainted with.*

ἐμ-περιπᾰτέω, *to walk about in*: *to tarry among.*

ἐμ-περονάω, f. ήσω, *to fasten with a brooch.* Hence

ἐμπερόνημα, Dor. **-ᾱμα**, ματος, τό, *a garment fastened with a brooch* or *buckle.*

ἔμπεσον, Ep. for ἐνέπεσον, aor. 2 of ἐμπίπτω.

ἐμπεσοῦμαι, fut. of ἐμπίπτω.

ἐμ-πετάννῡμι or **-ύω**, f. **-πετάσω** [ᾰ], *to unfold and spread on* or *out.*

ἐμπεφύασι, Ep. for ἐμπεφύκασι, 3 pl. pf. of ἐμφύω: **ἐμπεφυῖα**, Ep. part. fem.

ἐμ-πήγνῡμι or **-ύω**, fut. **-πήξω**: aor. 1 ἐνέπηξα:—*to fix* or *draft in,* c. dat.—Pass., aor. 2 ἐνεπάγην [ᾰ], with pf. act. ἐμπέπηγα, plqpf. -ήγειν:—*to stick in.*

ἐμ-πηδάω, f. ήσομαι, *to leap* or *jump in.*

ἔμ-πηρος, ον, *crippled, maimed, deformed.*

ἔμ-πης, Adv., Ion. and Hom. for ἔμπας.

ἐμπιεῖν, aor. 2 inf. of ἐμπίνω.

ἐμ-πικραίνω, f. ᾰνῶ, *to embitter*:—Pass. *to be bitter against.*

ἐμπίμπλημι, **ἐμπίμπρημι**, v. ἐμπίπ-.

ἐμ-πίνω, fut. -πίομαι: aor. 2 ἐνέπιον: pf. ἐμπέπωκα: *to drink in, drink up*; ἐμπίνειν τοῦ αἵματος *to drink of* the blood.

ἐμπίπληθι, imperat. of ἐμπίπλημι.

ἐμ-πίπλημι, f. -πλήσω: aor. 1 ἐνέπλησα:—*to fill full of* a thing:—Pass. and Med., **ἐμπίμπλαμαι**, aor. 1 ἐνεπλήσθην: Ep. aor. 2 ἐνεπλήμην, *to fill oneself, eat one's fill, be satisfied.* II. in Med. also trans. *to fill, satisfy*: metaph. *to have enough of, enjoy.*

ἐμ-πίπρημι, aor. 1 ἐνέπρησα:—*to set on fire.*

ἐμ-πίπτω, fut. -πεσοῦμαι: aor. 2 ἐνέπεσον Ep. ἔμπεσον:—*to fall upon*: *to break in, burst in*: aor. 2 part. ἐμπεσών, *rushing in violently*: also *to light on, fall in with.*

ἘΜΠΙ΄Σ, ίδος, ἡ, *a mosquito, gnat,* Lat. **culex.**

ἐμ-πίτνω, poët. for ἐμπίπτω, *to fall upon.*

ἐμπλᾰκῆναι, aor. 2 inf. of ἐμπλέκω.

ἐμ-πλάσσω Att. **-ττω**: f. άσω [ᾰ]: aor. 1 **ἐνέπλᾰσα**:—*to plaster up, daub over with* a thing.

ἔμ-πλειος, Ep. for ἔμ-πλεος.

ἐμ-πλέκω, f. ξω, *to plait* or *weave in, interweave,* Lat. *implicare*:—Pass. *to be entangled in* a thing. 2. metaph. *to weave artfully, to render perplexed.*

ἔμ-πλεος, α, ον, Ep. **ἔμπλειος** or **ἐνίπλειος**, η, ον, Att. **ἔμπλεως**, ων, *quite full of* a thing.

ἐμ-πλέω, f. -πλεύσομαι, *to sail in.*

ἐμπληγδην, Adv. (ἐμπλήσσω) *madly, rashly.*

ἔμπληκτος, ον, (ἐμπλήσσω) *stunned, amazed, stupified, senseless.* II. Att. *unsteady, rash*:—Adv. ἐμπλήκτως, *madly.*

ἐμπλήμενος, Ep. aor. 2 pass. part. of ἐμπίπλημι.

ἔμπλην, (ἐμπελάζω) Adv. *near, close by.*

ἔμ-πλην, Adv. strengthd. for πλήν, *besides, except.*

ἐμπλήσας, **-άμενος**, aor. 1 part. act. and med. of ἐμπίπλημι: **ἐμπλήσατο**, Ep. for ἐνεπλήσατο.

ἐμπλησθήσομαι, fut. pass. of ἐμπίπλημι.

ἐμ-πλήσσω Att. **-ττω** Ep. **ἐνιπλ-**: f. ξω:—*to strike against, stumble upon, fall upon* or *into.*

ἔμπλητο, for ἐνέπλητο, Ep. aor. 2 pass. of ἐμπίπλημι:—ἔμπλησο, imperat. of same tense.

ἐμπλοκή, ἡ, (ἐμπλέκω) *a plaiting* of the hair.

ἔμπνευσα, Ep. for ἐνέπνευσα, aor. 1 of ἐμπνέω.

ἐμ-πνέω, poët. **-πνείω**: f. -πνεύσομαι: aor. 1 ἐνέπνευσα:—*to blow* or *breathe on* or *in,* c. dat.: c. acc., ἱστίον ἐμπνεῖν *to swell* the sail: absol. *to breathe, live, be alive.* II. trans. *to breathe into, infuse, inspire*:—*to blow into, swell* the sail.

ἔμπνοια, ἡ, *in-breathing, inspiration.* From

ἔμ-πνοος, ον, contr. **-πνους**, ουν, (ἐν, πνοή) *having the breath in one, breathing, alive.*

ἐμ-ποδίζω, f. ίσω Att. ιῶ: (ἐν, πούς):—*to entangle the feet, fetter*; ἐμπ. ἰσχάδας *to tie together* figs *by their stalks.* II. generally, *to hinder, stop, check.*

ἐμ-πόδιος, ον, (ἐν, πούς) *in the way, obstructing.*

ἐμ-ποδών, Adv. for ἐν ποσὶν ὤν, *before the feet, in the way*; ἐμποδὼν εἶναι to be *in the way*:—with the Art., τὸ ἐμποδών *what is in the way, a hindrance.* II. also, *before one, patent.* Opp. to ἐκπόδων.

ἐμ-ποιέω, f. ήσω, *to make in, put in, insert.* 2. *to produce* or *create in, introduce, cause.*

ἐμπολαῖος, α, ον, (ἐμπολή) *of* or *concerned in traffic*, epith. of Hermes.

ἐμπολάω: impf. ἠμπόλων: f. ἐμπολήσω: pf. ἠμπόληκα: (ἐμπολή):—*to gain by traffic: to earn, gain*: Med., βίοτον πολὺν ἐμπολόωντο (Ep. for ἠμπολῶντο) *they were getting* much substance *by traffic.* II. absol. *to be a merchant, traffic.* III. *to purchase, buy.*

ἐμ-πολεμέω, f. ήσω, *to wage war in.*

ἐμ-πολέμιος, ον, *of belonging to war, hostile.*

ἐμπολεύς, έως, ὁ, (ἐμπολάω) *a merchant, trafficker.*

ἐμ-πολή, ἡ, (ἐν, πωλέω) *merchandise: traffic.* II. *gain made by traffic, profit.*

ἐμπόλημα, ατος, τό, (ἐμπολάω) *matter of traffic, a cargo*: in plur. *wares, merchandise.*

ἐμπολητός, ή, όν, (ἐμπολάω) *bought and sold.*

ἔμ-πολις, εως, ὁ, ἡ, (ἐν, πόλις) *in the city* or *state*: ὁ ἔμπολίς τινι one's *fellow-citizen.*

ἐμ-πολῑτεύω, f. σω, *to be a citizen in a state, hold civil rights in.*

ἐμπολόωντο, 3 pl. Ep. impf. pass. of ἐμπολάω.

ἐμπόρευμα, ατος, τό, *an article of commerce.* From

ἐμπορεύομαι, f. -εύσομαι: aor. 1 ἐνεπορεύθην: Dep.: (ἔμπορος):—*to be on a journey.* II. *to travel on business, be a merchant, to trade, traffic.* 2. c. acc. *to trade* or *traffic in* a thing. Hence

ἐμπορευτέον or **-έα**, verb. Adj. *one must go.*

ἐμπορία, ἡ, (ἔμπορος) *traffic, trade, commerce: a trade.* II. *goods trafficked in, merchandise.*

ἐμπορικός, ή, όν, (ἔμπορος) *of* or *for traffic, mercantile, commercial*; χρήματα ἐμπορικά *imported* goods.

ἐμπόριον, τό, (ἐμπόρος) Lat. *emporium, a trading-place, factory, mart.* II. ἐμπόρια, τά, *merchandise.* From

ἔμ-πορος, ον, (ἐν, πόρος) *a passenger on shipboard*, Lat. *vector.* II. *a traveller, wanderer.* III. *one who travels on business, a merchant*, Lat. *mercātor, instĭtor*; metaph., ἔμπορος βίου *a trader* in life.

ἐμ-πορπάω, f. ήσω, *to fix on with a brooch* or *buckle*:—Pass., εἵματα ἐνεπορπέατο (Ion. for -ηντο), *they wore* garments *buckled on the shoulder.*

Ἔμπουσα, ἡ, *Empusa, a hobgoblin* assuming various shapes. (Deriv. uncertain.)

ἔμπρακτος, ον, (ἐμπράσσω) *practicable.*

ἐμπρεπής, ές, *conspicuous in* or *by* a thing. From

ἐμ-πρέπω, *to be conspicuous in* or *among.* II. *to be conspicuous for.*

ἐμ-πρήθω, f. σω, *to blow up, inflate.* II. = ἐμπίπρημι, *to burn to ashes.*

ἔμπρησις, εως, ἡ, (ἐμπίπρημι) *a setting on fire.*

ἔμ-προθεν, Adv., poët. for ἔμπροσθεν.

ἔμ-προσθεν, poët. before a conson. -θε, Adv. and Prep. I. of Place, *before, in front of.* II. of Time, *before, earlier, of old.* Hence

ἐμ-πρόσθιος, ον, *front, fore*; οἱ πρόσθιοι (sub. πόδες) *the fore-feet* of a quadruped, opp. to οἱ ὀπίσθιοι.

ἐμπτύω, f. ύσω [ῠ], *to spit upon.*

ἐμ-πῠκάζω, f. άσω, *to wrap up closely*:—Pass., νόος οἱ ἐμπεπύκασται his mind *is veiled, wrapt in mystery.*

ἔμ-πῡος, ον, (ἐν, πῦον) *discharging matter.*

ἐμ-πῠρεύω, f. σω, (ἐν, πῦρ) *to set on fire.*

ἐμ-πῠρι-βήτης, ου, ὁ, (ἐν, πῦρ, βαίνω) *standing on* or *over the fire*, of a tripod, opp. to ἄπυρος.

ἔμ-πῠρος, ον, (ἐν, πῦρ) *in* or *on the fire.* II. *scorched, burnt.* III. *of sacrificial fire*; ἔμπυρος τέχνη the art *of divination by fire*:—as Subst., τὰ ἔμπυρα [ἱερά] *burnt sacrifices* or *omens from burnt sacrifices.*

ἔμῠκον, aor. 2 of μυκάομαι.

ἐμ-φᾰγεῖν, aor. 2 with no pres. in use (see ἐσθίω):—*to put in and eat, to eat up: to eat upon.*

ἐμ-φαίνω, f. -φᾰνῶ: aor. 1 ἐνέφηνα:—*to shew, make appear*:—Pass., with fut. med. ἐμφᾰνοῦμαι, *to be seen in, to be reflected: to appear, shew oneself.*

ἐμφᾰνῆναι, aor. 2 pass. of ἐμφαίνω.

ἐμφᾰνής, ές, (ἐμφανῆναι) *appearing in, visible, plain, manifest.* 2. *open, in public.* 3. *palpable, real, actual.* Hence

ἐμφᾰνίζω, f. ίσω Att. ιῶ, *to shew forth: to make clear, explain.*

ἐμφᾰνῶς Ion. **-έως**, Adv. of ἐμφανής, *visibly, openly*, Lat. *palam.*

ἔμφᾰσις, εως, ἡ, (ἐμφαίνομαι) *an appearing in, reflexion: outward appearance.*

ἐμφέρεια, ἡ, *resemblance.* From

ἐμφερής, ές, *resembling, similar.* Adv. **-ρῶς**, *similarly, just as.* From

ἐμ-φέρω, f. ἐν-οίσω, *to bear* or *bring in.* II. *to object to* one, *cast in* one's *teeth.*

ἐμ-φλέγω, f. ξω, *to light up in.*

ἔμ-φλοξ, ογος, ὁ, ἡ, *with fire in it.*

ἔμ-φοβος, ον, (ἐν, φόβος) *fearful, terrible.* II. pass. *frightened, afraid.*

ἐμ-φορβιόω, f. ώσω, (ἐν, φορβιά) *to put on the flute-player's mouthpiece.*

ἐμ-φορέω, f. ήσω, like ἐμφέρω, *to bear* or *bring in*:—Pass. *to be borne about* or *on.* II. in Med. and Pass. *to take one's fill of* a thing, *to make much use of.* III. *to inflict on.*

ἐμ-φράσσω Att. **-ττω**, f. ξω, *to stop up, block up.*

ἐμφρουρέω, f. ήσω, *to keep guard in.* From

ἔμ-φρουρος, ον, (ἐν, φρουρά) *on guard in* a place: *liable to serve.* II. pass. *guarded, garrisoned.*

ἔμ-φρων, ον, gen. ονος, (ἐν, φρήν) *in one's right mind: sensible, alive.* 2. *in one's senses, sensible, shrewd, prudent.*

ἐμφῠής, ές, (ἐμφύω) *implanted by nature, innate.*

ἔμ-φῡλος, ον, and **ἐμ-φύλιος**, ιον, (ἐν, φῦλον) *of the same tribe* or *race*; ἐμφύλιον αἷμα *kindred* blood; τοὔμφυλον αἷμα a *kinsman's* blood, i.e. murder *of a* *kinsman.* II. *in* or *among the people; στάσις ἔμφυλος intestine, civil* discord.

ἐμφύς, aor. 2 part. of ἐμφύω.

ἐμ-φῡσάω, f. ήσω, *to breathe in* or *into: breathe upon.*

ἔμφῠτος, ον, *inborn, innate.* From

ἐμ-φύω, f. ύσω [ῡ]: aor. 1 ἐνέφῡσα: in these tenses trans. *to implant.* II. intr. in Med. ἐμφύομαι, with act. pf. ἐμπέφῡκα, aor. 2 ἐνέφῡν, *to grow, be on* or *in: to be rooted in, cling closely to; ἐμφῦναι χειρί to cling fast to* his hand.

ἔμ-φωνος, ον, (ἐν, φωνή) *with a loud voice.*

ἔμ-ψοφος, ον, *noisy, sounding.*

ἔμ-ψῡχος, ον, (ἐν, ψυχή) *having life in one, alive, living.*

ἐμ-ψῡχόω, f. ώσω, (ἔμψυχος) *to animate.*

ἐν, Dor. and Aeol. for εἰς, *into.*

'EN poët. ἐνί Ep. εἰν, εἰνί, Prep. with dat. *IN:* I. Of place, *in, at; ἐν Ἀθήνῃσι, ἐν Τροίῃ.* 2. *on, upon; ἐν οὔρεσι on* the mountains, etc. 3. of clothing; ἐν ἐσθῆτι, *in* (i. e. *wearing*) a garment; ἐν ὅπλοις *in* or *under* arms. 4. *in the number of, amongst; ἐν τοῖς πρῶτοι among some of the very first:—in presence of, before.* 5. *within one's power, in one's hands; νίκης πείρατ' ἔχονται ἐν ἀθανάτοισι θεοῖσι* are *in* their *hands; ἐν ἐμοί ἐστι* it is *in* my *power.* 6. *according to, in accordance with.* II. Of the instrument or means, *with, by, by means of; ἐν πυρὶ πιμπράναι* to burn *with* fire; ἐν δεσμῷ δῆσαι to bind *with* a bond. III. Of time, *within; ἐν τούτῳ τῷ χρόνῳ within* this space; ἐν ᾧ (sub. χρόνῳ) *while, during the time* that; ἐν βραχεῖ *in* short time. IV. Ellipt. in such phrases as ἐν Ἀλκινόοιο, εἰν Ἀΐδαο Att. ἐν Ἅιδου, etc., where οἴκῳ or δόμοις is understood. V. Without case as adverb, *therein, thereat, thereby, moreover: especially.* VI. Position:—ἐν sometimes in Ep. follows its dative, but most freq. in the form ἐνί, then written ἔνι. VII. In compos., 1. with Verbs the Prep. retains its sense of being *near, at* or *in.* 2. with Adjs. it expresses either a modified degree, e. g. ἔμπικρος, ἔν-λευκος, *rather* harsh, whit*ish*, etc.; or else the possession of a quality, e. g. ἔν-αιμος, *with* blood *in it.* 2. in compos. ἐν- becomes ἐμ- before β μ π φ ψ; ἐγ- before γ κ ξ χ; ἐλ- before λ; and in a few words ἐρ- before ρ.

ἕν, neut. of εἷς; and **ἕνα**, acc. masc.

ἐν-αβρύνομαι, Pass. *to be vain of.*

ἐν-ᾰγής, ές, (ἐν, ἄγος) *in* or *under a curse, polluted, blood-guilty:* generally, *abominable, accurst.* Hence

ἐναγίζω, f. ίσω Att. ιῶ, *to offer sacrifice to the dead,* Lat. *parentare.* Hence

ἐνάγισμα, ατος, τό, *an offering to the dead.*

ἐν-αγκᾰλίζομαι, Med. *to take in one's arms.*

ἐν-αγκυλάω, f. ήσω, (ἐν, ἀγκύλη) *to fit thongs* to javelins to throw them with.

ἐν-αγρόμενος, Ep. aor. 2 part. pass. of ἐναγείρω.

ἔν-αγχος, Adv. (ἐν, ἄγχι) *just now, even now, lately.*

ἐν-άγω, f. ξω, *to lead in* or *into, lead on, urge, persuade.* 2. c. acc. rei, *to propose, suggest.*

ἐν-ᾰγωνίζομαι, Dep. *to contend* or *fight among:*—of a place, εὐμενὴς ἐναγωνίζεσθαι favourable *to fight in.*

ἐν-ᾰγώνιος, ον, (ἐν, ἀγών) *of* or *belonging to a contest, fight* or *game.* 2. ἐναγώνιοι θεοί the gods *who presided over the games,* esp. Hermes.

ἐν-αθλέω, f. ήσω, = ἀθλέω ἐν, *to contend in* or *among.*

ἐναιμήεις, εσσα, εν, = ἔναιμος.

ἔν-αιμος, ον, (ἐν, αἷμα) *with blood in it.*

ἐναιρέμεν, Ep. for ἐναίρειν, inf. of ἐναίρω.

ἐναίρω Ep. ἐνναίρω: fut. ἐνᾰρῶ: aor. 2 ἤνᾰρον, poët. also ἔνᾰρον: aor. 1 med. ἐνηράμην, Ep. 3 sing. ἐνήρατο: (ἔναρα):—*to slay, kill:* also of things, *to make away with, destroy.*

ἐν-αισῐμος and **ἐν-αίσιος**, ον, (ἐν, αἶσα) *fated, sent by destiny,* Lat. *fatalis:* in good sense, *seasonable.* II. *in accordance with fate, seemly, proper;* and of persons, *just, righteous:*—Adv. -ίμως, *fitly, becomingly.*

ἐν-αιχμάζω, f. σω, *to wield the spear in.*

ἐν-αιωρέομαι, Pass. *to float* or *drift about in*

ἐνάκις, Adv. = ἐννάκις.

ἐνᾰκόσιοι, αι, α, (ἐννέα) *nine hundred.*

ἐν-ᾰκούω, f. -ούσομαι, *to hear in* a place.

ἐν-αλείφω, f. ψω: pf. pass. ἐναλήλιμμαι:—*to anoint:* Med. *to anoint oneself* or *for oneself.*

ἐν-ᾰλίγκιος, ον, *like, resembling.*

ἐν-άλιος, α, ον, and ος, ον: Ep. and Lyr. also **εἰνάλιος**: (ἐν, ἅλς):—*in, on, of the sea,* Lat. *marinus.*

ἐναλλαγῆναι, aor. 2 inf. pass. of ἐναλλάσσω.

ἐναλλάξ, Adv. *crosswise: alternately,* Lat. *vicissim.* From

ἐν-αλλάσσω Att. -ττω: fut. ξω: aor. 1 -ήλλαξα: pf. -ήλλαχα, pass. -ήλλαγμαι:—*to exchange, receive in exchange:* also *to divert from* one thing *to* another. II. Pass. *to be changed, to differ from.* 2. *to have dealings with.*

ἐν-άλλομαι, f. -ᾰλοῦμαι: aor. 1 -ηλάμην: Dep.—*to leap in* or *on, to rush against.*

ἔν-αλλος, ον, *changed, contrary.*

ἔν-ᾰλος, ον, (ἐν, ἅλς) = ἐνάλιος.

ἐν-ᾰμέλγω, f. ξω, *to milk into.*

ἐν-άμιλλος, ον, (ἐν, ἅμιλλα) *engaged in equal contest with, a match for.*

ἐναμμένος, Ion. for ἐνημμένος, pf. part. pass. of ἐνάπτω.

ἔν-αντα, Adv. *opposite, over against,* c. gen.

ἔν-αντι, (ἐν, ἀντί) Adv., = ἐναντίον.

ἐν-αντίβιος, ον, *struggling against:* neut. ἐναντίβιον, *against, in opposition to.*

ἐν-αντίος, α, ον, *over against, opposite: face to face, in presence of.* 2. in hostile sense, *facing in fight, opposing.* II. *opposite, contrary, reverse;* τὸ ἐναντίον *the contrary, the reverse.* III. neut. ἐναντίον as Adv., *against* or *in presence of.* 2. ἐξ ἐναντίου, *over against, opposite.* 3. the regul. Adv. ἐναντίως, *contrariwise,* c. dat. Hence

ἐναντιόω, f. *ώσω*, *to place opposite*:—mostly as Dep. **ἐναντιόομαι**, f. *ώσομαι*: aor. 1 *ἠναντιώθην*: pf. *ἠναντίωμαι* poët. *ἐν-*:—*to set oneself against*, *oppose*, *withstand*· *to be adverse to*. 2. *to contradict*, *gainsay*, *deny*

ἐναντίωμα, *ματος*, *τό*, (*ἐναντιόω*) *an obstacle*.

ἐναντίωσις, *εως*, *ἡ*, (*ἐναντιόω*) *opposition*.

ἔναξα, aor. 1 of *νάσσω*.

ἐναπέθᾰνον, aor. 2 of *ἐναποθνήσκω*.

ἐναπῆπτε, Ion. for *ἐναφῆπτε*, 3 sing. impf. of *ἐναφάπτω*.

ἐναπῆκε, Ion. for *ἐναφῆκε*, 3 sing. aor. 1 of *ἐναφίημι*.

ἐν-αποδείκνῡμι, *to display in* a thing:—Pass. *to be distinguished* or *manifest*.

ἐν-αποθνήσκω, f. *-αποθᾰνοῦμαι*, *to die in*.

ἐν-αποκλάω, f. *-κλάσω* [ᾰ], *to break short off in*.

ἐν-απολείπω, f. *ψω*, *to leave behind in*.

ἐν-απόλλῡμι and **-ύω**: fut. *-ολέσω* Att. *-ολῶ*:—*to destroy in* or *among*.

ἐν-απομόργνῡμι, f. *-απομόρξω*:—*to rub or wipe off upon*; and so *to impart*

ἐν-απονίζω, f. *-απονιψω*, *to wash clean in* a thing.

ἐν-αποτίνω, f. *-αποτίσω*, *to pay as a penalty*.

ἐν-αποψύχω, f. *ξω*, *to give up the ghost*, *expire*.

ἐν-άπτω, f. *ψω*, *to bind* or *tie in*, *on* or *to*:—Pass. and Med., pf. *ἐνῆμμαι*, *to be clad in*. II. *to kindle*, *set on fire*: Med. *to get oneself a light*.

ἜΝΑ΄ΡΑ, *ων*, *τά*, used only in plur. *the arms of a slain foe*, Lat. *spolia*; *booty*, *spoil*.

ἐν-αραρίσκω, aor. 1 *ἐνῆρσα*, *to fit* or *fasten in*. II. intr. in pf. *ἐν-άρηρα*, *to be fitted in*.

ἐνάργει, Dor. for *ἐνήργει*, 3 sing. impf. of *ἐνεργέω*.

ἐναργής, *ές*, (*ἐν*, *ἀργός*) *distinct*, *visible*, *in bodily form*. 2. *bright*, *brilliant*. 3. of words, *distinct*, *plain*. Hence

ἐναργῶς Ion. **-έως**, Adv. *distinctly*, *visibly*.

ἐνάρεες or **ἐνάριες**, *οἱ*, a Scythian word, = Greek *ἀνδρόγυνοι*.

ἐνᾰρηρώς, *υῖα*, *ός*, part. pf. 2 of *ἐναραρίσκω*.

ἐνᾰρη-φόρος, *ον*, (*ἔναρα*, *φέρω*) *wearing the spoils*.

ἐνᾰρίζω, f. *ξω*: Ep. aor. 1 *ἐνάριξα*:—Pass., aor. 1 *ἠνᾰρίσθην*. pf. *ἠνάρισμαι*: (*ἔναρα*):—*to strip a slain foe*, Lat. *spoliare*, *ἐναρίζειν τινὰ ἔντεα*, *τεύχη to strip* one *of* his arms: hence *to slay in fight*, *to slay*:—Pass., *νὺξ ἐναριζομένα* night *being slain*, i.e. *brought to an end*.

ἐν-ᾰριθμέω, f. *ήσω*, *to count*, *reckon in* or *among*: generally, *to reckon*, *account*:—Med. *to make account of*, *value*.

ἐν-ᾰρίθμιος, *ον*, (*ἐν*, *ἀριθμός*) *reckoned in*, *counted among*. II. *taken into account*, *valued*, Lat. *in numero habitus*.

ἐνᾰρίμ-βροτος, *ον*, (*ἐναίρω*, *βρότος*) *slaying* men.

ἐν-αρμόζω and **-ττω**: f. *όσω* Dor. *όξω*:—*to fit in*: also *to fix* a weapon *in*. II. intr. *to fit*, *suit*, *to be adapted to*.

ἔνᾰρον, *τό*, see *ἔναρα*.

ἔνᾰρον, poët. for *ἤνᾰρον*, aor. 2 of *ἐναίρω*.

ἐν-άρχομαι, f. *ξομαι* Dep. *to begin with*. 2. in sacrifices, *ἐνάρχεσθαι τὰ κανᾶ to begin the offering*, by taking the barley (*οὐλοχύται*) from the baskets (*κανᾶ*, pl. of *κανοῦν*); cf. *κατάρχομαι*.

ἐν-ασελγαίνω, = *ἀσελγαίνω ἐν*, *to be insolent in*:—Pass. *to be treated with insult in* a thing

ἐν-ασπῐδόομαι, Pass. (*ἐν*, *ἀσπίς*) *to fit oneself with a shield*.

ἔνασσα, Ep. aor. 1 of *ναίω*

ἔνατος, Ep. and Ion. **εἴνατος**, *η*, *ον*, (*ἐννέα*) *ninth*, Lat. *nonus*. *τὰ ἔνατα* (sub. *ἱερά*) *offerings to the dead made nine days after the funeral*, Lat. *novendialia*.

ἐν-αυλᾰκο-φοῖτις, *ιδος*, *ἡ*, (*ἐν*, *αὖλαξ*, *φοιτάω*) *roaming in the fields*

ἐν-αυλίζω, f. *ίσω* Att. *ιῶ*, *to dwell* or *lodge in*:—Med. *to take up quarters for the night in* Hence

ἐναυλιστήριος, *ον*, *to be dwelt in*, *habitable*

ἔν-αυλον, *τό*, (*ἐν*, *αὐλή*) *an abode*.

ἔν-αυλος, *ὁ*, as Subst., I. (*ἐν*, *αὐλός*) *a hollow channel*: *a water-course*, *a torrent*. II. (*ἐν*, *αὐλή*) *a dwelling*, *shelter*; *haunt*.

ἔν-αυλος, *ον*, as Adj., I. (*ἐν*, *αὐλός*) *on* or *to the flute*: *still ringing in one's ears*, *fresh*. II. (*ἐν*, *αὐλή*) *dwelling in dens*: of men, *in one's den*, *at home*.

ἐν-αυξάνω, f. *-αυξήσω*, *to increase*, *enlarge*.

ἐν-αυχένιος, *ος*, *ον*, (*ἐν*, *αὐχήν*) *in* or *on the neck*

ἐν-αύω, aor. 1 inf. *ἐν-αῦσαι*, *to kindle* or *light a fire*. —Med. *to light oneself* a fire.

ἐν-αφάπτω, f. *ψω*, *to fasten up to* a thing.

ἐν-αφίημι, Ion. **ἐν-απ-**: f. *-αφήσω*, *to let drop in*.

ἔν-δαις, *αιδος*, *ὁ*, *ἡ*, (*ἐν*, *δαΐς*) *with lighted torch*.

ἐν-δαίω, *to kindle in*:—Med. *to burn in*.

ἐν-δάκνω, f. *δήξομαι*: aor. 2 *ἐνέδᾰκον*.—*to bite into*, *hold in the teeth*.

ἐν-δακρύω, f. *ύσω* [ῡ], *to weep in*.

ἐνδάπιος, *α*, *ον*, (*ἔνδον*) *native of the country*.

ἐν-δᾰτέομαι, Dep. *to divide*, *distribute*, esp. in speaking: hence II. *to speak of*; either in bad sense, *to upbraid*, *reproach*, *revile*: or in good sense, *to tell of*, *celebrate*.

ἐνδέδμημαι, pf. pass. of *ἐνδέμω*.

ἐνδεδῡμένος, pf. part. pass. of *ἐνδύω*

ἐνδεεστέρως, Adv. Comp. of *ἐνδεῶς*, *in a less degree*.

ἐνδεήσω, fut. of *ἐνδέω*. *to be in want*

ἐνδεής, *ές*, (*ἐνδέω*) *in need of*, *wanting* or *lacking in*: *inferior to*: absol. *in want*, *in need*, *deficient*, *poor*, *weak*:—*τὸ ἐνδεές lack*, *want*, *defect*. Hence

ἔνδεια, *ἡ*, *want*, *lack of* a thing: absol. *need*, Lat. *egestas*· in plur. *wants*, *needs*, *deficiencies*.

ἔνδειγμα, *ατος*, *τό*, (*ἐνδείκνυμι*) *a proof*

ἐν-δείκνῡμι or **-υω** f. *-δείξω*: aor. 1 *ἐνέδειξα*:—Pass., aor. 1 *ἐνεδείχθην*: pf. *ἐνδέδειγμαι*:—*to mark out*, Lat. *in-dicare*: as Att. law-term, *to inform against*. II. Med. *to declare oneself*: *to display*, *make a show of* a thing. 2. *to shew*, *give proof of*. Hence

ἔνδειξις, *εως*, *ἡ*, *a pointing out*: *a token*, *evidence*, *proof*: as Att. law-term, *a laying information against* one who undertook an office for which he was legally disqualified.

ἕν-δεκα, οἱ, αἱ, τά, (ἕν neut. of εἷς, δέκα) indecl., *eleven.* II. οἱ ἕνδεκα, *the Eleven* at Athens, i. e. the Commissioners of police.

ἑνδεκά-πηχυς, υ, gen. εος, *eleven cubits long.*

ἑνδεκά-πους, ὁ, ἡ, πουν, τό, gen. ποδος, *eleven feet long* or *broad.*

ἑνδεκάς, άδος, ἡ, (ἕν-δεκα) *the number eleven.*

ἑνδέκατος, η, ον, (ἕν-δεκα) *the eleventh.*

ἑνδεκ-ετής, οῦ, ὁ, fem. -έτις, ιδος, *eleven years old.*

ἐν-δέκομαι, Ion. for ἐνδέχομαι.

ἐνδελεχής, ές, *continual, constant.* Adv. ἐνδελεχῶς, *constantly.*

ἔνδεμα, τό, (ἐνδέω) *a thing bound on, band.*

ἐν-δέμω, f. μῶ, *to wall up*:—*to build in* a place.

ἐν-δεξιόομαι, Dep. *to grasp with the right hand, clasp, embrace.*

ἐν-δέξιος, α, ον, *on* or *towards the right hand, from left to right;* neut. pl. ἐνδέξια as Adv. 2. *propitious, favourable;* ἐνδέξια σήματα *right, good* omens.

ἔνδετος, ον, (ἐνδέω) *bound to* a thing, *entangled in.*

ἐν-δέχομαι, Ion. **-δέκομαι;** f. -δέξομαι: Dep.:—*to take upon oneself,* Lat. *suscipere.* II. *to accept, admit, believe:* also of things, *to admit, allow of:* hence 2. ἐνδέχεται, impers. *it may be, it is possible;* οὐκ ἐνδέχεται *it is* not *possible;* τὰ ἐνδεχόμενα *things possible;* ἐκ τῶν ἐνδεχομένων *by every possible means*:—Adv. ἐνδεχομένως, *possibly.*

ἐν-δέω, f. -δήσω: aor. 1 ἐνέδησα:—*to bind in,* *on* or *to: to entangle in, implicate* or *involve in*:—Med. *to tie* or *pack up.*

ἐν-δέω, f. -δεήσω, *to be in want of:* also *to be wanting, to fail.* II. impers. ἐνδεῖ, *there is need* or *want of: there is a deficiency;* πολλῶν ἐνέδει αὐτῷ he *was in want* of many things. III. Pass. *to be in want* or *need of.*

ἐνδεῶς, Adv. of ἐνδεής, *insufficiently.*

ἔν-δηλος, ον, (ἐν, δῆλος) *manifest, clear*:—Adv. ἐνδήλως, *clearly,* Sup. -ότατα.

ἐνδημέω, f. ήσω, (ἔνδημος) *to live in* or *at* a place.

ἔν-δημος, ον, *dwelling in* a place: esp. *at home: native,* opp. to ξένος: *attached to home:* of war, *civil, intestine.* II. *of* or *belonging to a state.*

ἐνδιάασκον, Ion. impf. of ἐνδιάω.

ἐν-διάγω, f. ξω, *to pass one's time in.*

ἐν-διαθρύπτομαι, Pass. *to play the coquet with, trifle with.*

ἐν-δῐαιτάομαι, Ion. -έομαι, f. ήσομαι, Dep. *to live* or *dwell in* a place.

ἐν-διατάσσω Att. **-ττω,** fut. ξω, *to arrange in order throughout.*

ἐν-διατρίβω [ῐ], f. ψω, *to spend* or *consume in* a place: absol. (sub. χρόνον) *to spend* or *waste time in:* also *to dwell upon.*

ἐν-δῐάω, (ἔνδιος) *to rest in the open air: to linger in* a place. II. trans. *to let go into the open air,* ποιμένες μῆλα ἐνδιάασκον (Ep. impf.) shepherds *let* their sheep *out into the air,* i. e. to feed.

ἐν-δῐδύσκω, = ἐνδύω, *to put on*:—Pass. *to wear.*

ἐν-δίδωμι, f. -δώσω: aor. 1 ἐνέδωκα:—*to give into one's hands, surrender: to give up* as lost, *throw up.* II. *to afford:* also *to allow, grant: to cause.* III. *to shew, exhibit, give proof of.* IV. intr. *to give in, give up, give way: to flag, fail:* of things, *to cease.* V. of a river, *to empty itself.*

ἐν-δίημι, (ἐν, δίω) found only in 3 pl. impf. ἐνδίεσαν, *to chase, pursue.*

ἔν-δῐκος, ον, (ἐν, δίκη) of things, *according to right, fair, right, just: legal.* II. of persons, *righteous, just, upright.* 2, *possessed of right.* III. Adv. ἐνδίκως, *with right, with justice:* Sup. ἐνδικώτατα.

ἔν-δῖνα, τά, (ἔνδον) *the entrails,* Lat. *intestina.*

ἐνδινεῦντι, Dor. for ἐνδινοῦσι, 3 pl. of ἐνδινέω.

ἐν-δῑνέω, f. ήσω, *to revolve in.*

ἔνδῐον, τό, *a seat in the air: a seat.* From

ἔν-διος, ον, *at midday, at noon.* II. *in the open air.* (From ἐν, Διός genit. of Ζεύς, Lat. *sub divo* or *dio,* Horace's *sub Jove.*)

ἐν-δίφριος, ον, (ἐν, δίφρος) *sitting on the same seat.*

ἔνδοθεν, Adv. (ἔνδον) *from within: from one's heart, of oneself.* II. *within,* c. gen.

ἔνδοθι, (ἔνδον) Adv. *within:* also, *at home.*

ἔνδοι, Adv. = ἔνδοθι.

ἐνδοιάζω, = ἐν δοιῇ εἶναι, *to be in doubt, at a loss: to waver:* of things, aor. 1 inf. pass. ἐνδοιασθῆναι, *to be matter of doubt.* Hence

ἐνδοιαστός, ή, όν, *doubtful.* Adv. -τῶς, *doubtfully.*

ἐνδο-μάχης, ου, ὁ, Dor. **-χας,** (ἔνδον, μάχομαι) *fighting* or *bold at home,* epith. of a dunghill cock.

ἐν-δόμησις, εως, ἡ, (ἐν, δόμος) *a thing built in, a building, structure.*

ἐνδό-μῠχος, ον, (ἔνδον, μυχός) *in the inmost part of a dwelling.*

ἔνδον, Adv., and Prep. governing gen., (ἐν) *within,* Lat. *intus: at home,* Lat. *domi: in one's own country;* οἱ ἔνδον *those of the house,* esp. *the domestics;* τὰ ἔνδον *household affairs.*

ἔν-δοξος, ον, (ἐν, δόξα) *held in repute, honoured.* 2. of things, *glorious.* Adv. -ξως.

ἐνδόσιμος, ον, (ἐνδίδωμι) *sounding the key-note:* τὸ ἐνδόσιμον (sub. μέλος) *a key-note.*

ἐνδότερος, α, ον, Comp. formed from ἔνδον, *inner:* Sup. **ἐνδότατος,** η, ον, *inmost.*

ἐν-δουπέω, f. ήσω, *to fall in with a heavy sound.*

ἐν-δρομέω, f. ήσω, (ἐν, δρόμος) *to run in, fall into.*

ἐν-δρομίς, ίδος, ἡ, (ἐν, δρόμος) *a thick cloak worn by runners* after exercise, for fear of cold.

ἔν-δροσος, ον, (ἐν, δρόσος) *dewy, dank.*

ἔν-δρῠον, τό, (ἐν, δρῦς) *the strong oaken pin* by which the yoke is fixed to the pole (ἱστοβοεύς).

ἐνδῠκέως, Adv. *zealously, heartily, earnestly.* The Adj. ἐνδυκής is not found. (Deriv. uncertain.)

ἐν-δῠνᾰμόω, f. ώσω, (ἐν, δύναμις) *to strengthen*:—Pass. *to acquire strength.*

ἐν-δυναστεύω, f. σω, *to have power in* or *among.* II. *to prevail by authority.*

ἐνδύς, ῦσα, ύν, aor. 2 part. of ἐνδύω.

ἐν-δυστυχέω, f. ήσω, *to be unlucky in* or *with.*

ἐν-δυτήρ, ῆρος, ὁ, (ἐνδύω) as Adj. *fit for putting on.*

ἐνδυτήριος, α, ον, (ἐνδύω) = ἐνδυτήρ.

ἐν-δυτός, όν, *put on:* as Subst., ἐνδυτόν, τό, *that which is put on, a garment, dress.* II. *clad in.* From

ἐν-δύω, f. ύσω [ῡ]: aor. 1 ἐνέδῡσα; in these tenses, trans., *to put on* another; ἐνδύσειν τινά τι *to put on* one, *clothe* one *in* II. intr. ἐνδύνω and in Med. ἐνδύομαι, with aor. 2 act. ἐνέδυν, pf. -δέδῡκα: *to put on oneself, put on, wear.* 2. *to go in, enter;* ἀκοντιστὺν ἐνδύσεαι *thou wilt enter* the contest of darting. 3. *to implicate oneself in* a matter: also *to insinuate oneself into.*

ἐνέβᾰλον, aor. 2 of ἐμβάλλω.

ἐνέβην, aor. 2 of ἐμβαίνω.

ἐνεγέγραπτο, 3 sing. plqpf. pass. of ἐγγράφω.

ἐνέγκαι and **ἐνεγκεῖν**, aor. 1 and 2 inf. of φέρω.

ἐνέγραψα, aor. 1 of ἐγγράφω.

ἐνεγύησα, ἐνεγύηκα, ἐνεγύων, see ἐγγυάω.

ἐνέδειξα, ἐνεδείχθην, aor. 1 act. and pass. of ἐνδείκνυμι.

ἐνέδησα, aor. 1 of ἐνδέω, *to bind in.*

ἐν-έδρα, ἡ, *a lying in wait, ambush,* Lat. *insidiae.*

ἐνεδρεύω, f. σω: (derived from ἐνέδρα: but in the augm. tenses, ἐνήδρευον, ἐνήδρευσα, ἐνηδρεύθην, ἐνήδρευμαι, as if compd. of ἐν, ἑδρεύω):—*to lie in wait for, lie in ambush,* Lat. *insidiari*:—Pass. *to be caught in an ambush: to be ensnared.* II. *to place in ambush:* Med. *to set an ambush:* Pass. *to be set in ambush.*

ἔν-εδρον, τό, = ἐνέδρα.

ἔν-εδρος, ον, (ἐν, ἕδρα) *an inmate, inhabitant.*

ἐνέδῡσα, ἐνέδυν, aor. 1 and 2 of ἐνδύω.

ἐν-έζομαι, f. -εδοῦμαι, Dep. *to sit down in, abide* or *reside in:* cp. ἐνῆμαι.

ἐνέηκα, Ep. for ἐνῆκα, aor. 1 of ἐνίημι.

ἐνέην, Ep. for ἐνῆν, impf. of ἔνειμι.

ἐνεθῡμήθην, aor. 1 of ἐνθυμέομαι.

ἐν-εῖδον, aor. 2 with no pres. in use, its place being supplied by ἐνοράω: *to see* or *observe in:* absol. *to observe, remark.* Cf. εἶδον.

ἔνεικα, Ep. for ἤνεικα (Ion. for ἤνεγκα), aor. 1 of φέρω: inf. ἐνεῖκαι.

ἐνεικέμεν, Ep. for ἐνεγκέμεν, aor. 2 inf. of φέρω.

ἐνείκεον, impf. of νεικέω.

ἐν-είλλω and **ἐν-ειλέω**, f. ήσω, *to wrap up in.*

ἔνειμα, aor. 1 of νέμω.

ἔν-ειμεν, Ep. for ἔνεσμεν, 1 pl. of ἔνειμι: but II. ἔνειμεν, 3 sing. aor. 1 of νέμω.

ἔν-ειμι, f. ἐνέσομαι, (ἐν, εἰμί *sum*) *to be in* a place, *to be within: to be in* or *among.* II. *to be possible;* impers., ἔνεστί τινι *it is in one's power, one may* or *can:* part. neut. ἐνόν used absol., *it being possible.*

ἐν-είρω: pf. pass. ἔνερμαι:—*to entwine, interweave.*

ἐνείς, ἐνεῖσα, aor. 2 part. of ἐνίημι.

ἕνεκα, Ion. and Ep. **ἕνεκεν**, poët. also **εἵνεκα, εἵνεκεν**: Prep. with gen., put both before and after its case, *on account of, for the sake of, for,* Lat. *gratia, causa.* II. *with respect to, as far as regards, as for;* ἕνεκα ἐμοῦ *as far as depends on* me. III. *by means of;* τέχνης εἵνεκα *by force of* art.

ἐνεκάλυψα, aor. 1 of ἐγκαλύπτω.

ἐνεκείμην, impf. of ἔγκειμαι.

ἐνεκέρᾱσα, aor. 1 of ἐγκεράννυμι.

ἐνέκρᾰγον, aor. 2 of ἐγκράζω.

ἐνέκρυψα, aor. 1 of ἐγκρύπτω.

ἐνέκυρσα, aor. 1 of ἐγκύρω.

ἐνέκυψα, aor. 1 of ἐγκύπτω.

ἐν-ελαύνω, f. -ελάσω Att. -ελῶ:—*to drive in* or *into.*

ἐνέλῐπον, aor. 2 of ἐλλείπω.

ἐν-ελίσσω, f. ξω, *to roll* or *wrap up in,* Lat. *involvo.*

ἐνεμαξάμην, aor. 1 med. of ἐμμάσσω.

ἐνέμεινα, aor. 1 of ἐμμένω.

ἐνεμέσσα, Ep. 3 sing. impf. of νεμεσάω.

ἐν-εμέω, f. έσω, *to vomit in.*

ἐνεμήθην, aor. 1 pass. of νέμω.

ἐνεμυήθην, aor. 1 pass. of ἐμμυέω.

ἐνένευον, impf. of ἐννεύω.

ἐνενήκοντα, οἱ, αἱ, τά, indecl., (ἐννέα) *ninety.*

ἐνένῑπε, 3 sing. Ep. redupl. aor. 2 of ἐνίπτω.

ἐνενώκᾱσι, Ion. for ἐνενοήκασι, 3 pl. pf. of ἐννοέω.

ἐνένωτο, Ion. for ἐνενόητο, 3 sing. plqpf. pass. of ἐννοέω.

ἐνέξομαι, fut. med. (with pass. sense) of ἐνέχω.

ἐνεός or **ἐννεός**, ά, όν, *dumb, speechless: deaf and dumb.*

ἐνεπάγην [ᾰ], aor. 2 pass. of ἐμπήγνυμι.

ἐνεπαίχθην, aor. 1 pass. of ἐμπαίζω.

ἐνέπαξα, Dor. for ἐνέπηξα, aor. 1 of ἐμπήγνυμι

ἐνέπασσα, Ep. for ἐνέπᾰσα, aor. 1 of ἐμπάσσω.

ἐνέπεσον, aor. 2 of ἐμπίπτω.

ἐνέπιον, aor. 2 of ἐμπίνω.

ἐνεπλάκην [ᾰ], aor. 2 pass. of ἐμπλέκω.

ἐνέπλησθεν, Ep. 3 pl. aor. 1 pass. of ἐμπίπλημι.

ἐνέπλησα, ἐνεπλήσθην, aor. 1 act. and pass. of ἐμπίπλημι.

ἐνέπνευσα, aor. 1 of ἐμπνέω.

ἐνεπορπέατο, Ion. for ἐνεπόρπηντο, plqpf. pass. of ἐκπορπάω.

ἐνέπρηθον, impf. of ἐμπρήθω.

ἐνέπρησα, aor. 1 of ἐμπίπρημι

ἐνέπτῠσα, aor. 1 of ἐμπτύω.

ἐνέπω, poët. also **ἐννέπω**: aor. 2 ἔνισπον, inf. ἐνισπεῖν: fut. ἐνισπήσω or ἐνίψω:—*to tell, tell of, describe, relate.* 2. *to speak to, address, accost.* 3. simply, *to speak, say.* 4. c. inf. *to bid.*

ἐν-εργάζομαι, fut. σομαι: pf. -είργασμαι: aor. 1 -ειργασάμην and -ειργάσθην: Dep.:—*to make* or *create in:* aor. 1 ἐνειργάσθην is also used in pass. sense. 2. *to labour, pursue a calling, work for hire.*

ἐνέργεια, ἡ, (ἐνεργής) *an action, operation, energy.*

ἐνεργέω, f. ήσω, (ἐνεργός) *to work, be active.* Hence

ἐνέργημα, ατος, τό, *an effect, work, operation.*

ἐν-εργής, ές, = ἐνεργός.

ἐν-εργός, όν, (ἐν, ἔργον) *working, active, busy:* of soldiers, *on service, fit for service:* of land, *in tillage, productive.* Hence

ἐνεργῶς, Adv. of ἐνεργής or ἐνεργός, *actively: productively.*

ἐν-ερείδω, f. σω, *to push in, to thrust in.*

ἐν-ερεύγω, aor. 2 ἐνήρῠγον, *to belch on* one.

ἔνερθε. before a vowel **-θεν**, *from beneath: beneath.* II. c. gen. *beneath.* 2. *below, in the power of.* From

ἔνεροι, ων, οἱ, (ἐν) Lat. *inferi, those in* or *beneath the earth,* of the dead and the gods below.

ἐνερμένος, pf. part. pass. of ἐνείρω.

ἐνερράφην [ᾰ], **ἐνερραψάμην**, aor. 2 pass. and aor. 1 med. of ἐνράπτω.

ἔνερσις, εως, ἡ, (ἐνείρω) *a fitting* or *fastening in.*

ἐνέρτερος, α, ον, Comp. of ἔνεροι, *deeper, lower.*

ἔνεσαν, Ep. for ἐνῆσαν, 3 pl. impf. of ἔνειμι.

ἐνεσία, ἡ, (ἐνίημι) *a suggestion, counsel.*

ἐνέσκληκα, pf. with pass. sense of ἐνσκέλλω.

ἐνέστακται, 3 sing. pf. pass. of ἐνστάζω.

ἐνέσταλμαι, pf. pass. of ἐνστέλλω.

ἐνεστεῶτος Ion. for ἐνεστῶτος, gen. of ἐνεστώς (for ἐνεστηκώς), pf. part. of ἐνίστημι.

ἐνεστήρικτο, 3 sing. plqpf. pass. of ἐνστηρίζω.

ἐνέσχετο, 3 sing. aor. 2 med. (in pass. sense) of ἐνέχω.

ἐνετάθην [ᾰ], aor. 1 pass. of ἐντείνω.

ἐνετειλάμην, aor. 1 med. of ἐντελλω.

ἐνετή, ἡ, (ἐνίημι) *a pin, brooch.*

ἐνέτρᾰγον, aor. 2 of ἐντρώγω.

ἐνετράπην [ᾰ], aor. 2 pass. of ἐντρέπω.

ἐνετράφην [ᾰ], aor. 2 pass. of ἐντρέφω.

ἐνετρίβην [ῐ], aor. 2 pass. of ἐντρίβω.

ἐνετύλιξα, aor. 1 of ἐντυλίσσω.

ἐνέτῠχον, aor. 2 of ἐντυγχάνω.

ἐν-ευδαιμονέω, f. ήσω, *to be happy in.*

ἐν-εύδω, fut. -ευδήσω, *to sleep in* or *on.*

ἐν-εύναιος, ον, (ἐν, εὐνή) *in* or *on which one sleeps;* δέρμα ἐνεύναιον a skin *to sleep on;* χήτει ἐνευναίων for want *of bed-clothes.*

ἔνευσα, aor. 1 both of νεύω and of νέω (B) *to swim.*

ἐνέφραξα, aor. 1 of ἐμφράσσω.

ἐνέφῡσα, **ἐνέφυν**, aor. 1 and 2 of ἐμφύω.

ἐνεφύσησα, aor. 1 of ἐμφυσάω.

ἐνέχεα, Ep. **ἐνέχευα**, aor. 1 med. of ἐγχέω.

ἐνεχείρησα, aor. 1 of ἐγχειρέω.

ἐνεχευάμην, Ep. aor. 1 med. of ἐγχέω.

ἐνεχθήσομαι, fut. pass. of φέρω.

ἐνεχθῆτι, **ἐνεχθείην**, **ἐνεχθῶ**, **ἐνεχθῆναι**, aor. 1 pass. imperat., optat., subj., and inf. of φέρω.

ἐνεχῠράζω, f. άσω, (ἐνέχῠρον) *to take a pledge from* one. 2. c. acc. rei, *to take in pledge:* Pass., ἐνεχυράζεσθαι τὰ χρήματα *to have one's goods seized for debt:* Med. *to have surety given one,* τόκου for interest.

ἐν-έχῠρον, τό, (ἐν, ἐχυρός) *a pledge, surety;* ἐνέχυρον τιθέναι τι to make a thing *a pledge.*

ἐν-έχω, f. ἐνέξω or ἐνσχήσω:—*to keep fast within: entertain, cherish.* II. Pass., with fut. med. ἐνέξομαι, aor. 2 ἐνεσχόμην, *to be held, caught, entangled in.* III. intr. *to enter, pierce into, penetrate: to press upon.*

ἐνεχώρησα, aor. 1 of ἐγχωρέω.

ἐν-ζεύγνῡμι, f. -ζεύξω, *to bind fast in, to involve in.*

ἔνη, ης, η, see ἔνος, η, ον.

ἐν-ηβάω, f. ήσω, *to spend one's youth in: to amuse oneself in, to be joyful in.* Hence

ἐνηβητήριον, τό, *a place of amusement.*

ἔν-ηβος, ον, (ἐν, ἥβη) *in the prime of youth.*

ἐνήδρευσα, **-εύθην**, aor. 1 act. and pass. of ἐνεδρεύω.

ἐνηείη, ἡ, (ἐνηής) *kindness, goodness.*

ἐνῆεν, Ep. for ἐνῆν, 3 sing. impf. of ἔνειμι.

ἐνηής, ές, gen. ἐνηέος, *kind, friendly, good-hearted.* (Connected with ἀπηνής and προσηνής.)

ἐνῆκα, aor. 1 of ἐνίημι.

ἐνήλατο, 3 sing. aor. 1 of ἐνάλλομαι.

ἐνήλᾰτον, τό, (ἐνελαύνω) *anything driven in:* in plur. *the rounds* of the ladder *fixed in* the poles or sides; ἀξόνων ἐνήλατα *the pins driven into* the axle, *linch-pins.*

ἐνήλλαγμαι, pf. pass. of ἐναλλάσσω.

ἐνήλλαξα, aor. 1 of ἐναλλάσσω.

ἐνήλλου, 2 sing. impf. of ἐνάλλομαι.

ἐν-ῆμαι, Pass. (really pf. of ἐν-έζομαι), *to be seated in.*

ἐν-ῆμμαι, pf. pass. of ἐνάπτω.

ἐνήνεγμαι, pf. pass. of φέρω.

ἐνήνοθε, 3 sing. pf., only found in this pers. and in compds. ἐπ-ενήνοθε, κατ-ενήνοθε, παρ-ενήνοθε, with the notion of *being upon* or *close to.* (The root ἐνέθω is not in use.)

ἐνήνοχα, pf. of φέρω.

ἐνήρατο, 3 sing. Ep. aor. 1 med. of ἐναίρω.

ἐνήσω, fut. of ἐνίημι.

ἔνθα, (ἐν) Adv., I. of Place, *there,* Lat. *ibi:* also as relat. to ὅθι, *where,* Lat. *ubi.* 2. *in this case* or *state.* 3. with a sense of Motion, *thither, hither,* Lat. *illuc.* II. of Time, *when.* Hence

ἐνθάδε, Adv. *thither,* Lat. *illuc:* also, *there:* of Time, *here, now.*

ἐν-θᾰκέω, f. ήσω, *to sit in* or *on.* Hence

ἐνθάκησις, εως, ἡ, *a sitting in;* ἐνθάκησις ἡλίου *a seat in* the sun.

ἐν-θάλπω, f. ψω, *to warm in:*—Pass., ἐνθάλπεσθαι ἔρωτι *to glow* with love.

ἐνθανεῖν, aor. 2 inf. of ἐνθνήσκω.

ἔνθᾰ-περ, (ἔνθα, περ) Adv. *there where, where.*

ἐν-θάπτω, f. ψω, *to bury in* a place.

ἐνθαῦτα, **ἐνθεῦτεν**, Ion. for ἐνταῦθα, ἐντεῦθεν.

ἐν-θεάζω, f. σω, (ἐν, θεός) *to be inspired.*

ἐνθέμεν, **ἐνθέμεναι**, Ep. aor. 2 inf. of ἐντίθημι.

ἔνθεν, (ἔνθα) Adv. *thence,* Lat. *illinc;* ἔνθεν καὶ ἔνθεν *on this side* and *on that:* also as relat. for ὅθεν, *whence, whereof,* Lat. *unde* II. of Time, *thereupon, after that.*

ἐνθένδε, (ἔνθεν) *hence.* Lat. *hinc.*

ἔνθεο, Ep. for ἔνθεσο, aor. 2 imper. med. of ἐντίθημι.

ἔν-θεος, ον, *full of the god, inspired, possessed: given by inspiration.*

ἐν-θερμαίνω, f. ανῶ, (ἐν, θερμός) *to heat*:—Pass., ἐντεθέρμανται πόθῳ *has been heated by* passion.

ἔνθεσις, εως, ἡ, (ἐντίθημι) *a putting in.* II. *a piece put in, a mouthful.*

ἔν-θετο, Ep. for ἐνέθετο, 3 sing. aor. 2 med. of ἐντίθημι.

ἔνθετος, ον, (ἐντίθημι) *put in, implanted.*

ἐνθεῦτεν, Adv., Ion. for ἐντεῦθεν.

ἔνθῃ, ἔνθῃς, ἔνθοι, ἔνθω, ἐνθών, Dor. for ἔλθῃ, ἔλθῃς, ἔλθοι, etc., aor. 2 of ἔρχομαι.

ἔν-θηρος, ον, (ἐν, θήρ) *full of wild beasts.* II. metaph. *savage, wild, rough, untended, undressed.*

ἐν-θνήσκω, f. -θανοῦμαι, *to die in: to grow rigid* or *torpid in.*

ἔνθορε, Ep. for ἐνέθορε, 3 sing. aor. 2 of ἐνθρώσκω.

ἐνθοῦ, Att. aor. 2 imperat. med. of ἐντίθημι.

ἐν-θουσιάζω, f. άσω, or **ἐν-θουσιάω**, f. ήσω, (ἔνθεος, contr. ἔνθους) *to be inspired.*

ἐνθρέψασθαι, aor. 1 inf. med. of ἐντρέφω.

ἐν-θριόω, f. σω, (ἐν, θρῖον) *to wrap in a fig-leaf, enwrap.*

ἐν-θρώσκω, f. -θοροῦμαι: aor. 2 ἐνέθορον Ep. ενθορον:—*to leap into, upon, among.*

ἐν-θυμέομαι, f. ήσομαι: aor. 1 ἐνεθυμήθην: pf. ἐντεθύμημαι: Dep.: (ἐν, θυμός):—*to lay to heart, consider well, ponder.* 2. *to take to heart, be concerned at.* 3. *to form a plan.* 4. *to infer, conclude.* Hence

ἐνθύμημα, ατος, τό, *a thought: invention, device, stratagem.* II. *an argument* in Rhetoric answering to the Syllogism in Logic: and

ἐνθύμησις, εως, ἡ, *consideration, esteem.*

ἐνθυμία, ἡ, (ἐνθυμέομαι) *consideration: suspicion.*

ἐν-θύμιος, ον, (ἐν, θυμός) *taken to heart, weighing upon the mind*; ἐνθύμιόν ἐστί μοι, Lat. *religio est mihi, I feel a scruple.*

ἐνθυμιστός, ή, όν, = ἐνθύμιος.

ἐν-θωρακίζω, f. ίσω, *to array in armour*: pf. pass. part. ἐντεθωρακισμένος, *armed in mail.*

ἐνί, poët. for ἐν. II. ἑνί, dat. of εἷς.

ἔνι, for ἔνεστι, *it is in*: also *it is allowed, possible.*

ἐνιαύσιος, ον, also α, ον, (ἐνιαυτός) *of a year, one year old.* II. *yearly, year by year.* III. *for a year, lasting a year*; ἐν. βεβὼς gone *for a year.*

ἐνιαυτός, ὁ, (ἔνος) *a year*; κατ' ἐνιαυτόν *yearly, every year.* 2. *any complete space of time*; ἔτος ἦλθε περιπλομένων ἐνιαυτῶν as *times* rolled on the year came.

ἐν-ιαύω, f. -ιαύσω, *to sleep in* or *among.*

ἐνιαχῇ, Adv. (ἔνιοι) *in some places.*

ἐνι-βάλλω, ἐνι-βλάπτω, Ep. for ἐμ-βάλλω, etc.

ἐνιβλαφθείς, Ep. aor. 1 pass. part. of ἐμβλάπτω.

ἐν-ιδεῖν, inf. of aor. 2 ἐνεῖδον.

ἐν-ιδρόω, f. ώσω, *to sweat in, labour at.*

ἐν-ιδρύνω, ἐν-ιδρύω, f. ύσω [ῡ], *to set, settle,* or *found in* a place:—Med. *to found for oneself.*

ἐνι ζεύγνυμι or -ύω, poët. for ἐνζ-.

ἐν-ίζω, f. -ιζήσω, (ἐν, ἵζω) *to sit in* or *on.*

ἐν-ίημι, fut. -ήσω: aor. 1 -ῆκα Ep. -έηκα: pf. -εῖκα, pass. -εῖμαι:—*to send in* or *into*: *to implant, inspire*: generally, *to throw in* or *among*: of ships, *to launch into* the sea: metaph. *to urge on, incite to* do a thing. 2. *to send in secretly.* II. rarely intr. *to enter.*

ἐνιθρέψας, poët. aor. 1 part. of ἐντρέφω.

ἐνι-κατατίθημι, Ep. for ἐγκ-: hence ἐνικάτθεο, Ep. aor. 2 med. imperat. for ἐγκατάθου.

ἐνι-κλάω, f. άσω [ᾰ], Ep. for ἐγκ-, *to break in, break off*, Lat. *infringo.*

ἐνι-κλείω, Ep. for ἐγ-κλείω.

ἐνι-ναιετάασκον, Ion. impf. of ἐν-ναιετάω.

ἔνι-οι, αι, α, (from ἔνι οἵ = εἰσὶν οἵ, as ἐνίοτε = ἔστιν ὅτε) *some*, Lat. *ali-qui.*

ἐνί-οτε, Adv. for ἔνι ὅτε = ἔστιν ὅτε, *at times, sometimes*: Dor. **ἐνι-όκα.**

ἐνιπή, ἡ, (ἐνίπτω) *a reproof, rebuke: abuse.*

ἐνί-πλειος, ον, Ep. for ἔμπλεος, *filled.*

ἐνι-πλήσασθαι, -πλησθῆναι, Ep. for ἐμ-πλ-, aor. 1 inf. med. and pass. of ἐμπίπλημι.

ἐνι-πλήξωμεν, -ωσι, Ep. 1 and 3 pl. for ἐμ-πλ-, aor. 1 subj. of ἐμπλήσσω.

ἐν-ιππεύω, f. σω, *to ride in, on* or *among.*

ἐνιπρῆσαι, Ep. aor. 1 inf. of ἐμπίπρημι.

ἐνίπτω, fut. ἐνίψω: Ep. redupl. aor. 2 ἠνίπαπον, or ἐνένιπον;—*to reprove, reproach, upbraid*, Lat. *objurgo.* II. = ἐνέπω, *to tell of, announce.*

ἐνι-σκήπτω, ἐνι-σκίμπτω, Ep. for ἐνσ-.

ἐνισπεῖν, ἐνισπήσω, aor. 2 inf. and fut. of ἐνέπω.

ἐν-ίσπω, aor. 2 subj. of ἐνέπω.

ἐνίσσω, collat. form of ἐνίπτω, *to reprove, reproach*: also *to maltreat, ill-use.*

ἐν-ίστημι, f. -στήσω: aor. 1 -έστησα: also fut. and aor. 1 med. -στήσομαι, -εστησάμην:—Causal in these tenses, *to put, set, place in.* 2. *to begin.* II. intrans. in Med., with aor. 2 act. ἐνέστην; pf. ἐνέστηκα; plqpf. ἐνειστήκειν:—*to be set in, to stand in* or *within.* 2. *to be appointed.* 3. *to be upon, be close upon, to be at hand*; τοῦ ἐνεστῶτος μηνὸς in the *present* month: of circumstances, *to arise, occur*, τὰ ἐνεστηκότα *present circumstances.* 4. *to oppose, resist, object.*

ἐν-ισχύω, f. ύσω [ῡ], *to strengthen.* II. intr. *to gain strength.*

ἐν-ίσχω, = ἐνέχω.

ἐνι-τρέφω, ἐνι-χρίμπτω, Ep. for ἐντ- and ἐγχ-.

ἐνιχριμφθείς, Ep. aor. 1 part. pass. of ἐγχρίμπτω.

ἐν-λαξεύω, f. σω, *to carve in* or *upon.*

ἐνναετήρ, ῆρος, ἡ, (ἐνναίω) *an inhabitant*:—fem. ἐνναέτειρα.

ἐννα-έτηρος, ον, = sq.

ἐννα-ετής, ές, (ἐννέα, ἔτος) *nine years old*: neut. ἐνναέτες, as Adv., *for nine years.*

ἐν-νᾰέτης, ου, ὁ, = ἐν-ναετήρ.

ἐννᾰ-έτις, ιδος, ἡ, fem. of ἐνναετής, *nine years old.*

ἐν-ναίω: Ep. fut. med. ἐννάσσομαι, aor. 1 ἐνενασσάμην :—*to dwell in : inhabit.*

ἐννάκις, Adv. (ἐννέα) *nine times*, Lat. *novies.*

ἐννᾰκόσιοι, v. ἐνακοσ–.

ἐννάσσαντο, Ep. 3 pl. aor. 1 med. of ἐνναίω.

ἔννᾰτος, false form for ἔνατος.

ἐν-ναυπηγέω, f. ήσω, *to build ships in.*

'ΕΝΝΕ'Α˘, indecl. *nine*, Lat. *novem.*

ἐννεά-βοιος, ον, (ἐννέα, βοῦς) *worth nine beeves.*

ἐννεα-καί-δεκα, indecl. *nineteen.* Hence

ἐννεακαιδεκά-μηνος, ον, (μήν) *nineteen months old.*

ἐννεακαιδεκ-ετής, ές, (ἔτος) *nineteen years old.*

ἐννεά-κρουνος, ον, *with nine springs*, a well at Athens, called also Καλλιρρόη.

ἐννεά-λῐνος, ον, (ἐννέα, λίνον) *of nine threads.*

ἐννεά-μηνος, ον, (ἐννέα, μήν) *of nine months.*

ἐννεά-πηχυς, υ, (ἐννέα, πῆχυς) *nine cubits long.*

ἐννεάς, άδος, ἡ, (ἐννέα) *the number nine : a number of nine.* II. *the ninth day of the month.*

ἐννεά-φωνος, ον, (ἐννέα, φωνή) *of nine tones* or *notes.*

ἐννεά-χῑλοι, αι, α, Ep. for ἐνάκις χίλιοι, *nine thousand.*

ἐννεά-χορδος, ον, (ἐννέα, χορδή) *of nine strings.*

ἐννενήκοντα, worse form for ἐνενήκοντα, *ninety.*

ἐννενηκοντα-εννέα, indecl. *ninety and nine.*

ἐννενώκασι, Ion. 3 pl. pf. of ἐννοέω.

ἔννεον, Ep. for ἔνεον, impf. of νέω, *to swim.*

ἐννε-όργυιος, ον, (ἐννέα, ὀργυιά) *nine fathoms long.*

ἐννεός, false form for ἐνεός.

ἐν-νεοσσεύω Att. **–ττεύω**, f. σω, *to make a nest* or *hatch young in :* c. acc. *to hatch.*

ἐννέπω, poët. lengthd. for ἐνέπω.

ἐννεσία, ἡ, see ἐνεσία.

ἐν-νεύω, f. σω, *to nod, beckon* or *make signs to.*

ἐννέ-ωρος, ον, (ἐννέα, ὥρα) *nine years old* or *long.*

ἐννήκοντα, Ep. for ἐνενήκοντα, *ninety.*

ἐνν-ῆμαρ, (ἐννέα, ἦμαρ) Adv. *for nine days.*

ἔννηφιν, Ep. for ἔνης, fem. gen. of ἔνος, as Adv.

ἐν-νοέω, f. ήσω : aor. 1 ἐνενόησα Ion. part. ἐννώσας : pf. ἐννενόηκα Ion. ἐννένωκα :—also in Med., with aor. 1 pass. ἐνενοήθην :—*to think of, have in one's mind, consider, ponder : to take thought, be anxious.* II. *to understand.* III. *to intend* to do, c. inf. IV *to devise, plan. invent*, Lat. *excogitare.* Hence

ἔννοια, ἡ, *a thought : an intent, design.*

ἔν-νομος, ον, (ἐν, νόμος) *within the pale of the law, lawful, right :* of persons, *just, upright :* also, *under the law.* II. (ἐν, νέμομαι) *feeding in, inhabiting.*

ἔν-νοος, ον, contr. **–νους**, ουν, (ἐν, νοῦς) *thoughtful, sensible :*—Comp. ἐννούστερος, Sup. –ούστατος.

ἐννοσί-γαιος, ὁ, poët. for ἐνοσίγ-, (ἔνοσις, γῆ) *the Earthshaker*, a name of Póseidon or Neptune.

ἐννοσί-φυλλος, ον, poët. for ἐνοσιφ–, (ἔνοσις, φύλλον) *with quivering leaves.*

ἐννοχλεῖς, poët. for ἐνοχλεῖς, 2 sing. of ἐνοχλέω.

ἕννῡμι or **ἐννύω**, from root ϜΕ'Ω, = ϜΕΣΘΩ, Lat. VESTIO : f. ἕσω Ep. ἕσσω ; Ep. aor. 1 ἕσσα :—Med. ἕννῠμαι : fut. ἕσομαι : aor. 1 ἑσάμην Ep. ἑσσάμην, 3 sing. ἑέσσατο :—Pass., pf. εἷμαι, εἷσαι, εἷται, but Ep. also ἕσσαι, ἕσται : plqpf. εἵμην, but 2 sing. ἕσσο, 3 sing. ἕστο Ep. ἕεστο, 3 dual ἕσθην, 3 pl. εἵατο :—*to put* clothes *on* another :—Med. c. acc. rei, *to put on oneself, clothe oneself in, put on :*—Pass. *to be clad in, to wrap* or *shroud oneself in* ; λάϊνον ἕσσο χιτῶνα *thou hadst been clad* in coat of stone, i. e. been buried.

ἕννυτο, 3 sing. impf. med. of ἕννῡμι.

ἐν-νῠχεύω, f. σω, (ἐν, νύξ) *to sleep* or *lodge in.*

ἐν-νύχιος, α, ον, or ος, ον, (ἐν, νύξ) *nightly, in the night, by night.* II. *dwelling in Night*, of the dead.

ἔν-νῠχος, ον, = ἐννύχιος.

ἐννῶσαι, **–νώσας**, Ion. for ἐννοῆσαι, –νοήσας, aor. 1 inf. and part. of ἐννοέω.

ἐν-όδιος, α, ον, Ep. **εἰν-όδιος**, η, ον, (ἐν, ὁδός) *in, on,* or *by the road ;* σφῆκες ἐνόδιοι wasps *that have their nests by the way-side.* II. *of* or *belonging to a journey.*

ἐν-οικέω, f. ήσω, *to dwell : to inhabit.* Hence

ἐνοίκησις, εως, ἡ, *a dwelling in* a place.

ἐν-οικίζω, fut. ίσω Att. ιῶ, *to make to dwell in* a place :—Pass. *to be settled* or *take up one's abode in.*

ἐν-οίκιος, ον, (ἐν, οἶκος) *in the house, keeping at home.*

ἐν-οικοδομέω, f. ήσω, *to build in* a place. II. *to build up, block up.*

ἔν-οικος, ον, *dwelling in :* as Subst. *a dweller in, an inhabitant.* II. pass. *dwelt in.*

ἐν-οινοχοέω, f. ήσω, *to pour in wine.*

ἐνόν, part. neut. of ἔνειμι, used absol., *it being possible.*

ἐνοπή, ἡ, (ἐνέπω) *a cry, scream, voice, sound :* esp. *a war-cry, battle-shout.*

ἐν-όπλιος, ον, (ἐν, ὅπλον) *in* or *with arms :* ὁ ἐνόπλιος (sub. ῥυθμός) the tune *for the war-dance.*

ἔν-οπλος, ον, (ἐν, ὅπλον) *in arms, armed.*

ἔνοπτρον, τό, (ἐνόψομαι) *a mirror.*

ἐν-οράω Ion. **–έω** : f. ἐνόψομαι (supplied from obsol. ἐνόπτομαι) : aor. 2 ἐνεῖδον, q. v. :—*to see* or *observe in* a person or thing. II. *to look at* or *upon.*

ἐνόρκιος, ον, = ἔνορκος.

ἔν-ορκος, ον, (ἐν, ὅρκος) *bound by oath, sworn.* II. *that to which one is sworn ;* ἔνορκον εἰπεῖν τι to speak *on oath.*

ἐν-ορμίτης [ῑ], ου, ὁ, (ἐν, ὅρμος) *one who is in harbour.*

ἐν-όρνῡμι, fut. ἐνόρσω : aor. 1 ἐνῶρσα : 3 sing. Ep. aor. 2 pass. ἐνῶρτο : (ἐν, ὄρω, ὄρνυμι) :—*to arouse* or *stir up in :*—Pass. *to arise in* or *among.*

ἐν-ορούω, f. σω, *to leap in* or *upon, assail, attack.*

ἐν-όρχης, ου, ὁ, and **ἔν-ορχις**, ιος, ὁ, ἡ, = ἔνορχος.

ἔν-ορχος, ον, (ἐν, ὄρχις) *uncastrated, entire.*

ἜΝΟΣ or **ἕνος**, ὁ, Lat. *ANNUS*, Subst. *a year :* hence ἐνιαυτὸς ἄφενος, δίενος, etc.

ἜΝΟΣ or **ἕνος**, η, ον, Adj. *a year old, last year's ;* ἕνος καρπός *last year's fruit :* generally, *old, bygone.* II. ἕνη καὶ νέα (sub. ἡμέρα), *the old and* *new day*, i.e. *the last day of the month*, so called because *this 30th day consisted of two halves; one belonging to the old, the other to the new moon.* 2. in obliquo cases of fem.: gen. ἕνης Ep. ἔννηφιν, = Lat. *perendie, the day after to-morrow*, αὔριον καὶ ἔννηφιν; so too, τῇ ἕνῃ, εἰς ἕνην.

ἑνός, gen. of εἷς and ἕν, *one.*

ἔνοσις, εως, ἡ, (*ἐνόθω) *a shaking, quake.*

Ἐνοσί-χθων, ονος, ὁ, (ἔνοσις, χθών) *the Earth-shaker*, a name of Poseidon or Neptune.

ἑνότης, ητος, ἡ, (εἷς) *unity, concord.*

ἐν-ουράνιος, ον, (ἐν, οὐρανός) *in heaven, heavenly.*

ἐν-ουρέω, f. ήσω, *to make water in.*

ἐν-οχλέω, f. ήσω: the augm. tenses take a double augm. impf. ἠνώχλουν, pass. ἠνωχλούμην; aor. 1 ἠνώχλησα: pf. ἠνώχληκα:—*to trouble, disturb*, Lat. *molesto:* absol. *to be an annoyance:*—Pass. *to be troubled* or *annoyed.*

ἔνοχος, ον, (ἐνέχομαι) *held in, bound by, liable* or *subject to* a penalty: *liable to be accused of* a crime.

ἐν-ράπτω, f. ψω, *to sew up in.*

ἐν-ριγόω, f. ώσω, = ῥιγόω ἐν, *to shiver* or *freeze in.*

ἐν-σείω, f. -σείσω: pf. pass. -σέσεισμαι:—*to shake in* or *into, to drive into, hurl* or *launch at.*

ἐν-σημαίνω, f. ἄνῶ, *to mean, imply:*—Med. *to give notice of, intimate.*

ἐν-σκέλλω, aor. 1 ἐνέσκηλα, *to dry up:*—Pass., with pf. act. ἐνέσκληκα, *to be dried up.*

ἐν-σκευάζω, f. άσω; *to get ready, prepare:*—Pass. *to be dressed* or *equipped:*—Med. *to dress oneself up.*

ἐν-σκήπτω, f. ψω: Ep. **ἐνισκ-**:—*to hurl, dart, launch in* or *upon.* II. intrans. *to fall in* or *on.*

ἐν-σκίμπτω, f. ψω: Ep. **ἐνισκ-**: poët. form of ἐνσκήπτω, *to dash in* or *upon:*—Pass. *to stick in.*

ἐν-σκιρρόω, f. ώσω, (ἐν, σκίρρος) *to harden:*—Pass. *to become callous, inveterate.*

ἔν-σοφος, ον, *wise in* a thing.

ἐν-σπείρω, f. -σπερῶ, *to sow among:*—Pass. *to be sown* or *spread among.*

ἔν-σπονδος, ον, (ἐν, σπονδή) *included in a treaty: in alliance with: under truce* or *safe-conduct.*

ἐν-στάζω, f. ξω, *to let drop in.*

ἐν-στἄλάζω, f. ξω, = ἐνστάζω.

ἐνστάτης, ου, ὁ, (ἐνίστημι) *one who withstands, an adversary.*

ἐν-στέλλω, f. -στελῶ:—*to dress in;*—Pass., ἱππάδα στολὴν ἐνεσταλμένος *clad in* a horseman's dress.

ἐν-στηρίζω, f. ξω, *to fix in.*

ἐν-στρἄτοπεδεύω, or **-εύομαι** as Dep., = στρατοπεδεύομαι ἐν, *to encamp in.*

ἐν-στρέφω, fut. ψω, *to turn about in:*—Pass. *to turn* or *move in.* 2. c. acc. loci, *to visit.*

ἐν-σφρᾱγίζω Ion. **ἐν-σφρηγ-**, *to impress on.*

ἐντἄθῆναι, aor. 1 inf. pass. of ἐντείνω.

ἐντἄκῆναι, aor. 2 inf. pass. of ἐντήκω.

ἔνταλμα, ατος, τό, (ἐντέλλω) *an injunction, precept.*

ἐν-τἄνύω, f. ύσω: aor. 1 inf. ἐντανύσαι:—poët. for ἐντείνω, *to stretch* or *strain tight: to bend* or rather *to string* a bow: also *to stretch on* or *over* a thing: *to extend, prolong.*

ἐν-τάσσω Att. **-ττω**, f. ξω, *to enrol, register in:*—Pass. *to be posted in battle.*

ἐνταῦθα Ion. **ἐνθαῦτα**, Adv. (ἐν) = ἔνθα: I. of Place, *here, there*, Lat. *hic:* also *hither, thither*, Lat. *huc.* II. of Time, *at the very time: then, now.* 2. like Lat. *deinde, thereupon, then.* Hence

ἐνταυθί [ῑ], Att. form for ἐνταῦθα.

ἐνταυθοῖ, Adv. *hither*, Lat. *huc.*

ἐντἄφιάζω, f. σω, (ἐντάφιος) *to bury.* Hence

ἐντἄφιασμός, ὁ, *burial.*

ἐν-τάφιος, ον, (ἐν, τάφος) *of* or *used in burial.* II. as Subst., ἐντάφιον, τό, *a shroud* or *winding-sheet;* τὰ ἐντάφια, *funeral honours, obsequies.*

ἜΝΤΕΑ, ων, τά, *instruments, gear, tools* of any kind: *arms, armour;* ἔντεα δαιτός *appliances* for a banquet; ἔντεα νηός *rigging, tackle* of a ship; ἔντεα ἵππεια horse-*trappings, harness.*

ἐντεθύμημαι, pf. of ἐνθυμέομαι.

ἐντεθωράκισμαι, pf. pass. of ἐνθωρακίζω.

ἐν-τείνω, fut. -τενῶ: aor. 1 ἐνέτεινα: pf. ἐντέτἄκα:—Pass., aor. 1 ἐνετάθην [ᾰ]: pf. ἐντέτᾰμαι:—*to stretch* or *strain tight*, Lat. *intendere;* δίφρος ἱμᾶσιν ἐντέταται the chariot board *is hung upon* straps: *to bend* a bow; γέφυραι ἐντεταμέναι a bridge of boats *with the cables all taut:*—ἐντείνασθαι ἁρμονίαν *to raise* it *to a higher pitch:*—ἐντείνειν ναῦν ποδί *to keep* a ship's sail *tight* by the sheet. II. *to stretch out at* or *against;* ἐντείνειν πλήγην Lat. *intendere plagam.* 2. *to entangle in.* III. *to strain, exert*, φωνὴν ἐντείνασθαι: hence in Pass., *to be eager* or *vehement*, ἐντεταμένοι εἰς τὸ ἔργον.

ἐν-τειχίζω, fut. ίσω Att. ῐῶ, *to wall in, fortify:*—Med., *to wall in*, i. e. *blockade.*

ἔν-τεκνος, ον, (ἐν, τέκνον) *having children.*

ἐν-τελευτάω, f. ήσω, *to end one's life in* a place.

ἐν-τελής, ές, = ἐν τέλει ὤν, *complete, entire, perfect:*—Adv. -λῶς, Sup. -λέστατα.

ἐν-τέλλω, mostly in Med., ἐν-τέλλομαι, *to enjoin, command:*—Pass., ἐντεταλμένα *commands.*

ἐντελοῦμαι, fut. med. of foreg.

ἐν-τέμνω Ion. **-τάμνω**: f. **-τεμῶ**: *to cut in, engrave* or *inscribe upon.* II. *to cut in pieces, to sacrifice.* 2. *to cut in, shred in.*

ἔντερον, τό, (ἐντός) *a piece of gut:*—in plur. *the guts, intestines, entrails, bowels.* Hence

ἐντερόνεια, ἡ, *timber for the ribs* of a ship, *belly-timber.*

ἐντεσι-εργός, όν, (ἔντεα, ἔργον) *working in harness.*

ἐντεταγμένος, pf. part. pass. of ἐντάσσω.

ἐντεταλμένος, pf. part. pass. of ἐντέλλω.

ἐντεταμένος, pf. part. pass. of ἐντείνω. Hence

ἐντετἄμένως, Adv. *vehemently, strongly.*

ἐντέτατο, for ἐνετέτατο, plqpf. pass. of ἐντείνω.

ἐντέτηκα, pf. with pass. sense of ἐντήκω.

ἐντετμημένος, pf. part. pass. of ἐντέμνω.

ἐντετῠλιγμένος, pf. part. pass. of ἐντυλίσσω.

ἐντεῦθεν Ion. **ἐνθεῦτεν,** Adv. (ἐνταῦθα) *hence* or *thence*, Lat. *hinc* or *illinc*. II. of Time, *henceforth, thenceforth, afterwards, thereupon.*

ἐντευθενί [ῑ], Att. for ἐντεῦθεν.

ἔντευξις, εως, ἡ, (ἐντυγχάνω) *a lighting upon.* 2. *converse, intercourse.* 3. *a petition, intercession, thanksgiving.* 4. *reading, study.*

ἐν-τευτλᾰνόω, f. ώσω, (ἐν, τεῦτλον) *to stew in beet.*

ἐν-τήκω, f. ξω, *to cause to melt in, to pour in while molten*:—Pass. with aor. 2 ἐνετάκην [ᾰ], and pf. act. ἐντέτηκα, *to be melted in, to sink deep into* one; μῖσος ἐντέτηκέ μοι; ἐντακῆναι τῷ φιλεῖν *to be wholly given up* to love.

ἐντί, Dor. for ἐστι and εἰσί, from εἰμί *sum.*

ἐν-τίθημι, fut. ἐνθήσω: aor. 2 ἐνέθην, Ep. inf. ἐνθέμεν:—*to put in*, Lat. *imponere*: metaph. *to inspire, instil*:—Med. *to put in for oneself, store up, lay by*: also ἐνθέσθαι τιμῇ *to hold in* honour.

ἐν-τίκτω, f. -τέξομαι: aor. 2 ἐνέτεκον:—*to bear* or *produce in*: *to create* or *cause in* II. pf. part. intr., ἐντετοκώς, *inborn.*

ἐν-τῑλάω, f. ήσω, *to squirt upon.*

ἐν-τῑμάω, f. ήσω, *to value in* or *among.*

ἔν-τῑμος, ον, (ἐν, τιμή) *in honour, honoured, prized*: τὰ θεῶν ἔντιμα *what is honoured in* the sight of the gods, their *ordinances* or *attributes*:—Adv., ἐντίμως ἔχειν or ἄγειν τινά to hold him *in honour.*

ἔντμημα, ατος, τό, (ἐντέμνω) *a cut, incision, notch.*

ἔντο, 3 pl. aor. 2 med. of ἵημι.

ἐντολή, ἡ, (ἐντέλλω) *an injunction, command.*

ἔντομος, ον, (ἐντέμνω) *cut in pieces, cut up*; ἔντομα ποιεῖν to offer *as victims.*

ἔντονος, ον, (ἐντείνω) *strained*: *intense, earnest, eager, violent.* Adv. -νως, *violently.*

ἐν-τόπιος, ον, = ἔντοπος.

ἔν-τοπος, ον, (ἐν, τόπος) *in* or *of a place.*

ἐντός, Adv. (ἐν) Lat. *intus, intrinsecus*, opp. to ἐκτός: I. of Place, *in, within, inside*; also as Prep. c. gen., ἐντὸς ἐμαυτοῦ *in* my *senses.* 2. *on this side*, Lat. *citra*, c. gen. II. of Time, *within, in less than*, c. gen., ἐντὸς εἴκοσι ἡμερῶν *within* 20 days. Hence

ἔντοσθε and before a vowel -θεν, Adv. *from within, within.*

ἐντρᾰγεῖν, aor. 2 inf. of ἐντρώγω.

ἐντρᾰπῆναι, aor. 2 inf. pass. of ἐντρέπω.

ἐντρᾰπήσομαι, fut. 2 pass. of ἐντρέπω.

ἐν-τρέπω, f. -τρέψω, *to turn about*: metaph. *to reprove, make ashamed*:—Med. and Pass. *to turn oneself, turn towards* a person: *to give heed to, listen to, respect* or *pay deference to*: *feel shame* or *fear.*

ἐν-τρέφω, f. -θρέψω, = τρέφω ἐν, *to bring up* or *train in*: of habits, etc., *to grow up with, become natural to*, c. dat.

ἐν-τρέχω, f. -θρέξομαι or -δρᾰμοῦμαι (from obsol. δρέμω):—*to run in, to move freely in.* II. *to slip in, enter.*

ἐντρῑβῆναι, aor. 1 inf. pass. of ἐντρίβω. Hence

ἐντρῑβής, ές, *rubbed in*: metaph. *skilled, versed in.*

ἐν-τρίβω [ῑ], f. ψω, *to rub in* unguents:—Pass. *to have rubbed in, to be anointed, painted.* II. *to rub away, wear by rubbing.*

ἐν-τρῑτωνίζω, f. ίσω, (ἐν, τρίτος) *to mix in a third part, temper with a third*, with allusion to Τριτογένεια.

ἔντριψις, εως, ἡ, (ἐντρίβω) *a rubbing in.*

ἔν-τρομος, ον, (ἐν, τρέμω) *trembling, fearful.*

ἐν-τροπᾰλίζομαι, Frequent. of ἐντρέπω, Pass. *to keep turning round, keep looking back.*

ἐντροπή, ἡ, (ἐντρέπομαι) *a turning towards*: *respect* or *reverence for* one: also *shame, reproach.*

ἐντροπία, ἡ, (ἐντρέπομαι) in pl. *tricks, artifices.*

ἔντροφος, ον, (ἐντρέφω) *brought up in, living in, among*, or *with*; ἔντρ. τινος *a nursling.*

ἐν-τρυλλίζω, f. ίσω, *to whisper in one's ear.*

ἐν-τρῠφάω, f. ήσω, (ἐν, τρυφή) *to revel in, play in*: absol. *to be luxurious.* II. *to make sport of.*

ἐν-τρώγω, f. -τρώξομαι: aor. 2 ἐνέτρᾰγον:—*to eat up greedily, to devour.*

ἐν-τυγχάνω, f. -τεύξομαι; aor. 2 ἐνέτῠχον: pf. ἐντετύχηκα:—*to light upon, fall in with, meet with.* 2. *to converse with*: *to intercede with.* 3. *to read.* II. also = τυγχάνω ὢν ἐν, *to happen* to be *in.*

ἐν-τῠλίσσω, f. ξω, *to roll* or *wrap up.*

ἔν-τῡνον, Ep. impf. of ἐντύνω; but also aor. 1 imperat.

ἐντύνω [ῡ]: f. ἐντῠνῶ: Ep. aor. 1 ἔντῡνα: (ἔντεα):—*to equip, deck out, get ready, furnish, prepare*: c. acc. pers., ἐντύνειν τινά *to make* one *ready, urge* him *on*: also c. inf. *to urge to* do a thing.

ἐν-τῠπάς, Adv. (ἐν, τύπτω) of Priam, ἐντυπὰς ἐν χλαίνῃ κεκαλυμμένος covered with his mantle *so as to shew the shape of his limbs.*

ἐν-τῠπόω, f. ώσω, (ἐν, τύπος) *to stamp, engrave.*

ἐν-τύφω, f. -θύψω, *to smoke.* [ῡ]

ἐντύω, Ep. impf. ἔντῠον, = ἐντύνω.

Ἐνῡάλιος, ὁ, (ἐνύω) *the Warlike*, epith. of Ares or Mars in the Iliad; but, in later authors, different from him. II. as Adj., *warlike, furious.* [ᾰ]

ἐν-υβρίζω, f. ίσω Att. ιῶ, *to insult* one *in* a thing.

ἔνυδρις, ιος, ἡ, *an otter.* From

ἐνυδρό-βιος, ον, *living in the water.*

ἔν-υδρος, ον, (ἐν, ὕδωρ) *with water in it, holding water.* II. *of water, watery.* III. *living in* or *by water.*

ἔνυξα, aor. 1 of νύσσω.

ἐνυπνιάζω, f. άσω, *to dream.* From

ἐνύπνιον, τό, *a thing seen in sleep.* 2. *a dream.* Properly neut. of ἐνύπνιος.

ἐνύπνιος, ον, (ἐν, ὕπνος) *appearing in sleep.*

ἔν-υπνος, ον, = ἐνύπνιος.

ἐνύσταξα, aor. 1 of νυστάζω.

ἐν-ῠφαίνω, f. ᾰνω, *to weave in as a pattern*:—Pass *to be inwoven.* Hence

ἐνῠφαντός, όν, *inwoven.*

ἘΝΥΩ΄, όος, contr. οῦς, ἡ, *Enyo*, goddess of war, answering to the Roman *Bellona.*

ἐνωμοτ-άρχης, ου, ὁ, *leader of an* ἐνωμοτία.

ἐνωμοτία, ἡ, (ἐνώμοτος) properly, *any band of sworn soldiers: a division of the Spartan army*, being *a subdivision of the* λόχος and containing 32 men.

ἐν-ώμοτος, ον, (ἐν, ὄμνυμι) *bound by oath: a conspirator.* Adv. -ότως, *on oath.*

ἐνωπᾰδίως, Adv. *to one's face.* From

ἐν-ωπή, ἡ, (ἐν, ὤψ) *the face, countenance:* dat. ἐνωπῇ as Adv. *before the face, openly*, Lat. *palam.*

ἐνώπια, ων, τά, *the inner walls fronting those who enter:* properly neut. of ἐνώπιος.

ἐνώπιον, *in the presence of*, Lat. *coram.* From

ἐν-ώπιος, ον, (ἐν, ὤψ) *in one's presence, face to face.*

ἐνῶρσα, aor. 1 of ἐνόρνυμι.

ἐνῶρτο, 3 sing. Ep. aor. 2 pass. of ἐνόρνυμι.

ἐνῶσα, Ion. for ἐνόησα, aor. 1 of νοέω.

ἐνωτίζομαι, Dep. (ἐν, οὖς) *to hearken to.*

ἘΞ, Lat. *EX*, put for ἐκ before a vowel.

ἝΞ, *οἱ, αἱ, τά*, indecl., Lat. *SEX*, our *SIX.*

ἐξαγαγεῖν, aor. 2 inf. of ἐξάγω.

ἐξ-αγγελία, ἡ, *information sent out to the enemy.* From

ἐξ-αγγέλλω, f. ελῶ, *to tell out, publish, report:* esp. *to send out information* to the enemy:—Med. *to promise to* do:—Pass. *to be reported as doing;* impers., ἐξαγγέλλεται *it is reported that.* Hence

ἐξ-άγγελος, ὁ, ἡ, *a messenger who brings news out:* esp. *an informer.* II. on the Greek stage the ἄγγελος came *to tell news from a distance*, but the ἐξάγγελος *told what was going on behind the scenes.*

ἐξάγγελτος, ον, (ἐξαγγέλλω) *told of, discovered.*

ἐξ-ᾰγίζω, f. ίσω Att. ιῶ, *to drive out as a pollution.*

ἐξ-ᾰγῑνέω Ion. for ἐξάγω.

ἐξάγιστος, ον, (ἐξαγίζω) *accursed, abominable.* II. of things, *devoted, mystical.*

ἐξ-αγκωνίζω, (ἐξ, ἀγκών) *to nudge with the elbow.*

ἐξ-άγνῡμι, f. -άξω, (ἐξ, ἄγνυμι) *to break and tear away, to rend.*

ἐξ-ᾰγοράζω, f. άσω, *to buy from: to redeem.*

ἐξ-ᾰγορεύω, f. σω, *to speak out, publish, divulge.*

ἐξ-αγριόω, f. ώσω, (ἐξ, ἄγριος) *to make wild* or *waste:* of living things, *to make savage, exasperate.*

ἐξ-άγω, f. -άξω: aor. 2 -ήγαγον:—*to lead* or *carry out of* or *away from.* 2. of things, *to carry out, export;* τὰ ἐξαγόμενα *exports.* 3. *to draw out from, set free from.* 4. *to drive out, expel.* II. *to bring forth, produce: to call forth, excite.* 2. of persons, *to lead on, excite, rouse:* also *to lead on, tempt.* III. intr. (sub. ἑαυτόν) *to go* or *march out.* Hence

ἐξᾰγωγή, ἡ, *a leading out, drawing out: exportation:* hence

ἐξᾰγώγιμος, ον, *carried out;* τὰ ἐξαγώγιμα *exports.*

ἐξ-ᾰγωνίζομαι, f. Att. ἴοῦμαι, Dep. *to struggle hard.*

ἑξάδ-αρχος, ον, (ἑξάς, ἄρχω) *leader of a body of six.*

ἐξ-ᾴδω, fut. -ᾴσομαι, *to sing away;* ἐξᾴδειν τὸν βίον *to sing away* one's life, *end* it *in song*, as the swan:—*to sing away a spell.* II. *to sing of. descant upon.*

ἐξ-ᾰείρω Ion. for ἐξαίρω.

ἑξᾰ-ετής, ές, gen. έος, (ἕξ, ἔτος) *six years old:* fem. ἑξαέτις, ιδος.—Adv. ἑξάετες, *for six years.*

ἐξ-αθροίζομαι, Med. *to collect out from.*

ἐξ-αιάζω, strengthd. for αἰάζω.

ἐξ-αιμάσσω Att. -ττω, f. ξω, *to make quite bloody.*

ἐξ-αίνῠμαι, Dep. *to take away, carry off.*

ἐξ-αίρεσις, εως, ἡ, (ἐξαιρέω) *a taking out:—a way of taking out.*

ἐξ-αιρετέον, verb. Adj. of ἐξαιρέω, *one must select.*

ἐξ-αίρετος, ον, *taken out, picked out, chosen.* 2. reversely, *taken out, rejected, expelled.* II. *that can be taken out.* From

ἐξ-αιρέω, f. ήσω: aor. 2 ἐξεῖλον Ep. ἔξελον (supplied from obsol. ἕλω):—Med., fut. ἐξελοῦμαι: aor. 2 ἐξειλόμην:—Pass., pf. ἐξῄρημαι Ion. ἐξαραίρημαι:—*to take out, take out of:*—Med. *to take out for oneself: to unlade, discharge one's cargo.* II. *to take from among* others, *to pick out, choose:*—Pass. *to be picked out* for a special gift: also *to be dedicated, devoted.* III. *to take away, remove:*—Med. *to take away from* one:—Pass. *to have* a thing *taken away.* IV. in Med. *to set free, deliver.* V. *to make away with: to destroy* or *demolish* a city.

ἐξ-αίρω, contr. of Ion. form ἐξ-αείρω: fut. ἐξ-ᾰρῶ: aor. 1 ἐξῆρα:—*to lift up, lift off the earth.* 2. *to raise, exalt, extol.* 3. *to arouse, stir up, excite.* II. Med. *to carry off for oneself, earn:*—ἐξαίρεσθαι νόσον *to take* a disease *on oneself, catch* it. III. Pass. *to be raised, to rise.* 2. *to be excited, agitated.*

ἐξ-αίσιος, ον, (ἐξ, αἶσα) *beyond what is right, transgressing right, lawless.* II. of things, *monstrous: violent.*

ἐξ-ᾱΐσσω Att. -ᾴσσω, -ᾴττω: fut. -αΐξω, -ᾴξω: aor. 1 -ῇξα:—*to rush forth, start out.*

ἐξ-ᾰϊστόω, f. ώσω, (ἐξ, ἄϊστος) *to bring to naught, utterly destroy, annihilate.*

ἐξ-αιτέω, f. ήσω: aor. 1 ἐξῄτησα:—*to demand from* another: ἐξ. τινά *to demand* that he *be given up, demand* his *surrender:*—Med. *to beg for oneself, to beg* a person *off, gain* his *release.* Hence

ἐξαίτησις, εως, ἡ, *a demanding from* another. 2. *a begging off, intercession.*

ἔξ-αιτος, ον, (ἐξ, αἰτέω) *chosen, choice, precious.*

ἐξ αίφνης, Adv. *on a sudden.*

ἐξ-ᾰκέομαι, fut. έσομαι: Dep.:—*to heal completely, apply a cure;* χόλον ἐξακέσασθαι, *to appease* it; ἐνδείας ἐξακέσασθαι *to make up for* deficiencies. Hence

ἐξάκεσις, εως, ἡ, *a thorough cure.*

ἑξάκῐς, Adv. (ἕξ) *six times*, Lat. *sexies.* Hence

ἑξακισ-χίλιοι, *six thousand;* and

ἑξακισ-μύριοι, *sixty thousand.*

ἐξ-ᾰκολουθέω, f. ήσω, *to follow up, imitate.*

ἐξ-ᾰκοντίζω, fut. ίσω Att. ιῶ, *to dart* or *shoot forth, launch.* 2. metaph. *to direct away from:* also *to stretch out to: to shoot forth from* one's mouth, *utter.*

ἑξᾰκόσιοι, αι, α, (ἕξ) *six hundred*, Lat. *sexcenti.* Hence

ἐξᾰκοσιοστός, ή, όν, *six-hundredth.*

ἐξ-ᾰκούω, f. -ακούσομαι: aor. 1 -ήκουσα:—*to hear a sound*, esp. *from a distance: to listen for.*

ἐξ-ακρῑβόω, f. ώσω, *to make accurately, finish carefully.* II. *to inquire accurately.* III. ἐξακριβοῦν λόγον *to speak distinctly.*

ἐξ-ακρίζω, f. ίσω Att. ιῶ, *to reach the top of;* ἐξακρίζειν αἰθέρα *to skim the upper* air.

ἐξακτέον, verb. Adj. of ἐξάγω, *one must march out.*

ἐξ-ᾰλᾰόω, f. ώσω, *to blind utterly;* ὀφθαλμὸν ἐξαλαῶσαι *to put out* his eye.

ἐξ-ᾰλᾰπάζω, f. ξω, of a city, *to sack, storm:* generally, *to ruin, destroy: to exhaust.*

ἐξάλατο, Dor. for ἐξήλατο, 3 sing. aor. 1 of ἐξάλλομαι.

ἐξᾰλέασθαι, Ep. aor. 1 med. inf. of ἐξαλέομαι.

ἐξάλειπτρον, τό, *a box for ointment.* From

ἐξ-ᾰλείφω, fut. ψω: aor. 1 -ήλειψα:—Pass., pf, ἐξήλιμμαι Att. ἐξαλήλιμμαι:—*to anoint thoroughly, plaster over.* II. *to wipe out, erase:* metaph. *to destroy utterly, blot out;* ἐξαλείφειν τινὰ ἐκ τοῦ καταλόγου *to strike* his name *off* the list:—Med., ἐξαλείψασθαι πάθος φρενός *to blot out* the suffering *from one's* mind.

ἐξ-ᾰλέομαι, Dep. *to beware of, shun, escape.*

ἐξ-ᾰλεύομαι, f. σομαι, = ἐξαλέομαι.

***ἐξ-ᾰλίνδω**, only found in aor. 1 part. ἐξαλίσας [ῐ], pf. ἐξήλῑκα:—*to roll out, roll well;* ἄπαγε τὸν ἵππον ἐξαλίσας οἴκαδε take him home *when you have given* him *a good roll* (see ἀλινδήθρα); ἐξήλικάς με ἐκ τῶν ἐμῶν *you have rolled, tumbled* me *out of* my all.

ἐξαλλᾰγή, ἡ, *a changing: difference.* From

ἐξ-αλλάσσω Att. -ττω: fut. ξω: aor. 1 -ήλλαξα: pf. -ήλλᾰχα:—Pass., aor. 1 and 2 -ηλλάχθην, -ηλλάγην: pf. -ήλλαγμαι:—*to change utterly* or *quite.* II. *to withdraw* or *remove from.* III. *to turn another way;* ποίαν [ὁδὸν] ἐξαλλάξω which way *shall I take;* ἐξαλλάσσειν κερκίδα *to ply* the shuttle *to and fro.*

ἐξ-άλλομαι, fut. -ᾰλοῦμαι: aor. 1 -ηλάμην: Ep. aor. 2 part. ἐξάλμενος: Dep.:—*to spring out of* or *forth from;* ἐξάλλεσθαι κατὰ τοῦ τείχους *to leap down from* it. II. *to leap up;* of horses, *to rear.*

ἐξ-ᾰλύσκω, f. ύξω: aor. 1 -ήλυξα: = ἐξαλέομαι.

ἐξ-ᾰμαρτάνω, f. -αμαρτήσομαι: aor. 2 -ήμαρτον:—*to mistake utterly, err greatly, commit a fault against:* —Pass. *to be mismanaged, wrongly treated.* Hence

ἐξᾰμαρτία, ἡ, *an utter mistake, error.*

ἐξ-αμάω, fut. ήσω or ήσομαι: pf. pass. ἐξήμημαι:—*to mow off, finish reaping:* metaph. *to cut off, destroy:*—Pass., γένους ἅπαντος ῥίζαν ἐξημημένος *having* the stock of all the race *cut off.*

ἐξ-αμβλόω, f. -αμβλώσω: pf. -ήμβλωκα:—*to make miscarry:* metaph., φροντίδ' ἐξήμβλωκας *you have made* my wit *miscarry.*

ἐξ-ᾰμείβω, fut. ψω: aor. 1 -ήμειψα:—*to exchange, alter:* hence *to put off, lay aside:*—Med. *to take the place of, follow close on.* II. of Place, *to change one for another, pass over* from one place to another, *withdraw from:*—Med. *to pass out.* III. in Med. also, *to requite, repay.*

ἐξ-ᾰμέλγω, f. ξω, *to milk* or *suck out.* II. *to press, as cheese.*

ἐξ-ᾰμελέω, f. ήσω, *to be utterly careless of.*

ἐξά-μετρος, ον, (ἕξ, μέτρον) *of six metres:* ἐξάμετρος (sub. τόνος), ὁ, *the heroic* or *hexameter verse.*

ἐξά-μηνος, ον, (ἕξ, μήν) *lasting six months*, Lat. *semestris:* as Subst., ἐξάμηνος, ὁ or ἡ, *a half-year.*

ἐξ-αμηχᾰνέω, f. ήσω, *to get out of a difficulty, extricate oneself from* it.

ἐξ-ᾰμιλλάομαι, f. ήσομαι: aor. 1 med. -ημιλλησάμην, pass. -ημιλλήθην: Dep.:—*to struggle vehemently;* ἁμίλλας ἐξαμιλληθεὶς *having gone through desperate* struggles. II. *to drive out of: to drive out of* one's *wits.* III. as Pass. *to be rooted out*, of the Cyclops' eye.

ἐξ-ᾰμύνομαι, Med. *to ward off from oneself, drive away.* [ῡ]

ἐξ-ᾰναγκάζω, f. άσω, *to force* or *compel utterly* II. *to force out, drive away.*

ἐξ-ανάγω, f. άξω: aor. 2 -ανήγαγον:—*to bring out of* or *up from:*—Pass. *to put out to sea, set sail.*

ἐξ-αναδύομαι, Med. with aor. 2 act. -ανέδυν:—*to rise out of, come from under, emerge from:* generally, *to escape from.*

ἐξ-αναζέω, fut. έσω, *to make to boil up* or *over:* metaph., ἐξαναζεῖν χόλον *to let* his fury *boil forth.*

ἐξ-αναιρέω, f. ήσω, *to take up out of.*

ἐξ-ανακρούω, f. σω, *to beat back:*—Med. of ships, *to retreat by backing water.*

ἐξ-ανᾱλίσκω, fut. -ανᾱλώσω: aor. 1 -ανήλωσα: pf. pass. -ανήλωμαι:—*to consume* or *destroy utterly:*—Pass. *to be quite used up*, Lat. *exhauriri.*

ἐξ-αναλύω, f. ύσω, *to set quite free.*

ἐξανάλωσις, εως, ἡ, (ἐξαναλίσκω) *exhaustion.*

ἐξ-αναπνέω, f. -πνεύσομαι, *to breathe again, revive.*

ἐξ-ανάπτω, f. ψω, *to hang up* a thing *from* or *by:* —Med. *to attach oneself.* II. *to rekindle.*

ἐξ-αναρπάζω, f. ξω and σω, *to snatch away.*

ἐξ-ανασπάω, f. άσω [ᾰ], *to tear away from.*

ἐξανάστᾰσις, εως, ἡ, (ἐξανίστημι) *a removal.* 2. intr. *an uprising from: the resurrection.*

ἐξ-αναστέφω, f. ψω, *to crown with wreaths.*

ἐξαναστήσω, ἐξαναστῆσαι, fut. and aor. 1 inf. of ἐξανίστημι.

ἐξ-αναστρέφω, f. ψω, *to turn upside down: to hurl headlong from.*

ἐξ-ανατέλλω, *to make spring up from.* II. intr. *to spring from.*

ἐξ-αναφανδόν, Adv. *quite openly.*

ἐξ-αναφέρω, f. -ανοίσω, *to bring up from the* water. II. intr. *to emerge from: to recover from* an illness.

ἐξ-αναχωρέω, f. ήσω, *to go out of the way, withdraw, retreat.* II. c. acc. *to evade.*

ἐξ-ανδρᾱποδίζω, and Med. **ἐξανδραποδίζομαι**, f.

-ίσομαι Att. -ιοῦμαι: (ἐξ, ἀνδράποδον):—*to sell for slaves, reduce to utter slavery*: the Att. fut. ἐξανδραποδιοῦμαι is also used in pass. sense, as are aor. 1 -ηνδραποδίσθην, pf. -ηνδραπόδισμαι. Hence

ἐξανδρᾰπόδῐσις, εως, ἡ, *a selling for slaves*.

ἐξ-ανδρόομαι, pf. ἐξήνδρωμαι: Pass.:—*to come to man's years*; λόχος ὀδόντων ὄφεος ἐξηνδρωμένος a band *having grown to men* from the dragon's teeth.

ἐξ-ανεγείρω, f. -εγερῶ, *to excite, stir up*.

ἐξανειλόμην, aor. 2 med. of ἐξαναιρέω.

ἐξ-άνειμι, *to rise out from*: *to go up in*. II. *to come back from*.

ἐξ-ᾰνεμόω, f. ώσω: aor. 1 -ηνέμωσα: (ἐξ, ἄνεμος):—*to inflate*: *puff up*. II. *to scatter to the winds, bring to nothing*.

ἐξ-ανέρχομαι, = ἐξάνειμι.

ἐξανέστηκα, **-ησα**, pf. and aor. 1 of ἐξανίστημι.

ἐξανέστραμμαι, pf. pass. of ἐξαναστρέφω.

ἐξανέτειλα, aor. 1 of ἐξανατέλλω.

ἐξ-ανευρίσκω, fut. -ανευρήσω, *to find out, invent*.

ἐξ-ανέχω, f. ξω, *to hold up* or *out*: intr. *to project*. II. Med., impf. and aor. 2 with double augm. ἐξ-ηνειχόμην, -ηνεσχόμην:—*to bear up against*.

ἐξανήγᾰγον, aor. 2 of ἐξανάγω.

ἐξανῆκα, aor. 1 of ἐξανίημι.

ἐξανήλωσα, aor. 1 of ἐξανᾱλίσκω: **ἐξανήλωμαι**, pf. pass.

ἐξ-ανθέω, f. ήσω: pf. -ήνθηκα:—*to put out flowers*. 2. *to bloom with, to be covered with, to break out with*, of sores. 3. metaph. *to burst forth, break out, flourish*.

ἐξ-ανθίζω, f. ίσω Att. ιῶ, (ἐξ, ἄνθος) *to deck as with flowers, adorn, paint*.

ἐξ-ανίημι, f. -ανήσω or -ανήσομαι: aor. 1 -ανῆκα:—*to send out* or *forth, let loose*: c. gen. *to send forth from*. 2. *to let go, dismiss*. 3. *to slacken, loosen*. II. intr. *to slacken, relax*, Lat. *remittere*.

ἐξ-ανίστημι, f. -αναστήσω, aor. 1 -ανέστησα: in these tenses Causal, *to make rise from one's seat*. 2. *to remove from* a settlement: *make to emigrate, expel*. 3. *to depopulate, destroy*. II. Pass. and Med., with aor. 2 act. -ανέστην, pf. -ανέστηκα, plqpf. -ειστήκειν, intrans. *to rise from one's seat* or *station*. 2. generally, *to arise and depart from* a place: *to be driven out* from one's home. 3. *to be depopulated*.

ἐξ-ανοίγω, *to lay open*.

ἐξ-ανορθόω, f. ώσω, *to set upright, restore*.

ἐξ-αντλέω, f. ήσω: aor. 1 -ήντλησα:—*to draw out*, Lat. *exhaurire*. II. metaph. *to endure to the end, see out*, Lat. *exantlare*.

ἐξ-ᾰνύω Att. **ἐξ-ᾰνύτω**, f. ύσω [ῡ]: aor. 1 ἐξήνῠσα:—*to accomplish, fulfil*. 2. *to dispatch, kill*, Lat. *conficere*. 3. of Time, *to bring to an end, accomplish*: hence *to finish one's way to* a place, *arrive at* it. 4. c. inf. *to manage* to do, Lat. *efficere ut* . . . 5. Med. *to finish for oneself*.

ἑξα-πάλαιστος, ον, (ἕξ, πᾰλαιστή) *of six hands breadths*.

ἐξ-απαλλάσσω Att. **-ττω**, f. ξω: aor. 1. -απήλλαξα:—*to free from, remove from*:—Med. *to remove oneself from, get rid of*.

ἐξ-ᾰπᾰτάω, f. ήσω: aor. 1 -ηπάτησα:—*to cheat* or *deceive thoroughly*: *to seduce*:—Pass., with fut. med. -ήσομαι, *to be utterly deceived*.

ἐξ-ᾰπάτη, ἡ, *a gross trick* or *deception*.

ἐξ-ᾰπᾰτητήρ, ῆρος, ὁ, (ἐξαπατάω) *a deceiver*.

ἐξ-ᾰπᾰτύλλω, Comic Dim. of ἐξαπατάω, *to cheat a little, impose upon*.

ἐξ-ᾰπᾰφίσκω, Ep. form of ἐξ-απατάω: aor. 2 ἐξήπᾰφον, part. ἐξαπαφών: also 3 sing. aor. 2 med. opt. ἐξαπάφοιτο occurs in act. sense.

ἑξά-πεδος, ον, (ἕξ, πούς) *six feet long*.

ἐξ-απεῖδον, inf. ἐξαπιδεῖν, aor. 2 (with no pres. in use), *to observe from afar*. Cf. εἶδον.

ἑξά-πηχυς, υ, (ἕξ, πῆχυς) *six cubits long*.

ἐξάπῖνα, Adv., later form of ἐξαπίνης.

ἐξαπίναιος, α, ον, = ἐξαιφνίδιος. From

ἐξᾰπίνης, Adv., collat. form for ἐξαίφνης. [ῐ]

ἑξα-πλάσιος, α, ον, Ion. **-πλήσιος**, η, ον, (ἕξ) *sixfold*.

ἑξά-πλεθρος, ον, (ἕξ, πλέθρον) *six πλέθρα long*, i. e. 1200 *feet long*.

ἐξ-απλόω, f. ώσω, *to unfold, roll out*: *to explain*.

ἐξ-αποβαίνω, f. -βήσομαι, *to step out of*.

ἐξ-αποδίομαι, Dep. *to chase away from*.

ἐξ-αποδύνω, *to put off*.

ἐξ-αποθνήσκω, *to be just on the point of death*.

ἑξά-πολις, εως, ἡ, (ἕξ, πόλις) *a league of six cities*.

ἐξ-απόλλῡμι, f. -απολέσω Att. -απολῶ:—*to destroy utterly*:—Med., with perf. 2 act. **ἐξαπόλωλα**, intr. *to perish utterly*: *to perish out of*.

ἐξ-απονέομαι, Pass. *to return out of*.

ἐξ-απονίζω, f. νίψω, *to wash thoroughly*.

ἐξ-αποξύνω, *to sharpen well*.

ἐξ-απορέω, also Med. **ἐξ-απορέομαι**, *to be utterly at a loss, be in great perplexity*.

ἐξ-αποστέλλω, *to send out* or *away*: *to divorce*.

ἐξ-αποτίνω, f. -αποτίσω [ῐ], *to atone fully*.

ἐξ-αποφθείρω, *to destroy utterly*.

ἐξ-άπτω, f. ψω: aor. 1 ἐξῆψα:—*to fasten from* or *to*: c. dat. *to attach to*. II. Med. *to hang from, cling to* a thing. 2. *to fasten about oneself, wear*.

ἐξαραίρημαι, Ion. pf. pass. of ἐξαιρέω.

ἐξ-ᾰράσσω Att. **-ττω**, fut. ξω: aor. 1 ἐξήραξα:—*to dash* or *knock out, shatter*: metaph. *to assail furiously*.

ἐξ-αργέω, f. ήσω, (ἐξ, ἀργός) *to be quite torpid*:—Pass. *to be quite neglected*.

ἐξ-αργῠρίζω, f. ίσω Att. ιῶ, and **ἐξ-αργῠρόω**, f. ώσω, *to turn into money, sell*.

ἐξ-ᾰρέσκομαι, f. -αρέσομαι, Dep. *to make oneself acceptable to*: also *to win over, conciliate*.

ἐξ-ᾰριθμέω, f. ήσω, *to count throughout*, Lat. *enumerare*. II. *to pay in ready money*.

ἐξ-αρκέω, f. έσω, *to be enough for*: impers., ἐξαρκεῖ μοι *it is enough for, satisfies* me, c. inf. II. *to* abound in, be content with: c. part. to be satisfied with doing. III. to assist, succour. Hence

ἐξαρκής, ές, enough, sufficient.

ἐξαρκούντως, Adv. pres. part. of ἐξαρκέω, enough, sufficiently.

ἐξ-αρνέομαι, f. ήσομαι: aor. 1 -ηρνησάμην and -ηρνήθην:—to deny strongly. Hence

ἐξαρνητικός, ή, όν, good at denying or disowning.

ἔξαρνος, ον, (ἐξαρνέομαι) denying, disowning.

ἐξ-αρπάζω, f. -αρπάξω and -αρπάσω or -αρπάσομαι: aor. 1 -ήρπαξα Att. -ήρπασα: pf. pass. -ήρπασμαι:—to snatch away from: to rescue from danger.

ἐξ-αρτάω, fut. ήσω, to hang from or upon. II. Pass., with fut. med. ἐξαρτήσομαι, pf. ἐξήρτημαι, to be hung upon, hang upon. 2. to have fastened to one, be equipt with: cf. ἐξάπτω. 3. to be exposed to view.

ἐξ-αρτίζω, fut. ίσω Att. ιῶ, to complete, finish:—Pass., pf. ἐξήρτισμαι, to be completely furnished.

ἐξ-αρτύω, f. ύσω [ῡ], to get ready: to fit out, equip:—Med. to get ready for oneself, fit out: to prepare, set about:—Pass., pf. ἐξήρτῡμαι, to be got ready.

ἐξᾶρχε, Dor. for ἐξῆρχε, 3 sing. impf. of ἐξάρχω.

ἔξ-αρχος, ον, beginning. II. as Subst., ἔξαρχος, ὁ, a leader, beginner, Lat. auctor. 2. the first in rank, chief, Lat. princeps. 3. the leader of the chorus, = κορυφαῖος.

ἐξ-άρχω, f. ξω, to begin, lead off; ἐξάρχειν παιᾶνά τινι to begin a hymn to one, address it to him: and reversely, ἐξάρχειν τινὰ λόγοις to address one with words:—so also in Med. **ἐξάρχομαι.**

ἐξ-ασκέω, f. ήσω: aor. 1 -ήσκησα:—to adorn, deck out. II. to train or exercise thoroughly:—Pass. to be well trained in.

ἐξ-ατῑμάζω, f. άσω, to dishonour utterly.

ἐξ-ᾴττω, Att. contr. for ἐξαΐσσω.

ἐξ-αυαίνω, aor. ἐξηύηνα: to dry up, parch up.

ἐξ-αυδάω, f. ήσω, to speak out:—also in Med.

ἐξ-αυλέω, f. ήσω, to wear out by piping.

ἐξ-αυλίζομαι, f. σομαι, Dep. to leave one's quarters.

ἐξ-αυτῆς, Adv., for ἐξ αὐτῆς [τῆς ὥρας], at the very point of time, at once.

ἐξ-αῦτις, Adv. for ἐξ-αῦθις, (ἐξ, αὖτις) over again, anew. II. of Place, back again, backwards.

ἐξ-αυτομολέω, f. ήσω, to desert from.

ἐξ-αυχέω, f. ήσω: aor. 1 ἐξηύχησα: to boast loudly.

ἐξ-ᾰΰω, aor. 1 ἐξήῡσα, to scream or cry out.

ἐξ-αφαιρέω, aor. 2 -αφεῖλον, med. -αφειλόμην (from obsol. ἕλω):—to take quite away:—Med., ψυχήν τινος ἐξαφελέσθαι to take his life from him.

ἐξ-αφίημι, fut. -αφήσω, to send forth, discharge: to set free from.

ἐξ-αφίστημι, to put away:—Med., with aor. 2 act. -έστην, pf. -έστηκα, plqpf. -εστήκειν, intrans. to depart or withdraw from.

ἐξ-αφρίζομαι, f. ίσομαι, Med. (ἐξ, ἀφρός) to foam away from oneself, Lat. despumare; ἐξαφρίζεσθαι μένος, to foam or fret away one's strength.

ἐξ-αφύσσω, f. ύσω [ῠ]: aor. 1 -ήφῠσα:—to draw forth.

ἐξάψαι, aor. 1 inf. of ἐξάπτω.

ἐξέβαλον, aor. 2 of ἐκβάλλω.

ἐξέβην, aor. 2 of ἐκβαίνω:—**ἔξεβαν**, Aeol. and Ep. 3 pl. for ἐξέβησαν.

ἐξ-εγγυάω, f. ήσω, (ἐξ, ἐγγύη) to free by giving bail:—Med. to give bail:—Pass. to be set free on bail. Hence

ἐξεγγύησις, εως, ἡ, a giving bail or surety.

ἐξ-εγείρω, f. -εγερῶ, to awaken: to raise from the dead: generally, to arouse, excite: to kindle:—Pass. with Ep. aor. 2 ἐξηγρόμην, inf. -εγρέσθαι, and pf. act. ἐξεγρήγορα, to be aroused, to wake up.

ἐξέγραψα, aor. 2 of ἐκγράφω.

ἐξέγροντο, 3 pl. Ep. aor. 2 pass. of **ἐξεγείρω.**

ἐξέδειξα, aor. 1 of ἐκδείκνυμι.

ἐξεδεξάμην, aor. 1 of ἐκδέχομαι.

ἐξεδίδαξα, aor. 1 of ἐκδιδάσκω.

ἐξέδοτο, 3 sing. aor. 2 med. of ἐκδίδωμι.

ἐξ-έδρα, ἡ, Lat. exbedra, a covered walk in front of a house.

ἐξέδρᾰμον, aor. 2 of ἐκτρέχω.

ἐξέδρᾱν, aor. 2 of ἐκδιδράσκω.

ἔξ-εδρος, ον, (ἐξ, ἕδρα) away from home: generally, strange, extraordinary. 2. c. gen. out of, away from; ἔξεδρος φρενῶν out of one's senses. II. of omens, in a bad quarter.

ἐξέδομαι, fut. of ἐξεσθίω.

ἐξέδῡν, aor. 2 (in intr. sense) of ἐκδύω.

ἐξέδῡσα, aor. 1 (in causal sense) of ἐκδύω.

ἐξέδωκα, aor. 1 of ἐκδίδωμι.

ἐξέθᾰνον, aor. 2 of ἐκθνήσκω.

ἐξεθέμην, aor. 2 med. of ἐκτίθημι.

ἐξέθηκα, aor. 1 of ἐκτίθημι.

ἐξέθορον, aor. 2 of ἐκθρώσκω.

ἐξέθρεψα, aor. 1 of ἐκτρέφω.

ἔξει, for ἔξιθι, imperat. of ἔξειμι exibo.

ἐξ-εῖδον, inf. ἐξιδεῖν, aor. 2 without any pres. in use, to look out, see far: also aor. 2 med. imperat., ἐξιδοῦ see well to it. Cf. ἔξοιδα.

ἐξείης, Adv. (ἔχω, ἕξω) poët. for ἑξῆς, in order, in a row, one after another.

ἐξ-εικάζω, fut. σω, to make like: to adapt: pf. part. pass. ἐξῃκασμένος, represented by a likeness or portrait.

ἐξ-ειλέω, f. ήσω, Lat. evolvere, to unfold.

ἐξείλλω, = ἐξίλλω.

ἐξεῖλον, **ἐξειλόμην**, aor. 2 act. and med. of ἐξαιρέω.

ἔξ-ειμι, 2 sing. ἔξεισθα (for ἔξει), inf. ἐξιέναι Ep. ἐξίμεναι: impf. ἐξῄειν: (ἐκ, εἶμι ibo):—to go out, come out: esp. to march out with an army; to come forward on the stage. II. of Time, to come to an end; expire; ὅταν τὸ κακὸν ἐξίῃ when the pain ceases.

ἔξ-ειμι (εἰμί sum), only in impers. ἔξεστι, q. v.

ἕξειν, fut. inf. of ἔχω.

ἐξεῖναι, inf. of ἔξεστι.

ἐξ-εῖπον, inf. *ἐξειπεῖν*, *to speak out, to utter, avow:* also, *to betray:* cf. *εἶπον*.

ἐξείρετο, 3 sing. impf. of *ἐξέρομαι*.

ἐξείρῠσα Ep. **-είρυσσα**, aor. 1 of *ἐξερύω*.

ἐξ-είρω, *to put forth, thrust out.* II. *to pull out.*

ἔξεισθα, for *ἔξει*, 2 sing. pres. of *ἔξειμι exibo*.

ἐξεκάθηρα, aor. 1 of *ἐκκαθαίρω*.

ἐξέκαμον, aor. 2 of *ἐκκάμνω*.

ἐξεκείνωσα, poët. aor. 1 of *ἐκκενύω*.

ἐξεκέχυντο, 3 pl. plqpf. pass. of *ἐκχέω*.

ἐξέκλεψα, aor. 1 of *ἐκκλέπτω*.

ἐξεκλησίαζον, **ἐξεκλησίασα**, irreg. impf. and aor. 1 of *ἐκκλησιάζω*.

ἐξέκλῑνα, aor. 1 of *ἐκκλίνω*.

ἐξεκόμισα, aor. 1 of *ἐκκομίζω*.

ἐξέκοψα, **ἐξεκόπην**, aor. 1 act. and aor. 2 pass. of *ἐκκόπτω*.

ἐξεκρέματο, 3 sing. aor. 1 med. of *ἐκκρεμάννυμι*.

ἐξέκρουσα, **ἐξεκρούσθην**, aor. 1 act. and pass. of *ἐκκρούω*.

ἐξεκύλῑσα, **-ίσθην**, aor. 1 act. and pass. of *ἐκκυλίνδω*.

ἐξέλᾰβον, aor. 2 of *ἐκλαμβάνω*.

ἐξελᾷς, **ᾷ**, 2 and 3 sing. fut. of *ἐξελαύνω*.

ἐξέλᾰσις, εως, ἡ, *a driving out, expulsion.* II. intr. *a marching out, expedition.* From

ἐξ-ελαύνω: f. *-ελάσω* Att. *-ελῶ*: pf. *-ελήλᾰκα*: also poët. pres. **ἐξελάω**, inf. *ἐξελάαν*:—*to drive out, chase out.* 2. *to beat out, hammer out,* of metals. II. *ἐξελαύνειν στρατόν to lead out* an army: hence (sub. *στρατόν*) intrans. *to set out on an expedition, march out.*

ἐξέλᾰχον, aor. 2 of *ἐκλαγχάνω*.

ἔξελε, poët. for *ἐξεῖλε*, 3 sing. aor. 2 act. of *ἐξαιρέω*: also 2 sing. imperat.

ἐξ-ελέγχω, f. *ξω*, *to search out, bring to the test: to convict, expose, confute:* of things, *to be proved against one.* 2. *οὐ τοῦτό γ' ἐξελέγχομαι I am* not *to blame* in this.

ἐξελεῖν, **ἐξελέσθαι**, aor. 2 act. and med. inf. of *ἐξαιρέω*.

ἐξέλῐπον, aor. 2 of *ἐκλείπω*.

ἐξ-ελευθεροστομέω, *to be very free of speech.*

ἐξελεύσομαι, **ἐξελθεῖν**, fut. and aor. 2 inf. of *ἐξέρχομαι*.

ἐξελήλακα, pf. of *ἐξελαύνω*.

ἐξελήλεγμαι, pf. pass. of *ἐξελέγχω*.

ἐξ-ελίσσω Att. **-ττω**, f. *ξω*, *to unroll, unfold:* metaph. *to explain.* II. = Lat. *explicare, to expand* the front by bringing up the rear men.

ἐξελκτέον, verb. Adj. *one must drag along.* From

ἐξ-έλκω, f. *-ελκύσω* [ῠ], as if from *-ελκύω*:—*to draw* or *drag out.* 2. *to draw out from, rescue from.* II. *to drag out, prolong, protract.*

ἐξέλῡσα, aor. 1 of *ἐκλύω*.

ἐξέμᾰθον, aor. 2 of *ἐκμανθάνω*.

ἐξεμάνην [ᾰ], aor. 2 pass. of *ἐκμαίνω*.

ἐξέμαξα, aor. 1 of *ἐκμάσσω*.

ἐξεμαργώθην, aor. 1 pass. of *ἐκμαργόω*.

ἐξέμαξα, **ἐξεμάγην** [ᾰ], aor. 1 act. and aor. 2 pass. of *ἐκμάσσω*.

ἐξέμεν, Ep. for *ἐξεῖναι*, aor. 2 inf. of *ἐξίημι*.

ἐξέμεν, Ep. for *ἕξειν*, fut. inf. of *ἔχω*.

ἐξ-εμέω, f. *-εμέσω*: aor. 1 *ἐξέμεσα*:—*to vomit forth, disgorge.* 2. absol. *to be sick.*

ἐξέμηνα, aor. 1 of *ἐκμαίνω*.

ἐξέμμορε, 3 sing. pf. of *ἐκμείρομαι*.

ἐξ-εμπεδόω, f. *ώσω*, *to keep fast* or *strictly, observe.*

ἐξ-εμπολάω Ion. *-έω*, f. *ήσω*, *to traffic; κέρδος ἐξεμπολᾶν to drive* a gainful *trade;* pf. pass. *ἐξημπόλημαι, I am bought and sold, betrayed.* II. *to sell off.*

ἐξ-εναίρω, aor. 2 inf. *ἐξεναρεῖν*, = *ἐξεναρίζω*.

ἐξ-ενᾰρίζω, f. *ίξω*, *to strip* or *spoil* a foe: *to slay in fight.*

ἐξενέγκατε, 2 pl. aor. 1 imperat. of *ἐκφέρω*.

ἐξ-ενέπω, *to speak out, proclaim.*

ἐξένευσα, aor. 1 of *ἐκνεύω* and also of *ἐκνέω*.

ἐξένθοις, **ἐξενθών**, Dor. for *ἐξέλθοις*, *ἐξελθών*, aor. 2 opt. and part. of *ἐξέρχομαι*.

ἐξενίκησα, aor. 1 of *ἐκνικάω*.

ἐξένιψα, aor. 1 of *ἐκνίζω*.

ἐξ-επᾴδω, f. *-επᾴσομαι*, *to charm away:*—Pass., *ἐξεπᾴδεσθαι φύσιν to be charmed out of* their nature.

ἐξ-επαίρω, f. *-επᾰρῶ*, *to stir up, elate.*

ἐξεπαίσα, aor. 1 of *ἐκπαίω*.

ἐξεπάταξα, aor. 1 of *ἐκπατάσσω*.

ἐξέπαυσα, aor. 1. of *ἐκπαύω*.

ἐξέπεισα, aor. 1 of *ἐκπείθω*.

ἐξεπειράθην [ᾱ], aor. 1 of *ἐκπειράομαι*.

ἐξέπεμψα, aor. 1 of *ἐκπέμπω*.

ἐξεπέρησα, Ion. aor. 1 of *ἐκπεράω*.

ἐξεπέτασσα, Ep. for *ἐξεπέτασα*, aor. 1 of *ἐκπετάννυμι*.

ἐξ-επεύχομαι, Dep. *to boast loudly.*

ἐξ-επι-και-δέκατος, η, ον, = *ἑκκαιδέκατος*.

ἐξ-επίσταμαι, Dep. *to understand, know thoroughly.* II. *to know by heart.*

ἐξ-επίτηδες, Adv., = *ἐπίτηδες, on purpose, carefully.*

ἐξεπλάγην [ᾰ], aor. 2 pass. of *ἐκπλήσσω*.

ἐξέπλησα, **ἐξεπλήσθην**, aor. 1 act. and pass. of *ἐκπίμπλημι*.

ἐξέπεσον, aor. 2 of *ἐκπίπτω*.

ἐξέπιον, aor. 2 of *ἐκπίνω*.

ἐξέπλευσα, aor. 1 of *ἐκπλέω*.

ἐξέπληξα, **ἐξεπλήχθην**, aor. 1 act. and pass. of *ἐκπλήσσω*.

ἐξέπνευσα, aor. 1 of *ἐκπνέω*.

ἐξεποίησα, aor. 1 of *ἐκποιέω*.

ἐξεπόνᾱσα, Dor. aor. 1 of *ἐκπονέω*.

ἐξεπόρευσα, **-εύθην**, aor. 1 act. and pass. of *ἐκπορεύω*.

ἐξεπόρισα, aor. 1 of *ἐκπορίζω*.

ἐξέπρᾰθον, aor. 2 of *ἐκπέρθω*.

ἐξεπτάμην or **-όμην**, aor. 2 of *ἐκπέταμαι* or *-ομαι*.

ἐξέπραξα, aor. 1 of *ἐκπράσσω*.

ἐξέπριον, aor. 2 of *ἐκπρίω*.

ἐξέπταξα, Dor. for *ἐξέπτηξα*, aor. 1 of *ἐκπτήσσω*.

ἐξέπτην, aor. 2 act. of ἐκπέταμαι.

ἐξέπτῠσα, aor. 1 of ἐκπτύω.

ἐξεπῠθόμην, aor. 2 of ἐκπυνθάνομαι.

ἐξέρᾱμα, τό, *a vomit, thing vomited.* From

ἐξ-εράω, f. άσω [ᾱ]: aor. 1 ἐξέρᾱσα:—*to vomit forth*, Lat. *evomere.* 2. metaph. *to disgorge, get rid of;* ἐξερᾶν τὰς ψήφους *to disgorge* the ballots *from* the urn.

ἐξ-εργάζομαι, f. -εργάσομαι: pf. -είργασμαι used both in med. and pass. sense: aor. 1 -ειργάσθην always in pass.: Dep.:—*to work out, finish, make complete.* 2. *to accomplish: to make, cause.* 3. *to work well, cultivate.* II. *to undo, destroy*, Lat. *conficere: to overwhelm, ruin:*—Pass., ἐξειργάσμεθα *we are undone;* τὰ ἐξειργασμένα *desperate* affairs; ἐπ' ἐξειργασμένοις *when all is over.* Hence

ἐξεργαστικός, ή, όν, *able to accomplish.*

ἐξ-έργω Att. -είργω, *to shut out, exclude from: to hinder, forbid: to drive away:*—Pass., ἀναγκαίῃ ἐξέργεσθαι *to be forced to* a thing.

ἐξ-ερεείνω, *to inquire into* or *after: search* or *try.*

ἐξ-ερεθίζω, **ἐξ-ερέθω**, strengthd. for ἐρεθίζω, ἐρέθω.

ἐξ-ερείπω, *to strike* or *hew off.* II. intr. in aor. 2 ἐξήρῐπον, inf. ἐξερῐπεῖν, and pf. ἐξήρῐπα:—*to fall to earth;* χαίτη ζεύγλης ἐξεριποῦσα the mane *streaming downwards from* the yoke: *to fall down.*

ἐξ-ερεύγομαι, Pass. of rivers, *to empty themselves.*

ἐξ-ερευνάω, f. ήσω, *to search out, examine.*

ἐξ-ερέω Att. contr. -ερῶ, (ἐξ, ἐρέω) fut. without any pres. in use, *I will speak out, proclaim:* hence pf. act. ἐξείρηκα; 3 plqpf. pass. ἐξείρητο; and fut. ἐξειρήσεται in pass. sense. The pres. in use is ἐξαγορεύω, the aor. ἐξεῖπον.

ἐξ-ερέω, Ep. for ἐξέρομαι, *to inquire into: inquire of.*

ἐξ-ερημόω, f. ώσω, *to make utterly desolate, desert utterly.*

ἐξ-ερίζω, f. ίσω, (ἐξ, ἔρις) *to be contumacious, resist.*

ἐξεριπεῖν, aor. 2 inf. of ἐξερείπω.

ἐξεριστής, οῦ, ὁ, (ἐξερίζω) *a stubborn disputant.*

ἐξ-έρομαι, fut. -ερήσομαι: Dep.: (ἐξ, ἔρομαι):—*to inquire of: to inquire into, examine:* cf. ἐξερέω.

ἐξ-έρπω, f. -έρψω: aor. 1 -είρπῠσα (as if from -ερπύω): *to creep out of:* absol. *to creep out.*

ἐξερράγην [ᾰ], aor. 2 pass. of ἐκρήγνυμι.

ἐξέρρᾱνα, aor. 1 of ἐκραίνω.

ἐξέρρηξα, aor. 1 of ἐκρήγνυμι.

ἐξέρριψα, aor. 1 of ἐκρίπτω.

ἐξερρύηκα, pf. of ἐκρέω.

ἐξερρύην, aor. 2 pass. (in act. sense) of ἐκρέω.

ἐξ-έρρω, (ἐξ, ἔρρω) *to go out:* only in imperat., ἔξερρε γαίας *away out* of the land.

ἐξ-ερύκω, *to ward off, repel.* [ῡ]

ἐξ-ερύω, f. ύσω [ῠ]: aor. 1 ἐξείρῠσα Ep. ἐξέρῠσα and ἐξείρυσσα:—*to draw out of, snatch out of, wrest from: to tear out.*

ἐξ-έρχομαι, Dep. with fut. -ελεύσομαι: aor. 2 -ήλῠθον contr. -ῆλθον: pf. -ελήλυθα:—*to go out, come out of, march off: to go through: to stand forth.* II. of Time, *to come to an end, expire.* III. of prophecies, etc., *to be accomplished, come true:* generally, *to reach* its end.

ἐξ-ερωέω, f. ήσω, *to swerve from the course, to shy.*

ἐξ-ερωτάω, f. ήσω, *to search out: to question.*

ἐξεσάωσα, aor. 1 of ἐκσαόω.

ἐξέσεισα, aor. 1 of ἐκσείω.

ἐξ-εσθίω, f. -έδομαι: pf. -εδήδοκα:—*to eat away.*

ἐξ-έσθω, collat. form of foreg.

ἐξεσία, ἡ, (ἐξίημι) *a sending out, mission.*

ἔξεσις, εως, ἡ, (ἐξίημι) *a dismissal: divorce.*

ἐξεσκέδᾰσα, aor. 1 of ἐκσκεδάννυμι.

ἐξέσμων, impf. of ἐκσμάω.

ἐξεσόβησα, aor. 1 of ἐκσοβέω.

ἐξέσσῠτο, 3 sing. plqpf. pass. (in aor. sense) of ἐκσεύω.

ἐξεστᾰκέναι, for ἐξεστηκέναι, pf. inf. or ἐξίστημι.

ἐξεστάναι, inf. pf. of ἐξίστημι, contr. for ἐξεστηκέναι.

ἐξέστειλα, aor. 1 of ἐκστέλλω.

ἐξεστεμμένος, pf. part. pass. of ἐκστέφω.

ἐξέστηκα, **ἐξέστην**, pf. and aor. 2 of ἐξίστημι.

ἔξ-εστι, impers., subj. ἐξῇ, optat. ἐξείη: inf. ἐξεῖναι: fut. ἐξέσται: impf. ἐξῆν: (ἐξ, εἰμί *sum*):—*it is allowed, it is in one's power, is possible:* part. ἐξόν Ion. ἐξεόν, absol. nom., *it being possible*, Lat. *quum liceat.*

ἐξεστράτευσα, aor. 1 of ἐκστρατεύω.

ἐξεστρατοπέδευμαι, pf. of ἐκστρατοπεδεύομαι.

ἐξέστρεψα, aor. 1 of ἐκστρέφω.

ἐξεσύρην [ῠ], aor. 2 pass. of ἐκσύρω [ῡ].

ἐξεσωρευόμην, impf. pass. of ἐκσωρεύω.

ἐξέσωσα, **ἐξεσώθην**, aor. 1 act. and pass. of ἐκσώζω.

ἐξ-ετάζω: f. ἐξετάσω Att. ἐξετῶ: aor. 1 ἐξήτασα Dor. ἐξήταξα: pf. ἐξήτακα:—Pass., aor. 1 ἐξητάσθην: pf. ἐξήτασμαι:—*to examine well* or *closely, to scrutinise:* hence *to question, esp. by the torture.* of things, *to search out, to inquire into, sift closely.* 2. of troops, *to inspect, review.* II. *to prove clearly, to test:* hence *to estimate, compare:*—Pass. *to be proved, to stand the trial: to be examined.*

ἐξετάθην [ᾰ], aor. 1 pass. of ἐκτείνω.

ἐξετάκην [ᾰ], aor. 2 pass. of ἐκτήκω.

ἐξέτᾰμον, aor. 2 of ἐκτέμνω.

ἐξετάνυσσα, Ep. aor. 1 of ἐκτανύω.

ἐξετᾰνύσθην, aor. 1 pass. of ἐκτανύω.

ἐξετάραξα, aor. 1 of ἐκταράσσω.

ἐξέτᾰσις, εως, ἡ, (ἐξετάζω) *a searching out: a military inspection* or *review.*

ἐξεταστικός, ή, όν, (ἐξετάζω) *skilful at examining:* absol. *inquiring.*

ἐξέτεινα, aor. 1 of ἐκτείνω.

ἐξέτεκον, aor. 2 of ἐκτίκτω.

ἐξετέλειον, Ep. impf. of ἐκτελέω.

ἐξετελεῦντο, Ep. 3 pl. impf. pass. of ἐκτελέω.

ἐξετετόξευτο, 3 sing. plqpf. pass. of ἐκτοξεύω.

ἐξετεχνησάμην, aor. 1 of ἐκτεχνάομαι.

ἐξετηκόμην, impf. pass. of ἐκτήκω.

ἐξ-έτης, ες, (ἕξ, ἔτος) *six years old.*

ἐξ-έτι, (ἐκ, ἔτι) Prep. with gen. *even until now.*

ἐξέτῑσα, aor. 1 of ἐκτίνω.

ἐξετόξευσα, aor. 1 of ἐκτοξεύω.

ἐξετρᾰπόμην, aor. 2 med. of ἐκτρέπω.

ἐξέτρεψα, aor. 1 of ἐκτρέπω.

ἐξέτριψα, aor. 1 of ἐκτρίβω.

ἐξέτρωσα, aor. 1 of ἐκτιτρώσκω.

ἐξ-ευλᾰβέομαι, Dep. *to be very cautious of.*

ἐξ-ευμᾰρίζω, (ἐκ, εὐμαρής) *to make easy, lighten.* II. Med. *to get ready, prepare,* Lat. *expedire.*

ἐξεύρεσις, εως, ἡ, (ἐξευρίσκω) *a searching out: a finding out, invention.*

ἐξεύρημα, ατος, τό, *a thing found out, an invention, contrivance.* From

ἐξ-ευρίσκω, f. –ευρήσω, aor. 2 –εὗρον :—*to find out, discover: to invent.* 2. *to seek out.* 3. *to find out, win, secure.*

ἐξ-ευτρεπίζω, *to prepare.*

ἐξ-εύχομαι, Dep. *to boast aloud, proclaim.* II. *to pray for.*

ἐξεφαάνθην Ep. for **ἐξεφάνθην**, aor. 1 pass. of ἐκφαίνω.

ἐξεφάνην [ᾰ], aor. 2 pass. of ἐκφαίνω.

ἐξεφθαρμένος, pf. pass. part. of ἐκφθείρω.

ἐξέφθινται, 3 pl. pf. pass. of ἐκφθίνω.

ἐξέφθῐτο, 3 plqpf. pass. of ἐκφθίνω.

ἐξ-εφίημι, mostly used in Med. **ἐξεφίεμαι**, *to enjoin, urge, bid.*

ἐξέφῠγον, aor. 2 of ἐκφεύγω.

ἐξέφῡσα, **ἐξέφῡν**, aor. 1 and 2 of ἐκφύω.

ἐξέχεα Ep. **ἐξέχευα**, aor. 1 of ἐκχέω.

ἐξεχορευσάμην, aor. 1 med. of ἐκχορεύω.

ἐξέχρησα, aor. 1 of ἐκχράω.

ἐξεχύθην [ῠ], aor. 1 pass. of ἐκχέω

ἐξ-έχω, f. –έξω, intr. *to stand out* or *project from:* of the sun, *to shine out, appear.*

ἐξέχωσα, aor. 1 of ἐκχώννυμι.

ἐξέψυξα, aor. 1 of ἐκψύχω.

ἐξ-έψω, f. –εψήσω, *to boil thoroughly.*

ἔξ-ηβος, ον, (ἐκ, ἥβη) *past one's youth.*

ἐξήγαγον, aor. 2 of ἐξάγω.

ἐξήγγειλα, **ἐξηγγέλθην**, aor. 1 act. and pass. of ἐξαγγέλλω.

ἐξ-ηγέομαι, fut. –ήσομαι: pf. –ήγημαι: Dep. :—*to be leader of,* c. gen. pers. 2. c. acc. pers. *to manage, direct, govern.* II. *to go first, lead the way:* 2. ἐξηγεῖσθαί τινι *to shew* one *the way* in a thing; and so *to guide:* also *to teach; to command.* III. like Lat. *praeīre verbis, to prescribe* a form of words :—*to expound, interpret.* IV. *to tell at length, narrate, describe.* Hence

ἐξηγητής, οῦ, ὁ, *a guide, director, counsellor:* generally, *a deviser.* II. *an interpreter* of oracles or sacred rites, Lat. *interpres religionum.*

ἐξηγρόμην, aor. 2 med. of ἐξεγείρω.

ἐξῄκασμαι, pf. pass. of ἐξεικάζω.

ἑξήκοντα, οἱ, αἱ, τά, indecl. (ἕξ) *sixty, sexaginta.*

ἑξηκοντα-έτης, ες, (ἑξήκοντα, ἔτος) *sixty years old.*

ἑξηκοντάκις poët. –άκι, (ἑξήκοντα) Adv. *sixty times.*

ἑξηκοντα-τᾰλαντία, ἡ, (ἑξήκοντα, τάλαντιον) *a sum of sixty talents.*

ἐξηκόντισα, aor. 1 of ἐξακοντίζω.

ἑξηκοστός, ή, όν, (ἑξήκοντα) *sixtieth, sexagesimus.*

ἐξ-ήκω, f. ήξω, *to have arrived at* a point:—of Time, *to have run out, expired:*—of prophecies, *to have turned out true.*

ἐξήλᾰσα Ep. **ἐξήλασσα**, aor. 1 of ἐξελαύνω.

ἐξήλᾰτος, ον, (ἐξελαύνω) *beaten out, hammered.*

ἐξηλέγχθην, aor. 1 pass. of **ἐξελέγχω**: **ἐξήλεγκτο**, 3 sing. plqpf.

ἐξήλειψα, aor. 1 of ἐξαλείφω.

ἐξῆλθον, aor. 2 of ἐξέρχομαι.

ἐξ-ηλῐάζω, f. άσω, (ἐξ, ἥλιος) *to set in the sun: to hang in the open air.*

ἐξήλλαξα, aor. 1 of ἐξαλλάσσω: **ἐξήλλαγμαι**, pf. pass.

ἐξήλῠσις, εως, ἡ, (ἐξήλῠθον aor. 2 of ἐξέρχομαι) *a going out: a way out.*

ἐξ-ῆμαρ, Adv. (ἕξ, ἦμαρ) *for six days, six days long.*

ἐξήμαρτον, **ἐξημάρτηκα**, aor. 2 and pf. of ἐξαμαρτάνω.

ἐξήμβλωκα, pf. of ἐξαμβλόω.

ἐξήμειψα, aor. 1 of ἐξαμείβω.

ἐξ-ημερόω, f. ώσω, *to tame* or *reclaim quite:* metaph. *to civilise, humanise.*

ἐξημημένος, pf. part. pass. of ἐξαμάω.

ἐξημιλλησάμην, –ήθην, aor. 1 med. and pass. of ἐξαμιλλάομαι.

ἐξημοιβός, όν, (ἐξαμείβω) *quite changed;* ἐξημοιβὰ εἵματα *changes of* raiment.

ἐξημπόλημαι, pf. pass. of ἐξεμπολάω.

ἐξηνδραποδίσθην, –ισμαι, aor. 1 and pf. pass. of ἐξανδραποδίζω.

ἐξήνδρωμαι, pf. pass. of ἐξανδρόομαι.

ἐξήνεγκα, **ἐξήνεγκον**, aor. 1 and 2 of ἐκφέρω.

ἐξηνειχόμην, **ἐξηνεσχόμην**, impf. and aor. 2 med. (with double augm.) of ἐξανέχω.

ἐξηνέμωσα, –ώθην, aor. 1 act. and pass. of ἐξανεμόω.

ἐξήνθηκα, –ησα, pf. and aor. 1 of ἐξανθέω.

ἐξήντληκα, –ησα, pf. and aor. 1 of ἐξαντλέω.

ἐξήνῠσα, aor. 1 of ἐξανύω or ἐξανύτω.

ἐξῇξα, Att. aor. 1 of ἐξαΐσσω, ἐξᾴσσω.

ἐξηπάτηκα, –ησα, pf. and aor. 1 of ἐξαπατάω.

ἐξήπᾰφον, aor. 2 of ἐξαπαφίσκω.

ἐξ-ηπεροπεύω, f. σω, *to cheat utterly.*

ἐξῆρα, aor. 1 of ἐξαίρω.

ἐξήραμμαι, pf. pass. of ξηραίνω.

ἐξηράνθην, aor. 1 pass. of ξηραίνω.

ἐξήραξα, aor. 1 of ἐξαράσσω.

ἐξήρᾰτο, 3 sing. aor. 1 med. of ἐξαίρω.

ἑξ-ήρετμος, ον, (ἕξ, ἐρέσσω) *with six oars.*

ἐξήρκουν, impf. of ἐξαρκέτο.

ἐξήρπαξα or –ασα, aor. 1 of ἐξαρπάζω.

ἐξήρτημαι, pf. pass. of ἐξαρτάω.

ἐξήρτισμαι, pf. pass. of ἐξαρτίζω.

ἐξήρτῡμαι, pf. pass. of ἐξαρτύω.

ἐξήρχετο, 3 sing. impf. med. of ἐξάρχω.

ἐξηρώησα, aor. 1 of ἐξερωέω.

ἐξήσκησα, aor. 1 of ἐξασκέω: **ἐξήσκημαι**, pf. pass.

ἑξῆς Ep. **ἑξείης**, Adv. (ἔχω, ἕξω) *one after another, in order:* also of Time, *thereafter, next.* II. c. gen. *next to.*

ἐξήτᾰσα Dor. **ἐξήταξα**, aor. 1 of ἐξετάζω.

ἐξῄτησα, aor. 1 of ἐξαιτέω.

ἐξηύηνα, aor. 1 of ἐξαναίνω.

ἐξηύχησα, -ηύχουν, aor. 1 and impf. of ἐξαυχέω.

ἐξήφῠσα Ep. **ἐξήφυσσα**, aor. 1 of ἐξαφύσσω.

ἐξ-ηχέω, f. ήσω, *to sound forth, publish.*

ἐξῆψα, ἐξήφθην, aor. 1 act. and pass. of ἐξάπτω.

ἐξ-ιάομαι, f. -ιάσομαι Ion. -ιήσομαι: Dep.:— *to cure thoroughly: to make full amends for.*

ἐξῐδεῖν, inf. of ἐξεῖδον.

ἐξ-ῐδῐόομαι, Dep. (ἐξ, ἴδιος) *to make one's own, to appropriate.*

ἐξ-ῐδίω, f. ίσω [ῐ], *to exude.*

ἐξ-ιδρύω, f. ύσω [ῡ], *to place in a resting posture:*— Med. *to establish oneself.*

ἐξῐέναι, inf. of ἔξειμι *exibo;* but **ἐξῑέναι**, of ἐξίημι.

ἐξ-ίημι, f. ήσω, *to send out, dispatch*, in Ep. aor. 2 inf. ἐξέμεν for ἐξεῖναι: of a sail or cable, *to let out* or *loose: to throw out* or *forth: to take out of:*—Med. *to put off from oneself, get rid of.* 2. *to send from oneself, divorce.*

ἐξ-ιθύνω [ῡ], *to make quite straight.*

ἐξ-ικετεύω, f. σω, *to beseech earnestly.*

ἐξ-ικνέομαι, f. ἐξίξομαι: aor. 2 ἐξικόμην [ῑ]: Dep.: —*to reach, arrive at.* 2. *to attain, come up to: to be sufficient for.* 3. *to accomplish, execute.*

ἐξ-ίκω, f. ξω, poët. for ἐξήκω.

ἐξ-ῐλάσκομαι, f. -ιλάσομαι [ᾰ], Dep. *to appease completely, propitiate.*

ἐξ-ίλλω, *to unravel, disentangle.* II. *to keep out from, bar from.*

ἐξίμεναι, for ἐξιέναι, inf. of ἔξειμι *exibo.*

ἐξ-ῑπόω, f. ώσω, *to press out, press heavily.*

ἐξ-ίπτᾰμαι, later form of ἐκπέτομαι.

ἕξις, εως, ἡ, (ἕξω fut. of ἔχω) *a being in a certain state, a permanent condition* or *habit*, of body or mind.

ἐξ-ίσης, Adv. for ἐξ ἴσης (sub. μοίρας), *equally;* also **ἐξ-ίσου** (sub. μέτρου).

ἐξ-ῐσόω, f. ώσω, *to make equal* or *even*, Lat. *exaequare:*—Med. *to make oneself equal:*—Pass. *to be equal, to be a match for.* 2. *to put on a level.* II. intr. *to be equal* or *like.*

ἐξ-ίστημι, f. ἐκστήσω, aor. 1 ἐξέστησα, in these tenses Causal, *to put out of its place, change, alter;* ἐξιστάναι τινὰ φρενῶν *to drive* one *out of* his senses: hence, simply, ἐξιστάναι τινά *to drive mad, to derange;* also *to astonish, to bewitch.* II. Pass., with aor. 2 act. ἐξέστην, pf. -έστηκα, plqpf. -εστήκειν, *to stand aside from: to stand out of the way: to make way for* one; also c. acc. *to shrink from, shun.* II. c. gen. rei, *to retire from: to be deprived of;* ἐκστῆναι πατρός *to lose* one's father. 2. φρενῶν ἐξεστάναι (pf. inf.) *to lose* one's senses: absol. *to be out of one's wits, be astonished.* 3. generally, *to give up one's* pursuits: also *to change one's opinion.*

ἐξ-ιστορέω, f. ήσω, *to inquire into: inquire of.*

ἐξ-ισχύω, f. ύσω [ῡ], *to be quite able.*

ἐξ-ίσχω,=ἐξέχω: trans. *to put forth:* intr. *to stand forth.*

ἐξῐσωτέον, verb. Adj. of ἐξισόω, *one must make equal.*

ἐξίτηλος, ον, (ἐξῐέναι) *going out, fading: extinct: forgotten.*

ἐξ-ῐτητέον, verb. Adj. of ἐξῐέναι, *one must go forth.*

ἐξ-ῐτός, ή, όν, verb. Adj. of ἐξῐέναι, *to be come out of;* τοῖς οὐκ ἐξιτόν ἐστι for whom there's no coming out.

ἐξ-ιχνεύω, f. σω, *to trace out.*

ἐξ-ιχνοσκοπέω, f. ήσω, *to seek by tracking out.*

ἐξ-μέδιμνος, ον, *of, holding six medimni.*

ἐξ-ογκόω, f. ώσω, *to make swell out;* μητέρα τάφῳ ἐξογκοῦν *to honour* her *by raising* a tomb:—Pass. *to be swelled out:* metaph. *to be puffed up, elated:* absol. *to swell, rise high.* Hence

ἐξόγκωμα, ατος, τό, *anything raised up: a mound, barrow, cairn.*

ἐξ-οδάω, f. ήσω, (ἔξοδος IV) *to sell.*

ἐξ-οδία, ἡ, (ἔξοδος) *a marching out, expedition.*

ἐξ-όδιος, ον, (ἔξοδος III) *of, belonging to an exit; to the finalé* of a play. II. as Subst., τὸ ἐξόδιον (sub. μέλος), *the finalé of a tragedy.* At Rome, *exodia* were *burlesques* acted after other plays, or *travesties* on the subject of the play itself, like some modern epilogues.

ἐξ-οδοιπορέω, f. ήσω, *to go out of.*

ἔξ-οδος, ἡ, *a going out.* 2. *a marching out, military expedition: a sally.* 3. *a solemn procession.* II. *a way out*, Lat. *exitus.* III. also like Lat. *exitus, an end, close: the close* of life, *decease.* 2. *the end of a tragedy.* 3. *a piece of music played at any one's exit.* IV. *an outgoing, payment of money:* hence ἐξοδάω.

ἐξ-οδῠνάω, f. ήσω, *to pain extremely.*

ἐξ-όζω, f. -οζήσω, *to smell strongly.*

ἔξ-οιδα, pf. without any pres. in use, Att. plqpf. **ἐξῄδη**, *to know thoroughly, know well:* cf. ἐξεῖδον.

ἐξ-οιδέω, f. ήσω: pf. -ῴδηκα:—*to be swollen up.*

ἐξ-οικέω, f. ήσω, *to leave one's home, to emigrate.* II. Pass. *to be thickly inhabited.* Hence

ἐξοικήσιμος, ον, *habitable, inhabited.*

ἐξ-οικίζω, f. ίσω Att. ιῶ: aor. 1 -ῴκισα:—*to remove* one *from his home, eject, expel:*—Pass. *to go from home, remove.* II. *to depopulate, empty.*

ἐξ-οικοδομέω, f. ήσω, *to build up, build from the ground, finish a building.*

ἐξ-οιμώζω, f. -οιμώξομαι, *to wail aloud.*

ἐξ-οινόομαι, pf. ἐξῴνωμαι, Pass. *to be quite drunk.*

ἐξ-οιστέος, α, ον, verb. Adj. of ἐκφέρω, *to be brought out.* II. ἐξοιστέον, *one must bring out.*

ἐξ-οιστράω or -έω, f. ήσω, *to drive quite wild.*

ἐξοίσω, fut. of ἐκφέρω:—med. **ἐξοίσομαι** also in pass. sense.

ἐξ-οιχνέω, f. ήσω, *to go out:* Aeol. 3 pl. **ἐξοιχνεῦσι.**

ἐξ-οίχομαι, Dep. *to have gone out.*

ἐξ-οκέλλω, aor. 1 -ώκειλα, *to thrust out of* the sea; *to run* a ship *aground:* intr. of the ship, *to run aground.* II. metaph. *to run* a person *aground, bring him into difficulties:*—Pass., δεῦρο **ἐξοκέλλεται** the thing *is brought to this pass.*

ἐξολέσαι, aor. 1 inf. of ἐξόλλυμι.

ἐξ-ολισθάνω, fut. -ολισθήσω: aor. 2 -ώλισθον:—*to slip off, to glance off* II. c. acc. *to slip out of, elude*

ἐξ-όλλῡμι and -ύω: fut. -ολέσω Att. -ολῶ: aor. 1 ἐξώλεσα:—*to destroy utterly.* II. Med. with perf. 2 ἐξόλωλα, *to perish utterly.*

ἐξ-ολοθρεύω, f. σω, *to destroy utterly.*

ἐξ-ολολύζω, f. ξω, *to howl aloud.*

ἔξομαι, fut. med. of ἔχω.

ἐξομήρευσις, εως, ἡ, *a demand of hostages.* From

ἐξ-ομηρεύω, f. σω, *to bind by taking hostages:* Med. *to take as hostages.*

ἐξ-ομῑλέω, f. ήσω, *to have intercourse, associate, live with.* II. Med. *to be away from one's friends, to be solitary.*

ἐξ-όμῑλος, ον, *away from intercourse with others: foreign, strange.*

ἐξ-ομμᾰτόω, f. ώσω, (ἐξ, ὄμμα) *to give sight to:*—Pass. *to be restored to sight.* 2. metaph. *to make clear* or *plain.* II. also *to bereave of sight.*

ἐξ-όμνῡμαι, f. -ομοῦμαι: aor. 1 -ωμοσάμην:—*to deny upon oath.* II. *to decline* an office *by an oath* that one has not means or health to discharge it.

ἐξ-ομοιόω, f. ώσω, *to make quite like:*—Pass. *to become* or *be like.*

ἐξ-ομολογέω, f. ήσω, and as Dep. **ἐξομολογέομαι**, f. ήσομαι, *to confess in full, admit.* 2. *to agree, promise.* II. *to make full acknowledgment for: praise, celebrate.*

ἐξ-ομόργνῡμι, f. -ομόρξω, *to wipe off from.* II. Med. *to wipe off from oneself:* hence *to impart to another:* *to wipe out* or *purge away* a pollution.

ἐξόν. part. from the impers. ἔξεστι.

ἐξ-ονειδίζω, fut. ίσω Att. ιῶ, *to cast in one's teeth, object to* one: also *to reproach bitterly.*

ἐξ-ονομάζω, f. σω, *to utter aloud, announce.*

ἐξ-ονομαίνω, aor. 1 -ονόμηνα, (ἐξ, ὄνομα) *to name, speak of by name.*

ἐξ-ονομακλήδην, Adv. *by name, calling by name.*

ἐξ-όπῑθεν and -θε, Adv., poët. for ἐξόπισθεν.

ἐξ όπιν, Adv. *behind.*

ἐξ-όπισθεν poët. -θε, Adv. *backwards, behind.* II. Prep. with gen. *behind, after.*

ἐξ-οπίσω, (ἐξ, ὀπίσω) Adv. of Place, *backwards, back again.* 2. Prep. with gen. *behind.* II. Adv. of Time, *henceforth, hereafter.* [ῐ]

ἐξ-οπλίζω, f. σω, *to arm completely, accoutre:*—Pass. and Med. *to arm oneself, go forth armed.* 2. generally, *to prepare;* pf. part. pass. ἐξωπλισμένος, *all ready* Hence

ἐξοπλῑσία, ἡ, *a being under arms:* and

ἐξόπλῑσις, εως, ἡ, *a getting under arms.*

ἐξ-οπτάω, f. ήσω, *to bake hard: to heat violently:*—metaph. *to scorch, consume.*

ἐξ-οράω, *to see from afar:* cf. ἐξεῖδον.

ἐξ-οργίζω, fut. ίσω Att. ιῶ, *to enrage:*—Pass. *to be furious.*

ἐξ-ορθιάζω, f. σω, *to lift up* the voice, *to cry aloud.*

ἐξ-ορθόω, f. ώσω, *to set upright:*—Pass. *to stand upright.* 2. metaph. *to amend, restore.*

ἐξ-ορίζω, f. ίσω Att. ιῶ: aor. 1 ἐξώρισα:—*to send beyond the frontier, banish: to expose* a child. II. ἄλλην ἀπ' ἄλλης ἐξορίζειν πόλιν *to wander* from one city to another. III. Pass. *to be an exile:* also *to pass the bounds, come forth.* Hence

ἐξ-ορίνω [ῑ], *to exasperate.*

ἐξ-όριστος, ον, *expelled, banished.*

ἐξ-ορκίζω, f. ίσω Att. ιῶ, *to swear* a person, *administer an oath to* him. II. *to exorcise,* i. e. *banish* an evil spirit. Hence

ἐξορκιστής, οῦ, ὁ, *one who administers an oath.* II. *an exorcist*

ἐξ-ορκος, ον, *bound by oath.*

ἐξ-ορκόω, f. ώσω, *to make one swear, bind by oath,* c. acc. pers.: c. acc. pers. et rei, *to make one swear by,* ἐξορκοῦν τινα τὸ Στυγὸς ὕδωρ. Hence

ἐξόρκωσις, εως, ἡ, *a binding by oath.*

ἐξ-ορμάω, f. ήσω, *to set out* or *start from:* of pain, *to break out.* II. trans. *to send forth;* ἐξορμᾶν τὴν ναῦν *to start* the ship: generally, *to excite, stir up:*—Pass. *to set out, start.*

ἐξ-ορμίζω, fut. ίσω Att. ιῶ, *to bring out of harbour;* ἐξορμίζειν ἐς πόντον *to let down* into the sea.

ἔξ-ορμος, ον, *sailing from a harbour.*

ἐξ-ορούω, f. σω, *to spring, leap forth.*

ἐξ-ορύσσω Att. -ττω: fut. ξω: aor. 1 ἐξώρυξα:—*to dig out;* ἐξορύσσειν τοὺς ὀφθαλμούς *to put out* the eyes. II. *to dig out of* the ground, *dig up.*

ἐξ-ορχέομαι, fut. ήσομαι, Dep. *to dance out, dance away:* also *to go through with a dance.* II. *to betray by indiscreet gestures.*

ἐξ-όσδω, Dor. for ἐξόζω.

ἐξ-οσιόω, f. ώσω, *to dedicate, devote.*

ἐξ-οστρᾰκίζω, f. ίσω, *to banish by ostracism.* Hence

ἐξοστρακισμός, οῦ, ὁ, *banishment by ostracism.*

ἐξότε, Adv. (ἐκ, ὅτε) *from the time when.*

ἐξ-οτρύνω, f. ὑνῶ, *to excite, arouse.*

ἐξ-ουδενόω, f. ώσω, = ἐξουθενέω.

ἐξ-ουθενέω, f. ήσω, (ἐκ, οὐθείς) *to set at naught;* pf. part. pass., τὰ ἐξουθενημένα *things of no account.*

ἐξούλης δίκη, ἡ, an action *against one who neglected an order of a court, an action for contempt of court.* The nom. ἐξούλη does not occur.

ἐξουσία, ἡ, (ἔξεστι) *power* or *authority* to do a thing:—absol. *authority.* 2. *a magistracy: the body of the magistrates, the authorities, powers.* II. *means, resources.* Hence

ἐξουσιάζω, f. σω, *to have authority over:*—Pass. *to have authority exercised over one.*

ἐξ-οφέλλω, *to increase exceedingly.*

ἐξ-όφθαλμος, ον, *with prominent eyes.*

ἐξοχή, ἡ, (ἐξέχω) *a standing out, prominence:* metaph. *eminence;* οἱ κατ' ἐξοχήν *the chief men.*

ἔξοχος, ον, (ἐξέχω) *standing out, prominent:* metaph. *eminent, excellent:* c. gen., ἔξοχος Ἀργείων *eminent* *among* or *above* them. Adv. neut. ἔξοχον and ἔξοχα; c. gen., ἔξοχα πάντων *far above* all.

ἐξ-υβρίζω, f. ίσω Att. ιῶ, *to break out into insolence, run riot, wax wanton*; ἐξυβρίζειν εἰς τόδε *to come to this pitch of* insolence; ἐξυβρίζειν παντοῖα *to commit* all kinds of *violence*.

ἐξυνῆκα ἐσυνῆκα, for ξυνῆκα συνῆκα, aor. 1 with dupl. augm. of συνίημι.

ἐξ-υπανίστημι, *to make to start up*. II. Pass., with aor. 2 act., intrans., σμῶδιξ μεταφρένου ἐξυπανέστη a weal *started up from under* the skin of the back.

ἐξ-ύπερθε, Adv. (ἐξ, ὕπερθε) *from above*.

ἐξ-υπηρετέω, f. ήσω, *to assist to the utmost*.

ἐξ-υπνίζω, f. ίσω, (ἐξ, ὕπνος) *to rouse from sleep*.

ἔξ-υπνος, ον, (ἐξ, ὕπνος) *awakened out of sleep*.

ἐξυπτιάζω, f. σω, *to turn upside down*.

ἐξῡράμην, aor. 1 med. of ξύρω.

ἐξύρημαι, pf. pass. of ξῠρέω.

ἔξυσμαι, pf. pass. of ξύω.

ἐξ-ῠφαίνω, f. ανῶ, *to finish weaving*, Lat. *pertexere*: metaph. *to complete, perfect*. Hence

ἐξύφασμα, ατος, τό, *a finished web*.

ἐξ-υφηγέομαι, f. ήσομαι, *to lead the way*.

ἔξω, Adv. (ἐξ, as εἴσω from εἰς) *without, on the outside*, Lat. *foris*. II. of Motion, *outwards, away out of the country*, Lat. *foras*. III. like ἐκτός, with gen., *outside of, out of reach of*; ἔξω βελῶν *out of* shot: Proverb., ἔξω τοῦ πηλοῦ πόδα ἔχειν to keep clear of difficulties. 2. *without, except*. IV. of Time, *beyond, over*.

ἕξω, fut. of ἔχω.

ἐξῴδηκα, pf. of ἐξοιδέω.

ἔξωθεν, Adv. (ἔξω) *from without*, c. gen., ἔξ. δόμων *from without* the house. II. also = ἔξω, *without*.

ἐξ-ωθέω, f. -ώθησω and -ώσω: aor. 1 ἐξέωσα:—*to thrust out*:—Pass. *to be thrust out*. II. *to thrust out of the sea, drive on shore*.

ἐξῴκισα, aor. 1 of ἐξοικίζω.

ἐξώλεια, ἡ, *utter destruction*. From

ἐξώλης, ες, (ἐξόλωλα) *utterly destroyed, ruined*. 2. act. *most destructive, ruinous*. II. of persons, *abandoned*.

ἐξωμῐδο-ποιΐα, ἡ, (ποιέω) *the making of an* ἐξωμίς.

ἐξωμίζω, f. σω, *to bare up to the shoulder*. From

ἐξ-ωμίς, ίδος, ἡ, (ἐξ, ὦμος) *a man's vest without sleeves*, leaving both shoulders bare, or *with one sleeve*, leaving one shoulder bare.

ἐξ-ωνέομαι, Dep. *to buy off*: generally, *to buy*.

ἐξ-ώπιος, ον, (ἐξ, ὤψ) *out of sight of, away from*.

ἐξωπλισμένος, pf. part. pass. of ἐξοπλίζω.

ἐξ-ωριάζω, (ἐξ, ὥρα) *to leave out of thought, neglect*.

ἐξώρισα, aor. 1 of ἐξορίζω.

ἐξώρμισαι, 2 sing. pf. pass. of ἐξορμίζω.

ἔξ-ωρος, ον, (ἐξ, ὥρα) *untimely*: *superannuated*.

ἐξῶρτο, 3 sing. Ep. aor. 2 pass. of ἐξόρνυμι.

ἐξῶσαι, aor. 1 inf. of ἐξωθέω.

ἐξώστης, ου, ὁ, (ἐξωθέω) *one who drives out*: ἐξῶσται ἄνεμοι winds *which drive ships ashore*.

ἐξώτατος, η, ον, Sup. of ἔξω: Adv. ἐξωτάτω *outermost*.

ἐξώτερος, α, ον, Comp. of ἔξω: Adv. ἐξωτέρω.

ἐξώφελλον, impf. of ἐξοφέλλω.

ἕο, Ep. for οὗ, gen. of 3rd pers. Pron. *his, of him*; ἀπὸ ἕο away from *him*.

ἑοῖ, Ep. for οἷ, dat. of 3rd pers. Pron. οὗ, *to him*.

ἔοι, Ep. for εἴη, 3 sing. opt. of εἰμί *sum*.

ἔοιγμεν, syncop. for ἐοίκαμεν, 1 pl. of ἔοικα.

ἔοικα, ας, ε, etc., pf. with pres. sense, from εἴκω, *to be like* (see εἴκω), Att. 1 pl. ἔοιγμεν (for ἐοίκαμεν), εἴξασι (for ἐοίκασι); Ep. 3 dual ἔϊκτον (for ἐοίκατον); inf. ἐοικέναι Att. εἰκέναι; part. ἐοικώς, υῖα, ός, lengthd. pl. nom. εἰοικυῖαι; Att. εἰκώς, εἰκυῖα, εἰκός, is also used by Hom.: Ion. **οἶκα**, ας, ε, part. οἰκώς: plqpf. ἐῴκειν, Ep. 3 pl. ἐοίκεσαν; of the plqpf. there is also an Ep. pass. form 3 sing. ἤϊκτο, and without augm. ἔϊκτο. I. *to be* or *look like*. II. *to be fit*: Homer has 3 sing. ἔοικε as impers., *it is fitting, right, seemly*. 2. Homer also uses part. ἐοικώς as an Adj. *meet, fitting, right*; ἐοικότι κεῖται ὀλέθρῳ he lies in *fitting* ruin; εἰκυῖα ἄκοιτις *a suitable* wife, 'a help *meet for him*.' III. Att. *to seem likely, seem*; ἔοικε *it seems*; ὡς ἔοικε, *as it seems, as is fitting*.

ἐοικότως Att. **εἰκότως** Ion. **οἰκότως**, Adv. of part. ἐοικώς, εἰκώς, οἰκώς, *similarly, like*: *reasonably, fairly, as was to be expected*.

ἔοιμι, ἔοις, ἔοι, Ion. for εἴην, εἴης, εἴη.

ἑοῖο, Ep. for ἑοῦ, gen. of ἑός.

ἑοῖς, dat. pl. of ἑός.

ἔοις, Ep. for εἴης, 2 sing. opt. of εἰμί *sum*.

ἐοῖσα, Dor. for ἐοῦσα, οὖσα, part. fem. of εἰμί *sum*.

ἔολπα, poët. pf. with pres. sense of ἔλπω: plqpf. **ἐώλπειν**.

ἔον, Ep. for ἦν, impf. of εἰμί *sum*; but **ἐόν** Ion. for ὄν, part. neut.

ἑόν, nom. or acc. neut. of ἑός.

ἔοντι, Dor. for εἰσί, 3 pl. of εἰμί *sum*.

ἔοργα, poët. pf. of ἔρδω; 3 pl. ἔοργαν for ἐόργασιν; part. ἐοργώς: Ion. 3 sing. plqpf. ἐόργεε.

ἑορτάζω Ion. **ὁρτάζω**, f. σω: impf., with irreg. augment, ἑώρταζον, and aor. 1 ἑώρτασα: (ἑορτή):—*to keep festival* or *holiday*: *to celebrate by a festival*.

ἙΟΡΤΗ', in Ion. Prose **ὁρτή**, ἡ, *a feast, festival, holiday*; ὁρτὴν ἄγειν to keep *a feast*.

ἑός, ἑή, ἑόν, Ion. and Ep. for ὅς, ἥ, ὅν, (ἕο for οὗ) possessive Adj. of 3 pers. sing., *his* or *her own*. II. in Poets after Hom. also 3 pers. pl. *their*; 2 sing. *thine*.

ἑοῦς, Boeot. for ἕο, οὗ, gen. of 3rd pers. Pron.

ἐπ-ᾰγάλλομαι, Pass. *to glory* or *exult in*.

ἐπαγγελία, ἡ, *an announcement, order*. 2. as Att. law-term, *a denunciation, information*. II. *a promise, an assurance*: also *the thing promised*. From

ἐπ-αγγέλλω, f. ελῶ: aor. 1 ἐπήγγειλα: pf. act. ἐπήγγελκα, pass. ἐπήγγελμαι:—*to tell, proclaim, announce, make known*. 2. *to give orders, command*: c. acc. rei, στρατιὰν ἐπαγγέλλειν *to order* an army, Lat. *imperare milites*. 3. *to denounce*. 4. *to* *demand, solicit, make application for* a thing. II. Med. *to promise, offer:* rarely so in Act. 2. *to make a show of, profess.* Hence

ἐπάγγελμα, ατος, τό, *an announcement, promise.*

ἐπ-ἄγείρω, f. -αγερῶ, *to gather together, collect:*—Pass., of men, *to assemble.* Hence

ἐπάγερσις, εως, ἡ, *a gathering, assemblage.*

ἐπάγην [ᾰ], aor. 2 pass. of πήγνυμι.

ἐπ-ἄγῖνέω, Ion. for ἐπάγω, *to bring to.*

ἐπ-αγλᾰΐζω, f. ίσω Att. ιῶ, *to honour still more:*—Pass. *to pride oneself on, exult in* a thing.

ἐπ-αγρυπνέω, f. ήσω, *to watch* or *brood over.*

ἐπ-άγω, f. ξω: aor. 2 ἐπήγαγον:—*to bring* or *lead to, bring upon.* 2. *to lead on, to set on, let loose:* hence *to instigate, impel:* metaph. *to bring* one *to* a thing, *lead* one *on.* 3. *to lay on;* ἐπάγειν κέντρον *to lay on, apply* the goad; ἔπαγε γνάθον *lay* your teeth *to* it. 4. *to bring in, supply, call in aid.* 5. *to bring in* a bill or lawsuit, *propose.* 6. *to bring in over and above: to add* or *intercalate* days in the year. II. Med. *to bring to oneself, procure for oneself:* metaph. *to devise, contrive.* 2. *to bring on oneself.* 3. *to bring in* as allies: in writing, *to adduce, quote, cite.* Hence

ἐπᾰγωγή, ἡ, *a bringing on, to* or *in: an invasion, attack.* II. in Logic, *the bringing a number of particular examples,* so as to lead to an universal conclusion, *the argument from induction.*

ἐπᾰγωγός, όν, (ἐπάγω) *bringing on, productive of.* II. *tempting, seductive.*

ἐπ-ᾰγωνίζομαι, f. ίσομαι Att. ιοῦμαι, Dep. *to contend against others.*

ἐπ-ᾰγώνιος, ον, (ἐπί, ἀγών) *presiding over the games.*

ἐπ-ᾴδω Ion. and poët. ἐπᾰείδω: f. -ᾴσομαι:—*to sing to* or *over.* 2. *to lead the song.* II. *to sing to, so as to charm:* hence *to use charms* or *incantations;* part. ἐπαείδων, *by incantations.*

ἐπ-ᾰείρω, Ion. and poët. for ἐπαίρω.

ἐπ-ᾰέξω, *to make to grow, enlarge.*

ἔπᾰθον, aor. 2 of πάσχω.

ἐπ-αθροίζω, f. σω, *to assemble besides.*

ἐπ-αιάζω, f. ξω, *to mourn over: to join in wailing.*

ἐπ-αιγίζω, f. σω, (ἐπί, αἰγίς 2) *to rush upon* or *over.*

ἐπ-αιδέομαι: fut. -αιδεσθήσομαι: aor. 1 -ῃδέσθην: *to be ashamed:* c. acc. *to reverence.*

ἐπαίνεσις, εως, ἡ, (ἐπαινέω) *praise:* and

ἐπ-αινέτης, ου, ὁ, *a praiser, eulogist.*

ἐπαινετός, ή, όν, *to be praised, praiseworthy:* τὸ ἐπαινετόν *the object of praise.* Adv. -τῶς. From

ἐπ-αινέω: fut. έσω Att. έσομαι Ep. ήσω: aor. 1 ἐπήνεσα Ep. -ησα: pf. ἐπήνεκα:—Pass., aor. 1 ἐπηνέθην: (ἐπί, αἰνέω):—*to approve, sanction:* c. dat. pers. *to agree with, assent to: to praise, commend, eulogize.* 2. = παραινέω, *to advise, recommend, bid.* II. in declining an offer, *I thank you,* Lat. *benigne;* κάλλιστ' ἐπαινῶ *I thank you* very kindly.

ἐπαίνημι, Aeol. for ἐπαινέω.

ἔπ-αινος, ὁ, (ἐπί, αἶνος) *approval, commendation.*

ἐπ-αινός, ή, όν, only in fem. ἐπαινή, strengthd. for αἰνή, *exceeding awful, dread.*

ἐπ-αίρω Ion. and poët. ἐπαείρω: fut. ἐπαρῶ: aor. 1 ἐπῆρα poët. ἐπάειρα:—Pass., aor. 1 ἐπήρθην: pf. ἐπῆρμαι:—*to lift up, raise: to exalt, magnify.* 2. *to stir up, rouse, excite: to induce* or *persuade* to do. II. intr. (sub. ἑαυτόν), *to rise up.* 2. (sub. στρατόν), *to set out:*—Pass. *to be roused, excited: to be elated* at a thing.

ἔπαισδον, Dor. for ἔπαιζον, impf. of παίζω.

ἐπ-αισθάνομαι, f. -αισθήσομαι: aor. 2 -ῃσθόμην: Dep.:—*to have a perception* or *feeling of* a thing, c. gen.: c. acc. *to perceive, learn:* c. part. *to perceive that.*

ἐπ-αΐσσω Att. -ᾴσσω or -ᾴττω: fut. -αΐξω Att. -ᾴξω:—*to rush at* or *upon:*—*to assail, assault, attack:*—Med., ἐπαΐξασθαι ἄεθλον *to rush upon, seize* the prize. II. ἐπᾴσσειν πόδα *to move* the foot *hastily:* Pass., χεῖρες ἐπαΐσσονται the hands *move violently.*

ἐπ-άϊστος, ον, (ἐπαΐω) *heard of, discovered.* [ᾱ]

ἐπ-αισχύνομαι, fut. -αισχυνθήσομαι, Dep. *to be ashamed of* or *at*

ἐπ-αιτέω, f. ήσω, *to ask in addition: to solicit.*

ἐπ-αιτιάομαι, f. άσομαι [ᾱ], Dep. *to bring a charge against* one, *accuse: to lay to one's charge.*

ἐπ-αίτιος, ον, (ἐπί, αἰτία) *blamed for* a thing, *blamable, culpable.*

ἐπ-ᾰΐω contr. ἐπ-ᾴω: f. ίσω: *to hear, perceive, feel.* 2. *to understand.* 3. *to profess, be a professor.*

ἐπ-αιωρέω, f. ήσω, *to keep in suspense:*—Pass. *to be buoyed up* or *float upon:* also *to overhang, threaten.*

ἐπ-ᾰκολουθέω, f. ήσω, *to follow close upon, follow after: to pursue* as an enemy. 2. *to follow* in one's mind, *understand.* 3. *to follow, obey.* Hence

ἐπακολούθημα, ματος, τό, *a consequence:* and

ἐπακολούθησις, εως, ἡ, *a following.*

ἐπᾰκουός, όν, (ἐπακούω) *listening to, attentive.*

ἐπ-ᾰκούω, f. -ακούσομαι: aor. 1 ἐπήκουσα:—*to listen* or *attend to.* II. *to listen to, obey.*

ἐπ-ακρίζω, f. σω, *to reach the top of* a thing; αἱμάτων ἐπήκρισε he *reached the highest point* in deeds of blood.

ἐπ-ακροάομαι, f. άσομαι [ᾱ], Dep. *to hearken to.*

ἐπακτήρ, ῆρος, ὁ, (ἐπάγω) *a hunter, a huntsman.*

ἐπ-άκτιος, α, ον, (ἐπί, ἀκτή) *on the strand* or *coast.*

ἐπακτός, όν, (ἐπάγω) *brought on* or *in from abroad, imported.* 2. *foreign, strange, alien, adventitious.*

ἐπακτρίς, ίδος, ἡ, (ἐπάγω) *a small row-boat, skiff.*

ἐπ-ᾰλᾰλάζω, f. ξω, *to raise the war-cry.*

ἐπᾰλαλκέμεν, Ep. aor. 2 inf. of ἐπαλέξω.

ἐπ-ᾰλάομαι, aor. 1 ἐπαλήθην, Dep. *to wander about, through, over.*

ἐπ-ᾰλαστέω, f. ήσω, *to be troubled at* a thing.

ἐπ-αλγέω, f. ήσω, *to grieve over.*

ἐπ-ᾰλείφω, f. ψω, *to smear over: to stop up by anointing.*

ἐπ-ᾰλέξω, f. ξήσω, *to defend, aid, help.* II. *to ward, keep off:* aor. 2 inf. ἐπαλαλκεῖν, Ep. -έμεν.

ἐπᾰληθείς, aor. 1 part. of ἐπ-αλάομαι.

ἐπαληθῇ, 3 sing. aor. 1 subj. of ἐπ-αλάομαι.

ἐπ-ᾰληθεύω, f. σω, *to prove true, verify.*

ἐπ-αλής, ές, (ἐπί, ἀλέα) *open to the sun, sunny.* [ᾱ]

ἐπ-αλκής, ές, (ἐπί, ἀλκή) *stout, strong.*

ἐπαλλᾰγή, ἡ, (ἐπαλλάσσω) *interchange, exchange.*

ἐπ-αλλάξ, Adv. = ἐναλλάξ, *crosswise, alternately.*

ἐπ-αλλάσσω Att. -ττω: fut. άξω: pf. -ήλλαχα:—Pass., aor. 1 -ηλλάχθην, aor. 2 -ηλλάγην [ᾰ]: pf. -ήλλαγμαι:—*to change over, interchange; πολέμοιο πεῖραρ ἐπαλλάξαντες making* the tug of war *go now this way, now that,* i. e. fighting with doubtful victory:—Pass. *to be closely joined.*

ἐπ-άλληλος, ον, (ἐπί, ἀλλήλων) *one upon another: continuous.*

ἐπ-άλμενος, ον, syncop. aor. 2 part. of ἐφάλλομαι.

ἔπαλξις, εως, ἡ, (ἐπαλέξω) *a means of defence: battlement, a parapet:*—generally, *a defence, protection.*

ἐπ-αλπνος, ον, (ἐπί, ἄλπνιστος) *happy.*

ἐπᾶλτο, 3 sing. Ep. aor. 2 of ἐφάλλομαι.

ἐπ-ᾰλώστης, ου, ὁ, (ἐπί, ἀλοάω) *one who drives the oxen in threshing.*

ἐπ-ᾰμάομαι, f. ήσομαι: Ep. aor. 1 ἐπαμησάμην: Med.:—*to scrape together for oneself, heap up together.*

ἐπαμβᾰτήρ, ῆρος, ὁ, poët. for ἐπαναβάτης, (ἐπαναβαίνω) *one that rises upon; νόσοι σαρκῶν ἐπαμβατῆρες* maladies *growing on* the flesh, leprous eruptions.

ἐπ-ᾰμείβω, f. ψω, *to exchange, barter:*—Med. *to change from one to another; νίκη ἐπαμείβεται ἄνδρας comes in turn* to men.

ἐπ-άμερος, ον, Aeol. for ἐφ-ήμερος.

ἐπ-αμμένος, Ion. for ἐφημμένος, pf. pass. part. of ἐφάπτω

ἐπ-αμμένω, poët. for ἐπ-αναμένω.

ἐπᾰμοιβᾰδίς, Adv. (ἐπαμείβω) *alternately.*

ἐπᾰμοίβιος, ον, and **ἐπᾰμοιβός**, όν, (ἐπαμείβω) *in turn, one upon another: in exchange.*

ἐπ-αμπέχω, f. -αμφέξω: aor. 2 ἐπήμπισχον, inf. ἐπαμπισχεῖν:—*to put on besides,* or *over all: to overwrap.*

ἐπᾰμύντωρ, ορος, ὁ, *a helper, defender.* From

ἐπ-ᾰμύνω, f. ῠνῶ, *to come to aid, defend, assist.*

ἐπ-αμφέρω, for ἐπαναφέρω.

ἐπ-αμφοτερίζω, fut. ίσω Att. ιῶ, (ἐπί, ἀμφότερος) *to be inclined to both sides, to play a double game: to halt between two opinions.*

ἐπάν, Conjunct., later form of ἐπήν.

ἐπ-αναβαίνω, f. -βήσομαι: pf. -βέβηκα:—*to get upon, mount on horseback* II. *to go up* inland.

ἐπ-αναβάλλω, f. -βᾰλῶ: pf. -βέβληκα:—*to throw on* or *over:*—Med. *to put on.* II. in Med., also, *to put off, delay.*

ἐπ-αναβῐβάζω, f. -βιβάσω Att. -βιβῶ:—Causal of ἐπαναβαίνω, *to make to mount upon.*

ἐπαναβληδόν, Adv. (ἐπαναβάλλω) *thrown over* another garment.

ἐπ-αναβοάω, f. ήσομαι, *to cry out at* a thing.

ἐπαναγαγεῖν, aor. 2 inf. of ἐπανάγω.

ἐπ-ᾰναγκάζω, f. άσω, *to compel by force.*

ἐπ-ᾰνάγκης, ες, (ἐπί, ἀνάγκη) only used in neut. ἐπάναγκες (sub. ἐστί), *it is necessary.* 2. neut also as Adv. *on compulsion; ἐπάναγκες κομῶντες* wearing long hair *by law.*

ἐπ-ανᾰγορεύω, *to proclaim publicly:* v. ἐπανεῖπον.

ἐπ-ανάγω, f. άξω: aor. 2 -ανήγᾰγον:—*to bring up, stir up, excite.* 2. *to exalt, elevate.* II. *to lead* or *draw back: to bring back, to refer to* one. III. intr. *to withdraw, retreat.* IV. *to put* ships *out to sea:*—Pass. *to put to sea against.* V. Pass. *to be carried to* a place. Hence

ἐπανᾰγωγή, ἡ, *a sailing out against, a naval attack.* II. *a recall, return.*

ἐπ-αναδιπλάζω, *to redouble, reiterate questions.*

ἐπ-αναθεάομαι, f. άσομαι [ᾱ], Dep. *to see again.*

ἐπ-αναίρω, *to lift up:*—Med. *to lift one against the other:*—Pass. *to rise up.*

ἐπ-ανάκειμαι, Pass. *to be laid upon* as a penalty.

ἐπ-ανακλαγγάνω, *to give tongue again and again.*

ἐπ-ανακρούω, *to drive back:*—Med. *to draw back.*

ἐπ-ανακύπτω, f. ψω, *to have an upward direction.*

ἐπ-αναλαμβάνω, f. -λήψομαι, *to take up again, resume, repeat.*

ἐπ-ανᾱλίσκω, f. -ανᾱλώσω, *to consume besides.*

ἐπ-αναμένω, f. -μενῶ, *to continue waiting, stay on.* II. *to wait for* one.

ἐπ-αναμιμνήσκω, f. -μνήσω, *to remind* one *of, mention again to* one.

ἐπ-ανανεόω, f. ώσω, *to renew, revive.*

ἐπ-αναπαύω, f. σω, *to make to rest upon:*—Med. *to rest upon.*

ἐπ-αναπηδάω, f. ήσω or ήσομαι, *to leap upon.*

ἐπ-αναπλέω, f. -πλεύσομαι; Ion. ἐπαναπλώω, f. -πλώσω:—*to sail up against.* II. *to float upon the surface; ἐπαναπλώει ὑμῖν ἔπεα κακά* ill language *floats up, rises to* the tongue. III. *to sail back again.*

ἐπ-αναρρίπτω and -έω, *to throw up in the air* (sub. ἑαυτόν) *to spring high in the air.*

ἐπανάσεισις, εως, ἡ, *a brandishing* of weapons. From

ἐπ-ανασείω, f. σω, *to lift up and shake, to brandish.*

ἐπανάστᾰσις, εως, ἡ, (ἐπανίστημι) *a rising up against, an insurrection.*

ἐπαναστήσομαι, fut. med. of ἐπανίστημι.

ἐπ-αναστρέφω, f. ψω, intr. *to turn back upon, resist:*—Med. *to wheel round, return to the charge.*

ἐπ-ανατείνω, f. -τενῶ, *to hold up towards; ἐπανατείνειν ἐλπίδας to hold out* hopes.

ἐπ-ανατέλλω, f. -ανατελῶ: aor. 1 -ανέτειλα:—*to lift up, raise.* II. intr. *to rise up, rise,* of the sun; ἐπαντέλλων χρόνος the time *which is coming to light*, the future.

ἐπ-ανατίθημι, f. –θήσω, *to lay upon.*

ἐπ-αναφέρω poët. **ἐπ-αμφέρω**, *to throw back upon* another, *ascribe* or *refer to.* 2. *to put into the account.* 3. *to bring back a message.* II. Pass. *to be borne up, rise*, as an exhalation.

ἐπ-αναφῡσάω, f. ήσω, *to play on the flute in accompaniment.*

ἐπ-αναχωρέω, f. ήσω, *to go back again, retreat, return.* Hence

ἐπαναχώρησις, εως, ἡ, *a return, retreat.*

ἐπ-άνειμι, *to go back, return.* II. *to go up, arise.*

ἐπανεῖναι, **ἐπανείς**, aor. 2 inf. and part. of ἐπανίημι.

ἐπανεῖπον, aor. 2, *to proclaim* or *promise openly*:—the pres. in use is ἐπαναγορεύω.

ἐπ-ανεί[illegible]ομαι, Ion. for ἐπανέρομαι.

ἐπανελθεῖν, **ἐπανελθών**, aor. 2 inf. and part. of ἐπανέρχομαι.

ἐπ-ανέρομαι Ion. **–είρομαι**, *to question again and again*: generally, *to question.*

ἐπ-ανέρχομαι, f. –ελεύσομαι: Dep., with aor. 2 act. –ῆλθον, pf. –ελήλυθα: (cf. ἔρχομαι):—*to go back, return*: *to go over, pass over.* II. *to go up, ascend.*

ἐπ-ανήκω, *to have come back, return.*

ἐπ-ανθέω, f. ήσω, *to bloom, be in flower*: metaph. of a salt crust *forming upon a surface*, or of down *on the cheeks*: generally, *to be upon the surface, appear plainly.*

ἐπ-ανθίζω, f. ίσω Att. ιῶ, (ἐπί, ἄνθος) *to deck with flowers*: generally, *to make to abound, to cover over with.*

ἐπανθρᾰκίδες, ων, αἱ, *small fish for frying.* From

ἐπ-ανθρακίζω, f. σω, *to broil on the coals.*

ἐπ-ανίημι, f. –ανήσω, *to let go back, relax, dismiss.* II. intr. with gen., *to relax from*: *to flag.*

ἐπ-ανῐσόω, f. ώσω, *to make equal, put on a par.*

ἐπ-ανίστημι, f. –στήσω, *to set up again*: *to make to rise.* II. Pass., with aor. 2 act. –ανέστην, pf. –ανέστηκα, intrans. *to stand up after* or *at the bidding of* another: generally, *to stand up, rise*; of things, *to be high, elevated.* 2. *to rise up against* one, *revolt.*

ἐπ-ανορθόω, f. ώσω: augm. tenses with double augm., impf. ἐπηνώρθουν, aor. 1 ἐπηνώρθωσα, etc.:—*to set up, set upright*: *to set up again*: generally, *to amend, improve.* Hence

ἐπανόρθωσις, εως, ἡ, *a correcting*: *amendment.*

ἐπ-αντέλλω, poët. and Ion. for ἐπανατέλλω.

ἐπ-άντης, ες, (ἐπί, ἄντα) *up-hill*, opp. to κατάντης.

ἐπ-αντιάζω, f. άσω, *to fall in with, meet.*

ἐπ-αντλέω, f. ήσω, *to pump over*: *to pour over*: Pass. *to be overflowed* or *filled.*

ἐπ-ᾰνύω, f. ύσω [ῠ], *to complete*:—Med. *to procure for.*

ἐπ-άνω, Adv. (ἐπί, ἄνω) *above, on the upper side*: with Art., ὁ ἐπάνω πύργος the *upper* tower. II. of Time, *before.* Hence

ἐπάνωθεν, poët. –θε, Adv. *from above, above*: οἱ ἐπ. *men of former time.*

ἐπ-άξιος, ον, and α, ον, (ἐπί, ἄξιος) *worthy, deserving of*, c. gen.: absol. *worthy, meet.* 2. *worth mentioning*:—Adv. –ίως. Hence

ἐπ-αξιόω, f. ώσω, *to think worthy, think right*, c. inf., Lat. *dignor.* II. *to expect, believe.*

ἐπ-αξόνιος, ον, (ἐπί, ἄξων) *upon an axle.*

ἐπάξω, Dor. 2 sing. aor. 1 med. of πήγνυμι.

ἐπᾰοιδή, ἡ, (ἐπαείδω) poët. and Ion. for ἐπῳδή.

ἐπᾰοιδός, ὁ, poët. for ἐπῳδός.

ἐπ-ᾰπειλέω, f. ήσω, *to hold out a threat to* one: *to add threats, to threaten besides.*

ἐπ-αποδύομαι, Med. *to strip and set to work at* a thing.

ἐπ-αποθνήσκω, f. –θανοῦμαι, *to die with* or *after.*

ἐπ-αποπνίγω, f. ξω, *to choke besides*; aor. 2 pass. ἐπαπεπνίγην [ῐ].

ἐπ-άπτω, Ion. for ἐφάπτω.

ἐπ-ᾱπύω, Dor. for ἐπηπύω.

ἐπ-αρά Ion. **ἐπ-αρή**, ἡ, (ἐπί, ἀρά) *a solemn curse, imprecation.* Hence

ἐπ-αράομαι: f. άσομαι Ep. ήσομαι; pf. ἐπήρᾱμαι: Dep.:—*to imprecate curses upon*; ἐπαρᾶσθαι λόγον to utter an imprecation.

ἐπ-αραρίσκω, f. ἐπάρσω: aor. 1 ἐπῆρσα:—*to fit to* or *upon, fasten to.* II. intr. in pf. med. ἐπάρηρα, *to fit well*: part. ἐπαρηρώς, *close-fitting*; so also ἐπάρμενος, η, ον.

ἐπάρας, aor. 1 part. of ἐπαίρω.

ἐπ-ᾰράσσω Att. **–ττω**, f. ξω, *to dash to.*

ἐπάρατος, ον, (ἐπαράομαι) *laid under a curse.*

ἐπ-άργεμος, ον, (ἐπί, ἄργεμος) of the eye, *with a white speck over it.* II. metaph. *dim, obscure.*

ἐπ-άργῠρος, ον, (ἐπί, ἄργυρος) *overlaid with silver.*

ἐπ-ᾰρήγω, f. ξω, *to come to aid, help.* Hence

ἐπάρηξις, εως, ἡ, *help, aid.*

ἐπάρηρα, –ειν, intr. pf. and plqpf. of ἐπαραρίσκω.

ἐπ-ᾰρίστερος, ον, (ἐπί, ἀριστερός) *on the left hand*: *left-handed, awkward*, French *gauche.*

ἐπάρκεσις, εως, ἡ, *aid, help, succour.* From

ἐπ-αρκέω, f. έσω: aor. 1 ἐπήρκησα:—*to ward off*, τινί τι something from one. 2. c. acc. rei only, *to hinder, prevent.* 3. c. dat. pers. only, *to help, aid, protect.* II. *to supply, furnish, impart.* III. absol. *to be sufficient, enough.* Hence

ἐπαρκούντως, Adv. pres. part., *sufficiently.*

ἐπάρμενος, Ep. aor. 2 part. pass. of ἐπαραρίσκω, *well-fitted, well-prepared.*

ἐπ-άρουρος, ον, (ἐπί, ἄρουρα) *on the soil, attached to the soil* as a serf, Lat. *adscriptus glebae.*

ἐπ-αρτάω, f. ήσω, *to hang on* or *over*:—Pass., φόβος ἐπήρτηται fear *hangs over, impends.*

ἐπ-αρτής, ές, (ἐπί, ἀρτέω) *ready, equipped.*

ἐπ-αρτύω and **–αρτύνω**, *to fit* or *fix on.* II. *to get ready, prepare*:—Med. *to prepare for oneself.*

ἐπαρχία, ἡ, *a prefecture, province.* From

ἔπ-αρχος, ον, (ἐπί, ἀρχή) *a commander: a governor of a country, prefect.*

ἐπ-άρχω, f. ξω, *to be an* ἔπαρχος, *governor of a province.* 2. *to rule in addition to* one's own dominions. II. Med. ἐπάρχομαι, *to begin anew, afresh;* ἐπάρξασθαι δεπάεσσιν *to begin with* the cups *again:* generally, *to supply, distribute.*

ἐπᾰρωγός, ὁ, (ἐπαρήγω) *a helper, aider.*

ἐπαρῴνουν, impf. of παροινέω.

ἐπᾰσάμην, aor. 1 of πατέομαι.

ἐπ-ασκέω, f. ήσω: aor. 1 -ήσκησα :—*to labour at, finish carefully.* II. *to adorn.* III. *to practise, practise oneself in, cultivate.*

ἐπ-ασσύτερος, α, ον, (ἐπί, ἆσσον) *one upon another, one after another.*

ἐπασσῦτερο-τρῐβής, ές, (ἐπασσύτερος, τρίβω) *following close one on the other.*

ἐπ-αστράπτω, f. ψω, *to lighten upon, flash.*

ἐπ-ᾴττω, Att. for ἐπαΐσσω, q. v.

ἐπ-αυδάω, f. ήσω, *to say besides*:—Med. *to call upon.*

ἐπαύθην or ἐπαύσθην, aor. 1 pass. of παύω.

ἐπ-αυλέω, f. ήσω: pf. pass. ἐπηύλημαι: (ἐπί, αὐλός): —*to play the flute to accompany*:—Pass. *to be played on the flute.*

ἐπ-αυλίζομαι, f. ισομαι, Dep. *to take up one's quarters at* a place.

ἔπ-αυλις, εως, ἡ, (ἐπί, αὖλις) *a place to pass the night in: quarters.*

ἔπ-αυλος, ὁ, (ἐπί, αὐλή) plur. ἔπαυλοι, οἱ, and ἔπαυλα, τά, *a fold for* cattle: generally, *a dwelling, home.*

ἐπ-αυξάνω or ἐπ-αύξω, f. -αυξήσω, *to increase, enlarge, augment*:—Pass. *to grow, increase.*

ἐπαυρεῖν Ep. -έμεν, aor. 2 inf. of ἐπαυρίσκομαι.

ἐπ-αυρέω, = ἐπαυρίσκομαι.

ἐπ-αύρεσις, εως, ἡ, (ἐπαυρίσκομαι) *the fruit, result of* a thing: *enjoyment, fruition.*

ἐπ-αύριον, Adv., for ἐπ' αὔριον, *on the morrow.*

ἐπ-αυρίσκομαι, Dep. (the Act. ἐπαυρίσκω occurs only once, and the simple αὐρίσκω or αὐρίσκομαι, *to take,* is not in use): fut. ἐπαυρήσομαι: aor. 2 act. ἐπηῦρον Dor. ἐπαῦρον, 3 sing. subj. ἐπαύρῃ, inf. ἐπαυρεῖν Ep. -έμεν: aor. 2 med. ἐπηυρόμην, Ep. 2 sing. subj. ἐπαύρηαι, 3 pl. -ωνται:—*to partake of, enjoy a share of: to reach, touch*:—Med. *to reap the fruits* of a thing, whether good or bad, c. gen.: more freq. in bad sense, ἵνα πάντες ἐπαύρωνται βασιλῆος that all *may have a benefit of their* king; ὀΐω μιν ἐπαυρήσεσθαι I think *he will feel the consequences.* 2. c. acc. *to bring upon oneself.*

ἐπάῦσον, aor. 1 imperat. of ἐπαΰω: ἐπαΰσας, part.

ἐπ-αῦτέω, f. ήσω, *to shout at* a thing: *to make a noise beside.* [ῡ]

ἐπ-αυτοφώρῳ, Adv., for ἐπ' αὐτοφώρῳ, Lat. *in ipso furto, in the very theft* or *very act.*

ἐπ-αυχένιος, ον, (ἐπί, αὐχήν) *on* or *for the neck.*

ἐπ-αυχέω, f. ήσω, *to boast of, exult in.*

ἐπ-ᾰΰω, f. -αύσω [ῡ], *to shout over* or *upon.*

ἐπ-αφαυαίνομαι, Pass. *to be dried up, worn out.*

ἐπ-ᾰφάω, f. ήσω, *to touch on the surface, stroke.*

ἐπᾰφή, ἡ, (ἐπαφάω) *a touch, handling.*

ἐπ-αφίημι, f. -αφήσω, *to throw at* a thing: *to let loose upon.*

ἐπ-αφρίζω, f. σω, *to foam up* or *on the surface:* metaph. *to babble, divulge.*

ἐπ-αφρόδῑτος, ον, (ἐπί, Ἀφροδίτη) *lovely, fascinating,* Lat. *venustus.*

ἐπ-αφύσσω, f. ύσω [ῠ], *to pour over* or *in addition.*

ἐπαχθής, ές, (ἐπί, ἄχθος) *heavy, ponderous: oppressive, grievous.*

ἐπ-άχθομαι, Pass. *to be distressed at* a thing.

ἐπ-αχλύω, f. ύσω [ῡ], (ἐπί, ἀχλύς) *to be obscure.*

ἐπαχύνθην, aor. 1 pass. of παχύνω.

ἐπεάν, Ion. for ἐπήν.

ἐπέβᾰλον, aor. 2 of ἐπιβάλλω.

ἐπέβην, ἐπέβησα, aor. 2 and 1 of ἐπιβαίνω.

ἐπεβίων, aor. 2 of ἐπιβιόω (as if from ἐπιβίωμι).

ἐπέβρῑσα, aor. 1 of ἐπιβρίθω.

ἐπ-εγγελάω, f. άσομαι [ᾰ], *to laugh at, deride.*

ἐπεγέγραπτο, 3 plqpf. pass. of ἐπιγράφω.

ἐπ-εγείρω, f. -εγερῶ, *to awaken, rouse up: to excite:* —Pass. *to be roused, rise:* ἐπέγρετο, ἐπεγρόμενος, 3 sing. ind. and part. Ep. aor. 2 pass. II. intrans. in pf. part. act. ἐπεγρηγορώς, *awake.*

ἐπ-εγκᾰλέω, f. έσω, *to bring a charge against.*

ἐπ-εγκάπτω, f. ψω, *to snap up, devour.*

ἐπ-εγκελεύω, f. σω, *to give an order* or *signal to* others.

ἐπέγρετο, 3 sing. Ep. aor. 2 pass. of ἐπεγείρω.

ἐπέγνων, aor. 2 of ἐπιγιγνώσκω.

ἐπεγρήγορα, see ἐπεγείρω II.

ἐπεγρόμενος, Ep. aor. 2 part. pass. of ἐπεγείρω.

ἐπ-εγχέω, f. -χεῶ, *to pour in upon* or *in addition.*

ἐπέδεξα, Ion. for ἐπέδειξα, aor. 1 of ἐπιδείκνυμι.

ἐπέδησα, aor. 1 of πεδάω.

ἐπεδόθην, aor. 1 pass. of ἐπιδίδωμι.

ἐπέδρᾰμον, aor. 2 act. of ἐπιτρέχω.

ἐπέδρη, ἡ, Ion. for ἐφέδρα.

ἐπέδῡν, aor. 2 of ἐπιδύω.

ἐπέθηκα, aor. 1 of ἐπιτίθημι.

ἐπεί Ep. also ἐπειή, (ἐπί) Conjunct.: I. OF TIME, *after that, when: from the time when* II. OF CAUSE, *since, seeing that, for that.* III. ἐπεὶ ἄρ, ἐπεὶ ἄρα, *when then, since then.* 2. ἐπεὶ οὖν *when then.* 3. ἐπεί περ *since really.*

ἘΠΕΙ΄ΓΩ, f. ξω: impf. ἤπειγον Ep. ἔπειγον: aor. 1 ἤπειξα:—Pass., fut. med. ἐπείξομαι (in pass. sense): aor. 1 ἠπείχθην:—*to press upon, weigh down*:—Pass. *to be weighed down.* 2. *to press hard, press upon,* in pursuit. II. *to drive on, urge forward, hasten, hurry on*:—Med. *to urge on for oneself:* Pass. *to haste to* do: also absol., *to hasten, hurry, speed:* part. ἐπειγόμενος as Adj., *swift, impetuous, eager.* III. intrans. = Pass. *to make haste.*

ἐπειδ-άν, Conjunction (ἐπειδὴ ἄν) *whenever, so soon as, after that.*

ἐπει-δή, (ἐπεὶ δή) Conjunction, I. of Time, *since, after that*, Lat *postquam*. II. of Cause, *seeing that, since, because*:—so **ἐπειδήπερ**, *since really, since now*.

ἐπ-εῖδον, inf. ἐπιδεῖν, aor. 2 without pres. in use (ἐφοράω being used instead), *to look upon, behold, see*. 2. *to continue to see, to live to see: to experience*.

ἐπειή or **ἐπεὶ ἦ**, Adv. *since certainly*.

ἐπείη, 3 sing. opt. of ἔπειμι.

ἐπ-εικάζω, f. σω, *to make like to* a thing; δάμαρτα τήνδ' ἐπεικάζων κυρῶ; am I right in *supposing* her his wife? II. generally, *to conjecture, infer, conclude*; ὡς or ὅσ' ἐπεικάσαι so far as *one may guess*.

ἐπείκεν, ἐπείκε, or **ἐπεί κεν, ἐπεί κε**, Ep. for ἐπεάν, ἐπήν.

ἐπείληφα, -ημμαι, pf. act. and pass. of ἐπιλαμβάνω.

ἔπ-ειμι, inf. ἐπεῖναι: impf. ἐπῆν: fut. ἐπέσομαι: (ἐπί, εἰμί *sum*):—*to be upon* or *at*. II. *to be upon, be fixed upon*: of rewards and penalties, *to be imposed*. III. of Time, *to be hereafter: to be coming on, to impend*. IV. *to be set over*, Lat. *praeesse*. V. *to be added, be over and above*.

ἔπ-ειμι, inf. ἐπιέναι: Ep. impf. ἐπήϊα, ας, ε, 3 pl. ἐπήϊσαν, ἐπῇσαν: fut. ἐπιείσομαι: aor. I med. part. ἐπιεισαμένη: (ἐπί, εἶμι *ibo*):—*to go* or *come to* or *towards: to come upon*: absol. *to come near, approach*. 2. *to come against, attack*; οἱ ἐπιόντες *the invaders, assailants*. 3. of events, *to come upon* one, *overtake*. 4. *to come on the stage*. II. of Time, *to come on* or *after, to follow, succeed*; ἡ ἐπιοῦσα ἡμέρα the *coming* day; ὁ ἐπιών, like ὁ τυχών, *the first comer*: τὸ ἐπιόν *what occurs* to one. III. *to traverse, pass over*. IV. *to go over*, i. e. *count over*.

ἐπ-είνῦμι, Ion. for ἐφέννυμι: inf. med. **ἐπείνυσθαι**, Ion. for ἐφέννυσθαι.

ἐπεί-περ, for ἐπεί περ, Conj. *since really, seeing that*.

ἐπ-εῖπον, aor. 2 without pres. in use, *to say besides: to say of* another:—inf. ἐπειπεῖν, part. ἐπείπων.

ἔπειρα, aor. I of πείρω.

ἐπείρομαι, Ion. for ἐπέρομαι.

ἐπειρυσάμενος, Ion. aor. I part. med. of ἐπερύω.

ἐπειρώατο, Ion. 3 pl. impf. of πειράομαι.

ἐπειρωτέω, Ion. for ἐπερωτάω.

ἐπ-ειρώτημα, -ησις, Ion. for ἐπερώτημα, -ησις.

ἔπεισα, aor. I of πείθω.

ἐπ-εισᾰγωγή, ἡ, (ἐπί, εἰσάγω) *a bringing in besides*. II. *a means of bringing* or *letting in*.

ἐπ-είσακτος, ον, (ἐπί, εἰσάγω) *brought in from abroad, alien: imported, foreign*.

ἐπ-εισβαίνω, f. -βήσομαι, *to go into upon: to enter*.

ἐπ-εισβάλλω, f. -βαλῶ, *to pour into besides*. II. intr. *to invade again*.

ἐπεισβάτης, ου, ὁ, (ἐπεισβαίνω) *an additional passenger, supernumerary on board* ship. [ᾰ]

ἐπ-είσειμι, *to come on besides: to come on the stage*.

ἐπ-εισέρχομαι, Dep., with aor. 2 act. -ῆλθον, pf. -ελήλυθα: *to come in upon* or *over: to come in after*. 2. *come into* or *enter besides*: of things, *to be imported*.

ἐπεισέφρησα, aor. I of ἐπεισφρέω.

ἐπ-εισκυκλέω, f. ήσω, *to roll in* or *on besides*.

ἐπεισόδιος, ον, *coming in besides, episodic*. From

ἐπ-είσοδος, ον, *a coming in besides, an entrance*.

ἐπ-εισπαίω, f. παιήσω, *to burst in*.

ἐπ-εισπηδάω, f. ήσω or ήσομαι, *to leap in upon*.

ἐπ-εισπίπτω, f. -πεσοῦμαι: aor. 2 -έπεσον:—*to fall* or *burst upon: to burst in*.

ἐπ-εισπλέω, f. -πλεύσομαι, *to sail in after: to sail at, attack*.

ἐπ-εισφέρω, f. -οίσω, *to bring in besides* or *after: to entail upon*: Med. *to bring in for oneself*.

ἐπ-εισφρέω, f. ήσω, *to introduce besides*.

ἔπ-ειτα, Adv. (ἐπί, εἶτα) marks the Sequence of one thing *upon* another: *thereupon, thereafter, then*, Lat. *deinde*. II. when a clause precedes it is emphatic: I. when a partic. of Time goes before, *then*; ἐπειδὴ σφαίρῃ πειρήσαντο, ὠρχείσθην δὴ ἔπειτα when they *finished* playing at ball, *then* they danced. 2. after εἰ, *then surely*; εἰ δ' ἐτεὸν δὴ ἀγορεύεις, ἐξ ἄρα δή τοι ἔπειτα θεοὶ φρένας ὤλεσαν if so, *then of a surety* have the gods infatuated thee. III. Interrog., when the question is founded on some supposition, after πῶς; εἰ μὲν δὴ ἕταρόν γε κελεύετέ μ' αὐτὸν ἑλέσθαι, πῶς ἂν ἔπειτ' Ὀδυσῆος λαθοίμην; how can I *in such a case* forget Ulysses? In Att., it begins the sentence, in an ironical sense, *And so? Indeed?* IV. *then, therefore*, much like οὖν. V. *and yet, nevertheless, still*. VI. with the Article, *the following, the future*; ὁ ἔπειτα χρόνος *the* time *to come*.

ἐπεί-τε, or **ἐπεί τε**, *since, for that, because*.

ἔπειτεν, Ion. for ἔπειτα, *thereupon, thereafter*.

ἐπεί-τοι, i. e. ἐπεί τοι, *for in truth, since truly*.

ἐπ-εκβαίνω, f. -βήσομαι, *to go out upon, disembark*.

ἐπ-εκβοηθέω, f. ήσω, *to rush out to aid*.

ἐπ-εκδῐκάσκω, f. άξω, *to teach in addition*.

ἐπ-εκδιηγέομαι, Dep. *to explain besides*.

ἐπεκδρομή, ἡ, (ἐπεκδραμεῖν, aor. 2 of ἐπεκτρέχω) *an excursion* or *expedition against*.

ἐπεκέατο, Ion. for ἐπέκειντο, 3 pl. impf. of ἐπίκειμαι.

ἐπ-έκεινα, Adv., for ἐπ' ἐκεῖνα, *on yonder side of, beyond*; οἱ ἐπέκεινα Εὐφράτου those *beyond* the Euphrates; τὸ ἐπέκεινα Att. τοὐπέκεινα, *the part beyond*; τὰ ἐπέκεινα *the parts beyond*. 2. of Time, οἱ ἐπέκεινα χρόνοι the times *beyond* or *before, earlier* times.

ἐπεκέκλετο, 3 sing. Ep. aor. 2 of ἐπικέλομαι.

ἐπέκελσα, aor. I of ἐπικέλλω.

ἐπέκερσα, aor. I of ἐπικείρω.

ἐπ-εκθέω, f. θεύσομαι, *to rush out against*.

ἐπέκλωσαν, ἐπεκλώσαντο, 3 pl. aor. I act. and med. of ἐπικλώθω.

ἐπ-εκπίνω, f. -πίομαι, *to drink off after*.

ἐπ-έκπλοος contr. **-έκπλους**, ὁ, *a sailing out against, an attack by sea*.

ἐπ-εκτείνω, f. -τενῶ, *to stretch out, lengthen*:—Pass. *to extend beyond*: also *to reach out towards, grasp at.*

ἐπ-εκτρέχω, f. -εκδρᾰμοῦμαι: aor. 2 -εξέδρᾰμον (from obsol. δρέμω):—*to rush out upon* or *against* one, *rush out to attack.*

ἐπ-εκφέρω, f. -οίσω, *to carry out far.*

ἐπ-εκχωρέω, f. ήσω, *to advance next* or *after.*

ἐπελάβετο, 3 sing. aor. 2 med. of ἐπιλαμβάνω.

ἐπελαθόμην, aor. 2 med. of ἐπιλανθάνω.

ἐπέλᾰσις, εως, ἡ, *an attack*, *assault.* From

ἐπ-ελαύνω: f. -ελάσω Att. -ελῶ: aor. 1 -ήλασα: pf. -ελήλακα: Pass., pf. -ελήλαμαι: 3 sing. plqpf. ἐπελήλατο:—*to drive upon: to lead on* or *against.* 2. seemingly intr. (sub. στρατόν), *to march against*: also *to sail against*: *to charge.* II. *to beat out thin upon*, as a plate of metal on a shield.

ἐπέλειβον, impf. of ἐπιλείβω.

ἐπελέλειπτο, 3 sing. plqpf. pass. of ἐπιλείπω.

ἐπελήκεον, impf. of ἐπιληκέω.

ἐπελήλᾰτο, 2 sing. plqpf. pass. of ἐπελαύνω.

ἐπελήλῠθα, pf. of ἐπέρχομαι.

ἐπέλησα, aor. 1 of ἐπιληθάνω.

ἐπελθεῖν, aor. 2 inf. of ἐπέρχομαι.

ἐπ-ελίσσω, **ἐπ-έλκω**, Ion. for ἐφελίσσω, ἐφέλκω.

ἐπέλλᾰβε, poët. aor. 2 of ἐπιλαμβάνω.

ἐπ-ελπίζω, f. σω, *to bring to hope, buoy up with hopes, cheat with false hopes.* II. *to hope*, = ἐλπίζω.

ἐπ-έλπομαι Ep. **ἐπι-έλπομαι**, Dep. *to have hopes of, to hope*: generally, *to expect.*

ἐπεμάνην [ᾰ], aor. 2 of ἐπιμαίνομαι.

ἐπεμάσσατο, 3 sing. Ep. aor. 1 of ἐπιμαίομαι.

ἐπ-εμβᾰδόν, Adv. *step upon step, ascendingly.*

ἐπ-εμβαίνω, f. -βήσομαι: aor. 2 ἐπενέβην, part. ἐπεμβάς:—*to step* or *tread upon*: *to stand on*, esp. in pf. ἐπεμβέβηκα Ep. -βέβαα, ας, οὐδοῦ ἐπεμβεβάως; also c. dat., πύργοις ἐπεμβάς. II. *to trample upon, insult.*

ἐπ-εμβάλλω, f. -βᾰλῶ, *to put on* or *over.* 2. *to throw down upon.* 3. *to put in besides, insert.* 4. *to put forward.* II. intr. *to flow in besides*, of rivers.

ἐπεμβάτης, ου, ὁ, (ἐπεμβαίνω) *one mounted, a horseman.*

ἐπεμβεβᾰώς, Ep. pf. part. of ἐπεμβαίνω.

ἐπέμεινα, aor. 1 of ἐπιμένω.

ἐπ-εμηλησάμην, **-εμηλήθην**, aor. 1 med. and pass. of ἐπιμελέομαι.

ἐπεμήνατο, 3 sing. aor. 1 med. of ἐπιμαίνομαι.

ἐπέμιξα, aor. 1 of ἐπιμίγνυμι.

ἐπ-εμπηδάω, f. ήσω or ήσομαι, *to leap upon, insult.*

ἐπ-εμπίπτω, f. -πεσοῦμαι, *to fall in* or *upon, to attack*; ἐπεμπίπτειν βάσιν τινί *to advance* one's foot *towards* a thing. 2. *to fall to, set to work.*

ἐπ-ενᾰρίζω, f. ξω, *to slay one upon another.*

ἐπενάχετο, Dor. 3 sing. impf. of ἐπινήχομαι.

ἐπ-ενδίδωμι, f. -δώσω, *to give over and above.*

ἐπενδύτης, ου, ὁ, *a tunic worn over* another, *an outer* or *over tunic.* From

ἐπ-ενδύνω, *to put on over*:—Pass. *to have on over.*

ἐπενεῖκαι, Ion. for ἐπενέγκαι, aor. 1 inf. of ἐπιφέρω.

ἐπένειμα, aor. 1 of ἐπινέμω.

ἐπένευσα, aor. 1 of ἐπινεύω.

ἐπενήνεον, impf. of ἐπινηνέω

ἐπ-ενήνοθε, (ἐπί, ἐνήνοθε) 3 sing. pf., with no pres. ἐπενέθω in use:—*there has grown upon, there is* or *was upon*; used three times by Hom.:—ψεδνὴ ἐπενήνοθε λάχνη thin downy hair *grew thereon*; οὔλη ἐπενήνοθε λάχνη a thick warm pile *was on it*: c. acc., οἷα θεοὺς ἐπενήνοθεν αἰὲν ἐόντας such as *appertains to* the gods.

ἐπένησα, aor. 1 of ἐπινέω (A).

ἐπ-ενθρώσκω, f. -ενθοροῦμαι: aor. 2 -ενέθορον, inf. -ενθορεῖν:—*to leap upon*; ἐπενθρώσκειν ἄνω *to leap* up *into.*

ἐπενθών, Dor. aor. 2 part. of ἐπέρχομαι.

ἐπεντᾰθείς, aor. 1 pass. part. of ἐπεντείνω.

ἐπ-εντᾰνύω, f. ύσω [ῠ], Ep. for ἐπεντείνω, *to stretch upon, bind fast to.*

ἐπ-εντείνω, f. -εντενῶ, *to stretch upon* or *over*; part. aor. 1 pass. ἐπεντᾰθεὶς *stretched upon* his sword. II. intr. *to press on*: *to gain ground*, of a report.

ἐπ-εντέλλω, *to command besides.*

ἐπ-εντύω and **-εντύνω**, *to get ready, equip*:—Med. *to train oneself for* a thing.

ἐπ-εξάγω, *to lead out* an army:—intr. *to march out.* Hence

ἐπεξᾰγωγή, ἡ, *a drawing out against, lengthening.*

ἐπ-έξειμι, inf. -εξιέναι: impf. ἐπεξῄειν:—*to go out against* an enemy. II. *to proceed against, prosecute.* III. *to go over, traverse, go through*: hence *to detail.* 2. ἐπεξιέναι τιμωρίας μείζους *to go through with, execute* greater vengeance.

ἐπ-εξελαύνω: f. -εξελάσω Att. -εξελῶ: pf. -εξελήλᾰκα:—*to drive on against*:—intr. *to ride on against.*

ἐπεξελθεῖν, aor. 2 inf. of ἐπεξέρχομαι.

ἐπ-εξεργάζομαι, f. άσομαι, Dep. *to effect besides* or *in addition*: *to consummate.* 2. *to slay over again.*

ἐπ-εξέρχομαι, f. -ελεύσομαι, Dep. with aor. 2 act. -εξῆλθον, pf. -εξελήλῠθα:—*to go out against* an enemy. 2. *to proceed against, prosecute.* II. *to go over, traverse.* 2. *to execute, accomplish.* 3. *to discuss, detail, investigate.* III. *to proceed to an extremity*; ὧδ' ἐπεξέρχεσθαι θρασύς *to reach* such *a pitch* of boldness.

ἐπ-εξέτᾰσις, εως, ἡ, *a review over again.*

ἐπ-εξευρίσκω, f. -ευρήσω, *to invent besides.*

ἐπ-εξῆς, Ion. for ἐφ-εξῆς.

ἐπ-εξιακχάζω, (ἐπί, ἐξ, Ἴακχος) *to shout in triumph over.*

ἐπ-εξόδιος, ον, *of a march* or *expedition*: τὰ ἐπεξόδια (sub. ἱερά), sacrifices *before the march of an army.* From

ἐπ-έξοδος, ἡ, *a march out against, expedition.*

ἐπ-έοικε, 3 sing. pf. with no pres. ἐπείκω in use:—*it is like, looks like, resembles.* II. *it is likely,* *reasonable, fitting*:—ἐπεικότα Att. for ἐπεοικότα, part. pf., *what is seemly, fit.*

ἐπέπεσον, aor. 2 of ἐπιπίπτω.

ἐπεπήγει, 3 sing. plqpf. of πήγνυμι.

ἐπέπιθμεν, for ἐπεποίθειμεν, 1 pl. plqpf. of πείθω.

ἐπέπλως, 2 sing. Ep. aor. 2 of ἐπιπλέω.

ἐπεποίθει, 3 sing. plqpf. of πείθω.

ἐπεπόνθει, 3 sing. plqpf. of πάσχω.

ἐπέπτᾰρον, aor. 2 of ἐπιπταίρω.

ἐπέπτᾰτο, 3 sing. aor. 2 of ἐπιπέταμαι.

ἐπέπυστο, 3 sing. plqpf. pass of πυνθάνομαι.

ἐπ-έπω, Ion. for ἐφέπω.

ἐπ-εργάζομαι, f. άσομαι, Dep. *to work upon* land, *till, cultivate.* Hence

ἐπεργᾰσία, ἡ, *a working* of another's land: *an encroachment.* II. *the right of mutual tillage* on each other's land.

ἐπ-ερεθίζω, f. σω, *to stimulate.*

ἐπ-ερείδω, f. -ερείσω, *to urge on with all one's force*; ἐπέρεισεν ἶν' ἀπέλεθρον he *applied* vast strength *to* it:—Pass. *to lean* or *bear heavily upon.*

ἐπ-ερέφω, f. ψω, *to cover with a roof*

ἐπερήρεισμαι, pf. pass. of ἐπερείδω.

ἐπ-έρομαι Ion. **-είρομαι**: f. -ερήσομαι Ion. -ειρήσομαι: aor. 2 ἐπηρόμην, inf. ἐπερέσθαι:—*to ask, to consult, question.*

ἐπέρριψα, aor. 1 of ἐπιρρίπτω.

ἐπερρώσαντο, 3 pl. aor. 1 of ἐπιρρώομαι.

ἐπερρώσθην, **ἐπέρρωσμαι**, aor. 1 and pf. pass. of ἐπιρρώννυμι.

ἐπέρυσσα, Ep. aor. 1 of ἐπερύω.

ἐπ-ερύω, f. -ερύσω [ῠ]: aor. 1 -είρῠσα:—*to draw on, pull to*: *to bring to* a place:—Med. *to draw on one's* clothes.

ἐπ-έρχομαι, f. -ελεύσομαι, Dep., with aor. 2 act. -ῆλθον Ep. -ήλῠθον, pf. -ελήλῠθα:—*to go* or *come to* or *towards*: *to come upon*, esp. *to come suddenly* or *unexpectedly upon.* 2. in hostile sense, *to come* or *go against, attack.* 3. *to come forward* to speak. II. *to come on, come about, return*; ἐπήλυθον ὧραι *the* seasons *came round again.* III. *to come in after* or *over the head of* another. IV. *to occur to one, come into one's mind.* V. *to go over* a space, *traverse, visit.* 2. *to go through* or *over discuss, recount.* 3. *to go through, execute.*

ἐπ-ερωτάω Ion. **ἐπειρ-**, fut. ήσω, *to consult, inquire of, question, ask about* a thing:—Pass. *to be questioned, asked.* Hence

ἐπερώτημα Ion. **ἐπειρ-**, ατος, τό, *a question*: and

ἐπερώτησις Ion. **ἐπειρ-**, εως, ἡ *a questioning.*

ἔπεσα, rare aor. 1 of πίπτω.

ἔπεσαν, Ep. 3 pl. impf. of ἔπειμι (εἰμί *sum*)

ἐπεσβαίνω, = ἐπεισβαίνω.

ἐπεσβολία, ἡ, *a using words at random, hasty speech, unseemly language.* From

ἐπεσ-βόλος, ον, (ἔπος, βάλλω) *throwing words about*: *rash-talking, scurrilous.*

ἐπ-εσθίω, f. ἐπέδομαι, *to eat after* or *in addition to.*

ἐπεσκεψάμην, aor. 1 of ἐπισκοπέω.

ἐπεσκίασμαι, pf. pass. of ἐπισκιάζω.

ἔπεσον, aor. 2 of πίπτω.

ἔπεσπον, aor. 2 of ἐφέπω.

ἐπέσσεται, Ep. 3 sing. fut. of ἔπειμι (εἰμί *sum*).

ἐπέσσευεν, Ep. 3 sing. impf. of ἐπισεύω.

ἐπεσσεύοντο, 3 pl. impf. med. of ἐπισεύω.

ἐπέσσῠμαι, pf. pass. of ἐπισεύω, part. ἐπεσσῠμένος.

ἐπέσσῠτο, poët. for ἐπέσυτο, 3 sing. Ep. syncop. plqpf. pass. of ἐπισεύω, in sense of aor. 2.

ἐπεστάλθην, **ἐπεστάλην** [ᾰ], aor. 1 and aor. 2 pass. of ἐπιστέλλω.

ἐπέσταλτο, 3 sing. plqpf. pass. of ἐπιστέλλω.

ἐπεστράφην [ᾰ], aor. 2 pass. of ἐπιστρέφω.

ἐπεστέως, Ion. pf. part. of ἐφίστημι.

ἐπέστην, aor. 2 of ἐφίστημι.

ἐπεσφέρω, Ion. for ἐπεισφέρω.

ἐπ-εσχάριος, ον, (ἐπί, ἐσχάρα) *on the hearth.*

ἐπ-έσχεθον, poët. aor. 2 of ἐπέχω.

ἐπ-έσχον, **-εσχόμην**, aor. 2 act. and med. of ἐπέχω.

ἐπέτᾰμον, aor. 2 of τέμνω.

ἐπέταξα, **ἐπετάχθην**, aor. 1 act. and pass. of ἐπιτάσσω.

ἐπ-έτειος, ον, and **ἐπ-έτεος**, ον, (ἐπί, ἔτος) *annual, yearly, every year*: *changeable as the seasons.* 2. *annual, lasting for a year.*

ἐπετετάχατο, Ion. 3 pl. plqpf. pass. of ἐπιτάσσω.

ἐπετήδευσα, aor. 1 of ἐπιτηδεύω.

ἐπέτης, ου, ὁ, (ἕπομαι) *a follower, attendant.*

ἐπ-ετήσιος, ον, = ἐπέτειος, *from year to year, lasting the whole year.*

ἔπετον, Aeol. for ἔπεσον, aor. 2 of πίπτω.

ἐπέτοσσε, a Dor. aor. 1 without any pres. in use, = ἐπέτυχε, *fell in* or *met with*; part. ἐπιτόσσαις = ἐπιτυχών, *having met with.* (Origin uncertain.)

ἐπετράπην [ᾰ], aor. 2 pass. of ἐπιτρέπω:—**ἐπετρᾰπόμην**, **ἐπετράπον**, aor. 2 med. and act.

ἐπετράφθην, Ion. aor. 1 pass. of ἐπιτρέπω.

ἐπέτῠχον, aor. 2 of ἐπιτυγχάνω.

ἕπευ, Ion. for ἕπου, imperat. of ἕπομαι.

ἐπ-ευθύνω, *to guide straight, direct.*

ἐπ-ευρίσκω, Ion. for ἐφ-ευρίσκω.

ἐπ-ευφημέω, f. ήσω: aor. 1 -ευφήμησα:—*to shout assent.* II. c. acc. *to accompany in singing*: *to sing in praise of.*

ἐπ-εύχομαι, f. ξομαι, Dep. *to pray to, make a vow*: *to pray* or *vow that*: in bad sense, *to pray a curse, imprecate upon.* II. *to exult* or *triumph over.*

ἐπέφαντο, 3 sing. plqpf. pass. of φαίνω.

ἔπεφνον, Ep. redupl. aor. 2 of *φένω.

ἐπεφόρβει, 3 sing. plqpf. of φέρβω.

ἐπέφρᾰδον, Ep. redupl. aor. 2 of φράζω.

ἐπεφράσω, 2 sing. aor. 1 med. of ἐπιφράζω.

ἐπέφρακτο, 3 sing. plqpf. pass. of φράσσω.

ἐπέφῡκον, Ep. for ἐπεφύκεσαν, 3 pl. plqpf. of φύω.

ἐπεφύσητο, 3 sing. plqpf. pass. of φυσάω.

ἐπεχευάμην, aor. 1 med. of ἐπιχέω

ἐπέχθην, aor. 1 pass. of πέκω.

ἐπέχυντο, 3 pl. Ep. aor. 2 pass. of ἐπιχέω.

ἐπ-έχω: fut. ἐφ-έξω: aor. 2 ἐπ-έσχον, inf. ἐπισχεῖν, poët. ἐπέσχεθον:—*to have* or *hold upon* or *to*, see ἐπώχατο:—*to hold, keep*:—Pass. and Med. *to keep hold of*. II. *to hold out, present, offer*. III. *hold towards, to keep aiming at*; τόξον σκοπῷ ἐπέχειν *to aim* the bow *at* the mark; τί μοι ὧδ' ἐπέχεις; why thus *launch out against me*? c. acc., ἐπέχειν τοὺς Τεγεήτας *to front them, face* them. 2. ἐπέχειν (sc. τοὺς ὀφθαλμούς, τὸν νοῦν) *to turn one's* eyes or mind *to, to intend, purpose*: *to attend to, be intent upon*. IV. *to keep in, hold back, check*: *to stop* or *hinder from*. 2. intrans. (sub. ἑαυτόν) *to stay, stop, wait, pause*, and then *to leave off doing*: c. gen. rei, *to cease from*. V. *to reach* or *extend over* a space:—Pass. *to be stretched, stretch oneself out, lie at length*. VI. *to have power over, command*: of a wind, *to prevail, continue*.

ἐπ-ηβάω, Ion. for ἐφ-ηβάω.

ἐπ-ήβολος, ον, (ἐπί, βάλλω, with η inserted) *having won* or *gained* a thing, Lat. *compos*: in bad sense, νόσου ἐπήβολοι *possessed by* a disease. II. *fitting* or *belonging to*.

ἐπήγἄγον, aor. 2 of ἐπάγω.

ἐπήγγειλα, ἐπήγγελκα, aor. 1 and pf. of ἐπαγγέλλω.

ἐπηγέρθην, aor. 1 pass. of ἐπεγείρω.

ἐπηγκενίδες, αἱ, *the long planks nailed along the upright ribs* (σταμίνες) of the ship: v. sub ἴκρια.

ἐπ-ηγορεύω or -έω, *to say against, object to* one.

ἐπῆεν, Ep. 3 sing. impf. of ἔπειμι (εἰμί *sum*).

ἐπ-ηετᾰνός, όν, and ή, όν, = ἐπέτειος, but always sed in a general sense, *sufficient, abundant, plentiful*; πηεταναὶ τρίχες *thick, full* fleeces.

ἐπήϊεν, Ep. 3 sing. impf. of ἔπειμι (εἶμι *ibo*), *he went after, followed upon*: ἐπήϊσαν 3 plur.

ἐπήϊσα, aor. 1 of ἐπαΐω.

ἐπήϊσσον, impf. of ἐπαΐσσω.

ἐπῆκαν, Ion. for ἐφ-, 3 pl. aor. 1 of ἐφίημι.

ἐπήκοος Dor. **ἐπάκοος**, ον, (ἐπακούω) *listening* or *giving ear to*: *within hearing*.

ἐπήκρισα, aor. 1 of ἐπακρίζω.

ἐπηκρόωντο, 3 pl. impf. of ἐπακροάομαι.

ἔπηλα, aor. 1 of πάλλω.

ἐπῆλθον, aor. 2 of ἐπέρχομαι.

ἐπ-ηλῠγάζω, (ἐπί, ἠλύγη) *to overshadow*: Med., φόβον ἐπηλυγάζεσθαι *to throw a shade over one's own* fear, *disguise* or *conceal* it.

ἐπήλῠθον, Ep. for ἐπῆλθον, aor. 2 of ἐπέρχομαι.

ἐπῆλυξ, ῠγος, ὁ, ἡ, (ἐπηλυγάζω) *overshadowing*; τὴν πέτραν ἐπήλυγα λαβεῖν to take the rock *as a shelter*.

ἔπηλῠς, ῠδος, ὁ, ἡ, (ἐπήλῠθον) *one who comes to* a place: *an incomer, stranger, foreigner*.

ἐπ-ηλῠσία Ion. -ίη, ἡ, (ἐπήλυθον) *a coming over*: *a bewitching*.

ἐπ-ήλῠσις, εως, ἡ, *an approach, assault*.

ἐπ-ηλύτης, ου, ὁ, = ἔπηλυς. [ῠ]

ἐπημαξευμένος, pf. part. pass. of ἐπαμαξεύω.

ἐπημοιβός, όν, (ἐπαμείβω) *in turn, alternate*; χιτῶνες ἐπημοιβοί changes of raiment.

ἐπ-ημύω, f. ύσω [ῡ], *to bend* or *bow down*.

ἐπήν Ion. **ἐπεάν** late Att. **ἐπάν**, Conjunct. (ἐπεί, ἄν) *whenever*, Lat. *quandocunque*.

ἐπ-ηνέμιος, ον, (ἐπί, ἄνεμος) *windy*. 2. *vain*.

ἐπήνεον, Ep. impf. of ἐπαινέω.

ἐπήνεσα Ep. **ἐπήνησα**, aor. 1 of ἐπαινέω.

ἐπήνθει, 3 sing. impf. of ἐπανθέω.

ἐπηνώρθουν, impf. with double augm. of ἐπανορθόω: so, **ἐπηνώρθωσα, -ώθην**, aor. 1 act. and pass.; **ἐπηνώρθωμαι**, pf. pass.

ἔπηξα, aor. 1 of πήγνυμι.

ἐπηξίωσα, aor. 1 of ἐπαξιόω.

ἐπ-ηόνιος, ον, (ἐπί, ἠών) *on the beach* or *shore*.

ἐπηπείλησα, aor. 1 of ἐπαπειλέω.

ἐπ-ηπύω, f. ύσω [ῡ], *to shout to, cheer on*.

ἐπ-ήρᾰτος, ον, (ἐπί, ἐράω) *lovely, pleasant*.

ἐπηρεάζω, f. σω, (ἐπήρεια) *to threaten abusively*: *to deal despitefully with, oppose wantonly*: absol. *to be insolent*.

ἐπήρεια, ἡ, *wanton insult, contumely*.

ἐπ-ηρεμέω, f. ήσω, (ἐπί, ἤρεμος) *to rest after*.

ἐπ-ήρετμος, ον, (ἐπί, ἐρετμός) *at the oar, rowing*. 2. equipped *with oars*.

ἐπ-ηρεφής, ές, (ἐπί, ἐρέφω) *covering, shading*. II. pass. *covered, sheltered*.

ἐπήρθην, aor. 1 pass. of ἐπαίρω.

ἐπήρκεσα, aor. 1 of ἐπαρκέω.

ἐπῆρσα, aor. 1 of ἐπαραρίσκω.

ἐπῆσαν, Ep. for ἐπήϊσαν, 3 pl. impf. of ἔπειμι (εἶμι *ibo*).

ἐπησθεῖεν, Ion. 3 pl. aor. 1 opt. of ἐφήδομαι.

ἐπήσθιον, impf. of ἐπεσθίω.

ἐπησθόμην, aor. 2 of ἐπαισθάνομαι.

ἐπήσκημαι, pf. pass. of ἐπασκέω.

ἐπητής, οῦ, ὁ, (ἔπος) *affable, kind, gentle*.

ἐπητιάσω, 2 sing. aor. 1 of ἐπαιτιάομαι.

ἐπ-ήτρῐμος, ον, (ἐπί, ἤτριον) *woven on* or *to*: hence *close, dense, thronged*.

ἐπητύς, ύος, ἡ, (ἐπητής) *a ready address*: generally, *courtesy, kindness*.

ἐπηῦρον, ἐπηυρόμην, aor. 2 act. and med. of ἐπαυρίσκομαι.

ἐπηύχησα, aor. 1 of ἐπαυχέω.

ἐπήφῠσα, aor. 1 of ἐπαφύσσω.

ἐπ-ηχέω, f. ήσω, *to resound, to reëcho*: *to accompany in shouting*.

ἐπί, PREP. WITH GEN., DAT., AND ACC. Radic. sense, *upon*: A. WITH GEN., I. of *rest at* a place, *on, upon, at, by, near*. 2. with the person. Pron.; ἐφ' ὑμείων *by* yourselves, alone; ἐφ' ἑαυτοῦ, ἐφ' ἑαυτῶν *by* himself, *by* themselves; τὸ ἐφ' ἑαυτῶν their own interest only. 3. with Cardinal Numbers; ἐπὶ τριῶν, τεττάρων etc., *by* three or four, three *deep* or *in file*; ἐπὶ κέρως in single file. 4. *before, in presence of*, Lat. *coram*. 5. *over*, of any one *set over* a special business; οἱ ἐπὶ τῶν πραγμάτων those *set over* the business. 6. *motion towards* a point; πλεῖν ἐπὶ Χίου to sail *for* Chios; ἀπελαύνειν ἐπ' οἴκου to go home-*wards*. II. of Time, *in* or *in the course of*; *ἐπ' εἰρήνης in time of* peace. III. of the Grounds on which a thing happens; *ἐπὶ μαρτυρίας on* evidence; *εἰπεῖν ἐπ' ὅρκου* to speak *on* oath; *ἐπ' ὅτευ on* what *ground*. B. WITH DAT., I. of Place; *ἐπὶ χώρᾳ on* the spot: esp. where hostility is implied, *opposite* or *against*. II. of the Time *in*, *on* or *at* which a thing happens; *ἐπὶ νυκτί in* the night; *ἐπ' ἤματι τῷδε on* this very day. 2. *upon* or *after* an event. III. *in addition, over and above, one on another*. IV. *for an object* or *purpose, with a view to; ἐπὶ δόρπῳ for* supper; *ἐπὶ κακῷ ἀνθρώπου for* mischief to man. V. of the Ground of doing a thing; *γελᾶν ἐπί τινι* to laugh *at* one; *μέγα φρονεῖν ἐπί τινι* to be proud *at* or *of* a thing. VI. of any condition *upon* which a thing happens; *ἐπὶ τούτῳ, ἐφ' ᾧτε* on condition, that . .; more briefly, *ἐφ' ᾧ* or *ἐφ' ᾧτε*; *ἐπ' οὐδενί* on no condition; *ἐπὶ πᾶσι δικαίοις with* strict justice; *ἐπ' ἴσοις on* reasonable terms. C. WITH ACCUS., I. of Place; *extending over; ἐπ' ἐννέα κεῖτο πέλεθρα over* nine acres he lay; *κλέος πάντας ἐπ' ἀνθρώπους* glory spread *among* all men. 2. *motion towards* or *to* a place; *πλεῖν ἐπ' Αἴγυπτον*: in hostile sense, *upon, against*:—metaph., *ἐπ' ἔργα, ἐπ' ἰθύν to* labour, *to* an enterprize: esp. *to gain* or *get* something, *for, after, in quest of; στέλλειν ἐπ' ἀγγελίην* to send *for* tidings: rarely of persons, *ἐπ' Ὀδυσσῆα ἤϊε*:—hence also to denote a *purpose*, *ἐπὶ τί*; for *what? wherefore?* 3. with Cardinal Numbers, *ἐπ' ἀσπίδας πέντε καὶ εἴκοσιν* eight-and-twenty deep or in file: with numbers, *up to* a certain number, *nearly, about*. II. of Time, *for* or *during* a certain time; *ἐπὶ χρόνον* for a time. 2. *up to* or *till* a certain time; *ἐπ' ἠῶ till* morning. III. more generally, *ἐπὶ στάθμην by* the line or rule; *τὸ ἐπ' ἐμέ for* me, as far as concerns me.

'Επί may follow its case, and then it is written ἔπι.

IN COMPOS. ἐπί denotes *rest at a place*, as in ἔπ-ειμι (εἰμί *sum*), ἐπι-βατεύω; or motion, esp. in a hostile sense, as in ἐπι-χειρέω, ἐπι-στρατεύω. II. of Time, *after*, as in ἐπι-βιόω, ἐπι-βλαστάνω. III. addition, accompaniment, as in ἐπί-κτητος, ἐπ-αυλέω. IV. a reciprocal action, as in ἐπ-εργασία, ἐπι-γαμία *intermarriage*. V. with Numerals, an integer and so much more, ἐπί-τριτος, *one and a third*, $=\frac{4}{3}$. VI. to strengthen the Compar., as in ἐπι-μᾶλλον, ἐπι-πλέον, etc.

ἔπι, for ἔπεστι, *it is there, ready, at hand*.

ἐπ-ῐάλλω, f. -ιᾰλῶ: aor. -ίηλα:—*to send upon, lay upon: to bring to pass*.

ἐπιάλμενος, Ep. aor. 2 part. of ἐφάλλομαι.

ἐπι-ανδάνω, poët. for ἐφανδ-, *to please, gratify*.

ἐπ-ῐαύω, *to sleep among*.

ἐπ-ιάχω [ᾰ], *to shout to, cheer: to shout aloud*.

ἐπίβᾱ, for ἐπίβηθι, aor. 2 imperat. of ἐπιβαίνω.

ἐπι-βάθρα, ἡ, (ἐπιβαίνω) *a ladder* or *steps to ascend by: a scaling-ladder: a gangway*.

ἐπίβαθρον, τό, (ἐπιβαίνω) *a roosting-place, perch*. II. (ἐπιβατής) *a passenger's fare*, Lat. *naulum*.

ἐπι-βαίνω, fut. -βήσομαι: pf. -βέβηκα: aor. 2 ἐπέβην: aor. 1 med. ἐπεβησάμην (Ion. 3 sing. ἐπεβήσετο, imperat. ἐπιβήσεο): I. c. gen. *to set foot on, tread* or *walk upon, to be* or *lie upon*. 2. *to get upon, mount: to arrive at, come to* a place: metaph. *to arrive at, reach unto; ἐπιβαίνειν εὐσεβίας to take one's stand on* piety. II. c. dat. *to mount upon, get on board of*:—also, *to set upon, attack, assault*. III. c. acc. *to light upon*, *Πιερίην ἐπιβαίνειν*, of gods descending upon it: simply, *to go to*. 2. *to attack*, like ἐπέρχομαι. 3. *ἐπιβαίνειν ἐπὶ ἵππον* to *mount* a horse. IV. absol. *to step forward* or *on, advance*:—*to get a footing*.

B. Causal in act. fut. ἐπιβήσω, aor. 1 ἐπέβησα, *to set* one *upon, make* him *mount*: metaph. *to bring to, make one arrive at*. Cf. ἐπιβιβάζω.

ἐπι-βάλλω, fut. -βᾰλῶ: aor. 2 -έβᾰλον: I. *to throw* or *cast upon: to put on: affix*. 2. *to lay on, apply: to lay on, impose*, as a tax or fine. 3. *to add: to add to, increase*. II. intrans., *ἐπιβάλλειν τινί* (sub. ἑαυτόν), *to throw oneself upon, go straight towards*. 2. *to fall upon: to attack*. 3. (sub. *νοῦν*), *to give one's attention to, think on, apply* one's *mind to*; aor. 2 part. ἐπιβαλών, absol., *when he thought on it*. 4. *to fall to one, come to* one's *share*: *τὸ ἐπιβάλλον* [sc. *μέρος*] *one's proper portion*; also impers. *it falls to one* to do a thing. III. Med. *to seize upon* a thing, *grasp at* it. 2. *to put upon oneself, put on*: metaph. *to take upon oneself, incur*. IV. Pass. *to be placed upon*; *τοξόται ἐπιβεβλημένοι having their* arrows *on the string*.

ἐπι-βᾰρέω, f. ήσω, (ἐπί, βαρύς) *to weigh heavily on*.

ἐπιβάς, aor. 2 part. of ἐπιβαίνω.

ἐπίβᾰσις, εως, ἡ, (ἐπιβαίνω) *a stepping upon* or *upwards*. 2. metaph. *a step* or *approach towards* a thing; *εἴς τινα ποιεῖσθαι ἐπίβασιν* to make *means of attacking* one.

ἐπι-βάσκω, poët. Causal of ἐπι-βαίνω, *κακῶν ἐπιβασκέμεν υἷας Ἀχαιῶν to lead* them *into* misery.

ἐπι-βαστάζω, f. σω, *to bear* or *weigh in the hand*.

ἐπι-βᾰτεύω, f. σω, *to take one's stand upon, to lay claim to, usurp*. II. *to be an ἐπιβάτης, passenger* or *soldier*. From

ἐπιβάτης [ᾰ], ου, ὁ, (ἐπιβαίνω) *one who mounts* or *embarks; οἱ ἐπιβάτοι* the *soldiers* on board a ship, *the fighting men*, as opp. to the rowers and seamen: *a passenger*. 2. *the warrior* in a chariot.

ἐπιβᾰτός, ή, όν, (ἐπιβαίνω) *that can be climbed, accessible*.

ἐπίβδᾱ, ας, ἡ, *the day after the festival*, Lat. *repotia*:—proverb., *ἕρπειν πρὸς τραχεῖαν ἐπίβδαν* to come to a hard reckoning, on the day after the feast. (Deriv. uncertain.)

ἐπιβέβηκα, pf. of ἐπιβαίνω.

ἐπιβείομεν, Ep. 1 pl. aor. 2 subj. of ἐπιβαίνω.

ἐπιβήμεναι, Ep. aor. 2 inf. of ἐπιβαίνω.

ἐπι-βήσεο, Ep. imperat. aor. 1 med. of ἐπιβαίνω.

ἐπι-βήσετο, Ep. for -ατο, 3 sing. aor. 1 med. of ἐπιβαίνω.

ἐπι-βήτωρ, ορος, ὁ, (ἐπιβαίνω) *one who mounts.* II. of male animals, e. g. a boar.

ἐπι-βιβάζω, f. -βιβάσω Att. -βιβῶ, Causal of ἐπιβαίνω, *to put one upon.*

ἐπι-βιόω, f. -βιώσομαι: aor. 2 ἐπεβίων:—*to survive.*

ἐπι-βλέπω, fut. ψομαι, later ψω, *to look upon, look to, regard.* 2. *to eye with envy,* Lat. *invidere.*

ἐπίβλημα, ατος, τό, (ἐπιβάλλω) *that which is thrown on* or *over: a cover: a patch.*

ἐπιβλής, ῆτος, ὁ, (ἐπιβάλλω) *a bolt* or *bar fixed in* or *on* a door.

ἐπι-βλώσκω, f. -μολοῦμαι: aor. 2 ἐπέμολον:—*to come upon, befall.*

ἐπι-βοάω, f. -βοήσομαι Ion. -βώσομαι:—*to call upon* or *to, cry out to.* 2. *to utter* or *sing aloud.* 3. *to cry out against.* 4. *to call upon, invoke; call to aid*:—so also in Med.

ἐπιβοήθεια, ἡ, *a helping, coming to aid, succour.* From

ἐπι-βοηθέω Ion. -βωθέω, *to come to aid, succour.*

ἐπιβόημα, ατος, τό, (ἐπιβοάω) *a call to* one.

ἐπιβόητος Ion. -**βωτος**, ον, (ἐπιβοάω) *cried out against, ill spoken of.*

ἐπιβολή, ἡ, (ἐπιβάλλω) *a throwing* or *putting on*; ἐπιβολαὶ πλίνθων *layers* or *courses* of bricks. II. *an infliction, penalty.* III. *a setting upon* a thing, *an attempt, enterprise: a hostile attempt.*

ἐπι-βομβέω, f. ήσω, *to roar in answer.*

ἐπι-βόσκω, f. -βοσκήσω, *to feed cattle upon*:—Med. of cattle, *to graze* or *feed upon.*

ἐπι-βουκόλος, ὁ, *an over-cowherd, herdsman.*

ἐπιβούλευμα, ατος, τό, (ἐπιβουλεύω) *a plan against, a plot, attempt, scheme.*

ἐπιβουλευτής, οῦ, ὁ, *one who plots against, a plotter.* From

ἐπι-βουλεύω, f. σω, *to plan* or *contrive against* one; ἐπιβουλεύειν θάνατόν τινι, c. dat. rei, *to lay plots for, to aim at*:—Pass. *to have snares laid for one.* Hence

ἐπιβουλή, ἡ, *a plan against* another, *a plot*; ἐξ ἐπιβουλῆς *by treachery.*

ἐπι-βουλία, ἡ, ἐπιβουλή.

ἐπί-βουλος, ον, (ἐπί, βουλή) *plotting against, treacherous.*

ἐπι-βραδύνω, f. ὑνῶ, *to loiter at* a place.

ἐπι-βραχύ, Adv. for ἐπὶ βραχύ, *for a short while.*

ἐπι-βρέμω, *to make to roar*:—Med. *to roar.* II. intr. *to roar* or *cry out to.*

ἐπι-βρῑθής, ές, *burdensome, grievous.* From

ἐπι-βρίθω, f. ίσω [ῑ], *to be heavy upon, weigh down.* II. metaph. *to press heavily.*

ἐπιβρίσειαν, 3 pl. aor. 1 opt. of ἐπιβρίθω.

ἐπι-βρόντητος, ον, = ἐμ-βρόντητος, *thunderstricken.*

ἐπι-βρύω, f. ύσω [ῠ], *to burst forth,* as water: of flowers, *to sprout, burst forth.*

ἐπι-βύω, f. ύσω [ῡ], *to stop, caulk tight.*

ἐπι-βωθέω, Ion. for ἐπι-βοηθέω.

ἐπι-βωμιο-στᾰτέω, f. ήσω, (ἐπί, βωμός, στῆναι) *to stand suppliant at the altar.*

ἐπι-βώμιος, ον, (ἐπί, βωμός) *on* or *at the altar.*

ἐπιβώσομαι, Ion. fut. of ἐπιβοάω.

ἐπι-βωστρέω, Ion. and Dor. for ἐπιβοάω, *to shout to, call upon, clamour for.*

ἐπί-βωτος, Ion. for ἐπιβόητος.

ἐπι-βώτωρ, ορος, ὁ, *an over-shepherd, shepherd.*

ἐπί-γαιος, ον, (ἐπί, γαῖα, = γῆ) *upon the earth*; τὰ ἐπίγαια *the parts on* or *near the ground.*

ἐπι-γαμβρεύω, f. σω, (ἐπί, γαμβρός) *to marry* a a widow *as her husband's next of kin.*

ἐπι-γᾰμέω, f. -γαμέσω Att. -γᾰμῶ:—*to marry besides*; ἐπιγαμεῖν τέκνοις μητρυιάν *to marry and set* a stepmother *over* one's own children. Hence

ἐπι-γᾰμία, ἡ, *an additional marriage.* II. *intermarriage, right of intermarriage,* between states.

ἐπί-γᾰμος, ον, (ἐπί, γάμος) *marriageable.*

ἐπι-γαυρόομαι, Pass. *to exult in.*

ἐπιγ-δουπέω, Ep. for ἐπι-δουπέω.

ἐπιγέγραμμαι, pf. pass. of ἐπιγράφω.

ἐπί-γειος, ον, (ἐπί, γέα = γῆ) *on* or *of the earth.*

ἐπι-γελάω, f. άσομαι [ᾰ], *to laugh to* or *with, to laugh in approval, to smile upon*: absol. *to laugh.*

ἐπι-γεραίρω, *to give honour to.*

ἐπι-γεύομαι, Med *to taste of.*

ἐπι-γηθέω, f. ήσω: pf. ἐπιγέγηθα:—*to rejoice* or *triumph over*: *to exult in.*

ἐπι-γίγνομαι, fut.—γενήσομαι: aor. 2 -εγενόμην: pf. -γέγονα or in pass. form -γεγένημαι:—*to be born after*; ἔαρος ἐπιγίγνεται ὥρη the season of spring *comes next*; οἱ ἐπιγιγνόμενοι *posterity*; χρόνου ἐπιγινομένου as time *was going on.* 2. *to come upon, fall upon*: in good sense, *to follow, ensue upon*: also *to fall upon, attack.* 3. *to happen after, come to pass.*

ἐπι-γιγνώσκω, fut. -γνώσομαι: aor. 2 -έγνων: pf. -έγνωκα:—*to look upon, observe.* II. *to recognise*: hence *to find out, discover*: *to become conscious of, come to a sense of.* III. *to come to a judgment, decide.*

ἐπι-γίνομαι, **ἐπι-γῑνώσκω**, Ion. and in late Gr. for ἐπιγιγν-.

ἐπι-γλωσσάομαι Att. -**ττάομαι**: fut. ήσομαι: Dep.: (ἐπί, γλῶσσα):—*to vent reproaches against, to upbraid.*

ἐπι-γναμπτός, ή, όν, *curved, twisted.* From

ἐπι-γνάμπτω, f. ψω, *to curve, bend.* II. metaph. *to bow* or *bend* another to one's purpose.

ἐπιγνοίην, aor. 2 opt. of ἐπιγιγνώσκω.

ἐπιγνούς, aor. 2 part. of ἐπιγιγνώσκω.

ἐπι-γνώμων, ονος, ὁ, ἡ, (ἐπί, γνώμη) *deciding upon*: as Subst. *an arbiter, judge.* II. *pardoning.*

ἐπι-γνωρίζω, fut. ίσω Att. ιῶ, *to make known, announce, signify.*

ἐπίγνωσις, εως, ἡ, (ἐπιγιγνώσκω) *full knowledge.*

ἐπιγνῶσι, Ep. 3 pl. aor. 2 subj. of ἐπιγιγνώσκω.

ἐπίγονος, *ον*, (*ἐπιγενέσθαι*) *born after*: generally, *offspring, posterity*:—*οἱ Ἐπίγονοι*, *the Afterborn*, sons of the chiefs who fell in the first war against Thebes.

ἐπιγουνίδιος, *ον*, *on, set upon the knee.* From

ἐπι-γουνίς, *ίδος*, *ἡ*, (*ἐπί*, *γούνατος*, Ion. gen. of *γόνυ*) *the region above the knee, the thigh.*

ἐπιγράβδην, Adv. (*ἐπιγράφω*) *scratching the surface, grazing.*

ἐπίγραμμα, *ατος*, *τό*, (*ἐπιγράφω*) *an inscription*, as of the name of the maker on a work of art, or of the dedicator on an offering. 2. *an epigram*, a poem of a few lines, mostly in Elegiacs.

ἐπιγρᾰφεύς, *έως*, *ὁ*, (*ἐπιγράφω*) *an inscriber*: esp. at Athens *a clerk who registered* property, etc.

ἐπιγρᾰφή. *ἡ*, (*ἐπιγράφω*) *an inscription.* II. at Athens, *a registration of* property.

ἐπι-γράφω f. *φω*; pf. *-γέγραφα*, pass. *-γέγραμμαι*:—*to mark the surface, graze*; *ἐπιγράψαι κλῆρον to put a mark on* a lot. II. later, *to write upon, inscribe*:—Pass., of the inscription, *to be inscribed upon.* III. *to enter in a public list* or *register*: esp. at Athens, *to register* the citizens' property: *ἐπιγράφειν τίμημα to lay* the damages at so much:—Med. *to register oneself*: but, *προστάτην ἐπιγράψασθαι to enter the name* of a patron *in the public register*, as all *μέτοικοι* at Athens were obliged to do.

ἐπί-γρῡπος, *ον*, *somewhat hooked*: *somewhat hook-nosed.*

ἐπι-δαίομαι, Dep. (*ἐπί*, *δαίω* B) *to distribute, offer.*

ἐπι-δαίσιος, *ον*, (*ἐπί*, *δαίω* B) *assigned, allotted.*

ἐπι-δακρύω, f. *ύσω* [ῡ], *to weep over* or *for.*

ἐπί-δᾱμος, *ον*, Dor. for *ἐπί-δημος.*

ἐπι-δαψῐλεύομαι, f. *σομαι*, Dep. *to lavish upon* a person, *give freely.*

ἐπιδέδρομα, pf. 2 of *ἐπιτρέχω.*

ἐπιδεής, *ές*, (*ἐπιδέομαι*) *in want of*: *deficient*: Att. neut. pl., *ἐπιδεᾶ.*

ἐπίδειγμα, *ατος*, *τό*, (*ἐπιδείκνυμι*) *a specimen*: *a pattern, example, lesson.*

ἐπι-δείελος, *ον*, (*ἐπί*, *δείλη*) *at, towards evening*; *ἐπιδείελα*, neut. pl. as Adv., *towards evening.*

ἐπι-δείκνῡμι and *-ύω*, f. *-δείξω*: aor. 1 *-έδειξα* Ion. *-έδεξα*:—*to exhibit as a specimen* or *pattern*: *to shew forth, display, parade*:—Med. *to display oneself, shew oneself off.* 2. *to shew, point out*:—*to shew, prove, demonstrate.* Hence

ἐπιδεικτικός, *ή*, *όν*, *fit for display*; *ἐπιδεικτικοὶ λόγοι* speeches *for display, set* orations, such as were frequent among the Athenian rhetoricians.

ἐπῐδεῖν, aor. 2 inf. of *ἐπεῖδον.*

ἐπιδεῖξαι, aor. 1 inf. of *ἐπιδείκνυμι.*

ἐπίδειξις Ion. **ἐπίδεξις**, *εως*, *ἡ*, (*ἐπιδείκνυμι*) *an exhibition, display*; *ἐς ἐπίδειξίν τινος ἀπικέσθαι* to come within one's *view*, to his *knowledge*. *pattern, example*, Lat. *specimen.*

ἐπι-δειπνέω, f. *ήσω*, (*ἐπίδειπνον*) *to eat after* dinner. II. *to eat as a second course, eat as a dainty.*

ἐπι-δείπνιος, *ον*, (*ἐπί*, *δεῖπνον*) *at* or *after dinner.*

ἐπί-δειπνον, *τό*, *an after-meal, second course* or *dessert.*

ἐπι-δέκᾰτος, *η*, *ον*, *one and one tenth*; $1 + \frac{1}{10} = \frac{11}{10}$. II. *one in ten, a tenth, tithe.*

ἐπι-δέμνιος, *ον*, (*ἐπί*, *δέμνιον*) *in* or *on the bed.*

ἐπι-δέξιος, *ον*, *from left to right, towards the right*, used chiefly in neut. pl. *ἐπιδέξια* as Adv., which therefore also means *auspiciously.* 2. = *δεξιός*, *on the right hand*; *τἀπιδεξία the right side.* II. of persons, *dexterous, skilful.*

ἐπί-δεξις, Ion. for *ἐπίδειξις.*

ἐπι-δέρκομαι, Dep. *to look upon, behold.*

ἐπι-δεσμεύω, f. *σω*, (*ἐπί*, *δεσμός*) *to bind up.*

ἐπι-δεσμός, *ὁ*, (*ἐπί*, *δεσμός*) *a band, bandage.*

ἐπιδεσμο-χᾰρής, *ές*, (*ἐπίδεσμος*, *χαίρω*) *bandage-loving*, epith. of gout.

ἐπι-δεσπόζω, f. *όσω*, *to be lord over.*

ἐπι-δευής, *ές*, poët. and Ion. for *ἐπιδεής*, *in need* or *want of, lacking.* II. *lacking, failing* in a thing, c. gen., *βίης ἐπιδευέες failing* in strength: also a compar. in sense, *βίης ἐπιδευέες Ὀδυσῆος inferior to* Ulysses in strength: absol., *πολλὸν δ' ἐπιδευέες ἦμεν* far *too weak* were we. From

ἐπι-δεύομαι, poët. for *ἐπιδέομαι* (*ἐπιδέω* B) *to be in want of, to lack*: *to need the help of.* II. *to be lacking in* a thing, *fail in* it.

ἐπι-δεύω, f. *σω*, *to moisten on the surface.*

ἐπι-δέχομαι, f. *ξομαι*, Dep. *to admit besides* or *in addition.*

ἐπι-δέω (A), f. *-δήσω*, *to bind* or *fasten on.* II. *to bind up, bandage.*

ἐπι-δέω (B), f. *-δεήσω*, *to want* or *lack* so much *of* a number:—impers. *ἐπιδεῖ*, *there is need of besides*:—Med. *to be in want of*, cf. *ἐπιδεύομαι.*

ἐπί-δηλος, *ον*, *quite evident, manifest*: *open.* 2. *distinguished.* II. *like, resembling.*

ἐπι-δημεύω, f. *σω*, *to live among the people.* From

ἐπιδημέω, f. *ήσω*, (*ἐπίδημος*) *to be at home, live at home*: *to sojourn among* people, *stay at* a place. II. *to come home*, from foreign travel. Hence

ἐπιδημία, *ἡ*, *a staying at home, stay at* a place.

ἐπι-δήμιος, *ον*, (*ἐπί*, *δῆμος*) *among the people*: *dwelling at home*; *πόλεμος ἐπιδήμιος civil* war; *ἐπιδήμιοι ἔμποροι native* merchants. II. *sojourning at* a place.

ἐπι-δημιουργοί, *ῶν*, *οἱ*, magistrates sent annually by Doric states to their colonies.

ἐπί-δημος, *ον*, = **ἐπιδήμιος**, *of the people, popular.*

ἐπι-διαβαίνω, fut. *-βήσομαι*, *to cross over besides* or *after* another.

ἐπι-διαγιγνώσκω Ion. **-γῑνώσκω**: fut. *-γνώσομαι*:—*to debate* or *decide afresh.*

ἐπι-διαιρέω, f. *ήσω*, *to divide over again*:—Med. of several, *to distribute among themselves.*

ἐπι-διαπλέω, f. *-πλεύσομαι*, *to sail across besides.*

ἐπι-διαρρήγνῡμι, f. *-ρήξω*, *to tear asunder after*:—Pass. *to burst in consequence of* a thing.

ἐπι-διατάσσομαι, Med. *to ordain* or *command besides.*

ἐπι-διαφέρομαι, Pass. *to go across after.*

ἐπι-διδάσκω, f. ξω, *to teach besides.*

ἐπι-δίδωμι, f. -δώσω, *to give besides, give freely: to give with, give in dowry.* II. ἐπιδιδόναι ἑαυτόν τινι *to give* oneself *up* or *devote* oneself *to* a thing. III. intr. *to increase, advance:* also *to improve, prosper.* IV. Med., θεοὺς ἐπιδώμεθα *let us give* or *take* the gods *as witnesses;* cf. περιδίδωμι II.

ἐπι-δίζημαι, Dep. *to seek* or *ask further: to seek for* or *demand besides.*

ἐπι-δικάζω, f. σω, *to adjudge to* one:—Med. of the claimant, *to sue for* a thing *at law, lay claim to.* Hence

ἐπι-δικάσιμος, *disputed at law:* generally, *much contested.*

ἐπι-δινέω, f. ήσω, *to whirl* or *swing round,* of one in act to throw:—Med. *to turn over in one's mind, revolve:*—Pass. *to wheel about,* as birds in the air; ἐπιδινηθέντε, aor. 1 part. dual.

ἐπι-διορθόω, f. ώσω, *to correct* or *set in order afterwards.*

ἐπι-διπλοΐζω or -οίζω, (ἐπί, διπλόος) *to redouble.*

ἐπι-διφριάς, άδος, ἡ, (ἐπί, δίφρος) *the rail in front of the chariot-board* (δίφρος), *the chariot-rail.*

ἐπι-δίφριος, ον, (ἐπί, δίφρος) *sitting on the car.*

ἐπί-διχα, Adv. for ἐπὶ δίχα.

ἐπι-διώκω, f. ξω, *to pursue after: follow up:*—as legal term, *to prosecute again.*

ἐπι-δοκέω, f. -δοκήσω and -δόξω, *to expect.*

ἐπ-ιδόντες, aor. 2 pl. nom. part. of ἐπεῖδον; but **ἐπι-δόντες**, of ἐπιδίδωμι.

ἐπί-δοξος, ον, (ἐπί, δόξα) *likely* or *expected to do* a thing; ἐπίδοξος γενέσθαι *likely to* prove so: of things, *likely, probable.* II. *well-known, illustrious.*

ἐπι-δόρπιος, ον, (ἐπί, δόρπον) *for* or *of the banquet.*

ἐπίδοσις, εως, ἡ, (ἐπιδίδωμι) *a giving over and above: a voluntary contribution* to the state. II. *increase, growth, progress.*

ἐπιδοῦναι, ἐπιδούς, aor. 2 inf. and part. of ἐπιδίδωμι.

ἐπι-δουπέω, f. ήσω, *to make a noise* or *clashing.*

ἐπιδοχή, ἡ, (ἐπιδέχομαι) *reception of something new.*

ἐπιδραμεῖν, aor. 2 inf. of ἐπιτρέχω; **ἐπιδραμέτην**, 3 dual indic.

ἐπιδρομή, ἡ, (ἐπιδραμεῖν) *a running over.* II. *a sudden inroad, raid,* or *attack.* III. *a place for ships to run to, a landing-place.*

ἐπί-δρομος, ον, *that may be run over* or *upon;* τεῖχος ἐπίδρομον a wall *that may be scaled.*

ἐπι-δύω and **-δύνω**, f. ύσω, *to go down* or *set upon.*

ἐπι-δώμεθα, 1 pl. aor. 2 med. subj. of ἐπιδίδωμι.

ἐπ-ιδών, part. of ἐπεῖδον.

ἐπιδώσω, fut. of ἐπιδίδωμι.

ἐπιείκεια, ἡ, (ἐπιεικής) *likelihood, reasonableness.* II. *fairness, clemency:* also *natural mildness.* 2. *equity, the spirit* as opposed to *the letter* of the law.

ἐπι-είκελος, ον, = εἴκελος, *like.*

ἐπι-εικής, ές, (ἐπί, εἰκός) *fitting, meet, suitable;* ὡς ἐπιεικές as is *meet;* ὅν κ' ἐπιεικὲς ἀκούειν whatever [word] is *meet* for you to hear. II. in Att. *fair, reasonable:* also *plausible:* of persons, *fair, kind, moderate.* 2. opp. to δίκαιος, *not insisting on strict justice, equitable.*

ἐπι-εικτός, ή, όν, (ἐπί, εἴκω) *yielding;* οὐκ ἐπιεικτός *that will never yield, unyielding;* πένθος οὐκ ἐπιεικτόν *unceasing* woe.

ἐπιεικῶς Ion. **έως**, Adv. of ἐπιεικής, *fairly, tolerably, moderately.* 2. *probably, reasonably.*

ἐπιειμένος, η, ον, Ion. for ἐφειμένος, pf. part. pass. of ἐπιέννυμι.

ἐπιεισάμενος, Ion. aor. 1 part. of ἔπειμι (εἶμι *ibo*).

ἐπιείσομαι, Ion. fut. of ἔπειμι (εἶμι *ibo*).

ἐπι-έλπομαι, poët. for ἐπέλπομαι. Hence

ἐπί-ελπτος, ον, *to be hoped* or *expected.*

ἐπι-έννυμι, Ion. for ἐφ-έννυμι; aor. 1 ἐπί-εσα Ep. ἐπί-εσσα: pf. pass. ἐπί-εσμαι or ἐπί-ειμαι:—*to put on besides* or *over:*—Pass., Ion. pf. part. ἐπιειμένος ἀλκήν, ἀναιδείην *clad in* strength, shamelessness; χαλκὸν ἐπιέσται (3 sing. pf.) it *was covered* in brass, *had* brass *upon* it:—Med. *to put on oneself besides:* generally, *to cover* or *shroud oneself in.*

ἐπιέσσαμεν, 1 pl. aor. 1 of ἐπιέννυμι.

ἐπιέσται, 3 sing. pf. pass. of ἐπιέννυμι.

ἐπι-ζαρέω, = ἐπιβαρέω.

ἐπι-ζάφελος, ον, (ἐπί, *ζάφελος from ζα- intens.) *vehement, violent:*—Adv. ἐπιζαφελῶς (as if from ἐπιζαφελής), *vehemently, furiously.*

ἐπι-ζάω, f. -ζήσω, *to outlive, survive.*

ἐπι-ζεύγνυμι and -ύω, f. -ζεύξω, *to join* or *fasten at top:* generally, *to tie together, bind fast.* II. *to yoke to.*

ἐπι-ζεφύριος, ον, = sq., epith. of Italian Locri.

ἐπι-ζέφυρος, ον, *lying towards the west.*

ἐπι-ζέω, f. -ζέσω, *to boil up* or *over;* ἡ νεότης ἐπέζεσέ μοι my youthful spirit *boiled over.* II. act. *to make to boil, heat.*

ἐπί-ζηλος, ον, *subject to envy: fortunate, prosperous.*

ἐπι-ζήμιος, ον, (ἐπί, ζημία) *bringing loss* or *penalty upon, hurtful.* II. *liable to punishment.* Hence

ἐπι-ζημιόω, f. ώσω, *to punish.*

ἐπι-ζητέω, f. ήσω, *to seek for, seek after, find wanting: to beat for game;* οἱ ἐπιζητοῦντες *the beaters.*

ἐπι-ζώννυμι, f. -ζώσω, *to bind* or *gird on:* Pass., pf. part. ἐπεζωσμένοι, *with their cloaks girt up.*

ἐπι-ζώω, Ion. for ἐπιζάω.

ἐπίηλα, aor. 1 of ἐπιάλλω.

ἐπ-ίημι, Ion. for ἐφίημι.

ἐπιήνδανε, Ep. 3 sing. impf. of ἐφανδάνω.

ἐπί-ηρα, τά, (ἐπί, ἦρα) *things acceptable, pleasing gifts.*

ἐπι-ήρανος, ον, (ἐπίηρα) *pleasing.* II. *warding off, assisting, governing.*

ἐπίηρος, *ον*, only in neut. pl. ἐπίηρα, q. v.

ἐπι-θᾰλάμιος, *ον*, (ἐπί, θάλαμος) *belonging to a bridal, nuptial;* τὸ ἐπιθαλάμιον (sub. μέλος), *the nuptial song, epithalamium,* sung in chorus before the bridal chamber.

ἐπι-θᾰλασσίδιος Att. **-ττίδιος**, *ον*, = sq.

ἐπι-θᾰλάσσιος Att. **-ττιος**, *α*, *ον*, (ἐπί, θάλασσα) *lying on the sea-shore, maritime.*

ἐπι-θᾰνάτιος, *ον*, (ἐπί, θάνατος) *condemned to death.*

ἐπι-θάνᾰτος, *ον*, *sick to death, like to die.*

ἐπι-θαρσύνω Att. **-θαρρύνω**, f. ῠνῶ, *to cheer on.*

ἐπι-θαυμάζω, f. *σω*, *to pay respect to, to compliment with a fee* (Lat. *honorarium*).

ἐπι-θειάζω, f. *άσω*, (ἐπί, θεός) *to call upon in the name of the gods, to adjure.* Hence

ἐπιθειασμός, *ὁ*, *an appeal to the gods, adjuration.*

ἐπι-θείην, **-θεῖναι**, aor. 2 opt. and inf. of ἐπιτίθημι.

ἐπιθείς, *-θεῖσα*, aor. 2 part. of ἐπιτίθημι.

ἐπι-θεῖτε, for *-θείητε*, 2 pl. aor. 2 opt. of ἐπιτίθημι.

ἐπι-θερᾰπεύω, f. *σω*, *to court* or *serve studiously: to work zealously for.*

ἔπι-θες, **-θέτω**, aor. 2 imperat. of ἐπιτίθημι.

ἐπίθεσις, *εως*, *ἡ*, (ἐπιτίθημι) *a laying on, imposition.* II. (from Med.) *a setting upon, attack.*

ἐπι-θεσπίζω, f. *σω*, *to prophesy upon.*

ἐπιθετικός, *ή*, *όν*, (ἐπιτίθεμαι) *ready to attack: enterprising.*

ἐπί-θετος, *ον*, (ἐπιτίθημι) *added, annexed: far-fetched, foreign.* II. as Subst., ἐπίθετον, τό, *an epithet.*

ἐπι-θέω, f. *-θεύσομαι*, *to run upon* or *at: to run after, chase, pursue.*

ἐπιθήκη, *ἡ*, (ἐπιτίθημι) *an addition, accession: something given in* or *over* in a bargain.

ἐπί-θημα, *ατος*, *τό*, (ἐπιτίθημι) *anything put on, a cover, lid.*

ἐπι-θοάζω, f. *σω*, *to sit as a suppliant at an altar, to pray the gods for aid:* cf. θοάζω.

ἐπιθορεῖν, aor. 2 inf. of ἐπιθρώσκω.

ἐπι-θορῠβέω, f. *ήσω*, *to shout in token of approval.*

ἐπι-θράσσω Att. **-ττω**, contr. for ἐπιταράσσω.

ἐπι-θραύω, f. *σω*, *to break besides.*

ἐπιθρέξας, aor. 1 part. of ἐπιτρέχω.

ἐπι-θρώσκω, f. *-θοροῦμαι*: aor. 2 ἐπέθορον:—*to spring* or *leap upon*, c. gen.; c. dat. *to insult over:* absol., τόσσον ἐπιθρώσκουσι so far *do they bound.*

ἐπι-θῡμέω, f. *ήσω*, (ἐπί, θυμός) *to set one's heart upon* a thing, *lust after, desire eagerly.* Hence

ἐπιθύμημα, *ατος*, *τό*, *the object of desire;* and

ἐπιθύμησις, *εως*, *ἡ*, *a longing desire;* and

ἐπιθῡμητής, *οῦ*, *ὁ*, *one who desires: a lover;* and

ἐπιθῡμητικός, *ή*, *όν*, *desiring, coveting.* Adv. *-κῶς.*

ἐπιθῡμία, *ἡ*, (ἐπιθυμέω) *a desire, yearning, longing:* in bad sense, *desire, lust.*

ἐπι-θῡμίᾱμα, *ατος*, *τό*, *an incense-offering:* from

ἐπι-θῡμιάω, f. *άσω* [ᾱ], *to offer incense.*

ἐπ-ῑθύνω, *to aim straight at: to direct, govern.*

ἐπῐ-θύω, f. *-θύσω* [ῡ], *to offer sacrifice upon* or *after:* —*to offer sacrifice, offer.*

ἐπι-θύω, f. *-θύσω* [ῡ], *to rush eagerly at.* 2. c. inf. *to strive vehemently to* do, *desire* or *long to* do, (v. θύω B.)

ἐπι-θωρᾱκίζομαι, Med. *to put on one's armour.*

ἐπι-θωΰσσω, f. *ξω*, *to shout* or *call out.*

ἐπι-ΐδμων, *ονος*, *ὁ*, = ἐπιΐστωρ.

ἐπι-ΐζομαι, Ion. for ἐφέζομαι.

ἐπι-ΐστωρ, *ορος*, *ὁ*, *ἡ*, *acquainted with, knowing.*

ἐπι-καθαιρέω, f. *ήσω*, *to pull down besides.*

ἐπι-καθέζομαι, f. *-εδοῦμαι*, Pass. *to sit down upon.*

ἐπι-κάθημαι Ion. **-κάτημαι**, *to sit upon: to press upon, be heavy upon.* II. *to sit down against* a place, *besiege it.*

ἐπι-καθίζω, f. *ίσω*, *to set upon.* II. intr. *to sit upon.*

ἐπι-καινόω, f. *ώσω*, *to innovate upon.*

ἐπι-καίριος, *ον*, (ἐπί, καιρός) *in due season, seasonable, opportune: important, critical;* οἱ ἐπικαίριοι *the chief persons.*

ἐπί-καιρος, *ον*, = ἐπικαίριος: c. gen. *fit, proper, convenient for* a thing.

ἐπι-καίω Att. **-κάω**: f. *καύσω*:—*to light* or *kindle on* a place: *to burn on an altar.*

ἐπι-κᾰλέω, f. *έσω*, *to call on, appeal to, adjure.* II. *to call in addition, give a surname to:*—Pass. *to be called by surname.* III. *to bring an accusation against, to lay to one's charge.* IV. Med. *to call to oneself, call to aid:* generally, *to invite:* also *to challenge*, Lat. *provocare.* 2. *to summon before one.*

ἐπικάλυμμα, *ατος*, *τό*, *a cover, covering: a veil, cloak, means of hiding.* From

ἐπι-κᾰλύπτω, f. *ψω*, *to cover up, shroud, hide.* II. *to put over.* Hence

ἐπικάλυψις, *εως*, *ἡ*, *a covering, concealment.*

ἐπικαμπή, *ἡ*, (ἐπικάμπτω) *a bend: the angle* of a building; ἐπικαμπὴν ποιεῖσθαι *to* draw up the wings *so as to form angles* with the centre.

ἐπικαμπής, *ές*, *curved, curling.* From

ἐπι-κάμπτω, f. *ψω*, *to bend into an angle:*—Pass. *to wheel round the wings*, so as to take the enemy in flank.

ἐπι-καμπύλος, *ον*, *bent forward.*

ἐπί-κᾰρ, (ἐπί, κάρα) Adv. *head-foremost.*

ἐπι-κάρσιος, *α*, *ον*, (ἐπίκαρ) properly *on the head, head forwards.* II. opp. to ὄρθιος, *crosswise, at an angle;* τὰ ἐπικάρσια the country *measured along the coast*, opp. to τὰ ὄρθια (measured inwards at right angles to the coast): c. gen., τριήρεις τοῦ Πόντου ἐπικάρσιαι triremes *forming an angle* with the current of the Pontus.

ἐπι-καταβαίνω, f. *-βήσομαι*, *to go down to* or *upon* a place. II. *to go down after* or *against.*

ἐπι-καταβάλλω, f. *-βᾰλῶ*, *to let fall down.*

ἐπι-κατάγω, *to bring down to land besides:*—Pass. *to come to land with* or *afterwards.*

ἐπι-καταδαρθάνω, f. *-δαρθήσομαι*: aor. 2 *-έδαρθον*: —*to fall asleep at* or *upon.*

ἐπι-κατακλύζω, f. -ύσω, *to overflow besides*.

ἐπι-κατακοιμάομαι, Dep. *to sleep at* or *upon* a place.

ἐπι-καταλαμβάνω, f. -λήψομαι, *to catch up, overtake.*

ἐπι-καταμένω, f. -μενῶ, *to stay yet longer.*

ἐπι-καταπίπτω, f. -πεσοῦμαι, *to throw oneself upon.*

ἐπι-κατάρᾱτος, ον, *yet more accursed.*

ἐπι-καταρριπτέω and -τω, *to throw down after* or *upon*

ἐπι-κατασφάζω and -ττω, f. ξω, *to slay upon* or *over.*

ἐπι-καταψεύδομαι, Dep. *to tell lies in addition.*

ἐπικατέδαρθον, aor. 2 of ἐπικαταδαρθάνω.

ἐπι-κατεῖδον, inf. -κατιδεῖν, aor. 2 with no pres. in use, *to look down upon*: cf. εἶδον.

ἐπι-κάτειμι, inf. -κατιέναι, *to go down upon* or *into.*

ἐπι-κατέχω, f. -καθέξω, *to detain still.*

ἐπί-καυτος, ον, (ἐπικαίω) *burnt at the end*, Lat. *praeustus.*

ἐπι-κάω, Att. for ἐπι-καίω. [ᾱ]

ἐπί-κειμαι, inf. -κεῖσθαι, serving as Pass. of ἐπιτίθημι, *to be laid upon*; of gates, *to be put to* or *closed.* 2. generally, *to be set on* or *in*: *to lie over against*; αἱ ἐπικείμεναι νῆσοι the islands *off the coast.* 3. *to hang over, impend.* II. *to press heavily upon*: *to press upon, be urgent.* III. of penalties, *to be laid on, imposed.* IV. *to have on one.*

ἐπι-κείρω, f. -κερῶ Ep. -κέρσω:—*to cut down, mow down.* II. metaph. *to cut short, baffle.*

ἐπικεκλόμην, aor. 2 of ἐπικέλομαι.

ἐπικεκλιμένος, pf. part. pass. of ἐπικλίνω.

ἐπι-κελᾰδέω, f. ήσω, *to shout in applause, to cheer.*

ἐπικέλευσις, εως, ἡ, *cheering, exhortation.*

ἐπι-κελεύω, also in Med. **ἐπι-κελεύομαι**, *to exhort* and *encourage, cheer on.*

ἐπι-κέλλω, fut. -κέλσω: aor. I ἐπέκελσα:—*to run aground* or *ashore*, of ships. 2. intrans. *to come to land, come ashore.*

ἐπι-κέλομαι, Dep. *to call to* or *upon, invoke.*

ἐπι-κεντρίζω, f. σω, *to apply the spur*

ἐπι-κεράννῡμι, f. -κεράσω [ᾰ]: aor. I ἐπεκέρᾰσα Ep. -έκρησα:—*to mix in, pour in again.*

ἐπι-κέρδια, ων, τά, (ἐπί, κέρδος) *profit on traffic.*

ἐπι-κερτομέω, f. ήσω, *to jeer at, insult, teaze.*

ἐπικέσθαι, Ion. aor. 2 impf. of ἐφικνέομαι.

ἐπι-κεύθω, f. σω, *to conceal, hide*; οὐ σ' ἐπικεύσω *I will* not *hide* it *from* thee

ἐπι-κήδειος, ον, (ἐπί, κῆδος) *of* or *at a burial.*

ἐπικηρῡκεία, ἡ, (ἐπικηρυκεύομαι) *the sending a herald* or *embassy* to treat for peace.

ἐπικηρύκευμα, ατος, τό, *a message* or *demand by herald.* From

ἐπι-κηρῡκεύομαι, Dep. *to send a message by a herald*: *to make proposals for a treaty*: generally, *to proclaim publicly.*

ἐπι-κηρύσσω Att. -ττω: f. ξω:—*to announce, proclaim*; ἀργύριον ἐπικηρύσσειν τινί or ἐπί τινι to *set* a price on his head: hence *to proscribe.*

ἐπι-κίδνημι, *to spread over*:—Pass. ἐπικίδνᾰμαι, *to be extended, spread over*; ὅσον τ' ἐπικίδναται ἠώς far as the morning light *is spread.*—Only used in pres.

ἐπι-κίνδῡνος, ον, *in danger, precarious, insecure.* II. *dangerous.* Adv. -νως.

ἐπι-κίρνημι, poët. and Ion. for ἐπικεράννυμι.

ἐπι-κλάζω, f. -κλάγξω, *to send forth* a sound *in answer.*

ἐπι-κλαίω Att. -κλάω: f. -κλαύσομαι:—*to weep upon* or *responsively.* Hence

ἐπίκλαυτος, ον, *tearful.*

ἐπι-κλάω, f. άσω [ᾰ], *to bend towards*:—Pass. *to be bent* or *broken in spirit*, Lat. *frangi animo.*

ἐπι-κλάω, Att. for ἐπικλαίω. [ᾱ]

ἐπι-κλεής, ές, (ἐπί, κλέος) *famous.*

ἐπι-κλείω (A), f. -κλείσω, *to shut up, close.*

ἐπι-κλείω (B), (ἐπί, κλέος) *to extol* or *praise the more.*

ἐπι-κληΐζω contr. -κλῄζω, Ion. for ἐπι-κλείω (B).

ἐπίκλημα, ατος, τό, (ἐπικαλέω) *an accusation.*

ἐπί-κλην, Adv. (ἐπικαλέω) *by surname* or *name.*

ἐπί-κληρος, ον, *succeeding to a patrimony*: as Subst. ἐπίκληρος, ἡ, *an only daughter and heiress*, who must by law marry her next of kin.

ἐπι-κληρόω, f. ώσω, *to assign by lot.*

ἐπίκλησις, εως, ἡ, (ἐπικαλέω) *a surname* or *additional name*, and generally, *a name*:—absol. acc. ἐπίκλησιν *by surname, by name*; but also *in name only, nominally.* II. *a reproach, imputation.*

ἐπίκλητος, ον, (ἐπικαλέω) *called upon, called in* as allies 2. *specially summoned*

ἐπι-κλῐνῆναι, aor. 2 inf. pass. of ἐπικλίνω.

ἐπικλῐνής, ές, (ἐπικλινῆναι) *sloping, slanting.*

ἐπί-κλιντρον, τό, *a thing to lean on*: *a couch, armchair.* From

ἐπι-κλίνω [ῑ]: f. -κλῐνῶ: pf. pass. -κέκλῐμαι:—*to lay upon so as to fit*:—Pass. *to be put to*; ἐπικεκλῐμέναι σανίδες *closed* doors. II. *to bend towards*: —Pass. *to be inclined at an angle*: pf. part. pass., ἐπικεκλιμένος *sloping, oblique.* III. Pass. *to lie over against* 2. *to recline at table.*

ἐπι-κλονέω, f. ήσω, *to stir up to commotion.*

ἐπί-κλοπος, ον, (ἐπί, κλοπή) *given to stealing, thievish, wily*: c. gen., ἐπίκλοπος μύθων *cunning in* speech.

ἐπι-κλύζω, f. ύσω, *to overflow, flood*: metaph. *to overwhelm, ruin.* Hence

ἐπίκλῠσις, εως, ἡ, *an overflow, flood.*

ἐπι-κλύω, *to listen to, hear.*

ἐπι-κλώθω, f. ώσω, *to spin to* one, *assign to* one *as one's destiny*, of the Fates:—so also in Med.

ἐπι-κνάμπτω, Att. for ἐπι-γνάμπτω

ἐπι-κνάω, inf. -κνῆν, *to scrape* or *grate upon* a thing.

ἐπ-ικνέομαι, Ion. for ἐφ-ικνέομαι.

ἐπι-κοιμάομαι, Pass. with fut. med. -ήσομαι, *to fall asleep over.*

ἐπί-κοινος, ον, (ἐπί, κοινός) *common to many, promiscuous*: neut. pl. ἐπίκοινα as Adv. *in common.*

ἐπι-κοινωνέω, f. ήσω, *to communicate with.* 2. *to share in common with.*

ἐπι-κομπάζω, f. σω, *to boast besides, add boastingly: to boast* or *exult in* a thing.

ἐπι-κομπέω, f. ήσω, *to add boastingly: to boast of.*

ἐπίκοπος, ον, (ἐπικόπτω) *cut short, lopped.*

ἐπι-κόπτω, f. ψω, *to strike upon, to knock down:*—Med. *to smite one's breast and wail for* another, Lat. *plangi.*

ἐπικός, ή, όν, (ἔπος) *Epic, of Epic poetry; οἱ ἐπικοί the epic poets.*

ἐπι-κοσμέω, f. ήσω, *to adorn with: to celebrate.*

ἐπί-κοτος, ον, *angry, vengeful: malicious, malignant.*

Ἐπικούρειος, ου, ὁ, (Ἐπίκουρος) *an Epicurean, a follower of the sect of Epicurus.*

ἐπικουρέω, f. ήσω, (ἐπίκουρος) *to come to aid, to help in war:* generally, *to help at need;* c. dat. rei, νόσοις ἐπικουρεῖν *to aid* one *against* them; ἐπικουρεῖν τινί τι *to keep off from* one. Hence

ἐπικούρημα, ατος, τό, *help, protection;* and

ἐπικούρησις, εως, ἡ, *aid, protection.*

ἐπικουρία, ἡ, (ἐπικουρέω) *a defence* or *protection against, aid, succour, assistance.* II. *an auxiliary* or *allied force.*

ἐπικουρικός, ή, όν, *auxiliary, allied.*

ἐπί-κουρος, ον, (ἐπί, κοῦρος) *helping, aiding, assisting:* as Subst. *an ally:*—οἱ ἐπίκουροι *the auxiliaries* or *mercenary troops*, opp. to the national army.

ἐπι-κουφίζω, f. ίσω Att. ιῶ, *to lighten: to relieve of* a burden. II. *to lift up, support.* 2. metaph. *to lift up, encourage:* in bad sense, *to puff up, elate.*

ἐπι-κράζω, f. ξω, *to shout to* or *at.*

ἐπι-κραίνω Ep. **-κραιαίνω**: f. -κρᾰνῶ: aor. 1 ἐπέκρᾱνα Ep. -έκρηνα, -εκρήηνα:—*to bring to pass, accomplish, fulfil;* νῦν μοι τόδ' ἐπικρήηνον ἐέλδωρ *grant* me now this prayer, *fulfil it:* generally, *to achieve, effect.*

ἐπί-κρᾱνον, τό, (ἐπί, κράνον) *a covering for the head, a head-dress.* II. *the capital of a column.*

ἐπικράτεια, ἡ, (ἐπικρᾰτής) *mastery, dominion. a government, dominion, province.*

ἐπι-κρᾰτέω, f. ήσω, *to rule over, govern*, c. dat.: absol. *to have power.* 2. *to prevail over: to get possession of*, Lat. *potiri*, c. gen.:—absol. *to prevail, conquer.*

ἐπικρατέως, *overbearingly, impetuously:* Adv. of

ἐπι-κρᾰτής, ές, (ἐπί, κράτος) *having control* or *mastery over* a thing: Comp. ἐπικρατέστερος, *superior.*

ἐπικράτησις, εως, ἡ, (ἐπικρατέω) *a conquest.*

ἐπι-κρεμάννυμι and **-ύω**: f. -κρεμάσω [ᾰ] Att. κρεμῶ:—*to hang over, cause to impend:*—Pass. *to overhang, impend over, threaten*, Lat. *imminere.*

ἐπι-κρεμής, ές, (ἐπικρεμάννυμι) *overhanging.*

ἐπικρήηνον, Ep. aor. 1 imperat. of ἐπικραίνω.

ἐπικρήνειε, Ep. 3 sing. aor. 1 opt. of ἐπικραίνω.

ἐπικρῆσαι, Ep. aor. 1 inf. of ἐπικεράννυμι.

ἐπι-κρίνω, f. -κρῐνῶ, *to give judgment upon, decide, determine.*

ἐπ-ίκριον, τό, (ἐπί, ἴκριον) *the sailyard* upon a ship's mast.

ἐπι-κροτέω, f. ήσω, *to rattle on* or *over.*

ἐπί-κροτος, ον, *trodden hard, beaten.*

ἐπι-κρούω, f. σω, *to hammer upon* or *in.* II. *to strike* or *smite upon.*

ἐπι-κρύπτω, f. ψω: aor. 2 -έκρῠφον:—*to throw a covering over:*—Med. *to disguise:*—Pass. *to conceal* or *disguise oneself.* Hence

ἐπί-κρῠφος, ον, *hidden, secret.*

ἐπι-κρώζω, f. σω, *to caw* or *croak at* one.

ἐπι-κτάομαι, f. -ήσομαι, Dep. *to gain, win besides;* ἐπικτᾶσθαι ἀρχήν *to gain additional* territory.

ἐπι-κτείνω, f. -κτενῶ, *to kill besides;* ἐπικτείνειν τον θανόντα *to slay* the slain *anew.*

ἐπίκτησις, εως, ἡ, (ἐπικτάομαι) *fresh gain.*

ἐπίκτητος, ον, (ἐπικτάομαι) *gained besides* or *in addition;* ἐπικτήτη γῆ *acquired* land, as the Delta of Egypt; ἐπικτήτη *a new* or *foreign* wife; ἐπίκτητοι φίλοι *newly acquired* friends.

ἐπι-κτῠπέω, f. ήσω, *to make a noise upon;* ἐπικτυπεῖν τοῖν ποδοῖν *to stamp* with the feet: *to resound with.*

ἐπι-κῡδής, ές, (ἐπί, κῦδος) *glorious: brilliant.*

ἐπι-κῠΐσκω, *to impregnate again:*—Pass. *to become doubly pregnant.*

ἐπι-κυκλέω, f. ήσω, *to come round in turn to.*

ἐπι-κῠλινδέω, f. -κυλίσω [ῐ]: aor. 1 -εκύλῖσα:—Pass., aor. 1 -εκυλίσθην:—*to roll down upon.*

ἐπι-κυμαίνω, *to flow in waves over.*

ἐπι-κύπτω, f. ψω, *to bend oneself over, to stoop down.*

ἐπι-κῠρέω and **-κύρω**: f. -κυρήσω and -κύρσω: aor. 1 -εκύρησα and -έκῠρσα: *to fall* or *light upon, fall in with:* c. gen. *to have a share of, partake in.*

ἐπι-κῡρόω, f. ώσω, (ἐπί, κῦρος) *to confirm, ratify: to determine.*

ἐπικύρσας, aor. 1 part. of ἐπικυρέω.

ἐπί-κυρτος, ον, (ἐπί, κυρτός) *humpbacked.* Hence

ἐπι-κυρτόω, f. ώσω, *to bend forward.*

ἐπι-κυψέλιος, ον, (ἐπί, κυψέλη) *guarding bee-hives.*

ἐπι-κωκύω, f. ύσω [ῡ], *to lament over.*

ἐπικώλῡσις, εως, ἡ, *a hinderance.* From

ἐπι-κωλύω, f. ύσω [ῡ], *to hinder, keep in check.*

ἐπι-κωμάζω, f. άσω, *to make a riotous assault upon.*

ἐπι-κώμιος, α, ον, (ἐπί, κῶμος) *of* or *for a festal procession.* 2. *laudatory.*

ἐπί-κωπος, ον, (ἐπί, κώπη) *at the oar, a rower.* 2. of a weapon, *up to the very hilt.*

ἐπιλᾰβέσθαι, aor. 2 med. inf. of ἐπιλαμβάνω.

ἐπιλᾰβή, ἡ, (ἐπιλαμβάνω) *a taking hold, grasping: a handle.*

ἐπιλᾰβόμενος, aor. 2 med. part. of ἐπιλαμβάνω.

ἐπι-λαγχάνω, f. -λήξομαι, *to receive by lot afterwards.* II. *to fall to one by lot, come afterwards.*

ἐπι-λάζῠμαι, Dep. *to lay hold of, hold tight.*

ἐπιλᾰθέσθαι, **ἐπιλάθωμαι**, aor. 2 med. inf. and subj. of ἐπιλανθάνω.

ἐπι-λαμβάνω, f. -λήψομαι: aor. 2 ἐπέλᾰβον: pf. -είληφα:—*to lay hold of, seize, attack.* 2. *to overtake, interrupt;* νυκτὸς ἐπιλαβούσης τὸ ἔργον. 3. *to attain to, reach, over-live.* 4. *to seize and stop;*

ἐπιλαμβάνειν τῆς ὀπίσω ὁδοῦ *to hinder from* getting back. II. metaph., πολὺν χῶρον ἐπιλαβεῖν *to get over* much ground. B. Med., with pf. pass. ἐπείλημμαι, *to hold oneself on by, lay hold of*; ἐπιλαμβάνειν προφάσιος *to lay hold of* a pretext. 2. *to attack*:—*to seize upon, arrest*:—*to get possession of, obtain*: *to come up to, reach*. Hence

ἐπίλαμπτος, ον, Ion. for ἐπίληπτος, *caught, detected*.

ἐπι-λάμπω, f. ψω, *to shine after* or *upon*; ἐπιλαμψάσης ἡμέρας when day *had dawned*.

ἐπι-λανθάνω, aor. 2 ἐπέλᾰθον, *to escape notice, be hidden*. II. **ἐπιληθάνω**, f. -λήσω: aor. 1 -έλησα: Causal, *to make to forget*. III. Med. **ἐπιλανθάνομαι**, fut. -λήσομαι, with pf. 2 act. -λέληθα, and pf. pass. -λέλησμαι, *to forget*; ὀφείλων ἐπιλέληθα *I forgot that* I owed:—Pass., aor. 1 -ελήσθην, *to be forgotten*.

ἐπί-λᾱσις, εως, ἡ, Dor. for ἐπίλησις.

ἐπι-λεαίνω, f. -λεᾰνῶ, *to smoothe over*; aor. 1 part., ἐπιλεήνας τὴν Ξέρξεω γνώμην *having smoothed over* the opinion of Xer--s, i. e. *making* it plausible.

ἐπι-λέγω, f. ξω, *to say in addition, to add further*. 2. *to call by name*. II. *to choose, pick out, select*: so also in Med.:—Pass., ἐπιλελεγμένοι or ἐπειλεγμένοι *chosen* men. III. in Med. also, *to read*. 2. *to think over, consider*.

ἐπι-λείβω, f. ψω, *to pour upon, make a libation over*.

ἐπι-λείπω, f. ψω: aor. 2 ἐπέλῐπον: pf. ᾿πιλέλοιπα: Pass., 3 sing. plqpf. ἐπελέλειπτο:—*to leave behind one*. II. *to fail one*, like Lat. *deficere*; ὕδωρ μιν ἐπέλιπε the water *failed* him; ἐπιλείπει με ὁ χρόνος time *fails* me: of rivers, ἐπιλείπειν τὸ ῥέεθρον, *to have* their stream *failing, to be dried up*; and so without ῥέεθρον, *to fail*: absol. *to fail, lack, be wanting*. Hence

ἐπίλειψις, εως, ἡ, *failure, lack*.

ἐπίλεκτος, ον, (ἐπιλέγω) *chosen, picked*; οἱ ἐπίλεκτοι *picked* soldiers.

ἐπιλέλησμαι, pf. pass. of ἐπιλανθάνω.

ἐπι-λέπω, f. ψω, *to peel, strip of* its *bark*.

ἐπι-λεύσσω, *to look towards, see before one*.

ἐπι-ληθάνω, see ἐπιλανθάνω II.

ἐπίληθος, ον, (ἐπιλανθάνω) *causing forgetfulness*.

ἐπι-λήθομαι, poët. for ἐπιλανθάνομαι, *to forget*.

ἐπι-ληΐς, ΐδος, ἡ, (ἐπί, λεία) *obtained as plunder*.

ἐπι-ληκέω, f. ήσω, *to shout in applause*.

ἐπι-λήνιος, ον, (ἐπί, ληνός) *of a winepress* or *the vintage*.

ἐπίληπτος, ον, (ἐπιλαμβάνω) *caught, detected*.

ἐπίλησις, εως, ἡ, (ἐπιλανθάνομαι) *forgetfulness*.

ἐπιλησμονή, ἡ, (ἐπιλανθάνομαι) *forgetfulness*.

ἐπιλήσμων, ον, gen. ονος, (ἐπιλανθάνομαι) *forgetful, having a bad memory*:—Comp. ἐπιλησμονέστερος: irreg. Sup. ἐπιλησμότατος.

ἐπιλήσομαι, fut. med. of ἐπιλανθάνω.

ἐπίληψις, εως, ἡ, (ἐπιλαμβάνω) *a laying hold of, seizure*: *a finding fault*.

ἐπι-λίγδην, Adv. *grazing, scratching*.

ἐπι-λιμνάζομαι, Pass. *to be flooded*.

ἐπι-λῖνευτής, οῦ, ὁ, (ἐπί, λινεύω) *one who uses nets, a fisherman* or *hunter*.

ἐπ-ιλλίζω, (ἐπί, ἴλλος) *to wink with the eyes, to make signs by winking*.

ἐπι-λογίζομαι: fut. ίσομαι Att. ἴοῦμαι: aor. 1 -ελογισάμην and -ελογίσθην: pf. -λελόγισμαι: Dep.:—*to reckon over, think on, consider*: *to make account of*.

ἐπίλογος, ὁ, (ἐπιλέγω) *a conclusion, inference*. II. *the concluding speech* of a play, *epilogue*: the *peroration* of a speech.

ἐπί-λογχος, ον, (ἐπί, λόγχη) *barbed*.

ἐπίλοιπος, ον, (ἐπιλείπω) *still left, remaining*: of Time, *to come, future*.

ἐπί-λουτρον, τό, *the price of a bath*.

ἐπι-λῡπέω, f. ήσω, *to trouble, grieve besides*. Hence

ἐπιλῡπία, ἡ, *trouble, grief*.

ἐπί-λῡπος, ον, (ἐπί, λύπη) *troubled, grieved*.

ἐπίλῠσις, εως, ἡ, (ἐπιλύω) *a release*.

ἐπι-λύω, f. ύσω, *to loose, untie*: *to let slip* dogs: generally, *to release*. 2. *to solve, explain*.

ἐπι-λωβεύω, f. σω, (ἐπί, λώβη) *to mock at*.

ἐπι-μάζιος, ον, (ἐπί, μαζός) *at the breast*.

ἐπι-μαίνομαι, Pass., with aor. 2 -εμάνην [ᾰ], aor. 1 med. -εμηνάμην, pf. act. -μέμηνα:—*to be mad after, dote upon*: *to be passionately in love with*.

ἐπι-μαίομαι, fut. -μάσομαι Ep. -μάσσομαι: Ep. aor. 1 -εμασσάμην: Dep.:—*to strive after, endeavour to obtain, aim at*. II. c. acc. *to lay hold of, grasp*: also *to touch, feel*.

ἐπι-μᾶλλον, Adv. for ἐπὶ μᾶλλον, *still more*.

ἐπιμανδᾰλωτόν, τό, (ἐπί, μανδαλωτός) *a wanton kiss*.

ἐπι-μανθάνω, f. -μᾰθήσομαι, *to learn besides* or *after*.

ἐπι-μαρτυρέω, f. ήσω, *to bear witness* or *depose to* a thing. Hence

ἐπιμαρτῠρία, ἡ, *a witness, testimony*

ἐπι-μαρτύρομαι, Dep. *to take to witness, to call on as witness, appeal to*: absol. *to call witnesses, call in evidence*. 2. *to call on earnestly, to conjure*, Lat. *obtestari*. 3. *to declare before witnesses*. Hence

ἐπι-μάρτῠρος, ὁ, *a witness to anything*.

ἐπι-μάρτυς, gen. -ῠρος, ὁ, = ἐπιμάρτυρος.

ἐπιμάσσομαι, Ep. fut. of ἐπιμαίομαι.

ἐπι-μάσσω, f. ξω, *to knead again*:—Med. *to stroke*.

ἐπι-μαστίδιος, ον, (ἐπί, μαστός) *at the breast*.

ἐπίμαστος, ον, (ἐπιμαίομαι) *seeking after* or *for*.

ἐπιμᾰχέω, f. ήσω, (ἐπίμαχος) *to fight for one*. Hence

ἐπιμᾰχία, ἡ, *a defensive alliance*.

ἐπί-μᾰχος, ον, (ἐπί, μάχομαι) *that may easily be attacked, assailable, open to attack*.

ἐπιμειδιάω, f. άσω [ᾱ], and **-μειδάω**, f. ήσω:—*to smile at* or *upon*.

ἐπιμεῖναι, aor. 1 inf. of ἐπιμένω.

ἐπιμέλεια, ἡ, (ἐπιμελής) *care, attention, diligence*; ἐπιμέλεια τινος *attention paid* to a thing.

ἐπι-μελέομαι and **ἐπι-μέλομαι**: Dep. with fut. med. -μελήσομαι, aor. 1 -εμελησάμην; also with fut. pass. -μεληθήσομαι, aor. 1 -εμελήθην: (ἐπί, μέλομαι):—

to take care of, have charge of: to have the management of: to pay attention to, cultivate, c. gen.: also c. acc. et inf. *to take care that.* Hence

ἐπιμέλημα, ατος, τό, *an object of care, a care.*

ἐπι-μελής, ές, (ἐπί, μέλομαι) *caring for, anxious about:* absol. *careful, attentive.* II. pass. *cared for, an object of care:* esp. in neut., as, ἐπιμελὲς τῷ Κύρῳ ἐγένετο it was *a care* to Cyrus; ἐπιμελές μοί ἐστι I have *to care* for it; τὸ ἐπιμελὲς τοῦ δρωμένου *the charge* of the execution of orders.

ἐπιμελητέον, verb. Adj. of ἐπιμελέομαι, *one must take care of, pay attention to* a thing.

ἐπιμελητής, οῦ, ὁ, (ἐπιμελέομαι) *one who is in charge, a manager, overseer, superintendent.*

ἐπι-μέλομαι, Dep. = ἐπιμελέομαι.

ἐπι-μέλπω, f. ψω, *to sing to.*

ἐπιμελῶς, Adv. of ἐπιμελής, *carefully.*

ἐπιμέμνημαι, pf. pass. of ἐπιμιμνήσκω.

ἐπι-μέμονα, Ion. and poët. pf. 2 with pres. sense, *to aim at, desire.*

ἐπι-μέμφομαι, f. ψομαι, Dep. *to impute to* one *as matter of blame, to object against* one *as matter of blame:* c. dat. pers. *to blame:* absol. *to find fault, complain.* Hence

ἐπίμεμψις, εως, ἡ, *blame, complaint.*

ἐπι-μένω, fut. -μενῶ: aor. 1 ἐπέμεινα:—*to stay on, to abide still.* 2. *to continue in* a pursuit 3. *to abide by.* II. *to wait for, await,* c. acc.

ἐπι-μεταπέμπομαι, Med. *to send for besides, send for a reinforcement.*

ἐπι-μετρέω, f. ήσω, *to measure out to, assign to:*— Pass., ὁ ἐπιμετρούμενος σῖτος the corn *measured out.* II. *to measure out* or *pay in addition.*

ἐπί-μετρον, τό, *something added to the measure, excess.*

ἐπι-μήδομαι, Dep. *to devise* or *concert against.*

Ἐπι-μηθεύς, έως, ὁ, (ἐπί, μῆδος) *Epimetheus,* i. e. *After-thought,* brother of *Prometheus* or *Fore-thought.*

ἐπι-μηθής, ές, (ἐπί, μῆδος) *thoughtful.*

Ἐπι-μηλίδες, ίδων, αἱ, (ἐπί, μῆλα) *Nymphs protectors of flocks.*

ἐπι-μήνιος, ον, (ἐπί, μήν) *monthly:* τὰ ἐπιμήνια (sub. ἱερά) *monthly offerings.*

ἐπι-μηνίω, f. ίσω [ῑ], *to be angry at* or *with.*

ἐπι-μηχᾰνάομαι, Dep. *to contrive against: to devise precautions.* II. *to devise besides.*

ἐπι-μήχᾰνος, ον, (ἐπί, μηχανή) *craftily devising;* κακῶν ἐπιμήχανος ἔργων *contriver* of ill deeds.

ἐπι-μίγνῡμι and -ύω, fut. -μίξω:—*to mix in* or *with:*—Pass. ἐπιμίγνῠμαι, *to mingle with, to have intercourse* or *dealings with.*

ἐπι-μιμνήσκω, f. -μνήσω, *to put in mind of.* II. Pass. and Med. ἐπι-μιμνήσκομαι, fut. -μνήσομαι and -μνησθήσομαι; aor. 1 -εμνησάμην and -εμνήσθην: —*to remember, recall to mind, think of:* ἐπιμνησαίμεθα χάρμης *let us think of* battle. II. later, *to make mention of:* also *to quote.*

ἐπι-μίμνω, poët. for ἐπιμένω.

ἐπιμίξ, Adv. (ἐπιμίγνυμι) *mixedly, confusedly, indiscriminately.*

ἐπιμιξία Ion. -ίη, (ἐπιμίγνῡμι) *a mixing with others, intercourse, dealings,* Lat. *commercium.*

ἐπί-μιξις, εως, ἡ, = ἐπιμιξία.

ἐπι-μίσγω, poët. and Ion. for ἐπι-μίγνυμι, *to have dealings with* one; in hostile sense, *to be brought in contact with, clash with:* absol. *to associate together.*

ἐπιμνάομαι, -μνῶμαι, Ion. for ἐπιμιμνήσκομαι.

ἐπιμνησαίμεθα, 1 pl. aor. 1 opt. med. of ἐπιμιμνήσκω.

ἐπιμνησθείς, aor. 1 part. pass. of ἐπιμιμνήσκω.

ἐπι-μοιχεύω, f. σω, *to commit adultery besides.*

ἐπι-μολεῖν, aor. 2 inf. of ἐπιβλώσκω. Hence

ἐπί-μολος, ον, *approaching, invading.*

ἐπιμομφή, ἡ, (ἐπιμέμφομαι) *blame, reproach.*

ἐπίμομφος, ον, (ἐπιμέμφομαι) *blameable, unlucky.*

ἐπιμονή, ἡ, (ἐπιμένω) *a staying on: delay.*

ἐπι-μύζω, f. ξω, *to mutter* or *murmur at.*

ἐπι-μύθιος, ον, (ἐπί, μῦθος) *coming after the story*: τὸ ἐπιμύθιον *the moral of a fable.*

ἐπί-μυκτος, ον, (ἐπιμύζω) *scoffed at.*

ἐπι-μύσσω Att. -ττω, = ἐπιμύζω, *to mutter.*

ἐπι-μύω, f. -μύσω [ῡ], *to close the eyes at* a thing: *to wink at,* in token of assent.

ἐπι-μωμάομαι Ion. -έομαι, Dep. *to find fault with.* Hence

ἐπιμωμητός, ή, όν, *blameworthy, blameable.*

ἐπί-μωμος, ον, *blamed, blameworthy.*

ἐπι-μώομαι, Dor. for ἐπιμαίομαι.

ἐπι-νάχομαι, Dor. for ἐπινήχομαι.

ἐπί-νειον -ό (ἐπί, ναῦς) *a sea-port for the navy, arsenal.*

ἐπι-νέμω, fut. -νεμῶ and -νεμήσω: aor. 1 -ένειμα: —*to allot, assign, distribute.* II. *to turn* cattle *to graze on another's land:*—Med., of cattle, *to feed over the boundaries, to go on grazing:* metaph. *to spread over;* πῦρ ἐπινέμεται τὸ ἄστυ the fire *spreads over* the town; so, ἡ νόσος ἐπενείματο τὰς Ἀθήνας.

ἐπινενησμένος, pf. part. pass. of ἐπινέω.

ἐπι-νεύσομαι, fut. of ἐπινέω.

ἐπι-νεύω, f. σω: aor. 1 -ένευσα:—*to nod forwards.* II. *to nod to,* in token of command or approval, *to nod assent, to make a sign* to another to do a thing: *to promise by nodding.* III. *to incline to* or *towards.*

ἐπι-νέφελος, ον, (ἐπί, νεφέλη) *clouded, overcast.*

ἐπι-νεφρίδιος, ον, (ἐπί, νεφρός) *upon the kidneys.*

ἐπι-νέω (A), f. νήσω, *to spin to,* esp. of the Fates.

ἐπι-νέω (B), = ἐπινηνέω, *to load with* a thing: pf. part. pass., ἐπινενησμένος *piled up with.*

ἐπι-νέω (C), f. -νεύσομαι, *to swim, float on the top.*

ἐπι-νήϊος, ον, (ἐπί, ναῦς) *on board ship.*

ἐπι-νηνέω, (ἐπί, νέω) *to heap* or *pile upon.*

ἐπι-νήφω, *to be sober at* or *for.*

ἐπι-νήχομαι, f. -νήξομαι, Dep. *to swim upon: to come to the top, float on the surface.* 2. *to swim to* or *over to.*

ἐπι-νίκιος, ον, (ἐπί, νίκη) *of victory.* II. as

Subst. τὸ ἐπινίκιον (sub. ᾆσμα or μέλος), *a song of victory, triumphal song* or *ode.* 2. (sub. θῦμα), *a feast in honour of a victory.*

ἐπί-νῑκος, ον, = ἐπινίκιος.

ἐπι-νίσσομαι, fut. –νίσομαι, *to go over: come upon.*

ἐπι-νίφω, *to snow upon.* [νῐ]

ἐπι-νοέω, f. ήσω: aor. 1 ἐπενόησα, but also with aor. 1 pass. ἐπενοήθην in same sense:—*to think on* or *of, contrive.* 2. c. inf. *to purpose, intend.* 3. absol. *to form a plan, design.* Hence

ἐπίνοια, ἡ, *a thinking of* or *over* a thing, *thought: power of thought, inventiveness.* 2. *a purpose, design.* II. *after-thought.*

ἐπίνομες, Dor. 1 pl. impf. of πίνω.

ἐπινομία, ἡ, (ἐπινέμομαι) *a grazing on* another's lands: *a right to pasture on each other's lands*, of the citizens of two neighbouring states.

ἐπίνομος, ον, (ἐπινέμομαι) *dwelling in the country.*

ἐπι-νύκτιος, ον, (ἐπί, νύξ) *by night, nightly.*

ἐπι-νυμφίδιος, ον, (ἐπί, νύμφα) *of* or *for a bride, bridal.*

ἐπι-νύσσω Att. **–ττω**, f. ξω, *to prick on the surface.*

ἐπι-νυστάζω, f. σω and ξω, *to drop asleep over.*

ἐπι-νωμάω, f. ήσω, *to bring* or *apply to.* II. *to distribute, assign.*

ἐπι-νωτίδιος, ον, (ἐπί, νῶτον) *on the back.*

ἐπι-νωτίζω, f. σω, (ἐπί, νῶτον) *to put on the back of, to cover with.*

ἐπι-νώτιος, ον, (ἐπί, νῶτον) *on the back.*

ἐπί-ξανθος, ον, *inclining to yellow, tawny*, of hares.

ἐπι-ξεινόω, f. ώσω, Ion. and poët. for ἐπιξενόω.

ἐπι-ξενόω, f. ώσω, (ἐπί, ξένος) *to entertain as a guest:*—Pass. *to be so entertained, to dwell abroad.* 2. Med., ἐπιξενοῦμαι ταῦτα *I claim* these offices *as a stranger.*

ἐπι-ξέω, f. –ξέσω, *to scrape on the surface.*

ἐπί ξηνον, τό, (ἐπί, ξηνός) *a chopping-block*, like ἐπικόπανον: *the executioner's block.*

ἐπί-ξῡνος, ον, poët. for ἐπίκοινος, *common to many;* ἐπίξυνος ἄρουρα a *common* field, i. e. in which *many* persons have rights.

ἐπι-οίνιος, (ἐπί, οἶνος) *at* or *over wine.*

ἐπι-οινοχοεύω, f. σω, *to pour out wine for.*

ἔπιον, aor. 2 of πίνω.

ἐπι-όπτης, ου, ὁ, poët. for ἐπόπτης.

ἐπιορκέω, f. ήσω: aor. 1 ἐπιώρκησα: (ἐπίορκος):—*to swear falsely, forswear oneself*, πρὸς δαίμονος by a deity; τὰς βασιληΐας ἱστίας ἐπιορκεῖν *to swear falsely by* the royal hearth. Hence

ἐπιορκία, ἡ, *a false oath*, Lat. *perjuria.*

ἐπί-ορκος, ον, (ἐπί, ὅρκος) *swearing falsely, forsworn*, Lat. *perjurus;* or of the oath, *sworn falsely;* ἐπίορκον ὀμνύναι to swear *falsely;* also, ἐπίορκον ἐπομνύναι to swear *a bootless oath.*

ἐπι-ορκοσύνη, ἡ, = ἐπιορκία.

ἐπι-όσσομαι, Dep. (ἐπί, ὄσσε) *to have before one's eyes, foresee.*

ἐπί-ουρος, ὁ, (ἐπί, οὖρος) *a watcher, guard:* c. dat., Κρήτῃ ἐπίουρος *guardian, chief over* Crete: c. gen., ὑῶν ἐπίουρος *chief* swine-*herd.*

ἐπ-ιοῦσα, ἡ, part. pres. fem. of ἔπειμι (εἶμι *ibo*), *the coming day* (sub. ἡμέρα). Hence

ἐπιούσιος, ον, *for the coming day, sufficient for the day;* ἐπιούσιος ἄρτος *daily* bread.

ἐπι-όψομαι, poët. for ἐπόψομαι.

ἐπί-παγχυ, Adv. *entirely, altogether.*

ἐπι-πάλλω, *to brandish at* or *against.*

ἐπι-πάμων, ον, gen. ονος, (ἐπί, πέπᾱμαι pf. of πάομαι) Dor. for ἐπίκληρος, *falling to one's share.*

ἐπί-παν, Adv. *upon the whole, generally, on the average.*

ἐπι-παρανέω, *to heap up besides.*

ἐπι-παρασκευάζω, f. σω, *to prepare besides:*—Med. *to provide oneself with besides.*

ἐπι-πάρειμι, inf. –εἶναι, *to be present at* or *near.* II. *to be present besides* or *in addition to.*

ἐπι-πάρειμι, inf. –ιέναι, *to come upon in flank, to march alongside of.* II. *to come on to assist.* III. *to come forward to speak.*

ἐπι-πάσσω Att. **–ττω**: fut. –πάσω [ᾰ]:—*to sprinkle upon* or *over.* Hence

ἐπί-παστος, ον, *sprinkled on* or *over:*—τὸ ἐπίπαστον a kind of cake *with comfits upon it:* also *a plaster.*

ἐπι-πᾰτᾰγέω, f. ήσω, *to make a noise at.*

ἐπί-πεδος, ον, (ἐπί, πέδον) *on the ground*, or *on a level with it, level, flat;* ἐν ἐπιπέδῳ on *a level:*—irreg. Comp. ἐπιπεδέστερος.

ἐπιπειθής, ές, *obedient, compliant.* From

ἐπι-πείθομαι, f. –πείσομαι, Pass. *to be persuaded, yield to persuasion;* c. dat. *to put faith in, comply with, obey.*

ἐπι-πέλομαι, Dep. (ἐπί, πέλω) *to come towards, approach;* Ep. syncop. aor. 2 part., ἐπιπλόμενον ἔτος *the coming* year.

ἐπί-πεμπτος, ον, *containing* 1 *and* $\frac{1}{5}=\frac{6}{5}$; δάνεισμα ἐπίπεμπτον a loan *at the rate of* $\frac{1}{5}$ *of the principal*, or 20 *per cent.*

ἐπι-πέμπω, f. ψω, *to send after* or *again.* 2. of the gods, to *send upon* or *to, let loose upon.* II. *to send besides: to send by way of supply.* Hence

ἐπίπεμψις, εως, ἡ, *a sending to a place.*

ἐπιπέπτωκα, pf. of ἐπιπίπτω.

ἐπιπέπωκα, pf. of ἐπιπίνω.

ἐπι-περκάζω, *to begin to turn dark*, of grapes ripening.

ἐπί-περκνος, ον, *somewhat dark*, properly of grapes ripening; then of the colour of hares.

ἐπιπεσοῦμαι, fut. med. of ἐπιπίπτω.

ἐπιπεσών, οῦσα, aor. 2 part. of ἐπιπίπτω.

ἐπι-πετάννῡμι, f. –πετάσω, *to spread over.*

ἐπι-πέταμαι or **–πέτομαι**, only found in aor. 2 ἐπεπτάμην or ἐπεπτόμην: Dep.:—*to fly over:* metaph. *to fly over, come to the knowledge of by flying.*

ἐπι-πήγνῡμι and **–ύω**, f. –πήξω, *to fix upon.* 2. *to make to freeze at top:*—Pass. *to congeal.*

ἐπι-πηδάω, f. ήσομαι, *to spring upon, rush at.*

ἐπί-πηχυς, υ, (ἐπί, πῆχυς) *above the elbow.*

ἐπι-πιέζω, f. σω, *to press upon.*

ἐπι-πίλνᾰμαι, Dep., used only in pres. and impf., *to approach, come near.*

ἐπι-πίμπλημι, f. -πλήσω, *to fill up with* a thing.

ἐπι-πίνω, f. -πίομαι: pf. -πέπωκα: aor. 2 -έπιον;—*to drink afterwards* or *besides: to tope after dinner.*

ἐπι-πίπτω, f. -πεσοῦμαι; pf. -πέπτωκα: aor. 2 -έπεσον:—*to fall upon:* also in hostile sense, *to fall upon, attack:* of accidents, *to befall* one.

ἔπιπλα (contr. from ἐπίπλοα), τά, *implements, furniture, movables,* as opp. to fixtures, Lat. *supellex.*

ἐπι-πλάζω, f. -πλάγξω, *to make to wander over, to drive about:*—Pass. with fut. med. -πλάγξομαι: aor. 1 pass. ἐπιπλάγχθην, *to wander about over.*

ἐπιπλάσας, aor. 1 part. of ἐπιπλάσσω.

ἐπι-πλάσσω Att. -ττω, f. -πλάσω [ᾰ]:—*to spread a plaster on, smear over.* Hence

ἐπίπλαστος, ον, *plastered over:*—*feigned, false.*

ἐπιπλαγχθείς, aor. 1 part. pass. of ἐπιπλάζω.

ἐπι-πλεῖον, Adv. = ἐπιπλέον.

ἐπί-πλειος, ον, Ep. for ἐπίπλεος.

ἐπι-πλείων, ον, gen. ονος, *still more.*

ἐπι-πλέκω, f. ξω, *to plait into a chaplet.*

ἐπι-πλέον, Adv., for ἐπὶ πλέον, *still more.*

ἐπί-πλεος, α, ον, Att. ἐπίπλεως, ων, (ἐπί, πλέος) *quite full of* a thing.

ἐπίπλευσις, εως, ἡ, *a sailing against:* ἐπίπλευσιν ἔχειν to have the power of *sailing against,* to have *the weather gage.* From

ἐπι-πλέω, f. -πλεύσομαι: Ion. ἐπιπλώω, f. -πλώσω: Ep. aor. 2 ἐπέπλων, part. ἐπιπλώς:—*to sail upon* or *over: to float upon.* II. *to sail against, to attack with a fleet.* III. *to sail on board a ship: to sail with* or *in charge of.*

ἐπί-πλεως, ων, Att. for ἐπίπλεος.

ἐπι-πληρόω, f. ώσω, *to fill up;* Med., ἐπιπληροῦσθαι τὴν ναῦν *to fill up one's* ship's crew, *to man* her *afresh.*

ἐπι-πλήσσω Att. -ττω, f. ξω, *to strike at:* of words, *to rebuke, reprove: to cast a reproach upon: to cast in* one's *teeth.*

ἐπί-πλοα, τά, fuller form of ἔπιπλα: properly neut. of ἐπίπλοος, ον, an Adj. formed from ἐπί, as ἅπλοος from ἅμα, δίπλοος from δίς.

ἐπιπλόμενος, Ep. for ἐπιπελόμενος, aor. 2 part. of ἐπιπέλομαι.

ἐπίπλοον, τό, (ἐπιπλέω) *the caul of the entrails,* Lat. *omentum:* also ἐπίπλοος, ὁ.

ἐπίπλοος contr. **ἐπίπλους**, ὁ, (ἐπιπλέω) *a sailing against the enemy, bearing down upon him, the attack* of a ship or fleet. 2. *a naval expedition against a place.*

ἐπι-πλώω, Ion. and Ep. for ἐπιπλέω.

ἐπι-πλώς, part. of ἐπέπλων, Ep. aor. 2 of ἐπιπλέω.

ἐπι-πλώσας, Ion. aor. 1 part. of ἐπιπλέω.

ἐπι-πνείω, Ep. for ἐπιπνέω.

ἐπι-πνέω Ep. -πνείω: fut. -πνεύσομαι: aor. 1 ἐπέπνευσα:—*to breathe* or *blow upon,* so as to revive:—metaph. *to excite, inflame: to blow favourably, to favour,* Lat. *adspiro.*

ἐπι-πνίγω, *to choke, stifle.* [πνῑ]

ἐπίπνοια, ἡ, (ἐπιπνέω) *a breathing upon: inspiration.*

ἐπι-πόδιος, α, ον, (ἐπί, πούς) *upon the feet.*

ἐπι-ποθέω, f. ήσω, *to yearn* or *long after, regret greatly,* Lat. *desidero.* Hence

ἐπιπόθησις, εως, ἡ, *a yearning after:* and

ἐπιπόθητος, ον, *longed for, earnestly desired:* and

ἐπι-ποθία, ἡ, = ἐπιπόθησις.

ἐπι-ποιμήν, ὁ, ἡ, *an over shepherd* or *shepherdess.*

ἐπιπολάζω, f. σω, (ἐπιπολή) *to be at the top, lie on the surface.* II. *to rise to the top:* metaph. *to be uppermost, to prevail.*

ἐπι-πόλαιος, ον, *on the surface: prominent, projecting.* 2. *superficial, ordinary.* From

ἐπι-πολή, ἡ, (ἐπί, πέλω) *a surface:* gen. ἐπιπολῆς as Adv., *at the top, atop:* c. gen. *on the top of, above.* II. αἱ Ἐπιπολαί, *a* piece of ground *with a sloping surface* near Syracuse.

ἐπι-πόλιος, ον, *growing hoary, grizzled.*

ἐπί-πολος, = πρόσπολος, *an attendant.*

ἐπι-πολύ, Adv., for ἐπὶ πολύ, *generally.*

ἐπι-πονέω, f. ήσω, *to toil on, persevere.*

ἐπί-πονος, ον, *painful, toilsome: wearisome:* of persons, *laborious, pains-taking:* of omens, *portending toil and suffering.* Adv. ἐπιπόνως, Lat. *aegré, with toil and trouble,* Sup. ἐπιπονώτατα.

ἐπι-πορεύομαι: f. med. -πορεύσομαι, aor. 1 pass. -επορεύθην: Dep.:—*to go, march to: to march over.*

ἐπι-πόρπᾱμα, ματος, τό, (ἐπί, πορπάω) *a mantle buckled on the shoulder.*

ἐπι-ποτάομαι, Dep., lengthd. for ἐπιπέτομαι, *to fly to* or *hover over.*

ἐπι-πρέπω, *to be conspicuous.* 2. *to beseem, be befitting.*

ἐπι-πρεσβεύομαι, Dep. *to go as ambassador any whither.* 2. *to send an embassy.*

ἐπι-πρηΰνω, Ion. for ἐπι-πραΰνω, = πραΰνω.

ἐπι-πρίω [ῑ], *to grind* [the teeth] *at* a thing.

ἐπι-προβάλλω, f. -βαλῶ, *to throw forward.*

ἐπιπροέηκα, Ep. aor. 1 of ἐπιπροΐημι.

ἐπιπροέμεν, Ep. aor. 2 inf. of ἐπιπροΐημι.

ἐπι-προϊάλλω, f. ἀλῶ: aor. 1 -προΐηλα:—*to set out* or *place before* one. 2. *to send out one before* or *after* another.

ἐπι-προΐημι, fut. -προήσω: aor. 1 -προῆκα Ep. -έηκα:—*to send forth towards* or *at: to shoot at.* II. νήσοισιν ἐπιπροέηκε [ναῦν] he *steered, made for* them.

ἐπί-προσθεν, rarely -θε, Adv. of Time and Place, *before:* also *in preference to.*

ἐπι-προσθέω (A), f. -θεύσομαι, *to run at* or *to.*

ἐπιπροσθέω (B), f. ήσω, (ἐπίπροσθεν) *to be before, be in the way;* ἐπιπροσθεῖν τοῖς πύργοις *to be in a line with* the towers, so as to cover one with the other.

ἐπι-προχέω, f. -χεῶ, *to pour forth over: to pour forth.*

ἐπι-πταίρω: aor. 2 ἐπέπτᾰρον:—*to sneeze at;* υἱός μοι ἐπέπταρε πᾶσιν ἔπεσσιν my son *sneezed* as I spoke the words,—a good omen: hence of the gods, *to be kindly to, favour*

ἐπιπτέσθαι, aor. 2 inf. of ἐπιπέτομαι.

ἐπιπτὔχή, ἡ, (ἐπί, πτύσσω) *an over-fold, a flap.*

ἐπι-πωλέομαι, Dep. *to go about, visit,* Lat. *obire:* of a general, *to inspect, review:* of an enemy, *to reconnoitre.* Hence.

ἐπιπώλησις, εως, ἡ, *a going round, visitation*

ἐπι-πωτάομαι, = ἐπι-ποτάομαι.

ἐπι-ραβδοφορέω, f. ήσω, of the rider, *to urge* a horse *by shaking the whip;* or of the horse, *to gallop*

ἐπιρ-ραθῦμέω, f. ήσω, *to be careless about* a thing.

ἐπιρραίνω, *to sprinkle upon* or *over.*

ἐπιρ-ράπτω, f. ψω, *to sew, stitch on.*

ἐπιρ-ράσσω Att. -ττω, Att. for ἐπιρρήσσω.

ἐπιρ-ρέζω, f. ξω, *to offer sacrifices at* a place; ἐπέρρεσκον Ion. impf. 2. *to sacrifice afterwards* or *besides.*

ἐπιρρεπής, ές, *leaning, inclined towards,* Lat. *proclivis.* From

ἐπιρ-ρέπω, f. ψω, *to lean towards,* of the balance: *to fall upon.* II. trans., ἐπιρρέπειν τάλαντον *to force down* one scale: hence *to weigh out to* one, *allot.*

ἐπιρρεπῶς, Adv. of ἐπιρρεπής, *favourably inclined.*

ἐπιρ-ρέω: f. -ρεύσομαι: aor. 2 pass. (in act. sense) ἐπερρύην:—*to flow upon the surface, float atop.* 2. *to flow to* or *into:* of men, *to stream on* or *towards;* οὑπιρρέων χρόνος *onward-streaming* time, i. e. the future

ἐπιρ-ρήγνῦμι, = ἐπιρρήσσω.

ἐπίρ-ρησις, εως, ἡ, (ἐπί, ῥῆσις) *a reproach.* II. *a spell, charm*

ἐπιρ-ρήσσω, f. -ρήξω: Att. **ἐπιρράσσω,** f. -ράξω:—*to dash against, force upon* or *to;* Ion. impf. ἐπιρρήσσεσκον. 2. *to rend at* or *on bearing* a thing. II. intr. *to burst forth,* of lightning

ἐπιρ-ρητορεύω, f. σω, (ἐπί, ῥήτωρ) *to speak as an orator to* or *over.*

ἐπίρ-ρητος, ον, *cried out against, infamous.*

ἐπίρ-ρικνος, ον, *shrunk up.*

ἐπιρ-ρίπτω and -έω: f. ψω: aor. 1 -έρριψα:—*to cast at* or *upon.* 2. metaph. *to commit to, give up to.* II. intr. *to fall upon.*

ἐπιρροή, ἡ, (ἐπιρρέω) *an afflux, influx, a flood.*

ἐπιρροθέω, f. ήσω, *to roar at,* of the waves: *to echo* or *answer to* a sound: *to shout applause at* a thing: *to repeat* or *second a prayer:* but also, *to inveigh against.* Hence

ἐπίρ-ροθος, ον, *hasting to the rescue, aiding:* generally, *helping in need, giving aid against.* II. ἐπίρροθα κακά reproaches *bandied back and forwards, abusive* language.

ἐπιρ-ροιβδέω, f. ήσω, *to forebode rain by croaking.* Hence

ἐπιρροίβδην, Adv. *with noisy fury.*

ἐπιρ-ροιζέω, f. ήσω, *to croak to* or *at:* c. acc. cognato, ἐπ. φυγάς τινι *to shriek* or *bode* flight to one.

ἐπιρρυείς, aor. 2 part. pass. of ἐπιρρέω.

ἐπιρ-ρύζω, f. ξω, (ἐπί, ῥύζω) *to set* a dog *on* one.

ἐπιρ-ρύομαι, Dep. *to save, preserve.*

ἐπίρρὔτος, ον, (ἐπιρρέω) *flowing in* or *to: coming in upon, adventitious.* 2. metaph. *overflowing, abundant.* II. *overflowed, moist.*

ἐπιρ-ρώννῦμι and -ύω: fut. -ρώσω: aor. 1 -έρρωσα:—*to add strength to, strengthen, encourage, cheer on in* a thing:—Pass. ἐπιρρώννυμαι; but the pf. ἐπέρρωμαι, plqpf. -ερρώμην are used as pres. and impf.: aor. 1 -ερρώσθην:—*to recover strength, be invigorated, be of good cheer:* also in aor. 1, impers., κείνοις ἐπερρώσθη λέγειν they *took courage* to speak.

ἐπιρ-ρώομαι, aor. 1 -ερρωσάμην: Dep.:—*to flow* or *stream downwards on* a thing: of hair, *to fall flowing.* II. *to apply one's strength to* a thing, *work lustily at;* ποσσὶν ἐπερρώσαντο they *moved nimbly* with their feet.

ἐπιρρωσθείς, aor. 1 pass. part. of ἐπιρρώννυμι.

ἐπι-ρύομαι, v. ἐπιρρ-

ἔπῖσα, aor. 1 of πιπίσκω, *to make to drink.*

ἐπίσαγμα, ατος, τό, (ἐπισάττω) *a pack-saddle:* metaph., ἐπίσαγμα νοσήματος *a burden* of disease.

ἐπι-σάττω, f. ξω, *to pile a load upon.* II. *to load* or *saddle* a horse.

ἐπι-σείω Ep. ἐπισσείω: 1. σω:—*to shake at* or *against.* 2. *to wave* or *beckon on:* hence *to set at* or *upon* one.

ἐπι-σεύω Ep. **ἐπισσεύω**;—*to put in motion against* one, *set on.* II. Pass. *to hurry, hasten towards:* in hostile sense, *to fall upon, rush at, attack:* esp. in pf. ἐπέσσῦμαι as pres., and plqpf. ἐπεσσύμην as impf. or aor. 2, part. ἐπεσσύμενος, *to rush on, hurry, hasten;* ἐπεσσύμενος πεδίοιο *hurrying over* the plain: of rapid motion, ἐπέσσυτο διώκειν *be hasted on* to follow:—metaph. *to be in excitement* or *agitation.*

ἐπί-σημα, ατος, τό, *device upon a shield.*

ἐπι-σημαίνω, f. ἀνῶ, *to set a mark* or *sign upon:*—Pass. *to be marked, bear a mark.* II. *to give a sign of approval:*—Med. *to give one's approval to* a thing.

ἐπί-σημος, ον, (ἐπί, σῆμα) *having a mark on* it, *bearing a mark* or *inscription:* of money, *stamped, coined* 2. *distinguished, famous, remarkable,* Lat. *insignis:* also in bad sense, *notorious.* II. ἐπίσημον, τό, as Subst. *any mark of distinction, a device: a device* or *bearing* on a shield: *the ensign* or *flag of* a ship.

ἐπ-ίσης, for ἐπ' ἴσης [sc. μοίρας], *equally.*

ἐπι-σίζω, *to set on,* as a dog.

ἐπί-σῖμος, ον, (ἐπί, σιμός) *somewhat flat-nosed.*

ἐπι-σῖμόω, f. ώσω, *to turn aside one's course.*

ἐπι-σῖτίζω, f. ίσω Att. ιῶ:—*to furnish with food:*—Med. *to furnish oneself with food, to forage:* c. acc., ἐπισιτίζεσθαι τὸ στράτευμα *to provision* the army; ἐπισιτίζεσθαι ἄριστον *to provide oneself with* a meal.

ἐπισίτισις, εως, ἡ, and **ἐπισίτισμα,** τό, = sq.

ἐπισιτισμός, ὁ, (ἐπισιτίζω) *a furnishing oneself with provisions: a stock of provisions*

ἐπι-σκάπτω, f. ψω, *to dig superficially.*

ἐπι-σκεδάννυμι, f. άσω [ᾰ], *to scatter* or *spread upon.*

ἐπι-σκελῐσις, εως, ἡ, (ἐπί, σκέλος) *the first spring* or *start* in a horse's gallop.

ἐπι-σκεπτέος, α, ον, verb. Adj. of ἐπισκέπτομαι, *to be considered, examined.*

ἐπι-σκέπτομαι, a pres. only used by late authors, which furnishes a fut. to ἐπισκοπέω.

ἐπι-σκέπω, *to cover over.*

ἐπι-σκευάζω, f. άσω, *to get ready: to equip, fit out:* ἐπισκευάσαι τὰ χρήματα *to pack the money upon.* II. *to equip anew, repair, restore.* Hence

ἐπισκευαστής, οῦ, ὁ, *one who restores.*

ἐπι-σκευή, ἡ, *a repair, restoration: materials for repairs, stores.*

ἐπίσκεψις, εως, ἡ, (ἐπισκέπτομαι) *a looking at, inspection.* 2. *consideration, reflexion: inquiry.*

ἐπί-σκηνος, ον, (ἐπί, σκηνή) *at* or *near a tent.*

ἐπι-σκηνόω, f. ώσω, *to lodge in a tent:* general'y, *to stay, abide at* a place.

ἐπι-σκήπτω, f. ψω, *to make to lean upon: make to light upon, impose upon:*—intr. *to fall uton,* like lightning:—Med. *to lean upon, rely upon.* II. *to enjoin solemnly upon, lay a strict charge upon, to command* one *to* do; τοσοῦτον σ' ἐπισκήπτω thus much *I command* thee. III. *to prosecute* or *indict.*

ἐπι-σκιάζω, f. άσω: pf. pass. ἐπεσκίασμαι:—*to throw a shade upon, overshadow,* Lat. *obumbrare:*—Pass., λαθραῖον ὄμμ' ἐπεσκιασμένη keeping a hidden watch.

ἐπί-σκιος, ον, (ἐπι, σκιά) *overshadowed.* 2. act. *shading,* c. gen.

ἐπι-σκοπέω, f. -σκέψομαι (from -σκέπτομαι): aor. 1 -εσκεψάμην: pf. -έσκεμμαι:—*to look upon* or *at, inspect, examine: to watch over, pay regard to.* ʔ. *to go to see, visit:*—Pass., ὀνείροις οὐκ ἐπισκοπούμενον un*visited* by dreams. 3. *to consider, reflect.* Hence

ἐπισκοπή, ἡ, *an overseeing: the office of an overseer* or *bishop:* also 2. *visitation, punishment.*

ἐπί-σκοπος, ὁ, (σκοπός 1) *an overseer, watcher, guardian:*—esp. a public officer sent by the Athenians as *inspector* or *overseer* of a subject state:—*a bishop.* II. *a scout, watch.*

ἐπί-σκοπος, ον, (σκοπός II) *hitting the mark: suitable to, coming up to:*—neut. pl. ἐπίσκοπα, as Adv., *successfully, with good aim.*

ἐπι-σκοτέω, f. ήσω, (ἐπί, σκότος) *to throw darkness* or *a shadow over.*

ἐπι-σκύζομαι, Pass. with fut. med. -σκύσομαι, *to be indignant at, brood over.*

ἐπι-σκῠθίζω, f. ίσω Att. ιῶ, *to ply with drink like a Scythian.*

ἐπι-σκυθρωπάζω, f. άσω, *to look savage.*

ἐπι-σκύνιον, τό, *the skin of the brows* which is knitted by frowning: hence, like ὀφρύς, Lat. *supercilium,* used for *arrogance, haughtiness.*

ἐπισκύσσαιτο, Ep. aor. 1 opt. med. of ἐπισκύζομαι.

ἐπι-σκώπτω, f. ψω, *to laugh at, turn into ridicule:* absol. *to joke, make fun.* Hence

ἐπίσκωψις, εως, ἡ, *raillery.*

ἐπι-σμάω, inf. -σμῆν, f. -σμήσω, *to rub* or *smear over.*

ἐπι-σμῠγερός, ά, όν, (ἐπί, σμυγερός = μογερός) *shameful, sad:*—Adv. ἐπισμυγερῶς, *sadly, to his cost.*

ἐπισπαστήρ, ῆρος, ὁ, (ἐπισπάω) *the handle by which a door is pulled to.* II. *a fishing-line, angle.*

ἐπίσπαστος, η, ον, *drawn upon oneself.* II. ἐπίσπαστος βρόχος *a tight-drawn* noose. From

ἐπι-σπάω, f. -σπάσω [ᾰ]: *to draw* or *drag after* one: *to bring on, cause.* 2. *to draw on, allure, induce:* so also in Med. 3. ἐπισπᾶν τὴν θύραν *to pull* the door *to.* 4. in Med. *to draw to oneself, win, obtain.*

ἐπισπεῖν, aor. 2 inf. of ἐφέπω.

ἐπι-σπείρω, f. ερῶ, *to sow with seed: to sow among.*

ἐπισπείσας, aor. 1 part. of ἐπισπένδω.

ἐπίσπεισις, εως, ἡ, *a libation at a sacrifice.* From

ἐπι-σπένδω, f. σπείσω, *to pour upon* or *over:* absol. *to make a libation.* II. Med. *to make a fresh treaty.*

ἐπισπερχής, ές, *hurried, eager:*—Adv. -χῶς. From

ἐπι-σπέρχω, f. ξω, *to urge on, hasten.* II. intr. *to hurry on, rage furiously.*

ἐπισπέσθαι, aor. 2 inf. med. of ἐφέπω.

ἐπι-σπεύδω, f. σω, *to urge on, promote, further.* II. intr. *to hasten onward.*

ἐπισπόμενος, aor. 2 part. med. of ἐφέπω.

ἐπισπονδή, ἡ, (ἐπισπένδομαι) *a renewed* or *renewable truce,* mostly in plur.

ἐπισπορία, ον, (ἐπισπείρω) *a sowing after.*

ἐπίσπορος, ον, (ἐπισπείρω) *sown afterwards:* οἱ ἐπίσποροι *posterity.*

ἐπι-σπουδάζω, f. άσω, *to urge on, to further.* II. intr. *to make haste in* a thing.

ἐπίσπω, ῃς, ῃ, **ἐπίσποιμι**, οις, οι, aor. 2 subj. and opt. of ἐφέπω:—**ἐπισπών**, οῦσα, όν, aor. 2 part.

ἐπισ-σείω, **ἐπισσεύω**, Ep. for ἐπισείω, ἐπισεύω.

ἐπίσ-σῠτος, ον, (ἐπέσσυμαι, pf. pass. of ἐπισεύω) *hurrying on, rushing, gushing: vehement:* also c. acc. *rushing upon.*

ἐπίσσωτρον, Ep. for ἐπίσωτρον, *a tire.*

ἐπίστα, for ἐπίστασαι, 2 sing of ἐπίσταμαι.

ἐπιστᾰδόν, Adv. (ἐπίσταμαι) *attentively, earnestly.*

ἐπι-στάζω, f. -στάξω, *to make to drop upon a thing:* ἐπιστάζειν χάριν *to shed* delight or honour.

ἐπι-σταθμάομαι, Dep. *to weigh well, ponder.*

ἐπί-σταθμος, ον, *at, belonging to a lodging* or *station.*

ἐπ-ίστᾰμαι, 2 pers. ἐπίστασαι poët. ἐπίστᾳ Ion. ἐπίστῃ: imperat. ἐπίστασο Ion. ἐπίσταο Att. ἐπίστω: impf. ἠπιστάμην Ep. ἐπιστάμην: fut. med. ἐπιστήσομαι: aor. 1 pass. ἠπιστήθην: Dep.: (ἐπί, ἵστημι). I. c. inf. *to know how* to do: *to be capable of* doing. II. c. acc. rei, *to understand, know, to be versed in* a thing: in Herodotus, *to be assurea of, to believe:* but in Att., *to know for certain, know well:*—pres. part. ἐπιστάμενος, η, ον, as an Adj., *knowing, skilful, wise:* c. gen., ἐπιστάμενος πολέμοιο *skilled* or *versed in* war.

ἐπισταμένως, Adv. (ἐπίσταμαι) *skilfully, expertly.*

ἐπιστάς, aor. 2 part. of ἐφίστημι.

ἐπίστασις, εως, ἡ, (ἐφίστημι) *a stopping, checking.* II. (ἐφίσταμαι) *a resting, staying: a halt* in a march. 2. *attention, care, diligence: anxiety.*

ἐπιστατεύω, f. σω, and

ἐπιστατέω, f. ήσω, (ἐπιστάτης) *to have charge of* a thing, *to be set over, preside over.* II. *to be chief President* (ἐπιστάτης) *in the assembly.* III. *to stand by, be present.*

ἐπιστάτης, ου, ὁ, (ἐφίσταμαι) *one who stands by, a suppliant.* 2. in battle-order, *one's rear-rank man, the man behind.* II. *one who is set over, a chief, master, lord: a manager, overseer;* ἐπιστάτης ἄθλων *president* or *steward* of the games. 2. at Athens, *the chief President* of the ἐκκλησία, cf. πρύτανις: *an inspector* or *commissioner* of any public works.

ἐπιστάτις, ιδος, ἡ, fem. of ἐπιστάτης.

ἐπιστέαται, Ion. for ἐπίστανται, 3 pl. of ἐπίσταμαι.

ἐπιστέατο, Ion. for ἠπίσταντο, 3 pl. impf. of ἐπίσταμαι.

ἐπι-στείβω, f. ψω, *to tread upon, stand upon.*

ἐπι-στείχω, *to go to, along,* or *over, to approach.*

ἐπι-στέλλω, f. -στελῶ: pf. -έσταλκα:—Pass., aor. 1 -εστάλθην, aor. 2 -εστάλην [ᾰ]: pf. -έσταλμαι:—*to send to, send by message* or *letter:* generally, *to bid, enjoin, command;* τὰ ἐπεσταλμένα *orders given.* 2. *to announce, give intelligence.* II. *to write letters;* cf. ἐπιστολή. III. *to draw in, tighten.*

ἐπι-στενάζω, f. άξω, *to groan over.*

ἐπι-στενάχω or -στενάχομαι, = ἐπιστένω.

ἐπι-στένω, *to groan* or *sigh at: lament over.*

ἐπι-στεφᾰνόω, f. ώσω, *to deck with a garland.*

ἐπιστεφής, ές, *crowned to the brim;* κρητῆρας ἐπιστεφέας οἴνοιο goblets *brimming over* with wine

ἐπι-στέφω, f. ψω, *to surround with* or *as with a chaplet:* Med., κρητῆρας ἐπεστέψαντο ποτοῖο they *crowned* the goblets *to the brim* with drink metaph., χοὰς ἐπιστέφειν τινί *to offer* libations *as an honour to* the dead.

ἐπιστέωνται, Ion. 3 plur. subj. of ἐπίσταμαι.

ἐπίστῃ, Ion. for ἐπίστασαι, 2 sing. of ἐπίσταμαι.

ἐπιστήμη, ἡ, (ἐπίσταμαι) *knowledge, understanding, skill, experience, wisdom.* 2. *scientific knowledge, science:* in plur. *the sciences.*

ἐπίστημι, Ion. for ἐφίστημι.

ἐπιστήμων, ον, gen. ονος, (ἐπίσταμαι) *wise, prudent: skilled in* or *acquainted with* a thing, c. gen.: generally, *learned, well-instructed, scientific.*

ἐπι-στηρίζω, f. ξω, *to make to lean upon:* hence *to confirm, establish:*—Pass. *to lean upon* a thing.

ἐπιστητός, ή, όν, (ἐπίσταμαι) *that can be scientifically known.*

ἐπι-στίλβω, *to glisten on the surface.*

ἐπ-ίστιος, ον, (ἐπί, ἱστίη) Ion. for ἐφέστιος:—as Subst., ἐπ-ίστιον, τό, *a dock for ships.*

ἐπιστολάδην, Adv. (ἐπιστέλλω) *girt up, neatly,* of dress. [ᾰ]

ἐπιστολεύς, έως, ὁ, (ἐπιστολή) *a letter-writer, secretary.* II. *a vice-admiral.*

ἐπιστολή, ἡ, (ἐπιστέλλω) *a message, command, commission,* whether verbal or in writing; ἐξ ἐπιστολῆς *by command.* 2. *a letter,* Lat. *epistola.*

ἐπι-στομίζω, f. ίσω Att. ιῶ, (ἐπί, στόμα) *to bridle, and so manage a horse:* metaph. *to curb* or *muzzle, silence, gag.* II. *to throw down on the face.*

ἐπι-στονᾰχέω, -ίζω, = ἐπιστένω, of the waves.

ἐπι-στορέννῡμι, shorter -στόρνῡμι or -στρώννυμι: f. -στρώσω: aor. 1 -εστόρεσα or -έστρωσα: pf. pass. -έστρωμαι:—*to strew* or *spread out upon.*

ἐπιστρᾰτεία Ion. -ηΐη, ἡ, (ἐπιστρατεύω) *a march* or *expedition against* one.

ἐπιστράτευσις, εως, ἡ, = ἐπιστρατεία. From

ἐπι-στρᾰτεύω, f. σω, *to march against, go on an expedition against:* in Prose mostly in Med.

ἐπι-στρᾰτηΐη, Ion. for ἐπιστρατεία.

ἐπι-στρᾰτοπεδεύω, f. σω, *to encamp over against.*

ἐπιστρᾰφείς, aor. 2 part. pass. ἐπιστρέφω: ἐπιστραφῆναι, inf.: ἐπιστραφῶ subj.

ἐπίστρεπτος, ον, (ἐπιστρέφω) *to be turned towards* or *looked at:* hence, *to be admired.*

ἐπι-στρεφής, ές, *turning towards: attentive, careful, sharp, shrewd.* Adv. ἐπιστρεφῶς Ion. -έως, *earnestly, sharply.* From

ἐπι-στρέφω, f. ψω: aor. 1 ἐπέστρεψα:—*to turn* or *direct towards.* 2. *to turn about, turn.* 3. *to turn* or *convert* from an error, *to correct, amend.* 4. *to curve, twist, make to writhe.* II. Med. and Pass. ἐπιστρέφομαι, aor. 2 -εστράφην [ᾰ]:—*to turn oneself round: to go backwards and forwards, to range* or *wander over: to visit.* 2. *to be turned* or *converted: to repent.* 3. *to look towards:* hence *to pay regard* or *deference to:* c. acc. *to allude to, mean.* III. intr. in Act. *to turn oneself in any direction: to return.* IV. pf. part. pass. ἐπεστραμμένος, η, ον, = ἐπιστρεφής, *earnest, pressing, vehement.*

ἐπιστροφάδην, Adv. (ἐπιστρέφω) *turning both ways, turning right and left.*

ἐπιστροφή, ἡ, (ἐπιστρέφω) *a wheeling about, return to the charge:* also of ships, *a tacking* or *putting about.* II. (ἐπιστρέφομαι) *attention, care, notice.* 2. *a moving about in a place;* δωμάτων ἐπιστροφαί *occupation* of the palace.

ἐπίστροφος, ον, (ἐπιστρέφω) *conversant with: concerned with* or *in.*

ἐπι-στρώννῡμι, shortened form of ἐπιστορέννυμι.

ἐπι-στρωφάω, f. ήσω, Frequent. of ἐπιστρέφω; but mostly intr., like Med. ἐπιστρέφομαι, *to visit* or *frequent* a place: *to occupy one's house:* also *to come to.*

ἐπίστω, for ἐπίστασο, 2 sing. imperat. of ἐπίσταμαι.

ἐπι-συνάγω, f. άξω, *to gather together again, collect and bring to* a place. Hence

ἐπισυνᾰγωγή, ἡ, *an assembling together at* a place.

ἐπισυνηγμένος, pf. part. pass. of ἐπισυνάγω.

ἐπι-συνίστημι, f. -συστήσω, *to set together*

against. II. Pass., with aor. 2 act. -έστην, pf. -έστηκα, *to conspire against.*

ἐπι-συντρέχω, f. -δραμοῦμαι, *to run together to.*

ἐπίσυρμα, ατος, τό, *anything trailed after* one: *the trail of a snake, the track made by dragging.* From

ἐπι-σύρω, *to drag* or *trail after* one. II. *to do anything in a careless way, to slur over.*

ἐπισύστἄσις, εως, ἡ, (ἐπισυνίσταμαι) *a being gathered together against, a riotous meeting, tumult.*

ἐπι-σφάζω, f. ξω, *to slaughter over* or *besides, immolate.*

ἐπι-σφἄλής, ές, (ἐπί, σφαλῆναι) *prone to fall, unsteady, precarious.*

ἐπι-σφάττω, f. ξω, later form of ἐπισφάζω.

ἐπι-σφίγγω, f. γξω, *to bind tight, fasten.*

ἐπι-σφρᾱγίζω, f. ίσω Att. ῐῶ, *to put a seal on, seal up.* 2. *to confirm, ratify.* Hence

ἐπισφρᾱγιστής, οῦ, ὁ, *one who seals* or *signs.*

ἐπι-σφύριον, τό, (ἐπί, σφυρόν) mostly in plur. *bands* or *clasps* which fastened the two plates of the greaves (κνημῖδες) *over the ancle: a covering for the ancle.*

ἐπι-σχεδόν, Adv. *near at hand.*

ἐπισχεθεῖν, poët. aor. 2 inf. of ἐπέχω.

ἐπισχεῖν, aor. 2 inf. of ἐπέχω.

ἐπι-σχερώ, Adv. (ἐπί, σχερός) *in a row, one after another.* II. of Time, *gradually, by degrees.*

ἐπισχεσία Ion. -ίη, ἡ, (ἐπέχω) *a pretext, excuse.*

ἐπίσχεσις, εως, ἡ, (ἐπέχω) *a checking, stopping, hindrance: delay, reluctance.*

ἐπ-ισχύω, f. ύσω [ῡ], *to make strong.* II. intr. *to be* or *grow strong:—to be urgent.*

ἐπ-ίσχω, collat. form of ἐπέχω, *to hold* or *direct towards.* II. *to keep in, hold in, check.* 2. intr. *to leave off, desist.*

ἐπισχών, aor. 2 part. of ἐπέχω.

ἐπι-σωρεύω, f. σω, (ἐπί, σωρός) *to heap, pile up.*

ἐπί-σωτρον Ep. ἐπίσσ-, τό, *the metal hoop laid upon the felloe of the wheel, the tire.*

ἐπιτᾰγή, ἡ, *an injunction, precept.* From

ἐπιτᾰγῆναι, aor. 2 inf. of ἐπιτάσσω.

ἐπίταγμα, ατος, τό, (ἐπιτάσσω) *an injunction, order.*

ἐπίτᾱδες, Dor. for ἐπιτηδές.

ἐπιτακτήρ, ῆρος, ὁ, and

ἐπιτάκτης, ου, ὁ, (ἐπιτάσσω) *a commander.*

ἐπίτακτος, ον, (ἐπιτάσσω) *enjoined, commanded.* II. *drawn up, behind;* οἱ ἐπίτακτοι, *the reserve* in an army.

ἐπι-τᾰλαιπωρέω, f. ήσω, *to labour* or *suffer yet more.*

ἐπιτάμης [ᾰ], 2 sing. aor. 2 subj. of ἐπιτέμνω.

ἐπι-τάμνω, Ion. for ἐπιτέμνω.

ἐπι-τᾰνύω, poët. for ἐπιτείνω, *to stretch over.*

ἐπίταξις, εως, ἡ, (ἐπιτάσσω) *an injunction, order;* ἐπίταξις τοῦ φόρου *the arrangement* of the tribute.

ἐπι-τᾰράσσω Att. -ττω, f. ξω, *to trouble* or *disquiet yet more.*

ἐπιτάρροθος, ὁ, lengthened for ἐπίρροθος, *a helper, defender, ally.*

ἐπίτᾰσις, εως, ἡ, (ἐπιτείνω) *a stretching, straining.*

ἐπι-τάσσω Att. -ττω, f. ξω: aor. 1 -έταξα:—Pass., aor. 1 -ετάχθην: pf. -τέταγμαι:—*to set over, put in command.* 2. *to enjoin, order;*—Pass. *to be under orders* to do a thing; of things, *to be ordered one:* τὰ ἐπιτασσόμενα *orders given.* II. *to place behind* or *in reserve:* also, *to place next* or *beside.*

ἐπι-τάφιος, ον, (ἐπί, τάφος) *on* or *over a tomb;* λόγος ἐπιτάφιος *a funeral oration* spoken at Athens yearly *over* the citizens who had fallen in battle; such as that of Pericles in Thuc. 2. 35 sqq.

ἐπι-τᾰχύνω, f. ῠνῶ, *to hasten on, urge forward.*

ἐπιτεῖλαι, aor. 1 inf. of ἐπιτέλλω.

ἐπι-τείνω, f. -τενῶ: Ion. impf. ἐπιτείνεσκον:—Pass., aor. 1 -ετάθην [ᾰ]: pf. -τέταμαι:—*to stretch upon* or *over.* 2. *to draw tight: to increase, heighten: to urge, excite:*—Pass. *to be stretched* as on the rack: generally *to be tortured, to be on the stretch, strained to the uttermost:—to endure.*

ἐπι-τειχίζω, f. ίσω Att. ιῶ, *to build a fort* or *occupy a fortified place against* one, esp. in the enemy's country: c. acc. loci, *to occupy with such a fort.* Hence

ἐπιτείχῐσις, εως, ἡ, *the building a fort on the enemy's country, the occupation of it:* and

ἐπιτείχισμα, ατος, τό, *a fort placed so as to command an enemy's country:* and

ἐπιτειχισμός, ὁ, = ἐπιτείχισις.

ἐπι-τελεστέον, verb. Adj. *one must accomplish.*

ἐπι-τελέω, f. έσω, *to complete, finish: to fulfil, accomplish,* esp. of vows or promises. 2. *to discharge a religious service.* 3. *to pay in full, discharge:* metaph. in Med., ἐπιτελεῖσθαι τὰ τοῦ γήρως *to have to pay, be subject to, the burdens* of old age; ἐπιτελεῖσθαι θάνατον *to pay the debt of* death.

ἐπι-τελής, ές, (ἐπί, τέλος) *brought to an end, accomplished, fulfilled.*

ἐπι-τέλλω fut. -τελῶ: aor. 1 -έτειλα: pf. -τέταλκα:—*to lay upon, enjoin, command, prescribe, ordain:* c. dat. pers. *to give orders to:*—so also in Med. II. intr. and in Med., *to rise,* of the sun or stars.

ἐπι-τέμνω Ion. -τάμνω: f. -τεμῶ: aor. 2 -έτᾰμον:—*to make a cut* or *incision into, gash.* II. *to cut short: to abridge.*

ἐπί-τεξ, εκος, ἡ, (ἐπί, τεκεῖν) *at the birth, about to bring forth.*

ἐπιτερπής, ές, *pleasing, delightful* From

ἐπι-τέρπομαι, Pass. *to rejoice* or *delight in.*

ἐπιτέτᾰμαι, pf. pass. of ἐπιτείνω.

ἐπιτετήδευκα, pf. of ἐπιτηδεύω.

ἐπιτέτραπται, 3 sing. pass. pf. of ἐπιτρέπω.

ἐπιτετράφαται, Ion. 3 pl. pf. pass. of ἐπιτρέπω.

ἐπι-τεύχω, f. ξω, *to make for.*

ἐπι-τεχνάομαι, Dep. *to contrive for* a purpose. II. *to contrive against.* Hence

ἐπιτέχνησις, εως, ἡ, *contrivance for a purpose.*

ἐπιτήδειος, α, ον, Ion. **ἐπιτήδεος**, η, ον, (ἐπιτηδές) *made for a special purpose, fit* or *adapted for it, convenient.* II. *useful, serviceable, necessary;* τὰ ἐπιτήδεια, *the necessaries of life.* 2. of persons, *serviceable, friendly, well-disposed:* as Subst., *an intimate friend,* Lat. *necessarius.*

ἐπιτηδειότης, ητος, ἡ, *fitness, suitableness, convenience for a purpose.*

ἐπιτηδείως Ion. **-έως**, Adv. of ἐπιτήδειος, *suitably, serviceably.*

ἐπι-τηδές, later **ἐπί-τηδες**, Adv. formed from ἐπὶ τάδε, *for a special purpose, for the purpose: on purpose, advisedly,* Lat. *consulto: designedly, artfully.*

ἐπιτήδευμα, ατος, τό, (ἐπιτηδεύω) *that which one pursues, one's pursuit in life, business, custom, practice,* Lat. *studium, institutum.*

ἐπιτήδευσις, εως, ἡ, *attention to a pursuit* or *business: the practising* or *studying* of a thing. From

ἐπιτηδεύω, f. σω, (ἐπιτηδές); but the tenses are formed as if it were a compd. of ἐπί with τηδεύω (which does not exist), aor. 1 ἐπετήδευσα, pf. ἐπιτετήδευκα:—*to pursue* or *practise* a thing, *make it one's business,* Lat. *studere rei:* also *to invent:* c. inf. *to take care to* do:—Pass. *to be practised, done with pains and care.*

ἐπίτηκτος, ον, *melted* or *luted to, overlaid:* metaph. *superficial, counterfeit.* From

ἐπι-τήκω, f. ξω, *to melt upon, pour upon when melted.*

ἐπι-τηρέω, f. ήσω, *to look out* or *watch for.*

ἐπι-τίθημι, f. -θήσω: aor. 1 -έθηκα: pf. -τέθεικα:—*to put* or *lay upon.* 2. *to set upon, turn* or *incline towards.* II. *to put to, close,* as a door or covering; ἠμὲν ἀνακλῖναι πυκινὸν νέφος ἠδ' ἐπιθεῖναι both to roll back the thick cloud and *put* it *to* III. *to put to besides, to add.* IV. *to put on,* as a last touch or finish. V. *to lay upon, impose, inflict,* esp. a penalty: also *to give a* name. VI. *to give an injunction* or *message: to send by message.* VII. Med. ἐπιτίθεμαι, aor. 2 -εθέμην: *to put on oneself* or *for oneself.* 2. *to set oneself to, apply oneself to, engage oneself in.* 3. *to set upon, make an attempt upon, attack.*

ἐπι-τιμάω, f. ήσω:—*to lay a value* or *set a price upon,* Lat. *aestimare: to value, honour, shew honour to.* 2. *to raise in price:*—Pass. *to rise in price.* II. *to lay* or *estimate the* amount of a penalty, *to appraise.* 2. *to object to* one *as blameable: to blame, reprove, find fault with.* Hence

ἐπιτίμησις, εως, ἡ, *a reproving, rebuking:* and

ἐπιτιμητής, οῦ, ὁ, *an estimator.* II. *a punisher, chastiser;* ἐπιτιμητὴς ἔργων *an appraiser* or *examiner* of what has been done. Hence

ἐπιτιμητικός, ή, όν, *censorious.*

ἐπιτιμήτωρ, ορος, ὁ, (ἐπιτιμάω) *an avenger.*

ἐπιτιμία, ἡ, (ἐπίτιμος) *the enjoyment of civil rights and privileges.* II. *rebuke: punishment.*

ἐπι-τίμιος, ον, (ἐπί, τιμή) *done in one's honour.* II. τὸ ἐπιτίμιον or τὰ ἐπιτίμια, as Subst., *the value* or *estimate of* a thing: *the honour due to a person.* 2. *the assessment of damages, penalty;* τἀπιτίμια τῆς δυσσεβείας *the wages* of ungodliness.

ἐπί-τιμος, ον, (ἐπί, τιμή) *in honour: in possession of one's* full rights and privileges as a citizen, opp. to ἄτιμος.

ἐπι-τίτθιος, ον, (ἐπί, τίτθη) *still at the breast, sucking.*

ἐπι-τιτρώσκω, f. -τρώσω, *to wound on the surface.*

ἐπι-τίω, f. -τίσω, *to lay a penalty upon, punish.*

***ἐπι-τλάω**, obsol. pres. (see ΤΛΑΩ): irr. aor. 2 ἐπέτλην inf. ἐπιτλῆναι:—*to bear patiently, submit.*

ἐπιτλήτω, 3 sing. aor. 2 imperat. of *ἐπιτλάω.

ἐπιτολή, ἡ, (ἐπιτέλλω) *the rising of a star: the season of a star's appearance in the heavens.*

ἐπι-τολμάω, f. ήσω, *to submit* or *endure* to do.

ἐπίτονος, ον, (ἐπιτείνω) *stretched, strained.* II. as Subst., ἐπίτονος (sub. ἱμάς), ὁ, *a rope* or *cord with which* a thing is *stretched* or *tightened, the back-stay* of the mast.

ἐπι-τοξάζομαι, Dep. *to shoot at.*

ἐπιτόσσαις, Dor. part. of ἐπέτοσσε.

ἐπιτρᾰπέουσι, Ep. 3 pl. of ἐπιτρέπω.

ἐπι-τράπω, Ion. for ἐπιτρέπω: ἐπέτραψα, ἐπιτράψομαι, Ion. aor. 1 act. and fut. med. of same.

ἐπι-τρεπτέον, verb. Adj. *one must permit.* From

ἐπι-τρέπω: f. ψω: aor. 1 -έτρεψα, aor. 2 -έτρᾰπον:—Med., f. Ion. -τράψομαι: aor. 2 -ετρᾰπόμην:—Pass., Ion. aor. 1 -ετράφθην: aor. 2 -ετράπην [ᾰ]:—*to turn to* or *towards:*—Med. *to incline to.* 2. *to give over, commit, entrust* to one's charge: *to put into another's hand, entrust oneself to:*—Pass. *to be entrusted;* ᾧ ἐπιτετράφαται λαοί (3 pl. pf., for ἐπιτετραμμένοι εἰσί) to whose charge they *have been committed;* Ὥραις μέγας οὐρανὸς ἐπιτέτραπται 3 sing. pf.); τὴν ἀρχὴν ἐπιτραφθείς *entrusted with* the command: Med. *to trust oneself* to a person. II. *to make over to one's heir, leave, bequeath.* III. *to give up, yield: to permit, suffer, allow.*

ἐπι-τρέφω, f. -θρέψω, *to bring up, maintain:*—Pass. *to grow up after:* generally, *to grow up.*

ἐπι-τρέχω, fut. 1 -θρέξομαι, aor. 1 -έθρεξα: also (from Root ἐπιδρέμω) fut. -δρᾰμοῦμαι, aor. 2 -έδρᾰμον: pf. -δεδράμηκα, pf. 2 ἐπιδέδρομα:—*to run at* or *upon: to assault, attack suddenly.* II. *to run over* a space: *to graze* as a lance does a shield: *to overspread, be shed abroad, be diffused.* 2. c. acc. *to overrun,* as an army does a country. 3. *to run over, treat lightly of,* Lat. *oratione percurrere.* III. *to run after: to grasp at, seek for.*

ἐπίτρεψον, ἐπιτρέψαι, aor. 1 imper. and inf. of ἐπιτρέπω.

ἐπι-τρίβω, f. ψω: aor. 2 pass. ἐπετρίβην [ῐ]:—*to rub on the surface: to grind down, afflict, destroy:*—Pass. *to be utterly destroyed.* Hence

ἐπίτριπτος, ον, *rubbed down, worn away:* metaph. *worn, practised, hackneyed.*

ἐπί-τριτος, ον, *one and one-third,* 1 + $\frac{1}{3}$, or $\frac{4}{3}$:—ἐπίτριτον (sub. δάνεισμα) was *a loan at the rate of* $\frac{1}{3}$ *of the principal,* i. e. 33$\frac{1}{3}$ *per cent. per annum.*

ἐπι-τροπαῖος, α, ον, (ἐπιτροπή) *entrusted, delegated.*

ἐπιτροπεία, ἡ, (ἐπιτροπεύω) *guardianship.*

ἐπι-τρόπευσις, εως, ἡ, = ἐπιτροπεία. Hence

ἐπιτροπευτικός, ή, όν, *fit for the office of guardian.*

ἐπιτροπεύω, f. σω, (ἐπίτροπος) *to be in charge, to be guardian, trustee, governor.*

ἐπιτροπή, ἡ, (ἐπιτρέπω) *a reference of* a thing *to* another: *a charge entrusted to a person.* 2. absol. *an arbitration.*

ἐπίτροπος, ὁ, (ἐπιτρέπω) *one to whom a charge is entrusted, a trustee, steward:* esp. *a guardian.*

ἐπιτροχάδην, Adv. (ἐπιτρέχω) *runningly, fluently.*

ἐπίτροχος, ον, (ἐπιτρέχω) *running easily:* metaph. *voluble.*

ἐπι-τρύζω, *to murmur beside* or *over.*

ἐπι-τρώγω, f. -τρώξομαι: aor. 2 -έτρᾰγον:—*to eat to, with,* or *after*, esp. as sauce or sweetmeat.

ἐπι-τυγχάνω, f. -τεύξομαι: aor. 2 -έτῠχον:—*to light upon, fall in with, meet with:* c. gen. rei, *to hit, reach, attain to:* c. part. *to succeed in* doing: in aor. 2 part., ὁ ἐπιτυχών, like ὁ τυχών, *the first one meets,* i. e. *a common, ordinary person, any one.*

ἐπι-τυμβίδιος, α, ον, (ἐπί, τύμβος) *at* or *over a tomb.* II. of the crested lark, *with a crest* or *top-knot.*

ἐπι-τύμβιος, ον, = ἐπιτυμβίδιος.

ἐπι-τύφω [ῡ], f. -θύψω:—*to kindle, inflame:*—Pass. *to be inflamed: to be furious.*

ἐπιτῠχεῖν, aor. 2 inf. of ἐπιτυγχάνω.

ἐπιτῠχής, ές, (ἐπιτυχεῖν) *hitting the mark, effective, successful.*

ἐπιφᾰγεῖν, aor. 2 inf. of ἐπεσθίω.

ἐπι-φαίνω, f. -φᾰνῶ: aor. 1 -έφηνα:—*to shew forth, display.* 2. intr. (sub. φῶς) *to shine upon.* II. Pass. and Med. *to shew oneself, come into light, shine forth, appear.*

ἐπιφάνεια, ἡ, *the appearance, manifestation.* II. *the surface, outside,* of anything.

ἐπιφᾰνείς, aor. 2 pass. part. of ἐπιφαίνω.

ἐπιφανέστερον, -έστατα, Comp. and Sup. of ἐπιφανῶς.

ἐπιφᾰνῆναι, aor. 2 inf. pass. of ἐπιφαίνω. Hence

ἐπιφᾰνής, ές, (ἐπιφανῆναι) *coming to light, appearing, conspicuous, open, manifest.* II. metaph. *famous,* Lat. *illustris:* of things, *remarkable.*

ἐπι-φάνια (sub. ἱερά), ων, τά, (ἐπιφανῆναι) the festival of *the Epiphany, the Manifestation* of Christ to the Gentiles.

ἐπί-φαντος, ον, (ἐπιφαίνομαι) *visible, alive.*

ἐπιφᾰνῶς, Adv. of ἐπιφανής, *openly.*

ἐπι-φατνίδιος, ον, (ἐπί, φάτνη) *at the manger.*

ἐπι-φαύω, f. σω, (ἐπί, φάος) *to shine upon.*

ἐπι-φέρω: f. -οίσω: aor. 1 -ήνεγκα: aor. 2 -ήνεγκον: (see φέρω):—*to bring, put* or *lay upon;* ἐπιφέρειν πόλεμον, Lat. *bellum inferre, to make* war *upon:* absol. *to attack, assail.* 2. *to throw a charge upon* one, *to impute to.* 3. *to confer upon,* also in bad sense *to inflict* or *impose upon:* also *to offer:*—Med. *to bring with oneself, bring as dowry.* 4. Pass., ἐπιφέρεσθαί τινι, *to rush upon, attack, assault, pursue:*—absol. *to ensue, follow upon, come after, to happen after.*

ἐπι-φημίζω, f. σω, (ἐπί, φήμη) *to utter words of omen to one, to promise in accordance with an omen.* Hence

ἐπιφήμισμα, τό, *a word of good* or *bad omen.*

ἐπι-φθάνω, f. άσω [ᾰ], *to arrive at, reach first.*

ἐπιφθάς, aor. 2 of ἐπιφθάνω, as if from ἐπίφθημι.

ἐπι-φθέγγομαι, f. -φθέγξομαι, Dep. *to utter after* or *in accordance, join in what is said.*

ἐπι-φθονέω, f. ήσω, *to grudge* or *withhold from jealousy.* II. *to bear hate against.*

ἐπί-φθονος, ον, *liable to envy* or *jealousy.* II. act. *bearing a grudge against, jealous of, hating: working mischief, malignant.* Hence

ἐπιφθόνως, Adv. *so as to provoke envy.* II. *at enmity.*

ἐπι-φθύζω, *to spit at:* Dor. part. fem. ἐπιφθύσδοισα.

ἐπι-φῐλοπονέομαι, Dep. *to labour willingly at.*

ἐπι-φλέγω, f. ξω, *to set on fire, burn up.* 2. metaph. *to inflame, excite:* also *to make brilliant* or *illustrious.* II. intr. *to blaze up, be brilliant.*

ἐπί-φοβος, ον, *frightful, terrible, fearful.* II. pass. *timid.*

ἐπι-φοιτάω, f. ήσω, *to come constantly to, go regularly to, visit periodically:* of foreign goods, *to be regularly imported.*

ἐπιφορά, ἡ, (ἐπιφέρω) *a bringing to* or *upon:* generally *an addition.*

ἐπι-φορέω, f. ήσω, = ἐπιφέρω, *to bring and put on.* Hence

ἐπιφόρημα, ατος, τό, mostly in pl., *that which is served up in addition: dessert.*

ἐπίφορος, ον, (ἐπιφέρω) *carrying towards.* II. of ground, *sloping.* III. *prone* or *inclined to* a thing.

ἐπι-φράζω, f. σω, *to say after* or *besides.* II. Med. and Pass., fut. -φράσομαι: aor. 1 -εφρᾰσάμην, and aor. -εφράσθην:—*to think of* doing, *be minded to* do. 2. *to reflect upon, devise, contrive.* 3. *to notice, observe, to recognise, take notice of.*

ἐπιφρασσαίατο, Ion. 3 pl. aor. 1 med. opt. of ἐπιφράζω.

ἐπι-φρονέω, f. ήσω, *to be shrewd, prudent.*

ἐπιφροσύνη, ἡ, (ἐπίφρων) *thoughtfulness*

ἐπί-φρουρος, ον, (ἐπί, φρουρά) *keeping watch by.*

ἐπί-φρων, ον, gen. ονος, (ἐπί, φρήν) *thoughtful.*

ἐπι-φύλιος, ον, (ἐπί, φῡλή) *distributed to tribes.*

ἐπι-φυλλίς, ίδος, ἡ, (ἐπί, φύλλον) *the small grapes left for gleaners:* a term applied by Aristophanes to poetasters, whose names are not mentioned until the list of true poets is exhausted.

ἐπι-φῠτεύω, f. σω, *to plant over* or *upon.*

ἐπι-φύω, f. ύσω [ῡ]:—*to make to grow upon.* II. Pass., with act. aor. 2 ἐπέφῡν, pf. ἐπιπέφῡκα, *to grow upon, to cling closely to.*

ἐπι-φωνέω, f. ήσω, *to tell of, mention.*

ἐπι-φώσκω, (ἐπί, φῶς) *to grow towards dawn.*

ἐπι-χαίνω, *to gape for.*

ἐπι-χαίρω, f. -χαιρήσω, *to rejoice over:* c. acc., σὲ

μὲν εὖ πράσσοντ' ἐπιχαίρω: but mostly in bad sense, *to shew malignant joy over*:—so also in aor. 2 pass. *ἐπιχαρῆναι*.

ἐπι-χᾰλαζάω, (*ἐπί, χάλαζα*) *to shower hail upon.*

ἐπι-χᾰλάω, f. *άσω* [ᾰ], *to relax, loosen.* II. intr. *to yield* or *relent in a thing.*

ἐπι-χαλκεύω, f. *σω, to forge upon an anvil: to work over again.* 2. metaph. *to forge to one's purpose.*

ἐπί-χαλκος, ον, *covered with copper, coppered over.*

ἐπιχᾰρῆναι, aor. 2 inf. pass. of *ἐπιχαίρω.*

ἐπιχᾰρής, ές, (*ἐπιχαίρω*) *gratifying, agreeable.*

ἐπι-χᾰρίζομαι, f. *ίσομαι* Att. *ἰοῦμαι*: Dep.:—*to grant freely besides, to oblige with a present*: aor. 1 imperat., *ἐπιχαρίτται* (Dor. for *ἐπιχαρίσαι*) *τῷ ξένῳ be gracious* to the stranger.

ἐπί-χᾰρις, ιτος, ὁ, ἡ, neut. *ἐπίχαρι, pleasing, agreeable, winning: giving pleasure*: the Comp. and Sup. are *ἐπιχαριτώτερος, -ιτώτατος,* as if from *ἐπιχάριτος, ον.*

ἐπιχαρίτται, Dor. aor. 1 imperat. for *ἐπιχαρίσαι.*

ἐπίχαρμα, ατος, τό, (*ἐπιχαίρω*) *an object of malignant joy: a feeling of such joy.*

ἐπίχαρτος, *ον,* (*ἐπιχαίρω*) *to be rejoiced at, delightful.* II. *to be exulted over; ἐχθροῖς ἐπίχαρτα matter of triumph* to enemies.

ἐπι-χειλής, ές, (*ἐπί, χεῖλος*) *full to the brim.*

ἐπι-χειμάζω, f. *σω, to stay the winter through.*

ἐπι-χειρέω, f. *ήσω,* (*ἐπί, χείρ*) *to put* one's *hand to* a thing: *to set to work at, make an attempt upon, endeavour to* do. 2. *to set upon, attack.* Hence

ἐπιχείρημα, *ατος, τό, an undertaking, attempt*: and

ἐπιχείρησις, *εως, ἡ, an attempt upon, attack*: generally, *an attempt*: and

ἐπιχειρητέον, verb. Adj. *one must attempt.*

ἐπιχειρητής, *οῦ, ὁ,* (*ἐπιχειρέω*) *an enterprising, adventurous person.*

ἐπί-χειρον, *τό,* (*ἐπί, χείρ*) only used in pl. *wages of manual labour.* 2. generally, *wages, pay, guerdon,* in good or bad sense, *reward* or *punishment.*

ἐπι-χειροτονέω, f. *ήσω, to ratify a proposed decree,* strictly, *by show of hands.* Hence

ἐπιχειροτονία, *ἡ, a decree passed by vote of the people,* esp. *by show of hands.*

ἐπιχεῦαι, Ep. for *ἐπιχέαι,* aor. 1 inf. of *ἐπιχέω.*

ἐπι-χέω, f. *-χεῶ,* aor. 1 *-έχεα*: Ep. pres. *ἐπιχεύω,* aor. 1 *-έχευα,* inf. *-χεῦαι*:—*to pour over* or *upon*: *shed upon.* II. Med. *to pour* or *spread over oneself* or *for oneself.* 2. *to have poured out for one to drink.* II. Pass., pf. *κέχῠμαι,* plqpf. *κεχύμην,* Ep. 3 pl. aor. 2 *ἐπέχυντο, to come as a torrent, to stream* or *flock to* a place:—*to spread over like a flood, inundate.*

ἐπι-χθόνιος, *ον,* or *α, ον,* (*ἐπί, χθών*) *upon the earth, earthy*: as Subst., *ἐπιχθόνιοι, οἱ, men on earth.*

ἐπί-χολος, *ον,* (*ἐπί, χολή*) *producing bile.*

ἐπι-χορεύω, f. *σω, to dance to* or *in honour of* a thing: *to come dancing on.*

ἐπι-χορηγέω, f. *ήσω, to furnish* or *supply besides*: generally, *to supply: to aid.* Hence

ἐπιχορηγία, *ἡ, a supply in addition.*

ἐπι-χραίνω, *to stain, colour.*

ἐπι-χράω (A), only used in aor. 2 *ἐπέχραον, to attack.*

ἐπι-χράω (B): f. *-χρήσω*: aor. 1 *-έχρησα*:—*to lend besides.* II. Med. *ἐπιχράομαι,* Ion. *-χρέομαι,* f. *-χρήσομαι, to make use of,* esp. *to have dealings, be friends with* one.

ἐπι-χρέμπτομαι, Dep. *to spit upon* or *at.*

ἐπι-χρίω, f. *ίσω* [ῑ], *to anoint, besmear*:—Med. *to anoint oneself.*

ἐπί-χρῡσος, *ον, overlaid* or *plated with gold.*

ἐπι-χρώννῡμι and *-ύω,* f. *-χρώσω, to rub* or *smear over*: esp. *to stain, colour.*

ἐπιχῠθείς, aor. 1 part. pass. of *ἐπιχέω.*

ἐπίχῠσις, *εως, ἡ,* (*ἐπιχέω*) *a pouring over: an overflow, flood.*

ἐπι-χωρέω, f. *ήσω, to yield, give way.* II. intr. *to come over to.*

ἐπι-χωριάζω, f. *άσω,* (*ἐπί, χωρίον*) *to visit often, to be in the habit of coming to,* Lat. *ventitare.*

ἐπι-χώριος, *α, ον,* also *ος, ον,* (*ἐπί, χώρα*) *in, of, belonging to the country*: *οἱ ἐπιχώριοι the people of the country, the natives*; *τὸ ἐπιχώριον the custom* or *fashion of the country.* Adv. *-ίως, in the fashion of the country.*

ἐπι-ψᾰκάζω, old Att. for *ἐπιψεκάζω.*

ἐπι-ψάλλω, *to accompany on a stringed instrument.*

ἐπι-ψαύω, f. *σω, to touch on the surface, glance over*: metaph. *to touch lightly on,* Lat. *strictim attingere.*

ἐπι-ψεκάζω old Att. **-ψακάζω**: *to pour drop by drop upon.*

ἐπι-ψεύδομαι, Dep. *to lie still more.*

ἐπι-ψηφίζω, f. *ίσω* Att. *ιῶ, to put to the vote, put the question*:—Med. *to confirm* or *decree by vote*:—Pass. *to be appointed by vote.*

ἐπί-ψογος, *ον, exposed to blame, blameable.* II. act. *blaming, censorious.*

ἐπ-ῑωγαί, *ῶν, αἱ,* (*ἐπί, ἰωγή*) *places sheltered from the wind, roadsteads.*

ἐπιών, part. of *ἔπειμι* (*εἶμι ibo*).

ἐπλάγχθην, aor. 1 pass. of *πλάζω.*

ἐπλάθην [ᾱ], aor. 1 pass. of *πελάζω.*

ἔπλᾰσα Ep. **ἔπλασσα,** aor. 1 of *πλάσσω.*

ἔπλε, for *ἔπελε,* 3 sing. aor. 2 of *πέλω*: so, **ἔπλεο** for *ἐπέλεο, ἐπέλου,* 2 sing. aor. 2 med.: **ἔπλευ** for *ἐπέλευ, ἐπέλου*; **ἔπλετο** for *ἐπέλετο.*

ἔπλεξα, aor. 1 of *πλέκω.*

ἐπλήγην, aor. 2 pass. of *πλήσσω.*

ἔπληντο, 3 pl. Ep. aor. 2 pass. of *πελάζω.*

ἐπλήσθην, aor. 1 pass. of *πίμπλημι.*

ἔπλων, aor. 2 of *πλέω,* as if from a verb in *μι.*

ἔπνευσα, ἐπνεύσθην, aor. 1 act. and pass. of *πνέω.*

ἐπ-όδια, ἐπ-οδιάζω, Ion. for *ἐφόδια, -ιάζω.*

ἐπ-οδύρομαι, Dep. *to lament over.*

ἐποδώκει, reputed to be Ion. for **ἐφ-ωδώκει,** 3 sing. plqpf. of **ἐφ-οδόω,** *to bring on the way.*

ἐπόθην, aor. 1 pass. of *πίνω.*

ἐπ-οικέω, f. *ήσω, to go as settler or colonist to* a place: *to settle in* a place, *inhabit* it. II. *to occupy against for offensive operations.* Hence

ἐπ-οικοδομέω, f. *ήσω, to build upon* or *besides.* II. *to build up, build again, rebuild.*

ἔπ-οικος, *ον, settling* or *sojourning among foreigners.* II. as Subst. *ἔποικος, ὁ, a sojourner, stranger.* 2. *a colonist, settler in a colony.* 3. *a neighbour.*

ἐπ-οικτείρω, *to have compassion on.*

ἐπ-οικτίζω, f. *σω*, = *ἐποικτείρω.* Hence

ἐποίκτιστος, *ον, to be pitied, pitiable, wretched.*

ἔπ-οικτος, *ον*, (*ἐπί, οἶκτος*) *piteous.*

ἐπ-οιμώζω, f. *-οιμώξομαι, to wail over,*

ἐπ-οίσω, fut. of *ἐπιφέρω.*

ἐπ-οιχνέω, f. *ήσω*, = *ἐποίχομαι.*

ἐπ-οίχομαι, f. *-οιχήσομαι*, Dep. *to go towards, approach: to draw near to.* 2. *to go against, attack.* II. *to go over, go round, visit in succession:* esp. of Apollo and Artemis, *to visit* with death. 2. *to go over, get through* one's work: *to set about; ἱστὸν ἐποίχεσθαι to ply* the loom, Lat. *percurrere telam.* 3. *to go over, traverse.*

ἐπ-οκέλλω, *to run* a ship *ashore:*—of the ship, *to run ashore.*

ἐπ-οκριόεις, *εσσα, εν, uneven, rugged.*

ἐπ-ολισθάνω, f. *-ολισθήσω, to glide upon.*

ἐπ-ολολύζω, f. *ξω, to raise a cry of triumph at.*

ἕπομαι, *to follow*, Dep. from *ἕπω*, q. v.

ἐπομβρέω, *ήσω, to rain upon;* and

ἐπομβρία, *ἡ, abundance of rain* or *moisture: wet weather*, opp. to *αὐχμός* (drought). From

ἔπ-ομβρος, *ον*, (*ἐπί, ὄμβρος*) *rainy: wet.*

ἐπ-όμνῡμι and **-ύω**: fut. *-ομοῦμαι*: aor. 1 *-ώμοσα*: —*to swear to* or *upon; ἐπομνύναι τοὺς θεοὺς to swear by* the gods: c. acc. rei, *to swear to* a thing:—aor. 1 part., with another Verb, **ἐπομόσας** εἶπε he said *with an oath, upon oath.*

ἐπομόσαι, aor. 1 inf. of *ἐπόμνυμι.*

ἐπ-ομφάλιος, *α, ον*, (*ἐπί, ὀμφᾰλός*) *upon the navel:* of a shield, *on the boss.*

ἐπόνᾱσα, Dor. aor. 1 of **πονέω.**

ἐπ-ονειδίζω, *to throw reproaches upon.* Hence

ἐπονείδιστος, *ον, to be reproached, disgraceful.* II. act. *reproachful.* Adv. *-τως, shamefully.*

ἐπ-ονομάζω, f. *σω, to give another name to, to surname:*—generally, *to call by a name; ἐπονομάζειν ὄνομά τινος to call upon by name:*—Pass. *to be named after* another.

ἔποπας, acc. pl. of **ἔποψ.**

ἐπ-οπίζομαι, Ep. imperat. *-οπίζεο*, Dep., only used in pres. and impf. *to regard with awe* or *reverence.*

ἐποποῖ, a cry to mimic that of the *hoopoe* (**ἔποψ**).

ἐποποιΐα, *ἡ, epic poetry.* From

ἐπο-ποιός, *όν*, (*ἔπος, ποιέω*) *writing epic poetry:*— as Subst., *ἐποποιός, ὁ, an epic poet.*

ἐπ-οπτάω, f. *ήσω, to roast besides* or *after.*

ἐπ-οπτεύω, f. *σω*: Ion. impf. *ἐποπτεύεσκον*: (*ἐπί, ὄψομαι*) :—*to look over, watch over, take charge of: to visit, punish.* II. *to become an ἐπόπτης, be initiated into the greater mysteries,* used proverbially of attaining to the highest earthly happiness.

ἐπ-οπτήρ, *ῆρος, ὁ*, = *ἐπόπτης*, of tutelary gods.

ἐπ-όπτης, *ου. ὁ*, (*ἐπόψομαι*) *an overseer, guardian, watcher.* II. *one initiated at the greater mysteries.*

ἐπ-οράω, Ion. for *ἐφοράω.*

ἐπ-ορέγω, f. *ξω, to hold out to, offer yet more.* II. Med., fut. *-ορέξομαι, to stretch oneself towards* a thing, *reach at* it; aor. 1 part. *ἐπορεξάμενος, having reached forward* to strike. 2. metaph. *to be desirous of more, rise in one's demands.*

ἐπ-ορέω, Ion. for *ἐφοράω.*

ἐπ-ορθιάζω, f. *σω*, (*ἐπί, ὄρθιος*) *to set upright:* intr. (sub. *φωνὴν*) *to lift up the voice, shout at;* but *ἐπορθιάζειν γόοις to lift up the voice* in wailing.

ἐπ-ορθοβοάω, f. *-βοήσομαι*, (*ἐπί, ὀρθοβόας*) *to utter with a loud shout.*

ἐπ-ορκίζω, Ion. for *ἐφορκίζω, to adjure.*

ἐπ-ορμέω, Ion. for *ἐφορμέω.*

ἐπ-όρνῡμι and **-ύω**: fut. *-όρσω*: aor. 1 *-ῶρσα*: (*ἐπί, ὄρνυμι*) :—*to stir up* or *rouse against: to stir up, excite:*—Pass. *to rise against, assault, fly upon* one.

ἐπ-ορούω, f. *σω, to rush violently at:* of sleep, *to come suddenly on.*

ἐπόρσειαν, 3 pl. aor. 1 opt. of *ἐπόρνυμι.*

ἔπορσον, aor. 1 imperat. of *ἐπόρνυμι.*

ἐπ-ορχέομαι, Dep. *to dance to* a tune.

ἜΠΟΣ, *εος, τό, a word; κατ' ἔπος word by word, accurately.* II. generally, *that which is spoken, uttered in words, a speech, tale:* also *a song.* III. it is used also of 1. *a prophecy, an oracle:* later also *a proverb, maxim* 2. *the meaning, substance of a speech.* 3. *ἔπη* in pl. meant *poetry in heroic verse, epic poetry*, opp. to *μέλη* or lyric poetry: then transferred to *elegiac verse;* and thence generally to *verses, poetry.*

ἐπότισα, aor. 1 of **ποτίζω.**

ἐπ-οτοτύζω, f. *σω, to yell out, utter lamentably.*

ἐπ-οτρύνω, f. *ὑνῶ, to stir up, urge on: to stir up against:*—Pass. *to hasten on.*

ἐπ-ουραῖος, *α, ον*, (*ἐπί, οὐρά*) *on the tail.*

ἐπ-ουράνιος, *α, ον*, (*ἐπί, οὐρανός*) *in heaven, heavenly.* 2. in plur. as Subst., = *θεοί.*

ἐπ-ουρίζω, f. *ίσω* Att. *ιῶ*: aor. 1 *-ούρισα*:—*to blow favourably upon:* metaph. *to help onward, to direct towards* a point. I. intr. *to sail with a fair wind.*

ἔπ-ουρος, *ον*, (*ἐπί, οὖρος*) *blowing favourably.*

ἐπ-οφείλω, *to remain a debtor, continue in debt.*

ἐπ-οχετεύω, f. *σω, to bring* water *by a channel to* a place, Lat. *derivare*

ἐποχέω, f. *ήσω*, (*ἔποχος*) *to carry towards* or *upon:* —Pass. with fut. med. *ἐποχήσομαι, to be carried upon, ride upon.*

ἐπ-οχθίδιος, *α, ον*, (*ἐπί, ὄχθη*) *on the mountains.*

ἔποχον, τό, *the saddlecloth, bousing.* From
ἔποχος, ον, (ἐπέχω) *mounted upon:* metaph., λόγοι μανίας ἔποχοι words *borne on* madness, i. e. frantic. 2. absol. *well-seated, mounted: keeping one's seat.*

ἜΠΟΨ, οπος, ὁ, *the hoopoe,* so called from its cry, Lat. *upŭpa.*

ἐπ-οψάομαι, Dep. (ἐπί, ὄψον) *to eat with* or *as sauce.*

ἐπ-οψίδιος, ον, (ἐπί, ὄψον) *used to eat with bread.*

ἐπ-όψιμος, ον, (ἐπόψομαι) *to be looked on.*

ἐπ-όψιος, ον, also α, ον, (ἐπί, ὄψις) *visible, seen afar, conspicuous: illustrious.* II. act. *overlooking all things.*

ἔπ-οψις, εως, ὁ, (ἐπί, ὄψις) *a view over;* ἔποψις τοῦ ἱροῦ *the view commanded by* the temple: generally, *the view* or *sight of* a thing.

ἐπόψομαι, fut. of ἐφοράω, formed from *ἐπόπτομαι.

ἐπράθην [ᾱ], aor. 1 pass. of πιπράσκω.

ἔπρᾰθον, aor. 2 of πέρθω.

ἔπρεσα, Ep. shortd. for ἔπρησα, aor. 1 of πρήθω.

ἐπρήθην, Ion. aor. 1 pass. of πιπράσκω.

ἔπρηξα, Ion. for ἔπραξα, aor. 1 of πράσσω.

ἔπρησα, aor. 1 of πρήθω.

ἐπριάμην, ίω, ίατο, aor. 2 of ὠνέομαι.

ἘΠΤΑ', οἱ, αἱ, τά, indecl., Lat. *SEPTEM, SEVEN,* Germ. *SIEBEN.*

ἑπτα-βόειος, ον, (ἑπτά, βοῦς) *of seven bulls'-hides.*

ἑπτά-βοιος, ον, (ἑπτά, βοῦς) *of seven bulls'-hides.*

ἑπτά-γλωσσος, ον, (ἑπτά, γλῶσσα) *seven-tongued, seven-toned.*

ἑπτά-δραχμος, ον, (ἑπτά, δραχμή) *worth seven drachms.*

ἑπτα-ετής, ές, (ἑπτα, ἔτος) *seven years old.* II. *of seven years:* neut. ἑπτάετες, as Adv., *for seven years.*

ἑπτά-ζωνος, ον, (ἑπτά, ζώνη) *seven-zoned,* of the planetary system.

ἔπταισμαι, pf. pass. of πταίω.

ἑπτᾰ-καί-δεκα, οἱ, αἱ, τά, indecl. *seventeen.*

ἑπτάκις, also ἑπτάκι, (ἑπτά) Adv. *seven times.*

ἑπτᾰκισ-μύριοι, αι, α, *seventy thousand.*

ἑπτακισ-χίλιοι, αι, α, *seven thousand.*

ἑπτά-κλῑνος, ον, (ἑπτά, κλίνη) *with seven couches* or *beds.*

ἑπτᾰκόσιοι, αι, α, (ἑπτά) *seven hundred.*

ἑπτα-κότῠλος, ον, (ἑπτά, κοτύλη) *holding seven cotylae.*

ἑπτά-κτῠπος, ον, *seven-toned, with seven chords.*

ἑπτά-λογχος, ον, (ἑπτά, λόγχη) *of seven lances, of seven troops of spear-men.*

ἑπτά-λοφος, ον, (ἑπτά, λόφος) *seven-hilled.*

ἐπτάμην [ᾰ], aor. 2 of πέταμαι.

ἑπτά-μηνος, ον, (ἑπτά, μήν) *born in the seventh month.*

ἑπτά-μῐτος, ον, (ἑπτά, μίτος) *of seven strings.*

ἑπτά-μῠχος, ον, *with seven recesses.*

ἔπταξα, Dor. aor. 1 of πτήσσω.

ἑπτά-πηχυς, υ, gen. εος, *seven cubits long.*

ἑπτα-πόδης, ου, ὁ, (ἑπτά, πούς) *seven feet long.*

ἑπτα-πορος, ον, *with seven tracks* or *paths.*

ἑπτά-πους, ὁ, ἡ, neut. πουν, *seven feet long.*

ἑπτά-πῠλος, ον, (ἑπτά, πύλη) *seven-gated:* epith. of *Boeotian* Thebes, in contradistinction to Egyptian Thebes, which was ἑκατόμπυλοι.

ἑπτά-πυργος, ον, *seven-towered.*

ἔπτᾰρον, aor. 2 of πταίρω.

ἑπτάρ-ροος, ον, contr. -**ρους**, ουν, *with seven channels* or *beds,* of the Nile.

ἑπτά-στολος, ον, *consisting of seven bodies of men.*

ἑπτά-στομος, ον, (ἑπτά, στόμα) *seven-mouthed.*

ἑπτα-τειχής, ές, (ἑπτά, τεῖχος) *with seven walls.*

ἔπτᾰτο, 3 sing. aor. 2 of πέταμαι.

ἑπτά-τονος, ον, *seven-toned.*

ἑπτά-φθογγος, ον, (ἑπτά, φθογγή) *seven-toned.*

ἑπτά-φωνος, ον, (ἑπτά, φωνή) *seven-voiced.*

ἔπτᾰχα, (ἑπτά) Adv. *in seven parts.*

ἑπτ-έτης, ες, fem. ἑπτέτις, ιδος, (ἑπτά, ἔτος) *seven years old.*

ἔπτην, aor. 2 act. of πέταμαι, as if from πτῆμι.

ἔπτηξα, aor. 1 of πτήσσω.

ἔπτῐκα, pf. act., **ἔπτισμαι**, pf. pass., of πτίσσω.

ἐπτοίηθεν, poët. 3 pl. aor. 1 pass. of πτοέω.

ἐπτοίημαι, poët. pf. pass. of πτοέω.

ἐπτοίησα, poët. aor. 1 of πτοέω.

ἐπτόμην, aor. 2 of πέτομαι.

ἔπ-υδρος, ον, Ion. for ἔφυδρος.

ἐπῠθόμην, aor. 2 of πυνθάνομαι.

ἐπύλλιον, τό, Dim. of ἔπος, *a versicle.*

ἝΠΩ, poët. impf. ἔπον: f. ἕψω: aor. 2 ἔσπον, inf. σπεῖν, part. σπών:—Med. ἕπομαι: impf. εἱπόμην Ep. ἑπόμην: fut. ἕψομαι: aor. 2 with aspirate ἑσπόμην, imperat. σποῦ Ion. σπέο Ep. σπεῖο, inf. σπέσθαι: I. Act. *to be engaged* or *with, to be busy about.* II. Med. *to follow,* Lat. *sequi: to attend, to obey.* 2. in hostile sense, *to pursue.* 3. *to follow with the mind, understand;* Lat. *mente assequi.*

ἐπῳδή, ἡ, contr. from ἐπαοιδή (ἐπᾴδω) *a song over: an enchantment, incantation, charm, spell.*

ἐπῴδιον, τό, Dim. of ἐπῳδή.

ἐπῳδός, όν, contr. of ἐπαοιδός, (ἐπᾴδω) *singing to* or *over: using songs* or *charms* to heal with: c. gen. *acting as a charm for* or *against.* 2. *sung* or *said after.* II. Subst., ἐπῳδός, ὁ, ἡ, *an enchanter* or *enchantress, wizard* or *witch.* III. ἐπῳδός, ἡ, *a lyric poem in couplets,* commonly of Iambic Trim. and Dim., but of any longer and shorter measure, *except Elegiac;* used by Horace.

ἐπ-ώδῠνος, ον, (ἐπί, ὀδύνη) *painful.*

ἐπ-ώζω, (ἐπί, ὦ) *to wail over.*

ἐπ-ωθέω, fut. -ώσω and -ωθήσω, *to push upon* or *into.*

ἐπώκειλα, aor. 1 of ἐποκέλλω.

ἐπ-ωλένιος, ον, (ἐπί, ὠλένη) *upon the arm.*

ἐπ-ωμάδιος, ον, (ἐπί, ὦμος) *on the shoulders.*

ἐπ-ωμίς, ίδος, ἡ, (ἐπί, ὦμος) *the upper part of the shoulder: the neck and shoulder.* 2. *the highest part of a ship.*

ἐπώμοσα, aor. 1 of ἐπόμνυμι.

ἐπώμοτος, ον, (ἐπόμνυμι) *on oath, sworn.* II. pass. *sworn by, invoked by oaths*, of Gods.

ἐπωνῠμία, ἡ, (ἐπώνυμος) *a name given after* some person or thing, Lat. *cognomen*; ἐπωνυμίαν ἔχειν ἐπί τινος to have *a name after* one:—but, ἐπωνυμίαν σχεῖν χώρας to have *the naming* of it, have it named after one. 2. *a name significant of fate.* II. generally, *a name.*

ἐπωνύμιος, α, ον, poët. for ἐπώνυμος.

ἐπ-ώνῠμος, ον, (ἐπί, ὄνυμα Aeol. for ὄνομα) *named after* some person or thing; ὄνομα ἐπώνυμον a name *given in commemoration* or *remembrance* of something; Ἀλκυόνην καλέεσκον ἐπώνυμον Alcyoné they called her *by name*: generally, *surnamed, called.* II. act. *giving one's name to* a thing or person: at Athens the first archon was called ἄρχων ἐπώνυμος, *as giving his name* to the current year.

ἐπωπάω, *to look over, observe.* From

ἐπ-ωπή, ἡ, (ἐπί, ὤψ) *a spot which commands a wide view, a look-out place.*

ἐπώπτων, impf. of ἐποπτάω.

ἐπώρα, Ion. for ἐφεώρα, 3 sing. impf. of ἐφοράω.

ἐπῶρσα, aor. 1 of ἐπόρνυμι.

ἐπῶρτο, 3 sing. Ep. aor. 2 pass. of ἐπόρνυμι.

ἐπωτίδες, ίδων, αἱ, (ἐπί; οὖς) *beams on each side of a ship's bows*, where the anchors were let down.

ἐπ-ωφελέω, f. ήσω, *to help in* a thing, *to be of use* or *service in.* Hence

ἐπωφέλημα, ατος, τό, *a succour, store.*

ἐπωφελία, ἡ, (ἐπωφελέω) *help, profit, advantage.*

ἐπώχᾰτο, 3 pl. Aeol. and Ion. plqpf. pass. of ἐπέχω, πᾶσαι γὰρ [πύλαι] ἐπώχατο all *were shut to.*

ἐπῳχόμην, impf. med. of ἐποίχομαι.

***ἜΡΑ**, ἡ, the Lat. *terra, earth*: only found in Adv. ἔραζε, *to earth.*

ἜΡᾼΜΑΙ, Ep. 2 pl. ἐράασθε: impf. ἠράμην:—Pass., fut. ἐρασθήσομαι: aor. 1 ἠράσθην: aor. 1 med. ἠρᾰσάμην:—*to love, desire, long after.*

ἐρᾰνίζω, f. σω, (ἔρανος) *to ask for contributions: to collect by way of contribution.* II. *to give a contribution.* III. *to combine.* Hence

ἐρᾰνιστής, οῦ, ὁ, *a contributor to an* ἔρανος or *club.*

ἐραννός, ή, όν, (ἐράω) *lovely, pleasant.*

ἔρᾰνος, ὁ, *a meal to which each contributed his share*, also συμβολή, Lat. *symbolum*: generally, *a feast, festival.* 2. *any subscription* or *contribution*: generally, *a kindness, service.* 3. *a club* or *society.*

ἔρασδε, Dor. for ἔραζε.

ἐρᾰσί-μολπος, ον, (ἐράω, μολπή) *loving song.*

ἐρᾰσι-χρήματος, ον, (ἐράω, χρήματα) *loving money, covetous, avaricious.*

ἐράσμιος, α, ον, also ος, ον, (ἐράω) *lovely, beloved.*

ἔρασσαι, Ep. for ἔρασαι, 2 sing. of ἔραμαι.

ἐράσσατο, Ep. for ἠράσατο, 3 sing. aor. 1 of ἔραμαι.

ἐραστεύω, f. σω, = ἐράω, *to love, desire.*

ἐραστής, οῦ, ὁ, (ἔραμαι) *a lover*: metaph. *an adherent, partizan*

ἐραστός, ή, όν, (ἐράω) *beloved, lovely.*

ἐρᾰτεινός, ή, όν, (ἐράω) *lovely: welcome.*

ἐρᾰτίζω, = ἐράω, *to desire extremely, be greedy for.*

ἐρᾰτός, ή, όν, poët. for ἐραστός, *beloved: lovely.*

ἐρᾰτό-χροος, ον, contr. -χρους, ουν, (ἐρατός, χρόα) *of face* or *complexion.*

ἐρᾱτύω, Dor. for ἐρητύω.

Ἐρᾰτώ, οῦς, ἡ, (ἐρατός) *Erăto, Lovely*, one of the nine Muses. 2. one of the Oceanides.

ἘΡΑ'Ω, only found in pres. and impf. with aor. 1 pass. ἠράσθην used in act. sense: see ἔραμαι:—*to love*: of things, *to long for, desire passionately*: absol., ἐρῶν *a lover*, ἡ ἐρωμένη *the beloved*:—Dep. ἐράομαι in same sense is very rare.

ἐργάζομαι, fut. ἐργάσομαι Dor. ἐργαξοῦμαι: aor. 1 εἰργασάμην: pf. εἴργασμαι Ion. ἔργασμαι, both in act. and pass. sense: but ἐργασθήσομαι, aor. 1 εἰργάσθην always in pass. sense: Dep.: (ἔργον):—*to be busy, to work, set to work*, esp. of husbandmen; τὸ χρῆμ' ἐργάζεται the matter *works*, i. e. *goes on.* II. trans. *to work, do, perform, carry out, accomplish.* 2. *to work at* or *in*; ἐργάζεσθαι χρυσόν *to work in* gold. 3. *to earn by working.* 4. *to make, build*: also *to produce, cause.* III. *to work at a trade, drive a trade.*

ἔργᾰθον, Ep. for εἴργαθον, poët. aor. 2 of εἴργω; inf. ἐργᾰθεῖν.

ἐργᾰλεῖον Ion. -ήϊον, τό, (ἔργον) *a tool, instrument.*

ἐργαξῇ, Dor. for ἐργάσει, 2 sing. fut. of ἐργάζομαι.

ἐργᾰσείω, Desiderat. of ἐργάζομαι, *to be about to do, intend to do.*

ἐργᾰσία, ἡ, (ἐργάζομαι) *work, toil*, Lat. *labor*: *daily labour, business, occupation*; ἐργασίαν δός take *pains to do.* II. *a working at* a thing; *husbandry, tillage*; ἐργασία μετάλλων *working* of mines. 2. *workmanship, art, craft*: also *a work of art.* 3. *gain, earnings, profit.*

ἐργάσιμος, ον, (ἐργάζομαι) *to be worked, that can be worked*: of land, *arable.*

ἔργασμαι, Ion. for εἴργασμαι, pf. of ἐργάζομαι.

ἐργαστέον, verb. Adj. of ἐργάζομαι, *one must work the land.* 2. *one must do.*

ἐργαστήρ, ῆρος, ὁ, (ἐργάζομαι) *a workman, farmer.*

ἐργαστήριον, τό, (ἐργάζομαι) *a workshop, manufactory, shop.*

ἐργαστικός, ή, όν, (ἐργάζομαι) *fit for working, hard-working, diligent, busy.*

ἐργάτης, ου, ὁ, (ἔργον) *a workman, husbandman*: *a practitioner, worker.* II. as Adj. *hard-working, diligent, energetic.* [ᾰ]

ἐργᾰτικός, ή, όν, (ἐργάζομαι) = ἐργαστικός.

ἐργᾰτίνης, ου, ὁ, = ἐργάτης. [ῐ]

ἐργάτις, ιδος, fem. of ἐργάτης, *a work-woman*: *a hireling, mercenary woman.* II. as Adj. *working at.* [ᾰ]

ἔργμα, ατος, τό, = ἔργον, *a work, deed.*

ἕργμα, ατος, τό, (εἴργω, ἕρκος) *a fence, enclosure.*

ἐργνύω and -νῡμι, poët. for εἴργω, ἕργω, *to enclose.*

ἐργο-δότης, ου, ὁ, (ἔργον, δίδωμι) *one who lets out work.*

ἐργολᾰβέω, *to contract for the doing of work*; ἐργολαβεῖν ἀνδριάντας, Lat. *statuas conducere faciendas.* From

ἐργο-λάβος, ον, (ἔργον, λαβεῖν) *contracting for work to be done*: as Subst., ἐργόλαβος, ὁ, *a contractor*, Lat. *conductor, redemptor.* [ᾰ]

ἔργον, τό, (*ἔργω = ἔρδω) *work*; *a man's business, employment*; τὰ σαυτῆς ἔργα κόμιζε mind your own *business.* 2. in the Il. mostly ἔργα, *works* or *deeds* of war; but in the Od. *works of industry, works of husbandry*: *tilled lands*; ἔργα Ἰθάκης *the tilled lands* of Ithaca: ἔργα βοῶν *the fields which* the oxen *plough*; so Virgil *boum labores*; ἔργα γυναικῶν *women's work, handiwork*, esp. *weaving*: of other *occupations*, as, θαλάσσια ἔργα *fishing* or, generally, *maritime pursuits*:—later of all kinds of works, e.g. of *mines*, like our iron-*works*, etc. 3. *a hard piece of work, a severe work.* 4. often in Hom. opp. to ἔπος, *deed, not word*; in Att. often opp. to λόγος. II. the following pecul. Att. phrases occur: ἔργον ἐστί, c. inf. *it is hard work, troublesome*; σὸν ἔργον ἐστί, c. inf. *it is your business* to do; ἔργα παρέχειν τινί, like πράγματα παρέχειν, to give one *trouble.*

ἜΡΓΩ, in Homer mostly ἐέργω, Ep. forms for Att. εἴργω or εἵργω: fut. ἔρξω or εἴρξω: aor. 1 εἶρξα: pf. ἔεργμαι, 3 pl. ἔρχᾰται: plqpf. ἐέργμην, 3 pl. ἔρχατο or ἐέρχατο: aor. 1 pass. part. ἐρχθείς:—*to shut in, confine, include*; ἐντὸς ἐέργειν *to enclose* within; γέφυραι ἐεργμέναι bridges *well-secured, strong-built, compact.* II. *to shut out*: *exclude* or *prohibit from* a thing:—also *to hinder* or *prevent from* doing:—Med. *to keep oneself from, to abstain from.*

***ἜΡΓΩ**, *to do work*, obsol. root, for which the pres. in use is ἔρδω:—hence fut. ἔρξω, aor. 1 ἔρξα, pf. ἔοργα, plqpf. ἐώργειν, which serve as the tenses of ἔρδω.

ἔρδεσκον, Ion. impf. of ἔρδω.

ἜΡΔΩ, fut. ἔρξω, etc., see *ἔργω:—*to work, do, accomplish*; c. dupl. acc., κακὰ ἔρδειν τινά or absol. ἔρδειν τινά, *to do* one *harm.* 2. like Lat. *sacra facere*, ἱερὰ ἔρδειν *to make, offer* a sacrifice: later, without ἱερά or θυσίας, like *facere* or *operari* in Latin.

ἐρεβεννός, ή, όν, (Ἔρεβος) *dark, gloomy.*

Ἐρέβεσφι, Ἐρέβευσφι, v. sub Ἔρεβος.

ἘΡΈΒΙΝΘΟΣ, ὁ, *a kind of pulse, vetch*, Lat. *cicer.*

ἐρεβο-δῐφάω, (ἔρεβος, διφάω) *to grope about in darkness.*

ἐρεβόθεν, Adv. *from Erebos.* From

Ἔρεβος, τό, gen. εος contr. ους, Ion. Ἐρέβευς, Ἐρέβευσφιν:—*Erebos*, a place of nether darkness, above the still deeper Hades.

Ἐρεβόσδε, Adv. *to* or *into Erebos.*

ἐρεείνω, like ἔρομαι, *to ask*; c. acc. pers. *to ask of* one: so also Med. ἐρεείνομαι.

ἐρεθίζω Dor. -ίσδω: f. ίσω Att. ιῶ: aor. 1 ἠρέθισα, later -ιξα: (ἐρέθω):—*to rouse to anger, provoke, irritate.* II. later *to excite, kindle*; φέψαλος ἐρεθιζόμενος the *kindled* spark. Hence

ἐρέθισμα, τό, *a stirring up, exciting.*

ἘΡΈΘΩ, like ἐρεθίζω, *to stir to anger*: *to raise, increase.*

ἘΡΕΙ´ΔΩ, f. ἐρείσω: aor. 1 ἤρεισα:—Pass., aor. 1 ἠρείσθην: pf. ἐρήρεισμαι: 3 sing. plqpf. ἠρήρειστο:—*to make* one thing *lean against* another: hence *to press, urge, force against*; ἐρείδειν πληγήν *to inflict* a *severe* blow. 2. *to prop, stay, support, strengthen*:—generally, *to fix firm, plant.* 3. *to press hard upon.* 4. *to dash, hurl.* 5. of wagers, *to match, set* one pledge *against* another, Lat. *deponere.* II. intr. *to lean against, withstand*; ἀλλήλῃσιν ἐρείδουσαι *crowding* one another: in Att. *to set upon, press hard on.* 2. *to go to work*; ἔρειδε *fall to* (*to eat*). III. Pass., and Med. *to prop* or *support oneself on* a thing, *lean on*: absol. in aor. 1 med. part., ἐρεισάμενος *having set himself firm, taken a firm stand*; οὔδεϊ χαῖται ἐρηρέδαται (3 pl. pf.) the hair *rested on* the ground. 2. *to be fixed firm*; λᾶε ἐρηρέδαται the stones *were firmly set.* 3. in Med. *to strive one with another, contend.*

ἘΡΕΙ´ΚΗ, ἡ, *heath, heather*, Lat. *erica.*

ἘΡΕΙ´ΚΩ, f. ξω: aor. 1 ἤρειξα:—*to break, tear, rend*; ἐρεικόμενος περὶ δουρί *rent, pierced* by the spear: generally, *to dash.* II. intr. in aor. 2 ἤρῐκον, *to shiver, fly in pieces.*

ἔρειο, Ep. for ἔρεο, ἔρου, imperat. of ἔρομαι.

ἐρειοί, οἱ, a word used as a term of insult to the Egyptians.

ἐρείομεν, Ep. for ἐρέωμεν, 1 pl. subj. of ἐρέω.

ἐρείπιον, τό, (ἐρείπω) *a fallen ruin*, in plur. *ruins*; ναυτικὰ ἐρείπια *wrecks, pieces of wreck*; νεκρῶν ἐρείπια *dead carcases*; πέπλων ἐρείπια *remnants* of robes.

ἘΡΕΙ´ΠΩ, f. ἐρείψω: aor. 1 ἤρειψα:—Pass., aor. 1 ἠρείφθην: pf. ἐρήριμμαι:—*to dash down, tear down*; ἐρείπει γένος θεῶν τις some god *dashes down* their race:—Pass. *to be dashed down, fall in ruins*; τεῖχος ἐρέριπτο (Ep. plqpf. for ἠρήριπτο):—Pind. has aor. 2 pass. part. ἐρῐπείς, dat. ἐριπέντι, *fallen.* II. intrans. in aor. 2 ἤρῐπον Ep. ἔρῐπον, pf. 2 ἐρήρῐπα, *to fall down, stumble*: *fall prostrate.*

ἐρεῖσαι, aor. 1 inf. of ἐρείδω.

ἐρεισθείς, aor. 1 part. pass. of ἐρείδω.

ἔρεισμα, ατος, τό, (ἐρείδω) *that which is fixed to support* a thing, *a prop, stay, support*; metaph. of persons, Θήρων' ἔρεισμ' Ἀκράγαντος Theron *pillar* of Agrigentum, like Lat. *colūmen.* II. = ἕρμα, *a sunken rock.*

ἐρείψιμος, ον, (ἐρείπω) *fallen down, in ruins.*

ἐρειψί-τοιχος, ον, (ἐρείπω, τοῖχος) *overthrowing walls.*

ἐρεμνός, ή, όν, contr. of ἐρεβεννός, *black, dark*; ἐρεμνὴ φάτις a *dark* (i.e. *obscure*) rumour.

ἔρεξα, aor. 1 of ῥέζω.

ἐρέομαι, Ep. and Ion. form of ἔρομαι, *to ask.*

ἐρέπτομαι, Dep. used only in pres. and impf., *to feed on*. (Deriv uncertain.)

ἐρέπτω, = ἐρέφω, *to roof over*: *to crown*.

ἐρέριπτο, Ep 3 sing. plqpf. pass of ἐρείπω.

ἐρέσθαι, aor. 2 inf. of ἔρομαι

ἘΡΕ'ΣΣΩ Att. -ττω fut. ἐρέσω: aor. 1 ἤρεσα:—*to row*. II. trans. *to urge by rowing*, metaph. of birds, πτερύγων ἐρετμοῖσιν ἐρεσσόμενοι *sped onward* by the oarage of their wings, Virgil's *remigio alarum*. 2. generally, *to ply, urge*:—Pass. of a bow, *to be plied, handled*.

ἐρέτης, ου, ὁ, (ἐρέσσω) *a rower*.

ἐρετμός, ὁ, or **ἐρετμόν**, τό, (ἐρέσσω) Lat. *remus, an oar*: in pl. only the neut. ἐρετμά is used. Hence

ἐρετμόω, f. ώσω, *to equip with oars, set to row*.

ἐρέττω, Att. for ἐρέσσω.

ἘΡΕΥ'ΓΟΜΑΙ, f. ἐρεύξομαι, Dep. *to spit* or *spew out, to disgorge*, Lat. *eructare*: absol. *to belch*, Lat. *ructare*. 2. metaph. of the sea, *to splash and foam* against the land, *break* upon the beach. II. in aor. 2 act. ἤρῠγον, inf. ἐρῠγεῖν, part. ἐρυγών, *to bellow, roar*.

ἐρευθέδᾰνον, τό, *madder*. From

ἐρευθέω, f. ήσω, *to be red*. From

ἔρευθος, εος, τό, *redness, bloom, blushing*: from

ἘΡΕΥ'ΘΩ, fut. ἐρεύσω, *to make red, stain red*.

ἔρευνα, ης, ἡ, (ἐρέω) *an inquiry, search*. Hence

ἐρευνάω, f. ήσω, *to seek* or *search for, search after*: *to search, examine*. 2. c. inf. *to seek* or *attempt* to do. Hence

ἐρευνητέον, verb. Adj. *one must search*.

ἐρεῦσαι, aor. 1 inf. of ἐρεύθω,

ἘΡΕ'ΦΩ, f. ψω: aor. 1 ἤρεψα:—*to cover* or *roof in* a building. II. *to cover with a crown, wreathe with garlands*:—Med. *to crown oneself*.

ἐρέχθω, *to rend, break, shiver*:—Pass., ναῦς ἐρεχθομένη ἀνέμοισι *a ship dashed hither and thither* by the storm, *shattered*. (Deriv. uncertain.)

ἔρεψα, aor. 1 of ἐρέφω.

ἐρέω, Ion. and Ep. for ἐρῶ.

ἐρέω, Ep. pres. for ἔρομαι, *to ask*.

ἐρημάζω, f. σω, (ἐρῆμος) *to be left lonely, go alone*: Ion. impf. ἐρημάζεσκον.

ἐρημαῖος, α, ον, poët. for ἐρῆμος.

ἐρημία, ἡ, (ἔρημος) *a solitude, desert, wilderness*. II. *solitude, loneliness*: of places, *a being laid waste, desolation*, Lat. *vastitas*: of persons, *desolateness, destitution*. 2. generally, *want of, absence*: also *exemption from* evil.

ἐρημιάς, άδος, ἡ, *a solitary devotee*.

ἐρημο-κόμης, ες, (ἔρημος, κόμη) *destitute of hair*.

ἐρημο-λάλος, ον, (ἔρημος, λᾰλέω) *chattering in the desert*.

ἐρημό-πολις, ι, gen. ιδος, (ἔρημος, πόλις) *reft of one's city*.

ἐρημο-νόμος, ον, (ἔρημος, νέμω) *haunting the desert*.

ἘΡΗ'ΜΟΣ, η, ον, also ος, ον: Att. **ἔρημος**:—of places, *lonely, lone, desert*: of persons, *lone, solitary, desolate*, also *destitute, helpless*. 3. c. gen. *reft of; destitute of, abandoned by*; στέγαι φίλων ἔρημοι. II. as Subst., ἐρῆμος (sub. γῆ, χώρα), ἡ, *a solitude, desert, wilderness*. III. ἐρήμη (sub. δίκη), ἡ, a trial *in which one party does not appear*, and lets judgment go *by default*; ἐρήμην δίκην ἑλεῖν to get judgment *by default*; ὀφλεῖν to let it go *by default*.

ἐρημοσύνη, ἡ, *solitude*. From

ἐρημόω, f. ώσω, (ἔρημος) *to make solitary* or *desert, lay waste, desolate, devastate*. 2. c. gen. *to bereave of*:—Pass. *to be bereft, deprived of*. II. *to leave, abandon*:—Pass. *to be left alone, deserted*. Hence

ἐρήμωσις, εως, ἡ, *desolation, devastation*: and

ἐρημωτής, οῦ, ὁ, *a desolator*.

ἐρηρέδαται, Ion. 3 pl. pf. pass. of ἐρείδω: **ἐρηρέδατο**, Ion. 3 pl. plqpf. pass.

ἐρήριμμαι, pf. pass. of ἐρείπω.

ἐρήριπα, intrans. pf. of ἐρείπω.

ἐρήτῡθεν, Aeol. 3 pl. aor. 1 pass. of ἐρητύω.

ἐρητύω, f. ύσω [ῡ]: aor. 1 ἐρήτῡσα: (ἐρύω):—*to hold back, restrain, to keep in check, repress*:—*to keep back from*.

ἐρητύσασκε, 3 sing. Ion. aor. 1 of ἐρητύω.

ἘΡΙ', insepar. Particle, like ἀρι–, used as a prefix to strengthen the sense of a word, *very, much*.

ἐρι-αύχην, ενος, ὁ, ἡ, *with high-arching neck*.

ἐρι-βόας, ου, ὁ, (ἐρι–, βοή) *clamorous, riotous*.

ἐρι-βρεμέτης, ου, ὁ, (ἐρι–, βρέμω) *loud-sounding, thundering, roaring*.

ἐρι-βρεμής, ές, = ἐρίβρομος.

ἐρί-βρομος, ον, (ἐρι–, βρέμω) *loud-shouting, roaring*.

ἐρι-βρύχης, ου, Ep. εω, ὁ, and **ἐρί-βρῡχος**, ον, (ἐρι–, βρυχάομαι) *loud-bellowing*.

ἐρι-βῶλαξ, ἄκος, ὁ, ἡ, and **ἐρί-βωλος**, ον, *with large clods*, of rich, loamy soil: hence *very fertile, fruitful*.

ἐρί-γδουπος, ον, = ἐρίδουπος, *thundering*.

ἐρῑδαίνω, f. ἐριδήσω, (ἐρίζω) *to wrangle, quarrel*: *to strive for*:—aor. 1 inf. med ἐρῑδήσασθαι.

ἐρίδιον, τό, Dim. of ἔριον.

ἐριδμαίνω, (ἐρίζω) *to provoke to strife, irritate*. II. intr. *to contend*.

ἐρίδμᾱτος, ον, (ἐρι–, δμητός) *strongly built*: hence *strong, excessive*.

ἐρί-δουπος, ον, (ἐρι–, δοῦπος) *loud-sounding*.

ἐριζέμεναι, Ep. inf. of ἐρίζω.

ἐρίζω Dor. **ἐρίσδω**: Ion. impf. ἐρίζεσκον: fut. ἐρίσω: aor. 1 ἤρισα, Ep. 3 sing. opt. ἐρίσσειε: (ἔρις):—*to strive, wrangle, quarrel*. 2. *to rival, strive*, or *vie with*: hence, *to be equal, be a match for*:—so also in Med.

ἐρί-ηρος, ον, (ἐρι–, *ἄρω) *fitting closely*: metaph. as epith. of ἑταῖρος, *loving, faithful, trusty*: so also in heterocl. plur., ἐρίηρες ἑταῖροι, acc. ἐρίηρας ἑταίρους.

ἐρῑθακίς, ίδος, ἡ, (ἔριθος) *a labouring woman*.

ἐρι-θᾱλής, ές, Dor. for ἐριθηλής.

ἐρῑθεία, ἡ, (ἐριθεύω) *labour for wages*. II. *intriguing*, Lat. *ambitus*: *party-spirit, faction*.

ἐρι-θηλής, ές, (ἐρι- τέθηλα) *very luxuriant, flourishing, fertile.*

ἔρῑθος, ὁ, also ἡ, *a day-labourer, hired servant;* in Homer, ἔριθοι, of men, are *mowers* or *reapers;* of women, *workers in wool.*

ἐρῐκεῖν, intrans. aor. 2 inf. of ἐρείκω.

ἐρι-κλάγκτης, ου, ὁ, (ἐρι-, κλάζω) *loud-sounding.*

ἐρί-κλαυστος and **-κλαυτος**, ον, (ἐρι-, κλαίω) *much-weeping.* II. pass. *much-wept, bewailed.*

ἐρί-κτῠπος, ον, *loud-sounding.*

ἐρι-κῡδής, ές, (ἐρι-, κῦδος) *very famous, glorious.*

ἐρι-κύμων [ῡ], ον, gen. ονος, (ἐρι-, κῦμα) *full of young, big with young.*

ἐρί-μῡκος, ον, (ἐρι-, μέμῡκα) *loud-bellowing.*

ἘΡΙ῀ΝΕΟ´Σ, ὁ, *the wild fig-tree,* Lat. *caprificus.*

ἐρίνεος, α, ον, (ἔριον) *of wool, woollen.*

ἘΡΙ῀ΝΥ´Σ (not Ἐριννύς), gen. ύος, ἡ: pl. nom. Ἐρινύες contr. -ῦς, acc. -ύας contr. -ῦς, gen. -ύων contr. -ῦν:—*the Erinys* or *Fury,* an avenging deity: the names *Tisiphone, Megaera, Alecto* do not occur till late. At Athens they were called Εὐμενίδες or Σεμναί, by an euphemism. II. as Appellat., μητρὸς ἐρινύες *curses from* one's mother; φρενῶν ἐρινύς *distraction, frenzy:* also, *blood-guiltiness.*

ἔριον Ep. and Ion. **εἴριον**, τό, (ἔρος) *wool,* Lat. *lana;* also in plur. 2. ἔρια ἀπὸ ξύλου *wool* from the tree, i. e. *cotton;* so in Germ., *baum-wolle.*

ἐριο-πώλης, ου, ὁ, (ἔριον, πωλέω) *a wool-dealer.* Hence

ἐριο-πωλικῶς, Adv. *like a wool-dealer, cheatingly.*

ἐριο-πώλιον, τό, *the wool-market.*

ἐριό-στεπτος, ον, (ἔριον, στέφω) *wreathed with wool.*

ἐρι-ούνιος, ὁ, Homeric epith. of Hermes, from ἐρι-, ὀνίνημι, *the helper, luck-bringer:* also absol. Ἐριούνιος, *Helper,* as a prop. n. of Hermes.

ἐρι-ουργέω, f. ήσω, *to make woollen stuff.*

ἐρι-ουργός, όν, (ἔριον, *ἔργω) *working wool.*

ἔριπε, Ep. for ἤριπε, 3 sing. intrans. aor. 2 of ἐρείπω.

ἐριπεῖν, intrans. aor. 2 inf. of ἐρείπω.

ἐρί-πλευρος, ον, (ἐρι-, πλευρά) *with sturdy sides.*

ἐρίπνη or **ἐρίπνα**, ἡ, (ἐρείπω) *a broken cliff, crag, scaur: any sheer ascent.*

ἐριπών, aor. 2 part. of ἐρείπω.

ἜΡΙΣ, ιδος, ἡ: acc. ἔριν and ἔριδα: pl. ἔριδες, later ἔρεις:—*strife, quarrel, debate:* esp. *rivalry, contention: discord, jealousy:* also in good sense, ἔρις ἀγαθῶν *zeal for* good II. as pr. nom., *Eris,* the Goddess of *Strife.*

ἐρίσδεν, Dor. inf. of ἐρίζω.

ἐρίσδομες, Dor. for ἐρίζομεν.

ἐρι-σθενής, ές, (ἐρι-, σθένος) *mighty in strength.*

ἔρισμα, ατος, τό, (ἐρίζω) *a cause of quarrel*

ἐρι-σμάρᾰγος, ον, (ἐρι-, σμᾰρᾰγή) *loud-thundering.*

ἐρίσσειε, -ειαν, Ep. 3 sing. and pl. aor. 1 opt. of ἐρίζω.

ἐρίσσεται, Ep. for ἐρίσηται, aor. 1 subj. med. of ἐρίζω.

ἐρι-στάφῠλος, ον, (ἐρι-, στᾰφυλή) *large-clustering, rich in grapes:* of wine, *made of fine grapes.*

ἐριστής, οῦ, ὁ, (ἐρίζω) *a wrangler, disputer.*

ἐριστός, ή, όν, (ἐρίζω), *to be disputed* or *contested.*

ἐρι-σφάρᾰγος, ον, = ἐρισμάραγος, *loud-roaring.*

ἐρί-τῑμος, ον, (ἐρι-, τιμή) *highly prized, precious*

ἐρίφειος, ον, (ἔρῐφος) *of* or *belonging to a kid.*

ἐρίφιον, τό, Dim. of ἔριφος, *a goat, kid.* [ῐ]

ἘΡΙ῀ΦΟΣ, ὁ, also ἡ, *a young goat, kid.* II. ἔριφοι, οἱ, Lat. *hoedi, a constellation* which brought storms; ἐπ' ἐρίφοις in stormy weather.

ἐρῐώλη, ἡ, *a whirlwind, hurricane, tornado:* Aristophanes gives a fanciful derivation from ἔριον and ὄλλυμι, *wool-consumption.*

ἑρκεῖος Att. **ἕρκειος**, ον, and α, ον, (ἕρκος) *belonging to the court* or *enclosure* in front of the house; Ζεὺς Ἑρκεῖος, the *household* god, because his statue stood in the ἕρκος; ἕρκειοι πύλαι the gates *of the court.*

ἑρκίον, τό, (ἕρκος) *a fence, enclosure.*

ἕρκος, εος, τό, (ἔργω, εἴργω) *an enclosure, hedge, fence, wall:* mostly of *the wall round the court-yard,* and so *a court-yard:* ἀγγέων ἕρκεα, periphr. for ἄγγη; σφραγῖδος ἕρκος, for σφραγίς; ἕρκος ὀδόντων *the ring-fence* of the teeth, for ὀδόντες the teeth themselves. II. *a net, snare: the coils* of the lasso. III. metaph. *any fence* or *defence, bulwark.*

ἑρκ-ουρος, ον, (ἕρκος, οὖρος) *watching an enclosure.*

ἑρκτή, ἡ, Ion. for εἱρκτή.

ἕρμα, ατος, τό, *a prop, support:* mostly of *the stays* or *beams* by which ships on shore were kept upright: metaph., ἕρμα πόληος *pillar* of the state, Lat. *columen.* 2. *a sunken rock* or *reef,* on which a vessel may strike: also *a mound, cairn, barrow* on land. 3. *ballast.* II. μελαινέων ἕρμ' ὀδυνάων, of a sharp arrow, *the foundation,* i.e. *cause,* of pangs. III. ἕρματα, *earrings,* akin to ὅρμος: generally, *a necklace, band: a chain.*

ἕρμαιον, τό, (Ἑρμῆς) *a windfall, godsend, lucky discovery,* Hermes being the reputed giver of such gifts, as in Latin *Hercules.*

Ἑρμαῖος, α, ον, Att. **Ἕρμαιος**, ον, (Ἑρμῆς) *of* or *from Hermes.* II. Ἕρμαια (sub. ἱερά), τά, a festival in his honour.

ἑρμᾰτίζω, (ἕρμα) *to ballast.*

Ἑρμ-αφρόδῑτος, ὁ, (Ἑρμῆς, Ἀφροδίτη) *an Hermaphrodite: an effeminate person.*

Ἑρμάων ωνος, ὁ. poët. esp. Dor. for Ἑρμῆς. [ᾱ]

Ἑρμέας, ὁ, poët. for Ἑρμῆς, dat. Ἑρμέᾳ.

Ἑρμείας, ὁ, Ep. for Ἑρμῆς; gen. Ἑρμείαο, -είω; dat. Ἑρμείᾳ; acc. Ἑρμείαν; voc. Ἑρμειᾶ.

ἑρμηνεία, ἡ, (ἑρμηνεύω) *interpretation, explanation.* II. *expression, power of speech.*

ἑρμήνευμα, ατος, τό, (ἑρμηνεύω) *an interpretation, explanation.* 2. *a sign, monument.*

ἑρμηνεύς, έως, ὁ, (Ἑρμῆς) *an interpreter, dragoman:* generally, *an expounder.* Hence

ἑρμηνεύω, f. σω, *to be an interpreter, to interpret, explain, make clear:* hence *to express, give utterance to.*

Ἑρμῆς, ὁ; Ep. gen. Ἑρμέω; dat. Ἑρμῇ; acc. Ἑρμῆν; voc. Ἑρμῆ:—*Hermes,* the Lat. *Mercurius.*

In Homer, as messenger of the gods, he is called διάκτορος; as giver of good luck, ἐριούνιος, ἀκάκητα; as god of all secret dealings, and cunning, δόλιος; as conductor of ghosts to Hades, ψυχοπομπός. Later, he was tutelary god of arts and sciences; also of heralds, traffic, markets, roads, whence he is ὅδιος, ἐνόδιος: hence any four-cornered post ending in a bust was called Ἑρμῆς.

Ἑρμίδιον, τό, Dim. of Ἑρμῆς, *a little figure of Hermes*: in vocat. *my dear little Hermes*.

ἑρμίς or **ἑρμίν**, ῖνος, ὁ, dat. pl. ἑρμῖσιν, (ἕρμα) *a prop, support*: *a bed-post*.

Ἑρμο-γλῠφεύς, έως, ὁ, (Ἑρμῆς, γλύφω) *a carver of Hermae*: generally, *a statuary*. Hence

ἑρμογλῠφικός, ή, όν, *of* or *for a statuary*: ἡ ἑρμογλυφική (sub. τέχνη), *the art of statuary*.

ἑρμο-γλύφος, ὁ, = ἑρμογλῠφεύς.

ἑρμο-κοπίδης, ου, ὁ, (Ἑρμῆς, κόπτω) *a mutilator of the Hermae*.

ἝΡΝΟΣ, εος, τό, *a shoot, scion*, of the olive and palm; ἀνέδραμεν ἔρνεϊ ἶσος he shot up like *a young plant* II. metaph. *a scion, a child*.

ἔρξα, aor. 1 of *ἔργω, = ἔρδω.

ἐρξείης or **ἐρξίης**, ὁ, translation of the Persian name Darius: from *ἔργω, ἔρδω, *the worker, doer*.

ἔρξω, fut. of *ἔργω, = ἔρδω.

ἐρόεις, εσσα, εν, (ἔρος) *lovely, pleasing*.

ἐροίην, for ἐροῖμι, pres. opt. of ἐρέω.

ἜΡΟΜΑΙ Ion. **εἴρομαι**: impf. εἰρόμην: fut. ἐρήσομαι Ion. εἰρήσομαι: aor. 2 ἠρόμην, imperat. ἔρου Ep. ἔρειο, subj. ἔρωμαι, opt. ἐροίμην, inf. ἐρέσθαι, part. ἐρόμενος:—*to ask, inquire*: *to ask after* or *for*. II. *to question, to ask advice of, consult*: c. dupl. acc. *to ask* one *about* a thing.

ἔρος, ὁ, poët. form of ἔρως, *love, desire*.

ἜΡΟΣ, εος, τό, *wool*, Lat. *lana*.

ἑρπετόν, τό, (ἕρπω) *a creeping thing, reptile*: esp. *a snake*; pl. ἑρπετά, as opp. to πετεινά, *any animals that move on the earth*.

ἑρπήστης, ου, ὁ, (ἕρπω) *a creeper, a mouse*.

ἑρπύζω, f. σω, (ἕρπω) *to creep, crawl, drag oneself along*: always with idea of difficulty or distress.

ἕρπυλλος, ὁ and ἡ, (ἕρπω) *creeping thyme*, Lat. *serpyllum*, an evergreen herb used for wreaths.

ἑρπύσαι, aor. 1 inf. of ἑρπύζω or ἕρπω.

ἑρπυστήρ, ῆρος, ὁ, and **ἑρπυστής**, οῦ, ὁ, (ἑρπύζω) *a reptile*: *a crawling child*.

ἝΡΠΩ, impf. εἷρπον: fut. ἕρψω Dor. ἑρψῶ: aor. 1 εἵρπῠσα, formed from ἑρπύζω (cf. ἕλκω, εἵλκῠσα):—*the* Lat. SERPO, REPO, *to creep, crawl, move slowly*: of men, *to creep, glide, slink about*: ἕρποντα *creeping things*. 2. metaph. *to creep on, spread*, as in Lat. *serpit rumor*.

ἕρπωμες, Dor. 1 pl. pres. subj. of ἕρπω.

ἐρράγην [ᾰ], aor. 2 pass. of ῥήγνυμι.

ἐρράδαται, Ep. 3 pl. pf. pass. of ῥαίνω: **ἐρράδατο**, Ep. 3 pl. plqpf.

ἐρραμμένος, pf. part. pass. of ῥάπτω.

ἐρράπισα, aor. 1 of ῥαπίζω

ἐρρέθεν and **ἐρρήθην**, aor. 1 pass. of ἐρέω, ἐρῶ.

ἔρρηξα, aor. 1 of ῥήγνυμι.

ἔρρῑγα, pf. 2 (with pres. sense) of ῥιγέω.

ἐρρίγησα, aor. 1 of ῥιγέω.

ἐρρίζωται, 3 sing. pf. pass. of ῥιζόω.

ἐρριμμένος, pf. part. pass. of ῥίπτω.

ἔρριψα, aor. 1 of ῥίπτω.

ἐρρύηκα, pf. of ῥέω;—**ἐρρύην**, aor. 2 pass.

ἔρ-ρυθμος, ον, *in rhythm, time* or *measure*.

ἘΡΡΩ, fut. ἐρρήσω: aor. 1 ἤρρησα: pf. ἤρρηκα:—*to go* or *walk slowly*; properly of a halting gait, whence Vulcan is called ἔρρων, *limping*. II. in a bad sense, *to go* or *come to ruin*; ἔρρων ἐκ ναός *gone* or *fallen from* a ship: imperat. ἔρρε, or ἔρρε ἐς κόρακας, Lat. *abi in malam rem, go with a plague* on thee; ἐρρέτω *let him pass, away with him*; ἐρρέτω Ἴλιον *let* Troy *perish!* ἔρρει τὰ καλά the luck *is gone!*

ἔρρωγα, pf. 2 of ῥήγνυμι.

ἐρρωμένος, pf. part. pass. of ῥώννυμι, as Adj., *in good health, vigorous, stout*: Adv. ἐρρωμένως, *stoutly*: irreg. Comp. ἐρρωμενέστερος, Sup. -έστατος.

ἐρρώοντο, 3 pl. impf. of ῥώομαι; **ἐρρώσαντο**, 3 pl. aor. 1 med.; **ἐρρώσθην**, aor. 1 pass.

ἐρρῶσθαι, pf. inf. pass. of ῥώννυμι.

ἔρρωσο, **ἔρρωσθε**, pf. imperat. pass. of ῥώννυμι.

ἕρση Ep. **ἐέρση**, ἡ, (ἄρδω) *dew*, Lat. *ros*; τεθαλυῖα ἐέρση plenteous *dew*: in pl. *rain-drops*. II. metaph. of any *young and tender thing*, esp. of *late-born lambs*, cp. μέτασσαι. Hence

ἑρσήεις Ep. **ἐερσήεις**, εσσα, εν, *dewy, dew-besprinkled*:—of a corpse, *fresh*.

ἔρσην, ενος, ὁ, Ion. for ἄρσην, ἄρρην.

ἐρυγγάνω, Att. form of ἐρεύγομαι, *to vomit*.

ἐρῠγεῖν, aor. 2 inf. of ἐρεύγομαι.

ἐρύγμηλος, η, ον, (ἐρεύγομαι) *loud-bellowing*.

ἐρυγών, aor. 2 part. of ἐρεύγομαι.

ἐρῠθαίνω, aor. 1 ἐρύθηνα, poët. for ἐρυθραίνω, *to redden, make to blush*:—Pass. *to become red*. Hence

ἐρύθημα, ατος, τό, *redness on the skin*: *a flush, blush*.

ἐρυθραίνω, f. ᾰνῶ, (ἐρυθρός) *to dye red*:—Pass. *to become red, to blush*.

ἐρυθριάω, f. άσω [ᾱ], (ἐρυθρός) *to be apt to blush*.

ἐρυθρο-βᾰφής, ές, (ἐρυθρός, βαφῆναι) *dyed red*.

ἐρυθρό-πους, ὁ, ἡ, gen. ποδος, (ἐρυθρός, πούς) *red-footed*: the name of a bird, *the red-shank*.

ἘΡΥΘΡΟ'Σ, ά, όν, *red*, Lat. *RUBER*. II. Ἐρυθρὴ θάλασσα, *the Erythraean sea*, our *Indian ocean*.

ἐρύκᾰκον, Ep. aor. 2 of ἐρύκω, inf. ἐρῡκᾰκέειν.

ἐρῡκᾰνάω, poët. for ἐρύκω, *to restrain, confine*.

ἐρυκανόωσι, Ep. for ἐρυκανῶσι, 3 pl. of ἐρυκανάω.

ἐρῡκάνω, poët. for ἐρύκω, *to restrain*. [ᾰ]

ἐρύκω, f. ξω: aor. 1 ἤρυξα Ep. ἔρυξα: Ep. aor. 2 ἠρύκᾰκον, or without augm. ἐρύκᾰκον, inf. ἐρῡκᾰκέειν: (ἐρύω):—*to keep in, hold back, restrain, hinder*: *to control, curb, keep in check*; γῆ ἐρύκει earth *confines* (the dead); μή με ἔρυκε μάχης *keep* me not *back from* fight. 2. *to detain* a guest. 3. *to ward off*, Lat. *arceo*. 4. *to keep apart, separate, divide*. II. Pass. *to be held back, detained: to be kept away*. 2. *to be guarded, safe.*

ἔρῦμα, ατος, τό, (ἐρύομαι) *a fence, guard: a bulwark, fort:* generally, *a defence, safeguard.*

ἐρῦμάτιον, τό, Dim. of ἔρυμα.

ἐρυμνό-νωτος, ον, *with impenetrable back.*

ἐρυμνός, ή, όν, (ἐρύομαι) *fenced, fortified.* Hence

ἐρυμνότης, ητος, ή, *strength, security*, of a place.

ἔρυντο, 3 pl. aor. 2 of ῥύομαι.

ἐρυσαίατο, Ion. 3 pl. aor. 1 opt. med. of ἐρύω.

ἐρῦσ-άρμᾰτος, ον, (ἐρύω, ἅρμα) *chariot-drawing:* Ep. heterocl. pl. ἐρυσάρματες, -τας.

ἐρῦσί-θριξ, τρῐχος, ὁ, ή, (ἐρύω, θρίξ) *for drawing through the hair*, epith. of a comb.

ἐρῦσῑ-νηΐς, ΐδος, ή, (ἐρύομαι, ναῦς) *preserving ships.*

ἐρῦσί-πτολις, ὁ, ή, (ἐρύομαι, πόλις) *protecting the city.*

ἔρῦσις, εως, ή, (ἐρύω) *a drawing.*

ἐρυσμός, ὁ, (ἐρύομαι) *a safeguard.*

ἐρύσσασθαι, Ep. aor. 1 inf. med. of ἐρύω.

ἐρύσσομεν, Ep. for ἐρύσωμεν, aor. 1 subj. of ἐρύω.

ἐρυστός, ή, όν, (ἐρύω) *drawn.*

ἔρῦτο, Ep. 3 sing. plqpf. (with sense of aor. 2) pass. of ἐρύω.

ἘΡΥ'Ω Ion. **εἰρύω**: fut. ἐρύσω or ἐρύω: aor. 1 εἴρῠσα Ep. εἴρυσσα or ἔρῠσα:—*to draw, drag;* νεκροὺς or νεκρὸν ἐρύειν, either of the friends, *to drag* the corpse *away, rescue* it, or of the enemy, *to drag* it *off for plunder, ransom*, etc.: *to drag about, treat roughly:* hence *to drag away, carry off violently; to tear off* or *down* χλαίνης ἐρύειν τινά *to pull* him *by* the cloak. II. Med. **ἐρύομαι** Ion. **εἰρύομαι**: fut. inf. ἐρύεσθαι but Ep. fut. also ἐρύσσομαι: aor. 1 εἰρῠσάμην Ep. εἰρυσσάμην or ἐρυσσάμην: the foll. forms are pass., pf. εἴρῠμαι both in med. and pass. sense, Ep. 3 pl. εἰρύᾰται; 3 sing. plqpf. (with sense of aor. 2) εἴρῡτο or ἔρῡτο, 3 pl. εἴρυντο or εἰρύατο:—*to draw to one's own side;* ξίφος ἐρύεσθαι *to draw one's* sword; ἐρύσασθαι τόξον *to draw one's* bow *to*, to string it; ἐρύεσθαι νῆας *to launch one's* ships, but in pass. sense, of the ships, *to be hauled ashore.* 2. from the sense of *drawing out from the press of battle*, comes the sense *to rescue, deliver*, and hence *to protect, guard.* 3. *to keep off, ward off;* ἡ δ' οὐκ ἔγχος ἔρῡτο *it kept* not *off* the spear: hence *to check, thwart, repress.* 4. *to keep guard upon, watch, to keep carefully, conceal:* also *to maintain, assert, hold in honour;* θέμιστας εἰρύαται *they maintain* laws.

ἔρχᾰται, Ion. 3 pl. pf. pass. of ἔργω, εἴργω:—**ἔρχᾰτο** (or **ἐέρχατο**), 3 pl. plqpf.

ἐρχᾰτάομαι, Pass. *to be shut up.* From

ἔρχᾰτος, ὁ, (ἔργω) *a fence, enclosure, hedge.*

ἐρχατόωντο, Ep. 3 pl. impf. of ἐρχατάομαι.

ἐρχθείς, aor. 1 part. pass. of ἔργω, εἴργω.

ἘΡΧΟΜΑΙ: impf. ἠρχόμην:—the tenses are formed from the Root **ἐλεύθω**: fut. ἐλεύσομαι: aor. ἤλῠθον, syncop. ἦλθον Dor. ἦνθον; later also aor. 1 ἦλθα: pf. ἐλήλῠθα Ep. εἰλήλουθα, 1 pl. εἰλήλουθμεν, part. εἰληλουθώς: 3 sing. plqpf., Ion. ἐληλύθεε Ep. εἰληλούθει:—*to come* or *go:*—*to come back, return:* —in Homer with cognate words, as, ὁδὸν or κέλευθον ἐλθεῖν; also poët., ἀγγελίην ἐλθεῖν, *to go on a* message. 2. c. gen. loci, πεδίοιο ἐλθεῖν *to go through* or *across* the plain 3. with fut. part., ἔρχομαι οἰσόμενος ἔγχος I come *to fetch* a spear: like an auxiliary Verb, ἔρχομαι ἐρέων *I am going to* tell, Fr. *je vais dire.* II. later phrases: εἰς λόγους ἔρχεσθαί τινι *to come* to speech, have an interview, converse with. 2. ἐπὶ πᾶν ἐλθεῖν to try everything. 3. παρὰ μικρὸν ἐλθεῖν, c. inf., *to come within a little of, be near* a thing. 4. with διά and its case, periphr. for a Verb, as. διὰ μάχης τινὶ ἔρχεσθαι for μάχεσθαί τινι, διὰ πολέμου ἔρχεσθαι for πολεμεῖν, etc.

ἑρψω, ἑρψοῦμες, Dor. 1 sing. and pl. fut. of ἕρπω

ἔρῳ, dat. of ἔρος, *love:* see ἔρως.

ἘΡΩ' Ion. and Ep. **ἐρέω**, fut. (φημί, λέγω and ἀγορεύω being used as pres. and εἶπον as aor. 2): from the same Root come pf. εἴρηκα, pass. εἴρημαι, plqpf. pass. εἰρήμην; aor. 1 pass. ἐρρήθην and ἐρρέθην, inf. ῥηθῆναι; fut. pass. ῥηθήσομαι, fut. 3 εἰρήσομαι:—*I will say, speak.* 2. *I will tell, proclaim, announce:* hence *I will promise.* 3. *I will tell, order* him *to do;* εἰρητό οἱ, c. inf., *it had been told* him to do. II. ἐρέω occurs sometimes in Hom. as a pres. = ἔρομαι, εἴρομαι, *to ask for* or *after.*

ἘΡΩΔΙΟ'Σ, ὁ, *the heron* or *hern*, Lat. *ARDEA.*

ἐρωείτω, 3 sing. pres. imperat. of

ἐρωέω, f. ήσω: aor. 1 ἠρώησα Ep. ἐρώησα:—*to flow, stream, burst out: to gush out by starts* or *at intervals.* 2. *to retreat, withdraw, cease from*, c. gen.: absol., νέφος οὔποτ' ἐρωεῖ the cloud never *leaves* it. II. trans. *to drive* or *force back.* (Akin to ῥώομαι.) Hence

ἐρωή, ή, *any quick, violent motion;* δουρὸς ἐρωή *the rush* or *flight* of a spear; λικμητῆρος ἐρωή *the force* or *swing* of the winnower's (shovel). 2. *an impulse, desire.* II. *a retreat from, rest from;* πολέμου ἐρωή.

ἐρωῆσαι, aor. 1 inf. of ἐρωέω: **ἐρωήσαιτε**, 2 pl. opt.

ἐρω-μανέω, f. ήσω, (ἔρως, μαίνομαι) *to be madly in love.* Hence

ἐρωμᾰνία, ή, *mad love.*

ἐρωμένιον, τό, *a little love, darling:* Dim. of

ἐρώμενος, ὁ, **ἐρωμένη**, ή, pres. part. pass. of ἐράω, *a loved one, one's love.*

ἔρως, ωτος, ὁ: heterocl. dat. ἔρῳ (from ἔρος), acc. ἔρων, for regular dat. ἔρωτι, acc. ἔρωτα: (ἔρος) —*love: desire for* a thing. II. as prop. n., *the god of love, Eros, Amor:* in plur. ἔρωτες the Loves. Hence

ἐρωτάριον, τό, Dim. *a little Cupid.*

ἐρωτάω Ion. **εἰρ-**, f. ήσω: aor. 1 ἠρώτησα: (ἔρομαι):—*to ask*, τινά τι something *of* one; τὸ ἐρωτη-

θέν the question. II. *to question* a person. III. *to ask, solicit, beg.* Hence

ἐρώτημα, *ατος, τό, a question; ἐρώτημα τοῦ ξυνθήματος the asking for* the watchword, *the challenge* of soldiers.

ἐρώτησις, *εως, ἡ,* (*ἐρωτάω*) *a questioning.*

ἐρωτιάς, *άδος, ἡ,* pecul. fem. of *ἐρωτικός.*

ἐρωτικός, *ή, όν,* (*ἔρως*) *of* or *caused by love; ἐρωτικὴ ξυντυχία* a *love* affair. 2. *given to love, fond.* Hence

ἐρωτικῶς, Adv. *lovingly, fondly.*

ἐρωτίς, *ίδος, ἡ,* (*ἔρως*) *a loved one, darling.* II. as Adj. *ἐρωτίδες νῆσοι,* islands *of love.*

ἐρωτο-γράφος, *ον,* (*ἔρως, γράφω*) *writing on love.*

ἐρωτο-πλάνος, *ον,* (*ἔρως, πλᾰνάω*) *beguiling love.*

ἐρωτο-πλοέω, f. *ήσω,* (*ἔρως, πλόος*) *to sail on love's ocean.*

ἐρωτύλος, *ὁ,* (*ἔρως*) *a darling, sweetheart.* II. as Adj., *ἐρωτύλα ἀείδειν* to sing *love-songs.* [ῠ]

ἐς, Ion. and old Att. form for *εἰς, to:* for all compounds with *ἐσ-* see under *εἰσ-.*

ἕς, aor. 2 imperat. of *ἵημι*

ἐσ-αγγελεύς, **ἐσ-αγγέλλω**, for *εἰσαγγ-.*

ἐσ-ᾰγείρω, v. *εἰσαγείρω;* in Homer only in 3 sing. Ep. impf. med. *ἐσαγείρετο,* Ep. aor. 1 med. *ἐσαγείρατο.*

ἐσ-άγω, v. *εἰσάγω.*

ἐσ-αιέν, (*ἐς, αἰέν*) Adv. *for ever.*

ἐσ-αθρέω, **ἐσ-ᾰκοντίζω**, **ἐσ-ᾰκούω**, v. sub *εἰσ-.*

ἐσαθρήσαιμι, aor. 1 opt. of *εἰσαθρέω.*

ἐσᾶλτο, 3 sing. Ep. aor. 2 of *εἰσάλλομαι.*

ἔσαν, Ep. and Ion. 3 pl. impf. of *εἰμί sum.*

ἕσαν, Ep. 3 pl. impf. of *ἕννυμι.*

ἐσάντα, v. *εἰσάντα.*

ἐσ-άπαξ, Ion. for *εἰσαπ-,* (*ἐς, ἅπαξ*) *at once.*

ἐσάπην [ᾰ], aor. 2 pass. of *σήπω.*

ἐσ-απικνέομαι, Ion. for *εἰσαφικνέομαι.*

ἐσ-ᾰράσσω, v. *εἰσαράσσω.*

ἕσατο, 3 sing. aor. 1 med. of *ἕννυμι.*

ἐσ-άχρι, Adv. for *εἰς ἄχρι, until,* c. gen.

ἐσάωθεν, 3 pl. aor. 1 pass. of *σαόω,* Ep. for *σώζω.*

ἐσάωσα, aor. 1 of *σαόω,* Ep. for *σώζω.*

ἐσβαίην, aor. 2 opt. of *εἰσβαίνω.*

ἐσ-βαίνω, **ἐσ-βάλλω**, v. *εἰσβαίνω, εἰσβάλλω.*

ἐσβάς, aor. 2 part. of *εἰσβαίνω.*

ἔσβην, aor. 2 of *σβέννυμι.*

ἐσ-βιβάζω, **ἐσ-βολή**, v. *εἰσβιβάζω, εἰσβολή.*

ἐσ-δέκομαι, Ion. for *εἰσδέχομαι.*

ἐσ-δίδωμι, **ἐσ-δύομαι**, **ἐσ-δύω**, v. *εἰσδ-.*

ἑσδόμενοι, **ἑσδώμεθα**, Dor. for *ἑζόμενοι, ἑζώμεθα.*

ἔσεαι, **ἔσεται**, poët. for *ἔσει* or *ἔσῃ, ἔσται,* 2 and 3 sing. fut. of *εἰμί sum.*

ἐσέδρᾰκον, aor. 2 of *εἰσδέρκομαι.*

ἐσέδρᾰμον, aor. 2 of *εἰστρέχω.*

ἔσ-ειμι, v. *εἴσειμι.*

ἐσελεύσομαι, fut. of *εἰσέρχομαι.*

ἐσελθεῖν, aor. 2 inf. of *εἰσέρχομαι.*

ἐσεμασσάμην, Ep. aor. 1 of *εἰσμαίομαι* (cf. *ἐπιμαίομαι*), *to touch; μάλα γάρ με θᾰνὼν ἐσεμάσσατο θυμόν* for by his death he very much *touched* me in *heart.*

ἐσέπτατο, 3 sing. aor. 2 of *εἰσπέταμαι.*

ἐσεργνύναι, Ion. inf. of *εἰσείργω, εἰσέργω.*

ἐσ-έρχομαι, v. *εἰσέρχομαι.*

ἐσεσάχατο, 3 pl. plqpf. pass. of *σάττω.*

ἐσέχυντο, 3 pl. Ep. aor. 2 pass. of *εἰσχέω.*

ἐσ-έχω, **ἐσ-ηθέω**, v. sub *εἰσέχω, εἰσηθέω.*

ἐσήλατο, 3 sing. aor. 1 med. of *εἰσάλλομαι.*

ἐσημήναντο, 3 pl. aor. 1 med. of *σημαίνω.*

ἔσηνα, aor. 1 of *σαίνω.*

ἕσθαι, aor. 2 inf. med. of *ἵημι.* 2. pf. inf. pass. of *ἕννυμι.*

ἐσθέσθαι, Ion. aor. 2 inf. med. of *εἰστίθημι.*

ἐσθέω, (*ἐσθής*) *to clothe:*—Pass. *to be clothed, dressed;* mostly in pf. *ἤσθημαι* Ion. *ἔσθημαι; ἐσθῆτα ἐσθημένος clad in* raiment. Hence

ἔσθημα, *ατος, τό, a garment, dress.*

ἕσθην, 3 dual plqpf. pass. of *ἕννυμι.*

ἐσθής, *ῆτος, ἡ,* (*ἕσθαι,* pf. inf. pass. of *ἕννυμι*) *a garment: dress, clothes, raiment,* Lat. *vestis.*

ἔσθησις, *εως, ἡ,* (*ἐσθέω*) *clothing, raiment.*

ἐσθίω, Ep. inf. *ἐσθιέμεν:* impf. *ἤσθιον:* fut. *ἔδομαι* (from Ep. pres. *ἜΔΩ*): pf. act. *ἐδήδοκα,* pass *ἐδήδεσμαι:* aor. 1 pass. *ἠδέσθην:* aor. 2 act. *ἔφᾰγον* (from Root *ΦΑΓΩ):—*the* Lat. *EDO, to eat:* metaph. *to devour, consume,* like fire or an *eating* disease; *ἐσθίειν ἑαυτόν to vex* or *annoy* oneself; *ἐσθίειν τὴν χελύνην to bite* the lip:—Pass. *to be eaten; οἶκος ἐσθίεται* the house *is eaten up.*

ἘΣΘΛΟ'Σ, *ή, όν,* Dor. **ἐσλός**, *ά, όν,* = *ἀγαθός, good* of his kind: *brave, stout:* also *noble, wealthy: kind, good.* 2. of omens, *good, lucky.* 3. as Subst., *ἐσθλά goods:* absol., *ἐσθλόν good luck.*

ἐσθλότερος, **-ατος**, Comp. and Sup. of *ἐσθλός.*

ἔσθορον Ep. aor. 2 of *εἰσθρώσκω.*

ἔσθος, *εος, τό,* = *ἐσθής, a dress, garment.*

ἐσθ' ὅτε, for *ἐστὶν ὅτε,* Lat. *est quum, there is a time when,* i. e. *now and then, sometimes.*

ἐσ-θρώσκω, v. *εἰσθρώσκω.*

ἔσθω, Ep. inf. *ἐσθέμεναι,* impf. *ἦσθον,* poët. form of *ἐσθίω, to eat, devour:* metaph. *to eat up* or *consume* one's means.

ἐσῑγάθην [ᾱ], Dor. aor. 1 pass. of *σιγάω.*

ἐσῐδεῖν, for *εἰσιδεῖν,* inf. of *εἰσεῖδον.*

ἐσιδέσθην, Ep. 3 dual aor. 2 med. of *εἰσεῖδον.*

ἐσῑέμεναι, fem. part. pres. med. of *εἰσίημι.*

ἐσίζηται, for *εἰσίζηται,* 3 sing. subj. of *εἰσίζομαι.*

ἐσ-ίημι, **ἐσ-ικνέομαι**, **ἐσ-ίπταμαι**, v. *εἰσ-.*

ἐσ-καταβαίνω, v. *εἰσκ-.*

ἐσκάτθετο, for *εἰσκατέθετο,* 3 sing. aor. 2 med. of *εἰσκατατίθημι.*

ἔσκε, Ep. and Ion. for *ἦν,* 3 sing. impf. of *εἰμί sum.*

ἐσκέδᾰσα, aor. 1 of *σκεδάννυμι.*

ἔσκεμμαι, pf. of *σκοπέω.*

ἐσκίδναντο, 3 pl. impf. pass. of *σκίδνημι.*

ἔσκληκα, intr. pf. of *σκέλλω:* **ἔσκλην**, aor. 2.

ἔσκον, Ep. and Ion. for *ἦν,* impf. of *εἰμί sum.*

ἐσλός, Dor. for ἐσθλός.

ἔσμηχον, impf. of σμήχω.

ἑσμός or ἐσμός, ὁ, (ἵημι) *a swarm of bees: any swarm or flock;* ἑσμοὶ γάλακτος *streams* of milk.

ἑσμο-τόκος, ον, (ἑσμός, τεκεῖν) *producing swarms of bees.*

ἕσο, Ep. for ἴσθι, imperat. of εἰμί.

ἐσ-οικέω, ἐσ-οικίζω, v. εἰσ-.

ἔσοπτος, v. εἴσοπτος. Hence

ἔσοπτρον, v. εἴσοπτρον.

ἐσ-οράω, v. εἰσοράω.

ἐσορῶμες, Dor. for εἰσορῶμεν.

ἐσοῦμαι, Dor. for ἔσομαι, fut. of εἰμί *sum.*

ἐσόψομαι, fut. of ἐσοράω, εἰσοράω.

ἐσπάθημαι, pf. pass. of σπαθάω.

ἔσπαρμαι, pf. pass. of σπείρω.

ἔσπεισα, aor. 1 of σπένδω.

ἙΣΠΕ΄ΡΑ, ἡ, Lat. *VESPERA*, fem. of the Adj. ἕσπερος: I. (sub. ὥρα), *evening;* ἑσπέρας (gen. of time) *at eve;* ἀπὸ ἑσπέρας after *evening, at night-fall;* εἰς or πρὸς ἑσπέραν towards *evening:* in plur. *the evening hours, eventide.* 2. (sub. χώρα), *the west,* Lat. *occidens;* τὸ πρὸς ἑσπέρης the *west* country. Hence

ἑσπερῖνός, ή, όν, = ἑσπέριος.

ἑσπέριος, α, ον, and ος, ον, (ἕσπερος) of Time, *in the evening, at eventide.* II. of Place, *western, towards the setting sun,* Lat. *occidentalis.*

ἑσπερίς, ίδος, ἡ, peculiar fem. of ἑσπέριος, *at evening.* II. as Subst., αἱ Ἑσπερίδες *the Hesperides, daughters of Evening,* who dwelt on a *western* island of the ocean, and guarded a garden with golden apples.

ἝΣΠΕΡΟΣ, ὁ, Lat. *VESPER, evening;* μένον ἐπὶ ἕσπερον ἐλθεῖν they waited for *even* to come on: irregul. plur. neut. ἕσπερα, τά, *the hours of evening, eventide.* 2. of Place, *Hesperus, the West,* i. e. *darkness, Hades.* II. as Adj. *of* or *at evening;* ἕσπερος ἀστήρ the *evening*-star. 2. of Place, *Western.*

ἔσπετε, for εἴπετε, 2 pl. Ep. imperat. of εἶπον.

ἑσπόμην, aor. 2 of ἕπομαι: Homer retains ἑ- in all the moods, imperat. ἑσπέσθω, subj. ἕσπωνται, opt. ἑσποίμην, inf. ἑσπέσθαι, part. ἑσπόμενος.

ἔσπον, aor. 2 of ἕπω.

ἔσσα, Ep. aor. 1 of ἕννυμι; ἕσσαι, inf. (but also 2 sing. pf. pass.): ἑσσάμενος, aor. 1 part. med.

'σσεῖται 3 sing. of ἐσσοῦμαι, Dor. fut. of εἰμί *sum.*

ἔσσεσθαι, for ἔσεσθαι, fut. inf. of εἰμί *sum.*

ἔσσευα, Ep. for ἔσευα, aor. 1 of σεύω.

ἐσσί, Ep. and Dor. for εἶς, εἶ, 2 sing. of εἰμί *sum.*

ἕσσο, Ep. for ἕσο, imperat. of ἕννυμι. II. Ep. 2 sing. plqpf. pass. of ἕννυμι.

ἔσσομαι, for ἔσομαι, Ep. fut. of εἰμί *sum:* but II. ἕσσομαι, Ep. fut. med. of ἕννυμι.

ἑσσόομαι, Ion. for ἡσσάομαι: impf. ἑσσούμην: aor. 1 ἑσσώθην: pf. ἕσσωμαι: Pass.: (ἕσσων, Ion. for ἥσσων):—*to be beaten.*

ἔσσῦμαι, pf. pass. of σεύω: ἐσσύμην, plqpf. with sense of aor. 2.

ἐσσύμενος, η, ον, part. pass. of σεύω (in sense and accent a pres., but redupl. as if pf.), *driven, hurried on, vehement: eager, yearning for:* hence Adv., ἐσσυμένως *hastily, vehemently.*

ἔσσῠο, ἔσσῠτο, 2 and 3 sing. Ep. plqpf. pass. of σεύω, with sense of aor. 2.

ἑσσωθῆναι, Ion. for ἡσσηθῆναι, v. ἑσσόω.

ἕσσω, Ep. fut. of ἕννυμι.

ἕσσων, Ion. for ἥσσων.

*ἕσταα, pf. 2 of ἵστημι with intrans. pres. sense, *to stand:* only in the following forms, dual ἕστᾰτον, plur. ἕστᾰμεν, ἕστᾰτε, ἑστᾶσι; inf. ἑστάναι Ep. ἑστάμεν, ἑστάμεναι; part. ἑσταώς Att. contr. ἑστώς Ion. ἑστεώς and ἑστηώς, fem. ἑστῶσα.

ἔσται, 3 sing. fut. of εἰμί *sum:* but II. ἕσται, 3 sing. pf. pass. of ἕννυμι.

ἐστάλᾰτο, Ion. 3 pl. plqpf. pass. of στέλλω.

ἐστάλην, aor. 2 pass. of στέλλω: ἔσταλκα, pf.

ἑστάμεν, ἑστάμεναι [ᾰ], see ἕσταα.

ἕστᾰμεν, 1 pl. of ἕσταα.

ἔσταν, Aeol. and Ep. 3 pl. aor. 2 of ἵστημι.

ἑστάναι, for ἑστηκέναι, v. ἕσταα.

ἑστᾰότες, plur. of ἑσταώς, v. ἕσταα.

ἕστᾰσαν, 3 pl. poët. plqpf. of ἵστημι, *they stood,* v. ἕσταα: but 2. ἔστᾰσαν, shortd. for ἔστησαν, 3 pl. aor. 1 of ἵστημι, *they placed.*

ἑστᾶσι, 3 pl. poët. pf. of ἵστημι; v. ἕσταα.

ἕστᾰτε, 2 plur., and ἕστᾰτον, 2 and 3 dual; see ἕσταα.

ἐσταυρωμένος, pf. part. pass. of σταυρόω.

ἔσ-τε Dor. ἔσ-τε: (ἐς, τε) Conjunct. *till, until,* Lat. *donec.* 2. *so long, so long as.* II. Adv. *even to,* Lat. *usque.*

ἔστειλα, aor. 1 of στέλλω.

ἐστεμμένος, pf. part. pass. of στέφω.

ἐστέρημαι, pf. pass. of στερέω.

ἐστεφάνωτο, 3 sing. plqpf. pass. of στεφανόω.

ἑστεώς, Ion. pf. part. of ἵστημι; v. ἕσταα.

ἕστηκα, ἑστήκειν, pf. and plqpf. intr. of ἵστημι.

ἔστην, aor. 2 intr. of ἵστημι.

ἑστήξω, ἑστήξομαι, fut. intr. of ἵστημι, *I shall* or *will stand:* cp. τεθνήξω, τεθνήξομαι from θνήσκω.

ἐστήρικται, 3 sing. pf. pass. of στηρίζω: ἐστήρικτο, plqpf.

ἔστησα, ἐστησάμην, aor. 1 act. and med. of ἵστημι.

ἑστηώς, Ion. pf. part. of ἵστημι; v. ἕσταα.

ἑστία Ion. ἱστίη, ἡ, (ἕζομαι) *the hearth of a house;* the shrine of the household gods, and hence a sanctuary for suppliants. 2. *the house itself, a dwelling, home.* 3. *the household, family.* II. as nom. pr., Ἑστία Ion. Ἱστίη, the Roman *Vesta,* daughter of Kronos (Saturn) and Rhea, *guardian of the hearth and home,* invoked first at festivals.

ἑστίᾱμα, ατος, τό, (ἑστιάω) *a banquet,*

ἑστιαρχέω, f. ήσω, *to be master of a house.* From

ἑστι-άρχης, ου, ὁ, (ἑστία, ἄρχω) *master of a house.*

ἑστίᾱσις, εως, ἡ, (ἑστιάω) *a feasting, banqueting.*

ἑστιάω impf. εἱστίων: f. ἑστιάσω [ᾱ]: aor. 1 εἱστίᾱσα: pf. εἱστίᾱκα:—Pass., f. (in med. form) ἑστιάσομαι: aor. 1 εἱστιάθην: pf. εἱστίᾱμαι: (ἑστία):—*to receive into one's home, to entertain hospitably, to feast:* —Pass. *to be a guest, be feasted:* c. acc. rei. *to feast on;* ἑστιᾶσθαι ἐνύπνιον *to have a* visionary *feast.*

ἑστι-οῦχος, ον, (ἑστία, ἔχω) *guarding the house* or *state.* 2. *having an altar* or *hearth.* 3. *on the hearth* or *altar.*

ἑστιόω, f. ώσω, (ἑστία) *to found a hearth* or *house:* —Pass., δῶμα ἑστιοῦται the family *is established.*

ἔστῐχον, aor. 2 of στείχω.

ἐστιχόωντο, 3 pl. Ep. impf. med. of στιχάω.

ἑστιώτης, ου, ὁ, fem. -ῶτις, ιδος, (ἑστία) *of* or *from the house.*

ἕστο, 3 sing. plqpf. pass. of ἕννυμι.

ἐσ-τοξεύω, = εἰσ-τοξεύω.

ἔστοργα, pf. of στέργω.

ἐστόρεσα, aor. 1 of στορέννυμι.

ἐστραμμένος, pf. part. pass. of στρέφω.

ἐστράφην [ᾰ], aor. 2 pass. of στρέφω.

ἐσ-τρίς, (ἐς, τρίς) Adv. *until three times, thrice.*

ἐστρωμένος, pf. part. pass. of στρώννυμι.

ἔστρωσα. -ώθην, aor. 1 act. and pass. of στρώννυμι.

ἔστρωτο, 3 sing. plqpf. pass. of στρώννυμι.

ἔστῠγον, aor. 2 of στυγέω.

ἕστωρ, ορος, ὁ, *a peg* or *nail at the end of the pole,* on which the ring, κρίκος, for fastening the harness was fixed. (Deriv. uncertain)

ἑστώς, -ῶσα, syncop. intr. pf. part. of ἵστημι; v. ἕσταα.

ἐσύλησα, aor. 1 of συλάω.

ἐσύνηκα, irreg. for συνῆκα, aor. 1 of συνίημι.

ἔσῡρα, aor. 1 of σύρω.

ἐσύρην [ῠ], aor. 2 pass. of σύρω.

ἐσ-υστερον, Adv. for εἰς ὕστερον, *for the future.*

ἐσφάγην [ᾰ], aor. 2 pass. of σφάζω, σφάττω.

ἔσφαγμαι, pf. pass. of σφάζω, σφάττω.

ἐσφαίρωτο, 3 sing. plqpf. pass. of σφαιρόω.

ἐσφάλην [ᾰ], aor. 2 pass. of σφάλλω.

ἔσφαλμαι, pf. pass. of σφάλλω.

ἔσφαξα, aor. 1 of σφάζω, σφάττω.

ἐσ-φέρω, v. εἰσ-φέρω.

ἐσφήκωντο, 3 pl. impf. pass. of σφηκόω.

ἔσφηλα, aor. 1 of σφάλλω.

ἐσ-φορέω, v. εἰσ-φορέω.

ἐσφρᾱγισμένος, pf. pass. part. of σφραγίζω.

ἘΣΧΑ΄ΡΑ Ion. ἐσχάρη, ἡ: Ep. gen. and dat. ἐσχαρόφιν:—*the hearth, fire-place,* like ἑστία; πυρὸς ἐσχάραι *watch-fires.* II. *an altar for burnt offerings.* III. *a pan of coals: a brasier.* Hence

ἐσχᾰρεών, ῶνος, ὁ, = ἐσχάρα I.

ἐσχάριος, ον, (ἐσχάρα) *of* or *on the hearth.*

ἐσχᾰρόφῐν, Ep. gen. and dat. sing. of ἐσχάρα.

ἔσχᾰσα, aor. 1 of σχάζω.

ἐσχᾰτάω, (ἔσχατος) *to be at the edge;* only used in Ep. part., ἐσχατόων, όωσα, of men, *lurking about the edge* of the camp; of cities, *lying on the border.*

ἐσχᾰτιά Ion. -ιή, ἡ, (ἔσχατος) *the furthest part, the edge, border, verge.* II. *a remote, retired spot.*

ἐσχάτιος, ον, poët. for ἔσχατος.

ἔσχᾰτος, η, ον, (ἐκ, ἐξ) *the furthest, uttermost, extreme;* ἔσχατοι ἀνδρῶν *most remote* of mankind:—*the furthest* each way: 1. *the uppermost, highest,* Lat. *summus.* 2. *the lowest,* Lat. *imus.* 3. *the innermost,* Lat. *intimus.* II. of sufferings, *the uttermost, utmost, last, worst:* as Subst., τὸ ἔσχατον, τὰ ἔσχατα, *the utmost, last, greatest extremity;* ἔσχατ' ἐσχάτων κακά worst of possible evils; Sup., τὰ ἐσχατώτατα *the extremest.* III. Adv. ἐσχάτως, *to the uttermost, extremely:* also neut. ἔσχατον as Adv. *for the last time:* Comp. ἐσχατώτερον *more extremely,* Sup. ἐσχατώτατα, *most utterly.*

ἐσχᾰτόων, όωσα, Ep. part. of ἐσχατάω.

ἔσχεθον, poët. for ἔσχον, aor. 2 of ἔχω; Ep. σχέθον; imper. σχεθέτω; subj. σχέθω; opt. σχέθοιμι; inf. σχεθεῖν Ep. -έειν; part. σχέθων.

ἐσ-χέω, for εἰσχέω.

ἔσχηκα, ἔσχημαι, pf. act. and pass. of ἔχω.

ἔσχῐσα, aor. 1 of σχίζω.

ἐσχίσθην, aor. 1 pass. of σχίζω.

ἔσχισμαι, pf. pass. of σχίζω.

ἔσχον, ἐσχόμην, aor. 2 act. and med. of ἔχω.

ἔσχων, impf. of σχάω.

ἕσω Ep. ἕσσω, fut. of ἕννυμι.

ἔσω, Adv. for εἴσω, *within:* Comp. ἐσωτέρω, *more within: inner:*—Sup. ἐσωτάτω, *most within.* Hence

ἔσωθεν and -θε, Adv. *from within: within, inside.*

ἐσώθην, aor. 1 pass. of σώζω

ἐσώτατος, η, ον, Sup. Adj. from ἔσω, *innermost,* Lat. *intimus.* Adv. ἐσωτάτω, v. ἔσω.

ἐσώτερος, α, ον, Comp. Adj. from ἔσω, *inner,* Lat. *interior:* Adv. ἐσωτέρω, v. ἔσω.

ἐτάγην [ᾰ], aor. 2 pass. of τάσσω.

ἐτάζω, f. σω, (ἐτεός) *to examine, test.*

ἐτάθην [ᾰ], aor. 1 pass. of τείνω.

ἑταίρα, ἡ, fem. of ἑταῖρος.

ἑταιρεία or -ία Ion. -ηΐη, ἡ, (ἑταῖρος) *companionship: an association, club, brotherhood.* II. at Athens, *a political club* or *union for party purposes.* III. generally, *friendship, intimacy.*

ἑταιρεῖος, α, ον, Ion. -ήϊος, η, ον, (ἑταῖρος) *of comrades* or *fellowship:* Ζεὺς ἑτ. *presiding over fellowship.*

ἑταιρέω, f. ήσω, (ἑταίρα) *to be a courtesan.*

ἑταιρηΐη, -ήϊος, Ion. for ἑταιρεία, -εῖος.

ἑταιρίζω, f. ίσω Att. ιῶ, (ἑταῖρος) *to be one's comrade* or *companion in arms.* 2. = ἑταιρέω, *to be a courtesan.* II. Med. *to choose for one's comrade.*

ἑταιρικός, ή, όν, = ἑταιρεῖος, *of* or *like a comrade, social;* τὸ ἑταιρικόν = ἑταιρεία.

ἑταιρίς, ίδος, ἡ, = ἑταίρα, *a courtesan.*

ἑταιρίσσαι, Ep. aor. 1 inf. of ἑταιρίζω.

ἑταῖρος Ep. and Ion. ἕτᾰρος, ὁ, (ἔτης) *a companion, comrade, fellow, mate: a brother-in-arms, a shipmate;*

a messmate: also *a fellow-slave:*—as Adj. *associated;* Sup. ἑταιρότατος. II. **ἑταίρα** Ion. **ἑταίρη** Ep. **ἑτάρη**, ἡ, *a female companion, helper, friend.* 2. in Att. *opp. to a lawful wife, a concubine: a courtesan, harlot.* Hence

ἑταιρόσυνος, η, ον, *friendly:* as Subst. *a friend.*

ἐτάκευ, ἐτάκετο, Dor. for ἐτήκου, ἐτήκετο, 2 and 3 sing. impf. med. of τήκω.

ἐτάκην [ᾰ], aor. 2 pass. of τήκω.

ἔτᾱκον, -όμην, Dor. impf. act. and pass. of τήκω.

ἐτᾰλάσσας, Ep. 2 sing. aor. 1 of ταλάω.

ἔτᾰμον, aor. 2 of τέμνω.

ἔταξα, aor. 1 of τάσσω.

ἐτάραξα, aor. 1 of ταράσσω.

ἑτᾰρίζομαι, Ep. for ἑταιρίζομαι.

ἕτᾰρος, ἑτάρη, Ep. and Ion. for ἑταῖρος, ἑταίρα.

ἐτάρπην, aor. 2 pass. of τέρπω.

ἐτάρφθην, Ep. aor. 1 pass. of τέρπω.

ἔτας, acc. pl. of ἔτης.

ἐτάτυμος, Dor. for ἐτήτυμος.

ἐτάφην [ᾰ], aor. 2 pass. of θάπτω.

ἐτάχθην, aor. 1 pass. of τάσσω.

ἐτέθαπτο, 3 sing. plqpf. pass. of θάπτω.

ἐτέθην, aor. 1 pass. of τίθημι.

ἐτεθήπεα, Ep. plqpf. of τέθηπα.

ἐτέθῠτο, 3 sing. plqpf. pass. (in med. sense) of θύω.

ἔτειος, α, ον, (ἔτος) *yearly, annual.* II. *of one year, yearling.*

ἔτεκον, ἐτεκόμην, aor. 2 act. and med. of τίκτω.

ἐτελείετο, Ep. for ἐτελεῖτο, 3 sing. impf. pass. of τελέω.

ἐτελέσθην, aor. 1 pass. of τελέω.

ἐτέλεσσα, Ep. aor. 1 of τελέω.

ἔτεμον, aor. 2 of τέμνω.

Ἐτεό-κρητες, οἱ, (ἐτεοί, Κρῆτες) *true Cretans.*

ἘΤΕΌΣ, ά, όν, (perhaps from εἰμί *sum*) *true, real, genuine:* in neut. ἐτεόν as Adv., *in truth, in sooth, really, truly, verily,* Lat. *revera:*—Att. in ironical questions, ἐτεόν; *so! indeed!* Lat. *itane?* Ion. dat. fem. ἐτεῇ is also used as Adv., *in truth.*

ἑτερ-αλκής, ές, (ἕτερος, ἀλκή) *giving strength to one of two;* Δαναοῖσι μάχης ἑτεραλκέα νίκην δοῦναι to give victory in battle *decided in favour of* the Danaans; νίκη ἑτεραλκής a *decisive* victory; δῆμος ἑτεραλκής a body of men *which decides the victory.* II. *inclining first to one side then to the other, doubtful,* Lat. *anceps.*

ἑτερ-ήμερος, ον, (ἕτερος, ἡμέρα) *on alternate days, day and day alternately.*

ἑτέρηφι, Ep. dat. fem. of ἕτερος.

ἑτερό-γλωσσος Att. -ττος, ον, (ἕτερος, γλῶσσα) *of other tongue,* i. e. *of foreign, strange tongue.*

ἑτερό-γνᾰθος, ον, *with one side of the mouth harder than the other,* of a horse.

ἑτερο-δῐδασκᾰλέω, (ἕτερος, διδάσκαλος) *to teach other than the truth, to teach errors.*

ἑτερό-δοξος, ον, (ἕτερος, δόξα) *of another opinion, differing in opinion.* 2. *of other than the true opinion, heterodox.*

ἑτερό-ζηλος, ον, (ἕτερος, ζῆλος) *zealous for one side, partial:* Adv. -λως, *unfairly.* II. *devoted to another pursuit.*

ἑτεροζῠγέω, f. ήσω, *to be yoked with an animal of a different kind: be at variance with.* From

ἑτερό-ζῠγος, ον, (ἕτερος, ζυγόν) *unevenly yoked: different.* 2. *unequally balanced.*

ἑτεροῖος, α, ον, (ἕτερος) *of a different nature* or *kind.* Adv. -οίως. Hence

ἑτεροιόω, f. ώσω, *to make otherwise, alter:*—Pass. *to become changed, alter.*

ἑτερο-κλῑνής, ές, (ἕτερος, κλινῆναι) *leaning to one side:* of ground, *sloping.*

ἑτερο-μήκης, ες, (ἕτερος, μῆκος) *with unequal sides, oblong, rectangular.*

ἑτερο-μήτωρ, ορος, ὁ, ἡ, (ἕτερος, μήτηρ) *born of another mother.*

ἑτερό-πλοος, ον, contr. -πλους, ουν, (ἕτερος, πλέω) *lent on the security of a ship and her cargo, with the risk of the outward,* but not of the homeward, *voyage,* of money.

ἑτερορ-ρεπής, ές, and **ἑτερόρ-ροπος**, ον, (ἕτερος, ῥέπω) *inclined to one side;* ἑτερορρεπὴς Ζεύς *who makes now one side and now another preponderate.*

ἝΤΕΡΟΣ, α, ον, Lat. *ALTER, the other, one of two;* χειρὶ φέρειν ἑτέρῃ to carry in *one* of his hands; ἕτεροι ἑτέρων ἄρχουσι *the one* rule *the other;* ἕτερος τοιοῦτος *another such;* ἕτερα τοσαῦτα as *many more,* Lat. *alterum tantum;* δεύτερος ἕτερος *yet* a second. 2. also like Lat. *alter,* for δεύτερος, *second:* ἡ ἑτέρα (sub. ἡμέρα), *the second* day, i. e. the day *after to-morrow.* II. put loosely for ἄλλος, Lat. *alius,* opp., not to *one,* but to *many.* III. *other* (than usual), *different: of other kind,* like ἀλλοῖος; *other* (than good), Lat. *sequior, evil.* IV. as Adv. in dat. fem., τῇ ἑτέρᾳ, θατέρᾳ (sub. ὁδῷ) *otherwise, in another way, place,* or *manner;* also (sub. χειρί) *with one hand,* i. e. *with the left hand;* and (sub. ἡμέρᾳ) *on the next day.* 2. also neut., τὸ ἕτερον, τὰ ἕτερα, as ἐπὶ θάτερα *one or the other way;* ἐκ τοῦ ἐπὶ θάτερα from *the one side,* opp. to εἰς τὰ ἐπὶ θάτερα to *the other side.* [The Dor. used ἅτερος [ᾰ] for ἕτερος: whereas in Att. ἅτερος [ᾱ] was (by crasis) for ὁ ἕτερος: gen. θατέρου, dat. θατέρῳ, acc. θάτερον.]

ἑτερό-τροπος, ον, (ἕτερος, τρόπος) *of different sort* or *fashion: of different turn* or *temper.* II. *turning another way: uncertain, inconstant.*

ἑτερό-φωνος, ον, (ἕτερος, φωνή) *of different voice* or *speech, barbarous.*

ἐτέρσετο, 3 sing. impf. of τέρσομαι.

ἐτέρφθην, aor. 1 pass. of τέρπω.

ἑτέρωθεν, (ἕτερος) Adv. *from the other side.* II. *on the other side, opposite.*

ἑτέρωθι, (ἕτερος) Adv. *on the other side: elsewhere:* ἑτέρωθι τοῦ λόγου *in another part* of my story. II. *at another time.*

ἑτερῶς, Adv. of ἕτερος, *differently, otherwise.*

ἑτέρωσε, (ἕτερος) Adv. *to one side, to the other side:* hence *to another place.*

ἑτερῶτα, Aeol. for ἑτέρωθι, *at another time.*

ἐτέταλτο, 3 sing. plqpf. pass. of τέλλω.

ἐτετεύχατο, Ep. 3 pl. plqpf. pass. of τεύχω.

ἐτετεύχεε, Ion. 3 sing. plqpf. of τυγχάνω.

ἐτετήκειν, intr. plqpf. of τήκω.

ἐτέτραπτο, 3 sing plqpf. pass. of τρέπω.

ἔτετμον, impf. of τέτμω.

ἐτέτυξο, -υκτο, 2 and 3 sing. plqpf. pass. of τεύχω.

ἔτευξα, aor. 1 of τεύχω.

ἐτεύχετον, 3 dual impf. of τεύχω.

ἐτέχθην, aor. 1 pass. of τίκτω.

ἔτηξα, aor. 1 of τήκω.

ἜΤΗΣ, οῦ, ὁ, *a kinsman, clansman, cousin.* II. Att. *a townsman, neighbour: a private citizen.* III. for ὦ τάν or ὦ 'τάν, v. sub τάν.

ἐτησίαι (sub. ἄνεμοι), ων, οἱ, (ἔτος) *periodical winds,* such as the Egyptian *monsoons,* which blow from the North during the whole summer: so too of northerly winds in Greece, which blew in the Aegean for forty days from the rising of the dog-star.

ἐτήσιος, ον, (ἔτος) *a year long, for a year.* 2. *yearly, annual.*

ἐτητυμία, ἡ, *truth.* From

ἐτήτυμος, ον, lengthd. for ἔτυμος, *true, genuine, real,* Lat. *sincerus.* Adv. ἐτητύμως, also neut. ἐτήτυμον as Adv., *in truth, really.*

ἜΤΙ, Adv., I. of the Present or Past, *yet, as yet, still,* Lat. *adhuc.* II. of the Future, *yet longer, still.* III. generally, *yet, still, besides, moreover,* Lat. *praeterea;* ἔτι δέ nay *more;* ἔτ' ἄλλος *yet* another; ἔτι μᾶλλον *yet* more.

ἐτίθεις, ἐτίθει, 2 and 3 sing. impf. of *τιθέω = τίθημι.

ἔτιλα, aor. 1 of τίλλω.

ἐτίμᾱσα, Dor. aor. 1 of τιμάω.

ἐτίναχθεν, Ep. 3 pl. aor. 1 pass. of τινάσσω.

ἔτῐσα, aor. 1 of τίνω.

ἔτλην Dor. **ἔτλᾱν**, aor. 2 of the root *τλάω: but ἔτλᾰν, Ep. for ἔτλησαν, 3 plur.

ἐτμάγην [ᾰ], aor. 2 pass. of τμήγω.

ἐτμήθην, aor. 1 pass. of τέμνω.

ἐτν-ήρῠσις, εως, ἡ, (ἔτνος, ἀρύω) *a soup-ladle.*

ἜΤΝΟΣ, εος, τό, *a thick soup of peas* or *beans: soup, pudding.*

ἑτοιμάζω, f. άσω, aor. 1 ἡτοίμασα: (ἑτοῖμος):—*to make* or *get ready, prepare:*—Med., with pf. pass. ἡτοίμασμαι, *to prepare for oneself, make one's arrangements, get oneself ready:* c. inf. *to make one ready* to do. Hence

ἑτοιμᾰσία, ἡ, *a being prepared, preparation: readiness.*

ἑτοιμασσαίατο, Ep. 3 pl. aor. 1 opt. med. of ἑτοιμάζω.

ἙΤΟΙ̃ΜΟΣ or **ἕτοιμος**, η, ον, or ος, ον, *at hand, ready, prepared;* ἐξ ἑτοίμου *immediately, off hand.* II. τὰ ἕτοιμα, 1. Lat. *quae in promptu sunt;* ἐπὶ τὰ ἕτοιμα μᾶλλον τρέπονται betake themselves rather to *that which is close at hand.* 2. one's *property,* Lat. *parata.* II. of persons, *ready, active, prompt.* 2. of the mind, *ready, quick, active, versatile.* III. of things, *real, actual, carried into effect.*

ἑτοιμότης, ητος, ἡ, *a being prepared, readiness.*

ἑτοιμο-τόμος, ον, (ἑτοῖμος, τεμεῖν) *ready for cutting.*

ἑτοίμως, Adv. of ἕτοιμος, *readily:* Comp. and Sup., ἑτοιμότερον, -ότατα.

ἔτορον, aor. 2 of τορέω.

ἜΤΟΣ, εος, τό, *a year;* κατὰ ἔτος every year; ἀνὰ πᾶν ἔτος every *year;* δι' ἔτους πέμπτου every fifth *year;* ἔτος εἰς ἔτος *year* after *year.*

ἐτός, Adv., = ἐτωσίως, *without reason, for nothing, in vain:* mostly with a negat., οὐκ ἐτός *not without reason:*—mostly in questions, οὐκ ἐτὸς ἄρ' ὡς ἔμ' ἦλθεν οὐδεπώποτε; it was not *for nothing* then? (Deriv. uncertain.)

ἔτρᾰγον, aor. 2 of τρώγω.

ἔτρᾰπον, ἐτράπην, aor. 2 act. and pass. of τρέπω.

ἐτράφθην, Ion. aor. 1 of τρέπω.

ἔτρᾰφον, ἐτράφην, aor. 2 act. and pass. of τρέφω.

ἔτρεσα, aor. 1 of τρέω.

ἔτρεψα, aor. 1 of τρέπω.

ἔτριψα, ἐτρίφθην, aor. 1 act. and pass. of τρίβω.

ἔτρωσα, ἐτρώθην, aor. 1 act. and pass. of τιτρώσκω.

ἐτύθην [ῠ] aor. 1 pass. of θύω.

ἐτυμο-λογία, ἡ, (ἔτυμος, λόγος) *the true account* or *analysis of a word: its derivation, etymology.*

ἔτῠμος, ον, rarely η, ον, (ἐτεός) *true, real, actual:* neut. pl. ἔτυμα, *truths, the truth:* neut. ἔτυμον is used as an Adv. like ἐτεόν, *indeed, of a truth, truly, actually.*

ἐτύπην [ῠ], Dor. aor. 2 pass. of τύπτω

ἐτύφην [ῠ], aor. 2 pass. of τύφω.

ἐτύφθην, aor. 1 pass. of τύπτω.

ἐτύχησα, ἔτῠχον, aor. 1 and 2 of τυγχάνω.

ἐτύχθην, aor 1 pass. of τεύχω.

ἐτωσιο-εργός, όν, (ἐτώσιος, ἔργον) *working in vain.*

ἐτώσιος, ον, (ἐτός, Adv.) *fruitless, idle, useless.*

εὖ Ep. also **ἐΰ**, Adv., properly neut. of ἐΰς, *well,* opp. to κακῶς; εὖ καὶ ἐπισταμένως *well* and knowingly: sometimes, *luckily, happily:* εὖ ἔχειν or ἥκειν to be *well off,* c. gen., εὖ ἥκειν τοῦ βίου to be *well off* for living: εὖ γεγονώς *well* born. II. as Subst., τὸ εὖ good luck: but also *the right, the good cause;* τὸ εὖ νικάτω may *the right* prevail. III in Compos. it commonly implies *greatness, abundance* or *easiness.*

εὗ, Ion. for **οὗ**, gen. of reflexive Pron. of 3rd pers.

εὐαγγελίζομαι, f. ίσομαι Att. ιοῦμαι, Dep. (εὐάγγελος):—*to bring good news, announce them.* 2. *to preach* or *proclaim as glad tidings: to preach the gospel:*—so also in Act., and then in Pass., *to have the gospel preached to* one:—in Pass. also of the gospel, *to be preached.*

εὐαγγέλιον, τό, (εὐάγγελος) *the reward of good*

tidings :—Att. always in plur., εὐαγγέλια στεφανοῦν or ἀναδῆσαί τινα to crown one for *good news brought;* εὐαγγέλια θύειν to offer a sacrifice for *them.* II. *the glad tidings, the gospel.*

εὐαγγελιστής, οῦ, ὁ, (εὐαγγελίζομαι) *a bringer of good tidings: an evangelist, preacher of the gospel.* 2. esp. *a writer of one of the four Gospels.*

εὐ-άγγελος, ον, (εὖ, ἀγγέλλω) *bringing good news.*

εὐ-ἄγέω, f. ήσω, *to be pure, holy.* From

εὐ-ἄγής, ές, (εὖ, ἄγος) *guiltless, pure, undefiled,* Lat. *castus,* of persons and actions:—poët. Adv. εὐᾰγέως.

εὐ-ᾱγής, ές, (ἄγω) *moving well, nimble.*

εὐ-ᾱγής, ές, = εὐαυγής, *far-seen, conspicuous;* ἕδρα εὐαγὴς στρατοῦ a seat *in full view of* the army.

εὐ-άγητος, ον, = εὐᾱγής, *bright, clear.* [ᾱ]

εὐ-άγκᾰλος, ον, (εὖ, ἀγκάλη) *easy to bear in the arms.*

εὐ-αγκής, ές, (εὖ, ἄγκος) *with fair valleys* or *glades.*

εὐ-ᾱγορέω, Dor. for εὐηγορέω.

εὐαγρεσία, ἡ, *good sport in hunting.* From

εὐ-αγρέω, (εὖ, ἄγρα) *to have good sport.* Hence

εὐαγρία, ἡ, *good sport in hunting, fishing,* etc.

εὔ-αγρος, ον, (εὖ, ἄγρα) *lucky in the chase, successful.*

εὐ-αγωγός, όν, (εὖ, ἄγω) *easily led, docile.*

εὐ-άγων, ωνος, ὁ, ἡ, (εὖ, ἀγών) *belonging to prosperous* or *glorious contests.* [ᾰ]

εὐᾰδε, Ep. for ἕαδε, 3 sing. aor. 2 of ἁνδάνω.

εὐάζω or **εὐἁζω**, (εὖα) *to cry* εὖα *in honour of Bacchus:*—also in Med. εὐάζομαι.

εὐ-ᾱής, ές, (εὖ, ἄημι) *with a good breeze, airy.* II. act. *blowing fair:*—metaph. *prosperous, favourable.*

εὔ-αθλος, ον, (εὖ, ἆθλος) *successful in contests.*

εὐ-αίνητος, ον, (εὖ, αἰνέω) *much-extolled.*

εὐ-αίρετος, ον, (εὖ, αἱρέω) *easy to be taken.*

εὐ-αίων, ωνος, ὁ, ἡ, (εὖ, αἰών) *of happy life,* generally, *happy;* εὐαίων ὕπνος *blessed* sleep.

εὐ-ᾱκοέω, **εὐάκοος**, Dor. for εὐηκ-.

εὐ-ᾱλάκατος, ον, Dor. for εὐηλ-.

εὐ-αλδής, ές, (εὖ, ἀλδαίνω) *well-grown, luxuriant.*

εὐ-άλιος, ον, Dor. for εὐήλιος. [ᾱ]

εὐ-άλφῐτος, ον, (εὖ, ἄλφιτον) *of good meal.*

εὐ-άλωτος, ον, (εὖ, ἁλῶναι) *easy to be taken.* [ᾰ]

εὐ-άμπελος, ον, (εὖ, ἄμπελος) *with fine vines.*

εὐάν, *evan!* a cry of Bacchanalians, like εὖα, εὐοῖ.

εὐ-ανάκλητος, ον, (εὖ, ἀνακαλέω) *easy to call back.*

εὐανδρία, ἡ, *abundance of men, store of good men.* II. *manhood, manliness, courage, spirit.* From

εὔ-ανδρος, ον, (εὖ, ἀνήρ) *abounding in good men and true.* II. *prosperous to men.*

εὐ-άνεμος [ᾱ], ον, Dor. for εὐήνεμος.

εὐ-άνθεμος, ον, (εὖ, ἄνθεμον) *with fair flowers, flowery.*

εὐανθέω, f. ήσω, *to be flowery* or *blooming.* From

εὐ-ανθής, ές, (εὖ, ἄνθος) *blooming, budding.* II. *rich in flowers, flowery:* metaph. *flowery, gay.* 2. also *blooming, fresh.*

εὐ-άνιος, ον, Dor. for εὐήνιος, [ᾱ]

εὐ-ᾱνορία, ἡ, Dor. for εὐηνορία.

εὐ-άντητος, ον, (ἀντάω) *easy to meet, gracious.*

εὐ-άνωρ, ορος, ὁ, ἡ, Dor. for εὐήνωρ. [ᾱ]

εὐ-απάλλακτος, ον, (εὖ, ἀπαλλάσσω) *easily got rid of: easy to dispose of.*

εὐ-ἄπάτητος, ον, (εὖ, ἀπᾰτάω) *easily cheated.*

εὐ-απήγητος, ον, Ion. for εὐαφήγητος.

εὐ-απόβᾰτος, ον, *convenient for disembarking.*

εὐ-αποτείχιστος, ον, (εὖ, ἀποτειχίζω) *easy to be walled off* or *blockaded.*

εὐᾰρεστέω, f. ήσω, *to be well-pleasing.* From

εὐ-άρεστος, ον, *well-pleasing, acceptable.* Adv. εὐαρέστως, Comp. -οτέρως.

εὐ-αρίθμητος, ον, (εὖ, ἀριθμέω) *easy to be counted.*

εὔ-αρκτος, ον, (εὖ, ἄρχω) *well-governed: submissive.*

εὐ-άρματος, ον, (εὖ, ἅρμα) *with good* or *beautiful chariot: victorious in the chariot-race.*

εὐαρμοστία, ἡ, *easiness of temper, good nature.* From

εὐ-άρμοστος, ον, (εὖ, ἁρμόζω) *well-adapted, accommodating.* II. *well-tuned, harmonious.*

εὔ-αρνος, ον, (εὖ, ἀρνός gen.) *rich in sheep.*

εὐ-άροτος, ον, (εὖ, ἀρόω) *well-ploughed, easy to be ploughed.*

εὔ-αρχος, ον, (εὖ, ἄρχομαι) *beginning well: making a good beginning.*

εὐάς, άδος, ὁ, ἡ, (εὖα) *Bacchic, Bacchanalian.*

εὔασμα, ατος, τό, (εὐάζω) *a Bacchanalian shout.*

εὐασμός, ὁ, (εὐάζω) *the cry of* εὖα, *a shout of revelry,* esp. of *Bacchic revelry.*

εὐάστειρα, ἡ, fem. of εὐαστήρ.

εὐαστήρ, ῆρος, ὁ, and **εὐαστής**, οῦ, ὁ, (εὐάζω) *a Bacchanal.*

εὐάτριος, Dor. for εὐήτριος.

εὐ-αυγής, ές, (εὖ, αὐγή) *well-lit, bright, conspicuous.*

εὐ-αύχην, ενος, ὁ, ἡ, (εὖ, αὐχήν) *with beautiful neck.*

εὐ-αφήγητος Ion. **εὐαπήγητος**, ον, (εὖ, ἀφηγέομαι) *easy to describe.*

εὐ-ᾱχής, **εὐ-άχητος** [ᾱ], Dor. for εὐηχής, εὐήχητος.

εὐ-βάστακτος, ον, (εὖ, βαστάζω) *easy to carry* or *bear.*

εὔ-βᾰτος, ον, (εὖ, βατός) *accessible: passable.*

εὐ-βλέφᾰρος, ον, (εὖ, βλέφαρον) *with beautiful eyelids.*

Εὔβοια, as Ion. ης, ἡ, *Euboea,* now *Negropont,* an island lying along the coast of Boeotia and Attica.

εὐβολέω, f. ήσω, *to make a good throw.* From

εὔ-βολος, ον, (εὖ, βαλεῖν) *throwing luckily.* Adv. εὐβόλως, *luckily;* εὐβόλως ἔχειν to be *well off.*

εὐβοσία, ἡ, (εὔβοτος) *good feeding.*

εὐ-βόστρῠχος, ον, *with beautiful locks.*

εὔ-βοτος, ον, (εὖ, βόσκω) *feeding well, with good pasture.* II. *well-fed, thriving.*

εὐ-βότρῠος, ον, and **εὔ-βοτρυς**, υ, gen. υος, (εὖ, βότρυς) *rich in grapes.*

εὐβουλία, ἡ, *good counsel: prudence.* From

εὔ-βουλος, ον, (εὖ, βουλή) *well-advised, prudent.*

εὔ-βους, ουν, gen. οος, (εὖ, βοῦς) *rich in cattle.*

εὔ-βροχος, ον, (εὖ, βρόχος) *well-knit.*

εὐ-γᾱθής, ές, and **εὐ-γάθητος**, ον, Dor. for εὐγηθ-.

εὖ-γε, Adv. for εὖ γε, Lat. *euge! well done! well said! capital! bravo!*

εὔ-γειος, ον, (εὖ, γῆ) *of* or *with good soil: fertile.*

εὐγένεια, ἡ, (εὐγενής) *nobility of birth, high descent.* II. *nobility of soul, generosity.*

εὐ-γένειος Ep. **ἠΰ-**, ον, (εὖ, γένειον) *well-bearded.*

εὐ-γενέτης, ου, ὁ, = sq.

εὐ-γενής Ep. **εὐη-γενής** and **ἠϋ-γενής**, ές, (εὖ, γένος) *well-born, of noble race, of high descent:* also *denoting nobility.* II. *noble-minded, generous.* III. of animals, *high-bred, noble.*

εὐ-γενία Ion. -ίη, ἡ, = εὐγένεια.

εὔ-γεως, ων, (εὖ, γῆ) Att. for εὔγειος.

εὐ-γηθής, ές, and **εὐ-γήθητος**, ον, (εὖ, γηθέω) *joyous, cheerful.*

εὐγηρία, ἡ, (εὔγηρως) *happy old age.*

εὔ-γηρυς, υ, *sweet-sounding.*

εὔ-γηρως, ων, (εὖ, γῆρας) *happy in old age.*

εὐ-γλάγετος, ον, **εὐ-γλᾰγής**, ές, and **εὔ-γλᾰγος**, ον, (εὖ, γλάγος) *abounding in milk;* irreg. dat. εὔγλαγι, as if from εὖ-γλαξ.

εὔ-γλυπτος, ον, and **εὐ-γλῠφής**, ές, (εὖ, γλύφω) *well carved* or *engraved.*

εὐγλωσσία Att. -ττία, ἡ, *fluency of speech.* From

εὔ-γλωσσος Att. -ττος, ον, (εὖ, γλῶσσα) *with good and ready tongue, sweet-sounding, eloquent.* II. act. *loosing the tongue, making fluent.*

εὖγμα, ατος, τό, (εὔχομαι) like εὖχος, *a boast.* II. = εὐχή, *a prayer.*

εὔ-γναμπτος Ep. **ἐΰγν-**, ον, (εὖ, γνάμπτω) *well-bent, easily bent.*

εὐγνωμοσύνη, ἡ, *good feeling, candour.* From

εὐ-γνώμων, ον, gen. ονος (εὖ, γνώμη) *of good feeling, indulgent, fair, charitable.* II. *sensible, prudent:*—Adv. εὐγνωμόνως, *prudently.*

εὔ-γνωστος, ον, (εὖ, γιγνώσκω) *well-known, familiar.*

εὔ-γομφος, ον, (εὖ, γόμφος) *well-nailed* or *fastened.*

εὐγονία, ἡ, *fruitfulness, fertility.* From

εὔ-γονος, ον, (εὖ, γονή) *fruitful, prolific.*

εὔ-γραμμος, ον, (εὖ, γραμμή) *well-drawn.*

εὐ-γρᾰφής, ές, (εὖ, γράφω) *well painted.* II. act. *writing* or *drawing well.*

εὐ-γώνιος, ον, (εὖ, γωνία) *well-cornered, regular.*

εὐ-δαίδαλος, ον, *beautifully wrought.*

εὐδαιμονέω, f. ήσω, (εὐδαίμων) *to be prosperous, well off* or *happy.* Hence

εὐδαιμόνημα, ατος, τό, *a piece of good fortune.*

εὐδαιμονία, ἡ, (εὐδαιμονέω) *prosperity, happiness.*

εὐδαιμονίζω, f. σω, (εὐδαίμων) *to account happy*

εὐδαιμονικός, ή, όν, (εὐδαίμων) *of* or *tending to happiness:* of persons, *happy.* Adv. -κῶς, *happily.*

εὐδαιμόνως, Adv. of εὐδαίμων, *happily:* Comp. and Sup. εὐδαιμονέστερον, -έστατα.

εὐ-δαίμων, ον, gen. ονος, (εὖ, δαίμων) *with a good genius* or *destiny, fortunate, prosperous,* Lat. *felix:* also *wealthy,* like Lat. *beatus: happy.*

εὐ-δάκρῡτος, ον, (εὖ, δακρύω) *much to be wept, lamentable.*

εὐ-δείελος, ον, (εὖ, δέελος for δῆλος) *very clear, far-seen.*

εὔ-δειπνος, ον, (εὖ, δεῖπνον) *honoured with rich feasts.* II. εὔδαιτοι δαῖτες *luxurious feasts.*

εὑδέμεναι, Ep. inf. of εὕδω.

εὔ-δενδρος, ον, (εὖ, δένδρον) *abounding in fair trees.*

εὕδεσκον, Ion. impf. of εὕδω.

εὔ-δηλος, ον, (εὖ, δῆλος) *very clear, manifest.*

εὕδησθα, Ep. 2 sing. subj. of εὕδω.

εὐδία, ἡ, (εὔδιος) *fair weather:* metaph. *tranquillity, prosperity.*

εὐ-διάβᾰτος, ον, *easy to be crossed, practicable.*

εὐ-διαίτερος, α, ον, irreg. Comp. of εὔδιος.

εὐ-δίαιτος, ον, (εὖ, δίαιτα) *living temperately.*

εὐ-διᾱνός, ή, όν, = εὔδιος, *warm.*

εὐδιάω, f. ήσω, (εὐδία) *to be calm.*

εὐ-δικία, ἡ, (εὖ, δίκη) *righteous dealing: justice.*

εὐ-δίνητος, ον, (εὖ, δῑνέω) *easily turning* or *turned.*

εὔ-διος, ον, (εὖ, Διός gen. of Ζεύς) *calm, fine, clear: genial:* of persons, *cheerful:*—irreg. Comp. and Sup. εὐδιέστερος, -έστατος; also εὐδιαίτερος.

εὔ-δμητος Ep. **ἐΰδ-**, ον, (εὖ, δέμω) *well built* or *fashioned.*

εὐ-δοκέω, f. ήσω: aor. 1 εὐδόκησα: (εὖ, δοκέω):—*to be content* or *well pleased, to approve of* or *acquiesce in* a thing: c. inf. *to consent* to do. Hence

εὐδοκία, ἡ, *satisfaction, approval.*

εὐδοκῐμέω, f. ήσω impf. and aor. 1 ηὐδοκίμουν, ηὐδοκίμησα, but often without augm. εὐδ-: (εὐδόκιμος):—*to be of good repute, be in esteem, famous, popular;* εὐδοκιμεῖν ἔν τινι *to be distinguished for* a thing. Hence

εὐδοκῐμία, ἡ, *good repute, credit.*

εὐ-δόκῐμος, ον, *in good repute, highly esteemed.*

εὐδοξέω, f. ήσω, (εὔδοξος) *to be in good repute, be thought well of, be famous.* Hence

εὐδοξία, ἡ, *good report, a good name, credit, glory.*

εὔ-δοξος, ον, (εὖ, δόξα) *of good report, glorious.*

εὐ-δρᾰκής, ές, (εὖ, δρακεῖν) *sharp-sighted.*

εὔ-δροσος, ον, *well-bedewed, abounding in water.*

ΕΥ᾿ΔΩ, impf. ηὗδον Ep. εὗδον: fut. εὑδήσω:—*to sleep, lie down to sleep:* also *to sleep* in death. II. metaph. *to rest, be still* or *hushed: to cease.*

εὐ-έᾰνος, ον, (εὖ, ἑᾰνόν) *richly-dight, well-clad.*

εὔ-εδρος, ον, (εὖ, ἕδρα) *well-seated: with a fair throne.* II. pass. *easy to sit,* of a horse.

εὐ-έθειρος, ον, (εὖ, ἔθειρα) *fair-haired.*

εὐ-ειδής, ές, (εὖ, εἶδος) *well-shaped, graceful.*

εὔ-ειλος, ον, (εὖ, εἵλη) *sunny, warm,* Lat. *apricus.*

εὐ-είμων, ον, gen. ονος, (εὖ, εἷμα) *well-dressed.*

εὔ-ειρος Att. **εὔερος**, ον, (εὖ, εἶρος) *with* or *of good wool, fleecy.*

εὐ-έλεγκτος, ον, (εὖ, ἐλέγχω) *easy to be refuted.*

εὔ-ελπις, ὁ, ἡ, neut. εὔελπι, gen. ιδος, *of good hope, hopeful, cheerful, sanguine;* εὔελπίς εἰμι, c. inf. to be *of good hope that.*

εὐ-εξάλειπτος, ον, *easy to blot out* or *erase.*

εὐ-εξᾰπάτητος, ον, (εὖ, ἐξαπατάω) *easily deceived.*

εὐ-εξία, ἡ, (εὖ, ἕξις) *a good habit of body, good state of health:* generally, *good condition, good case.*

εὐ-έξοδος, *ον, easy to get out of* or *escape from.*

εὐέπεια, ἡ, *beautiful language, eloquence.* II. = εὐφημία, *words of good omen.* From

εὐ-επής, ές, (εὖ, ἔπος) *well-speaking, eloquent.* 2. *making eloquent, inspiring.* II. *well-spoken.*

εὐ-επία, ἡ, Ion. and poët. for εὐέπεια.

εὐ-επιβούλευτος, *ον*, (εὖ, ἐπιβουλεύω) *easy to plot against: exposed to treachery.*

εὐ-επίθετος, *ον*, (εὖ, ἐπιτίθεμαι) *easy to be set upon* or *attacked;* εὐεπίθετόν ἐστί τινι it is *easy* for one *to make an attack.*

εὐ-επίτακτος, *ον*, (εὖ, ἐπιτάσσω) *easy to arrange: tractable.*

εὐεργεσία, ἡ, *well-doing, good conduct.* II. *a doing good, a good deed, service, kindness.* From

εὐεργετέω, f. ήσω: in the augm. tenses, sometimes εὐηργέτουν, εὐηργέτησα, sometimes εὐεργ- with no augm.: (εὐεργέτης):—*to do well, do good.* II. *to do* one *good, shew kindness to, confer a benefit upon:*—Pass., **εὐεργετεῖσθαί τι** *to have a kindness done* one. Hence

εὐεργέτημα, *ατος, τό, a good deed, a service, kindness.*

εὐ-εργέτης, *ου*, ὁ, (εὖ, *ἔργω) *a well-doer, a benefactor:* a title of honour of such *as had done the state service.* II. as Adj. *beneficent.*

εὐεργετητέον, verb. Adj. of εὐεργετέω, *one must do good* or *shew kindness to.*

εὐεργετικός, ή, όν, (εὐεργετής) *disposed to do good.*

εὐ-εργέτις, ιδος, fem. of εὐεργέτης.

εὐ-εργής, ές, (εὖ, *ἔργω) *well-wrought, well-made, well-built:* of gold, *well-wrought, refined.* II. *well-done:* hence in plur. εὐεργέα, *good deeds, benefits.*

εὐ-εργός, όν, (εὖ, *ἔργω) *doing good, upright, virtuous.* II. pass. *well-wrought, well-tilled:* also *easy to work.*

εὐ-ερκής, ές, (εὖ, ἕρκος) *well-fenced, well-protected: shutting close:* of cities, *well-guarded.*

εὐ-έρκτης, οῦ, ὁ, poët. for εὐεργέτης.

εὐ-ερνής, ές, (εὖ, ἔρνος) *sprouting well, flourishing.*

εὔ-ερος, Att. for εὔειρος.

εὐ-εστώ, οῦς, ἡ, (εὖ, εἰμί *sum*) *well-being, prosperity.*

εὐετηρία, ἡ, (εὖ, ἔτος) *a good season.*

εὐ-ετία, ἡ, = εὐετηρία.

εὐ-εύρετος, *ον*, (εὖ, εὑρίσκω) *easy to find.*

εὐ-έφοδος, *ον, easy to assail.*

εὔ-ζηλος, *ον, emulous in good:*—Adv. -ζήλως.

εὔ-ζῠγος Ep. **ἐΰζυγος**, *ον*, (εὖ, ζυγόν III) of a ship, *well-benched.*

εὔ-ζυξ, ῠγος, ὁ, ἡ, (εὖ, ζεύγνυμι) *well paired* or *matched.*

εὐ-ζῳά, Dor. for εὐζωΐα.

εὔ-ζωνος Ep. **ἐΰζωνος**, *ον*, (εὖ, ζώνη) *well-girded,* of women. II. *girt up for exercise, with one's loins girded, active,* as in Horace *alte praecinctus: unencumbered,* Lat. *expeditus.*

εὔ-ζωρος, *ον*, (εὖ, ζωρός) *quite pure, unmixed,* of wine: Comp. -ζωρότερος, also irreg. -έστερος.

εὐη-γενής, Ep. for εὐγενής.

εὐ-ηγεσία, ἡ, (εὖ, ἡγέομαι) *good government.*

εὐ-ηγορέω, f. ήσω, (εὖ, ἀγορεύω) *to speak well of, praise.*

εὐήθεια or **εὐηθία** Ion. -ίη, ἡ, *goodness of disposition, singleness of heart, simplicity:* also in bad sense, *simplicity, silliness.* From

εὐ-ήθης, ες, (εὖ, ἦθος) *well-disposed, single-hearted, simple-minded:* in bad sense, *simple, silly:*—Adv. εὐηθῶς, Sup. -έστατα.

εὐηθίη, ἡ, Ion. for εὐήθεια.

εὐηθικός, ή, όν, (εὐήθης) *of mild, gentle character:* hence *simple, foolish.* Adv. -κῶς, *in simple fashion.*

εὐ-ήκης, ες, (εὖ, ἀκή) *well-pointed, keen-edged.*

εὐ-ήκοος, *ον*, (εὖ, ἀκούω) *hearing well: ready to hear.*

εὐ-ηλάκᾰτος Dor. **εὐᾱλακ-**, *ον*, (εὖ, ἠλακάτη) *with quick spindle, spinning beautifully.*

εὐ-ήλᾰτος, *ον*, (εὖ, ἐλαύνω) *easy to drive* or *ride over;* πεδίον εὐήλατον a plain *fit for cavalry operations.*

εὐ-ήλιος Dor. **εὐάλιος**, *ον*, (εὖ, ἥλιος) *well-sunned, sunny, warm,* Lat. *aprīcus:*—Adv. -ίως, *with bright, sunny weather.*

εὐ-ημερέω, f. ήσω, (εὐήμερος) of weather, *to be fair.* 2. of persons, *to spend the day cheerfully: to be happy: to be successful in* a thing. Hence

εὐημερία, ἡ, *fineness of the day, fine weather.* II. *good times, health and wealth, honour and glory.*

εὐ-ήμερος, *ον*, (εὖ, ἡμέρα) *of a fine day: propitious.* 2. *cheerful, happy.*

εὐηνεμία, ἡ, *a fair wind.* From

εὐ-ήνεμος, *ον*, (εὖ, ἄνεμος) *with fair wind.* 2. *unvexed by winds, sheltered, serene.*

εὐ-ήνιος, *ον*, (εὖ, ἡνία) *obedient to the rein:* generally, *obedient, docile.*

εὐηνορία, ἡ, *manliness, manly virtue.* From

εὐ-ήνωρ, *ορος*, ὁ, ἡ, (εὖ, ἀνήρ) *giving manhood, inspiriting.* II. of cities, *abounding in brave men.*

εὐ-ήρᾰτος, *ον*, (εὖ, ἔραμαι) *much-loved, lovely*

εὐ-ήρετμος, *ον*, (εὖ, ἐρετμός) *well fitted to the oar: well-rowed, well-pulled.*

εὐ-ήρης, ες, (εὖ, ἀρᾰρεῖν) *well-fitted* or *put together: well-poised, easy to handle.*

εὐ-ήτριος, *ον*, (εὖ, ἤτριον) *well-woven.* II. act *weaving well.*

εὐ-ήχης, ες, (εὖ, ἦχος) *well-sounding, tuneful.*

εὐ-ήχητος, *ον, well-sounding: loud-sounding.*

εὐ-θάλασσος, *ον*, (εὖ, θάλασσα) *prosperous by sea.*

εὐ-θᾰλής, ές, (εὖ, θάλος) *growing well, flourishing*

εὐ-θᾱλής, ές, Dor. for εὐθηλής.

εὐθαρσέω, f. ήσω, *to be of good courage.* From

εὐ-θαρσής, ές, (εὖ, θάρσος) *of good courage:*—Adv. -σῶς. 2. *giving courage, safe.*

εὐθενέω, older form of εὐθηνέω.

εὐ-θεράπευτος, *ον*, (εὖ, θεραπεύω) *easily healed.* II. *easily won by kindness* or *attention*

εὐθετέω, f. ήσω, (εὔθετος) *to be well-arranged, convenient.* 2. trans. *to set in order, arrange well.* **εὐθετίζω**, *to set in order, arrange orderly.* From

εὔ-θετος, ον, (εὖ, τίθημι) *well-arranged, well-disposed: easily stowed* or *disposed of: convenient for use.*

εὐθέως, Adv. of εὐθύς, *straightway.*

εὐ-θηγής, ές, (εὖ, θήγω) *sharpening well.*

εὐ-θηλήμων, ον, gen. ονος, rare form for **εὐθηλής**.

εὐ-θηλής Dor. **-θᾱλής**, ές, (εὖ, θηλή) *well-suckled: well-fed, thriving.*

εὔ-θηλος, ον, (εὖ, θηλή) *with distended udder.*

εὐθημοσύνη, ἡ, *good order, good management: a habit of good order.* From

εὐ-θήμων, ον, gen. ονος, (εὖ, τίθημι) *well-arranged, well-made.* II. act. *orderly, setting in order.*

εὐθηνέω and **εὐθενέω**, *to be well off, thrive, flourish: to abound in:*—so also in Pass., aor. 1 εὐθηνήθην. Hence

εὐθηνία, ἡ, *abundance.*

εὐ-θήρᾱτος, ον, (εὖ, θηράω) *easily caught* or *won.*

εὔ-θηρος, ον, (εὖ, θήρα) *lucky in the chase.* II. (θῆρες) *abounding in game.*

εὐ-θήσαυρος, ον, *well-stored, precious.*

εὐ-θνήσιμος, ον, (εὖ, θνήσκω) *with easy death.*

εὔ-θοινος, ον, (εὖ, θοίνη) *with rich banquet: copious.*

εὐ-θορύβητος, ον, (εὖ, θορυβέω) *easily confounded.*

εὔ-θριγκος, ον, (θριγκός) *with good coping* or *cornice.*

εὔ-θριξ Ep. **ἐΰ-θριξ**, -τρῐχος, ὁ, ἡ, (εὖ, θρίξ) *with fine hair:* of horses, *with flowing mane:* of birds, *well-plumed.* II. *made of stout hair*, of a fishing-line.

εὔ-θρονος Ep. **ἐΰθρονος**, ον, (εὖ, θρόνος) *with beautiful seat* or *throne.*

εὔ-θροος, ον, (εὖ, θρόος) *loud-sounding.*

εὐθύ, neut. of εὐθύς, used as Adv.

εὐθύ-γλωσσος Att. **-ττος**, ον, (εὐθύ, γλῶσσα) *of straight tongue, honest of tongue.*

εὐθῠδικία, ἡ, *an open, fair trial.* From

εὐθύ-δῐκος, ον, or η, ον, (εὐθύ, δίκη) *judging righteously.*

εὐθυδρομέω, f. ήσω, *to run straight:* of ships, *to sail in a straight course.* From

εὐθύ-δρομος, ον, *running a straight course.*

εὐθυ-εργής, ές, (εὐθύ, ἔργον) *accurately wrought.*

εὐθυ-μάχης, ου, ὁ, and **εὐθύ-μᾰχος**, ον, (εὐθύς, μάχομαι) *fighting straightforward, fair-fighting*

εὐθῡμέω, f. ήσω, (εὔθυμος) *to be of good cheer.* II. trans. *to make cheerful, cheer:*—Pass. **εὐθυμέομαι**, *to be of good cheer.* Hence

εὐ-θυμητέον, verb. Adj., *one must be cheerful.*

εὐθῡμία, ἡ, (εὐθυμέω) *cheerfulness, festivity.*

εὔ-θῡμος, ον, (εὖ, θυμός) *well-disposed, generous, kind.* II. *of good cheer, cheerful:* of horses, *spirited.* III. Adv. **εὐθύμως**, *cheerfully;* Comp. -ότερον; Sup. -ότατα.

εὔθῡνα, ἡ, but mostly used in pl. **εὔθῡναι**, αἱ, (εὐθύνω) *an examination of accounts, audit;* εὐθύνας ἀπαιτεῖν to call for one's *accounts;* εὐθύνας διδόναι to give *them* in, submit to a scrutiny; εὐθύνας ὀφλεῖν to be bound to do so. II. *correction, chastisement.* Hence

εὔθῡνος, ὁ, *an investigator, auditor*, who examined and passed *the accounts* of magistrates: at Athens there were ten. II. *a corrector, chastiser.*

εὐθυντήρ, ῆρος, ὁ, (εὐθύνω) *a director, corrector.* II. as Adj., εὐθυντὴρ οἴαξ *the guiding* rudder.

εὐθυντηρία, ἡ, *the part of a ship wherein the rudder was fixed:* fem. from

εὐθυντήριος, α, ον, (εὐθύνω) *directing, ruling.*

εὐθυντής, οῦ, ὁ, = εὐθυντήρ.

εὐθύνω, fut. ῠνῶ, (εὐθύς) = the Homeric ἰθύνω, *to guide straight: to steer straight.* 2. *to direct, govern.* 3. *to keep straight, preserve.* II. *to make straight*, as a bent piece of wood: metaph. *to rectify, revise.* III. at Athens, *to call to account, scrutinise the accounts* (εὔθυναι) *of* a magistrate: Pass. *to be called to account*, and so *to be corrected.*

εὐθύ-πνοος, ον, contr. **-πνους**, ουν, (εὐθύ, πνέω) *straight-blowing.*

εὐθύ-πομπος, ον, (εὐθύ, πέμπω) *guiding straight.*

εὐθῠπορέω, f. ήσω, *to go straight forward;* πότμος εὐθυπορῶν *unswerving, inflexible* fate: c. acc. cognato, εὐθυπορεῖν δρόμον *to go a straight* course. From

εὐθύ-πορος, ον, (εὐθύ, πορεύομαι) *going straight:* metaph. *straightforward, plain-sailing, honest.*

εὔ-θυρσος, ον, *with beautiful thyrsus.*

ΕΥ'ΘΥ'Σ, εὐθεῖα, εὐθύ, = the Ion. form ἰθύς, *straight, direct:*—in moral sense, *straightforward, plain, honest:*—in Adverb. usages, εἰς τὸ εὐθὺ βλέπειν to look *straight forward;* ἀπὸ τοῦ εὐθέος λέγειν to speak *straight out;* ἐκ τοῦ εὐθέος *at once, immediately.* II. as Adv. **εὐθύς** and **εὐθύ**, of Place, *straight to, direct for:* also c. gen. *straight towards* .., εὐθὺ Πελλήνης. 2. of Time, *straightway, forthwith, at once;* τοῦ θέρους εὐθὺς ἀρχομένου *immediately* at the beginning of summer.— So also the regular Adv. εὐθέως.

εὐ-θύσᾰνος, ον, (εὖ, θύσανος) *well-fringed.*

εὐθύτης, ητος, ἡ, (εὐθύς) *straightness.* II. metaph. *honesty, justice.* [ῠ]

εὐθύ-τομος, ον, (εὐθύ, τεμεῖν) *cut straight, straight.*

εὐθύ-φρων, ον, (εὐθύ, φρήν) *right-minded.*

εὐθύ-ωρος, ον, also α, ον, (εὐθύ, ὥρα) *in a straight direction:* neut. εὐθύωρον as Adv., = εὐθύς II.

εὐ-θώρηξ, ηκος, ὁ, ἡ, (εὖ, θώραξ) *well-mailed.*

εὐιάζω, v. εὐάζω.

εὐιᾰκός, ή, όν, (εὔιος) *Bacchic:* fem. **εὐιάς**, άδος.

εὐ-ίερος, ον, (εὖ, ἱερός) *very holy, hallowed.*

Εὔιος, ὁ, *Evius*, epith. of Bacchus, from the cry εὖα, εὐοῖ. II. **εὔιος**, ον, Adj. *Bacchic, inspired by Bacchus.*

εὔ-ιππος, ον, of persons, *delighting in horses, having fine horses:* of places, *famed for horses.*

εὔ-ιστος, ον, (εὖ, ἴσημι) *of good knowledge.*

εὐ-ίσχιος, ον, (εὖ, ἰσχίον) *with beautiful hips.*

εὐ-καθαίρετος, ον, (εὖ, καθαιρέω) *easy to overthrow.*

εὐ-κάθεκτος, ον, (εὖ, κατέχω) *easy to keep down.*

εὐκαιρέω, f. ήσω, (εὔκαιρος) *to have good opportu-*

nity, have leisure:—εὐκαιρεῖν εἴς τι, to devote one's leisure to a thing, spend one's time in it.

εὐκαιρία, ἡ, *good season, opportunity, leisure.* II. *prosperity.* From

εὔ-καιρος, ον, (εὖ, καιρός) *in season, seasonable, well-timed, opportune:* of places, *convenient.* Adv. εὐκαίρως *opportunely; at leisure;* Comp. -ότερον; Sup. -ότατα.

εὔ-κᾱλος, εὐ-κᾱλία, Dor. for εὐκηλ-.

εὐ-κάμᾰτος, ον, (εὖ, κάματος) *of easy labour, easy.* 2. *well-wrought: won by noble toils.* [ᾰ]

εὐ-καμπής, ές, (εὖ, κάμπτω) *well-bent, curved.*

εὐ-κάρδιος, ον, (εὖ, καρδία) *good of heart, stout-hearted,* Lat. *egregie cordatus:* of a horse, *spirited, of good courage.* Adv. ίως, *with stout heart.*

εὔ-καρπος, ον, *rich in fruit, fruitful: prolific.*

εὐ-κατάλλακτος, ον, (εὖ, καταλλάσσω) *easy to appease.*

εὐ-κατάλῠτος, ον, (εὖ, καταλύω) *easy to overthrow.*

εὐ-κατάφορος, ον, (εὖ, καταφέρομαι) *prone towards,* Lat. *proclivis.*

εὐ-καταφρόνητος, ον, (εὖ, καταφρονέω) *easy to despise, despicable.*

εὐ-κατέργαστος, ον, (εὖ, κατεργάζομαι) *easy to work,* of land:—*easy to digest:*—*easy to effect* or *subdue.*

εὐ-κατηγόρητος, ον, (εὖ, κατηγορέω) *easy to blame.*

εὐ-κέᾰτος, ον, Ep. for εὐ-κέαστος, (εὖ, κεάζω) *easily cleft* or *split.*

εὐ-κέλᾰδος, ον, *sounding well, melodious.*

εὔ-κεντρος, ον, (εὖ, κέντρον) *well-pointed.*

εὐ-κέραος, ον, and **εὔκερως**, ων, gen. ωτος, (εὖ, κέρας) *with goodly horns.*

εὐκηλήτειρα, ἡ, *she that lulls, soothes.* From

εὔκηλος Dor. **εὔκᾱλος**, ον, lengthd. form of ἕκηλος, *tranquil, free from care* or *fear,* Lat. *securus.*

εὔ-κισσος, ον, (εὖ, κισσός) *ivied.*

εὐ-κίων, ον, gen. ονος, *with goodly pillars.* [ῑ]

εὐ-κλεής, ές, acc. εὐκλεέα contr. εὐκλεᾶ; also (as if from εὐκλής) acc. sing. εὐκλέᾰ, pl. εὐκλέας Ep. ἐϋκλεῖας: (εὖ, κλέος):—*of good fame, glorious, noble.* Hence

εὔκλειᾰ Ep. **ἐϋκλείη**, and in late Poets **εὐκλείη**, ἡ, *good fame, renown.* Hence

εὐκλεΐζω Ion. **εὐκληΐζω**, f. σω, *to praise, laud.*

ἐϋκλειής, ές, Ep. for εὐκλεής: Adv. ἐϋκλειῶς.

εὔ-κλεινος, ον, *much-famed.*

εὐ-κληΐς or **ἐϋ-κληΐς**, ῖδος, ἡ, (εὖ, κλείω) *well-closed, fast-shutting.*

εὐκληρέω, f. ήσω, *to have a good lot.* From

εὔ-κληρος, ον, *with a good lot* or *portion.*

εὔ-κλωστος Ep. **ἐΰκλ-**, ον, (εὖ, κλώθω) *well-spun.*

εὐ-κνήμῑς, ῖδος, ὁ, ἡ, (εὖ, κνημίς) *well-equipped with greaves, with well-wrought greaves:* Ep. nom. and acc. pl. ἐϋκνήμῑδες, ἐϋκνήμῑδας. [ῑ]

εὔ-κνημος, ον, (εὖ, κνήμη) *with beautiful legs.*

εὐ-κοινόμητις, ὁ, ἡ, *taking common counsel.*

εὔ-κολλος, ον, (εὖ, κόλλα) *gluing well, sticky.*

εὔ-κολος, ον, (εὖ, κόλον) *of good digestion:* generally, *contented, easy,* Lat. *făcilis: good-natured, popular.*

εὔ-κολπος, ον, *swelling beautifully, in goodly folds.* 2. *with beautiful bays.*

εὐκόλως, Adv. of εὔκολος, *contentedly, calmly.*

εὐ-κομῐδής, ές, (εὖ, κομιδή) *well-cared for.*

εὔ-κομος Ep. **ἠΰκ-**, ον, (εὖ, κόμη) *thick-haired.*

εὔ-κομπος, ον, *loud-sounding.*

εὔ-κοπος, ον, *with easy labour, easy.*

εὐ-κόσμητος, ον, (εὖ, κοσμέω) *well-adorned.*

εὐκοσμία, ἡ, *orderly behaviour, good order.* From

εὔ-κοσμος, ον, *well-ordered, orderly, decorous:*—Adv. -μως, *in good order.* II. *well-adorned, graceful.*

εὔ-κραιρος, ον, or α, ον, (εὖ, κραῖρα) *with fine horns.*

εὐ-κράς, ᾶτος, ὁ, ἡ, (εὖ, κεράννυμι) *well-tempered:* of climate, *temperate, mild, moderate.* II. *mixing readily with.*

εὐ-κρασία, ἡ, *good mixture* or *temperament.* From

εὔ-κρᾱτος, ον, (εὖ, κεράννυμι) *well-tempered, temperate:* of wine, *mixed for drinking:*—metaph. *temperate, mild.*

εὔ-κρεκτος, ον, (εὖ, κρέκω) *well-struck, well-played,* of stringed instruments. II. *well-woven.*

εὔ-κρηνος, ον, (εὖ, κρήνη) *well-watered.*

εὔ-κρητος, ον, Ion. for εὔκρατος.

εὔ-κρῑθος, ον, (εὖ, κριθή) *rich in barley.*

εὐκρῑνέω, f. ήσω, *to keep distinct and in order.* From

εὐ-κρῑνής, ές, (εὖ, κρίνω) *well-separated, distinct, regular: well-arranged, in good order.* Adv. -νως Ion. -νέως.

εὔ-κρῐτος, ον, (εὖ, κρίνω) *easy to judge* or *decide: easily discerned, plain, manifest.*

εὐ-κρότᾰλος Ep. **ἐϋκρ-**, ον, (εὖ, κρόταλον) *accompanied by castanets, lively, rattling.*

εὐ-κρότητος, ον, (εὖ, κροτέω) *well-welded, well-wrought,* of metal.

εὔ-κρυπτος, ον, (εὖ, κρύπτω) *easy to hide.*

εὐκταῖος, α, ον, (εὔχομαι) *of* or *for prayer, votive:* τὰ εὐκταῖα, *wishes, prayers, vows:*—of the gods, *invoked in prayer:* of things, *prayed for.*

εὐ-κτέᾰνος, ον, (εὖ, κτέανον) *with fine possessions.*

εὐ-κτήμων, ον, gen. ονος, (εὖ, κτῆμα) *with fair possessions.*

εὔ-κτητος, ον, (εὖ, κτάομαι) *easily gotten.*

ἐϋ-κτίμενος, η, ον, (εὖ, κτίζω) *well-built: well-made: full of goodly buildings.*

ἐΰ-κτῐτος, ον, Ep. and Ion. for εὔκτιστος, = ἐϋκτίμενος.

εὐκτός, ή, όν, (εὔχομαι) *prayed for: to be prayed for.*

εὔ-κυκλος, ον, *well-turned, well-rounded.* II. *moving in a circle, circling.*

εὐ-κύλῐκος, ον, (εὖ, κύλιξ) *suited to the wine-cup.*

εὐλάβεια Ion. **εὐλαβίη**, ἡ, *discretion, caution, circumspection.* 2. *fear of the gods, piety.* From

εὐ-λᾰβέομαι, fut. med. -ήσομαι or pass. -ηθήσομαι: aor. 1 pass. ηὐλαβήθην or εὐλ-: Dep.: (εὐλαβής):—*to be cautious, circumspect, discreet:*—*to have a* *care, beware, fear.* II. c. acc. *to beware of* 2. *to watch for, await quietly.*

εὐλαβήθητι, 2 sing. aor. 1 imperat. of foreg.

εὐ-λᾰβής, ές, (εὖ, λαβεῖν) *taking in hand cautiously, cautious, circumspect, discreet.* 2. *fearing the gods, pious, devout.*

εὐ-λᾰβίη, see εὐλάβεια.

εὐλᾰβῶς, Adv. of εὐλαβής, *cautiously:* Comp. -εστέρως.

εὐλάζω, f. ξω, old Dor. Verb, *to plough.*

εὐ-λᾶϊγξ, ιγγος, ὁ, ἡ, = εὔλιθος.

εὐλάκα, ἡ, old Dor. word for *a ploughshare.*

εὔ-λᾰλος, ον, (εὖ, λαλέω) *sweet-spoken.*

εὐ-λάχᾰνος, ον, (εὖ, λάχανον) *fruitful in herbs.*

εὔ-λειμος, ον, and **εὐ-λείμων**, ον, gen. ονος, (εὖ, λειμών) *with fair meadows.*

εὔ-λεκτρος, ον, (εὖ, λέκτρον) *blessing marriage: happy in marriage.*

εὔ-λεξις, ι, (εὖ, λέξις) *with good choice of words.*

εὐ-λεχής, ές, (εὖ, λέχος) *well-wedded, blessed in one's marriage-bed.*

ΕΥ'ΛΗ', ἡ, *a worm, maggot.*

εὐ-ληκτος, ον, (εὖ, λήγω) *soon-ceasing.*

εὔ-ληπτος, ον, (εὖ, λαμβάνω) *easy to take hold of; easy to be taken, seized, conquered.* Adv. εὐλήπτως, *so that one can easily take hold:* Sup. -ότατα.

εὔληρα, ων, τά, old Ep. word for ἡνία, *reins.*

εὐ-λίμενος, ον, (εὖ, λῑμήν) *with good harbours.*

εὐλογέω, f. ήσω: in augm. tenses, impf. εὐλόγουν or ηὐλ-, aor. 1 εὐλόγησα or ηὐλ-: (εὔλογος):—*to speak well of, praise.* 2. *to bless.* Hence

εὐλογητός, ή, όν, *blessed.*

εὐλογία, ἡ, (εὐλογέω) *good-speaking, fair-speaking.* II. *praise, eulogy: glory.* 2. *blessing* or *a blessing, bounty:* also *almsgiving.*

εὐ-λόγιστος, ον, (εὖ, λογίζομαι) *easy to reckon.* II. *rightly reckoning, prudent.*

εὔ-λογος, ον, (εὖ, λόγος) *reasonable, sensible: reasonable, probable, fair:* τὸ εὔλογον *a fair reason:*—Adv., εὐλόγως ἔχειν to be *reasonable;* Comp. -ωτέρως.

εὐ-λοέτειρα, ἡ, (εὖ, λουτρόν) *with fine baths.*

εὔ-λοφος, ον, *well-plumed.*

εὔ-λοχος, ον, (εὖ, λοχεύω) *helping in childbirth.*

εὐ-λύρης, ου, Dor. **εὐλύρας**, α, ὁ, = εὔλυρος.

εὔ-λῠρος, ον, (εὖ, λύρα) *with beautiful lyre, playing beautifully on the lyre.*

εὔ-λῠτος, ον, (εὖ, λύω) *easy to untie, easy to loose.* 2. metaph. *easy to dissolve* or *break.*

εὐμάθεια, ἡ, *docility.*

εὐ-μᾰθής, ές, (εὖ, μαθεῖν) *ready* or *quick at learning*, Lat. *docilis:*—Adv. εὐμαθῶς, *readily:* Comp. -έστερον. II. pass. *easy to learn* or *know, intelligible: well-known, familiar.*

εὐ-μαθία Ion. -ιη, ἡ, = εὐμάθεια.

εὐ-μάκης, Dor. for εὐμήκης.

εὔ-μαλλος, ον, *of fine wool.*

εὔ-μᾶλος, Dor. for εὔμηλος.

εὐ-μάρᾰθος, ον, (εὖ, μάραθον) *abounding in fennel.*

εὐμάρεια, ἡ, *easiness, ease, convenience;* εὐμαρείᾳ χρῆσθαι *to be in comfort,* but also = Lat. *alvum exonerare, to ease oneself.* From

εὐ-μᾰρής, ές, (εὖ, μάρη = χείρ) *easy, convenient, without trouble.* 2. rarely of persons, *easy, gentle.*

εὐ-μᾰρίη, Ion. for εὐμάρεια.

εὐμᾱρίς, ίδος, ἡ, but acc. εὐμαρίν, *an Asiatic shoe* or *slipper.* (Foreign word.)

εὐμᾰρῶς poët. -έως, Adv. of εὐμαρής, *gently.*

εὐ-μεγέθης, ες, (εὖ, μέγεθος) *of good size, well-grown.*

εὐ-μέλᾰνος, ον, (εὖ, μέλαν) *well-blackened, inky.*

εὐ-μελής, ές, (εὖ, μέλος) *melodious, musical.*

εὐμένεια, ἡ, (εὐμενής) *good will, kindness, favour.*

εὐμενέτης, ου, ὁ, poët. for εὐμενής, *a well-wisher, friend:* fem. εὐμενέτειρα

εὐμενέω, f. ήσω, *to be propitious, kind.* II. c. acc. *to be kind to, deal kindly with.* From

εὐ-μενής, ές, (εὖ, μένος) *well-disposed, kind, gracious, favourable:* of men, *friendly,* also *acceptable.* 2. of things, *favourable, propitious:* also *bounteous, abundant.*

εὐ-μενία, ἡ, poët. collat. form of εὐμένεια.

Εὐμενίδες (sub. θεαί), αἱ, (εὐμενής) *the gracious goddesses,* appellation of *the Furies,* instead of the ill-omened name Ἐρινύες.

εὐμενία, ἡ, poët. for εὐμένεια.

εὐμενίζομαι, f. ίσομαι Att. ιοῦμαι, Med., (ευμενής) *to make propitious, propitiate.*

εὐμενῶς Ion. -έως, Adv. of εὐμενής, *kindly, graciously:* Comp. -έστερον or -εστέρως.

εὐ-μετάβλητος, ον, and **εὐ-μετάβολος**, ον, (εὖ, μεταβάλλω) *easy to change.*

εὐ-μετάδοτος, ον, (εὖ, μεταδίδωμι) *readily imparting, bountiful.*

εὐ-μεταχείριστος, ον, (εὖ, μεταχειρίζω) *easy to manage.* 2. *easy to deal with* or *master.*

εὔ-μετρος, ον, (εὖ, μέτρον) *moderate, well-proportioned.*

εὐ-μήκης, ες, (εὖ, μῆκος) *of good length, tall.*

εὔ-μηλος, ον, (εὖ, μῆλον) *rich in sheep.*

εὐ-μήρῡτος, ον, (εὖ, μηρύω) *easy to spin* or *draw out.*

εὐμηχᾰνία, ἡ, *skill in devising means, fertility of resources.* From

εὐ-μήχᾰνος, ον, (εὖ, μηχανή) *good at expedients, skilful in devising:* absol. *inventive, ready, ingenious.*

εὐ-μίσητος, ον, (εὖ, μῑσέω) *exposed to hatred.*

εὔ-μῐτος, ον, *with fine* or *stout threads.*

εὔ-μιτρος, ον, (εὖ, μίτρα) *with beautiful girdle.*

ἐϋμ-μελίης, ὁ, Ion. gen. ἐϋμμελίω, Dor. -ίας, gen. -ία: (εὖ, μελία) *armed with good ashen spear.*

εὐ-μνήμων, ον, (εὖ, μνήμη) *easy to remember:* comp. Adv., εὐμνημονεστέρως ἔχειν to be *easier to remember.*

εὐ-μνηστος, ον, (εὖ, μιμνήσκομαι) *well-remembering, mindful.*

εὔ-μοιρος, ον, (εὖ, μοῖρα) *well off for fortune, wealthy.*

εὐμολπέω, f. ήσω, *to sing well.* From

εὔ-μολπος, (εὖ, μολπή) *sweetly-singing.*

εὐμορφία, ἡ, *beauty of form, symmetry.* From

εὔ-μορφος, ον, (εὖ, μορφή) *fair of form, comely.*

εὐμουσία, ἡ, *accomplishments.* From

εὔ-μουσος, ον, (εὖ, Μοῦσα) *skilled in the arts of the Muses: accomplished in poetry, music, and dancing: musical, melodious.*

εὔμοχθος, ον, *industrious, laborious.*

εὔ-μῦθος, ον, *well-spoken, eloquent.*

εὔ-μῡκος, ον, (εὖ, μυκάομαι) *loud-bellowing.*

εὐνάζω, f. άσω: in augm. tenses, aor. 1 εὔνασα or ηὐν–, pass. εὐνάσθην or ηὐν–: (εὐνή):—*to lay in bed, put to sleep:* also *to lay in ambush:* of animals, *to lay* their young *in a form:* of death, *to lay asleep.* 2. metaph. *to lull to sleep, soothe, assuage.* II. Pass. *to go to bed, lie asleep, sleep:* of birds, *to roost.* III. intr. in Act. *to sleep.*

εὐ-ναιετάων, ουσα, ον, (εὖ, ναιετάω) *well-peopled* or *well-situated.*

εὐ-ναιόμενος, η, ον, (εὖ, ναίω) *well-peopled* or *well-situated.*

εὐναῖος, α, ον, (εὐνή) *in one's bed* or *couch;* εὐναῖος λαγὼς a hare *in its form;* εὐναῖαι πτέρυγες wings *over the nest.* 2. *wedded.* 3. of pain, *making one keep one's bed.* II. (εὐνή II) *of* or *for anchorage:* hence *steadying* or *guiding a ship.*

εὐνάσιμος, ον, (εὐνάζω) *convenient for sleeping in.*

εὐναστήρ, ῆρος, ὁ, (εὐνάζω) *a bedfellow.* Hence

εὐνάτειρα, **εὐνατήρ**, **εὐνάτωρ**, Dor. for εὐνητ–.

εὐνᾱτήριον, τό, *a bed-chamber.*

εὐνάω, f. ήσω:—Pass., aor. 1 εὐνήθην: pf. εὔνημαι: (εὐνή):—*to lull to sleep:* also *to lay in ambush.* 2. metaph. *to lull to sleep, soothe, assuage.* II. Pass. *to go to bed: go to sleep:* also *to be bedded with:* of storms, *to be lulled, assuaged.*

εὐνέτης, ου, ὁ, (εὐνή) = εὐναστήρ or εὐνήτηρ.

ΕΥ'ΝΗ', ἡ, *a bed, any sleeping-place: the lair* of a deer, *the seat* or *form* of a hare, *the nest* of a bird:—also *the grave.* 2. *the marriage-bed, wedlock, marriage.* II. in plur. εὐναί, *stones used as anchors,* and thrown out from the prow, while the stern was made fast to land; ἐκ δ' εὐνὰς ἔβαλον κατὰ δὲ πρυμνήσι' ἔδησαν.

εὐνηθείς, aor. 1 part. pass. of εὐνάω.

εὐνῆθεν, (εὐνή) Adv. *out of bed.*

εὐνηθῆναι, aor. 1 inf. pass. of εὐνάω.

εὔνημα, ατος, τό, (εὐνάω) *marriage, wedlock.*

εὐνήτειρα, fem. of εὐνητήρ, *a wife.*

εὐνητήρ, ῆρος, ὁ, (εὐνάω) *a bedfellow, husband.*

εὔ-νητος Ep. **ἐΰν-νητος**, ον, (εὖ, νέω) *well-spun* or *woven, of fine texture.*

εὐνήτρια, ἡ, = εὐνήτειρα.

εὐνήτωρ, ορος, ὁ, = εὐνητήρ.

εὐνῆφι, –φιν, Ep. gen. sing. and pl. of εὐνή.

εὖνις, ὁ, ἡ, gen. ιος; in pl. εὔνιες or εὔνιδες:—*reft of, bereaved of.* II. absol. *bereaved, desolate.*

εὖνις, ιδος, ἡ, (εὐνή) *a bedfellow, wife.*

ἐΰν-νητος, Ep. for εὔνητος.

εὐνοέω, f. ήσω, (εὔνοος) *to be well-disposed* or *friendly:*—Pass. *to be kindly treated.*

εὔνοιᾰ, ἡ, poët. also **εὐνοίᾱ** Ep. **εὐνοΐη**, (εὔνοος) *good will, kindness;* in pl. *kindnesses, kind feelings:*—κατ' εὐνοίαν *out of kindness, favourably;* so, μετ' εὐνοίας, ὑπ' εὐνοίας, εὐνοίᾳ. Hence

εὐ-νοϊκός, ή, όν, *of kind, benevolent character.* Adv., εὐνοϊκῶς ἔχειν to be *kindly disposed.*

εὐνομέομαι: f. med. εὐνομήσομαι: aór. 1 pass. εὐνομήθην: (εὔνομος):—*to have good laws, enjoy a good constitution, to be orderly.* Hence

εὐνομία Ion. –ίη, ἡ, *good order, order.* From

εὔ-νομος, ον, (εὖ, νόμος) *under good laws, well-ordered, orderly.*

εὔ-νοος, ον, Att. contr. **εὔ-νους**, ουν, pl. εὖνοι: (εὖ, νόος, νοῦς):—*well-minded, well-affected, kindly, benevolent:*—Comp. εὐνούστερος Ion. –οέστερος; Sup. –ούστατος.

εὐνουχίζω, f. ίσω, *to make an eunuch of.* From

εὐν-οῦχος, ὁ, (εὐνή, ἔχω) *an eunuch:* employed in Asia as *chamberlains* (whence the name, οἱ τὴν εὐνὴν ἔχοντες, *guardians of the bed*).

εὖντα, Dor. for ἐόντα, ὄντα, neut. pl. part. of εἰμί *sum.*

εὐ-νώμας, ου, ὁ, (εὖ, νωμάω) *swiftly moving.*

εὔ-νως, Adv. of εὔνοος, εὔνους, *kindly.*

εὐξαίμην, aor. 1 opt. of εὔχομαι.

εὔ-ξαντος, ον, (εὖ, ξαίνω) *well-carded,* of wool.

εὔ-ξενος Ion. **εὔ-ξεινος**, ον, (εὖ, ξένος) *kind to strangers, hospitable;* ἀνδρὼν εὔξενος *the guest*-chamber: πόντος εὔξεινος *the Euxine,* now *the Black sea,* called, before the Greek settlements upon it, ἄ-ξενος *the inhospitable.*

εὔ-ξεστος Ep. **ἐΰξεστος**, ον, or η, ον, *well-polished.*

εὔ-ξοος Ep. **ἐΰξοος**, ον, Ep. gen. ἐΰξου, (εὖ, ξέω) = εὔξεστος.

εὐ-ξύμβλητος, **εὐ-ξύμβολος**, **εὐ-ξύνετος**, Att. for εὐσ–.

εὐοδέω, f. ήσω, (εὔοδος) *to have a free passage,* of running water. Hence

εὐοδία, ἡ, *a good journey, fair voyage.*

εὔ-οδμος, ον, (εὖ, ὀδμή) *sweet-smelling, fragrant.*

εὔ-οδος, ον, (εὖ, ὁδός) *easy to travel through: with free passage:*—Sup. εὐοδώτατος. Hence

εὐ-οδόω, f. ώσω: Pass., f. –οδωθήσομαι: aor. 1 –ωδώθην:—*to put in the right way, help on the way:* Pass. *to prosper, be successful.*

εὐοῖ, Bacchanalian exclamation, Lat. *evoe!*

εὔ-ολβος, ον, (εὖ, ὄλβος) *wealthy, prosperous.*

εὐοπλέω, f. ήσω, (εὔοπλος) *to be well-equipt.*

εὐοπλία, ἡ, *the being well armed, a good state of arms and equipments.* From

εὔ-οπλος, ον, (εὖ, ὅπλον) *well-armed, well-equipt.*

εὐοργησία, ἡ, *gentleness, mildness of temper.* From

εὐ-όργητος, ον, (εὖ, ὀργή) *good-tempered, free from passion.* Adv. –τως, *with good temper.*

εὐορκέω, f. ήσω, (εὔορκος) *to swear truly, take a true oath, to keep one's oath.* Hence

εὐορκησία, ἡ, *an abiding by one's oath, good faith.*

εὐορκία, ἡ, (εὐορκέω) = εὐορκησία. From

εὔ-ορκος, ον, (εὖ, ὅρκος) *true to one's oath:* of oaths, ὀμνύναι εὔορκα (as Adv.) to swear *truly;* **εὔορκόν** [ἐστι] 'tis *according to one's oath.* Hence

εὐόρκωμα, ατος, τό, *a faithful oath.*

εὐόρκως, Adv. of εὔορκος, *according to one's oath.*

εὔ-ορμος, ον *with good anchorage:* of ships, *safe at anchor.*

εὔ-ορνις, ῖθος, ὁ, ἡ, (εὖ, ὄρνις) *of good augury, auspicious.* II. *abounding in birds.*

εὐ-όροφος, ον, (εὖ, ἐρέφω) *well-roofed.*

εὐ-όφθαλμος, ον, *with beautiful eyes.* II. *pleasing to the eyes.* III. *specious.*

εὔ-οφρυς, υ, (εὖ, ὀφρύς) *with fine eyebrows.*

εὐ-οχέω, f. ήσω, (εὖ, ἔχω) *to treat, tend well.*

εὐοχθέω, f. ήσω, *to be in plenty.* From

εὔ-οχθος, ον, *with goodly banks, fruitful, rich.*

εὐ-πᾰγής, ές, (εὖ, παγῆναι) *well put together, compact.*

εὐπάθεια Ion. **εὐπαθίη**, ἡ, *enjoyment of good things, the being in good case, comfort:* in plur. *enjoyments, luxuries;* ἐν εὐπαθίῃσι εἶναι *to enjoy oneself, make merry.* [ᾰ] From

εὐπᾰθέω, f. ήσω, *to be well off, enjoy oneself, make merry, live comfortably.* From

εὐ-πᾰθής, ές, (εὖ, παθεῖν) *well off, in good case, comfortable.*

εὐ-πᾰθίη, Ion. for εὐπάθεια.

εὐπαιδία, ἡ, *a goodly race of children.* From

εὔ-παις, παιδος, ὁ, ἡ, (εὖ, παῖς) *blest with children, with many* or *good children;* γόνος εὔπαις, *a noble son.*

εὔ-πακτος, Dor. for εὔπηκτος.

εὐ-πάλᾰμος, ον, (εὖ, πᾰλάμη) *handy, ingenious: inventive.*

εὐ-παράγωγος, ον, (εὖ, παράγω) *easy to lead away.*

εὐ-πάρᾱος, ον, Dor. for εὐπάρειος, –ηος.

εὐ-παράπειστος, ον, *easily led aside.*

εὐ-πάρεδρος, ον, *constantly attending on, devoted to.*

εὐ-πάρειος, ον, (εὖ, παρειά) *with beauteous cheeks.*

εὐ-πάρθενος, ον, *famed for fair maidens.* II. εὐπάρθενος Δίρκη Dircé, *happy maid!*

εὐ-παρόξυντος, ον, (εὖ, παροξύνω) *easily irritated.*

εὐ-πάρῠφος, ον, (εὖ, παρυφή) *with a handsome border.*

εὐ-πᾰτέρεια, ἡ, (εὖ, πατήρ) *daughter of a noble sire: belonging to a noble father.*

εὐ-πατρίδης, ου, ὁ, (εὖ, πατηρ) *of good* or *noble father, of noble family.* II. at Athens, *the* Εὐπατρίδαι, Lat. *Optimates,* were the first class the γεωμόροι the second, the δημιουργοί the third.

εὔ-πατρις, ῐδος, ὁ, ἡ, (εὖ, πατήρ) *born of a noble sire.*

εὐ-πάτωρ, ορος, ὁ, ἡ, = εὔπατρις.

εὐ-πειθής, ές, (εὖ, πείθομαι) *ready to obey, obedient, tractable.* II. act. *persuasive, convincing.*

εὔ-πειστος, ον, (εὖ, πείθομαι) *easily persuaded.*

εὐ-πέμπελος, ον, (εὖ, πέμπω) *gently leading.*

εὐ-πένθερος, ον, *with a good father-in-law.*

εὔ-πεπλος, ον, *beautifully attired.*

εὐ-περιάγωγος, ον, (εὖ, περιάγω) *easily turned round.*

εὐ-περίγραπτος, ον, (εὖ, περιγράφω) *easy to sketch out.*

εὐ-περίγραφος, ον, (εὖ, περιγραφή) = foreg.

εὐ-περίπᾰτος, ον, (εὖ, περιπατέω) *easy to walk on.*

εὐ-περίσπαστος, ον, (εὖ, περισπάω) *easy to pull off.*

εὐ-περίστᾰτος, ον, (εὖ, περιίσταμαι) *easily besetting.*

εὐ-περίτρεπτος, ον, (εὖ, περιτρέπω) *easily turned round, changeable, inconstant.*

εὐ-πέτᾰλος, ον, (εὖ, πέταλον) *with beautiful leaves.*

εὐ-πέτεια, ἡ, *ease;* δι' εὐπετείας *easily.* 2. *easiness of getting* or *having,* Lat. *copia.* From

εὐ-πετής, ές, (εὖ, πεσεῖν) *falling well* or *easily:* hence *easy, without trouble,* Lat. *facilis: abundant, plentiful.*

εὔ-πετρος, ον, (εὖ, πέτρα) *of good, hard stone.*

εὐπετῶς Ion. –έως, Adv. of εὐπετής, *easily, amply:* Comp. εὐπετέστερον and –ρως.

εὐ-πηγής, ές, (εὖ, πήγνυμι) *well-made, stout.*

εὔ-πηκτος, ον, (εὖ, πήγνυμι) *well put together, well-built, compact:* of cheese, *well-curdled, solid.*

εὐ-πήληξ, ηκος, ὁ, ἡ, *with beautiful helmet.*

εὔ-πηνος, ον, (εὖ, πήνη) *of fine texture.*

εὔ-πηχυς, υ, *with beautiful arms.*

εὐ-πῖδαξ, ᾰκος, ὁ, ἡ, *abounding in fountains.*

εὐπῑθέω, = εὐπειθέω. From

εὐ-πῑθής, ές, = εὐπειθής, *obedient, submissive.*

εὔ-πιστος, ον, *easy to believe, trustworthy, credible.* II. act. *easily believing, credulous:*—Adv. –τως.

εὐ-πίων, ον, gen. ονος, *very fat, rich.* [ῑ]

εὐ-πλᾰτής, ές, (εὖ, πλάτος) *of a good breadth.*

εὔ-πλειος, α, ον, *well filled.*

εὐ-πλεκής Ep. **ἐϋ-πλεκής**, ές, (εὖ, πλέκω) *well-plaited;* δίφροι ἐϋπλεκέες, see **εὔπλεκτος**,

εὔ-πλεκτος Ep. **ἐΰ-πλεκτος**, ον, (εὖ, πλέκω) *well-plaited, well-netted;* εὔπλεκτος δίφρος a chariot *with sides of wicker-work.*

εὔπλοια Ep. **εὐπλοΐη**, ἡ, (εὔπλοος) *a fair voyage.*

εὐ-πλόκᾰμος Ep. **ἐϋπλ–** ον, *with goodly locks:* pecul. fem. **ἐϋπλοκαμίς**, ῖδος.

εὔ-πλοκος, ον, = εὔπλεκτος.

εὔ-πλοος, ον, contr. **εὔ-πλους**, ουν, (εὖ, πλέω) *sailing well, having a fair voyage.*

εὐ-πλῠνής Ep. **ἐϋπλ–**, ές, (εὖ, πλύνω) *well-washed.*

εὔ-πλωτος, ον, (εὖ, πλώω) *favourable to sailing.*

εὔπνοια poët. **εὐπνοΐη**, ἡ, *easiness of breathing.* II. *fragrance.* From

εὔ-πνοος Ep. **ἐΰ-πνοος**, ον, contr. **εὔ-πνους**, ουν, (εὖ, πνέω) *breathing well* or *freely: good to breathe through.* II. *sweet-smelling, fragrant,*—Comp. εὐπνώτερος, also irreg. –πνούστερος

εὐποδία, ἡ, (εὔπους) *strength* or *speed of foot.*

εὐποιητικός, ή, όν, (εὖ, ποιέω) *disposed to be kind, beneficent.*

εὐ-ποίητος, ον, also η, ον, (εὖ, ποιέω) *well-made, well-wrought.*

εὐ-ποιΐα, ἡ, (εὖ, ποιέω) *beneficence.*

εὐ-ποίκῐλος, ον, (εὖ, ποικίλος) *much-variegated.*

εὔ-ποκος, ον, (εὖ, πόκος) *with fine wool; fleecy.*

εὐ-πόλεμος, ον, *good at war.*

εὔ-πομπος, ον, (εὖ, πέμπω) *well-conducting, propitious.*

εὐπορέω, f. ήσω: aor. 1 εὐπόρησα: (εὔπορος):—*to be prosperous, be well off: to be well off for* a thing, *have plenty of* it. 2. *to find a way, be able.* II. *to supply, provide:* Pass. *to have plenty of, abound in.* Hence

εὐπορία, ἡ, *facility in moving, facility in doing.* 2. *readiness of supply: means, resources.* 3. *plenty, store: wealth.* II. opp. to ἀπορία, *the solution of doubts* or *difficulties.*

εὔ-πορος, ον, (εὖ, πόρος) *easy to pass through* or *over.* II. *easy, ready.* 2. of persons, *well-provided with resources, ingenious, inventive.* III. *abounding in, rich in:* absol. *plentiful;* of persons, *wealthy.*

εὐπόρως, Adv. of εὔπορος, *easily: in abundance.*

εὔ-ποτμος, ον, *well-fated, happy.*

εὔ-ποτος, ον, (εὖ, ποτόν) *pleasant to drink.*

εὔπους, ὁ, ἡ, –πουν, τό, gen. –ποδος, (εὖ, ποῦς) *with good feet, strong* or *swift of foot.*

εὐπρᾱγέω, f. ήσω, *to fare well, be well off, prosper.* From

εὐ-πρᾱγής, ές, (εὖ, πρᾶγος) *faring well, flourishing.*

εὐπρᾱγία, ἡ, (εὐπραγέω) *well-doing, welfare.*

εὔ-πρακτος, ον, (εὖ, πράσσω) *easy to be done.*

εὐπραξία Ion. **εὐπρηξίη**, ἡ, = εὐπραγία, *good fortune, success.* II. *good conduct.*

εὔ-πραξις, ἡ, poët. for εὐπραξία.

εὔ-πρεμνον, ον, (εὖ, πρέμνον) *with good stem.*

εὐπρέπεια, ἡ, *fair appearance: beauty, comeliness.* II. *speciousness, plausibility.* From

εὐ-πρεπής, ές, (εὖ, πρέπω) *well-looking, goodly, comely:* hence, 2. *fitting, becoming: glorious.* 3. *specious, plausible.*

εὔ-πρεπτος, (εὖ, πρέπω) *conspicuous.*

εὐπρεπῶς Ion. **–έως**, Adv. of εὐπρεπής, *becomingly: speciously:* Comp. εὐπρεπέστερον; Sup. –έστατα.

εὐπρηξίη, Ion. for εὐπραξία.

εὐπρήσσω, (εὖ, πρήσσω) *to arrange* or *order well:* Ion. impf. ἐϋπρήσσεσκον.

εὔ-πρηστος, ον, (εὖ, πρήθω) *strong-blowing.*

εὐ-πρήων, ωνος, ὁ, ἡ, (εὖ, πρήων) *with fair headlands.*

εὐ-πρόσδεκτος, ον, (εὖ, προσδέχομαι) *acceptable.*

εὐ-πρόσεδρος, ον, = εὐπάρεδρος, *assiduous, diligent.*

εὐ-προσήγορος, ον, (εὖ, προσηγορέω) *of easy address, affable, courteous.*

εὐ-πρόσιτος, ον, (εὖ, πρόσειμι) *easy of access.*

εὐ-πρόσοδος, ον, *of good* or *easy access, affable,* Lat. *qui faciles aditus habet.* II. of places, *accessible;* εὐπροσώτατον *the easiest way of approach.*

εὐ-πρόσοιστος, ον, (εὖ, προσφέρω) *easy to be got: attainable, easy.*

εὐπροσωπέω, f. ήσω, (εὐπρόσωπος) *to make a fair show, be specious, plausible.*

εὐπροσωπό-κοιτος, η, ον, (εὐπρόσωπος, κοίτη) *lying* or *placed cheerfully;* τύχῃ εὐπροσωποκοίτῳ πεσεῖν to fall with *a cheerful posture* of fortune.

εὐ-πρόσωπος, ον, (εὖ, πρόσωπον) *well-looking, with fair face:* metaph. *specious.* 2. *cheerful, friendly-looking.*

εὐ-προφάσιστος, ον, (εὖ, προφασίζομαι) *with a good pretext, excusable, plausible.*

εὔ-πρυμνος, ον, (εὖ, πρύμνα) of ships, *with handsome stern.*

εὔ-πρῳρος, ον, (εὖ, πρῷρα) of ships, *with handsome prow.*

εὔ-πτερος, ον, (εὖ, πτερόν) *well-winged, well-plumed:* metaph., εὔπτεροι γυναῖκες *high-plumed* dames of quality.

εὐ-πτέρυγος, ον, (εὖ, πτέρυξ) = **εὔπτερος.**

εὐ-πτόρθος, ον, *finely branching.*

εὔ-πυργος, ον, *with goodly towers.*

εὐ-πώγων, ον, gen. ωνος, *well-bearded.*

εὔ-πωλος, ον, *with fine colts: breeding fine horses.*

εὐράμην, aor. 1 med. of εὔρω.

εὐράξ, (εὖρος) Adv. *from one side, sideways.* II. εὐρὰξ πατάξ, an exclamation to frighten away birds.

εὐρέα, acc. masc. or neut. pl. of εὐρύς; also Ion. fem.

εὑρέθην, aor. 1 pass. of εὑρίσκω.

εὑρεῖν Ep. **εὑρέμεναι**, aor. 2 inf. of εὑρίσκω.

εὑρετέος, α, ον, verb. Adj. of **εὑρίσκω**, *to be discovered, found out.*

εὑρετής, οῦ, ὁ, fem. **εὑρέτις**, ιδος, (εὑρίσκω) *a finder, inventor, discoverer.*

εὕρετο, 3 sing. aor. 2 med. of **εὑρίσκω.**

εὑρετός, ή, όν, verb. Adj. of **εὑρίσκω**, *discovered: to be found out* or *discovered.*

εὕρηκα, **εὕρημαι**, pf. act. and pass. of **εὑρίσκω.**

εὕρημα, ατος, τό, (εὑρίσκω) *that which is found, an unexpected gain, windfall:* hence generally, *a gain, advantage.* 2. of a child, *a foundling.* II. *an invention, discovery: a remedy.*

εὑρῆν, Dor. for εὑρεῖν.

εὑρησι-επής, ές, (εὑρίσκω, ἔπος) *inventive of words, fluent: wordy, sophistical.*

εὑρήσω, fut. of εὑρίσκω.

εὑρήτωρ, ορος, ὁ, (εὑρίσκω) *an inventor, discoverer.*

εὔ-ρῑνος, ον, (εὖ, ῥινός) *of good leather.*

εὔρῑνος, gen. of **εὖρις.**

εὔ-ρῑπος, ὁ, (εὖ, ῥιπίζω) *any strait of the sea, where the tide is violent:* esp. of the strait which separates Euboea from Boeotia; the ancients believed that this ebbed and flowed seven times a day.

εὔ-ρῑς, ῖνος, ὁ, ἡ, (εὖ, ῥίς, ῥίν) *with a good nose, keen-scented:* metaph. *keen at tracking out* a thing.

ΕΥ῾ΡΙ´ΣΚΩ: fut. εὑρήσω: pf. εὕρηκα or ηὕρ–: aor. 2 εὗρον or ηὗρον, imperat. εὑρέ, inf. εὑρεῖν:—Med., f. εὑρήσομαι: aor. 2 εὑρόμην or ηὑρ–, later aor. 1 εὑράμην:—Pass., fut. εὑρεθήσομαι and (in same sense) med. εὑρήσομαι: aor. 1 εὑρέθην or ηὑρέθην: pf. εὕρημαι or ηὕρ–. I. *to find, find out, discover:* c. acc. cognato, **εὕρημα εὑρίσκειν** *to make* an unexpected *discovery* or *gain*. 2. *to devise, invent*. II. *to find, gain, get, win, obtain*:—Med. *to find* or *get for oneself, procure, obtain*. 2. of merchandise, etc., *to fetch* so much money: hence, *to be worth, to sell for*.

εὐροέω, f. ήσω, (εὔροος) *to flow well*. II. metaph. *to flow* or *go on well*. III. *to be fluent*.

εὐ-ροίζητος, ον, (εὖ, ῥοιζέω) *loud-whizzing*.

εὑροίμην, εὕροιμι, aor. 2 opt. med. and act. of εὑρίσκω.

εὐρο-κλύδων, ωνος, ὁ, (Εὖρος, κλύδων) a tempestuous wind mentioned in Act. Apost. 27. 14: the name seems to mean *a storm from the East*.

εὕρομες, Dor. 1 pl. aor. 2 of εὑρίσκω.

εὗρον, aor. 2 of εὑρίσκω.

εὔ-ροος, ον, contr. εὔρους, ουν, (εὖ, ῥέω) *flowing well, fair-flowing*. II. of words, *flowing, fluent*.

εὔ-ροπος, ον, (εὖ, ῥέπω) *easily inclining* or *slipping*.

Εὖρος, ὁ, *the South-East wind*, Lat. *Eurus*.

εὖρος, τό, (εὐρύς) *breadth, width*, opp. to μῆκος: εὖρος, *in breadth*, opp. to ὕψος, *in height*.

ἐϋρ-ραφής, Ep. for εὐρραφής. (εὖ, ῥάπτω) *well-stitched*.

εὐρ-ρεής, ές, Ep. gen. ἐϋρρεῖος (for εὐρρεοῦς), *fair-flowing*.

ἐϋρ-ρείτης, ου, ὁ, = εὐρρεής·

ἐΰρ-ροος, Ep. for εὔροος.

εὐρύ, neut. of εὐρύς, often used as Adv.

εὐρῠ-άγυιος, α, ον, (εὐρύ, ἀγυιά) *with wide streets*, epith. of great cities, in Il. usually of Troy and Athens.

εὐρυ-αίχμας, ὁ, (εὐρύ, αἰχμή) *with stout lance*.

εὐρυ-βίας Ion. and Ep. –βίης, ου, ὁ, (εὐρύ, βία) *ruling widely, of far-extended power*.

εὐρυ-θέμεθλος poët. –θέμειλος, ον, (εὐρύ, θέμεθλον) *with broad foundations, spacious, extensive*.

εὐῤῥυθμία, ἡ, *good time* or *proportion*: *orderliness, gracefulness, graceful*. From

εὔ-ρυθμος, ον, *in good time* or *measure, rhythmical*, Lat. *numerosus*:—of persons, *orderly*: *well-proportioned, graceful*.

εὐρύθμως, Adv. of ευρυθμος, *in good order, gracefully*.

εὐρύ-κολπος, ον, *with spacious bosom*.

εὐρυ-κρείων, οντος, ὁ, *wide-ruling*.

εὐρυ-λείμων, ον, gen. ωνος, *with broad meadows*.

εὐρυ-μέδων, οντος, ὁ, *wide-ruling*.

εὐρυ-μέτωπος, ον, (εὐρύ, μέτωπον) *broad-fronted*.

εὐρῦναι, aor. 1 inf. of εὐρύνω.

εὐρύνω, f. ὔνῶ, (εὐρύς) *to make wide* or *broad*; εὐρῦναι ἀγῶνα *to make room for* the dance; τὸ μέσον εὐρύνειν *to leave a wide space* in the middle.

εὐρύ-νωτος, ον, (εὐρύ, νῶτος) *broad-backed, stout*.

εὐρυ-όδεια, ἡ, (εὐρύ, ὁδός) *with broad, open ways*.

εὐρυ-όπης Aeol. εὐρύοπᾰ, ὁ, (εὐρύ, ὄψομαι) *the far-glancing, far-seeing*, Homeric epith. of Jove.

εὐρύ-οψ, ὁ, acc. εὐρύοπα, = εὐρυόπης.

εὐρύ-πεδος, ον, (εὐρύ, πέδον) *with broad surface*.

εὐρύ-πορος, ον, *with broad ways*, of the sea.

εὐρυ-πρωκτία, ἡ, *the character of a lewd fellow*.

εὐρύ-πρωκτος, ον, (εὐρύ, πρωκτός) *lewd, obscene*: also *an adulterer*.

εὐρυ-πύλης, ές, (εὐρύ, πύλη) *with wide gates*.

εὐρυ-ρέεθρος, ον, (εὐρύ, ῥέεθρον) *with broad channel*.

εὐρυ-ρέων, ουσα, ον, (εὐρύ, ῥέω) *broad-flowing*.

ΕΥ'ΡΥ'Σ, εὐρεῖα, εὐρύ: gen. εὐρέος, είας, έος: acc. sing. εὐρύν, and sometimes εὐρέᾰ Ion. fem. nom. εὐρέα:—*wide, broad, spacious, far-reaching, wide-spread*:—Comp. εὐρύτερος; see εὐρύ.

εὐρυ-σάκης, ές, (εὐρύ, σάκος) *with broad shield*. [ᾰ]

εὐρυ-σθενής, ές, (εὐρύ, σθένος) *wide-ruling, mighty*.

εὐρύ-σορος, ον, *with wide bier* or *tomb*.

εὐρύ-στερνος, ον, (εὐρύ, στέρνον) *broad-breasted*.

εὐρυτέρως, Adv., Comp. of εὐρύ, *more widely*.

εὐρύ-τῑμος, ον, (εὐρύ, τιμή) *far-honoured*.

εὔ-ρῠτος, ον, (εὖ, ῥέω) *full-flowing*.

εὐρυ-φᾰρέτρης, ου, ὁ, (εὐρύ, φαρέτρα) *with wide quiver*.

εὐρυ-φυής, ές, (εὐρύ, φύω) *growing widely*.

εὐρυ-χᾰδής, ές, (εὐρύ, χαδεῖν) *wide-gaping, wide-mouthed*, of cups.

εὐρυ-χαίτης, ου, ὁ, (εὐρύ, χαίτη) *with wide-spread hair*.

εὐρύ-χορος, ον, shortened Ep. for εὐρύχωρος.

εὐρυχωρία, ἡ, *free space, plenty of room*; ἐν εὐρυχωρίᾳ in *the open sea*. From

εὐρύ-χωρος, ον, (εὐρύ, χώρα) *roomy, spacious*.

εὐ-ρώγης, (εὖ, ῥώξ) *rich in grapes*.

εὐρώδης, ες, poët. for εὐρύς.

εὐρώεις, εσσα, εν, (εὐρώς) *mouldering, dank and dark, squalid*; οἴκια εὐρώεντα, Virgil's *loca senta situ*.

εὑρών, οῦσα, όν, aor. 2 part. of εὑρίσκω.

ΕΥ'ΡΩ'ΠΗ, ἡ, *Europa, Europe*, as a geographic name first in the Homeric hymn to Apollo.

εὐρωπός, ή, όν, = εὐρύς.

ΕΥ'ΡΩ'Σ, ῶτος, ὁ, *mould, dank, decay*, Lat. *situs, squalor*.

εὐρωστία, η, *stoutness, strength*. From

εὔ-ρωστος, ον, (εὖ, ῥώννυμι) *stout, strong*. Adv. –τως.

εὐρῶτι, dat. sing. of εὐρώς.

εὐ-ρωτιάω, (εὐρώς) *to become* or *to be mouldy, to decay*; βίος εὐρωτιῶν *a coarse, unpolished* life.

ΕΥ'Σ, ὁ, *good, brave, noble*; gen. sing. ἑῆος; gen. plur. neut. ἐάων [ᾱ], as if from nom. ἐά, θεοί, δωτῆρες ἐάων the gods, givers *of good things*.

εὖσα, Dor. for ἐοῦσα, οὖσα, part. fem. of εἰμί *sum*.

εὗσα, aor. 1 of εὕω.

εὐσέβεια, ἡ, (εὐσεβής) *reverence towards the gods, piety, religion* Lat. *pietas*, 2. *credit* or *character for piety*.

εὐσεβέω, f. ήσω, (εὐσεβής) *to live* or *act piously*: *to be pious in* a thing: c. acc. pers. *to reverence*.

εὐ-σεβής, ές, (εὖ, σέβω) Lat. *pius, pious, religious, reverent*: of things, *holy, hallowed*.

εὐ-σεβία Ion. –ίη, poët. for εὐσέβεια.

εὔ-σελμος Ep. ἐΰσσ–, ον, (εὖ, σέλμα) *with good banks of oars, well-rowed*.

εὔ-σεπτος, ον, (εὖ, σέβω) *much reverenced, holy*.

εὔ-σημος, ον, (εὖ, σῆμα) *of good omen, auspicious.* II. *manifest, remarkable, conspicuous.*

εὐσθενέω, f. ήσω, *to be strong, healthy.* From

εὐ-σθενής, ές, (εὖ, σθένος) *stout: strong, firm.*

εὐ-σίπυος, ον, (εὖ, σιπύα) *with full pantry* or *larder.*

εὐ-σκάνδιξ, ῐκος, ὁ, ἡ, *abounding in chervil.*

εὔ-σκαρθμος, ον, (εὖ, σκαίρω) *swift-springing, high-bounding.*

εὐ-σκέπαστος, ον, (εὖ, σκεπάζω) *well-covered:* Sup. *-ότατος, serving as the best covering.*

εὐσκευέω, *to be well equipped.* From

εὔ-σκευος, ον, (εὖ, σκεῦος) *well-equipped.*

εὐ-σκίαστος, ον, (εὖ, σκιάζω) *well-shaded, shadowy.*

εὔ-σκιος, ον, (εὖ, σκιά) *shadowy.*

εὔ-σκοπος Ep. **ἐΰ-σκοπος**, ον, (εὖ, σκοπέω) *keen-sighted, watchful.* 2. of a place, *far-seeing* or *far-seen, commanding a wide view.* II. (εὖ, σκοπός) *shooting well, of unerring aim.*

εὔ-σοια, ἡ, *a healthy state, prosperity.* From

εὔ-σοος, ον, *well-secured, safe and well, happy.*

εὐ-σπειρής, ές, and **εὔσπειρος**, ον, (εὖ, σπεῖρα) *well-turned: wreathing, winding.*

εὐσπλαγχνία, ἡ, *goodness of heart.*

εὔ-σπλαγχνος, ον, (εὖ, σπλάγχνον) *with bowels of compassion, compassionate.*

εὔ-σπορος, ον, (εὖ, σπείρω) *well-sown: rich in seed.*

ἐΰσ-σελμος, Ep. for εὔσελμος.

ἐΰσ-σωτρος, Ep. for εὔσωτρος.

εὐστάθεια, ἡ, (εὐσταθής) *goodness of health.*

εὐστᾰθέω, f. ήσω, *to be steady, firm: to be calm,* of the sea. From

εὐ-στᾰθής Ep. **ἐϋσταθής**, ές, (εὖ, ἵσταμαι) *well-based, steadfast, firm: sound, healthy.*

εὐσταθίη, Ep. for εὐστάθεια.

εὐ-στᾰλής, ές, (εὖ, σταλῆναι) *well-arrayed: ready for action, serviceable.*

εὔ-σταχυς, υ, *rich in ears of corn: fruitful.*

εὐ-στέφανος Ep. **ἐϋστ-**, ον, *well-girded* or *well-crowned:* of a city, *circled with towers.*

εὐ-στέφιος, ον, poët. form for εὐστέφανος.

εὐ-στῐβής, ές, (εὖ, στιβεῖν) *well-trodden.*

εὔ-στολος, ον, (εὖ, στέλλω) = εὐσταλής.

εὐστομέω, f. ήσω, *to sing sweetly.* II. *to use words of good omen,* or *to preserve a religious silence* so as to avoid words of ill omen, = εὐφημέω. From

εὔ-στομος, ον, (εὖ, στόμα) *with good mouth:* of horses, *well-bitted.* II. *speaking* or *singing well, eloquent.* 2. *speaking auspicious words,* or *keeping silence* to avoid words of ill omen; neut. plur. as Adv., περὶ τούτων μοι εὔστομα κείσθω on this let me keep *a religious silence;* εὔστομ' ἔχε peace, be still!

εὔ-στοος, ον, (εὖ, στοά) *with goodly colonnades.*

εὐ-στόρθυγξ, υγγος, ὁ, ἡ, *from a good trunk.*

εὐστοχία, ἡ, *skill in shooting at a mark, good aim: quickness at guessing, wit, cleverness.* From

εὔ-στοχος, ον, *aiming well, hitting the mark.* 2. pass. *well aimed.* II. metaph. *guessing well, sharp, witty, clever.*

εὔστρα, ἡ, (εὕω) *a place for singeing swine.*

εὔ-στρεπτος Ep. **ἐΰστρ-**, ον, (εὖ, στρέφω) *well-twisted: easily turned, lissom.*

εὐ-στρεφής Ep. **ἐϋστρ-**, ές, (εὖ, στρέφω) *well-twisted.*

εὐ-στρόφᾰλιγξ, ιγγος, ὁ, ἡ, *well-curled, curly.*

εὔ-στροφος Ep. **ἐΰστρ-**, ον, (εὖ, στρέφω) *well-twisted: easily turning, nimble.*

εὔ-στρωτος, ον, (εὖ, στρώννυμι) *well spread with rugs* or *clothes,* Lat. *bene stratus.*

εὔ-στῡλος, ον, *with goodly pillars.*

εὐ-σύμβλητος old Att. **εὐ-ξύμβλ-**, ον, (εὖ, συμβάλλω) *easy to infer by comparison, easy to guess.*

εὐ-σύμβολος old Att. **εὐ-ξύμβ-**, ον, (εὖ, συμβολή) *easy to infer by comparison, easy to guess.* II. *easy to deal with, honest, upright.*

εὐ-σύνετος old Att. **εὐ-ξυν-**, ον, (εὖ, συνίημι) *quick of apprehension, intelligent.* II. *easily understood, intelligible.*

εὐσυνέτως, Adv. of εὐσύνετος, *with quickness of apprehension:* Comp. εὐσυνετώτερον.

εὐ-σύνοπτος, ον, *easily seen at a glance.*

εὔ-σφῡρος Ep. **ἐΰσφ-**, ον, (ἐΰς, σφυρόν) *with beautiful ankles.*

εὐσχημονέστερος, **-έστατος**, Comp. and Sup. of εὐσχήμων.

εὐσχημόνως, Adv. of εὐσχήμων, *with grace, like a gentleman:* Comp. εὐσχημονέστερον.

εὔ-σχημος, ον, = εὐσχήμων.

εὐσχημοσύνη, ἡ, *grace of manner, elegance.* From

εὐ-σχήμων, ον, gen. ονος, (εὖ, σχῆμα) *of good bearing, graceful, elegant, becoming:* in bad sense, *good in outward show, specious.*

εὐσχήμως, = εὐσχημόνως.

εὐ-σχῐδής, ές, and **εὔ-σχιστος**, ον, (εὖ, σχίζω) *easy to split* or *cleave.*

εὐσωμᾰτέω, f. ήσω, *to be sound in limb.* From

εὐ-σώμᾰτος, ον, (εὖ, σῶμα) *sound in limb.*

εὔ-σωτρος Ep. **ἐΰσσ-**, ον, (εὖ, σῶτρον) *with good felloes: with good wheels.*

εὐ-τᾰκής, ές, (εὖ, τακῆναι) *easy to melt.*

εὐτακτέω, f. ήσω, *to be orderly, behave well.* From

εὔ-τακτος, ον, (εὖ, τάσσω) *well-ordered, well-behaved:* of soldiers, *well-disciplined.* Hence

εὐτάκτως, Adv. *in good order.*

εὐταξία, ἡ, (εὐτακτέω) *good order, discipline.*

εὔ-ταρσος, ον, *delicate-footed.*

εὖτε, Adv. of Time, a poët. form of ὅτε, *when, at the time when: seeing that, since.* II. εὖτ' ἄν, like ὅταν, *so often as, whensoever, in the case that.*

εὐ-τειχής, ές, **εὐ-τείχεος**, ον, and **εὐ-τείχητος**, ον, (εὖ, τεῖχος) *well-walled, well-fortified, strong.*

εὐτεκνέω, (εὔτεκνος) *to have good* or *fine children.*

εὐτεκνία, ἡ, *the having good* or *fine children.*

εὔ-τεκνος, ον, (εὖ, τέκνον) *having many* or *fine children, blest with a goodly progeny;* εὔτεκνος ξυνωρίς a pair *of fair children.*

εὐτέλεια Ion. εὐτελίη, ἡ, *cheapness,* Lat. *vilitas:*

πρὸς εὐτελίην cheaply; χῆν εἰς εὐτέλειαν γεγραμμένος a goose painted on cheap terms. II. thrift, frugality, economy; ἐπὶ εὐτελείᾳ for economy.

εὐ-τελής, ές, (εὖ, τέλος) easily paid for, cheap, Lat. vilis. II. mean, paltry, worthless. III. thrifty, frugal.

εὐτελίη, ἡ, Ion. for εὐτέλεια.

εὐτελῶς, Adv. of εὐτελής, cheaply, at a cheap rate.

εὐ-τερπής, ές, (εὖ, τέρπω) delightful, charming.

εὐ-τέχνητος, ον, (εὖ, τεχνάομαι) wrought with skill.

εὐτεχνία, ἡ, skill in art. From

εὔ-τεχνος, ον, (εὖ, τέχνη) skilful, ingenious.

εὐ-τλήμων, ον, gen. ονος, much-enduring, steadfast.

εὔ-τμητος Ep. **εὔτμ-**, ον, (εὖ, τέμνω) well-cut.

εὐτοκέω, f. ήσω, (εὔτοκος) to bring forth easily. Hence

εὐ-τοκία, ἡ, an easy childbirth, happy birth.

εὔ-τοκος, ον, (εὖ, τεκεῖν) bringing forth easily.

εὐτολμέω, f. ήσω, (εὔτολμος) to be daring. Hence

εὐτολμία, ἡ, courage, boldness.

εὔ-τολμος, ον, (εὖ, τόλμα) brave-spirited, courageous.

εὔ-τονος, ον, (εὖ, τείνω) well-stretched, well-strung, sinewy, nervous. Hence

εὐτόνως, Adv. with main strength.

εὔ-τοξος, ον, (εὖ, τόξον) with good arrows.

εὐ-τόρνευτος, ον, (εὖ, τορνεύω) well-rounded.

εὔ-τορνος, ον, well-turned, round

εὐ-τράπεζος, ον, (εὖ, τράπεζα) with a good table, hospitable, luxurious, sumptuous.

εὐτρᾰπελία, ἡ, wit, liveliness, politeness, Lat. urbanitas. 2. coarse jesting, ribaldry. From

εὐ-τράπελος, ον, (εὖ, τρέπω) easily turning: hence versatile, ingenious, clever. 2. witty, lively, Lat. facetus. 3. tricky, dishonest.

εὐ-τρᾰφής, ές, (εὖ, τραφῆναι) well-grown, thriving. II. act. nourishing.

εὐ-τρεπής, ές, (εὖ, τρέπω) ready to turn, prepared, ready. Hence

εὐ-τρεπίζω, f. ίσω Att. ιῶ: Pass., pf. ηὐτρέπισμαι: —to make ready, get ready, prepare: to make friendly, conciliate:—Pass. to be ready:—Med. to get oneself ready.

εὔ-τρεπτος, ον, easily turned, changeable.

εὐτρεπῶς, Adv. of εὐτρεπής, in a state of preparation.

εὐ-τρεφής Ep. **ἐϋτρ-**, ές, (εὖ, τρέφω) well-fed.

εὔ-τρητος Ep. **ἐΰτρ-**, ον, well bored or pierced.

εὐ-τρίαινα, Dor. for -ης, ὁ, (εὖ, τρίαινα) with goodly trident.

εὔ-τρῐχες, nom. pl. of εὔθριξ.

εὔ-τρῐχος, ον, = εὔθριξ.

εὐτροπία, ἡ, versatility, Lat. versutia. From

εὔ-τροπος, ον, (εὖ, τρέπω) easily turning, versatile.

εὐ-τρόχᾰλος Ep. **ἐϋτρ-**, ον, (εὖ, τρέχω) running well, quick-moving. 2. (εὖ, τροχός) well-rounded.

εὔ-τροχος Ep. **ἐΰτρ-**, ον, (εὖ, τροχός) well-wheeled or well-rounded. II. running easily.

εὔ-τῡκος, ον, rare poët. form for εὔτυκτος.

εὔ-τυκτος, ον, (εὖ, τεύχω) well-made, well-wrought, εὔτυκτον ποιεῖσθαί τι to make ready.

εὐτῠχέω, f. ήσω: in augm. tenses, impf. εὐτύχουν or ηὐτ-, aor. 1 εὐτύχησα or ηὐτ-, etc.: (εὐτυχής):—to be lucky, to be well off, to succeed. 2. of things, to turn out well, prosper: pf. pass. impers., εὐτύχηταί τινι things have gone well with him. Hence

εὐτυχέως, Ion. for εὐτυχῶς.

εὐτύχημα, ατος, τό, a piece of good luck, success.

εὐ-τῠχής, ές, (εὖ, τυχεῖν) well-off, successful, lucky, fortunate, prosperous.

εὐτῠχία, ἡ, (εὐτυχέω) success, good luck, prosperity: in plur. successes.

εὐτῠχῶς Ion. -έως, Adv. of εὐτυχής, with good fortune, successfully: Comp. εὐτυχέστερον, Sup. -έστατα.

εὐ-ὕᾰλος, ον, (εὖ, ὕαλος) with or of good glass.

εὔ-υδρος, ον, (εὖ, ὕδωρ) well-watered, abounding in water: of a river, with good water: Comp. εὐυδρότερος.

εὔ-υμνος, ον, celebrated in many hymns.

εὐ-υφής, ές, (εὖ, ὑφή) well-woven.

εὐ-φᾱμία, **εὔ-φᾱμος**, Dor. for εὐφημ-.

εὐ-φᾰρέτρης, ου, ὁ, Dor. -ας, α, (εὖ, φαρέτρα) with beautiful quiver.

εὐ-φεγγής, ές, (εὖ, φέγγος) with clear light, bright.

εὐφημέω, f. ήσω, (εὔφημος) to use words of good omen or to abstain from words of ill omen: hence I. to keep silence, to observe a solemn silence; in imperat. εὐφήμει, εὐφημεῖτε, hush! be silent! Lat. favete linguis. II. to shout in honour of any one, or in triumph. III. to sound auspiciously. Hence

εὐφημία, ἡ, the use of words of good omen or the avoidance of words of bad omen: hence I. solemn silence during religious rites. II. praise, worship: in plur. songs of praise.

εὔ-φημος, ον, (εὖ, φήμη) of good sound or omen, auspicious: of persons, using only words of good omen or avoiding words of ill omen:—hence, I. religiously silent. II. interpreting favourably; πρὸς τὸ εὔφημον in a good sense.

εὔ-φθογγος, ον, (εὖ, φθέγγομαι) well-sounding, sweet-voiced.

εὐ-φῐλής, ές, (εὖ, φιλέω) well-beloved. II. act. loving well.

εὐ-φίλητος, ον, also η, ον, (εὖ, φιλέω) well-beloved.

εὐ-φῐλό-παις, παιδος, ὁ, ἡ, (εὖ, φιλέω, παῖς) fond of children, or pass. beloved of children.

εὔ-φλεκτος, ον, (εὖ, φλέγω) easily set on fire.

εὐφορέω, f. ήσω, (εὔφορος) to bring forth abundantly.

εὐ-φόρητος, ον, (εὖ, φορέω) easily borne, tolerable.

εὐ-φόρμιγξ, ιγγος, ὁ, ἡ, with beautiful lyre: playing beautifully on it.

εὔ-φορος, ον, (εὖ, φέρω) well or patiently borne. 2. easily worn, convenient, manageable. II. act. bearing well, hence of a breeze, favourable: of the body, sound, healthy.

εὔ-φορτος, ον, well freighted or laden.

εὐφόρως, Adv. of *εὔφορος*, *patiently*, *readily*.

εὐφράδεια, ἡ, (εὐφραδής) *correctness of language*.

εὐ-φρᾰδής, ές, (εὖ, φράζω) *speaking well* or *eloquently*:—Ep. Adv. **εὐφραδέως**, *in set terms*, *eloquently*.

εὐφρᾰδίη, ἡ, poët. for **εὐφράδεια**.

εὐ-φραίνω Ep. **ἐϋφρ-**: f. *εὐφρᾰνῶ* Ep. *εὐφρανέω*: aor. 1 *εὔφρᾱνα* Ep. *εὔφρηνα*:—Pass., f. *εὐφρανθήσομαι*, but also with f. med. *εὐφρανοῦμαι* in same sense, Ion. 2 sing. *εὐφράνεαι*: aor. 1 *εὐφράνθην*: (*εὔφρων*):—*to cheer*, *gladden*. II. Pass. *to rejoice*; c. part., *ὁρῶν εὐφραίνεται is rejoiced at* seeing. Hence

εὐ-φραντικός, ή, όν, *cheering*, *delightful to*.

εὐφρῆναι, Ep. aor. 1 inf. of *εὐφραίνω*.

εὐ-φρονέων Ep. **ἐϋφρ-**, participial Adj. (εὖ, φρονέω) *well-meaning*, *well-judging*, *kindly-disposed*.

εὐ-φρόνη, ἡ, (εὔφρων) *the kindly time*, i. e. *night*, euphemism for *νύξ*. Hence

εὐφρονίδης, ου, ὁ, *son of Night*.

εὐφρόνως, Adv. of *εὔφρων*, *with good cheer*: *graciously*.

εὐ-φροσύνη Ep. **ἐϋφρ-**, ἡ, (εὔφρων) *cheerfulness*, *mirth*, *merriment*: of a banquet, *good cheer*: in pl. *glad thoughts*, *festivities*. [ῠ]

εὐ-φρόσυνος, ον, (εὔφρων) poët. form, *cheery*.

εὔ-φρων Ep. **ἐΰφρ-**, ον, (εὖ, φρήν) *cheerful*, *gladsome*, *merry*, *light-hearted*. 2. act. *cheering*, *making glad* or *merry*, *comforting*. II. *well-minded*, *well-disposed*, *gracious*.

εὐ-φυής, ές, (εὖ, φυή) *well-grown*, *shapely*, *goodly*: *graceful*. II. *of good natural parts*: *clever*, *witty*; also *of good disposition*. Hence

εὐφυΐα, ἡ, *goodness of shape*. II. *goodness of disposition* or *good natural parts*, *cleverness*.

εὐ-φύλακτος, ον, (εὖ, φυλάσσω) *easy to keep* or *guard*; *εὐφυλακτότερα γίγνεται* it is *easier to keep watch*.

εὔ-φυλλος, ον, (εὖ, φύλλον) *with thick foliage*.

εὐφυῶς, Adv. of *εὐφυής*, *cleverly*: Comp. *-νέστερον*.

εὐφωνία, ἡ, *goodness of voice*. F^ro^m

εὔ-φωνος, ον, (εὖ, φωνή) *sweet-voiced*; *loud-voiced*.

εὐ-χαίτης, ου, ὁ, (εὖ, χαίτη) *with beautiful hair*: of plants, *with beautiful leaves*.

εὔ-χαλκος, ον, (εὖ, χαλκός) *wrought of fine brass*, or *well wrought in brass*.

εὐ-χάλκωτος, ον, *well wrought of brass*.

εὔ-χᾰρις, neut. εὔχαρι, gen. ιτος, (εὖ, χάρις) *pleasing*, *engaging*: *agreeable*: *popular*, Lat. *gratiosus*.

εὐχᾰριστέω, f. *ήσω*, *to be thankful*, *return thanks*: hence *to requite*. Hence

εὐχᾰριστία, ἡ, *thankfulness*, *gratitude*. II. *a giving of thanks*, *thanksgiving*: *the holy Eucharist*.

εὐ-χάριστος or *-ιτος*, ον, (εὖ, χαρίζομαι) *winning*, *agreeable*, *pleasant*. II. *grateful*, *thankful*, Lat. *gratus*: Adv., *εὐχαρίστως διακεῖσθαι πρός τινα* to be *gratefully* disposed towards him.

εὔ-χειρ, ειρος, ὁ, ἡ, *ready of hand*, *handy*, *dexterous*.

εὐ-χείρωτος, ον, (εὖ, χειρόω) *easy to overcome*.

εὐχέρεια, ἡ, *readiness of hand*, *dexterity*, *readiness*, *skill*. 2. *proneness* or *inclination for* a thing. 3. in bad sense, *recklessness*. From

εὐ-χερής, ές, (εὖ, χείρ) *quick* or *ready of hand*, *handy*, *dexterous*, *expert*. 2. in bad sense, *reckless*. II. *easy to handle* or *manage*, *manageable*. Hence

εὐχερῶς. Adv. *readily*: *recklessly*.

εὐχετάομαι, Ep. for *εὔχομαι*, only used in pres. and impf.; Ep. inf. *εὐχετάασθαι*, 3 pl. impf. *εὐχετόωντο*: Dep.:—*to pray*, *offer one's vows*. II. *to boast oneself*, *vaunt*, *profess*.

εὐχή, ἡ, (εὔχομαι) *a prayer*, *wi•h* or *vow*, Lat. *votum*. 2. *a prayer for evil*, *a curse*, *imprecation*.

εὔ-χῑλος, ον, *rich in fodder*. II. of a horse, *well-fed*, *in good condition*.

εὐ-χίμᾰρος, ον, (εὖ, χίμαρος) *rich in goat‹*

εὔ-χλοος, ον, contr. **χλους**, *ουν* (εὖ, χλοά) *making fresh and green*.

ΕΥ῞ΧΟΜΑΙ: impf. *εὐχόμην* or *ηὐ* fut. *εὔξομαι*: aor. 1 *εὐξάμην* or *ηὐ* : aor. 1 part. *εὐχθεὶς* in pass. sense; so also pf. *ηὖγμαι*; but 3 sing. plqpf. *ηὖκτο* in act. sense: Dep.:—*to pray*, *pay one's vows*, Lat. *precari*: c. acc. pers. *to pray to*, *pray* or *beseech* one. 2. c. inf. *to pray that*. 3. c. acc. objecti, *to pray for*, *long* or *wish for*. II *to vow* or *promise to* do; *εὔχεσθαι κατὰ χιμάρων to make a vow of* goats, i. e. vow to offer them. 2. c. acc. rei, *to vow* or *devote* a thing to some god. III. *to vow loudly*, *make great* promises, *boast*, *vaunt oneself*: but often, *to profess*, *maintain*, *assert*.

εὔ-χορδος, ον, (εὖ, χορδή) *well-strung*, *harmonious*.

εὖχος, εος, τό, (εὔχομαι) *a thing prayed for*, *vow*, Lat. *votum*. 2. *a votive offering*. II. *one's boast* or *pride*.

εὔ-χρηστος, ον, (εὖ, χράομαι) *easy to make use of*, *serviceable*. Adv. *-τως*.

εὐ-χροέω, f. *ήσω*, *to be of a good complexion*. From

εὐ-χροής, ές, poët. for *εὔχροος*, *of good complexion*.

εὔ-χροος, ον, contr. **-χρους**, *ουν*, (εὖ, χρόα) *of good complexion*, *fresh-looking*, *healthy*:—Comp. **εὐχροώτερος** or *-ούστερος*.

εὔ-χρῡσος, ον, *rich in gold*.

εὔ-χρως, ων, — *εὔχροος*.

εὐχωλή, ἡ, (εὔχομαι) poët. form of **εὐχή**, *a prayer*, *vow*, Lat. *votum*. II. *boasting*: *a boast*, *vaunt*, *matter of boasting*. Hence

εὐχωλῐμαῖος, α, ον, *bound by a vow*.

εὐ-ψάμᾰθος, ον, *with good sands*, *sandy*.

εὐψῡχέω, f. *ήσω*, (εὔψυχος) *to be of good courage*. II. *εὐψύχει farewell!* inscr. on tombs, like Lat. *have pia anima!* Hence

εὐψῡχία, *good courage*, *stoutness of heart*.

εὔ-ψῡχος, ον, (εὖ, ψυχή) *of good courage*, *stout of heart*, Lat. *animosus*. Adv. **-χως**, *with good courage*.

ΕΥ῞Ω, f. **εὕσω**: aor. 1 **εὗσα**:—*to singe*: metaph. of a scolding wife, **εὕει ἄτερ δαλοῦ ἄνδρα** *she roasts* her husband without the help of a fire.

εὐώδης, ες, (εὖ, ὄδωδα pf. of ὄζω) *sweet-smelling.* Hence

εὐωδία, ἡ, *a sweet smell, fragrance.*

εὐωδώθην, aor. 1 pass. of εὐοδόω.

εὐ-ώλενος, ον, (εὖ, ὠλένη) *fair-armed.*

εὐ-ώνυμος, ον, (εὖ, ὄνομα) *of good name, honourable: of good omen.* II. euphemistic for the ill-omened word ἀρίστερος, *left, on the left hand or side;* ἐξ εὐωνύμου (sub. χειρός) on *the left* hand.

εὐ-ῶπις, ιδος, fem. of εὐώψ, *fair-eyed* or *fair-faced.*

εὐ-ωπός, όν, (εὖ, ὤψ) *fair to look on, friendly.*

εὐ-ωχέω, f. ήσω, (εὖ, ἔχω) *to treat well: to entertain hospitably, feast:*—Pass., with fut. med. -ήσομαι, aor. and pf. pass., εὐωχήθην, -ημαι, *to be well entertained, to be regaled, fare sumptuously;* c. acc., κρέα εὐωχοῦ *make merry on* your meat: generally, *to relish, enjoy.* Hence

εὐωχία, η, *good cheer, feasting.*

εὐ-ώψ, ῶπος, ὁ, ἡ, (εὖ, ὤψ) *fair-eyed* or *fair-faced, goodly.*

ἔφᾱ, Dor. 3 sing. impf. of φημί.

ἐφᾰάνθην, Ep. aor. 1 pass. of φαίνω.

ἐφ-ᾱβος, **ἐφαβικός**, Dor. for ἐφηβ–.

ἐφ-ᾰγιστεύω, f. σω, (ἐπί, ἅγος) *to perform sacred rites* over a thing.

ἐφ-αγνίζω, f. ίσω Att. ιῶ, *to make offerings on* a grave.

ἔφᾰγον, aor. 2 of ἐσθίω: see φαγεῖν.

ἐφ-αιρέομαι, Pass. *to be chosen in addition* or *in succession to* another.

ἐφ-άλιος, ον, (ἐπί, ἅλς) = ἔφαλος.

ἐφ-άλλομαι, fut. ἐφαλοῦμαι: Ep. 3 sing. aor. 2 ἐπᾶλτο part. ἐπιάλμενος or ἐπάλμενος: Dep.:—*to spring upon, to assail:* without hostile sense, ἐπιάλμενος ἵππων *having leaped upon* or *into* the chariot: absol., κύσσε μιν ἐπιάλμενος he kissed him *having leaped upon* him.

ἔφ-ᾰλος, ον, (ἐπί, ἅλς) *on* or *by the sea.*

ἐφᾱλόω, Dor. for ἐφηλόω.

ἔφᾰμαν [ᾰ], Dor. for ἐφάμην, aor. 2 med. of φημί.

ἐφ-αμαξεύω, (ἐπί, ἅμαξα) *to drive wains over:* Ion. pf. part. pass. ἐπημαξευμένος *traversed by wains.*

ἐφᾱμέριος, **ἐφάμερος** [ᾱ], Dor. for ἐφήμ–.

ἐφ-άμιλλος, ον, (ἐπί, ἅμιλλα) *a match for, rivalling, vying with.* 2. pass. *to be striven, contended for.*

ἔφᾰν, 3 pl. aor. 2 of φημί.

ἐφ-ανδάνω, impf. -ανον, *to please, be grateful* or *welcome to:* Ep. also ἐπιανδάνω, impf. ἐπιήνδανον.

ἐφάνην [ᾰ], aor. 2 pass. of φαίνω.

ἐφάνθην, aor. 1 pass. of φαίνω.

ἔφαντο, 3 pl. aor. 2 med. of φημι.

ἐφ-άπαξ, Adv. *once for all: at once.*

ἐφ-απλόω, f. ώσω, *to fold* or *spread over.*

ἐφ-άπτω Ion. **ἐπάπτω**: f. ἐφάψω: aor. 1 ἐφῆψα: pf. pass. ἐφῆμμαι:—*to fasten on* or *to:* hence *to fix firmly, decree.* II. Pass. *to be hung over, impend over,* in pf. and plqpf. ἐφῆπται, ἐφῆπτο, like Lat. *imminet, imminebat;* Τρώεσσι κήδε' ἐφῆπται woes *impend over* the Trojans. III. Med. *to lay hold of, grasp, touch: to seize hold upon, claim.* 2. *to reach, attain to,* Lat. *attingere;* so Ion. pf. part. pass., εἴδεος ἐπαμμένος *possessed of* beauty. Hence

ἐφ-αρμόζω, f. σω, *to fit on* or *to, to suit, coincide with.* II. trans. *to fit* one thing *on* or *to* another, *to adapt, accommodate.*

ἐφαρμόσδων, Dor. for ἐφαρμόζων.

ἐφαρμόσσειε, 3 sing. Ep. aor. 1 opt. of ἐφαρμόζω.

ἐφ-αρμόττω, Att. for ἐφαρμόζω.

ἐφαρξάμην, **ἐφάρχθην**, Att. for ἐφραξάμην, ἐφράχθην, aor. 1 med. and pass. of φράσσω.

ἔφᾰτο, **ἔφαντο**, 3 sing. and pl. aor. 2 med. of φημί.

ἐφ-έδρα Ion. ἐπέδρη, ἡ *a sitting at* or *by: a siege, blockade,* Lat. *obsessio.*

ἐφ-εδράω, f. ήσω, (ἐπί, ἕδρα) *to sit* or *rest upon.*

ἐφ-εδρεία, ἡ, *a sitting upon.* II. *a lying in wait,* Lat. *insidiae.* From

ἐφεδρεύω, f. σω, *to sit* or *rest upon.* II. *to lie by, lie in wait: to watch for:*—also *to halt.* From

ἔφ-εδρος, ον, (ἐπί, ἕδρα) *sitting on;* λεόντων ἔφεδρος *seated on* a chariot drawn by lions *lying by* or *near.* II. *lying by and watching, lying in wait for* an enemy. III. *posted in reserve,* of a third combatant who sits by to fight the conqueror: *an avenger, a successor.*

ἐφ-έζομαι, fut. -εδοῦμαι: Dep.:—*to sit upon.* 2. *to sit by* or *near.*

ἐφέηκα, Ep. aor. 1 of ἐφίημι.

ἐφείην, ης, η, aor. 2 opt. of ἐφίημι.

ἐφειμένος, pf. pass. part. of ἐφέννυμι.

ἐφεῖναι, aor. 2 inf. of ἐφίημι.

ἐφεισάμην, aor. 1 of φείδομαι.

ἐφείω, ῃς, ῃ, Ep. aor. 2 subj. of ἐφίημι.

ἔφ-εκτος, ον, (ἐπί, ἕκτος) $1 + \frac{1}{6} = \frac{7}{6}$: τόκος ἔφεκτος interest *at the rate of* $\frac{1}{6}$ *of the principal,* = $16\frac{2}{3}$ p. cent.

ἐφ-ελίσσω, f. ξω, *to roll on* or *along.*

ἐφελκύσαι [ῠ], aor. 1 inf. of ἐφέλκω.

ἐφ-ελκυστικός, ή, όν, *drawing on, attractive.* From

ἐφ-έλκω Ion. ἐπέλκω: fut. ἐφέλξω, but the aor. 1 in use is ἐφείλκῠσα (formed from *ἐφελκύω):—*to draw on* or *towards: to drag* or *trail after* one: of a ship, *to tow after.* 2. *to drink off, drain.* II. Pass., πόδες ἐφελκόμενοι feet *dragged* or *trailing along;* οἱ ἐπελκόμενοι *the stragglers* of an army. III. Med. *to draw* or *drag after* one; ἐφέλκετο μείλινον ἔγχος *he trailed along* the spear (which was stuck in his foot); ἐφέλκεται ἄνδρα σίδηρος iron *draws* men *after it,* i. e. *attracts* them, *tempts* them; ἐφέλκεσθαι τὴν θύραν *to pull to* the door. . *to bring on, entail* consequences 3. *claim, assume.*

ἐφέμεν, Ep. for ἐφεῖναι, aor. 2 inf. of ἐφίημι.

ἐφ-έννῡμι, = more freq. ἐπιέννυμι.

ἐφ-εξῆς Ion. **ἐπεξῆς** poët. **ἐφεξείης**, Adv. (ἐπί, ἔχομαι) *in order, one after another, in a line.* II. of Time, *successively: thereupon.*

ἔφεξις, εως, ἡ, (ἐπέχω) *an excuse, pretext.*

ἐφ-έπω: impf. ἐφεῖπον Ep. ἔφεπον Ion. ἐφέπεσκον: fut. ἐφέψω: aor. 2 ἐπέσπον: inf. ἐπισπεῖν: part. ἐπισπάν:—*to go after, follow upon, pursue.* 2. *to drive on, urge on.* 3. *to follow* a pursuit, *busy oneself about, manage.* 4. *to seek out, search, traverse.* 5. πότμον ἐπισπεῖν, θάνατον καὶ πότμον ἐπισπεῖν, θανέειν καὶ πότμον ἐπισπεῖν *to seek out* one's fate or death, *bring it on* oneself, *incur* it. II. Med., impf. ἐφειπόμην: fut. ἐφέψομαι: aor. 2 ἐφεσπόμην, inf. ἐπισπέσθαι:—*to follow, pursue: to accompany, attend upon: to obey, comply with.*

ἐφ-ερπύζω, late form for ἐφέρπω.

ἐφ-έρπω, f. ἐφέρψω: aor. 1 ἐφείρπυσα, inf. -ερπύσαι (formed from ἐφερπύζω):—*to creep upon* or *towards.* II. *to come upon gradually* or *stealthily:* absol., χρόνος ἐφέρπων *advancing* time.

ἔφες, aor. 2 imperat. of ἐφίημι.

ἐφέσιμος δίκη, a suit, *in which there was the right of appeal* to another court. From

ἔφεσις, εως, ἡ, (ἐφίημι) *a throwing at.* 2. as Att. law-term, *an appeal to another court.*

ἐφ-έσπερος, ον, (ἐπί, ἑσπέρα) *western.*

ἐφ-έσπομαι, poët. for ἐφέπομαι.

ἐφέσσαι, Ep. for ἐφέσαι, aor. 1 inf. of ἐφίζω.

ἔφεσσαι, Ep. aor. 1 imperat. med. of ἐφίζω.

ἐφεσσάμενος, Ep. aor. 1 part. med. of ἐφίζω.

ἐφέσσομαι, Ep. fut. med. of ἐφίζω.

ἐφεσταότες Att. -ῶτες, nom. pl. pf. part. of ἐφίστημι.

ἐφεστᾶσιν, for ἐφεστήκασιν, 3 pl. pf. of ἐφίστημι.

ἐφ-έστιος Ion. ἐπίστιος, ον, (ἐπί, ἑστία) *by one's own hearth* or *fireside: having a hearth and home:* with Verbs of motion, *towards home.* 2. *sitting at* or *by the hearth,* of suppliants; ἐφέστιος δμώς a suppliant *inmate* of the house. II. *of the house* or *household:* hence, ἐφέστιον Ion. ἐπίστιον, τό, *a household, family;* θεοὶ ἐφέστιοι *the household* gods, Lat. *Lares* or *Penates:* also of gods, *presiding over hospitality.*

ἐφ-εστρίδιον, τό, Dim. of ἐφεστρίς.

ἐφ-εστρίς, ίδος, ἡ, (ἐφέννυμι) *an upper garment, wrapper, cloak, mantle.*

ἐφεστώς, for ἐφεστηκώς, pf. part. of ἐφίστημι.

ἐφέτης, ου, ὁ, (ἐφίημι) *a commander.* II. οἱ ἐφέται, at Athens, *a special court to try criminal cases.*

ἐφετμή, ἡ, (ἐφίημι) *a command, behest.*

ἔφευξα, aor. 1 of φεύζω (not of φεύγω).

ἐφευρετής, οῦ, ὁ, *an inventor, contriver.* From

ἐφ-ευρίσκω Ion. ἐπ-: fut. ἐφευρήσω: aor. 2 ἐφεῦρον:—*to find by chance, find anywhere:* generally, *to discover, invent, find out:* also *to detect* one doing.

ἐφεψάσθω, poët. aor. 1 imperat. med. of ἐφέπω.

ἐφ-εψιάομαι, Dep. *to mock* or *scoff at, ridicule.*

ἐφεώρᾱτο, 3 sing. plqpf. of ἐφοράω.

ἐφεώρων, Ion. impf. of ἐφοράω.

ἐφ-ηβάω, f. ήσω, *to come to man's estate.*

ἐφηβεία, ἡ, (ἐφηβεύω) *manhood, man's estate.*

ἐφήβειος, α, ον, (ἔφηβος) *youthful.*

ἐφηβικός, ή, όν, Dor. ἐφαβικός, ά, όν, *of* or *for a young man:* τὸ ἐφηβικόν *the body of youth.* From

ἔφ-ηβος Dor. ἔφᾱβος, ον, (ἐπί, ἥβη) *arrived at manhood* or *man's estate,* which was, at Athens, *eighteen.* Hence

ἐφηβοσύνη, ἡ, *the age of an* ἔφηβος, *manhood.*

ἐφ-ηγέομαι, Dep. *to lead against* one. II. *to lead to* a place, *give information.*

ἐφ-ήδομαι, Pass. *to exult over.*

ἐφῆκα, aor. 1 of ἐφίημι.

ἐφ-ήκω, *to have arrived at:*—*to extend* or *reach to.*

ἐφ-ῆλιξ, ικος, ὁ, ἡ, = ἔφηβος.

ἐφ-ηλόω, f. ώσω, (ἐπί, ἧλος) *to nail on, nail firmly:* metaph. in Pass., *it is fixed* or *determined.*

ἔφ-ημαι, Pass. *to sit on, at,* or *by.*

ἐφημερία, ἡ, *a daily order* or *course.* From

ἐφ-ημέριος Dor. ἐφᾱμ-, ον, also α, ον, (ἐπί, ἡμέρα) *for* or *during the day, the whole day through;* ἐφημέρια φρονεῖν to take no thought for the morrow: of men, ἐφημέριοι *creatures of a day, ephemeral:* hence generally, *lasting but a day, short-lived.*

ἐφ-ήμερος Dor. ἐφᾱμ- Aeol. ἐπᾱμ-, ον, (ἐπί, ἡμέρα) *lasting* or *living but a day, short-lived.* II. *daily.*

ἐφημοσύνη, ἡ, (ἐφίημι) *a command, behest.*

ἔφηνα, aor. 1 of φαίνω.

ἐφῆπται, ἐφῆπτο, 3 sing. pf. and plqpf. pass. of ἐφάπτω.

ἔφησα, aor. 1 of φημί.

ἔφησθα, for ἔφης, 2 sing. aor. 2 of φημί.

ἐφήσω, fut. of ἐφίημι.

ἔφθαξα, Dor. for ἔφθᾰσα, aor. 1 of φθάνω.

ἔφθαρμαι, pf. pass. of φθείρω; 3 pl. ἐφθάραται.

ἔφθᾰσα, aor. 1 of φθάνω.

ἐφθέγξατο, 3 sing. aor. 1 of φθέγγομαι.

ἔφθειρα, aor. 1 of φθείρω.

ἐφθ-ημιμερής, (ἑπτά, ἡμιμερής) *containing seven halves,* i. e. $3\frac{1}{2}$: esp. in metre, *of three feet and a half,* as the first $3\frac{1}{2}$ feet of a Hexameter or Iambic Trimeter: cf. πενθημιμερής.

ἔφθην, aor. 2 of φθάνω (as if from φθημι).

ἐφθίατο, Ion. 3 pl. plqpf. or aor. 2 pass. of φθίνω.

ἔφθιεν, 3 sing. impf. of φθίω = φθίνω.

ἔφθιθεν, Ep. 3 pl. aor. 1 pass. of φθίνω.

ἔφθῑτο, 3 sing. Ep. aor. 2 med. of φθίνω.

ἔφθορα, pf. med. of φθείρω.

ἐφθός, ή, όν, verb. Adj. of ἕψω, *boiled, dressed.*

ἐφ-ιζάνω, = ἐφίζω, only used in pres. and impf.

ἐφίζω Dor. ἐφίσδω: impf. ἔφιζον Ion. ἐφίζεσκον: intr. *to sit upon, at,* or *by.* II. Causal in Ep. fut. med. ἐφέσσομαι, aor. 1 inf. act. and med. ἐφέσσαι, ἐφέσσασθαι, *to make to sit upon, set upon.*

ἐφ-ίημι, fut. ἐφήσω: aor. 1 ἐφῆκα Ion. and Ep. ἐφέηκα: aor. 2 imperat. ἔφες, Ep. subj. ἐφείω: there is also a 3 sing. impf. ἐφίει (as if from *ἐφιέω):—*to send to* one. 2. *to send against, launch,* or *send at: to set on, to do* a thing; ἐφιέναι χεῖράς τινι *to lay hands on* him. 3. of events, *to send upon* one; ἐφιέναι νόστον τινί *to permit* one a return. II. *to let go, loosen:* metaph. *to give a rein to: to give* *up, yield:* also intr. (sub. ἑαυτόν), *to give oneself up to.* 2. *to permit, allow.* III. *to put* the male *to* the female, Lat. *admittere.* IV. as law-term, *to refer to* a higher judge, *to appeal;* cf. ἔφεσις. V. Med. ἐφίεμαι, fut. ἐφήσομαι, *to lay one's command* or *behest upon: to enjoin, command: to intrust* to one: *to allow* one *to do* a thing. ^ *to* ~·~ *it, long after, desire.*

ἐφ-ικνέομαι Ion. ἐπ–: fut. ἐφίξομαι: aor. 2 ἐφῑκόμην: pf. ἐφῖγμαι: Dep.:—*to come up to, reach, attain to,* c. gen.: of things, *to hit exactly:* metaph., ἐφικέσθαι λέγων or λόγῳ, *to touch the right point in speaking:* absol. *to extend.* II. *to come upon, visit,* c. acc.; ἐπικέσθαι (Ion. aor. 2 inf.) μάστιγι πληγὰς τὸν Ἑλλήσποντον *to visit* the Hellespont *with* blows. Hence

ἐφικτός, ή, όν, verb. Adj., *easy to reach.*

ἐφίλαθεν, ἐφίλασα, Dor. for ἐφίλησα, ἐφίληθεν.

ἐφίλᾰτο, 3 sing. Ep. aor. 1 med. of φιλέω.

ἐφίληθεν, Ep. 3 plur. aor. 1 pass. of φιλέω.

ἐφ-ίμερος, ον, (ἐπί, ἵμερος) *longed for, desired: delightful, agreeable.* [ῑ]

ἐφιμώθην, aor. 1 pass. of φιμόω.

ἐφ-ίππιος, ον, (ἐπί, ἵππος) *of* or *for a horse* or *riding:* τὸ ἐφίππιον (sub. στρῶμα), Lat. *ephippia, a saddle-cloth, a horse's harness.*

ἔφ-ιππος, ον, (ἐπί, ἵππος) *on horseback:* κλύδων ἔφιππος a rushing wave *of horses.*

ἐφ-ίπτᾰμαι, late form of ἐπιπέτομαι.

ἐφ-ισδάνω, ἐφ-ίσδω, Dor. for ἐφίζανω, ἐφίζω.

ἐφ-ίστημι Ion. ἐπ–: A. Causal in pres., impf., fut., and aor. 1 ἐπέστησα:—*to set* or *place upon: to impose.* 2. *to set* one person *over* another: *to appoint to* an office 3. ἐφιστάναι τινὶ ἀγῶνα *to found* or *institute* games *in honour of* a person. II. *to set by* or *near.* III. *to check, make halt.* IV. ἐφιστάναι τὸν νοῦν, *to attend to,* Lat. *animum advertere:* absol., ἐφιστάναι *to attend.*

B. Intrans. in Pass. and in aor. 2 act. ἐπέστην, pf. ἐφέστηκα, plqpf. ἐφεστήκειν:—*to stand upon: to be imposed.* 2. *to stand* or *float on the top;* τὸ ἐφιστάμενον τοῦ γάλακτος, i. e. cream. 3. *to be set over,* Lat. *praeesse;* pf. part. Ion. οἱ ἐπεστεῶτες Att. οἱ ἐφεστῶτες, *those in authority.* II. *to stand by* or *near:* absol. *to stand by.* 2. *to stand over against, oppose:* metaph. *to impend, be close at hand,* Lat. *instare;* Κῆρες ἐφεστᾶσιν θανάτοιο the fates of death *are close at hand.* III. *to halt, stop.* IV. *to attend to.*

ἔφλᾰδον, aor. 2 of φλάζω.

ἐφόβηθεν, Ep. 3 pl. aor. 1 pass. of φοβέω.

ἐφ-οδεύω, f. σω, (ἐπί, ὁδός) *to visit, go the rounds, patrol:* also of an officer who visited yearly at Satrapies of Persia: generally, *to superintend, watch over.*

ἐφ-όδια, τά, see ἐφόδιος.

ἐφοδιάζω Ion. ἐπ–, f. άσω, *to furnish with supplies* or *stores for a journey:*—Med. *to supply oneself with* or *receive for one's supplies.* From

ἐφ-όδιος, ον, (ἐπί, ὁδός) *of* or *for a journey:*—as Subst., ἐφόδιον, τό, Lat. *viaticum, supplies for travelling* (mostly in pl., ἐφόδια);—an ambassador's *travelling expenses:* generally *ways and means, supplies.*

ἔφ-οδος, ἡ, (ἐπί, ὁδός) *a way towards, approach: a means of reaching, access.* II. *an onset, attack.*

ἔφ-οδος, ὁ, *one who goes the rounds, an inspector.*

ἔφ-οδος, ον, (ἐπί, ὁδός) *accessible:* Sup. -ώτατος.

ἐφοίτη, Dor. 3 sing. impf. of φοιτάω.

ἐφόλκαιον, τό, (ἐφέλκω) *a rudder.*

ἐφόλκιον, τό, (ἐφέλκω) *a small boat towed after a ship:*—generally, *an appendage.*

ἐφολκίς, ἡ, (ἐφέλκω) *a burdensome appendage.*

ἐφολκός, όν, (ἐφέλκω) *drawing on* or *towards, attractive, enticing.* II. *drawling:* absol. *a laggard.*

ἐφ-ομαρτέω, f. ήσω, *to follow close upon.*

ἐφ-οπλίζω, f. σω: Ep. aor. 1 inf. ἐφοπλίσσαι:—*to equip, get ready, prepare:* so also in Med.

ἐφορᾱτικός, ή, όν, *looking over, watchful of.* From

ἐφ-οράω Ion. ἐπ–: impf. ἐφεώρων Ion. 3 sing. ἐπώρα: f. ἐπόψομαι Ep. ἐπιόψομαι: aor. 2 ἐπεῖδον:—*to look over, oversee, observe.* 2. generally *to look on, view:*—Pass., ὅσον ἐφεώρατο τῆς νήσου as much of the island as *was in view* 3. *to look out for, choose.*

ἐφορεία, ἡ, (ἐφορεύω) *an overlooking:*—*the office* or *dignity of* ἔφορος, *the ephoralty*

ἐφορεῖον, τό, *the court of the ephori.* From

ἐφορεύω, f. σω, = ἐφοράω. II. (ἔφορος) *to be an ephor.*

ἐφορικός, ή, όν, (ἔφορος) *of* or *for the ephori.*

ἐφ-όριος, α, ον, (ἐπί, ὅρος) *on the frontier.*

ἐφ-ορμαίνω, *to rush on.*

ἐφ-ορμάω Ion. ἐπ–: f. ήσω: aor. 1 -ώρμησα:—*to stir up, rouse against* one, *urge on, set in motion.* 2. intr. *to rush upon, attack.* II. Pass. and Med., aor. 1 ἐφωρμησάμην and ἐφωρμήθην:—*to be stirred up, roused: to rush furiously on: to hurry, rush forward.* 2. *to make a dash at.*

ἐφ-ορμέω Ion. ἐπ–, f. ήσω, *to lie at anchor over against, to blockade* an enemy: generally, *to watch:*—Pass. *to be blockaded.*

ἐφ-ορμή, ἡ, (ἐπί, ὁρμή) *an entrance, access an attempt* upon a place, *attack.*

ἐφορμηθεῖεν, 3 pl. aor. 1 opt. pass. of ἐφορμάω.

ἐφόρμησις, εως, ἡ, (ἐφορμέω) *the lying at anchor so as to blockade* an enemy, *a blockade.*

ἐφ-ορμίζω, f. ίσω Att. ιῶ, (ἐπί, ὅρμος) *to bring* a ship *to her moorings:*—Med. and Pass., *to come to anchor.*

ἔφ-ορμος, ον, (ἐπί, ὅρμος) *at anchor.*

ἔφ-ορμος, ὁ, = ἐφόρμησις, *a blockade.*

ἔφορος, ον, (ἐφοράω) *overseeing.* as Subst., ἔφορος, ὁ, *an overseer, guardian, ruler* 2. at Sparta, οἱ ἔφοροι *the Ephori* or *Overseers,* a body of five magistrates, who controlled even the kings.

ἐφ-όσον, Adv. for ἐφ' ὅσον, *in so far as.*

ἐφρασάμαν, Dor. aor. 1 med. of φράζω.

ἔφραξα, aor. 1 of φράσσω.

ἔφριξα, aor. 1 of φρίσσω.

ἐφρύαξα, aor. 1 of φρυάσσω.

ἔφρυξα, aor. 1 of φρύγω.

ἐφ-υβρίζω, f. ίσω Att. ιῶ, *to insult over one, add insult to injury:* also in Med.

ἔφῠγον, aor. 2 of φεύγω.

ἐφ-υδριάς, άδος, ἡ, (ἐπί, ὕδωρ) *of the water.*

ἔφ-υδρος Ion. ἐπ-, ον, (ἐπί, ὕδωρ) *wet, rainy, bringing rain.* 2. *abounding in water.*

ἐφ-υμνέω, f. ήσω, *to sing* or *chant after: to chant over.* II. *to sing a dirge* or *mournful strain.* III. *to sing of, descant on.*

ἔφῡν, aor. 2 of φύω: also Ep. 3 pl. ἔφῦσαν.

ἐφ-ύπερθε, before a vowel -θεν, Adv. *from above: above, on atop, over.*

ἘΦΎΡΑ Ion. -ρη, ἡ, *Ephўrē*, old name of Corinth.

ἔφυρσα, aor. 1 of φύρω.

ἔφῡσαν, 3 pl. aor. 1 of φύω. 2. 3 pl. aor. 2 of φύω.

ἐφύση, Dor. for ἐφύσᾱ, 3 sing. impf. of φυσάω. [ῡ]

ἐφ-υστερίζω, f. σω, (ἐπί, ὕστερος) *to be later, come after another.*

ἐφ-ύω, f. ύσω [ῡ], (ἐπί, ὕω) *to rain upon:*—Pass. *to be rained upon, exposed to the rain:* pf. part. ἐφυσμένος.

ἐφ' ᾧ, ἐφ' ᾧτε, i. e. ἐπὶ τούτῳ ὥστε, *on the condition that.*

ἐφ-ώριος, ον, (ἐπί, ὥρα) *in season, ripe, mature.*

ἔχᾰδον, aor. 2 of χανδάνω.

ἔχᾰνον, aor. 2 of χαίνω or χάσκω.

ἐχάρην [ᾰ], aor. 2 pass. of χαίρω.

ἐχᾰρισάμην, ἐχᾰρίσθην, aor. 1 med. and pass of χαρίζομαι.

ἔχεα, aor. 1 of χέω.

ἐχ-έγγυος, ον, = ἔχων ἐγγύην, i. e. I. *having given security, responsible: trustworthy, faithful.* II. *having received security, secure.*

ἐχέ-θῡμος, ον, (ἔχω, θυμός) *controlling one's temper, under self-control.*

ἐχέ-μῡθέω, (ἔχω, μῦθος) *to hold one's peace.* Hence

ἐχεμυθία, ἡ, *silence.*

ἐχε-νηΐς, -νηΐδος, contr. **ἐχε-νῇς**, -νῇδος, ἡ, (ἔχω, ναῦς) *holding ships fast.*

ἐχε-πευκής, ές, (ἔχω, πευκή) epith. of a dart, *bitter* or *sharp, piercing.*

ἐχέ-σαρκος, ον, (ἔχω, σάρξ) *fitting to the body.*

ἔχεσκον, Ion. impf. of ἔχω.

ἐχέ-στονος, ον, (ἔχω, στόνος) *bringing sorrows.*

ἐχέτλη, ἡ, (ἔχω) *the plough-handle*, Lat. *stiva.* Hence

ἐχετλήεις, εσσα, εν, *of the plough-handle.*

ἔχευ, Dor. imperat. pass. of ἔχω.

ἔχευα, Ep. aor. 1 of χέω: med. ἐχευάμην.

ἐχεφρονέω, (ἐχέφρων) *to be sensible* or *shrewd.*

ἐχεφροσύνη, ἡ, *good sense, shrewdness.* From

ἐχέ-φρων, ον, gen. ονος, (ἔχω, φρήν) *sensible, shrewd.*

ἔχησθα, Ep. 2 sing. subj. of ἔχω.

ἐχθαίρω, f. ἐχθᾰρῶ: aor. 1 ἤχθηρα: fut. med. ἐχθᾰροῦμαι in pass. sense: (ἔχθος):—*to hate, be an enemy to*: c. acc. cognato, ἔχθος ἐχθαίρειν *to bear* hate:—pass., ἐχθαίρεσθαι ἔκ τινος *to be hated* by one.

ἐχθαρτέος, α, ον, verb. Adj. of ἐχθαίρω, *to be hated.*

ἐχθές, Adv., = χθές, *yesterday.*

ἔχθιστος, η, ον, irreg. Sup. of ἐχθρός, formed from Subst. ἔχθος, as κέρδιστος from κέρδος:—*most hated, most hateful*: as Subst. *one's bitterest enemy.*

ἐχθίων, ον, gen. ονος, irreg. Comp. of ἐχθρός, formed from Subst. ἔχθος, as κερδίων from κέρδος:—*more hated: more hostile.*

ἐχθοδοπέω, f. ήσω, *to cause hatred.* From

ἐχθοδοπός, ή, όν, (ἔχθος) *hateful, hostile.*

ἜΧΘΟΣ, εος, τό, *hate, hatred, enmity*, Lat. *odium;* ἔχθος τινός *hatred for* one. II. *a hated object*

ἔχθρα Ion. **ἔχθρη**, ἡ, *hatred, enmity*; ἔχθρα τινός *hatred for* one; δι' ἔχθρας μολεῖν or ἀφικέσθαι τινί to become *at enmity* with one.

ἐχθραίνω, f. ᾰνῶ, (ἐχθρός) *to hate: to be at enmity with.*

ἐχθρο-δαίμων, ον, gen. ονος, (ἐχθρός, δαίμων) *hated of the gods: ill-fated, miserable.*

ἐχθρό-ξενος, ον, (ἐχθρός, ξένος) *unfriendly to guests, inhospitable.*

ἐχθρός, ά, όν, (ἔχθος) *hated, hateful.* II. act. *hating, hostile, at enmity with.* III. as Subst. ἐχθρός, ὁ, *one's enemy*, Lat. *inimicus.*—Besides ἐχθρότερος, ἐχθρότατος, the irreg. Comp. and Sup. ἐχθίων, ἔχθιστος, were in common use.

ἜΧΘΩ, *to hate.*—Pass. *to be hated, hateful.* Only used in pres. and impf.

ἔχιδνα, ἡ, (ἔχις) *a viper, adder.* Hence

ἐχιδναῖος, α, ον, *of* or *like a viper.*

ἘΧΙ͂ΝΑΙ, ῶν, αἱ, *islands in the Ionian sea*, afterwards called Ἐχινάδες.

ἐχινέες, οἱ, *a kind of mice with rough bristling hair*, in Libya. (Deriv. unknown.)

ἘΧΙ͂ΝΟΣ, ὁ, *the urchin, hedgehog:* also *the sea-urchin.* 2. *the shell of the sea-urchin*, often used as *a jar:* hence, II. like Lat. *testa, a jug, pitcher, vase*, Lat. *echinus.* 2. *the vase* in which the notes of evidence were sealed up. III. *part of the bit of a bridle*, studded over with points to make it severe.

ἜΧΙΣ, εος and εως, ὁ, *a viper, adder.*

ἔχμα, ατος, τό, (ἔχω) *that which holds:* I. *a hindrance, obstacle.* 2. c. gen. *a bulwark, defence against.* II. *a hold-fast, stay, support;* ἔχματα νηῶν *props, cradles for ships;* ἔχματα πέτρης *supports* of rock, i. e. solid rock; ἔχματα πύργων *supporting* towers.

ἔχοισα, Dor. for ἔχουσα.

ἔχουν, impf. of χόω: see χώννυμι.

ἔχρᾱνα, aor. 1 of χραίνω.

ἔχρησα, aor. 1 of χράω.

ἐχρήσθην, aor. 1 pass. of χράομαι.

ἔχρισα, aor. 1 of χρίω.

ἐχύθην [ῠ], aor. 1 pass. of χέω.

ἔχυντο, ἔχῠτο, 3 pl. and sing. Ep. aor. 2 pass. of χέω.

ἐχῠρός, ά, όν, (ἔχω) *firm, strong, secure, safe;* ἐν ἐχυρῷ εἶναι to be *in safety:* also *trustworthy.* Hence

ἐχῠρῶς, Adv. *securely:*—Comp. ἐχυρώτερον.

ἜΧΩ: impf. εἶχον Ep. ἔχον Ion. ἔχεσκον: fut.

ἴξω, or (in the sense of *holding*) σχήσω: pf. ἔσχηκα 1 p. ὄχωκα (in compd. συνοχωκότε): aor. 2 ἔσχον, imperat. σχές, subj. σχῶ, opt. σχοίην, inf. σχεῖν Ep. σχέμεν, part. σχών; poët. also ἔσχεθον, inf. σχεθεῖν: Pass. and Med. ἔχομαι: impf. εἰχόμην: fut. ἕξομαι and σχήσομαι: aor. 2 ἐσχόμην Ep. 3 sing. σχέτο, imperat. σχοῦ, inf. σχέσθαι, part. σχόμενος.

A. Trans.: Radic. sense, *to have, hold;* I. *to have, possess; οἱ ἔχοντες* those that *have*, i. e. *the wealthy:*—Pass. *to be possessed by, belong to.* 2. *to have to wife: to have in one's house, to entertain:* c. acc. loci, *to dwell in, inhabit:* ἐν γαστρὶ ἔχειν (sub. βρέφος), *to be pregnant, be with child.* 3. of a State or Condition; γῆρας ἔχειν *to have reached* old age, = the simple Verb γηράσκειν, etc.; so, ἐν στόματι ἔχειν *to be always talking of.* 4. *to imply, infer;* αἰσχύνην ἔχειν *to imply* disgrace. 5. like Lat. *teneo, to know, understand, comprehend.* II. *to hold, keep: to hold fast: to keep with one, retain, detain: to hold tight, grip, grasp,* of the hold of wrestlers. 2. *to hold up, bear up, sustain:* hence *to hold out* or *bear up against, to resist,* in which sense Homer uses fut. σχήσειν and med. σχήσεσθαι. 3. *to direct to, aim: to guide, steer:* in fut. σχήσω and aor. σχεῖν, *to land.* 4. *to hold in, check, stop:* also *to keep fast* or *close,* as a bar does a gate: *to allay* pain: c. gen. *to stop* or *hinder from* a thing. 5. *to keep, ward off:* hence *to guard, keep safe:* of armour, *to protect.* 6. *to keep doing* or *making, cause.* III. *to have means* or *power to* do a thing, *to be able,* like Lat. *habeo:* οὐκ ἔχω, followed by ὅπως, πῶς, ποῦ, etc., *I know not how, know not where,* etc.

B. Intrans., *to hold oneself, to be* or *keep* in a certain state: esp. with Advs., εὖ ἔχει, καλῶς or κακῶς ἔχει, Lat. *bene, male se habet, it is going on well,* etc.; a gen. modi is often added, εὖ ἔχειν τινός *to be well off for* a thing, *abound in* it; καλῶς ἔχειν τῆς μέθης to be pretty *well off for* drink. 2. *to be so and so, be;* λόγος ἔχει the story *goes, prevails.* 3. *to keep* one's *ground, stand fast* or *firm.* 4. *to stand up, jut out, rise, project;* κίονες ὕψοσ' ἔχοντες pillars *rising* high. 5. *to point towards, glance at, be directed towards;* ἔχθρα ἔχουσα ἐς Ἀθηναίους enmity *directed towards* the Athenians: of Place, *to extend, reach unto:* also, ἔχειν ἀμφί or περί τι *to be about, busy, occupied with.* 6. in Att., ἔχω is joined with aor. part. of another Verb; κρύψαντες ἔχουσι for κεκρύφασι; ἀποκλείσας ἔχεις for ἀποκέκλεικας. 7. the part. ἔχων with the pres., adds a notion of *duration* to what is *being done;* τί δῆτα διατρίβεις ἔχων; why then *keep* wasting time? ληρεῖς ἔχων *you keep on* trifling.

C. Med. *to hold oneself to, hold on by, cling to, make fast to:* metaph. *to hold to one, depend upon, be closely connected with:* hence *to lay hold on, claim, take possession of:* 2. of Place, *to be close, border on, next to;* ὁ ἐχόμενος that comes *next* or *nearest;* τὸ ἐχόμενον ἔτος the year *next ensuing.* II. *to bear, wear, carry for oneself,* or *what is one's own:* also *to carry* or *conduct oneself;* ἔχεο κρατερῶς *bear thyself* resolutely. II. *to keep oneself back, abstain, refrain from:* absol., σχέο, σχέσθε *hold! cease!*

ἔχωντι, Dor. for ἔχωσι.

ἔχωσα, aor. 1 of χώννυμι.

ἐχώσατο, 3 sing. aor. 1 of χώομαι.

ἐχώσθην, aor. 1 pass. of χώννυμι.

ἐψάλαται, Ion. 3 pl. pf. pass. of ψάλλω.

ἕψ-ανδρα, ἡ, (ἕψω, ἀνήρ) *boiling men,* epith. of Medea, from her *restoring old Aeson to youth.*

ἔψαυσα, aor. 1 of ψαύω.

ἔψεξα, aor. 1 of ψέγω.

ἐψευσάμην, aor. 1 of ψεύδομαι.

ἔψημαι, pf. pass. of ψάω.

ἕψησις, εως, ἡ, (ἕψω) *a boiling:* generally, *cookery.*

ἑψήσω, fut. of ἕψω.

ἑψητήρ, ῆρος, ὁ, (ἕψω) *a pipkin, pan for boiling.*

ἑψητός, ή, όν, (ἕψω) *boiled, sodden.*

ἐψία Ion. ἐψίη, ἡ, (ψιά, ψειά) *a game played with pebbles:* generally, *amusement, pastime.* Hence

ἐψῐάομαι, Dep. *to play with pebbles:* generally, *to disport, amuse oneself: to entertain oneself with.*

ἐψιθυρίσδομες, Dor. 1 pl. impf. of ψιθυρίζω.

ἐψισμένος, pf. pass. part. of ψίζω.

ἐψύγην [ῠ], aor. 2 pass. of ψύχω.

ἝΨΩ: impf. ἧψον (Ion. ἕψεον as if from ἑψέω): fut. ἑψήσω: aor. 1 ἥψησα:—Med., fut. ἑψήσομαι:—Pass., aor. 1 ἡψήθην: pf. ἥψημαι:—*to boil, seethe,* opp. to ὀπτάω: of metals, *to smelt, refine:* metaph. *to cherish, nurse.*

ἔω, Ion. for ὦ, pres. subj. of εἰμί *sum.*

ἐῶ, contr. for ἐάω.

ἐῷ, contr. for ἐάοι, 3 sing. opt. of ἐάω.

ἑῷ, dat. of ἑός.

ἕω, Ion. for ὧ, aor. 2 subj. of ἵημι.

ἕω, gen. and acc. sing. of ἕως, *the dawn.*

ἔῳγα, pf. 2 of οἴγνυμι, *to open.*

ἔῳγμαι, pf. pass. of οἴγνυμι.

ἔωθα, ἐώθεα, Ion. pf. 2 and plqpf. of ἔθω.

ἕωθεν Dp. ἠῶθεν, Adv. (ἕως) *from morn, at earliest dawn, at break of day.*

ἑωθῐνός, ή, όν, (ἕως) *in the morning, early;* τὸ ἑωθινόν as Adv. *early in the morning;* ἐξ ἑωθινοῦ = ἕωθεν.

ἐώθουν, impf. of ὠθέω.

ἐῴκειν, plqpf. of ἔοικα.

ἑωλο-κρᾱσία, ὁ, (ἕωλος, κρᾶσις) *a mixture* or *compound of dregs of wine:* metaph., ἑωλοκρασίαν τῆς πονηρίας κατασκεδάσαι τινός to empty *the stale dregs* of his villany over one.

ἕωλος, ον, (ἕως) *a day old, kept till the morrow:* of food, *stale:* hence *out of date, obsolete.*

ἐώλπει, 3 sing. plqpf. of ἔλπω.

ἕωμεν, in Il. 19. 404, ἐπεί χ' ἕωμεν πολέμοιο, when *we have enough* of war:—commonly considered as aor. 2 subj. of ἵημι, but sometimes referred to ἕω = ἄω, *to satiate.*

ἐῶμεν, contr. from ἐάομεν, 1 pl. of ἐάω.

ἐῷμι, contr. from ἐάοιμι, 1 sing. opt. of ἐάω.

ἐών, Hom. and Ion. for ὤν, pres. part. of εἰμί *sum*.

ἐώνημαι, ἐωνήμην, pf. and plqpf. of ὠνέομαι.

ἐῳνοχόει, 3 sing. impf. with double augm. of οἰνοχοέω.

ἔῳξα, aor. 1 of οἴγνυμι.

ἑῷος, *α, ον*, also *ος, ον*, poët. **ἑώϊος** Ep. **ἠοῖος**. (ἕως) *in the morning, at early dawn, at day-break.* 2. *eastern*, Lat. *Eöus*.

ἑώρα, ἡ, collat. form of αἰώρα, *a being suspended, hanging in the air, oscillation.* II. *a noose for hanging.*

ἑώρα, 3 sing. impf. of ὁράω.

ἑώρᾱκα, ἑώρᾱμαι, pf. act. and pass. of ὁράω.

ἐώργει, for ἐόργει, 3 sing. plqpf. of *ἔργω.

ἐωρέω, collat. form of αἰωρέω, whence aor. 1 part. fem., ἐωρήσασα τοὐμὸν ὄμμα *having raised aloft* mine eye.

ἑώρταζον, ἑώρτασα, impf. and aor. 1, with irreg. augm., of ἑορτάζω.

ἕωρτο, for ἤορτο, 3 [illegible]. plqpf. pass. of ἀείρω.

ἑώρων, impf. of ὁράω.

ἕως, Att. for Ion. ἠώς, *morn*.

ἝΩΣ Ion. and Ep. **εἵως** Ep. **εἷος**: I. as Conjunction, *while, so long as*, Lat. *donec*, properly relative to the antec. τέως Ep. τείως. 2. = τέως, *for a time.* 3. *till, until, until such time as.* 4. = ὡς, ὅπως, ἵνα, *that, in order that.* II. as Adv., ἕως ὅτε, Lat. *usque dum, till the time when*: so too, ἕως οὗ; ἕως ποτε; Lat. *quousque? how long?* 2. with Advs. of Place, ἕως ὧδε, ἕως ἔσω or ἔξω, *up to* this point, *till* within, etc.

ἕωσα, ἑωσάμην, aor. 1 act. and med. of ὠθέω.

ἕωσι, Ion. for ὦσι, 3 pl. pres. subj. of εἰμί *sum*.

ἐῶσι, contr. for ἐάουσι, 3 pl. pres. of ἐάω.

ἕωσμαι, pf. pass. of ὠθέω.

ἕωσ-περ, strengthd. for ἕως, *even until*.

ἑωσ-φόρος, *ον*, (ἕως, φέρω) *morn-bringing*: as Subst., ὁ Ἑωσφόρος *the Morning-star*, Lat. *Lucifer*.

ἑωυτοῦ, ἑωυτέων, Ion. for ἑαυτοῦ, ἑαυτῶν.

Z

Z, ζ, ζῆτα, τό, indecl., sixth letter of Gr. Alphabet: as numeral ζ′ = ἑπτά and ἕβδομος (the obsol. ϛ′, i. e. Ϝ or *vau*, being retained to represent ἕξ), but ͵ζ = 7000. Z is compounded of σ and δ, = σδ, whence in Aeol. and Dor. μουσίσδω ψιθυρίσδω are written for μουσίζω ψιθυρίζω. In Ion. δ was changed into ζ; and ζ easily passed into δ, as appears in παίζω παιδνός, ἀλαπάζω ἀλαπαδνός etc.: it also melted into ι, e. g. ζόρξ ἴορκος, ζυγόν *jugum*.

Zeta, being a double conson., makes a short vowel before it long by position. But there are two proper names in Homer, before which the vowel is retained short, ἄστυ Ζελείης, ὑλήεσσά Ζάκυνθος.

ZA-, Aeol. for διά: also as insep. Prefix with intensive sense, like ἀρι-, ἐρι-, ἀγα-, as in ζά-θεος, ζα-μενής, etc.

ζάγκλον, τό, *a reaping-hook* or *sickle*, Lat. *falx* (Old Sicilian word.)

ζᾱ-ής, *ές*, (ζα-, ἄημι) *strong blowing, stormy, gusty*. ζαῆν, irreg. acc. for ζαέα, ζαῆ.

ζά-θεος, *α, ον*, also *ος, ον*, *very divine, holy, hallowed.*

ζᾰ-θερής, *ές*, (ζα-, θέρος) *very hot.*

ζαῖεν Att. **ζῷεν**, 3 pl. opt. of ζάω.

ζάκορος, ὁ, = διάκτορος, διάκονος, *a minister, servant.*

ζά-κοτος, *ον*, *very wrathful.*

ζάλη, ἡ, (ἅλς) *surge, spray: a storm*: metaph. *trouble, distress.* (Akin to σάλος, Lat. *salum*.)

ζᾱλοῖσα, Dor. for ζηλοῦσα.

ζᾶλος, ζᾱλόω, ζᾱλωτός, Dor. for ζηλ-.

ζᾰμενέω, f. ήσω, *to be very violent, exert all one's strength.* From

ζᾰ-μενής, *ές*, (ζα-, μένος) *very strong* or *mighty, raging, violent.*

ζᾱμία, Dor. for ζημία.

Ζάν, Ζανός, ὁ, Dor. for Ζήν, Ζηνός, old form of Ζεύς, q. v. Hence Lat. *Janus*.

ζά-πεδον, τό, = δάπεδον.

ζα-πληθής, *ές*, (ζα-, πλῆθος) *very full*: ζαπληθής γενειάς *a bushy* beard: *full-sounding.*

ζά-πλουτος, *ον*, *very rich.*

ζά-πῡρος, *ον*, (ζα-, πῦρ) *very fiery.*

ζατεῦσα, Dor. for ζητοῦσα.

ζᾱτεύω, ζατρεῖον, ζατρεύω, Dor. for ζητ-.

ζα-τρεφής, *ές*, (ζα-, τρέφω) *well-fed, fat.*

ζα-φλεγής, *ές*, (ζα-, φλέγω) *full of fire, fiery.*

ζά-χολος, *ον*, *very wrathful.*

ζά-χρειος, *ον*, (ζα-, χρεία) *very needy*, ζάχρειος ὁδοῦ *one who wants to know* the way.

ζα-χρηής, *ές*, (ζα-, χράω B) *attacking violently, furious*: of warriors, *eager, fiery.*

ζά-χρῡσος, *ον*, *rich in gold.*

ZA'Ω Ep. **ζώω**, in later Poets **ζόω**, Att. contr. **ζῶ**, ζῇς, ζῇ; imperat. ζῆ or ζῆθι; opt. ζῴην; inf. ζάειν contr. ζῆν: impf. ἔζην (as if from ζῆμι), ἔζης, ἔζη, but 3 pl. ἔζων: fut. ζήσω and ζήσομαι: aor. 1 ἔζησα: pf. ἔζηκα:—*to live, breathe*; ζῶν alive: ζῆν ἀπό τινος *to live off* or *on a* thing, cf. ἀποζῆν: c. acc. cognato, ζῆν ζόην, βίον. II. metaph. *to be in full vigour, to be fresh, strong, efficient*: part. ζῶν, as Adj., *active, powerful, efficacious.*

-ζε, insepar. enclitic Particle, denoting *motion towards a place*, ζ being written for σδ, as, Ἀθήναζε, θύραζε, for Ἀθήνασδε, θύρασδε.

ζεγέριες, a Libyan word, a kind of *mice.*

ZEIA', ἡ, *zea*, a sort of *grain*, used as fodder for horses, prob. *a coarse wheat, spelt.*

ζεί-δωρος, *ον*, (ζειά, δωρέομαι) *zea-giving, fruitful.*

ζειρά, ἡ, *a wide upper garment*, girded about the loins and falling over the feet. (Foreign word.)

ζείω, poët. for ζέω, as πνείω for πνέω.

ζέσσα, Ep. for ἔζεσα, aor. 1 of ζέω.

ζεστός, *ή, όν*, (ζέω) *boiled, boiling, hot.*

ζευγάριον, τό, Dim. of ζεῦγος, *a puny team* of oxen.

ζευγηλᾰτέω, f. ήσω, *to drive a yoke of oxen.* From

ζευγ-ηλάτης, ου, ὁ, (ζεῦγος, ἐλαύνω) *a driver of a yoke of oxen.*

ζευγίτης [ῑ], οῦ, ὁ, (ζεῦγος) *yoked together, two and two, in pairs.* II. ζευγῖται, οἱ, *yeomen*, the third of Solon's four classes of Athenian citizens, so called from *their being able to keep a team* (ζεῦγος) *of oxen:* the first class being called πεντακοσιομέδιμνοι, the second ἱππεῖς, and the fourth θῆτες.

ζεύγλη poët. **ζεῦγλᾰ**, ἡ, *the collar* or *loop of the yoke* (ζυγόν), through which the oxen's heads were put, so that the ζυγόν had two ζεῦγλαι. II. *the rudder-bands*; see πηδάλιον.

ζεῦγμα, ατος, τό, (ζεύγνυμι) *that which is linked together, a band, bond:* ζεῦγμα τοῦ λιμένος *a boom* or *chain across* the mouth of the harbour.

ζευγνύμεν, -ύμεναι, Ep inf. of ζεύγνυμι.

ΖΕΥ'ΓΝΥΜΙ or **-ύω**: impf. 3 pl. ἐζεύγνῠσαν (Ep. ζεύγνυσαν) or ἐζεύγνυον (Ep ζεύγνυον): fut. ζεύξω: aor. 1 ἔζευξα:—Pass., aor. 1 ἐζεύχθην, more frequent aor. 2 ἐζύγην [ῠ]:—*to join* or *link together, yoke:*—Med., ἵππους ζεύγνυσθαι *to yoke* horses *for oneself, put to one's* horses; also *to harness.* II. generally, *to join* or *fasten together, make fast;* σανίδες ἐζευγμέναι *close-shut* doors. 2. *to join in wedlock, marry, unite:*—Med. of the husband, *to wed:*—Pass. *to be married.* 3. *to join by bridges, throw a bridge across.* 5. *to undergird* ships with ropes.

ζεῦγος, εος, τό, (ζεύγνυμι) *a yoke* or *team of beasts, a pair of horses.* 2. *the carriage drawn by a team, a chariot, plough: any pair* or *couple.* II. of *more than two things* or *persons joined together*, e. g. ζεῦγος τριπάρθενον three maiden sisters.

ζευκτηρία, *a fastening, band;* see πηδάλιον. From

ζευκτήριος, α, ον, (ζεύγνυμι) *fit for joining* or *yoking;* τὸ ζευκτήριον *a yoke.*

ζεῦξαι, aor. 1 inf. of ζεύγνυμι: **ζεύξειεν**, 3 sing. opt.; **ζεῦξον**, imperat.

ζεῦξις, εως, ἡ, (ζεύγνυμι) *a yoking* or *manner of yoking* oxen. 2. *a joining* by a bridge.

ΖΕΥ'Σ, ὁ, voc. Ζεῦ; but genit. Διός, dat. Διΐ, acc. **Δία** as if from *Δίς: poët. Ζηνός, Ζηνί, Ζῆνα, Dor. **Ζάνος**, etc., as if from *Ζήν, Ζάν:—*Zeus, Jupiter*, king and father of gods and men, son of Kronos (or Saturn) and Rhea, hence called Κρονίδης, Κρονίων: ruler of the lower air (ἀήρ); hence rain and storms come from him, as Ζεὺς ὕει.

Ζεφῠρίη (sub. πνοή), ἡ, = Ζέφυρος, *the west wind.*

Ζέφῠρος, ὁ, *Zephyrus, the west wind*, or properly *the north-west.* (From ζόφος, *darkness* or *the West*, as Εὖρος from ἕως, *morn* or *the East.*)

ΖΕ'Ω, fut. ζέσω: aor. 1 ἔζεσα Ep. ζέσσα:—*to boil, seethe:* generally, *to boil up*, esp. of hot springs: also simply *to be hot, throb with heat;* χθὼν ἔζεε the earth *was hot:* metaph. *to boil with passion*, like Lat. *fervere.* II. trans. *to make to boil, heat.*

ζῆ, ζῆθι, imperat, of ζάω.

ζηλαῖος, α, ον, (ζῆλος) *jealous.*

ζηλήμων, ον, gen. ονος, (ζηλέω) *jealous.*

ζηλο-δοτήρ, ῆρος, ὁ, (ζῆλος, δίδωμι) *giver of bliss.*

ζηλο-μᾰνής, ές, (ζῆλος, μανῆναι) *mad with jealousy.*

ζῆλος, ὁ, (ζέω) *eager rivalry, emulation*, in good sense, opp. to φθόνος (envy). 2. *any strong passion*, esp. *jealousy: zeal* or *emulous desire for* a thing. II. pass. *the object of emulation* or *rivalry, happiness, blessedness*

ζηλοσύνη, ἡ, poët. for ζῆλος

ζηλοτῠπέω, f. ήσω, (ζηλοτυπος) *to emulate, rival, be jealous of.* 2. *to envy.* 3. *to affect, pretend to.* Hence

ζηλοτῠπία, ἡ, *rivalry, jealousy, envy.*

ζηλό-τῠπος, ον, (ζῆλος, τύπτω) *jealous*

ζηλόω, f. ώσω, (ζῆλος) *to rival, vie with, emulate.* Lat. *aemulari:* c. acc. rei, *to desire emulously, strive after.* 2. *to be jealous of, envy.* 3. *to emulate, envy, admire, commend.* Hence

ζήλωμα, ατος, τό, *the object of emulation:* in pl. *high fortunes.* II. *rivalry, emulation.*

ζήλωσις, εως, ἡ, (ζηλόω) *emulation, imitation.*

ζηλωτής, οῦ, ὁ, (ζηλόω) *a rival, zealous imitator.* 2. *a zealot.*

ζηλωτός, ή, όν, (ζηλόω) *to be emulated, worthy of imitation.* 2. *enviable, happy, blessed.*

ζημία, ἡ, *loss, damage*, Lat. *damnum*, opp. to κέρδος: φανερὰ ζημία *a* clear *loss.* II. *a penalty*, esp. in money, *a fine;* θάνατον ζημίαν προτιθέναι to make death *the penalty.* (Deriv. uncertain.) Hence

ζημιόω, f. ώσω, *to cause loss to* one, *do* one *damage* or *hurt:* *to punish;* esp. in money, *to fine.*—Pass., with fut. med. ζημιώσομαι or pass. ζημιωθήσομαι, aor. 1 ἐζημιώθην, *to be fined.*

***Ζήν**, ὁ, gen. Ζηνός, poët. for Ζεύς, q. v.

Ζηνο-δοτήρ, ῆρος, ὁ, (Ζήν, δίδωμι) = Ζηνόφρων.

Ζηνό-φρων, ον, gen. ονος, (Ζήν, φρήν) *knowing the mind of Zeus, revealing the will of Jove*, of oracles.

ζήσομαι, fut. of ζάω.

ζητεύω, poët. for ζητέω.

ΖΗΤΕ'Ω, f. ήσω, *to seek, seek for, seek after.* 2. *to search out, inquire into, examine, investigate:* c. inf. *to seek to* do. 3. *to have to seek.* Hence

ζήτημα, ατος, τό, *that which is sought: an inquiry, question.*

ζητήσιμος, ον, (ζητέω) *to be searched;* τὰ ζητήσιμα *places to be beaten* for game.

ζήτησις, εως, ἡ, (ζητέω) *a seeking for, searching after: a searching out, inquiry, investigation.*

ζητητέος, α, ον, verb. Adj. of ζητέω, *to be sought.* II. ζητητέον, *one must seek out.*

ζητητής, οῦ, ὁ, (ζητέω) *a seeker, searcher, inquirer, examiner.* II. at Athens, the ζητηταί were *commissioners to inquire into state-offences.*

ζητητός, ή, όν, verb. Adj. of ζητέω, *sought for.*

ζιζάνιον, τό, *a weed that grows in wheat, darnel*, Lat. *zizanium, lolium.* (Eastern word.)

ζόη, Ion. for ζωή.

ζοΐα, Aeol. for ζωή.
ζοός, ά, όν, poët. for ζωός, ζώς.
ζορκάς, άδος, ή, = δορκάς: also **ζόρξ**, ζορκός, ή.
ζοφερός, όν, (ζόφος) *dark, dusky, murky, gloomy.*
ΖΌΦΟΣ, ὁ, *darkness, dusk, gloom:* esp. *of the nether world:* hence *the land of darkness, the nether world itself:*—Homer divides the world into a light and dark side, where ζόφος *the dark* or *night side, the west,* is opposed πρὸς Ἠῶ τ' Ἠέλιόν τε, *the light side, the east.* Hence.
ζοφόω, f. ώσω, *to darken:*—Pass. *to be dark.*
ζοφ-ώδης, ες, (ζόφος, εἶδος) *dusky, gloomy.*
ζόω, for ζάω.
ζύγαστρον, τό, (ζεύγνυμι) *a chest* or *box of boards strongly fastened together.*
ζῠγείς, aor. 2 part. pass. of ζεύγνυμι.
ζῠγῆναι, aor. 2 inf. pass. of ζεύγνυμι.
ζῠγη-φόρος, ον, poët. for ζυγοφ–, *bearing the yoke.*
ζύγιος, α, ον, (ζῠγόν) *of* or *for the yoke;* ζύγιος ἵππος *a draught-horse, wheeler.*
ζῠγίτης, ου, ὁ, (ζυγόν) *one of the rowers who sat on the second of the three banks* or *benches,* those on the lowest being θαλαμῖται, those on the highest θρανῖται. [ῑ]
ζῠγό-δεσμον, τό, (ζυγόν, δεσμός) *a yoke-band* or *band for binding the yoke* to the pole.
ζῠγο-μᾰχέω, f. ήσω (ζυγόν, μάχομαι) *to struggle with one's yoke-fellow, to quarrel.*
ΖΥΓΟ'Ν, τό, also **ζῠγός**, ὁ, but in pl. always ζυγά:—Lat. *jŭgum, the yoke* or *cross-bar* tied by the ζυγόδεσμος to the end of the pole, and having ζεῦγλαι (collars or loops) at each end, by which two horses, mules or oxen were put to the plough or carriage: metaph., τὸ δούλιον ζυγόν *the yoke* of slavery; κατὰ ζυγά, *in pairs.* II. *the cross-bar,* Lat. *transtillum, joining* the two horns of the φόρμιγξ. III. *the cross-planks of a ship, joining* the two opposite sides, *the benches* or *thwarts,* Lat *transtra.* IV. *the beam of the balance,* in pl. *the balance itself.* V. *the cross-straps* of sandals.
ζῠγός, v. sub ζυγόν
ζῠγόφιν, Ep. gen. of ζυγόν.
ζῠγόω, f. ώσω, (ζυγόν) *to yoke a pair, join together:* metaph. *to bring under the yoke, subdue, tame*
ζῠγωθρίζω, *to lock up.* From
ζύγωθρον, τό, (ζυγόω) *the bar* or *bolt of a door.*
ζῠγωτός, ή, όν, (ζυγόω) *drawn by a pair* of horses.
ζύμη, ή, (ζέω) *leaven.* [ῡ] Hence
ζῡμίτης, ου, Adj. masc *leavened.* [ῑ]
ζῡμόω, f. ώσω, (ζύμη) *to leaven, make to ferment.*
ζωάγρια, ων, τα, (ζωός, ἄγρα) *a reward for life saved:* also like θρεπτήρια, *a reward for nursing and rearing one, offerings to Aesculapius for recovery from illness.*
ζωάγριος, ον, (ζωός, ἄγρα) *for saving life.*
ζῳάριον, τό, Dim. of ζῷον, *an animalcule.* [ᾰ]
ζω-αρκής, ές, (ζωή, ἀρκέω) *maintaining life.*
ζωγρᾰφέω, f. ήσω, (ζωγράφος) *to paint from life.*
ζωγρᾰφία, ή, *the art of painting, painting.*
ζωγραφικός, ή, όν, *skilled in painting.* From
ζω-γράφος, ον, (ζῷον, γράφω) *painting animals, painting from nature:* as Subst., ζωγράφος, ὁ, *a painter.*
ζώγρει, **ζωγρεῖτε**, pres. imperat. of
ζω-γρέω, f. ήσω, (ζωός, ἀγρεύω) *to take alive, take prisoner* in war, *to give quarter to.* II. *to restore to life and strength, revive.* Hence
ζωγρία Ion. –ίη, ή, *a taking alive, taking prisoner.*
ζωδιακός, ή, όν, (ζῴδιον) *of* or *containing animals;* ὁ ζωδιακός (sub. κύκλος) *the Zodiac.*
ζῴδιον, τό, Dim. of ζῷον, *a small figure, painted* or *carved.*
ζωέμεν, **ζωέμεναι**, for ζώειν, inf. of ζώω = ζάω.
ζώεσκον, Ion. impf. of ζάω.
ζωή Dor. **ζωά** Ion. and poët. **ζόη** Aeol. **ζοΐα**, ή, (ζάω) *a living, means of living, subsistence, goods, property.* II. *life.*
ζω-θάλμιος, ον, (ζωή, θάλλω) *giving vigour of life.*
ζωϊκός, ή, όν, (ζῷον) *of* or *for animals.*
ζῶμα, ατος, τό, (ζώννυμι) *that which is girded: the girded tunic* worn under the armour: *the armour* girded by the ζωστήρ. II. also = ζώνη, or ζωστήρ, *a girdle, belt.*
ζώμευμα, ατος, τό, *broth, soup.* From
ζωμεύω, f. σω, (ζωμός) *to boil for broth, seethe.*
ζωμίδιον, τό, Dim. of ζωμός, *a little sauce.*
ζωμός Dor. **δωμός**, ὁ, (ζέω) *broth, soup,* esp. *sauce* to eat with other dishes.
ζώνη, ή, (ζώννυμι) *a belt, girdle,* properly *the lower of the two girdles worn by women, the man's belt* being ζωστήρ; φέρειν ὑπὸ ζώνην and τρέφειν ἐντὸς ζώνης to bear or nourish under *the girdle,* i. e. in the womb. Later, the girdle was used to keep money in, whence in Horace, *zonam perdere* to lose one's *purse.* II. *the part round which the girdle passed, the waist, loins.* III. *anything that one girds on, a garment, armour.*
ΖΩ'ΝΝΥΜΙ or –ύω; fut. ζώσω: aor. ἔζωσα:—Med. ζώννῦμαι, fut. ζώσομαι: aor. 1 ἐζωσάμην:—Pass., aor. 1 ἐζώσθην: pf. ἔζωσμαι:—*to gird,* esp. *to gird for battle.* II. Med. *to gird oneself, gird up one's loins for battle* or *for work:* c. acc., ζώνην, χαλκὸν ζώννυσθαι *to gird on* one's belt, sword.
ζωννύσκετο, Ion. 3 sing. impf. med. of ζώννυμι.
ζωο-γλύφος, ον, (ζῷον, γλύφω) *carving animals:* as Subst., ζωογλύφος, ὁ, *a sculptor:* cf. ζωγράφος.
ζωογονέω, f. ήσω, *to produce, propagate animals.* II. *to preserve alive.* From
ζωο-γόνος, ον, (ζῷον, γείνομαι) *producing animals: life-giving.*
ζωο-γράφος, ον, poët. for ζωγ–.
ζῷον, τό, properly contr. from ζώϊον, *a living being, animal,* Lat. *animal.* II. *the figure of an animal,* but also *any figure* or *image;* ζῷα γράφειν or γράφεσθαι, for ζωγραφεῖν, *to paint,* and in Herodotus, with a second acc. of the thing painted, as, ζῷα γράψασθαι τὴν ζεῦξιν τοῦ Βοσπόρου *to have* the passage of the Bosporus *painted.*

ζωο-ποιέω, ήσω, (ζωός, ποιέω) *to make alive, quicken.*

ζωός, ή, όν, (ζάω) *alive, living;* ζωὸν ἑλεῖν τινα to take one prisoner, i. e. give quarter to him.

ζωό-σοφος, ον, (ζωή, σοφός) *wise in life.*

ζωο-φόρος, ον, (ζωός, φέρω) *lifegiving.* II. (ζῷον, φέρω) *bearing animals;* ὁ ζωοφόρος (sub κύκλος) = ὁ ζωδιακός.

ζωοφῠτέω, f. ήσω, *to put forth live shoots.* From

ζωό-φῠτος, ου, (ζωός, φύω) *producing plants.*

ζω-πονέω, f. ήσω, (ζωός, πονέω) *to represent alive.*

ζωπῠρέω, f. ήσω, *to kindle into flame:* metaph. *to set on fire, provoke.* From

ζώ-πῠρον, τό, (ζωός, πῦρ) *a spark, a piece of hot coal: a match to light a fire with.*

ζωροποτέω, f. ήσω, *to drink sheer wine.*

ζωρο-ποτής, οῦ, ὁ, (ζωρός, πίνω) *drinking sheer wine, drunken.*

ζωρός, όν, *sheer, unmixed,* of wine without water:—as Subst. **ζωρός** (sub. οἶνος), ὁ, or as neut., ζωρόν, τό, Lat. *merum, sheer wine:* Homer uses only Comp., ζωρότερον κέραιε mix *purer wine,* i. e. pour in less water. As the Greeks used to dilute their wine with water, ζωρότερον πίνειν came to mean not only *to drink purer wine than common,* but generally *to drink hard, be a drunkard.* (Prob. for ζωερός from ζωός.)

ζώς, neut. ζών, gen. ζώ, rarer form for ζωός.

ζῶσαι, aor. 1 med. imperat. of ζώννυμι.

ζωστήρ, ῆρος, ὁ, (ζώννυμι) *the warrior's belt* or *baldric,* which secured the body-armour, ζώνη being the woman's girdle: but later, *any belt* or *girdle.*

ζῶστρον, τό, (ζώννυμι) *a belt, girdle.*

ζωτῐκός, ή, όν, (ζάω) *of* or *for life.* II. *full of life, lively, vivid,* Lat. *vivax:* of works of art, *true to life;* τὸ ζωτικὸν φαίνεσθαι πῶς ἐνεργάζῃ τοῖς ἀνδριᾶσιν; how do you make *that look of life* appear in your statues?

ζωΰφιον, τό, Dim. of ζῷον, = ζῴδιον.

ζώ-φῠτος, ον, (ζωός, φύω) *producing plants, fruitful.*

ζώω, Ep. and Ion. for ζάω, *to live.*

H

H, η, ἦτα, τό, indecl., seventh letter of the Greek alphabet; as numeral η′—ὀκτώ and ὄγδοος, but ͵η = 3000. The uncial form of Eta (H) was a double EI, and prob. it was so pronounced, as δῆλος, ζῆλος, from δέελος, ζέελος. The old alphabet had only one sign (ε) for the sound of *e* both long and short, till the long vowel η, with ω, was introduced from the Samian into the Athenian alphabet in the archonship of Euclides (B. C. 403) together with ω, ξ, ψ. The sign H, before it represented long ε, was used for the rough breathing, as HOΣ for ὅς, which usage remains in the Latin H. When the same H became a vowel, it was divided, so that ⊢ represented the rough, ⊣ the smooth breathing, whence came the present signs for the breathings. η was most in use among the Ion.; in the Attic dialect, it often passed into ᾱ, as Ion. πρήσσω, θώρηξ are in Att. πράσσω, θώραξ. In later Att., ει and ηϊ were not seldom changed into ῃ, e. g. κλεῖθρον κλῇθρον, Νηρηΐδες Νηρῇδες.

ἤ poët. **ἠέ**, Conjunction with three chief signfs., disjunctive, interrogative, comparative: I. ἤ DISJUNCTIVE, *or,* Lat. *aut;* and doubled, ἤ.., ἤ.., *either.., or..,* Lat. *aut.., aut...* II. ἤ INTERROGATIVE: in indirect questions in a subjoined clause, εἰπὲ ἤ.. say *whether..;* and doubled ἤ.., ἤ.., *whether.., or..?* Lat, *utrum.., an..?* 2. also with direct questions, like Lat. *an;* τίπτ' εἰλήλουθας; ἦ ἵνα ὕβριν ἴδῃ Ἀγαμέμνονος; why hast thou come? *is it* that thou may'st see..? III. ἤ COMPARATIVE, *than, as,* like Lat. *quam,* after a Comp. Adj.: also after positive Adjs. which have a comp. force, ἄλλο τι ἤ.., some other thing *than..;* ἐνάντιος ἤ.., contrariwise *than..;* οὐδ' ὅσον ἤ.., not so much *as..;* so after Verbs, βούλομαι ἤ.. to wish *rather than..;* φθάνω ἤ.. to come *sooner than...* 2. ἤ sometimes joins two Comparatives, when they both refer to the same subject; πάντες κ' ἀρησαίατ ἐλαφρότεροι πόδας εἶναι, ἢ ἀφνειότεροι all would then pray to be light of foot *rather than* rich; ταχύτερα ἢ σοφώτερα *more* quickly *than* wisely.

[When ἢ οὐ, ἢ οὐκ come together in a verse, the two words coalesce into one syll.: so too μὴ οὐ.]

ἦ, an exclamation, to call one's attention to a thing; ἤ, ἤ, σιώπα *what ho,* be silent!

ἦ, Adv., with two signfs., strengthening and questioning: I. TO STRENGTHEN or CONFIRM, *in truth, truly, verily, of a surety;* ἦ μήν, Ion. ἦ μέν, introduces *the very words* of an oath, to give greater solemnity. II. in INTERROG. sentences, = Lat. *num?* sometimes it may be rendered, *what? pray?* or *can it be?* ἦ οὐ..; Lat. *nonne..?*

ἦ, for ἔφη, 3 sing. impf. of ἠμί.

ἦ, for ἦν, 1 sing. impf. of εἰμί *sum.*

ᾖ, 3 sing. pres. subj. of εἰμί *sum.*

ἡ, fem. of Artic. ὁ.

ἥ, fem. of relat. Pron. ὅς, ἥ, ὅ, *who, what?*

ᾗ, dat. fem. of possess. Pron. ὅς, ἥ, ὅν, *his, her.*

ᾗ, dat. sing. fem. of relat. Pron. ὅς, ἥ, ὅ: also used adverbially: 1. of Place, *which way, where, whither, in* or *at what place.* 2. of Manner, *how, as;* ᾗ θέμις ἐστί, *as* is lawful and right. 3. joined with Sup., ᾗ μάλιστα or ᾗ δυνατὸν μάλιστα as much, as far *as possible;* ᾗ τάχιστα as quick *as possible.*

ἦα, ἦεν, Ep. for ἦν, 1 and 3 sing. impf. of εἰμί *sum.*

ᾖα, contr. of ἤϊα, for ᾔειν, Ep. impf. of εἶμι *ibo.*

ἥατο, Ion. for ἧντο, 3 pl. impf. of ἧμαι.

ἠβαιός, ά, όν, Ion. for βαιός, *little, small, poor, slight:* mostly with a negat., οὔ οἱ ἔνι φρένες, οὐδ' ἠβαιαί no sense is in [illegible], no, not *the slightest:* in neut. as Adv., οὐδ' ἠβαιόν not *in the least,* not *in the slightest degree;* without a negat., ἠβαιὸν ἀπὸ σπείους *a little* from the cave.

ἡβάσκω, Inceptive of ἡβάω, *to come to man's estate, come to one's strength*, Lat. *pubescere*.

ἡβάω, f. ήσω: aor. 1 ἥβησα: pf. ἥβηκα: (ἥβη):—*to be at man's estate, to be in the flower* or *prime of youth*, Lat. *pubescere*; ἀνὴρ μάλα ἡβῶν a man *in the full vigour of youth*; so of plants, ἡμερὶς ἡβώωσα *a young, luxuriant* vine. II. metaph. *to be young, fresh, vigorous*: also *to be full of youthful joy, to be full of passion*.

ἭΒΗ, ἡ, *man's estate, manhood, youth*, Lat. *pubertas*: also *the strength and freshness of youth*:—as a legal term ἥβη was *the time just before manhood*, at Sparta fixed at 18, so that οἱ δέκα ἀφ' ἥβης were men of 28, οἱ τετταράκοντα ἀφ' ἥβης men of 58. 2. metaph. *freshness, vigour, youthful passion, fire, spirit*. 3. *a body of youth, the youth*. Lat. *juventus*. II. as fem. prop. n. Ἥβη, *Hebé*, wife of Hercules, cup-bearer of the gods. Hence

ἡβηδόν, Adv. *in the manner of youth*. 2. πάντες ἡβηδόν all *from the youth upwards*.

ἡβητήρ, ῆρος, ὁ, **ἡβητής**, οῦ, ὁ, (ἡβάω) *in the prime of youth*.

ἡβητικός, ή, όν, (ἡβάω) *of* or *fit for youth, youthful*, Lat. *juvenilis*.

ἡβός, ή, όν, (ἥβη) *youthful*.

ἠβουλήθην, **ἠβουλόμην**, for ἐβ , aor. 1 and impf. of βούλομαι.

ἡβυλλιάω, Comic Dim. of ἡβάω, *to be youngish*.

ἡβῴην, Att. opt. of ἡβάω.

ἡβῷμι Ep. **ἡβώοιμι**, opt. of ἡβάω.

ἡβώων, **ἡβώωσα**, Ep. part. of ἡβάω.

ἠγάασθε, **ἠγάμην**, v. sub ἄγαμαι.

ἤγαγον, **ἠγαγόμην**, aor. 2 act. and med. of ἄγω.

ἠγάθεος, η, ον, (ἄγαν, θεός) *hallowed, most holy*.

ἤγᾰνον, τό, Ion. for τήγανον.

ἠγάπευν, Dor. for ἠγάπων, impf. of ἀγαπάω.

ἠγάσσατο, 3 sing. aor. 1 of ἀγάομαι.

ἤγγειλα, aor. 1 of ἀγγέλλω.

ἤγγῐκα, **ἤγγισα**, pf. and aor. 1 of ἐγγίζω.

ἠγγύηκα, -ημαι, pf. act. and pass. of ἐγγυάω.

ἠγγύησα, -ήθην, aor. 1 act. and pass. of ἐγγυάω.

ἠγγύων, impf. of ἐγγυάω.

ἤγειρα, aor. 1 of ἀγείρω.

ἡγεμόνευμα, τό, (ἡγεμονεύω) *a leading*: *a leader*.

ἡγεμονεύς, gen. έως Ep. ῆος, ὁ, poët. for ἡγεμών.

ἡγεμονεύω, f. σω, (ἡγεμών) *to go before*: *to lead the way, guide on the way*. II. *to lead* in *war, to rule, command*, c. gen. pers.: absol. *to be ruler*.

ἡγεμονία, ἡ, (ἡγεμών) *a leading the way, going first*. II. *chief command, sovereignty*: *the supremacy of one state over a number of subordinates*; ἡγεμονία τῆς Ἑλλάδος *the supremacy* of Greece.

ἡγεμονικός, ή, όν, (ἡγεμών) *fit for guiding, ready to guide*. II. *fit for commanding, chief, leading*, Lat. *princeps*.

ἡγεμόνιος, α, ον, (ἡγεμών) *of* or *belonging to a guide*: ὁ ἡγεμόνιος, name of Hermes, as *the guide* of departed souls.

ἡγεμόσυνος, η, ον, *belonging to a leader*: τὰ ἡγεμόσυνα (sub. ἱερά), *thank-offerings for safe-conduct*.

ἡγεμών, όνος, ὁ, *a leader*, Lat. *dux*: I. *a guide* to shew one the way, ἡγεμὼν ὁδοῦ;—generally, *one who does a thing first*, Lat. *princeps, auctor*; ἡγεμὼν γίγνεσθαί τινι to be one's *guide* or *authority*. 2. *the leader* of an army, *a commander, captain, chief*. From

ἡγέομαι, f. ἡγήσομαι: aor. 1 ἡγησάμην: pf. ἥγημαι (sometimes used in pass. sense): Dep.: (ἄγω):—*to go before, lead the way*, opp. to ἕπομαι: *to shew the way, guide, conduct*. 2. *to lead* an army, and so *to command, rule*:—with dat. it has the orig. sense of *going before*, with gen. the derived one of *leading, commanding*:—absol. *to be the first, to be a guide, leader, chief*; ὁ ἡγούμενος *a leader, ruler, chief*. II. like Lat. *ducere, to suppose, believe, hold*; ἡγεῖσθαί τινα βασιλέα *to hold* or *regard* as king; ἡγεῖσθαι θεούς *to believe in* gods, like νομίζειν.

ἠγερέθομαι, Ep. form of ἀγείρομαι Pass., *to be gathered together*, only in 3 pl. pres. and impf. ἠγερέθονται, ἠγερέθοντο.

ἠγερέομαι, Ep. form of ἀγείρομαι Pass., *to gather, come together*, only in pres. inf. ἠγερέεσθαι.

ἤγερθεν, Ep. 3 pl. aor. 1 pass. of ἀγείρω.

ἡγηλάζω, Ep. form of ἡγέομαι, *to guide*; also, like Lat. *agere*, κακὸν μόρον ἡγηλάζειν *to lead* a wretched life.

ἥγημαι, pf. of ἡγέομαι.

ἡγητέον, verb. Adj. of ἡγέομαι, *one must lead*. II. *one must suppose*.

ἡγητήρ, ῆρος, ὁ, **ἡγητής**, οῦ, ὁ, **ἡγήτωρ**, ορος, ὁ, (ἡγέομαι) *a leader, guide*. 2. *a leader, commander, chief*; ἡγήτορες ἠδὲ μέδοντες *chiefs* in field and council.

ἡγιασμένος, pf. part. pass. of ἁγιάζω.

ἠγίνεον, impf. of ἀγῑνέω.

ἠγκαλισάμην, **ἠγκάλισμαι**, aor. 1 med. and pf. pass. of ἀγκαλίζομαι.

ἠγκύρισα, aor. 1 of ἀγκυρίζω.

ἠγλάϊσα, aor. 1 of ἀγλαΐζω.

ἦγμαι, pf. pass. of. ἄγω.

ἠγνόηκα, **ἠγνόησα**, pf. and aor. 1 of ἀγνοέω.

ἥγνισαι, 2 sing. pf. pass. of ἁγνίζω.

ἠγνόουν, impf. of ἀγνοέω.

ἦγξα, aor. 1 of ἄγχω.

ἦγον, impf. of ἄγω.

ἠγοράασθε, -όωντο, Ep. lengthd. for ἠγορᾶσθε, -ῶντο, 2 and 3 pl. impf. of ἀγοράομαι.

ἠγόρᾰκα, **ἠγόρᾰσα**, pf. and aor. 1 of ἀγοράζω.

ἠγόρευκα, **ἠγόρευσα**, pf. and aor. 1 of ἀγορεύω.

ἤγουν, Conj. (ἤ, γοῦν) *that is to say*, Lat. *scilicet*.

ἠγρίᾱνα, aor. 1 of ἀγριαίνω.

ἠγρίωκα, **ἠγρίωσα**, pf. and aor. 1 of ἀγριόω.

ἠγρύπνησα, aor. 1 of ἀγρυπνέω.

ἠγρόμην, Ep. for ἠγερόμην, aor. 2 med. of ἐγείρω.

ἦγχον, aor. 2 and impf. of ἄγχω.

ἠγωνίᾱκα, -ίᾱσα, -ίων, pf., aor. 1 and impf. of ἀγωνιάω.

ἠγωνισάμην, aor. I med. of *ἀγωνίζομαι*.

ἠγωνίσθην, ἠγώνισμαι, aor. I and pf. pass. of *ἀγωνίζομαι*.

ἠ-δέ, (ἤ, δέ) *and:* if *καί* follows ἠδέ, it takes the sense also, e. g. *ἠδὲ καί and* also. II when it answers to *ἠμέν* it means, *as also*.

ἥδε, fem. of *ὅδε*.

ᾔδεα, Ion. resolved form of *ᾔδη*, plqpf. of **εἴδω*.

ᾔδειν, *ειs*, *ει*, plqpt. (with impf. sense) of **εἴδω*: 3 pl. *ᾔδεισαν* or *ᾔδεσαν*.

ᾐδεσάμην, aor. I of *αἰδέομαι*.

ἠδέσθην, aor. I pass. of *ἐσθίω*.

ᾐδέσθην, aor. I pass. of *αἰδέομαι*.

ἡδέως, Adv. of *ἡδύς*, *sweetly, pleasantly, gladly*, *ἡδέως ἔχειν to be kind:* Comp. *ἥδιον*, Sup. *ἥδιστα*.

ἬΔΗ, Adv. of Time, like Lat. *jam, already, by*, or *from this time, now, presently, forthwith:* also of Place, *ἀπὸ ταύτης ἤδη Αἴγυπτος* after this lake *directly* begins Egypt.

ᾔδη, *ᾔδησθα*, *ᾔδη* Att. for **ᾔδειν**, plqpf. (with impf. sense) of **εἴδω*.

ἠδίκεον, ἠδίκηκα, ἠδίκησα, impf., pf., and aor. I of *ἀδικέω*.

ἡδίων, ἥδιστος, *η*, *ον*, Comp. and Sup. of *ἡδύς*.

ἠδολέσχεον, impf. of *ἀδολεσχέω*.

ἭΔΟΜΑΙ, fut. *ἡσθήσομαι*: aor. 1 *ἥσθην*, rarely in med. form *ἡσάμην*: Dep.:—*to enjoy oneself, take one's pleasure:* with partic., *ἥσθη ἀκούσας he was glad to have heard:* often used in dat. of partic., *ἡδομένῳ γίγνεταί μοί τι* I am well pleased at the thing happening, like *ἀσμένῳ, βουλομένῳ*. Hence

ἡδομένως, Adv. pres. part. of *ἥδομαι*, *gladly*.

ἡδονή, *ἡ*, (*ἧδος*, *ἥδομαι*) *delight, enjoyment, pleasure*, Lat. *voluptas; πρὸς* or *καθ' ἡδονὴν λέγειν* to speak so *as to please another*.

ἧδος, *εος*, *τό*, (*ἥδομαι*) *delight, enjoyment, pleasure*.

ἦ δ' ὅs, *said he*. for *ἔφη ἐκεῖνος*. v. *ἠμί*.

ἡδῠ-βόης, *ου*, Dor. **-βόας**, *α*, *ὁ*, (*ἡδύς*, *βοή*) *sweet-sounding*.

ἡδύ-γᾰμος, *ον*, (*ἡδύς*, *γαμος*) *sweetening marriage*.

ἡδύ-γελως, *ων*, gen. *ω*, (*ἡδύς*. *γέλως*) *sweetly-laughing*.

ἡδύ-γλωσσος, *ον*, (*ἡδύς*, *γλῶσσα*) *sweet-tongued*.

ἡδυ-γνώμων, *ον*, gen. *ονος*, (*ἡδύς*, *γνώμη*) *of pleasant mind, of kindly sentiments*.

ἡδυ-επής, *ές*, (*ἡδύς*, *ἔπος*) *sweet-speaking · sweet-sounding:*—poet. fem. **ἡδυέπεια**.

ἡδύ-θροος, *ον*, contr. **-θρους**, *ουν*, (*ἡδύς*, *θρόος*) *sweet-strained*.

ἡδύ-ληπτος, *ον*, (*ἡδύς*, *λαμβάνω*) *taken with pleasure*.

ἡδύ-λογος, *ον*, (*ἡδύς*, *λέγω*) *sweet-speaking: flattering, fawning*.

ἡδῠ-λύρης, *ου*, *ὁ*, (*ἡδύς*, *λύρα*) *singing sweetly to the lyre*.

ἡδῠ-μελής, *ές*, (*ἡδύς*, *μέλος*) *sweet-singing*.

ἡδῠ-μελί-φθογγος, *ον*, (*ἡδύς*, *μελί*, *φθόγγος*) *with honey-sweet voice*.

ἡδῠ-μῐγής, *ές*, (*ἡδύς*, *μιγῆναι*) *sweetly-mixed*.

ἥδῠμος, *ον*, poët. for *ἡδύς*, *sweet, pleasant*.

ἠδυνάμην, Att. for *ἐδυνάμην*, impf. of *δύναμαι*.

ἠδυνήθην, Att. aor. I pass. of *δύναμαι*.

ἡδύνω, f. *ῠνῶ*: aor. I *ἥδῡνα*: (*ἡδύς*):—*to sweeten, season*.

ἡδύ-οινος, *ον*, (*ἡδύς*, *οἶνος*) *producing sweet wine*.

ἡδύοσμον, *τό*, *the sweet-smelling herb, mint*. From

ἡδύ-οσμος, *ον*, (*ἡδύς*, *ὀσμή*) *sweet-smelling*.

ἡδῠπάθεια, *ἡ*, *pleasant living, luxury*. From

ἡδῠπᾰθέω, f. *ησω*, (*ἡδυπαθής*) *to live pleasantly enjoy oneself, be luxurious*. Hence

ἡδυπάθημα, *ατος*, *τό*, *enjoyment*. [ᾰ]

ἡδυ-πᾰθής, *ές*, (*ἡδύς*, *παθεῖν*) *living pleasantly*

ἡδύ-πνευστος, *ον*, (*ἡδύς*, *πνέω*) = *ἡδύπνοος*.

ἡδύ-πνοος, *ον*, contr. **-πνους**, *ουν*, (*ἡδύς*, *πνοή*) *sweet-breathing: sweet-smelling*.

ἡδύ-πολις, *ιος*, and *εως*, also *εος*. *ὁ*. *ἡ*, (*ἡδύς*, *πόλις*) *dear to the people*.

ἡδυ-πότης, *ου*, (*ἡδύς*, *πίνω*) *fond of drinking*.

ἡδύ-ποτος, *ον*, (*ἡδύς*, *πίνω*) *sweet to drink*.

ἡδύς, *ἡδεῖα*, *ἡδύ*; Ion. fem. *ἡδέᾰ* Dor. *ἁδεά*; Dor. acc sing. *ἁδέα*, for *ἡδύν*:—Comp. *ἡδίων*, Sup. *ἥδιστος*: later, also, *ἡδύτερος*, *ἡδύτατος* · (*ἥδομαι*):—*sweet* to the taste, smell, or hearing: metaph. *sweet, pleasant*. II. of persons, *pleasant. welcome, dear, glad*.

ἥδυσμα, *ατος*, *τό*, (*ἡδύνω*) *that which sweetens* or *flavours, seasoning, spice, sauce*.

ἡδῠ-σώμᾰτος, *ον*, (*ἡδύς*, *σῶμα*) *of sweet form*.

ἡδῠ-φᾰής, *ές*, (*ἡδύς*, *φάος*) *sweetly-shining*.

ἡδύ-φρων, *φρονος*, *ὁ*, *ἡ*, (*ἡδύς*, *φρήν*) *sweet-minded*.

ἡδυφωνία, *ἡ*, *sweetness of voice*. From

ἡδύ-φωνος, *ον*, (*ἡδύς*, *φωνή*) *sweet-voiced*.

ἡδῠ-χᾰρής, *ές*, (*ἡδύς*, *χαρῆναι*) *sweetly joyous*.

ἡδύ-χροος, *ον*, contr. **-χρους**, *ουν*, (*ἡδύς*, *χρόα*) *of sweet complexion:* **ἡδύχρουν**, *τό*, as Subst., *a kind of perfume*.

ἠέ, Ep. for *ἤ*, *or*.

ᾖε, Ep. for *ᾔει*, 3 sing. impf. of *εἶμι ibo*.

ᾔει, 3 sing impf. of *εἶμι*.

ἤειδον, ἤεισα, impf. and aor. I of *ἀείδω*.

ἠείδειν, Ep. plqpf. (with impf. sense) of **εἴδω*.

ἠέλιος, *ὁ*, poet. and Ion. for *ἥλιος*.

ἠελιῶτις, Ep. for *ἡλιῶτις*.

ἦεν, Ep. 3 sing. impf. of *εἰμί sum*.

ἠέ-περ, poët. for *ἤπερ*.

ἠέρα, Ion. and Ep. acc. of *ἀήρ*.

ἠερέθομαι, lengthd. form of *ἀείρομαι* Pass., *to hang floating* or *waving in the air:* metaph., *ὁπλοτέρων φρένες ἠερέθονται* young men's minds *are flighty*.

ἠέρθην, aor. I pass. of *ἀείρω*.

ἠέρι, Ion. and Ep. dat. of *ἀήρ*.

ἠέριος, *α*, *ον*. Ep. for *ἀέριος* (*ἀήρ*) *early, at morn, at day-break, when all things are yet wrapt in mist* (*ἀήρ*). 2. *high in air*.

ἤερμαι, pf. pass. of *ἀείρω*.

ἠερο-δίνης, *ες*, (*ἀήρ*, *δινέω*) *wheeling in mid-air*. [ῑ]

ἠερο-ειδής, *ές*, Ion. and Ep. for *ἀερ-*, (*ἀήρ*, *εἶδος*) *of* *cloudy look, clouded, dark, murky: cloud-capped*, of hills: *dim, gray.*

ἠερόεις, εσσα, εν, Ion. and Ep. for ἀερ-, (ἀήρ) *clouded, dark, murky.*

ἠερόθεν, Adv., Ion. and Ep. for ἀερ-, (ἀήρ) *from air.*

ἠέρος, Ion. and Ep. gen. of ἀήρ.

ἠερο-φοῖτις, ιδος, ἡ, fem. Adj. (ἀήρ, φοιτάω) *walking in darkness.*

ἠερό-φωνος, ον, (ἀήρ, φωνή) *sounding through air, loud-voiced.*

ἠέρταζον, impf. of ἀερτάζω.

ἠέρτησα, ἠέρτημαι, aor. I act. and pf. pass. of ἀερτάω.

ἤεσαν 3 pl. impf. of εἶμι *ibo.*

ἤην, Ep. 3 sing. impf. of εἰμί *sum.*

ἠήρ, ἡ, a late nom. formed after ἠέρος, ἠέρι, ἠέρα, the Ep. and Ion. cases of ἀήρ.

ἠθαῖος, α, ον, Dor. for ἠθεῖος.

ἠθάς, άδος, ὁ, ἡ, Ion. for ἐθάς, (ἦθος) *used, accustomed, habituated to* a thing II. *wonted, accustomed.*

ἠθεῖος, α, ον, (ἦθος) *honoured, respected*: voc. ἠθεῖε, *Sir*, as a term of respect from a younger to an elder brother.

ἠθέληκα, ἠθέλησα, pf. and aor. I of ἐθέλω.

ἤθελον, impf. of ἐθέλω.

ἤθεος, ὁ, ἡ, Att. for ἠίθεος.

'ΗΘΕ'Ω, f. ήσω, *to sift* or *strain.*

ἠθικός, ή, όν, (ἦθος) *of* or *for morals, ethical, moral*, opp. to intellectual (διανοητικός). II. *expressive of moral character.*

ἤθληκα, ἤθλησα, pf. and aor. I of ἀθλέω.

ἠθμός, ὁ, (ἠθέω) *a strainer.*

ἦθος, εος, τό, (ἔθος) *an accustomed place*: hence in plur. ἤθεα, *seats, haunts, abodes*, first, *of beasts*, but afterwards *of men.* II. *custom, usage, habit*: in pl., like Lat. *mores, the disposition, temper, character.*

ἦθον, imp. of αἴθω.

ἤθροισα, aor. I of ἀθροίζω.

ἠθροίσθην, ἤθροισμαι, aor. I and pf. pass. of ἀθροίζω.

ἤϊα contr. ᾖα, τά, (ἤϊα, contr. ᾖα, impf. of εἶμι *ibo*) *provisions for a journey*, Lat. *viaticum*: generally, *food, meat.* II. *chaff, husks.* [ῐ]

ἤϊα, Ion. for ᾔειν, impf. of εἶμι *ibo*: 3 sing. ἤϊε, 3 pl. ἤϊον or ἤϊσαν.

ἠίθεος Att. contr. ἤθεος, ὁ, *a youth* come to manhood, but not yet married, *a bachelor*, answering to the fem. παρθένος:—rarely in fem. ἠϊθέη, *a young girl.*

ἤϊκτο, 3 sing. Ep. plqpf. of ἔοικα (as if from ἠίγμην).

ἦϊξα, aor. I of ἀίσσω.

ἠϊόεις, εσσα, εν, (ἠϊών) *with high, steep banks.*

ἤϊον, Ep. 3 pl. impf. of εἶμι *ibo.*

ἤϊος, ὁ, epith. of Phoebus, from the cry ἤ, ἤ.

ἤϊσαν, Ep. for ᾔεσαν, 3 pl. impf. of εἶμι *ibo.*

ἤϊσκον, impf. of εἴσκω.

ἤϊσσον, impf. of ἀίσσω.

ἠΐχθην, aor. I pass. of ἀίσσω.

'ΗΙΩ'Ν Att. ᾐών Dor. αἰών, όνος, ἡ, *a sea-bank, the shore, beach*: also a *river-bank.* [ῐ]

ἠϊών, ονος, ἡ, (ἀίω) *a hearing, report.*

'ΗΚΑ, Adv. of Sound, *low, tranquilly.* II. of Motion, *slightly, a little*: *softly, gently.* III. of Sight, *smoothly, sleekly.* [ᾰ]

ἧκα, aor. I of ἵημι.

ᾔκαζον, Att. impf. of εἰκάζω.

ᾐκαιρεῖσθε, 2 pl. impf. of ἀκαιρέομαι.

ᾔκασα, ᾐκάσθην, Att. aor. I act. and med. of εἰκάζω.

ᾔκασμαι, Att. pf. pass. of εἰκάζω.

ἤκᾰχε, 3 sing. aor. 2 of ἀχέω.

ἠκέσατο, 3 sing. aor. I of ἀκέομαι.

ἤ-κεστος, η, ον, for ἄ-κεστος, (α privat., κεντέω) *ungoaded*: *free from labour.*

ἠκή, ἡ, Ion. for ἀκή, ἀκωκή.

ᾐκισάμην, aor. I med. of αἰκίζω.

ᾐκίσθην, ᾔκισμαι, aor. I and pf. pass. of αἰκίζω.

ἥκιστος, η, ον, Sup. Adj. from the Adv. ἦκα, *gentlest, slowest.*

ἥκιστος, η, ον, Sup. of Comp. ἥσσων, *the worst, least, poorest, meanest*:—Adv. ἥκιστα, *least* (κακός or μικρός is used as positive).

ἤκμᾰσα, aor. I of ἀκμάζω.

ἠκολούθησα, aor. I of ἀκολουθέω.

ἠκόντισα, aor. I of ἀκοντίζω.

ἤ-κου, Ion. and Dor. for ἤπου.

ἤκουσα, aor. I of ἀκούω.

ἤκουσμαι, pf. pass. of ἀκούω.

ἠκροώμην, ἠκροᾱσάμην, impf. and aor. I of ἀκροάομαι.

ἠκρωτηρίασα, ἠκρωτηρίασμαι, aor. I act. and pf. pass. of ἀκρωτηριάζω.

'ΗΚΩ, impf. ἧκον: fut. ἥξω:—properly *I have come, am here.* Lat. *adsum*: the impf. taking a plqpf. sense, *I had come, was here*, Lat. *aderam*:—then loosely *to come.* II. *to have come to, reached a point*; εἰς τοῦτο τόλμης ἥκειν *to have reached* this pitch of audacity. 2. with gen. and an Adv., εὖ **ἥκειν** τινός *to be* well *off for* a thing, *have plenty of* it. 3. *to have come to. to relate* or *belong to.*

ἠλάθην [ᾰ], aor. I pass. of ἐλαύνω.

ἠλαίνω, Ion. and poët. for ἀλαίνω. (ἀλάομαι) *to wander, stray*: *to wander in mind, be mad.*

ἠλακᾰτα, ων, τά, *the wool on the distaff.*

ἠλᾰκάτη, ἡ, *a distaff*, Lat. *colus*: also *a spindle*: later of things of the same shape, as II. *the joint of a reed* or *cane.* III. *an arrow*, like ἄτρακτος, Lat. *arundo.*

ἠλάλαξα, aor. I of ἀλαλάζω.

ἤλαλκον, poët. aor. 2 of ἀλέξω.

ἡλάμην, aor. I med. of ἅλλομαι.

ἤλᾰσα, ἠλάσθην, aor. I act. and pass. of ἐλαύνω.

ἠλασκάζω, (ἀλάομαι) *to wander away from*; ἐμὸν μένος ἠλασκάζει *he flees from* or *shuns* my wrath. II. trans. *to drive to and fro.*

ἠλάσκω, Ep. form of ἀλάομαι, ἀλαίνω, *to wander, stray, roam about.*

ἠλάστεον, impf. of ἀλαστέω.

ἠλᾶτο, 3 sing. impf. of ἀλάομαι.

ἠλάττωσα, ἠλαττώθην, aor. 1 act. and pass. of *ἐλασσόω.*

ἤλγησα, aor. 1 of *ἀλγέω.*

ἤλγῡνα, ἠλγύνθην, aor. 1 act. and pass. of *ἀλγύνω.*

ἤλδᾰνε, 3 sing. aor. 2 of *ἀλδαίνω.*

ἤλειψα, ἠλείφθην, aor. 1 act. and pass. of *ἀλείφω.*

ἠλεάμην, aor. 1 of *ἀλέομαι.*

ἠλέγχθην, aor. 1 pass. of *ἐλέγχω.*

ἤλεκτρον, *τό,* and **ἤλεκτρος,** *ὁ* and *ἡ,* (*ἠλέκτωρ*) *electron,* mentioned in the Odyssey along with copper, gold, silver, and ivory, *a metallic substance* consisting of *gold* alloyed with *silver*:—in Ar. Eq. 532 *ἐκπιπτουσῶν τῶν ἠλέκτρων,* it seems to mean, *the pegs of his lyre inlayed with electron.* II. *amber.*

ἠλεκτρο-φᾰής, *ές,* (*ἤλεκτρον, φάος*) *amber-gleaming.*

ἠλέκτωρ, *opos, ὁ, the beaming sun:* as Adj., *ἠλέκτωρ Ὑπερίων beaming* Hyperion. (Deriv. uncertain.)

ἠλεός, *ή, όν,* (*ἠλός*) *wandering in mind, distracted, crazed.* II. act. *distracting, crazing.*

ἠλέμᾰτος Dor. **ἀλ–,** *ον,* (*ἠλεός, ἠλός*) *distraught, silly, trifling, vain.*

ἤλεσα, aor. 1 of *ἀλέω, to grind.*

ἠλεύατο, Ep. for *ἠλεύσατο,* 3 sing. aor. 1 med. of *ἀλεύομαι = ἀλέομαι.*

ἠλήλαντο, 3 pl. plqpf. pass. of *ἐλαύνω.*

ἠλήλατο, 3 sing. plqpf. pass. of *ἐλαύνω.*

ἠληλίμμην, plqpf. pass. of *ἀλείφω.*

ἦλθον, contr. of *ἤλυθον,* aor. 2 of *ἔρχομαι.*

ἡλιάζω, = *ἡλιόω,* (*ἥλιος*) *to warm in the sun.* II. Med. *ἡλιάζομαι, to sit in the court* Ἡλιαία.

ἡλιαία, *ἡ,* (*ἁλής, ἁλία*) at Athens *a hall* in which the chief law-court was held: *the Heliaea* or *supreme law-court.*

ἡλιάξει Dor. 2 sing. fut. of *ἡλιάζομαι.*

ἡλιαστής, *οῦ, ὁ,* (*ἡλιάζομαι*) *a juryman in the court Heliaea, a Heliast.* Hence

ἡλιαστικός, *ή, όν, of* or *belonging to a Heliast.*

ἠλίβᾰτος, *ον, steep, abrupt, precipitous: high, huge, enormous.* II. like Lat. *altus, deep, profound.* (Deriv. uncertain.)

ἅλῐθα, Adv. (*ἅλις*) *enough, sufficiently: abundantly.*

ἠλῐθιάζω, *to speak* or *act idly, foolishly.* From

ἠλίθιος Dor. **ἀλίθ–,** *α, ον,* (*ἠλός, ἠλεός*) *idle, trifling, vain, foolish, silly.* Adv. *–ίως.* Hence

ἠλῐθιόω, f. *ώσω, to make foolish, to distract, craze.*

ἡλῐκία, *ἡ,* (*ἧλιξ*) *time of life, age.* 2. *the vigour* or *prime of life, manhood; οἱ ἐν ἡλικίᾳ* men *of age fit for service*:—*youthful heat and passion.* II. as Subst., = *οἱ ἥλικες, those of the same age, fellows, comrades, mates.* III. generally, *age, time:* later *an age,* Lat. *seculum.* IV. of the body, *stature, growth, bulk.* Hence

ἡλῐκιώτης, *ου, ὁ,* fem. **–ῶτις,** *ιδος, an equal in age, fellow, comrade,* Lat. *aequalis.*

ἡλίκος, *η, ον,* Relat. to *τηλίκος* or *τηλικοῦτος,* as Lat. *quantus* to *tantus, as big as, as tall as, as great as.* 2. in indirect *questions, how great* or *strong*: also *how old, at what age: as old as.* [ῐ] From

ἩΛΙΞ, *ῐκος, ὁ, ἡ, of the same age,* Lat. *aequalis*:—as Subst. *a fellow, comrade, mate.*

ἡλιό-βλητος, *ον,* (*ἥλιος, βάλλω*) *sun-burnt.*

ἡλιο-κᾱής, *ές,* (*ἥλιος, κάω, καίω*) *sun-burnt.*

ἡλιό-καυστος, *ον,* = *ἡλιοκάης.*

ἡλιο-μᾰνής, *ές,* (*ἥλιος, μανῆναι*) ***doting on the sun,*** *mad for love of the sun.*

ἥλιος Dor. **ἅλιος** poët. **ἠέλιος,** *ὁ,* (*ἕλη* Lat. *sol*) *the sun; πρὸς Ἠῶ τ' Ἠέλιόν τε* toward the morn and *rising sun,* i. e. *the East,* opp. to *πρὸς ζόφον,* the land of darkness or West; so also Herodotus opposes *πρὸς ἠῶ τε καὶ ἡλίου ἀνατολάς* to *πρὸς ἑσπέρην.* 2. *day,* like Lat. *sol.* 3. *οἱ ἥλιοι the sun-beams,* like Lat. *soles.* II. as prop. n. *Helios, the sun-god,* who after the time of Aeschylus was identified with Apollo or Phoebus.

ἡλιο-στερής, *ές,* (*ἥλιος, στερέω*) *shading from the sun.*

ἡλιο-στῐβής, *ές,* (*ἥλιος, στιβεῖν*) *sun-trodden, exposed to the sun.*

ἡλιόω, f. *ώσω,* (*ἥλιος*) *to warm in the sun*:—Pass. *to bask in the sun, be lighted and heated by the sun.*

ἥλῐσα, ἡλίσθην, aor. 1 act. and pass. of *ἁλίζω.*

ἤλῐσα, ἤλῐκα, aor. 1 and pf. of *ἀλίνδω.*

ἤλῐτον, aor. 2 of *ἀλιταίνω.*

ἠλῐτο-εργός, *όν,* (*ἀλιταίνω, ἔργον*) *missing the work, failing in one's end* or *aim.*

ἠλῐτό-μηνος, *ον,* (*ἀλιταίνω, μήν*) *missing the right month, untimely born.*

ἠλίφην [ῐ], aor. 2 pass. of *ἀλείφω.*

ἨΛΙΨ, *ῖπος, ὁ,* said to be *a Dorian shoe.*

ἡλίωσα, aor. 1 both of *ἁλιόω* and of *ἡλιόω.*

ἡλιώτης, *ου, ὁ,* fem. **–ῶτις,** *ιδος,* poët. **ἠελ–,** (*ἥλιος*) *of* or *belonging to the sun.*

ἥλκησα, aor. 1 of *ἑλκέω.*

ἡλκωμένος, pf. part. pass. of *ἑλκόω.*

ἠλλάγην, –χθην, aor. 2 and 1 pass. of *ἀλλάσσω.*

ἠλλαγμένος, pf. part. pass. of *ἀλλάσσω.*

ἤλλαξα, aor. 1 of *ἀλλάσσω.*

ἠλλοίωσα, ἠλλοίωμαι, aor. 1 act. and pf. pass. of *ἀλλοιόω.*

ἠλόησα, Ep. *ἠλοίησα,* aor. 1 of *ἀλοάω.*

ἠλόκισμαι, pf. pass. of *ἀλοκίζω.*

ἩΛΟΣ, *ὁ, a nail, stud:* more for ornament than use.

ἠλός, *ή, όν,* (*ἄλη*) *wandering, crazy, silly.*

ἤλπετο, 3 sing. impf. of *ἔλπομαι.*

ἤλπῐσα, ἠλπίσθην, aor. 1 act. and pass. of *ἐλπίζω.*

ἠλσάμην, aor. 1 med. of *εἵλω.*

ἠλύγη [ῠ], *ἡ,* (*ἦλυξ*) *shadow, darkness:* metaph., *δίκης ἠλύγη the darkness* or *obscurity* of a law-suit

ἤλῠθον, Ep. for *ἦλθον,* aor. 2 of *ἔρχομαι.*

ἦλυξ, *ῠγος, ὁ, darkness,* only found in compd. *ἐπῆλυξ.* (Formed from *λύγη,* with a prefix.)

ἤλυξα, aor. 1 of *ἀλύσκω.*

Ἠλύσιον πεδίον, *τό,* (*ἐλεύσομαι,* fut. of *ἔρχομαι*) *the Elysian fields:* later without *πεδίον, Elysium.* Homer places it on the west border of the earth; Hesiod and Pindar in the *μακάρων νῆσοι.*

ἠλύσιος, *α, ον, coming:* or *Elysian.* [ῠ] From

ἤλῠσις, εως, ἡ, (ἐλεύσομαι, fut. of ἔρχομαι) *a coming: a step.* 2. *a coming event, the future.*

ἦλφον, aor. 2 of ἀλφαίνω.

ἥλωκα, Ion. for ἑάλωκα, pf. of ἁλίσκομαι.

ἥλων, Ion. for ἑάλων, aor. 2 of ἁλίσκομαι.

ἠλώμην, impf. of ἀλάομαι.

ἧμα, τό, (ἵημι) *that which is thrown, a dart, javelin.*

ἠμᾰθόεις, εσσα, εν, (ἄμαθος) Ion. for ἀμ–, *sandy.*

ἧμαι, ἧσαι, ἧται, 3 pl. ἧνται Ion. ἕᾰται Ep. εἵᾰται; imperat. ἧσο, ἥσθω, etc.; inf. ἧσθαι; part. ἥμενος; impf. ἥμην, ἧσο, ἧστο, 3 pl. ἧντο Ion. ἕᾰτο Ep. εἵᾰτο:—only used in pres. and impf. (which are properly pf. and plqpf. of ἕζομαι), *to be set, to sit:* often with collat. sense *to tarry, linger, loiter:* ἥμενος χῶρος, like εἱαμένη, *a low, sunken* place. It is rarely used c. acc., ἧσθαι σέλμα *to sit on* a bench.

ἦμαρ Dor. **ἆμαρ**, ἄτος, τό, poët. for ἡμέρα, *day;* αἴσιμον ἦμαρ, μόρσιμον ἦμαρ *the day* of destiny, *day* of death; ἐλεύθερον, δούλιον ἦμαρ *the day* of freedom, of slavery, i. e. freedom, slavery itself; of the seasons, ὀπωρινόν, χειμέριον ἦμαρ autumn, winter *time;* ἐπ' ἤματι *day by day, daily,* but ἐπ' ἦμαρ *by day;* κατ' ἦμαρ, *day by day;* παρ' ἦμαρ *every other day,* Lat. *alternis diebus:* also, ἦμαρ as Adv., *by day,* opp. to νύκτωρ.

ἡμάρτηκα, ἡμάρτησα, pf. and aor. 1 of ἁμαρτάνω.

ἤμαρτον, aor. 2 of ἁμαρτάνω.

ἠμάτιος, α, ον, (ἦμαρ) poët. for ἡμερήσιος, *by day: day by day, daily.*

ᾑμάτωμαι, pf. pass. of αἱματόω.

ἤμβλωκα, ἤμβλωσα, pf. and aor. 1 of ἀμβλίσκω.

ἤμβροτον, inf. ἀμβροτεῖν, Ep. aor. 2 of ἁμαρτάνω.

ἡμεδᾰπός, ή, όν, (ἡμεῖς) *of our land* or *country, native,* Lat. *nostras.*

ἡμεῖς, ἡμᾶς, nom. and acc. pl. of ἐγώ.

ἤμελγον, impf. of ἀμέλγω.

ἠμελημένως, Adv. pf. pass. part. of ἀμελέω, *in a neglectful manner.*

ἤμελλον, Att. impf. of μέλλω.

ἠ-μέν.., ἠ-δέ.., (ἤ, μέν) poët. for καί.., καί.., *as well.., as also..*, Lat. *et.., et..:* also disjunctive, *if..,* or *if..*, *whether.., whether..*, Lat. *vel.., vel..,* or *sive.., sive...*

ἦμεν, 1 pl. impf. of εἰμί *sum.*

ἦμεν, Dor. for εἶναι, inf. of εἰμί *sum.*

ἩΜΕ'ΡΑ Ion. **ἡμέρη** Dor. **ἁμέρα**, ἡ, *day: the light of day;* ἅμ' ἡμέρᾳ or ἅμα τῇ ἡμέρᾳ with *dawn of day,* with *day-break;* δι' ἡμέρας *all day long;* διὰ τρίτης ἡμέρας every third day, Lat. *tertio quoque die;* ἐφ' ἡμέραν *sufficient for the day,* or *daily;* καθ' ἡμέραν *day by day;* μεθ' ἡμέραν by *day,* Lat. *interdiu;* ὀψὲ τῆς ἡμέρας late *in the day;* πρὸς ἡμέραν *towards* or *near* day. II. metaph. *life:* παλαιὰ ἡμέρα old *age;* νέα ἡμέρα youth. Hence

ἡμερεύω, f. σω, *to pass the day;* ἡμερεύειν μακρᾶς κελεύθου *to rest the day* after a long journey. 2. *to pass one's days, live.*

ἡμερήσιος, α, ον, also ος, ον, (ἡμέρα) *of* or *for the day, by day.* II. *a day long;* ἡμερησία ὁδὸς *a day's* journey.

ἡμερία, ἡ, = ἡμέρα.

ἡμερῐνός, ή, όν, = ἡμερήσιος. *by day,* opp. to νυκτερινός by night; ἄγγελος ἡμερινὸς *a day-*messenger. II. = ἐφήμερος, *for the day, perishable.*

ἡμέριος, ον, also α, ον, (ἡμέρα) *of a day, lasting* or *living but a day.*

ἡμερίς, ίδος, ἡ, fem. of ἥμερος, *cultivated,* opp. to ἄγριος, wild:—as Subst. *the vine.*

ἡμερο-δρόμος, ον, (ἡμέρα, δραμεῖν *running the livelong day:*—as Subst. *a day-runner, a courier.*

ἡμερο-θᾱλής, ές, Dor. for sq.

ἡμερο-θηλής, ές, (ἥμερος, θάλλω) *gently-sprouting*

ἡμερό-κοιτος, ον, (ἡμέρα, κοίτη) *sleeping by day,* i. e. *awake by night,* epith. of a thief.

ἡμερο-λεγδόν, Adv. (ἡμέρα, λέγω) *counting every day, day by day, every day.*

ἡμερο-λογέω, (ἡμέρα, λέγω) *to count by days, register.*

ἡμερο-λόγιον, τό, (ἡμέρα, λέγω) *a calendar, almanack.*

'ΗΜΕΡΟΣ, ον, also α, ον, *tame, reclaimed, domestic,* of animals; of trees, *cultivated:* — opp. to ἄγριος, wild. II. metaph. of men, *gentle, civilised.*

ἡμερο-σκόπος, ὁ, (ἡμέρα, σκοπέω) *watching by day.* as Subst. *a day-watcher.*

ἡμερό-φαντος, ον, (ἡμέρα, φαίνομαι) *appearing by day.*

ἡμερο-φύλαξ, ἄκος, ὁ, (ἡμέρα, φύλαξ) *watching by day*

ἡμερό-φωνος, ον (ἡμέρα, φωνέω) epith. of the cock, *herald of day.*

ἡμερόω, f. ώσω, (ἥμερος) *to tame, make tame, reclaim:* of trees, *to cultivate.* 2. metaph. of men *to soothe, conciliate:* also *to tame by conquest, subdue*

ἧμες, Dor inf. of εἰμί *sum.*

ἡμετέρειος, α, ον, = ἡμεδαπός.

ἡμέτερος, α, ον, (ἡμεῖς) *our,* Lat. *noster;* εἰς ἡμέτερον (sub. δῶμα) *to our house*

ἡμέων, Ion and Ep. gen. pl. of ἐγώ.

ἤμην, rare Att. form for ἦν, impf. of εἰμί *sum.*

ἥμην, impf. of ἧμαι.

ἠμί, the same as φημί, *I say,* Lat. *inquam;* παῖ, ἠμί, παῖ, boy, *I say,* boy!—impf. 1 and 3 sing., ἦν δ' ἐγώ *said I,* ἦ δ' ὅς *said he,* are freq. in Att. Homer has only 3 sing. impf. ἦ, *he spoke.*

'ΗΜΙ–, freq. as a prefix, *half,* Lat. *semi* the Adj. is ἥμισυς.

ἡμί-ανδρος, ὁ, (ἡμι–, ἀνήρ) *a half-man, eunuch*

ἡμι-άνθρωπος, ὁ, = ἡμιάνδρος.

ἡμι-βρεχής, ές, (ἡμι–, βρέχομαι) *half-watered*

ἡμι-βρώς, ῶτος, ὁ, ἡ, and **ἡμί-βρωτος**, ον, (ἡμι–, βιβρώσκω) *half-eaten.*

ἡμι-γένειος, ον, (ἡμι–, γένειον) *with but half a beard.*

ἡμί-γυμνος, ον, (ἡμι–, γυμνός) *half-naked.*

ἡμι-δᾱής, ές, (ἡμι–, δαίω) *half-burnt*

ἡμι-δᾱρεικόν, τό, (ἡμι–, δαρεικός) *a half-daric.*

ἡμι-δεής, ές, (ἡμι–, δέω) *wanting half, half-full.*

ἡμι-διπλοΐδιον Att. contr. **–οίδιον**, τό, (ἡμι–, διπλοΐς) *a half-shawl,* or *shawl doubled in half.*

ἡμί-δουλος, ον, *a half-slave.*

ἡμι-εκτεόν, τό, *a half-ἑκτεύς*, i. e. *a twelfth part* of a medimnus.

ἡμι-έλλην, ηνος, ὁ, ἡ, *a half-Greek*.

ἡμι-εργής, ές, and **ἡμι-έργος**, ον, (ἡμι–, *ἔργω) *half-made*.

ἡμί-εφθος, ον, (ἡμι–, ἕψω) *half-boiled, half-cooked*.

ἡμι-θᾰλής, ές, (ἡμι–, θαλεῖν) *half-green*.

ἡμι-θᾰνής, ές, (ἡμι–, θανεῖν) *half-dead*.

ἡμί-θεος Dor. ἁμ–, ὁ, *half a god, demigod*.

ἡμιθνής, ῆτος, ὁ, ἡ, (ἡμι–, θᾰνεῖν) *half-dead*.

ἡμί-θραυστος, ον, (ἡμι–, θραύω) *half-broken*.

ἡμί-κᾰκος, ον, *a rogue by halves, half a villain*.

ἡμι-κλήριον, τό, (ἡμι–, κλῆρος) *half the inheritance*.

ἡμί-κραιρα, ἡ, *half the head* or *face*.

ἡμί-λεπτος, ον, (ἡμι–, λέπω) *half-peeled, half-hatched*.

ἡμί-λευκος, ον, *half-white*.

ἡμιλλήθην, **ἡμίλλημαι**, aor. 1 and pf. of ἁμιλλάομαι.

ἡμι-μᾰνής, ές, (ἡμι–, μανῆναι) *half-mad*.

ἡμι-μάραντος, ον, (ἡμι–, μαραίνομαι) *half-withered* or *faded*. [ᾰ]

ἡμι-μεθής, ές, (ἡμι–, μέθη) *half-drunk*.

ἡμι-μναῖος, α, ον, (ἡμι–, μνᾶ) *of, amounting to a half-mina*: ἡμιμναῖον, τό, as Subst. *a half-mina*.

ἥμιν or **ἡμῖν**, dat. pl. of ἐγώ.

ἡμί-ξηρος, ον, *half-dry*.

ἡμιολία (ναῦς), ἡ, *a light ship with one and a half bank of oars*. Fem. from

ἡμι-όλιος, α, ον, (ἡμι–, ὅλος) *one and a half, half as much again*; ἡμιόλια τοῦ τοτε καθεστῶτος μέτρου *half as large again* as the customary size; ἡμιόλιον οὗ πρότερον ἔφερον *one half more* than they used to receive before.

ἡμιόνειος, α, ον, (ἡμίονος) *of a mule*; ἅμαξα ἡμιονεία a car *drawn by mules*; ζυγὸν ἡμιόνειον a team *of mules*.

ἡμιονικός, ή, όν, = ἡμιόνειος.

ἡμί-ονος, ἡ or ὁ, (ἡμι–, ὄνος) *a half-ass, a mule*. II. as Adj., βρέφος ἡμίονον *a mule*-foal.

ἡμί-οπος, ον, (ἡμι–, ὀπή) *with half its proper number of holes*; ἡμίοποι αὐλοί flutes *with only three holes*.

ἡμί-οπτος, ον, *half-roasted*.

ἡμι-πέλεκκον, τό, (ἡμι–, πέλεκυς) *a half-axe, a single edged axe*, opp. to ἀμφιπέλεκκον.

ἡμί-πλεθρον, τό, *a half-πλέθρον*. i. e. 50 *feet*.

ἡμι-πλίνθιον, τό, (ἡμι-πλίνθος) *a half-plinth, a brick*, Lat. *semilaterium*.

ἡμί-πνοος, ον, contr. **–πνους**, ουν, (ἡμι–, πνέω) *half-breathing, half-choked*.

ἡμι-πύρωτος, ον, (ἡμι–, πυρόω) *half-burnt*. [ῠ]

ἡμίσεες, nom. pl. of ἥμισυς

ἡμίσεια, ἡ, *a half*, fem. of ἥμισυς.

ἡμί-σοφος, ον, *half-wise*.

ἡμί-σπαστος, ον, (ἡμι–, σπάω) *half torn down*.

ἡμι-στᾰδιαῖος, α, ον, (ἡμι–, στάδιον) *of half a stadium*.

ἡμι-στρᾰτιώτης, ου, ὁ, *a half-soldier*.

ἡμι-στρόγγῠλος, ον, *half-round*.

ἩΜΙΣΥΣ, εια, υ; Ion. fem. ἡμισέα: gen. ἡμίσεος rarely –εως, fem. ἡμισείας Ion. –έας: nom. pl. ἡμίσεες Att. –εις:—*half*, Lat. *SEMIS*: in plur. it sometimes agrees with the Subst., as ἡμίσεις λαοί *half* the people; in Att. the Subst. is commonly in genit., but gives its gender and number to the Adj., as αἱ ἡμίσειαι τῶν νεῶν *half* the ships; so also, ἥμισυς λόγος *half* the tale; ἥμισυ τεῖχος *half* the wall; neut. sing. ἥμισυ as Subst. *a half, half*, ἥμισυ τιμῆς.

ἡμῐ-τάλαντον, τό, *a half-talent*, as a weight; τρίτον ἡμιτάλαντον *two talents and a half* (cf. Lat. *sestertius*); but, τρία ἡμιτάλαντα *three half-talents*.

ἡμῐτέλεια, ἡ, (ἡμιτελής) *a remission of half*.

ἡμῐ-τέλεστος, ον, (ἡμι–, τελέω) *half-finished*.

ἡμῐ-τελής, ές, (ἡμι–, τέλος) *half-finished, half-accomplished, half-perfect*; δόμος ἡμιτελής a house *but half complete*, i. e. *wanting its master*.

ἡμί-τομος, ον, (ἡμι–, τεμεῖν) *half cut through*: *cut in two*: τὸ ἡμίτομον *a half*.

ἡμιτύβιον, τό, *a strong linen cloth, towel, napkin*. (Prob. an Egypt. word.)

ἡμι-φᾰής, ές, (ἡμι–, φάος) *half-shining*.

ἡμι-φάλακρος, ον, *half-bald*.

ἡμί-φαυλος, ον, *half-knavish*.

ἡμί-φλεκτος, ον, (ἡμι–, φλέγω) *half-burnt*.

ἡμιωβολιαῖος, α, ον, *worth half an obol*. From

ἡμι-ωβόλιον or **-ωβέλιον**, τό, *a half-obol*. From

ἡμι-ώβολον, τό, (ἡμι–, ὀβελός) *a half-obol*.

ἡμι-ώριον, τό, (ἡμι–, ὥρα) *a half-hour*.

ἧμμαι, pf. pass. of ἅπτω.

ἦμος Dor. **ἆμος**, poët. Adv., relat. to τῆμος as ὅτε to τότε: *when, while, so long as*.

ἠμπεσχόμην, aor. 2 med. of ἀμπέχω.

ἡμός, ή, όν, Aeol. **ἀμός**, for ἡμέτερος.

ἤμουν, impf. of ἐμέω.

ἠμπέδουν, impf. of ἐμπεδόω.

ἠμπόληκα, **–ησα**, pf. and aor. 1 of ἐμπολάω.

ἠμπόλων, impf. of ἐμπολάω.

ἤμπλακον, aor. 2 of ἀμπλακίσκω.

ἤμῡνα, aor. 1 of ἀμύνω.

ἠμύσειε, 3 sing. aor. 1 opt. of ἠμύω.

ἠμύστικα, pf. of ἀμυστίζω.

ἠμύω, f. ύσω [ῡ]: aor. 1 ἤμῡσα: (μύω):—*to sink, droop, bow down*; ἤμυσε κάρη his head *dropped*, of a dying man; of a corn-field, ἠμύει ἀσταχύεσσι *it bows down* with its ears; of cities, *to totter to their fall*: later *to fall, perish*.

ἠμφεγνόησα, **ἠμφεγνόουν**, aor. 1 and impf. of ἀμφιγνοέω.

ἠμφεσβήτουν or **ἠμφισ–**, impf. of ἀμφισβητέω.

ἠμφεσβήτησα or **ἠμφισ–**, aor. 1 of ἀμφισβητέω.

ἠμφίεσα, aor. 1 of ἀμφιέννυμι.

ἠμφίεσμαι, pf. pass. of ἀμφιέννυμι.

ἤμων, contr. impf. of ἀμάω.

ἥμων, ονος, ὁ, (ἵημι) *a thrower, darter, slinger*.

ἤν, contr. from ἐάν, conditional Conj., always followed by Subj. *if, in case that*; ἢν μή *unless*: in indirect questions, *if, whether*.

ἦν, Interject. *see! see there!* Lat. *en!*
ἦν, 1 and 3 sing. impf. of εἰμί *sum.*
ἦν, impf. of ἠμί = φημί.
ἥν, acc. fem. of relat. Pron. ὅς. *who.*
ἥν, acc. fem. of possess. Pron. ὅς, ἑός, *his.*
ἠναίνετο, 3 sing. impf. of ἀναίνομαι.
ἠνάλωσα, ἠνάλωκα, later forms for ἀναλ-, aor. 1 and pf. of ἀναλίσκω.
ἤνᾰρον, aor. 2 of ἐναίρω.
ἥνδανε, 3 sing. impf. of ἁνδάνω.
ἠνδραπόδισα, -ίσθην, -ισμαι, v. ἀνδραποδίζω.
ἠναντιώθην, -ωμαι, aor. 1 and pf. pass. of ἐναντιόω.
ἠναρίσθην, -ισμαι, aor. 1 and pf. pass. of ἐναρίζω.
ἤνεγκα, aor. 1 of φέρω.
ἤνεγκον, aor. 2 of φέρω.
ᾐνέθην, aor. 1 pass. of αἰνέω.
ἤνεικα, Ion. aor. 1 of φέρω.
ἠνειχόμην, impf. med. of ἀνέχω.
ᾔνεκα, Att. pf. of αἰνέω.
ἠνεκής, ές, (*ἐνέκω, v. φέρω) *continuous, long.*
ἠνεμόεις, εσσα, εν, (ἄνεμος) *windy, airy, high, elevated.* II. *light as air, subtle;* φρόνημα ἠνεμόεν *airy, winged* thought.
ᾔνεον, ᾔνεσα, Att. impf. and aor. 1 of αἰνέω.
ἠνεσχόμην, aor. 2 med. of ἀνέχω.
ἤνετο, 3 sing. impf. pass. of ἄνω.
ἠνέχθην, aor. 1 pass. of φέρω.
ἠνέῳγα, Att. pf. of ἀνοίγνυμι.
ᾔνημαι, pf. pass. of αἰνέω.
ἠνηνάμην, aor. 1 of ἀναίνομαι.
ᾔνησα, aor. 1 of αἰνέω.
ἠνθισμένος, pf. part. pass. of ἀνθίζω.
ἤνθομες, Dor. 1 pl. aor. 2 of ἔρχομαι.
ἦνθον, Dor. aor. 2 of ἔρχομαι.
ἠνθράκωμαι, pf. of ἀνθρακόομαι.
ἠνί, Interject., = ἦν, cf. ἠνίδε.
ἠνία, 3 sing. impf. of ἀνιάω.
ἡνία, ίων, τά, *the reins:* Homer uses this neut. form only, and always in plur.: cf. ἡνία, ἡ.
ἩΝΙ'Α, ἡ, *a bridle, a rein:* metaph., χαλάσαι τὰς ἡνίας τοῖς λόγοις to *give a free rein* to one's words, Lat. *immittere habenas.* II. *any leathern thong, a shoe-string.*
ᾔνιγμαι, pf. pass. of αἰνίσσομαι.
ἠν-ίδε, Interject., (ἦν, ἴδε) *see! see there!*
ἡνίκᾰ, Adv., relat. to τηνίκα or τοτηνίκα, *when, at which time, at the time when;* c. optat. *whenever.*
ᾐνιξάμην, aor. 1 of αἰνίσσομαι.
ἡνιοποιεῖον, τό, *a saddler's shop.* From
ἡνιο-ποιός, ὁ, (ἡνία, ποιέω) *a bridle-maker, saddler.*
ἡνιοστροφέω, f. ήσω, *to guide by reins, to drive.* From
ἡνιο-στρόφος, ον, (ἡνία, στρέφω) *guiding by reins:* —as Subst. *a charioteer.*
ἡνι-οχεύς, έως Ion. ῆος, poët. for ἡνίοχος.
ἡνι-οχεύω and -έω, *to be charioteer, hold the reins, drive.* II. *to bridle, govern, control.* From
ἡνί-οχος, ὁ, (ἡνία, ἔχω) *holding the reins, a driver, charioteer,* who drove while the warrior (παραιβάτης) fought. 2. metaph. *one who guides* or *controls.*
ἤνῐπᾰπε, 3 sing. aor. 2 of ἐνίπτω.
ἦνῖς, ιος, ἡ, nom. pl. ἦνῖς, (ἔνος) *a year old, yearling* [acc. ἦνῖν.]
ᾐνίχθην, aor. 1 pass. of αἰνίσσομαι.
ἦνον, impf. of ἄνω.
ἠνορέα Ep and Ion. έη, ἡ, (ἀνήρ) *manhood.*
ἦνοψ, οπος. ὁ, ἡ, in Hom. always in phrase, ἤνοπι χαλκῷ with *glittering, flashing* brass. (Deriv. uncertain.)
ἠντεβόλησα, aor. 1 of ἀντιβολέω.
ἤντεον, Ion. impf. of ἀντάω.
ἠντίαζον, ἠντίᾰσα, impf. and aor. 1 of ἀντιάζω.
ἠντληκώς, pf. part. of ἀντλέω.
ἦντο, 3 pl. impf. of ἧμαι.
ἤνῠκα, ἤνυσμαι, pf. act. and pass. of ἀνύω, ἀνύτω
ἤνυστρον, τό, (ἀνύω) *the fourth stomach of ruminating animals,* in which the digestion was *completed.*
ἤνῠτο, 3 sing. impf. pass. of ἄνυμι.
ἠνώγεα, Ion. plqpf. of ἄνωγα.
ἠνώγειν, plqpf. (with impf. sense) of ἄνωγα.
ἠνώρθουν, impf. of ἀνορθόω.
ἠνώχληκα, ἠνώχλησα, pf. and aor. 1 of ἐνοχλέω.
ἠνώχλουν, -ούμην, impf. act. and pass. of ἐνοχλέω.
ἦξα, aor. 1 both of ἄγω *to lead,* and ἄγνυμι *to break.*
ᾖξα, aor. 1 of ᾄσσω (contr. from ἀΐσσω).
ἡξεῖς, ἡξῶ, Dor. for ἥξεις, ἥξω, fut. of ἥκω.
ἠξίωμαι, pf. pass. of ἀξιόω.
'Ηοῖ, dat. of 'Ηώς.
ἠοῖος, α, ον, ('Ηώς) = ἠῷος, ἑῷος. *in the morning: toward morning, eastern,* Lat. *orientalis,* opp. to ἑσπέριος. II. as Subst., ἠοίη (sub. ὥρα), ἡ, *the morning;* πᾶσαν ἠοίην all *the morning.*
ἤομεν, 1 pl. impf. of εἶμι *ibo.*
ἠόνιος, α, ον, (ἠϊών) contr. from ἠϊόνιος, *on the shore.*
ἠπάομαι, aor. 1 inf. of ἠπήσασθαι *to mend.*
'ΗΠΑΡ, ᾰτος, τό, *the liver,* Lat. *jecur:* represented as the seat of the passions, esp. anger and love.
ἠπάτηκα, ἠπάτησα, pf. and aor. 1 of ἀπατάω.
ἡπάτιον, τό, Dim. of ἧπαρ.
ἤπᾰφε, 3 sing. aor. 2 of ἀπᾰφίσκω.
ἠπεδᾰνός, ή, όν, *weak, infirm: maimed, halting:* c. gen. *void of.* (Deriv. uncertain.)
ἠπείλησα, aor. 1 of ἀπειλέω.
ἠπειρο-γενής, ές, (ἤπειρος, *γένω) *living on the mainland.*
ἠπειρόνδε, Adv. (ἤπειρος) *to the mainland.*
ἤ-πειρος, for ἄπειρος (sc. γῆ), ἡ, *the mainland, continent, of the land,* as opp. to *the sea;* κατ' ἤπειρον by *land;* hence even *an island* is called ἤπειρος. II. the *mainland of Greece,* as opp. to its *islands:* part of which was afterwards called 'Ἤπειρος as n. pr.: Asia was specially called ἡ ἤπειρος *the* Continent; and αἱ δισσαὶ ἤπειροι, the two *continents,* are Europe and Asia. Hence
ἠπειρόω, f. ώσω, *to make into mainland:*—Pass. *to become so,* when an island is joined to the mainland

ἠπειρώτης, ου, ὁ, fem. -ῶτις, ιδος, (ἤπειρος) *of the mainland, born* or *living thereon*; ἠπειρῶτις ξυμμαχία alliance *with a military power*, opp. to ναυτικὴ ξυμμαχία. II. *of* or *on the mainland of Asia, Asiatic.*

ἠπειρωτικός, ή, όν, (ἠπειρώτης) *of* or *for the inhabitants of the mainland, continental.*

ἤ-περ poët. **ἠέ-περ**, Conj. (ἤ, περ) *than, than even.*

ᾗ-περ, Adv., properly dat. of ὅσπερ, *in the same way as, just as.*

ἠ-περοπεύς, gen. έως Ion. ῆος, ὁ, = ἠπεροπευτής.

ἠπεροπευτής, οῦ, ὁ, *a cheat, deceiver.* From

ἠπεροπεύω, f. σω, *to cheat, deceive, cozen*

ἠπητής, οῦ, ὁ, (ἠπάομαι) *a mender, cobbler.*

ἠπἴᾰλέω, *to have a fever* or *ague.* From

ἠπίᾰλος (sub. πυρετός), ὁ, *a fever attended with shivering, ague.* II. *the nightmare.*

ἠπἴο-δίνητος, ον, (ἤπιος, δινέω) *softly-rolling.*

ἠπιό-δωρος, ον, (ἤπιος, δῶρον) *giving welcome gifts.*

ἠπιό-θῡμος, ον, (ἤπιος, θυμός) *gentle of mood.*

ἬΠΙΌΣ, *α*, *ον*, Att. *ος*, *ον*, *gentle, mild, kind.* II. act. *soothing, assuaging, calming.*

ἠπιό-χειρ, ὁ, ἡ, (ἤπιος, χείρ) *with soothing hand.*

ἠπίως, Adv. of ἤπιος, *gently, mildly.*

ἤπλακον, for ἤμπλακον, aor. 2 of ἀμπλακίσκω.

ἤ-που, or ἤ που, Adv. *or, as, or perhaps, as perhaps.*

ἦπου or ἦ που, Adv. *of a truth, doubtless, I presume*: after a negat., *much less.* II. in a question, *is it then?*

ἧπται, 3 sing. pf. pass. of ἅπτω.

ἠπύτᾰ [ῠ], ὁ, Adj. masc. *calling, crying*; ἠπύτα κῆρυξ *the loud-voiced* herald: in form like ἱππότα. From

ἠπύω Dor. **ἀπύω** [ᾱ]: f. ύσω [ῡ]: aor. 1 ἤπῡσα: (ἔπος, εἰπεῖν):—*to call on, call out* or *forth, invoke.* II. absol. *to call aloud, shout, speak*; of the lyre, *to sound*; of the wind, *to howl, roar.*

ἜΡ, τό, poët. for ἔαρ, *spring*, Lat. *VER*: gen. and dat. ἦρος, ἦρι are the only cases used in Prose.

ἤρᾱ, 3 sing. impf. of ἐράω.

ἦρᾰ, 1 sing. aor. 1 of αἴρω.

ἦρα (ἤρᾰρον aor. 2 of ἀραρίσκω) always joined with φέρειν or its compds., to bring *what is pleasant*, to do *a kindness*; cp. ἐπίηρα.

ἭΡΑ Ion. Ἥρη, ἡ, *Hera*, the Roman *Juno*, queen of the gods, sister and wife of Zeus. Hence

Ἡραῖος, α, ον, *of* or *belonging to Hera*: τὸ Ἡραῖον, (ἱερόν) *the temple of Hera, Heraeum*: τὰ Ἡραῖα, (ἱερά) *her festival.*

ἩΡΑΚΛΈΗΣ contr. **Ἡρακλῆς**, ὁ: gen. Ἡρακλέεος contr. Ἡρακλέους Ep. Ἡρακλῆος: dat. Ἡρακλέεϊ contr. Ἡρακλέει Ἡρακλεῖ Ep. Ἡρακλῆϊ: acc. Ἡρακλέεα contr. Ἡρακλέᾱ Ep Ἡρακλῆα rarely Ἡρακλῆ later also Ἡρακλῆν: voc. Ἡράκλεες, Ἡράκλεις: in Ion. also declined Ἡρακλέος -κλεῦς, Ἡρακλέϊ, Ἡρακλέᾰ:—*Heracles*, Lat. *Hercules*, son of Zeus and Alcmena, the most famous of the Greek heroes: the vocat. Ἡράκλεις is commonly an exclamation of surprise or disgust. Hence

Ἡράκλειος, α, ον, also ος, ον, Ep. **Ἡρακλήειος**, η, ον:—*of* or *belonging to Hercules*; βίη Ἡρακληείη the might *of Hercules*, i. e. *Hercules himself*; Ἡράκλειαι στῆλαι the pillars *of Hercules*, the opposite headlands of Gibraltar and Ceuta:—τὸ Ἡράκλειον Ion. -ήϊον, *the temple of Hercules*; τὰ Ἡράκλεια *his festival.* II. Ἡράκλεια λουτρά *hot baths.*

Ἡρακλῆς, contr. from Ἡρακλέης.

ἠράμην, aor. 1 med. of αἴρω:—also impf. of ἔραμαι.

ἤρᾰρον, ες, ε, aor. 2 of ἀραρίσκω.

ἠρᾰσάμην, aor. 1 med. of ἐράομαι.

ἠράσθην, aor. 1 pass. (in med. sense) of ἐράομαι.

ἠράσσατο, Ep. for ἠράσατο, 3 sing. aor. 1 of ἐράομαι.

ἤρᾰτο, 3 sing. aor. 1 med. of αἴρω.

ἠρᾶτο, 3 sing. impf. of ἀράομαι.

ᾑρέθην, aor. 1 pass. of αἱρέω.

ἤρεθον, impf. of ἐρέθω.

ᾕρει, 3 sing. impf. of αἱρέω.

ἤρεισα, aor. 1 of ἐρείδω.

ἠρέμᾰ and **ἠρέμᾰς**, Adv. *gently, quietly, calmly, softly*: *a little, slightly*: *slow.* The old Adj. ἤρεμος, from which it is derived, is only found in Comp. ἠρεμέστερος; ἠρεμαῖος being used instead.

ἠρεμαῖος, α, ον, (ἠρέμα) *soft, gentle, quiet.* Adv. -ως.

ἠρεμέστερος, α, ον, irreg. Comp. of ἠρεμαῖος, see ἠρέμα: Adv. ἠρεμεστέρως

ἠρεμέω, f. ήσω, (ἤρεμα) *to be still, keep quiet.*

ἠρεμί [ῐ], Adv. for ἠρέμα, *gently.*

ἠρεμία, ἡ, (ἠρέμα) *stillness, calmness, rest.*

ἠρεμίζω, f. σω, (ἠρέμα) *to calm, quiet*:—Pass. *to be still, at rest.* II. intr. *to be at rest.*

ἤρεσα, aor. 1 of ἀρέσκω.

ᾑρέτῐσα, aor. 1 of αἱρετίζω.

ᾕρευν, Ion. for ᾕρουν, impf. of αἱρέω.

Ἥρη, Ion. for Ἥρα.

ᾕρημαι, pf. pass. of αἱρέω.

ἠρήμωσα, aor. 1 of ἐρημόω.

ἠρήρει, 3 sing. plqpf. of ἀραρίσκω.

ἠρήρειστο, 3 sing. plqpf. pass. of ἐρείδω.

ἤρθην, aor. 1 pass. of αἴρω.

ἦρι, (ἦρ) Adv. *early, at early morn*; ἅμα ἦρι τοῦ θέρους *early in* the summer.

Ἠρῐδᾰνός, ὁ, *Eridanus*, a river, first mentioned in Hesiod. Later authors took it mostly for *the Po*; others also for *the Rhone* or *the Rhine.*

ἠρίθμεον, impf. of ἀριθμέω.

ἠρίθμημαι, pf. pass. of ἀριθμέω.

ἤρῐκε, 3 sing. intrans. aor. 2 of ἐρείκω.

ἠρῐνός, ή, όν, (ἦρ) = ἐαρινός, *of* or *in the spring*: neut. ἠρινόν and ἠρινά as Adv., *in spring.*

ἩΡΊΟΝ, τό, *a mound, barrow, tomb.*

ἤρῐπον, aor. 2 of ἐρείπω.

ἠρι-πόλη, ἡ, fem. Adj. (ἦρι, πολέω) *early-stirring*: as Subst. *the morn, dawn.*

ἤρῐσα, aor. 1 of ἐρίζω.

ἧρκα, **ἧρμαι**, pf. act. and pass. of αἴρω.

ἡρμένος, pf. part. pass. of ἀραρίσκω.
ἠρνεῖτο, 3 sing. impf. of ἀρνέομαι.
ἠρνησάμην, aor. 1 of ἀρνέομαι.
ἠρόθην, aor. 1 pass. of ἀρόω.
ἠρόμην, impf. med. of αἴρω.
ἥρπαξα or **ἥρπασα**, aor. 1 of ἁρπάζω.
ἤρρησα, aor. 1 of ἔρρω.
ἦρσα, aor. 1 of ἀραρίσκω. II. also of ἄρδω.
ἠρτημένος, pf. part. pass. of ἀρτάω.
ἠρτύναντο, 3 pl. aor. 1 med. of ἀρτύνω.
ἤρῠγον, intrans. aor. 2 act. of ἐρεύγομαι.
ἠρύκᾰκε, 3 sing. aor. 2 of ἐρύκω.
ἠρχόμην, impf. of ἔρχομαι: also impf. med. of ἄρχω.
ἠρῶ, 2 sing. impf. of ἀράομαι.
ἥρῳ, poët. for ἥρωι, dat. of ἥρως; ἥρω, acc.
ἡρῷειον, τό, = ἡρῷον.
ἠρώτησα, aor. 1 of ἐρωτάω.
ἡρωϊκός, ή, όν, (ἥρως) *of* or *for heroes, heroic*: ἡρωϊκὸν μέτρον, *the heroic* verse, *hexameter*.
ἡρωΐνη [ῑ], contr. **ἡρῴνη**, fem. of ἥρως *a heroine*.
ἡρώϊος, α, ον, = ἡρωϊκός.
ἡρωΐς, ΐδος, ἡ, = ἡρωΐνη, *a heroine*.
ἠρώμην, impf. of ἀράομαι.
ἡρῷον, τό, *the temple* or *shrine of a hero*: neut. from
ἡρῷος, α, ον, contr. of ἡρώϊος, *of* or *for heroes, heroic*: ὁ ἡρῷος (sub. ῥυθμός), *the heroic measure, hexameter*. From
ἥρως, ὁ: gen. ἥρωος Att. ἥρω: dat. ἥρωι contr. ἥρῳ: acc. ἥρωα contr. ἥρω: pl. nom. and acc. ἥρωες, rarely contr. ἥρως:—*a hero*: in Homer not restricted to *warriors*, but applied to all *free men* of that age, as to the minstrel, the herald, the leech, etc. II. Hesiod makes *the Heroes* the Fourth Age of men, who fell before Thebes and Troy, and superior to the present race. III. Pindar represents them as a race between gods and men, *demigods*, ἡμίθεοι, whether those born of one divine parent, as Hercules or Aenaeas, or those who, like Theseus, had done great service to mankind. IV. the heroes were in later times *inferior local deities*, patrons of tribes, cities, etc.; as at Athens, the ἥρωες ἐπώνυμοι were the heroes after whom the ten φυλαί were named. The founders of a city were worshipped under this name.
ἦς, Dor. for ἦν, 3 sing. impf. of εἰμί *sum*.
ᾖσα, Att. aor. 1 of ᾄδω.
ἦσα, aor. 1 of ἥδω.
ἧσαι, 2 sing. of ἧμαι.
ἦσαν, 3 pl. impf. of εἰμί *sum*.
ᾖσαν, Att. for ᾔδεσαν, 3 pl. plqpf. (in impf. sense) of οἶδα. II. for ἤϊσαν, 3 pl. impf. of εἶμι *ibo*.
ἥσατο, 3 sing. Ep. aor. 1 of ἥδομαι.
ἥσειν, fut. inf. of ἵημι.
ἦσθα, Aeol. for ἦς, 2 sing. impf. of εἰμι *sum*.
ἧσθαι, inf. of ἧμαι.
ἠσθένουν, impf. of ἀσθενέω.
ἥσθην, aor. 1 pass. of ἥδομαι.
ᾔσθην, Att. aor. 1 pass. of ἀείδω.
ἤσθιον, impf. of ἐσθίω.
ᾐσθόμην, aor. 2 of αἰσθάνομαι.
ἦσθον, impf. of ἔσθω.
ἡσι-επής, ές, (ἵημι, ἔπος) *a babbler*.
ἤσκειν, contr. for ἤσκεεν, 3 sing. impf. of ἀσκέω.
ᾖσμαι, Att. pf. pass. of ἀείδω.
ᾔσμεν, Att. for ᾔδειμεν, 1 pl. plqpf. of οἶδα.
ἧσο, 2 sing. imperat. of ἧμαι.
ἧσσα Att. **ἧττα**, ης, ἡ, *a defeat, discomfiture*: c. gen. *defeat by, yielding to*. From
ἡσσάομαι Att. **ἡττάομαι**: fut. both med. and pass. ἡττήσομαι, ἡσσηθήσομαι: aor. 1 ἡσσήθην: pf. ἥττημαι:—Ion. **ἑσσόομαι**, see the word: Pass.: (ἥσσων)—*to be less, weaker, inferior to* another: *to be beaten worsted, discomfited*: *to give way, submit*: absol. *to be beaten* or *defeated*: as law-term, *to lose one's cause* Hence
ἡσσητέος, α, ον, and, in neut. plur. ἡσσητέα, verb. Adj.: *one must be beaten, submit*.
ᾖσσον, Att. impf. of ἀΐσσω.
ἥσσων, ἧσσον, gen. ονος: Att. **ἥττων**: Ion. **ἕσσων**:—*less, weaker, inferior*: c. gen. pers. *weaker than* another, *unable to contend with, yielding* to a thing. (Used as irreg. Comp. of Positive κακός: probably formed from ἧκα, ἥκιστος being the Sup.)
ἧσται, 3 sing. of ἧμαι.
ᾖστε, Att. for ᾔδειτε, 2 pl. plqpf. of *εἴδω.
ἤστην, for ἤτην, 3 dual impf. of εἰμί *sum*.
ᾔστην, Att. for ᾐδείτην, 2 and 3 dual plqpf. of *εἴδω.
ἧστο, 3 sing. impf. of ἧμαι.
ἦστον, for ἦτον, 2 dual impf. of εἰμί *sum*.
ᾔστωσα, aor. 1 of ἀϊστόω.
ἥσῠχα, neut. pl. of ἥσυχος, used like ἡσυχῇ.
ἡσῠχάζω, f. σω, (ἥσυχος) *to be still, quiet, at rest*; τὸ ἡσύχαζον τῆς νυκτὸς *the quiet time* of night, *dead* of night.
ἡσῠχαῖος, α, ον, poet. for ἥσυχος, *still, quiet, at rest*.
ἡσῠχαίτερος, α, ον, irr. Comp. of ἥσυχος, ἡσυχαῖος.
ἡσῠχῇ Dor. **ἁσυχᾶ**, Adv. of ἥσυχος, *quietly, gently*.
ἡσῠχία Dor. **ἁσυχ-**, ἡ. (ἥσυχος) *stillness, quiet, peace*; ἡσυχίαν ἄγειν or ἔχειν to keep *quiet*, be at *peace* or *at rest* 2. *rest, leisure*, Lat. *otium*.
ἡσύχιμος Dor **ἁσύχ-**, ον, poët. for ἥσυχος.
ἡσύχιος, ον, rarely α, ον, poët. for ἥσυχος.
ἩΣΥΧΟΣ Dor. **ἅσῠχος**, ον, *still, quiet, at rest*; ἔχ' ἥσυχος keep *quiet*. 2. *quiet, gentle*. II. Comp. and Sup. were irreg. ἡσυχαίτερος, -αίτατος; but also -ώτερος. III. Adv. **-χως**, also ἡσυχῇ and neut. pl. ἥσυχα as Adv. [ῠ]
ᾔσχυγκα, pf. of αἰσχύνω.
ᾔσχυμμαι, pf. pass. of αἰσχύνω.
ᾔσχῡνα, aor. 1 of αἰσχύνω.
ἥσω, fut. of ἵημι.
ἤ-τε or **ἤ τε**, Conj. *or also*.
ἦ-τε or **ἦ τε**, Adv. *surely, doubtless*.
ᾖτε, for ᾔειτε, 2 pl. impf. of εἶμι *ibo*.
ᾔτηκα, **ᾔτησα**, pf. and aor. 1 of αἰτέω.
ἤτην, 3 dual impf. of εἰμί *sum*.
ᾐτιάασθε, **ᾐτιόωντο**, Ep. 2 and 3 pl. impf. of αἰτιάομαι.

ἠτιᾱσάμην, ἠτίᾱμαι, aor. 1 med. and pf. pass. of *αἰτιάομαι.*

ἤ-τοι, Conjunct.: II. = ἤ τοι, *full, surely, verily.* III. = ἤ τοι, *either in truth,* followed by *ἤ .., either .., or ...*

ἡτοίμασμαι, pf. pass. of ἑτοιμάζω, in med. sense.

ἮΤΟΡ, *τό,* only used in nom. or acc.:—*the heart.*

ἮΤΡΙΟΝ Dor. **ἄτριον,** *τό,* *the warp in a web* of cloth (the woof being *κρόκη*): in pl. *ἥτρια, a thin, fine cloth:* hence, *ἥτρια βύβλων* leaves *made of strips* of papyrus *joined crosswise.*

ἦτρον, *τό,* (ἦτορ) *the belly,* Lat. *abdomen.*

ἧττα, ἡττάομαι, ἥττων, etc., Att. for *ἡσσ-.*

ἤτω, for *ἔστω,* 3 sing. imperat. of *εἰμί sum.*

ἠΰ· neut. from *ἠΰς.* In compds. with *εὐ-* or *ἐϋ-,* this is often lengthd. Ep. into *ἠϋ-*; v. sub *εὐ-.*

ηὔδησα, ηὔδηκα, aor 1 and impf. of *αὐδάω.*

ηὐδοκίμουν, impf. of *εὐδοκιμέω.*

ηὔδων, Att. impf. of *αὐδάω.*

ηὔξανον, impf. of *αὐξάνω.*

ηὔλησα, aor. 1 of *αὐλέω.*

ηὐλίσθην, aor. 1 pass. of *αὐλίζω.*

ηὐξάμην, aor. 1 of *εὔχομαι*

ηὐξήθην, ηὔξημαι, aor. 1 and pf. pass. of *αὐξάνω.*

ηὔξηκα. ηὔξησα, pf and aor. 1 of *αὐξάνω.*

ηὗρον, ηὑρέθην, aor. 2 act. and aor. 1 pass. of *εὑρίσκω.*

ἠΰς. neut. *ἠΰ,* Ep. for *ἐΰς, good, brave.*

ἤϋσα, aor. 1 of *ἀΰω.* [ῡ]

ἠΰτε, Ep. Conjunct. *as, like as.* II. for *ἤ, than;* only once in Homer. *νέφος μελάντερον ἠΰτε πίσσα,* blacker *than* pitch. [ῠ]

ηὐτρέπισμαι, pf. pass. of *εὐτρεπίζω.*

ηὐχόμην, impf. of *εὔχομαι.*

Ἡφαίστειος, *α, ον,* (Ἥφαιστος) *of* or *for Vulcan,* Lat. *Vulcanius:* τὸ Ἡφαιστεῖον or Ἡφαίστειον (sub. *ἱερόν*) *the temple of Vulcan:* τὰ Ἡφαίστεια (sub. *ἱερά*), *his festival,* Lat. *Vulcanalia.*

Ἡφαιστό-πονος, *ον,* (Ἥφαιστος, *πονέω*) *wrought by Vulcan*

Ἥφαιστος, *ου, ὁ, Hephaistos,* the Lat. *Vulcanus,* son of Zeus and Hera, lame from his birth, god of fire, master of the arts which need the aid of fire, esp. of working in metal.

Ἡφαιστό-τευκτος, *ον,* and **Ἡφαιστο-τευχής,** *ές,* (Ἥφαιστος, *τεύχω*) *wrought by Vulcan.*

ἥφθα, Dor. 3 sing. aor. 1 pass. of *ἅπτω.*

ἦφι, Ep. for *ᾗ.*

ἤφιε, for *ἀφίει,* 3 sing. impf. of *ἀφίημι* (as if from *ἀφίω*).

ἠφίουν, impf. of *ἀφίημι* (as if from *ἀφιέω*).

ἤφυσα, aor. 1 of *ἀφύσσω.*

ἠφυσσόμην, impf. med. of *ἀφύσσω.*

ἦχα, pf. of *ἄγω.*

ἠχεσκον, Ion. impf. of *ἠχέω.*

ἠχέτης, *ου, ὁ,* Ep. **ἠχέτᾰ,** (ἠχέω) *clear-sounding, chirping,* epith. of the grasshopper:—as Subst. *the chirper,* i. e. *the grasshopper,* Lat. *cicāda.*

ἠχέω Dor. **ἀχέω** [ᾱ]: f. *ήσω*:—*to sound, ring, peal;* c. acc. cognato, *ἀχεῖν ὕμνον, κωκυτόν to utter, send forth* a hymn or wail. From

ἨΧΗ´ Dor. **ἄχα,** *ἡ, a sound: the tumultuous noise* of a crowd, *the roar* of the sea, etc.; in Trag. usu. like *ἰαχή, a cry of sorrow, wail.*

ἠχήεις, *εσσα, εν,* (ἠχή) *sounding, roaring, echoing.*

ἤχημα, *ατος, τό,* (ἠχέω) *a sound.*

ἠχητής, *οῦ, ὁ,* and **ἠχητικός,** *ή, όν,* = *ἠχέτης.*

ἦχι, Ep. for *ᾗ,* Adv. *where.*

ἤχθετο, 3 sing. impf. both of *ἄχθομαι* and *ἔχθομαι.*

ἤχθημαι, pf. pass. of *ἔχθομαι.*

ἤχθην, aor. 1 pass. of *ἄγω.*

ἤχθηρα, aor. 1 of *ἐχθαίρω.*

ᾔχμᾱσα, aor. 1 of *αἰχμάζω.*

ἦχος, *ὁ,* = *ἠχή.*

ἠχώ Dor. **ἀχώ,** *ἡ,* gen. *-όος* contr. *-οῦς,* = *ἠχή, a reverberated sound, an echo.* II. as prop. n. Ἠχώ, *Echo,* personified as an Oread.

ἥψατο, 3 sing. aor. 1 of *ἅπτομαι.*

ἥψησα, ἡψήθην, aor. 1 act. and pass. of *ἕψω.*

ἠῶθεν Dor. **ἀῶθεν** Att. **ἕωθεν,** Adv. (ἠώς) *from morn. from peep of day, at dawn.*

ἠῶθι, old Ep. gen. of *ἠώς, ἠῶθι πρό* before *dawn.*

ᾐών, *όνος, ὁ,* Att. contr. for *ἠϊών.*

ἠῷος, *α, ον, at morn, at break of day.* II. *eastern.* From

ἨΩ´Σ, *ἡ,* gen. *ἠόος* contr. *ἠοῦς*: dat. *ἠόϊ* contr. *ἠοῖ*: acc. *ἠόα* contr. *ἠῶ*:—Att. **ἕως,** gen. **ἕω,** acc. **ἕω** or **ἕων**:—Dor. **ἀώς**:—Aeol. **αὔως**:—*the day-break, dawn, morning,* opp. to *μέσον ἦμαρ* mid-day, and *δείλη* evening; acc., *ἠῶ the whole morning long; ἅμ' ἠοῖ* at *day-break.* 2. *the East,* opp. to *ζόφος.* 3. as the Greeks counted by mornings, *ἠώς* came to mean *a day:* also *the light of day.* II. as prop. n. **Ἠώς,** *Eos, Aurora, the goddess of morn.*

Θ

Θ, θ, θῆτα, *τό,* indecl., eighth letter of the Greek alphabet: as numeral *θ´* = *ἐννέα, ἔνατος,* but *͵θ* = 9000. In Doric, *θ* was often changed into *σ,* as Lacon. *σεῖος Ἀσάνα σάω,* for *θεῖος Ἀθάνα θάω*: so also in Ion., *βυσσός* for *βυθός.* Θ was also changed, Aeol. and Dor., into *φ,* as *φήρ φλάω φλίβω* for *θήρ θλάω θλίβω.* Lastly, *θ* sometimes stood for the rough breathing, as *θαμά* for *ἅμα, θάλασσα* for *ἅλς.*—On the ballots of the judges at Athens, Θ stood for *θάνατος.*

θᾱάσσω, Ep. for *θάσσω, to sit,* only in pres. and Ep. impf. *θάασσον.*

θαεῖτο, 3 sing. impf. of Dor. *θαέομαι.*

θάεο, imperat. of *θάομαι.*

θᾱέομαι, Dor. for Att. *θεάομαι* Ion. *θηέομαι.* Hence

θάημα, *τό,* Dor. for *θέαμα, a sight, spectacle.*

θᾱητός, *ή, όν,* Dor. for *θηητός, θεατός.*

θαἰμάτια, crasis for *τὰ ἱμάτια.*

ΘΑΙΡΟ´Σ, *ὁ, the hinge of a door* or *gate.*

θᾱκέω, f. *ήσω,* (θᾶκος) *to sit,* esp. *as a suppliant, to* *take a seat*: c. acc. cognato, ἕδρας παγκρατεῖς θακεῖν *to sit* on imperial throne. Hence

θάκημα, ατος, τό, *a sitting* as a suppliant: *a seat.*

θάκησις, εως, ἡ, (θᾰκέω) *a sitting, seat.*

θᾶκος, ὁ, (θάσσω) *a seat*: Ion. θῶκος.

θᾰλάμαξ, ᾶκος, ὁ, = θαλαμίτης.

θᾰλάμευμα, ατος, τό, = θάλαμος, *a dark chamber* or *dwelling-place.*

θᾰλάμη, ἡ, (θάλαμος) *a lair, den, hole.* [ᾰ]

θᾰλᾰμήϊος, η, ον, (θάλαμος) *of* or *for a chamber* or *dwelling*: *fit for building one.*

θᾰλᾰμη-πόλος, ον, (θάλαμος, πολέομαι) *waiting in the lady's chamber.* II. as Subst., θαλαμηπόλος, ὁ or ἡ, *a bridegroom* or *bridesmaid.*

θᾰλάμιος, α, ον, (θάλᾰμος) *belonging to the chamber.* As Subst.: I. θαλάμιος, ὁ, = θαλαμίτης. II. θαλαμία Ion. -ίη (sub. κώπη), *the oar of the* θαλαμίτης. 2. (sub. ὀπή) *the hole in the ship's side through which this oar worked, the port-hole.*

θᾰλᾰμίτης, ου, ὁ, (θάλαμος) *one of the rowers on the lowest bench* of a trireme, who had the shortest oars and the least pay: cf. ζυγίτης, θρανίτης. [ῑ]

θάλαμόνδε, (θάλαμος) Adv. *to the bed-chamber.*

ΘΑ'ΛΑΜΟΣ, ὁ, *an inner room* or *chamber*: 1. *the women's apartment, inner part of the house.* 2. *a bed-room, bride-chamber.* 3. *the storeroom.* II. *any chamber* or *abode*: *a fold, pen* for sheep. III. *the lowest part* or *hold of the ship*, in which the θαλαμῖται sat.

θάλασσα Att. **ττα**, ἡ, (ἅλς) *the sea*: Herodotus calls the Mediterranean ἥδε ἡ θάλασσα, ἡ καθ' ἡμᾶς θάλασσα, ἡ ἔσω θάλασσα, (as the Latins called it *nostrum mare*), and the Ocean ἡ ἔξω θάλασσα: metaph., θάλασσα κακῶν '*a sea* of troubles.' 2. *a well of salt* or *brackish water.* Hence

θᾰλασσαῖος, α, ον, = θαλάσσιος.

θᾰλασσεύω, (θάλασσα) *to be at sea, go by sea.*

θᾰλάσσιος, α, ον, also ος, ον, (θάλασσα) *of, in* or *on the sea, belonging to it*, Lat. *marinus*; θαλάσσια ἔργα *sea-affairs, the sea*, also *fishing*: θαλάσσια animals *living in the sea*, opp. to χερσαῖα. 2. *skilled in the sea, nautical, maritime.*

θᾰλασσο-κοπέω, f. ήσω, (θάλασσα, κόπτω) *to strike the sea with the oar, make a splash*: metaph. *to make much ado about nothing.*

θᾰλασσο-κρᾰτέω, f. ήσω, (θάλασσα, κρατέω) *to be master of the sea.*

θᾰλασσο-κράτωρ, ορος, ὁ, ἡ, (θάλασσα, κρατέω) *master of the sea.*

θᾰλασσό-πλαγκτος, ον, (θάλασσα, πλάζω) *sea-driven, tempest-tossed.*

θᾰλασσό-πληκτος, ον, (θάλασσα, πλήσσω) *sea-beaten.*

θᾰλασσο-πόρος, ον, (θάλασσα, πόρος) *sea-faring.*

θᾰλασσ-ουργός, όν, (θάλασσα, *ἔργω) *working at sea*: as Subst., θαλασσουργός, ὁ, *a fisherman.*

θάλαττα, θαλάττιος, Att. for θάλασσ-.

θάλεα, τά, (θᾰλεῖν) *good cheer, comforts, delights.*

θᾰλέθω, poët. for θάλλω, *to bloom, flourish.*

θάλεια, ἡ, *blooming, luxuriant, bounteous*, ἐν δαιτὶ θαλείῃ at the *bounteous* feast. It is fem. of an obsol. Adj. θάλυς, derived from θαλεῖν. II. as prop. n. Θάλεια, ἡ, one of the Muses, *the blooming one*: later esp. the Muse of Comedy.

θᾰλεῖν, aor. 2 inf. of θάλλω.

θᾰλερός, ά, όν, (θαλεῖν) *blooming, fresh*: *vigorous, active.* II. *luxuriant, copious, large, abundant.*

θᾰλερ-ῶπις, ιδος, ἡ, (θαλερός, ὤψ) *with bright eyes.*

θᾰλέω, Dor. for θηλέω.

Θᾰλῆς, ὁ, gen. Θαλέω, dat. Θαλῇ, acc. Θαλῆν: but also Θάλητος, ητι, ητα, and Θαλοῦ: *Thales* of Miletus, one of the Seven reputed Wise Men of Greece.

θᾰλία, ἡ, (θαλεῖν) *bloom*: metaph. *good cheer, wealth, plenty*: in plur. *festivities, a feast.*

θαλλήσω, a doubtful fut. of θάλλω, for θηλήσω from θηλέω.

θαλλός, ὁ, (θάλλω) *a young shoot, twig*: ὁ τῆς ἐλαίας θαλλός *the olive-branch used at festivals*; also, ἱκτὴρ θαλλός the *branch* carried by suppliants.

θαλλο-φόρος, ον, (θαλλός, φέρω) *carrying olive-branches*, as the old men did at the Panathenaea.

ΘΑ'ΛΛΩ, fut. θᾰλῶ: aor. 2 ἔθᾰλον: pf. τέθηλα (in pres. sense), part. τεθηλώς, Ep. fem. τεθᾰλυῖα; 3 sing. plqpf. τεθήλει:—*to bloom, flourish, to shoot out, to swell, be rich in* a thing: the part. τεθηλώς is used absol. as Adj. *swelling, rich, abundant.* 2. metaph. *to bloom, flourish, prosper*: *to be at the height.*

ΘΑ'ΛΟΣ, εος, τό, like θαλλός, *a young shoot* or *branch, twig*, esp. *an olive-branch*: metaph. *a child, scion*, Lat. *stirps.*

θαλπιάω, Ep. part. θαλπιόων, (θάλπω) *to be* or *become warm, warm oneself.*

θαλπνός, ή, όν, *warming, fostering.* From

θάλπος, εος, τό, (θάλπω) *warmth, heat*, esp. *summer-heat*; τὰ θάλπη *the sun's rays*, Lat. *soles.* 2. metaph. *a sting, smart, tingling.*

θαλπτήριος, ον, *warming.* From

ΘΑ'ΛΠΩ, f. ψω: aor. 1 ἔθαλψα:—Pass., aor. 1 ἐθάλφθην: pf. inf. τεθάλφθαι:—*to warm, heat.* II. metaph. *to heat, inflame.* 2. *to foster, cherish, warm in one's bosom*: in bad sense, *to cheat.* Hence

θαλπωρή, ἡ, *a warming*: metaph. *a comfort.*

θᾰλυκρός, ά, όν, (θάλπω) *warm, glowing.*

θᾰλύσια (sub. ἱερά), ίων, τά, (θαλεῖν) *the firstlings of the harvest, offering of first-fruits.* [ῠ] Hence

θᾰλῠσιάς, άδος, ἡ, fem. Adj., *of* or *for the offering of first-fruits.*

θαμά, Adv. (ἅμα) *together in crowds, close, thick.* II. of Time, *often, oft-times, frequent*

θᾰμάκις, Adv. = θαμά II

θαμβαίνω, *to be astonished at.* From

θαμβέω, f. ήσω: pf. τεθάμβηκα: (θάμβος):—*to be astonished* or *amazed*: c. acc. *to marvel at* a thing.

θάμβος, εος, τό, *astonishment, amazement*, Lat. *stupor.* (From Root ΤΑΦ-, see τέ-θηπα.)

θᾰμέες, οἱ, αἱ, dat. θᾰμέσι, acc. θᾰμέας, (θαμά)

poët. pl. Adj. (with no sing. *θαμύς*), *crowded, close, thick.*

θᾰμειός, *ά, όν*, (*θαμά*) *crowded, close, thick.*

θᾰμίζω, f. *σω*, (*θαμά*) *to come often*, Lat. *frequentare*:—*to be often* or *constantly engaged with* a thing. c. dat.: *to be wont* to do, c. part.

θᾰμῐνά, neut. plur. of *θαμινός*, as Adv., = *θαμά.*

θᾰμῐνός, *ή, όν*, = *θαμειός.*

θάμνος, *ὁ*, (*θαμινός*) *a bush, shrub.*

θᾰνάσῐμος, *ον*, (*θάνατος*) *deadly*:—Adv. -*μως*, *with deadly blow, mortally.* 2. *of, belonging to death.* II. pass. *subject to death, mortal*: also *dead.*

θανατάω, Desiderat. of *θνήσκω*, *to wish to die.*

θᾰνᾰτηφορία, *ἡ*, *a causing of death.* From

θᾰνᾰτη-φόρος, *ον*, (*θάνατος, φέρω*) *death-bringing*

θᾰνᾰτιάω, Desiderat. of *θνήσκω*, *to wish to die.*

θᾰνᾰτόεις, *εσσα, εν*, (*θάνατος*) *deadly.*

θάνατόν-δε, Adv. *to death.*

θάνᾰτος, *ὁ*, (*θᾰνεῖν*) *death*; *θάνατον καταγιγνώσκειν τινός* to pass *sentence of death* on one:—pl. *θάνατοι*, *kinds of death*, usually of *violent death.* II. as prop. n., *Θάνατος*, *Death*, the twin-brother of Sleep. III. *a corpse.*

θᾰνᾰτούσια (sub. *ἱερά*), *ίων, τά*, (*θάνατος*) *a feast of the dead.*

θᾰνᾰτόω, f. *ώσω*, (*θάνατος*) *to put to death*: metaph. *to mortify.* II. *to condemn to death*

θάνον, Ep. aor. 2 of *θνήσκω.*

θᾰνεῖν Ep. **θανέειν**, aor. 2 inf. of *θνήσκω.*

θανεῖσθαι Ep. **θανέεσθαι**, fut. inf. of *θνήσκω.*

θανοῖσα, Dor. fem. part. aor. 2 of *θνήσκω.*

θανοῦμαι, fut. of *θνήσκω.*

ΘΑ'ΟΜΑΙ: f. *θήσομαι* Dor. *θάσομαι*: inf. *ἐθησάμην*: Dep.:—*to wonder at, admire* II. *to gaze upon, look at, see.*

θαπτέον, verb Adj. of *θάπτω*, *one must bury*

ΘΑ'ΠΤΩ, fut. *θάψω*: aor. 1 *ἔθαψα*· pf. *τέτᾰφα*: Pass., fut. 2 *τᾰφήσομαι*, fut. 3 *τεθάψομαι*: aor. 1 *ἐθάφθην*, aor. 2 *ἐτάφην* [ᾰ]: pf. *τέθαμμαι*, Ion. 3 pl. *τεθάφαται*: 3 sing. plqpf. *ἐτέθαπτο*:—*to perform funeral rites* to the dead: *to bury, inter, entomb.*

Θαργήλια, *ων, τά*, a festival of Apollo and Artemis, held at Athens in the month Thargelion. Henc

Θαργηλιών, *ῶνος, ὁ*, the 11th month of the Attic year, from middle of May to middle of June

θαρρᾰλέος, θαρρέω, θάρρος, etc., Att. for *θαρσ*–.

θαρσᾰλέος, *α, ον*, (*θάρσος*) *bold, daring, courageous, confident*: in bad sense, *over-weening, presumptuous*: *τὸ θαρσάλεον confidence, safety*: of things, *cheering, encouraging*:—Comp. *θαρσαλεώτερος.* Adv *έως*, *with confidence.*

θαρσεῦσα, Dor. fem. part. of *θαρσέω.*

θαρσέω Att. **θαρρέω**: f. *ήσω*: (*θάρσος*):—*to be of good courage, be of good cheer, be confident, assured*; *θάρσει take courage! be of good heart!*—in bad sense, *to be over-weening, presumptuous*:—c. acc. rei, *to feel confident about, have no fear for*:—c. inf. *to believe confidently that.* Hence

θάρσησις· *εως, ἡ*, *confidence in, reliance on.*

ΘΑ'ΡΣΟΣ or **ΘΡΑ'ΣΟΣ** Att. **θάρρος**, *τό*, *courage boldness, confidence*: in bad sense, *over-boldness, daring, presumption*: in pl., *τὰ θάρση grounds of confidence.*

θαρσούντως Att. **θαρρούντως**. Adv. of pres. part. of *θαρσέω*, *boldly. courageously*

θαρσύνεσκον, Ion. impf. of *θαρσύνω.*

θάρσῠνος. *ον*, *relying on* a thing.

θαρσύνω Att. **θαρρύνω**. f. *ῠνῶ*, (*θάρσος*) *to encourage, cheer.* II. intr. = *θαρσέω*, *to be of good courage.* [ῠ]

θᾶσαι, Dor. aor. 1 imperat. of *θάομαι.*

θάσασθαι, Dor. aor. 1 inf. of *θάομαι.*

θασόμενος, Dor. for *θησόμενος*, fut. part. of *θάομαι.*

Θάσιος, *α, ον*. (*Θάσος*) *from Thasos. Thasian*: *ἡ Θασία* (sub. *ἅλμη*), *pickled sea-fish*; *ἀνακυκᾶν* **Θασίαν** to mix *this pickle.*

ΘΑ'ΣΣΩ Ep. **θαάσσω**, *to sit, sit idle.*

θάσσων Att. **θάττων**, *ον*, Comp. of *ταχύς*, *quicker, swifter*: *θᾶσσον* as Adv., *more quickly.*

θάτερον, θατέρᾳ, see *ἕτερος.*

θάττων, Att. for *θάσσων.*

θαῦμα Ion. **θώυμα** or **θῶμα**, *ατος, τό*, (*θαομαι*) *a wonder, marvel, wondrous thing*; *θαῦμα ἰδέσθαι a wonder* to behold; so, *θαῦμα ἀκοῦσαι, μαθεῖν*: *τὰ θαύματα jugglers' tricks, strange gambols.* II. *wonder, surprise, astonishment.*

θαυμάζω Ion. **θωῦμ**– or **θωμ**–: fut. –*άσομαι* Ep. -*άσσομαι*, later in act. form –*άσω*: aor. 1 *ἐθαύμᾰσα*: pf. *τεθαύμακα*:—Pass., fut. *θαυμασθήσομαι*: aor. 1 *ἐθαυμάσθην*: (*θαῦμα*):—*to wonder, be astonished.* 2. c. acc. *to wonder at*: like Lat. *mirari*, *to regard with wonder* or *esteem, to admire.* 3. c. gen. *to wonder at.* II. Pass. *to be looked at with wonder*: c. part., *θαυμάζομαι μὴ παρών* my absence *is wondered at.*

θαυμαίνω, fut. *ᾰνῶ* Ep. *ᾰνέω*, (*θαῦμα*) *to wonder at.*

θαυμάσιος, *α, ον*, Ion. **θωῦμ**– or **θωμάσιος**, (*θαυμάζω*) *wondrous, wonderful, marvellous*:—*admirable, excellent* Adv. -*ίως*, *marvellously.*

θαυμᾰσι-ουργέω, f. *ήσω*, (*θαυμάσιος, εργον*) *to work wonders, perform curious tricks*, of jugglers.

θαυμάσσομαι, Ep. fut. of *θαυμάζω*

θαυμαστέον, verb. Adj. of *θαυμάζω*, *one must wonder, marvel.*

θαυμαστός Ion. **θωυμ**– or **θωμ**–, *ή, όν*, (*θαυμαζω*) *to be wondered at, wondrous, wonderful, marvellous*:—*admirable, excellent.* Adv. –*τῶς*, *wonderfully.*

θαυμᾰτόομαι, Pass. (*θαῦμα*) *to be regarded as a wonder.*

θαυμᾰτοποιέω, f. *ήσω*, *to do wonders.* From

θαυμᾰτο-ποιός, *όν*, (*θαῦμα, ποιέω*) *wonder-working*: as Subst. *a conjurer, juggler.*

θαυμᾰτός, *ή, όν*, Ep. for *θαυμαστός.*

θαυμᾰτουργέω, f. *ήσω*, *θαυματοποιέω.* From

θαυμᾰτ-ουργός, *όν*, (*θαῦμα*, **ἔργω*) = *θαυματοποιός.*

θάψαι, aor. 1 inf. of *θάπτω.*

θάψῐνος, *η, ον*, *yellow-coloured, sallow.* From

θάψος, ἡ, *a plant* or *wood used for dyeing yellow*, from the island of Thapsos.

***ΘΑ'Ω**, Ep. for the prose θηλάζω: aor. 1 inf θῆσαι: —*to suckle, feed*:—Med., pres. inf. θῆσθαι, *to suck, milk*, ἐπηετανὸν γάλα θῆσθαι milk *to milk* the year round: 3 sing. aor. 1, θήσατο μαζόν *he sucked* the breast.

***θάω**, Lacon. σάω, *to see*:—see θάομαι.

θεά, ἡ, fem. of θεός, *a goddess*: τὰ θεά (Att. τὼ θεώ), in dual, are always Ceres and Proserpine: αἱ σεμναὶ θεαί the Eumenides or Furies.

θέᾱ, ἡ, (θεάομαι) *a looking at, view*. II. *a thing seen, sight, spectacle*.

θεᾱθῆναι, ἡ, aor. 1 inf. pass. of θεάομαι.

θέαινᾰ, ἡ, poët. for θεά, *a goddess*.

θε-αίτητος, ον, (θεός, αἰτέω) *asked of the gods*.

θέᾱμα Ion. **θέημα**, ατος, τό, (θεάομαι) *a sight, spectacle*.

θεάμων, ονος, ὁ, ἡ, (θεάομαι) *a spectator*. [ᾱ]

θεάομαι: f. θεάσομαι [ᾱ], Ion. θεήσομαι: aor. 1 ἐθεᾱσάμην: pf. τεθέᾱμαι: Dep.: (θάομαι):—*to view, gaze at, behold*; οἱ θεώμενοι *the spectators* in a theatre:—aor. 1 ἐθεάθην in pass sense, *to be seen*. See θάομαι, θηέομαι.

θεᾱρός, ὁ, Dor. for θεωρός.

θεᾱτής Ion. **θεητής**, οῦ, ὁ, (θεάομαι) *a spectator*.

θεᾱτός, ή, όν, (θεάομαι) *to be seen*.

θεατρίζω, f. σω, (θέατρον) *to bring on the stage: to make a show of, hold up to ridicule* or *shame*.

θέατρον Ion. **θέητρον**, τό, (θεάομαι) *a place for seeing, a theatre*. 2. collectively, *the spectators, the audience*. 3. = θέαμα, *the piece represented, a show*. [ᾱ]

θε-ειδής, ές, (θεός, εἶδος) = θεοειδής.

θέειον, τό, poët. for θεῖον, *brimstone*.

θέειος, η, ον, Ep. for θεῖος, *divine*.

θεειοῦται, 3 sing. pres. pass. of θεειόω.

θεειόω, Ep. for θειόω, *to smoke with brimstone*.

θέεσκον, Ion. impf. of θέω.

θέη, ἡ, Ion. for θέα.

θεήϊος, η, ον, Ion. for θέειος, θεῖος, *divine*.

θε-ήλᾰτος, ον, (θεός, ἐλαύνω) *driven* or *pursued by a god*. 2. *sent, caused by a god*. II. *built by a god* or *for the gods*.

θέημα, τό, Ion. for θέαμα.

θεη-μᾰχία, ἡ, **θεη-μάχος**, ον. poët. for θεομ-.

θεήμων, ονος, ὁ, ἡ, Ion. for θεάμων.

θεη-πολέω, **θεη-πολός**, όν. poët. for θεοπ-.

θεήσεαι, Ion. 2 sing fut. of θεάομαι.

θέῃσι, Ep. 3 sing. subj. of θέω.

θεητής, οῦ, ὁ, Ion. for θεατής.

θεητός, **θέητρον**, **θεήτωρ**, Ion. for θεατ-.

θεία, ἡ, fem. of θεῖος, *one's father's* or *mother's sister, aunt*, Lat. *amita* and *matertera*.

θειάζω, f. σω. (θεῖος) *to practise divinations*. Hence

θειασμός, ὁ, *practice of divinations*.

Θείβᾱθεν, **Θείβᾱθι**, Aeol. for Θηβ-.

θεῖεν, 3 pl. aor. 2 opt. of τίθημι.

θείην, aor. 2 opt. of τίθημι.

θείκελος, = θέσκελος.

θειλό-πεδον, τό, (εἵλη, πέδον) *a place in the sunshine, where things were put to dry*.

θεῖμεν, for θείημεν, 1 pl. aor. 2 opt. of τίθημι.

θεῖναι, aor. 2 inf. of τίθημι:—also aor. 1 inf. of θείνω.

ΘΕΙ'ΝΩ, fut. θενῶ: aor. 1 ἔθεινα: aor. 2 ἔθενον, only in imperat. θένε, subj. θένω, inf. θενεῖν, part. θενών:—*to strike, dash*.

θειό-δομος, ον, (θεῖος, δέμω) *god-built*.

θείομεν, Ep. for θέωμεν, θῶμεν, 1 pl. aor. 2 subj. of τίθημι.

θεῖον Ep. **θέειον**, τό, (θεῖος) *brimstone*, Lat. *sulfur*.

θεῖον, τό, neut. of θεῖος, used as Subst., *the Divine Being, Deity*. II. τὰ θεῖα, *the acts* or *attributes of the gods*. 2. *religious observances*.

θεῖος, α, ον, (θεός) *of* or *from the gods*, Lat. *divinus, sent* or *caused by a god, appointed of God*. 2. *in honour of a god, holy, sacred*. 3. *godlike, superhuman, extraordinary, excellent*.

ΘΕΙ'ΟΣ, ὁ, *one's father's* or *mother's brother, uncle*, Lat. *patruus* and *avunculus*: fem. θεία.

θειοτέρως, Adv. Comp. of θείως.

θειότης, ητος, ἡ, (θεῖος) *divine nature, divinity*.

θειό-χροος, ον, contr. **-χρους**, ουν, (θεῖον, χρόα) *brimstone-coloured*.

θειόω Ep. **θεειόω**: f. ώσω: (θεῖον):—*to smoke with brimstone, fumigate*: hence *to purify*.

θείς, θεῖσα, aor. 2 part. of τίθημι.

θεῖτε, θεῖσαν, 2 and 3 pl. aor. 2 opt. of τίθημι.

θεῖτο, 3 sing. aor. 2 opt. of τίθημι.

θείω, poët. for θέω, *to run*.

θείω, Ep. for θέω, θῶ, aor. 2 subj. of τίθημι.

θείως, Adv. of θεῖος, *by divine providence*: Comp. θειοτέρως, *by more special providence*.

θει-ώδης, ες, (θεῖον, εἶδος) *brimstone-like*, Lat. *sulfureus*.

θελγεσί-μῡθος, ον, (θέλγω, μῦθος) *of soft, persuasive speech*.

θέλγεσκον, Ion. impf. of θέλγω.

θέλγητρον, τό, (θέλγω) *a charm* or *spell*.

ΘΕ'ΛΓΩ, f. ξω: aor. 1 ἔθελξα:—Pass., aor. 1 ἐθέλχθην:—*to stroke with magic power, to charm, enchant, spell-bind*, Lat. *mulceo*: *to cheat, cozen*.

θέλεος, ον, (θέλω) *willing, voluntary*.

θέλημα, ατος, τό, (θέλω) *will*.

θέλησις, εως, ἡ. (θέλω) *a willing, will*.

θελκτήρ, ῆρος, ὁ, (θέλγω) *a charmer*. Hence

θελκτήριον, τό, *a charm, spell, enchantment, means* or *power of charming*: neut. from

θελκτήριος, ον, (θέλγω) *charming, enchanting*.

θέλκτρον, τό, = θελκτήριον, *a charm*.

θέλκτωρ, ορος, ὁ, ἡ, = θελκτήρ.

θέλξαι, aor. 1 inf. of θέλγω.

θελξεῖ, Dor. for θέλξει, 3 sing. fut. of θέλγω.

θελξί-νοος, ον, contr. **-νους**, ουν, (θέλγω, νόος) *charming* or *witching the heart*.

θελξί-πικρος, ον, (θέλγω, πικρός) *deliciously bitter*.

θελξί-φρων, ον, gen. ονος, (θέλγω, φρήν) = θελξίνοος.

θέλοισα, Dor. for *θέλουσα*, fem. part. of *θέλω*.

θέλυμνα, *τά*, = *θέμεθλα*.

ΘΕ'ΛΩ, impf. *ἔθελον*: fut. *θελήσω*: aor. 1 *ἠθέλησα*: shortened form of *ἐθέλω*.

θέμεθλα, *τά*, (*τίθημι*) *the foundation, the base* or *bottom* of a thing, *the roots* of a mountain, etc.; *Ἄμμωνος θέμεθλα the shrine* of Ammon.

θεμείλια, *τά*, Ep. for *θεμέλια*, = *θέμεθλα*; *θεμείλια θέσαν* or *προβάλοντο* they laid *the foundations*.

θεμελιόθεν, Adv. *from the bottom*, Lat. *funditus*.

θεμέλιον, *τό*, as sing. of *θεμείλια*, *the foundation*: *τὰ θεμέλια* = *θεμείλια*, *θέμεθλα*. From

θεμέλιος, *ον*, (*τίθημι*) *belonging to the foundation*. II. as Subst., *θεμέλιος* (sub. *λίθος*), *ὁ*, *a foundation stone; οἱ θεμέλιοι*, *the foundations*. Hence

θεμελιόω, f. *ώσω*, *to lay the foundation, found firmly*: —Pass. *to have the foundations laid*.

θέμεν. **θέμεναι**, Ep. for *θεῖναι*, aor. 2 inf. of *τίθημι*.

θέμενος, aor. 2 med. part. of *τίθημι*.

θεμερός, *όν*, (*τίθημι*) *grave, serious, steadfast*.

θεμερ-ῶπις, *ιδος*, *ἡ*, (*θεμερός*, *ὤψ*) *of serious countenance, honest*.

θεμίζω, (*θέμις*) *to regulate, punish, control*: Med., poët. aor. 1 *θεμίσσασθαι to regulate for oneself, control*.

θεμί-πλεκτος, *ον*, (*θεμίς*, *πλέκω*) *woven of right; θεμίπλεκτος στέφανος a well-earned* crown.

ΘΕ'ΜΙΣ, *ἡ*, Ep. gen. *θέμιστος*, acc. *θέμιν*:—in Homer as prop. n. **Θέμις**, *Θέμιστος*, acc. *Θέμιστα*: but Att. gen. *Θέμιτος*, sometimes also *Θέμιδος*, acc. *Θέμιν*; Ion. gen. *Θέμιος*, voc. *Θέμι*: I. *law, right*, agreed on by common consent or prescription, opposed to *statute-law*, Lat. *jus* or *fas*, as opp. to *lex*; *θέμις ἐστί* 'tis *meet and right*, Lat. *fas est*; *ᾗ θέμις ἐστί* as 'tis *right*, as *the custom* is. II. pl. *θέμιστες*, *sanctions, laws, ordinances*. 2. *the rights* of the chief, *prerogative, privilege, authority*: hence *dues, tribute*, etc. 3. *existing laws* or *ordinances* 4. *law-suits*: also *courts to administer justice*: *judicial sentences*. III. *Θέμις* as prop. n., *Themis, goddess of law and order, Justice*.

θεμι-σκοπός, *όν*, (*θέμις*, *σκοπέω*) *keeping order*.

θεμισ-κρέων, *οντος*, *ὁ*, *reigning by right*.

θέμιστα, **-ας**, Ep. acc. sing. and pl. of *θέμις*.

θεμιστεῖος, **α**, *ον*, (*θέμις*) *lawful, righteous*.

θεμιστεύω, f. *σω*, (*θεμιστός*) *to give law, lay down ordinances, give oracles*: *to order, govern*.

θεμιστέων, Ep. gen. pl. of *θέμις*

θεμιστο-πόλος, *ον*, (*θέμις*, *πολέω*) *ministering law and right*

θεμιστός, *ή*, *όν*, (*θεμίζω*) *sanctioned by law, lawful*.

θεμἴτός, *ή*, *όν*, Ep. for *θεμιστός*

ΘΕΜΟ'Ω, an Ep. Verb only occurring once in aor. 1, *νῆα θέμωσε χέρσον ἱκέσθαι he forced* the ship to come to land, or *set* it so as to come.

-θεν, insep. Particle, affixed to Nouns denoting *motion from* a place, opp. to *-δε*, as, *οἴκοθεν*, *οὐρανόθεν*, *from* home, *from* heaven: more rarely affixed to names of persons, as *Διόθεν*, *θεόθεν*, *from* Zeus, *from* the gods. Originally *-θεν* was the genit. termination, as appears from *ἐμέθεν*, *σέθεν*, *ἕθεν*

θένἄρ, *ἄρος*, *τό*, (*θένω*, *θείνω*) *the part of the hand with which one strikes, the flat of the hand*: *ἁλὸς θέναρ the surface of the sea*.

θέο, Ep. 2 sing. aor. 2 med. imperat. of *τίθημι*

θεοβλἄβέω, *to sin against the gods*. From

θεο-βλἄβής, *ές*, (*θεός*, *βλαβῆναι*) *stricken of God, visited with judicial blindness, reckless*.

θεο-γεννής, *ές*, (*θεός*, *γέννα*) *begotten of a god*.

θεό-γλωσσος, *ον*, (*θεός*, *γλῶσσα*) *with the tongue of a god*.

θεογονία, *ἡ*, *the generation* or *genealogy of the gods*, the title of a poem of Hesiod. From

θεό-γονος, *ον*, (*θεός*, **γένω*) *born of God*.

θεο-δέγμων, *ον*, gen. *ονος*, (*θεός*, *δέχομαι*) *receiving a god*.

θεο-δήλητος, *ον*, (*θεός*, *δηλέομαι*) *hurtful to the majesty of the gods*.

θεο-δίδακτος, *ον*, (*θεός*, *διδάσκω*) *taught of God*. [ῐ]

θεό-δμητος, *ον*, Dor. **-δμᾱτος**, *α*. *ον*, (*θεός*, *δέμω*) *god-built, made* or *founded by the gods*.

θεό-δοτος, *ον*, = *θεόσδοτος*.

θεο-ειδής, *ές*, (*θεός*, *εἶδος*) *divine of form, beauteous as the gods, godlike*: irreg. Sup. *θεαιδέστατος*

θεο-είκελος, *ον*. (*θεός*, *εἴκελος*) *godlike*.

θεοεχθρία, *ἡ*, *a being hated by the gods*. From

θεό-εχθρος, *ον*, (*θεός*, *ἐχθρός*) *hated by the gods*.

θεόθεν, old gen. of **θεός**, used as Adv., *from the god*. Lat. *divinitus*.

θέοισα, Dor. for *θέουσα*, fem. part. of *θέω*.

θεοκλῦτέω, f. *ήσω*, *to call the gods to aid*. *to invoke divine vengeance*: *to call on, conjure*. From

θεό-κλῦτος, *ον*, (*θεός*, *κλύω*) *calling on the gods*.

θεό-κραντος, *ον*, (*θεός*, *κραίνω*) *wrought by the gods*.

θεό-κρῖτος, *ον*, (*θεός*, *κρίνω*) *judging between gods*.

θεό-κτιστος, *ον*, and **θεό-κτῐτος**, *ον*, (*θεός*, *κτίζω*) *created by God*.

θεο-μᾰνής, *ές*, (*θεός*, *μανῆναι*) *maddened by the gods*; *λύσσα θεομανής* madness *caused by the gods*.

θεό-μαντις, *εως*, *ὁ*, (*θεός*, *μάντις*) *one who has a spirit of prophecy*.

θεομᾰχέω, *to fight against God*: and

θεομᾰχία, *ἡ*, *the battle of the gods*, as certain books of the Iliad were called, esp. the 19th. From

θεο-μάχος, *ον*, (*θεός*, *μάχομαι*) *fighting against God*.

θεο-μήστωρ, *ορος*, *ὁ*, (*θεός*, *μήσταρ*) *like the gods in counsel*.

θεο-μῖσής, *ές*, (*θεός*, *μισέω*) *hated of the gods*.

θεό-μορος Dor. **θεύμ-**, *ον*, (*θεός*, *μόρος*) *destined* or *allotted by the gods*. II. *blessed by the gods*.

θεό-μορφος, *ον*, (*θεος μορφή*) *of form divine*.

θεο-μῠσής, *ές*, (*θεός*, *μύσος*) *abominable before the gods*

θεό-παις, *παιδος*, *ὁ*, *ἡ*, (*θεός*, *παῖς*) *child of the gods*.

θεό-πεμπτος, *ον*, (*θεός*, *πέμπω*) *sent by the gods*.

θεό-πνευστος. *ον*, (*θεός*, *πνέω*) *inspired of God*.

θεοποιέω, *to make into gods, deify*. From

θεο-ποιός, όν, (θεός, ποιέω) *making statues of gods.*

θεό-πομπος, ον, (θεός, πέμπω) *god-sent.*

θεο-πόνητος, ον, (θεός, πονέω) *wrought by a god.*

θεο-πρεπής, ές, (θεός, πρέπω) *befitting a god.* Adv. -πῶς.

θεοπροπέω, *to prophesy*, in part. *θεοπροπέων*; and

θεοπροπία, ἡ, or -ιον, τό, *a prophecy.* From

θεο-πρόπος, (θεός, πρέπω) *prophetic, boding, divining:* as Subst., *θεοπρόπος, ὁ, a prophet.* II. *a public messenger sent to inquire of the oracle*, cf. *θεωρός.*

θεό-πτυστος, ον, (θεός, πτύω) *abhorred by the gods.*

θεό-πῦρος, ον, (θεός, πῦρ) *kindled by the gods.*

θέ-ορτος, ον, (θεός, ὄρνυμαι) *sprung from the gods.*

ΘΕΟ'Σ, ὁ, Lat. *DEUS, God:* in Homer either *God*, as, *Θεὸς δώσει God* will grant; or, *θεός τις a god, some particular god:* later *the Deity*, like *τὸ θεῖον*:—*σὺν θεῷ, σὺν θεοῖς. οὐκ ἄνευθε θεοῦ.* Lat. *non sine diis, by the will of God; ὑπὲρ θεόν against his will:* —as an oath, *πρὸς θεῶν* by *the gods*, in God's name. II. fem. *θεός*, for *θεά, θέαινα, a goddess:* esp. in **Att.** phrase *τὼ θεώ. the two goddesses*, i. e. Ceres and Proserpine. III. as Adj. in Comp. *θεώτερος, more divine.*

θεόσ-δοτος, ον, (θεός, δίδωμι) *given by the gods.*

θεόσ-δωρος, ον, poët. for *θεοδώρητος.*

θεοσέβεια, ἡ, *the worship* or *fear of God.* From

θεο-σεβής, ές, (θεός, σέβομαι) *worshipping* **God**, *religious, devout.* Adv. *-βῶς, religiously.*

θεό-σεπτος, ον, (θεός, σέβομαι) *worshipped as a god.*

θεο-σέπτωρ, ορος, ὁ, = *θεοσεβής.*

θεοσ-εχθρία, ἡ, (θεός, ἐχθρός) *hatred of the gods, ungodliness, impiety.*

θεόσ-σῦτος, ον, poët. for *θεόσυτος, sent by the gods.*

θεο-στήρικτος, ον, (θεός, στηρίζω) *supported by God.*

θεο-στῐβής, ές. (θεός, στιβεῖν) *trodden by God.*

θεο-στῠγής, ές, (θεός, στυγέω) *hated of the gods* or *of God, abominable.* II. act. *hating God.*

θεο-στύγητος, ον *hated of the gods.*

θεό-σῠτος, poët. also **θεόσ-συτος**, ον. (θεός. σεύω) *sent by the gods.*

θεό-ταυρος, ὁ, (θεός, ταῦρος) *the god-bull*, a name for Zeus changed into a bull.

θεο-τείχης, ες, (θεός, τεῖχος) *walled by the gods.*

θεό-τευκτος, ον, (θεός, τεύχω) *made by God.*

θεότης, ητος, ἡ, (θεός) *divinity, divine nature.*

θεο-τίμητος, ον, (θεός, τιμάω) *honoured of God.*

θεό-τῑμος, ον, *honoured of God.*

θεό-τρεπτος, ον, (θεός, τρέπω) *directed by the gods.*

θεο-τρεφής, ές, (θεός, τρέφω) *feeding the gods.*

θεουδεία. ἡ, *the fear of God, holiness.*

θεουδής, ές, (θεός, δέος) *fearing god, godly.* Hence

θεο-φάνια (sub. ἱερά), τά, (θεός, φανῆναι) a festival at Delphi, *at which the images of the gods were shewn to the people.*

θεο-φῐλής, ές, (θεός, φιλέω) *beloved of the gods.*

θεόφιν, Ep. gen. and dat. sing. and pl. of *θεός*: esp. in phrase, *θεόφιν μήστωρ ἀτάλαντος.*

θεο-φόρητος, ον, (θεός, φορέω) *inspired by a god.* II. act. *carrying a god* or *goddess.*

θεο-φόρος, ον, (θεός. φέρω) *bearing a god.* II. *θεόφορος, ον, borne* or *possessed by a god, inspired.*

θεό-φρων, ον, gen. ονος, (θεός, φρήν) *godly-minded. godly, devout*, Lat. *pius.*

θεόω, f. *ώσω*, (θεός) *to make into a god, deify.*

θεράπαινα and -νίς, ίδος, ἡ, fem. of *θεράπων, a waiting-maid, handmaid.*

θερᾰπεία Ion. -ηΐη, ἡ, (θεραπεύω) *a waiting on, service attendance; θεραπεία θεῶν* divine *worship*, 2. *a fostering, nurture: tending in sickness, medical treatment.* 3. *a courting paying court.* II. *a body of attendants, suite, retinue.*

θεράπευμα, *ματος, τό*, (θεραπεύω) *service done. attendance, nurture: medical treatment*

θερᾰπευτέον, verb. Adj. of *θεραπεύω, one must cultivate:* also *one must cure.*

θερᾰπευτήρ, *ῆρος, ὁ*, and **θεραπευτής**, *οῦ*, (θεραπεύω) *an attendant, servant.* 2. *one who attends to anything: a worshipper of the gods: a physician.*

θερᾰπευτικός, ή, όν, (θεραπεύω) *inclined to serve. attentive, obedient: courteous.* 2. *able to cure; ἡ θεραπευτική* (sc. *τέχνη*) *the healing art.*

θερᾰπεύω, f. *σω*, (θεράπων) *to wait on, attend, serve: to be an attendant: to do service to* the gods, *to worship: to serve, attend, pay observance to.* 2. *to pay court to, to flatter:* also of things, *to consult, attend to*, Lat. *inservire commodo.* 3. c. acc. rei, *to take care of, provide for; θεραπεύειν τὸ παρόν, to provide for* the present; *θεραπεύειν ἡμέρην to observe* a day, *keep* it *holy.* 4. *to tend* the sick, *to treat medically, to heal, cure.* 5. of land, *to cultivate, till.*

θερᾰπηΐη, Ion. for *θεραπεία.*

θερᾰπήϊος, *η, ον*, Ion. and poët. for *θεραπευτικός.*

θεράπνη, ἡ, poët. for *θεράπαινα, a handmaid:*—and, **θεραπνίς**, ίδος, ἡ, poët. contr. from *θεραπαινίς.*

θερᾰποντίς, ίδος. ἡ, (θεράπων) *of a waiting-maid.*

ΘΕΡΑ'ΠΩΝ, *οντος, ὁ, an attendant, servant*, differing from *δοῦλος*, as implying free service: in Homer, *a companion in arms, comrade*, though inferior in rank, as Patroclus was the *θεράπων* of Achilles; so, kings were *Διὸς θεράποντες*, warriors *θεράποντες Ἄρηος*, poets *Μουσάων θεράποντες.* II. *in Chios*, the *θεράποντες* were *slaves.*

θέραψ, ὁ, rare form for *θεράπων*, only found in accus. *θέραπα*, nom. pl. *θέραπες.*

θέρειος, α. ον, (θέρος) *of, belonging to summer, in summer; αὐχμὸς θ. summer*-drought; *ἡ θέρεια*, Ion. *θερείη* (with or without *ὥρα*), *summer-time, summer.*

θερέω, Ep. for *θερῶ*, aor. 2 pass. subj. of *θέρω.*

θερίζω, f. *ίσω* Att. *ιῶ*: aor. 1 *ἐθέρισα* syncop. *ἔθρισα*:—Pass., aor. 1 *ἐθερίσθην*: pf. *τεθέρισμαι*: (*θέρος*):—*to mow, reap, cut, harvest* corn:—metaph. *to mow down, cut off, slay:* also *to cut* the hair. 3. also *to pack up.* II. intr. *to pass the summer*; cf. *ἐαρίζω, χειμάζω.*

θερίνεος, α, ον, = θέρειος; τροπαὶ θερίνεαι *the summer solstice*, i. e. the 21st of June. [ῐ]

θερῐνός, ή, όν, (θέρος) prose form for θέρειος, *of, in*, or *during summer*.

θερισμός, ὁ, (θερίζω) *a mowing, reaping, harvesting.*

θεριστής, οῦ, ὁ, (θερίζω) *a mower, reaper, harvest-man.*

θερίστριον or **θέριστρον**, τό, (θερίζω) *a light summer-garment*, opp. to χειμάστριον.

θερμαίνω, f. ἄνῶ: aor. 1 ἐθέρμηνα: (θερμός):—*to warm, heat*:—Pass. *to become warm* or *hot, grow hot, glow*: metaph., θερμαίνεσθαι ἐλπίσι *to glow* with *hope*.

θέρμη, ἡ, (θερμός) *heat, feverish heat.* II. θέρμαι, αἱ, *hot-springs*, Lat. *thermae*.

θερμό-βλυστος, ον, (θερμός, βλύω) *hot-bubbling.*

θερμό-βουλος, ον, (θερμός, βουλή) *hot in counsel, rash.*

θερμο-δότης, ου, ὁ, fem. **θερμό-δοτις**, ιδος, ἡ, (θερμός, δίδωμι) *one who brought the hot water* (Lat. *calda*) *at baths* or *sacrifices*, Lat. *caldarius*.

θερμο-εργός, όν, = θερμουργός.

θερμό-νους, ουν, (θερμός, νοῦς) *heated in mind.*

Θερμο-πύλαι, ῶν, αἱ, (θερμός, πύλη) *Hot-Gates*, a narrow pass, in which were hot-springs, the name of the famous pass from Thessaly to Locris; also called simply **Πύλαι** [ῠ]

θερμός, ή, όν, also poët. ός, όν, (θέρω): *warm, hot, boiling* II. metaph. *hot, hasty, rash, reckless.* 2. *active, ready.* III. τὸ θερμόν, *heat*, Lat. *calor*: also, θερμὸν (sub. ὕδωρ), *hot drink*, Lat. *calda*: τὰ θερμά (sub. χωρία), *hot places*, or (sub. λουτρά), *hot baths.*

ΘΕΡΜΟΣ, ὁ, *the lupine.*

θερμο-τρᾰγέω, f. ήσω, (θέρμος, τρώγω) *to eat lupines.*

θερμ-ουργός, όν. (θερμός, *ἔργω) *doing hot and hasty acts, rash, reckless, impetuous.*

θέρμω, only used in pres. imperat. and in impf. (θέρω) *to warm, heat, make hot*:—Pass. *to grow hot.*

θέρος, τό, (θέρω) *summer, summer-time*: *summer-heat*: τὸ θέρος, absol., *during summer*; τοῦ θέρεος *in the course of* summer. II. *a harvest, a crop.*

ΘΕ΄ΡΩ, fut. θέρσω, *to warm, heat*:—Homer uses only Pass. **θέρομαι**, with fut. med. θέρσομαι, aor. 2 ἐθέρην in subj. θερέω for θερῶ: *to become warm, grow hot, warm oneself*; πυρὸς θέρεσθαι *to be burnt with fire.*

θές, aor. 2 imperat. of τίθημι.

θέσαν, Ep. 3 pl. aor. 2 of τίθημι.

θέσθαι, aor. 2 inf. med. of τίθημι.

θέσθω, θέσθε, 3 sing. and 2 pl. aor. 2 imperat. med. of τίθημι.

θέσις, εως, ἡ, (τίθημι) *a setting, placing, arranging*; ἐπέων θέσις *a setting* of words in verse. poetry. II. *a deposit* of money, *earnest-money.* III. *adoption* as the child of some one; cf. θετός. IV. (from Pass. τίθεσθαι) *a being placed, position, situation.* 2. *a position* or *thesis* to be proved. V. in metre *the last half of the foot*, in which the voice falls, opp. to the *first* half (ἄρσις), in which it rises.

θέσ-κελος, ον, (θεός, εἴσκω, ἴσκω) *godlike*: but generally, *marvellous, wondrous*, always of things, θεοείκελος being used of persons; θέσκελα ἔργα works *of wonder*; neut. as Adv., ἔικτο δὲ θέσκελον αὐτῷ he was *wondrous* like him.

θέσμιος Dor. **τέθμιος**, ον, (θεσμός) *according to law, lawful, legitimate*: θέσμια, τά, as Subst. *laws, customs, rites.*

θεσμο-θέτης, ου, ὁ, (θεσμός, τίθημι) *a lawgiver.* II. the θεσμοθέται at Athens were *the six junior archons*: after their year expired they became members of the Areopagus.

θεσμο-ποιέω, f. ήσω, (θεσμός, ποιέω) *to make laws.*

θεσμο-πόλος, ον, (θεσμός, πολέω) *conversant with laws* or *customs.*

θεσμός Dor. **τεθμός**, ὁ: irreg. pl. θεσμά, τά: (τίθημι):—*a law, rule, ordinance*, Lat. *institutum*: *a rite, form, institution.* 2. at Athens, Draco's laws were called θεσμοί, because each began with the word θεσμός; Solon's laws were named νόμοι. Hence

θεσμοσύνη, ἡ, *justice*, like δικαιοσύνη.

θεσμοφόρια, ων, τά, (θεσμοφόρος) *the Thesmophoria*, an ancient festival held by the Athenian women in honour of Demeter Θεσμοφόρος: it lasted three days from the 11th of Pyanepsion. Hence

θεσμοφοριάζω, f. σω, *to keep the Thesmophoria*; αἱ Θεσμοφοριάζουσαι, a play of Aristophanes.

θεσμοφόριον, τό, *the temple of Demeter* Θεσμοφόρος.

θεσμο-φόρος, ον, (θεσμός, φέρω) *law-giving*: epith. of Demeter, Lat. *Ceres*, as the goddess of tillage and civilised life; τὰ θεσμοφόρω Ceres and Proserpine, who were worshipped together at the Thesmophoria.

θεσμο-φύλαξ, ἄκος, ὁ, mostly in pl., θεσμο-φύλακες, like νομο-φύλακες, *guardians of the law*, a magistracy at Elis. [ῠ]

θεσ-πέσιος, α, ον, also ος, ον, (θεός, ἔπος) of the voice, *divinely sweet.* II. *more than mortal* or *human*: *unspeakable, ineffable*, and generally = θεῖος, *divine*: dat. fem. θεσπεσίῃ (sub. βουλῇ) as Adv., *by the will of God.* 2. *wondrous, marvellous, excellent.* 3. of anything *sent by God*, and so, *awful, fearful.* Hence

θεσπεσίως, Adv. *in divine manner*; θεσπεσίως ἐφόβηθεν they trembled *unspeakably.*

θεσπῐ-δαής, ές, (θέσπις, δαίω A) *kindled by a god*; θεσπιδαὲς πῦρ, *supernatural, furious* fire.

θεσπι-έπεια, fem. Adj. (θέσπις, ἔπος) *prophetic.*

θεσπίζω: fut. ίσω Att. ιῶ, Ion. inf. θεσπιέειν: aor. 1 ἐθέσπισα Dor -ιξα: (θέσπις):—*to declare by oracle, prophesy, divine.*

θεσπίξασα, Dor. for θεσπίσασα, aor. 1 part. fem. of foreg.

θέσπιος, ον, = θεσπέσιος.

θέσ-πις, ιος, ὁ, ἡ, (θεός, ἔπος) *inspired, prophetic, sacred.* II. = θεῖος II, *divine, wondrous awful.*

θέσπισμα, ατος, τό, (θεσπίζω) *an oracle.*

θεσπιῳδέω, f. ήσω, *to sing in prophetic strain.* From

θεσπι-ῳδός, όν, (θέσπις, ᾠδή) *singing in prophetic train, prophetic.*

Θεσσᾰλός Att. **Θετταλός**, ὁ, fem. **Θεσσαλίς**, ίδος, *a Thessalian:* also as Adj., Θεσσαλὸν σόφισμα *a Thessalian trick*, from the faithless character of the people.

θέσσασθαι, *to pray for:* a defect. poët. aor. 1, of which we find only 3 pl. θέσσαντο, part. θεσσάμενος. (Origin uncertain.)

θεσφᾰτη-λόγος, ον, (θέσφατος, λέγω) *prophetic.*

θέσ-φᾰτος, ον, (θεός, φημί) *spoken by God, decreed, appointed, destined,* Lat. *fatalis:* as Subst., θέσφατα, τά, *oracles.* II. like θεῖος, *made by God, divine.*

Θετίδειον, τό, *the temple of Thetis.* From

Θέτις, ιδος, ὁ, *Thetis*, one of the Nereids, wife of Peleus, mother of Achilles.

θέτο, Ep. 3 sing. aor. 2 med. of τίθημι.

θετός, ή, όν, verb. Adj. of τίθημι, *placed, set.* II. *adopted as one's child.*

θεῦ, Dor. and Ion. aor. 2 imperat. med. of τίθημι.

θεύ-μορος, ον, Dor. for θεόμορος.

θεῦς, ὁ and ἡ, Dor. for θεός, *a god.*

θεύσομαι, *I will run*, fut. of θέω.

θευ-φορία, ἡ, Dor. for θεοφορία.

ΘΕ'Ω Ep. also **θείω**: fut. θεύσομαι:—*to run; θέειν πεδίοιο to run over* the plain; περὶ τρίποδος θέειν *to run for* a tripod; περὶ ψυχῆς Ἕκτορος θέειν *to run for* Hector's life; later also, θέειν τὸν περὶ τῆς ψυχῆς (sc. δρόμον) *to run* for one's life. II. of birds, *to fly:* of ships, *to run;* of the *running* wheel, of a *rolling* stone. III. of things which *run* in a continuous line, though not actually in motion; of anything circular, which seems *to run round into itself*, ἄντυξ ἣ πυμάτη θέεν ἀσπίδος the rim which *ran round* at the verge of the shield.

θεῶ, contr. for θεάου, imperat. of θεάομαι.

θέωμεν, Ion. for θῶμεν, 1 pl. aor. 2 subj. of τίθημι.

θεωρέω, f. ήσω, (θεωρός) *to look at, view, behold, observe:* esp. *to be a spectator at the public games and festivals.* 2. of the mind, like Lat. *contemplari, to contemplate, consider.* II. *to be a* θεωρός or *state ambassador to the oracle* or *at the games.* III. Causal in Soph. O. C. 1084, θεωρήσασα τοὐμὸν ὄμμα *having made* my eyes *behold;* but see ἑωρέω. Hence

θεώρημα, ατος, τό, *a sight, spectacle.* II. *a thing contemplated* by the mind, *a principle deduced:* in Mathematics, *a theorem.*

θεωρητήριον, τό, (θεωρέω) *a seat in a theatre.*

θεωρητικός, ή, όν, (θεωρέω) *of* or *for speculation, theoretic.*

θεωρία, ἡ, (θεωρέω) *a looking at, viewing, beholding, observing;* θεωρίας εἵνεκεν for the purpose of *seeing the world:* esp. *the being a spectator* at the public games. 2. of the mind, *contemplation, reflection.* II. *the sending of* θεωροί or *state-ambassadors* to the oracle or games: also *the* body of θεωροί themselves. 2. *the office of* θεωρός. III. pass. *a sight, spectacle.*

θεωρικός, ή, όν, (θεωρός) *of* or *belonging to spectators* or *to the sacred ambassadors* (θεωροί). II. τὰ θεωρικά (sub. χρήματα) *the money*, which, from the time of Pericles, was given from the treasury to the poor citizens, *to pay for their seats at the theatre* (at 2 obols the seat), but also for other purposes.

θεωρίς, ίδος, ἡ, with and without ναῦς, *a sacred ship which carried the* θεωροί to their destination; used also for other state-purposes. From

θεωρός, ὁ, (θεός, ὥρα) *a spectator, observer, one who travels to see* men and things. II. *an ambassador, sent by the state to consult an oracle:*—the Athenians sent θεωροί to the Delphic oracle, to Delos, and to the four great Hellenic games, the Olympian, Pythian, Nemean, and Isthmian.

θεώτερος, α, ον, Comp. of θεός, *more divine.*

Θηβᾱ-γενής, ές, (Θήβη, γενέσθαι) *sprung from Thebes, born at Thebes, Theban.*

Θήβᾱθι, Adv. *at Thebes.*

Θήβαζε, Adv. *to* or *towards Thebes.* From

ΘΗ~ΒΑΙ, ων, αἱ, poët. also **Θήβη**, ἡ, *Thebes*, the name of several cities, of which the most famous are the Egyptian, the Boeotian, and another in the Troad, all in Homer, who uses both sing. and plur. of all. Hence

Θηβαι-γενής, ές, = Θηβαγενής: and

Θηβαιεύς, έως Ion. έος, epith. of Jove, *Theban:*—so **Θηβαῖος**, α, ον, and **Θηβαϊκός**, ή, όν, *Theban.*

Θηβαΐς, ΐδος, ἡ, (Θῆβαι) *the Thebaïs*, i. e. territory of Thebes. II. *the Thebaïd*, a poem on the siege of Thebes.

Θήβασδε, poët. Adv., = Θήβαζε.

Θήβη, v. Θῆβαι.

Θήβησιν poët. **Θήβησι**, (Θῆβαι) Adv. *at Thebes.*

θηγᾰλέος, α, ον, (θήγω) *pointed, sharp.* II. act. *sharpening.*

θηγάνη, ἡ, (θήγω) *a whetstone:* metaph. *anything to whet one's fury, a provocative to rage.* [ᾰ]

θηγάνω, = θήγω.

ΘΗ'ΓΩ, f. θήξω: aor. 1 ἔθηξα:—Pass., pf. τέθηγμαι:—*to sharpen, whet:*—Med., δόρυ θήξασθαι *to whet one's* spear. II. metaph. *to sharpen, provoke, irritate.*

θηεῖτο, 3 sing. impf. of θηέομαι.

θηέομαι, f. -ήσομαι, Ion. form of θεάομαι: Dor. **θᾱέομαι**:—*to look on, gaze at, observe, admire:* impf., 3 sing. ἐθηεῖτο Ep. θηεῖτο, Ion. 3 pl. ἐθηεῦντο Ep. θηεῦντο; ἐθηεύμεσθα Ion. 1 pl.; θηεύμενος Ion. part.: θηήσαιο, -αιτο 2 and 3 pl. aor. 1 opt.: cf θάομαι.

θήῃς, Ep. for θῇς, 2 sing. aor. 2 subj. of τίθημι.

θηητήρ, ῆρος, ὁ, Ion. for θεατής, (θηέομαι) *one who gazes at, an admirer.*

θηητός, ή, όν, Ion. for θεατός, *gazed at, to be looked at* or *admired, wondrous.*

θήϊον, τό, Ep. for θεῖον, *brimstone.*

θήϊος, Ep. for θεῖος, *divine.*

θῆκα, Ep. aor. 1 of τίθημι.

θηκαῖος, α, ον, *like a chest* or *coffin, belonging to a* *sepulchre of the dead; οἴκημα θηκαῖον a burial* vault. From

θήκη, ἡ, (τίθημι) *a case to put anything in, a box, chest: a place for putting corpses in, a grave, vault.*

θηκτός, ή, όν, verb. Adj. of θήγω, *sharpened.*

θηλάζω, fut. άσω Dor. άξω: (θηλή) :—*to give suck, suckle.* II. of the child, *to suck; θηλάζων sucking,*

θήλεα, Ion. fem. of θῆλυς.

θηλέω Dor. **θᾱλέω**, f. ήσω, (θηλή) *to flourish, abound;* c. gen., λειμῶνες ἴου ἠδὲ σελίνου θήλεον the meadows *were rich with* violets and parsley. II. *to make to bloom.*

θηλή, ἡ, (τέθηλα) *the part of the breast which gives suck, the teat, nipple.*

θηλυ-γενής, ές, (θῆλυς, γενέσθαι) *of female sex.*

θηλύ-γλωσσος, ον, (θῆλυς, γλῶσσα) *with woman's tongue.*

θηλυδρίας, ου, ὁ, Ion. -ίης, (θῆλυς) *an effeminate person.*

θηλυδρι-ώδης, ες, (θηλυδρίας, εἶδος) *of womanish kind, effeminate.*

θηλυ-κρᾰτής, ές, (θῆλυς, κρατέω) *swaying women.*

θηλυ-κτόνος, ον, (θῆλυς, κτείνω) *slaying by women's hands.*

θηλυ-μᾰνής, ές, (θῆλυς, μανῆναι) *mad for women.*

θηλυ-μελής, ές, (θῆλυς, μέλος) *singing in soft strain.*

θηλυ-μίτρης, ου, ὁ, (θῆλυς, μίτρα) *with a woman's head-dress:* fem. θηλύμιτρις, ιδος, ὁ, ἡ.

θηλύ-μορφος, ον, (θῆλυς, μορφή) *woman-shaped.*

θηλύ-νοος, νοον, contr. **θηλύνους**, ουν, (θῆλυς, νοῦς) *of womanish mind.*

θηλύνω, f. ὕνῶ: aor. 1 ἐθήλῡνα :—*to make weak and womanish:*—Pass. *to become so.*

θηλύ-πους, ὁ, ἡ, -πουν, τό, gen. -ποδος, (θῆλυς, πούς) θηλύπους βάσις the tread *of female foot.*

θηλυ-πρεπής, ές, (θῆλυς, πρέπω) *befitting a woman.*

θῆλυς, εια, υ, also fem. θῆλυς: Ep. and Ion. fem. θήλεᾰ, acc. θηλεᾰν, pl. θήλεαι, -εας: (τέθηλα) :—*of female sex, female,* opp. to ἄρρην; θήλεια θεύς a goddess; θήλειαι ἵπποι mares. 2. generally, *of* or *belonging to women; τὸ θῆλυ the female* sex. II. of things, 1. *fruitful, prolific, nourishing.* 2. *tender, delicate:* in bad sense, *womanish, weak, effeminate.* III. the Comp. θηλύτερος, α, ον [ῠ], is used like the Positive in the phrases θηλύτεραι θεαί or γυναῖκες.

θηλύ-σπορος, ον, (θῆλυς, σπείρω) *born of woman;* γέννα θηλύσπορος a race *of females.*

θηλύτερος, α, ον, v. θῆλυς sub fin.

θηλυ-τόκος, ον, (θῆλυς, τεκεῖν) *bearing girls.*

θηλύ-φρων, ον, (θῆλυς, φρήν) *of woman's mind.*

θηλῠ-χίτων, gen. ωνος, ὁ, ἡ, (θῆλυς, χιτών) *with a woman's frock* or *dress.* [ῐ]

θἠμέρᾳ, by crasis for τῇ ἡμέρᾳ.

θἠμετέρου, by crasis for τοῦ ἡμετέρου.

θἤμισυ, by crasis for τὸ ἥμισυ.

θημών, ῶνος, ὁ, (τίθημι) like θωμός, *a heap*

θήν, an Ep. enclitic Particle, rare in Att. Poets, *surely now; ἦ θην in very truth; οὐ θην surely not.*

θηξάσθω, 3 sing aor. 1 imperat. med. of θήγω.

θηοῖο, Ep. for θεῷο, 2 sing. opt. of θηέομαι.

ΘΗΡ, θηρός, Ep. dat. pl. θήρεσσι, ὁ, *a wild beast, a beast of prey:* joined with a Subst., as θὴρ λέων. 2 any *monster,* as the sphinx; often of *the centaurs:* also *satyrs.*

θήρα Ion. **θήρη**, ἡ, (θήρ) *a hunting, pursuit of wild beasts, the chase:—eager pursuit* of anything. II. in collective sense, *the beasts, the game, quarry.*

θηρ-αγρέτης, ου, ὁ, (θήρα, ἀγρεύω) *a hunter.*

θήρᾱμα, ατος, τό, (θηράω) *that which is caught, prey, booty.*

θηράσιμος, ον, (θηράω) *to be caught* or *won.*

θηρᾱτέος, α, ον, verb. Adj. of θηράω, *to be caught* or *won.* II. θηρατέον, *one must catch* or *win.*

θηρᾱτής, οῦ, ὁ, (θηράω) *a hunter, hunter after.*

θηρᾱτικός, ή, όν, *of* or *for the chase, devoted to hunting; τὰ θηρατικὰ τῶν φίλων the arts for winning* friends.

θήρᾱτρον, τό, (θηράω) *a thing to catch with, a net, trap.*

θηράω, f. άσω or θηράσομαι: (θήρα) :—*to hunt wild beasts, to chase, pursue, catch.* 2. metaph., like Lat. *venari, to hunt after* a thing, *pursue, seek it eagerly.* II. the Med. θηρῶμαι is used in Act. sense, *to hunt after, seek for.* also in Pass. *to be hunted, pursued.*

θῆρε, dual. nom. of θήρ

θήρειος, ον, (θήρ) *of, belonging to wild beasts,* Lat. *ferinus:* θηρεία βία, periphr. for ὁ θήρ, *the centaur*

θήρεσσι, Ep. for θηρσί, dat. pl. of θήρ.

θήρευμα, ατος, τό, (θηρεύω) *spoil, prey, game* II *hunting.*

θήρευσις, εως, ἡ, (θηρεύω) *a hunting, the chase:* metaph. *a hunting after.*

θηρευτής, οῦ, ὁ, (θηρεύω) *a hunter;* κύνεσσι καὶ ἀνδράσι θηρευτῇσιν with hounds and *huntsmen* also *a fisher.* Hence

θηρευτικός, ή, όν, *of, belonging to the chase* or *hunting:* κύνες θ. *hunting* dogs, *hounds:* ἡ θηρευτικὴ with and without τέχνη), *the art of hunting, the chase*

θηρεύω, f. σω (θήρ) = θηράω, *to hunt, run down, catch: to hit, strike:* metaph. *to hunt* or *seek after* Pass. *to be hunted:* also *to be preyed upon*

θηρέω, Ion. and Dor. for θηράω

θήρημα, τό, Ion. for θήραμα.

θηρητήρ, ῆρος, and **θηρήτωρ**, ορος, ὁ, Ep. and Ion. for θηρατής, *a hunter.*

θηριομᾰχέω, f ήσω, (θηρίον, μάχομαι) *a fight with wild beasts.* From

θηριο-μάχος, ον, *fighting with wild beasts*

θηρίον, τό, in form a Dim. of θήρ, but used for it almost always in Prose, *a wild animal, beast:* esp. of *such as are hunted, game: a beast, brute,* as opp to birds and men. II. as real Dim. of θήρ, *a little animal.* III. as a term of reproach, *beast!* like Lat. *bellua,* ὦ δειλότατον σὺ θηρίον.

θηρι-ώδης, ες, (θηρίον, εἶδος) *full of wild beasts, infested by them*, Lat. *belluosus*. II. *brutal* in manners or nature, *wild, savage*, Lat. *belluinus*.

θηροβολέω, f. ήσω, *to strike* or *kill wild beasts*. From

θηρο-βόλος, ον, (θήρ, βάλλω) *killing wild beasts*.

θηρο-βότος, ον, (θήρ, βόσκω) *fed on by wild beasts*.

θηρό-θῡμος, ον, (θήρ, θυμός) *with brutal mind, brutal*.

θηρο-κτόνος, ον, (θήρ, κτείνω) *killing wild beasts*.

θηρ-ολέτης, ου, ὁ, (θήρ, ὄλλυμι) *a slayer of beasts*.

θηρο-νόμος, ον, (θήρ, νέμω) *feeding wild beasts*.

θηρο-σκόπος, ον, (θήρ, σκοπέω) *looking out for wild beasts*.

θηροσύνη, ἡ, (θήρ) *hunting, the chase*.

θηρο-τόκος, ον, (θήρ, τεκεῖν) *producing wild beasts*.

θηρο-τρόφος, ον, (θήρ, τρέφω) *feeding wild beasts*. II. proparox. θηρότροφος, pass. *fed by beasts, feeding on them*.

θηρο-φόνος, ον, also η, ον, (θήρ, *φένω) *slaying wild beasts*.

θηρσί, dat. pl. of θήρ.

θήρῳον, crasis for τὸ ἡρῷον.

ΘΗ'Σ, θητός, ὁ, *a serf* or *villain*, who is bound to the soil, Lat. *ascriptus glebae*: also *a hired labourer*. They formed the last of Solon's four tribes, the other three being the πεντακοσιομέδιμνοι, ἱππεῖς, ζευγῖται. This class took in all whose property in land yielded less than 150 medimni: they were generally excluded from public service, but were employed as light-armed troops and seamen, and, in case of need, as heavy-armed. II. fem. **θῆσσα** Att. **θῆττα**, ἡ, *a labouring girl*. 2. as Adj., θῆσσα τράπεζα *a menial's* fare.

θῆσαι, aor. 1 inf. of θάω, *to suckle*.

θησαίατο, Ep. 3 pl. aor. 1 opt. of θάομαι = θεάομαι.

θησάμενος, aor. 1 part. med. of θάω, *to suckle*.

θήσατο, 3 sing. aor. 1 med. of θάω, *to suckle*.

θησαυρίζω, f. ίσω, (θησαυρός) *to store* or *treasure up, lay by*: of fruits, *to lay up in store, preserve* Hence

θησαύρισμα, ατος, τό, *a store, treasure*.

θησαυρός, ὁ, (θήσω, fut. of τί-θημι) *a store laid up, treasure*. II. *a store* or *treasure-house*: *any receptacle* for valuables, *a chest, casket*.

Θησεῖον, τό, (Θησεύς) *the temple of Theseus*, a sanctuary for runaway slaves. II. τὰ Θησεῖα (sub. ἱερά), *the festival of Theseus*.

θησεῖς, θησῶ, Dor. 2 and 1 sing. fut. of τίθημι.

θησείω, Desiderat. of τίθημι, *I wish to place*.

θησέμεναι, θησέμεν, Ep. fut. inf. of τίθημι.

θησεύμεθα, Dor. 1 pl. fut. med. of τίθημι.

Θησεύς, έως, ὁ, *Theseus*, the most famous of the heroes of Athens. (Prob. from τί-θημι, *the Settler, Civiliser*.)

θῆσθαι, pres. inf. pass. of θάω, *to suckle*.

θῆσσα Att. **θῆττα**, fem. of θής.

θήσω, fut. of τίθημι.

θητεία, ἡ, (θητεύω) *hired service*.

θητεύω, f. σω, (θής) *to be a menial, serve for hire*.

θητικός, ή, όν, (θής) *fit for menial service, menial*.

θῆττα, Att. for θῆσσα.

-θῐ, insep. affix, added to several Nouns, denoting *the place at which*, as, ἀγρόθι, οἴκοθι, *in* the fields, *at* home. Like -θεν, it was originally a genitive termination, as in Ἰλιόθι πρό, ἠῶθι πρό.

θῐᾰσ-άρχης, ου, ὁ, (θίασος, ἄρχω) *the chief* or *leader of a sacred band of revellers*.

θῐᾰσεία, ἡ, *revelling*. From

θῐᾰσεύω, (θίασος) *to honour with sacred revelry*:—Pass., θιασεύεται ψυχάν *he has* his soul *imbued with Bacchic revelry*.

ΘΙ'ΑΣΟΣ, ὁ, *a company* or *procession of persons dancing and singing in honour of a god*, esp. of Bacchus, *a band of Bacchic revellers*. 2. *any company* or *troop*. Hence

θῐᾰσόω, *to make into a festive company*.

θιάσως, Dor. acc. pl. of θίασος.

θῐᾰσώτης, ου, ὁ, (θιασόω) *the member of a company of revellers*; c. gen., θιασῶται τοῦ Ἔρωτος *worshippers* or *followers* of Love.

θιγγάνω, lengthd. form of Root ΘΙΓ- (which appears in aor. 2 and in *te-tigi*, pf. of *tango*): fut. θίξομαι: aor. 2 ἔθῐγον:—*to touch lightly, just touch*, less strong than ἅπτομαι; then generally *to touch*: *to touch, attempt*: *to reach, gain*.

θιγεῖν Ep. **θιγέμεν**, aor. 2 inf. of θιγγάνω.

θίγημα, ματος, τό, (θῐγεῖν) *a touch*.

θίξομαι, fut. of θιγγάνω

ΘΙ'Σ, gen. θινός, Ep. ὁ, later ἡ:—*a heap of sand* on the beach: hence *the beach, shore, strand*: in pl. θῖνες, *sand-heaps, sand-banks*:—then *any heap*; θῖνες νεκρῶν *heaps* of dead; ὀστεόφιν θίς *a heap* of bones. 2. *the sand at the bottom of the sea*; θὶς κελαινά a dark, muddy *bottom*: metaph., ὥς μου τὸν θῖνα ταράττεις how thou troublest *the very bottom* of my heart.

θλαστός, ή, όν, *crushed, bruised*. From

ΘΛΑ'Ω, inf. θλᾶν: fut. θλάσω [ᾰ]: aor. 1 ἔθλᾰσα Ep. θλάσσα:—Pass., pf. τέθλασμαι:—*to crush, bruise, pound, bray*.

ΘΛΙ'ΒΩ [ῑ]: fut. θλίψω: aor. 1 ἔθλιψα:—Pass., aor. 1 ἐθλίφθην, aor. 2 ἐθλίβην [ῐ]: pf. τέθλιμμαι:—*to press, press hard, gall*:—Med., θλίψεται ὤμους *he will rub his* shoulders. 2. metaph. *to oppress, afflict, distress*: pf. part. **τεθλιμμένος**, *hemmed in, confined, narrow*. Hence

θλῖψις, εως, ἡ, *a pressing, pressure*. 2. metaph. *oppression, affliction*.

θνάσκω, Dor. for θνήσκω.

θνατός, Dor. for θνητός.

θνήσκω, lengthd. from Root ΘΑΝ-: fut. θᾰνοῦμαι. Ep. inf. θανέεσθαι: aor. 2 ἔθανον, Ep. inf. θανέειν: pf. **τέθνηκα**, whence syncop. pl. τέθνᾰμεν, τέθνᾰτε, **τεθνᾶσι**; imperat. **τέθνᾰθι**; opt. **τεθναίην**; inf. **τεθνάναι** [ᾰ] Ep. **τεθνάμεν, τεθνάμεναι** [ᾰ], rarely **τεθνᾶναι**; part. **τεθνεώς, τεθνεῶσα, τεθνεώς** (or **τεθνεός**) Ep. **τεθνηώς**, gen. **ῶτος** Ep. also **τεθνηότος**; 3 pl. plqpf. ἐτέθνᾰσαν:—from **τέθνηκα** arose the Att. future forms **τεθνήξω, τεθνήξομαι**:—*to be dying, to die*, Lat.

morior:—perf. τέθνηκα *I have died, am dead;* so too aor. 2 ἔθανον, *I died, am dead;* part. θανών, *dead,* Lat. *mortuus.* II. metaph. of things, *to die, perish.*

θνητο-γενής, ές, (θνητός, γενέσθαι) *born of mortals, of mortal race.*

θνητο-ειδής, ές, (θνητός, εἶδος) *of mortal nature.*

θνητός, ή, όν, also ός, όν: Dor. **θνατός**, ά, όν, (θνήσκω):—*mortal*, opp. to ἀθάνατος; θνητοί *mortals.* 2. of things, *befitting mortals, human.*

θοάζω, (θοός) trans. *to move quickly, ply rapidly, dispatch.* 2. intr. *to move oneself quickly, hurry along.* II. = θάσσω, θωκέω, *to sit.*

θοἰματίδιον, by crasis for τὸ ἱματίδιον.

θοἰμάτιον, by crasis for τὸ ἱμάτιον.

θοινάζω, (θοίνη) = θοινάω, *to feast.* Hence

θοίνᾱμα, ατος, τό, *a meal, feast.*

θοινᾱτήρ, ῆρος, ὁ, (θοινάω) *a feaster.*

θοινᾱτήριος, ον, (θοινάω) *of* or *for a feast.*

θοινᾱτικός, ή, όν, (θοινάω) *of* or *for a feast.*

θοινάτωρ, ορος, ὁ, = θοινατήρ. [ᾱ]

θοινάω, f. ήσω, *to feast on, eat.* II. *to feast, entertain*:—hence in Med. or Pass., with fut. med. θοινάσομαι, aor. 1 pass. ἐθοινήθην, pf. τεθοίνᾱμαι:—*to feast: to feast on, eat.* From

ΘΟΙ'ΝΗ, ἡ, *a meal, feast, banquet, dinner:* generally, *food, provender.*

θοινήτωρ, ὁ, Ion. for θοινάτωρ.

θοινίζω, f. σω, (θοίνη) *to feast, entertain.*

θοῖτο, for θεῖτο, 3 sing. aor. 2 opt. med. of τίθημι.

θολερός, ά, όν, (θολός) *muddy, thick, troubled,* Lat. *turbidus*, properly of water. II. metaph. *troubled by passion, turbid, agitated.*

θολία, ἡ, (θόλος) *a round hat* to keep the sun off.

ΘΟ'ΛΟΣ, ἡ, *a dome* or *circular vault:* generally, *any round* or *vaulted building.* 2. at Athens, *the round chamber* in which the Prytanes dined.

ΘΟΛΟ'Σ, ὁ, *mud.* II. *the dark juice of the cuttle-fish (sepia)*, which it emits to hide itself, Lat. *loligo.* Hence

θολόω, f. ώσω, *to make muddy, turbid:* metaph. like Lat. *perturbare, to trouble, disquiet.*

θοός, ή, όν, (θέω) *quick, active, ready;* θοὴ νύξ *quickly-passing* night; θοὴ δαίς *a hasty* meal. II. *sharp, pointed,* of rocky islands or headlands.

θοόω, f. ώσω, (θοός) *to make sharp* or *pointed.*

θόρε, Ep. 3 sing. aor. 2 of θρώσκω.

θορεῖν, aor. 2 inf. of θρώσκω.

θορή, ἡ, = θορός.

θόρνυμαι and **θορνύομαι**, Dep., collat. form, of θρώσκω, *to leap,* esp. *to pair, mate, couple.*

θορός, ὁ, (θορεῖν) *the semen genitale of the male.*

θοροῦμαι, fut. of θρώσκω.

θορυβεῦσιν, Dor. 3 pl. of θορυβέω.

θορῠβέω, f. ήσω, (θόρυβος) *to make an uproar,* mostly of a crowded assembly, *in token either of approbation* or *the contrary:* hence, 1. *to cheer, applaud.* 2. *to groan, murmur at* one. II. trans. *to trouble, disturb* with noise or tumult:—Pass. *to be troubled: to be in disorder* or *confusion.* Hence

θορῠβητικός, ή, όν, *inclined to riot, tumultuous.*

ΘΟ'ΡΥΒΟΣ, ὁ, *the noise of a crowded assembly,* 1. in token of approbation, *applause, cheers.* 2. the contrary, *a clamour, uproar, groaning.*

θορών, aor. 2 part. of θρώσκω.

θοῦ, Att. imperat. aor. 2 med. of τίθημι.

θοὔδωρ, **θοὔδατος**, by crasis for τὸ ὕδωρ, τοῦ ὕδατος.

Θουριό-μαντις, εως, ὁ, (Θούριον, μάντις) *a Thurian prophet,* generally *a soothsayer.*

θοῦρις, ιδος, ἡ, fem. of sq.

θοῦρος, ὁ, (θορεῖν) *leaping, rushing, impetuous, eager*:—fem. **θοῦρις**, ῖδος, mostly as epith. of ἀλκή, *impetuous* might; θουρὶς ἀσπίς shield *of impetuous warrior.*

θόωκος, ὁ, Ep lengthd. from θῶκος, *a seat.* 2. *a sitting, assembly.*

θοῶς, Adv. of θοός, *quickly, soon.*

Θρᾴκη Ion. **Θρηΐκη** poët. **Θρῄκη**, ἡ, *Thrace.*

Θρᾴκιος, α, ον, Ion. **Θρηΐκιος** poët. **Θρῄκιος**, (Θρᾷξ) *of* or *belonging to the Thracians, Thracian.*

θρᾱνεύω, f. σω, (θρᾶνος) *to stretch on the tanner's board, to tan:* θρανεύσομαι, fut. med. in pass. sense, *to be tanned.*

θρᾱνίον, τό, Dim. of θρᾶνος, *a small bench, stool.*

θρᾱνίτης, ου, ὁ, (θρᾶνος) *one of the rowers on the topmost of the three benches* in a trireme, who had the longest oars and most work; cf. ζυγίτης, θαλαμίτης. [ῑ]

θρᾱνῖτις, ιδος, ἡ, fem. of θρανιτης.

ΘΡΑ'ΝΟΣ, ὁ, *a bench, form:* esp. *the topmost of the three benches* in a trireme.

Θρᾷξ, Θρᾳκός, ὁ; Ion. **Θρήϊξ**, Θρήῖκος, poët. **Θρῄξ**, Θρῃκός, *a Thracian.*

θρᾶξαι, **θρᾶξον**, aor. 1 inf. and imper. of θράσσω.

θράσεως, Adv. of θρασύς, *boldly:* Comp. θρασύτερον, Sup. -ύτατα.

ΘΡΑ'ΣΟΣ, εος, τό, = θάρσος, *courage, confidence:* in bad sense, *over-boldness, daring, rashness, presumption, impudence.* [ᾰ]

Θρᾷσσα Att. **Θρᾷττα**, ἡ, Ion. and poët. **Θρῇσσα** Dor. **Θρέϊσσα**, *a Thracian woman.*

θράσσω Att. **θράττω**, fut. ξω, Att. contr. from ταράσσω, *to trouble, disquiet, disturb.*

θρᾰσύ-γυιος, ον, (θρασύς, γυῖον) *relying on strength of limb.*

θρᾰσῠ-κάρδιος, ον, (θρασύς, καρδία) *bold of heart, stout-hearted.*

θρᾰσῠ-μέμνων, ον, gen. ονος, (θρασύς, μένω) *bravely patient;* cf. Μέμνων.

θρᾰσῠ-μήδης, ες, (θρασύς, μῆδος) *bold of device, daring, resolute.*

θρᾰσύ-μητις, ιδος, ὁ, ἡ, (θρασύς, μῆτις) = θρασυμήδης.

θρᾰσῠ-μήχᾰνος Dor. **-μάχανος**, ον, (θρασύς, μηχανή) *bold in scheming* or *contriving.*

θρᾰσύ-μῡθος, ον, (θρασύς, μῦθος) *bold of speech.*

θρᾰσύνω, f. ὑνῶ (θρασύς) like θαρσύνω, *to make bold, encourage*:—Pass. and Med. *to be bold, ready, courageous*; θρασύνεσθαί τινι *to rely on* one.

θρᾰσῠ-πόλεμος poët. **θρασυπτόλεμος**, ον, (θρασύς, πόλεμος) *bold in war*.

θρᾰσύ-πονος, ον, (θρασύς, πόνος) *bold at work*.

ΘΡΑ´ΣΥ´Σ, εῖα, ύ, *bold, spirited, resolute*: in bad sense, *rash, venturous, presumptuous*. II. of things, *causing confidence, safe*.

θρᾰσύ-σπλαγχνος, ον, (θρασύς, σπλάγχνον) *bold-hearted*.

θρᾰσυστομέω, *to be over-bold of tongue*. Hence

θρᾰσυστομία, ἡ, *licence of speech, insolence*. From

θρᾰσύ-στομος, ον (θρασύς, στόμα) *over-bold of tongue, insolent*.

θρᾰσύτης, ητος, ἡ, (θρασύς) *over-boldness, rashness, audaciousness*. [ῠ]

θρᾰσύ-χειρ, χειρος, ὁ, (θρασύς, χείρ) ἡ, *bold of hand*.

Θρᾷττα, Att. for Θρῇσσα.

θράττω, Att. for θράσσω.

θραυσ-άντυξ, ῠγος, ὁ, ἡ, (θραύω, ἄντυξ) *breaking wheels*.

θραῦσμα, τό, *that which is broken, a fragment*. From

ΘΡΑΥ´Ω, f. σω: aor. 1 ἔθραυσα:—*to break, break in pieces, shiver, shatter*. II. metaph. *to break down, enfeeble*.

θρέμμα, ατος, τό, (τρέφω) *that which is reared* or *tended, a nursling: a creature*.

θρέξασκον, Ion. for ἔθρεξαν, 3 pl. aor. 1 of τρέχω.

θρέξομαι, fut. of τρέχω.

θρέπτειρα, ἡ, fem. of θρεπτήρ.

θρεπτέος, έα, έον, verb. Adj. of τρέφω, *to be fed*. II. **θρεπτέον**, *one must feed*. 2. (from Pass.) *one must be fed*.

θρεπτήρ, ῆρος, ὁ, (τρέφω) *a feeder, rearer*. Hence

θρεπτήριος, ον, *able to feed, feeding, nourishing*. II. θρεπτήρια, τά, *rewards for rearing*, esp. *the returns made by children for their rearing*. 2. *food, support*.

θρέπτρα, τά, (τρέφω) like θρεπτήρια, *the returns made by children for their bringing up, filial duty*.

θρεττᾰνελό, *a sound imitative of the cithara*.

θρέττε, τό,—τὸ θαρραλέον or θάρσος, barbarism in Ar. Eq. 17, οὐκ ἔνι μοι τὸ θρέττε, *the spirit's* not in me.

θρεφθῆναι, aor. 1 pass. inf. of τρέφω.

θρέψα, poët. for ἔθρεψα, aor. 1 of τρέφω.

θρέψαιο, 2 sing. aor. 1 med. opt. of τρέφω.

θρέψω, fut. of τρέφω.

ΘΡΕ´Ω, only used in pres. and impf. med., *to cry aloud, shriek out, wail, lament*.

Θρηϊκίη, ἡ, Ep. for Θρᾴκη.

Θρηΐκιος, η, ον, Ep. for Θρήκιος, Θρᾴκιος.

Θρῆϊξ, ῑκος, ὁ, Ion. for Θρῇξ, Θρᾷξ.

Θρήϊσσα, ἡ, Ion. for Θρῇσσα, Θρῇσσα.

Θρῄκη, ἡ, Ion. for Θρᾴκη. Hence

Θρῄκηθεν, Adv. *from Thrace*: and

Θρῄκηνδε, Adv. *to Thrace*.

Θρῄκιος, η, ον, Ion. for Θρᾴκιος, *Thracian*.

θρηνέω, f. ήσω, (θρῆνος) *to wail, lament, mourn*: ἀοιδὴν θρηνεῖν *to sing* a dirge or lament. Hence

θρήνημα, ατος, τό, *a lament*; and

θρηνητήρ, ῆρος, ὁ, **θρηνητής**, οῦ, *a mourner, wailer*.

θρῆνος, ὁ, (θρέω) *a wailing, lamenting*: *a funeral-song, dirge*, like the Gaelic *coronach*.

θρῆνυς, υος, ὁ, (θρᾶνος) *a footstool*. 2. *a bench*: θρῆνυς ἑπταπόδης, the seven-foot *bench*, the seat of the helmsman or the rowers.

Θρῇξ, ῃκός, ὁ, Ion. for Θρᾷξ.

θρησκεία Ion. -ηΐη, ἡ, (θρησκεύω) *religious worship, service, observance: religion*.

θρησκεύω, f. σω, (θρῆσκος) *to observe religiously, hold scrupulously*.

θρησκηΐη, Ion. for θρησκεία.

ΘΡΗ˜ΣΚΟΣ, ον, *religious*.

Θρῇσσα, Ion. for Θρᾷσσα.

Θρῖαί, ῶν, αἱ, *the Thriae*, Parnassian nymphs nurses of Apollo.

θρῐαμβεύω, f. σω, (θρίαμβος) *to triumph*. II. *to lead in triumph*. III. *to make to triumph*.

θριαμβικός, ή, όν, *triumphal*. From

θρίαμβος, ὁ, *a hymn to Bacchus*: also *a name of Bacchus*. II. used to express the Roman *triumphus, a triumph*.

θριγκίον, τό, Dim. of θριγκός.

ΘΡΙΓΚΟ´Σ, ὁ, *the coping, eaves, cornice*, which projects beyond the rest of the wall; θριγκὸς κυάνοιο *a cornice* of blue metal:—metaph. *the coping-stone, last finish*. II. generally *a wall, fence*. Hence

θριγκόω, f. ώσω, *to surround with a coping*; αὐλὴν ἐθρίγκωσεν ἀχέρδῳ *he fenced* it *at top* with thorn-bushes:—metaph. *to build up even to the coping-stone, to put the finishing stroke to*. Hence

θρίγκωμα, τό, *a coping, cornice*.

ΘΡΙ´ΔΑΞ, ᾰκος, ἡ, *lettuce*, Lat. *lactūca*. [ῐ]

θρίζω, poët. syncop. for θερίζω.

Θρῑν-ακία Ep. -ίη, ἡ, and **Θρῑν-ακρίς**, ίδος, ἡ, (θρῖναξ) *the trident-land*, sub. γῆ or νῆσος, an old name of Sicily from its *three promontories*, Lat. *Trinacria*.

θρῖναξ, ᾰκος, ὁ, (for τρῖναξ, from τρίς) *a trident, three-pronged fork*.

ΘΡΙ´Ξ, ἡ, gen. τρῐχός, dat. pl. θριξί:—*the hair*, both of man and beast: sheep's *wool*: also of *the beard*:—Proverb., θρὶξ ἀνὰ μέσσον *only a hair's breadth off*.

ΘΡΙΟ˜Ν, τό, *a fig-leaf*. I. a kind of *omelette*, so called because it was wrapped in fig-leaves.

ΘΡΙ´ΟΣ, ὁ, *one of the reefs* or *little ropes on the lower part of the sail*, used to take it in.

θρῑπ-ήδεστος, ον, (θρίψ, ἔδω) *worm-eaten*.

θρίψ, gen. θρῑπός, ὁ, (τρίβω) *a wood-worm*.

θροέω, f. ήσω, (θρόος) *to cry aloud, shriek forth*: generally, *to speak, declare*. II. *to frighten*:—Pass. *to be frightened* or *troubled*.

ΘΡΟ´ΜΒΟΣ, ὁ, *a lump, piece*, Lat. *grumus*: *a clot* or *gout of blood*.

θρομβ-ώδης, ες, (θρόμβος, εἶδος) *curdled, clotted*.

θρόνον, τό, only in plur. θρόνα, *flowers* or *patterns embroidered on cloth.* II. later, θρόνα are *flowers* or *herbs used as charms.* (Deriv. uncertain.)

ΘΡΟ'ΝΟΣ, ὁ, *a seat, chair.* II. *a chair of state, throne: the chair of a judge, teacher,* etc.: in pl. *the king's estate* or *dignity.*

θρόος Att. contr. θροῦς, ὁ, (θρέω) *a confused noise, tumult, murmuring.* II. *a report,* Lat. *rumor.*

θρυαλλίδιον, τό, Dim. of θρυαλλίς.

ΘΡΥ'ΑΛΛΙ'Σ, ίδος, ἡ, *a wick.*

θρῡλέω (vulgo θρυλλέω): f. ήσω: pass. pf. τεθρύλημαι: (θρῦλος):—*to make a noise, to keep babbling.* II. c. acc. rei, *to keep talking about a thing, make a great talk of:*—Pass. *to be the common talk,* τὸ θρυλουμένον or τεθρυλημένον *what is in every one's mouth.*

θρῡλίζω (vulgo θρυλλίζω), f. ίσω: (θρῦλος):—*to make a false note in playing on the cithara.*

θρυλίσσω (vulgo θρυλλίσσω) *to break in pieces:* —Pass. *to be shivered;* Ep. aor. 1 θρυλίχθην. (Akin to θραύω, θρύπτω.) Hence

ΘΡΥ'ΛΟΣ (vulgo θρύλλος), ὁ, *a confused noise, shouting, tumult, murmuring.*

θρύμμα, ατος, τό, (θρύπτω) *a piece broken off, a bit, piece, morsel.*

ΘΡΥ'ΟΝ, τό, *a rush,* Lat. *juncus.*

θρυπτικός, ή, όν, *breaking, crushing.* II. pass. *easily broken:* metaph. *effeminate, enervated.* From

ΘΡΥ'ΠΤΩ, f. θρύψω: aor. 1 ἔθρυψα:—Pass., fut. med. in pass. sense, θρύψομαι: aor. 2 ἐτρύφην [ῠ]: pf. τέθρυμμαι:—*to break in pieces, crush:*—Pass. *to be broken, crushed.* II. metaph. in Pass. *to be enfeebled, enervated.* III. in Pass. also, *to be affected, give oneself airs, look languishing:* generally, *to be conceited;* θρύπτεσθαί τινι, *to feel pride in a thing.* Hence

θρύψις, εως, ἡ, *a breaking in pieces.* II. metaph. *softness, weakness, effeminacy.*

θρώσκω, lengthd. from the Root ΘΟΡ-, which appears in fut. and aor. 2: fut. θοροῦμαι Ion. θορέομαι: aor. 2 ἔθορον, inf. θορεῖν Ep. θορέειν:—*to leap, spring,* as the arrow from the string, or the lot from the helmet. 2. foll. by Prep., *to leap* or *spring upon* one, *to attack, assault.* II. trans. *to mount, impregnate.*

θρωσμός, ὁ, (θρώσκω) *a springing* or *rising,* as of a hill from the plain.

Θυβριάς, άδος, ἡ, and Θύβρις, ιδος, ἡ, = Θυμβ–.

ΘΥΓΑ'ΤΗΡ, ἡ, gen. θυγᾰτέρος contr. θυγατρός, dat. θυγᾰτέρι θυγατρί, acc. θυγᾰτέρα Ep. θύγατρα, voc. θύγᾰτερ: *a daughter.* Hence

θυγατριδῆ, ἡ, *a daughter's daughter, grand-daughter.*

θῠγατρῖδοῦς, οῦ, Ion. -ιδέος, έου, ὁ, *a daughter's son, grandson.*

θῠγάτριον, τό, Dim. of θυγάτηρ, *a little girl.*

θῠεία, ἡ, (θύω) *a mortar.* Hence

θῠείδιον, τό, Dim. of θυεία.

θύελλα, ἡ, (θύω) *a storm, a hurricane, whirlwind, tempest;* πυρὸς θύελλαι *storms of lightning;* ἄτης θύελλαι *storms* of woe.

θυέων, gen. pl. of θύος.

θυη-δόχος, (θύος, δέχομαι) *receiving incense.*

θῠήεις, εσσα, εν, (θύος) *smoking with incense, fragrant.*

θῠηλή, ἡ, (θύω) *the part of the victim burned: a burnt-offering* or *sacrifice.*

θυηπολέω, f. ήσω, *to busy oneself with sacrifices:* —Pass. *to be filled with sacrifices.* And

θυηπολία, ἡ, *a sacrificing.* From

θῠη-πόλος, ον, (θύω, πολέω) *busy about sacrificing, sacrificial:* as Subst. *a sacrifice, a priest.*

θῠη-φάγος, ον, (θύος, φαγεῖν) *consuming offerings.*

θυία or θύα [ῠ], ὁ, (from θύω to smell): *a sweet-scented African tree,* perhaps *a* kind of *cedar.*

θυῖαι, ῶν, αἱ, = θυιάδες.

θυιάς or θῠάς, gen. άδος, ἡ, (θύω) *a frantic* or *inspired woman, Bacchante.*

θύϊνος, η, ον, *made of the wood of the tree* θυία.

θυίω, = θύω, *to rage, be inspired.*

θῡλάκιον, τό, Dim. of θύλακος, *a small bag.*

ΘΥ'ΛΑ'ΚΟΣ, ὁ, *a bag, pouch,* commonly of leather. II. in pl. *the loose trousers* worn by Eastern nations.

θυλέομαι, f. -ήσομαι, (θυηλή) Dep. *to offer.* Hence

θύλημα, τό, *that which is offered;* θυλήματα *cakes, incense,* etc. [ῡ]

θῦμα, ατος, τό, (θύω) *a sacrifice, offering;* πάγκαρπα θύματα *offerings* of all fruits.

θῡμαίνω, f. ᾰνῶ, (θυμός) *to be wroth* or *angry.*

θῡμ-αλγής, ές, (θυμός, ἀλγέω) *heart-grieving.*

θῡμάλωψ, ωπος, ὁ, (τύφω) *a piece of burning wood* or *charcoal, a hot coal* or *ember.*

θῡμᾱρέω, *to be well-pleased.* From

θῡμ-άρης [ᾱ], ες, (θυμός, ἀρ-αρεῖν) *suiting one's mind, well-pleasing.*

ΘΥ'ΜΒΡΑ, ἡ, a bitter herb, *savory.*

θυμβρ-επί-δειπνος, ον, (θύμβρα, ἐπί, δεῖπνον) *eating the herb savory, living poorly.*

Θυμβριάς, άδος, ἡ, *a nymph of the Tiber.* From

Θύμβρις, ιδος, ἡ, *the Tiber,* Lat. *Tiberis.*

θυμβρο-φάγος, ον, (θύμβρα, φαγεῖν) *eating the herb savory;* θυμβροφάγον βλέπτειν to look *as if one had eaten savory,* make *a wry face.*

θῠμέλη, ἡ, (θύω) *a place for sacrifice, an altar.* II. in the Athen. theatre, *an altar-shaped platform* in the middle of the orchestra: *a raised stage* or *seat.* Hence

θυμελικός, ή, όν, *of* or *for the thymelé, scenic.*

θῡμ-ηγερέω, f. ήσω, (θύμος, ἀγείρω) *to collect one's spirit, recover courage, be oneself again.*

θῡμ-ηδής, ές, (θύμος, ἧδος) *well-pleasing, dear.*

θῡμίᾱμα Ion. -ημα, ατος, τό, (θυμιάω) *that which is burnt as incense, incense.*

θῡμιᾱτήριον Ion. -ητήριον, τό, (θυμιάω) *a censer.*

θῡμιάω, f. άσω, [ᾱ]: Ion. aor. 1 ἐθῡμίησα: (θῦμα, θύω):—*to burn so as to produce smoke:*—*to burn as incense*:—Pass., Ion. 3 sing. **θυμιῆται**, for -ᾶται, *to be burned.*

θῡμίδιον, τό, Dim. of θυμός. [ῐδ]

θῡμίημα, Ion. for θυμίαμα.

θῡμιῆται, Ion. 3 sing. pres. pass. of θυμιάω.

θῡμιητήριον, τό, Ion. for θυμιατήριον.

θύμῐνος, η, ον, (θύμος) *made of* or *with thyme.* [ῠ]

θῡμίτης, ου, ὁ, (θύμος) *seasoned with thyme.*

θῡμο-βᾰρής, ές, (θυμός, βαρύς) *heavy at heart.*

θῡμοβορέω, f. ήσω, *to gnaw* or *vex the heart.* From

θῡμο-βόρος, ον, (θυμός, βιβρώσκω) *heart-eating.*

θῡμο-δᾰκής, ές, (θυμός, δακεῖν) *biting the heart.*

θυμο-ειδής, ές, (θυμός, εἶδος) *high-spirited, courageous*, Lat. *animosus.* II. *hot-tempered, passionate*: of horses, *restive, wild.*

θῡμο-λέων, οντος, ὁ, (θυμός, λέων) *lion-hearted.*

θῡμό-μαντις, εως, ὁ, ἡ, (θυμός, μάντις) *of prophetic soul.*

θῡμο-μᾰχέω, f. ήσω, (θυμός, μάχομαι) *to fight with all one's heart and soul.*

θῡμο-πληθής, ές, (θυμός, πλῆθος) *wrathful.*

θῡμο-ρᾰϊστής, οῦ, ὁ, (θυμός, ῥαίω) *life-destroying.*

θῡμός, ὁ, (θύω) *the soul*; also, *the life, breath*, Lat. *anima*; θυμὸν ἀφελέσθαι, ὀλέσαι to take away, destroy *the life.* II. *the soul, heart*, Lat. *animus*; ἀνώγει με θυμός, ἤθελε θυμός *my heart* bids me; κατὰ θυμόν after *my heart's desire*; ἀπὸ θυμοῦ against one's *heart's desire*; ἐκ θυμοῦ or θυμῷ φιλέειν to love *with all one's heart*; ἐμῷ κεχαρισμένε θυμῷ most precious to my *soul.* 2. of any vehement passion, *anger, wrath*, and in good sense, *spirit, courage.* III. *the mind, will, purpose*; ἐδαΐζετο θυμός *his mind* or *purpose* wavered.

θύμος [ῠ], ου, ὁ, or εος, τό, (θύω) *thyme*, Lat. *thymus.* 2. *a mixture of thyme with honey and vinegar.*

θῡμοσοφικός, ή, όν, *of* or *like a man of genius, clever.* From

θῡμό-σοφος, ον, (θυμός, σοφός) *naturally clever, a man of genius.*

θῡμοφθορέω, f. ήσω, *to break the heart.* From

θῡμο-φθόρος, ον, (θυμός, φθείρω) *life-destroying*; θυμοφθόρα γράμματα *deadly characters*, i. e. *fatal* to the bearer; θυμοφθόρα φάρμακα *poisonous, deadly* drugs: of persons, *heart-breaking, most irksome.*

θῡμόω, f. ώσω, (θυμός) *to make angry*:—Pass., with fut. med. -ώσομαι, aor. 1 ἐθυμωσάμην and ἐθυμώθην: pf. τεθύμωμαι:—*to be wroth* or *angry*: *to be wild* or *restive*; τὸ θυμούμενον, *passion.*

θυμώδης, ες, = θυμοειδής.

θυμωθείς, aor. 1 part. pass. of θυμόω.

θύμωμα, ατος, τό, (θυμόω) *wrath, passion.* [ῡ]

θῡνέω, = θύνω.

θυννάζω, f. άσω, (θύννος) *to spear a tunny-fish*: *to strike with a harpoon.*

θύννειος, α, ον, (θύννος) *of the tunny-fish.*

θυννευτικός, ή, όν, *fit for tunny-fishing.* From

θύννος, ὁ, (θύνω, θύω) *the tunny-fish*, Lat. *thunnus.*

θυννοσκοπέω, f. ήσω, *to watch for tunnies.* From

θυννο-σκόπος, ον, (θύννος, σκοπέω) *watching for tunnies*; esp. of a man on a high place who *looked out* for the shoals of tunnies.

θυνν-ώδης, ες, (θύννος, εἶδος) *like a tunny-fish, simple.*

θύννως, Dor. for θύννους, acc. pl. of θύννος.

θύνω, (θύω B) *to rush* or *dart along.* [ῡ]

θῠο-δόκος, ον, (θύος, δέχομαι) *receiving incense, fragrant with incense.*

θῠόεις, εσσα, εν, (θύος) *laden with incense, fragrant.*

θύον, τό, (θύω) a tree, prob. the same as θυία.

θύοντι, Dor. 3 pl. of θύω. [illegible] dat. sing. of part. θύων.

θύος, εος, τό, (θύω) *a sacrifice, offering.*

θῠοσ-κέω, (θύος, κέω = καίω) *to offer burnt-sacrifices.* Hence

θῠοσκόος, ου, ὁ, *the sacrificing priest.*

θῠόω, f. ώσω, (θύος) *to make fragrant*: pf. part. pass. ἔλαιον τεθυωμένον *fragrant* oil.

ΘΥΡΑ Ion. **θύρη**, ἡ, Germ. *THUR*, our *DOOR*; θύρην ἐπιτιθέναι to put to *the door*, opp. to ἀνακλίνειν; κόπτειν, κρούειν θύραν, Lat. *januam pulsare*, to knock at the *door*; ἐπὶ ταῖς θύραις *at the doors*, i. e. *close at hand.* 2. *the door* of a carriage. 3. θύρη καταπακτή *a* trap-*door.* II. generally, *an entrance, access.* III. *boards put together like a door, a frame, raft.* Hence

θύραζε, for θύρασδε, Adv. *to the door, outside the door*: then like Lat. *foras, out*; ἐκ μηροῦ δόρυ ὦσε θύραζε he wrenched the spear *out* of his thigh.

θύρᾱθεν Ep. -ηθε, (θύρα) Adv. *from without, without, outside*; οἱ θύραθεν *foreigners, aliens.*

θῠραῖος, α, ον, also ος, ον, (θύρα) *outside the door, abroad*; θυραῖος οἰχνεῖν to go *out of the door*; θυραῖος ἐλθεῖν to come *from abroad*; ἄνδρες θυραῖοι *stranger* men; ὄλβος θυραῖος the good fortune *of other men.*

θύρᾱσι, -σιν, Adv. (θύρα) *at the door, outside the door, abroad*, Lat. *foris.*

θῠραυλέω, *to be out of doors, live in the air.* And

θῠραυλία, ἡ, *a living out of doors.* From

θύρ-αυλος, ον, (θύρα, αὐλή) *living out of doors* or *in the open air, keeping the field.*

θῠρέ-ασπις, ιδος, ἡ, (θυρεός, ἀσπίς) *a large shield.*

θῠρέος, ὁ, (θύρα) *a great stone put against a door* to keep it shut. II. *a large oblong shield*, Lat. *scutum.*

θύρετρον, τό, = θύρα, *a door.* [ῠ]

θύρη, ἡ, Ion. and Ep. for θύρα.

θύρηθε, Adv., Ep. for θύραθεν.

θύρηφι, Ep. dat. of θύρα: also used as Adv. *outside, without.*

θῠρίδιον, τό, Dim. of θύρα.

θύριον, τό, Dim. of θύρα, *a little door, wicket.*

θῠρίς, ίδος, ἡ, Dim. of θύρα, *a small door*: *window.*

θῠροκοπέω, f. ήσω, *to break a door open.* From

θῠρο-κόπος, ον, (θύρα, κόπτω) *knocking at the door*, esp. *for alms.*

θῠρόω, f. ώσω, (θύρα) *to furnish with doors, bar close.*

θυρσάζω, Lacon. inf. *θυρσαδδοᾶν*, (*θύρσος*) *to bear* or *brandish the thyrsus.*

θυρσο-μᾰνής, *ές*, (*θύρσος, μανῆναι*) *raving with the thyrsus*

θύρσος, *ὁ*, with heterog. pl. *θύρσα, τά*, (*θύω*) *any light, straight shaft:* commonly *the thyrsus*, a wand wreathed in ivy and vine-leaves with a pine-cone at the top, carried by the devotees of Bacchus.

θυρσοφορέω, f. *ήσω*, *to bear the thyrsus; θ. θιάσους to assemble* companies *with the thyrsus.* From

θυρσο-φόρος, *ον*, (*θύρσος, φέρω*) *thyrsus-bearing.*

θυρσο-χᾰρής, *ές*, (*θύρσος, χαρῆναι*) *delighting in the thyrsus.*

θύρωμα, **ατος**, *τό*, (*θυρόω*) *a room with doors to it.* II. *a door with its frame.*

θῠρών, *ῶνος*, *ὁ*, (*θύρα*) *the door-way: a hall, antechamber*, Lat. *atrium, vestibulum.*

θῠρωρός, *ὁ*, *ἡ*, (*θύρα, ὤρα*) *a door-keeper, porter.*

θῦσαι, aor. 1 inf. of *θύω.*

θῠσᾰνόεις Ep. **θυσσ–**, *εσσα, εν*, *tasseled, fringed.* From

θύσᾰνος, *ὁ*, (*θύω*) *a tassel, tuft*, or *tag:* in pl. *tassels, fringe.* esp. *of the αἰγίς.* [ῠ]

θῠσᾰνωτός, *ή*, *όν*, (*θυσανόω*) *tasseled, fringed.*

θύσθλα, **ων**, *τά*, (*θύω*) *the sacred implements of Bacchic worship: Bacchic worship.*

θῠσία, *ἡ*, (*θύω*) *sacrificing, the mode of sacrificing:* in pl. *θυσίαι, sacrifices.* II. *the victim* itself.

θῠσιαστήριον, *τό*, (*θυσία*) *an altar.*

θύσῐμος, *ον*, (*θύω*) *fit for sacrifice.* [ῠ]

θυσσανόεις, *εσσα, εν*, Ep. for *θυσανόεις.*

θυστάς, *άδος*, *ἡ*, (*θύω*) *of* or *for sacrifice, sacrificial; θυστὰς βοή* the cry *uttered in sacrificing; θυστάδες λιταί* the prayers *offered with a sacrifice.*

θυσῶ, Dor. fut. of *θύω.*

θῠτέον, verb. Adj. of *θύω one must sacrifice.*

θῠτήρ, *ῆρος*, *ὁ*, (*θύω*) *a sacrificer, slayer.* Hence

θῠτήριον, *τό*, = *θῦμα.*

θύψαι, **θύψω**, aor. 1 inf. and fut. of *τύφω.*

ΘΥ'Ω (A), fut. *θύσω* [ῡ]: aor. 1 *ἔθῡσα:* pf. *τέθῠκα:*—Med., fut. *θύσομαι*, also used in pres. sense:—Pass., aor. 1 *ἐτύθην* [ῠ]: pf. *τέθῠμαι*, also used in med. sense:—*to offer, sacrifice, slay a victim:* also absol., *θύειν θεοῖς to sacrifice* to the gods: later, *to celebrate* with sacrifices, *γαμους θυειν, εὐαγγέλια θυειν ἕκατον βοῦς to acknowledge* the good news *by sacrificing* a hundred oxen. II. Med. *to have a victim slain:* hence *to take the auspices.*

ΘΥ'Ω (B), f. *θύσω* [ῡ], like *θύνω, θυνεω*, of any violent motion, *to rush on* or *along, dart along:* generally, *to storm, rage.*

θῠ-ώδης, *ες*, (*θύος, εἶδος*) *like incense, sweet-smelling.*

θύωμα, *ατος*, *τό*, (*θυόω*) *that which is burnt as incense*, in pl. *spices.*

θῶ, *θῇς*, *θῇ*, aor. 2 subj. of *τίθημι*

θωή, *ἡ*, (*τίθημι*) *a penalty; θωὴ 'Αχαιῶν a penalty* imposed by the Achaeans.

θωκέω, Ion. for *θακέω*, *to sit.* From

θῶκος, Ep. lengthd. **θόωκος**, *ὁ*, Ion. for *θᾶκος*, *a seat, chair.* II. *a sitting, assembly; θῶκόνδε to the sitting.*

θῶμα, **θωμάζω**, **θωμάσιος**, Ion. for *θαυμ–.*

ΘΩ'ΜΙΓΞ, *ιγγος*, *ὁ*, *a cord, string*, esp. *a bowstring.*

θωμίσω, f. *ξω*, *to whip with small cords, scourge.*

θὤμισυ, by crasis for *τὸ ἥμισυ*, *the half.*

θωμός, *ὁ*, (*τίθημι*) *a heap.*

θωπεία, *ἡ*, (*θωπεύω*) *a flattering, flattery.*

θώπευμα, *ατος*, *τό*, (*θωπεύω*) *a piece of flattery, a caress.*

θωπευμάτιον, *τό*, Dim. of *θωπευμα*, *a bit of flattery.*

θωπεύω, f. *σω*, (*θώψ*) *to flatter, fawn on, cajole, wheedle.*

θωπικός, *ή*, *όν*, (*θώψ*) *fawning, flattering.*

θὦπλα, crasis for *τὰ ὅπλα.*

θώπτω, f. *ψω*, = *θωπεύω.*

θωρᾱκεῖον, *τό*, (*θώραξ*) *a breastwork.*

θωρᾱκίζω, f. *ίσω*, (*θώραξ*) *to arm with breastplate.* II. generally, *to sheath in armour, cover with armour.*

θωρᾱκο-ποιός, *όν*, (*θώραξ, ποιέω*) *making breastplates.*

θωρᾱκο-φόρος Ion. **θωρηκ–**, *ον*, (*θώραξ, φέρω*) *wearing a breastplate, a cuirassier.*

θώραξ, *ᾱκος*, Ion. **θώρηξ**, *ηκος*, *ὁ*, *a breastplate, cuirass; διπλόος θώρηξ a* double *cuirass*, consisting of breast and back piece joined with clasps, Lat. *lorica.* 2. *the part covered by the breastplate, the chest.* II. *the breastwork* of a wall: also *the strong, outer wall.*

θωρηκο-φόρος, *ον*, Ion. for *θωρακοφόρος.*

θωρηκτής, *οῦ*, *ὁ*, (*θωρήσσω*) *armed with breastplate* or *cuirass.*

θώρηξ, *ηκος*, *ὁ*, Ion. and Ep. for **θώραξ.**

θωρῆξαι, aor. inf. of sq.

θωρήξομεν, 1 pl. fut. of *θωρήσσω*; but also Ep. for *θωρήξωμεν*, aor. 1 subj.

θωρήσσω, f. *ξω*, (*θώραξ*) *to arm with a breastplate* or *cuirass*, generally, *to arm, harness:*—Pass. *θωρήσσομαι*, f. *-ξόμαι*; aor. 1 *ἐθωρήχθην*: *to arm oneself, put one's armour on.* II. in Act. also, in Ion. and Poets, *to make drunk:*—Med. *to get drunk.* Hence

θωρηχθείς, **θωρηχθῆναι**, aor. 1 pass. part. and inf.

ΘΩ'Σ, **θωός**, *ὁ* or *ἡ*, *the jackal.*

θωῠκτήρ, *ῆρος*, *ὁ*, (*θωΰσσω*) *a barker, roarer.*

θωῦμα, **θωυμάζω**, **θωυμάσιος**, **θωυμάστης**, **θωυμαστός**, less correct Ion. forms for *θῶμα, θωμάζω*, etc.

θωΰσσω, f. *ξω*, of a dog, *to bark, bay, growl;* of a gnat, *to buzz, hum:* generally, *to cry aloud, shout out:* c. acc., *to call on, call.*

ΘΩ'Ψ, gen. *θωπος*, *ὁ*, *a flatterer, fawner, cajoler.*

I

I, ι ἰῶτα, *τό*, indecl., ninth letter of the Greek alphabet. As numeral, $ι' = 10$, but $͵ι = 10{,}000$.

The ι *subscriptum* was always *adscriptum* or written by the side, not under (as τῶι, not τῷ), till the 13th century In Capitals it is still so written, as ΤΩΙ.

ῐ was easily exchanged with ει, whence forms like εἴλω ἴλλω, εἴλη ἴλη: ῐ was sometimes exchanged with ε, as ἑστία ἱστίη: but more frequently it is inserted to lengthen the syll., as in εἰν εἰς ξεῖνο· κεινός διαί παραί for ἐν ἐς ξένος κενός διά παρά.

The Quantity of ι varies.

-ί, *iota demonstrativum*, is attached to all cases of demonstr. Pronouns in Attic, to strengthen their force, e. g. οὑτοσί, αὑτηΐ, τουτί, Latt. *bicce, baecce, bocce*, ἐκεινοσί, ὁδί, τουτογί, etc.: also demonstr. Advs., as οὑτωσί, ὡδί, ἐνθαδί. Those that end in σί take the ν ἐφελκυστικόν before a vowel, as οὑτοσίν, ἐκεινοσίν, οὑτωσίν. In all these, the last syll. is long, and takes the accent; a long vowel or diphthong in penult. is shortened, e. g. αὑτηΐ, οὑτοιΐ.

ΙΑ' Ion. **ἰή**, ἡ, = βοή, *a voice, cry.*

ἴα, ἰῆς, ἰῇ, ἴαν, old Ion. fem. of εἷς for μία, μίας, etc.

ἰά, τά, irreg. pl. of ἰός, *an arrow.* [ῐ]

ἴα, τά, pl. of ἴον, *a violet*

ἰαί, exclam of triumph.

ἰᾱθήσομαι fut. pass. of ἰαομαι

ἰαιβοῖ, strengthd. form of αἰβοῖ, to express disgust.

ΙΑΙ'ΝΩ, fut. ἰᾰνῶ: aor. 1 ἴηνα: aor. 1 pass. ἰάνθην: —*to warm, beat.* 2. *to melt, soften* by heat: metaph., θυμὸν ἰαίνειν *to melt* the heart 3. *to warm, cheer, refresb, recruit*: c. dat. *to take delight in* a thing

Ἰακχάζω, (Ἴακχος) *to raise the cry of Iacchus*

Ἰακχέω, f. ήσω, = Ἰακχάζω

Ἴακχος, ὁ, (ἰαχω) *Iacchos, mystic name of Bacchus*, as the god of shouting and revelry 2. *the Bacchanalian shout*

ἰᾰλεμίζω Ion. **ἰηλ-**, f. ίσω, (ἰάλεμος) *to bewail.* Hence

ἰᾰλεμίστρια Ion. ἰηλ-, ἡ, *a wailing woman.*

ἰάλεμος [ᾰ] Ion. **ἰήλεμος**, ὁ, (ἰά) *a wail, lament, dirge* II. as Adj. *melancholy, plaintive.*

ἰάλλω, f. ἰᾰλῶ · aor. 1 ἴηλα, inf. ἰῆλαι:—*to send forth*; ἐπ' ὀνείατα χεῖρας ἴαλλον *they put forth* their hands to the dishes; περὶ χειρὶ δεσμὸν ἴηλα I *put* chains *on* thy hands. 2. *to attack, assail*; ἀτιμίησιν ἰάλλειν τινά *to assail* one with insults. 3. *to send.* II. intr (sub ἑαυτόν), *to send oneself on, to flee, run, burry* [ῐ] Hence

ἰαλτός, ή, όν, verb. Adj. *sent, dispatched*

ἴᾱμα Ion. **ἴημα** ατος. τό. (ἰάομαι) *a means of bealing, treatment, remedy*

ἰαμβεῖος, ον, (ἴαμβος) *in iambics*; τὸ ἰαμβεῖον *iambic verse*

ἰαμβιάζω, f. ασω, and **ἰαμβίζω**, f. ίσω, (ἴαμβος), *to assail in iambics*: generally, *to lampoon.*

ἼΑΜΒΟΣ, ὁ, *an iambus*, a metrical foot consisting of a short and long. syll., as ἐγώ. II *an iambic verse*, the *trimeter* or *senarius*, first used by the sarcastic writers Archilochus and Hipponax; and then in the *Attic Drama.*

Ἰάν, ὁ, pl. Ἰᾶνες, contr. for Ἰάων Ἰάονες, *an Ionian.*

ἰάνθην, aor. 1 pass. of ἰαίνω.

ἸΑ'ΟΜΑΙ: fut. ἰάσομαι Ion. ἰήσομαι: aor. 1 ἰασάμην Ion. ἰησάμην: Dep.:—*to beal, cure*: metaph. *to remedy, beal, correct.* II. aor. 1 ἰάθην [ᾱ], and pf. ἴᾱμαι, in pass. sense, *to be bealed, to recover.*

Ἰάοναῦ, barbarism for the vocat. of Ἰάων·

Ἰάονες, pl. of Ἰάων·

ἸΑ'ΠΤΩ, f. ψω, *to send, drive*; of missiles, *to send forth, shoot, discharge*: *to set in motion*; ἰάπτειν ὀρχήματα *to begin* the dance. 2. *to assail, bandle roughly, burt.* II. intr. (sub. ἑαυτόν), *to rush, burry, speed.*

ἸΑ'ΠΥΞ Ion. **Ἰῆπυξ**, ὔγος, ὁ, *the north-west* or *west-north-west wind.*

Ἰάς, άδος, ἡ, Adj fem. of Ἴων *Ionic.* II. as Subst. (sub. γυνή), *an Ionian woman.* 2. (sub. γλῶσσα or διάλεκτος), *the Ionic dialect.*

ἴᾱσι, 3 pl. pres. of εἶμι *ibo.*

ἰᾶσι, for ἱέασι, 3 pl. of ἵημι.

ἰάσιμος, ον, (ἰάομαι) *admitting of cure, remediable*: —*appeasable*

ἴᾱσις Ion. **ἴησις**, εως, ἡ, (ἰάομαι) *a cure, remedy.*

ἼΑΣΠΙΣ, ιδος, ἡ, *a precious stone, jasper.*

Ἰαστί, Adv. (Ἰάς) *in the Ionic fashion* or *dialect.*

Ἰᾱσώ, gen. όος, contr. οῦς, ἡ, (ἰάομαι) *Iāso, the goddess of bealing and bealth.*

ἰᾱτήρ Ep. **ἰητήρ**, ῆρος, ὁ, poët. for ἰατρός, *a chirurgeon, surgeon, leech, physician.* [ῑ]

ἰᾶτο, 3 sing. impf. of ἰάομαι.

ἰᾱτορία, ἡ, (ἰάτωρ) *the art of medicine.*

ἰᾱτός, ή, όν, (ἰάομαι) *curable.*

ἰᾱτρεῖον, τό, (ἰατήρ) *a surgery.*

ἰατρικός, ή, όν, (ἰατρός) *of* or *for the art of bealing*· ἡ ἰατρική (sub. τέχνη), *surgery, the art of bealing.*

ἰατρό-μαντις, εως, ἡ, (ἰατρός, μάντις) *the physician-seer*, of Apollo and Aesculapius.

ἰατρός Ion. **ἰητρός**, ὁ, (ἰάομαι) = ἰατήρ, *a surgeon, leech, physician*: metaph., ἰατρὸς κακῶν, ὀργῆς, etc., *a bealer.*

ἰατρο-τέχνης, ου, ὁ, (ἰατρός, τέχνη) *a practiser of the bealing art.*

ἰατταταῖ, ἰαττᾰταιάξ, Interj. *ab, woe is me!*

ἰάτωρ, ορος, ὁ, Ion. ἰήτωρ, poët. for ἰατρός. [ῑᾱ]

ἰαῦ, a shout in answer, *bo! bolla!*

ἰαυοῖ, exclamation of joy, *bo! bo!* [ῑ]

ἰαύω, f. σω: aor. 1 ἴαυσα: (αὔω):—*to sleep, to pass the night*: hence *to dwell in* a place:—ἰαύειν πόδα *to rest* the foot.

ἰ-ᾰφέτης, ου, ὁ, (ἰός, ἀφίημι) *an archer.* [ῑ]

ἰάφθην, aor. 1 pass. of ἰάπτω.

ἰαχαῖος, α, ον, (ἰαχή) *glad-sounding.*

ἰᾰχέω, f. ήσω, = ἰάχω, *to shout, cry aloud.*

ἰαχή, ἡ, (ἰάχω) *a cry, shout*: *a wail, sbriek*: generally, *any loud sound.* [ῐᾰ]

ἰάχημα, ατος, τό, (ἰαχέω) *a cry, shout.* [ῐᾰ]

ἰάχω, f. ἰαχήσω: pf. ἴαχα, fem. part. ἰαχυῖα: (ἰά):

—*to cry, shout*, either in sign of joy or lamentation: c. acc. *to sound, proclaim*. II. of things, *to resound, reecho*; of the waves, *to roar*; of hot iron in water, *to hiss*. [ῐᾰ]

Ἰάων, ονος, ὁ, Ep. for Ἴων, *an Ionian*.

ἶβις, gen. Ion. ἴβιος Att. ἴβιδος, acc. ἶβιν, ἡ, *the ibis*, an Egyptian bird, to which divine honours were paid. It is scarlet, of the stork kind.

ἼΓΔΗ or ἴγδις, ἡ, *a mortar*.

ἶγμαι, part. ἰγμένος, pf. of ἱκνέομαι.

ἰγνύη, ἡ, (γόνυ) *the hollow* or *hinder part of the knee*, Lat. *poples*. [ῡ]

ἰγνύς, ύος [ῠ], ἡ, = ἰγνύη, acc. ἰγνύα or ἰγνύν.

Ἴδα Ion. **Ἴδη**, ἡ, *Ida*, a mountain in Phrygia near Troy: also another in Crete. II. *a thick wood, wood, copse*. 2. *timber*; ἴδη ναυπηγήσιμος *timber* for ship-building. [ῑ]

ἰδάλιμος, ον, (ἶδος) *causing sweat*.

ἰδέ, Ion for ἠδέ, *and*. [ῐ]

ἴδε or **ἰδέ**, imperat. of εἶδον, aor. 2 of *εἴδω, *lo, behold*. [ῐ]

ἴδε, Ep. 3 sing. of εἶδον, aor. 2 of *εἴδω. [ῐ]

ἰδέα Ion. -έη, ἡ, (ἰδεῖν) *form*. 2. generally, *the look* or *appearance* of a thing, as opp. to its reality, Lat. *species*. 3. *a nature, kind, sort; a way, manner, fashion*. [ῐ]

ἰδεῖν Ep. **ἰδέειν**, inf. of εἶδον, aor. 2 of *εἴδω.

ἰδέσθαι, inf. med. of εἶδον, aor. 2 of *εἴδω.

ἴδεσκον, Ion. for εἶδον, aor. 2 of *εἴδω. [ῐ]

ἰδέω, Ion. subj. of εἶδον, aor. 2 of *εἴδω.

ἴδηαι, Ep. 2 sing. of εἰδόμην, aor. 2 med. of *εἴδω. [ῐ]

ἰδησῶ, for εἰδήσω, Dor. fut. of *εἴδω. [ῐ]

ἰδίᾳ, v. sub ἴδιος.

ἰδιαίτερος, **ἰδιαίτατος**, Comp. and Sup. of ἴδιος, formed from ἰδίᾳ.

ἰδιο-βουλεύω, f. σω, (ἴδιος, βουλεύω) *to follow one's own counsel, take one's own way*.

ἼΔΙΟΣ, α, ον, Att. also ος, ον: *one's own, personal, private*, Lat. *privus, privatus*: opp. to public (δημόσιος). 2. *one's own*, opp. to ἀλλότριος; τὸ ἴδιον or τὰ ἴδια *private property* or *concerns*. 3. *peculiar, separate, distinct*: hence *strange*. II. dat. ἰδίᾳ is used as Adv. *privately*, opp. to δημοσίᾳ; ἰδίᾳ φρενός *away from* one's senses. 2. *on one's own account*. III. irreg. Comp. and Sup. ἰδιαίτερος, ἰδαίτατος (formed from ἰδίᾳ).

ἰδιο-συγκρἶσία, ἡ, (ἴδιος, συγκρίνω) *a peculiar temperament* or *habit of body, idiosyncrasy*.

ἰδίω, f. ίσω [ῑ]: aor. 1 ἴδῑσα: (ἶδος):—*to sweat: to sweat* with fear: in Prose usually ἱδρόω.

ἰδίως, Adv. of ἴδιος, *privately*.

ἰδιωτεία, ἡ, (ἰδιώτης) *private life, a business*.

ἰδιωτεύω, f. σω, *to live as a private man*. II. *to be without professional knowledge, be a layman*. From

ἰδιώτης, ου, ὁ, (ἴδιος) *a private person, one in a private station*, opp. to στρατηγός, *a private soldier*: also an *individual*, opp. to πόλις. II. *one who has no professional knowledge, a layman*, opp. to one who has; ἰατρὸς καὶ ἰδιώτης a mediciner or *an unprofessional man*; ποιητὴς ἢ ἰδιώτης a poet or *a prose-writer*: c. gen. rei, *unskilled* or *unversed in* a thing. 2. *an ill-informed, common-place fellow*. III. ἰδιῶται *one's countrymen*, opp. to ξένοι. Hence

ἰδιωτικός, ή, όν, *of* or *for a private man, private* or *personal*, opp. to public. 2. *commonplace, trivial, awkward*.

ἴδμεν, Ion. and Dor. for ἴσμεν, 1 pl. of οἶδα. II. Ep. for εἰδέναι, inf. of οἶδα.

ἴδμεναι, Ep. for εἰδέναι, inf. of οἶδα.

ἰδμοσύνη, ἡ, *knowledge, skill*. From

ἴδμων, ον, gen. ονος, (ἴδμεναι = εἰδέναι) *practised, skilled, versed in* a thing.

ἸΔΝΟ'Ω, f. ώσω, *to crook, bend*:—Pass. *to double oneself up, writhe*, esp. for pain.

ἰδνώθην, aor. 1 pass. of ἰδνόω.

ἰδοίατο, Ion. for ἴδοιντο, 3 pl. aor. 2 opt. of *εἴδω.

ἰδοῖσα, Dor. for ἰδοῦσα, aor. 2 part. fem. of *εἴδω.

ἴδον, Ep. for εἶδον, 1 sing. and 3 pl. aor. 2 of *εἴδω.

ἼΔΟΣ, εος, τό, *sweat, perspiration*. 2. *violent heat*.

ἰδοῦ, imperat. med. of εἶδον. II. as Adv. written ἰδού, *lo! behold! see there!* in giving a thing, *there! see there!* 2. *well! as you please!* 3. ironically in repeating another's words, ἰδού γ' ἄκρατον, *yes to be sure*, sheer wine.

ἰδρεία Ion. **ἰδρείη** or **ἰδρίη** [ῐ], ἡ, (ἴδρις) *knowledge, practice, skill*; ἰδρείῃ πολέμοιο *skill in* war.

ἴδρις, gen. ἴδριος Att. ἴδρεως, ὁ, ἡ, neut. ἴδρι, (ἴδμεναι, = εἰδέναι) *experienced, skilful*: as Subst., ἴδρις *the provident creature* = μύρμηξ, *the ant*.

ἰδρός, ὁ, poët. for ἱδρώς. [ῐ] Hence

ἱδρόω f. ώσω, *to sweat, perspire*, generally from toil, but also from pain or fear. This Verb, like ῥιγόω, is contracted into ω and ῳ instead of ου and οι (as if it were ἱδράω), hence 3 pl. pres. ἱδρῶσι, 3 sing. opt. ἱδρῴη, fem. part. ἱδρῶσαι.

ἵδρῡμα, τό, (ἱδρύω) *a thing founded, built: a temple, a statue, image*; ἵδρυμα πόλεως the *stay, support* of the city, like Lat. *columen rerum*.

ἱδρύθησαν, 3 pl. aor. 1 pass. of ἱδρύω.

ἱδρῡτέον, verb. Adj. of ἱδρύω, *one must found, establish*: *one must inaugurate* a statue. II. pass. οὐχ ἱδρυτέον *one must* not *sit still, loiter*.

ἱδρύω, f. ύσω [ῡ]: aor. 1 ἵδρῡσα:—Pass., aor. 1 ἱδρύθην [ῡ] not ἱδρύνθην: pf. ἵδρῡμαι: (ἵζω):—Causal of ἕζομαι, *to make to sit down*; ἱδρῦσαι στρατιήν *to encamp* an army:—Pass. *to be seated, sit still*: pf. part. pass. ἱδρῡμένος *firmly seated, steady, secure*. II. *to fix, found, establish*: *to set up* statues, *dedicate* temples:—Med., with pf. pass., ἵδρῡμαι, *to found* or *set up* for oneself. III. *to fix, settle, establish* persons in a place; Ἄρη ἐμφύλιον ἱδρῦσαι *to give footing to, introduce*, intestine war:—pf. pass. ἵδρῡμαι, *to be placed, situated*; ἱδρῦσθαι εἰς τόπον *to settle* in a place:—Med. *to found* or *establish for oneself*.

ἱδρῶ, ἱδρῷ, Ep. for ἱδρῶτα, ἱδρῶτι, acc. and dat. of ἱδρώς.

ἱδρῴην, opt. of ἱδρόω.

ἱδρώς, ῶτος, ὁ: Ep. dat. and acc. ἱδρῷ, ἱδρῶ: (ἶδος): *sweat, perspiration.* 2. *the sweat of trees, resin* or *gum.* II. metaph. *anything earned by the sweat of one's brow.*

ἱδρῶσαι, pres. part. fem. of ἱδρόω.

ἰδυῖα, ἡ, Ep. for εἰδυῖα, part. fem. of οἶδα (v. *εἴδω), always in phrase ἰδυίῃσι πραπίδεσσιν, with *knowing, sensible* heart.

ἴδω Ep. **ἴδωμι**, aor. 2 subj. of *εἴδω.

ἰδών, ἰδοῦσα, aor. 2 part. of *εἴδω.

ἴε, ἴεν, Ep. 3 sing. impf. of εἶμι *ibo.*

ἵει, 3 sing. Ion. and Att. impf. of ἵημι (as if from ἱέω).

ἱείη, Ep. for ἴοι, 3 sing. opt. of εἶμι *ibo.*

ἱείς, ἱεῖσα, ἱέν, pres. part. of ἵημι.

ἱεῖσι, 3 pl. of ἵημι.

ἵεμαι, pres. pass. and med. of ἵημι.

ἵεμεν, ἱεμέναι, Ep. for ἱέναι, inf. of ἵημι.

ἱέμενος, η, ον, pres. part. pass. of ἵημι.

ἵεν, Aeol. for ἵεσαν, 3 pl. impf. of ἵημι.

ἰέναι, pres. inf. of εἶμι *ibo.*

ἱέναι, pres. inf. of ἵημι.

ἱερᾱκίσκος, ὁ, Dim. of ἱέραξ, *a small hawk.*

ἹΕ'ΡΑΞ, ᾱκος, Ion. **ἱέρηξ** contr. **ἴρηξ**, ηκος, ὁ, *a hawk, falcon.*

ἱεράομαι Ion. **ἱρ-**, Pass. (ἱερός) *to be a priest* or *priestess.*

ἱερᾱτεία, ἡ, (ἱερατεύω) *the priest's office, priesthood.*

ἱεράτευμα, ατος, τό, (ἱερᾱτεύω) *the priesthood, body of priests.*

ἱερᾱτεύω, f. σω, (ἱερεύς) *to be priest* or *priestess.*

ἱέρεια Ion. **ἱρεια**, ἡ, fem. of ἱερεύς, *a priestess.*

ἱερεῖον Ion. **ἱερήϊον** or **ἱρήϊον**, τό, (ἱερός) *a victim, sacrifice:* generally, *a slaughtered animal.*

ἱερεύς, έως Ion. **ἱρεύς, ῆος**, ὁ, (ἱερός) *a priest, sacrificer.*

ἱέρευτο, for ἱερεύετο, 3 sing. impf. pass. of

ἱερεύω Ion. **ἱρεύω**, f. σω, (ἱερός) *to offer, sacrifice.* 2. *to kill, slaughter.* II. intr. *to be a priest.*

ἱερή, ἡ, = ἱέρεια.

ἱερήϊον, τό, Ion. for ἱερεῖον.

ἱερία, ἡ, Att. poët. form of ἱέρεια.

ἱερο-γλῠφικός, ή, όν, (ἱερός, γλύφω) *hieroglyphic, expressing ideas by sacred symbols* instead of letters.

ἱερο-γραμματεύς, έως, ὁ, (ἱερός, γραμματεύς) *a sacred scribe,* one of a lower order of the Egyptian priesthood.

ἱερο-δόκος, ον, (ἱερόν, δέχομαι) *receiving sacrifices.*

ἱερό-θῠτος, ον, (ἱερός, θύω) *sacrificed to a god;* ἱερόθυτος καπνός smoke *from the sacrifices.*

ἱερο-λογέω, (ἱερός, λέγω) *to discuss sacred things.*

ἱερο-λογία Ion. **ἱρολογίη**, ἡ, *mystic language.*

ἱερο-μηνία, ἡ, or **ἱερο-μήνια**, τά, (ἱερός, μήν or μήνη) *the holy moon,* or *the holy-day of the month.*

ἱερομνημονέω, f. ήσω, *to be* ἱερομνήμων. From

ἱερο-μνήμων, ονος, ὁ, (ἱερός, μνήμων) *mindful of sacred things.* II. Subst. *the sacred recorder sent by each Amphictyonic state* to their Council along with the πυλαγόραι.

ἱερόν, τό, v. ἱερός II.

ἱερο-νίκης, ου, ὁ, (ἱερός, νῑκάω) *conqueror in the games.*

ἱερο-ποιός, όν, (ἱερός, ποιέω) *managing sacred rites:* at Athens, the ἱεροποιοί were *ten* officers, one from each tribe, *who saw that the victims were without blemish.*

ἱερο-πρεπής, ές, (ἱερός, πρέπω) *beseeming a sacred place, person* or *matter: holy, reverend.*

ἹΕΡΟ'Σ, ά, όν, also ός, όν: Ion. and Ep. also **ἱρός**, ή, όν:—*of* or *relating to the gods,* Lat. *sacer.* 2. *holy, hallowed, consecrated,* of any place, person or thing under the protection of a god; ἱερὸς καὶ ὅσιος, *sacred* and profane; v. sub ὅσιος. II. as Subst.: 1. ἱερόν Ion. ἱρόν, τό, *a temple.* 2. ἱερά Ion. ἱρά, τά, *offerings, sacrifices, victims:* ἱερὰ ῥέζειν, Lat. *sacra facere* or *operari,* to do or offer *sacrifice:* afterwards, *the entrails of a victim,* and so *the auspices:* generally, *sacred things* or *rites,* Lat. *sacra.* III. special phrases: 1. ἱερὰ νόσος, *the sacred,* i. e. *the great* or *mysterious disease,* prob. *the epilepsy.* 2. ἡ ἱερὰ ὁδός, *the sacred* road to Delphi; also that from Athens to Eleusis. 3. ἡ ἱερὰ τριήρης *the sacred ship* sent from Athens to Delos.

ἱερό-στεπτος, ον, (ἱερόν, στέφω) *wreathed in holy fashion.*

ἱεροσῡλέω, f. ήσω, (ἱερόσυλος) *to rob a temple, steal sacred things, commit sacrilege.* Hence

ἱεροσῡλία, ἡ, *temple-robbery, sacrilege.*

ἱερό-σῡλος, ον, (ἱερόν, συλάω) *robbing temples, sacrilegious:* as Subst. *a sacrilegious person,* Lat. *sacrilegus.*

ἱερουργέω, f. ήσω, (ἱερουργός) *to perform sacred rites;* ἱερουργεῖν τὸ εὐαγγέλιον *to minister* the gospel. Hence

ἱερουργία Ion. **ἱροεργίη**, ἡ, *religious service, worship, sacrifice.*

ἱερ-ουργός, όν, (ἱερός, ἔργον) *sacrificing:* esp. as Subst. *a sacrificing priest.*

ἱεροφαντέω, f. ήσω, *to be an initiating priest.* From

ἱερο-φάντης Ion. **ἱρ-**, ου, ὁ, (ἱερός, φαίνω) *one who expounds sacred things: an initiating priest.* Hence

ἱεροφαντικός, ή, όν, *of* or *for an initiating priest.* Adv. -κῶς.

ἱερο-φύλαξ, ᾰκος, ὁ, (ἱερός, φύλαξ) *a keeper of a temple* or *of the sacred vessels in it,* Lat. *aedituus.* [ῠ]

ἱερό-χθων Ion. **ἱρ-**, ὁ, ἡ, (ἱερός, χθών) *of hallowed soil.*

ἱερόω, f. ώσω, (ἱερός) *to hallow, dedicate.*

ἱερ-ώνῠμος, ον, (ἱερός, ὄνομα) *of holy name.*

ἱερωστί, (ἱερός) Adv. *in holy manner, piously.*

ἱερωσύνη Ion. **ἱρ-**, ἡ, (ἱερός) *the office of priest, priesthood: a priest's salary.*

ἱέσθην, 3 dual impf. med. of ἵημι.

ἰεῦ, an ironical exclamation, Lat. *hui!*

ἱζάνω, (ἵζω) Causal, *to make to sit, seat.* II.

intr. *to sit*. 2. of soil, *to settle down, sink in*, Lat. *sidere*.

ἽΖΩ, impf. ἷζον Ion. ἵζεσκον: for the aor. 1, v. εἷσα: later fut. ἱζήσω, aor. 1 ἵζησα: I. Causal, *to make to sit*: see εἷσα. II. intr. *to sit, sit down*; ἵζειν ἐς θρόνον to take one's seat: ἵζειν of soldiers, *to place themselves in ambush, to encamp*: also *to sit still*:—Pass. ἵζομαι also occurs in same sense; ἵζεσθαι ἐν τῷ Τηυγέτῳ or ἐς τὸ Τηΰγετον *to take post* at Taygetus. 2. of earth, *to settle down, sink in*, Lat. *sīdĕre*.

ἰή, *io!* exclam. of joy. [ῑ]

ἰή, ἡ, Ion. for ἰά, *voice, sound*.

ἰήϊος, α, ον, also ος, ον, (ἰή) *wailing, mournful, plaintive*; ἰήϊος βοά a cry *of woe*. II. epith. of Apollo, the god *invoked with the cry* ἰή.

ἶηλα, inf. ἶῆλαι, aor. 1 of ἰάλλω.

ἰήλεμος, ἰηλεμίζω, ἰηλεμίστρια, Ion. for ἰάλεμ–.

ἴημα, τό, = ἴαμα.

ἵημι, ἵης, ἵησι, 3 pl. ἱᾶσι or ἱεῖσι; imperat. ἵει; subj. ἱῶ; opt. ἱείην; inf. ἱέναι Ep. ἱέμεναι or ἱέμεν; part. ἱείς:—impf. ἵην, Aeol. 3 pl. ἵεν:—fut. ἥσω:—aor. 1 ἧκα Ep. ἕηκα:—aor. 2 ἧν, of which the ind. is only used in compds.; imperat. ἕς, subj. ὧ, opt. εἵην, inf. εἷναι, part. εἵς:—pf. εἷκα: plqpf. εἵκειν. Pass. and Med., pres. ἵεμαι: impf. ἱέμην: aor. 1 pass. ἕθην, also εἵθην: aor. 1 med. ἡκάμην: aor. 2 med. εἵμην or ἕμην: pf. pass. εἷμαι: plqpf. εἵμην. Causal of εἶμι (*ibo*), *to make to go, set agoing*: hence 1. *to send, send away, let go, dismiss*. 2. of sounds, *to send forth, utter, emit*. 3. of things at rest, *to set in motion, send, let fly, throw, hurl*: c. gen. pers. *to throw at* one:—the acc. is often omitted, so that ἵημι is seemingly intr. *to throw, shoot*. 4. of water, *to let flow, let burst forth*: and without acc., ποταμὸς ἐπὶ γαῖαν ἵησιν the river *flows* over the land: of tears, *to let fall*: metaph., κὰδ δὲ κάρητος ἧκε κόμας *she let* her hair *flow* down from her head. 5. generally, *to put, place*. II. Med. *to feel an impulse towards* a thing, *long for, yearn after*; part. ἱέμενος, *longing for*: c. inf. *to desire to do*. 2. the 3 pl. aor. 2 med. ἕντο is used by Homer only in phrase ἐπεὶ πόσιος καὶ ἐδητύος ἐξ ἔρον ἕντο, when *they had put away*, i. e. *satisfied*, desire of meat and drink.

ἶηνα, aor. 1 of ἰαίνω.

Ἰη-παιήων, ονος, ὁ, epith. of Apollo from the cry ἰὴ παιάν: also *a hymn* sung to him. Hence

ἰη-παιωνίζω, f. ίσω, *to cry* ἰὴ παιών or παιάν!

ἰήσασθαι, Ion. aor. 1 inf. of ἰάομαι.

ἴῃσι, Ep. for ἴῃ, 3 sing. pres. subj. of εἶμι *ibo*.

ἵησι, 3 sing. pres. ind. of ἵημι.

ἰήσιμος, ἴησις, Ion. for ἰασ–.

Ἰησοῦς, οῦ, dat. also οῦ, acc. οῦν, Greek form of the Hebrew *Joshua, Saviour*.

ἰητήρ, ῆρος, ὁ, Ion. for ἰατήρ.

ἰητορίη, ἰητρός, ἰήτωρ, Ion. for ἰατ–.

ἰθᾱ-γενής poët. **ἰθαιγενής**, ές, (ἰθύς, γένος) *of honest birth, lawfully begotten, legitimate*; of a nation, *genuine, of the good old stock*. II. of some mouths of the Nile, *naturally formed, original*, opp. to ὀρυκτά.

ἸΘΑ΄ΚΗ, ἡ, *Ithăca*, the home of Ulysses, an island on the West coast of Greece. Hence

Ἰθάκηνδε, Adv. *to Ithaca*: and

Ἰθακήσιος, α, ον, *of Ithaca, an Ithacan*.

ἰθέα, ἡ, Ion. fem. for ἰθεῖα, v. ἰθύς [ῐ]

ἰθέως, Adv. of ἰθύς, *directly, straight*, Lat. *recta via*.

ἴθι, imperat. of εἶμι, *come, go, begone*:—as Adv. *come on! forward!*

ἴθμα, ατος, τό, (εἶμι) *a step, movement*.

ἰθύ, neut. of ἰθύς; used as Adv., like ἰθέως.

ἰθυ-δίκης, ου, ὁ, (ἰθύς, δίκη) *giving simple justice*.

ἰθυ-δρόμος, ον, (ἰθύς, δραμεῖν) *straight-running*.

ἰθύ-θριξ, τρῐχος, ὁ, ἡ, (ἰθύς, θρίξ) *straight-haired*, opp. to οὐλόθριξ, woolly-haired. [ῐθ]

ἰθυμᾰχία, ἡ, *a fair, stand-up fight*. From

ἰθυ-μάχος, ον, (ἰθύς, μάχομαι) *fighting fairly and honestly*.

ἰθύ-νοος, ον, (ἰθύς, νόος) *honest*.

ἰθύντατα, Ep. Sup. of ἰθέως, *most straight, most rightly*.

ἰθύνω, f. ῠνῶ: aor. ἴθῡνα:—Pass., aor. 1 ἰθύνθην:—Ion. and Ep. for εὐθύνω, *to make straight, straighten, direct, rule*:—Pass. *to become straight* or *even*; τὼ δ' ἰθυνθήτην they *ran even with one another*. 2. *to guide in a straight line, to direct* or *steer straight, to send* or *shoot straight*; ἰθύνειν ἵππους, *to drive* the horses *straight*:—Pass. of a boat, *to be guided, steered*. 3. *to guide, rule*: of a judge, *to rectify, correct*: also *to chastise*.

ἰθῠ-πόρος, ον, (ἰθύς, πορεύομαι) *going straight on*.

ἰθῠ-πτίων, ωνος, ὁ, ἡ, (ἰθύς, πέτομαι) *straight-flying*, of an ashen spear-shaft. [πῐ]

ἸΘΥ΄Σ, ἰθεῖα, ἰθύ, Ion. fem. ἰθέα: Ion. and Ep. form of the Att. εὐθύς:—of motion, *straight, direct, going straight*:—in moral sense, *straight, upright, just, true*:—Comp. and Sup. ἰθύτερος, ἰθύτατος:—in Adverbial usage, acc. fem. τὴν ἰθεῖαν (sub. ὁδόν), *straight on*, Lat. *recta via*: so, ἐκ τῆς ἰθείης, *straightforward, openly*. II. as Adv., ἰθὺς or ἰθὺ *straight at, straight towards*; ἰθὺς μαχέσασθαι to fight *fair, openly and aboveboard*. 2. of Time, *straightway*. Hence

ἰθύς, ύος, ἡ, Homer only in acc. ἰθύν, *an impulse, purpose, plan, undertaking, endeavour*: but also ἀν' ἰθύν, = ἀν' ὀρθόν, *straight upwards*. [ῐ]

ἰθῠ-τενής, ές, (ἰθύς, τείνω) *stretched out, straight*. [ῐ]

ἰθύ-τονος, ον, (ἰθύς, τείνω) = ἰθυτενής.

ἰθύ-τρῐχες, οἱ, αἱ, plur. from ἰθύθριξ.

ἰθύω, f. ύσω: aor. 1 ἴθῡσα: [ῡ]: (ἰθύς):—*to go straight, press right on*: c. gen., ἴθυσε νεός drove *right against* the ship. II. *to be eager to do, bent upon doing*: hence *to desire, purpose*.

ἱκᾰνός, ή, όν, (ἱκ-έσθαι) *befitting, becoming*: I. of persons, *sufficient, competent, able to do* a thing; ἱκανὸς ἰατρικήν *sufficiently versed in* medicine: absol.

considerable, respectable, tolerable. II. of things, *sufficient, enough: large* or *long enough;* ἱκανὸν χρόνον *a long* time; τὸ ἱκανὸν λαμβάνειν to take *security* or *bail,* Lat. *satis accipere.* Hence

ἱκᾰνότης, ητος, ἡ, *sufficiency, fitness.*

ἱκᾰνόω, f. ώσω, *to make fit, make sufficient, qualify.*

ἱκάνω [ᾱ], Ep. lengthd. for ἵκω, = ἱκνέομαι, only used in pres. and impf., *to come: to come to, arrive at, reach:* also Med. ἱκάνομαι.

ἱκᾰνῶς, Adv. of ἱκανός, *sufficiently,* Lat. *satis;* ἱκανῶς ἔχειν to be *sufficient:* Sup. ἱκανώτατα.

Ἰκάριος, α, ον, (Ἴκᾰρος) *Icarian,* name of that part of the Aegaean sea which is between the Cyclades and Caria, where Icarus the son of Daedalus was said to have been drowned.

ἴκελος, η, ον, poët. form for **εἴκελος,** *like.* [ῐ] Hence

ἱκελόω, f. ώσω, *to make like.*

ἱκέσθαι, aor. 2 inf. of *ἱκνέομαι.*

ἱκέσθω, 3 sing. aor. 2 imperat. of *ἱκνέομαι.*

ἱκεσία, ἡ, (ἱκέτης) *the prayer of a suppliant.* II. as fem. of ἱκέσιος, *a female suppliant.*

ἱκέσιος, α, ον, also **ος,** ον, (ἱκέτης) *of, for* or *presiding over suppliants,* epith. of Zeus. II. *suppliant, supplicating.*

ἱκετα-δόκος, ον, (**ἱκέτης, δέχομαι**) *receiving* or *protecting suppliants.*

ἱκετεία, ἡ, = ἱκεσία, q. v.

ἱκέτευμα, ατος, τό, (ἱκετεύω) *a mode of supplication.*

ἱκετευτέος, α, ον, *proper to be supplicated.* From

ἱκετεύω, f. σω: aor. 1 ἱκέτευσα [ῐ Att., ῑ Ep.]: (ἱκέτης):—*to approach as a suppliant, to supplicate, entreat, beseech.*

ἱκετήριος sync. **ἱκτήριος,** α, ον, (ἱκέτης) *of* or *fit for suppliants.* II. ἡ ἱκετηρία (sub. ἐλαία), *the olive branch which a suppliant held in his hand.*

ἱκέτης, ου, ὁ, (**ἱκέσθαι**) *one who comes* to seek protection, *a suppliant* or *fugitive* II. *the protector of the suppliant.* Hence

ἱκετήσιος, α, ον, *protecting the suppliant,* of Zeus.

ἱκέτις, ιδος, ἡ, fem. of **ἱκέτης.**

ἵκηαι, Ep. for ἵκῃ, 2 sing. aor. 2 subj. of ἱκνέομαι.

ἰκμάζω and **ἰκμαίνω,** *to moisten.* From

ἸΚΜΑ'Σ, άδος, ἡ, *moisture* of any kind.

ἴκμενος or **ἵκμενος,** only in the phrase ἴκμενος οὖρος *a fair* breeze, (from ἱκνέομαι), a *following* and so *favourable,* wind, Lat. *ventus secundus.*

ἱκνέομαι, lengthd. from ἽΚΩ [ῐ]: fut. ἵξομαι Dor. ἰξοῦμαι: aor. 2 ἱκόμην: pf. ἷγμαι, part. ἱγμένος:—*to come: to come to, arrive at, reach.* 2. *to come as a suppliant* (ἱκέτης) to one, *to beseech, entreat* him. 3. impers. in pres. and impf., *it becomes, befits, beseems;* τοὺς μάλιστα ἱκνέεται whom *it* most *concerns;* τὸ ἱκνεύμενον *that which is fitting, proper.*

ἱκνεῦνται, Dor. for ἱκνοῦνται, 3 pl. of ἱκνέομαι.

ἱκνουμένως Ion. **ἱκνεομ–, ἱκνευμ–.** Adv. part. pres. of ἱκνέομαι, *fittingly, aright.*

ἱκοίμαν, Dor. for ἱκοίμην, aor. 2 opt. of ἱκνέομαι.

ἼΚΡΙΑ, τά, *the half-deck* of an Homeric ship: generally, *a boarded platform, scaffold, benches.*

ἴκταρ, Adv. (ἵκω) *at once, close together.* II. of Place, *close to, hard by,* c. gen.

ἱκτήρ, ῆρος, ὁ, (ἵκω) *a suppliant.* II. **Ζεὺς** ἱκτήρ, *the protector of the suppliant.*

ἱκτήριος, α, ον, syncop. for **ἱκετήριος.**

ἰκτίδεος, α, ον, (ἴκτις) *of a weasel, of weasel-skin,* in Homer κτίδεος. II. as Subst., ἰκτιδέα, contr. ἰκτιδῆ (sub. δορά), ἡ, *weasel-skin.*

ἸΚΤΙ΄ΝΟΣ, ὁ, *a kite,* Lat. *milvus.*

ἼΚΤΙΣ, ἴδος, ἡ, *the yellow-breasted marten-cat.*

ἶκτο, 3 sing. plqpf. of ἱκνέομαι.

ἽΚΩ, impf. ἶκον: aor. 2 ἶξον: root of **ἱκνέομαι,** a form used in Ep. poetry:—*to come: to come to, arrive at, reach* a certain point, whether of Place or Time; τὰ σὰ γοῦνα ἱκόμεθα *we come to* thy knees, in token of supplication (cf. ἱκνέομαι 2, ἱκέτης):—metaph. *to reach, arrive at,* manhood, old age, etc.; ὕβρις τε βίη τε σιδήρεον οὐρανὸν ἵκει violence and force *are reaching* even to heaven. 2. conversely of circumstances, conditions; χρειὼ ἵκει με necessity *is upon* me; ὕπνος, γῆρας, ἱκάνει με *come upon* or *over* me.

ἵκωμαι, aor. 2 subj. of ἱκνέομαι.

ἴλᾱ, Dor. for ἴλη. [ῑ]

ἰλᾰδόν, Adv. (ἴλη) *in troops, in bodies, in companies,* Lat. *turmatim: in abundance.* [ῑ]

ἴλᾰθι, pres. imperat. of ἵλημι.

ἱλάομαι, Ep. for ἱλάσκομαι.

ἽΛΑΟΣ, ον, Att. **ἵλεως,** ων, nom. pl. ἵλεῳ, neut. ἵλεα:—of gods, *propitious, gracious:* of men, *gracious, kindly, gentle:* also *cheerful, gay.* 2. ἵλεως σοί, (sc. ἔστω ὁ Θεός) God *be gracious* to thee, i. e. be it far from thee.

ἱλᾰρία, ἡ, *cheerfulness, gaiety.* From

ἱλᾰρός, ά, όν, (ἵλαος) *cheerful, gay, joyous, mirthful,* Lat. *hilaris.* Adv -ρῶς. Hence

ἱλᾰρότης, ητος, ἡ, *gaiety,* Lat. *hilaritas.*

ἱλάσκομαι: fut. ἱλάσομαι [ᾰ] Ep. ἱλάσσομαι Dor ἱλάξομαι: aor. 1 ἱλασάμην: Dep.: (ἵλαος):—*to appease, propitiate, reconcile to oneself,* of gods:—but also *to conciliate* a man. II. *to expiate, atone for.* III aor. 1 imperat. pass. ἱλάσθητι, in pass. sense, *be gracious.* Hence

ἱλασμός, ὁ, *a means of appeasing: a propitiation, sacrifice.* [ῑ]

ἱλασσάμενος, Ep. aor. 1 part. of ἱλάσκομαι.

ἱλάσσεαι, Ep. for ἱλάσῃ, 2 sing. aor. 1 subj. of ἱλάσκομαι.

ἱλαστήριος, α, ον, (ἱλάσκομαι) *propitiatory;* esp. II. as Subst., ἱλαστήριον, τό, *propitiation* or *the mercy seat.*

ἵλεα, Att. neut. pl. of ἵλαος.

ἵλεως, Att. for ἵλαος.

ἴλη or **εἴλη** Dor. **ἴλα,** ἡ, (ἴλλω, εἴλω) *a crowd, band, troop, company.* 2. *a troop of horse, squadron,* Lat. *turma, ala,* strictly of 64 men: generally, *a troop,* *company.* 3. at Sparta, *a certain division* of the youths.

ἴληθι, imperat. of ἵλημι.

ἱλήκω, (ἵλαος) *to be gracious, propitious*, in 3 sing. subj. ἱλήκῃσι, and 2 sing. opt. ἱλήκοις.

ἵλημι, = ἱλήκω, esp. in imperat. ἵληθι Dor. ἵλᾰθι, *be gracious, propitious!*

Ἰλιάς, άδος, ἡ, pecul. fem. of Ἰλιακός. II. as Subst. Ἰλιάς, 1. (sub. γῆ) *the land of Ilium.* 2. (sub. γυνή), *a woman of Ilium.* 3. (sub. ποίησις), *the Iliad*, of Homer.

ἰλιγγιάω, f. σω: aor. 1 ἰλιγγίᾱσα:—*to have a swimming in the head.* From

ἴλιγγος, ὁ, (ἴλλω, εἴλω) *a spinning round: a swimming* in the head, Lat. *vertigo: a swoon.* [ῐ]

ἴλιγξ, ιγγος, ἡ, (ἴλλω) *a whirling, whirlpool.*

Ἰλιόθεν, Adv. (Ἴλιος) *from Troy.*

Ἰλιόθι, old Ep. gen. of Ἴλιος, Adv. *at Troy.*

Ἰλιορ-ραίστης, ὁ, (Ἴλιος, ῥαίω) *destroyer of Troy.*

Ἰλιόφι, old Ep. gen. of Ἴλιος.

ἼΛΙΟΣ, ου, ἡ, or **Ἴλιον**, τό, *Ilios* or *Ilium, the city of Ilus*, also called *Troy.*

ἰλλάς, άδος, ἡ, (ἴλλω, εἴλω) *a rope, band.*

ἰλλός, ὁ, (ἴλλω) *squinting.*

ἼΛΛΩ, v. sub εἴλω.

ἼΛΥΣ, ύος, ἡ, *mud, slime, dirt.* [genit. ἰλῠος Homer, later ἰλῡος.]

ἱμάντεσσι, Ep. dat. pl. of ἱμάς.

ἱμαντίδιον, τό, Dim. of ἱμά

ἱμάντῐνος, η, ον, (ἱμάς) *of leathern thongs.*

ἱμάντιον, τό, Dim. of ἱμάς.

ἱμαντο-πέδη, ἡ, (ἱμάς, πέδη) *a leathern band:* metaph. *one of the feelers of the polypus.*

ἹΜΆΣ, άντος, ὁ, dat. pl. ἱμᾶσι Ep. ἱμάντεσσι:—*a leathern strap* or *thong;* in pl. *the straps* or *harness* of a chariot: *the thong* or *lash* of a whip. 2. *the cestus* of boxers, consisting of *leathern straps* put round the hand: 3. the magic *girdle* of Aphrodité, Lat. *caestus.* 4. *a latch*, by which the bolt was shot home into the socket: also *a shoe-latchet:* later *the rope of a draw-well.*—Proverb., ἱμὰς κύνειός ἐστι he's as tough as *a thong* of dogskin.

ἱμάσθλη, ἡ, (ἱμάς, ἱμάσσω) *the thong* or *lash* of a whip, generally *a whip.* [ῐ]

ἱμάσσω, fut. ἱμάσω [ᾰ]: aor. 1 ἵμασα: (ἱμάς):—*to flog, scourge:* also *to smite.*

ἱμᾰτιδάριον, τό, Dim. of ἱμάτιον. [ῑμ-δᾰ]

ἱμᾰτίδιον, τό, Dim. of ἱμάτιον.

ἱμᾰτίζω, f. ίσω, (ἱμάτιον) *to clothe:* pf. part. pass. ἱματισμένος, *clothed.*

ἱμᾰτιο-κάπηλος, ὁ, (ἱμάτιον, κάπηλος) *a dealer in clothes.*

ἱμάτιον, τό, in form only a Dim. of εἷμα, *an outer garment, cloak* or *mantle* worn above the χιτών, answering to Homer's χλαῖνα; ἱμάτια, τά, generally, *clothes.* II. *a cloth.*

ἱμᾰτι-φῠλᾰκέω, f. ήσω, (ἱμάτιον, φυλακέω) *to take care of clothes.*

ἱμᾰτισμός, ὁ, (ἱματίζω) *clothing, apparel.* [ῐ]

ἱμείρω Aeol. **ἱμέρρω**, (ἵμερος) *to long for, yearn for* or *after, desire;* c. inf. *to long* or *wish* to do.—More freq. **ἱμείρομαι** as Dep., with aor. 1 med. ἱμειράμην, pass. ἱμέρθην.

ἵμεν, 1 pl. of εἶμι *ibo.*

ἴμεν, ἴμεναι, Ep. for ἰέναι, inf. of εἶμι *ibo.*

ἱμερο-δερκής, ές, (ἵμερος, δέρκομαι) *looking longingly.*

ἱμερόεις, εσσα, εν, (ἵμερος) *exciting love* or *desire, lovely; charming.*

ἱμερο-θᾱλής, ές, (ἵμερος, τέθηλα) Dor. for ἱμεροθηλής) *sweetly growing* or *blooming.*

ἽΜΕΡΟΣ [ῑ], ὁ, *a longing* or *yearning after* a person or thing, Lat. *desiderium:* absol. *love, desire.*

ἱμέρρω, Aeol. for ἱμείρω.

ἱμερτός, ή, όν, (ἱμείρω) *longed for, lovely.*

ἴμμεναι, poët. for ἴμεναι, ἰέναι, inf. of εἶμι *ibo.*

ἱμονιά, ἡ, (ἱμάς) *the rope of a draw-well:* acc. ἱμονιάν, absol., *a rope's length*, i. e. as long as a bucket takes to go down and come up a well.

ἵν, Dor. for ἵ, acc. of Pron. of 3rd pers.

ἽΝΑ, Conjunction:—*that, in order that*, = ὅπως, Lat. *ut:* I. *with Subj. mood after tenses of present time;* ἥκεις, ἵν' ἴδῃς thou art come *that thou mayest* see. 2. *with Optat. after tenses of past time;* Παλλὰς ἔδωκε μένος, ἵν' ἔκδηλος γένοιτο Pallas gave him strength, *that he might* become conspicuous. 3. *with the past tenses of the Indicat.*, to imply a consequence which is *now* impossible; ἵν' ἦν τυφλὸς *in which case he would have been* blind. II. ἵνα μή, *that not, lest*, Lat. *ut ne.* III. elliptic with other Particles, ἵνα δή, ἵνα περ, ἵνα τι (sub. γένηται); *to what end?*

Adverb., I. of Place, = ὅπου, Lat. *ubi, in what place, where;* ἵν' ἐτράφεν ἠδ' ἐγένοντο *where* they were bred and born: c. gen. loci, ἵνα γῆς, χώρας, etc., Lat. *ubi terrarum.* 2. = ὅποι, Lat. *quo, to what place, whither;* ἵν' οἴχεται *whither* he is gone.

ἰνδάλλομαι, Dep., only used in pres. and impf.: (εἴδαλιμος, εἰδάλλομαι):—*to appear, to appear like;* with double dat., ἰνδάλλετο σφίσι Πηλείωνι he *seemed* to them *like* the son of Peleus: absol. *to appear, seem.*

Ἰνδικός, ή, όν, (Ἰνδός) *Indian.*

Ἰνδ-ολέτης, ου, ὁ, (Ἰνδός, ὀλέσθαι) *the Indian-killer*, epith. of Bacchus.

ἸΝΔΟΎΣ, ὁ, *an Indian:*—as Adj. = Ἰνδικός, *Indian.* II. the river *Indus.*

Ἰνδῷος, α, ον, = Ἰνδικός.

ἶνες, pl. nom. of ἴς.

ἰνίον, τό, (ἴς) *the muscles at the back of the neck:* generally, *the back of the head, nape of the neck.* [ῐν]

ἽΝΙΣ, ὁ, *a son, child.*

Ἰνώ, όος, contr. οῦς, ἡ, *Ino*, daughter of Cadmus, afterwards worshipped as a sea-goddess by the name of Leucothea.

ἰν-ώδης, ες, (ἴς, εἶδος) *sinewy, fibrous.* [ῑ]

ἴξαλος, ον, (from ἀΐσσω, as if contracted from ἀΐξαλος) epith. of the wild goat, *bounding, springing.*

ἴξεσθαι, fut. inf. of ἱκνέομαι.

ἰξευτής, οῦ, ὁ, (ἰξεύω) *a fowler, bird-catcher, snarer.*

ἰξεύω, f. σω, (ἰξός) *to catch birds by birdlime.*

ἰξοβολέω, f. ήσω, *to catch birds with lime-twigs.* From

ἰξο-βόλος, ον, (ἰξός, βάλλω) *setting lime-twigs.*

ἰξο-εργός, ὁ, (ἰξός, *ἔργω) *one who uses birdlime, a fowler*

ἴξομαι, fut. of ἱκνέομαι.

ἶξον, Ep. aor. 2 of ἵκω

ἸΞΟ΄Σ, ὁ. Lat. *VISCUM, misseltoe:* also, *the misseltoe-berry* II. *birdlime* prepared from *the misseltoe-berry*, Lat. *viscus.*

ἰξο-φορεύς, έως, ὁ, (ἰξός, φέρω) *bearing misseltoe.*

ἸΞΥ΄Σ, ύος, ἡ: dat. ἰξύϊ contr ἰξυῖ: *the waist.*

Ἰό-βακχος, ὁ, (ἰώ, βάκχε) *Bacchus invoked with the cry of ἰώ:—a song beginning ἰὼ* Βάκχε!

ἰο-βλέφᾰρος, ον, (ἴον, βλέφαρον) *violet-eyed.*

ἰοβολέω, f. ήσω, *to shoot arrows.* From

ἰο-βόλος, ον, (ἰός, βάλλω) *shooting arrows.*

ἰο-βόστρῠχος, ον, (ἴον, βόστρυχος) *dark-haired.*

ἰό-δετος, ον, (ἴον, δέω) *violet-twined.*

ἰο-δόκος, ον, (ἰός, δέχομαι) *holding arrows.*

ἰο-ειδής, ές, (ἴον, εἶδος) *violet-coloured*, of the sea.

ἰόεις, εσσα, εν, (ἴον) *violet-coloured, dark.*

ἰοίην, Att. for ἴοιμι, opt. of εἶμι *ibo.*

ἰοῖσαι, Dor. for ἰοῦσαι, part. fem of εἶμι *ibo.*

ἴομεν, Ep. for ἴωμεν, 1 pl. subj. of εἶμι *ibo.*

ἰο-μῐγής, ές, (ἰός, μιγῆναι) *mixed with poison.*

ἰό-μωρος, ον, (ἴον, μόρος) *dark-fated, miserable.*

ἼΟΝ, τό, *the violet*, Lat. *viola.* [ῐ]

ἴον, Ep. form of impf. of εἶμι *ibo.*

ἰονθάς, άδος, ἡ, *shaggy, hairy.* From

ἴονθος, ὁ, *the down on the face.* (Deriv. uncertain.) [ῐ]

Ἰόνιος, α, ον, (Ἰώ) *of Io;* Ἰόνιος κόλπος *the Iŏnian sea*, the sea between Epirus and Italy, at the mouth of the Adriatic sea, across which she was said to have swum,—not to be confounded with the Iōnian sea.

ἰόντες, part. pl. of εἶμι.

ἰο-πλόκᾰμος, ον, (ἴον, πλόκαμος) *with violet locks, dark-haired.* [ῐ]

ἰός [ῑ], ὁ, with irreg. pl. ἰά, (ἰέναι inf. of εἶμι *ibo*) *an arrow.*

ἸΟ΄Σ, ὁ, *rust, verdigris*, Lat. *aerugo.*

ἸΟ΄Σ, ὁ, *poison*, esp. of serpents.

ἴος, ἴα, Ep. for εἷς, μία; dat. ἰῷ for ἑνί.

ἰο-στέφᾰνος, ον, (ἴον, στέφανος) *violet-crowned.*

ἰότης, ητος, ἡ, *will, resolve;* mostly in dat., θεῶν ἰότητι *by the will* or *pleasure* of the gods.

ἰο-τῠπής, ές, (ἰός, τυπῆναι) *struck by an arrow.*

ἰοῦ, a cry of woe, Lat. *heu!* seldom, like ἰώ, a cry of joy. [ῠ]

Ἰουδαΐζω, f. σω, *to live as a Jew.* From

Ἰουδαϊκός, ή, όν, *of* or *for the Jews.* Adv. -κῶς. From

Ἰουδαῖος, α, ον, *of the tribe of Judah:* as Subst.: 1. *a Jew.* 2. Ἰουδαία (sc. γῆ) *the land of Judaea.*

Ἰουδαϊσμός, ὁ, (Ἰουδαῖος) *Judaism.*

ἰουλίς, ίδος, ἡ, *a red fish.*

ἴουλος, ον, (οὖλος) *down, the first growth of the beard:* ὑπὸ κροτάφοισιν ἴουλοι *the young hair* beneath the temples, i. e. *the whiskers.*

ἰο-χέαιρα, ἡ, (ἰός, χαίρω) *delighting in arrows*, or (from χέω) *showering arrows.*

ἰπνο-κᾱής, ές, (ἰπνός, καῆναι) *baked in the oven*

ἰπνο-λέβης, ητος, ὁ, (ἰπνός, λέβης) *a boiler, caldron.*

ἰπνο-ποιός, όν, (ἰπνός, ποιέω) *working in an oven* or *furnace;* as Subst. *a potter*

ἸΠΝΟ΄Σ, ὁ, *an oven* or *furnace*, Lat. *furnus.* II. *the place of the oven, kitchen.* III *a lantern.*

ἶπος, ὁ or ἡ, (ἴπτομαι) in a mouse-trap, *the piece of wood that falls and catches* the mouse; generally, *a trap; a heavy* weight. Hence

ἰπόω, f ώσω. *to press down:*—Pass. *to be pressed down* or *crushed;* εἰσφοραῖς ἰπούμενος *squeezed* hard by taxes. [ῑ]

ἱππ-αγρέται, ῶν, οἱ, (ἱππεύς, ἀγείρω) three officers at Lacedaemon, *who chose* 300 *youths to serve as ἱππεῖς* or *body-guard for the kings.*

ἱππ-ᾰγωγός, όν, (ἵππος, ἄγω) *carrying horses:* ἱππαγωγοί (sub. ναῦς) αἱ, *transport-ships for horses.*

ἱππάζομαι, fut. άσομαι Dep. (ἵππος) *to drive* or *guide a horse, to drive a chariot:* later, *to ride;* ἱππάζεσθαι χώραν *to ride over* a country. II. as Pass. of a horse, *to be driven* or *ridden;* also *to be broken in.*

ἵππ-αιχμος, ον, (ἵππος, αἰχμή) *fighting on horseback.*

ἱππ-ᾰλεκτρῠών, όνος, ὁ, (ἵππος, ἀλεκτρυών) *a horse-cock: a gryphon, dragon.*

ἱππᾰλίδας, ου, ὁ, poët. form for ἱππεύς.

ἱππᾰπαί, (ἵππος) cry of *the knights* to each other in comic imitation of the seaman's cry ῥυππαπαί.

ἱππάριον, τό, Dim. of ἵππος, *a little horse, pony.*

ἱππ-αρμοστής, οῦ, ὁ, (ἵππος, ἁρμοστής) Lacedaemonian word for ἵππαρχος.

ἱππαρχέω, f. ήσω, *to be a general of cavalry, to command the cavalry.* Hence

ἱππαρχία, ἡ, *the command of the cavalry.*

ἱππαρχικός, ή, όν, *of* or *for cavalry.* From

ἵππ-αρχος, and **ἱππ-άρχης**, ου, ὁ, (ἵππος, ἄρχω) *ruling the horse*, epith of Neptune. II. *a general of cavalry;* at Athens there were two.

ἱππάς, άδος, ἡ, fem. of ἱππικός; ἱππὰς στολή *a riding*-dress, *horseman's cloak.* II. as Subst. (sub. τάξις), *the order of knights: the knights' tax.*

ἱππᾰσία, ἡ, (ἱππάζομαι) *riding, horse-exercise.* 2. *chariot-driving.*

ἱππάσιμος, η, ον, (ἱππάζομαι) *fit for horses* or *for riding: easily ridden.*

ἱππαστήρ, ῆρος, and **ἱππαστής**, οῦ, ὁ, (ἱππάζομαι) *a horseman.* II as Adj. *fit for riding.*

ἱππεία, ἡ, (ἱππεύω) *horsemanship, riding, driving*, esp. *racing.* II. *cavalry.*

ἵππειος, α, ον, (ἵππος) *of a horse* or *horses;* ἵππειος λόφος a crest *of horse-hair.*

ἵππ-ερος, ὁ, (ἵππος, ἔρος) *love for horses, a horse-fever.*

ἵππευμα, ατος, τό, (ἱππεύω) *a ride on horseback, expedition in a chariot.*

ἱππεύς, έως Ion. ῆος, ὁ, (ἵππος) in Homer, either *a driver of horses, charioteer*, or *the warrior fighting from the chariot.* 2. *a horseman, rider.* II. at Athens the ἱππεῖς Att. ἱππῆς. *Horsemen* or *Knights*, were the 2nd class, according to Solon's constitution: they were required to possess 300 medimni and a horse: see πεντακοσιομέδιμνοι. 2. at Sparta, 300 chosen men, who formed *the king's body-guard*, but did not serve on horseback: see ἱππαγρέται.

ἱππευτήρ, ῆρος, ὁ, and **ἱππευτής**, οῦ, ὁ, *a rider, horseman.* from

ἱππεύω, f. σω: aor. 1 ἵππευσα: (ἱππεύς):—*to be a horseman, to ride:* metaph. of the wind, Ζεφύρου πνοαῖς ἱππεύσαντος when Zephyr *rode with* his gales, as in Horace, *Eurus equitavit per undas.* II. *to serve on horseback.*

ἱππῆας, Ep. pl. acc. of ἱππεύς.

ἱππηδόν, Adv. (ἵππος) *like a horse.* II. *like a horseman.*

ἱππήεσσι, Ep. for ἱππεῦσι, pl. dat. of ἱππεύς.

ἱππ-ηλάσιος, α, ον, (ἵππος, ἐλαύνω) *fit for riding* or *driving;* ἱππηλασία ὁδός *a chariot* road.

ἱππ-ηλάτα, ὁ, Ep. form for ἱππηλάτης.

ἱππηλᾰτέω, f. ήσω, *to ride* or *drive.* From

ἱππ-ηλάτης, ου, ὁ, Ep. **ἱππηλάτα**, (ἵππος, ἐλαύνω) *a driver of horses, one who fights from a chariot*, epith. of honour, like our *Knight.* [ᾰ]

ἱππ-ήλᾰτος, ον, (ἵππος, ἐλαύνω) *fit for horsemanship* or *driving.*

Ἱππ-ημολγοί, ῶν, οἱ, (ἵππος, ἀμέλγω) *the Mare-milkers*, a Scythian or Tartar tribe:—as Adj. *milking mares.*

ἱππι-άναξ, ακτος, (ἵππος, ἄναξ) *chief of horsemen.*

ἱππικός, ή, όν, (ἵππος) *of a horse* or *horses;* ἀγὼν ἱππικός *a horse* or *chariot* race. II. *of* or *for riding* or *horsemen, equestrian: skilled in riding.* 2. ἡ ἱππική (sub. τέχνη), *horsemanship, riding.* III. τὸ ἱππικόν, *the cavalry.* IV. Adv. -κῶς, *like a horseman.*

ἵππιος, α, ον, (ἵππος) *of a horse* or *horses.*

ἱππιο-χαίτης, ου, ὁ, (ἵππιος, χαίτη) *shaggy with horse-hair.*

ἱππιο-χάρμης, ου, ὁ, (ἵππιος, χάρμη) *one who fights from a chariot.* 2. *a horseman, rider.*

ἱππο-βάμων [ᾰ], ον, gen. ονος, (ἵππος, βαίνω) *going on horseback, equestrian.* 2. metaph., ῥήματα ἱπποβάμονα *high-paced* words, *bombast.*

ἱππο-βάτης [ᾰ], ου, ὁ, (ἵππος, βαίνω) *a horseman.*

ἱππο-βότης, ου, ὁ, (ἵππος, βόσκω) *a feeder of horses:* in Chalcis of Euboea, the Ἱπποβόται were *the knights, nobles.*

ἱππό-βοτος, ον, (ἵππος, βόσκω) *fed on by horses, good for grazing, rich in cattle.*

ἱππο-βουκόλος, ὁ, (ἵππος, βουκόλος) *a horsekeeper.*

ἱππο-γέρᾰνοι, οἱ, (ἵππος, γέρανος) *crane-cavalry.*

ἱππό-γῡποι, οἱ, (ἵππος, γύψ) *vulture-cavalry.*

ἱππό-δᾰμος, ον, (ἵππος, δαμάω) *horse-taming:* as Subst. *a tamer of horses.*

ἱππο-δάσεια, as fem., without any masc. ἱππόδασυς in use, (ἵππος, δασύς) epith. of κόρυς, *thick with horse-hair, with rough horse-hair crest.*

ἱππό-δεσμα, ων, τά, (ἵππος, δεσμός) *reins, a halter.*

ἱππο-δέτης, ου, ὁ, (ἵππος, δέω) *a halter.*

ἱππο-διώκτης, ου, ὁ, Dor. **-τας**, (ἵππος, διώκω) *a driver* or *rider of horses.*

ἱππο-δρομία, ἡ, (ἱππόδρομος) *a horse-race* or *chariot-race.* Hence

ἱππο-δρόμιος, ον, *of the horse-race.* II. epith. of Poseidon, *delighting in the speed of horses.*

ἱππό-δρομος, ὁ, (ἵππος, δρόμος) *a race-course.*

ἱππο-δρόμος, ὁ, (ἵππος, δραμεῖν) *a horse-courier.*

ἱππόθεν, Adv. (ἵππος) *forth from the horse.*

ἵπποιϊν, Ep. dual gen. of ἵππος.

ἱππο-κάνθαρος, ὁ, (ἵππος, κάνθαρος) *a horse-beetle, monstrous beetle.*

ἱππο-κέλευθος, ον, (ἵππος, κέλευθος) *driving horses:* as Subst. *a charioteer, rider.*

ἱππο-κένταυρος, ὁ, (ἵππος, κένταυρος) *a horse-centaur, half-horse half-man.*

ἱππο-κομέω, f. ήσω, *to keep* or *groom horses;* ἱπποκομεῖν κάνθαρον *to groom one's* beetle. From

ἱππο-κόμος, ον, (ἵππος, κομέω) *keeping* or *grooming horses.* II. as Subst., ἱπποκόμος, ὁ, *a groom, one who attended the* Athenian ἱππεύς *in war.*

ἱππό-κομος, ον, (ἵππος, κόμη) *decked with horse-hair.*

ἱππο-κορυστής, οῦ, ὁ, (ἵππος, κορύσσω) *one who is furnished with a horse, a horseman, knight.*

ἱππο-κρᾰτέω, f. ήσω, (ἵππος, κρατέω) *to be superior in horse:* Pass. *to be inferior in horse.* Hence

ἱπποκρᾰτία, ἡ, *victory in a skirmish of horse.*

ἱππό-κρημνος, ον, (ἵππος, κρημνός) *tremendously steep;* ἱππόκρημνον ῥῆμα *a neck-breaking* word.

ἱππό-κροτος, ον, (ἵππος, κροτέω) *sounding with the tramp of horses.*

ἱππό-λοφος, ον, (ἵππος, λόφος) *with horse-hair crest.*

ἱππο-μᾰνής, ές, (ἵππο, μανῆναι) *mad for horses: luxuriant.* II. as Subst., ἱππομανές, έος, τό, an Arcadian plant, *which makes horses mad.* 2. *an excrescence on the forehead of new-born foals*, used as a charm: also *a humour which falls from mares.* Hence

ἱππο-μᾰνία, ἡ, *a mad love for horses, racing*, etc.

ἱππομᾰχέω, f. ήσω, (ἱππομάχος) *to fight on horseback.* Hence

ἱππομᾰχία, ἡ, *a horse-fight, skirmish of horse.*

ἱππο-μάχος, ον, (ἵππος, μάχομαι) *fighting on horseback:* as Subst., ἱππομάχος, ὁ, *a trooper.*

ἱππο-νώμας, ου, ὁ, (ἵππος, νωμάω) *driving horses.*

ἱππο-πόλος, ον, (ἵππος, πολέομαι) *busied with horses:* as Subst., ἱπποπόλος, ὁ, *a rider* or *driver of horses.*

ἱππο-πότᾰμος, ὁ, (ἵππος, ποταμός) *the river-horse* of Egypt, *hippopotamus:* in Herodotus, ἵππος ποτάμιος.

ἽΠΠΟΣ, ὁ, ἡ, *a horse, mare*, Lat. *equus, equa:* the pl. ἵπποι is *the pair of horses in the chariot*, and hence also *the chariot* itself; ἀφ' ἵππων from *the chariot; λαός τε καὶ ἵπποι* the foot-soldiers and *those who fought in chariots; ἵπποι καὶ πεζοί horse* and foot. II. ἡ ἵππος, *the horse, cavalry*, Lat. *equitatus*, always in sing., as, χιλίη ἵππος, *a thousand* horse. III. ἵππος ποτάμιος *the hippopotamus*. IV. in Compos., *anything large* or *coarse*, as in our *horsechestnut, horselaugh*, v. ἱππό-κρημνος, etc.

ἱππο-σόας, ου, ὁ, (ἵππος, σεύω) *driver of horses*.

ἱππο-σόος, α, ον, *horse-driving*.

ἱππό-στᾰσις, εως, ἡ, (ἵππος, στάσις) *a stable:* metaph., Ἀελίου κνεφαία ἱππόστασις the dark *stabling-place* of the sun, i. e. *the West*.

ἱπποσύνη, ἡ, (ἵππος) *the art of driving* or, later, *of riding: the art of horsemanship*. II. *the horse* of an army, *cavalry*.

ἱππόσῠνος, η, ον, = ἱππικός.

ἱππότᾰ, Ep. for ἱππότης.

ἱππότης, ου, ὁ, (ἵππος) *a driver* or *rider of horses, a horseman, knight:* Homer always uses Ep form ἱππότα, esp. of Nestor. II. as Adj., λεὼς ἱππότης *the horse-folk, horsemen*.

ἱππο-τοξότης, ου, ὁ, (ἵππος, τοξότης) *a mounted bowman, horse-archer*.

ἱπποτροφέω, f. ήσω, *to breed* or *keep horses*. And

ἱπποτροφία, ἡ, *a breeding* or *keeping of horses*, esp. for racing. From

ἱππο-τρόφος, ον, (ἵππος, τρέφω) *horse-feeding: breeding* or *keeping horses*.

ἱππο-τῡφία, ἡ, (ἵππος, τῦφος) *excessive pride*.

Ἱππου-κρήνη, ἡ, *Hippocrene, the horse's well* on Helicon, sacred to the Muses, said to have sprung out where the hoof of Pegasus struck the earth.

ἵππ-ουρις, ιδος, ἡ, (ἵππος, οὐρά) fem. Adj. *decked with a horse-tail, with crest of horse-hair*.

ἱππο-φόρβιον, τό, (ἵππος, φέρβω) *a stable*. II. *a troop of horses*.

ἱππο-φορβός, όν, (ἵππος, φέρβω) *a horse-keeper, trainer*.

ἱππο-χάρμης, ου, ὁ, (ἵππος, χάρμη) = ἱππιοχάρμης.

ἱππ-ώδης, ες, (ἵππος, εἶδος) *horse-like*.

ἱππών, ῶνος, ὁ, (ἵππος) *a place for horses, a stable: a halting-place, station*.

ἱππωνεία, ἡ, *a buying of horses* From

ἱππωνέω, f. ήσω, *to buy horses*. From

ἱππ-ώνης, ου, ὁ, (ἵππος, ὠνέομαι) *a buyer of horses*.

ἵπτᾰμαι, a late form for πέτομαι, *to fly*.

ἵπτομαι, f. ἴψομαι: (ἶπος): Dep.:—*to press hard, oppress:* generally, *to hurt, harm*.

ἱρά, τά, Ion. for ἱερά.

ἵραξ, ᾱκος, ὁ, contr. for ἱέραξ, *a hawk*.

ἱράομαι, Ion. for ἱεράομαι.

ἱρεία, Ion. for ἱέρεια.

ἱρεύεσκον, Ion. impf. of ἱερεύω.

ἱρεύς, ῆος, ὁ, Ion. for ἱερεύς.

ἱρεύω, Ion. for ἱερεύω.

ἱρήϊον, Ion. for ἱερεῖον.

ἱρήν, ένος, ὁ, Ion. for εἰρήν.

ἵρηξ, ηκος, ὁ, Ion. for ἱέραξ.

ἱρία, Dor. for ἱέρεια.

ἶρις, ιδος, ἡ: acc. ἶριν as well as ἴριδα:—*the rainbow*, in Homer, as in the Bible, a sign to men (τέρας μερόπων ἀνθρώπων) II. impersonated **Ἶρις**, ιδος, ἡ, acc. Ἶριν, voc. Ἶρι, *Iris, the Rainbow*, as a messenger of the gods, esp. from the gods to men: Hesiod makes her daughter of Thaumas (*the Wonderer*).

ἵρισσιν, Ep. for ἶρισιν, dat. pl. of ἶρις.

ἱρο-δρόμος, ὁ, (ἱρός, δραμεῖν) Ion. for ἱεροδρ., *running in the sacred races*. [ῑ]

ἱρο-εργίη, Ion. for ἱερουργία.

ἱρόν, τό, Ion. for ἱερόν. [ῑ]

ἱρός, ή, όν, Ion. for ἱερός. [ῑ]

ἱρο-φάντης, ὁ, Ion. for ἱεροφ-.

ἱρωσύνη, Ion. for ἱερωσύνη, *priesthood*.

ἼΣ, ἡ, gen. ἰνός, acc. ἶνα: pl. nom. ἶνες, dat. ἴνεσι Ep. ἴνεσσι:—Lat. *VIS, strength, force, nerve, thew and sinew:* very freq. in periphr. like βίη, as, ἲς Τηλεμάχοιο the strong Telemachus. II. *a muscle: the neck*. [ῑ]

ἶσα, ἴσα, neut. pl. of ἶσος, ἴσος, used as Adv.

ἰσ-άγγελος, ον, (ἴσος, ἄγγελος) *like an angel*.

ἰσ-άδελφος, ον, (ἴσος, ἀδελφός) *like a brother*.

ἰσάζω, f. άσω, (ἴσος) *to make equal:*—Med. *to make* or *hold equal* to another, c. dat.

ἴσᾱμι, Dor. for ἴσημι.

ἰσ-άμιλλος, ον, (ἴσος, ἅμιλλα) *equal in the race*.

ἴσαν, 3 pl. Ep. impf. of εἶμι *ibo*. II. Ep. for ᾔσαν, ᾔδεισαν, 3 pl. plqpf. of εἴδω.

ἰσ-άνεμος, ον, (ἴσος, ἄνεμος) *swift as the wind*. [ᾰ]

ἴσαντι, Dor. for ἴσασι, 3 pl. of ἴσημι.

ἰσ-άργῠρος, ον, (ἴσος, ἄργυρος) *as good as silver, worth its weight in silver*.

ἴσας, Dor. part. of ἴσημι.

ἴσᾱσι, 3 pl. of ἴσημι, and of οἶδα (v. εἴδω B).

ἰσάσκετο [ῑ], Ion. for ἰσάζετο, 3 sing. impf. med. of ἰσάζω, *she likened herself*.

ἴσᾱτι, Dor. for ἴσησι, 3 sing. of ἴσημι.

ἰσ-ηγορέω and Med. -έομαι, (ἴσος, ἀγορεύω) *to speak on equal terms, with equal freedom*. Hence

ἰσηγορία, ἡ, *equal right of speech:* generally, *equality in the eye of the law*.

ἰσ-ῆλιξ, ῐκος, ὁ, ἡ, (ἴσος, ἧλιξ) *of the same age with*.

ἰσ-ημέριος, α, ον, (ἴσος, ἡμέρα) *lasting an equal time*.

ἼΣΗΜΙ, *I know:*—a pres. only used in the Dor. forms, sing. ἴσᾱμι, ἴσᾱτι; pl. ἴσᾰμεν, ἴσᾱσι or ἴσαντι; part. ἴσας.

ἰσ-ήρετμος, ον, (ἴσος, ἐρετμός) *with as many oars*

ἰσ-ήρης, ες, (ἴσος, ἀραρεῖν) *equally fitted, equal*.

ἴσθι, *know*, imperat. pf. of *εἴδω. II. ἴσθι, *be*, imperat. of εἰμί *sum*.

Ἴσθμια (sub. ἱερά), ων, τά, (ἰσθμός) *the Isthmian games*, holden on the Isthmus of Corinth. Hence

Ἰσθμιάζω, f. άσω, *to attend the Isthmian games*.

Ἰσθμῐᾰκός, ή, όν, (ἴσθμιον) *of the Isthmus*.

Ἰσθμιάς, άδος, pecul. fem. of Ἴσθμιος: αἱ Ἰσθμιάδες (sub. ἑορταί), *the Isthmian games.*
ἴσθμιον, τό, (ἰσθμός) *a necklace.*
Ἴσθμιος, α, ον, also ος, ον, (ἰσθμός) *of the Isthmus, Isthmian.*
Ἰσθμόθεν, Adv. *from the Isthmus;* and
Ἰσθμόθι, Adv. *on the Isthmus;* and
Ἰσθμοῖ, Adv. *on the Isthmus.* From
ἰσθμός, οῦ, ὁ, (εἶμι ibo) *a neck: any narrow passage.* 2. *a neck of land* between two seas, *an isthmus:* esp. as prop. n. *the Isthmus* of Corinth.
ἰσθμ-ώδης, ες, (ἰσθμός, εἶδος) *like an isthmus.*
Ἰσιάς, άδος, fem. Adj. *of* or *belonging to Isis.* From
Ἶσις, ἡ, gen. Ἴσιδος Ion. Ἴσιος: dat. Ἴσῖ: acc. Ἶσιν:—*Isis*, an Egyptian goddess, answering to the Greek Demeter, Lat. *Ceres.*
ἼΣΚΩ or **ἐΐσκω**, *to make like;* ἴσκε ψεύδεα πολλὰ λέγων ἐτύμοισιν ὁμοῖα speaking many lies *be made* them *like* truths. II. *to hold* or *think like;* ἐμὲ σοὶ ἴσκοντες *thinking* me *like* you: absol., ἴσκειν ἕκαστος ἀνὴρ each man *imagined* or *supposed.* III. in late Poets, ἴσκε, ἴσκεν, = ἔλεγεν, *be spake, said.*
ἴσμεν, 1 pl. of οἶδα, for which Homer always uses ἴδμεν; v. εἴδω B.
ἰσο-βᾰρής, ές, (ἴσος, βάρος) *of equal weight.*
ἰσο-δαίμων, ον, gen. ονος, (ἴσος, δαίμων) *godlike, equal to a god.* II. *equal in fortune* or *happiness.*
ἰσο-δίαιτος, ον, (ἴσος, δίαιτα) *living on an equal footing.*
ἰσοζῠγής, ές, (ἴσος, ζυγῆναι) *equally balanced: equal.*
ἰσό-θεος, ον, (ἴσος, θεός) *equal to the gods, godlike.*
ἰσο-κίνδῡνος, ον, (ἴσος, κίνδυνος) *equal to the danger.*
ἰσό-κληρος, ον, (ἴσος, κλῆρος) *equal in property.*
ἰσο-κρᾰτής, ές, (ἴσος, κράτος) *of equal might* or *power, possessing equal privileges with* others. Hence
ἰσοκρᾰτία, ἡ, *equality of power and rights, political equality.*
ἰσ-όμᾰλος, ον, (ἴσος, ὁμαλός) *equally level, nearly equal.*
ἰσο-μάτωρ, Dor. for ἰσο-μήτωρ, ορος, ὁ, ἡ, (ἴσος, μήτηρ) *like one's mother.*
ἰσό-μᾰχος, ον, (ἴσος, μάχη) *equal in the fight.*
ἰσο-μεγέθης, ες, (ἴσος, μέγεθος) *equal in size.*
ἰσο-μέτωπος, ον, (ἴσος, μέτωπον) *with equal forehead* or *front.*
ἰσο-μήκης, ες, (ἴσος, μῆκος) *equal in length.*
ἰσομοιρέω, f. ήσω, (ἰσόμοιρος) *to have an equal share: to take a share in* a thing *with* another. Hence
ἰσομοιρία Ion. -ίη, ἡ, *a sharing equally, equal partnership.*
ἰσό-μοιρος, ον, (ἴσος, μοῖρα) *having an equal share of* a thing; γῆς ἰσόμοιρος ἀήρ earth's *equal partner* air. 2. generally, *equal, close, resembling;* φάος σκότῳ ἰσόμοιρον light *close akin to* darkness.
ἰσό-μορος, ον, (ἴσος, μόρος) = ἰσόμοιρος, *resembling.*
ἰσ-όνειρος, ον, (ἴσος, ὄνειρος) *dream-like, vacant.*
ἰσό-νεκυς, υος, ὁ, ἡ, (ἴσος, νέκυς) *dying the same death.*
ἰσονομέομαι, Pass. (ἰσόνομος) *to have equal rights.* Hence
ἰσονομία, ἡ, *equality of rights, political equality.*
ἰσό-νομος, ον, (ἴσος, νόμος) *having equal rights, enjoying freedom.*
ἰσό-παις, παιδος, ὁ, ἡ, (ἴσος, παῖς) *like a child.*
ἰσο-πάλαιστος, ον, (ἴσος, παλαιστή) *a span long.*
ἰσοπᾰλέω, f. ήσω, *to be a match for.* From
ἰσο-πᾰλής, ές, (ἴσος, πάλη) *equal in the struggle, well-matched, on a par with: equal.*
ἰσό-πᾰλος, ον, = ἰσοπαλής.
ἰσό-πεδον, τό, *level ground, a flat:* neut. from
ἰσό-πεδος, ον, (ἴσος, πέδον) *of even surface, level.*
ἰσο-πλᾰτής, ές, (ἴσος, πλάτος) *equal in breadth.*
ἰσο-πλάτων, ωνος, ὁ, (ἴσος, Πλάτων) *a second Plato.*
ἰσο-πληθής, ές, (ἴσος, πλῆθος) *equal in number* or *quantity.*
ἰσό-πρεσβυς, υ, (ἴσος, πρέσβυς) *like an old man.*
ἰσορροπία, ἡ, *equipoise, equilibrium.* From
ἰσόρ-ροπος, ον, (ἴσος, ῥοπή) *equally balanced, in equipoise: equally matched.*
ἼΣΟΣ, ἴση, ἴσον, Att. **ἴσος** [ῐ], ἴση, ἴσον, Ep. also **ἐΐσος** [ῑ]:—*equal to, the same as, like;* ἴσα πρὸς ἴσα *measure* for *measure;* ἴσος καὶ.., *equally* with; ἴσον ἐμοί *equally with* me. II. *equally divided* or *distributed, equal;* ἴση μοῖρα an *equal portion*, also ἴση alone (sub. μοῖρα); τὸ ἴσον and τὰ ἴσα, *an equal share, fair measure;* προστυχεῖν τῶν ἴσων to obtain *one's dues:* hence *fair, reasonable,* ἴσος ἀνήρ *a fair, upright* man. 2. at Athens, of *the equal division of all civic rights;* τὸ ἴσον *equality*, ἡ ἴση (sub. τιμωρία) punishment *equal to the offence, condign* punishment; ἴσαι (sub. ψῆφοι) votes *equally divided.* III. of Place, *even, level, flat,* Lat. *aequus;* εἰς τὸ ἴσον καταβαίνειν, Lat. *in aequum descendere;* δι' ἴσου at an *equal* distance or *interval.* IV. Adv. ἴσως, q. v.: but neut. sing. and pl. ἶσον Att. ἴσον, ἶσα Att. ἴσα, are also used adverbially: in Att. ἴσα generally means *equally*, ἴσως *perhaps:*—so also ἐξ ἴσου *equally;* ἐκ τοῦ ἴσου *on an equal footing;* ἐν ἴσῳ *equally;* cp. ἐπίσης. V. Att. Comp. ἰσαίτερος.
ἰσοσκελής, ές, (ἴσος, σκέλος) *with equal legs;* ἰσοσκελὲς τρίγωνον a triangle *with two sides equal.*
ἰσοτέλεια, ἡ, (ἰσοτελής) *equality of taxation.*
ἰσο-τέλεστος, ον, (ἴσος, τελέω) *accomplished for all alike.*
ἰσο-τελής, ές, (ἴσος, τέλος) *paying alike, paying the same taxes:* at Athens the ἰσοτελεῖς were a favoured class of μέτοικοι, who needed no patron (προστάτης), and paid no alien-duty (μετοίκιον), but had to pay taxes with the citizens.
ἰσο-τενής, ές, (ἴσος, τείνω) *equally stretched.*
ἰσότης, ητος, ἡ, (ἴσος) *equality.*
ἰσοτῑμία, ἡ, *equality of honour* or *privilege.* From
ἰσό-τῑμος, ον, (ἴσος, τιμή) *held in equal honour: having the same privileges.*
ἰσο-φᾰρίζω, (ἴσος, φέρω) Ep. Verb only used in pres. *to match oneself with, cope with, vie with;* ἰσοφαρίζειν

τινὶ ἔργα *to vie with* one in accomplishments: generally, *to be equal to.*

ἰσοφαρίσδεν, Dor. inf. of ἰσοφαρίζω.

ἰσο-φόρος, ον, (ἴσος, φέρω) *bearing equal weights, equal in strength.*

ἰσο-χειλής, ές, or **ἰσό-χειλος**, ον, (ἴσος, χεῖλος) *level with the edge* or *brim.*

ἰσό-χνοος, ον, (ἴσος, χνόος) *equally woolly with.*

ἰσοχρονέω, f. ήσω, *to be contemporary with.* From

ἰσό-χρονος, ον, (ἴσος, χρόνος) *equal in age* or *time.*

ἰσοψηφία, ἡ, *equal right to vote.* From

ἰσό-ψηφος, ον, (ἴσος, ψῆφος) *having an equal number of votes.* II. *having an equal vote with* others, *equal in deciding:* of states, *equal in franchise.* III. *equal in numerical value,* of words the letters of which make up the same sum.

ἰσό-ψῡχος, ον, (ἴσος, ψυχή) *of equal spirit* or *soul:* κράτος ἰσόψυχον power *of like spirit with men.*

ἰσόω, f. ώσω, (ἴσος) *to make equal;* ἰσώσας ταφέσει τὰ τέρματα *having made* the winning-post *even with* the starting-post, i. e. *having* run the whole course:—Med., ὄνυχας χεῖράς τε ἰσώσαντο *they made* their nails and hands *alike,* i. e. used them in like manner:—Pass. *to be made like* or *equal to.*

ἱστάμεν, ἱστάμεναι, Ep. for ἱστάναι, inf. of ἵστημι.

ἵστασο, pres. imperat. pass. of of ἵστημι.

ἱστάω, rare collat. form of ἵστημι, in 3 sing. pres. ἱστᾷ, and 3 sing. impf. ἵστα.

ἴστε, 2 pl. of οἶδα, v. *εἴδω B.

ἱστέαται, Ion. for ἵστανται.

ἵστημι (lengthd. from *ΣΤΑ'Ω):—the tenses of ἵστημι are divided into causal and intrans.:—A. Causal, *to make to stand,* pres. ἵστημι, impf. ἵστην, fut. στήσω, and aor. 1 ἔστησα, of Act. B. Intrans. *to stand,* in aor. 2 ἔστην, pf. ἕστηκα, plqpf ἑστήκειν, together with pres. pass. ἵσταμαι, impf. ἱστάμην, fut. σταθήσομαι (as also fut. med. στήσομαι, fut. 3 ἑστήξομαι), aor. 1 ἐστάθην [ᾰ], pf. ἕστᾰμαι, plqpf. ἐστάμην. But the pres. ἵσταμαι, impf. ἱστάμην, as well as aor. 1 ἐστησάμην, must also be regarded as *med.*, in which case they take a causal sense, *to place.*

Epic forms: 3 sing. impt. ἵστασκε: 3 pl. aor. 1 Ep. ἔστᾰσαν for ἔστησαν: syncop. dual and plur. perf. ἕστᾰτον, ἕστᾰμεν, ἕστᾰτε (or ἑστήκατε), ἑστᾶσι; imperat. ἕστᾰθι; subj. ἑστῶ; opt. ἑσταίην; inf. ἑστάναι Ep. ἑστάμεν, ἑστάμεναι [ᾰ]; part. ἑστώς ἑστῶσα, ἑστώς (or ἑστός), gen. ἑστῶτος; Ion. ἑστεώς, ῶτος, also ἑστηώς (Homer uses gen. ἑστᾰότος, acc. ἑστᾰότα, nom. pl. ἑστᾰότες): aor. 2 στάσκον, ες, ε, 3 pl. ἔσταν, στάν [ᾰ]; 2 and 3 sing. subj. στήῃς, στήῃ for στῇς, στῇ, 1 plur. στέωμεν and στείομεν for στῶμεν: inf. στήμεναι for στῆναι.

A. Causal, *to make to stand, set, place.* II. *to make to stand still, stop, check: to make fast, fix.* III. *to set up, set upright, to raise up,* as the mast in a ship: *to raise* or *erect* buildings, *to set up* a statue in one's honour; ἱστάναι τινὰ χαλκοῦν *to set up* a person in brass, raise a brasen statue to him. 2. *to raise, raise up, stir;* ἔριν στῆσαι *to begin* a quarrel. 3. *to set up, appoint, establish.* IV. *to place in the balance, weigh;* τι πρός τι one thing against another.

B. Intrans. *to stand, be set* or *placed;* with an Adv. *to be in a* certain *state* or *condition;* ἵνα χρείας ἕσταμεν in what need *we are:*—στῆναι εἰς .. or παρὰ .., *to set oneself towards, go to.* 2. *to lie, be situated.* II. *to stand still, take one's stand: to stand firm, remain fast, be fixed: to cease.* III. *to stand upright, rise up, be set up:* of a horse, ἵστασθαι ὀρθός to rear up. 2. generally, *to arise, begin;* ἔαρος νέον ἱσταμένοιο as spring *was just beginning;* τοῦ μὲν φθίνοντος μηνός τοῦ δ' ἱσταμένοιο as one month ends and the next *begins:*—thus in Homer the month is divided into *two* parts, μὴν ἱστάμενος and φθίνων; in the Attic Calendar the month, which consisted of 30 days, was divided into three parts of ten days each, called respectively, μὴν ἱστάμενος, μεσῶν, φθίνων. 3. *to be appointed.*

ἱστίη, Ion. for ἑστία.

ἱστιῆσθαι, Ion for εἱστιᾶσθαι, pf. inf. pass. of ἑστιάω.

ἱστιητόριον, τό, Ion. for ἑστιατ

ἱστίον, τό, (ἱστός) *a thing woven, a web, cloth, sheet: a sail,* ἄκροισι χρῆσθαι ἱστίοις to keep *the sails* reefed.

ἱστιορ-ράφος, ον, (ἱστίον, ῥάπτω) *sail-patching* metaph. *a meddling, cheating fellow.*

ἱστιο-φόρος, ον, (ἱστίον, φέρω) *carrying sails.*

ἱστο-βοεύς, gen. -έως Ion. -ῆος, ὁ, (ἱστός, βοῦς) *the plough-tree* or *pole.*

ἱστο-βόη, ἡ, = foreg.

ἱστο-δόκη, ἡ, (ἱστός, δέχομαι) *the mast-holder, a* rest on which the mast was laid when let down.

ἴστον, 2 and 3 dual pf. of *εἴδω

ἱστο-πέδη, ἡ, (ἱστός, πέδη) *a hole* in the keel *for fixing the mast in.*

ἱστο-πόνος, ον, (ἱστός, πονέω) *working at the loom.*

ἱστορέω, f. ήσω, (ἵστωρ) *to learn by inquiry: to inquire of, question,* c. acc. pers.: of things, *to inquire about* something. II. *to narrate what one has learnt, narrate historically.* Hence

ἱστορία, ἡ, *a learning by inquiry: knowledge* or *information obtained by inquiry.* II. *a narration of what one has learnt, historical narrative*

ἱστός, ὁ, (ἵστημι) *a ship's mast,* ἱστὸν στῆσαι or στήσασθαι to set up *the mast:* generally, *a rod* or *pole* II. *the web-beam* of the loom (which in ancient looms *stood upright*), *the loom;* ἱστὸν ἐποίχεσθαι to be busy about *the beam,* and so to weave 2. *the warp that was fixed to the beam: the web.*

ἱστό-τονος, ον, (ἱστός, τείνω) *stretched on the web-beam.*

ἱστ-ουργέω, f. ήσω, (ἱστός, *ἔργω) *to work at the loom.*

ἴστω, 3 sing. imperat. pf. of *εἴδω.

ἱστῶ, Dor. gen. of ἱστός: but **ἱστῷ**, dat. of the same.

ἴστωρ or **ἵστωρ**, ορος, ὁ, ἡ, *knowing, acquainted*

with, versed in: as Subst. *one who knows law and right, a judge.*

ἰσχάδιον, τό, Dim. of ἰσχάς. [ᾰ]

ἰσχᾰδό-πωλις, ιδος, ἡ, (ἰσχάς, πωλέω) *a woman who sells figs.*

ἴσχ-αιμος, ον, (ἴσχω, αἷμα) *quenching blood*: ἴσχαιμον, τό, *a styptic.*

ἰσχαίνω, f. l. for ἰσχναίνω.

ἰσχᾰλέος, α, ον, poët. for ἰσχνός, *dry, dried.*

ἰσχανάᾳ, Ep. 3 sing. of ἰσχανάω.

ἰσχᾰνάω, Ep. lengthd. form of ἰσχάνω, ἴσχω, *to hold back, check, hinder*:—Pass. *to check oneself, wait.* II. intrans. *to hold on by, cling to* a thing, and so *to desire eagerly.*

ἰσχάνω, = ἰσχανάω, *to check, hinder*: c. gen. *to keep back from* a thing. [ᾰ]

ἰσχάς, άδος, ἡ, (ἰσχνός) *a dried fig.*

ἰσχέμεν, ἰσχέμεναι, Ep. inf. of ἴσχω.

ἴσχεο, imperat. med. of ἴσχω.

ἰσχίον, τό, (ἴς, ἰσχύς) *the socket in which the thigh-joint turns, the hip-joint*:—in pl. *the hips* or *loins.*

ἰσχναίνω, (ἰσχνός) *to make thin, dry, withered*:—Pass. *to become* so:—metaph., σφριγῶντα θυμὸν ἰσχναίνειν *to bring down* the proud stomach.

ἰσχνο-πάρειος, ον, (ἰσχνός, παρειά) *with withered cheeks.*

ἰσχνός, ἡ, όν, (ἴσχω) *thin, lean, withered, meagre.* II. of style, *poor, meagre.*

ἰσχνό-φωνος, ον, (ἰσχνός, φωνή) *with thin or weak voice.* II. *stuttering, stammering.*

ἰσχῡρίζομαι, f. ίσομαι Att. ἰοῦμαι: aor. 1 ἰσχῡρισάμην: (ἰσχυρός): Dep.:—*to use all one's strength, to insist strongly, contend stoutly*: esp. *to affirm obstinately*:—Pass. *to be strengthened, gain greater force.*

ἰσχῡρός, ά, όν, (ἰσχύω) *strong, mighty, powerful.* 2. *stiff, firm, lasting, hard.* 3. *severe, great, excessive*: κατὰ ἰσχυρόν *by violence, force*, opp. to δόλῳ. Hence

ἰσχυρῶς, Adv. *strongly, stiffly, exceedingly*, Lat. *vehementer*:—Sup. ἰσχυρότατα, *most certainly.*

ἰσχύς, ύος, ἡ, (ἴς, ἴσχω) *strength, force, might*, esp. *bodily strength.* 2. *a force of soldiers.*

ἰσχύω, impf. ἴσχυον: f. ἰσχύσω: aor. 1 ἴσχῡσα [ῡ]: (ἰσχύς):—*to be strong, mighty, powerful*: *to have one's full powers, be in health and strength.*

ἴσχω, a form of ἔχω, only found in pres., and in impf. ἴσχον:—*to hold, check, restrain*: intr. *to stop*:—Med. *to hold oneself in, check oneself*: ἴσχεο *hold! be still!* c. gen., ἴσχεσθαί τινος *to desist from* a thing; ἴσχετο ἐν τούτῳ (impers.) here *it stopped.* II. later like ἔχω, *to hold* or *possess.* 2. *to have to wife.*

ἰσ-ωνία, ἡ, (ἴσος, ὠνή) *a fair price.*

ἰσ-ώνῠμος, ον, (ἴσος, ὄνομα) *bearing the same name.*

ἴσως, Adv. of ἴσος, *equally, in like manner.* II. *fairly, equitably.* III. *probably, perhaps*: in Att. often joined with ἄν or τάχ' ἄν. IV. with numerals, *about.*

ἰσωσαίμην, aor. 1 med. opt. of ἰσόω.

Ἰταλία Ion. -ίη, ἡ, *Italy.* [first syll. long in hexam.]

Ἰτᾰλίδης, ου, ὁ, poët. for Ἰταλιώτης.

Ἰτᾰλικός, ή, όν, (Ἰταλός) *Italian.*

Ἰτᾰλίς, ίδος, pecul. fem. of Ἰταλικός.

Ἰτᾰλιώτης, ου, ὁ, *an Italiote, one of the Greek inhabitants of Italy*: fem. **Ἰταλιῶτις**, ιδος, *Italian.*

ΙΤΑ˘ΛΟ´Σ, ὁ, *an Italian*:—as Adj. *Italian.*

ἰτᾰμός, ή, όν, (ἴτης) *headlong, hasty.*

ΙΤΕ´Α Ion. -έη and -είη, ἡ, *a willow*, Lat. *salix.* II. *a wicker shield, a target.* Hence

ἰτέϊνος, η, ον, *of willow, made of willow, wicker.*

ἰτέον, verb. Adj. of εἶμι *ibo, one must go.*

ἴτην, Ep. 3 dual impf. of εἶμι *ibo.*

ἴτης, ου, ὁ, (εἶμι *ibo*) *hasty, impetuous*: *impudent.*

ἰτός, ή, όν, (εἶμι *ibo*) *passable.*

ἰτρίνεος, α, ον, *like honey-cake.* From

ἴτριον, τό, *a cake*, made of sesamé and honey.

ἴττω, Boeot. for ἴστω, 3 sing. pf. of *εἴδω; ἴττω Ζεύς, Zeus *be witness!*

ἼΤΥ˘Σ, υος, ἡ, *the edge* or *rim of* anything round, *the felloe* of wheels: *the outer edge of* the shield: *the round shield* itself.

ἴτω, 3 sing. imperat. of εἶμι *ibo.*

ἴτων, 3 dual and Att. 3 pl. of εἶμι *ibo.*

ἰῡγή, ἡ, (ἰύζω) *a howling, shrieking, yelling.*

ἰυγμός, ὁ, (ἰύζω) *a shouting, shout of joy*: also *a cry of pain, scream, shriek.*

ἴυγξ or **ἰυγξ**, ἴυγγος, ἡ, (ἰύζω) *the wryneck*, so called from its cry: the ancient witches used to bind it to a wheel, which they turned round, believing that they drew men's souls along with it and charmed them to obedience; it was used to recover unfaithful lovers: hence metaph. *a love-charm, witchery*: *strong desire.*

ἸΥ˘´ΖΩ, fut. ἰύξω: aor. 1 ἴυξα:—*to shout, holla*: also *to howl, shriek.* (Formed from the sound.)

ἰυκτής, οῦ, ὁ, (ἰύζω) *one who shouts* or *cries*: *a singer, whistler, piper.* [ῐ]

ἴφθῑμος, η, ον, also ος, ον, (ἶφι) *strong, mighty, stout, stalwart*: of women, *goodly, comely.*

ἾΦΙ, Ep. Adv. *strongly, stoutly, with might* or *force, valiantly*: old poët. dat. from ἴς.

Ἰφῐ-γένειᾰ, ἡ, (ἶφι, γένω) *Iphigeneia*, Agamemnon's daughter, called by Homer Ἰφιάνασσα.

ἴφιος, α, ον, (ἶφι) *strong, mighty*: of sheep, *goodly.*

ἼΦΥΟΝ, τό, a kind of *pot-herb.*

ἰχθυάζομαι, Dep. = ἰχθυάω.

ἰχθυάω, f. άσω, (ἰχθύς) *to fish, angle*: Ep. 3 sing. ἰχθυάᾳ, impf. ἰχθυάασκον.

ἰχθῠβολέω, f. ήσω, *to strike fish, spear them.* From

ἰχθῠ-βόλος, ον, (ἰχθύς, βάλλω) *striking* or *spearing fish*; ἰχθ. θήρα a spoil of *speared fish*:—as Subst., ἰχθυβόλος, ὁ, *an harpooner, spearer.*

ἰχθύ-βοτος, ον, (ἰχθύς, βόσκω) *fed on by fish.*

ἰχθύδιον, τό, Dim. of ἰχθύς, *a little fish.*

ἰχθῠ-δόκος, ον, (ἰχθύς, δέχομαι) *holding fish.*

ἰχθυηρός, ά, όν, (ἰχθύς) *fishy, scaly, foul.*

ἰχθυο-βολέω, ἰχθυο-βόλος, = ἰχθυβ–.

ἰχθῠο-ειδής, ές, (ἰχθύς, εἶδος) *fish-shaped, fish-like.*

ἰχθυόεις, εσσα, εν, (ἰχθύς) *full of fish, fishy.* II. *consisting of fish.*

ἰχθυο-θηρητήρ, ῆρος, ὁ, (ἰχθύς, θηράω) *a fisherman.*

ἰχθυο-λύμης, ου, ὁ, (ἰχθύς, λύμη) *the plague* or *destruction of fish.*

ἰχθυο-φάγος, ον, (ἰχθύς, φαγεῖν) *fish-eating;* οἱ Ἰχθυοφάγοι ἄνδρες *the Fish-eaters*, a tribe.

ἰχθυ-πἄγής, ές, (ἰχθύς, παγῆναι) *fish-piercing.*

ΙΧΘΥΣ, ύος, ὁ: acc. ἰχθύν and later ἰχθύα: the nom. and acc. pl. ἰχθύες, ἰχθύας are contr. into ἰχθῦς:—*a fish*, Lat. *piscis.* II. plur. οἱ ἰχθύες, *the fish-market.* [ῡ in sing. nom. and acc., ὔ in genit. and in all compds.]

ἰχθυσι-ληϊστήρ, ῆρος, ὁ, (ἰχθύς, λῃστής) *a stealer of fish.*

ἰχθυ-φἄγος, ον, = ἰχθυοφάγος. [ᾰ]

ἰχθυ-ώδης, ες, (ἰχθύς, εἶδος) = ἰχθυοειδής: *full of fish.*

ἰχναῖος, α, ον, (ἴχνος) *following on the track.*

ἰχνεία, ἡ, (ἰχνεύω) *a casting about for the scent.*

ἰχν-ελάτης, ου, ὁ, (ἴχνος, ἐλαύνω) *one who follows in the track, a tracker out.*

ἰχνεύμων, ονος, ὁ, (ἰχνεύω) *the tracker:* an Egyptian animal of the weasel kind, *the ichneumon* or *Pharaoh's rat, which hunts out* crocodiles' eggs.

ἴχνευσις, εως, ἡ, (ἰχνεύω) *a tracking.*

ἰχνευτής, οῦ, ὁ, *a tracker, hunter.* 2. *the ichneumon:* and

ἰχνευτικός, ή, όν, *good at tracking.* From

ἰχνεύω, f. σω, (ἴχνος) *to track* or *trace out, hunt after.*

ἴχνιον, τό, (ἴχνος) *a track, trace, footstep.*

ἰχνο-πέδη, ἡ, (ἴχνος, πέδη) a kind of *fetter* or *trap.*

ἼΧΝΟΣ, εος, τό, *a track, footstep:* metaph. *a track, trace, mark, clue.*

ἰχνο-σκοπέω, (ἴχνος, σκοπέω) *to examine the track.*

ΙΧΩΡ, ῶρος, ὁ, *ichor*, the fluid that flows in the veins of gods: Ep. acc. ἰχῶ, for ἰχῶρα.

ἴψ, ὁ, gen. ἰπός, nom. pl. ἶπες: (ἴπτομαι):—*a worm that eats horn and wood.* [ῐ]

ἴψαο, 2 sing. aor. 1 of ἴπτομαι.

ἴω, subj. of εἶμι *ibo.*

ἰῶ, contr for ἰάου, imperat. of ἰάομαι.

ἰώ, *io! O!* an exclamation of joy, as in Lat. *io triumphe!* but Att. also of fear, sorrow, etc., *oh!*

ἰώ, **ἰών**, **ἰώγα** and **ἰώνγα**, Boeot. for ἐγώ, ἐγών, and ἔγωγε.

ἰωγή, ἡ, (ἰέναι) *shelter;* Βορέω ὑπ' ἰωγῇ under *shelter from* the north wind.

ἰωή, ἡ, (ἰά, ἰώ) *any loud sound;* *the sound* of the lyre; *the roaring* or *whistling* of the wind; *the sound* of footsteps.

ἰῶκα, heterocl. acc. of ἰωκή, as if from ἰώξ.

ἰωκή, ἡ, (διώκω) *the battle-din, the rout, pursuit.*

ἰών, **ἰώνγα**, v. ἰώ, ἰών.

ἼΩΝ, ωνος, ὁ, *Ion*, son of Xuthus (or Apollo) and Creüsa, from whom sprung the Ionian race; οἱ Ἴωνες *the Ionians.* [ῑ]

ἰωνιά, ᾶς, ἡ, (ἴον) *a violet-bed*, Lat. *violarium.*

Ἰωνικός, ή, όν, (Ἴων) *Ionic, Ionian:*—Adv. -κῶς, *in the Ionic fashion, softly, effeminately.*

ἰῶτα, the smallest letter in the Greek alphabet, hence in N. T. *an iota, a jot.*

ἰωχμός, ὁ, = ἰωκή, ἀν' ἰωχμόν in *chase, pursuit.*

K

K, κ, κάππα, τό, indecl., tenth letter in Greek Alphabet. As numeral κ' = 20, but ˏκ = 20,000. κ is near akin to γ and χ; hence the older Att. changed χνόος into κνόος, γνάπτω into κνάπτω, ῥέγχω into ῥέγκω; so the Ion. χιτών into κιθών, δέχομαι into δέκομαι, etc.—γ before κ, as in ἄγκαθεν, is pronounced like our *ng.*

κᾶ, Dor. for the Ion. κε, = the Att. ἄν.

κάββἄλε, Ep. for κατέβαλε, aor. 2 of καταβάλλω.

καββάς, poët. for καταβάς, aor. 2 part. of καταβαίνω.

Κάβειροι, οἱ, *the Cabeiri*, divinities worshipped by the Pelasgians in Lemnos and Samothrace: they were represented as dwarfs, and were called sons of Hephaistos or Vulcan, as being masters in the art of working metals.

κάγ, Ep. for κατά before γ, as κὰγ γόνυ.

κάγκἄνος, ον, (καίω) *fit for burning, dry.*

καγχάζω, fut. άσω, = καχάζω. Hence

καγχἄλάω, *to laugh aloud*, Lat. *cachinnor;* Ep. 3 pl. καγχαλόωσιν; Ep. part. καγχαλόων, -όωσα.

κάγχρυς, see κάχρυς.

κἀγώ, crasis for καὶ ἐγώ.

κάδ, Ep. for κατά before δ, as κὰδ δέ.

καδδρἄθέτην, Ep. for κατεδραθέτην, 3 dual aor. 2 of καταδαρθάνω.

καδδύναμιν, Ep. for κατὰ δύναμιν.

καδδῦσαι, Ep. for καταδῦσαι, nom. pl. aor. 2 part. fem. of καταδύω.

καδεμών, Dor. for κηδέμων.

κἄδίσκος, ὁ, Dim. of κάδος: *the balloting-urn.*

Καδμεῖος, α, ον, (Κάδμος) *Cadmean*, οἱ Καδμεῖοι *the Cadmeans* or ancient inhabitants of Thebes; ἡ Καδμεία *the citadel of Thebes.* Proverbial, Καδμεία νίκη a *Cadmean* victory, i. e. dear-bought victory (from the story of Polynices and Eteocles).

Καδμείων, ωνος, ὁ, (Κάδμος) *a descendant of Cadmus, Theban.*

Καδμήϊος, η, ον, Ep. and Ion. for Καδμεῖος.

Καδμηΐς, ΐδος, Ep. and Ion. fem. of Καδμεῖος.

Κάδμος, ὁ, *Cadmos;* son of the Phoenician king Agenor, brother of Europa, founder of Thebes in Boeotia, who brought from Phoenicia the old Greek alphabet of sixteen letters, hence called Καδμήϊα γράμματα, which was afterwards increased by the eight Ionic, η ω θ φ χ ζ ξ ψ.

κάδος, ὁ, (χαδεῖν) *a pail, jar, cask*, Lat. *cadus*. II. *an urn* or *box for collecting the votes*. [ᾰ]

κᾶδος, εος, τό, Dor. for κῆδος.

Κάειρα, ἡ, fem. of Κάρ, *a Carian woman*. II. Adj. fem. for Καρική, *Carian*.

κᾰείς, aor. 2 part. pass. of καίω.

κᾰήμεναι, Ep. aor. 2 pass. inf. of καίω.

καήσομαι, fut. 2 pass. of καίω.

κᾰθά, Adv., contr. from κατά, ἅ, *according as*.

καθ-ᾰγίζω, f. ίσω Att. ιῶ, (κατά, ἁγίζω) *to devote* or *dedicate by fire*. II. *to burn as a sacrifice, burn as incense: devour*. Hence

καθᾰγισμός, ὁ, *a devoting* or *dedication by fire*. II. *a burning of a dead body: funeral rites*.

καθ-αγνίζω, f. ίσω Att. ιῶ, (κατά, ἁγνός) *to make pure, cleanse, hallow*. II. *to offer as an atonement* or *expiation*.

καθαιμακτός, όν, *bloodstained, bloody*. From

καθ-αιμάσσω, f. ξω, (κατά, αἱμάσσω) *to make bloody, stain with blood*.

καθ-αιμᾰτόω, = καθαιμάσσω.

καθαίρεσις, εως, ἡ, (καθαιρέω) *a putting down, destroying: a pulling down, demolishing*.

καθαιρετέος, έα, έον, and **καθαιρετός**, ά, όν, verb. Adj. of καθαιρέω, *to be put down: to be accomplished*.

καθαιρέτης, ου, ὁ, *a destroyer*. From

καθ-αιρέω Ion. **καταιρέω**: fut. ήσω: fut. 2 καθελῶ: aor. 2 καθεῖλον, inf. καθελεῖν:—*to take down*; καθελεῖν ἱστία *to lower* the sails; ὀφθαλμοὺς καθελεῖν *to close* the eyes of the dead; καθαιρεῖν σελήνην *to bring down* the moon, Lat. *coelo deducere lunam*: generally, *to take down* anything *hung up*; hence Med., καθαιρεῖσθαι τὰ τόξα *to take down* one's bow from the peg. 2. *to take down by force, pull down, overpower*: also *to demolish, destroy*: also *to humble, reduce*; esp. *to depose*: of a decree or resolution, *to cancel, rescind* it: as law-term, *to condemn*. 3. *to bring to an end, accomplish, achieve*: Med., καταιρέεσθαι μεγάλα πράγματα *to achieve* great feats. 4. like αἱρεῖν, *to take and carry off, seize*.

κᾰθαίρω, fut. κᾰθᾰρῶ: aor. 1 ἐκάθηρα:—Pass., aor. 1 ἐκαθάρθην: pf. κεκάθαρμαι: (καθαρός):—*to make pure* or *clean, cleanse*:—in religious sense, *to cleanse, purify, purge*: Med. *to have oneself purified*. II. *to purge off, wash away, to cleanse away, atone for, expiate*.

κᾰθ-άλλομαι, fut. -αλοῦμαι: aor. 1 καθηλάμην: Dep.:—*to leap down*, Lat. *desilire*: of a storm, *to rush down*.

κάθαμμα, ατος, τό, (καθάπτω) *anything tied, a knot*, κάθαμμα λύειν λόγου to untie a knotty point.

καθ-ανύω, Att. for κατανύω.

καθ-άπαξ, Adv. *once for all: altogether*.

καθά-περ Ion. **κατάπερ**, Adv. = καθά with enclit. περ, *even as, just as*.

καθαπτός, ή, όν, *fastened on* or *to*; καθαπτὸς δοραῖς *clad in* skins. From

καθ-άπτω, f. ψω: aor. 1 καθῆψα: (κατά, ἅπτω):—*to tie* or *fasten on*:—Pass., βρόχῳ καθημμένος (pf. part.) *fastened* or *attached to* a noose. 2. = καθάπτομαι, *to lay hold of*. II. Med. καθάπτομαι, fut. -άψομαι:—*to lay hold of, fasten upon*, esp. *to accost* one. 2. *to assail, attack, upbraid*. 3. *to appeal to one as witness, claim as a witness*, Lat. *antestari*.

κᾰθᾰρευτέον, *one must keep clean, be pure*, τινός from a thing; verb. Adj. from

κᾰθᾰρεύω, f. σω, (καθαρός) *to be clean* or *pure*: esp. *to be clear* or *free from guilt*.

κᾰθᾰρίζω, fut. ίσω Att. ιῶ, = καθαίρω, *to cleanse, purify, make clean*.

κᾰθάριος, ον, (καθαρός) *cleanly, neat*. Hence

κᾰθᾰριότης, ητος, ἡ, *cleanliness, neatness*.

κᾰθᾰρισμός, ὁ, (καθαρίζω) *a cleansing, purifying*.

κάθαρμα, ατος, τό, (καθαίρω) *that which is thrown away in cleansing*: in pl. *off-scourings, defilement*. II. metaph. *a worthless fellow, castaway, outcast*. III. *a space purified with proper rites*; ἐντὸς καθάρματος within *the purified ground*.

καθ-αρμόζω, f. σω, *to join* or *fit to*.

κᾰθαρμός, ὁ, (καθαίρω) *a cleansing, purifying*. 2. *an atonement, expiation*.

ΚᾸΘᾸΡΟ΄Σ, ά, όν, *clean, pure, spotless, unsoiled*, of garments. II. *clear, open, free*; ἐν καθαρῷ (sub. τόπῳ) in *an open* space, in a place *clear from dead bodies*; ἐν καθαρῷ ἡλίῳ in the *open* sun, opp. to the shade. III. in moral sense, *with clean hands, pure, free from offence*. IV. *pure, bright, clear*; hence *genuine, true*. V. generally, *perfect, complete, effective*; τὸ καθαρὸν τοῦ στρατοῦ *the portion* of the army *fit for service*. Hence

κᾰθᾰρότης, ητος, ἡ, *cleanness, purity*.

καθ-αρπάζω, fut. άσω or άξω, *to tear* or *snatch down*.

κᾰθάρσιος, ον, (καθαίρω) *cleansing, purifying, expiatory*. II. as Subst., τὸ καθάρσιον (sub. ἱερόν), *an expiatory sacrifice: purification, expiation*.

κάθαρσις, εως, ἡ, (καθαίρω) *a cleansing, purification*.

κᾰθαρτής, οῦ, ὁ, (καθαίρω) *a cleanser, purifier*.

καθεδοῦμαι, fut. of καθέζομαι.

καθ-έδρα, (κατά, ἕδρα) ἡ, *a seat*; ἡ καθέδρα τοῦ λαγῶ the hare's *seat* or *form*. II. *a sitting still, lounging, delaying*.

καθ-έζομαι: impf. καθεζόμην, but also ἐκαθεζόμην (as if the Verb were not a compd.): fut. καθεδοῦμαι: aor. 1 part. καθεσθείς: Dep.:—*to sit down, sit still, to linger, tarry*: *to sit* as suppliants: of an army, *to sit down in a country, take up a position*.

καθέηκα, Ep. and Ion. aor. 1 of καθίημι.

καθείατο, Ep. for ἐκάθηντο, 3 pl. impf. of κάθημαι.

καθεῖλον, aor. 2 of καθαιρέω.

καθεῖμαι, pf. pass. of καθίημι.

καθ-είργνῡμι and **καθείργω**, Att. for κατ-: f. -είρξω; aor. 1 -εῖρξα: (κατά, εἵργω):—*to shut up, enclose, confine*.

καθ-εῖς, for καθ' εἷς, *one by one, one after another*; also εἷς καθεῖς, for εἷς καθ' ἕνα.

καθεῖσα, Ep. aor. 1 of καθίζω.

καθεκτός, ή, όν, (κατέχω) *to be held back.*

καθελεῖν, aor. 2 inf. of καθαιρέω.

καθ-ελίσσω, f ξω, *to wrap round, infold:* Ion. plqpf. pass. κατειλίχατο, for καθειλιγμένοι ἦσαν.

καθ-έλκω, f. -έλξω or -ελκύσω (as if from -ελκύω): aor. 1 καθείλκὕσα: pf. καθείλκὕκα:—Pass., aor. 1 καθειλκύσθην: pf. καθείλκυσμαι:—*to draw down,* esp. of ships, *to launch*, Lat. *deduco.*

καθελοῖσα, Dor. for καθελοῦσα, fem. of καθελών.

καθελῶ, fut. of καθαιρέω.

καθελών, aor. 2 part. of καθαιρέω.

καθ-έννῡμι, *to clothe;* see καταέννυμι.

καθεξῆς, Adv. (κατά, ἔχω) *in order, in succession.*

κάθεξις, εως, ἡ, (κατέχω) *a holding, keeping hold of.*

καθέξω, fut. of κατέχω.

κάθ-ερμα, ατος, τό, (κατά, ἕρμα) *a necklace.*

καθ-έρπω, f. -ερπύσω (as if from -ερπύω): aor. 1 καθείρπὕσα: (κατά, ἕρπω):—*to creep* or *steal down:* metaph. of the first down, *to steal down the cheek.*

κάθες, aor. 2 imperat. of καθίημι.

καθεσθείς, aor. 1 part. pass. of καθέζομαι.

καθέσταμεν, Ep. 1 pl. pf. of καθίστημι.

καθεστηκώς, υῖα, ός, pf. part. of καθίστημι.

καθεστήξω, fut. 3 of καθίστημι, with intr. sense.

καθεστῶτα, ων, τά, syncop. part. pf. plur. neut. of καθίστημι, *existing laws, customs, usages.*

καθ-εύδω: impf. Ep. καθεῦδον, Att. also καθηῦδον and ἐκάθευδον: fut. καθευδήσω:—*to lie down to sleep, sleep, slumber:* metaph. *to rest, be at rest.*

καθ-ευρίσκω, f. -ρήσω, *to find out, discover.*

καθ-εψιάομαι, f. -ήσομαι, (κατά, ἐψιάομαι): Dep.: —*to mock at, deride;* Ep. 3 pl. κατεψιόωνται.

καθ-έψω, fut. -εψήσω, (κατά, ἕψω) *to boil down, digest.* II. metaph. *to soften, temper.*

κάθῃ, Att. for κάθησαι, 2 sing. of κάθημαι.

καθηγεμών, όνος, ὁ, ἡ, (κατά, ἡγεμών) *a leader, guide.*

καθ-ηγέομαι, f. -ήσομαι: (κατά, ἡγέομαι): Dep.: —*to lead the way, be guide:* hence *to shew the way in doing a thing, to establish, ordain, to dictate, prescribe,* Lat. *praeire verbis.* Hence

καθηγητής, οῦ, ὁ, *a leader, guide, teacher.*

καθήγισα, aor. 1 of καθαγίζω.

καθήγνισα, aor. 1 of καθαγνίζω.

καθ-ηδῠπᾰθέω, f. ήσω, (κατά, ἡδυπαθέω) *to squander in luxury.*

καθῆκα, aor. 1 of καθίημι.

καθ-ήκω, f. ξω, (κατά, ἥκω) *to come* or *go down, go down to fight.* 2. *to come down to, come* or *reach to, extend to.* II. *to reach as far as, to suffice* or *be enough for* a thing: *to be meet, proper.* 2. part., τὸ καθῆκον, οντος. and τὰ καθήκοντα, *that which is meet* or *proper, one's duty:* but also τὰ καθήκοντα = τὰ καθεστῶτα, *the present state of things, circumstances.*

καθ-ηλιάζω, (κατά, ἥλιος) *to bring the sun in upon, to illuminate.*

κάθ-ημαι: imperat. κάθησο; subj. κάθωμαι; opt. καθοίμην; inf. καθῆσθαι; part. καθήμενος: impf. ἐκαθήμην:—properly perf. of καθέζομαι, *to have seated oneself, to be seated, sit:* of judges, *to have taken their seats in court:* generally, *to take up one's abode, sojourn, dwell:* in bad sense, *to sit idle, be listless, lie unemployed:* of an army, *to encamp: to lie in wait.*

καθ-ημέριος, α, ον, also **καθημερινός**, ή, όν, (καθ' ἡμέραν) *happening every day, daily.*

κάθηρα, Ep. for ἐκάθηρα, aor. 1 of καθαίρω.

κάθησθε, 2 pl. of κάθημαι: but **καθῆσθε**, 2 pl. Ep. impf. of same.

κάθησο, imperat. of κάθημαι:—**καθῆστο**, 3 sing. impf.

καθηῦδον, impf. of καθεύδω.

καθ-ιδρύω, f. ύσω [ῡ]:—Causal of καθέζομαι, *to make to sit down, set down: to establish, institute:* of sacred things, *consecrate:*—Pass. *to sit down, settle.*

καθ-ίεμαι, Pass. of καθίημι.

καθ-ῑερόω, f. ώσω, *to dedicate, consecrate, devote, hallow.*

καθ-ιζάνω, (κατά, ἵζω) *to sit down.*

καθίζεο, Dor. for καθίζου, med. imperat. of sq.

καθ-ίζω: impf. καθῖζον or κάθιζον Att. ἐκάθιζον (as if the Verb were not a compd.): fut. καθίσω Att. καθιῶ Dor. καθίξω: aor. 1 ἐκάθῑσα Dor. κάθιξα, Ep. part. καθίσσας: another Ep. form of aor. 1 is καθεῖσα, also written καθῖσα, always used in Causal sense: (κατά, ἵζω): I. Causal, *to make to sit down;* ἀγορὰς καθίσαι *to make* an assembly *be seated*, i. e. *open* one: generally, *to set, appoint, constitute.* 2. *to place* or *settle in* a place, *establish.* 3. *to place* one *in a certain condition, make* one so *and* so. II. intr. *to sit down, be seated, sit,* esp. *to sit at meals:* of an army, *to sit down in a country, encamp.*

καθ-ίημι, fut. καθήσω: aor. 1 καθῆκα Ep. καθέηκα: pf. καθεῖκα, pass. καθεῖμαι: (κατά, ἵημι):—*to send down, let down, let fall,* Lat. *demitto;* καθιέναι τὴν ἄγκυραν *to let go* the anchor; καθιέναι καταπειρητηρίην, *to let down* a sounding-line, hence absol., καθιέναι *to sound:*—metaph. *to put forward, attempt:* —Pass. *to be carried down, reach* or *stretch down seawards;* καθεῖτο τὰ τείχη the walls *were carried down to the sea.* II. *to send down into the place of contest, enter for a contest.* III. intr. *to come down upon, attack.*

καθίκεο, 2 sing. aor. 2 of καθικνέομαι.

καθ-ῑκετεύω, *to intreat earnestly.*

καθ-ικνέομαι, fut. -ίξομαι: aor. 2 -ῑκόμην: (κατά, ἱκνέομαι): Dep.:—*to come down, come to, reach to:* hence *to touch, probe.*

καθ-ιμάω, f. ήσω, (κατά, ἱμάω) *to let down by a rope.*

καθίξας, Dor. for καθίσας, aor. 1 part. of καθίζω.

καθίξῃ, Dor. for καθίσῃ, 2 sing. aor. 1 of καθίζω.

καθ-ιππάζομαι, f. -άσομαι: Dep.:—*to ride down, overrun with horse:* generally, *to trample down.*

καθ-ιππεύω, f. σω, *to ride down, trample under foot.*

καθῖσα, Att. aor. 1 of καθίζω.

καθίστα or **-τη**, for καθίσταθ imperat. of καθίστημι.

καθ-ιστάνω and **καθ-ιστάω**, forms of the pres. καθίστημι.

καθ-ίστημι. I. in Causal sense. pres. *καθί-στημι*, impf. *καθίστην*, fut. *καταστήσω*, aor. 1 *κατέ-στησα*: so also of the Med., pres. *καθιστάμαι*, impf. *καθιστάμην*, aor. 1 *κατεστησάμην*:—*to set down, put down: bring down to* a place *and set* there; *κατα-στῆσαι νῆα to bring* a ship *to land, put in.* 2. *to settle, ordain, appoint, establish, put in train:* generally, *to set in order, arrange:* also *to restore:*—Med. *to appoint for oneself, choose: to make* or *render so and so, bring into a certain state.* II. Intrans. in aor. 2 *κατέστην*, pf. *καθέστηκα*, plqpf. *καθεστήκειν*, and in all tenses of Pass.:—*to be placed, set down: to settle oneself.* 2. *to be set, established, appointed.* 3. *to stand quiet* or *calm; πνεῦμα καθ-εστηκὸς* a calm: of persons, *to become calm and composed.* 4. *to be in a certain state; εὖ καταστῆναι to come to a* good *issue.* 5. *to be usual* or *customary; to be* or *become: καθεστηκώς* Ion. *κατεστεώς, existing, established; τὰ καθεστῶτα existing laws, customs, usages.*

καθιστῶντες, pres. part. pl. of *καθιστάω*.

καθ-ό, Adv. for *καθ' ὅ, in so far as, according as.*

καθολικός, *ή, όν*. (*κάθολος*) *general, universal.*

καθ-όλου, for *καθ' ὅλου*, as Adv. *on the whole, in general, generally.*

καθ-ομολογέω, f. *ήσω*, (*κατά. ὁμολογέω*) *to confess.* II. *to promise, engage.*

καθ-οπλίζω, f. *ίσω* Att. *ιῶ. to equip* or *array fully.*

καθ-οράω: f. *κατόψομαι* formed from *κατόπτομαι*: pf. *καθεόρακα*: aor. 2 *κατεῖδον*, inf. *κατιδεῖν* (cf. *εἶ-δον*):—*to look down* II. trans. *to look down upon:* generally, *to view, see, behold: to perceive, observe.*

καθ-ορμάω, f. *ήσω*, *to set in motion, impel.*

καθ-ορμίζω, f. *ίσω* Att. *ιῶ*:—*to bring into harbour, bring to anchor* or *moorage:* and in Pass., with aor. 1 med. *καθωρμισάμην, to come into harbour, put in.* 2. generally, *to bring into* a certain condition.

καθ-οσιόω, f. *ώσω*. (*κατά, ὅσιός*) *to offer sacrifice:* —so also in Med. *to offer on one's own part.*

καθ-ότι, used as Adv. for *καθ' ὅτι, in what manner.*

καθοῦ, for *καθέσο*, aor. 2 med. imperat. of *καθίημι*.

καθ-υβρίζω, f. *ίσω* Att. *ιῶ, to treat despitefully, to insult wantonly.* II. absol. *to wax insolent.*

κάθ-υδρος, *ον*, (*κατά, ὕδωρ*) *full of water; κάθυδρος κρατήρ* a cup *of water*, periphr. for *water* itself.

καθ-υμνέω, f. *ήσω*, *to sing of, to descant upon*

καθ-υπερἄκοντίζω. f. *ίσω*, (*κατά, ὑπερ-ακοντίζω*):—*to shoot beyond* another, *excel in shooting.*

καθ-ύπερθε, before a vowel **-θεν**, (*κατά, ὕπερθε*) Adv. *from above, down from above* 2. *on the upper side, above;* c. gen., *καθύπερθε Χίου above* Chios. 3. of Time, *before.*

καθ-ὑπέρτερος. *α, ον*, Comp. of *καθύπερθε, upper, higher, above:* of persons, *having the upper hand, superior.* Sup. **καθυπέρτατος**, *η, ον*, *highest, uppermost*

καθ-υπισχνέομαι, Dep. *to promise earnestly.*

καθ-υπνόω. f. *ώσω*, *to be fast asleep:* also in Med.

καθ-υποκρίνομαι: Dep. (*κατά, ὑποκρίνομαι*):—*to deceive by false appearances.* II. c. inf. *to pretend to be other than* one is, *personate* some person or thing.

καθ-υφίημι, fut. *-υφήσω*: (*κατά, ὑφίημι*):—*let loose, let go,* hence *to give up, betray.* 2. intr. *to slacken one's exertions.* 3. Med., *καθυφίεσθαί τινι to give way, yield:* also *to slacken in one's exertions.*

κάθωμαι, subj. of *κάθημαι*,

καθώς, Adv. (*κατά, ὡς*) *according as, as.*

ΚΑΙ', Conjunct., *and, also* I. joining words and sentences, like Lat. *et*, while enclit. *τε* answers to Lat. *que:* when in Prose two words or clauses are closely combined, *τε καί* are often used, *ἄρκτοι τε καὶ λέοντες* bears and lions, *both as creatures of one kind; θαυμάζονται ὡς σοφοί τε καὶ εὐτυχεῖς γεγενη-μένοι* they are admired *both* as wise *and* fortunate. II. *also*, used to make a single word or clause emphatic, *ἔπειτά με καὶ λίποι αἰών* then let life *also* forsake me. 2. with Participles or Adjectives, *καί* may be rendered by *though, although, albeit*, as, *Ἕκτορα, καὶ μεμαῶτα, μάχης σχήσεσθαι ὀΐω*, Hector will I keep away, *how much soever* or *although* he rage. 3. *even*, to increase or diminish the force of words, esp. with a Comp., as, *θεὸς καὶ ἀμείνονας ἵππους δωρήσαιτο*; *καί* is often used in this way before *οὗτος*; with neut. pl., *καὶ ταῦτα and that, and besides, especially; τί γὰρ δεινότερον δικαστοῦ, καὶ ταῦτα γέροντος*; for what is worse than a judge, *and that* an old one (i. e. *especially* an old one). 4. so also in diminishing, *ἱέμενος καὶ καπνὸν ἀποθρώσκοντα νοῆ-σαι* he longs to see *even* the smoke rising, i. e. *were it but* the smoke, *only* the smoke; *οἷς ἡδὺ καὶ λέγειν* with whom 'tis sweet *only* to speak. III. *as*, after *ὅμοιος, ἴσος, ὁ αὐτός*, like Lat. *ac, atque* after *aeque, simul, perinde*, etc.; *γνώμῃσι ἐχρέοντο ὁμοίῃσι καὶ σύ* they held the same opinion *as* you. IV. of number, *about*; *καὶ ἐς ἑβδομήκοντα about* to the number of 70.

καιάδας, *ου*, Dor. *α, ὁ*, *a chasm* or *underground cavern* at Sparta, into which state-criminals were thrown, like the Athenian *βάραθρον*. (Lacon. word.)

καὶ γάρ, *for truly*, to confirm a prop. which of itself is tolerably certain; *καὶ γὰρ δή for of a surety.*

καί . . γε, *and indeed.* Lat. *et .. quidem*, to introduce something more emphatic; *καὶ λίην κεῖνός γε ἐοι-κότι κεῖται ὀλέθρῳ and indeed* very deserved. **Γε** is always separated from *καί* by one or more words.

καὶ δή, *and even. also even.* II. *and indeed, certainly:* in answers. *yes indeed, by all means.* Lat. *et certe, et vero.* III. *supposing it to be the case*, Lat. *fac ita esse.* IV. *καὶ δὴ καί, and besides that also, and moreover.*

καὶ εἰ, *even if, although, supposing that*, where the thing may really exist or not: whereas with *εἰ καί* the thing is supposed as existing.

καιέμεν, Ep. for *καίειν*.

καί κε, καί κεν, Ep. for *καὶ ἄν, κἄν.*

καικίας, ου, ὁ, *the north-east wind.*

καὶ μάλα, καὶ μάλα γε, *aye and very much.*

καὶ μήν, *and verily, and certainly*, Lat. *et vero.* II. *and further, and besides.* III. in answers, *well, be it so.*

καινίζω, f. ίσω Att. ιῶ, (καινός) *to make new, to have new; καί τι καινίζει στέγη* the house *has something new* about it; *καίνισον ζυγόν bear* thy *new* yoke; *καινίσαι εὐχάς to offer strange, new-fangled prayers.*

καινο-πᾰθής, ές, (καινός, παθεῖν) *newly suffered, never before suffered.*

καινο-πηγής, ές, (καινός, πήγνυμι) *newly fastened, new-made.*

καινο-πήμων, ον, gen. ονος, (καινός, πῆμα) *newly suffering, new to suffering.*

καινο-ποιέω, f. ήσω, (καινός, ποιέω) *to make new, renew:* in Pass., τί καινοποιηθὲν λέγεις; what *new phrases* art thou using? Hence

καινοποιητής, οῦ, ὁ, *an inventor of new pleasures.*

ΚΑΙΝΟ'Σ, ή, όν, *new, fresh*, Lat. *recens; καινοὶ λόγοι news; ἐκ καινῆς* (sub. ἀρχῆς) *anew, afresh*, Lat. *de novo.* II. *newly introduced, new-fangled, strange; καινοὶ θεοὶ strange* gods.

καινό-τᾰφος, ον, (καινός, τάφος) *of a new tomb.*

καινότης, ητος, ἡ, (καινός) *newness, freshness: novelty.*

καινοτομέω, f. ήσω, (καινοτόμος) *to cut fresh into;* in mining, *to open a new vein:* metaph. *to begin something new, institute anew; to make innovations* in the state, Lat. *res novas tentare.* Hence

καινοτομία, ἡ, *a cutting anew: innovation.*

καινο-τόμος, ον, (καινός, τεμεῖν) *cutting newly: beginning something new, innovating.*

καινουργέω, f. ήσω, (καινουργός) *to make new.* II. *to innovate, make innovations.* Hence

καινουργία, ἡ, *innovation.*

καιν-ουργός, όν, (καινός, *ἔργω) *making new, innovating: τὸ καινουργόν a novelty.*

καινόω, f. ώσω, (καινός) *to make new, innovate:*—Pass. *to become fond of novelty* or *innovation.* II. *to devote anew, consecrate, dedicate.*

καί νύ κε, *and now perhaps.*

ΚΑΙ'ΝΥΜΑΙ, impf. ἐκαινύμην [ῠ]: pf. (in pres. sense) κέκασμαι Dor. κέκαδμαι, plqpf. (in impf. sense) ἐκεκάσμην, formed as if from κάζω:—*to surpass, excel; ἐκαίνῠτο φῦλ' ἀνθρώπων κυβερνῆσαι he surpassed* mankind in steering; ἐγχείῃ ἐκέκαστο Πανέλληνας *he excelled* all the Greeks in throwing the spear; so in part., δόλοισι κεκασμένος *surpassing all* in wiles; but κεκασμένος also *well-furnished.*

καὶ νῦν, *and now, even now.*

ΚΑΙ'ΝΩ, fut. κᾰνῶ: aor. 2 ἔκᾰνον, inf. κᾰνεῖν: pf. κέκονα:—*to kill, slay, slaughter.*

καί-περ, (καί περ) *although, albeit.*

καὶ πῶς; *and how? but how?* when a thing is supposed to be impossible: only interrog.

καί ῥα, Ep. *and then, and so.*

καίριος, α, ον, also ος, ον, (καιρός): *in season, seasonable, happening at the right* or *critical time*, Lat. *opportunus:*—also *lasting for a season.* II. of Place, *in* or *at the right* or *critical place;* of the parts of the body, *vital; ἐν καιρίῳ* or *κατὰ καίριον in a vital part:*—of wounds, *deadly, mortal; καιρία* (sub. πληγή) *a mortal wound:* generally, τὰ *καίρια accidents.* Hence

καιρίως, Adv. *seasonably.* II. *mortally.*

ΚΑΙΡΟ'Σ, ὁ, *due measure, right proportion, fitness; καιροῦ πέρα* beyond *measure, unduly.* II. of Time, *the right season, the right time for action, the critical moment*, Lat. *opportunitas:* generally, *convenience, advantage, profit; πρὸς καιρόν*, or absol. *καιρόν, at the right* or *proper time, in season, opportunely; ἐν καιρῷ τινι εἶναι* or *γίγνεσθαι* to suit one's convenience, be of service to him; *κατὰ καιρόν in due season*, Lat. *dextro tempore;* but, ἀπό or ἄνευ καιροῦ or παρὰ καιρόν, *out of season*, Lat. *alieno tempore.* III. of Place, *the right point, right spot:* also *a vital part* of the body.

ΚΑΙ'ΡΟΣ, ὁ, *the webbing* or *thrums to which the threads of the warp are fastened.* Hence

καιροσέων, a gen. pl. in Od. 7. 107, καιροσέων ὀθονέων ἀπολείβεται ὑγρὸν ἔλαιον from *the close-woven* linen-cloths trickles off the liquid oil. It seems to be for καιροέσσων, gen. pl. fem. of καιρόεις.

καιρο-φῠλᾰκέω, f. ήσω, (καιρός, φυλακή) *to watch for the right time*, Lat. *tempora observare.*

καὶ ταῦτα, *and that, and besides, especially.*

καί τοι or **καί-τοι**, *and indeed: and yet, although.*

ΚΑΙ'Ω Att. **κάω** [ᾱ]: impf. ἔκαιον Att. ἔκᾱον Ep. κεῖον: fut. καύσω: aor. 1 ἔκαυσα, Att. also ἔκεα, Ep. ἔκηα or ἔκεια (or without augm. κῆα, κεῖα):—Pass., aor. 1 ἐκαύθην: aor. 2 ἐκάην: pf. κέκαυμαι: I. *to burn, kindle, set on fire:*—Med. *to kindle fires for oneself:*—Pass. *to be set on fire, take fire, burn.* II. *to burn up, consume: to scorch, shrivel up.*

κάκ, Ep. for κατά before κ, as in κὰκ κεφαλῆς.

κἀκ, crasis for καὶ ἐκ.

κᾰκ-άγγελος, ον, (κακά, ἀγγέλλω) *bringing ill tidings.*

κᾰκ-άγγελτος, ον, (κακά, ἀγγέλλω) *caused by ill tidings; κακάγγελτα ἄχη* the sorrow *of ill tidings.*

κακ-άγορος, Dor. for κακήγορος.

κακ-ανδρία, ἡ, (κακός, ἀνήρ) *unmanliness, cowardice.*

κἀκεῖ, by crasis for καὶ ἐκεῖ, *and there, there also.*

κἀκεῖνος, κἀκεῖνον, by crasis for καὶ ἐκεῖνος, etc.

κᾰκ-εστώ, οῦς, ἡ, (κακός, εἰμί *sum*), *ill-being*, opp. to εὐεστώ *well-being.*

κάκη, ἡ, (κακός) *badness, baseness: cowardice.*

κᾰκηγορέω, f. ήσω, (κακήγορος) *to speak ill of, abuse, slander.* Hence

κᾰκηγορία, ἡ, *evil-speaking, abuse, slander, calumny; κακηγορίας δίκη* an action *for defamation.*

κᾰκ-ήγορος, ον, (κακός, ἀγορεύω) *evil-speaking, abusive, slanderous, calumnious:*—irreg. Comp. and Sup. κακηγορίστερος, -ίστατος.

κᾰκία, ἡ, (κακός) *badness, baseness, cowardice*, **Lat.**

malitia. 2. wickedness vice. Lat. pravitas. II. disgrace, dishonour.

κᾰκίζω, f. ίσω Att. ιῶ, (κακός) to make or think bad, to abuse, blame, reproach. II. to make cowardly:—Pass. to behave basely, play the coward:—to be worsted.

κάκιστος, η, ον, irreg. Sup. of κακός.

κᾰκίων, ον, gen. ονος, irreg. Comp. of κακός. [ῐ Ep., ῑ in Att. poets.]

κακκάω, (κάκκη) the Lat. cacare.

κακκεῖαι, Ep. for κατακεῖαι, aor. 1 inf. of κατακαίω.

κακκείοντες, Ep. κατακείοντες, part. of κατακείω.

κακ-κεφᾰλῆς, better divisim κὰκ κεφαλῆς, Ep. for κατὰ κεφαλῆς

ΚΑ'ΚΚΗ, ἡ, human ordure, dung.

κακκῆαι Ep. κατακῆαι, aor. 1 inf. of κατακαίω.

κακκόρυθα, κακκορυφήν, better divisim κὰκ κόρ-, Ep. for κατὰ κορύθα, κατὰ κορυφήν.

κακ-κρύπτω, Ep. for κατα-κρύπτω.

κακ-κῠνηγέτις, ιδος, ἡ, for κατακυνηγέτις.

κᾰκό-βῐος, ον, (κακός, βίος) living badly, living a hard life, faring hardly.

κᾰκοβουλεύομαι, Med. to act unwisely. From

κᾰκό-βουλος, ον, (κακός, βουλή) ill-advised, unwise.

κᾰκο-γείτων, ον, gen. ονος, (κακός, γείτων) a bad neighbour, or a neighbour in misery.

κᾰκό-γλωσσος, ον, (κακός, γλῶσσα) ill-tongued; βοὴ κακόγλωσσος a cry full of misery 2. slanderous.

κᾰκοδαιμονάω, (κακοδαίμων) to be tormented by an evil genius, be like one possessed.

κᾰκοδαιμονέω, f. ήσω, (κακοδαίμων) to be unhappy or unfortunate. Hence

κᾰκοδαιμονία ἡ, unhappiness, misfortune. II. a being possessed by a demon, raving madness.

κᾰκο-δαίμων, ον, gen. ονος, (κακός, δαίμων) having an evil genius, ill-starred, ill-fated, unhappy, wretched. II as Subst. an evil genius.

κᾰκοδοξέω, f. ήσω, (κακόδοξος) to be in ill repute.

κᾰκοδοξία, ἡ, (κακόδοξος) ill repute, infamy.

κᾰκό-δοξος, ον, (κακός, δόξα) in ill-repute. without fame, unknown. II. infamous.

κᾰκο-δρομία, ἡ, (κακός, δρόμος) a bad passage.

κᾰκο-είμων, ον, gen. ονος, (κακός, εἷμα) ill-clad.

κᾰκοεργία, ἡ, poët. for κακ-ουργία, ill-doing. From

κᾰκο-εργός, όν, (κακός, *ἔργω) doing ill; κακόεργος γαστήρ the importunate stomach, like Lat. fames improba.

κᾰκο-ζοΐα, ἡ, (κακός, ζοΐα poët. for ζωή) a miserable life.

κᾰκοήθεια, ἡ, badness of disposition, maliciousness II. bad manners or habits. From

κᾰκο-ήθης, ες, (κακός, ἦθος) of ill habits, ill-disposed, malicious: τὸ κακόηθες an ill habit, Lat. scribendi cacoëthes, an itch for writing.

κᾰκοθημοσύνη, ἡ, disorderliness. From

κᾰκο-θήμων, ον, gen. ονος, (κακός, τίθημι) ill-arranged, disorderly, careless.

κᾰκό-θροος, ον, contr. -θρους, ουν, (κακός, θρόος) speaking ill; λόγος κακόθρους a slanderous word.

Κᾰκο-ΐλιος, ἡ, = κακὴ Ἴλιος, evil or unhappy Ilium.

κᾰκοκέρδεια, ἡ, base love of gain. From

κᾰκο-κερδής, ές, (κακός, κέρδος) making base gain.

κακό-κνᾱμος, ον, (κακός, κνήμη) Dor. form, thin-legged.

κᾰκο-κρῐσία, ἡ, (κακός, κρίνω) a bad judgment.

κᾰκο-λογέω, (κακολόγος) to speak ill of rail at. Hence

κᾰκολογια, ἡ, evil-speaking, railing, abuse.

κᾰκο-λόγος, ον, (κακός, λέγω) evil-speaking, railing, slanderous, abusive.

κᾰκό-μαντις, εως, ὁ, ἡ, = κακὸς μάντις, prophet of ill.

κᾰκο-μέλετος, ον, (κακός, μέλος) ill-sounding.

κᾰκομετρέω, f. ήσω, to give bad measure. From

κᾰκό-μετρος, ον, (κακός, μέτρον) in bad measure.

κᾰκο-μηδής, ές, (κακός, μῆδος) contriving ill, crafty.

κᾰκο-μήτης, ου, ὁ, (κακός, μῆτις) = κακομηδής.

κᾰκομηχανέω, f. ήσω, (κακομήχανος) to practise base arts. Hence

κᾰκομηχᾰνία, ἡ, a practising of base arts, ingenuity in mischief.

κᾰκο-μήχᾰνος, ον, (κακός, μηχανή) mischief-plotting, mischievous, malicious.

κᾰκό-μοιρος, ον, (κακος, μοιρα) ill-fated.

κᾰκό-μορφος, ον, (κακός, μορφή) ill-shapen.

κακό-νοιᾰ, η, (κακόνους) illwill, malice, opp. to εὔνοια.

κᾰκονομια, ἡ, a bad system of laws, a bad constitution, bad government. From

κᾰκό-νομος, ον, (κακός, νόμος) with bad laws, with a bad constitution, ill-governed.

κᾰκό-νοος, ον; contr. -νους, ουν, pl. κακόνοι; (κακός, νόος) ill-disposed: disaffected: bearing malice against one. Comp. and Sup. κακονούστερος, -νούστατος.

κᾰκο-νυμφος, ον, (κακός, νύμφη) ill-wedded. II. as Subst., κακόνυμφος, ὁ, a bad or unhappy bridegroom.

κᾰκό-ξενος Ion. -ξεινος, ον, (κακός, ξένος) having ill guests: irreg. Ep. Comp. κακοξεινώτερος. II. unfriendly to guests, inhospitable.

κᾰκο-ξύνετος, ον, (κακός, ξυνετός) wise only for evil.

κᾰκοπάθεια, ἡ, (κακοπαθής) ill plight, distress.

κᾰκοπᾰθέω, f. ήσω, to suffer ill; to be distressed. From

κᾰκο-παθής, ές, (κακός, παθεῖν) suffering ill, distressed.

κᾰκο-πᾰρθενος, ον, (κακός, παρθένος) unbecoming a maid.

κᾰκό-πατρις, ιδος, ὁ, ἡ, (κακός, πατήρ) having a low-born father, of low descent.

κᾰκο-πῖνής, ές, (κακός, πίνος) foul and loathsome.

κᾰκοποιέω, f. ήσω, (κακοποιός) to do ill, be a rogue. II. trans. to hurt, spoil, lay waste. Hence

κᾰκοποιΐα, ἡ, ill doing, damage.

κᾰκο-ποιός, όν, (κακός, ποιέω) doing ill, mischievous.

κᾰκό-ποτμος, ον, (κακός, πότμος) ill-fated.

κό-πους, ὁ, ἡ, πουν, τό, gen. ποδος, (κακός, πούς) bad feet, weak in the feet.

κο-πρᾶγέω, f. ήσω, (κακός, πρᾶγος) to be ill off, badly, fail in an enterprise. Hence

κοπρᾶγία, ἡ, ill-success, failure.

κο-πράγμων, ον, gen. ονος, (κακός, πρᾶγμα) doing, mischievous.

κό-πτερος, ον, (κακός, πτερόν) ill-omened.

κορ-ρᾰφία, ἡ, (κακός, ῥάπτω) contrivance of ill, chievousness. 2. ill contrivance, unskilfulness.

κορ-ρήμων, ον, (κακός, ῥῆμα) evil-speaking. II. ng of ill, ill-omened.

κορ-ροθέω, f. ήσω, (κακός, ῥόθος) to speak evil: peak evil of a person, abuse, revile him.

κόρ-ρῡπος, ον, (κακός, ῥύπος) foul and filthy.

ΑΚΟ΄Σ, ή, όν, bad, ill, evil, bad in its kind, worth-: ugly, as opp. to καλός. 2. bad at one's trade; ὸς ἀλήτης a bad beggar: cowardly, faint-hearted; κάκη. 3. of low birth, mean, vile. 4. in a ral sense, bad, evil, wicked. 5. of things, bad, , mischievous: of omens, unlucky, ill-boding: of rds, evil, abusive, foul. II. as Subst. κακόν, evil, ill, mischief: also woe, distress, loss: bodily ill, injury. 2. in moral sense, evil, , wickedness; κακόν τι ἔρδειν to do evil or to any one. III. Degrees of Comparison:— g. Comp. κακίων, ον, Sup. κάκιστος, η, ον: but ρων χείριστος, ἥσσων ἥκιστος are also used as mp. and Sup. of κακός. IV. in Compos. it netimes expresses the fault of excess, and so = ν, Lat. nimis: but commonly it gives a collat. ion of hurtful, unlucky, = δυσ-, as in κακό-σιvος: netimes it marks defect of a property, as in κακό-τος: sometimes it is used like the simple Adj., as κο-ίλιος for κακὸς Ἴλιος.

ικο-σκελής, ές, (κακός, σκέλος) with bad legs.

ικο-σκηνής, ές, (κακός, σκῆνος) of a bad, mean body.

ικ-οσμος, ον, (κακός, ὀσμή) ill-smelling,

ικό-σπλαγχνος, ον, (κακός, σπλάγχνον) faint-rted, cowardly.

ικο-σπορία, ἡ, (κακός, σπόρος) a bad crop.

ικοστομέω, f. ήσω, to speak evil of. From

ικό-στομος, ον, (κακός, στόμα) evil-speaking, foul-uthed.

ακό-στρωτος, ον, (κακός, στρώννυμι) ill-spread, gged.

ακο-σύνθετος, ον, (κακός, συντίθημι) ill put toge-r, ill composed:

ακό-σχολος, ον, (κακός, σχολή) inactive, idle, y. II. act., κακόσχολοι πνοαί winds that ar men out in idleness.

ακοτεχνέω, f. ησω, (κακότεχνος) to practise bad ts, be guilty of mal-practices, act basely, Lat. male ago. Hence

ακοτεχνία, ἡ, the practice of bad arts, mal-practice, . forgery, malversation.

ακό-τεχνος, ον, (κακός, τέχνη) using bad arts or l-practices, artful, wily.

κᾰκότης, ητος, ἡ, (κακός) badness, baseness, cowardice, like κάκη. II. moral badness, wickedness, worthlessness. III. evil, distress, suffering.

κᾰκοτροπία, ἡ, bad habits, maliciousness, wickedness. From

κᾰκό-τροπος, ον, (κακός, τρόπος) of ill habits, mischievous, malignant.

κᾰκοτῠχέω, f. ήσω. to be unfortunate. From

κᾰκο-τῠχής, ές, (κακός, τύχη) unfortunate.

κᾰκουργέω, f. ήσω, (κακοῦργος) to do evil or mischief, to be an evil-doer: c. acc. to do evil to one, to damage, hurt, harm: to ravage a country. Hence

κᾰκουργία Ep. **κακοεργίη** [ῑ], ἡ the character of an evil-doer, wickedness, villany. From

κᾰκ-οῦργος Ep. **κακό-εργος**, ον, (κακός, *ἔργω) doing ill, knavish, villanous: as Subst. an evil-doer, knave: an offender, criminal. II. doing harm to one, damaging, hurtful.

κᾰκ-ουχέω, f. ήσω, (κακός. ἔχω) to treat ill, wrong, hurt, injure. Hence

κᾰκουχία, ἡ, ill-treatment, ill-conduct; κακουχία χθονός the devastation of a country.

κᾰκό-φᾰτις, ιδος, ἡ, (κακός, φάτις) sounding ill, ill-omened.

κᾰκο-φρᾰδής, ές, (κακός, φράζομαι) devising ill, thoughtless, foolish. Hence

κᾰκο-φρᾰδία Ion. -ίη, ἡ, folly, thoughtlessness.

κᾰκο-φρονέω, f. ήσω, to be ill disposed, to bear ill-will or malice. From

κᾰκό-φρων, ον, gen. ονος, (κακός, φρήν) evil-minded, malicious, malignant. II. thoughtless, heedless.

κᾰκό-χαρτος, ον, (κακός, χαίρω) rejoicing in the ills of others, malicious.

κᾰκο-χράσμων, ον, gen. ονος, (κακός, χράομαι) with scanty means, poor.

κᾰκό-ψογος, ον, (κακός, ψέγω) malignantly blaming.

κᾰκόω, f. ώσω, (κακός) to treat badly, ill-use, maltreat: of things, to harm, destroy:—Pass. to be ill-treated, distressed, to suffer: in pf. pass. part. κεκακωμένος, disfigured, befouled.

κακτάμεναι, Ep. for κατακτάμεναι, κατακτάναι, inf. of κατέκτην, aor. 2 of κατακτείνω.

κάκτᾰνε, Ep. for κατάκτανε, aor. 2 imperat. of κατακτείνω; also for κατέκτανε, 3 sing. ind.

κάκτεινε, Ep. for κατέκτεινε, 3 sing. impf. of κατακτείνω,

ΚΑ΄ΚΤΟΣ, ἡ, the cactus, a prickly plant.

κᾰκύνω, f. ῠνῶ, (κακός) to damage, injure:—Pass. to behave badly, act basely; of soldiers, to mutiny. II. to revile, reproach:—Pass to be reproached.

κακχεῦαι, Ep. for καταχέαι, aor. 1 inf. of καταχέω.

κακῶς, Adv. of κακός, ill, badly: with difficulty, scarcely. Comp. κάκιον, Sup. κάκιστα.

κάκωσις, εως, ἡ, (κακόω) ill-treatment: a distressing, wearing out: damage, misfortune.

κακώτερος, Ep. Comp. of κακός: cf. κακίων.

κᾰλᾰθίσκος, ὁ, Dim. of κάλαθος, a small basket.

ΚΑ΄ΛΑ˘ΘΟΣ, ὁ, a basket, a wicker hand-basket,

Lat. *calathus* II. *a cooling-vessel, cooler:* also a kind of *cup*.

κᾰλάϊνος, η, ον, *coloured like the κάλαϊς, between blue and green, of changeful hue.* From

κάλαϊς, ὁ, a precious stone of a greenish blue, *the topaz* or *chrysolite*

κᾰλᾰμαία, ἡ, (καλάμη) *a* kind of *grasshopper*.

κᾰλᾰμευτής, οῦ, ὁ, (κάλαμος) *a reaper, mower.* II. *an angler.*

ΚΑΛΑ'ΜΗ, ἡ, *a stalk of reed* or *corn*, Lat. *calamus, stipula: a fishing-rod.* II. *stubble:* metaph. *the residue, remnant, remains:* of an old man, καλάμην γέ σ' οἴομαι εἰσορόωντα γιγνώσκειν thou may'st still, I ween, perceive *the stubble* (i. e. *the relics*) of former strength.

κᾰλᾰμητομία, ἡ, *a cutting of stalks, reaping.* From

κᾰλᾰμη-τόμος, ον, (καλάμη, τεμεῖν) *cutting stalks, reaping.*

κᾰλᾰμη-φάγος, ον, (καλάμη, φᾰγεῖν) *devouring stalks, mowing* or *cutting them.*

κᾰλᾰμη-φόρος, ον, (καλάμη, φέρω) *carrying reeds* or *canes.*

κᾰλαμίνθη, ἡ, (καλός, μίνθα) *mint.* Hence

Κᾰλᾰμίνθιος, ὁ, *Minty*, name of a frog.

κᾰλάμῐνος, η, ον, (κάλαμος) *made of reed* or *cane.*

κᾰλᾰμίς, ίδος, ἡ, (κάλαμος) *a fishing-rod.*

κᾰλᾰμίσκος, ὁ, Dim. of κάλαμος.

κᾰλᾰμῖτις, ιδος, ἡ, (κάλαμος) *a* kind of *grasshopper.*

κᾰλᾰμόεις, εσσα, εν, *of reed;* καλαμόεσσα ἰαχά the sound *as of a reed-flute.* From

ΚΑ'ΛΑ'ΜΟΣ, ὁ, Lat. *calamus, a reed* or *cane*, Lat. *arundo: an arrow of reed: a reed-pipe, reed-flute: a writing-reed*, used as a pen; generally, *a pen, a fishing-rod.* II. generic term for any plant, which is neither bush (ὕλη), nor tree (δένδρον).

κᾰλᾰμο-στεφής, ές, (κάλαμος, στέφω) *crowned* or *covered with reed.*

κᾰλᾰμό-φθογγος, ον, (κάλαμος, φθέγγομαι) *played on a reed.*

καλάσῑρις, ιος, ἡ, *a long Egyptian garment* with a border of tassels or fringe. (Egyptian word.)

κᾰλαῦροψ, οπος, ἡ, *a shepherd's staff* or *crook*, thrown so as to drive back the cattle.

κᾰλέεσκον, Ion. impf. of καλέω; Ep. 3 sing. impf. med. **καλέσκετο**.

καλέοντι, Dor. for καλέουσι, 3 pl. of καλεω.

καλέσας, aor. 1 part. of καλέω.

καλέσασθε, 2 pl. aor. 1 med. imperat. of καλέω.

κάλεσσα, Ep. aor. 1 of καλέω.

καλεῦνται, Dor. for καλοῦνται.

καλεῦντο, Ep. and Dor. for ἐκαλοῦντο, 3 pl. impf. pass. of καλέω.

ΚΑ'ΛΕ'Ω: Ion. impf. καλέεσκον: fut. καλέσω Ion. and Ep. καλέω Att. καλῶ: aor. 1 ἐκάλεσα Ep. ἐκάλεσσα or καλέσσα: pf. κέκληκα (for κεκάληκα):—Med., fut. καλέσομαι Att. καλοῦμαι: aor. 1 ἐκαλεσάμην poët. καλεσσάμην:—Pass., fut. κληθήσομαι, paullo-post f. κεκλήσομαι: aor. 1 ἐκλήθην: pf. κέκλημαι. I. *to call, summon:* c. inf. *to call on, summon to do* a thing. 2. *to call to one's house, to invite*, Lat. *vocare ad coenam.* 3. *to call on* or *invoke* the gods. 4. as law-term, in Act. of the judge, καλεῖν τινα *to cite, summon* before the court; in Med. of the plaintiff, καλεῖσθαί τινα *to sue* at law, Lat. *vocare in jus.* II. *to call by name, address by name*, generally, *to name;* καλεῖν τινα ἐπίκλησιν *to call* by name:—Pass., *to be named, receive a name;* and in pf. κέκλημαι, *to have been named*, and so *to be called:* the pf. pass. freq. means simply *to be;* as, τάδε μὲν Περσῶν πιστὰ καλεῖται these *are called* (i. e. *are*) the faithful counsellors of the Persia.

κᾰλήμεναι, poët. for καλεῖν, inf. of καλέω.

κᾰλήτης, Dor. and Att. for κηλήτης.

κᾰλήτωρ, ορος, ὁ, (καλέω) *a crier.*

κᾰλιά Ion. -ιή, ἡ, (κᾶλον) *a wooden house, hut, cabin, cot: a barn, granary:* a bird's *nest: a wooden shrine* for a statue.

κᾰλιάς, άδος, ἡ, = καλιά, *a hu..*

κᾰλινδέομαι, Pass., with fut. med. καλινδήσομαι, = ἀλινδέομαι, κυλινδέομαι, *to lie rolling* or *wallowing:* metaph. *to be busy with* a thing, *to be constantly engaged with it.* Hence

κᾰλινδήθρα, ἡ, = ἀλινδήθρα, *a place for horses to roll in after exercise.*

κάλλαια, τά, *a cock's wattles*, Lat. *palea:* also *a cock's tail.*

καλλείπω, Ep. for καταλείπω.

καλλι-, in compd. words, either gives the additional idea of *beautiful* to the simple word; or is like a mere Adj. with its Subst., as καλλίπαις = καλὴ παῖς.

καλλι-βλέφαρος, ον, (καλλι-, βλέφαρον) *with beautiful eyelids* or *eyes.*

καλλι-βόας, ου, ὁ, (καλλι-, βοή) *beautiful-sounding.*

καλλί-βοτρυς, υ, gen. υος, (καλλι-, βότρυς) *with beautiful clusters.*

καλλί-βωλος, ον, (καλλι-, βῶλος) *with rich soil.*

καλλι-γάληνος, ον, (καλλι-, γᾰλήνη) *sweetly-tranquil*

καλλί-γᾰμος, ον, *happy in marriage.*

καλλιγένεια, ἡ, (καλλι-, γένος) *bearer of a fair offspring, mother of beauteous things*, the name by which Ceres was invoked in the Thesmophoria.

καλλι-γύναιξ, gen. αικος, ὁ, ἡ, (καλλι-, γυνή) *with beautiful women* or *maidens:* the nom. seems never to have been used. [ῠ]

καλλῐ-δίνης, ου, ὁ, (καλλι-, δίνη) *flowing with beautiful eddies.* [δῑ]

καλλί-διφρος, ον, *with beautiful chariot.*

καλλι-δόναξ, ακος, ὁ, *with beautiful reeds.*

καλλι-έλαιος, ὁ, (καλλι-, ἐλαία) *the cultivated olive*, opp. to ἀγριέλαιος.

καλλι-επέω, f. ήσω, *to speak in fair set terms, in high-flown phrases;* κεκαλλιεπημέναι λόγοι *high-wrought* speeches. From

καλλι-επής, ές, (καλλι-, ἔπος) *beautifully speaking, elegant.*

καλλ-ιερέω Ion. **καλλ-ιρέω**, f. ήσω, (καλλι-, ἱερόν): —to have favourable signs in sacrifice, Lat. litare, perlitare:—c. acc. to sacrifice with good omens. 2. of the offering, to give good omens, be favourable, propitiou

καλλι-ζῠγής, ές, (καλλι-, ζυγῆναι) beautifully-yoked.

καλλί-ζωνος, ον, (καλλι-, ζώνη) with beautiful girdles.

καλλί-θριξ, τρῐχος, ὁ, ἡ, (καλλι-, θρίξ) with beautiful hair or mane: of sheep, with fine wool.

καλλιθῠτέω, f. ήσω, to offer auspiciously. From

καλλί-θῠτος, ον, (καλλι-, θύω) with beautiful or auspicious sacrifices.

καλλί-καρπος, ον, with fine fruit, rich in fine fruit.

καλλί-κερως, ατος or ω, ὁ, ἡ, (καλλι-, κέρας) with beautiful horns

Καλλι-κολώνη, ἡ, Fair-hill, a district near Troy.

καλλι-κόμης Dor. **-μας**, ὁ, ἡ, and **καλλίκομος**, ον, (καλλι-, κόμη) beautiful-haired.

καλλι-κρήδεμνος, ον, (καλλι-, κρήδεμνον) with beautiful fillets or hair-bands.

καλλί-κρηνος Dor. **-κρᾱνος**, ον, (καλλι-, κρήνη) with a beautiful spring.

καλλι-λαμπέτης, ου, ὁ, (καλλι-, λάμπω) beautiful-shining.

καλλι-λογέω, (καλλι-, λέγω) to express a thing elegantly:—Med. to give a fair name to a thing.

καλλί-μορφος, ον, (καλλι-, μορφή) beautifully shaped.

κάλλῐμος, ον, poët. for καλός, beautiful.

καλλί-νᾱος, ον, (καλλι-, νάω) beautifully flowing.

καλλί-νῑκος, ον, (καλλι-, νίκη) with glorious victory, triumphant. II. crowning or ennobling victory; τὸ καλλίνικον the glory of victory.

κάλλιον, neut. of καλλίων, Comp. of καλός: used also of Adv., more beautifully.

Καλλι-όπη poët. **Καλλι-όπεια**, ἡ, (καλλι-, ὄψ) Calliŏpé, first of the nine Muses, the beautiful-voiced.

καλλί-παις, παιδος, ὁ, ἡ, with beautiful children. II. = καλὴ παῖς, a beautiful child

καλλι-πάρῃος, ον, (καλλι-, παρειά) beautiful-cheeked.

καλλι-πάρθενος, ον, of, with beautiful maidens or nymphs.

κάλλῐπον, Ep. aor. 2 of καταλείπω: inf. καλλιπέειν.

καλλι-πέδῑλος, ον, (καλλι-, πέδιλον) with beautiful sandals.

καλλί-πεπλος, ον, beautifully robed.

καλλι-πέτηλος, ον, (καλλι-, πέτηλον) with beautiful leaves.

καλλί-πηχυς, υ, gen. εως, with beautiful elbows.

καλλι-πλόκᾰμος, ον, with beautiful locks.

καλλί-πλουτος, ον, adorned with riches.

καλλί-πολις, εως, ἡ, beautiful city.

κάλλῐπον, Ep. for κατέλιπον, aor. 2 of καταλείπω.

καλλί-πονος, ον, beautifully wrought.

καλλι-πότᾰμος, ον, of beautiful rivers.

καλλί-πρῳρος, ον, (καλλι-, πρῷρα) with beautiful prow, of ship: metaph. of men, with beautiful face.

καλλί-πῠλος, οι (καλλι-, πύλη) with beauteous gates.

καλλί-πυργος, ον, with beautiful towers, towering.

καλλι-πύργωτος, ον, (καλλι-, πυργόω) built with beauteous towers

καλλί-πωλος, ον, with beautiful steeds or colts.

καλλι-ρέεθρος, ον, (καλλι-, ῥέεθρον) beautifully flowing.

καλλ-ιρέω, Ion. for καλλ-ιερέω.

καλλί-ροος, poët. for καλλίρ-ροος.

καλλίρ-ροος, ον, contr. **καλλίρ-ρους**, ουν, (καλλι-, ῥέω) beautifully flowing.

κάλλιστα, Adv. Sup. of καλῶς, most beautifully.

καλλι-στάδιος, ον, (καλλι-, στάδιον) with a fine race-course.

καλλιστεῖον, τό, (καλλιστεύω) the prize of beauty or excellence: in pl., = ἀριστεῖα, the meed of valour.

καλλίστευμα, τό, the prime of beauty: the first-fruits of beauty, the offering of choicest beauty.

καλλιστεύω, f. σω, (κάλλιστος) to be the most beautiful, be esteemed so: generally, to be the most beautiful among others, exceed in beauty.

καλλι-στέφᾰνος, ον, beautifully crowned: of cities, crowned with beauteous towers.

κάλλιστος, η, ον, Sup. of καλός.

καλλί-σφῠρος, ον, (καλλι-, σφυρόν) with beautiful feet or ankles.

καλλί-τοξος, ον, (καλλι-, τόξον) with beautiful bow.

καλλίτριχας, acc. pl. of καλλίθριξ.

κάλλιφ', for κάλλιπε, Ep. for κατέλιπε.

καλλι-φεγγής, ές, (καλλι-, φέγγος) beautiful-shining.

καλλί-φθογγος, ον, (καλλι-, φθέγγομαι) beautiful-sounding.

καλλί-φλοξ, φλογος, ὁ, ἡ, beautiful-blazing.

καλλί-φυλλος, ον, (καλλι-, φύλλον) with beautiful leaves.

καλλί-χορος, ον, Ep. for καλλι-χῶρος, with beautiful places. II. (χόρος) of or for beautiful dances: beautiful in the dance.

καλλίων, ον, gen. ονος, Comp. of καλός.

καλλονή, ἡ, (κάλλος) beauty.

κάλλος, gen. εος Att. ους, τό, (καλός) beauty. II. a beauty, beautiful object: in pl. κάλλεα, κάλλη, beautiful works; κάλλεα κηροῦ beautiful works of wax.

καλλοσύνη, ἡ, poët. for κάλλος, beauty.

καλλύνω, f. ῠνῶ, (καλός) to beautify; metaph. to gloss, colour over:—Med. to adorn oneself, plume oneself on a thing.

καλλ-ωπίζω, f. ίσω Att. ιῶ, (κάλλος, ὤψ) to make the face beautiful, to beautify, embellish, give a fair appearance to a thing:—Med. to adorn oneself, to pride oneself, glory in a thing: absol. to make a display. Hence

καλλώπισμα, ατος, τό, embellishment; and

καλλωπισμός, ὁ, an embellishing or adorning oneself, making a display.

καλο-διδάσκαλος, ὁ, = καλοῦ διδάσκαλος, *a teacher of virtue.*

καλοκἀγαθία, ἡ, *nobleness and goodness.* From

κᾰλο-κᾰγᾰθός, ον, i. e. καλὸς καὶ ἀγαθός, *beautiful and good, noble and good.*

κᾶλον, τό, (καίω) *dry, seasoned wood.*

κᾶλο-πέδῐλα, τά, (κᾶλον, πέδιλον) *wooden shoes,* used to keep a cow still while milking.

κᾰλο-ποιέω, f. ήσω, (καλός, ποιέω) *to do good.*

κᾰλό-πους, ὁ, ἡ, πουν, τό, gen. ποδος, (καλός, πούς) *with beautiful feet.*

ΚΑΛΟ'Σ, ή, όν, *beautiful, fair,* Lat. *pulcer;* Ἀλκιβιάδης ὁ καλός Alcibiades *the fair;* τὸ καλόν, like κάλλος *beauty.* II. *serving a good purpose, fair, good;* καλὸς λιμήν a *fair* harbour; ἐν καλῷ (sub. τόπῳ or χρόνῳ) *in good* time or place. 2. of sacrifices, *good, auspicious.* III. *morally beautiful, good, right, noble:* τὸ καλόν *moral virtue,* Lat. *honestum.* IV. Degrees of Comparison:—Comp. καλλίων, ον, Sup. κάλλιστος, η, ον. V. Adv. καλῶς, q. v.:—but neut. καλόν is often used as Adv. by Poets, *beautifully.*

κάλος, Ep. and Ion. for κάλως, *a rope.*

καλοῦμαι, εῖ, εῖται, Att. fut. med. of καλέω.

ΚΑ'ΛΠΙΣ, ιδος, ἡ, acc. κάλπιν or κάλπιδα:—*a vessel for drawing water, a pitcher, urn: a drinking-cup: an urn for drawing lots: an urn for the ashes of the dead.*

κᾰλύβη, ἡ, (καλύπτω) *a hut, cabin, cell.* [ῠ]

καλύβιον, τό, Dim. of καλύβη, *a small hut.*

καλύκεσσι, poët. for κάλυξι, dat. pl. of κάλυξ.

κᾰλῠκο-στέφᾰνος, ον, (κάλυξ, στέφανος) *crowned with flower-buds.*

κᾰλῠκ-ῶπις, ιδος, ἡ, (κάλυξ, ὤψ) *like a flower-bud, blushing, roseate.*

κάλυμμα, ατος, το, (καλύπτω) *a covering, a hood* or *veil.* 2. *a grave.*

κάλυξ, ῠκος, ἡ, (καλύπτω) *the cup* or *calyx of a flower, a flower-bud;* κάλυκος ἐν λοχεύμασι when *the fruit* is setting. II. in pl., κάλυκες are *women's ornaments,* made of metal, so called from their shape.

κᾰλύπτειρα, ἡ, like καλύπτρα, *a veil.*

κᾰλυπτός, ή, όν, verb. Adj. of καλύπτω, *covered.* II. *wrapped round: enveloping.*

κᾰλύπτρα Ion. -πτρη, ἡ, *a woman's veil;* δνοφερὰ καλύπτρα *the mantle* or *veil of* darkness. From

ΚΑΛΥ'ΠΤΩ, f. ύψω: aor. 1 ἐκάλυψα:—*to cover,* νυκτὶ καλύψας *having covered* with night; γαῖα ἐκάλυψέ νιν earth *covered* him 2. *to cover, conceal.* 3. *to cover with dishonour.* II. *to put over as a covering, throw over* or *around.*

καλύψατο, Ep. 3 sing. aor. 1 med. of καλύπτω.

Κᾰλυψώ, gen. -όος contr. -οῦς, ἡ, *Calypso,* a nymph, daughter of Atlas, who lived in the island Ogygia, and *concealed* (ἐκάλυψε) Ulysses on his way back from Troy.

καλχαίνω, (κάλχη) *to search for the purple-fish:* metaph. *to search in the depths of one's mind, to ponder deeply.*

Κάλχας, αντος, ὁ, *Calchas,* the Greek Seer at Troy, properly *the Searcher.*

ΚΑ'ΛΧΗ, ἡ, also **χάλκη**, *the murex, purple limpet,* from which a purple dye was obtained.

καλῶ, εῖς, εῖ, Att. fut. of καλέω.

κᾰλώδιον, τό, Dim. of κάλως, *a small cord* or *rope.*

καλῶς, Adv. of καλός, *beautifully, well;* καλῶς ἔχειν or πράττειν, to be *well off,* fare *well;* c. gen., καλῶς ἔχειν τινός to be *well off for* a thing. 2. = πάνυ, *right well, altogether, entirely.* 3. in answers, *well said! bravo!* Lat. *euge:* but also to decline an offer, *thank you!* like Lat. *benigne.*

ΚΑ'ΛΩΣ, ὁ, gen. κάλω, acc. κάλων: Ep. and Ion. **κάλος**, ου, ὁ:—*a rope, a cable;* ἀπὸ κάλω πλεῖν to sail *at a cable's end,* i. e. to have the ship towed: κάλων κατεῖναι to let down *a sounding-line:*—also *a sail-rope, reef;* proverb., πάντα κάλων ἐξιάσι they are letting out every *reef,* i.e. are using every effort.

καλω-στρόφος, ὁ, (κάλως, στρέφω) *a rope-twister.*

κάμ, Ep. for κατά before μ, as κὰμ μέν for κατὰ μέν.

κᾰμάκῖνος, ον, *made of brittle wool.* From

ΚΑ'ΜΑΞ, ᾰκος, ἡ or ὁ, *a pole, stake, a vine-prop.* II. *the shaft of a spear.*

ΚΑΜΑ'ΡΑ, ἡ, Lat. *camera, anything with a vaulted* or *arched covering, a covered carriage.* [κᾰμᾰ]

καμασῆνες, οἱ, *a kind of fish.*

κᾰμᾰτηρός, ά, όν, *toilsome, troublesome, wearisome.* II. pass. *broken down, worn out.* From

κάμᾰτος, ὁ, (κάμνω) *toil, trouble, labour.* 2. *weariness, distress.* II. *that which is hardly earned;* ἡμέτερος κάματος our *hard-won earnings.* [κᾰ]

κᾰμᾰτ-ώδης, ες, (κάματος, εἶδος) *toilsome.*

καμ-βαίνω, Ep. for καταβαίνω.

κάμε, Ep. for ἔκαμε, 3 sing. aor. 2 of κάμνω.

κἀμέ, crasis for καὶ ἐμέ.

καμεῖν, aor. 2 inf. of κάμνω.

καμεῖται, 3 sing. fut. of κάμνω.

κάμηλος, ὁ and ἡ, *a camel:*—ἡ κάμηλος, like ἡ ἵππος, *the camels in an army.* (From Hebr. *Gāmal.*)

κᾰμῑνευτήρ, ῆρος, ὁ, (κάμινος) *one that works at a furnace;* αὐλὸς καμινευτῆρ the pipe *of a smith's bellows.*

κᾰμῑνευτής, οῦ, ὁ, = καμινευτήρ.

καμινοῖ, dat. of καμινώ.

κάμῑνος, ἡ, (καίω) *an oven, furnace,* or *kiln.* Hence

κᾰμῑνώ, οῦς, dat. οῖ, ἡ, *a furnace-woman.*

καμμέν, or better κὰμ μέν, Ep. for κατὰ μέν.

κάμμες, crasis for καὶ ἄμμες, Aeol. for καὶ ἡμεῖς.

κὰμ μέσσον, Ep. for κατὰ μέσον

καμμίξας, Ep. for καταμίξας, aor. 1 part. of καταμίγνυμι.

καμ-μονίη, ἡ, Ep. for καταμονή, *staunchness in battle, patience, endurance.*

κάμ-μορος, ον, Ep. for κατάμορος, *ill-fated*

καμ-μύω, Ep. for καταμύω.

ΚΑ'ΜΝΩ: fut. κᾰμοῦμαι, εῖ, εῖται: aor. 2 ἔκᾰμον, inf. καμεῖν, Ep. redupl. subj. κεκάμω: pf. κέκμηκα,

Ep. pf. part. κεκμηώς, κεκμηῶτι, κεκμηῶτα, acc. pl. κεκμηότας: I. intr. *to be weary, tired, exhausted,* or *worn out:* c. part., κάμνει πολεμίζων, ἐλαύνων, *one is weary* of fighting, rowing. 2. *to feel trouble* or *annoyance; οὐκ ἔκαμον τανύων I found* no *trouble* in bending the bow 3. *to be worsted* or *beaten.* 4. *to be sick* or *ill,* generally, *to be afflicted, distressed, harassed.* 5. οἱ καμόντες and οἱ κεκμηκότες Ep. κεκμηότες or κεκμηῶτες, Lat. *defuncti, those who have finished their labours, the dead:* but, οἱ κάμνοντες *the sick;* and κεκμηκότες are also *the spirits of the dead,* Lat. *dii manes.* II. trans. *to work hard at, to bestow labour upon.* 2. *to work out, earn by toil;* in aor. 2 med., νῆσον ἐκάμοντο *they worked, tilled* the island *for themselves.*

κἀμοί, by crasis for καὶ ἐμοί.

ΚΑΜΠΗ', ἡ, (κάμπτω) *a bending, winding,* as of a river. II. *the turning* in a *race-course, turning-post:* metaph., μῦθον ἐς καμπὴν ἄγειν to bring a speech to *its middle* or *turning-point.* III. καμπαί, in Music, *turns, tricks, quavers.*

κάμπιμος, η, ον, (καμπή) *bent, turning, double.*

καμπτήρ, ῆρος, ὁ, *a bend, an angle.* II. *the turning-point in a race-course.*

ΚΑ'ΜΠΤΩ, fut. κάμψω: aor. 1 ἔκαμψα: Pass., aor. 1 ἐκάμφθην:—*to bend, bow:*—esp., 1. γόνυ and γούνατα κάμπτειν, *to bend* the knees so as to sit down and rest, *to take rest.* 2. γόνυ κάμπτειν *to bend* the knee in prayer. 3. γόνυ κάμπτειν *to bend* the knee in running, *to run.* II. *to bend, turn, guide* anything. 2. absol. *to turn round* a point; κάμπτειν ἄκρην *to double* a headland; κάμπτειν κόλπον *to skirt* the bay: metaph., κάμπτειν βίον *to turn the middle point* of life, i. e. to draw near to its close; cf. καμπή. III. like Lat. *flecto, to bend, move by entreaties, soften, make relent:* generally, *to bend, humble.*

καμπύλος, η, ον, (κάμπτω) *bent, curved.* [ῠ]

καμφθείς, καμφθῆναι, aor. 1 pass. part. and inf. of κάμπτω.

καμψέμεν, Ep. fut. inf. of κάμπτω.

καμψί-πους, ὁ, ἡ, πουν, τό, gen. ποδος, (κάμπτω, πούς) *bending the foot, swift-running.*

κάμψις, εως, ἡ, (κάμπτω) *a bending, curving.*

καμών, aor. 2 part. of κάμνω.

κἄν, crasis for καὶ ἄν:—also for καὶ ἤν, *and if, even if.*

κἀν, crasis for καὶ ἐν, *and in.*

κάν, Ep. for κατά before ν, as κὰν νόμον for κατὰ νόμον.

κάναθρον or **κάνναθρον**, τό, (κάνη) *the body of a wicker carriage: a cane* or *wicker carriage.*

Κανανίτης, ου, ὁ, Syriac word, of which the Greek Ζηλωτής, *Zealot,* is a translation: not to be confounded with Χαναναῖος, *a Canaanite.*

ΚΑΝΑ'ΣΣΩ, f. ξω, *to make a gurgling sound with water.* (Formed from the sound.)

κάναστρον, τό, (κάνη) *a wicker basket,* Lat. *canistrum.* II. *an earthen vessel, dish.*

κανᾱ-φόρος, Dor. for κανηφόρος.

κᾰνᾰχέω, f. ήσω, *to ring* or *clash, clang,* of metal: *to plash,* of water. From

κᾰνᾰχή, ἡ, (κανάσσω) *a sharp, ringing sound,* esp. *the ring* or *clash* of metal; also of *the tramp* of mules; καναχὴ ὀδόντων *the gnashing* of teeth; καναχαὶ αὐλῶν *the shrill sound* of flutes. Hence

κᾰνᾰχηδά, Adv. *with a sharp, ringing noise.*

κᾰνᾰχής, ές, (κανάσσω) *making a sharp, ringing noise:* of water, *plashing.*

κανάχησε, Ep. 3 sing. aor. 1 of καναχέω.

κανάχιζε, Ep. 3 sing. impf. of καναχίζω.

κᾰνᾰχίζω, f. ίσω, = καναχέω.

κάνδυς, υος, ὁ, *a Median garment with sleeves,* also κανδύκη. (Median word.)

κάνεον Ion. **κάνειον** Att. contr. **κανοῦν**, τό, (κάννη) *a basket of reed* or *cane, a wicker basket: a bread-basket,* Lat. *canistrum,* used esp. for carrying the sacred barley (οὐλαί) at sacrifices.

κᾰνεῖν, aor. 2 inf. of καίνω.

κάνη, ἡ, a rarer form of κάννα. [ᾰ]

κανῆν, Dor. for κανεῖν, aor. 2 inf. of καίνω.

κᾰνηφορέω, f. ήσω, *to carry the sacred basket in procession.* From

κᾰνη-φόρος, ον, (κανεον, φέρω) *carrying a basket:* ἡ Κανηφόρος *the Basket-bearer,* in Athens a maiden who carried on her head a basket containing the sacred things in processions at the feasts of Demeter, Bacchus, and Athena.

ΚΑ'ΝΘΑ'ΡΟΣ, ὁ, Lat. *cantharus,* a kind of *beetle,* worshipped in Egypt. II. *a sort of drinking-cup,* Lat. *cantharus.* III. *a* kind of *Naxian boat.* IV. *a mark* or *knot resembling a beetle,* on the tongue of the Egyptian god Apis.

κανθήλια, ων, τά, Lat. *clitellae, a pack-saddle,* or *the large panniers* of a pack-saddle.

κανθήλιος, ὁ, *a large sort of ass* for carrying burdens, *a pack-ass.*

κάνθων, ωνος, ὁ, (κανθος) = κανθήλιος, *a pack-ass.*

ΚΑ'ΝΝΑ or **κάννη**, ης, ἡ, *a reed* or *cane,* Lat. *canna:* hence *anything made of reeds, a reed-mat, a reed-fence.*

καννάβῐνος, η, ον, *hempen, made of hemp.* From

ΚΑ'ΝΝΑ'ΒΙΣ, ἡ, gen. ιος, acc. ιδα, also gen. εως: —*hemp,* Lat. *cannabis.* II. *anything made of it, tow.*

καννεύσας, Ep. for κατανεύσας.

κάννη, ἡ, = κάννα.

καννόμον, better κὰν νομον, Ep. for κατὰ νόμον.

κᾰνονίς, ῐδος, ἡ, (κανών) *a ruler.*

κᾰνόνισμα, τό, poët. for κανών, *a rule:* also *a ruler.*

κᾰνοῦν, Att. contr. of κάνεον.

κᾰνεῖν, aor. 2 inf. of καίνω.

κᾰνῶ, fut. of καίνω.

Κάνωβος or **Κάνωπος**, ὁ, *Canobus,* a town in Lower Egypt, notorious for its luxury.

κᾰνών, όνος, ὁ, (κάνη, κάννα) *any straight rod* or *bar:* in Homer, κανόνες are *two rods* running across the hollow of the shield, through which the arm was passed, to hold it by. 2. *a rod used in weaving; the shuttle* or *quill* by which the threads of the woof (πηνίον) were passed between the threads of the warp (μίτος). 3. *a carpenter's rule:* metaph. *a rule* or *level ray of light.* 4. *the beam* or *tongue of the balance:* pl. *the keys* or *stops* of a flute. II. metaph. like Lat. *norma, a rule* or *standard* of excellence:—so, the old Greek authors were called κανόνες, *rules* or *models* of excellence, *classics;* and the books received by the Church *as the rule of faith and practice* are called *the Canon* or *canonical* scriptures.

καυών, aor. 2 part. of καίνω.

Κάνωπος, ὁ, see Κάνωβος.

κάξ, crasis for καὶ ἐξ.

κάπ, Ep. for κατά before π or φ, as κὰπ πεδίον for κατὰ πεδίον.

κἄπειτα, by crasis for καὶ ἔπειτα, *and then, and next.*

κάπετος, ἡ, (σκάπτω, for σκάπετος) *a ditch, trench,* Lat. *fossa: a vault, grave:* generally, *a hole.*

ΚΑ'ΠΗ, ἡ, *a crib, manger.*

κᾰπηλεῖον, τό, *the shop of a* κάπηλος, *a tavern,* Lat. *caupona.* From

κᾰπηλεύω, f. σω, (κάπηλος) *to be a retail-dealer, drive a petty trade:* metaph. *to hawk about, higgle in;* καπηλεύειν μάχην *to make a trade* of war, Ennius' *bellum cauponari:*—also, *to adulterate, give out as genuine, palm off.*

κᾰπηλικός, ή, όν, (κάπηλος) *of* or *like a petty trader: tricky, knavish.* Adv., καπηλικῶς ἔχειν to play *roguish tricks.*

καπηλίς, ίδος, fem. of κάπηλος, Lat. *copa.*

κάπηλος, ὁ, (κάπτω) *a retail-dealer, petty tradesman, huckster, higgler,* Lat. *caupo,* opp. to ἔμπορος: esp. *a tavern-keeper.* II. *a cheat, rogue, knave.*

κἀπί, by crasis for καὶ ἐπ'

καπίθη, ἡ, (κάπτω) *a measure containing two* χοίνικες.

κάπνη, ἡ, (καπνός) *a smoke-hole, chimney.*

καπνίζω, f. ίσω Att. ιῶ, (καπνός) *to cause smoke: to make* or *light a fire.* II. *to smoke, blacken with smoke.* Hence

κάπνισμα, ματος, τό, *a smoke-offering: incense.*

κάπνισσαν, Ep. 3 pl. aor. 1 of καπνίζω.

καπνο-δόχη Ion. -δόκη, ἡ, (καπνός, δέχομαι) *a smoke-receiver: a hole in the ceiling* or *roof for the smoke to pass through.*

ΚΑΠΝΟ'Σ, ὁ, *smoke,* Lat. *fumus.* Hence

καπνόω, f. ώσω, *to turn into smoke:*—Pass. *to be burned into smoke, burnt to ashes.*

καπν-ώδης, ες, (καπνός, εἶδος) *like smoke, smoky:* generally, *dark, dusky.*

κᾶποι, Dor. for κῆποι.

κᾶπος, ὁ, Dor. for κῆπος.

κάππα, τό, v. sub Κ.

Καππᾰδοκίζω, f. σω, *to favour the Cappadocians.* II. *to play the Cappadocian,* i. e. *play the rogue.* From

Καππάδοξ, οκος, ὁ, *a Cappadocian.*

κάππεσον, Ep. for κατέπ-, aor. 2 of καταπίπτω.

καππο-φόρος, ον, (κάππα, φέρω) of a horse, *marked with a* κάππα: cf. κοππατίας.

καπ-πυρίζω, poët. for καταπυρίζω, (κατά, πῦρ) *to catch fire.*

καπράω, (κάπρος) *to be lewd* or *lecherous.*

κάπριος, ὁ, poët. for κάπρος *a wild boar.* II. as Adj. *like a wild boar.*

ΚΑ'ΠΡΟΣ, ὁ, Lat. *APER, the wild-boar.*

καπρο-φόνος, ον, (καπρός, *φένω) *killing wild boars.*

ΚΑ'ΠΤΩ, fut. κάψω: aor. 1 ἔκαψα: Ep. pf. part. κεκαφηώς, for κεκᾰφώς —*to eat quick, swallow greedily, gulp down.* II. κάπτειν θυμόν *to gasp for* breath.

κᾰπῦρός, ά, όν, (καπύω) *dry, dried.* 2. act. *drying, parching.* II. metaph. of sound, *loud and clear, distinct.*

κάπυσσα, Ep. aor. 1; see ἀποκαπύω.

καπ-φάλαρα, better κὰπ φάλαρα, for κατὰ φάλαρα.

κάρ, Ep. for κατά before ῥ, as κὰρ ῥόον for κατὰ ῥόον.

ΚΑ'Ρ, κᾶρός, τό, *the hair of the head,* akin to κάρα; τίω δέ μιν ἐν καρὸς αἴσῃ I value him but at *a hair's worth.* II. also for κάρα, κάρη, *head,* as in ἐπὶ κάρ *head*-long.

Κάρ, ὁ, gen. Κᾶρός, pl. Κᾶρες:—*a Carian,* in later times despised as mercenaries:—Proverb., ἐν Καρὶ or ἐν τῷ Καρὶ διvδυνεύειν to make the risk on *a Carian,* Lat. *experimentum facere in corpore vili:*—Fem. Κάειρα.

ΚΑ'ΡΑ Ion. **κάρη** [ᾰ], τό, indecl. *the head:* generally, *the head, top, summit* of anything: *the brim* of a cup: it is used, like κεφαλή, Lat. *caput,* to express *a person,* as Οἰδίπου κάρα for Οἰδίπους:—used by Hom. only in nom. and acc sing.; later, the defective cases were supplied, viz. κάρης, κάρῃ, κάρην. In Ep. we find lengthd. forms of gen. and dat. κάρητος κάρητι, κᾰρήατος κᾰρήατ

κᾰρᾰβο-πρόσωπος, ον, (κάραβος, πρόσωπον) *with the face of a crab.*

ΚΑ'ΡΑΒΟΣ, ὁ, *a kind of beetle, the stag-beetle,* Lat. *scarabaeus.* II. *a* prickly kind of *crab.*

κᾰρᾰ-δοκέω, f. ήσω, (καρά, δοκεύω) *to watch with outstretched head, watch eagerly* or *expectantly.*

κᾰρᾰνιστήρ, ῆρος, ὁ, (κάρα) *touching the head, beheading.*

κάρᾱνον, τό, Dor. and Att. for κάρηνον.

κάρᾱνος, ὁ, (κάρα) *a head, chieftain, chief.* Hence

κᾰρᾱνόω, f. ώσω, like κεφαλαιόω, (κάρανον) *to accomplish, achieve, complete.*

κᾰρά-τομος, ον, (κάρᾱ, τεμεῖν) *with the head cut off, beheaded.* 2. *cut from the head.*

κάρβᾰνος, ον,= βάρβαρος, *outlandish, foreign, barbarous.* (Foreign word.)

ΚΑΡΒΑ'ΤΙΝΑΙ or **καρπάτιναι**, αἱ, *shoes of undressed leather, brogues, mocassins.*

καρδᾰμίζω, f. ίσω Att. ιῶ, (κάρδαμον) *to be like cress;* metaph. *to look sharp* or *pungent;* τί καρδαμίζεις; why *chatter so much about cress* (i. e. about nothing)?

ΚΑ'ΡΔΑΜΟΝ, τό, *a* kind of *cress,* Lat. *nastur-*

tium: also *the seed,* which was eaten by the Persians like mustard:—metaph. κάρδαμον βλέπειν to look *cress,* i. e. to look sharp and bitter.

ΚΑΡΔΙ'Α, poët. **κρᾰδία** Ion. **καρδίη, κρᾰδίη,** ἡ, *the heart,* Lat. *cor;* ἀπὸ καρδίας λέγειν, like Lat. *ex animo,* to speak from *the heart.* II. *the stomach.*

καρδῐᾰκός, ή, όν, (καρδία) *of the heart* or *stomach:* hence II. *dyspeptic.*

καρδιο-γνώστης, ου, ὁ, (καρδια, γιγνώσκω) *knower of hearts.*

καρδιό-δηκτος, ον, (καρδία, δάκνω) *gnawing the heart.*

καρδι-ουλκέω, (καρδία, ἕλκω) *to draw the heart out of a victim* at a sacrifice.

καρδοπεῖον, τό, *the cover of a kneading-trough.* II. *a muzzle.* From

ΚΑ'ΡΔΟΠΟΣ, ἡ, *a kneading-trough, any trough.*

Κάρεσσι, dat. pl. of Κάρ.

κάρη, Ion. and Ep. for κάρα, *the head.*

καρήατος, καρήατι, Ep. gen. and dat. of κάρα.

κᾰρηβάρεια Ion. -ίη, ἡ, *heaviness in the head: top-heaviness.* From

κᾰρηβαρέω, f. ήσω, *to be heavy in the head, top-heavy.* From

κᾰρη-βαρής, ές, (κάρη, βάρος) *heavy in the head.*

κᾰρη-κομόωντες, or better **κάρη κομόωντες,** οἱ, *with hair on the head, long-haired,* of the Achaians, opp. to the Abantes, who wore their hair only at the back of the head, and so were called ὄπιθεν κομόωντες. κομόωντες is Ep. part. pl. of κομάω; but there is no Verb καρηκομάω.

κᾰρῆναι, aor. 2 pass. inf. of κείρω.

κάρηνον, τό, mostly in pl. κάρηνα, (κάρη) *the head;* ἀνδρῶν κάρηνα, = ἄνδρες; βοῶν κάρηνα so many *head* of cattle. II. metaph. *a mountain-top, peak, crest* of a hill: also of a town, *the citadel.*

κάρητος, κάρητι, Ep. gen. and dat. of κάρη.

Κᾶρικο-εργής, ές, (Καρικός, ἔργον) *of Carian work.*

Κᾶρῐκός, ή, όν, (Κάρ) *Carian:* Καρική μοῦσα, ἡ, a kind of *funeral song, a wail* or *dirge.*

ΚΑΡΙ'Σ, gen. ῖδος or ίδος, ἡ, Dor. also κουρίς or κωρίς, *a shrimp* or *prawn,* Lat. *squilla.* [ᾱ]

καρκαίρω, *to ring* or *quake,* of the earth. (Formed from the sound.)

ΚΑΡΚΙ'ΝΟΣ, ὁ, with heterog. pl. καρκίνα, τά, *a crab,* Lat. *cancer:* also *Cancer, the Crab,* as a sign in the zodiac. II. *a pair of tongs.* [ῐ]

καρκῐνό-χειρες, ων, pl. Adj. (καρκίνος, χείρ) *with crab's claws for hands.*

ΚΑ'ΡΝΕΙΑ or **Κάρνεα,** τά, *a festival held in honour of Apollo* Κάρνειος by the Spartans, during nine days of the Attic month Metageitnion, hence called Καρνεῖος μήν.

καρός, Dor. for κηρός.

Κάρπᾰθος, ἡ, an island between Crete and Rhodes, called in Homer Κράπαθος.

καρπαία, ἡ, *a mimic dance* of the Thessalians.

καρπάλῐμος, ον, (ἁρπάζω, Lat. *carpo*) *tearing, swift, rapid.* Adv. καρπαλίμως, *rapidly.*

κάρπᾰσος, ἡ, with heterog. pl. κάρβασα, τά, *a fine flax* grown in Spain, Lat. *carbasus.* (Eastern word.)

καρπίζω, f. ίσω Att. ιῶ (καρπός) *to pluck* or *gather fruit:* — Med. *to enjoy the fruits of, reap the return.* II. *to make fruitful, fertilise*

κάρπιμος, η, ον, (καρπός) *bearing fruit, fruitful.*

καρπο-γένεθλος, ον, (καρπός, γενέθλη) *producing fruit.*

καρπό-δεσμα, ων, τά, (καρπός, δεσμός) *chains for the wrists* or *arms, armlets.*

καρπο-ποιός, όν, (καρπός, ποιέω) *producing fruit.*

ΚΑΡΠΟ'Σ, ὁ, *fruit;* καρπὸς ἀρούρης, corn, but also of wine; οἱ καρποί *the fruits of the earth, corn.* II. metaph. *the fruits, produce, returns, profit of* a thing.

ΚΑΡΠΟ'Σ, ὁ, *the joint of the arm and hand, the wrist,* Lat. *carpus.*

καρπο-τελής, ές, (καρπός, τελέω) *bringing fruit to perfection: fruitful, prolific.*

καρπο-τόκος, ον, (καρπός, τεκεῖν) *bearing fruit.*

καρπο-φάγος, ον, (καρπός, φᾰγεῖν) *eating fruit.*

καρπο-φθόρος, ον, (καρπός, φθείρω) *spoiling fruit.*

καρποφορέω, f. ήσω, *to bear fruit.* From

καρπο-φόρος, ον, (καρπός, φέρω) *fruit-bearing.*

καρπο-φύλαξ, ᾰκος, ὁ, (καρπός, φύλαξ) *a watcher of fruit.* [ῠ]

καρπόω, f. ώσω, (καρπός) *to bear fruit:* later *to offer fruit.* II. Med. καρπόομαι *to gather fruit* or *reap crops from* land:—*to exhaust, plunder.* 2. *to enjoy the interest of* money: *to reap the fruits of, enjoy* a thing.

κάρπωμα, ατος, τό, (καρπόω) *fruit: produce, profit.*

κάρπωσις, εως, ἡ, (καρπόομαι) *a reaping the fruit of: use, profit.*

καρρέζουσα, Ep. for καταρρέζουσα.

κάρτᾰ, Adv. (κάρτος) *very, very much,* Lat. *valde;* καὶ τὸ κάρτα, *very much indeed, really and truly.*

καρτερέω, f. ήσω, (καρτερός) *to be steadfast* or *patient.* 2. c. acc. *to endure manfully.* 3. with a Prep. *to hold out* or *bear up against* a thing. 4. with part. *to persevere, persist in* doing. Hence

καρτέρησις, εως, ἡ, *a bearing patiently, patience, endurance.*

καρτερία, ἡ, = καρτέρησις.

καρτερικός, ή, όν, (καρτερός) *enduring, patient.*

καρτερό-θῡμος, ον, (καρτερος, θυμός) *stout-hearted.*

καρτερός, ά, όν, (κάρτος) = κρατερός, *strong, staunch, brave,* mostly of persons, but also of things; καρτερὰ ἔργα *valiant* deeds; κάρτερος ὅρκος a *binding* oath. 2. of places, *strong,* in a military sense. 3. *master of* a thing, *lord of.* 4. *master of oneself; steadfast, patient, constant:* also *obstinate.* II. Besides the regul. Comp. and Sup., the forms most in use are κρείσσων, κράτιστος.

καρτερό-χειρ, ὁ, ἡ, (καρτερός, χείρ), *strong of hand.*

καρτερῶς, Adv. of κάρτερος, *strongly;* καρτερῶς ὑπνοῦσθαι *to sleep sound.*

κάρτιστος, η, ον, Ep. for κράτιστος.

κάρτος, εος, τό, Ep. and Ion. for κράτος, *strength, vigour, courage.* Hence

καρτύνω, Ep. for κρατύνω, *to strengthen;* aor. 1 med., ἐκαρτύνατο φάλαγγας *they strengthened their* ranks; χεῖρας ἐκαρτύναντο *they strengthened* or *armed their* hands.

Κᾰρυάτιδες, ων, αἱ, (Καρυαί) *the women of Caryae* in Laconia. II. in Architecture, *Caryatides* are *female figures used as bearing shafts.* [ᾱ]

κᾰρύκη, ἡ, *a rich Lydian sauce made of blood and rich spice.* [ῡ] Hence

κᾰρύκινος, η, ον, *of the colour of* καρύκη, *blood-red.*

κᾰρῡκο-ποιέω, f. ήσω, (καρύκη, ποιέω) *to make a rich savoury sauce.*

κάρυξ, Dor. for κῆρυξ.

ΚΑ'ΡΥΟΝ, *the nut;* κ. Περσικόν *the walnut;* κ. Εὐβοϊκόν *the chestnut;* κ. Ποντικόν *the filberd.*

κᾰρῠο-ναύτης, ου, ὁ, (κάρυον, ναύτης) *one who goes to sea in a nutshell.*

καρύσσω, Dor. for κηρύσσω.

καρφᾰλέος, α, ον, (κάρφω) *dry, parched:* of sound, *hollow.*

κάρφη, ἡ, (κάρφω) *a dry blade of grass.*

καρφηρός, ά, όν, (κάρφος) *of dry straw.*

καρφίτης [ῑ], ου, ὁ, (κάρφος) *built of dry straw.*

κάρφος, εος, τό, (κάρφω) *any dry particle, a dry stalk* or *chip*, Lat. *palea: dry twigs, straws, bits of wool*, such as birds make their nests of: in pl. *husks, chaff*, Lat. *quisquiliae.* 2. *the dry sticks of cinnamon* were also called κάρφ

ΚΑ'ΡΦΩ, f. κάρψω, *to make dry* or *withered:*—Pass. *to wither away.*

καρχᾰλέος, α, ον, (κάρχαρος) *rough in throat with thirst*, Virgil's *siti asper.*

καρχαρ-όδους or –όδων, όδοντος, ὁ, ἡ, (κάρχαρος, ὀδούς) *with sharp jagged teeth.*

κάρχᾰρος, ον, (χαράσσω) *sharp-pointed* or *jagged:* generally, *sharp, biting.*

Καρχηδών, όνος, ἡ, *Carthage:* **Καρχηδόνιος**, α, ον, and **Καρχηδονιακός**, ή, όν, *Carthaginian.*

καρχήσιον, τό, *a drinking-cup* or *goblet* narrower in the middle than at top and bottom. II. *the masthead of a ship.* (Deriv. uncertain.)

κάρψε, Ep. 3 sing. aor. 1 of κάρφω.

καρῷ, Dor. for κηρῷ.

κἀς, by crasis for καὶ εἰς or καὶ ἐς.

κᾰσαλβάζω, f. σω, *to abuse in harlot's language.* From

κᾰσαλβάς, άδος, ἡ, *a harlot, strumpet.*

κάσας, **κασᾶς** or **κασῆς**, ου, ὁ, *a horse's caparison* or *housing, a carpet* or *skin to sit upon.* (Akin to κῶς, κῶας.)

ΚΑ'ΣΙ'Α Ion. –ίη, ἡ, *cassia*, an Arabian spice, an inferior kind of cinnamon.

κᾰσι-γνήτη, ἡ, *a sister:* fem. of κασίγνητος.

κᾰσί-γνητος, ὁ, (κάσις, γεννάω) *a brother:*—then *any blood-relation, a nephew* or *niece.* II. as Adj. κασίγνητος, η, ον, *brotherly, sisterly.*

ΚΑ'ΣΙΣ, ιος, ὁ or ἡ: vocat. κάσι: *a brother* or *sister.* [ᾰ]

Κασσιτερίδες, ων, αἱ, *the Cassiterides* or *tin-islands.*

ΚΑΣΣΙ'ΤΕΡΟΣ Att. **καττίτερος**, ὁ, *tin*, Lat. *stannum;* χεῦμα κασσιτέροιο a plating of *tin.*

κάσσῡμα Att. **κάττ**–, ατος, τό, *anything stitched* or *sewed, the sole of a shoe* or *sandal:* generally, *a leather sole* or *shoe.* From

ΚΑΣΣΥ'Ω Att. **καττύω**, *to stitch, sew together.* II. metaph. *to stitch up*, i. e. *to concoct, a plot.* [ῡ]

κἀστόν, by crasis for καὶ ἐστόν.

Καστόρειος, ον, (Κάστωρ) *of* or *for Castor;* καστόρειος νόμος, a warlike air for the flute, mostly used in Sparta.

καστορίδες, αἱ, (Κάστωρ) a famous Laconian breed of *hounds*, said to be first reared by Castor: also καστόριαι κύνες.

καστορνῦσα, Ep. for καταστορνῦσα, pres. part. fem. of καταστόρνυμι.

Κάστωρ, ορος, ὁ, *Castor*, son of Zeus (or Tyndarus) and Leda, brother of Pollux.

ΚΑ'ΣΤΩΡ, ορος, ὁ, *the beaver.*

κάσχεθε, Ep. for κατέσχεθε, 3 sing. Ep. aor. 2 of κατέχω.

κᾰσώρῐον, τό, *a brothel.* From

κᾰσωρίς, ίδος, ἡ, = κασάλβη, *a harlot.*

ΚΑΤΑ', Prep. with gen. and acc.: A. GENIT.: I. denoting *motion from above, down from.* II. *down towards, down upon;* κατὰ χθονὸς ὄμματα πῆξαι to fix the eyes *down upon* the ground; of a dart, κατὰ γαίης ᾤχετο it went *down to the ground:*—so, τοξεύειν κατά τινος to shoot *at* one (because the arrow falls *down upon* its mark); παίειν κατά τινος to strike *at* one; ὀμόσαι κατά τινος to swear *upon* a thing. III. *against, in opposition to;* λόγος κατά τινος, Lat. oratio *in* aliquem, a speech *against* one accused; but, πρός τινα, Lat. *adversus* aliquem, a speech *in answer to* an opponent.

B. Accus.: I. of motion *downwards*, κατὰ ῥόον *down* the stream. 2. of motion or extension, *over, throughout, among, at, about, over*, as κατὰ γαῖαν, πόντον: *throughout, all along:* also of Place, *upon*, βάλλειν κατ' ἀσπίδα. 3. generally, of Place, as, κατὰ γῆν καὶ κατὰ θάλατταν *by* land and sea. II. *distributively*, of a whole divided into parts; κατὰ φῦλα, κατὰ φρήτρας *by* tribes and clans; κατὰ σφέας *by* themselves; so, of time, κατ' ἐνιαυτόν year *by* year; and of numbers, κατ' ὀλίγους few *at* a time. III. of object or purpose, πλεῖν κατὰ πρῆξιν to sail *on* a business; πλάζεσθαι κατὰ ληΐδα to rove *in search of* booty. IV. of fitness, *according to, answering to;* κατα θυμόν *according to* one's mind; so, καθ' ἡμέτερον νόον *after* our liking; κατ' ἄνθρωπον *according to* the capacity of a man; κατὰ φύσιν naturally; κατὰ δύναμιν to the best of one's power; κατὰ τὰ συγκείμενα *according to* the terms agreed upon. 2. *in relation to, concerning;* τὰ κατὰ πόλεμον all *that belongs to* war; τὸ καθ' ὑμᾶς as far as concerns you; *κατὰ τοῦτο in* this way; *κατὰ ταὐτά in* the same way. V. of numbers, *nearly, about; κατὰ ἑξηκόσια ἔτεα about* 600 years. VI. of Time, *throughout, during, in the course of; κατὰ τὸν πόλεμον in the course of* the war; *κατὰ Ἄμασιν about the time* of Amasis; *οἱ καθ' ἡμᾶς* those that live *about* our time, our contemporaries. VII. the Comp. is followed by *ἢ κατά..*, when the *qualities* of things are compared; *μεῖζον ἢ κατ' ἄνθρωπον* greater than *is suited to* man, too great for man; *μείζω ἢ κατὰ δάκρυα* greater *than to call for* tears, too great to weep for.

Position: when *κατά* follows its case, it is written *κάτα*.

As Adv., like *κάτω, downwards, from above, down.*

In compos.: I. *downwards, down,* as in *κατα-βαίνω.* II. *over against, in answer to,* as in *κατ-ᾴδω,* Lat. *occino.* III. *against,* in hostile sense, as in *κατ-ηγορέω.* IV. often only to strengthen the simple word, as in *κατα-κόπτω, κατα-φαγεῖν.*

Κατά as a Prep. was shortened by Poets into *κάγ* before *γ*, *κάκ* before *κ*, *κάμ* before *μ*, *κάν* before *ν*, *κάπ* before *π* or *φ*, *κάρ* before *ρ*, *κάτ* before *τ* or *θ*. In compd. Verbs, *κατά* sometimes changes into *καβ, καλ, καρ, κατ,* as *κάββαλε, κάλλιπε, καρρέζουσα, κάτθανε.*

κατά, Ion. for *καθ' ἅ.*

κᾆτα, crasis for *καὶ εἶτα, and then.*

κατάβα, for *κατάβηθι*, aor. 2 imperat. of *καταβαίνω.*

καταβάδην, Adv. (*καταβαίνω*) *going down: below, down-stairs,* opp. to *ἀναβάδην.* [βᾰ]

καταβαθμός, ὁ, (*καταβαίνω*) *a descent:* the name of *the steep slope* which separates Egypt and Libya.

καταβαίην, aor. 2 opt. of

κατα-βαίνω, f. *-βήσομαι*: pf. *-βέβηκα*; aor. 2 *κατέβην*, Ep. 1 pl. subj. *καταβείομεν*, for *καταβῶμεν*; *κατάβᾰ* imperat. (for *κατάβηθι*): aor. 1 med. *κατεβησάμην*, Ep. 3 sing. *κατεβήσετο*, Ep. imperat. *καταβήσεο*:—*to go* or *come down,* Lat. *descendere:* c. gen. *to go down from; καταβαίνειν δίφρου to come down from* a chariot: c. acc. *to go down to; θάλαμον κατεβήσατο* she *came down to* her chamber; but also, *κλίμακα καταβαίνειν to come down* the ladder; and absol. *to come down stairs.* 2. *to go down to the sea.* 3. *to go down into the arena, to fight, contend.* 4. metaph. *to come to* a thing, *arrive at,* e. g. in speaking. II. rarely in Pass., *ἵππος καταβαίνεται* the horse *is dismounted from.*

κατα-βακχιόομαι, Pass. (*κατά, Βακχιόω*) *to be full of Bacchic frenzy.*

κατα-βάλλω, fut. *-βᾰλῶ*: aor. 2 *κατέβᾰλον*, Ep. 3 sing. *κάββαλε*: pf. *-βέβληκα*, pass. *-βέβλημαι*:—*to throw down, cast down, overthrow, lay low; καταβάλλειν εἰς γόνυ to throw* on the knee, of wrestling: *to let fall, drop down:* also *to lay* or *put down.* 2. *to strike down,* and so *to slay.* 3. *to bring* or *carry down,* esp. *to the sea.* 4. *to put down, pay down:* hence *to pay off, discharge.* 5. *to put down into a place and leave there:*—Med. *to lay as a foundation, ground, found.*

κατα-βάπτω, f. *ψω*, (*κατά, βάπτω*) *to dip down* or *into.*

κατα-βᾰρέω, f. *ήσω*, (*κατά, βάρος*) *to weigh down, overload.*

καταβάς, aor. 2 part. of *καταβαίνω.*

κατάβᾰσις, εως, ἡ, (*καταβαίνω*) *a going down, descending.* 2. *a way down, a descent: the entrance to a cave.*

κατα-βασμός, Att. for *καταβαθμός.*

καταβάτω [ᾰ], 3 sing. aor. 2 imperat. of *καταβαίνω.*

κατᾰβαΰζω, f. *ξω*, *to bark* or *bay at, τινός.*

κατα-βεβαιόομαι, Dep. *to affirm positively.*

καταβεβλημένος, pf. pass. part. of *καταβάλλω.*

καταβείομεν, Ep. for *καταβῶμεν*, 1 pl. aor. 2 subj. of *καταβαίνω.*

καταβήμεναι, Ep. for *καταβῆναι*, aor. 2 inf. of *καταβαίνω.*

καταβήσεο, Ep. for *κατάβησαι*, 2 sing. aor. 1 med. imperat. of *καταβαίνω.*

καταβήσομαι, fut. of *καταβαίνω.*

κατα-βῐβάζω, f. *-βιβάσω* Att. *-βιβῶ*, Causal of *καταβαίνω, to make to go down, bring down.*

κατα-βιβρώσκω, fut. *-βρώσομαι*: aor. 2 *κατέβρων*: —Pass., aor. 1 *κατεβρώθην*: pf. *-βέβρωμαι*:—*to eat up, devour.*

κατα-βῐόω, f. *-ώσομαι*: aor. 2 *κατεβίων*:—*to bring life to an end, pass life.*

κατα-βλᾱκεύω, f. *σω*, *to treat carelessly, mismanage.*

κατα-βλάπτω, f. *βλάψω*, *to damage.*

κατα-βλητικός, ή, όν, (*καταβάλλω*) *likely to throw off.*

κατα-βληχάομαι, f. *ήσομαι*, Dep. *to bleat aloud.*

κατα-βλώσκω, f. *-μολοῦμαι*: aor. 2 *κατέμολον*;—*to go down* or *through, pass through.*

κατα-βοάω, fut. *-βοήσομαι* Ion. *-βώσομαι*:—*to cry down, cry out against, exclaim against,* c. gen. II. c. acc. *to outcry, silence.* Hence

καταβοή, ῆς, ἡ, *a cry* or *outcry against* one: and

καταβόησις, εως, ἡ, *a crying out against.*

καταβολή, ἡ, (*καταβάλλω*) *a laying down: a foundation, beginning.* 2. *a paying down.* 2. *a periodical attack of illness, a fit.*

κατα-βόσκω, f. *-βοσκήσω*, (*κατά, βόσκω*) *to feed flocks upon* a place:—Med. *to feed upon.*

κατα-βόστρῠχος, ον, *with long flowing locks.*

κατα-βρᾰβεύω, f. *σω*, *to decide against one, deprive one of one's right*:—Pass. *to be unfairly cast in a suit.*

κατα-βρέχω, f. *-βρέξω*: Pass., aor. 1 *κατεβρέχθην*: —*to wet through, drench.*

κατα-βρίθω [ῑ], f. *-βρίσω*:—*to weigh* or *press down:* metaph. *to outweigh.* II. intr. *to be heavily laden, weighed down by* a thing. [ῑ]

***καταβρόχω**, aor. 1 *κατέβροξα*, opt. *καταβρόξεια*, *to gulp* or *swallow down:* cf. *ἀναβρόχω.*

κατα-βροχθίζω, f. *ίσω* Att. *ιῶ*, (*κατά, βρόχθος*) *to gulp down.*

κατα-βρύκω [ῡ], f. *ξω*, *to bite in pieces, eat up.*

καταβρώσομαι, fut. of *καταβιβρώσκω*.

κατα-βυρσόω, (*κατά, βύρσα*) *to cover over with hides.*

καταβώσομαι, Ion. fut. of *καταβοάω*

κατά-γαιος Att. **-γειος**, *ον*, (*κατά, γαῖος*) *underground, subterraneous.* II. *on the ground; κατάγαιοι στρουθοί* birds *that run* instead of flying, *ostriches.*

καταγγελεύς, *έως, ὁ*, (*καταγγέλλω*) *a proclaimer.*

κατ-αγγέλλω, f. *ελῶ*, *to announce, proclaim, declare; καταγγέλλειν πόλεμον to declare* war. 2. *to denounce, disclose, betray.* Hence

κατ-άγγελτος, *ον*, *denounced, betrayed.*

κατά-γειος, Att. for *κατάγαιος*.

Κατα-γέλα, *ἡ*, (*κατά, γελάω*) Comic name of a supposed town, **Γέλα** *καὶ* **Καταγέλα**.

κατα-γέλαστος, *ον*, *ridiculous.* From

κατα-γελάω, f. *άσομαι* [ᾰ]: aor. 1 *κατεγέλᾰσα*:—Pass., aor. 1 *κατεγελάσθην*: pf. *γεγέλασμαι*:—*to laugh at:* absol. *to laugh scornfully, mock.*

κατά-γελως, *ωτος, ὁ*, (*κατά, γέλως*) *ridicule, mockery:* also *absurdity.*

καταγῆναι, aor. 2 inf. pass. of *κατάγνυμι*.

κατα-γηράσκω, f. *γηράσω* or *άσομαι*. aor. 1 *κατεγήρᾱσα* or *εγήρᾱνα*, pf. *-γεγήρᾱκα*—*to grow old, pass one's old age*, Lat. *senesco*, 3 sing. impf. *κατεγήρα* (from *καταγηράω*), or aor. 2 (as if from a Verb in *μι*, cf. *γηράσκω*). *to grow old*, Lat. *senesco.*

κατα-γιγαρτίζω, f. *ίσω*, (*κατά, γίγαρτον*) *to take out the kernel:* metaph. for *stuprare.*

κατα-γίγνομαι, f. *γενήσομαι*: *to stay* or *reside at.* also *to busy oneself about* a thing.

κατα-γιγνώσκω, f. *γνώσομαι*. aor. 2 *κατέγνων*:—*to remark, observe, discover*, esp. with a view to finding fault. 2. *to lay* something *to one's charge*, c. gen pers. et acc. rei, as, *καταγιγνώσκειν τινὸς ἀνανδρίην to lay a charge* of cowardice *against* him —Pass., *καταγνωσθεὶς πρήσσειν being thought* or *suspected to be* doing. 3. *to give judgment* or *sentence against* a person; *καταγιγνώσκειν τινὸς θάνατον to pass sentence* of death on one, Lat. *damnare aliquem mortis; καταγιγνώσκειν δίκην to adjudge* or *decide* a suit.

κατ-ᾰγίζω, Ion. for *καθαγίζω*.

κατ-ᾰγῑνέω, Ion. for *κατάγω*, *to lead* or *carry down.* II. *to bring back.*

κατα-γίνομαι, **γῑνώσκω**, later forms for *καταγιγ-*.

κατ-αγλᾰΐζω, f. *ίσω*, strengthd. for *ἀγλαΐζω*.

κατα-γλωττίζω: f. *ίσω* Att. *ιῶ*. pf. pass. *κατεγλώττισμαι*. (*κατά, γλῶττα*).—*to kiss by joining tongues: μέλος κατεγλωττισμένον a wanton, licentious* song. II. *to use the tongue* or *speak against* one. III. *to talk* one *down, silence* him. Hence

καταγλώττισμα, *τό*, *a wanton kiss.*

κάτ-αγμα, *ατος, τό*, (*κατάγω*) *wool spun out: a piece* or *flock of wool*

κατα-γνάμπτω, f. *ψω*, *to bend down.*

καταγνοίην, aor. 2 opt. of *καταγιγνώσκω*.

καταγνούς, aor. 2 part. of *καταγιγνώσκω*.

κατ-άγνῡμι; fut. *κατάξω*: aor. 1 *κατέαξα*, part. *κατάξας*: pf. (in pass. sense) *κατέᾱγα* Ion. *κατέηγα*. aor. 2 pass. *κατεάγην* [ᾰ], inf. *καταγῆναι*:—*to break in pieces, shatter, shiver: to break, weaken.* II. in Pass., and in pf. act *κατέᾱγα*, *to be broken, κατεᾱγέναι* or *καταγῆναι τὴν κεφαλήν to have* the head *broken.*

κατάγνωσις, *εως, ἡ*, (*καταγιγνώσκω*) *an unfavourable opinion.* II. *condemnation.*

κατα-γοητεύω, f. *σω*, *to enchant, bewitch to cheat, impose upon.*

κατ-ᾰγορεύω, f. *σω*, *to denounce.*

κατάγρᾰφος, *ον*, *engraved, embroidered.* From

κατα-γράφω, f. *ψω*, *to mark* or *scratch deeply: to engrave: to paint over, fill with letters.* II. *to write down: to register, enroll.*

κατ-αγρέω, f. *ήσω*, *to catch, overtake.*

κατα-γυμνάζω, fut. *άσω*, *to exercise constantly.*

κατ-άγω, f. *άξω*: aor 2 *κατήγᾰγον*:—*to lead* or *carry down*, Lat. *deducere to lead* or *carry to* a place, esp. *to the sea-coast.* 2. *to bring down from the high sea to land*:—Pass. *to come to land*, opp. to *ἀνάγεσθαι* (*to put out to sea*) 3. *to draw out, spin.* 4. *to bring down, lower.* II. *to bring back*, esp. from banishment, *to recall, restore.* Hence

καταγωγή, *ἡ*, *a bringing down.* II. *a putting a ship into harbour, landing.* 2. *a landing-place:* hence 3. *a resting-place, lodging-place.*

καταγώγιον, *τό*, (*κατάγω*) *a place to lodge in, resting-place, inn.*

κατ-ᾰγωνίζομαι, fut. *-ίσομαι* Att. *-ιοῦμαι*, Dep. *to struggle against, prevail against.*

κατα-δαίνῡμαι, f. *δαίσομαι*, Pass *to devour.*

κατα-δάκνω, fut. *δήξομαι*, *to bite in pieces.*

κατα-δακρυχέων, *ουσα*, better divisim, *κατὰ δάκρυ χέων*, *shedding tears.*

κατα-δακρύω, f. *σω*, *to bewail* or *lament bitterly:* absol. *to weep bitterly.*

κατα-δᾰμάζω, f. *άσω*: aor 1 inf. med. *καταδαμάσασθαι*:—*to subdue utterly.*

καταδάμναμαι, *καταδαμάζω*.

κατα-δᾰπᾰνάω, f. *ήσω*, *to squander, waste utterly.*

κατα-δάπτω, f. *δάψω*, *to rend in pieces, devour.*

κατα-δαρθάνω: aor 2 *κατέδαρθον*, by poët. metath. *κατέδρᾰθον*; also, in same sense, aor 2 pass. *κατεδάρθην*, poet. subj. *καταδραθῶ*, part. *καταδαρθείς*:—*to sleep soundly, fall asleep.*

κατα-δατέομαι, f. *δάσομαι*, Med. *to divide among themselves.*

καταδεής, *ές*, (*καταδέω*) *wanting* or *failing in something, lacking of*: hence *poor, needy*; Comp. *καταδεέστερος*, *weaker, inferior*, see *καταδεῶς*.

κατα-δεῖ, impers. *there is wanting*: see *καταδέω*.

κατα-δείδω, f. *-δείσω*. aor. 1 *κατέδεισα*:—*to fear very much, be in great terror of.*

κατα-δείκνῡμι and *-ύω*, f. *-δείξω*: aor. 1 *κατ-έδειξα* Ion. *-έδεξα*:—*to shew clearly, point out, make known:* c. inf. *to shew how to do: to establish, prove.*

κατα-δειλιάω, f. άσω [ᾱ]:—*to shew signs of fear* or *cowardice.*

καταδέξαι, Ion. aor. 1 inf. of καταδείκνυμι.

κατα-δέομαι, f. –δεήσομαι, Dep. *to want* or *need very much: to intreat earnestly*, Lat. *deprecari.*

κατα-δέρκομαι, aor. 2 act. κατέδρᾰκον, and in same sense pass. κατεδέρχθην: Dep.:—*to look down, to look down upon.*

κατά-δεσμος, ὁ, *a tie* or *band: a magic knot, love-knot.*

κατα-δεύω, f. σω, aor. 1 κατέδευσα, *to wet through: to water.*

κατα-δέχομαι, f. –δέξομαι: Dep.:—*to receive, admit.* 2. *to receive back, take home again.*

κατα-δέω (A), f. –δήσω, *to bind on* or *to, bind fast:* Med. *to bind to* or *for oneself.* 2. *to put in bonds, imprison.* 3. metaph. *to convict of* a crime. II. *to tie down, shut up, close, check.*

κατα-δέω (B), f. –δεήσω, *to want, lack, need, be lacking in* a thing, esp. of numbers: καταδεῖ, impers. *there is need.*

καταδεῶς, Adv. of καταδεής, *in defect:* Comp. καταδεεστέρως ἔχειν to be *very ill off.*

κατά-δηλος, ον, *very plain* or *manifest.*

κατα-δημοβορέω, f. ήσω, (κατά, δημοβόρος) *to consume publicly.*

κατα-δῐαιτάω, f. ήσω, *to decide as arbitrator against, to give arbitration against*, τινός.

κατα-διαλλάσσω Att. –ττω, fut. –άξω, *to reconcile again.*

κατα-δίδωμι, f. –δώσω, of rivers, intr., *to flow* or *empty themselves into.*

κατα-δῐκάζω, f. άσω: Pass., aor. κατεδικάσθην: pf. καταδεδίκασμαι:—*to give judgment against, pass sentence upon*, τινός: absol. *to condemn:*—Med. *to get sentence given against* another, *procure* his *condemnation:*—Pass., καταδεδικασμένος *one who has judgment given against him.*

κατα-δίκη, ἡ, (κατά, δίκη) *judgment given against one, condemnation, sentence: a fine.* [ῐ]

κατά-δικος, ον, (κατά, δίκη) *condemned.*

κατα-δῐώκω, f. ξω or ξομαι, *to pursue closely.*

κατα-δοκέω, f. –δόξω, *to suppose* a thing *against* or *to the prejudice of* another, *to suspect: to think, suppose:* also in aor. 1 part. pass. καταδοχθείς *being suspected.*

καταδοξάζω, fut. άσω, = καταδοκέω.

κατα-δουλόω, f. ώσω, *to reduce to slavery, enslave:* also as Dep., with fut. and aor. 1 med. –δουλώσομαι, –εδουλωσάμην, pf. pass. –δεδούλωμαι. Hence

καταδούλωσις, εως, ἡ, *a reducing to slavery, enslaving.*

κατα-δουπέω, f. ήσω, *to fall with a heavy sound.*

Κατά-δουποι, ων, οἱ, (κατά, δοῦπος) *the Cataracts* of the Nile: also the parts of Ethiopia in which they are called by Cicero *Catadupa* as neut. pl.

καταδοχή, ἡ, (καταδέχομαι) *a receiving, admitting.*

καταδρᾰθῶ, aor. 2 subj. pass. of καταδαρθάνω.

καταδρᾰμεῖν, aor. 2 inf. of κατατρέχω.

κατα-δρέπω, f. –δρέψω, *to strip off.*

καταδρομή, ἡ, (καταδραμεῖν) *an overrunning, inroad, raid.* Hence

κατάδρομος, ον, *overrun, wasted by a raid.*

κατά-δρυμμα, ατος, τό, *a tearing* or *rending.* From

κατα-δρύπτω, f. –δρύψω, *to tear in pieces, rend.*

καταδῦναι, aor. 2 inf. of καταδύω.

κατα-δῠναστεύω, f. σω, *to exercise lordship* or *sovereignty over, overpower, oppress.*

κατα-δύνω, = καταδύω in intrans. sense.

καταδύς, aor. 2 part. of καταδύω.

κατάδῠσις, εως, ἡ, (καταδύω) *a going down under water:* of the stars, *a setting:* generally, *a descent.*

κατα-δυσωπέω, *to put quite to the blush*, esp. by earnest intreaty.

κατα-δύω and **κατα-δύνω**: fut. –δύσω: aor. 1 κατέδῡσα: aor. 2 κατέδῡν: I. Causal, in pres. καταδύω, fut. –δύσω, aor. 1 –έδῡσα:—*to make to sink*, Lat. *mergere;* καταδῦσαι ναῦν *to sink* or *disable* a ship. II. intrans. in pres. act. καταδύνω and in med. καταδύομαι, with aor. 2, pf., plqpf. act., κατέδυν, –δέδῡκα, –δεδύκειν:—*to go under water, sink, set*, of the sun; ἅμ' ἠελίῳ καταδύντι with sunset. 2. *to go down into, to steal* or *creep into: to get into the midst of;* τεύχεα καταδῦναι *to get under*, i. e. *put on* arms. 3. *to keep hidden, lie hid.*

κατ-ᾴδω Ion. –ᾰείδω: f. –ᾴσομαι: rarely –ᾴσω:—*to sing to, to charm by singing*, Lat. *occinere:* absol. *to sing a spell, charm.* II. *to deafen by singing.*

κατα-δωροδοκέω, f. ήσω, *to accept presents* or *bribes.*

κατ-αείδω, Ion. for κατᾴδω.

κατα-ειμένος, pf. part. pass. of καθέννυμι, *clothed, clad, covered.* II. pf. part. pass. of καθίημι, *let down, hanging down.*

καταείνῠσαν, 3 pl. impf. of καθέννυμι.

καταείσατο, Ep. for καθείσατο, 3 sing. aor. 1 med. of καθέζω.

κατα-έννῡμι, poët. for καθέννυμι: impf. καταείνυον: *to clothe, cover, overspread.*

κατ-αζαίνω: Ion. aor. 1 καταζήνασκον: (κατα, ἀζαίνω, ἄζω):—*to make quite dry, parch up.*

κατα-ζάω, inf. καταζῆν, *to live one's life out.*

κατα-ζεύγνῡμι and –ύω, f. –ζεύξω:—*to tie* or *yoke together, yoke:*—Pass. *to be bound fast, straitened: to be imprisoned.*

καταζήνασκε, 3 sing. Ion. aor. 1 of καταζαίνω.

κατα-ζώννῡμι and –ύω, f. –ζώσω, *to gird fast:* Med. *to gird oneself.*

καταθᾰνεῖν, aor. 2 inf. of καταθνήσκω.

κατα-θάπτω, f. ψω, *to bury, inter.*

κατα-θαρσύνω, *to embolden* or *encourage against:*—Pass. *to take courage, behave boldly.* [ῡ]

κατα-θεάομαι, f. άσομαι [ᾱ], Dep. *to look down upon, watch from above, observe.*

καταθεῖναι, aor. 2 inf. of κατατίθημι.

καταθεῖο, 2 sing. aor. 2 opt. med. of κατατίθημι.

καταθείομαι, Ep. for –θέωμαι, aor. 2 subj. med. of κατατίθημι.

καταθείομεν, Ep. for -θέωμεν, 1 pl. aor. 2 subj. of κατατίθημι.

κατα-θέλγω, f. ξω, *to subdue by charms.* Hence

κατάθελξις, εως, ἡ, *enchantment.*

κατάθεμα, ατος, τό, (κατατίθημι) *an accursed thing.*

κατα-θεματίζω, f. σω, (κατάθεμα) *to curse.*

καταθέσθαι, aor. 2 med. inf. of κατατίθημι.

κατάθεσις, εως, ἡ, (κατατίθημι) *a putting down: a paying down, discharging.*

κατα-θέω, f. -θεύσομαι:—*to run down:* of ships, *to run into harbour.* II. *to make inroads* or *incursions:* c. acc., καταθεῖν χώραν *to overrun a* country.

κατα-θεωρέω, f. ήσω, *to contemplate from above.*

κατα-θήγω, f. ξω, *to sharpen, whet.*

κατα-θηλύνω, (κατά, θῆλυς) *to make womanish.*

καταθησῶ, Dor. for καταθήσω, fut. of κατατίθημι.

κατα-θνήσκω, fut. -θᾰνοῦμαι: aor. 2 κατέθᾰνον Ep. κάτθᾰνον: pf. -τέθνηκα, part. -τεθνηκώς Ep. -τεθνηώς, ῶτος, inf. -τεθνάναι Ep. -τεθνάμεν [ᾰ]:—*to die away, be dying:* in aor. 2 and pf. *to be dead, deceased.* Hence

καταθνητός, ή, όν, *mortal.*

καταθορεῖν, aor. 2 inf. of καταθρώσκω.

κατα-θορυβέω, f. ήσω, *to cry down.*

κατα-θρηνέω, f. ήσω, *to bewail, lament.*

κατα-θρώσκω, f. -θοροῦμαι: aor. 2 κατέθορον, inf. -θορεῖν:—*to leap* or *jump down:* c. acc., καταθρώσκειν τὴν αἱμασίην *to leap down from* the wall.

κατ-αθῡμέω, f. ήσω, (κατά, ἀθυμέω) *to lose all heart, to be very much dejected.*

κατα-θύμιος, ον, also η, ον, *in* or *upon the mind, at heart;* μηδέ τί τοι θάνατος καταθύμιος ἔστω let not death sit *heavy at thy heart.* II. *according to one's mind, welcome, well-pleasing.*

κατα-θύω, f. ύσω [ῡ], *to sacrifice: to offer, dedicate.* II. Med., καταθύεσθαί τινα *to compel* one's *love by magic sacrifices.*

κατα-θωρᾱκίζω, f. ίσω Att. ιῶ, *to cover with a coat of mail, arm at all points.*

καταί-βᾰσις, εως, ἡ, poët. for κατάβασις.

καται-βάτης, ου, ὁ, poët. for καταβάτης, (καταβαίνω) *one who comes down* or *descends,* of Zeus *descending in thunder and lightning:* also of the thunder-bolt, *hurled down, descending.* 2. epith. of Ἀχέρων, *to which one descends, downward, infernal.*

καται-βᾰτός, ή, όν, poët. for καταβατός, *giving a passage downwards;* θύραι καταιβαταὶ ἀνθρώποισι gates *by which* men *descend.*

κατ-αιδέομαι, Dep. with fut. med. -αιδέσομαι, aor. 1 pass. -ῃδέσθην:—*to feel shame* or *reverence before* another, *to reverence, respect:* c. inf. *to be ashamed to do* a thing.

κατ-αιθαλόω, f. ώσω, *to burn to ashes.*

κατ-αιθύσσω, f. ξω, of motion, *to float* or *hover over;* πλόκαμοι νῶτον καταίθυσσον his locks *floated down* his back.

κατ-αίθω, *to burn down, burn to ashes.* 2. *to light up, ignite, illumine.*

κατ-αικίζω, f. ίσω Att. ιῶ, *to wound severely: to ill-treat, disfigure.*

κατ-αινέω, f. έσω poët. ήσω:—*to agree to, assent to, approve of;* καταινεῖν ἐπί τινι *to agree* to a thing on certain conditions. II. *to grant, promise: to promise in marriage, betroth.*

κατ-αιρέω, Ion. for καθαιρέω.

κατ-αίρω, fut. -ἀρῶ, (κατά, αἴρω):—*to take* or *put down.* 2. intr. *to put into port:* of birds, *to go down to* a place, *light upon* it.

κατ-αισθάνομαι, f. -αισθήσομαι, Dep. *to comprehend fully.*

κατ-αίσιος, ον, (κατά, αἴσιος) *righteous.*

καταισχυντήρ, ῆρος, *a disgracer.* From

κατ-αισχύνω, f. ὑνῶ, *to shame, disgrace, dishonour.* III. Med. *to feel shame before* another, *to reverence.*

κατα-ΐσχω, poët. for κατίσχω.

κατ-αιτιάομαι, f. άσομαι [ᾱ], Dep. *to accuse, arraign, blame, find fault with:* c. acc., *to lay to one's charge, object to* one: *impute.* II. the aor. 1 part. καταιτιαθείς occurs in pass. sense, *accused, put on one's defence.*

καταῖτυξ, ῠγος, ἡ, *a low helmet* or *skull-cap* without a crest. (Deriv uncertain.)

κατ-αιωρέομαι, Pass. (κατά, αἰωρέω) *to hang down.*

κατα-καγχάζω, f. άσω, *to laugh loudly at.*

κατακαῆμεν, Dor. and Lacon. for κατακαῆναι, aor. 2 inf. pass. of κατακαίω.

κατακαιέμεν, Ep. for κατακαίειν.

κατα-καίνω, fut. -κᾰνῶ, aor. 2 κατέκᾰνον:—like κατακτείνω, *to slay.*

κατα-καίω Att. -κάω [ᾱ]: fut. -καύσω: aor. 1 κατέκαυσα Ep. κατέκηα: aor. 1 pass. κατεκαύθην, aor 2 κατεκάην:—*to burn, burn down, consume by burning:*—Pass., κατὰ πῦρ ἐκάη the fire *had burned down* or *out.*

κατα-κᾰλέω, f. έσω, *to call down, summon, invite.* II. *to call upon, invoke.*

κατα-κᾰλύπτω, f ψω, *to cover up, envelope:*—Med. *to veil oneself.*

κατα-κάμπτω, f. -κάμψω, *to bend down: to bend* or *turn by entreaty;* κατακάμπτειν ἐλπίδας *to bend down, break down* hopes.

κατα-κάρφω, *to dry up, parch:*—Pass. *to wither, fall into the sere.*

κατακαύσας, aor. 1 part. of κατακαίω.

κατα-καυχάομαι, f. ήσομαι, Dep *to boast against exult over, vaunt at.*

κατακεῖαι, Ep. aor. 1 inf. of κατακαίω.

κατακειέμεν, Ep. pres. inf. of κατακαίω.

κατακείετε, 2 pl. of κατακείω.

κατά-κειμαι, f. -κείσομαι, Dep. *to lie down: to lie hid: to lie stored up, to be laid by.* 2. *to lie sick.* 3. *to recline at meals.*

κατακείομεν, another form of κατακήομεν, q. v.:—but also Ep. for κατακείωμεν, pres. subj. of κατακείω.

κατα-κείρω, f. -κερῶ, *to cut down, waste, consume.*

κατα-κείω, Desiderat. of *κατάκειμαι, to wish to lie down: κακκείοντες*, Ep. part. for *κατακείοντες*.

κατακέκλῐσο, 2 sing. plqpf. pass. of *κατακλίνω*.

κατακεκράκτης, *ου, ὁ*, (*κατακράζω*) *a brawler*.

κατα-κελεύω, f. *σω, to give the word of command*: of the *κελευστής, to give the time in rowing*.

κατα-κεντέω, f. *ήσω, to pierce through, sting severely*.

κατα-κεραυνόω, f. *ώσω, to strike down by thunder*.

κατα-κερδαίνω, f. *ᾰνῶ* or *ήσω, to make a gain of* a thing *wrongly* or *meanly*.

κατα-κερτομέω, f. *ήσω, to rail violently: to mock at*.

κατακηέμεν, Ep. pres. inf. of *κατακαίω*.

κατα-κηλέω, f. *ήσω, to soothe by charms: to enchant*.

κατακήομεν, Ep. for *κατακήωμεν*, 1 pl. aor. 1 subj. of *κατακαίω*.

κατα-κηρόω, f. *ώσω*, (*κατά, κηρός*) *to cover with wax*.

κατα-κηρύσσω Att. **-ττω**, f. *ύξω, to proclaim* or *command by herald*.

κατα-κίρνημι, poët. for *κατακεράννυμι, to mix well*:—Pass. *to be well mixed*.

κατά-κισσος, *ον*, (*κατά, κισσός*) *ivy-wreathed*.

κατα-κλαίω Att. **-κλάω** [ᾱ]: fut. *-κλαύσομαι*:—*to bewail* or *lament loudly*: absol. *to wail aloud*.

κατακλᾳξασθαι, Dor. aor. 1 inf. med. of *κατακλείω*.

κατα-κλάω, f. *άσω* [ᾰ]: aor. 1 *κατέκλᾰσα*:—Pass., aor. 1 *κατεκλάσθην*:—*to break down, break short off, snap*. II. metaph. *to break down, overcome, enfeeble*, of sorrow, fear, or illness.

κατακλαχθῆναι, Dor. aor. 1 pass. inf. of *κατακλείω*.

κατα-κλάω, Att. for *κατακλαίω*. [ᾱ]

κατακλείς, *εῖδος*, Ion. and Ep. **κατακληΐς**, *ηῖδος, ἡ*, (*κατακλείω*) *a fastening for doors*.

κατα-κλείω Ion. **-κληΐω** old Att. **-κλῄω**: f. *-κλείσω* Dor. *-κλᾳξω*:—Med., aor. 1 *κατεκλεισάμην* Dor. *κατεκλᾳξάμην*:—Pass., aor. *κατεκλείσθην* Ion. *-εκληΐσθην* Dor. *-εκλάχθην* (not *-εκλάσθην*):—*to shut up, shut fast*. 2. *to shut up in* a fortress, *to blockade*.

κατα-κληροδοτέω, f. *ήσω*, (*κλῆρος, δίδωμι*) *to distribute by lot*.

κατα-κληρονομέω, f. *ήσω, to inherit, obtain by inheritance*.

κατα-κληρουχέω, f. *ήσω, to receive as one's allotment*. II. *to assign* to another *as his lot, give to inherit*.

κατακλῐθῆναι, aor. 2 inf. pass. of *κατακλίνω*.

κατακλῐνής, *ές*, (*κατακλινῆναι*) *lying down, stretched at length*. II. *sloping, steep*.

κατα-κλῑνο-βάτης, *ές*, (*κατά, κλίνη, βαίνω*) *making one lie abed*.

κατα-κλίνω [ῑ], f. *-κλῐνῶ*: aor. 1 *κατέκλῑνα*:—*to lay down, to make to lie down* or *sit at table*: also *to lay upon a couch, to lay* the sick *on couches* in the temple of Aesculapius:—Pass. *to lie down*, esp. at table. II. *to lay low, overthrow*. Hence

κατάκλῐσις, *εως, ἡ, a making to lie down* or *sit at table; ἡ κατάκλισις τοῦ γάμου the celebration* of a marriage.

κατα-κλύζω, f. *ύσω* [ῠ]: aor. 1 *κατέκλῠσα*:—*to wash over, deluge, inundate: to fill full of water*. II. *to wash down* or *away*: also *to wash out, efface*. Hence

κατακλυσμός, *ὁ, a deluge, flood*.

Κατα-κλῶθες, *αἱ*, (*κατακλώθω*) *the weird women who spin thread*, a name of the goddesses of Fate, *Μοῖραι*, Lat. *Parcae*.

κατα-κλώθω, f. *-κλώσω, to spin out*, of the Fates.

κατα-κνάω, f. *-κνήσω*: aor. 1 *κατέκνησα*:—*to scrape* or *grate down: to cut piecemeal*.

κατα-κνήθω, = *κατακνάω*.

κατα-κνίζω, f. *ίσω*: aor. 1 *κατέκνῐσα*:—*to pull to pieces*, Lat. *vellĭco*:—Pass. *to itch*.

κατα-κοιμάω, f. *ήσω*, like *κατακοιμίζω, to put to sleep, lull to sleep*: aor. 1 inf. pass. *κατακοιμηθῆναι, to go to sleep, fall asleep, sleep*. II. *to sleep through, sleep out; κατακοιμῆσαι τὴν φυλακὴν to sleep out* the watch.

κατα-κοιμίζω, f. *ίσω*, = *κατακοιμάω, to lull to sleep*.

κατα-κοινωνέω, f. *ήσω to make one a sharer, give one a share*.

κατ-ᾰκολουθέω, f. *ήσω, to follow closely*.

κατα-κολπίζω, f. *ίσω* Att. *ιῶ*, (*κατά, κόλπος*) *to run into a bay* or *gulf*.

κατα-κομῐδή, *ἡ, a bringing down to the sea-shore, exportation*. From

κατα-κομίζω, f. *ίσω* Att. *ιῶ*:—*to bring down*, esp. *to the sea*. 2. *to bring to land* or *into barbour*: *to bring into a place of refuge*.

κατά-κομος, *ον*, (*κατά, κόμη*) *with falling hair*.

κατ-ᾰκονά, *ἡ*, (*κατά, ἀκονή*) *destruction*.

κατα-κονδῠλίζω, f. *ίσω, to buffet severely*.

κατ-ᾰκοντίζω, f. *ίσω* Att. *ιῶ*, (*κατά, ἀκοντίζω*) *to strike down with darts*.

κατα-κόπτω, f. *ψω*: aor. 1 *κατέκοψα*:—Pass., p. post f. *κατακεκόψομαι*: aor. 2 *κατεκόπην*:—*to cut in pieces, cut up: to kill, slay*. II. *to stamp with a die, coin into money*

κατα-κοσμέω, f. *ήσω, to arrange, set in order; ἐπὶ νευρῇ κατακοσμεῖν to fit* the arrow on the string: generally, *to furnish, adorn*.

κατ-ᾰκούω, f. *-ακούσομαι, to hear and obey, be subject to*. II. *to hearken to, give ear to, hear plainly*.

κατα-κράζω, fut. *-κεκράξομαι, to cry down, outdo in crying*.

κατα-κρᾰτέω, f. *ήσω, to prevail over, subdue*:—absol. *to prevail, become master: to become current*.

κατα-κρέμᾰμαι, Pass. *to hang down, hang suspended*.

κατα-κρεμάννυμι or *-ύω*, fut. *-κρεμάσω* [ᾰ]: aor. 1 *κατεκρέμᾰσα*:—*to hang to* or *upon, hang up, attach to* or *by*.

κατα-κρεουργέω, f. *ήσω, to cut up like a butcher*.

κατα-κρῆθεν, (*κατά, κάρα*) Adv. *from the head downwards, from top to bottom*:—metaph. *entirely, utterly*.

κατα-κρημνάμαι or *-άομαι*, = *κατακρέμαμαι*.

κατα-κρημνίζω, f. *ίσω* Att. *ιῶ*, (*κατά, κρημνός*) *to throw down a precipice, throw headlong down*.

κατά-κρημνος, *ον, precipitous*.

κατάκρῐμα, *ατος, τό, condemnation, sentence*. From

κατα-κρίνω, f. -κρῐνῶ: aor. 1 κατέκρῖνα:—*to give judgment against: to condemn, sentence.* [ῑ] Hence

κατάκρῐσις, εως, ἡ, *condemnation.*

κατα-κρύπτω, f. ψω, *to bide away, conceal, keep bidden*: part. κακκρύπτων Ep. for κατακρύπτων. II. intr. *to use concealment, dissemble.* Hence

κατα-κρῠφή, ἡ, *a biding*: metaph. *a subterfuge.*

κατα-κρώζω, f. -κρώξω, *to croak at.*

κατα-κτάμεν and **-κτάμεναι**, Ep. aor. 2 inf. of κατακτείνω.

κατα-κτάομαι, fut. -κτήσομαι: aor. 1 -εκτησάμην: Dep. *to get* or *gain for oneself*: in pf. κατακέκτημαι. *to possess.*

κατακτάς, Ep. aor. 2 act. part. of κατακτείνω: pass. κατακτάμενος.

κατα-κτείνω: fut. -κτενῶ Ion. -κτᾰνῶ Ep. -κτᾰνέω: aor. 1 κατέκτεινα: aor. 2 κατέκτᾰνον poët. κατέκταν, ας, α, Ep. imperat. κάκτανε, inf. κατακτάμεν. -άμεναι, part. κατακτάς: pf. κατέκτονα:—Pass., aor. 1 κατεκτάθην: Ep. aor. 2 κατεκτάμην, part. κατακτάμενος: 2 pl. fut. med. (in pass. sense) κατακτενέεσθε.—*to kill, slay, put to deatb.*

κατα-κῠβεύω, f. σω, (κατά, κύβος) *to lose by tbe dice, gamble away.*

κατα-κῠλίνδω, f. ίσω [ῐ]:—Pass., aor. 1 εκῠλίσθην: pf. -κεκύλισμαι:—*to roll down*:—Pass. *to be rolled down* or *off.*

κατα-κύπτω, f. ψω: aor. 1 κατέκυψα:—*to bend down, s'oop: to stoop and peep into.*

κατα-κῡριεύω, f. σω, *to exercise autbority over.*

κατα-κῡρόω, (κατά, κῦρος) *to ratify*: aor. 1 part. κατακυρωθείς = κατακριθείς, *condemned to* something.

κατα-κωλύω, f. ύσω [ῡ]: *to binder from* doing: *to detain, keep back.*

κατα-κωμάζω, f. άσω, *to burst riotously in upon, to attack witb a drunken band.*

κατακωχή, incorrect form for κατοκωχή.

καταλαβεῖν, aor. 2 inf. of καταλαμβάνω.

κατ-ᾰλαζονεύομαι, (κατα, ἀλαζών) Dep. *to boast* or *br ig largely.*

κατα-λᾰλέω, f. ήσω, *to babble, cbatter.* II. *to talk* or *r ul at. slandr.* Hence

καταλᾰλία, ἡ, *evil report, slander* · and

κατάλᾰλος, ον, *slanderous.*

κατα-λαμβάνω: f. -λήψομαι Ion. -λάμψομαι · aor. 2 κατέλαβον: pf. κατείληφα Ion. καταλελάβηκα:—Pass., aor. 1 κατελήφθην Ion. κατελάμφθην: *to seize upon, iay bold of, take possession of: to seize*:—Med. *to seize for oneself: to preoccupy.* II. *to bold in, keep down* or *under, check*: hence *to put an end to, stop: to settle, conclude.* 2. *to bind* by oath. III. *to catch, overtake, come up with*: hence *to discover, detect, find.* 2. of events, *to come upon, befall, bappen* to one: impers., καταλαμβάνει *it bappens* to one; τὰ καταλαβόντα = τὰ σύμβαντα, *wbat bad bappened, the circumstances* of the case. Hence

καταλαμπτέος, α, ον, verb. Adj, *to be cbecked.*

κατα-λάμπω, f. -λαμψω, *to sbine upon: to sbine.*

κατ-αλγέω, f. ήσω, *to suffer greatly, be in great pain.*

κατα-λέγω, f. -λέξω: aor. 1 pass. κατελέχθην, aor. 2 κατελέγην:—*to lay down, put to bed, make lis down*:—Med., with aor. 1 κατελεξάμην, *to lie down, sleep*: in this sense occur κατελέκτο. 3 sing. of Ep aor. 2 pass. κατελέγμην, inf. καταλέχθαι, part. καταλέγμενος. II. *to pick out, cboose out* of many, *to cboose* as soldiers, *levy, enlist, enrol.* III. *to tell* or *count up, recount, reckon up: to go over, repeat, detail*, e. g. a pedigree.

κατα-λείβω, f. ψω, *to pour down, let drop: to sbed tears*:—Pass. *to run cr drop down.*

κατάλειμμα, τό, (καταλείπω) *a remnant, residue.*

κατάλειπτος, ον, (καταλείφω) *anointed.*

κατα-λείπω. f. ψω: Ep. form pres. **καλλείπω**, fut. καλλείψω · aor. 2 κάλλῐπον:—*to leave bebind, leave as an beritage, bequeatb.* II. *to forsake, abandon: to leave* or *give up to* another. III. *to suffer, allow*

κατα-λειτουργέω, f. ήσω, *to spend one's substance in bearing public burtbens.*

κατ-ᾰλείφω, f. ψω, *to smear on* or *over.*

καταλεξῶ, Dor. for καταλέξω, fut. of καταλέγω.

κατα-λεπτολογέω, f. ήσω, *to wear away by fine distinctions.*

κατα-λεύω, f. σω, (κατά, λεύω) *to stone to deatb.*

κατα-λέχθαι, Ep. aor. 2 inf. pass. of καταλέγω.

κατ-ᾰλέω, f. έσω, *to grind down.*

κατα-λήγω, f. ξω, *to leave off, stop, cease.*

κατα-λήθομαι, Pass. *to forget utterly.*

καταληπτικός, ή, όν, (καταλαμβάνω) *able to grasp* or *cbeck, able to keep down*

καταληπτός, ή, όν, verb. Adj. of καταλαμβάνω, *to be grasped* or *seized, witbin reacb, attainable.* II. act. *seizing upon.*

κατάληψις, εως, ἡ, (καταλαμβάνω) *a grasping, seizing, winning.* II. *an attacking, assaulting.*

κατα-λῐθάζω, f. άσω, (κατά, λίθος) *to stone to deatb.*

κατα-λῑπᾰρέω, f. ήσω, *to entreat earnestly.*

καταλλᾰγή, ἡ, *exchange, profit made on exchange.* II *a change from enmity to friendsbip reconciliation.* mostly in plur. From

κατ-αλλάσσω Att. -ττω: f. άξω: aor. 1 κατήλλαξα:—*to change*: Med. *to exchange, give in exchange.* II. *to change from enmity to friendsbip, reconcile*.—Pass., with aor. 1 κατηλλάχθην, aor. 2 κατηλλάγην [ᾰ], *to become reconciled.*

κατ-ᾰλοάω, f. ήσω, *to crusb in pieces, destroy.*

κατα-λογίζομαι, fut. -ίσομαι Att. -ῐοῦμαι: Dep.:—*to count up, reckon, consider*: also *to impute* a thing to one II. *to count* or *reckon among.*

κατάλογος, ὁ, καταλέγω) *a counting up, enrolment: tbe catalogue* or *list of persons liable to serve in tbe army*; οἱ ἐκ καταλόγου those *on tbe list for service.*

κατά-λοιπος, ον, *left, remaining.*

κατ-ᾰλοκίζω, f. ίσω, *to cut into furrows.*

κατα-λούω, f. σω, *to wash completely*:—Med., καταλούειν τὸν βίον *to spend one's* life *in bathing*.

κατα-λοφάδεια, Adv. = κατὰ λόφον, *on the neck*.

κατα-λοχίζω, f. σω, *to distribute into troops*. Hence

καταλοχισμός, ὁ, *distribution into troops*.

κατα-λόω, old Att. pres. for καταλούω.

κατά-λῦμα (κατα, λυω) *an inn, lodging*.

κατα-λῦμαίνομαι, Dep. *to ravage, destroy*.

καταλύσιμος, ον (καταλύω) *to be made an end of*.

κατάλῠσις, εως, ἡ, (καταλύω) *a dissolving, putting down, making an end of*: of an army, *a disbanding*: κατάλυσις τοῦ πολέμου *an ending* of the war: generally, *a conclusion, finishing*. II. *a resting, lodging*: also = κατάλυμα, *a resting-place, inn*.

καταλῠτής, οῦ, *one who lodges in a place*. From

κατα-λύω, f. λύσω: aor. 1 κατέλῡσα: *to dissolve, put down, make an end of, destroy, cancel*: *to put down* a form of government: *to depose* from command: *to dissolve, dismiss, disband*. 2. *to bring to an end, terminate*, καταλύειν πόλεμον *to end a war*:—Med. *to come to terms with* one, *make peace with* him. II. *to unloose, unyoke*: hence absol. *to take up one's quarters, halt, rest, lodge*.

κατα-λωφάω, f. ήσω, *to rest from* a thing.

κατα-μᾰγεύω, f. σω, (κατά, μάγος) *to bewitch*.

κατα-μαλᾰκίζω, f. ίσω Att. ιῶ:—*to make soft* or *effeminate*:—Pass. *to be* or *become so*.

κατα-μᾰλάσσω Att. -ττω, f. άξω, *to soften much, appease, pacify*.

κατα-μανθάνω, fut. -μᾰθήσομαι: aor. 2 -έμᾰθον: pf. -μεμάθηκα:—*to learn* or *observe well*, *to understand*: *to consider well*.

κατα-μαργάω Ion. -έω, f. ήσω,—*to be stark mad*.

κατα-μάρπτω, f. -μάρψω, *to catch hold of, catch*.

κατα-μαρτῠρέω, f. ήσω, *to bear witness against*:—Pass. *to have evidence given against one*.

κατα-μάσσομαι, Med. *to wipe off*.

κατ-αμάω, f. ήσω, (κατά, ἀμάω) *to pile up, heap up*: Ep. aor. 1 med. κατᾱμησάμην.

κατ-αμβλύνω, (κατά, ἀμβλύνω) *to take the edge off, make blunt* or *dull*.

κατα-μεθύσκω, f. -μεθύσω [ῠ], *to make drunk with sheer wine*.

καταμεῖναι, aor. 1 inf. of καταμένω.

κατ-ᾰμελέω, f. ήσω, *to give no heed to, neglect*: absol. *to be heedless*:—Pass. *to be neglected*.

κατα-μελῐτόω, f. ώσω, (κατά, μέλι) *to shed honey over*, of the nightingale's voice.

κατάμεμπτος, ον, *blamed by all, abhorred*: neut. pl. as Adv. *so as to give cause for blame*. From

κατα-μέμφομαι, f. -μέμψομαι: aor. 1 med. -εμεμψάμην, pass. -εμέμφθην: Dep.:—*to blame, accuse, find fault with*. Hence

καταμεμψις, εως, ἡ, *a blaming, finding fault, accusing*.

κατα-μένω, f. -μενῶ, *to stay behind*: *to remain, continue in* a state.

κατα-μερίζω, f. ίσω Att. ιῶ, *to cut in pieces*: *to distribute*.

κατα-μετρέω, f. ήσω, *to measure* or *mete out to*: *to measure*.

κατα-μηλόω, f. ώσω, (κατά, μήλη) *to put in the probe*: metaph., κημὸν καταμηλοῦν *to put* the ballot-box *like a probe* down another's throat, i. e. *make* him *disgorge* stolen goods.

κατα-μηνύω, f. ύσω [ῡ], *to give information against*. 2. *to intimate, make known*.

καταμήσατο, 3 sing. Ep. aor. 1 med. of καταμάω.

κατα-μιαίνω, f. ᾰνῶ, *to taint, defile, pollute*:—Pass. *to wear unwashen garments* in sign of grief, Lat. *squalere*.

κατα-μίγνῡμι or -ύω, f. -μίξω: aor. 1 κατέμιξα, Ep. part. καμμίξας:—*to mix, mix up, compound*.

κατα-μίσγω, = καταμίγνυμι.

κατα-μισθοφορέω, f. ήσω, *to spend in paying publ.c officers*.

κατάμομφος, ον, (καταμέμφομαι) *faulty*.

κατα-μόνᾱς, (κατά, μόνος) Adv. *alone, apart*.

κατα-μονομαχέω, f. ήσω, *to conquer in single combat*.

κατ-αμπέχω and -αμπίσχω, *to encompass, cover*.

καταμύξατο, 3 sing. Ep. aor. 1 med. of καταμύσσω.

κατάμῠσις, εως, ἡ, (καταμύω) *a closing of the eyes*.

κατ-ᾰμύσσω Att. -ττω, f. ξω, *to tear, scratch, rend*.

κατα-μυττωτεύω, f. σω, (κατά, μυττωτόν) *to make mincemeat of*.

κατα-μύω, f. ύσω [ῡ]: aor. 1 κατέμυσα, poët. inf. καμμῦσαι:—*to shut* or *close the eyes*: *to nod, drop asleep, dose*: also *to die*.

κατ-ᾰναγκάζω, f. άσω, *to force down into a place*. II. *to overpower by force, constrain, confine*: *coerce*.

κατ-ανάθεμα, ατος, τό, *a curse*. Hence

καταναθεμᾰτίζω, f. ίσω, *to curse*.

κατα-ναίω, *to make to dwell, settle*: only used in Ep. aor. 1 act. κατένασσα med. κατενασσάμην:—Pass. *to take up one's abode, dwell*, only in aor. 1 κατενάσθην.

κατ-ανᾱλίσκω, f. -ανᾱλώσω: aor. 1 κατηνάλωσα:—*to spend lavishly*, εἴς τι *upon* a thing:—Pass., with pf. act. κατανάλωκα, *to be lavished*.

κατα-ναρκάω, *to be slothful towards, press heavily upon*.

κατα-νάσσω, f. -νάξω, *to beat down firmly*.

κατα-ναυμᾰχέω, fut. ήσω, *to conquer in a sea-fight, beat at sea*.

κατα-νέμω, f. -νεμῶ, *to distribute, allot, assign among*. II. Med. and Pass. *to divide among themselves, partition out*: hence *to take possession of*. 2. *to feed* or *graze land* with cattle, Lat. *depasci*.

κατάνευσις, εως, ἡ, *a nodding to, assent*. From

κατα-νεύω, f. -νεύσομαι: Ep. aor. 1 part. καννεύσας:—*to nod assent*, opp. to ἀπονεύω; ὑπέσχετο καὶ κατένευσεν he promised and *confirmed* his promise *by a nod*: *to make a sign by nodding the head*.

κατα-νεφόω, f. ώσω, *to overcloud*.

κατα-νέω Ion. -νήω, f. -νήσω, *to heap* or *pile up*.

καταυῆσαι, aor. 1 inf. of καταυέω.

κατ-ανθρᾰκίζω, f. ίσω, and **κατ-ανθρᾰκόω**, f. -ώσομαι: (κατά, ἄνθραξ) :—*to burn to cinders* :—Pass. *to be burnt to ashes.*

κατα-νίφω, *to snow upon* or *over:* impers., καταυίφει *it snows;* κατένιψε χιόνι τὴν Θράκην *snow fell all over* Thrace.

κατα-νοέω, f. ήσω, *to remark, observe, perceive: to understand, learn, know: to consider.*

κατ-άνομαι, Pass. (κατά, ἄνω) *to be used up or wasted.* The Act is supplied by κατανύω

κατα-νοτίζω, f. ίσω Att. ιῶ, *to bedew.*

κάτ-αντᾰ, Adv. of κατάντης, *downwards.*

κατ-αντάω, f. ήσω, *to come down to, arrive at.*

κατ-άντης, ες, (κατά, ἄντα) *down-hill* opp. to ἀνάντης.

κατ-άντηστιν, Adv. (κατά, ἀντάω) *opposite.*

κατ-αντικρύ, (κατά, ἀντικρύ) *straight down from.* II. *over against, right opposite, facing.* 2. absol. *outright, downright.* [ι of the penult. long in Hom., short in Att.]

κατ-αντίον, Adv. *over against, opposite, fronting.*

κατ-αντιπέρας, Adv. *right over against, opposite.*

κατ-αντλέω, f. ήσω, *to pour upon* or *over.*

κατάνυξις, εως, ἡ, *stupefaction, slumber.* From

κατα-νύσσω Att. -ττω, f. ξω, *to prick* :—Pass. *to be pricked at heart.* II. in Pass. also *to lie in a deep sleep, to slumber.*

κατ-ᾰνύω Att. -ύτω: f. ύσω [ῠ]: aor. 1 κατήνῠσα: —*to bring to an end, finish* a journey: *to arrive at* a place; c. gen., φίλης προξένου κατηνύσαν *they have reached the house of* a kind hostess. 2. *to accomplish, perpetrate.*

κατα-νωτίζομαι, fut. -ίσομαι, Dep. (κατα, νωτίζω): —*to carry on one's back.*

κατα-ξαίνω: f. -ξανῶ: aor. 1 κατέξηνα :—Pass., aor. 1 κατεξάνθην: pf. κατέξαμμαι :—*to card* or *comb well: to tear in pieces, wear away, reduce to nothing.*

καταξέμεν, Ep. for κατάξειν, fut. inf. of κατάγω.

κατα-ξενόω, f. ώσω, (κατά, ξένος) *to receive as a guest, entertain.*

κατ-άξιος, ον, *quite worthy of.* Adv. -ίως. Hence

καταξιόω, f. ώσω, *to deem worthy, esteem, honour.* II. *to bid;* πολλὰ χαίρειν ξυμφοραῖς καταξιῶ I *bid* a long farewell to calamities. 2. *to resolve* or *determine on* a thing.

κατα-ξύω, f. ύσω [ῡ]: Pass., pf. -έξυσμαι :—*to scrape down, to scratch* or *mark.*

κατῄορος, Dor. for κατήορος.

κατα-παίζω, f. -παίξομαι, *to jest at.*

καταπακτός, ή, όν, (καταπήγνυμι) *fastened down* or *downwards;* καταπακτὴ θύρα *a trap-*door.

κατα-πᾰλαίω, f. σω, *to throw in wrestling.*

κατα-πάλλω, *to shake down* :—Pass., in 3 sing. Ep. aor. 2 κατέπαλτο, *to vault* or *leap down.*

κατα-πάσσω Att. -ττω, f. -πάσω [ᾰ]: aor. 1 κατέπᾰσα :—*to besprinkle: to sprinkle* or *strew over.* Hence

κατάπαστος, ον, *besprinkled with, embroidered.*

κατα-πᾰτέω, f. ήσω, *to trample down, trample under foot:* metaph. *to trample on.*

κατάπαυμα, ατος, τό, *a check, hindrance;* and

κατάπαυσις, εως, ἡ, *a putting a stop to, putting down, deposing.* II. (from Pass.) *a calm.* From

κατα-παύω poët. **καπ-παύω**: f. σω:—*to put to rest, calm, assuage.* 2. *to make* one *stop from* a thing, *hinder* or *check from: to stop, hinder, keep in check:* —*to put down, depose* one *from power.* II. Pass. and Med. *to leave off, cease, rest.*

κατ-ᾰπειλέω, f. ήσω, *to threaten loudly;* καταπειλεῖν ἔπη *to use threatening* words.

κατα-πειρᾱτηρία Ion. **-πειρητηρίη**, ἡ, (κατά, πειράω) *a sounding-line.*

κατα-πελτάζω, fut. -άσομαι, *to overrun with light-armed troops* (πελτασταί).

καταπεμπτέος α ον, verb. Adj. of καταπέμπω, *to be sent down.*

κατα-πέμπω, f. ψω, *to send down to the sea.*

κατα-πενθέω, f. ήσω, *to mourn for.*

καταπέπηγα, intr. pf. of καταπήγνυμι.

καταπεπτηυῖα, Ep. pf. part. fem. of καταπτήσσω.

κατ-άπερ, Ion. for καθάπερ.

κατα-πέρδω, mostly in Med. **-πέρδομαι**: aor. 2 κατέπαρδον: pf. καταπέπορδα —*to break wind at* one.

κατα-πέσσω Att. -ττω: fut. -πέψω:—*to boil down* or *digest:* metaph. *to digest, keep from rising.*

καταπεσών, aor. 2 part. of καταπίπτω.

κατα-πετάννῡμι or -ύω, fut. -πετάσω [ᾰ] :—*to spread out over.* II. *to spread* or *cover with.* Hence

καταπέτασμα, ατος, τό, *a curtain, veil.*

κατα-πέτομαι, fut. -πτήσομαι: aor. 2 κατεπτάμην, part. καταπτάμενος :—*to fly down.*

κατα-πετρόω, f. ώσω, (κατά, πέτρα) *to stone to death.*

κατα-πέττω, Att. for καταπέσσω.

καταπέφνων, part. of aor. 2 κατέπεφνον.

καταπέψῃ, 3 sing. aor. 1 subj. of καταπέσσω.

κατα-πήγνῡμι and -ύω: fut. -πήξω: aor. 1 κατέπηξα :—*to stick fast in the ground, fix firmly* :— Pass., with intr. pf. act. κατα-πέπηγα, 3 sing. Ep. aor. 2 κατέπηκτο, *to stand fast* or *firm in, be firmly fixed in.*

κατα-πηδάω, f. -ήσομαι, *to leap down from.*

κατα-πίμπλημι, f. -πλήσω, *to fill quite full.*

κατα-πίμπρημι, f. -πρήσω, *to burn to ashes.*

κατα-πίνω, fut. -πίομαι: aor. 2 κατέπιον Ep. κάππιον :—*to gulp* or *swallow down, absorb.* 2. metaph. *to drink in, imbibe.* 3. *to swallow up, use up, consume.*

κατα-πιπράσκω, *to sell outright.*

κατα-πίπτω, fut. -πεσοῦμαι: aor. 2 κατέπεσον Ep. κάππεσον: pf. -πέπτωκα :—*to fall down:* metaph. *to fall, sink, subside.*

κατα-πισσόω Att. -ττόω: f. -ώσω, *to cover with pitch, pitch over* to keep out the air.

κατάπλασμα, ατος, τό, *that which is spread* or *smeared over, a plaster.* From

κατα-πλάσσω Att. -ττω: f. -πλάσω [ᾰ]: aor. 1

κατέπλᾰσα:—*to spread* or *smear over, plaster with*: —Med., καταπλάσσεσθαι τὴν κεφαλήν *to plaster one's own* head. Hence

καταπλαστός, ή, όν, *plastered over.*

κατα-πλαστύς, ύος, ή, Ion. for κατάπλασμα.

κατα-πλέκω, f. ξω, *to entwine, plait*: metaph. *to implicate, entangle.* 2. *to finish twisting*, and so *to bring to an end, finish.*

κατά-πλεος, ον, also α, ον: Att. **-πλεως**, ων, gen. ω: (κατά, πλέος):—*quite full of* a thing: *soiled* or *stained with* it.

κατα-πλέω, f. -πλεύσομαι: aor. 1 κατέπλευσα:—Ion. pres. -πλώω:—*to sail down*, as, *to sail from the high sea to shore, put into port, put in*:—*to sail down stream.* II. *to sail back.*

κατά-πλεως, ων, gen. ω, Att. for κατάπλεος.

κατάπληξ, ῆγος, ὁ, ἡ, (καταπλήσσω) *terror-stricken.*

κατάπληξις, εως, ἡ, *amazement, consternation.* From

κατα-πλήσσω Att. -ττω: f. ξω: aor. 1 κατέπληξα: —Pass., aor. 2 κατεπλάγην [ᾰ] Ep. κατεπλήγην:—pf. -πέπληγμαι:—*to strike down*: metaph. *to strike with amazement, astound, confound*:—Pass. *to be panic-stricken, be amazed.*

κατά-πλοος contr. **-πλους**, ὁ, (καταπλέω) *a sailing down to land, a putting ashore, putting into harbour.* II. *a sailing back, return.*

κατα-πλουτίζω, fut. ίσω Att. ιῶ, *to make very rich, enrich.*

κατα-πλύνω [ῡ], *to bathe with water.* Hence

κατάπλῠσις, εως, ἡ, *a bathing in water.*

κατα-πλώω, Ion. for καταπλέω.

κατα-πνείω, Ep. for καταπνέω.

κατα-πνέω, f. πνεύσομαι: aor. 1 κατέπνευσα:—*to breathe upon* or *over.* 2. *to inspire, instil.* Hence

καταπνοή, ἡ, *a breathing* or *blowing.*

κατα-πόδα and **κατα-πόδας**, Adv., for κατὰ πόδα, κατὰ πόδας, *upon the track, quickly, straightway.*

καταποθῇ, 3 sing. aor. 1 subj. pass. of καταπίνω.

κατα-πολεμέω, f. ήσω, *to war down, wear down* or *overcome in war*, Lat. *debellare.*

κατα-πονέω, f. ήσω, *to wear out by toil* or *suffering.*

κατα-ποντίζω, f. ίσω Att. ιῶ, (κατα, πόντος) *to throw into the sea, plunge* or *drown therein.* Hence

καταποντιστής, οῦ, ὁ, *one who throws into the sea*, of pirates.

κατα-ποντόω, f. ώσω, = καταποντίζω.

κατα-πορνεύω, f. -εύσω, *to prostitute.*

κατα-πράσσω Att. -ττω, f. -πράξω, *to effect, accomplish, achieve.*—Med. *to achieve for oneself.*

κατα-πρηνής, ές, *head foremost, with the forepart downwards*, χειρὶ καταπρηνεῖ with the hand *moved downwards*, i. e. *with the flat of* the hand. Hence

καταπρηνόω, f. ώσω, *to throw down headlong.*

κατα-πρίω [ῑ]: aor. 1 κατέπρῑσα:—*to saw up* or *in pieces*: *to cut* or *tear in pieces.*

κατα-προδίδωμι, f. -προδώσω, *to betray.*

κατα-προΐσσομαι, f. -προΐξομαι Att. προΐξομαι:—*to do for nothing*, i. e. *with impunity*, always with negat., and in bad sense: 1. absol., οὐ καταπροΐξεσθαι ἔφη he said *they should* not *get off free, with impunity*; οὐ καταπροΐξει you shan't *do* it *for nothing.* 2. also with part., οὐ λωβησάμενος ἐμὲ καταπροΐξεται *he shall* not *escape for having* thus insulted me; οὐ καταπροΐξει τοῦτο δρῶν *thou shalt* not *escape* or *get off for doing* this. 3. c. gen. pers., ἐμεῦ δ' ἐκεῖνος οὐ καταπροΐξεται *he shall* not *use* me *ill for nothing.*

κατά-πρωκτος, ον, = καταπύγων.

καταπτᾰκών, όντος, aor. 2 part. of καταπτήσσω.

κατά-πτερος, ον, (κατά, πτερόν) *winged.*

καταπτήσομαι, fut. of καταπέτομαι.

κατα-πτήσσω, fut. -πτήξω: Ep. aor. 2 κατάπτην, 3 dual καταπτήτην; another poët. aor. 2 part. καταπτᾰκών occurs: pf. κατέπτηκα or -χα, Ep. part. καταπεπτηώς:—*to crouch* or *cower down, to lie crouching* or *cowering.*

κατ-άπτομαι, Ion. for καθάπτομαι.

κατάπτυστος, ον, also η, ον, (καταπτύω) *to be spat upon, abominable, despicable.*

κατα-πτυχής, ές, (κατά, πτύχη) *with ample folds.*

κατα-πτύω, f. ύσω [ῠ]: aor. 1 κατέπτῠσα:—*to spit upon* or *at*, as a mark of abhorrence and contempt.

κατα-πτώσσω, = καταπτήσσω.

καταπῡγοσύνη, ἡ, *lewdness.* From

κατα-πύγων, ονος, ἡ, neut. -πύγον, (κατά, πυγή) *lewd, lustful, brutal.*

κατα-πύθω, f. ύσω [ῡ]: aor. κατέπῡσα:—*to make rotten*:—Pass. *to become rotten.*

κατά-πυκνος, ον, *very thick.*

κατα-πῠρίζω, f. ίσω, (κατά, πῦρ) *to catch fire.*

κατα-πυρπολέω, f. ήσω, *to consume with fire.*

κατ-άρα Ion. -άρη [ᾰ], ἡ, *an imprecation, curse.*

καταραιρημένος, Ion. for καθῃρημένος, pf. part. pass. of καθαιρέω.

κατ-αράομαι: f. -άσομαι Ion. -ήσομαι: Dep.:—*to invoke upon* one, mostly in bad sense; πολλὰ κατηρᾶτο *he uttered* many *curses*: *to pray for evil* to one, *curse, utter imprecations upon*:—pf. part. κατηρᾱμένος, in pass. sense, *accursed.*

κατ-ᾰράσσω Att. -ττω, f. ξω, *to dash down, smash, break in pieces, to hurl down.*

κατάρᾱτος, ον, (καταράομαι) *accursed, abominable.*

κατ-αργέω, f. ήσω, (κατά, ἀργός) *to leave unemployed*: hence *to make barren.* II. *to make useless* or *void*:—Pass. *to be abolished*: *to be set free.*

κατ-αργίζω, f. ίσω, (κατά, ἀργός) *to make to tarry.*

κάταργμα, ατος, τό, (κατάρχομαι):—in pl. τὰ κατάργματα, *the beginnings of the sacrifice, introductory rites.*

κατ-αργῠρόω, f. ώσω, *to cover* or *plate with silver.* II. *to buy* or *bribe with silver.*

κατ-άρδω, f. άρσω, *to water*: esp. metaph. *to besprinkle with praise.*

κατ-ᾱρέομαι or **-έωμαι**, Ion. for καταράομαι.

κατα-ρῑγηλός, ή, όν, (κατά, ῥιγέω) *making one shudder, horrible.*

κατ-ἄριθμέω, f. ήσω, *to count* or *reckon among.* 2. *to count up* :—Med. *to recount.*

κατ-αρκέω, f. ήσω, *to be fully sufficient.*

κατ-αρμόζω, Ion. for *καθαρ–*.

κατ-αρνέομαι: Dep. with fut. med. *–αρνήσομαι*, aor. 1 pass. *–ηρνήθην* :—*to deny stoutly.*

κατ-ἄρόω, f. *–αρόσω*, *to plough up.*

καταρρἄγῆναι, aor. 2 pass. inf. of *καταρρήγνυμι.*

καταρ-ρᾳθῦμέω, f. ήσω, *to lose* or *miss from carelessness* :—Pass., pf. part. **τὰ** *κατερρᾳθυμημένα things carelessly lost.* II. intr. *to be very careless* or *idle.*

καταρ-ρἄκόω, f. ώσω, (*κατά, ῥάκος*) *to tear into shreds* : Pass., pf. part. *κατερρακωμένος*, *in rags* or *tatters.*

καταρράκτης, ου, (*καταρρήγνυμι*) as Adj. *broken, precipitous.* II. as Subst., *καταρράκτης, ὁ, a waterfall*, Lat. *cataracta.*

καταρ-ράπτω, f. ψω, *to stitch up, to cover over* : metaph. *to plot, devise, compass.* Hence

κατάρρἄφος, *ον*, *sewn together, patched.*

καταρ-ρέζω, f. ξω: Ep. aor. 1 *κατέρεξα* :—*to pat with the hand, to stroke, fondle, caress* :—*καρρέζουσα*, Ep. for *καταρρέζουσα.*

καταρ-ρέπω, f. ψω, *to make to sink* or *fall.*

καταρ-ρέω, f. *–ρεύσομαι* and (in pass. form) *–ρυήσομαι*: pf. *–ερρύηκα*: aor. 2 in pass. form *κατερρύην*: —*to flow down* : c. dat. *to run down* or *drop with a* thing: metaph. *to rush down.* 2. *to fall* or *slip down* : aor. 2 part. pass. *καταρρυείς, fallen.* 3. *to come to, fall to the lot of.* II. *to run down with* wet; and in Pass. *to be wet with* a thing.

καταρ-ρήγνῡμι and **–ύω**: f. *–ρήξω* :—*to break down.* 2. *to tear in pieces, rend* :—Med., *καταρρήξαντο τοὺς κιθῶνας they rent their* coats. 3. *to break up, put to confusion*, of armies. II. Pass., esp. in aor. 2 *κατερράγην* [ᾰ], *to fall* or *rush down* : *to break* or *burst out, gush forth* :—so also intrans. in pf. act. *κατέρρωγα to break out, burst forth.*

καταρ-ρινάω or **–έω**, f. ήσω, *to file down* : *κατερρινημένον τι λέγειν* to say anything *polished* or *well-turned.*

καταρ-ρίπτω, f. ψω, *to throw down, overthrow.*

κατάρροος contr. **κατάρρους**, ου, ὁ, (*καταρρέω*) *a running from the head, a catarrh.*

καταρ-ροφέω, f. ήσω, *to gulp* or *swallow down.*

καταρρυῆναι, aor. 2 inf. pass. of *καταρρέω.* Hence

καταρρῠής, ές, *flowing down, falling away, ebbing.*

κατάρρῠτος, ον, (*καταρρέω*) *overflowed, watered, irrigated.* II. *carried down by water* : *formed by depositions from water, alluvial.*

κατ-αρρωδέω, f. ήσω, Ion. for *κατορρωδέω.*

καταρρώξ, ῶγος, ὁ, ἡ, (*κατέρρωγα*) *broken, rugged.*

κάταρσις, εως, ἡ, (*καταίρω*) *a landing-place.*

κατ-αρτάω, f. ήσω, (*κατά, ἀρτάω*) *to fasten, attach*, or *adjust fitly* ; *χρῆμα κατηρτημένον* (pf. part. pass.) *a well-adjusted, fit*, or *convenient* thing.

κατ-αρτίζω, f. ίσω, *to adjust, put in order again, restore, repair* : *to settle by mediation, reform.* II. *to furnish completely* : *κατηρτισμένος* (pf. part. pass.) *well furnished, complete.* Hence

κατάρτισις, εως, ἡ, *a restoring, restoration* : *a making perfect, educating.*

καταρτιστήρ, ῆρος, ὁ, (*καταρτίζω*) *one who adjusts* : *a mediator, reformer.*

κατ-αρτύω, f. ύσω [ῡ]: pf. *–ήρτῠκα* pass. *–ήρτῠμαι* : aor. 1 pass. *–ηρτύθην* [ῠ] :—*to prepare, dress* : *to arrange, put in order* :—Pass. *to be trained* or *disciplined.* II. *κατηρτύκως*, pf. part. act. in intrans. sense, of suppliants, *having performed all the rites.*

κατά-ρῠτος, *ον*, poët. for *κατάρρυτος.*

κατ-αρχάς, Adv. for *κατ' ἀρχάς, in the beginning.*

κατ-άρχω, f. ξω, (*κατά, ἄρχω*) *to make a beginning* of a thing: c. gen., *ὁδοῦ κατάρχε lead* the way: c. acc. *to begin* a thing; *κατάρχειν τὸν λόγον.* 2. Med. *to begin the rites of sacrifice* ; **Νέστωρ** *χέρνιβά τ' οὐλοχύτας τε κατήρχετο* Nestor *began* [the sacrifice] *with* the washing of hands and sprinkling the barley on the victim's head: later c. gen., *κατάρχεσθαι τοῦ ἱερείου to make a beginning of* the victim, *consecrate* him *for sacrifice* by cutting off the hair of his forehead: *to sacrifice, immolate.* 3. *to lead the dance in honour of* one, *to celebrate, honour.*

κατα-σβέννῡμι and **–ύω**: f. *–σβέσω*: aor. 1 *κατέσβεσα* :—*to put out, quench, extinguish* : metaph., *θάλασσαν κατασβέσαι to dry up* the sea; *κατασβέσαι βοήν, ἔριν to quell* noise and strife. II. Pass., with intrans. aor. 2 act. *κατέσβην* and pf. *κατέσβηκα*, *to be quenched, go out.*

κατα-σείω, f. *–σείσω*: pf. *–σέσεικα* :—*to shake* and *throw down* ; *κατασείειν τῇ χειρί to sign* with *the hand, beckon.*

κατασέσηπα, intr. pf. of *κατασήπω.*

κατα-σεύομαι: Ep. aor. 2 *κατεσσύμην*: Pass. (*κατά, σεύω*) *to rush down* or *back into.*

κατα-σήπω, *to make rotten, let rot.* II. Pass., aor. 2 *κατ-εσάπην* [ᾰ], with intr. pf. act. *κατασέσηπα*, *to grow rotten, rot away.*

κατ-ασθενέω, f. ήσω, (*κατά, ἀσθενέω*) *to weaken.*

κατ-ασθμαίνω, *to pant* or *snort against.*

κατα-σῑγάω, f. ήσομαι, *to become silent.*

κατα-σῐκελίζω, f. σω, (*κατά, Σικελός*) *to Sicilise*, i. e. *make away with.*

κατα-σῑτέομαι, f. *–ήσομαι*, Dep. *to eat up, feed on.*

κατα-σῐωπάω, f. *–ήσομαι*, *to be silent about* a thing: c. acc. rei, *to keep silent, pass over.* II. trans. *to make silent, silence*, c. acc. pers.

κατα-σκάπτω, f. ψω, *to dig down, rase to the ground, demolish* : aor. 2 pass. *κατεσκάφην.* Hence

κατασκᾰφή, ἡ, *a rasing to the ground, demolishing.* II. in plur., *burial* : also *a grave.*

κατασκᾰφῆναι, aor. 2 inf. pass. of *κατασκάπτω.* Hence

κατασκᾰφής, ές, *dug down, deep-dug.*

κατα-σκεδάννῡμι and **–ύω**, f. *–σκεδάσω* [ᾰ]: aor. 1 *κατεσκέδᾰσα* :—*to scatter upon* or *over* : also in bad sense; **κατασκέδασαι φήμην τινός** *to spread* a report *against* one.

κατα-σκέλλω, *to parch up.* II. Pass., with pf. act. κατέσκληκα, *to wither away.*

κατα-σκέπω, (κατά, σκέπας) *to shelter, cover up.*

κατα-σκευάζω, f. άσω, *to prepare, furnish, equip again* or *anew.* 2. *to get ready, build*:—Med. *to build, construct a house*:—Pass. *to be furnished* or *provided* with a thing. 3. *to put in a certain state, render so and so*:—Med. *to prepare oneself for* doing, *be ready* to do. Hence

κατασκεύασμα, ατος, τό, *a contrivance, device*: and

κατασκευασμός, ὁ, *contrivance.*

κατα-σκευή, ἡ, (κατά, σκευή) *any artificial preparation*, Lat. *apparatus*: *any kind of furniture that is fixed* or *lasting*, opp. to what is movable or temporary (παρασκευή); *a building*: also *any furniture*, as *the baggage* of an army. II. *the state* or *constitution* of a thing.

κατα-σκηνάω, f. ήσω, = κατασκηνόω.

κατα-σκηνόω, f. ώσω, (κατά, σκηνή) *to pitch one's camp, take up one's quarters, encamp*: *to rest, settle.* Hence

κατασκήνωμα, ατος, τό, *a covering, veil*: and

κατασκήνωσις, εως, ἡ, *an encamping, an encampment*: *a resting-place, a nest.*

κατα-σκήπτω, f. ψω, *to rush down* or *fall upon, light upon, be hurled down upon*: of lightning, of sudden attacks of sickness, etc. II. λιταῖς κατασκήπτειν *to assail* or *importune* with prayers.

κατα-σκιάζω, f. -σκιάσω, *to overshadow, cover over.*

κατα-σκιάω, poët. for κατασκιάζω.

κατα-σκίδνᾰμαι, used as Pass. of κατασκεδάννυμι.

κατά-σκιος, ον, (κατά, σκιά) *overshadowed.* II. *overshadowing.*

κατα-σκοπέω (tenses formed from κατα-σκέπτομαι): f. -σκέψομαι: aor. 1 -εσκεψάμην; pf. -έσκεμμαι:—*to view closely*: *to spy out*: *to reconnoitre.* Hence

κατασκοπή, ἡ, *a viewing closely, spying.*

κατά-σκοπος, ον, (κατά, σκοπός) *spying, exploring*: as Subst. *a scout, spy.*

κατα-σκώπτω, fut. -σκώψομαι, *to make jokes upon, banter*: *to jeer* or *mock.*

κατα-σμικρύνω, f. ὔνῶ, *to lessen, abridge*:—Pass. *to become less.*

κατα-σμύχω, f. ξω:—*to burn with a slow fire*:—Pass. *to smoulder away.*

κατα-σοφίζομαι, f. -ίσομαι Att. -ιοῦμαι, Dep. *to conquer by trickery, circumvent, outwit*:—also as Pass. *to be outwitted.*

κατα-σπᾰράσσω Att. -ττω, f. ξω, *to pull to pieces.*

κατα-σπαταλάω, f. ήσω, *to live wantonly.*

κατα-σπάω, f. άσω [ᾰ], *to draw* or *pull down*; κατασπᾶν τινα τῶν τριχῶν *to drag* one *down by* the hair: of ships, *to haul down, set afloat.* II. *to quaff* or *swallow down.*

κατα-σπείρω, f. -σπερῶ: aor. 1 κατέσπειρα:—*to sow* or *plant thickly*: metaph. *to beget.* II. *to besprinkle.*

κατα-σπένδω, f. -σπείσω: aor. 1 κατέσπεισα: pf. -έσπεικα:—Pass., aor. 1 -εσπείσθην: pf. -έσπεισμαι:—*to pour as a drink-offering* or *libation*: absol. *to pour drink-offerings*: generally, *to pour upon* one. II. *to honour with libations.*

κατα-σπέρχω, f. ξω, *to urge on, stimulate.*

κατα-σποδέω, f. ήσω, (κατά, σποδός) *to throw down in the dust, make bite the dust.*

κατα-σπουδάζομαι, Dep., with aor. 1 pass. -εσπουδάσθην, pf. -εσπούδασμαι; (κατά, σπουδάζω):—*to be earnest about* a thing: absol. *to be very serious.*

κατα-στάζω, f. ξω, *to let fall in drops upon, pour upon*: *to let drop, shed.* II. intr. *to drop down, trickle*; νόσῳ καταστάζειν πόδα *to have* one's foot *running* with a sore. 2. *to bedew, wet, moisten.*

καταστᾰθείς, aor. 1 part. pass. of καθίστημι.

καταστάς, aor. 1 part. of καθίστημι.

κατα-στᾰσιάζω, f. άσω, *to form a counter-party.* II. Pass. *to be beaten by party* or *faction.*

κατάστᾰσις, εως, ἡ, *a settling, appointing, establishing*: *an appointment, institution.* 2. *a bringing* of ambassadors *before* the assembly, *a presentation.* II. intrans. *a standing fast, a fixed* or *settled condition*: *a state, condition*: *the nature of* a thing: *the constitution* of a state.

καταστᾰτέον, verb. Adj. of καθίστημι, *one must appoint.*

καταστάτης, ου, ὁ, (καθίστημι) *an establisher.*

κατα-στεγάζω, f. άσω, *to cover over.* Hence

καταστέγασμα, ατος, τό, *a covering.*

κατά-στεγος, ον, (κατά, στέγη) *covered in, roofed.*

κατα-στείβω, f. ψω, *to tread on.*

καταστεῖλαι, aor. 1 inf. of καταστέλλω.

κατα-στέλλω, f. -στελῶ, *to put in order, arrange*: *clothe, dress, array.* 2. *to keep down, check.*

κατα-στένω, *to sigh over* or *lament*, c. acc. 2. *to sigh for* or *about* one, c. gen.

κατα-στεφανόω, f. ώσω, *to crown.*

καταστεφής, ές, *wreathed, crowned.* From

κατα-στέφω, f. ψω: aor. 1 κατέστεψα:—*to wreathe, crown.*

κατα-στηλῑτεύω, f. σω, (κατά, στήλη) *to expose* one *to infamy by posting up his name.*

κατάστημα, ατος, τό, (καθίστημι) *a state, condition.*

κατα-στηρίζω, f. ίξω, *to support, prop, sustain.*

καταστῆσαι, **κατάστησον**, aor. 1 inf. and imperat. of καθίστημι: **καταστήσω**, fut. of same.

κατα-στίζω, f. ξω, *to cover with punctures.* Hence

κατά-στικτος, ον, *spotted, speckled, brindled, dappled.*

κατα-στίλβω, *to beam brightly.*

καταστολή, ἡ, (καταστέλλω) *an arranging, dressing*: *equipment, dress.* II. *quietness, moderation.*

κατα-στονᾰχέω, f. ήσω, *to sigh over, bewail.*

κατα-στορέννῡμι and -ύω, fut. -στορέσω: aor. 1 κατεστόρεσα:—*to spread* or *cover with* a thing. II. *to spread* or *strew on the ground*: *to overthrow, lay* *low;* καταστορέσαι κύματα *to smooth* the waves, Lat. *sternere aequor.*

κατ-αστράπτω, f. ψω, *to hurl down lightning, flash lightning:* absol., καταστράπτει *it lightens.*

κατα-στρᾰτοπεδεύω, f. σω, *to make to encamp, station:*—Med. *to take up one's quarters, encamp.*

κατα-στρέφω, f. ψω, *to turn over* the soil, Lat. *aratro vertere.* II. *to upset, overturn.* 2. Med. *to subject to oneself, subdue:*—Pass. *to be subdued;* κατέστραμμαι ἀκούειν *I am compelled* to hear. III. *to bring to an end, close:* intrans. *to come to an end, end.*

καταστρέψας, aor. 1 part. of καταστρέφω.

καταστρέψοντι, Dor. 3 pl. fut. of καταστρέφω.

κατα-στρηνιάω, *to behave insolently towards.*

καταστροφή, ἡ, (καταστρέφω) *an overturning, overthrowing.* 2. *a subduing, reduction.* II. *a sudden turn: an end, close:*—in the drama, *the catastrophé* or *turn* of the plot.

κατάστρωμα, ατος, τό, *that which is spread upon* or *over:* in a ship, *the deck.* From

κατα-στρώννῡμι and -ύω, f. -στρώσω: aor. 1 κατέστρωσα: = καταστορέννυμι.

κατα-στῠγέω, f. ήσω: aor. 2 κατέστῠγον:—*to be horror-struck:*—c. acc. rei, *to shudder at, abhor.*

κατα-στύφελος, ον, *very hard* or *rugged.*

κατα-στωμύλλω, *to have a glib tongue:* pf. part. pass. in act. sense κατεστωμυλμένος, *a chattering fellow.*

κατα-σύρω, aor. 1 -έσῡρα, *to pull down and carry off, to ravage and plunder* a country, Lat. *diripere.*

κατασφᾰγή, ἡ, *a slaughtering* or *killing.* From

κατα-σφάζω or -σφάττω: f. ξω: aor. 2 pass. -εσφάγην [ᾰ]:—*to slaughter, murder.*

κατα-σφρᾱγίζω, f. ίσω Att. ιῶ, *to seal up, put under seal:* pf. part. pass. κατεσφραγισμένος, *sealed up, secured.*

κατασχεθεῖν Ep. -έειν, poët. aor. 2 inf. of κατέχω.

κατασχεῖν, aor. 2 inf. of κατέχω.

κατάσχεσις, εως, ἡ, (κατέχω) *a holding back, hindering.* II. *a holding fast, possession.*

κατᾰσχετος, ον, (κατέχω) *held back, kept back.* II. *possessed.*

κατα-σχίζω, f. ίσω, *to cleave asunaer;* κατασχίζειν τὰς πύλας *to burst* the gates *open.*

κατα-σχολάζω, f. άσω, *to loiter, tarry:* c. acc., χρόνον τι κατασχολάζειν *to tarry somewhat too long.*

κατασχῶμεν, 1 pl. aor. 2 subj. of κατέχω.

κατασχών, κατασχόμενος, aor. 2 part. act. and med. of κατέχω.

κατα-σώχω, *to rub in pieces, bruise, pound, bray*

κατα-τάμνω, Ion. and Dor. for κατα-τέμνω.

κατα-τᾰνύω, f. ύσω [ῠ], = κατα-τείνω.

καταταξεῖς, Dor. for κατατήξεις, 2 sing. fut. of κατατήκω.

κατα-τάσσω Att. -ττω, f. ξω, *to draw up in order, arrange: to put in its proper place, classify, digest.* 2. *to appoint.*

κατατεθναίη, 3 sing. pf. opt. of καταθνήσκω.

κατατεθνεώς and -ηώς, Ep. gen. ῶτος, pf. part. of καταθνήσκω.

κατατέθνηκα, pf. of καταθνήσκω.

κατα-τείνω, fut. -τενῶ: pf. -τέτᾰκα:—*to stretch* or *draw tight:* metaph. *to strain, force:* also *to strain* or *exert.* II. intrans. *to stretch* or *strain oneself. to stretch* or *extend towards,* Lat. *tendere in* . . . 2. *to strain* or *exert oneself, strive earnestly.*

κατα-τέμνω Ion. and Dor. -τάμνω: f. -τεμῶ: aor. 2 κατέτᾰμον: pf. κατατέτμηκα, pass. κατατέτμημαι:—*to cut in pieces, cut up;* κατατέμνειν τινὰ καττύματα *to cut* him *into* strips; κατατέτμηντο τάφροι trenches *had been cut.*

κατά-τεχνος, ον, (κατά, τέχνη) *artificial.*

κατα-τήκω, f. ξω: aor. 1 κατέτηξα.—*to make melt away, to thaw: to dissolve, make liquid.* II. Pass., with pf. act. κατατέτηκα, *to melt* or *be melting away, to thaw: to pine away.*

κατα-τίθημι, f. -θήσω: pf. -τέθηκα: aor. 2 κατέθην, Ep. pl. κάτθεμεν, κάτθετε, κάτθεσαν; καταθείομεν, Ep. subj. for καταθῶμεν; Ep. inf. κατθέμεν; and in Med., κατθέμεθα, καταθέσθην, κατθέμενοι, Ep. for κατέθεμεν, etc.; καταθείομαι, Ep. subj. for καταθῶμαι:—*to place, put* or *lay down;* καταθεῖναι ἄεθλον *to put down, propose* a prize. 2. *to pay down:* generally, *to make good, to perform.* 3. καταθεῖναι τισί τι ἐς μέσον *to communicate* a thing to others, *give* them *a common share of* it. II. Med. *to lay down for* or *from oneself, put down, lay aside: to put away, get rid of.* 2. *to deposit, lay up in store:* metaph., κατατίθεσθαι κλέος *to lay up a store of* glory; χάριν κατατίθεσθαί τινι *to lay up a store of* gratitude *for oneself* with one. 3. *to lay up in memory.*

κατα-τιλάω, f. ήσω, *to befoul,* Lat. *concacare.*

κατα-τιτρώσκω, f. -τρώσω, *to cover with wounds, wound mortally.*

κατᾰτομή, ἡ, (κατατέμνω) *a cutting into: outward, fleshly circumcision.*

κατα-τοξεύω, f. σω, *to strike down with arrows, shoot down, slay with arrows: shoot through.*

κατατρᾰγεῖν, aor. 2 inf. of κατατρώγω

κατα-τραυματίζω Ion. -τρωματίζω· f. ίσω Att. ιῶ:—*to cover with wounds, wound all over.* of ships. *to disable utterly, cripple.*

κατα-τρέχω, f. -δρᾰμοῦμαι: aor. 2 κατέδρᾰμον (formed from obsol. δρέμω):—*to run down:* of a ship, *to run into port.* II. *to run down upon, attack.* III. *to run over: to overrun, ravage, lay waste.*

κατα-τρίβω, f. ψω: aor. 2 pass. -ετρίβην [ῐ]: pf. -τέτριμμαι:—*to rub down. wear away with rubbing:* of persons, *to wear out, weary, exhaust:* of property. *to waste, squander:*—Pass. *to be worn out.* 2. of Time, *to wear away, get rid of it,* Lat. *diem terere:*—Pass., esp. in pf. -τέτριμμαι, *to spend one's life, live one's whole time.* [ῑ]

κατα-τρίζω, *to squeak, scream shrilly.*
κατα-τροχάζω, f. άσω, *to run down* or *over.*
κατα-τρύζω, f. ύσω, *to chatter against.*
κατα-τρύχω, *to rub down, wear out, exhaust.* [ῡ]
κατα-τρώγω, fut. -τρώξομαι: aor. 2 κατέτρᾰγον:—*to gnaw in pieces, eat up.*
κατα-τρωματίζω, Ion. for καταтραυμ-.
κατα-τυγχάνω, fut. -τεύξομαι, *to hit one's mark, reach, gain, obtain:* absol. *to be successful.*
κατ-αυαίνω, *to dry, parch,* or *wither up.*
κατ-αυγάζω, f. άσω, *to illumine* or *light up:*—Med. *to gaze at.*
κατ-αυδάω, f. ήσω, *to speak aloud, declare.*
κατ-αῦθι, or better **κατ' αὖθι**, Adv. *on the spot.*
κατ-αυλέω, f. ήσω, *to play upon the flute to one:*—Pass. *to have the flute played to one: to resound with the flute.* II. c. acc. *to overpower by flute-playing:* generally, *to strike dumb.*
κατ-αυλίζομαι, f. ίσομαι: aor. 1 med. κατηυλισάμην and pass. κατηυλίσθην: Dep.:—*to take up one's quarters, encamp, settle, lodge.*
κατ-αυτίκα, better **κατ' αὐτίκα.**
κατ-αυτόθι, Adv. *on the spot,* for κατ' αὐτόθι.
κατ-αυχένιος, α, ον, (κατά, αὐχήν) *on* or *over the neck.*
κατ-αυχέω, f. ήσω, *to exult much in.*
κατα-φᾰγεῖν, aor. 2 inf. of κατεσθίω, *to eat up, devour.* 2. *to consume in eating.*
κατα-φαίνω, f. -φᾰνῶ, *to make visible.* II. Pass. *to become visible, appear.* 2. *to be clear* or *plain.*
καταφᾰνῆναι, aor. 2 inf. pass. of καταφαίνω. Hence
καταφᾰνής, ές, *clearly seen, conspicuous.* 2. *manifest, clear.*
κατάφαρκτος, ον, old Att. for κατάφρακτος.
κατα-φαρμᾰκεύω, f. σω, *to anoint with drugs: to charm, bewitch.*
κατα-φαρμάσσω, f. ξω, *to poison.*
κατα-φαυλίζω, f. σω, *to depreciate.*
καταφερής, ές. (καταφέρομαι) *sloping, slanting;* εὖτε ἂν καταφερὴς γίγνηται ὁ ἥλιος when the sun is *near setting.* II. *inclined to* a thing.
κατα-φέρω: f. κατοίσω or κατοίσομαι: aor. 1 κατήνεγκα:—*to bring down:*—Pass. *to be brought down,* as by a river: *to be weighed down* by sleep. II. *to bring down* from the high sea. *bring to land:*—Pass. *to be carried* or *driven down to* a place.
κατα-φεύγω, f. ξομαι: aor. 2 κατέφῠγον:—*to flee for refuge* or *betake oneself to. to have recourse to.* Hence
κατα-φευκτέον. verb. Adj. *one must betake oneself.*
κατά-φευξις. εως. ἡ, *flight for refuge.* 2. *a place of refuge*
κατά-φημι, *to say yes. assent to.*
κατα-φημίζω. f. σω and ξω. *to spread a report, announce. proclaim.*
κατα-φθᾰτέομαι. Dep. (κατά. φθατέω or φθατάω = φθάνω):—*to take first possession of. occupy.*
κατα-φθείρω, f. -φθερῶ, *to bring to nothing, ruin.*
κατα-φθῐνύθω, = καταφθίω. [ῠ]
κατα-φθίνω: aor. 1 κατεφθίνησα: pf. κατεφθίνηκα:—*to waste away, decay, perish.*
κατα-φθίω, I. Causal in fut. καταφθίσω [ῑ], aor. 1 κατέφθῑσα, *to ruin, destroy, kill.* II. intrans. in pf. pass. κατέφθῐμαι, Ep. aor. 2 κατεφθίμην [ῐ], inf. -φθίσθαι:—*to be destroyed, ruined, waste away, perish;* ὡς καταφθίσθαι ὤφελες O that thou *badst perished:* part. καταφθίμενος, *dead, departed.*
καταφθορά, ἡ, (καταφθείρω) *destruction, ruin, death:* metaph. *confusion, distraction.*
κατα-φῐλέω, f. ήσω, *to kiss tenderly, caress.*
κατα-φλέγω, f. ξω, *to burn down, consume.*
καταφλεξί-πολις, ὁ, ἡ, (καταφλέγω, πόλις) *inflamer of cities.*
κατά-φλεξις, εως, ἡ, (καταφλέγω) *a burning*
κατα-φοβέω, f. ήσω, *to strike with fear* or *dismay:*—Pass., with fut. med. φοβήσομαι, aor. 1 κατεφοβήθην, *to be afraid of.*
κατα-φοιτάω Ion. -έω, *to come down regularly.*
κατα-φονεύω, f. σω, *to slaughter, butcher, slay.*
κατα-φορέω, f. ήσω, *to carry down* or *along:* of a river, *to carry down with the stream:*—Pass. *to be so carried down.*
κατα-φράζω, f. σω, *to declare.* II. Med., with fut. -φράσομαι, aor. 1 med. -εφρασάμην, pass. -εφράσθην:—*to think upon, reflect upon: to remark, observe.*
κατάφρακτος, ον, *covered, decked: shut up in.* From
κατα-φράσσω Att. -ττω, f. ξω, *to cover, fence in.*
κατα-φρονέω, f. ήσω, *to think slightly of, disdain, despise: to scorn, contemn.* II. *to fix one's thoughts upon, think of:* also *to aim at,* Lat. *affectare.* III. *to think arrogantly, to presume:* and simply *to think, suppose.* Hence
καταφρόνημα, ατος, τό, *contempt* of others; μὴ φρόνημα μόνον, ἀλλὰ καταφρόνημα not only spirit, but *a spirit of disdain:* and
καταφρόνησις, εως, ἡ, *a low opinion of others: presumption:* and
καταφρονητής, οῦ, ὁ, *a despiser:* and
καταφρονητικός, ή, όν, *contemptuous, disdainful.* Adv. -κῶς, *scornfully.*
κατα-φροντίζω, f. ίσω Att. ιῶ, *to think* or *study* a thing *away.*
κατα-φρύγω, f. ξω, *to burn away.*
κατα-φυγγάνω, = καταφεύγω.
καταφῠγεῖν, aor. 2 inf. of καταφεύγω. Hence
καταφῠγή, ἡ, *a refuge, place of refuge.*
κατα-φῠλᾰδόν, Adv., for κατὰ φυλάς, *in tribes, by tribes* or *clans.*
κατα-φῠλάσσω Att. -ττω, f. ξω, *to guard well.*
κατα-φυλλορoέω, f. ήσω, *to shed leaves: to decay.*
κατά-φῠτος, ον, (κατά, φυτόν) *well-planted.*
κατα-φωράω, f. άσω [ᾱ], *to catch in a theft:* generally, *to catch in the act, detect, discover.*
κατα-φωτίζω, f. ίσω Att. ιῶ, *to illuminate, light up.*
κατα-χαίρω, f. -χαρήσω, *to exult over* one.

κατα-χᾰλαζάω, f. ήσω, *to shower down like hail on* one.

κατά-χαλκος, ον, (κατά, χαλκός) *covered with brass;* κατάχαλκον πεδίον the plain *gleaming with brasen armour.* Hence

κατα-χαλκόω, f. ώσω, *to cover with brass.*

κατα-χᾰρίζομαι, f. ίσομαι Att. ιοῦμαι, *to do* or *give up* a thing *out of courtesy:* generally. *to flatter, curry favour.*

κατάχαρμα, ατος, τό, (καταχαίρω) *a mockery*, Lat. *ludibrium.*

κατα-χέζω, f. -χέσομαι, *to befoul*, Lat. *concacare.*

κατα-χειροτονέω, f. ήσω, *to vote by show of hands against* generally, *to vote against.* Hence

καταχειροτονία, ἡ, *condemnation by show of hands.*

καταχεῦαι, Ep. aor. 1 inf. of καταχέω.

κατα-χέω Ep. -χεύω: fut. χεῶ: aor. 1 κατέχεα Ep. κατέχευα:—Pass., aor. 1 κατεχύθην [ῠ]: Ep. aor. 2 κατεχύμην [ῠ], 3 sing. and pl. κατέχῠτο, χατέχυντο:—*to pour down. shed upon* or *over. to shower down: to throw, cast down: to let fall upon.* 2. *to melt down* II. Med. *to let flow down*, esp. of the hair. 2 *to have* or *cause to be melted down;* χρυσὸν καταχέασθαι.

καταχήνη, ἡ, (καταχαίνω) *derision, mockery.*

κατα-χηρεύω, f. σω, *to pass in widowhood.*

κατ-ᾱχής, ές. Dor. for κατηχής.

κατ-άχθομαι, Pass. *to be grieved* or *distressed.*

κατα-χθόνιος, ον, (κατά, χθών) *subterranean, infernal*

κατα-χορδεύω, f. σω, *to cut in strips.*

κατα-χραίνομαι, Dep. *to spot* or *sprinkle.*

κατα-χράομαι, f. -χρήσομαι: Dep.:—*to make use of, apply: to use to the uttermost, use up, consume.* 2. *to misuse. misapply.* 3. of persons, *to make away with, destroy, despatch.* II. the Act. καταχράω is only used impers. in 3 sing., καταχρᾷ, *it is enough, it suffices;* so impf. κατέχρα *it sufficed;* fut. καταχρήσει *it will suffice:* once with a nom., ἀντὶ λόφου ἡ λοφιὴ κατέχρα the name *sufficed, served* as a crest.

κατα-χρειόομαι, Pass. *to be ill treated.*

κατα-χρέμπτομαι. Dep. *to spit upon* or *at*, in sign of contempt.

κατα-χρηστέον, verb. Adj. of καταχράομαι, *one must use* or *abuse.*

κατά-χρυσος. ον, *covered with gold, gilded.* Hence

καταχρῡσόω, f. ώσω, *to cover with gold, to gild.*

κατα-χρώζω. also -χρώννυμι and -ύω: f. -χρώσω: *to colour, tinge: to soil, tarnish.*

καταχύδην, (καταχέω) Adv. *pouring down*, i. e. *profusely, lavishly.* [ῠ]

κατάχυσμα, ατος, τό, (καταχέω) *that which is poured on* or *over:* in pl. *handfuls of nuts and figs*, which were *showered over* a bride, or any new-comer, in sign of welcome.

κατα-χωνεύω, f. σω, *to melt down.*

κατα-χώννῡμι or -ύω, fut. -χώσω, *to cover with a heap* or *mound, bury, inter.*

κατα-χωρίζω, f. ίσω Att. ιῶ, *to set* or *place in, establish in a place* or *spot.*

καταχῶσαι, aor. 1 inf. of καταχώννυμι.

κατα-ψακάζω, Att. for καταψεκάζω.

κατα-ψάω, f. -ψήσω, *to stroke with the hand.*

κατα-ψεκάζω Att. -ψακάζω, f. άσω, *to drop down on, bedew.*

κατα-ψεύδομαι, f. σομαι, Dep. *to feign, invent;* καταψεύδεσθαί τινος *to tell lies against* one: *to say falsely, pretend.*

κατα-ψευδομαρτῠρέω, f. ήσω, *to bear false witness against:*—Pass. *to be borne down by false witness.*

κατάψευστος, ον, (καταψεύδομαι) *feigned, fabulous.*

κατα-ψηφίζομαι, fut. ίσομαι Att. ιοῦμαι, *to vote against* or *in condemnation of:*—as Pass. *to be condemned.*

κατα-ψήχω. f. -ψήξω, *to rub* or *grate down:*—Pass. *to crumble away.* II. metaph. = καταψάω.

κατα-ψύχω, f. ξω, *to cool, refresh.* [ῡ]

κατέᾱγα, pf. of κατάγνυμι:—**κατεάγην** [ᾰ], aor. 2 pass.

κατεᾰγῶσιν, 3 pl. aor. 2 subj. pass. of κατάγνυμι.

κατέαξα, aor. 1 of κατάγνυμι.

κατεάξω, late fut. of κατάγνυμι.

κατέαται, Ion. for κάθηνται, 3 pl. of κάθημαι.

κατέατο, Ion. for ἐκάθηντο, 3 pl. impf. of κάθημαι.

κατέβα, Dor. 3 sing. aor. 2 of καταβαίνω.

κατέβαν, for κατέβησαν, 3 pl. aor. 2 of καταβαίνω.

κατέβην, aor. 2 of καταβαίνω.

κατεβήσετο, Ep. for -ατο, 3 sing. aor. 1 med. of καταβαίνω.

κατεβλᾱκευμένως, Adv. pf. pass. part. of καταβλᾱκεύω, *slothfully, sluggishly.*

κατ-εγγῠάω, f. ήσω: (κατά, ἐγγύη):—*to pledge, betroth.* II. as Att. law-term, *to make responsible, compel to give security* or *bail.*

κατ-εγγύη, ἡ, *bail, security given.*

κατεγέλων, impf. of καταγελάω.

κατεγήρα, 3 sing. impf. or aor. 2; see γηράσκω.

κατ-εγχέω, f. -χεῶ, *to pour down into.*

κατέδησα, aor. 1 of καταδέω (A).

κατέδομαι, fut. of κατεσθίω.

κατέδραθον, for κατέδαρθον, aor. 2 of καταδαρθάνω.

κατέδραμον, aor. 2 of κατατρέχω.

κατέδυν, aor. 2 of καταδύνω.

κατ-έδω, Ep. for κατεσθίω.

κατεηγώς, Ion. pf. part. of κατάγνυμι.

κατέθεντο, 3 pl. aor. 2 med. of κατατίθημι.

κατέθηκα, aor. 1 of κατατίθημι.

κατ-είβω, poët. for καταλείβω, *to let flow down, shed:*—Med. *to flow apace, trickle down:* metaph., αἰὼν κατείβετο life *ebbed* or *passed away.*

κατειδέναι, inf. pf. of *κατείδω.

***κατ-είδω**, I. in aor. 2 κατεῖδον, inf. κατιδεῖν (which serves as aor. 2 to καθοράω), *to look down upon, contemplate, observe;* so also in aor. 2 med. κατειδόμην, inf. κατιδέσθαι. II. in pf. κάτοιδα, inf. κατειδέναι, *to know well, to be assured of.*

κατ-είδωλος, *ον*, (*κατά*, *εἴδωλον*) *given to idols.*

κατ-εικάζω, f. *άσω*, *to liken to*:—Pass. *to be* or *become like.* II. *to guess, surmise, conjecture*: of evil, *to suspect.*

κατ-ειλέω, f. *ήσω*, *to force into a place, coop up*:—Pass. *to be cooped up.*

κατείληφα, **κατείλημμαι**, pf. act. and pass. of *καταλαμβάνω.*

κατ-ειλίσσω, Ion. for *καθελίσσω.*

κατειλίχἄτο, Ion. 3 pl. plqpf. pass. of *καθελίσσω.*

κατ-ειλύω, f. *ύσω* [ῡ], *to cover up, wrap up.*

κάτ-ειμι: Ep. aor. 1 med. *καταεισάμην*: (*κατά*, *εἶμι ibo*) *to go* or *come down*: *to go down* to the sea; but also, *to sail down from* the high sea to land: of a river, *to flow down*: of a wind, *to sweep down.* II. *to come back, return*: of exiles, *to return home.*

κατεῖναι, Ion. for *καθεῖναι*, aor. 2 inf. of *καθίημι.*

κατ-είνῡμι, Ion. for *καθέννυμι.*

κατεῖπα, aor. 1 = *κατεῖπον.*

κατεῖπον, inf. *κατειπεῖν*, without any pres. in use: (*κατά*, *εἶπον*): *to speak against, to accuse, charge.* II. *to speak out, declare, tell plainly.* 2. *to denounce, tell, to inform of.*

κατειργαθόμην, poët. aor. 2 med. of *κατείργω.*

κατ-είργνῡμι and **-ύω**, = *κατείργω.*

κατ-είργω Ion. **-έργω**, f. *ξω*, *to shut in, enclose, confine*:—*to press hard, reduce to straits.* II. *to hinder.*

κατ-ειρύω, Ion. for *κατερύω.*

κατ-ειρωνεύομαι, Dep. *to use irony towards, banter*: *to dissemble*

κατ-εισάγω, f. *άξω*, *to bring in to one's own loss.* [ᾰ]

κατέκειρα, aor. 1 of *κατακείρω.*

κατέκηα, aor 1 of *κατακαίω.*

κατέκλᾰσα, aor. 1 of *κατακλάω.*

κατεκλάσθην, aor. 1 pass of *κατακλάω.*

κατεκλάχθην, Dor. aor. 1 pass. of *κατακλείω.*

κατέκλῠσα, aor. 1 of *κατακλύζω.*

κατέκλων, contr. impf. of *κατακλάω.*

κατεκρίθην, aor. 1 pass. of *κατακρίνω*

κατέκταν, Ep. aor. 2 of *κατακτείνω.*

κατέκτᾰθεν, Aeol. and Ep. 3 pl. aor. 1 pass of *κατακτείνω*

κατέκτᾰνον, aor. 2 of *κατακτείνω.*

κατέλᾰβον, aor 2 of *καταλαμβάνω*

κατ-ελαύνω: fut. *ελάσω* Att. *-ελῶ*: aor 1 *κατήλασα*. *to drive down*: *to master*

κατ-ελέγχω, f. *γξω*, *to convict of falsehood*: *to belie.*

κατέλεκτο, 3 sing. Ep. aor. 2 pass. of *καταλέγω.*

κατ-ελεύσομαι, fut. of *κατέρχομαι.*

κατελήφθην, aor. 1 pass. of *καταλαμβάνω.*

κατελθεῖν Ep. **-θέμεν**, aor. 2 inf. of *κατέρχομαι.*

κατ-ελίσσω, Ion. for *καθελίσσω.*

κατ-ελκύω, Ion. for *καθελκύω*

κατ-ελπίζω, f. *ίσω*, *to hope confidently*

κάτεμεν, Ion. 1 pl. aor 2 of *καθίημι*

κατ-εναίρομαι, Dep., with aor. 1 med. *κατενηράμην*, and also aor 2 act *κατήναρον*: *to kill, slay, slaughter.*

κατ-εναντίον, also **κατ-έναντι**, Adv. (*κατά*, *ἐναντίος*) *over against, opposite, fronting.*

κατ-εναρίζω, f. *ξω*, strengthd. for *ἐναρίζω*, *to kill.*

κατένασσα, Ep. aor. 1 of *καταναίω.*

κατενεχθείς, aor. 1 part. pass. of *καταφέρω.*

κατ-ενήνοθε, pf. with no pres. in use, *it was upon, it lay upon*, *κόνις κατενήνοθεν ὤμους*: cf. *ἐπ-ενήνοθε*, *παρ-ενήνοθε*; the simple *ἐνήνοθε* does not occur.

κατενήρατο, 3 sing. aor. 1 of *κατεναίρομαι.*

κατενθεῖν, Dor. aor. 2 inf. of *κατέρχομαι.*

κατενύγησαν [ῠ], 3 pl. aor. 2 pass. of *κατανύσσω*

κατ-ένωπᾰ and **κατ-ενώπιον**, Adv. (*κατά*, *ἐνωπή*) *right over against, right opposite, fronting.*

κατ-εξανίστᾰμαι, Pass., with aor. 2 act. *-εξανέστην*, *to rise up against, contend against.*

κατέξανται, 3 sing. pf. pass. of *καταξαίνω.*

κατεξενωμένος *ὁ*, *received as a guest*, pf. part. pass. of *καταξενόω.*

κατ-εξουσιάζω, f. *άσω*, *to exercise authority over.*

κατ-επαγγέλλομαι, Med. *to make a contract* or *engagement with* one.

κατ-επάγω, f. *άξω*, *to bring down upon, bring* one thing *quickly upon* another.

κατεπάλμενος, Ep. aor. 2 part. of *κατεφάλλομαι.*

κατέπαλτο, 3 sing. Ep. aor. 2 pass. of *καταπάλλω.*

κατ-επείγω, f. *ξω*, *to press down, oppress.* 2. *to urge, impel, stimulate, hasten*; *τὸ κατεπεῖγον urgent necessity.* II. intr. *to hurry, make haste.*

κατέπεσον, aor. 2 of *καταπίπτω.*

κατεπέστην, aor. 2 of *κατεφίστημι.*

κατέπεφνον, redupl. aor. 2 of *καταφένω.*

κατέπηκτο, 3 sing. Ep. aor. 2 pass. of *καταπήγνυμι.*

κατέπηξα, aor. 1 of *καταπήγνυμι.*

κατέπλᾰσα, aor. 1 of *καταπλάσσω.*

κατέπλευσα, aor. 1 of *καταπλέω.*

κατεπλήγην, aor. 2 pass. of *καταπλήσσω.*

κατέπτῠσα, aor. 1 of *καταπτύω.*

κατ-εργάζομαι, fut. *-άσομαι*: aor. 1 *κατειργάσθην*: pf. *κατείργασμαι*: Dep. (but aor. 1 and pf. are also used in pass. sense):—*to effect, accomplish, achieve.* 2. like Lat. *conficere*, *to make an end of, destroy, despatch*: hence *to overpower, conquer*:—pf. in pass. sense, *to be overcome.* 3. in good sense, *to prevail upon, persuade, influence*:—aor. 1 in pass. sense, *to be prevailed on.* II. *to work in, make*; *κατεργάζεσθαι μέλι to make honey*: also *to manufacture.* III. of things, *to earn, to acquire by labour*: absol. *to go to work.*

κατ-έργω, Ion. for *κατείργω.*

κατερεικτός or **-ερικτός**, *όν*, *bruised.* From

κατ-ερείκω, *to tear, rend*:—Med. *to rend one's garments* II. *to bruise* or *grind down*; metaph., *κατερείκειν θυμόν to wear away* one's mind.

κατ-ερείπω, f. *ψω*, *to throw* or *cast down*: *to demolish, dismantle, lay waste.* II. intr. in aor. 2 *κατήριπον*, pf. *κατερήριπα*, *to fall down, fall in.*

κατέρεξα, Ep aor. 1 of *καταρρέζω.*

κατ-ερεύγω, f *ξω*, *to belch at* or *upon.*

κατ-ερέφω, f. ξω, *to cover, roof*:—Med. *to roof over for oneself*.

κατ-ερέω, Ion. for κατερῶ, serving as fut. (with pf. κατείρηκα), of the aor. κατεῖπον:—*to speak against, accuse*, c. gen.: also c. acc. *to denounce, impeach, arraign*. 2. *to say plainly, speak out*: Pass., κατειρήσεται *it shall be declared*.

κατερήριπα, intr. pf. of κατερείπω.

κατ-ερητύω, f. ύσω [ῡ]:—*to keep in, detain, confine*.

κατερρίβην [ῐ], aor. 2 pass. of κατατρίβω.

κατέρρωγα, intrans. pf. of καταρρήγνυμι.

κατερῡκάνω, poët. for κατερύκω. [ᾰ]

κατ-ερύκω [ῡ]; f. ξω, *to hold back, detain*.

κατ-ερύω Ion. -**ειρύω**: f. ύσω [ῠ]: aor. 1 κατείρῠσα: Pass., pf. κατείρυσμαι:—*to draw* or *haul down*: of ships, *to draw down to the water, launch*, Lat. *deducere naves*.

κατ-έρχομαι, fut. κατελεύσομαι: aor. 3 κατήλῠθον contr. κατῆλθον, inf. κατελθεῖν: Dep.:—*to go down*, esp. to the coast. of things, *to fall down*: of a river, *to flow* or *run down*. II. *to come back, return*: of exiles, *to return home*.

κατερῶ, v. sub κατερέω.

κατέσβεσα, aor. 1 of κατασβέννυμι.

κατέσβηκα, **κατέσβην**, intrans. pf. and aor. 2 of κατασβέννυμι.

κατ-εσθίω, f. κατέδομαι, pf. κατεδήδοκα Ep. κατέδηδα pf. pass. κατεδήδεσμαι:—*to eat up, devour, prey upon*.

κατέσκαμμαι, pf. pass. of κατασκάπτω.

κατεσκεύασμαι, pf. pass. of κατασκευάζω.

κατεσκεψάμην, aor. 1 med. of κατασκοπέω.

κατέσκληκα, intr. pf. of κατασκέλλω.

κατέσπειρα, aor. 1 of κατασπείρω.

κατέσπεισα, aor. 1 of κατασπένδω.

κατέσσῠτο, 3 sing. Ep. aor. 2 pass. of κατασεύομαι.

κατέστᾰθεν, Aeol. and Ep. 3 pl. aor. 1 pass. of καθίστημι.

κατέσταλμαι, pf. pass. of καταστέλλω.

κατέστειψα, aor 1 of καταστείβω.

κατεστεώς, Ion. pf. part. of καθίστημι.

κατέστην, aor. 2 of καθίστημι: **κατέστησα**, aor. 1.

κατεστήσαντο, 3 pl. aor. 1 med. of καθίστημι.

κατεστόρεσα, aor. 1 of καταστορέννυμι.

κατεστράφατο, Ion. for κατεστραμμένοι ἦσαν, 3 pl. plqpf. pass. of καταστρέφω.

κατέστρωσα, aor. 1 of καταστρώννυμι.

κατέστυγον, aor. 2 of καταστυγέω.

κατετάκετο, Dor. 3 sing. impf. pass. of κατατήκω.

κατέτηξα, aor. 1 of κατατήκω.

κάτευγμα, ατος, τό, (κατεύχομαι) *a vow, wish, prayer*: esp. for evil, *an imprecation, curse*. II. *a votive offering*.

κατ-ευθύ or -**ευθύς**, Adv. *straight forward*.

κατ-ευθύνω, f. ῠνῶ, *to make straight, set right*: *to guide, direct, conduct*.

κατ-ευνάζω, fut. άσω, *to lull to sleep*:—Pass. *to lie down to sleep*; Aeol. 3 pl. aor. 1 κατεύνασθεν.

κατευνάω, f. ήσω, *to put to sleep, compose to sleep*.—Pass. *to fall asleep*.

κατευνήσαιμι, aor. 1 opt. of κατευνάω.

κατ-ευτρεπίζω, f. σω, *to get ready, set in order, prepare*.

κατ-ευφημέω, f. ήσω, *to praise loudly, extol*.

κατ-ευφραίνω, f. ᾰνῶ, *to gladden* or *delight much*.

κατευχή, ἡ, *a wish, prayer, vow*. From

κατ-εύχομαι, f. -ξομαι, Dep. *to pray earnestly*: *to pray to* one: absol. *to make a vow, pray*. 2. *to pray for evil on* one, *invoke a curse*. II. *to boast*.

κατ-ευωχέομαι, Pass. *to feast, make merry*.

κατέφᾰγον, used as aor. 2 of κατεσθίω.

κατ-εφάλλομαι, Dep. *to spring down upon, rush upon*; κατεπάλμενος, Ep. aor. 2 part.

κατέφθῐτο, 3 sing. Ep. aor. 2 pass. of καταφθίω.

κατ-εφίσταμαι, Pass., with aor. 2 act. κατεπέστην, pf. κατεφέστηκα, *to rise up again*.

κατέφῠγον, aor. 2 of καταφεύγω.

κατέχῠτο, **κατέχυντο**, 3 sing. and pl. Ep. aor. 2 pass. of καταχέω.

κατ-έχω: fut. καθέξω and κατασχήσω: aor. 2 κάτεσχον poët. -έσχεθον: I. trans. *to hold, keep back, withhold*: *to check, restrain*:—Pass. *to stop, cease*. II. *to possess, occupy, keep, dwell in*: *to seize, take possession of, occupy* with soldiers. 2. *to cover, encompass*: also in Med., πρόσωπα κατέσχετο she *covered her* face: generally, *to hide, keep concealed*. III. intrans. *to check oneself*: *to hold, stop, cease*. 2. *to come from the high sea to shore, land, touch, put in*. 3. *to come to pass, happen*; εὖ κατασχήσει it *will turn out* well. 4. of a report, *to prevail, be frequent*: *to have the upper hand*. IV. Med. *to keep back from oneself, embezzle*: also *to blind*.

κατήγαγον, aor. 2 of κατάγω.

κατηγγέλην, aor. 2 pass. of καταγγέλλω.

κατηγεμών, **κατηγέομαι**, etc., Ion. for καθηγ-.

κατήγετο, 3 sing. impf. pass. of κατάγω.

κατ-ηγορέω, f. ήσω, (κατήγορος) *to speak against, to accuse, arraign*. 2. *to lay* a thing *to one's charge*:—Pass., κατηγορεῖταί τι τινός *a charge is brought against* him. 3. absol. *to be an accuser, appear as prosecutor*. 4. generally, *to signify, indicate, prove, intimate*. Hence

κατηγορία, ἡ, *an accusation, charge*.

κατήγορος, ὁ, (κατά, ἀγορεύω) *an accuser*: *betrayer*.

κατῴκισμαι, pf. pass. of κατοικίζω.

κατήκοος, ον, (κατακούω) *listening to, attentive*: as Subst. *a listener, spy, eavesdropper*. II. *hearkening to, obeying*: as Subst. *a subject*. III. *hearkening to, giving ear to*.

κατ-ήκω, Ion. for καθήκω.

κατῆλθον, aor. 2 of κατέρχομαι.

κατῆλιψ, ῐφος, ἡ, *the upper story* of a house: a *staircase* or *ladder*. (Deriv. uncertain.)

κατηλλάχθην, **κατηλλάγην** [ᾰ], aor. 1 and 2 pass. of καταλλάσσω.

κατ-ηλογέω, f. *ήσω*, (*κατά, λόγος*) *to make of small account, slight, despise.*

κατήλυθον, uncontr. form of *κατῆλθον*. Hence

κατήλῠσις, *εως, ἡ, a going down, descent.*

κάτημαι, Ion. for *κάθημαι.*

κατημελημένος, pf. part. pass. of *καταμελέω.*

κατηναρίσθην, -ίσμαι, aor. 1 and pf. pass. of *κατεναρίζω.*

κατήνεγκα, aor. 1 of *καταφέρω.*

κατηνθρακώθην, -ωμαι, aor. 1 and pf. pass. of *κατανθρακόω.*

κατήνῠσα, aor. 1 of *κατανύω.*

κατήορος or **κατῄορος**, *ον*, Dor. **-άορος**, (*κατά, αἰωρέω*) *hanging down: hanging on* or *to.*

κατ-ηπιάω, f. *άσω*, (*κατά, ἤπιος*) *to soothe, assuage:* —Ep. 3 pl. impf. pass. *κατηπιόωντο.*

κατηρᾰμένος, pf. part. of *καταράομαι.*

κατηράσω [ᾱ], 3 sing. aor. 1 of *καταράομαι.*

κατηρᾶτο, 3 sing. impf. of *καταράομαι.*

κατ-ηρεμίζω, f. *ίσω*, *to calm, appease, quiet.*

κατ-ηρεφής, *ές*, (*κατά, ἐρέφω*) *covered over, overhanging, overarched; δάφνῃσι κατηρεφές overshadowed* with laurels; *κατηρεφῆ πόδα τιθέναι* to keep the foot *covered* by the fall of the robe, of one who stands still, opp. to *ὀρθὸν πόδα τιθέναι.* 2. c. gen. *covered with, laden with.*

κατ-ήρης, *ες*, (*κατά, ἀρᾰρεῖν*) *fitted out, furnished, supplied:* of ships, *furnished with oars.*

κατηριθμημένος, pf. pass. part. of *καταριθμέω.*

κατήρῐπον, aor. 2 of *κατερείπω.*

κατηρτίσω, 2 sing. aor. 1 med. of *καταρτίζω.*

κατήρτισμαι, pf. pass. of *καταρτίζω.*

κατῆστο, Ion. 3 sing. impf. of *κάθημαι.*

κατήφεια Ion. **-είη**, *ἡ*, (*κατηφής*) *a casting the eyes downwards: dejection, sorrow, shame.*

κατηφέω, f. *ήσω*, *to be downcast, struck dumb.* From

κατη-φής, *ές*, (*κατά, φάος*) *with downcast eyes, dejected, downcast, struck dumb.* Hence

κατηφών, *όνος, ὁ, one who causes shame, a disgrace.*

κατ-ηχέω, f. *ήσω*, *to resound.* II. *to sound* a thing *in one's ears, din* it *into* one:—Pass. *to be informed of* a thing. 2. *to teach by word of mouth, teach the elements of religion:*—Pass. *to be instructed in these elements;* aor. 1 *κατηχήθην*, pf. *κατήχημαι.*

κατ-ηχής, *ές*, (*κατά, ἦχος*) *sounding, resounding.*

κατήχθην, aor. 1 pass. of *κατάγω.*

κάτθᾰνον, Ep. aor. 2 of *καταθνήσκω.*

κατθᾰνοῦμαι, fut. of *καταθνήσκω.*

κατθάψαι, Ep. aor. 1 inf. of *καταθάπτω.*

κατ-θείην, poët. aor. 2 opt. of *κατατίθημι.*

κατθέμεν, Ep. for *καταθεῖναι*, aor. 2 inf. of *κατατίθημι*: but **κάτθεμεν**, Ep. 1 plur. of same.

κάτθετε, κάτθεσαν, Ep. 2 and 3 pl. aor. 2 of *κατατίθημι.*

κατθέμεθα, Ep. and 1 pl. aor. 2 med. of *κατατίθημι.*

κατθέμενος, Ep. aor. 2 part. med of *κατατίθημι.*

κάτθεο, Ep. for *κατάθου*, aor. 2 imperat. med. of *κατατίθημι.*

κατθέσθην, Ep. 2 pl. aor. 2 med. of *κατατίθημι*

κατ-ῐάπτω, f. *ψω*, *to harm, hurt, damage.*

κατίᾱσι, 3 pl. of *κάτειμι* (*εἶμι ibo*).

κατιᾶσι, Ion. for *καθιᾶσι*, 3 pl. of *καθίημι.*

κατῐδεῖν, aor. 2 inf. of *καθοράω.*

κατῐδέσθαι, aor. 2 inf. med. of *καθοράω.*

κατ-ίζω, Ion. for *καθίζω.*

κατ-ίημι, Ion. for *καθίημι.*

κατ-ῑθύνω, Ion. for *κατευθύνω.*

κατ-ῐκετεύω, Ion. for *καθικετεύω.*

κατ-ῑλύω, f. *ύσω* [ῡ], (*κατά, ἰλύς*) *to fill with mud* or *dirt.*

κατίμεν, Ep. inf. of *κάτειμι* (*εἶμι ibo*).

κατιππάζομαι, κατῑρόω, κατίστημι, Ion. for *καθ-*.

κάτισθι, 2 sing. imperat. of *κάτοιδα*, v. **κατείδω.*

κατ-ισχναίνω, *to make to waste away, bring down.*

κατ-ισχύω, f. *ύσω* [ῡ], *to have power over, prevail against, overpower*, c. gen. II. intr. *to come to one's full strength, be in full vigour.*

κατ-ίσχω, collat. pres. form of *κατέχω*, *to hold back, hold in, restrain*, Lat. *detineo:*—Med. *to keep by one.* II. *to possess, occupy.* III. *to guide* or *steer* for a place. IV. intr. *to light upon; σέλας κατίσχει ἐξ οὐρανοῦ* the light *comes down upon* the place from heaven.

κατιών, *οῦσα, όν*, aor. 2 part. of *κάτειμι* (*εἶμι ibo*).

κάτ-οδος, Ion. for *κάθοδος.*

κάτ-οιδα, pf. of **κατείδω.*

κατ-οικέω, f. *ήσω*, *to dwell in, inhabit:*—Pass. *to be dwelt in, inhabited:* of persons, *to be settled in a* place. 2. of a state, *to be administered, regulated* Hence

κατοίκησις, *εως, ἡ, a settling in a place: dwelling.*

κατοικητήριος, *α, ον*, (*κατοικέω*) *fit for inhabiting; κατοικητήριον* (sub. *χωρίον*), *τό*, *a dwelling-place.*

κατοικία, *ἡ*, (*κατοικέω*) *a dwelling, habitation.* II. *a colony.*

κατ-οικίζω, fut. *ίσω* Att. *ιῶ*, *to bring* or *remove into a dwelling* persons *as colonists*:—Pass. *to be placed, settled.* II. *to colonise* a place:—Pass., of places, *to have colonies planted there, to be colonised* or *established.* III. *to bring home, restore to one's country.* Hence

κατοίκῐσις, *εως, ἡ, a planting with inhabitants, colonisation.*

κατ-οικοδομέω, f. *ήσω*, *to build on* or *in* a place.

κάτ-οικος, *ον*, (*κατά, οἶκος*) *dwelling in, inhabiting:* as Subst., *κάτοικος, ὁ, an inhabitant.*

κατ-οικτείρω, *to have compassion on.* II. intr. *to feel compassion, shew pity.*

κατ-οικτίζω, f. *ίσω* Att. *ιῶ*, *to have compassion on* another:—Med., with aor. 1 pass. *κατῳκίσθην*, *to pity oneself, to bewail, lament.* II. *to cause* or *excite pity.* Hence

κατοίκτῐσις, *εως, ἡ, a pitying, compassion.*

κατ-οιμώζω, fut. *-ώξομαι*, *to bewail, lament.*

κάτ-οινος, *ον*, (*κατά, οἶνος*) *drunken with wine.*

κατοίσομαι, fut. of *καταφέρω.*

κατ-οίχομαι, fut. -οιχήσομαι, Dep. *to have gone down*; οἱ κατοιχόμενοι, *the departed.*

κατ-οκνέω, f. ήσω, *to shrink from doing* a thing.

κατοκωχή, ἡ, (κατέχω) *a being possessed, possession.* Hence

κατοκώχιμος, ον, *held in possession, detained.* II. *capable of being possessed, frantic.*

κατ-ολισθάνω, f. -ολισθήσω, *to slip down.*

κατ-όλλῠμαι, Pass., with pf. act. -όλωλα: (κατά, ὄλλυμι) :—*to perish utterly.*

κατ-ολολύζω, f. ύξω, *to shriek over.*

κατ-ολοφύρομαι, Dep. *to bewail, lament.* [ῡ]

κατ-ομβρέω, f. ήσω, (κατά, ὄμβρος) *to rain upon*: —Pass. *to be rained upon*: *to be wet as with rain.*

κατ-όμνῡμι and -ύω: fut. -ομοῦμαι: aor. 1 -ώμοσα: —*to swear to, confirm by oath.* 2. c. acc. pers. *to call to witness, swear by.* 3. c. gen. pers. *to take an oath against, accuse on oath.*

κατ-ονίνημι, fut. -ονήσω, *to be of use, profit, advantage*:—Med. *to have the benefit of, enjoy.* [νῐ]

κατ-όνομαι, Dep. *to blame, slight.*

κάτ-οξυς, εια, υ, (κατά, ὀξύς) *very sharp, piercing.*

κατ-οπάζω, f. άσω, *to follow after.*

κατ-όπιν, Adv., = κατόπισθε.

κατ-όπισθε, and before a vowel -θεν, (κατά, ὄπισθε) Adv. of Place, *behind, after, in the rear.* II. of Time, *hereafter.*

κατ-οπτεύω, f. σω, (κατόπτης) *to spy out, observe.*

κατ-οπτήρ, ῆρος, ὁ, (κατά, ὀπτήρ) *a spy, scout.*

κατ-όπτης, ου, ὁ, = κατοπτήρ.

κάτ-οπτος, ον, (κατά, ὄψομαι) *to be seen, visible*: c. gen. *to be seen from* a place, *within sight of.*

κατοπτρίζω, f. ίσω Att. ιῶ, *to shew as in a mirror*: Med. *to behold oneself in a mirror.* 2. in Med. also *to reflect as in a mirror.* From

κάτοπτρον, τό, (κάτοπτος) *a mirror*, Lat. *speculum*, anciently of polished metal.

κατ-οράω, Ion. for καθοράω.

κατ-οργᾰνίζω, f. ίσω, *to sound with music through.*

κατ-ορθόω, f. ώσω: aor. 1 κατώρθωσα :—*to set upright, erect.* 2. metaph. *to keep straight, set right*: *to direct* or *manage well*: absol. *to be right in* a thing:—Pass. *to succeed, prosper*: also *to be well determined* or *purposed.* II. intr. *to be successful, go on prosperously.* Hence

κατόρθωμα, ατος, τό, *that which is done rightly*: *a right action.* 2. *a success.*

κατ-ορούω, f. σω, *to rush downwards.*

κατ-ορρωδέω Ion. **καταρρ-**, f. ήσω, *to be dismayed at, dread.* II. absol. *to be afraid.*

κατ-ορύσσω Att. **-ττω**: f. ξω: fut. 1 pass. -ορυχθήσομαι, fut. 2 -ορῠχήσομαι:—*to bury, inter*: *to hide in the ground.*

κατ-ορχέομαι, f. -ήσομαι, Dep. *to dance in triumph over*, Lat. *insultare*: hence *to treat despitefully, insult.* II. *to charm by dancing.*

κατ-όσσομαι, Dep. *to contemplate, behold.*

κατ-ότι, Adv. Ion. for καθ' ὅ τι.

κατ-ουδαῖος, ον, (κατά, οὖδας) *under the earth.*

κατ-ουλόω, f. ώσω, (κατά, οὐλή) *to make to cicatrise* or *form a scar over*:—Pass. *to cicatrise, heal over.*

κατ-ουρέω, f. ήσω, *to make water upon.*

κατ-ουρίζω, f. ίσω Att. ιῶ, *to waft with a fair wind.* II. intr. *to sail before the wind, come safe to port.*

κατ-ουρόω, f. ώσω, = κατουρίζω.

κατ-οφρυόομαι, (κατά, ὀφρύς) *to contract the eyebrows, frown.*

κατοχή, ἡ, (κατέχω) *a holding fast, detention.* 2. *possession* by a god.

κατόχῐμος, ον, incorrect form of κατοκώχιμος.

κάτοχος, ον, (κατέχω) *holding fast.* II. pass. *held fast, overpowered, constrained.* 2. *possessed, inspired.*

κατ-όψιος, ον, (κατά, ὄψις) *full in sight, opposite.*

κατόψομαι, used as fut. of καθοράω.

κατ-τά, κατ-τάδε, Dor. for κατὰ τά, κατὰ τάδε.

κατ-τάνῠσαν, Ep. for κατετάνυσαν, 3 pl. aor. 1 of καταταννύω.

καττίτερος, Att. for κασσίτερος, *tin.*

κάττῡμα, καττύω, Att. for κάσσυμα, κασσύω.

κατ-τῶ, Dor. for κατὰ τοῦ.

κατ-υβρίζω, κατ-ύπερθε, κατ-υπέρτερος, Ion. for καθ-.

κατ-υπνόω, Ion. for καθυπνόω.

κάτω, Adv. (κατά) *down, downwards.* II. *beneath, below, underneath*, opp. to ἄνω. 2. *οἱ κάτω, those in the nether world, the dead*: also, *dwellers on the coast* or *in the plain*, as opp. to those inland or on the hills. 3. *ἄνω καὶ κάτω*, or *ἄνω κάτω upside down.* III. c. gen. *under, below*: *down from.* IV. Comp. κατωτέρω: Sup. κατωτάτω.

κατ-ώγειος, ον, Att. **κατώγεως**, ων, gen. ω, = κατάγειος.

κάτωθε, before a vowel **-θεν**, Adv. (κάτω) *from below, up from below.* II. *below, beneath.*

κατ-ωθέω, f. -ήσω: aor. 1 -έωσα, *to thrust down.*

κᾰτω-κάρα, Adv. (κάτω, κάρα) *head downwards.* [κᾰ]

κατῴκησα, aor. 1 of κατοικέω.

κατῴκισθεν, 3 pl. aor. 1 pass. of κατοικίζω.

κατ-ωμάδιος, α, ον, (κατά, ὦμος) *down from the shoulder*, δίσκος κατωμάδιος a quoit *thrown down from the shoulder.* II. *borne on the shoulder.*

κατ-ωμᾰδόν, Adv. (κατά, ὦμος) *from the shoulder, with the whole arm.*

κατωμοσία, ἡ, (κατόμνυμι) *an oath taken against* one, *accusation on oath.*

κατω-νάκη, ἡ, (κάτω, νάκος) *a coarse frock with a border of sheepskin* (νάκος). [νᾰ]

κατ-ωρᾰΐζομαι, Ion. for καθωραΐζομαι.

κατώρθωσα, aor. 1 of κατορθόω: but **κατώρθωσαι**, 2 sing. pf. pass.

κατ-ῶρυξ, ῠχος, ὁ, ἡ, (κατορύσσω) *imbedded* in the earth. II. *buried, hidden in the ground, under ground.* III. as Subst., κατῶρυξ, ἡ, *a pit, cavern.*

κατώτατος, η, ον, (κάτω) *the lowest.*

κατωτάτω, Adv. Sup. of *κάτω*, *at the lowest part.*
κατώτερος, α, ον, (*κάτω*) *lower:* of Time, *later.*
κατωτέρω, Adv. Comp. of *κάτω*, *lower than, further downwards.*
κατω-φᾰγᾶς, οῦ or ᾶ, ὁ, (*κάτω*, *φαγεῖν*) *glutton*, the name of a bird in Aristophanes.
κατω-φερής, ές, (*κάτω*, *φέρομαι*) *hanging downwards, precipitous.*
κατ-ωχράω, f. ήσω, (*κατά*, *ὠχρός*) *to turn very pale.*
κανάξαις, for *καϝϝάξαις* (with the digamma), 2 sing. Ep. aor. 1 opt. of *κατάγνυμι.*
καυλῖνος, η, ον, *made of stalk* or *stick.* From
ΚΑΥΛΟ'Σ, ὁ, *a stalk, stem.* 2. *a handle, shaft: spear-shaft: the hilt* of a sword.
καῦμα, ατος, τό, (*καίω*) *burning heat*, as of the sun; *καύματος*, absol. *in the heat.* II. *feverish heat.* Hence
καυμᾰτίζω, f. ίσω, *to scorch, wither by heat.*
καυνάκης, ου, ὁ, *a Persian garment.* [ᾰ] (Foreign word.)
ΚΑΥΝΟ'Σ, ὁ, *a lot.*
καυσία, ἡ, (*καίω*) *a heat-shade*, name of a broad-brimmed Macedonian hat.
καύσῐμος, ον, (*καίω*) *fit for burning, combustible.*
καῦσις, εως, ἡ, (*καίω*) *a burning: burning heat.* Hence
καυσόομαι, Pass. *to be on fire, intensely hot.*
καύστειρα, fem. Adj. with no masc. in use, *burning.*
καυστήριον, see *καυτήριον.*
καύσω, fut. of *καίω.*
καύσων, ωνος, ὁ, (*καίω*) *burning heat: a scorching wind.*
καυτήρ, ῆρος, ὁ, (*καίω*) *a burner.*
καυτηριάζω, f. άσω, *to sear with red-hot iron:*—metaph. in Pass. *to be seared* in conscience. From
καυτήριον, τό, (*καίω*) *a branding-iron.*
καύτης, ου, ὁ, = *καυτήρ.*
καὐτός, by crasis for *καὶ αὐτός.*
καυχάομαι, fut. -ήσομαι: pf. *κεκαύχημαι*: Dep.:—*to boast* or *vaunt oneself.* (Akin to *αὐχέω*, *εὔχομαι.*)
καυχᾶσαι, for *καυχᾷ*, 2 sing. of *καυχάομαι.*
καύχη, ἡ, = *καύχησις*, *a boasting, vaunting.*
καύχημα, ατος, τό, (*καυχάομαι*) *a vaunt, boast.* 2. *a subject of boasting.*
καυχήμων, ονος, ὁ, ἡ, (*καυχάομαι*) *boastful.*
καύχησις, εως, ἡ, (*καυχάομαι*) *a boasting, cause of boasting.*
κᾰχάζω, f. άξω Dor. αξῶ, *to laugh loud*, Lat. *cachinnor: to laugh scornfully.* (Formed from the sound.)
κᾰχασμός, ὁ, (*καχάζω*) *a loud* or *mocking laugh.*
κᾰχ-εταιρεία, ἡ, (*κακός*, *ἑταῖρος*) *ill company.*
καχ-ήμερος, ον, (*κακός*, *ἡμέρα*) *living sad days, wretched.*
καχλάζω, f. άσω, redupl. from *χλάζω*, *to dash, plash, bubble*, of the sound of liquids.
κάχληξ, ηκος, ὁ, *a pebble:* collectively, *gravel, shingle.* (Akin to *χάλιξ.*)

καχ-ορμισία, ἡ, (*κακός*, *ὁρμίζω*) *ill harbourage.*
κάχρυς, ῠος, ἡ, = *κάγχρυς*, *parched barley.*
κᾰχ-ύποπτος, ον, (*κακός*, *ὕποπτος*) *suspecting evil, meanly suspicious.*
ΚΑ'ΨΑ, ἡ, *a box, chest, case*, Lat. *capsa.*
κάω [ᾱ], Att. for *καίω*, *to burn.*
ΚΕ, and before a vowel **κεν**, Ep. and Ion. for *ἄν*, Dor. **κᾱ**: *ἄν κε*, *κεν ἄν*, are sometimes found together: *κε* is always enclit.
κεάζω, f. άσω: aor. 1 *ἐκέᾰσα* Ep. *ἐκέασσα*, *κέασα*, and *κέασσα*: Pass., aor. 1 *ἐκεάσθην* Ep. *κεάσθην*: (*κέω*, *κείω*):—*to split, cleave:* of lightning, *to shiver, shatter:* generally, *to sever, separate, divide forcibly.*
κέᾰρ, ᾰρος, τό, Lat. *cor*, *the heart:*—contr. **κῆρ**, q. v.
κέας, part. of Att. aor. 1 of *καίω.*
κέασα, **κέασσα**, Ep. aor. 1 of *κεάζω.*
κέᾰται, **κέᾰτο**, Ep. and Ion. 3 pl. pres. and impf. of *κεῖμαι.*
κέβλη or **κεβλή**, ἡ, contr. for *κεφαλή*, *the head.*
κεβλή-πῡρις, (*κεβλή*, *πῦρ*) a bird called *the redcap.*
κεγχριαῖος, α, ον, (*κέγχρος*) *of the size* or *shape of a grain of millet.*
κεγχρίτης [ῑ], ου, ὁ, fem. **-ῖτις**, ιδος, (*κέγχρος*), *like millet, full of small grains.*
κεγχρο-βόλος, ον, (*κέγχρος*, *βάλλω*) *scattering millet.*
ΚΕ'ΓΧΡΟΣ, ὁ, and ἡ, *millet*, Lat. *milium:* hence *any small grain:* also *the spawn of fish.*
κεγχρώματα, ων, τά, (*κέγχρος*) *things of the size of millet-grains: eyelet-holes* in the rim of the shield.
κεδάννῡμι: f. *κεδάσω*: Ep. aor. 1 *ἐκέδασσα*: aor. 1 pass. *ἐκεδάσθην*:—poët. for *σκεδάννυμι*, *to scatter, disperse, break up, break in pieces.*
κεδασθείς, aor. 1 pass. part. of *κεδάννυμι.*
κεδνός, ή, όν, (*κῆδος*) *careful, discreet, trusty.* II. pass. *cared for, dear:* of things, *valued, prized.*
κέδρῐνος, η, ον, (*κέδρος*) *of cedar, made of cedar.*
κεδρίς, ίδος, ἡ, (*κέδρος*) *the cone of the cedar-tree:* also *a juniper-berry.*
ΚΕ'ΔΡΟΣ, ἡ, *the cedar-tree*, Lat. *cedrus.* II. *anything made of cedar; a cedar coffin* or *chest.*
κεδρωτός, ή, όν, (*κέδρος*) *made of*, or *inlaid with, cedar-wood.*
κέεσθαι, Ion. inf. of *κεῖμαι.*
κέεται, Ion. 3 sing. of *κεῖμαι.*
κεῖα, Ep. aor. 1 of *κείω.*
κειάμενος, Ep. aor. 1 med. part. of *καίω.*
κείαντες, Ep. aor. 1 part. pl. of *καίω.*
κείᾰται, **κείᾰτο**, Ep. 3 pl. pres. and impf. of *κεῖμαι.*
κεῖθεν, Adv., Ion. and Ep. for *ἐκεῖθεν*, *thence.*
κεῖθι, Adv., Ion. and Ep. for *ἐκεῖθι*, *there: thither.*
ΚΕΙ'ΜΑΙ, *κεῖσαι*, *κεῖται* Ion. *κέεται*; 3 pl. *κεῖνται*, Ion. and Ep. *κέᾰται*, Ep. also *κείαται* and Ion. *κέονται*: so 3 pl. impf. *ἔκειντο* Ion. *ἐκέατο* Ep. *κείᾰτο*, *κέᾰτο*; subj. *κέωμαι*, *κέῃ*, *κέηται* Ep. *κῆται*: opt. *κεοίμην*: inf. *κεῖσθαι* Ion. *κέεσθαι*: part. *κείμενος*:—fut. *κείσομαι* Dor. *κεισεῦμαι*. Used as Pass. to *τίθημι.*

Radic. sense, *to be laid, to lie: to lie down, lie asleep.* 2. *to lie idle* or *at ease, be inactive:* also *to lie still, rest;* κακὸν κείμενον *abated, allayed* evil. 3. of many conditions, as *to lie sick, lie in weakness* or *old age: to lie dead,* like Lat. *jacēre:* of things, *to be destroyed, overthrown, lie in ruins.* 4. of a corpse, *to lie unburied:* also *to lie uncared for, neglected.* II. of places, *to lie, be situated.* 2. of things, *to be in* or *at a place,* where continuance is implied. III. generally, *to be in a position, be laid* or *placed, stand.* IV. *to be laid up, laid in store;* τὰ κείμενα *deposits.* V. *to be fixed, settled, laid down;* κεῖται νόμος the law *is fixed, laid down;* κεῖται ζημία the penalty *is fixed;* κεῖται ἄεθλον the prize *lies ready, is proposed.* 2. freq. in Homer, ταῦτα θεῶν ἐν γούνασι κεῖται these things *rest* on the knees of the gods, i. e. depend upon the gods; κεῖσθαι ἔν τινι *to be dependent on* a person.

κείμᾱν, Dor. for ἐκείμην, impf. of κεῖμαι.

κειμήλιον, τό, (κεῖμαι) *anything stored up, a treasure* or *valuable: heirloom.*

κείμην, Ep. impf. of κεῖμαι.

κεῖνος, κείνη, κεῖνο, Ion. and poët. for ἐκεῖνος, *that, he, she, it;* dat. fem. κείνῃ, as Adv. *on that road:* also *in that way* or *manner.*

κεινός, ή, όν, Ion. and poët. for κενός, *empty.*

κείνως, Adv., Ion. for ἐκείνως, *in that way.*

Κεῖος, ὁ, (Κεώς) *a Ceian, a man from the island Ceos:* see Χῖος.

κείρασθαι, aor. 1 inf. med. of κείρω.

κειρία, ἡ, (κείρω) *a bandage, roller, a swathing-band.* II. *the cord* or *sacking of a bedstead.*

κειρύλος, ὁ, for κηρύλος, *a kingfisher.* [ῠ]

ΚΕΙ'ΡΩ: fut. κερῶ Ion. κερέω Ep. κέρσω: aor. 1 ἔκειρα Ep. ἔκερσα:—Med., fut. κεροῦμαι:—Pass., aor. 1 ἐκέρθην: aor. 2 ἐκάρην [ᾰ]: pf. κέκαρμαι:—*to clip, cut short,* esp. the hair:—Med. *to cut off one's own* hair or *have* it *cut off:*—Pass., κεκάρθαι τὰς κεφαλάς *to have* their heads *shorn.* 2. *to cut out, hew off.* II. *to ravage, waste* a country, esp. *by cutting down* the fruit-trees. 2. generally, *to cut up, devour, waste, consume, destroy.*

κεὶς, contr. for καὶ εἰς.

κεῖσε, Adv., Ion. and Ep. for ἐκεῖσε, *thither.*

κεισεῦμαι, Dor. fut. of κεῖμαι.

κεῖσο, κείσθω, 2 and 3 sing. imperat. of κεῖμαι.

κείσομαι, fut. of κεῖμαι.

κείω, Ep. Desiderat. of κεῖμαι, *to wish to lie down* or *sleep;* βῆ κείων he went *to lie down.*

ΚΕΙ'Ω, *to cleave,* radic. form of κεάζω.

κεκαδήσομαι, Ep. fut. pass. of κήδω.

κεκᾰδήσω, Ep. fut. of χάζω.

κέκαδμαι, Dor. for κέκασμαι, q. v.

κεκάδοντο, 3 pl. Ep. aor. 2 med. of χάζω.

κεκᾰδών, Ep. aor. 2 part. of χάζω.

κεκαλυμμένος, pf. part. pass. of καλύπτω.

κεκάλυπτο, Ep. 3 sing. plqpf. pass. of καλύπτω.

κέκᾰμον, Ep. redupl. aor. 2 of κάμνω:—subj. κεκάμω, 3 pl. κεκάμωσι.

κεκάρθαι, pf. inf. pass. of κείρω.

κεκαρμένος, pf. part. pass. of κείρω.

κέκασμαι Dor. κέκαδμαι, pf. pass. (in pres. sense) of καίνυμαι.

κέκαυμαι, pf. pass. of καίω.

κεκαύχημαι, pf. of καυχάομαι.

κεκᾰφηώς, Ep. pf. part. of κάπτω.

κεκείνωμαι, Ion. pf. pass. of κενόω.

κεκεύθει, 3 sing. Ep. plqpf. of κεύθω.

κέκλαυμαι, pf. pass. of κλαίω.

κεκλέαται, Ion. 3 pl. of κέκλημαι, pf. of καλέω.

κέκλειμαι or **-σμαι**, pf. pass. of κλείω.

κεκλείσομαι, paullo-p. fut. pass. of κλείω, *to shut.*

κέκλεμμαι, pf. pass. of κλέπτω.

κέκλετο, Ep. 3 sing. aor. 2 of κέλομαι.

κεκλήᾰτο, Ion. and Ep. for ἐκέκληντο, 3 pl. plqpf. pass. of καλέω.

κέκληγα, part. κεκληγώς, pf. of κλάζω, whence is formed a pres. part. κεκλήγοντες, as if from κεκλήγω.

κέκληκα, pf. of καλέω.

κέκλημαι, pf. pass. of καλέω: opt. κεκλῄμην, -ῇο, -ῇτο: inf. κεκλῆσθαι: part. κεκλημένος.

κέκλῃμαι, Att. pf. pass. of κλείω, κλῄω.

κεκλήσομαι, paullo-p. fut. pass. of καλέω.

κεκλίᾰται, Ion. and Ep. for κέκλινται, 3 pl. pf. pass. of κλίνω.

κέκλῐμαι, pf. pass. of κλίνω.

κέκλῐτο, Ep. 3 sing. plqpf. pass. of κλίνω.

κεκλόμενος, poët. aor. 2 part. of κέλομαι, *calling out to* one, to cheer him on, c. dat.: but c. acc. *calling on* one, *calling* him for help.

κέκλοφα, pf. act. of κλέπτω.

κέκλῠθι, Ep. redupl. aor. 2 imperat. of κλύω.

κεκλυσμένος, pf. part. pass. of κλύζω.

κέκλῠτε, 2 pl. poët. aor. 2 imperat. of κλύω.

κέκμηκα, pf. of κάμνω.

κεκμηώς, gen. ῶτος or ότος, Ep. pf. act. part. of κάμνω.

κέκναισμαι, pf. pass. of κναίω.

κέκομμαι, pf. pass. of κόπτω.

κεκονιᾱμένος, pf. pass. part. of κονιάω.

κεκονῑμένος, pf. part. pass. of κονίω.

κεκόνῑτο, Ep. 3 sing. plqpf. of κονίω.

κεκοπώς, pf. part. of κόπτω.

κεκόρημαι, Ion. for κεκόρεσμαι, pf. pass. of κορέννυμι.

κεκορηώς, ότος, Ep. and Ion. pf. part. (with pass. sense) of κορέννυμι; hence dual κεκορηότε.

κεκορυθμένος, Ion. and Ep. for κεκορυσμένος, pf part. pass. of κορύσσω.

κεκοτηώς, gen. ότος, Ep. pf. act. part. of κοτέω.

κεκράανται, κεκράαντο, Ep. 3 sing. pf. and plqpf. pass. of κραίνω, κρααίνω.

κέκρᾱγα, pf. (with pres. sense) of κράζω. Hence

κέκραγμα, ατος, τό, (κράζω) *a scream, cry.*

κεκραγμός, *a screaming, crying.*

κεκράκτης, ου, ὁ, (κράζω) *a crier, bawler.*

κέκρᾱμαι, pf. pass. of κεράννυμι.

κεκραξι-δάμας, αντος, ὁ, (κέκρᾱγα, δᾰμάω) *he who conquers all in bawling, the blusterer.*

κεκράξομαι, paullo-p. fut. (with act. sense) of κράζω.

κέκραχθι, imperat. of κέκρᾱγα, pf. of κράζω.

κέκρῑγα, pf. 2 of κρίζω.

κεκρῐμένος, pf. pass. part. of κρίνω.

Κεκρόπιδαι, ων, οἱ, *the sons* or *descendants of Cecrops*, i. e. the Athenians.

Κεκρόπιος, α, ον, (Κέκροψ) *Cecropian*, i. e. Athenian; **Κεκροπία** (γῆ), ἡ, *Attica;* οἱ Κεκρόπιοι, *the Athenians.*

Κεκροπίς, ίδος, pecul. fem. of Κεκρόπιος.

κεκροταμένος, Dor. pf. part. pass. of κροτέω.

Κέκροψ, οπος, ὁ, *Cecrops*, an ancient king of Athens.

κεκρυμμένος, pf. part. pass. of κρύπτω.

κεκρύφᾰλος, ὁ, (κρύπτω) *a woman's head-dress*, made of net, to confine the hair, Lat. *reticulum.* II. *the pouch* or *belly of a hunting-net.* III. *part of the headstall of a bridle.*

κεκρύφαται, Ion. and Ep. 3 pl. pf. pass. of κρύπτω.

κέκτημαι, pf. of κτάομαι: inf. κεκτῆσθαι.

κεκύθωσι [ῠ], Ep. 3 pl. redupl. aor. 2 subj. of κεύθω.

κεκύλισμαι, pf. pass. of κυλίνδω.

κέκῡφα, pf. of κύπτω.

κελᾰδεινός, ή, όν, Dor. **κελαδεννός**, ά, όν, (κέλαδος) *murmuring, noisy, boisterous:* also *clear-toned.*

κελᾰδέω, f. ήσω also ήσομαι. Ep. aor. 1 κελάδησα: (κέλαδος):—*to murmur, roar*, like the rushing of water. 2. *to utter a cry* or *sound.* II. trans. *to sing of, celebrate loudly: to call to, invoke.* Hence

κελάδημα, ατος, τό, *a murmur, din, roaring.*

κελᾰδητής, οῦ, ὁ, fem. -ῆτις, ιδος, (κελαδέω) *loud-sounding, vocal, harmonious.*

ΚΕ'ΛΑΔΟΣ, ὁ, *a noise, as of the wind* or *of rushing waters: the din* or *tumult of battle, a shouting:* rarely of *the sound of music.* Hence

κελάδω, = κελαδέω, *to murmur, roar*, esp. of water.

κελαιν-εγχής, ές, (κελαινός, ἔγχος) *with dark, bloody spear.*

κελαι-νεφής, ές, (κελαινός, νέφος) *black with clouds: cloud-wrapt.* 2. *cloud-black, livid.*

κελαινό-βρωτος, ον, (κελαινός, βιβρώσκω) *gnawed black.*

κελαινός, ή, όν, cognate form of μέλας, *black, swart: dark, gloomy: murky.*

κελαινο-φᾰής, ές, (κελαινός, φάος) *dark-shining, murky.*

κελαινό-φρων, ον, (κελαινός, φρήν) *black-hearted.*

κελαινο-χρώς, ῶτος, ὁ, ἡ, (κελαινός, χρῶς) *black-coloured.*

κελαινόω, (κελαινός) *to make black:*—Pass. *to become black.*

κελαιν-ώπης, ου, Dor. -ώπᾱς, ὁ, fem. -ῶπις, ιδος: (κελαινός, ὤψ):—*black-faced, swarthy, gloomy.*

κελαιν-ώψ, ῶπος, ὁ, ἡ, = κελαινώπης.

κελᾰρύζω Dor. -σδω, = κελαδέω, *to babble, murmur.*

κελάρυσδεν, Dor. 3 sing. impf. of κελαρύζω.

κέλεαι, Ep. 2 sing. of κέλομαι.

κελέβη, ἡ, *a drinking vessel: an urn* or *pail.*

κελέοντες, ων, οἱ, (κᾶλον, κῆλον) *the beams in the loom* between which the web was stretched.

κέλετο, Ep. 3 sing. impf. of κέλομαι.

κελευθήτης, ου, ὁ, (κέλευθος) *a wayfarer.*

κελευθο-ποιός, όν, (κέλευθος, ποιέω) *road-making.*

κελευθο-πόρος, ον, (κέλευθος, πόρος) *a wayfarer.*

κέλευθος, ἡ, with neut. pl. κέλευθα, but also κέλευθοι:—*a road, way, path, track*, either by land or water; κέλευθοι νυκτός τε καὶ ἤματος *the ways of* night and day, i. e. night and day. II. *a travelling, journey, voyage: an expedition.* III. *a mode of walking, gait:* metaph. *a way* or *walk* of life: also *a way* or *course* of doing.

κέλευσμα or **κέλευμα**, ατος, τό, (κελεύω) *an order, command: the word of command* in war: *the call of the* κελευστής, which gave the time to the rowers.

κελευσμός, ὁ, (κελεύω) *an order, command.*

κελευσμοσύνη, ἡ, Ion. for κελευσμός.

κελευστής, οῦ, ὁ, (κελεύω) *a commander, fugleman* on board ship, *the man who* by his *call* (κέλευσμα) *gives the time to the rowers, a boatswain.*

κελευστός, ή, όν, (κελεύω) *ordered, commanded.*

κελευτιάω, Frequentat. of κελεύω, *to be continually bidding* or *urging on.*

κελεύω, f. σω: Ep. aor. 1 κέλευσα. (κέλλω):—*to urge on: to exhort, bid, command, order: to beseech urgently:* of the κελευστής, *to give time* to the rowers *by his call.* II. c. dat. pers. *to call to, order.*

κελέων, ὁ, obsol. sing. of κελέοντες.

κέλης, ητος, ὁ, (κέλλω) *a courser, race-horse*, driven or ridden singly. II. *a fast-sailing vessel* with one bank of oars, Lat. *celes, celox.*

κελήσομαι, fut. of κέλομαι.

κελητίζω, f. ίσω, (κέλης) *to ride a race-horse*, generally, *to ride:* esp. of a man who rode two or more horses leaping from one on another.

κελήτιον, τό, Dim. of κέλης.

ΚΕ'ΛΛΩ, f. κέλσω: aor. 1 ἔκελσα. I. trans. of seamen, *to drive on, push ashore*, νῆα κέλσαι *to run a ship ashore.* II. intr. of ships, *to run ashore, put into harbour:*—generally, *to reach a haven.*

κέλομαι, f. κελήσομαι: aor. 2 κεκλόμην and ἐκεκλόμην, 3 sing. κέκλετο, ἐκέκλετο, part. κεκλόμενος: (κέλλω):—poet. for κελεύω, *to urge on, exhort, cheer on, command.* II. also like καλεῖν, *to call, call to: to call by name.*

κέλσαι, aor. 1 inf. of κέλλω.

Κελτοί, οἱ, *the Kelts* or *Celts;* later Κέλται. Hence

Κελτιστί, Adv. *in Keltic* or *Celtic, in the language* or *after the manner of the Kelts.*

κέλῡφος, εος, τό, *a husk, rind, pod, shell:* metaph. of old δικασταί, ἀντωμοσιῶν κελύφη mere affidavit-husks. (Deriv. uncertain.)

ΚΕ'ΛΩΡ, ωρος, ὁ, *a son.*

κεμάς and **κεμμάς**, άδος, ἡ, *a young deer.*

κέν, before a vowel for κε.

κεν-αγγής, ές, (κενός, ἄγγος) *emptying vessels, breeding famine, hungry.*

κενανδρία, ἡ, *lack of men, dispeopled state.* From

κέν-ανδρος, ον, (κενός, ἀνήρ) *empty of men, dispeopled.*

κεν-αυχής or **κενε-αυχής**, ές, (κενός or κενεός, αὐχή) *vain-boasting, braggart.*

κενέβρειος, ον, *dead:* in pl., κενέβρεια, τά, *carrion.* (Deriv. uncertain.)

κεν-εμβᾰτέω, f. ήσω, (κενός, ἐμβάτης) *to step into a hole, stumble.*

κενεός, ή, όν, Ion. for κενός, *empty.*

κενεό-φρων, ον, (κενεός, φρήν) *empty-minded.*

κενεών, ῶνος, ὁ, (κενός) *the hollow between the ribs and the hip, the flank.* II. *any hollow space.*

κεν-οδοντίς, ίδος, fem. of κενόδους.

κενοδοξία, ἡ, *vainglory, vanity.* From

κενό-δοξος, ον, (κενός, δόξα) *vain-glorious.*

κεν-όδους, οντος, ὁ, ἡ, (κενός, ὀδούς) *toothless.*

ΚΕΝΟ´Σ Ion. **κεινός**, ή, όν; Ep. **κενεός** :—*empty: empty-handed.* II. *fruitless, vain, idle:* κενεά as Adv. *in vain.* III. *exhausted:* c. gen. *void, destitute, bereft of:* absol. of a lioness, *bereaved of her young.* IV. Comp. and Sup. κενότερος, -ότατος: but also regular κενώτερος, -ώτατος.

κενο-τᾰφέω, (κενός, τάφος) *to honour with a cenotaph.*

κενο-τάφιον, τό, (κενός, τάφος) *an empty tomb, cenotaph.*

κενό-φρων, ον, (κενός, φρήν) *empty-minded.*

κενοφωνία, ἡ, *vain talk, babbling.* From

κενό-φωνος, ον, (κενός, φωνή) *empty-sounding, prating.*

κενόω Ion. **κεινόω**: f. ώσω, aor. 1 ἐκένωσα :—Pass., aor. 1 ἐκενώθην: pf. κεκένωμαι: (κενός) :—*to empty out, drain: forsake, desert:*—Pass. *to be emptied of* a thing, c. gen.: also *to be left empty, deserted.* II. *to make void* or *of no account:*—Pass. *to become vain, of none effect.*

κένσαι, Ep. aor. 1 act. inf. of κεντέω, as if from *κέντω. II. also aor. 1 med. imperat. of κεντέω.

κέντᾱσε, Dor. 3 sing. aor. 1 of κεντέω.

Κενταύρειος, α, ον, (Κένταυρος) *Centaurian, of* or *for Centaurs.*

Κενταυρίδης, ου, ὁ, (Κένταυρος) *descended from Centaurs.*

Κενταυρικός, ή, όν, (Κένταυρος) *like a Centaur: savage, brutal.* Adv. -κῶς.

Κενταυρο-πληθής, ές, (Κένταυρος, πλῆθος) *full of Centaurs.*

Κέν-ταυρος, ὁ, (κεντέω) *a Centaur,* properly *a Piercer, Spearman:* they were a race of savage horsemen, dwelling between Pelion and Ossa in Thessaly, extirpated in a war with their neighbours the Lapithae. II. later, they were believed to be monsters of double shape, *half man and half horse.*

ΚΕΝΤΕ´Ω: f. ήσω: aor. 1 ἐκέντησα: inf. κένσαι as if from *κέντω :—*to prick, goad, sting: to wound, stab, pierce.*

κέντο, Dor. for ἐκέλετο: cf. γέντο, ἦνθον.

κεντόω, false form for κεντρόω.

κεντρ-ηνεκής, ές, (κέντρον, *ἐνέγκω) *goaded on.*

κεντρίζω, f. ίσω, (κέντρον) *to prick, goad, spur.*

κεντρο-δήλητος, ον, (κέντρον, δηλέομαι) *goaded.* 2. act. *goading, stinging.*

κεντρο-μᾰνής, ές, (κέντρον, μανῆναι) *spurring to madness.*

κέντρον, τό, (κεντέω) *a point, prickle, spike, sting: a horse* or *ox-goad: a spur:* proverb., πρὸς κέντρα λακτίζειν to kick against *the pricks.* 2. *an instrument of torture.* 3. metaph. *a spur, incentive.* II. *the point* round which a circle is described, the *centre.*

κεντρο-τῠπής, ές, (κέντρον, τυπῆναι) *struck by a spur.*

κεντρόω, f. ώσω, *to furnish with a sting:*—Pass. *to be so furnished.* 2. *to strike with a goad.*

κέντρων, ωνος, ὁ, (κέντρον) *a rogue that has been branded, a spur-galled jade.*

κεντυρίων, ωνος, ὁ, the Lat. *centurio.*

κέντωρ, ορος, ὁ, (κεντέω) *a goader, driver.*

κενῶς, Adv. of κενός, *vainly, idly.*

κεοίμην, opt. of κεῖμαι.

κέομαι, Ep. and Ion. collat. form of **κεῖμαι**, whence 3 sing. κέεται, 3 pl. κέονται.

Κέος, ἡ, Ion. for **Κέως**.

ΚΕΠΦΟΣ, ὁ, *a light sea-bird of the petrel kind:* metaph. *a light-headed simpleton, a noddy.*

κεράασθε, Ep. 2 pl. pres. med. of κεράω.

κεράεσσι, Ep. dat. pl. of κέρας.

κεραία, ἡ, (κέρας) *a horn.* II. *anything like a horn, a yard-arm,* Lat. *cornu antennarum: a projecting beam* or *timber.* 2. *a horn* or *promontory of land.* 3. *a small dot* in writing, '*a tittle.*' 4. *anything made of horn,* e. g. *a bow.*

κερᾰΐζω, f. ΐσω, later ΐξω: aor. 1 ἐκεράϊσα: (**κέρας**): —*to lay waste, ravage.* II. of persons, *to kill, slaughter: to disable* ships.

κερᾰΐς, ΐδος, ἡ, (κέρας) *a worm that eats horn.*

κερᾰϊστής, οῦ, ὁ, (κεραΐζω) *a ravager, robber.*

κεραίω, Ep. for κεράω, the Root of **κεράννυμι**, *to mix;* ζωρότερον κέραιε *mix* the wine stronger.

κερᾰμεικός, ή, όν, (κέραμος) *earthen.*

Κερᾰμεικός, ὁ, (κεραμεύς) *the Potters' Quarter* in Athens, where two places were called *Cerameicus,* one within and the other without the Thriasian Gate.

κεράμειος, α, ον, (κέραμος) *of clay, earthen.*

κερᾰμεύς, έως, ὁ, (κέραμος) *a potter:*—proverb., κεραμεὺς κεραμεῖ κοτέει *potter* envies *potter.*

κερᾰμεύω, f. σω, (κέραμος) *to be a potter, work in earthenware:* metaph. *to botch* or *patch up* the state.

κερᾰμήϊος, η, ον, Ion. and Ep. for **κεράμειος**.

κερᾰμηΐς, ΐδος, pecul. Ep. fem. of **κεράμειος**.

κεράμῐνος, η, ον, and **κεραμικός**, ή, όν, = κεράμειος, *of earthenware* or *clay.*

κεράμιον, τό, (κέραμος) *an earthenware vessel, a pot, jar, pipkin,* Lat. *testa.*

κερᾱμίς, ῖδος Att. ίδος [ĭ], ἡ, (κέραμος) *a tile:* also *a tiled roof.*

ΚΕ´ΡΑ˘ΜΟΣ, ὁ, *potter's earth, potter's clay.* II. *any earthen vessel, a pot, jar:* also in collective sense, *earthenware, pottery.* III. *a tile;* collectively, *the tiles;* τῷ κεραμῷ βάλλειν to strike *with tiles,* never in plur. IV. χαλκέῳ ἐν κεράμῳ seems to be in a brasen *prison.*

κεράννυμι and -ύω: fut. κεράσω [ᾰ]: aor. 1 ἐκέρᾰσα Ep. κέρασσα:—Med., Ep. 3 sing. aor. 1 κεράσσατο: —Pass., aor. 1 ἐκεράσθην and ἐκράθην [ᾱ]: pf. κεκέρασμαι and κέκρᾱμαι: (κεράω):—*to mix, mingle,* often of diluting wine: more freq. in Med., as, κρητῆρα κεράσασθαι *to mix oneself* a bowl; Pass., κύλιξ ἴσον ἴσῳ κεκραμένη a cup *mixed* half and half. 2. *to temper* or *cool.* 3. metaph. *to blend together, temper, regulate, tone down.* II. generally, *to mix, compound,* Lat. *attemperare.*

κερᾰο-ξόος, ον, (κέρας, ξέω) *polishing horn, working in horn;* esp. for bows.

κερᾰός, ά, όν, (κέρας) *horned.* II. *made of horn.*

κερα-οῦχος, ον, (ἔχω) = κερ-οῦχος.

κέρας, τό; gen. κέρᾱτος Ep. κέραος Att. contr. κέρως; dat. κέρᾱτι, κέραϊ, κέρᾳ:—dual κέραε; κέρᾱ, gen. and dat. κεράοιν, κερῷν: plur. κέραα, κέρᾱ; gen. κεράων, κερῶν; dat. κέρᾱσι Ep. κέρᾰσι and κεράεσσι: —Ion. declension κέρας, κέρεος, κέρεϊ: (akin to κάρα):—*the horn of an animal:* hence *horn,* as a material for working. II. *anything made of horn;* esp. *a bow:* later, *a horn for blowing:* also *a drinking-horn,* or *a goblet in the shape of a horn.* III. *a horn* or *guard* at the end of a fishing-line, to prevent the fish from biting it. IV. *an arm* or *branch of a river,* so called from its shape. V. *the wing of an army* or *fleet;* ἐπὶ κέρας Att. ἐπὶ κέρως, *in single file, in column,* i.e. one after another, not abreast. VI. *the sail-yard* of a ship. VII. *any projection* or *elevation,* as *a mountain-peak, horn.*

κέρασσε, Ep. 3 sing. aor. 1 of κεράννυμι.

κεραστής, οῦ, ὁ, (κέρας) *horned.*

κεραστός, ή, όν, (κεράννυμι) *mingled, tempered.*

κερασ-φόρος, ον, (κέρας, φέρω) *horn-bearing.*

κερατέα or -ία, ἡ, (κέρας) *the locust-tree:* its fruit was κεράτιον.

κεράτῐνος, η, ον, (κέρας) *of horn, made of horn.*

κεράτιον, τό, Dim. of κέρας, *a little horn.* II. *the fruit of the* κερατέα or *locust-tree.*

κερ-αύλης, ου, ὁ, (κέρας, αὐλέω) *a horn-blower.*

κεραύνειος, ον, (κεραυνός) *thundering.*

κεραύνιος, α, ον, also ος, ον, (κεραυνός) *of a thunderbolt.* II. *thunder-stricken.*

κεραυνοβολέω, f. ήσω, *to hurl the thunderbolt: to strike with thunderbolts.* From

κεραυνο-βόλος, ον, (κεραυνός, βάλλω) *hurling the thunderbolt, smiting with it.*

κεραυνο-βρόντης, ου, ὁ, (κεραυνός, βροντάω) *the lightener and thunderer.*

κεραυνο-μάχης, ου, ὁ, (κεραυνός, μάχομαι) *fighting with the thunderbolt.*

ΚΕΡΑΥΝΟ´Σ, ὁ, *a thunderbolt, thunder and lightning,* Lat. *fulmen: thunder* by itself was βροντή, Lat. *tonitru,* and *the flash of lightning* ἀστεροπή, στεροπή, Lat. *fulgur:* plur. κεραυνοί, *thunderbolts.*

κεραυνο-φᾰής, ές, (κεραυνός, φάος) *flashing like the thunderbolt.*

κεραυνόω, f. ώσω, (κεραυνός) *to strike with a thunderbolt.*

ΚΕΡΑ´Ω, Ep. Radic. form of κεράννυμι, *to mix.*

Κέρβερος, ὁ, *Cerberus,* the dog which guarded the gate of the nether world; acc. to Hesiod, the fifty-headed son of Typhaon and Echidna; later, represented with three heads.

κερδαίνω, f. κερδανῶ Ion. -έω: aor. 1 ἐκέρδανα Ion. ἐκέρδηνα: fut. also κερδήσω. κερδήσομαι: aor. 1 ἐκέρδησα: (κέρδος):—*to gain, make gain* or *profit from:* absol. *to gain advantage, be benefited.* 2. hence *to traffic, make merchandise.* II. in bad sense, like ἀπολαύω, *to gain* a loss.

κερδᾰλέος, α, ον, (κέρδος) *with an eye to gain, crafty, cunning: shrewd.* 2. of things, *gainful, profitable:* Adv. κερδαλέως, *to one's profit.*

κερδᾰλεό-φρων, ον, (κερδαλέος, φρήν) *crafty-minded.*

κερδάνῃς, 2 sing. aor. 1 subj. of κερδαίνω.

κέρδιστος, η, ον, Sup. of κερδίων (with no Positive in use), formed from κέρδος, *most cunning* or *crafty.* II. *most profitable.*

κερδίων, ον, gen. ονος, Comp. (with no Positive in use), formed from κέρδος, *more profitable.*

ΚΕ´ΡΔΟΣ, εος, τό, *gain, profit, advantage: desire of gain.* II. in pl. *cunning arts, wiles, tricks.*

κερδοσύνη, ἡ, (κέρδος) *cunning, craft, shrewdness:* dat. κερδοσύνῃ as Adv. *cunningly, shrewdly.*

κερδώ, όος contr. οῦς, ἡ, (κέρδος) *the wily one.* or *the thief,* name of *a fox.*

κερδῷος, α, ον, (κέρδος) *bringing gain.*

κέρεα, Ion. for κέραα, κέρατα, pl. of κέρας.

κερέω, Ion. for κερῶ, fut. of κείρω.

κερκίζω, f. ίσω, *to close the web with the* κερκίς. From

κερκίς, ίδος, ἡ, (κέρκω, κρέκω) = σπάθη, *a staff* or *rod* to make the web close: *the weaver's comb: the shuttle containing the spindle,* Lat. *radius.* II. *any taper rod, of wood, ivory,* etc., as *the quill* with which stringed instruments were struck, Lat. *plectrum.* 2. *a measuring-rod,* Lat. *radius.*

ΚΕ´ΡΚΟΣ, ἡ, *the tail* of a beast, Lat. *cauda.*

κέρκουρος or **κερκοῦρος**, ὁ, *a boat, pinnace.*

Κέρκῡρα, ἡ, the island *Corcyra,* now *Corfu:* hence **Κερκυραῖος**, ὁ, *a Corcyraean:* Adj. **Κερκυραϊκός**, ή, όν, *of* or *for Corcyra.*

κέρκω, rarer collat. form for κρέκω

κέρμα, ατος, τό, (κείρω) *a slice:* in plur. *small coin, small change: small wares.* Hence

κερμᾰτίζω, f. ίσω Att. ιῶ, *to mince up.* II. *to coin into small money: to change large coin for small.* Hence

κερματιστής, οῦ, ὁ, *a money-chang..*

κερο-βάτης [ᾰ], ου, ὁ, (κέρας, βαίνω) *horn-footed, horn-hoofed*, epith. of Pan.

κερο-βόας, ου, ἡ, (κέρας, βοάω) *sounding with horn*, of a flute tipped with horn.

κερό-δετος, ον, (κέρας, δέω) *bound with horn.*

κερόεις, όεσσα contr. οῦσσα, οεν, (κέρας) *horned.*

κερ-οίαξ, ᾶκος, ὁ, (κέρας, οἴαξ) *a rope belonging to the sailyards;* cf. κέρας VI.

κερο-τυπέω, f. ήσω, (κέρας, τύπτω) *to butt with the horn;* generally, *to dash* or *knock about.*

κερ-ουλκός, ή, όν, (κέρας, ἕλκω) *drawing a bow of horn.* 2. of the bow, *drawn by the horns.*

κερουτιάω, (κέρας) *to toss the horns* or *head.*

κερ-ουχίς, ίδος, fem. of sq.

κερ-οῦχος, ον, (κέρας, ἔχω) *having horns, horned.*

κερο-φόρος, ον, (κέρας, φέρω) *horned.*

κέρσας, Ep. aor. 1 part. of κείρω.

κέρσε, Ep. 3 sing. aor. 1 of κείρω.

κερτομέω, f. ήσω, (κέρτομος) *to taunt, to mock* or *jeer at* a person: absol. *to sneer, scoff.* Hence

κερτόμησις, εως, ἡ, *jeering, mockery.*

κερτόμια, ἡ, = κερτόμησις.

κερ-τόμιος and **κέρ-τομος**, ον, (κέαρ, τέμνω) *heart-cutting, stinging;* κερτόμια ἔπη or absol. κερτόμια, *stinging, reproachful words.* II. *mocking, delusive.*

κέρχνη, ἡ, (κέρχνω) *a* kind of *hawk*, so called from its hoarse voice, *the kestrel.*

κερχνηΐς, ηΐδος, and **κερχνῇς**, ῇδος, ἡ, collat. forms of κέρχνη.

ΚΕ΄ΡΧΝΩ, *to make rough* or *hoarse.* II. intr. and in Pass. *to be hoarse*, of the voice.

κερῶ, fut. of κείρω.

κερῶν, part. of κεράννυμι.

κέρωνται, Ep. 3 pl. subj. pass. of κεράω.

κές, v. sub κάς.

κέσκετο, Ion. 3 sing. impf. of κεῖμαι.

κεστός, ή, όν, (κεντέω) *worked, embroidered;* κεστὸς ἱμάς of the girdle of Venus: hence II. as Subst. κεστός, ὁ, *a girdle*, Lat. *cestus.*

κέστρα, ἡ, (κεντέω) *a pickaxe, poleaxe.* II. *a* kind of *fish, a pike*, or *a conger.*

κευθάνω, poët. for κεύθω.

κεῦθμα, ατος, τό, and **κευθμός**, ὁ, = κευθμών.

κευθμών, ῶνος, ὁ, (κεύθω) *any secret place, hole, hiding-place, den; the lair* of a beast. 2. of the nether world, *the abyss.* 3. = ἄδυτον, *the inmost place, sanctuary.*

κεύθοισα, Dor. for κεύθουσα, part. fem. of κεύθω.

κεῦθος, εος, τό, (κεύθω) = κευθμών: in pl., κεύθεα γαίης *the depths* of the earth.

ΚΕΥ΄ΘΩ, fut. κεύσω: aor. 2 ἔκῠθον, Ep. redupl. subj. κεκύθω: pf. κέκευθα: plqpf. ἐκεκεύθειν Ep. κεκεύθειν:—*to cover up, hide, conceal, shroud*:—Pass. *to lie hidden.* 2. *to keep hidden* or *secret, conceal, disguise:* with dupl. acc., κεύθει τινά τι *to keep* a thing *concealed from* one. 3. the pf. κέκευθα is used as pres., *I keep concealed;* and plqpf. ἐκεκεύθειν as impf., *I concealed, contained.* II. intrans. *to be concealed, lie hidden.*

κεφαλᾷ, Dor. dat. of κεφαλή.

κεφάλαιος, α, ον, (κεφαλή) *of* or *belonging to the head:* metaph., like Lat. *capitalis, principal, chief.* II. κεφάλαιον, τό, as Subst., like κεφαλή, *the head*, as κεφάλαιον ῥαφανῖδος *the head* of a radish: *the chief* or *main point:* in money, *the capital-sum.* 2. *a summary, the sum of the matter;* ἐν κεφαλαίῳ or ἐν κεφαλαίοις εἰπεῖν to speak *summarily.* 3. generally, *the crown, completion, finish* of a thing. Hence

κεφᾰλαιόω, f. ώσω, *to bring under heads, sum up, state summarily* II. *to smite on the head, slay.*

κεφᾰλαι-ώδης, ες, (κεφαλή, εἶδος) *principal, capital.*

κεφᾰλαίωμα, ατος, τό, (κεφαλαιόω) *the sum total.*

κεφᾰλ-αλγής, ές, (κεφαλή, ἄλγος) *causing pains in the head.* Hence

κεφαλαλγία, ἡ, *head-ache.*

ΚΕΦΑ΄ΛΗ΄, ἡ, *the head*, Lat. *caput;* ἐς πόδας ἐκ κεφαλῆς from *head* to foot; ἐπὶ κεφαλήν *head fore-most.* 2. *the head*, as the noblest part, for *the whole person*, just as Lat. *caput* is used: esp. in salutation, φίλη κεφαλή, Lat. *carum caput;* in bad sense, ὦ κακαὶ κεφαλαί. 3. *the life*, Lat. *caput*, as we use *head;* παρθέμενοι κεφαλάς setting *their heads* on the cast; εἰς κεφαλὴν τρέποιτ' ἐμοί on my *head* be it! II. *the head* or *upper part* of anything: *the coping* of a wall: in pl. *the head* or *source* of a river. III. κεφαλὴ περίθετος *a wig* or *head-dress.* IV. metaph. *the point, sum, conclusion.*

κεφᾰλῆφι, κεφαλῆφι, Ep. gen. and dat. of κεφαλή.

κεφᾰλίς, ίδος, ἡ, Dim. of κεφαλή, *a little head* or *bulb* II. *a head, chapter, division.*

Κεφαλλήν, ῆνος, ὁ, *a Cephallenian*:—hence

Κεφαλληνία, ἡ, *Cephallenia*, an island in the Ionian sea, now *Cefalonia.*

κεχάλασμαι, pf. pass. of χαλάω.

κέχανδα, pf. of χανδάνω, whence part. neut. pl. κεχανδότα, 3 plqpf. Ep. κεχάνδει.

κεχαραγμένος, pf. part. pass. of χαράσσω.

κεχάρηκα, pf. of χαίρω.

κεχάρημαι, pf. pass. of χαίρω.

κεχᾰρησέμεν, Ep. fut. inf. of χαίρω.

κεχᾰρήσομαι, Ep. paullo-post fut. of χαίρω

κεχάρητο, κεχάρηντο, Ep. 3 sing. and pl. plqpf. pass. of χαίρω.

κεχᾰρηώς, Ep. pf. part. of χαίρω.

κεχᾰρισμένος, pf. part. of χαρίζομαι, *agreeable, winning, charming:* Adv. κεχαρισμένως, *charmingly, gracefully.*

κεχάριστο, 3 sing. plqpf. of χαρίζομαι.

κεχᾰρῑτωμένος, pf. part. pass. of χαριτόω. Adv. κεχαριτωμένως, *agreeably, welcome.*

κέχαρμαι, pf. pass. of χαίρω.

κεχᾰροίατο, Ep. for κεχάροιντο, 3 pl. Ep. redupl. aor. 2 med. opt. of χαίρω.

κεχάροντο, 3 pl. Ep. redupl. aor. 2 med. of χαίρω.

κέχηνα, pf. of χαίνω or χάσκω, *to gape.* Hence Κεχηναῖοι, ων. οἱ, *Gapers*, comic for Ἀθηναῖοι.

κεχλᾰδώς, pf. part. of χλάζω: there is also an acc. pl. κεχλάδοντας, as if from κεχλάδω, like κεκλήγοντας from κεκληγώς.

κεχλίαγκα, pf. of χλιαίνω.

κεχλῐδώς, pf. part. of χλίω.

κεχολώσθαι, pf. inf. pass. of χολόω.

κεχολώσομαι, paullo-post fut. of χολόω.

κεχρηματισμένος, pf. part. pass. of χρηματίζω.

κεχρημένος pf. part. of χράομαι.

κέχῠμαι, pf. pass. of χέω.

κέχῠτο, κέχυντο, 3 sing. and pl. Ep. plqpf. pass. of χέω.

κεχωρίδαται, Ion. 3 pl. pf. pass. of χωρίζω.

κεχωσμένος, pf. part. pass. of χώννυμι.

κέω, Ep. collateral form of κείω.

Κέως Ion. **Κέος**, *Ceos*, an island in the Archipelago.

κέωμαι, subj. of κεῖμαι.

κῇ, Ion. for πῇ (interrog.): but **κη** enclit. for πη.

κῆαι, Ep. aor. 1 inf. καίω; but **κήαι**, 3 sing. opt.

κηάμενος, Ep. aor. 1 part. of καίω.

κἠγώ or **κἠγών**, Dor. for κἀγώ, i. e. καὶ ἐγώ.

κηδεία, ἡ, (κῆδος) *care* for the dead: *obsequies.* II. *affinity, connexion by marriage.*

κήδειος, ον, (κῆδος) *cared for, dear, beloved.* 2. *careful for.* II. *of* or *for a funeral, sepulchral.*

κηδεμονεύς, έως, ὁ, (κηδέω) = κηδεμών.

κηδεμών, όνος, ὁ, (κηδέω) *one that has charge of* a person, *one who cares for the dead, a mourner*:—*a protector, guardian.* II. *a relation by marriage*, Lat. *affinis.*

κήδεος, ον, = κήδειος.

κήδεσκον, Ion. impf. of κήδω.

κηδέσκετο, 3 sing. Ion. impf. pass. of κήδω.

κηδεστής, οῦ, ὁ, (κῆδος) *a connexion by marriage*, Lat. *affinis: a son-in-law*, also *a father-in-law, brother-in-law.* Hence

κηδεστία, ἡ, *connexion by marriage, affinity.*

κήδευμα, ατος, τό, (κηδεύω) *alliance by marriage, affinity.* 2. *one who is so connected, a connexion*, Lat. *affinis.*

κηδεύω, f. σω, (κῆδος) *to take charge of, care for, tend.* 2. *to pay the last offices of the dead*:—Pass. *to have these last offices paid one.* II. *to ally oneself in marriage to* a person:—Pass. *to be so allied.* 2. *to make* a person *one's kinsman by marriage.*

κηδήσω, fut. of κήδω (as if from κηδέω).

κήδιστος, η, ον, Sup. formed from κῆδος, like κέρδιστος from κέρδος, *most cared for, dearest, most beloved.* II. *most nearly allied by marriage.*

κῆδος Dor. **κᾶδος**, εος, τό, (κήδω) *care, concern, regard for* another. 2. *trouble, sorrow, affliction, distress*:—*mourning for one dead*: hence *a funeral.* 3. *an object of care, a care.* II. *connexion by marriage*, Lat. *affinitas.*

κηδόσυνος, ον, (κῆδος) *anxious.*

ΚΗ'ΔΩ, f. κηδήσω, *to make anxious, give concern*: hence *to trouble, annoy, distress.* II. in Pass., with Ep. fut. κεκᾰδήσομαι, pf. act. κέκηδα:—*to be troubled, distressed, annoyed*: part. κηδόμενος, η, ον, *distressed, in trouble*: c. gen. *to be anxious* or *concerned for*; οὐκέτι Δαναῶν κεκαδησόμεθα.

κἤδωκε, by crasis for καὶ ἔδωκε.

κῆεν, 3 sing. Ep. aor. 1 of καίω.

κηθάριον, τό, *a vessel into which the lots were cast, a ballot-box.* (Deriv. uncertain.)

κἠκ, Dor. for κἀκ, by crasis for καὶ ἐκ.

ΚΗΚΙ'Σ, ῖδος, ἡ, *matter that oozes* or *exudes* from a burnt sacrifice: *juice, moisture*: *ink.* Hence

κηκίω, Ep. impf. κήκιον:—*to gush* or *ooze forth*: also in Med., αἱμὰς κηκιομένα ἑλκέων clotted blood *oozing* from his wounds. [ῐ Ep., ῑ Att.]

κήλεος or **κήλειος**, ον, (καίω) *burning, blazing.*

ΚΗΛΕ'Ω, f. ήσω, *to charm, bewitch, fascinate*: generally, *to wheedle, beguile, seduce.*

ΚΗ'ΛΗ, ἡ, *a rupture*, Lat. *hernia.*

κηληθμός, ὁ, (κηλέω) *rapture, fascination.*

κήλημα, ατος, τό, (κηλέω) *a magic charm, spell.*

κήλησις, εως, ἡ, (κηλέω) *an enchanting, charming.*

κηλητήριος, ον, (κηλέω) *charming*: *appeasing.*

κηλῑδόω, f. ώσω, (κηλίς) *to stain, sully*: metaph. *to stain, dishonour, disgrace.*

ΚΗΛΙ'Σ, ῖδος, ἡ, *a stain, spot*: *a blemish, disgrace.*

ΚΗ'ΛΟΝ, τό, *the shaft* of an arrow: *an arrow.*

κήλων, ωνος, ὁ, (κῆλον) *a swipe* or *machine for drawing water from* a well.

κηλώνειον Ion. -ήϊον, τό, = κήλων.

κἠμαυτόν, Dor. by crasis for καὶ ἐμαυτόν.

κἠμέ, Dor. by crasis for καὶ ἐμέ.

ΚΗΜΟ'Σ, ὁ, *a muzzle* or *halter*, put on a led horse. 2. *the funnel-shaped top* to the voting urn (κάδος) in the Athenian law-courts, through which the ballots (ψῆφοι) were dropped in the urn.

κημόω, f. ώσω, (κημός) *to muzzle* a horse.

κἠν, Dor. for κἀν, i. e. καὶ ἐν: but **κἤν** for καὶ ἄν.

κἦνθε, Dor. by crasis for καὶ ἦνθε (i. e. καὶ ἦλθε).

κῆνος, Aeol. for κεῖνος, ἐκεῖνος.

κῆνσος, ὁ, the Lat. *census, an assessment*: *tribute.*

ΚΗ'Ξ, κηκός, ἡ, *a sea-gull, sea-mew.*

κήομεν, Ep. for κήωμεν, 1 pl. aor. 1 subj. of καίω.

κἦπε, Dor. by crasis for καὶ εἶπε.

κἠπεί, κἤπειτα, Dor. for κἀπεί, κἄπειτα, i. e. καὶ ἐπ-.

κήπευμα, ατος, τό, (κηπεύω) *that which is reared in a garden, a garden-herb* or *flower.*

κηπεύς, έως, τό, (κῆπος) *a gardener.*

κηπεύω, f. σω, (κῆπος) *to rear in a garden*: metaph. *to tend, cherish, foster.*

κἠπί, Dor. for κἀπί, i. e. καὶ ἐπί.

κηπίον, τό, Dim. of κῆπος, *a small garden, parterre*: metaph. *a decoration, ornament.*

κηπο-λόγος, ον, (κῆπος, λέγω) *teaching in a garden.*

ΚΗ'ΠΟΣ Dor. **κᾶπος**, ὁ, *a garden, an orchard* or *plantation*; also *the enclosure* for the Olympic games: **οἱ Ἀδώνιδος κῆποι**, cresses and other plants grown quickly in pots :—hence proverb. of amusements and pastimes.

κηπ-ουρός, ὁ, (κῆπος, οὖρος) *a gardener.*

ΚΗ´Ρ, ἡ. gen. Κηρός, acc. Κηρα, *the goddess of death* or *of fate:* hence *doom, death, destruction.* 2. *the goddess of mischief* or *evil:* hence *bane, mischief, evil* itself. II. any evil *fate; disease;* and, of moral evil, *disgrace*

ΚΗ῀Ρ, τό, gen. κῆρος, acc. κῆρ, contr from κέαρ, *the heart*, Lat. *cor.* The dat. κῆρι is in Homer freq. used as Adv., like κηρόθι, *with all the heart, heartily.*

κηραίνω, f. ἄνῶ, (κήρ, ἡ) *to harm, hurt, destroy.*

κηραίνω, f. ἄνῶ, (κῆρ, τό) *to be alarmed, disquieted.*

Κηρεσσι-φόρητος, ον, (Κήρ, φορέω) *borne on by the* Κῆρες or *fates*

κήρῐνος, η, ον, (κηρός) *of wax, waxen.*

κηριο-κλέπτης, ου, ὁ, (κηρίον, κλέπτω) *stealer of honeycombs*

κηρίον, τό, (κηρός) *a honeycomb*, Lat. *favus.* II. *a waxen tablet.*

κηρι-τρεφής, ές, (κήρ, τρέφω) *born to die.*

κηρο-δέτης, ου, ὁ, Dor. **κηροδέτας**, = κηρόδετος.

κηρό-δετος, ον, (κῆρος, δέω) *bound together by wax.*

κηρο-δομέω, f. ήσω, (κηρός, δέμω) *to build with wax.*

κηρόθεν, Adv. (κῆρ) *from the heart.*

κηρόθι, Adv. (κῆρ) *in the heart, with all the heart, heartily*

κηρο-πἄγής, ές, (κηρός, παγῆναι) *fastened with wax.*

κηρο-πλάστης, ου, ὁ, (κηρός, πλάσσω) *a modeller in wax.*

κηρό-πλαστος, ον, (κηρός, πλάσσω) *moulded of wax, waxen.* II. = κηρόδετος.

ΚΗΡΟ´Σ, ὁ, *bees-wax, wax.* Lat. *cera.*

κηρο-τρόφος, ον, (κηρός, τρέφω) *wax-producing.*

κηρο-χίτων, ωνος, ὁ, ἡ, (κηρός, χιτών) *clad with wax.*

κηροχῠτέω, f. ήσω, *to mould in melted wax: to make waxen cells.* From

κηρό-χῠτος, ον, (κηρός, χέω) *moulded of* or *in wax.*

κήρυγμα, ατος, τό, (κηρύσσω) *a proclamation by herald, public notice;* ἐκ κηρύγματος by *proclamation.*

κηρύκαινα, ἡ, fem. of κήρυξ, *a female herald.*

κηρυκεία Ion. **-ηΐη**, ἡ, (κῆρυξ) *the office of herald.*

κηρύκειον Ion. **-ήϊον**, τό, *a herald's wand*, Lat. *caduceus.* [ῡ] Properly neut. from

κηρύκειος, α, ον, (κῆρυξ) *of* or *for a herald.* [ῡ]

κηρύκεσσι, Ep. for κήρυξι, dat. pl. of κῆρυξ.

κηρύκευμα, ατος, τό, (κηρυκεύω) *a herald's proclamation, public notice.* [ῡ]

κηρῡκεύω, f. σω, (κῆρυξ) *to be a herald, give public notice.* II. trans. *to proclaim, give notice of.*

κηρῡκηΐη, **-κήϊον**, Ion. for -εία, -ειον

κηρύλος Att. **κειρύλος**, ὁ, *a sea-bird, the halcyon.* [ῠ]

κῆρυξ, ῡκος, ὁ, (κηρύσσω) *a herald* or *pursuivant*, whose chief duties were to summon the assembly, to separate combatants, to carry to and fro messages between enemies. They carried wands (σκῆπτρα): their persons were inviolable, and they were regarded as the messengers and under the protection of Jove.

ΚΗΡΥ´ΣΣΩ Att. **-ττω**: f. ξω: pf. κεκήρῡχα:—Pass., fut. κηρυχθήσομαι, but also fut. med. κηρύξομαι in pass. sense: pf. κεκήρυγμαι :—*to be* or *act as herald: to make proclamation as a herald, summon, convene as herald.* 2. impers., κηρύσσει (sc. ὁ κῆρυξ) *notice is given, proclamation is made.* II. *to proclaim, announce: to extol* 2. *to put up* or *advertise* for sale. 3. *to call on, invoke.* III. *to preach* or *teach publicly.*

κηρυχθῆναι, aor. 1 inf. pass. of κηρύσσω.

κήρωμα, ατος, τό, (κηρόω) *anything waxed over: a waxed tablet* for writing. 2. *an unguent used by wrestlers.* Hence

κηρωμἄτικός, ή, όν, *anointed with* κήρωμα.

κηρωτός, ή, όν, (κηρόω) *waxed:*—hence, as Subst., **κηρωτόν**, τό, or **κηρωτή**, ἡ, *a cerate* or *ointment.*

κῇς, Dor. for καὶ εἰς

κῆται, Ep. for κέηται, 3 sing. subj. of κεῖμαι.

κήτειος, α, ον, (κῆτος) *of sea-monsters*

ΚΗ῀ΤΟΣ, εος, τό, *any sea-monster* or *huge fish:* in Odyssey, *a seal* or *sea-calf:* later *a whale*, Lat. *cete.*

κητο-φόνος, ον, (κῆτος, *φένω) *killing sea-monsters.*

κητώεις, εσσα, εν, only as epith. of Lacedaemon, κοίλη Λακηδαίμων κητώεσσα, either (from κῆτος as implying hugeness) *vast, spacious;* or (from κῆτος as if = καιάδας, *a gulf, abyss*) *sunken, hollow.*

κηὖ, by crasis for καὶ εὖ

κήϋξ, ῡκος [ῡ], ὁ, (κήξ) *a sea-gull.*

κἤφᾱ, Dor. by crasis for καὶ ἔφη

ΚΗΦΗ´Ν, ῆνος, ὁ, *a drone-bee, drone*, Lat. *fucus:* metaph. *a drone* or *lazy fellow*, who will do nothing for his bread; also of *an old, decrepit person.*

Κηφῆνες, οἱ, *Cephenes*, old name of the Persians

κἤφθᾱ, Dor. by crasis for καὶ ἤφθη.

Κηφῑσός, ὁ, *the Cephisus*, a river in Boeotia; hence fem. λίμνη Κηφισίς. II. a famous river of Athens: also a river in Argolis and in other places.

κηώδης, ες, (καίω) *fragrant, sweet-scented.*

κηώεις, εσσα, εν, = κηώδης, *fragrant.*

κῐάθω, Att. lengthd. for κίω, *to go.* [ᾰ]

κιβδηλεύω, f. σω, (κίβδηλος) *to adulterate, alloy.* II. metaph. *to pass off, palm off.*

κιβδηλία, ἡ, (κίβδηλος) *alloy, base metal:* metaph. *fraud, dishonesty*

κίβδηλος ον, (κίβδος) *adulterated, spurious, base.* II. metaph. of men, *base, false.* 2. *base-born, bastard.* 3. *deceitful, ambiguous*, of oracles.

ΚΙ´ΒΔΟΣ, ἡ, *dross, alloy.*

κίβῑσις, ἡ, *a pocket, wallet, scrip.*

κῑβωτάριον and **κῑβώτιον**, τό, Dim. of κιβωτός.

ΚΙΓΒΩΤΟ´Σ, ἡ, *a wooden box, chest, coffer.*

κιγκλίζω, f. ίσω, (κίγκλος) *to wag the tail* like the κίγκλος: metaph. *to change constantly.*

ΚΙΓΚΛΙ´Σ, ίδος, ἡ, the Lat. *cancelli, a latticed gate* or *partition*, fencing off the courts of justice or council chamber, *the bar.*

ΚΙ´ΓΚΛΟΣ, ὁ, *a water-bird*, a kind of *wagtail.*

κιγχάνω [ᾰ], Att. for κιχάνω [ᾱ].

κίδνᾰμαι, Pass., poët. for *σκεδάννυμαι*, *to be spread.*

ΚΙ´ΘΑ´ΡΑ Ion. -η, also **κίθαρις**, ιος, ἡ, Lat. *cithara. a lyre, harp* or *lute*, like the *φόρμιγξ* or *λύρα.*

κῐθᾰρ-αοιδός contr. -ῳδός, ὁ, (*κιθάρα, ἀοιδός*) *one who plays and sings to the lyre* or *harp, a harper* :—Sup. *κιθαραοιδότατος.* [ᾰ]

κῐθᾰρίζω, f. *ίσω* Att. *ιῶ*, (*κίθαρις*) *to play the lyre* or *lute:* it is also used of the *φόρμιγξ* and *λύρα*, so that the *κιθάρα, λύρα*, and *φόρμιγξ* must have been nearly the same.

κίθᾰρις, ιος, ἡ, acc. *κίθαριν*, = *κιθάρα* : also *music, harping, playing.*

κῐθᾰριστής, οῦ, ὁ, (*κιθαρίζω*) *a player on the lyre* or *harp, a harper.* Hence

κῐθᾰριστρίς, ίδος, ἡ, fem. of *κιθαριστής.*

κῐθᾰριστύς, ύος, ἡ, (*κιθαρίζω*) *a playing the lyre* or *harp, the art of playing it.*

κῐθᾰρῳδικός, ή, όν, *of* or *for harp-playing.* From

κῐθᾰρ-ῳδός, ὁ, contr. for *κιθαραοιδός.*

κιθών, ῶνος, ὁ, Ion. for *χιτών.*

κῐκεῖν, inf. of a poët. aor. 2 *ἔκικον* ; see *κίκω.*

κίκι, τό, = *κρότων.* II. *the berry of the κρότων, castor-berry.*

ΚΙ´ΚΙΝΝΟΣ, ὁ, *a curled lock of hair, a ringlet of hair*, Lat. *cincinnus.*

κικκᾰβαῦ, a cry in imitation of the screech-owl's note, *toowhit, toowhoo.*

ΚΙ´ΚΚΟΣ, ὁ, *the husk, shell* of fruit, Lat. *ciccus.*

κικλήσκω, poët. redupl. form of *καλέω, to call, summon, invite: to call on, invoke:* also in Med. II. *to accost, address.* III. *to name, call by name.*

κικράω, Dor. for *κεράννυμι, κιρνάω.*

ΚΙ´ΚΥΣ, ἡ, *strength, vigour.*

***ΚΙ´ΚΩ**, a verb only found in aor. 2 *ἔκῐκον*, inf. *κικεῖν*, and Dor. aor. 1 *ἔκιξα*, med. *ἐκιξάμην* :—*to make to go, move, toss.* (Akin to *κίω* and *διωκεῖν.*)

Κιλίκιος, α, ον, *Cilician.* From

Κίλιξ, ῐκος, ὁ, *a Cilician.* [ῐ] Hence

Κίλισσα, ης, ἡ, *a Cilician woman.* 2. as Adj., fem. of *Κιλίκιος.*

κιλλί-βας, αντος, ὁ, *a trestle, stand* or *support* for anything, esp. for a shield. (From *κίλλος, ass, βαίνω* : so Germ. *esel*, our *easel* and *horse.*) [ῐ]

ΚΙ´ΛΛΟΣ, ὁ, *an ass.* (Dor. word.)

Κιμμέριοι, οἱ, *the Cimmerians*, a people supposed to dwell in perpetual darkness : later, a people about the Palus Maeotis.

Κῑμωλία (*γῆ*), ἡ, *Cimolian earth*, a kind of white clay, like *fuller's earth*, from Cimōlus in the Cyclades.

ΚΙ´ΝΑ´ΒΡΑ, ἡ, *the rank smell of a goat.* Hence

κῐναβράω, *to smell like a goat.*

κίνᾰδος, εος, τό : vocat. *κίναδε*, as if it were masc., —Sicil. word, *a fox* : metaph. *a wily fellow, a cheat.*

κῐνάθισμα, ατος, τό, *a rustling motion, rustling.* (From *κιναθίζω*, = *κινέω.*) [νᾰ]

κῐν-ᾰχύρα, ἡ, (*κινέω, ἄχῠρον*) *a kind of bag* or *sieve* for bolting flour.

κινδῦνευμα, ατος, τό, *a risk, venture, enterprise;* and

κινδῦνευτέον, verb. Adj. *one must venture;* and

κινδῦνευτής, οῦ, ὁ, *an adventurous person* :—from

κινδῦνεύω, f. *σω*, *to be daring, venture into danger, run a risk, hazard.* 2. absol. *to make a venture, do a daring thing:* so with acc. of the danger, *κ. κινδύνευμα to venture* the risk. II. from the notion of *running a risk*, *κινδυνεύω* c. inf. comes to mean, *to run a risk* or *chance of doing, be likely to do so and so;* *κινδυνεύουσι οἱ ἄνθρωποι οὗτοι γόητες εἶναι* *they run a risk of being reputed* conjurers : hence *κινδυνεύει* as impers. *it seems to be, is likely* :—Pass. *to be hazarded, exposed to danger.* From

ΚΙ´ΝΔΥ´ΝΟΣ, ὁ, *a danger, risk, hazard, venture,* Lat. *periculum: an experiment, trial;* *κίνδυνον ποιεῖν*, Lat. *periculum facere*, to make *an experiment.*

κινεῦ, Dor. for *κινοῦ*, pres. imperat. pass. of *κινέω.*

κῑνέω, f. *ήσω*, (*κίω*) *to move, set in motion, set a-going, urge on: to move* a thing from its place; hence, *to meddle with* things sacred: *to change, innovate.* 2. *to set in motion, originate, be the author* or *contriver of* a thing. 3. *to stir up, arouse: to move to anger, provoke.* 4. *κινεῖν πᾶν χρῆμα to set* every engine *at work, turn* every stone. II. Pass., with fut. med. *κινήσομαι* and pass. *κινηθήσομαι*, aor. 1 *ἐκινήθην* : *to be put in motion, to be moved, to move;* of an earthquake, as, *ἐκινήθη Δῆλος.*

κινήθην, Ep. aor. 1 pass. of *κινέω.*

κῑνηθμός, ὁ, = *κίνησις, motion.*

κίνησις, εως, ἡ, (*κινέω*) *a moving* or *being moved* ; *motion.* II. *excitement, commotion* : *a movement, disturbance.* [κῑ]

κῑνητήρ, ῆρος, ὁ, = *κινητής.* Hence

κῑνητήριος, α, ον, *liable to move* or *excite.*

κῑνητής, οῦ, ὁ, (*κινέω*) *a mover, author.*

κῑνητικός, ή, όν, (*κινέω*) *putting in motion, stirring up, exciting.*

κιννάμωμον, τό, *cinnamon*, a word introduced by the Greeks from the Phoenicians.

κίνυγμα, ατος, τό, (*κινύσσομαι*) *a floating* or *hovering body, a phantom.* [ῐ]

κίνῠμαι, Ep. Pass. (from an obsol. Act. *κίνῡμι*), = *κινέομαι, to be in motion, go, move, march.* [ῐ]

κίνυντο, Ep. for *ἐκίνυντο*, 3 pl. impf. of *κίνυμαι.*

κῑνύρομαι [ῠ], Dep. *to utter a plaintive* sound, *moan, lament:* c. acc. cognato, *χαλινοὶ κινύρονται φόνον* the bridles *ring* or *clash* murderously. From

κῑνῠρός, ά, όν, *wailing, plaintive.* (Formed from the sound.)

κῑνύσσω, = *κινέω, to put in motion* :—Pass. *to waver, be swayed to and fro.*

κῑνώ, οῦς, ἡ, Dor. for *κίνησις.*

κῑό-κρᾱνον, τό, = *κιονόκρανον.*

κίομεν, Ep. for *κίωμεν*, 1 pl. subj. of *κίω.*

κίον, Ep. for *ἔκιον*, impf. of *κίω.*

κῑονό-κρᾱνον, τό, (*κίων, κρανίον*) *the capital of a column.*

κίοσι, dat. pl. of *κίων, a pillar.*

Κίρκη, ἡ, *Circé*, an enchantress who changed

Ulysses' companions to swine, v. Odyss. lib. 10, Hor. Epist. 1. 2, 23.

κιρκ-ήλᾰτος, ον, (κίρκος, ἐλαύνω) *chased by a hawk.*

ΚΙ'ΡΚΟΣ, ὁ, *a* kind of *hawk* or *falcon*, which flies in *wheels* or *circles*. 2. *a circle, ring*, mostly in form κρίκος. Hence

κιρκόω, f. ώσω, *to hoop in, secure by rings.*

κιρνάω and **-ημι**, poët. forms of κεράννυμι, *to mix* wine with water:—from κιρνάω comes 3 sing. pres. κιρνᾷ, 3 sing. impf. ἐκίρνα: from κίρνημι, Ep. 3 sing. impf. κίρνη, part. κιρνάς.

ΚΙ'Σ, ὁ, gen. κιός, acc. κίν, *a worm in wood* or *in corn, the weevil*, Lat. *curculio.*

κίσηρις, εως, ἡ, (κίς) *the pumice-stone*, Lat. *pumex.*

ΚΙ'ΣΣΑ Att. **κίττᾰ**, ἡ, *a chattering bird, the jay.* II. *the longing of pregnant women, a craving for strange food.* Hence

κισσᾰβίζω Att. **κιτταβίζω**, f ίσω, *to scream like a jay.*

κισσάω Att. **κιττάω**, f. ήσω, (κίσσα II) *to crave for strange food:* generally, *to long* or *yearn after.*

κισσήρης, ες, (κισσός) *ivy-clad.*

κίσσηρις, εως, ἡ, = κίσηρις, q. v.

κίσσῐνος, η, ον, (κισσός) *of ivy.*

κισσο-δέτης, ου, ὁ, Dor. **-δέτας**, (κισσός, δέω) *bound* or *crowned with ivy.*

κισσο-κόμης, ου, ὁ, (κισσός, κόμη) *ivy-tressed, crowned with ivy.*

ΚΙΣΣΟ'Σ Att. **κιττός**, ὁ, *ivy*, Lat. *hedera.*

κισσο-στέφᾰνος, ον, and **κισσο-στεφής**, ές, (κισσός, στέφανος, στέφω) *ivy-wreathed.*

κισσοφορέω Att. **κιττ-**, *to be decked with ivy.* From

κισσο-φόρος, ον, (κισσός, φέρω) *wearing ivy, ivy-crowned: luxuriant with ivy.*

κισσόω Att. **κιττ-**, f. ώσω, (κισσός) *to deck with ivy.*

κισσύβιον [ῠ], τό, (κισσός) *a drinking-cup* either made of *ivy-wood* or *with ivy-leaves carved on it.*

κισσωτός, ή, όν, (κισσόω) *decked with ivy.*

ΚΙ'ΣΤΗ, ἡ, *a box, chest*, Lat. *cista.*

κιστίς, ίδος, ἡ, Dim. of κίστη, *a little chest.*

ΚΙΤΡΕ'Α or **κιτρία**, ἡ, *the citron-tree.*

κίτρῐνος, η, ον, (κίτρον) *of citron.*

κίτρον, τό, *the fruit of the* κιτρέα, *citron.*

κίττα, κιττᾰβίζω, κιττάω, Att. for κισσ-.

κιττός, ὁ, Att. for κισσ-.

κιχάνω [ᾰ], used only in pres. and impf. indic., in inf. κιχάνειν, and Med. κιχάνομαι: most of the other moods and tenses being formed as if from κίχημι;—Ep. subj. κιχείω, opt. κιχείην, inf. κιχῆναι Ep. κιχήμεναι, part. κιχείς and Med. κιχήμενος: so impf. ἐκίχην, 2 sing. ἐκίχεις (as if from κιχέω); 1 pl. κίχημεν, 3 dual κιχήτην: fut. κιχήσομαι: aor. 2 ἔκιχον Ep. κίχον, part. κιχών: aor. 1 med. ἐκιχησάμην: Att. κιγχάνω [ᾰ], q. v.:—*to light upon, meet with, find: to arrive at.*

κιχείην, opt. of κιχάνω.

κιχείς, pres. part. of κίχημι, = κιχάνω.

κιχείομεν, Ep. for κιχῶμεν, Ep. 1 pl. subj. of κίχημι.

κίχηλα, ἡ, Dor. for κίχλη.

κιχήμεναι, κιχήμενος, v. sub κιχάνω

***κίχημι**, v. sub κιχάνω.

κιχήσομαι, fut. of κιχάνω.

κίχον, aor. 2 of κιχάνω.

ΚΙ'ΧΛΗ, ἡ, *a thrush* or *fieldfare*, Lat. *turdus.*

κιχλίζω, f. ίσω Att. ιῶ, *to titter, giggle*, formed like καγχλάζω from the sound. II. (κίχλη) *to eat* κίχλαι, *to live daintily.*

κιχλίσδοντι, Dor. for κιχλίζουσι, 3 pl. of κιχλίζω.

κιχλισμός, ὁ, (κιχλίζω) *a tittering, giggling.* II. (κίχλη) *dainty living.*

κίχρημι, fut. χρήσω: aor. 1 ἔχρησα: (see χράω C. II): —*to lend.* II. Mod. κίχρᾰμαι, fut. χρήσομαι: aor. 1 ἐχρησάμην:—*to have lent to one, to borrow.*

***ΚΙ'Ω**, *to go*, pres. not used in indicat.; subj. κίω, Ep. 1 pl. κίομεν; opt. κίοιμι, part. κιών, κιοῦσα: impf. ἔκιον Ep. κίον:—*to go:* of ships, *to sail.*

ΚΙ'ΩΝ, ονος, ὁ and ἡ, *a pillar, column.* II. = στήλη, *a gravestone*, Lat. *cippus.* [ῑ]

κλαγγάνω, collat. form of κλάζω, of hounds, *to give tongue:* of birds, *to scream, screech.*

κλαγγεῦντι, Dor. for κλαγγοῦσι, 3 pl. of

κλαγγέω, = κλάζω, of hounds, *to give tongue.*

κλαγγή, ἡ, (κλάζω) *any sharp, quick sound*, as *the twang* of the bow, *the scream* of birds, *the hissing* of serpents, *the barking* or *baying* of dogs: also the *grunting of swine.* Hence

κλαγγηδόν, Adv. *with a clang, noise, din.*

κλᾰγερός, ά, όν, (κλάζω) *screaming, screeching.*

κλάγξας, aor. 1 part. of κλάζω.

κλᾰδᾰρός, ά, όν, (κλάω) *broken, fragile, brittle.*

κλάδας, irreg. acc. pl. of κλάδος.

κλᾷδας, Dor. for κλεῖδας, acc. pl. of κλείς.

κλᾳδί, Dor. for κλειδί, dat. of κλείς.

κλᾰδίον, τό, Dim. of κλάδος.

κλᾰδίσκος, ὁ, Dim. of κλάδος.

κλάδος, ου, ὁ, (κλάω) *a young slip* or *shoot* of a tree: *a young branch* or *shoot*, esp. *an olive-branch*, which was wound round with wool and presented by suppliants.

ΚΛΑ'ΖΩ, f. κλάγξω: aor. 1 ἔκλαγξα: Ep. aor. 2 ἔκλᾰγον, inf. κλαγεῖν: pf. with pres. sense κέκλαγγα and κέκληγα, part. **κεκληγώς**, ότος, also **κεκλήγων**, οντος (as if from a new pres. κεκλήγω):—Pass., paullo-p. fut. κεκλάγξομαι:—*to make a sharp, quick sound;* of arrows in the quiver, *to clash, clang, rattle;* of birds, *to scream, screech:* of dogs, *to bark* or *bay:* of the wind, *to rustle:* of men, *to shout aloud, halloo, shriek forth, cry out.*

κλαίεσκον, Ion. impf. of κλαίω.

κλαΐς, gen. κλαΐδος, ἡ, Dor. for κληΐς, κλείς, Lat. *clavis*

κλαΐστρον, Dor. for κλεῖστρον, κλεῖθρον.

ΚΛΑΙ'Ω Att. **κλάω** [ᾱ]: f. κλαύσομαι Dor. κλαυσοῦμαι: also κλαιήσω Att. κλᾱήσω: aor. 1 ἔκλαυσα Ep. κλαῦσα:—Pass., paullo-p. fut. κεκλαύσομαι: pf. κέκλαυμαι and κέκλαυσμαι:—*to weep, lament, wail:* hence Att. phrase, κλαύσεται *he shall weep*, i. e. *he shall repent it, have cause to rue it:* so, **κλαίων ἄν**

your peril, to your sorrow; κλάειν σε λέγω, Lat. *plorare te jubeo.* II. transit. *to bewail, mourn, deplore:*—Pass. *to be mourned for* or *lamented;* also κεκλαυμένος *bathed in tears, weeping.*

κλᾴξ, ᾳκός, ἡ, Dor. for κλείς, *a key.*

κλᾳξῶ, Dor. fut. of κλείω, *to shut.*

κλᾰπῆναι, aor. 2 inf. pass. of κλέπτω.

κλάριος, ον, (κλᾶρος) *apportioning by lot.* [ᾱ]

κλᾶρος, κλᾱρόω, κλᾱρονομέω, Dor. for κληρ-.

κλάσε, Ep. for ἔκλᾰσε, 3 sing. aor. 1 of κλάω.

κλᾰσῐ-βῶλαξ, ἄκος, ὁ, ἡ, (κλάω, βῶλαξ) *clod-breaking.*

κλάσις, εως, ἡ, (κλάω) *a breaking.* [ᾰ]

κλάσμα, ατος, τό, (κλάω) *that which is broken off, a fragment, piece, morsel.*

κλάσσε, κλάσσατο, Ep. 3 sing. aor. 1 act. and med. of κλάω.

κλαστάζω, f. άσω, (κλάω) *to prune a vine,* Lat. *pampinare:* metaph. *to bring down, humble.*

κλαστός, ή, όν, (κλάω) *broken in pieces.*

κλᾰσῶ, Dor. for κλάσω, fut. of κλάω.

κλαυθμός, ὁ, (κλαίω), *a weeping, wailing.* Hence

κλαυθμῠρίζω, f. σω, *to make to weep.* Hence

κλαυθμῠρισμός, ὁ, *a crying like a child.*

κλαῦμα, ατος, τό, (κλαίω) *a weeping, wailing.* II. *a trouble, misfortune.*

κλαύσᾱρα, by crasis for κλαύσει ἄρα. [σᾱ]

κλαῦσε, Ep. 3 sing. aor. 1 of κλαίω

κλαυσιάω, (κλαῦσις) *to wish to weep;* τὸ θύριον φθεγγόμενον ἄλλως κλαυσιᾷ the door *is like to weep,* i. e. *shall suffer,* for creaking without cause.

κλαυσί-γελως, ωτος, and ω, ὁ, (κλαίω, γέλως) *smiles and tears.* [ῐ]

κλαυσί-μᾰχος, ον, (κλαίω, μάχη) parody on the name of *Lamachus, Rue-the-fight.*

κλαύσομαι, fut. of κλαίω:—Dor. **κλαυσοῦμαι.**

κλαυστός or **κλαυτός**, ή, όν, (κλαίω) *wept, bewailed: to be bewailed, mournful.*

ΚΛΑ´Ω: f. κλάσω [ᾰ]: aor. 1 ἔκλᾰσα Ep. κλάσα, κλάσσα: aor. 2 part. κλάς, as if from κλῆμι:—Pass., aor. 1 ἐκλάσθην: pf. κέκλασμαι:—*to break, break off, break in pieces:* of plants, *to prune*:—metaph. *to weaken, enervate.*

κλάω, Att. for κλαίω, as κάω for καίω. [ᾱ]

κλέα, Ep. shortd. form of κλέεα, plur. of κλέος.

κλεεινός or **κλεεννός**, ή, όν, poët. for κλεινός, *famous.*

κλεηδών, Ep. for κληδών

κλεῖα, contr. of κλέεα, nom. and acc. pl. of κλέος.

κλειδίον, τό, Dim. of κλείς, *a little key.*

κλειδουχέω Att. **κληδ-**, *to hold the keys, have the charge* or *custody of;* κλειδουχεῖν θεᾶς *to be priestess* of a goddess:—Pass. *to be watched.* From

κλειδ-οῦχος Att. **κληδ-**, ον, (κλείς, ἔχω) *holding the keys, having charge* or *custody of:* of a goddess, *tutelary.*

κλειδο-φύλαξ, ᾰκος, ὁ, ἡ, (κλείς, φύλαξ) = foreg.

κλεΐζω, f. κλεΐζω Dor. for κλῄζω.

κλεῖθρον Att. **κλῇθρον** Ion. **κληΐθρον**, τό, (κλείω) *a bolt* or *bar for closing a door.*

κλεινός, ή, όν, (κλέος) *famous, renowned, illustrious.*

κλεΐξαι, aor. 1 inf. of κλεΐζω, Dor. for κλῄζω.

κλείς, ἡ, gen. κλειδός: acc. κλεῖδα Att. κλεῖν: pl. nom. κλεῖδες, acc. κλεῖδας contr. κλεῖς: Ion. **κληΐς**, gen. κληῖδος, acc. κληῖδα: old Att. **κλῄς**, gen. κλῃδός, acc. κλῇδα:—*a thing to close the door with:* I. *a key*, by which the bolt (ὀχεύς) was shot or unshot *from the outside:* if the door was fastened *on the inside*, there was a latch (ἱμάς) by which the bolt was made fast to the handle (κορώνη). 2. *a bar* or *bolt*, commonly of wood, drawn across the door. 3. metaph. of silence, κλῄς ἐπὶ γλώσσῃ *a key* on the tongue, as if from some weight pressing it down; κλῇδας ἔχειν, like κληδουχεῖν, *to watch, have the charge of.* II. *the hook* or *tongue* of a clasp. III. *the collar-bone,* Lat. *jugulum;* κληῒς ἀποέργει αὐχένα τε στῆθός τε *locks* the neck and breast *together.* IV. *a bench for rowers.* V. *a narrow strait* or *pass,* such as we call *the key* of a country; mostly in pl., as, Κλεῖδες τῆς Κύπρου.

κλεῖς, contr. nom. and acc. pl. of κλείς, κλειδός.

κλειστός, old Att. **κλῃστος**, Ion. **κληϊστός**, ή, όν, *to be shut* or *closed.*

κλεῖστρον, τό, (κλείω) *a bolt, bar,* Lat. *claustrum.*

κλειτός, ή, όν, (κλείω B), *renowned, famous:* of things, *splendid, excellent.*

ΚΛΕΙ´Ω (A); f. κλείσω: aor. 1 ἔκλεισα:—Pass., aor. 1 ἐκλείσθην: pf. κέκλεισμαι and κέκλειμαι:—Ion. and Ep. pres. **κληΐω**: f. κληΐσω: aor. 1 ἐκλήϊσα Ep. κλήϊσα:—old Att. **κλῄω**, f. κλῄσω: aor. 1 ἔκλῃσα: pf. pass. κέκλῃμαι:—Dor. fut. κλᾳξῶ. Lat. *CLAUDO, to shut, shut up, close, keep fast: to confine:*—Pass. *to be shut up.*

κλείω (B), poët. for κλέω, *to celebrate.*

Κλειώ, οῦς, ἡ, (κλέος) *Clio, the Celebrator,* the Muse of Epic Poetry and History

κλέμμα, ατος, τό, (κλέπτω) *a thing stolen: a theft.* 2. *a trick, device, stratagem.*

κλέος, τό, only used in nom. and acc.: Ep. pl. κλέα, κλεῖα for κλέεα:—*a rumour, report, common fame, news;* σὸν κλέος *news* of thee:—*a mere report,* opp. to certainty; ἡμεῖς δὲ κλέος οἶον ἀκούομεν, οὐδέ τι ἴδμεν we hear *a rumour* only, but know not anything. II. *good report, fame, glory:* also *repute,* whether *good* or *bad:*—in plur., κλέα ἀνδρῶν ἀείδειν to sing the *glorious deeds* of heroes; κλέος ἀρέσθαι to win *honour.*

κλέπταν, Dor. for κλέπτην, acc. of κλέπτης.

κλεπτέον, verb. Adj. of κλέπτω, *one must withhold*

κλέπτεσκον, Ion. impf. of κλέπτω.

κλεπτήρ, ῆρος, ὁ, and **κλέπτης**, ου, ὁ, (κλέπτω) *a thief:* generally, *a rogue, deceiver.*

κλεπτίστᾰτος, η, ον, Att. Sup. formed from κλέπτης *the most arrant thief.*

κλέπτον, v. κλέπτω.

κλεπτοσύνη, ἡ, *thievishness, knavery.* From

ΚΛΕ´ΠΤΩ: f. ψω, or med. κλέψομαι: aor. 1 ἔκλεψα: pf. κέκλοφα:—Pass., aor. 1 ἐκλέφθην: aor. 2

ἐκλάπην [ᾰ], inf. κλαπῆναι: pf. κέκλεμμαι:—*to steal, filch, purloin*: of women, *to carry off*: part. κλέπτων, ουσα, ον, *thievish*; κλέπτον βλέπει he has *a thief's* look. II. *to cozen, cheat, beguile, deceive*: hence *to mislead*. III. *to withhold, conceal, keep secret, disguise*. IV. generally, *to do* a thing *stealthily* or *treacherously*: so c. part., κλέπτων ποιεῖ he does it *secretly*.

κλεψί-φρων, ον, gen. ονος, (κλέπτω, φρήν) *of deceptive mind, dissembling*

κλεψί-χωλος, ον, (κλέπτω, χωλός) *disguising lameness*. [ῐ]

κλεψ-ύδρα, ἡ, (κλέπτω, ὕδωρ) *a water-clock*, with a narrow orifice through which the water trickled, (instead of sand, as in our glasses);—used to time speeches in law-courts.

ΚΛΕ'Ω Ep. **κλείω** (κλέος) = κλῄζω, *to tell of, celebrate, glorify, extol*:—Pass. *to be famous*. II. = καλέω, *to call*.

κλῇδες, Att. for κλεῖδες, nom. pl. of κλῄς.

κλήδην, Adv. (καλέω) *by name*.

κληδόνισμα, ατος, τό, (κληδών) *a sign* or *omen*.

κληδ-ουχέω, κληδ-οῦχος, Att. for κλειδ-.

κληδών, όνος, ἡ, Ep. **κλεηδών** and **κληηδών**: (κλέω): *an omen, presage, boding*. II. *a rumour, report*: *reputation, glory*. III. *a calling, invocation*.

κλῄζω (A), f. ήσω: aor. 1 ἔκλησα: pf. pass. κέκλησμαι:—Ion. pres. **κληΐζω** Dor. **κλεΐζω**: (κλέος):—*to make famous, to celebrate*. II. *to name, call*:—Pass. *to be spoken of, be mentioned*.

κλῄζω (B), f. σω, late form for κλῄω, κλείω, *to shut*.

κληηδών, Ep. for κληδών.

κληθῆναι, aor. 1 inf. pass. of καλέω.

ΚΛΗ'ΘΡΑ Ion. **κλήθρη**, ἡ, *the alder*, Lat. *alnus*.

κλῇθρον, τό, Att. for Ion. κλήϊθρον, = κλεῖθρον.

κληΐδεσσι, Ep. for κληῖσι, dat. pl. of κληΐς.

κληΐζω, f. ίσω, Ion. for κλῄζω.

κλήϊθρον, τό, Ion. for κλῇθρον, κλεῖθρον.

κληΐς, ῖδος, ἡ, Ion. for κλείς.

κλήϊσα, Ep. aor. 1 of κληΐω, κλείω.

κληϊστός, ή, όν, Ion. for κληστός, κλειστός.

κληΐω, f. ίσω, Ion. for κλείω, *to shut*.

κλῆμα, ατος, τό, (κλάω) *a shoot* or *twig broken off* to be grafted on another tree, *a slip, cutting*: esp. *a vine-twig*, Lat. *palmes*. Hence

κλημάτινος, η, ον, *made of vine-twigs*.

κληματίς, ίδος, ἡ, Dim. of κλῆμα: mostly in pl. *brushwood, fagot-wood*.

κληρίον, τό, Dim. of κλῆρος, *a small portion*.

κληρονομέω, f. ήσω, (κληρονόμος) *to obtain a portion* or *lot*: *to receive a share of an inheritance, to inherit*. Hence

κληρονόμημα, ατος, τό, *an inheritance*: an

κληρονομία, ἡ, (κληρονομέω) *an inheritance, patrimony*: generally, *possession, property*.

κληρο-νόμος, ον, (κλῆρος, νέμομαι) *receiving one's portion*: as Subst., κληρόνομος, ὁ, *an inheritor, heir*.

κληρο-πᾰλής, ές, (κλῆρος, πάλλω) *distributed* [b]y *shaking the lots*.

κλῆρος Dor. **κλᾶρος**, ου, ὁ, *a lot*: twigs, potsherds or even a clod of earth was used for the purpose. In Homer each hero marks his own lot, and they are thrown into a helmet: the first which came out was the winning lot. 2. *a casting lots, drawing lots*. II. *an allotment, portion*, often of conquered land: *an inheritance, estate, property*: generally, *lands*. III. *the clergy*, as opp. to *the laity*.

κληρουχέω, fut. ήσω, (κληροῦχος) *to possess* or *hold by allotment, to have allotted to one*. Hence

κληρουχία, ἡ, *the allotment* or *portioning out of land in a foreign country among the citizens* of a state. 2. *the body of citizens among whom it was divided*.—An Athenian κληρουχία differed from a colony (ἀποικία), in that the κληροῦχοι were still citizens of the mother-country, instead of forming an independent state.

κληρουχικός, ή, όν, (κληρουχία) *of* or *for a κληρουχία* or *apportionment of land*.

κληρ-οῦχος, ον, (κλῆρος, ἔχω) *holding* or *possessor of an allotment of land*; esp. *of land in a foreign country portioned out among the citizens* as Subst. κληροῦχος, ὁ, *a portion-holder*. 2. metaph., πολλῶν ἐτῶν κληροῦχος *possessed of* many years, i.e. advanced in years.

κληρόω, f. ώσω, (κλῆρος) *to choose by lot*, and generally, *to choose*: of the lot, *to fall on* one, *designate*.—Pass. *to be chosen by lot*:—Med. *to cast lots for* a thing, *to have* a thing *allotted one*. II. *to allot, assign, apportion*:—Pass., κληροῦσθαι δούλη *to be allotted* as a slave, *to have* slavery *for one's lot*. Hence

κλήρωσις, εως, ἡ, *a choosing by lot*.

κληρωτός, ή, όν, (κληρόω) *appointed by lot*.

κλῄς, κλῃδός, old Att. for **κλείς, κλειδός**.

κλῆσις, εως, ἡ, (καλέω) *a calling*: *a calling into court, legal summons, citation*: hence *an indictment, impeachment*. 2. *a calling* or *invitation to a feast*. 3. *a name, appellation*.

κλῇσις, εως, ἡ, (κλῄω = κλείω) *a shutting up, closing, blockading*.

κλῄσω, fut. of κλῄω = κλείω:—also of κλῄζω.

κλητεύω, f. σω, (καλέω, κλητός) *to cite* or *summon into court*. II. *to be a witness, give evidence*.

κλητήρ, ῆρος, ὁ, (καλέω) *one who calls, a summoner*. II. *a witness, called to prove that legal summons has been served*.

κλητός, ή, όν, (καλέω) *called, invited*: ... *called out, chosen*.

κλῄω, old Att. for κλείω, *to shut*.

κλῑβᾰνίτης, κλίβᾰνος, v. sub κριβαν-.

κλῐθῆναι, aor. 1 pass. inf. of κλίνω.

κλίμα [ῐ], τό, (κλίνω) *an inclination, slope*. *a region* or *zone* of the earth, *clime*: *climate*.

κλῑμάκιον, τό, Dim. of κλῖμαξ, *a small staircase, ladder, a flight of steps*.

κλῑμακτήρ, ῆρος, ὁ, (κλῖμαξ) *the step of a staircase, round of a ladder.*

κλῖμαξ, ἄκος, ἡ, (κλίνω) *a ladder* or *staircase, flight of steps*, from its *leaning aslant: a scaling-ladder: a ship's ladder.* II. *an instrument like a ladder*, on which persons were tortured. III. in Soph. Trach., κλίμακες ἀμφίπλεκτοι seem to be *twistings* or *grapplings* of two bodies entangled with each other. IV. in Rhetoric, *a climax*, a gradual ascent from weaker expressions to stronger, as in Cicero against Catiline, *abiit evasit erupit.*

κλῖναν, Ep. for ἔκλιναν, 3 pl. aor. 1 of κλίνω.

κλίνη, ἡ, (κλίνω) *that on which one lies, a couch, bed:* also *a bier.* [ῑ]

κλῐνῆναι, aor. 2 inf. pass. of κλίνω.

κλῑνήρης, ες, (κλίνη, ἀρᾰρεῖν) *bed-ridden.*

κλίνθην, Ep. aor. 1 pass. of κλίνω.

κλῑνίδιον, τό, Dim. of κλίνη, *a small couch.*

κλῑνίς, ίδος, ἡ, Dim. of κλίνη, *a small couch.*

κλῑνο-πετής, ές, (κλίνη, πεσεῖν) *bedridden.*

κλῑνο-χᾰρής, ές, (κλίνω, χαρῆναι) *fond of bed.*

κλιντήρ, ῆρος, ὁ, (κλίνω) *a couch, bed, sofa.*

ΚΛΙ'ΝΩ [ῑ]: fut. κλῐνῶ: aor. 1 ἔκλῑνα: pf. κέκλῐκα:—Med., aor. 1 ἐκλῑνάμην:—Pass., aor. 1 ἐκλίνθην and ἐκλίθην [ῐ], aor. 2 ἐκλίνην [ῐ]: pf. κέκλῐμαι:—*to make slope* or *slant, incline.* 2. *to make* one thing *slope* against another, *prop* or *rest* it against. 3. *to turn aside;* ὄσσε πάλιν κλίνειν *to turn* back the eyes. 4. *to make recline* or *sit down*, esp. at meat. II. Pass. *to be bent: to bend aside, swerve.* 2. *to lean, rest, support oneself* against a thing. 3. *to lie down*, [illegible] meals, La[illegible]*bere.* 4. of Places, *to be sloping;* λίμνη κεκλιμένη *sloping towards* the lake. 5. *to wander from the right course.* III. Med. *to decline, verge:* so later in Act., ὁ ἥλιος κλίνει the sun *declines;* κλίνειν ἐπὶ τὸ χεῖρον *to fall away* for the worse.

κλῐσία Ion. -ίη, ἡ, (κλίνω) *a place for lying down: a hut, tent, cot,* or *cabin*, used by herdsmen in time of peace, and by soldiers in time of war: as they were of wood, an army on breaking up did not strike the κλισίαι, but burned them on the spot: the collected κλισίαι formed *a camp.* II. *a couch, bed.* III. *a company of* people *sitting at meals.*

κλισιάδες, ων, αἱ, (κλίνω) *folding-doors* or *gates:* metaph. *an entrance.* Prob. better κλεισιάδες, from κλείω *to shut.*

κλῐσίηθεν, Adv. (κλισία) *out of a cot* or *tent.*

κλῐσίηνδε, Adv. *to a cot* or *tent.*

κλίσιον, τό, (κλῐσία) *the outbuildings round a herdsman's lodge.*

κλίσις, εως, ἡ, (κλίνω) *a bending, inclination.* II. *a lying down, reclining.* [ῐ]

κλισμός, ὁ, (κλίνω) *a couch* or *chair for reclining.*

κλίτος, τό, = κλίμα II, *a clime.* [ῐ]

κλῐτύς, ύος, ἡ, acc. pl. κλιτῦς: (κλίνω) *a sloping place, slope, hill-side*, Lat. *clivus.*

κλοιός, ὁ, with irreg. pl. κλοιά, as well as κλοιοί: Att. κλῳός: (κλείω):—*a dog-collar:* esp. *a large wooden collar:* hence also *a pillory.*

κλονέω, f. ήσω, (κλόνος) *to drive in confusion, to confound, agitate, distract:*—Pass. *to flee in confusion, rush wildly: to be beaten by the waves.*

ΚΛΟ'ΝΟΣ, ὁ, *any violent motion*, esp. *the press of battle, the battle-rout:* generally, *a tumult, throng.*

κλοπαῖος, α, ον, (κλώψ) *stolen: furtive, stealthy.*

κλοπεύς, έως, ὁ, (κλέπτω) *a thief: a secret doer.*

κλοπή, ἡ, (κλέπτω) *theft.* II. *a stealthy act, fraud;* ποδοῖν κλοπὰν ἀρέσθαι to steal away on foot.

κλόπιος, α, ον, (κλοπή) *thievish, artful.*

κλοπός, ὁ, (κλέπτω) *a thief.*

κλοτοπεύω, *to deal subtly:* a lengthd. form of κλέπτω, κλοπεύω.

κλύδων, ωνος, ὁ, (κλύζω) *a wave, billow, surge.* II. metaph., κλύδων κακῶν *a flood* of ills. Hence

κλῠδωνίζομαι, Pass. *to be tossed by the waves.*

κλῠδώνιον, τό, Dim. of κλύδων, *a little wave, ripple:* but often like κλύδων, *a wave: a surging sea.*

ΚΛΥ'ΖΩ: Ion. impf. κλύζεσκον: fut. κλύσω [ῠ] Ep. κλύσσω: Pass., aor. 1 ἐκλύσθην: pf. κέκλυσμαι:—*to wash* or *dash against, break over:*—Pass. of the sea, *to be stormy, dash high:* so intr. in Act., κύματα κλύζεσκον ἐπ' ἠϊόνος the waves *dashed, broke* against the shore. II. *to wash off* or *away: to wash out.* 2. κισσύβιον κεκλυσμένον κηρῷ a wooden vessel *washed* or *coated* with wax.

κλῦθι, aor. 2 imperat. of κλύω.

κλύμενος, η, ον, (κλύω) = κλυτός, *famous.* [ῠ]

κλύσμα, τό, (κλύζω) *a liquid used for washing out: a clyster* or *drench.* II. *the part washed by the waves, the beach.*

κλυστήρ, ῆρος, ὁ, (κλύζω) *a clyster-pipe, syringe.*

κλῦτε, 2 pl. aor. 2 imperat. of κλύω.

κλῠτό-δενδρος, ον, (κλυτός, δένδρον) *famed for trees.*

κλῠτο-εργός, όν, (κλυτός, ἔργον) *famous for work.*

κλῠτό-καρπος, ον, (κλυτός, καρπός) *famous with fruit.*

κλῠτό-μητις, ι, (κλυτός, μῆτις) *famous for skill.*

κλῠτό-μοχθος, ον, (κλυτός, μόχθος) *famous for toils.*

κλῠτό-νοος, ον, contr. -νους, ουν, (κλυτός, νόος) *famous for wisdom.*

κλῠτό-παις, παιδος, ὁ, ἡ, (κλυτός, παῖς) *with famous children.*

κλῠτό-πωλος, ον, (κλυτός, πῶλος) *famous for horses.*

κλῠτός, ή, όν, also ός, όν, (κλύω) *heard of, to be heard of, famous, glorious, renowned.* 2. of things, *glorious, noble, splendid, beauteous.*

κλῠτο-τέχνης, ου, ὁ, (κλυτός, τέχνη) *famous for art, renowned artist.*

κλῠτό-τοξος, ον, (κλυτός, τόξον) *famous for the bow, renowned archer.*

ΚΛΥ'Ω: impf. or aor. 2 ἔκλυον, imperat. sing. and pl. (as if from κλῦμι), κλῦθι, κλῦτε, Ep. redupl. κέκλῠθι, κέκλῠτε:—*to hear, to give ear to, listen to, hearken to:* but also c. gen. *to obey.* 3. *to hear, learn by hearing, ascertain.* 4. generally, *to per-*

ceive. II. *to bear oneself called, be called* so and so, like ἀκούω. Lat. *audio;* κακῶς κλύειν *to be ill spoken of.*

ΚΛΩΒΟ'Σ, ὁ, *a cage, bird-cage.*

κλωγμός, ὁ, (κλώζω) *the whistle* or *sound* which a rider uses to his horse.

ΚΛΩ'ΖΩ, f. κλώξω, *to croak, have a hoarse note,* properly of jackdaws.

ΚΛΩ'ΘΩ, fut. κλώσω, *to twist, spin,* esp. of the goddesses of fate. Hence

Κλωθώ, οῦς, ἡ, Lat. *Klotho,* one of the three Μοῖραι or Fates, who span the thread of life.

κλωμᾰκόεις, εσσα, εν, *stony, rocky, rugged.* From

ΚΛΩ'ΜΑΞ or κρώμαξ, ᾱκος, ος, *a heap of stones.*

κλών, gen, κλωνός, ὁ, (κλάω) = κλάδος, *a young shoot, sprout, twig,* Lat. *surculus.*

κλωνίον, Dim. of κλών.

κλῳός, Att. for κλοιός.

κλωπεύω, f. σω, = κλοπεύω, *to steal.*

κλωπικός, ή, όν, (κλώψ) *thievish, furtive.*

κλωπο-πάτωρ, ορος, ὁ, ἡ, (κλώψ, πατήρ) *of a thievish* or *unknown father.* [ᾰ]

κλωστήρ, ῆρος, ὁ, (κλώθω) *a thread, yarn, line.*

κλωστός, ή, όν, (κλώθω) *spun, twisted.*

κλώψ, κλωπός, ὁ, (κλέπτω) *a thief,* Lat. *fur.*

κναίω, = Att. κνάω, like καίω for Att. κάω, etc.

κνᾰκων, ωνος, ὁ, Dor. for κνήκων, *the goat:* see κνηκός.

κνάμα, Dor. for κνήμη.

κνᾱμός, Dor. for κνημός.

κνάμπτω, old Att. for γνάμπτω.

κνάπτω or γνάπτω: f. ψω: (κνάω): *to scratch:* esp. *to tease, card* or *comb* wool, *to full* cloth, from the teasel or comb (κνάφος) which was used. II. metaph. *to mangle tear, lacerate.*

κνάσαιο, 2 sing. aor. 1 opt. med. of κνάω.

κνάσω, κνᾶσαι, Dor. for κνήσω, κνῆσαι, fut. and aor. 1 inf. of κνάω.

κνᾰφεῖον Ion. ήϊον, τό, (κνάπτω) *a fuller's shop.*

κνᾰφεύς or γναφεύς, έως, ὁ, Lat. *fullo, a fuller, cloth-carder* or *dresser, clothes-cleaner.*

κνᾰφεύω, f. σω, (κναφεύς) *to full* or *card cloth.*

κνᾰφήϊον, Ion. for κναφεῖον.

κνάφος, ὁ, (κνάω) *the prickly teasel,* Lat. *spina fullonica,* a plant used by fullers to card or clean cloth: hence also *a carding-comb;* also used as an instrument of torture.

ΚΝΑ'Ω, Att. 2 and 3 sing. κνῇς, κνῇ, inf. κνῆν; impf. 3 sing. ἔκνη Ep. κνῆ (used in the sense of aor. 2): fut. κνήσω: aor. 1 ἔκνησα:—*to scrape* or *grate,* Lat. *radere: to scrape off:* metaph. *to wear down, scrape away:*—Med., κνᾶσθαι τὰ ὦτα *to tickle one's ears.*

κνεφάζω, f. άσω, (κνέφας) *to cloud over.*

κνεφαῖος, α, ον, also ος, ον, (κνέφας) *dark, gloomy, murky.* 2. *in the dark,* either *at nightfall* or *before daybreak.*

κνέφᾰς, τό, Att. gen. κνέφους; dat. κνέφᾳ poët. κνέφει: (νέφος) *darkness, dusk at nightfall,* also *the morning twilight* or *dawn,* Lat. *diluculum.*

κνῆ, Ep. for ἔκνη, 3 sing. impf. of κνάω.

κνήθω, f. κνήσω, (κνάω) *to scratch.* II. *to tickle:*—Pass. *to itch.*

κνηκίας, ου, ὁ, v. sub κνηκός.

ΚΝΗ'ΚΟΣ, ἡ, Lat. *cnēcus* or *cnīcus,* a plant of the *thistle* kind.

κνηκός, ή, όν, Dor. κνᾱκός, ά, όν, (κνῆκος) *pale yellow, whitish yellow,* hence the goat is called ὁ κνάκων, and the wolf ὁ κνηκίας.

κνήμ-αργος, ον, (κνήμη, ἀργός) *white-legged.*

ΚΝΗ'ΜΗ, ἡ, *the part of the leg between the knee and ancle, the leg,* Lat. *tibia.*

κνημῑδο-φόρος, ον, (κνημίς, φέρω) *wearing greaves* to protect the leg.

κνημίς, ῖδος, ἡ, (κνήμη) *a greave, leg-armour,* reaching from knee to ancle; the κνημῖδες consisted of two parts, and were fastened with silver clasps (ἐπισφύρια); but βόειαι κνημῖδες are *boots* or *leggings* of ox-hide, to protect the legs.

κνημός, ὁ, (κνήμη) *the slope* or *shoulder* of a mountain; as it were *the leg,* opp. to πούς (the foot).

κνησιάω, f. άσω, Desiderat. of κνάω, *to wish to scratch, to itch.*

κνῆσμα, τό, (κνάω) *an itching*

κνησμονή, ἡ, = κνῆσμα.

κνῆστις, εως and ιος, ἡ; contr. dat. κνήστῑ: (κνάω) *a knife for scraping, a rasp, grater.*

κνίδη, ἡ, (κνίζω) *a nettle,* Lat. *urtica.* [ῑ]

Κνίδιος, α, ον, *Cnidian, of* or *from Cnidos.* From

Κνίδος, ἡ, *Cnidus.*

κνίζη, ης, ἡ, = κνίδη. From

κνίζω: f. κνίσω: aor. 1 ἔκνισα Dor. ἔκνιξα:—Pass., aor. 1 ἐκνίσθην: (κνάω): —*to scrape* or *grate, rasp.* II. *to make to itch:* hence metaph. *to nettle, tease, chafe, vex:*—Pass. *to be teased, chafed, fretted.*

κνῑπός, όν, (κνίζω) *scraping, niggardly, miserly.*

ΚΝΙ'ΣΑ Ep. κνίσση, ης, ἡ, Lat. *nidor, the smell* or *savour of a victim, steam of a burnt sacrifice.* II. *the fat-caul,* in which the flesh of the victim was wrapped: *the fat* itself. Hence

κνῑσάεις, εσσα, εν, Dor. for κνισήεις.

κνῑσᾶντι, Dor. for κνισάεντι, dat. of κνισάεις.

κνῑσάω, f. ήσω, (κνῖσα) *to fill with the steam* or *savour of a burnt sacrifice.* II. intr. *to raise the steam of sacrifice.*

κνίσδω, Dor. for κνίζω.

κνῑσήεις Dor. κνισάεις, εσσα, εν, (κνῖσα) *full of the steam of sacrifice, steaming.*

κνίσμα, τό, (κνίζω) *that which is caused by itching: a scratch, scraping.*

κνισμός, ὁ, (κνίζω) *an itching of the skin, tickling, irritation, fretting.*

κνῑσο-διώκτης, ου, ὁ, (κνῖσα, διώκω) *hunting after the smell of roast meat,* name of a mouse.

κνίσσα, κνισσάεις, less correct forms for κνῖσα, κνισάεις, etc.

κνῑσωτός, ή, όν, (κνισόω) *steaming with burnt sacrifice.*

κνίψ, ὁ, also ἡ, gen. κνῑπός, pl. **κνῖπες**, (κνίζω) *a kind of emmet*, which gnaws figs.

κνύζᾰ, contr. for κόνυζα.

κνυζάομαι and **-έομαι**, Dep. only used in pres., *to whine, whimper*, of a dog; also of children. (Formed from the sound.) Hence

κνυζηθμός, ὁ, *a whining, whimpering*.

κνύζημα, τό, = κνυζηθμός.

κνυζόω, f. ώσω, *to disfigure, make dim and dark*.

κνύω, f. ύσω [ῡ]: (κνάω) *to scratch* or *touch gently*.

κνώδᾰλον, τό, *any dangerous animal, a monster, beast*. (Deriv. uncertain.)

κνώδων, οντος, ὁ, (ὀδούς) *a sword*: pl. κνώδοντες, *two projecting teeth* on the blade of a hunting spear; ξίφους διπλοῖ κνώδοντες a cross-hilted sword.

ΚΝΩ'ΣΣΩ, only used in pres. *to nod, slumber, sleep*.

κοάλεμος, ὁ, *a stupid fellow, booby*. [ᾱ]

κοάξ, Comic word formed to imitate the croaking of frogs βρεκεκεκὲξ κοὰξ κοάξ.

κοάω, v. κοέω.

κοβᾰλίκευμα, τό, *a knavish trick*. From

κοβᾰλῑκεύω, *to play the knave*. From

κόβᾰλος, ὁ, *an impudent rogue, an arrant knave*: neut. Adj. κόβαλα, *knavish tricks, rogueries*. (Deriv. uncertain.)

ΚΟΓΧΗ, ἡ, *a muscle* or *cockle*, Lat. *concha*: also *a muscle-shell*. II. *the case round a seal* attached to documents: (hence ἀνακογχυλιάζω), to unseal).

κόγχος, ὁ, also ἡ, = κόγχη, *a muscle* or *cockle*.

κογχύλη, ἡ, = κόγχη. [ῠ] Hence

κογχῠλιάτης (sub. λίθος), ου, ὁ, *a shelly marble*. [ᾱ]

κογχύλιον, τό, (κογχύλη) *a muscle* or *cockle*: also its *shell*, generally, *a bivalve-shell*. [ῠ]

κοδράντης, ου, ὁ, Greek form of the Lat. *quadrans*, = ¼ *of an as*, about ½d. English.

ΚΟΕ'Ω or **κοάω** contr. **κοῶ**, Ion. for νοέω, νοῶ, *to mark, perceive, hear, observe*.

κόθεν, Ion. for πόθεν.

κόθορνος, ὁ, Lat. *cothurnus*, *a buskin* or *high boot*, covering the whole foot and reaching to the middle of the leg, laced in front, and with thick soles. 2. the κόθορνος was worn by tragic actors: thus it became the emblem of Tragedy, as the *soccus* of Comedy. 3. since the buskins might be worn on either foot, ὁ Κόθορνος was a nickname for a *trimmer* or *time-server* in politics.

κόθουρος, ον, = κόλουρος, *without a sting*.

ΚΟΙ', sound to express *the grunting* of young pigs.

κοΐζω, f. ίσω, (κοΐ) *to grunt like a young pig*.

κοίῃ, Ion. for ποίᾳ, dat. sing. of ποῖος, Ion. κοῖος, used as Adv. *how? in what manner? in what respect?*

κοιλαίνω, fut. ᾰνῶ: aor. 1 ἐκοίλῆνα, inf. κοιλῆναι, Att. ἐκοίλᾱνα, inf. κοιλᾶναι: pf. pass. κεκοίλασμαι: (κοῖλος):—*to make hollow, scoop, hollow out*.

κοίλη, ἡ, *a hollow*, properly fem. of κοῖλος; the name of a δῆμος or borough in Attica.

κοιλία Ion. **-ίη**, ἡ, (κοῖλος) *the hollow of the belly, the belly*, Lat. *venter*. 2. *the contents of the belly, the bowels: tripe: black-puddings*.

κοιλιο-πώλης, ου, ὁ, (κοιλία, πωλέω) *a tripe* or *black-pudding seller*.

κοιλο-γάστωρ, ορος, ὁ, ἡ, (κοῖλος, γαστήρ) *hollow-bellied*: hence *hungry, ravenous*.

κοιλό-πεδος, ον, (κοῖλος, πέδον) *lying in a hollow*.

ΚΟΙ'ΛΟΣ, η, ον, *hollow, hollowed*; κοῖλαι νῆες, for the early ships were hollowed out, like canoes; later, κοίλη ναῦς or κοίλη alone was *the hollow* or *hold* of the ship: of Places, *lying in a hollow* or *vale*: of a road, *cut deep, overhung*: κοῖλον, τό, *a hollow place, hollow, recess*; κοῖλος χρυσός gold *made into hollow vessels*, i. e. plate.

κοιλ-όφθαλμος, ον, (κοῖλος, ὀφθαλμός) *hollow-eyed*.

κοιλο-χείλης, ες, (κοῖλος, χεῖλος) *hollow to the rim*.

κοιλόω, f. ώσω, (κοῖλος) *to make hollow*.

κοιλ-ώδης, ες, (κοῖλος, εἶδος) *hollow-looking*.

κοίλωμα, ματος, τό, (κοιλόω) *a hollow*.

κοιλ-ῶνυξ, ῠχος, ὁ, ἡ, (κοῖλος, ὄνυξ) *hollow-hoofed*.

κοιλ-ώπης, ου, ὁ, fem. **κοιλῶπις**, ιδος, = κοιλωπός.

κοιλ-ωπός, όν, (κοῖλος, ὤψ) *hollow-looking*.

κοιμᾶτο, Ep. 3 sing. impf. pass. of κοιμάω.

κοιμάω Ion. **-έω**, fut. ήσω, (κεῖμαι) *to lull to sleep, put to sleep, put to bed*. 2. generally, *to lull, still, calm, tranquillise, soothe, assuage*. II. Med. and Pass., fut. κοιμήσομαι, aor. 1 med. ἐκοιμησάμην, pass. ἐκοιμήθην:—*to fall asleep, go to bed*: of animals, *to lie down*; κοιμήσατο χάλκεον ὕπνον *he slept* a brasen sleep, i. e. the sleep of death. 2. *to sleep the sleep of death, be fallen asleep*.

κοιμέω, Ion. for κοιμάω.

κοιμηθῆναι, aor. 1 inf. pass. of κοιμάω.

κοίμημα, τό, (κοιμάω) *sleep*; κοιμήματα αὐτογέννητα *intercourse* of the mother with her own son.

κοιμήσατο, Ep. 3 sing. aor. 1 med. of κοιμάω.

κοίμησις, εως, ἡ, (κοιμάω) *a sleeping*. also 2 *rest, repose*.

κοιμίζω, f. ίσω Att. ιῶ, = κοιμάω, *to put to sleep*:—*to lay asleep*, of the sleep of death. 2. generally, *to lay to rest, to quench; to appease, assuage*. Hence

κοιμιστής, οῦ, ὁ, *one putting to sleep*.

κοινᾶν ᾶνος, ὁ, Dor. for κοινών, κοινωνός.

κοινᾱνέω, Dor. for κοινωνέω.

κοινάσομαι, Dor. for κοινώσομαι, fut. of κοινόω.

κοινάσαντες, Dor. for κοινώσαντες, aor. 1 part. of κοινόω.

κοινῇ, dat. fem. of κοινός used as Adv., *in common, by common consent*. 2. *publicly*.

κοινο-βουλέω, (κοινός, βουλή) *to deliberate in common*.

κοινο-βωμία, ἡ, (κοινός, βωμός) *community of altars*, of gods who are worshipped at one common altar.

κοινό-λεκτρος, ον, (κοινός, λέκτρον) *having a common bed, a bedfellow, consort*.

κοινο-λεχής, ές, (κοινός, λέχος) *sharing the same bed, a paramour*.

κοινο-λογέομαι, Dep., with fut. med. -ήσομαι, aor. 1

med. ἐκοινολογησάμην and pass. -ήθην: pf. κεκοινολόγημαι: (κοινός, λόγος):—*to take common counsel with, to consult together.*

κοινό-πλοος, ον, contr. **-πλους**, ουν, (κοινός, πλέω) *sailing in common: making a joint expedition.*

κοινό-πους, ὁ, ἡ, πουν, τό, gen. ποδος, (κοινός, πούς) *with common foot, coming together.*

ΚΟΙΝΟ'Σ, ή, όν, also ός, όν, *common, shared in common.* II. *common to all the people, public;* τὸ κοινὸν ἀγαθόν the *common* weal. 2. τὸ κοινόν *the state,* Lat. *respublica;* ἀπὸ τοῦ κοινοῦ *by public authority, on the part of the state:* also *the public treasury;*—τὰ κοινά *the public moneys, public affairs.* III. of persons, *impartial, affable, accessible.* 2. *of common origin, kindred.* IV. of forbidden meats, *common, profane.* Hence

κοινότης, ητος, ἡ, *a sharing in common, fellowship.* II. *affability.*

κοινό-τοκος, ον, (κοινός, τεκεῖν) *born of common parents.*

κοινο-φῐλής, ές, (κοινός, φιλέω) *loving in common.*

κοινό-φρων, ον, gen. ονος, (κοινός φρήν) *like-minded.*

κοινόω, f. ώσω: Dor. fut. κοινάσομαι, aor. 1 ἐκοίνᾱσα: (κοινός):—*to make common, communicate, impart: to make a sharer in.* 2. *to make common* or *unclean, to pollute:* Med. *to deem common* or *unclean.* II. Med. *to communicate,* like the Act. 2. *take counsel, consult.* 3. *to be partaker* or *sharer in* a thing, c. gen.: also c. acc. rei, *to take part* or *share in.* III. Pass. *to hold communion, have intercourse with.*

κοινών, ῶνος, Dor. **κοινᾶν**, ᾶνος, ὁ, = κοινωνός.

κοινωνέω, f. ήσω, (κοινωνός) *to be a partaker, have a share of, to take part in;* κοινωνεῖν τινι *to have dealings with* a man. Hence

κοινώνημα, ματος, τό, *a communication:* and

κοινωνία, ἡ, *communion, fellowship, intercourse.*

κοινωνικός, ή, όν, *communicative, social.* From

κοινωνός, ὁ, also ἡ, (κοινός) *a companion, partner, fellow, associate.* II. as Adj. = κοινός.

κοινῶς, Adv. of κοινός, *in common, jointly: by common consent.* 2. *publicly.*

κοῖος, η, ον, Ion. for ποῖος, α, ον.

κοιρᾰνέω, f. ήσω, (κοίρανος) *to be lord* or *master, to rule, command.* 2. c. acc. *to lead, arrange.* Hence

κοιρανία Ion. -ίη, ἡ, *lordship, rule.*

κοιρᾰνίδης, ου, ὁ, = κοίρανος.

ΚΟΙ'ΡΑ˘ΝΟΣ, ὁ, *a ruler, leader, commander,* either in war or peace: generally, *a lord, master.*

Κοισῡρόομαι, Pass. (Κοισύρα) *to live like Coesura* (wife of Alcmaeon), i. e. *live a gay, fashionable life.*

κοιτάζω, (κοίτη), *to put to bed:* Med., with Dor. aor. 1 κοιταξάμην, *to go to bed, sleep.*

κοιταῖος, α, ον, (κοίτη) *lying in bed, abed, asleep,* 2. as Subst., τὸ κοιταῖον *the lair* of a wild beast.

κοίτη, ἡ, (κεῖμαι) *a place to lie down in, bed, couch: the marriage-bed;* κοίτην ἔχειν to be pregnant; **κοῖται** in pl. *lewdness.* 2. of animals, *a lair, den, nest.* II. *sleep, the act of going to bed;* τῆς κοίτης ὥρη *bed*-time.

κοῖτος, ὁ, = κοίτη. 2. *a going to bed: sleeping, sleep.* Hence

κοιτών, ῶνος, ὁ, = (κοίτη) *a bed-room, bed-chamber.*

κόκκῐνος, η, ον, *scarlet,* Lat. *coccineus.* From

ΚΟ'ΚΚΟΣ, ἡ, *a kernel, a berry:* esp. *the kermes-berry used to dye scarlet*

κόκκῠ, properly of the bird's cry, *cuckoo:* hence *a cry* or *call to a person;* κόκκυ, μεθεῖτε, *quick,* let go.

κοκκύζω Dor. **κοκκύσδω**: f. ύσω: pf. κεκόκκῡκα; (κόκκυξ):—*to cry cuckoo:* of the cock, *to crow.* II. *to cry like a cuckoo* or *cock, give a signal by such cry.*

κόκκυξ, ῠγος, ὁ, (κόκκυ) *a cuckoo,* from its cry.

κοκκύσδω, Dor. for κοκκύζω.

κόκκων, ωνος, ὁ, (κόκκος) *a pomegranate-seed.*

κοκύαι, οἱ, *ancestors.* (Deriv. uncertain.)

κολᾷ, 2 sing. fut. med. of κολάζω.

κολάζω f. κολάσω: aor. 1 ἐκόλασα: also in Med., fut. κολάσομαι, Att. contr. κολῶμαι, κολᾷ: aor. 1 ἐκολασάμην:—Pass., fut. κολασθήσομαι: aor. 1 ἐκολάσθην: pf. κεκόλασμαι: (κόλος, akin to κολούω): —*to prune, retrench:* metaph. *to hold in check, keep in, confine:* then *to chastise, correct, punish:*—Pass. *to be punished.*

Κολαινίς, ίδος, ἡ, epith of Artemis. (Deriv. and meaning uncertain.)

κολᾰκεία, ἡ, (κολακεύω) *flattery, fawning.*

κολάκευμα, τό, (κολακεύω) *a piece of flattery.* [ᾰ]

κολᾰκευτέος, α, ον, verb. Adj. of κολακεύω, *to be flattered.*

κολᾰκευτικός, ή, όν, (κολακεύω) *flattering, fawning.*

κολᾰκεύω, f. σω, (κόλαξ) *to flatter, fawn on:*—Pass. *to be flattered.*

Κολᾰκ-ώνῠμος, ὁ, (κόλαξ, ὄνομα) *parasite-named,* Comic distortion of a real name Kleonymos.

ΚΟ'ΛΑΞ, ᾰκος, ὁ, *a flatterer, fawner.*

κολαπτήρ, ῆρος, ὁ, *a chisel, graver.* From

ΚΟΛΑ'ΠΤΩ, f. ψω, *to hew, cut, chisel:* of birds *to peck.*

κόλᾰσις, εως, ἡ, (κολάζω) *a pruning: a checking, punishing, correction, chastening.*

κόλασμα, τό, (κολάζω) *chastisement, punishment.*

κολάστειρα, ἡ, fem. of **κολαστήρ**.

κολαστήριος, ον, (κολαστήρ) *fit for punishing.* II. as Subst., **κολαστήριον**, τό, *a prison.* 2. *a punishment, punishing.*

κολαστήρ, ῆρος, ὁ, = κολαστής.

κολαστής, οῦ, ὁ, (κολάζω) *a chastiser, punisher.*

κολάστρια, ἡ, fem. of κολαστήρ.

κολᾰφίζω, f. ίσω Att. ιῶ, (κόλαφος) *to give one a box on the ear, buffet, cuff.*

κόλᾰφος, ὁ, (κολάπτω) *a box on the ear, cuff.*

κολέον Ion. **κουλεόν**, τό, = κολεός, *a sheath.*

κολεός, ὁ, or **κόλεον**, τό, **κουλεόν**, τό, (κοῖλος) *a sheath* or *scabbard* of a sword.

κολετράω, f. ήσω, *to trample on.*

κόλλα Ion. **κόλλη**, ης, ἡ, *glue,* Lat. *gluten.*

κόλλᾰβος, ὁ, = κόλλοψ. II. *a kind of wheaten cake*, named from its shape.

κολλάω, f. ήσω, (κόλλα) *to glue, cement.* 2. *to inlay: to weld.* II. *to join together, unite*:— Pass. *to be joined to, to attach oneself to, cleave to.*

κολλήεις, εσσα, εν, (κόλλα) *glued together, close-joined.*

κόλλησις, εως, ἡ, (κολλάω) *a gluing, cementing*: κόλλησις σιδήρου *a welding* of iron.

κολλητός, ή, όν, (κολλάω) *glued together, cemented, closely joined, well-fastened.*

κολλῑκο-φάγος, ον, (κόλλιξ, φαγεῖν) *roll-eating.*

ΚΟ'ΛΛΙΞ, ῑκος, ὁ, *a long roll of coarse bread.*

ΚΟ'ΛΛΟΨ, οπος, ὁ, *the peg* or *screw* of a lyre, by which the strings are tightened: metaph., κόλλοπα ὀργῆς ἀνεῖναι to unscrew your passion.

κολλῠβιστής, οῦ, ὁ, (κόλλυβος) *a money-changer.*

ΚΟ'ΛΛΥΒΟΣ, ὁ, *a small coin.* 2. in plur., κόλλυβα, τά, *small round cakes.* [ῠ]

κολλύρα, ἡ, = κόλλιξ. [ῡ]

κολλύριον, τό, Dim. of κολλύρα, *eye-salve*, Lat. *collyrium*, so called because it was made up *in small cakes.* [ῠ]

κολοβός, όν, (κόλος) *docked, curtal*, Lat. *curtus*: of animals, *short-horned*: also *maimed, mutilated.* Hence

κολοβόω, f. ώσω, *to dock, curtail, shorten*

κολοι-άρχος, ου, ὁ, (κολοιός, ἄρχω) *a leader of jackdaws, a jackdaw-general.*

κολοιάω, f. άσω, (κολοιός) *to scream like a jackdaw.*

κολοιός, ὁ, *a jackdaw*, Lat. *graculus*: proverb., κολοιὸς ποτὶ κολοιόν = 'birds of a feather flock together.'

κολοκῡσία, ἡ, or **κολοκάσιον**, τό, *the colocasia* or *Egyptian bean*, a plant resembling the water-lily, found in the marshy parts of Egypt.

κολό-κῡμα, τό, (κόλος, κῦμα) *a large heavy wave* before it breaks, *the heavy swell* before a storm.

κολοκύνθη or **-κύντη**, ης, ἡ, *the round gourd* or *pumpkin*, Lat. *cucurbĭta* Hence

κολοκυνθιάς, άδος, ἡ, *food prepared from pumpkins.*

κολοκύνθινος, η, ον, *made from pumpkins.*

κόλον, τό, *the colon* or *lower part of the bowels.* From

ΚΟ'ΛΟΣ, ον, *docked, curtailed, stunted*, Lat. *curtus*; κόλον δόρυ a *spear broken short off*: esp. of oxen, etc., *hornless, short-horned.*

κολοσσός, ὁ, *a colossus, gigantic statue*, also simply *a statue.* The most famous Colossus was that of Apollo at Rhodes seventy cubits high, made in the time of Demetrius Poliorcĕtes.

κολοσυρτός, ὁ, *a rabble* or *noisy crowd.* *uproar.*

κολούω, f. σω: aor. 1 ἐκόλουσα:—Pass., aor. 1 ἐκολούθην and -ούσθην: pf. κεκόλουμαι and ουσμαι: (κόλος):—*to dock, clip, curtail, cut short, abridge*: metaph., ἔπος μεσσηγὺ κολούειν *to cut short* a word in the middle, Lat. *praecidere*, i.e. leave it unfinished; δῶρα κολούειν *to abridge, limit* gifts. also 2. like κολάζω, *to check, restrain, put down.*

κολοφών, ῶνος, ὁ, *a top, finishing, end.*

κολπίας, ου, ὁ, (κόλπος) *swelling in folds.*

ΚΟ'ΛΠΟΣ, ὁ, *the bosom, lap*. later also *the mother's womb.* II. *the lap* or *fold formed by a loose garment*, sometimes used for a pocket. III. *any lap* or *hollow*, θαλάσσης κόλπον ὑποδῦναι to go under *the lap* of ocean, i e. *the deep hollow* between two waves. 2. *a bay* or *creek* of the sea.—It corresponds in all senses to the Lat. *sinus.* Hence

κολπόω, f ώσω, *to form into a lap* or *fold: to make* a sail *belly* or *swell.*

κολπ-ώδης, ες, (κόλπος, εἶδος) *embosomed, embayed.*

ΚΟΛΥΜΒΑ'Ω, f. ήσω, *to dive: to swim.* Hence

κολυμβήθρα, ἡ, *a place for diving, a swimming-bath*: and

κολυμβητήρ, ῆρος, ὁ, and **κολυμβητής**, οῦ, ὁ, (κολυμβάω) *a diver, swimmer.*

κολυμβίς, ίδος, ἡ, (κολυμβάω) a sea-bird, *a diver.*

κόλυμβος, ὁ, (κολυμβάω) *a diver, swimmer.* II. = κολύμβησις.

Κόλχος, ὁ, *a Colchian*:—hence Adj **Κολχικός**, ή, όν, *Colchian*; pecul. fem. **Κολχίς**, ίδος.

κολῳάω Ion. -έω, f. ήσω, (κολῳός) *to brawl, scold.*

κολώμενος, Att. contr. fut. part. med. of κολάζω.

ΚΟΛΩ'ΝΗ, ἡ, *a hill, mound*: esp. *a sepulchral mound, barrow, cairn*, Lat. *tumulus.*

κολωνία, ἡ, the Lat. *colonia, a colony*

κολωνός, ὁ, (κολώνη) *a hill*; κολωνὸς λίθων *a heap* of stones. II. *Colonos*, a demos of Attica lying on and round a hill, sacred to Poseidon, the scene of the Oedipus Coloneüs of Sophocles.

κολῳός, οῦ, ὁ, (κολοιός) *a brawling, wrangling.*

ΚΟ'ΜΑΡΟΣ, ὁ, and ἡ, *the strawberry-tree, arbŭtus.*

κομᾰρο-φάγος, ον, (κόμαρος, φαγεῖν) *eating the fruit of the arbŭtus.*

κομάω Ion. -έω, Ep. part. κομόων: fut. ήσω: aor. 1 ἐκόμησα: (κόμη):—*to let the hair grow long, wear long hair*: as long hair was a sign of birth, it meant *to plume oneself, to be proud, haughty, arrogant*; οὗτος ἐκόμησε ἐπὶ τυραννίδι *he aimed at* the monarchy. Originally the Greeks seem generally to have worn their hair long, whence κάρη κομόωντες Ἀχαιοί in Homer. At Sparta the citizens continued to wear long hair; but at Athens it was worn only by youths until the 18th year. II. of horses, *to be decked with manes.* III. metaph. of trees, plants, etc., *to have leaves* or *foliage.*

κομέεσκε, 3 sing. Ion impf. of κομέω.

ΚΟΜΕ'Ω, f. ήσω, *to take care of, attend to, tend.*

κομέω, Ion. for κομάω

ΚΟ'ΜΗ, ἡ, *the hair* Lat. *coma*; κείρασθαι κόμην to have one's *hair* cut close in sign of mourning. II. metaph. like *coma, the foliage, leaves*, of trees.

Κομητ-ᾰμῡνίας, ου, ὁ, (κομήτης, Ἀμυνίας) *Coxcomb-Amynias.*

κομήτης, ου, ὁ, (κομάω) *long-haired*; ἰὸς κομήτης *a feathered* arrow. 2 *leafy, grassy.* II. *a comet.*

κομιδή, ἡ, (κομίζω) *attendance, attention, care*: also

the management, care of a garden. II. *a bringing* or *carrying of supplies, a procuring of supplies,* Lat. *commeatus frumenti, a gathering in* of harvest:—also *provisions, stores.* 2. (from Med. κομίζομαι) *a carrying away for oneself, a rescue, recovery.* 3. (from Pass. κομίζομαι) *a going* or *coming: a return, means of getting back.*

κομῐδῇ, dat. of κομιδή used as Adv., *with care, carefully, exactly: wholly, altogether: absolutely, quite:* in answers, κομιδῇ μὲν οὖν *very much so indeed, just so,* ay *and more than that.*

κομιεύμεθα, Dor. for κομιούμεθα, 1 pl. contr. fut. med. of κομίζω.

κομίζω: f. ίσω Att. ιῶ: aor. 1 ἐκόμισα Ep. ἐκόμισσα and κόμισσα:—Med., Att. fut. κομῐοῦμαι: Ep. aor. 1 ἐκομισσάμην and κομισσάμην:—Pass., f. κομισθήσομαι: aor. 1 ἐκομίσθην: pf. κεκόμισμαι: (κομέω):—*to take care of, provide for, supply*:—Med. *to receive hospitably.* 2. of things, *to take care of, take heed to, mind,* τὰ σ' αὐτῆς ἔργα κόμιζε *mind* thine own affairs. II. *to carry away,* in order to save; νεκρὸν κομίζειν *to carry away* a corpse:—Med. *to carry with one, rescue, save,* cf. ἐρύομαι; κόμισαί με *convey* me *away, rescue* me. 2. *to carry off* or *away, bear off*:—Med. *to carry off as a prize:* also *to get, gain, receive.* 3. *to bring to* a place: *to gather in* corn; *to introduce, import.* 4. *to conduct, escort.* 5. *to fetch back, redeem*:—Med. *to get back, recover.* III. Pass. *to be carried, to convey oneself, journey, travel, voyage: to betake oneself.* 2. *to come back, return.*

κομιοῦμαι, Att. contr. fut. med. of κομίζω.

κομίσαιο, 2 sing. aor. 1 med. opt. of κομίζω.

κόμισα and **κόμισσα**, Ep. aor. 1 of κομίζω.

κομιστέος, α, ον, verb. Adj. of κομίζω, *to be taken care of, to be gathered in.*

κομιστήρ, ῆρος, ὁ, = κομιστής.

κομιστής, οῦ, ὁ, (κομίζω) *one who takes care of, a protector, guardian.* II. *a bringer, conductor.*

κόμιστρα, τά, (κομίζω) *rewards* or *payment for saving.*

κομιῶ, Att. contr. fut. of κομίζω.

κόμμα, τό, (κόπτω) *that which is struck* or *cut, the stamp* or *impression of a coin:* proverb., πονηροῦ κόμματος of bad *stamp.* 2. generally, *coin.* II. *a short clause* in a sentence, Lat. *comma.* Hence

κομματικός, ή, όν, *framed in short clauses.*

ΚΟ'ΜΜΙ, τό, *gum,* Lat. *gummi;* indecl.

κομμός, οῦ, ὁ, (κόπτω) *a striking:* esp. like Lat. *planctus, a beating* of the breasts, *in sign of lamentation,* hence *a lament, wail, dirge.* II. in the Att. Drama, *a song sung alternately by an actor and the chorus,* mostly *a mournful dirge.*

κομόωντε, κομόωντες, Ep. part. dual and pl. of κομάω.

κομόωντι, Dor. for κομῶσι, 3 pl. of κομάω.

κομπάζω, f. άσω, (κόμπος) *to vaunt, boast, brag:* c. acc., κομπάζειν λόγον *to speak big* words; κομπάζειν τέχνην *to boast* one's art:—Pass. *to be made a boast, be renowned.*

Κομπασεύς, ὁ, Comic word, *one of the borough* Κόμπος, *a Bragsman.*

κόμπασμα, τό, (κομπάζω) *a boast:* in pl. *boasts, vaunts, braggart words.*

κομπέω, f. ήσω, (κόμπος) *to ring, clash, rattle.* II. metaph. *to utter high-sounding words, talk by boast, vaunt*:—Pass. *to be boasted of.*

κομπο-λᾰκέω, f. ήσω, (κόμπος, λακέω) *to talk big, be an empty braggart.* Hence

κομπολᾰκύθης, ου, ὁ, *braggart, boaster.* [ῡ]

ΚΟ'ΜΠΟΣ, ὁ, *a noise, din, clash,* as of a boar's tusks: *the stamping* of dancers' feet: *the ringing* of metal. II. metaph. *big words, boasting: a boast, vaunt.*

κομπός, ὁ, (κομπέω) *a boaster.*

κομπο-φᾰκελορ-ρήμων, ον, gen. ονος, (κόμπος, φάκελος, ῥῆμα) *pomp-bundle-worded,* epith. of Aeschylus, because of his long compound words.

κομπ-ώδης, ες, (κόμπος, εἶδος) *boastful.*

κομψεία, ἡ, (κομψεύω) *elegance, refinement: affectation.*

κομψ-ευρῑπικῶς, Adv. (κομψός, Εὐριπίδης) *with the prettiness* or *affectation of Euripides.*

κομψεύω, f. σω, (κομψός) *to make elegant, refine;* κόμψευε τὴν δόξαν *refine on* your suspicion, like Lat. *argutari*:—Med. *to refine overmuch*:—Pass. *to play the exquisite.*

κομψο-πρεπής, ές, (κομψός, πρέπω) *dainty-seeming.*

κομψός, ή, όν, (κομέω) *well-dressed, neat, fine,* Lat. *comptus:* hence *a pretty fellow,* Lat. *bellus homo.* 2. of words and things, *elegant, pretty, clever, witty, exquisite, affected.* Hence

κομψῶς, Adv. *prettily, exquisitely:* Comp., κομψοτέρως ἔχειν *to be better* in health.

κονᾰβέω, f. ήσω, (κόναβος) *to resound, clash, ring: to re-echo.* Hence

κονᾰβηδόν, Adv. *with a clash, ringing.*

κονᾰβίζω, f. ίσω, = κοναβέω.

ΚΟ'ΝᾸΒΟΣ, ὁ, *a clashing, ringing.*

ΚΟ'ΝΔΥ'ΛΟΣ, ὁ, *a knuckle:* in pl. *the knuckles.*

κονέω, f. ήσω, (κόνις) *to raise dust, to hasten.*

κονία Ion. and Ep. **κονίη**, ἡ, (κόνις) *dust, a cloud of dust,* as stirred up by men's feet; ποδῶν ὑπένερθε κονίη ἵστατ' ἀειρομένη from beneath their feet *the dust* stood rising:—freq. in plur. κονίαι, in collective sense, like Lat. *arenae;* πίπτειν ἐν κονίῃσι, to fall in the *dust.* 2. *dust* or *sand.* II. *cinders* or *ashes,* also in plur., like Lat. *cineres.* III. *a fine powder,* sprinkled over wrestlers' bodies after being oiled, to make them more easily grasped by the opponent. [ῑ in Homer; in Att. mostly ῐ.]

κονῑᾱτός, ή, όν, *plastered, whitewashed.* From

κονιάω, pf. pass. κεκονίᾱμαι: (κονία):—*to plaster with lime, to plaster,* Lat. *dealbare;* τάφοι κεκονιαμένοι *plastered, whited* sepulchres.

κονίζω, a mistaken form, originating in the wrong forms ἐκόνισσα, κεκόνισμαι; see κονίω.

κονι-ορτός, ὁ, (κόνις, ὄρνυμι) *dust stirred up, a cloud of dust:* κονιορτὸς ὕλης κεκαυμένης *a cloud* of wood-ashes. II. metaph. *a dirty fellow.*

κόνιος, α, ον, (κόνις) *dusty.*

ΚΟ'ΝΙΣ, ιος Att. εως, ἡ: dat. κόνῑ for κόνιϊ: = κονία, *dust.* II. *the dust of ashes, ashes.* III. *the powder with which wrestlers were* sprinkled after being oiled, cf. κονία: metaph. of toil. [ῐ]

κονισάλος [ῐ], ὁ, (κόνις) *dust, a cloud of dust.*

κονίω: fut. ίσω [ῑ]: aor. 1 ἐκόνῑσα:—Pass., pf. κεκόνῑμαι: Ep. 3 sing. plqpf. κεκόνῑτο: (κόνις):—*to make dusty, cover, fill with dust:*—Pass., κεκονιμένος *all covered with dust,* i. e. in the greatest haste; so in Med., κονίσαι λαβών *make haste and* take. 2. *to sprinkle* or *cover* as with dust, *strew over.* II. intr. *to raise dust, make haste, speed.*

κοννέω, contr. κοννῶ, = γιγνώσκω.

ΚΟ'ΝΝΟΣ, ὁ, *the beard.* 2. Κόννος, as the pr. n. of an insignificant person; Κόννου ψῆφος, proverb. of something worthless.

κοντός, οῦ, ὁ, *a pole,* esp. *a punting-pole,* Lat. *contus.* 2. *the shaft of a pike.*

κοντο-φόρος, ον, (κοντός, φέρω) *carrying a pole* or *pike: hurling a pike.*

ΚΟ'ΝΥΖΑ contr. **κνύζα**, ης, ἡ, *fleabane, pulicaria.*

κοπάζω, f. άσω: aor. 1 ἐκόπασα: (κόπος):—*to grow tired* or *weary*: generally, *to abate, lull.*

κόπᾰνον, τό, (κόπτω) *an instrument for braying, a pestle:* also 2. = κοπίς, *an axe.*

κοπεῖν, aor. 2 inf. of κόπτω: κοπείς, aor. 2 part. pass.

κοπετός, ὁ, (κόπτομαι) *a wailing, mourning.*

κοπεύς, έως, ὁ, (κόπτω) *a chisel.*

κοπή, ἡ, (κόπτω) *a striking: a cutting in pieces, slaughter.*

κοπιάω, f. άσω [ᾱ]: aor. 1 ἐκοπίᾱσα. pf. κεκοπίᾱκα: (κόπος):—*to work hard, work till one is weary.* II. *to be tired, grow weary;* κοπιᾶν ὑπὸ ἀγαθῶν *to be exhausted* by good things.

κόπις, εως, ὁ, (κόπτω) *a babbler, wrangler.*

κοπίς, ίδος, ἡ, (κόπτω) *a chopper, cleaver, bill-hook.*

κόπος, ου, ὁ, (κόπτω) *a striking, beating.* II. *toil and trouble, suffering, pain, weariness.* Hence

κοπόω, f. ώσω, *to weary*:—Pass. = κοπιάω.

κόππα, τό, a letter of the ancient Greek alphabet, which was not received into the later Athenian alphabet: its sign was Ϙ, cf. κοππατίας. In the alphabet *Koppa* stood between π and ρ, like the Lat. *q,* and was retained as a numeral = 90, as were also σταῦ and σάμπι, qq. v. Hence

κοππᾰτίας, ου, ὁ, ἵππος, *a horse branded with the letter Koppa* (Ϙ) as a mark. Cf. σαμφόρας.

κοπρᾰγωγέω, f. ήσω, *to carry dung.* From

κοπρ-ᾰγωγός, όν, (κόπρος, ἄγω) *carrying dung.*

κόπρειος, α, ον, (κόπρος) *full of dung, filthy.*

κοπρία, ἡ, (κόπρος) *a dunghill.*

κοπρίζω, f. ίσω Ep. ίσσω, (κόπρος) *to dung, manure.*

κοπρο-λόγος, ον, (κόπρος, λέγω) *collecting dung* or *manure:* hence *a dirty fellow.*

ΚΟ'ΠΡΟΣ, ἡ, *dung: manure: filth, dirt.* II. *a dung-yard, a cattle-stall* or *stable.*

κοπροφορέω, f. ήσω, *to carry dung: to cover with dung* or *dirt.* From

κοπρο-φόρος, ον, (κόπρος, φέρω) *carrying dung:* κόφινος κοπροφόρος a *dung*-basket.

κοπρών, ῶνος, ὁ, (κόπρος) *a place for dung, privy.*

κόπτοισα, Dor. for κόπτουσα, part. fem. of κόπτω.

κοπτός, ή, όν, (κόπτω) *beaten, bruised, pounded.*

ΚΟ'ΠΤΩ: κόψω: aor. 1 ἔκοψα: pf. κέκοφα, Ep. part. κεκοπώς:—Pass., aor. 2 ἐκόπην: pf. κέκομμαι:—*to strike, smite, cut.* 2. *to knock down, fell, slay.* 3. *to cut off, chop off;* δένδρα κόπτειν *to cut down, fell* trees; hence absol., κόπτειν τὴν χώραν *to lay* a country *waste by cutting down the trees: to damage, hurt;* φρενῶν κεκομμένος, *deprived* of sense or reason. 4. *to hammer, forge:* also *to stamp, coin* money, Lat. *percutere nummos:*—Med. *to coin oneself* money. 5. κόπτειν τὴν θύραν *to knock* or *rap at* the door, Lat. *pulsare.* 6. *to cut small, chop up.* 7. of birds, *to peck at, strike with the beak:* of a horse, *to jolt, shake:* also, *to tire, stun, deafen.* II. Med. κόπτομαι, *to beat* or *strike oneself,* in sign of grief, like Lat. *plangere:* also, κόπτεσθαί τινα *to mourn for* any one, Lat. *plangere aliquem.*

κορᾰκῖνος, ὁ, (κόραξ) *a young raven.*

ΚΟ'ΡΑΞ, ᾰκος, ὁ, *a raven* or *crow:* Proverb., λευκοὶ κόρακες, like 'black swans,' of anything unusual; ἔρρ᾽ ἐς κόρακας, or ἐς κόρακας alone, like Lat. *pasce corvos,* go and be hanged! βάλλ᾽ ἐς κόρακας hang him! hang it! II. *anything hooked like a raven's beak,* as, 1. *an engine for grappling ships.* 2. *a hooked handle of a door,* like κορώνη. 3. *an instrument of torture.*

κοράσιον, τό, Dim. of κόρη, *a little girl, damsel.*

κόραυνα, ἡ, a barbarism for κόρη.

κορβᾶν, ὁ, indecl., Hebrew word, *a gift offered to God, a consecrated offering.* 2. *the treasury of the Temple.*

κορδᾰκίζω, f. ίσω, (κόρδαξ) *to dance the* κόρδαξ.

κορδᾰκισμός, ὁ, *the dancing the* κόρδαξ.

ΚΟ'ΡΔΑΞ, ᾰκος, ὁ, *the cordax,* a low dance belonging to the Old Comedy; κόρδακα ἑλκύσαι to dance the cordax, from its slow, trailing movement.

ΚΟΡΔΥ'ΛΗ [ῠ], ἡ, *a cudgel, truncheon:* also *a swelling.* II. *a covering for the head, bead-dress;* ἐγκεκορδυλημένος *wrapt* or *rolled up.*

κορέει, Ep. 3 sing. fut. of κορέννυμι.

κορέννῡμι: f. κορέσω Ep. κορέω: aor. 1 ἐκόρεσα Ep. κόρεσσα:—Med., aor. 1 ἐκορεσάμην Ep. ἐκορεσσάμην and κορεσσάμην:—Pass., aor. 1 ἐκορέσθην: pf. κεκόρεσμαι Ion. κεκόρημαι; also pf. act. part. with pass. sense, κεκορηώς, ότος: (κόρος):—*to satisfy, glut,* or *fill with* a thing:—Pass. and Med. *to be glutted with* a thing, *have one's fill of* a thing, c. gen.; φυλόπιδος κορέσασθαι *to have one's fill of* strife.

κορεσαίατο, 3 pl. aor. 1 med. opt. of κορέννυμι.

κορεσθείς, aor. 1 part. pass. of κορέννυμι.

κορέσσατο, Ep. 3 sing. aor. 1 med. of κορέννυμι.

κόρευμα, τό, *maidenhood.* From

κορεύομαι, f. κορευθήσομαι: Pass.: (κόρη):—*to be a maid, grow up to maidenhood.*

ΚΟΡΕ'Ω, f. ήσω, *to sweep, brush*; κορεῖν τὴν Ἑλλάδα *to sweep* Greece *clean*, empty her of people.

κορέω, Ep. fut. of κορέννυμι.

κόρη Ion. **κούρη** Dor. **κώρα**, ἡ, fem. of κόρος, κοῦρος, *a maiden, maid, girl, damsel*, Lat. *puella:* sometimes of *a newly-married woman, young wife.* like νύμφη, Lat. *puella, nympha.* 2. with the gen. of a pr. name added, *a daughter*, as Νύμφαι, κοῦραι Διός II. *a puppet, doll*, Lat. *pupa.* 2. *the pupil* of the eye from the small images seen in it, Lat. *pupa, pupilla.* III. *a long sleeve* reaching over the hand.

Κόρη Ion. **Κούρη**, ἡ, was the name under which Proserpine was worshipped in Attica, *the Daughter* (of Demeter); hence the two are often mentioned together, as τῇ Μητρὶ καὶ τῇ Κούρῃ.

κόρηθρον, τό, (κορέω) *a besom, broom.*

κόρημα, τό, (κορέω) *sweepings, refuse.* 2. *a besom, broom*

κορθύνω, κορθύω [ῡ]

κόρθυς, υος ἡ, (κορυς) *a rising, heap.*

κορθύω or -ύνω, (κόρθυς) *to lift up, raise, shew its crest:*—Pass., κῦμα κορθύεται the wave *is lifted up, rears its crest.*

ΚΟΡΙ'ΑΝΝΟΝ, τό, *coriander*, the plant or seed.

κορίδιον, τό, Dim. of κόρη = κοράσιον.

κορίζομαι, f. -ίσομαι, (κόρη, κόριον): Dep.:—*to fondle, caress, coax.*

Κορίνθιος, α, ον, also **Κορινθιακός**, ή, όν, and fem. **Κορινθιάς**, άδος, ἡ:—*Corinthian.* From

Κόρινθος, ἡ, *Corinth*, the city and country: anciently Ἐφύρη: Adv. **Κορινθόθι**, *at Corinth.*

κόριον, τό, Dim. of κόρη, *a little girl.*

ΚΟ'ΡΙΣ, ιος Att. εως, ὁ, *a bug:* pl. κόρεις, οἱ.

κορίσκιον, τό, Dim. of κόρη.

κόρκορος or **κόρχορος**, ὁ, a poor vegetable, growing wild in the Peloponnesus, *a* kind of *pimpernel.* (Deriv. uncertain.)

κορκορυγή, ἡ, *the rumbling* or *grumbling* of the empty bowels: *any hollow sound, din, tumult.* (Formed from the sound.)

κορμός, ὁ, (κείρω) *the trunk* of a tree with the boughs *lopped off, a log.*

ΚΟ'ΡΟΣ, ου, ὁ, *one's fill, satiety, surfeit*, Lat. *satietas;* κόρον ἔχειν τινός to have enough or too much of a thing: in bad sense, *satiety, surfeit:* hence II. *insolence, petulance;* πρὸς κόρον *insolently.*

κόρος, ου, ὁ, Ion. **κοῦρος** Dor. **κῶρος**, (κείρω) *a boy, lad, youth, stripling.* 2. with genit. of pr. names, *a son.* Cf. κόρη.

κόρος, ὁ, the Hebrew *cor*, a dry measure containing ten Attic medimni, or about 120 gallons.

κόρση, ἡ, later Att. **κόρρη** Dor. **κόρρα**, (κάρα) *the side of the forehead;* ἐπὶ κόρρης πατάσσειν to slap on *the face.* II. *the hair on the temples.*

Κορυβάντειος, α, ον, (Κορύβας) *Corybantian.*

Κορυβαντιάω, f. άσω, (Κορύβας) *to celebrate the rites of the Corybantes: to start up like a Corybant.*

Κορυβαντίζω, f. ίσω, (Κορύβας) *to purify by the rites of the Corybantes.*

Κορυβαντ-ώδης, ες, (Κορύβας, εἶδος) *Corybant-like, frantic.*

Κορύβας, αντος, ὁ, *a Corybant priest of Cybelé in Phrygia.* [ῠ]

κορυδαλλή, -αλλίς, -αλλός, = κόρυδος.

κόρυδος, ὁ, and **κορυδός**, ἡ, (κόρυς) *the crested* or *tufted lark*, Lat. *alauda cristata.*

κόρυζα, ης, ἡ, (κόρρη, κόρυς) *a cold in the head, a running at the nose, catarrh*, Lat. *pituita.* II. metaph. *drivelling, stupidity.* Hence

κορυζάω, *to have a running at the nose, to have a cold.*

κόρυθα, **κόρυθας**, acc. sing. and pl. of κόρυς.

κορυθ-άϊξ, ϊκος, (κόρυς, ἀΐσσω) *helmet-shaking, with waving plume.* [ᾰ]

κορυθ-αιόλος, ον, (κόρυς, αἰόλος) *with glancing helm.*

κόρυμβος, ὁ, pl. κόρυμβα as well as κόρυμβοι: (κόρυς, κορυφή):—*the top, peak, summit;* κόρυμβα νηῶν *the high poops* of the ships. II. *the cluster of the ivy flower:* generally, *a cluster of fruit* or *flowers.*

κορυνάω, f. ήσω, *to put forth knobs* or *buds.* From

κορύνη, ἡ, (κόρυς) *a club*, often shod with iron for fighting, *a mace:* also *a shepherd's staff.* [ῠ]

κορυνήτης, ου, ὁ, (κορυνάω) *a club-bearer, one who fights with a club* or *mace.*

κορυνη-φόρος, ον, (κορύνη, φέρω) *club-bearing:* κορυνηφόροι, οἱ, *club-bearers*, the body-guard of Peisistratus, instead of δορυφόροι.

κορυνιάω, = κορυνάω: in Ep. part., **κορυνιόωντα** πέτηλα *sprouting* leaves.

κορυπτίλος, ὁ, *one that butts with the head.* [ῐ] From

κορύπτω, f. ψω, *to butt with the head.* From

κόρυς, υθος, ἡ, acc. κόρυθα and κόρυν, (κάρα) *a helmet, helm, casque.* II. *the head.* Hence

κορύσσω, fut. κορύξω:—Med., aor. 1 ἐκορυσσάμην, part. κορυσσάμενος:—Pass., pf. κεκόρυθμαι:—*to arm with a helmet:* generally, *to arm, equip, array:*—Pass. and Med. *to arm oneself; to do battle, fight:* also of things, δοῦρε κεκορυθμένα χαλκῷ spears *headed with* brass. 2. generally, *to furnish, provide.* II. *to make crested;* κόρυσσε κῦμα the river *reared* his wave *to a crest:*—Pass. *to come to a crest* or *head, rear its head*, as a wave does. Hence

κορυστής, οῦ, ὁ, *a man armed with a helmet, an armed warrior.*

κορυφαία, ἡ, (κορυφή) *the head-stall of a bridle.*

κορυφαῖον, τό, *the upper rim of a hunting-net:*—strictly neut. from sq.

κορυφαῖος, α, ον, (κορυφή) *at the head:*—ὁ κορυφαῖο; *the foremost man, leader, chief*; in the Att. Drama, *the leader of the chorus*.

κορῠφή, ἡ, (κόρυς) *the head, top, summit: the crown* or *top of the head*. 2. *the top* or *peak* of a mountain. 3. metaph. *the highest point, acme, prime*.

κορῠφόω, f. ώσω, (κορυφή) *to bring to a head, make peaked*:—Pass., κῦμα κορυφοῦται the wave *rises to a crest*. II. like κεφαλαιόω, *to bring to an end, sum up*.

κορων-εκάβη, ἡ, (κορώνη, Ἑκάβη) *an old woman as old as a crow and Hecuba*. [ᾰ]

κορωνέως, ω, ἡ, *of a raven-grey colour*. From

κορώνη, ἡ, (κοραινος) *a* kind of *sea-fowl, sea-crow* 2. *a crow* or *raven*, Lat. *cornix*. II. *anything hooked* like a crow's bill, as, 1. *the handle on a door* 2. *the tip of a bow*, on which the bowstring was hooked. 3. *the tip* or *projection of the plough-beam*, upon which the yoke is hooked. Cf. κόραξ.

κορωνιάω, f. άσω, (κορώνη II) *to bend, curve*. of a horse, *to arch the neck*.

κορωνίς, ίδος, ἡ, (κορώνη II) as Adj *crook-beaked*: generally, *crooked, curved, bent, hooked*. 2. of kine, *with crumpled horns* II. as Subst. *anything curved*: 1. *a wreath* or *garland*, Lat. *corona*. 2. *a flourish with the pen* at the end of a book: generally, *the end, completion*.

κορωνο-βόλος, ον, (κορώνη, βαλεῖν) *shooting crows*:—as Subst., κορωνοβόλον, τό, *a sling* or *cross-bow for crow-shooting*.

κορωνός, ή, όν, (κόραξ) *curved, bent*: of kine, *with crumpled horns*.

κοσκῖνηδόν, Adv. (κόσκινον) *as in a sieve*.

κοσκῖνό-μαντις, ιος Att. εως, ὁ, and ἡ, (κόσκινον, μάντις) *a diviner by a sieve*.

ΚΟ'ΣΚΙΓΝΟΝ, τό, *a sieve*.

κοσκυλμάτια, ων, τά, (σκύλλω) *parings* or *shreds of leather*: metaph. *of the scraps of flattery of the tanner* Cleon.

κοσμέω, f. ήσω, (κόσμος) *to order, arrange*: esp. *to set* an army *in array, marshal* it; and in Med., κοσμησάμενος πολιήτας *having marshalled his* countrymen; δόρπον κοσμεῖν *to arrange a* repast. II. *to order, rule, govern*. III. *to deck, adorn, trick out, embellish*. 2. of persons, *to honour* them, *adorn, be an honour* or *ornament to*. IV. in Pass. *to be assigned to, be classed under*.

κόσμηθεν, Aeol. 3 pl. aor. 1 pass. of κοσμέω.

κοσμῆν, Dor. inf. of κοσμέω.

κοσμητής, οῦ, ὁ, (κοσμέω) *an orderer, arranger*. 2. *an adorner*.

κοσμητός, ή, όν, (κοσμέω) *well-arranged, regular*.

κοσμήτωρ, ορος, ὁ, (κοσμέω) *a commander*.

κοσμικός, ή, όν, (κόσμος) *of the world, earthly, worldly*.

κόσμιος, α, ον, also ος, ον, (κόσμος) *well-ordered, moderate, regular*: of persons, *orderly, well-behaved, modest*; τὸ κόσμιον *order, decorum*. Hence

κοσμιότης, ητος, ἡ, *propriety, decorum, orderly behaviour*.

κοσμίως, Adv. of κόσμιος, *regularly, decently*: Comp. κοσμιώτερον; Sup. -ώτατα.

κοσμο-κόμης, ου, ὁ, (κοσμέω, κόμη) *dressing the hair*.

κοσμο-κράτωρ, ορος, ὁ, (κόσμος, κρατέω) *ruler of this world*. [ᾰ]

κοσμο-πλόκος, ον, (κόσμος, πλέκω) *framing* or *holding together the world*.

κόσμος, ου, ὁ, (κομέω) *order*: κατὰ κόσμον or κόσμῳ *in order, duly*; οὐδένι κόσμῳ in no sort of *order*. 2. *good order, good behaviour, decency*. 3. *a set form* or *order*: of states, *government*. 4. *the mode* or *fashion* of a thing. II. *an ornament, decoration, dress, raiment*: plur. *ornaments*. 2. *an honour, credit*. III. *the world* or *universe*, from its perfect *arrangement*, Lat. *mundus*.

κοσμο-φθόρος, ον, (κόσμος, φθείρω) *world-destroying*.

κόσος, η, ον, Ion. and Aeol. for πόσος.

κόσσᾰβος, ὁ, Ion. for κότταβος.

κόσσῠφος Att. κόττ-, ὁ, *a blackbird*.

κοταίνω, = κοτέω, *to bear hatred against*.

κότε and **κοτέ**, Ion. for πότε and ποτέ.

κότερον, κότερα, Ion. for πότερον, πότερα.

κοτέω, Ep. aor. 1 κοτέσα: Ep. pf. part. κεκοτηώς:—Med., **κοτέομαι**: Ep. 3 pl. impf. κοτέοντο, Ep. fut. κοτέσσομαι: Ep. aor. 1 ἐκοτεσσάμην, κοτεσσάμην: (κότος):—*to bear a grudge* or *spite, bear malice against, envy*, Lat. *invideo*: proverb., κεραμεὺς κεραμεῖ κοτέει. cf. κεραμεύς.

κοτήεις, εσσα, εν, (κοτέω) *angry, wrathful, jealous*.

κοτῖνη-φόρος, ον, (κότινος, φέρω) *producing wild olive-trees*.

ΚΟ'ΤΙΓΝΟΣ, ὁ or ἡ, *the wild olive*, Lat. *oleaster*.

κοτῖνο-τράγος, ον, (κότινος, τρᾰγεῖν) *eating the wild olive*.

κότορνος, ὁ, Ion. for κόθορνος.

ΚΟ'ΤΟΣ, ου, ὁ, *a grudge, spite, rancour, ill-will*: also, *anger, wrath*: later, *envy, jealousy*.

κοττᾰβίζω, f. ίσω Att. ιῶ, (κότταβος) *to play at the cottabus*.

κότταβος Ion. and old Att. **κόσσαβος**, ὁ, *the cottabus*, a Sicilian game, much in vogue at the drinking-parties of young men at Athens. The simplest mode was when each threw the wine left in his cup smartly into a metal basin; if all fell inside the basin, and the sound was clear, it was a favourable sign. The game was played in various ways. (Deriv. uncertain.)

ΚΟ'ΤΤΑ˘ΝΟΝ, τό, *a small fig*, Lat. *cottănum*.

ΚΟΤΥ˘ΛΗ, ἡ, *a small cup* or *vessel*. 2. *a liquid measure* containing 6 κύαθοι or *a* ½ ξέστης, nearly *a* ½ *pint*. II. *the cup* or *socket of the hip-bone*. Hence

κοτῠληδών, όνος, ἡ, *any cup-like hollow*: in pl. *the*

suckers on the feelers of the polypus, Ep. dat. κοτυληδονόφιν. II. *the socket of a joint*

κοτῠλ-ήρῠτος, ον, (κοτύλη, ἀρύω) *that can be drawn in cups*, i. e. *flowing copiously*.

κοτῠλίς, ίδος, ἡ, -ίσκιον, τό, and **-ίσκος, ὁ**, Diminutives of κοτύλη, *a small cup*.

κότῠλος, ὁ, = κοτύλη.

κοὐ, by crasis for καὶ οὐ.

κοῦ and **κου**, Ion. for ποῦ and **πού.**

κοὐκέτι, by crasis for καὶ οὐκέτι.

κουλεόν, κουλεός, Ion. for κολεόν, **κολεός.**

κοῦμι, Hebrew word, *arise.*

κουρά, ᾶς, ἡ, (κείρω) *a clipping* or *cropping* of the hair or beard, as a sign of mourning. II. *a lock cut off.*

κουρεῖον, τό, (κουρά) *a barber's shop.*

κουρεύς, έως, ὁ, (κείρω) *a barber*, *hair-cutter*, Lat. *tonsor:* hence *a tatler, gossip.*

κούρη, ἡ, Ion. for κόρη. II. also Ion. for κουρά.

κουρήϊος, η, ον, Ion. for κόρειος, *youthful.*

κούρητες, ων, οἱ, (κόρος, κοῦρος) *young men, young warriors.*

Κουρῆτες, ων, οἱ, *the Curētes*, inhabitants of Pleuron in Aetolia

κουρίας, ου, ὁ, (κουρά) *one who wears his hair short.*

κουριάω, f. άσω, (κουρά) *to wear untrimmed hair.* 2. of the hair, *to need clipping.*

κουρίδιος, α, ον, (κοῦρος, κούρη) *wedded, lawfully wedded;* κουρίδιος πόσις her *wedded* husband; then, as Subst., (without πόσις), κουρίδιος φίλος her dear *husband.* 2. more frequently of the wife, κουριδίη ἄλοχος his *lawful, wedded wife*, as opp. to a concubine (παλλακίς); so, 3. κουρίδιον λέχος the bed *of lawful marriage.* 4. *nuptial, bridal;* κουρίδιος χιτών the *bridal* robe.

κουρίζω, f. ίσω, (κόρος, κοῦρος) intr. *to be a youth.* II. trans. *to bring up to manhood.*

κούριμος, η, ον, also ος, ον, (κουρά) *fit for cutting* or *shaving hair, trenchant.* II. pass. *shorn, cropped, clipped:*—as Subst., κούριμος, ἡ, *a mask with the hair cut shor..*

κουρίξ, Adv. (κουρά) *by the hair.*

κουρο-βόρος, ον, (κοῦρος, βιβρώσκω) *devouring children;* κουροβόρος πάχνη the blood *of eaten children.*

κοῦρος, ὁ, Ion. for κόρος, *a boy, youth, son.*

κουροσύνη, ἡ, (κοῦρος) *youthful prime, youth:* hence *youthful spirits, mirthfulness.*

κουρότερος, α, ον, Comp. of κοῦρος, *younger, more youthful.*

κουρο-τόκος, ον, (κοῦρος, τεκεῖν) *bearing boy-children.*

κουρο-τρόφος, ον, (κοῦρος, τρέφω) *rearing boys:* so Ithaca is called ἀγαθὴ κουροτρόφος a good *nursing-mother of boys.*

κουστωδία, ἡ, the Lat. *custodia, a watch, guard.*

κουφίζω, fut. ίσω Att. ιῶ, (κοῦφος): I. intr. *to be light* II. trans. *to lighten: to lift up, raise:* κουφίζειν ἅλμα *to make a light* leap. 2. metaph. *to lighten, assuage, relieve:* of persons, *to relieve* them *from* burthens. Hence

κούφῐσις, εως, ἡ, *a relief, alleviation.*

κούφισμα, ατος, τό, (κουφίζω) *that which is lifted up.* 2. *a lightening, relief.*

κουφολογία, ἡ, *light talking.* From

κουφο-λόγος, ον, (κοῦφος, λέγω) *lightly-talking.*

ΚΟΥ'ΦΟΣ, η, ον, *light, nimble:* neut. pl. κοῦφα as Adv., *lightly.* 2. metaph. *easy, light:—empty, vain, idle.* Hence

κούφως, Adv. *lightly:* Comp. κουφότερον, *more lightly, with lighter heart:* Sup. κουφότατα, *most lightly.*

ΚΟ'ΦΙΝΟΣ, ὁ, *a basket.*

κοχλίας, ου, ὁ, (κόχλος) *a snail with a spiral shell*, Lat. *cochlea.* II. *anything twisted spirally, a screw: a spiral stair.*

κοχλίον, τό, Dim. of κόχλος, *a small snail.*

ΚΟ'ΧΛΟΣ, ου, ὁ, *a shell-fish with a spiral shell: the shell itself.* sometimes used as a trumpet, like Lat *concha.*

κοχῠδέω, Ion. impf. κοχύδεσκε:—*to stream forth copiously.* (Reduplicated from χέω, χύδην.)

ΚΟΧΩ'ΝΗ, ἡ, dual κοχώνā, *the hams.*

κόψατο, Ep. 3 sing. aor. 1 med. of **κόπτω.**

κόψῐχος, ὁ, = κόσσυφος, *a blackbird.*

Κόωνδε, Adv. (Κόως Ep. for Κῶς) *to Cos.*

κράατος, κράατι, κράατα, lengthd. forms of κρᾶτος, κρᾶτι, κρᾶτα, gen., dat., acc. of κράς = κάρα, *a head.*

κράββᾰτος, ὁ, *a couch*, Lat. *grăbātus.* (Maced. word.)

κρᾱγόν. Adv. (κράζω) *with loud cries.*

κρᾰδαίνω, (κραδάω) *to swing, brandish, shake:*—Pass. *to vibrate, quiver.*

ΚΡΑ'ΔΑ'Ω, *to brandish, shake.*

κράδη, ἡ, (κραδάω) *the light quivering spray at the end of a branch:* generally, *a branch*, esp. *of a fig-tree:* hence *a fig-tree.* [ᾰ]

κρᾰδία, ἡ, Dor. for **κραδίη, καρδία.**

κραδίη, ἡ, Ion. and Ep. for **καρδία.**

ΚΡΑ'ΖΩ: fut. κράξω, but Att. in paullo-post form κεκράξομαι: aor. 1 ἔκραξα: aor. 2 ἔκρᾰγον: pf with pres. sense κέκρᾱγα, 1 pl. contr. κέκραγμεν. imperat. κέκραχθι, part. κεκρᾱγώς, inf. κεκρᾱγέναι:—*to croak*, properly of the raven: generally, *to scream, screech, cry:* hence c. acc. *to call out* or *clamour for* a thing.

κρᾱθείς, aor. 1 part. pass. of κεράννυμι.

ΚΡΑΙ'ΝΩ, fut. κρᾰνῶ: aor. 1 ἔκρᾱνα Ep. ἔκρηνα:—Pass., fut. κρανθήσομαι, but also Ep. fut. inf. in pass. sense κρανέεσθαι: aor. 1 ἐκράνθην: Homer mostly uses the Ep. form κραιαίνω, 3 sing. impf. ἐκραίαινεν: aor. 1 imperat. κρήηνον κρηήνατε, inf. κρηῆναι: 3 sing. pf. pass. κεκράανται, and plqpf. κεκράαντο:—*to accomplish, bring to pass, fulfil, execute:*—Pass. *to be accomplished, brought to pass;* οὔ μοι δοκέει τῇδέ γ' ὁδῷ κρανέεσθαι it seems to me that it *will* not *be accomplished* by this journey; κέκρανται ψῆφος the vote *hath been determined;* also of workmanship, χρυσῷ ἐπὶ χεῖλεα κεκράανται the edges *are finished off* with gold. II. intr. *to have the ruling power:* later c. gen. *to reign over, govern:* c. acc. cognato, κραίνειν σκῆπτρα *to sway* the sceptre. II. intr. also *to come to an end* or *result in* a thing.

ΚΡΑΙΠΑ'ΛΗ [ᾰ], ἡ, *a debauch and its consequences, nausea, sickness, and headache*, Lat. *crapula; ἐκ κραιπάλης* after *the debauch was over.*

κραιπᾰλό-κωμος, ον, (κραιπάλη, κῶμος) *rambling in drunken revelry.*

κραιπνός, ή, όν, (ἁρπ-άζω, like *rapidus* from *rap-io*) *tearing, sweeping, rushing:* cf. καρπάλιμος. 2. *swift, rapid.* 3. metaph., *hasty, hot, impetuous.*

κραιπνό-σῦτος, ον. (κραιπνός, σεύομαι) *swift-rushing.*

κραιπνο-φόρος, ον, (κραιπνός, φέρω) *swift-bearing.*

κρακτικός, ή, όν, (κράζω) *clamorous.*

ΚΡΑ'ΜΒΗ, ή, *cabbage, kail*, Lat. *crambe.*

ΚΡΑ'ΜΒΟΣ, η, ον, *dry, parched, shrivelled.* 2. metaph. *clear, loud.*

κραμβο-φάγος, ον, (κράμβη, φᾰγεῖν) *Cabbage-eater*, name of a frog.

κρᾰνᾱή-πεδος, ον, (κραναός, πέδον) *with stony soil*

κρᾶναι, Dor. pl. of κρήνη.

ΚΡΑ'ΝΑ'Ο'Σ, ή, όν, *hard, rugged, rocky, stony*, of Athens, from its soil, cf. λεπτόγεως: οἱ Κραναοί *the people of Attica.*

κρᾰνέεσθαι, Ep. fut. inf. med. (with pass. sense) of κραίνω.

κράνεια Ion. -είη, ή, (κράνον) *the cornel-tree*, Lat *cornus:* it was used for spear-shafts and bows: hence *a spear.*

κρᾰνέϊνος, η, ον, (κράνον) *made of cornel-wood*, κρανέϊνον ἀκόντιον, cf. Virgil's *spicula cornea.*

κράνα, ή, Dor for κρήνη. [ᾱ]

κρανθῆναι, aor. I inf. pass. of κραίνω.

Κρᾱνιάς, Κρᾱνίς, Dor. for Κρηνιάς, Κρηνίς.

κρᾱνίον, τό, (κάρα) *the upper part of the head, skull.*

ΚΡΑ'ΝΟΝ, τό, *the cornel-tree*, Lat. CORNUS.

κρᾰνοποιέω, f. ήσω, *to make helmets: to talk big and warlike.* From

κρᾰνο-ποιός, όν, (κράνος, ποιέω) *making helmets:* as Subst., κρανοποιός, ὁ, *a helmet-maker.*

κράνος, εος, τό, (κάρα) *a helmet.* [ᾰ]

κράντειρα, ή, fem. of κραντήρ.

κραντήρ, ῆρος, ὁ, (κραίνω) *one that accomplishes, a doer, performer.*

κράντωρ, ορος, ὁ, (κραίνω) *a ruler, sovereign.*

ΚΡΑ'Σ, ὁ, collat. form of κόρα, gen κρᾱτός (which is sometimes fem.), dat κρᾱτί, acc. κρᾶτα: plur., gen. κράτων, dat. κρᾱσί Ep κράτεσφι: in Hom. also a lengthd. gen and dat., κράατος, κράατι, pl nom. κράατα:—*the head:* metaph *a top, peak, height.*

κρᾶσις, εως, ή, (κεράννυμι) *a mixing, compounding, blending.* II. *the temperature* of the air, *climate*, Lat. *temperies* III. in Gramm., *crasis*, when the consecutive vowels of two words melt into one, e. g. τοὔνομα for τὸ ὄνομα, ἀνήρ for ὁ ἀνήρ.

ΚΡΑ'ΣΠΕΔΟΝ, τό, *the edge, border, margin, hem* of a thing. Hence

κρασπεδόω, f. ώσω, *to surround with a border* or *fringe.*

κράσσων, ον, Dor. for κρείσσων, κρείσσων.

κρᾶτα, τό, indecl., = κάρα:—but also κρᾶτα, τόν, acc of κράς.

κρᾱτα-βόλος, ον, (κραταιός, βάλλω) *hurled with violence*

κρᾰται-γύᾰλος, ον, (κραταιός, γύαλον) *with strong back and breast piece, strongly arched*, of a corslet

κρᾰταιΐς, ή, = κράτος, only of the stone of Sisyphus, τότ' ἀποστρέψασκε κραταιΐς αὖτις then did *mighty force* turn it back again. II. Κρᾰταιΐς, as pr. n. *Crataeïs, the mighty one*, name of the mother of the sea-monster Scylla

κρᾰταί-λεως, ων. gen. ω, (κραταιός, λᾶς) *stony, rocky, rugged.*

κρᾰταιός, ά, όν, (κράτος) poët. for κρατερός, *mighty, strong, resistless.*

κρᾰταιόω, f. ώσω, later form for κρατύνω.

κρᾰταί-πεδος, ον, (κραταιός, πέδον) *with hard ground* or *soil.*

κρᾰταί-πους, ὁ, ή, -πουν, τό, gen. -ποδος: also **καρταίπους**: (κραταιός, πούς): *stout-footed sure-footed.*

κρᾰταί-ρῑνος, ον, (κραταιός, ῥινός) *strong-shelled*

κρᾰτερ-αίχμης, ου, ὁ, also καρτ-, (κρατερός, αἰχμή) *mighty with the spear, warlike.*

κρᾰτερός poët. **καρτερός**, ά, όν, (κράτος, κρατέω) *strong, stout, mighty, valiant;* but also *hard-hearted, cruel, harsh, rough:* so, χῶρος κρατερός *hard, solid*, ground. 2. also *strong, violent.*

κρᾰτερό-φρων, ον, gen. ονος, (κρατερός, φρήν) *stout-hearted, dauntless.*

κρᾰτερό-χειρ, χειρος. ὁ. ή, (κρατερός, χείρ) *stout of hand*

κρᾰτερ-ῶνυξ, ῠχος, ὁ, ή, (κρατερός, ὄνυξ) *strong-hoofed, solid-hoofed:* of lions, *with strong claws.*

κρατερῶς, Adv. of κρατερός, *strongly, stoutly: sternly, roughly*

κράτεσφι, Ep. dat. pl. of κράς. [ᾰ]

ΚΡΑ'ΤΕΥΤΑΙ', ῶν, οἱ, *the forked stand* or *frame on which a spit turns.*

κρᾰτέω. f. ήσω: (κράτος):—*to be strong and mighty: to rule, hold sway:* c. dat. *to rule among*, ἀνδράσι καὶ θεοῖσι κρατεῖν. 2. c. gen. *to lay hold of, become master of, to be lord of, ruler over;* also *to conquer, subdue:* absol. *to prevail, get the upper hand;* of reports, *to prevail, become current.* II. c. acc. pers. *to prevail against, vanquish, master:* also *to surpass, excel* III. c. acc. rei, *to hold fast, seize, secure.* IV. *to order, command:*—Pass. *to obey.*

κρατήρ Ion. **κρητήρ**, ῆρος, ὁ, (κεράννυμι) *a mixing vessel, a bowl, in which the wine was mixed with water*, and from which the cups were filled; κρητῆρα κεράσασθαι to mix *a bowl.* II. *any hollow, a basin* in a rock: *the mouth* of a volcano, *crater.*

κρᾰτησί-μᾰχος, ον, (κρατέω, μάχη) *victorious in the fight.*

κρᾰτησί-πους, ο, ἡ, πουν, το, gen. ποδος, (κρατέω, πούς) *victorious in the foot-race.*

κρᾰτήσ-ιππος, ον, (κρατέω, ἵππος) *victorious in the horse-race.*

κρᾱτί, dat. sing. of κράς.

κρᾰτιστεύω, f. σω, (κράτιστος) *to be best, most excellent, supreme: to excel.*

κράτιστος Ep. **κάρτιστος**, η, ον, and as irreg. Sup. of ἀγαθός, being formed from κράτος, as κέδιστος from κέρδος:—*strongest, mightiest, fiercest.* 2. *best, most excellent.*—The Comp. in use is κρείσσων. [ᾰ]

ΚΡΑ'ΤΟΣ poët. **κάρτος**, εος, τό, *strength, might, prowess: force, violence;* πόλιν ἑλεῖν κατὰ κράτος to take a city *by open force, by storm;* also, κατὰ κράτος with *all one's might;* so also, ἀνὰ κράτος up to *one's full power,* with *all one's might.* II. generally, *might, power, rule, sway, dominion:* c. gen. *power over.* III. *mastery, victory.*

κρᾱτός, gen. of κράς.

κρᾰτύνω Ep. **καρτύνω**: f. ῠνῶ: (κράτος):—*to strengthen, confirm:* Med. *to strengthen for oneself,* ἐκαρτύναντο φάλαγγας *they strengthened their* ranks:—Pass. *to become strong, be strengthened.* 2. *to harden.* II. *to rule, govern,* c. gen. 2. *to become master, get possession of: to conquer.* [ῡ]

κρᾰτύς, masc. Adj., only found in nom., (κράτος) *strong, mighty.* [ῠ]

κραυγάζω, fut. άσω, (κραυγή) *to scream, shriek.*

Κραυνᾰσίδης, ου, ὁ, (κραυγή) *Croaker,* name of a frog.

κραυγή, ἡ, (κράζω) *a crying, screaming, shrieking.*

κρε-άγρα, ὁ, (κρέας, ἀγρέω) *a flesh-hook.*

κρε-αγρίς, ίδος, ἡ, = κρεάγρα.

κρεάδιον, τό, Dim. of κρέας, *a slice of flesh.*

κρεᾱνομέω, f. ήσω, (κρεανόμος) *to distribute flesh, to divide the flesh* of a victim amongst the guests:—Med. *to divide among themselves.* Hence

κρεᾱνομία, ἡ, *a distribution of the flesh of a victim amongst the guests,* Lat. *visceratio.*

κρεᾱ-νόμος, ον, (κρέας, νέμω) *distributing the flesh of victims:* as Subst., κρεανόμος, ὁ, *a carver,* Lat. *dispensator.*

ΚΡΕ'ΑΣ Dor. **κρῆς**, τό; gen. κρέως: plur. κρέᾰ· gen. κρεῶν Ep. κρειῶν; dat. κρέᾰσι Ep. κρέεσσι:—*flesh, a piece of meat: meat.* 2. *a carcase: a body, person.*

κρεη-δόκος, ον, and **κρειο-δόκος**, ον, (κρέας, δέχομαι) *containing flesh.*

κρεῖον, τό, (κρέας) *a meat-tray, dresser.*

κρείουσα, fem. of κρείων, q. v.

κρεισσό-τεκνος, ον, (κρείσσων, τέκνον) *dearer than children.*

κρείσσων, ον, gen. ονος, Att. **κρείττων** Ion. **κρέσσων** Dor. **κάρρων**:—*stronger, mightier: better, braver:* used with εἰμί *sum* and part., as κρείσσων γὰρ ἦσθα μηκέτ' ὢν ἢ ζῶν τυφλὸς thou wert *better* not alive, than living blind. II. *too great for, exceeding;* ὕψος κρεῖσσον ἐκπηδήματος a height *too great for* leaping out; of evil deeds, κρείσσον' ἀγχόνης *too bad for* hanging. III. *superior to master of;* κρείσσων χρημάτων *superior to* bribes. IV. in moral sense, *better, more excellent.* (κρείσσων is used as irreg. Comp. of ἀγαθός, κράτος being the Root, whence also Sup. κράτιστος.)

κρείττων, Att. form of foreg.

ΚΡΕΙ'ΩΝ, όντος, ὁ: fem. **κρειουσα**, ἡ:—*a ruler, lord, master:* a general title of honour, like ἄναξ.

κρειῶν, Ep. for κρεῶν, gen. pl. of κρέας.

κρεκάδια, ων, τά, (κρέκω) *a* kind *of tapestry.*

κρεκτός, ή, όν, *struck so as to sound,* of stringed instruments; *played, sung.* From

ΚΡΕ'ΚΩ, f. ξω: aor. 1 ἔκρεξα:—*to strike, beat: to strike* the web with the shuttle, *to weave.* 2. *to strike* with the plectrum, *to play on* an instrument. 3. generally, *to make any sharp sound, to rustle.*

κρεμάθρα, ἡ, (κρεμάννυμι) *a basket to hang things up in.*

κρέμᾰμαι, shortd. pres. pass. of κρεμάννυμι; subj. κρέμωμαι; opt. κρεμαίμην; inf. κρέμασθαι: impf. ἐκρεμάμην: fut. (in pass. sense) κρεμήσομαι.

κρεμάννῡμι rarely -ύω: fut. κρεμάσω [ᾰ] Att. κρεμῶ, ᾷς, ᾷ, Ep. lengthd. κρεμόω: aor. 1 ἐκρέμᾰσα Ep. κρέμᾰσα:—Med., aor. 1 ἐκρεμᾰσάμην:—Pass., κρεμάννῠμαι: fut. κρεμασθήσομαι: aor. 1 ἐκρεμάσθην:—*to hang, hang up, let hang down: to hang up by* a thing, c. gen.; κρεμάσαι τὴν ἀσπίδα *to hang up* one's shield, i. e. give up war: so in Med., πηδάλιον κρεμάσασθαι *to hang up* one's rudder, i. e. give up the sea II. Pass. *to be hung up* or *suspended, to swing from, hang down from* 2. metaph. *to be in suspense.*

κρεμάσας, aor. 1 part. of κρεμάννυμι.

κρεμασθείς, aor. 1 part. pass. of κρεμάννυμι.

κρεμαστός, ή, όν, (κρεμάννυμι) *hung up, hung, hanging:* c. gen. *hung from* or *on* a thing; κρεμαστὸς αὐχένος *hung by* the neck

κρεμάστρα, ἡ, = κρεμάθρα.

κρεμάω, Root of κρεμάννυμι, *to hang, hang up.*

κρεμβᾰλιάζω, f. άσω, (κρέμβαλα) *to keep time with castanets.* Hence

κρεμβᾰλιαστύς, ύος, ἡ, *a rattling with castanets,* to give the time in dancing.

ΚΡΕ'ΜΒΑ'ΛΑ, τά, *castanets.*

κρεμήσομαι, fut. med. (in pass. sense) of κρέμαμαι.

κρεμόω, Ep. for Att. κρεμῶ, fut. of κρεμάννυμι.

κρέξ, ἡ, gen. κρεκός, Lat. *crex,* (κρέκω) *a bird with a sharp notched bill, a rail.*

κρεό-βοτος, ον, (κρέας, βόσκω) *fed on flesh.*

κρεο-δαίτης, ου, ὁ, (κρέας, δαίω) *the carver at a public meal.*

κρεοκοπέω, Att. for κρεωκοπέω.

κρεο-πώλης, ου, ὁ, (κρέας, πωλέω) *a butcher.*

κρεουργέω, f. ήσω, (κρεουργός) *to cut up meat like a butcher: to butcher.* Hence

κρεουργηδόν, Adv. *like a butcher: in joints* or *pieces:* and

κρεουργία, ἡ, *a cutting up like a butcher, butchering.*

κρε-ουργός, όν, (κρέας, ἔργον) *cutting up meat:* as Subst., κρεουργός, ὁ, *a butcher* or *a carver:*—κρεουργὸν ἦμαρ a day *of feasting.*

κρεο-φάγος, ον, (κρέας, φᾰγεῖν) *eating flesh, carnivorous.*

κρέσσων, ον, gen. ονος, Ion for κρείσσων.

κρέων, οντος, = κρείων.

κρεῶν, gen. pl. of κρέας.

κρήγυος, ον, *good, agreeable.* II. *true, real.*

κρή-δεμνον Dor. **κρά-δεμνον**, τό, (κάρα, δέω) *a sort of head-dress,* like *a veil* or *mantilla with lappets.* II. metaph. in plur. *the battlements* which *crown* the walls. III. *the lid* of a vessel.

κρηῆναι, aor. 1 inf. of κραιαίνω, Ep. for κραίνω.

κρήηνον, aor. 1 imperat. of κραιαίνω, Ep. for κραίνω.

κρῆθεν, Adv. (κρᾶς) *from the head, from above.*

κρημνάς, part. of κρήμνημι.

κρημνάω and **κρήμνημι**, = κρεμάννυμι, *to let down from a height, cast down, hang down:*—Pass. κρήμνᾰμαι, *to hang down, be suspended: to float* or *hover in air.*

κρήμνη, for κρῆμναθι, imperat. of κρήμνημι.

κρημνο-βάτης [ᾰ], ου, ὁ, (κρημνός, βαίνω) *haunter of the steeps.*

κρημνο-ποιός, όν, (κρημνός, ποιέω) *talking precipices, using big rugged words,* of Aeschylus.

κρημνός, ὁ, (κρεμάννυμι) *an overhanging steep, a beetling crag:* also *the steep bank* or *edge* of a river or trench

κρημν-ώδης, ες, (κρημνός, εἶδος) *precipitous, steep.*

κρῆναι, aor. 1 inf. of κραίνω.

κρηναῖος, α, ον, (κρήνη) *of* or *from a spring* or *fountain;* κρηναῖον ὕδωρ *spring water.*

ΚΡΗ′ΝΗ Dor. **κράνα**, ἡ, *a well, spring,* Lat. *fons:* in pl. *water.* II. *a source, fountain-head.* Hence

κρήνηθεν, Adv. *from a well* or *spring;* and

κρήνηνδε, Adv. *to a well* or *spring.*

κρηνιάς, άδος, ἡ, pecul. fem. of κρηναῖος, *of* or *from a well* or *spring:* Dor. **Κρᾱνιάδες**, *Nymphs of a spring:* so too Κρᾱνίδες.

κρηνίς, ῖδος, ἡ, Dim. of κρήνη. [ῐ]

κρῆνον, aor. 1 imperat. of κραίνω.

ΚΡΗΠΙ′Σ, ῖδος, ἡ, *a* kind of *man's boot:* in Theocritus, κρηπῖδες poët. for *booted men.* II. generally, *a groundwork, foundation, basement,* of a temple or altar: metaph., ἡ ἐγκράτεια ἀρετῆς κρηπίς self-command is *the founddtion* of virtue. 2. *the side* of a river *with a coping* to it, *a quay,* Lat. *crepīdo; generally, an edge.* [ῑ]

κρῆς, Dor. for κρέας.

Κρής, ὁ, gen. Κρητός: pl. Κρῆτες, gen. Κρητῶν:—*a Cretan:* fem. **Κρῆσσα.** Hence

Κρήσιος, α, ον, *Cretan.*

κρῆσαι, Ep. for κεράσαι, aor. 1 inf. of κεράννυμι.

κρησφύγετον, τό, *a place of refuge* or *security, retreat, resort.*

Κρήτη, ἡ, *the island Crete,* now *Candia.* Hence

Κρήτηθεν, Adv *from Crete;* and

Κρήτηνδε, Adv. *to Crete.*

κρητήρ, Ep. for κρατήρ: dat. pl. κρητῆρσι.

Κρητίζω, f. σω, (Κρής) *to lie like a Cretan.*

Κρητικός, ή, όν, (Κρήτη) *Cretan, of the island of Crete:*—Adv. -κῶς, *in Cretan fashion.* II. κρητικὸν (sub. ἱμάτιον), τό, a garment *of Cretan fashion.* III. κρητικὸς (sub ποὺς), ὁ, a metrical foot, e. g. Ἀντιφῶν [—⏑—] called also amphimacer (ἀμφίμακρος).

κρητισμός, οῦ, ὁ, (Κρητίζω) *lying.*

κρῖ, τό, Ep. shorter form for κριθή, *barley.*

κρῑβᾰνίτης [ῑ], ου, ὁ, *baked under a pot* or *pan:*—κριβανίτης (sub. ἄρτος), ὁ, *a loaf* so *baked.* From

κρίβᾰνος, ὁ, Att. for κλίβανος, *a covered earthen vessel, a pot, pan* or *pipkin,* in which bread was baked by putting hot embers round it. [ῑ] Hence

κρῑβᾰνωτός, ή, όν, = κριβανίτης.

ΚΡΙ′ΖΩ, f. ξω: aor. 2 ἔκρῐκον: pf. κέκρῑγα:—*to creak,* Lat. *stridēre: to screech, squeak.* (Formed from the sound.)

κρῑηδόν, Adv. (κριός) *like a ram.*

κρῑθαία, ἡ, (κριθή) *a mess of barley pottage.*

κρῑθάω, f. ήσω, (κριθή) *to be over-fed with barley, to be restive.*

κρῐθείς, aor. 1 pass. part. of κρίνω.

κρίθεν, Aeol. 3 pl. aor. 1 pass. of κρίνω.

ΚΡΙΘΗ′, ἡ, and in plur. κριθαί, αἱ, *barley;* οἶνος ἐκ κριθέων (Ion. gen. pl.) wine made from *barley,* i. e. *a* kind of *beer:* also *roasted barley.* [ῑ]

κρῐθῆναι, aor. 1 inf. pass. of κρίνω.

κρῑθίᾱσις, εως, ἡ, (κριθή) *a disease of horses,* caused by feeding them *with barley,* Lat. *hordeatio.*

κριθίζω, f. σω, (κριθή) *ta feed with barley.*

κρίθῐνος, η, ον, (κριθή) *made of barley.*

κρῑθο-τράγος, ον, (κριθή, τρᾰγεῖν) *barley-eating.*

κρῐθῶ, aor. 1 subj. pass. of κρίνω.

κρίκε, Ep. for ἔκρῐκε, 3 sing. aor. 2 of κρίζω.

κρίκος, ὁ, = κίρκος, *a ring, circle:* also *an eyelet-hole, a deadeye,* in the corner of a sail.

κρῖμα, not **κρίμα**, ατος, τό, (κρίνω) *a judgment, sentence.* 2. *a matter for judgment: an accusation, charge,* Lat. *crimen.*

κρίμνον, τό, (κρῖ, κριθή) *coarse barley-meal.*

κριμν-ώδης, ες, (κρίμνον, εἶδος) *like coarse meal;* κατανίφει κριμνώδη it snows *thick as meal.*

κρίνας, aor. 1 part. of κρίνω.

ΚΡΙ′ΝΟΝ, τό, *a lily:* irreg. pl. κρίνεα, dat. κρίνεσι, as if from a nom. κρίνος, εος, τό. [ῐ]

ΚΡΙ′ΝΩ [ῑ]: fut. κρῐνῶ: aor. 1 ἔκρῑνα: pf. κέκρῐκα:—Med., fut. κρινοῦμαι: aor. 1 ἐκρῑνάμην:—Pass., fut. κρῐθήσομαι: aor. 1 ἐκρίθην [ῐ], older ἐκρίνθην, whence part. κρινθείς: pf. κέκρῐμαι, inf. κεκρίσθαι:—the Lat. *CERNO, to separate, divide, put apart:* hence *to pick out, choose;* and in Med. *to pick out* *for oneself, choose, prefer*:—Pass. *to be chosen* or *distinguished.* 2. *to decide* a contest or dispute, e. g. for a prize; σκολιὰς θέμιστας κρίνειν *to judge* crooked judgments. i. e. to judge unjustly:—Pass. and Med. κρίνομαι, *to be at variance, contend, fight: to dispute, quarrel.* 3. *to judge of, estimate*: hence *to expound, explain*: c. inf. *to judge, pronounce that* a thing is. III. *to question, examine, bring to trial, accuse, arraign*: — Pass. *to be brought to trial, tried.* 2. *to pass sentence upon, to condemn*:—Pass. *to be judged, condemned.*

κριξός, ὁ, Dor. for κρισσός, κιρσός.

κρῖο-βόλος, ον, (κριός, βάλλω) *ram-slaying.*

κρῖο-πρόσωπος, ον, (κριός, πρόσωπον) *ram-faced.*

ΚΡΙΟ΄Σ, ὁ, *a ram*, Lat. *aries.* 2. *a battering-ram*, because it butted like a ram; generally finished in the shape of *a ram's head.*

Κρῖσα, ης, ἡ, *Crisa* or *Crissa*, a city in Phocis, not far from Delphi:—Adj. **Κρισαῖος**, α, ον, *Crissaean.*

κρίσις [ῐ], εως, ἡ, (κρίνω) *a separating, putting apart*: hence *a picking out, choosing.* 2. *a deciding, determining; a judgment, sentence.* 3. *a trial.* II. *a dispute, quarrel.* III. *the event, issue, decision.*

κρῑτήριον, τό, (κριτής) *a means for judging* or *trying, a standard, test.* 2. *a court of judgment, tribunal.*

κρῐτής, οῦ, ὁ, (κρίνω) *a discerner, judge, arbiter*: at Athens of *the judges in the poetic contests.* 2. κριτὴς ἐνυπνίων, *an interpreter, expounder* of dreams. Hence

κρῐτικός, ή, όν, *able to discern and decide, critical.*

κρῐτός, ή, όν, verb. Adj. of κρίνω, *picked out, chosen: choice, excellent.*

κροαίνω, Ep. for κρούω, of a horse, *to stamp* or *strike with the hoof.*

κρόκα, heterocl. acc. sing. of κρόκη.

κροκάλη, ἡ, = κρόκη II: in pl. *the sea-shore, beach, strand.* [ᾰ]

κρόκεος, ον, (κρόκος) *saffron-coloured.*

κρόκες, αἱ heterocl. nom. pl. of κρόκη.

κρόκη, ἡ, with heterocl. acc. κρόκα and nom. pl. κρόκες, as if from a nom. κρόξ: (κρέκω):—*the woof* or *weft*, Lat. *subtemen*, opp. to στήμων the warp: generally, *a thread*: in pl. *wool.* II. *a rounded stone* or *pebble.*

κροκήϊος, η, ον, poët. for κρόκεος, *saffron-coloured.*

κροκό-βαπτος, ον, (κρόκος, βάπτω) *saffron-dyed.*

κροκο-βᾰφής, ές, (κρόκος, βαφῆναι) *crocus-dyed*, of *crocus-hue*, i. e. *purple, red*, not *yellow* (see κρόκος).

κροκόδειλος, ὁ, *a lizard.* II. name given by the Ionians to *the crocodile* or *alligator* of the Nile: in full, ὁ κροκόδειλος ὁ ποτάμιος, called by the natives χάμψα.

κροκόεις, εσσα, εν, (κρόκος) *saffron-coloured.* II. as Subst., κροκόεις (sub. πέπλος) ὁ, *a robe of saffron.*

κροκό-πεπλος, ον, (κρόκος, πέπλος) *saffron-robed.*

ΚΡΟ΄ΚΟΣ, ου, ὁ, *the purple crocus.* II. *saffron* (which is made from its stamens).

κροκύς [ῠ], ύδος, ἡ, (κρόκη) *the flock, nap, pile* of cloth: generally, *a piece* or *flock of wool*

κροκωτίδιον, τό, Dim. of κροκωτός, *a short, saffron robe.*

κροκωτός, ή, όν, (κροκόω) *saffron-dyed* or *coloured.* II. as Subst., κροκωτός (sub. πέπλος), ὁ, *a saffron-coloured robe for state occasions*, as for the festivals of Bacchus.

κροκωτοφορέω, f. ήσω, *to wear a saffron robe.* From

κροκωτο-φόρος, ον, (κροκωτός, φέρω) *wearing a saffron robe.*

κρομμῠ-οξῠ-ρεγμία, ἡ, (κρόμμυον, ὄξος, ἐρευγμός) *a belch of onions and vinegar.*

ΚΡΟ΄ΜΜΥΟΝ or κρόμμυον, τό, *an onion.*

Κρονίδης, ου, ὁ, patronym. from Κρόνος, *son of Cronos* or *Saturn*, i. e. Zeus: cf. Κρονίων, Κρόνος. [ῐ]

Κρονικός, ή, όν, (Κρόνος) *old-fashioned, antiquated, out of date*, cf. sq.

Κρόνιος, α, ον, (Κρόνος) *of Cronos* or *Saturn*; τὰ Κρόνια (sub. ἱερά), τά, his festival celebrated at Athens on the twelfth of the month Hecatombaeon; Κρονίων ὄζειν to smell of *old times*, to smack of *antiquity.*

Κρόν-ιππος, ὁ, (Κρόνος, ἵππος) *an old fool, old dotard.*

Κρονίων, ὁ, gen. ίονος [ῑ], but also Κρονίωνος, patronym. from Κρόνος, *son of Cronos* or *Saturn, Zeus.*

Κρόνος, ὁ, *Cronos*, Lat. *Saturnus*, son of Uranos and Gaia, husband of Rhea, father of Zeus: his time was the golden age. II. a name given at Athens to *a superannuated dotard.*

ΚΡΟ΄ΣΣΑΙ, ῶν, αἱ, *battlements* on walls. 2. *the courses* or *steps* in which the Pyramids rose from bottom to top.

κροτᾰλίζω, f. ίσω, (κρόταλον) *to rattle castanets*: generally, *to make to rattle.*

κρότᾰλον, τό, (κροτέω) *a rattle, castanet* II. metaph. *a rattling, chattering fellow.*

κρότᾰφος, ὁ, (κροτέω) *the side of the forehead*: in pl. *the temples*, Lat. *tempora*: also *the sides of the face.* 2. metaph. *the brow* of a mountain.

κροτέω, fut. ήσω: (κρότος):—*to make to rattle* or *clash.* II. *to knock, beat, strike*: of a smith, *to hammer* or *weld together, forge*:—Pass. *to be worked with the hammer, welded, forged*; εὐθὺς τὸ πρᾶγμα κροτείσθω, *let* the matter *be struck* at once, i. e. 'strike while the iron is hot.' 2. *to strike together, clap* the hands, in token of applause: absol. *to clap, to applaud.* III. intr. in Act. *to rattle, make a clatter.* Hence

κροτησμός, ὁ, *a striking, beating.*

κροτητός, ή, όν, verb. Adj. of κροτέω, *stricken, smitten, sounding with blows.* 2. *rattled* or *whirled rattling along.* 3. *played with the plectrum.*

κρότος, ου, ὁ, (κρούω) *the sound of striking; κρότος χειρῶν a clapping* of hands: generally, *a loud rattling* or *noise.*

κροτών, ῶνος, ὁ, *a tick*, Lat. *ricinus.* II. the

palma Christi or *ricinus*, which bears the castor-oil berry.

κροῦμα, ατος, τό, (κρούω) *a beat, stroke.* 2. *a sound produced by striking a string, a note.*

κρούνισμα, ατος, τό, *a gushing* or *stream.* From

ΚΡΟΥΝΟΣ, οῦ, ὁ, *a spring, well-head:* in pl. *streams:* metaph. *a torrent of words.* Hence

κρουνο-χυτρο-λήραιος, ὁ, (κρουνός, χύτρα, λῆρος) *a pourer forth of weak, washy twaddle.*

κρουσι-δημέω, f. ήσω, (κρούω, δῆμος) *to play upon the people, impose* upon them.

κροῦσις, εως, ἡ, (κρούω) *a striking: a playing on a stringed instrument.*

κρουστέον, verb. Adj. of κρούω, *one must knock at.*

κρουστικός, ή, όν, *fit for striking* II. metaph. *striking, astonishing, forcible;* τὸ κρουστικόν *striking eloquence.* From

ΚΡΟΥΏ, f. σω: aor. 1 ἔκρουσα:—Pass., pf. κέκρουμαι and -σμαι:—*to knock, strike, smite;* κρούειν χεῖρας *to clap* the hands; κρούειν πόδα, *to strike* the foot against the ground in dancing. 2. *to strike with a plectrum;* generally, *to play* any instrument. 3. κρούειν τὴν θύραν *to knock at* the door. 4. Med. κρούεσθαι -ύμναν *to back* stern foremost; cf. ἀνακρούω.

κρύβδα, Adv. (κρύπτω) *without the knowledge of,* κρύβδα Διός, Lat *clam Jove*

κρύβδην Dor. -δαν, Adv. (κρύπτω) *secretly, covertly:* —also, like κρύβδα, *without the knowledge of*

κρυβῆναι, aor. 2 inf. pass. of κρύπτω.

κρυερός, ά, όν, (κρύος) *icy, chill, chilling.*

κρυμός, ὁ, (κρύος) *icy cold, chill, frost.*

κρυμ-ώδης, ες, (κρυμός, εἶδος) *icy-cold: frozen, icy.*

κρυόεις, εσσα, εν, = κρυερός, *icy-cold, chilling.*

ΚΡΥΌΣ, τό, *icy cold, chill, frost:* metaph. *an inward chill, shudder, horror.*

κρυπτάδιος, α, ον, also ος, ον: (κρύπτω): *secret, hidden, clandestine.*

κρυπτάζω, f. άσω, collateral form of κρύπτω.

κρύπτασκε, 3 sing. Ion. impf. of κρύπτω.

κρυπτεία, ἡ, (κρυπτεύω) *a secret service* or *commission;* at Sparta intrusted to the young men, to season them against fatigue.

κρυπτέον, verb. Adj. of κρύπτω, *one must conceal.*

κρυπτεύω, f. σω, (κρύπτω) *to conceal, hide.* II. *to hide oneself, lie concealed.* III. Pass. κρυπτεύομαι, *to have snares laid for* one.

κρύπτη, ἡ, *a covered place, vault, crypt.* From

κρυπτός, ή, όν, verb. Adj. of κρύπτω, *hidden, secret.*

ΚΡΥΠΤΩ: Ion. impf. κρύπτασκον: fut. κρύψω: aor. 1 ἔκρυψα: pf. κέκρυφα:—Pass., fut. 2 κρυβήσομαι, paullo-p. fut. κεκρύψομαι: aor. 1 ἐκρύφθην: aor. 2 ἐκρύβην [ῠ]: pf. κέκρυμμαι:—*to hide, cover, conceal:*—Pass. *to hide oneself, lie hidden.* II. metaph. *to conceal, keep secret* or *covered over;* with dupl. acc., μή με κρύψῃς τοῦτο do not *hide* this from me.

κρυσταλλίζω, f. ίσω, (κρύσταλλος) *to be like crystal.*

κρυστάλλινος, η, ον, (κρύσταλλος) *of crystal.*

κρυσταλλό-πηκτος, ον, or **κρυσταλλο-πήξ**, ῆγος, ὁ, ἡ, (κρύσταλλος, πήγνυμι) *congealed to ice, frozen.*

κρύσταλλος, ὁ, (κρύος) *clear ice, ice,* Lat. *glacies.* 2. *extreme cold, torpor.* II. ὁ and ἡ, *crystal, rock-crystal.*

κρύφα, Adv. (κρύπτω) *secretly from, without the knowledge of,* like κρύβδα, c. gen. [ῠ]

κρυφαῖος, α, ον, and ος, ον, (κρύπτω) *secret, hidden, covert.* Adv. -ως.

κρυφῇ Dor -φα, Adv. (κρύπτω) *secretly, in secret.*

κρυφηδόν, Adv. = foreg.

κρύφθη, Ep. 3 sing. aor. 1 pass. of κρύπτω.

κρύφιος, α, ον, also ος, ον, (κρύπτω) *secret, hidden, clandestine.* [ῠ]

κρυφός, ὁ, (κρύπτω) *concealment, obscurity.*

κρύφω, late form of κρύπτω.

κρύψαι, aor. 1 inf. of κρύπτω.

κρυψι-μέτωπος, ον, (κρύπτω, μέτωπον) *hiding the forehead.*

κρυψί-νοος, ον, contr. -νους, ουν: (κρύπτω, νόος): *hiding one's thoughts, reserved, dissembling.*

κρύψις, εως, ἡ, (κρύπτω) *a hiding, concealment: the art* or *means of concealing.*

ΚΡΩΒΥΛΟΣ, ὁ, *a roll of hair gathered to a knot on the crown of the head.* II. *the crest* on a helmet. [ῠ]

κρωγμός, ὁ, (κρώζω) *the croaking* or *cawing of a crow.*

ΚΡΩΖΩ, f. κρώξω, *to croak* or *caw like a crow,* Lat. *crocitare.* II. of men, *to croak out.* (Formed from the sound.)

κρῶσσαι, Ion. for κρόσσαι.

κρωσσίον, τό, Dim. of κρωσσός.

ΚΡΩΣΣΟΣ, οῦ, ὁ, *a water-pail, pitcher, jar.* 2. *a cinerary urn.*

κτά, for ἔκτα, Ep. 3 sing. aor. 2 of κτείνω: optat. **κταίην**; inf. **κτάναι**; part. **κτάς**.

κταίνω, Dor. for κτείνω.

κτάμεν, **κτάμεναι**, Ep. aor. 2 inf. of κτείνω. [ᾰ]

κτάμενος aor. 2 part. med. (with pass. sense) of κτείνω.

κτάνε, Ep. 3 sing. aor. 2 of κτείνω. [ᾰ]

κτάνθεν, Aeol. and Ep. 3 pl. aor. 1 pass. of κτείνω.

ΚΤΑΟΜΑΙ Ion. κτέομαι: fut. κτήσομαι: paullo-p. fut. κεκτήσομαι: aor. 1 ἐκτησάμην: pf. κέκτημαι Ion. ἔκτημαι, subj. κέκτωμαι, opt. κεκτήμην or -ῴμην: plqpf. ἐκεκτήμην: Dep.:—*to get for oneself, gain, be in the course of acquiring* or *procuring:* also *to bring upon oneself, incur.* II. in pf. κέκτημαι or ἔκτημαι, and paullo-p. fut. κεκτήσομαι, *to have acquired* or *got,* and so, *to possess, to have* or *hold;* ὁ κεκτημένος *an owner, master:* hence as Subst. c. gen., ὁ ἐμοῦ κεκτημένος my *master;* ἡ ἐμὴ κεκτημένη my *mistress.* III. aor. 1 ἐκτήθην is used in pass. sense, *to be gotten, obtained, acquired.*

κτάσθαι, Ep. aor. 2 inf. med. (with pass. sense) of κτείνω; but, II. κτᾶσθαι, inf. of κτάομαι.

κτέανον, ὁ, (κτάομαι) = κτῆμα: but mostly in pl.

possessions, property; Ep. heterocl. dat. κτεάτεσσι, as if from κτέαρ.

κτεάτειρα, ἡ, fem. of κτεάτηρ, *she that puts one in possession of.* [ᾰ]

κτεάτηρ, ηρος, ὁ, (κτάομαι) *a possessor.*

κτεᾰτίζω, f. ίσω: Ep. aor. 1 κτεάτισσα: (κτεαρ):—*to get, gain, win:* pf. pass. with med. sense, ἐκτεάτισμαι *to get for oneself.* Hen

κτεᾰτιστός, ή, όν, *gotten, won, acquired.*

κτείνω: Ion. impf. κτείνεσκον: f. κτενῶ Ep. κτενέω or κτανέω: aor. 1 ἔκτεινα: aor. 2 ἔκτᾰνον: pf. ἔκτονα:—Pass., aor. 1 ἐκτάνθην: pf. ἔκτᾰμαι:—the following Ep. forms are freq. in Homer, 3 sing. and pl. aor. 2 ἔκτᾰ, ἔκτᾰν (as if from κτῆμι); subj. κτέω, 1 pl. κτέωμεν; inf. κτάμεν, κτάμεναι [ᾰ], for κτάναι; part. κτάς: aor. 2 med. (with pass. sense) ἐκτάμην [ᾰ], inf. κτάσθαι: part. κτάμενος: also Aeol. 3 pl. aor. 1 pass. ἔκτᾰθεν:—*to kill, slay:* of animals, *to slaughter.*

κτείνωμι, Ep. pres. subj. for κτείνω.

ΚΤΕΙ'Σ, ὁ, gen. κτενός, *a comb.* 2. *the weaver's comb,* Lat. *pecten* or *radius.* 3. *a rake, barrow.* 4. *the band, with the fingers spread open.* Hence

κτενέω, Ion. fut. of κτείνω.

κτενίζω, f. ίσω, *to comb: to curry* horses:—Med., κτενίζεσθαι κόμας *to comb one's* hair.

κτενίον, τό, Dim. of κτείς, *a small comb.*

κτενισμός, ὁ, (κτενίζω) *a combing.*

κτέομαι, Ion. for κτάομαι.

κτέρας, ατος, τό, (κτάομαι) = κτέανον, κτῆμα.

κτέρεα, τά, (κτάομαι) properly = κτήματα, *possessions, property:* but mostly of *favourite possessions,* such as pieces of armour, *burnt with the dead:* generally, *funeral honours, obsequies;* see κτερεΐζω, κτερίζω.

κτερεΐζω, f. ΐξω, lengthd. for κτερίζω, *to bury with due honours:*—with acc. of cognate sense, κτέρεα κτερεΐζειν *to pay* funeral honours; see κτερίζ.

κτερίζω: fut. κτεριῶ: aor. 1 ἐκτέρῐσα: (κτέρεα):—*to bury with due honours:*—with acc. of cognate sense, κτέρεα κτερίζειν *to pay* funeral honours, Lat. *justa facere, exequias facere.*

κτεριοῦσι, 3 pl. fut. of κτερίζω.

κτερίσματα, τά, (κτερίζω) = κτερέα.

κτέω, κτέωμεν, 1 sing. and pl. Ep. aor. 2 subj. of κτείνω.

κτηθῆναι, aor. 1 inf. of κτάομαι, used in pass. sense.

κτῆμα, ατος, τό, (κτάομαι) *anything gotten, a piece of property, possession:*—in pl. κτήματα, *possessions, property, goods.* II. *a thing,* like χρῆμα.

κτηνηδόν, Adv. (κτῆνος) *like beasts.*

κτῆνος, εος, τό, (κτάομαι) properly, like κτῆμα, *a piece of property;* chiefly used in pl. κτήνεα, contr. κτήνη, *property in herds* or *flocks, cattle:* rarely in sing. of *a single head of cattle, an ox* or *sheep.*

κτήσαιτο, 3 sing. aor. 1 opt. of κτάομαι.

κτήσιος, α, ον, also ος, ον, (κτῆσις) *of* or *from one's property;* κτήσιον βοτόν a sheep *of one's own flock.* II. *belonging to one's own house, domestic,* Lat. *penetralis;* κτήσιοι θεοί *household* gods.

κτῆσις, εως, ἡ, (κτάομαι) *an acquiring, getting.* II. (from pf. pass. κέκτημαι) *possession:*—as collective, *possessions, property.*

κτητός, ή, όν, verb. Adj. of κτάομαι, *that may be gotten* or *gained.* II. *acquired, held as property, possessed.*

κτήτωρ, ορος, ὁ, (κταομαι) *a possessor, owner.*

κτίδεος, α, ον, (κτίς) = ἰκτίδεος, *of a marten-cat, made of its skin.*

ΚΤΙ'ΖΩ, f. ίσω: aor. 1 ἔκτῐσα Ep. ἔκτισσα, κτίσσα:—Pass., aor. 1 ἐκτίσθην: pf. ἔκτισμαι:—*to people* or *occupy* a country: of a city, *to found, plant, build:*—of a festival, *to institute, establish.* II. *to produce, create.* 2. generally, *to make* or *render* so and so. 3. *to perpetrate* a deed.

ΚΤΙ'ΛΟΣ, ον, *gentle, tame.* II. as Subst., κτίλος, ὁ, *a ram.* [ῐ] Hence

κτῐλόω, f. ώσω: aor. 1 med. ἐκτιλωσάμην:—*to tame, civilise: to win the affections of.*

κτίμενος, η, ον, Ep. part. aor. 2 pass. of κτίζω, *built, founded:* only in compd. ἐΰ-κτίμενος. [ῐ]

κτίς, ἡ, = ἰκτίς, *a marten-cat, marten.*

κτίσις, εως, ἡ, (κτίζω) *a founding, settling, foundation.* 2. *a making, creating: the creation* of the universe. II. *the world* or *universe itself.* 2. *a created thing, creature.* [ῐ]

κτίσμα, ατος, τό, (κτίζω) *a created thing, creature.*

κτίσσα, Ep. aor. 1 of κτίζω.

κτίστης, ου, ὁ, (κτίζω) *a founder, establisher.*

κτιστύς, ύος, ἡ, Ion. for κτίσις.

κτίστωρ, ορος, ὁ, = κτίστης.

κτίτης [ῐ] ου, ὁ, (κτίζω) *a founder, colonist:* generally, *an inhabitant.*

κτῠπέω, f. ήσω: aor. 1 ἐκτύπησα poët. κτύπησα: aor. 2 ἔκτῠπον Ep. κτύπον: (κτύπος): I. intr. *to crash,* as trees falling: *to ring, resound, echo.* II. trans. *to make to resound:*—Pass *to ring, resound.* Hence

κτύπημα, ατος, τό, *a sound, a crashing: a clapping* of the hands. [ῠ]

κτύπος, ου, ὁ, (τύπτω) *any loud noise, the crash* of thunder, *rattling* of chariots, *clash* of arms. [ῠ]

κύᾰθος, ὁ, (κύω) *a cup* for drawing wine out of the κρατήρ or bowl. II. *an Attic measure holding two κόγχαι, about* $\frac{1}{12}$ *of a pint.* III. *a cupping-glass.*

κῠᾰμευτός, ή, όν, (κυαμεύω) *chosen by beans,* i. e. *by lot.*

κῠᾰμεύω, f. σω, (κύαμος) *to choose by beans* or *lot.*

κῠᾰμιαῖος, α, ον, (κύαμος) *of the size of a bean.*

ΚΥ'Α'ΜΟΣ, ὁ, *a bean.* II. *the lot* by which public officers were elected at Athens; ὁ κυάμῳ λαχών an officer chosen *by lot,* = κληρωτός.

κῠᾰμο-τρώξ, ῶγος, ὁ, (κύαμος, τρώγω) *bean-eater.*

κῠᾰμο-φᾰγία, ἡ, (κύαμος, φαγεῖν) *eating of beans, a bean-diet.*

κῠᾰν-αιγίς, ίδος, ἡ, (κύανος, αἰγίς) *with dar..egis.*

κῠᾰν-άμπυξ, ῠκος, ὁ, ἡ, (κύανος, ἄμπυξ) *with dark blue band* or *margin.*

κῠᾰν-αυγής, ές, (κύανος, αὐγή) *dark-gleaming, murky.*

Κῠάνεαι (sc. νῆσοι or πέτραι), αἱ, *the Dark Rocks,* two small islands at the entrance of the Euxine; also, κυάνεαι Συμπληγάδες. [ᾰ]

κῠᾰν-έμβολος, ον, (κυάνεος, ἔμβολον) *with dark blue prow* or *peak.*

κυάνεος, α, ον, (κύανος) *dark blue:* generally, *dark, dusky, murky.* [ῠ]

κῠᾰνο-βλέφᾰρος, ον, (κύανος, βλέφαρον) *dark-eyed.*

κῠᾰνο-ειδής, ές, (κύανος, εἶδος) *dark blue, deep blue.*

κῠανό-θριξ ριχος, ὁ, ἡ, (κύανος, θρίξ) *dark-haired.*

κυᾰνό-πεζα, ἡ, (κύανος, πέζα) *with feet of cyanus.*

κυᾰνό-πεπλος, ον, (κύανος, πέπλος) *dark-veiled.* [κῡ-, metri grat.]

κῠᾰνο-πρώρειος and **κυᾰνό-πρῳρος**, ον, (κύανος, πρῷρα) *with dark blue prow, dark-prowed.*

κῠᾰνό-πτερος, ον, (κύανος, πτερόν) *with dark blue* or *black feathers, dark-winged.*

ΚΥ´ΑΝΟΣ, ου, ὁ, *cyanos, a dark blue substance, used* in the Heroic age to adorn works in metal, perhaps *blue steel.* II. *the blue corn-flower.*

κῠᾰνο-στόλος, ον, (κύανος, στολή) *dark-robed.*

κῠᾰν-όφρυς. υ, gen. υος, (κύανος, ὀφρύς) *dark-browed.*

κῠᾰνο-χαίτης, ου, ὁ, (κύανος, χαίτη) *dark-haired;* of a horse, *dark-maned.*

κῠᾰνό-χροος, ον, -χρως, ωτος, ὁ, ἡ, (κύανος, χρόα, χρώς) *dark-looking, of dark colour* or *complexion.*

κῠᾰν-ώπης, ου, ὁ, (κύανος, ὤψ) *dark-eyed:* fem. **κῠᾰν-ῶπις**, ιδος.

κύβδᾰ, Adv. (κύπτω) *with the head forwards, stooping.*

κῠβεία, ἡ, (κυβεύω) *dice-playing, dicing, gambling:* hence *sleight, trickery, deceit.*

Κῠβέλη, ἡ, *Cybelé,* a Phrygian goddess, worshipped throughout Asia Minor, also at Greece, and later at Rome, under the name of *the Idaean Mother.*

ΚΥ´ΒΕΡΝΑ´Ω, fut. ήσω, Lat. *guberno, to steer:* metaph. *to hold the helm of the state, guide, govern.* Hence

κῠβέρνησις Dor. -ᾱσις, εως, ἡ, *a steering, pilotage:* metaph. *a guiding, governing.*

κῠβερνῆτα, voc. of κυβερνήτης.

κῠβερνήτειρα, ἡ, fem. of κυβερνητήρ.

κῠβερνητήρ, ῆρος, ὁ, rarer form for κυβερνήτης.

κῠβερνήτης, ου, ὁ, (κυβερνάω) *a steersman, helmsman,* Lat. *gubernator:* metaph. *a guide, governor.* Hence

κῠβερνητικός, ή, όν, *skilled in steering* or *governing.*

κῠβεύω, f. σω, (κύβος) *to play at dice: to run a hazard, take the chances.* 2. trans. *to set upon a throw.*

κῠβιστάω, f. ήσω, (κύπτω) *to throw oneself head-foremost, tumble headlong: to plunge headlong into water, dive: to tumble, turn heels over head, turn a summerset,* of mountebanks. Hence

κῠβίστημα, ατος, τό, *a summerset.*

κῠβιστητήρ, ῆρος, ὁ, (κυβιστάω) *a jumper headforemost, a diver: a mountebank, tumbler.*

ΚΥ´ΒΟΣ, ὁ, Lat. *cubus, a solid square, a cube.* II. *a cubical die,* marked on all six sides for the game of dice: the Greeks threw three dice; τρὶς ἓξ βαλεῖν to throw three sixes, i. e. to throw the highest throw, have complete success; κρίνειν τι ἐν κύβοις to decide a thing *by the dice,* i. e. by chances.

κῡδάζω, no fut. in use, (κῦδος), *to revile, abuse:*—Pass. *to be mocked, insulted.* (κυδάζω is used in bad, κυδαίνω in good sense.)

κῡδαίνω, f. ᾰνῶ: aor. 1 ἐκύδᾱνα Ep. κύδηνα: (κῦδος): —*to honour, do honour to, glorify, praise:* also of the outward appearance, *to beautify, adorn: to gladden by marks of honour* II. seldom in bad sense, *to flatter.* See κυδάζω.

κυδάλιμος, ον, (κῦδος) *glorious, renowned, famous;* κυδάλιμον κῆρ *noble* heart.

κῡδάνω [ᾰ], = κυδαίνω, *to honour, hold in honour.* II. intr. = κυδιάω, *to vaunt aloud, boast.*

κυδῆναι, aor. 1 inf. of κυδαίνω.

κύδηνεν, Ep. 3 sing. aor. 1 of κυδαίνω.

κῠδήεις, εσσα, εν, (κῦδος) *glorious, noble.*

κῡδι-άνειρα, ἡ, (κῦδος, ἀνήρ) fem. Adj. like ἀντιάνειρα, as if from a masc. in -άνωρ, *man-ennobling, bringing glory to men.*

κῡδῐάω, Ep. part. κυδιόων, no fut. in use: (κῦδος): —*to vaunt* or *pride oneself,* Lat. *gloriari:* hence *to exult, rejoice.*

κύδῐμος, ον, κυδάλιμος.

κυδιόων, Ep. part. of κυδιάω.

κύδιστος, η, ον, Sup. of κυδρός (formed from κῦδος, as αἴσχιστος from αἶσχος), *most glorious, most honoured, noblest: the greatest.*

κῡδίων [ῐ], ον, gen. ονος, Comp. of κυδρός (see κύδιστος), *more glorious, nobler:* generally, *better.*

κυδνός, ή, όν, = κυδρός.

κῠδοιδοπάω, f. ήσω, (κυδοιμός) *to make a hubbub* or *uproar.*

κῠδοιμέω, fut. ήσω, (κυδοιμός) *to make an uproar, spread confusion and alarm.* II. trans. *to drive in confusion.*

ΚΥΔΟΙΜΟ´Σ, ὁ, *uproar, confusion, tumult, hubbub.*

ΚΥ´ΔΟΣ, εος, τό, *glory, fame, renown,* esp. *in war:* κῦδος ἀρέσθαι to win *glory;* of a hero, μέγα κῦδος Ἀχαιῶν the great *glory* or *pride* of the Achaeans, like Lat. *decus.*

κυδρός, ά, όν, (κῦδος) *glorious, illustrious, noble:* of a horse, *proud, stately.*

Κύδων or **Κῠδωνία**, ἡ, *Cydonia,* a city of Crete

Κῠδωνιάω, *to swell like a quince.* From

Κῠδώνιος, α, ον, (Κύδων) *Cydonian,* i. e. *Cretan;* μῆλον Κυδώνιον the *quince.* II. metaph. *swelling like a quince, round and plump.*

κῠέω, older form for κύω, impf. ἐκύουν: fut. κυήσω: aor. 1 ἐκύησα: I. trans. *to bear in the womb, to be pregnant of,* Lat. *gestare.* II. intr. *to be pregnant, to conceive.*

κύθε, Ep. for ἔκυθε, 3 sing. aor. 2 of κεύθω.

Κῦθέρεια, ἡ, *Cytherea*, surname of Venus, from the city Κύθηρα in Crete, or from the Island Κύθηρα.

Κύθηρα, ων, τά, *Cythera*, an island on the south of Laconia, now *Cerigo*.

Κυθηρο-δίκης, ου, ὁ, (Κύθηρα, δίκη) *a Spartan magistrate sent annually to govern the island of Cythera.*

Κῦθηρόθεν, Adv. (Κύθηρα) *from Cythera.*

κύθρα, -θρινος, -θρος, Ion. for χύτρ-.

κυΐσκω, only used in pres. (κύω, κυέω) *to impregnate*:—Pass. *to become pregnant, conceive.*

κυκᾰνάω, collat. form of κυκάω, *to confound.*

ΚΥ'ΚΑ'Ω, f. ήσω, *to mix up, beat up and mix.* II. like Lat. *miscere, to stir up, mix together: to throw into confusion, confound*:—Pass. *to be confounded, panic-stricken:* also of the mind, *to be disquieted, agitated.*

κῠκεών, ῶνος, ὁ: acc. κυκεῶνα, shortd. Ep. κυκεῶ and κυκειῶ: (κυκάω):—*a mixture, a mixed drink, refreshing draught, tankard,* compounded of barley-meal, grated cheese and wine.

κῠκήθησαν, 3 pl. aor. 1 pass. of κυκάω.

κύκηθρον, τό, (κυκάω) *a ladle for stirring:* metaph. *a turbulent fellow, agitator.* [ῠ]

κῠκησί-τεφρος, ον, (κυκάω, τέφρα) *mixed up with ashes.*

κυκλάμῑνος, ἡ, *cyclamen, sow-bread,* a bulbous plant, with a fragrant flower used for garlands.

κυκλάς, άδος, ἡ, (κύκλος) *encircling:* αἱ Κυκλάδες (sub. νῆσοι), *the Cyclades,* islands in the Aegaean sea, which *encircle* Delos. II. of Time, *circling, revolving.*

κυκλέω, f. ήσω, (κύκλος) *to move* a thing *round and round, wheel along;* πόδα κυκλεῖν *to walk round and round*:—Pass. *to surround, encircle.* II. intr. *to revolve, come round and round.*

κυκλιάς, άδος, ἡ, (κύκλος) fem. Adj. *round, circular.*

κυκλικός, ή, όν, (κύκλος) *circular.* II. those Epic poets were called οἱ Κυκλικοί, whose writings collectively formed a *cycle* or *series* of heroic legends down to the death of Ulysses.

κυκλιο-δῑδάσκᾰλος, ὁ, (κύκλιος, διδάσκω) *a teacher of the cyclic chorus, a dithyrambic poet.*

κύκλιος, α, ον, also ος, ον, (κύκλος) *round, circular:* neut τὸ κύκλιον, as Subst. *a circle.* II. κύκλιοι χοροί, οἱ, *circular* or *cyclic choruses, dancing in a ring round* the altar of the god; chiefly appropriated to those of Bacchus, *dithyrambic choruses;* hence, κύκλια μέλη *dithyrambs.*

Κυκλοβορέω, f. ήσω, *to roar like the torrent of Cycloborus.*

Κυκλο-βόρος, ὁ, (κύκλος, βιβρώσκω) *a mountain-torrent* in Attica.

κυκλο-δίωκτος, ον (κύκλος, διώκω) *driven round in a circle.* [ῐ]

κυκλόεις, εσσα, εν, (poët. for κυκλικός) *circular.*

κυκλόθεν, Adv. (κύκλος) *in a circle all around.*

κυκλο-μόλιβδος, ὁ, (κύκλος, μόλιβδος) *a round lead-pencil.*

κυκλο-ποιέω, f. ήσω, (κύκλος, ποιέω) *to make into a circle, form like a circle.*

ΚΥ'ΚΛΟΣ, ου, ὁ, also with irreg. pl. κύκλα, *a ring, round, circle:* κύκλῳ as Adv. *in a circle, round about:* also like a Prep., c. acc., κύκλῳ σῆμα *round about* the monument; and c. gen., κύκλῳ τοῦ στρατοπέδου. II. *any circular body:* as, 1. *a wheel.* 2. *a place of assembly:* also like Lat. *corona, a crowd of people standing round, a ring* or *circle of people* 3. *the vault* of the sky: *the moon's disk.* 4. *the circle* or *walls surrounding a* city, esp. of Athens. 5. *a shield.* 6. in pl. *the balls of the eye.* III. *any circular motion, orbit* or *revolution.*

κυκλόσε, Adv. (κύκλος) *in* or *into a circle, around.*

κυκλο-σοβέω, f. ήσω, (κύκλος, σοβέω) *to drive round in a circle, whirl round.*

κυκλο-τερής, ές, (κύκλος, τείρω) made *round by rubbing* or *turning, circular;* κυκλοτερὲς τόξον ἔτεινεν he bent the bow *into a circle.*

κυκλόω, f. ώσω, (κύκλος) *to encircle, surround;* but in this sense mostly in Med. II. *to drive round and round whirl round.* III. *to form into a circle*:—Pass. *to form a circle, be bent round;* also of a fleet *wheeling into a crescent* shape.

κύκλωμα, ατος, τό, (κυκλόω) *anything made into a circle,* as *a wheel.* 2. βυσσότονον κύκλωμα *a circle* with hide stretched over it, i. e. *a drum.*

Κυκλώπειος, α, ον, (Κύκλωψ) *Cyclopean, of* or *befitting the Cyclopes,* commonly used of the ancient architecture attributed to them (also called Πελασγικός).

Κυκλωπικός, ή, όν, *of* or *like the Cyclops.* Adv. -κῶς.

Κυκλώπιον, τό, Dim. of Κύκλωψ.

Κυκλώπιος, α, ον, = Κυκλώπειος:—pecul. fem. Κυκλωπίς, ίδος.

κύκλωσις, εως, ἡ, (κυκλόω) *a surrounding, enclosing.*

κυκλωτός, ή, όν, (κυκλόω) *rounded, round.*

Κύκλωψ, ωπος, ὁ, (κύκλος, ὤψ) *a Cyclops,* i.e. *Round-eye;* as Hesiod says. Κύκλωπες δ' ὄνομ' ἦσαν ἐπώνυμον, οὕνεκ' ἄρα σφέων κυκλοτερὴς ὀφθαλμὸς εἷς ἐνέκειτο μετώπῳ:—in sing. of *Polyphemus;* but Hesiod mentions three Cyclopes, *Brontes, Steropes,* and *Arges,* who forged the thunderbolts for Zeus.

κύκνειος, α, ον, (κύκνος) *of* or *like a swan.*

κυκνό-μορφος, ον, (κύκνος, μορφή) *swan-shaped.*

ΚΥ'ΚΝΟΣ, ὁ, *a swan,* Lat. *cycnus.* II. metaph. from the swan's dying song, *a poet.*

κύκν-οψις, εως, ὁ, ἡ, (κύκνος, ὄψις) *like a swan.*

ΚΥ'ΛΑ, ων, τά, *the parts under the eyes.*

κῠλινδέω, f. ήσω, late form of κυλίνδω. Hence

κῠλινδήθρα, ἡ, = ἀλινδήθρα: and

κυλίνδησις, εως, ἡ, *a rolling, wallowing.* *ercise, practice.*

ΚΥ'ΛΙ'ΝΔΩ: fut. κυλίσω [ῑ]: aor. 1 ἐκύλῖσα, inf. κυλῖσαι: aor. 1 pass. ἐκυλίσθην:—older form of κυλινδέω, *to roll, roll on* or *along.* II. Pass. κυλίνδομαι, *to be rolled* or *roll along, to roll* or *toss,* like a ship at sea: *to roll* or *wallow* in the dirt. 2. *to be circulated, be much talked of, like* Lat. *jactari*. 3. *to be employed* on a thing, like Lat. *versari*.

ΚΥ'ΛΙΞ [ŭ], ῐκος, ἡ, *a cup, drinking-cup.*

κυλίσθη, 3 sing. Ep. aor. 1 pass. of *κυλίω*.

κύλισμα, ατος, τό, (*κυλίνδω*) *a roll:* also *a place to roll in.* [ŭ]

κῠλίχνη, ἡ, (*κύλιξ*) *a small cup.*

κῠλίχνιον, τό, *a little cup* or *box.*

κῠλίω [ῑ], late form for *κυλίνδω*.

κύλλαστις Ion. **κύλληστις**, ιος, ὁ, *Egyptian bread made from ὀλύρα.*

κυλλή, ἡ, see *κυλλός*.

Κυλλήνη, ἡ, *Cyllené, a mountain in Arcadia:* whence Hermes was called **Κυλλήνιος**, ὁ.

Κυλλο-ποδίων [ῐ], ονος, ὁ, (*κυλλός, πούς*) *maimed of foot, halting,* Ep. name of Vulcan.

κυλλός, ή, όν, *crooked, crippled, halt.* 2. *κυλλὴ χείρ* is *the hand with the fingers bent to make a hollow for alms; ἔμβαλε κυλλῇ* (sub. *χειρί*) put it into *the hollow of the hand.*

κῠλ-οιδιάω, (*κύλα, οἰδάω*) *to have a swelling below the eye,* from blows or from sleepless nights.

κῦμα, ατος, τό, (*κύω*) *anything swoln, the swell* of the sea, *a wave, billow, surge:* collectively, *ὡς τὸ κῦμα ἐστρωτο* when *the waves* abated. II. like *κύημα, the foetus in the womb, embryo.*

κῡμαίνω, f. ἄνῶ, (*κῦμα*) *to swell* or *rise in waves, surge, seethe:* so also, metaph., of passion. Hence

κῡμᾰτίας, ου, ὁ, Ion. *ίης*, (*κῦμα*) *surging, billowy.* 2. act. *causing waves, stormy.*

κῡμᾰτο-ᾱγής, ές, (*κῦμα, ἄγνυμι*) *breaking like waves, stormy.*

κῡμᾰτόεις, εσσα, εν, poët. for *κυματίας*.

κῡμᾰτο-πλήξ, ῆγος, ὁ, ἡ, (*κῦμα, πλήσσω*) *wave-beaten.*

κῡμᾰτόω, f. ώσω, (*κῦμα*) *to drive the waves over*:— Pass. *to rise in waves, to swell,* of the sea.

κῡμᾰτ-ωγή, ἡ, (*κῦμα, ἄγνυμι*) *a place where the waves break, beach, strand.*

κυμβᾰλίζω, f. ίσω, (*κύμβαλον*) *to play the cymbals.*

κύμβᾰλον, τό, (*κύμβος*) *a cymbal,* Lat. *cymbalum.*

κύμβᾰχος, ον, (*κύπτω*) *head-foremost,* Lat. *pronus.* II. *κύμβαχος*, ὁ, as Subst. *the crown* or *top of a helmet,* in which the plume is placed.

ΚΥ΄ΜΒΗ, ὁ, *a hollow vessel:* 1. *a drinking vessel, cup, bowl.* II. *a boat,* Lat. *cymba.* Hence

κυμβίον, τό, Dim. *a small cup.*

κύμινδις, Ion. name of the bird *χαλκίς, the night-hawk; χαλκίδα κικλήσκουσι θεοί, ἄνδρες δὲ κύμινδιν.*

κῡμῑνεύω, f. σω, (*κυμινον*) *to strew with cummin.*

ΚΥΜΙ΄ΝΟΝ, τό, *cummin,* Lat. *cuminum.*

κῡμῑνο-πρίστης, ου, ὁ, (*κύμινον, πρίω*) *a cummin-splitter,* i. e. *a skinflint, niggard, churl.*

κῡμῑνο-πριστο-καρδᾰμο-γλύφος, ον, (*κυμινοπρίστης, καρδαμογλύφος*) *a cummin-splitting cress-scraper,* of an excessive miser. [ŭ]

κῡμο-δέγμων, ον, gen. ονος, (*κῦμα, δέχομαι*) *receiving* or *meeting the waves.*

κύνα, κύνας, acc. sing. and pl. of *κύων*.

κυνᾱγεσία, κυνᾱγέτας, Dor. for *κυνηγ-*.

κῠν-ᾱγός, ον, Dor. for *κυνηγός*, but the Dor. form is always used in Att. poets: (*κύων, ἄγω*):—*dog-leading:* hence as Subst. *a hunter, huntsman.*

κῠν-άγχη, ἡ, (*κύων, ἄγχομαι*) *cynanché,* a bad kind of *sore throat.* II. *a dog-collar.*

κῠν-ᾰγωγός, ὁ, (*κύων, ἄγω*) *a dog leader, huntsman.*

κῠν-ᾰλώπηξ, εκος, ἡ, (*κύων, ἀλώπηξ*) *a fox-dog, mongrel between dog and fox:* applied as a nickname to Cleon.

κῠνά-μυια, ἡ, (*κύων, μυῖα*) *dog-fly, shameless fly.*

κῠνάριον, τό, Dim. of *κύων*, *a little dog, whelp, puppy.* [ᾰ]

κῠνάς, άδος, fem. Adj. *of a dog,* Lat. *caninus.* II. as Subst., *κυνάς* (sub. *θρίξ*), ἡ, *dog's hair,* of a bad fleece.

κῠνάω, f. ήσω, (*κύων*) *to play the Cynic.*

κῠνέη, Att. contr. **κυνῆ**, (properly fem. of *κύνεος*, sub. *δορά*), ἡ, *a dog's skin, a leather cap* or *bonnet, a soldier's cap: a helmet* of any kind: *a bonnet.*

κύνει, Ep. for *ἐκύνει*, 3 sing. impf. of *κυνέω*.

κύνειος, α, ον, also ος, ον, (*κύων*) *of a dog.*

κύνεος, α, ον (*κύων*) *of* or *like a dog:* metaph. *shameless, unabashed.*

κύνες, nom. pl. of *κύων*.

ΚΥΝΕ΄Ω: fut. *κυνήσομαι*, but also *κύσω* [ῠ], poët. *κύσσω*: aor. 1 *ἔκῠσα* Ep. *κύσα, ἔκυσσα, κύσσα*:—*to kiss:* of doves, *to bill.* 2. *to intreat, beseech.*

κῠνῆ, ἡ, Att. contr. for *κυνέη*.

κυνηγεσία, ἡ, = *κυνηγέσιον*.

κῠνηγέσιον, τό, *a hunting establishment, huntsman and hounds, a pack of hounds.* II. *the hunt, chase: a hunting-ground.* III. *that which is taken in hunting, the game.* From

κῠνηγετέω, f. ήσω, *to hunt: to chase, pursue.* 2. *to persecute, harass.* From

κῠν-ηγέτης, ου, ὁ, Dor. **κυνᾱγέτας**, (*κύων, ἡγέομαι*): *a hunter, huntsman.* Hence

κῠνηγετικός, ή, όν, *of* or *for hunting.*

κῠν-ηγέτις, ιδος, ἡ, fem. of *κυνηγέτης*, *a huntress.*

κῠνηγία, ἡ, *a hunt, chase.* From

κῠνηγός, v. sub *κυναγός*.

κῠνηδόν, Adv. (*κύων*) *like a dog, greedily.*

κῠνήποδες, οἱ, (*κύων* vi, *πούς*) *the fetlocks* of a horse.

Κύνθος, ὁ, *Cynthus,* a mountain in Delos, birthplace of Apollo and Artemis; whence Apollo is called **Κύνθιος**, *Cynthian,* and **Κυνθο-γενής**, *Cynthos-born.*

κῠνίδιον, τό, Dim. of *κύων*, *a little dog.*

κῠνικός, ή, όν, (*κύων*) *of* or *like a dog,* Lat. *caninus.*

κῠνίσκη, ἡ, (*κύων*) *a bitch-puppy.*

κῠνίσκος, ὁ, (*κύων*) *a young dog, whelp, puppy:* metaph. *a little Cynic.*

κῠνο-δρομέω, f. ήσω, (*κύων, δραμεῖν*) *to run down, chase with dogs:* metaph. *to hunt after.*

κῠνο-θαρσής or **-θρασής**, ές, (*κύων, θαρρέω*) *impudent as a dog.*

κῠνο-κέφᾰλος, ον, (κύων, κεφαλή) *dog-headed.* 2. as Subst., κυνοκέφαλος, ὁ, *the dog-headed ape.*

κῠνο-κλόπος, ον, (κύων, κλέπτω) *dog-stealing.*

κῠνο-κοπέω, f. ήσω, (κύων, κόπτω) *to beat like a dog.*

κυνόμυια, = κυνάμυια.

κῠνο-πρόσωπος, ον, (κύων, πρόσωπον) *dog-faced.*

κῠνο-ραιστής, οῦ, ὁ, (κύων, ῥαίω) *a dog-tick.*

κύνος, gen. of κύων·

Κῠνόσαργες, εος, τό, *Cynosarges*, a gymnasium outside the city of Athens, sacred to Hercules, for the use of those who were not of pure Athenian blood.

κῠνόσ-ουρα, ἡ, (κυνός, οὐρά) *a dog's-tail:* esp. *the Cynosure*, name of the constellation *Ursa Minor.*

κῠνο-σπάρακτος, ον, (κύων, σπαράσσω) *torn by dogs.*

κυν-οῦχος, ὁ, (κύων, ἔχω) *a dog-holder, dog-leash, slip.* II. *a dog-skin sack*, used in hunting.

κῠνό-φρων, ον, gen. ονος, (κύων, φρήν) *dog-minded, sordid* or *shameless of soul.*

κῠνόσ-βᾰτος, ἡ, (κύων, βάτος) *dog-thorn*, a kind of *wild rose.*

κύντερος, α, ον, Comp. Adj. formed from κύων, *more dog-like*, i. e. *more shameless, more audacious:*—Sup. **κύντατος**, η, ον, *most shameless.*

κυνώ, οῦς, ἡ, (κύων) *a she-dog, bitch.*

κῠν-ώπης, ου, ὁ, (κύων, ὤψ) = κυνὸς ὄμματ' ἔχων, *the dog-eyed*, i. e. *shameless one:*—fem. **κῠν-ῶπις**, ιδος, ἡ, *the shameless woman;* also *fierce-eyed, terrible.*

κύπαιρος, Dor. for κύπειρος.

κῠπᾰρίσσῐνος Att. -ττῐνος, η, ον, (κυπάρισσος) *made of cypress wood.*

ΚΥ͂ΠΑ΄ΡΙΣΣΟΣ Att. -ττος, ἡ, *a cypress*, Lat. *cupressus.*

ΚΥ͂ΠΕΙΡΟΝ, τό, or **κύπειρος**, ὁ, a marsh-plant, used to feed horses, *galingal.*

κῠπελλο-μάχος, ον, (κύπελλον, μάχομαι) *at which they fight with cups*, cf. Horace's *scyphis pugnare.*

κύπελλον, τό, (κύπη) *a capacious drinking-vessel, a beaker, goblet.* [ῠ]

κύπερος, ὁ, Ion. for κύπειρος.

κύπη, ἡ, = γύπη· *a hole, hollow.*

Κυπρίδιος, α, ον, (Κύπρις) *of* or *like Cypris, lovely, tender, delicate.* [ῐδ]

Κύπριος, α, ον, (Κύπρος) *of Cyprus, Cyprian.*

Κύπρις, ῐδος, ἡ, acc. Κύπριν and Κύπριδα, *Cypris*, a name of Venus, from the island of Cyprus, where she was most worshipped. II. *love.*

Κυπρο-γενής, ές, (Κυπρος, *γένω) *Cyprus-born:* fem. **Κυπρο-γένεια** Ep. -γενέα, ἡ.

Κυπρόθεν, Adv. *from Cyprus:* and

Κύπρονδε, Adv. *to Cyprus.* From

Κύπρος, ου, ἡ, *Cyprus*, a Greek island on the southern coast of Asia Minor. (Hence Lat. *cyprium*, our *copper.*)

κυπτάζω, f. άσω: Frequentative from κύπτω, *to keep stooping, to go poking* or *pottering* about a thing.

ΚΥ͂ΠΤΩ, f. κύψω: aor. 1 ἔκυψα: pf. κέκῡφα:—*to bend forward, stoop: to bow down* under a burden; κέρεα κεκυφότα ἐς τὸ ἔμπροσθεν horns *growing bent forward;* often in aor. 1 part. with another Verb, θέει κύψας runs *with the head down;* κύψας ἐσθίει eats *stooping*, i. e. *greedily.*

Κύρβας, αντος, ὁ, shortd. form of Κορύβας

κυρβᾰσία, ἡ, *a Persian bonnet* or *hat*, with a peaked crown. The king alone wore it upright.

ΚΥ΄ΡΒΕΙΣ or **κύρβιες**, gen. κύρβεων, dat. κύρβεσι, *triangular tables*, forming a three-sided pyramid turning round on a pivot; the few early laws of Athens were written on the three sides. II. later, any *pillars* or *tablets with inscriptions.* III. the sing. κύρβις is used later of *a pettifogging lawyer.*

ΚΥΡΕ΄Ω and **ΚΥ΄ΡΩ** [ῡ]: impf. ἐκύρουν [ῠ] and ἔκῡρον with Ep. 3 sing. κῦρε: fut. κύρήσω and κύρσω: aor. 1 ἐκύρησα [ῠ], inf. κῠρῆσαι, part. κῠρήσας; and Ep. ἔκυρσα, inf. κύρσαι, part. κύρσας: I. followed by a case, 1. dat. *to hit, light upon, reach, attain: to meet with, fall in with;* as λέων σώματι κύρσας. 2. dat. with ἐπί or ἐν, as, λέων ἐπὶ σώματι κύρσας = λέων σώματι κύρσας. 3. gen. *to reach to, as far as: to arrive at, gain, win, obtain.* 4. acc. *to reach, obtain;* also *to find by chance.* II. intrans. *to happen, come to pass, turn out.* 2. absol. *to be right, hit the exact truth;* with part., τόδ' ἂν λέγων κυρήσαις *you would be right* in saying this. 3. as auxil. Verb, like τυγχάνω with partic. *to turn out, prove, happen* to be so and so; κυρεῖ ὤν *he happens* to be.

κῠρηβάζω, f. άσω, (akin to κυρίσσω) *to butt with the horns:* generally, *to strike.* Hence

κῠρηβᾰσία, ἡ, *a butting: fighting.*

ΚΥ͂ΡΗ΄ΒΙΑ, ων, τά, *chaff, husks, bran.*

Κυρηναῖος, α, ον, *of Cyrene.* From

Κυρήνη, ἡ, *Cyrene*, the name of a Greek colony in Africa, famous for its breed of horses.

κῡρία, ἡ, *the mistress, lady.*

κῡριᾰκός, ή, όν, (κύριος) *of, belonging to a lord* or *master;* esp. *belonging to the LORD (CHRIST):* hence ἡ κυριακή (sub. ἡμέρα), *the Lord's day, dies dominica:* τὸ κυριακόν, *the Lord's house*, whence our *kyrk, church.*

κυριεύω, f. σω, *to be lord* or *master of.* From

κύριος, α, ον, also ος, ον, (κῦρος): 1. of men, *having power* or *authority* over, *lord* or *master of*, c. gen.: κύριός εἰμι c. inf., *I have the right* or *am entitled* to do. II. of things, *decisive, valid: critical.* 2. *authorised, ratified.* 3. of times, *fixed, appointed, regular:* at Athens, κυρία ἐκκλησία an *ordinary* assembly, opp. to σύγκλητος ἐκκλησία (one specially summoned.) 4. *principal, chief.* 5. esp. of language, *strict, literal.* III. as Subst., κύριος, ὁ, *a lord, master: an owner, possessor:* 2. ὁ Κύριος = Hebr. *JEHOVAH, THE LORD:* in N.T. of CHRIST. Hence

κῡριότης, ητος, ἡ, *power, rule, dominion.*

κῡρίσσω Att. -ττω, fut. ίξω, (κόρυς) *to butt with the horns:* also *to strike* or *dash against*, of floating bodies.

κῡρίως, Adv. of κύριος, *like a lord* or *master, authoritatively.* 2. *rightfully, fitly.*

κυρκᾰνάω, rare form for κυκανάω.

κύρμα, ατος, τό, (κύρω) *that which one lights upon, a godsend, booty, prey, spoil.*

ΚΥ'ΡΟΣ, εος, τό, *supreme power, authority.* II. *validity, security.* III. as pr. n. Κῦρος, ὁ, *Cyrus*, the founder of the Persian empire. Hence

κῡρόω, f. ώσω: aor. 1 ἐκύρωσα:—Pass., aor. 1 ἐκυρώθην: pf. κεκύρωμαι:—*to make valid* or *sure*, Lat. *ratum facere: to settle, accomplish: to confirm, ratify:*—Pass. *to be ratified, fixed, settled;* c. inf., ἐκεκύρωτο συμβάλλειν *it had been decided* to engage.

κύρσαι, κύρσας, aor. 1 inf. and part. of κύρω.

κύρσω, fut. of κύρω.

κυρτευτής, οῦ, ὁ, (κυρτή) *a fisherman.*

ΚΥ'ΡΤΗ, ἡ, *a fishing-basket, weel*, Lat. *nassa.*

κύρτος, ὁ, = κύρτη.

ΚΥΡΤΟ'Σ, ή, όν, *curved, bent, arched;* ὤμω κυρτώ *round, humped* shoulders:—*convex*, opp. to concave.

κυρτόω, (κυρτός) *to curve, bend, arch.*

ΚΥ'ΡΩ, = κυρέω, of which it is the Radic. form.

κύρωσις, εως, ἡ, (κυρόω) *a ratification:* hence *execution, accomplishment.* [ῡ]

κύσα, Ep. for ἔκῠσα, aor. 1 of κυνέω; inf. κύσαι.

κῡσαμένη, aor. 1 part. med. of κύω.

κύσθος, ὁ, (κύω) *any hollow.*

κῠσί, dat. pl. of κύων.

κύσσα, Ep. for ἔκῠσα, aor. 1 of κυνέω.

κύστις, εως and ιος, ἡ, (κύω) = κύστη, *the bladder:* generally, *a bag, pouch.*

κύσω, fut. of κυνέω.

ΚΥ'ΤΙΣΟΣ, ὁ, *cytisus, a shrubby* kind of *clover.*

κυτμίς, ίδος, ἡ, a kind of *plaster.*

κῠτο-γάστωρ, ορος, ὁ, ἡ, (κύτος, γαστήρ) *with capacious belly, capacious.*

κύτος, εος, τό, (κύω) *a hollow: a hollow vessel, a vase, jar, pot, urn.* II. *the body, the skin*, Lat. *cutis.*

κύτρα, κύτρος, Ion. for χύτρ–.

κύττᾰρον, τό, = sq., *a pine-cone.*

κύττᾰρος, ὁ, (κύτος) *any hollow* or *cavity;* κύτταρος οὐρανοῦ, *the vault* of heaven, Lat. *cavum coeli: the cell of a honeycomb: the cup* of an acorn: *a pine-cone.*

κῡφ-ᾰγωγός, ὁ, (κυφός, ἄγω) *with arching neck.*

κῡφᾰλέος, α, ον, poët. for κυφός.

κῡφός, ή, όν, (κέκῡφα, pf. of κύπτω) *bent* or *bowed forwards, stooping.* Hence

κύφων, ωνος, ὁ, *a crooked piece of wood*, esp. *the bent yoke of the plough.* II. *a sort of pillory in which animals were fastened by the neck.* 2. *one who has been in the pillory*, Lat. *furcifer.*

κῦψαι, κύψας, aor. 1 inf. and part. of κύπτω.

κυψέλη, ἡ, (κύπη) *any hollow vessel: a chest, box, bin* (whence Cypselus was called).

Κυψελίδαι, οἱ, *the descendants of Cypselus.*

ΚΥ'Ω, *to hold, contain:*—1 c. acc., like κυέω, *to carry in the womb*, Lat. *gestare.* 2. absol. *to be big with young, be pregnant, conceive:* metaph. *to be in labour with a thought.* II. Causal in aor. 1 act. ἔκῡσα, of the male, *to impregnate make to conceive:* but in aor. 1 med. ἐκῡσάμην, *to conceive.*

ΚΥ'ΩΝ, ὁ and ἡ, gen. κυνός, dat. κυνί, acc. κύνα, voc. κύον:—plur. nom. κύνες, gen. κυνῶν, dat. κυσί Ep. κύνεσσι, acc. κύνας:—*a dog* or *bitch;* κύνες τραπεζῆες house-*dogs*, that fed while their master was at table; κύνες θηρευταί *hounds*, of which the Laconian breed was famous, and later the Molossian. II. *a dog, bitch*, as *a word of reproach*, to denote *shamelessness* or *audacity.* III. this term is often applied to the *faithful* or *watchful servants* of the gods; so the eagle is Διὸς πτηνὸς κύων; the griffins also are Ζηνὸς κύνες. IV. *a sea-dog.* V. *the dog-star.* VI. *the fetlock-joint of a horse.*

κω, Ion. for πω.

κῶας, later contr. κῶς, τό: irreg. pl. nom. and acc. κώεα, dat. κώεσι: (κεῖμαι):—*a soft fleece, sheepskin.*

κωδάριον, τό, Dim. of κώδιον. [ᾰ]

κώδεια, ἡ, *the head: the head of a poppy.*

κώδιον, τό, Dim. of κῶας, *a fleece, sheepskin.*

ΚΩ'ΔΩΝ, ωνος, ὁ Att. ἡ, *a bell:* in fortified towns a bell was passed round at night from sentinel to sentinel to secure their being at their post; τοῦ κώδωνος παρενεχθέντος as *the bell* went its rounds. 2. *an alarm-bell:* metaph. *a noisy rattling fellow.* II. *the mouth of a trumpet:* also *the trumpet* itself. Hence

κωδωνίζω, f. ίσω Att. ιῶ, *to try* or *prove by ringing.*

κωδωνό-κροτος, ον, (κώδων, κροτέω) *ringing* or *jingling as with bells.*

κωδωνο-φᾰλᾰρό-πωλος, ον, (κωδων, φαλαρα, πῶλος) *with bells on his horses' trappings.*

κωδωνο-φορέω, f. ήσω, (κώδων, φέρω) *to carry bells: to go the rounds* (cf. κώδων):—so in Pass., ἅπαντα κωδωνοφορεῖται everywhere *the bell goes round*, i. e. the sentinels are challenged.

κώεα, κώεσι, Ep. nom. and dat. pl. of κῶας.

ΚΩ'ΘΩΝ, ωνος, ὁ, *a Laconian earthen drinking-vessel:* generally, *a cup, goblet.*

κωθώνιον, τό, Dim. of κώθων.

κῶῐλος, α, ον, Aeol. for κοῖλος.

Κώϊος, α, ον, contr. Κῷος, q. v.

κώκῡμα, ατος, τό, (κωκύω) *a shriek, wail, lament.*

κωκῡτός, ὁ, (κωκύω) *a shrieking, wailing.* II. as pr. n., Κωκῡτός, ὁ, *Cocytus*, the river *of wailing*, one of the rivers of hell.

ΚΩΚΥ'Ω, f. ύσω [ῡ] or ύσομαι: aor. 1 ἐκώκῡσα Ep. κώκῡσα:—*to shriek, cry, wail, lament.*

κωλ-αγρέτης or –ακρέτης, ου, ὁ, (so called ἐκ τοῦ ἀγείρειν τὰς κωλᾶς):—*the collector of the fragments at a sacrifice*, name of an ancient magistracy at Athens, originally entrusted with the charge of the finances: afterwards they only had to see after the public table in the Prytaneium, and the payment of the dicasts.

κωλάριον, τό, Dim. of κῶλον.

κωλῆ, ἡ, contr. from κωλεά or κωλέα, (κῶλον), *the thigh-bone with the flesh, hind-quarter, ham.*

κώληψ, ηπος, ἡ, (κῶλον, κωλῆ) *the hollow* or *bend of the knees.*

Κωλιάς (sub. ἄκρα), άδος, ἡ, *Colias*, a promontory of Attica, with a temple of Venus there.

ΚΩ͂ΛΟΝ, τό, *a limb, member* of a body. II. generally, *a member* or *part* of anything. 1. of a building, *the side* or *front.* 2. *one limb* or *half of the race-course.* 3. *a member* or *clause* of a sentence.

κώλῡμα, ατος, τό, (κωλύω) *a hindrance, obstruction*, Lat. *impedimentum.* II. *a defence* or *precaution against* a thing.

κωλύμη, ἡ, = κώλυμα, [ῡ]

κωλῡσί-δρομος, η, ον, (κωλύω, δρόμος) *checking the course.*

κωλῡτέον, verb. Adj. of κωλύω, *one must hinder.*

κωλῡτής, οῦ, ὁ, (κωλύω) *a hinderer.*

κωλῡτικός, ή, όν, (κωλύω) *hindering, preventive.*

κωλύω [ῡ]: f. ύσω [ῡ]: aor. 1 ἐκώλυσα:—Pass., fut. κωλυθήσομαι, but also f. med. κωλύσομαι in pass. sense: aor. 1 ἐκωλύθην: pf. κεκώλῡμαι: (κόλος):—akin to κολούω, *to cut short:* hence *to let, hinder:* 1. c. inf. *to hinder* one *from* doing, *forbid to* do. 2. c. gen. rei, *to let* or *hinder* one *from* a thing. 3. c. acc. rei, *to hinder, prevent* a thing. 4. absol., esp. in part., ὁ κωλύσων *one to hinder, a preventer;* τὸ κωλῦον *a hindrance;* also οὐ κωλύει *there is no hindrance.* II. Pass. *to be hindered.*

κῶμα, ατος, τό, (κεῖμαι, κοιμάω) *a deep, sound sleep*, Lat. *sopor.* 2. *a lethargy, a trance.*

κωμάζω: fut. άσω or άσομαι: aor. 1 ἐκώμασα: pf. κεκώμακα: Dor. pres. κωμάσδω, f. άξομαι, aor. 1 ἐκώμαξα: (κῶμος):—*to go about with a company of revellers, revel, make merry.* 2. *to celebrate a* κῶμος or *merrymaking*, in honour of the victor at the games, *to join in these festivities: to honour* or *celebrate in* or *with the* κῶμος. 2. generally, *to visit* or *break in upon in the manner of revellers: to burst in, force a way in.*

κωμ-άρχης, ου, ὁ, (κώμη, ἄρχω) *the head of a village.*

κωμάσδω, Dor. for κωμάζω.

κωμαστής, οῦ, ὁ, (κωμάζω) *a reveller, merrymaker:*—of Bacchus, *the jolly god.*

κωμάστωρ, ορος, ὁ, poët. for κωμαστής.

ΚΩ͂ΜΗ, ἡ, = Lat. *vicus, an unwalled village* or *country town*, a Dor. word = the Att. δῆμος; κατὰ κώμας οἰκεῖσθαι to dwell in *villages*, as opp. to walled towns. II. of a city, *a quarter, ward, district.* Hence

κωμηδόν, Adv. *in villages*, Lat. *vicatim.*

κωμήτης, ου, ὁ, (κώμη) *a villager, countryman.* II. in a city, *one of the same ward*, Lat. *vicinus:* generally, *an inhabitant.*

κωμῆτις, ιδος, fem. of κωμήτης.

κωμῐκεύομαι, Dep. *to speak like a comic poet.* From

κωμῐκός, ή, όν, (κῶμος) *of* or *for comedy, comic.*

κωμό-πολις, εως, ὁ, (κώμη, πόλις) *a village-town. a town built in a straggling way.*

κῶμος, οῦ, ὁ, (κώμη) *a revel, carousal, merrymaking*, Lat. *comessatio*, with music and dancing: it ended in the party parading the streets with crowned heads, and with torches, singing and dancing: there were also κῶμοι, *festal processions*, in honour of several gods, as Bacchus, and also in honour of the victors at the games. II. *the band of revellers;* metaph. *any riotous band* or *company.* III. *the Ode sung* at one of these festive processions.

κωμῳδέω, f. ήσω, (κωμῳδός) *to represent in a comedy: to ridicule, caricature:*—Pass. *to be so satirised.*

κωμῳδία, ἡ, (κωμῳδέω) *a comedy: a mirthful spectacle* or *exhibition.* There were three periods of Attic Comedy, the Old, the Middle, and the New. Hence

κωμῳδικός, ή, όν, *of* or *for comedy, comic.*

κωμῳδό-γελως, ωτος, ὁ, (κωμῳδός γέλως) *a comic actor.*

κωμῳδο-γράφος, ὁ, (κωμῳδος, γράφω) *a comic writer.*

κωμῳδοδῐδασκᾰλία, ἡ, *the rehearsing a comedy with the actors:* generally, *the comic poet's art.* From

κωμῳδο-δῐδάσκᾰλος, ὁ, (κωμῳδός, διδάσκαλος) *a comic poet*, because he had the charge of teaching and training the actors, chorus, etc.

κωμῳδο-λοιχέω, f. ήσω, (κωμῳδός, λείχω) *to play the parasite and buffoon.*

κωμῳδο-ποιητής, οῦ, ὁ, and

κωμῳδο-ποιός, ὁ, (κωμῳδός, ποιέω) *a maker of comedies, comic poet.*

κωμ-ῳδός, ὁ, (κώμη, ἀοιδός) *a comedian:* 1. *a comic actor.* 2. *a comic poet.*

κωμῳδο-τρᾰγῳδία, ἡ, (κωμῳδός, τραγῳδια) *a tragicomedy.*

ΚΩ͂ΝΕΙΟΝ, τό, *hemlock*, Lat. *cicūta.* 2. *hemlock juice*, a poison by which criminals were put to death at Athens.

κωνίον, τό, Dim. of κῶνος, *a small cone.*

κωνίτης [ῑ], ου, ὁ, fem. -ῖτις, ιδος, *extracted from pine-cones.*

ΚΩ͂ΝΟΣ, ου, ὁ, *a pine-cone, fir-cone:*—as fem. *a pine* or *fir tree.* 2. *the cone* or *peak* of a helmet.

κωνο-φόρος, ον, (κῶνος, φέρω) *cone-bearing*, as pines, etc.: also of the thyrsus, which had *a pine-cone* on the point.

κωνωπεῖον, τό, = κωνωπεών, Lat. *conopium.*

κωνωπεών, ῶνος, ὁ, (κώνωψ) *an* Egyptian *bed* or *litter with mosquito-curtains.*

ΚΩ͂ΝΩΨ, ωπός, ὁ, *a gnat*, Lat. *culex.*

Κῷος, α, ον, *of, from the island Cos, Coan.* II. ὁ **Κῷος**, often written **κῶος** (sub. βόλος), *the highest throw with the dice, counting six*, opp. to Χῖος, which *counted one:* hence the proverb, Κῷος πρὸς Χῖον.

κωπεύς, έως, ὁ, (κώπη) *a piece of wood fit for an oar, a spar for an oar.*

κωπεύω, f. σω, (κώπη) *to propel with oars.* 2. *to fit out with oars.*

κώπη, ἡ, (from κάπτω, *capio*, as λαβή from λαμβάνω) *any handle*, as *the handle of an oar:* then, *the oar* itself. 2. *the handle* or *haft of a sword, the* *bilt*, Lat. *manubrium*. 3. *the handle of a key*. 4. *the handle* or *haft of a torch*. Hence

κωπήεις, εσσα, εν, *hilted*.

κωπηλᾰτέω, f. ήσω, *to row: to move like an oar, move backwards and forwards*. From

κωπ-ηλάτης, ου, ὁ, (κώπη, ἐλαύνω) *a rower*, Lat. *remex*.

κωπ-ήρης, ες, (κώπη, ἀραρεῖν) *furnished with oars*. II. *holding the oar*.

κωπίον, τό, Dim. of κώπη, *a small oar*.

κώρα, Dor. for κούρη, κόρη.

κώριον. Dor. for κούριον, κόριον.

κῶρος, κώρος, Dor. for κοῦρος, κούρη.

ΚΩΡΥ͂ΚΟΣ, ὁ, *a leathern sack* or *wallet with provisions:* also *a large stuffed sack* or *bag for tilting at*, like the quintain.

Κώρῠκος, ὁ, *Corycus, a promontory of Cilicia*, with a famous cavern; there was another at Delphi.

Κῶς Ep. **Κόως**, ἡ, gen. Κῶ, the island *Cos*, in the Aegaean sea, opposite Caria.

κῶς, Ion. for πῶς: but enclit. **κώς**, Ion. for πώς.

κωτιλλοίσαι, Dor. part. pl. fem. of κωτίλλω.

ΚΩΤΙ´ΛΛΩ, *to prate, chatter*, Lat. *garrire: to wheedle, coax*. II. trans. *to chatter to, talk over*. Hence

κωτίλος, η, ον, *chattering, prattling:* of a swallow, *twittering*. II. *coaxing, wheedling*. [ῐ]

κωφάω, f. άσω, (κωφός) *to make deaf* or *dumb*. II. *to dull, blunt*.

κωφός, ή, όν, (κόπτω) *blunt*, opp. to ὀξύς. II. of the senses, 1. *dumb*, Lat. *mutus;* κωφὸν κῦμα *a noiseless* wave, before it breaks; of men, *dumb, mute, speechless;* also *insensate, unmeaning*. 2. also *dull of hearing, deaf*, Lat. *surdus*. 3. *dull of mind, stupid, obtuse*.

κᾦχετο, by crasis for καὶ ᾤχετο, impf. of οἴχομαι.

κᾦψον, by crasis for καὶ ὄψον.

Λ

Λ, λ, λάμβδα or **λάβδα**, τό, indecl., eleventh letter of the Greek alphabet: as a numeral λ′ = 30, but ͵λ = 30,000. The Lacedaemonians bore Λ upon their shields, as the Sicyonians Σ, the Messenians Μ.

Changes of λ: I. Dor. into ν, as ἦνθον φίντατος for ἦλθον φίλτατος: whereas the Att. prefers λ, as, λίτρον πλεύμων for νίτρον πνεύμων II. Ion., λ beginning a word is dropped, as εἴβω for λείβω, αἰψηρός for λαιψηρός. III. Ep. poets use λλ for λ, esp. after the augment, as ἔλλαβε for ἔλαβε; and in compds., where the latter part begins with λ, as in τρίλλιστος. IV. Att., λ is sometimes changed into ρ, as κρίβανος for κλίβανος, ναύκραρος for ναύκληρος. V. Aeol., δ is sometimes changed into λ, as Lat. *lacryma* corresponded to δάκρυον, *olere* to ὄζειν, ὀδ-ωδέναι. VI. in some words γ and λ are interchanged, as in μόγις and μόλις. VII. ν before λ becomes λ, as in συλλαμβάνω σύλλογος ἐλλείπω.

ΛΑ˘, insep. Prefix with *intensive* force (like λαι-, λι-, δα-, ζα-), e. g. in λά-μαχος *very* warlike, λα-κατάρατος *much* accursed.

ΛΑ˘ΑΣ, ὁ, gen. λᾶος, dat. λᾶϊ, acc. λᾶαν: plur., gen. λάων, dat. λάεσι Ep. λάεσσι:—in Att. also contr. nom. λᾶς, acc. λᾶν:—a gen. λάου also occurs: Lat. *LAPIS, a stone*. II. *a rock, crag*.

λᾰβεῖν Ion. **λαβέειν**, aor. 2 inf. of λαμβάνω.

λαβέν, Dor. for λαβεῖν, aor. 2 inf. of λαμβάνω: but **λάβεν**, Ep. 3 sing.

λάβεσκον, Ion. aor. 2 of λαμβάνω.

λᾰβή, ἡ, (λαβεῖν) *the part to hold by, a handle, haft, hilt;* λαβὴν δοῦναι to give one *a grip* or *hold*, metaph., to give one *a handle, something to lay hold of*, Lat. *ansam praebere*. II. *the act of grasping, a taking, acceptance*.

λαβῆν, Dor. for λαβεῖν, aor. 2 inf. of λαμβάνω.

λάβησι, Ep. 3 sing. aor. 2 subj. of λαμβάνω.

λαβοῖσα, Dor. aor. 2 part. fem. of λαμβάνω.

λαβρ-ᾰγόρης, ου, ὁ, Att. **-αγόρας**, (λάβρος, ἀγορεύω) *a bold, rash talker, braggart*.

λάβραξ, ακος, ὁ, (λάβρος) *a sea-wolf*.

λαβρεύομαι, Dep. (λάβρος) *to talk boldly, brag, vaunt*.

λαβρο-πόδης, ου, ὁ, (λάβρος, πούς) *rapid of foot, impetuous*.

λαβροποτέω, f. ήσω, *to drink hard*. From

λαβρο-πότης, ου, ὁ, (λάβρος, πίνω) *a hard drinker*.

ΛΑ´ΒΡΟΣ, ον, *furious, boisterous, blustering, vehement*. 2. of persons, *boisterous, furious, turbulent:* also *gluttonous, greedy*.

λαβροστομέω, (λαβρόστομος) *to talk boldly*. Hence

λαβροστομία, ἡ, *bold, rash talking*.

λαβρό-στομος, ον, (λάβρος, στόμα) *talking rashly*.

λαβροσύνη, ἡ, (λάβρος) *boisterousness:* also *greediness*.

λαβρό-σῠτος, ον, (λάβρος, σεύω) *rushing furiously*.

λάβρως, Adv. of λάβρος, *violently, greedily*.

λᾰβύρινθος, ὁ, *a labyrinth, maze*, a large building with intricate passages intersecting each other: the earliest was that of Crete. II. *anything of spiral* or *twisted shape*. (Foreign word.)

λαβῠρινθ-ώδης, ες, (λαβύρινθος, εἶδος) *like a labyrinth, intricate*.

λάβω, λαβών, aor. 2 subj. and part. of λαμβάνω.

λᾰγᾰρίζω, f. σω, (λαγαρός) *to make slack* or *hollow:*—Med. *to become hollow* or *gaunt* from hunger.

λᾰγᾰρός, ά, όν, *slack, hollow, sunken*. II. *slack, pliant, flexible*. (Akin to λαπαρός.) Hence

λᾰγᾰρόω, = λαγαρίζω: Pass. *to become slack* or *loose*.

λάγδην, Adv. (λάζω, λακτίζω) = λάξ, *with the heel*.

λάγειος, ον, also α, ον, (λαγός, λαγώς) *of* or *from a hare*.

λᾱ-γέτης, *ου*, Dor. **λᾱγέτας**, *α*, *ὁ*, (λαός, ἡγέομαι) *leader of the people.*

ΛΑ'ΓΗΝΟΣ, *ὁ*, *a flagon*, Lat. *lagena.*

λάγῐνος, *η*, *ον*, (λαγώς) *of* or *from a hare.*

λᾰγίον, *τό*, Dim. of λαγώς, *a leveret.*

λαγνεία, *lewdness, lust, desire.* From

ΛΑ'ΓΝΟΣ, *ον*, *lewd, lustful.*

λᾰγο-δαίτης, *ου*, *ὁ*, (λαγός, δαίω) *hare-devourer.*

λᾰγο-θήρας, *ου*, *ὁ*, (λαγός, θηράω) *a hare-hunter.* Hence

λᾰγοθηρέω, *to hunt hares.*

λᾰγοκτονέω, f. *ήσω*, *to kill hares.* From

ΛΑΓΟ'Σ, *οῦ*, *ὁ*, collat. form of λαγώς, *a hare.*

λάγῡνος, *ὁ*, also *ἡ*, = λάγηνος. [Later also ῠ.]

ΛΑΓΧΑ'ΝΩ: fut. λήξομαι Ion. λάξομαι: aor. 2 ἔλᾰχον Ep. ἔλλᾰχον: pf. εἴληχα, poët. λέλογχα:—Pass., aor. 1 ἐλήχθην: pf. εἴληγμαι:—*to obtain by lot* or *fate*: generally, *to obtain, get possession of*: c. acc. cognato, *πάλον λαχεῖν to have* a post *assigned* one *by lot.* 2. *to have assigned to one, to have for one's share*; esp. of the gods, Κὴρ λάχε γεινόμενον Fate *had* him *given over to* her at his birth: hence *to protect* as *the tutelary deity* of a place: also of men, *to obtain for one's share*: later, *to obtain by inheritance, succeed to.* 3. absol. *to draw lots*: *to obtain an office by lot, to cast lots for*: c. inf., ὁ λαχὼν πολεμαρχέειν *he who had the lot* to be polemarch: absol., *οἱ λαχόντες those on whom the lot fell.* 4. as Att. law-term, *λαγχάνειν δίκην τινί* to sue one at law: hence, *λαγχάνειν τοῦ κλήρου* (sc. *δίκην*) *to sue* for one's inheritance. II. with partitive gen., *to receive a share of, become possessed of* a thing. III. Causal, in Ep. redupl. aor. 2 λέλᾰχον, *to put in possession of*; *λελαχεῖν τινὰ πυρός to grant* one *the right of* funeral fire. IV. intr. *to fall to one's lot* or *share*: *to be assigned by lot.*

λᾰγω-βόλον, *τό*, (λαγώς, βάλλω) *a staff for flinging at hares*, also used as *a shepherd's crook*, Lat. *pedum*: and

λᾰγωδάριον and **λᾰγῴδιον**, *τό*, Dim. of λαγώς, *a leveret.*

ΛΑΓΩ'Ν, *όνος*, *ἡ*, also *ὁ*, poët. dat. pl. λαγόνεσσι, *any hollow*: esp. like *κενεών*, *the hollow part below the ribs, the flank*: in pl. λαγόνες, *the flanks, loins.*

λᾰγωο-βόλος, *ον*, (λαγωός, βαλεῖν) *hitting hares.*

ΛΑΓΩΟ'Σ, *οῦ*, *ὁ*, Ep. for λαγώς, λαγός, *a hare.*

λᾰγῷος, *α*, *ον*, contr. for λαγώειος, (λαγώς) *of* or *from a hare*:—τὰ λαγῷα (sub. *κρέα*) *hare-flesh, roast hare*, and generally, *dainties, delicacies.*

ΛΑΓΩ'Σ, *ὁ*, gen. λαγώ, acc. λαγών and λαγώ: Ep. nom. **λᾰγωός**, *οῦ*, Ion. also **λαγός**:—Lat. LEPUS, *a hare.*

λάδᾰνον, *τό*, = λήδανον.

λάε, Ep. 3 sing. impf. of λάω, *to see.*

λᾶε, dual nom. of λᾶας *a stone.*

λάεσσι, Ep. dat. pl. of λᾶας *a stone.*

λαζεῦ, Dor. imperat. of λάζομαι.

λάζομαι, Dep. poet. for λαμβάνω, *to take, seize, grasp, catch, hold*; *λάζεσθαί τινα ἀγκάς to take* one in the arms: metaph., *μῦθον πάλιν λάζεσθαι to take* back one's words, retract.

λάζῠμαι, collat. form of λάζομαι.

λάθα, *ἡ*, Dor. for λήθη.

λᾱθ-άνεμος, *ον*, (λήθη, ἄνεμος) Dor. for **ληθάνεμος**, *escaping the wind.*

λάθε, Ep. 3 sing. aor. 2 of **λανθάνω**.

λᾰθέμεν, Ep. aor. 2 inf. of **λανθάνω**.

λᾰθέσθαι, aor. 2 inf. med. of **λανθάνω**.

λᾰθῐ-κηδής, *ές*, (λαθεῖν, κῆδος) *banishing care.*

λᾱθί-πονος, *ον*, (λήθω, πόνος) *forgetful of sorrow, grief*; *βίοτος ὀδυνᾶν λαθίπονος*, a life *forgetting*, i.e. *exempt from*, pain.

λᾰθί-φθογγος, *ον*, (λαθεῖν, φθογγή) *robbing of voice, striking dumb*, epith. of death.

λαθοίατο, 3 pl. aor. 2 med. opt. of λανθάνω.

λᾶθος, *εος*, *τό*, Dor. for λῆθος, = λήθη.

λάθρα, v. sub λάθρῃ. Hence

λαθραῖος, *α*, *ον*, also *ος*, *ον*, *secret, hidden, stealthy, covert.* Adv. *-ως*, Sup. λαθραιότατα.

λάθρῃ, Ep. and Ion. Adv., Att. **λάθρᾱ**: (λαθεῖν): *secretly, by stealth, covertly, insensibly*: c. gen. *without* one's *knowledge*; Καδμείων λάθρα *without the knowledge of* the Cadmeans.

λᾰθρηδόν, Adv. = λάθρῃ.

λαθρίδιος, *α*, *ον*, poët. for λάθριος. Adv. **-ως**. [Ῐ]

λάθριος, *ον*, (λάθρα) *stealthy, secret, furtive.*

λαθρο-βόλος, *ον*, (λάθρα, βαλεῖν) *hitting secretly.*

λαθρο-δάκνης, *ου*, *ὁ*, (λάθρα, δάκνω) *biting secretly.*

λαθρό-πους, *ὁ*, *ἡ*, *-πουν*, *τό*, gen. *-ποδος*, (λάθρα, πούς) *stealthy-paced, silent-footed.*

λάθω, **λᾰθών**, aor. 2 subj. and part. of λανθάνω.

λαι-, insep. Prefix, with intens. force, like **λα-** or λι-, found in few compds., as λαί-μαργος.

λᾶϊγξ, *ϊγγος*, *ἡ*, Dim. of λᾶας, *a pebble.*

λαίθ-αργος, *ον*, = λήθαργος.

λαικάζω, f. *άσομαι*, (ληκω) *to wench.*

λαικαστής, *οῦ*, *ὁ*, (λαικάζω) *a wencher*: fem. **λαικάστρια**, *a harlot.*

ΛΑΙ'ΛΑΨ, *ᾰπος*, *ἡ*, *a tempest, storm, hurricane.*

λαῖμα, *τό*, Comic word coined as a pun on λῆμα, αἷμα, and λαιμός.

λαί-μαργος, *ον*, (λαι-, μάργος) *greedy, gluttonous.* II. *talkative.*

λαιμάσσω Att. *-ττω*, (λαιμός) *to swallow greedily, bolt, devour*: intr. *to be greedy.*

λαιμη-τόμος, *ον*, poët. for λαιμοτόμος.

λαιμο-δᾰκής, *ές*, (λαιμός, δακεῖν) *throat-biting.*

λαιμοπέδη, *ἡ*, (λαιμός, πέδη) *a dog-collar.* II. *a springe for catching birds.*

λαιμο-ρῠτός, *ον*, (λαιμός, ῥέω) *gushing from the throat.*

ΛΑΙΜΟ'Σ, *οῦ*, *ὁ*, *the throat, gullet.*

λαιμό-τμητος, *ον*, (λαιμός, τμητός) *with the throat cut* or *severed.*

λαιμο-τόμος, *ον*, (λαιμός, τεμεῖν) *throat-cutting.* II.

pass. **λαιμότομος**, ον, *with the throat cut, severed by the throat.*

λᾱΐνεος, α, ον, = λάϊνος. [ῑ]

λάϊνος, η, ον, (λᾶας) *of stone, stony; λάϊνον ἕσσο χιτῶνα* thou hadst put on coat *of stone*, i. e. thou hadst been buried in stones, stoned to death.

λαῖον, τό, Dor. for λήϊον.

λαιός, ά, όν, *left;* λαιᾶς χειρός on *the left* hand; so πρὸς λαίᾳ χερί; ἐπὶ λαίου on *the left.*

λαιο-τομέω, f. ήσω, (λαῖον, τεμεῖν) *to plough land.*

λαισήϊον, τό, (λάσιος) *a shield* or *target* lighter than the ἀσπίς, covered with raw hides.

ΛΑΙΓΜΑ, τό, *the deep sea.*

ΛΑΙΦΟΣ, τό, *a tattered garment*, generally, *a garment:* also *a piece of cloth, a sail.*

λαιψηρό-δρομος, ον, (λαιψηρός, δραμεῖν) *swift-running.*

λαιψηρός, ά, όν, (λαι-, ψαίρω) *light-footed, swift.*

λᾰκάζω, = λακέω, λάσκω, *to shout, howl.*

Λάκαινα, ἡ, fem. of Λάκων, Lat. *Lacaena, Laconian.* 2. (sub. γυνή), *a Laconian woman.*

Λακαινᾶν, Dor. gen. pl. of Λάκαινα.

λᾰκάνη, late form for λεκάνη.

λᾱ-καταπύγων, ον, (λα-, καταπύγων) *very lustful.* [ῡ]

λάκε, 3 sing. Ep. aor. 2 of λάσκω.

Λᾰκεδαίμων, ονος, ἡ, *Lacedaemon*, the capital of Laconia; also *Laconia* itself.

λᾰκεῖν, aor. 2 inf. of λάσκω.

λᾰκέρυζα, ἡ, (λακέω) *one that cries;* λακέρυζα κορώνη a *cawing* crow; λακέρυζα κύων a *yelping* dog.

λᾱκέω, Dor. for ληκέω.

λᾰκήσω, fut. of λάσκω.

λᾰκίζω, f. ίσω Att. ιῶ, *to rend, tear.*

λᾰκίς, ίδος, ἡ, (λάσκω) *a rent, tearing, rending;* λακίδες πέπλων *ragged robes, tatters.*

λάκισμα, ατος, τό, (λᾰκίζω) *that which is torn:* in pl. *rags, tatters.*

λᾰκιστός, ή, όν, (λακίζω) *torn, rent;* μόρος λακιστός death *by rending.*

λακκό-πρωκτος, ον, (λάκκος, πρωκτός) *a lewd person, an adulterer.*

λακκό-πῡγος, ον, (λάκκος, πυγή) = λακκόπρωκτος.

ΛΑΚΚΟΣ, ὁ, *any hollow, a hole, pit: a cistern, tank:* also *a cellar, storehouse: a pond:* also *a stew* for water-fowl, Lat. *vivarium.*

λάκος, wrong form of λάκκος.

λακ-πάτητος, ον, (λάξ, πατέω) *trampled under foot, trodden down.* [πᾰ]

λακτίζω, f. ίσω Att. ιῶ, (λάξ) *to kick with the heel* or *foot, stamp* or *trample on;* λακτίζειν τὸν πεσόντα *to trample on* the fallen. 2. absol. *to kick;* λακτίζειν πρὸς κέντρα *to kick* against the pricks: also *to struggle convulsively, throb.* Hence

λάκτισμα, τό, *a kick: a trampling on.*

λακτιστής, οῦ, ὁ, (λακτίζω) *one who tramples;* λακτιστὴς ληνοῦ *a treader* of the wine-press.

Λάκων, ωνος, ὁ, *a Laconian* or *Lacedaemonian;* and as Adj. *Laconian:* fem. Λάκαινα. Hence

Λᾰκωνίζω, f. ίσω, *to imitate the Lacedaemonians in manners, dress*, etc.: hence *to speak laconically.* II. *to be in the Lacedaemonian interest.* Hence

Λᾰκωνικός, ή, όν, *Laconian;* τὸ Λακωνικόν *the Laconian people:*—ἡ Λακωνική, 1. (sub. γῆ), *Laconia.* 2. (sub. κρηπίς), *a* kind of *man's shoe.*

Λᾰκωνίς, ίδος, fem. of Λακωνικός, 1. (sub. γυνή), *a Laconian woman.* 2. (sub. γῆ), *the Laconian land.*

Λᾰκωνισμός, ὁ, (Λακωνίζω) *the imitation of the Lacedaemonians in manners, dress*, etc. II. *a being in the Lacedaemonian interest, Laconism.*

Λᾰκωνιστής, οῦ, ὁ, (Λακωνίζω) *one who imitates* or *takes part with the Lacedaemonians, a Laconizer.*

Λᾰκωνο-μᾰνέω, (Λάκων, μανῆναι) *to be mad after the Lacedaemonians, to have a Laconomania.*

λαλαγεῦντες, **λαλαγεῦντι**, Dor. for λαλαγοῦντες, λαλαγοῦσι, pres. part. and ind. of λαλαγέω.

λᾰλᾰγέω, f. ήσω, (λαλέω) *to prattle, babble:* of birds, *to chirrup, chirp.* Hence

λαλάγημα, ατος, τό, (λαλαγέω) *a prattling, babbling.*

λᾰλάζω, *to prattle, babble*, of water. From

λάλαξ, (λαλέω) *a prattler, babbler.*

λαλεῦμες, Dor. pres. ind. of λαλέω.

ΛΑ˘ΛΕ´Ω, f. ήσω, *to prate, chatter, babble:* of birds, *to twitter, chirp:* properly, *to make an inarticulate sound*, opp. to articulate speech: but also, generally, *to talk, talk of.* Hence

λάλημα, τό, *talk.* II. *a talker, prater.*

λᾰλητέος, α, ον, verb. Adj. of λαλέω, *to be talked of.*

λᾰλητής, οῦ, ὁ, (λαλέω) *a talker, prater.*

λᾰλητικός, ή, όν, (λαλέω) *given to talking.*

λᾰλητρίς, ίδος, ἡ, fem. of λαλητής, *a gossip.*

λᾰλιά, ἡ, (λαλέω) *talking, chat, gossip.* II. *a form of speech, dialect.*

λάλιος, α, ον, poët. for λάλος.

λάλλαι, αἱ, (λαλέω) *pebbles*, from their *babbling* in the stream.

λάλος, ον, (λαλέω) *talkative, chattering:* of wings, *flapping.*—Irreg. Comp. λαλίστερος, Sup. λαλίστατος.

λαμά, Heb. for *what? why?*

Λαμαχ-ίππιον, τό, (Λάμαχος, ἱππίον) name for Lamachus, *little jockey Lamachus.*

Λά-μᾰχος, ον, (λᾱ-, μάχη) *very warlike*, name of an Athenian general.

λαμβάνω. fut. λήψομαι Ion. λάμψομαι Dor. λαψοῦμαι, -εῦμαι:—aor. 2 ἔλᾰβον Ep. ἔλλαβον Ion. λάβεσκον, imperat. λᾰβέ, inf. λαβεῖν, part. λαβών, οῦσα, όν:—pf. εἴληφα Ion. λελάβηκα: plqpf. εἰλήφειν:—Med., aor. 2 ἐλαβόμην, Ep. redupl. inf. λελαβέσθαι: Pass., fut. ληφθήσομαι: aor. 1 ἐλήφθην Ion. ἐλάμφθην: pf. εἴλημμαι poët. λέλημμαι Ion. λέλαμμαι. *To take, take hold of, grasp, seize;* when this action refers to *a part*, the part is put in genit., as, τῆς πτέρυγος λάβεν he *caught* her *by* the wing:—metaph., φρενὶ λαβεῖν *to grasp* with the mind; also, absol. *to understand, comprehend:* — Med. *to keep hold of, grasp tight:* also *to get hold of, make one's own:* metaph., λαβέσθαι τῶν ὀρῶν *to take to* the hills. II.

to catch, come upon, overtake: of things, *to take away, carry off.* 2. Att. *to meet with, find, find out, detect.* III. *to take in, receive hospitably, entertain.* IV. *to gain, win, procure, acquire.* V. λαμβάνειν τινὰ ὁρκίοισι *to bind* one by oath. VI. metaph. *to take* a thing in a particular sense. VII. *to have given one, receive, get:* in Med. *to have to wife.* 2. of a woman, *to conceive.* 3. δίκην λαβεῖν *to receive*, i. e. *exact*, a penalty, Lat. *sumere poenas:* but also in the opposite sense, *to suffer* punishment, Lat. *dare poenas.*

λάμβδα, τό, indecl., v. sub **λ.**

Λάμια, ἡ, (λάμος) *a fabulous monster said to feed on man's flesh, a vampire,* a bugbear to children.

λαμπᾰδη-δρομία, ἡ, (λαμπάς, δρόμος) *the torch-race,* an Athenian ceremony at the festivals of Prometheus, Vulcan and Minerva, in which the runners carried lighted torches from the joint altar of these gods in the outer Cerameicus to the Acropolis. After the Persian war Pan received a like honour.

λαμπᾰδηφορία, ἡ, *a carrying of torches,* = **λαμπαδηδρομία.** From

λαμπᾰδη-φόρος, ον, (λαμπάς, φέρω) *torch-bearing:* as Subst., λαμπαδηφόρος, ὁ, *a torch-bearer.*

λαμπάδιον, τό, Dim. of λαμπάς, *a small torch.* II. *a bandage* for wounds.

λαμπᾰδ-οῦχος, ον, (λαμπάς, ἔχω) *torch-carrying, bright-beaming, flashing.*

λαμπάς, άδος, ἡ, (λάμπω) *a torch:* also *a light, lantern, lamp.* 2. *the torch-race,* like λαμπαδηδρομία. II. as Adj., poët, fem. of λαμπρός, *gleaming with torches.*

λάμπεσκε, 3 sing. Ion. impf. of **λάμπω.**

λαμπετάω, poët. for λάμπω, *to shine, flash,* only in Ep. part. λαμπετόων.

λαμπέτης, ου, ὁ, fem. **λαμπέτις**, ιδος, (λάμπω) *the lustrous one.*

ΛΑ'ΜΠΗ, ἡ, *the scum or coating* which gathers on liquors left to stand.

λαμπηδών, όνος, ἡ, (λάμπω) *lustre.*

Λάμπος, ὁ, (λάμπω) one of the horses of Morn, *Bright.*

λάμπ-ουρος, ον, (λάμπω, οὐρά) *bright-tailed:* as a dog's name, *Firetail.*

λαμπρός, ά, όν, (λάμπω) *bright, brilliant, radiant;* λαμπρὸν ὕδωρ *limpid* water. 2. of the voice, *clear, distinct.* 2. of the wind, *fresh, keen.* 3. metaph. *evident, clear, manifest.* II. of men, *illustrious, brilliant, magnificent, splendid.* Hence

λαμπρότης, ητος, ἡ, *brilliancy, splendour.* II. metaph. *distinction, splendour: munificence.*

λαμπροφωνία, ἡ, *loudness of voice.* From

λαμπρό-φωνος, ον, (λαμπρός, φωνή) *loud-voiced.*

λαμπρύνω, f. ῠνῶ: Med., aor. 1 ἐλαμπρῡνάμην:—Pass., 3 sing. pf. λελάμπρυνται:—(λαμπρός):—*to make bright* or *brilliant.* II. Med. *to pride oneself* on a thing: *to distinguish oneself* in. III. Pass. *to become bright;* λαμπρύνεσθαι ὄμμασιν to become clear-sighted. 2. *to be* or *become clear, evident, notorious.*

λαμπρῶς, Adv. of λαμπρός, *brilliantly:* Sup. λαμπρότατα.

λαμπτέος, ον, Ion. for ληπτέος, verb. Adj. of λαμβάνω, *to be taken.*

λαμπτήρ, ῆρος, ὁ, (λάμπω) *a stand* or *grate* for burning wood in: *a beacon-light, watch-fire: a torch, lamp.*

λαμπτηρ-ουχία, ἡ, (λαμπτήρ, ἔχω) *a holding of torches;* λαμπτηρουχίαι *the beacon-watches.*

λαμπτῆρσι, dat. pl. of λαμπτήρ.

ΛΑ'ΜΠΩ, f. ψω: aor. 1 ἔλαμψα: pf. λέλαμπα:—*to shine, to be bright, brilliant, radiant.* 2. of sound, *to be clear, ring loud and clear.* 3. metaph. *to shine forth, be conspicuous* or *illustrious.* II. trans. *to make to shine, light up:* Pass. *to shine.*

λᾰμῠρός, ά, όν, (λάμος) *yawning, profound.* II. *voracious, gluttonous.* III. metaph. *bold, wanton:* of women, *coquettish; wayward, arch.* Hence

λαμυρῶς, Adv. *greedily:* Comp. λαμυρότερον.

λαμφθῆναι, Ion. aor. 1 pass. inf. of **λαμβάνω.**

λάμψομαι, Ion. for λήψομαι, fut. of **λαμβάνω.**

λανθάνω or **ΛΗ'ΘΩ**, whence the tenses are formed: fut. λήσω Dor. **λᾱσῶ**: aor. 2 **ἔλᾰθον**: pf. λέληθα: plqpf. **ἐλελήθειν**:—*to escape* or *elude notice, to be unseen, unnoticed;* c. acc. pers., **λάθεν Ἕκτορα** he *escaped the notice* of Hector. 2. with part., λανθάνει κλέπτων *he escapes notice* while stealing, i. e. he steals *without being seen,* (where λανθάνω is best expressed by an Adverb, *unawares, secretly*): also with a pass. part., as, μὴ διαφθαρεὶς λάθῃ lest he perish *without himself knowing it;* also with the acc. of the pers. pron. added, as, ἕως σαυτὸν λάθῃς διαρραγείς until *thou mayest not observe* thyself having burst in twain, i. e. mayest burst *without being thyself aware of it.* II. Causal, in pres. **ληθάνω**, aor. 1 ἔλησα, redupl. Ep. aor. 2 λέλᾰθον, subj. λελάθῃ:—*to make to forget:* hence, III. Med. and Pass. **λανθάνομαι** or **λήθομαι**: fut. λήσομαι Dor. λᾱσεῦμαι paullo-post fut. λελήσομαι: aor. 2 med. ἐλᾰθόμην: aor. 1 pass. ἐλήσθην: pf. λέλησμαι, Ion. and Ep. λέλασμαι part. λελασμένος:—*to forget, lose the memory of.*

λανός, λανῶ, Dor. for ληνός, ληνοῦ.

ΛΑ'Ξ, Adv. *with the heel* or *foot;* **λὰξ πατεῖσθαι** to be trodden *under foot.*

λαξευτός, ή, όν, *hewn in stone.* From

λαξεύω, (λᾶς, ξέω) *to cut stones: to hew in stone.*

λάξις, (λάζομαι) *an allotment of land.*

λᾶξις, ιος, ὁ, Dor. for λῆξις, *cessation.*

λάξομαι, Ion. for λήξομαι, fut. of **λαγχάνω.**

λᾱο-δάμᾱς, αντος, ὁ, (λαός, δαμάω) *man-subduing.*

λᾱο-ξόος, ον, (λᾶας, ξέω) *stone-cutting:* as Subst., λαοξόος, ὁ, *a sculptor.*

λᾱο-πᾰθής, ές, (λαός, παθεῖν) *suffered by the people.*

λᾱο-πόρος, ον, (λαός, πόρος) *conveying the people.*

ΛΑΟ'Σ, οῦ, ὁ, Ion. **ληός** Att. **λεώς**:—*the people:*

—in the Il. *the soldiery, host, army;* also *a land-army* opp. to a fleet; also *the common men* opp. to their leaders. II. in plur. λαοί, *the subjects* of a prince.

λᾶος, irreg. gen. of λᾶας, *a stone.*

λᾱο-σεβής, ές, (λαός, σέβομαι) *revered by the people.*

λᾱοσ-σόος, ον, (λαός, σεύω) *rousing* or *stirring nations.*

λᾱο-τέκτων, ονος, ὁ, (λᾶας, τέκτων) *a worker in stone, mason.*

λᾱο-τίνακτος, ον, (λᾶας, τινάσσω) *stirred by a stone.*

λᾱο-τρόφος, ον, (λαός, τρέφω) *nourishing the people.*

λᾱο-τύπος, ον, (λᾶας, τύπτω) *cutting stones:* as Subst., λαοτύπος, ὁ, *a stone-cutter, stone-mason.*

λᾱο-φθόρος, ον, (λαός, φθείρω) *ruining the people.*

λᾱο-φόνος, ον, (λαός, *φένω) *slaying the people.*

λᾱο-φόρος Att. **λεω-φόρος**, ον, (λαός, φέρω) *bearing people;* λαοφόρος ὁδός a road, highway.

λᾰπάζω, f. ξω, = ἀλαπάζω, *to plunder, spoil, pillage:* also, *to carry off.*

λᾰπάρᾱ Ion. **-ρη**, ἡ, *the soft part of the body* between the ribs and hips, *the flank, loins,* Lat. *ilia.* Properly fem. of λαπαρός.

λᾰπᾰρός, ά, όν, (λαπάζω) *slack, loose, relaxed.*

ΛΑ'ΠΗ, ἡ, *phlegm,* Lat. *pituīta:* metaph., ἀνηλίῳ λάπᾳ in sunless *damp,* cf. Virgil's *loca senta situ.* [ᾰ]

λᾰπῆναι, aor. 2 pass. inf. of λάπτω.

Λᾰπίθαι, οἱ, the *Lapithae,* a Thessalian people in the heroic age, conquerors of the Centaurs. [ῐ]

λάπτω, fut. ψω: aor. 1 ἔλαψα: pf. λέλᾰφα:—*to lap with the tongue,* like Lat. *lambo:* generally, *to drink, drain, suck.* (Formed from the sound.)

λᾱρῑνός, ή, όν, (λαρός) *fatted, fat.*

λᾰρίς, ίδος, ἡ, = λάρος, *a gull.*

Λάρῑσα Ion. **Ληρ-**, ἡ, *Larissa,* name of many old Greek cities, esp. of one in Thessaly. Hence

Λᾱρῑσαῖος, α, ον, *Larissaean, of* or *from Larissa.*

λαρκίδιον, τό, Dim. of λάρκος. [κῐ]

ΛΑ'ΡΚΟΣ, ὁ, *a basket* for charcoal, *a coal-basket.*

ΛΑ'ΡΝΑΞ, ᾰκος, ἡ, *a coffer, box, chest: a cinerary urn: an ark.*

ΛΑ'ΡΟΣ, ὁ, a ravenous sea-bird, *the gull, a cormorant.* [ᾰ, except in one passage.]

ΛΑΡΟ'Σ, ά, όν, *dainty, sweet, pleasant:*—irreg. Sup. λαρώτατος: but the reg. Comp. λαρότερον occurs as Adv.

λᾰρυγγιάω, (λάρυγξ) *to scream, screech.*

λᾱρυγγίζω, Att. fut. ιῶ, (λάρυγξ) *to bawl, bellow.* II. *to outdo in shouting.*

ΛΑ'ΡΥΓΞ, gen. υγγος, ὁ, *the larynx* or *upper part of the windpipe:* also *the gullet, throat.*

λᾶς, λᾶος, ὁ, *a stone,* Att. contr. for λᾶας.

ΛΑ'ΣΑΝΟΝ, τό, always in pl. *a trivet* or *stand for a pot, a gridiron.* II. Lat. *lasanum, a night-stool.* [λᾰ]

λάσδεο, Dor. for λάζου, imperat. of λάζομαι.

λᾱσεῦμαι, Dor. for λήσομαι, fut. med. of λανθάνω: 1 pl. **λασεύμεσθα**, for λησόμεθα.

ΛΑ'ΣΘΗ, ἡ, *mockery, insult.*

λασθῆμεν, Dor. for λασθῆναι, λησθῆναι, aor. 1 pass. inf. of λανθάνω.

λᾰσι-αύχην, ενος, (λάσιος, αὐχήν) *with shaggy neck.*

λᾰσιό-θριξ, τρῐχος, ὁ, ἡ, (λάσιος, θρίξ) *shaggy-haired.*

λάσιος, α, ον, Att. ος, ον, *shaggy with hair* or *wool, hairy.* II. *shaggy with bushes, bushy.* (Akin to δασύς.) [ᾰ] Hence

λασιό-στερνος, ον, (λάσιος, στέρνον) *with hairy chest.*

ΛΑ'ΣΚΩ, (the tenses formed from obsol. *λᾰκέω, λάκω): fut. λᾰκήσομαι: aor. 1 ἐλάκησα [ᾰ]: aor. 2 ἔλᾰκον, inf. λᾰκεῖν: pf. λέλᾱκα Ion. λέληκα, Ep. part. fem. λελᾰκυῖα:—Med., aor. 2 ἐλᾰκόμην, Ep. redupl. λελακόμην, whence 3 plur. λελάκοντο [ᾰ]:—*to ring, clash, crash, crackle:* of axles, *to creak:* commonly of things, but also II. of animals, *to shriek, scream:* of dogs, *to howl, bay.* III. of men, *to speak loud, shout, shout forth:* rarely *to sing.*

λᾱσῶ, Dor. for λήσω, fut. of λανθάνω.

ΛΑ'ΤΑΞ, ᾰγος, ἡ, *a drop of wine.*

Λατο-γενής, ές, (Λατώ, *γένω) *born of Latona.*

λᾱτομέω, f. ήσω, (λατόμος) *to quarry stones.* Hence

λᾱτομία, ἡ, *a stone-quarry.*

λᾱ-τόμος, ὁ, (λᾶς, τέμνω) *a stone-cutter, quarry-man.*

λατρεία, ἡ, (λατρεύω) *hired labour, service, servitude:* esp. *the service of the gods, worship.*

λάτρευμα, τό, *hired service, servitude:* esp. *service paid to the gods, worship.* II. *a slave.* From

λατρεύω, f. σω, (λάτρις) *to work for hire* or *pay.* 2. *to serve, be bound* or *enslaved to,* c. dat. pers.: but also c. acc. pers. *to serve.* 2. *to serve* the gods, c. dat.

λάτριος, α, ον, *of a servant* or *service.* From

λάτρις, ιος, ὁ and ἡ, *a hired servant,* Lat. *latro:* generally, *a servant, slave.*

ΛΑ'ΤΡΟΝ, τό, *pay, hire;* λάτρων ἄτερθε without *rent* or *quittance.*

λαυκᾰνίη, ἡ, = λαιμός, *the throat.* (Deriv. uncertain.)

ΛΑΥ'ΡΑ Ion. **λαύρη**, ἡ, *an alley, lane, narrow passage between houses:* also *a pass between rocks, ravine, defile.* II. *a sewer, drain.*

λαφυγμός, ὁ, (λαφύσσω) *greediness, gluttony.*

ΛΑ'ΦΥΡΑ, τά, *spoils* taken in war, Lat. *spolia.*

λαφῡρ-αγωγέω, f. ήσω, *to make booty of.* From

λᾰφῡρ-αγωγός, όν, (λάφυρα, ἄγω) *carrying off booty.*

λᾰφῡροπωλέω, f. ήσω, *to sell booty.* From

λᾰφῡρο-πώλης, ου, ὁ, (λάφυρα, πωλέω) *a retailer of booty,* Lat. *sector.*

λᾰφύσσω Att. **-ττω**, fut. ξω, (λάπτω) *to swallow greedily, eat up, devour:* of men, *to eat gluttonously, gorge,* Lat. *belluari.* Hence

λᾰφύστιος, α, ον, *gluttonous.*

ΛΑΧΑΙ'ΝΩ, f. ᾰνῶ: aor. 1 ἐλάχηνα:—*to dig.*

λᾰχᾰνεύω, f. σω, (λάχανον) *to plant with potherbs:* —Med. *to gather herbs.*

λᾰχᾰνη-λόγος, ον, (λάχανον, λέγω) *gathering h[erbs]*

λᾰχᾰνίζομαι, Dep. (λάχανον) *to gather herbs.* Hence

λᾰχᾰνισμός, ὁ, *a gathering of herbs.*

λάχᾰνον, τό, (λᾰχαίνω) mostly in pl. λάχανα, τά, *garden-herbs*, opp. to wild plants *potherbs, vegetables, greens, garden-stuff*, Lat. *olera*. 2. τὰ λάχανα *the vegetable-market, the green-market.*

λᾰχᾰνο-πώλης, ου, ὁ, (λάχανον, πωλέω) *a green-grocer*: fem. **λᾰχᾰνο-πωλήτρια**, and **λᾰχᾰνό-πωλις**, ιδος, ἡ, *a woman who sells garden-stuff*

λάχε, Ep. for ἔλᾰχε, 3 sing. aor. 2 of λαγχάνω.

λάχεια, either for ἐλάχεια, fem. of ἐλαχύς, *small*; or fem. of an Adj. λαχύς (from λαχαίνω) *well-tilled, fertile.*

λᾰχεῖν, aor. 2 inf. of λαγχάνω.

Λάχεσις, gen. εως Ion. ιος, ἡ, (λᾰχεῖν) *Lachesis*, one of the three Fates, *the disposer of lots.* II. *lot, destiny, fate.*

λάχη, ἡ, (λαχαίνω) *a digging.*

λαχναῖος, α, ον, *woolly, hairy, downy.* From

ΛΑ'ΧΝΗ, ἡ, *soft woolly hair, down*: *the soft nap* or *pile* on cloth: *sheep's-wool.* Hence

λαχνήεις, εσσα, εν, *woolly, hairy.*

λαχνό-γυιος, ον, (λάχνη, γυῖον) *with hairy limbs.*

λάχνος, ὁ, = λάχνη, *wool.* Hence

λαχνόω, f. ώσω, *to make hairy*:—Pass. *to grow downy.*

λαχν-ώδης, ες, (λάχνη, εἶδος) *like down, downy.*

λᾰχοίην, Att. for λάχοιμι, aor. 2 opt. of λαγχάνω.

ΛΑ'ΧΟΣ, τό, (λᾰχεῖν) *one's lot, fate, destiny.* II. *the portion obtained by lot, a lot, share, portion.* [ᾰ]

λᾰχών, aor. 2 part. of λαγχάνω.

λαψεῦμαι and **λαψοῦμαι**, Dor. fut. of λαμβάνω.

λάψων, fut. part. of λάπτω.

λαψῇ, Dor. 2 sing. aor. 1 med. subj. of λαμβάνω.

ΛΑ'Ω, = βλέπω, *to see, behold, look at*; old Ep. word used by Hom. in part. λάων and Ep. 3 sing. impf. λάε. [ᾰ]

***ΛΑ'Ω**, = θέλω, *to wish*: see λῶ.

λέαινα, ἡ, fem. of λέων, *a lioness.*

λεαίνω, f. λεᾰνῶ Ep. λειᾰνέω: aor. 1 ἐλέηνα Ep. λέηνα: (λεῖος) :—*to smooth, polish, work smooth*; λεαίνειν κελεύθον *to smooth* the way. II. *to rub smooth, bray* or *pound in a mortar*: *to destroy.* III. metaph. *to smooth away, smooth* or *soften down*

λεάντειρα, ἡ, fem. of λεαντήρ.

λεαντήρ, ῆρος, ὁ, (λεαίνω) *a polisher.*

λέβης, ητος, ὁ, (λείβω) *a kettle, caldron.* II. *the basin* in which the purifying water (χέρνιψ) was handed round: but also, a sort of *basin* which was struck like a cymbal at the funerals of the Spartan kings. III. *a cinerary urn.*

λεγεών, ῶνος, ὁ, Gr. form of the Lat. *legio, a legion.*

λέγομες, λέγοντι, Dor. for λέγομεν, λέγουσι, 1 and 3 pl. of λέγω.

ΛΕ'ΓΩ, f. λέξω: aor. 1 ἔλεξα: pf. εἴλοχα :—Med., f. λέξομαι: aor. 1 ἐλεξάμην :—Pass., fut. λεχθήσομαι: paullo-post fut. λελέξομαι: aor. 1 pass. ἐλέχθην, aor. 2 ἐλέγην: Ep. aor. 2 pass. ἐλέγμην, 3 sing. λέκτο: pf. εἴλεγμαι or λέλεγμαι: I. Act. *TO LAY, to lay asleep, lull to sleep*:—Pass. and Med. *TO LIE, to lie down.* II. *to lay in order, arrange*, and so *to gather, pick up*:—Med. *to gather for oneself*: hence *to choose, pick out* III. *to reckon, count, tell* or *reckon up.* IV. *to recount, tell, relate*: hence *to speak, say, utter*: also of oracles, *to say, declare*: it is used later to express any communication *by word of mouth*; λέγειν κατά τινος *to accuse* one; c. inf., λέγειν τινὰ ποιεῖν τί *to tell, bid, command*; λέγειν τί, *to say something*, i. e. *to speak to the purpose*; opp. to λέγειν οὐδέν, *to say nothing to the purpose*: also, like Lat. *dicere, to speak of, mean, refer to*, as, εἴσω κομίζου σύ, Κασάνδραν λέγω, go thou within, *I mean* Cassandra :—Pass. λέγεται, *it is said, on dit*; τὸ λεγόμενον, absol. *as the saying goes.*

λεηλᾰσία, ἡ, *a driving off booty, pillaging.* From

λεηλᾰτέω, f. ήσω, *to drive away booty, drive cattle, to make booty*: hence *to plunder, despoil.* From

λε-ηλάτης, ου, ὁ, (λεία, ἐλαύνω) *one who drives off booty, a plunderer, marauder.* [ᾰ]

ΛΕΙ'Α Ion. **ληΐη**, ἡ, *booty, plunder*, esp. of cattle; hence *what can be driven off as booty.*

λειαίνω, fut. λειᾰνέω, Ion. and Ep. for λεαίνω.

ΛΕΙ'ΒΩ, ψω: aor. 1 ἔλειψα :—*to pour, pour forth*: mostly like σπένδω, *to pour a libation.* II. *to let flow, shed*:—Med. *to flow, run, trickle*; λείβεσθαι δακρύοις *to melt into* tears: hence *to melt* or *pine away*:—Pass. *to be moistened, bedewed.*

λεΐζομαι, Ion. and poët. for ληΐζομαι.

λείηναν, Ep. 3 pl. aor. 1 of λειαίνω.

λειήνας, Ep. aor. 1 part. of λεαίνω.

λεῖμαξ, ᾰκος, ἡ, = λειμών, *a meadow*: *a garden.*

λεῖμμα, ατος, τό, (λείπω) *a remnant, remains*

λειμών, ῶνος, ὁ, (λείβω) *any moist grassy place, a meadow, mead*, Lat. *pratum.*

λειμωνιάς, άδος, poët. fem. of λειμώνιος; νύμφη λειμωνιάς a *meadow*-nymph.

λειμώνιος, α, ον, (λειμών) *of a meadow*

λειμωνίς, ίδος, poët. fem. of λειμώνιος.

λειμωνόθεν or -θε, Adv. (λειμών) *from a meadow.*

λειο-γένειος, ον, (λεῖος, γένειον) *smooth-chinned.*

λειο-κύμων, ον, (λεῖος, κῦμα) *with gentle waves.*

λειό-μιτος, ον, (λεῖος, μίτος) *smoothing the threads of the warp.*

λειοντῆ, ἡ, poët. for λεοντῆ, *a lion's skin.*

λειοντο-μάχης, ου, ὁ, (λέων, μάχη) poët. for λεοντ-, *a lion-fighter.*

λειοντο-πάλης, ου, ὁ, (λέων, πάλη) poët. for λεοντ-, *wrestler with a lion.*

ΛΕΙ'ΟΣ, α, ον, or ος, ον, Lat. *LAEVIS, smooth*: of the ground, *smooth, level, flat*; of the sea, *smooth*: c. gen., λεῖος πετράων *level and free from* rocks. 2. *with a smooth chin, beardless.* 3. metaph. *smooth, soft, gentle.*

λειότης, ητος, ἡ, (λεῖος) *smoothness.*

λείουσι, poët. for λέουσι, dat. pl. of λέων.

λειπτέον, verb. Adj. of λείπω, *one must leave.*

ΛΕΙ'ΠΩ, f. λείψω: aor. 2 act. ἔλῐπον, inf. λῐπεῖν; (aor. 1 ἔλειψα only in late writers): pf. λέλοιπα:—Med., fut. λείψομαι in pass. sense:—Pass., fut. λειφθήσομαι, paullo-post. fut. λελείψομαι: aor. 1 ἐλείφθην: aor. 2 ἐλίπην [ῐ]: pf. λέλειμμαι: plqpf. ἐλελείμμην:—Lat. *LINQUO, to leave, leave remaining:* of dying persons, *to leave behind, bequeath:*—so in Med. *to leave behind one, bequeath, leave as a memorial.* 2. *to desert in danger, abandon, forsake.* II. Pass. *to be left, left behind, left remaining.* 2. *to be left behind in a race:* pf. part. λελειμμένος, *left behind, lingering behind, inferior to:* absol. *to stay behind.* 3. c. gen. *to be left without: to come short of.., be inferior, worse, weaker than* another. 4. *to be wanting* or *lacking.* III. intr. in Act. *to be gone, fail, disappear: to be wanting, cease,* Lat. *deficere.*

λειριόεις, εσσα, εν, (λείριον) *of* or *like a lily, lily-white, delicate.*

ΛΕΙ'ΡΙΟΝ, τό, *a lily, the white lily,* Lat. *lilium.*

λεϊστός, see ληϊστός.

λέϊτος or **λεῖτος**, ον, (λαός, λεώς) *of the people,* Ion. for Att. δημόσιος.

λειτουργέω, f. ήσω, (λειτουργός) *to perform public duties, to do the state service:*—at Athens, *to serve public offices at one's own cost:* cf. λειτουργία. II. *to minister* as a priest, *officiate.* Hence

λειτουργία, ἡ, *a public service:*—at Athens *a liturgy,* i. e. *a burdensome public office* or *charge,* which the richer citizens discharged at their own expense, properly in rotation, but also voluntarily or by appointment. II. *divine service,* whence our word *Liturgy.*

λειτουργικός, ή, όν, *performing public service, ministering.* From

λειτ-ουργός, όν, (λέϊτος or λεῖτος, ἔργον) *performing public duties, serving the state.* II. *a priest, minister of God.*

ΛΕΙΧΗ'Ν, ῆνος, ὁ, *a tree-moss, lichen.* II. hence *a lichen-like eruption* on the skin, *scurvy:* of the ground, *a blight, canker.*

ΛΕΙ'ΧΩ, f. ξω: aor. 1 ἔλειξα:—Lat. *LINGO, to lick: to lick up:* hence irreg. pf. part. λελειχμότες.

λείψας, aor. 1 part. of λείβω.

λειψᾰνη-λόγος, ον, (λείψανον, λέγω) *gathering remnants.*

λείψᾰνον, τό, (λείπω) *a piece left, remnant, relic, wreck:* in plur. *remains, remnants,* Lat. *reliquiae.*

Λειψ-ύδριον, τό, (λείπω, ὕδωρ) *an ill-watered district* near mount Parnes in Attica.

λείων, ὁ, poët. for λέων, hence Ep. dat. λείουσι.

λεκάνη, ἡ, (λέκος) *a dish, pot, pan.* [ᾰ] Hence

λεκᾰνίς, ἡ, **λεκάνιον**, τό, **λεκᾰνίσκη**, ἡ, Diminutives of λεκάνη:—*a little dish* or *pan, platter.*

λεκῐθο-πώλης, ου, ὁ, fem. **-πωλις**, ιδος, (λέκιθος, πωλέω) *a pulse-porridge seller.*

ΛΕ'ΚΙΘΟΣ, ὁ, *pulse-porridge.*

ΛΕ'ΚΟΣ, εος, τό, *a dish, plate, pot, pan.*

λεκτικός, ή, όν, (λέγω) *good at speaking, fluent, eloquent.* II. *suited for speaking.*

λέκτο, 3 sing. Ep. aor. 2 pass. of λέγω.

λεκτός, ή, όν, (λέγω) *gathered, chosen, picked out.* II. *uttered, spoken, said: to be spoken.*

λέκτρον, τό, (λέγω) *a couch, bed,* Lat. *lectus:* λέκτρονδε *to bed.* 2. in pl. *the marriage-bed, marriage.*

λελᾰβέσθαι, Ep. redupl. aor. 2 inf. med. of λαμβάνω.

λελάβηκα, Ion. pf. of λαμβάνω.

λελάθη, 3 sing. Ep. redupl. aor. 2 subj. of λανθάνω.

λελάθοντο, **λελᾰθέσθω**, **λελᾰθέσθαι**, 3 pl. indic., 3 sing. imperat., and inf., aor. 2 med. of λανθάνω.

λέλᾱκα, pf. of λάσκω.

λελάκοντο, 3 pl. Ep. redupl. aor. 2 med. of λάσκω.

λελᾰκυῖα, Ep. pf. part. fem. of λάσκω.

λέλεμμαι, Ion. pf. pass. of λαμβάνω.

λέλασμαι, Ion. and Ep. pf. pass. of λανθάνω.

λέλᾰχον, Ep. redupl. aor. 2 of λαγχάνω.

λελάχω, Ep. redupl. aor. 2 subj. of λαγχάνω.

λέλειπτο, Ep. 3 sing. plqpf. pass. of λείπω.

λελεῖφθαι, pf. pass. inf. of λείπω.

λελειχμότες, nom. pl. irreg. pf. part. of λείχω.

λέλευσμαι, pf. pass. of λεύω.

λελέχᾰται, Ion. 3 pl. pf. pass. of λέγω.

λέληθα, pf. of λανθάνω.

λέληκα, Ion. pf. of λάσκω: part. λεληκώς.

λέλημμαι, poët. pf. pass. of λαμβάνω.

λέλησμαι, Ion. pf. pass. of λανθάνω: but **λέλησμαι**, pf. pass. of ληΐζομαι.

λελίημαι, old Ep. pf. of λιλαίομαι, (and therefore properly λελίλημαι), *to strive eagerly, long for, be zealous for:* part. λελῑημένος, *zealous, hasty, eager.*

λελιμμένος, pf. pass. part. of λίπτω.

λέλογα, pf. of λέγω.

λελογισμένως, Adv. pf. pass. part. of λογίζομαι, *deliberately, advisedly.*

λέλογχα, pf. of λαγχάνω.

λελόγχη, poët. for ἐλελόγχει, 3 sing. plqpf. of λαγχάνω.

λέλοιπα, pf. of λείπω.

λελουμένος, pf. part. pass. of λούω.

λελύμασμαι, pf. pass. of λυμαίνομαι. [ῠ]

λέλυνται, 3 pl. pf. pass. of λύω:—**λέλυντο**, Ep. for ἐλέλυντο, 3 pl. plqpf. pass.

λελῦτο, Ep. for λελύοιτο, 3 sing. pf. opt. pass. of λύω.

λελώβημαι, pf. in pass. sense of λωβάομαι.

ΛΕ'ΜΒΟΣ, ὁ, *a small boat with a sharp prow, a felucca.*

λέμμα, ατος, τό, (λέπω) *that which is peeled off, peel, husk, skin, scale.*

λέντιον, τό, the Lat. *linteum, a linen cloth, napkin.*

λέξεο, Ep. for λέξαι, aor. 1 imperat. med. of λέγομαι, *to lie down.*

λέξις, εως, ἡ, (λέγω) *a speaking, speech.* 2. *a way of speaking, diction, style.*

λέξο, Ep. for λέξαι, aor. 1 med. imperat. of λέγομαι, *to lie down.*

λεοντέη contr. **λεοντῆ** (sub. δορά), ἡ, *a lion's skin*, properly fem. of λεόντεος

λεόντειος, α, ον, (λέων) *of a lion: lion-like.*

λεοντό-διφρος, ον, (λέων, δίφρος) *in chariot drawn by lions.*

λεοντο-κέφᾰλος, ον, (λέων, κεφαλή) *lion-headed.*

λεοντό-πους, ὁ, ἡ, πουν, τό, (λέων, πούς) *lion-footed.*

λεοντο-φόνος, ον, (λέων, *φένω) *lion-killing.*

λεοντο-φόρος, ον, (λέων, φέρω) *lion-bearing.*

λεοντο-φυής, ές, (λέων, φυή) *of lion nature.*

λεοντό-χλαινος, ον, (λέων, χλαῖνα) *clad in lion's skin.*

ΛΕ'ΠΑΔΝΟΝ, τό, *a broad leather strap* or *band*, fastening the yoke round the neck, and passing between the fore legs to join the girth (μασχαλιστήρ).

λεπαῖος, α, ον, (λέπας) *of a scaur* or *crag: craggy.*

λέπ-αργος, ον, (λέπος, ἀργός) *with white skin* or *feathers.*

λέπας, τό, (λέπω) *a bare rock, scaur, crag.*

λεπάς, άδος, ἡ, *a limpet*, Lat. *patella*, from its clinging to the rock (λέπας).

λεπαστή, ἡ, (λέπας) *a limpet-shaped drinking-cup.*

λεπιδόομαι, Pass. (λεπίς) *to be covered with scales.* Hence

λεπῐδωτός, ή, όν, *scaly, covered with scales;* λεπιδωτὸς θώρηξ *scale-armour.* II. Subst. *a fish with large scales.*

λεπίς, ίδος, ἡ, (λέπας) *a scale, husk, shell.*

λέπρα Ion. **λέπρη**, ἡ, (λέπρος) *the leprosy.*

λεπράς, άδος, ἡ, poët. fem. of λεπρός, *rough.*

λεπρός, ά, όν, (λέπος) *scaly, rough: leprous, mangy.*

λεπτᾰκῐνός, ή, όν, poët. for λεπταλέος.

λεπτᾰλέος, α, ον, (λεπτός) *fine, slender, delicate.*

λεπτ-επί-λεπτος, ον, *thin upon thin, thin as can be.*

λεπτό-γειος, ον, Att. **λεπτό-γεως**, ων, (λέπτος, γαῖα, γῆ) *of a thin* or *poor soil*

λεπτο-γνώμων, ον, gen. ονος, (λεπτός, γνώμη) *subtle in mind*

λεπτό-γραμμος, ον, (λέπτος, γραμμή) *drawn fine.*

λεπτό-γραφος, ον, (λέπτος, γράφω) *written fine.*

λεπτό-δομος, ον, (λέπτος, δέμω) *slightly built: slight.*

λεπτολογέω, f. ήσω, *to speak subtly, to chop logic, quibble:* so too **λεπτολογέομαι**, as Dep. From

λεπτο-λόγος, ον, (λεπτός, λέγω) *speaking subtly, subtle, quibbling.*

λεπτό-μῐτος, ον, (λέπτος, μίτος) *of fine threads*

λεπτόν (sub. νόμισμα), τό, *a very small coin*, about a fourth of a farthing, *a mite.*

λεπτός, ή, όν, (λέπω) *peeled, cleaned of the husks:* —hence, generally, *thin, fine, slender, delicate:* in bad sense, *thin, lean, meagre.* II. *strait, narrow.* III. *slight, small, insignificant;* τὰ λεπτὰ τῶν προβάτων *small* cattle, i. e. *sheep and goats;* λεπτὰ πλοῖα *small* craft: of sound, *light, slight.* IV. metaph. *fine, subtle, refined ingenious:* of the voice, *fine, delicate.*

λεπτοσύνη, ἡ, = λεπτότης.

λεπτότης, ητος, ἡ, (λεπτός) *thinness, fineness, slightness, leanness.* II. metaph. *subtlety.*

λεπτουργέω, f. ήσω, (λεπτουργός) *to do fine work:* hence *to refine overmuch, deal subtly, quibble.*

λεπτ-ουργής, ές, (λεπτός, ἔργον) *finely worked.*

λεπτ-ουργός, όν, (λεπτός, ἔργον) *producing fine work.*

λεπτο-ῡφής, ές, (λεπτός, ὑφαίνω) *finely woven.* [ῡ]

λεπτο-ψάμαθος, ον, (λεπτός, ψάμαθος) *with fine sand.*

λεπτύνω, f. υνῶ, (λεπτός) *to make thin: to thrash, beat out:*—Pass. *to grow lean.*

λεπτῶς, Adv. of λεπτός, *slightly: subtly*

λεπύριον, τό, Dim. *a small husk, thin rind.* From

λέπῡρον, τό, (λέπος) *a shell, husk, rind.*

ΛΕ'ΠΩ, fut. ψω: aor. 1 ἔλεψα:—*to strip off the husks* or *rind, to peel* or *bark.*

Λέρνα, ἡ, *Lerna*, a marsh in Argolis, the abode of the Hydra:—hence **Λερναῖος**, α, ον, *Lernaean.*

Λεσβιάζω, *to imitate the Lesbian women.* From

Λεσβιάς, άδος, ἡ, (Λέσβος) *a Lesbian woman.*

Λεσβίζω, = λεσβιάζω.

Λέσβιος, α, ον, (Λέσβος) *Lesbian of Lesbos.*

Λεσβόθεν, Adv. *from Lesbos.* From

Λέσβος, ἡ, *Lesbos*, a large island on the coast of Asia Minor.

λεσχάζω, (λέσχη) *to chatter, gossip.*

λέσχη, ἡ, (λέγω) *a place where people resorted to talk and hear the news, a lounge, place of public resort:* also *a council-hall.* II. *talking, gossip:* in good sense, *conversation, discussion, debate;* πρὸς ἐμὴν λέσχην to *conversation* with me. Hence

λεσχηνεύω, f. σω, *to chat* or *converse with.*

λευγᾰλέος, α, ον, (akin to λυγρός) *in sorry plight, wretched, pitiful, melancholy, dismal.*

Λευΐτης, ου, ὁ, *one of the tribe of Levi* (Λευΐ), *a Levite.* [ῑ] Hence

Λευῑτικός, ή, όν, *Levitical.*

λευκαίνω, (λευκός) *to whiten, blanch, bleach.* 2. *to make bright* or *light.*

λευκᾶν, Dor. for λευκῶν, gen. pl. of **λευκός.**

λευκᾶναι, aor. 1 inf. of λευκαίνω.

λευκ-ανθής, ές, (λευκός, ἄνθος) *white-blossoming, white, blanched, pale;* λευκανθὲς κάρα a *white* head.

λευκ-ανθίζω, (λευκός, ἄνθος) *to have white blossoms:* generally, *to be white.*

λευκάς, άδος, poët. fem. of **λευκός**, *white, chalky:* hence the promontory of Epirus was called Λευκάς

λευκᾶς, Dor. gen. fem. of λευκός.

λεύκ-ασπις, ῐδος, ὁ, ἡ, (λευκός, ἀσπίς) *white-shielded.*

λεύκη, ἡ, (λευκός) *the white leprosy.* II. *the white poplar*, Lat. *populus alba*, used for chaplets.

λευκ-ήρετμος, ον, (λευκός, ἐρετμός) *with white* or *foaming oars.*

λευκ-ήρης, ες, (λευκός, ἀραρεῖν) *white, blanched.*

Λευκιππίδες, αἱ, *daughters of Leucippus*, nymphs worshipped at Sparta.

λεύκ-ιππος, ον, (λευκός, ἵππος) *riding* or *driving white horses: famous for white horses.*

λευκίτης [ῑ], ου, ὁ, = λευκός.

Λευκο-θέα, ἡ, (λευκή, θεά) *the white goddess;* the name by which Ino was worshipped as a propitious sea-goddess.

λευκό-θριξ, τρῐχός, ὁ, ἡ, (λευκός, θρίξ) *white-haired.*

λευκο-θώραξ, ᾱκος, ὁ, ἡ, (λευκός, θώραξ) *with white cuirass.*

λευκό-ϊον, τό, (λευκός, ἴον) *the stock* or *wall-flower.*

λευκο-κύμων, ον, gen. ονος, (λευκός, κῦμα) *white with waves, surfy.* [ῡ]

λευκό-λῐνον, τό, (λευκόν, λίνον) *white flax* for ropes and rigging, used by the Phoenicians.

λευκο-λόφας, ου, ὁ, and **λευκό-λοφος**, ον, (λευκός, λόφος) *white-crested:*—**λευκόλοφον**, τό, *a white hill.*

λευκο-όπωρος, ον, (λευκός, ὀπώρα) *with white autumn fruits.*

λευκο-πάρειος Ion. -**πάρῃος**, ον, (λευκός, παρειά) *fair-cheeked.*

λευκό-πεπλος, ον, (λευκός, πέπλος) *white-robed.*

λευκό-πηχυς, υ, gen. εως, (λευκός, πῆχυς) *white-armed.*

λευκο-πληθής, ές, (λευκός, πλῆθος) *filled with white* or *with persons in white.*

λευκό-πους, ὁ, ἡ, πουν, τό, gen. ποδος, (λευκός, πούς) *white-footed: barefooted.*

λευκο-πρεπής, ές, (λευκός, πρέπω) *white-looking.*

λευκό-πτερος, ον, (λευκός, πτερόν) *white-winged.*

λευκό-πωλος, ον, (λευκός, πῶλος) *with white horses: riding a white horse.*

ΛΕΥΚΟ'Σ, ή, όν, *light, bright, brilliant, clear:* of water, *bright.* II. *white, gray, hoary:* of the skin, *white, fair,* but also, *blanched, pale, wan.* 2. λευκὸς χρυσός, *pale* (i. e. *alloyed*) gold, opp. to ἄπεφθος or refined. 3. metaph. *fair, happy, joyful, gay* 4. of sound, *clear,* like λαμπρός.

λευκο-στεφής, ές, (λευκός, στέφω) *white-wreathed.*

λευκό-στικτος, ον, (λευκός, στίζω) *speckled with white, grizzled.*

λευκό-σφῠρος, ον, (λευκός, σφυρόν) *white-ankled.*

λευκό-τροφος, ον, (λευκός, τρέφω) *white-growing.*

λευκο-φᾰής, ές, (λευκός, φάος) *white-gleaming.*

λευκο-φόρος, ον, (λευκός, φέρω) *white-robed.*

λεύκ-οφρυς, υ, (λευκός, ὀφρύς) *white-browed.*

λευκο-χίτων, ωνος, ὁ, ἡ, (λευκός, χιτών) *white-coated.* [ῐ]

λευκό-χροος, ον, contr. -**χρους**, ουν, (λευκός, χρόα) *white-coloured:* heterocl. acc. λευκόχροα.

λευκό-χρως, ωτος, ὁ, ἡ, (λευκός, χρώς) *white-skinned.*

λευκόω, f. ώσω, (λευκός) *to whiten: to paint white:* —Med., λευκοῦσθαι ὅπλα *to whiten their* shields. II. λευκοῦν πόδα *to bare* the foot.

λευκ-ώλενος, ον, (λευκός, ὠλένη) *white-armed.*

λεύκωμα, τό, (λευκός, λευκόω) *anything whitened: a white tablet* for public notices, Lat. *album.*

λευρός, ά, όν, (λεῖος) *smooth, level, even.* II. *smooth, polished.*

***ΛΕΥ'Σ**, ὁ, = λᾶας, *a stone:* hence

λεύσῐμος, ον, *stoning; λεύσιμος θάνατος* death *by stoning;* λεύσιμοι ἀραί curses *that will end in stoning;* λεύσιμος δίκη the penalty *of death by stoning.*

λευσμός, οῦ, ὁ, (λεύς, λεύω) *a stoning.*

λεύσσω, fut. λεύσω (only in late authors), *to look* or *gaze upon, see, behold.* 2. absol. *to look;* ὁ μὴ λεύσσων, he *that sees* not, i. e. one *that is dead.*

λευστήρ, ῆρος, ὁ, (λεύς, λεύω) *one who stones* or *deserves stoning:*—as Adj., λευστὴρ μόρος death *by stoning.*

λεύω, f. σω, aor. 1 pass. ἐλεύσθην: (λεύς):—*to stone.*

λεχε-ποίη, ἡ, (λέχος, ποία) *with grassy couch, grassy, meadowy.*

λεχ-ήρης, ες, (λέχος, ἀραρεῖν) *bed-ridden.*

λεχθείς, aor. 1 part. pass. of λέγω.

λέχος, εος, τό, (λέγω I) *a couch, bed.* 2. *a bier.* II. *the marriage-bed: a marriage.* Hence

λέχοσδε, Adv. *to bed.*

λέχριος, α, ον, *slanting crosswise, oblique.* From

ΛΕ'ΧΡΙΣ, Adv. *slanting, crosswise, athwart.*

λεχώ, όος contr. οῦς, ἡ, (λέχος) *a woman in child-bed.*

λεχώϊος, ον, (λεχώ) *of, belonging to child-bed*

Λεω-κόριον, τό, (Λεώς, κόρα) *the temple of the daughters of Leos.*

ΛΕ'ΩΝ, οντος, ὁ, Ep. dat. pl. λείουσι, Lat. *LEO, a lion:* metaph. of Artemis, Ζεύς σε λέοντα γυναιξὶ θῆκε Zeus made thee *a lion* toward women, i. e. their destroyer.

λε-ωργός, όν, (Adv. λέως, ἔργον) *all-daring, audacious:* as Subst., λεωργός, ὁ, *a knave, villain.*

λεώς, ώ, ὁ, Att. for λαός, nom. pl. λεῴ, *people;* ἀκούετε λεῴ hear *O people,* the beginning of Athenian proclamations.

λέως, Adv., Ion. for λίαν, *entirely, wholly.*

λεω-σφέτερος, ον, (λεώς, σφέτερος) only in Hdt. 9. 33, λεωσφέτερον ἐποιήσαντο Τισαμένου they made him *one of their own people.*

λεω-φόρος, ον, (λεώς, φέρω) *bearing people, frequented:* λεωφόρος (sub. ὁδός), ἡ, *a thoroughfare.*

λῇ, 3 sing. of *λάω, λῶ.

ληγέμεναι, ληγέμεν, Ep. inf. of λήγω.

ΛΗ'ΓΩ, f. ξω, *to LAY, allay, abate,* like παύω: c. gen., λήγειν χεῖρας φόνοιο *to stay* one's hands *from* murder. II. more freq. intr., *to leave off,* or *cease from,* λήγειν ἔριδος *to cease from* strife; c. part., λήγω ἐναρίζων *I cease slaying:*—also absol. *to cease, make an end.*

λήδᾰνον, τό, (λῆδον) *gum ladanum, gum mastich.*

ληδάριον, τό, Dim. of λῆδος, *a light dress.* [ᾰ]

ΛΗ'ΔΟΝ, τό, *the mastich,* a shrub on the leaves of which the gum λήδανον is found.

λῆδος, εος, τό, (λεῖος) *a thin cloth, light dress.*

λῄζομαι, Att. for ληΐζομαι.

λήθαιος or **ληθαῖος**, α, ον, (λήθη) *of* or *for forgetfulness, oblivious.* II. *of* or *from Lethe, Lethean.*

ληθάνω, Causal of λανθάνω: see λανθάνω II.

ληθαργικός, ή, όν, *drowsy, slothful.* From

λήθαργος, ον, (λήθη) *forgetting,* c. gen.: absol. *forgetful, lethargic.*

ληθεδᾰνός, ή, όν, (ληθάνω) *causing forgetfulness.*

ληθεδών, όνος, ή, poët. for λήθη.

λήθη Dor. **λάθα**, ή, (λήθομαι) *a forgetting, forgetfulness*, Lat. *oblivio*. II. *Lethé, the river of oblivion* in the lower world.

λῆθος, τό, Dor. λᾶθος, = λήθη.

ΛΗ'ΘΩ, λήθομαι, older form of λανθάνω, λανθάνομαι, whence the tenses are formed; see λανθάνω.

ληι-άνειρα, ή, (ληΐς, ἀνήρ) *making prey of men.*

ληιάς, άδος, poët. fem. of ληΐδιος, *captive.*

ληι-βοτήρ, ῆρος, ὁ, fem. **ληϊ-βότειρα**, (λήιον, βόσκω) *crop-devouring.*

ληίδιος, α, ον, (ληΐς) *taken as booty, captive.*

ληίζομαι Att. **λῄζομαι**: fut. ληίσομαι Ep. ληίσσομαι: aor. 1 ἐληισάμην Att. ἐλῃσάμην, Ep. 3 sing. ληίσσατο:—Pass., pf. λέλῃσμαι: Dep.: (ληΐς):—*to seize as booty, make spoil of:* generally, *to get* or *gain by force.* II. *to plunder, ravage* a country. III. pf. λελῄσομαι occurs in pass. signf., *to be spoiled, taken as booty.*

ληίη, Ion. for λεία.

ληι-νόμος, ον, (λήϊον, νέμω) *dwelling among the corn-fields.*

ΛΗ'ΙΟΝ, τό, *a crop, crop of corn:* later, *a corn-field.*

ληίς, ίδος, ή, Ion. for λεία, *booty, spoil.* 2. *a herd* or *flock, cattle.*

ληίσσατο, Ep. 3 sing. aor. 1 of ληίζομαι.

ληιστήρ, ῆρος, ὁ, (ληίζομαι) Ep. for Att. **λῃστής**.

ληιστής, οῦ, ὁ, Ion. for λῃστής.

ληίστωρ, ορος, ὁ, = ληϊστήρ.

ληιστός or **λεϊστός**, ή, όν, (ληΐζομαι) *carried off as booty, to be won by force.*

ληιστύς, ύος, ή, (ληίζομαι) *plundering, spoiling.*

ληῗτις, ιδος, ή, (ληΐς) *she who makes* or *dispenses booty*, epith. of Athena.

λήιτον [ῐ], τό, Achaian name for the Athen. πρυτανεῖον, *the town-hall.* Properly, neut. of λήϊτος.

λήιτος, η, ον, (λεώς, λαός) *of the people, public.*

ΛΗΚΕ'Ω Dor. **λᾱκέω**, *to sound*, = λάσκω. Hence

ληκίνδα, Adv. *sounding;* παίζειν λ. *to beat time.*

ληκύθιον, τό, Dim. of λήκυθος, *a small oil-flask.*

ΛΗ'ΚΥΘΟΣ, ή, *an oil-flask, oil-bottle: a casket.* [ῠ]

λῆμα, τό, (*λάω, λῶ) *wish, will, purpose:* in good sense, *spirit, courage:* in bad sense, *pride, arrogance.*

λημᾰλέος, α, ον, (λήμη) *bleared, purblind*, of the eyes, Lat. *lippus.*

λημᾰτιάω, (λῆμα) *to be spirited* or *resolute.*

λημάω, (λήμη) *to be bleared: to be purblind.*

ΛΗ'ΜΗ, ή, Lat. *gramia, a humour that gathers in the eye, rheum:* αἱ λῆμαι, *sore eyes.*

λῆμμα, τό, (εἴλημμαι) *anything received, income, receipts: gain, profit*, Lat. *lucrum.*

Λήμνιος, α, ον, *of Lemnos, Lemnian.* From

Λῆμνος, ή, *Lemnos*, an island in the north Aegaean sea, sacred to Vulcan, because of its volcanic fires.

Ληνᾰϊκός, ή, όν, (Λήναια) *belonging to the* Λήναια.

ληναῖος, α, ον, (ληνός) *belonging to the wine-press:* 1. Ληναῖος, Lat. *Lenaeus*, epith. of Bacchus as *god of the wine-press.* 2. Λήναια (sub. ἱερά), τά, *the Lenaea*, an Athenian festival held in the month Ληναιών in honour of Bacchus, at which there were dramatic contests, esp. of the Comic poets 3. Λήναιον, τό, *the Lenaeum*, or place at Athens *where the Lenaea were held.*

Ληνᾱΐτης, ου, ὁ, = Ληναϊκός.

Ληναιών, ῶνος, ὁ, old name of the Att. month Γαμηλιών *in which the Athenian Lenaea were held*, the latter part of Jan. and former of Feb.: the seventh month of the Attic year.

ΛΗΝΟ'Σ Dor. **λᾱνός**, οῦ, ή or ὁ, *a trough*, Lat. *alveus:* 1. *a wine-vat.* 2. *a trough* for watering cattle. 3. *a kneading-trough.*

ΛΗ'ΝΟΣ Dor. **λᾶνος**, εος, τό, Lat. *LANA, wool.*

λήξαιμι, aor. 1 opt. of λήγω.

λῆξις, εως, ή, (λήγω) *a cessation, end.*

λῆξις, εως, ή, (λήξομαι *appointment by lot, allotment.* II. as law-term, *a written complaint lodged with the archons, a plea* or *accusation.* 2. λῆξις τοῦ κλήρου *an application for one's lawful inheritance.*

λήξομαι, fut. of λαγχάνω.

ληός, rare Ion. form for λαός.

ληπτέος, α, ον, verb. Adj. of λαμβάνω, *to be taken.* II. neut. ληπτέον, *one must take hold: one must take* or *accept.*

ληπτός, ή, όν, verb. Adj. of λαμβάνω, *to be taken* or *comprehended.*

ληρέω, f. ήσω, (λῆρος) *to be foolish* or *silly, behave foolishly;* ληρεῖ ἔχων *he keeps on acting foolishly.*

ΛΗ'ΡΟΣ, ὁ, *idle talk: frivolousness, nonsense.*

ληρός, οῦ, ὁ, *a small trinket*, Lat. *leria.*

λῇς, 2 sing. of *λάω, λῶ.

λησίμ-βροτος, ον, (λήθω, βροτός) *taking men unawares, a cheat.*

λησμοσύνη, ή, *forgetfulness.* From

λήσμων, ον, gen. ονος, (λήθω) *forgetting, unmindful.*

λήσομαι, fut. med. of λανθάνω.

λῃστεία, ή, (λῃστεύω) *a course of plundering, robbery, piracy*, Lat. *latrocinium.*

λῃστεύω, f. σω, (λῃστής) *to be a robber* or *pirate:* c. acc. *to plunder, sack.*

λῃστήριον, τό, *a band of robbers.* From

λῃστής Ion. **ληϊστής**, οῦ, ὁ, (λῄζομαι) *a robber, plunderer:* esp. *a pirate.*

λῃστικός, ή, όν, (λῃστής) *inclined to rob, piratical:* τὸ λῃστικόν *piracy.* Adv. -κῶς, *in the manner of pirates:* Comp. λῃστικώτερον *more after the manner of pirates.*

λῆστις, ή, (λήθω) *a forgetting.*

λῃστο-κτόνος, ον, (λῄστης, κτείνω) *slaying robbers.*

λῃστρικός, ή, όν, = λῃστικός, *piratical;* τὸ λῃστρικόν *a pirate-vessel.*

λῃστρίς, ίδος, pecul. fem. of λῃστρικός.

λήσω, fut. of λανθάνω.

Λητο-γενής, ές, Dor. **Λᾱτ-**, (Λητώ, *γένω) *born of Latona*, of Apollo and Diana: fem. Λατογένεια, of Diana

Λητοΐδης Dor. **Λᾱτ-**, ου, ὁ, (Λητώ) *son of Leto*, of Apollo. [ῐ]

Λητώ, όος contr. οῦς, ἡ, *Leto*, Lat. *Latona*, mother of Apollo and Diana; gen. Λητοῦς, dat. Λητοῖ, acc. Λητώ, voc. Λητοῖ.

Λητῷος Dor. **Λᾱτ-**, α, ον, (Λητώ) *of* or *born of Latona*: fem. also Λητωΐς, ΐδος.

ληφθείς, aor. 1 pass. part. of λαμβάνω.

λῆψις, ἡ, (λήψομαι, fut. of λαμβάνω) *a taking, seizing*. 2. *an accepting, receiving*.

λήψομαι, fut. of λαμβάνω.

ΛΙ-, insep. Prefix with intens. force, cf. λα-, λαι-.

ΛΙ´Α´ΖΟΜΑΙ, aor. 1 ἐλιάσθην: Pass.:—*to bend sidewards, swerve, withdraw*: of the waves, *to retire, recede*: *to vanish*, of a vision II. *to bend downwards, slip down, fall*; part. λιασθείς *having fallen*; πτερὰ πυκνὰ λίασθεν the thick wings *drooped*.

λίαν Ion. **λίην**, Adv. (λι-) *too much, over-much*, like the later ἄγαν, Lat. *nimis*. II. *very much, exceeding, right well*. [ι both long and short.]

λῐαρός, ά, όν, = χλιαρός, *warm, lukewarm*: generally, *soft, mild*.

λιασθείς, aor. 1 part. pass. of λιάζομαι.

λίασθεν, Ep. 3 pl. aor. 1 of λιάζομαι.

λῐβάζω, f. σω, (λιβάς) *to let fall in drops*:—Med. *to run out in drops, trickle*

λίβᾰνος, ὁ, *the frankincense-tree*, producing λιβανωτός. II. = λιβανωτός, *frankincense*.

λῐβᾰνο-φόρος, ον, = λιβανωτοφόρος.

λῐβᾰνωτός, οῦ, ὁ, (λίβανος) *frankincense, the gum of the tree* λίβανος. II. *a censer*.

λῐβᾰνωτο-φόρος, ον, (λιβανωτός, φέρω) *bearing frankincense*.

λῐβάς, άδος, ἡ, (λείβω) *anything that drops* or *trickles*: *a spring, fount* or *stream*: in pl. *water*; δακρύων λιβάδες *streams* of tears.

λιβερτῖνος, ὁ, the Lat. *libertinus*, and **λίβερτος**, ο, the Lat. *libertus, a freedman*.

λίβος, τό, = λιβάς, *tears*: but **λιβος**, gen. of λίψ.

λιβρός, ά, όν, (λείβω) *dripping, wet*.

Λιβύη, ἡ, *Libya, the north part of Africa*, west of Egypt, first mentioned in the Odyssey.

Λίβῠς, ῠος, ὁ, fem. **Λίβυσσα**, (Λιβύη) *a Libyan*: also as Adj. *Libyan*. Hence

Λιβυστικός, ή, όν, *of* or *for Libya, African*.

ΛΙ´ΓΑ˘, Adv. of λιγύς, as ὦκα of ὠκύς, *loudly, clearly, thrillingly, shrilly*. [ῐ]

λῐγαίνω, (λιγύς) *to cry out with clear loud voice*: *to shriek, scream*: also *to sound, play, sing*

λίγγω, (λιγύς) only found in Ep. aor. 1, λίγξε βιός the bowstring *twanged*.

λίγδην, Adv. (λίζω) *scraping, grazing*, Lat. *strictim*.

λιγεῶν, poët. for λιγειῶν, gen. pl. fem. of λιγύς.

λῐγέως, Adv. of λιγύς, *loudly, clearly, shrilly*.

ΛΙΓΝΤ´Σ, ύος, ἡ, *smoke mixed with flame, murky flame*.

λίγξε, 3 sing. Ep. aor. 1 of λίγγω.

λῐγῠ-ηχής, ές, (λιγύς, ἠχή) *clear-sounding*.

λῐγυ-ροος, ον, contr. **-θρους**, ουν, (λιγυς, θρόος) *clear-singing*.

λῐγύ-μολπος, ον, (λιγυς, μολπή) *clear-*[illegible]*ing*.

λῐγύ-μῦθος, ον, (λιγύς, μῦθος) *clear-speaking*.

λῐγυ-πνείων, οντος, (λιγύς, πνέω) *shrill-blowing, whistling, rustling*.

λῐγύ-πνοιος, ον, (λιγύς, πνοή) = λιγυπνείων.

λῐγυ-πτέρῠγος, ον, (λιγύς, πτέρυξ) *chirping with the wings*, of the cicada.

λῐγῠρίζω, f. σω, (λιγυρός) *to sing loud* or *clear*.

λῐγῠρός, ά, όν, (λιγύς) *shrill, sharp, piercing*, of sound: also *clear, sweet clear-toned* II. later, *pliant, flexible*.

λῐγῠρῶς, Adv. *loudly, clearly*.

ΛΙΓΤ´Σ, λιγεῖα, λιγύ, of sound, *clear, sharp, piercing, shrill*: also *clear-toned, sweet*: also of grief, *clamorous*: and of the nightingale, *thrilling*. [ῐ]

Λίγυς, υος, ὁ, ἡ, *a Ligurian*, one who lived in Liguria (north of Genoa).

λῐγύ-φθογγος, ον, (λιγυς, φθογγή) *clear-voiced, clear-toned*.

λῐγύ-φωνος, ον, (λιγύς, φωνή) *clear-voiced, screaming*.

ΛΙ´ΖΩ, f. ξω, (akin to λείχω) *to graze, scratch, wound slightly*: hence λίγδην and ἐπι-λίγδην.

λίην, Adv., Ion. for λίαν.

λῐθάζω, f. σω, (λίθος) *to throw stones*. 2. *to stone*.

λίθαξ, ακος, ὁ, ἡ, (λίθος) *stony, rocky*. II. as Subst. λίθαξ, ἡ, *a stone*.

λῐθάς, άδος, ὁ, (λίθος) *a stone*: collectively, *a shower of stones*.

λίθεος, α, ον, (λίθος) *made of stone, stony*.

λῐθ-ηλογής, ές, (λίθος, λέγω II) *built of stones*.

λῐθίδιον, τό, Dim. of λίθος, *a small stone, pebble*.

λίθινος, η, ον, (λίθος) *made of stone, stony*. Adv. -νως, *like stone, with stony look*.

λῐθό-βλητος, ον, (λίθος, βάλλω) *stone-throwing, pelting*. II. *set with stones*.

λῐθοβολέω, f. ήσω, *to pelt with stones, stone*. From

λῐθο-βόλος, ον, (βαλεῖν) *throwing stones, pelting with stones*; οἱ λιθοβόλοι *stone-throwers, slingers*. II. λιθόβολος, ον, pass. *struck with stones, stoned*.

λῐθο-γλύφος, ον, (λίθος, γλύφω) *carving stone*; as Subst., λιθογλύφος, ὁ, *a sculptor*. [ῠ]

λῐθο-δερκής, ές, (λίθος, δέρκομαι) *with stony look, looking one to stone*.

λῐθό-δμητος, ον, (λίθος, δέμω) *stone-built*.

λῐθο-δόμος, ον, (λίθος, δέμω) *building with stone*: as Subst., λιθοδόμος, ὁ, *a mason*.

λῐθο-εργός, όν, (λίθος, *ἔργω) *turning to stone*.

λῐθο-κόλλητος, ον, (λίθος, κολλάω) *wrought with stone, inlaid with precious stones*: *hard as stone*.

λῐθο-κτονία, ἡ, (λίθος, κτείνω) *death by stoning*.

λῐθό-λευστος, ον, ὁ, (λίθος, λεύω) *stoned with stones*; λιθόλευστος Ἄρης death *by stoning*.

λῐθολόγημα, ατος, τό, *a stone building*. From

λῐθο-λόγος, ον, (λίθος, λέγω II) *picking out stones and laying them together* not shaped or hewn; cf.

λογαυγῆν ;—as Subst., λιθολόγοι, ὁ, *a mason*, = λιθόδομος.

λἴθο-ξόος, ον, (λίθος, ξέω) *polishing stone*: as Subst., λιθόξοος, ὁ, *a marble-mason*.

λἴθο-ποιός, όν, (λίθος, ποιέω) *turning to stone*.

λἴθόρ-ρῖνος, ον, (λίθος, ῥινός) *with stony skin*.

ΛΙ'ΘΟΣ [ἴ], ου, ὁ, *a stone*: of stupid people, λίθοι, *blocks, stones*: proverb., λίθον ἕψειν to boil *a stone*, i. e. to lose one's labour. 2. *stone* as a substance. II. λίθος, ἡ, mostly of *some special stone*, as *marble* or *the magnet*; ἡ διαφανὴς λίθος a transparent *crystal* used for a burning-glass. III. at Athens, λίθος was a name for various *blocks of stone used for rostra* or *pulpits*, to speak from; as the Bema of the Pnyx. IV. *the piece on a draught-board*.

λἴθο-σπᾰδής, ές, (λίθος, σπάω) *rent in the stone, made by tearing out a piece of rock*.

λἴθό-στρωτος, ον, (λίθος, στρώννυμι) *paved with stones, inlaid with stones*: as Subst., λιθόστρωτον, τό, *a tesselated pavement*.

λἴθοτομία, ἡ, *a cutting* or *quarrying of stones*: *a stone-quarry*. From

λἴθο-τόμος, ον, (λίθος, τέμνω) *cutting stone*.

λἴθουργέω, f. ήσω, *to work in stone*: *turn into stone*.

λἴθ-ουργός, όν, (λίθος, *ἔργω) *working in stone*: as Subst., λιθουργός, ὁ, *a stone-mason*, also *a sculptor*: hence, σιδήρια λιθουργά a *stone-mason's* tools.

λἴθοφορέω, f. ήσω, *to carry stones*. From

λιθο-φόρος, ον, (λίθος, φέρω) *carrying stones*.

λἴθ-ώδης, ες, contr. for λιθοειδής, (λίθος, εἶδος) *like stone, stony*.

λικμαῖος, α, ον, *of* or *for winnowing*. From

λικμάω, f. ήσω, (λικμός) *to winnow corn*. 2. metaph. *to scatter like chaff*. Hence

λικμητήρ, ῆρος, ὁ, *a winnower* of corn

λικμητός, ὁ, (λικμάω) *a winnowing*.

ΛΙΚΜΟ'Σ, οῦ, ὁ, = λίκνον.

ΛΙ'ΚΝΟΝ, τό, *a wicker fan* or *basket* for throwing the corn against the wind, so as to separate the chaff from the grain, *a winnowing-fan*. II. *a fan-shaped basket*, used at the feast of Bacchus, called by Virg. *mystica vannus Iacchi*. III. *a cradle* of wicker-work.

λικνο-φόρος, ον, (λίκνον, φέρω) *carrying the sacred winnowing-fan in procession*.

λἴκρῖφίς, Adv. *crosswise, sideways, athwart*. (From λέχρις, λέχριος.)

λἴλαίομαι, (λι-, λελίημαι) Dep. *to long, crave*; of a lance, λιλαιομένη χροὸς ἄσαι *longing* to taste flesh: c. gen. *to long* or *thirst for* a thing.

λῑμαίνω, (λιμός) *to hunger, be starved, famished*.

λιμένεσσιν, Ep. for λιμέσιν, Dat. pl. of λιμήν.

λἴμενίτης [ῑ], ου, ὁ, fem. -ῖτις, ιδος, (λιμήν) *of the harbour*: *presiding over the harbour*.

λἴμεν-ορμίτης [ῑ], ου, ὁ, (λιμήν, ὁρμίζω) *stationed in the harbour*.

ΛΙΜΗ'Ν, ένος, ὁ, *a harbour, haven*. 2. metaph. *a haven, retreat, refuge*. 3. *a gathering-place, receptacle*.

λῑμηρός, ά, όν, (λιμός) *hungry, starved, famished*.

Λίμναι, αἱ, (λίμνη) *a quarter of Athens* near the Acropolis, in which stood the Lenaeum.

λιμναῖος, α, ον, (λίμνη) *marshy, of* or *from the mere*, ὄρνιθες λιμναῖοι *water*-fowl: *stagnant*.

λιμνάς, άδος, ἡ, poët. fem. of λιμναῖος

λιμνάτης [ᾱ], fem. -ᾶτις, Dor. for λιμνήτης, -ῆτις.

λίμνη, ἡ, (λείβω) *a large pool of standing water*: *a lake, mere*, esp. *a marshy lake*. 2. in Homer, *the sea*. 3. *a basin* or *artificial reservoir for water*.

λιμνήτης, ου, ὁ, fem. -ῆτις Dor. -ᾶτις, ιδος, (λίμνη) *living* or *growing in marshes*.

λιμνο-φυής, ές, (λίμνη, φύω) *marsh-born*.

λιμν-ώδης, ες, (λίμνη, εἶδος) *like a marsh, marshy*.

λῑμο-θνής, ῆτος, ὁ, ἡ, (λιμός, θνήσκω) *dying of hunger*.

ΛΙΜΟ'Σ, οῦ, ὁ, also ἡ, *hunger, famine*.

λῑμο-φορεύς, ὁ, (λιμός, φέρω) *a bringer of hunger*.

λίμ-ώδης, ες, (λῑμός, εἶδος) *like hunger, famished*.

λῑμώσσω Att. -ττω, (λιμός) *to be famished*.

λίνεος, α, ον, contr. -οῦς, ῆ, οῦν, (λίνον) *of flax, flaxen, linen*, Lat. *lineus*.

λἴνευτής, οῦ, ὁ, (λίνον) *a hunter with nets*.

λἴνό-δεσμος, ον, (λίνον, δεσμός) = λινόδετος.

λἴνό-δετος, ον, (λίνον, δέω) *bound with flaxen bonds* or *bands* 2. *tied by a thread*.

λἴνο-θήρας, ου, ὁ, (λίνον, θηράω) *a hunter with nets*.

λἴνο-θώρηξ, ηκος, ὁ, ἡ, Ion. for λινοθώραξ, (λίνον, θώραξ) *wearing a linen cuirass*.

λἴνό-κλωστος, ον, (λίνον, κλώθω) *spinning flax*.

λἴνό-κροκος, ον, (λίνον, κρέκω) *flax-woven*.

ΛΙ'ΝΟΝ, τό, *anything made of flax*: *a flaxen cord*: metaph. *the thread* spun by the Fates. 2. *a net, fishing-net*. 3. *linen, linen cloth*: in pl. *sail-cloth*; *linen garments*. 4. *the wick* of a lamp. II. *the plant that produces flax, lint*, Lat. *linum*; λίνου σπέρμα *lint*-seed. [ἴ]

λἴνό-πεπλος, ον, (λίνον, πέπλος) *with linen robe*.

λἴνο-πόρος, ον, (λίνον, πορεύω) *sail-wafting*.

λινοπτάομαι, Dep. (λινόπτης) *to watch the nets*.

λἴνό-πτερος, ον, (λίνον, πτερόν) *sail-winged*.

λἴν-όπτης, ου, ὁ, (λίνον, ὄψομαι) *one who watches nets to see whether anything is caught*.

λἴνορ-ρᾰφής, ές, (λίνον, ῥάπτω) *sewed of flax*; δόμος λινορραφής a ship *having her sails of linen*.

Λίνος, ου, ὁ, *Linos*, a minstrel, son of Apollo and Urania. II. as appellat., Λίνος, ὁ, *the song* or *lay of Linos*; in Homer sung by a boy while the vintage is going on. Cf. αἴλινον.

λἴνοστᾰσία, ἡ, *a laying of nets*. From

λινο-στατέω, f. ήσω, (λίνον, ἵστημι) *to lay nets*.

λἴνοῦς, ῆ, οῦν, contr. for λίνεος.

λἴνο-φθόρος, ον, (λίνον, φθείρω) *linen-wasting*.

λίπα, τό, an old word used by Homer in the phrases ἀλείψαι and ἀλείψασθαι λίπ' ἐλαίῳ, probably used as an Adv. *unctuously, richly*. (Cf. λίπος.) [ἴ]

λῐπαίνω, f. ἄνῶ, (λίπας, λίπος) *to oil, anoint*: metaph. *to make fat, enrich*:—Med. *to anoint oneself.*

λῐπᾰρ-άμπυξ, ῦκος, ὁ, ἡ, (λιπαρός, ἄμπυξ) *with bright fillet* or *tiara.*

λῐπᾰρέω, f. ήσω, *to persist, hold out, persevere*; c. dat. *to persist in* a thing. II. *to beg* or *pray earnestly, to be importunate, ask pertinaciously*: c. inf., λιπαρεῖς τυχεῖν *thou art earnest* to obtain. From

ΛΙ͂ΠΑ͂ΡΗ͂Σ, ές, *persisting* or *persevering in* a thing, *earnest, pertinacious.* II. *earnest in praying, importunate.*

λῐπᾰρητέον, verb. Adj. of λιπαρέω, *one must be importunate, beg hard.*

λῐπᾰρία, ἡ, (λιπαρέω) *perseverance, importunity.*

λῐπᾰρό-ζωνος, ον, (λιπαρός, ζώνη) *bright-girdled.*

λῐπᾰρό-θρονος, ον, (λιπαρός, θρόνος) *bright-throned.*

λῐπᾰρο-κρήδεμνος, ον, (λιπαρός, κρήδεμνον) *with bright head-band* or *fillet.*

λῐπᾰρο-πλόκᾰμος, ον, (λιπαρός, πλόκαμος) *with shining locks.*

λῐπᾰρός, ά, όν, (λίπας or λίπος) *oily, shining, anointed with oil*: later *fat, greasy.* II. of the skin, *shining, sleek, in good case*, Lat. *nitidus*: metaph. *sleek, comfortable, easy.* III. of things, *bright, brilliant, costly*: *ample* IV. of soil, *fat, rich.*

λῐπᾰρο-χροος, ον, contr. -χρους, ουν, and -χρως, ωτος, ὁ, ἡ, (λιπαρός, χρόα, χρώς) *with sleek, shining body* or *skin.*

λῐπᾰρῶς, Adv. of λῐπᾰρός, *sleekly, comfortably.*

λῐπᾰρῶς, Adv. of λῐπᾰρής, *earnestly, importunately.*

ΛΙ͂ΠΑ͂Σ, αος, τό, = λίπος, *fat, oil.* [ĭ]

λῐπ-αυγής, ές, (λιπεῖν, αὐγή) *deserted by light, blind.*

λῐπάω, (λίπας, λίπος) *to be fat and sleek.*

λίπε, λίπεν, Ep. 3 sing. aor. 2 of λείπω.

λιπεῖν, aor. 2 inf. of λείπω.

λιπερνήτης, ου, ὁ, fem. -ῆτις, ιδος, (λιπεῖν, φέρνη) *without dowry, destitute.*

λῐπό-γᾰμος, ον, (λιπεῖν, γάμος) *leaving a wife* or *husband, adulterous*: ἡ λιπογάμος *the adulteress.*

λῐπο-γνώμων, ον, gen. ονος, (λιπεῖν, γνώμων) of horses, *without the tooth which marks their age*: hence generally, *of unknown age.*

λῐπό-γυιος, ον, (λιπεῖν, γυῖον) *wanting a limb, maimed.*

λιποῖσα, λιποῖσαν, Dor. for λιποῦσα, λιποῦσαν, aor. 2 part. of λείπω.

λῐπο-μήτωρ, ορος, ὁ, ἡ, (λιπεῖν, μήτηρ) *without a mother, orphan.*

λῐπό-ναυς Dor. also **λῐπό-νᾱς**, ὁ, ἡ, (λιπεῖν, ναῦς) *leaving the ship, deserting the fleet.*

λῐπο-ναύτης, ου, ὁ, (λιπεῖν, ναύτης) *leaving the sailors.*

λῐπό-νεως, ων, = λιπόναυς.

λῐπο-πᾰτρις, ιδος, ὁ, ἡ, (λιπεῖν, πατρίς) *causing to forget one's country.*

λῐπο-πάτωρ, ορος, ὁ, ἡ, (λιπεῖν, πατήρ) *a deserter, forsaker of one's father.*

λῐπό-πνοος, ον, contr. -πνους, ουν (λιπεῖν, πνοή) *scant of breath, breathless, dead.*

ΛΙ͂ΠΟΣ, τό, *grease*, whether animal, as *fat, lard, tallow*; or vegetable, as *oil*: metaph., λίπος αἵματος *a clot* of blood.

λῐπο-σαρκής, ές, (λιπεῖν, σάρξ) *wanting flesh, meagre.*

λῐπο-στέφᾰνος, ον, (λιπεῖν στέφανος) *falling from the wreath.*

λῐπο-στρᾰτία, ἡ, and **λῐπο-στράτιον**, τό, (λιπεῖν, στρατιά) *desertion of the army.*

λῐπο-ταξία, ἡ, and **λῐπο-τάξιον**, τό, (λιπεῖν, τάξις) *a leaving one's post, desertion.*

λῐπο-τρῐχής, ές, (λιπεῖν, θρίξ) *scant of hair, bald.*

λῐπο-ψῡχέω, f. ήσω, (λιπεῖν, ψυχή) *to be lifeless* i. e. *senseless, to faint, swoon*: *to die.* II. *to lack spirit*

λιπόων, Ep. part. of λιπάω.

λίπτομαι, Dep. with pf. pass. λέλιμμαι: (formed from prefix λι-):—*to be eager*: c. gen. *to be eager for, long for*: in pf. part., λελιμμένοι μάχης *eager for* battle.

λιπών, οῦσα, όν, aor. 2 part. of λείπω.

λῖς, ὁ, acc. λῖν, Ep. for λέων, *a lion*:—later nom. and dat. plur. λῖες, λίεσσι.

λίς, ἡ, Ep. apocopate form for λισσή, *smooth*; λὶς πέτρη *a bare, smooth rock.*

λίσαι, aor. 1 imperat. of λίσσομαι. [ĭ]

λίσῃ, 2 sing. fut. of λίσσομαι. [ĭ]

λίσπος, η, ον, (λισσός, λεῖος) *smooth, polished.*

λίσσαι, Ep. aor. 1 imperat. of λίσσομαι.

λισσάς, άδος, pecul. fem. of λισσός, *smooth*:—as Subst., λισσάς, ἡ, *a smooth bare cliff*; cf. λισσός.

λισσέσκετο, 3 sing. Ion. impf. of λίσσομαι.

ΛΙ͂ΣΣΟΜΑΙ: aor. 1 ἐλῐσάμην Ep. ἐλλῐσάμην: aor. 2 ἐλῐτόμην, opt. λιτοίμην, inf. λιτέσθαι: Dep.: —*to beg, pray, intreat, beseech*, either absol., or c. acc. pers.: c. inf., λίσσεσθαι μὴ προδοῦναι *to pray* one *not* to betray.

λισσός, ή, όν, (λεῖος, λίσπος) *smooth*; λισσὴ πέτρη *a smooth, bare cliff*; cf. λισσά

λιστός, ή, όν, (λίσσομαι) *to be moved by prayer.*

λιστρεύω, f. σω, *to dig, hoe*; φυτὸν λιστρεύειν *to dig round* a plant. From

λίστρον, τό, (λισσός) *a tool for levelling* or *smoothing, a shovel, spade, hoe.*

λῖτα, τά, in Homer, *smooth, plain clothes*; v. sub λὶς II.

λῐταίνω, (λιτή) *to pray, entreat*: *supplicate.*

λιτανεύσομεν, Ep. for -ωμεν, aor. 1 subj. of λιτανεύω.

λῐτᾰνεύω, f. σω:—the augm. tenses are used in Ep. with λλ metri grat., impf. ἐλλιτάνευον, aor. 1 ἐλλιτάνευσα: (λιτή):—*to pray, entreat, beseech, conjure, supplicate.*

λῐτᾰνος, η, ον, (λιτή) *praying, suppliant*: as subst., λίτανα, τά, = λιταί, *prayers.*

λῐταργίζω, f. σω, *to hasten, run, hurry.* From

λίτ-αργος, ον, (λι-, ἀργός) *running quick.*

λῐτέσθαι, aor. 2 inf. of λίσσομαι.

λῐτή, ἡ, (λίσσομαι) *a prayer, entreaty, supplication.* II. Λιταί, *Prayers*, personified as goddesses, in Il. 9. 502, sq.

λῐτοίμην, aor. 2 opt. of λίσσομαι.

λίτομαι [ῐ], rarer pres. for λίσσομαι, *to pray.*

λῑτός, ή, όν, (λεῖος) *smooth, plain*, Lat. *simplex.*

λῐτός, ή, όν, (λίσσομαι) *praying, supplicatory.*

λίτρα, ας, ἡ, Lat. *libra, a pound:* as a weight, = 12 ounces. Hence

λιτραῖος, α, ον, *worth a λίτρα.*

λίτρον, τό, Att. for νίτρον.

Λῑτῠέρσης, ου, ὁ, Dor. **-σας**, *Lityerses*, a son of Midas, from whom was named a song sung by reapers; cf. Λίνος, Μανέρως.

λίτυον, τό, the Roman *lituus* or augur's rod.

λῐχᾰνός, ον, (λείχω) *licking:* as Subst., λίχανος (sub. δάκτυλος), ὁ, *the fore-finger.*

λιχήν, ῆνος, ὁ, v. sub λειχήν.

λιχμάζω, f. άσω, (λείχω) *to lick.*

λιχμάομαι, Dep. (λείχω) *to lick, to play with the tongue*, esp. of snakes.

λιχνεία, ἡ, *daintiness, greediness.*

λιχνο-βόρος, ον, (λίχνος, βορά) *nice in eating, dainty.*

λίχνος, η, ον, (λείχω) *dainty, lickerish, greedy.* 2. metaph. *curious, eager.*

λίψ, ὁ, gen. λῐβός, (λείβω) *the SW. wind*, Lat. *Africus.*

λίψ, ὁ, gen. λῐβός, acc. λίβα, (λείβω) *any liquid poured forth, a drop, libation, drink-offering.*

λό', for λόε; see λούω.

λοβός, οῦ, ὁ, (λέπω) *the lobe* or *lower part of the ear:—the lobe of the liver.* 2. *a pool.*

λογάδην, Adv. (λογάς) *picking out*, esp. of stones *picked out* for building, without being squared. [ᾰ]

λογάς, άδος, ὁ and ἡ, (λέγω) *gathered: picked, chosen*, esp. of soldiers.

λογάω, (λόγος, λέγω) *to be fond of talking.*

λογεῖον, τό, (λόγος) *a speaking-place:* in the Att. theatre the front of the stage occupied by the *speakers* or *actors*, Lat. *pulpitum.*

λογία, ἡ, (λέγω) *a collection for the poor.*

λογίδιον, τό, Dim. of λόγος, *a little fable.* [ῐ]

λογίζομαι, f. ίσομαι Att. ιοῦμαι: aor. 1 med. ἐλογισάμην, pass. ἐλογίσθην: pf. λελόγισμαι: Dep. (λόγος):—*to count, reckon, calculate, compute;* ἀπὸ χειρὸς λογίζεσθαι *to calculate* off hand. II. *to take into account, consider:* c. acc. *to count* or *consider* as so and so. 2. c. inf. *to count* or *reckon upon* doing. 3. *to calculate, reason:* also, *to conclude by reasoning, infer.* III. the pres., and the aor. 1 and pf. ἐλογίσθην, λελόγισμαι, are also used in pass. sense, *to be computed* or *calculated.*

λογῐκός, ή, όν, (λόγος) *belonging to speech* or *speaking.* II. *belonging to the reason, rational.* 2. *fit for reasoning:* hence ἡ λογική (sub. τέχνη), *Logic.*

λόγιμος, η, ον, also ος, ον, (λόγος) *worth mention, remarkable, considerable.*

λόγιον, τό, *a declaration, oracle:* neut. of λόγιος.

λόγιος, α, ον, (λόγος) *skilled in words:* I. *learned*, esp. *learned in history:* as Subst., λόγιος, ὁ, *a writer of annals, chronicler, prose-writer*, as opp. to ποιητής. II. *eloquent.*

λογισμός, ὁ, (λογίζομαι) *reckoning, computation.* II. *consideration, reasoning, reflexion: a conclusion.*

λογιστής, οῦ, ὁ, (λογίζομαι) *a calculator, computer.* II. in pl. *auditors:* at Athens, a board of ten, to whom magistrates going out of office submitted their accounts.

λογιστικός, ή, όν, (λογιστής) *skilled in calculating.* II. *skilled in reasoning* or *arguing.*

λογογρᾰφία, ἡ, *prose-writing*, opp. to poetry. From

λογο-γράφος, ον, (λόγος, γράφω) *writing prose:* as Subst., λογογράφος, ὁ, *a chronicler, annalist.* II. *writing speeches*, esp. for others to deliver.

λογο-λέσχης, ου, ὁ, (λόγος, λέσχω) *a prater.*

λογομαχέω, (λογομάχος) *to strive about words.* Hence

λογομᾰχία, ἡ, *a war about words.*

λογο-μάχος, ον, (λόγος, μάχη) *warring about words.*

λογοποιέω, (λογοποιός) *to make words, invent stories, fabricate reports.* Hence

λογοποιία, ἡ, *invention of stories, tale-telling.*

λογο-ποιός, όν, (λόγος, ποιέω) *word-making:*—as Subst., λογοποιός, ὁ, *a writer of prose, a chronicler, annalist, prose-writer.* 2. *a writer of fables.* II. at Athens, *one who wrote speeches* for others to deliver. 2. *an inventor of stories, tale-teller, newsmonger.*

λόγος, ὁ, (λέγω) I. *the word by which the inward thought is expressed:* also II. *the inward thought* or *reason itself.*

I. Lat. *oratio, vox, that which is said* or *spoken:* 1. *a word*, in pl. *words, language;* ὡς εἰπεῖν λόγῳ in *a word:*—in Att., *talk, pretence;* τῷ λόγῳ in *pretence*, opp. to ἔργῳ *in reality.* 2. *a saying, expression: an oracle, maxim, proverb.* 3. *conversation, discussion;* εἰς λόγους ἐλθεῖν, to have *a conference* or *interview.* 4. *a speaking* or *talking* about a thing; λόγου ἄξιος worth *talking of*, worth *mention:*—*a report, rumour;* λόγος ἐστί or ἔχει, so *the story* goes, Lat. *fama fert.* 5. *a tale, story*, opp. both to mere fable (μῦθος) and to regular history (ἱστορία): a. *fictitious story, fable*, such as those of Aesop. b. *a story, narrative*, mostly in pl., *history, chronicles:* in sing. *one part of the narrative.* 6. λόγοι, *prose-writing, prose*, opp. to ποίησις, *a book.* b. at Athens, *speeches: a speech; the power of speaking, oratory, eloquence.* 7. *the right* or *privilege of speaking*, Lat. *copia dicendi*, λόγον τινὶ διδόναι to give one *the right of speaking*, i. e. a hearing. 9. like ῥῆμα, *the thing spoken of, the subject of the* λόγος.

II. Lat. *ratio, thought, reason;* κατὰ λόγον *agreeable to reason: reflexion, deliberation:* λόγον ἑαυτῷ διδόναι to allow himself *reflexion*, i. e. *to think over a thing.* 2. *account, consideration, esteem.*

regard; λόγου ποιεῖσθαί τινα to make one of *account;* λόγον τινὸς ἔχειν to make *account* of a person; opp. to ἐν οὐδενὶ λόγῳ ποιεῖσθαί τινα to make one of no *account;* ἐν ἀνδρὸς λόγῳ ἔχειν to regard *in the light* of a man. 3. *calculation, reckoning: the account* or *reckoning:* λόγον διδόναι to give *an account.* 4. *relation, proportion, analogy.* 5. *a reasonable ground, a condition,* esp. in the phrase ἐπὶ τῷ λόγῳ or ἐπὶ τοῖς λόγοις upon *condition;* ὁ λόγος αἱρεῖ *it stands to reason that,* Lat. *ratio evincit.*

III. in N. T., Ὁ ΛΟΓΟΣ, *the* LOGOS or WORD, comprising both senses of *Word* and *Reason.*

ΛΟΓΧΗ, ἡ, *a spear-head, javelin-head,* Lat. *spiculum:* in pl. *the point with its barbs.* II. *a* LANCE, *spear, javelin,* Lat. *lancea.* III. *a troop of spearmen.*

λογχ-ήρης, ες, (λόγχη, ἀραρεῖν) *armed with a spear.*

λογχίδιον, τό, Dim. of λόγχη.

λόγχῐμος, ον, (λόγχη) *of* or *with a spear.*

λογχο-ποιός, όν, (λόγχη, ποιέω) *making spears.*

λογχο-φόρος, ον, (λόγχη, φέρω) *spear-bearing:*— as Subst., λογχοφόρος, ὁ, *a spearman, pikeman.*

λογχωτός, ή, όν, (λόγχη) *lance-headed.*

λόγως, Dor. acc. pl. of λόγος.

λόε, 3 sing. Ep. impf. of λούω.

λοέσσας, λοεσσάμενος, Ep. for λούσας, λουσάμενος, aor. 1 part. act. and med. of λούω.

λοέσσομαι, Ep. for λούσομαι, fut. med. of λούω.

λοετρόν, λοετρο-χόος, oldest form of λουτρ–.

λοέω, Ep. form of λούω.

λοιβή, ή, (λείβω) *a pouring, a drink-offering, libation,* Lat. *libatio.*

λοίγιος, ιον, (λοιγός) *pestilent, deadly.*

ΛΟΙΓΟΣ, οῦ, ὁ, *ruin, mischief, death: plague.*

λοιδορέω, f. ήσω: aor. 1 ἐλοιδόρησα:—Med. and Pass., f. -ήσομαι: aor. 1 ἐλοιδορησάμην and ἐλοιδορήθην: (λοίδορος):—*to rail at, abuse, revile:* against the gods, *to blaspheme:*—Med. *to rail at one another;* but the med. and pass. forms are commonly used in same sense as Act. Hence

λοιδορησμός, οῦ, ὁ, *a railing at, abusing.*

λοιδορία, ἡ, (λοιδορέω) *railing, abuse, reproach.*

λοίδορος, ον, *railing, abusive.*

ΛΟΙΜΟΣ, οῦ, ὁ, *a plague, pestilence,* Lat. *pestis.*

λοιπός, ή, όν, (λείπω) *remaining, surviving,* Lat. *reliquus;* τοῦ λοιποῦ (sub. χρόνου), *for the rest of the time, henceforward;* οἱ λοιποί *all the rest,* Lat. *ceteri;* τὸ λοιπόν *the remainder,* Lat. *quod superest;* τὰ λοιπά *the rest, residue,* Lat. *cetera.*

λοισθήϊος, ον, Ep. for λοίσθιος, λοῖσθος; λοισθήϊον ἄεθλον the prize *for the last* in the race.

λοίσθιος, α, ον or ος, ον, = λοῖσθος.

λοῖσθος, ον, (λοιπός) *left behind, last:* Sup. λοισθότατος, *last of all.*

λόκκη (not λόκη), ἡ, *a cloak.*

Λοκρίς, ίδος, fem. Adj. *Locrian.* II. as Subst. (sub. γῆ) *Locris.* From

Λοκροί, οἱ, *the Locrians: the Opuntian Locrians* opp. Euboea; *the Epicnemidian,* on the Maliac Gulf; *the Epizephyrian,* in the South of Italy

Λοξίας, ου, ὁ, epith. of Apollo, from λέγειν, λόγος, as being the Interpreter of Zeus.

λοξο-βάτης, ου, ὁ, (λοξός, βαίνω) *walking sideways.*

ΛΟΞΟΣ, ή, όν, *slanting, crosswise,* Lat. *obliquus:* λοξὸν or λοξὰ βλέπειν τινί to look *askance* at one, Lat. *limis oculis spectare;* αὐχένα λοξὸν ἔχειν to hang down the head, Lat. *stare capite obstipo.*

λοξο-τρόχις, ιδος, fem. Adj. (λοξός, τρέχω) *oblique-running.*

λόον, Ep. 3 pl. impf. of λούω.

λοπᾰδ-αρπᾰγίδης, ου, ὁ, (λοπάς, ἁρπάζω) *a dish-snatcher.*

λοπάδιον, τό, Dim. of λοπάς, *a little dish, platter.* [ᾰ]

ΛΟΠΑΣ, άδος, ἡ, *a flat dish, plate* or *platter.*

λοπίς, ίδος, ἡ, = λεπίς.

λοπός, οῦ, or **λόπος**, ου, ο, (λέπω) *a shell, husk, bark, peel.*

λουέω, Ep. for λούω.

λοῦμαι, Att. for λούομαι, Pass. of λούω.

λούσαντο, Ep. 3 pl. aor. 1 med. of λούω

λοῦσεν, Ep. 3 sing. aor. 1 of λούω.

λοῦσθαι, contr. inf. pass. of λούω.

λουσῶ, Dor. fut. of λούω.

λουτιάω, Desiderat. of λούω, *to wish to bathe.*

λούτριον, τό, (λούω) *water that has been used in a bath.*

λουτρο-δάϊκτος, ον, (λουτρόν, δαΐζω) *slain in the bath.*

λουτρόν Ep. **λοετρόν**, τό, (λοέω, λούω) *a bath, bathing-place.* II. *water for bathing;* ἐν λουτρῷ while *bathing.* III. *libations*

λουτρο-φόρος, ον, (λουτρόν, φέρω) *bringing water for bathing* or *washing,* esp. at a marriage; λουτροφόρος χλιδή *the marriage-ceremony.*

λουτροχοέω, *to pour water into the bath.* From

λουτρο-χόος, ον, Hom. **λοετρ–**, (λουτρόν, λοετρόν, χέω) *pouring water into the bath, preparing it.*

λουτρών, ῶνος, ὁ, (λουτρόν) *a bathing-room, bath.*

ΛΟΥΩ: fut. λούσω Dor. λουσῶ: aor. 1 ἔλουσα Ep. λοῦσα:—Med., f. λούσομαι: aor. 1 ἐλουσάμην, Ep. 3 pl. λούσαντο:—Pass., aor. 1 ἐλούσθην:—pf. λέλουμαι.—From the uncontr. form **λοέω** come the Ep. impf. λόεον, aor. 1 inf. and part. λοέσσαι, λοέσσας: Med., fut. λοέσσομαι: 3 sing. aor. 1 ind. and part. λοέσσατο, λοεσσάμενος.—Several forms also come from λόω, Ep. 3 sing. and pl. impf. λόε, λόον; Ion. and old Att., pl. impf. ἐλοῦμεν (contr. from ἐλόομεν), pres. med. λοῦμαι, λοῦνται; impf. ἐλοῦτο, ἐλοῦντο, inf. λόεσθαι, λοῦσθαι. *To wash,* esp. *to wash the body:* Med. and Pass. *to wash oneself, bathe;* c. gen., λελουμένος Ὠκεανοῖο (of a star just risen) *fresh bathed* in Ocean. II. *to wash off* or *away.*

λοφάω, f. ήσω, (λόφος) *to have a crest.* 2. *to be sick, ill of a crest.*

λοφεῖον, τό, (λόφος) *a crest-case: any case.*

λοφιά Ion. **-ιή**, ἡ, (λόφος) *the mane* of animals, esp. of horses, *the bristly back* of boars; ἀντὶ λόφου ἡ λοφιὴ κατέχρα *the mane* served for a *crest*. II. *the ridge of a hill, a hill*.

λοφιήτης, ου, ὁ, (λόφος) *a dweller on the hills*.

λοφνίς, ίδος, ἡ, (λέπω) *a torch of vine-bark*.

λοφο-ποιός, όν, (λοφός, ποιέω) *making crests*: as Subst., λοφοποιός, ὁ, *a crest-maker*.

ΛΟ'ΦΟΣ, ου, ὁ, *the back of the neck, the neck*. esp. of draught-cattle: metaph., ὑπὸ ζυγῷ λόφον ἔχειν to have *the neck* under the yoke II. *a ridge of ground, the brow of a hill*, Lat. *jugum, dorsum*: *a hill*. III. *the crest* of a helmet, Lat. *crista*, commonly of horse-hair. 2. *a tuft of hair* on the crown: *the crest* or *tuft on the head* of birds, Lat. *crista, a cock's comb*.

λόφωσις, ἡ, (λόφος) *the wearing a crest*: *the crest itself*.

λοχ-ᾱγέτης, ου, ὁ, Dor. and Att. for λοχηγέτης, = λοχαγός, q. v.

λοχᾱγέω, Dor. and Att. for λοχηγέω, (λοχαγός) *to lead a* λόχος or *company* Hence

λοχᾱγία, ἡ, Dor. and Att. for λοχηγία, *the rank* or *office of* λοχαγός.

λοχ-ᾱγός, οῦ, ὁ, (λόχος, ἄγω) Dor. and Att. for λοχηγός, *the leader of a* λόχος, *the captain of a company*, Lat. *centurio*.

λοχάζω, = λοχάω.

λοχάω, f. -ήσω and -ήσομαι: aor. 1 ἐλόχησα: 3 pl. Ep. pres. λοχόωσι, part. pl. λοχόωντες: (λόχος):—*to waylay, lie in wait, lay wait for*, c. acc. pers. II. absol. *to lie in wait* or *ambush* III. c. acc. loci, *to beset with an ambush*.

λοχεία, ἡ, (λοχεύω) *child-birth*. II. *a child*.

λοχεῖος, α, ον, (λόχος) *of* or *for child-birth*. II. τὰ λοχεῖα (sub. χωρία), *a birth-place*.

λοχεός, οῦ, ὁ, = λόχος, *an ambush*.

λόχευμα, τό, (λοχεύω) *that which is born, a child*. II. *child-birth*: metaph., κάλυκος λοχεύματα *the bursting* of the bud.

λοχεύω, f. σω, (λόχος II) *to bring forth, bear*. 2. *to attend in child-birth, bring to the birth*. II. Pass. *to travail, bear children* 2. *to be brought forth, born* 3. generally, *to lie imbedded*.

λοχηγέτης, -ηγέω, -ηγός, Ion. for λοχαγ-.

λοχῆσαι, aor. 1 inf. of λοχάω

Λοχία, ἡ, fem. of λόχιος, name of Diana, as *the goddess of child-birth*.

λοχίζω, f. ίσω, (λόχος) *to waylay, lie in wait* or *lay wait for*. 2. *to place in ambush*. II. *to arrange men in companies, draw up in order of battle*.

λόχιος, α, ον, = λοχεῖος, *of* or *for child-birth*.

λοχίτης [ῑ], ου, ὁ, fem. -ῖτις, ιδος, (λόχος) *one of the same company, a fellow-soldier, comrade*.

λοχμαῖος, α, ον, *haunting the woods*. From

λόχμη, ἡ, (λόχος) *a thicket, lair* of wild beasts: generally, *copse-wood, a coppice*. Hence

λόχμιος, ον, also α, ον, *dwelling in the coppice*. 2. as Subst., λόχμια, τά, *a thicket, coppice*.

λοχμ-ώδης, ες, (λόχμη, εἶδος) *overgrown with copse-wood, bushy*.

λόχονδε, Adv. *to ambush, for ambuscade*. From

λόχος, ὁ, (λέγω I, λέγομαι) *a place for lying in wait, ambush* or *ambuscade*: *the lair* of wild beasts. 2. *the act of lying in wait* or *the men that form the ambush*; λόχον εἷσαι to place *an ambuscade*; λόχονδε κρίνειν ἄνδρας ἀριστῆας to pick out the best men for an *ambuscade*. 3. *any armed band, a company*, commonly reckoned at 100 men:—among the Spartans a λόχος was *the fourth* or *fifth part of a* μόρα (q. v.): generally, *any body* or *company of people*. II. *a lying in*: *child-birth*, like λοχεία.

λοχόωντες, λοχόωσι, Ep. pres. part. and 3 pl. ind. of λοχάω.

λόω, = λούω; from it come several Ion. and old Att. forms; v. λούω.

λύα, ἡ, (λύω) *dissolution*: *faction, riot, sedition*.

Λῠαῖος, ὁ, (λύω) *the looser* or *deliverer* from care, epith. of Bacchus, *Lyaeus*; cp. Lat. *Liber*.

λύγδην, Adv. (λύζω) *with sobs*.

λυγδίνεος, α, ον, and **λύγδῐνος**, η, ον, *of white marble*. 2. *white as marble, dazzling white*. From

ΛΥ'ΓΔΟΣ, ὁ, *a dazzling white stone, white marble*.

ΛΥ'ΓΗ, ἡ, *shadow, darkness, gloom*. [ῡ]

λῠγίζω: f. ίσω Dor. λυγιξῶ: Pass., aor. 1 pass. ἐλυγίχθην: pf. λελύγισμαι: (λύγος):—*to bend, twist, to throw in wrestling*. II. Pass. *to bend* or *twist oneself, to writhe*. 2. *to be thrown* or *mastered*.

λύγῐνος, η, ον, (λύγος) *of willow* or *withy*, Lat. *vietus*.

λυγιξεῖν, Dor. fut. inf. of λυγίζω.

λῠγισμός, οῦ, ὁ, (λυγίζω) *a bending, twisting*: metaph. *the winding and twisting* of a sophist.

λύγκειος, α, ον, (λύγξ, ὁ) *lynx-like*.

ΛΥ'ΓΞ, λυγκός, ὁ, *a lynx*.

λύγξ, λυγγός, ἡ, (λύζω) *a hiccough* or *hiccup*.

ΛΥ'ΓΟΣ, ἡ, *any pliant twig* or *rod, a willow twig, with*, Lat. *vimen*. II. *a willow-like tree, a withy*, Lat. *vitex agnus castus*. [ῠ]

λῠγο-τευχής, ές, (λύγος, τεύχω) *made of withs*.

λῠγόω, ώσω, = λυγίζω.

ΛΥΓΡΟ'Σ, ά, όν, *mournful, sad, gloomy, dismal*: φάρμακα λυγρά *baneful* drugs; εἵματα λυγρά *sorry* garments; and neut. pl. alone, λυγρά, *bane, misery, ruin* II. of men, *baneful, mischievous*. 2. *sorry, weak, cowardly*. Hence

λυγρῶς, Adv. *sadly, sorely*.

Λῡδία, ἡ, *Lydia*, the kingdom of Croesus in Asia Minor, afterwards a Persian satrapy.

Λυδίζω, f. ίσω, (Λυδός) *to imitate the Lydians*.

Λυδίος, α, ον, (Λυδίς) *Lydian*; ἡ Λυδία λίθος, a stone used to test gold, like βάσανος.

Λυδιστί, Adv. (Λυδός) *in the Lydian tongue* or *fashion*.

Λῡδο-πᾰθής, ές, (Λυδός, παθεῖν) *luxurious as a Lydian.*

Λῡδός, οῦ, ὁ, *a Lydian.*

ΛΥ´ΖΩ, f. ξω, *to have the hiccough* or *hiccup* II. *to sob*, Lat. *singultire : to whine, whimper.*

λύθεν, Aeol. and Ep. 3 pl. aor. 1 pass. of λύω. II. λῠθέν, aor. 1 part. neut. pass.

λῠθῆναι, aor. 1 pass. inf. of λύω.

λύθρον, τό, or **λύθρος**, ὁ, *filth, defilement*, esp. *of blood : gore, impure blood.* (Akin to λύμη.)

λυθρώδης, ες, (λύθρον, εἶδος) *like gore, defiled with gore.*

λῠκά-βας, αντος, ὁ, (*λύκη, βαίνω) *the path of light, the sun's course the year.* II. as Adj. *making up the year*, λυκαβαντίδες ὧραι.

λύκαινα, ἡ, (λύκος) *a she-wolf.* [ῠ]

Λῠκαῖον, τό, *Mount Lycaeus* in Arcadia.

Λῠκαῖος, α, ον, *Lycaean, Arcadian*, epith. of Jupiter. II. as Subst., Λυκαῖος, ὁ, or Λυκαῖον, τό, a mountain in Arcadia. 2. Λύκαια (sub. ἱερά), τά, *the festival of Lycaean Jupiter* :—also the Roman *Lupercalia.*

Λυκαονιστί, Adv. *in the Lycaonian language.*

λῠκ-αυγής, ές, (*λύκη, αὐγή) *of* or *at the gray twilight :* as Subst., λυκαυγές, τό, *early dawn.*

Λυκάων, ονος, ὁ, *a Lycaonian, inhabitant of Lycaonia*, in the South of Asia Minor

λῠκέη, Att. contr. λυκῆ (sub. δορα), ἡ, *a wolf's-skin : a helmet of it*, cf. κυνέη.

Λύκειον, τό, *the Lyceum*, a gymnasium with covered walks in the Eastern suburb of Athens, named after the neighbouring temple of Apollo Λύκειος.

λύκειος, α, ον, (λύκος) epith. of Apollo, of doubtful meaning, either, 1. from λύκος, *wolf-slaying*, like λυκοκτόνος ; 2. from Λυκία, *the Lycian god*, like Λυκηγενής ; or, 3. from *λυκή (*light*), *the god of day.*

λῠκῆ, ἡ, Att. contr. for λυκέη.

***ΛΥ´ΚΗ**, *light*, an obsol. Root, whence come λυκάβας, λυκόφως, λευκός, Lat. *luceo, lux*, etc.

Λῠκη-γενής, ές (Λυκία, γένος) epith. of Apollo, *Lycian-born.*

λῠκηδόν, Adv. (λύκος) *wolf-like.*

Λῠκία, ἡ, *Lycia*, in the South of Asia Minor :—**Λυκίηθεν**, Adv. *from Lycia :* **Λυκίηνδε**, Adv. *to Lycia.*

Λῠκιο-εργής contr. **-ουργής**, ές, (Λυκία, ἔργον) *of Lycian workmanship.*

λῠκο-εργής, ές, (λύκος, ἔργον) *wolf-destroying*, Lat. *lupos conficiens ;* πρόβολοι λυκοεργέες javelins *for killing wolves.*

λῠκο-θαρσής, ές, (λύκος, θάρσος) *bold as a wolf.*

λῠκο-κτόνος, ον, (λύκος, κτείνω) *wolf-slaying :* epith. of Apollo, *the wolf-slayer.*

λῠκορ-ραίστης, ου, ὁ, (λύκος, ῥαίω) *a wolf-worrier.*

ΛΥ´ΚΟΣ, ὁ, *a wolf :*—proverb., λύκον ἰδεῖν *to see a wolf*, i.e. *to be struck dumb*, as was believed of those at whom a wolf *got the first look ;* so in Virgil, *Moerim lupi videre priores.* II. in pl. st[illegible]es *on the bits* of hard-mouthed horses, Lat. *lupi, lupata*, from their resemblance to the jagged teeth of a wolf.

λῠκό-φως, ωτος, ὁ, (λύκη, φῶς) *twilight*, both of morning and evening, *the gloaming*, Lat. *diluculum.*

λῠκόω, f. ώσω, (λύκος) *to tear like a wolf :*—Pass. *to be torn by wolves.*

λῦμα, ματος, τό, *filth* or *dirt removed by washing :* also *the dirty water, washings, offscourings.* II. *moral defilement, disgrace, infamy.* III. *an abandoned man.* (From λούω, Lat. *luo.*)

λῡμαίνομαι, f. λυμᾰνοῦμαι : aor. 1 ἐλυμηνάμην : also aor. 1 pass. ἐλυμάνθην : pf. λελύμασμαι, but 3 sing. λελύμανται : Dep. : (λύμη) :—*to treat with indignity* or *contumely, outrage :*—*to maltreat, maim, mutilate, spoil, destroy :* also, *to persecute.* II. the pres. λυμαίνομαι, with aor. 1 and pf. pass. are sometimes used in pass. sense, *to be maltreated, destroyed.* Hence

λῡμαντήρ, ῆρος, ὁ, *a spoiler, destroyer :* and

λῡμαντήριος, α, ον, *injurious, destructive :* c. gen., *ruining* another.

λῡμαντής, οῦ, ὁ, = λυμαντήρ.

λύμασις, ἡ, = λύμη. [ῡ]

λῡμεών, ῶνος, ὁ, (λύμη) *a destroyer, spoiler.*

ΛΥ´ΜΗ [ῡ], ἡ, *outrage* by word or deed, *an affront, disgrace :* generally, *maltreatment, maiming, mutilation, destruction ;* ἐπὶ λύμῃ for the sake of *insult.*

λύμην, Ep. aor. 2 pass. of λύω.

λῡμηνάμενος, aor. 1 part. of λυμαίνομαι.

λύντο, 3 pl. Ep. aor. 2 pass. of λύω.

λῡπέω, f. ήσω, (λύπη) *to give pain to, to pain, distress, grieve, annoy :* of light troops, *to harass, annoy :*—Pass.. with f. med. λυπήσομαι, *to be sad, to be grieved.*

ΛΥ´ΠΗ [ῡ], ἡ, *pain*, either of body or mind, Lat. *dolor : grief, distress, suffering, sad plight.*

λύπημα, ατος, τό, (λῡπέω) *pain, distress.*

λῡπῆν, Dor. inf. of λυπέω.

λῡπηρός, ά, όν, (λυπέω) *painful*, Lat. *molestus.*

λῡπητέον, verb. Adj. of λυπέομαι, *one must feel pain.*

λῡπρός, ά, όν, (λυπέω, λυπηρός) *wretched, distressed, poor, sorry.* II. *painful, distressing.*

ΛΥ´ΡΑ [ῠ], ἡ, Lat. *lyra, a lyre*, a Greek musical instrument *of seven strings*, like the κιθάρα and φόρμιγξ.

λῠρ-ᾰοιδός, ὁ, (λύρα, ἀοιδός) *one who sings to the lyre.*

λῠρίζω, f. ίσω, (λύρα) *to play the lyre.*

λῠρικός, ή, όν, (λύρα) *singing to the lyre :* as Subst., λυρικός, ὁ, *a lyric poet.*

λύριον, τό, Dim. of λύρα.

λῠρο-γηθής, ές, (λύρα, γηθέω) *delighting in the lyre.*

λῠρο-θελγής, ές, (λύρα, θέλγω) *charmed by the lyre.*

λῠρο-κτῠπία, ἡ, (λύρα, κτυπέω) *a sounding the lyre.*

λῠρο-ποιός, όν, (λύρα, ποιέω) *making lyres.*

λῠρ-ώδης, ες, (λύρα, εἶδος) *adapted to the lyre, lyrical.*

λῠρῳδός, ὁ, contr. for λυραοιδός.

λῡσ-ᾰνίας, ου, ὁ, (λύω, ἀνία) *ending sadness.*

λύσειαν, 3 pl. aor. 1 opt. of λύω.

λῡσί-γᾰμος, ον, (λύω, γάμος) *dissolving marriage.*
λῡσί-ζωνος, ον, or η, ον, (λύω, ζώνη) *loosing the zone*: epith. of Diana, *who lightened the pangs of travail.*
λῡσί-κᾰκος, ον, (λύω, κακόν) *ending evil.*
λῡσί-μᾰχος, ον, or η, ον, (λύω, μάχη) *ending strife.*
λῡσι-μελής, ές, (λύω, μέλος) *limb-relaxing.*
λῡσι-μέριμνος, ον, (λύω, μέριμνα) *driving care away.*
λύσιμος, ον, (λύσις) *able to loose* or *relieve.*
λῡσί-ποθος, ον, (λύω, πόθος) *delivering from love.*
λῡσί-πονος, ον, (λύω, πόνος) *freeing from toil.*
λύσις [ῠ], gen. εως Ion. ιος, ἡ: (λύω): *a loosing, setting free*, esp. of a prisoner, *release, ransoming*: *deliverance*; λύσις χρειῶν *liquidation of* debt. 2. *means* or *power of releasing* or *loosing.*
λῡσιτελέω, f. ήσω, = λύω τέλος (which is found in Sophocles) *to pay dues* or *tribute to*: *to be useful* or *advantageous to*: impers., λυσιτελεῖ, *it profits, benefits*: with a comp. force, τεθνάναι λυσιτελεῖ ἢ ζῆν *it is better* to be dead than alive; οὐ λυσιτελεῖ μοι *it profits* me not; neut. part. τὸ λυσιτελοῦν, τὰ λυσιτελοῦντα *profit, gain, advantage.* From
λῡσι-τελής, ές, (λύω, τέλος) *paying dues, indemnifying*: *profitable, advantageous*: also, *cheap.* Comp. -έστερος, Sup. -έστατος.
λῡσιτελούντως, Adv. pres. part. of λυσιτελέω, *usefully, profitably.*
λῡσι-φλεβής, ές, (λύω, φλέψ) *opening the veins.*
λῡσί-φρων, ονος, ὁ, ἡ, (λύω, φρήν) *setting free the mind.*
ΛΥ'ΣΣΑ˘ Att. **λύττᾰ**, ἡ, *rage, fury*, esp. in war, *martial rage*: *raging madness, raving, frenzy.* Hence
λυσσαίνω, *to be raging-mad, to rave.*
λυσσάς, άδος, ἡ, (λύσσα) *raging-mad, raving.*
λυσσάω Att. **λυττάω**, (λύσσα) *to be raging, furious*, esp. in battle. 2. *to be raging-mad, to rave.*
λύσσημα, τό, (λυσσάω) *a fit of madness*: in pl. *ravings.*
λυσσῆν, Dor. inf. of λυσσάω.
λυσσητήρ, ῆρος, and **λυσσητής**, οῦ, ὁ, (λυσσάω) *one that is raging* or *raving-mad*: *a madman.*
λυσσο-μᾰνής, ές, (λύσσα, μανῆναι) *raging-mad.*
λυσσ-ώδης, ες, (λύσσα, εἶδος) *like madness*: *raging-mad, raving.*
λυτέον, verb. Adj. of λύω, *one must loose.*
λῠτήρ, ῆρος, ὁ, (λύω) *one who looses, a deliverer, releaser.* II. *an arbitrator, settler.*
λῠτήριος, α, ον, or ος, ον, (λύω) *loosing, releasing*: c. gen. *delivering* or *setting free from.*
λύτο [ῠ], Ep. 3 sing. Ep. aor. 2 pass. of λύω; but **λῦτο**, contr. for λύετο, Ep. impf. pass. of λύω.
λύτρον, τό, (λύω) *the price paid*: 1. *a ransom, price of redemption*, mostly in pl. 2. *an atonement.*
λυτρόω, f. ώσω, (λύτρον) *release on receipt of ransom, to hold to ransom.* 2. Med. *to release by payment of ransom, to ransom, redeem.* 3. Pass. *to be ransomed.*
λύτρωσις, εως, ἡ, (λυτρόω) *a ransoming.* 2. *Redemption.*
λυτρωτής, οῦ, ὁ, (λυτρόω) *a ransomer, redeemer.*
λύττα, λυττάω, Att. for λύσσα, λυσσάω.
λύχνα, τά, irreg. pl. of λύχνος.
λυχνεῖον or **λυχνίον**, τό, (λύχνος) = λυχνία.
λυχνέων, ῶνος, ὁ, (λύχνος) *a place to keep lamps in.*
λυχνία, ἡ, (λύχνος) *a lamp-stand.*
λυχνίδιον, τό, Dim. of λύχνος, *a small lamp.*
λυχνο-καΐα, ἡ, (λύχνος, καίω) *a lighting of lamps, illumination*, a festival at Sais in Egypt in honour of Minerva, like the Chinese Feast of Lanterns.
λυχνο-ποιός, όν, (λύχνος, ποιέω) *making lamps* or *lanterns.*
λυχνό-πολις, ἡ, (λύχνος, πόλις) *city of lamps.*
λυχνο-πώλης, ου, ὁ, (λύχνος, πωλέω) *a dealer in lamps* or *lanterns.*
ΛΥ'ΧΝΟΣ, ὁ, pl. λύχνοι and λύχνα, *a light, lamp*: περὶ λύχνων ἁφάς about the time for *lamp-lighting*, i. e. at dusk.
λυχνοφορέω, f. ήσω, (λυχνοφόρος) *to carry a lantern*: Lacon. part. λυχνοφορίοντες.
λυχνο-φόρος, ον, (λύχνος, φέρω) *carrying a lamp.*
ΛΥ'Ω, fut. λύσω [ῡ], aor. 1 ἔλῡσα: pf. λέλῠκα:—Pass., fut. λῠθήσομαι and paullo-post. fut. λελύσομαι [ῡ]: aor. 1 ἐλύθην [ῠ]: Ep. aor. 2 pass. λύμην [ῠ], 3 sing. λύτο, 3 pl. λύντο: pf. λέλῠμαι, plqpf. ἐλελύμην [ῠ], 3 sing. Ep. opt. λελῦτο, for λελύοιτο.—*To loose*: *to loosen, unfasten, untie, slacken*; λύειν ὀφρῦν *to unbend* the brow; λ. στόμα *to open* the mouth; etc.:—Med. *to loosen* or *undo for oneself.* 2. of horses, *to unyoke, unharness.* 3. generally, *to loose, release, set free.* 4. *to release a captive on receipt of ransom, to hold to ransom, release*:—Med. *to release by payment, ransom, redeem.* II. *to loosen, weaken, relax*; λύειν γυῖα, γούνατα *to loose* the limbs, knees, i. e. *unnerve, enfeeble*, and often in Homer, *to slay, kill.* III. *to dissolve, break up.* 2. *to break down, lay low, demolish.* 3. generally, *to undo, do away with*: of disputes, *to put down*: of laws, *to repeal, annul*; λύειν σπονδάς *to break* a treaty. 4. *to dismiss, assuage, calm.* 5. *to undo, atone, make up for*, Lat. *luere, rependere*; so λύειν ἁμαρτίας. IV. in Att., τέλη, μισθοὺς λύειν *to pay* rates or taxes: hence, 2. λύειν τέλη = λυσιτελεῖν, *to profit, avail*; οὐ λύει τέλη *it boots* not; also λύειν, absol. without τέλη, *to profit.*
λῶ, contr. from λάω, *I will, wish* or *desire*, a Doric defect. Verb. only used in sing. λῶ, λῇς, λῇ, 3 pl. λῶντι; subj. λῇς, λῇ; opt. λῴη; inf. λῆν; also part. dat. τῷ λῶντι.
λωβάομαι Ion. -έομαι: f. -ήσομαι Dor. λωβᾱσοῦμαι: aor. 1 med. ἐλωβησάμην: (but aor. 1 ἐλωβήθην and pf. λελώβημαι in pass. sense): Dep.: (λώβη):—*to treat despitefully, to insult, maltreat*: *to maim, mutilate*: *to dishonour.* 2. absol. *to act outrageously* or *despitefully.* II. pf. part. λελωβημένος, in pass. sense, *mutilated.*

λωβεύω, f. σω, (λώβη) *to mock, make a mock of.*

ΛΩ'ΒΗ, ἡ, *ill-usage* by word or deed, *despiteful treatment outrage, contumely, indignity: mutilation, maiming.* 2. of a person, *a disgrace, opprobrium.*

λωβηθῆναι, aor. 1 inf. of λωβάομαι.

λωβήτειρα, fem. of λωβητήρ.

λωβητήρ, ῆρος, ὁ, (λωβάομαι) *one who treats despitefully, a foul slanderer:* generally, *a destroyer: mutilator, murderer.* II. pass. *a worthless wretch.*

λωβητής, οῦ, ὁ, = λωβητήρ; λωβητὴς τέχνης *a disgrace to* his trade.

λωβητός, ή, όν, (λωβαομαι) *ill-treated, outraged, dishonoured.* II. act. *insulting, abusive: baneful.*

λωβήτωρ, ορος, ὁ, = λωβητήρ.

λῶα, λωίτερος, v. λωίων.

λωίων, ονος, ὁ, ἡ, λώιον, τό: Att. contr. λῴων, λῷον: neut. pl. λωίονα, syncop. λώια: (λῶ *to wish*): —*more desirable; better*:—Sup. λώιστος, η, ον, contr. λῷστος.—There is also a second Comp. λωίτερος, ον.

ΛΩ'ΜΑ, ατος, τό, *the hem* or *border of a robe.* Hence

λωμάτιον, τό, Dim. *a fringe, flounce.*

λῶντι, 3 pl. of Dor. verb λῶ, *to wish.*

λώπη, ἡ, (λέπω, λοπός) *a covering, mantle.* 2. *a skin, husk, shell.*

λωπίζω, f. ίσω, (λώπη) *to cover, wrap up.*

λωποδυτέω, f. ήσω, *to steal clothes:* hence trans. *to rob, plunder.* From

λωπο-δύτης [ῠ], ου, ὁ, (λῶπος, δύω) *one who slips into another's clothes* or *strips him of them, a clothes-stealer:* generally *a thief, robber, footpad.*

λῶπος, ὁ, = λώπη.

λῷστος, η, ον, Att. contr. from λώιστος, Sup. of λωίων, *most desirable, best.*

λωτεῦντα, Ion. acc. neut. pl. of λωτόεις.

λωτίζω, f. ίσω, (λωτός) *to pluck flowers*:—Med. λωτίζομαι, *to cull flowers for oneself, choose the best.*

λώτῐνος, η, ον, (λωτός) *of lotus.*

λώτισμα, τό, (λωτίζω) *a flower:* metaph. *the flower, choicest, best.*

λωτόεις, εσσα, εν, (λωτός) *overgrown with lotus;* πεδία λωτεῦντα, Ion. for λωτόεντα, *lotus*-plains.

ΛΩΤΟ'Σ, οῦ, ὁ, *the lotus*, name of several plants:—I. *the Greek lotus*, a kind of *clover* or *trefoil*, on which horses fed. II. *the Cyrenean lotus* or *jujube*, an African shrub, the fruit of which was eaten by certain tribes on the coast, hence called *Lotophagi:* the fruit was *honey-sweet*, μελιηδής: *in size* as large as the olive, and in taste resembling the date. III. *the Egyptian lotus, the lily of the Nile.* IV. there was also a *lotus-tree* growing in Africa, distinguished by its hard, black wood, of which flutes were made: hence λωτός is used poët. for *a flute.*

λωτο-τρόφος, ον, (λωτός, τρέφω) *growing lotus.*

λωτο-φάγος, ον, (λωτός, φᾰγεῖν) *eating lotus:* as Subst., Λωτοφάγοι, οἱ, *the Lotus-eaters*, a peaceful nation on the coast of Cyrenaica.

λωτρόν, λωτρο-χόος, Dor. for λουτρ-.

λωτῶ, Dor. for λωτοῦ, gen. of λωτός.

λωφάω Ion. -έω, f. ήσω, (λόφος) *to rest from toil, take rest:* c. gen. *to have rest, abate from.* 2. *to abate*, of a disease or of wind. II. trans. *to lighten, relieve, release.*

λωφήσειε, 3 sing. aor. 1 opt. of λωφάω.

λώφησις, ἡ, (λωφάω) *rest from*:—*remission, cessation.*

λῴων, neut. λῷον, Att. contr. for λωίων, λώιον.

M

M, μ, μῦ Ion. μῶ, τό, indecl., twelfth letter of the Gr. alphabet: as numeral, μ′ = 40, but ‚μ = 40,000.

Changes of μ, esp. in the dialects: I. Aeol. and Lacon. into π, as μετά into πεδά. II. Aeol. μ doubled, e. g. ἄμμες ὔμμες, for ἡμεῖς ὑμεῖς. III. μ becomes ν, as, μίν Dor. νίν μή, Lat. *ne.* IV. μ is often added or left out, 1. at the beginning of a word, as ἴα μία, ὄσχος μόσχος, ὀχλεύς μοχλεύς, Ἄρης Lat. *Mars.* 2. in the middle of a word, as πίμπλημι πίπλημι, πίμπρημι πίπρημι, ἄμβροτος ἄβροτος, ὄμβριμος ὄβριμος, etc. V. μ sometimes has α or ο prefixed, as, μέλγω ἀμέλγω, μέργω ἀμέργω, μόργνυμι ὀμόργνυμι. VI. σ is added or left out before μ, as, σμάραγδος μάραγδος, σμάω μάω, σμικρός μικρός, σμυγερός μογερός.

μ', apostr. for με. II. very rarely for μοι.

μά, a Particle used in strong protestation and oaths, either affirmative or negative acc. to the context: I. *in affirmation;* ναὶ μὰ τόδε σκῆπτρον yea *by* this sceptre. II. *in negation;* οὐ μὰ γὰρ Ἀπόλλωνα nay *by* Apollo. III. Att. μά is used absol., μὰ Δία, *by Zeus!* IV. in common discourse, the name of the deity sworn by was often suppressed, ναὶ μὰ τόν, οὐ μὰ τόν (sub. Δία). V. μά is sometimes omitted after οὐ; as, οὐ τὸν Δία, οὐ τὸν θεόν, no *by* Jove, etc.

μᾶ, Aeol. and Dor. shortd. for μάτηρ μήτηρ, as μᾶ γᾶ for μῆτερ γῆ: cf. βᾶ, δῶ, λῖ.

μαγάδιον, τό, *the bridge of the magadis.* [ᾰ] From

μάγαδῐς, ἡ, gen. ιδος: irreg. dat. μαγάδι: acc. μάγαδιν:—*the magadis, a harp with twenty strings.*

μαγγάνευμα, τό, *a piece of jugglery:* pl. *juggleries, mountebank's tricks:* and

μαγγᾰνευτής, οῦ, ὁ, *a juggler, mountebank.* From

μαγγᾰνεύω, f. σω, (μάγγανον) *to cheat by sleight of hand: to bewitch.* 2. intr. *to play tricks.*

ΜΑ'ΓΓΑΝΟΝ, τό, *any means for tricking* or *bewitching, a philtre, drug: a juggler's apparatus.* II. = γάγγαμον, *a hunting-net.*

μᾰγεία, ἡ, (μαγεύω) *the religion of the Magi.* 2. *magic, art.*

μαγειρεῖον, τό, (μάγειρος) *a place for cooking, a cook-shop.* II. Maced. *a pot, kettle.*

μᾰγειρικός, ή, όν, (μάγειρος) *fit for a cook* or *cookery:* ἡ μαγειρική (sub. τέχνη), *cookery*. Hence **μαγειρικῶς**, Adv. *in a cook-like way, artistically.*

μάγειρος, ὁ. *a cook:* also *a butcher*. (From μάσσω, μᾶζα, because the baking of bread was originally the chief business of the cook.)

μάγευμα, τό, (μᾰγεύω) *a piece of magic art:* in pl. *charms, spells.*

μᾰγεύω, f. σω, (Μάγος) *to be a Magus* or *a magician:* μαγεύειν μέλη to sing incantations. II. trans. *to enchant, bewitch, charm.*

Μάγνης, ητος, ὁ, fem. **Μάγνησσα**, *a Magnesian*, a dweller in Μαγνησία in Thessaly: also **Μαγνήτης**, fem. Μαγνῆτις. II. λίθος **Μαγνῆτις**, ἡ, *the magnet*, also called λίθος Ἡρακλεία.

ΜΑΓΟΣ, ου, ὁ. *a Magus, Magian*, one of a Median tribe. II. *one of the wise men* or *seers in Persia* who interpreted dreams. III. *any enchanter, wizard: magician:* in bad sense *a juggler, quack.* [ᾰ]

μᾰγο-φόνια, τά, (Μάγος, φόνος) *the slaughter of the Magi*, a Persian festival.

μαγώτερος, α, ον, Comp. Adj. formed from μάγος, *more magical.*

μᾰδᾰρός, ά, όν, (μαδάω) of flesh, *flaccid, loose:* of the head, *bald.*

μᾰδάω, f. ήσω, (μαδός) *to be moist* or *wet, to melt away:* of hair, *to fall off*, Lat. *defluere:* hence *to be bald.*

μάδδα, Dor. for μᾶζα.

***ΜΑΔΟ'Σ**, ή, όν, the Root of μαδάω, etc., = μαδαρός.

μᾶζα, ἡ, (μάσσω, *to knead*) *barley-bread, a barley-cake*, opp. to ἄρτος, *wheaten* bread; μᾶζαν μεμᾰχώς having baked him *a cake*, with a pun on μάχη.

μαζίσκη, ἡ, Dim. of μᾶζα, *a barley-scone.*

μαζο-νόμος, ὁ, (μᾶζα, νέμω) *a wooden trencher for serving barley-cakes on:* generally, *a large platter* or *charger*, Lat. *mazonomus.*

ΜΑΖΟ'Σ, οῦ, ὁ, *one of the breasts* (στέρνον being *the whole breast* or *chest*), mostly of *women*, but also of men. μαστός differs from μαζός only in dialect.

μᾰθεῖν, aor. 2 inf. of μανθάνω.

μᾰθεῦμαι, Dor. for μαθήσομαι, fut. of μανθάνω.

μάθημα, ατος, τό, (μᾰθεῖν) *that which is learnt, a lesson.* 2. *learning, knowledge:*—in pl., τὰ μαθήματα *mathematics.* Hence

μᾰθημᾰτικός, ή, όν, *fond of learning.* II. *belonging to the sciences*, esp. *to mathematics:* ἡ μαθηματική (sub. ἐπιστήμη), *mathematics:* ὁ μαθηματικός *a mathematician.*

μάθησις, ἡ, (μᾰθεῖν) *the act of learning, acquiring information.* 2. *desire* or *power of learning.*

μᾰθήσομαι, fut. of μανθάνω.

μᾰθητέος, α, ον, verb. Adj. of μανθάνω, *to be learnt.* II. neut. μαθητέον, *one must learn.*

μᾰθητεύω, f. σω, *to be a pupil* or *scholar.* II. trans. *to make a disciple of* one, *instruct.* From

μᾰθητής, οῦ, ὁ, (μαθεῖν) *a learner, pupil*, Lat. *discipulus: a disciple.*

μᾰθητιάω, Desiderat. of μανθάνω, *to wish to become a disciple.* II. *to be a disciple* or *pupil.*

μᾰθητός, ή, όν, (μαθεῖν) *learnt, that may be learnt.*

μᾰθήτρια, ἡ, fem. of μαθητής, *a female pupil.*

μᾰθοῖσι, Dor. fem. of μαθών, aor. 2 part. of μανθάνω.

μάθον [ᾰ], Ep. aor. 2 of μανθάνω.

μάθος [ᾰ], τό, poët. and Ion. for μάθησις.

μᾰθών, aor. 2 part. of μανθάνω.

ΜΑΙ͂Α, ἡ, *good mother, dame.* II. *a nurse, foster-mother, mother.* III. *a midwife.*

Μαῖα, ἡ, *Maia*, daughter of Atlas, mother of Hermes: also **Μαιάς**, άδος, ἡ.

Μαίανδρος, ὁ, *Maeander*, a river in Caria noted for its windings.

μαιεύομαι, f. σομαι, Dep. (μαῖα III) *to serve* as a midwife: trans. *to batch.*

Μαιμακτηριών, ῶνος, ἡ, *the fifth Attic month*, answering to the end of November and beginning of December, so called from the festival of Zeus Μαιμάκτης held in it.

Μαιμάκτης, ου, ὁ, (μαιμάσσω) epith. of Jupiter, *the boisterous, stormy*, in whose honour the Maemacteria were kept at Athens in the first winter month, as being *the god of storms*, etc.

μαιμάσσω, = μαιμάω, *to burst forth.*

μαιμάω, Ep. 3 pl. μαιμώωσι, part. μαιμώων, -ώωσα: f. ώσω: Ep. aor. 1 μαίμησα: (redupl. of μάω, as παιφάσσω from φάω):—*to be very eager, to pant* or *quiver with eagerness:* c. gen. *to be eager for.*

μαινάς, άδος, ἡ, (μαίνομαι) *mad, raving, frantic.* 2. as Subst. *a mad woman: a Bacchanal, a Maenad.* II. act. *causing madness.*

ΜΑΙ'ΝΗ, ἡ, *maena, a small sea-fish*, like our herring.

μαινίς, ίδος [ῐ], ἡ, Dim. of μαίνη, *a sprat.*

μαινόλης, ου, ὁ, fem. **μαινόλις**, ιδος, (μαίνομαι) *raving, frenzied.*

μαινόλιος, α, ον, = μαινόλης.

μαίνομαι, fut. μᾰνήσομαι and μᾰνοῦμαι: pf. with pres. sense μέμηνα, also (in pass. form) μεμάνημαι: aor. 1 med. ἐμηνάμην, aor. 2 pass. ἐμάνην, part. μᾰνείς, inf. μᾰνῆναι: (*μάω) :—*to rage, to be furious*, in war: also *to rave* with anger: *to be mad with wine, be madly drunk*, and of Bacchic frenzy, μαινόμενος Διόνυσος the *frenzied* Dionysus: metaph. of things, *to rage, riot*—μαίνεσθαι ὑπὸ τοῦ θεοῦ *to be driven mad* by the god:—Att. phrase, πλεῖν ἢ μαίνομαι, more than *madness*, i. e. utter distraction. II. Causal in aor. 1 act. ἔμηνα, *to make mad, madden.*

ΜΑΙ'ΟΜΑΙ, fut. μάσομαι [ᾰ], Dep. *to endeavour, strive: to seek, seek to compass:* cf. ἐπιμαίομαι.

μαιόομαι, f. =ώσομαι, Dep. = μαιεύομαι.

Μαῖρα, ἡ, (μαρ-μαίρω) *the Sparkler*, i. e. the dog-star.

Μαιωτιστί, Adv. *in Maeotic* (i. e. Scythian) *fashion.*

ΜΑ'ΚΑΡ [μᾰ], ᾰρος, ὁ: fem. μάκαρ or μάκαιρα:—*blessed, happy*, properly of the gods, opp. to *mortal* men: absol. μάκαρες, *the blessed ones*, i. e. *the gods.* II. of men, *supremely blest, fortunate;*

but also, *prosperous, wealthy.* III. the dead were esp. called μάκαρες, *the blessed,* as being beyond the reach of pain:—μακάρων νῆσοι the islands *of the blest,* (placed by the later Greeks in the ocean at the extreme West).—Comp. and Sup., μακάρτερος, –τατος.

μακάρεσσι, Ep. dat. pl. of μάκαρ.

μᾰκᾰρία, ἡ, (μάκαρ) *happiness, bliss.* II. *the abode of the blessed.*

μᾰκᾰρίζω, fut. ίσω Att. ιῶ, (μάκαρ) *to call* or *esteem happy: to bless.*

μάκαριος, α, ον, or ος, ον, collat. form of μάκαρ, *blessed, happy, fortunate:*—in Att. *one of the upper classes:*—Comp. and Sup. μακαριώτερος, –τατος.

μᾰκᾰρισμός, οῦ, ὁ, (μακαρίζω) *a pronouncing* or *esteeming happy, a blessing.*

μᾰκᾰριστός, ή, όν, (μακαρίζω) *deemed* or *pronounced happy* by others: absol. *enviable.* Adv. –τως.

μᾰκᾰρίτης [ῑ], ου, ὁ, like μάκαρ III, *one in a state of bliss,* i. e. *one dead:* fem. **μᾰκᾰρῖτις,** ιδος.

μᾰκαρτός, ή, όν, = μακαριστός.

μᾰκεδνός, ή, όν, (μῆκος) *tall, taper.*

Μᾰκεδονίζω, f. σω, (Μακεδών) *to be on the Macedonian side:* or, *to speak Macedonian.*

Μακεδόνιος, α, ον, and **–ονικός,** ή, όν, *Macedonian.* From

Μᾰκεδών, όνος, ὁ, *a Macedonian.*

μάκελλα, poët. also **μακέλη,** ἡ, (μία, κέλλω, as δίκελλα from δίς, κέλλω) *a pick-axe with one point.*

μάκελλον, τό, Lat. *măcellum, a slaughter-house, shambles, market.*

μᾱκεστήρ, ῆρος, ὁ, (μᾶκος) used as Adj., μῦθος μακεστήρ *a long, tedious* tale.

Μᾰκηδών, όνος, ὁ, poët for Μακεδών.

μάκιστος, Dor. for μήκιστος, (μῆκος) irreg. Sup. of μακρός, = μέγιστος, *greatest.*

μακκοάω, f. άσω, [ᾱ], *to be stupid:* pf. part. μεμακκοακώς, *dreaming, mooning.*

μᾶκος, τό, Dor. for μῆκος, *length:* acc. μᾶκος as Adv., = μακράν, *afar.*

μακρά (sub. γραμμή), ἡ, *the long line* which the δικαστής drew upon his tablet in token of condemnation, opp. to the short line (βραχεῖα), which was in token of acquittal.

μακρ-αίων, ωνος, ὁ, ἡ, (μακρός, αἰών) *lasting long:* of persons, *long-lived;* οἱ μακραίωνες *the immortals.*

μακράν Ion. **μακρήν,** acc. fem. of μακρός, used as Adv. *at a distance, afar off, far:* Comp. μακροτέραν, *farther, to a greater distance.* 2. also of Time, *at length, tediously;* μακρὰν εἰπεῖν to speak *at great length:* also *long,* μακρὰν ζῆν to live *long.*

μακρ-αύχην, ενος, ὁ, ἡ, (μακρός, αὐχήν) *long-necked.*

μακρ-ηγορέω, f. ήσω, (μακρός, ἀγορεύω) *to speak at great length.* Hence

μακρηγορία Dor. **μακραγ–,** ἡ, *long-windedness, prolixity, prosing.*

μακρ-ημερία, ἡ, (μακρός, ἡμέρα) *the season of long days.*

μακρό-βῐος, ον, (μακρός, βίος) *long-lived:* οἱ Μακρόβιοι an Ethiopian people south of Egypt.

μακρο-βίοτος, ον, (μακρός, βίοτος) *long-lived, of long duration.*

μακρό-γηρως, ων, gen. ω, (μακρός, γῆρας) *very old, in advanced age.*

μακρο-δρόμος, ον, (μακρός, δραμεῖν) *far-running.*

μακρόθεν, Adv. (μακρός) *from afar.*

μακροθῡμέω, f. ήσω, (μακρόθυμος) *to be long-suffering, patient;* μακροθυμεῖν εἴς τινα *to be forbearing* or *long-suffering* towards one. Hence

μακροθυμία, ἡ, *long-suffering.*

μακρό-θῡμος, ον, (μακρός, θυμός) *long-suffering, forbearing: patient.* Adv. –μως, *patiently.*

μακρολογέω, f. ήσω, (μακρολόγος) *to speak at length:* c. acc. rei, *to speak long on* a subject. Hence

μακρολογία, ἡ, *a speaking at length.*

μακρο-λόγος, ον, (μακρός, λέγω) *speaking at length.*

μακρό-πνοος, ον, contr. **–πνους,** ουν, (μακρός, πνέω) *long-breathed: long-lived, lasting long.*

μακρός, ά, όν, (μᾶκος, μῆκος) *long,* whether of Space or Time: I. of Space, *long, far-stretching.* 2. *tall, lofty:* also *deep.* 3. *far, far distant;* μακραὶ ἐπιβοήθειαι succours *from a distance:* ἐπὶ μακρόν *far, for a long way;* ὅσον ἐπὶ μακρότατον *as far as possible.* 4. dat. μακρῷ is often used, like πολύ, *by far, much;* μακρῷ πρῶτος *by far* the first. II. of Time, *long: long-lasting, enduring;* διὰ μακροῦ (sc. χρόνου) after *a long time;* εἰς μακρόν *for a long time.* 2. *long, tedious;* διὰ μακρῶν *at great length.* III. regul. Comp. μακρότερος; Sup. μακρότατος; Irreg. Comp. μάσσων, μᾶσσον; Sup. μήκιστος Dor. μάκιστος, formed from μῆκος, as αἴσχιστος from αἶσχος. IV. the neut. pl. μακρά is used as Adv., μακρὰ βιβάς taking *long* strides; μακρὰ μεμυκώς *loudly* bellowing; μακρὰ προσεύχεσθαι to make *long* prayers:—so also neut. sing., μακρὸν αὐτεῖν to shout *aloud.*

μάκρος, εος, τό, = μᾶκος, μῆκος, *length.*

μακρο-τένων, οντος, ὁ, ἡ, (μακρός, τείνω) *far-stretched, long drawn out.*

μακροτέραν, Comp. of μακράν, q. v.

μακρό-τονος, ον, (μακρός, τείνω) = μακροτένων.

μακρο-φάρυγξ, υγγος, ὁ, ἡ, (μακρός, φάρυγξ) *with long throat* or *gullet.*

μακρο-φλυᾱρήτης, ου, ὁ, (μακρός, φλυαρέω) *a tedious prater.*

μακρο-χρόνιος, ον, (μακρός, χρόνος) *long-enduring.*

μάκτρα, ἡ, (μάσσω) *a kneading-trough.*

μάκτρον, τό, (μάσσω) *a towel, napkin.*

μακύνω, Dor. for μηκύνω.

μᾰκών, old poët. aor. 2 part. of μηκάομαι.

μάκων [ᾱ], ωνος, Dor. for μήκων, ωνος.

ΜΑ'ΛΑ˘, Adv. *very, very much, exceedingly, quite:* 1. strengthening the word with which it stands; μάλα πολλά *very* many; μάλ' εὖ *right* well; μάλ' αὐτίκα *quite* directly; μάλα διαμπερές *right* through; οὐ μάλα *by no means, on no account.* 2.

strengthening a whole sentence; ἦ μάλα δή.., now *in very truth*..; so, with a part., μάλα περ μεμαώς though desiring *never so much*. II. Comp. μᾶλλον, *more, more strongly*: also *rather*, Lat. *potius*. 2. *too much, far too much*. 3. μᾶλλον is sometimes joined to another Comp.; ῥηίτερος μᾶλλον *more* easier; ἐχθίων μᾶλλον; etc. 4. μᾶλλον ἤ is often followed by οὐ (where οὐ seems redundant), as, πόλιν ὅλην διαφθείρειν μᾶλλον ἢ οὐ τοὺς αἰτίους: in this case μᾶλλον ἢ οὐ is preceded by another negat. 5. παντὸς μᾶλλον *more* than anything, i. e. *by all means*. III. Sup. μάλιστα, *most, most strongly: most of all, especially*; ἐν τοῖς μάλιστα (sc. οὖσι), Lat. *imprimis, as much as any*; ἐς τὰ μάλιστα *for the most part, mostly*: μάλιστα is sometimes added to another Sup., as ἔχθιστος μάλιστα. 2. in numbers, μάλιστα is often added to shew that they are not exact, *at the most, at most*; πεντήκοντα μάλιστα fifty *at most*, where the real number is *forty-nine*: hence *about, pretty near*, ἐς μέσον μάλιστα *about* the middle. 3. καὶ μάλιστα *most certainly*, Lat. *vel maxime*.

μᾰλάβαθρον or **μαλόβαθρον**, τό, *malobathrum*, the aromatic leaf of an Indian plant, *the betel* or *areca*.

μᾰλᾰκαί-πους, ὁ, ἡ, πουν, τό, gen. ποδος, (μαλακός, πούς) *softly treading*.

μᾰλᾰκία, ἡ, (μαλακός) *softness, tenderness*: of men, *effeminacy, weakness*.

μᾰλᾰκιάω, (μαλακία) *to be soft* or *tender*.

μᾰλᾰκίζω, f. σω, (μαλακός) *to make soft, enervate*. II. Pass. and Med. μαλακίζομαι, f. -ίσομαι Att. -ιοῦμαι: aor. 1 med. ἐμαλακισάμην, pass. ἐμαλακίσθην:—*to be soft* or *tender, weak* or *effeminate*. 2. *to be softened* or *appeased*.

μᾰλᾰκίων, ωνος, ὁ, (μαλακός) *a darling*. [κῐ]

μᾰλᾰκο-γνώμων, ον, gen. ονος, (μαλακός, γνώμη) *gentle of mood*.

ΜΑ˘ΛΑ˘ΚΟ'Σ, ή, όν, Lat. *MOLLIS, soft*; μαλακὸς λείμων *a soft, grassy* meadow. II. *soft, gentle, mild*. 2 in bad sense, *soft, effeminate: easy, careless, remiss*.

μᾰλᾰκό-χειρ, χειρος, ὁ, ἡ, (μαλακός, χείρ) *soft-handed, soothing*.

μᾰλᾰκύνω, = μαλακίζω, *to soften*:—Pass. *to be soft* or *weakly, to flag*.

μᾰλᾰκῶς, Adv. of μαλακός, *softly: easily, carelessly*: Sup. μαλακώτατα.

μᾰλάσσω Att. -ττω, fut. ξω, (μαλακός) *to make soft, soften*: of leather, *to make supple, curry*: and metaph., μαλάσσειν τινά *to give* one *a dressing, curry* him. II. metaph. *to soften by entreaties, to pacify*: also *to relieve*.—Pass. *to be softened*: c. gen. *to be relieved from*.

μαλάχη, ἡ, (μᾰλᾰκός) *a mallow*, Lat. *malva*.

μᾰλερός, ά, όν, (μάλα) *very strong, mighty, raging*, of fire: metaph. *glowing, vehement*.

ΜΑ'ΛΗ, ἡ, *the arm-pit*, Lat. *ala*: only in the phrase ὑπὸ μάλης or ὑπὸ μάλην, under *the arm*.

ΜΑ'ΛΘΑ˘ or **μάλθη**, ἡ, *a mixture of wax and pitch* for calking ships. 2. *the wax* laid over writing-tablets.

μαλθᾰκίζω, f. ίσω Att. ιῶ, = μαλακίζω, *to soften*:—Pass. *to be softened: to be remiss*.

μαλθάκινος, η, ον, poët. for μαλθακός.

μαλθᾰκιστέον or -έα, verb. Adj. of μαλθακίζομαι, *one must be remiss*.

μαλθᾰκός, ή, όν, = μαλακός (with θ inserted), *soft*. II. *soft, gentle, mild*: in bad sense, *soft, weakly, effeminate*.

μαλθᾰκῶς, Adv. *softly: gently, mildly*.

μαλθάσσω, f. ξω, = μαλάσσω, *to soften, soothe*:—Pass., μαλθαχθῆναι ὕπνῳ *to be unnerved* by sleep.

μάλινος, α, ον, Dor. for μήλινος.

μάλιον, τό, (μαλλός) *hair, a lock of hair*. [ᾰ]

Μαλίς, ίδος, ἡ, Dor. for **Μηλίς**, (μᾶλον, = μῆλον) *a nymph who protects the flocks* (μῆλα).

μάλιστα, Adv., Sup. of μάλα: v. μάλα III.

μᾶλλο, by crasis for μὴ ἀλλά, *nay but*.

μαλλό-δετος, ον, (μαλλός, δέω) *bound with wool*.

μᾶλλον, Adv., Comp. of μάλα: v. μάλα II.

ΜΑΛΛΟ'Σ, οῦ, ὁ, *a lock of wool, the wool of sheep, a fleece*: of men, *a lock* or *braid of hair*.

μαλόβαθρον, v. μαλάβαθρον.

μᾶλον, Dor. for μῆλον B.

μαλο-πάρῃος, ον, Dor. for μηλοπάρῃος.

μᾱλός, ή, όν, *white*. (Origin uncertain.)

μαλο-φόρος, **μαλο-φύλαξ**, Dor. for μηλοφ—.

μάμμᾰ and **μάμμη**, ἡ, a child's attempt to call to its *mother*; like ἄππα, ἀπφά, ἄττα, πάππα. II. = μήτηρ, *mother*. III. later *a grandmother*.

Μαμμάκῡθος, ὁ, proverb. word for *a blockhead*.

μαμμᾶν αἰτεῖν, *to cry for the mother's breast*, of young children before they can articulate.

μαμμία, ἡ, (μάμμα) *a mother*.

Μαμμωνᾶς or **Μαμωνᾶς**, οῦ, ὁ, *Mammon*, the Syrian god of riches, = Greek **Πλοῦτος**: hence generally, *wealth, riches*.

μάν, affirm. Particle, Dor. and old Ep. for μήν.

ΜΑ'ΝΔΡΑ, ἡ, *a fold, byre, stable*, Lat. *mandra*: also 2. *the setting of a seal*, Lat. *pala, funda*.

μανδρᾰγόρας, ου, ὁ, *mandrake*, a narcotic plant.

μᾰνείς, εῖσα, έν, aor. 2 part. of μαίνομαι.

Μανέρως, ὁ, *Maneros*, only son of the first king of Egypt: also a national dirge named after him, identical with the Greek Λίνος.

μᾶνες, Dor. for μῆνες, pl. of μήν.

μᾰνῆναι, aor. 2 inf. of μαίνομαι.

ΜΑΝΘΑ'ΝΩ: fut. μᾰθήσομαι Dor. μᾰθεῦμαι: aor 2 ἔμᾰθον, in Homer either without augm. μάθον, or with double μ, ἔμμαθες, ἔμμαθε: pf. μεμάθηκα:—*to learn by inquiry, to ascertain*: in aor. *to have learnt*, i. e. *to understand, be acquainted with*. II. of the attempt, *to ask, inquire about*. III. *to perceive, understand, comprehend*, like Lat. *teneo*; μανθάνεις; *do you understand?* Answ., πάνυ μανθάνω, *perfectly!*—c. part., μάνθανε ὤν, *know that* you are. IV.

in Att.; τί παθών; comes to mean *wherefore?* properly, *having ascertained* what? *for* what *fresh reason?* almost = τί παθών;

μᾰνία Ion. **-ίη**, ἡ, (μαίνομαι) *madness, frenzy.* II. generally, *mad passion, rage, fury.* III. *enthusiasm, Bacchic frenzy.*

μᾰνῐάς, άδος, (μαίνομαι) fem. Adj. *frantic, mad, frenzied:* joined with a neut. pl. Subst., μανιάσιν λυσσήμασι with *mad* fits of raving, like *victricia arma.*

μᾰνῐκός, ή, όν, (μανία) *inclined to madness mad;* βλέπειν μανικόν to look *mad.* Hence

μανικῶς, Adv. *in mad fashion, madly.*

μᾶνις, ῐδος, Dor. for μῆνις.

μανίω, Dor. for μηνίω.

μᾰνι-ώδης, ες, (μανία, εἶδος) *mad-like, mad:* τὸ μανιῶδες *madness.*

ΜΑ'ΝΝΑ˘, ἡ, *a morsel, grain.* 2. *manna.*

ΜΑ'ΝΝΟΣ or **μάνος**, ὁ, Lat. *monile, a necklace, collar.*

μαννο-φόρος, ον, (μάννος, φέρω) *wearing a collar.*

ΜΑΝΟ'Σ, ή, όν, Lat. *rarus, thin, loose, slack, flaccid.* II. of number, *few, scanty.* See μανῶς.

μαντεία Ion. **-ηίη**, ἡ, (μαντεύομαι) *prophesying, power of divination:* also *the mode of divination.* II. *an oracle, prophesy.*

μαντεῖον Ion. **-ήιον**, τό, (μαντίς) *an oracle,* i.e., I. *an oracular response.* II. *the seat of an oracle.*

μαντεῖος, α, ον, or ος, ον, Ion. **-ήιος**, η, ον, (μάντις) *oracular, prophetic.*

μάντευμα, ατος, τό, *an oracle.* From

μαντεύομαι, f. -σομαι: aor. 1 ἐμαντευσάμην: pf. μεμάντευμαι: Dep.: (μάντις):—*to divine, prophesy, deliver an oracle.* 2. *to presage, forebode, surmise:* of animals, *to scent.* 3. *to seek divinations: to consult an oracle.* II. aor. 1 ἐμαντεύθη, impers. in pass. sense, *an oracle was given:* and pf. part. τὰ μεμαντευμένα, *the oracles delivered.* Hence

μαντευτέον, verb. Adj. *one must divine, prophesy.*

μαντευτός, ή, όν, (μαντεύομαι) *foretold* or *ordained by an oracle.*

μαντηίη, **-τήιον**, **-τήιος**, Ion. for μαντεία, etc.

μάντι, voc. of μάντις.

μαντικός, ή, όν, *of* or *for a soothsayer* or *diviner, prophetic:* as Subst., μαντική (sub. τέχνη), ἡ, *the art* or *faculty of divination.* Adv. -κῶς.

μαντῐπολέω, f. ήσω, *to prophesy.* From

μαντῐ-πόλος, ον, (μάντις, πολέω) *inspired, frenzied.*

μάντῐς, ὁ, gen. εως Ion. ιος: (μαίνομαι): *a diviner, soothsayer, seer, prophet:* also as fem., *a prophetess.* 2. metaph. *a foreboder.* II. *a* kind of *locust* or *grasshopper.*

μαντοσύνη, ἡ, *the art of divination, divining.* [ῠ]

μαντόσῠνος, η, ον, (μάντις) *oracular, prophetic.*

μαντῷος, α, ον, = μαντεῖος.

μᾱνύω, **μᾱνῡτής**, **μάνῡσις**, Dor. for μην—.

μανῶς, Adv. of μανός, *rarely:* comp. μανότερον, *less often.*

μάομαι, see μαίομαι.

μᾰπέειν, Ep. aor. 2 inf. of μάρπτω.

μάραγνα, ἡ, = σμάραγνα, *a lash, whip, scourge.* [μᾰ]

μάρᾰθον, τό, Dor. and Att. form of μάραθρον.

ΜΑ˘ΡΑΘΡΟΝ, τό, *fennel,* Lat. *marathrum.* [μᾰ]

Μᾰρᾰθών, ῶνος, ἡ, *Marathon,* a plain on the east coast of Attica, celebrated for the defeat of the Persians, so called from its being overgrown with fennel (μάραθον).

Μᾰρᾰθωνο-μάχης, ου, ὁ, (Μαραθών, μάχομαι) *one who fought at Marathon:* hence *a brave veteran.*

ΜΑ˘ΡΑΙ'ΝΩ, f. ᾰνῶ: aor. 1 ἐμάρηνα Att. -ᾱνα:—Pass., aor. 1 ἐμᾰράνθην: pf. μεμάραμμαι or μεμάρασμαι:—*to put out, quench, extinguish:*—Pass. *to die away, burn low.* II. metaph. *to quench: to weaken, make to waste* or *pine away:*—Pass. *to die away, waste away, languish.*

μαρὰν ἀθά, Syriac, *the Lord cometh,* sc. to judgment.

μαργαίνω, only in pres., (μάργος) *to rage furiously.*

μαργᾰρίτης [ῑ], ου, ὁ, *a pearl,* Lat. *margarita.*

μαργάω, only in part., (μάργος) *to rage furiously.*

Μαργίτης [ῑ], ου, ὁ, (μάργος) *Margites,* hero of a mock-heroic poem ascribed to Homer.

ΜΑ˘ΡΓΟΣ, η, ον, or ος, ον, *raging mad,* Lat. *furiosus.* 2. *greedy, gluttonous.* 3. *lustful.* Hence

μαργότης, ητος, ἡ, *rage, madness.* 2. *greediness, gluttony.* 3. *lust.*

ΜΑ'ΡΗ, ἡ, = χείρ, *a hand.* (Hence εὐ-μαρής.)

ΜΑ˘ΡΙ'ΛΗ, ἡ, *the embers of charcoal.* [ῑ]

μᾰρῑλο-πότης, ου, ὁ, (μαρίλη, ΠΟ– Root of some tenses of πίνω) *gulper of coal-dust.*

ΜΑΡΜΑΙ'ΡΩ, only in pres. and impf., *to flash, sparkle, glisten, gleam,* mostly of metal; ὄμματα μαρμαίροντα *sparkling* eyes. Hence

μαρμάρεος, α, ον, (μαρμαίρω) *flashing, sparkling, glistening,* of metals: also of the sea.

μαρμάρῐνος, η, ον, (μάρμαρος) *of marble.*

μαρμᾰρόεις, εσσα, εν, = μαρμάρεος, *bright, gleaming.*

μάρμᾰρον, τό, = μάρμαρος.

μάρμᾰρος, ου, ὁ, (μαρμαίρω) any *stone* or *rock,* with *sparkling* crystals in it: also as Adj., πέτρος μάρμαρος a *sparkling* stone. II. μάρμαρος, ἡ, Lat. *marmor, marble:* also *a work in marble, a slab* or *tablet of marble.*

μαρμᾰρῠγή, ἡ, (μαρμαρύσσω) *a flashing, sparkling:* of any quick motion, μαρμαρυγαὶ ποδῶν *the quick twinkling* of the dancers' feet.

μαρμᾰρ-ωπός, όν, (μάρμαρος, ὤψ) *with sparkling eyes.*

ΜΑ˘ΡΝΑ˘ΜΑΙ, ασαι, αται, imperat. μάρναο, subj. μάρνωμαι, opt. μαρνοίμην, inf. μάρνασθαι, part. μαρνάμενος; impf. ἐμαρνάμην, αο, ατο, dual ἐμαρνάσθην: no other tenses in use: Dep.:—*to fight, do battle, contend:*—of boxers, *to contend, encounter.* 2. *to quarrel, wrangle.* 3. metaph. *to struggle, strive.*

μαρναμένοιϊν, Ep. part. gen. dual of μάρναμαι.

μάρνατο, **μάρναντο**, Ep. 3 sing. and pl. impf. of μάρναμαι.

μαρπτίς, ὁ, (μάρπτω) *a seizer, ravisher.*

ΜΑ'ΡΠΤΩ, fut. *μάρψω*: aor. 1 *ἔμαρψα*: Ep. redupl. aor. 2 *μέμαρπον*: and a shortd. aor. 2 *ἔμᾰπον*, inf. *μᾰπέειν*, whence 3 pl. opt. *μεμάποιεν*: pf. part. *μεμαρπώς*:—*to grasp, bold, catch: to lay bold of, seize: to embrace, clasp: to reach, overtake, catch*

ΜΑ'ΡΣΙ'ΠΟΣ, *a bag, pouch*, Lat. *marsupium*.

ΜΑ'ΡΤΥ'Ρ, ῠρος, ὁ and ἡ, Aeol. for *μάρτυς*. Hence

μαρτῠρέω, f. *ήσω*:—Pass., fut. 1 *μαρτῠρηθήσομαι*, but also f. med. in pass. sense, *μαρτῠρήσομαι*: aor. 1 *ἐμαρτυρήθην*: pf. *μεμαρτύρημαι*:—*to be a witness: to bear witness: μαρτυρεῖν τινί to bear witness in favour of* another: c. acc. rei, *to bear witness to* a thing, *testify to*: c. inf. *to testify* or *declare* that a thing is:—Pass. *to bave witness borne to one.* II. later, *to be* or *become a martyr*. Hence

μαρτύρημα, ατος, τό, *testimony*.

μαρτῠρία, ἡ, (*μαρτυρέω*) *a bearing witness.* 2. *witness, testimony, evidence*.

μαρτύριον, τό, *a testimony, proof*: in pl., *μαρτύρια, τά, evidence*. [ῠ] From

μαρτύρομαι [ῡ]: f. ῠροῦμαι: aor. 1 *ἐμαρτῠράμην*: Dep.: (*μάρτυς*):—*to call to witness, invoke*: absol. *μαρτύρομαι, I call witnesses, I protes*.

μάρτῠρος, ὁ, Ep. form of *μάρτυς, a witness*.

ΜΑ'ΡΤΥ'Σ, ὁ or ἡ, gen. *μάρτῠρος*, acc. *μάρτῠρα*, as if from *μάρτυρ*, but also acc. *μάρτῠν*: pl. *μάρτῠρες*, dat. *μάρτῠσι* poët. *μάρτυσσι*:—*a witness*.

μαρυκάομαι, μᾱρύκημα, Dor. for *μηρυκ-*.

μαρύομαι, Dor. for *μηρύομαι*.

μάρψαι, aor. 1 inf. of *μάρπτω*.

μᾰσάομαι, f. *ήσομαι*, Dep., (*μάω, μάσσω*) *to chew*.

μάσασθαι [ᾰ], aor. 1 inf. of Root **μάω, to touch*.

μάσδα, μασδός, Dor. for *μᾶζα, μαζός*.

μάσθλη, ἡ, = *ἱμάσθλη, a leathern thong*. Hence

μάσθλης, ητος, ὁ, *a leathern thong.* II. metaph. *a supple, slippery knave*.

μασθός, ὁ, a Dor. form of *μαστός, μαζός*.

μασί, Dor. for *μησί*, dat. pl. of *μήν*.

μάσομαι [ᾰ], fut. of **μάω* II.

Μασσαλία, ἡ, Lat. *Massilia, Marseilles*. Hence

Μασσαλιώτης, ου, ὁ, *a man of Marseilles*.

μασσάομαι, etc., = *μασάομαι*.

μάσσω Att. **μάττω**: fut. *μάξω*: aor. 1 *ἔμαξα*: pf. *μέμᾰχα*:—Pass., aor. 1 *ἐμάχθην*: pf. *μέμαγμαι*: (**μάω*) :—*to touch, handle* II. *to work with the hands, to knead* dough, Lat. *pinso*:—Pass., *σῖτος μεμαγμένος* dough *ready kneaded*

μάσσων, ὁ, ἡ, neut. *μᾶσσον*, gen. *μάσσονος*, irreg. Comp. of *μακρός* for *μακρότερος, longer, larger*

μάσταξ, ᾰκος, ἡ, (*μασάομαι*) *that with which one chews* or *eats, the jaws, mouth.* II. *that which is chewed, a mouthful, morsel*.

μαστᾰρύζω or **-ίζω**, *to mumble*, of an old man. (Formed from the sound.)

μάστειρα, ἡ, fem. of *μαστήρ*

μαστεύω, f. *σω*, = *ματεύω, to seek: to seek* or *endeavour to do: to seek* or *search after*.

μαστήρ, ῆρος, ὁ, (**μάω*) *a seeker, searcher*. Hence

μαστήριος, α, ον, *searching*.

μαστῑγέω, false form for *μαστιγόω*.

μαστῑγίας, ου, ὁ, (*μάστιξ*) *one who deserves whipping, a worthless slave, sorry knave*, Lat. *verbero*.

μαστῑγο-φόρος, ον, (*μάστιξ, φέρω*) *carrying a whip*: as Subst., *μαστιγοφόρος*, ὁ, a sort *of constable*.

μαστῑγόω, f. *ώσω*: pf. aor. 1 *ἐμαστίγωσα*:—Pass., fut. med. in pass. sense *μαστιγώσομαι*: pf. *μεμαστίγωμαι*: (*μάστιξ*):—*to whip, flog, beat*. Hence

μαστῑγώσῐμος, ον, *that deserves whipping*.

μαστῑγωτέος, α, ον, verb. Adj. of *μαστιγόω, to be whipped, deserving a whipping*.

μαστίζω, f. *ξω*: aor. 1 *ἐμάστιξα* Ep. *μάστιξα*: (*μάστιξ*):—*to whip, flog*.

μαστίκτωρ, ορος, ὁ, (*μαστίζω*) *a scourger*.

μάστιξ, ῑγος, ἡ, (*μάω, μάσσω*) *a whip, scourge; ἵππου μάστιξ a* horse-*whip* II. metaph. *a scourge, plague; μάστιξ Πειθοῦς the lash* of eloquence.

μαστῑόων, Ep. part. of *μαστίω*.

μάστῑς, ῖος, ἡ, Ion. for *μάστιξ*; dat. *μάστῑ*.

μαστίσδω, Dor. for *μαστίζω*.

μαστῑχάω, (*μάσταξ*) *to gnash the teeth*, only in Ep. part. dat. *μαστιχόωντι*.

μαστίω, collat. form of *μαστίζω, to whip, scourge, beat, lash*:—Med., *μαστίεται πλευρὰς οὐρῇ* [the lion] *lashes* his sides with his tail.

μαστό-δετον, τό, (*μαστός, δέω*) *a breast-band*.

μαστός, οῦ, ὁ, *one of the breasts* of a woman, later form for Hom. *μαζός*. II. metaph. *a round hill, knoll*. III. *a piece of wool* fastened to the edge of the nets.

μαστροπεία, ἡ, *a pandering*. From

μαστροπεύω, f. *σω*, (*μαστροπός*) *to be a pander, play the pander*: c. acc. *to seduce*.

μαστροπός, ὁ and ἡ, (*μάω, μαστήρ*) *a pander, pimp*, Lat. *leno, lena*.

μασχάλη, ἡ, (*μάλη*) *the armpit*, Lat. *ala, axilla*. [χα]

μασχᾰλίζω, f. *ίσω*, (*μασχάλη*) *to put under the armpits: to mutilate* a corpse, since murderers fancied that by cutting off the extremities, and placing them under the armpits, they would avert vengeance. Hence

μασχᾰλιστήρ, ῆρος, ὁ, *a broad strap passing behind the horse's shoulders* and fastened to the yoke by the *λέπαδνον*: generally, *a girdle, band*.

μᾰτάζω, (*μάτην*) *to act unmeaningly* or *foolishly*.

μᾰταιάζω, (*μάταιος*) = *ματάζω*.

μᾰταιολογία, ἡ, *idle talking*. From

μᾰταιο-λόγος, ον, (*μάταιος, λέγω*) *idly talking*.

μάταιος [ᾰ], α, ον, or ος, ον, (*μάτη*) *idle, foolish, unmeaning, trifling* II. *thoughtless, rash, wanton, profane*. Hence

μᾰταιότης, ητος, ἡ, *folly, vanity*.

μᾰταίως, Adv. of *μάταιος, idly, without reason*.

ΜΑ'ΤΑ'Ω, f. *ήσω*, (*μάτη*) *to be idle, to loiter, linger, lag; οὐ ματᾷ τοὔργον* the work *lags* not. II. *to be in vain, fruitless*

μᾰτεύω, f. *σω*: aor. 1 *ἐμάτευσα*: (**μάω*):—*to seek, search: to seek to do.* 2. *to seek* or *search after: to search, explore*.

μᾰτέω, rare form for *ματεύω*. II. Aeol. form of πατέω, *to tread on*.

ΜΑΤΗ, ἡ, = *ματία*, *a folly, a fault*. [ᾰ] Hence

μάτην Dor. **μάταν** [ᾰ], Adv. *in vain, idly, foolishly*, Lat. *frustra*. 2. *senselessly, at random*, Lat. *temere*.—3. *idly, falsely*, Lat. *falso*. Originally acc. of *μάτη*, hence εἰς *μάτην* at *random*. [ᾰ]

μάτηρ, Dor. for *μήτηρ*, Lat. *mater*. [ᾱ]

ματῆς, Dor. for *ματᾶς*.

μᾰτία Ion. -ίη, ἡ, (μάτην) *a vain attempt*.

ματρ-αδελφέος, **ματρο-δόκος**, etc., Dor. for *μητρ-*.

ματτύη, ἡ, *a rich, high-seasoned dish*, Lat. *mattea* and *mattya*. (Foreign word.)

ματτυο-λοιχός, όν, (ματτύα, λείχω) *licking up dainties*.

μάττω, f. ξω, Att. for *μάσσω*.

μαῦλις, ιδος or ιος, ἡ, *a knife*.

μαυρόω, like ἀμαυρόω, *to darken*: metaph. *to make powerless, to make obscure* or *forgotten*:—Pass. *to become dark* or *obscure*.

μάχαιρα [μᾰ], ἡ, *a large knife*, worn like a dirk next the sword-sheath. II. as a weapon, *a short sword* or *dagger*: *a sabre* or *scimitar*, opp. to ξίφος (the straight sword). III. a kind of *rasor*; διπλῆ *μάχαιρα scissors*. Hence

μᾰχαιρίδιον, τό, Dim. *a short sword* or *dagger*.

μᾰχαιρίς, ίδος, ἡ, Dim. of *μάχαιρα*, *a small knife*. 2. *a small rasor*.

μᾰχαιροποιεῖον, τό, *a sword* or *knife factory*. From

μᾰχαιρο-ποιός, όν, (μάχαιρα, ποιέω) *a cutler*.

μᾰχαιρο-φόρος, ον, (μάχαιρα, φέρω) *wearing a sabre*.

μᾰχατάς, ὁ, Dor. for *μαχητής*.

Μᾰχάων [ᾱ], ονος, ὁ, *Machaon, son of Aesculapius*.

μᾰχειόμενος, Ep. part. of *μάχομαι*.

μᾰχέομαι, Ion. for *μάχομαι*.

μᾰχεούμενος, Ep. part. of *μάχομαι*.

μαχέσκετο, 3 sing. Ion. impf. of *μάχομαι*.

μάχευ, Dor. for *μάχου*, pres. imperat. of *μάχομαι*.

ΜΑ'ΧΗ [ᾰ], ἡ, *a battle, fight, combat*; properly *an engagement between armies*, but also, *a single combat*; *μάχην νικᾶν* to win *a battle*; but *μάχῃ νικᾶν τινά* to conquer one *in battle*. II. *a quarrel, strife, wrangling*. III. *an amicable contest*, as for a prize in the games. IV. *a mode of fighting, way of battle*. V. *a field of battle*. Hence

μᾰχήμων, ον, gen. ονος, *warlike*.

μᾰχητής, οῦ, ὁ, (μάχη) *a fighter, warrior*; as Adj. *warlike*. Hence

μᾰχητικός, ή, όν, of or fo. *fighting, pugnacious*.

μάχῐμος, η, ον, (μάχη) *disposed for battle, warlike*: οἱ *μάχιμοι* or τὸ *μάχιμον the soldiery, the effective force*.

μᾰχῐμ-ώδης, ες, (μάχιμος, εἶδος) *warlike, contentious*.

μαχλάς, άδος, poët. fem. of *μάχλος*.

ΜΑ'ΧΛΟΣ, ον, *lewd, lustful*: *wanton*. Hence

μαχλοσύνη, ἡ, *lewdness, lust, wantonness*.

μαχοίατο, Ion. for *μάχοιντο*, 3 pl. opt. of

μάχομαι Ion. **μαχέομαι** [ᾰ], Ep. part. *μαχειόμενος* and *μαχεούμενος*: fut. *μαχέσομαι* Ep. *μαχέσσομαι* or *μαχήσομαι* Att. *μαχοῦμαι*: aor. 1 ἐμαχεσάμην, Ep. inf. *μαχέσσασθαι* or *μαχήσασθαι*: pf. *μεμάχημαι*: Dep.: (μάχη):—*to fight, contend in battle*; c. dat. pers. *to fight with*, i. e. *against*; but, σύν τινι *with the sanction of*; κατὰ σφέας *μάχεσθαι to fight* by themselves: but, καθ' ἕνα *μάχεσθαι to fight* one against one, in single combat. II. generally, *to quarrel, wrangle, dispute*: hence, *to oppose, withstand one*. III. *to contend for the prize* in the games: *to measure oneself with*.

ΜΑ'Ψ, Adv. *in vain, idly, fruitlessly*; μὰψ ὀμόσαι to swear *lightly, unmeaningly*. II. *thoughtlessly, rashly, indecorously*.

μαψ-αῦραι, ῶν, αἱ, (μάψ, αὔρα) *squalls, gusts of wind*.

μαψίδιος, ον, (μάψ) *vain, false, idle, useless*. Hence

μαψῐδίως, Adv., = μάψ, *foolishly, thoughtlessly*: *without reason*: *recklessly*.

μαψῐ-λόγος, ον, (μάψ, λέγω) *idly talking*.

μαψῐ-τόκος, ον, (μάψ, τεκεῖν) *bringing forth in vain*.

μαψ-ῠλάκας, ου, ὁ, (μάψ, ὑλακτῶ) *idly yelping, repeating again and again*. [λᾰ]

***ΜΑ'Ω**, a Root, only used in pf. act. and in Med.: I. *μέμαα*, pf. with pres. sense, 3 pl. *μεμάασι*, often in the syncopate forms, dual *μέμᾰτον*, *μέμᾰμεν*, *μέμᾰτε*; 3 sing. imperat. *μεμάτω* [ᾰ]; 3 pl. plqpf. *μέμᾰσαν*; but most often in part. *μεμᾰώς*, *μεμᾰυῖα*, *μεμᾰῶτος*, *μεμᾰῶτες*, but also *μεμᾰότες*, *μεμᾰότε*:—*to strive after, long for, desire eagerly*, mostly c. inf.: also absol., πρόσσω *μεμανῖαι pressing forward*; *μεμαότες* ἐγχείῃσι *pressing forward* with their spears. 2. *to wish* or *claim to be*. II. Med., *μάομαι*, *μῶμαι*, part. *μώμενος*, inf. **μῶσθαι**, imperat. *μώεο*, *to seek after, covet*.

μέ, enclit. acc. of ἐγώ.

μέγᾰ, neut. of *μέγας*.

μεγᾰ-θαρσής, ές, (μέγας, θάρσος) *very bold*.

μέγᾰθος, Ion. for *μέγεθος*.

μεγά-θῡμος, ον, (μέγας, θυμός) *high-minded, magnanimous*.

μεγαίρω, aor. 1 ἐμέγηρα, (μέγας) *to look on* a thing *as too great*: hence, *to grudge* a thing to another *as too great* for him, and generally, *to refuse* or *deny*, *withhold* from envy: *to object, complain*.

μεγᾰ-κήτης, ες, (μέγας, κῆτος) *huge, unwieldy*.

μεγα-κλεής, ές, declined (as if from *μεγακλής*) *μεγακλέος*, -εῖ, -έα, -έες, cf. εὐκλεής: (μέγας, κλέος):—*very famous*. 2. pr. n. of several of the family of the Alcmaeonidae at Athens.

μεγᾰ-κύδης, ές, (μέγας, κῦδος) *much renowned*.

μεγάλα, neut. pl. of *μέγας*.

μεγᾰλ-ᾱνορία, **μεγᾰλ-άνωρ**, Dor. for *μεγαλην-*.

μεγᾰλ-αυχέω, f. ήσω, (μέγας, αὐχέω) *to boast highly, speak haughtily*:—Med. *to boast oneself*.

μεγᾰλ-αύχητος and **μεγάλ-αυχος**, ον, (μέγας, αὐχέω) *very boastful, vaunting, arrogant*.

μεγᾰλεῖος, α, ον, (μέγας) *magnificent, splendid:* of men, *haughty.* Hence

μεγᾰλειότης, ητος, ἡ, *grandeur, splendour, majesty.*

μεγαλείως, Adv. of μεγαλεῖος, *magnificently.*

μεγᾰληγορέω, f. ήσω, (μεγαλήγορος) *to talk big, boast.* Hence

μεγᾰληγορία, ἡ, *big talking.*

μεγᾰλ-ήγορος, ον, (μέγας, ἀγορεύω) *talking big, vaunting, boastful.*

μεγᾰληνορία, ἡ, *manliness, courage.* 2. in bad sense, *haughtiness.* From

μεγᾰλ-ήνωρ, ορος, ὁ, ἡ, (μέγας, ἀνήρ) *heroic, high-minded.* 2. in bad sense, *haughty.*

μεγᾰλ-ήτωρ, ορος ὁ, ἡ, (μέγας, ἦτορ) *great-hearted: magnanimous.*

μεγᾰλίζω, (μέγας) *to magnify:*—Pass. *to be exalted, to bear oneself haughtily.*

μεγᾰλογνωμοσύνη, ἡ, *loftiness of sentiment.* From

μεγᾰλο-γνώμων, ον, gen. ονος, (μέγας, γνώμη) *of lofty sentiments, high-minded.*

μεγᾰλό-δοξος, ον, (μέγας, δόξα) *very glorious.*

μεγᾰλοδωρία, ἡ, *munificence, liberality.* From

μεγᾰλό-δωρος, ον, (μέγας, δῶρον) *making rich presents: munificent.*

μεγάλ-οιτος, ον, (μεγας, οἶτος) *very wretched.*

μεγᾰλο-κευθής, ές, (μέγας, κεύθω) *concealing much:* hence *capacious.*

μεγᾰλο-κρᾰτής, ές, (μέγας, κράτος) *far-ruling.*

μεγᾰλό-μητις, ι, (μέγας, μῆτις) *of high design, ambitious.*

μεγᾰλό-μισθος, ον, (μέγας, μισθός) *receiving large pay.*

μεγᾰλό-πετρος, ον, (μέγας, πέτρα) *on the vast rock.*

μεγᾰλό-πολις, ι, gen. ιος Att. εως, (μέγας, πόλις) joined with the name of a place, as, Ἀθῆναι μεγαλοπόλιες *the great city* of Athens.

μεγᾰλο-πράγμων, ον, gen. ονος, (μέγας, πρᾶγμα) *disposed to do great deeds, forming great designs.*

μεγᾰλοπρέπεια, ἡ, *splendour, magnificence.* From

μεγᾰλο-πρεπής, ές, (μέγας, πρέπω) *befitting greatness: magnificent, splendid, sumptuous.* Hence

μεγᾰλοπρεπῶς Ion. -έως, Adv. *magnificently:* Comp. μεγαλοπρεπέστερον, Sup. -έστατα.

μεγάλος, v. μέγας.

μεγᾰλο-σθενής, ές, (μεγας, σθένος) *of great strength.*

μεγᾰλό-σπλαγχνος, ον, (μέγας, σπλάγχνον) *high-spirited.*

μεγᾰλό-στονος, ον, (μέγας, στένω) *very piteous.*

μεγᾰλοσύνη, ἡ, = μέγεθος.

μεγᾰλο-σχήμων, ον, gen. ονος, (μέγας, σχῆμα) *of large form, magnificent.*

μεγᾰλό-τολμος, ον, (μέγας, τόλμα) *greatly daring, enterprising, adventurous.*

μεγᾰλοφρόνως, Adv. of μεγαλόφρων, *generously, proudly.*

μεγᾰλοφρονέω, f. ήσω, (μεγαλόφρων) *to be high-minded;* in bad sense, *to be proud, haughty.* Hence

μεγᾰλοφροσύνη, ἡ, *greatness of mind:* in bad sense, *pride, haughtiness.*

μεγᾰλό-φρων, ονος, ὁ, ἡ, (μέγας, φρήν) *high-minded, noble, generous:* in bad sense, *proud, haughty.*

μεγᾰλοφωνία, ἡ, *big talking, vaunting.* From

μεγᾰλό-φωνος, ον, (μέγας, φωνή) *loud-talking.*

μεγᾰλοψῡχία, ἡ, *greatness of soul, magnanimity:* in bad sense, *arrogance.* From

μεγᾰλό-ψῡχος, ον, (μέγας, ψυχή) *high-souled, great-hearted, magnanimous.*

μεγᾰλύνω, (μέγας) *to make great* or *powerful:*—Pass. *to be exalted.* II. *to extol, magnify.* *to exaggerate* or *aggravate* a crime.

μεγᾰλ-ώνῠμος, ον, (μέγας, ὄνομα) *giving a great name, conferring glory.*

μεγάλως, Adv. of μέγας, *greatly.*

μεγᾰλωστί, Adv. of μέγας, *over a large space: greatly, hugely:* also *magnificently.*

μεγᾰλωσύνη, ἡ, (μέγας), *greatness.*

μέγαν, acc. masc. of μέγας.

μεγ-άνωρ, ορος, ὁ, ἡ, (μέγας, ἀνήρ) *manly, heroic.* [ᾱ]

Μέγᾰρα, ων, τά, *Megara:*—**Μεγαρεύς**, έως, ὁ, *a Megarian.* Hence

Μεγᾰρίζω, f. ίσω Att. ιῶ, *to take part with the Megarians, speak their dialect:* cf. Λακωνίζω.

Μεγᾰρικός, ή, όν, (Μέγαρα) *Megarian.*

Μεγαρίς, ίδος, fem. Adj. *Megarian:*—as Subst. (sub. γῆ), *the Megarian territory, Megarid.*

Μεγαρόθεν, Adv. (Μέγαρα) *from Megara:* and

Μεγαροῖ, Adv. *at Megara.*

μέγᾰρον, τό, (μέγας) *a large room* or *chamber, the hall* 2. *a woman's apartment* 3. *a bed-chamber.* II. *a house, mansion,* mostly like Lat. *aedes, a house* in plur. III. *the sacred chamber in the temple at Delphi, the sanctuary, shrine:* in this sense always in sing., like Lat. *aedes, a temple.* Hence

μεγᾰρόνδε, Adv. *homewards, home.*

ΜΕ´ΓΑΣ, μεγάλη [ᾰ], μέγᾰ: gen. μεγάλου, ης, ου: dat. μεγάλῳ, ῃ, ῳ, acc. μέγᾰν, μεγάλην, μέγᾰ: dual μεγάλω, α, ω: plur. μεγάλοι, αι, α, etc., like a regul. Adj. in ος: but the regul. form ΜΕ´ΓΑΛΟΣ is never used in sing. nom. and acc. masc. and neut.: *large, big, great:*—hence, 1. *great, vast, tall.* 2. *spacious, wide.* 3. *long.* II. of degree, *great, powerful, mighty: weighty, important.* 2. *strong, violent.* 3. of sounds, *loud.* 4. in bad sense, *over-great, excessive;* μέγα φρονεῖν to have *too high, presumptuous* thoughts. III. besides the Adv. μεγάλως and μεγαλωστί, the neut. sing. and pl. μέγα and μεγάλα are used as Adv., *very much, exceedingly.* 2. of Space, *far.* 3. with Adjs., *far,* μέγ' ἀμείνων, *far* better. IV. Comp. μείζων, neut. μεῖζον, gen. μείζονος; in Ion. prose μέζων, ον; Dor. μέσδων, Boeot. μέσσων: *greater, larger:* also *too great, more than enough.*—Sup. μέγιστος, η, ον, *greatest, largest.*

μεγα-σθενής, ές, (μέγας, σθένος) *very mighty.*

μεγ-αυχής, ές, (μέγας, αὐχέω) *vaunting, braggart.*

μέγεθος Ion. **μέγαθος**, εος, τό, (μέγας) *greatness, height: magnitude, bulk, size;* μεγάθεϊ σμικρὸς small *in size;* μεγάθεϊ μέγας large *in size:*—the acc. μεγάθος is used absol. as Adv., *in size*, or like μεγάλως, *greatly*, λάμποντες μέγαθος shining *greatly:* so too in pl., ποταμοὶ οὐ κατὰ τὸν Νεῖλον ἐόντες μεγάθεα rivers not bearing any proportion to the Nile *in size.*

μεγήρας, aor. 1 part. of μεγαίρω.

μεγ-ήρᾰτος, ον, (μέγας, ἐρατός) *passing lovely.*

μεγιστᾶνες, οἱ, (μέγιστος) *the nobles, chief men.*

μεγιστό-πολις, ι, gen. ιος Att. εως, (μέγιστος, πόλις) *making cities greatest* or *most blest.*

μέγιστος, η, ον, Sup. of μέγας.

μεγιστό-τῑμος, ον, (μέγιστός, τιμή) *greatest in honour.*

μεδέων, οντος, ὁ, = μέδων, *one that cares for* or *rules, a guardian, ruler*, of guardian gods; Ἴδηθεν μεδέων *guardian* of Ida. 2. fem. μεδέουσα, = μέδουσα, always of *guardian goddesses: ruling, presiding over.* Properly the part. of an oid Verb, μέδέω, *to rule.*

μεδήσομαι, fut. of μέδομαι.

ΜΕ´ΔΙΜΝΟΣ, ὁ, Ion. also ἡ, *the medimnus* or common Attic corn-measure, containing 6 ἑκτεῖς, 48 χοίνικες, and 192 κοτύλαι, = 6 Roman modii = nearly 12 gallons.

ΜΕ´ΔΟΜΑΙ, fut. μεδήσομαι: Dep.: *to give heed to, attend to, think on;* c. gen., πολέμοιο μέδεσθαι, *to be thinking of, preparing for* battle. II. *to plan, contrive* or *devise.*

μέδουσα, fem. of μέδων, like μεδέουσα, *a ruler:* hence as name of the Gorgon, *Medusa.*

μέδων, οντος, ὁ, *one who rules over: a guardian, lord.* Properly part. of an old Verb μέδω, *to rule.*

μέζεα, ων, τά, = μήδεα, *the genitals.*

μεζόνως, Ion. Adv. of μέζων.

μέζων, ον, Ion. for μείζων, Comp. of μέγας.

μεθ-αιρέω, aor. 2 μεθεῖλον Ion. μεθέλεσκον:—*to catch in turn.*

μεθ-άλλομαι: Ep. syncop. aor. 2 part. pass. μετάλμενος:—*to leap* or *rush upon.* II. *to rush after, overtake.*

μεθ-ᾱμέριος, Dor. for μεθ-ημέριος.

μεθ-αρμόζω, f. σω: aor. 1 μεθήρμοσα:—*to dispose differently, to correct, reform:*—Med., with pf. pass. μεθήρμοσμαι, *to alter one's way of life;* μεθάρμοσαι (aor. 1 imperat.) νέους τρόπους *adopt new* habits.

μεθέηκα, Ep. for μεθῆκα, aor. 1 of μεθίημι.

μεθείην, aor. 2 opt. of μεθίημι.

μεθεῖλον, aor. 2 of μεθαιρέω.

μεθεῖναι, **μεθείς**, aor. 2 inf. and part. of μεθίημι.

μεθείω, Ep. for μεθέω, μεθῶ, aor. 2 subj. of μεθίημι.

μεθεκτέον, verb. Adj. of μετέχω, *one must share in.*

μεθέλεσκε, Ion. for μεθεῖλε, 3 sing. aor. 2 of μεθαιρέω.

μεθέμεν, Ep. for μεθεῖναι, aor. 2 inf. of μεθίημι.

μέθεν, Dor. for ἐμέθεν = ἐμοῦ, gen. of ἐγώ.

μεθέξομαι, fut. of μετέχω.

μεθ-έπω, impf. μεθεῖπον Ep. μέθεπον: fut. μεθέψω: poët. aor. 2 μετέσπον, inf. μετασπεῖν, part. μετασπών: aor. 2 med. μετεσπόμην:—*to follow after, follow closely, hard upon, chase*, Lat. *insequi.* 2. *to seek* or *search after.* 3. *to visit.* 4. metaph. *to manage, dispose;* ἄχθος νώτῳ μεθέπων *disposing* a burden on his back. II. trans., Τυδείδην μέθεπεν ἵππους *he turned* the horses *in pursuit of* Tydides.

μεθ-ερμηνεύω, f. σω, *to translate.*

μεθέστηκα, pf. of μεθίστημι.

μέθη, ἡ, (μέθυ) *strong drink.* II. *drunkenness.*

μεθῆκα, aor. 1 of μεθίημι.

μεθ-ήκω, *to have come in quest of.*

μέθ-ημαι, properly pf. of μεθ-έζομαι, *to be seated among.*

μεθ-ημερῑνός, ή, όν, (μετά, ἡμέρα) *happening by day, in open day-light*, Lat. *diurnus.*

μεθ-ημέριος, ον, = μεθημερινός.

μεθημοσύνη, ἡ, *remissness, carelessness.* From

μεθ-ήμων, ον, gen. ονος, (μεθίημι) *remiss, careless.*

μεθήρμοσμαι, pf. pass. (in med. sense) of μεθαρμόζω.

μεθησέμεναι, **μεθησέμεν**, Ep. fut. inf. of μεθίημι.

μεθίεν, Ep. for μεθίεσαν, 3 pl. impf. of μεθίημι. [ῐ]

μεθ-ίημι, inf. μεθιέναι part. μεθιείς: fut. μεθήσω: aor. 1 μεθῆκα Ep. μεθέηκα: aor. 2 inf. μεθεῖναι part. μεθείς:—Med. μεθίεμαι: f. μεθήσομαι: 3 sing. aor. 2 μεθεῖτο, inf. μεθέσθαι.—Homer uses 2 and 3 sing. pres. μεθιεῖς, μεθιεῖ (as if from μεθιέω), Ep. inf. μεθιέμεν, μεθιέμεναι: 2 and 3 sing. impf. μεθίεις, μεθίει (as if from μεθιέω), 3 pl. μεθίεν (for μεθίεσαν): aor. 1 μεθῆκα and μεθέηκα: aor. 2 subj. μεθείω for μεθῶ, inf. μεθέμεν for μεθεῖναι:—Herodotus has 3 sing. pres. μετίει (not μετιεῖ), and also 3 sing. impf. pass. μετίετο or ἐμετίετο (for μεθίετο); fut. pass. μετήσομαι; pf. pass. part. μεμετιμένος (for μεθειμένος). I. trans. *to set loose, let go,* 1. c. acc. pers. *to let loose, release: to set* or *leave at liberty.* 2. c. acc. rei, *to let go, let fall, throw;* μεθίεναι χόλον *to let go, give up* one's wrath; μεθιέναι δάκρυα *to let* tears *flow*, i.e. *shed* them; μεθιέναι γλῶσσαν Περσίδα *to let drop, utter* Persian words. 3. *to release* or *relieve from.* 4. *to give up, resign:* also c. dat. pers. et acc. rei, *to give up to* or *for another.* 5. *to neglect, regard lightly.* 6. *to forgive, excuse* one a fault. II. Med. μεθίεσθαι, *to loose oneself from, let go hold of*, παιδὸς οὐ μεθήσομαι; the Act. takes the acc. *to let go*, παῖδα οὐ μεθήσω. III. intrans. in Act. *to relax one's efforts:* in war, *to slacken, be lukewarm:* generally, *to be remiss* or *careless, to be idle, loiter.* 2. c. gen. rei, *to cease from, abandon:* c. gen. pers. *to abandon* or *neglect* one. 3. c. part., κλαύσας καὶ ὀδυράμενος μεθέηκε having wept and bewailed *he left off.* [ῑ in Att.; ῐ in Ep., except metri gratia.]

μεθ-ιστάνω, collat. form of μεθίστημι.

μεθ-ίστημι, I. Causal: in pres. and impf., fut. μετα-στήσω: aor. 1 act. μετέστησα and med. -εστησάμην:—*to place in another way: to substitute, change.* 2. *to put away, remove:* generally, *to remove from one place to another:* so too in aor. 1 med. *to remove from oneself.* II. intrans. in Med. and Pass., pres. μεθίστἄμαι impf. μεθιστάμην; aor. 1 μετεστάθην [ᾰ]; and in intr. tenses of Act., aor. 2 μετέστην, pf. μεθέστηκα, plqpf. μεθεστήκειν:—*to change one's place, withdraw, retire;* δαίμων στρατῷ μεθέστηκε fortune *hath changed* for the army: *to go over to another party, to revolt:* hence generally *to change,* either *for the better* or *for the worse.*

μεθοδεία, ἡ, *craft, artifice.* From

μεθοδεύω, f. σω, (μέθοδος) *to work by method:* hence *to deal craftily with.*

μέθ-οδος, ἡ, (μετά, ὁδός) *a following after: a scientific inquiry* or *treatise: method, system.*

μεθ-ομῑλέω, f. ήσω, *to associate with, mix with.*

μεθ-όριος, α, ον, (μετά, ὅρος) *bordering on, forming a boundary;* τὰ μεθόρια (sub. χωρία), *the borders, frontier.*

μεθ-ορμάω, f. ήσω, (μετά, ὁρμάω) *to urge in pursuit:*—Pass., aor. 1 μεθωρμήθην, *to follow closely, pursue eagerly;* μεθορμηθεὶς *following close.*

μεθ-ορμίζω, f. ίσω Att. ιῶ, *to remove* ships *from one anchorage to another,* properly trans., but often intr. with νέας omitted: metaph. *to remove from one place to another:*—Pass. *to sail from one place to another.*

ΜΕ'ΘΥ, ὕος, τό, *wine,* Lat. *merum.*

μεθ-υδριάς, άδος, ἡ, (μετά, ὕδωρ) *of* or *from the water,* epith. of Nymphs.

Μεθ-ύδριον, τό, (μετά, ὕδωρ) *a place between waters,* a place in the heart of Arcadia, whence the waters *ran different ways:* cf. Lat. *Interamnia.*

μεθῠ-πῖδαξ, ᾰκος, ὁ, ἡ, (μέθυ, πῖδαξ) *gushing with wine.*

μεθύ-πληξ, ῆγος, ὁ, ἡ, (μέθυ, πλήσσω) *wine-struck, drunken.*

μεθ-υποδέομαι, Med. (μετά, ὑποδέομαι) *to change shoes, put on another person's shoes.*

μέθυσις, ἡ, (μεθύω) *drunkenness.*

μεθύσκω, f. ύσω (ῠ), aor. 1 ἐμέθῠσα:—Causal of μεθύω, *to make drunk with wine, to intoxicate:*—Pass., in pres. *to get drunk;* in aor. 1 ἐμεθύσθην, *to be drunk.*

μεθῠσο-κότταβος, ον, (μέθυσος, κότταβος) *drunk with playing at the* κότταβος.

μέθῠσος, η, ον, also ος, ον, (μέθυ) *drunken.*

μεθ-ύστερος, α, ον, *later, living after;* οἱ μεθύστεροι *posterity:* neut. μεθύστερον as Adv. *afterwards, later.*

μεθυ-σφᾰλής, ές, (μέθυ, σφαλῆναι) *reeling-drunk.*

μεθυστής, οῦ, ὁ, (μεθύω) *a drunkard.*

μεθυ-τρόφος, ον, (μέθυ, τρέφω) *producing wine.*

μεθύω, only used in pres. and impf., the other tenses being supplied by the Pass. of μεθύσκω: (μέθυ):—*to be drunken, be given to drinking.* II. metaph. *to be drenched, steeped in* any liquid. 2. *to be intoxicated* with passion: *to be stupefied* with blows.

μεθῶμεν, 1 pl. aor. 2 sub. of μεθίημι.

μει-ᾰγωγέω, f. σω, (μεῖον, ἀγωγός) *to bring too little;* μειαγωγεῖν τὴν τραγῳδίαν *to weigh* tragedy *by scruples, weigh scrupulously:* see μεῖον.

ΜΕΙΔΑ'Ω, f. ήσω: aor. 1 ἐμείδησα Ep. μείδησα:—*to smile:* for Σαρδάνιον μειδῆσαι, see Σαρδάνιος. Hence

μείδημα and **μειδίᾱμα**, ατος, τό, *a smile, smiling.*

μειδιάω, f. άσω [ᾰ], collat. form of μειδάω, *to smile:* Ep. part. μειδιόων.

μειζόνως, Adv. of μείζων, *in a greater degree.*

μειζότερος, later form for μείζων.

μείζων, ον, irreg. Comp. of μέγας, *greater.*

μείλανι, Ep. for dat. of μέλας.

μείλια, ίων, τά, (μειλίσσω) *anything that pacifies* or *pleases, bridal gifts, a bridal dowry.*

μείλιγμα, ατος, τό, (μειλίσσω) *anything to soothe* or *gladden;* μειλίγματα θυμοῦ *scraps to appease* hunger. 2. in pl. *a propitiation* offered to the dead, Lat. *inferiae.* 3. *a fondling, darling,* Lat. *deliciae.* 4. *a soothing song.*

μειλικτήριος, ον, (μειλίσσω) *able to soothe, propitiatory;* μειλικτήρια (sub. ἱερά), τά, *atonements.*

μείλῐνος, η, ον, poët. for μέλινος, *ashen.*

μειλίσσω, f. ξω: (μέλι):—*to make mild, to soothe, please: to treat kindly: to appease, propitiate:*—Pass. *to be soothed, grow calm:*—Med. *to use soothing words;* μηδέ τί μ' αἰδόμενος μειλίσσεο μηδ' ἐλεαίρων *extenuate* not aught from respect or pity.

μειλῐχία Ion. -ίη, ἡ, (μείλιχος) *mildness, gentleness:* but also *backwardness, lukewarmness* in battle.

μειλίχιος, α, ον, also ος, ον, (μειλίσσω) *mild, gentle, soothing:* in neut. pl., προσαυδᾶν μειλιχίοισι (sub. ἐπέεσσι) to address with *soothing words:* cf. κερτόμια. II. of persons, *mild, gracious.*

μειλῐχό-γηρυς, υ, (μείλιχος, γῆρυς) *soft-voiced.*

μειλῐχό-δωρος, ον, (μείλιχος, δῶρον) *giving pleasing gifts.*

μείλῐχος, ον, (μειλίσσω) *mild, gentle, kind.*

μεῖναι, aor. 1 inf. of μένω.

μεῖναν, **μεῖνε**, Ep. 3 pl. and sing. aor. 1 of μένω.

μεῖον, ονος, τό, neut. of μείων, *less, too small.* II. μεῖον, τό, name of *the lamb which was offered at the Athenian Apaturia;* since, if not of a certain weight, it was rejected as μεῖον, *too light!* see μειαγωγέω.

μειον-εκτέω, f. ήσω, (μεῖον, ἔχω) *to have too little, to be poor:* c. gen. rei, *to be scant of* a thing. Hence

μειονεξία, ἡ, *disadvantage.*

μειόνως, Adv. of μείων, *in a less degree;* μειόνως ἔχειν *to be too mean.*

μειόω, f. ώσω, (μείων) *to make smaller, lessen, diminish.* 2. *to lessen in honour, degrade.* 3. *to extenuate.* II. Pass. *to become smaller, to decrease.* 2. *to become worse* or *weaker;* c. gen. *to fall short of.*

μειρᾰκι-εξᾰπάτης, ου, ὁ, (μειράκιον, ἐξ-απατάω) *a boy-cheater.* [ᾰ]

μειρᾰκιεύομαι, Dep. (μεῖραξ) *to be a boy: to be idle* or *mischievous*, Lat. *adolescenturire.*

μειράκιον, τό, Dim. of μεῖραξ, *a lad, stripling.*

μειρᾰκιόομαι, Dep. (μεῖραξ) *to be a boy* or *lad.*

μειρᾰκίσκη, ἡ, Dim. of μεῖραξ, *a little girl.*

μειρᾰκίσκος, ὁ, Dim. of μεῖραξ, *a lad, stripling.*

μειρᾰκύλλιον, τό, Dim. of μεῖραξ, *a mere lad.*

ΜΕΙ'ΡΑΞ, ὁ, and ἡ, *a boy* or *girl, lad* or *lass.*

ΜΕΙ'ΡΟΜΑΙ: pf. ἔμμορα pass. εἵμαρμαι: Dep. I. in pres. *to receive as one's portion* or *due;* c. acc., ἥμισυ μείρεο τιμῆς *take* half the honour *as thy due.* II. in pf. ἔμμορα, *to have* or *obtain one's share of* a thing; c. gen., ἔμμορε τιμῆς *he hath gotten his share of* honour. III. the pf. pass. is used as impers. εἵμαρται, *it is allotted* or *decreed by fate;* plqpf. εἵμαρτο *it was so decreed:*—also in part. εἱμαρμένος, η, ον, *allotted, decreed;* ἡ εἱμαρμένη (sub. μοῖρα), *that which is allotted, destiny,* like πεπρωμένη from πέπρωται.

μείς, ὁ, Ion. and Aeol. for μήν, *a month.*

μείωμα, ατος, τό, (μειόω) *a diminution: a fine.*

μείων, neut. μεῖον gen. μείονος, used as Comp. of μικρός and ὀλίγος.

μελάγ-γαιος, ον, **μελάγ-γειος**, ον, and **μελάγ-γεως**, ων, gen. ω, (μέλας, γαῖα = γῆ) *with black soil, loamy.*

μελάγ-κερως, gen. ω, (μέλας, κέρας) *black-horned.*

μελαγ-κόρῠφος, ὁ, (μέλας, κορυφή) *with a black head:* as Subst., μελαγκόρυφος, ὁ, a bird, *the blackcap.*

μελάγ-κροκος, ον, (μέλας, κρέκω) *woven with black:* of a ship, *with black sails.*

μελαγ-χαίτης, ου, ὁ, (μέλας, χαίτη) *black-haired.*

μελάγχειμα, ων, τά, *dark spots in snow.* From

μελάγχῐμος, ον, *black, dark.* (Formed from μέλας with termination -χιμος, as δυσ-χιμος from δυσ-).

μελαγ-χίτων, ωνος, ὁ, ἡ, (μέλας, χίτων) *with black raiment:* hence *gloomy, dark-brooding.*

μελάγ-χλαινος, ον, (μέλας, χλαῖνα) *black-cloaked:* οἱ Μελάγχλαινοι a Scythian nation.

μελαγχολάω, (μελάγχολος) *to be jaundiced* or *melancholy.*

μελάγ-χολος, ον, (μέλας, χολή) *with black bile, jaundiced.* II. *dipped in black bile.*

μελαγ-χροιής, ές, (μέλας, χροιά) = μελάγχροος.

μελάγ-χροος, ον, contr. **-χρους**, ουν, (μέλας, χρόα) *black-skinned, sun-burnt, bronzed, swarthy:* there is an irreg. nom. pl. μελάγχροες.

μελαγ-χρώς, ῶτος, ὁ, ἡ, (μέλας, χρώς) = μελαγχροος.

μέλαθρον, τό, (μέλας) *the cross-beam* or *rafter in a room,* so called from *being blackened* with smoke, hence *the ceiling:* also *the projecting beam* outside a house, *the cornice.* II. generally, *a roof:* in pl., like Lat. *tecta, a house.*

μελαθρόφιν, poët. gen. of μέλαθρον.

μελαίνω, f. ανῶ:—Pass., aor. 1 ἐμελάνθην: pf. μεμέλασμαι: (μέλας):—*to blacken, make black:*—Pass. *to grow black* or *dark, turn black.*

μελαμ-βᾰθής, ές, (μέλας, βάθος) *deep in darkness.*

μελαμ-βᾰφής, ές, (μέλας, βαφῆναι) *dark-dyed.*

μελάμ-βωλος, ον, (μέλας, βῶλος) *with black soil.*

μελαμ-πᾱγής, ές, Dor. for μελαμπηγής, (μέλας, πήγνυμι) *black-clotted:* generally, *black, discoloured.*

μελάμ-πεπλος, ον, (μέλας, πέπλος) *black-robed.*

μελαμ-πέτᾰλος, ον, (μέλας, πέταλον) *dark-leaved.*

μελάμ-πτερος, ον, (μέλας, πτερόν) *black-winged.*

μελαμ-φᾰής, ές, (μέλας, φάος) *with darkness for light.*

μελάμ-φυλλος, ον, (μέλας, φύλλον) *dark-leaved: with dark foliage, dark-wooded.*

μέλᾰν, ἄνος, τό, (neut. of μέλας) *black dye, ink.*

μελᾰν-αιγίς, ίδος, ὁ, ἡ, (μέλας, αἰγίς) *with dark aegis.*

μελᾰν-αυγής, ές, (μέλας, αὐγή) *dark-gleaming.*

μελάν-δετος, ον, (μέλας, δέω) *bound* or *mounted with black;* σάκος μελάνδετον *an iron-rimmed* shield.

μελαν-δόκος, ον, (μέλαν, δέχομαι) *holding ink;* κίστη μελανδόκος an *ink*-stand.

μελάν-δρυον, τό, (μέλας, δρῦς) *heart of oak.*

μελᾰν-είμων, ον, (μέλας, εἷμα) *with black raiment.*

μελάνει or **μελανεῖ**, a 3 sing. without any other part of the Verb in use, either *to make dark* (from μελάνω = μελαίνω), or *to grow dark* (from μελανέω).

μελ-ανθής, ές, (μέλας, ἄνθος) *with black blossoms:* generally, *black-coloured.*

μελᾰνία, ἡ, (μέλας) *a black cloud.*

μελᾰνό-ζυξ, ῠγος, ὁ, ἡ, (μέλας, ζεύγνυμι) *with black benches.*

μελᾰνο-κάρδιος, ον, (μέλας, καρδία) *black-hearted.*

μελᾰν-όμμᾰτος, ον, (μέλας, ὄμμα) *black-eyed.*

μελᾰνο-νεκῠο-είμων, ον, gen. ονος, (μέλας, νέκυς, εἷμα) *clad in black shroud.*

μελᾰνό-πτερος, ον, and **μελᾰνο-πτέρυξ**, ῠγος, ὁ, ἡ, (μέλας, πτερόν, πτέρυξ) *black-winged.*

μελάν-οσσος, ον, (μέλας, ὄσσε) *black-eyed.*

μελάν-οστος, for μελᾰνόστεος, ον, (μέλας, ὀστέον) *black-boned.*

μελάν-ουρος, ον, fem. **μελᾰν-ουρίς**, ίδος, (μέλας, οὐρά) *black-tailed.*

μελᾰνό-χροος, ον, = μελάγχροος.

μελᾰνό-χρως, οος, ὁ, ἡ, = μελάγχρως.

μελαν-τειχής, ές, (μέλας, τεῖχος) *with black walls.*

μελάντερος, α, ον, Comp. of μέλας.

μελαν-τρᾰγής, ές, (μέλας, τραγεῖν) *black when eaten.*

μελάν-υδρος, ον, (μέλας, ὕδωρ) *with black water.* [ᾰ]

ΜΕ'ΛΑ˘Σ, Aeol. **μέλαις**, μέλαινα, μέλᾰν: gen. μέλανος, μελαίνης, μέλανος; etc.: cf. τάλας:—*black, dark, gloomy, dusky, murky.* II. Comp. μελάντερος, α, ον.

ΜΕ'ΛΔΩ, only used in pres. *to melt, make liquid:*—Pass. μέλδομαι, *to melt, grow liquid.*

μέλε, Ep. 3 sing. impf. of μέλω.

μέλε, ὦ μέλε, as a familiar address, *my friend, my dear:* Ep. vocat., of which no other part remains in use.

μελεδαίνω, (μέλω) *to care for, be cumbered* or *anxious about,* c. gen. II. *to tend, attend upon,* c. acc. Hence

μελέδημα, ατος, τό, *care, anxiety, concern.* II. *the thing cared for*, Hence

μελεδήμων, ον, gen. ονος, *caring for, anxious about.* II. *busy.*

μελεδών, ῶνος, ἡ, = μελεδώνη.

μελεδωνεύς, ὁ, poët. for μελεδωνός.

μελεδώνη, ἡ, like μελεδών, (μελεδαίνω) *care, sorrow.*

μελεδωνός, ὁ, and ἡ, (μελεδαίνω) *one who takes care of, a guardian, steward: a keeper* or *tender.*

μέλει, impers., see μέλω

μελεϊστί, Adv. (μελείζω) *limb from limb.*

μελεο-πᾰθής, ές, (μέλεος, παθεῖν) *suffering misery.*

μελεό-πονος, ον, (μέλεος, πόνος) *labouring in misery.*

μέλεος, α, ον, also ος, ον, (μέλω) *fruitless, vain, empty:* neut. μέλεον as Adv. *in vain.* 2. *unhappy, wretched.*

μελεό-φρων, ονος, ὁ, ἡ, (μέλεος, φρήν) *wretched in mind.*

μελεσί-πτερος, ον, (μέλος. πτερόν) *singing with its wings.*

μέλεται, 3 sing. pres. med. of μέλω.

μελετάω, f. ήσω:—*to care for*, c. gen. II. c. acc. *to study, prosecute diligently*, Lat. *excolere: to court: to practise, exercise;* μελετᾶν σοφίαν *to practise* wisdom; also c. dat. rei, μελετᾶν τόξῳ *to practise with* the bow: absol. *to practise, exercise oneself;* ἐν τῷ μὴ μελετῶντι (dat. part. for inf.) by want *of practice:* absol. *to take heed, take thought.* 2. c. acc. pers. *to exercise* or *train* one. From

μελέτη, ἡ, (μέλομαι) *care, attention* 2. *practice, exercise.* II. *care, anxiety.*

μελέτημα, ατος, τό, (μελετάω) *a practice, study.*

μελετηρός, ά, όν, (μελετάω) *practising diligently.*

μελετητέον, verb. Adj. of μελετάω, *one must practise.*

μελέτωρ, ορος, ὁ, (μέλω) *one who cares for, a guardian, avenger.*

μεληδών, όνος, ἡ, = μελεδών, μελεδώνη.

μέλημα, ατος, τό, (μέλω) *an object of care: a beloved object* II. *a charge, duty: care, anxiety.*

μελησέμεν, Ep. for μελήσειν, fut. inf. of μέλω.

μελησίμ-βροτος, ον, (μέλησις, βροτός) *cared for by men.*

Μελητίδης [ῐ], ου, ὁ, proverbial name at Athens for a *blockhead*, as if patronym. from Μέλητος.

ΜΕ'ΛΙ, ῐτος, τό, Lat. *MEL, honey.*

μελία Ion. -ίη, ἡ, *the ash*, Lat. *fraxinus:* from its toughness it was used for *spears* II. *a spear*

μελῐ-βόας, ὁ, (μέλι, βοή) *with honey-tone.*

μελί-βρομος, ον, (μέλι, βρέμω) *honey-toned.*

μελί-γδουπος, ον, (μέλι, δουπέω) *sweet-sounding.*

μελί-γηρυς Dor. **-γαρυς**, υος, ὁ, ἡ, (μέλι. γῆρυς) *honey-voiced, musical.*

μελί-γλωσσος, ον, (μέλι, γλῶσσα) *honey-tongued.*

μέλιγμα, ατος, τό, (μελίζω) *song: a pipe.*

μελίζω Dor. **μελίσδω**, (μέλος) *to modulate, warble, play:* so also in Med., with Dor. fut. μελίξομαι. 2. trans. *to sing of, celebrate in song.*

μελι-ηδής, ές, (μέλι, ἡδύς) *honey-sweet:* metaph. *sweet to the soul, pleasing.*

μελί-θρεπτος, ον, (μέλι, τρέφω) *honey-fed.*

μελί-θροος, ον, contr. **-θρους**, ουν, (μέλι, θροέω) *sweet-sounding.*

μελί-κηρον, τό, (μέλι, κηρός) *a honeycomb.*

μελί-κομπος, ον, (μέλι, κομπέω) *sweet-sounding.*

μελί-κρᾱτος Ion. **-κρητος**, ον, (μέλι, κεράννυμι) *mixed with honey:* μελί-κρητον Att. -κρᾱτον, τό, *a drink of honey and milk* offered as a libation.

μελικτής, οῦ, Dor. **μελικτάς**, ᾶ, ὁ, (μελίζω) *a singer, player*, esp. *a flute-player.*

μελί-λωτον, τό, also **μελί-λωτος**, ο, (μέλι, λωτός) *melilot*, a kind of clover, so called from the quantity of honey it contained.

ΜΕΛΙ'ΝΗ, ἡ, *millet*, Lat *panĭcum:* in pl. *millet-fields.* [ῐ]

μέλινος Ep. **μείλινος**, η, ον, (μελία) *ashen*, Lat. *fraxineus.*

Μελῐνο-φάγοι, οἱ, (μελίνη, φᾰγεῖν) *the Millet-eaters*, name of a Thracian tribe.

μελί-παις, παιδος, ὁ and ἡ, (μέλι, παῖς) *with honey-children*, epith. of the bee-hive.

μελί-πνοος, ον, contr. **-πνους**, ουν, (μέλι, πνέω) *honey-breathing, sweet-breathing.*

μελίρ-ροος, ον, (μέλι, ῥέω) *flowing with honey.*

μελίρ-ρῠτος, ον, = μελίρροος.

μελίσδω, Dor. for μελίζω: **μελίσδεν**, Dor. inf.

μέλισμα, ατος, τό, (μελίζω) *a song, chant: a tune.*

μέλισσα Att. **μέλιττα**, ης, ἡ, (μέλι) *a bee.* 2. *a priestess* of Delphi. II. *honey* itself.

μελίσσειος, not μελίσσιος, α, ον, (μέλισσα) *of, belonging to bees;* μελίσσειον κηρίον a *honey*comb

μελισσό-βοτος, ον, (μέλισσα, βόσκω) *fed on by bees.*

μελισσο-νόμος, ον, (μέλισσα, νέμω) *keeping bees.* II. (μέλισσα I. 2) *a priestess.*

μελισσο-πόνος, ον, (μέλισσα, πονέω) *tending bees.*

μελισσο-σόος, ον, (μέλισσα, σόος) *guardian of bees.*

μελισσό-τοκος, ον, (μέλισσα, τεκεῖν) *produced by bees, honied.*

μελισσο-τρόφος, ον, (μελισσα, τρέφω) *feeding bees.*

μελισσών Att. **μελιττών**, ῶνος, ὁ, (μέλισσα) *a bee-house, apiary.*

μελι-στᾰγής, ές, (μελι, σταγῆναι) *dropping honey.*

μελί-στακτος, ον, = μελιστάγης.

μελίτεια, ἡ, (μέλι) a herb, *baulm*, Lat. *apiastrum.*

μελῐ-τερπής, ές, (μέλι, τέρπω) *honey-sweet*

Μελῑτίδης, false form for Μελητίδης.

μελῐτόεις, εσσα, εν, (μέλι) *honied, sweet.* II. *made of honey:* as Subst., μελιτόεσσα Att. μελιτοῦττα (sub. μᾶζα), ἡ, *a honey-cake.*

μελῐτο-πώλης, ου, ὁ, (μέλι, πωλέω) *a dealer in honey.*

μελῐτοῦττα, v. μελιτοεις.

μελῐτόω, f. ώσω, (μέλι) *to sweeten with honey.*

μέλιττα, ἡ, Att. for μέλισσα, *a bee.*

μελίττιον, τό, Dim. of μέλιττα, *a small bee.*

μελιττο-τρόφος, Att. for μελισσοτρ-

μελιττ-ουργός, **–ουργέω**, **–ουργία**, ἡ, Att. for μελισσ–.

μελἴτ-ώδης, ες, (μέλος, εἶδος) *like honey.*

μελίτωμα, ατος, τό, (μελιτόω) *a honey-cake.* [ῐ]

μελί-φθογγος, ον, (μέλι, φθογγή) *honey-voiced, sweet-toned, honied.*

μελί-φρων, ονος, ὁ, ἡ, (μέλι, φρήν) *sweet to the mind, delicious.*

μελί-φυρτος, ον, (μέλι, φύρω) *mixed with honey.*

μελί-χλωρος, ον, (μέλι, χλωρός) *yellow* or *pale as honey, tawny.*

μελί-χροος, ον, contr. **–χρους**, ουν, (μέλι, χρόα) *honey-coloured, tawny.*

μελιχρ-ώδης, ες, (μελίχρους, εἶδος) *yellow as honey.*

μελί-χρως, ωτος, ὁ, ἡ, (μέλι, χρώς) = μελίχροος.

μέλλημα, ατος, τό, (μέλλω) *a delay:* in pl. *delays.*

μέλλησα, Ep. for ἐμέλλησα, aor. 1 of μέλλω.

μέλλησις, ἡ, (μέλλω) *a being about to* do, *intending* or *threatening to do: an intention.* II. *an unfulfilled intention, a delaying, delay.*

μελλητέον, verb. Adj. of μέλλω, *one must delay.*

μελλητής, οῦ, ὁ, (μέλλω) *a delayer.*

μελλό-γἄμος, ον, (μέλλω, γαμέω) *betrothed.*

μελλο-δειπνικός, ή, όν, (μέλλω, δεῖπνον) *played at the beginning of dinner,* of music.

μελλο-νικιάω, (μέλλω, νικάω) *to put off conquering;* with a pun upon the name of Nicias.

μελλό-νυμφος, ον, (μέλλω, νύμφη) *about to be wedded:* also, in wider sense, *whoever is of marriageable age.*

ΜΕ'ΛΛΩ, impf. ἔμελλον: fut. μελλήσω: aor. 1 ἐμέλλησα: in Att. the augm. is doubled, ἤμελλον, ἠμέλλησα:—*to be on the point of doing, to be about to do* or *suffer:* hence *to intend, design, purpose.* II. *to be fated, destined to do;* τὰ οὐ τελέεσθαι ἔμελλον which *were* not *destined to be* accomplished. 2. *to be likely, to be certain,* often best rendered by *must:* μέλλω που ἀπέχθεσθαι Διὶ πατρί *it must be that* I am hated by father Zeus. 3. to mark *a probability;* τὰ δὲ μέλλετ' ἀκουέμεν *you are likely* to have heard of it; ὅθι που μέλλουσιν ἄριστοι βουλὰς βουλεύειν where the best *are likely* to be holding counsel. III. *to be always going to do, meaning to do,* without doing: hence *to delay, put off, hesitate, scruple.* IV. μέλλω often stands without its infin., and so seems to govern an acc., which depends on the inf. omitted; ὅ τι μέλλετε [sc. πράττειν] εὐθὺς πράττετε, what you are about [to do], do quickly: the part. μέλλων is also used so, as ὁ μέλλων χρόνος *the future* time; ἡ μέλλουσα αὐτοῦ δύναμις his *future* power: esp. in neut., τὸ μέλλον, τὰ μέλλοντα *things to come, the issue, result.*

μελλώ, οῦς, ἡ, poët. for μέλλησις.

μελογρἄφία, ἡ, *song-writing.* From

μελο-γράφος, ον, (μέλος, γράφω) *writing songs.*

μελοποιέω, f. ήσω, (μελοποιός) *to make lyric poems.*

μελοποιητής, οῦ, ὁ, = μελοποιός.

μελο-ποιός, όν, (μέλος, ποιέω) *making lyric poems:* as Subst., μελοποιός, ὁ, *a lyric poet.*

ΜΕ'ΛΟΣ, εος, τό, *a limb;* κατὰ μέλεα *limb by limb.* II. *a song, strain;* plur. μέλη *lyric poetry, choral songs.* 2. *the music to which a song is set, an air, melody.*

μελο-τῠπέω, f. ήσω, (μέλος, τύπτω) *to strike up a strain, chant.*

μέλπηθρον, τό, (μέλπω) *the song and dance, festivity, sport;* μέλπηθρα κυνῶν *a sport for* dogs.

Μελπομένη, ἡ, *Melpomené, the Songstress,* the Muse of Tragedy. From

μέλπω, f. ψω: aor. 1 ἔμελψα: (μέλος):—*to sing, celebrate.* 2. intr. *to sing.* II. so also **μέλπομαι**, fut. –ψομαι, as Dep.; μέλπεσθαι κιθαρίζων *to sing to* the harp; μέλπεσθαι *to dance* in honour of Mars, i. e. to fight bravely. 2. c. acc. *to sing, celebrate.*

μελύδριον, τό, Dim. of μέλος, *a ditty.*

ΜΕ'ΛΩ, fut. μελήσω:—*to be an object of care* or *thought;* πᾶσι μέλω *I am a care* to all. 2. mostly in 3 sing. μέλει, impf. ἔμελε, fut. μελήσει, pres. and fut. inf. μέλειν and μελήσειν:—something *is a care to me, an object of thought, anxiety,* Lat. *curae est mihi;* of a pursuit, μέλει μοι πόλεμος war is *a care to* me: so in inf., σοὶ χρὴ τάδε μέλειν it is right that these things *should be a care* to thee. 3. μέλει is often impers.; μέλει μοι τοῦδε *there is a care* to me *for* this, I *care* for this. II. pres. and fut. Med. μέλεται, μελήσεται, are also used in 3 sing. for μέλει, μελήσει; as ἐμοὶ δέ κε ταῦτα μελήσεται but these things *shall be* my *care.* 2. pf. act. μέμηλε with pres. sense, for Att. μεμέληκε, and the plqpf. μεμήλει, with impf. sense, *to be a care, be thought of;* μεμηλότα ἔργα *carefully tended* works. 3. Ep. pf. and plqpf. pass. μέμβλεται, μέμβλετο, shortd. for μεμέληται, ἐμεμέλητο, also occur in pres. and impf. sense; ἤ νύ τοι οὐκέτι μέμβλετ' Ἀχιλλεύς surely Achilles *is* no longer *a care* to thee; μέμβλετο οἱ τεῖχος the wall *was a care* to him. III. the Act. μέλω, Med. μέλομαι are also found in trans. sense, *to care for, take care of, tend,* c. gen., μέλειν βροτῶν *to take care of* mortals; so in pf. part., πτολέμοιο μεμηλώς *busied with* war: also in aor. 1 pass. μεληθῆναι, *to care for, take care of.*

μελῳδέω, f. ήσω, (μελῳδός) *to sing.* Hence

μελῳδία, ἡ, *a singing.*

μελ-ῳδός, όν, (μέλος, ᾠδή) *singing, musical.*

μέμαα, pf. of *μάω: 3 pl. μεμάᾶσι.

μεμάθηκα [μᾰ], pf. of μανθάνω.

μεμᾰκυῖα, Ep. pf. part. fem. of μηκάομαι.

μέμᾰμεν, Ep. for μεμάομεν, 1 pl. pf. of *μάω.

μεμάνημαι [μᾰ], pf. of μαίνομαι, formed as if from *μανέομαι.

μεμᾱότες, pf. part. pl. of *μάω.

μεμάποιεν [μᾰ], 3 pl. Ep. aor. 2 opt. of μάρπτω.

μεμαρπώς, pf. part. of μάρπτω.

μέμᾰτε, Ep. for μεμάετε, 2 pl. pf. of *μάω.

μέμᾰχα, pf. of μάσσω.

μεμᾱώς, μεμᾰυῖα, pf. part. of *μάω: **μεμαῶτες, μεμαῶτας**, lengthd. for μεμαότες, μεμαότας, nom. and acc. plur.

μέμβλεται, μέμβλετο, Ep. for μεμέληται, ἐμεμέλητο, 3 sing. pf. and plqpf. pass. of μέλω.

μέμβλωκα, pf. of. βλώσκω.

μεμβράνα, ἡ, Lat. *membrāna, a parchment, skin.*

ΜΕΜΒΡΑ'Σ, άδος, ἡ, a small kind of *anchovy.* [ᾰ]

μεμέληκα, pf. of μέλω.

μεμένηκα, pf. of μένω.

μεμετιμένος, Ion. for **μεθειμένος**, pf. pass. part. of μεθίημι.

μεμηκώς, pf. part. of μηκάομαι.

μέμηλε, Ep. 3 sing. pf. of μέλω, with pres. sense, also **μεμήλει**, plqpf. with impf. sense.

μέμηνα, pf. of μαίνομαι.

μεμηχᾰνημένως, Adv. pf. part. of μηχανάομαι, *craftily, by stratagem.*

μεμίασμαι, pf. pass. of μιαίνω.

μέμιγμαι, pf. pass. of μίγνυμι: inf. **μεμίχθαι.**

μεμνᾱμένος, Dor. pf. part. of μιμνήσκω.

μέμνεο, Ion. pf. pass. imperat. of μιμνήσκω.

μεμνέῳτο, Ion. for **μέμνῳτο**, 3 pl. pf. opt. pass. of μιμνήσκω.

μέμνημαι, pf. pass. of μιμνήσκω, inf. μεμνῆσθαι.

μεμνῄμην, μεμνῴμην, pf. opt. pass. of μιμνήσκω.

μεμνηστευμένος, pf. part. pass. of μνηστεύω.

μεμνῶμαι, pf. subj. pass. of μιμνήσκομαι.

Μέμνων, ονος, ὁ, (μένω) *Memnon*, properly *the Resolute.*

μεμόλυγκα, -υσμαι, pf. act. and pass. of μολύνω.

μέμονα, poët. and Ion. pf. with pres. sense, without any pres. in use: (*μάω):—*to wish, long, yearn, strive;* διχθὰ δέ μοι κραδίη **μέμονε** my heart *longs* with a twofold wish.

μεμόρηται, poët. 3 sing. pf. pass. of μείρομαι.

μεμορυγμένος, pf. part. pass. of μορύσσω.

μεμούνωμαι, Ion. pf. pass. of μονόω.

μεμπτός, ή, όν, (μέμφομαι) *to be blamed, blameworthy, contemptible.* II. act. *blaming, bearing a grudge against.*

μέμῡκα, pf. of μυκάομαι: also of μύω.

ΜΕ'ΜΦΟΜΑΙ, fut. μέμψομαι: aor. 1 med. ἐμεμψάμην, pass. ἐμέμφθην: Dep.:—*to blame, upbraid, reproach, find fault with*, c. acc. pers. or rei; c. gen. rei, *to complain of* a thing; c. acc. rei et gen. pers., ὃ μάλιστα μέμφονται ἡμῶν which is the chief *complaint they make* against us. II. c. dat. pers. et acc. rei, *to object* a thing *to* another: *reproach* him with it: c. dat. pers. *to find fault with.*

μεμψί-μοιρος, ον, (μέμφομαι, μοῖρα) *complaining of one's fate, repining, discontented.*

μέμψις, εως, ἡ, (μέμφομαι) *a blaming, reproach, reproof.* 2. *a complaint.*

ΜΕ'Ν, conjunctive Particle, used to distinguish the word or clause with which it stands from something that is to follow, and commonly answered by δέ in the corresponding clause. Generally, μέν and δέ may be expressed by *on the one hand.., on the other; as well.. as, while;* μέν, like δέ, can never stand first in a clause: μέν is not always answered by δέ, but by other Particles, as by ἀλλά, ἀτάρ, ἔπειτα, αὖτε, αὖθις; also by μέντοι, εἶτα. Μέν is often found without δέ expressed, as, ὡς μὲν λέγουσι as they *say*, (*but* as I do not believe). Μέν was orig. the same as μήν, and ἦ μέν is retained in Ion. for ἦ μήν as a form of protestation. II. μέν before other Particles: 1. μὲν ἄρα, Ep. μέν ῥα, *accordingly, and so.* 2. μέν γε or μὲν .. γε, *yet at least, certainly*, Lat. *certe.* 3. μὲν δή *however.* 4. μὲν οὖν or μενοῦν, Lat. *imo vero, ay indeed: rather, nay rather:* so too, μὲν οὖν γε or μενοῦνγε, *yea rather.* 5. μέν τοι Ep., Att. μέντοι, *certainly, at any rate.* b. to recall what has gone before, *now.* c. to mark an objection, or exception, *yet, however, still, nevertheless.*

μεναίχμης, ου, ὁ, (μένω, αἰχμή) *sustaining the fight, resolute, unflinching.*

μενεαίνω, only used in pres. and impf., (μένος) *to desire earnestly, to be bent on* doing: c. gen., μενεαίνειν μάχης *to long for* battle. II. *to be angry, rage, be furious:—to be convulsed* in death.

μεν-έγχης, ες, (μένω, ἔγχος) *steadfast in fight.*

μενε-δήϊος, ον, (μένω, δήϊος) *standing one's ground against the enemy, staunch, unflinching.*

μενεήνᾰμεν, Ep. 1 pl. aor. 1 of μενεαίνω.

Μενέ-λᾱος, Att. **Μενέλεως** Dor. **Μενέλας**, ὁ, pr n. (μένω, λαός) *Menelaus*, i. e. *withstanding men.*

μενε-πτόλεμος, ον, (μένω, πόλεμος) *staunch in battle, steadfast, resolute.*

Μενεσθεύς, έως, Ion. ῆος, ὁ, (μένω) *Menestheus*, i. e. the *Abider.*

μενετέον, verb. Adj. of μένω, *one must abide.*

μενετός, ή, όν, (μένω) *standing one's ground, steadfast:* also *patient, longsuffering;* οἱ καιροὶ οὐ μενετοί opportunities *will* not *wait.*

μενε-φύλοπις, ιος, ὁ, ἡ, (μένω, φύλοπις) = μενεπτόλεμος. [ῠ]

μενε-χάρμης, ου, ὁ, and **μενέ-χαρμος**, ον, (μένω, χάρμη) *staunch in battle, resolute.*

μενο-εικής, ές, (μένος, εἰκός from *εἴκω) *suited to the desires, satisfying, plentiful:* generally, *agreeable, pleasant, suiting one's taste.*

μενοινάω, f. ήσω: Ep. impf. μενοίνεον: Ep. pres. μενοινώω, 3 sing. μενοινάα: Ep. aor. 1 μενοίνησα, 3 sing. opt. μενοινήσειε: (μενοινή):—*to desire eagerly, long for, to strive for.* 2. *to purpose, intend.*

μενοινή, ἡ, *eager desire.*

μενοινώω, Ep. for μενοινάω.

ΜΕ'ΝΟΣ, εος, τό, *force, strength of body, prowess.* 2. of animals, *strength, fierceness, spirit.* 3. of things, *strength, might, force:* hence of the blood as giving strength; μέλαν μένος *a flow of* **black** *blood.* II. *spirit, ardour:* μένει, dat. *with fury, violently.* 2. *wish, bent, purpose.* 3. generally, *temper, disposition.* III. μένος is also used in periphr. like βίη, ἴς; as ἱερὸν μένος Ἀλκινόοιο the sacred *Alcinoüs* himself.

μενοῦν, μέντοι, etc., v. sub μέν II. 4, 5.

ΜΕ'ΝΩ: Ion. impf. μένεσκον: fut. μενῶ, Ep. uncontr. μενέω: aor. 1 ἔμεινα: pf. μεμένηκα:—*to stay, wait*, Lat. *MANEO*: *to abide, stand one's ground*. 2. *to stay at home, tarry*. 3. *to stay behind, linger, dally*. 4. of things, *to be lasting, to remain, stand*. 5. of condition, *to be unchanged, continue, hold good*. 6. *to abide* or *stand by* an opinion. II. trans. *to await, expect, abide, await steadfastly*:—*to await for*; μένον δ' ἐπὶ ἕσπερον ἐλθεῖν *they waited for* evening's coming on: also *to watch for*.

μερίζω, f. ίσω Att. ιῶ: Dor. μερίσδω, f. ξω: (μερίς): —*to divide into parts*. II. *to divide, distribute*: —Med. *to divide among themselves*.

μέριμνα, ἡ, (μερίς, μερίζω) *care, thought*: *anxious care* or *thought, trouble, disquietude*. II. *the thought, mind*. Hence

μεριμνάω, f. ήσω, *to care for, be anxious about, think earnestly upon*; πολλὰ μεριμνᾶν *to be cumbered with* many *cares*. Hence

μερίμνημα, ατος, τό, *anxious thought, care*: and

μεριμνητής, οῦ, ὁ, *one who is careful about* things.

μεριμνο-τόκος, ον, (μέριμνα, τεκεῖν) *giving birth to care*.

μεριμνο-φροντιστής, οῦ, ὁ, (μέριμνα, φροντίζω) *an over-careful thinker*.

μερίς, ίδος, ἡ, (μέρος) *a part, portion, share*. II. *a part, class*: *a party, faction*, Lat. *partes*.

μερισμός, ὁ, (μερίζω) *a partition, dividing, distributing*.

μεριστής, οῦ, ὁ, (μερίζω) *a divider* or *distributer*.

μερίτης, ου, ὁ, (μερίς) *a partaker*. [ῑ]

μέρμερος, ον, (μέριμνα) *full of care, causing anxiety, mischievous, baneful*: neut. pl. μέρμερα, *mischiefs, troubles*. Hence

μέρμηρα, ἡ, poët. for μέριμνα, *care, trouble*. Hence

μερμηρίζω, f. ίξω: Ep. aor. 1 μερμήριξα:—*to be anxious, thoughtful, to ponder, think earnestly*: hence, *to be perplexed, to hesitate*. II. trans. *to think of, devise*.

ΜΕ'ΡΜΙΣ, ῑθος, ἡ, *a cord, string, rope, line*.

μεροπήϊος, ον, (μέροψ) *human*.

ΜΕ'ΡΟΣ, εος, τό, *a part, share*: *a portion, heritage, lot*. 2. *a share in* a thing with others, hence, *each person's turn*; ἐν μέρει in *turn*; so, ἀνὰ μέρος or κατὰ μέρος *in turn, successively*; κατὰ τὸ ἐμὸν μέρος as far as concerns me, Lat. *pro rata*; but τοὐμὸν or τὸ σὸν μέρος *as to me*, Lat. *quod ad me attinet*. 3. ἐν μέρει τινὸς τιθέναι, to put *in the class of* .., consider *as so and so*, like ἐν λόγῳ ποιεῖσθαι, Lat. *in numero habere*.

μέρ-οψ, οπος, ὁ, (μείρομαι, ὄψ) *dividing the voice*, i. e. *endowed with speech, articulate-speaking*, epith. of human beings.

μές, Dor. for μέν.

μέσα-βον, τό, (μέσος, βοῦς) *a leathern strap*, by which the yoke was fastened to the pole, Lat. *subjugium*.

μεσ-άγκυλον, τό, (μέσος, ἀγκύλη) *a javelin with a thong* for throwing it by.

μεσαι-πόλιος, ον, (μέσος, πολιός) poët. for μεσοπόλιος, *half-gray, grizzled, middle-aged*.

μεσαίτατος, η, ον, Ion. Sup. of μέσος, *the midst, middlemost*:—Comp. μεσαίτερος, η, ον, *more in the middle*.

μέσ-ακτος, ον, (μέσος, ἀκτή) *midway between two shores, in mid-sea*.

μεσ-αμβρίη, ἡ, Ion. for μεσημβρία.

μεσ-αμβρινός, μεσ-αμέριος, Dor. for μεσημ–.

μεσάτιος, ον, μέσατος, η, ον, poët. for μέσος: so also Ep. μέσσατος and μεσσάτιος.

μέσ-αυλος Ep. μέσσαυλος Att. μέταυλος, ον, *inside the* αὐλή or *hall*:—as Subst., μέσσαυλος, ὁ, or μέσσαυλον, τό, *the inner court*. II. in Att. μέταυλος (sc. θύρα), ἡ, *the door between the court-yard and inner part of the house, the inner door*.

μέσδων, ον, Dor. for μέζων, μείζων.

μεσηγύ, and before a vowel –ύς, Ep. μεσσηγύ, –ύς, Adv. of Space: (μέσος):—*in the middle between*. 2. c. gen. *in the middle of, betwixt*. II. of Time, *meanwhile, meantime*. III. as Subst., μεσηγύ, τό, *the part between, interval*: τὸ μεσηγὺ ἤματος *midday, noon*.

μεσήεις, εσσα, εν, (μέσος) *middle, middling*.

μεσ-ημβρία Ion. μεσ-αμβρίη, ἡ, (for μεσημερία, from μέσος, ἡμέρα) *midday, noon*, when the sun is at the meridian; μεσημβρία ἵσταται 'tis high *noon*. II. *the country towards the meridian, the South*. Hence

μεσ-ημβριάζω and –άω, *to pass the noon*, Lat. *meridiari*.

μεσημβρινός, ή, όν, commoner form for μεσημεριός, (μεσημβρία) *belonging to noon, noontide*; θάλπη μεσημβρινή *noonday* heat. II. *southern*.

μεσημέριος, ον, = μεσημβρινός.

μεσ-ήρης poët. μεσσήρης, ες, (μέσος, ἀρᾰρεῖν) *set in the middle, midmost*; Σείριος ἔτι μεσήρης Sirius is still *in mid-heaven*.

μεσιτεύω, f. σω, *to be* or *act as a mediator*. From

μεσίτης, ου, ὁ, (μέσος) *a mediator, intercessor*. [ῑ]

μεσῖτις, ιδος, fem. of μεσίτης.

μεσό-γαιος or –γειος, ον, also α, ον, also μεσό-γεως, ων, (μέσος, γῆ, γαῖα) *inland, in the heart of a country*: as Subst., ἡ μεσογεία (sub. χώρα), *the interior*.

μεσό-δμη, ἡ, (μέσος, δέμω, as if for μεσοδόμη) properly, *something built between*; hence *the part between two upright beams, a panel*. 2. κοίλη μεσόδμη *the cross-plank* of a ship, with a pole through it, for the mast.

μέσοι, poët. μέσσοι, Adv. (μέσος) *in the middle*.

μεσο-λαβής, ές, (μέσως, λαβεῖν) *held by the middle firm-grasped*.

μεσό-λευκος, ον, (μέσος, λευκός) *middling white, half white.*

μεσ-όμφᾰλος, ον, (μέσος, ὀμφαλός) *in mid-navel, central, midmost*, of Apollo's shrine at Delphi, from the prevalent notion that it was the centre of the earth.

μέσον, τό, see μέσος III.

μεσο-νύκτιος, ον, (μέσος, νύξ) *of* or *at midnight*: neut. μεσονύκτιον as Adv., *at midnight.*

μεσο-πᾰγής Ep. **μεσσοπ–**, ές, (μέσος, παγῆναι) *driven to the middle.*

μεσο-πᾰλής, ές, Ep. **μεσσοπ–**, (μέσος, παλῆναι) *swung* or *poised by the middle.*

μεσο-πόρος, ον, (μέσος, πορεύομαι) *in the midway, traversing the centre.*

μεσο-ποτάμιος, α, ον, (μέσος, ποταμός) *between rivers*: as Subst., ἡ Μεσοποταμία (sub. χώρα), *Mesopotamia, the land between the two rivers* Tigris and Euphrates.

μεσο-πύλη, ἡ, = μέση πύλη, *the middle gate.* [ῠ]

ΜΕ'ΣΟΣ Ep. **μέσσος**, η, ον: I. *middle, in the middle*, Lat. *medius*; μέσον ἦμαρ *mid*-day: in Att. also c. gen. *between, midway between*:—proverb. from the wrestling ring, ἔχεται μέσος he is caught *by the middl* II. *middle* or *mean between two extremes, middling, moderate, of middle rank.* III. as Subst., μέσον, τό, *the middle, the space between*: also, *common ground*; ἐς μέσον τιθέναι τινί τι to set a prize *before all, in public*, Lat. *in medio ponere*; so, ἐς μέσον ἀμφοτέροις δικάζειν to judge *fairly* or *impartially* for both; ἐκ τοῦ μέσου καθέζεσθαι to remain *neutral*; διὰ μέσου, *between*; and of Time, *meanwhile, in the meantime.* IV. neut. μέσον, as Adv. *in the middle*, like μέσως, *moderately.* V. poët. Comp. μεσαίτερος, Sup. μεσαίτατος.

μεσο-σχῐδής, ές, (μέσος, σχίζω) *split in two.*

μεσότης, ητος, ἡ, (μέσος) *a middle, a mean between two extremes*, Lat. *mediocritas.*

μεσό-τοιχον, τό, (μέσος, τοῖχος, *a partition-wall.*

μεσοτομέω, *to cut through the middle, bisect.* From

μεσό-τομος, ον, (μέσος, τεμεῖν) *cut through the middle, cut in twain.*

μεσ-ουράνημα, ατος, τό, (μέσος, οὐρανός) *the meridian* or *zenith.* 2. *the mid-heaven.*

μεσόω, f. ώσω, (μέσος) *to be in the middle, be half over, to reach the height, culminate*; ἡμέρα μεσοῦσα midday, *noon*; θέρος μεσοῦν *mid*summer. 2. c. gen. *to be in the middle of*, μεσοῦν τῆς ἀναβασιος *to be in the middle of* the ascent.

ΜΕ'ΣΠΙΛΟΝ, τό, the *medlar-tree*: *a medlar.*

μέσσᾰτος, η, ον, = μέσατος, poët. for μέσος.

μέσσ-αυλος, ὁ, or **μέσσ-αυλον**, τό, poët. for μέσαυλ–.

μεσσηγύ, μεσσηγύς, poët. for μεσηγ–.

μεσσ-ήρης, ες, poët. for μεσήρης.

Μεσσίας, ου, ὁ, Heb. *the Messiah*, i.e. *the Anointed.*

μεσσόθεν, Ep. for μεσόθεν, Adv. (μέσος) *from the middle.*

μεσσόθι, Ep. for μεσόθι, Adv. (μέσος) *in the middle.*

μεσσο-πᾰλής, μεσσο-πόρος, poët. for μεσοπ–.

μέσσος, η, ον, poët. for μέσο

ΜΕΣΤΟ'Σ, ή, όν, *full, filled, filled full*:—c. gen. *full of, filled with* a thing: metaph. *sated, disgusted with* a thing: c. part., μεστὸς ἦν θυμούμενος he *had his fill* of anger.

μεστόω, f. ώσω, (μεστός) *to fill full, glut, cram*: —Pass. *to be filled* or *full of.*

μέσφᾰ, poët. Adv. for μέχρι, *till, until*, c. gen.; μέσφ' ἠοῦς *till* morn:—μέσφ' ὅτε *unt*

μέσως, Adv. of μέσος, *middlingly, moderately.*

ΜΕΤΑ', poët. **μεταί**, Dor. **πεδά** or **πέδα**:—when placed after its Subst., it is written μέτα:—Prep. with gen., dat., et acc.

WITH GEN. *in the midst* of, *among, between.* II. *in common with, with the help* or *favour of*; μετ' Ἀθηναίης *with the help of* Athena. III. *with, by means of*; as μετ' ἀρετῆς πρωτεύειν.

WITH DAT. only poët. properly of persons, *among, in company with*: sometimes, *besides, over and above*; πύματος μετὰ οἷς ἑταιροῖσιν last *over and above* his companions. 2. of things, *in the midst of, with*, as, μετὰ νηυσί, κύμασι, ἀστράσι; so also, μετὰ πνοιῇς ἀνέμοιο *in company with* the winds.

WITH ACCUS. of motion, *coming into* or *among*, as μετὰ φῦλα θεῶν, μετὰ λαόν: generally, *after, in quest* or *pursuit of*, either in hostile or friendly sense: hence *with a view to, looking to*; πόλεμον μέτα θωρήσσοντο they armed *for* the battle. II. of Place, *after, next after, behind*; μετὰ κτίλον ἕσπετο μῆλα the sheep followed *after* the bell-wether. 2. of Time, *after, next to*; μετὰ ταῦτα *thereafter*:—also, μεθ' ἡμέραν *in the course of* the day, Lat. *interdiu.* 3. of order of Rank, *next to, next after, after*; κάλλιστος ἀνὴρ μέτ' ἀμύμονα Πηλείωνα the fairest man *after* the son of Peleus. III. *after, according to*; μετὰ σὸν καὶ ἐμὸν κῆρ *as* you and I *wish* IV. *among, in, between*, as with dat.; μετὰ πάντας ἄριστος best *of all, among all.*

AS ADV. *among them, with them.* II. *and then, next afterwards.* III. *thereafter, afterwards*; μετὰ γὰρ καὶ ἄλγεσι τέρπεται ἀνήρ one feels pleasure even in troubles *afterwards.*

Μέτα is often used for μέτεστι, q. v.

IN COMPOS. μετά implies *community* or *participation*, as in μετα-δίδωμι. II. *interval* of space or time, *between, during*, as in μετ-αίχμιον. III. *succession* of time, as in μετ-αυτίκα IV. *towards, in pursuit, following*, as in μετα-διώκω, μετ-οίχομαι. V. *letting go*, as in μεθ-ίημι. VI. *after, behind*, as in μετά-φρενον. VII. *backwards, back again, reversely*, as in μετα-τρέπω, μετα-στρέφω. VIII. most freq. of *change* of place, condition, mind, etc. as in μετα-βαίνω, μετα-βάλλω, μετα-γιγνώσκω, etc.

μετάβᾰ, for μετάβηθι, aor. 2 imperat. of μεταβαίνω.

μετα-βαίνω, f. –βήσομαι, aor. 2 μετέβην: pf. μεταβέβηκα:—*to pass over, to pass on*: generally, *to pass* *from one place to another.* II. Causal in aor. 1 μετέβησα, inf. μεταβῆσαι, *to carry over* or *away.*

μετα-βάλλω, f. -βᾰλῶ: aor. 2 μετέβαλον: pf. μεταβέβληκα, pass. -βέβλημαι:—*to turn quickly* or *suddenly; μεταβάλλειν γῆν to turn,* i. e. *plough,* the earth, Lat. *novare.* 2. *to turn about, change, alter, reverse; μεταβάλλειν τὰ ὕδατα to change the course of* the water; *μεταβάλλειν δίαιταν to change* one's diet or way of life. II. intr. *to undergo a change, become changed, alter: to change one's purpose.* III. Med. *to change for oneself, exchange, traffic.* 2. *to turn oneself, turn about: to change one's mind* or *purpose.* 3. *to turn one's back, turn* or *wheel round.*

μετα-βάπτω, f. ψω, *to change by dyeing: to stain, dye:* metaph. *to change one's complexion.*

μεταβάς, ᾶσα, άν, aor. 2 part. of μεταβαίνω.

μετάβᾰσις, ἡ, (μεταβαίνω) *a passing over, shifting, changing.* II. *change, alteration.*

μετα-βέβηκα, pf. of μεταβαίνω.

μετάβηθι, aor. 2 imperat. of μεταβαίνω.

μεταβήσομαι, fut. of μεταβαίνω.

μετα-βῐβάζω, f. -βιβάσω Att. -βιβῶ, Causal of μεταβαίνω, *to carry* or *convey over, bring into another place.*

μεταβολή, ἡ, (μεταβάλλω) *a change, changing:* in plur. *changes, vicissitudes;* but c. gen. *change from* a thing, as μεταβολὴ κακῶν: *change to* another party, μεταβολὴ ἐς τοὺς Ἕλληνας *going over* to the Greeks. 2. μεταβολὴ τῆς ἡμέρης *an eclipse.*

μετα-βουλεύω, or as Dep. **μεταβουλεύομαι**, *to alter one's plans, change one's mind.*

μετά-βουλος, ον, (μετά, βουλή) *changing one's mind, changeful, fickle.*

μεταβῶ, ῇς, ῇ, aor. 2 subj. of μεταβαίνω.

μετ-άγγελος, ου, ὁ and ἡ, *a messenger between two parties, a go-between,* Lat. *internuncius.*

Μετα-γειτνιών, ῶνος, ὁ, (μετά, γείτων) the second month of the Athenian year, answering to the Laconian Καρνεῖος, the latter half of August and first of Sept.; so called because then people *flitted and changed their neighbours.*

μετα-γιγνώσκω Ion. and in late Gr. **-γῑνώσκω**: f. -γνώσομαι: aor. 2 μετέγνων:—*to ascertain after* or *too late.* II. *to change one's mind:* c. acc. *to alter, repeal* a decree. 2. *to repent:* c. acc. *to repent* of a thing.

μετά-γνοιᾰ, ἡ, = μετάνοια, *repentance, remorse.*

μετάγνωσις, εως, ἡ, (μεταγνῶναι) *change of mind.*

μετα-γράφω, ψω, *to write differently: to alter, correct:* also, *to interpolate, falsify* 2. *to translate:* Med. *to get* a letter *translated.*

μετ-άγω, f. -άξω: aor. 2 μετήγαγον:—*to convey from one place to another.* II. seemingly intr. *to change one's course.*

μετα-δαίνῡμι, f. -δαίσομαι Dep. *to share the feast:* generally, *to partake of.*

μεταδέδογμαι, pf. pass. of μεταδοκέω.

μετα-δέω, f. -δήσω, *to tie differently: to untie.*

μετα-δήμιος, ον, (μετά, δῆμος) *in the midst of* or *among the people:* hence, *native, at home.*

μετα-δῐαιτάω, f. ήσω, (μετά, δίαιτα) *to change one's way of life.*

μετα-δίδωμι, fut. -δώσω, *to give part of, give a share.* II. *to give after.*

μετα-δίομαι, Dep., = μεταδιώκω.

μεταδίωκτος, ον, *chased, overtaken.* From

μετα-δῐώκω, f. -διώξομαι later -διώξω, *to give chase to, pursue closely.* II, intr. *to follow close after.*

μετα-δοκέω, f. -δόξω: aor. 1 -έδοξα: pf. pass. -δέδογμαι:—*to change one's opinion:* impers. **μεταδοκεῖ**, μετέδοξε, *one changes, one changed one's plans* or *purpose:* absol. in pf. pass. part., **μεταδεδογμένον μοι** μὴ στρατεύεσθαι *my purpose* is *changed* so as not to march.

μετα-δόρπιος, ον, (μετά, δόρπον) *during supper,* or *after supper.*

μεταδός, aor. 2 imperat. of μεταδίδωμι.

μετάδοσις, ἡ, (μεταδίδωμι) *the giving a share, imparting.*

μεταδοῦναι, aor. 2 inf. of μεταδίδωμι.

μετά-δουπος, ον, (μετά, δουπέω) *falling between, useless.*

μετα-δρομάδην, Adv. (μετά, δρομος) *running after, following close upon.*

μετα-δρομή, ἡ, (μετά, δραμεῖν) *a running after, pursuit, chase.*

μετα-δρόμος, ον, (μετα, δραμεῖν) *running after, pursuing, hunting down, taking vengeance of.*

μέταζε, Adv. (μετά) *afterwards.*

μετα-ζεύγνυμι, f. -ζεύξω, *to unyoke and put to another carriage.*

μετάθεσις, ἡ, (μετατίθημι) *transposition. change of opinions, a going over.* II. *the power* or *right of changing.*

μετα-θέω, f. -θευσομαι, *to run after, chase.*

μεταί, poët. for μετά.

μετα-ΐζω, poët. for μεθίζω, *to take one's seat beside.*

μεταΐξας, aor. 1 part. of μεταΐσσω.

μετ-αίρω, *to lift up and remove;* ψήφισμα μεταίρειν *to repeal* a statute II. intr. (sub. ἑαυτόν) *to go away, depart.*

μετ-αΐσσω, f. ξω, *to rush after, rush upon: to rush upon, attack.*

μετ-αιτέω, f. ήσω, *to demand one's share of* a thing: *to beg.* 2. *to beg of, ask alms of,* τινά.

μετ-αίτιος, ον, also ος, ον, (μετά, αἴτιος) *being in part the cause;* μεταίτιος φόνου *an accomplice in, accessory to,* the murder.

μετ-αίχμιος, ον, Aeol. **πεδ-**, (μετά, αἰχμή) *between two armies:* μεταίχμιον, τό, *the space between two armies;* also, *a disputed frontier, debateable ground.* 2. generally, *midway between, in mid air.*

μετα-καθέζομαι, f. -εδοῦμαι, Med. *to change one's seat* or *place.*

μετα-καινίζω, f. σω, *to model anew.*

μετα-κᾰλέω, f. έσω, *to call away: to call back, recall.*

μετᾰ-κῐάθω, only used in impf., *to follow after*: either absol. *to give chase*, or c. acc. *to chase*. II. *to go to visit*, c. acc. III. πᾶν πεδίον μετεκίαθον *they were marching over* the whole field.

μετα-κῑνέω, f. ήσω, *to remove*: *to change, alter*:—Med. *to go from one place to another*. Hence

μετακῑνητός, ή, όν, *transposed, changed*: *to be changed* or *disturbed*.

μετα-κλαίω, f. -κλαύσομαι, *to weep* or *wail afterwards*. 2. *to weep fo*.

μετα-κλάω, *to break and so change*.

μετα-κλίνω, f. -κλῐνῶ, *to turn in a new direction*:—Pass. *to take another course, set the other way*.

μετα-κοιμίζω, f. σω, *to lull to sleep*.

μετά-κοινος, ον, (μετά, κοινός) *sharing in common, partaking*.

μετα-κομίζω, f. ίσω, *to transport, carry over*.

μετα-κῠλινδέω, f. ήσω, *to roll away*; μετακυλινδεῖν αὐτόν *to roll* oneself *over*.

μετα-κύμιος, ον, (μετά, κῦμα) *between the waves*; ἄτας μετακύμιον *between two waves* of woe, i.e. *bringing a short lull* or *pause* from woe. [ῡ]

μετα-λαγχάνω, f. -λήξομαι, *to get a share of*.

μετα-λαμβάνω, f. -λήψομαι: pf. -είληφα: pass. -είλημμαι:—*to have* or *get a share of*, to *partake in*:—Med., μεταλαμβάνεσθαί τινος *to claim* a thing *to oneself, assume*. II. *to take instead, take in exchange*, as πόλεμον ἀντ' εἰρήνης; μεταλαμβάνειν παλτόν *to take a fresh dart*. 2. *to interchange*.

μετ-αλγέω, f. ήσω, *to feel remorse, to repent*.

μετα-λήγω Ep. **μεταλλήγω**, fut. ξω, *to leave off, cease from*.

μετάληψις, ή, (μεταλαμβάνω) *a partaking of, communion in* a thing.

μεταλλᾰγή, ή, (μεταλλάσσω) *a taking in exchange, a changing, change*: μεταλλαγὴ τὰς ἡμέρας *an eclipse*.

μεταλλακτός, ή, όν, verb Adj of μεταλλάσσω, *changed, altered*.

μετάλλαξις, ή, = μεταλλαγή, *a change*.

μετ-αλλάσσω Att. -ττω: f. ξω: aor. 1 μετήλλαξα: *to exchange, to change, alter*. 2. *to change to, take in exchange*. 3. *to change from, leave, quit*. 4. intr. *to undergo a change, change*.

μετ-άλλατος, Dor. for μετάλλητος.

μετ-αλλάω, f. ήσω, (μετ' ἄλλα) *to search after other things, to explore, inquire curiously*: *to question*: also *to ask about, ask after*. Cf. μέταλλον.

μεταλλεύω, f. σω, (μέταλλον) *to produce by mining*: *to dig mines*. II. = μεταλλάω, *to explore*.

μεταλ-λήγω, Ep. for μεταλήγω.

μεταλλῆσαι, aor. 1 inf. of μεταλλάω.

μετάλλητος, ον, verb. Adj. of μεταλλάω, *to be searched, sought out*.

μεταλλικός, ή, όν, *of* or *for mines*. From

μέτ-αλλον, τό, *a mine, quarry*; ἁλὸς μέταλλον a salt-*pit*, salt-*mine*: mostly in pl., χρύσεα καὶ ἀργύρεα μέταλλα gold and silver *mines*. (From μετ' ἄλλα, *in quest of other things*; cf. μεταλλάω.)

μεταλλό-χρῡσος, ον, (μέταλλον, χρυσός) *containing gold ore*.

μετάλμενος, Ep. aor. 2 part. pass. of μεθάλλομαι.

μετα-μάζιος, ον, (μετά, μαζός) *between the breasts*: μεταμάζιον, τό, *the part between the breasts, chest*.

μετα-μαίομαι, Dep. *to search after, chase*.

μετα-μανθάνω, f. -μᾰθήσομαι: aor. 2 μετέμαθον: *to learn differently*: *to unlearn one thing and learn another*, Lat. *dediscere*.

μετ-ᾰμείβω, f. ψω, *to exchange*, ἀγαθὸν κακοῦ good *for* evil; also in Med. 2. *to change, remove*. II. Med. *to change one's condition, escape from*; μεταμειβόμενοι *in turns*.

μετα-μέλει, fut. -μελήσει: aor. 1 μετεμέλησε: I. impers. *it repents* me, *rues* me, c. dat. pers. et gen. rei, μεταμέλει μοι τοῦ πεπραγμένου, Lat. *poenitet me facti*: also, μεταμέλει μοι οὕτως ἀπολογησαμένῳ *I repent of* having so defended myself: absol., μεταμέλει μοι *it repents* me; and in part., μεταμελόν μοι, Lat. *quum poeniteat me*. 2. also with a nom., τῷ Ἀρίστωνι μετέμελε τὸ εἰρημένον what had been said *caused sorrow* to Ariston. Hence

μεταμέλεια, ή, *change of purpose, regret, repentance*: and

μετα-μέλομαι, fut. med. μεταμελήσομαι, aor. 1 pass. μετεμελήθην: Dep.: (μετά, μέλω):—*to feel repentance, to rue, regret*: absol. *to change one's purpose*.

μετά-μελος, ὁ, (μετά, μέλομαι) *repentance, regret*.

μετα-μέλπομαι, Dep. *to sing* or *dance among*

μετα-μελητικός, ή, όν, *full of repentance, repentant*.

μετα-μίγνυμι, f. -μίξω, *to mix among, confound with*.

μετα-μίσγω, = μεταμίγνυμι.

μετα-μορφόομαι, Pass. (μετά, μορφή) *to be transformed*: *to be transfigured*.

μετ-αμφιάζω, f. σω, *to change* another's *dress, to transform*: Med. *to change one's own dress*.

μετ-ᾰμώνιος, ον, (μετά, ἄνεμος) *borne by the wind*: *vain, idle, bootless*; μεταμώνια βάζειν to talk *idly*.

μετ-αναγιγνώσκω, *to persuade* one *to change his purpose*:—Pass. *to be changed in purpose*.

μετα-ναιετάω, *to dwell with*.

μετα-ναιέτης, ου, ὁ, (μετά, ναίω) *a settler in a new place, a wanderer*.

μετ-ανάστᾰσις, ή, (μετανίσταμαι) *migration*.

μετα-νάστης, ου, ὁ, (μετά, ναίω) *one who has changed his home, a wanderer, emigrant*, opp. to an original inhabitant. Hence

μετανάστιος, ον, *like a wanderer, wandering*.

μετανάστρια, fem. of μετανάστης.

μετανεγνώσθην, aor. 1 pass. of μεταγιγνώσκω.

μετ-ανέστηκα, -ανέστην, pf. and aor. 2 of μετανίστημι.

μετα-νίσσομαι, Dep. *to go over, pass over to the other side*. II. trans. *to go after, pursue*.

μετ-ανίστημι, f. -στήσω, *to remove* another *from* his *country* II. in Pass, with intr. tenses of Act.

aor. 2 *μετανέστην*, pf. **μετανέστηκα**, *to move off elsewhere, to migrate.*

μετα-νοέω, f. *ήσω*, *to perceive afterwards* or *too late.* 2. *to change one's mind* or *opinion.* 3. *to repent.* Hence

μετάνοια, *ἡ*, *after-thought: change of mind on reflection, repentance.*

μετ-αντλέω, f. *ήσω*, *to draw from one vessel into another.*

μεταξύ, Adv. (*μετά*) Adv. of Place, *betwixt, between; τὸ μεταξύ the space between*:—of Time, *between-whiles, afterwards.* II. as Prep., with gen., *between*:—of Time, *during.*

μετα-παιδεύω, f. *σω*, *to educate differently.*

μετα-παύομαι, Pass. *to rest between times.* Hence

μετα-παυσωλή, *ἡ*, *rest between times.*

μετα-πείθω, f. *σω*, *to change by persuasion, win over.*

μετα-πειράομαι, Dep. *to try in a different way.*

μεταπεμπτέος, *α, ον*, *to be sent for*: and

μετάπεμπτος, *ον*, *sent for*: verb. Adjectives from

μετα-πέμπω, f. *ψω*, *to send for, summon*, Lat. *arcessere*: the Med. is more frequent in same sense.

μετα-πέτομαι, f. *-πτήσομαι*: aor. 2 *-επτάμην*: Dep. *to fly away.*

μετα-πηδάω, f. *ήσομαι*, *to leap from one to another.*

μετα-πίπτω, f. *-πεσοῦμαι*: aor. 2 *-έπεσον*: pf. *πέπτωκα*:—*to fall differently, undergo a change, change suddenly.* 2, of votes, *to change sides.* 3. of conditions, *to change for the worse, to decline*: but also *to change for the better.*

μετα-πλάσσω, f. *-πλάσω* [ᾰ], *to mould differently, remodel.*

μετα-ποιέω, f. *ήσω*, *to remodel, cast anew, alter*:—Med. *to pretend to, make pretence of* a thing, c. gen.

μετα-ποίνιος, *ον*, (*μετά, ποινή*) *punishing afterwards.*

μετα-πορεύομαι, fut. med. *-εύσομαι*: aor. 1 pass. *μετεπορεύθην*: Dep.:—*to go after* or *in quest of*: *to follow up, punish.* II. *to emigrate.*

μεταπρεπής, *ές*, *distinguished among.* From

μετα-πρέπω, only used in pres. and impf. *to be conspicuous* or *distinguished among.*

μεταπτάμενος, aor. 2 part. of *μεταπέτομαι.*

μετα-πτοιέω, f. *ήσω*, (*μετά, πτοιέω*) intr. *to cower* or *crouch from fear.*

μετα-πύργιον, *τό*, (*μετά, πύργος*) *the wall between the towers, the curtain.*

μετ-ᾰρίθμιος, *ον*, (*μετά, ἀριθμός*) *counted among.*

μεταρ-ρίπτω, *ψω*, *to turn upside down.*

μεταρ-ρυθμίζω, f. *ίσω*, *to change the form* or *fashion* of a thing, *to remodel*: esp. *to reform, correct.*

μεταρσιο-λεσχέω, f. *ήσω*, (*μετάρσιος, λέσχης*) *to talk on lofty subjects.* Hence

μεταρσιολεσχία, *ἡ*, *a talking on lofty subjects.*

μετάρσιος, *ον*, also *α, ον*, Dor. **πεδάρσιος**: (*μεταίρω*) *raised aloft, high in air*: metaph. *scattered to the winds.* 2. *floating in air, unsteady*: also *airy, empty.* II. like *μετέωρος*, *out at sea.* Hence

μεταρσιόω, f. *ώσω*, *to raise aloft, lift up.*

μετα-σεύομαι Ep. **μετασ-σεύομαι**: Ep. aor. 2 *μετεσσύμην*, 3 sing. *μετέσσῦτο*: Pass.:—*to go along with.* II. *to rush after*: c. acc. *to rush upon.*

μετα-σκευάζω, f. *άσω*, *to fashion differently*: *to transform*: *to disguise.*

μετα-σπάω, f. *άσω* [ᾰ], *to draw over from one side to another, persuade, convince.*

μετασπόμενος, aor. 2 part. med. of *μεθέπω.*

μετασπών, aor. 2 part. act. of *μεθέπω.*

μέτασσαι, *αἱ*, *lambs coming midway between* the *πρόγονοι* and *ἕρσαι*, *the middle-born lambs, summer lambs.* (From *μετά*, as *περισσός* from *περί*.)

μετασ-σεύομαι, Ep. for *μετασεύομαι.*

μετασταθῶ, aor. 1 subj. pass. of *μεθίστημι.*

μεταστάς, *ᾶσα, άν*, aor. 2 part. of *μεθίστημι.*

μετάστᾰσις, *εως*, *ἡ*, (*μεθίσταμαι*) *a removal from one place to another*; *μετάστασις ἡλίου* an eclipse. 2. *μετάστασις βίου departure* from life: absol. *decease.* II. *a changing, change.* 2. *a change of political constitution, revolution.*

μετα-στείχω, *to go after* or *in quest of, pursue.*

μετα-στέλλομαι, Dep. *to send for, summon.*

μετα-στένω, *to bewail* or *lament afterwards*: so also in Med.

μεταστήσας, **μεταστήσω**, aor. 1 part., and fut., of *μεθίστημι.*

μετα-στοιχεί or *-ί*, Adv. (*μετά, στοῖχος*) *in a line one after* another.

μετα-στονᾰχίζω, *to sigh* or *wail afterwards.*

μετα-στρᾰτοπεδεύω, and Med. **-εύομαι**, *to shift one's camp.*

μεταστρᾰφήσομαι, fut. pass. of *μεταστρέφω.*

μεταστρεφθείς, aor. 1 pass. part. of *μεταστρέφω.*

μετα-στρέφω, f. *ψω*, *to turn about, turn round*:—Pass., aor. 1 *μετεστρέφθην*, aor. 2 *μετεστράφην* [ᾰ], *to turn oneself round*, whether *to rally* or *to flee*; often in aor. 1 part. *μεταστρεφθείς.* 2. *to turn round upon, retort.* 3. *to change, alter.* II. intr. *to change one's course.* 2. *to care for, regard*, c. gen. 3. *to turn round upon, to visit with vengeance.*

μετασχεῖν, aor. 2 inf. of *μετέχω.*

μετάσχεσις, *εως*, *ἡ*, (*μετέχω*) *a participation, sharing in.*

μετα-σχημᾰτίζω, f. *ίσω* Att. *ιῶ*, (*μετά, σχῆμα*) *to change the form of, alter, transform.*

μετα-τάσσω Att. *-ττω*, f. *σω*, *to change the order of, arrange differently*:—Med. *to change one's order of battle*: *to go over to* the enemy.

μετα-τίθημι, f. *-θήσω*: aor. 1 *μετέθηκα*:—*to place among.* II. *to place differently, change, alter*:—Med. *to change for oneself*: *to change one's opinion, retract*; *μετατίθεσθαι τὴν γνώμην to change to* a new opinion.

μετα-τίκτω, f. *-τέξομαι*, *to bring forth after.*

μετα-τρέπω, f. *ψω*, *to turn round*:—Med. *to turn*

oneself round, turn back. 2. *to turn and look after, to care for, regard, take care of.*

μετα-τρέχω, f. -θρέξομαι aor. 2 μετέδρᾰμον (from obsol. δρέμω) :—*to run after.*

μετα-τροπᾰλίζομαι, Pass. (μετά, τρέπω) *to keep turning about*, in a retreat.

μετατροπή, ἡ, (μετατρέπω) *a turning round* or *back: a visiting, vengeance for* a thing.

μετατροπία, ἡ, = μετατροπή.

μετάτροπος, ον, (μετατρέπω) *turning round* or *about:* of an enemy, *turning round upon;* ἔργα μετάτροπα deeds *that are visited with vengeance.*

μετα-τρωπάω, f. ήσω, poët. for μετατρέπω.

μετ-αυγάζω Dor. -πεδ–, *to look about for.*

μετ-αυδάω, f. ήσω, *to speak among, to address*, c. dat. plur. II. later, *to accost, address*, c. acc.

μετ-αῦθις Ion. -αῦτις, Adv. *afterwards, thereupon.*

μετ-αυτίκα, Adv. *forthwith, thereupon.*

μετα-φέρω, f. μετοίσω, *to carry from one place to another, transfer.* 2. *to change, alter: to pervert:* —Pass. *to change one's course.*

μετά-φημι, impf. or aor. 2 μετέφην, *to speak among.*

μεταφορά, ἡ, (μεταφέρω) *a carrying from one place to another.* II. in Rhetoric, *a transferring to one word the sense of another, a metaphor, trope.*

μετα-φορέω, = μεταφέρω.

μετα-φράζομαι, f. σομαι, Med. *to consider after.*

μετά-φρενον, τό, (μετά, φρήν) properly, *the part behind the midriff* (φρένες), *the broad of the back.*

μετα-φωνέω, f. ήσω, *to speak among, address.*

μετα-χειρίζω, f. ίσω, or more often as Dep. **μεταχειρίζομαι**, f. ίσομαι Att. ιοῦμαι: aor. 1 μετεχειρισάμην :—*to have in one's hands, handle.* 2. *to take in hand, manage*, Lat. *administrare;* μεταχειρίζεσθαι πρᾶγμα *to conduct* an affair. 3. *to have in hand, pursue, practice*, Lat. *exercere.* 4. *to handle, treat* in a certain way.

μετα-χρόνιος, α, ον, = μετάχρονος. II. in Poets, = μετάρσιος, *aloft, on high.*

μετά-χρονος, ον, (μετά, χρόνος) *after the time, done afterwards.*

μετα-χωρέω, f. ήσω, *to go to another place, withdraw: to migrate*, of birds of passage.

μετα-ψαίρω, *to brush against.*

μετέᾱσι, Ep. for μέτεισι, 3 pl. of **μέτειμι.**

μετέβᾰλον, aor. 2 of μεταβάλλω.

μετέβην, aor. 2 of μεταβαίνω

μετ-εγγράφω, f. ψω, *to enroll* or *enter on a new register*, in fut. 2 pass. μετεγγραφήσεται.

μετέγνων, aor. 2 of μεταγιγνώσκω.

μετέδοξα, aor. 1 of μεταδοκέω.

μετέδωκα, aor. 1 of μεταδίδωμι.

μετέειπε, **μετέειπον**, Ion. and Ep. for μετεῖπε, etc.

μετέῃσι, Ion. for μετῇ, 3 sing. subj. of μέτειμι.

μετέθηκα, aor. 1 of μετατίθημι.

μετείληφα, -ημμαι, pf. act. and pass. of μεταλαμβάνω.

μέτ-ειμι, f. μετέσομαι Ep. -έσσομαι: (μετά, εἰμί sum) :—*to be among, live with, associate with.* II. impers., μέτεστί τοί τινος *I have a share* of a thing; part. neut. absol., μετόν *there being a share* or *claim:* —sometimes with a nom., μέτεστ' πᾶσι τὸ ἴσον equality *is shared* by all.

μέτ-ειμι, (μετά, εἶμι ibo) *to go between* or *among.* II. *to go after* or *behind, follow* 2. *to go after* or *for, fetch.* 3. *to pursue, visit with vengeance.* 4. *to go to, approach, draw near to.* III. *to pass over, go over to the other side.*

μετ-εἶπον Ep. μετέειπον, used as aor. 2 of μετάφημι: (μετά, εἶπον) :—*to speak among.* 2. *to speak thereafter, afterwards.*

μετείς, Ion. for μεθείς, aor. 2 part. of **μεθίημι.**

μετεισάμενος, Ep. aor. 1 part. med. of μέτειμι (εἶμι ibo).

μετείω, Ep. for μετῶ, subj. of μέτειμι (εἰμί sum).

μετ-εκβαίνω, *to step out of one thing into another.*

μετεκίαθον, impf. of μετακῑάθω.

μετέλᾰβον, aor. 2 of μεταλαμβάνω.

μετέλᾰχον, aor. 2 of μεταλαγχάνω.

μετελεύσομαι, fut. of μετέρχομαι.

μέτελθε, **μετελθών**, aor. 2 imperat. and part. of μετέρχομαι.

μετέμᾰθον, aor. 2 of μεταμανθάνω.

μετ-εμβαίνω, f. -βήσομαι, *to go on board another* ship.

μετ-εμβῐβάζω, f. -βιβάσω Att. -βιβῶ, Causal of μετεμβαίνω, *put on board another* ship.

μετέμελε, **μετεμέλησε**, impf. and aor. 1 of μεταμέλει.

μετέμμεναι, Ep. pres. int. of μέτειμι (εἰμί sum).

μετ-έμφῠτος, ον, (μετά, ἐμφύω) *engrafted afresh.*

μετ-ενδύω, f. δύσω, *to put other clothes on* a person. II. Med., with aor. 2 **μετ-ενέδυν**, *to put on other clothes.*

μετενήνοχα, Att. pf. of μεταφέρω.

μετενίσσετο, 3 sing. impf. of μετανίσσομαι.

μετ-εννέπω, *to speak among.*

μετ-εξαιρέομαι, Med. *to take out and put elsewhere.*

μετ-εξανίσταμαι, Pass. *to move from one place to another.*

μετ-εξ-έτεροι, αι, α, (μετά, ἐξ, ἕτεροι) *some others.*

μετέον, Ion. for μετόν, neut. part. of μέτειμι (εἰμί sum)

μετ-έπειτα, Adv. *afterwards, thereafter.*

μετέπεσον, aor. 2 of μεταπίπτω

μετ-έρχομαι, f. μετελεύσομαι: Dep., with aor 2 act. -ῆλθον, pf. -ελήλυθα :—*to come among.* 2 *to go between the ranks* 3. *to go in among, attack.* II. *to go to another place, go away.* III. c. acc. *to go after, to go to seek, go in quest of:* hence *to seek for, aim at* 2. of things, *to go after, attend to, manage.* 3. *to pursue, visit as an avenger:* in legal sense, *to prosecute.* 4. *to approach with prayers, supplicate.* 5. *to court* or *woo.*

μετέσσῠτο, 3 sing. Ep. aor. 2 of μετασεύομαι.

μετέσχηκα, pf. of μετέχω.

μετ-εύχομαι, f. -εύξομαι, Dep. *to change one's wish or prayer, to wish something else.*

μετέφη, 3 sing. impf. or aor. 2 of μετάφημι.

μετ-έχω, f. μεθέξω, *to partake of, have a share of*, c. gen.: also c. acc. rei, μετέχειν ἴσον (sc. μέρος) ἀγαθῶν τινι *to enjoy* an equal *share* of good with another.

μετέω, Ion. and Ep. subj. of μέτειμι (εἰμί *sum*).

μετεωρίζω, f. ίσω, (μετέωρος) *to raise to a height, raise, lift up*: Pass., μετεωρισθεὶς ἐν τῷ πελάγει *keeping out* on the *high* sea. II. metaph. *to buoy up* or *excite*: *to buoy up with false hopes.*

μετεωρο-κοπέω, f. ήσω, (μετέωρος, κόπτω) *to prate about the heavenly bodies.*

μετεωρο-λέσχης, ου, ὁ, = μετεωρο-λόγος.

μετεωρολογέω, f. ήσω, (μετεωρολόγος) *to talk of high things*, or *of the heavenly bodies.* Hence

μετεωρολογία, ἡ, *a treatise on the heavenly bodies.*

μετεωρο-λόγος, ον, (μετέωρος, λέγω) *talking* or *treating of the heavenly bodies.*

μετ-έωρος Ep. **μετ-ήορος**, ον, (μετά, ἑώρα or αἰώρα) *suspended in mid air, aloft, raised on high, high in air.* 2. of a ship, *on the high sea, out at sea.* II. metaph. of the mind, *excited, in suspense*, Lat. *spe erectus*: hence *wavering, fluctuating.* III. τὰ μετέωρα, *things in the air, the heavenly bodies, meteors, natural phenomena*; generally, *abstruse, lofty* speculations.

μετεωρο-σοφιστής, ὁ, *a meteorological philosopher.*

μετεωρο-φέναξ, ᾶκος, ὁ, *a meteorological quack.*

μετήγαγον, aor. 2 of μετάγω.

μετῆλθον Ep. **μετήλυθον**, aor. 2 of μετέρχομαι.

μετήλλαξα, aor. 1 of μεταλλάσσω.

μετ-ηνέμιος, ον, (μετά, ἄνεμος) *swift as the wind.*

μετ-ήορος, older Ep. form for μετέωρος.

μετῆρα, aor. 1 of μεταίρω.

μετήσεσθαι, Ion. for μεθήσεσθαι, fut. inf. med. of μεθίημι.

μετηύδων, ας, α, impf. of μεταυδάω.

μετίει, Ion. 3 sing. impf. of μεθίημι; also 3 sing. pres.

μετίετο, Ion. 3 sing. impf. med. of μεθίημι.

μετ-ίημι, μετ-ίστημι, Ion. for μεθ-.

μετ-ίσχω, = μετέχω.

μετοικεσία, ἡ, = μετοικία I. 2. *the Captivity* of the Jews. From

μετοικέω, f. ήσω, (μέτοικος) *to change one's abode, remove to* a place, c. acc.: c. dat. loci, *to settle in.* absol. *to be a μέτοικος* or *settler.* Hence

μετοίκησις, εως, ἡ, = μετοικία I: and

μετοικία, ἡ, *change of abode, migration.* II. *a settling as μέτοικος, a settlement: society.* 2. *the condition* of a μέτοικος or *sojourner.*

μετ-οικίζω, f. ίσω Att. ιῶ, *to lead to another abode*: —Pass. *to be led to another country, to emigrate.*

μετοικικός, ή, όν, (μέτοικος) *of* or *for a μέτοικος*: τὸ μετοικικὸν *the list of μέτοικοι* or *aliens.*

μετοίκιον, τό, *the tax of twelve drachmae paid by the μέτοικοι* at Athens. From

μέτ-οικος, ον, (μετά, οἶκος) *changing one's abode, settling elsewhere.* II. at Athens, μέτοικος, ὁ and ἡ, *a foreign settler, an alien who was suffered to settle in the city* on payment of a tax (μετοίκιον), yet without enjoying civic rights, Lat. *inquilinus.*

μετοικο-φύλαξ, ᾰκος, ὁ, ἡ, *the guardian of the μέτοικοι* or *aliens* at Athens.

μετ-οίχομαι, f. -οιχήσομαι, Dep. *to have gone after, to be gone in pursuit.* 2. *to have gone among* or *through.*

μετοίσω, fut. of μεταφέρω.

μετ-οκλάζω, f. σω, *to keep shifting one's knees*, of a coward crouching in ambush.

μετ-ονομάζω, f. σω, *to change the name, call by a new name*:—Pass. *to take a new name.*

μετ-όπιν, Adv. = μετόπισθε.

μετ-όπισθε, and before a vowel -θεν, Adv. of Place *from behind, backwards*:—of Time, *after, afterwards.* II. as Prep. with gen. *behind.*

μετοπωρινός, ή, όν, *of* or *like the end of autumn, verging on winter, autumnal.* From

μετ-όπωρον, τό, (μετά, ὀπώρα) *the season after ὀπώρα, late autumn*; cp. φθινόπωρον.

μετ-ορμίζω, Ion. for μεθορμίζω.

μετ-όρχιον τό, (μετά, ὄρχος) *the space between rows of vines.*

μετ-ουσία, ἡ, (μετοῦσα part. fem. of μέτειμι *intersum*) *participation, communion: possession, enjoyment.*

μετοχή, ἡ, (μετέχω) *a partaking of, communion.*

μετ-οχλίζω, f. ίσω, (μετά, ὀχλος) *to remove by a lever, hoist out of the way.*

μετοχλίσσειε, Ep. 3 sing. aor. 1 opt. of μετοχλίζω.

μέτοχος, ον, (μετέχω) *partaking of*:—as Subst. *a partaker, partner, accomplice.*

μετρέω, f. ήσω, (μέτρον) *to measure.* I. of Space, *to measure*, i. e. *pass over*, Lat. *metiri, emetiri*:—Med., μετρεῖσθαι ἴχνη *to measure* the footmarks with the eyes. II. of Number, *to count: to measure out, dole out.* 2. of Size, Value, etc., *to measure, estimate, compute.* Hence

μέτρημα, ατος, τό, *that which is measured out*: 1. *a measured distance.* 2. *a measure, dole.*

μέτρησις, ἡ, (μετρέω) *a measuring, measurement.*

μετρητής, οῦ, ὁ, (μετρέω) = ἀμφορεύς, Lat. *metrēta*, at Athens the common liquid measure, holding 12 χόες, or 144 κοτύλαι, about 9 gallons English: the Roman amphora held ⅔ of a μετρητής.

μετρητός, ή, όν, (μετρέω) *measured, measurable.*

μετριάζω f. σω, (μέτριος) *to be moderate*: *to be of an even temper, be calm, unruffled.* II. trans. *to moderate.*

μετριοπαθέω, f. ήσω, *to be moderate* or *merciful towards.* From

μετριο-πᾰθής, ές, (μέτριος, παθεῖν) *bearing moderately.*

μετριο-πότης, ου, ὁ, (μέτριος, ΠΟ- Root of some tenses of πίνω) *a moderate drinker, moderate in potations*: Sup. μετριοποτίστατος.

μέτριος, *α, ον*, also *ος, ον*, (*μέτρον*) *within measure, moderate*: of Size, *of average* or *ordinary height*. II. of Number, *few*. III. of Degree, *holding to the mean, moderate*: of *middle condition* or *rank*: *τὸ μέτριον the mean*. 2. *tolerable*. 3. of Persons, *moderate, temperate*. also *fair, reasonable*. 4. *suitable*.—The neut. *μέτριον, μέτρια* are often used. Adv. = *μετρίως*.

μετρίως, see *μέτριος*.

μετριότης, *ητος, ἡ*, (*μέτριος*) *moderation*.

μετρίως, Adv of *μέτριος, moderately, in due limits* or *measure*. 2. *modestly, temperately*: *on fair terms*.—Comp. *μετριώτερον*, Sup. *-ώτατα*.

ΜΕ'ΤΡΟΝ, *τό, a measure or rule; a standard*. 2. *the contents* or *thing measured*, as well as *the measure itself*. 3. *any space measured* or *measurable*; *μέτρον ὅρμου the size* of the harbour; *μέτρον ἥβης the full measure* or *prime* of youth. II. *the mean between two extremes, proportion, due measure: fitness*. III. *metre*, opp. to *μέλος* (tune) and *ῥυθμός* (time).

μετῴκισα, aor. 1 of *μετοικίζω*.

μετ-ωνυμία, *ἡ*, (*μέτα, ὄνομα*) *change of name*: in Rhetoric, *the use of one word for another, metonymy*.

μετ-ωπηδόν, Adv. (*μέτωπον*) *with the forehead foremost, fronting*: of ships, *in line*; opp. to *ἐπὶ κέρως*, in column.

μετωπίδιος, *ον*, (*μέτωπον*) *on* or *of the forehead*.

μετ-ώπιον, *τό*, = *μέτωπον, the forehead*.

μέτ-ωπον, *τό*, (*μετά, ὤψ*) *the space between the eyes, the forehead, front*. II. *the front* or *fore part* of anything: *the front* or *face* of a building: *the front* of an army.

μετωπο-σώφρων, *ον*, gen. *ονος*, (*μέτωπον, σώφρων*) *with ingenuous countenance*.

μεῦ, Ep. and Ion. gen. of *ἐγώ*.

ΜΕ'ΧΡΙ, rarely **μέχρις** even before a vowel: I. Prep. with gen. *until, unto, to a given point*, 1. of Place, *μέχρι θαλάσσης as far as* the sea. 2. of Time, *τέο μέχρις until* when? *μέχρις οὗ; μέχρις ὅσου; until* when? how long? *μέχρι τινός for* a space; *μέχρι τοῦδε until* now. II. in Ion., *μέχρι οὗ* is sometimes followed by another gen., as, *μέχρι οὗ ὀκτὼ πύργων, as far as* eight towers, instead of *μέχρις οὗ ὀκτὼ πύργοι εἰσίν*. III. Conjunct. *until*, with indic., *μέχρι ἕως ἐγένετο till* morning came; with *ἄν* and subj., *μέχρι ἂν τοῦτο ἴδωμεν till* we see this: also, *μέχρι οὗ* in same sense.

ΜΗ', Adv. *not*, used where the Negation depends on some Condition, either expressed or implied, while *οὐ* denies absolutely: *μή* expresses that one *thinks* a thing *is not*, *οὐ* that it *is not*: hence *μή* always follows *εἰ, ἐάν, ἤν, ὅταν, ἐπειδάν, ἕως ἄν*, because these speak of a thing *not as a fact, but as a supposition*: whereas *ἐπεί, ἐπειδή* are joined with *οὐ*, because they refer to *a fact*. 2. *μή* also is used after the final Conjunctions *ἵνα, ὡς, ὅπως, ὥστε*, because these are in their nature contingent, as, *ὡς μή .. ὄλωνται that they perish not*. 3. with infin., as, *τὸ μὴ πυθέσθαι μ' ἀλγύνειεν ἄν* the *not*-knowing would grieve me. 4. with the Participle, as, *μὴ ἀπενείκας* = *εἰ μὴ ἀπήνεικε*, if he had *not* carried away. II. *μή* is freq. in INDEPENDENT clauses containing *a command*, when, like Lat. *ne*, it stands first in the sentence: 1. with the pres. imperat, *μὴ λέγε*. 2. with the subjunctive aorist, *μὴ λέξῃς*. 3. with the optat. aor. to express a *wish*, *μὴ γὰρ ὅγ' ἔλθοι ἀνήρ* O that he may *not* come!

B. **μή**, CONJUNCTION, *that not, lest*, Lat. *ne*: I. with aor. subjunct. subjoined to a Verb in pres. or fut., as, *φεύγω μὴ ληφθῶ* I flee *lest* I may be caught. II. with optat. after principal Verb in past tense, as, *ἔφυγον μὴ ληφθείην* I fled *lest* I might be caught. III. after Verbs expressing *fear*, as, *δέδοικα μὴ γένηται*, Lat. *vereor ne fiat*, I fear *lest* it happen, i. e. I fear *it will* happen.—For this subj., the Att. also use indic. fut. IV. *μή* is used with inf. after vehement negations or affirmations; *ἴστω Ζεὺς μὴ μὲν χεῖρ' ἐπενεῖκαι* Jove be witness *that* I have *not* laid on hand: so after negat. wishes, *δὸς μὴ Ὀδυσσῆα οἴκαδ' ἱκέσθαι*. V. *μή* is used after all Verbs which have a negative sense, such as *ἀρνεῖσθαι, κωλύειν, εἴργειν, φεύγειν*, as, *ἀρνεῖσθαι τὸ μὴ ποιεῖν* to deny the doing a thing; also after Nouns of like sense, as *κώλυμα*; or Adverbs, as *ἐμποδών*.

C. As INTERROGAT., in direct questions, where a negative answer is expected, *ἦ μή που .. φάσθε; surely ye did not* say? 2. *μή* is also used with the indicative subjoined to another Verb, when it may be expressed by *whether*, as, *δείδω μὴ δὴ πάντα νημερτέα εἶπεν* I fear as to *whether* she has spoken all too true, i. e. I fear she has spoken all too true.

μὴ γάρ, an elliptic phrase, used in emphatic denial, *no certainly*, Lat. *nullo modo*, where an imperat. or optat. Verb must be supplied from the foregoing passage to which the denial refers, as, *μὴ λεγέτω τὸ ὄνομα*, let him *not* say the name; Answ. *μὴ γὰρ* [*λεγέτω*], *no*, certainly.

μή γε, *not at least*, strengthd. for *μη*.

μηδ-ἀμά and **μηδ-ἀμῆ**, Adv. of *μηδαμός, nowhere*. II. *in nowise, not at all*.

μηδἄμόθεν, Adv. (*μηδαμός*) *from no place*; *μηδαμόθεν ἄλλοθεν from no* other *place*.

μηδἄμόθι, Adv. *nowhere*: and

μηδαμοῖ, Adv. *nowhither*. From

μηδ-ἄμός, *ή, όν*, for *μηδὲ ἀμός, not even one not any one, no one, none*. Hence

μηδἄμοῦ, Adv. *nowhere*.

μηδἄμῶς, Adv. of *μηδαμός, in no way, not at all*.

μη-δέ, Adv. (*μή, δέ*) *but not, and not, nor*, Lat. *neque, nec*. 2. at the beginning of two following clauses, *μηδέ .. μηδέ ..*, *neither .. nor ..*, Lat. *neque .. neque ..* II. strengthening the negative, which is always the sense when joined with a single word or phrase, *not even*, Lat. *ne .. quidem*.

μηδ-είς, *μηδ-εμίἄ, μηδ-έν*, gen. *μηδενός, μηδεμιᾶς*,

μηδενός, etc.:—declined like εἷς μία ἕν, (μηδέ, εἷς) *not even one, no one, none*, Lat. *nullus*. 2. ὁ or ἡ μηδέν (sc. ὤν, οὖσα), one who is a *mere nothing, a nobody*:—τὸ μηδέν *a nothing, a useless* or *worthless person*. 3. neut. μηδέν often as Adv., *not at all, by no means*.

μηδέ-ποτε, Adv. *not* or *nor at any time, never*.

μηδέ-πω, Adv. *nor as yet* or *not as yet*.

μηδε-πώποτε, Adv. *not yet at any time, never yet*.

μηδ-έτερος, α, ον, (μηδέ, ἕτερος) *neither of the two*.

μηδ-ετέρωσε, Adv. *to neither side*.

μὴ δή, *nay do not*.

Μηδίζω, f. σω, (Μῆδος) *to imitate the Medes in manners, language*, or *dress*: esp. *to side with the Medes*, opp. to Ἑλληνίζω.

Μηδικός, ή, όν, (Μῆδος) *Median*: τὰ Μηδικά (sc. πράγματα) *the Median affairs*, esp. *the great Median* or *Persian war*. II. Μηδικὴ ποία, *herba Medica*, a kind of *clover, lucerne*.

Μηδίς, ίδος, ἡ, fem. of Μηδικός, *a Median woman*.

Μηδισμός, ὁ, (Μηδίζω) *a leaning towards the Medes, the being in their interest*.

Μηδο-κτόνος, ον, (Μῆδος, κτείνω) *Mede-slaying*.

μήδομαι, f. μήσομαι: aor. 1 ἐμησάμην: Dep.: (μῆδος):—*to devise, resolve, counsel, advise*. 2. *to plot, scheme, bring about, contrive*.

μηδ-οπότερος, α, ον, (μηδέ, ὁπότερος) *neither of the two*.

ΜΗ'ΔΟΣ, εος, τό, only used in plur. μήδεα, *counsels, plans, schemes: cunning, craft*. 2. like μῆτις, *care, anxiety*; σὰ μήδεα *care* for thee. II. in pl. also, like Lat. *virilia, the genitals*.

μηδ-οστισοῦν, neut. μηδοτιοῦν, for μηδὲ ὅστις οὖν, μηδὲ ὅ τι οὖν, *no one whatever, nothing whatever*.

μηδοσύνη, ἡ, (μῆδος) *counsel, prudence*.

Μηδο-φόνος, ον, = Μηδοκτόνος.

μηθείς, neut. μηθέν, a later form for μηδείς, μηδέν.

ΜΗΚΑ'ΟΜΑΙ, Dep., with aor. 2 part. μακών: Ep. pf. with pres. sense, μέμηκα, part, μεμηκώς, shortd. fem. μεμᾰκυῖα (so βέβρῡχα, μέμῡκα from βρυχάομαι, μυκάομαι): also impf., formed from pf., ἐμέμηκον:—*to bleat*, of sheep: of fawns and hares, *to scream, shriek, cry*.

μηκάς, άδος, ἡ, (μηκάομαι) fem. Adj. *bleating*, epith. of she-goats: as Subst. *a bleater, she-goat*.

μηκ-έτι, Adv. (μή, ἔτι) *no more, no longer, no further*.

μήκιστος, η, ον, Dor. and Att. **μάκιστος**, [ᾱ], α, ον, (μῆκος), Sup. of μακρός, but formed from μῆκος, as αἴσχιστος from αἶσχος, *the longest, tallest*, or generally, *greatest*. II. neut. μήκιστον, pl. μήκιστα, as Adv., *for a very long time* or *in the highest degree: very far*:—also *at length, at last*.

ΜΗ'ΚΟΣ, εος, τό, *length*: also *height, tallness, stature*. 2. of Time, *a long space, length*. 3. of Size or Degree, *greatness, magnitude*. II. τὸ μῆκος or μῆκος, absol. as Adv., *in length* or *greatness*.

μή-κοτε, Adv., Ion. for μήποτε.

μηκύνω, f. -ῠνῶ Ion. -ῠνέω: Dor. **μᾱκύνω**: (μῆκος):—*to lengthen, prolong*. 2. *to protract: to delay, put off*; μηκύνειν λόγον *to speak at length*; also without λόγον, *to be lengthy* or *prolix*. 3. μηκύνειν βοήν *to raise a loud* cry. 4. Med. ἐμᾱκύναντο κόλοσσον *erected a tall* statue.

ΜΗ'ΚΩΝ Dor. **μάκων**, ωνος, ἡ, *the poppy*. 2. *the head of a poppy*. 3. *poppy-seed*, prepared for food.

μηλέα, ἡ, (μῆλον) *an apple-tree*, Lat. *malus*.

μήλειος, ον, also α, ον, (μῆλον) *of* or *belonging to a sheep*.

Μηλιακός, ή, όν, *of* or *for Melis* or *Malia*.

Μηλιάδες or **Μηλίδης**, αἱ, (μῆλον A or B) *nymphs of the flocks* or *of the fruit-trees*. 2. *nymphs of Melis* or *Malia* in Trachis: cf. Μηλιεύς.

Μηλιεύς, έως, ὁ, *an inhabitant of Melis* or *Malia* in Trachis. II. as Adj., Μηλιεὺς κόλπος *the Maliac gulf*.

μήλῐνος, η, ον, Dor. **μάλινος**, α, ον, (μῆλον B) *of an apple-tree*.

Μήλιος, α, ον, *of* or *from the island of Melos, Melian*.

Μηλίς, ίδος, ἡ, with or without γῆ, *Melis* or *Malia* in Trachis.

μηλο-βοτήρ, ῆρος, ὁ, and **μηλο-βότης**, ου, ὁ, Dor. -τας, (μῆλον, βόσκω) *a shepherd*.

μηλό-βοτος, ον, (μῆλον, βόσκω) *grazed by sheep*.

μηλο-δόκος, ον, (μῆλον, δέχομαι) *sheep-receiving*.

μηλο-θύτης, [ῠ], ου, ὁ, (μῆλον, θύω) *a sacrificer of sheep, a priest*; βωμὸς μηλοθύτης a *sacrificial* altar.

μηλολόνθη, ἡ, a kind of *beetle* or *cockchafer*.

ΜΗ'ΛΟΝ, ου, τό, (A) *a sheep* or (sometimes) *a goat*: ἄρσενα μῆλα *rams, wethers*: the pl. μῆλα means *flocks of sheep* or *goats, small cattle*, opp. to βόες.

ΜΗ'ΛΟΝ, ου, τό, (B) Dor. **ΜΑ'ΛΟΝ**, Lat. *MALUM, an apple*; generally, *any tree-fruit*, as, μῆλον Κυδώνιον *the quince*, μῆλον Περσικόν *the peach*, μῆλον Μηδικόν *the orange* or *citron*. II. metaph. in pl. of a *woman's breasts*; or of *the cheeks*, Lat. *mālae*.

μηλο-νομεύς, έως, or **μηλο-νόμης**, ου, Dor. -μας, α, ὁ, (μῆλον A, νέμω) *a shepherd, goatherd, herdsman*.

μηλο-νόμος, ον, (μῆλον A, νέμω) *feeding sheep* or *goats*.

μηλο-πάρειος, ον, Dor. **μαλοπάρῃος**, (μῆλον B, παρειά) *apple-cheeked, ruddy-cheeked*.

μηλό-σκοπος, ον, (μῆλον B, σκοπέω) *fit for watching sheep from*.

μηλό-σπορος, ον, (μῆλον B, σπείρω) *planted with fruit-trees*.

μηλοσ-σόος, ον, poët. for μηλοσόος, (μῆλον A, σώζω) *sheep-protecting*.

μηλοσφᾰγέω, f. ήσω, *to slay sheep*; ἱερὰ μηλοσφαγεῖν *to offer sheep* in sacrifice. From

μηλο-σφάγος, ον, (μῆλον A, σφάζω) *slaying sheep*.

μηλο-τρόφος, ον, (μῆλον A, τρέφω) *sheep-feeding*.

μηλ-οῦχος, ὁ, (μῆλον B. II, ἔχω) *a girdle that confines the breasts*.

μηλο-φόνος, ον, (μῆλον A, *φένω) *sheep-slaying.*

μηλοφορέω, f. ήσω, *to carry apples.* From

μηλο-φόρος, ον, (μῆλον B, φέρω) *bearing apples.*

μηλο-φύλαξ, ἄκος, ὁ, and ἡ, (μῆλον A or B, φύλαξ) *one who watches sheep* or *apples.* [ῠ]

μηλωτή, ἡ, (μῆλον A) *a sheep's skin.*

μήλ-ωψ, οπος, ὁ, ἡ, (μῆλον B, ὤψ) *looking like an apple, yellow, golden*

μὴ μάν, *nay verily.*

μὴ μέν, Ion. for μὴ μάν.

μήν, Dor. and Ep. **μάν**, a Particle strengthening affirmation, *yea, indeed, verily, truly, in sooth;* ἦ μήν or ἦ μάν, in *very* truth, *yea verily,* used at the beginning of an oath: καὶ μήν, Lat. *et vero, and yet, nay more:* ἀλλὰ μήν *yet truly,* Lat. *verum enimvero:* οὐ μήν *assuredly* not, so too μὴ μήν; τί μήν; *what then? i.* e. *of course* II. = μέντοι, *however.*—Μήν was orig. the same as μέν, but after the introduction of the long vowel η it became the more emphatic form: but ἦ μέν, μὴ μέν, were retained in Ep. and Ion., = Att. ἦ μήν, μὴ μήν.

ΜΗ'Ν, ὁ, gen. μηνός: dat. pl. μησί, Aeol. and Dor. **μεῖς**:—Lat. *MEN-SIS, A MON-TH:* κατὰ μῆνα *month by month, monthly.* In earlier times the month was divided into two parts, μὴν ἱστάμενος, the *month rising,* and μὴν φθίνων the *month waning.* The Attic division was into three, μὴν ἱστάμενος, μεσῶν, φθίνων: the last division was sometimes reckoned backwards, as μηνὸς τετάρτῃ φθίνοντος the fourth day from the end of the month; sometimes onwards, as τῇ τρίτῃ ἐπ' εἰκάδι on the three-and-twentieth day of the month II. = μηνίσκος II.

μηνάς, άδος, ἡ, = μήνη, *the moon.*

μήνατο, Ep. 3 sing. aor. 1 med. of μαίνομαι.

μήνεσι, corrupt form of μησί, dat. pl. of μήν, μηνός.

μήνη, ἡ, (μήν) *the moon,* Lat. *luna.* Hence

μηνιαῖος, α, ον, *monthly.*

μηνιθμός, οῦ, ὁ, (μηνίω) *wrath.*

μήνῐμα, ατος, τό, (μηνίω) *the cause of anger;* μήνιμα θεῶν *the cause of* divine *wrath.* 2. *guilt* of blood, *blood-guiltiness.*

ΜΗ^ΝΙΣ Dor. **μᾶνις**, ιος ἡ, Att. gen. μήνῐδος, *wrath, anger:* also, *malice.*

μηνίσκος, ὁ, Dim. of μήνη, *a crescent,* Lat. *lunula.* II. *a crescent-shaped body, to protect the head of statues*

μηνίω Dor. **μανιω**: f. μηνίσω [ῑ]: aor. 1 ἐμήνῑσα: (μῆνις):—*to cherish wrath, be wroth against:* also *to declare one's wrath against* a person.

μηνο-ειδής, ές, (μήνη, εἶδος) *crescent-shaped,* Lat. *lunatus:* of the sun and moon *when partially eclipsed.*

μήνῡμα, ατος, τό, (μηνύω) *an information.*

μηνῡτήρ, ῆρος, ὁ, (μηνύω) *an informer, guide.*

μηνῡτής, οῦ, ὁ, (μηνύω) masc. Adj. *bringing to light.* II. as Subst. *an informer,* Lat. *delator.*

μήνῡτρον, τό, (μηνύω) *the price paid for information, reward:* almost always used in plur.

μηνύτωρ, ορος, ὁ, = μηνυτήρ. [ῠ] From

ΜΗΝΥ'Ω Dor. **μᾱνύω**: f. μηνύσω [ῡ]: aor. 1 ἐμήνῡσα:—Pass., aor. 1 ἐμηνύθην [ῡ]: pf. μεμήνῡμαι:—*to disclose, reveal, make known: betray.* II. at Athens, *to inform* or *lay public information against* another: impers. in Pass., μηνύεται *information is laid:* but in Pass. also of persons, *to be informed against.*

μὴ ὅπως (an ellipse for μὴ ὑπολάβητε ὅπως..), followed by ἀλλά, *do not suppose that.., but..; not only not so.., but...*

μὴ ὅτι, = μὴ ὅπως, followed by ἀλλα, *not only not* so.., *but..; not to mention that* , *let alone,* Lat. *ne dicam.*

μὴ οὐ, are joined I. with the subjunctive, after Verbs of fearing, doubting, and the like, as δέδοικα μὴ οὐ γένηται I fear *it will not* be, opp. to δέδοικα μὴ γένηται I fear *it will* be. Here both negatives have their proper force: but II. with the Infinitive, after Verbs of denying, doubting, etc., as οὐδείς σοι ἀντιλέγει τὸ μὴ οὐ λέξειν no one disputes your right to speak (where μὴ οὐ may be translated by Lat. *quin, quominus*), *nemo te impediet quin dicas.* 2. generally, after all clauses in which a negat. is expressed or implied, as, after οὐ δύναμαι, οὐκ ἔστι etc.; as οὐ οἰκός ἐστι Ἀθηναίους μὴ οὐ δοῦναι δίκας it is *not* reasonable that the Athenians should *not*... Lat. *non potest fieri quin..;* so also, with a negat. implied, as, δεινὸν ἐδόκει . μὴ οὐ λαβεῖν it seemed strange *not* to take. III. with a Participle, δυσάλγητος γὰρ ἦν, μὴ οὐ κατοικτείρων for I were unfeeling, *did I not* pity.—In II. and III. μή might stand without οὐ

μὴ πολλακίς, *lest perchance,* Lat. *ne forte.*

μή-ποτε, = μή ποτε, 1. with subj. *that at no time, lest ever,* Lat. *ne quando* 2. with infin. *never.*

μή που, *lest anywhere: lest perchance.*

μή-πω, = μή πω, *not yet,* Lat. *nondum:* μήπω γε, *nay, not yet.*

μὴ πώποτε, *never yet.*

μή-πως, = μή πως, *lest in any way, lest any how, lest perchance.* II. in case of doubt, *whether or no.*

μηρά, τά, = μηρία, *thigh-bones.*

μηρίᾰ, τά, never used in sing., (μηρός) *the thigh-bones,* which by old usage they cut out from the leg (ἐκ μηρία τάμνον), and wrapped in two folds of fat (μηρία κνίσῃ ἐκάλυψαν, δίπτυχα ποιήσαντες): they were then laid on the altar and burnt. II. = μηροί, *the thighs.*

μηριαῖος, α, ον, (μηρός) *of* or *belonging to the thigh,* Lat. *femoralis:* ἡ μηριαία, *the thigh.*

μήρινθος, ου, ἡ, (μηρύω) *a cord, line, string;* proverb., ἡ μήρινθος οὐδὲν ἔσπασε *the line* caught nothing, i. e. it was of no avail.

ΜΗΡΟ'Σ, οῦ, ὁ, *the upper part of the thigh, the ham.*

μηρο-τρᾰφής, ές, (μηρός, τραφῆναι) *nursed in the thigh,* epith. of Bacchus.

μηρο-τύπής, ές, (μηρός, τυπῆναι) *striking the thigh.*

μηρῡκάομαι, Dep. *to chew the cud,* Lat. *ruminare.*

ΜΗΡΥ'ΟΜΑΙ, f. *-ύσομαι* [ῡ]. aor. 1 *ἐμηρῡσάμην*:—*to draw up* or *furl* sails: *to draw up* an anchor. 2. in weaving, *κρόκα ἐν στήμονι μηρύσασθαι to weave* the woof into the warp. II. *μηρύομαι* is sometimes used as Pass., *κισσὸς μηρύεται περὶ χεῖλη* ivy *is twined* around the edge.

μήσαο, μήσατο, Ep. 2 and 3 sing. aor. 1 of *μήδομαι*.

μήσεαι, Ep. 2 sing. of *μήσομαι*, fut. of *μήδομαι*.

μῆστο, Ep. 3 sing. contr. aor. 2 of *μήδομαι*.

μήστωρ, *ωρος*, *ὁ*, (*μήδομαι*) *an adviser, counseller; μήστωρ μάχης the adviser* or leader of battle.

μή-τε, = *τή τε*, *and not.* II. repeated, *μήτε .. μήτε, neither .. nor.*

ΜΗ'ΤΗΡ Dor. **ΜΑ'ΤΗΡ**, *ἡ*, gen. *μητέρος*, contr. *μητρός*: acc. *μητέρα*, pl. *μητέρας*:—Lat. *MATER, MOTHER*: of animals, *a dam*: metaph. of lands, *μήτηρ μήλων mother* of flocks; *γῆ μήτηρ Mother* Earth:—*ἡ Μητήρ* sometimes *Ceres*, sometimes *Rhea* or *Cybelé*.

μῆτῐ, neut. of *μή-τις*, *μήτινος*.

μῆτῐ, contr. for *μήτιϊ*, dat. of *μῆτις*, *μήτιος*.

μητιάασθαι, μητιάασθε, Ep. for *μητιᾶσθαι*, *μητιᾶσθε*, pres. inf. and 2 pl. pres. ind. of *μητιάω*.

μητῐάω, f. *μητιάσω*: (*μῆτις*):—*to meditate, intend, plan* a thing: absol. *to deliberate*, and in Med. *to debate in one's own mind.* II. *to devise, contrive, bring about.*

μητῐέτης Ep. **μητιετᾰ**, *ου*, *ὁ*, (*μῆτις*) *counseller.*

μητῐόεις, *εσσα*, *εν*, (*μῆτις*) *wise in counsel*: also, *skilful, skilfully chosen.*

μητῐομαι, f. *-ίσομαι* [ῑ]: aor. 1 *ἐμητῑσάμην*: Dep.: (*μῆτις*):—*to invent, contrive, devise.*

μητῐόων, Ep. for *μητιῶν*, part. of *μητιάω*.

μητιόωσι, -όωντο, Ep. 3 pl. pres. act. and impf. med. of *μητιάω*.

ΜΗ'ΤΙΣ, *ιος*, *ἡ*; Att. gen. *ῐδος*; Ep. dat. *μήτι* for *μήτιϊ*; acc. *μῆτιν*:—*counsel, wisdom, skill, cunning, craft.* II. *a plan, enterprise.*

μή-τῐς, *ὁ*, *ἡ*, *μή-τῐ*, *τό*, gen. *μήτῐνος*: (*μή*, *τὶς*):—*lest any one, lest anything; that no one, that nothing,* Lat. *ne quis, ne quid.* II. *μήτι* is freq. as Adv. *lest by any means, that by no means*: also separately, *μή τι*: in an indirect question, *whether perchance.*

μή-τοι, stronger form of *μή*, *in nowise, nay*: *μήτοι γε, nay upon no account.*

μήτρα, *ἡ*, (*μήτηρ*) Lat. *matrix, the womb.*

μητρ-ᾱγύρτης, *ου*, *ὁ*, (*μήτηρ*, *ἀγύρτης*) *a begging priest of Cybelé, a sort of mendicant friar.*

μητρ-ᾱδελφεός or **μητρ-άδελφος**, *ὁ* and *ἡ*, Dor. **ματρ-**, (*μήτηρ*, *ἀδελφός*) *a mother's brother* or *sister, an uncle* or *aunt.*

μητρ-ᾱλοίας or **μητρ-αλῴας**, *ου*, *ὁ*, (*μήτηρ*, *ἀλοιάω*) *striking one's mother, a matricide.*

μήτρη, *ἡ*, Ion. for *μήτρα*.

μητριάς, *άδος*, *ἡ*, pecul. fem. of *μήτριος*.

μητρίδιος, *α*, *ον*, (*μήτρα*) *fruitful, prolific.*

μητρό-δοκος Dor. **ματρ-**, *ον*, (*μήτηρ*, *δέχομαι*) *received by the mother.*

μητρόθεν Dor. **ματρόθεν**, Adv. (*μήτηρ*) *from the mother, by the mother's side.*

μητρο-κασιγνήτη, *ἡ*, (*μήτηρ*, *κασιγνήτη*) *a mother's sister.*

μητροκτονέω, f. *ήσω*, *to kill one's mother, to be a matricide.* From

μητρο-κτόνος, *ον*, (*μήτηρ*, *κτείνω*) *killing one's mother, a matricide.* II. *μητρόκτονος*, *ον*, pass. *killed by one's mother.*

μητρο-μήτωρ Dor. **-μάτωρ** [ᾰ], *ορος*, *ἡ*, = *μητρὸς μήτηρ*, *one's mother's mother, grandmother.*

μητρο-πάτωρ [ᾰ], *ορος*, *ὁ*, = *μητρὸς πατήρ*, *one's mother's father, grandfather.*

μητρό-πολις Dor. **ματρ-**, *εως*, *ἡ*, (*μήτηρ*, *πόλις*) *the mother-state*, from which colonies were sent out. [illegible]. generally, *a metropolis, a capital.* III. *one's mother-city, mother-country, home.*

μητρο-πόλος, *ον*, (*μήτηρ*, *πολέομαι*) *tending mothers.*

μητρόρ-ριπτος, *ον*, (*μήτηρ*, *ῥίπτω*) *rejected by one's mother.*

μητρο-φθορος, *ον*, (*μήτηρ*, *φθείρω*) *mother-murdering.*

μητρο-φόνος, *ον*, also *η*, *ον*, (*μήτηρ*, **φένω*) *mother-murdering, matricidal.*

μητρο-φόντης, *ου*, *ὁ*, (*μήτηρ*, **φένω*) *a matricide.*

μητρυιά, *ᾶς*, Ion. **μητρυιή**, *ῆς*, *ἡ*, (*μήτηρ*) *a step-mother*, Lat. *noverca*: metaph. a rocky coast is called *μητρυία νεῶν*.

μητρῷος Ep. **μητρώϊος**, *α*, *ον*, (*μήτηρ*) *of* or *belonging to a mother, maternal.*

μήτρως, *ὁ*; gen. *μήτρωος* and *ω*; acc. *μήτρωα* and *ων*; (*μήτηρ*) *a maternal uncle* 2. *any relation by the mother's side.*

μηχανάασθαι, -άασθε, Ep. for *μηχανᾶσθαι -ᾶσθε*, pres. inf. and 2 pl. ind. of *μηχανάομαι*.

μηχανάομαι, f. *-ήσομαι*: aor. 1 *ἐμηχανησάμην*: pf. *μεμηχάνημαι*: Dep.: (*μηχανή*):—Lat. *machinari, to make by art, put together, construct, prepare.* 2. *to contrive, devise, scheme.* II. as Med. *to procure for oneself.*

μηχανάω, = *μηχανάομαι*, found in act. voice in Ep. part. *μηχανόωντας*: but perf. *μεμηχάνημαι* is used in pass. sense.

μηχανοῴμην, *-όῳο*, *-όῳτο*, Ep. for *μηχανῴμην*, pres. opt. of *μηχανάομαι*.

μηχανέομαι, Ion. for *μηχανάομαι*.

μηχᾰνή, *ἡ*, (*μῆχος*) Lat *machĭna, an instrument* or *machine* for lifting weights:— 2. *an engine* of war. II. *any artificial means, a contrivance, device*; generally, *a way, means*:—*μηχαναί, arts, wiles*: c. gen., *μηχανὴ κακῶν a contrivance against* ills: *μηδεμιῇ μηχανῇ* by no *means* whatsoever, by no *contrivance.*

μηχάνημα, *ατος*, *τό*, (*μηχανάομαι*) *an engine.* II. *a subtle contrivance* or *device, art, trick.*

μηχανητέον, verb. Adj. of *μηχανάομαι*, *one must contrive.*

μηχᾰνητικός, *ή*, *όν*, (*μηχανάομαι*) = *μηχανικός*.

μηχᾰνικός, ή, όν, (μηχανή) *inventive, ingenious, clever.* II. as Subst., ἡ μηχανική (sub. τέχνη), *mechanics.*

μηχᾰνιώτης, ου, ὁ, poët. for μηχανητής.

μηχᾰνο-δίφης, ου, ὁ, (μηχανή, δῑφάω) *inventing contrivances* or *artifices, ingenious.*

μηχᾰνόεις, εσσα, εν, (μηχανή) *inventive, ingenious.*

μηχᾰνο-ποιός, όν, (μηχανή, ποιέω) *making machines:* as Subst., μηχανοποιός, ὁ, *an engineer, maker of war-engines.*

μηχᾰνορρᾰφέω, f. ήσω, *to contrive craft, deal subtly, craftily.* From

μηχᾰνορ-ράφος, ον, (μηχανή, ῥάπτω) *contriving devices, crafty-dealing, craft-contriving.*

μηχᾰν-ουργός, όν, (μηχανή, ἔργον) = μηχανοποιός. II. pass. *cunningly contrived.*

μηχανόωνται, -όωντο, 3 pl. pres. and impf. of μηχανάομαι.

μῆχαρ, τό, = μῆχος, *a means, contrivance.*

ΜΗ͂ΧΟΣ, τό, *a means, expedient, contrivance.*

μίᾰ, ἡ; gen. μιᾶς Ion. μιῆς; dat. μιᾷ, μιῇ; acc. μίᾰν :—fem. of εἷς, *one.*

ΜΙΑΙ΄ΝΩ, f. μιᾰνῶ: aor. 1 ἐμίηνα Att. ἐμίᾱνα: pf. μεμίαγκα :—Pass., aor. 1 ἐμιάνθην : pf. μεμίασμαι or -αμμαι :—*to paint over, stain, dye, colour,* Lat. *violare.* 2. *to stain, defile, soil.* 3. metaph. *to taint, defile, pollute.*

μῐαιφονέω, f. ήσω, (μιαιφόνος) :—*to be blood-stained, bloody, murderous.* Hence

μιαιφονία, ἡ, *bloodguiltiness.*

μῐαι-φόνος, ον, (μιαίνω, *φένω) *blood-stained, bloody: defiled with blood, blood-guilty* :—Comp. -ώτερος; Sup. -ώτατος.

μιάνθην, Ep. for ἐμιάνθην, aor. 1 pass. of μιαίνω.

μῐᾰρία, ἡ, (μιαρός) *brutality.* II. *defilement.*

μῐᾰρό-γλωσσος, ον, (μιαρός, γλῶσσα) *foul-mouthed.*

μῐᾰρός, ά, όν, (μιαίνω) *defiled with blood.* 2. generally, *polluted, abominable, foul,* Lat. *impurus: brutal, coarse, disgusting.* Adv. μιαρῶς, *brutally.*

μίασμα, ατος, τό, (μιαίνω) *a stain, defilement;* of persons, *a pollution.*

μῐασμός, οῦ, ὁ, (μιαίνω) *pollution.*

μῐάστωρ, ορος, ὁ, (μιαίνω) *a guilty wretch, one who brings pollution,* Lat. *homo piacularis.* II. ἀλάστωρ, *an avenger* of such guilt.

μίγα, Adv. (μίγνυμι) *mixed* or *blended with.*

μῐγάζομαι, Dep. poët. for μίγνυμαι.

μῐγάς, αδος, ὁ, ἡ, (μίγα) *mixed up, promiscuous.*

μίγδᾰ and **μίγδην**, Adv. *promiscuously.*

μιγείην, aor. 2 opt. pass. of μίγνυμι.

μιγείς, aor. 2 part. pass. of μίγνυμι.

μίγεν, for ἐμίγησαν, 3 pl. aor. 2 pass. of μιγνυμι.

μιγήμεναι, Ep. aor. 2 inf. pass. of μίγνυμι.

μῐγῆναι, aor. 2 inf. pass. of μίγνυμι.

μῖγμα, ατος, τό, (μίγνυμι) *a mixture, compound.*

ΜΙ΄ΓΝΥΜΙ and -ύω, also **ΜΙ΄ΣΓΩ** : f. μίξω : aor. 1 ἔμιξα, inf. μῖξαι :—Med. and Pass. μίγνῠμαι and μίσγομαι : fut. med. μίξομαι, fut. 1 pass. μιχθήσομαι, f. 2 μῐγήσομαι, f. 3 μεμίξομαι : aor. 1 ἐμίχθην, aor. 2 ἐμίγην [ῐ]; 3 sing. Ep. aor. pass. ἔμικτο, μῖκτο : pf. μέμιγμαι : Ep. 3 sing. plqpf. μέμικτο :—Lat. *MISCEO, to mix, mix up, mingle,* properly of liquids, e. g. οἶνον καὶ ὕδωρ. generally, *to join, bring together, bring in contact with.* 3. *to make acquainted with, unite with:* also, μῖξαί τινα ἄνθεσι *to cover* one *with* flowers. II. Med. and Pass. *to be brought into contact with, to be mingled with, to reach;* κλισίῃσι μιγῆναι *to reach* the tents : *to come to, to be present at:* hence *to meet, live, associate with:* but also in hostile sense, *to encounter:* more rarely μίσγεσθαι ἐς Ἀχαιούς, *to go to join* the Achaeans. 2. *to lie with: to have intercourse with, to be united to.*

μιγνύω, = μίγνυμι.

μιήνῃ, 3 sing. aor. 1 subj. of μιαίνω.

μῐη-φόνος, ον, = μιαιφόνος.

μικκός, ά, όν, Dor. for μικρός, *little.*

μῑκρ-αῦλαξ, ᾰκος, ὁ, ἡ, (μικρός, αὖλαξ) *with small furrows:* hence *small, scanty.*

μῑκρ-έμπορος, ὁ, (μικρός, ἔμπορος) *a pedlar.*

μῑκρολογέομαι, f. -ήσομαι, Dep., (μικρολόγος) *to examine* or *discuss with extreme minuteness.* Hence

μικρολογία, ἡ, *minute discussion, frivolity.*

μῑκρο-λόγος, ον, (μικρός, λέγω) *reckoning trifles: caring about petty expenses, penurious, mean.* 2. *cavilling about trifles, captious.*

μῑκρο-πολίτης [ῑ], ου, ὁ, fem. **-ιτις**, ιδος, ἡ, (μικρός, πολίτης) *a citizen of a petty town* or *state.*

ΜΙ͂ΚΡΟ΄Σ, Ion. and old Att. **σμικρός** Dor. **μικκός**, ά, όν, *small, little: petty, mean, trivial, insignificant:* of Time, *little, short.* II. Adv. usages : gen. μικροῦ (sub. δεῖ) it wants *but little, almost* :—dat. μικρῷ *by a little:* acc. μικρόν *a little.* 2. with Preps., ἐπὶ μικρόν *for a little, but a little;* κατὰ μικρόν *little by little,* or *into small parts;* μετὰ μικρόν *after a little;* παρὰ μικρόν within *a little, almost.*—Besides the regular Comp. and Sup. μικρότερος, μικρότατος, the irr. forms ἐλάσσων, ἐλάχιστος, μείων μεῖστος, μειότερος μειότατος are used.

μῑκροφῐλοτῑμία, ἡ, *petty ambition.* From

μῑκρο-φῐλότῑμος, ον, (μικρός, φιλότιμος) *ambitious of petty distinctions.*

μῑκροψῡχία, ὁ, *littleness of soul, meanness of spirit.* From

μῑκρό-ψυχος, ον, (μικρός, ψυχή) *little-souled, narrow-minded, paltry.*

μίκτο, 3 sing. Ep. aor. 2 pass. of μιγνυμι.

μικτός, ή, όν, (μίγνυμι) *mixed, compound.*

μῖλαξ, ᾰκος, ἡ, Att. for σμῖλαξ, *the yew-tree.* II *a convolvulus.*

Μῑλήσιος, α, ον, *of* or *from Miletus.* From

Μίλητος, ἡ, *Miletus,* a famous Greek city in Caria.

μιλιάριον, τό, *a milestone,* the Lat. *milliarium.* II. *a copper vessel* for boiling water in.

μίλιον, τό, *a Roman mile,* Lat. *mille passus,* = 8 stades, = 1680 yards, i. e. 80 yards less than our mile.

μιλτεῖον, τό, *a vessel for keeping* μίλτος in.

μιλτ-ηλἴφής, ές, (μίλτος, ἀλιφῆναι) *painted red.*

μιλτο-πάρῃος, ον, (μίλτος, παρειά) *red-cheeked:* of ships, *with the bows painted red.*

ΜΙ´ΛΤΟΣ, ἡ, *red earth, red chalk* or *ochre, ruddle,* Lat. *rubrīca.* II. *vermilion,* Lat. *minium.*

μιλτο-φὕρής, ές, (μίλτος, φυρῆναι) *smeared with ochre.*

μιλτόω, f. ώσω: pass. pf. μεμίλτωμαι; (μίλτος):—*to colour with ochre, paint red;* σχοινίον μεμιλτωμένον a rope *smeared with red paint,* with which they swept the Agora at Athens, and drove the idlers to the Pnyx.

μιλτ-ώδης, ες, (μίλτος, εἶδος) *of the nature* or *colour of* μίλτος.

μίμαρκυς, ἡ, a kind of *hare-soup.* (A foreign word.)

Μίμας, αντος, ὁ, *a rocky promontory of Ionia.*

ΜΙ¯ΜΕ´ΟΜΑΙ, f. -ήσομαι: aor. 1 ἐμιμησάμην: pf. μεμίμημαι: Dep.:—*to imitate, mimic, copy:* pf. part. μεμιμημένος, in pass. sense, *made exactly like, made in imitation of.* II. of the fine arts, *to represent by means of imitation.* Hence

μιμηλός, ή, όν, *imitative.*

μίμημα, ατος, τό, (μιμέομαι) *an imitation, copy.*

μίμησις, ἡ, (μιμέομαι) *imitation.*

μιμητέος, α, ον, verb. Adj. of μιμέομαι, *to be imitated.* II. μιμητέον, *one must imitate.*

μῑμητής, οῦ, ὁ, (μιμέομαι) *an imitator, copyist.*

μῑμητικός, ή, όν, (μιμέομαι) *imitative.*

μῑμητός, ή, όν, (μιμέομαι) *to be imitated* or *copied.*

μιμνάζω, Frequent. of μίμνω, μένω, *to keep staying, to stay, remain.* II. trans. *to expect, await.*

μιμνήσκω, fut. μνήσω: aor. 1 ἔμνησα: (μνάω):—*to remind, put in mind.* 2. *to recall to the memory* of others. II. Med. and Pass. μιμνήσκομαι, with the older form ΜΝΑ´ΟΜΑΙ, μνῶμαι, whence the tenses are formed: fut. med. μνήσομαι, f. 1 pass. μνησθήσομαι, f. 3 μεμνήσομαι: aor. 1 med. ἐμνησάμην, pass. ἐμνήσθην:—the pf. μέμνημαι is both med. and pass., in Att. with pres. sense like Lat. *memini,* 2 sing. μέμνῃ, shortened from μέμνησαι; imperat. μέμνησο Ion. μέμνεο; subjunct. μέμνωμαι; optat. μεμνῄμην, but also μεμνῴμην, ῳο, ῳτο, Ion. μεμνέῳτο: infin. μεμνῆσθαι: Ion. 3 pl. plqpf. ἐμεμνέατο:—*to remind oneself, remember:* c. gen. ἀλκῆς μνήσασθαι *to bethink one* of one's strength: also, c. part., μέμνημαι ἐλθών *I remember having* come. 2. *to mention, make mention of.* 3. *to give heed to, judge of.*

μίμνοντι, Dor. for μίμνουσι, 3 pl. of μίμνω. 2. dat. pres. part. of the same Verb.

μίμνω, for **μῐ-μένω**, redupl. form of μένω, *to remain, stay, wait:* c. acc. *to await.*

μῑμο-λόγος, ον, (μῖμος, λέγω) *mocking one's words.* II. as Subst. *a writer of mimes.*

ΜΙ¯ΜΟΣ, ου, ὁ, *an imitator, copyist: an actor, mime.* II. *a mime,* a kind of drama.

μίν [ῐ], Ion. acc. sing. of the Pron. of the 3rd pers. through all genders, for αὐτόν, αὐτήν, αὐτό: always enclitic: Dor. and Att. νιν: μὶν αὐτὸν *himself;* but, αὐτόν μιν *oneself,* for ἑαυτόν. II. rarely as 3 pers. pl., for αὐτούς, αὐτάς, αὐτά. III. = the reflex. Pron. ἑαυτόν.

ΜΙ´ΝΘΟΣ, ὁ, *human ordure, dung.* Hence

μινθόω, f. ώσω, *to befoul with dung.*

Μῐνύαι, οἱ, *the Minyans,* a race of nobles in Orchomenos: Adj. **Μινύειος**, α, ον, Ep. **Μινυήιος**, *of the Minyans.*

ΜΙ¯ΝΥ´ΘΩ [ῠ], Ion. impf. μινύθεσκον, Lat. *minuo, to diminish, lessen, curtail, weaken.* II. intr. *to decrease, decline, fall away, be wasted.* Hence

μίνυνθᾰ, Adv. *a little, very little:* of Time, *a short time.* Hence

μῐνυνθάδιος, α, ον, *lasting a short time, short-lived:* Comp. μινυνθαδιώτερος.

μῐνῠρίζω, f. ίσω, (μινυρός) *to moan, whine:* also *to hum, chant in a low tone,* Lat. *minurīre.* Hence

μῐνύρισμα, ατος, τό, *a warbling, humming.*

μῐνῠρισμός, ὁ, (μινυρίζω) *a moaning: warbling.*

μῐνύρομαι, Dep. = μινυρίζω, of the nightingale, *to warble:* generally, *to hum a tune, chant in a low tone.* [ῡ]

ΜΙ¯ΝΥ¯ΡΟ´Σ, ά, όν, *complaining in a low tone, moaning, whining, whimpering.*

μῐνῠ-ώριος and **μινύ-ωρος**, ον, (μινύθω, ὥρα) *short-lived.*

Μίνως, ὁ, *Minos,* king of Crete: gen. Μίνωος and Μίνω; dat. Μίνωϊ, Μίνῳ; acc. Μίνωα, also Μίνω and Μίνων:—hence Adj. **Μῑνώϊος** Att. **Μινῷος**, α, ον, *of Minos.*

μῖξαι, aor. 1 inf., **μίξεσθαι**, fut. inf. med. of μίγνυμι.

μῖξις, εως, ἡ, (μίξω fut. of μίγνυμι), *a mixing, mingling.* II. *intercourse* or *commerce with* others.

μιξο-βάρβᾰρος, ον, (μίξω fut. of μίγνυμι, βάρβαρος) *half barbarian half Greek.*

μιξό-θηρ, ὁ, ἡ, (μίξω, θήρ) *half beast.*

μιξό-θροος, ον, (μίξω, θρόος) *with mingled cries.*

μιξό-λευκος, ον, (μίξω, λευκός) *mixed with white.*

μίξομαι, fut. med. of μίγνυμι.

μιξόμ-βροτος, ον, for μιξό-βροτος, (μίξω, βροτός) *half mortal.*

μιξο-νόμος, ον, (μίξω νέμω) *feeding promiscuously.*

μιξο-παρθενος, ον, (μίξω, παρθένος) *half a maiden, half woman.*

μίξω, fut. of μίγνυμι.

μῑσαγαθία, ἡ, *hatred of good.* From

μῑσ-άγαθος, η, ον, (μῖσος, ἀγαθός) *hating good.*

μῑσ-ᾰθήναιος, ον, (μῖσος, Ἀθηναῖος) *hating the Athenians.*

μῑσ-ᾰλάζων, ον, gen. ονος, (μῖσος, ἀλάζων) *hating boasters.*

μῑσ-ᾰλέξανδρος, ον, (μῖσος, Ἀλέξανδρος) *hating Alexander.*

μισ-άμπελος, ον, (μῖσος, ἄμπελος) *hating the vine.*

μῑσ-άνθρωπος, ον, (μῖσος, ἄνθρωπος) *hating mankind, misanthropic.*

μισγ-άγκεια, ἡ, (μίσγω, ἄγκος) *a place where several mountain glens* (ἄγκη) *meet, a meeting of glens.*

μίσγεσθαι, pres. inf. pass. of μίσγω.

μίσγοισαι, Dor. pres. part. pl. fem. of μίσγω.

ΜΙ'ΣΓΩ, see μίγνυμι.

μῑσ-έλλην, ηνος, ὁ, ἡ, (μῖσος, Ἕλλην) *a hater of the Greeks.*

μῑσέω, f. ήσω: pf. μεμίσηκα:—Pass., f. med. in pass. sense μισήσομαι: aor. 1 ἐμισήθην: pf. μεμίσημαι: (μῖσος):—*to hate*:—Pass. *to be hated.*

μίσηθρον, τό, (μισέω) *a charm for producing hatred*, opp. to φίλτρον (from φιλέω), *which caused love.*

μίσημα, ατος, τό, (μισέω) *an object of hate.*

μισητέος, verb. Adj. of μισέω, *to be hated.*

μῑσητία, ἡ, (μισέω) *hateful lewdness* or *greediness.*

μῑσητός, ή, όν, (μισέ[ω]) *[h]ated, hateful, odious.*

μίσητρον, τό, = μίση[θρον].

μισθαποδοσία, ἡ, *payment of wages, recompense.* From

μισθ-αποδότης, ου, ὁ, (μισθός, ἀποδίδωμι) *one who pays wages, a rewarder, recompenser.*

μισθάριον, τό, Dim. of μισθός, *a small fee.*

μισθαρνέω, f. ήσω, (μίσθαρνος) *to work* or *serve for hire, receive pay.* Hence

μισθαρνία, ἡ, *a receiving of wages, hired service.*

μίσθ-αρνος, ὁ, (μισθός, ἄρνυμαι) *a hired servant.*

μισθ-αρχίδης, ου, ὁ, (μισθός, ἀρχή) a Comic Patronymic, *son of a placeman.*

μίσθιος, α, ον, also ος, ον, (μισθός) *hired, salaried.*

μισθοδοσία, ἡ, *payment of wages.* From

μισθοδοτέω, f. ήσω, *to pay wages.* From

μισθο-δότης, ου, ὁ, (μισθός, δίδωμι) *one who pays wages, a paymaster.*

ΜΙΣΘΟ'Σ, οῦ, ὁ, *wages, pay, hire:* μισθὸς ῥητός fixed *wages;* ἐπὶ μισθῷ for *hire;* διδόναι τάλαντον μηνὸς μισθόν to give a talent as a month's *pay.* 2. at Athens *the pay* of the soldiery: also, μισθὸς βουλευτικός *the pay* of the council of 500, a drachma each for every day of sitting; μισθὸς δικαστικός or ἡλιαστικός *the wages* of a dicast or juror (at first *one obol*, from the time of Cleon *three*) for every day he sat on a jury; μισθὸς συνηγορικός *the pay* of a public advocate, one drachma for every court-day. 3. generally, *recompense, reward:* in bad sense, *punishment, retribution.*

μισθοφορά, ἡ, (μισθοφόρος) *receipt of wages: wages received, wages, pay, salary.*

μισθοφορέω, f. ήσω, (μισθοφόρος) *to receive wages, to serve for hire:* c. acc. rei, *to receive as pay.* Hence

μισθοφορητέον, verb. Adj. *one must keep in pay.*

μισθοφορία, ἡ, (μισθοφορέω) *service for wages* or *pay, hired service.*

μισθο-φόρος, ον, (μισθός, φέρω) *receiving wages, serving for hire;* οἱ μισθοφόροι *hireling soldiers, mercenaries;* μισθοφόροι τριήρεις galleys *manned with mercenaries.*

μισθόω, f. ώσω: aor. 1 ἐμίσθωσα: pf. μεμίσθωκα: (μισθός):—*to let out for hire, farm out*, Lat. *locare:* c. inf., μισθοῦν τὸν νηὸν τριηκοσίων ταλάντων ἐξεργάσασθαι *to let out* the building of the temple for 300 talents, Lat. *locare aedem exstruendam.* II. Med., f. μισθώσομαι: aor. 1 ἐμισθωσάμην: pf. (in med. sense) μεμίσθωμαι:—*to engage* or *hire at a price*, Lat. *conducere: to retain*, as an advocate or physician; μισθοῦσθαί τινα ταλάντου *to engage his services* at a talent; c. inf., μισθοῦσθαι νηὸν ἐξοικοδομῆσαι *to contract* for the building of the temple, Lat. *conducere aedem aedificandam.* III. Pass., aor. 1 ἐμισθώθην: pf. (in pass. sense) μεμίσθωμαι:—*to be hired for pay.* Hence

μίσθωμα, ατος, τό, *that which is let for hire, a hired house.* II. *the price agreed on, the contract-price: rent.*

μισθώσιμος, ον, (μισθόω) *that can be hired.*

μίσθωσις, εως, ἡ, (μισθόω) *a letting for hire.* II. (μισθόομαι) *a hiring.* III. = μίσθωμα, *rent.*

μισθωτής, οῦ, ὁ, (μισθόω) *one who pays rent, a tenant.*

μισθωτικός, ή, όν, (μισθόω) *mercenary.*

μισθωτός, ή, όν, (μισθόω) *hired* or *to be hired:* as Subst. *a hireling, mercenary*, of soldiers.

μῑσό-γάμος, ον, (μῖσος, γάμος) *marriage-hating.*

μῑσό-γελως, ωτος, ὁ, ἡ, (μῖσος, γέλως) *laughter-hating.*

μῑσο-γόης, ου, ὁ, (μῖσος, γόης) *hating imposture.*

μῑσοδημία, ἡ, *hatred of democracy.* From

μῑσό-δημος, ον, (μῖσος, δῆμος) *hating the commons hating democracy.*

μῑσό-θεος, ον, (μῖσος, θεός) *hating the gods, godless.*

μῑσό-θηρος, ον, (μῖσος, θήρα) *hating the chase.*

μῑσο-καῖσαρ, ἄρος, ὁ, (μῖσος, Καῖσαρ) *hating Caesar.*

μῑσο-λάκων, ωνος, ὁ, (μῖσος, Λάκων) *a Laconian-hater.* [ᾰ]

μῑσο-λάμᾰχος, ον, (μῖσος, Λάμαχος) *hating Lamachus.* [λᾰ]

μῑσολογία, ἡ, *hatred of argument.* From

μῑσό-λογος, ον, (μῖσος, λόγος) *hating argument.*

μῑσό-νοθος, ον, (μῖσος, νόθος) *hating bastards.*

μῑσό-παις, παιδος, ὁ, ἡ, (μῖσος, παῖς) *hating children.*

μῑσο-πέρσης, ου, ὁ, (μῖσος, Πέρσης) *a Persian hater.*

μῑσό-πολις, ιος, ὁ, ἡ, (μῖσος, πόλις) *hating the state.*

μῑσοπονηρέω, f. ήσω, *to hate the bad.* From

μῑσο-πόνηρος, ον, (μῖσος, πονηρός) *hating the bad.*

μῑσο-πονία, ἡ, (μῖσος, πόνος) *hatred of work.*

μῑσο-πόρπαξ, ᾱκος, ὁ, ἡ, (μῖσος, πόρπαξ) *hating the shield-handle*, i. e. *hating war:* Sup. μισοπορπᾱκίστατος.

μῑσό-πτωχος, ον, (μῖσος, πτωχός) *hating the poor.*

μισο-ρώμαιος, ον, (μῖσος, Ῥωμαῖος) *Roman-hating.*

ΜΙ'ΣΟΣ, τό, *hate, hatred:* I. pass. *hate borne one.* 2. act. *a hating, a grudge, strong dislike.* II. *a hateful object*, = μίσημα.

μῖσο-σύλλας, *ου*, *ὁ*, (*μῖσος*, *Σύλλας*) *bating Sylla.*

μῖσο-τύραννος, *ον*, (*μῖσος*, *τύραννος*) *tyrant-bating.*

μῖσο-φίλιππος, *ον*, (*μῖσος*, *Φίλιππος*) *bating Philip.*

μῖσό-χρηστος, *ον*, (*μῖσος*, *χρηστός*) *bating the good.*

μῖσο-ψευδής, *ές*, (*μῖσος*, *ψεῦδος*) *bating lies.*

ΜΙΣΤΥ´ΛΛΩ, f. ὔλῶ, *to cut up meat before roasting.*

μῐτο-εργός, *όν*, (*μίτος*, **ἔργω*) *working the thread.*

μῐτορ-ρᾰφής, *ές*, (*μίτος*, *ῥαφῆναι*) *sewn with thread, baving mesbes of thread.*

ΜΙ´ΤΟΣ, *ου*, *ὁ*, *a thread of the warp*, Lat. *tela* :—generally, *a thread : a web.* [ῐ] Hence

μῐτόω, f. *ώσω*, *to stretch the warp* in the loom :—Med. *to ply the loom ;* metaph., *φθόγγον μιτώσασθαι to let* one's voice *sound like a barp-string.*

μίτρα, Ep. and Ion. **μίτρη**, *ἡ*, (*μίτος*) *a linen girdle* or *band*, worn below the *θώραξ* : generally *a girdle, zone.* II. *a beadband, a snood.* 2. *a Persian cap*, like *κυρβασία.*

Μίτρα, *ης*, *ἡ*, the Persian Aphroditê or Venus.

μιτρη-φόρος, *ον*, (*μίτρα*, *φέρω*) *wearing a μίτρα, whether girdle* or *bead-dress*

μιτρό-δετος, *ον*, (*μίτρα*, *δέω*) *bound with a μίτρα.*

μιτροφορέω, f. *ήσω*, *to wear a μίτρα.* From

μιτρο-φόρος, *ον*, = *μιτρηφόρος.*

ΜΙ´ΤΥ˜ΛΟΣ or **μύτιλος**, *η*, *ον*, Lat. *mutilus, curtailed*, esp. *bornless.* [ῐ]

μῐτ-ώδης, *ες*, (*μίτος*, *εἶδος*) *like thread, of linen.*

μιχθῆναι, aor. 1 inf. pass. of *μίγνυμι.*

μίχθη, Ep. 3 sing. aor. 1 pass. of *μίγνυμι.*

μιχθήμεναι, Ep. aor. 1 pass. inf. of *μίγνυμι.*

ΜΝΑ͂ Ion. **μνέα**, *ἡ* ; gen. *μνᾶς* ; nom. pl. *μναῖ* :—the Lat. *MINA*, I. a weight, = 100 drachmae = 15 oz. $83\frac{3}{4}$ grs. II. a sum of money, also = 100 drachmae, = *4l.* 1s. *3d.* :—60 *μναῖ* made a talent.

μνᾶμα, μνᾱμεῖον, μναμοσύνη, Dor. for *μνημ–.*

ΜΝΑ´ΟΜΑΙ (A), contr. *μνῶμαι*, used in the contr. forms 3 sing., 1 and 3 pl, *μνᾶται*, *μνώμεθα*, *μνῶνται* ; imperat. 3 sing. *μνάσθω* ; inf. *μνᾶσθαι* ; part. *μνώμενος* ; also in Ep. resolved forms, 2 sing. *μνάᾳ* inf. *μνάασθαι* ; 3 sing. Ion. impf. *μνάσκετο* for *ἐμνᾶτο*, Ep. 3 pl. *μνώοντο*, part. *μνωόμενος* :—*to woo to wife, woo, court.* II. generally, *to court, sue for, solicit, canvass for*, Lat. *ambire.*

ΜΝΑ´ΟΜΑΙ (B), contr. *μνῶμαι*, *to remember*, Ep. and Ion. for *μιμνήσκομαι.*

μνᾶσθαι, inf. of *μνάομαι to*

μνάσθω, 3 sing. pres. imperat. of *μνάομαι to woo.*

μνάσομαι, Dor. for *μνήσομαι*, fut. med. of *μιμνήσκω.*

μναστήρ, *ὁ*, fem. **μνάστειρα**, Dor. for *μνηστ–.*

μνᾶστις, *ἡ*, Dor. for *μνῆστις*, q. v.

μνέα, Ion. for *μνᾶ.*

μνεία, *ἡ*, (*μνάομαι* B) *remembrance, memory.* II. *mention ; μνείαν ποιεῖσθαί τινος*, Lat. *mentionem facere.*

μνῆμα Dor. **μνᾶμα**, *ατος*, *τό*, (*μνάομαι* B) Lat. *monimentum, a memorial, remembrance, record* of a person or thing : *a memorial of one dead, a monument.* II. = *μνήμη, memory.*

μνημεῖον Ion. **-ήῐον** Dor. **μνᾱμεῖον**, *τό*, (*μνῆμα*) Lat. *monimentum, a memorial, remembrance, record of* a person or thing : of one dead, *a monument.*

μνήμη, *ἡ*, (*μνάομαι* B) *remembrance, memory, recollection.* 2. *the faculty of memory ; μνήμης ὕπο* from *memory.* 3. *a memorial, monument.* II. *mention* or *notice* of a thing.

μνημήῐον, *τό*, Ion. for *μνημεῖον.*

μνημονεύω, f. *σω*, (*μνήμων*) *to remember, call to mind, recollect.* 2. *to call to* another's *mind, mention, say*, Lat. *memorare.* II. Pass., with 1. med. *-εύσομαι* and pass. *-ευθήσομαι* : aor. 1 *ἐμνημονεύθην*. —*to be remembered, bad in memory, mentioned.*

μνημονῐκός, *ή*, *όν*, (*μνήμων*) *of* or *for remembrance* or *memory ; τὸ μνημονικόν* = *μνήμη, memory.* II. of persons, *of good* or *ready memory.*

μνημονικῶς, Adv. *from* or *by memory, readily.*

μνημοσύνη, *ἡ*, (*μνήμων*) *remembrance, memory*, Lat. *memoria.* II. as prop. n. *Mnemosyné*, the mother of the Muses; because before the invention of writing *memory* was the Poet's chief gift.

μνημόσῠνον Dor. **μνᾱμ–**, *τό*, (*μνήμων*) *a remembrance, memorial, record* of a thing: also *a reminder, refresber.* 2. *bonourable mention, fame.*

μνήμων, *ὁ*, *ἡ*, neut. *μνῆμον*, (*μνάομαι* B) *mindful, remembering :* c. gen. *mindful of.* 2. *ever mindful, unforgetting.*

μνῆσαι, aor. 1 inf. and aor. 1 med. imperat. of *μιμνήσκω.*

μνησαίατο, Ion. for *μνήσαιντο*, 3 pl. aor. 1 med. opt. of *μιμνήσκω.*

μνήσασθαι, aor. 1 inf. med. of *μιμνήσκω.*

μνησάσκετο, Ion. for *ἐμνήσατο*, 3 sing. aor. 1 med. of *μιμνήσκω.*

μνησθῆναι, aor. 1 pass. inf. of *μιμνήσκω.*

μνήσθητι, 2 sing. aor. 1 imperat. pass. of *μιμνήσκω.*

μνησῐ-δωρέω Dor. **μνᾱσ–**, f. *ήσω*, (*μνῆσις*, *δῶρον*) *to bring presents in token of gratitude : to be grateful.*

μνησῐκᾰκέω, f. *ήσω*, *to remember old injuries : to bear ill-will* or *malice ; οὐ μνησικακεῖν to bear* no *malice, pass an act of amnesty.* II. also c. acc. rei, *τὴν ἡλικίαν μνησικακεῖν to remind of* the ills of age. From

μνησί-κᾰκος, *ον*, (*μνάομαι* B, *κακόν*) *remembering old injuries, bearing malice.*

μνησῐ-πήμων, *ον*, gen. *ονος*, (*μιμνήσκω*, *πῆμα*) *reminding of misery.*

μνῆσις Dor. **μνᾶσις**, *εως*, *ἡ*, (*μνάομαι* B) *remembrance, memory.*

μνήσομαι, fut. med. of *μιμνήσκω.*

μνήστειρα, *ἡ*, fem. of *μνηστήρ*, (*μνάομαι* A) *a bride.* II. fem. Adj. (*μνάομαι* B) *reminding of.*

μνήστευμα, *ατος*, *τό*, (*μνηστεύω*) *courtship, wooing:* in plur., *espousals.*

μνηστεύω, f. *σω* : aor. 1 *ἐμνήστευσα* : (*μνάομαι* B) :—Pass., aor. 1 *ἐμνηστεύθην* :—*to woo, court, seek in marriage ; to espouse :* Pass. *to be courted.* II. *to promise in marriage, betroth :* Pass. *to be betrothed.*

μνηστήρ Dor. **μναστήρ**, ῆρος, ὁ, (μνάομαι A) *a wooer, suitor:* later, *a bridegroom.* II. (μνάομαι B) *calling to mind, mindful of.*

μνηστήρεσσι, Ep. for μνηστῆρσι, dat. pl. of foreg.

μνῆστις Dor. **μνᾶστις**, ιος, ἡ, (μνάομαι B) *a remembering, remembrance.* II. *reputation, fame.*

μνηστός, ή, όν, (μνάομαι) *wooed, wedded.*

μνηστύς, ύος, ἡ, Ion. for μνηστεία, *a wooing, courting, seeking in marriage.*

μνήστωρ, ορος, ὁ, (μνάομαι) *mindful of.*

μνήσω, fut. of μιμνήσκω.

μνιᾰρός, ά, όν, *mossy; soft as moss.* From

ΜΝΙ'ΟΝ, τό, *moss, sea-weed.*

μνόος contr. **μνοῦς**, ὁ, *fine down.*

μνώμενος, part. of μνάομαι, *to woo.*

μνῶνται, 3 pl. of μνάομαι *to woo.*

μνωόμενος, Ep. part. of μνάομαι, *to remember.*

μνώοντο, Ep. 3 pl. impf. of μνάομαι A and B.

μογερός, ά, όν, of persons, *labouring, distressed, wretched:* of things, *toilsome, grievous.* From

μογέω, f. ήσω, (μόγος) *to toil, labour, be in trouble* or *distress:* pres. part. μογέων = μόγις, *with trouble, hardly; μογέων ἀποκινήσασκε with much toil* he moved, *hardly* he moved. II. *to labour at.*

μογῐ-λάλος, ον, (μόγις, λᾰλέω) *speaking with difficulty, stammering* or *dumb.*

μόγῐς, Adv. (μόγος, μογέω) *with toil and trouble: hardly, scarcely:* like the later μόλις. Hence

ΜΟ'ΓΟΣ, ου, ὁ, *toil, trouble: hardship, pain, sorrow.*

μογοσ-τόκος, ον, (μόγος, τεκεῖν) *helping women in hard travail.*

μόδιος, ὁ, a dry measure, Lat. *modius*, = $\frac{1}{6}$ of a medimnus, = 2 gallons.

ΜΟ'ΘΟΣ, ὁ, *battle, the battle-din; μόθος ἵππων the noise* or *trampling* of horses.

μόθων, ωνος, ὁ, at Sparta, a name for the *child of a Helot:* such children being brought up as foster-brothers of the young Spartans. 2. from their insolence, μόθων meant *an impudent fellow:* hence invoked as the *god of impudence.* 3. *a rude dance.*

μοί, enclit. dat. sing. of ἐγώ.

μοῖρα, gen. as Ion. ης, ἡ: (μείρομαι):—*a part, portion, division,* as opp. to the whole: *a division* of an army. II. *a part* or *party* in a state, Lat. *partes.* III. *the part* or *portion* which falls to one, esp. *one's portion* of the spoil: *one's inheritance, patrimony.* 2. one's *portion in life, lot, destiny:* esp. like μόρος, one's *fate, doom.* 3. *that which is* one's *due;* generally, *that which is meet and right; κατὰ μοῖραν ἔειπες* thou hast spoken *fitly, rightly; μοῖραν νέμειν τινί* to give one *his due:* hence 4. *due reverence, consideration; ἐν μοίρῃ ἄγειν τινά* to hold one *in proper respect.*

Μοῖρα, as prop. n., *Moira, the goddess of fate:* later there were three, *Clotho, Lachesis, Atropos.*

μοιράω, f. άσω [ᾱ], Ion. ήσω: (μοῖρα):—*to share, distribute:* Med. *to share among themselves.*

μοιρη γενής, ές, (μοῖρα, γένος) *fated from birth.*

μοιρίδιος, α, ον, also ος, ον, (μοῖρα) *allotted by fate* or *doom, destined, fated,* Lat. *fatalis.*

μοιρό-κραντος, ον, (μοῖρα, κραίνω) *ordained by fate, fated, destined.*

Μοῖσα, ἡ, Aeol. for Μοῦσα: **Μοισᾶν**, Aeol. for Μουσῶν, pl. gen.

Μοισαῖος, α, ον, Aeol. for Μούσειος.

μοιχ-άγρια, τά, (μοιχός, ἄγρα) only in pl. *the fine imposed on one taken in adultery.*

μοιχᾰλίς, ίδος, ἡ, irreg. fem. of μοιχός, *an adulteress,* Lat. *moecha:* as fem. Adj. *adulterous.*

μοιχάς, άδος, ἡ, fem. of μοιχός, *an adulteress.*

μοιχάω, f. ήσω, (μοιχός) trans. *to commit adultery with; μοιχᾶν τὴν θάλατταν to hold dalliance with* the sea. II. intr. *to commit adultery,* Lat. *moechari.*

μοιχεύω, f. σω, *to commit adultery with, to seduce,* c. acc. II. intr. *to commit adultery,* Lat. *moechari.*

μοιχίδιος, α, ον, (μοιχός) *born in adultery.*

μοίχιος, α, ον, *adulterous.* From

ΜΟΙΧΟ'Σ, οῦ, ὁ, *an adulterer, paramour, seducer,* Lat. *moechus; κεκάρθαι μοιχὸν μιᾷ μαχαίρᾳ* to have the head shaven with a rasor *like an adulterer's;* since persons taken in adultery had their heads close shaven by way of punishment.

ΜΟΛΕΙ'Ν, aor. 2 inf. of βλώσκω.

μολῐβ-αχθής, ές, (μόλιβος, ἄχθος) *loaded with lead.*

μόλῐβος, ου, ὁ, poët. for μόλυβδος, *lead.*

μόλῐς, Adv., later form for μόγις, *hardly, scarcely, with difficulty; οὐ μόλις not scarcely,* i. e. *quite, utterly.*

μολοβρός, οῦ, ὁ, *a glutton, greedy beggar.*

μολοῖσα, Dor. for μολοῦσα, fem. of μολών.

Μολοσσός Att. -ττός, όν, *Molossian; κύων Μολοττικός* the *Molossian* dog, a kind of wolf-dog used by shepherds. II. ὁ μολοσσός (sub. ποῦς), in Prosody, *the Molossus,* a foot consisting of three long syllables, e. g. πρυμνήτης.

μολοῦμαι, fut. of βλώσκω.

μολπάζω, (μολπή) *to sing of,* Lat. *canere.* Hence

μολπαστής, οῦ, ὁ, *a minstrel* or *dancer.*

μολπή, ἡ, (μέλπω) in Hom. *dancing to music: anything done in time:* generally, *play, sport,* properly when singing and dancing formed part of it. II. generally, *singing, song,* opp. to dancing. Hence

μολπηδόν, Adv. *with singing.*

μολπῆτις Dor. -ᾶτις, ιδος, ἡ, (μολπή) *a songstress.*

μολύβδαινα, ἡ, (μόλυβδος) *a piece of lead,* esp. *the lead* to sink a fishing-line. 2. *a plummet, a leaden ball* or *bullet.*

μολύβδῐνος, η, ον, (μόλυβδος) *leaden, of lead.*

μολυβδίς, ίδος, ἡ, (μόλυβδος) like μολύβδαινα, the *leaden weight* on a net. II. *a leaden ball* or *bullet.*

ΜΟ'ΛΥΒΔΟΣ, ου, ο, *lead.* II. *plumbago, black lead:* hence *a blacklead pencil.*

μολυβδο-χοέω, f. ήσω, (μόλυβδος, χέω) *to fix with melted lead.*

μολῠνο-πραγμονέομαι, Pass. (μολύνω, πρᾶγμα);—*to be mixed up in a dirty quarrel.*

ΜΟΛΥΝΩ [ῡ]: f. ῠνῶ: pf. pass. μεμόλυσμαι:—*to stain, sully, defile, corrupt:* also *to seduce* a woman:—Pass. *to be* or *become vile, wallow.*

μολυσμός, ὁ, (μολύνω) *defilement, pollution.*

μολών, οῦσα, όν, aor. 2 part. of βλώσκω.

μομφή, ἡ, (μέμφομαι) *blame, reproof, complaint:*—*a cause of complaint.*

μόνα, Dor. for μόνη.

μονάζω, f. σω, (μόνος) *to be alone, live in solitude.*

μοναμπῠκία, ἡ, for ὁ μονάμπυξ, *a race-horse that runs single.*

μον-άμπυξ, ῠκος, ὁ, ἡ, (μόνος, ἄμπυξ II) *having one frontlet;* μονάμπυκες πῶλοι horses *that run single, racehorses:* also of a bull, *having no yokefellow.*

μοναρχέω Ion. μουν-: f. ήσω: (μόναρχος):—*to be monarch* or *sovereign;* ἐπὶ τούτου μουναρχέοντος in this king's *reign.* Hence

μοναρχία Ion. μουν-, ἡ, *absolute rule, sovereignty, monarchy.*

μόν-αρχος Ion. μουν-, ον, (μόνος, ἄρχω) *ruling alone, sovereign.*

μονάς Ion. μουνάς, άδος, ἡ, (μόνος) properly a fem. Adj., *solitary, single:* also masc. of a man, *alone, by oneself.* II. as Subst., μονάς, ἡ, *a unit.*

μονᾰχῇ, Adv. properly dat. fem. of μοναχός, *in one way only: singly* or *alone.*

μονᾰχός, ή, όν, (μόνος) *solitary;*—as Subst. μοναχός, ὁ, *a monk.*

μον-ερέτης Ion. μουν-, ου, ὁ, (μόνος, ἐρέτης) *one who rows singly, a sculler.*

μονή, ἡ, (μένω) *a staying, abiding, tarrying.* 2. *a place to stay in, mansion.*

μον-ημέριον, τό, (μόνος, ἡμέρα) *a hunt of one day.*

μον-ήρης, ες, (μόνος, ἀρᾰρεῖν) *single;* ναῦς μονήρης a ship *with one bank of oars.*

μόνῐμος, ον, or η, ον, (μονή) *staying, fixed:* of persons, *steadfast, constant.* 2. of conditions, *abiding, lasting,* Lat. *stabilis.*

μόν-ιππος, ον, (μόνος, ἵππος) *with one horse, a horseman,* opp. to a charioteer.

μονο-βάμων, ον, gen. ονος, (μόνος, βαίνω) *walking alone:* of metre, *consisting of one foot.* [βᾰ]

μονό-γᾰμος, ον, (μόνος, γαμέω) *marrying one wife.*

μονο-γένεια Ion. μουνογ-, ἡ, pecul. fem. of sq.

μονο-γενής Ep. and Ion. μουνογ-, ές, (μόνος, γένος) *only-begotten: born from one and the same mother.*

μονό-γληνος, ον, (μόνος, γλήνη) *one-eyed.*

μονο-δάκτῠλος, ον, (μόνος, δάκτυλος) *one-fingered.*

μονο-δέρκτης, ου, ὁ, (μόνος, δέρκομαι) *one-eyed.*

μονό-δουπος, ον, (μόνος, δοῦπος) *of unvaried sound, monotonous.*

μον-όδους, -όδοντος, ὁ, ἡ, (μόνος, ὀδούς) *one-toothed.*

μονό-δροπος, ον, (μόνος, δρέπω) *plucked from one stem: cut* or *carved from one block.*

μονο-ειδής, ές, (μόνος, εἶδος) *of one kind, simple.*

μονο-ζῠγής, ές, and **μονόζυξ**, ῠγος, ὁ, ἡ, (μόνος, ζυγῆναι) *having one horse yoked:* generally, *single, alone.*

μονο-ήμερος, ον, (μόνος, ἡμέρα) *lasting but one day.*

μονο-κέλης Ion. μουνο-κ-, ητος, ὁ, (μόνος, κέλης) *a single horse.*

μονό-κερως, ων, gen. -κερω, acc. -κερων, (μόνος, κέρας) *one-horned:* as Subst. *a unicorn.*

μονό-κλαυτος, ον, (μόνος, κλαίω) *with one mourner.*

μονό-κλῑνον, τό, (μόνος, κλίνη) *a bed for one only, a coffin.*

μονο-κοιτέω, f. ήσω, (μόνος, κοιτέω) *to sleep alone.*

μονο-κρηπῑς, ῖδος, ὁ, ἡ, (μόνος, κρηπίς) *with but one sandal.*

μονό-κροτος, ον, (μόνος, κροτέω) *with one bank of oars.*

μονό-κωλος Ion. μουν-, ον, (μόνος, κῶλον) *with but one limb:* of buildings, *with but one room:* περίοδος μονόκωλος a sentence *consisting of one clause.*

μονό-κωπος, ον, (μόνος, κώπη) *with a single oar: with a single ship.*

μονό-λῐθος Ion. μουν-, ον, (μόνος, λίθος) *made out of one stone.*

μονο-μάτωρ, ορος, Dor. for μονομήτωρ. [ᾱ]

μονομᾰχέω Ion. μουν-, f. ήσω, (μονομάχος) *to fight in single combat:* of the Athenians at Marathon, μοῦνοι μουνομαχήσαντες τῷ Πέρσῃ *having fought single-handed* with the Persian. Hence

μονομᾰχία Ion. μουνομαχίη, ἡ, *single combat.*

μονομάχιον, τό, = μονομαχία.

μονο-μάχος, ον, (μόνος, μάχομαι) *fighting in single combat: wielded in single combat.*

μονο-μήτωρ, ορος, ὁ, ἡ, (μόνος, μήτηρ) *left alone by one's mother, deprived of one's mother.*

μονο-νυχί Ion. μουν-, Adv. (μόνος, νύξ) *in a single night.*

μονό-ξῠλος, ον, (μόνος, ξύλον) *made from a single log.* II. *made of wood only.*

μονό-παις, -παιδος, ὁ, ἡ, (μόνος, παῖς) act. *having but one child.* II. pass. = μόνος παῖς, *an only child.*

μονο-πάλης Ion. μουν-, ου, ὁ, (μόνος, πάλη) *one who conquers alone in wrestling.* [ᾰ]

μονό-πελμος, ον, (μόνος, πέλμα) *with but one sole.*

μονό-πεπλος, ον, (μόνος, πέπλος) *left without a robe, clad in a tunic only:* v. ἄπεπλος.

μονό-πους, ὁ, ἡ, -πουν, τό, gen. -ποδος, (μόνος, πούς) *one-footed.*

μονό-πωλος, ον, (μόνος, πῶλος) *with one horse.*

μον-ορύχης, ου, ὁ, (μόνος, ὀρυγῆναι) *digging with one point.* [ῠ]

ΜΟΝΟΣ Ion. μοῦνος, η, ον, Dor. μῶνος, α, ον, *alone, left alone, forsaken:* c. gen., μόνος σοῦ *reft of, deprived of* thee. II. *alone, only:* often with gen. added, μοῦνος πάντων ἀνθρώπων *alone of* all men. III. like Lat. *unus* for *unicus, standing alone, single in its kind, unique.* IV. Sup. μονώτατος, *the one only person, one above all others,* cf. αὐτότατος. V. neut. μόνον as Adv., *alone, only, merely;* μόνον οὐ, Lat. *tantum non, all but, well nigh.*

μονο-σίδηρος, ον, (μόνος, σίδηρος) *made of iron only.*

μονοσῑτέω, f. ήσω, *to eat but once in the day.* From

μονό-σῑτος, ον, (μόνος, σῖτος) *eating but once a day.*

μονο-σκηπτρος, ον, (μόνος, σκῆπτρον) *wielding the sceptre alone, absolute.*

μονο-στἴβής, ές, (μόνος, στιβεῖν) *walking alone, unaccompanied.*

μονό-στῐχος, ον, (μόνος, στίχος) *consisting of one verse.*

μονό-στολος, ον, (μόνος, στολή) *going alone*: generally, *alone, single.*

μονο-στόρθυγξ, υγγος, ὁ, ἡ, (μόνος, στόρθυγξ) *carved out of a single block.*

μονο-σύλλᾰβος, ον, (μόνος, συλλαβή) *of one syllable, dealing with monosyllables.*

μονό-τεκνος, ον, (μόνος, τέκνον) *with but one child.*

μονο-τράπεζος, ον, (μόνος, τράπεζα) *at a solitary board, eaten apart.*

μονό-τροπος, ον, (μόνος, τρόπος) *solitary, unsocial.*

μον-ούᾰτος, ον, (μόνος, οὖς) *one-eared*: *with one handle.*

μονο-φάγος, ον, (μόνος, φᾰγεῖν) *eating alone* or *once a day*: irreg. Sup. μονοφαγίστατος.

μον-όφθαλμος Ion. μουν-, ον, (μόνος, ὀφθαλμός) *one-eyed.*

μονό-φρουρος, ον, (μόνος, φρουρά) *watching alone.*

μονό-φρων, ον, gen. ονος, (μόνος, φρήν) *single in one's opinion, standing alone, single.*

μονο-φυής Ion. μουν-, ές, (μόνος, φυή) *of simple nature*: *made of one piece.*

μονό-χηλος Dor. **-χαλος**, ον, (μόνος, χηλή) *solid-hoofed.*

μονό-ψηφος Dor. -ψαφος, ον, (μόνος, ψῆφος) *voting alone*: *singular in one's vote or purpose.*

μονόω Ion. **μουν-**: f. ώσω: aor. 1 ἐμόνωσα Ep. μούνωσα:—Pass., aor. 1 ἐμονώθην, Ion. part. μουνωθείς: pf. μεμόνωμαι Ion. μεμούνωμαι: (μόνος):—*to make single* or *solitary*; μουνοῦν γενεήν *to give an only* son in each generation:—Pass. *to be left alone, to be forsaken*: also *to be taken apart, without witnesses*: c. gen., μεμουνωμένοι συμμάχων *deserted* by allies.

μονῳδέω, f. ήσω, (μονῳδός) *to sing alone, to sing a monody.* Hence

μονῳδία, ἡ, *a song sung alone, a monody, solo*, opp. to the song of the chorus.

μον-ῳδός, όν, (μόνος, ᾠδή) *singing alone.*

μονωθείς, aor. 1 pass. part. of μονόω

μόνως, Adv. of μόνος, *only.*

μον-ώψ poët. μοῦν-, ῶπος, ὁ, ἡ, (μόνος, ὤψ) *one-eyed.*

μόρα, ἡ, (μείρομαι) = μοῖρα. 2. *one of the six divisions of the Spartan infantry.*

μορίαι (sc. ἐλαῖαι), αἱ, *the sacred olives* in the Academy, so called because they were supposed *to be parted* or *propagated* (μειρόμεναι, μεμορημέναι) from the original olive-stock that grew in the Acropolis. Hence Ζεὺς **Μόριος** as *the guardian of these sacred olives* II. μορία [ῑ], = μωρία, *folly.*

μόρῐμος, ον, poët. for μόρσιμος.

μόριον, τό, Dim of μόρος, *a small piece*, generally, *a piece, portion.*

μόριος, α, ον, poët. for μόρσιμος.—For Ζεὺς Μόριος, see μορίαι.

μορμολῠκεῖον, το, *a bugbear, bogoblin.* From

μορμολύττομαι, Dep. (μορμώ) *to fright, scare.*

μορμορ-ωπός, όν, (μορμώ, ὤψ) *hideous to behold.*

μορμύρω [ῡ], formed from μύρω, as πορφύρω from φύρω, of water, *to roar, boil*, Lat. *murmuro.*

ΜΟΡΜΩ', gen. όος, contr. οῦς, ἡ, *a hideous shemonster*, to frighten children with; *a bugbear, hobgoblin.* II. in Aristophanes, a mere exclamation. μορμὼ τοῦ θράσους *a fig* for his courage!

μορόεις, εσσα, εν, *skilfully* or *richly wrought*; or *glistening, shining.* (Deriv. unknown.)

ΜΟ'ΡΟΝ, τό, *the black mulberry.*

μόρος, ὁ, (μείρομαι) like μοῖρα, *one's appointed lot, fate, doom, destiny*; ὑπὲρ μόρον beyond *one's doom, against fate.* 2. esp. *an unhappy lot, ruin, death.* Lat. *fatum*, in Homer always *a violent* death.

μόρσῐμος, ον, (μόρος) *appointed by fate, doomed, destined*, Lat. *fatalis*: *foredoomed, destined to die*: hence μόρσιμον ἦμαρ *the fated* day, the day *of doom*: τὸ μόρσιμον *fate, doom, destiny.*

ΜΟΡΥ'ΣΣΩ, *to soil, stain, defile, sully*: pf. pass. part. μεμορυγμένος, *soiled, defiled.*

μορφᾷ, μορφάν, Dor. for μορφῇ, μορφήν.

μορφάζω, (μορφή) *to make gesticulations.*

μορφάω, f. ήσω, (μορφή) *to shape, fashion, mould.*

Μορφεύς, έως, ὁ, *Morpheus*, son of Sleep, god of dreams: properly *the fashioner, moulder*, so called from the shapes he calls up before the sleeper. From

ΜΟΡΦΗ', ἡ, *form, shape, figure*: *a beautiful form, beauty*, Lat. *forma* 2. generally, *form, fashion, appearance* 3. *a form, kind, sort.* Hence

μορφήεις, εσσα, εν, *formed, fashioned, shaped*: *well-shaped, comely*, Lat. *formosus.*

μόρφνος, ον, (epith. of the eagle) of colour, *dusky, dark*, = ὀρφνός (from ὄρφνη), Lat. *furvus*

μορφόω, f. ώσω, (μορφή) *to form, give shape to.* Hence

μόρφωμα, ατος, το, *form, shape, figure*: *the outline of a figure.*

μόρφωσις, ἡ, (μορφόω) *a shaping*: *form, semblance.*

μορφωτήρ, ῆρος, ὁ, (μορφόω) *one who shapes*:—fem. **μορφώτρια**; συῶν μορφώτρια *changing men into* swine.

μόσσυν or **μόσυν**, ῡνος, ὁ, *a wooden house* or *tower.*

Μοσσύν-οικοι or **Μοσύν-οικοι**, οἱ, (μόσσυν or μόσυν, οἰκέω) an Asiatic race near the Black Sea, neighbours of the Colchians, *living in wooden houses.*

μόσχειος, α, ον, (μόσχος) *of a calf*; μόσχειος κυνοῦχος *a calf-skin* leash: as Subst., μόσχειον, τό, *a calf-skin.*

μοσχεύω, f. σω, (μόσχος) *to plant a sucker, propagate.*

μοσχίδιον, τό, Dim. of μόσχος, *a young sucker.* [ῐ]

μόσχιος, α, ον, (μόσχος) like μόσχειος, *of a calf.*

μοσχο-ποιέω, f. ήσω, (μόσχος, ποιέω) *to make a calf.*

μόσχος, ὁ, also ἡ, *the young shoot of* a plant, *a sprout, sucker, scion.* II. metaph. of the young of animals, *a calf:* also *a young bull: a heifer.* 2. *a boy:* more often *a girl, maid,* L^t. *iuvenca.* 3. *any young animal.*

μουνάξ, Adv. (μοῦνος) *singly, alone.*

μουναρχέω, Ion. for μοναρχέω.

μοῦνος, Ion. for μόνος. For all Ion. forms beginning with μουν-, see under μον-.

Μουνῠχία, ἡ, *Munychia,* a harbour at Athens, adjoining Piræeus. II. epith. of Diana, who was worshipped there. Hence

Μουνῠχίαζε, Adv. *to Munychia:* and

Μουνῠχίᾱσι, Adv. *at Munychia.*

Μουνῠχιών, ῶνος, ὁ, *Munychion,* tne tenth Attic month, in which was held the festival of Munychian Artemis, = the latter part of April and beginning of May.

μουνωθείς, Ion. aor. I part. pass. of μονόω.

μουν-ώψ, Ion. for μονώψ.

ΜΟΥ῀ΣΑ, ης, Aeol. Μοῖσα Dor. Μῶσα Lacon. Μῶα, ας, ἡ, *the Muse,* goddess of song, music, poetry, dancing, and the fine arts. There were *nine* Muses,—Clio, Euterpē, Thalia, Melpomĕnē, Terpsichŏrē, Erăto, Polymnia or Polyhymnia, Urania, and Calliŏpē. II. later *music, song:* also *eloquence;* and in pl. *arts, accomplishments.*

Μουσ-ᾱγέτης, ου, ὁ, Dor. for Μουσηγ-, (Μοῦσα, ἡγέομαι), *the leader of the Muses,* i. e. Apollo.

Μουσεῖον, τό, *the temple of the Muses, seat* or *haunt of the Muses:* hence *a school of arts and learning, a Museum:* metaph., μουσεῖα θρηνήμασι ξυνῳδά *halls* resounding with lamentations; μουσεῖα χελιδόνων *places* where swallows *twitter.* Properly. neut. of Μούσειος.

Μούσειος Dor. Μοισαῖος, α, ον, also ος, ον, (μοῦσα) *of* or *belonging to the Muses, sacred to the Muses.*

μουσίζομαι, Dep. (μοῦσα) *to sing* or *play.*

μουσῐκός, ή, όν, (μοῦσα) *of the Muses* or *the fine arts, devoted to the Muses.* II. as Subst., I. μουσικός, ὁ, *a musician, poet, a lyric-poet:* generally, *a man of letters, a scholar, an accomplished person,* opp. to ἄμουσος. 2. μουσική (sc. τέχνη), ἡ, *any art over which the Muses presided,* esp. *music* or *lyric poetry set and sung to music,*—one of the three branches of Athenian education, the other two being γράμματα, γυμναστική:—generally, *arts, letters, accomplishments.* III. Adv. -κῶς, *harmoniously, elegantly:* Sup. -κώτατα.

μουσίσδω, Dor. for μουσίζω.

μουσό-δομος, ον, (μοῦσα, δέμω) *built by song.*

μουσομᾰνέω, f. ήσω, *to be Muse-mad, smitten by the Muses.* From

μουσο-μᾰνής, ές, (μοῦσα, μανῆναι) *smitten by the Muses.*

μουσό-μαντις, εως, ὁ, ἡ, (μοῦσα, μάντις) *of prophetic song.*

μουσο-μήτωρ, ορος, ἡ, (μοῦσα, μήτηρ) *the mother of the Muses and arts.*

μουσο-ποιέω, f. ήσω, *to write poetry about.* From

μουσο-ποιός, όν, (μοῦσα, ποιέω) *making poetry:* μουσοποιός, ἡ, *a poetess:* also *singing* or *playing.*

μουσο-πόλος, ον, (μοῦσα, πολέω) *serving the Muses:* as Subst., μουσοπόλος, ὁ, *a minstrel.*

μουσο-πρόσωπον, ον, (μοῦσα, πρόσωπον) *musical-looking.*

μουσουργία, ἡ, *a making poetry, singing.* From

μουσ-ουργός, όν, contr. for μουσο-εργός, (μοῦσα, ἔργον) *devoted to the service of the Muses, playing, singing:*—as Subst., μουσουργός, ἡ, *a singing-girl.*

μουσο-φίλης, ου, ὁ, and μουσό-φῐλος, ον, (μοῦσα, φιλέω) *loving the Muses.*

μουσο-χᾰρής, ές, (μοῦσα, χαίρω) *delighting in the Muses, delighting in music* or *poetry.*

μουσόω, f. ώσω, (μοῦσα) *to devote to the Muses:*—Pass. *to be well educated, accomplished, elegant.*

μοχθεῦντας, Dor. part. acc. pl. of μοχθέω.

μοχθέω, f. ήσω, (μόχθος) *to be weary with toil, be sore troubled* or *distressed, to suffer greatly:* c. acc. cognato, μοχθεῖν μόχθους, πόνους *to undergo hardship, toils;* μοχθεῖν μαθήματα *to toil at* learning. Hence

μόχθημα, ατος, τό, *toil, hardship.*

μοχθηρία, ἡ, *wretchedness, poor condition:* mostly in moral sense, *badness, wickedness.* From

μοχθηρός, ά, όν, (μοχθέω) *in sore distress, wretched* 2. of things, *toilsome, laborious:* but also *in sorry plight.* II. in moral sense, *knavish, villainous, rascally,* Lat. *pravus.* Hence

μοχθηρῶς, Adv. *in sorry plight, miserably.*

μοχθητέον, verb. Adj. of μοχθέω, *one must labour.*

μοχθίζω, f. σω, = μοχθέω, *to toil, labour:* also *to suffer greatly.*

μόχθος, ὁ, (μογέω) *toil, hardship, distress, trouble:* in pl. *toils, troubles, hardships:*—μόχθος differs from πόνος, in that μόχθος always implies *distress, hardship,* Lat. *aerumna,* while πόνος is merely *work, labour,* Lat. *labor.*

μοχλευτής, οῦ, ὁ, *one who heaves up by a lever;* θαλάσσης μοχλευτής *he who makes* the sea *to heave;* καινῶν ἐπῶν μοχλευτής *one who heaves up* new words. From

μοχλεύω, f. σω, (μοχλός) *to prise up, to heave up* or *wrench by a lever.*

μοχλέω, f. ήσω, Ion. for μοχλεύω.

μοχλίον, τό, Dim. of μοχλός.

ΜΟΧΛΟ´Σ, οῦ, ὁ, *a lever* or *bar for prising* or *heaving up, a crowbar,* Lat. *vectis.* II. *any bar* or *stake:*—*the bar* or *bolt* of a door, Lat. *obex.*

ΜΥ´ or ΜΥ῀, an imitation of the sound made *by murmuring* or *muttering with closed lips.* II. to *imitate the sound of sobbing.*

μῦ ἄγρα, ἡ, (μῦς, ἄγρα) *a mouse-trap.*

μῠάω, (μῦ) *to bite* or *compress the lips.*

μῡ-γᾰλῆ, (μῦς, γαλέη) *the field-mouse, shrew-mouse,* Lat. *mus araneus.*

μυγμός, οῦ, ὁ, (μύζω) *a moaning, muttering.*

μῠδᾰλέος, *α, ον*, *wet, dripping, soaked*. II. *damp, mouldy*. From

μῠδάω, f. ήσω, (μύδος) *to be damp, wet, dripping*. II. *to be damp* or *clammy* from decay.

ΜΥ´ΔΟΣ, ὁ, *damp: clamminess, decay*, Lat. *situs*. [ῠ]

μυδροκτῠπέω, f. ήσω, *to forge red-hot iron*. From

μυδρο-κτύπος, ον, (μύδρος, κτῠπέω) *forging* or *welding red-hot iron*.

ΜΥ´ΔΡΟΣ [ῡ], ὁ, *any red-hot mass*; μύδρους αἴρειν χεροῖν to lift *masses of red-hot iron* in the hands, as an ordeal: also *any lump* or *mass of metal*.

μυέλῐνος, η, ον, (μυελός) = μυελόεις.

μυελόεις, εσσα, εν, (μυελός) *full of marrow*.

ΜΥΕΛΟ´Σ, οῦ, ὁ, Lat. *MEDULLA*, *marrow*: metaph. of *strengthening food*, as wine and barley, which are called μυελὸς ἀνδρῶν. 2. *the marrow of the skull, the brain*. 3. generally, *the inmost part, core*. [ῡ in Hom., ῠ in Att.]

μῠέω, f. ήσω: aor. 1 ἐμύησα:—Pass., aor. 1 ἐμυήθην: pf. μεμύημαι: (μύω):—*to initiate into the mysteries*.—Pass. *to be initiated*; c. acc. cognato, μυεῖσθαι τὰ Καβείρων ὄργια *to be initiated* in the mysteries of the Cabiri; μυεῖσθαι τὰ μεγάλα *to be initiated in* the great mysteries. 2. generally, *to instruct*.

μύζω, f. μύξω, (μῦ) *to murmur with closed lips, moan: to mutter*. II. *to drink with closed lips, to suck in*.

μῡθέομαι, Ep. 2 sing. μυθεῖαι, contr. for μυθέεαι, and omitting one ε, μυθέαι: 3 pl. Ion. impf. μυθέσκοντο: f. μυθήσομαι: aor. 1 ἐμυθησάμην, Ep. 3 sing. μυθήσατο: Dep.: (μῦθος):—*to say, speak, tell, name*. II. *to say over to oneself*, like φράζομαι, *con over, consider*.

μυθεῦ, Dor. for μυθοῦ, imperat. of μυθέομαι.

μυθεῦμαι, Dor. for μυθέομαι.

μῡθεύω, = μυθέομαι:—Pass., *to be the subject of a story, to be talked of*.

μυθησαίμην, aor. 1 med. opt. of μυθέομαι.

μῡθιάζομαι, Dep. = μυθέομαι.

μῡθίδιον, τό, Dim. of μῦθος, *a short tale* or *fable*.

μῡθίζω Dor. -ίσδω, later form for μυθέομαι.

μῡθικός, ή, όν, (μῦθος) *mythic, legendary*.

μυθίσδω, Dor. for μυθίζω.

μῡθο-λογεύω, (μῦθος, λέγω) *to tell word for word*.

μῡθο-λογέω, f. ήσω, (μυθολόγος) *to tell mythic tales* or *legends*: also *to tell as a legend*:—Pass. *to be* or *become mythical*. 2. *to tell tales, talk*. Hence

μυθολογητέον, verb. Adj. *one must tell legends*.

μῡθολογία, ἡ, (μυθολογέω) *a telling of mythic tales* or *legends, mythology*. Hence

μῡθολογικός, ή, όν, *versed in mythology*.

μῡθο-λόγος, ον, (μῦθος, λέγω) *dealing in mythic legends*: as Subst., μυθόλογος, ὁ, *a teller of legends*.

μῡθο-πλόκος, ον, (μῦθος, πλέκω) *weaving tales*.

ΜΥ῀ΘΟΣ, ὁ, *anything delivered by word of mouth, word, speech*: as opp. to ἔργον, *a mere word*, without the deed: *a speech*. II. *talk, conversation*: also, *the subject of conversation, the matter itself*. III. *advice, a command, order*. IV. *a purpose, design, plan*. V. *a tale, story*: afterwards, μῦθος was *the poetic* or *legendary tale*, as opposed to the *historical* account. 2. *a tale, story, fable*, such as Aesop's fables.

μῡθ-ώδης, ες, (μῦθος, εἶδος) *like a fable, legendary, fabulous*.

ΜΥ῀ΙΑ Att. **μύα**, ἡ, *a fly*, Lat. *musca*.

μυιο-σόβη, ἡ, (μυῖα, σοβέω) *a fly-flap*.

μυιο-σόβος, ον, (μυῖα, σοβέω) *flapping away flies*.

ΜΥ῀ΚΑ´ΟΜΑΙ, f. -ήσομαι: Ep. aor. 2 ἔμῠκον: Ep. pf. μέμῡκα (so βέβρυχα, μέμηκα from βρυχάομαι, μηκάομαι): Dep.:—Lat. *MUGIRE*, of oxen, *to bellow*: also of other animals, as of asses, *to bray*, of dogs, *to growl*, etc.: of things, *to grate, jar, roar*: also *to groan* from exertion. (Formed from the sound of oxen, as βληκάομαι, μηκάομαι from that of sheep and goats, βρυχάομαι from that of bulls, etc., βρωμάομαι from that of asses.)

μύκε, Ep. 3 sing. aor. 2 of μυκάομαι.

μῡκηθμός, ὁ, (μυκάομαι) *a bellowing*: and

μύκημα, ατος, τό, *a bellowing*: *the roar* of thunder. [ῡ]

Μῠκηναῖος, ον, *of* or *from Mycenae*. From

Μῠκήνη, ἡ, and **Μῠκῆναι**, αἱ, *Mycenè, Mycenae*, an ancient Pelasgic city, superseded by the Doric Argos: —Adv. **Μυκήνηθεν**, *from Mycenae*.

Μῠκηνίς, ίδος, ἡ, pecul. fem. of Μυκηναῖος.

ΜΥ´ΚΗΣ, ητος, ὁ, also **μύκης**, ου, ὁ, *a mushroom*, Lat. *fungus*. II. *any round body*, shaped like a mushroom, as, 1. *the cap at the end of a sword's scabbard*. 2. *the snuff* of a lamp-wick, supposed to forebode rain; cf. Virgil's *putres concrescere fungos*.

μῠκήτῐνος, η, ον, (μύκης) *made of mushrooms*.

μυκτήρ, ῆρος, ὁ, (μύζω) *the nose, snout*: in pl. *the nostrils*. Hence

μυκτηρίζω, f. ίσω, *to turn up the nose* or *sneer at*, Lat. *naso adunco suspendere*.

μυκτηρόθεν, Adv. (μυκτήρ) *out of the nose*.

μυκτηρό-κομπος, ον, (μυκτήρ, κόμπος) *sounding from the nostril*.

μῠλαῖος, ον, (μύλη) *working in a mill*.

μῠλακρίς, ίδος, ἡ, (μύλη) *of a mill*;—μυλακρὶς λᾶας *a millstone*.

μύλαξ, ἄκος, ὁ, (μύλη) *a millstone, any large round stone*.

μῠλ-εργάτης, ου, ὁ, (μύλη, ἐργάτης) *one who works in a mill, a miller*. [ᾰ]

μύλη [ῠ], ἡ, *a mill*, Lat. *mŏla, a hand-mill*. II. *the nether millstone*.

μυλή-φᾰτος, ον, (μύλη, πέφαμαι pf. pass. of *φένω) *bruised* or *crushed in a mill*.

μῠλιάω, (μύλη) *to gnash* or *grind the teeth*.

μῠλικός, ή, όν, (μύλη) *of* or *for a mill*; λίθος μυλικός *a millstone*.

μύλλω, (μύλη) *to crush, pound*, Lat. *mŏlĕre*.

μῠλο-ειδής, ές, (μύλος, εἶδος) *like a millstone*.

μυλος, ὁ, (μύλη) *a millstone;* Ep. ὀνικός. [ῠ]

μύλωθρος, ὁ, (μύλη) *a miller, a master miller.*

μῠλών, ῶνος, ὁ, *a mill-house, mill,* Lat. *pistrinum;* βάλλειν εἰς μυλῶνα, Lat. *detrudere in pistrinum,* to condemn [a slave] to work the *mill.*

μύνη, ἡ, (ἀμύνω) *an excuse, pretence, pretext.* [ῡ]

μύνομαι, Dep. (μύνη) *to make excuses: to put off.*

μύξα, ἡ, (μύζω, μύξω) *the discharge from the nose, mucus, phlegm.*

μυξωτήρ, ῆρος, ὁ, = μυκτήρ, *a nose, nostril.*

μῠο-κτόνος, ον, (μῦς, κτείνω) *mouse-killing.*

μύραινα, ἡ, (μύρος) Lat. *muraena, a sea-eel* or *lamprey:* also *a sea-serpent.*

μῡριάκις, Adv. (μυρίος) *ten thousand times.*

μῡρι-άμφορος, ον, (μυρίος ἀμφορεύς) *holding ten thousand measures* (ἀμφορεῖς).

μῡρι-άρχης, ου, ὁ, and **μῡρί-αρχος**, ὁ, (μυρίος, ἄρχω) *a commander of* 10,000 *men.*

μῡριάς, άδος, ἡ, Att. gen. plur. μυριαδῶν, (μυρίος) *the number* 10,000, *a myriad:*—when μυριάς, μυριάδες are used alone of *money,* δραχμῶν must be supplied; when of *corn,* μεδίμνων.

μῡρι-ετής, ές, gen. έος, (μυρίος, ἔτος) *lasting ten thousand years: of countless years.*

μῡρίζω, f. ίσω: pf. pass. μεμύρισμαι: (μύρον):—*to anoint.*

ΜΥΡΙ´ΚΗ [ῑ], ἡ, Lat. *myrica, the tamarisk.* Hence

μῡρῑκίνεος, α, ον, *of the tamarisk;* and

μῡρίκῑνος, η, ον, *of the tamarisk.* [ῑ]

μῡριό-βοιος, ον, (μυρίος, βοῦς) *with ten thousand oxen.*

μῡρι-όδους, όδοντες, ὁ, ἡ, (μυρίος, ὀδούς) *having immense teeth.*

μῡριό-καρπος, ον, (μυρίος, καρπός) *bearing countless fruit.*

μῡριό-κρᾱνος, ον, (μυρίος, κρᾶνον) *with numberless heads, many-headed.*

μῡριό-λεκτος, ον, (μυρίος, λέγω) *said ten thousand times.*

μῡριό-μορφος, ον, (μυρίος, μορφή) *of countless shapes.*

μῡριό-μοχθος, ος, (μυρίος, μόχθος) *of endless toil.*

μῡριό-ναυς, αος, ὁ, ἡ, (μυρίος, ναῦς) *of numberless ships.*

μῡριόντ-αρχος, ον, = μυρίαρχος.

μῡριο-πάλαι, Adv. (μυρίος, πάλαι) *time out of mind.*

μῡριο-πλᾰσίων, ον, gen. ονος, (μυρίος) *ten thousand fold: infinitely more than.*

μῡριο-πληθής, ές, (μυρίος, πλῆθος) *of infinite number, countless.*

ΜΥΡΙ´ΟΣ, α, ον, *numberless, countless,* of Number mostly in pl., but often in sing., as μύριον αἷμα, χαλκός, etc. 2. of Size, *huge, vast, immense, infinite;* ἄχος μυρίον *infinite* sorrow. 3. of Time, *endless, infinite.* II. as a definite Numeral in pl., μύριοι, αι, α, *ten thousand:* in some phrases the sing. may be used, as, ἵππος μυρίη 10,000 horse. [ῡ]

μῡριοστός, ή, όν, (μύριος) *the* 10,000*th.*

μῡριοστύς, ύος, ἡ, (μύριοι) *a body of ten thousand.*

μῡριο-τευχής, ές, (μύριοι, τεῦχος) *with ten thousand armed men.*

μῡριο-φόρος, ον, (μυριοι, φέρω) *of ten thousand talents burthen.*

μῡριο-φόρτος, ον, = μυριοφόρος

μῡριό-φωνος, ον, (μυρίος, φωνή) *with countless voices.*

μῡρί-πνοος, ον, contr. **-πνους**, ουν, (μύρον, πνέω) *breathing of unguents* or *essence.*

μῡρι-ωπός, όν, (μυρίος, ὤψ) *with countless eyes.*

μυρμηκιά, ᾶς, ἡ, (μύρμηξ) *an ant's nest, ant-hill.*

μυρμηκίας, ου, ὁ, (μύρμηξ) *got from ant-hills.*

ΜΥ´ΡΜΗΞ, ηκος, ὁ, *the ant,* Lat. *FORMICA.* I. *a beast of prey* in India. III. *a sunken rock* on the Thessalian coast between Sciathus and Magnesia.

Μυρμῐδόνες, οἱ, *the Myrmidons,* a warlike people of Thessaly, subjects of Peleus and Achilles.

μῠρο-βόστρῠχος, ον, (μύρον, βόστρυχος) *with perfumed locks.*

μῠρόεις, εσσα, εν, (μύρον) *anointed, scented.*

μύρομαι, v. sub μύρω. [ῠ]

ΜΥ´ΡΟΝ [ῠ], τό, *sweet oil extracted from plants:* generally, *sweet oil, an unguent, perfume, balsam.* II. *the* place where unguents were sold, *the perfume-market* III. metaph. *anything sweet* or *charming.*

μυρό-πνοος, ον, contr. **-πνους**, ουν, (μύρον, πνέω) *breathing of unguent.*

μῠρο-πώλης, ου, ὁ, fem. **-πωλις**, ιδος, ἡ, (μύρον, πωλέω) *a dealer in unguents, a perfumer.*

μῠρόρ-ραντος, ον, (μύρον, ῥαίνω) *wet with unguent.*

μῠρο-φεγγής, ές, (μύρον, φέγγος) *shining with unguent.*

μῠρό-χριστος, ον, (μύρον, χριστός) *anointed with sweet oil.*

μῠρόω, f. ώσω, (μύρον) *to rub with unguent, anoint.*

ΜΥ´ΡΡΑ, ἡ, *the juice of the Arabian myrtle,* Lat. *myrrha, murrha.*

μυρρίνη [ῐ], ἡ, later Att. for μυρσ–, *a myrtle twig* or *wreath.* II. μυρρίναι, αἱ, *the myrtle-market.*

μύρρῐνος, η, ον, (μυρρίνη) *of myrtle,* Lat. *myrteus.*

μυρρῐνών, ῶνος, ὁ, (μυρρίνη) *a myrtle-grove,* Lat. *myrtetum.*

ΜΥΡΣΙ´ΝΗ [ῐ] later Att. μυρρίνη, ἡ, *the myrtle.* II. *a myrtle-branch.* [ῐ]

μυρσῐνο-ειδής, ές, (μυρσίνη, εἶδος) *myrtle-like.*

μύρτον, ου, τό, *the fruit of the myrtle* (μύρτος), *the myrtle-berry,* Lat. *myrtum.*

ΜΥ´ΡΤΟΣ, ἡ, *the myrtle,* Lat. *myrtus.*

ΜΥ´ΡΩ [ῠ], only used in pres. and impf., *to flow, run, trickle, stream.* II. Med. μύρομαι, *to melt into tears: to shed tears, weep.* 2. trans. *to weep for, bewail, lament.*

μύρωμα, ατος, τό, (μυρόω) *plaster.*

ΜΥ͂Σ, ὁ, gen. μυός, acc. μῦν, voc. μῦ, *a mouse,* Lat. *MUS:* μῦς ἀρουραῖος, *a field-mouse.* II. *a muscle* of the body, Lat. *musculus.*

μύσαγμα, ατος, τό, (μυσάττομαι) = μυσος.

μύσαν [ῠ], Ep. 3 pl. aor. 1 of μύω.

μῠσᾰρός, ά, όν, (μύσος) *foul, loathsome, abominable*, Lat. *impurus*: τὸ μύσαρον *an abomination*.

μῠσάττομαι, f. μυσαχθήσομαι: aor. 1 ἐμυσάχθην: Dep.: (μύσος):—*to loathe, abominate*.

μύσος [ῠ], τό, (μύζω) *anything that causes disgust*: metaph. *an abomination, defilement*, Lat. *piaculum*.

Μῡσός, ὁ, *a Mysian*.

μυσ-πολέω, (μῦς, πολέω) *to run about like a mouse*.

μυστηρῐκος, ή, όν, *for mysteries, mystical*. From

μυστήριον, τό, (μύστης) *a mystery, secret rite*: mostly in pl. μυστήρια, τά, *the mysteries*, religious celebrations, the most famous of which were the Eleusinian *mysteries of Demeter* or *Ceres*. 2. *any mystery* or *secret thing*: *a mystic history* or *dispensation*.

μυστηρίς, ίδος, pecul. fem. of μυστηρικός.

μυστηριώτης, ου, ὁ, fem. **-ῶτις**, ιδος, (μυστήριον) *belonging to the mysteries*.

μύστης, ου, ὁ, (μυέω) *one initiated*. Hence

μυστῐκός, ή, όν, *of* or *for the mysteries*: *secret, mystical*.

μυστῐλάομαι, Dep. *to sop bread in soup* or *gravy to eat it with*. From

ΜΥΣΤΙ'ΛΗ [ῐ], ἡ, *a crust of bread hollowed out as a spoon*, to sup soup or gravy with.

μυστῐ-πόλος, ον, (μύστης, πολέω) *solemnising the mysteries*.

μυστο-δόκος, ον, (μύστης, δέχομαι) *receiving the mysteries, receiving the initiated*.

μυστο-δότης, ου, ὁ, (μύστης, δίδωμι) *initiating, introducing into the mysteries*.

μυτίλος [ῐ], ὁ, (μῦς) the fish *muscle*, Lat. *mytilus*.

μυττωτεύω, f. σω, *to make into mince-meat*. From

ΜΥΤΤΩΤΟ'Σ, ὁ, *a mess of cheese, honey, garlic* beaten up together, *mince-meat*.

μύχᾰτος, η, ον, irreg. Sup. of μύχιος, formed from μυχός, as μέσατος from μέσος. [ῠ]

μυχθίζω, f. σω, Dor. **μυχθίσδω**, (μύζω) *to breathe hard through the nostrils, to snort* or *moan* from passion. 2. *to make mouths at, sneer*. Hence

μυχθισμός, ὁ, *a snorting*: *sneering*.

μύχῐος, α, ον, (μυχός) *inward, inmost, most retired*, Lat. *intimus*: irreg. Sup. μῠχοίτατος.

μυχμός, ὁ, (μύζω) *moaning, groaning*.

μῠχόθεν, Adv. (μύχος) *from the inmost part of the house, from the women's chambers*.

μῠχοίτατος, η, ον, (μυχός) irreg. Sup. of μύχιος; μυχοίτατος ἶζε he sat *in the farthest corner*.

μῠχόνδε, Adv. (μυχός) *to the far corner*.

μῠχός, οῦ, ὁ, (μύω) *the innermost place, inmost nook* or *corner, a recess*, Lat. *sinus*: *the inmost part of a house, the women's apartments*, Lat. *penetralia*. 2. *a bay* or *creek* running far inland

ΜΥ'Ω, f. μύσω: aor. ἔμῦσα: pf. μέμῦκα: I. intr. *to be shut* or *closed*, esp. of the lips and eyes; but also of wounds; σὺν δ' ἕλκεα πάντα μέμυκεν all his wounds *have closed*. 2. of persons, *to shut the eyes, keep one's eyes shut*: absol., μύσας *with one's eyes shut*. 3. metaph. *to be lulled to rest, to abate*. II. trans. *to shut, close*.

μῡών, ῶνος, ὁ, (μῦς) *a knot of muscles, a muscular part of the body*.

μυῶν, gen. plur. of μύς.

μῠωπάζω, (μυώψ) *to be purblind, to see dimly*.

μῠωπίζω, (μύωψ) *to spur, prick with the spur, goad*. II. Pass. *to be teased by flies*.

μῠ-ωπός, όν, (μύω, ὤψ) = μυώψ 1.

μυ-ώψ, ῶπος, ὁ, ἡ, (μύω, ὤψ) *closing the eyes, short-sighted*. II. as Subst., μύωψ, ωπος, ὁ, *the horse-fly* or *gad-fly*. 2. *a goad, spur*. [ῠ]

Μῶα, ἡ, Lacon. for **Μοῦσα**.

μῶλος, ὁ, *a toil*, esp. *the toil* or *tug of war*: *battle, war*: *a struggle, contest*: generally, *a quarrel, broil*.

ΜΩ'ΛΥ, ῠος, το, *moly*, a magic herb with a black root and white blossom, given by Hermes to Ulysses, as a counter-charm to the spells of Circé.

ΜΩ'ΛΩΨ, ωπος, ὁ, *the mark of a blow, a weal, bruise*.

μωμάομαι, Ion. **-έομαι**: f. -ήσομαι: aor. ἐμωμησάμην, Dor. poët. 3 sing. μωμάσατο: Dep.: (μῶμος):—*to find fault with, blame, chide*, c. acc.:—aor. pass. ἐμωμήθην in pass. sense, *to be blamed*.

μωμεύω, f. σω, (μῶμος) *to blame, chide, find fault with*.

μωμητός, ή, όν, (μωμάομαι) *blamed, blamable*.

μῶμος, ου, ὁ, (μέμφομαι) *blame, censure, disgrace*. II. personified, *Momus*, the god of *blame*.

μῶν, Adv., Dor. contr. for μὴ οὖν, used in questions to which a negative answer is expected, *it is not, is it?* Lat. *num?* e. g. μῶν ἐστι . . ; Answ. οὐ δῆτα. Sometimes however it asks doubtingly, Lat. *num forte?* and may be answered in the affirmative.

μῶνος, α, ον, Dor. for μοῦνος, μόνος.

μῶ-νυξ, ῠχος, ὁ, ἡ, (μόνος, ὄνυξ) *with single, solid, uncloven hoof*, Lat. *solipes*, epith. of the horse.

μώνυχος, ον = μῶνυξ.

μωραίνω, f. ᾰνῶ: aor. 1 ἐμώρᾱνα: (μωρός):—*to be silly, foolish, to play the fool*: c. acc., πεῖραν μωραίνειν *to make a senseless* attempt. II. *to make foolish, convict of folly*. 2. *to make tasteless*: Pass. *to become* so.

μωρανθείς, aor. 1 pass. part. of μωραίνω.

μωρῐ́α, ἡ, (μῶρος) *silliness, folly, absurdity*.

μωρολογία, ἡ, *a speaking foolishly, idle talk*. From

μωρο-λόγος, ον, (μωρός, λέγω) *speaking foolishly*.

ΜΩΡΟ'Σ, ά, όν, *dull, heavy*: generally, *stupid, silly, foolish*. 2. *tasteless, insipid*.

μωρό-σοφος, ον, (μῶρος, σοφός) *foolishly wise*.

μώρως, Adv. of μωρός, *foolishly*.

Μῶσα, ἡ, Dor. for **Μοῦσα**.

μῶσθαι, inf. of μῶμαι, v. sub. *μάω C.

N

N, **ν**, **νῦ**, *τό*, indecl., thirteenth letter of Gr. alphabet: as numeral, ν′ = 50, but ͵ν = 50,000.

Changes of *ν*: I. into *γ* before the gutturals *γ*, *κ*, *χ*, *ξ*, as *ἔγ-γονος*, *ἔγ-καιρος*, *ἐγ-χώριος*, *ἐγ-ξέω*. II. into *μ* before the labials *β*, *π*, *φ*, *μ*, *ψ*, as *σύμ-βιος*, *συμ-πότης*, *συμ-φυής*, *ἐμ-μανής*. *ἔμ-ψυχος*. III. into *λ*, before *λ*, as *ἐλ-λείπω*. IV. into *ρ* before *ρ*, as *συρ-ράπτω*. V. into *σ* before *σ*, as *σύσ-σιτος*. VI. *ν* is inserted in aor. 1 pass. of some pure Verbs, as *ἱδρύνθην* from *ἱδρύω*.

The *νῦ ἐφελκυστικόν* or final *ν* is found with dat. pl. in *σι*, as *ἀνδράσιν* for *ἀνδράσι*; 3 pers. pl. of verbs in *σι*, as *εἰλήφασιν* for *εἰλήφασι*; 3 pers. sing. in *ε* and *ι*, as *ἔκτανεν δείκνυσιν*, for *ἔκτανε δείκνυσι*: with the local termin. *-σι*, as Ἀθήνῃσιν Ὀλυμπίασιν; the Epic termin. *φι*, as *ὀστεόφιν*; with the numeral *εἴκοσιν* for *εἴκοσι*; the Advs. *νόσφιν πέρυσιν*, for *νόσφι πέρυσι*; with the enclit. Parts. *κέν*, *νύν*, for *κέ νύ*. It is used to avoid hiatus where a vowel follows.

νᾶες, **νᾶας**, Dor. nom. and acc. pl. of *ναῦς*.

νᾰετήρ, ῆρος, ὁ, and **νᾰέτης**, *ου*, *ὁ*, (*ναίω*) *an inhabitant*, *dweller*.

Ναζαρηνός and **Ναζωραῖος**, ὁ, *a Nazarene inhabitant of Nazareth*.

ναί, Adv., used in strong affirm., *yea*, *verily*, Lat. *nae*: with an affirmative clause: but in answers the Att. use *ναί* by itself, *yea*, *yes*, *aye*.

νᾶϊ, Dor. and Att. poët. dat. of *ναῦς*.

Νᾱϊᾰκός, *ή*, *όν*, (Ναϊάς) *of* or *for a Naiad*.

Νᾱϊάς, *άδος*, *ἡ*, mostly in pl. **Ναϊάδες** Ion **Νηϊάδες**, (*νάω*) *a Naiad*, *a river* or *water-nymph*.

ναίεσκε, 3 sing. Ion. impf. of *ναίω*.

ναιετάασκε, 3 sing. Ion. impf. of *ναιετάω*.

ναιετάω: Ep. part. fem. *ναιετάωσα*, Ion. impf. *ναιετάεσκον*: (*ναίω*): 1. of persons, *to dwell*, *inhabit*: generally, *to live*, *be*:—c. acc. loci, *to dwell in*, *inhabit*. 2. of places, *to be situated*, *lie*: and so in pass. sense, *to be inhabited*.

ναῖον, Ep. impf. *ναίω* B.

νάϊος, *α*, *ον*, Dor. for *νήϊος*.

ναίοισα, Dor. for *ναίουσα*, pres. part. fem. of *ναίω*.

Νᾱΐς, *ΐδος*, *ἡ*, Ion. **Νηΐς**, (*νάω*) = **Ναϊάς**. [ῐ]

ναίχι, Adv. for *ναί*, like *οὐχί* for *οὐ*.

ΝΑΙ'Ω (A): I. intr. in pres. and impf., 1. of persons, *to dwell*:—c. acc. loci, *to dwell in*, *inhabit*. 2. of places, *to lie*, *be situated*. II. Causal, in Ep. aor. 1 *ἔνασσα* or *νάσσα*, for *ἔνᾰσα*, *to make inhabited*, *give to dwell in*; *καί κέ οἱ Ἄργεϊ νάσσα πόλιν I would have given him* a town in Argos *for his home*. 2. *to make* a person *dwell* in a place, *to settle* him:—in Ep. aor. 1 pass. and med., *to settle*, *dwell*; *πατὴρ ἐμὸς Ἄργεϊ νάσθη* my father *settled* at Argos; *νάσσατο ἄγχ' Ἑλικῶνος he settled* near Helicon.

ναίω (B), = *ναω*, *to flow*, *overflow*.

ΝΑ'ΚΗ, *ἡ*. *a goat-skin*: *a sheep's fleece*, Lat. *vellus*. [ᾰ]

νάκος, *τό*, later form of *νάκη*. [ᾰ]

νᾶμα, *ατος*, *τό*, (*νάω*) *anything flowing*, *a current*, *stream*, *spring*; *ν. πυρός a stream* of fire. Hence

νᾱμᾰτιαῖος, *α*, *ον*, *flowing*, *running*.

ναμερτής, **ναμέρτεια**, Dor. for *νημ-*.

νᾶν, Dor. for *ναῦν*, acc. of *ναῦς*.

ΝΑ͂ΝΟΣ, *ὁ*, *a dwarf*, Lat. *nānus*.

νᾱνο-φῠής, *ές*, (*νᾶνος*, *φυή*) *of dwarfish stature*.

Νάξιος, *α*, *ον*, (*Νάξος*) *from the isle of Naxos*: Νάξιοι, οἱ, *the Naxians*: **Ναξία** *λίθος* or *πέτρα* a kind of *whetstone*, Lat. *cos Naxia*.

Ναξι-ουργής, *ές*, (*Νάξιος*, *ἔργον*) *of Naxian work*.

Νάξος, *ἡ*, *Naxos*, one of the Cyclades, anciently called *Dia*.

νᾱο-πόλος Ion. **νηο-πόλος**, *ον*, (*ναός*, *πολέω*) *dwelling* or *busied in a temple*: as Subst., *ναοπόλος*, *ὁ*, *the keeper of a temple*, Lat. *aedituus*.

νᾱός Ion. **νηός** Att. **νεώς**, *ὁ*, (*ναίω*) *the dwelling of a god*, *a temple*, Lat. *aedes* (in sing.). II. *the inner part of a temple*, *the cell*, *the shrine* in which the image of the god was placed.

νᾱός, Dor. and Att. poët. gen. of *ναῦς*.

ναπαῖος, *α*, *ον*, (*νάπη*) *of*, *in a wooded vale* or *dell*.

ΝΑ'ΠΗ, *ἡ*, *a woody dell* or *glen*, Lat. *saltus*. [ᾰ]

νάπος, *τό*, later form of *νάπη*.

ΝΑ͂ΠΥ, *υος*, *τό*, = *σίναπι*, *mustard*.

ναρδο-λῐπής, *ές*, (*νάρδος*, *λίπος*) *anointed with nard-oil*.

νάρδος, *ἡ*, *nard*, *spikenard*, Lat. *nardus*. II. *nard-oil*.

ναρθηκο-πλήρωτος, *ον*, (*νάρθηξ*, *πληρόω*) *filling the hollow of the νάρθηξ* or *reed*.

ναρθηκο-φόρος, *ον*, (*νάρθηξ*, *φέρω*) *carrying a staff of reed* (*νάρθηξ*), = *θυρσοφόρος*: *a rod-bearer*.

ΝΑ'ΡΘΗΞ, *ηκος*, *ὁ*, a tall umbelliferous plant, Lat. *ferŭla*, with a pithy stalk, in which Prometheus conveyed the spark of fire from heaven to earth: *a reed*. The stalks were used for *wands*, *canes*, *rods*: also, as *splints*.

ναρκάω, f. *ήσω*: Ep. aor. 1 *νάρκησα*:—*to grow stiff*, *numb* or *dead*, Lat. *torpere*, *to be rigid*. From

ΝΑ'ΡΚΗ, *ἡ*, *stiffness*, *numbness*, Lat. *torpor*.

νάρκισσος, *ὁ*, *the narcissus*. (From *ναρκάω*, because of its *narcotic* properties.)

νᾱρός, *ά*, *όν*, (*νάω*) *flowing*, *liquid*.

νᾶς, *ἡ*, Dor. for *ναῦς*.

νάσθη, Ep. 3 sing. aor. 1 pass. of *ναίω*; v. *ναίω* II. 2.

νᾱσιώτας, Dor. for *νησιώτης*.

νασμός, *ὁ*, (*νάω*) *a flowing current*: *a stream*, *spring*.

νᾱσός, Dor. for *νῆσος*.

νάσσα, Ep. for *ἔνᾰσα*, aor. 1 of *ναίω*.

νᾶσσα, Dor. for *νῆσσα*, *νῆττα*, *a duck*.

νάσσατο, Ep. for *ἐνάσατο*, 3 sing. aor. 1 med. of *ναίω*: v. *ναίω* II. 2.

ΝΑ'ΣΣΩ, f. *νάξω*: aor. 1 *ἔναξα*: pf. pass. *νένασμαι*:

or νέναγμαι:—*to press* or *squeeze close, stamp down, compress: to pile up.*

ναστός, ή, όν, (νάσσω) *close-pressed, firm, well-kneaded.* II. as Subst., ναστός, ὁ, *a well-kneaded cake.*

νάττω, Att. for νάσσω.

ναυᾱγέω Ion. **ναυηγ** : f. ήσω: (ναυαγός):—*to suffer shipwreck, be shipwrecked: to crash, smash*, of chariots. Hence

ναυᾱγία Ion. **ναυηγίη**, ἡ, *shipwreck, wreck.*

ναυάγιον Ion. **ναυήγιον**, τό, *a piece of a wreck, wreck;* ναυάγια ἱππικα *the wreck* of a chariot. From

ναυ-ᾱγός Ion. **ναυηγός**, όν, (ναῦς, ἄγνυμι) *shipwrecked, stranded*, Lat. *naufrăgus:* generally, *ruined, wrecked.*

ναυαρχέω, f. ήσω, (ναύαρχος) *to be admiral of a fleet.* Hence

ναυαρχία, ἡ, *the command of a fleet, office of admiral.* 2. *the period of his command.*

ναύ-αρχος, ὁ, (ναῦς, ἄρχω) *the commander of a fleet, an admiral.*

ναυάτης, ου, ὁ, poët. for ναύτης. [ᾰ]

ναυ-βάτης [ᾰ], ου, ὁ, (ναῦς, βαίνω) *one who embarks in a ship, a seaman.* II. as Adj. *nautical, of sailors.*

ναύ-δετον, τό, (ναῦς, δέω) *a ship's cable.*

ναυηγός, ναυηγέω, ναυηγία, Ion. for ναυᾱγ–.

ναυκληρέω, f. ήσω, (ναύκληρος) *to be a ship-owner, master of a ship.* II. metaph. *to manage, govern.* Hence

ναυκληρία, ἡ, *the life and calling of a master of a ship, a seafaring life.* 2. poët. *a voyage:* generally, *an enterprise.* 3. also *a ship.*

ναυκληρικός, ή, όν, (ναύκληρος) *of* or *for the master of a ship.*

ναύ-κληρος, ὁ, (ναῦς, κλῆρος) *the owner* or *master of a ship*, who carried goods or passengers. 2. poët. *a seaman.*

ναύ-κρᾱρος, ὁ, the same with ναύκληρος. II. at Athens, *the member of a division* (ναυκραρία) *of the citizens:* in Solon's time there were 12 in each of the 4 tribes, 48 in all: when Cleisthenes increased the number of the tribes to 10, there were 5 ναυκοαροί belonging to each tribe, 50 in all.

ναυκρᾰτέω, f. ήσω, *to have the mastery at sea, to command the sea:*—Pass. *to be mastered at sea.* From

ναυ-κράτης, εος, ὁ, ἡ, (ναῦς, κρᾰτέω) *having the mastery at sea, commanding the sea.*

ναυ-κράτωρ, ορος, ὁ, ἡ, (ναῦς, κρατέω) *commanding the sea.* II. as Subst. *the master of a ship.* [ᾰ]

ναῦλος, ὁ, or **ναῦλον**, τό, (ναῦς) *passage-money, fare*, Lat. *naulum.* 2. also *a freight.*

ναυλοχέω, f. ήσω, (ναύλοχος) *to lie in a harbour* or *creek: to lie in wait*, so as to sally out upon ships passing: c. acc. *to lie in wait for.*

ναύ-λοχος, ον, (ναῦς, λόχος) *affording safe anchorage, having a good roadstead.* II. as Subst., ναύλοχος, ὁ, with irreg. pl. **ναυλοχα**, *an anchorage*, Lat. *statio navium.*

ναυμᾰχέω, f. ήσω, (ναυμαχος) *to fight in a ship, to fight by sea:* generally, *to fight* or *contend with.* Hence

ναυμᾰχία, ἡ, *a sea-fight.*

ναύ-μᾰχος, ον, (ναῦς, μάχομαι) *of, for* or *suited to a sea-fight;* ξυστὰ ναύμαχα *boarding* pikes.

ναυπηγέω, f. ήσω, (ναυπηγός) *to build ships:*—Med., ναῦς ναυπηγέεσθαι *to build oneself* ships:—Pass. of the ships, *to be built.*

ναυπηγήσιμος, ον, (ναυπηγέω) *suited for ship-building.*

ναυπηγία, ἡ, (ναυπηγέω) *ship-building.*

ναυπήγιον, τό, *a place for ship-building, a dock-yard.* From

ναυ-πηγός, όν, (ναῦς, πήγνυμι) *building ships:* as Subst., ναυπηγός, ὁ' *a ship-builder, shipwright.*

ναύ-πορος, ον, (ναῦς, πόρος) *traversed by ships, naval.* II. parox. ναυπόρος, ον, *propelling a ship.*

ΝΑΥ͂Σ, ἡ, Lat. *NAV-IS, a ship;* ναῦς μακρά, *a long ship, ship of war.*—Att. declens., ναῦς, νεώς, νηΐ, ναῦν; dual gen. νεοῖν; pl. νῆες, νεῶν or νηῶν, ναυσί, ναῦς:—Ion., νηῦς, νεός, νηί, νέα, pl. νέες, νεῶν, νηυσί, νέας:—Ep. νηῦς, νηός, νηί, νῆα, pl. νῆες, νηῶν, νηυσί or νήεσσι, νῆα, (but also gen. and acc. νεός, νέα, pl. νέες, νεῶν, νέεσσι, νέας):—Dor. ναῦς, νᾱός, νᾱί, ναῦν, pl. νᾶες, νάων, ναυσί or νάεσσι, νᾶας.

ναυσθλόω, contr. for ναυστολέω, *to carry by sea.* Med. *to take with one by sea: to hire a ship for oneself:*—Pass., with fut. med. ναυσθλώσομαι, *to go by sea.*

ναυσία Att. **ναυτία**, ἡ, (ναῦς) *sea-sickness, qualmishness, retching*, Lat. *nausea.* Hence

ναυσιάω Att. **ναυτιάω**, (ναυσία) *to be qualmish, to retch, suffer from sea-sickness.*

ναυσι-κλειτός, ή, όν, (ναῦς, κλειτός) *renowned for ships, famous by sea.*

ναυσι-κλῠτός, όν, = ναυσικλειτός.

ναυσῐ-πέδη, ἡ, (ναῦς, πέδη) *a ship-cable.*

ναυσῐ-πέρᾱτος Ion. **νηυσιπέρητος**, ον, (ναῦς, περάω) *to be crossed by a ferry* or *traversed by ships, navigable.*

ναυσι-πόμπος, ον, (ναῦς, πέμπω) *ship-wafting;* ναυσιπόμπος αὔρα *a fair* breeze. [ῐ]

ναυσί-πορος, ον, (ναῦς, πόρος) = ναυπορος, *traversed by ships*, of a river, *navigable* II. parox. **ναυσιπόρος**, ον, act. *going in ships, sea-faring.* 2. *propelling a ship, ship-speeding.*

ναυσί-στονος, ον, (ναῦς, στένω) *lamentable to the ship.*

ναυσῐ-φόρητος, ον, (ναῦς, φορέω) *carried in a ship, going by ship.*

ναύ-σταθμον, τό, (ναῦς, σταθμός) *a harbour, anchorage, roadstead*, Lat. *statio navium.*

ναυστολέω, f. ήσω, (ναυστόλος) trans. *to carry* or *convoy by sea:*—Pass., with fut. med. ναυστολήσομαι, *to go by sea.* 2. *to guide, govern.* II. intr., like Pass., *to go by sea, sail.* Hence

ναυστόλημα, ατος, τό, *a voyage.*

ναυστολία, ἡ, (ναυστολέω) *a going by ship.*

ναυ-στόλος, ον, (ναῦς, στέλλω) *sending by ship.* II. *voyaging, sailing.*

ναύτης, ου, ὁ, (ναῦς) Lat. *nauta, a seaman, sailor.* II. *one who goes on shipboard, a companion by sea.*

ναυτία, ναυτιάω, Att. for ναυσία, ναυσιάω.

ναυτικός, ή, όν, (ναῦς, ναύτης) *of* or *for a ship;* ναυτικὸς στρατός *a sea*-force, opp. to πεζός: also, ναυτικόν, τό, *a fleet;* ναυτικά, τά, *naval affairs, naval power.* 2. of persons, *skilled in seamanship, nautical.*

ναυτιλία, ἡ, (ναυτίλος) *sailing, seamanship:* in pl. *voyages.* Hence

ναυτίλλομαι, Dep. only found in pres. and impf. *to go by sea, make a voyage, sail.*

ναυτίλος [ῐ], ὁ, (ναύτης) *a seaman, sailor.* 2. Adj. *of a ship, naval.* II. *the nautilus,* a shell-fish, furnished with a membrane which serves it for a sail.

ναυτο-λογέω, f. ήσω, (ναύτης, λέγω) *to enlist seamen, take on board:* generally, *to receive.*

ναυφθορία, ἡ, *shipwreck, loss of ships.* From

ναύ-φθορος, ον, (ναῦς, φθείρω) *shipwrecked;* ναύφθορος στολή the garb *of shipwrecked men.*

ναῦφι, ναῦφιν, Ep. gen. and dat. pl. of ναῦς.

ναύ-φρακτος Att. **ναύ-φαρκτος**, ον, (ναῦς, φράσσω) *ship-fenced, ship-girt;* ναύφρακτον βλέπειν to look *like a ship of war.*

ΝΑ'Ω, only found in pres. and impf. *to flow*

νέα, Ion. acc. sing. from ναῦς.

νε-άγγελτος, ον, (νέος, ἀγγέλλω) *newly told.*

νεᾱ-γενής, ές, (νέος, *γένω) *newly born.*

νεάζω, only found in pres. (νέος), intr. *to be young* or *new: to be the younger of two.* 2. *to act* or *think like a youth.* 3. *to grow young, grow young again.*

νε-αίρετος, ον, (νέος, αἱρέω) *newly caught.*

νεαίτερος, irreg. Comp. of νέος: **νεαίτατος** and **νέατος**, irreg. Sup.

νε-ᾱκόνητος, ον, (νέος, ἀκονάω) *newly-whetted, keen-edged.*

νεᾱλής, ές, (νέος) *fresh with youth:* generally, *fresh, vigorous.*

νε-άλωτος, ον, (νέος, ἁλῶναι) *newly caught.* [ᾰ]

νε-ανθής, ές, (νέος, ἀνθέω) *new-budding, blooming.*

νεᾱνίας, ου, Ep. and Ion. **νεηνίης**, εω, ὁ, (νέος) *a young man, youth:* often with another Subst., as, ἄνδρες νεηνίαι, παῖς νεηνίης. II. as masc. Adj. *youthful: fresh, vigorous, impetuous.*

νεᾱνιεύομαι, Dep. (νεανίας) *to be a youth: to act like a youth, behave wilfully* or *impetuously, to make youthful boasts.*

νεᾱνικός, ή, όν, (νεανίας) *youthful: fresh, impetuous, vigorous.* 2. *high-spirited, noble.* 3. in bad sense, *hasty, wanton, insolent.* 4. generally, *great, mighty, strong.*

νεᾱνικῶς, Adv. of νεανικός, *vigorously.*

νεᾶνις Ion. **νεῆνις**, gen. ιδος, acc. νεάνιδα and νεάνιν, fem. of νεανίας, *a young woman, girl, maiden.* II. as Adj. *youthful: new.*

νεᾱνισκεύομαι, Dep. (νεανίσκος) *to be in one's youth, be a stripling.*

νεᾱνίσκος Ion. **νεηνίσκος**, ὁ, (νεανίας *a youth, young man.*

νε-ᾱοιδός, όν, (νέος, ἀοιδός) *singing youthfully.*

νεᾰρός, ά, όν, (νέος) *young, youthful: fresh, new, recent, late.*

νεᾰρο-φάης, ες, (νεαρός, φαός) *coming fresh to light, new-appearing.*

νέας, Ion. and Ep. acc. pl. of ναῦς.

νέᾰτος Ion. **νειᾰτος**, η, ον, irreg. Sup. of νέος, as μέσατος from μέσος, *the last, uttermost, lowest, extreme;* πόλις νεάτη Πύλου a city *lying on the border* of Pylos. II. of Time, *latest,* Lat. *novissimus.*

νέᾰτος, ὁ, *the ploughing up of fallow land.* From

νεάω, f. άσω, (νέος) *to plough up fallow land, to till anew:* νεωμένη (sc. γῆ), ἡ, *land ploughed anew.*

νεβρῐδό-πεπλος, ον, (νεβρίς, πέπλος) *clad in a fawn-skin.*

νεβρίζω, f. σω, *to wear a fawn-skin, to run about at the feast of Bacchus.* From

νεβρίς, ίδος, ἡ, (νεβρός) *a fawn-skin,* worn at the feasts of Bacchus.

ΝΕΒΡΟ'Σ, οῦ, ὁ, *the young of the deer, a fawn.*

νέες, Ion. and Ep. nom. pl. of ναῦς.

νέεσσι, rarer Ep. dat. pl. of ναῦς.

νέηαι, Ion. for νέῃ, 2 sing. pres. subj. of νέομαι.

νεη-γενής Att. and Dor. **νεαγενής**, ές, (νέος, γένος) *new-born, just born.*

νεη-θᾰλής, ές, (νέος, θαλεῖν) *fresh-shooting, fresh-blown.*

νε-ηκής Dor. **νεᾱκής**, ές, (νέος, ἀκή) *newly whetted* or *sharpened.*

νε-ηκονής, ές, (νέος, ἀκόνη) = νεηκής.

νε-ήλᾰτος, ον, (νέος, ἐλαύνω) *newly pounded, fresh ground;* as Subst., νεήλατα, τά, *cakes of fresh flour.*

νέ-ηλῠς, ῠδος, ὁ, ἡ, (νέος, ἤλυσις) *one newly come, a new-comer,* Lat. *advĕna.*

νεηνίης, νεῆνις, Ion. for νεανίας, νεᾶνις.

νεηνίσκος, Ion. for νεανίσκος.

νεή-φᾰτος, ον, (νέος, φημί) *fresh-uttered, new-sounding.*

νεί, Boeot. for νή.

νεῖαι, Ep. 2 sing. pres. of νέομαι.

νείαιρᾰ Ion. **νειαίρη**, ἡ, irr. fem. Comp. of νέος, as νειᾰτος for νέατος in Sup., *latter, lower;* νειαίρῃ ἐν γαστρί in *the lower part of* the belly.

νειᾰτος, η, ον, Ion. for νέατος, Sup. of νέος.

νεικείω, νεικείῃσι, νεικείεσκον, v. νεικέω.

νεικεστήρ, ῆρος, ὁ, (νεικέω) *a wrangler, disputer, brawler:* c. gen. *one who wrangles with.*

νεικεῦσι, Aeol. for νεικοῦσι, 3 pl. of νεικέω.

νεικέω, Ion. and Ep. **νεικείω**, Ep. 3 sing. subj. νεικείῃσι, Ion. impf. νείκειον and νεικείεσκον: Ep. fut. νεικέσσω, Ep. aor. 1 νείκεσσα: (νεῖκος):—*to quarrel,* *wrangle, dispute with:* also c. acc. cognato, νείκεα νεικεῖν: part. νεικέων, *holding out obstinately, contentiously.* II. trans. *to vex, annoy,* esp. by word, *to taunt, upbraid, to accuse, criminate.*

νείκη, ἡ, = νεῖκος.

ΝΕΙ͂ΚΟΣ, τό, *a quarrel, wrangle, dispute: strife:* esp. *railing, a taunt, reproach.* 2. *a strife at law, debate, dispute before a judge.* 3. also, *battle, fight.* II. *the cause of strife, matter* or *ground of quarrel.*

Νειλαιεύς, ὁ, (Νεῖλος) *a native of the Nile.*

Νειλαῖος, α, ον, (Νεῖλος) *of* or *from the Nile.*

Νειλο-γενής, ές, (Νεῖλος, γενέσθαι) *Nile-born.*

Νειλο-θερής, ές, (Νεῖλος, θέρω) *fostered by the Nile.*

Νειλόρ-ρῠτος poët. Νειλό-ρῠτος, ον, (Νεῖλος, ῥέω) *watered by the Nile.*

Νεῖλος, ὁ, *the Nile,* the great river of Egypt, called in Homer Αἴγυπτος.

Νειλωΐς, ΐδος, ἡ, (Νεῖλος) *built on* or *by the Nile.*

Νειλώτης, ου, ὁ, fem. -ῶτις, ιδος, (Νεῖλος) *living in* or *on the Nile;* χθὼν Νειλῶτις the land *of Nile.*

νείμας, aor. 1 part. of νέμω.

νεῖμεν, 3 sing. Ep. aor. 1 of νέμω: νεῖμαν, 3 pl.: νεῖμον 2 sing. imperat.

νειόθεν, Ion. for νεόθεν, Adv. (νέος) *from the bottom;* νειόθεν ἐκ κραδίης *from the bottom* of his heart. II. *anew.*

νειόθι, Ion. for νεόθι, Adv, (νέος) *at the bottom, in the inmost part.*

νειο-κόρος, ὁ, ἡ, Ion. for νεωκόρος.

νείομαι, Ion. for νέομαι.

νειο-ποιέω, f. ήσω, (νειός, ποιέω) *to let a field lie fallow,* or *to take a green crop* off it, so to prepare it for corn.

νειός, οῦ, ἡ, (νέος) *new land, land ploughed up anew, a fallow, fallow ground,* Lat. *novāle.*

νειός, Ion. for νέος: Sup. νειότατος, η, ον.

νειο-τομεύς, ὁ, (νειός, τεμεῖν) *one who breaks up a fallow.*

νεῖρα or νείρα, ἡ, contr. for νείαιρα, *the belly, stomach.*

νεῖται, contr. for νέεται, 3 sing. of νέομαι.

νεκάς, άδος, ἡ, (νέκυς) *a heap of slain:* Ep. dat. pl. νεκάδεσσι.

νεκρ-άγγελος, ον, (νεκρός, ἄγγελος) *messenger to the dead.*

νεκρᾰγωγέω, f. ήσω, *to conduct the dead.* From

νεκρ-ᾰγωγός, όν, (νεκρός, ἄγω) *conducting the dead.*

νεκρ-ᾰκᾰδημεία, ἡ, (νεκρός, Ἀκαδημεία) *a school of the dead.*

νεκρῐκός, ή, όν, (νεκρός) *of* or *for the dead.*

νεκρο-βᾰρής, ές, (νεκρός, βάρος) *laden with corpses.*

νεκρο-δέγμων, ον, gen. ονος, (νεκρός, δέχομαι) *receiving the dead.*

νεκρο-δόκος, Ion. for Att. -δόχος, ον, (νεκρός, δέχομαι) *receiving the dead.* Hence

νεκρο-δοχεῖον, τό, *a receptacle for the dead, cemetery.*

νεκρο-θήκη, ἡ, (νεκρός, θήκη) *a receptacle for a corpse, coffin.*

νεκρο-πομπός, όν, (νεκρός, πέμπω) *conducting the dead, ferrying the dead over* the Styx.

νεκρός, οῦ, ὁ, (νέκυς) *a dead body, carcase, corpse, corse:* in pl. *the dead.* II. as Adj., νεκρός, ά, όν, *dead.*

νεκρο-στολέω, (νεκρός, στέλλω) *to ferry over the dead.*

νεκρόω, f. ώσω, (νεκρός) *to make dead:*—Pass. *to be put to death, become lifeless.* 2. metaph. *to deaden, mortify.*

νεκρών, ῶνος, ὁ, (νεκρός) *a place for dead bodies, a burial-place.*

νέκρωσις, ἡ, (νεκρόω) *a making dead.* II. pass. *a becoming dead, death: deadness.*

ΝΕ΄ΚΤᾸΡ, ἄρος, τό, *nectar,* the drink of the gods, as ambrosia was their food: in Homer *the nectar* is red (ἐρυθρόν), poured like wine by Hebé, and, like it, drunk mixed with water. Hence

νεκτάρεος, α Ion. η, ον, *like nectar, scented, fragrant:* generally, *divine.* [ᾰ]

νεκῠ-ηγός, όν, (νέκυς, ἄγω) = νεκροπομπός, *conducting, guiding the dead.*

νεκῠο-μαντεῖον Ion. -ήιον, τό, (νέκυς, μαντεῖον) *an oracle of the dead,* a place where the ghosts of the dead were called up and questioned.

νεκῠο-στόλος, ον, (νέκυς, στέλλω) *ferrying the dead.*

ΝΕ΄ΚΥΣ, ῠος, ὁ, Ep. dat. sing. νέκυϊ: Ep. dat. pl. νεκύεσσι contr. νέκυσσι: acc. pl. νέκυας contr. νέκῡς: —*a dead body, a corpse:* in pl. *the dead.* II. as Adj. *dead, lifeless.* [ῠ]

Νεμέα Ion. -έη, ἡ, *Nemea,* a place between Argos and Corinth; cp. Νέμεα, τά.

Νέμεα poët. Νέμεια, τά, *the Nemean games,* celebrated in the second and fourth years of each Olympiad.

Νέμεος or Νέμειος, α, ον, *of* or *from Nemea.*

νεμέθω, poët. for νέμω, in 3 pl. impf. med. νεμέθοντο, Ep. for ἐνέμοντο, *they grazed, fed.*

νεμεσάω, Ion. impf. νεμέσασκον: fut. ήσω: Ep. aor. 1 νεμέσησα:—Ep. pres. νεμεσσάω, f. νεμεσσήσω, etc.: (νέμεσις): —*to feel just indignation,* properly *at undeserved good fortune,* generally, *to be angry, vexed.* II. Med. and Pass., νεμεσῶμαι: f. -ήσομαι: aor. 1 pass. ἐνεμεσήθην Ep. νεμεσσήθην; Ep. aor. 1 med. opt. νεμεσσήσαιτο:—*to be displeased* or *vexed with oneself: to be ashamed, be filled with shame.* 2. c. acc. rei, νεμεσσᾶται κακὰ ἔργα *he shews just displeasure at, visits, punishes* evil deeds.

Νεμέσεια, (sub. ἱερά), τά, *the feast of Nemesis.*

νεμεσητός Ep. νεμεσσητός, ή, όν, (νεμεσάω) *causing indignation* or *wrath, worthy of it;* οὔτοι νεμεσητόν it is not a thing *fit to raise indignation.* II. *to be regarded with awe, awful.*

νεμεσίζομαι, Dep. only found in pres. and impf. *to become* or *be displeased with: to chafe* or *chide at* a thing: absol. *to be angry, surprised.* II. like νεμεσάομαι, *to be ashamed, feel dread* or *awe:* c. acc., θεοὺς νεμεσίζετο *he stood in awe of* the gods. From

νέμεσις Ep. **νέμεσσις, εως**, ἡ, (νέμω) *just* or *deserved indignation, anger at anything unjust, righteous resentment.* 2. *indignation at undeserved good fortune: jealousy, vengeance*, esp. of the gods: of men, *grudging, envy.* II. *that which causes* or *deserves just indignation, the object of just resentment*; οὐ νέμεσίς [ἐστι] there is not *cause for indignation.* III. in one's own person, *a sense of sin, remorse.*

Νέμεσις, ἡ, as prop. n., voc. Νέμεσι: *Nemesis*, personified as *the goddess of Retribution*, who brings down all immoderate good fortune.

νεμεσσατά, Dor. for νεμεσσητή.

νεμέσσα, Ep. for νεμέσα, imperat. of νεμεσάω.

νεμεσσάω, f. ήσω, Ep. for νεμεσάω.

νεμεσσηθείς, Ep. aor. 1 part. pass. of νεμεσάω.

νεμεσσηθῶμεν, Ep. 1 pl. aor. 1 subj. pass. of νεμεσάω.

νεμεσσητός, ή, όν, Ep. for νεμεσητός.

νέμεσσις, ἡ, Ep. for νέμεσις.

νεμέτωρ, ορος, ὁ, (νέμω) *a dispenser* of justice, *a judge, arbiter.*

νέμος, εος, τό, (νέμω) *a wooded pasture, grove*, Lat. *nemus.*

NE'MΩ: fut. νεμῶ, later νεμήσω: aor. 1 ἔνειμα Ep. νεῖμα: pf. νενέμηκα:—Med. νέμομαι: f. νεμοῦμαι, later νεμήσομαι:—Pass., aor. 1 ἐνεμήθην: pf. νενέμημαι (but these tenses are also used in med. sense): —*to deal out, distribute: to apportion, assign, allot.* II. Med. νέμομαι, c. acc., *to distribute among themselves*, hence *to possess, enjoy, have in use.* 2. also *to dwell in, inhabit, occupy.* III. later also in Act. *to hold, possess:* Pass. of places, *to be inhabited.* 2. *to sway, manage, wield, control.* 3. like νομίζω, *to esteem, consider.*

B. νέμω, of herdsmen, *to pasture, drive to pasture*, Lat. *pascere:* more freq. in Med. νέμεσθαι, of cattle, *to feed, go to pasture, graze*, Lat. *pasci:* hence *to eat, feed on:* metaph. of fire, *to feed on, devour, consume:* also Pass., πυρὶ χθὼν νέμεται the land *is consumed by* fire. II. later in Act., ὄρη νέμειν *to graze* the hills (with cattle): metaph., πυρὶ νέμειν πόλιν *to waste* a city by fire. III. in Med. also of ulcers, *to spread.*

νένασμαι, pf. pass. of νάσσω.

νενέαται, Ion. 3 pl. pf. pass. of νέω, *to heap.*

νενέμηκα, pf. of νέμω.

νένηκα, pf. of νέω, *to spin.*

νένιμμαι, νένιπται, 1 and 3 sing. pf. pass. of νίζω.

νενόμισμαι, pf. pass. of νομίζω.

νένωμαι, νενωμένος, Ion. and Dor. for νενόημαι, νενοημένος, pf. pass. ind. and part. of νοέω.

νεο-άλωτος, ον, (νέος, ἁλῶναι) = νεάλωτος.

νεο-αρδής, ές, (νέος, ἄρδω) *newly watered.*

νεό-γᾰμος, ον, (νέος, γαμέω) *new-married:* as Subst., νεόγαμος, ὁ or ἡ, *a bridegroom* or *bride.*

νεο-γενής, ές, (νέος, γενέσθαι) *new-born.*

νεογῑλός, ή, όν, *new-born, young.* (Deriv. uncertain.)

νεο-γνής, ές, = νεογνός.

νεο-γνός, όν, contr. for νεόγονος, *new-born.*

νεό-γονος, ον, (νέος, γενέσθαι) *new-born.*

νεό-γραπτος and **νεό-γρᾰφος**, ον, (νέος, γράφω) *newly painted* or *written.*

νεό-γυιος, ον, (νέος, γυῖον) *with young, fresh limbs.*

νεο-δᾱμώδης, ες, a Spartan word, *lately made one of the people* (νέος, δᾶμος = δῆμος), *newly enfranchised:* hence those Helots were called Νεοδαμώδεις, who were set free in reward for services in war.

νεό-δαρτος, ον, (νέος, δέρω) *newly stripped off, newly flayed.*

νεο-δίδακτος, ον, (νέος, διδάσκω) *newly taught:* of a play *newly brought out, newly exhibited.*

νεο-δμής, ῆτος, ὁ, ἡ, and **νεό-δμητος**, ον, (νέος, δαμάω) *newly tamed* or *broken in:* metaph. *newly-wedded.*

νεό-δμητος Dor. **-δματος**, ον, (νέος, δέμω) *new-built.*

νεό-δρεπτος, ον, (νέος, δρέπω) *fresh plucked* or *cropped: wreathed with fresh leaves.*

νεό-δρομος, ον, (νέος, δρᾰμεῖν) *just having run.*

νεό-δροπος, ον, = νεόδρεπτος.

νεό-ζευκτος, ον, (νέος, ζεύγνυμι) = νεοζυγής.

νεο-ζῠγής, ές, and **νεό-ζῠγος**, ον, (νέος, ζυγῆναι) *newly yoked:* metaph. *newly married.*

νεό-ζυξ, ῠγος, ὁ, ἡ, = νεοζυγής.

νεο-θᾱλής, ές, Dor. for νεοθηλής.

νεόθεν, Adv. (νέος) *anew: newly, lately.*

νεο-θηλής, ές, (νέος, τέθηλα) *fresh budding* or *sprouting:* metaph. *fresh, cheerful.*

νεό-θηλος, ον, = νεοθηλής.

νεο-θήξ, ῆγος, ὁ, ἡ, (νέος, θήγω) *newly sharpened.*

νεο-θλῑβής, ές, (νέος, θλιβῆναι) *newly pressed.*

νεοίη, ἡ, (νέος) poët. for νεότης, *youthful spirit.*

νέ-οικος, ον, (νέος, οἰκέω) *newly built on.*

νεο-κατάστᾰτος, ον, (νέος, καθίστημι) *lately established* or *settled.*

νεο-κηδής, ές, (νέος, κῆδος) *having a fresh grief.*

νεο-κληρόνομος, ον, *having lately inherited.*

νεό-κλωστος, ον, (νέος, κλώθω) *newly spun* or *woven.*

νεο-κόνητος, ον, (νέος, καίνω) *newly shed*; νεοκόνητον αἷμα χεροῖν ἔχειν to have *newly-shed* blood upon his hands.

νεό-κοπτος, ον, (νεος, κοπτω) *fresh-chiselled.*

νεόκοτος, ον, (νέος) *strange, unheard of:*—generally, *fresh, new.*

νεο-κράς, ᾶτος, ὁ, ἡ, (νέος, κεράννυμι) *newly mixed*; νεόκρας φίλος *a newly made* friend.

νεό-κτιστος, ον, also η, ον, (νέος, κτίζω) *newly founded* or *built: new-made.*

νεό-κτονος, ον, (νέος, κτείνω) *just killed.*

νεο-λαία, ἡ, (νέος, λαός) *a band of youth, the youth* of a nation, Lat. *juventus.*

νεό-λουτος poët. **νεόλλουτος**, ον, (νέος, λούομαι) *just bathed.*

NE'OMAI contr. νεῦμαι, 2 and 3 sing. νεῖαι, νεῖται: inf. νέεσθαι contr. νεῖσθαι: Dep., only used in pres. and impf. :—*to go* or *come:* commonly with a fut. sense, *to go away* or *back:* also *to go to the war:* of a stream, *to flow back.*

νεο-μηνία contr. νουμηνία, ἡ, (νέος, μήν) *the time of the new moon, the beginning of the month.*

νεο-παθής, ές, (νέος, παθεῖν) *suffering from a late calamity.*

νεο-πενθής, ές, (νέος, πένθος) *fresh-mourning.* II. pass. *lately mourned*

νεο-πηγής, ές, (νέος, πήγνυμι) *newly congealed* or *frozen.*

νεό-πλουτος, ον, (νέος, πλοῦτος) *newly enriched, vainglorious, ostentatious;* opp. to ἀρχαιόπλουτος.

νεό-πλῠτος, ον, (νέος, πλύνω) *newly washen*

νεό-ποκος, ον, (νέος, πέκω) *newly shorn.*

νεό-πριστος, ον, (νέος, πρίω) *fresh-sawn.*

Νεο-πτόλεμος, ον, (νέος, πτόλεμος) *New-to-war,* surname of Pyrrhus son of Achilles, because he *came late to Troy.*

νεό-πτολις, ἡ, (νέος, πτόλις) *newly founded.*

νεόρ-ραντος, ον, (νέος, ῥαίνω) *newly sprinkled: fresh-reeking.*

νεόρ-ρῠτος, ον, (νέος, ῥέω) *fresh-flowing.*

νεόρ-ρῡτος, ον, (νέος, ῥύω) *just drawn.*

νέ-ορτος, ον, (νέος, ὄρνυμι) *newly risen,* generally, *new, late.*

ΝΕ'ΟΣ, νέα Ion. νέη, νέον, Att. also ος, ον: Ion. νεῖος, η, ον:—of men, *young, youthful:* as Subst., νέοι, *young men, youths;* ἐκ νέου from *a youth,* from *youth upwards,* Lat. *a puero.* 2. *suited to a youth, youthful,* Lat. *juvenilis.* 3. of things, *new, fresh, recent:* but also, *strange, unexpected.* 4. of Time, ἐκ νέου and ἐκ νέας *anew, afresh,* Lat. *denuo:* hence νέον Ion. νεῖον, as Adv., *newly, lately, anew:* ἡ νέα (sub. σελήνη) *the new* moon: for ἕνη καὶ νέα, see ἕνη. III. the degrees of Comp. are νεώτερος, νεώτατος Ion. νειότατος, v. νεῖος. Hence

νεός (sub. γῆ), ἡ, *fresh land, fallow,* Lat. *novāle.*

νεός, Ion. gen. of ναῦς.

νεο-σίγᾰλος, ον, (νέος, σιγαλόεις) *new and sparkling, glossy.*

νεο-σκύλευτος, ον, (νέος, σκυλεύω) *newly plundered.*

νεό-σμηκτος, ον, (νέος, σμήχω) *newly cleaned.*

νεο-σπᾰδής, ές, and **νεο-σπάς**, άδος, ὁ, ἡ, (νέος, σπάω) *newly plucked* or *gathered.*

νεό-σπορος, ον, (νέος, σπείρω) *newly sown.*

νεοσσεύω Att. **νεοττεύω** or **νοττεύω**: f. σω: (νεοσσός) :—*to hatch;* pf. part. pass. νενοσσευμένος.

νεοσσιά Ion. -ιή-Att. **νεοττιά**, ἡ, (νεοσσός) *a nest of young birds, a nest: the brood of young birds.*

νεόσσιον Att. **νεόττιον** or **νόττιον**, τό, Dim. of νεοσσός, *a young bird, nestling, chicken.*

νεοσσίς Att. **νοττίς**, ίδος, ἡ, fem. of νεοσσός, *a chicken.*

νεοσσο-κόμος Att. **νεοττ-**, ον, (νεοσσός, κομέω) *rearing young birds* or *chickens.*

νεοσσός Att. **νεοττός**, ὁ, (νέος) *a young bird, nestling, chicken.* 2. *any young animal,* as *the young of a crocodile: a young child:* in pl. *a swarm of young bees.*

νεοσσώς, Dor. for νεοσσούς.

νεό-στροφος, ον, (νέος, στρέφω) *newly twisted.*

νεο-σφᾰγής, ές, (νέος, σφαγῆναι) *newly slaughtered.*

νεότᾱς, ᾶτος, ἡ, Dor. for νεότης.

νεό-τευκτος, ον, and **νεο-τευχής**, ές, (νέος, τεύχω) *newly wrought* or *fashioned.*

νεότης, ητος, ἡ, (νέος) *youth:* also 2. *youthful spirit, rashness.* II. *a body of youth, the youth,* Lat. *juventus.*

νεό-τμητος Dor. **-τματος**, ον, (νέος, τέμνω) *newly cut.*

νεό-τοκος, ον, (νέος, τεκεῖν) *new-born.* II. νεοτόκος, ον, act. *having just brought forth.*

νεό-τομος, ον, (νέος, τεμεῖν) *fresh cut* or *ploughed;* νεότομα πλήγματα blows *newly inflicted.* II. *fresh cut off, plucked.*

νεο-τρεφής, ές, (νέος, τρέφω) *newly reared, young.*

νεοττεύω, νεοττιά, νεόττιον, νεοττός, Att. for νεοσσ-.

νεοττο-τροφέω, (νεοττός, τρέφω) *to rear young birds.*

νεουργέω, f. ήσω, *to make new, renew.* From

νε-ουργός, όν, (νέος, *ἔργω) *making new, renewing.*

νε-ούτᾰτος, ον, (νέος, οὐτάω) *lately wounded.*

νεό-φοιτος, ον, (νέος, φοιτάω) *newly trodden.*

νεό-φονος, ον, (νέος, *φένω) *lately killed: fresh-shed.*

νεό-φῠτος, ον, (νέος, φύω) *newly planted.* II. *a new convert, neophyte.*

νεο-χάρακτος, ον, (νέος, χᾰράσσω) *newly impressed* or *imprinted.*

νεοχμός, όν, (νέος) *new, fresh.* 2. *novel, unusual, strange, revolutionary.* Hence

νεοχμόω, f. ώσω, *to make new,* esp. *to make political innovations.*

νεό-χνοος, ον, (νέος, χνόος) *with the first down.*

νεόω, f. ώσω, (νέος) *to renew, renovate, change.*

νέποδες, ων, οἱ, *children;* an old Epic word.

νέρθε and **νέρθεν**, Adv., = ἔνερθε, *under, beneath:* also *from below* II. c. gen. *under, beneath.*

νερτέριος, α, ον, (νέρτερος) *underground,* Lat. *inferus.*

νερτερο-δρόμος, ου, ὁ, (νέρτερος, δρόμος) *the courier of the dead.*

νέρτερος, α, ον, = ἐνέρτερος, *lower, nether,* Lat. *inferior,* a Comp. without any Posit. in use: but also as a Posit. = νερτέριος, *nether, infernal, underground;* οἱ νέρτεροι *the dwellers in the nether world, the gods below* or *the dead,* Lat. *inferi.*

ΝΕ'ΡΤΟΣ, ὁ, *a bird of prey.*

νεῦμα, ατος, τό, (νεύω) *a nod* or *sign: a command.*

νεῦμαι, Ep. and Ion. contr. pres. for νέομαι.

ΝΕΥΡΑ' Ion. νευρή, ἡ, *a sinew, tendon.* II. *a string* or *cord of sinew;* 1. *a bow-string.* 2. *a musical string* or *chord.*

νευρειή, ἡ, poët. for νευρά.

νευρή, ἡ, Ion. for νευρά.

νευρῆφι, νευρῆφιν, Ep. gen. and dat. of νευρή.

νευρο-λάλος, ον, (νεῦρον, λαλέω) *with sounding strings.*

ΝΕΥ῀ΡΟΝ, τό, Lat. *nervus, a sinew, tendon:* esp. in pl. νεῦρα, *the tendons* of the feet; νεῦρα τέμνειν to hamstring, disable. 2. metaph. *strength, vigour, nerve.* II. *a string, cord, lace made of sinew:* hence 2. *a bowstring:* also *cord of a sling.* 3. *a musical string* or *chord.*

νευρο-πλεκής, ές, (νεῦρον, πλέκω) *plaited with sinews.*

νευρορραφέω, f. ήσω, *to stitch with sinews: to mend shoes.* From

νευρο-ράφος, ον, (νεῦρον, ῥάπτω) *stitching with sinews:* as Subst. *a cobbler.*

νευρο-σπᾰδής, ές, (νεῦρον, σπάω) *drawn* or *strained back with a sinew* or *string;* νευροσπαδὴς ἄτρακτος the arrow *drawn back with the string,* i. e. *just ready to fly.*

νευρό-σπαστος, ον, (νεῦρον, σπάω) *drawn by strings;* ἀγάλματα νευρόσπαστα puppets *moved by strings.*

νευρο-τενής, ές, (νεῦρον, τείνω) *stretched by sinews.*

νευρο-χᾰρής, ές, (νεῦρον, χαρῆναι) *delighting in the bowstring*

νεύσομαι or **νευσοῦμαι**, fut. of νέω B.

νευστάζω, (νεύω) *to nod,* Lat. *nūto;* νευστάζειν κόρυθι *to nod with* the crest, stride with nodding crest; νευστάζειν κεφαλῇ *to nod* with the head, of one fainting; νευστάζειν ὀφρύσι *to make signs* with the eyebrows.

ΝΕΥ'Ω, f. νεύσω, *to nod, beckon,* as a sign or command. 2. in token of assent, *to nod, bow, promise, confirm by a nod.* 3. generally, *to nod, bend forward;* νεύειν κάτω *to stoop;* νεύειν κεφαλὰς *to bow down, droop* the head; νεύειν εἴς τι *to incline towards* a thing. 4. metaph. *to decline, fall away.*

νεφέλη, ἡ, (νέφος) *a cloud, mass of clouds,* Lat. *nebula:* metaph. *the cloud of death;* ἄχεος νεφέλη *a cloud* of sorrow. II. *a fine bird-net.*

νεφελ-ηγερέτα, Ep. for -της, ὁ, only used in nom. and gen. νεφεληγερέταο, (νεφέλη, ἀγείρω) *cloud-gatherer, cloud-compeller.*

Νεφελο-κένταυρος, ὁ, (νεφέλη, Κένταυρος) *a cloud-centaur.*

Νεφελο-κοκκῡγία, ἡ, (νεφέλη, κόκκυξ) *Cloud-cuckoo-town,* built by the birds in Aristoph. Aves. Hence

Νεφελο-κοκκῡγιεύς, ὁ, *citizen of Cloud-cuckoo-town.*

νεφελόω, f. ώσω, (νεφέλη) *to make cloudy.* Hence

νεφελωτός, ή, όν, *made of clouds.*

νεφο-ειδής, ές, (νέφος, εἶδος) *like a cloud.*

ΝΕ'ΦΟΣ, εος, τό, *a cloud, mass of clouds,* Lat. *nebula:* metaph. *the cloud of death,* θανάτου μέλαν νέφος; so, νέφος ὀφρύων *a cloud upon* the brow. 2. metaph. also, *a cloud* or *dense throng* of men, birds, etc.

νεφρῖτις, ιδος, (νεφρός) fem. Adj. *of* or *in the kidneys;* ἡ νεφρῖτις (sc. νόσος), *a disease in the kidneys.*

ΝΕΦΡΟ'Σ, οῦ, ὁ, mostly in pl. *the kidneys.*

ΝΕ'Ω (A), *to go,* v. sub νέομαι.

ΝΕ'Ω (B), impf. ἔνεον Ep. ἔννεον: fut. νεύσομαι and νευσοῦμαι: aor. 1 ἔνευσα:—*to swim,* Lat. *nāre.* 2. of shoes that are too large; νεῖν ἐν ἐμβάσιν *to swim* or *slip about* in one's shoes.

ΝΕ'Ω (C), fut. νήσω: Ep. 3 pl. aor. 1 med. νήσαντο: aor. 1 pass. ἐνήθην:—*to spin,* Lat. *nēre.*

ΝΕ'Ω (D), fut. νήσω: Ion. **νήω, νηέω, νηνέω**: pf. pass. νένημαι or νένησμαι:—*to pile, heap, heap up.*

νεωκορέω, f. ήσω, (νεωκόρος) *to be a bedel, to have charge of a temple.* II. metaph. *to keep clean and pure.* Hence

νεωκορία, ἡ, *the office of a bedel*

νεω-κόρος, ὁ, (νεώς, κορέω) properly *one who sweeps a temple:* hence *one who has charge of a temple, a bedel, verger,* Lat. *aedituus.* II. a title of cities, *which had built a temple in honour of* their patron-god: hence Ephesus was called νεωκόρος Ἀρτέμιδος.

νέως, gen. pl. of νέος: but **νεῶν**, gen. pl. of ναῦς.

νεών, ῶνος, ὁ, (ναῦς) *a dock* or *basin for ships.*

νε-ώνητος, ον, (νέος, ὠνέομαι) *newly bought.*

νε-ωρής, ές, (νέος, ὥρα) *new, fresh, late.*

νε-ώριον, τό, (νεωρός) *a place where ships are overhauled, a dock-yard, arsenal.*

νεώς, ώ, ὁ, Att. for ναός, *a temple,* like λεώς for λαός.

νεώς, Att. gen. of ναῦς.

νεώσ-οικος, ὁ, (νεώς gen. of ναῦς, οἶκος) literally *a ship's house, a slip* or *dock in which a ship was built* or *repaired: a store-house,* being a part of the νεώριον.

νεωστί, Adv. of νέος, *lately, just now, recently.*

νέωτα, Adv. of νέος, Aeol. for νέωσε, νέωτε, *next year, for next year;* also, εἰς νέωτα.

νεώτατος, η, ον, Sup. of νέος: Adv. νεώτατα, *most recently.*

νεωτερίζω, f. ίσω Att. ιῶ, (νεώτερος) *to make changes* or *alterations: to make innovations* or *revolutionary movements.* II. trans. *to change entirely;* νεωτερίζειν τὴν πολιτείαν *to revolutionise* the state.

νεωτερικός, ή, όν, (νέος) *natural to a youth, youthful.*

νεωτερισμός, οῦ, ὁ, (νεωτερίζω) *innovation.*

νεωτεροποιΐα, ἡ, *innovation, revolution.* From

νεωτερο-ποιός, όν, (νεώτερος, ποιέω) *innovating, revolutionary.*

νεώτερος, α, ον, Comp. of νέος, *younger: newer, fresher:* in bad sense, *strange, unusual;* τὰ νεώτερα or νεώτερα πράγματα, *revolutionary* movements, Lat. *res novae.* Adv. νεωτέρως, *more recently.*

νη-, insep. Prefix, being a strengthd. form of ἀνα- privat., as in νη-πενθής; cf. Lat. *ne-* in *ne-fas,* etc.

ΝΗ', Att. Particle affirming strongly, with acc. of the person invoked; νὴ Δία or νὴ τὸν Δία, also νὴ μὰ τὸν Δία, *yea* by Zeus!

νῆα, νῆας, Ion. acc. sing. and pl. of ναῦς.

νηγάτεος, η, ον, (for νεηγάτος by transposition of ε and η, from νέος, γέγαα,) *new-made.*

νή-γρετος, ον, (νη-, ἐγείρω) *unwaking;* νήγρετος ὕπνος a sleep *that knows no waking, a sound deep sleep:* later also of death: neut. as Adv., νήγρετον *without waking.*

νήδυια, *ων, τά*, (*νηδύς*) *the entrails, bowels*, Lat. *intestina.*

νηδυιόφιν, for *νηδυόφιν*, Ep. gen. of *νηδύς*.

νήδῠμος, *ον*, Homeric epith. of *ὕπνος*: either like *νήγρετος*, *sound, deep* sleep; or from *ἡδύς*, *sweet, delightful*, as if for *ἥδυμος*.

ΝΗΔΥ'Σ, *ύος, ἡ*, *the stomach*, or *the belly, paunch*: *the womb*:—also *the bowels, entrails*; *ἐξελεῖν τὴν νηδύν* to take out *the entrails*, disembowel.

νήεον, Ep. impf. of *νηέω*.

νῆες, nom. pl. of *ναῦς*.

νήεσσι, Ep. dat. pl. of *ναῦς*.

νηέω, fut. *νηήσω*, Ion. and Ep. for *νέω*, *to heap* or *pile up*. II. *to pile, load.*

νήησαν, Ep. 3 pl. aor. 1 of *νηέω*:—**νηησάσθω**, 3 sing. aor. 1 imper. med.

νήθω, (*νέω* C) *to spin.*

νηΐ, Ion. dat. sing. of *ναῦς*.

Νηϊάς, *άδος, ἡ*, Ion. for **Ναϊάς**.

νήϊος, *η, ον*, Dor. **νάϊος**, *α, ον*, also *ος, ον*, *of, belonging to a ship*; *δόρυ νήϊον ship*-timber.

Νηΐς, *ΐδος, ἡ*, Ion. for **Ναΐς**.

νῆϊς, *ιδος, ὁ, ἡ*, (*νη-, ἰδεῖν*) *unknowing, unlearned*: c. gen. *unskilled in* a thing.

νηΐτης, *ου, ὁ*, (*ναῦς*) *of* or *belonging to a ship, consisting of ships.* [ῑ]

νη-κερδής, *ές*, (*νη-, κέρδος*) *without gain, unprofitable.*

νή-κερως, *ωτος, ὁ, ἡ*, Ep. **νή-κερος**, *ον*, (*νη-, κέρας*) *not horned, without horns.*

νή-κεστος, *ον*, (*νη-, ἀκέομαι*) *incurable.*

νη-κουστέω, (*νη-, ἀκούω*) *to give no heed to, disobey*: Ep. aor. 1 *νηκούστησα*.

νη-λεής, *ές*, dat. and acc. *νηλέϊ, νηλέα*, as if from *νηλής*, (*νη-, ἔλεος*) *without pity, pitiless, ruthless, remorseless*; *νηλεὲς ἦμαρ* the *ruthless* day, i. e. the day *of death.* II. *unpitied.*

νηλειής, *ές*, Ep. for *νηλεής*. Adv. *νηλειῶς*.

νηλεό-θῡμος, *ον*, (*νηλεής, θυμός*) *of ruthless spirit.*

νηλεό-ποινος, *ον*, (*νηλεής, ποινή*) *punishing ruthlessly.*

νηλεῶς, Adv. of *νηλεής*, *without pity.*

νηλής, *ές*, see *νηλεής*.

νηλίπους, *ὁ, ἡ, -πουν, τό*, gen. *-πόδος*, = *ἀν-ηλίπους*, *unshod, barefooted*: hence *needy, abject.* [ῐ]

νη-λῑτής, *ές*, (*νη-, ἀλῐτεῖν*) *guiltless, harmless, unoffending.*

νῆμα, *ατος, τό*, (*νέω to spin*) *that which is spun, thread, yarn*: *the thread of a* spider's *web*: *the thread* of the Fates.

νη-μερτής, *ές*, (*νη-, ἁμαρτεῖν*) *unfailing, unerring, infallible*; *νημερτὲς ἐνισπεῖν, νημερτέα εἰπεῖν* to speak *infallible* truths.

νηνεμία Ion. *-ίη, ἡ*, *stillness in the air, a calm*:—*γαλήνη ἔπλετο νηνεμίη* there was a calm and *perfect stillness.* From

νή-νεμος, *ον*, (*νη-, ἄνεμος*) *without wind, breezeless, calm, tranquil.*

νηνέω, = *νηέω*, Ion. and Ep. for *νέω*, *to heap.*

νῆνις, *ιος, ἡ*, contr. for *νεᾶνις*, *a girl, maiden.*

νῆξις, *εως, ἡ*, (*νήχω*) *a swimming.*

νήξομαι, fut. of *νήχομαι*.

νηο-βάτης, *ου, ὁ*, Ion. for *ναυ-βάτης*. [ᾰ]

νηο-πόλος Att. **ναο-**, *ον*, (*νηός* = *ναός, πολέω*) *busying oneself in a temple*: as Subst., *νηοπόλος, ὁ*, *a priest, temple-keeper*, Lat. *aedituus.*

νηο-πορέω, f. *ήσω*, (*ναῦς, πόρος*) *to go in a ship*

νηός, *οῦ, ὁ*, Ion. for *ναός*, *a temple.*

νηός, Ion. gen. of *ναῦς*.

νηό-σοος poët. **νηόσ-σοος**, *ον*, (*ναῦς, σαόω*) *protecting ships.*

νηο-φόρος, *ον*, (*ναῦς, φέρω*) *bearing ships.*

νη-όχος, *ον*, (*ναῦς, ἔχω*) *holding ships.*

νη-πενθής, *ές*, (*νη-, πένθος*) *free from sorrow.* II. act. *soothing* or *assuaging sorrow.*

νηπία Ep. **νηπιάα** and **νηπιέη**, *ἡ*, (*νήπιος*) *childhood, infancy*: in plur. *childishness, folly.*

νηπιάζω, f. *ήσω*, = *νηπιαχεύω*.

νηπῐᾰχεύω, *to be childish, play like a child.* From

νηπίᾰχος, *ον*, poët. for *νήπιος*, *childish.*

νηπῐέη, *ἡ*, Ion. for *νηπία*.

νήπῐος, *α* Ion. *η, ον*, Att. also *ος, ον*, (*νη-, ἔπος*) properly, *not speaking*, Lat. *infans*; *νήπια τέκνα infant* children: also *νήπια* alone, *the young* of an animal. II. metaph. *childish, senseless*: *without forethought, weak, helpless.*

νηπιότης, *ητος, ἡ*, = *νηπία*.

νή-πλεκτος, *ον*, (*νη-, πλέκω*) *not plaited*: *with unbraided hair.*

νη-ποινεί or **-ί**, Adv. of *νήποινος*, Lat. *impune, with impunity.*

νή-ποινος, *ον*, (*νη-, ποινή*) *unpunished, unavenged, with impunity*: but, *φυτῶν νήποινος without share of, unblest with*, fruitful trees.

νηπῠτῐεύομαι, Dep. *to behave childishly.* From

νη-πύτιος, *α, ον*, (*νη-, ἀπύω*) *childish, infantine*; and as Subst. *a child*, like *νήπιος*, Lat. *infans*:—metaph. *childish, thoughtless, heedless.*

Νηρεΐς Ion. **Νηρηΐς**, *ΐδος, ἡ*, *a daughter of Nereus*, hence *a Nereïd* or *Nymph of the sea*, always in pl. *Νηρηΐδες*: they were fifty in number. Cf. **Ναϊάς**.

Νηρεύς, gen. *έως* Ion. *ῆος, ὁ*, *Nereus*, an ancient sea-god. He was eldest son of Pontus (*the sea*), husband of Doris and father of the Nereïds. Hence

Νηρή, poët. for **Νηρηΐς**.

Νηρηΐς, *ΐδος, ἡ*, Ion. for **Νηρεΐς**.

νή-ριθμος, *ον*, (*νη-, ἀριθμός*) *countless, numberless.*

νή-ρῑτος, *ον*, poët. form of *νήριθμος*.

νῆσαι, aor. 1 inf. both of *νέω* (C) *to spin*, and *νέω* (D) *to pile up.*

νησαῖος, *α* Ion. *η, ον*, (*νῆσος*) *of* or *for an island, insular.*

νήσαντο, Ep. 3 pl. aor. 1 med. of *νέω* (C) *to spin.*

νησίδιον, *τό*, Dim. of *νῆσος*, *an islet.*

νησίον, *τό*, Dim. of *νῆσος*, *an islet.*

νησίς, *ῖδος, ἡ*, Dim. of *νῆσος*, *an islet.*

νησίτης, ου, ὁ, (νῆσος) *of* or *for an island*: fem. **νησῖτις**, ιδος, ἡ. [ῑ]

νησιώτης, ου, ὁ, fem. **-ῶτις**, ιδος, ἡ, (νῆσος) *an islander.* II. as Adj. *of an islander: insular, living, situated on an island.* Hence

νησιωτικός, ή, όν, *of* or *for an island* or *an islander*; τὸ νησιωτικόν *insular situation.*

νησο-μᾰχία, ἡ, (νῆσος, μάχη) *an island-fight.*

ΝΗ͂ΣΟΣ Dor. **νᾶσος**, οῦ, ἡ, *an island*, Lat. *insula*: also, *a peninsula*, applied to the Peloponnese

νῆσσα Att. **νῆττα**, ἡ, (νέω *to swim*) *a duck*, Lat. *anas.*

νησσάριον Att. **νηττ-**, τό, Dim. of νῆσσα, *a duckling.*

νηστεία, ἡ, (νηστεύω) *fasting, a fast.*

νηστεύω, f. σω, (νῆστις) *to fast*; νηστεύειν τινός *to fast from, abstain from* a thing

νῆστις, ιος or έως, ὁ, and ἡ: nom. pl. νήστιες or νήστεις: (νη-, ἐσθίω):—*not eating, fasting.* 2. act. *causing hunger, starving.*

νησύδριον, τό, Dim. of νῆσος, *an islet.*

νή-τῑτος, ον, (νη-, τίνω) *unavenged, unpunished.*

νητός, ή, όν, (νέω *to heap*) *heaped up, piled up*

νητός, ή, όν, (νέω *to spin*) *spun, twisted.*

νῆττα, ἡ, **νηττάριον**, τό, Att. for νησσ-.

νηῦς, ἡ, Ion. for ναῦς.

νηυσί, Ion. dat. pl. of ναῦς.

νηυσι-πέρητος, ον, v. ναυσι-πέρατος.

νή-υτμος, ον, (νη-, ἀϋτμή) *breathless.*

νηφᾰλιεύς, ὁ, = νηφάλιος.

νηφάλιος, α, ον, also ος, ον, (νήφω) of persons, *drinking no wine, sober*: of drink, *without wine*; νηφάλια μειλίγματα, of the offerings to the Eumenides, which were composed of water, milk, and honey. [ᾰ]

νήφοσι, poët. for νήφουσι, dat. pl. part.

ΝΗ΄ΦΩ, f. νήψω, *to drink no wine, to be sober, live soberly.*

νή-χῠτος, ον, (νη-, χέω) *not merely poured, full-flowing.*

νήχω Dor. **νάχω**, f. ξω, (νέω) *to swim*: also as Dep. **νήχομαι**, f. ξομαι, aor. 1 ἐνηξάμην.

νηῶν, Ion. gen. pl. of ναῦς.

νηώς, Dor. for ναούς, acc. pl. of ναός.

νίγλᾰρος, ὁ, *a small fife, pipe* or *whistle*, used by the κελευστής to give the time in rowing.

ΝΙ΄ΖΩ, f. νίψω: aor. 1 ἔνιψα:—Med., f. νίψομαι: aor. 1 ἐνιψάμην: pf. νένιμμαι —*to wash*, esp. the hands and feet; νίψασθαι ἁλός *to wash one's hands* with sea water: generally, *to purge, cleanse, purify.* II. *to wash off.*—νίζω is properly used of *washing part* of the body, λούομαι of *bathing*, πλύνω of *washing clothes.*

νικαξῶ, Dor. for νικήσω, fut. of νικάω.

νικασεῖν, Dor for νικήσειν, fut. inf. of νικάω.

νῑκατήρ, ὁ, Dor. for νικητήρ.

νῑκάτωρ, ορος, ὁ, Dor. for νικήτωρ.

νῑκάω, f. ήσω, (νίκη) *to conquer, prevail, get the upper hand*; τὰ χερείονα νικᾷ the worse *prevails*; τὸ εὖ νικάτω let the good *prevail*; νικᾶν τινι *to win* in the judgment of another. 2. of opinions, *to prevail, carry the day*; ἡ νικῶσα γνώμη *the prevailing* opinion, vote of the majority. 3. as law-term, *to win in a suit, gain a cause.* II. trans. *to conquer, vanquish, overcome, overpower*:—Pass., νικᾶσθαι *to be vanquished, overcome by* another: *to be inferior to, give way to.* III. c. acc. cognato, νικήν νικᾶν *to gain* a victory; ναυμαχίαν ναυμαχεῖν *to win* a sea-fight.

νίκειος, ον, (νῖκος) *victorious.*

ΝΙ΄ΚΗ [ῑ], ἡ, *victory, conquest*, Lat. *victoria*: *the fruits of victory.*

νίκη, Aeol. and poët. for ἐνίκα, 3 sing. impf. of νικάω.

νῑκήεις Dor. **νικάεις**, εσσα, εν, (νίκη) *victorious, conquering.*

νικηθείς, aor. 1 part. pass. of νικάω.

νίκημι, Aeol. for νικάω. [ῑ]

νικησέμεν, Ep. for νικήσειν, fut. inf. of νικάω.

νικητέον, verb. Adj. of νικάω, *one must conquer.*

νῑκητήρ, ῆρος, ὁ, like νικητής, *a conqueror.* Hence

νικητήριος, α, ον, *belonging to a conqueror* or *to victory.* II. as Subst. νικητήριον (sub. ἆθλον), τό, *the prize of victory* 2. νικητήρια (sub. ἱερά), τά, *a festival in honour of victory*; νικητήριον ἑστιᾶν to celebrate *the feast of victory.*

νῑκητής, οῦ, ὁ, (νικάω) *a conqueror.*

νῑκητικός, ή, όν, (νικάω) *likely to conquer, conducing to victory.*

νῑκήτωρ, ορος, ὁ, poët. for νικητήρ, *a conqueror.*

νῑκηφορέω, f. ήσω, (νικηφόρος) *to carry off as prize, win.* Hence

νῑκηφορία, ἡ, *a conquering, victory.*

νῑκη-φόρος, ον, (νίκη, φέρω) *bringing victory.* II. *bearing off the prize, conquering, victorious.*

νῑκό-βουλος, ον, (νικάω, βουλή) *prevailing in the Council.*

νῑκο-μάχᾱς, ου, ὁ, (νικάω, μάχη) *conqueror in the fight.*

νῖκος, εος, τό, later form for νίκη, *victory.*

νικῷεν, Att. contr. for νικάοιεν, 3 pl. opt of νικάω.

νίν, Dor. and Att. enclit. acc. of 3rd pers. Pron., for αὐτόν, αὐτήν, αὐτό, *him, her, it*; never used reflexively: of all genders, both sing. and pl., but the pl. is much more rare: Hom., and Ion. writers use μίν.

νιπτήρ, ῆρος, ὁ, (νίζω) *a washing vessel, basin, laver.*

νίπτρον, τό, (νίζω) *water for washing*: mostly in plur.

νίπτω, later form for νίζω.

νίσσομαι, f. νίσομαι [ῑ] = νέομαι, *to go, to go away.*

ΝΙ΄ΤΡΟΝ, τό, in Herodotus and Att. **λίτρον**, *carbonate of soda, soda.*

νίφα, τήν, *snow*, irreg. acc. of νιφάς, as if from a nom. *νίψ.

νῐφάς, άδος, ἡ, (νίφω) *a snow-flake*: in pl. *snow-flakes, a storm of snow.* 2. generally, *a shower*:—metaph., νιφὰς πολέμου *the storm* or *sleet* of war. II. as Adj., fem. of νιφόεις, *snowy, snow-capt.*

νῐφέμεν, Ep. inf. of νίφω.

νῐφετός, οῦ, ὁ, (νίφω) *a shower of snow, a snow-storm.*

νῐφό-βολος, (νίφα, βάλλω) *snow-beaten, wintry.*

νῐφόεις, εσσα, εν, (**νίφα**) *snow-covered, snow-capt.*

νῐφο-στῐβής, ές, (νίφα, στιβεῖν) *thick with snow.*

ΝΙ'ΦΩ [ῐ], f. νίψω, intrans. *to snow;* ὁ θεὸς νίφει, or νίφει alone, *it snows.* II. trans. *to cover with snow:* Pass. *to be snowed on, covered with snow.* Cf. ὕω, ὕομαι.

νίψαι, νίψασθαι, aor. 1 inf. act. and med. of νίζω.

νίψω, fut. of νίζω, and also of νίφω.

νοερός, ά, όν, (νόος, νοῦς) *intellectual.*

νοέω, f. νοήσω: Ion. νώσω: aor. 1 ἐνόησα Ion. ἔνωσα: pf. νενόηκα Ion. νένωκα:—Med., Ep, 3 sing. aor. νοήσατο Ion. part. νωσάμενος:—Pass., aor. 1 ἐνοήθην:—Pass., aor. 1 ἐνοήθην: pf. νενόημαι Ion. νένωμαι: Ion. plqpf. ἐνενώμην: (νόος):—*to see so as to remark* or *discern*, distinguished from merely seeing, as, τὸν δὲ ἰδὼν ἐνόησε when he saw him *he perceived who he was: to notice, remark.* II. *to think:* absol. *to be minded:* hence, *to purpose, intend:* c. inf. *to intend to do* a thing: in part. νοέων, *discreet, thoughtful.* 2. of words or expressions, *to mean, imply, have a certain sense.* III. *to think out, devise, contrive.* IV. *to think* or *deem* that a thing is so and so.

νόημα, ατος, τό, (νοέω) *that which is thought, a thought.* II. *a purpose, design, resolve.* III. generally, *thought, understanding, mind.* Hence

νοήμων, ον, gen. ονος, *thoughtful, sensible:* also *in ones right mind*, opp. to παραφρονέων.

νόησις, εως, ἡ, (νοέω) *thought, intelligence.*

νοητικός, ή, όν, (νοέω) *intelligent.*

νοητός, ή, όν, (νοέω) *perceptible, intelligible.*

νοθᾱ-γενής, ές, Dor. for νοθηγενής, (νόθος, γενέσθαι) *base-born.*

νοθο-καλλοσύνη, ἡ, (νόθος, κάλλος) *spurious charms.*

ΝΟ'ΘΟΣ, η, ον, Att. also ος, ον, *illegitimate, born out of wedlock;* νόθος υἱός a *natural* son, opp. to γνήσιος, Lat. *legitimus.* II. generally, *spurious, counterfeit, adulterated.*

νοΐδιον, τό, Dim. of νόος, νοῦς, *a little thought, a notion.*

νομαῖος, α, ον, (νομός) *roaming, roving, ranging.*

νόμαιος, α, ον, (νόμος) *customary, conventional:* τὰ νόμαια, like νόμιμα, *customs, usages,* Lat. *instituta.*

νομ-άρχης, ου, ὁ, (νομός, ἄρχω) *the chief of an Egyptian province* (νομός): also among the Scythians.

νομάς, άδος, ὁ, ἡ, (νόμος) *roaming, ranging, wandering from one place to another:* Νομάδες, οἱ, *pastoral tribes that roved about* with their flocks, *Nomads;* and as prop. n. *Numidians,* Lat. *Numidae.* II. *grazing, feeding.*

νόμευμα, ατος, τό, (νομεύω) *that which is put to graze, a flock* or *herd.*

νομεύς, έως Ep. ῆος, ὁ, (νέμω, νομός) *a shepherd* or *herdsman.* II. *a dispenser, distributer.* III. plur. νομέες = ἐγκοίλια, are *the ribs of a ship.*

νομεῦσι, dat. pl. of νομεύς.

νομευσῶ, Dor. for νομεύσω, fut of νομεύω.

νομεύω, (νομεύς) *to pasture, feed, drive afield;* βοῦς νομοὺς νομεύειν *to feed down* the pastures with oxen, Lat. *depascere.*

νομή, ἡ, (νέμω) *a pasture, pasturage: fodder, food.* 2. *a feeding, grazing.* II. *division, distribution;* esp. of an inheritance.

νομῆες, Ep. for **νομεῖς**, nom. pl. of νομεύς.

νομίζω: fut. νομίσω Ion. νομιέω Att. νομιῶ: pf. νενόμικα:—Pass., aor. 1 ἐνομίσθην: pf. νενόμισμαι: (νόμος):—*to hold* or *own as a custom* or *usage:* said of things *recognised by convention* or *prescriptive right;* νομίζειν τοὺς θεούς *to recognise* the gods acknowledged by the state; but, νομίζειν θεούς *to recognise* the existence of the gods generally:—Pass. *to be in esteem;* νομίζεται *it is the custom, is customary, is usually recognised;* τὰ νομιζόμενα or νενομισμένα, *customs, usages, laws,* Lat. *instituta.* 2. *to adopt, practise a custom* or *usage;* Ἕλληνες ἀπ' Αἰγυπτίων ταῦτα νενομίκασι the Greeks *have adopted* these *customs* from the Egyptians. 3. *to own, acknowledge, recognise as;* τοὺς κακοὺς χρηστοὺς νομίζειν:—in Pass., τοῦ θεῶν νομίζεται; to which of the gods *is it held sacred?* 4. absol. *to be accustomed.* 5. Pass. *to be governed after old laws and customs.* II. c. dat., like χρῆσθαι, *to be accustomed to* a thing, *practise* it; hence *to make common use of, use;* and in Att., *to use as a current coin.* III. c. acc. et inf. *to expect that* a thing will be.

νομῐκός, ή, όν, (νόμος) *of* or *for the laws: resting on the authority of law.* II. *learned in the law:* as Subst., νομικός, ὁ, *a lawyer.*

νόμῐμος, η, ον, (νόμος) *conformable to usage* or *law:* hence 1. *conventional, prescriptive.* 2. *lawful, legal.* 3. in neut. pl. νόμιμα, *usages, customs;* νόμιμα ποιεῖν, of funeral rites, to pay *the customary offices,* Lat. *justa facere.* II. of persons, *observant of law.* Hence

νομίμως, Adv. *according to law:* Comp. νομιμώτερον.

νόμιος, α, ον, also ος, ον, (νομός, νομή) *belonging to shepherds, pastoral.*

νόμῐσις, ἡ, (νομίζω) *usage, prescription:* also, *a mode of esteeming.*

νόμισμα, ατος, τό, (νομίζω) *anything recognised by established usage,* viz., 1. *the current coin* of a state, Lat. *nummus:* cf. νομίζω, fin. 2. *an established weight* or *measure, legal measure.* 3. *any institution* or *custom.*

νομο-γράφος, ον, (νόμος, γράφω) *writing laws:* as Subst., νομογράφος, ὁ, *a lawgiver.*

νομο-δείκτης, ου, ὁ, (νόμος, δείκνυμι) *an explainer of the laws.*

νομο-δῐδάσκᾰλος, ὁ, (νόμος, διδάσκαλος) *a teacher of the law:* so, **νομο-διδάκτης**, ου, ὁ.

νομοθεσία, ἡ, *law-giving, legislation.* From

νομοθετέω, f. ήσω, (νομοθέτης) *to be a law-giver, make laws:*—Pass. *to have a code of laws:*—Med. *to make laws for oneself.* II. *to ordain by law.* Hence

νομοθέτημα, ματος, τό, *a law, ordinance.*

νομο-θέτης, ου, ὁ, (νόμος, τίθημι) *a lawgiver.*

νομόνδε, Adv. (νομός) *to the pasture.*

νομός, οῦ, ὁ, (νέμω) *a pasture, place for cattle to graze; νομὸς ὕλης a* woodland *pasture.* 2. *pasturage, herbage:* generally, *food.* 3. metaph., ἐπέων πολὺς νομός ample *pasture*, a wide *range* for words. II. *an abode allotted* to one, *a district, department, province, satrapy,* Lat. *praefectura.*

νόμος, ου, ὁ, (νέμω) *anything assigned* or *apportioned*, viz., I. *an usage, custom, convention: a positive enactment, law, ordinance,* Lat. *institutum; νόμῳ, conventionally,* opp. to φύσει, *naturally*:—at Athens νόμοι was the name given to *Solon's* laws, in contradistinction to those of *Draco*, which were called θεσμοί. 2. χειρῶν νόμος *the law of force* or *might*, opp. to δίκης νόμος; ἐν χειρῶν νόμῳ διαφθείρεσθαι to die *in the fight* or *scuffle*; ἐς χειρῶν νόμον ἀπικέσθαι to come *to blows.* II. *a musical strain: a song, ode; νόμοι πολεμικοί* war-*songs.*

νομο-φύλαξ, ἄκος, τό, (νόμος, φύλαξ) *a guardian of the laws.* [ῠ]

νοό-πληκτος, ον, (νόος, πλήσσω) *striking the mind, mind-distracting.*

ΝΟ'ΟΣ, νόου, contr. **νοῦς**, νοῦ, ὁ; later also gen. νοός, dat. νοΐ, acc. νόα, nom. pl. νόες:—*mind*, Lat. *mens; νόῳ* or σὺν νόῳ *mindfully, prudently; πάρεκ νόον without sense; ἀνθρώπων νόος the mood* or *temper* of men; ἐκ παντὸς νόου with all his *heart; κατὰ νόον* according to one's *mind.* II. *a thought, purpose, resolve.* III. *the sense* or *meaning* of a word or expression.

νοσερός, ά, όν, (νόσος) *sickly, ill.*

νοσέω, f. ήσω, (νόσος), *to be sick, ill, sickly, to ail,* whether in body or mind. 2. metaph. *to be distressed, suffer, be afflicted.*

νοσηλεία, ἡ, (νοσηλεύω) *matter discharged* from a running sore.

νοσηλεύω, (νοσέω) *to tend a sick person.*

νόσημα, ατος, τό, (νοσέω) *a sickness, disease, plague, malady.* 2. metaph. *a disease, disorder, affliction.*

νοσηματ-ώδης, ες, (νόσημα, εἶδος) *sickly.*

νοσηρός, ά, όν, (νοσέω) *unhealthy, unwholesome,* of places.

ΝΟ'ΣΟΣ Ion. **νοῦσος**, ἡ, *sickness, disease: a malady, ailment.* II. metaph. *distress, affliction, evil.* 2. *disease of mind,* esp. madness. 3. generally, *a plague, bane, mischief.*

νοσο-φόρος Ion. **νουσ-**, ον, (νόσος, φέρω) *bringing sickness* or *disease.*

νοσσεύω, contr. for νεοσσεύω, *to hatch.*

νοσσιά, ἡ, and **νοσσίον**, τό, Att. contr. for νεοσσ–.

νοσσίς, ίδος, ἡ, Dim. of νοσσός, Att. contr. for νεοσσίς, *a little bird:* also *a young girl.*

νοσσο-τροφέω, contr. for νεοσσοτροφέω.

νοστέω, f. ήσω, (νόστος) *to return, come, or go back,* to one's home or country. 2. *to return safe after danger.* 3. generally, *to go, come, travel.*

νοστήσειε, Aeol. 3 sing. opt. aor. I. of νοστέω.

νοστησέμεν, Ep. inf. fut. of νοστέω.

νόστιμος, ον, (νόστος) *of* or *belonging to a return;* νόστιμον ἦμαρ the day *of return.* 2. *returning, that will* or *may return, surviving, safe,* Lat. *salvus.*

νόστος, ου, ὁ, (νέομαι) *a return home* or *homeward:* c. gen. loci, *return to* a place. 2. generally, *travel, journey; νόστος φορβῆς a journey to bring* food *home,* i. e. *in search, in quest of* food.

νόσφι, before a vowel or metri grat. **νόσφιν**: I. as Adv. of Place, *afar, aloof, apart;* hence *aside, secretly, furtively:* νόσφιν ἀπό, c. gen., like νόσφι II, *aloof from.* II. as Prep. c. gen. *far from, aloof* or *away from,* mostly of Place: hence *without, separate from.* 2. of mind or disposition, νόσφιν Ἀχαιῶν *apart from* the Achaeans, i. e. *differing from* them. 3. *besides, except.*

νοσφίδιος, α, ον, (νόσφι) *taken away, abstracted.*

νοσφίζω, f. ίσω Att. νοσφιῶ, (νόσφι) *to put away, remove, part.* II. Med. and Pass. **νοσφίζομαι**, f. -ίσομαι: aor. I med ἐνοσφισάμην Ep. νοσφισάμην, Ep. part. νοσφισσάμενος: aor. I pass. ἐνοσφίσθην:—*to remove oneself, withdraw, retire:* and in act. sense, *to leave, forsake, abandon.* 2. metaph. of the mind, *to become estranged* or *alienated.* III. act. *to abstract, steal:* c. dupl. acc., *to rob* one *of* a thing:—Med. *to appropriate.* 2. *to make away with, kill, despatch.*

νοσφισθείς, aor. I part. pass. of νοσφίζω.

νοσφισσάμενος, Ep. aor. I part. med. of νοσφίζω.

νοσ-ώδης, ες, (νόσος, εἶδος) *sickly, ailing:* generally, *diseased.* II. act. *unwholesome, unhealthy.*

νοτερός, ά, όν, (νότος) *wet, damp, moist; νοτερὸς χειμών* a storm *of rain.*

νοτία, ἡ, *wet, damp, moisture, rain; νοτίαι εἰαριναί* spring *rains.*

νοτίζω, f. ίσω, (νότιος) *to moisten*:—Pass. *to be wet.*

νότιος, α, ον, also ος, ον, (νότος) *wet, damp, rainy;* ὑψοῦ δ' ἐν νοτίῳ τήν γ' ὥρμισαν they moored her [the ship] far from land *in the sea,* opp. to the beach. II. *southern, southerly.*

νοτίς, ίδος, ἡ, (νότος) *moisture, damp, wet.*

ΝΟ'ΤΟΣ, ου, ὁ, *the south* or *south-west wind,* Lat. *Notus.* II. *the south* or *south-west quarter.*

νοττεύω, **νοττίον**, etc., contr. for νεοττ–.

νου-βυστικός, ή, όν, (νοῦς, βύω) *choke-full of wit, crammed with cleverness, clever.* Adv. -κῶς, *cleverly.*

νουθεσία, ἡ, *a warning, admonishing: reproof.* From

νου-θετέω, f. ήσω, (νοῦς, τίθημι) *to bring to mind: to remind, warn, advise, admonish, chastise.* Hence

νουθέτημα, ατος, τό, *an admonition, warning.*

νουθετητέος, α, ον, verb. Adj. of νουθετέω, *to be warned, advised.*

νουθετικός, ή, όν, (νουθετέω) *admonitory.*

νου-μηνία, ἡ, Att. contr. for νεομηνία, *the new moon: the time of the new moon, the first of the month.*

νουν-έχης, ές, (νοῦς, ἔχω) *having understanding, sensible, discreet.* Adv. -χῶς, *discreetly, prudently.*

νοῦς, ὁ, contr. for *νόος*, *mind.*

νοῦσος, ἡ, Ion. for *νόσος*.

νουσο-φόρος, *ον*, Ion. for *νοσοφόρος*.

νύ, see *νῦν*, *νύν*.

νύγδην, Adv. (*νύσσω*) *by pricking*, Lat. *punctim.*

νῠγείς, aor. 2 part. pass. of *νύσσω*.

νυκτερείσιος, *ον*, = *νυκτερήσιος*, *nightly.*

νυκτ-ερέτης, *ου*, ὁ, (*νύξ*, *ἐρέσσω*) *one who rows by night.*

νυκτερευτικός, *ή*, *όν*, *fit for watching by night*, *fit for hunting by night.* From

νυκτερεύω, f. *σω*, (*νύκτερος*) *to pass the night*: *to keep watch*, *mount guard by night*, *bivouac*: also *to hunt*, *fish*, etc., *by night.*

νυκτερήσιος, *ον*, (*νύκτερος*) *nightly.*

νυκτερῐνός, *η*, *όν*, (*νύξ*) *nightly*, *by night*, Lat. *nocturnus.*

νυκτερίς, *ίδος*, ἡ, (*νύξ*, *νύκτερος*) *a night-bird*, *a bat*, Lat. *vespertilio.*

νύκτερος, *ον*, (*νύξ*) *nightly.*

νυκτερ-ωπός, *όν*, (*νύκτερος*, *ὤψ*) *night-faced*, *dusky.*

νυκτ-ηγορέω or in Med. **νυκτ-ηγορέομαι**, (*νύξ*, *ἀγορά*) *to assemble by night.* Hence

νυκτηγορία, ἡ, *a nightly assembly* or *discourse.*

νυκτ-ηρεφής, *ές*, (*νύξ*, *ἐρέφω*) *shrouded by night*, *gloomy.*

νυκτί-βρομος, *ον*, (*νύξ*, *βρέμω*) *roaring by night.*

νυκτί-γᾰμος, *ον*, (*νύξ*, *γαμέω*) *marrying by night* or *clandestinely.*

νυκτι-κλέπτης, *ου*, ὁ, = *νυκτοκλέπτης*.

νυκτῐ-κόραξ, *ἄκος*, ὁ, (*νύξ*, *κόραξ*) *the night-jar*, *goat-sucker*. also *the screech-owl.*

νυκτῐ-λαθραιο-φάγος, *ον*, (*νύξ*, *λαθραῖος*, *φᾰγεῖν*) *eating secretly by night.*

νυκτῐ-λάλος, *ον*, (*νύξ*, *λᾰλέω*) *nightly-sounding*, *serenading.*

νυκτῐ-λαμπής, *ές*, (*νύξ*, *λάμπω*) *illumined by night alone*, i. e. *gloomy*, *murky.*

νύκτιος, *α*, *ον*, (*νύξ*) *nightly.*

νυκτῐ-πᾰται-πλάγιος, *ον*, (*νύξ*, *πατέω*, *πλάγιος*) *roaming about by night.* [ᾰ]

νυκτί-πλαγκτος, *ον*, (*νύξ*, *πλάζω*) *making to wander by night*, *disquieting*, *disturbing*: also 2. pass. *νυκτίπλαγκτος εὐνή* a bed *from which one wanders by night*, a *restless* bed.

νυκτι-πλᾰνής, *ές*, and **νυκτί-πλᾰνος**, *ον*, (*νύξ*, *πλανάω*) *wandering*, *rambling about by night.*

νυκτῐ-πόλος, *ον*, (*νύξ*, *πολέω*) *roaming by night.*

νυκτί-σεμνος, *ον*, (*νύξ*, *σεμνός*) *solemnised by night.*

νυκτι-φανής, *ές*, (*νύξ*, *φανῆναι*) *shining* or *appearing by night.*

νυκτί-φαντος, *ον*, (*νύξ*, *φαίνομαι*) *appearing by night*: *nightly.*

νυκτι-φρούρητος, *ον*, (*νύξ*, *φρουρέω*) *keeping night-watches.*

νυκτο-θήρας, *ου*, ὁ, (*νύξ*, *θηράω*) *one who hunts by night.*

νυκτο-κλέπτης, *ου*, ὁ, (*νύξ*, *κλέπτω*) *a thief of the night.*

νυκτο-μᾰχέω, f. *ήσω*, (*νύξ*, *μάχη*) *to fight by night.* Hence

νυκτομᾰχία, ἡ, *a night battle*, *a battle in the dark.*

νυκτο-περιπλάνητος, *ον*, (*νύξ*, *περιπλᾰνάω*) *rambling about at night.*

νυκτοπορέω, f. *ήσω*, *to go* or *travel by night.* From

νυκτο-πόρος, *ον*, (*νύξ*, *πόρος*) *travelling by night.*

νυκτο-φᾰής, *ές*, (*νύξ*, *φάος*) *giving light by night*, *shining by night.*

νυκτοφῠλᾰκέω, f. *ήσω*, *to keep guard by night*, *to be a night-watch.* From

νυκτο-φύλαξ, *ᾰκος*, ὁ, ἡ, (*νύξ*, *φύλαξ*) *one that keeps watch by night*, *a warder*, Lat. *excubitor.*

νυκτῷον, *τό*, (*Νύξ*) *a temple of Night.*

νυκτ-ωπός, *όν*, (*νύξ*, *ὤψ*) *with the look of night*, i. e. *murky*, *obscure.*

νύκτωρ, Adv. (*νύξ*) *by night*, Lat. *noctu.*

νύμφᾰ, poët. for *νύμφη*, in voc. *νύμφα φίλη*.

νύμφᾱ, Dor. for *νύμφη*.

νυμφ-ᾰγωγός, *όν*, (*νύμφη*, *ἄγω*) *the leader of the bride*; esp. *one who leads her from her home to the bridegroom's house*: *the friend of the bridegroom.*

νυμφαῖον, *τό*, *a temple of the Nymphs*, Lat. *Nymphaeum.* From

νυμφαῖος, *α*, *ον*, (*νύμφη*) *of* or *sacred to the Nymphs.*

νυμφᾶν, Dor. gen. pl. of *νύμφα*.

νυμφεῖος, *α*, *ον*, (*νύμφη*) *belonging to a bride*, *bridal*, *nuptial.* II. as Subst., *νυμφεῖον* (sub. *δῶμα*), *τό*, *the bridechamber.* 2. *νυμφεῖα* (sub. *ἱερά*), *τά*, *nuptial rites*, *marriage*:—but, also, *the bride herself.*

νύμφευμα, *τό*, (*νυμφεύω*) *marriage*, *espousal.* II. *the person married*, *a match.*

νυμφευτήριος, *α*, *ον*, (*νυμφεύω*) *bridal*, *nuptial.*

νυμφευτής, *οῦ*, ὁ, (*νυμφεύω*) *the friend of the bridegroom*, = *παρανύμφιος*. II. *a bridegroom*, *husband.*

νυμφεύτρια, ἡ, (*νυμφευτής*) *a bridesmaid.* II. *the bride* herself.

νυμφεύω, f. *σω*, (*νύμφη*) *to give a daughter in marriage*, *to betroth*, *lead to the bridechamber.* 2. *to marry*, mostly of the woman, Lat. *nubere*: but also of the man, Lat. *ducere.* II. Pass., with fut. med. *νυμφεύσομαι*, aor. 1 both med. and pass. *ἐνυμφευσάμην*, *ἐνυμφεύθην*:—*to be given in marriage*, *marry*, of the woman. III. Med., of the man, *to take to wife.*

ΝΥ͂ΜΦΗ, ἡ, voc. also *νύμφᾰ*: *a bride*, Lat. *nupta*: hence, 2. *a young wife.* 3. *any married woman*, like Lat. *nympha.* 4. *a marriageable maiden.* II. as prop. name, *a Nymph*, a goddess of lower rank, called in Homer *θεαὶ* **Νύμφαι**: they presided over springs, trees, seas, mountains, etc., and were distinguished by special names: *spring*-nymphs were Naiads, **Ναΐδες**: *sea*-nymphs, **Νηρηΐδες**: *mountain*-nymphs, **Νύμφαι** *ὀρεστιάδες* or *ὀρεάδες*; *tree*-nymphs, from the oak their favourite tree, **Δρυάδες**, **Ἁμαδρυάδες**, **Ἀδρυάδες**; *rain*-nymphs, **Νύμφαι** *ὑάδες*; *meadow*-nymphs, **Νύμφαι** *λειμωνιάδες*; *rock*-nymphs, **Νύμφαι** *πετραῖαι*. 2. the Muses are often called Nymphs: hence all persons in a state of *rapture* were said to be caught by the Nymphs, *νυμ-*

φόληπτοι, Lat. *lymphati*. III. *the chrysalis* or *pupa* of moths.

νυμφίδιος, α, ον, (νύμφη) *of* or *belonging to bridal, nuptial.*

νυμφικός, ή, όν, = νυμφίδιος.

νυμφίος, ὁ, (νύμφη) *a bridegroom, husband.* II. as Adj., **νύμφιος**, ιον, *newly-wedded: bridal.*

νυμφό-κλαυτος, ον, (νύμφη, κλαίω) *deplored by brides* or *wives.*

νυμφοκομέω, f. ήσω, *to dress oneself as a bride.* II. *to dress a bride, lead home as bride.* From

νυμφο-κόμος, ον, (νύμφη, κομέω) *dressing* or *taking care of a bride: bridal.*

νυμφό-ληπτος, ον, (νύμφη, λαμβάνω) *possessed by Nymphs,* i. e. *rapt, entranced,* Lat. *lymphatus.*

νυμφο-στολέω, f. ήσω, (νύμφη, στέλλω) *to escort the bride.*

νυμφό-τῑμος, ον, (νύμφη, τιμάω) *honouring the bride;* μέλος νυμφότιμον the song *in honour of the bride.*

νυμφών, ῶνος, ὁ, (νύμφη) *the bridechamber.*

ΝΥ͂Ν, enclit. **νυν** Ep. **νυ**, Adv. *now, at this very time,* Lat. *nunc;* οἱ νῦν ἄνθρωποι men *of the present day;* ὁ νῦν χρόνος the time *present.* 2. with the Article, τὸ νῦν or τὰ νῦν, τονῦν or τανῦν, *as to the present,* i. e. *at the present moment,* a stronger form of νῦν. II. νῦν also denotes the immediate following of one thing *upon* another in point of Time, *then, thereupon.* 2. also an Inference, *then, therefore;* μὴ νῦν μοι νεμεσήσετε *now* do not, do not *then,* be wroth with me. 3. in enclit. form νυν, used to strengthen a command, as, δεῦρό νυν quick *then!* φέρε νυν, ἄγε νυν come *then.*

νυνί Att. **νῦν**, strengthd. like οὑτοσί for οὗτος, *now, at this moment.*

νῦν ὅτε, = ἔστιν ὅτε, *at times, sometimes.*

ΝΥ͂Ξ, νυκτός, ἡ, *NIGHT,* Lat. *NOX,* whether *the night-season* or *a night;* νυκτός *by night,* Lat. *noctu;* νύκτα *during the night, the night long:*—so also with preps., ἀνὰ or διὰ νύκτα *all night* long; διὰ νυκτός in the course of *the night;* ἐκ νυκτός just after *night-fall;* so also ὑπὸ νύκτα; πόρρω τῆς νυκτός far into *the night.* II. *gloom, darkness, murkiness.* 2. *the night of death,* i. e. *death* itself. 3. *the nether world.* III. Νύξ, as prop. n., *the goddess of Night,* daughter of Chaos. IV. pl. νύκτες, *the hours* or *watches* of the night: from Homer downwards, the Greeks divided the night into three watches; μέσαι νύκτες *midnight.* V. *the quarter of night, the evening-quarter of heaven,* i. e. *the West,* as opp. to the dayspring in the *East.*

νύξε, Ep. for ἔνυξε, 3 sing. aor. 1 of νύσσω.

ΝΥΟ΄Σ, οῦ, ἡ, *a daughter-in-law:* generally, *any female connected by marriage,* as γαμβρός meant *a man* connected by marriage. II. generally, *a bride, mistress.*

νύσσα, ης, ἡ, (νύσσω) *a post* or *pillar on a racecourse,* viz., 1. *the turning-post* so placed at the end of the course, that the chariots driving up the right side turned round it and returned by the left side; the same as καμπτήρ, Lat. *meta:* as the near horse was turned sharp round this post, ἐν νύσσῃ ἐγχριμφθῆναι meant to make a sharp turn, graze *the turning-post.* 2. *the starting-post, pillar.* 3. generally, *a partition-wall.*

ΝΥ΄ΣΣΩ Att. **νύττω**: f. νύξω: aor. 1 ἔνυξα:—Pass., aor. 2 ἐνύγην, inf. νῠγῆναι:—*to prick, spur, pierce, puncture.*

νυστάζω, fut. άσω and άξω:—*to nod,* esp. in sleep, hence *to slumber, sleep:* also *to be sleepy, drowsy,* Lat *dormito:* also *to hang down the head.* Hence

νυστακτής, οῦ, ὁ, as Adj. *nodding, drowsy.*

νύττω, Att. for νύσσω.

νύχᾰ, Adv. (νύξ) = νύκτωρ, *by night.* [ῠ]

νῠχ-εγρεσία, ἡ, (νύξ, ἐγείρω) *the being roused at night, rising by night.*

νύχευμα, ατος, τό, *a nightly watch,* Lat. *pervigilium.* [ῠ] From

νῠχεύω, f. σω, (νύξ) *to watch the night through.*

νυχθ-ήμερον, τό, (νύξ, ἡμέρα) *a day and night.*

νύχιος [ῠ], α, ον, also ος, ον, (νύξ): 1. act. *doing a thing by night: as if asleep.* 2. *dark as night, murky.*

νώ, for νῶϊ, nom. and acc. dual of ἐγώ, *we two.*

νω-δός, ή, όν, (νη-, ὀδούς) *toothless,* Lat. *e-dentulus.*

νωδῠνία, ἡ, *ease* or *relief from pain.* From

νώδῠνος, ον, (νη-, ὀδύνη) = ἀνώδυνος, *without pain, pleasing, grateful.* II. act. *soothing pain.*

νῶε, poët. for νῶϊ.

ΝΩΘΗ΄Σ, ές, gen. έος, *sluggish, lazy, torpid: dull. stupid.* Comp. νωθέστερος.

νώθητι, Ion. contr. for νοήθητι, aor. 1 pass. imperat. of νοέω.

νωθρός, ά, όν, = νωθής, *sluggish, lazy, dull.*

ΝΩ͂Ι, nom. and acc. dual of ἐγώ, *we two, us two,* Att. νώ: poët. **νῶε**: gen. and dat. dual νῶϊν, *of us two, to us two;* Att. νῷν. Hence

νωΐτερος, α, ον, *of, from,* or *belonging to us two.* [ῑ]

νωλεμές, Adv. *unceasingly, continually, without intermission.* (Deriv. uncertain.)

νωλεμέως, Adv. = νωλεμές.

νῶμα, τό, Ion. for νόημα.

νωμάω, f. ήσω, (νέμω) *to deal out, distribute, dispense.* II. *to direct, guide, control:* 1. of weapons, *to manage skilfully, wield, sway, ply.* 2. of the limbs, *to ply nimbly.* 3. metaph. *to revolve in the mind: to think on, observe, remark.*

νῷν, Att. for νῶϊν; see νῶϊ.

νώνυμνος, ον, Ep. collat. form of νώνυμος, like δίδυμνος for δίδυμος, ἀπάλαμνος for ἀπάλαμος.

νώνῠμος, ον, (νη-, ὄνυμα Aeol. for ὄνομα) *without name,* i. e. *unknown, inglorious.* II. c. gen. *without the name of,* i. e. *without knowledge of.*

νῶροψ, οπος, ὁ, ἡ, only in dat. and acc., νώροπι χαλκῷ, νώροπα χαλκόν *flashing, gleaming* brass.

νωσάμενος, νώσασθαι, Ion. aor. 1 med. part. and inf. of νοέω.

νωτ-ᾰγωγέω, f. ήσω, (νῶτον, ἀγωγός) *to carry on the back.*

νων-άκμων, ονος, ὁ, ἡ, (νῶτον, ἄκμων) *with mailed back.*

νωτῐαῖος, α, ον, (νῶτον) *of* or *belonging to the back;* νωτιαῖα ἄρθρα the joints *of the back*, the vertebrae.

νωτίζω, f. ίσω, (νῶτον) *to make to turn the back, put to flight.* II. intr. *to turn one's back, turn and flee.* III. *to cover the back of* another :—πόντον νωτίσαι *to skim* the sea.

νωτο-βᾰτέω, f. ήσω, (νῶτον, βαίνω) *to mount the back.* II. *to walk on the back* or *ridge of.*

ΝΩ͂ΤΟΝ, τό, τά, *the back*, Lat. *tergum;* the pl. νῶτα often used for the sing., like Lat. *terga*, e. g. τὰ νῶτα δοῦναι to turn the back, flee, like Lat. *dare terga;* κατὰ νώτου from behind. II. metaph. any *wide surface;* εὐρέα νῶτα θαλάσσης the broad *back* or *surface* of the sea: also *large tracts of land, plains.* 2. *any back* or *ridge.*

νωτο-φόρος, ον, (νῶτον, φέρω) *carrying on the back.*

νωχελής, ές, *moving sluggishly, slothful, inactive.* (Deriv. uncertain.) Hence

νωχελία Ep. -ίη, ἡ, *laziness, sluggishness.*

Ξ

Ξ, **ξ**, **ξῖ**, τό, indecl., fourteenth letter of the Greek alphabet: as numeral ξ΄, 60, but ͵ξ, 60,000.—It was a double consonant, compounded of γσ, κσ, χσ. In Att. Greek, ξ came in with the Samian alphabet (see H, η); before this it was represented by χσ. II. ξ in Aeol. and Att. is interchanged with κ and σ, as, κοινός ξυνός; and Dor. fut. and aor. κλᾳξῶ for κλῄσω, παῖξαι for παῖσαι, etc. III. ξ also is often interchanged with σσ or ττ, not only in the fut. of Verbs in -σσω and -ττω, e. g. ἀνάσσω, ἀνάξω, but also in words like δισσός τρισσός Ion. διξός τριξός.—ξ was most. freq. in Dor. and old Att. dialect. [Vowels before ξ are always long by position.]

ΞΑΙ΄ΝΩ, f. ξᾰνῶ: aor. 1 ἔξηνα :—Pass., aor. 1 ἐξάνθην: pf. ἔξαμμαι :—*to scratch, comb:* esp. of wool, *to card*, so as to make it fit for spinning. 2. of cloth, *to full, clean.* II. metaph. *to treat as in fulling, to thresh, mangle, lacerate.*

ξανθᾶς, Dor. for ξανθῆς, fem. gen. of ξανθός.

ξανθίζω, f. ίσω Att. ιῶ, (ξανθός) *to make yellow* or *brown: to roast* or *fry brown.*

ξάνθισμα, ατος, τό, (ξανθίζω) *that which is dyed yellow.*

ξανθό-γεως, ων, (ξανθός, γῆ) *of yellow soil.*

ξανθό-θριξ, τρῐχος, ὁ, ἡ, (ξανθός, θρίξ) *yellow-haired.*

ξανθο-κόμης, ου, ὁ, (ξανθός, κόμη) = ξανθόθριξ.

ξανθός, ή, όν, *yellow* of various shades, *golden* or *pale yellow;* also *red-yellow, chestnut, auburn*, Lat. *flavus;* ξανθαὶ τρίχες *golden* hair; ξανθὰς ἵππους *chestnut* mares. II. Ξάνθος paroxyt., as prop. n., 1. a stream of the Troad, so called by gods, by men Scamander. 2. a horse of Achilles.

ξανθο-φῠής, ές, (ξανθός, φυή) *yellow by nature.*

ξανθο-χίτων, ωνος, ὁ, ἡ, (ξανθός, χῑτών) *with yellow coat.*

ξανθό-χροος, ον, (ξανθός, χρώς) *with yellow skin.*

ξάντης, ου, ὁ, fem. **ξάντριᾰ**, (ξαίνω) *a wool-carder.*

ξειν-ᾰπάτης, ου, ὁ, Ion. for ξεναπάτης.

ξείνη, ἡ, Ion. for ξένη.

ξεινη-δόκος, ον, poët. for ξεινοδ-.

ξεινήιον, τό, (ξεῖνος) Ion. for ξενεῖον, *a host's gift*, presented on parting, mostly in pl.: also *provision made for a guest*, and generally, *friendly gifts.*

ξεινίζω, Ion. for ξενίζω.

ξεινίη, **ξεινικός**, Ion. for ξεν-.

ξείνιον, τό, **ξείνιος**, η, ον, Ion. for ξεν-.

ξεινίσαι, Ep. for ξενίσαι, aor. 1 inf. of ξενίζω.

ξείνισσεν, Ep. for ἐξένισεν, 3 sing. aor. 1 of ξενίζω.

ξεινο-δοκέω, **ξεινο-δόκος**, ον, Ion. for ξενοδ-.

ξεινο-κτονέω, Ion. for ξενοκτονέω.

ξεῖνος, η, ον, Ion. for ξένος. Hence

ξεινοσύνη, ἡ, Ion. for ξενοσύνη.

ξεινόω, Ion. for ξενόω.

ξεν-ᾱγέτης, ου, ὁ, (ξενός, ἀγέτης) *one who takes charge of guests.*

ξενᾱγέω, f. ήσω, (ξεναγός) *to be a guide of strangers:* —Pass. *to be conducted to see sights.* II. *to levy* or *lead mercenary troops.*

ξεν-ᾱγός, όν, (ξένος, ἡγέομαι) *conducting strangers* or *guests.* II. as Subst., ξεναγός, ὁ, *the leader of a body of mercenaries.*

ξεν-ᾰπάτης ου, ὁ, poët. **ξειν-**, (ξένος, ἀπατάω) *one who deceives guests* or *strangers.* [ᾰ]

ξεν-αρκής, ές, (ξένος, ἀρκέω) *aiding strangers.*

ξένη, ἡ, fem. of ξένος: 1. (sub. γυνή), *a female guest: a foreign woman.* II. (sub. χώρα or γῆ), *a foreign country.*

ξενηλᾰσία, ἡ, at Sparta, *a measure for keeping foreigners out of the country.* From

ξεν-ηλᾰτέω, (ξένος, ἐλαύνω) *to banish foreigners.*

ξενία Ep. **ξενίη** Ion. **ξεινίη**, ἡ, (ξένος) *the state* or *privileges of a guest, hospitality: hospitable reception, entertainment.* 2. *a friendly relation between* two princes or states. II. *the state* or *rights of a foreigner*, as opp. to a citizen: ξενίας φεύγειν (sc. γραφήν) to be indicted as an alien for usurping civic rights.

ξενίζω Ion. **ξεινίζω**: fut. ξενίσω Ep. ξεινίσσω: aor. 1 ἐξένισα Ep. ἐξείνισσα or ξείνισσα: (ξένος):—*to receive a guest* or *stranger, to entertain hospitably*, Lat. *hospitio excipere:*—Pass. *to be entertained as a guest.* II. *to be* or *speak like a foreigner.*

ξενικός, ή, όν, also ός, όν, Ion. **ξεινικός**: (ξένος): —*of* or *for a stranger, foreign.* 2. of soldiers, *mercenary, hired for foreign service;* τὸ ξενικόν, = οἱ ξένοι, *a body* or *army of mercenaries.* II. *strange, foreign, outlandish.*

ξένιος, *α*, *ον*, Att. also *ος*, *ον*, Ion. **ξείνιος** (*ξένος*, *ξεῖνος*) :—*belonging to a guest, hospitable, belonging to hospitality; ξένιός τινι bound to* one *by ties of hospitality.* II. *ξένια* (sub. *δῶρα*), *τά*, *a guest's gifts: friendly gifts.*

ξένισις, *ἡ*, (*ξενίζω*) *the entertainment of a guest.*

ξενισμός, *οῦ*, *ὁ*, = *ξένισις*.

ξενῐτεύω, (*ξένος*), or **ξενιτεύομαι** as Dep., *to be a foreigner: to be a mercenary in foreign service.*

ξενο-δᾰΐκτης, *οῦ*, *ὁ*, (*ξένος*, *δαΐζω*) *a murderer of a guest.*

ξενο-δαίτης, *ου*, *ὁ*, (*ξένος*, *δαίω*) *a devourer of guests* or *strangers.*

ξενο-δοκεῖον and **-χεῖον**, *τό*, *a place for strangers to lodge in, an inn:* from

ξενοδοχέω Ion. **ξεινοδοκέω**, (*ξενοδόχος*) *to entertain, lodge guests* or *strangers.* Hence

ξενοδοχία, *ἡ*, *the entertainment of a guest* or *stranger.*

ξενο-δόχος, *ον*, Ion. **ξεινο-δόκος**, (*ξένος*, *δέχομαι*) *entertaining guests* or *strangers:* as Subst., *ξεινοδόκος*, *ὁ*, *the host*, opp. to *ξεῖνος*, *the guest.*

ξενο-δώτης, *ου*, *ὁ*, (*ξένος*, *δίδωμι*) *the host.*

ξενόεις, *εσσα*, *εν*, (*ξένος*) *full of strangers.*

ξενοκτονέω Ion. **ξεινοκτ-**, f. *ήσω*, *to slay guests* or *strangers.* From

ξενο-κτόνος, *ον*, (*ξένος*, *κτείνω*) *slaying guests* or *strangers.*

ΞΕ'ΝΟΣ Ion. **ξεῖνος**, *ὁ*, *a guest* or *host*, Lat. *hospes:* either as I. *the friend*, with whom one has a treaty of hospitality: in this sense both parties are *ξένοι*, and the relation was hereditary. II. in Homer mostly *the guest*, as opp. to *the host.* 2. *any stranger*, as being entitled to the rights of hospitality. 3. later, *ὦ ξένε*, *O stranger*, was a common term of address. 4. from meaning *a stranger ξένος* came to signify *a hireling*, who entered into *foreign* service, *a mercenary soldier*, e. g. of the Greeks in Persian pay. 5. simply for *βάρβαρος a foreigner.*

As Adj. **ξένος**, *η*, *ον*, Att. *ος*, *ον*, Ion. **ξεῖνος**, *η*, *ον*, *foreign, strange.* 2. c. gen. rei, *strange to* a thing, *unacquainted with, ignorant of* it.

ξενό-στᾰσις, *ἡ*, (*ξένος*, *ἵστημι*) *a lodging for guests* or *strangers.*

ξενοσύνη Ion. **ξειν-**, *ἡ*, (*ξένος*, *ξεῖνος*) *hospitality, the ties* or *rights of hospitality.*

ξενό-τῑμος, *ον*, (*ξένος*, *τιμάω*) *honouring guests* or *strangers.*

ξενοτροφέω, f. *ήσω*, *to entertain* or *maintain guests:* esp. *to maintain mercenary troops.* From

ξενο-τρόφος, *ον*, (*ξένος*, *τρέφω*) *entertaining guests:* esp. *maintaining mercenaries.*

ξενοφονέω, f. *ήσω*, *to murder guests* or *strangers.* From

ξενο-φόνος, *ον*, (*ξένος*, **φένω*) *murdering strangers.*

ξενόω Ion. **ξεινόω**, f. *ώσω*, (*ξένος*) *to make* or *treat as one's guest: to entertain.* II. Pass., with fut. med. *ξενώσομαι*: aor. 1 *ἐξενώθην*; *to enter into a treaty of hospitality with* one. 2. *to be lodged as a guest, to be entertained.* 3. *to be in foreign parts, to be abroad: to go into banishment.*

ξενών, *ῶνος*, *ὁ*, (*ξένος*) *a guest-chamber.*

ξένως, Adv. of *ξένος*, *strangely: ξένως ἔχειν* to be *strange.*

ξένωσις, *ἡ*, (*ξενόω*) *estrangement: innovation.*

ΞΕΡΟ'Σ, *ά*, *όν*, Ion. for *ξηρός*, *dry; ποτὶ ξερόν* to *dry land.*

ξέσμα, *ατος*, *τό*, (*ξέω*) *that which is smoothed, polished:* hence = *ξόανον*, *a statue* or *image.*

ξεσμάω, (*ξέω*) *to rub off, wipe out.*

ξέσσε, Ep. for *ἔξεσε*, 3 sing. aor. 1 of *ξέω.*

ξέστης, *ου*, *ὁ*, a liquid and dry measure, corrupted from the Lat. *sextarius*, nearly = a pint English.

ξεστός, *ή*, *όν*, (*ξέω*) *scraped, planed, smoothed, polished.*

ΞΕ'Ω: f. *ξέσω* Ep. *ξέσσω*: aor. 1 *ἔξεσα* Ep. *ξέσσα*: —*to scrape, to polish by scraping* or *planing.* II. *to carve* or *work* in wood or stone.

ξήνας, part. aor. 1 of *ξαίνω.*

ξηραίνω, f. *ᾰνῶ*: aor. 1 *ἐξήρᾱνα*:—Pass., aor. 1 *ἐξηράνθην*: pf. *ἐξήρασμαι* or *ἐξήραμμαι*: (*ξηρός*):—*to parch up, dry up*:—Pass. *to become* or *be dry, parched.* 2. *to empty, drain, dry*, Lat. *siccare.*

ξηρ-ᾰλοιφέω, f. *ήσω*, (*ξηρός*, *ἀλείφω*) *to rub with dry unguents, to use oil unmixed with water:* a term used by wrestlers.

ξηρ-αμπέλῐνος, *η*, *ον*, (*ξηρός*, *ἄμπελος*) *of the colour of withered vine-leaves*, a sort of *scarlet*, hence Lat. *vestes xerampelinae.*

ξηρανθείς, aor. 1 pass. part. of *ξηραίνω.*

ΞΗΡΟ'Σ, *ά*, *όν*, *dry, parched*, of the channel of a river, also of the air: of persons, *withered, haggard.* II. like Lat. *siccus*, *fasting, sober, austere, harsh.* III. generally, *drained, exhausted.* IV. as Subst., *ξηρά* (sub. *γῆ*), *ἡ*, *dry land*, opp. to *ὑγρά*; so also *τὸ ξηρόν.*

ξηρότης, *ητος*, *ἡ*, (*ξηρός*) *dryness* or *soundness* of timber.

ξηρο-φᾰγέω, f. *ήσω*, (*ξηρός*, *φαγεῖν*) *to eat dry food.*

ξῐφ-ήρης, *ες*, (*ξίφος*, *ἀρᾰρεῖν*) *armed with a sword, sword in hand.*

ξῐφη-φόρος, *ον*, (*ξίφος*, *φέρω*) *bearing a sword: sword in hand.*

ξῐφίδιον, *τό*, Dim. of *ξίφος*, *a small sword, a dagger, dirk.* [ῐ]

ξῐφο-δήλητος, *ον*, (*ξίφος*, *δηλέομαι*) *slain by the sword:* of wounds, *inflicted by the sword.*

ξῐφο-κτόνος, *ον*, (*ξίφος*, *κτείνω*) *slaying with the sword.* II. proparox. *ξιφόκτονος*, *ον*, pass. *slain by the sword.*

ξῐφο-μάχαιρα, *ἡ*, (*ξίφος*, *μάχαιρα*) *a sword slightly curved, between a straight sword and sabre:* cf. sq. [ᾰ]

ΞΙ'ΦΟΣ Dor. **σκίφος**, *εος*, *τό*, *a sword:* in Homer described as large and sharp, and two-edged: later, *ξίφος* was distinguished as the *straight sword*, from the *sabre*, *μάχαιρα.* [ῐ]

ξῐφ-ουλκός, όν, (ξίφος, ἕλκω) *drawing a sword.*

ξῐφ-ουργός, όν, (ξίφος, ἔργον) *making swords.*

ξόᾰνον, τό, (ξέω) *an image carved* of wood: *the statue of a god.*

ξοᾰνο-ποιΐα, ἡ, (ξόανον, ποιέω) *a carving of images.*

ξοΐς, ΐδος, ἡ, (ξέω) *a sculptor's chisel.*

ξουθό-πτερος, ον, (ξουθός, πτερόν) *having dusky wings.*

ΞΟΥΘΟ΄Σ, ή, όν, akin to ξανθός, *a colour between* ξανθός and πυῤῥός, *yellowish, tawny, dusky,* mostly of *colour;* but also of sound, *shrill, thrilling;* τέττιξ ξουθὰ λαλῶν the cicada with its *shrill* note.

ξυγγ–, for all words so beginning, v. sub συγγ–.

ξύγκλησις, εως, ἡ, old Att. for σύγκλεισις.

ξυγκλῄω, f. ήσω, old Att. for συγκλείω.

ξυήλη, ἡ, (ξύω) = κνῆστις, *a tool for scraping* or *filing wood, a plane* or *rasp.* II. *a curved dagger,* used by the Spartans.

ξῠληγέω, f. ήσω, *to carry wood* or *timber.* From

ξῠλ-ηγός, όν, (ξύλον, ἄγω) *carrying wood.*

ξῠλίζομαι, Dep. (ξύλον) *to carry* or *gather wood,* Lat. *lignari.*

ξύλινος, η, ον, (ξύλον) *of wood, wooden.* [ῠ]

ξυλλ–, for all words so beginning, v. sub συλλ–.

ξῠλο-κόπος, ον, (ξύλον, κόπτω) *hewing, felling wood.* 2. as Subst., ξυλοκόπος, ὁ, *a wood-cutter.*

ξύλον, τό, (ξύω) *wood* ready for use, *firewood, timber,* etc.: in pl., ξύλα νήϊα ship-*timber.* II. *a stick* or *piece of wood: a stick, cudgel.* 2. *a collar of wood,* put on the neck of the prisoner to confine him, δῆσαί τινα ἐν ξύλῳ: the πεντεσύριγγον ξύλον consisted of a wooden collar with stocks to confine the arms and legs. 3. *a bench, table,* esp. *a money-changer's table.* 4. πρῶτον ξύλον, *the front bench* of the Athenian theatre, and so nearest the actors. III. later, *a tree;* cp. εἴριον.

ξῠλο-τόμος, ον, (ξύλον, τεμεῖν) *cutting wood:* as Subst., ξυλοτόμος, ὁ, *a wood-cutter.*

ξῠλουργέω, f. ήσω, (ξυλουργός) *to work wood.* Hence

ξῠλ-ουργία, ἡ, *the working of wood.*

ξῠλ-ουργός, όν, (ξύλον, ἔργον) *working in wood:* as Subst., ξυλουργός, ὁ, *a joiner, carver of images.*

ξῠλοχίζομαι Dor. **ξυλοχίσδομαι**, Dep. *to gather wood.* From

ξύλ-οχος, ἡ, (ξύλον, ἔχω) *a thicket, copse:* hence *the lair of a wild beast.*

ξῠλόω, f. ώσω, (ξύλον) *to make of wood.* Hence

ξύλωσις, ἡ, *the wood-work, framework of a house.*

ξυμβαίη, 3 sing. aor. 2 opt. of ξυμβαίνω.

ξυμβλήμεναι, Ep aor. 2 pass. inf. cf. συμβάλλω; **ξύμβλητο**, **ξύμβληντο**, 3 sing. and pl. Ep. aor. 2 pass. ind.

ξυμμ–, for all words so beginning, v. sub συμμ–.

ΞΥ΄Ν, used in old Att. for the later and more common σύν; ξύν seldom occurs in Homer. For all compds. of ξυν–, v. sub συν–.

ξυνᾰγείρατο, Ep. for συνηγείρατο, 3 sing. aor. 1 med. of συναγείρω.

ξῡνάν, ᾶνος, ὁ, = ξυνάων, ξυνήων, q. v.

ξῡνᾱ́ων, ονος, ὁ, Dor. for ξυνήων. [ᾰ]

ξυνέαξα, aor. 1 of συνάγνυμι.

ξῠν-εείκοσι, Ep. for ξυνείκοσι, συνεικοσι, (ξύν, εἴκοσι) *twenty at a time, twenty together.*

ξυνέηκα, Ep. for ξυνῆκα, aor. 1 of ξυνίημι.

ξυνέκλῃον, old Att. impf. of συγκλείω.

ξυνελάσαι, aor. 1 inf. of ξυνελαύνω.

ξύνες, aor. 2 imperat. of ξυνίημι.

ξυνεών, ῶνος, ὁ, Ion. for ξῡνήων.

ξῡνῇ, Adv., = κοινῇ, *in common,* properly dat. fem. of ξυνός.

ξῡνήϊος, η, ον, Ep. for ξύνειος, (ξυνός) *public, common:* as Subst., ξυνήϊα, τά, *public property.*

ξυνῆκα, aor. 1 of ξυνίημι.

ξῡνήων, ονος, ὁ, Dor. **ξῡνάων** [ᾱ], Ion. **ξῡνεών** Dor. ξῡνάν: (ξυνός): *a joint owner, part proprietor, partner:* ἅλς ξυνάων, the salt *on the common table.*

ξύνῐε, pres. imperat. of ξυνίημι, as if from *ξυνίω.

ξῠνίει, pres. imperat. of ξυνίημι, as if from *ξυνιέω. [ῐ]

ξύνῑον, Ep. for ξυνίεσαν, 3 pl. impf. of ξυνίημι. [ῠ]

ξῡνός, ή, όν, (ξύν) = κοινός, from which it only differs in dialect, *common, public, general, belonging to all in common;* ξυνὰ λέγειν to speak *for the common good:* dat. fem. ξυνῇ as Adv. = κοινῇ, *in common;* so too neut. pl. ξυνά. Hence

ξῡνό-φρων, ονος, ὁ, ἡ, (ξυνός, φρήν) *like-minded.*

ξῡνο-χᾰρής, ές, (ξυνός, χαρῆναι) *rejoicing with all alike.*

ξῡνωνία, ἡ, = κοινωνια, *partnership, fellowship.*

ξῦον, Ep. for ἔξυον, impf. of ξύω.

ξῠράω or -έω: f. ήσω: (ξυρόν):—*to shave;* proverb., ξυρεῖν ἐν χρῷ *to shave* to the quick.—Med., with pf. pass. ἐξύρημαι: *to shave oneself* or *get oneself shaved:* also c. acc., ξυρεῖσθαι κεφαλήν *to shave one's* head or *get it shaved.*

ξῠρ-ήκης, ες, (ξυρόν, ἀκή) *keen as a rasor, with a rasor's edge.* II. *close-shaven.*

ξῠρο-δόκη and **ξῠρο-δόχη**, ἡ, (ξύρον, δέχομαι) *a rasor-case.*

ξῠρόν, τό, (ξύω) *a rasor:* proverb. of critical situations, ἐπὶ ξυροῦ ἵσταται ἀκμῆς.. .. ὄλεθρος ἠὲ βιῶναι death or life stands on *a rasor's* edge; so, ἐπὶ ξυροῦ τῆς ἀκμῆς ἔχεται ἡμῖν τὰ πράγματα our affairs rest on *a rasor's* edge.

ξῠρο-φορέω, f. ήσω, (ξυρόν, φέρω) *to carry a rasor.*

ξυρρ–, for all words so beginning, v. sub συρρ–.

ξύρω, = ξυράω: aor. 1 med. ἐξυράμην.

ξῦσαι, aor. 1 inf. of ξύω.

ξυσθείς, aor. 1 pass. part. of ξύω.

ξύσμα, ματος, τό, and **ξυσμή**, ἡ, (ξύω) *that which is scraped* or *planed off, filings, shavings.*

ξυστήρ, ῆρος, ὁ, (ξύω) *a graving tool,* Lat. *scalprum.*

ξυστίς, ίδος, Att. **ξύστις**, ιδος, ἡ, (ξύω) *a robe with a sweeping train.*

ξυστο-βόλος, *ον*, (*ξυστόν*, *βαλεῖν*) *spear-darting, hurling the javelin.*

ξυστόν, *τό*, (*ξύω*) *the polished shaft of a spear*, in Homer once mentioned as twenty-two cubits long. 2. like *δόρυ*, *a spear, dart, javelin*; generally, *a pole, shaft.* (Properly neut. of the Adj. *ξυστός*.)

ξυστός, *ὁ*, (*ξύω*) *a covered colonnade* in gymnasia or schools of exercise, where athletes exercised in winter, serving also for a walking-place, so called from its smooth and polished floor. II. in Roman villas, *a terrace with a colonnade*, also *xystum*. (Properly masc. of the Adj. *ξυστός*, sub. *δρόμος*.)

ξυστός, *όν*, (*ξύω*) *scraped, polished*, Lat. *rasus*.

ξυστο-φόρος, *ον*, (*ξυστόν*, *φέρω*) *carrying a spear.*

ξύστρα, *ἡ*, = *ξυστρίς*.

ξυστρίς, *ίδος*, *ἡ*, (*ξύω*) *a tool for scraping* or *rubbing off, the scraper* or *strigil* used after bathing.

ΞΥ'Ω: impf. *ἔξυον* Ep. *ξῦον*: f. *ξύσω*: aor. 1 *ἔξῦσα*: —Pass., aor. 1 *ἐξύσθην*: pf. *ἔξυσμαι*:—*to scrape, plane, smooth* or *polish.* 2. generally, *to make smooth* or *fine, to work finely or delicately.* 3. *ξῦσαι ἀπὸ γῆρας ὀλοιόν to rub away, get rid of* sad old age.

O

O, **ο**, **ὂ μικρόν**, *little*, i. e. *short o*, (in opp. to *ὢ μέγα great*, i. e. *long and double o*, *ω* being for *oo*): fifteenth letter in the Greek alphabet: as numeral *ο'*, 70, but *,ο*, 70,000.

O came very near to diphth. *ου*, as appears from their frequent interchange; as in Aeol. *βόλομαι* for *βούλομαι*, and Ion. *μοῦνος νοῦσος* for *μόνος νόσος*.

Aeol., *ο* is often changed into *ῠ*, as *ὄνυμα μύγις* for *ὄνομα μόγις*. II. Dor. often for *οι*, as *ἀγνοιέω πτοιέω πνοιά* for *ἀγνοέω πτοέω πνοά*. III. like *α*, *ο* is often rejected or prefixed, as *κέλλω ὀκέλλω*, *δύρομαι ὀδύρομαι*. IV. in compds., esp. Adjectives, *ο*, if it comes before the second member, is changed by Poets metri grat. into a long vowel, usu. *η* as *θεογενής θεοδόκος ξιφοφόρος*, into *θεηγενής* (Dor. *θεᾱγενής*) *θεηδόκος ξιφηφόρος*.

'Ο' Ἡ, ΤΟ', is, A. *demonstr. Pronoun;* B. *the definite Article;* C. accentuated in masc. and fem. sing. and plur. *ὅ*, *ἥ*, *τό*, *relative Pronoun* for *ὅς*, *ἥ*, *ὅ*.

Gen. *τοῦ*, *τῆς*, *τοῦ*: dat. *τῷ*, *τῇ*, *τῷ*: acc. *τόν*, *τήν*, *τό*:—dual nom. and acc. *τώ*, *τά*, *τώ*: gen. and dat. *τοῖν*, *ταῖν*, *τοῖν*:—plur. nom. *οἱ*, *αἱ*, *τά*: gen. *τῶν*. dat. *τοῖς*, *ταῖς*, *τοῖς*: acc. *τούς*, *τάς*, *τά*. Homer has also gen. sing. *τοῖο* for *τοῦ*, nom. pl. *τοί*, *ταί*, gen. pl. fem. *τάων* [ᾱ], dat. pl. *τοῖσι*, *τῆς* and *τῇσι*, as demonstr. Pronouns.

A. *ὁ*, *ἡ*, *τό*, DEMONSTR. PRONOUN, for *ὅδε*, *ἥδε*, *τόδε*, in Homer the usual sense. Homer uses the Pronoun chiefly in two ways: I. joined with a Subst. not as the Article, but like Lat. *ille*, *ὁ Τυδείδης the famous* son of Tydeus; **Νέστωρ ὁ γέρων** Nestor, *that* aged man. II. without a Subst., *he, she, it*, as, *ὁ γὰρ ἦλθε* for *he* came. III. peculiar uses as Pronoun: 1. before relat. Pronouns *ὅς*, *ὅσος*, *οἷος*, it serves to recall the attention to the foregoing noun, as, *ἐφάμην σε περὶ φρένας ἔμμεναι ἄλλων, τῶν, ὅσσοι Λυκίην ναιετάουσιν* I thought that thou wert in sense far above the rest, *namely those who*, etc. 2. *ὁ μέν.., ὁ δέ..*, from Homer downwards a very common phrase, *sometimes* in opposition (where *ὁ μέν* refers to *the former*, *ὁ δέ* to *the latter*), sometimes expressing different parts of a thing, *the one.., the other..*, Lat. *hic.., ille..*: in neut. *τὸ μέν.., τὸ δέ..*, in adverbial sense, *partly.., partly..*: also *τὰ μέν.., τὰ δέ*.—'Ο δέ.. often occurs without *ὁ μέν..* before. On the other hand *οἱ μέν..* is often answered by some similar word, as *ἀλλά*, or by *ἕτερος δέ..*, *ἔνιοι δέ..*, etc.

B. *ὁ*, *ἡ*, *τό*, THE DEFINITE ARTICLE, *the*, the indefin. Pron. being *τὶς*, *τὶ*. The use of *ὁ*, *ἡ*, *τό*, as the Article, is later than its use as the Pronoun, and sprang from it, as *τὸν ἄριστον*, *him that was* bravest, came to mean simply *the* bravest; *φίλους ποιεῖσθαι* to make friends, but *τοὺς φίλους ποιεῖσθαι* to make *the* friends *one does make*.

Peculiar usages of the Article. 1. it may stand with prop. names, as *ὁ Σωκράτης*; but not when some attribute with the Article follows, as *Σωκράτης ὁ φιλόσοφος*. 2. before the Infinitive, used as a neut. Subst., in all cases, as, *τὸ εἶναι the* being, *τοῦ εἶναι*, etc. 3. before Adverbs, which thus take an Adject. sense, as, *τὸ νῦν the* present; *οἱ τότε ἄνθρωποι the* men of that time. The Subst. is often omitted, as, *οἱ τότε* (sc. *ἄνθρωποι*), *ἡ αὔριον* (sc. *ἡμέρα*) the morrow. 4. before any word or phrase cited, the Art. is used in neut. gend., as, *τὸ ἄνθρωπος the word* or *notion* man; *τὸ λέγω the word λέγω*, etc.; so before a whole sentence, as, *τὸ μηδένα εἶναι τῶν ζωόντων ὄλβιον the fact* or *statement* that no living man is happy. 5. absol. with Adverbs of time and place, where the Adv. retains its adverbial force, and the Art. only serves to strengthen it, as *τὰ νῦν now*, *τὸ πρίν formerly*. 6. before the interrog. Pron., *τίς* or *ποῖος*, mostly in neut. sing., *τὸ τί*; *τὸ ποῖον*; to make the question more precise. II. in elliptic expressions: 1. before gen. of a prop. name, *ὁ Διός the son of* Jupiter, *ἡ Λητοῦς the daughter of* Latona, where *υἱός* or *θυγάτηρ* is to be supplied: but this form also includes other persons, which must be supplied from the context, as *brother, wife*, etc. 2. before a neut. gen. it indicates any relation to a thing, and often alters the meaning but little, as *τὸ τῆς πόλεως that which belongs to* the state, nearly the same as *ἡ πόλις*; so, *τὰ τῶν Ἑλλήνων*, *τὰ τῶν Περσῶν the affairs* or *power* of the Greeks, Persians, etc.; *τὰ τῶν Ἀθηναίων φρονεῖν* to hold *the sentiments* of the Athenians, i. e. be on their side: so, with neut. of possess. Pron., *τὸ ἐμόν*, *τὸ σόν what regards* me or thee, my or thy part, often put for ἐγώ, σύ, etc.

ABSOL. USAGE OF SINGLE CASES: I. τῇ of Place, *there, that way, here, this way*, Lat. *hac.* 2. with a notion of motion towards *thither.* 3. of Manner, τῇπερ *in this way, thu* 4. repeated τῇ μέν.., τῇ δέ.., of Place, *here*.; *there*..: also *on the one part*.., *on the other*... 5. relative, *where*, for ᾗ, only Ep II. τῷ, dat. neut., *therefore, on this account.* 2. *thus, so, in this wise*, only Ep. III. τό, acc. neut. (like Att. ὅ neut. from ὅs), *wherefore.* IV. τοῦ, gen. neut. *wherefore* V. with Prepositions, of Time, ἐκ τοῦ *ever since*, τῷ *whilst.*

C. ὅ, ἥ, τό, accentuated through all cases, RELATIVE PRONOUN, for ὅs, ἥ, ὅ: very freq. in Homer, also Ion.

D. the enclitic gen. and dat. του, τῳ, are used for τινός, τινί, from the INDEFINITE PRONOUN τὶs τί. So Ion. τεο, contr. τευ: dat. τεῳ: gen. and dat. pl. τεων, τεοις τεοισι:—but τοῦ; Ion. τέο; τεῦ; for τίνος; interrog., *wherefore?* dat. τέῳ for τινί; pl. gen. τέων; dat. τέοις, τέοισι.

ὃ, Ion. and Dor. relat. Pron. for ὅs; v. ὅ, ἥ, τό C.

ὅ, neut. of relat. Pron. ὅs.

ὀά, *woe!* Lat. *vae!* [ŏᾱ]

ὈΑ΄Ρ, ὄᾰρος, ἡ, *a consort, mate, wife*: gen. pl. ὀάρων: contr. nom. ὦρ, with dat. pl. ὤρεσσι. Hence

ὀᾰρίζω contr. ὠρίζω, f. σω, *to converse familiarly, bold converse with.* Hence

ὀᾰρισμός, οῦ, ὁ, *familiar converse, fond discourse.*

ὀᾰριστής, οῦ, ὁ, (ὀαρίζω) *a companion, mate, bosom-friend.*

ὀᾰριστύς, ύος, ἡ, Ion. for ὀάρισμα, (ὀαρίζω) *familiar converse, fond discourse.* 2. generally, *intercourse.* 3. *a band* or *company.*

ὌΑ΄ΡΟΣ, ὁ, = ὀαρισμός, *familiar converse, fond discourse*, and generally, *converse, discourse, words*, mostly in plur.; but also in sing. *talk, discourse.*

Ὄᾰσις, ἡ, *Oăsis*, a name of the fertile spots in the Libyan desert.

ὀβελίσκος, ὁ, Dim. of ὀβελός, *a small spit: any pointed instrument, the leg of a compass* II. *a pointed pillar, obelisk.*

ὀβελός Aeol. and Dor. **ὀδελός**, οῦ, ὁ, *a spit*: also *any pointed instrument.* II. *a pointed pillar, obelisk.* (ὀβελός, = βέλος with ο prefixed.)

ὀβολός, οῦ, ὁ, collat. form of ὀβελός, *an obol*, a coin worth 8 χαλκοῖ, ⅙th of a δραχμή, rather more than three halfpence. II. also as *a weight*, the sixth part of a drachma.

ὀβολοστατέω, f. ήσω, *to practise petty usury.* From

ὀβολο-στάτης, ου, ὁ, (ὀβολός, ἵστημι) *a weigher of obols: a petty usurer, pawnbroker.* [ᾰ]

ὌΒΡΙΑ, τά, *the young* of animals.

ὀβρίκᾰλα, τά, = ὄβρια. [ῐ]

ὀβρῐμο-εργός, όν, (ὄβριμος, ἔργον) *doing deeds of violence* or *wrong.*

ὀβρῐμό-θῡμος, ον, (ὄβριμος, θυμός) *strong-minded.*

ὀβρῐμο-πάτρη, ἡ, (ὄβριμος, πατήρ) *daughter of a mighty father*, epith. of Minerv

ὌΒΡΙ΄ΜΟΣ, ον, also η, ον, *strong, mighty*

ὀγδοάς, άδος, ἡ, (ὀκτώ) *the number eight.*

ὀγδόᾰτος, η, ον, poët. for ὄγδοος (like τρίτατος for τρίτος), *the eighth*:—ἡ ὀγδοάτη (sub. ἡμέρα), *the eighth day.*

ὀγδοήκοντα, οἱ, αἱ, τά, indecl. (ὀκτώ) *eighty.*

ὀγδοηκοντᾰ-ετής, ές, or **ὀγδοηκοντ-ούτης**, ες, (ὀγδοήκοντα, ἔτος) *eighty years old.*

ὀγδοηκοστός, ή, όν, (ὀγδοήκοντα) *the eightieth.*

ὄγδοος, η, ον, (ὀκτώ) *the eighth*, Lat. *octavus.*

ὀγδώκοντα, οἱ, αἱ, τά, indecl., contr. for ὀγδοήκοντα, *eighty*, Lat. *octoginta.*

ὀγδωκοντᾰ-ετής, ές, contr. for ὀγδοηκονταετής, *eighty years old.*

ὅ-γε, ἥ-γε, τό-γε, the demonstr. Pron. ὁ, ἡ, τό, made more emphat. by the addition of γε, Lat. *hicce, haecce, hocce, he, she, it.* 2. fem. dat. τῇγε, used as Adv. of place, *here, on this spot* 3. acc. neut. τόγε *on this account, for this very reason.*

Ὄγκᾱ poët. **Ὀγκαίη**, ἡ, a name of Minerva in Thebes: a gate in that city was called from her Ὀγκαῖοι or Ὀγκαΐδης.

ὀγκάομαι, f. -ήσομαι, Dep. *to bray.* Hence

ὀγκηθμός, ὁ, *a braying.*

ὀγκηρός, ά, όν, (ὄγκος) *bulky, swollen.* II. metaph. *stately, pompous.* 2. *grievous, troublesome.* Lat. *molestus.*

ὀγκητής, οῦ, ὁ, (ὀγκάομαι) *a br r*, i. e. *an ass.*

ὄγκιον, τό, (ὄγκος) *a case* for barbed arrows, etc.

ὌΓΚΟΣ, ὁ, (A), (ἄγκος) *a bend, curve*, hence *a hook, barb*, esp. of an arrow or spear-head.

ὌΓΚΟΣ, ὁ, (B), *bulk, mass*; ὄγκος φρυγάνων *a heap* or *pile* of faggots. 2. a particular way of dressing the hair; which was gathered up into a *bushy knot* or *roll*, to give the appearance of height to the persor II. metaph. *bulk, weight, importance, dignity*: but also in bad sense, *arrogance, conceit.* 2. *trouble, difficulty.*

ὀγκόω, .. ώσω: aor. 1 ὤγκωσα:—Pass., aor. 1 ὠγκώθην: pf. ὤγκωμαι: (ὄγκος B):—*to make bulky, enlarge*:—Pass. *to be heaped up, swollen* II. metaph. *to exalt, raise to honour*: but also, *to puff up with pride*:—Pass. *to be puffed up, swol.., elated.*

ὀγκύλλομαι, Pass., = ὀγκόομαι.

ὀγκ-ώδης, ες, (ὄγκος B, εἶδος) *bulky, su rounded: turgid.*

ὀγκωτός, ή, όν, (ὀγκόω) *heaped up.*

ὀγμεύω, f. -εύσω, *to trace a straight line*, ploughers, reapers, or mowers; of an army, *to defile*, ὤγμευον αὐτῷ *they were marching in file* before him: metaph., ὀγμεύειν στίβον *to trail one's weary way*, of a lame man From

ὄγμος, ὁ, (ἄγω) *anything traced in a straight line; a furrow* in ploughing; *a swathe* in reaping: *a row* or *line*: *a path*; esp. *the path* of the heavenly bodies.

'ΟΓΧΝΗ, ἡ, *a pear-tree*. II. *a pear*.

ὀδ-αγός, ὁ, Dor. for ὁδηγός.

ὁδαῖος, α, ον, (ὁδός) *belonging to a way* or *journey*. II. ὁδαῖα, τά, *goods with which a merchant travels, merchandise*.

ὀδάξ, Adv. (δάκνω with ο euphon.) *with the teeth, by biting*, Lat. *mordicus*. Hence

ὀδάξω or as Dep. **ὀδάξομαι**: impf. ὤδαξον: pf. pass. ὤδαγμαι:—*to feel a biting pain, feel irritation*. II. in act. sense, *to bite, nibble, sting*.

ὁδάω, f. ήσω, (ὁδός) *to export and sell, traffic in*:—Pass. *to be carried away and sold*.

ὅ-δε, ἥ-δε, τό-δε, demonstr. Pron., formed by adding the enclit. -δε to the old demonstr. Pron. ὁ, ἡ, τό, and declined like it: Ep. dat. pl. masc. and fem. τοῖσδεσσι, τοῖσδεσσιν, as well as τοῖσδε: Att. more emphat. ὁδί, ἡδί, τοδί, etc. [ῑ]:—ὅδε, ἥδε, τόδε is much the same as οὗτος, *this*, but is more emphatic, *this one here*, Lat. *hicce, haecce, hocce*: as opposed to οὗτος, ὅδε marks *what is to follow*, while οὗτος refers to *what has been before mentioned*. II. it often seems to stand, like Lat. *hic*, as Adv. of Place, *here, there*, but always agreeing with its noun, as, ἔγχος μὲν τόδε κεῖται ἐπὶ χθονός *here* lies the lance upon the ground; Ἀχιλλεὺς ἐγγὺς ὅδε κλονέων *here* is Achilles nigh at hand routing. 2. with a pers. Pron., ὅδ' εἰμί, ὅδ' ἐγὼ ἤλυθον *here* am I. 3. with τίς, τίς ὅδε Ναυσικάᾳ ἕπεται; who is *here* following Nausicaa? 4. also with Verbs of motion, like δεῦρο, *hither*. III. to Advs. of Place and Time this Pron. adds precision, *just, very*; αὐτοῦ τῷδ' ἐνὶ δήμῳ *here* amid *this very* people. IV. ὅδ' αὐτός, stronger form for ὁ αὐτός, *the very same, this very*; τοῦδ' αὐτοῦ λυκάβαντος *this very* year. V. in Att. dialogue, the masc. and fem. Pron. often refer to the speaker, ὅδ' ἀνήρ, or ὅδε alone, *this man here, the man before you*, i. e. myself, emphatic for ἐγώ. VI. ellipt. with gen., ἐς τόδε χρόνου *to this point* of time.

B. absol. usage of some cases: τῇδε of Place, *here, on the spot*, Lat. *hac*. 2. of the Way or Manner, *thus*. II. acc. neut. τόδε, *hither, to this spot*. 2. *therefore, on this account*. III. acc. neut. pl. τάδε, *on this account*. 2. *thus, so*. IV. dat. neut. pl. τοῖσδε, τοισίδε *on this wise, after this fashion*; also *with these words*.

ὀδελός, ὁ, Aeol. and Dor. for ὀβελός and ὀβολός.

ὁδευτής, οῦ, ὁ, *a wayfarer, traveller*. From

ὁδεύω, f. σω, (ὁδός) *to go, journey, travel*.

ὁδηγέω, f. ήσω, *to lead* one *upon his way, to shew* one *the way, guide, act as guide*. From

ὁδ-ηγός Dor. ὁδ-αγός, ὁ, (ὁδός, ἄγω) *a guide*.

ὁδί, ἡδί, τοδί, Att. for ὅδε, ἥδε, τόδε, q. v. [ῑ]

ὅδιος, ον, (ὁδός) *belonging to a way* or *journey*: *auspicious for the journey*.

ὅδισμα, ατος, τό, (ὁδός) *a means of passing, way*.

ὁδίτης, ου, ὁ, (ὁδός) *a wayfarer, traveller*: Dor. acc. ὁδίταν. [ῑ]

ὀδμή Ion. ὀσμή, ἡ, (ὄζω) *a smell, scent, a sweet odour*: also *a bad smell, stench, stink*.

ὁδοιπλανέω, f. ήσω, *to stray from the road, wander about, lose one's way*. From

ὁδοι-πλανής, ές, (ὁδός, πλανάομαι) *straying from the road, wandering about, roaming*.

ὁδοιπορέω: impf. ὡδοιπόρουν: f. ήσω: pf. ὡδοιπόρηκα: (ὁδοιπόρος):—*to be a wayfarer, to travel, journey, walk*. Hence

ὁδοιπορία, ἡ, *a journey, way*: *a journey by land*, opp. to a sea-voyage.

ὁδοιπορικός, ή, όν, *of* or *for a journey*. Adv. -κῶς, *like a traveller*.

ὁδοιπόριον, τό, *provision for a journey*. From

ὁδοι-πόρος, ον, (ὁδός, πόρος) *travelling, journeying*: as Subst., ὁδοιπόρος, ὁ, *a wayfarer, foot-traveller*: also, *a fellow-traveller* or *guide*.

ὀδόντα, ὀδόντας, acc. sing. and pl. of ὀδούς.

ὀδοντο-φόρος, ον, (ὀδούς, φέρω) *bearing teeth*; κόσμος ὀδ. an ornament *consisting of strings of teeth*.

ὀδοντο-φυής, ές, (ὀδούς, φύω) *sprung from teeth*.

ὀδοντόω, f. ώσω, (ὀδούς) *to furnish with teeth*. Hence

ὀδοντωτός, ή, όν, *furnished with teeth*.

ὁδοποιέω: impf. ὡδοποίουν: f. ήσω: pf. pass. ὡδοποίημαι: (ὁδοποιός):—*to make* or *level a road*: *to make a path for oneself*:—Pass., of roads, *to be made fit for use*. 2. *to make practicable* or *passable*. 3. *to put* one *in the way, guide, to set forward on a journey*:—Pass. *to make one's way, advance*, Lat. *progredi*.

ὁδοποιΐα, ἡ, *road-making, the duty of a pioneer*. From

ὁδο-ποιός, όν, (ὁδός, ποιέω) *making roads*: as Subst., ὁδοποιός, ὁ, *a road-maker, pioneer*: *a road-surveyor*.

ὀδός, οῦ, ὁ, Att. for Ion. οὐδός, *a threshold*.

'ΟΔΟ'Σ Aeol. **οὐδός**, οῦ, ἡ, *a way, path, road, highway*: *a track, pathway*: *an entrance, approach*: *the course, channel* of a river: *the path* of the heavenly bodies: πρὸ ὁδοῦ *further on the way*; κατ' ὁδόν by *the way*. II. *a travelling, journey*, or *voyage*: also *a march* or *expedition*: οἰωνῶν ὁδοί *the flight* of birds; λογίων ὁδός *the way*, i. e. *meaning*, of the oracles. III. metaph. *the way, means*, or *manner* of doing a thing. 2. *a way* or *method*: also, *a way of thinking, mode of belief*, esp. used of *the Christian Faith*.

ὁδ-οῦρος, ον, (ὁδός, οὖρος) *watching* or *guarding the road*: as fem. Subst., ὁδοῦρος, ἡ, *a conductress*.

'ΟΔΟΥ'Σ, in Ion. Prose ὀδών, ὁ, gen ὀδόντος: dat. pl. ὀδοῦσι:—*a tooth*, Lat. *dens*; ἕρκος ὀδόντων, see ἕρκος.

ὁδο-φύλαξ, ἄκος, ὁ, (ὁδός, φύλαξ) *a watcher, patrol of the roads*. [ῠ]

ὁδόω, f. ώσω: aor. 1 ὥδωσα: (ὁδός):—*to lead into the right way*: *to put in the way*; c. inf., ὥδωσε βροτοὺς φρονεῖν *he guided* mortals to be wise; also *to* *bring, send*:—Pass. *to be brought on the way, advance, succeed.*

ὀδυνᾶσαι, for ὀδυνᾷ, 2 sing. pres. pass. of ὀδυνάω.

ὀδῠνάω, f. ήσω, *to cause pain, to pain, distress*:—Pass. *to feel pain, suffer.* From

'ΟΔΥ'ΝΗ, ἡ, Lat. *dolor, pain* of body, but also, 2. of mind, *grief, distress.* [ῠ]

ὀδῠνηρός Dor. **–ᾱρός**, ά, όν, (ὀδύνη) *painful.* 2. *grievous: distressing.* Adv. –ρῶς.

ὀδῠνή-φᾰτος, ον, (ὀδύνη, πέφαται, 3 sing. pf. of φένω) *killing* (i. e. *stilling, assuaging*) *pain.*

ὄδυρμα, ατος, τό, *wailing, lamentation*: and

ὀδυρμός, ὁ, *a wailing, lamenting.* From

'ΟΔΥ'ΡΟΜΑΙ, Trag. also **δύρομαι**: Ion. 3 sing. impf. ὀδυρέσκετο: fut. ὀδῡροῦμαι: aor. 1 ὠδῡράμην, part. ὀδυράμενος:—*to bewail, mourn for, lament*, c. acc.: c. gen. pers. *to mourn for, for the sake of*: c. dat. pass. *to wail to* or *in answer to* another: absol. *to wail, mourn.* [ῡ] Hence

ὀδυρτός, ή, όν, *mourned for, lamentable*: ὀδυρτά, as Adv., *lamentably*

ὀδύσαντο, Ep. for ὠδύσαντο, 3 pl. aor. 1 of ὀδύσσομαι.

'Οδυσσεία, ἡ, *the story of Ulysses, the Odyssey.* From

'Οδυσσεύς, έως, ὁ, Lat. *Ulysses* or *Ulixes*, king of Ithaca, whose return from Troy to Ithaca forms the subject of the Odyssey: Ep. declens., 'Οδυσσεύς, –ῆος, –ῆι, –ῆα: Ep. nom also 'Οδῠσεύς: Aeol. gen. 'Οδῠσεῦς.

***'ΟΔΥ'ΣΣΟΜΑΙ**, Dep., used only in aor. 1 med. ὠδῠσάμην, Ep. 2 and 3 sing. ὠδύσαο, ὠδύσατο, Ep. 3 pl. ὀδύσαντο, part. ὀδυσσάμενος, and 3 sing. pf. pass. ὀδώδυσται (redupl. for ὤδυσται):—*to be grieved* or *wroth at*, c. dat.

ὄδωδα, pf. (with pres. sense) of ὄζω.

ὀδώδει, 3 sing. plqpf. (with impf. sense) of ὄζω.

ὀδωδή, ή, (ὄζω) *smell, scent, odour* also *the sense of smell.*

ὀδώδυσται, 3 sing. pf. (with pres. sense) of ὀδύσσομαι.

ὀδών, όντος, ὁ, Ion. for ὀδούς, *a tooth.*

ὁδωτός, ή, όν, (ὁδόω) *passable: practicable.*

ὄεσσι, Ep. dat. plur. of ὄϊς, οἷς.

ὀζᾰλέος, α, ον, (ὄζος) *branching.*

ὀζήσω, fut. of ὄζω.

'Οζόλαι, οἱ, *the Ozolae*, a tribe of the Locrians.

"ΟΖΟΣ, ου, ὁ, *a bough, branch, twig, shoot.* II. metaph. *an offshoot, scion*; ὄζος Ἄρηος *scion* of Mars: cf. ἔρνος, θάλος.

ὀζό-στομος, ον, (ὄζω, στόμα) *with bad breath.*

"ΟΖΩ, fut. ὀζήσω: pf. with pres. sense ὄδωδα: plqpf. with impf. sense ὠδώδειν, Ep. 3 sing. ὀδώδει:—*to smell, to have a smell*, whether *pleasant* or *not*: c. gen. *to smell of* a thing, ὄζειν ἴων *to smell* of violets: metaph. *to smell* or *savour of* a thing, Lat. *sapere aliquid*; Κρονίων ὄζειν *to smell of* antiquities: c. dupl. gen., τῆς κεφαλῆς ὄζω μύρου *I smell* of ointment from the head. II. often used impers., ὄζει ἡδὺ τῆς χρόας *there is a sweet smell from* the skin; ἱματίων ὀζήσει δεξιότητος *there will be an odour* of wit from your clothes.

ὅθεν, Adv. (ὅς) *whence, from whence*, Lat. *unde*: also of persons, *from whom* or *which.* 2. also like οὗ, as an Adv. of Place, = ὅθι, ὅπου, *where*, but only as relative to a word implying motion from. II. in Att. also, *wherefore, on which account.*

ὅθι, relat. Adv., poët. for οὗ, *where*, Lat. *ubi.*

ὀθνεῖος, α, ον, also ος, ον, (ἔθνος) *strange, foreign.*

"ΟΘΟΜΑΙ, Dep., only used in pres. and impf., *to have a care* or *concern for, take heed, regard*: c. part., οὐκ ὄθετο ῥέζων *he recked* not that he was doing: c. gen. pers., οὐδ' ὄθομαι κοτέοντος *I do* not *heed him* when he is angry.

'ΟΘΟ'ΝΗ, ἡ, mostly in plur., *fine white linen: a fine linen veil, a linen garment*: also, *sail-cloth, a sail*: also, *a sheet, linen cloth.* Hence

ὀθόνῐνος, η, ον, *made of linen.*

ὀθόνιον, τό, Dim. of ὀθόνη, *a piece of fine linen*, in pl. *linen bandages* for wounds, or *lint.*

ὁθ-ούνεκα, for ὅτου, ἕνεκα, *because*: sometime also for ὅτι, *that*, Lat. *quod.*

ὅ-θριξ, gen. ὄτρῐχος, poët. for ὁμό-θριξ, ὁ, ἡ, (ὁμοῦ, θρίξ) *with like hair.*

OI', exclam. of pain, grief, pity, astonishment, *oh! ah!* Lat. *heu* or *vae*: sometimes c. nom., οἴ ἐγώ: mostly c. dat., οἴ μοι.

οἱ, nom. pl. masc. of Art. ὁ.

οἵ, nom. pl. masc. of relat. Pron. ὅς.

οἱ, dat. sing. of third pers. Pron., masc. and fem., for αὐτῷ αὐτῇ, *to him, to her*: more rarely used in the reflexive sense *himself*, as the Ep. ἑοῖ is always used; often also οἱ αὐτῷ, *to himself.* The Nom is wanting, gen. οὗ, acc. ἕ.

οἷ, relat. Adv., properly dat. of relat. Pron. ὅς, *whither, how far*, Lat. *quo*: often c. gen., οἷ κακῶν *to what a height of* miseries.

οἰᾱκίζω Ion. **οἰηκ–**, f. σω, (οἴαξ) *to steer, manage.*

οἰάκισμα, τό, (οἰακίζω) *the act of steering* or *governing.* [ᾰ]

οἰᾱκο-νόμος, ον, (οἴαξ, νέμω) *holding the helm steering*: as Subst. *a pilot, ruler.*

οἰᾱκοστροφέω, f. ήσω, *to turn the helm, steer.* From

οἰᾱκο-στρόφος, ον, (οἴαξ, στρέφω) *guiding the helm, steering.*

ΟΙ'ΑΞ, ᾱκος, Ion. **οἴηξ**, ηκος, ὁ, *the tiller, handle of the rudder, the helm.* . pl. οἴηκες, *the rings of the yoke*, through which pass the cords for guiding the oxen.

Οἰᾶτις νόμος, a pasture *in the Attic deme* Οἴα.

οἴγνυμι or **–ύω**, lengthd. from **ΟΙ'ΓΩ**: f. οἴξω: aor. 1 ᾦξα Ep. ὤιξα, part. οἴξας:—Pass., Ep. 3 pl. impf. ὠίγνυντο: aor. 1 ῴχθην:—*to open, unlock*: of a cask, *to broach.*

οἶδα, *I know*, pf. with pres. sense of *εἴδω, v. εἴδω B.

οἰδάνω [ᾰ] or **οἰδαίνω**, (οἰδέω) *to make to swell*,

swell, Lat. tumefacere: Pass. *to be swoln, swell*, Lat. *tumere*. II. intr. = οἰδέω.

οἶδας, 2 sing. of οἶδα, for the Att. οἶσθα.

οἰδέω, f. **ήσω**: aor. 1 ᾤδησα: pf. ᾤδηκα: (οἶδος):—intr. *to swell, swell up, become swoln*, Lat. *tumere, turgere*; **οἰδεῖν τὼ πόδε** *to swell* in the feet, i. e. to have swollen feet. II. metaph. *to be inflamed* or *troubled*; **πράγματα οἰδέοντα**, *unsettled, disordered* circumstances. Hence

οἴδημα, τό, *a swelling, tumour*.

Οἰδι-πόδης, ου, ὁ, properly patronym. of Οἰδίπους, *son* or *descendant of Oedipus*: but commonly poët. for Οἰδίπους, *Oedipus himself*.

Οἰδί-πους, ποδος, ὁ: acc. -ποδα and -πουν: voc. -πους, more rarely -που: (οἰδέω, πούς):—*Oedipus*, i. e. *the swoln-footed*: poët. **Οἰδίπος**, ου, ὁ. [ῐ]

οἶδμα, ατος, τό, (οἰδέω) *the swell of the sea, a wave, billow*. II. *the swelling* of the wind.

ΟΙ͂ΔΟΣ, τό, *a swelling, tumour*.

οἴεος, α, ον, (οἶς) *of* or *from a sheep*; ἡ οἰέη (sub. δορά) *a sheepskin*.

ὀΐεσσι, Ep. dat. pl. of ὄϊς.

οἰ-έτης, ες, (ὁμός, ἔτος) contr. for ὁμοέτης, *equal in years, of the same age*: cf. ὄθριξ.

ὀϊζύος, ον, = ὀϊζυρός.

ὀϊζῠρός Att. **οἰζυρός**, ά, όν, (ὀϊζύς) *woful, pitiable, miserable, woe-begone*: of things, *toilsome, dreary, painful*: also *sorry, wretched, poor*. Ep. Comp. and Sup. ὀϊζυρώτερος, -ώτατος, for -ότερος, -ότατος.

ὀϊζύς Att. **οἰζύς**, ύος, ἡ, as dissyll.: contr. dat. ὀϊζυῖ for ὀϊζύϊ: (οἴ):—*woe, misery, distress, hardship*. [ῡ in trisyll. cases, in dissyll. ῠ.] Hence

ὀϊζύω Att. **οἰζύω** (as trisyll.): f. ύσω [ῡ]: aor. 1 ὀΐζυσα:—*to wail, mourn, lament*. II. c. acc. rei, *to suffer*: absol. *to be miserable*, or *to suffer*.

οἰηθῆναι, aor. 1 inf. of οἴομαι.

οἰήιον, τό, = οἴηξ, οἴαξ, *a rudder, helm*. [ῐ]

οἰηκίζω, Ion. for οἰακίζω.

οἴηξ, ηκος, Ion. for οἴαξ, ἄκος.

οἰήσομαι, fut. of οἴομαι.

ὀΐς, ΐδος, ἡ, poët. for ὄϊς, *a sheep*: acc. οἶϊδα.

οἶκα, ας, ε, Ion. for ἔοικα.

οἴκαδε Dor. **οἴκαδις**, Adv. (οἶκος) = οἶκόνδε, *to one's house, home*, or *country, home, homewards*. II. = οἴκοι, *at home*.

οἰκέαται Ion. for ᾤκηνται, 3 pl. pf. pass. of οἰκέω.

οἰκεῖος, α, ον, also ος, ον: Ion. **οἰκήιος**, η, ον, (οἶκος):—*belonging to a house* or *household affairs, domestic*:—**τὰ οἰκεῖα** *household affairs, a household*; also, *household goods*, Lat. *res familiaris*. II. *belonging to a family, akin, intimate*, Lat. *familiaris*; οἱ οἰκεῖοι *friends, relations, connexions*; Ion. Sup., οἱ οἰκηιώτατοί τινος one's *most intimate friends*: τὸ οἰκεῖον *relationship*. III. *belonging to one's house* or *family, one's own, private*: so of possessions, *one's own, peculiar*; ἡ οἰκεία ἡ οἰκηίη (sub. γῆ), *one's own land, one's country*: hence of corn, *home-grown*, opp. to imported. IV. *proper to* a thing, *fitting, suitable*: *naturally suited* to a thing: τὸ οἰκεῖον = τὸ καθῆκον, *what is suitable, befitting*.

οἰκειότης Ion. **οἰκηιότης**, ητος, ἡ, *relationship*: *intimacy, friendship*: also *marriage*.

οἰκειόω Ion. **οἰκηιόω**: f. ώσω: (οἰκεῖος):—*to make one's own*: hence *to make* a person *one's friend*: Med. *to make* a person *one's friend, win* his *regard*. 2. *to make one's own, appropriate*: Med. *to claim, reckon as one's own*.

οἰκείως, Adv. of οἰκεῖος, *in a friendly manner, familiarly*; οἰκείως ἔχειν πρός τινα to be *intimate* with one. 2. *as if it was one's own*. 3. *properly, naturally*: *dutifully*.

οἰκείω, poët. for οἰκέω.

οἰκείωσις, ἡ, (οἰκειόω) *a taking as one's own, appropriation*.

οἰκετεία, ἡ, *the household, the servants*, Lat. *familia*. From

οἰκετεύω, f. σω, *to inhabit*. From

οἰκέτης, ου, ὁ, (οἰκέω) *an inmate of* one's *house*: *a house-slave, menial, domestic*, Lat. *verna*:—in pl. οἰκέται, *one's family, women and children*.

οἰκέτις, ῐδος, ἡ, fem. of οἰκέτης, *a female domestic* or *slave*. II. *the mistress of the house, housewife*.

οἰκεῦντες, Dor. for οἰκοῦντες, part. pl. of οἰκέω.

οἰκεύς, έως Ion. ῆος, ὁ, (οἰκέω) *an inmate of one's house*. II. *a domestic servant*.

οἰκέω, impf. ᾤκεον contr. -οῦν Ion. οἴκεον: fut. οἰκήσω: aor. 1 ᾤκησα: pf. ᾤκηκα:—Med., f. οἰκήσομαι in pass. sense:—Pass., aor. 1 ᾠκήθην: pf. ᾤκημαι Ion. οἴκημαι: (οἶκος): I. trans. *to inhabit*: hence *to possess, occupy*:—ἡ οἰκουμένη (sub. γῆ), *the civilised world, the whole habitable globe*. 2. like οἰκίζω, *to place* or *settle* persons in a place; in Pass., *to be settled*: the pf. pass. ᾤκημαι Ion. οἴκημαι is used as pres. *to be settled*; c. acc. *to inhabit*; of cities, *to be placed* or *situated*. 3. like διοικέω, *to manage, govern*. II. intr. *to dwell, live, to have as* one's *abode*. 2. of states, *to be settled, situated, lie*:—also *to be managed, governed*, ἡ πόλις οἰκεῖ κακῶς the state *is* ill *managed*.

οἰκῆας, Ep. for οἰκεῖς, acc. pl. of **οἰκεύς**.

οἰκήιος, η, ον, Ion. for οἰκεῖος.

οἰκηιότης, ητος, ἡ, Ion. for οἰκειότης.

οἰκηιόω, Ion. for οἰκειόω.

οἴκημα, τό, (οἰκέω) *a dwelling-place, a dwelling-house, a chamber in a house, the story of a house*. 2. *a cage* or *pen* for animals. 3. *a temple, fane*. 4. *a prison*.

οἰκῆν, Dor. for οἰκεῖν, pres. inf. of οἰκέω.

οἰκήσιμος, ον, *habitable*. From

οἴκησις, ἡ, (οἰκέω) *the act of dwelling*. II. *a place for dwelling, a house, dwelling*.

οἰκητήρ, ῆρος, = οἰκητής.

οἰκητήριον, τό, (οἰκέω) *a dwelling*.

οἰκητής, οῦ, ὁ, (οἰκέω) *an inhabitant, dweller*.

οἰκητός, ή, όν, (οἰκέω) *inhabited*: *habitable*.

οἰκήτωρ, ορος, ὁ, = οἰκητήρ, -τής, *an inhabitant*.

οἰκία Ion. -ίη, ἡ, (οἶκος) *a house, dwelling.* II. *a household:* also *the inmates of the house,* Lat. *familia.* III. *a house* or *family from which one is descended.* Hence

οἰκῐᾰκός, ή, όν, *of one's own house, domestic.*

οἰκίδιον, τό, Dim. of οἶκος, *a small house.*

οἰκίζω, f. ίσω Att. ιῶ: aor. 1 ᾤκισα Ion. οἴκισα:—Med., fut. οἰκιοῦμαι:—Pass., fut. οἰκισθήσομαι: aor. 1 ᾠκίσθην: pf ᾤκισμαι Ion. οἴκισμαι: (οἶκος):—*to build a house: to found* or *establish* a new settlement: *to people* a country, *to colonise.* II. *to settle* or *fix as a colonist* or *inhabitant: to remove, transplant:* —Pass. *to settle* or *establish oneself in a place:* also c. acc. *to inhabit.*

οἰκίον, τό, (οἶκος) always used in pl. **οἴκια,** τά, like Lat. *aedes, a house, dwelling, abode:* esp. *a palace* containing ranges of buildings. 2. *a den, lair.* etc., of animals: *a nest.*

οἴκῐσις, ἡ, (οἰκίζω) *the building* or *settlement* of a colony: *colonisation.*

οἰκίσκος, ὁ, Dim. of οἶκος, *a small house* or *room: a cage, coop, pen.*

οἴκισται, Ion. for ᾤκισται, 3 sing. pf. pass. of οἰκίζω.

οἰκιστήρ, ῆρος, poët. for οἰκιστής.

οἰκιστής, οῦ, ὁ, (οἰκίζω) *a settler, colonist.*

οἰκο-γενής, ές, (οἶκος, γενέσθαι) *born in the house, home-bred, domestic:* of animals, *tame.*

οἰκοδεσποτέω, f. ήσω, *to be master of a house, to manage the household.* From

οἰκο-δεσπότης, ου, ὁ, (οἶκος, δεσπότης) *the master of a house* or *family: the good-man of the house.*

οἰκοδομέω, f. ήσω, (οἰκοδόμος) *to build a house.* 2. generally, *to build, construct:*—Med., οἰκοδομεῖσθαι οἴκημα *to build oneself* a house. 3. metaph. *to build* or *found upon.* 4. metaph. *to edify.* Hence

οἰκοδομή, ἡ, = οἰκοδόμησις, *the act of building:*—*a building, edifice.* 2. metaph. *edification, improvement, instruction.*

οἰκοδόμημα, τό, (οἰκοδομέω) *a house built, building.*

οἰκοδόμησις, ἡ, = οἰκοδομία.

οἰκοδομία, ἡ, (οἰκοδομέω) *the building of a house; a way of building, structure.* 2. *a building, edifice.*

οἰκοδομικός, ή, όν, (οἰκοδόμος) *skilful in building:* ἡ οἰκοδομική (sub. τέχνη) *architecture.*

οἰκο-δόμος, όν, (οἶκος, δέμω) *building a house:*—as Subst., οἰκοδόμος, ὁ, *a builder, an architect.*

οἴκοθεν, Adv. (οἶκος) *from one's own house, from home.* 2. *from one's own fortune* or *means, from one's own nature, of oneself;* οὐκ εἶχον οἴκοθεν I had it not *of my own.*

οἴκοθι, Adv. (οἶκος) *at home,* Lat. *domi.*

οἴκοι, Adv. (οἶκος) *at home,* Lat. *domi:* τὰ οἴκοι *one's own affairs.*

οἰκόνδε, poët. for οἴκαδε, (οἶκος) *homeward, home.*

οἰκονομέω, f. ήσω, (οἰκονόμος) *to be a householder* or *steward.* 2. c. acc. *to manage, order, arrange.*

οἰκονομία, ἡ, (οἰκονομέω) *the management of a household* or *family:* generally, *administration, government* of a state.

οἰκονομικός, ή, όν, *conversant with the management of a household* or *family:* generally, *practised in managing, thrifty, economical:* ἡ οἰκονομική (sub. τέχνη) *domestic economy;* also τὰ οἰκονομικά, *domestic affairs.* Adv. -κῶς. From

οἰκο-νόμος, ον, (οἶκος, νέμω) *managing a household* or *family:* as Subst. οἰκονόμος, ὁ, *a house-keeper, manager, steward.*

οἰκό-πεδον, τό, (οἶκος, πέδον) *the site of a house,* Lat. *area domus.* II. *the house itself.*

οἰκο-ποιός, ός, (οἶκος, ποιέω) *making* or *constituting a house.*

οἰκόριος, α, ον, Dor. for οἰκούριος.

ΟΙ͂ΚΟΣ, ου, ὁ, *a house, abode, dwelling: any place to live in;* κατ' οἶκον or κατ' οἴκους at *home.* 2. *part of a house, a room, chamber:* hence οἶκοι in pl. often stands for *a single house,* like Lat. *aedes.* 3. *a temple.* II. *household affairs, house-wifery: household property, house and goods.* III. *a household, family.* IV. *a house, race, family.*

οἰκός, Ion. for ἐοικός, part. neut. of ἔοικα.

οἰκό-σῖτος, ον, (οἶκος, σῖτος) *feeding at home, living at one's own cost.* II. *living in a house.*

οἰκο-τρῐβής, ές, (οἶκος, τρῐβῆναι) *ruining a house* or *family.*

οἰκό-τριψ, ῐβος, ὁ, (οἶκος, τρίβω) *a slave born and bred in the house,* Lat. *verna.*

οἰκο-τύραννος, ὁ, (οἶκος, τύραννος) *a domestic tyrant.*

οἰκότως, Ion. for ἐοικότως, Adv. of ἐοικώς (part. of ἔοικα), *reasonably, probably.*

οἰκουμένη (sub. γῆ), ἡ, v. sub οἰκέω.

οἰκουρέω, f. ήσω, (οἰκουρός) *to watch* or *keep the house:* c. acc. *to guard, order, govern.* II. *to keep within doors, stay at home.* Hence

οἰκούρημα, τό, *the watch of a house:* generally, *watch and ward;* οἰκούρημα ξένων *watch kept* by strangers. II. *one who keeps house, a stay-at-home.*

οἰκουρία, ἡ, (οἰκουρέω) *a keeping at home: inactivity.*

οἰκούριος, ον, *belonging to housekeeping;* hence τὰ οἰκούρια (sub. δῶρα), *wages for housekeeping.* II. *keeping within doors:* ἑταῖραι οἰκόριαι (Dor. for οἰκούρ-) *female house-mates.* From

οἰκ-ουρός, όν, (οἶκος, οὖρος) *watching* or *keeping the house.* II. *staying at home, domestic:* as Subst., οἰκουρός, ἡ, *the mistress of the house.*

οἰκοφθορέω, f. ήσω, (οἰκοφθόρος) *to ruin a house* or *family, consume one's substance:*—Pass. *to lose one's fortune, to be ruined, undone.* Hence

οἰκοφθορία, ἡ, *ruin of a house* or *family.*

οἰκο-φθόρος, ον, (οἶκος, φθείρω) *ruining a house:* as Subst., οἰκοφθόρος, ὁ, *a prodigal.*

οἰκο-φύλαξ, ᾰκος, ὁ, ἡ, (οἶκος, φύλαξ) *a house-guard.*

οἰκτείρημα, τό, and **οἰκτείρησις,** ἡ, *pity.* From

οἰκτείρω: impf. ᾤκτειρον Ion. οἴκτειρον: fut. οἰκτερῶ: aor. 1 ᾤκτειρα, (οἶκτος):—*to pity, have pity or com-*

passion upon, commiserate, c. acc. pers.; οἰκτ. τινά τινός *to pity* one *for* or *because of* a thing

οἰκτίζω, f. ίσω Att. ιῶ: aor. 1 ᾤκτισα: (οἶκτος):—*to grieve for, pity, commiserate*:—Med. *to express grief, mourn*: *to bewail, lament*.

οἰκτιρμός, οῦ, ὁ, (οἰκτείρω) *pity, compassion*.

οἰκτίρμων, ον, gen. ονος, (οἰκτείρω) *merciful*.

οἴκτισμα, ατος, τό, (οἰκτίζω) *lamentation*.

οἰκτισμός, οῦ, ὁ, (οἰκτίζω) *lamentation*.

οἴκτιστος, η, ον, irreg. Sup. of οἰκτρός (formed from οἶκτος, cf. αἰσχρός, αἴσχιστος; but the Comp. is οἰκτρότερος):—*most pitiable, miserable, lamentable*: neut. pl. οἴκτιστα as Adv. *most miserably*

ΟἿΚΤΟΣ, ου, ὁ, *pity, compassion*. 2. *the expression of pity* or *grief, weeping, wailing*

οἰκτρό-βιος, ον, (οἰκτρός, βίος) *leading a pitiable life*.

οἰκτρός ά, όν, (οἶκτος) *pitiable, lamentable*: *piteous, mournful*. Comp. and Sup. οἰκτρότερος, οἰκτρότατος, also irreg. Sup. οἴκτιστος

οἰκτρο-χοέω, (οἰκτρός, χέω) *to pour forth piteously*.

οἰκτρῶς, Adv of οἰκτρός, *piteously*: Sup. οἰκτρότατα.

οἰκώς, υῖα, ός, Ion. for ἐοικώς, part. of ἔοικα.

οἰκ-ωφελής, ές, (οἶκος, ὠφελέω) *profitable to a house*.

οἰκωφελία Ion. -ίη, ἡ, (οἰκωφελής) *profit to a house*: hence *thrift* or *carefulness in household* matters, of a *home-life*, as opp. to the life of a warrior.

οἶμα, ατος, τό, (*οἴω = φέρω) *an impetuous attack, the spring* of a lion, *swoop* of an eagle, Lat. *impetus*.

οἶμαι, Att. contr. from οἴομαι.

οἰμάω, f. ήσω, (οἶμα) = ὁρμάω, *to dart upon, to pounce* or *swoop*, of a bird of prey

ΟἸΜΗ, ἡ, = οἶμος, *a way, path*: metaph. *the course* of a tale or poem: *the tale* or *poem* itself

οἴμοι, exclam. of pain, fright, pity, anger, surprise, *woe's me!* οἴμοι is used with a nom., as, οἴμοι ἐγώ *ah me! woe's me!* or with a gen., as, οἴμοι τῶν κακῶν *alas for* my misfortunes!

ΟἾΜΟΣ, ου, ὁ, *a way, road, course, path*. 2. *a stripe, layer* 3. *a strip of land* 4. metaph. like οἴμη, οἶμος ἀοιδῆς *the course* or *strain* of song, *a song, lay*.

οἰμωγή, ἡ, (οἰμώζω) properly *a crying* οἴμοι, *weeping and wailing, lamentation*.

οἴμωγμα, ατος, τό, *a cry of lamentation, wail*: and **οἰμωγμός**, ὁ, *a lamenting*. From

οἰμώζω, fut. οἰμώξομαι later οἰμώξω: aor. 1 ᾤμωξα: (οἴμοι):—*to cry* οἴμοι, (as αἰάζω *to cry* αἴ, αἴ), *to wail, lament*; οἴμωζε as a curse, *go howl! plague take you!* Lat. *abi in malam rem!* so, οὐκ οἰμώξεται; shall he not *have to cry out?* i. e. *shall he not rue it?* II. trans. *to pity, bewail*, c. acc.

οἰμωκτός, ή, όν, (οἰμώζω) *to be pitied* or *bewailed*.

οἰμώξειε, 3 sing Ep aor. 1 opt. of οἰμώζω.

οἰν-άνθη, ἡ, (οἴνη, ἄνθη) *the first shoot* or *bud of the vine*: then, like Lat. *pampinus, the vine-stock, the vine*. 2. *the down of the vine-leaf*: metaph. *the down on the cheek*, Lat. *lanugo*.

οἰν-ανθίς, ίδος, ἡ, = οἰνάνθη.

οἰνάρεον, τό, = οἴναρον.

οἰναρίζω, f. σω, (οἴναρον) *to strip off vine-leaves*.

οἰνάριον, τό, Dim. of οἶνος, *weak, poor wine*.

οἴναρον, τό, (οἴνη) *a vine-leaf*, Lat. *pampinus*.

ΟἼΝΗ, ἡ, *the vine*, Lat. *vitis*. 2. = οἶνος, *wine*.

οἰνηρός, ά, όν, (οἶνος) *of wine, addicted to wine*, Lat. *vinosus*. II. *containing wine*. III. of countries, *rich in wine*.

οἰν-ήρυσις, ἡ, (οἶνος, ἀρύω) *a vessel for drawing wine*

οἰνίζω, (οἶνος) *to smell of wine* II. Med. *to procure wine by barter, buy wine*.

οἰνο-βαρείων, ὁ, an Ion. participial form (as if from οἰνο-βαρέω) = οἰνοβαρής. From

οἰνο-βαρής, ές, (οἶνος, βαρύς) *heavy* or *drunken with wine*, Lat. *vino gravis*.

οἰνο-βρεχής, ές, (οἶνος, βρέχω) *soaked in wine*, i. e. *drunken*.

οἰνο-δόκος, ον, (οἶνος, δέχομαι) *receiving* or *holding wine*.

οἰνο-δότης, ου, Dor. -δότας, α, ὁ, (οἶνος, δίδωμι) *giver of wine*, epith. of Bacchus.

οἰνόεις, -όεσσα, -όεν, contr. **οἰνοῦς**, -οῦσσα Att. -οῦττα, -οῦν, (οἶνος) *made of* or *with wine*. II. as Subst., οἰνοῦττα, ἡ, *a cake* or *porridge of pearl-barley, water, oil and wine*, esp. for rowers.

οἰνό-μελι, ιτος, τό, (οἶνος, μέλι) *honey mixed with wine, mead*.

οἰνό-πέδη, ἡ, and **οἰνό-πεδον**, τό, (οἶνος, πέδον) *land fit for growing wine, a vineyard*.

οἰνό-πεδος, ον, (οἶνος, πέδον) *fit for the growth of the vine, abounding in wine*

οἰνο-πέπαντος, ον, (οἶνος, πεπαίνω) *ripe for making wine*.

οἰνο-πίπης [ῐ], ου, ὁ, (οἶνος, ὀπιπτεύω) *gaping after wine*, formed like the Homeric παρθενοπίπης.

οἰνο-πληθής, ές, (οἶνος, πλήθω) *abounding in wine*.

οἰνο-πλήξ, ῆγος, ὁ, ἡ, (οἶνος, πλήσσω) *wine-stricken*, i. e. *drunk*.

οἰνοποτάζω and **οἰνοποτέω**, (οἰνοπότης) *to drink wine*.

οἰνο-ποτήρ, ῆρος, ὁ, and **οἰνο-πότης**, ου, ὁ, fem. **οἰνο-πότις**, ιδος, (οἶνος, ΠΟ- Root of some tenses of πίνω) *a wine-drinker, wine-bibber*.

ΟἾΝΟΣ, ου, ὁ, Lat. *VINUM, wine*; ἐν οἴνῳ, ἐπ' οἴνῳ, παρ' οἴνῳ, over *wine*, Lat. *inter pocula*. 2. the fermented juice of apples, pears, etc., *cider, perry*: οἶνος ἐκ κριθῶν barley-*wine*, a kind of *beer*: *palm-wine, lotus-wine*, also occur as distinguished from *grape-wine* (οἶνος ἀμπέλινος)

οἰνο-τρέφος, ον, (οἶνος, τρέφω) *producing wine*.

οἰνοῦς, οἰνοῦσσα Att. -οῦττα, -οῦν, contr. for οἰνόεις, εσσα, εν.

οἰνο-φαγία, ἡ, (οἶνος, φαγεῖν) *a consuming of wine*.

οἰνοφλυγία, ἡ, *a love of drinking, drunkenness*. From

οἰνό-φλυξ, υγος, ὁ, ἡ, (οἶνος, φλύω) *given to drinking, drunken*.

οἰνο-φόρος, ου, (οἶνος, φέρω) *carrying, holding wine*, as Subst., *οἰνοφόρος*, ὁ, Lat. *oenophorus, a wine-cask.*

οἰνο-χᾰρής, *ές*, (οἶνος, χαρῆναι) *rejoicing in wine.*

οἰνο-χάρων, *οντος*, ὁ, (οἶνος, Χάρων) *the Wine-Charon*, a nickname of Philip of Macedon, because he killed his enemies by poisoning their wine.

οἰνοχοεύω, Ep. form of *οἰνοχέω, to pour out wine.*

οἰνοχοέω: 3 sing. impf. *ᾠνοχόει* Ep. *ἐῳνοχόει*; f. *ήσω*: aor. 1 inf. *οἰνοχοῆσαι*: (*οἰνοχόος*):—*to be a cup-bearer: to pour out wine* or *like wine; νέκταρ ἐῳνοχόει she was pouring out* nectar *for wine.*

οἰνο-χόη, ἡ, (οἶνος, χέω) *a cup* or *can for ladling wine from the bowl* (*κρατήρ*) into the cups.

οἰνο-χόος, *ον*, (οἶνος, χέω) *pouring out wine to drink*: as Subst., *οἰνοχόος*, ὁ, *a cup-bearer.*

οἰνό-χῠτος, *ον*, (οἶνος, χέω) *poured of* or *with wine; πῶμα οἰνόχυτον* a draught *of wine.*

οἰν-οψ, *οπος*, ὁ, = *οἶνοψ, wine-coloured, wine-dark.*

οἰνόω, f. *ώσω*:—Pass., aor. 1 *ᾠνώθην*: pf. *ᾤνωμαι* Ion. *οἴνωμαι*: (*οἶνος*):—*to make drunk with wine*:— Pass. *to get drunk, be drunken.*

οἰνών, *ῶνος*, ὁ, (*οἶνος*) *a wine-cellar, wine-shop.*

οἰν-ωπός, *ή, όν*, or *ός, όν*, and **οἰν-ώψ**, *ῶπος*, ὁ, ἡ, (*οἶνος, ὤψ*) *wine-coloured.*

οἴξας, aor. 1 part. of *οἴγνυμι.*

οἶο, Ep. for *οὗ*, gen. of possess. Pron. *ὅς, his, her.*

οἰό-βᾰτος, *ον*, (*οἶος, βαίνω*) *walking alone: lonesome.*

οἰο-βουκόλος, *ον*, (*οἶος, βουκόλος*) *herdsman of a single cow.*

οἰο-βώτας, ὁ, (*οἶος, βόσκω*) *one who feeds alone; φρενὸς οἰοβώτας feeding* his mind *apart, self-willed.*

οἰό-γᾰμος, *ον*, (*οἶος, γαμέω*) *married only to one.*

οἰό-ζωνος, *ον*, (*οἶος, ζώνη*) *with one girdle*, i. e. *single-handed, alone.*

οἰόθεν, Adv. (*οἶος*) *from one side alone*, hence generally, *alone; οἰόθεν οἶος all alone.*

ΟΙ'ΟΜΑΙ Ep. **ὀΐομαι**: impf. *ᾠόμην*, Ep. 3 sing. *ὠΐετο*: fut. *οἰήσομαι*: aor. 1 Ep. *ὠΐσθην* part. *ὀϊσθείς*, Att. *ᾠήθην* inf. *οἰηθῆναι* part. *οἰηθείς*: Ep. aor. 1 med. *ὠισάμην*, 3 sing. *ὀΐσατο* part. *ὀϊσάμενος*. The Act. *οἴω* or *ὀΐω* is also found: Dor. pres. *οἰῶ*. The Att. also use a contr. pres. **οἶμαι**, impf. *ᾤμην.*

To suppose, think, believe, as opp. to *knowing*, always of the fut.: of good, *to hope, anticipate*; of evil, *to fear*:—often used absol., *αἰεὶ ὀΐεαι thou art* ever *suspecting*; and so in the sense *to deem, believe, expect; θυμὸς ὀΐσατό μοι* my heart *foreboded* it: it is also once found impersonal, *ὀΐεταί μοι ἀνὰ θυμόν there comes a boding* into my heart. 2. *to be minded, to mean, purpose to* do a thing. 3. also used parenthetically in first person, *ἐν πρώτοισιν* (*ὀΐω*) *κείσεται* among the first (*methinks*) will he be lying: so in Att., the contr. *οἶμαι* impf. *ᾤμην, I think, I suppose, I believe*, is put without any grammat. construction in the sentence: also in phrase, *πῶς οἴει; πῶς οἴεσθε*; how *think you?*

[When the diphthong is resolved Ep., the ι is long in all tenses, *ὀΐω, ὀΐσατο*, etc.: only the act, pres. *ὀΐω* has sometimes ῐ in the middle of the verse.]

οἱον-εί, for *οἷον εἰ, as if*: Dor. *οἷον αἰ.*

οἰο-νόμος, *ον*, (*οἶος, νέμω*) *feeding alone: lonely.*

οἰο-νόμος, *ον*, (*οἶς, νέμω*) *feeding sheep*: as Subst. *a shepherd.*

οἱόν-τε, *possible; οὐχ οἷόντε impossible*: v. *οἷος* III.

οἰό-ποκος, *ον*, (*οἶς, πέκω*) *shorn from a sheep.*

οἰοπολέω, f. *ήσω, to roam* or *haunt alone.* From

οἰο-πόλος, *ον*, (*οἶος, πέλομαι*) *being alone: lonely, solitary.* B. (*οἶς, πολέω*) *tending sheep.*

οἰόρ, Scyth. for *ἀνήρ*. Hence

οἰόρ-πατα, Scyth. word in Herodotus. = *ἀνδροκτόνοι.*

ΟΙ'ΟΣ, *οἴη, οἶον, alone, by oneself, lone, lonely*: it can often only be rendered by an Adv., *alone, only*: strengthd., *εἷς οἶος, μία οἴη one alone, one only*: also in dual, *δύο οἴω*, and in pl., *δύο οἴους*. 2. c. gen., *τῶν οἶος left alone* by them; *οἶος θεῶν alone of all* the gods; *οἶος Ἀτρειδῶν apart from* the sons of Atreus. II. *singular, peculiar of its kind, unique*, Lat. *unicus.*

οἷος, *οἵα* Ion. *οἵη, οἷον*, (*ὅς*) *such as, of such sort, manner* or *kind as . .*, Lat. *qualis*; relat. Pronoun, answering to *ποῖος* interrog. and indef., and to demonstr. *τοῖος; ὅσσος οἷός τε*, Lat. *qualis quantusque*: c. acc., *οἷος ἀρετήν what a man for* virtue: often only to be rendered by an Adv., as, *οἷος μέτεισι πόλεμόνδε how* he rushes into war.

Οἷος in an independent sentence often expresses astonishment, being often strengthd. by *δή, οἷον δὴ τὸν μῦθον ἔειπας what* a word hast thou spoken!— the neut. *οἷον* is often used as an Adv., *οἷον δή νυ θεοὺς βροτοὶ αἰτιόωνται how* do men now find fault with gods! II. implying a Comparison, the anteced. *τοῖος* or *τοιόσδε* being often omitted; *οἷος ἀστὴρ εἶσι like as* a star wanders; and so as an exclam., *οἷ' ἀγορεύεις what* art thou saying! *οἷά μ' ἔοργας what* hast thou done to me! 2. *οἷος* often introduces a reason for what has gone before, *δή* being sometimes added to express certainty; *οἷος δή, οἷον δή, such as all know.* 3. if the Comparison is general, Homer uses *οἷός τε, in some such way as, οἷός τε πελώριος ἔρχεται Ἄρης some such one as* Ares; so, *οἷός τις the sort of person.* 4. when a Comparison involves Time, *οἷος ὅτε* is used, *like as when.* 5. *οἷος* is used in many brief Att. expressions, as, *οὐδὲν οἷον ἀκούειν αὐτοῦ τοῦ νόμου* there's nothing *like*, i. e. *so good as*, hearing the law itself: —it adds force to the Superl., *χωρίον οἷον χαλεπώτατον*, in full *τοιοῦτον οἷόν ἐστι χωρίον*, ground the most difficult *possible.* III. *οἷος* c. inf. implies Fitness or Ability, *οἷος ἔην τελέσαι ἔργον τε ἔπος τε how able* was he to make good both deed and word; *οἷος ἔην βουλευέμεν ἠδὲ μάχεσθαι how able* was he to counsel and to fight: in this sense *οἷός τε* is more usual, *οἷός τε εἰμὶ ποιεῖν I am such a man as* to do it, i. e. *I am able* to do it: in neut. sing. and pl., *οἷόν τέ ἐστι* and *οἷά τέ ἐστι*, it is *possible.* 2. absol.

in neut., οἷόν τε ἐστι it is *possible*; οὐχ οἷόν τε ἐστί it is im-*possible*. IV. οἷος is in Att. often repeated in the same clause, as, οἷ' ἔργα δράσας οἷα λαγχάνει κακά having done *what kind* of actions, *what kind of* sufferings he receives! οἵαν ἀνθ' οἵων θυμάτων χάριν *what* thanks, *for what* offerings! V. as Adv. in neut. sing. οἷον, also in pl. οἷα, *how*; also with Adj. οἷον ἐερσήεις *how* fresh. 2. in Comparisons, *as, like as, just as*: οἷον ὅτε, *as when*. 3. *as, like, for instance*. 4. *about, hard upon*, Lat. *quasi*, οἷον δέκα σταδίους *about* ten stades.

οἰός, ὀϊός, gen. of οἶς ὄϊς.

οἰό-φρων, ονος, ὁ, ἡ, (οἶος, φρήν) *single, in one's opinion*: generally, *lonely*.

οἰο-χίτων, ωνος, ὁ, ἡ, (οἶος, χιτών) *with nothing but a tunic on, lightly clad*.

οἰόω, (οἶος) *to leave alone*: Pass. οἰόομαι, Ep. aor. I οἰώθην, *to be forsaken*.

*ΟΙ'Σ, ὁ and ἡ, gen. ὄϊος acc. ὄϊν; plur., nom. ὄϊες gen. ὀΐων, dat. οἴεσι Ep. ὀΐεσσι shortened ὄεσσι; acc. ὄϊας; contr. nom. and acc. pl. ὄϊς:—Att. nom. οἶς gen. οἰός, dat. οἰί acc. οἶν: pl. nom. οἶες gen. οἰῶν, dat. οἰσί acc. οἶας; nom. and acc. pl. also οἶς. Lat. *OVIS, a sheep*, whether *ram* or *ewe*; though sometimes the gender is marked by a word added, as, ὄϊς ἀρνειός or ἄρσην *a ram*; ὄϊς θῆλυς *a ewe*.

ὀΐσατο, ὀϊσάμενος, Ep. aor. I med. of οἴομαι. [ῑ]

οἶσε -έτω, -ετε, fut. imperat. of φέρω.

οἰσέμεν, οἰσέμεναι, Ep. for οἴσειν, fut. inf. of φέρω.

οἰσεῦμες, Dor. for οἴσομεν, I pl. fut. of φέρω.

οἶσθα, *thou knowest*, 2 sing. of οἶδα.

ὀϊσθείς, aor. I pass. part. of οἴομαι.

οἰσθήσομαι, fut. pass. of φέρω.

οἴσομαι, fut. med., with pass. sense, of φέρω.

ΟΙ'ΣΠΗ, ἡ, *the grease in unwashen wool, greasy wool*.

οἰσ-πώτη, ἡ, (ὄϊς, οἶς, πάτος) *the dirt on the hinder part of a sheep*.

οἰστέος, α, ον, verb. Adj. of φέρω, *to be borne*. neut. οἰστέον *one must bear*.

ὀϊστευτήρ, ῆρος, ὁ, and ὀϊστευτής, οῦ, ὁ, (ὀϊστεύω) *a bowman, an archer*.

ὀϊστεύω, f. σω, (ὀϊστός) *to shoot arrows*: aor. I part. ὀϊστεύσας. II. trans. *to shoot with an arrow*.

ὀϊστο-δέγμων, ον, gen. ονος, (ὀϊστός, δέχομαι) *holding arrows*.

οἰστός, ή, όν, (οἴσω) *that must be borne, endurable*.

ὀϊστός Att. οἰστός, οῦ, ὁ, (οἴσω, fut. of φέρω) *an arrow*, Lat. *sagitta*.

οἰστράω or οἰστρέω: f. ήσω: aor. I act. ᾤστρησα inf. οἰστρῆσαι:—Pass., aor. I ᾠστρήθην inf. οἰστρηθῆναι: (οἶστρος):—properly of a gadfly, *to torment by stinging*: generally, *to sting* or *goad to madness*: Pass. *to be driven mad*. II. intr. *to go mad, run wild, rage*.

οἰστρ-ήλατος, ον, (οἶστρος, ἐλαύνω) *driven by the gadfly, driven mad*.

οἴστρημα, ατος, τό, (οἰστράω) *the smart of a gadfly's sting*: *a fit of madness, raving*.

οἰστρο-βολέω, f. ήσω, (οἶστρος, βαλεῖν) *to strike with a sting*, esp. of love.

οἰστρο-δίνητος, ον, (οἶστρος, δινέω) *driven round and round by the gadfly*: *driven wild*.

οἰστρο-δόνητος, ον, and -δονος, ον, (οἶστρος, δονέω) *driven by the gadfly*: *driven wild*.

οἰστρο-πλήξ, ῆγος, ὁ, ἡ, (οἶστρος, πλήσσω) *stung by a gadfly, driven mad*.

ΟΙ'ΣΤΡΟΣ, ου, ὁ, *the gadfly, breese*, Lat. *asilus*, an insect which infests cattle: in Poets of the fly that tormented Io. II. metaph. *a sting, goad, anything that torments*: *the smart of pain, agony*. 2. *any vehement passion*: *madness, frenzy*.

οἰστρο-φόρος, ον, (οἶστρος, φέρω) *maddening*.

ΟΙΣΥ'Α, ἡ, a tree of the *osier* kind. Hence

οἰσύϊνος, η, ον, *of osier, made of wicker-work*.

οἰσύπη, ἡ, = οἴσπη.

οἰσυπηρός, ά, όν, (οἴσυπος) *greasy, dirty*, esp. of *unwashed* wool, Lat. *lana succida*.

οἴσυπος, ὁ, (οἶς) = οἴσπη, οἰσύπη.

οἴσω Dor. οἰσῶ, fut. of φέρω, from Root *οἴω; whence is formed Ep. imperat. οἶσε, inf. οἰσέμεν, οἴσειν.

ΟΙ'ΤΟΣ, ου, ὁ, *fate, lot, doom*; in Homer *ill fate, doom, ruin, death*; κακὸν οἶτον ἀπόλλυσθαι to die a sad *death*.

Οἰτόσυρος, ὁ, the Scyth. name of Apollo.

οἰχέομαι, = οἴχομαι, q. v.

οἰχνέω, Ion. impf. οἴχνεσκον, = οἴχομαι, *to go, come*; of birds, *to fly*:—generally, *to walk, live*.

ΟΙ'ΧΟΜΑΙ, Dep.: impf. ᾠχόμην: fut. οἰχήσομαι: pf. ᾤχημαι Ion. οἴχημαι: also pf. med. ᾤχωκα Ion. οἴχωκα: Ion. 3 sing. plqpf. οἰχώκεε. The pres. οἰχέομαι Ion. οἰχεῦμαι also occurs: I. of persons, *to be gone, to have gone*, and so opp. to ἥκω *to have come*: c. part., οἴχεται φεύγων he has fled *and gone*; οἴχεται θανών *he* is dead *and gone*: c. acc. cognato, ὁδὸν οἴχεσθαι *to be gone* on a journey: c. acc. pers. *to have escaped from*. 2. for θνήσκω, *to be gone hence, to have departed, be deceased*; Att. part. οἰχόμενος *the departed*. 3. pf. ᾤχωκα, like ὄλωλα, *to be undone, ruined*. II. of things, as of darts, etc., *to rush, sweep along*. 2. of strength, *to be gone, lost, vanished*.

οἴω and ὀΐω, used by Ep. Poets for οἴομαι.

*οἴω, see φέρω.

οἰώθην, aor. I pass. of οἰόω.

οἰωνίζομαι, Att. fut. ιοῦμαι: Dep.: (οἰωνός):—*to take omens from the flight and screams of birds*, Lat. *augurium capere*. II. *to look upon as an omen, forebode*, Lat. *augurari*.

οἰώνισμα, ατος, τό, (οἰωνίζομαι) *divination by the flight* or *cries of birds*, Lat. *augurium*.

οἰωνιστήριον, τό, (οἰωνίζομαι) *a place for watching the flight of birds*, Lat. *templum augurale*. II. *the omen* or *augury itself*.

οἰωνιστής, οῦ, ὁ, (οἰωνίζομαι) *one who foretells from the flight and cries of birds, an augur, diviner.*

οἰωνο-θέτης, ου, ὁ, (οἰωνός, τίθημι) *an interpreter of auguries, an augur.*

οἰωνό-θροος, ον, (οἰωνός, θρόος) *of the cry of birds.*

οἰωνο-κτόνος, ον, (οἰωνός, κτείνω) *killing birds*

οἰωνό-μαντις, εως, ὁ, and ἡ, (οἰωνός, μάντις) *an interpreter of the flight and cries of birds, an augur.*

οἰωνο-πόλος, ον, (οἰωνός, πολέω) *observing the flight and cries of birds:* as Subst., οἰωνοπόλος, ὁ, *an augur.*

οἰωνός, οῦ, ὁ, (οἶος) *a solitary bird,* esp. *a bird of prey,* such as *a vulture* or *eagle.* II. *a bird of omen* or *augury,* because the greater birds of prey were observed for the sake of omens; and so distinguished from the common birds, ὄρνιθες. III. *an omen, presage,* Lat. *auspicium* or *augurium;* εἷς οἰωνὸς ἄριστος, ἀμύνεσθαι περὶ πάτρης the one best *omen* is, to fight for one's country; οἰωνοὶ ἀγαθοί good *omens.*

οἰωνοσκοπέω, f. ήσω, *to watch the flight* or *cries of birds, to take auguries, practise augury.* From

οἰωνο-σκόπος, ον, (οἰωνός, σκοπέω) *watching birds, taking omens from their flight* or *cries:* as Subst., οἰωνοσκόπος, ὁ, *an augur, soothsayer.*

οἴως, Att. Adv. of οἷος, οἷος ἂν οἴως ἔχεις· being such a man *in what a state* art thou!

ὄκᾱ poët. ὄκκᾱ, Dor. for ὅτε, *when.*

'ΟΚΕ'ΛΛΩ, aor. 1 ὤκειλα, inf. ὀκεῖλαι, = κέλλω, nautical term, I. trans. of the sailors, *to run a* ship *aground, run* it *on shore, strand* it. II. intr. of the ship, *to run aground.*

ὄκη, Ion. for ὅπη.

ὄκκᾱ poët. for ὄκα.

ὄκ-κᾱ or **ὄκ κα**, for ὅτε κεν, like κὰκ κεφαλῆς for κατὰ κεφαλῆς.

ὀκλᾰδίας (sub. δίφρος), ου, ὁ, (ὀκλάζω) *a seat with folding joints, a folding-chair, camp-stool.*

'ΟΚΛΑ'ΖΩ, f. σω: aor. 1 ὤκλασα:—*to sink on one's knees, to crouch down, cower:* generally, *to bend, sink down: to sink from weariness, to sit down to rest.* 2. *to leave off through weariness, to flag, slacken, abate.* II. c. acc. *to let sink, to bend, lower.*

ὀκνᾰλέος, α, ον, (ὄκνος) poët. for ὀκνηρός.

ὀκνείω, poët. for ὀκνέω.

ὀκνέω poët. ὀκνείω: impf. ὤκνειον: f. ήσω: (ὄκνος): —*to shrink* from doing, *scruple* or *hesitate* to do a thing.

ὀκνηρός, ά, όν, (ὄκνος) *shrinking, hesitating, unready.* II. of things, *grievous, troublesom*

'ΟΚΝΟΣ, ὁ, *a shrinking, hesitation, unreadiness: cowardice.*

ὀκόθεν, ὀκοῖος, ὀκόσος, ὀκότε, ὀκότερος, ὄκου, Ion. for ὁπόθεν, ὁποῖος, etc.

ὀκρῑάω, (ὄκρις) *to make rough* or *jagged:* metaph. in Pass. *to be exasperated.*

ὀκρῑόεις, εσσα, εν, (ὄκρις) *rugged, jagged,* of unhewn stone.

ὀκριόωντο, Ep. for ὀκριῶντο, 3 pl. impf. of ὀκριάω.

ὄκρῖς, ιος, ἡ, like ἄκρις, ἄκρα, *a jagged point, a crag.* II. as Adj. ὀκρίς, ῖδος, ὁ, ἡ, *rugged, jagged.*

ὀκρῠόεις, εσσα, εν, (κρυόεις, with ο euphon.) = κρυερός, *cold, chilling: fearful, dreadful, horrible.*

ὀκτά-βλωμος, ον, (ὀκτώ, βλωμός) *consisting of eight mouthfuls;* ὀκτάβλωμος ἄρτος a kind of loaf which *was scored in eight equal parts.*

ὀκτᾰ-δάκτῠλος, ον, (ὀκτώ, δάκτυλος) *eight-fingered.*

ὀκτᾰ-ήμερος, ον, (ὀκτώ, ἡμέρα) *for eight days* · *on the eighth day.*

ὀκτάκις, Adv. (ὀκτώ) *eight times.* [ᾰ]

ὀκτᾰκισ-μύριοι, αι, α, *eighty thousand.*

ὀκτᾰκισ-χίλιοι, αι, α, *eight thousand:* it is also used in sing., ἵππος ὀκτακισχιλίη = ὀκτακισχίλιοι ἱππεῖς, '8000 horse.'

ὀκτά-κνημος, ον, (ὀκτώ, κνήμη) *with eight spokes.*

ὀκτᾰκόσιοι, αι, α, (ὀκτώ) *eight hundred.*

ὀκτά-μηνος, ον, (ὀκτώ, μήν) *eight months old, in the eighth month.* [ᾰ]

ὀκτά-πεδος, ον, Dor. for ὀκτάπους.

ὀκταπλάσιος, α, ον, and **ὀκταπλᾰσίων**, ον, gen. ονος, (ὀκτώ) *eightfold,* Lat. *octuplus.*

ὀκτᾰ-πόδης, ου, ὁ, (ὀκτώ, πούς) *eight feet long.*

ὀκτά-πους, ὁ, ἡ, πουν, τό, gen. ποδος, (ὀκτώ, πούς) *eight-footed.* II. *eight feet long.*

ὀκτάρ-ρῐζος, ον, (ὀκτώ, ῥίζα) *with eight roots:* of a stag's horns, *with eight points* or *tynes.*

ὀκτάρ-ρῡμος, ον, (ὀκτώ, ῥυμός) *drawn by eight pairs.*

ὀκτά-τονος, ον, (ὀκτώ, τείνω) *eight-stretched;* ἕλικες ὀκτάτονοι *the eight arms* which the cuttle-fish *stretches out* to catch its prey.

'ΟΚΤΩ', οἱ, αἱ, τά, indecl. *eight,* Lat. OCTO.

ὀκτω-δάκτῠλος, ον, *with eight fingers.*

ὀκτω-καί-δεκα, οἱ, αἱ, τά, indecl. *eighteen.*

ὀκτωκαιδεκά-δραχμος, ον, (ὀκτωκαίδεκα, δραχμή) *weighing* or *worth eighteen drachmae.*

ὀκτωκαιδέκᾰτος, η, ον, *the eighteenth:* ὀκτωκαιδεκάτη (sub. ἡμέρα), *the eighteenth day.*

ὀκτωκαιδεκ-έτης, ου, ὁ, (ὀκτωκαίδεκα, ἔτος) *eighteen years old:*—fem. **ὀκτωκαιδεκ-έτις**, ιδος.

ὀκχέω, poët. form of ὀχέω, *to bear, convey, carry.*

ὄκχος, ὁ, poët. form of ὄχος, *a chariot.*

ὄκως, Ion. for ὅπως.

ὄκωχα, old pf. of ἔχω, whence the compd. dual συνοχωκότε.

ὀλβίζω, f. ίσω Att. ιῶ: aor. 1 ὤλβισα:—Pass., aor. 1 ὠλβίσθην: pf. ὤλβισμαι: (ὄλβος):—*to make happy: to deem* or *pronounce happy,* like μακαρίζω and εὐδαιμονίζω.

ὀλβιο-δαίμων, ονος, ὁ and ἡ, (ὄλβιος, δαίμων) *of blessed lot* or *fortune.*

ὀλβιό-δωρος, ον, (ὄλβιος, δῶρον) *bestowing bliss, bounteous.*

ὀλβιο-δώτης or **-δότης**, ου, ὁ, fem. **-δῶτις**, ιδος, (ὄλβιος, δίδωμι) *bestower of bliss.*

ὀλβιο-εργός, όν, (ὄλβιος, ἔργον) *making happy.*

ὀλβιό-μοιρος, ον, (ὄλβιος, μοῖρα) *of happy fate.*

ὄλβιος, ον, or α, ον, (ὄλβος) *happy, blest*, esp. with worldly goods, *prosperous, wealthy, rich*, Lat. *beatus:* generally, *happy, blessed:* Homer only uses neut. pl., as ὄλβια δοῦναι to bestow *rich* gifts; δῶρα ὄλβια ποιεῖν to make gifts *blessed:* so in Adv. ὄλβια ζώειν to live *happily.* Irreg. Sup. ὀλβιστος, η, ον, formed directly from ὄλβος, as αἴσχιστος, κέρδιστος from αἶσχος, κέρδος: the reg. Sup. ὀλβιώτατος also occurs. Adv. -ίως.

ὀλβιό-φρων, ονος, ὁ, ἡ, (ὄλβιος, φρήν) *leaning towards the rich.*

ὄλβιστος, η, ον, irreg. Sup. of ὄλβιος.

ὀλβίως, Adv. of ὄλβιος, *happily, blissfully.*

ὀλβο-δοτήρ, ῆρος, ὁ, and **ὀλβο-δότης**, ου, ὁ, fem. **ὀλβο-δότειρα**, (ὄλβος, δίδωμι) *giver of bliss* or *prosperity.*

ὌΛΒΟΣ, ου, ὁ, *happiness, bliss, wealth.*

ὀλβο-φόρος, ον, (ὄλβος, φέρω) *bringing bliss.*

ὀλέεσθαι, Ion. for ὀλεῖσθαι, fut. med. inf. of ὄλλυμι.

ὀλέεσκε, Ion. 3 sing. aor. 2 of ὄλλυμι.

ὀλέθριος, ον, also α, ον, (ὄλεθρος) *destructive, deadly;* ὀλέθριον ἦμαρ the day *of destruction:* c. gen., γάμοι ὀλέθριοι φίλων a marriage *destructive to* one's friends. II. pass. *lost, undone.*

ὄλεθρος, ὁ, (ὄλλυμι) *ruin, destruction, undoing;* οὐκ εἰς ὄλεθρον (sc. ἐρρήσεις); wilt thou not go to *perdition?* i. e. *ruin* seize thee, answering to Comic phrase οὐκ ἐς κόρακας; II. like Lat. *pernicies, that which causes destruction, a bane, plague, pest.*

ὀλεῖ, ὀλεῖται, 2 and 3 sing. fut. of ὄλλυμι.

ὀλέκρᾶνον, τό, = ὠλέκρανον.

ὈΛΕ΄ΚΩ, only used in pres. and impf. ὄλεκον (without augm.), collat. form of ὄλλυμι:—*to ruin, destroy, kill:*—Pass. *to perish, die.*

ὀλέσαι, ὀλέσας, aor. 1 inf. and part. of ὄλλυμι.

ὀλέσειε, 3 sing. aor. 1 opt. of ὄλλυμι.

ὀλεσ-ήνωρ, ορος, ὁ, ἡ, (ὄλλυμι, ἀνήρ) *man-destroying.*

ὀλέσθαι, aor. 2 inf. med. of ὄλλυμι.

ὀλεσί-θηρ, ῆρος, ὁ, ἡ, (ὄλλυμι, θήρ) *destroying wild beasts.*

ὀλεσίμ-βροτος, ον, (ὄλλυμι, βροτός) *man-destroying.*

ὀλεσι-τύραννος, ον, poët. **ὀλεσσιτ-**, (ὄλλυμι, τύραννος) *destroying tyrants.*

ὀλέσκω, collat. form of ὄλλυμι.

ὀλέσσαι, ὀλέσσας, Ep. for ὀλέσαι, ὀλέσας.

ὄλεσσε, Ep. for ὤλεσε, 3 sing. aor. 1 of ὄλλυμι.

ὀλέσσει, Ep. for ὀλέσει, 3 sing. fut. of ὄλλυμι.

ὀλέσω, fut. of ὄλλυμι.

ὀλέτειρα, ἡ, fem. of ὀλετηρ, *a murderess.*

ὀλετήρ, ῆρος, ἡ, (ὄλλυμι) *a destroyer, murderer.*

ὀλέτις, ιδος, ἡ, = ὀλέτειρα.

ὄληαι, ὄληται, 2 and 3 sing. aor. 2 subj. med. of ὄλλυμι.

ὀλῐγάκῐς, Adv. (ὀλίγος) *but few times, seldom.* [ᾰ]

ὀλῐγ-άμπελος, ον, (ὀλίγος, ἄμπελος) *scant of vines.*

ὀλιγανδρέω, (ὀλίγανδρος) *to be scant of men.* Hence

ὀλιγανδρία, ἡ, *fewness of men.*

ὀλίγ-ανδρος, ον, (ὀλιγος, ἀνήρ) *scant of men.*

ὀλῐγανθρωπία, ἡ, *scantiness of people.* From

ὀλῐγ-άνθρωπος, ον, (ὀλίγος, ἄνθρωπος) *scant of people.*

ὀλῐγ-αρχέομαι, Pass. (ὀλίγοι, ἄρχω) *to be governed by a few, be subject to an oligarchy.* Hence

ὀλῐγαρχία, ἡ, *an oligarchy, government by a few families* or *persons.* Hence

ὀλῐγαρχικός, ή, όν, *oligarchical: inclined to oligarchy.*

ὀλῐγ-αῦλαξ, ἄκος, ὁ, ἡ, (ὀλίγος, αὖλαξ) *having few furrows, having but little land for ploughing.*

ὀλῐγᾰχόθεν, Adv. (ὀλίγος) *from few parts* or *places:* c. gen., ὀλιγαχόθεν τῆς Ἀσίης *from few parts* of Asia.

ὀλῐγηπελέων, εουσα, (participial form, as if from a pres. ὀλιγηπελέω), *having little power, powerless.* From

ὀλῐγη-πελής, ές, (ὀλίγος, πέλομαι) *powerless.* Hence

ὀλῐγηπελία Ion. -ίη, ἡ, *feebleness.*

ὀλῐγήριος, ον, = ὀλίγος, *small, little.*

ὀλῐγ-ηροσίη, ἡ, (ὀλίγος, ἄροσις) *want of arable land.*

ὀλῐγη-σίπῡος, ον, (ὀλίγος, σιπύα) *with a small cornbin: with little corn.*

ὀλίγιστος, η, ον, irreg. Sup. of ὀλίγος, *least.*

ὀλιγογονία, ἡ, *scantiness of produce, barrenness,* From

ὀλῐγό-γονος, ον, (ὀλίγος, *γένω) *producing little, unfruitful, barren.*

ὀλῐγοδρᾰνέων, εουσα, participial form, as if from a pres. ὀλιγοδρανέω, *able to do little, feeble, powerless.* From

ὀλῐγο-δρᾰνής, ές, (ὀλιγος, δραίνω) *of little strength, powerless.* Hence

ὀλῐγοδρᾰνία, ἡ, *feebleness.*

ὀλῐγο-έτης, ες, (ὀλίγος, ἔτος) *of few years.* Hence

ὀλῐγοετία, ἡ, *fewness of years, youthfulness.*

ὀλῐγό-ξῠλος, ον, (ὀλίγος, ξύλον) *with little wood.*

ὀλῐγό-πιστος, ον, (ὀλίγος, πίστις) *of little faith.*

ὈΛΙ΄ΓΟΣ, η, ον, of Number or Quantity, *few, little,* opp. to πολύς.—The governing body in Oligarchies was called οἱ ὀλίγοι, *the Few,* opp. to τὸ πλῆθος or οἱ πολλοί (*the Many, the People*). 2. c. inf. *too few to* do a thing. II. of Size, *small, little,* opp. to μέγας: the neut. ὀλίγον as Adv., *little, a little, in a small degree:* so also dat. ὀλίγῳ. III. special phrases: ὀλίγου δεῖ there wants *but little,* i. e. *almost;* c. inf., ὀλίγου ἐδέησε καταλαβεῖν it wanted *but little* to overtake, *all but* overtook: hence ὀλίγου alone (δεῖ being omitted), *within a little, all but, nearly, almost.* 2. δι' ὀλίγου, *at a short distance;* or of Time *after a short space, shortly after:*—but δι' ὀλίγων *in few words.* 3. ἐν ὀλίγῳ, *in a small compass;* and of Time, *in short, briefly:* also, like ὀλίγου, *almost.* 4. ἐς ὀλίγον, = παρ' ὀλίγον. 5. κατ' ὀλίγον *by little and little:* but the Adj. is often put in the gender and number of its Subst., as, οὗτοι κατ' ὀλίγους γιγνόμενοι ἐμάχοντο these fought forming themselves *into small parties.* 6. παρ' ὀλίγον, *within a little, all but, almost.* IV. Degrees of Comparison:—μείων, ον, gen. ονος, as also ἐλάσσων, is used for the Comp- 2. Sup. ὀλίγιστος, η, ον: ὀλιγίστου, genit. used Adv. (see ὀλίγος III) *very nearly*.

ὀλῐγοστῐχία, ἡ, *the consisting of few lines*. From

ὀλῐγό-στῐχος, ον, (ὀλίγος, στίχος) *consisting of few lines* or *verses*.

ὀλῐγοστός, ή, όν, (ὀλίγος) *one out of a few*, opp. to πολλοστός.

ὀλιγότης, ητος, ἡ, (ὀλίγος) *fewness, smallness*.

ὀλιγοτροφέω, *to give little nourishment*. From

ὀλιγο-τρόφος, ον. (ὀλίγος, τρέφω) *giving little nourishment*.

ὀλιγο-φιλία, ἡ, (ὀλίγος, φίλος) *fewness of friends*.

ὀλῐγο-χρόνιος, ον, also α, ον, (ὀλίγος, χρόνος) *lasting but little time, of short duration*.

ὀλιγοψυχέω (ὀλιγόψυχος), *to be faint-hearted*. Hence

ὀλιγοψυχία, ἡ, *faint-heartedness*.

ὀλῐγό-ψῡχος, ον, (ὀλίγος, ψυχή) *faint-hearted*.

ὀλῐγ-ῶλαξ, ἄκος, ὁ, ἡ, = ὀλιγαύλαξ.

ὀλῐγωρέω, f. ήσω, (ὀλίγωρος) *to regard lightly, make small account of*, c. gen. Hence

ὀλῐγωρία, ἡ, *a regarding lightly, slighting, contempt*.

ὀλίγ-ωρος, ον, (ὀλίγος, ὥρα) *little caring, lightly regarding, slighting, despising, contemptuous*. Hence

ὀλιγώρως, Adv. *carelessly*; ὀλιγώρως ἔχειν or διακεῖσθαι to be *careless, heedless*. [ῐ]

ὀλίγως, Adv. of ὀλίγος, *a little*.

ὀλισθάνω and later -αίνω: fut. ὀλισθήσω: aor. 1 ὠλίσθησα: pf. ὠλίσθηκα: aor. 2 ὤλισθον, part. ὀλισθών, inf. ὀλισθεῖν: (ὄλισθος):—*to slip, slide, fall suddenly*; νηὸς ὀλισθὼν *having slipped* from the ship.

ὄλισθε, Ep. for ὤλισθε, 3 sing. aor. 2 of ὀλισθάνω.

ὀλισθεῖν, aor. 2 inf. of ὀλισθάνω.

ὀλισθήεις, εσσα, εν, = ὀλισθηρός.

ὀλίσθημα, ματος, τό, (ὀλισθεῖν) *a slip, fall*.

ὀλισθηρός, ά, όν, (ὀλισθεῖν) *slippery, sliding*.

ὀλισθο-γνωμονέω (ὀλισθεῖν, γνώμη), *to make a slip* or *error in judgment*.

ὌΛΙΣΘΟΣ, ὁ, *slipperiness: a slip*.

ὁλκάς, άδος, ἡ, (ἕλκω, ὁλκή) *a ship which is towed, a ship of burthen, merchantman, trading vessel*.

ὁλκή, ἡ, (ἕλκω) *a drawing, trailing, dragging*. II. *a being drawn towards* a thing, *attraction*.

ὁλκός, ή, όν, (ἕλκω) *attractive*.

ὁλκός, οῦ, ὁ, (ἕλκω) as an Instrument, *that which draws* or *hauls*; ὁλκοί *machines for hauling* ships on land. 2. *a strap* or *trace for drawing*. II. *a track made by drawing, a furrow, track*, Lat. *sulcus: the trail* of a serpent. III. periphr., ὁλκοὶ δάφνης *drawings of* laurel, i. e. laurel-boughs *drawn along*.

ὌΛΛΥΜΙ and **ὀλλύω**: impf. ὤλλυν: f. ὀλέσω Ep. ὀλέσσω Ion. ὀλέω Att. ὀλῶ: aor. 1 ὤλεσα Ep. ὤλεσσα, ὄλεσσα: pf. ὀλώλεκα:—Med. ὄλλῠμαι, Ion. fut. ὀλέομαι Att. ὀλοῦμαι: aor. 2 ὠλόμην: pf. 2 ὄλωλα: plqpf. ὠλώλειν:—οὐλόμενος, properly aor. 2 part. med. for ὀλόμενος, became a mere Adj., v. sub voce. I. Act. *to destroy, make an end of, to kill*. 2. *to lose*.—The Act. corresponds in its two senses to Lat. *perdere*. II. Med. *to perish, come to an end, die*: ὄλοιο, ὄλοιτο, ὄλοισθε, etc., *may'st thou, may he, may ye perish!*—*to be undone, ruined*. 2. so pf. 2 ὄλωλα, *I am undone, ruined*; οἱ ὀλωλότες *the dead*.

ὀλλύς, ῦσα, ύν, pres. part. of ὄλλυμι.

ὅλμος, ὁ, (εἴλω, Lat. *volvo*) *a round smooth stone, a roller*. 2. *a mortar*. 3. *a kneading-trough*.

ὀλόεις, εσσα, εν, = ὀλοός, *destructive*.

ὀλοθρευτής, οῦ, ὁ, (ὀλοθρεύω) *a destroyer*.

ὀλοθρεύω, f. εύσω, (ὄλεθρος) *to destroy*.

ὀλοίῐος, ον, poët. for sq., like ὁμοίῐος for ὅμοιος.

ὀλοιός, όν, poët. for ὀλοός, *destructive*.

ὀλοί-τροχος or **ὁλοί-τροχος**, ὁ, Ep. **ὀλοοί-τροχος**, (prob. from εἴλω *volvo*, τρόχος) *a rolling stone, a round stone*, such as the besieged rolled down on the enemy: also as Adj. *round, globular*.

ὁλοκαυτέω, f. ήσω, *to bring a burnt-offering*. From

ὁλό-καυτος, ον, (ὅλος, καίω) *burnt whole*: as Subst., ὁλόκαυτον, τό, *a burnt-offering*. Hence

ὁλοκαυτόω, f. ώσω, *to burn whole: to make a burnt-offering*. Hence

ὁλοκαύτωμα, ατος, τό, *a whole burnt-offering*.

ὁλοκληρία, ἡ, *soundness in all parts*. From

ὁλό-κληρος, ον, (ὅλος, κλῆρος) *complete in all parts, entire, sound, perfect*, Lat. *integer*.

ὀλολῡγή, ἡ, (ὀλολύζω) *any loud crying*, esp. of women, Lat. *ululatus*: usually *a cry of joy*; but also of *lamentation*.

ὀλόλυγμα, ατος, τό, (ὀλολύζω) *a loud cry*, usually of *joy*.

ὀλολυγμός, οῦ, ὁ, (ὀλολύζω) *a loud crying*, usually in honour of the gods, expressive of joy.

ὀλολῡγών, όνος, ἡ, an animal, named from its note, *the tree-frog*. From

ὀλολύζω, f. -ύξομαι: aor. ὠλόλυξα:—*to cry aloud to the gods*, usually of female voices, Lat. *ululare*. II. *to utter a loud cry*, usually in sign of joy. (Formed from the sound.)

ὀλόμην, ὄλοντο, Ep. for ὠλ-, aor. 2 med. of ὄλλυμι.

ὀλοοί-τροχος, ὁ, poët. form of ὀλοίτροχος.

ὀλοός poët. **ὀλοιός**, **ὀλοίϊος**, η, ον, (ὄλλυμι) *destructive, destroying, hurtful, deadly*; ὀλοὰ φρονεῖν to design *ill*:—Comp. and Sup. **ὀλοώτερος**, ὀλοώτατος. II. pass. *destroyed, lost, undone*, Lat. *perditus*.

ὀλοό-φρων, ονος, ὁ and ἡ, (ὀλοός, φρήν) *meaning mischief, baleful*. II. *crafty, sagacious*.

ὀλόπτω, f. ψω, *to pull, pluck out: to strip off*. (Akin to λοπός, λέπω.)

ὍΛΟΣ Ep. **οὖλος**, η, ον, *whole, entire, complete*, Lat. *solus, solidus*; τὰ ὅλα *one's all*. 2. *entire, utter*; ὅλον ἁμάρτημα an *utter* blunder: in neut., as Adv., ὅλον and τὸ ὅλον *altogether*. II. *whole*, i. e. *safe and sound*, Lat. *integer*.

ὁλο-σφύρητος Dor. -σφύρᾱτος, ον, (ὅλος, σφύρα) *hammered all through, made of solid metal*, opp. to cast.

ὀλο-σχερής, *ές*, (ὅλος, σχερός) *whole, entire, sound, complete*, Lat. *integer*. 2. *relating to the whole, important, considerable.* II. Adv. -ρῶς, *completely, entirely.*

ὀλο-τελής, *ές*, (ὅλος, τέλος) *quite complete, perfect.*

ὀλοῦμαι, fut. med. of ὄλλυμι.

ὀλο-φυγδών, *όνος*, ἡ, (ὅλος, φύω) *a large pimple, pustule.*

ὀλοφυδνός, ή, όν, (ὀλοφύρομαι) *lamenting, wailing:*—neut. pl. ὀλοφυδνά, as Adv., *miserably.*

ὀλοφυρμός, οῦ, ὁ, *a lamenting, lamentation.* From

'ΟΛΟΦΥ'ΡΟΜΑΙ [ῠ], Dep.: f. ὀλοφῠροῦμαι: aor. 1 ὠλοφυράμην, Ep. 2 and 3 sing. ὀλοφύραο, ὀλοφύρατο: aor. 1 part. pass. ὀλοφυρθείς, in same sense. I. intr. *to lament, wail, moan, weep.* 2. *to lament* or *mourn for others, to feel pity:* c. gen. *to have pity upon.* 3. *to beg with tears and lamentations.* II. c. acc. *to lament over, bewail, weep for, mourn.* 2. *to pity.* Hence

ὀλόφυρσις, ἡ, *lamentation.*

ὀλοφώιος, *ον*, lengthd. for ὀλοός, ὀλοιός, *destructive, deadly;* ὀλοφώια εἰδώς versed in *pernicious* arts

ὌΛΠΗ, ἡ, *a leathern oil-flask*, used in the *palaestra.*

ὌΛΠΙΣ, *ιος* and *ιδος*, ἡ, = ὄλπη.

'Ολυμπία, ἡ, *Olympia*, a district of Elis round the city of Pisa, where the Olympic games were held: properly fem. of 'Ολύμπιος (sub. γῆ or χώρα).

'Ολύμπια, *τά, the Olympic games*, established by Hercules and renewed by Iphitus, held at intervals of four years in honour of *Olympian Zeus* by the Greeks assembled at *Olympia* in Elis; 'Ολύμπια νικᾶν to conquer *at the Olympic games:* also, 'Ολύμπια ἀνελέσθαι or ἀναιρηκέναι to have carried off the prize *at the Olympic games.*

'Ολυμπιάζε, Adv. ('Ολυμπία, η) *to Olympia.*

'Ολυμπίαθεν, Adv. ('Ολυμπία, ἡ) *from Olympia.*

'Ολυμπιάς, *άδος*, ἡ, pecul. fem. of 'Ολύμπιος, *Olympian*, epith. of the Muses: generally, *a dweller on Olympus, a goddess.* 2. 'Ολυμπιὰς ἐλαία the olive-crown *of the Olympic games.* II. as Subst., 1. *the Olympic games.* 2. *a victory at Olympia* (sub. νίκη); 'Ολυμπιάδα ἀναιρεῖσθαι, νικᾶν to gain a victory in the *Olympic games.* 3. *an Olympiad*, i. e. the space of four years between the celebrations of the Olympic games: the first Olympiad begins 776 B. C.

'Ολυμπίασι, Adv. ('Ολυμπία, ἡ) *at Olympia:* cf. θύρᾱσι.

'Ολυμπιασι [ᾰ], dat. pl. of 'Ολυμπιάς.

'Ολυμπιεῖον or **'Ολυμπίειον**, *τό*, ('Ολύμπιος) *the temple of Olympian Zeus.*

'Ολυμπικός, ή, όν, ("Ολυμπος) *Olympic;* ὁ 'Ολυμπικὸς ἀγών *the Olympic* games.

'Ολυμπῐο-νίκης, *ου*, ὁ, ('Ολύμπια, νικάω) *a conqueror in the Olympic games.* [νῑ]

'Ολυμπιό-νῑκος, *ον*, ('Ολύμπια, νικάω) *conquering in the Olympic games.*

'Ολύμπιος, *ον*, ("Ολυμπος) *Olympian, dwelling on Olympus*, epith. of the gods above, esp. of Jove, who is called also simply 'Ολύμπιος; 'Ολύμπια δώματα the mansions of *Olympus.*

"Ολυμπόνδε Ep. Οὔλ-, Adv. *to* or *towards Olympus.*

"Ολυμπος Ep. and Ion. **Οὔλυμπος**, ὁ, *Olympus*, a high wall on the Macedonian frontier of Thessaly. It was believed to be the abode of the gods, and that the approach was guarded by a thick cloud.

'ΟΛΥΝΘΟΣ, ὁ, *a fig* which grows during the winter, but seldom ripens: *an untimely fig*, Lat. *grossus.*

"ΟΛΥΡΑ, ἡ, mostly in pl., *a kind of grain, spelt*, mentioned as food for horses along with barley (κρῖ); used in Egypt for *making bread.*

ὀλώιος, collat. form of ὀλοός, ὀλοιός.

ὄλωλα, pf. med. of ὄλλυμι.

ὀλώλεκα, pf. of ὄλλυμι.

ὅλως, Adv. of ὅλος, *wholly, altogether, on the whole: in short*, Lat. *denique:* οὐχ ὅλως *not at all*, Lat. *omnino non.*

ὁμᾶ, Adv. Dor. for ὁμῆ.

ὁμᾰδέω, f. ήσω, (ὅμαδος) *to make a noise* or *din.*

ὅμᾰδος, ὁ, (ὁμός) *a noise, din, made by many voices together.* II. *a tumultuous crowd, throng.* III. *the din of battle, the battle-throng.*

ὁμαίμιος, *ον, related by blood, kindred.* From

ὅμ-αιμος, *ον*, (ὁμός, αἷμα) *of the same blood, related by blood, akin*, Lat. *consanguineus:* as Subst., ὅμαιμος, ὁ, ἡ, *a brother* or *sister.* Hence

ὁμαιμοσύνη, ἡ, *relationship by blood.*

ὁμ-αίμων, *ον*, gen. *ονος*, = ὅμαιμος:—Comp. ὁμαιμονέστερος, *more nearly akin.*

ὁμαιχμία, ἡ, *a fighting together: a defensive alliance, league.* From

ὅμ-αιχμος, *ον*, (ὁμός, αἰχμή) *fighting together:* as Subst., ὅμαιχμος, ὁ, *an ally.*

ὁμᾰλής, *ές*, (ὁμαλός) *even, level:* τὰ ὁμαλῆ *level ground.*

ὁμᾰλίζω, .. σω, (ὁμαλός) *to make even* or *level, to level: to equalise.*

ὁμᾰλός, ή, όν, (ὁμός) *even, level;* τὸ ὁμαλόν *level ground.* 2. *of equal, like degree;* ὁμαλὸς γάμος marriage *with one of like degree.* 3. metaph. *middling, average, ordinary.* Hence

ὁμαλότης, *ητος*, ἡ, *evenness, equality.*

ὁμαλῶς (ὁμαλός), Adv. *evenly;* ὁμαλῶς βαίνειν to march *in even line.*

ὁμ-αρτέω: impf. ὡμάρτουν Ion. -ευν: f. ὁμαρτήσω: aor. 1 ὡμάρτησα: (ὁμοῦ, ἀρτάω):—*to meet;* 1. in hostile sense, *to meet in fight:*—Med. *to attack in fight* 2. *to walk together*, esp. in part., βῆσαν ὁμαρτήσαντες they walked *in company: to keep pace, equal in speed:* c. dat. *to walk beside, accompany* 3. *to pursue.*

ὁμαρτῇ or **ὁμαρτῆ**. Adv. *together, jointly*, another form of ἁμαρτῇ, ἁμαρτῆ.

ὁμάρτη, Dor. for ὁμάρτει, 3 sing. impf. of ὁμαρτέω.

ὁμαρτήσαντο, Ep. for ὡμ-, 3 pl. aor. 1 med. of ὁμαρτέω.

ὁμαρτήσειεν, 3 sing. Ep. aor. 1 opt. of ὁμαρτέω.

ὁμαρτήτην, Ep. for ὡμ–, 3 dual impf. of ὁμαρτέω.

ὅμ-ασπις, ιδος, ὁ, ἡ, (ὁμοῦ, ἀσπίς) *allied in arms:* as Subst., ὅμασπις, ὁ, *a comrade, fellow-soldier.*

ὁμ-αῦλαξ, ἄκος, ὁ, ἡ, (ὁμοῦ, αὖλαξ) *with adjoining furrows* or *lands.*

ὁμαυλία, ἡ, *a dwelling together, union.* From

ὅμ-αυλος, ον, (ὁμοῦ, αὐλή) *living together:* hence, *neighbouring.*

ὅμ-αυλος, ον, (ὁμοῦ, αὐλός) *playing together on the flute, harmonious, blending, in unison.*

ὀμβρέω, f. ήσω, (ὄμβρος) *to rain.* II. trans. *to rain* or *shower down upon: to bedew, wet.*

ὀμβρηρός, ά, όν, (ὄμβρος) *rainy, watery.*

ὀμβρῖμος, ον, = ὄβριμος.

ὄμβριος, ον, also α, ον, (ὄμβρος) *rainy: of* or *belonging to rain,* Lat. *pluvialis;* ὕδωρ ὄμβριον rain-water.

ὀμβρο-δόκος, ον, (ὄμβρος, δέχομαι) *holding* or *receiving rain.*

ὀμβρο-κτύπος, ον, (ὄμβρος, κτυπέω) *striking with rain.*

ὌΜΒΡΟΣ, ὁ, Lat. *IMBER, a storm of rain, a thunder-shower, rain.* 2. generally *water.* II. metaph. *a storm* or *shower* of tears, darts, etc.

ὀμβρο-φόρος, ον, (ὄμβρος, φέρω) *rain-bringing.*

ὀμεῖται, 3 sing. fut. of ὄμνυμι.

ὁμ-έστιος, ον, (ὁμοῦ, ἑστία) *sharing the same hearth.*

ὁμ-ευνέτης, ου, ὁ, fem. **ὁμευνέτις**, ιδος, = ὅμευνος.

ὅμ-ευνος, ον, (ὁμοῦ, εὐνή) *sleeping together:* as Subst., ὅμευνος, ὁ, ἡ, *a bedfellow, consort.*

ὁμ-έψιος, ὁ, ἡ, (ὁμοῦ, ἑψία) *a playmate.*

ὁμῆ or **ὁμῇ**, Adv. (ὁμός) poët. for ὁμοῦ.

ὁμ-ηγερής, ές, (ὁμός, ἀγείρω) *assembled together.*

ὁμηγυρίζομαι, f. ίσομαι, Dep. *to assemble, call together.* From

ὁμ-ήγυρις Dor. **ὁμάγ–**, ιος, ἡ, (ὁμός, ἄγυρις) *an assembly, meeting: a throng, company.*

ὁμηλικία Ion. –ίη, ἡ, (ὁμῆλιξ) *equality of age:*— as Collective Subst. *those of the same age, one's friends, playmates, comrades.* II. of a single person, = ὁμῆλιξ.

ὁμ-ῆλιξ, ικος, ὁ, ἡ, (ὁμοῦ, ἧλιξ) *of the same age,* esp. of young persons: as Subst. *an equal in age, comrade, playmate.* II. *of like stature.*

ὁμηρεία, ἡ, (ὁμηρεύω) *a giving hostages* or *securities: a security, pledge.*

Ὁμήρειος, α, ον, (Ὅμηρος) *of Homer, Homeric.*

ὁμηρεῦσαι, Ion. for ὁμηροῦσαι, part. fem. pl. of ὁμηρέω.

ὁμηρεύω, f. σω, (ὅμηρος) *to be a hostage, serve as a pledge* or *hostage.* II. trans. *to give as a hostage, pledge* or *security.*

ὁμηρέω, f. ήσω, (ὅμηρος) *to meet.* 2. metaph. *to accord, agree.*

Ὁμηρίδης, ου, ὁ, mostly in plur. Ὁμηρίδαι, οἱ, *the Homerids,* a family of poets in Chios, who pretended to trace their descent from Homer, and recited his poems: generally, *the admirers of Homer.*

ὅμ-ηρος, ον, (ὁμοῦ, ἀραρεῖν) *joined together, united, wedded.* II. as Subst., ὅμηρος, ὁ, *a pledge to preserve peace, a surety, security, hostage.*

ὁμῑλᾰδόν, Adv. (ὅμιλος) *in groups, bands,* Lat. *turmatim: in crowds.*

ὁμῑλέω, f. ήσω: aor. 1 ὡμίλησα: (ὅμιλος):—*to be together* or *in company with;* μετ' Ἀχαιοῖς ὁμιλεῖν *to associate* with the Achaeans; ἐνὶ πρωτοῖσιν ὁμιλεῖν *to be in company* among the foremost; περὶ νεκρὸν ὁμιλεῖν *to throng* about the corpse. 2. absol. *to come* or *live together.* II. in hostile sense, *to meet in battle, encounter:* absol. *to meet one another.* III. of social intercourse, *to hold converse: to live familiarly with, associate with: to have dealings with.* 2. absol. *to be friends.* IV. of pursuits or business, *to be conversant with, engaged in, attend to.* 2. of things, *to be present to one, to be at hand.* V. of a place, *to come into, be in: to haunt, frequent* a spot.

ὁμῑληδόν, Adv. = ὁμιλαδόν.

ὁμῑλήσειν, fut. inf. of ὁμιλέω.

ὁμῑλητής, οῦ, ὁ, (ὁμιλέω) *a scholar, hearer.*

ὁμῑλητός, ή, όν, (ὁμιλέω) *to be conversed with;* οὐχ ὁμιλητός *unapproachable, savage.*

ὁμῑλία, ἡ, (ὅμιλος) *a being* or *living together, intercourse, converse, dealings with another;* ἡ ἐμὴ ὁμιλία *converse* with me; ὁμιλία χθονός *intercourse with* a country. 2. *instruction.* II. *a meeting, assembly;* ναὸς ὁμιλία ship-*mates.*

ὅμ-ῑλος, ὁ, (ὁμοῦ, ἴλη) *an assembled crowd, a throng of people, mob, multitude.* II. *the throng of battle, tumult.*

ὀμιχέω, f. ήσω, = ὀμίχω.

ὈΜΙ´ΧΛΗ Ion. ὀμίχλη Dor. **ὀμίχλα**, ἡ, *misty air, a mist, fog.* II. also *smoke, steam.* Hence

ὀμιχλήεις Ion. **ὀμιχλ–**, εσσα, εν, *misty.*

ὈΜΙ´ΧΩ, *to make water,* Lat. *MINGO.* [ῐ]

ὄμμα, ατος, τό, (ὦμμαι, pf. pass. of ὁράω) *the eye;* ὄμματι λοξῷ ἰδεῖν to look *with eye* askance at; opp. to ὀρθοῖς ὄμμασιν ὁρᾶν or ἐξ ὀρθῶν ὀμμάτων, Lat. *rectis oculis videre,* to look straight at; κατ' ὄμμα *face to face, in full sight;* ὡς ἀπ' ὀμμάτων to judge by *the eye,* Lat. *ex obtutu;* ἐν ὄμμασι, Lat. *in oculis,* before one's *eyes;* so also παρ' ὄμμα, πρὸ ὀμμάτων; ἐξ ὀμμάτων out of *sight.* II. *that which one sees, a sight.* 2. *a phantom, image of fancy.* III. ὄμμα νυκτός, i. e. *the moon;* so ὄμμα αἰθέρος, of *the sun;* generally, *light;* ὄμμα φήμης *the light* of happy tidings. IV. metaph. *anything dear* or *precious.* V. periphr. of the person, ὄμμα πελείας for πελεία, ὄμμα νύμφας for νύμφα; cf. κάρα. Hence

ὀμμάτιον, τό, Dim. of ὄμμα, *a little eye.*

ὀμμᾰτο-στερής, ές, (ὄμμα, στερέω) *deprived of eyes.* II. act. *depriving of eyes: blighting, cankering,* esp. the buds of plants.

ὀμμᾰτόω, f. ώσω: pf. pass. ὠμμάτωμαι: (ὄμμα):—*to give eyes to:*—Pass., φρὴν ὠμματωμένη a mind *quick of sight.* II. metaph. *to make distinct, explain.*

ΌΜΝΥΜΙ or **ὀμνύω**, imperat. ὄμνυθι or ὄμνυ, 3 pl. ὀμνύντων: impf. ὤμνυν or ὤμνυον: fut. ὀμοῦμαι, εῖ, εῖται, inf. ὀμεῖσθαι, later fut. ὀμόσω: aor. 1 ὤμοσα Ep. ὄμοσα, ὄμοσσα: pf. ὀμώμοκα: plqpf. ὀμωμόκειν: —Pass., aor. 1 ὠμόσθην or ὠμόθην: pf. ὀμώμοσμαι, 3 pers. ὀμώμοσται or ὀμώμοται:—*to swear; ὅρκον ὀμόσαι to swear* an oath: *to swear to* a thing, *affirm, confirm by oath:* foll. by inf. *to swear that one will ..:* ἦ μήν is often inserted before the inf. for the sake of emphasis; freq. in part., as, εἰπεῖν ὀμόσας to say *with an oath.* II. *to call as witness of an oath, invoke, swear by.*

ὁμο-βώμιος, ον, (ὁμοῦ, βωμός) *having one common altar,* like Ceres and Proserpine.

ὁμο-γάλαξ, ακτος, ὁ, ἡ, (ὁμός, γάλα) *suckled with the same milk: a clansman.*

ὁμό-γᾰμος, ον, (ὁμοῦ, γαμέω) *married together,* as Subst. *a husband* or *wife.*

ὁμο-γάστριος, ον, (ὁμός, γαστήρ) *from the same womb, born of the same mother; κασίγνητος ὁμόγαστρος* an *uterine* brother.

ὁμο-γενέτωρ, ορος, ὁ, *born of the same parents a brother.* From

ὁμο-γενής, ές, (ὁμοῦ, *γένω) *of the same family:* generally, *kindred, akin.* II. act. *engendering with.*

ὁμο-γέρων, οντος, ὁ, (ὁμοῦ, γέρων) *a contemporary in old age.*

ὁμογλωσσέω Att. **-γλωττέω**, *to speak the same tongue.* From

ὁμό-γλωσσος Att. **-γλωττος**, ον, (ὁμός, γλῶσσα) *speaking the same tongue* or *language with.*

ὁμό-γνιος, ον, contr. for ὁμογένιος, (ὁμοῦ, γένος) *of the same race.* II. *presiding over kindred; ὁμόγνιοι θεοί* gods *who protect a race* or *family,* Lat. *Dii gentilitii.*

ὁμογνωμονέω, f. ήσω, *to be of one mind, to league together: to agree with, assent to.* From

ὁμο-γνώμων, ον, gen. ονος, (ὁμοῦ, γνώμη) *of one mind, like-minded.* Adv. -μόνως.

ὁμό-γονος, ον, (ὁμοῦ, γονή) *of the same family.*

ὁμό-γραμμος, ον, (ὁμοῦ, γραμμή) *of* or *with the same letters.*

ὁμό-δᾱμος, Dor. for ὁμόδημος.

ὁμο-δέμνιος, ον, (ὁμοῦ, δέμνιον) *sharing one's bed,*

ὁμό-δημος Dor. **-δαμος**, ον, (ὁμός, δῆμος) *of the same people* or *race.*

ὁμοδοξέω, *to be of the same opinion, to agree.* From

ὁμό-δοξος, ον, (ὁμοῦ, δόξα) *of the same opinion.*

ὁμό-δουλος, ον, (ὁμοῦ, δοῦλος) *a fellow-slave.*

ὁμο-δρομία, ἡ, (ὁμοῦ, δρόμος) *a running together* or *meeting.*

ὁμο-εθνής, ές, (ὁμοῦ, ἔθνος) *of the same nation.*

ὁμό-ζῠγος, ον, (ὁμοῦ, ζυγῆναι) *yoked together:* as Subst. *a yoke-fellow.* II. *yoked in wedlock, married.*

ὁμο-ήθης, ές, (ὁμοῦ, ἦθος) *of the same character.*

ὁμο-ῆλιξ, ῐκος, ὁ, ἡ, (ὁμοῦ, ἧλιξ) *of the same age,* Lat. *aequalis.*

ὁμόθεν, Adv. (ὁμός) *from the same place, of the same origin: ὁ ὁμόθεν a brother.* II. *from near at hand, hand to hand: close upon.*

ὁμό-θρονος, ον, (ὁμοῦ, θρόνος) *sharing the same throne, partner of one's throne.*

ὁμοθῡμᾰδόν, Adv. *with one accord.* From

ὁμό-θῡμος, ον, (ὁμοῦ, θυμός) *of one mind, unanimous.*

ὁμοιάζω, f. σω, (ὅμοιος) *to be like, resemble.*

ὁμοίῐος, Ep. for ὅμοιος. [ῐ Ep.]

ὁμοιο-κατάληκτος, ον, (ὅμοιος, καταλήγω) *ending alike,* of verses.

ὁμοιοπᾰθέω, f. ήσω, *to be in like case, to be similarly affected, sympathise.* From.

ὁμοιο-πᾰθής, ές, (ὅμοιος, πάθος) *being in like case, having like affections, sympathising.*

ὁμοιο-πρεπής, ές, (ὅμοιος, πρέπω) *of like appearance with.*

ὅμοιος, α, ον, Ion. and old Att. **ὁμοῖος**, η, ον, Att. also ος, ον; Ep. **ὁμοίῐος**, ον: (ὁμός):—*like, resembling,* Lat. *similis:* Proverbs, ὡς αἰεὶ τὸν ὁμοῖον ἄγει θεὸς ὡς τὸν ὁμοῖον 'birds of a feather flock together;' τὸ ὁμοῖον ἀνταποδιδόναι, Lat. *par pari referre,* to give *like for like,* pay *tit for tat.* 2. *shared alike, common, mutual.* 3. *equal in force, a match for* one, Lat. *par.* 4. *in unison with, agreeing.* . ἡ ὁμοία (sub. δίκη or χάρις), τὴν ὁμοίαν διδόναι, ἀποδιδόναι to pay any one *like for like,* to make *a like* return; τὴν ὁμοίαν φέρεσθαι to have *a like return* made one; ἐπ' ἴσῃ καὶ ὁμοίᾳ on fair and *equal* terms. 6. ἐν ὁμοίῳ ποιεῖσθαί τι to hold a thing *in like esteem.* II. *of the same rank* or *station;* οἱ ὅμοιοι, all citizens *with equal privileges: peers.*—*The person* or *thing to which another is like* is commonly in dat., but also like Lat. *similis* in genit.:—also followed by a Relat., ὅμοιος ὥσπερ .., *like* as ..; ὅμοιος καὶ .., Lat. *aeque ac* .., *like as* ..; cf. ὁμοίως.

ὁμοιότης, ητος, ἡ, (ὅμοιος) *likeness, similitude.*

ὁμοιό-τροπος, ον, (ὅμοιος, τρόπος) *of like manners and life.* Adv. -πως, *in like manner with.*

ὁμοιόω, f. ώσω: aor. 1 ὡμοίωσα:—Pass. and Med., ὁμοιώσομαι and -ωθήσομαι (in same sense): aor. 1 ὡμοιώθην: (ὅμοιος):—*to make like, assimilate:* esp. *to liken, compare:*—Pass. *to be made like, become like,* ὁμοιωθήμεναι ἄντην *to be made like* before one. II. Med. *to make a like return.* Hence

ὁμοιωθήμεναι, Ep. for ὁμοιωθῆναι, aor. 1 inf. pass. of ὁμοιόω.

ὁμοίωμα, ατος, τό, *that which is made like, a likeness, image.*

ὁμοίως, Adv. of ὅμοιος, *in like manner, like, alike:* the neuters ὅμοιον and ὅμοια, Ion. ὁμοῖον, ὁμοῖα, were also common as Adv.:—ὁμοίως ὡς .., *like as* ..; so, ὁμοίως καὶ .., Lat. *aeque ac* .. *perinde ac* ..; ὅμοιον ὥστε .., *like* as; ὅμοια τοῖς μάλιστα *on a par* with the best.

ὁμοίωσις, ἡ, (ὁμοιόω) *a making like, likening.* I. *a becoming like.* 2. *a likeness, image.*

ὁμό-κλαρος, Dor. for ὁμόκληρος.

ὁμο-κλάω, 3 sing. impf. ὁμόκλᾱ, = ὁμοκλέω.

ὁμοκλέω, f. ήσω: aor. 1 ὁμόκλησα, Ion. 3 sing. ὁμοκλήσασκε :—*to call out, shout to*, either *to encourage, cheer on*, or *to upbraid, chide;* mostly in latter sense: c. inf. *to command with a loud shout, call to* one *to do.* From

ὁμο-κλή, ἡ, (ὁμοῦ, καλέω) *a calling out together, shouting of several persons: the harmony* or *concert* of flutes: *any loud calling* or *shouting*, whether *to encourage* or *upbraid.*

ὁμό-κληρος, ον, (ὁμοῦ, κλῆρος) *having an equal lot, share* or *portion*, esp. of an inheritance: as Subst., ὁμόκληρος, ὁ, *a coheir*, Lat. *consors.*

ὁμοκλήσασκε, 3 sing. Ion. aor. 1 of ὁμοκλέω.

ὁμοκλητήρ, ῆρος, ὁ, (ὁμοκλέω) *one who calls out to, a cheerer on, encourager.*

ὁμό-κλῑνος, ον, (ὁμοῦ, κλίνη) *reclining on the same couch* at table.

ὁμό-λεκτρος, ον, (ὁμοῦ, λέκτρον) *sharing the same bed.*

ὁμολογέω, f. ήσω: aor. 1 ὡμολόγησα: pf. ὡμολόγηκα:—Pass., aor. 1 ὡμολογήθην: pf. ὡμολόγημαι: (ὁμόλογος):—*to speak together, to speak one language.* 2. *to hold the same language, to agree with:* of things, *to be in accordance with.* *to make an agreement, come to terms*, esp. of a surrender; ἐπί τισι on certain terms. *to agree to a thing, allow, admit, confess;* ὁμολογῶ σοι *I grant you.* 5. *to agree, promise to* do. 6. *to be connected with, bear affinity to.* II. Med. *to agree, assent to;* much like the Act. III. Pass. *to be allowed* or *granted;* esp. in part. pres. τὰ ὁμολογούμενα and pf. part. ὡμολογημένα, *things granted, acknowledged principles.* Hence

ὁμολόγημα, ματος, τό, *a thing agreed on, a postulate;* and

ὁμολογία, ἡ, *agreement.* 2. *an agreement made, compact:* in war, *terms of surrender.* 3. *an assent, admission, confession.*

ὁμό-λογος, ον, (ὁμοῦ, λέγω) *assenting, agreeing, admitting.* 2. of things, *suitable, in accordance with:*—Adv. -γως, *confessedly, avowedly.*

ὁμολογουμένως, Adv. pres. part. pass. of ὁμολογέω, *agreeably, conformably to: confessedly, avowedly.*

ὁμο-μαστῑγίας, ου, ὁ, (ὁμοῦ, μάστιξ) *one flogged with another, a fellow-slave.*

ὁμο-μήτριος, α, ον, (ὁμοῦ, μήτηρ) *born of the same mother, an uterine brother* or *sister.*

ὁμό-νεκρος, ον, (ὁμοῦ, νεκρός) *companion in death.*

ὁμονοέω, f. ήσω, (ὁμόνοος) *to be of one mind, agree together, have sentiments in common.* Hence

ὁμονοητικός, ή, όν, *conducing to agreement.*

ὁμόνοια, ἡ, *sameness of mind, agreement in sentiments, unity*, Lat. *concordia.* From

ὁμό-νοος, ον, contr. **-νους**, ουν, (ὁμοῦ, νόος) *of one mind, agreeing in sentiments, unanimous*, Lat. *concors.* Adv., ὁμονόως, *unanimously.*

ὁμο-παθής, ές, (ὁμοῦ, πάθος) *having the same passions.*

ὁμο-πάτριος, ον, (ὁμοῦ, πατήρ) *by the same father.*

ὁμο-πλεκής, ές, (ὁμοῦ, πλέκω) *inter-laced.*

ὁμό-πλοος, ον, contr. **-πλους** ουν, (ὁμοῦ, πλόος) *sailing together* or *in company.*

ὁμό-πολις poët. **ὁμόπτολις**, εως, ὁ, ἡ, (ὁμοῦ, πόλις) *from the same city* or *state.*

ὁμό-πτερος, ον, (ὁμοῦ, πτέρον) *with the same plumage: of like feather, akin, alike:* generally, οἱ ὁμόπτεροι *birds of the same feather, comrades;* νᾶες ὁμόπτεροι *consort*-ships, i. e. *that sail in company.*

ὁμό-πτολις, poët. for ὁμόπολις.

ὀμοργάζω, = ὀμόργνυμι, *to wipe off.*

ὀμόργνυ, Ep. for ὠμόργνυ, 3 sing. impf. of

ὈΜΟ΄ΡΓΝΥ͂ΜΙ, fut. ὀμόρξω:—Med., aor. 1 ὠμορξάμην:—*to wipe, to wipe off, dry up:*—Med. *to dry for oneself;* δάκρυα ὀμόρξασθαι *to dry one's* tears.

ὀμορξάμενος, aor. 1 part. med. of ὀμόργνῡμι.

ὁμορέω Ion. **ὁμουρέω**, *to have the same boundaries with, to border on.* From

ὅμ-ορος Ion. **ὅμουρος**, ον, (ὁμοῦ, ὅρος) *having the same borders, bordering on*, Lat. *finitimus:*—as Subst., ὅμορος, ὁ, *a neighbour, borderer:* τὸ ὅμορον *neighbourhood.*

ὁμορροθέω, f. ήσω, *to row together:* generally, *to agree with, agree together.* And

ὁμορρόθιος, ον, *rowing* or *swimming together.* From

ὁμόρ-ροθος, ον, (ὁμοῦ, ῥοθέω) *rowing together:* generally, *acting together.*

ὉΜΟ΄Σ, ή, όν, *one and the same: belonging to two or more jointly, common, joint*, Lat. *communis.* (Akin to ἅμα: hence ὅμοιος, ὁμῶς, ὅμως, ὁμοῦ, ὁμῇ, ὁμόθεν, ὁμόσε.)

ὀμόσαι, **ὀμόσας**, aor. 1 inf. and part. of ὄμνυμι.

ὁμόσε, Adv. (ὁμός) *to one and the same place, to the same spot:* ὁμόσε ἰέναι, in hostile sense, to come *to close quarters*, Lat. *cominus pugnare;* ὁμόσε ἰέναι τοῖς ἐχθροῖς to go *to meet* the enemy.

ὁμο-σθενής, ές, (ὁμοῦ, σθένος) *of equal might.*

ὁμοσῑτέω, f. ήσω, *to eat* or *live together with.* From

ὁμό-σῑτος, ον, (ὁμοῦ, σῖτος) *eating together.*

ὁμό-σκευος, ον, (ὁμοῦ, σκευή) *arrayed in the same way.*

ὁμοσκηνία, ἡ, *a living in the same tent.* From

ὁμό-σκηνος, ον, (ὁμοῦ, σκηνή) *living in the same tent*, Lat. *contubernalis.*

ὁμο-σκηνόω, f. ώσω, *to live in the same tent with.*

ὁμό-σπλαγχνος, ον, (ὁμοῦ, σπλάγχνα) *from the same womb. of the same mother.*

ὁμό-σπονδος, ον, (ὁμοῦ, σπονδή) *sharing in the drink-offering, sharing the same cup: bound by treaty.*

ὁμό-σπορος, ον, (ὁμοῦ, σπείρω) *sown together sprung from the same parents* or *ancestors.*

ὀμόσσαι, **ὀμόσσας**, Ep. for ὀμόσαι, ὀμόσας.

ὁμο-στῐχάω, (ὁμοῦ, στείχω) *to walk together with.*

ὁμό-στολος, ον, (ὁμοῦ, στέλλω) *sent together with.*

in company with. II. (ὁμοῦ, στολή) *clad alike: of the same kind.*

ὁμό-τἄφος, ον, (ὁμοῦ, τάφος) *buried together.*

ὁμό-τεχνος, ον, (ὁμοῦ, τέχνη) *practising the same craft:* as Subst., ὁμότεχνος, ὁ, *a fellow-workman.*

ὁμό-τῑμος, ον, (ὁμοῦ, τιμή) *equally honoured, held in equal honour:* οἱ ὁμότιμοι among the Persians, *the chief nobles who were equal among themselves, the peers of the realm.*

ὁμό-τοιχος, ον, (ὁμοῦ, τοῖχος) *having one common wall, separated by a party wall:* metaph. *hardly different from.*

ὁμο-τράπεζος, ον, (ὁμοῦ, τράπεζα) *sitting* or *eating at the same table with*

ὁμό-τροπος, ον, (ὁμοῦ, τρόπος) *of the same habits:* ὁμότροπα ἤθεα *like* habits:—as Subst., ὁμότροπος, ὁ, *a comparison.*

ὁμό-τροφος, ον, (ὁμοῦ, τρέφω) *brought up* or *bred together with;* ὁμότροφα τοῖσι ἀνθρώποισι θηρία beasts *brought up with* men.

ὁμοῦ, Adv. (properly neut. gen. of ὁμός), *together,* of Place:—also *together, at once;* γαῖαν ὁμοῦ καὶ πόντον earth and sea *together* 2. *together with, along with;* c. dat., ὁμοῦ νεκύεσσι *with* or *among* the dead. 3. *near, hard by: nearly, almost.* 4. ὁμοῦ καί, *in like manner as, just like as,* Lat. *aeque ac.*

ὁμοῦμαι, fut. of ὄμνυμι.

ὁμουρέω, ὅμουρος, Ion. for ὁμορέω, ὅμορος.

ὁμό-φοιτος, ον, (ὁμοῦ, φοιτάω) *going together with:* as Subst., ὁμόφοιτος, ὁ, *a companion.*

ὁμοφρονέω, f. ήσω, (ὁμόφρων) *to be of one mind with;* πόλεμος ὁμοφρονέων a war *resolved on unanimously.*

ὁμοφροσύνη, ἡ, *a being of the same mind, unity.* From

ὁμό-φρων, ονος, ὁ, ἡ, (ὁμοῦ, φρήν) *of one mind, agreeing in sentiments, united.*

ὁμο-φυής, ές, (ὁμοῦ, φυή) *of the same age* or *nature.*

ὁμό-φῡλος, ον, (ὁμοῦ, φῦλον) *of the same race* or *people:* as Subst., ὁμόφυλοι, οἱ, *men of the same race:* τὸ ὁμόφυλον *sameness of race.*

ὁμοφωνέω, f. ήσω, *to speak the same language with.* 2. *to chime in with.* From

ὁμό-φωνος, ον, (ὁμοῦ, φωνή) *speaking the same language with.* 2. *agreeing in tone, in unison with.*

ὁμο-χροία, ἡ, (ὁμοῦ, χρόα) *sameness of colour.* II. *smoothness of surface: the surface, skin.*

ὁμοχρονέω, f. ήσω, *to keep time with.* From

ὁμόχρονος, ον, (ὁμοῦ, χρόνος) *of the same time with.*

ὁμό-χροος, ον, contr. **-χρους**, ουν, (ὁμοῦ, χροιά) *of the same colour.*

ὁμό-ψηφος, ον, (ὁμοῦ, ψῆφος) *voting with.* II. *having an equal right to vote with.*

ὁμόω, f. ώσω, (ὁμός) *to join together, unite:*—Pass., aor. 1 ὡμώθην, *to be united.*

ὈΜΠΝΗ, ἡ, *corn, food.*

ὀμπνιακός, ή, όν, = ὄμπνιος.

ὄμπνιος, α, ον, (ὄμπνη) *of* or *from corn, nourishing, thriving, large:*—Ὀμπνιά [ᾰ], ἡ, a name of Ceres, as *the mother of corn.*

ὀμφᾰκίας, ου, ὁ, (ὄμφαξ) *wine made from unripe grapes.* II. metaph. as masc. Adj. *harsh, austere, bitter, crabbed.*

ὀμφᾰκο-ράξ, ᾶγος, ὁ, ἡ, (ὄμφαξ, ῥάξ) *with sour* or *unripe grapes.*

ὀμφάλιος, ον, (ὀμφαλός) *belonging to the navel:* as Subst., ὀμφάλιον, τό, = ὄμφαλος. 2. *having a boss, like a boss.*

ὀμφᾰλόεις, εσσα, εν, (ὀμφαλός) *having a navel* or *boss;* ἀσπὶς ὀμφαλόεσσα a shield *with a central boss.*

ὈΜΦᾸΛΌΣ, οῦ, ὁ, *the navel,* Lat. *umbilīcus.* II. *anything like a navel: the raised knob* or *boss in the middle* of the shield, Lat. *umbo.* 2. *a knob* on the horse's yoke to fasten the reins to. 3. *the centre:* so Calypso's island Ogygia is called ὀμφαλὸς θαλάσσης, *the navel* or *centre* of the sea: and Delphi was called ὀμφαλός as *the navel* or *centre of Earth.*

ὌΜΦΑΞ, ᾰκος, ἡ, *an unripe grape.* 2. metaph. *a young girl.*

ὀμφή, ἡ, *a divine voice,* opp. to αὐδή: *a prophecy, oracle, warning voice: any token conveying divine intimation:* later, *tuneful voice, melody.* II. *fame, report;* σὴ ὀμφή *the report about* thee.

ὁμωθῆναι, aor. 1 inf. pass. of ὁμόω.

ὁμ-ῶλαξ, ακος, ὁ, ἡ, = ὁμαῦλαξ.

ὀμώμοκα, pf. of ὄμνυμι.

ὀμώμοσμαι, 3 sing. ὀμώμοται, pf. pass. of ὄμνυμι.

ὁμ-ωνύμιος, α, ον, and **ὁμ-ώνῠμος**, ον, (ὁμός, ὄνομα) *having the same name:*—as Subst., ὁμώνυμος, ὁ, ἡ, *a namesake.* II. *ambiguous, equivocal.*

ὁμ-ωρόφιος, ον, and **ὁμ-ώροφος**, ον, (ὁμοῦ, ὀροφή) *living under the same roof with.*

ὁμῶς, Adv. of ὁμός, *equally, alike, in equal parts,* Lat. *pariter.* 2. like ὁμοῦ, *together, at once, alike.* II. c. dat. *like as, equally with,* Lat. *pariter ac;* ἐχθρὸς ὁμῶς Ἀΐδαο πύλῃσι hated *like* the gates of Hell.

ὅμως, Conj. (ὁμός) *nevertheless, notwithstanding, yet, still,* Lat. *tamen;* ὅμως μήν or μέντοι *but still, for all that:*—ὅμως is in Att. often joined with a part., Lat. *quamvis,* κλῦθί μου νοσῶν ὅμως hear me *although* thou art diseased.

ὁμ-ωχέτης, ου, ὁ, (ὁμός, ἔχω) *holding* or *dwelling together;* θεοὶ ὁμωχέται gods *worshipped in the same temple.*

ὀν-ᾱγός, ὁ, Dor. and Att. for ὀνηγός.

ὄν-αγρος, ὁ, (ὄνος, ἄγριος) *the wild ass.*

ὀναίμην, ὄναιο, ὄναιτο, aor. 2 med. opt. of ὀνίνημι.

ὌΝᾸΡ, τό, *a dream, vision in sleep,* opp. to a waking vision (ὕπαρ): only used in nom. and acc. (ὄνειρος and ὄνειρον being used in the other cases):—proverb. of anything fleeting or unreal, σκιᾶς ὄναρ *the dream* of a shadow. II. in Att., ὄναρ was mostly used as an Adv., *in a dream, in sleep;* οὐδὲ ὄναρ not even *in a dream:* often opp. to ὕπαρ, ὄναρ ἢ ὕπαρ ζῆν to live *in a dream* or awake.

ὀνάριον, τό, Dim. of ὄνος, *a young ass.*

ὀνασεῖ, Dor. for ὀνήσει, 3 sing. fut. of ὀνίνημι.

ὄνασθαι, aor. 2 med. inf. ὀνίνημι.

ὄνασις, Dor. for ὄνησις.

ὄνειαρ, τό, gen. ὀνείᾰτος, (ὀνίνημι) *anything that profits* or *is helpful, advantage, succour: a refreshment, refection:* plur. ὀνείᾰτα, *food, victuals.*

ὀνείδειος, ον, (ὄνειδος) *reproachful: disgraceful.*

ὀνειδίζω, f. ίσω Att. ιῶ: aor. 1 ὠνείδισα: pf. ὠνείδικα:—Pass., with fut. med. ὀνειδιοῦμαι: (ὄνειδος):—*to throw a reproach upon, cast in one's teeth, object* or *impute* something to one, Lat. *objicere.* 2. *to reproach, upbraid.*

ὀνείδισμα, τό, (ὀνειδίζω) *a reproach.*

ὀνειδισμός, ὁ, (ὀνειδίζω) *a reproaching: reproach.*

ὀνειδιστήρ, ῆρος, ὁ, (ὀνειδίζω) *a reproacher, upbraider:* as masc. Adj. *reproachful.*

ὌΝΕΙΔΟΣ, τό, *any report* or *character,* whether *good* or *bad,* like Lat. *fama:* but commonly, *reproach, blame.* 2. *matter of reproach, a reproach, disgrace.*

ὄνειος, ον, (ὄνος) *of an ass;* **ὄνειον γάλα** *ass's* milk.

ὀνείρᾰτα, τά, used as pl. of ὄνειρον.

ὀνείρειος, α, ον, (ὄνειρος) *dreamy, of dreams;* ἐν ὀνειρείῃσι πύλῃσι at the gates *of dreams.*

ὀνειρο-κρίτης, ου, ὁ, (ὄνειρος, κριτής) *an interpreter of dreams.*

ὀνειρό-μαντις, εως, ὁ, ἡ, (ὄνειρος, μάντις) *an interpreter of dreams.*

ὄνειρον, τό, collat. form of ὄνειρος, *a dream:* the pl. mostly in use is ὀνείρατα, -άτων, -ασι: and from these a sing. gen. and dat., ὀνείρατος, -ατι were formed, as if from a nom. ὄνειραρ.

ὀνειροπολέω, f. ήσω, *to be absorbed in dreams:* c. acc. *to dream of,* as, ἵππους of horses. II. *to cheat by dreams.* From

ὀνειρο-πόλος, ον, (ὄνειρος, πολέω) *versed in dreams:* as Subst., ὀνειροπόλος, ὁ, *an interpreter of dreams.*

ὌΝΕΙΡΟΣ, ὁ, *a dream:* also *the subject of a dream:* cf. ὄναρ, ὄνειρον. 2. as prop. n., Ὄνειρος, *god of dreams.*

ὀνειρο-σκόπος, ον, (ὄνειρος, σκοπέω) *an interpreter of dreams.*

ὀνειρό-φαντος, ον, (ὄνειρος, φαίνομαι) *appearing in dreams, haunting one's dreams.*

ὀνειρό-φρων, ονος, ὁ, ἡ, (ὄνειρος, φρήν) *understanding dreams.*

ὀνειρώσσω Att. -ττω, (ὄνειρος) *to dream.*

ὀνεύω, (ὄνος II) *to draw up with a windlass, to haul up.*

ὀν-ηγός Dor. **ὀν-αγός**, ὁ, (ὄνος, ἡγέομαι) *an ass-driver.*

ὀν-ηλάτης [ᾰ], ου, ὁ, (ὄνος, ἐλαύνω) *an ass-driver.*

ὀνήμενος, aor. 2 part. med. of ὀνίνημι; **ὄνησα**, Ep. for ὤνησα, aor. 1; **ὀνήσει**, 3 sing. fut.

ὀνήσιμος, ον, (ὄνησις) *useful, profitable: aiding, succouring.*

ὄνησις, εως, ἡ, (ὀνίνημι) *profit, advantage, service: enjoyment, delight.*

ὌΝΘΟΣ, ὁ, *dirt, dung.*

ὀνία, ἡ, Aeol. for ἀνία.

ὀνίδιον, τό, Dim. of ὄνος, *a little ass, donkey.*

ὀνῐκός, ή, όν, (ὄνος) *of* or *for an ass;* ὀνικὸς μύλος a mill-stone *turned by an ass,* larger than the stones of the common hand-mills.

ὀνίνημι, ὀνίνης, ὀνίνησι, inf. ὀνῐνάναι [ᾰ], part. ὀνίνας: fut. ὀνήσω: aor. 1 ὤνησα: as if from obsol. *ὈΝΈΩ:—Med. and Pass. ὀνίνᾰμαι, impf. ὠνινάμην: fut. ὀνήσομαι: aor. 2 ὠνήμην, -ησο, -ητο, or ὠνάμην; imperat. ὄνησο, opt. ὀναίμην, inf. ὄνασθαι, part. ὀνήμενος: aor. 1 ὠνήθην. I. Act. *to profit, benefit, help, support;* and, like Lat. *juvo, to gratify, delight.* II. Med. *to have profit* or *advantage, to enjoy help;* esp. *to have delight* or *enjoyment:* c. gen. *to enjoy, have enjoyment* or *pleasure of* a thing. 2. freq. in aor. 2 opt. ὀναίμην, αιο, αιτο, to express good wishes, οὕτως ὀναίμην so *may I thrive!* ὄναιο, Lat. *sis felix! mayest thou be happy!* also with χάριν, ὄναιο τοῦ γενναίου χάριν bless thee for thy noble spirit: so also in phrase ἐσθλός μοι δοκεῖ εἶναι, ὀνήμενος (sub. εἴη or ἔστω), he seems brave, *may he be fortunate!*:—also ironical, ὄναιο μέντἄν εἴ τις ἐκπλύνειέ σε you *would* however *be the better* for it, if one were to wash you.

ὀνίς, ίδος, ἡ, (ὄνος) *ass's dung.*

ὄνοιτο, 3 sing. pres. opt. of ὄνομαι.

ὌΝΟΜΑ, ᾰτος, τό, Ion. **οὔνομα** Aeol. **ὄνῠμα**:—Lat. *NOMEN, a name:* ὄνομα θεῖναί τινι to give one *a name;* ὄνομα φέρεσθαι to bear *a name;* ὄνομα καλεῖν τινα to call one *by a name.* II. *name, fame, report,* whether *good* or *bad.* III. *name,* as opp. to reality, esp. opp. to ἔργον, like λόγος. 2. *a false name, pretence, pretext;* ἐπ' ὀνόματι under *the pretence.* IV. ὄνομα is also used with the names of persons, for the person, like κάρα, as ὦ φίλτατον ὄνομα Πολυνείκους. V. *a word, expression: a saying.* VI. in Grammar, *a noun,* Lat. *nomen,* opp. to ῥῆμα, Lat. *verbum, a verb.*

ὀνομάζω Ion. **οὐνομάζω**: fut. ὀνομάσω Aeol. ὀνυμάξω: aor. 1 ὠνόμασα: pf. ὠνόμακα:—Pass., aor. 1 ὠνομάσθην: pf. ὠνόμασμαι: (ὄνομα):—*to name, speak of, call* or *address by name.* 2. *to name* or *speak of,* as opp. to doing, as ὄνομα opp. to ἔργον. 3. *to call* one *by a* name, ὀνομάζειν τινά τι; also σοφιστὴν ὀνομάζουσιν τὸν ἄνδρα εἶναι they *call* the man a sophist *by name:* ὀνομάζειν ἀπό or ἔκ τινος *to name* or *call from* or *after* another; so also ἐπί τινος or τινι:—Med. *to have* one *called by a name. name:*—Pass. *to be called by a name.*

ὌΝΟΜΑΙ, 2 sing. ὄνοσαι, 3 pl. ὄνονται; imperat. ὄνοσο, 3 sing. opt. ὄνοιτο: fut. ὀνόσομαι Ep. ὀνόσσομαι: aor. 1 ὠνοσάμην, opt. ὀνοσαίμην, αιο, αιτο, Ep. inf. ὀνόσσασθαι; also aor. 1 pass. ὠνόσθην: Homer has also Ep. 2 pl. pres. οὔνεσθε, 3 sing. aor. 1 ὤνατο: Dep.:—*to blame, reject, find fault, be discontented with, scorn:* c. gen., οὐδ' ὥς σε ἔολπα ὀνόσσεσθαι κακότητος not even thus do I fancy that thou *wilt be discontented with* thy ill fortune.

ὀνομαίνω: fut. ὀνομᾰνῶ Ion. οὐνομανέω: aor. 1 ὠνόμηνα Ep. ὀνόμηνα: (ὄνομα):—poët. for. ὀνομάζω, *to name, call by name*, Lat. *nomino*: also, *to give a name to, call by a name*. 2. *to promise* to do. 3. *to name, appoint*. 4. *to pronounce, utter*.

ὀνομα-κλήδην, Adv. (ὄνομα, καλέω) *calling by name, by name*, Lat. *nominatim*.

ὀνομα-κλῠτός, όν, (ὄνομα, κλυτός) *of famous name, renowned*. II. act. *celebrating*.

ὀνομαστί, Adv. (ὀνομάζω) *by name*, Lat. *nominatim*.

ὀνομαστός Ion. οὐν-, ή, όν, (ὀνομάζω) *named*: *to be named, to be mentioned*. II. *of name* or *note, famous, glorious*: of things, *memorable*.

ὀνοματο-λόγος, ὁ, (ὄνομα, λέγω) *one who tells people's names*, Lat. *nomenclator*.

ὀνόμηνα, Ep. aor. 1 of ὀνομαίνω.

ὌΝΟΣ, ὁ and ἡ, *an ass*, Lat. *asinus, asina*: Proverbs: περὶ ὄνου σκιᾶς for *an ass's shadow*, like Lat. *de lana caprina*, i. e. for a mere trifle: ὄνου πόκαι ass's wool, like ὀρνίθων γάλα, of something not existing. II. from the ass being a beast of burden, the name was applied to, 1. *a windlass, crane, pulley*. 2. *the upper millstone*. III. *a beaker, wine-cup*, prob. from its shape.

ὀνοσσάμενος, Ep. aor. 1 med. part. of ὄνομαι.

ὀνόσσεσθαι, Ep. for ὀνόσεσθαι, fut. inf. of ὄνομαι.

ὀνοστός, ή, όν, (ὄνομαι) *to be blamed* or *scorned*.

ὀνοτάζω, like ὄνομαι, *to blame, rail at*.

ὀνοτός, ή, όν, for ὀνοστός.

ὀνο-φορβός, όν, (ὄνος, φέρβω) *an ass-keeper*.

ὄντα, τά, pl. part. neut. of εἰμί, *the things which actually exist, the present*, opp. to the past and future: —also *reality, truth*. II. *that which one has, property, fortune*.

ὄντως, Adv. part. of εἰμί sum, *really, actually*.

ὄνῠμα, τό, Aeol. for ὄνομα. Hence

ὀνῠμάζω, ὀνυμαίνω, Aeol. for ὀνομ-.

ὄνυξ, ῠχος, ὁ, dat. pl. ὄνυξι Ep. ὀνύχεσσι: 1. in pl. *the talons* of a bird of prey: also in sing., of beasts of prey, *a claw*; of human beings, *a nail*, Lat. *unguis*; of cattle, *a hoof*; ὄνυχας ἐπ' ἄκρους στῆναι to stand *on tiptoe*, Lat. *summis digitis*. 2. ἐξ ἁπαλῶν ὀνύχων, Horace's *de tenero ungui*, from a tender age. II. *a gem streaked with veins, an onyx*: also *any vessel made of it*.

ὀνύχεσσι, Ep. dat. pl. of ὄνυξ.

ὀξ-άλμη, ἡ, (ὄξος, ἅλμη) *a sauce made of vinegar and brine*.

ὀξέα, Ion. for ὀξεῖα, fem. of ὀξύς:—ὀξέσι, dat. pl.

ὀξέως, Adv. of ὀξύς, *sharply*.

ὀξηρός, ά, όν, (ὄξος) *of* or *for vinegar*; κέραμος ὀξηρός a jar *for vinegar*.

ὀξίνης [ῐ], ου, ὁ, (ὄξος) *sour*, of wine. 2 metaph. *sour-tempered, crabbed*.

ὀξίς, ίδος, ἡ, (ὄξος) *a vinegar-cruet*, Lat. *acetabulum*. II. a sort of *shrimp*.

ὄξος, εος, τό, (ὀξύς) *sour wine*: *vinegar*, Lat. *acētum*.

ΟΞΥ'Α or ὀξύη, ἡ, a kind of *beech*. II. *a spear-shaft* made from its wood: generally, *a spear*.

ὀξῠ-βάφων, τό, (ὀξύς, βάπτω) *a vinegar-saucer*, Lat. *acetabulum*: *a shallow dish* or *saucer*.

ὀξῠ-βελής, ές, (ὀξύς, βέλος) *sharp-pointed*: generally, *pointed, rough*.

ὀξῠ-βόας and **ὀξῠ-βόης**, ου, ὁ, (ὀξύς, βοάω) *shrill-screaming*: *sharp-buzzing*.

ὀξύ-γοος, ον, (ὀξύς, γόος) *shrill-wailing*.

ὀξῠ-δερκής, ές, (ὀξύς, δέρκομαι) *sharp-sighted, quick-sighted*: Sup. ὀξυδερκέστατος.

ὀξύ-δουπος, ον, (ὀξύς, δοῦπος) *sharp-sounding, shrill-sounding*.

ὀξῠ-έθειρος, ον, (ὀξύς, ἔθειρα) *with sharp, pointed hair*: irreg. plur. ὀξυέθειρες.

ὀξύ-θηκτος, ον, (ὀξύς, θήγω) *sharp-edged, sharp-pointed*: metaph. *sharply goaded*.

ὀξῠθῡμέω, f. ήσω, (ὀξύθυμος) *to be quick to anger, quick-tempered*:—also as Pass. *to be provoked*. Hence

ὀξῠθῡμία, ἡ, *quickness to anger, choler*.

ὀξύ-θῡμος, ον, (ὀξύς, θυμός) *quick to anger, quick-tempered, passionate, choleric*.

ὀξῠ-κάρδιος, ον, (ὀξύς, καρδία) *quick-tempered*.

ὀξῠ-κίνητος, ον, (ὀξύς, κινέω) *moved quickly*. [ῐ]

ὀξύ-κομος, ον, (ὀξύς, κόμη) *with pointed hair*: of plants, *with prickly leaves*.

ὀξῠ-κώκῡτος, ον, (ὀξύς, κωκύω) *loudly wailed*.

ὀξῠλᾰβέω, (ὀξυλαβής) *to seize quickly*: *to seize the opportunity*.

ὀξῠ-λᾰβής, ές, (ὀξύς, λαβεῖν) *seizing quickly*.

ὀξῠ-λάλος, ον, (ὀξύς, λᾰλέω) *glib-tongued*.

ὀξῠ-μελής, ές, (ὀξύς, μέλος) *clear-singing*.

ὀξῠ-μέριμνος, ον, (ὀξύς, μέριμνα) *keenly laboured* or *studied*.

ὀξῠ-μήνῑτος, ον, (ὀξύς, μηνίω) *quickly roused to wrath*; φόνος ὀξυμήνιτος murder *in hot blood*.

ὀξύ-μολπος, ον, (ὀξύς, μολπή) *clear-singing*.

ὀξύ-μωρος, ον, (ὀξύς, μωρός) *pointedly foolish*:—as Subst., ὀξύμωρον, τό, *a remark that seems to contradict itself, a paradox*, such as, *insaniens sapientia* or *concordia discors*.

ὀξυνθείς, aor. 1 part. pass. of ὀξύνω.

ὀξυντήρ, ῆρος, ὁ, *a sharpener*. From

ὀξύνω, f. ῠνῶ, (ὀξύς) *to make sharp* or *pointed, to sharpen*. 2. metaph. *to spur on, stimulate, sharpen*: also *to provoke*:—Pass. *to be provoked*.

ὀξῠόεις, εσσα, εν, poët. for ὀξύς, *sharp-pointed*; or from ὀξύα *with beechen shaft*.

ὀξῠ-όστρᾰκος, ον, (ὀξύς, ὄστρακον) *with a sharp jagged shell*.

ὀξυ-παγής, ές, (ὀξύς, παγῆναι) *sharp-pointed*.

ὀξῠ-πευκής, ές, (ὀξύς, πεύκη) *sharp-pointed*.

ὀξύ-πους, ὁ, ἡ, πουν, τό, gen. ποδος, (ὀξύς, πούς) *swift-footed*.

ὀξύ-πρῳρος, ον, (ὀξύς, πρῷρα) *having a sharp prow*: generally, *with a sharp front* or *point*.

ὀξῠ-ρεπής, ές, poët. for ὀξυρρεπής, = ὀξύρροπος.

ὀξύρ-ροπος, ον, (ὀξύς, ῥέπω) *quick-turning, nicely*

poised, of a delicate balance; *easily swayed:* metaph. *easily roused* or *led on*, Lat. *propensus.*

'ΟΞΥ'Σ, ὀξεῖα Ion. ὀξέα, ὀξύ, *sharp, keen, pointed;* λίθος ὀξύς a *sharpened* stone for a knife; ἐς ὀξὺ ἀπηγμένον brought to *a point;* τὸ ὀξύ *the sharp point*, or *vertex* of a triangle. II. of impressions on the senses, *sharp, keen, piercing;* of the sun, like *rapidus sol* in Virgil, *dazzling.* 2. of sight, *keen, piercing;* ὀξύτατον δέρκεσθαι to be *most keen* of sight; ὀξὺ ἀκούειν *to be quick* of hearing. 3. of sound, *sharp, shrill*, opp. to βαρύς. 4. of taste, *sharp, pungent.* 5. of pain or grief, *sharp, piercing.* III. *quick, sharp, keen, hasty*, esp. *quick to anger.* IV. of motion, *quick, swift.*—Besides Adv. ὀξέως, the neut. ὀξύ, and pl. ὀξέα, are often used as Adv. *sharply*, etc.

ὀξύ-στομος, ον, (ὀξύς, στόμα) *sharp-toothed;* of the gad-fly, *sharp-stinging;* of a sword, *keen-edged.*

ὀξυ-τενής, ές, (ὀξύς, τείνω) = ὀξύτονος.

ὀξύτης, ητος, ἡ, (ὀξύς) *sharpness, pointedness.* II. of sound, *highness of pitch* or *tone.* 2. of taste, *pungency.* III. metaph. *sharpness, cleverness.* 2. of action, *quickness, haste.*

ὀξῠ-τόμος, ον, (ὀξύς, τεμεῖν) *sharp-cutting, keen.*

ὀξύ-τονος, ον, (ὀξύς, τόνος) *stretched to a point: sharp, piercing: violent.* II. *having the acute accent*, i. e. accent on the last syllable, *oxytone.*

ὀξῠ-τόρος, ον, (ὀξύς, τείρω) *piercing, pointed, prickly.*

ὀξύ-φθογγος, ον, (ὀξύς, φθόγγος) = ὀξύφωνος.

ὀξύ-φρων, ονος, ὁ, ἡ, (ὀξύς, φρήν) *sharp-witted.*

ὀξύ-φωνος, ον, (ὀξύς, φωνή) *with clear, shrill voice.*

ὀξύ-χειρ, χειρος, ὁ, ἡ, (ὀξύς, χείρ) *quick of hand.* 2. ὀξύχειρ κτύπος a sound of *quick-beating with the hands.*

ὀξύ-χολος, ον, (ὀξύς, χόλος) *quick to anger.*

ὀξῠ-ωπής, ές, (ὀξύς, ὤψ) *sharp-sighted.*

ὅου, Ep. for οὗ, gen. of ὅς or ὅ.

ὅπα, Dor. for ὅπη.

ὀπαδέω, ὀπαδός, Dor. for ὀπηδέω: **ὀπηδός**, *an attendant.*

'ΟΠΑ'ΖΩ, f. ὀπάσω Ep. ὀπάσσω: aor. 1 ὤπᾰσα Ep. ὄπασσα:—Med., Ep. fut. ὀπάσσομαι, Ep. aor. 1 ὀπασσάμην:—*to make to follow, give as a companion* or *follower;* πολὺν λαὸν ὀπάζειν τινί *to give* him much people *to follow*, i. e. *make* him *leader over* many:—Med. *to make* another *follow* one, *take as a companion* or *follower.* II. of things, κῦδος ὀπάζειν τινί to *give* him glory *to follow:*—*to add, attach, annex to:*—generally, *to give, grant, bestow;* ἔργον πρὸς ἀσπίδι ὀπάζειν *to put* a work of art *on* the shield. III. *to follow, pursue, press hard:* absol. *to force one's way:*—Pass., χειμάρρους ὀπαζόμενος Διὸς ὄμβρῳ a torrent *forced on* (i. e. *swoln* with) the rain.

ὀπαῖος, α, ον, (ὀπή) *with a hole* or *opening:* as Subst., ὀπαῖον, τό, *a hole in the roof.*

ὁπανίκα, Dor. for ὁπηνίκα.

ὀπάσαιμι, aor. 1 opt. of ὀπάζω.

ὄπασσε, ὀπάσσατο, 3 sing. Ep. aor. 1 act. and med. of ὀπάζω.

ὀπάσσεαι, Ep. for ὀπάσει, 2 sing. fut. med. of ὀπάζω.

ὅ-πατρος, ον, for ὁμό-πατρος, (ὁμός, πατήρ) *by the same father.*

ὀπάων [ᾱ], ονος, Ion. **ὀπέων**, -έωνος, ὁ, (ὀπάζω) like ὀπηδός, *a companion, comrade*, esp. in war: later *a servant, attendant.*

"ΟΠΕΑ'Σ, ᾰτος, τό, *an awl*, Lat. *subula:* Aeol. **ὕπεας**, which is the usual form.

ὅπερ, Ep. for ὅσπερ.

ὀπέων, ωνος, ὁ, Ion. for ὀπάων.

'ΟΠΗ', ῆς, ἡ, *an opening, hole: a hole in the roof*, for a chimney.

ὅπη Ep. **ὅππη** Dor. **ὅπᾱ** Ion. **ὅκη**, Adv. of Place, *by which way*, Lat. *qua*, and so *where*, like ὅπου, Lat. *ubi:* also like ὅποι, *whither*, Lat. *quo.* 2. c. gen., ὅπη γᾶς, Lat. *quo terrarum? to which part* of the land? also like Lat. *ubi terrarum? where?* II. of Manner, *in what way? how?*

ὀπηδέω, Dor. ὀπαδέω, *to follow, accompany, attend, go with* another. From

ὀπηδός, όν, Dor. ὀπαδός, (ὀπάζω) *accompanying, attending:* and as Subst. ὀπηδός, ὁ, *an attendant.*

ὁπηνίκᾰ, Adv. *when, at what time.* II. *since*, Lat. *quoniam.*

ὀπίας, ου, ὁ, (ὀπός) *cheese made from milk curdled with fig-juice* (ὀπός): in full τυρὸς ὀπίας.

ὀπίζομαι, f. -ίσομαι: Dep.: (ὄπις):—*to have respect for, care for, regard: to stand in awe of, dread, fear:* also *to reverence, honour, obey.*

ὄπῐθε and **ὄπῐθεν**, Adv., poët. for ὄπισθε, ὄπισθεν.

ὀπῐθόμ-βροτος, ον, poët. for ὀπισθόμβροτος, (ὄπιθε, βροτός) *coming after a mortal;* ὀπιθόμβροτον αὔχημα the glory *that lives after men.*

'Οπικοί, οἱ, *the Opicans*, an ancient people of Italy: Adj. **'Οπικός**, ή, όν, *ancient, barbarous, Gothic.*

ὀπιπτεύω, f. σω, (*ὄπτομαι) *to look around after, gaze curiously at:* generally, *to observe, watch.*

ὄπῐς, ῐδος, ἡ, acc. ὄπῐν or ὄπῐδα, (ὄψ) *regard paid to* a person or thing; 1. in bad sense, *vengeance, punishment;* ὄπις θεῶν *the vengeance* of the gods. 2. in good sense, *reward, favour, regard.* 3. *awe, veneration, respect*, Lat. *reverentia.*

ὄπισθα, Adv., Aeol. and Dor. for ὄπισθε.

ὄπισθε, and before a vowel **ὄπισθεν**, Ep. **ὄπῐθε, ὄπῐθεν**: (ὄπις): Lat. *pone:* I. of Place, *after, behind*, opp. to πρόσθε in front; οἱ ὄπισθε *those left behind;* οἱ ὄπισθε λόγοι *the remaining* books; τὸ or τὰ ὄπισθεν *the hinder parts, rear, back;* εἰς τοὔπισθεν *back, backwards.* 2. as Prep. with gen., *behind:* also *inferior, second to.* II. of Time, *after, in future, hereafter.*

ὀπίσθιος, α, ον, also ος, ον, (ὄπισθε) *hinder*, Lat. *posticus:* ὀπ. σκέλεα *the hind*-legs.

ὀπισθο-βάμων, ον, gen. ονος, (ὄπισθε, βαίνω) *walking backwards.* [ᾰ]

ὀπισθό-γρᾰφος, ον, (ὄπισθε, γράφω) *written on the back* or *cover.*

ὀπισθό-δετος, ον, (ὄπισθε, δέω) *bound behind* or *backwards.*

ὀπισθό-δομος, ὁ, (ὄπισθε, δόμος) *the back chamber of a temple*: at Athens *the cella* of the old temple of Athena in the citadel, used as the treasury.

ὀπισθο-νόμος, ον, (ὄπισθε, νέμω) *grazing backwards*, of certain cattle with large horns slanting forwards.

ὀπισθο-νυγής, ές, (ὄπισθε, νυγῆναι) *pricking from behind.*

ὀπισθό-πους, ὁ, ἡ, πουν, τό, gen. ποδος, (ὄπισθε, πούς) *walking behind, following, attendant.*

ὀπισθοφυλακέω, f. ήσω, (ὀπισθοφύλαξ) *to guard the rear, form the rear-guard.* II. *to command the rear-guard.* Hence

ὀπισθοφυλακία, ἡ, *the command of the rear.*

ὀπισθο-φύλαξ, ἄκος, ὁ, ἡ, (ὄπισθε, φύλαξ) *one who watches behind*: οἱ ὀπισθοφύλακες *the rear-guard* of an army.

ὀπίσσω, Adv., Ep. for ὀπίσω.

ὀπίστατος, η, ον, (ὄπισθε) *hindmost*, Lat. *postremus.*

ὀπίσω Ep. **ὀπίσσω**, Adv. (ὄπις) of Place, *behind, backwards*: τὸ ὀπίσω, contr. τοὐπίσω, also εἰς τοὐπίσω, *backwards.* 2. as Prep. with gen. *after, behind.* II. of Time, *afterwards, hereafter.* III. *over again, again.* [Ĭ]

ὁπλᾶς, Dor. for ὁπλῆς, gen. of ὁπλή.

ὁπλέω, (ὅπλον) poët. for ὁπλίζω, *to make ready.*

ὁπλή, ἡ, (ὅπλον) *a hoof*, properly *the solid hoof* of a horse: but also *the cloven hoof* of horned cattle.

ὁπλήεις, εσσα, εν, (ὅπλον) *armed.*

Ὅπλητες, οἱ, = ὁπλῖται, name of one of the four old tribes at Athens.

ὁπλίζω, f. ίσω Att. ιῶ: aor. ὥπλισα Ep. ὥπλισσα:—Med., Ep. aor. 1 ὡπλισσάμην:—Pass., aor. 1 ὡπλίσθην, Ep. 3 pl. ὅπλισθεν: pf. ὥπλισμαι:—*to make* or *get ready*: of meats, *to dress*: so in Med., δόρπον ὁπλίζεσθαι *to prepare one* a meal: of horses, *to get ready, harness*: of soldiers, *to equip, arm, harness*: also, *to train, exercise.* 2. *to arm as* ὁπλῖται. II. Pass. *to get ready, be ready*: *to arm, prepare for battle.* Hence

ὅπλισις, ἡ, *a preparing* for war, *equipment, accoutrement, arming.*

ὅπλισμα, ατος, τό, (ὁπλίζω) *equipment, armour* II. *an army, armament.*

ὁπλισμός, ὁ, (ὁπλίζω) = ὅπλισις.

ὁπλιστέον, verb. Adj. of ὁπλίζω, *one must arm*

ὁπλιστής, οῦ, ὁ, (ὁπλίζω) *of a warrior.*

ὁπλῖτ-ἀγωγός, όν, (ὁπλίτης, ἄγω) *commanding the heavy-armed.*

ὁπλιτεύω, f. σω, *to be an* ὁπλίτης, *serve as a heavy-armed soldier.* From

ὁπλίτης [ῑ], ου, ὁ, (ὅπλον II. 2) *heavy-armed, armed in full armour*; ὁπλίτης στρατός *an armed* host. II. as Subst., ὁπλίτης, ου, ὁ, *a heavy-armed foot-soldier*, who carried a pike (δόρυ), and a large shield (ὅπλον), *a man-at-arms*: opp. to light-armed troops, ψιλοί or γυμνῆτες, γυμνῆται. Hence

ὁπλιτικός, ή, όν, *of* or *for a heavy-armed soldier*; τὸ ὁπλιτικόν, = οἱ ὁπλῖται.

ὅπλομαι, Med. (ὅπλον) poët. for ὁπλίζομαι, *to get ready for oneself.*

ὁπλομανέω, f. ήσω, *to be madly fond of arms, have a mania for war.* From

ὁπλο-μανής, ές, (ὅπλον, μανῆναι) *madly fond of arms.*

ὁπλομαχία, ἡ, *the art of using heavy arms*: generally, *the art of war, tactics.* From

ὁπλο-μάχος, ον, (ὅπλα, μάχομαι) *fighting in heavy arms.* II. *one who drills soldiers.*

ὍΠΛΟΝ, τό, *any tool* or *implement*: I. a ship's *tackling, cordage, cables, ropes, cords*; ὅπλα χαλκήια a blacksmith's *tools*; ἀρούρης ὅπλον a sickle; ὅπλον γεροντικόν a staff. II. mostly in plur. *implements of war, arms* whether offensive or defensive, *harness, armour*; rarely in sing. *a weapon*: ἐν ὅπλοις μένειν to remain *under arms.* 2. in sing. mostly *the heavy shield* used by Greek foot-soldiers, whence the name ὁπλῖται. 3. τὰ ὅπλα, = ὁπλῖται, *heavy-armed* soldiers. 4. τὰ ὅπλα also, *the camp, quarters.*

ὁπλότερος, α, ον, and **ὁπλότατος**, η, ον, Comp. and Sup. without any Posit. in use: poët. for νεώτερος, νεώτατος: (ὅπλα):—*those more* or *most capable of bearing arms, the youth, the men fit for service*, opp. to the old men and children:—then, generally, of age, ὁπλότερος γενεῇ *younger* by birth, Lat. *minor natu*:—also, ἄνδρες ὁπλότεροι men *of later days.*

ὁπλοφορέω, f. ήσω, *to bear heavy arms, be a heavy-armed soldier*:—Pass. *to have a body-guard.* From

ὁπλο-φόρος, ον, (ὅπλα, φέρω) *bearing arms, armed*: as Subst., ὁπλοφόρος, ὁ, *an armed man, a warrior.* II. *one of the body-guard.*

ὁποδαπός, ή, όν, (ποδαπός) relat. Adj. *what sort of a person*, esp. *of what country*, Lat. *cujas.*

ὁπόθεν Ep. **ὁππόθεν** Ion. **ὁκόθεν**, relat. Adv. *whence, from what place.*

ὁπόθι Ep. **ὁππόθι**, relat. Adv. (πόθι) *where.*

ὅποι Ion. **ὅκοι**, relat. Adv. of Place, *whither, thither where*; ὅποι ποτέ *whithersoever*; μέχρι ὅποι up *to what place*, how far. 2. c. gen., ὅποι γῆς *whither* in the world, Lat. *quo terrarum.* II. of Manner, for ὅπως, *how, how far.*

ὁποῖος, α, ον, Ep. **ὁπποῖος**, η, ον, Ion. **ὁκοῖος**, η, ον: (ποῖος) relat. Adj. *of what sort, kind*, or *quality*, Lat. *qualis.* II. the correlat. of ὁποῖος is τοῖος; τοῖος .. ὁποῖος such *as*; ὁπποῖόν κ' εἴπῃσθα ἔπος, τοῖόν κ' ἐπακούσαις *such* word *as* thou hast spoken, such shalt thou hear again. III. ὁποῖός τις refers to a special subject; ὁποῖός τις ἦ *what manner of man* was he. IV. ὁποῖος οὖν *of what kind soever*, Lat. *qualiscunque.* V. Adv. **ὁποίως**: also in neut. pl ὁποῖα, *like as*, Lat. *qualiter.*

ὈΠΟ'Σ, οῦ, ὁ, *juice*, esp. of trees or plants, *the milky* *juice, resin*, or *gum*: *the acid juice of the fig-tree*:— metaph., ὀπὸς ἥβης *the juicy freshness* of youth

ὀπός, gen. of ὄψ.

ὁποσάκῐς, Adv. (ὁπόσος) *as many times as .. as often as* ... [ᾰ]

ὁποσᾰχῆ, Adv. (ὁπόσος) *at as many places as* ...

ὁπόσε Ep. **ὁππόσε**, Adv., poët. for ὅποι, *whither*.

ὁπόσος, η, ον, Ep. ὁππόσος, ὁπόσσος, ὁππόσσος Ion. **ὁκόσος**: (πόσος): relat. Adj., I. of Number, *as many, as many as* .., Lat. *quot*. II. of Space, *as large, as large as* .., Lat. *quantus*.

ὁπότ-ᾰν Ep. **ὁππότ-ᾰν**, for ὁπότ' ἄν, (πότε): Conj. followed by subjunctive, *whensoever*, Lat. *quandocunque*.

ὁπότε Ep. **ὁππότε** Ion. **ὁκότε**, relat. Conj. *when*, Lat. *quando*. II. in causal sense, *for that, because, since*.

ὁπότερος, α, ον, Ep. **ὁππότερος**, η, ον: (πότερος): —*which of two, whither of the twain*, Lat. *uter*: also *which of us two, which of you two*. 2. ὁποτεροσοῦν and ὁπότερος δήποτε, *whichever of the two*, Lat. *utervis, uterlibet, utercunque*. 3. neut. ὁπότερον and ὁπότερα as Adv., for ὁποτέρως, *in whichever of two ways*: also for πότερον, *whether*, Lat. *utrum*, when there is choice of two things. II. *one of two*, Lat. *alteruter*. Hence

ὁποτέρωθε, **–ωθεν** Ep. **ὁππoτ–**, relat. Adv. *from which of the two, from whether of the twain*

ὁποτέρως, relat. Adv. *in whichever of two ways*.

ὁποτέρωσε, relat. Adv. (ὁπότερος) *to which* or *whichever of two sides; in which of two ways*.

ὅπου Ion. **ὅκου**, relat. Adv. *where*, Lat. *ubi*. 2. also c. gen., ὅπου γῆς *where in the world*, Lat. *ubi terrarum*. 3. ἔσθ' ὅπου *there are places, where* .., i. e. *in some places, somewhere*, as Lat. *est ubi* .., for *alicubi*. 4. ὅπου ἄν or ὅπουπερ ἄν, *wherever*:— ὁπουοῦν, ὁπουδή, ὁπουδήποτε, *wheresoever*, Lat. *ubicunque*. II. of Time, like Lat. *ubi, when, at the time when*. III. of Manner, *how*. IV. Causal, *because, since*, Lat. *quando, quoniam*. (Really gen. of an old Pron. *ὅπος.)

ὅππα, Adv. poët. for ὅπα, Dor. for ὅπῃ.

ὄππατα, Dor. for ὄμματα.

ὅππῃ, Adv., Ep. for ὅπῃ.

ὁππόθεν, **ὁππόθῐ**, Ep. for ὁπόθεν, ὁπόθι.

ὁπποῖος, **ὁππόσε**, Ep. for ὁποῖος, ὁπόσε.

ὁππόκᾰ, Dor. for ὁπότε

ὁππόσος, η, ον, Ep. for ὁπόσος.

ὁππόταν, **ὁππότ' ἄν**, Ep. for ὁπόταν, ὁπότ' ἄν.

ὁππότε, Ep. for ὁπότε.

ὁππότερος, **ὁπποτέρωθεν**, Ep. for ὁποτ–.

ὅππως, Ep. for ὅπως.

ὀπτᾰλέος, α, ον, (ὀπτάω) *roasted*: also *baked*.

ὀπτάνιον, τό, (ὀπτάω) *a kitchen*.

ὀπτᾰσία, ἡ, (ὄψομαι) *a sight, a vision*.

'ΟΠΤΑ'Ω, impf. ὤπτων: f. ὀπτήσω:—Pass., aor. 1 ὠπτήθην: pf. ὤπτημαι:—*to roast* or *broil* meat, opp. to ἕψω, *to boil*. 2. *to bake* bread; also of pottery, *to bake* or *burn*. 3. *to bake, harden* by exposure to the sun. 4. metaph. of love, *to scorch, burn*.

ὀπτεύμενος, Dor. for ὀπτώμενος, pres. pass. part. of ὀπτάω.

ὀπτεύω, = ὁράω, *to see*.

ὀπτήρ, ῆρος, ὁ, (ὄψομαι) *one who looks after* a thing, *a spy*, Lat. *speculator*.

ὀπτήριος, α, ον, (ὄψομαι) *of* or *belonging to sight*; τὰ ὀπτήρια (sub. δῶρα), *presents made by the bridegroom on seeing the bride without the veil*: generally, *presents upon seeing* or *to see* a person.

ὀπτίλος [ῐ], ὁ, (ὄψομαι) *the eye*; Dor. also ὀπτίλλος.

***ὄπτομαι**, obsol. pres. whence the tenses of ὁράω are formed: see ὁράω.

ὀπτός, ή, όν, (ὀπτάω) *roasted*: generally, *prepared by fire, baked*; ἑφθὰ καὶ ὀπτά boiled meats and *roast*: also of pottery, etc., *baked* or *burned*.

'ΟΠΥΙ'Ω Att. **ὀπύω**, f. ύσω [ῡ]: I. Act. of the man, *to marry, wed, take to wife, have to wife*: ὀπυίοντες *married men*, opp. to *the unmarried* (ἠίθεοι). II. Pass., of the woman, *to be married, become a wife*.

ὄπωπα, Ion. pf. med. of ὁράω: Dor. 3 sing. ὀπώπη.

ὀπωπή, ἡ, (ὄπωπα) poet. for ὄψις, *a sight, view, vision*. II. *sight, power of seeing*.

ὀπωπητήρ, ῆρος, ὁ, (ὄπωπα) *a spy, looker out*.

'ΟΠΩ'ΡΑ Ion. **ὀπώρη**, ἡ, properly *the part of the year between the rising of Sirius and of Arcturus, the end of summer*: it was *the rainy* and *stormy season*. II. from being the *fruit-time*, ὀπώρα also means *the fruit itself*, esp. *tree-fruit*. III. metaph. *the vigour of life, ripe manhood*.

ὀπωριεῦντες, Ion. for ὀπωριοῦντες, part. Att. fut. of ὀπωρίζω.

ὀπωρίζω, f. ίσω Att. ιῶ, (ὀπώρα) *to gather fruits*. II. *to gather fruits off* a tree.

ὀπωρῑνός, ή, όν, (ὀπώρα) *of* or *at the time of early autumn, autumnal*; ἀστὴρ ὀπωρινός *the summer*-star, *dog*-star, also Σείριος, whose rising marked the beginning of ὀπώρα. [ι is long Ep., when last syll. is long.]

ὀπωροφορέω, f. ήσω, *to bear fruit*. From

ὀπωρο-φόρος, ον, (ὀπώρα II, φέρω) *bearing fruit*.

ὅπως Ep. **ὅππως** Ion. **ὅκως**:—relat. Conj. of Manner, *how, in what way* or *manner*, Lat. *quomodo*. 2 sometimes put for οἷος, as, τοῖόν με ἔθηκεν, ὅπως ἐθέλει, for οἷον ἐθέλει, he has made me such *as* he wills. 3. ὅπως ἔχω *as I am*, i. e. *immediately, on the spot*. 4. c. gen., σοῦσθε ὅπως ποδῶν (sub. ἔχετε), run *as you are off for feet*, i. e. as quick as you can. 5. ὁπωσδή, ὁπωσοῦν, ὁπωσδηποτοῦν, ὁπωστιοῦν, *howsoever, in what manner soever*; so, οὐδ' ὁπωστιοῦν, *not in any way whatever, not in the least*. 6. οὐκ ἔσθ' ὅπως it is not (i. e. cannot be) *that* ..; but, οὐκ ἔσθ' ὅπως οὐ, Lat. *non fieri potest quin* .., it cannot but be *that* .. II. like Lat. *ut*, of Time, *when, as, so soon as*; Τρῶες ἐρρίγησαν, ὅπως ἴδον αἰόλον ὄφιν the Trojans shuddered *when* they saw. III. like ὡς and ὅτι, Lat. *quam*, with Sup.

of Adv. ὅπως τάχιστα *as* quickly *as possible*, Lat. *quam celerrime*; ὅπως ἄριστα *as* well *as possible*.

B. ὅπως as final Conjunction, denoting an end or purpose, *that, in order that, so that*, Lat. *quo, ut*, followed, I. by the Subjunct. when the anteeed. Verb is of pres. time, as, ὁρᾷ ὅπως γένηται he is looking *that* he may be; πεῖρα, ὅπως κεν ἵκηαι keep trying *that* thou mayest come:—also elliptically (sub. ὅρα, ὁρᾶτε, etc.) to express a caution, usually with μή, as, ὅπως τοῦτό γε μὴ ποιήσῃς, [see] thou do it not; so also with indicat. fut., ὅπως ἄνδρες ἔσεσθε see *that* ye be men! II. by the Optat., if the anteced. Verb be of past time, whether imperf. or aor., as, ἔλεγον (εἶπον) ὅπως γένοιτο I kept speaking (spoke) *that* it might be done. III. by the Indicat. of fut.; θέλγει ὅπως Ἰθάκης ἐπιλήσεται she beguiles him *with the view that* he should forget Ithaca: also to convey a caution, δεῖ σ' ὅπως δείξεις. IV. in Att. occurs the phrase οὐχ ὅπως, ἀλλά or ἀλλὰ καί .. *not only not so, but* .., οὐχ ὅπως χάριν αὐτοῖς ἔχεις, ἀλλὰ καὶ κατὰ τουτωνὶ πολιτεύει you *not only are not* grateful to them, *but* you are even taking measures against them;—in full, οὐ λέγω ὅπως I do not say *that*, etc.; so, οὐχ ὅπως, ἀλλ' οὐδέ *not only not so, but* not at all. V. ὅπως μή, = the Conjunction μή: generally used only with aor. 2 subj., or with indicat. fut.

ὁράας, Ep. for ὁρᾷς, 2 sing. of ὁράω.

ὅρᾱμα, τό, (ὁράω) *that which is seen, a view, sight*.

ὅραμνος, ὁ, later form of ὀρόδαμνος.

ὅρᾱσις, εως, ἡ, (ὁράω) *seeing, the sense of sight*.

ὁρᾱτός, ή, όν, (ὁράω) *to be seen, visible*; τὰ ὁρατά *visible objects*.

‘ΟΡΑ΄Ω, impf. Att. ἑώρων: Ion. **ὁρέω** impf. ὥρεον: Ep. also **ὁρόω**: pf. **ἑόρᾱκα** later ἑώρᾱκα, pass. ἑόρᾱμαι later ἑώρᾱμαι. Other tenses are supplied from the Root *ΟΠΤ-ΟΜΑΙ, fut. ὄψομαι, with a rare aor. 1 ὠψάμην: Pass., fut. ὀφθήσομαι: aor. 1 ὤφθην inf. ὀφθῆναι: pf. ὦμμαι, ὦψαι, ὦπται, inf. ὦφθαι: there is also in Ep. a perf. med. ὄπωπα, plqpf. ὀπώπειν from the same Root. Lastly, from the Root *ἼΔΩ are formed also aor. 2 act. εἶδον inf. ἰδεῖν: aor. 2 med. εἰδόμην, inf. ἰδέσθαι: pf. with pres. sense οἶδα, οἶσθα, *I know*, etc., inf. εἰδέναι (see οἶδα).

To see, to look; κατ' αὐτοὺς αἰὲν ὅρα (3 Ep. impf.) *be kept looking* continually at them 2. *to have sight*, like βλέπω, opp. to μὴ ὁρᾶν to be blind; ὅσ' ἂν λέγοιμι, πάνθ' ὁρῶντα λέξομαι my words *shall have eyes*, i. e. shall have meaning; ἐν σκότῳ ὀψοίατο *may they have sight* in darkness, i. e. may they be blind. 3. *to see, look to, take heed, beware*, mostly in Imperat. ὅρα εἰ ... 4. c. acc. cognato, ὁρᾶν ἀλκάν *to look* prowess, look like a warrior. 5. trans. *to see, look at, behold, perceive, observe*, c. acc.; ὁρᾶν φάος Ἠελίοιο (Hom.), and φῶς ὁρᾶν (Att.) *to see* the light, i. e. to be alive. II. Pass. *to be seen, also to appear*; c. part., ὤφθημεν ὄντες ἄθλιοι *we were seen to be* wretched: τὰ ὁρώμενα *things visible*. III. of the mind, *to discern, perceive*.

ὀργάζω, f. άσω: aor. 1 ὤργασα: p. pass. ὤργασμαι: (ὀργάω):—*to soften, knead, mould*, Lat. *subig*.

ὀργαίνω, f. ᾰνῶ: aor. 1 ὤργᾱνα: (ὀργή):—*to make angry, enrage*. II. intr. *to grow* or *be angry*.

ὀργάνιον, τό, Dim. of ὄργᾰνον, *a small tool* or *instrument*.

ὄργᾰνον, τό, (ἔργον) *an instrument, implement, tool, engine*; λαΐνεα Ἀμφίονος ὄργανα, the stony *works* of Amphion, i. e. the walls of Thebes. II. *a musical instrument*. III. *the material* of a work. IV. *the work, product itself*.

ὀργᾰνος, η, ον, (*ἔργω) *working, fashioning*.

ὀργάς (sub. γῆ), άδος, ἡ, (ὀργάω) *a well-watered, fertile tract of land, a meadow*.

ὀργάω, (ὀργή) *to swell* or *teem with moisture*: of soil, *to abound, swell* with produce: of fruit, *to swell as it ripens*; c. inf., ὀργᾷ ἀμᾶσθαι [the crop] *is ripe* for cutting. II. of animals, *to swell with lust, wax wanton, be at heat*: *to be excited, passionate*. 2. c. gen. *to yearn* or *long for*.

ὀργεών, ῶνος, Ep. **ὀργείων**, ονος, ὁ, (ὄργια) *a priest*.

ὀργή, ἡ, (ὀρέγω) *impulse, feeling*: *the temperament, disposition, temper*, esp. in pl., ὀργαὶ ἀστυνόμοι social *dispositions*. II. *any violent emotion* or *passion, anger, wrath*; ὀργῇ χρᾶσθαι to indulge one's *anger*; ὀργὴν ἄκρος prone *to anger*, passionate: ὀργῇ as Adv. *in anger, in a passion*: so also δι' ὀργῆς, κατ' ὀργήν, μετ' ὀργῆς, πρὸς ὀργήν. 2. Πανὸς ὀργαί panic *passions, terrors*.

ὄργια, ίων, τά, (ἔργον) only used in pl., *secret rites, secret worship*, practised by the initiated alone at the secret worship of Demeter at Eleusis: also *the rites of Bacchus, orgies* II. *any rites, worship, sacrifice*. 2. *any mysteries*, without reference to religion. Hence

ὀργιάζω, f. άσω, *to celebrate orgies*. II. *to solemnise* or *celebrate any sacred rites*.

ὀργίζω, f. ίσω Att. ιῶ: aor. 1 ὤργισα: (ὀργή):—*to make angry, provoke to anger, irritate*. II. Pass., with fut. med. ὀργιοῦμαι, but also pass. ὀργισθήσομαι: aor. 1 ὠργίσθην: pf. ὤργισμαι:—*to grow angry, be wroth*.

ὀργίλος [ῐ], η, ον, (ὀργή) *prone to anger, passionate*.

ὀργιο-φάντης, ου, ὁ, (ὄργια, φαίνω) *one who initiates* others *into orgies*.

ὄργυιᾰ or **ὀργυιά**, ἡ, (formed from ὀρέγω, as ἀγυιά from ἄγω) *the length of the outstretched arms*. 2. as a measure of length, = 4 πήχεις or 6 *feet* 1 *inch*, about our *fathom*: 100 ὀργυιαί make one stadium. Hence

ὀργυιαῖος, α, ον, *a fathom long* or *large*.

ὄρεγμα, ατος, τό, (ὀρέγω) *a stretching out*: *a holding out, offering*.

ὀρέγνυμι, = ὀρέγω, whence ὀρεγνύς (part. pres.)

’ΟΡΕ΄ΓΩ, fut. ὀρέξω: aor. 1 ὤρεξα:—*to reach, stretch out, extend*, Lat. *porrigo*: *to stretch out the* hands in entreaty. 2. *to reach out, hand, offer, give.* II. Med. ὀρέγομαι, with aor. 1 med. ὠρεξάμην, and pass. ὠρέχθην: pf. pass. ὀρώρεγμαι:—*to stretch oneself out, reach out;* χερσὶ ὀρέξασθαι *to reach with* the hands; ὀρέξασθαι ἔγχεϊ *to lunge, thrust out with* the spear; ποσσὶν ὀρωρέχαται (pf.) πολεμίζειν of horses, *they stretched themselves* with their feet (i. e. went at full gallop) to the fight; ὀρέξατ' ἰὼν *he stretched himself* as he went, i. e. went at *full stride.* 2. c. gen. *to reach at* or *to* a thing, *grasp at: to reach at, aim a blow at:* metaph. *to reach after, grasp at, desire.* 3. c. acc. *to reach, gain one's end:* also *to reach with a weapon, strike, wound: to hand to oneself, reach for oneself.*

ὀρει-άρχης, ου, ὁ, (ὄρος, ἄρχω) *lord of the mountains.*

ὀρειάς, άδος, ἡ, (ὄρος) pecul. fem. of ὄρειος, *of* or *belonging to mountains.* II. sub. Νύμφη, *an Oread, mountain-nymph.*

ὀρειβᾰτέω, *to roam the mountains.* From

ὀρει-βάτης, ου, ὁ, (ὄρος, βαίνω) *mountain-ranging.*

ὀρειδρομία, ἡ, *a running wild over the hills.* From

ὀρει-δρόμος, ον, (ὄρος, δραμεῖν) *running on the hills.*

ὀρει-νόμος, ον, (ὄρος, νέμω) *feeding on the mountains, mountain-ranging.*

ὀρεινός, ή, όν, (ὄρος) *mountainous, hilly.* II. *on* or *of a mountain:* as Subst., ὀρεινός, ὁ, *a mountaineer.*

ὀρειο-νόμος, ον, = ὀρεινόμος.

ὄρειος, α, ον, also ος, ον, Ion. **οὔρειος**, (ὄρος) *mountainous, hilly:* also, *living on the mountains.*

ὀρειο-χᾰρής, ές, (ὄρος, χαρῆναι) *delighting in the hills.*

ὀρεί-πλαγκτος, see ὀρίπλαγκτος.

ὀρει-τύπος, ον, (ὄρος, τύπτω) *working in the mountains,* i. e. *felling timber,* or *quarrying stone.*

ὀρει-φοίτης, ου, (ὄρος, φοιτάω) *mountain-ranging.*

ὀρεί-χαλκος, ὁ, (ὄρος, χαλκός) Lat. *orichalcum, fine copper ore* and *the brass made from it:* also, *fine brass.*

ὀρειώτης, ου, ὁ, (ὄρος) *a mountaineer.*

ὀρεκτός, ή, όν, (ὀρέγω) *stretched out, presented:* also, *to be presented.*

ὀρεξάμενος, **ὀρέξας**, aor. 1 part. med. and act. of ὀρέγω.

ὄρεξις, εως, ἡ, (ὀρέγω) *a longing* or *yearning after* a thing, *desire for* it.

ὀρεό-κομος, ον, incorrect form of ὀρεωκόμος.

ὀρέοντο, 3 pl. Ep. aor. 2 med. of ὄρνυμι.

ὀρεοπολέω, *to haunt the mountains.* From

ὀρεο-πόλος, ον, (ὄρος, πολέω) *mountain-haunting.*

ὀρεσί-τροφος, ον, (ὄρος, τρέφω) *mountain-bred* or *reared,* epith. of the lion.

ὀρέ-σκιος, ον, (ὄρος, σκιά) *shadowed by mountains.*

ὀρέσ-κοος Ep. **ὀρεσ-κῷος**, ον, (ὄρος, κεῖμαι) *lying on mountains, mountain-bred, wild.*

ὀρέσσ-αυλος, ον, (ὄρος, αὐλή) *dwelling in the mountains.*

ὄρεσσι, Ep. for ὄρεσι, dat. pl. of ὄρος.

ὀρεσσῐ-βάτης, ου, ὁ, = ὀρειβάτης. [ᾰ]

ὀρεσσῐ-γενής, ές, and **ὀρεσσί-γονος**, ον, (ὄρος, γένος, γόνος) *mountain-born.*

ὀρεσσῐ-νόμος, ον, (ὄρος, νέμω) Ep. for ὀρεινόμος, *feeding on the mountains, mountain-haunting.*

Ὀρεστεία, ἡ, *the tale of Orestes,* the general name for the Agamemnon, Choëphoroe and Eumenides of Aeschylus, being the only extant Trilogy.

ὀρέστερος, α, ον, (ὄρος) poët. for ὀρεινός, *mountainous, dwelling in the mountains.*

ὀρεστιάς, άδος, ἡ, (ὄρος) = Ὀρειάς; Νύμφαι ὀρεστιάδες, *the mountain-nymphs, the Oreads.*

ὄρεσφι, -φιν, Ep. gen. and dat. sing. and pl. ὄρος.

ὀρεύς Ion. **οὐρεύς**, έως, ὁ, (ὄρος *a mountain*) *a mule.*

ὄρευς, Dor. for ὄρεος, gen. of ὄρος.

ὀρεχθέω, f. ήσω, = ὀρέγομαι, *to stretch oneself;* also, *to beat fast, pant, quiver,* of the heart, etc.; βόες ὀρέχθεον σφαζόμενοι the steers *lay stretched,* or *quivered convulsively,* as they were slain: θάλασσαν ἔα ποτὶ χέρσον ὀρεχθῆν (Dor. inf. for ὀρεχθεῖν) let the sea *stretch itself* (i. e. *roll up*) *to* the beach.

ὁρέω pl. **ὁρέομεν**, Ion. for ὁράω, ὁράομεν.

ὅρηαι or **ὁρῆαι**, poët. 2 sing. pres. med. of ὁράω.

ὅρημι, Aeol. for ὁράω, inf. ὁρῆν, part. ὁρείς.

ὁρητός, ή, όν, Ion. for ὁρατός.

ὄρθαι, inf. of ὤρμην, Ep. aor. 2 pass. of ὄρνυμι.

ὀρθεύω, f. σω, (ὀρθός) = ὀρθόω, *to set upright: set straight.*

Ὀρθία, ἡ, name of Diana in Laconia and Arcadia.

ὄρθια, neut. pl. of ὄρθιος: used also as Adv. *aloud.*

ὀρθιάδε, Adv. (ὄρθιος) *straight up, upwards.*

ὀρθιάζω, f. άσω (ὄρθιος) *to speak in a high tone of voice* or *in a high key, speak loud.* II. *to set upright.*

ὀρθίασμα, ατος, τό, (ὀρθιάζω) *a high pitch of the voice, a loud shout* or *cry.*

ὄρθιος, α, ον, Att. also ος, ον, (ὀρθός) *straight up, rising upwards, steep;* ὄρθιον πορεύεσθαι or πρὸς ὄρθιον ἰέναι to march *up hill;* τὰ ὄρθια the country *from the coast upwards.* 2. *upright:* of animals, *standing upright, rearing.* 3. *straight, right.* II. of the voice, *high-pitched, loud, shrill, clear;* νόμος ὄρθιος, *a stirring, thrilling air:* in neut. pl. as Adv., ὄρθια ἤυσε she cried *aloud.* III. ὄρθιοι λόχοι, Livy's *recti ordines,* as a military term, battalions *in column* or *file,* whereas in φάλαγξ the men stood *in line;* ὀρθίους τοὺς λόχους ἄγειν to bring the companies up *in column.* IV. generally, like ὀρθός, *straight,* opp. to crooked.

ὀρθο-βᾰτέω, (ὀρθός, βαίνω) *to go straight on* or *upright.*

ὀρθό-βουλος, ον, (ὀρθός, βουλή) *right-counselling.*

ὀρθο-δᾱής, ές, (ὀρθός, δαῆναι) *knowing rightly how to do,* c. inf.

ὀρθο-δίκαιος, ον, (ὀρθός, δίκαιος) *righteously judging.*

ὀρθο-δίκας, Dor. for ὀρθοδίκης, ου, ὁ, (ὀρθός, δικάζω) *a righteous judge.* [ῐ]

ὀρθοδρομέω, *to run straight forward.* From

ὀρθο-δρόμος, ον, (ὀρθός, δραμεῖν) *running straight forward.*

ὀρθο-έπεια, ἡ, (ὀρθός, ἔπος) *correct language.*

ὀρθό-θριξ, τρῐχος, ὁ, ἡ, (ὀρθός, θρίξ) *with hair upstanding*, or *making the hair stand on end.*

ὀρθό-κραιρος, α, ον, (ὀρθός, κραῖρα) *with straight* or *upright horns*, epith. of horned cattle: *with upright beaks*, of the two ends of a galley which turned up so as to resemble horns: Ep. gen. pl. fem. ὀρθοκραιράων.

ὀρθό-κρᾶνος, ον, (ὀρθός, κρᾶνον) *having a high head* or *crown*: *with a lofty mound.*

ὀρθομαντεία, ἡ, *true prophecy.* From

ὀρθό-μαντις, εως Ion ιος, ὁ, ἡ, (ὀρθός, μάντις) *a true prophet.*

ὀρθο-πάλη, ἡ, (ὀρθός, πάλη) *wrestling upright.* [ᾰ]

ὀρθό-πλοος, ον, contr. -πλους, ουν, (ὀρθός, πλέω) *sailing straight before the wind*: generally, *successful.*

ὀρθοποδέω, (ὀρθόπους) *to walk straight* or *uprightly.*

ὀρθό-πολις, εως, ὁ, ἡ, (ὀρθος, πόλις) *upholding cities.*

ὀρθό-πους, ὁ, ἡ, -πουν, τό, gen. -ποδος, (ὀρθός, πούς) *with straight feet*: *standing upright.* II. *uphill, steep.*

ʼΟΡΘΟ΄Σ, ή, όν, *straight*, Lat. *rectus*: in height, *upright, standing erect.* II. in line, *straight, straight forward, in a straight line*; ὀρθὸς ἀντ' ἠελίοιο τετραμμένος turned *straight* to front the sun; ὀρθὸν πόδα τιθέναι *to put the foot straight out*, as in walking, opp. to κατηρεφής when it is covered with the robe from not being in motion; βλέπειν ὀρθά to see *straight* or *well.* III. metaph. *right, safe, prosperous.* 2. *right, true, exact*; ὀρθ' ἀκούειν to be *rightly* called: ὀρθῷ λόγῳ in *strict* terms, *in very truth*: so Adv., ὀρθῶς λέγειν to speak *true.* 3. *true, genuine, real.* 4. *upright, righteous, just*, Lat. *rectus*; κατὰ τὸ ὀρθὸν δικάζειν to judge *righteously.* 5. *on tiptoe, in eager expectation*, Lat. *erectus animo.* IV. ἡ ὀρθή (sub. πτῶσις) *the nominative*, Lat. *casus rectus*, as opp. to the oblique cases.

ὀρθο-στάδην, Adv. (ὀρθός, στῆναι) *standing upright, in a standing posture.*

ὀρθο-στάτης, ου, ὁ, (ὀρθός, στῆναι) *one who stands upright* II. *an upright shaft, pillar*: as Adj., κλίμακες ὀρθοστάται *upright* ladders. III. a sort of *cake* used in funeral oblations. [ᾰ]

ὀρθότατα, Adv. Sup. of ὀρθῶς.

ὀρθότης, ητος, ἡ, (ὀρθός) *straightness, upright posture.* II. metaph. *rightness, fitness*: *the right sense.*

ὀρθο-τομέω, (ὀρθός, τέμνω) *to cut straight*: *handle aright.*

ὀρθόω, f. ώσω: aor. 1 ὤρθωσα:—Pass., aor. 1 ὠρθώθην:—(ὀρθός):—*to set straight*: 1. in height, *to set upright, set up*: of buildings, *to raise, restore, repair*: hence, ὀρθωθεὶς *raised up, set on one's legs again*:—Pass. *to stand* or *sit upright.* 2. in a line, *to set straight*:—Pass. *to be aimed straight.* II. metaph. *to raise up, restore to health, safety*, etc. 2. *to exalt, honour, extol.* 3. ὀρθῶσαι ὕμνον *to raise the lofty* song. 4. *to guide aright.* III. Pass. of actions, *to succeed*; *prosper*; τὸ ὀρθούμενον *success*: of persons and places, *to flourish, prosper.* 2. *to be right, be true.* 3. *to be upright, deal justly* or *uprightly.*

ὀρθρεύοισα, Dor. for -εύουσα, part. fem. of

ὀρθρεύω, f. σω, (ὄρθρος) *to rise* or *wake early.*

ὀρθρίδιος, α, ον, poët. for ὄρθριος. [ῐ]

ὀρθρίζω, f. σω, (ὄρθρος) *to rise, wake early.*

ὀρθρινός [ῑ], ή, όν, (ὄρθρος) later form for ὄρθριος.

ὄρθρῐος, α, ον, also ος, ον, (ὄρθρος) *at daybreak, at dawn, in the morning, early*: irreg. Comp. and Sup. ὀρθριαίτερος, -αίτατος:—Neut. τὸ ὄρθριον or ὄρθριον, as Adv. *in the morning, early.*

ὀρθρο-βόας, ου, ὁ, (ὄρθρος, βοάω) *the early caller, Chanticleer*, i. e. the cock.

ὀρθρο-γόη, ἡ, (ὄρθρος, γοάω) *early-wailing*, of the swallow.

ὀρθρο-λάλος, ον, (ὄρθρος, λαλέω) *early-twittering.*

ʼΟΡΘΡΟΣ, ὁ, *the time about daybreak, dawn, early morn*; τὸν ὄρθρον, absol., *in the morning*; so, ὄρθρου γενομένου *at dawn*; and ἅμα ὄρθρῳ, ἐς ὄρθρον, κατ' ὄρθρον, περὶ ὄρθρον; but πρὸς ὄρθρον towards *dawn*: ὄρθρος βαθύς early *morn.*

ὀρθρο-φοιτο-σῡκοφαντο-δῐκο-τᾰλαίπωρος, ον, (ὄρθρος, φοιτάω, συκοφάντης, δίκη, ταλαίπωρος) ὀρθ. τρόποι *early-prowling base-informing sad-litigious plaguy* ways.

ὀρθωθείς, aor. 1 pass. part. of ὀρθόω.

ὀρθ-ώνῠμος, ον, (ὀρθός, ὄνομα) *rightly-named.*

ὀρθῶς, Adv. of ὀρθός, *rightly*: *uprightly, justly*: *truly, really.*

ʼΟρθωσία, ἡ, = Ὀρθία.

ὀρθωτήρ, ῆρος, ὁ, (ὀρθόω) *one who sets upright, a restorer.*

ὀρῐ-βάτης, ου, ὁ, dub. for ὀρειβατής.

ʼΟΡΙ΄ΓΑ΄ΝΟΝ, τό, and ὀρίγᾰνος, ἡ, an acrid herb, *marjoram*: ὀρίγανον βλέπειν to look *origanum*, i. e. to look *sour* or *crabbed.* [ῐ]

ὀριγνάομαι, Med., with fut. -ήσομαι, aor. 1 pass. ὠριγνήθην: (ὀρέγομαι):—*to stretch oneself out.* 2. c. gen. *to stretch oneself after* a thing, *reach at, grasp at.*

ὁρίζω: fut. ὁρίσω Att. ὁριῶ: aor. 1 ὥρισα Ion. οὔρισα: pf. ὥρικα:—Med., fut. ὁριοῦμαι: aor. 1 ὡρισάμην:—Pass., fut. ὁρισθήσομαι: aor. 1 ὡρίσθην: pf. ὥρισμαι (sometimes used in med. sense): (ὅρος):—*to divide* or *separate* one part *from* another. *to divide as a boundary*; ποταμὸς οὐρίζει τήν τε Σκυθικὴν καὶ τὴν Νευρίδα γῆν a river *is the boundary between* Scythia and Neuris;—Pass., of a country, *to be bounded.* 2. ὁρίζειν τινὰ ἀπὸ γῆς *to part, banish* one from the land. II. *to mark out by boundaries, lay down, mark out*: *to limit, define*:—Med. *to mark out for oneself, set up, dedicate.* III. generally, *to deter-*

mine, appoint: to settle. 2. to define a word. 3. to assign, ὁρίζειν ψῆφον to give a vote. IV. intr. to border upon.

ὀρῑκός, ή, όν, (ὀρεύς) of or for a mule.

ὀρινθείην, aor. 1 pass. opt. of ὀρίνω.

ὀρίνω: aor. 1 ὤρῑνα Ep. ὄρῑνα:—Pass. 3 sing. impf. ὠρίνετο: aor. 1 ὠρίνθην Ep. ὀρίνθην: (ὄρνυμι):—to stir, raise, Lat. agitare: metaph. to move, excite, affect the mind:—Pass. to be stirred, roused, disquieted: to be affrighted, thrown into confusion.

ὅριον, τό, = ὅρος, a bound, goal: ὅρια, τά, boundaries, borders, frontier.

ὅριος, ον, (ὅρος) of or presiding over boundaries.

ὅρισμα Ion. **οὔρ-**, τό, (ὁρίζω) a boundary: in plur. the borders, frontier.

ὁριστής, οῦ, ὁ, (ὁρίζω) one who marks boundaries: one who determines.

ὀρί-τροφος, ον, (ὄρος, τρέφω) mountain-bred.

ὀρκάνη, ἡ, = ἑρκάνη, ἕρκος, from ἔργω, εἴργω, an enclosure, fence: a trap or pitfall. [ᾰ]

ὀρκ-ᾰπάτης, ου, ὁ, (ὅρκος, ἀπατάω) an oath-breaker. [ᾰ]

ὁρκίζω, f. ίσω, (ὅρκος) to make one swear, adjure.

ὅρκιον, τό, (ὅρκος) an oath: also a pledge, surety. II. mostly in plur., ὅρκια, τά, things sworn to, articles of a treaty, a treaty; ὅρκια πιστὰ ταμεῖν to conclude a binding treaty, Lat. foedus ferire, icisse foedus: of two parties, in Med., ὅρκια τάμνεσθαι to make a treaty between them; ὅρκια δηλήσασθαι, ὑπὲρ ὅρκια δηλήσασθαι to violate a solemn treaty: so too, ὅρκια συγχεῦαι, ὅρκια ψεύσασθαι, opp. to ὅρκια φυλάσσειν or τηρεῖν. 2. the victims sacrificed on taking these solemn oaths, like ἱερά.

ὅρκιος, ον, more rarely α, ον, (ὅρκος) of or for an oath: sworn, bound by oath. 2. that is sworn by, adjured as witness to an oath; ὅρκιοι θεοί the gods invoked at an oath; ξίφος ὅρκιον a sword which is sworn by.

ὍΡΚΟΣ, ου, ὁ, an oath; ὅρκον ὀμόσαι to swear an oath; ὅρκος θεῶν an oath by the gods; ὅρκον λαμβάνειν to accept an oath from another; ἀποδιδόναι to take it oneself. 2. the witness of the oath, the power or object adjured, as the Styx by the gods. II. Ὅρκος, personified, son of Eris, who visits the transgression of an oath. (ὅρκος was orig. equiv. to ἕρκος, as ὀρκοῦρος to ἑρκουρος.)

ὀρκ-οῦρος, ὁ, = ἑρκοῦρος.

ὁρκόω, f. ώσω, (ὅρκος) to make one swear, bind by oath:—Pass. to be bound by oath, to swear.

ὅρκωμα, τό, (ὁρκόω) an oath.

ὁρκωμοσία, ἡ, (ὁρκωμοτέω) a swearing, an oath.

ὁρκωμόσιον, τό, the place of an oath. II. in pl. asseverations on oath. From

ὁρκωμοτέω, f. ήσω, to take an oath, swear: ὁρκωμοτεῖν θεούς to swear by the gods. From

ὁρκ-ωμότης, ου, ὁ, (ὅρκος, ὄμνυμι) = ὁρκωτής.

ὁρκωτής, οῦ, ὁ, (ὁρκόω) one who administers an oath.

ὁρμᾰθεῖν, an aor. 2 form of ὁρμάω, to rush, whence subj. ὁρμᾰθῶ: but ὁρμᾰθῇ is Dor. for ὁρμηθῇ, 3 sing. aor. 1 subj. pass. of ὁρμάω.

ὁρμᾰθός, οῦ, ὁ, (ὅρμος) a row, chain, cluster or string of things hanging one from the other.

ὁρμαίνω: impf. ὥρμαινον: aor. 1 ὥρμηνα: (ὁρμάω): —to move or stir violently; to turn over or revolve a plan in the mind, to ponder or muse upon it: to debate, consider. 2. to long for, desire. II. later, 1. trans. to drive, urge on: to excite, inflame. 2. intr. to hasten, hurry, be impatient.

ὁρμάω, f. ήσω: aor. 1 ὥρμησα: pf. ὥρμηκα: (ὁρμή): I. trans. to set in motion, urge on, rouse: to stir up. II. intr. to hurry or rush on: c. inf. to be eager to do, to start or essay to do: absol. to be eager or foremost. 2. to rush headlong, esp. at one, c. gen. III. Pass. with fut. med. ὁρμήσομαι; aor. 1 med. ὁρμήσασθαι and pass. ὁρμηθῆναι; pf. pass. ὥρμημαι:—in same sense as intr. act.: 1. to hurry, hasten, start off eagerly: generally, to be eager, to long or purpose to do. 2. to set off or proceed from a place, to begin from; of a general, to make a place his base of operations: ἀπ' ἐλασσόνων ὁρμώμενος setting out from or beginning with smaller means. 3. absol. to rush on, make a desperate attack, to be eager: generally, to make a start, go; ὁ λόγος ὥρμηται the report flies abroad.

ὁρμέατο, Ion. for ὥρμηντο, 3 pl. plqpf. pass. of ὁρμάω.

ὁρμειά, ἡ, = ὁρμιά.

ὄρμενος, aor. 2 part. med. of ὄρνυμι.

ὁρμέω, f. ήσω, (ὅρμος):—to be moored, lie at anchor, of a ship: proverbial, ἐπὶ δυοῖν ἀγκυραῖν ὁρμεῖν to ride two anchors, as we say 'to have two strings to your bow:' metaph. to anchor one's hopes upon, depend upon.

ὁρμεώμενος, Ion. part. pass. of ὁρμάω.

ὁρμή, ἡ, (ὄρνυμι) an assault, attack, the first shock or onset in war, Lat. impetus; mostly of things, as, ἔγχεος ὁρμή the force of a spear; πυρὸς ὁρμή the rage of fire; κύματος ὁρμή the shock of a wave. 2. the beginning or first start in a thing: a struggle or effort to reach a thing. 3. eagerness, violence, passion, impulse; μιᾷ ὁρμῇ with one accord; c. gen. eager desire for a thing. 4. a start, setting out on a march, etc.

ὁρμηθείς, εῖσα, έν, aor. 1 pass. part. of ὁρμάω.

ὅρμημα τό, (ὁρμάω) any violent impulse, passionate desire.

ὁρμήσειε, 3 Ep. aor. 1 opt. of ὁρμάω.

ὁρμητήριον, τό, (ὁρμάω) any means of exciting, a stimulant, incentive. II. a starting-place, station, head-quarters.

ὁρμιά, ἡ, (ὅρμος) a fishing-line of horse-hair Lat. linea. [ῑ]

ὁρμίζω: fut. -ίσω Ep. -ίσσω Att. -ιῶ: aor. 1 ὥρμισα: (ὅρμος);—to bring to anchorage, bring into harbour, to moor, anchor. 2. generally, to make fast or sure. II. Med., with fut. med. ὁρμιοῦμαι, aor. 1 med. ὡρμισάμην and pass. ὡρμίσθην: pf. pass. ὥρμισμαι:—*to come to anchor, anchor; ὁρμίζεσθαι πρὸς πέδον to come to* a place *and anchor* there. 2. metaph. *to be in haven, to reach the barbour,* i. e. *to be at rest; ὁρμίζεσθαι ἔκ τινος to be dependent on* a thing.

ὁρμῑη-βόλος, ον, (ὁρμιά, βάλλω) *throwing a line, angling.*

ὁρμο-δοτήρ, ῆρος, ὁ, (ὅρμος, δίδωμι) *a bringer into harbour, a pilot.*

ὅρμος, ὁ, (εἴρω) *a cord, chain, necklace, collar; στεφάνων ὅρμος a string* of crowns. 2. a kind of *dance performed in a ring.* II. *a roadstead, anchorage,* Lat. *statio navalis: the inner part of a harbour,* as opp. to λιμήν. 2. generally, *a haven, place of shelter* or *refuge.*

ὀρνῡπέτιον, τό, Boeot. for ὄρνεον.

ὄρνεον, τό, = ὄρνις. II. τὰ ὄρνεα, *the bird-market.*

ὀρνεό-φοιτος, ον, (ὄρνεον, φοιτάω) *haunted by birds.*

ὀρνίθ-αρχος, ὁ, (ὄρνις, ἀρχός) *king of birds.* [ῐ]

ὀρνίθειος, α, ον, also ος, ον, (ὄρνις) *of* or *belonging to a bird; κρέα ὀρνίθεια birds'* flesh.

ὀρνῑθευτής, οῦ, ὁ, *a bird-catcher, fowler.* From

ὀρνῑθεύω, f. σω, (ὄρνις) *to catch, net, snare birds.*

ὀρνῑθίας, ου, (ὄρνις) masc. Adj., a name given to the north wind in spring, *which brought the birds of passage; χειμὼν ὀρνιθίας* a storm *of birds.*

ὀρνῑθικός, ή, όν, (ὄρνις) *of* or *for birds.*

ὀρνίθιον, τό, Dim. of ὄρνις, *a little bird: a nestling, chicken.* [νῐ]

ὀρνῑθό-γονος, ον, (ὄρνις, *γένω) *sprung from a bird.*

ὀρνῑθο-θήρας, ου, ὁ, (ὄρνις, θηράω) *a bird-catcher, fowler.*

ὀρνῑθο-λόχος Dor. **ὀρνῑχ-**, ὁ, (ὄρνις, λοχάω) *a bird-catcher, fowler.*

ὀρνῑθομᾰνέω, f. ήσω, *to be mad for birds.* From

ὀρνῑθο-μᾰνής, ές, (ὄρνις, μανῆναι) *mad after birds.*

ὀρνῑθο-πέδη, ἡ, (ὄρνις, πέδη) *a snare* or *gin for birds.*

ὄρνιθος, gen. of ὄρνις: Ep. dat. pl. ὀρνίθεσσι.

ὀρνῑθο-σκόπος, ον, (ὄρνις, σκοπέω) *observing the flight and cries of birds,* Lat. *augur, auspex; θᾶκος ὀρνιθοσκόπος an augur's* seat, Lat. *templum augurale.*

ὀρνῑθο-τροφία, ἡ, (ὄρνις, τρέφω) *bird-keeping.*

ὄρνῖος, ον, also ος, ον, poët. for ὀρνίθειος.

ὌΡΝΙΣ, ὁ, but also ἡ: gen. ὄρνῑθος, etc.: acc. sing. ὄρνῑθα and ὄρνιν: pl. ὄρνῑθες, etc.: Att. pl. ὄρνεις, gen. ὀρνέων, acc. ὄρνεις: Dor. forms, gen. ὄρνῑχος, pl. ὄρνῑχες, etc., as if from a Nom. ὄρνιξ:—*a bird:* often added to the names of birds, as ὄρνις ἀηδών, ὄρνις πέρδιξ, the nightingale, the partridge. II. also like οἰωνός, *a bird of omen, ὄρνις κακός a bird of* evil *augury:* hence, like Lat. *avis* for *augurium, the omen* or *prophecy taken from the flight* or *cries of birds:* in bad sense, *an omen, fateful presage.* III. in Att., ὄρνις, ὁ, *a cock; ὄρνις, ἡ, a hen.* IV. in pl. sometimes *the bird-market,* cf. ὄρνεον. V. poët. Μουσῶν ὄρνιθες, *the birds* of the Muses, i. e. *poets.* VI. proverb., ὀρνίθων γάλα 'pigeon's milk,' i. e. any marvellous good-fortune.

ὄρνῑχος, -χα, Dor. gen. and acc. of ὄρνις: poët. dat. pl. ὀρνίχεσσι.

ὄρνῠθι, ύτω, pres. imperat. of ὄρνυμι.

ὀρνύμεν, ὀρνύμεναι, Ep. for ὀρνύναι, pres. inf. of ὄρνυμι.

ὀρνύμενος, η, ον, pres. med. part. of ὄρνυμι.

ὄρνῡμι or **ὀρνύω** [ῠ], lengthd. form of Root *ὈΡΩ: imperat. ὄρνῠθι, ύτω, etc.: impf. ὤρνυον: fut. ὄρσω: aor. 1 ὦρσα, part. ὄρσας, Ion. 3 sing. ὄρσασκε: 3 sing. redupl. aor. 2 ὄρωρε:—Med. ὄρνῠμαι, imperat. ὄρνυσο, ύσθω, υσθε, part. ὀρνύμενος: impf. ὠρνύμην, 3 sing. and pl. ὤρνῠτο, ὤρνυντο: fut. ὄρσομαι, also ὀροῦμαι, 3 sing. ὀρεῖται: aor. 2 ὠρόμην, 3 sing. ὤρετο contr. ὦρτο, 3 pl. without augm. ὄροντο also ὀρέοντο; 3 sing. subj. ὄρηται; imperat. ὄρσο or ὄρσεο Ion. contr. ὄρσευ; inf. ὄρθαι, contr. for ὀρέσθαι; part. ὄρμενος, η, ον, for ὀρόμενος:—pf. ὄρωρα, in intr. sense 3 sing. subj. ὀρώρῃ: 3 sing. plqpf. ὀρώρει, also ὠρώρει I. Act., *to rouse, stir, stir up: to set on, let loose upon:*—Med., with pf. ὄρωρα, *to move, stir oneself; εἰσόκε μοι φίλα γοῦνατ' ὀρώρῃ* while my limbs *have power to move.* 2. Act. *to make to arise, call forth:* of animals, *to rouse, put up, start, chace:*—Med. *to start up, arise:* esp. *to wake out of sleep, to spring up:* also c. inf. *to rise to do* a thing, *set about.* 3. Act. *to stir up, rouse, encourage, cheer on:*—Pass. and Med. *to be roused, stirred in mind, excited, inflamed.* 4. Act. of things, *to call forth, cause, excite,* Lat. *ciēre:*—Med. *to come on, to arise,* Lat. *oriri.*

ὄρνῠτο, ὄρνυντο, Ep. for ὤρνυτο, ὤρνυντο, 3 sing. and pl. impf. of ὄρνυμι.

ὈΡΟΒΟΣ, ὁ, *the vetch,* Lat. ERVUM.

ὀρόγυια, ἡ, poët. for ὀργυιά.

ὀροδαμνίς, ίδος, ἡ, Dim. of ὀρόδαμνος, *a sprig.*

ὀρόδαμνος, ὁ, *a bough, branch.*

ὀρο-θεσία, ἡ, (ὅρος, τίθημι) *the fixing of boundaries, boundaries.*

ὀροθύνω: Ep. impf. ὀρόθυνον: also aor. 1 imperat. ὀρόθυνον:—like ὄρνυμι, *to stir up, rouse, urge on.*

ὀροί-τυπος, ον, = ὀρείτυπος.

ὄρομαι, Dep. (οὖρος *a guard*) *to watch, keep watch and ward, be on guard.*

ὀρο-μᾱλίδες, αἱ, (ὄρος, μῆλον) Dor. for ὀρομηλίδες, a kind of *wild apples.*

ὈΡΟ'Σ or **ὀρρός**, ὁ, *whey, the watery* or *serous part of milk,* Lat. *serum.* 2. *the watery parts of the blood.*

ὌΡΟΣ Ion. **οὖρος**, εος, τό, *a mountain, hill: a range* or *chain of hills.*

ὍΡΟΣ Ion. **οὖρος**, ου, ὁ, *a boundary, limit, frontier, border:* esp. *a land-mark.* 2. οὖροι, plur., are *marking* or *monumental stones* bearing inscriptions, *tables set up on mortgaged property,* to serve as evidence of the debt. II. *a rule, standard, limit, measure* III. *the definition* of a word.

Ὀροσάγγαι, οἱ, Persian word for *the Benefactors of the King,* = εὐεργέται.

ὀρούω, fut. σω: aor. 1 ὄρουσα: (ὄρνυμι):—intr. *to*

rush violently on or *forward, to hasten, dart* or *start forward.*

ὀροφή, ἡ, (ἐρέφω) *the roof* or *ceiling of a room: the roof of a house.*

ὀροφη-φάγος, ον, (ὀροφή, φαγεῖν) *roof-devouring.*

ὀροφη-φόρος, ον, (ὀροφή, φέρω) *bearing a roof.*

ὀροφίας, ου, ὁ, *living under a roof;* μῦς ὀροφίας the *domestic* mouse, opp. to μῦς ἀρουραῖος (the field mouse); ὀροφίας ὄφις a *tame* snake.

ὄροφος, ὁ, (ἐρέφω) *the reeds used for thatching houses* II. *a roof:* in pl. *a house, temple.*

ὀρόω, Ep. for ὁράω: part. ὀρόων for ὁρῶν.

ὀρόωντι, Dor. for ὁρῶσι, 3 pl. of ὁράω.

ὌΡΠΗΞ Att. ὅρπηξ, ηκος, Dor. ὅρπαξ, ᾶκος, ὁ:—*a sapling, young shoot* or *plant: a rod* or *pole: a lance.* II. metaph. *a scion, descendant.*

ὀρρᾰνός, ὁ, Aeol. for οὐρανός.

ὀρρο-πύγιον, τό, (ὄρρος, πυγή) *the tail* or *tail-feathers* of birds. 2. *the tail-fin of fish.* 3. *the tail* or *rump* of any animal. [ῡ]

ὈΡΡΟΣ, ὁ, *the end of the os sacrum: the tail, rump.*

ὈΡΡΟ΄Σ, ὁ, = ὀρός, *whey, serum.*

ὀρρωδέω Ion. ἀρρωδ–: f. ήσω:—*to shudder at, shrink from, dread,* Lat. *horreo,* c. acc.: c. gen. rei, *to fear for* or *because of* a thing. Hence

ὀρρωδία, ἡ, *a shuddering at, shrinking from, affright*

ὄρσας, aor. 1 part. of ὄρνυμι.

ὄρσασκε, Ion. for ὦρσε, 3 sing. aor. 1 of ὄρνυμι.

ὄρσεο, ὄρσευ, Ep. for ὄρσαι, aor. 1 med. imperat. of ὄρνυμι.

ὀρσέ-κτῠπος, ον, (ὄρνυμι, κτύπος) *noise-arousing;* Ζεὺς ὀρσέκτυπος *the rouser of thunder.*

ὀρσῐ-νεφής, ές, (ὄρνυμι, νέφος) *cloud-raising.*

ὀρσί-πους, -ποδος, ὁ, ἡ, (ὄρνυμι, πούς) *raising the foot, light-footed.*

ὄρσο, Ep. for ὄρσαι, aor. 1 med. imperat. of ὄρνυμι, *bestir thee! up! arouse thee!*

ὀρσο-θύρη, ἡ, (ὄρνυμι, θύρα) *a raised door approached by steps.* [ῠ]

ὀρσολοπεύω and -έω, *to provoke, attack:*—Pass., θυμὸς ὀρσολοπεῖται my heart *is troubled.* From

ὀρσόλοπος, ον, *provoking strife, turbulent.* (Deriv. uncertain.)

ὀρσός, Lacon. for ὀρθός.

ὀρσο-τρῐαίνης Dor. -τριαίνας, α, ὁ; a poët. nom. -τρίαινα: (ὄρνυμι, τρίαινα):—*wielder of the trident.*

ὄρσω, fut. of ὄρνυμι.

ὀρτάζω, Ion. for ἑορτάζω.

ὀρτᾰλίς, ίδος, ἡ, (ὄρνῡμι) *the young* of any animal, Lat. *pullus: a young bird, a chicken.* Hence

ὀρτᾰλῐχεύς and ὀρτάλῐχος, ὁ, *a bird, fowl: a domestic fowl, chicken.*

ὀρτή, ἡ, Ion. for ἑορτή.

Ὀρτῠγία, ἡ, (ὄρτυξ) properly *Quail-island,* the ancient name of Delos: also part of the city of Syracuse, called also Νᾶσος or *the Island.*

ὀρτῠγο-κόπος, ον, (ὄρτυξ, κόπτω) *playing at knocking down quails.*

ὀρτῠγο-μήτρα, ἡ, (ὄρτυξ, μήτηρ) *a bird which migrates with the quails:* applied to Leto *the Ortygian mother:* cf. Ὀρτυγία.

ὌΡΤΥΞ, ῠγος, ὁ, *the quail,* Lat. *coturnix,* -*īcis.*

ὀρῠγῆναι, aor. 2 inf. pass. of ὀρύσσω.

ὄρυγμα, τό, (ὀρύσσω) *a place dug out, a pit, ditch, hole, trench,* Lat. *scrobs: a mine, tunnel:* at Athens = βάραθρον, *the pit* into which criminals were thrown. II. = ὄρυξις.

ὀρυγμᾰδός, ὁ, late form for ὀρυμαγδός.

ὀρυκτός, ή, όν, (ὀρύσσω) *dug, formed by digging.* II. *dug out, quarried, mined.*

ὀρῠμαγδός, ὁ, *a loud noise, rumbling, roaring, any tumultuous sound,* not of the human voice.

ὄρυξ, ῠγος, ὁ, (ὀρύσσω) a kind of *gazelle* or *antelope,* in Egypt and Lybia, so called from its *pointed horns.*

ὀρύξαι, aor. 1 inf. of ὀρύσσω.

ὄρυξις, εως, ἡ, (ὀρύσσω) *a digging.*

ὄρυς, υος, ὁ, an unknown wild animal in Lybia.

ὈΡΥ΄ΣΣΩ Att. -ττω: fut. ὀρύξω: aor. 1 ὤρυξα Ep. ὄρυξα: pf. ὀρώρῠχα: plqpf. ὠρωρύχειν:—Pass., aor. 1 ὠρύχθην: pf. ὀρώρυγμαι: plqpf. ὠρωρύγμην:—*to dig,* Lat. *fodio.* 2. *to dig up:* Med., λίθους ὀρύξασθαι *to have* stones *dug* or *quarried:* Pass., ὁ ὀρυσσόμενος χοῦς the soil *that was dug up.* 3. *to dig through, make a passage through, burrow.* 4. *to bury.*

ὀρφάνευμα, τό, *orphan state.* From

ὀρφᾰνεύω, f. σω, (ὀρφανός) *to take care of orphans, tend, rear them:*—Pass. with fut. med. -εύσομαι, *to be an orphan, be in an orphan state.*

ὀρφᾰνία, ἡ, (ὀρφανός) *orphanhood:* generally, *bereavement, destitution.*

ὀρφᾰνίζω, f. σω, (ὀρφανός) *to make orphan: to bereave, deprive:*—Pass. *to be left an orphan.*

ὀρφᾰνῐκός, ή, όν, (ὀρφανός) *orphan, fatherless;* ἦμαρ ὀρφανικός the day *which makes one an orphan.*

ὀρφάνιος, ον, = ὀρφανικός.

ὀρφᾰνιστής, οῦ, ὁ, (ὀρφανίζω) *one who takes care of orphans, a guardian.*

ὈΡΦΑΝΟ΄Σ, ή, όν, Att. ός, όν, Lat. *ORBUS, left orphan, without father* or *mother, fatherless.* 2. c. gen. *reft* or *bereft of* a thing; ὀρφανοὶ γενεᾶς *reft of* offspring, childless.

ὀρφᾰνο-φύλαξ, ἄκος, ὁ, (ὀρφανός, φύλαξ) *the guardian of an orphan.* [ῠ]

ὀρφᾰνόω, f. ώσω, (ὀρφανός) *to make orphan:*—Pass. *to be bereft of* a thing.

Ὀρφειος, α, ον, *of Orpheus.* From

Ὀρφεύς, έως, ὁ, *Orpheus,* a famous Thracian bard.

ὀρφναῖος, α, ον, (ορφνη) *dark, dusky, murky.* II. *nightly, by night.*

ὌΡΦΝΗ Dor. ὄρφνα, ἡ, *darkness, night: gloom.* Hence

ὄρφνῐνος, η, ον, *dark, dusky;* ὄρφνινον χρῶμα a colour *mixed of black, red and white,* between πορφύρεος and φοινίκινος.

ὀρφνίτης, ου, ὁ, (ὄρφνη) *dusky*. [ῑ]

ὌΡΦΟΣ Att. **ὀρφώς**, ὁ, *a* kind of *sea-perch*.

ὄρχᾰμος, ὁ, (ὄρχος) *the first of a row, a file-leader, fugle-man: the Coryphaeus* or *leader of the chorus*.

ὄρχᾰτος, ὁ, = ὄρχος, *a row of trees*. II. *a piece of land enclosed and planted*, Milton's *orchat, an orchard, garden*. (From ὄρχος, like μέσατος from μέσος.)

ὀρχέομαι, f. ήσομαι: aor. 1 ὠρχησάμην: Dep.: (ὄρχος):—*to dance:* c. acc. *to represent by dancing* or *gestures; ὀρχεῖσθαι* Κύκλωπα, Lat. *Cyclopa moveri, to dance* the Cyclops. 2. *to leap*.

ὀρχηδόν, Adv. (ὄρχος) *one after another, all in a row, man by man*, Lat. *virītim*.

ὀρχηθμός Ion. **ὀρχησμός**, ὁ, (ὀρχέομαι) *a dancing, the dance*.

ὄρχημα, τό, (ὀρχέομαι) *a dance, dancing*.

ὄρχησις, ἡ, (ὀρχέομαι) *dancing, the dance: pantomimic dancing*.

ὀρχησμός, ὁ, Att. for ὀρχηθμός.

ὀρχηστήρ, ῆρος, ὁ, and **ὀρχηστής**, οῦ, ὁ, (ὀρχέομαι) *a dancer*. Hence

ὀρχηστικός, ή, όν, *of, fit for dancing*.

ὀρχηστο-δῐδάσκᾰλος, ὁ, (ὀρχέομαι, διδάσκαλος) *a dancing-master*.

ὀρχηστο-μᾰνέω, f. ήσω, (ὀρχέομαι, μανῆναι) *to be dancing-mad*.

ὀρχήστρα, ἡ, (ὀρχέομαι) *an orchestra*, in the Attic theatre *a large semicircular space on which the chorus danced*. II. generally, *a place for dancing*.

ὀρχηστρίς, ίδος, ἡ, fem. of ὀρχηστής, *a dancing girl*.

ὀρχηστύς, ύος, ἡ, Ion. for ὄρχησις, (ὀρχέομαι) *the dance, dancing;* contr. dat. ὀρχηστυῖ.

ὈΡΧΙ'ΛΟΣ, ὁ, a bird, prob. *the wren*. [ῐ]

ὀρχῐπεδάω, f. ήσω, (ὀρχίπεδον) *to seize the testicles*.

ὀρχῐ-πέδη, ἡ, (ὄρχις, πέδη) *impotence*.

ὀρχί-πεδον, τό, in pl. ὀρχίπεδα, τά, (ὄρχις, πέδον) *the testicles*, Lat. *testiculi*.

ὌΡΧΙΣ, ιος and εως, ὁ, pl. ὄρχεις or ὄρχῑς Ion. ὄρχιες, *a testicle, the testicles*.

Ὀρχομενός, ἡ, the name of several Greek cities, the most famous of which was Ὀρχόμενος Μινύειος in Boeotia.

ὌΡΧΟΣ, ὁ, *a row of trees;* cf. ὄρχατος.

ὄρωρα, pf. of ὄρνυμι.

ὀρώρει, 3 sing. Ep. plqpf. of ὄρνυμι.

ὀρώρεται, Ep. 3 sing. pres. pass. of ὄρνυμι, equiv. to ὄρωρε: subj. ὀρώρηται.

ὀρωρέχαται, Ion. 3 pl. pf. pass. of ὀρέγω.

ὀρωρέχατο, Ion. 3 pl. plqpf. pass. of ὀρέγω.

ὀρώρυκτο, 3 sing. plqpf. pass. of ὀρύσσω.

ὀρώρῠχα, pf. of ὀρύσσω.

ὍΣ, ἥ, ὅ; gen. οὗ, ἧς, οὗ, dat. ᾧ, ᾗ, ᾧ; acc. ὅν, ἥν, ὅ: pl., nom. οἵ, αἵ, ἅ; gen. ὧν; dat. οἷς, αἷς, οἷς; acc. οὕς, ἅς, ἅ. There is also an Ion. gen. ὅου, fem. ἕης; and Ep. fem. dat. pl. ᾗς and ᾗσι.

A. Relat. Pronoun, *who, which* or *that*, Lat. *qui:* the Relat. Pron. often takes the case of the Anteced. by attraction, as, τῆς γενεῆς, ἧς Ζεὺς δῶκε, for ἥν Ζεὺς δῶκε: the neut. ὅ is used to refer to sentences where no antecedent is expressed, as, ὃ δὲ πάντων μέγιστον, ὃ δὲ πάντων δεινότατον, etc., but *what* is greatest of all, *what* is most strange of all, etc. The Relat. Pron. also stands for ἵνα, as in Lat. *qui* for *ut*, to express an end or intention, as, ἄγγελον ἧκαν, ὃς ἀγγείλειε γυναικί they sent a messenger *to* tell, Lat. *nuncium miserunt, qui nunciaret*.

The Relat. Pronoun is used absol. in some cases: I. gen. sing., of Time, ἐξ οὗ (sub. χρόνου) *from the time when, since:* also οὗ alone, *when;* ἔστιν οὗ, *sometimes, at times*. 2. of Place, *of which place*, i. e. *where;* ἔστιν οὗ *in some places*. II. dat. sing. fem. ᾗ, of Place, Lat. *qua, at which place, where:*—later, of *motion to* a place, *whither:*—in full τῇ, ᾗ .. *there, where* .., *thither, whither* ... 2. of the Way or Manner, like ὅπως, as Lat. *quomodo;* ᾗ θέμις ἐστίν *as* is right: *so far as*, Lat. *qua, quatenus*. 3. with Sup. Adv., ᾗ μάλιστα, ᾗ ἄριστον, etc., like ὡς μάλιστα, etc., Lat. *quam maxime*, etc. III. acc. sing. neut. ὅ, for δι' ὅ, *that, because*, Lat. *quod*. 2. *wherefore*, Lat. *quapropter*.

The Relat. Pron. is modified by having particles joined with it: I. ὅς γε, Lat. *qui quidem* or *quippe qui*, gives the Relat. a limiting force, *who at least, since it was he who* ... II. ὅς κε or κέν Att. ὃς ἄν, is used in case of uncertainty, Lat. *quicunque, whosoever, who if any* ...

B. Ὅς is also used as a Demonstr. Pron., for οὗτος or ὅδε, *this, that;* chiefly in nom. masc. ὅς or οἵ, sometimes in fem. ἥ and neut. ὅ: this is chiefly found in Homer, and later in dialogues of Plato, ἦ δ' ὅς said *he*. II. in opposition, οἵ .., οἵ .. *these* .., *those* .., *the one party, the other:* Att. ὃς μέν .., ὃς δέ .. *the one* .., *the other:* ἃ μέν .., ἃ δέ .. *partly* .., *partly* ... III. ὃς καὶ ὅς *such and such a person, so and so*.

C. There is also a Possessive Pron., ὅς, ἥ, ὅν, mostly of the third person, for ἑός, *his, her:* Ep. gen. οἷο. II. of the second person, for σός, *thy, thine*. III. of the first person, for ἐμός, *my, mine*.

ὁσάκι Ep. **ὁσσάκι**, Adv. (ὅσος) *as many times as, as often as*, Lat. *quoties*.

ὁσάτιος, α, ον, Ion. **ὁσσάτιος**, poët. for ὅσος. [ᾰ]

ὁσᾰχοῦ, Adv. (ὅσος) *in as many places as*.

ὅσδος, Aeol. for ὄζος.

ὅσδω, Dor. for ὄζω.

ὁσ-ημέραι, Adv., for ὅσαι ἡμέραι, *as many days as are*, i. e. *daily, day by day*, like Lat. *quotidie* for *quot dies*.

ὁσία Ion. **-ίη**, ἡ, properly fem. of ὅσιος, *divine law, the law of nature*, answering to Lat. *fas:* hence οὐχ ὁσίη Att. οὐχ ὁσία, c. inf., *it is against the law of nature* to do; πολλὴν ὁσίαν τοῦ πράγματος νομίσαι to hold the full *lawfulness* of a thing. II. *the service of God, rites, offering;* ὁσίης ἐπιβῆναι to perform *the due rites*. III. proverb., ὁσίας ἕνεκα ποιεῖσθαί τι to do a thing *for form's sake*, for the sake of the *propriety of* the thing, Lat. *dicis caussa*. [ῐ]

ὅσῐος, α, ον, *sanctioned* or *approved by the law of nature*, opp. to δίκαιος (established by human law); τὰ ὅσια καὶ δίκαια *things of divine and human ordinance*. 2. as opp. to ἱερός (sacred, reserved to the gods), ὁσιός means *what is not so reserved*, i. e. *appropriated* or *permitted to man's use*; ἱερὰ καὶ ὅσια the property *of* gods and *men*, Lat. *sacra et profana*; ὅσιον χωρίον a place *not set apart to the gods*, *lawful for man to enter*, and so = βέβηλος, Lat. *profanus*. II. more rarely of persons, *pious*, *devout*, *scrupulous*, *religious*; c. gen., ἱερῶν πατρῴων ὅσιος *scrupulous in discharging* the sacred rites of his forefathers; ὅσιαι χεῖρες *pure*, *clean* hands.

ὁσῐότης, ητος, ἡ, (ὅσιος) *observance of divine law*, *religiousness*, *piety*, *holiness*.

ὁσῐόω, f. ώσω, (ὅσιος) *to make holy*, *to hallow*, *purify*, *make atonement for*, Lat. *expiare*:—Med., στόμα ὁσιοῦσθαι *to keep one's* tongue *from evil*.

ὁσίως, Adv. of ὅσιος, *religiously*, *piously*: Comp. ὁσιώτερον, Sup. -ώτατα.

ὀσμάομαι, Dep., like ὀδμάομαι, *to smell*, *scent*: generally, *to perceive*. From

ὀσμή, ἡ, (ὄζω) like ὀδμή, *a smell*, *scent*, *odour*, whether *good* or *bad*. 2. *a scent*, *perfume*.

ὁσον-ῶν, Ion. for ὅσον οὖν, *however little*, Lat. *quantulumcunque*.

ὍΣΟΣ, ὅση, ὅσον, Ep. ὅσσος, ὅσση, ὅσσον, Lat. *quantus*:—of Size, *as great as*, *how great*: of Quantity, *as much as*, *how much*: of Space, *as far as*, *how far*: of Time, *as long as*, *how long*: of Number, *as many as*, *how many*: of Sound, *as loud as*, *how loud*:—its Antecedent is τόσος, after which ὅσος must be simply rendered *as*; ὅσα πλεῖστα or πλεῖστα ὅσα as much *as* possible. In plur. *all that*, *as many as*, often after πάντες. 2. of Time, ὅσοι μῆνες, ὅσαι ἡμέραι *every month*, *day*, *monthly*, *daily*, Lat. *quot menses*, *quot dies*; cf ὁσημέραι. 3. ὅσος δή and ὁσοσδήποτε, *how great soever he be*, Lat. *quantuscunque*; ὅσος ἄν *how great* soever. II. neut. ὅσον as Adv. *as greatly as*, *as loudly*, as, etc. 2. Ep. and Ion., ὅσον τε *about as far as*; the Noun is often added, ὅσον τ' ὄργυιαν *about* a fathom; ὅσον τ' ἐπὶ ἥμισυ to *about* half. 3. ὅσον μόνον, Lat. *tantum non*, *all but*; so also, ὅσον οὐ; but Att. ὅσον and ὅσον μόνον *only so far as*, *only just*; ὅσον ὅσον *only just*. 4. ὅσσον ἐπί and ὅσσον τ' ἐπί *as far as*, Att. ἐφ' ὅσον. 5. with Comp. and Sup., ὅσον βασιλεύτερός ἐστι *so far as*, *inasmuch as* he is a greater king. 6. ὅσον τάχος *as quick as possible*: more usu. ὅσον τάχιστα. 7. ὅσον αὐτίκα, also, ὅσον οὐκ ἤδη *all but* now, *instantly*. 8. οὐχ ὅσον *not only not*, Lat. *ne dicam*. III. ὅσῳ *inasmuch as*, with Comp. ὅσῳ πλέον, ὅσῳ μᾶλλον the more *since*, especially *since*. 2. ὅσῳ with Comp. followed by another Comp. with τοσούτῳ, *the more* . ., *so much the more* . ., like Lat. *quo* or *quanto melior*, *eo* . ., etc. 3. ὅσῳπερ *by how much*, *in so far as*.

ὅσοσ-περ, ὅση-περ, ὅσον-περ, *however great* or *much*, *as great* or *as much as*.

ὅσ-περ, ἥ-περ, ὅ-περ, (Ep. also ὅπερ masc., as ὅ τε masc. for ὅστε), *who*, *which*, *indeed*. *the very man who* or *thing which*, Lat. *qui quidem*.

ὌΣΠΡῙΟΝ, τό, *pulse*, *beans*: *vegetables*.

ὌΣΣᾸ, ἡ, *a rumour*, Lat. *fama*: *a divine voice* or *sound*. II. generally, *a voice*. III. *a sound*, *tone*, of the harp: the *din* of battle. IV. *an ominous* or *warning voice*, *prophecy*, *boding*: cf. ὀμφή.

ὅσσα, Ion. neut. plur. of ὅσος.

ὁσσάκῐ, Adv., Ion. for ὁσάκι. [ᾰ]

ὁσσάτιος, Ion. for ὁσάτιος. [ᾰ]

ὌΣΣΕ, τώ, neut. dual, *the two eyes*, often with pl Adj., as, ὄσσε φαεινά, ὄσσε αἱματόεντα: the gen. and dat. took the plur. form of 2nd decl., ὄσσων, ὄσσοις, ὄσσοισι.

ὁσσῐχος, η, ον, Dim. of ὅσος, ὅσσος, *as little*, *how little*, Lat. *quantulus*.

ὈΣΣΟΜΑΙ, (ὄσσε) Dep., only used in pres. and impf. (without augm.):—*to see*. II. *to see in one's mind's eye*, *to presage*, *forebode*, *foretell*.

ὅσσος, η, ον, Ep. and Ion. for ὅσος.

ὀστάριον, τό, Dim. of ὀστέον, *a little bone*.

ὅσ-τε, ἥ-τε, ὅ-τε, (Ep. also ὅ τε for masc., as ὅπερ masc. for ὅσπερ) *who*, *which*.

ὀστέϊνος, η, ον, (ὀστέον) *made of bone*, *bony*.

'ΟΣΤ[illegible]Ν Att. contr. ὀστοῦν, τό, pl. ὀστέα Att. contr. [illegible], —*a bone*, Lat. *OS*, *OSSIS*.

ὀστε[illegible]ν, Ep. gen. pl. of ὀστέον.

ὅστινος, η, ον, (ὀστέον) = ὀστέϊνος, *bony*, *of bone*: neut. pl. ὅστινα, τά, as Subst.. Lat. *tibiae*, *bone pipes*.

ὅσ-τις, ἥ-τις, ὅ τι or ὅ, τι; gen. οὗτινος, ἧστινος; dat. ᾧτινι, ᾗτινι, etc.: pl. οἵτινες, αἵτινες, ἅτινα, etc.; (Ep. also ὅ-τις for masc., as ὅπερ for ὅσπερ, ὅ τε for ὅστε); neut. ὅ ττι. II. also declined, gen. ὅτου, dat. ὅτῳ: Ep. gen. ὅττεο contr. ὅττευ and ὅτευ, dat. ὅτεῳ: acc. ὅτινα:—plur., nom. neut. ὅτινα; gen. ὅτεων Att. ὅτων; dat. ὁτέοισιν, also fem. ὁτέῃσιν; neut. acc. Ep. and Ion. ἅσσα Att. ἅττα. *Whosoever*, *whichsoever*, *any one who*, *anything which*, differing from ὅς, as Lat. *quisquis*, *quicunque*, from *qui*; ὅ τις κ' ἐπίορκον ὀμόσσῃ *whoso* forswears himself; οὐδεὶς ὅστις οὐ there is none *who* does not, i. e. *every one*; οὐδὲν ὅ τι οὐκ everything. 2. in Att. Poets sometimes used simply for ὅς, *qui*. II. neut. ὅ τι or ὅ, τι absol. as Adv. *wherefore*, *for what reason*.

ὀστο-λογέω, f. ήσω, (ὀστέον, λέγω) *to gather the bones* after the burning of the body.

ὀστοῦν, τό, Att. contr. for ὀστέον.

ὀστο-φυής, ές, (ὀστέον, φυή) *of bony nature*.

ὀστρᾰκεύς, έως, ὁ, (ὄστρακον) *a potter*

ὀστρᾰκίζω, f. ίσω Att. ιῶ, (ὄστρακον) *to banish by potsherds*, *ostracise*; see ὀστρακισμός.

ὀστρᾰκίνδα, Adv. (ὄστρακον) *played with potsherds*, of a game in which potsherds black on one side and white on the other were tossed up, as in our 'heads or tails.'

ὀστράκἴνος, η, ον, (ὄστρακον) *like earthenware: earthen, made of clay*, Lat. *testaceus.*

ὀστρακισμός, ὁ, (ὀστρακίζω) *banishment by potsherds, ostracism*, which was practised at Athens to get rid of a citizen whose power was considered too great for the liberty of the state. Each person wrote on a potsherd the name of him who was to be banished.

ὀστρᾰκό-δερμος, ον, (ὄστρακον, δέρμα) *with a skin or shell like a potsherd.*

ὀστρᾰκόεις, εσσα, εν, poët. for ὀστράκινος.

ὈΣΤΡΑ'ΚΟΝ, τό, *a piece of earthenware, a tile, potsherd*, Lat. *testa: the earthen tablet used in voting.* 2. a sort of *castanet made of earthenware.* II. *the hard shell of testacea*, as snails, tortoises.

ὀστρᾰκό-χροος, ον, contr. -χρους, ουν, (ὄστρακον, χρόα) *with a hard skin, shell* or *rind.*

ὀστρειο-γραφής, ές, (ὄστρειον, γράφω) *purple-painted.*

ὄστρεον or -ειον, τό, (ὀστέον) *an oyster*, Lat. *ostrea.* II. *a purple used in dying*, Lat. *ostrum.*

ὀστ-ώδης, ες, (ὀστέον, εἶδος) *like bone, bony.*

ὀσφραίνομαι, fut. ὀσφρήσομαι: aor. 2 ὠσφρόμην, part. ὀσφρόμενος: Dep.: (ὄζω):—*to smell, scent, track by scent*, c. gen.: c. acc. cognato, ὀσφραίνεσθαι ὀδμήν. Hence

ὀσφραντήριος, α, ον, *smelling, that can be smelt.* II. act. *able to smell, sharp-smelling.*

ὀσφρέσθαι, aor. 2 inf. of ὀσφραίνομαι.

ὄσφρησις, εως, ἡ, (ὀσφρέσθαι) *a smelling, sense of smelling.*

ὀσφρόμενος, aor. 2 part. med. of ὀσφραίνομαι.

ὄσφροντο, 3 pl. aor. 1 med. of ὀσφραίνομαι.

ὈΣΦΥ'Σ, ύος, acc. ὀσφύν and ὀσφύα, ἡ, *the hip*, Lat. *coxa.*

ὌΣΧΟΣ, ου, ὁ, = μόσχος I, *a sucker, shoot: a vine-branch.*

ὅτα, Aeol. for ὅτε, like πότα for πότε.

ὅτᾶν, for ὅτ' ἄν, equivalent to Ep. ὅτε κεν, (ὅτε, ἄν):—Adv. of Time, *whenever*, Lat. *quandocunque*, foll. by subj.

ὅτε, Adv. of Time, *when*, Lat. *quando*:—the proper Antec. is τότε, sometimes ἔνθα, or any Adv. of Time. 2. sometimes in causal sense, *since, seeing that*, Lat. *quandoquidem.* 3. ὅτε μή is used for εἰ μή, *unless, except, save when*; οὔτέ τεῳ σπένδεσκε θεῶν, ὅτε μὴ Διὶ πατρί nor did he pour a libation to any of the gods, *save* to father Jove. III. πρίν γ' ὅτε *ere the time when, before that.* 2. εἰς ὅτε κεν *against the time when.* IV. ἔσθ' ὅτε or ἔστιν ὅτε, like Lat. *est ubi, there are times when, sometimes.* V. ὅτε is also used without any conjunctive force in two corresponding clauses, ὅτε μέν .., ὅτε δέ .., *now* .., *now* ..; *sometimes* .., *sometimes* ..; *at one time* .., *at another time* ..; but in Il. often answered by ἄλλοτε, as, ὅτε μὲν κακός, ἄλλοτε δ' ἐσθλός.

ὅτε, neut. of ὅστε, also Ep. and Ion. masc. of ὅστε.

ὁτέοισιν, Ep. for οἵστισιν, dat. pl. of ὅστις.

ὅτευ, Ion. for οὗτινος, gen. of ὅστις.

ὅτεῳ, Ep. for ᾧτινι, dat. of ὅστις.

ὅτεων, Ep. for ὧντινων, gen. pl. of ὅστις.

ὅτῐ Ep. ὅττῐ, Conjunction, *that*, being originally neut. of ὅστις, as Lat. *quod, that*, of *qui.* II. Att. ὅτι is used like our *that* in quoting another's words: and especially in the N. T., often introduces the very words of a speech, when it need not be rendered in English. III. ὅτι in Att. often represents a whole sentence, as in οἶδ' ὅτι (sub. οὕτως ἔχει) I know *that it is so*; so οἶσθ' ὅτι, ἴσθ' ὅτι: so also δηλονότι as Adv., *manifestly*, for δῆλον ὅτι οὕτως ἔχει. IV. ὅτι μή, *unless, except, except that*, Lat. *nisi, nisi quod*, like εἰ μή. V. μὴ ὅτι .., ἀλλά .., like μὴ ὅπως and μὴ ἵνα, *not that so and so is the case* .., *but* ..; *not only so, but* .., Lat. *non modo non* .., *sed ne quidem* ... VI. μὴ ὅτι alone, without an answering ἀλλά, Lat. *ne dicam, not to mention that* .., *not to say that* ...

B. ὅτι, as a Causal Particle, *for that, because*, Lat. *quod.* 2. in Ep. sometimes for τούνεκα, *therefore.* II. with Sup. of Adv. in Ep. ὅττι τάχιστα *as* quick *as possible*, Lat. *quam* celerrime. 2. in Att. also with Sup. of Adj., as, ὅτι πλεῖστον χρόνον *as* long a time *as possible*; ὅτι πλεῖστοι, Lat. *quam* plurimi, *as* many *as possible.* 3. with a Subst. only in phrase ὅτι τάνος for ὅτι τάχιστα, *as* quickly *as possible.*

ὅ τι, neut. of ὅστις, *anything which*; often written ὅ, τι, to distinguish it from ὅτι, *that.*

ὀτῐή, Conjunct., (ὅτι) *because.*

ὅτινα, Ep. for ὅντινα and ἅτινα, acc. masc. sing. and neut. pl. of ὅστις.

ὅτινας, Ep. for οὕστινας, ἅστινας, acc. pl. of ὅστις.

ὅ-τις, Ep. and Ion. for ὅστις.

ὀτλεύω, f. -εύσω, or **ὀτλέω**, f. ήσω, *to suffer, endure.* From

ὄ-τλος, ὁ, *suffering, distress.* (ὄτλος is formed from τλῆμι, with ο euphon.)

ὀτοβέω, f. ήσω, *to sound loud, sound wildly.* From

ὄτοβος, *any loud, wild noise, the din* of battle: *the rattling* of chariots: also of *the sound* of the flute. (Formed from the sound.)

ὀτοτοῖ, an exclamation of pain and grief, *ah! woe!* also lengthd. ὀτοτοτοῖ, ὀτοτοτοτοῖ.

ὀτοτύζω, (from ὀτοτοῖ, as αἰάζω from αἰαῖ) *to cry* ὀτοτοῖ, *to wail, lament*:—Pass. *to be bewailed.* Hence

Ὀτοτύξιοι, οἱ, Com. pr. n., *the Wailers.*

ὅτου, **ὅτῳ**, gen. and dat. sing., **ὅτων**, **ὅτοις**, gen. and dat. pl. of ὅστις.

ὀτρᾰλέως, Adv. of an obsol. Adj. ὀτραλέος = ὀτρηρός, *nimbly, actively, zealously.*

ὀτρηρός, ά, όν, (ὀτρύνω) *quick, nimble, busy, zealous.*

ὄτρῐχες, nom. pl. of ὄθριξ.

ὀτρῦναι, aor. 1 inf. of ὀτρύνω.

ὀτρύνεια, Ep. aor. 1 opt. of ὀτρύνω.

ὀτρῡνέμεν, Ep. pres. inf. of ὀτρύνω.

ὀτρύνεσκον, Ep. impf. of ὀτρύνω.

ὀτρυνέω, Ep. and Ion. fut. of ὀτρύνω.

ὀτρυντύς, ύος, ἡ, Ion. for ὄτρυνσις, *a stirring up, rousing, encouragement.* From

'ΟΤΡΥ'ΝΩ [ῡ]: impf. ὤτρῡνον Ion. ὀτρύνεσκον: fut. ὑνῶ Ep. and Ion. ὑνέω: aor. 1 ὤτρῡνα:—*to stir up, rouse, prompt, cheer, urge on, encourage: to rouse from sleep, wake up*:—Pass. *to rouse oneself, bestir oneself, to hasten.* 2. of animals, *to spur, goad, cheer on.* 3. of things, *to urge forward, quicken, speed.*

ὅττα, ἡ, Att. for ὅσσα.

ὅττεο contr. **ὅττευ**, Ep. for οὗτινος, gen. of ὅστις.

ὅττι, Ep. for ὅτι, *that.*

ὅ ττι, Ep. for ὅ τι, neut. of ὅστις.

ὀττοβέω, ὅττοβος, wrong forms for ὀτοβέω, ὄτοβος.

ὅττομαι, Att. for ὄσσομαι.

ὅτῳ, Att. for ᾧτινι, dat. of ὅστις.

ΟΥ', before a vowel with smooth breathing **οὐκ**, before one with rough breathing **οὐχ**: in Att. also **οὐχί** [ῐ] Ep. **οὐκί** [ῐ]: negat. Adv., *not*, Lat. *non*, used in independent clauses, whereas μή is used in dependent; οὐκ ἀγαθόν ἐστι it is *not* good; οὐ δοκεῖ it seems *not.* II. οὐ may be used in dependent clauses, after the definite Relative ὅς, after the Conjunctions ὅτι *because*, ἐπεί, ἐπειδή *since*, and others which introduce a positive fact. 2. οὐ is joined with a Participle when it can be expressed in English by *though* or *since* with a verb, but μή is used when the Participle is expressed by *if* or *unless*, as, οὐ λέγων = ὅτι οὐ λέγω; but μὴ λέγων = εἰ μὴ λέγω. 3. οὐ is often joined to an Adj. or Adv., as, οὐ πάνυ *not by any means*, οὐχ ἥκιστος *not the least*, i.e. *the greatest.* III. when a negative sentence is strengthened by *any, even, anywhere*, etc., these words also are compounded with the negative, e.g. οὐκ ἐποίησε τοῦτο οὐδαμοῦ οὐδείς *no one ever* did it. IV. οὐ is foll. by acc. in solemn asseverations for οὐ μά, as, οὐ τὸν Ὄλυμπον *no*, by Olympus.

Οὐ in questions expresses a question to which an affirm. answer is expected, as, οὔ νυ καὶ ἄλλοι ἔασι; are there *not* others too? implying *that there are.* II. the fut. with οὐ is used interrog. instead of the imperat., as, οὐ δράσεις; wilt thou *not* do it? i.e. *do it.*

Οὔ takes the ACCENT, I. when it is the last word in the clause, as, ἦν καλὸς μέν, μέγας δ' οὔ. II. when it is repeated singly after a negative clause, and so is emphatic, as, θεοῖς τέθνηκεν οὗτος, οὐ κείνοισιν, οὔ· he is dead to the gods, not to them, *no.* III. when οὐ is a simple negat. answer, *no.*

Prosody:—if the vowel η precede οὐ, the two vowels coalesce into one syllable, as in ἢ οὐ, μὴ οὐ: so also ἐγὼ οὐ.

οὗ, gen. of relat. Pron. ὅς, q. v.

οὗ, Lat. *sui*, gen. of 3 pers. Pron. masc. and fem. for αὑτοῦ, αὑτῆς, and αὐτοῦ, αὐτῆς.

οὐά, exclam. of astonishment or abhorrence, Lat. *vah!*

οὐαί, exclam. of pain and anger, Lat. *vae, ah! woe!*

οὖας, ατος, τό, poët. for οὖς, *the ear.* Hence

οὐᾰτόεις, εσσα, εν, *with ears, long-eared.* 2. *with ears* or *handles.*

οὐ γάρ, *for not.* II. in answers, to express a strong negative; οὐ γάρ, *no—why should you?*

οὐ γὰρ ἀλλά, an ellipt. phrase, expressing a negation and adding the reason, as, μή σκῶπτέ μ'· οὐ γὰρ ἀλλ' ἔχω κακῶς, which in full would be μὴ σκῶπτέ με· οὐ γὰρ σκωπτικῶς, ἀλλὰ κακῶς ἔχω do not jest at me, *for I am not* in a jesting mood, *but* badly off.

οὐ γὰρ οὖν, a negat. answer, *why no, certainly not.*

οὐ γάρ ποτε, *for never.*

οὐ γάρ που, *for in no manner.*

οὑγώ, Att. crasis for ὁ ἐγώ.

οὐδᾰμά and **οὐδᾰμῇ**, Adv. of οὐδαμός, *nowhere, in no place; to no place, no way.* II. *in no way, in no wise.*

οὐδᾰμόθεν, Adv. (οὐδαμός) *from no place, from no side.*

οὐδᾰμόθῐ, Adv. (οὐδαμός) poët. and Ion. for οὐδαμοῦ, *nowhere, in no place*: c. gen., οὐδαμόθι τῆς Εὐρώπης *in no part of* Europe.

οὐδ-ᾰμός, ή, όν, for οὐδὲ ἀμός, *not even one*, i.e. *none.*

οὐδᾰμόσε, Adv. (οὐδαμός) *to no place, no way.*

οὐδᾰμοῦ, Adv. of οὐδαμός, *nowhere*: c. gen., οὐδαμοῦ γῆς *in no part of* the earth; οὐδαμοῦ λέγειν, or οὐδαμοῦ ποιεῖσθαί τινα to esteem *as naught*, Lat. *nullo loco habere.* II. of manner, *in no way, not at all.*

οὐδᾰμῶς, Adv. (οὐδαμός) *in no wise.*

ΟΥ'ΔΑΣ, τό, gen. οὔδεος, dat. οὔδεϊ, οὔδει:—*the surface of the earth, ground*; οὖδας ὀδὰξ ἑλεῖν to bite *the dust*; οὖδάσδε *to the ground, to earth.* 2. *the floor* or *pavement* in houses.—Proverb., ἐπ' οὔδει καθίζειν τινά to bring a man *to the ground*, strip him of all he has.

οὐ-δέ, Adv. (οὐ, δέ) *but not, and not, nor*, connecting two *whole clauses.* 2. doubled οὐδέ.., οὐδέ.. at the beginning of two following clauses, *not even*.., *nor yet*..; as, καὶ μὴν οὐδ' ἡ ἐπιτείχισις οὐδὲ τὸ ναυτικὸν ἄξιον φοβηθῆναι and so *not even* their building forts, *nor yet* their navy, is worth fearing:—οὐδέ often follows the simple negat. οὐ.., as, οὐκέτι μένος ἔμπεδον οὐδέ τις ἀλκή. II. strengthening the negat., *not even*; which is always the sense when attached to a single word or phrase; Homer joins it with Advs., as οὐδ' ἠβαιόν, οὐδέ τυτθόν, οὐδὲ μίνυνθα, etc. *not even* a little, *not even* for a short space.

οὐδ-είς, οὐδε-μία, οὐδ-έν, gen. οὐδενός, οὐδεμιᾶς, οὐδενός, etc. declined like εἷς, μία, ἕν: (οὐδὲ εἷς):—*and not one*, i.e. *no one, none, no*, as Lat. *nullus* for *ne ullus*: the neut. οὐδέν is used as Adv., *in nothing.*

by no means, in no wise. 2. in plur. οὐδένες, gen. οὐδένων, dat. οὐδέσιν, for οὐδαμοί, *none.* 3. ὁ and ἡ οὐδέν (sub. ὤν, οὖσα), *a good-for-nothing, worthless* person: so in masc. οὐδείς, *a nobody, one who goes for nothing.* 4. οὐδὲν ὅ τι οὐ, Lat. *nibil non, every, all;* so in masc. οὐδεὶς ὅστις οὐ, Lat. *nemo non, every one.*

οὐδέ-κοτε, Ion. for *οὐδέποτε.*

οὐδενόσ-ωρος, ον, (οὐδείς, ὥρα) *not worth notice* or *regard, contemptible.*

οὐδέ πῃ, Adv. *in no wise, by no means.*

οὐδέ-ποτε Ion. **οὐδέ-κοτε**, Adv. *and not ever, not at any time, never*

οὐδέ-πω, Adv. *and not yet, nor as yet, not yet.*

οὐδε-πώ-ποτε, Adv. *not yet at any time, never yet.*

οὐδ-έτερος, α, ον, (οὐδέ, ἕτερος) *neither of the two,* Lat. *neuter* II. **τὸ οὐδέτερον** (sub. γένος), Lat. *genus neutrum, the neuter gender.*

οὐδ-ετέρως, Adv. of οὐδέτερος, *in neither of two ways.*

οὐδ-ετέρωσε, Adv. *to* or *towards neither of two sides, nowhither.*

οὐδ' ἔτι, Adv. *and no more, no longer.*

οὐ δή, Adv. *certainly not,* Lat. *non sane.*

οὐ δή που or **οὐ δήπου**, *no I surely imagine not.*

οὐδός, ὁ, Ion. for ὀδός (ὁ), *the threshold of a house, the threshold* or *sill of a door:* metaph., ἐπὶ γήραος οὐδῷ *on the threshold* or *verge* of old age.

οὐδός, ἡ, Aeol. for ὁδός (ἡ), *a way.*

ΟΥ̓͂ΘΑΡ, ἄτος, τό, properly of animals, *the UDDER:* later of women, *the breast.* II. metaph. *fruitfulness, milkiness, exuberance;* οὖθαρ ἀρούρης *the most fertile* land, Lat. *uber arvi.*

οὔθατα, neut. pl. of *οὖθαρ.*

οὐθάτιος, α, ον, (οὖθαρ) *of the udder.*

οὐθ-είς, οὐθ-έν, later form for οὐδείς, οὐδέν.

οὐ θην, *surely not, certainly not.*

οὐκ, for οὐ before a vowel with smooth breathing, and in Ion. (for οὐχ) before a rough breathing.

οὑκ, crasis of ὁ ἐκ.

οὐκ ἄρα, *so not, not then: surely not.*

οὐκ-έτι, Adv. *no more, no longer, no further.*

οὐκί, Ion. Adv. for οὐχί, = οὐκ. [ῐ]

οὔκ-ουν, Adv. *not therefore,* so *not,* Lat. *non ergo.* 2. in interrog., *not therefore? not then? and so not?* like Lat. *nonne ergo? is it not?*

οὐκ-οῦν, Adv. *therefore, then, accordingly,* Lat. *ergo.* When the word has this accent, the negat. sense vanishes, and the force of οὖν only remains.

οὔ-κω or **οὔ κω**, Ion. for *οὔπω, not yet.*

οὔκ-ων, οὐκ-ῶν, Ion. for *οὔκουν, οὐκοῦν.*

οὔ-κως or **οὔ κως**, Ion. for *οὔπως, by no means.*

οὐλαί Att. **ὀλαί**, αἱ, *bruised* or *coarsely-ground barley,* which was sprinkled on the head of the victim before the sacrifice, *like the mola salsa* of the Romans. (Commonly derived from οὖλος, ὅλος, as if οὐλαί or ὀλαί were *the whole, unground barleycorns.*)

οὐλαμός, οῦ, ὁ, (εἴλεω) *a band* or *throng of warriors.*

ΟΥ̓ΛΗ΄, ἡ, *a wound healed* or *scarred over a scar,* Lat. *cicātrix.*

οὔλιος, α, ον, (οὖλος, ὀλεῖν) *baneful, deadly*

οὐλό-θριξ, -τρῐχος, ὁ, ἡ, (οὖλος, θρίξ) *with curly hair.*

οὐλο-κάρηνος, ον, (οὖλος, κάρηνον) *with thick, curling hair.*

οὐλόμενος, η, ον, properly an Ep. form of ὀλόμενος, aor. 2 med. part. of ὄλλυμι; but commonly used as Adj. *destructive, baneful, deadly, fatal.*

ΟΥ̓͂ΛΟΝ, τό, mostly in plur. οὖλα, *the gums.*

οὐλοός, ἡ, όν, Ep. for ὀλοός.

ΟΥ̓͂ΛΟΣ, η, ον, Ep. and Ion. form of ὅλος, *whole, entire, perfect, complete,* Lat. *integer;* οὖλος ἄρτος *a whole* loaf 2. *of full force, able, substantial.* 3. of sound, *continuous, incessant;* οὖλον κεκλήγοντες screaming *incessantly.* 4. of sight or touch, *fine, thick, fleecy;* οὖλαι κόμαι *a thick* head of hair: later, *twined, crooked.* II. Ep. Adj. of ὄλλυμι, = οὐλόμενος, οὐλοός (for ὀλόμενος, ὀλοός), *destructive, baneful, deadly, fatal.*

οὐλό-χῠται, αἱ, (οὐλαί, χέω) *bruised* or *coarsely-ground barley sprinkled* over the victim and the altar before a sacrifice; οὐλοχύτας κατάρχεσθαι to begin the sacred rites by *sprinkling the barley.*

Οὔλυμπος, ὁ, Ion. for Ὄλυμπος: Οὐλυμπίνδε ιοι Ὀλυμπόνδε, *to Olympus.*

οὔλω, (οὖλος 1) *to be whole* or *sound, to be hale* or *well:* imperat. οὖλε, as a salutation, like χαῖρε, *health to thee, hail,* Lat. *salvē.*

οὐ μάν, Dor. for οὐ μήν, *in truth not, assuredly not.*

οὐ μέν, *no truly, nay verily;* old form for οὐ μήν.

οὐ μὲν δή, *in truth not, nay verily.*

οὐ-μεν-οῦν, for οὐ μὲν οὖν, *then not.*

οὐ μέν πως, like οὔπως, *by no means, in nowise.*

οὐ μέν-τοι, *not however.*

οὐ μή, in independent sentences often used to strengthen the simple negative, mostly with indicat. fut., also with aor. 2 subj.: I. when used with fut. indic., the clause must be interrog. II. with aor. subj. there seems to be an ellipse of δεινόν ἐστι or the like, as, οὐ μὴ ληφθῶ I shall *not* be taken, i. e. οὐ δεινόν ἐστι, μὴ ληφθῶ there is *no* danger *lest* I be taken.

οὐ μήν, *indeed not, surely not.*

οὐ μὴν ἀλλά, also **οὐ μὴν ἀλλὰ καί**, *nevertheless, notwithstanding, yet still.*

οὐ μήν γε, after a negat., *no nor even yet,* Lat. *nedum.*

οὐ μὴν οὐδέ, *nay not even.*

οὑμός, by Att. crasis for ὁ ἐμός.

ΟΥ̓͂Ν Ion. **ὦν**, Adv. *then,* denoting the sequence of one clause upon another. II. *therefore, accordingly, consequently,* to mark the result or consequence of what has been said, as at the end of a speech. 2. when a speech has been interrupted, οὖν serves *to resume.* 3. in repetitions οὖν implies the truth of what is repeated, *surely, of a truth,* as, εἰ δ' ἔστιν, ὥσπερ οὖν ἔστι, θεός if he is, as he *surely* is, a god: ἀλλ' οὖν introduces an objection, *certainly, but .., but still ...* 4. attached to a relat. Pron. or Adv., οὖν makes it less definite, as, ὅστις *whoever*, ὁστισοῦν *whosoever*; ὅπως *how*, ὁπωσοῦν *howsoever*.

οὕνεκα, before a vowel **οὕνεκεν**, Adv., for οὗ ἕνεκα, *on which account, wherefore.* 2. the anteced. τοῦ-νεκα being omitted, *therefore since, for that, because.* 3. after certain Verbs, *so far as, how* or *so that.* 4. *that*, like ὅτι. II. **οὕνεκα** (in this sense never οὕνεκεν), Prep. with gen., equiv. to ἕνεκα, *on account of*, mostly following its case.

οὔνεσθε, Ion. for ὄνεσθε, 2 pl. pres. of ὄνομαι.

οὔνομα, οὐνομάζω, οὐνομαίνω, οὐνομαστός, Ion. for ὄνομα, ὀνομάζω, etc.

οὔξ, contr. for ὁ ἐξ.

οὐξιών, by crasis for ὁ ἐξιών, part. of ἔξειμι *exibo.*

οὖπα, Dor. for οὔπω.

οὔ περ or **οὔ-περ**, Adv. *by no means.*

οὔ πῃ, Adv. *nowhere, in no wise.*

οὔ ποθι, Adv. *nowhere.*

οὔ-ποτε Dor. **οὔ-ποκα**, Adv. *not ever, never.*

οὔποψ, by crasis for ὁ ἔποψ.

οὔ-πω, Adv. *not yet*, Lat. *nondum.*

οὐ-πώ-ποτε, Adv. *not yet at any time, never yet.*

οὔ-πως, Adv. *no how, in nowise, by no means.*

ΟΥ'ΡΑ' Ion. **οὐρή**, ἡ, *the tail*, Lat. *cauda.* II. generally, *the hinder parts, the after part* of anything; of a ship, *the stern.* 2. of an army, *the rear-guard, rear: the rear-rank;* κατ' οὐράν *in rear, behind;* ὁ κατ' οὐράν *the rear-rank-man;* ἐπὶ or κατ' οὐράν *to the rear, backwards.*

οὖρα, τά, for οὖροι, ὅροι, *boundaries:* see οὖρον.

οὐρ-ᾱγός, όν, (οὐρά, ἡγέομαι) *leading the rear* of an army: as Subst., οὐρᾱγός, ὁ, *leader of the rear-guard.*

οὐραῖος, α, ον, (οὐρά) *in* or *of the tail;* τρίχες οὐραῖαι the hairs *of the tail.* 2. generally, *hindward, hindmost,* οὐραῖοι πόδες *the hind* feet; τὰ οὐραῖα *the hinder parts.*

Οὐρᾰνία, ἡ, (οὐρανός) *Urania*, i. e. *the heavenly one*, name of one of the Muses, the Muse of Astronomy. II. epith. of Aphrodité or Venus, *the heavenly.*

Οὐρανίδης, ου, ὁ, (οὐρανός) *son of Uranus:* generally, *a dweller in heaven*, Lat. *coelicola*, like Οὐρανίων.

οὐράνιος, α, ον, Att. also ος, ον, (οὐρανός) *heavenly, of* or *in heaven, dwelling in heaven;* θεοὶ οὐράνιοι, or οὐράνιοι alone, like Οὐρανίωνες, Οὐρανίδαι, Lat. *coelītes, coelicŏlae, the dwellers in heaven, heavenly beings.* II. *coming from heaven*, of rain. III. *reaching to heaven, high as heaven.* 2. metaph. *enormous, awful, stupendous;* οὐράνιον ὅσον, like θαυμάσιον ὅσον, Lat. *immane quantum:*—neut. pl. οὐράνια, as Adv., *vehemently, tremendously.*

Οὐρᾰνίων ωνος, ὁ, (οὐρανός) like Οὐρανίδης, *the heavenly one:* in plur. Οὐρανίωνες θεοί or Οὐρανίωνες, *the gods*, Lat. *coelītes:* fem. **Οὐρανιῶναι.**

οὐρᾰνο-γνώμων, ον, (οὐρανός, γνῶναι) *skilled in the heavens.*

οὐρᾰνό-δεικτος, ον, (οὐρανός, δείκνυμι) *shewn from heaven, shewing itself in heaven.*

οὐρᾰνόθεν, Adv. of οὐρανός, *from heaven, down from heaven:* properly an old gen. of οὐρανός, and therefore used with Preps., ἀπ' οὐρανόθεν, ἐξ οὐρανόθεν.

οὐρᾰνόθῐ, Adv. of οὐρανός, *in heaven, in the heavens:* but οὐρανόθι πρό is for πρὸ οὐρανοῦ, where οὐρανόθι is gen. for οὐρανοῦ, as ὄρεσφι for ὄρεος.

οὐρᾰνο-μήκης, ες, (οὐρανός, μῆκος) *as high as heaven, reaching to heaven.* 2. *enormous, stupendous.*

οὐρᾰνό-νῑκος, ον, (οὐρανός, νικάω) *conquering heaven.*

ΟΥ'ΡΑ'ΝΟ'Σ Dor. **ὠρανός** Aeol. **ὀρανός**, ὁ, *heaven*, Lat. *coelum:* in Homer *the vault* or *firmament of heaven, the sky* represented as a concave hemisphere, on which the sun performed his course; the stars too were fixed upon it, and revolved with it; οὐρανὸς ἀστερόεις the starry *firmament.* 2. *heaven*, as the seat of the gods, above this vault or hemisphere; πύλαι οὐρανοῦ *Heaven*-gate, i. e. a thick cloud, which the Hours lifted or put down. II. as masc. prop. n. *Uranus*, son of Erebus and Gaia.

οὐρᾰν-οῦχος, ον, (οὐρανός, ἔχω) *holding heaven.*

οὔρεα, τά, nom. and acc. pl. of **οὖρος**, Ion. for ὄρος, τό, *a mountain.*

οὐρεί-θρεπτος, v. l. for **οὐρί-θρεπτος**, q. v.

οὔρειος, η, ον, Ion. for ὄρειος, (ὄρος, τό) *of the mountain;* Νύμφη οὐρείη *a mountain*-nymph.

οὐρεό-φοιτος, ον, (οὖρος, τό, φοιτάω) *mountain-roaming:*—fem. **οὐρεο-φοιτάς**, άδος.

οὐρεσι-βώτης, ου, ὁ, (οὖρος, τό, βόσκω) poët. for ὀρεσιβώτης, *feeding on the mountains.*

οὐρεσί-οικος, ον, (οὖρος, τό, οἰκέω) *mountain-dwelling.*

οὐρεσι-φοίτης, ου, ὁ, and **-φοίτος**, ον, = οὐρεόφοιτος.

οὐρεύς, ῆος, ὁ, Ion. for ὀρεύς, *a mule.*

οὐρέω, impf. ἐούρουν: f. οὐρήσω or -ήσομαι: aor. 1 ἐούρησα: (οὖρον):—*to make water.*

οὐρῆας, Ep. acc. pl. of οὐρεύς: **οὐρήων**, gen. pl.

οὐρησείω, Desiderat. of οὐρέω, *to want to make water.*

οὐρητιάω, = οὐρησείω.

οὐρίᾰχος, ὁ, (οὐρά) *the hindmost part, lowest part;* ἔγχεος οὐρίαχος *the butt-end* of a spear.

οὐρι-βάτας, ου, ὁ, poët. for ὀρειβάτης, *mountain-walking.*

οὐρίζω, Ion. for ὁρίζω, *to bound, limit.*

οὐρίζω, f. ίσω Att. ιῶ, (οὖρος) *to waft with a fair wind: to speed on the way, guide prosperously.* II. intr. *to blow fairly, give a fair passage.*

οὐρί-θρεπτος, η, ον, (οὖρος, τό, τρέφω) poët. for ὀρείθρεπτος, *mountain-bred.*

οὔριος, α, ον, also ος, ον, (οὖρος) *with a fair wind*, Lat. *vento secundo*, esp. of a ship. 2. of a voyage, *prosperous, fair:* generally, *prosperous, successful:*—neut. plur. as Adv., οὔρια θεῖν to run *before the wind:* but ἐξ οὐρίων δραμεῖν (sub. πνευμάτων), to run *with a fair breeze.* II. *prospering, favouring, propitious.* 2. οὐρία (sub. πνοή), ἡ, = οὖρος, *a fair wind.*

οὐριο-στάτης, ου, ὁ, (οὔριος, ἵστημι) *standing prosperous* or *secure*. [ᾰ]

οὐριόω, (οὔριος) *to give to the winds, let flow.*

οὔρισμα, ατος, τό, Ion. for ὅρισμα, *a boundary line.*

οὖρνις, by crasis for ὁ ὄρνις.

ΟΥ̓ΡΟΝ, τό, Lat. *URINA*, *urine.*

οὖρον, τό, poët. for οὖρος, ὅρος, ὁ, *a boundary;* found in three places of Homer; (1) ὅσα δίσκου οὖρα πέλονται as far as *the boundaries* of the quoit reach, i. e. the distance of *a quoit's throw*: (2) ὅσσον τ' ἐν νειῷ οὖρον πέλει ἡμιόνοιιν τόσσον ὑπεκπροθέων .. ἵκετο; and (3) ὅσσον τ' ἐπὶ οὖρα πέλονται ἡμιόνων; in which two passages, a certain distance is expressed by οὖρον ἡμιόνοιιν and οὖρα ἡμιόνων, and the distance meant is *that by which mules would beat oxen in ploughing a furrow of given length in a given time.*

οὐρός, οῦ, ὁ, (εἴρω) *a trench* or *channel* for hauling up ships on shore and launching them again.

ΟΥ̓ΡΟΣ, ου, ὁ, *a fair wind*, right astern; πέμπειν κατ' οὖρον to send *down* (i. e. *with*) *the* wind, to speed on its way: metaph., οὖρος [ἐστι], like καιρός [ἐστι], it is *a fair time.*

ΟΥ̓ΡΟΣ, ου, ὁ, *a watcher, warder, guard.*

οὖρος, ου, ὁ, Ion. for ὅρος, *a boundary.*

οὖρος, εος, τό, Ion. for ὄρος, *a mountain.*

ΟΥ̓ΡΟΣ, ὁ, *a wild bull*, Lat. *URUS.*

ΟΥ̓Σ, τό, gen. ὠτός, dat. ὠτί: pl. nom. ὦτα, gen. ὤτων, dat. ὠσίν: Ion. and Ep. **οὖας**, οὔατος: Dor. **ὦς**, ὠτός:—Lat. *AURIS*, *the ear;* εἰς οὖς, εἰς ὦτα in or into one's *ear*, i. e. *secretly.* II. *an ear* or *handle*, of pitchers, urns, etc.

οὐσία, ἡ, (οὖσα, part. fem. of εἰμί sum) *that which is one's own, one's property, substance: state, condition;* τὰς ἄπαιδας ἐς τὸ λοιπὸν οὐσίας her childless *state* for the future, i. e. her bearing no children for the future. II. *the being, substance, essence* of a thing.

οὖτᾰ, 3 sing. Ep. aor. 2, but **οὔτᾱ**, 3 sing. impf., of οὐτάω.

οὔταε, imperat. of οὐτάω.

οὐτάζω, f. οὐτάσω: aor. 1 οὔτᾰσα: pf. pass. οὔτασμαι:—like οὐτάω, *to wound;* οὔταζον σάκος *they hit, shattered* the shield; c. acc. cognato, ἕλκος, ὅ με βροτὸς οὔτασεν ἀνήρ the wound which a man *struck* me *withal.*

οὐτάμεν, οὐτάμεναι, Ep. aor. 2 inf. of οὐτάω.

οὔτασται, 3 sing. pf. pass. of οὐτάζω.

οὐτάω, imperat. οὔταε: Ion. impf. οὔτασκον: fut. οὐτήσω: aor. 1 οὔτησα Ion. οὐτήσασκον: aor. 1 pass. οὐτήθην:—Ep. 3 sing. aor. 2 οὖτᾰ (as if from οὔτημι), inf. οὐτάμεναι and οὐτάμεν, part. (in pass. sense) οὐτάμενος [ᾰ]:—*to wound, to wound by striking* with a spear or sword, opp. to βάλλειν (to strike with a missile):—Pass., οὐταμένη ὠτειλή the wound *inflicted.*

οὔ-τε, Adv., *and not.* II. repeated οὔτε .., οὔτε.., *neither.., nor..*, Lat. *neque.., neque..:* but τε is often used in the second clause answering to οὔτε in the first, *both not... and..*

οὔτερος, Ion. for ὁ ἕτερος: neut. τοὔτερον.

οὐτηθείς, aor. 1 pass. part. of οὐτάω

οὐτήσασκε, Ion. 3 sing. aor. 1 of οὐτάω.

οὐτήτειρα, ἡ, fem. of οὐτητήρ.

οὐτητήρ, ῆρος, (οὐτάω) *one who wounds.*

οὔ-τι, neut. of οὔτις.

οὐτῐδᾰνός, ή, όν, Att. also ός, ον, (οὔτις) *useless, worthless, good for naught.*

οὔ-τι-πω, Adv., for οὔ τί πω, like οὔπω, *not at all yet.*

οὔ-τις, gen. οὔτινος, *no one, nobody*, Lat. *ne ullus, nullus;* neut. οὔ-τι, *nothing*, Lat. *nihil:*—neut. also as Adv. *by no means, not at all:* hence II. with changed accent, Οὖτις, ὁ, acc. Οὖτιν, *Noman, Nobody*, a name assumed by Ulysses to deceive Polyphemus.

οὔ-τοι, Adv. (οὐ, τοί) *indeed not*, Lat. *non sane.*

οὗτος, αὕτη, τοῦτο, gen. τούτου, ταύτης, τούτου, etc., demonstr. Pron., *this*, as opp. to ἐκεῖνος, *the nearer* of two things, opp. to the more remote, like Lat. *hic* opp. to *ille.* II. when opp. to ὅδε, οὗτος generally refers to what has gone before, ὅδε to what is to follow. III. οὗτος, αὕτη are used to call a slave or an inferior, generally in a contemptuous sense, Lat. *heus! you there! hollo you!* also οὗτος σύ, *heus tu!* but also in a solemn call, as to Oedipus, ὦ οὗτος, οὗτος Οἰδίπους! IV. τοῦτο μέν.., τοῦτο δέ.., or ταῦτα μέν.., ταῦτα δέ.., stronger than μέν.., δέ.., *on the one hand.., on the other..; partly.., partly..* V. καὶ ταῦτα, to add something with emphasis, *and that too, and more than that*, often without a Verb, as, καὶ ταῦτα τηλικοῦτος and *that too* being such an one; τί γὰρ δεινότερον δικαστοῦ καὶ ταῦτα γέροντος; for what is more to be feared than a judge, and *that too* an old one? VI. καὶ ταῦτα μὲν δὴ ταῦτα, like εἶεν, *so much for this*, Lat. *haec hactenus.* VII. neut. pl. ταῦτα as Adv. *for this reason*, like διὰ ταῦτα, ταῦτ' ἄρα, ταῦτ' οὖν *for this reason then, accordingly.* 2. ταῦτα (sub. δράσω), in affirm. answers, ταῦτ', ὦ δέσποτα *yes*, master. VIII. dat. fem. sing. ταύτῃ was also used as Adv., 1. of Place (sub. χώρᾳ), *in this spot, here.* 2. of Manner, *in this way*, so. 3. *in this respect, so far, for the matter of that.* IX. οὗτος is often strengthd. in Att. by the demonstr. ῑ, οὑτοσί, αὑτηί, τουτί, gen. τουτουΐ, nom. pl. οὑτοιί, neut. ταυτί, etc., *this man here*, Lat. *hicce:*—before a vowel ι becomes ῑν, as οὑτοσίν: neut. τουτογί, ταυταγί.

οὕτως, before a conson. **οὕτω**, Adv. of οὗτος, *in this way* or *manner, so thus*, Lat. *sic* II. with a qualifying power, *so, only so, simply, no more than.* III. *in wishes*, with optat., εἰ γὰρ ἐγὼν οὕτω γε Διὸς παῖς εἴην would I were the son of Jove so [truly] as... 2. *in protestations*, as, ἔγωγ' οὕτως ὀναίμην τῶν τέκνων, μισῶ τὸν ἄνδρα I, so help me my children, hate the man. IV. οὕτω μέν.., οὕτω δέ.., *partly.., partly.., on the one hand.., on the other..;* cf. οὗτος IV. V. in beginning a story, *οὕτω ποτ' ἦν μῦς καὶ γαλῆ* so there were once upon a time a mouse and a marten-cat.

οὑτωσί, οὑτωσίν, = *οὕτως.* [ῑ]

οὐχί, Adv. for *οὐ, not.* [ῐ]

οὑχῖνος, by crasis for *ὁ ἐχῖνος.*

ὀφειλέτης, *ου, ὁ,* fem. **ὀφειλέτις,** *ιδος, ἡ,* (*ὀφείλω*) *a debtor.*

ὀφειλή, *ἡ,* (*ὀφείλω*) *a debt: one's due.*

ὀφείλημα, *τό,* (*ὀφείλω*) *that which is owed, a debt.*

'ΟΦΕΙ'ΛΩ, impf. *ὤφειλον*: fut. *ὀφειλήσω*: aor. 1 *ὠφείλησα*: aor. 2 *ὤφελον* Ion. *ὄφελλον* Ep. *ὤφελλον, ὄφελλον*: pf. *ὠφείληκα*:—*to owe, be indebted for, have to pay*: absol. *to be in debt*:—Pass. *to be owed, to be due*: part. *ὀφειλόμενος, bounden, due, fitting; τὸ ὀφειλόμενον one's due.* 2. *ζημίαν ὀφείλειν to be liable to, be in danger of* a penalty, etc.: *of retribution, βλάβην ὀφείλειν τινί to owe* one an ill turn. II. *to be under an obligation, to be bound to do* a thing. 2. aor. 2 *ὤφελον, I ought..*, of what one has *not* done; *ὤφελεν ἀθανάτοισιν εὔχεσθαι* he *ought* to have prayed to the gods: hence this aor. comes to express the wish that a thing had happened which has not, as, *τὴν ὄφελ' ἐν νήεσσι κατακτάμεν Ἄρτεμις would that* Diana had slain her! Lat. *utinam eam interfecisset!* properly, Diana *ought* to have slain her: mostly with the Conjunction *εἴθε* Ep. *αἴθε*, as, *αἴθ' ὄφελες ἄγονος ἔμεναι O that thou hadst* been unborn! *εἴθ' ὤφελ' Ἀργοῦς μὴ διαπτάσθαι σκάφος would that* the Argo *had* not sped through: also with *ὡς, ὡς ὄφελον* or *ὤφελλον O that I had ..!* also with negat., *μὴ ὄφελες would thou hadst not..!* III. of anything binding upon us, esp. in Pass.; *πᾶσιν ἡμῖν τοῦτ' ὀφείλεται παθεῖν* this is a debt *due* for us all to pay; so, *πᾶσιν ἡμῖν κατθανεῖν ὀφείλεται*, Horace's *debemur morti*, we *must* all pay the debt of nature.

'ΟΦΕ'ΛΛΩ, Ep. for *ὀφείλω*, impf. *ὤφελλον* or *ὄφελλον, to owe*: Pass., *χρεῖός μοι ὀφέλλεται* a debt *is due* to me. II. *to be obliged, bound.*

'ΟΦΕ'ΛΛΩ, f. *ὀφελῶ*: aor. 1 *ὤφειλα*, Aeol. 3 sing. opt. *ὀφέλλειεν*:—poët. word, *to increase, enlarge, augment, strengthen; μῦθον ὀφέλλειν to multiply* words; *ὀφέλλειν τινὰ τιμῇ to raise* one in honour, Lat. *honore augere*: generally, *to help, make to thrive*:—Pass. *to wax, grow, thrive, increase.*

ὄφελον, Ep. aor. 2 of *ὀφείλω.*

ὄφελος, *τό,* (*ὀφέλλω*) *advantage, help, profit, usance*; c. gen., *τῶν ὄφελος οὐδέν* whose *use* was nothing, i. e. who were of no use; so, *ὅ τι ὄφελος στρατεύματος* what was really *serviceable* of the army.

ὀφθαλμία, *ἡ,* (*ὀφθαλμός*) a disease of the eyes accompanied by the discharge of humours, *ophthalmia.*

ὀφθαλμιάω, (*ὀφθαλμία*) *to have the ophthalmia, to have sore eyes.*

ὀφθαλμίδιον, *τό,* Dim. of *ὀφθαλμός.* [ῐ]

ὀφθαλμο-δουλεία, *ἡ,* (*ὀφθαλμός, δουλεία*) *eye-service.*

ὀφθαλμός, *οῦ, ὁ,* (*ὀφθῆναι*) *the eye; ἐς ὀφθαλμούς τινος* before one's *eyes* or *face*; *ἐν ὀφθαλμοῖς* Lat. *in oculis*, before *the eyes; ἐξ ὀφθαλμῶν* out of *sight*; *κατ' ὀφθαλμούς* to one's *face.* II. like *ὄμμα* and *ἄνθος, the dearest, choicest, best* of anything, as the eye is the most precious part of the body; *ὀφθαλμὸς στρατιᾶς the flower* of the army, as we say, the *apple of the eye.* III. in Persia, *ὀφθαλμοὶ βασιλέως*, the king's *eyes*, were confidential officers, through whom he beheld his subjects.

ὀφθαλμό-τεγκτος, *ον,* (*ὀφθαλμός, τέγγω*) *wetting the eyes.*

ὀφθαλμ-ώρυχος, *ον,* (*ὀφθαλμός, ὀρύσσω*) *tearing out the eyes.*

ὀφθαλμώς, Dor. for *ὀφθαλμούς.*

ὀφθείς, aor. 1 pass. part. of *ὁράω.*

ὀφθῆναι, aor. 1 pass. inf. of *ὁράω.*

ὀφθήσομαι, fut. pass. of *ὁράω.*

ὀφίεσσι, Ep. for *ὄφισι*, dat. pl. of *ὄφις.*

ὀφιο-βόλος, *ον,* (*ὄφις, βαλεῖν*) *serpent-slaying.*

ὀφιό-πους, *ποδος,* (*ὄφις, πούς*) *with snakes for legs.*

'ΟΦΙ'Σ, gen. *εως* Ion. *ιος, ὁ, a serpent, snake.*

ὀφι-ώδης, *ες,* (*ὄφις, εἶδος*) *of serpent shape, snaky.*

ὀφλεῖν, aor. 2 act. inf. of *ὀφλισκάνω.*

ὄφλημα, *ατος, τό,* (*ὀφλεῖν*) *a debt* or *a fine incurred in a lawsuit, damages.*

ὀφλήσω, fut. of *ὀφλισκάνω.*

ὀφλισκάνω, fut. *ὀφλήσω*: pf. *ὤφληκα*: aor. 2 *ὦφλον*, inf. *ὀφλεῖν*, part. *ὀφλών*:—*to owe, incur a debt*, but mostly used in the technical phrase *δίκην ὀφλεῖν* or *ὀφλισκάνειν, to be cast* in a suit, *lose* one's cause; as, *ὀφλὼν ἁρπαγῆς τε καὶ κλοπῆς δίκην being cast* in a suit of robbery and theft; also, *θανάτου δίκην ὀφλισκάνειν to be found guilty* of a capital crime: often without *δίκην, ὀφλισκάνειν ἀστρατείας* (sub. *δίκην*) *to be found guilty* of not serving: absol. *to be cast, be found guilty, convicted*: also, *ζημίαν ὀφλεῖν to incur* a penalty. II. generally, of anything one *brings on oneself; γέλωτα* or *αἰσχύνην ὀφλεῖν to bring* laughter or shame *on oneself, incur* them: so also, *δειλίαν ὀφλισκάνειν to incur the charge* of cowardice; *μωρίαν ὀφλισκάνειν τινί to bring on oneself the imputation* of folly in any one's estimation.

ὀφλών, *οῦσα, όν,* aor. 2 part. of *ὀφλισκάνω.*

'ΟΦΡΑ, Conjunction, marking end or intention, *that, in order that, to the end that*, Lat. *ut.* II. Adv. of Time, like Lat. *donec, so long as, while: until.*

ὀφρύη, *ἡ,* Ion. for *ὀφρύς, the brow* or *edge of a hill.* [ῠ]

ὀφρυόεις, *εσσα, εν,* (*ὀφρύς*) *on the brow* or *edge of a rock, beetling.* 2. metaph. *towering, pompous.*

'ΟΦΡΥ'Σ, *ύος, ἡ*; acc. *ὀφρύν* later *ὀφρύα*; acc. pl. *ὀφρυάς, ὀφρῦς*:—*the eyebrow*, Lat. *supercilium*, used in many phrases to denote grief, rage, scorn or pride; as, *τὰς ὀφρῦς ἀνασπᾶν* to draw up *the eyebrows* in token of grief; *τὰς ὀφρῦς συνάγειν to knit*, contract *the brows, frown*; opp. to *λύειν* and *μεθιέναι τὰς ὀφρῦς to smoothe* or *unknit the brow.* 2. *ὀφρύς*, like Lat. *supercilium, gravity, dignity: scorn,* *pride,* II. metaph. *the brow of a hill, the edge of a cliff, a beetling* or *overhanging crag.*

ὀφρῦς, contr. for ὀφρύας, acc. pl. of ὀφρύς.

ὄχᾰ, (ἔχω) Ep. Adv. *by far, eminently,* always with Sup. ἄριστος: later ἔξοχα.

ὀχάνη, ἡ, and **ὄχᾰνον**, τό, (ὀχέω, ἔχω) *the handle of a shield,* consisting of two bands fastened crosswise on the under side of the shield, through which the bearer passed his arm.

ὀχέεσκον, Ion. impf. of ὀχέω.

ὀχέεσσι, Ep. for ὄχεσι, dat. pl. of ὄχος.

ὀχεία, ἡ, (ὀχεύω) *a covering,* of the horse.

ὄχεσφι, -ιν, Ep. for ὄχεσι, dat. pl. of τὸ ὄχος.

ὀχετεύω, f. σω, (ὀχετός) *to carry off by a ditch* or *channel: to divert by a canal* or *aqueduct:*—Pass., ὕδωρ ὀχετευόμενον water *carried off by a canal.*

ὀχετ-ηγός, όν, (ὀχετός, ἄγω) *drawing off water by a conduit* or *canal.*

ὀχετός, οῦ, ὁ, (ὀχέω) *a conduit, ditch, canal, aqueduct, drain: any channel for water, the bed of a river.* 2. metaph. *a channel* or *means of escape.*

ὀχεύς, gen. έως Ion. ῆος, ὁ, (ἔχω) *any fastening*· 1. *the band* or *strap for fastening the helmet* under the chin. 2. in pl. *the clasps of the belt.* 3. *a bolt which fastened the door* within.

ὀχευτής, οῦ, ὁ, (ὀχεύω) *a stallion: a lewd person.*

ὀχεύω, f. σω, (ὀχέω) *to ride:* of male animals, *to cover.*

ὀχέω, f. ήσω, (ὄχος, ὁ) collat. form of ἔχω, as φορέω of φέρω, *to bear, endure, support, hold;* φρουρὰν ὀχεῖν *to keep* watch. 2. *to let ride, mount* II. in Pass., with fut. med. ὀχήσομαι, *to be borne* or *carried;* κύμασιν, νηυσὶν, ἵπποισιν ὀχεῖσθαι *to be carried* by the waves, by ships, etc.: hence without any Subst. after it, like Lat. *vehi, to drive, ride, sail;* ἐπ' ἀγκύρας ὀχεῖσθαι *to ride* at anchor.

ὀχῆα, Ep. acc. of ὀχεύς: **ὀχῆες**, nom. pl.

ὄχημα, τό, (ὀχέω) *that which bears* or *supports, a support, stay.* II. *a carriage, a chariot,* Lat. *vehiculum:* also *a vessel, ship.*

ὀχθέω, f. ήσω, *to be heavy laden:* metaph. *to be heavy* or *oppressed in mind, to be vexed at heart;* ὤχθησαν *they were heavy at heart.* (From ἄχθομαι, as ὀχέω from ἔχω.)

ὌΧΘΗ, ἡ, older form of ὄχθος, *any raised ground,* natural or artificial, *a hill, mound, dyke, dam:* in pl. *the banks of a river* or *trench, dyke,* etc.: also, *crags* by a river. Hence

ὀχθηρός, ά, όν, *raised, hilly.*

ὄχθος, ὁ, later form of ὄχθη, *rising ground, a hill.*

ὀχλέω, = μοχλεύω, *to heave* or *move by a lever:*— Pass. *to be rolled, roll along;* ψηφῖδες ἅπασαι ὀχλεῦνται (Aeol. for ὀχλοῦνται) all the pebbles *are rolled* or *swept away* by the water.

ὀχλέω, f. ήσω, (ὄχλος) *to disturb by a mob* or *tumult;* generally, *to trouble* or *importune,* c. acc.: absol. *to be troublesome.*

ὀχληρός, ά, όν, (ὀχλέω) *troublesome, importunate.*

ὀχλίζω, f. ίσω, = ὀχλέω, ὀχλεύω, *to move* or *heave by a lever,* generally, *to move a great weight, roll it away by dint of strength.*

ὀχλίσσειαν, 3 pl. Ep. aor. 1 opt. of ὀχλίζω.

ὀχλο-ποιέω, f. ήσω, (ὄχλος, ποιέω) *to make a riot:* ὀχλοποιεῖν τὴν πόλιν *to set* the city *in an uproar.*

ὌΧΛΟΣ, ὁ, *a throng of people, an irregular crowd, mob, multitude: the populace, mob,* Lat. *turba,* opp. to δῆμος (*the people* in a constitutional sense). II. *noise made by a crowd, a riot, tumult,* Lat. *turba:* —generally, *disturbance, trouble, annoyance, importunity.*

ὀχλ-ώδης, ές, contr. for ὀχλο-ειδής, (ὄχλος, εἶδος) *like a mob, turbulent, riotous;* τὸ ὀχλῶδες *troublesomeness, turbulence.*

ὄχμα, ατος, τό, (ἔχω) *a hold, fastening.* Hence

ὀχμάζω, f. άσω, *to grip, hold fast: to bind, fetter:* of horses, *to rein in, make obedient to the bit.*

ὄχνη, ἡ, *a wild pear,* late form of ὄγχνη.

ὄχος, εος, τό, (ἔχω) *a chariot,* always in pl., and mostly in Ep. dat. ὄχεσφι, ὄχεσφιν, for ὄχεσι.

ὄχος poët. **ὄκχος**, ου, ὁ, (ἔχω) *that which holds:* νηῶν ὄχοι *places to hold* ships, i. e. harbours, roadsteads. II. *that which bears, a carriage, chariot car;* but, ὄχοι ἀπήνης *bearers* of the chariot, i. e. the wheels.

ὀχῠρός, ά, όν, (ἔχω) like ἐχυρός, *firm, lasting, stout strong:* esp. of places, *firm, secure: strong, tenable* of a fortress or the like.

ὀχῠρόω, f. ώσω, (ὀχυρός) *to make fast, fortify* Hence

ὀχύρωμα, ατος, τό, *a stronghold, fortress.*

ὀχῠρῶς, Adv. of ὀχυρός, *firmly, strongly.*

ὄχωκα, by metath. for ὄκωχα, perf. of ἔχω.

ὄψ, ἡ, gen. ὀπός, dat. ὀπί, acc. ὄπα (εἰπεῖν, ἔπος) *a voice.* II. *a discourse, word.*

ὀψ-ᾱμάτης [μᾱ], ου, ὁ, voc. ὀψᾱμᾶτα, (ὀψέ, ἀμάω) *one who mows till late at even;* cf. ὀψαρότης.

ὄψᾰνον, τό, (ὄψομαι) = ὄψις, *a sight, vision.*

ὀψάριον, τό, Dim. of ὄψον, esp. *fish: a small fish.*

ὀψ-ᾰρότης, ου, ὁ, (ὀψέ, ἀρόω) *one who ploughs late;* cf. ὀψαμάτης.

ὈΨΕ', Adv. *after a long time, at length, late,* Lat. *sero;* ὀψὲ μανθάνειν to learn *too late.* 2. *late in the day, at even,* opp. to πρωΐ: *late in the season,* ὀψὲ ἦν it was *late:* c. gen., ὀψὲ τῆς ἡμέρας *late* in the day, Lat. *serum diei:* also, ὀψὲ τῶν Τρωικῶν *long after* the Trojan war.—Att. irreg. Comp. ὀψιαίτερον *later;* Sup. ὀψιαίτατα, *latest*

ὀψείω, Desiderat. of ὁράω, formed from fut. ὄψομαι, *to wish to see.*

ὄψεσθαι, fut. inf. of ὁράω.

ὄψι, Aeol. for ὀψέ.

ὀψία (sub. ὥρα), ἡ, properly fem. of ὄψιος, *the latter part of the day, evening,* often joined with δείλη. Opp. to ὄρθρος: see δείλη.

ὀψῐαίτερος, -τατος, irreg. Comp. and Sup. of ὄψιος: see ὀψέ.

ὀψί-γονος, *ον*, (ὀψέ, γενέσθαι) *late-born, after-born, born in a later age.* 2. of a son, *late-born, born in one's old age.* 3. *later-born*, i. e. *younger.* [ῐ]

ὀψῐέστερος, -τατος, Comp. and Sup. of ὄψιος.

ὀψίζω, f. ίσω, (ὀψέ) *to do, go* or *come late: to be too late in doing:* Pass. *to be belated, benighted.*

ὀψί-κοιτος, *ον*, (ὀψέ, κοίτη) *going late to bed, late watching* or *wakeful.*

ὀψῐμᾰθέω, f. ήσω, *to learn late* or *too late.* From

ὀψι-μᾰθής, *ές*, (ὀψέ, μαθεῖν) *late in learning, late to learn*, Lat. *serus studiorum: too late* or *too old to learn*, c. gen.

ὄψῐμος, *ον*, (ὀψέ) poët. for ὄψιος, *late, slow, tardy:* τέρας ὄψιμον a prognostic *late of fulfilment.*

ὀψί-νοος, *ον*, (ὀψέ, νόος) *late of thought, inobservant.*

ὄψιος, *α, ον*, (ὀψέ) *late*, Lat. *serus*, opp. to πρώιος.—Att. Comp. ὀψιαίτερος, *α, ον*, Sup. ὀψιαίτατος, *η, ον*: Neut. ὀψιαίτερον, -τατα, Adv. as Comp. and Sup. of ὀψέ. The forms ὀψιέστερος and ὀψιέστατος also occur.

ὄψις, gen. εως Ion. ιος, ἡ, (ὄψομαι) *a sight, appearance; a vision, apparition:*—ὄψις οἰκοδομημάτων *a show* of buildings. 2. *outward appearance, look: the face, visage.* II. *the power of sight* or *seeing, eyesight.* 2. *a viewing, seeing, view, sight*, Lat. *conspectus;* ἀπικέσθαι ἐς ὄψιν τινί to come into one's *sight* or *presence.*

ὀψῐ-τέλεστος, *ον*. (ὀψέ, τελέω) *late of fulfilment, to be late fulfilled.*

ὄψομαι, fut. of ὁράω, formed from *ὄπτομαι.

ὄψον, *τό*, (ἕψω) properly, *boiled meat:* generally, *meat, flesh.* II. *anything eaten with bread*, to give it flavour: hence onions are called ὄψον ποτῷ, *a zest* or *relish* to drink. III. generally, *sauce, seasoning:* metaph. of hunger or toil, οἱ πόνοι ὄψον τοῖς ἀγαθοῖς labour is *a sauce* to good things IV. *any dainty food, rich fare:* in pl. *dainties.* V. at Athens, mostly of *fish*, the chief dainty of the Athenians. 2. *the market-place*, esp. *the fish-market.*

ὀψοποιέω, Dep. (ὀψοποιός) *to dress meat delicately:* Med. *to eat meat* or *fish with bread.* Hence

ὀψοποιΐα, *ἡ*, *the art of cookery:* and

ὀψοποιϊκός, *ή, όν*, *of* or *for delicate cookery.*

ὀψο-ποιός, *όν*, (ὄψον, ποιέω) *cooking food skilfully:* as Subst., ὀψοποιός, ὁ, *a cook.*

ὀψο-πόνος, *ον*, (ὄφον, πονέω) *dressing food elaborately.*

ὀψοφᾰγέω, f. ήσω, (ὀψοφάγος) *to eat* or *live upon dainties alone, to fare delicately.* Hence

ὀψοφᾰγία, *ἡ*, *dainty living: eating delicacies.*

ὀψο-φάγος, *ον*, (ὄψον, φᾰγεῖν) *eating dainties* or *delicacies:* as Subst., ὀψόφαγος, ὁ, *an epicure, gourmand.*—Irreg. Att. Comp. and Sup. ὀψοφαγίστερος, ὀψοφαγίστατος.

ὀψ-ωνέω, f. ήσω, (ὄψον, ὠνέομαι) *to buy* or *purvey fish:* generally, *to buy victuals.* Hence

ὀψώνιον, *τό*, properly, *provisions, supplies for an army:* generally, *recompense, wages.*

Π

Π, **π**, **πῖ**, indecl.: sixteenth letter of Gr. alphabet: as numeral π′ = 80, but ͵π = 80,000.

Changes of π: it is often interchanged with β, as in πάλλω βάλλω: often also in Ion. for φ, as ἀπικέσθαι for ἀφικ-, ἀπηγέεσθαι for ἀφηγ-; and so before an aspirate, π was retained by the Ion., e. g., ἀπ' ἡμῶν, ὑπ' ἡμῶν for ἀφ' ἡμῶν, ὑφ' ὑμῶν. II. in Ion. Prose, π becomes κ in relatives and interrogatives, e. g. κῶς ὅκως κοῖος ὁκοῖος κόσος ὁκόσος for πῶς ὅπως ποῖος ὁποῖος ὅσος ὁπόσος. III. in Aeol. π is used for μ, as ὄππα for ὄμμα, πεδά for μετά. IV. in Aeol. and Dor. π is for τ, as πέμπε for πέντε. V. π is sometimes interchanged with γ, as in λαπαρός λαγαρός. VI. π is often redupl. in relatives, metri grat. esp. in Aeol. e. g. ὅππη, ὅππως, ὁπποῖος, ὁππόσος for ὅπη, etc. VII. Poët., τ is sometimes inserted after π, esp. in πτόλις, πτόλεμος for πόλις, πόλεμος with their derivatives.

πᾶ, πᾶ, Dor. for πῆ, πη.

πᾶα, Lacon. for πᾶσα.

πᾱγά, Dor. for πηγή.

παγγενέτειρα, *ἡ*, *mother of all.* From

παγ-γενέτης, *ου, ὁ*, (πᾶς, γενέσθαι) *father of all.*

παγ-γλῠκερός, *ά, όν*, (πᾶς, γλυκερός) *sweetest of all.*

παγ-γλωσσία, *ἡ*, (πᾶς, γλῶσσα) *wordiness.*

πᾰγείς, *εῖσα, έν*, aor. 2 pass. part. of πήγνυμι.

πάγεν [ᾰ], Aeol. and Ep. for ἐπάγησαν, 3 pl. aor. 2 pass. of πήγνυμι.

πᾰγετός, *ὁ*, (πάγος) *frost, ice.*

πᾰγετ-ώδης, *ες*, (παγετός, εἶδος) *frosty, icy-cold.*

πάγη [ᾰ], 3 sing. Ep. aor. 2 pass. of πήγνυμι.

πάγη [ᾰ], *ἡ*, (παγῆναι) *anything that fixes* or *holds fast: a snare, noose, trap: the toils used in fowling: a fowling-net.* 2. metaph. *a snare, stratagem.*

πᾰγῆναι, aor. 2 inf. pass. of πήγνυμι.

πᾰγῐδεύω, f. σω, (παγίς) *to lay a snare for, entrap.*

πάγιος, *α, ον*, (πᾰγῆναι) *fixed, firm, solid, steadfast.* Adv. -ίως, *firmly, steadily.*

πᾰγίς, *ίδος, ἡ*, (παγῆναι) like πάγη, *a snare, trap, gin:*—ἄγκυρα παγὶς νεῶν the anchor *which holds* ships *like a trap.*

παγ-καίνιστος, *ον*, (πᾶς, καινός) *all new* or *fresh.*

πάγ-κᾰκος, *ον*, (πᾶς, κακός) *quite* or *utterly bad: most unlucky* or *unfortunate:* in moral sense, *utterly bad* or *depraved:* Sup. παγκάκιστος. Adv. παγκάκως, *all miserably.*

πάγ-κᾰλος, *ον*, (πᾶς, καλός) *all-beautiful, all-good.*

παγκαρπία, *ἡ*, *an offering of all kinds of fruit.* From

πάγ-καρπος, *ον*, (πᾶς, καρπός) *of* or *consisting of all kinds of fruit: rich in every fruit.*

παγ-κᾰτάρᾱτος, *ον*, (πᾶς, καταράομαι) *all-accursed.*

παγ-κευθής, *ές*, (πᾶς, κεύθω) *all concealed.* II. act. *all-concealing.*

πάγ-κλαυστος and **-κλαυτος**, ον, (πᾶς, κλαίω) *all-lamented, most woeful.* II. act. *all-tearful.*

παγκληρία, ἡ, *a sole inheritance, full possession.* From

πάγ-κληρος, ον, (πᾶς, κλῆρος) *held in full possession.*

πάγ-κοινος, ον, (πᾶς, κοινός) *common to all.*

παγ-κοίτης, ου, ὁ, (πᾶς, κοίτη) *giving rest to all;* θάλαμος παγκοίτης the chamber *in which all must rest*, i. e. the grave.

παγ-κόνῑτος, ον, (πᾶς, κονίω) *coverea all over with dust;* ἄεθλα παγκόνιτα prizes *gained by all kinds of contests.*

παγ-κρᾰτής, ές, (πᾶς, κράτος) *all-powerful, all-mighty, all-ruling: all-conquering.*

παγκρᾰτιάζω, f. σω, *to perform the exercises of the pancratium.*

παγκράτιον, τό, (παγκρᾰτής) *a complete contest*, i. e. *an exercise which combined both wrestling* (πάλη) *and boxing* (πυγμή), *the pancratium.*

παγ-κρότως, Adv. (πᾶς, κρότος) *sounding all at once*, of rowers *who keep good time.*

πάγος, ὁ, (πᾰγῆναι) *a firm-set rock: a peak, crag, rocky hill:* ὁ Ἄρειος πάγος *the Areopagus* at Athens. [ᾰ]

πάγος, ὁ, (πᾰγῆναι) *anything stiffened* or *hardened: frozen water, ice, frost.* [ᾰ]

πάγ-ουρος, ὁ, (πᾰγῆναι, οὐρά) *a* kind of *crab.*

παγ-χάλεπος, ον, (πᾶς, χαλεπός) *very difficult and dangerous.* Adv. -πως.

παγ-χάλκεος and **πάγ-χαλκος**, ον, (πᾶς, χαλκός) *all-brasen, all of brass.*

πάγ-χρηστος, ον, (πᾶς, χρηστός) *good for all work.*

πάγ-χριστος, ον, (πᾶς, χριστός) *all-anointed;* πάγχριστον πειθοῦς *the all-anointed* of persuasion, of the robe anointed with the blood of Nessus, to be used as a love-charm.

παγ-χρύσεος, ον, and **πάγ-χρῡσος**, ον, (πᾶς, χρυσός) *all gold, of solid gold.* [ῡ]

πάγχῠ, Adv. (πᾶς, πᾶν) Ion. for πάνυ, *quite, wholly, entirely, altogether.*

πᾰγῶ, aor. 2 subj. pass. of πήγνυμι.

πᾱδάω, Dor. for πηδάω.

πάθε [ᾰ], Ep. for ἔπαθε, 3 sing. aor. 2 of πάσχω.

πᾰθεῖν Ep. **πᾰθέειν**, aor. 2 inf. of πάσχω. Hence

πάθη [ᾰ], ἡ, *anything that befals one: suffering, misfortune.*

πάθημα, ατος, τό, = πάθος, *a suffering, misfortune;* τὰ παθήματα μαθήματα *sufferings* are lessons to learn by.

πάθησθα, Ep. 2 sing. aor. 2 subj. med. of πάσχω.

πᾰθητός, ή, όν, (παθεῖν) *having suffered: subject to suffering, destined to suffer*

πάθος, εος, τό, (πᾰθεῖν) *anything that befals one, a suffering, misfortune, calamity.* 2. *a passive condition: a passion, affection.* 3. *an incident.*

πάθω [ᾰ], aor. 2 subj. of πάσχω.

πᾰθών, οῦσα, όν, aor. 2 part. of πάσχω

παῖ, Ep. πάϊ, vocat. of παῖς.

Παιάν, ᾶνος, ὁ, Ep. and Ion. **Παιήων**, ονος, later Παιών, ῶνος, *Paeon* or *Paean*, the physician of the gods; Παιήονος γενέθλη the race *of Paeon*, i. e. physicians. 2. later the name was transferred to Apollo, who was invoked by the cry ἰήιε Παιάν; also to his son Aesculapius. 3. *a physician:* and more generally, *a saviour, deliverer.* II. as appellat. **παιάν** Ion. **παιήων**, *a paean*, i. e. *a choral song, a hymn* or *chant*, addressed to Apollo, as Παιάν. 2. *a song of triumph* after victory, properly to Apollo: also *a triumphant song* before battle, *a war-song.* 3. *any solemn song* or *chant.* 4. in pl., παιήονες *paean-singers.* Hence

παιᾱνίζω, f. σω, *to chant the paean, sing a song of triumph.*

Παιάων, ονος, ὁ, Dor. for Παιήων. [ᾱ]

παῖγμα, ατος, τό, (παίζω) *play, sport;* λωτοῦ π. flute-*playing.*

παιγνιά, ἡ, (παίζω) *play, sport, a game, pastime.* II. *a feast, festival.*

παιγνια-γράφος, ον, (παιγνιά, γράφω) *writing sportive poetry.*

παιγνιήμων, ον, gen. ονος, (παιγνιά) *fond of a joke.*

παίγνιον, τό, (παίζω) *a plaything, toy:* impl. of a person, like Lat. *deliciae, a darling.* II. in Theocritus, the Egyptians are called κακὰ παίγνια, roguish *cheats.* III. *a sportive poem: merry noise.*

παίγνιος, ον, (παιγνιά) *sportive, droll, done in play.*

παιγνι-ώδης, ες, (παιγνιά, εἶδος) *playful, sportive, merry;* τὸ παιγνιῶδες *playfulness.*

παιδ-ᾰγωγεῖον, τό, (παιδαγωγός) *a school-room.*

παιδᾰγωγέω, f. ήσω, (παιδαγωγός) *to attend boys: to lead like a child, to train, educate.* Hence

παιδᾰγωγία, ἡ, *an attending boys, education:—attendance.*

παιδ-ᾰγωγός, όν, (παῖς, ἄγω) *attending or training boys:* as Subst., παιδαγωγός, ὁ, *the slave who went with a boy from home to school and back again:* hence generally, *a tutor, teacher, instructor.*

παιδάριον, τό, Dim. of παῖς, *a young child, a little boy* or *girl.* II. *a young slave.*

παίδδω, **παιδδοᾶν**, Lacon. for παίζω, παίζειν.

παιδεία, ἡ, (παιδεύω) *the rearing* or *bringing up of a child: teaching, education, discipline, correction.* II. *youth, childhood.* III. *handiwork.*

παίδειος, ον, (παῖς) *childish, concerning* or *suited to children;* ὕμνοι παίδειοι hymns *sung by the boys.*

παιδεραστέω, f. ήσω, *to love boys.* From

παιδ-εραστής, οῦ, ὁ, (παῖς, ἐράω) *a lover of boys.*

παιδεραστία, ἡ, (παιδεραστέω) *love of boys.*

παίδεσσι, Ep. for παισί, dat. pl. of παῖς.

παίδευμα, ατος, τό, (παιδεύω) *that which is reared* or *educated, a nursling, scholar, pupil.* II. *that which is taught, lesson.*

παίδευσις, ἡ, (παιδεύω) *a rearing, training, education.* II. *a place of teaching, school;* ἡ ἡμετέρα πολις Ἑλλάδος παίδευσις our city is *the school* of Greece.

παιδευτέος, α, ον, verb. Adj. of παιδεύω, *to be educated:* neut. παιδευτέον, *one must educate.*

παιδευτής, οῦ, ὁ, *an educator, instructor.* II. *a corrector, chastiser.* From

παιδεύω, f. σω: aor. 1 ἐπαίδευσα: pf. πεπαίδευκα:—Pass., aor. 1 ἐπαιδεύθην: pf. πεπαίδευμαι: (παῖς): —*to rear* or *bring up a child:* usu. 2. *to teach, educate, instruct;* ὁ πεπαιδευμένος *a man of education,* opp. to ἀπαίδευτος:—Med. *to have any one taught* or *educated,* applied to parents. 3. *to accustom* or *inure to* a thing. 4. *to correct, chasten.*

παιδήιος, η, ον, Ion. for παίδειος.

παιδιά, ᾶς, ἡ, (παίζω) *child's play, sport, pastime: a game.*

παιδία, ἡ, worse form for παιδεία.

παιδικά, ῶν, τά, *a darling, love,* relating to a single person, Lat. *deliciae.* II. παιδικά (sub. μέλη), *songs to* or *about a beloved boy.* Neut. from

παιδικός, ή, όν, (παῖς) *of* or *fit for a boy, childish, boyish,* Lat. *puerilis.* 2. *playful, sportive.* II. *belonging to a beloved youth.*

παιδιόθεν, Adv. *from childhood, from a child.* From

παιδίον, τό, Dim. of παῖς, *a young child.* II. *a young slave.*

παιδισκάριον, τό, Dim. of παιδίσκη, *a little girl.*

παιδίσκη, ἡ, Dim. of παῖς (ἡ), *a young girl, maiden, damsel.* II. *a young female slave: a courtesan.*

παιδίσκος, ὁ, Dim. of ὁ παῖς, *a young son, boy, lad.*

παιδνός, ή, όν, also ός, όν, (παίζω) *childish, silly, playful* II. as Subst. παιδνός, ὁ, = ὁ παῖς, *a boy, lad:* παιδνή, ἡ, *a girl.*

παιδο-βόρος, ον, (παῖς, βορά) *child-eating.*

παιδο-γόνος, ον, (παῖς, *γένω) *begetting children.* II. *making fruitful* or *prolific.*

παιδο-κομέω, (παῖς, κομέω) *to take care of a child.*

παιδο-κόραξ, ακος, ὁ, (παῖς, κόραξ) *a boy-raven.*

παιδοκτονέω, f. ήσω, *to murder children.* From

παιδο-κτόνος, ον, (παῖς, κτείνω) *child-murdering.*

παιδ-ολετήρ, ῆρος, ὁ, and **παιδ-ολέτωρ**, ορος, ὁ, (παῖς, ὄλλυμι) *a child-murderer:*—fem. **παιδολέτειρα** and **παιδόλετις**, ιδος, *a child-murderess.*

παιδο-λύμας, ου, ὁ, ἡ, (παῖς, λύμη) *destroying children.* [ῡ]

παιδο-νόμος, ον, (παις, νεμω) *controlling boys:* as Subst., Παιδονόμοι, οἱ, magistrates *who superintended the education of youths,* at Sparta.

παιδοποιέω, f. ήσω, (παιδοποιός) of men, *to beget children;* of women, *to bear children:* so also in Med., with pf. pass. πεπαιδοποίημαι. Hence

παιδοποιΐα, ἡ, *a begetting* or *bearing of children.*

παιδο-ποιός, όν, (παῖς, ποιέω) *begetting* or *bearing children: generative.*

παιδο-πόρος, ον, (παῖς, πειρω) *through which a child passes.*

παιδοσπορέω, f. ήσω, *to beget children.* From

παιδο-σπόρος, ον, *begetting children.*

παιδοτρῐβέω, *to teach boys wrestling:* generally, *to train, exercise, practise.* From

παιδο-τρίβης, ου, ὁ, (παῖς, τρῐβῆναι) *a training-master for boys, a master of exercises:* ἐν παιδοτρίβου in the house or school *of the trainer:* generally, *a teacher, master.* [ῐ] Hence

παιδοτρῐβικός, ή, όν, *of* or *fit for a training-master* or *his art.* Adv. -κῶς, *like a gymnastic master*

παιδό-τριψ, ῖβος, ὁ, (παῖς, τρῐβῆναι) *a slave that attends upon the children.*

παιδοτροφέω, f. ήσω, (παιδοτρόφος) *to rear children.* Hence

παιδοτροφία, ἡ, *the rearing of children.*

παιδο-τρόφος, ον, (παῖς, τρέφω) *feeding* or *rearing children:* as Subst., παιδοτρόφος, ἡ, *a mother.*

παιδό-τρωτος, ον, (παῖς, τιτρώσκω) *wounded by children;* of wounds, *inflicted by children.*

παιδ-ουργέω, f. ήσω, (παῖς, ἔργον) = παιδοποιέω. Hence

παιδουργία, η, *a begetting children:* also of *the wife herself.*

παιδοφῐλέω, f. ήσω, *to be fond of boys.* From

παιδο-φίλης, ου, ὁ, (παῖς, φιλέω) *fond of boys.*

παιδο-φόνος, ον, (παῖς, *φένω) *killing children:* συμφορὰ παιδοφόνος the calamity *of having killed a son;* παιδοφόνον αἷμα the blood *of slain children.*

παιδο-φορέω, (παῖς, φορέω) *to waft away a boy.*

παίζω: f. παίξομαι or παιξοῦμαι, rarely παίξω: aor. 1 ἔπαισα and ἔπαιξα: pf. πέπαικα:—Pass., aor. 1 ἐπαίχθην: pf. πέπαισμαι, also πέπαιγμαι: (παῖς):—*to play like a child, to sport, play: to jest, joke, be merry: to trifle.* 2. *to dance:* also, *to sing.* 3. *to play at a game;* σφαίρῃ or σφαῖραν παίζειν *to play* at ball. 4. *to play* (on an instrument). 5. *to make sport of, mock at, to jest* upon a thing. 6. transit. *to treat jocosely.*

Παιηόνιος, α, ον, also fem. **Παιηονίς**, ίδος, (Παιήων) *healing.*

παιήσω, fut. of παίω *to strike.*

Παιήων, ονος, ὁ, Ion. for Παιάν, Παιών, *Paeon,* the physician of the gods. II. παιήων as appellat. for παιάν, *a festal song;* cf. Παιάν.

Παιήων, ονος, ὁ, ἡ, as Adj. = Παιηόνιος.

παίκτης, ου, ὁ, (παίζω) *a dancer* or *player.*

παίξομαι or **παιξοῦμαι**, Att. fut. of παίζω.

παιπάλη, ἡ, (redupl. from πάλη or παλή) *the finest flour* or *meal,* Lat. *pollen: any fine dust:* metaph. *a subtle rogue.* [ᾰ] Hence

παιπάλημα, ατος, τό, *a subtle fellow.*

παιπᾰλόεις, εσσα, εν, an old Ep. word, *steep, craggy, rugged.* (Deriv. uncertain.)

ΠΑΙ'Σ, παιδός, ὁ and ἡ; gen. pl. παίδων Dor. παιδῶν; dat. pl. παισί, παίδεσσι: the Ep. preferred the dissyll. nom. πάϊς, vocat. πάϊ: I. of Descent, *a child, a son* or *a daughter;* παῖς παιδός *a child's child, grandchild.* 2. periphr., Λυδῶν παῖδες *sons* of the Lydians, i. e. the Lydians themselves. II. of Age, *a child:* παῖς, ὁ, *a boy, youth, lad;* παῖς, ἡ, *a* *maiden, girl*:—ἐκ παιδός, ἐκ παίδων *from a child, from childhood.* III. also like Lat. *puer*, ὁ or ἡ, *a slave, servant.*

πάϊς, ὁ, Ep. for παῖς.

παίσατε, 2 pl. aor. 1 imperat. of παίζω.

παῖσδα, Dor. for παῖδα, acc. of παῖς.

παίσδω, Dor. for παίζω.

παιφάσσω, (redupl. from ΦΑ-, the Root of φαίνω) *to look wildly, stare wildly about*; later *to quiver, palpitate.*

ΠΑΙ'Ω, fut. παίσω and παιήσω: aor. 1 ἔπαισα: pf. πέπαικα:—Pass., aor. 1 ἐπαίσθην: pf. πέπαισμαι:—*to strike* or *smite* a person:—Med., ἐπαίσατο τὸν μηρόν *he smote his* thigh. 2. *to strike* a weapon against a person. 3. *to drive away.* 4. *to hit hard in speaking.* II. intr. *to strike against, to dash against* or *upon*, Lat. *illido.*

Παιών, ῶνος, ὁ, like Παιάν, *Paeon*, the god of medicine, of Aesculapius: generally, *a physician, healer.* II. like παιάν, *a solemn song* or *chant.* III. in Prosody, *a paeon*, a foot consisting of three short and one long syll., with four variations, – ∪ ∪ ∪, ∪ – ∪ ∪, ∪ ∪ – ∪ and ∪ ∪ ∪ –.

Παιωνιάς, άδος, fem. of Παιώνιος, *medicinal, healing.*

παιωνίζω, f. σω, = παιανίζω, *to raise the Paean.*

Παιώνιος, α, ον, (Παιών) *belonging to Paeon* or *medicine, medicinal, healing.* II. as Subst., Παιωνία, ἡ, Παιωνιάς, άδος· ἡ, and Παιωνίς, ίδος, ἡ, with and without τέχνη, *the healing art, medicine*: τὰ Παιώνια *a festival of Paeon*

παιωνισμός, ὁ, = παιανισμός, *a chanting of the paean.*

πακτά, πακτίς, πακτός, Dor. for πηκτή, etc.

πακτόω, f. ώσω, (πακτός) *to fasten, make fast* or *close*; δῶμα πακτοῦν *to make fast* the house. 2. *to stop, to stop up, caulk.* 3. *to bind fast.*

ΠΑ˘ΛΑ'ΘΗ, ἡ, *a sort of cake made of preserved fruit*, mostly of figs melted together. [λᾰ]

ΠΑ'ΛΑΙ, Adv. *long ago, in olden time, of old.* II. *formerly, erst, before*: also of time *just past*, opp. to the present: also τὸ πάλαι.

πᾰλαι-γενής, ές, (πάλαι, γενέσθαι) *born long ago, aged, full of years.*

πᾰλαί-γονος, ον, (πάλαι, γενέσθαι) = παλαιγενής.

πᾰλαιμονέω, f. ήσω, = παλαίω, *to wrestle, fight.*

παλαιο-γενής, ές, = παλαιγενής.

παλαιό-γονος, ον, = παλαίγονος.

πᾰλαιο-μήτωρ Dor. **-μάτωρ**, ορος, ὁ, (παλαιός, μήτηρ) *ancient mother.*

πᾰλαιό-πλουτος, ον, (παλαιός, πλοῦτος) = ἀρχαιόπλουτος, *rich of old, rich in hereditary wealth*, opp. to νεόπλουτος.

πᾰλαιορ-ρίζος, ον, (παλαιός, ῥίζα) *with aged roots.*

πᾰλαιός, ά, όν, (πάλαι) *old, aged.* 2. *ancient, of olden time*; οἱ παλαιοί *the ancients*; παλαιὸς χρόνος time *long past*: τὸ παλαιόν, as Adv., *anciently, formerly*: ἐκ παλαιοῦ from *of old.* 3. of things, in good sense, *ancient, time-honoured, venerable*: in bad sense, *antiquated, obsolete, out of date.* II. regul. Comp. and Sup. παλαιότερος, παλαιότατος; more often παλαίτερος, παλαίτατος, formed from the Adv. πάλαι; ἐκ παλαιτέρου *from the older time.* Hence

πᾰλαιότης, ητος, ἡ, *age, length of time, antiquity*: *old-fashioned ways*: also *dotage.*

πᾰλαιό-φρων, ονος, ὁ, ἡ, (παλαιός, φρήν) *old in mind, with the experience of age.*

πᾰλαιόω, f. ώσω, (παλαιός) *to make old*: hence *to abrogate, annul*, Lat. *antiquare*:—Pass. *to become obsolete.*

πάλαισμα, ατος, τό, (παλαίω) *a bout* or *fall in wrestling*: generally, *a struggle.* II. *any trick* or *artifice, a subterfuge.*

πᾰλαισμοσύνη, ἡ, (παλαίω) poët. for πάλη, *wrestling, the wrestler's art.*

πᾰλαιστή, ἡ, = παλάμη, *the palm of the hand.* II. a measure of length, *a palm, four fingers breadth* (a little more than three inches).

πᾰλαιστής, οῦ, ὁ· (παλαίω) *a wrestler*: generally, *one who contends for a prize, a rival, candidate.* 2. metaph. *a trickster, cunning fellow.*

πᾰλαιστιαῖος, α, ον, (παλαιστή) *a palm long* or *broad.*

παλαιστικός, ή, όν, (παλαιστής) *of* or *for wrestling.*

πᾰλαίστρα, ἡ, (παλαίω) *a palaestra, wrestling-school*: generally *a school.* Hence

παλαιστρίτης [ῑ], ου, ὁ, *presiding over the palaestra.*

πᾰλαίτερος and **πᾰλαίτατος**, irreg. Comp. and Sup. of παλαιός, formed from the Adv. πάλαι.

πᾰλαί-φᾰτος, ον, (πάλαι, φημί) *spoken long ago*, epith. of ancient oracles. II. *spoken of long ago, legendary.* III. *primitive, ancient, olden.*

πᾰλαί-χθων, ονος, ὁ, ἡ, (πάλαι, χθών) *long in the land*: as Subst., παλαίχθων, ὁ, *an old inhabitant*, Lat. *indigena.*

πᾰλαίω, f. αίσω: aor. 1 ἐπάλαισα: (πάλη):—*to wrestle*, Lat. *luctare.* II. metaph. *to wrestle with, struggle against*:—Pass. *to be wrestled with.* 2. absol. *to labour* or *be distressed* in battle, Lat. *laborare.*

πᾰλᾰμάομαι, f. ήσομαι: Dep.: (παλάμη):—*to manage, work, bring about.* II. *to devise skilfully, contrive cunningly*; τόλμημα παλᾰμήσασθαι *to plan* a daring deed.

ΠΑ˘ΛΑ'ΜΗ, ἡ, Ep. gen. and dat. παλάμηφι, παλάμηφιν:—the Lat. *PALMA, the palm of the hand, the hand*: metaph. *force of hand, violence, murder.* II. metaph. *a device, skilful plan* or *method, means, contrivance.* 2. *a thing made by art, an instrument.*

πᾰλαμναῖος, ὁ, (παλάμη) *a murderer, one defiled by blood, a blood-guilty man*: *the suppliant not yet purified.* II. *the avenger of blood.*

παλαξέμεν, Ep. for παλάξειν, fut. inf. of **παλάσσω.**

πᾰλάσιον, τό, = παλάθη.

πᾰλάσσω, f. ξω: pf. pass. πεπάλαγμαι: (πάλλω):—*to besprinkle*:—Pass. *to be besprinkled, smeared, defiled*; but also, ἐγκέφαλος πεπάλακτο (3 plqpf.) the brain *was scattered about.* II. *to shake the lots* *in a helmet*; and so, *to draw lots*: hence pf. pass., κλήρῳ πεπάλαχθε (2 pl. perf. imperat.) *be ye decided* by lot, i. e. *decide the matter* by lot.

πᾰλαστή, ή, and **παλαστιαῖος**, α, ον, more correct forms for παλαιστή, παλαιστιαῖος.

ΠΑ˘ΛΕΥ'Ω, f. σω, *to catch by decoy-birds*.

παλέω, Ion. aor. 1 πάλησα, *to be disabled*.

πάλη, ή, (πάλλω) *wrestling*, Lat. *lucta*; generally, *a struggle, contest*.

πάλη, ή, (πάλλω) *the finest meal* or *flour*, Lat. *pollen*: hence παιπάλη.

πᾰλῆναι, aor. 2 inf. pass. of πάλλω.

πάλησειε, 3 sing. Aeol. aor. 1 opt. of παλέω.

πάλῐ, shortd. poët. form of πάλιν. [ᾰ]

πᾰλιγ-γενεσία, ή, (πάλιν, γένεσις) *a being born again, new birth, regeneration*. II. *resurrection*.

πᾰλίγ-γλωσσος, ον, (πάλιν, γλῶσσα) *double-tongued, contradictory, false*. II. *of strange* or *foreign tongu*

πᾰλιγκᾰπηλεύω, *to sell over again, sell by retail*. From

πᾰλιγ-κάπηλος, ὁ, (πάλιν, κάπηλος) *one who buys and sells again, a retailer, petty dealer, huckster*.

πᾰλίγκοτος, ον, (πάλιν) properly of wounds, *breaking out afresh*, Lat. *recrudescens*. II. metaph. *malignant, spiteful, inveterate*; παλίγκοτος τύχη *adverse* fortune; οἱ παλίγκοτοι *adversaries*.

πᾰλίγ-κραιπνος, ον, (πάλιν, κραιπνός) *very swift*.

πᾰλιλλογέω, f. ήσω, *to say again, reïterate*. From

πᾰλίλ-λόγος, ον, (πάλιν, λέγω) *collected again*.

πᾰλίμ-βᾱμος, ον, (πάλιν, βαίνω) *going backwards*.

πᾰλιμ-βλαστής, ές, (πάλιν, βλαστεῖν) *shooting up again*.

πᾰλιμβολία, ή, *change of mind, repentance*: in bad sense, *fickleness*. From

πᾰλίμ-βολος, ον, (πάλιν, βάλλω) *throwing back again*: metaph. *changeable, fickle*.

πᾰλιμ-μήκης, ες, (πάλιν, μῆκος) *as long again*: generally, *very long*.

πᾰλίμ-παις, –παιδος, ὁ, ή, (πάλιν, παῖς) *one who is a child again, in one's second childhood*.

πᾰλιμ-πετής, ές, (πάλιν, ΠΕΤ– Root of πίπτω) *falling back*: neut. παλιμπετές as Adv. *back, back again*.

πᾰλίμπλαγκτος, ον, *tost to and fro, wandering back again*. From

πᾰλιμ-πλάζομαι, Pass. (πάλιν, πλάζομαι) aor. 1 part. παλιμπλαγχθείς: *to wander back*

πᾰλιμ-πλᾰνής, ές, (πάλιν, πλάνη) *wandering to and fro*.

πᾰλίμ-πλῠτος, ον, (παλιν, πλυνω) *washed again, vamped up*. II. act. *vamping up old wares*

πᾰλίμ-ποινος, η, ον, (πάλιν, ποινή) *requiting, revenging*: τὸ παλίμποινον *requital, retribution*.

πᾰλίμ-πους, ποδος, ὁ, ή, (πάλιν, πούς) *going back, returning*.

πᾰλιμ-πρυμνηδόν, Adv. (πάλιν, πρύμνη) *stern foremost*.

πᾰλίμ-φημος Dor. **–φᾱμος**, ον, (πάλιν, φήμι) *dissonant, discordant*.

πᾰλιμ-φῠής, ές, (πάλιν, φύομαι) *growing again*.

ΠΑ'ΛΙΝ, Adv. *back, backwards*; πάλιν δοῦναι to give *back, restore*: sometimes c. gen., πάλιν κίε θυγατέρος ἧς she went *back from* her daughter. 2. πάλιν also implies opposition, *on the contrary, reversely*; πάλιν ἐρεῖν to say *to the contrary*, i. e. *gainsay*; πάλιν ποίησε γέροντα she made him *reversely* an old man, i. e. *trans*formed him into an old man. II. of Time, *again, once more, anew*.

πᾰλῐν-άγρετος, ον, (πάλιν, ἀγρέω) *taken back, to be taken back* or *recalled* · ἔπος οὐ παλινάγρετον an *irrevocable* word

πᾰλῐν-αυξής, ές, (πάλιν, αὔξω) *growing again*.

πᾰλῐν-αυτόμολος, ον, *deserting back again*: as Subst. *a double deserter*.

πᾰλιν-δίνητος, ον, (πάλιν, δῑνέω) *whirling to and fro, eddying*. [ᾰ]

πᾰλινδρομέω, f. ησω, (παλινδρόμος) *to run back again*. Hence

πᾰλινδρομία, ή, *a running back, going backwards*.

παλιν-δρόμος, ον, (πάλιν, δραμεῖν) *running back again, recurring*.

παλι-νηνεμία, ή, (πάλιν, νήνεμος) *a returning calm*.

πᾰλῐν-όρμενος, η, ον, *rushing back*: cf. sq.

πᾰλίν-ορσος Att. **–ορρος**, ον, (πάλιν, ὄρνυμαι) *hastening* or *darting back*. II. *recurring, inveterate*.

πᾰλίν-σκῐος, ον, = παλίσκιος.

πᾰλίν-σοος, ον, *safe again, recovered*.

πᾰλιν-στομέω, f. ήσω, (πάλιν, στόμα) *to speak again*.

πᾰλίν-τῖτος, ον, (πάλιν, τίνω) *requited, repaid*: *avenged, punished*.

πᾰλίν-τονος, ον, (πάλιν, τείνω) *stretched back*: epith. of the bow, παλίντονα τόξα, 1. *of the strung* or *bent bow*, when the archer pulls the two ends to him to discharge the arrow with more force. 2. *of the unstrung bow*, which *bends back* in the contrary direction.

πᾰλιν-τράπελος, ον, (πάλιν, τρέπω) = παλίντροπος.

πᾰλιν-τρῐβής, ές, (πάλιν, τριβῆναι) *rubbed again and again*: *hardened, obdurate, villainous*.

πᾰλίν-τροπος, ον, (πάλιν, τρέπω) *turned back* or *away, averted*, Lat. *retortus*. II. *turning back*. III. *turned the contrary way, reverse*

πᾰλιν-τῠχής, ές, (πάλιν, τύχη) *with a reverse of fortune*.

πᾰλῐν-ῳδέω, f. ήσω, (πάλιν, ᾠδή) *to recant what had been said in an ode*: generally, *to recant*. Hence

πᾰλῐνῳδία, ή, *a recantation, palinode*.

ΠΑ˘ΛΙ'ΟΥΡΟΣ, ή, a kind of thorny shrub, *rhamnus paliurus*.

πᾰλῐουρο-φόρος, ον, (παλίουρος, φέρω) *with a bundle of paliurus-wood*.

πᾰλιρ-ρόθιος, α, ον, (πάλιν, ῥόθος) *back-flowing*; κῦμα παλιρρόθιον a wave *dashing to and fro, ebbing and flowing*.

πᾰλίρ-ροθος, ον, (πάλιν, ῥόθος) *ebbing and flowing.*

παλίρροια, ἡ, (παλίρροος) *the reflux of water, backwater, ebb.*

πᾰλίρ-ροιος, η, ον, Ep. for παλίρροος.

πᾰλίρ-ροος, ον, contr. **παλίρρους**, ουν, (πάλιν, ῥέω) *flowing backwards, refluent: ebbing and flowing.* II. metaph. *returning on one's head, retributive.*

πᾰλίρ-ροπος, ον, (πάλιν, ῥέπω) *sliding back, sinking.*

πᾰλί-σκιος, ον, (πάλιν, σκιά) *shadowed over, gloomy, dusky.*

πᾰλίσ-σῠτος, ον, (πάλιν, σεύω) *rushing hurriedly back;* δρόμημα παλίσσυτον *a backward* course.

πᾰλ-ίωξις, ἡ, (πάλιν, ἰωκή) *a pursuit back again, pursuit in turn after a rally.*

πάλλαγμα, ατος, τό, (πάλλαξ) *concubinage.*

Παλλάδιον, τό, (Πάλλας) *the statue of Pallas.*

Παλλάδιος, α, ον, (Πάλλας) *of* or *sacred to Pallas.*

παλλᾰκεύομαι, Dep. (πάλλαξ) *to keep as a concubine.*

παλλᾰκή, ἡ, (πάλλαξ) *a concubine.*

παλλᾰκίς, ίδος, ἡ, = πάλλαξ, *a concubine.*

ΠΑ'ΛΛΑΞ, ἄκος, ἡ, *a concubine*, Lat. *pellex*, opp. to the lawful wife (ἄκοιτις, ἄλοχος).

Παλλάς, άδος [ᾰ], ἡ, (πάλλω) *Pallas*, name of Minerva, in Homer always Παλλὰς Ἀθήνη or Παλλὰς Ἀθηναίη, but later used alone, = Ἀθήνη.

Πάλλᾱς, αντος, ὁ, *Pallas*, masc. prop. n.

πάλ-λευκος, ον, (πᾶν, λευκός) *all white.*

ΠΑ'ΛΛΩ: aor. 1 ἔπηλα Ep. πῆλα: Ep. aor. 2 part. πεπᾰλών (in compd. ἀμπεπαλών):—Pass., pf. πέπαλμαι: Ep. 3 sing. aor. 2 pass. πάλτο:—*to wield, brandish, sway, whirl, swing: to toss with the arms*:—Pass. *to make a spring, move swiftly: to leap, bound: to quiver*, as fish on land: *to quiver* or *quake* for fear or from any kind of agitation: *to dash oneself.* 2. κλήρους πάλλειν *to shake* the lots together till one *leapt forth:* hence πάλλειν, absol., *to cast lots*:—in Med. πάλλεσθαι *to draw lots.* II. πάλλω, intr. like πάλλομαι, *to leap, bound: to quiver, quake.*

παλμός, ὁ, (πάλλω) intr. *a quivering: the beating of the* heart or pulse.

πάλος, ὁ, (πάλλω) *the lot cast from an helmet*, generally, *a lot;* ἀρχὰς πάλῳ ἄρχειν to hold public offices *by lot.*

πάλτο, 3 sing. Ep. aor. 2 pass. of πάλλω.

παλτόν, τό, *anything brandished* or *thrown, a dart* or *javelin, the jerreed:* properly neut. from παλτός.

παλτός, ή, όν, (πάλλω) *brandished, hurled.*

παλύνας, aor. 1 part. of παλύνω.

πᾰλύνω, f. ῠνῶ: aor. 1 ἐπάλῡνα: (πάλλω):—*to strew* or *scatter upon.* II. *to bestrew, besprinkle.*

πᾶμα, ατος, τό, (πάομαι) *property*

παμ-βᾰσίλεια, ἡ, (πᾶς, βασίλεια) *queen of all, all-powerful queen.*

παμ-βδελῠρός, ά, όν, (πᾶς, βδελυρός) *all-loathsome* or *abominable.*

παμ-βίας, ου, ὁ, (πᾶς, βία) *all-subduing.*

πάμ-βοτος, ον, (πᾶς, βόσκω) *all-nourishing.*

παμ-βῶτις, ιδος, ἡ, fem. Adj. (πᾶς, βώτης) *all-feeding, all-nourishing.*

παμ-μάταιος, ον, (πᾶς, μάταιος) *all-vain, all-useless.*

πάμ-μᾰχος, ον, (πᾶς, μάχη) *all-conquering, triumphant.* II. = παγκρατιαστής.

παμ-μέγας, -μεγάλη, -μεγα, (πᾶς, μέγας) *very great.*

παμ-μεγέθης, ές, (πᾶς, μέγεθος) *of enormous size*

παμ-μέλᾱς, αινα, ᾰν, (πᾶς, μέλας) *all black.*

παμ-μήκης, ες, (πᾶς, μῆκος) *very long, prolonged.*

πάμ-μηνος, ον, (πᾶς, μήν) *through every month, through the live-long year.*

παμ-μήτειρα, ἡ, = παμμήτωρ.

παμμῆτις, ιδος, ὁ, ἡ, (πᾶς, μῆτις) *all-knowing, all-planning.*

παμ-μήτωρ, ορος, ἡ, (πᾶς, μήτηρ) *mother of all.* II. *altogether a mother, a very mother.*

παμ-μίᾰρος, ον, (πᾶς, μιαρός) *all-abominable.*

παμ-μῐγής, ές, (πᾶς, μιγῆναι) *all-blended, all-confounded, promiscuous.*

πάμ-μῑκρος, ον, (πᾶς, μικρός) *very small.*

πάμ-μικτος, ον, = παμμιγής.

πάμ-μορος, ον, (πᾶς, μόρος) *all-hapless.*

παμ-μῠσᾰρός, ά, όν, (πᾶς, μύσος) παμμίαρος.

πάμπᾰν, Adv. (πᾶς) like πάνυ, *quite, wholly, altogether;* οὐ πάμπαν *not at all, by no means.*

παμ-πειθής, ές, (πᾶς, πείθω) *all-persuasive.*

παμπήδην, Adv. (πᾶς) like πάμπαν, *entirely, totally.*

παμ-πησία, ἡ, (πᾶς, πέπᾱμαι) *entire possession.*

παμπληθεί, Adv. *with the whole multitude* From

παμ-πληθής, ές, (πᾶς, πλῆθος) *of* or *with the whole multitude.* II. *very numerous.* III. neut. παμπληθές as Adv. *entirely.*

πάμ-πληκτος, ον, (πᾶς, πλήσσω) *in which all kinds of blows are inflicted.*

παμ-ποίκῐλος, ον, also η, ον, (πᾶς, ποικίλος) *all-variegated, of rich and varied work.*

πάμ-πολις, εως, ὁ, ἡ, (πᾶς, πόλις) *prevailing in all cities, universal.*

πάμ-πολυς, -πόλλη, -πολυ, (πᾶς, πολύς) *very much, very great*, and in pl. *very many*:—neut. πάμπολυ as Adv. *very much.*

παμ-πόνηρος, ον, (πᾶς, πονηρός) *all-depraved, utterly base* or *bad.*

παμ-πόρφῠρος, ον, (πᾶς, πορφύρα) *all-purple.*

παμ-πότνια, ἡ, (πᾶς, πότνια) *all-venerable.*

πάμ-πρεπτος, ον, (πᾶς, πρέπω) *all-conspicuous, splendid, refulgent.*

παμπρόσθη, corrupt word in Aesch. Agam.

πάμ-πρωτος, η, ον, (πᾶς, πρῶτος) *the very first, first of all:* πάμπρωτον and πάμπρωτα as Adv., *first of all.*

παμ-φαής, ές, (πᾶς, φάος) *all-beaming, all-blazing; also transparent, translucent.* Adv. -ῶς.

παμφαίνω, redupl. form of φαίνω, *to shine* or *beam brightly:* Ep. 3 sing. pres παμφαίνησι, as if from παμφαίνημι; πρῶτον παμφαίνων, of a star first *rising.*

παμφᾰνόων, fem. -όωσα, gen. -όωντος, Ep. part. of παμφαίνω (as if from παμφᾰνάω) *all-shining, bright-beaming, glistening.*

παμ-φάρμᾰκος, ον, (πᾶς, φάρμακον) *skilled in all charms or simples.*

παμ-φεγγής, ές, (πᾶς, φέγγος) *all-shining, resplendent.*

πάμ-φθαρτος, ον, (πᾶς, φθείρω) *all-destroying.*

πάμ-φλεκτος, ον, (πᾶς, φλέγω) *all-burnt, all-blazing.*

πάμ-φορβος, ον, also η, ον, (πᾶς, φορβή) *all-feeding.*

παμ-φόρος, ον, (πᾶς, φέρω) *all-bearing, all-productive.* II. *bearing all things with it.*

πάμ-φῡλος, ον, (πᾶς, φυλή) *of all tribes* or *sorts.*

πάμ-φωνος, ον, (πᾶς, φωνή) *with all tones, full-toned:* generally, *expressive.*

παμ-ψηφεί, Adv. (πᾶς, ψῆφος) *with all the votes.*

πάμψῡχος, ον, (πᾶς, ψυχή) *in all life, in full possession of life.*

πᾶν, neut. of πᾶς.

Πάν, gen. Πᾱνός, ὁ, *Pan*, an Arcadian rural god, drawn with goat's feet, horns, and shaggy hair: at Athens the worship of Pan did not begin till after the battle of Marathon:—plur. Πᾶνης, = Lat. *Fauni.*

πάν-αβρος, ον, (πᾶς, ἁβρός) *quite* or *very soft.*

παν-ᾰγής, ές, (πᾶς, ἄγος) *all-hallowed*, Lat. *sacrosanctus.*

παν-άγρετος, ον, (πᾶς, ἀγρέω) *all-catching.*

πᾰν-αγρεύς, έως, ὁ, (πᾶς, ἀγρέω) *one who catches everything.*

πάν-αγρος, ον, (πᾶς, ἄγρα) *catching all.*

πᾰν-άγρυπνος, ον, (πᾶς, ἄγρυπνος) *quite sleepless, wakeful, watchful.*

παν-άγυρις, Dor. for πανήγυρις.

Πᾰν-ᾰθήναια (sub. ἱερά), τά, (πᾶς, Ἀθήνη) *the Panathenaea*, two festivals of the Athenians, τὰ μεγάλα and τὰ μικρά, in honour of Athena or Minerva. Hence

Πᾰνᾰθηναϊκός, ή, όν, *of* or *for the Panathenaea, Panathenaïc.*

πᾰν-άθλιος, α, ον, (πᾶς, ἄθλιος) *all-wretched.*

πᾰν-αιγλήεις, εσσα, εν, (πᾶς, αἴγλη) *all-shining.*

πάν-αιθος, η, ον, (πᾶς, αἴθω) *all-blazing.*

πᾰν-αίολος, ον, (πᾶς, αἰόλος) *all-variegated, glittering, glancing.* II. metaph. *manifold.*

πάν-αισχρος, ον, (πᾶς, αἰσχρός) *utterly ugly* or *shameful:* Sup. παναίσχιστος.

πᾰν-αίτιος, ον, (πᾶς, αἰτία) *the cause of all: to whom all the guilt belongs*, opp. to μεταίτιος.

παν-άκεια, ἡ, (πᾶς, ἄκος) *a panacēa, universal remedy:* also **πανάκη**, ἡ.

πᾰν-ᾰλάστωρ, ορος, ὁ, (πᾶς, ἀλάστωρ) *an all-avenging genius.*

πᾰν-ᾰληθής, ές, (πᾶς, ἀληθής) *quite true: all too true.* Adv. -θῶς, *all truly.*

πᾰν-αλκής, ές, (πᾶς, ἀλκή) *all-powerful.*

πᾰν-άλωτος, ον, (πᾶς, ἁλωτός) *all-catching, all-encompassing.* [ᾰ]

πᾰν-άμερος, -αμέριος, Dor. for παν-ήμερος, -ημέριος.

πᾰν-άμμορος, ον, (πᾶς, ἄμμορος) *without any share in.* II. *all-luckless.*

πᾰν-άμωμος, ον, (πᾶς, ἄμωμος) *all-blameless.*

παν-ᾰοίδιμος, ον, (πᾶς, ἀοίδιμος) *sung by all.*

παν-άπᾰλος, ον, (πᾶς, ἁπαλός) *all-tender* or *delicate.*

πᾰν-ᾰπενθής, ές, (πᾶς, α privat., πένθος) *wholly without grief, sorrowless.*

πᾰν-ᾰπήμων, ον, gen. ονος, (πᾶς, ἀπήμων) *all-harmless, all free from hurt.*

πᾰν-άποτμος, ον, (πᾶς, ἄποτμος) *all-hapless.*

πᾰν-άργῠρος, ον, (πᾶς, ἄργυρος) *all of silver.*

παν-άρετος, ον, (πᾶς, ἀρετή) *all-virtuous.*

πᾰν-άριστος, ον, (πᾶς, ἄριστος) *best of all.*

πᾰν-αρκέτας, gen. fem. of πανάρκετος, *all-sufficing, all-powerful.*

πᾰν-αρμόνιος, α, ον, (πᾶς, ἁρμονία) *embracing all modes* or *tones, of full compass.* 2. *harmonising with all, all-harmonious.*

πάν-αρχος, ον, (πᾶς, ἄρχω) *all-powerful, ruling all.*

παν-ατρεκής, ές, (πᾶς, ἀτρεκής) *all-exact, infallible.*

πᾰν-ᾰφῆλιξ, ῐκος, ὁ, ἡ, (πᾶς, ἀπό, ἧλιξ) *all away from the friends of one's youth.*

πᾰν-άφθῐτος, ον, (πᾶς, ἄφθιτος) *all-imperishable.*

πᾰν-άφυκτος, ον, (πᾶς, ἄφυκτος) *all-inevitable.*

πᾰν-άφυλλος, ον, (πᾶς, ἄφυλλος) *all-leafless.*

Πᾰν-ᾰχαιοί, οἱ, = πάντες Ἀχαιοί, *all the Achaians.*

πᾰν-άχραντος, ον, (πᾶς, ἄχραντος) *all-unstained.*

πᾰν-ᾰώριος, ον, (πᾶς, ἄωρος) *all-untimely, doomed to an all-untimely fate.*

παν-δαισία, ἡ, (πᾶς, δαίς) *a complete banquet, a banquet at which nothing fails.*

παν-δάκρῡτος, ον, (πᾶς, δακρύω) *all in tears, all-tearful.* II. *all-bewept, most lamentable.*

παν-δᾰμάτωρ, ορος, ὁ, (πᾶς, δαμάω) *all-subduer* [ᾰ]

παν-δαμεί, Dor. for πανδημεί.

πάν-δεινος, ον, (πᾶς, δεινός) *all-dreadful, frightful.*

πανδελέτειος, α, ον, (Πανδέλετος) *knavish like Pandeletus.*

παν-δερκέτης, ου, masc. Adj. and **πανδερκής**, ές, (πᾶς, δέρκομαι) *all-seeing, observing all.*

παν-δημεί and **–δημί**, Adv. of πάνδημος, *with the whole people, in a mass* or *body, en masse.*

πανδημία, ἡ, *the whole people:* in dat. πανδημίᾳ as Adv., *altogether.* From

παν-δήμιος, ον, (πᾶς, δῆμος) *of all the people*, hence *public, general, common.*

πάν-δημος, ον, (πᾶς, δῆμος) *of, belonging to all the people*, hence *public, common, accessible to all;* πάνδημος πόλις *the whole body of* the city.

Πάν-δῐα (sub. ἱερά), τά, (πᾶς, Δίς gen. Δῖος) *a festival of Jupiter* in Athens.

πάν-δῐκος, ον, (πᾶς, δίκη) *all-righteous.* Adv. πανδίκως, *all-justly.*

Πανδῑονίς, ίδος, ἡ, fem. patronym., *daughter of Pandion*, i. e. the swallow. II. (sub. φυλή), one of the Athen. tribes, named from Pandion.

παν-δοκεῖον, τό, *a house for the reception of strangers, an inn.* From

παν-δοκεύς, έος, ὁ, = πάνδοκος, *a host:* hence fem.

παν-δοκεύτρια, ἡ, *a hostess.*

παν-δοκεύω, f. σω, (πάνδοκος) *to receive all, to entertain as a host, to keep an inn.*

παν-δοκέω, = πανδοκεύω.

πάν-δοκος, ον, (πᾶς, δέχομαι) *all-receiving: common to all:* esp. *receiving guests, hospitable:*—as Subst., πάνδοκος, ὁ, *an innkeeper, host.*

πανδοξία, ἡ, *unblemished fame, perfect glory.* From

πάν-δοξος, ον, (πᾶς, δόξα) *all-glorious.*

πάν-δουλος, ον, (πᾶς, δοῦλος) *all a slave, an utter slave.*

πανδοχεῖον, **πανδοχευς**, etc., v. πανδοκ–.

πάν-δυρτος, ον, poët. for πανόδυρτος, (πᾶς. ὄδυρτος) *all-lamentable, all-plaintive.*

παν-δῠσία, ἡ, (πᾶς, δύω) *the total setting of a star.*

παν-δώρα, ἡ, (πᾶς, δῶρον) *giver of all*, epith. of the earth II. as fem. prop. n., *Pandora*, a beautiful woman made by Vulcan, *who received presents from all the gods.*

πάν-δωρος, ον, (πᾶς, δῶρον) *all-giving, all-bounteous.*

πᾰν-ελεύθερος, ον, (πᾶς, ἐλεύθερος) *entirely free.*

Πᾰν-έλληνες, οἱ, = πάντες Ἕλληνες, *all the Hellenes* or *Greeks.*

πᾰν-επήρᾰτος, ον, (πᾶς, ἐπήρατος) *all-lovely.*

παν-επίσκοπος, ον, (πᾶς, ἐπισκοπέω) *all-surveying.*

πᾰν-επ-όρφνιος, (πᾶς, ἐπί, ὄρφνη) *all night long.*

πᾰν-εργέτης, ου, ὁ, (πᾶς, ἐργάτης) *all-effecting.*

παν-έρημος, ον, (πᾶς, ἔρημος) *all-desolate.*

πᾰν-έσπερος, ον, (πᾶς. ἑσπέρα) *lasting the whole evening.*

παν-έστιος, ον, (πᾶς, ἑστία) *with the whole household.*

πᾰν-έτης, ες, (πᾶς, ἔτος) *lasting the whole year:* neut. πάνετες, as Adv., *the whole year long.*

παν-εύτονος, ον (πᾶς. εὔτονος) *much-strained, very active.*

πάν-εφθος, ον, (πᾶς, ἑφθός) *quite boiled*: of metals *quite refined* or *unalloyed.*

πᾰν-ηγῠρίζω, f. σω, (πανήγυρις) *to keep* or *attend a public festival;* πανηγυρίζειν ἐς πόλιν *to go* to a city *to attend a festival* there. II. *to make a set speech in a public assembly, to deliver a panegyric.*

πᾰν-ηγῠρικός, ή, όν, *fit for a public festival* or *assembly; solemn, festive:* ὁ πανηγυρικός (with or without λόγος), *a festival, oration, a panegyric, eulogy.* Adv. –κῶς, *pompously.* From

πᾰν-ήγῠρις Dor. πανάγυρις, εως, ἡ; Ion. nom. and acc. pl. πανηγυρῖς: (πᾶς, ἄγυρις Aeol. for ἀγορά):—*an assembly of a whole nation*, esp. for a public festival, *a high festival, a solemn assembly;* πανηγύρις πανηγυρίζειν to hold *such festivals.*

πᾰν-ῆμαρ, Adv. *all day long, the livelong day.*

πανημερεύω, f. σω, (πανήμερος) *to spend the whole day in* a thing.

πᾰν-ημέριος, α, ον, (πᾶς, ἡμέρα) *lasting all day, doing* a thing *all day;* νηῦς πανημερίη a ship *which sails all day;* πανημέριος χρόνος *all the day long:*—neut. πανημέριον as Adv., *all day long, the livelong day.*

πᾰν-ήμερος, ον, (πᾶς, ἡμέρα) *doing all the day long;* πανήμερος μολεῖν to be *a whole day* in coming: neut. πανημερόν as Adv., *all day long* or *every day.*

παν-θελκτήρ, ῆρος, ὁ, fem. **–κτειρα**, ἡ, (πᾶς, θέλγω) *charmer of all.*

παν-θηλής, ές, (πᾶς, τέθηλα) *growing of all kinds*, esp. *shooting with all sorts of trees.*

ΠΑ'ΝΘΗΡ, ηρος, ὁ, *a panther*, Lat. *panthēra.*

παν-θῡμᾰδόν, Adv. (πᾶς, θυμός) *in high wrath.*

πάν-θῠτος, ον, (πᾶς, θύω) *celebrated with all kinds of sacrifices.*

Πᾱνικός, ή, όν, (Πᾶν) *of* or *fit for Pan:* Πανικόν (sub. δεῖμα), τό, *panic fear*, such fear being supposed to originate with Pan.

πᾰν-ίμερος, ον, (πᾶς, ἵμερος) *all-lovely, all-desired.* [ῑ]

πᾱνίσδομαι, Dor. for πηνίζομαι.

Πᾰν-ιώνιον, τό, = πᾶν Ἰώνιον, *the whole body* or *community of Ionians: their place of meeting* at Mycalé, *their common temple.* II. τὰ Πανιώνια (sub. ἱερά), *the festival of the united Ionians.*

παν-λώβητος, ον, (πᾶς, λωβάομαι) *all-disfigured, hideous.*

παννῠχίζω, f. σω, (παννυχίς) *to celebrate a festival by night.* II. *to watch* or *do* anything *the livelong night;* παννυχίζειν τὴν νύκτα *to spend* the *livelong* night.

παννυχικός, ή, όν, (παννυχίς) *of* or *for a vigil.*

παν-νύχιος, α, ον, Att. also ος, ον, (πᾶς, νύξ) *all night long, lasting* or *doing something the whole night;* παννυχίη νηῦς πεῖρε κέλευθον the ship continued her course *all night long.*

παν-νῠχίς, ίδος, ἡ, (πᾶς, νύξ) *a night-festival, vigil*, Lat. *pervigilium.* II. *a watching, keeping awake all night.*

πάν-νῠχος, ον, = παννύχιος: neut. pl., πάννυχα as Adv., *the livelong night.*

πᾰν-όδυρτος, ον, (πᾶς, ὀδύρομαι) *all-bewailed, all-lamentable.*

παν-οιζύς, υ, gen. ύος, (πᾶς, οἰζύς) *all unhappy, most melancholy.*

παν-οικεί and **–οικί**, Adv., = πανοικίᾳ.

πᾰν-οικίᾳ Ion. **–ίῃ** (πᾶς, οἶκος) dat. used as Adv., without any nom. πανοικία in use, *with all the house, household and all.*

παν-οίμοι, Interj. (πᾶς, οἴμοι) *oh utter woe!*

πᾰν-όλβιος, ον, (πᾶς, ὄλβιος) *truly happy, with unalloyed happiness.*

πᾰν-ομῑλεί, Adv. (πᾶς, ὅμιλος) *in whole troops.*

παν-όμματος, ον, (πᾶς, ὄμμα) *all eyes.*

πᾰν-όμοιος Ep. –ομοίῖος [ῑ], ον, (πᾶς, ὅμοιος) *exactly like.*

πᾰν-ομφαῖος, ὁ, (πᾶς, ὀμφή) *author of all ominous voices, all-oracular.*

πᾰνοπλία, ἡ, (πάνοπλος) *the full armour of a heavy-armed soldier*, i. e. shield, helmet, breastplate, greaves, sword, and lance, *a full suit of armour, panoply;* πανοπλίῃ *in full armour, cap-a-pie.* Hence

πᾰν-οπλίτης, ου, ὁ, *a man in full armour.* [ῑ]

πάν-οπλος, ον, (πᾶς, ὅπλον) *in full armour, 'with all his harness on.'*

πᾶν-όπτης, ου, ὁ, (πᾶς, ὄψομαι) *the all-seeing.*

πάν-ορμος, ον, (πᾶς, ὅρμος) *always fit for landing.*

πᾶνός, ὁ, Aeol. for φανός, (φαίνω) *a torch, beacon.*

πᾶνουργέω, f. ήσω, (πανοῦργος) *to play the knave* or *villain, act like a rogue;* ὅσια πανουργεῖν *to do a* holy deed *in an unholy way.* Hence

πᾶνούργημα, ατος, τό, *a knavish, roguish act.*

πᾶνουργία, ἡ, (πανουργέω) *villany, knavery, trickery:* in plur. *knavish tricks.*

πᾶνουργ-ιππαρχίδας, ου, ὁ, (πανοῦργος, ἵππαρχος) *a captain of rascals:* or = πανοῦργος Ἱππαρχίδης, *knave Hipparchides.*

πᾶν-οῦργος, ον, (πᾶν, ἔργον) *ready to do anything:* mostly in bad sense, *ready for all crimes, unscrupulous, knavish, villanous, treacherous:* as Subst., πανοῦργος, ὁ, ἡ, *a knave, villain, rogue;* πανοῦργον, τό, = πανουργία.—Sup. πανουργότατος, *most rascally.*—Adv. πανούργως, *villainously;* Sup. -ότατα.

πᾶν-όψιος, ον, (πᾶς, ὄψις) *seen by all,* epith. of a spear.

παν-σᾶγία, ἡ, (πᾶς, σάγη) = πανοπλία: dat. as Adv. πανσαγίᾳ, like πανοπλίᾳ, *in full armour.*

παν-σέληνος, ον, (πᾶς, σελήνη) of the moon, *at the full;* ὥρα πανσέληνος the time *of full moon:* ἡ πανσέληνος (sub. νύξ), *the time of full moon, the full moon;* ἡ αὔριον πανσέληνος to-morrow's *full moon.*

πάν-σεμνος, ον, (πᾶς, σεμνός) *very stately.*

πάν-σκοπος, ον, (πᾶς, σκοπέω) *all-surveying.*

πάν-σοφος, ον, (πᾶς, σοφός) *all-wise, very wise.*

πάν-σπερμος, ον, (πᾶς, σπέρμα) *composed of all sorts of seeds.*

παν-στρᾶτιᾷ Ion. -ιῇ, (πᾶς, στρατός) dat. used as Adv., without any nom. πανστρατιά in use (but gen. πανστρατιᾶς occurs), *with the whole army.*

πᾶνσῠδίᾳ Ion. -ίῃ, (πᾶς, σεύω) dat. used as Adv., without any nom. πανσυδία in use, *with all speed.*

πάν-συρτος, ον, (πᾶς, σύρω) *swept together from every side, accumulated.*

παντᾶ, Adv., Dor. for πάντῃ.

πᾶντακῇ, Adv., Ion. for πανταχῇ.

παν-τάλᾱς, αινα, ἄν, (πᾶς, τάλας) *all-wretched.*

παντάπᾱσι, before a vowel -σιν, Adv. (πᾶς) *entirely, wholly, altogether:* in replying it affirms strongly, *by all means, undoubtedly.*

παντάρβη, ἡ, name of *a precious stone.*

παντ-αρκής, ές, (πᾶς, ἀρκέω) *all-prevailing.*

παντ-άρχας, Dor. for παντάρχης, ου, ὁ, (πᾶς, ἀρχή) *ruler of all.*

πάντ-αρχος, ον, (πᾶς, ἄρχω) *all-ruling, absolute.*

παντᾰχῇ, Ion. παντακῇ, Adv. (πᾶς) of Place, *everywhere: in every direction, every way.* II. of Manner, *by all means, absolutely: in all respects.*

παντᾰχόθεν, Adv. (πᾶς) *from all places* or *sides.*

παντᾰχοῖ, Adv. (πᾶς) *in all directions, every way.*

παντᾰχόσε, Adv. (πᾶς) *to all places, every way.*

παντᾰχοῦ, Adv. (πᾶς) *everywhere.*

παντᾰχῶς, Adv. (πᾶς) *in all ways.*

παν-τελής, ές, (πᾶς, τέλος) *all-complete, all-perfect: entire, absolute.* 2. *fully accomplished.* 3. *comprising all, the whole,* Lat. *universus.* II. act. *all-accomplishing.* Hence

παντελῶς Ion. -έως, Adv., also παντελές, *completely, entirely, absolutely: outright.*

πάντεσσι, Ep. for πᾶσι, dat. pl. of πᾶς.

παν-τευχία, ἡ, (πᾶς, τεῦχος) = παν-οπλία, *complete armour;* ξὺν or ἐν παντευχίᾳ *in full armour.*

πάν-τεχνος, ον, (πᾶς, τέχνη) *assisting all the arts.*

πάντῃ Dor. **παντᾶ**, Adv. (πᾶς) *everywhere, on every side, every way.* II. *in every way, by all means;* οὐ πάντῃ not *quite.*

πάν-τῑμος, ον, (πᾶς, τίμη) *all-honourable.*

παντό-γηρως, ων, gen. ω, (πᾶς, γῆρας) *making all old, enfeebling all.*

παντο-δᾱής, ές, (πᾶς, *δάω) *all-knowing.*

παντοδᾰπός, ή, όν, (πᾶς) *of every kind, of all sorts, manifold.* Adv. -πῶς, *in all kinds of ways.*

πάντοθεν, Adv. (πᾶς) *from all quarters, from every side,* Lat. *undique.*

πάντοθῐ, Adv. (πᾶς) *everywhere.*

παντοῖος, α, ον, (πᾶς) *of all sorts* or *kinds, manifold;* παντοῖος γενέσθαι *to take all shapes,* i. e. to try every expedient, turn every stone, in order to effect any object. Hence

παντοίως, Adv. *in every kind of way.*

παντο-κράτωρ, ορος, ὁ, (πᾶς, κρᾰτέω) *all-mighty.*

παντ-ολῐγοχρόνιος, ον, (πᾶς, ὀλιγοχρόνιος) *utterly short-lived.*

πάν-τολμος, ον, (πᾶς, τόλμα) *all-daring, shameless.*

παντο-μῑσής, ές, (πᾶς, μῖσος) *all-hateful.*

παντο-πᾰθής, ές, (πᾶς, παθεῖν) *all-suffering.*

παντο-πόρος, ον, (πᾶς, πόρος) *all-inventive.*

παντ-όπτας, Dor. for παντόπτης, ου, ὁ, (πᾶς, ὄψομαι) *all-seeing.*

πάντοσε, Adv. (πᾶς) *in all ways, every way.*

παντό-σεμνος, ον, (πᾶς, σεμνός) *all-reverend, august.*

πάντοτε, Adv. *at all times, always.*

παντό-τολμος, ον, (πᾶς, τόλμα) *all-daring.*

παντ-ουργός, όν, (πᾶς, ἔργον) = πανοῦργος.

παντο-φάγος, ον, (πᾶς, φαγεῖν) *all-devouring.*

παντό-φυρτος, ον, (πᾶς, φύρω) *all-confused, commingled.*

πάν-τροπος, ον, (πας, τρεπω) *utterly routed.*

παν-τρόφος, ον, (πᾶς, τρέφω) *all-nourishing.*

πάντως, Adv. (πᾶς) *wholly, altogether:* οὐ πάντως *in nowise, by no means, not at all,* Lat. *omnino non.* II. in strong affirmation, *at all events, at any rate, at least:* in answers, *yes, by all means.*

πάνῠ, Adv. (πᾶς) *altogether: at all, in all,* Lat. *omnino.* 2. *very, very much, exceedingly.* 3. ὁ πάνυ with some Adj. omitted, *the well-known,* the *thorough;* οἱ πάνυ τῶν στρατιωτῶν *the thorough soldiers,* i. e. the veterans; ὁ πάνυ Περικλῆς *the famous* Pericles. II. in answers, *yes by all means, certainly.* [ᾰ]

παν-υπείροχος, ον, (πᾶς, υπείροχος) *eminent above all.*

πᾰν-ῡπέρτατος, η, ον, (πας, ερτατος) *uppermost; highest of all.*

παν-υστάτιος, ον, and **πᾰν-ύστᾰτος**, η, ον, (πᾶς, ὕστατος) *last of all.*

πᾰνωλεθρία, ἡ, *utter destruction, utter ruin.* From

πᾰν-ώλεθρος, ον, (πᾶς, ὄλεθρος, ὄλλυμι) *utterly ruined, destroyed, undone.* 2. in moral sense, *utterly abandoned.* II. act. *all-destructive, all-ruinous.*

πᾰν-ώλης, ες, (πᾶς, ὄλλυμι) *utterly ruined, destroyed.* 2. in moral sense, *utterly abandoned.* II. act. *all-destructive.*

πᾰν-ωπήεις, εσσα, εν, (πᾶς, ὤψ) *visible to all.*

πάν-ωρος, ον, (πᾶς, ὥρα) *in every season.*

πάξ, Lat. *pax! hush! still!*

πᾶξαι, πάξαιμι, Dor. for πῆξαι, πήξαιμι, aor. 1 inf. and opt. of πήγνυμι.

ΠΑ'ΟΜΑΙ, f. πάσομαι [ᾱ]; aor. 1 ἐπᾱσάμην: pf. πέπᾱμαι, inf. πεπᾶσθαι: Dep.:—*to get, acquire*, Lat. *potior*:—the pf. is also used as a pres., *to possess, to have in possession.*

πᾰπαῖ, Interj. of suffering, Lat. *vae! oh! alas!* II. of surprise, *ah!*

πᾰπαιάξ, lengthd. for παπαῖ.

Παπαῖος, ὁ, a Scythian name of Jupiter.

παπαπαπαῖ, an exclam. of surprise.

παππάζω, (πάππας) *to call papa*, as a child: *to coax* or *wheedle by calling papa.*

ΠΑ'ΠΠΑΣ, ου, ὁ, *papa*, childish pronunciation of πατήρ, as μάμμα, *mamma*, of μήτηρ.

παππίας, ου, ὁ, Dim. of πάππας, *dear little papa.*

παππίδιον, τό, = παππίας. [ῐ]

παππίζω, = παππάζω.

ΠΑ'ΠΠΟΣ, ὁ, *a grandfather.*

παππῷος, α, ον, (πάππος) *of* or *for one's grandfather, appointed by him.*

πάπραξ, ακος, ὁ, *a fish found in the Thracian lake Prasia.* (Foreign word.)

παπταίνοισα, Dor. for -νουσα, part. fem. of

ΠΑΠΤΑΙ'ΝΩ, fut. ᾰνῶ: aor. 1 ἐπάπτηνα:—*to look cautiously* or *timidly round, to peer about: to look eagerly.* II. c. acc. *to look round for, look earnestly after.*

παπτήνας, aor. 1 part. of παπταίνω.

πάπῡρος, ὁ and ἡ, *the papyrus*, a kind of rush, of which writing-paper was made in Egypt by cutting its inner rind (βύβλος) into strips: it was also used for making ropes.

πάρ, poët. abbrev. for παρά. II. it is also used for πάρα in sense of πάρεστι.

ΠΑΡΑ' Ep. **πάρ, παραί**, Prep. with gen., dat., et acc.: Radical sense, *beside:*

I. WITH GENIT. *from beside, from alongside of*, whether of Place or Person: metaph. *issuing, derived, proceeding from;* παρ' ἑαυτοῦ διδόναι to give *from* oneself, *from* one's own *means.* In Att. Prose, παρά is used like ὑπό, Lat. *a* or *ab, by*, with pass. Verbs to denote the agent, as, παρά τινος τυφθῆναι to be struck *by* any one.

II. WITH DAT. *by the side of, beside, alongside of, by*, both of Places and Things, as also of Persons, Lat. *apud* and *coram;* παρ' ἐμοί, Lat. *me judice, before* me; παρὰ Δαρείῳ κριτῇ *before* Darius as judge; παρ' ἑωυτῷ *at* one's *home*, Lat. *apud se.*

III. WITH ACCUS., 1. of Place, *running along, beside* 2. of Motion to, *to, towards*, mostly of persons. 3. *going by, leaving on one side;* παρὰ τὴν Βαβυλῶνα παριέναι to go *past* Babylon: metaph. *going by, beyond* or *beside* the mark; παρὰ δύναμιν *beyond* one's strength: *contrary to, against;* παρὰ μοῖραν *contrary to* destiny; παρὰ δόξαν *contrary to* opinion. 4. *beside, beyond, except;* οὐκ ἔστι παρὰ ταῦτ' ἄλλα *besides* this, there is nothing else; so, παρὰ ἓν πάλαισμα ἔδραμε νικᾶν 'Ολυμπιάδα he was *within* one conflict of winning the Olympic prize; παρὰ μικρόν, παρ' ὀλίγον *within* little, i. e. *well-nigh, almost;* παρὰ πολύ *by much;* παρὰ τοσοῦτον *by* so much; παρ' ὅσον *by* how much, Lat. *quatenus;*—so, παρὰ μικρὸν ἦλθεν ἀποθανεῖν he came *within a little* of dying; παρὰ τοσοῦτον κινδύνου ἐλθεῖν to come *within* so great a nearness of danger, i. e. to escape danger by so little. 5. *in comparison with;* αὐτὸς παρ' ἑαυτόν himself *compared with* himself; παρ' οὐδέν ἐστι it is *compared with* (i. e. *as*) nothing; παρ' οὐδὲν ἡγεῖσθαι to consider *as* nothing:—also, παρ' ἡμέραν day *as compared with* day, day *by* day; παρὰ τὰ ἄλλα ζῷα ὥσπερ θεοὶ οἱ ἄνθρωποι βιοτεύουσι men *as compared with* all other animals live like gods; παρὰ τοὺς ἄλλους πονεῖν to labour *in comparison of* all the rest, i. e. *more than* the rest. II. of Time, *during;* παρὰ τὸν πόλεμον *in the course of* the war.

Παρά may follow its Subst. in all three cases, but is then written πάρα: so also when it stands for πάρειμι or πάρεστι.

Παρά absol., AS ADV., *near, together, at once.*

IN COMPOS., παρά retains its chief usages as Prep., I. *alongside of, beside*, as in παρά-κειμαι, παρ-έζομαι. II. from one *to* another, as in παρα-δίδωμι, παρ-έχω. III. *passing by*, as in παρ-έρχομαι, παρ-οίχομαι. 2. metaph. *swerving aside*, i.e. *amiss, wrong*, as in παρα-βαίνω, παρ-ακούω: also, *contrary to, against*, as in παρ-αίσιος. IV. of alteration or change, as in παρά-φημι, παρα-πείθω.

παραβᾰθῆναι, aor. 1 pass. inf. of παραβαίνω.

παρα-βαίνω, f. -βήσομαι: pf. -βέβηκα, part. -βεβώς Ep. παρβεβᾰώς: aor. 2 παρέβην:—*to go by* or *by the side of: to stand beside*, c. dat. II. *to pass beside* or *beyond*, i. e. *to overstep, transgress;* ὁ παραβάς *the transgressor:*—Pass., with aor. 1 πᾰρεβάθην [ᾰ], pf. παρα-βέβασμαι, *to be transgressed* or *offended against.* III. *to pass over, omit: to let pass, let slip:* οὔ με παρέβα it escaped me not. IV. in Comedy, παραβαίνειν ἐς or πρὸς τὸ θέατρον *to step forward* to address the spectators.

παρά-βακτρος, ον, (παρά, βάκτρον) *like a staff. as of a staff.*

παρά-βακχος, ον, (παρά, Βάκχος) *like a Bacchanal.*

παρα-βάλλω, f. -βᾰλῶ: aor. 2 παρέβᾰλον: pf. -βέβληκα:—Pass., aor. 1 -εβλήθην: pf. -βέβλημαι:—*to throw beside, put before*, as fodder before horses, Lat. *objicere, projicere: to hold out as a bait:* also *to object* or *cast in one's teeth*, Lat. *objicere.* II. *to set side by side, to stake* one thing *against* another, as in games of chance; then generally, *to venture, hazard, stake:*—Med. *to expose oneself to danger;* ἐμὴν ψυχὴν παραβαλλόμενος πολεμίζειν *setting my* life *upon a cast* in war: so, παραβάλλεσθαι τὰ τέκνα *to stake one's own* children. 2. *to set side by side*, so as *to compare* one with another:—Med., παραβαλλόμενοι *vying with one another:* Pass., ἀπάτα δ' ἀπάταις παραβαλλομένα one piece of treachery *set against* another. III. *to bring to the side of:* esp. in Med., παραβάλλεσθαι τὴν ἄκατον *to bring* the boat *alongside;* and absol. in aor. 2 imperat. παραβαλοῦ, *put to land.* IV. *to throw* or *turn sideways;* ὄμμα παραβάλλειν *to cast* one's eye *askance:* παραβάλλειν τὼ ὀφθαλμὼ *to cast* both eyes *sideways*, i. e. to squint. V. *to deposit with* one, *entrust to* him. VI. *to deceive, betray.* VII. intr. in Act. *to come near, approach.* 2. *to pass over* by sea, like Lat. *trajicio.*

παραβάς, ᾶσα, άν, aor. 2 part. of παραβαίνω.

παράβᾰσις Ep. **παραίβασις**, εως, ἡ, (παραβαίνω) *an overstepping, transgression.* II. *the parabasis* or *digression*, a part of the old Comedy, in which the Chorus came forward and addressed the audience in the Poet's name.

παραβάτης [ᾰ], ου, ὁ, (παραβαίνω) *one who stands beside: the warrior* or *combatant who stands beside the charioteer.* II. *a transgressor*, in poët. form παρβάτης.

παραβᾰτός poët. **παρβατος**, ή, όν, (παραβαίνω) *transgressed.* II. *to be gone beyond, surpassed.*

παραβέβᾰσμαι, pf. pass. of παραβαίνω.

παραβέβασθαι, pf. inf. pass. of παραβαίνω.

παραβῆναι, aor. 2 inf. of παραβαίνω.

παρα-βιάζομαι, f. άσομαι: Dep.:—*to do* a thing *by force contrary to law.* 2. *to use violence towards* any one, *to constrain, compel.*

παρα-βλέπω, f. ψω, *to look aside* or *askance, take a side look;* παραβλέπειν θατέρῳ *to wink* with one eye. 2. *to see wrong.*

παραβλήδην, Adv. (παραβάλλω) *thrown in by the side:* metaph., παραβλήδην ἀγορεύειν to speak *with a side meaning*, i. e. *maliciously, invidiously.*

παράβλημα, ατος, τό, (παραβάλλω) *something hung beside, a curtain* or *skreen used to cover* the sides of ships.

παρα-βλώσκω: f. -μολοῦμαι: aor. 2 παρέμολον: pf. παραμέμβλωκα Ep. παρμέμβλωκα:—*to go beside*, for the purpose of aiding or protecting.

παραβλητέος, α, ον, and **παραβλητός**, ή, όν, verb. Adj. of παραβάλλω, *comparable.*

παραβλώψ, ῶπος, ὁ, ἡ, (παραβλέπω) *looking sideways* or *askance, squinting.*

παρα-βοάω, f. -βοήσομαι, *to call* or *cry out to.*

παρα-βοηθέω, f. ήσω, *to come to help* another: absol. *come to the rescue.*

παραβολεύομαι, Dep. (παράβολος), *to expose oneself to danger, run hazard.*

παραβολή, ἡ, (παραβάλλω II) *a placing beside, comparison: illustration, parable.*

παράβολος, ον, (παραβάλλομαι) *staking, risking: hazarding:* of persons, *venturesome, reckless* 2. of things, *hazardous, perilous.*

παρα-βουλεύομαι, Dep. *to shew disregard.*

παράβυστος, ον, (παραβύω) *stuffed in.*

παρα-βύω, f. σω, *to stuff in, insert.* [ῡ]

παραγαγεῖν, aor. 2 inf. of παράγω.

παραγγελία, ἡ, *a command issued to soldiers: the word of command.* 2. *the summoning one's partisans.* 3. *instruction, doctrine.* From

παρ-αγγέλλω, f. -αγγελῶ: aor. 1 παρήγγειλα: pf. παρήγγελκα: pass. παρήγγελμαι:—*to pass an announcement from one to another.* II. as military term, *to give the watchword*, which was *passed* from man to man, Lat. *imperium per manus tradere:*—also *to give the word of command, give orders:*—then 2. generally, *to recommend, charge, exhort.* 3. c. acc. rei, *to order;* παραγγέλλειν σιτία *to order* provisions, like Lat. *imperare frumentum:* τὰ παραγγελλόμεν *orders given.* III. also *to encourage, cheer on* IV. *to summon to one's help, to summon one's partisans* or *clients.* Hence

παράγγελμα, ατος, τό, *an announcement passed from one to another.* II. *an order, word of command.* III. *instruction.*

παράγγελσις, ἡ, (παραγγέλλω) *an announcing.* II. in war, *a giving orders, giving the word of command.*

παρα-γεύω, f. σω, *to give just a taste of* a thing:—Med. *to taste slightly of* a thing.

παρα-γηράω, f. άσομαι, *to be the worse for old age.*

παρα-γίγνομαι later **-γίνομαι** [ῑ]: fut. -γενήσομαι: aor. 2 παρεγενόμην:—*to be at hand, by* or *near, be present: to stand by, to second, support.* 2. of things, *to be at hand, to come, happen, belong to.* II. *to come to, arrive at:* absol. *to arrive at one's destination.* 2. *to come to maturity.*

παρα-γιγνώσκω later **-γῑνώσκω**: fut. -γνώσομαι: aor. 2 παρέγνων:—*to decide beside the right*, i. e. *to decide unfairly, err in one's judgment.*

παρ-αγκάλισμα, ατος, τό, (παρά, ἀγκάλη) *that which is taken in the arms, the object of one's embrace.*

παρ-αγκωνίζομαι, Dep. (παρά, ἀγκών) *to push aside with the elbows, elbow.*

παραγνούς, **παραγνῶναι**, aor. 2 part and inf. of παραγιγνώσκω.

παράγραμμα, ατος, τό, (παραγράφω) *that which one writes beside, an additional clause, codicil.*

παραγρᾰφή, ἡ, (παραγράφω) *any thing written beside, a marginal note.* II. *an exception taken* by the defendant *to the indictment* (γραφή).

παρα-γράφω, f. ψω, *to write beside, to add, subjoin, annex* a clause or codicil. II. Med., with pf. pass. παραγέγραμμαι, *to have* a thing *written by the side: to have* a person *registered* 2. παραγράφειν γραφήν *to take an exception to an indictment* (γραφή); absol., παραγράφεσθαι *to demur:* cf. παραγραφή.

παρα-γυμνόω, f. ώσω, *to lay bare at the side:* metaph. *to lay open, disclose.*

παρ-άγω, f. ξω: aor. 2 -ήγαγον:—*to lead beside, to lead by* or *past.* 2. as military term, *to make* the men *file off, to wheel* them *from column into line.* II. *to lead aside from the way, lead away:* absol. *to mislead, deceive:* generally, *to persuade, bring over,* but in bad sense 2. *to lead aside, divert, alter the course of, to distort, pervert.* III. *to bring beside* or *in front, to bring forward* as a speaker, witness, etc. IV. *to bring in stealthily.* V. intrans. *to pass by, pass on one's way: pass away.* Hence

παρᾰγωγή, ἡ, *a leading by* or *past, carrying across.* 2. of soldiers, *a wheeling from column into line.* 3. *a sliding motion* of the oars so as to make no splash (πίτυλος) in coming out of the water. II. *a leading aside* or *away, misleading: a fallacy, quibble.* III. *an alteration, change, variety.*

παρα-δακρύω, f. ύσω [ῡ], *to weep beside* or *along with.*

παρα-δαρθάνω, f. -δαρθήσομαι: aor. 2 παρέδαρθον Ep. παρέδρᾰθον, inf. παραδραθέειν:—*to sleep beside* or *by.*

παράδειγμα, τό, (παραδείκνυμι) *a pattern, model, plan,* Lat. *exemplar: a copy, representation.* 2. *a precedent, example;* ἐπὶ παραδείγματος by way of *example:* also *an example, lesson, warning.* 3. *an illustration, proof from example.* Hence

παρα-δειγμᾰτίζω, f. σω, *to make an example of, make a show of, put to sham*

παραδειγμᾰτώδης, ες, (παράδειγμα, εἶδος) *like an example.*

παρα-δείκνυμι and -ύω: f. -δείξω:—*to shew by the side of: to exhibit, bring forward.* 2. *to represent* as so and so, *to represent, pourtray.* 3. *to hand over* or *assign mone*

παρα-δειπνέομαι, Dep. (παρά, δεῖπνον) *to go without one's dinner.*

παράδεισος, ὁ, *a park* or *pleasure-grounds;* an Eastern word used in the Septuagint for *the garden of Eden.*

παρα-δέχομαι Ion. **-δέκομαι**: f. -δέξομαι: pf. -δέδεγμαι: Dep.:—*to take* or *receive from another, to have by right of succession,* as hereditary. 2. c. inf. *to take upon oneself* or *engage* to do. 3. *to admit, let in:* hence *to admit, allow.*

παρα-δηλόω, f. ώσω, *to disclose by a side hin.*

παρα-διᾱκονέω, f. ήσω, *to attend and serve.*

παρα-διατρῐβή, ἡ, *useless disputation.*

παρα-δίδωμι, f. -δώσω, *to give* or *hand over,* Lat. *tradere: to commit, consign.* 2. *to give into another's hands* as an hostage, Lat. *dedere, to deliver up, surrender: to hand over to justice:* also *to betray.* 3. *to hand down, transmit to posterity.* II. *to grant, bestow, offer:* c. inf. *to grant, allow, concede.*

παραδοθῶ, ῇς, ῇ, aor. 1 pass. subj. of παραδίδωμι.

παραδοξο-λογία, ἡ, (παράδοξος, λόγος) *a strange story, marvel.*

παρά-δοξος, ον, (παρά, δόξα) *contrary to opinion, unexpected, strange, marvellous.* Adv. -ξως.

παράδοσις, ἡ, (παραδίδωμι) *a handing down, bequeathing, transmission* 2. *a giving up, surrender.* 3. *the transmission* or *handing down* of legends, doctrines, etc., *tradition:*—also *that which is handed down, a tradition.*

παραδοτέος, α, ον, or **παραδοτός**, ή, όν, verb. Adj of παραδίδωμι, *to be handed down,* etc.:—neut. παραδοτέον or -δοτέα (plur.) *one must give up.*

παραδούς, aor. 2 part. of παραδίδωμι.

παραδοχή, ἡ, (παραδέχομαι) *the act of receiving from another.* 2. *that which has been so received, a custom.*

παραδρᾰθεῖν Ep. -έειν, aor. 2 inf. of παραδαρθάνω.

παραδρᾰμεῖν, aor. 2 inf. of παρατρέχω.

παρα-δράω Ep. **παρα-δρώω**: fut. -δράσω:—*to be near as a servant, to serve.*

παραδρομή, ἡ, (παραδραμεῖν) *a running beside* or *by;* ἐκ παραδρομῆς *cursorily, by the way,* Lat. *obiter.*

παράδρομος, ον, (παραδραμεῖν) *running beside.* II. *that may be run through;* τὰ παράδρομα *spaces for getting through, gaps.*

παρα-δρώω, Ep. for παραδράω.

παραδύμεναι, Ep. for παραδῦναι, aor. 2 inf. of παραδύω.

παρα-δῠναστεύω, f. σω, (παρά, δυνάστης) *to govern* or *reign with one.*

παράδῠσις, ἡ, *a slinking in beside.* From

παρα-δύομαι, Med., with aor. 2 act. παρέδῡν, inf. παραδῦναι Ep. παραδύμεναι:—*to creep* or *slink past* 2. *to creep in underhand, slink* or *steal in.*

παραδωσείω, Desiderat. of παραδίδωμι *to be disposed* or *ready to deliver up.*

παρ-ᾰείδω, f. σω, *to sing beside* or *to* one.

παρ-ᾰείρω contr. **παραίρω** (παρά, ἀείρω contr. αἴρω) *to lift up and set beside:*—Pass. *to hang on one side:* Ep. aor. 1 pass. παρηέρθην Att. παρᾱέρθην.

παρα-ζεύγνυμι and -ύω, f. -ζεύξω, *to yoke beside, couple: to set beside:*—Pass. *to be joined side by side, coupled together.*

παρα-ζηλόω, f. ώσω, *to provoke to jealousy.*

παρα-ζώννυμι and -ύω, f. -ζώσω, *to gird to the side, hang to the girdle.*

παρα-θᾰλασσίδιος Att. **-ττίδιος**, ον, = παραθαλάσσιος.

παρα-θᾰλάσσιος Att. **-ττιος**, α, ον, also ος, ον (παρά, θάλασσα) *beside the sea, lying on the seaside.*

S 5

παρα-θάλπω, f. ψω, *to cherish, comfort.*

παρα-θαρσύνω later –θαρρύνω, *to embolden. cheer on, inspire with confidence.*

παραθεῖεν, 3 pl. aor. 2 opt. of *παρατίθημι.*

παραθείς, παράθες, aor. 2 part. and imperat. of *παρατίθημι.*

παρα-θέλγω, f. ξω, *to soften, assuage, soothe.*

παρα-θερμαίνω, *to heat* or *inflame to excess.*

παράθεσις, εως, ἡ, (*παρατίθημι*) *a putting beside, juxtaposition, comparison.* II. *suggestion, advice.*

παρα-θέω, f. –*θεύσομαι, to run beside* II. *to run to one side of, deviate from.* III. *to run beyond, outrun.*

παρα-θεωρέω, f. ήσω, *to observe* one thing *beside* another, *compare.* II. *to overlook, slight.*

παρα-θήγω, f. ξω, *to whet* or *sharpen upon :* metaph. *to encourage.*

παραθήκη, ἡ, (*παρατίθημι*) *anything lodged with* one, *a deposit :* of persons, *a hostage.*

παραθήσομαι, fut. med. of *παρατίθημι.*

πᾰραί, poët. for *παρά.*

παραιβᾰσίη, ἡ, poët. for *παραβασία, transgression.*

παραι-βᾰτέω, παραι-βάτης, poët. for *παραβ–.*

παραίβολος, *ον*, poët. for *παράβολος*, (*παραβάλλω*) *thrown in by the way, sneering, malicious :* see *παραβλήδην.*

παρ-αιθύσσω, f. ξω, *to stir up, kindle.* II. intr. of words, *to fall from one by chance.*

παραίνεσις, ἡ, (*παραινέω*) *advice, counsel.*

παρ-αινέω, f. *–έσω* or *–έσομαι*: aor. 1 *παρῄνεσα*: pf. *παρῄνεκα*: Pass., aor. 1 *παρῃνέθην*: pf. *παρῄνημαι*:—*to advise, recommend, counsel.*

παραιπεπίθῃσιν, παραιπεπιθοῦσα, Ep. for *παραπίθῃ, παραπιθοῦσα*, 3 sing. aor. 2 subj., and part. fem. aor. 2 of *παραπείθω.*

παραίρεσις, ἡ, *a taking away from beside, a withdrawing of, curtailing.* From

παρ-αιρέω, f. *ήσω*: aor. 2 *παρεῖλον*: pf. *παρῄρηκα*: Pass., aor. 1 *παρῃρέθην*: pf. *παρῄρημαι*:—*to take away from beside.* 2. *to draw aside on one, to divert to; παραιρεῖν ἀρὰν εἰς παῖδα to draw aside* the curse on thy son. II. Med. *to draw off* or *away from, draw over to one's own side, detach.* 2. generally, *to take away from :* also *to lessen, damp.* Hence

παραίρημα, *ατος, τό, that which is taken off from the side, the selvage of cloth :* generally, *a band, strip.*

παρ-αίρω, contr. for poët. *παρ-αείρω.*

παρ-αισθάνομαι, f. *–αισθήσομαι* : Dep.:—*to hear of by the way.*

παρ-αίσιος, *ον*, (*παρά, αἴσιος*) *of ill omen, ominous, portentous.*

παρ-αΐσσω, f. ξω: Ep. aor. 1 *παρήϊξα*:—*to dart past.*

παρ-αιτέομαι, f. *–ήσομαι*: pf. *παρῄτημαι*: Dep.—*to beg of* or *from* another : . c. acc. rei, *to obtain by prayer* or *entreaty.* 2. c. acc. pers. *to move by entreaty obtain leave from :* also *to intercede with, beg earnestly.* 3. *to entreat* one *to* do. II. like Lat. *deprecari, to avert by entreaty, beg off.* Hence

παραίτησις, ἡ, *an obtaining by prayer : earnest supplication.* II. *a deprecating.* III. *an interceding for. begging off.*

παρ-αίτιος. *ον*, also *α. ον*, (*παρά, αἰτία*) *being in part the cause · accessory to.*

παραι-φάμενος, *η, ον*, Ep. for *παραφάμενος*, pres. med. part. of *παράφημι. exhorting, encouraging.*

παραί-φᾰσις. ἡ, poët. for *παράφασις*. (*παράφημι*) *encouragement, persuasion :* also. *a beguiling.*

παραι-φρονέω, poët. for *παραφρονέω.*

παρ-αιωρέω, f. *ήσω, to hang up beside :*—Pass. *to be hung* or *hang beside.*

παρακάββᾱλε, Ep. for *παρακατέβαλε*, 3 sing. aor. 2 of *παρακαταβάλλω.*

παρακαθεζέσθαι, aor. 2 inf. med. of *παρακαθίζω.*

παρα-κάθημαι, inf. *–καθῆσθαι*, Dep. *to sit beside* or *near.*

παρα-καθίζω, f. *–καθιζήσω* Att. *–καθιῶ*, *to set beside* or *near.* II. Med., fut. *–καθεδοῦμαι* : aor. 2 *–εκαθεζόμην*: also aor. 1 *ἐκαθισάμην* :—*to sit down beside.*

παρα-καθίημι, f. *–καθήσω, to let down by the side :* so also in Med. *παρα-καθίεμαι.*

παρα-καθίστημι, f. *–καταστήσω, to put, place, set down beside* or *near.* II. in Med. and intr. tenses of Act., aor. 2 *–κατέστην*, pf. *–καθέστηκα, to stand beside* or *near.*

παρα-καίριος and **παρά-καιρος**, *ον*, (*παρά, καιρός*) *untimely, ill-timed, unseasonable.*

παρα-καίω, f. *–καύσω, to light, kindle, burn beside* or *near*

παρα-κᾰλέω, f. *–καλῶ* later *–καλέσω*: pf. *–κέκληκα*, pass. *–κέκλημαι* :—*to call to* one, i. e., I. *to call to aid, send for, summon*, Lat. *arcessere : to call as witness, to invoke* the gods : *to invite.* II. *to call to, cheer on, encourage, exhort : to excite.* III. *to demand, require.*

παρακάλυμμα, *τό, a covering :* metaph. *a cloak, veil.* From

παρα-κᾰλύπτω, f. ψω, *to cover by hanging something beside, to veil, cloak, disguise.*

παρα-καταβάλλω, f. *–καταβᾰλῶ*: Ep. aor. 2 *παρακάββαλον* for *παρακατέβαλον*:—*to throw* or *put down beside*; *παραβάλλειν ζώνην τινί to put* a girdle *beside* one, i. e. gird it around one. II. as law-term, *to make a deposit, pay a sum into court.* Hence

παρακαταβολή, ἡ, *money deposited* in suits for recovery of an inheritance, to be forfeited in case of failure, Lat. *sacramentum.*

παρακαταθήκη, ἡ, (*παρακατατίθημι*) *anything lodged in one's hands*, esp. *a deposit, trust.*

παρα-καταθνήσκω, f. *–καταθανοῦμαι*: aor. 2 *–κατέθανον* Ep. *–κάτθανον* :—*to die beside* or *near.*

παρα-κατάκειμαι, inf. *–κατακεῖσθαι*, Pass. *to lie beside* or *near*, esp. *to sit by* at meals, Lat. *juxta accumbere.*

παρα-κατακλίνω, f. *ῐνῶ, to lay down beside.*

παρα-καταλέγομαι, f. ξομαι, Pass. *to lie down beside, to lie with*: Ep. 3 sing. aor. 2 παρκατέλεκτο.

παρα-καταλείπω, f. ψω, *to leave behind in one's hands.*

παρα-καταπήγνυμι, f. -καταπήξω, *to fix* or *drive in alongside.*

παρα-κατατίθημι, f. -καταθήσω, *to deposit* or *lodge in* a person's *hands*:—Med. *to deposit one's* property *with* another, *give* it *in trust, entrust to his keeping.*

παρα-κατέχω, f. -καθέξω, *to keep back, restrain.*

παρα-κατοικίζω, f. σω, *to make to dwell beside*:—Med. *to settle* another *near oneself.*

παρα-καττύω, Att. for παρα-κασσύω, *to sew on* or *to*:—metaph. in Med. *to set all straight.*

παρά-κειμαι, inf. -κεῖσθαι: 3 sing. Ep. impf. παρεκέσκετο: Pass.:—*to lie beside, near* or *before*: generally, *to be ready, lie close at hand*: metaph. *to be presented* or *proposed to one*; τὰ παρακείμενα *things before one* or *present.*

παρακέλευμα, ματος, τό, = παρακέλευσμα.

παρα-κελεύομαι, Med. *to exhort, advise, recommend, prescribe.* II. *to exhort, encourage, cheer on by shouting*: 3 sing. plqpf. παρακεκέλευστο is used in pass. sense, *orders had been given.* Hence

παρακέλευσις, ἡ, *a calling out to, cheering on.*

παρακέλευσμα, ατος, τό, (παρακελεύομαι) *an exhortation, encouragement.*

παρακελευσμός, ὁ, = παρακέλευσις.

παρακελευστός, ή, όν, (παρακελεύομαι) *cheered on, summoned.*

παρα-κελητίζω, f. σω, *to ride by* or *past.*

παρακινδύνευσις, ἡ, *a desperate venture.* From

παρα-κινδῡνεύω, f. σω, *to make a rash venture, to dare recklessly*: c. acc. rei, *to venture* or *hazard* a thing: c. inf. *to have the hardihood to* do: absol. *to venture, run the risk, stand the hazard*: in Pass., ἔπος παρακεκινδυνευμένον *a hardy, venturous phrase.*

παρα-κινέω, f. ήσω, trans. *to move aside*: *to excite, disturb violently*, Lat. *commovere.* II. intr. *to shift one's ground, alter.* 2. *to be impassioned*: *to be distraught, mad.* 3. *to raise troubles* or *commotions.*

παρα-κίω, *to pass by.*

παρα-κλαίω, f. -κλαύσομαι and -κλαυσοῦμαι:—*to weep beside* or *at.*

παρα-κλείω Ion. **-κληιω**, *to bar* or *shut out.*

παρα-κλέπτω, f. ψω, *to steal from the side* or *in passing, filch underhand.*

παρακληθήσομαι, fut. pass. of παρακαλέω.

παρα-κληίω, Ion. for παρακλείω.

παράκλησις, ἡ, (παρακαλέω) *a calling to one, summons to assist.* 2. *a calling upon, imploring.* 3. *exhortation, encouragement.*

παρακλητέος, α, ον, = παράκλητος: neut. παρακλητέον, *one must call on.*

παρακλητικός, ή, όν, (παρακαλεω) *of* or *for exhorting, hortatory.*

παράκλητος, ον, verb Adj. of **παρακαλέω**, *called to one's aid*, esp. in a court of justice, Lat. *advocatus*. as Subst., παράκλητος, ὁ, *an advocate.* 2. generally, *a helper*; hence in N. T., ὁ Παράκλητος *the Helper, Comforter.*

παρακλῐδόν, Adv. (παρακλίνω) *bending sideways, turning aside, averting.*

παρακλίντωρ, ορος, ὁ, = παρακλίτης. From

παρα-κλίνω [ῑ], f. -κλῐνῶ, *to turn* or *bend aside*; παρακλίνειν τὴν θύραν *to set* the gate *ajar.* 2. metaph. *to make to swerve, distort*; ἄλλῃ παρακλίνουσι δίκας *they turn* righteous judgments *aside.* II. Pass. and Med., aor. 2 παρεκλίθην [ῐ]: pf. παρακέκλῐμαι: *to lie down beside, lie near*, esp. at meals, Lat. *juxta accumbere.* III. intr. in Act., *to turn aside, slip away, escape.* Hence

παρακλίτης, ου, ὁ, *one who lies beside* at meals. [ῐ]

παρα-κλύω, *to hear beside* or *amiss*: *to hear wrong.*

παρ-ακμάζω, f. άσω, *to be past the prime*: *to be faded, withered*

παρα-κοάω, Ion. for παρα-νοέω.

παρᾰκοή, ἡ, (παρακούω) *hearing amiss*: *unwillingness to hear, disobedience.*

παρα-κοινάομαι, Med. (παρά, κοινός) *to take counsel with* another, Lat. *communicare.*

παρα-κοίτης, ου, ὁ, (παρά, ἀκοίτης) *one who sleeps beside, a bedfellow, husband.*

παρ-άκοιτις, ιος, ἡ, acc. ιν: Ep. dat. παρακοίτῑ: (παρά, ἄκοιτις) *a wife, consort.*

παρ-ᾰκολουθέω, f. ήσω, *to follow close* or *hard upon one*: *to attend studiously*: of rules, *to hold good throughout.* II. metaph. *to follow in one's mind, to understand.*

παρακομῐδή, ἡ, (παρακομίζω) *a carrying across, transporting, conveying* II. (from Pass.) *a going* or *sailing across.*

παρα-κομίζω, f. ίσω Att. ιῶ: *to carry beside* or *along with, escort*: *carry across*: generally *to carry* or *convey*:—Med. *to have* a thing *brought one*:—Pass. *to sail beside, coast along.*

παρ-ᾰκονάω, f. ήσω, *to sharpen* or *whet besides.*

παρ-ᾰκοντίζω, f. ίσω, *to throw the dart with* others.

παρακοπή, ἡ, (παρακόπτω) *a striking falsely, a coining falsely*: metaph. *madness, frenzy.*

παράκοπος, ον, (παρακόπτω) *struck falsely, counterfeit*: metaph. *deranged, mad.*

παρα-κόπτω, f. ψω, *to strike amiss*, esp. of money, *to forge, counterfeit*; ἀνδράρια παρακεκομμένα (pf. pass. part.) men *of a false stamp.* II. Med. *to cheat, swindle out of* a thing, c. gen.: absol. *to cheat*:—Pass. *to be cheated.* III. metaph. *to drive mad, derange, distract.*

παρ-ᾰκούω, f. -ακούσομαι, (παρά, ἀκούω) *to hear beside* or *by the way, to hear talk of.* II. *to hear* or *learn underhand.* III. *to hear wrong, misunderstand.*

παρα-κρεμάννυμι, f. -κρεμάσω Att. -κρεμῶ:—*to let hang on the side.*

παρακρεμάσας, aor. 1 part. of παρακρεμάννυμι.

παρα-κρίνω [ῑ], f. -κρῐνῶ: aor. I παρέκρῑνα: pf. παρακέκρῐκα: Pass., aor. I παρεκρίθην [ῐ]: pf. παρακέκρῐμαι:—*to separate and place beside*:—Pass. *to be drawn up along, extend over a space.*

παρα-κροτέω, f. ήσω, *to pat, touch on the side.*

παράκρουσις, ἡ, (παρακρούω) *a striking beside, striking a false note: an error.* II. *a cheating, fraud.*

παρα-κρούω, f. σω: pf. παρακέκρουκα: Pass., aor. I παρεκρούσθην: pf. παρακέκρουσμαι:—*to strike beside*, esp. *to strike a wrong note* in music. II. *to lead aside, mislead, deceive.*

παρα-κτάομαι, f. ήσομαι, Dep. *to get over and above*: in pf. παρακέκτημαι, *to have over and above.*

παρ-ακτίδιος, ον, and **παρ-άκτιος**, α, ον, (παρά, ἀκτή) *on the seaside, on the shore.*

παρα-κύπτω, f. ψω: aor. I παρέκυψα:—*to stoop aside, put one's head on one side affectedly.* 2. generally, *to take a side glance at, look carelessly at.* 3. *to lean forward and peep out of* a door, window, etc.: also *to peep in.*

παρακωχή, see παροκωχή.

παρα-λαμβάνω: f. -λήψομαι Ion. -λάμψομαι: aor. 2 -έλαβον, inf. -λαβεῖν: pf. -είληφα, pass. -είλημμαι:—*to receive from another, to succeed to* an office or to property. 2. *to take possession of, to take in pledge*: also *to take by force, seize forcibly.* 3. *to take to oneself*, as to wife:—*to produce* or *bring forward* as a witness. II. *to receive* or *entertain* as a friend, *to invite.* III. *to receive by hearsay* or *tradition, to learn, hear*, Lat. *accipere.* IV. *to take upon oneself, undertake*, Lat. *suscipere.* V. *to wait for, intercept*, Lat. *excipere.*

παρα-λέγω, f. ξω, *to put, lay beside* or *near*:—Med., f. -λέξομαι: aor. I παρελεξάμην: 3 sing. Ep. aor. 2 παρ-έλεκτο: *to lie beside* or *with one, to lie down beside.* II. παραλέγεσθαι γῆν *to sail by* or *along* the land, *to coast along.*

παραλειπτέον, verb. Adv. *one must omit.* From

παρα-λείπω, f. ψω, *to leave on one side, leave remaining.* 2. *to leave on one side, leave unnoticed, pass by*, Lat. *praetermittere.* 3. *to neglect*, Lat. *omittere.*

παρ-αλείφω, f. ψω, *to smear with ointment.*

παραλέλῠμαι, pf. pass. of παραλύω.

παρα-λεύσσω, = παροράω.

παραληπτέον, verb. Adj. of παραλαμβάνω, *one must take to oneself.*

παραληπτός, ή, όν, verb. Adj. of παραλαμβάνω, *to be accepted.*

παρα-ληρέω, f. ήσω, *to talk great nonsense, to be in one's dotage*, Lat. *delirare.*

παραληφθήσομαι, **παραλήψομαι**, fut. pass. and med. of παραλαμβάνω.

παράληψις, εως, ἡ, (παραλαμβάνω) *a receiving from another, succession.*

παραλία (sub. χώρα), ἡ, *the sea-coast, coastland.* From

παρ-άλιος, ον, also α, ον, (παρά, ἅλς) *by the sea, on the sea shore.*

παραλλᾰγή, ἡ, (παραλλάσσω) *a passing from hand to hand, transfer.* II. *alternation: change, variation.*

παράλλαγμα, ματος, τό, (παραλλάσσω) *an exchange.*

παραλλάξ, Adv. (παραλλάσσω) *alternately: in alternating rows.*

παρ-αλλάσσω Att. -ττω: f. ξω: aor. I παρήλλαξα: Pass., aor. I -ηλλάχθην: aor. 2 -ηλλάγην [ᾰ]: pf. -ήλλαγμαι:—*to make* things *alternate.* 2. *to change* or *alter a little*, esp. *for the worse, to corrupt.* 3. of Place, *to pass by* or *beyond.* II. intr. *to pass by one another.* 2. *to pass aside, turn from the path, to deviate, vary*:—hence *to slip aside, escape.*

παρ-άλληλος, ον, (παρά, ἀλλήλοι) *beside one another, side by side, parallel.*

παρα-λογίζομαι, f. ίσομαι, Dep. *to reckon wrong, misreckon, miscalculate.* 2. *to reason falsely.* II. *to cheat by false reasoning.* Hence

παραλογισμός, ὁ, *false reckoning: a fallacy.*

παρά-λογος, ον, (παρά, λόγος) *beyond calculation, unexpected, unaccountable.* Hence

παρά-λογος, ὁ, as Subst. *that which is beyond all calculation, an unexpected issue: miscalculatio.*

πάρ-ᾰλος, ον, (παρά, ἅλς) *by* or *near the sea, naval, maritime.* II. οἱ Πάραλοι in Attica, *the people of the sea-coast* (Παραλία); opp. to the dwellers on the plain, and the mountaineers. 2. *the crew of the ship Paralos.* III. ἡ Πάραλος (sub. ναῦς or τριήρης), *the Paralos*, one of the Athenian state-galleys, reserved for religious missions, embassies, etc.: the other was called Σαλαμινία

παρα-λυπέω, f. ήσω, (παρά, λυπέω) *to grieve along with* something else: οἱ παραλυποῦντες, *the refractory.*

παραλῠτικός, ή, όν, (παραλύω) *affected with palsy, paralytic.*

παρα-λύω, f. -λύσω [ῡ]: aor. I παρέλῡσα: pf. -λέλῠκα: Pass., aor. I παρελύθην [ῠ]: pf. -λέλῠμαι:—*to loose from the side, loose and take off, detach from.* 2. *to separate, part from*:—Pass. *to be parted from.* 3. *to release* or *set free from*:—Pass. *to be exempt from* a thing. 4. *to discharge, dismiss, depose from* command: also *to set free.* 5. *to undo, put an end to.* II. *to relax at the side*:—Pass. *disabled on one side, to be palsied*; pf. part. παραλελυμένος, like παραλυτικός, *palsied, paralytic*: generally, *to be enfeebled* or *exhausted, to flag.*

παρ-ᾰμείβω, f. ψω: aor. I παρήμειψα: (παρά, ἀμείβω):—*to change* or *alter a little.* 2. *to leave on one side, pass by*: hence *to exceed, excel.* II. Med. *to pass beside, pass by: outrun.* 2. *to pass over, omit, make no mention of.* 3. of Time, *to pass, go by.* 4. *to change for oneself.* 5. *to lead aside from the road.*

παρ-ᾰμελέω, pf. -ημέληκα: Ion. 3 sing. plqpf. παρημελήκεε: (παρά, ἀμελέω):—*to pass by and disregard, pay no heed to.*

παραμέμνημαι, pf. of *παραμιμνήσκομαι.*

παρα-μένω, f. *-μενῶ*: aor. 1 *παρέμεινα*:—*to stay beside* or *near, stand by.* II. absol. *to stand one's ground, stand fast* 2. *to stay* at a place, *stay behind* 3. *to survive, remain alive*: of things, *to endure, last.*

παρ-άμερος, *ον*, Dor. for *παρήμερος.* [ᾱ]

παρα-μετρέω, f. *ήσω*, *to measure* one thing *by* another, *to compare.* II. *to measure out.*

παρ-ἄμεύω, Dor. = *παραμείβω*:—Med., *παραμεύεσθαί τινος μορφῇ to surpass* one in beauty.

παρα-μηρίδιος, *ον*, (*παρά, μηρός*) *at the side of* or *along the thighs*: **τὰ** *παραμηρίδια armour for the thighs, cuisses.*

παρα-μίγνυμι and **-ύω** Ion. **-μίσγω**: f. *-μίξω*: pf. pass. *-μέμιγμαι*:—*to mingle, intermix with, τινί τι.* 2. *to mix in, add by mixing.*

παρ-άμιλλος, *ον*, (*παρά, ἅμιλλα*) *vying* or *racing with.*

παρα-μιμνήσκομαι, fut. *-μνήσομαι*: pf. *-μέμνημαι*: Dep.:—*to mention besides* or *by the way, to make mention of* one thing *along with* another.

παρα-μίμνω, poët. for *παραμένω* absol., *to tarry, stay.*

παρα-μίσγω, Ion. for *παραμίγνυμι.*

παρα-μνάομαι, Ion. for *παραμιμνήσκομαι.*

παραμολεῖν, aor. 2 inf. of *παραβλώσκω.*

παραμόνιμος, *ον*, also *η, ον*, (*παραμένω*) *abiding by, lasting, steadfast, faithful.* Neut. *παρμόνιμον*, as Adv., *steadfastly.*

παρά-μονος poët. **πάρμονος**, *ον*, (*παραμένω*) *lasting.*

παρά-μουσος, *ον*, (*παρά*, **Μοῦσα**) *averse to the Muses* or *music, discordant with*: hence *harsh, horrid.*

παρ-αμπέχω or **-αμπίσχω**: f. *παραμφέξω*: aor. 2 *παρήμπισχον*: (*παρά, ἀμπέχω*):—*to cover with a cloak* or *robe*; hence *to cloak* or *disguise.*

παρ-αμπῠκίζω Lacon. **-πυκίδδω**: (*παρά, ἄμπυξ*): —*to bind the hair with a fillet* or *head-band*

παρα-μῡθέομαι, f. *-ήσομαι*: aor. 1 *-εμῡθησάμην*: Dep.:—*to address* with *soothing* or *cheering words*: *to encourage, exhort, advise.* 2. *to console, appease.* Hence

παραμῡθία, *ἡ*, *encouragement*: also *persuasion.*

παραμύθιον, *τό*, (*παραμυθέομαι*) *an address, exhortation.* 2. *a consolation, relief, assuagement.*

παρα-μῡκάομαι, f. *ήσομαι*, Dep. *to bellow beside* or *near.*

παρ-αναγιγνώσκω later **-αναγῑνώσκω**: f. *-αναγνώσομαι*: (*παρά, ἀναγιγνώσκω*):—*to read beside* or *near*: *to read side by side, compare, collate.*

παρα-ναιετάω, *to dwell beside* or *near.*

παρ-ἄνᾱλίσκω, f *-ανᾱλώσω*, *to spend beside* or *amiss, to waste, lavish.*

παρ-ανατέλλω, *to arise beside* or *near.*

παρα-νέω, f. *-νεύσομαι* and *-νευσοῦμαι*, (*παρά, νέω to swim*) *to swim beside* or *by.*

παρανέω, f. *-νήσω*, (*παρά, νέω to heap*) *to heap* or *pile up beside*. Ion. *παρα-νηέω* and *-νηνέω.*

παρα-νήχομαι, f. *ξομαι*, Dep. *to swim beside, to swim along the shore.*

παρα-νῑκάω, f. *ήσω*, *to corrupt by conquest.*

παρα-νίσσομαι, Dep. = *παρανέομαι*, *to pass beside* or *near.*

παρ-ανίσχω, *to raise up beside* or *in answer.* II. intr. *to stand forth beside.*

παρα-νοέω, f. *ήσω*, *to think amiss* or *wrongly.* II. *to be deranged, senseless*: *to go mad.* Hence

παράνοιᾰ, *ἡ*, *derangement, madness, folly.*

παρ-ανοίγνυμι and **-ανοίγω**: f. *-ανοίξω*, (*παρά, ἀνοίγω*) *to open at the side* or *a little.*

παρα-νομέω: impf. *παρενόμουν*: aor. 1 *παρενόμησα*: pf. *παρανενόμηκα*: Pass., aor. *παρενομήθην*: pf. *παρανενόμημαι*: (*παράνομος*):—*to transgress the law, act illegally.* 2. *to commit an outrage*: c. acc. pers. *to commit an outrage* upon one; so in Pass., *to be ill-used, maltreated.* Hence

παρανόμημα, *ατος, τό*, *an illegal act, transgression.*

παρανομία, *ἡ*, (*παρανομέω*) *transgression of law, habitual law-breaking.*

παρά-νομος, *ον*, (*παρά, νομος*) *contrary to law and custom, unlawful, illegal*: generally, *lawless, unjust, violent.* II. as Att. law-terms, *παράνομα γράφειν* to propose *unconstitutional measures*; but, *παρανόμων γράφεσθαί τινα* to indict one *for proposing unconstitutional measures.*

παρά-νοος, *ον*, contr. **παρά-νους**, *ουν*, (*παρα, νόος*) *distraught, frenzied.*

πάρ-αντα, Adv. (*παρά, ἀντίος*) *sideways, sidewards.*

παρ-αντέλλω, poët. for *παραν ατέλλω.*

παρά-νυμφος, *ἡ*, (*παρά, νύμφη*) *the bride's-maid*, who conducts her to the bridegroom.

παρα-νύσσω Att. **-ττω**, f. *ξω*, *to prick beside*: metaph. *to prick on* or *stimulate* to do a thing.

παρά-ξενος, *ον*, *with a false claim to friendship* or *hospitality*: generally, *false, spurious.*

παρα-ξέω, f. *έσω*, *to scrape beside*: *to graze in passing.*

παρ-αξόνιος, *ον*, (*παρά, ἄξων*) *beside* or *near the axle*: *παραξόνια, τά*, as Subst. *rapid whirlings.*

παρα-ξύω, f. *-ξύσω* [ῠ], *to shave at the side*: metaph. *to graze, keep close beside.*

παρα-παίω, f. *-παιήσω*, *to strike on the side.* II. intrans. *strike aside*: *to fall aside, fall out from*, Lat. *excidere*; *παραπαίειν φρενῶν to wander from* one's *senses, lose* one's wits.

παρα-πάλλω, *to hurl beside*:—Med. *to vault* or *bound aside.*

παρά-παν. Adv., for *παρὰ πᾶν*, *on the whole, altogether, absolutely*: in reckoning, *ἐπὶ διηκόσια τὸ παράπαν* up to two hundred *altogether, on the average.*

παρ-ἄπᾰτάω, f. *ήσω*, *to mislead, cajole.*

παρ-ἄπᾰφίσκω: fut. *-απαφήσω*: aor. 2 *παρήπᾰφον*: —poet. for *παραπατάω*, *to mislead*: *to persuade* one to do a thing *by craft* or *fraud.*

παρα-πείθω, f. *-πείσω*, *to win by persuasive arts, to prevail upon, win over*: Homer often uses an Ep. redupl. aor. 2 subj. in 3 sing. *παραιπεπίθησι*; part. *παρπεπιθών, παραιπεπιθοῦσα, παρπεπιθόντες.*

παρα-πειράομαι, f. άσομαι [ᾱ], Dep. *to make trial of.*

παρα-πέμπω, f. ψω: aor. 1 παρέπεμψα:— *to send by* or *beyond*, *make to pass through*: of sound, *to send* or *echo back.* 2. *to send by* or *along the coast*: generally *to send along.* 3. *to escort*, *convoy*: so in Med., *to convoy* ships. II. *to send besides* or *in addition.* III. metaph. *to let pass take no heed of.* Lat. *praetermitter*

παραπεσών, aor. 2 part. of παραπίπτω.

παρα-πέτᾰμαι, = παραπέτομαι.

παρα-πετάννῡμι and -ύω, f. -πετάσω: pf. -πεπέτασμαι:—*to stretch a curtain before.* Hence

παραπέτασμα, ατος, τό, *that which is spread out before*, *a curtain*, *veil.*

παρα-πέτομαι: f. -πετήσομαι, syncop. -πτήσομαι: Dep.:—*to fly beside*, *near*, *by*: *to fly along*, *fly over*: *to fly to.*

παρα-πήγνῡμι and -ύω, f. -πήξω, *to fix* or *plant beside* or *near*:—Pass., with pf. med. -πέπηγα, *to be fixed* or *planted beside.*

παρα-πηδάω, f. ήσομαι, *to spring by* or *beyond*: c. acc. *to overleap*, *transgress.*

παρα-πικραίνω, *to embitter*, *provoke.* Hence

παραπικρασμός, ὁ, *provocation*: *contumacy.*

παρα-πίμπρημι, f. -πρήσω, *to kindle*, *burn beside* or *near*:—Pass. *to be inflamed.*

παρα-πίπτω, f. -πεσοῦμαι: aor. 2 -έπεσον: pf. -πέπτωκα:—*to fall beside.* II. *to fall in one's way*, *fall in with*:—of things, *to befal*, *happen*, *offer itself.* III. *to fall aside*: hence *to mistake*, *err.*

παραπλάγξας, aor. 1 part. of παραπλάζω.

παρα-πλάζω, f. -πλάγξω: aor. 1 παρέπλαγξα: Pass., aor. 1 παρεπλάγχθην:—*to make* a person *wander from the right way*, *lead astray*, *to drive out of the course*:—Pass *to wander*, *go astray*, *wander away from.* II. metaph. *to mislead*:—Pass. *to be misled*, *err*, *be wrong.*

παρα-πλευρίδια, τά, (παρά, πλευρά) *covers for the sides of war-horses.*

παρα-πλέω Ion. **-πλώω**: f. -πλεύσομαι and -πλευσοῦμαι: 3 sing. Ep. aor. 2 παρέπλω (as if from a Verb in -μι):—*to sail beside*, *near* or *alongside*: *to sail along* a coast: *to sail past.*

παραπλῆγας, acc. pl. of παραπλήξ.

παράπληκτος, ον, (παραπλήσσω) *stricken aside*: metaph. *frenzy-stricken.*

παραπλήξ, ῆγος, ὁ, ἡ, (παραπλήσσω) *struck sideways*; ἠιόνες παραπλῆγες *a shelving* beach, *on which the waves break obliquely*, and not directly (as against a cliff). II. metaph. = παράπληκτος, *mad.*

παρα-πλήσιος, ον, also α, ον, (παρά, πλησίος) *coming close beside*, *resembling*, *near akin to*, *about the same*, *about equal*:—Sup. -ώτατος.—Neut. παραπλήσιον, παραπλήσια as Adv., but also regul. Adv. παραπλησίως, *nearly*, *almost*; παραπλησίως ἀγωνίζεσθαι to fight *with nearly equal advantage.*

παρα-πλήσσω Att. **-ττω**, f. ξω, *to strike on the side*:—Pass. *to be stricken on one side*, *to be palsied*, *deranged*, *frenzied.*

παραπλόμενος, η, ον, *coming to a place*, Ep. syncop. part. from an obsol. pres. παραπέλομαι.

παράπλοος contr. **-πλους**, ὁ, (παραπλέω) *a sailing beside.* 2. *a passage* over the sea, Lat. *trajectus.*

παρα-πλώω, Ion. for παραπλέω.

παρέπλω, 3 sing. Ep. aor. 2, as if from a Verb in -μι.

παραπνεύσας, aor. 1 part. of παραπνέω.

παρα-πνέω, f. -πνεύσομαι, *to blow beside* or *by the side*, *to escape by the side.*

παρα-πόδιος, poët. **παρπόδιος**, ον, (παρά, πούς) *at the feet*, *close by*, *present.*

παρα-ποιέω, f. ήσω, *to make falsely*:—Med. *to make falsely for oneself*, *get* a thing *made falsely*

παρ-απόλλυμι, f. -απολέσω Att. -απολῶ, *to destroy*, *ruin beside*:—Pass., with fut. med. -απολοῦμαι, pf., -απόλωλα, plqpf. -ολώλειν, *to perish beside* or *near.*

παραπομπή, ἡ, (παραπέμπω) *a convoying*, *procuring.* II. *that which is procured*, *supplies*, *provisions.*

παρα-πόντιος, ον, (παρά, πόντος) *by the sea.*

παρα-πορεύομαι, Pass. *to go beside* or *past.*

παρα-ποτάμιος, α, ον, (παρά, ποταμός) *beside* or *near a river*, *situated* or *dwelling on a river*; οἱ παραποτάμιοι *people who live on a river.*

παρα-πράσσω Att. **-πράττω** Ion. **-πρήσσω**, f. ξω, *to do beside* or *beyond* the main purpose. II. *to do with* another, *join* or *help in doing.*

παραπρεσβεία, ἡ, *a false* or *dishonest embassage.* From

παρα-πρεσβεύω, Act. and Med. *to execute an embassy faithlessly* or *dishonestly.*

παράπρισμα, ατος, τό, *that which falls off in sawing*, *saw-dust.* From

παρα-πρίω, f. -πριοῦμαι, *to saw beside* or *gently.* [ῑ]

παρ-άπτω, f. ψω, *to fasten beside*, *near* or *alongside*:—Pass., παραπτομένα χερσὶ πλάτα the oar *grasped* by the hands:—Med. *to touch beside* or *at the side.*

παράπτωμα, ατος, τό, (παραπίπτω) *a fall beside*: metaph. *a transgression.*

παρα-πύθια, τά, (παρά, Πύθια) *a sickness which prevented one from being victor at the Pythian games* (Πύθια).

παρα-ρρᾳθυμέω, **παρα-ραίνω**, etc., v. παραρρ-.

πάρ-ᾱρος Ion. **πάρηρος**, ον, like παρήορος, (παρά, ἀείρω) *deranged in mind.*

πάρᾱρος, ον, Dor. and poët. for παρήορος, *distraught.*

παρ-αρπάζω, fut. άσω, later άξω, *to take away from the side*, *filch.*

παραρ-ράπτω, ψω, *to sew beside* or *along*:—Pass. *to be sewn on as a fringe* or *border.*

παραρ-ρέω, f. -ρεύσομαι: pf. παρερρύηκα: aor. 2 in pass. form παρερρύην: (παρά, ῥέω):—*to flow beside*, *by* or *past*, c. acc. 2. c. dat., παραρρεῖν τινι *to slip off* it. II. *to slip away*, *to slip* from one's memory. III. *to slip in unawares.*

παραρ-ρήγνυμι, f. -ρήξω: aor. 1 παρέρρηξα: (παρά, ῥήγνυμι):—*to break at the side*, esp. *to break* a line of battle:—Pass. of the line, *to be broken.* II. Pass., with pf. med. παρέρρωγα, *to break* or *burst out beside* or *from*; **παρέρρωγεν ποδὸς φλέψ** a vein *bas burst out* from his foot.

παραρ-ρητός, ή, όν, (παρά, ρητός) of persons, *that may be moved by words.* II. of words, *persuasive.*

παραρ-ρῑγόω, (παρά, ῥιγόω) *to freeze beside* or *near.*

παραρ-ρίπτω and -έω, *to throw beside*, esp. *to throw down one's stake:* hence *to run the risk* of doing a thing. II. *to throw aside* or *away, reject.*

παραρρυείην, aor. 2 opt. of παραρρέω.

παράρ-ρυθμος poët. **παράρυθμος**, ον (παρά, ῥυθμός) *out of time* or *tune: discordant.*

παράρρῡμα, ατος, τό, *anything drawn along the side for shelter: a curtain stretched along* the sides of ships to protect the men. From

παραρ-ρύομαι Dep. (παρά, ῥύομαι) *to draw along the side.*

παρ-αρτάω Ion. -έω: f. ήσω: pf. pass. παρήρτημαι:—*to hang* or *attach alongside* or *upon.* II. Ion. παραρτέομαι, 1. Med. *to fit out, equip, get ready.* 2. Pass. *to be* or *get ready, hold oneself in readiness.* Hence

παρ-άρτημα, τό, *anything hanging at the side.*

παρασάγγης, ου, ὁ, *a parasang*, the Persian *farsang*, a measure of distance equal to thirty stadia.

παρα-σάττω, f. ξω, *to stuff* or *cram in beside.*

παρά-σειρος, ον, (παρά, σειρά) *fastened beside with a thong* or *cord;* παράσειρος ἵππος a horse *fastened alongside* of the regular pair *by a rein* or *trace, an outrigger* (σειραφόρος), opp. to ζύγιος:—metaph. *a yokefellow, comrade.*

παρα-σείω, f. σω, *to swing beside* one.

παρα-σημαίνω, f. ανῶ, *to seal by the side:*—Med. *to seal for oneself, seal up: to counterseal.*

παρά-σημον, τό, *a mark of distinction; the ensign of a ship:* properly neut. of παράσημος.

παρά-σημος, ον, (παρά, σῆμα) *stamped amiss* or *falsely:* of money, *base, counterfeit, spurious.* II. *marked in any way, conspicuous.*

παρασιτέω, f. ήσω, (παράσιτος) *to eat at another's table, to be a parasite.* II. *to have a seat at the public table.*

παρα-σῑτικός, ή, όν, *of* or *for a parasite* or *flatterer:* ἡ παρασιτική (sub. τέχνη), *the trade of a parasite.* From

παρά-σῖτος, ον, (παρά, σῖτος) *eating at the table of another:* as Subst., παράσιτος, ὁ, *one who lives at another's table, a parasite, flatterer.*

παρα-σκευάζω, f. σω: aor. 1 παρεσκεύασα: Pass., pf. παρεσκεύασμαι: Ion. 3 pl. plqpf. παρασκευάδατο:—*to get ready, prepare: to hold ready;* also *to procure, provide, furnish.* 2. *to make* or *render* so and so. II. Med. *to get ready, prepare* or *furnish for oneself:* absol. *to make preparations.* 2. *to procure* by fair means or foul, as witnesses, partisans, etc.: *to manage:* absol. *to form a party: to bring over to one's party.* III. Pass. *to get oneself ready, prepare:* in pt. παρεσκεύασμαι *to be ready, be prepared.* 2. of things, *to be got ready, prepared,* ὡς παρεσκεύαστο when *preparations had been made;* παρεσκευάδατο τοῖς Ἕλλησι *preparations had been made* by the Greeks. Hence

παρασκεύασμα, ατος, τό, *anything got ready* or *prepared.*

παρασ-κευή, ἡ, *a getting ready, preparing, preparation, provision: preparation, practice:* ἀπὸ or ἐκ παρασκευῆς, *of set purpose*, Lat. *ex instituto;* δι' ὀλίγης παρασκευῆς with short *practice*, i. e. at short notice. 2. *a plan, scheme, plot, intrigue.* II. *that which is prepared, furniture, garniture,* Lat. *apparatus: pomp.* 2. of warlike preparation, *a force, power, equipment:* generally, *means, resources.*

παρα-σκηνέω, f. ήσω, (παρά, σκηνή) *to pitch one's tent beside* or *near.*

παρα-σκήνια, τά, (παρά, σκηνή) *the space at the sides of the stage, the side scenes;* or, *the side entrances to the theatre.*

παρα-σκηνόω, f. ώσω, (παρά, σκηνή) *to throw over* one *like a curtain* or *tent.*

παρα-σκήπτω, f. ψω, *to light* or *fall beside* or *near.*

παρα-σκιρτάω, f. ήσω, *to leap beside* or *near.*

παρα-σκοπέω, f. -σκέψομαι, *to look aside from, miss the sense of.*

παρα-σκώπτω, f. ψω, *to jeer, jest beside* or *indirectly.*

παρα-σπάω, f. άσω [ᾰ], *to wrest aside, distort:*—Med. *to draw off* or *away from* a thing: *to detach from a party.*

παρ-ασπίζω, f. ίσω, (παρά, ἀσπίς) *to bear a shield beside, to fight* or *stand by* another. Hence

παρασπιστής, οῦ, ὁ, *one who bears a shield beside one, a companion in arms.*

παρασπονδέω, f. ήσω, *to act contrary to engagements: to break a treaty.* From

παρά-σπονδος, ον, (παρά, σπονδή) *contrary to a compact* or *treaty.* 2. of persons, *faithless, forsworn.*

παραστᾰδόν, Adv. (παρίσταμαι) *stepping beside going up to.* II. *standing beside* or *at the side.*

παρασταίην, **παραστάς**, ᾶσα, άν, aor. 2 opt. and part. of παρίστημι.

παραστάς, άδος, ἡ, (παρίσταμαι) properly, *anything that stands beside, a door-post, pillar:* plur. παραστάδες, αἱ, *pillars that stand in line, a colonnade, the portico* of a house or temple, Lat. *vestibulum.* See the shortened form παστάς.

παράστᾰσις, εως, ἡ, (παρίστημι) *a putting aside, banishing.* II. (παρίσταμαι) *a being beside, a position* or *post near* a king.

παραστᾰτέω, f. ήσω, *to stand by* or *near.* From

παραστάτης, ου, ὁ, (παρίσταμαι) *one who stands by* or *near:* in line of battle, *one's comrade on the flank,* as προστάτης is one's front-rank-man, ἐπιστάτης one's rear-rank-man: generally *a comrade in battle.* Hence

παρα-στᾰτίς, ίδος, ἡ, *a helper, assistant, ally.*

παρα-στείχω, aor. 2 παρέστῐχον, *to go by, past* or *beyond, pass by: pass into.*

παρα-στῆναι, -στῆσαι, aor. 2 and 1 inf. of παρίστημι.

παρα-στορέννυμι, f. -στορέσω Att. -στορῶ :—*to stretch beside* or *along, lay flat.*

παρα-στρέφω, f. ψω, *to turn* or *twist aside.* 2. *to turn aside, prevent, divert.*

παρα-συγγρᾰφέω, f. ήσω, (παρά, συγγραφή) *to break contract with.*

παρα-συλλέγομαι, Pass. without Act. in use, *to assemble beside* or *with others.*

παρα-σύρω [ῡ], f. -σῠρῶ, *to drag* or *sweep away, hurry along,* as a flood. 2. παρασύρειν ἔπος *to drag, force* a word *in.*

παρα-σφάλλω, fut. -σφᾰλῶ: aor. 1 παρέσφηλα :—*to push* or *thrust off sideways* : *make to glance* or *slide off:* of an arrow, *to make miss* or *swerve aside.*

παράσχε, -έτω, aor. 2 imperat. of παρέχω.

παρασχεθεῖν, poët. aor. 2 inf. of παρέχω.

παρασχεῖν Ep. παρασχέμεν, aor. 2 inf. of παρέχω.

παρα-σχίζω, f. -σχίσω, *to rip up lengthwise.*

παρασχόν, aor 2 part. neut. of παρέχω, used absol., see παρέχω IV.

παράταξις, ἡ, *an arranging* soldiers *in order of battle: an army in array;* ἐκ παρατάξεως *in battle-array.* From

παρα-τάσσω Att. -ττω : f. ξω : aor. 1 παρέταξα : Pass., pf. παρατέταγμαι : Ion. 3 pl. plqpf. pass. παρατετάχατο :—*to post beside others,* esp. in order of battle :—Med. *to draw up one's* men *in order of battle* :—Pass. *to be set* or *posted beside in array* : *to be drawn up in order of battle.* II. Med. *to meet one another in battle* : absol. *to stand side by side in battle.*

παρα-τείνω, fut. -τενῶ : aor. 1 παρέτεινα : pf. παρατέτᾰκα : Pass., aor. 1 παρετάθην : pf. παρατέταμαι :—*to stretch out along, beside* or *near* : *to stretch out in a line;* παρατείνειν τάφρον *to draw* a *long* trench. 2. of time, *to protract, prolong, wear out by delay.* 3. *to stretch on the rack, torture* :—Pass. of a corpse, *to be laid along, lie dead;* πολιορκίᾳ παρατείνεσθαι *to hold out to the last* in a siege. II. intr. *to stretch out, extend along, run along.*

παρα-τείχισμα, ατος, τό, (παρά, τειχίζω) *a wall* or *fort built beside* : *a side* or *cross wall.*

παρα-τεκταίνομαι, aor. 1 παρετεκτηνάμην : Med. : —*to work into another form* : generally, *to fashion anew, transform, alter.* 2. *to alter from the truth, falsify.*

παρα-τέμνω, f. -τεμῶ poët. -τᾰμῶ :—*to cut off at the side, cut off.*

παρατετάχατο, Ion. 3 pl. plqpf. pass. of παρατάσσω.

παρα-τηρέω, f. ήσω, *to watch closely* or *narrowly* : *to observe superstitiously.* Hence

παρατήρησις, ἡ, *an observing closely, observation.*

παρα-τίθημι, with 3 sing. pres. παρατιθεῖ, and 2 and 3 sing. impf. παρετίθεις, -ει (as if from παρατιθέω) : fut. -θήσω : aor. 1 παρέθηκα : Med., aor. 2 παρεθέμην : Pass., pf. παρατέθειμαι :—*to place beside* or *before, set before* : generally, *to provide, furnish, supply.* 2. *to lay before* one, *represent, declare* : *to allege.* 3. *to place side by side, compare.* II. Med. *to set before oneself, have set before one* : esp. *to take to oneself.* 2. *to deposit* in a person's hands, *to commit to his charge.* 3. *to venture, stake, hazard.*

παρα-τίλλω, f. -τῐλῶ, *to pluck the hair off* :—Med. *to pluck hairs from one's own person* :—Pass., pf. part. παρατετιλμένος *with one's hair plucked out.*

παράτονος, ον, (παρατείνω) *stretched out beside* or *along, hanging down by the side.*

παρατρᾰγεῖν, aor. 2 inf. of παρατρώγω.

παρα-τρέπω, f. -τρέψω, *to turn aside, to turn from the right way, mislead;* ποταμὸν παρατρέπειν *to divert* a river *from* its channel, Lat. *derivare* : metaph. *to pervert, falsify* : generally, *to alter.* 2. *to turn* one *from* his *opinion, to mislead* :—Pass. *to let oneself be diverted from* a thing.

παρα-τρέφω, f. -θρέψω, *to rear beside* or *with* :—Pass. *to live with* or *at the expense of* another.

παρα-τρέχω, f. -θρέξομαι or -δρᾰμοῦμαι : aor. 2 παρέδρᾰμον :—*to run, rush by* or *past* : c. acc. *to escape.* 2. *to outrun, overtake, run down.* 3. *to run through* or *over.* II. *to run up to, run quickly to.*

παρα-τρέω, f. τρέσω, *to start, swerve aside from fear.*

παρα-τρίβω, f. ψω, *to rub beside;* παρατρίβειν χρυσὸν ἀκήρατον ἄλλῳ χρυσῷ (sc. εἰς βάσανον) *to rub* pure gold *by the side of* other gold on the lapis Lydius and see the difference of the marks they leave; Pass. *to be rubbed beside* baser *metal* and so *tested.* [ῑ]

παρα-τροπέω, = παρατρέπω, *to turn aside, turn from the right way, mislead.*

παρατροπή, ἡ, (παρατρέπω) *a turning off* or *away, averting, means of averting.*

παράτροπος, ον, (παρατρέπω) *turned aside, turned from the right way* II. act. *turning away* or *averting* a thing.

παρα-τροχάζω, poët. for παρατρέχω.

παρα-τρώγω, fut. -τρώξομαι : aor. 2 παρέτρᾰγον : —*to gnaw at the side, nibble at, take a bite of,* c. gen.

παρα-τρωπάω, poët. for παρατρέπω, *to turn away, divert.*

παρα-τυγχάνω, f. -τεύξομαι : aor. 2 παρέτῠχον :—*to happen to be by* or *at hand, come to* : *to be present at,* Lat. *interesse* : of a thing, *to offer* or *present itself,* Lat. *praesto esse.* 2. ὁ παρατυχών *whoever chanced to be by, any chance person;* τὸ παρατύγχανον or τὸ παρατυχόν, *whatever happens.* 3. παρατυχόν, absol. like παρόν, παρασχόν, *it being in one's power.*

παρά-τῡπος, ον, (παρά, τύπτω) *marked with a false stamp, base, counterfeit.*

παρατῠχών, οῦσα, όν, aor. 2 part. of παρατυγχάνω.

παρ-αυδάω, f. ήσω, *to speak to, address.* 2. *to make light of in speaking.* 3. *to try to persuade* one *of* a thing, *talk over* to a thing.

παρ-αυλίζω, or in Med. **παραυλίζομαι**, *to dwell or lie near.*

πάρ-αυλος, ον, (παρά, αὐλή) *dwelling* or *lodging beside; generally, neighbouring, near.*

πάρ-αυλος, ον, (παρά, αὐλός) *out of tune.*

πάρ-αυτᾰ, Adv. for παρ' αὐτά (sc. τὰ πράγματα), like παραχρῆμα, *immediately, on the spot.* II. *in like manner*, Lat. *perinde.*

παρ-αυτίκᾰ, Adv. (παρά, αὐτίκα) *immediately, on the instant:* with the Art., αἱ παραυτίκα ἡδοναί *present, momentary* pleasures.

παρ-αυχένιος, ον, also α, ον, (παρά, αὐχήν) *beside* or *on the neck.*

παραφᾰγεῖν, aor. 2 inf. of παρεσθίω.

παρα-φαίνω poët. **παρφ-**: f. -φᾰνῶ: *to shew* or *make appear beside: to produce, present;* παραφαίνειν τοῦ σώματος *to give a glimpse of* the body. 2. *to shew a light at the side, to light* one *to* a place. II. Pass. *to shew oneself* or *appear beside.*

παράφᾰσις poët. **παραίφασις** and **πάρφασις**, η, (παράφημι) *a speaking to, an address, consolation, assuagement.* 2. *allurement, persuasion*

παρα-φέρω, f. παρ-οίσω:—*to bear, bring* or *carry along to: to hand to, serve up:* Pass. *to be set on table.* 2. generally, *to bring forward, produce: to allege, mention;* παραφέρειν νόμον *to propose* a law. 3. *to turn aside* or *away: to avert.* 4. *to carry away:* Pass. *to be carried away.* II. *to carry past* or *beyond:*—Pass. *to be carried past* or *round:* metaph. *to go past* or *beside the truth, to err.* III. intrans. in Act., like Pass. *to go past, pass,* of Time. 2. *to be beyond, be over and above.*

παρα-φεύγω, f. -φεύξομαι and ουμαι, *to flee close by, past, beyond.*

παρά-φημι, f. -φήσω, *to speak to:* also *to talk over, exhort, persuade.* II. *to speak deceitfully*

παραφθαίην, aor. 2 opt. of παραφθάνω.

παραφθάμενος, aor. 2 med. part. of παραφθάνω.

παρα-φθάνω [ᾰ], f. -φθάσω [ᾰ] and -φθήσομαι: aor. 2 παρέφθην part. παραφθάς:—*to anticipate, overtake, be beforehand with, surpass.*

παρα-φθέγγομαι, f. -φθέγξομαι, *to say beside* or *by the way.*

παρα-φθῇσι, Ep. for παραφθῇ, aor. 2 subj. of παραφθάνω.

παραφορά, ἡ, (παραφέρομαι) *a being carried aside, distraction, madness.*

παραφορέω, = παραφέρω, *to bring forward, produce, present.*

παράφορος, ον, (παραφέρω) *carried aside* or *out of the way; reeling, staggering.*

παράφραγμα, ατος, τό, (παραφράσσω) *a fence, breastwork: a low screen:* in a ship, *the bulwarks.*

παρα-φράσσω Att. -ττω, f. ξω, *to run a fence beside* or *round* a place: *to enclose with a fence.*

παρα-φρονέω, f. ήσω, *to be beside oneself, to be distraught.* Hence

παραφρόνησις, εως, ἡ, **παραφρονία**, ἡ, and **παραφροσύνη**, ἡ, (παράφρων) *derangement of mind.*

παρα-φρόνιμος, ον, = παράφρων.

παρα-φρυκτωρεύομαι, Dep. (παρά, φρυκτωρός) *to make signals to the enemy underhand.*

παρά-φρων, ον, gen. ονος, ὁ, ἡ, (παρά, φρήν) *beside one's right mind, out of one's wits.* 2. *false, foolish.*

παρα-φῠλάσσω Att. -ττω, f. ξω, *to watch* or *keep guard beside, to watch narrowly.*

παρα-φῡσάω, f. ήσω, *to puff up.*

παρα-φύω, f. -φύσω [ῡ], *to make grow beside.* II. Med., with act. pf. πέφῡκα, aor. 2 παρέφῡν, intr. *to grow beside* or *at the side.*

παρα-χᾰλάω, f. άσω [ᾰ], *to slacken:* of a ship, *to let in water, to leak.*

παρα-χειμάζω, f. άσω, *to winter at* a place. Hence

παρα-χειμᾰσία, ἡ, *a wintering in a place.*

παρα-χέω, f. -χεῶ: aor. 1 παρέχεα: pf. -κέχῠκα: —*to pour in beside, pour in: to heap up beside.*

παρα-χορδίζω, f. σω, (παρά, χορδή) *to strike beside the right string, to strike a wrong note.*

παρα-χράομαι, f. ήσομαι, Dep. *to use amiss, abuse, misuse: to act wrongly* or *ill: to disregard, neglect, slight:* absol. in Ion. part. παραχρεώμενοι, *regardless of their lives, fighting desperately.*

παρα-χρῆμα, Adv. for παρὰ τὸ χρῆμα, *on the spot, forthwith, straightway;* ἡ παραχρῆμα ἀνάγκη the *immediate* necessity; ἐκ τοῦ παραχρῆμα *off-hand, on the spur of the moment.*

παρά-χροος, ον contr. -χρους, ουν, (παρά, χρόα) *changing its colour, colourless, faded.*

παρα-χώννῡμι, f. -χώσω, *to throw up a mound near* or *beside.*

παρα-χωρέω, f. ήσω, *to go aside so as to make room, to give place: to retire* or *withdraw from* a place. Hence

παραχωρητέον, verb. Adj. *one must give way.*

παραψῡχή, ἡ, *a cooling, refreshment, comfort.* From

παρα-ψύχω, *to cool, refresh, comfort.* [ῡ]

παρ-βάτης, ου, ὁ, poët. for παραβάτης. [βᾰ]

παρβεβᾰώς, poët. for παραβεβαώς, pf. part. of παραβαίνω.

ΠΑ'ΡΔΑΚΟΣ [ᾰ], ον, *wet, damp.*

παρδᾰλέη Att. contr. **παρδαλῆ** (sub. δορά), ἡ, *a leopard-skin.* From

πάρδᾰλις, εως Ion. ιος, η, = πάρδος, Lat. *pardalis a pard, leopard* or *panther.*

παρδᾰλωτός, ή, όν, (πάρδαλις) *spotted like the pard.*

παρδεῖν, **παρδήσομαι**, aor. 2 inf. and fut. of πέρδω.

ΠΑ'ΡΔΟΣ, ὁ, like πάρδαλις, πάνθηρ, *a pard, leopard* or *panther.*

πάρδω, aor. 2 subj. of πέρδω.

παρέᾱσι, Ep. for παρεῖσι, 3 pl. of πάρειμι (εἰμί *sum*).

παρεβάθην [ᾰ], aor. 1 pass. of παραβαίνω.

παρέβᾰλον, aor. 2 of παραβάλλω.

παρέβην, aor. 2 of παραβαίνω.

παρ-εγγράφω [ᾰ], f. ψω, *to add at the side, interpo-*

late: to enroll illegally among the citizens; παρεγγρᾰφείς, aor. 2 pass. part. *illegally registered.*

παρ-εγγυάω, f. ήσω, *to hand on to one's neighbour;* παρεγγυᾶν τὸ ξύνθημα *to pass on* the watchword or word of command. 2. *to command suddenly, to exhort, encourage.* 3. *to pledge one's word to another.* II. *to hand over, commit* or *commend to another.* Hence

παρ-εγγυή, ἡ, and παρ-εγγύησις, ἡ, *a passing on* the watchword or word of command.

παρεδόθην, aor. 1 pass. of παραδίδωμι.

παρέδρᾰθεν, 3 sing. aor. 2 of παραδαρθάνω.

παρέδρᾰμον, aor. 2 of παρατρέχω.

παρεδρεύω, f. σω, (πάρεδρος) *to sit constantly beside, to be ever with* or *by,* Lat. *assidēre.* II. *to be an assessor* (πάρεδρος) to one.

παρ-εδρία, ἡ, (πάρεδρος) *a sitting beside.* II. *the office* or *dignity of assessor.*

πάρ-εδρος, ον, (παρά, ἕδρα) *sitting beside:* generally, *beside, next to, near* II. as Subst. πάρεδρος, ὁ, *an assessor, assistant:*—in Prose, *the assessor* or *coadjutor* of a magistrate.

παρέδωκα, παρέδων, aor. 1 and 2 of παραδίδωμι.

παρ-έζομαι, f. -εδοῦμαι, Dep. *to sit beside:* but παρέζεο, παρεζόμενος are aor. 2 med. imperat. and part. of παρίζω.

παρεθῆναι, aor. 1 pass. inf. of παρίημι

παρέθηκα, aor. 1 of παρατίθημι.

πᾰρειά, ἡ, (παρά) *the cheek,* used by Homer always in plur.; in sing. he uses Ion. form παρήιον. II. *the cheek-piece* of a helmet.

πᾰρείας, ου, ὁ, = παρώας.

παρ-εῖδον, aor. 2 with no pres. in use, παρ-οράω being used instead, (παρά, εἶδον) *to observe by the way, to remark, notice.* II. *to overlook, disregard.*

παρείθην, aor. 1 pass. of παρίημι.

παρ-είκω, f. ξω: poët. aor. 2 παρεικᾰθον, inf. -αθεῖν: —*to yield on one side, give way: to permit, allow.* II. impers., παρείκει μοι *it is in my power, allowable;* ὅπῃ παρείκοι wherever *it was practicable;* κατὰ τὸ ἀεὶ παρεῖκον as it was *practicable* from time to time.

παρ-ειλίσσω, poët. for παρελίσσω.

παρεῖμαι, pf. pass. of παρίημι.

πάρ-ειμι inf. παρεῖναι: impf. παρῆν: f. παρέσομαι: (παρά, εἰμί *sum*):—*to be by, to be present.* 2. *to be by* or *near* one, c. dat.: also *to be present in* or *at.* 3. *to be present to help, to stand by,* like Lat. *adesse.* 4. *to have arrived at* a place. 5. impers., πάρεστί μοι *it is in* my *power:* absol. *it is possible, it may be done, it is allowed:* part. παρόν Ion. παρεόν, *it being possible, since it is allowed,* Lat. *quum fieri possit.* 6. τὰ παρόντα *present circumstances, the present state* or *condition;* also τὸ παρόν.

πάρ-ειμι inf. παριέναι: impf. παρῄειν: (παρά, εἶμι *ibo*):—*to go by, beside* or *near, to pass: to go alongside.* 2. *to pass by, overtake, surpass.* 3. of Time, *to pass on, pass.* II. *to pass on towards, to go to* or *near, enter:* absol. *to approach.* III. generally, *to come, put oneself forward, present oneself.*

παρεῖναι, inf. of πάρειμι (εἰμί *sum*).

παρ-εῖπον, (παρά, εἶπον) aor. 2 with no pres. in use, παρά-φημι being used instead: c. acc. pers. *to talk over, persuade:* hence *to overreach.* [In Hom., part. πᾱρειπών, πᾱρειποῦσα, metri grat.]

παρ-ειρύω, Ion. for παρερύω.

παρ-είρω, (παρά, εἴρω) *to fasten* or *attach beside, insert;* νόμους παρείρων seems to mean *adding observance* of the laws.

πάρεις, 2 sing. of πάρειμι (εἰμί *sum*).

πᾰρείς, εἶσα, έν, aor. 2 part. of παρίημι.

παρ-εισάγω, f. ξω, *to bring in beside: to bring forward, introduce, exhibit.* II. *to introduce secretly.* Hence

παρείσακτος, ον, *brought in beside, introduced secretly.*

παρ-εισδέχομαι, f. ξομαι, Dep. *to take in besides* or *along with.*

παρ-εισδύομαι, Pass. and Med., with act. aor. 2 -έδυν pf. -δέδῡκα, and plqpf. -δεδύκειν, intr.:—*to get in by the side, to slip* or *creep in.*

παρ-εισέρχομαι, Dep. with act. aor. 2 -ῆλθον, pf. -ελήλυθα:—*to come in secretly* or *wrongfully.*

παρ-εισφέρω, *to bring in beside;* παρεισφέρειν νόμον *to introduce* a law *inconsistent with* another. II. *to add* or *apply besides.*

παρεῖται, 3 sing. pf. pass. of παρίημι.

πᾰρ-έκ, before a vowel πᾰρ-έξ, (παρά, ἐκ) as Prep., 1. c. gen. *outside, before:*—*besides, except, exclusive of.* 2. c. acc. *out along, beyond, alongside of;* παρὲκ νόον *out of* reason, foolishly; also, παρὲξ Ἀχιλῆα *without the knowledge of* Achilles. II. as Adv. of Place, *out beside, out and away.* 2. metaph. *beside the mark, senselessly, foolishly.* 3. *beside, except,* παρὲκ ἢ ὅσον.., *except* so long as ..

παρ-εκβαίνω, f. -εκβήσομαι, *to step out past* or *beyond, to deviate from: to overstep, transgress* a rule: absol. *to deviate, to make a digression.* Hence

παρέκβᾰσις, ἡ, *a stepping out beyond, deviation:* also *a digression.*

παρ-εκδύομαι, Pass. *to slip out by the side, steal away*

παρεκέσκετο, 3 sing. Ion. impf. of παράκειμαι.

παρ-εκκλίνω, *to turn a little aside: to deviate.*

παρ-εκλέγω, f. ξω, *to collect covertly, to embezzle.*

παρ-εκπροφεύγω, *to flee out away from before, to elude;* προεκπροφῠ́γῃσι, Ep. for -φύγῃ, 3 sing. aor. 2 subj.

παρ-εκτᾰνύω, f. υσω, = παρεκτείνω.

παρ-εκτείνω, f. τενῶ, *to stretch out along, to deploy.*

παρ-εκτελέω, f. έσω, *to accomplish against a wish.*

παρ-εκτέον, verb. Adj. of παρέχω, *one must furnish.*

παρ-εκτός, Adv. (παρά, ἐκτός) *out of, without, besides.*

παρ-εκτρέπω, f. ψω, *to turn aside, divert from the way.*

παρ-εκτρέχω, *to run out past.*

παρέλᾰβον, aor. 2 of παραλαμβάνω.

παρ-ελαύνω: f. -ελάσω [ᾰ], Ep. -ελάσσω Att. -ελῶ: aor. 1 παρήλᾰσα Ep. παρέλασσα:—*to drive by* or *past.* II. as if intr. (sub. δίφρον, ἵππους, etc.) *to drive past;* then with a new acc. *to drive past* a person, *overtake* him; also, παρελαύνειν ἐφ' ἅρματος, ἐφ' ἵππου *to drive* on a chariot, or *ride* on horseback. 2. *to row* or *sail by, past* (sub. ναῦν): then with an acc. loci, *to sail by, past* a person or place. 3. later also *to ride by, run by:—to ride to, advance towards:—to ride on one's way.*

παρέλεκτο, 3 sing. Ep. aor. 2 pass. of παραλέγω.

παρελεῦντα, Dor. for παρελῶντα, fut. part. acc. of παρελαύνω.

παρελεύσομαι, rare fut. of παρέρχομαι; πάρειμι (εἶμι *ibo*) being so used in Att.

παρ-έλκω: f. παρέλξω or παρελκύσω [ῠ]: aor. 1 παρείλκῠσα: pf. pass. παρείλκυσμαι: (παρά, ἕλκω): —*to draw aside* or *to the side:*—Med. *to draw aside for oneself, intercept.* 2. *to lead alongside,* of led horses; of boats, παρέλκειν ἐκ γῆς *to tow* from the bank. 3. *to distort, twist.* II. *to spin out, prolong, put off:* intr. *to delay.*

παρ-εμβάλλω, f. -εμβᾰλῶ, *to put in beside* or *between, interpolate:* hence *to throw in by the way, insinuate.* II. *to draw up* troops *in battle order, to encamp.*

παρ-εμβλέπω, f. ψω, *to look askance.*

παρεμβολή, ἡ, (παρεμβαλεῖν) *a putting in beside, insertion, interpolation.* II. *a drawing up in battle-order: an army so drawn up, a regular camp:* hence *any fortified place, a castle, camp.*

παρ-εμβύω, f. ύσω [ῡ], *to push* or *stuff in.*

παρέμμεναι, Ep. inf. of πάρειμι (εἰμί *sum*).

παρ-εμπίπλημι, f. -εμπλήσω, *to fill secretly full of.*

παρ-εμπίπτω, f. -εμπεσοῦμαι, *to fall in by the way, creep in.*

παρ-εμπολάω, f. ησω, *to traffic underhand in* a thing, *to smuggle in, bring about fraudulently.*

παρεμπόρευμα, ατος, τό, *an article of small value.* From

παρ-εμπορεύομαι, Dep. (παρά, ἔμπορος) *to traffic in besides.* II. metaph. *to yield* or *afford besides.*

παρ-εμφύομαι, Pass. *to grow in beside, hang upon.*

παρενεγκεῖν, aor. 2 inf. of παραφέρω.

παρ-ενεῖδον, inf. -ιδεῖν, aor. 2 with no pres. in use, *to take a side look at.*

παρενήνεον, impf. of παρανηνέω (see παρανέω).

παρενθεῖν, παρένθω, Dor. for παρελθεῖν, παρέλθω, aor. 2 inf. and subj. of παρέρχομαι.

παρενθήκη, ἡ, (παρεντίθημι) *something put in beside, an appendix;* παρενθήκη λόγου *a digression.*

παρ-ενοχλέω, f. ήσω, *to trouble* or *annoy* one *while about something:* Pass., pf. παρηνώχλημαι, *to be troubled besides.*

παρ-ενσᾰλεύω, f. σω, intr. *to swing to and fro.*

πᾰρ-έξ or **πάρ-εξ**, v. παρέκ.

παρ-εξάγω, f. ξω, *to lead out beside* or *past:* hence *to mislead.*

παρ-εξαυλέω, f. ήσω, *to wear out with playing upon:* pf. pass. part. παρεξηυλημένος *worn out by being played upon,* generally, *worn out, exhausted.*

παρεξέβην, aor. 2 of παρεκβαίνω,

παρ-έξειμι, inf. παρεξιέναι, (παρά, ἔξειμι) *to go out beside, pass by* or *alongside.* 2. *to overstep, transgress.*

παρ-εξ-ειρεσία, ἡ, (παρά, ἐκ, εἰρεσία) *the part of the ship out beyond the rowers, either end of the ship, the bows* or *the stern.*

παρ-εξελαύνω, f. -εξελάσω Att. -εξελῶ:—seemingly intr. (sub. ἵππον, etc.), *to drive out past, to drive past:* (sub. ναῦν) *to row past:* (sub. στρατόν) *to march by.*

παρεξελθών, οῦσα, όν, aor. 2 part. of παρεξέρχομαι.

παρεξέμεν, Ep. aor. 2 inf. of παρεξίημι.

παρ-εξέρχομαι, f. -εξελεύσομαι: Dep. with act. aor. 2 παρεξῆλθον pf. παρεξελήλυθα:—*to go out beside, to slip past, elude: to pass out over,* c. gen.; but also c. acc. *to pass by* one. II. *to overstep, transgress.*

παρ-εξετάζω, f. άσω, *to search out by comparison.*

παρ-εξευρίσκω, f. -εξευρήσω, *to find out besides.*

παρ-εξίημι, f. -εξήσω, *to let out beside:*—of Time, *to let pass.*

παρεξίμεν [ῐ], Ep. inf. of παρέξειμι (εἶμι *ibo*).

παρ-εξίστημι, f. -εκστήσω, *to remove aside, change:* —Pass., with intr. tenses of Act., *to undergo a change.*

παρεοῖσα, Dor. fem. part. of πάρειμι (εἰμί *sum*).

παρέπεισα, aor. 1 of παραπείθω.

παρ-επάλλομαι, Ion. for παρεφάλλομαι.

παρ-επιδείκνυμι, f. -επιδείξω, *to point out beside.* II. Med. *to exhibit out of season, make a display.*

παρ-επίδημος, ον, *sojourning at a strange place:* as Subst. *a stranger, sojourner.*

παρ-επισκοπέω, f. -επισκέψομαι, *to inspect beside.*

παρεπιστροφή, ἡ, (παρεπιστρέφω) *a turning round in passing.*

παρεπλάγχθην, aor. 1 pass. of παραπλάζω.

παρέπλω, 3 sing. Ep. aor. 2 of παραπλέω, as if a Verb in -μι.

παρ-έπομαι, f. ψομαι, Dep. *to follow by the side, follow close: to follow as an escort.*

παρεργάτης, ου, ὁ, (πάρεργον) *a doer of trifles, a trifler.* [ᾰ]

πάρ-εργος, ον, (παρά, ἔργον) *beside the main subject, subordinate, incidentally.* II. as Subst., πάρεργον, τό, *a by-work, subordinate business;* ἐν παρέργῳ *as a by-work, as subordinate* or *secondary,* Lat. *obiter;* ἐκ παρέργου ποιεῖσθαι to do *by the way:* hence 2. *a useless addition, appendage.*

παρέργως, Adv. of πάρεργος, *incidentally.*

παρέρπω, f. παρερπύσω [ῠ]: aor. 1 παρείρπῠσα:—*to creep in at the side: to creep up to.* II. *to pass by.*

παρ-ερύω Ion. **παρειρύω**, f. ύσω, (παρά, ἐρύω) *to draw along the side.* [ῠ]

παρ-έρχομαι: fut. -ελεύσομαι, but the Att. fut. is πάρειμι (εἶμι *ibo*): Dep., with aor. 2 -ῆλθον Ep. -ήλυθον pf. -ελήλυθα:—*to go by, beside* or *past,* *pass by, pass away.* 2. of Time, *to pass; ὁ παρελθὼν χρόνος* time *past; τὸ παρελθόν* and *ἐν τῷ παρελθόντι in time past, of old.* II. *to pass by, outstrip, surpass:* metaph. *to outwit, overreach, circumvent.* III. *to pass by without heeding, pass over, slight:* also of things, *to escape one's notice, be passed over* 2. also *to transgress.* IV. *pass on and to come to* a place, *arrive at:* esp. *to pass into* a house. V. *to come forward,* esp. to speak in public.

πάρεσαν, Ep. 3 pl. impf. of πάρειμι (εἰμί *sum*).

παρ-εσθίω, f. -έδομαι: aor. 2 -έφἄγον, inf. -φἄγεῖν: —*to eat besides.* II. *to eat a piece of, gnaw* or *nibble at,* c. gen.

πάρεσις, ἡ, (παρίημι) *a letting pass, a letting go:* also *remission, forgiveness.*

παρεσκευάδᾶται, παρεσκευάδᾶτο, Ion. 3 pl. pf. and plqpf. pass. of παρασκευάζω.

παρεστάμεν, παρεστάμεναι, Ep. pf. inf. of παρίστημι.

παρέστηκα, pf. of παρίστημι: part. παρεστηκώς, contr. παρεστώς:—neut. παρεστηκός used absol., see παρίστημι, at end.

παρεστήν, aor. 2 of παρίστημι.

παρ-έστιος, ον, (παρά, ἑστία) *by* or *at the hearth.*

παρέσχον, aor. 2 of παρέχω.

παρετήρουν, impf of παρατηρέω.

πάρετος, ον, verb. Adj. of παρίημι, *relaxed, palsied.*

παρέτρεσσαν, Ep. 3 pl. aor. 1 of παρατρέω.

παρ-ευδοκιμέω, f. ήσω, *to surpass in reputation.*

παρ-ευθύνω, *to guide* one *from the right way, to constrain.* [ῡ]

παρ-ευκηλέω, f. ήσω, (παρά, εὔκηλος) *to calm, soothe.*

παρ-ευνάζομαι, fut. -άσομαι, Med. *to lie* or *sleep beside.*

πάρ-ευνος, ον, (παρα, ευνη) *lying beside* or *with.*

παρ-ευρίσκω, f. -ευρήσω: aor. 2 -εῦρον:—*to find out* or *discover besides: to invent.*

παρ-ευτρεπίζω, f. ίσω, *to put in order, arrange.* 2. *to arrange amiss, neglect.*

παρέχον, part. neut. of παρέχω used absol., see παρέχω IV.

παρέχοντι, Dor. for παρέχουσι, 3 pl. of παρέχω. II. pres. part. dat. of παρέχω.

παρ-έχω: f. παρέξω or παρασχήσω: pf. παρέσχηκα: aor. 2 παρέσχον poët. παρέσχεθον:—*to hold beside, hold in readiness: to furnish, supply.* II. of things, *to afford, grant, cause, render.* III. *to offer* or *present* for a purpose: also *to make oneself over to* another, *put oneself at* his *disposal:* also *to make* or *render* so and so: *to put forward, represent, produce,* esp. as parties to an agreement. IV. *to allow, grant.* V. impers., παρέχει τινί *it is allowed* one, *is in* one's *power to do* so and so, Lat. *licet:* hence neut. part. pres. and aor. 2 παρέχον and παρασχόν (used absol. like παρόν, ἐξόν, etc.), *it being or having been in one's power,* Lat. *quum liceat* or *liceret.* VI. absol. in imperat., πάρεχ' ἐκποδών *get yourself* out of the way.

B. Med. παρέχομαι, f. παρέξομαι or παρασχήσομαι: pf. παρέσχημαι:—*to offer* or *supply of oneself* or *from one's own means: to produce* or *display on one's own part; παρέχεσθαί τινα μάρτυρα to bring forward* as a witness. II. generally, *to have as one's own, produce as one's own; παρέχεσθαί τινα ἄρχοντα to acknowledge* as *one's* general; of an ambassador, παρέχεσθαι πόλιν μεγίστην *to represent* the greatest city. III. *to make* or *render* so and so. IV. of Numbers, *to make up, amount to, give the sum of.*

παρ-ηβάω, f. ήσω, *to be past one's prime, to be verging towards old age.*

πάρ-ηβος, ον, (παρά, ἥβη) *past one's prime.*

παρήγγειλα, aor. 1 of παραγγέλλω.

παρῆγον, impf. of παράγω.

παρηγορέω, impf. παρηγόρουν, rarely ἐπαρηγόρουν: f. ήσω: aor. 1 παρηγόρησα: (παρήγορος):—*to address, exhort, encourage: to advise, exhort.* II. *to console, comfort, soothe.*—The Med. παρηγορέομαι is also used like the Act. Hence

παρηγορία, ἡ, *an addressing, exhortation, persuasion.* 2. *a consolation.*

παρ-ήγορος, ον, (παρά, ἀγορεύω) *addressing, encouraging, cheering.* 2. *consoling.*

παρηέρθην, aor. 1 pass. of παραείρω.

πᾰρήιον, τό, used in Homer as sing. for παρειά (which he only uses in plur.), *the cheek: the jaw* of a wild beast. II. *the cheek-ornament* of a bridle.

πᾰρηΐς, -ηΐδος, contr. Att. **παρῇς**, -ῇδος, ἡ, = παρήιον, *the cheek.*

παρῆκα, aor. 1 of παρίημι.

παρ-ήκω, f. ξω, *to have come alongside: to lie beside, stretch along.* 2. *to reach* or *extend to* or *towards.* II. *to come forth, appear.* III. of Time, *to be gone by, past.*

παρήλᾶσα, aor. 1 of παρελαύνω.

παρῆλθον, aor. 2 of παρέρχομαι.

παρ-ῆλιξ, ῐκος, ὁ, ἡ, like πάρηβος, *past one's prime.*

πάρ-ημαι, inf. -ῆσθαι: properly the pf. pass. of παρίζω, *to be seated by, beside,* or *at,* c. dat.: *to sit by* one: *to dwell with* one: *to be present at* or *near.*

παρ-ήμερος Dor. **παράμερος**, ον, (παρά, ἡμέρα) *coming day by day, daily.*

παρῄνουν, impf. of παραινέω.

παρῆξαι, aor. 1 of παραΐσσω.

πάρηξις, ἡ, (παρήκω) *arrival alongside, coming to shore.*

παρ-ηονίτης, ου, ὁ, fem. -ῖτις, ιδος, ἡ, (παρά, ἠών) *lying on the shore.* [ῑ]

παρηορία, ἡ, (παρήορος) *the reins by which the outside horse* or *outrigger was fastened beside* a pair of horses in the yoke.

παρ-ήορος Dor. **παρ-άορος**, ον, (παρά, ἀείρω) *hanging beside: παρήορος* (sub. ἵππος) *a horse which draws by the side of the regular pair* (ξυνωρίς) *an outrigger,* also called παράσειρος or σειραφόρος, opp. to ζυγίτης or ζύγιος. II. *lying along, sprawling, helpless:* —also *beside oneself, distraught, silly.*

παρήπαφε, 3 sing. aor. 2 of παραπαφίσκω.

παρῇς, -ῇδος, ἡ, Att. contr. for παρηίς, -ηίδος.

παρῆσθα, Ep. 2 sing. impf. of πάρειμι (εἰμί *sum*).

παρῄσθευ, Dor. 2 sing. aor. 2 of παραισθάνομαι.

παρῄτημαι, pf. pass. of παραιτέω.

παρθέμενος, poët. aor. 2 med. part. of παρατίθημι.

παρθενεία and -ία, ἡ, (παρθενεύω) *maidenhood, virgin estate* or *condition.*

παρθένεια, τά, = παρθένια, τά.

παρθένειος Ion. -ήιος, ον, (παρθένος) *maidenly, maiden, virgin.*

παρθένευμα, ατος, τό, (παρθενεύω) *virgin estate* or *condition:* in plur. *the pursuits of a virgin.*

παρθενεύω, f. σω, (παρθένος) *to bring up a virgin:* —Pass. παρθενεύομαι, *to lead a maiden life, remain a maid.*

παρθενία, ἡ, = παρθενεία.

παρθένια (sub. μέλη), τά, *songs sung by maidens* to the flute with dancing:—properly neut. from παρθένιος.

παρθενικη (sub. κόρη), ἡ, poët. for παρθένος, *a virgin, maid:* strictly fem. from sq.

παρθενικός, ή, όν, (παρθένος) *of* or *for a maiden, maidenly.*

παρθένιος, α, ον, also ος, ον, (παρθένος) *of a maiden* or *virgin, maiden.* παρθένιος, ὁ, as Subst., *the son of an unmarried woman* II. metaph. *virgin, pure, chaste, unsullied.*

παρθεν-οπίπης [ῐ], ου, (παρθένος, ὀπιπτεύω) *one who looks after maidens, a seducer.*

ΠΑΡΘΕ'ΝΟΣ, ἡ, *a maid, maiden, virgin,* Lat. *virgo:*—sometimes masc., *an unmarried youth.* 2. Παρθένος, as a name of several goddesses, of Minerva at Athens; of Diana and the Tauric Iphigenia. II. as Adj. *maiden, virgin, pure, chaste.*

παρθενό-σφᾰγος, ον, (παρθένος, σφαγῆναι) *from the sacrifice of a maiden.*

παρθενό-χρως, ωτος, ὁ, ἡ, (παρθένος, χρώς) *of maidenly, delicate colour.*

παρθενών, ῶνος, ὁ, (παρθένος) *the young women's chamber,* in a house, mostly in plur. II. *the temple of Athena Parthenos* in the citadel at Athens, *the Parthenon,* rebuilt by Pericles.

παρθεν-ωπός, όν, (παρθένος, ὤψ) *of virgin aspect.*

πάρθεσαν, poët. for παρέθεσαν, 3 pl. aor. 2 of παρατίθημι.

παρθεσίη, ἡ, (παρατίθημι) *a deposit, pledge.*

παρ-ῑαύω, (παρά, ἰαύω) *to sleep beside* or *with.*

παρῐδεῖν, inf. of παρεῖδον.

παρ-ῑδρύω, f. σω, *to set up beside:*—so also in Med.

παρ-ίζω, *to place* or *make to sit beside.* . intrans. *to seat oneself beside, sit beside,* but this sense is more common in Med. παρίζομαι, aor. 2 παρεζόμην, inf. παρεζέσθαι.

παρ-ίημι, fut. παρήσω: aor. 1 παρῆκα: pf. παρεῖκα: Med., aor. 2 παρείμην: Pass., aor. 1 παρείθην, inf. παρεθῆναι: pf. παρεῖμαι, part. παρειμένος:—*to let drop beside* or *at the side, let fall.* II. *to let by, past, through.* 2. metaph. *to let pass, disregard, neglect,* Lat. *praetermittere.* 3. of Time, *to let pass.* III. *to unloose, relax,* Lat. *remittere.* 2. c. gen., τοῦ ποδὸς παριέναι *to let go one's hold of, slack away* the sheet: metaph. *to yield, give way:*—Med. and Pass. *to be relaxed, weakened,* hence pres. part. παριέμενος, aor. 2 παρέμενος, pf. παρειμένος, *exhausted,* Lat. *remissus.* 2. *to remit,* Lat. *condonare:* hence *to forgive, pardon.* IV. *to yield, give up,* Lat. *concedere:* *to allow, permit:* hence *to admit, let in.* V. Med. παρίεσθαι, *to win* a person *over:* *to beg off* a thing, *beg to be excused:* *to ask pardon.*

παρ-ίκω, old. poët. form of παρήκω. [ῑ]

παρ-ιππεύω, f. σω, *to ride alongside.* 2. *to ride along* or *over.*

πάρ-ῐσος, ον, (παρά, ἴσος) *almost equal, just like.*

παρ-ῐσόω, f. ώσω, *to make just like:*—Pass., aor. 1 παρισώθην, *to measure oneself with, vie with.*

παρίστᾰσο, pres. med. imperat. of

πάρ-ίστημι, f. παραστήσω: I. trans. in pres., impf., fut. and aor. 1, *make to stand beside, to place by, beside,* or *near, to present, offer* to one. 2. *to set before the mind, present, offer, suggest:*—*to prove, shew.* 3. the Med., esp. fut. -στήσομαι, and aor. 1 -εστησάμην, have peculiar usages, *to set by one's side, produce:*—*to bring to one's side, to bring over by force, overcome, subdue:* also *to win over, persuade:* hence also *to dispose for one's own views.* II. intrans. in Pass. -ίσταμαι, with act. aor. 2 -έστην, pf. -έστηκα, plqpf. -ειστήκειν, *to stand by, beside,* or *near:* hence *to stand by, to help* or *defend.* 2. of events, *to be near, be close at hand:* τὸ παριστάμενον *present circumstances:* so too, τὸ παρεστὼς or παρεστός, contr. pf. part. for παρεστηκός. 3. *to come to the side of* another: metaph. *to come over to* his *opinion:* absol. *to come to terms, surrender, submit.* 4. *to come into one's head, suggest itself to* one. 5. of events, *to take place, occur, happen:* so too in fut. med. -στήσομαι. 6. *to be in one's power,* hence absol., pf. part. παρεστηκός, = παρόν, ἐξόν, *it being in one's power to* do, Lat. *quum liceat.*

παρ-ιστίδιος, α, ον, (παρά, ἱστός) *by* or *at the loom.*

παρ-ίσχω, collat. form of παρέχω, *to have by, hold in readiness:* *to present, offer.*

παρ-ῑτητέον and -έα, verb. Adj. of πάρειμι (εἶμι *ibo*), *one must approach* or *go.*

παρκατέλεκτο, Ep. 3 sing. aor. 2 pass. of παρακαταλέγω, as if from παρακατελέγμην.

παρκείμενος, Ep. part. of παράκειμαι.

παρ-κλίνω, Ep. for παρακλίνω.

παρ-κύπτω, Ep. for παρακύπτω; Dor. part. fem. παρκύπτοισα, for παρακύπτουσα.

παρμέμβλωκε, Ep. 3 sing. pf. of παραβλώσκω.

παρ-μένω, Ep. for παραμένω.

παρ-μόνιμος, poët. for παραμόνιμος.

πάρ-μονος, ον, poët. for *παράμονος*.

Παρνάσιος [ᾰ], α, ον, Ion. **Παρνήσιος**, η, ον, also ος, ον, *of* or *from Parnassus:* Ion. fem. **Παρνησιάς**, άδος, and **Παρνησίς**, ίδος. From

Παρνᾶσός Ion. **Παρνησός**, ὁ, *Parnassus*, a mountain of Phocis: later Παρνασσός (with double σ).

Παρνήθιος, α, ον, *of* or *from Parnes.* From

Πάρνης, ηθος, ἡ or ὁ, *Parnes*, a mountain of Attica.

Παρνησός, ὁ, Ion. for Παρνᾶσός.

ΠΑ'ΡΝΟΨ, οπος, ὁ, a kind of *locust.*

παρ-οδεύω, f. σω, *to journey by.*

παροδίτης [ῑ], ου, ὁ, voc. -ῖτα: fem. **παροδῖτις**, ιδος: (πάροδος) :—*a passer by, traveller, wayfarer.*

πάρ-οδος, ἡ, (παρά, ὁδός) *a way past, passage.* 2. *a going by* or *past, passing; ἐν παρόδῳ in passing.* II. *a side-entrance, a narrow entrance* or *approach.* III. *a coming forward to speak* before the assembly. 2. *the first entrance* of a chorus into the orchestra, which was made *from the side.*

παρ-οίγνυμι and **παρ-οίγω**: f. -οίξω: aor. 1 -έῳξα: —*to open at the side* or *a little, set ajar:* c. gen., *παροίξας τῆς θύρας having opened a little of* the door.

πάροιθε and before a vowel **-θεν**, (πάρος) Prep. with gen. *before, in the presence of*, Lat. *ante, coram.* 2. of Time, *before.* II. Adv. of Place, *before, in front.* 2. of Time, *before this, erst, formerly, heretofore; πάροιθε πρίν*, Lat. *priusquam.*

παρ-οικέω, f. ήσω, *to dwell by, beside*, or *near.* II. *to sojourn.* Hence

παροικησία and **παροίκησις**, ἡ, *a dwelling beside* or *near, neighbourhood.*

παροικία, ἡ, (πάροικος) *a dwelling* in a place *as πάροικος, sojourning.*

παροικίζω, f. ίσω, (πάροικος) *to place* or *settle near* another:—Pass. *to settle* or *live near.*

παρ-οικοδομέω, f. ήσω, *to build beside* or *near, build a wall along* or *across.* II. *to keep off by a wall* or *bank.*

πάρ-οικος, ον, (παρά, οἰκέω) *dwelling beside* or *near, neighbouring.* II. as Subst., *πάροικος*, ὁ, *a neighbour:*—also *an alien, foreigner*, who dwells in the land, *a sojourner*, Lat. *inquilinus.*

παροιμία, ἡ, (πάροιμος) *a by-word, proverb, adage, saw.* 2. *a parable*, in St. John's Gospel; elsewhere in N. T. called *παραβολή.* Hence

παροιμιακός, ή, όν, *proverbial:*—as metrical term, *παροιμιακός* (sub. στίχος), ὁ, *a paroemiac*, an Anapaestic dimeter catalectic, mostly at the end of an Anapaestic system.

πάρ-οιμος, ον, (παρά, [illegible]) *by the way-side.*

παρ-οινέω: impf. ἐπαρῴνουν and aor. 1 ἐπαρῴνησα, with dupl. augm.: pf. πεπαρῴνηκα, with augm. and redupl.: so in Pass., aor. 1 ἐπαρῳνήθην: pf. πεπαρῴνημαι: (πάροινος) :—*to behave ill in one's cups, play drunken tricks.* II. trans. *to maltreat one in drunkenness:* generally, *to maltreat and abuse, like a drunken man.*

παροινία, ἡ, (πάροινος) *drunken violence: a drunken frolic.*

παροινικός, ή, όν, *disposed to drunkenness.* From

παρ-οίνιος, ον, and **πάρ-οινος**, ον, (παρά, οἶνος) *drunken with wine, quarrelsome over one's cups.*

πᾰροίτατος, η, ον, Sup. of *πάροιθε, πάρος*, of Place, *the foremost.*

πᾰροίτερος, α, ον, Comp. of *πάροιθε, πάρος, the one before* or *in front.*

παρ-οίχομαι, f. -οιχήσομαι: pf. παρῴχηκα Ion. παροίχωκα, and in late writers pass. παρῴχημαι: Dep.: *to have past by, pass on.* 2. of Time, *to be gone by, spent; ἡ παροιχομένη νύξ the bygone* night; ἄνδρες παροιχόμενοι men *of bygone times.* II. *to be gone, be dead*, like *οἴχομαι.* III. c. gen. *to shrink from.* 2. *to wander, depart from; ὅσον μοίρας παροίχῃ* how *art thou fallen from* thy high estate.

παροκωχή, ἡ, (παρέχω) Att. redupl. form of **παροχή**, *a furnishing.*

παρ-ολισθάνω, later **-αίνω**: fut. -ολισθήσω:—*to slip in secretly.*

παρ-ομοιάζω, f. άσω, *to be like, to resemble.*

παρ-όμοιος, ον, also α, ον, (παρά, ὅμοιος) *nearly like, much alike: nearly equal.*

παρόν, όντος, τό, pres. part. **neut.** of **πάρειμι** (εἰμί *sum*), used absol., see *πάρειμι* 5.

παροξυντικός, ή, όν, *fit for inciting, provoking.* From

παρ-οξύνω, f. ὑνῶ: aor. 1 παρώξῡνα:—*to make keen for* a thing: metaph. *to urge, prick*, or *spur on: to provoke, irritate, excite.* Hence

παροξυσμός, ὁ, *irritation: a provoking, inciting.*

παρόρᾱσις, ἡ, (παροράω) *an overlooking: carelessness.*

παρ-οράω, f. παρόψομαι: aor. 2 παρεῖδον (v. sub ὁράω) :—*to look at by the way, notice, remark.* II. *to look past, overlook:* to *slight, make light of.* III. *to look sideways.*

παρ-οργίζω, f. ίσω, *to provoke to anger:*—Pass. *to be* or *be made angry at.* Hence

παροργισμός, ὁ, *provocation to anger.*

παρ-ορίζω, f. ίσω, *to pass one's own boundaries, encroach on a neighbour.* Hence

παροριστής, οῦ, ὁ, *an encroacher.*

παρ-ορμάω, f. ήσω, *to put in motion, urge on:*—Pass., with fut. med. -ήσομαι, *to pass rapidly, rush at.*

παρ-ορμίζω, fut. ίσω Att. -ιῶ, *to bring to anchor side by side.*

πάρ-ορνις, ῑθος, ὁ, ἡ, *ill-omened, with evil auspices.*

παρ-ορύσσω Att. **-ττω**: f. ξω: aor. 1 παρώρυξα:—*to dig beside* or *along.* II. *to dig one against another*, as was done in training for the Olympic games.

παρ-ορχέομαι, f. -ήσομαι, Dep. *to dance amiss, dance the wrong dance*

ΠΑ'ΡΟΣ, Adv., I. of Time, *before, erst, formerly:* also with the Att., τὸ πάρος or τοπάρος, *formerly.* 2. with inf., like *πρίν*, Lat. *priusquam*, *πάρος ἦν γαῖαν ἱκέσθαι before* he should reach his own land. 3. παρός, followed by πρίν γε as relat., Lat. *prius .., quam, rather .., than.* 4. *too soon.* 5. *rather, sooner.* II. of Place, *before, in front.*

B. Prep., poët. for πρό, *before,* both of Time and Place. II. *before, rather than:* also *for, instead of.*

Πάριος, α, ον, *of the island of Paros, Parian;* Πάριος λίθος *Parian* marble. From

Πάρος, ἡ, *Paros,* one of the Cyclades, famous for its white marble.

παρ-οτρύνω, f. ὑνῶ, *to urge* or *excite to mischief.*

παρ-ουσία, ἡ, (παρών, παροῦσα) *a being present, presence;* ἀνδρῶν παρουσία = ἄνδρες οἱ παρόντες; παρουσίαν ἔχειν = παρεῖναι. 2. *arrival.* II. like τὰ παρόντα, *present circumstances.*

παρ-οχετεύω, f. σω, *to turn off into a side channel:* metaph. *to turn off* or *divert* an inquiry.

παρ-οχέω, f. ήσω, (παρά, ὀχέω) *to carry by* or *beside:*—Med. *to sit beside in a chariot.*

παροχή, ἡ, (παρέχω) *a supplying, furnishing.*

παρ-οχλίζω, f. ίσω, *to move aside with a lever, remove.*

πάρ-οχος, ὁ, (παρά, ὄχος) *one who rides beside in a chariot.*

παρ-οψίς, ίδος, ἡ, (παρά, ὄψον) *a dainty side-dish.*

παρόψομαι, fut. of παροράω, formed from obsol. παρόπτομαι.

παρ-οψωνέω, f. ήσω, *to buy a dainty dish to set before* one. Hence

παροψώνημα, ατος, τό, *an additional dainty set before one:* metaph., παροψώνημα τῆς χλιδῆς *a fresh relish* to the pleasure.

παρπεπιθών, redupl. aor. 2 part. of παραπείθω.

παρ-ρησία, ἡ, (πᾶς, ῥῆσις) *freedom of speech:* in bad sense, *licence of tongue.* Hence

παρ-ρησιάζομαι, f. -άσομαι, Dep. *to speak freely.*

παρσένος, Lacon. for παρθένος.

παρσταίην, παρστᾶσα, Ep. for παρασταίην, παραστᾶσα, aor. 2 opt. and part. fem. of παρίστημι.

παρστήετον, Ep. for παραστῆτον, 2 dual aor. 2 subj. of παρίστημι.

παρταμεῖν, poët. for παραταμεῖν, aor. 2 of παρατέμνω.

παρτέμνω, poët. for παρατέμνω.

παρτιθεῖ, poët. for παρατιθεῖ, = παρατίθησιν.

παρ-ὑφαίνω, f. ἀνῶ: pf. pass. παρύφασμαι:—*to weave beside* or *along, attach to the side* or *hem:* metaph., ὅπλα παρυφασμένα armed men *hemming in* a crowd.

πάρφαινε, poët. pres. imperat. of παραφαίνω.

παρφάμενος, παρφάσθαι, poet. aor. 2 med. part. of παράφημι.

παρ-φάσία, ἡ, poët. for παραφασία.

πάρ-φἄσις, ἡ, poët. for παράφασις.

παρ-φέρομαι, poët. for παραφέρομαι.

παρ-φῠγέειν, poët. for παραφυγεῖν, aor. 2 inf. of παραφεύγω.

πάρφυκτος, ον, poët. for παράφυκτος, verb. Adj. of παραφεύγω, *to be avoided.*

πᾰρώας, ου, ὁ, (παρωός) *a snake of a colour between red and brown,* sacred to Aesculapius.

παρῳδία, ἡ, *a burlesque, parody.* From

παρ-ῳδός, όν, (ᾠδή) *singing a song in a different style, burlesquing* a song. II. *intimating obscurely.*

παρ-ωθέω, fut. -ώσω and -ωθήσω:—*to push aside* or *away, repulse from* one: *to put on one side, keep secret:*—Med. *to push away from oneself, reject, renounce.*

παρών, οὖσα, όν, part. of πάρειμι (εἰμί *sum*).

παρ-ώνῠμος, ον, (πάρα, ὄνυμα Aeol. for ὄνομα) *formed by a slight change from a word.*

πᾰρωός, όν, *reddish brown* or *bay,* of horses.

παρ-ωρείτης, ου, ὁ, (παρά, ὄρος) *one who dwells a mountain-side.*

πάρ-ωρος, ον, (παρά, ὥρα) *out of season, untimely:* neut. pl. πάρωρα as Adv., *unseasonably.*

παρ-ωροφίς, ίδος, ἡ, (παρά, ὀροφή) *the part of the roof stretching beyond the wall, the eaves, cornice.*

παρῴχετο, 3 sing. impf. of παροίχομαι.

παρῴχημαι, pf. of παροίχομαι; part. παρῳχημένος.

ΠΑ͂Σ, πᾶσα, πᾶν: gen. παντός, πάσης, παντός: gen. pl. masc. and neut. πάντων, fem. πασῶν Ion. πασέων, Ep. also πασάων: dat. pl. masc. and neut. πᾶσι poët. πάντεσσι, fem. πάσαις:—*all,* Lat. *omnis:* of one person or thing, *the whole, entire, all;* of each of a number, *every;* in plur. *all:* ἡ πᾶσα βλάβη she who is *all mischief;* ἐς πᾶν κακοῦ *to the uttermost* of evil: —ὅσοι, not οἵ properly follows πάντες as relat., πάντες, ὅσοι.., Lat. *omnes quicunque.., all* whosoever! πᾶς τις *every one* taken one by one, *every single* one: παντὸς μᾶλλον more *than anything,* above *everything.* II. with Numerals it marks an exact number; τὰ πάντα δέκα ten *in all.* III. in dat. pl. masc. πᾶσι, *in the judgment of all;* ὁ πᾶσι κλεινός the renowned *in the judgment of all.* 2. πᾶσι as neut., *in all things, altogether.* IV. the neut. is used in various senses:—πάντα γίγνεσθαι, like παντοῖος γίγνεσθαι, to become *all things,* to try *every expedient:* but, πάντα εἶναί τινι to be *everything* to one. 2. τὸ πᾶν *the whole,* and as an Adv. *altogether;* οὐ τὸ πᾶν, *not at all;* so also εἰς τὸ πᾶν, ἐπὶ πᾶν, *on the whole;* ἐς πᾶν κακοῦ to *every* extremity of evil; περὶ παντὸς ποιεῖσθαί τινα to esteem one above *all.* 3. πάντα as Adv. for πάντως, *entirely, utterly, wholly:* but, τὰ πάντα *in every way, by all means.* 4. διὰ παντός *continually, always.*

πασᾶν, Dor. for πασῶν, gen. pl. fem. of πᾶς.

πάσασθαι [ᾰ], aor. 1 inf. of πατέομαι.

πάσασθαι [ᾱ], aor. 1 inf. of πάομαι.

πᾶσι-μέλουσα, ἡ, (πᾶς, μέλει) *a care to all:* generally, *known to all, famous.*

πάσομαι [ᾰ], fut. of πατέομαι.

πάσομαι [ᾱ], fut. of πάομαι.

πασπάλη [ᾰ], ἡ, = παιπάλη, *the finest meal: a*

morsel, scrap· ὕπνου οὐδὲ πασπάλη not even *a wink* of sleep.

πασσᾰλευτός, ή, όν, *pinned down*. From

πασσᾰλεύω Att. **ππατταλεύω**, f. σω (πάσσαλος) *to pin to* 2. *to drive in like a bolt*.

πάσσᾰλος Att. **πάτταλος**, ὁ, (πήγνυμι) *a peg*, to hang anything upon: often in Ep. genit. πασσαλόφι; αἱρεῖν ἀπὸ πασσαλόφι to take down from *a peg*; κρεμάσαι ἐκ πασσαλόφι to hang upon *a peg*· the form πασσαλόφιν is also dat. II. *a gag*.

πασσᾰλόφι, old Ep. gen. and dat. of πάσσαλος.

πασσάμενος, **πάσσασθαι**, Ep. for πᾰσάμενος, πάσασθαι, aor. 1 part. and inf. med. of πατέομαι.

πάσσαξ, ᾱκος, ὁ, rarer collat. form of πάσσαλος.

πάσσε, Ep. for ἔπασσε, 3 sing. impf. of πάσσω.

πάσ-σοφος, ον, for πάνσοφος.

πασ-σῠδεί, **πασ-σῠδίῃ**, Adv. for πανσυδεί, etc.

ΠΑ'ΣΣΩ Att. **πάττω**: f. πάσω [ᾰ]: aor. 1 ἔπᾰσα: Pass., aor. 1 ἐπάσθην: pf. πέπασμαι:—*to sprinkle upon*:—metaph. *to sprinkle in* or *upon, interweave, work in embroidery*. II. *to besprinkle with* a thing.

πάσσων, ον, gen. ονος, irr. Comp. of παχύς, for παχύτερος and παχίων, like γλύσσων from γλυκύς: *thicker, broader, stouter*.

παστάς, άδος, ή, shortened from παραστάς (q. v.) *a porch in front of the house, a colonnade*, Lat. *porticus*. II. *an inner chamber: a bridal chamber*.

παστέος, α, ον, verb. Adj. of πάσσω, *to be besprinkled*.

παστός, ὁ, = παστάς, *a bridal chamber* or *bridal bed: a shrine*.

Πάσχα, τό, indecl. *the Passover, paschal lamb*: also *the time* or *feast of the Passover*. (Hebrew word.)

ΠΑ'ΣΧΩ, fut. πείσομαι: aor. 2 ἔπᾰθον: pf. πέπονθα, 2 pl. πέποσθε, Ep. for πεπόνθατε: fem. part. pf. πεπᾰθυῖα, Ep. for πεπονθυῖα:—*to suffer* or *be affected by anything* whether good or bad, opp. to acting of oneself; εἴ τι πάθοιμι or ἤν τι πάθω *if* aught *were to happen* to me, Lat. *si quid mihi acciderit*, was used to imply death: τί πάθω; what *is to become of me*? so, τί πάσχω; τί πάσχεις; what *is the matter with* me or you? so in part. τί παθών; implying something amiss, τί παθόντε λελάσμεθα θούριδος ἀλκῆς; *what ails us* that we have forgotten our impetuous prowess? II. πάσχειν with other words; κακῶς πάσχειν *to be ill off, in evil plight*; κακῶς πάσχειν ὑπό τινος *to be ill used, evilly entreated* by any one; opp. to εὖ πάσχειν *to be well off, in good case*; εὖ πάσχειν ὑπό τινος *to be well used, well treated by.., receive kindness from* a person. III. πάσχειν is also used of states or conditions; ἵνα μὴ ταὐτὸ πάθητε τῷ ἵππῳ that *ye be not in* the same *case* with the horse: so, of Things, *to be liable to certain affections*; πάσχειν ταὐτὸν ὅπερ ἄλλοι *to be liable to the* same as others; so, πάσχει τοῦτο καὶ κάρδαμα this is just the way with cress.

πατά, Scythian word, = κτείνειν.

πᾰτᾰγέω, f. ήσω, (πάταγος) *to clatter, clash, crash*, of the noise caused by the collision of two bodies: of the waves, etc. *to dash, plash*: hence *to chatter, scream*, as *birds*.

ΠΑ'ΤΑΓΟΣ, ὁ, *a clattering, clashing, any sharp noise* made by the collision of two bodies; πάταγος ὀδόντων *a chattering* of the teeth; πάταγος κυμάτων *the plash* of waves. (Formed from the sound.)

Πάταικοι or **Παταϊκοί**, οἱ, Phoenician deities of dwarfish shape, whose images formed the figure-heads of Phoenician ships.

πατάξαι, **πατάξας**, aor. 1 inf. and part. o

πᾰτάσσω, f. ξω: aor. 1 ἐπάταξα:—intr. *to beat, knock, throb*; Ἕκτορι θυμὸς ἐνὶ στήθεσσι πάτασσεν his heart *was beating, throbbing* in his breast. 2. *to clap* the hands. II. trans. *to strike, wound, beat, smite*.

ΠΑ'ΤΕ'ΟΜΑΙ, f. πάσομαι [ᾰ]: aor. 1 ἐπᾰσάμην, Ep. part. πασσάμενος: pf. πέπασμαι:—*to feed on. eat, taste*

πατεοντι, Dor. for πατέουσι, 3 pl. of πατέω: also part. sing. dat.

πᾰτερίζω, f. ίσω, (πατήρ) *to say, call father*

πᾰτέω, f. ήσω, (πάτος) *to tread, walk, step*. II. trans. *to tread on, tread*; πορφύρας πατεῖν *to walk on* purple carpets. 2. *to tread constantly, frequent, traverse* a place: metaph., like Lat. *terere, to thumb with using*, as, πατεῖν Αἴσωπον *to be always thumbing* Aesop. 3. *to tread under foot, trample on*.

ΠΑ'ΤΗ'Ρ, ὁ, gen. πατέρος contr. πατρός, dat. πατέρι contr. πατρί, acc. πατέρα: in dual and pl. ε is retained, except that in gen. pl. πατρῶν is used as well as πατέρων, and dat. pl. is always πατράσι [ᾰ]:—*a father*; πατρὸς πατήρ *a grandfather*. II. among the gods Jove is emphat. called πατήρ. III. πατήρ is used like ἄπφα, ἄττα, as a mode of address to an older person. IV. in plur., *forefathers, ancestors*.

πατησεῖς, Dor. for πατήσεις, 2 sing. fut. of πατέω.

πᾰτησμός, ὁ, (πατέω) *a treading on*.

πάτνη, ή, Dor. for φάτνη.

ΠΑ'ΤΟΣ, ὁ, *a trodden* or *beaten way, path*. [ᾰ]

πάτρᾱ, ας Ion. **πάτρη**, ης, ή: (πατήρ) *one's fatherland, native land, country*, like πατρίς. II. *a body of persons claiming the same race* or *descent, a house, clan*, Lat. *gens*.

πατρ-ᾰδελφεός, ὁ, poët. for πατρ-άδελφος.

πατρ-άδελφος, ὁ, = πατρὸς ἀδελφός, *a father's brother, uncle by the father's side*.

πάτρᾱθε, Adv., Dor. for πάτρηθε.

πατρ-ᾱλοίας, gen. α and ου, voc. -αλοῖα, ὁ, (πατήρ, ἀλοιάω) *one who strikes* or *slays his father, a parricide*.

πάτρη, ή, Ion. for πάτρα. Hence

πάτρηθε and -θεν Dor. **πάτρᾱθε**, Adv., = ἐκ πάτρας, *from one's native land*. II. *from a race* or *lineage*.

πατριά, ᾶς Ion. **πατριή**, ῆς, ή (πατήρ) *lineage, descent*. II. *a house, clan*.

πατρι-άρχης, ου, ὁ, (πατριά, ἀρχή) *the father* or *chief of a family, a patriarch*.

πατρίδιον, τό, coaxing Dim. of *πατήρ*, *daddy*, *papa*.

πατρῐκός, ή, όν, (*πατήρ*) *from one's fathers* or *ancestors*, *patriarchal*, *hereditary*. II. *of* or *from one's father*; ἡ πατρική (sc. οὐσία) *one's patrimony*; so τὰ πατρικά (sc. χρήματα).

πάτριος, α, ον, also ος, ον, (*πατήρ*) *of* or *belonging to one's father*, Lat. *paternus*. II. *of* or *from one's forefathers*, *hereditary*, *customary*, *national*: τὰ πάτρια, *the manners*, *customs*, *institutions of ancestors*, Lat. *instituta majorum*.

πατρίς, ίδος, poët. fem. of *πάτριος*, *of one's fathers*; πατρὶς γαῖα, *one's father-land*, *country*; πατρὶς πόλις one's *native* city:—also as Subst., πατρίς, ἡ, like πάτρα.

πατριώτης, ου, ὁ, (*πάτριος*) *one of the same country*, *a fellow-countryman*.

πατριῶτις, ιδος, fem. of *πατριώτης*; πατριῶτις γῆ, = πατρίς, *one's native land*; πατριῶτις στολή a dress *of the country*.

πατρο-δώρητος, ον, (*πατήρ*, δωρέω) *given by a father*.

πατρόθεν, Adv. (*πατήρ*) *from* or *after a father*, *by one's father's name*; ἀναγραφῆναι πατρόθεν ἐν στήλῃ to have one's name inscribed on a tablet *with one's father's name added*.

πατρο-κᾰσίγνητος, ὁ, = πατρὸς κασίγνητος, *a father's brother*, *uncle by the father's side*.

Πάτροκλος, ὁ, *Patroclus*, the friend of Achilles: the gen. Πατροκλῆος, acc. Πατροκλῆα, voc. Πατρόκλεις occur in Hom.; but there is no nom. Πατροκλεύς.

πατροκτονέω, f. ήσω, *to murder one's father*. From

πατρο-κτόνος, ον, (*πατήρ*, κτείνω) *murdering one's father*, *parricidal*.

πατρο-νομία, ή, (*πατήρ*, νόμος) *a father's authority*.

πατρο-παράδοτος, ον, (*πατήρ*, παραδίδωμι) *handed down* or *inherited from one's fathers*.

πατρο-πάτωρ, ορος, ὁ, = πατρὸς πατήρ, *a father's father*, *grandfather*.

πατρο-στερής, ές, (*πατήρ*, στερέω) *reft of one's father*, *fatherless*.

πατρ-οῦχος, ον, (*πατήρ*, ἔχω) *having her father's property*: as Subst., πατροῦχος (sub. παρθένος), ἡ, *a sole-heiress*, opp. to *a coheiress*.

πατρο-φονεύς, έως Ep. ῆος, ὁ, (*πατήρ*, φονεύς) *the murderer of one's father*.

πατρο-φόνος, ον, (*πατήρ*, *φένω) *murdering one's father*, *parricidal*.

πατρο-φόντης, ου, ὁ, (*πατήρ*, *φένω) *murderer of one's father*, *a parricide*.

πατρώιος, η Dor. α, ον, poët. form of *πατρῷος*.

πατρ-ωνύμιος, ον, (*πατήρ*, ὄνυμα Aeol. for ὄνομα) *named after one's father*, *by the father's side*.

πατρῷος, α, ον, also ος, ον, poët. πατρώιος, η Dor. α, ον: (*πατήρ*):—*of a father*, *coming* or *inherited from a father*, Lat. *paternus*: *transmitted from one's father*; ἔχθρα πατρῴα *hereditary* feud.

πάτρως, ὁ, gen. ωος and ω, dat. ῳ, acc. ωα and ων: (*πατήρ*):—πατροκασίγνητος, πατράδελφος, *an uncle by the father's side*, Lat. *patruus*; opp. to *μήτρως*, one by the *mother's* side.

παττᾰλεύω, **πάττᾰλος**, Att. for πασσ—.

παύεσκον, Ion. impf. of *παύω*:—**παυέσκετο**, Ion. 3 sing. impf. med.

παῦλα, ή, (*παύω*) *a resting-point*, *pause*, *rest*; παῦλα κακῶν *rest from* ills. II. *a bringing to an end*: *means of stopping*.

παυράκις or -κι [ᾰ], Adv. (*παῦρος*) like ὀλιγάκις, *few times*, *seldom*.

παυρίδιος, α, ον, poët. for *παῦρος*, *little*, *very short*: neut. παυρίδιον, as Adv., *a very little*.

παυρο-επής, ές, (*παῦρος*, ἔπος) *of few words*.

παῦρος, α, ον, *little*, *small*: of Time, *short*, *brief*. 2. mostly in pl. παῦροι, of Number, *few*; so with a collective Subst., παῦρος λαός *few* people:—Comp. παυρότερος, *fewer*. 3. neut. pl. παῦρα as Adv. *seldom*.

παυσ-άνεμος, ον, (*παύω*, ἄνεμος) *calming the wind*.

παύσειεν, 3 sing. Aeol. aor. 1 opt. of *παύω*.

παυσῐ-κάπη [ᾰ], ή, (*παύω*, κάπη) *a projecting collar worn by slaves* while grinding or kneading, to prevent their eating any of the corn.

παυσί-λῡπος, ή, (*παύω*, λύπη) *ending pain* or *grief*.

παυσί-νοσος, ον, (*παύω*, νόσος) *checking sickness*.

παυσί-πονος, ον, (*παύω*, πόνος) *ending toil*.

παυστέον, verb. Adj. of *παύω*, *one must stop* or *put an end to*. II. of *παύομαι*, *one must cease*.

παυστήρ, ῆρος, ὁ, (*παύω*) *one who stays* or *calms*, *an allayer*, *assuager*. Hence

παυστήριος, ον, *fit for allaying* or *relieving*.

παυσωλή, ή, like παῦλα, *rest*.

ΠΑΥ'Ω: f. παύσω: aor. 1 ἔπαυσα: pf. πέπαυκα: Med. and Pass., fut. παύσομαι, pass. παυσθήσομαι, and paullo-p. fut. πεπαύσομαι: aor. 1 med. ἐπαυσάμην, pass. ἐπαύθην or ἐπαύσθην: pf. πέπαυμαι:—*to make to cease*, *to stop*, *bring to an end*: of a king, *to depose*, *put down*: *to stop from* a thing, c. gen. 2. of things, *to make an end of*: of suffering, etc., *to abate*, *allay*. II. Med. and Pass. *to come to an end*, *cease*, *rest*, *leave off*: also of a magistrate, *to be deposed* from office: c. gen. *to cease from*. III. intr. in Act., like *παύομαι* or λήγω, but only in imperat., παῦε, *stop! have done!*

Παφλᾰγών, όνος, ὁ, *a Paphlagonian*.

παφλάζω, f. άσω: (redupl. from φλάζω, like πιπνύω from πνέω):—*to bubble*, *froth*, *foam*: of the wind, *to storm*, *bluster*. II. metaph. *to splutter*, *fret*, *fume*, *chafe*, of the angry Cleon, with allusion to Παφλαγών. Hence

πάφλασμα, ατος, τό, *a frothing*, *foaming*, of the sea, etc. II. metaph., παφλάσματα *spluttering words*.

Πάφος, ον, ή, *Paphos*, a town in Cyprus celebrated for its temple of Venus.

πάχετος, irreg. Ep. form for *παχύτερος*, *thicker*.

πάχετος, τό, (*παχύς*) poët. for *πάχος*, *thickness*.

παχθῇ, Dor. for πηχθῇ, 3 sing. aor. 1 pass. subj. of πήγνυμι.

πάχιστος, η, ον, irreg. Sup. of παχύς.

παχίων, gen. ονος, irreg. Comp. of παχύς.

πάχνη, ἡ, (πήγνυμι) *boar-frost, rime*, Lat. *pruina.* 2. metaph. *clotted blood.* Hence

παχνόω, f. ώσω, *to cover with boar frost* or *rime* :—Pass. *to be so covered* II. metaph. *to strike chill, to freeze* ; ἐπάχνωσεν φίλον ἦτορ he *made* his heart's blood *run cold* :—Pass. *to be struck with chill, to be frozen.*

πάχος, εος, τό, (παχύς) *thickness* : acc. πάχος is used absol., *in thickness*, as μῆκος *in length*, εὖρος *in breadth*, etc. [ᾰ]

πᾰχύ-κνημος, ον, (παχύς, κνήμη) *with stout calves.*

πᾰχύνω [ῡ], f. ῠνῶ : aor. 1 ἐπάχῡνα : pf. pass. πεπάχυσμαι :—*to thicken, to fatten* : also *to make dull* or *gross of understanding* :—Pass. *to become thick* : *to grow fat, to be swollen* : also *to look large*, of objects seen in a mist: metaph., ὄλβος ἄγαν παχυνθεὶς wealth '*when it has waxed fat.*'

πᾶχυς, Dor. for πῆχυς.

ΠΑ'ΧΥ'Σ, εῖα, ύ, *thick, large, stout* : παχὺς λᾶας *a large heavy* stone : of linen, etc., *thick, coarse.* 2. of the consistence of a mass, *thick, curdled, clotted.* 3. later, *stout, fat*, Lat. *pinguis.* 4. generally, *great, large, considerable.* II. οἱ παχέες, opp. to δῆμος, *the men of substance, the wealthy.* III. *thick-witted, dense, stupid*, Lat. *pinguis.* IV. Comp. πάσσων, ον : also πᾰχίων, ον, gen. ονος :—Sup. πάχιστος : later the regul. πᾰχύτερος (Ep. πάχετος) and πᾰχύτατος.

πᾰχύτης, ητος, ἡ, (παχύς) *thickness*, of the skin, etc. : *the sediment* or *lees* of liquor. [ῠ]

πέδᾰ, Aeol. for μετά.

πεδάᾳ, Ep. 3 sing. pres. of πεδάω.

πεδάασκον, Ion. impf. of πεδάω.

πεδ-αίρω, Aeol. for μεταίρω.

πεδ-αίχμιος, ον, Aeol. for μεταίχμιος.

πεδ-ᾰμείβω, Aeol. for μεταμείβω.

πεδ-άορος, ον, Aeol. for μετήορος. [ᾰ]

πεδ-άρσιος, ον, Aeol. for μετάρσιος.

πεδ-αυγάζω, Aeol. for μεταυγάζω.

πεδά-φρων, ον, gen. ονος, Aeol. for μετάφρων, (μετά, φρήν) *wise too late.*

πεδάω, f. ήσω : Ep. aor. 1 πέδησα : (πέδη) :—*to bind with fetters, to bind fast, make fast* : generally, *to shackle, trammel, constrain*

πεδ-έρχομαι, Aeol. for μετέρχομαι.

πεδ-έχω, Aeol. for μετέχω.

πεδέω, Ion. for πεδάω.

πέδη, ἡ, (πέζα) *a fetter*, Lat. *pedica, compes* ; ζεῦγος πεδῶν a pair *of fetters.* II. *a mode of breaking in a horse.*

πεδητής, οῦ, ὁ, (πεδάω) *one who fetters* : *a hinderer.*

πεδιάς, άδος, fem. Adj. (πεδίον) *flat, even, level* ; ἡ πεδιάς (sub. γῆ), *the plain country.* II. *on a plain* or *level country* : λόγχη πεδιὰς the spear (i. e. battle) *on a fair field.*

πεδιεύς, έως, ὁ, (πεδίον) *a man of the plain.*

πεδι-ήρης, ες, (πεδίον, ἀραρεῖν) *abounding in plains.*

πέδῑλον, τό, (πέδη) mostly in plur. *sandals, a pair of sandals.* II. *any covering for the feet, shoes, slippers* ; also *boots, brogues.* III. *a tie for cows* at milking time. IV. metaph., Δωρίῳ πεδίλῳ φωνὰν ἐναρμόξαι to suit one's voice to the Dorian *march*, i. e. to write in Doric rhythm.

πεδινός, ή, όν, (πεδίον) *flat, level, even.* II. *of, from the plain, living in* or *on the plain.*

πεδίον, τό, (πέδον) *a plain, flat, open country, an open plain, a field*, Lat. *campus* ; πεδία πόντου the *fields* of the sea, Lat. *Neptunia arva.* Hence

πεδίονδε, Adv. *to the plain.*

πεδῐο-νόμος, ον, (πεδίον, νέμομαι) *haunting the fields.*

πεδο-βάμων [ᾱ], ον, gen. ονος, Dor. for πεδοβήμων, (πέδον, βαίνω) *walking upon earth, of the earth.*

πεδόθεν, Adv. (πέδον) *from the ground* : metaph. *from the ground* or *bottom of the heart.*

πέδοι, Adv. (πέδον) *on the ground, on earth.*

πέδοικος, ον, Aeol. for μέτοικος.

πεδο-κοίτης, ου, ὁ, (πέδον, κοίτη) *making one's bed* or *lair on the ground.*

ΠΕ'ΔΟΝ, ου, τό, *the ground, earth* : generally *land, soil.* Hence

πέδονδε, Adv. *to the ground, earthwards.*

πεδόσε, Adv. = πέδονδε.

πεδο-στῐβής, ές, (πέδον, στείβω) *treading, pacing the earth.* 2. *on foot*, opp. to ἱππηλάτης.

πεδό-τριψ, ῐβος, ὁ and ἡ, (πέδη, τρίβω) *wearing out fetters*, of good-for-nothing slaves.

πεδ-ώρῠχος, ον, (πέδον, ὀρύσσω) *digging the soil.*

πέζᾰ, ης, ἡ, (πέδον) *the foot* : metaph. *the bottom* of anything : ἐπὶ ῥυμῷ πέζῃ ἔπι πρώτῃ on the pole *at the* very *end* : *the hem* or *border* of a garment

πεζ-αρχος, ον, (πεζός, ἄρχω) *leading infantry* or *land-army* : as Subst., πέζαρχος, ὁ, *a leader of foot.*

πεζ-έταιροι, οἱ, (πεζός, ἑταῖρος) *the foot-guards* in the Macedonian army.

πεζεύω, f. σω, (πεζός) *to go* or *travel on foot, walk*, opp. to riding or driving. 2. *to go* or *travel by land*, opp. to going by sea : Pass. *to be traversed by travellers.*

πεζῇ, v. sub πεζός.

πεζικός, ή, όν, (πεζός) *on foot* or *by land*, πεζικὸς λεὼς *foot*-soldiers. *infantry* as opp. to horse, or *an army* as opp. to a fleet.

πεζο-βόας, α, ὁ, Dor. for -βόης, (πεζός, βοή) *one who shouts on foot, a foot-soldier, a soldier.*

πεζομᾰχέω, f. ήσω, *to fight by land.* From

πεζο-μάχης, ου, ὁ, (πεζός, μάχομαι) *fighting on foot*, as opp. to cavalry. 2. *fighting on land*, as opp. to sea. Hence

πεζομαχία, ἡ, *a battle by land*, opp. to ναυμαχία.

πεζο-νόμος, ον, (πεζός, νέμω) *commanding by land.*

πεζοπορέω, *to go on foot.* 2. *to go by land.* From

πεζο-πόρος, ον, (πεζός, πορεύω) *going on foot, walking.* 2. *going by land.*

πεζός, ή, όν, (πέζα) *on foot, walking*; πεζοί *foot-soldiers*, opp. to **ἱππεῖς**; so, πεζὸς στρατός is sometimes *foot-soldiery*, opp. to cavalry; but also *a land-army*, opp. to a sea-force; ὁ πεζός, and τὸ πεζόν are also so used. II. *on land, going* or *travelling by land;* Dat. fem. πεζῇ as Adv. (sub. ὁδῷ), *on foot* or *by land;* πεζῇ ἕπεσθαι to follow *by land.*

πεῖ, Dor. for πῇ, ποῦ.

πειθ-άνωρ Ion. **πειθήνωρ**, ορος, ὁ, ἡ, (πείθομαι, ἀνήρ) *obeying men, obedient.*

πειθαρχέω, f. ήσω, also Med. **-έομαι**, (πείθαρχος) *to obey one in authority, be obedient.* Hence

πειθαρχία, ἡ, *obedience.*

πείθ-αρχος, ον, (πείθομαι, ἀρχή) *obeying one in authority, obedient.*

πείθημι, Aeol. for **πείθω**.

πειθός, ή, όν, (πείθω) = **πιθανός**, *persuasive.*

ΠΕΙ'ΘΩ, fut. πείσω: aor. 1 ἔπεισα: aor. 2 ἔπῐθον Ep. redupl. πέπῐθον, 1 pl. subj. πεπίθωμεν, opt. πεπίθοιμεν, inf. πεπῐθεῖν, part. πεπιθών: pf. πέπεικα:—Med. and Pass. πείθομαι: fut. πείσομαι: aor. 2 ἐπῐθόμην Ep. πιθόμην, imperat. πίθου, Ep. redupl. opt. πεπίθοιτο, inf. πῐθέσθαι: pf. med. πέποιθα; plqpf. πεποίθεα, contr. 1 pl. ἐπέπιθμεν: pf. pass. πέπεισμαι. Homer has also a fut. πῐθήσω and aor. 1 part. πιθήσας, intr. as if from πιθέω: but the redupl. aor. 1 subj. πεπῐθήσω is transit.: I. Act. *to prevail upon, win over, talk over, persuade:* in bad sense, *to mislead, over-persuade, cheat.* 2. *to prevail on by entreaty, to appease, propitiate;* πείθειν **τινὰ** χρήμασι *to bribe* one. 3. *to impel, stir up.* 4. c. dupl. acc., πείθειν **τινά** τι *to persuade* one of a thing. 5. c. acc. rei only, *to argue* a point. II. Med. and Pass. *to be won over, prevailed on, persuaded to comply.* 2. πείθεσθαί τινι *to listen to* a person, *obey, comply with;* γήρᾳ πείθεσθαι *to yield to* old age. 3. πείθεσθαί τινι *to believe* or *trust in* a thing; also c. neut. acc., ταῦτ' ἐγώ σοι οὐ πείθομαι *I do* not *take* this *on your word;* c. acc. et inf. *to believe that* ... III. pf. med. πέποιθα, inf. πεποιθέναι, *to trust, rely, have confidence in.* IV. pf. pass. πέπεισμαι *to be fully persuaded, believe, trust:* of things, *to be believed.* Hence

Πειθώ, όος contr. οῦς, ἡ, *Persuasion* personified as a goddess, Lat. *Suada, Suadēla.* II. *the faculty of persuasion, eloquence, persuasiveness.* 2. *a persuasion* in the mind. 3. *a means of persuasion, inducement;* dat. πειθοῖ *by fair means*, opp. to βίᾳ by force. 4. *obedience.*

ΠΕΙ'ΝΑ or **πείνη**, ἡ, *hunger, famine*, Lat. *fames.* 2. metaph. *hunger* or *longing for* a thing. Hence

πεινάλεος, α, ον, *hungry, empty.* [ᾰ]

πεινᾶμες, Aeol. for πεινῶμεν, 1 pl. of πεινάω.

πεινᾶντι, Dor. for πεινῶντι, dat. pres. part. of πεινάω: also for πεινῶσι 3 pl. pres.

πεινάω contr. **πεινῶ**, ῇς, ῇ; inf. πεινῆν Ep. πεινήμεναι; fut. πεινήσω, later πεινάσω [ᾱ]: (πεῖνα): aor. 1 ἐπείνησα, later -ᾱσα: pf. πεπείνηκα:—*to be hungry, suffer hunger, be famished.* II. c. gen. *to hunger after:* metaph. *to hunger after* or *for, crave after.*

πεινέω, Ion. for πεινάω.

πείνη, = πεῖνα.

πεινῆν, inf. of πεινάω; Ep. **πεινήμεναι**.

ΠΕΙ'ΡΑ, ἡ, *a trial, attempt, essay, experiment:* hence *experience;* πεῖραν ἔχειν to have *experience*, to make *proof* of; ἐπὶ πείρᾳ by way of *test* or *trial.* II. *an attempt, plot* or *design against* one. III. generally, *an attempt, plan, enterprise.*

πεῖρα, Ep. for ἔπειρα, aor. 1 of πείρω.

πειρά, ἡ, (πείρω) *a point, edge.*

πειράζω, f. άσω: Pass., aor. 1 ἐπειράσθην: pf. πεπείρασμαι:—like πειράω, *to make proof* or *trial of* one:—*to tempt, make trial of, seek to seduce.* II. *to attempt* a thing.

Πειραιεύς or **Πειρᾶεύς**, ὁ, *Peiræeus*, the most famous harbour of Athens, from which it was distant about five English miles: gen. **Πειραιέως** or -αιῶς; dat. -αιεῖ; acc. -αιᾶ.

Πειραιοῖ, Adv. *at* or *in Peiræeus.*

πειραίνω, f. ᾰνῶ: aor. 1 ἐπείρηνα: (πεῖραρ):—*to bind, tie on* or *to, fasten on by a knot;* σειρὴν ἐξ αὐτοῦ πειρήναντε *tying* a rope *from* or *to* it. II. lengthd. for περαίνω, *to end, complete, finish;* in Pass., πάντα πεπείρανται (3 sing. pf.) all *has been completed.*

πεῖραν, Ep. 3 pl. aor. 1 of πείρω.

ΠΕΙ'ΡΑΡ, ᾰτος, τό, poët. for **πέρας**, *an end;* in plur., πείρατα γαίης *the ends* of the earth: *the ends of ropes, knotted ropes.* II. *the end* or *issue* of a thing: *the furthest point, the utmost verge; the chief* or *most important object.* III. act. *that which finishes;* a goldsmith's tools are called **πείρατα τέχνης**, *the finishers* of art.

πείρᾰσις, ἡ, (πειράω) *a trying: an attempt.*

πειρασμός, ὁ, (πειράζω) *a tempting, temptation.*

πειρᾰτέον, or in plur. -έα, verb. Adj. of πειράω, *one must make trial, attempt.*

πειρᾱτήρ, ῆρος, ὁ, collat. form of **πειρατής**.

πειρᾱτήριον Ion. **πειρητ-**, τό, (πειράω) *a means of trying* or *proving, ordeal;* φόνια πειρατήρια the murderous *ordeal*, i. e. *torture.* II. *a pirate's nest.*

πειρᾱτής, οῦ, ὁ, (πειράω) *one who attempts: a pirate*, Lat. *pirāta.*

πειρᾱτικός, ή, όν, *piratical.*

πειράω, f. άσω Ion. ήσω: more freq. as Dep. **πειράομαι**, with fut. med. πειράσομαι, Dor. 2 pl. πειρασεῖσθε: aor. 1 med. ἐπειρᾱσάμην Ion. ἐπειρησάμην; pass. ἐπειράθην [ᾱ] Ion. ἐπειρήθην: pf. pass. πεπείρᾱμαι Ion. πεπείρημαι: (πεῖρα):—*to attempt, undertake, try.* 2. c. gen. pers. *to make trial of* a person; *to try to persuade* him: also *to make an attempt on, attack:* also c. acc. *to make an attempt on.* 3. absol. *to try one's skill* or *luck* in a thing. II. the Dep. πειράομαι is mostly used with gen. pers., *to make trial* *of* one, *put* him to *the proof;* hence *to examine, question:* also *to try oneself against another, to match oneself with* him 2. c. gen. rei, *to make trial* or *proof of* a thing, *have experience of.* 3. absol. *to try one's strength, make a trial:* *to make a trial* or *attempt with* words; πεπείρημαι μύθοις *I have tried myself,* i. e. *I am versed* or *skilled,* in words.

πειρηθείην, πειρηθῆναι, aor. 1 opt. and inf. pass. of πειράω, πειράομαι.

πειρητήριον, τό, Ion. for πειρᾱτήριον.

πειρητίζω, f. ίσω, = πειράω, *to attempt, try, prove.* II. c. gen. pers. *to make trial of, put to the proof:* also *to try* another *in battle:* c. acc. *to attempt, attack, assail.*

πεῖρινς, ινθος, ἡ: acc. πείρινθα:—*the wicker-basket* used in Greece as *the body of a cart* upon the ἅμαξα or carriage.

ΠΕΙ'ΡΩ, fut. περῶ: aor. 1 ἔπειρα Ep. πεῖρα: Pass., aor. 2 ἐπάρην [ᾰ] pf. πέπαρμαι: (πέρας):—*to pierce quite through, to run through, pierce,* of meat, *to spit;* κρέα ἀμφ' ὀβελοῖσιν ἔπειραν *they stuck* the meat on the spits:—pf. part., ἥλοισι πεπαρμένον *stuck close* or *studded* with nails; metaph., ὀδύνῃσι πεπαρμένος *pierced* with pain. II. metaph., κύματα πείρειν *to cleave* the waves; πεῖρε κέλευθον *clave* her way (through the waves).

πεῖσα, ης, ἡ, (πείθω) poët. for πειθώ, *persuasion* or *obedience, subjection.*

πείσειε, 3 sing. Aeol. aor. 1 opt. of πείθω.

πεισί-βροτος, ον, (πείθω, βροτός) *persuading* or *controlling mortals.*

πεισέμεν, Ep. for πείσειν, fut. inf. of πείθω.

πεῖσμα, ατος, τό, (πείθω) *the cable* by which the ships were secured by the stern to the land: generally, *a cable, rope.* II. *that on which one may trust.*

πεισμονή, ἡ, (πείθω) *earnest persuasion, solicitation.*

πείσομαι, fut. med. of πείθω.

πείσομαι, irreg. fut. of πάσχω.

πειστέον, verb. Adj. of πείθω, *one must persuade.* II. (from Pass.) *one must obey:* cf. ἀρκτέον.

πειστήριος, α, ον, (πείθω) *fit for persuading, persuasive, winning.*

πειστικός, ή, όν, (πείθω) *persuasive.*

πείσω, fut. of πείθω.

πέκος, τό, (πέκω) *wool, a fleece.*

πεκτέω, f. ήσω, (πέκω) *to shear, clip.*

ΠΕ'ΚΩ Ep. **πείκω:** f. πέξω: aor. 1 med. ἐπεξάμην, part. πεξάμενος; aor. 1 pass. ἐπέχθην:—*to comb* or *card* wool, Lat. *pectere:* med., χαίτας πεξαμένη *having combed her* hair 2. *to shear, clip.*

πελᾰγίζω, f. ίσω, (πέλαγος) *to form a sea* or *lake:* of a river, *to overflow:* of places, *to be flooded, swamped.* II. *to be out at sea.*

πελάγιος, α, ον, also ος, ον, (πέλαγος) *of, on* or *by the sea:* *living in the sea,* Lat. *marinus:* *out at sea, on the open sea.*

πελᾰγίτης [ῑ], ου, ὁ, fem. **-ῖτις,** ιδος, (πέλαγος) *of* or *on the sea.*

ΠΕ'ΛΑΓΟΣ, εος, τό: Ep. dat. pl. πελάγεσσι:—*the sea, the high sea, open sea, the main,* Lat. *pelagus:* *any large expanse of water* is so called: metaph. of anything huge or excessive, as, πέλαγος κακῶν *a 'sea of troubles.'*

πελάζω: f. πελάσω Att. πελῶ: aor. 1 ἐπέλᾰσα Ep. πέλασα, ἐπέλασσα and πέλασσα: aor. 1 med. ἐπελασάμην: Pass., aor. 1 ἐπελάσθην poet. ἐπλάθην [ᾱ]: Ep. aor. 2 pass. ἐπλήμην, 3 sing. and pl. πλῆτο, πλῆντο and ἔπληντο: pf. pass. πέπλημαι part. πεπλημένος:—πελάω, πελάθω, πλάθω are collat. forms: (πέλας): I. intrans. *to approach, draw near to* any point: absol. *to come near, draw near* or *nigh.* II. trans. *to bring near* or *to, make to approach* or *draw nigh;* πελάζειν νευρὴν μαζῷ *to draw* the bowstring *to* one's breast:—metaph., πελάζειν τινὰ ὀδύνῃσι *to bring* him *near to* anguish; so, ἔπος ἐρέω, ἀδάμαντι πελάσσας I will speak a word, *having made* it *firm as* adamant; φυγᾷ μ' οὐκέτ' ἀπ' αὐλίων πελᾶτε (sc. ὑμῖν) no more *will ye draw* me *after* you in flight from my cave: c. gen. pro dat., πάρα πελάσαι φάος νεῶν thou may'st *bring* light *near* the ships. III. in Pass. like the intr. Act. *to be brought near* or *close to, come nigh, approach;* ἐπεὶ τὰ πρῶτα πέλασθεν when *they* first *drew near:* so in Ep. aor. 2, ἀσπίδες ἔπληντ' ἀλλήλῃσι the shields *were brought close* to each other; πλῆτο χθονὶ *be came near,* i. e. *sank to* earth; so also, πελασθῆναι ἐπὶ τὸν θεόν *to draw nigh* to the god. 2. *to approach* or *wed* a woman.

πελάθω [ᾰ], collat. form of πελάζω, always intr.

πέλᾰνος, ὁ, *any half-liquid mixture,* of various consistency; *a mixed mass* or *gruel,* applied to *oil, honey, foam, clotted blood.* II. of *a mixture offered to the gods,* of meal, honey and oil, *poured out.* (Deriv. uncertain.)

πελαργῐδεύς, ὁ, (πελαργός) *a young stork.*

πελαργικός, ή, όν, *of* or *for a stork.* From

πελ-αργός, ὁ, (πελός, ἀργός) *the stork.*

ΠΕ'ΛΑ¯Σ, Adv. *near, hard by, close, nigh to,* mostly c. gen., but also c. dat.: c. gen. it answers to Lat. *prope ab aliquo loco,* c. dat. to Lat. *prope ad aliquem locum.* II. absol. *near, nigh at hand:* οἱ πέλας *one's neighbours, fellow-creatures, mankind:* rare in sing., ὁ πέλας *one's neighbour.*

πελασαίατο, Ep. for πελάσαιντο, 3 pl. aor. 1 opt. med. of πελάθω.

Πελασγικός, ή, όν, *of* or *for the Pelasgians:* τὸ Πελασγικόν name of *the northern side* of the Acropolis at Athens. From

Πελασγός, ὁ, *a Pelasgian;* Πελασγοί, οἱ, *the Pelasgians,* placed in Thessaly by Homer, but among the allies of the Trojans; also in Crete and about Dodona: contrasted by Herodotus with the Hellenes.

πελάτης [ᾰ], ου, ὁ, fem. **-ᾶτις,** ιδος, (πελάζω) *one who approaches* or *comes near, a neighbour,* Lat. *accŏla:* also *an invader, intruder.* II. *a client.*

πελάω, shorter form of πελάζω, trans. and intrans., 1. *to bring near.* 2. *to come* or *draw near.*

πέλεθος or **σπέλεθος**, ὁ, (πηλός) *ordure, dung.*

πέλεθρον, τό, lengthd. poët. form for πλέθρον.

πέλεια, ἡ, (πελός) *the wood-pigeon, ring-dove, cushat,* from its dark colour. II. πέλειαι, αἱ, name of the prophetic priestesses, derived from the prophetic doves of Dodona.

πελειάς, άδος, ἡ, = πέλεια.

Πελειάδες, αἱ, = Πλειάδες, *the Pleiads:* also in sing. **Πελειάς**, άδος, ἡ, *a Pleiad.*

πελειο-θρέμμων, ον, (πέλεια, τρέφω) *pigeon-feeding.*

πελεκάν, ᾶνος, or **πελεκᾶς**, ᾶντος, Dor. **πελεκᾶς**, ᾶ, ὁ, (πελεκάω) *the woodpecker, the joiner-bird.* II. *the pelican.*

πελεκάω, f. ήσω, (πέλεκυς) *to hew* or *shape with an axe, rough-hew,* Lat. *dolare.*

πελεκίζω, f. ίσω, (πέλεκυς) *to strike with an axe, to behead,* Lat. *securi percutere.*

πελεκῖνος, ὁ, = πελεκάν II, a water-bird of the *pelican* kind.

πελέκκησε, for ἐπελέκησε, Ep. 3 sing. aor. 1 of πελεκάω.

πέλεκκον, τό, (πέλεκυς) *an axe-handle.*

πέλεκῠς, εως Ion. εος, ὁ: dat. pl. πελέκεσι Ep. πελέκεσσι:—*a double-edged axe, an axe;* οὐ δόρασι μάχεσθαι, ἀλλὰ καὶ πελέκεσι to fight not with spears only, but also *with axes,* i. e. not soldiers only, but every man.

πελεμίζω, fut. ξω: Ep. aor. 1 πελέμιξα: aor. 1 pass. ἐπελεμίχθην: (πάλλω):—*to swing, shake, to make to shake, quiver* or *tremble:*—Pass. *to be shaken, to tremble, quake: to be driven away, flee trembling.*

πελεμίχθην, Ep. for ἐπελεμίχθην, aor. 1 pass. of πελεμίζω.

πελέσκεο, Ion. and Ep. 2 sing. impf. of πέλομαι.

πέλευ, Ep. 2 sing. imperat. of πέλομαι.

πεληιάς, άδος, ἡ, Ion. for πελειάς.

πελιδνός or **πελιτνός**, ή, όν, (πελιός) *livid.*

πελιός, ά, όν, (πελός) of the body, *discoloured by a bruise, livid.*

ΠΕ'ΛΛΑ Ion. **πέλλη**, ης, ἡ, *a wooden bowl, milk-pail,* Lat. *mulctra.* II. *a drinking-cup.*

ΠΕΛΛΟ'Σ or **πελός**, ή, όν, Lat. *PULLUS, dark-coloured, blackish, dusky.*

πέλομες, Dor. for πέλομεν, 1 pl. of πέλω.

Πελοποννήσιοι, οἱ, *the Peloponnesians.*

Πελοποννησιστί, Adv. *in the Peloponnesian* (i. e. *Dorian*) *dialect.* From

Πελοπόν-νησος, ἡ, = Πέλοπος νῆσος, *the Peloponnesus,* now the Morea.

πελός, ή, όν, v. πελλός.

Πέλοψ, οπος, ὁ, (πελός, ὄψ) *Pelops,* i. e. *dark-face,* son of Tantalus, said to have migrated from Lydia, and to have given his name to the Peloponnesus.

πελτάζω, f. σω, (πέλτη) *to serve as a targeteer.*

πελταστής, οῦ, ὁ, (πελτάζω) *one who bears a target* or *light shield* (πέλτη) instead of the large shield (ὅπλον), *a targeteer,* Lat. *cetratus:* they held a place between the ὁπλῖται or heavy-armed infantry, and the ψιλοί or light-armed troops. Hence

πελταστικός, ή, όν, *skilled in the use of the target:* τὸ πελταστικόν, = οἱ πελτασταί, *the body of targeteers.*

ΠΕ'ΛΤΗ, ἡ, *a small light shield without a rim* (ἴτυς), orig. used by the Thracians. 2. *a body of targeteers* (πελτασταί), as ἀσπίς for ἀσπισταί, ὅπλον for ὁπλῖται. II. *a shaft, pole* III. *a horse's ornament.*

πελτο-φόρος, ον, (πέλτη, φέρω) *bearing a target.*

ΠΕ'ΛΩ, more common as Dep. **πέλομαι**, only used in pres. and impf., which latter is used in syncop. forms, as 3 sing. impf., act. ἔπλεν for ἔπελεν; 2 sing. impf. med. ἔπλεο, ἔπλευ, for ἐπέλου; 3 sing. ἔπλετο for ἐπέλετο: the impf. is also lengthd. Ion. in 2 and 3 sing. πελέσκεο, πελέσκετο: imperat. πέλευ: the pres. part. is syncop. in the compds. ἐπιπλόμενος, περιπλόμενος, for ἐπιπελόμενος, περιπελόμενος, but does not occur in the simple form:—orig. *to be in motion, to go* or *come, rise;* κλαγγὴ πέλει οὐρανόθι πρό the cry *goes up* to heaven; γῆρας καὶ θάνατος ἐπ' ἀνθρώποισι πέλονται old age and death *come* upon men. II. *to be,* implying continuance, *to be used* or *wont to be: to become.*

ΠΕ'ΛΩΡ, τό, undeclined, *a monster,* of anything huge, but mostly in bad sense. Hence

πελώριος, α, ον, also ος, ον, = πελώρος, *monstrous, huge, immense;* τὰ πρὶν πελώρια *the mighty ones* of old.

πέλωρον, τό, = πέλωρ, *a monster;* πέλωρα θεῶν *portents* sent by the gods; strictly neut. of

πέλωρος, η, ον, (πέλωρ) *monstrous, prodigious, huge, portentous;* and so, *terrible:* neut. pl. as Adv., πέλωρα, *hugely, portentously.*

πέμμα, ατος, τό, (πέπεμμαι) *any kind of dressed food:* esp. in plur. *cakes, sweetmeats.*

πεμμᾰτ-ουργός, ὁ, (πέμμα, ἔργον) *a pastry-cook.*

πεμπάδ-αρχος, ὁ, (πεμπάς, ἄρχω) *a commander of a body of five.*

πεμπάζω, f. άσω, *to count on the five fingers, count by fives:* generally, *to count.* From

πεμπάς. άδος, ἡ, Aeol. for πεντάς, *the number five: a body of five.*

πεμπαστής, οῦ, ὁ, (πεμπάζω) *one who counts by fives:* generally, *one who counts,* μύρια πεμπαστής *reviewing by* tens of thousands.

πέμπε, Aeol. for πέντε, *five.*

πεμπέμεναι, **πεμπέμεν**, Ep. for πέμπειν.

πεμπταῖος, α, ον, (πέμπτος) *in five days, on the fifth day.*

πεμπτ-άμερος, ον, (πέμπτος, ἡμέρα) Dor. for πενθήμερος, *of five days.*

πεμπτέον, verb. Adj. of πέμπω, *one must send.*

πέμπτος, η, ον, (πέντε) *the fifth;* ἡ πέμπτη (sub. ἡμέρα) *the fifth day.*

πεμπτός, ή, όν, verb. Adj. of πέμπω, *sent.*

ΠΕ'ΜΠΩ fut. πέμψω: aor. 1 ἔπεμψα Ep. πέμψα: pf. πέπομφα:—Pass., aor. 1 ἐπέμφθην: pf. πέπεμμαι,

3 sing. πεπεμπται :—*to send, despatch.* II. *to send off* or *away, dismiss, send home;* χρὴ ξεῖνον παρεόντα φιλεῖν, ἐθέλοντα δὲ πέμπειν 'welcome the coming, *speed* the parting guest.' 2. of things, *to throw from one,* of missiles, *to shoot, dart, discharge.* III. *to convoy, attend, escort, conduct;* ὁ πέμπων *the conductor,* of Mercury; πομπὴν πέμπειν *to conduct* a procession 2. *to send with* one, esp. *to take* on a journey. IV. *to send up:* of the earth, *to produce.* V. Med., πέμπεσθαί τινα, *to send for* one. 2. *to send one's own* or *in one's own service.*

πεμπ-ώβολον, τό, (πέμπε, ὀβολός) *a five-pronged fork.*

πέμψειας, 2 sing. Aeol. aor. 1 opt. of πέμπω.

πεμψέμεναι, Ep. for πέμψειν, fut. inf. of πέμπω.

πέμψις, εως, ἡ, (πέμπω) *a sending: a mission.*

πεμψῶ, πεμψεῖ, Dor. for πέμψω, πέμψει.

πενέστερος, πενέστατος, Comp. and Sup. of πένης.

πενέστης, ου, ὁ, *a servant, labourer;* the πενέσται were the Thessalian *serfs* or *villains,* like the Εἵλωτες in Laconia, orig. a conquered tribe, afterwards increased by prisoners of war. II. generally, *any slave, bondsman, poor man.*

πένης, ητος, ὁ, (πένομαι) *one who earns his daily bread, a day-labourer,* hence *a poor man.* II. as Adj. *poor:* c. gen., like Lat. *egens,* πένης χρημάτων *poor in* money.—Comp. πενέστερος, Sup. πενέστατος.

πενητο-κόμος, ον, (πένης, κομέω) *tending the poor.*

πενθᾰλέος, α, ον, (πένθος) *sad, mourning.*

πένθεια, ἡ, collat. form of πένθος.

πενθείετον, Ep. for πενθεῖτον, 3 dual of πενθέω.

πενθερά, ἡ, fem. of πενθερός, *a mother-in-law,* Lat. *socrus.*

ΠΕΝΘΕΡΟ'Σ, ὁ, *a father-in law,* Lat. *socer;* also ἑκυρός. II. generally, *a connexion by marriage, brother-in-law.*

πενθέω, f. ήσω: Ep. 3 dual πενθείετον for πενθέετον, πενθεῖτον: pres. inf. πενθήμεναι for πενθεῖν: (πένθος) :—*to bewail, lament, mourn for.* Pass. *to be mourned for.* 2. *to deplore* a thing.

πένθημα, τό, (πενθέω) *lamentation, mourning.*

πενθήμεναι, Ep. inf. pres. of πενθέω.

πενθ-ήμερος, ον, (πέντε, ἡμέρα) *of, lasting five days:* πενθήμερον, τό, *a space of five days.*

πενθ-ημῐμερής, ές, (πέντε, ἡμιμερής) *consisting of five halves,* i. e. *of two and a half;* hence in Prosody, τομὴ πενθημιμερής the caesura *after two feet and a half,* as in Iamb. Trim., opp. to τομὴ ἑφθημιμερής the caesura *after three feet and a half.*

πενθ-ημῐποδιαῖος, α, ον, (πέντε, ἡμιπόδιον) *consisting of five half feet,* i. e. *of* $2\frac{1}{2}$ *feet.*

πενθήμων, ον gen. ονος, (πενθέω) *mournful, sorrowful, sad.*

πενθήρης, ες, (πένθος, ἀρᾰρεῖν) *lamenting, mourning.*

πενθητήρ, ῆρος, ὁ, ἡ, (πενθέω) *a mourner, wailer.*

πενθητήριος, α, ον, (πενθέω) *in sign of mourning.*

πενθήτρια, ἡ, fem. of πενθητήρ.

πενθῐκός, ή, όν, (πένθος) *of* or *for grief, mourning, sorrowful.* Adv., πενθικῶς ἔχειν τινός to be *in mourning* for a person.

πένθῐμος, ον, *in token of grief, mourning sorrowful.* II. *mournful, wretched.* From

ΠΕ'ΝΘΟΣ, εος, τό, *grief, sorrow: mourning for* the dead. II. *a misfortune.*

πενία Ion. -ίη, ἡ, (πένομαι) *poverty, need.*

πενιχρᾰλέος, α, ον, collat. form of πενιχρός, *poor.*

πενιχρός, ά, όν, like πένης, *poor, needy.*

ΠΕ'ΝΟΜΑΙ, only used in pres. and impf.: Dep. I. intr. *to work for one's living, to toil, work, labour:*— *to be poor* or *needy:* c. gen. *to be poor in, have need of.* II. trans. *to work at, prepare, be busy with.*

πενταδραχμία, ἡ, *five drachms.* From

πεντά-δραχμος, ον, (πέντε δραχμή) *of the weight* or *value of five drachms.*

πεντ-άεθλιον, τό, poët. for πεντάθλιον.

πέντ-αεθλον, τό, poët. for πένταθλον

πεντ-άεθλος, ὁ, poët. for πένταθλος.

πεντᾰετηρίς, ίδος, ἡ, *five years, a space of five years.* II. as Adj. *coming every five years, recurring at intervals of five years.* From

πεντᾰ-έτηρος, ον, poët. for πενταετής, *five years old.*

πεντᾰ-ετής, ές or **πεντα-έτης**, ες, (πέντε, ἔτος) *five years old.* II. of Time, *lasting five years:* hence πενταέτες, as Adv. *for five years.*

πεντ-άθλιον, τό, collat. form of πένταθλον.

πέντ-αθλον Ion. **πεντ-άεθλον**, τό, (πέντε, ἆθλον) *the contest of the five exercises;* πεντάεθλον ἀσκεῖν to practise *the five exercises.* These were ἅλμα, δίσκος, δρόμος, πάλη, πυγμή: but for the last the ἀκόντισις or ἄκων was substituted: the five are comprised in one Pentameter line,—ἅλμα, ποδώκειαν, δίσκον, ἄκοντα, πάλην.

πέντ-αθλος Ion. **πεντ-άεθλος**, ὁ, (πέντε, ἆθλον) *one who practises the* πένταθλον or *five exercises, the conqueror in them.* II. metaph. *one who tries his hand at everything, a 'jack-of-all-trades.'*

πέντ-αιχμος, ον, (πέντε, αἰχμή) *five-pointed.*

πεντάκις, Adv. (πέντε) *five times.*

πεντᾰκισ-μύριοι, αι, α, *five times* 10,000 = 50,000

πεντᾰκισ-χίλιοι, αι, α, *five times* 1000 = 5000.

πεντᾰκόσιοι Ep. **πεντηκόσιοι**, αι, α, (πέντε) *five hundred:* also in sing. with a collective noun, πεντακοσία ἵππος *five hundred* horse. II. at Athens, οἱ πεντακόσιοι, = ἡ βουλή, *the council of* 500, i. e. the senate chosen by lot (οἱ ἀπὸ κυάμου), fifty from each of the ten tribes.

πεντᾰκοσιο-μέδιμνος, ον, (πεντακόσιοι, μέδιμνος) *possessing land that produced* 500 *medimni yearly:* acc. to Solon's distribution of the Athenian citizens the πεντακοσιομέδιμνοι formed the first class the other three being the ἱππεῖς, ζευγῖται, θῆτες.

πεντᾰκοσιοστός, ή, όν, (πεντακόσιοι) *the five hundredth.*

πεντᾰ-κῡμία, ἡ, (πέντε, κῦμα) *the fifth wave,* supposed to be larger than the four preceding; cf. *τρικυμία*, *δεκακυμία*.

πεντᾰ-πάλαστος, *ον*, (*πέντε, παλαστή*) *five handbreadths wide.*

πεντά-πηχυς, *υ*, gen. *εος*, (*πέντε, πῆχυς*) *five cubits long* or *broad.*

πένταπλάσιος [ᾰ], *α, ον*, (*πέντε*) *fivefold.*

πενταπλήσιος, *η, ον*, Ion. for *πενταπλάσιος*.

πεντά-πολις, *ἡ*, (*πέντε, πόλις*) *a state of five towns*, as *Τρίπολις* was a state of three, *Δεκάπολις* of ten.

πεντάρ-ρᾱγος, *ον*, (*πέντε, ῥάξ*) *with five berries.*

πεντα-σπίθᾰμος, *ον*, (*πέντε, σπιθαμή*) *five spans long* or *broad.* [ῐ]

πεντά-στῖχος, *ον*, (*πέντε, στίχος*) *of five lines* or *verses.*

πεντά-στομος, *ον*, (*πέντε, στόμα*) *with five mouths* or *openings*, of the Nile and Danube.

πεντά-τευχος, *ον*, (*πέντε, τεῦχος*) *consisting of five books in one volume:* as Subst., *πεντάτευχος* (sc. *βίβλος*), *ἡ*, *the five books of Moses, Pentateuch.*

πεντᾰ-φῠής, *ές*, (*πέντε, φυή*) *five in nature* or *number.*

πένταχᾰ, Adv. (*πέντε*) *fivefold, five-ways, in five divisions.*

πενταχοῦ, Adv. (*πέντε*) *in five places.*

ΠΕ'ΝΤΕ Aeol. *πέμπε*, *οἱ, αἱ, τά*, indecl. *five.* Lat. *quinque.* In Compos. it takes the form *πεντα-* as well as *πεντε-*.

πεντε-καί-δεκα, *οἱ, αἱ, τά*, indecl. *fifteen.*

πεντεκαιδεκᾰ-νᾱΐα, *ἡ*, (*πεντεκαίδεκα, ναῦς*) *a squadron of fifteen ships.*

πεντεκαιδεκα-τάλαντος, *ον*, (*πεντεκαίδεκα, τάλαντον*) *of fifteen talents worth* or *weight.*

πεντε-και-δέκᾰτος, *η, ον*, *fifteenth.*

πεντεκαιδεκ-ήρης, *ες*, *with fifteen banks of oars.*

πεντε-σύριγγος, *ον*, (*πέντε, σύριγξ*) *with five pipes* or *holes; ξύλον πεντεσύριγγον* a wooden machine *furnished with five holes*, through which the head, arms, and legs of criminals were passed, a sort of *pillory.*

πεντε-τάλαντος, *ον*, (*πέντε, τάλαντον*) *worth five talents: for the recovery of five talents*, of a law-suit.

πεντ-ετηρίς, *ίδος, ἡ*, *a term* or *space of five years; διὰ πεντετηρίδος at intervals of five years, every five years.* II. *a festival celebrated every five years*, such as the *Panathenaea* at Athens. From

πεντ-έτης, *ες*, (*πέντε, ἔτος*) *of five years, lasting five years.*

πεντε-τρῐάζω, *to conquer five times.*

πεντήκοντα, *οἱ, αἱ, τά*, indecl. (*πέντε*) *fifty.*

πεντηκοντά-ετις, *ιδος, ἡ*, fem. of

πεντηκοντᾰ-ετής, *ές* or *-έτης, ες*, contr. *-ούτης*, (*πεντήκοντα, ἔτος*) *of fifty years, lasting for fifty years.*

πεντηκοντᾰ-κάρηνος, *ον*, (*πεντήκοντα. κάρηνον*) *fifty-headed.*

πεντηκοντᾰ-κέφᾰλος, *ον*, (*πεντήκοντα, κεφαλή*) = *πεντηκοντακάρηνος*.

πεντηκοντά-παις, *-παιδος, ὁ, ἡ*, *consisting of fifty children.*

πεντηκόντ-αρχος, *ὁ*, (*πεντήκοντα, ἄρχω*) *the commander of fifty men.* II. *one who commands a πεντηκόντορος, the captain of a penteconter.*

πεντηκόντερος, *ἡ*, = *πεντηκόντορος*.

πεντηκοντήρ, *ῆρος, ὁ*, (*πεντήκοντα*) *the commander of fifty men*, a title peculiar to the Spartan army.

πεντηκοντό-γῠος, *ον*, (*πεντήκοντα, γύα*) *of fifty acres of corn-land.*

πεντηκοντ-όργυιος, *ον*, (*πεντήκοντα, ὄργυια*) *fifty fathoms deep, high*, etc.

πεντηκόντορος, *ἡ*, with and without *ναῦς*, (*πεντήκοντα*) *a ship of burden with fifty oars.*

πεντηκοντ-ούτης, *ες*, contr. for *πεντηκονταέτης*.

πεντηκόσιοι, *αι, α*, Ep. for *πεντᾰκόσιοι*.

πεντηκοστεύω, f. *σω*, (*πεντηκοστή*) *to collect the tax πεντηκοστή* or *two per cent:*—Pass. *to pay the tax.*

πεντηκοστή, *ἡ*, see *πεντηκοστός*.

πεντηκοστήρ, *ῆρος, ὁ*, = *πεντηκοντήρ*.

πεντηκοστο-λόγος, *ον*, (*πεντηκοστή, λέγω*) *collecting the tax πεντηκοστή:* as Subst., *πεντηκοστολόγος, ὁ, the collector of the πεντηκοστή.*

πεντηκοστό-παις, *-παιδος, ὁ, ἡ*, (*πεντήκοντα, παῖς*) *with fifty children.*

πεντηκοστός, *ή, όν*, (*πεντήκοντα*) *fiftieth.* II as Subst., *πεντηκοστή, ἡ*, 1. (sub. *μερίς*), *the fiftieth part*, at Athens, *the tax of the fiftieth*, or *two per cent.*, imposed on all exports and imports. 2. (sub. *ἡμέρα*), *the fiftieth day after the Passover, the day of Pentecost.* Hence

πεντηκοστύς, *ύος, ἡ*, *the number fifty, a number of fifty*, as a division of the Spartan army.

πεντ-ήρης, *ες*, (*πέντε, ἐρέσσω*) *with five banks of oars:* as Subst., *πεντήρης* (sub. *ναῦς*), *ἡ*, *a quinquereme.*

πέντ-οζος, *ον*, (*πέντε, ὄζος*) *having five branches* or *points:* Hes. calls the hand *πέντοζον, the five-pointed.*

πεντ-όργυιος, *ον*, (*πέντε, ὄργυια*) *of five fathoms.*

πεντ-ώβολος, *ον*, (*πέντε, ὀβολός*) *of* or *worth five obols:* as Subst., *πεντώβολον, τό, a five-obol piece; πεντώβολον ἡλιάσασθαι* to sit in the court Heliaea *at five obols a day.*

πεξαμένη, aor. 1 med. part. fem. of **πέκω**.

πεξῶ. Dor. for *πέξω*, fut. of *πέκω*.

ΠΕ'ΟΣ, *εος, τό*, *membrum virile*, Lat. *penis.*

πεπᾰθυῖα, Ep. for *πεπονθυῖα*, pf. part. fem. of *πάσχω*.

πεπαίνω, f. *ᾰνῶ:* aor. 1 *ἐπέπᾱνα:* Pass., fut. *πεπανθήσομαι:* aor. 1 *ἐπεπάνθην:* pf. inf. *πεπάνθαι:* (*πέπων*):—*to ripen, make ripe* or *mellow:* of pain, etc., *to soothe, assuage, soften:*—Pass. *to become ripe, soft, mellow: to be softened.* II. intr. *to become ripe, mellow.*

πεπαίτερος, **πεπαίτατος**, irreg. Comp. and Sup. of *πέπων*.

πεπᾰλαγμένος, **πεπᾰλάχθαι**, pf. pass. part. and inf. of *παλάσσω*.

πεπάλακτο, 3 sing. plqpt. pass. of **παλάσσω**.

πεπάλαισμαι, pf. pass. of **παλαίω**.

πέπαλμαι, pf. pass. of **πάλλω**.

πεπᾰλών, Ep. redupl. aor. 2 part. of **πάλλω**.

πεπαμαι, pf. of πάομαι.

πέπᾰνος, ον, collat. form of πέπων, *ripe, mellow.*

πεπᾰρεῖν, an old aor. 2 inf. *to display, manifest.*

πέπαρμαι, pf. pass. of πείρω: inf. πεπάρθαι.

πεπαρμένος, pf. pass. part. of πείρω.

πεπάσθαι, pf. inf. of πατέομαι.

πεπᾶσθαι, pf. inf. of πάομαι, *to possess.*

πέπασμαι, πεπάσμην, pf. and plqpf. of πατέομαι.

πεπάχυσμαι, pf. pass. of παχύνω.

πεπείθαται, Ion. 3 pl. pf. pass. of πείθω.

πέπεικα, pf. of πείθω.

πέπειρος, ον, also fem. πέπειρᾰ, = πέπων, *ripe, mellow,* Lat. *maturus:* metaph. *mild, softened.*

πέπεισθῐ, 2 sing. pf. pass. imperat. of πείθω.

πέπεισμαι, pf. pass. of πείθω.

πεπέρασμαι, pf. pass. of περαίνω.

πεπερημένος, Ep. pf. part. pass. of περάω.

πέπηγα, pf. med. of πήγνυμι.

πεπίεσμαι, pf. pass. of πιέζω.

πεπῐθέσθαι, redupl. aor. 2 med. inf. of πείθω.

πεπῐθήσω, Ep. fut. of πείθω.

πέπῐθον, Ep. redupl. aor. 2 of πείθω; πεπίθωμεν 1 pl. subj.; πεπίθοιμεν, πεπίθοιεν 1 and 3 pl. opt.: inf. πεπῐθεῖν, fem. part. πεπῐθοῦσα.

πεπλᾰνημένως, Adv. pf. pass. part. of πλανάω, *roaming, wandering.*

πέπλασμαι, pf. pass. of πλάσσω.

πέπλευσμαι, pf. pass. of πλέω.

πεπληγέμεν, Ep. aor. 2 inf. of πλήσσω.

πέπληγον, πεπληγόμην, Ep. redupl. aor. 2 act. and med. of πλήσσω.

πεπληγώς, pf. part. of πλήσσω.

πέπλημαι, pf. pass. of πελάζω.

ΠΕΠΛΟΣ, ὁ, in Poets also with irreg. pl. πέπλα, τά, Lat. *peplum, any woven cloth* used for a covering, *a sheet, hanging, curtain.* II. *a large full robe* or *shawl* worn by women: esp. *the robe of Minerva,* which was carried in procession at the Panathenaic festival. III. also *a man's cloak* or *robe,* of the long Eastern dress.

πέπλῠμαι, pf. pass. of πλύνω: inf. πεπλύσθαι.

πέπλωμα, ατος, τό, (πέπλος) *a flowing robe, garment.*

πέπνῡμαι, poët. pf. pass. of πνέω, used as pres., *to have breath* or *soul;* metaph. *to be wise, discreet, prudent, sage;* 2 sing. πέπνῡσαι; inf. πεπνῦσθαι; 2 sing. plqpf. πέπνῡσο:—part. πεπνῡμένος used as Adj. *sage, wise, prudent.*

πεπνῡμένος, part. of πέπνυμαι.

πέποιθα, perf. med. of πείθω, *to trust, rely on.* Hence

πεποίθεα, Ep. for ἐπεποίθειν, plqpf. med. of πείθω.

πεποίθησις, ἡ, *trust, reliance, boldness.*

πεποιθοίην, opt. of πέποιθα.

πεποίθομεν, Ep. for πεποίθωμεν, 1 pl. subj. of πέποιθα.

πεποίθω, subj. of πέποιθα.

πεπόλιστο, Ep. 3 sing plqpf. pass. of πολίζω.

πέπομαι, pf. pass. of πίνω.

πεπόνητο, Ep. 3 sing. plqpf. pass. of πονέω.

πέπονθα, pf. 2 of πάσχω.

πέπορθα, pf. med. of πέρθω.

πέποσθε, Ep. for πεπόνθατε, 2 pl. pf. of πάσχω.

πεποτήαται, Ep. for πεποτήνται, 3 pl. pf. of ποτάομαι: **πεποτῆσθαι**, inf. of same.

πέπρᾱγα, pf. 2 of πράσσω.

πέπραγμαι, pf. pass. of πράσσω.

πέπρᾱκα, πέπρᾱμαι, pf. act. and pass. of πιπράσκω.

πέπρισμαι, pf. pass. of πρίω.

πέπρωται, πέπρωτο, 3 sing. pf. and plqpf. pass. of an obsol. Verb *πόρω (from which also comes aor. 2 ἔπορον):—*it has, had been fated;* part. πεπρωμένος, *fated:* ἡ πεπρωμένη (sub. μοῖρα), *that which is fated, fate, destiny,* like εἱμαρμένη.

πέπτᾰμαι, pf. pass. of πετάννυμι: part. πεπταμενος.

πεπτέαται, for πέπτανται, 3 pl. pf. pass. of πετάννυμι.

πεπτεῶτα, for πεπτῶτα, pf. part. nom. and acc. neut. of πίπτω.

πεπτηώς, Ep. for πεπτηκώς, pf. part. of πτήσσω, *frightened, timid, shy.*

πέπτωκα, pf. of πίπτω.

πεπτώς, Att. pf. part. of πίπτω.

πέπτω, see πέσσω.

πεπύθοιτο [ῠ], 3 sing. Ep. redupl aor. 2 opt. of πυνθάνομαι.

πεπῠκασμένος, pf. pass. part. of πυκάζω.

πέπυσμαι, pf. of πυνθάνομαι: inf. πεπύσθαι.

πέπυστο, Ep. 3 sing. plqpf. of πυνθάνομαι.

πέπωκα, pf. of πίνω.

ΠΕΠΩΝ, ον, gen. ονος; Comp. and Sup. πεπαίτερος, -τατος:—of fruit, *ripe, mellow,* Lat. *mitis, maturus.* II. metaph. *soft, tender, gentle:* also *softened, assuaged:* often used in addressing a person, ὦ πέπον, as Subst., *oh my friend:* so, κριὲ πέπον my *pet* ram: in bad sense, ὦ πέπονες *ye weaklings, ye dastards.*

ΠΕΡ, enclit. Particle, adding force to the word to which it is annexed: *much, very,* often with an Adj. and the part. of εἰμί, ἐπεί μ' ἔτεκές γε μινυνθάδιόν περ ἐόντα since you have given birth to me *all* short-lived as I am: also with an Adj. only, κρατερός περ strong *as he is;* or with an Adv., μίνυνθά περ, for a *very* little time; ὀλίγον περ little *as it is.* 2. to call attention to something objected to, *albeit, though, however;* so, λιγύς περ ἐὼν ἀγορητής *however* loud-tongued a talker he be. 3. also to strengthen a negation, οὐδέ περ, *no, not even, not at all,* where, as in Lat. *ne .. quidem,* οὐδέ is divided by one or more words from περ. II. to call attention to one or more things, *however, at any rate, yet,* as, ἄλλους περ ἐλέαιρε pity others *at any rate.* III. περ is often attached to a relat. Pron., Adj. or Adv., as ὅσπερ, ἧπερ, διόπερ, ὥσπερ, etc.

πέρᾱ, Adv. *beyond, across* or *over, further,* Lat. *ultra;* μέχρι τοῦ μέσου πέρα δ' οὔ as far as the middle, but no *further.* II. of Time, *beyond, longer:* c. gen., πέρα μεσούσης ἡμέρας *beyond* midday. III. metaph. *beyond measure, excessively:* c. gen., πέρα δίκης *beyond all* justice. IV. absol. expressing *something greater*; ἄπιστα καὶ πέρα κλύων hearing things incredible, and *more than that.*

περᾶαν, Ep. for περᾶν, pres. inf. of περάω.

περάασκε, Ion. 3 sing. impf. of περάω.

πέρᾱθεν Ion. **πέρηθεν**, Adv. (πέρα) *from beyond, from the far side.*

περαίνω: aor. 1 ἐπέρᾱνα: Pass., aor. 1 ἐπεράνθην: pf. πεπέρασμαι, inf. πεπέρανθαι: (πέρας) :—*to bring to an end, finish, complete: to bring about, accomplish*:—Pass. *to be brought to an end, be finished; to be fulfilled, accomplished.* 2. περαίνειν λόγον *to end* a discourse: hence absol. *to conclude, come to an end.* II. intr. *to extend, reach,* or *penetrate.*

περαῖος, α, ον, (πέραν) *being* or *dwelling beyond*, esp. *beyond the sea* or *river.* II. ἡ περαίη (sub. γῆ or χώρα) as Subst., *the country beyond the sea* or *river*: *the country over against* or *opposite.* Hence

περαιόω, f. ώσω: aor. 1 ἐπεραίωσα: Pass., f. περαιωθήσομαι: aor. 1 ἐπεραιώθην: pf. πεπεραίωμαι:—*to carry* or *convey to the opposite country* or *bank, carry over* or *across*:—Pass. *to pass over, cross.* II. intr. in Act. *to cross, pass over.*

περαίτερος, α, ον, Comp. of πέρα, *beyond, further*; ὁδοὶ περαίτεραι roads *leading further*: Adv. περαιτέρω: also neut. περαίτερον, *further, beyond.*

πέρᾱν Ion. and Ep. **πέρην**, Adv. (πέρα) *on the other side of, across*, Lat. *trans*, c. gen. 2. absol. *over, to* or *on the opposite side*; πέραν εἰς τὴν Ἀσίαν διαβῆναι to cross *over* into Asia. II. *over against*, c. gen., as, Χαλκίδος πέραν. III. sometimes = πέρα, *out beyond.*

περαντικός, ή, όν, (περαίνω) *conclusive.*

περ-άπτω, Aeol. for περιάπτω.

πέρᾰς, ᾰτος, τό, (πέρα) *an end, extremity: an end, issue, termination*: as Adv., *at last.* 2. in a racecourse, *the goal*, Lat. *meta.* II. metaph. *accomplishment, the power of accomplishing.*

περάσιμος, ον, (περάω) *that may be crossed* or *traversed, passable.* [ᾱ]

πέρᾱσις, ἡ, (περάω) *a going beyond, passing*; βίου πέρασις *passage* from life (to death).

πέρᾰτος, η, ον, (πέρα) *on the opposite side*, Lat. *ulterior.* II. ἡ περάτη (sub. γῆ or χώρα) as Subst., *the opposite country*, also *the opposite quarter of the heavens*, esp. of *the west*, as opp. to the east.

περᾱτός Ion. **περητός**, ή, όν, (περάω) like περάσιμος, *that may be crossed* or *passed over.*

περάω (A), inf. περᾶν Ep. περάαν: Ion. impf. περάασκον: fut. περάσω [ᾱ] Ion. περήσω, Ep. inf. περησέμεναι: aor. 1 ἐπέρᾱσα Ion. ἐπέρησα: pf. πεπέρᾱκα (πέρα): I. trans. *to drive right across* or *through.* 2. *to pass across* or *through, to pass over, cross, traverse*; τάφρος ἀργαλέη περάαν a ditch hard *to pass*; metaph., κίνδυνον περᾶν *to pass through* a danger; περᾶν ὅρκον *to go through* or *recite* the terms of an oath. 2. *to let go through.* II. intr. *to penetrate* or *pierce right through: to extend, reach.* 2 *to pass right across* or *through, pass, traverse, go through,* or *over.* 3. c. gen. *to exceed, go beyond in.*

περάω (B): fut. περάσω [ᾰ] Ep. περάσσω Att. περῶ: aor. 1 ἐπέρᾰσα Ep. ἐπέρασσα: pf. pass. πεπέρημαι: (πέρα) :—*to carry beyond seas for sale*, hence *to sell*, mostly *to sell as slaves*; περᾶν τινὰ Λῆμνον *to sell* one *to* Lemnos.

Περγᾰμία, ἡ, = Πέργαμι

Πέργᾰμος, ἡ, *Pergamos*, the citadel of Troy: also in pl. Πέργαμα, τά. II. πέργαμα, τά, as appellat., like ἀκρόπολις, *the citadel* of any town.

ΠΕΡΔΙΞ, ῑκος or ῐκος, ὁ and ἡ, *the partridge*, Lat. *perdix, -icis.*

ΠΕ'ΡΔΟΜΑΙ, Dep., with act. aor. 2 ἔπαρδον, pf. πέπορδα:—*to break wind.*

πεοεμμένον, Aeol. for πεοιειμένον, pf. pass. part. of περιέννυμι.

πέρηθεν, Adv., Ion. for πέραθεν.

πέρην, Adv., Ion. for πέραν.

περησέμεναι, Ep. for περήσειν, fut. inf. of περάω.

περητός, ή, όν, Ion. for περᾱτός.

πέρθαι, Ep. aor. 2 pass. inf. of πέρθω.

ΠΕ'ΡΘΩ, fut. πέρσω: pf. πέπορθα: aor. 1 ἔπερσα: aor. 2 ἔπρᾰθον, inf. πρᾰθεῖν Ep. πρᾰθέειν:—Pass. with fut. med. πέρσομαι: Ep. aor. 2 inf. πέρθαι, like δέχθαι from δέχομαι:—*to waste, ravage, sack, rase.* 2. of persons, *to destroy, kill, slay.* 3. of things, *to destroy.* II. *to get by plunder.*

ΠΕΡΙ', Prep., with gen., dat., et acc.: Radic. sense, *all around, about.*

With Genitive: I. of Place, *around, about, near.* II. Causal, *about, concerning, on, of*; περὶ νόστου ἄκουσα I have heard *of* his return; λέγειν περί τινος to speak *of* a subject. 2. *about, for, on account of*; βουλεύειν περὶ φόνου to lay plans *for* the slaying. 3. of *contending for* an object; περὶ θανόντος *for* the dead; θεῖν περὶ ψυχῆς to run *for* one's life; μάχεσθαι περὶ πτόλιος to fight *for* the city. 4. of the *motive*; περὶ ἔριδος μάρνασθαι to fight *for* very enmity's *sake.* 5. with a Subst., *as to, in reference to, with regard to, about*; ἀριθμοῦ πέρι *as to* number. III. like Lat. *prae, before, above, beyond*; περὶ πάντων ἔμμεναι ἄλλων to be *above* or *before* all the rest: in this sense, the Prep. is often divided from its gen. IV. the following phrases are of common occurrence: περὶ πολλοῦ ἐστιν ἡμῖν, it is *of* much consequence to us; περὶ πολλοῦ ποιεῖσθαι or ἡγεῖσθαί τι, to reckon a thing *worth* much; περὶ πλείονος, περὶ ὀλίγου, περὶ οὐδενὸς ποιεῖσθαι to reckon a thing *of* more, *of* little, *of* no *consequence.*

With Dative of the object, about, or near which a thing is, *around, about*: I. of Place, *around, round about*; περὶ χροΐ *close round* the skin; χεὶρ περὶ ἔγχεϊ the hand *round, grasping* the spear; ἀσπαίρειν περὶ δουρί to quiver *round* or *on* the spear. 2. *hard by, near*, always of several, as encompassing *round about* one. II. Causal, of an object *for* which one fights; μάχεσθαι περὶ οἷσι κτεάτεσσι to fight *for* one's own possessions. 2. of anxiety, care, or confidence about a thing, *for, about, on account* of. 3. *by reason of*, like Lat. *prae;* περὶ φόβῳ *for* fear; περὶ χάρματι *for* joy.

With Accus. of the object round about which a thing goes or moves: I. of Place, *about, around, near, by;* ἡ περὶ Κνίδον ναυμαχία the sea-fight *off* Cnidos; περὶ τὰ ἕλεα οἰκέουσι they dwell *all about* the marshes; πλεῦνες περὶ ἕνα many *round about* one, many *to* one. II. of persons *who are about one*, as attendants, comrades, like οἱ ἀμφί τινα; τὰ περί τι all that *belongs to* a thing. III. of the object *with which one is occupied*, esp. of the place; περὶ δόρπα πονεῖσθαι to be busy *about* supper: metaph., ἡ φιλοσοφία περὶ ἀλήθειάν ἐστι philosophy is occupied *about* or *with* truth. 2. *in relation* or *reference to, with regard to;* τὰ περὶ τὸν Κῦρον οὕτως ἐγένετο the circumstances *relating to* Cyrus turned out thus. IV. of Time, *about*, Lat. *circa;* περὶ τούτους χρόνους: also of numbers, περὶ τρισχιλίους *about* 3000.

In Position, περί may follow its Subst. in all cases, and then it becomes paroxyt. πέρι.

As Adv., περί, *around, about*, also *near, by*. II. also πέρι, with accent thrown back, *before, above, exceedingly, above measure:* so in phrases, πέρι κῆρι, πέρι θυμῷ *beyond measure in* heart or soul; where πέρι must not be taken as Prep. with the dat.

Πέρι sometimes stands for περίεστι.

In Compos. all its chief senses recur: *around, about*, as in περι-βάλλω, περι-έχω, περι-βαίνω. II. *a going beyond, exceeding*, as in περι-γίγνομαι, περι-εργάζομαι. III. *beyond measure, very, exceedingly*, as in περι-καλλής, περι-δείδω, like Lat. *per-* in *per-multus, per-gratus*.

Quantity. Though ι in περί is short, yet it is not properly elided before a vowel.

περι-αγγέλλω, f. -αγγελῶ, *to announce by a message sent round:* absol. *to send* or *carry a message round.* II. c. dat. et inf. *to send round orders for* people *to* do something; π. παρασκευάζεσθαι *to send orders round* to make ready; π. ναῦς *to order* ships.

περι-āγής, , (περί, ἔāγα) *broken in pieces.* II. Dor. for περιηγής.

περι-άγνῡμι and -ύω, f. -άξω, *to break all round, break in pieces:*—Pass., ὀψ περιάγνυται the voice *is echoed all round.*

περι-άγω, f. -άξω, *to lead round, drive round;* c. acc. loci, περιάγουσι τὴν λίμνην κύκλῳ *they drive round* the lake in a circle. 2. *to lead about with one:* so also in Med. 3. *to turn round:* also *to twist* or *wrench round.* II. intr. *to go round;* περιάγειν τὰς πόλεις *to go round* the cities. [ᾰ] Hence

περιᾰγωγεύς, έως, ὁ, *a machine for twisting round, a tourniquet.*

περιαγωγή, ἡ, (περιάγω) *a turning round, revolution.*

περιαιρετός, ή, όν, *able to be taken off.* From

περι-αιρέω: f. περιαιρήσω: aor. 2 περιεῖλον, inf. περιελεῖν:—*to take away all round*, as the walls of a city, or the earthen mould in which gold has been cast: generally, *to take off* or *away:* c. gen. pass. *to strip* a thing *off* one. II. Med. *to take off from oneself;* περιαιρεῖσθαι κυνέην *to take off* one's helmet; βιβλίον περιαιρεόμενος *taking the cover off* one's letter; but it is often used just like the Act. III. Pass. *to be stripped off* or *taken away from* one· also *to have* a thing *taken away from one.*

περι-αλγέω, f. ήσω, *to be greatly distressed.*

περι-αλείφω, f. ψω, *to anoint* or *smear all over.*

περι-άλλος, ον, (περί, ἄλλος) *beyond* or *before others*.—neut. pl. περίαλλα as Adv., *before all: exceedingly.*

περι-ᾰλουργός, όν, (περί, ἁλουργός) *dyed with purple all round:* metaph., κακοῖς περιαλουργός *double-dyed* in villany.

περίαμμα, ατος, τό, (περιάπτω) *anything fastened round one, an amulet.*

περι-αμπέχω, f. -αμφέξω: aor. 2 περιήμπεσχον:—*to put round about:*—Med. *to put around one, to put on.* II. *to cover all round.*

περι-αμπίσχω, impf. -ήμπισχον, = περιαμπέχω.

περίαπτος, ον, *hung about* or *upon:*—as Subst., περίαπτον, τό, = περίαμμα. From

περι-άπτω, f. ψω, *to fasten about, attach to:*—Med. *to put round oneself, to gain for oneself*

περι-αρμόζω Att. -όττω, f. όσω, *to fasten* or *fit on all round:*—Pass. *to have fastened round* or *fitted on.*

περι-αστράπτω, f. ψω, *to lighten* or *flash all round.*

περι-ασχολέω, f. ήσω, *to be busy about a thing.*

περι-αυχένιος, ον, (περί, αὐχήν) *worn round the neck;* as Subst., περιαυχένιον, τό, *a necklace.*

περίᾰχον, Ep. for περίαχον, impf. of περιάχω.

περι-βαίνω, f. -βήσομαι: aor. 2 περιέβην: pf. περιβέβηκα:—*to go round about* or *to bestride* one who has fallen, so as to defend him: c. gen., περιβῆναι ἀδελφειοῦ κταμένοιο *to stand over* his slain brother: of sound, *to float around.*

περι-βάλλω, f. -βᾰλῶ: aor. 2 περιέβᾰλον: pf. περιβέβληκα:—*to throw round, about*, or *over, put on* or *over, invest with;* περιβάλλειν τινὰ χαλκεύματι *to fix* him *round* a sword, i. e. to stab him. 2. Med., with pf. pass. περιβέβλημαι, *to throw round* or *over oneself, put on:* *to throw round oneself for defence, enclose around:* c. dupl. acc., τεῖχος περιβάλλεσθαι πόλιν, *to build* a wall *round* a city. II. metaph. *to put round* or *upon* a person, *invest* with. 2. *to attribute* or *ascribe* to a person. 3. *to surround, encompass, enclose with* a thing: metaph. *to involve* or *implicate* in evils, etc. 4. c. acc only, *to embrace, encompass, surround;* περιβάλλει με σκότος darkness *encompasses* me. 5. of ships, *to fetch a compass round, double.* 6. *to frequent, be fond of* a place. III. in Med. *to embrace for oneself, to compass, aim at*, Lat. *affectare:* pf. pass. *to be in* *possession of.* IV. *to throw beyond: beat in throwing:* generally, *to beat, excel.*

περι-βᾱρίδες, αἱ, (περί, βᾶρις) a sort of *women's shoes.*

περί-βᾰρυς, υ, gen. εος, *exceeding heavy.*

περιβάς, ᾶσα, άν, aor. 2 part. of περιβαίνω.

περιβέβλημαι, pf. pass. of περιβάλλω

περίβη, Ep. for περιέβη, 3 sing. aor. 2 of περιβαίνω.

περιβῆναι, aor. 2 inf. of περιβαίνω.

περίβλεπτος, ον, (περιβλέπω) *looked at from all sides, gazed at, notable.*

περι-βλέπω, f. ψω, intr. *to look round about, gaze around.* II. trans. *to look at on all sides, look much at:* hence *to gaze on, survey, admire:*—Pass. *to be looked at, admired, looked up to.*

περίβλητος, ον, (περιβάλλω) *put round* or *on.*

περιβόητος, ον, (περιβοάω) *noised abroad, notorious,* in good or bad sense: hence either *famous, extolled:* or *exclaimed against.* I. act. *with loud cries.*

περιβόλαιον, τό, (περιβάλλω) *that which is put round one, a covering, garment.*

περιβολή, ἡ, (περιβάλλω) *anything thrown* or *put round;* περιβολὴ ξίφεος *the sheath* of a sword: *walls thrown round* a town. II. *a space enclosed, compass.* III. *a circumference, circuit.* IV. metaph. *a compassing, aiming at.*

περίβολος, ον, (περιβάλλω) *going round, compassing, encircling.* II. as Subst., περίβολος, ὁ, = περιβολή, *anything thrown round;* οἱ περίβολοι *walls thrown round a town.* 2. *an enclosure, circuit, compass.*

περι-βομβέω, f. ήσω, *to hum round.*

περί-βουνος, ον, *surrounded by hills.*

περι-βρᾰχῑόνιον, τό, (περί, βραχίων) *an armlet* or *piece of armour for the arm.*

περι-βρύχιος, α, ον, (περί, βρύχιος) *surging all round.* [ῠ]

περί-βωτος, ον, Ion. for περιβόητος.

περι-γίγνομαι, Ion. and later form **-γίνομαι** [ῑ]: fut. -γενήσομαι: aor. 2 -εγενόμην:—*to be over* or *above:* I. *to be superior, prevail over, overcome, excel: to be better* or *more advantageous,* c. gen. II. *to live over; to survive, get over, escape from.* 2. of things, *to remain over and above.* 3. also *to remain as a result* or *consequence, to result* or *proceed from:* cf. περίειμι (εἰμί *sum*).

περι-γλᾰγής, ές, (περί, γλάγος) *full of milk.*

περι-γληνάομαι, Dep. (περί, γλήνη):—*to turn round the eyeballs, glare around.*

περί-γλωσσος, ον, (περί, γλῶσσα) *eloquent.*

περι-γνάμπτω, f. ψω, *to bend round, fetch a compass round, double* a headland.

περι-γογγύζω, f. σω, *to mutter* or *whisper round about.*

περίγραμμα ατος, τό, (περιγράφω) *anything marked round by a line, an enclosure, ring.*

περιγραπτός όν, (περιγράφω) *marked round, fenced in, enclosed.*

περιγρᾰφή, ἡ, *a marking round: an outline, sketch: an impression, print.* From

περι-γράφω, f. ψω, *to draw a line round, mark round, circumscribe;* περιγράφειν κύκλον *to draw* a circle *round.* 2. *to define, determine.* II. *to draw in outline, sketch out,* Lat. *delineare.* III. *to enclose within brackets, to strike out, cancel.*

περίδδεισα, Ep. for περιέδεισα, aor. 1 of περιδείδω.

περι-δέδρομα, pf. of περιτρέχω.

περι-δεής, ές, (περί, δέος) *very timid* or *fearful:* Adv. -ῶς, *in great fear.*

περιδείδια, Ep. pf. of περιδείδω.

περι-δείδω, f. -δείσομαι: aor. 1 περιέδεισα Ep. περίδδεισα, part. περιδδείσας: pf. περιδέδοικα Ep. περιδείδια:—*to fear very much, be in great fear* or *dread about* one.

περί-δειπνον, τό, (περί, δεῖπνον) *a funeral feast.*

περι-δέξιος, ον, like ἀμφιδέξιος, *using both hands alike,* Lat. *ambi-dexter.* II. generally, *very dexterous, versatile,* or *expert.*

περι-δέρκομαι, Dep. I. intr. *to look round about, gaze about.* II. trans. *to look earnestly at.*

περι-δέω, f. -δήσω, *to bind, tie round* or *on:*—Med. *to bind round oneself, put on.*

περι-δήρῑτος, ον, (περί, δηρίω) *fought for, disputed.*

περι-δίδωμι, Ion. 2 and 3 sing. -διδοῖς, -διδοῖ: f. -δώσω:—*to give round.* II. Med. περιδίδομαι, fut. -δώσομαι: aor. 2 -εδόμην:—*to stake* or *wager,* c. gen. rei; τρίποδος περιδώμεθον *let us make a wager of* a tripod; ἐμέθεν περιδώσομαι αὐτῆς *I will wager for* myself, i. e. *pledge* myself; περιδίδομαι περὶ τῆς κεφαλῆς *I stake* my head: absol., περίδου νῦν ἐμοί come now, *lay a wager* with me.

περι-δῑνέω, f. ήσω, *to whirl* or *wheel round:*—Pass. *to whirl oneself round, run round and round: to spin round,* like a top; περιδινηθήτην, Ep. 3 dual aor. 1.

περῐ-δῑνής, ές, (περιδινέω) *whirled round.*

περι-δίω, old Ep. form for περιδείδω: *to be much afraid* about one.

περίδου, aor. 2 imper. med. of περιδίδωμι.

περίδρᾰμον, Ep. for περιέδραμον, aor. 2 of περιτρέχω.

περι-δράσσομαι, Dep. *to grasp round with the hand.*

περι-δρομάς, άδος, fem. of περίδρομος, *surrounding, encompassing.*

περιδρομή, ἡ, (περίδρομος) *a running round and round, a circuit.* 2. *a revolution, orbit.*

περίδρομος, ον, (περιδραμεῖν) *running round, surrounding: circular.* 2. *going about, roaming.* 3. pass. *that can be run round, standing detached.* II. as Subst., περίδρομος, ὁ, like περιδρομή, *that which surrounds* or *encompasses:* as 1. *the string that runs round a net for closing it.* 2. *a gallery running round a building.* 3. *the rim of a shield.*

περι-δρύπτω, f. ψω, *to tear all round about:*—Pass., Ep. 3 sing. aor. 1 περιδρύφθη, *he had the skin torn off all round.*

περι-δύω, f. -ύσω, *to pull off from around, strip off*

περιδώμεθον, 1 dual aor. 2 med. subj. of περιδίδωμι.

περι-εδέετο, 3 sing. plqpf. pass. of περιδέω.

περι-έζωσμαι, pf. pass. of περιζώννυμι.

περι-εῖδον, aor. 2 with no pres. in use, περιοράω being used instead:—*to look about for, await.* 2. *to overlook, neglect, disregard,* hence also *to let pass, allow, suffer.* II. pf. περίοιδα with pres. sense; plqpf. περιῄδειν with impf. sense, Att. περιῄδη; inf. περιειδέναι Ep. περιίδμεναι: *to know* or *understand better; βουλῇ περιίδμεναι ἄλλων to be better* in counsel *than* others.

περιειλάς, άδος, ἡ, (περιείλω) *wound round, encircling.*

περι-ειλίσσω, Ion. for περιελίσσω.

περιεῖλον, aor. 2 of περιαιρέω.

περι-είλλω or -ειλέω, *to fold* or *wrap round*:—Pass. *to be wrapped round.* 2. *to wrap up.*

περί-ειμι, (περί, εἰμί sum) *to be around; τὰ περιόντα circumstances.* II. *to be better than* or *superior to* another, *surpass.* 2. *to exceed in number, outnumber.* III. *over-live, outlive*: absol. *to survive*: of things, *to be extant.* 2. of property, *to be over and above, to remain in hand.* IV. *to remain as a result* or *consequence, come about, ensue*: cf περιγίγνομαι.

περί-ειμι, (περί, εἶμι ibo) *to go round* or *about, fetch a compass.* 2. c. acc. *to go round, compass; περιιέναι φυλακάς to go the rounds* of the guards. II. *to come round to* in turn. III. of Time, χρόνου περιιόντος as time *came round.*

περι-είρω, *to insert* or *fix round.*

περιέκρῠβεν, 3 sing. aor. 2 act. or 3 pl. aor. 2 pass. of περικρύπτω.

περιέλᾰσις, εως, ἡ, *a driving* or *riding round*: *a place for driving round.* From

περι-ελαύνω, fut. -ελάσω: aor. 1 -ήλᾰσα: pf. -ελήλᾰκα:—*to drive round, push about,* of cups. 2. *to drive about, harass, distress.* II. (sub. ἅρμα, ἵππον, etc.) *to drive* or *ride round.*

περιελεῖν, aor. 2 inf. of περιαιρέω.

περι-ελίσσω Att. -ττω Ion. -ειλίσσω:—f. ξω:—*to roll* or *wind round*:—Med. *to roll round oneself.*

περι-έλκω, f. -ελκύσω [ῠ], *to drag round* or *about.*

περι-έννῡμι, *to put round*:—Med. *to draw round one.*

περιεπατήκει, 3 sing. plqpf. of περιπατέω.

περιέπεσον, aor. 2 of περιπίπτω.

περι-έπω: impf. περιεῖπον: fut. περιέψω: aor. 2 περιέσπον, inf. περισπεῖν: fut. med. inf. περιέψεσθαι: aor. 1 pass. inf. περιεφθῆναι:—*to be busy about, tend diligently, take care of*: of persons, *to treat with attention; εὖ περιέπειν τινά to treat* a man well; but, τρηχέως περιέπειν *to handle* roughly:—so in Pass., τρηχέως περιεφθῆναι ὑπό τινας *to be* roughly *handled* by one; καλῶς περιέπεσθαι *to be* well *treated*:—also, περιέπειν τινὰ ὡς or ἅτε πολέμιον *to treat* one as an enemy.

περι-εργάζομαι, f. -σομαι: pf. -είργασμαι: Dep.:—*to waste one's labour; to be employed overmuch* about a thing, *to be over-officious; τῷ θυλάκῳ περιειργάσθαι* (pf. inf.) *that they had overdone it* with their 'sack' (i. e. need not have used the *word*). 2. *to meddle, interfere, be officious.*

περί-εργος, ον, (περί, ἔργον) *over-careful, taking needless trouble*: *τὰ περίεργα curious arts.* 2. *meddling, interfering, officious* II. pass. *overwrought, elaborate, expensive.* 2. *superfluous.*

περι-έργω Att. -είργω, f. ξω, *to enclose all round, encompass.*

περι-ερρύην, aor. 2 pass. of περιρρέω.

περι-έρρω, *to wander* or *ramble about.*

περι-έρχομαι, impf. περιηρχόμην: f. -ελεύσομαι: aor. 2 -ῆλθον: pf. -ελήλυθα:—*to go round, go about*: esp. *to go about canvassing,* like Lat. *ambire*: c. acc. loci, *to go round, visit in succession.* 2. of Time, *to come round.* II. *to go round and return* to a spot, *to come round to; ἡ τίσις περιῆλθε τὸν Πανιώνιον* vengeance *came at last upon* him. III. c. acc. pers., like Lat. *circumvenire, to come round, overreach, cheat.*

περι-εσθίω, f. -έδομαι, *to gnaw round about.*

περιέσκεμμαι, pf. pass. of περισκοπέω.

περιεσπᾶτο, 3 sing. impf. pass. of περισπάω.

περί-εσσι, Ep. for περί-ει, 2 sing. of περίειμι (εἰμί sum).

περιεστώς, pf. part. of περιΐστημι.

περιέσχον, aor. 2 of περιέχω

περι-έσχᾰτος, η, ον, *about the last.*

περι-έφθος, ον, (περί, ἑφθός,) *thoroughly boiled.*

περι-έχω: f. περιέξω and περισχήσω: aor. 2 περιέσχον, inf. περισχεῖν: aor. 2 med. περιεσχόμην, inf. περισχέσθαι:—*to hold around, encompass, embrace, surround*: of a city, *to beleaguer* or *blockade.* II. like περίειμι (εἰμί sum) II, *to be superior to, surpass, overcome*: esp. *to outnumber, to outflank.* III. Med. *to clasp round,* and so *to take charge of, to protect.* 2. *to hold fast on by, to cling to, cleave to.* 3. *to be pressing, urgent with.*

περι-ζᾰμενῶς, Adv. (περί, ζαμενής) *very powerfully* or *violently.*

περι-ζέω poët. -ζείω, f. -ζέσω, *to boil round about*

περί-ζῠγος, ον, also **περίζυξ**, ῠγος, ὁ, ἡ, (περί, ζυγόν) *over and above a pair, more than a pair*: so, of horses' harness, περίζυγα are *spare straps.*

περίζωμα, ατος, τό, *an apron.* From

περι-ζώννῡμι or -ύω: f. -ζώσω: *to gird round*:—Med. *to gird round oneself, put on as a belt* or *apron.* Hence

περιζωσάμενος, aor. 1 med. part.

περι-ζώστρα, ἡ, (περί, ζῶστρον) *a girdle, apron.*

περι-ηγέομαι, f. -ήσομαι, Dep. *to lead round about, shew the way round.* Hence

περιηγής, ές, (περιάγω) *drawn round, lying in a circle, forming a circle*: *circular.*

περιήγησις, εως, ἡ, like περιγραφή, *a sketch, outline*: generally, *a form, figure.*

περιῄδη, Att. plqpf. of περιοίδα: see περιεῖδον.

περι-ήκω, f. ξω, *to have come round to one, to have*

arrived at last: c. acc., τὰ σὲ περιήκοντα *that which has come round to* thee, *fallen upon* thee.

περιῆλθον, aor. 2 of περιέρχομαι.

περιήλῠσις, ἡ, (περιέρχομαι) *a coming round, revolution.*

περι-ημεκτέω, f. ήσω, *to be greatly aggrieved* or *disconcerted* at a thing, c. dat.: c. gen. pers. *to be greatly aggrieved at* or *with him.* (The deriv. of ἡμεκτέω is uncertain.)

περιήνεικα, Ion. aor. 1 of περιφέρω.

περι-ηχέω, f. ήσω, *to echo* or *ring all round.*

περι-θαλπής, ές, (περί, θάλπος) *very warm* or *hot.*

περιθείς, εῖσα, έν, aor. 2 part. of περιτίθημι.

περίθεσις, εως, ἡ, (περιτίθημι) *a placing* or *putting round, putting on.*

περιθετός, ή, όν, and **περίθετος**, ον, (περιτίθημι) *put round, put on, assumed,* of false hair.

περι-θέω, f. -θεύσομαι, *to run round.*

περι-θεωρέω, f. ήσω, *to go round and observe.*

περί-θῡμος, ον, (περί, θυμός) *very wrathful.* Adv., περιθύμως ἔχειν to be *very angry.*

περι-ιάπτω, f. ψω, *to wound all round.*

περι-ιάχω [ᾰ], *to ring around, re-echo:* Ep. 3 sing. impf. περίαχε [ῐ] for περιίαχε.

περιιδεῖν, inf. of aor. 2 περιεῖδον.

περιίδμεναι, Ep. for περιειδέναι, inf. of περίοιδα.

περι-ίζομαι, Dep. *to sit round about.*

περι-ίστημι, f. περιστήσω: aor. 1 -έστησα;—*to place* or *set round* a person or thing: metaph. *to bring round to* a certain state. 2. aor. 1 med. περιεστησάμην is also trans., *to place round oneself.* II. Pass., with intr. tenses of Act., aor. 2 -έστην: pf. -έστηκα: plqpf. -εστήκειν:—*to stand round about: to encircle, surround, encompass.* 2. *to come round to, devolve upon:* of events, *to come round to be* so and so, *turn out,* esp. *for the worse.* 3. *to go round so as to avoid, to shun.*

περι-ίσχω, = περιέχω.

περιιών, οῦσα, όν, aor. 2 part. of περίειμι (εἶμι)

περι κάθαρμα, ατος, τό, *an offscouring, defilement:* hence *a polluted wretch.*

περι-καθέζομαι, Dep. *to sit down round about,* esp. *to invest, beleaguer* a town.

περι-κάθημαι Ion. -**κάτημαι**, inf. -ῆσθαι: (properly pf. pass. of περικαθέζομαι):—*to be seated round, to sit round;* περικαθῆσθαι πόλιν *to beleaguer* or *invest* a town: of ships, *to blockade:* c. acc. pers. *to sit beside* one as a companion.

περι-καίω, fut. -καύσω, *to set on fire, burn round about:*—Pass. *to be scorched all round:* metaph. *to be inflamed.*

περι-καλλής, ές, (περί, κάλλος) *very beautiful.*

περι-κᾰλύπτω, f. ψω, *to put round as a covering, throw as a veil over.* II. *to cover all round, cover completely.*

περι-κατάγνυμι, f. άξω, *to break all round.*

περι-καταλαμβάνω, f. -λήψομαι, *to embrace all round.* 2. *to overtake.* 3. *to constrain, compel.*

περι-καταρρέω, f. -ρεύσομαι, *to fall down all round, go to ruin.*

περι-καταρρήγνῡμι, f. -ρήξω, *to tear down round about, rend off:*—Med. *to rend one's own* garment.

περι-κάτημαι, Ion. for περικάθημαι.

περι-κάω, Att. for περικαίω. [ᾱ]

περί-κειμαι, inf. -κεῖσθαι, used as Pass. of περιτίθημι, with f. med. -κείσομαι:—*to be put round, to lie round* or so as *to embrace:* absol., τεῖχος περίκειται a wall *is round about.* 2. metaph. *to be over and above, profit;* οὔ τι μοι περίκειται *there is* no *advantage* for me. II. *to have round one, to have on one;* περικείμενος ὕβριν *clad in* arrogance.

περι-κείρω, f. -κέρσω, *to shear* or *clip all round:*—Med., περικείρεσθαι τρίχας *to clip* one's hair.

περικεκλῃμένος, Ion. pf. pass. part. of περικλείω.

περι-κεφαλαία, ἡ, (περί, κεφαλή) *a helmet.*

περι-κήδομαι, Dep. *to be very anxious* or *concerned about* one.

περί-κηλος, ον, (περί, κῆλον) *exceeding dry, well-dried.*

περι-κίδναμαι, Pass. *to spread round about.*

περι-κλάω, f. -κλάσω, *to break around.*

περι-κλεής, ές, (περί, κλέος) *far-famed.*

περί-κλειτος, ον, *famous all round, far-famed.*

περι-κλείω Ion. -**κληίω** old Att. -**κλῄω**: f. -κλείσω or -κλῄσω: (περί, κλείω):—*to shut in all round, enclose, environ: to surround,* of ships.

περι-κλύζω, f. -ύσω, *to wash all round:*—Pass. *to be washed all round,* of an island. Hence

περίκλυστος, η, ον, Att. also ος, ον, *washed all round by the sea sea-washed, sea-girt.*

περι-κλῠτός, ή, όν, *heard of all round, famous, renowned,* Lat. *inclytus:* of things, *excellent, noble, glorious.*

περι-κνίδιον, τό, *a stalk* or *sprig.*

περι-κνίζω, f. -ίσω, *to scratch all round:*—Med., poët. aor. 1 περιεκνιξάμην, *to gnaw all round.*

περι-κοκκύζω, f. σω, *to cry cuckoo all round.*

περι-κομίζω, f. -ίσω, *to carry round:*—Pass. *to be conveyed round,* hence *to go round.*

περίκομμα, ατος, τό, (περικόπτω) *that which is cut off all round, the clippings, trimmings;* περικόμματα ἐκ σοῦ σκευάσω I will make *minced meat* of you.

περικομμάτιον, τό, Dim. of περίκομμα.

περί-κομψος, ον, *very elegant, exquisite.*

περι-κονδῠλο-πωρο-φίλα, ἡ, (περί, κόνδυλος, πῶρος, φιλέω) fem. Adj., epith. of the gout, *exceeding fond of swelled knuckles.*

περικοπή, ἡ, *a cutting all round, mutilation.* From

περι-κόπτω, f. ψω, *to cut all round, clip, mutilate.* 2. *to cut down the fruit-trees* in an enemy's country, *to lay waste, plunder.*

περι-κρᾰτής, ές, (περί, κράτος) *having full command of.*

περι-κρεμάννῡμι: f. -κρεμάσω [ᾰ], Att. -κρεμῶ:—*to hang up all round:*—Pass. *to be hung about, cling to,* c. dat. Hence

περι-κρεμής, ές, *hung round with* a thing.

περι-κρούω, f. σω, *to strike* or *knock all round.*

περι-κρύβω [ῠ], late form of περικρύπτω.

περι-κρύπτω, f. ψω, *to cover all round, conceal: to hide oneself.*

περι-κτίονες, ὀνων, οἱ, Ep. dat. pl. περικτιόνεσσι, (περί, κτίζω) like ἀμφι-κτίονες, *the dwellers around, neighbours.*

περι-κτίται [ῑ], ῶν, οἱ, = περικτίονες.

περι-κυκλέομαι, f. -ήσομαι: Dep. *to encircle, encompass, enclose*

περι-κυκλόω, f. ώσω, *to encircle, encompass.* Hence

περικύκλωσις, ἡ, *an encircling.*

περι-κῠλινδέω: f. -κυλίσω [ῑ]:—*to roll round:* Pass. *to be rolled about.*

περι-κύμων, ον, gen. ονος, (περί, κῦμα) *surrounded by the waves.*

περι-κωμάζω, f. άσω, *to go about with a party of revellers* (κῶμος): *to carouse around.*

περι-κωνέω, f. ήσω, (περί, κῶνος) *to smear all over with pitch:* περικωνεῖν τὰ ἐμβάδια *to black* shoes.

περι-λᾰλέω, f. ήσω, *to chatter on all sides* or *beyond measure.*

περι-λαμβάνω, f. -λήψομαι: aor. 2 περιέλᾰβον:—*to seize around, embrace.* 2. *to encompass, surround:* hence *to get possession of, catch, secure:*—Pass. *to be caught.* II. *to comprehend, take in.* III. *to constrain, compel.*

περι-λάμπω, f. ψω, *to shine* or *beam round about.*

περι-λείβομαι, Pass. *to be shed all over.*

περι-λείπω, f. ψω, *to leave remaining:*—Pass. *to be left remaining, survive.*

περι-λείχω, f. ξω, *to lick all round: lick clean.*

περίλεξις, ἡ, (περιλέγω) *circumlocution.*

περι-λέπω, f. ψω, *to strip off all round.*

περι-λεσχήνευτος, ον, (περί, λεσχηνεύω) *talked about on all sides, much discussed.*

περι-λιμνάζω, f. άσω, (περί, λίμνη) *to surround with water, insulate.*

περι-λιχμάομαι, Dep. = περιλείχω.

περί-λοιπος, ον, *left remaining.*

περι-λούω, f. σω, *to wash all round, wash carefully.*

περί-λῡπος, ον, (περί, λύπη) *exceeding sorrowful.*

περι-μαιμάω, *to gaze eagerly round:* Ep. part. fem. περιμαιμώωσα.

περι-μαίνομαι, Dep. *to rage round about*

περι-μακής, ές, Dor. for περιμηκής.

περι-μάρναμαι, Dep. *to fight round about:* also *to fight for a thing.*

περι-μάσσω Att. -ττω: f. ξω:—*to wipe all round:* metaph. *to purify by magic arts.*

περιμάχητος, ον, *fought about, fought for;* and so, *to be desired.* From

περι-μάχομαι [ᾰ], Dep. *to fight around.*

περῐ-μένω, *to wait for one, await, expect.* II. intr. *to wait, abide.*

περί-μεστος, ον, *full all round, very full.*

περί-μετρον, τό, (περί, μέτρον) *the circumference.*

περί-μετρος, ον, (περί, μέτρον) *above measure, very large, immense.* II. *measuring round:* as Subst., περίμετρος (sub. γραμμή), ἡ, *a circumference.*

περι-μήκετος, ον, poët. for περιμήκης.

περι-μήκης, ες, (περί, μῆκος) *very tall, high* or *long.*

περι-μηχᾰνάομαι, f. -ήσομαι: Ep. 3 pl. impf. -μηχανόωντο: Dep.:—*to contrive cunningly, scheme craftily for.*

περι-μυκάομαι, Dep. *to bellow around.*

περι-ναιετάω, *to dwell round about* or *near,* 2. in pass. sense *to be inhabited.*

περιναιέτης, ου, ὁ, *a neighbour.* From

περι-ναίω and Med. -ναίομαι, *to dwell round.*

περι-νέφελος, ον, (περί, νεφέλη) *overclouded.*

περι-νέω, f. ήσω: aor. 1 inf. περινῆσαι Ep. -νηῆσαι: (περί, νέω):—*to pile round.*

περί-νεως, ὁ, gen. -νεω, nom. pl. περίνεῳ: (περί, νεώς gen. of ναῦς): *a supernumerary in a ship, a passenger,* as opp. to a rower (πρόσκωπος).

περινήσας Ep. -νηήσας, aor. 1 part. of περινέω.

περι-νίσσομαι, Dep. *to go round:* of Time, *to recur.*

περι-νοέω f. ήσω, *to consider on all sides: to contrive cunningly.*

περίνοιᾰ, ἡ, *intelligence.* II. *over-wiseness.* From

περί-νοος, ον, (περί, νόος) *exceeding wise.*

περι-νοστέω, f. ήσω, *to go round* or *about.*

πέριξ, strengthd. for περί. I. Prep. *round about, all round;* c. gen., but mostly c. acc. II. Adv. *round about.*

περι-ξεστός, ή, όν, *polished all round.*

περι-ξέω, f. -ξέσω, *to polish all round.*

περι-ξῠράω Ion. -έω, f. ήσω, *to shave all round.*

περί-οδος, ἡ, *a going round, the making a circuit round.* II. *a way round: a circuit, compass;* τὴν περίοδον absol., *in circumference.* III. *a book of travels, account of countries travelled over:* also *a map* or *chart.* IV. *a going round in a circle, a cycle of years, a period of time.* 2. *a course at dinner;* περίοδος λόγων *table-talk.* 3. *the orbit of a heavenly body.* 4. *a fit* that recurs at intervals. V. *a well-rounded sentence, period.*

περίοιδα, pf. of περιεῖδον: see περιεῖδον II.

περι-οικέω, f. ήσω, *to dwell round about:* c. acc. *to dwell round* a person or slave.

περι-οικίς, ίδος, ἡ, fem. of περίοικος, *dwelling* or *lying round about, neighbouring.* II. as Subst., περιοικίς (sub. γῆ or χώρα), ἡ, *the country round:* also *the suburbs, outskirts.*

περι-οικοδομέω, f. ήσω: pf. pass. -ῳκοδόμημαι Ion. -οικοδόμημαι:—*to build round about.* II. *to enclose by building round:*—Pass. *to be built up, walled in.*

περί-οικος, ον, (περί, οἰκέω) *dwelling round about* or *near, neighbouring.* II. οἱ περίοικοι were, in Laconia, *the free inhabitants of the country-towns,* the remains of the original inhabitants, who enjoyed civil but not political privileges, opp. on the one hand to the Spartans, and on the other to the Helots.

περιοίσω, fut. of περιφέρω.

περι-ολισθάνω, f. -ολισθήσω, *to slip about.*

περιόντα, part. neut. pl. of περίειμι (εἰμί *sum*).

περι-οπτέος, α, ον, verb. Adj. of περιοράω (see περιόψομαι), *to be overlooked, suffered* or *disregarded.* II. neut. περι-οπτέον, *one must overlook* or *suffer.*

περί-οπτος, ον, (περιόψομαι) *seen from all sides: admired, admirable.*

περι-οράω: impf. περιεώρων Ion. περιώρων: pf. περιεόρᾱκα or -εώρακα: pass. περιεόρᾱμαι:—f. περιόψομαι, from an obsol. verb περιόπτομαι; whence also aor. 1 pass. περιώφθην, pf. περιῶμμαι:—(for aor. 2 περι-εῖδον, pf. περίοιδα, see περι-εἶδον):—*to look around for, wait for.* II. *to overlook, to disregard, suffer to be* or *do.* III. Med. *to look about* before doing a thing, *to be circumspect, delay, wait: to shrink from.* 2. c. gen. *to look about for,* Lat. *respicere.*

περι-οργής, ές, (περί, ὀργή) *very angry, wrathful:* Adv. -γῶς, *very wrathfully.*

περί-ορθρον, τό, (περί, ὄρθρος) *daybreak, dawn.*

περι-ορίζω, f. σω, *to mark out by boundaries.* Hence

περιορισμός, οῦ, ὁ, *a marking out by boundaries.*

περι-ορμέω, f. ήσω, *to be moored* or *anchor round* so as to blockade.

περι-ορμίζω, f. ίσω, *to bring round a ship to anchor:* —Med. and Pass. *to come to anchor round.*

περι-ορύσσω Att. -ττω, f. ξω, *to dig round.*

περιουσία, ἡ, (περίειμι) *that which is over and above: a surviving.* 2. *that which remains over and above, the residue, surplus, abundance, plenty.* 3. *superiority, advantage.* Hence

περιούσιος, ον, *more than enough, abundant.* 2. *peculiar, proper.*

περιοχή, ἡ, (περιέχω) *the full meaning* or *contents.* II. *a section* of a book.

περιόψομαι, used as fut. of περιοράω, formed from *περιόπτομαι.

περι-παπταίνω, *to look timidly round.*

περι-πᾰτέω, f. ήσω, *to walk round, walk about: to walk, live.* Hence

περιπᾰτητικός, ή, όν, *given to walking about,* esp. while teaching: hence Aristotle and his followers were called Περιπατητικοί, *Peripatetics.*

περί-πᾰτος, ὁ, (περί, πατέω) *a walking about, strolling,* Lat. *ambulatio.* II. *a place for walking, a covered walk.* III. *a conversation during a walk:* generally, *a philosophical discussion.*

περι-πείρω, *to put round a spit, to pierce through.*

περι-πέλομαι, Dep.: syncop. Ep. part. περιπλόμενος: (περί, πέλω):—*to move round, to be round* or *about.* 2. of Time, *to come round, revolve, recur.*

περίπεμπτος, ον, verb. Adj. of περιπέμπω, *sent round.*

περι-πέμπω: f. ψω: aor. 1 pass. περιεπέμφθην:—*to send round, despatch in different directions.*

περιπέπτᾰμαι, pf. pass. of περιπετάννυμι.

περι-πέσσω Att. -ττω: f. -πέψω: aor. 1 pass. -επέφθην:—*to bake all round:* metaph. *to crust* or *gloss over: to cajole,* aor. 1 pass. part. περιπεφθείς *cajoled.*

περιπεσεῖν, περιπεσών, aor. 2 inf. and part. of περιπίπτω.

περι-πετάννῡμι or -ύω: f. -πετάσω [ᾰ]: pf. pass. -πέπτᾰμαι or -πέπτασμαι:—*to spread* or *stretch around: to spread out.* Hence

περι-πεταστός, ή, όν, *spread round, outspread.*

περιπέτεια, ἡ, (περιπετής) *a sudden change* of fortune, *a reverse,* on which the plot of a Tragedy turns.

περιπετής, ές, (περιπίπτω) *falling round, with arms clasped round.* 2. *enfolded, encompassed;* but, ἔγχος περιπετές the sword *on which he had fallen.* II. *falling in with.* III. *changing suddenly, reversed;* περιπετῆ πρήγματα *a sudden reverse of* circumstances.

περι-πέτομαι: f. -πετήσομαι syncop. -πτήσομαι: Dep.:—*to fly around.*

περι-πευκής, ές, (περί, πεύκη) *very sharp* or *keen.*

περι-πήγνῡμι or -ύω: f. -πήξω:—*to fix round, to put as a fence round.* II. *to make to congeal round:*—Pass. *to grow stiff round:* of shoes, *to be frozen on the feet.*

περι-πηδάω, f. -ήσομαι, *to leap round about.*

περι-πίμπλημι, f. -πλήσω, *to fill entirely:*—Pass. *to be quite filled.*

περι-πίμπρημι, *to set on fire round about:* impf. 3 sing. and pl. περι-επίμπρα, -επίμπρασαν.

περι-πίπτω, f. -πεσοῦμαι: aor. 2 -έπεσον: pf. -πέπτωκα:—*to fall around,* so as to *embrace* 2. *to fall round* or *upon* a sword. II. *to fall in with,* esp. of ships: also *to fall foul of, be dashed* or *wrecked against.* 2. metaph. *to fall into, be betrayed into;* ἑαυτῷ περιπίπτειν *to be caught in* one's own snare. II. of a thing, *to befall* one.

περι-πίτνω, = περιπίπτω, *to come over* or *upon.*

περι-πλᾰνάω, *to make to wander about:*—Pass. *to wander* or *roam about:* metaph. *to flutter* or *hover round about: to be in a state of uncertainty.* Hence

περιπλάνιος, ον, *wandering, roving about.*

περιπλέγδην, Adv. *closely twined, in close embrace.* From

περι-πλέκω, f. ξω, *to twine round about.* 2. *to intertwine, interweave:*—Pass., aor. 1 -επλέχθην, pf. -πέπλεγμαι: *to fold oneself round, cling to, clasp,* c. dat.; ἱστῷ περιπλεχθείς *folded round* the mast.

περί-πλευρος, ον, (περί, πλευρά) *covering the side.*

περιπλέχθη, Ep. 3 sing. aor. 1 pass. of περιπλέκω.

περι-πλέω, f. -πλεύσομαι and -πλευσοῦμαι: aor. 1 -έπλευσα: Ion. -πλώω:—*to sail* or *swim round, to circumnavigate,* c. acc.

περί-πλεως, ων, nom. pl. -πλεῳ, -πλεα: Ion. **περι-πλέος**, ον:—*quite full, over-full.*

περι-πληθής, ές, (περί, πλῆθος) *very full: very populous:* also *very large.*

περιπλοκάδην, Adv. (περίπλοκος) *twined round.*

περιπλοκή, ἡ, (περιπλέκω) *a twining round.* 2. *entanglement, intricacy.*

περίπλοκος, ον, (περιπλέκω) *enfolded; entangled.*

περιπλόμενος, Ep. syncop. pres. part. of περιπέλομαι.

περί-πλοος, ον, contr. -πλους, ουν, (περιπλέω) act. *sailing round.* II. pass. *that may be sailed round.*

περί-πλοος, ὁ, contr. -πλους, gen. -πλου; nom. pl. -πλοι: (περιπλέω): *a sailing round,* c. gen.: *a circumnavigating.* 2. *the account of a coasting voyage.*

περι-πλύνω [ῡ], *to wash all round, wash clean.*

περι-πλώω, Ion. for περιπλέω.

περι-πνείω, poët. for περιπνέω.

περι-πνέω, f. -πνεύσομαι, *to breathe round.*

περι-πόθητος, ον, (περί, ποθέω) *desired on all sides, much beloved.*

περι-ποιέω, f. ήσω, *to make to remain over and above, to preserve, keep safe, protect.* 2. *to save up, lay by: to lay up in store, procure.* II. Med. *to keep* or *get for oneself, to compass, acquire, gain possession of.* Hence

περιποίησις, εως, ἡ, *a keeping safe: an acquiring, gaining possession.*

περιπολ-άρχης, ου, or -αρχος, ου, ὁ, (περίπολος, ἄρχω) *a superintendant of guards* or *patrols.*

περι-πολέω, f. ήσω, *to go round, wander about, range about.* 2. c. acc. *to traverse.* 3. *to walk round,* as a patrol.

περι-πόλιον, τό, *a station for περίπολοι, a guard-house.* From

περί-πολος, ον, (περί, πολέω) *going round, going the rounds.* II. as Subst., 1. περίπολοι, οἱ, *the patrol: at Athens young citizens between 18 and 20 who were employed on home service, to guard the frontier,* Lat. *publici custodes.* 2. generally, περίπολος, ὁ, *an attendant, follower.*

περι-πόνηρος, ον, *very villainous.*

περι-πόρφυρος, ον, (περί, πορφύρα) *edged with purple,* Lat. *praetextatus.*

περι-ποτάομαι, poët. for περιπέτομαι, *to hover about.*

περι-πρό, Adv., = περὶ πρό, *very, especially.*

περι-προχέω, f. -χεῶ: aor. 1 -έχεα: pf. -κέχῠκα:—*to pour forth round* or *over:* Pass. aor. 1 part., ἔρος θυμὸν περιπροχυθεὶς ἐδάμασσε love *gushing forth over* his soul overcame it.

περίπτισμα, ατος, τό, *a husk, skin.* From

περι-πτίσσω, *to strip off the husk* or *skin:* pf. pass. part. περιεπτισμένος *free from chaff, clean winnowed.*

περίπτυγμα, ατος, τό, (περιπτύσσω) *anything folded round, a covering.*

περιπτύξας, ασα, αν, aor. 1 part. of περιπτύσσω.

περι-πτύσσω, f. ξω: aor. 1 περιέπτυξα:—*to enfold, enwrap, enshroud: to clasp, embrace:* as military term, *to outflank.* II. *to fold round:* Pass. *to be folded round, coil round.* Hence

περιπτῠχή, ἡ, *something enfolding, a cloak, fence:* τειχέων περιπτυχαί *the fence* or *circuit* of walls; Ἀχαιῶν ναύλοχοι περιπτυχαί the naval *fence* or *bulwark* of the Achaeans. 2. *an enfolding, embracing.*

περιπτῠχής, ές, (περιπτύσσω) *folded round;* φασγάνῳ περιπτυχὴς *fallen round* (i. e. *upon*) his sword.

περι-πτώσσω, *to fear very much.*

περιρρᾰγής, ές, (περιρραγῆναι) *broken* or *rent round about.*

περιρ-ραίνω, f. ᾰνῶ, *to besprinkle* or *wet round about.* Hence

περιρρᾰγῆναι, aor. 2 pass. inf. of περιρρήγνυμι.

περιρραντήριον, τό, *a vessel for sprinkling* water at sacrifices: *a vessel for lustral water.*

περιρ-ρέω, f. -ρεύσομαι: pf. -ερρύηκα: aor. 2 pass. (in act. sense) -ερρύην:—*to flow round,* c. acc.:—Pass. *to be surrounded by water.* II. *to slip from off* a thing; ἡ ἀσπὶς περιερρύη εἰς τὴν θάλασσαν his shield *slipped off* into the sea. 2. *to overflow on all sides: to run over, to be in abundance.*

περιρ-ρήγνῡμι and -ύω, f. -ρήξω: aor. 1 -έρρηξα: Pass., aor. 2 -ερράγην [ᾰ]: intr. pf. -έρρωγα:—*to break off round: to rend all round, to rend and tear off:*—Pass. *to be rent and torn off: to be broken* or *parted all round;* κατὰ τὸ ὀξὺ τοῦ Δέλτα περιρρήγνυται ὁ Νεῖλος at the apex of the Delta the Nile *is broken round* it, i. e. *breaks into several branches.*

περιρρηδής, ές, (περιρρέω) *falling round* or *upon.*

περιρροή, ἡ, (περιρρέω) *a flowing round about.*

περίρροος, ον, contr. -ρους, ουν, (περιρρέω) like περίρρυτος, *surrounded with water.*

περίρρῠτος, ον, also η, ον, (περιρρέω) *surrounded with water, sea-girt.* 2. act. *flowing round,* c. gen., πεδία περίρρυτα Σικελίας the waters *that flow round* Sicily.

περι-σαίνω Ep. περισ-σαίνω, *to wag the tail round, fawn upon.*

περι-σείω poët. περισσείω, f. σω, *to shake all round:*—Pass. *to be shaken all round, wave about, float upon the air.*

περί-σεμνος, ον, also η, ον, *very solemn.*

περί-σεπτος, ον, also η, ον, (περί, σέβομαι) *much revered, greatly honoured.*

περί-σημος, ον, (περί, σῆμα) *very famous* or *distinguished,* Lat. *insignis.*

περισθενέω, f. ήσω, *to be exceedingly powerful, to be strong above measure.* From

περι-σθενής, ές, (περί, σθένος) *exceeding strong* or *powerful.*

περι-σκελής, ές, (περί, σκέλλω) *dried* or *hardened all round, rigid.* 2. metaph. *obstinate, stubborn, unbending.*

περι-σκελίς, ίδος, ἡ, (περί, σκέλος) *a band for the leg, a garter* or *anklet.*

περί-σκεπτος, ον, (περί, σκέπτομαι) *to be seen on all sides, far-seen, conspicuous: admired*

περισκέψομαι, fut. of περισκοπέω.

περι-σκιάζω, f. σω, *to overshadow.*

περι-σκιρτάω, f. ήσω, *to leap round* or *about.*

περι-σκοπέω: f. –σκέψομαι: aor. 1 –εσκεψάμην: pf. –έσκεμμαι, formed from *περισκέπτομαι:—*to look round.* 2. *to consider on all sides* or *well, to look at from all points: to watch and see: to look about one, be circumspect.*

περι-σκῠλακισμός, οῦ, ὁ, (περί, σκύλαξ) *a sacrifice in which a puppy was sacrificed and carried round.*

περι-σμᾰρᾰγέω, f. ήσω, *to rattle all round.*

περι-σμύχω, *to consume by a smouldering fire.* [ῡ]

περι-σοβέω, f. ήσω, *to chase* or *push about.* II. intr. *to run round about,* c. acc.

περι-σοφίζομαι, Dep. *to overreach, trick.*

περι-σπάω, f. άσω [ᾰ], *to draw off from around, strip off:*—Med. *to strip oneself of* a thing. II. *to wheel round.* III. Pass. *to be drawn different ways, distracted.*

περισπεῖν, aor. 2 inf. of περιέπω.

περισπερχέω, = περισπερχὴς εἰμι, *to be very indignant.* From

περι-σπερχής, ές, (περί, σπέρχω) *very hasty* or *hurried;* **περισπερχὲς πάθος** an *over-hasty* death.

περί-σπλαγχνος, ον, (περί, σπλάγχνον) *greathearted.*

περισ-σαίνω, Ep. for περισαίνω.

περισσεία, ἡ, (περισσεύω) *superfluity, abundance.* II. *superiority, preeminence.*

περισ-σείω, poët. for περισείω.

περίσσευμα, τό, *superabundance, that which is left* or *is over, a remnant.* From

περισσεύω later Att. **–ττεύω**: impf. ἐπερίσσευον: (περισσός):—*to be over and above, outnumber, be too many for,* c. gen. II. *to be more than enough;* **τὰ περιττεύοντα** *what remains over, the surplus;* **τοσοῦτον τῷ Περικλεῖ ἐπερίσσευε** such *an abundance of reason* had Pericles. 2. in bad sense, *to be overmuch* or *superfluous.* III. *to have more than enough of* a thing, c. gen. IV. later in causal sense, *to make to abound.*

περισσο-λογία, ἡ, (περισσός, λόγος) *useless talking, wordiness, verbiage.*

περισσός later Att. **περιττός,** ή, όν, (περί) *above measure, more than the average, above the common: uncommon:* c. gen. *beyond, greater than;* περισσὸς ἄλλων πρός τι *beyond* others in a thing. 2. *strange, unusual:* in bad sense, *monstrous;* in good, *extraordinary.* II. *more than sufficient;* τὸ περισσόν *a surplus, residue;* περισσαὶ σκηναί *spare* tents. III. in bad sense, *superfluous, excessive;* περισσὰ δρᾶν to be *over*-busy; περισσὰ φρονεῖν to be *over*-wise. 2. of speeches, *over-subtle, refined over much: artificial.* IV. of numbers, *odd, uneven,* Lat. *impar,* opp. to ἄρτιος.

περισσότης later Att. **περιττότης,** ητος, ἡ, (περισσός) *superfluity, excess.*

περισσό-φρων, ονος, ὁ, ἡ, (περισσός, φρήν) *over-wise.*

περισσῶς, Adv. of περισσός, *exceedingly:* Comp. περισσότερον *more abundantly.* 2. **οὐδὲν περισσότερον,** Lat. *nihil aliud, nothing else;* so, **οὐδὲν περισσότερον** ἢ εἰ .. no *otherwise* than if.

περι-στᾰδόν, Adv. (περιίστημι) *standing round about.*

περι-στάζω, f. ξω, *to drop* or *trickle round about.*

περιστάθη, Ep. 3 sing. aor. 1 pass. of περιίστημι. [ᾰ]

περισταίην, aor. 2 opt. of περιίστημι.

περιστάς, –στᾶσα, –στάν, aor. 2 part. of περιίστημι.

περί-στᾰτος, ον, (περιίστημι) *surrounded, admired by the crowd.*

περι-σταυρόω, f. ώσω, *to fence about with a palisade, fortify* or *fence round:*—Med. *to fortify oneself with a palisade.*

περιστείλας, aor. 1 part. of περιστέλλω.

περι-στείχω, f. ξω, *to go round about.*

περιστείωσι, Ep. for περιστῶσι, 3 pl. aor. 2 subj. of περιίστημι.

περι-στέλλω, f. –στελῶ: aor. 1 –έστειλα:—*to dress, clothe, to wrap round: to lay out* a corpse, Lat. *componere;* hence *to bury.* II. *to wrap up, cover, cloak.* III. *to take care of, protect, maintain;* περιστέλλειν ἀοιδάν *to uphold* minstrelsy; περιστέλλειν ἔργα *to attend to* agriculture.

περι-στενᾰχίζω, f. ίσω, *to sigh, groan about* or *over, bemoan:*—Med. *to echo around.*

περι-στένω, *to cram full all round:* Pass. *to be crammed full.* II. *to groan around.*

περίστεπτος, ον, (περιστέφω) *crowned, wreathed.*

ΠΕΡΙΣΤΕΡΑ΄, ἡ, *a dove, pigeon.*

περιστερεών, ῶνος, ὁ, *a dove-cote.* From

περι-στεφᾰνόω, f. ώσω, (περί, στέφανος) *to encircle, surround as with a crown.*

περιστεφής, ές, *wreathed, crowned;* ἀνθέων περιστεφὴς *with a crown* of flowers. II. act. *twining, encircling.* From

περι-στέφω, f. ψω, *to surround as with a crown, enwreathe.*

περίστησαν, Ep. for περιέστησαν, 3 pl. aor. 2 of περιίστημι.

περιστήσαντο, Ep. for περιεστήσαντο, 3 pl. aor. 1 med. of περιίστημι.

περιστήωσι, Ep. for περιστῶσι, 3 pl. aor. 2 subj. of περιίστημι.

περι-στίζω, f. ξω: aor. 1 –έστιξα:—*to dot at equal intervals,* hence *to place round at equal distances.* 2. c. dat. *to stick round with* things.

περι-στίλβω, f. ψω, *to beam* or *flash round about.*

περι-στῐχίζω, f. σω, (περί, στίχος) *to put all round.*

περι-στοιχίζω, f. σω, (περί, στοῖχος) *to surround with toils* or *nets:*—Med. *to hedge in.*

περί-στοιχος, ον, (περί, στοῖχος) *set round in rows.*

περι-στονᾰχίζω, *to groan all round.*

περι-στρᾰτοπεδεύομαι, f. σομαι: aor. 1 –εστρατοπεδευσάμην: Dep.:—*to encamp about, invest, besiege, beleaguer.*

περι-στρέφω, f. ψω, *to whirl round*, of one preparing to throw a stone :—Pass. *to be turned round, to spin round.* Hence

περιστροφή, ἡ, *a turning round: an orbit* or *revolution.*

περι-στρωφάω, f. ήσω, *to turn round often* :—Pass. *to go round about to*: περιστρωφώμενος πάντα τὰ χρηστήρια *going round to* all the oracles.

περί-στῦλος, ον, (περί, στῦλος) *with pillars set round, surrounded with a colonnade*:—as Subst., περίστυλον, τό, *a colonnade round a building.*

περι-σφᾰλής, ές, (περί, σφαλῆναι) *very slippery.*

περι-σφύριος, ον, (περί, σφῠρόν) *round the ankle*: —as Subst., περισφύριον, τό, *an anklet.*

περί-σφῠρος, ον, = περισφύριος.

περισχέμεν, Ep. for περισχεῖν, aor. 2 inf. of περιέχω.

περίσχεο, Ep. for περίσχου, aor. 2 med. imperat. of περιέχω.

περι-σχίζω, f. ίσω, *to slit all round, cut off.* II. Pass., of a river, *to split into two branches*, so as *to enclose* a space.

περι-σχοινίζω, f. ίσω, (περί, σχοῖνος) *to part off by a rope*, as in the Athenian law-courts, to keep the judges apart from the people.

περι-σώζω, f. σω, *to save alive, save from death* :—Pass. *to escape with one's life.*

περι-τάμνω, Ion. for περιτέμνω.

περι-ταφρεύω, f. σω, (περί, τάφρος) *to dig a trench round, surround with a trench.*

περι-τείνω, f. -τενῶ, (περί, τείνω) *to stretch all round* or *over.*

περι-τειχίζω, f. ίσω, *to wall all round, fortify.* 2. *to build a wall round, invest, beleaguer, blockade* :—Pass. *to be built round.* Hence

περιτείχῐσις, ἡ, *a walling round, an investing, beleaguering.*

περιτείχισμα, τό, (περιτειχίζω) *a wall built round, blockading wall.*

περιτειχισμός, ὁ, (περιτειχίζω) *a walling round, blockading.*

περι-τελέω, f. έσω, *to finish completely.*

περι-τέλλομαι, Pass. (περί, τέλλω) *to go* or *run round*; of Time, *to revolve.*

περιτεμεῖν, inf. fut. of περιτέμνω.

περι-τέμνω Ion. and Ep. περιτάμνω: f. -τεμῶ: aor. 2 -έτεμον :—*to cut round, clip round about* :—Med., περιτάμνεσθαι τὰ αἰδοῖα *to practise circumcision*; περιτάμνεσθαι βραχίονας *to make incisions all round* one's arms. II. *to cut off* the extremities: Pass., περιτέμνεσθαι γῆν *to be curtailed* or *cut short of* certain land. III. *to cut off, intercept*; Med. *to intercept for oneself*: Pass. *to be cut off* or *intercepted.*

περι-τέρμων, ον, (περί, τέρμα) *bounded all round.*

περι-τέχνησις, ἡ, (περί, τέχνη) *eminent art* or *cunning.*

περι-τίθημι, f. -θήσω: aor. 1 -έθηκα: aor. 2 -έθην, imperat. -θες :—*to place round about, put round* or *on* :—Med. *to put round oneself, put on.* II. *to bestow* or *confer upon, invest with*: also *to impose upon.*

περι-τίλλω, *to pluck* or *strip all round.*

περι-τῑμήεις, εσσα, εν, (περί, τιμή) *much honoured.*

περιτομή, ἡ, (περιτέμνω) *circumcision.*

περι-τοξεύω, f. σω, *to overshoot, outshoot.*

περι-τραχήλιον, τό, (περί, τράχηλος) *a necklace.*

περι-τρέπω, f. -τρέψω: aor. 1 -έτρεψα :—*to turn round about, to turn upside down, to overturn.* II. intr. *to turn* or *go round, revolve.*

περίτρεσαν, 3 pl. Ep. aor. 1 of περιτρέω.

περι-τρέφω, f. -θρέψω: aor. 1 -έθρεψα :—*to make to congeal around* :—Pass. *to congeal* or *stiffen round about.*

περι-τρέχω, f. -θρέξομαι: other tenses formed from *περι-δρέμω,—f. -δρομοῦμαι: aor. 2 -έδρᾰμον: pf. -δέδρομα :—*to run round, spin* or *whirl round.* II. c. acc. *to run round about, make the circuit of*: *to run round in quest of.* 2. metaph. *to come round, overreach.*

περι-τρέω, f. -τρέσω, *to tremble round about.*

περιτρῐβής, ές, (περιτριβῆναι) *worn all round.* From

περι-τρίβω, f. ψω: aor. 1 -έτριψα :—Pass, aor. 2 -ετρίβην [ῐ]: pf. -τέτριμμαι :—*to wear down all round.* Hence

περίτριμμα, ατος, τό, *anything worn smooth by rubbing*: metaph *a practised knave.*

περι-τρομέω, (περί, τρέμω) *to tremble* or *quiver all round*: Pass, σάρκες περιτρομέοντο μέλεσσιν *all the flesh quivered on* his limbs.

περι-τροπέω, Ep. collat. form of περιτρέπω, intr. *to turn oneself round*; of Time, *to revolve.* 3. c. acc. *to drive about, harass.*

περιτροπή, ἡ, (περιτρέπω) *a turning about, revolution*; ἐν περιτροπῇ or ἐκ περιτροπῆς *by turns.*

περι-τρόχᾰλος, ον, = περίτροχος; neut. pl. as Adv., περιτρόχαλα κείρεσθαι to have one's hair *clipt round about.*

περι-τροχάω, collat. form of περιτρέχω, *to run round*: *to crowd round about.*

περίτροχος, ον, (περιτρέχω) *running round, round.*

περι-τρώγω, f -τρώξομαι: aor. 2 -έτρᾰγον :—*to gnaw round about, nibble, carp at*: *to nibble off, purloin.*

περιττεύω, **περιττός**, etc., later Att. for περισσεύω, περισσός, etc.

περι-τυγχάνω, f. -τεύξομαι: aor. 2 -έτῠχον: pf. -τετύχηκα :—*to happen to be about, at* or *near*: *to light upon, fall in with, meet with, encounter*: also *to happen to* one, *befall.*

περι-τύμβιος, ον, (περί, τύμβος) *round about the grave.*

περι-υβρίζω, f. ίσω, *to treat with great insult, to insult very wantonly* :—Pass. *to be wantonly ill-treated.*

περι-φαίνομαι, Pass. *to be visible all round*; ἐν περιφαινομένῳ (sc. χώρῳ) on a spot *seen far around*

περιφάνεια, ἡ, *a being seen all round: full knowledge, notoriety*. [ᾰ] From

περι-φᾰνής, ές, (περιφαίνομαι) *seen all round: manifest*: Comp. and Sup., περιφανέστερος, -έστατος.

περίφαντος, ον, (περιφαίνομαι) *seen all round, manifest*: also 2. *famous, renowned*, Lat. *illustris*.

περιφᾰνῶς, Adv. of περιφανής, *manifestly*.

περι-φείδομαι, Dep. *to spare so that he survives*, c. gen.

περιφέρεια, ἡ, *a circumference: a round figure*. From

περιφερής, ές, (περιφέρω) *carried round about: revolving, rolling: surrounding* 2. *surrounded by*.

περι-φέρω, f. περιοίσω: aor. 1 περιήνεγκα:—*to carry round* or *about: to carry about* with one. 2. *to move* a thing *round in a circle: to hand round*. II. οὔ με περιφέρει οὐδὲν εἰδέναι τούτων [sc. ἡ μνήμη] my memōry does not *carry me back* to know any of these things. III. *to endure, hold out*. IV. Pass. *to move round, revolve*, esp. of time. 2. *to wander* or *range about*.

περι-φεύγω, f. -φεύξομαι and -φευξοῦμαι:—*to flee from, avoid, elude*, c. acc. 2. *to escape from illness, get over an attack*.

περι-φλεύω, pf. pass. περιπέφλευσμαι:—*to scorch* or *burn all round*.

περί-φλοιος, ον, (περί, φλοιός) *with bark all round*.

περι-φλύω [ῡ], = περιφλεύω.

περι-φοβέομαι, Pass. *to fear greatly*.

περί-φοβος, ον, (περί, φόβος) *in great fear, fearful above measure, terrified*.

περί-φοιτος, ον, (περί, φοιτάω) *wandering about*.

περιφορά, ἡ, (περιφέρω) *a carrying* or *handing round*: also *the meals handed round*. II. (from Pass.) *a going* or *turning round, circuit, revolution*.

περι-φορέω, = περιφέρω. Hence

περιφορητός, όν, *carried about*. II. *going* or *ranging about*. III. *notorious, infamous*.

περιφρᾰδής, ές, *very thoughtful, very careful, considerate*. Adv. -δέως, *carefully*. From

περι-φράζομαι, Med. *to think over, consider on all sides*.

περίφρακτος, ον, *fenced round*:—as Subst., περίφρακτος, τό, *an enclosure*. From

περι-φράσσω Att. -ττω, f. ξω, *to fence round*.

περι-φρονέω, f. ήσω, *to compass in thought, speculate about*. II. *to have thoughts above* or *beyond, to contemn, despise*.

περι-φρουρέω, f. ήσω, *to guard on all sides, blockade*.

περί-φρων, ονος, ὁ, ἡ, voc. πέριφρον, (περί, φρήν) *very thoughtful, very careful*. II. like ὑπέρ-φρων, *haughty, overweening*: c. gen. *despising* a thing.

περιφῠγή, ἡ, (περιφυγεῖν) *a place of refuge*.

περιφύς, ῦσα, ύν, aor. 2 part. of περιφύω.

περι-φύσητος, ον, (περί, φῡσάω) *blown upon from all sides*.

περι-φύω, fut. -φύσω [ῡ]: aor. 1 -έφῡσα:—trans. *to make to grow round* or *upon, make to cling to* or *adhere*. II. intr. in Med. περιφύομαι: fut. -φύσομαι [ῡ]: with pf. act. περιπέφῡκα: aor. 2 περιέφῡν, inf. περιφῦναι, part. περιφύς [ῡ]:—*to grow round about* or *upon*, c. dat.: *to cling to, clasp*, c. dat.

περι-χᾰρᾰκόω, f. ώσω, (περί, χάραξ) *to surround with a palisade*: generally, *to fortify*.

περι-χᾰράσσω Att. -ττω, fut. ξω, *to scratch* or *cut all round*.

περιχάρεια, ἡ, *exceeding great joy*. From

περι-χᾰρής, ές, (περί, χαρῆναι) *exceeding glad* or *joyous*: τὸ περιχαρές = περιχάρεια.

περι-χειλόω, f. ώσω, (περί, χεῖλος) *to surround with a rim* or *border*.

περι-χέω, f. -χεῶ: aor. 1 περιέχεα: Ep. pres. περιχεύω, aor. 1 περιχεῦα: Pass., aor. 1 -εχύθην [ῠ]: pf. -κέχῠμαι:—*to pour round about, over* or *upon*; περιχέειν χρυσὸν κέρασι *to put* gold *round* the horns: —Pass. *to be poured* or *spread all about*: of persons, *to pour* or *crowd round*.

περι-χθών, όνος, ὁ, ἡ, *round about the earth*.

περι-χορεύω, f. σω, *to dance round* or *about*.

περι-χρῡσόω, f. ώσω, *to gild all over*.

περι-χώομαι, f. -χώσομαι: Ep. aor. 1 περιχωσάμην: —*to be exceeding angry* or *wroth*.

περι-χωρέω, f. ήσω, *to go round about*. II. *to come round to, come to in succession*.

περί-χωρος, ον, (περί, χῶρος) *round about a place*; as Subst., περίχωρος (sub. γῆ), ἡ, *the country round about*.

περι-ψάω, inf. -ψῆν: fut. -ψήσω:—*to wipe all round: to wipe* the eyes. Hence

περίψημα, τό, *anything wiped off, offscouring*.

περι-ψῑλόω, f. ώσω, (περί, ψιλός) *to make bald all round: to strip* or *peel off all round*: Pass., περιψιλωθῆναι τὰς σάρκας *to have* the flesh *all stripped off*.

περι-ῳδέω, f. ήσω, (περί, ᾠδή) *to subdue by spells*.

περιωδῠνία, ἡ, *excessive pain*. From

περι-ώδῠνος, ον, (περί, ὀδύνη) *exceeding painful* II. *suffering great pain*.

περι-ωθέω, f. -ωθήσω and -ώσω, *to push* or *thrust about*:—Pass. with pf. περιέωσμαι, *to be thrust away* or *pushed on one side, to be repulsed*.

περι-ωπή, ἡ, (περί, ὤψ) *a place commanding a wide view*: ἐκ περιωπῆς *by a bird's-eye view*. II. *circumspection, caution*.

περι-ώσιος, ον, Ion. for περιούσιος. *immense, vast*, as Adv. περιώσιον, *exceeding, beyond measure*: also as Comp., περιώσιον ἄλλων *far beyond* the rest.

περκάζω, f. σω, (περκός) *to turn dark*, of grapes ripening.

πέρκη, ἡ, *the perch*, Lat. *perca*.

ΠΕΡΚΝΟ'Σ, ή, όν, *dark-coloured*, of grapes ripening: *dark, dusky*, name of a kind of eagle.

πέρκος, η, ον, = περκνός.

πέρνα, ἡ, *a ham*, Lat. *perna*.

πέρνημι, 3 pl. περνᾶσι, part. περνάς: 3 sing. Ion. impf. πέρνασκε: (περάω):—*to carry beyond seas for sale, to export, sell*:—Pass. *to be offered for sale*.

πέρ-οδος, ἡ, Aeol. for περίοδος.

περόναμα, -ατρίς, Dor. for περόνημα, -ητρίς.

περονάω, f. ήσω, (περόνη) *to pierce, pin:* Med., χλαῖναν περονήσασθαι *to pin* or *buckle one's* cloak.

περόνη, ἡ, (πείρω, περάω) *anything pointed for piercing: a large pin* for fastening a cloak, *a buckle, brooch*, Lat. *fibula.* II. *the small bone* of the arm or leg, Lat. *radius, fibula.*

περόνημα Dor. -αμα, ατος, τό, = περονητρίς.

περονητρίς Dor. -ατρίς, ίδος, ἡ, (περονάω) *a robe fastened on the shoulder with a buckle* or *brooch.*

περονίς, ίδος, ἡ, = περόνη.

περπερεύομαι, Dep. *to boast* or *vaunt oneself, be a braggart.* From

ΠΕ'ΡΠΕΡΟΣ, ον, *vainglorious, braggart.*

πέρρ-οχος, ον, Aeol. for περίοχος.

πέρσα, Ep. for ἔπερσα, aor. 1 of πέρθω.

περσέ-πολις poët. **περσέπτολις**, εως, ὁ, ἡ, (πέρθω, πόλις) *destroyer of cities.* II. (Πέρσαι, πόλις) *Persepolis*, the ancient capital of Persia.

Περσεύς, έως Ep. ῆος later Ion. έος, ὁ, *Perseus*, son of Jove and Danaë, one of the most famous Grecian heroes.

Περσεφόνη, ἡ, poët. **Περσεφόνεια** also **Περσέφασσα**:—*Persephonē, Proserpine*, Lat. *Proserpĭna*, daughter of Jupiter and Ceres. Pluto carried her off, and as his consort she reigned in the lower world.

Πέρσης, ου, ὁ, acc. Πέρσην or Πέρσεα, voc. Πέρσᾰ or Πέρση, *a Persian, native of Persia.* (The Greeks derived the name of the people from Perseus.)

Περσίζω, f. σω, (Πέρσης) *to side with* or *imitate the Persians.* 2. *to speak Persian.*

Περσικός, ή, όν, (Πέρσης) *Persian:* hence 1. αἱ Περσικαί a sort of *thin shoes* or *slippers.* 2. Περσικὸς ὄρνις *the common cock.* 3. τὸ Περσικόν *a Persian dance.* 4. ὁ Περσικός or τὸ Περσικὸν (sub. μῆλον), *the peach.*

Περσίς, ίδος, poët. fem. of Περσικός, *Persian.* II. as Subst. 1. (sub. γῆ), *Persis, Persia.* 2. (sub. γυνή), *a Persian woman.* 3. (sub. χλαῖνα), *a Persian cloak.*

Περσιστί, Adv. (Περσίζω) *in Persian fashion, in the Persian tongue.*

Περσο-διώκτης, ου, ὁ, (Πέρσης, διώκω) *pursuer of the Persians.*

Περσο-νομέομαι, Pass. *to be governed by the Persian laws* or *by Persians.* From

Περσο-νόμος, ον, (Πέρσης, νέμω) *ruling Persians.*

πέρῠσι or -ιν, Adv. (πέρας) *a year ago, last year;* ἡ πέρυσι κωμῳδία the comic play *of last year.* Hence

περῠσινός, ή, όν, *of last year, last year's.*

Πέρφερες, οἱ, the name of the five officers who escorted the Hyperborean maidens to Delos.

πεσδᾷ, Adv., Dor. for πεζῇ.

πέσε, Ep. for ἔπεσε, 3 sing. aor. 2 of πίπτω.

πεσεῖν Ep. **πεσέειν**, aor. 2 inf. of πίπτω.

πέσημα, ατος, τό, (πεσεῖν) *a fall: a falling* or *fallen body.*

πέσος, τό, = πέσημα, πτῶμα, *a fall, slaughter.*

πεσοῦμαι, fut. med. of πίπτω.

πεσσεία Att. **πεττ-**, ἡ, *the game of draughts.* From

πεσσεύω Att. **πεττ-**, (πεσσός) *to play at draughts.*

πεσσο-νομέω, f. ήσω, (πεσσός, νέμω) *to set the* πεσσοί *in order for playing: to arrange, dispose, adjust.*

ΠΕΣΣΟ'Σ Att. **πεττός**, ὁ, pl. πεσσοί and πεσσά, *an oval-shaped stone for playing a game like our draughts*, mostly in plur. 2. in pl. also *the board on which the game was played:* it was divided by five lines both ways, and so into thirty-six squares: the middle line was called ἱερὰ γραμμή. 3. πεσσοί, οἱ, also, *the place* in which the game was played: *the game* itself.

ΠΕ'ΣΣΩ Att. **πέττω**, later also **πέπτω**: fut. πέψω: aor. 1 ἔπεψα:—Pass., aor. 1 ἐπέφθην: pf. πέπεμμαι, inf. πεπέφθαι:—*to soften, make soft:* of the sun, *to ripen.* II. *to boil:* generally, *to cook, dress:* also *to bake;* Med., πέσσεσθαι πέμματα *to bake oneself* cakes. III. of the stomach, *to digest*, Lat. *coquere, concoquere.* 2. metaph. *to stomach* or *digest* an affront, or rather *to brood over* it; so γέρα πεσσέμεν (Ep. for πέσσειν) *to brood over* or *dwell on* one's honours; βέλος πέσσειν *to nurse* or *have to heal* the wound of a dart.

πεσών, οῦσα, όν, aor. 2 part. of πίπτω.

πετᾰλισμός, ὁ, *petalism*, a mode of banishing citizens practised in Syracuse, like the ὀστρακισμός of Athens, except that the name of the obnoxious citizen was written on *olive-leaves* instead of potsherds. From

πέτᾰλον Ion. **πέτηλον**, τό, *a leaf:* hence 2. used for voting, *a vote, ballot;* cf. ψῆφος. (Properly neut. from πέταλος.)

πέτᾰλος Ion. **πέτηλος**, η, ον, (πετάννυμι) *spread out, unfolded, broad, flat.* II. metaph. *full-grown.*

πέτᾰμαι, = πέτομαι, q. v.

ΠΕΤΑ'ΝΝΥ'ΜΙ or -ύω: f. πετάσω [ᾰ] Att. πετῶ: aor. 1 ἐπέτασα Ep. πέτᾰσα and πέτασσα: Pass., aor ἐπετάσθην Ep. πετάσθην: pf. πεπέτασμαι Ep. πέπταμαι: Ep. plqpf. ἐπεπτάμην, πεπτάμην:—*to spread, stretch out, unfold, unfurl, expand:* metaph., θυμὸν πετάσαι *to open* one's heart:—pf. pass. πέπταμαι, *to be spread on all sides, to be widely extended;* part. πεπταμένος, η, ον, *spread wide, opened wide*, of folding doors.

πέτασε, Ep. 3 sing. aor. 1 of πετάννυμι.

πέτασμα, ατος, τό, (πετάννυμι) *anything spread out:* in plur. *hangings, curtains, carpets.*

πετάσσας, Ep. aor. 1 part. of πετάννυμι.

πέτ-αυρον or **πέτ-ευρον**, τό, (πέδαυρος Aeol. for μετέωρος) *a pole* or *perch* for fowls to roost on.

πετεινός, ή, όν. Ep. **πετεεινός**, Ion. **πετηνός** and **πετεηνός**, *able to fly, winged, flying:* **πετηνά**, πετεηνά *winged creatures, fowls of the air.* 2. of young birds, *fledged.*

πέτευρον, τό, = πέταυρον.

πέτηλον, τό, Ion. for πέταλον.

πετοῖσαι, Dor. for πεσοῦσαι, aor. 2 part. nom. pl. of πίπτω.

ΠΕ'ΤΟΜΑΙ: impf. ἐπετόμην Ep. πετόμην: f. πετήσομαι, shortd. πτήσομαι: sync. aor. 2 ἐπτόμην, inf. πτέσθαι, part. πτόμενος; also ἐπτάμην, Ep. 3 sing. subj. πτῆται for πτᾶται, inf. πτάσθαι, part. πτάμενος: Dep.:—but there is also an act. aor. 2 ἔπτην, inf. πτῆναι, part. πτάς, as if from ἵπτημι:—there is also a present πέταμαι: ποτάομαι, πωτάομαι are lengthd. forms:—*to spread the wings in flight, to fly*: of any quick motion, *to fly, dart, rush, speed*: imperat., πέτου *fly!* i. e. *make haste.* II. metaph. *to be on the wing, flutter*, Lat. *volitare*; ὄρνις πετόμενος a bird *ever on the wing.* 2. *to fly abroad, be bruited abroad.*

πετόντεσσι, Aeol. and poët. for πεσοῦσι, aor. 2 part. dat. pl. of πίπτω.

ΠΕ'ΤΡΑ Ion. πέτρη, ἡ, *a rock, crag*, Lat. *rupes, scopulus*; πέτρος being *a stone*, Lat. *saxum*: *a ledge* or *shelf of rock* (in the sea), λεῖος πετράων free from *rocks*:—pl. πέτραι, *masses of rock*: δίστομος πέτρα *a rock* or *cave* with double entrance. Hence

πετραῖος, α, ον, *rocky, of* or *belonging to a rock, living among the rocks.*

πετρη-γενής, ές, (πέτρα, γενέσθαι) *rock-born.*

πετρήεις, εσσα, εν, (πέτρα) *rocky.*

πετρηρεφής, ές, (πέτρα, ἐρέφω) *over-arched with rock.*

πετρήρης, ες, (πέτρα) *of rock, rocky.*

πετρίδιον, τό, Dim. of πέτρα. [ῐ]

πέτρῐνος, η, ον, (πέτρα) *of rock, rocky.*

πετροβολία, ἡ, *a stoning.* From

πετρο-βόλος, ον, (πέτρα, βαλεῖν) *throwing stones.*

πετρό-κοιτος, ον, (πέτρα, κοίτη) *sleeping on rock.*

πετρορ-ρῐφής, ές, (πέτρα, ῥιφῆναι) *hurled from a rock.*

ΠΕ'ΤΡΟΣ, ὁ, *a piece of rock, a stone*; cp. πέτρα.

πετρο-τόμος, ον, (πέτρα, τεμεῖν) *cutting* or *hewing stones*: as Subst., πετροτόμος, ὁ, *a stone-cutter.*

πετρόω, f. ώσω, (πέτρος) *to stone*:—Pass. *to be stoned.*

πετρ-ώδης, ες, (πέτρα or πέτρος, εἶδος) *like rock* or *stone, rocky, stony.*

πέτρωμα, ατος, τό, (πετρόω) *a piece of stone* or *rock.* II. *a stoning*; λευσίμῳ πετρώματι θανεῖν to die *by stoning.*

πεττεία, πεττεύω, πεττός, Att. for πεσσ-.

πέττω, Att. for πέσσω.

ΠΕΥ'ΘΟΜΑΙ, poët. for the prose πυνθάνομαι: impf. ἐπευθόμην. Hence

πευθώ, οῦς, ἡ, *tidings, news.*

πευκάεις, Dor. for πευκήεις.

πευκάλιμος [ᾰ], η, ον, lengthd. Ep. form of πυκινός (cf. λευγάλεος, λυγρός), *wise, prudent.*

πευκεδᾰνός, ή, όν, (πεύκη) *keen, piercing.*

ΠΕΥ'ΚΗ, ἡ, *the fir*, Lat. *picea.* II. *anything made from the wood* or *resin of the fir, a torch of fir-wood.* Hence

πευκήεις Dor. **πευκάεις**, εσσα, εν, *of* or *made of fir*, πεύκηεν σκάφος, a boat *of fir-wood.* II. metaph. *sharp, keen, piercing.*

πεύκῐνος, η, ον, (πεύκη) *of* or *made of fir-wood*; πεύκινα δάκρυα tears *of the fir*, i. e. the gum or resin that exudes from it

πεύσομαι Dor. **πευσοῦμαι**, fut. of πυνθάνομαι

πευστήριος, α, ον, *of* or *for enquiry*: ἡ πευστηρία (sub. θυσία) a sacrifice *for learning the will of the gods.*

πεφάνθαι, pf. pass. inf. of φαίνω.

πέφανται, 3 sing. pf. pass. of φαίνω. II. 3 plur. pf. pass. of *φένω.

πέφαργμαι, Att. for πέφραγμαι, pf. pass. of φράσσω.

πέφασμαι, pf. pass. of φαίνω and of φημί: part. πεφασμένος, η, ον, *brought to light, made manifest.*

πεφευγώς, pf part. of φεύγω.

πέφηνα, pf. of φαίνω.

πεφήσομαι, poët. paullo-p. fut. of φαίνω.

πεφήσομαι, poët. paullo-p. fut. of *φένω.

πεφῐδέσθαι, Ep. redupl. aor. 2 inf. of φείδομαι.

πεφῐδήσομαι, Ep. paullo-p. fut. of φείδομαι.

πεφῐδοίμην, Ep. aor. 2 opt. of φείδομαι.

πεφῐλᾰμένος, Dor. for πεφιλημένος, pf. pass. part. of φιλέω

πεφίμωσο, pf. pass. imperat. of φῑμόω.

πέφνε, πεφνέμεν, πέφνων, etc., v. sub *φένω.

πεφοβήατο, Ep. 3 pl. plqpf. of φοβέομαι

πεφοβημένος, η, ον, pf. part. pass. of φοβέω: Adv. πεφοβημένως, *timorously.*

πεφορτισμένος, pf. pass. part. of φορτίζω.

πέφραγμαι, pf. pass. of φράσσω.

πέφρᾰδον, Ep. redupl. aor. 2 of φράζω: Ep. inf. πεφρᾰδέειν and πεφρᾰδέμεν.

πέφρῑκα, pf. of φρίσσω: poët. part. πεφρίκοντες.

πεφύᾱσι, Ep. for πεφύκασι, 3 pl. pf. of φύω.

πεφυγμένος, η, ον, pf. pass. part. of φεύγω.

πεφυζότες, Ep. for πεφευγότες, nom. pl. pf. part. from pres. *φύζω, = φεύγω.

πέφῡκα, pf. of φύω.

πεφύκω, Ep. pres. formed from pf. πέφῡκα: Ep. impf. πέφῡκον.

πεφῠλαγμένος, η, ον, pf. pass. part. of φυλάσσω: —Adv. πεφυλαγμένως, *cautiously, guardedly.*

πεφυρμένος, pf. pass. part. of φύρω.

πεφῠυῖα, Ep. for πεφυκυῖα, pf. part. fem. of φύω.

πεφῠῶτες, Ep. for πεφυκότες, pf. part. pl. of φύω.

πη Ion. **κη** Dor. **πᾶ**, enclit. Particle: of Manner, *in some way* or *other, somehow*: οὐδέ πη in no *way at all*, not *at all*: of numbers, *about.* 2. of Space, *by some way, to some place.* 3. πῇ μὲν.., πῇ δὲ.. now *one way, now another*; *partly*... *partly*... II. πῇ; Ion. κῇ; Dor. πᾷ; interrog. Particle; 1. of Manner, *how?* also *why?* in Att. *how?* 2. of Space, *which way?* Lat. *qua?* also *where?*

πηγάζω, f. άσω, (πηγή) *to spring, well,* or *gush forth.* II. trans. *to make to gush forth.*

πηγαῖος, α, ον, also ος, ον, (πηγή) *from a well* or *spring.*

ΠΗΓΑ'ΝΟΝ, τό, *rue*, Lat. *ruta:* proverb., οὐδ' ἐν σελίνῳ οὐδ' ἐν πηγάνῳ, not even at the parsley nor *the rue*, i. e. scarcely at the beginning of a thing, because these herbs were planted for *borders* in gardens.

πηγάς, άδος, ἡ, (πήγνυμι) *anything congealed* or *hardened: boar-frost, rime.*

Πηγάσιον, τό, Dim. of Πήγᾰσος. [ᾰ]

Πηγᾰσίς, ίδος, fem. Adj. of *Pegasus;* Πηγασὶς κρήνη = Ἵππου κρήνη: see Πηγασος.

Πήγᾰσος, ὁ, *Pegasus*, a horse sprung from the blood of Medusa, and named from *the springs* (πηγαί) of Ocean, near which she was killed. Later he was supposed to be the winged horse which Bellerophon rode when he slew Chimaera, under whose hoof the fountain *Hippocrene* (ἵππου κρήνη) sprang up on Helicon.

πηγεσί-μαλλος, ον, (πήγνυμι, μαλλός) *thick-fleeced.*

ΠΗΓΗ' Dor. **παγά**, ἡ, *a spring, well*, Lat. *fons;* in pl. *the springs* or *source* of rivers; but also, πηγαὶ ποταμῶν river *waters:* metaph. of anything liquid, πηγαὶ δακρύων the *source* or *fount* of tears, i. e. the eyes; also, πηγὴ ἀκούουσα *the fount* of hearing, i. e. the ear; πηγαὶ γάλακτος *streams* of milk; πηγὴ πυρός *the source* of fire; also, πηγὴ ἀργύρου *a well* (i. e. rich vein) of silver. 2. metaph. *the fount, source, origin* of anything.

πῆγμα, ατος, τό, (πήγνυμι) *anything fastened together:* metaph. *a bond, obligation.*

ΠΗΓΝΥ'ΜΙ or -ύω: fut. πήξω: aor. 1 ἔπηξα Ep. πῆξα: Pass., pres. πήγνῠμαι: fut. πᾰγήσομαι: aor. 1 ἐπήχθην, aor. 2 ἐπάγην [ᾰ]: pf. πέπηγμαι, but the pf. med. πέπηγα is mostly used in this sense:—*to stick* or *fix in, make firm* or *fast in:* of plants, *to set* or *plant:* σκηνὴν πηγνύναι *to fix* or *pitch* a tent; and Med., σκηνὰς πήξασθαι *to fix their* tents:—Pass. *to be fixed:* of persons, *to be impaled.* 2. *to stick* or *fix on:* metaph. *to fix* or *fasten upon.* II. *to fasten together, put together, construct, build:* Med., ἅμαξαν πήξασθαι *to build oneself* a wagon. III. *to make solid, stiff: to congeal, freeze:*—Pass. *to be* or *become stiff, be frozen.* IV. metaph. *to make fast, fix*, Lat. *pangere;* ὅρκος παγείς *a sure and steadfast* oath.

πηγός, ή, όν, (πήγνυμι) *firm, solid: compact, strong.*

πηγῠλίς, ίδος, ἡ, (πήγνυμι) *covered with boar-frost, frozen, icy.*

πηδάλιον, τό, (πηδόν) *a rudder:* a Greek ship had two, hence mostly in pl. πηδάλια: they were moved like *large oars* or *sweeps;* and the two were often joined by cross-bars or rudder-bands (ζεῦγλαι or ζευκτήριαι): the upper part with the tiller being called οἴαξ. 2. metaph. of a horse's *reins* or *bridle.* [ᾰ]

ΠΗΔΑ'Ω, Ion. inf. πηδέειν: fut. ήσω or -ήσομαι: aor. 1 ἐπήδησα:—*to spring, bound, leap:* of things, *to dart, spring:* c. acc. cognato, πήδημα πηδᾶν *to take* a leap; hence πηδᾶν μείζονα (sub. πηδήματα) to take a greater *leap:* but πεδία πηδᾶν *to bound over* the plains. II. *to leap, throb, beat*, esp. of the pulse.

πήδημα, ατος, τό, (πηδάω) *a leaping, bounding: a beating* or *throbbing* of the heart.

ΠΗΔΟ'Σ, ὁ, or **ΠΗ'ΔΟΝ**, τό, *the flat* or *blade of an oar:*—*an oar.*

πηκτίς, ίδος, ἡ, (πήγνυμι) *an ancient* sort of *harp* with twenty strings, mostly used by the Lydians, also called μαγάδις. 2. *a shepherd's pipe.*

πηκτός, ή, όν, verb. Adj. of πήγνυμι, *fixed* or *fastened in:* of trees, *planted.* II. *well put together, compact.* 2. ἡ πηκτή *a* sort of *cage* to catch birds. 3. τὰ πηκτὰ (Dor. πακτὰ) τῶν δωμάτων *the barriers* of the house, *the door.* III. *solid, thick, congealed, curdled:* ἡ πηκτή Dor. πακτά, *cream*-cheese.

πῆλαι, **πήλας**, aor. 1 inf. and part. of πάλλω.

πῆλε, Ep. for ἔπηλε, 3 sing. aor. 1 of πάλλω.

Πηλείδης, ου Ep. εω and αο, ὁ, patronymic of Πηλεύς, *son of Peleus, Achilles.*

Πηλείων, ωνος, ὁ, the same as Πηλείδης: Adv. **Πηλείωνάδε**, *to the son of Peleus.*

Πηλεύς, έως Ep. ῆος, ὁ, *Peleus*, son of Aeacus, husband of Thetis, father of Achilles, prince of the Myrmidons in Thessaly.

Πηληιάδης, εω, ὁ, Ep. for Πηλείδης.

Πηλήιος, η, ον, Ep. Adj (Πηλῆος, Ep. gen. of Πηλεύς) *of* or *belonging to Peleus.*

πήληξ, ηκος, ἡ, (πῆλαι) *a helmet, casque.*

Πηλιᾰκός, ή, όν, *of Mount Pelion.*

Πηλιάς, άδος, ἡ, (Πήλιον) *of* or *from Mount Pelion.*

πηλίκος [ῐ], η, ον, interrog. of τηλίκος, ἡλίκος. *how great? how much? how old?* Lat. *quantus?*

πήλῐνος, η, ον, (πηλός) *of clay, earthen*, Lat. *luteus.*

Πήλιον, τό, *Pelion*, a mountain in Thessaly. Hence

Πηλιώτης, ου, ὁ, fem. **-ῶτις**, ιδος, *of* or *from Pelion.*

πηλο-βάτης [ᾰ], ου, ὁ, (πηλός, βαίνω) *mud-walker*, name of a frog.

πηλοδομέω, f. ήσω, *to build of clay.* From

πηλό-δομος, ον, (πηλός, δέμω) *clay-built.*

πηλο-πλάθος [ᾰ], ον, (πηλός, πλάσσω) *moulding clay:* as Subst., πηλοπλάθος, ὁ, *a potter.*

ΠΗΛΟ'Σ, ὁ, *clay*, such as was used by the potter, Lat. *lutum:* also *mud*, Lat. *coenum.*

πηλ-ουργός, όν, (πηλός, ἔργον) *working in clay:* as Subst, πηλουργός, ὁ, *a worker in clay.*

πηλοφορέω, f. ήσω, *to carry clay.* From

πηλο-φόρος, ον, (πηλός, φέρω) *carrying clay.*

πηλό-χῠτος, ον, (πηλός, χέω) *cast in clay, earthen.*

πηλ-ώδης, ες, (πηλός, εἶδος) *like clay, clayey, of the consistency of clay.*

πῆμα, ατος, τό, (πήσομαι, fut. of πάσχω) *suffering misery, woe:* also of a person, πῆμά τινι *a bane* or *sorrow to* ... Hence

πημαίνω: f. ᾰνῶ Ion. ᾰνέω: aor. 1 ἐπήμηνα: Med., fut. πημᾰνοῦμαι (in pass. sense): Pass., aor. 1 ἐπημάνθην Ep. πημάνθην:—*to make suffer, bring into misery:* also *to grieve, distress: to harm, injure:* absol. *to do mischief.* Hence

πημαντέος, α, ον, *possible to be injured.*

πημήνειαν, 3 pl. Aeol. aor. 1 opt. of πημαίνω.

πημονή, ἡ, poët. for πῆμα, *suffering.*

πημοσύνη, ἡ, = πημονή, πῆμα, *suffering.*

Πηνελόπη Ep. **Πηνελόπεια**, ἡ, *Penelopé*, daughter of Icarius, wife of Ulysses: (called from her weaving the *web*, πήνη.)

πηνέλοψ, οπος, ὁ, *a* kind of *duck.*

ΠΗ΄ΝΗ, ἡ, like πῆνος, *the thread* on the shuttle, *the woof;* in plur. *the web.*

πηνίζομαι Dor. **πανίσδομαι**: Dep.: (πηνίον):—*to wind thread off a reel:* generally, *to wind off.*

ΠΗΝΙ΄ΚΑ [ῐ], Adv. *at what point of time? at what hour?* πηνίκ' ἐστὶ τῆς ἡμέρας; *what hour* of day is it?

πηνίον, τό, Dim. of πῆνος or πήνη, *the thread of the woof:* or *the quill on which the thread is wound.*

πήνισμα, ατος, τό, (πηνίζω) *the thread wound on a spindle, the thread of the woof.*

πῆξαι, aor. 1 inf. of πήγνυμι.

πῆξε, Ep. for ἔπηξε, 3 sing. aor. 1 of πήγνυμι.

πηός Dor. **πᾱός**, οῦ, ὁ, (πάομαι) *a kinsman* by marriage, *a connexion*, Lat. *affinis.*

ΠΗ΄ΡΑ Ion. πήρη, ἡ, *a leathern pouch, a wallet, scrip, knapsack*, Lat. *pera.*

πηρίδιον, τό, Dim. of πήρα, *a little wallet.*

πηρό-δετος, ον, (πήρα, δέω) *tying a wallet.*

ΠΗΡΟ΄Σ, ά, όν, *disabled in a limb, maimed*, Lat. *mancus.*

πηρόω, f. ώσω, (πηρός) *to maim, disable:* metaph. *to incapacitate.*

πήσομαι, Ion. fut. of πάσχω.

πηχυαῖος, α, ον, *a cubit long.*

πηχύνομαι, Med. *to take into one's arms.*

ΠΗ΄ΧΥΣ, εως, ὁ: gen. pl. πήχεων:—*the fore-arm*, from the wrist to the elbow, Lat. *ulna:* generally *the arm.* II. *the centre-piece, which joined the two horns of the bow.* III. in pl., πήχεες are *the horns* or *sides of the lyre*, opp. to ζυγόν the bridge. IV. as a measure of length, *the space from the point of the elbow to the end of the little finger*, Lat. *cubitus, a cubit*, orig. containing 24 δάκτυλοι, or about 18 inches: the πῆχυς βασιλήιος was longer by three δάκτυλοι, being = 27 δάκτυλοι or about 20 inches. V. *a cubit-rule.*

πιάζω, f. άσω and άξω: aor. 1 part. πιάξας: Dor. form of πιέζω, *to press: to lay hold of, apprehend.*

πιαίνω, f. ᾰνῶ: aor. 1 ἐπίᾱνα, pass. ἐπιάσθην: pf. pass. πεπίασμαι: (πίων):—*to make fat, fatten;* of the soil, *to fatten, enrich:* metaph. *to increase, enlarge.* 2. metaph. *to make wanton:*—Pass. *to become fat, wax wanton.*

πιάξας, Dor. aor. 1 part. of πιάζω.

πῖαρ, τό, indecl. (πίων) *fat, tallow, suet:* also *oil, cream:* hence *fatness:* metaph. *the fat of the land, the cream* of a thing, *the choicest, best.*

πῖᾰρός, ά, όν, (πῖαρ) *fat, rich.*

πίασμα, τό, (πιαίνω) *that which makes fat* or *rich, an enricher, fattener*, of a river.

πῖδᾰκῖτις, ιδος, ἡ, (πῖδαξ) *of the spring* or *fountain.*

πῖδᾰκόεις, εσσα, εν, (πῖδαξ) *gushing.*

πῖδᾰκ-ώδης, ες, (πῖδαξ, εἶδος) *like a fountain, gushing with spring-water.*

ΠΙ΄ΔΑΞ, ᾰκος, ἡ, *a spring, fountain.* Hence

πῖδήεις, εσσα, εν, *rich in springs.*

πῖδύω, *to gush out.*

πίε, Ep. 2 sing. aor. 2 imperat. of πίνω: but also Ep. for ἔπιε, 3 sing. indic.

πιέειν, Ep. for πιεῖν, aor. 2 inf. of πίνω.

πιεζέω, = πιέζω: and hence Ep. impf. πιέζευν and Ion. part. pass. πιεζεύμενος.

ΠΙΕ΄ΖΩ, f. πιέσω: aor. 1 ἐπίεσα: Pass., aor. 1 ἐπιέσθην or ἐπιέχθην: pf. πεπίεσμαι or πεπίεγμαι:—*to press, squeeze, crush, press hard upon.* II. *to lay hold of.*

πιεῖν, aor. 2 inf. of πίνω.

πίειρα [ῐ], ἡ, pecul. fem. of πίων, *fat, rich:* of cities, *prosperous, wealthy:* δαὶς πίειρα *a plentiful* meal:—of pine-wood, *resinous, juicy, unctuous.*

πιέμεν, Ep. for πιεῖν, aor. 2 inf. of πίνω.

Πῑερίδες, αἱ, *the Pierides*, name of the Muses, from mount Pierus in Thessaly.

Πῑερίηθεν, Adv. *from Pieria* in Thessaly.

πιέσαι, for πίει, 2 sing. fut. of πίνω.

πιεσθείς, εῖσα, έν, aor. 1 pass. part. of πιέζω.

πῑήεις, εσσα, εν, poët. for πίων, *fat, rich.*

πίησθα, 2 sing. aor. 2 med. subj. of πίνω.

πιθάκνη Att. **φῐδάκνη**, ἡ, (πίθος) *a wine-cask, wine-jar.*

πίθᾰκος, Dor. for πίθηκος, *an ape.*

πιθᾰνολογέω, f. ήσω, (πιθανολόγος) *to use probable arguments.* Hence

πιθᾰνολογία, ἡ, *the use of probable arguments.*

πιθᾰνο-λόγος, ον, (πιθανός, λέγω) *speaking persuasively, using probable arguments.*

πιθᾰνός, ή, όν, (πείθω) act. *calculated to persuade:* 1. of persons, *persuasive.* 2. of manners, *winning.* 3. of reports, *plausible, credible:* hence *reasonable, likely.* 4. of works of art, *producing illusion, natural.* II. pass. *easy to persuade, credulous.* 2. *obedient.*

πιθᾰνῶς, Adv. of πιθανός, *persuasively:* Comp. πιθανώτερον, *more persuasively.*

πιθέσθαι, aor. 2 med. inf. of πείθω.

πιθεών, ῶνος, ὁ, (πίθος) *a place for casks, a cellar.*

πιθηκίζω, f. ίσω, (πίθηκος) *to play the ape.* Hence

πιθηκισμός, ὁ, *a playing the ape, aping.*

πίθηκος Dor. **πίθακος**, ὁ, (πείθω) *an ape*, Lat. *simius:* hence, *one who plays ape's tricks, a jackanapes.*

πιθηκο-φᾰγέω, (πίθηκος, φαγεῖν) *to eat ape's flesh.*

πιθηκο-φόρος, ον, (πίθηκος, φέρω) *carrying apes.*

πιθήσας, aor. 1 part. of πείθω, as if from πιθέω.

πίθι, irreg. 2 sing. aor. 2 imperat. of πίνω.

πιθ-οιγία, ἡ, (πίθος, οἴγνυμι) *an opening of casks.*

πιθοίγια, τό, (πίθος, οἴγνυμι) *the cask-opening*, a festival on the first day of the Anthesteria.

πῐθόμην, Ep. for ἐπιθόμην, aor. 2 med. of πείθω.

πίθος, ὁ, *a wine-jar* made of *earthenware.* [ῐ]

πίθων, ὁ, = πίθηκος, *an ape.* [ῐ]

πῐθών, οῦσα, όν, aor. 2 part. of πείθω.

πικραίνω, f. ἄνῶ, (πικρός) *to make sharp* or *bitter:* metaph. *to embitter, anger:*—Pass. *to grow angry.*

πῐκρία, ἡ, (πικρός) *bitterness:* of temper, *bitterness, malice, venom, spleen.*

πῐκρό-γᾰμος, ον, (πικρός, γαμέω) *embittered in marriage, unhappily wedded*

πῐκρό-γλωσσος, ον, (πικρός, γλῶσσα) *of sharp* or *bitter tongue.*

πῐκρό-καρπος, ον, (πικρός, καρπός) *bearing bitter fruit.*

ΠΙ'ΚΡΟ'Σ, ά, όν, also ός, όν, *sharp, keen, piercing:* of taste, *sharp, pungent, bitter:* of sound, *sharp, piercing, shrill.* 2. of persons, words, acts, etc., *bitter, cruel, harsh, stern, morose, severe:* also *hateful, hostile.* II. Comp. and Sup. πικρότερος, -ότατος, never πικρώτερος, -ώτατος. Hence

πῐκρότης, ητος, ἡ, *bitterness: harshness, cruelty.*

πῐκρό-χολος, ον, (πικρός, χολή) *with bitter gall: splenetic.*

πῐκρῶς, Adv. of πικρός, *sharply, harshly, bitterly, cruelly.*

πῖλέω, = πιλόω:—Pass. *to be close pressed.*

πιλίδιον, τό, Dim. of πῖλος, *a little felt-hat*, Lat. *pileolus.* [λῐ]

πῑ-λῐπής, ές, (πῖ, λιπεῖν) *wanting the letter πῖ.*

πιλνάω, = πελάζω, *to bring near to:*—Pass. πίλναμαι, *to draw near to, approach, encounter*, c. dat.

ΠΙ'ΛΟΣ, ὁ, *wool* or *hair wrought into felt, felt, felt-cloth.* II. *a felt-cap, hat;* πῖλος χαλκοῦς a brasen *hat*, i. e. helmet: also *a felt cuirass.*

πῖλοφορικός, ή, όν, *used to wear a felt-hat.* From

πῖλο-φόρος, ον, (πῖλος, φέρω) *wearing a felt-hat.*

πῖλόω, f. ώσω, (πῖλος) *to press wool so as to make it into felt, to felt wool:* hence *to press close, squeeze tight.*

πῖμελή, ἡ, (πίων, πῖαρ) *fat*, Lat. *adeps.* Hence

πῖμελής, ές, *fat*, Lat. *pinguis.*

πίμπλαντο, Ep. 3 pl. impf. pass. of πίμπλημι.

πιμπλάνω, poët. for πίμπλημι, hence pres. med. πιμπλάνεται for πίμπλαται.

πιμπλέω, = πίμπλημι: Ion. part. pl. fem. πιμπλεῦσαι.

ΠΙ'ΜΠΛΗΜΙ, inf. πιμπλάναι [ᾰ]: 3 pl. impf. ἐπίμπλασαν: (tenses formed from πλήθω): fut. πλήσω: aor. 1 ἔπλησα, med. ἐπλησάμην: Pass., aor. 1 ἐπλήσθην: pf. πέπλησμαι:—also, Ep. aor. 2 pass. ἐπλήμην, 3 sing. and pl. πλῆτο, πλῆντο, imperat. πλῆσο, opt. πλήμην or πλείμην:—*to fill, fill up, fill full of* a thing, c. acc. pers. et gen. rei; or *to fill with* a thing, c. dat. rei. 2. c. acc. pers. only, *to fill full, satisfy, glut.* 3. *to fulfil, discharge* an office. II. Med. *to fill for oneself*, or *what is one's own.* III. Pass. *to become* or *be full of: to be filled, satisfied, have enough of* a thing.

ΠΙ'ΜΠΡΗΜΙ, inf. πιμπράναι [ᾰ]: (tenses formed from πρήθω); fut. πρήσω: aor. 1 ἔπρησα: Pass., aor. ἐπρήσθην: pf. πέπρησμαι:—*to kindle, burn, set on fire:*—Pass. πίμπραμαι, *to be burnt, set on fire, consumed.*

πῖν, poët. inf. of ἔπιον, aor. 2 of πίνω.

πῐνᾰκηδόν, Adv. (πίναξ) *like planks.*

πῐνάκιον, τό, Dim. of πίναξ, *a little tablet*, esp. that on which the judges (δικασταί) wrote their verdict of guilty or not guilty, Lat. *tabella.*

πῐνᾰκίσκος, ὁ, = πινάκιον.

πῐνᾰκο-πώλης, ου, ὁ, (πίναξ, πωλέω) *one who sells small birds ranged upon a board.*

ΠΙ'ΝΑΞ, ᾰκος, ὁ, *a board, plank: a writing-tablet: a votive tablet.* 2. *a wooden trencher, dish, plate,* or *platter.* 3. *a board* for painting on, *a picture,* Lat. *tabula.* 4. *a plate engraved* or *written upon: a chart* or *map.* 5. *a board for public notices: a register, list.*

πῐνᾰρός, ά, όν, (πίνος) *dirty, squalid.*

πῐνάω, (πίνος) *to be dirty.*

πῐνέμεν, πῐνέμεναι, Ep. inf. of πίνω.

πίνεσκον [ῐ], Ion. impf. of πίνω.

πῐνηρός, ή, όν, Ion. for πιναρός.

ΠΙ'ΝΝΑ and **πίννη**, ἡ, a kind of *muscle, the pinna.*

πιννο-τήρης, ου, ὁ, (πίννα, τηρέω) *a small crab* that lives in the pinna's shell: metaph. *a little parasite.*

πῐνόεις, εσσα, εν = πιναρός.

ΠΙ'ΝΟΣ, ὁ, *dirt, filth*, Lat. *squalor.* [ῐ]

πῐνύσκω: aor. 1 ἐπίνυσσα; pass. ἐπινύσθην: (πέπνυμαι, pf. pass. of πνέω):—*to make wise* or *prudent, admonish, instruct, inform.* Hence

πῐνῠτή, ἡ, *understanding, wisdom.*

πῐνῠτής, ῆτος Dor. ᾶτος, ἡ, = πινυτή.

πῐνῠτός, ή, όν, (πινύσσω) *wise, understanding.*

πῐνῠτό-φρων, ονος, ὁ, ἡ, (πινυτός, φρήν) *of wise* or *understanding mind.*

ΠΙ'ΝΩ [ῑ]: fut. πίομαι: aor. 2 ἔπιον, imperat. πίε, also πῖθι, inf. πιεῖν: from Root ΠΟ- come pf. πέπωκα, aor. 1 pass. ἐπόθην: pf. pass. inf. πεπόσθαι:—*to drink*, Lat. *bibo;* c. gen. *to drink of* a thing: metaph. *to drink up, absorb:* pf. πέπωκα, *to have drunk, to be drunken.*

πῐν-ώδης, ες, (πίνος, εἶδος) *dirty, squalid.*

πίοιμι, aor. 2 opt. of πίνω.

πίομαι, fut. of πίνω: but also used as pres. med.

πίον, Ep. aor. 2 of πίνω.

πῖος, α, ον, poët. for πίων.

πῑότης, ητος, ἡ, (πῖος, πίων) *fatness, richness.*

πῑπίσκω, f. πίσω [ῑ]: aor. 1 ἔπῖσα: Causal of πίνω, *to give to drink*, c. dupl acc.; πίσω σφε Δίρκας ὕδωρ *I will give* them the water of Dircé *to drink.*

πίπλω, poët. for πίμπλημι, impf. ἔπιπλον, *to fill.*

πιππίζω, f. ίσω, *to chirp like young birds.* (Formed from the sound.)

πῐπράσκω Ion. **πιπρήσκω**, redupl. form of περάω:

pf. πέπρᾶκα: Pass., fut. 1 πρᾱθήσομαι, paullo-p. fut. πεπράσομαι [ᾱ]: aor. 1 pass. ἐπράθην [ᾱ]: pf. πέπρᾱμαι Ion. -ημαι: (περάω):—*to sell beyond seas*, like περάω: generally, *to sell*:—Pass. *to be sold*: metaph. *to be bought and sold*, i. e. *betrayed*.

πίπτω, for πι-πέτω, redupl. from Root ΠΕΤ-: Ep. impf. πίπτον: fut. πεσοῦμαι Ion. πεσέομαι: aor. 2 ἔπεσον, inf. πεσεῖν: pf. πέπτωκα, Ep. part. πεπτεώς and πεπτεώς, -εῶτος Att. πεπτώς, -ῶτος, syncop. from πεπτωκώς:—*to fall, fall down*; c. acc. cognato, πίπτειν πτώματα, πεσήματα: absol. in pf. πέπτωκα, *to be fallen, lie low*. II. Special usages: πίπτειν ἔν τινι *to fall upon* a thing *violently, to attack*. 2. πίπτειν ἔκ τινος *to fall out of* or *lose* a thing, Lat. *decidere de*..; ἐκ θυμοῦ πίπτειν τινί *to fall out of* or *lose* one's favour. 3. πίπτειν μετὰ ποσσὶ γυναικός *to fall* between the feet of a woman, i. e. to be born. 4. *to fall* in fight. 5. *to fall, sink, leave off*; ἄνεμος πέσε the wind *fell*. 6. πίπτειν ὑπό τινος *to fall by* another's hand, *to be overthrown, overcome*; ὁ στρατὸς αὐτὸς ὑπ' ἑωυτοῦ ἔπεσε the army failed of itself, Lat. *mole sua corruit*. 7. *to fall short, fail*: of a play, *to fail*, Lat. *cader*. 8. of the dice, to *fall* in a certain position; τὰ δεσποτῶν εὖ πεσόντα θήσομαι I shall count my master's throws lucky: generally, εὖ or καλῶς πίπτειν, *to be lucky*:—so also, *to fall, turn out, happen*.

πίρωμις, an Egypt. word = καλὸς κἀγαθός, *noble*.

πίσῐνος, η, ον, (πίσος) *made of peas*, ἔτνος πίσινον *pea-soup*.

ΠΙ'ΣΟΣ, a kind of *pulse, the pea*, Lat. *pisum*. [ῐ]

πῖσος, τό, (πίσω fut. of πιπίσκω) only in nom. and acc. pl. πίσεα, *moist lands, meadows*.

ΠΙ'ΣΣΑ˘ Att. πίττᾰ, ἡ, *pitch*, Lat. *pix*: proverb., μελάντερον ἠύτε πίσσα blacker than *pitch*.

πισσήρης, ες, (πίσσα) *of* or *like pitch, pitchy*.

πισσῖνος Att. **πιττινος**, η, ον, (πίσσα) *pitched over, coated with pitch*.

πισσόω Att. πιττ-, f. ώσω, *to pitch, cover with pitch*.

πίστευμα, τό, (πιστεύω) *a pledge of good faith*.

πιστευτικός, ή, όν, *disposed to trust, confiding*. From

πιστεύω, f. σω, (πίστις) *to believe, trust in, put faith in, confide in, rely on* a person or thing: absol., χαλεπὸν πιστεύειν hard *to believe*; πιστεύειν εἰς τινα *to believe on* a person:—Pass. *to be believed* or *trusted*. 2. *to believe, comply, obey*. II. c. inf. *to believe that, feel sure* or *confident that* a thing is: also c. dat. et inf. *to trust to* one, *rely on* one to do so and so. III. *to entrust* or *confide* something to another.

πιστικός, ή, όν, (πίνω) *drinkable, liquid*.

πιστικός, ή, όν, (πίστις) *trusty, faithful*. 2. *persuasive*. 3. *pure, genuine*.

πίστις, εως, ἡ, (πείθω, πείθομαι) *trust*, in others, *faith, belief*; Lat. *fides, fiducia*; πίστις θεῶν *faith in* the gods: *persuasion* of a thing, *confidence, assurance*. 2. *good faith, faithfulness, honesty*, Lat. *fides*. 3. *credit, trust*; εἰς πίστιν διδόναι to give *in trust*. II. *that which gives trust* or *confidence, an assurance, pledge of good faith, warrant*; πίστιν καὶ ὅρκια ποιεῖσθαι to exchange *assurances* and oaths. 2. *a means of persuasion, an argument, proof*.

πιστός, ή, όν, (πίνω) *drinkable, liquid*; τὰ πιστά *liquid medicines, draughts*.

πιστός, ή, όν, (πείθω) of persons, *faithful, trusty, true*: in Persia οἱ πιστοί or τὰ πιστά were *confidential* officers about the court, *privy-councillors*; πιστὰ πιστῶν, like ἔσχατ' ἐσχάτων, = πιστότατοι, *most trusty*. 2. *believed, trusted*. II. of things, *trustworthy, sure, deserving belief*: *credible*. 2. τὸ πιστόν, as Subst., *a pledge, security, warrant*; πιστὸν or πιστὰ δοῦναι καὶ λαβεῖν to give and receive *pledges*: also τὸ πιστόν = πίστις, *good faith*. III. act. *believing, relying on*. 2. *obedient*. Hence

πιστότης, ητος, ἡ, *good faith, honour, faithfulness*.

πιστόω, f. ώσω, (πιστός) *to make faithful* or *trustworthy, bind by a pledge* or *engagement*. II. Pass. *to be made trustworthy, give a pledge* or *warrant*; ὅρκῳ πιστωθῆναι *to pledge oneself* by oath. 2. *to feel trust, to be persuaded*; πιστωθείς, *trusting, confiding*. III. Med. *to give one another pledges* or *guarantees, exchange troth*. 2. πιστοῦσθαί τινα ὑφ' ὅρκων *to secure* his *good faith, bind* him by oaths.

πίστρα, ἡ, (πίνω) *a drinking-trough* or *cup*.

πίστρον, τό, (πίνω) = πίστρα.

πίστωμα, ατος, τό, (πιστόω) *an assurance, guarantee, pledge*. 3. γηραλέα πιστώματα = πιστοὶ γέροντες, as πιστὰ Περσῶν is used for πιστοὶ Περσῶν.

πιστῶς, Adv. of πιστός, *faithfully*: *persuasively*.

πιστώσαντο, Ep. 3 pl. aor. 1 med. of πιστόω.

πίσῠνος, η, ον, (πείθω) *trusting on, relying* or *depending on, confiding in*, c. dat.

πίσῠρες, οἱ, αἱ, πίσυρα, τά, Aeol. for τέσσαρες, τέσσαρα.

πίσω [ῑ], fut. of πιπίσκω.

πίτνα, Ep. for ἐπίτνα, 3 sing. impf. of πίτνημι.

πιτνάς, ασα, αν, part. of πίτνημι.

πίτνημι, collat. form of πετάννυμι, *to spread out, extend, expand*.

πιτνώ, = πετάννυμι, *to spread out*: impf. ἐπίτνον.

πίτνω [ῐ], poët. form of πίπτω, used metri grat. when the penult. is required to be short, as μίμνω is used for μένω, when the penult. is to be long.

πίττᾰ, ἡ, Att. for πίσσα.

πιττῖνος, η, ον, Att. for πίσσινος.

πιττόω, Att. for πισσόω.

πιτῠ-κάμπτης, ου, ὁ, = πιτυο-κάμπτης.

πιτῠλεύω, f. σω, (πίτυλος) *to ply the plashing oar*.

ΠΙ'ΤΥ˘ΛΟΣ [ῐ], ὁ, *the measured plash of oars*; ἑνὶ πιτύλῳ with one *stroke*. II. *the plash of* falling drops; πίτυλος σκύφου *the plash* of wine poured into a cup. 2. *the noise made by a quick succession of blows*, as, *the beating of the breast, clapping of the hands, repeated blows* with the fist, with the spear. 3. metaph. of any *violent gestures, frantic passion*.

πῐτῠο-κάμπτης, ου, ὁ, (πίτυς, κάμπτω) *the pine-bender*, epith. of the robber Sinis, who killed travellers by tying them between two pine-trees bent down so as nearly to meet, and then let go.

πῐτῠο-τρόφος, ον, (πίτυς, τρέφω) *growing pines*.

πίτῡρον, τό, (πτίσσω) *bran, the husk of corn:* generally, *refuse*, Lat. *furfur, furfura;* mostly used in pl.

ΠΙ'ΤΥ'Σ, υος, ἡ, poët. dat. pl. πίτυσσιν: *the pine-tree*, Lat. *pinus:* proverb., πίτυος δίκην ἐκτρίβεσθαι to be destroyed like *a pine-tree*, i. e. *utterly*, because the pine-tree once cut down never grows again.

πῐτῠ-στεπτος, ον, (πίτυς, στέφω) *pine-crowned*.

πιφαύσκω, (redupl. form of φαίνω, akin to φάσκω, as διδάσκω to δαίω), only used in pres. and impf. *to let be seen, shew, reveal by a token:* mostly, *to shew by words, to make known, tell, declare, reveal.* 2. πιφαύσκομαι as Dep. *to make manifest, make known, declare.*

πίω, aor. 2 subj. of πίνω.

ΠΙ'ΩΝ [ῑ], ὁ, ἡ, neut. πῖον, gen. πίονος:—Lat. *PINGUIS, fat, plump, sleek*, of animals: *oily, rich.* II. of soil, *fat, rich, fertile:* also *wealthy.* III. Comp. and Sup. πῑότερος, πῑότατος (as if from πῖος).

πιών, οῦσα, όν, aor. 2 part. of πίνω.

πλαγά, Dor. for πληγή.

πλᾰγιάζω, f. άσω, (πλάγιος) *to turn sideways* or *slanting, turn aside: to tack to and fro.*

πλᾰγί-αυλος, ὁ, (πλάγιος, αὐλός) *the cross flute, German flute.*

πλάγιος, α, ον, also ος, ον, *placed sideways, slanting, athwart;* εἰς πλάγιον *sideways;* τὰ πλάγια *the sides*, in military sense, *the flanks* of an army; εἰς τὰ πλάγια *right and left;* κατὰ πλάγια in *flank;* ἐκ πλαγίου on *the flank;* πλαγίους λαβεῖν τοὺς πολεμίους to take the enemy *in flank.* II. metaph. *sideways, askance, treacherous.*

πλᾰγιόω, (πλάγιος) *to turn* or *move sideways.*

πλᾰγίως, Adv. of πλάγιος, *aslant.*

πλαγκτήρ, ῆρος, ὁ, (πλάζω) act. *he that leads astray, a misleader.* 2. pass. *a wanderer, rover.*

πλαγκτός, ή, όν, also ός, όν, (πλάζω) *wandering, roaming.* II. metaph. *wandering in mind, distraught, unsettled.* Hence

πλαγκτοσύνη, ἡ, *a wandering, roaming.*

πλάγξομαι, fut. med. of πλάζω.

πλαγχθῆναι, **-θείς**, aor. 1 pass. inf. and part. of πλάζω.

πλᾰδᾰρός, ά, όν, *wet, moist.* From

ΠΛΑ'ΔΟΣ, ὁ, *moisture.*

ΠΛΑ'ΖΩ: Ep. impf. πλάζον: f. πλάγξω: aor. 1 ἔπλαγξα:—*to make to wander* or *roam, drive from the right course, cast away:* metaph. *to lead astray:* generally, *to mislead, seduce.* II. Pass., with fut. med. πλάγξομαι, aor. 1 pass. ἐπλάγχθην Ep. πλάγχθην, *to wander, go astray: to glance* or *slide off.*

πλᾰθάνη, ἡ, (πλάσσω) *a platter* or *mould* to bake in.

πλάθᾰνον, τό, πλάθανος, ὁ, = πλαθάνη.

πλᾰθῆναι, **-θείς**, aor. 1 pass. inf. and part. of πελάζω.

πλάθω, collat. form of πελάζω, intr. *to approach, draw near, come nigh.* [ᾰ]

ΠΛΑΙ'ΣΙΟΝ, τό, *an oblong figure* or *body;* ἰσόπλευρον πλαίσιον *a square:* of an army, ἐν πλαισίῳ τετάχθαι to be drawn up in *square*, Lat. *agmine quadrato*, as opp. to marching order, *agmine longo.*

πλακείς, εῖσα, έν, aor. 2 pass. part. of πλέκω.

πλᾰκερός, ά, όν, (πλάξ) = πλατύς, *broad.*

πλάκῐνος, η, ον, (πλάξ) *made of a board* or *plank, wooden.* [ᾰ]

πλᾰκοῦς, οῦντος, ὁ, contr. from πλακόεις, (πλάξ) *a flat cake.*

πλάκτωρ, ορος, ὁ, Dor. for πλήκτωρ.

πλάν, Dor. for πλήν.

πλᾰνάω Ion. -έω, f. ήσω, (πλάνη) *to lead astray, lead wandering about:* of ships, *to drive from* their course: generally, *to mislead, lead into error.* II. Pass. πλανάομαι, with fut. med. πλανήσομαι, aor. 1 pass. ἐπλανήθην, pf. πεπλάνημαι:—*to wander, roam about, stray:* c. acc., πλανᾶσθαι χθόνα *to wander over* a land, Lat. *oberrare:* πλανᾶσθαι ἐν λόγῳ *to be at a loss* in one's story: *to wander in mind, be at a loss.*

ΠΛΑ'ΝΗ, ἡ, *a wandering* or *roaming about, straying: erring, error.* [ᾰ]

πλάνημα, ατος, τό, (πλᾰνάω) *a wandering, going astray.*

πλάνης, ητος, ὁ, (πλάνη) *a wanderer, roamer, rover,* Lat. *erro;* πλάνητες ἀστέρες *wandering* stars, *planets.*

πλάνησις, εως, ἡ, (πλανάω) *a leading astray: a dispersing.* [ᾰ]

πλανητέον, verb. Adj. of πλανάομαι, *one must wander.*

πλᾰνήτης, ου, ὁ, fem. **-ῆτις**, ιδος, (πλαναω) = πλάνης, *a wanderer.* 2. *a planet.*

πλάνιος, α, ον, poët. for πλάνος.

πλαν-οδία, ἡ, (πλάνος, ὁδός) *a wrong way, by-way.* [πλᾱ- metri grat.]

ΠΛΑ'ΝΟΣ [ᾰ], η, ον, also ος, ον, act. *leading astray, deceiving:* as Subst., πλάνος, ὁ, *a deceiver.* 2. pass. *wandering, roaming.*

ΠΛΑ'ΝΟΣ, ὁ, = πλάνη, *a wandering about, roaming, straying:* φροντίδος πλάνοι *wanderings* of thought.

πλᾰνο-στῑβής, ές, (πλάνος, στείβω) *trodden by wanderers.*

πλᾰνύττω, = πλαναομαι, *to wander about.*

ΠΛΑ'Ξ, ἡ, gen. πλᾰκός, *anything flat and broad, flat land, a plain;* πόντου πλάξ the ocean *plain:* the *flat top of a hill, table-land:*—also *a flat stone, tombstone.*

πλᾶξεν, Dor. for ἔπληξεν, 3 sing. aor. 1 of πλήσσω.

πλάξ-ιππος, ον, Dor. for πλήξιππος.

πλάσμα, ατος, τό, (πλάσσω) *anything moulded* or *modelled* in clay or wax, *an image, figure;* πλάσματα πηλοῦ *vessels* of clay. II. *that which is imitated, a forgery.*

ΠΛΑ'ΣΣΩ Att. **-ττω**: f. πλασω [ᾰ]: aor. 1 ἔπλᾰσα Ep. ἔπλασσα, πλάσσα: pf. πέπλᾰκα: Pass., aor. 1 ἐπλάσθην: pf. πέπλασμαι:—*to form, mould,* *shape, fashion*, Lat. *fingere*, of the statuary who works in clay or wax.—Pass. *to be moulded, made, fashioned.* II. generally, *to mould, shape*, of the mind and body:—Med., πλασάμενος τῇ ὄψει *having formed himself* in face, i. e. having composed his countenance III. metaph. *to make up, fabricate, forge:* absol., δόξω πλάσας λέγειν I shall seem to speak *from invention;* κόμπος οὐ πεπλασμένος no *false* boast. Hence

πλαστής, οῦ, ὁ, fem. **πλάστειρα**, *one who moulds* or *models, a modeller.*

πλάστιγξ Ion. **πλῆστιγξ**, ιγγος, ἡ, (πλήσσω) *the tongue* or *scale of a balance.* II. *a pair of scales, balance:* also *a yoke for horses.* III. *a whip.*

πλαστός, ή, όν, doubtful form of πελαστός.

πλαστός, ή, όν, (πλάσσω) *formed, moulded, modelled.* II. metaph. *made up, forged, counterfeit, unreal;* πλαστὸς πατρί *a supposititious* son.

πλᾰτᾰγέω, f. ήσω, *to clap the hands loudly:* *to clash, crack.* II. *to beat*, so as to make a loud noise. From

πλᾰτάγη, ἡ, (πλατάσσω) *a rattle.*

πλᾰτάγημα, ατος, τό, (πλαταγέω) *a clapping.*

πλᾰτᾰγών, ῶνος ὁ (πλαταγέω) *anything that rattles* or *cracks.*

πλᾰτᾰγώνιον, τό, Dim. of πλαταγών, *the broad petal of the poppy*, which they used to lay on the hand and strike smartly; it was a good omen if it burst *with a loud crack.*

Πλάταια, ἡ, mostly in plur. **Πλαταιαί**, ῶν, αἱ, *Plataea*, a city in Boeotia: adverbial dat., Πλαταιᾶσι *at Plataea.* Hence

Πλαταιεῖς Ion. **-έες** Att. **-ῆς**, οἱ, *the Plataeans.*

πλᾰτᾰμών, ῶνος, ὁ, (πλατύς) *any broad flat body:* *a flat stone, a flat beach.*

πλᾰτάνιστος, ἡ, = πλάτανος. Hence

πλᾰτᾰνιστοῦς, οῦντος, ὁ, contr. for πλατανιστόεις, *a plane-tree grove.*

πλάτᾰνος, ἡ, (πλᾰτύς) *the oriental plane, the plane-tree*, Lat. *platanus*, so called from its *broad, flat* leaf.

πλᾰτεῖα, ἡ, see πλατύς.

πλᾰτειάζω Dor. **-άσδω**: f. άσω: (πλατύς):—*to speak* or *pronounce broadly*, esp. *with a Doric accent.*

πλατέως, Adv. of πλατύς, *broadly.*

πλάτη Dor. **πλάτα**, ἡ, (πλᾰτύς) *the flat* or *broad part* of anything, *the blade of an oar*, Lat. *palmula remi:* *the whole oar.* 2. *a sheet of paper.*

πλᾰτίον, Adv., Dor. for πλησίον.

πλᾶτις, ιδος, ἡ, (πελάζω) poët. for πελάτις, *a wife.*

πλάτος, εος, τό, (πλᾰτύς) *breadth, width:* absol. in acc., τὸ πλάτος or πλάτος *in breadth*

πλᾱτός, ή, όν (πελάζω) = πλαστός, πελαστός.

πλᾰτόω, f. ώσω, (πλάτη) *to form the flat of oars*

πλᾰτῠγίζω, f. σω, (πλατύς) *to beat the water with the blade of an oar:* *to splash about:* metaph *to make a splash, splutter, swagger*

πλᾰτῠ-λέσχης, ου, ὁ, (πλατύς, λέσχη) *a babbler.*

πλατυντέον, verb. Adj. of πλατύνω, *one must widen.*

πλᾰτύνω, f. ῠνῶ, (πλατύς) *to make broad, widen, extend:*—Med., πλατύνεσθαι τὴν γῆν *to widen one's* territory. 2. *to open wide:* 3 sing. pf. pass. πεπλάτυνται *has been opened.*

πλᾰτύ-νωτος, ον, (πλατύς, νῶτος) *broad-backed.*

πλᾰτύρ-ροος, ον, contr. **-ρους**, ουν, (πλατύς, ῥέω) *broad-flowing.*

ΠΛΑΤΥ'Σ, εῖα, ύ, Ion. fem. πλατέα:—*flat, wide, broad:*—metaph., πλατὺς κατάγελως *flat* mockery 2. as Subst., ἡ πλατεῖα (sub. ὁδός), *a street:* also (sub. χείρ), *the flat of the hand.* II. *salt, brackish*, because πλατὺ ὕδωρ was originally used of *the sea.* III. Comp. and Sup., πλατύτερος, πλατύτατος.

πλᾰτύτης, ητος, ἡ, (πλατύς) *breadth, width:* generally, *size, bulk.* [ῠ]

πλέας, acc. of πλέες, q. v.

πλέγδην, Adv. (πλέκω) *in plaits* or *braids.*

πλέγμα, ατος, τό, (πλέκω) *anything twined* or *plaited, a net:* in pl. *wreaths, chaplets.*

πλέες, οἱ, acc. πλέᾰς, Ep. for πλείονες, Comp. of πολύς, *more:* Dor. contr. πλεῖς.

πλεθρῐαῖος, α, ον, *of the size of a* πλέθρον.

ΠΛΕ'ΘΡΟΝ Ep. **πέλεθρον**, τό, as measure of length, *a plethron*, being 100 Greek or 101 English feet, the sixth part of a stade. 2. *a race-course* or *race of this length.* II. as a square measure, 10,000 square feet, about 37 perches.

Πλειάς, άδος, ἡ, in plur. **Πλειάδες** Ion. **Πληιάδες**, αἱ, *the Pleiads*, seven daughters of Atlas and Pleïonē, who were placed among the stars.

πλείμην, εῖο, εῖτο, aor. 2 med. opt. of πίμπλημι.

πλεῖν, Att. for πλέον, like δεῖν for δέον *more.* inf. of πλέω *to sail.*

πλεῖος, η, ον, Ion. and Ep. for πλέος, *full.*

πλειότερος, η, ον, Comp. of πλεῖος, *fuller.*

πλειστάκις, Adv. (πλεῖστος) *most times, mostly, very often.*

πλειστήρης, ες, (πλεῖστος) *manifold;* ἅπας πλειστήρης χρόνος the whole *extent* of time. Hence

πλειστηρίζομαι, Dep. *to assign as the chief agent* of a thing, *to accuse of being the author* of a thing.

πλειστο-βόλος, ον, (πλεῖστος, βαλεῖν) *throwing the most, throwing the highest.*

πλειστόμ-βροτος, ον, (πλεῖστος, βροτός) *thronged with people, crowded.*

πλεῖστος, η, ον, Sup. of πολύς, *most*, Lat. *plurimus:* *very much;* also, *very great:*—οἱ πλεῖστοι *the greatest number;* τὸ πλεῖστον *the greatest part;* so also agreeing with its Noun, ὁ πλεῖστος τοῦ βίου *the most part* of life:—ἡ πλείστη γνώμη ἦν his opinion was *mostly;* πλεῖστός εἰμι τῇ γνώμῃ I am *mostly* of opinion; ὅσοι πλεῖστοι *the most* possible; ἐν τοῖς πλεῖστοι *about the most*, like ἐν τοῖς πρῶτοι:—neut. πλεῖστον as Adv. *most:* τὸ πλεῖστον *for the most part:*—with Preps., διὰ πλείστου at *the greatest* distance; ἐπὶ πλεῖστον to *the greatest* extent; περὶ πλείστου of *the greatest* importance or value.

πλείω, Ep. pres. for πλέω, *to sail.*

πλείων or **πλέων**, ὁ, ἡ, neut. πλεῖον or πλέον, gen. ονος; Ep. nom. and acc. pl. πλέες πλέᾰς, Dor. πλεῖς: πλεῦν, πλεῦνος, πλεῦνες etc., are Ion. and Dor. for πλέον, πλέονος, etc.: πλεῖν Att. for πλέον, like δεῖν for δέον: Ep dat. pl. πλεόνεσσι: Comp. of πολύς:—*more:* also *greater, larger,* of size as well as number: —οἱ πλέονες Ion. and Dor. οἱ πλεῦνες, *the greater number,* and so, like οἱ πολλοί, *the many, the people,* opp. to the chief men; τὸ πλεῖον *the greater part;* so also agreeing with its Noun, πλέων νύξ *the greater part of* night. II. the neut. πλέον has various usages, *more* of a thing, Lat. *plus;* τὸ πλέον, Ion. and Dor. τὸ πλεῦν, as Adv. *mostly;* οὐ τὸ πλέον not *so much;* πλέον ἤ.. *more* than..; but the ἤ may be omitted, πλείω ἑβδομήκοντα *more than* seventy:—πλέον ἔφερε οἱ ἡ γνώμη his opinion *rather* tended; πλέον ἔχειν to have *the best* of it, opp. to ἔλαττον ἔχειν to be beaten:—with Preps., ἐπὶ πλέον as Adv. *more, further;* ἐς πλέον *more;* περὶ πλείονος of *more* importance, of *higher* value.

πλειών, ῶνος, ὁ, (πλεῖος, πλέος) *a full space of time, a year.*

πλέκος, εος, τό, (πλέκω) *anything twined* or *plaited, wickerwork.*

πλεκτᾰνάω, f. ήσω, *to twist into wreaths, coil.* From

πλεκτάνη, ἡ, (πλέκω) *anything twined* or *plaited, a coil, wreath;* πλεκτάνη καπνοῦ *a wreath* of smoke. [ᾰ]

πλεκτή, ἡ, fem of πλεκτός, *a coil, wreath.* 2. *a twisted rope, cord, string.*

πλεκτικός, ή, όν, (πλέκω) *of* or *for plaiting.*

πλεκτός, ή, όν, (πλέκω) *plaited, twisted, twined;* πλεκταὶ στέγαι *wicker* coverings, i.e. cars; τὰ πλεκτά *any plaited instruments, ropes.*

ΠΛΕ'ΚΩ, f. ξω: aor. 1 ἔπλεξα: pf. πέπλεχα: Pass., aor. 1 ἐπλέχθην, and aor. 2 ἐπλάκην [ᾰ]: pf. πέπλεγμαι:—*to twine, twist, weave, braid, enfold,* Lat. *plico, plecto:* also *to knit;* Med., πλέξασθαι πεῖσμα *to twist oneself a rope.* 2. metaph. *to plan, devise, contrive.* II. Pass. *to be plaited* or *woven.* 2. *to twist oneself round,* and so *to clasp, embrace.*

πλέον, neut. of πλέων, *more:* also neut. of πλέος, *full.*

πλεονάζω, f. άσω: pf. πεπλεόνᾰκα: (πλέον):—*to be more than enough, to go too far, take* or *claim too much: to presume on,* c. dat. II. *to exaggerate, overstate.*

πλεονάκις, Adv. (πλέων) *more frequently, oftener: too often.* [ᾰ]

πλεον-εκτέω, f. ήσω or ήσομαι, = πλέον ἔχω *to have* or *take more than another, to have* or *claim a larger share; to claim more than is one's due, to be grasping: to gain some advantage.* 2. c. gen. *to have* or *gain the advantage over* another:—Pass. *to be overreached, defrauded.* 3. c. gen. rei, *to have a greater share of* a thing; πλεονεκτεῖν ψύχους *to bear more* cold. Hence

πλεονέκτημα, ατος, τό, *an advantage, gain:* in pl. *gains, successes.*

πλεον-έκτης, ου, ὁ, = ὁ πλέον ἔχων, *one who has* or *claims more than his share,* hence *greedy, grasping, selfish:* also as Adj., λόγος πλεονέκτης *a grasping, overbearing* speech. And

πλεονεκτικός, ή, όν, *disposed to take more than one's share:* From

πλεονεξία Ion. -ίη, ἡ, *a disposition to take more than one's share, a grasping temper, greediness, covetousness, a claiming more than one's share.* 2. *advantage, superiority;* πλεονεξία τινός *advantage over* another; ἐπὶ πλεονεξίᾳ for one's *advantage* or *gain.*

πλεόνως, Adv. of πλέων, *too much.*

ΠΛΕ'ΟΣ, α, ον, Ion. **πλεῖος**, η, ον, Att. **πλέως**, έα, έων; pl. πλέῳ, πλέᾳ (for πλέαι), πλέᾱ:—*full, filled,* c. gen.: hence *satisfied, cloyed:* of Time, *full, complete.* Comp. πλειότερος.

πλέτο, poët. for ἔπλετο, 3 sing. impf. of πέλομαι.

πλεῦν, Ion. and Dor. for πλέον: so **πλεῦνος, πλεῦνες**, for πλέονος, πλέονες, etc.

πλεύνως, Adv. Ion. for πλεόνως, *too much.*

ΠΛΕΥΡΑ', ᾶς, ἡ, *a rib,* Lat. *costa:* in pl. *the ribs, the side* or *sides.* II. later, *the page* of a book.

πλευρῖτις, ιδος, ἡ, (πλευρά) *pain in the side, pleurisy.*

πλευρόθεν, Adv. (πλευρά) *from the side.*

πλευρο-κοπέω, f. ήσω, (πλευρά, κόπτω) *to smite the ribs.*

ΠΛΕΥΡΟ'Ν, τό, *a rib,* an older poët. form of πλευρά: in pl. *the ribs, the side.*

πλευρο-τῠπής, ές, (πλευρόν, τύπτω) *striking the sides.*

πλεύρωμα, ατος, τό, like πλευρόν, *the side.*

πλεύσομαι or **πλευσοῦμαι**, fut. med of **πλέω.**

πλευστέον, verb. Adj. of πλέω, *one must sail.*

πλευστικός, ή, όν, (πλέω) *fit for sailing, fair.*

ΠΛΕ'Ω Ep. **πλείω**: fut. πλεύσομαι or πλευσοῦμαι: aor. 1 ἔπλευσα: pf. πέπλευκα; Pass., aor. 1 ἐπλεύσθην: pf. πέπλευσμαι: cp. the Ion. form **πλώω**:—*to sail, go by sea;* c. acc. cognato, ὑγρὰ κέλευθα πλεῖν *to sail* the watery ways:—*to swim, float;*—metaph., πλεῖν κατ' ὀρθόν *to go on* prosperously.

πλέω, Att. nom. and acc. neut. pl. of **πλέων**, *more.*

πλέων, neut. πλέον, for πλείων, q. v.

πλέως, πλέᾱ, **πλέων**, pl. πλέῳ, πλέᾳ (for πλέαι), πλέᾱ, *full,* Att. for πλέος.

πληγείς, εῖσα, έν, aor. 2 pass. part. of πλήσσω.

πληγή, ἡ, (πλήσσω) *a blow, stroke, stripe:*—also *a wound,* Lat. *plāga:* also *a beating* or *fighting with clubs:* metaph. *a blow, stroke, shock.*

πλῆγμα, ατος, τό, = πληγή.

πλῆθος, εος, τό, (πίμπλημι) *a great number, a mass, throng, crowd: the greater part, the mass, main body;* hence *the people, the commons:* also *the government of the people, democracy.* II. *number* or *quantity:* also *magnitude, size, bulk.* III. sometimes *length, duration* of Time.

πληθύνω [ῡ], f. ῠνῶ, (πληθύς) *to make full: to increase, multiply:* Pass. *to increase* (intr.), *to be completed;* of persons, *to be fully resolved.* II. intr. = πληθύω.

πληθύς, ύος, ἡ, Ep. dat. πληθυῖ. Ion. for πλῆθος, *a throng, crowd.*

πληθύω, (πληθύς) *to be* or *become full;* ἀγορῆς πληθυούσης when the market-place *becomes full:* of rivers, *to swell, rise.* 2. *to abound: to increase in number: to spread, prevail;* ὁ πληθύων λόγος *the current* story.

πλήθω, pf. πέπληθα: (πλέος):—*to be* or *become full;* πλήθουσα σελήνη the moon *at the full:* of rivers, *to be full, to swell, rise.* 2. *to complete* a space of time.

πληθώρη, ἡ, (πλήθω) *fulness: satiety.*

πλήκτης, ου, ὁ, (πλήσσω) *a striker, brawler, quarrelsome person.*

πληκτίζομαι, Dep. (πλήσσω) *to fight, combat.* II. *to beat one's breast for grief.* Lat. *plangere.* III. *to engage in dalliance.*

πληκτισμός, ὁ, (πληκτίζομαι) *dalliance.*

πλῆκτρον, τό, (πλήσσω) *an instrument to strike with, an instrument for striking the lyre,* Lat. *plectrum.* 2. *a spear-point.* 3. *a cock's spur,* Lat. *calcar.* 4. *a punting-pole* or *paddle.*

πλήκτωρ, ορος, ὁ, (πλήσσω) *a striker, brawler.*

πλήμενος, Ep. aor. 2 pass. part. of πίμπλημι.

πλημμέλεια, ἡ, (πλημμελής) *a mistake in music, false note:* generally, *a fault, error, offence.*

πλημμελέω, f. ήσω, (πλημμελής) *to make a false note in music: to err, offend:*—Pass. *to be neglected, to be ill-treated* or *insulted.* Hence

πλημμέλημα, ατος, τό, = πλημμέλεια.

πλημ-μελής, ές, (πλήν, μέλος) *out of tune, making a false note:* generally, *erring, faulty, offending:* of things, *unpleasant, harsh.* Adv. -λῶς.

πλήμμη, ἡ, = πλήσμη.

πλήμμῡρα, ἡ, = πλημμυρίς, *flood-tide: a flood.* Hence

πλημμῡρέω, f. ήσω, *to overflow.*

πλημμυρίς, ίδος, ἡ, (πλήμμη) *the flow of the sea, the flood-tide;* πλημμυρὶς ἐκ πόντοιο *the flood* setting in towards land: generally, *a flood, deluge.* [ῠ Ep., ῡ Att.]

πλήμνη, ἡ, (πλήθω) *the nave of a wheel.*

πλήν, (properly contr. from πλέον, *more than*), *beyond:* I. as Prep., with gen. *except, save.* II. as Adv. *besides, unless, save, except;* πλὴν ὅσον *except* so far as: it is often followed by some conjunct.; πλὴν ὅταν *save* when; πλὴν ὅτι *except* that; πλὴν εἰ or ἐάν, Lat. *nisi si, only* if; etc.; when apparently followed by an acc, there is an ellipse, οὐκ οἶδα πλὴν ἕν (sc. οἶδα) I know not, *only* one thing (I know).

πλῆντο, 3 pl. Ep. aor. 2 pass. of πίμπλημι. II. 3 pl Ep aor. 2 pass. of πελάζω.

πλῆξα, Ep. for ἔπληξα, aor. 1 of πλήσσω.

πλήξ-ιππος, ον, (πλήσσω, ἵππος) *striking* or *driving horses.*

πληρεῦντες, -εύμεναι, Ion. part. act. and pass. of πληρόω

πλήρης, ες, gen. εος contr. ους. (πλέος) *full of,* c. gen.; rarely c. dat. *filled with:* absol. *full, filled to the brim.* 2. generally, *full, complete, sufficient.* 3. of persons, *satisfied, satiated, cloyed with* a thing.

πληρο-φορέω, f. ήσω, (πλήρης, φέρω) *to bring full confirmation, to fulfil:*—Pass. *to be fully assured:* of things, *to be fully believed.* Hence

πληροφορία, ἡ, *full conviction, certainty.*

πληρόω, f. ώσω: pf. πεπλήρωκα: fut. med. πληρώσομαι mostly used in pass. sense: fut. pass. πληρωθήσομαι: (πλήρης):—*to fill, make full:* πληροῦν ναῦν *to man* a ship: πληροῦτε θωρακεῖα *man* the walls. 2. *to fill full* of good, *to satiate, satisfy.* 3. πληροῦν τὴν χρείαν *to supply* the need. II. of numbers, *to make full, complete, make up.* III. *to fulfil a duty:* generally, *to perform* or *discharge a task.* IV. intr. *to be complete.* Hence

πλήρωμα, ατος, τό, *that which fills up, a full measure, complement:* of the men in a ship, *a ship's complement, her crew:* of number, *the sum.* II. *a filling up, completing.*

πλήρωσις, ἡ, (πληρόω) *a filling up, filling: the completing a number: the manning* a ship.

πλησαίατο, Ep. for πλήσαιντο, 3 pl. aor. 1 med. opt. of πίμπλημι.

πλήσας, aor. 1 part. of πιμπλημι.

πλῆσθεν, Ep. for ἔπλησθεν, 3 pl. aor. 1 pass. of πίμπλημι.

πλησθήσομαι, fut. pass. of πιμπλημι.

πλησιάζω, f. άσω: pf. πεπλησίακα: (πλησίος):—*to bring near:*—Pass. *to be brought near, approach.* II. intr. *to be near: to approach:* c. dat. also, *to be always near, associate with.*

πλησιαίτερος, -αίτατος, Att. Comp. and Sup. of πλησίος: Adv. Comp. πλησιαιτέρω, *nearer.*

πλησιέστερος, -έστατος, Comp. and Sup. of πλησίος.

πλησιος, α, ον, (πέλας, πελάζω) *near, hard by, close to.* II. as Subst, πλήσιος, ὁ, *a neighbour.* III. Adv. πλησίον, *near, nigh, hard by;* ὁ πλησίον (sub. ὤν) *one's neighbour:* so Dor. ὁ πλᾱτίον. IV. Comp. πλησιέστερος, Sup. -έστατος, also πλησιαίτερος, -αίτατος, *nearer, nearest.*

πλησιό-χωρος, ον, (πλησίος, χώρα) *near a country, bordering upon,* Lat. *finitimus:* as Subst. *one who lives near, a neighbour*

πλησ-ίστιος, ον, (πίμπλημι, ἱστίον) *filling* or *swelling the sails.*

πλήσμη, ἡ, (πίμπλημι) *the swelling* or *rising* of a river.

πλησμονή, ἡ, (πίμπλημι) *a filling up* or *being filled up, satiety:* generally, *fulness, repletion, plenty.*

ΠΛΗ'ΣΣΩ Att. -ττω: f. ξω: aor. 1 ἔπληξα Ep. πλῆξα: pf. πέπληγα: Pass., fut. πληγήσομαι, paullo-p. fut. πεπλήξομαι: aor. 2 ἐπλήγην, in compds. ἐπλάγην [ᾰ]: pf. πέπληγμαι:—Ep. redupl. aor. 2 act. πέπληγον, inf. πεπληγέμεν, med. πεπληγόμην:—*to strike, smite, wound,* of a direct blow, as opp. to βάλλειν (*to strike with a missile*): of Jove, *to strike* with lightning: *to strike back, drive away*:—Med., πλήξασθαι *to smite* or *beat oneself* in sign of grief:—Pass. *to be struck, stricken, smitten*: also *to be beaten*: *to be stricken* by misfortune: but, πλήσσεσθαι δώροισι *to be touched* by bribes. II. metaph. of violent emotions, *to strike, amaze, confound, stun*; πληγεὶς ἔρωτι *smitten* with love.

πλῆστιγξ, ἡ, Ion. for πλάστιγξ.

πλῆτο, 3 sing. Ep aor. 2 pass. of πίμπλημι. II. 3 sing. Ep. aor. 2 of πελάζω, *be came near*.

πλινθεύω, f. σω, (πλίνθος) *to make into bricks*. absol. *to make bricks*. II. *to build of brick*.

πλινθηδόν, Adv. (πλίνθος) *in the shape of a brick*.

πλίνθῐνος, η, ον, (πλίνθος) *made* or *built of brick*.

πλινθίον, τό, Dim. of πλίνθος, *a small brick*.

πλινθίς, ίδος, ἡ, Dim. of πλίνθος: *a whetstone*.

πλινθο-ποιέω, f. ήσω, (πλίνθος, ποιέω) *to make bricks*:

πλίνθος, ἡ, *a brick*, Lat. *later*; πλίνθοι ὀπταί baked *bricks*; πλίνθους ἑλκύσαι or εἰρύσαι Lat. *ducere lateres*, to make *bricks*: δόμοι πλίνθου layers of *brick*. 2. *anything shaped like a brick, a plinth, an ingot* of metal. 3. *the plinth* of a column.

πλινθουργέω, f. ήσω, *to make bricks*. From

πλινθ-ουργός, όν, (πλίνθος, *ἔργω) *making bricks*: as Subst., πλινθουργός, ὁ, *a brick-maker*.

πλινθοφορέω, f. ήσω, *to carry bricks*. From

πλινθο-φόρος, ον, (πλίνθος, φέρω) *carrying bricks*.

πλινθόω, f. ώσω, (πλίνθος) *to make of brick*: Med. *to build for oneself*.

πλινθ-ῠφής, ές, (πλίνθος, ὑφαίνω) *brick-built*.

ΠΛΙ'ΣΣΟΜΑΙ, f. πλίξομαι: pf. πέπλιγμαι: Dep.:—*to cross one's legs in walking*: *to walk briskly, trot*.

πλοη-τόκος, ον, (πλόος, τεκεῖν) *producing navigation*.

πλοιάριον, τό, Dim. of πλοῖον, *a skiff, boat*.

πλοῖον, τό, (πλέω) *a floating vessel, a ship* of any kind; πλοῖα λεπτά small *craft*; πλοῖα ἱππαγωγά transport-*vessels*; πλοῖα μακρά *ships* of war, Lat. *longae naves*; πλοῖα στρογγύλα *ships* of burthen, Lat. *naves onerariae*:—as distinguished from ναῦς (*a ship of war*), πλοῖον was a *merchant-ship* or *transport*.

πλοκᾰμίς, ῖδος, ἡ, (πλόκαμος) *a braid, lock*, or *curl of hair*: also *curly hair*. [ῐ]

πλόκᾰμος, ὁ, (πλέκω) *a braid, lock* or *curl of hair*: in pl. *the locks, the hair*. II. *a twisted rope*.

πλοκή, ἡ, (πλέκω) *anything plaited* or *woven, a web*: metaph. *a web of deceit*.

πλόκος, ὁ, (πλέκω) *a lock* or *curl of hair*. II. *a wreath* or *chaplet*.

πλόμενος, Ep. syncop. pres. part. of πέλομαι.

πλόος Att. contr. **πλοῦς**, ὁ, plur. πλοῖ, πλῶν, etc.: (πλέω):—*a sailing voyage*: *time* or *tide for sailing*:—proverb., δεύτερος πλοῦς the next best way.

πλουθ-ῠγίεια, ἡ, (πλοῦτος, ὑγίεια) *health and wealth*.

πλοῦς, ὁ, Att. contr. for πλόος.

πλούσιος, α, ον, (πλοῦτος) *rich, wealthy*: c. gen. rei, *rich in* a thing Lat. *dives opum*. II. *ample, abundant*. III. Adv. ίως, *like a rich man*.

Πλουτεύς, έως, ἡ, poët for Πλούτων.

πλουτέω, f. ήσω, (πλοῦτος) *to be rich, wealthy*: c. gen. *to be rich, abound in* a thing. Hence

πλουτηρός, ά, όν, *enriching*.

πλουτίζω, f. ίσω, (πλοῦτος) *to enrich, make wealthy*.

πλουτο-γᾱθής, ές, Dor. for πλουτογηθής, (πλοῦτος, γηθέω) *delighting by* or *in riches*

πλουτο-δοτήρ, ῆρος, ὁ, and **πλουτο-δότης**, ου, ὁ, (πλοῦτος, δίδωμι) *giver of rich*.

πλουτο-κρᾰτία, ἡ, (πλοῦτος, κρατέω) *an oligarchy of wealth*.

ΠΛΟΥ͂ΤΟΣ, ὁ, *wealth, riches*. II. as masc. prop. n. *Plutus*, god of riches, represented as blind.

πλουτό-χθων, ονος, ὁ, ἡ, (πλοῦτος, χθών) *rich in the treasures of the land*.

Πλούτων, ωνος, ὁ, *Pluto*, god of the nether world: a name of Ἅιδης, derived from πλοῦτος, because corn, the *wealth* of early times, was sent from beneath the earth as his gift.

πλοχμός, οῦ, ὁ, (πλέκω) mostly in pl. *locks, hair*.

πλῦναν, Ep. for ἔπλυναν, 3 pl. aor. 1 of πλύνω.

πλύνεσκον [ῡ], Ion. impf. of πλύνω.

πλῠνός, ὁ, (πλύνω) *a trough* or *pit to wash clothes in*: *a washing trough* or *tub*:

πλυντήριος, ον, (πλύνω) *of* or *for washing*: τὰ Πλυντήρια (sub. ἱερά) a festival at Athens, *in which the robes of the statue of Minerva were washed*.

ΠΛΥ'ΝΩ [ῡ]: fut. πλῠνῶ Ion. πλυνέω: aor. 1 ἔπλῡνα Ep. πλῦνα: Pass., aor. 1 ἐπλύνθην: pf. πέπλῠμαι:—*to wash clean*, esp. linen, opp. to λούομαι (*to bathe*), or νίζω (*to wash the hands* or *feet*). 2. *to wash off* dirt. II. metaph., πλύνειν τινά *to give* him *a dressing, to beat* or *cudgel*. Hence

πλύσις, εως, ἡ, *a washing*. [ῠ]

πλωάς, άδος, (πλέω) fem. Adj. *floating*.

πλωΐζω, f. σω, (πλώω) *to sail on the sea, use ships, practise navigation*.

πλώϊμος, ον, (πλώω) *fit for sailing*: of a ship, *fit for sea, sea-worthy, serviceable*. 2. of the sea, *to be sailed over, navigable*: in neut., πλωϊμωτέρων γενομένων or ὄντων as circumstances became or were *more favourable to navigation*.

πλώσιμος, ον, = πλώϊμος, *to be sailed over*.

πλωτήρ, ῆρος, ὁ, (πλώω) *a seaman, sailor*. II. *a swimmer*.

πλωτός, ή, όν, (πλώω) *sailing, floating, swimming*. II. *that can be sailed on, navigable*.

πλώω, f. ώσω: aor. 1 ἔπλωσα: pf. πέπλωκα: Ep. and Ion. for πλέω, *to sail, float*: there is also (as if from a Verb in μι) an Ep. aor. 2 ἔπλων, ως, ω, part. πλώς, gen. πλῶντος.

πνείω, Ep. pres. for πνέω, *to breathe*.

πνεῦμα, ατος, τό, (πνέω) *wind, air*. II. *breath*, πνεῦμα βίου *the breath* of life; πνεῦμα ἀφιέναι to give up *the ghost*:—spend one's *spirit, life*. 2. *spirit, inspiration*. III. *a Spirit, spiritual Being*:—

Πνεῦμα and ἅγιον Πνεῦμα the *Holy Spirit, Holy Ghost.* Hence

πνευμᾰτικός, ή, όν, *belonging to wind* or *breath.* II. *of the spirit, spiritual:* Adv. -κῶς, *spiritually.*

πνευματόω, f. ώσω, (πνεῦμα) *to turn into wind* or *air: to inflate.* 2. *to agitate with wind.*

πνεύμων common Att. **πλεύμων**, ονος, ὁ, (πνέω, πνεῦμα) used both in sing. and pl. *the organs of breathing, the lungs.*

πνεύσομαι, fut. of πνέω.

ΠΝΕ'Ω Ep **πνείω**: f. πνεύσομαι and πνευσοῦμαι, later πνεύσω: aor. 1 ἔπνευσα: Pass., aor. 1 ἐπνεύσθην: pf. πέπνῦμαι, part. πεπνῦμένος (v. sub. πέπνυμαι):—*to blow, breathe,* of the wind. II *to breathe, send forth an odour, exhale:* c. gen. rei, *to smell of* a thing, *be redolent of;* rarely c. dat. rei, *to smell with* it. III. of animals, *to breathe hard, pant, gasp.* IV. *to draw breath, breathe: to live.* V. metaph., c. acc. cognato, μένεα πνείοντες *breathing* spirit; Ἄρεα πνεῖν, Lat. *Martem spirare;* μέγα πνεῖν to be of a high spirit. VI *to breathe favourably* or *graciously on* one, Lat. *aspirare alicui.*

πνῖγεύς, έως, ὁ, (πνίγω) *an oven:* or 2. *a cover* or *damper put on coals to smother the flame.*

πνῖγηρός, ά, όν, (πνίγω) *choking, stifling,* of throttling or heat.

πνῖγίζω, = πνίγω.

πνῖγμα, ατος, τό, (πνίγω) *a choking.*

πνιγμός, ὁ, (πνίγω) *a choking, stifling heat.*

πνιγόεις, εσσα, εν, *choking, stifling.* From

πνῖγος, τό, (πνίγω) *a choking, stifling,* of heat.

ΠΝΙ'ΓΩ [ῑ]: fut. πνίξω or med. πνίξομαι: aor. 1 ἔπνιξα, inf. πνῖξαι: Pass., fut. πνῐγήσομαι: aor. 2 ἐπνίγην [ῐ]:—*to stifle, choke: to seize by the throat, throttle:*—Pass. *to be stifled* or *choked:* also *to be drowned.* II. *to cook in a covered vessel, to seethe, stew.*

πνῖγώδης, ες, (πνῖγος, εἶδος) *stifling.*

πνικτός, ή, όν, (πνίγω) *stifled, strangled.*

πνοή, ῆς, ἡ, Ep. and Ion. **πνοιή** Dor. **πνοά, πνοιά**: (πνέω):—*a wind, blast, air;* ἅμα πνοιῇς ἀνέμοιο along with (i. e. swift as) *blasts* of wind; πυρὸς πνοαί *blasts* of fire: metaph., πνοαί Ἄρεος *blasts* of Ares. II. *a hard-drawn breath, breath.* III *a breathing odour, fragrance: a vapour, exhalation.* IV. *the breath* of a wind-instrument.

ΠΝΥ'Ξ, gen. πυκνός (not πνυκός), ἡ, *the Pnyx, the place* at Athens where the ἐκκλησίαι or meetings of the people were held: it was cut out of a small hill just west of the Acropolis, of semicircular form like a theatre.

ΠΟ'Α, ἡ, Ion. **πόη** and **ποίη** Dor. **ποία**:—*grass:* ποία Μηδική, Lat. *herba Medica, sainfoin* or *lucerne.* II. *a grassy place, meadow.* III. *grass-time, summer.*

ποδ-αβρός, όν, (πούς, ἁβρός) *soft of foot.*

ποδ-ᾱγός, όν, Dor. and Att. for ποδηγός, *guiding the foot:* as Subst., ποδαγός, ὁ, *a guide, an attendant.*

ποδ-άγρα, ἡ, (πούς, ἄγρα) *a trap* or *snare for the feet.* II. *gout in the feet,* opp. to χειράγρα (gout in the hands). Hence

ποδαγράω, *to have gout in the feet.*

ποδαγρικός, ή, όν, (ποδάγρα) *liable to gout, gouty.*

ποδαγρός, όν, (ποδάγρα) *gouty.*

ποδᾰ-νιπτήρ, ῆρος, ὁ, (πούς, νίζω) *a vessel for washing the feet in, foot-pan.*

ποδά-νιπτρον, τό, (πούς, νίζω) *water for washing the feet in.*

ποδᾰπός, ή, όν, interrog. Adj. = ποῦ (or πόθεν) ἀπο; *from what country?* Lat. *cujas?*

πόδ-αργος, ον, (πούς, ἀργός) *swift-* or *white-footed.*

ποδ-άρκης, ες, (πούς, ἀρκέω) *able of foot, swift-footed.*

ποδ-ένδῠτος, ον, (πούς, ἐνδύω) *drawn upon the foot.* 2. as Subst., ποδένδυτον, τό, *a robe* or *garment reaching to the feet.*

ποδεών, ῶνος, ὁ, (πούς) in plur. *the ragged ends formed by the feet and tail,* in the skins of animals; δέρμα λέοντος ἀφημμένον ἄκρων ἐκ ποδεώνων a lion's skin hung round one's neck by *the ends.* II. *the neck* or *mouth of a wine-skin,* which was formed by one of these ends, the other being sewn up. III. *any similar extremity;* ποδεὼν στεινός a narrow *strip of land.* 2. *the lower end* or *corner of a sail, the sheet.*

ποδ-ηγός, όν, see ποδ-ᾱγός.

ποδ-ηνεκής, ές, (πούς, *ἐνέγκω) *reaching down to the feet.*

ποδ-ήνεμος, ον, (πούς, ἄνεμος) *swift as the wind.*

ποδ-ήρης, ες, (πούς, ἀρᾰρεῖν) *reaching down to the feet;* πέπλος ποδήρης a robe *that falls over the feet:* hence, ποδήρης στῦλος a *tall straight* pillar; ποδήρης ἀσπίς the large shield *which quite covered the body:*—τὰ ποδήρη, *the feet.*

ποδιαῖος, α, ον, (πούς) *of the measure of a foot, a foot long, broad,* or *high.*

ποδίζω, f. ίσω, (πούς) *to bind the feet, tether:*—Pass., of horses *to have the feet tied, be tethered.*

ποδί-κροτος, ον, (πούς, κροτέω) *fixed on* or *to the feet.*

ποδιστήρ, ῆρος, ὁ, (ποδίζω) *reaching over the feet:* πέπλος ποδιστήρ a long garment *that entangles the feet in it.*

ποδίστρα, ἡ, (ποδίζω) *a strap* or *snare for the feet.*

ποδοῖϊν, Ep. gen and dat. dual for ποδοῖν.

ποδο-κτύπη, ἡ, (πούς, κτυπέω) *a dancing-girl.*

ποδορ-ρᾰγής, ές, (πούς, ῥαγῆναι) *bursting forth at a stamp of the foot.*

ποδο-στράβη, ἡ, (πούς, στράβη) *a snare* or *trap to catch the feet.*

ποδό-ψηστρον, τό, (πούς ψάω) *a cloth to rub the feet on, a foot-cloth, mat.*

ποδώκεια, ἡ, *swiftness of foot, fleetness.* From

ποδ-ώκης, ες, (πούς, ὠκύς) *swift-footed, fleet of foot:* generally *swift, quick.*

πόη, ἡ, Ion. for πόα, *grass.*

ποθέεσκε, 3 sing. Ion. impf. of ποθέω.

ποθεινός, ή, όν, also ός, όν, (ποθέω) *longed for, desired, missed, regretted*: hence *mourned for*.

πόθεν Ion. **κόθεν**, interrog. Adv. *whence? from what place?* Lat. *unde?* τίς, πόθεν εἰς ἀνδρῶν; who, *whence* art thou of men? πόθεν τῆς Φρυγίης; *from what part* of Phrygia? II. in Att. to express surprise, *whence can it be? how possibly?* III. for ποῦ; *where?*

ποθέν, enclit. Adv. *from some place* or *other*.

ποθ-έρπω, Dor. for προσέρπω.

ποθ-έσπερος, ον, Dor. for προσέσπερος.

ποθεῦντες, Dor. and Aeol. part. pl. of ποθέω.

ποθεῦντι, Dor. 3 pl. of ποθέω.

ποθέω, fut. ποθήσω or ποθέσομαι: aor. 1 act. ἐπόθησα or ἐπόθεσα Ep. πόθεσα: pf. πεπόθηκα, pass. πεπόθημαι: (ποθή or πόθος):—*to desire what is absent* or *lost, to desire* or *regret fondly, yearn after, long for*; and so *to miss, regret*, Lat. *desiderare*: τὸ ποθοῦν = πόθος, one's *desiring*, one's *desire*. 2. c. inf. *to long* or *be anxious to do*. II. as Dep., ποθουμένη φρήν the *longing* soul.

ποθή, ή, Ep. = πόθος, *fond desire of, regret for*; σὴ ποθή *a longing after* thee.

ποθήμεναι, Ep. pres. inf. of ποθέω (as if from πόθημι).

ποθητός, ή, όν, (ποθέω) *desired, longed for, regretted*.

πόθι, interrog. Adv., poët. for ποῦ, *where?* II. for ποῖ, *whither?*

ποθί, enclit. Adv., poët. for που, *anywhere, somewhere*: also *anyhow, perhaps*. II. of Time, *some time*: *at length*.

ποθό-βλητος, ον, (πόθος, βάλλω) *love-stricken*.

πόθ-οδος, ή, Dor. for πρόσ-οδος.

ποθ-οράω, **ποθ-όρημι**, Dor. for προσ-οράω.

ποθορεῦσα, for προσορῶσα, part. fem. of προσουράω.

ΠΟ΄ΘΟΣ, ὁ, *desire for what is absent* or *lost, fond desire* or *regret, a yearning after, longing for*, Lat. *desiderium*; σὸς πόθος *a yearning after* thee: *love*.

ποῖ, interrog. Adv. *whither?* Lat. *quo?* c. gen., ποῖ χθονός: *to what spot* of earth? 2. for ποῦ; Lat. *ubi? where?* II. *to what end?* Lat. *quorsum?*

ποι, enclitic Adv. *somewhither*.

ποία, ή, Dor. for πόα, *grass*.

ποιεύμενος, Ep. pres. med. part. of ποιέω.

ποιεύμην, Ep. impf. med. of ποιέω.

ποιεῦντα, Dor. for ποιοῦντα, pres. part. acc. of

ΠΟΙΕ΄Ω, f. ήσω: I. *to make, produce, execute*, esp. of works of art:—Med. *to make for oneself*, of bees, οἰκία ποιήσασθαι *to make themselves* houses: also *to have* a thing *made*. 2. *to bring to pass, bring about, cause, effect*; ποιεῖν ἱρά, Lat. *sacra facere, to do* sacrifice, *perform* the rites of sacrifice; ποιεῖν Ἴσθμια *to celebrate* the Isthmian games 3. *to make, shape, create*: *to beget*: of corn, etc., *to produce, grow, raise*: also *to make* or *render* so and so:—Pass. *to be made* so *and* so, *to become*:—Med. *to make* so and so *for oneself*, ποιεῖσθαί τινα ἑταῖρον *to make* him *one's* friend: ποιεῖσθαί τινα υἱόν *to make* a person *one's* son, i. e. to adopt him as son; ἑαυτοῦ ποιεῖσθαί τι *to make* a thing *one's own*: generally *to hold, reckon, esteem* a thing as .., συμφορὰν ποιεῖσθαί τι *to take, reckon* a thing for a visitation; δεινὸν ποιεῖσθαί τι *to esteem* it a grievous thing; περὶ πολλοῦ ποιεῖσθαι, Lat. *magni facere, to esteem* a thing of great moment. 4. *to compose, write*, esp. in verse, *to make*: also *to invent*:—also *to make, represent in poetry* (whence ποιητής a poet): periphr. in Med., ὀργὴν ποιεῖσθαι for ὀργίζεσθαι, θαῦμα ποιεῖσθαι for θαυμάζειν: also ποιεῖσθαι δι' ἀγγέλου, for ἀγγέλλειν. II. *to do*; Σπαρτιητικὰ ποιέειν *to act* like a Spartan: c. acc. dupl. *to do* something to another, κακά or ἀγαθὰ ποιεῖν τινα *to do* one good or evil. 2. *to put*. III. intr. *to be doing, to do*; ποιέειν ἢ παθέειν *to do* or have done to one. 2. there is also a pecul. usage, ἡ εὔνοια παρὰ πολὺ ἐποίει ἐν τοὺς Λακεδαιμονίους, good-will *made* greatly for or towards the Lacedaemonians. [Att. Poets, esp. Comic, often use the penult. short, ποῐ-.]

ποίη, ή, Ion. for πόα, *grass*.

ποιήεις, εσσα, εν, (ποίη) *grassy, rich in grass*.

ποίημα, ατος, τό, (ποιέω) *anything made* or *done*: 1. *a work, piece of workmanship*. 2. *a poetical work, poem*. 3. *an act, deed*.

ποιημάτιον, τό, Dim. of ποίημα, *a little poem*.

ποιηρός, ά, όν, (ποίη) *grassy*.

ποιήσειαν, 3 pl. Aeol. aor. 1 opt. of ποιέω.

ποίησις, εως, ή, (ποιέω) *a making*: *a forming, creating*. II. *the art of poetry*. 2. *a poem*.

ποιητέος, α, ον, verb. Adj. of ποιέω, *to be made* or *done*. II. neut. ποιητέον *one must make* or *do*.

ποιητής, οῦ, ὁ, (ποιέω) *one who makes, a maker*. II. *a maker*, i. e. *a poet*.

ποιητικός, ή, όν, (ποιέω) *capable of making, productive*: *poetical*:—ἡ ποιητική (sub. τέχνη) *the art of poetry, poetry*. Adv. -κῶς.

ποιητός, ή, όν, (ποιέω) *made, fabricated, worked*. II. *made by oneself, invented*.

ποιη-φᾰγέω, (ποίη, φαγεῖν) *to eat grass*.

ποικιλ-άνιος, ον, Dor. for ποικιλ-ήνιος, (ποικίλος, ἡνία) *with broidered reins*.

ποικῐλ-είμων, ον, gen. ονος, (ποικίλος, εἷμα) *with party-coloured robe, with spangled garb*.

ποικῐλία, ή, (ποικίλος) *an embroidering, embroidery*. *a piece of embroidery*: metaph. *cunning*.

ποικίλλω, f. ιλῶ. ἐποίκιλα. Pass., pf. πεποίκιλμαι: (ποικίλος):—*to broider, work in embroidery* II. *to embroider*: *to diversify, vary*: metaph. *to trick out with fair words, embellish*. Hence

ποίκιλμα, ατος, τό, *anything wrought in various colours*. 2. *broidered work, broidery*.

ποικῐλό-βουλος, ον, (ποικίλος, βουλή) *of changeful* or *subtle counsel*.

ποικῐλό-γηρυς Dor. -γαρυς, υος, ὁ, ή, (ποικίλος, γῆρυς) *of varied voice, many-toned*.

ποικιλό-δειρος, ον, (ποικίλος, δείρα) *with variegated neck*.

ποικῐλο-δέρμων, ον, gen. ονος, (ποικίλος, δέρμα) *with spotted* or *dappled skin.*

ποικῐλο-εργός, όν, (ποικίλος, ἔργον) *of varied work.*

ποικῐλό-θριξ, -τρῐχος, ὁ, ἡ, (ποικίλος, θρίξ) *with spotted hair, spotted, b* [illegible]*dled.*

ποικῐλο-μήτης, ου, ὁ, and **ποικῐλό-μητις**, ιδος, ὁ, ἡ, (ποικίλος, μῆτις) *full of various wiles.*

ποικῐλο-μήχᾰνος, ον, (ποικίλος, μηχανή) *full of various devices.*

ποικῐλό-μορφος, ον, (ποικίλος, μορφή) *of variegated form, variegated.*

ποικῐλό-μῡθος, ον, (ποικίλος, μῦθος) *of various discourse.*

ποικῐλό-νωτος, ον, (ποικίλος, νῶτος) *with back of varied hues.*

ποικῐλό-πτερος, ον, (ποικίλος, πτερόν) *with wing of changeful hue.*

ΠΟΙΚΙ'ΛΟΣ, η, ον, *many-coloured, spotted, pied, dappled.* II *worked in various colours, of varying colour;* τεύχεα ποικίλα χαλκῷ arms *inwrought* with brass. III. generally *changeful, various:* hence *of various art, elaborate, inlaid, variegated.* 2. *changeful, varying,—intricate, riddling, ambiguous;* hence *artful, cunning.*

ποικῐλο-σάνδᾰλος Aeol. -σάμβᾰλος, ον, (ποικίλος, σάνδαλον) *with broidered sandals.*

ποικῐλό-στολος, ον, (ποικίλος, στολή) *with variegated robe:* of a ship, *with painted prow.*

ποικῐλο-τερπής, ές (ποικίλος, τέρπω) *with varied delights: delighted by variety.*

ποικῐλό-τευκτος, ον, (ποικίλος, τεύχω) *curiously wrought.*

ποικῐλό-τραυλος, ον, (ποικίλος τραυλός) *twittering* or *singing in various notes.*

ποικῐλο-φόρμιγξ, ιγγος, ὁ, η, (ποικίλος, φόρμιγξ) *accompanied by the various notes of the harp.*

ποικῐλό-φρων, ονος, ὁ, ἡ, (ποικίλος, φρήν) *with manifold counsel, wily-minded.*

ποικιλτής, οῦ, ὁ, fem. **ποικίλτρια**, ἡ, (ποικίλλω) *one who embroiders: a broiderer.*

ποικῐλ-ῳδός, όν, (ποικίλος, ᾠδή) *of riddling song.*

ποικίλως, Adv. of ποικίλος, *variously;* ποικίλως **ἔχειν** to be *different.*

ποιμαίνω, f. ᾰνῶ, (ποιμήν) *to feed, tend,* Lat. *pascere:* absol. *to keep flocks, be a shepherd.* 2. metaph. *to tend, cherish foster:—to guide, lead, govern:* —also *to soothe, lull, beguile,* like Lat. *pascere:* hence *to deceive.* II. Pass. *to graze,* Lat. *pasci: to range over in grazing, to stray;* πᾶς πεποίμανται τόπος every place *has been ranged over, traversed.*

ποιμάν, ὁ, Dor. for ποιμήν.

ποιμᾰνόριον, τό, (ποιμάνωρ) *a herd:* metaph. *an army under its leader.*

ποιμανῶ, fut. of ποιμαίνω.

ποιμάνωρ [ᾱ], ορος, ὁ, (ποιμαίνω) = ποιμήν, *a herdsman, shepherd: a shepherd of the people, prince, chief.*

ποιμήν, ένος, ὁ, (ποία) *a herdsman, a shepherd;* **ποιμὴν λαῶν** *a shepherd* of the people, i. e. *a prince, chief.*

ποίμνη, ἡ, (ποιμήν) *a herd of cattle, a flock of sheep.*

ποιμνήιος, η, ον, (ποίμνη) *of* or *for a flock* or *herd.*

ποίμνιον, τό, Dim. of ποίμνη, *a little flock.*

ποιναῖος, α, ον, (ποινή) *punishing, avenging.*

ποινάτωρ, ορος, ὁ, ἡ, *an avenger, punisher.* [ᾱ]

ποινάω, f. άσω [ᾱ] Ion. ήσω, *to avenge, punish:*— Med. *to avenge oneself on one.* From

ποινή, ἡ, *a ransom* paid for the shedding of blood; generally, *a price paid, redemption, requital:* also *the price exacted, vengeance, penalty,* Lat. *poena;* ἀνελέσθαι ποινὴν τῆς ψυχῆς to take *vengeance for* his life: ποινὴν τῖσαι Ξέρξῃ τῶν κηρύκων ἀπολωλμένων to give Xerxes *satisfaction for* the death of his heralds: often in phrase, ποινὰς δοῦναι, like δίκην δοῦναι, to suffer *punishment,* Lat. *dare poenas;* ποίνας λαμβάνειν to inflict it, Lat. *sumere poenas.* 2. in good sense, *recompense, reward.* II. personified, Ποίνη, ἡ, *the goddess of vengeance, vengeance.*

ποινήτης, ου, ὁ, fem. -ῆτις, ιδος, *one that punishes* or *avenges, an avenger.*

ποίνῐμος, ον, (ποινή) *avenging, punishing.*

ποιολογέω, f. ήσω, *to gather herbs:* also *to put up corn in sheaves.* From

ποιο-λόγος, ον, (ποία, λέγω) *gathering herbs.*

ποιο-νόμος, ον, (ποία, νέμω) *feeding on grass* or *herbs.* II. **ποιό-νομος**, ον, (ποία, νομή) *with grassy pastures.*

ΠΟΙ'ΟΣ α, ον Ion. **κοῖος**, η, ον, interrog. Adj. *of what nature? of what sort?* Lat. *qualis?* in Homer expressing surprise and anger; ποῖον τὸν μῦθον ἔειπες! *what manner of* speech hast thou spoken! II. in Att. also with the Art. when it stands alone, ὁ ποῖος; III. fem. dat. ποίᾳ Ion. κοίῃ (sub. ὁδῷ): as Adv., = πῶς; Lat. *quomodo? how? in what manner?*

ποιός, ά, όν, indef. Adj. *of a certain nature, kind* or *quality.*

ποιότης, ητος, ἡ, (ποῖος) *quality.*

ποιπνύω, f. ύσω [ῠ], (redupl. from πνέω), *to be out of breath;* hence generally, *to hasten, hurry, bustle:* also *to work hard, be busy.*

ποίφυγμα, ατος, τό, *a blowing, snorting.* From

ποιφύσσω, f. ξω, (redupl. from φυσάω) *to blow, puff, snort.* II. *to blow out, puff up.*

ποι-ώδης, ες, (ποία, εἶδος) *like grass, grassy.*

πόκᾰ or **ποκά**, Dor. for πότε or ποτέ.

ποκάς, άδος, ἡ, (πόκος) *wool, hair.*

ποκίζω, f. ίσω Dor. ίξω, (πόκος) *to shear wool:*— Med. *to shear* or *clip for oneself.*

πόκος, ὁ, (πέκω) *wool uncombed, a fleece:* also *a flock* or *tuft of wool.* II. *a sheep-shearing.* III. an irreg. pl. act. occurs in the proverb εἰς ὄνου πόκας, to an *ass-shearing,* i. e. to a place where nothing is to be got. Hence

ποκόω, f. ώσω, *to cover with wool:* Pass. *to be covered* or *clothed in wool.*

πόκως, Dor. for πόκους, acc. pl. of πόκος.

πολέες, έων, έεσσι, έας, Ep. plur. of πολύς.

πολεμᾱδόκος, Dor. for πολεμηδόκος.

πολεμαρχεῖον, *τό*, *the Polemarch's residence:* and

πολεμαρχέω, f. *ήσω*, *to be Polemarch.* From

πολέμ-αρχος, *ὁ*, (*πόλεμος*, *ἄρχω*) *one who begins* or *leads the war, a leader, chieftain.* II. at Athens *the Polemarch* was *the third archon*, who originally commanded in battle; he was present at the battle of Marathon: later he presided in the court in which the causes of the *μέτοικοι* were tried. 2. in Sparta *the commander of a division* or *μόρα.* 3. at Thebes it was the name of two officers of chief rank after the Boeotarchs.

πολεμέω, f. *ήσω*: Pass., aor. 1 *ἐπολεμήθην*: (*πόλεμος*):—*to be at war, wage war with:* also *to fight, give battle:* generally, *to quarrel, dispute with* one. II. c. acc. *to make war upon, treat as an enemy, attack:*—Pass. *to have war made upon* one; so fut. med. *πολεμήσομαι* in pass. sense. III. in Pass. also of war, *to be waged* or *carried on; ὅσα ἐπολεμήθη* whatever *hostilities were committed.*

πολεμη-δόκος Dor. **πολεμα-δόκος**, *ον*, (*πόλεμος*, *δέχομαι*) *undertaking war: warlike.*

πολεμήιος, *ον*, Ion. form of *πολέμειος*, (*πόλεμος*) *warlike.* II. *hostile.*

πολεμησείω, Desiderat. of *πολεμέω*, *to wish for war.*

πολεμητέον, verb. Adj. of *πολεμέω*, *one must go to war.*

πολεμίζω poët. **πτολ-**: fut. *ίσω* Dor. *ίξω*: (*πόλεμος*):—poët. for *πολεμέω*, *to wage war, fight with* or *against* one; *μετά τινι* in conjunction with another: later *to quarrel, wrangle, dispute.* II. trans *to make war upon, fight with.*

πολεμικός, *ή*, *όν*, (*πόλεμος*) *of* or *for war, warlike;* *τὰ πολεμικά*, *warlike exercises, warlike usages, the art of war:* so, *ἡ πολεμική* (sub. *τέχνη*), *the art of war, war.* 2. *τὸ πολεμικόν the signal for battle.* II. *hostile:* also *causing hostility.* Hence

πολεμικῶς, Adv. *in hostile fashion: πολεμικῶς ἔχειν* to be *hostile.*

πολέμιος, *α*, *ον*, also *ος*, *ον*, (*πόλεμος*) *of* or *belonging to war; τὰ πολέμια the business of war.* 2. rarely like *πολεμικός*, *warlike.* II. *hostile:*—as Subst., *πολέμιοι*, *οἱ*, the *enemy.* 2. *ἡ πολεμία* (sub. *γῆ*, *χώρα*), *the enemy's country.* 3. *τὸ πολέμιον*, *hostility.*

πολεμιστά, *ὁ*, Ep. for **πολεμιστής**: *a warrior.*

πολεμιστήριος, *α*, *ον*, also *ος*, *ον*, *of* or *belonging to a warrior; πολεμιστήρια ὅρματα war*-chariots. II. *τὰ πολεμιστήρια the business of war.* From

πολεμιστής Ep **πτολ-**, *οῦ*, *ὁ*, (*πολεμίζω*) *a warrior, combatant; ἵπποι πολεμισταί war*-horses.

πολεμό-κλονος, *ον*, (*πόλεμος*, *κλόνος*) *raising the din of war.*

πολεμό-κραντος, *ον*, (*πόλεμος*, *κραίνω*) *finishing war.*

πολεμο-λᾱμ-ᾰχᾰϊκός, *ή*, *όν*, compd. of *πόλεμος*, *Λάμαχος* and *Ἀχαϊκός*, *like a Greek Lamachus in war.*

πόλεμόνδε Ep. **πτόλ-**, Adv. of *πόλεμος*, *to the war, into the fight.*

πολεμο-ποιέω, f. *ήσω*, (*πόλεμος*, *ποιέω*) *to stir up war.*

ΠΟ´ΛΕΜΟΣ Ep. **πτόλεμος**, *ὁ*, *a battle, fight:* generally, *war; πόλεμον αἱρεσθαί τινι* to levy *war* against one. II. personified, *War, Battle.*

πολεμο-φθόρος, *ον*, (*πόλεμος*, *φθείρω*) *wasting by war.*

πολεμόω, f. *ώσω*, (*πόλεμος*) *to make hostile, make an enemy of:*—Pass. *to be made an enemy of.*

πολεύω, (*πόλος*) intr. *to go* or *range about*, Lat. *versari.* II. trans. *to turn up, till, plough.*

πολέω, (*πόλος*) *to go about, range, haunt.* II. trans. *to turn up, to turn* the soil *with the plough, to plough.*

πόλεων, gen. pl. of *πόλις*: but **πολέων**, Ion. for *πολλῶν*, gen. pl. of *πολύς*.

πόληες, *ων*, *ας*, Ion. for *πόλεες*, *πόλεις*, plur. of *πόλις*: Ion. gen. and dat. sing. *πόληος*, *πόληι*.

πολιαίνομαι, Pass. (*πολιός*) *to grow gray* or *white.*

πολιά-οχος, *ον*, Dor. for *πολιήοχος*, *πολιοῦχος*, q. v.

πολί-αρχος, *ὁ*, (*πόλις*, *ἄρχω*) *prince of a city* or *state.*

Πολιάς, *άδος*, *ἡ*, (*πόλις*) *guardian of the city*, epith. of Athena (Minerva) in her *oldest* temple on the Acropolis of Athens, as distinguished from *Ἀθηνᾶ Παρθένος* and *Ἀθηνᾶ Πρόμαχος*.

πόλιες, **πολίεσσιν**, Ep nom. and dat. pl. of *πόλις*.

πολίζω, f. *ίσω*, aor. 1 *ἐπόλισα* Ep *πόλισσα*: Pass., pf. *πεπόλισμαι*: (*πόλις*):—*to build* or *found a city:* generally, *to build, found, lay the foundation of.* II *to colonise by building a city.*

πολιή-οχος, Dor. *πολιάοχος* = *πολιοῦχος*.

πολιήτης, *εω*, *ὁ*, Ion. for *πολίτης*, *a citizen:* also *a fellow-citizen, countryman.*

πολιῆτις, *ιδος*, fem. of *πολιήτης*.

πόλινδε, Adv. of *πόλις*, *into* or *to the city.*

πολιο-κρότᾰφος, *ον*, (*πολιός*, *κρόταφος*) *with gray hair on the temples, growing gray*

πολι-ορκέω, f. *ήσω*: aor. 1 *ἐπολιόρκησα*: Pass, fut. *πολιορκηθήσομαι*, and in med. form *πολιορκήσομαι*: aor. 1 *ἐπολιορκήθην*: (*πόλις*, *εἴργω*, or *ἕρκος*):—*to hem in a city, blockade, beleaguer besiege:* metaph. *to besiege, importune.* Hence

πολι-ορκητέος, *α*, *ον*, verb. Adj. *that must* or *can be taken by siege.*

πολιορκία, *ἡ*, (*πολιορκέω*) *a beleaguering* or *besieging a city, a siege.*

ΠΟΛΙΟ´Σ, *ά*, *όν*, also *ός*, *όν*:—*gray, white;* of hair, *gray* or *hoary; αἱ πολιαί* (sub. *τρίχες*), *gray* or *white hair; ἅμα ταῖς πολιαῖς κατιούσαις* as the *gray hairs* come lower down (i. e. from the head and temples to the beard): *πολιός* absol. *a gray-headed man.* II. metaph. *bright, serene.* III. metaph. *hoary, venerable.*

πολι-οῦχος, *ον*, (*πόλις*, *ἔχω*) *protecting a city.*

πολιό-χρως, *ωτος*, *ὁ*, *ἡ*, (*πολιός*, *χρώς*) *with white skin: white.*

πολι-πόρθης, *ου*, (*πόλις*, *πέρθω*) *sacker of cities.*

ΠΟ´ΛΙΣ Ep. **πτόλις**, *εως*, *ἡ*; Ion. gen. *πόλιος* Att.

poët. also πόλεος Ep. πόληος, πόλευς: dat. πόλει Ep. πόλῃι: acc. πόλιν, but Ep. acc. πόληα also occurs:—Plur., nom. πόλεες Att. πόλεις Ion. πόλιες: gen. πολίων: dat. πόλισι Ep. πολίεσσι Dor. πολίεσι: acc. πόλιας, πόλεις Ion. πόλῖς:—*a city*: πόλις ἄκρη, = ἀκρόπολις, *the fortress of the city, citadel*, which at Athens was sometimes called πόλις, while the rest of the city was called ἄστυ. II. *a whole country, state*. III. when πόλις and ἄστυ are joined, πόλις is the *body of citizens*, ἄστυ *their dwellings*: hence πόλις *the state, the citizens* who form the state, *a free state, republic*. 2. *the right of citizenship*.

πόλισμα, ατος, τό, (πολίζω) *a collection of buildings, a city, town*.

πολισσο-νόμος, ον, (πόλις, νέμω) *managing* or *ruling a city*.

πολισ-σόος, ον, (πόλις, σώζω) *guarding a city*.

πολισσ-οῦχος, ον, poët. for πολιοῦχος.

πολῑτ-άρχης, ου, ὁ, (πολίτης, ἄρχω) *a ruler of citizens* or *a state, a chief magistrate*.

πολῑτεία Ion. -ηίη, ἡ, (πολιτεύω) *the relation of a citizen to the state, the condition and rights of a citizen, citizenship*, Lat. *civitas*. 2. *the life of a citizen*. II. *the life of a statesman, government, administration*. III. *civil polity, the condition of a state, a state, constitution*. 2. *a commonwealth: a republic*.

πολίτευμα, ατος, τό, (πολῑτεύω) *a measure of government, political act*. II. *a state, community*.

πολῑτεύω, f. σω, (πολίτης) *to be a citizen* or *freeman, live in a free state*. 2. *to have a certain form of government, have public affairs administered in a certain way*: Pass. *to be governed*. II. Dep. πολιτεύομαι, fut. med. πολιτεύσομαι: aor. 1. med. ἐπολιτευσάμην and pass. ἐπολιτεύθην: pf. pass. πεπολίτευμαι:—*to be a free citizen, have the qualifications of a free citizen*: generally, *to live in a state*. 2. *to take part in the government*. III. trans. *to administer* or *govern*: absol. *to conduct the government*.

πολῑτηίη, ἡ, Ion. for πολιτεία.

πολίτης [ῑ], ου, Ion. **πολιήτης**, εω, ὁ, (πόλις) *the member of a city* or *state, a citizen, freeman*, Lat. *civis*. 2. also *a fellow-citizen, fellow-countryman*: also used with another Subst., θεοὶ πολῖται gods *our fellow-citizens*, gods *of the city*.

πολῑτικός, ή, όν, (πολίτης) *of* or *for a citizen, befitting a citizen, like a citizen, constitutional*, Lat. *civilis*: τὸ πολιτικόν *the body of citizens, the community*. II. *belonging to* or *befitting a statesman*: as Subst., πολιτικός, ὁ, *a statesman*. III. *belonging to the state* or *its administration, concerning the body politic*: τὸ πολιτικόν *the commonwealth*; but ἡ πολιτική (sc. τέχνη) *the science of politics*; τὰ πολιτικά, *state-affairs*. IV. generally, *public*. as opp. to private.

πολῑτικῶς, Adv. of πολῑτικός, *in a manner befitting a citizen, constitutionally*, Lat. *civiliter*.

πολίχνη, ἡ, (πόλις) *a small town*.

πολίχνιον, τό, Dim. of πολίχνη, *a very small town*.

πολλάκις poët. **πολλάκι** [ᾰ], Adv. (πολύς) *many times, often, oft*. II. in Att. εἰ πολλάκις *perhaps, perchance*, Lat. *si forte*; μὴ πολλάκις Lat. *ne forte*.

πολλαπλάσιος, α, ον, also ος, ον, (πολύς) *many times as many, many times more, many times larger*; followed by ἤ . , ἤπερ . . , or by a gen.: neut. pl. πολλαπλάσια as Adv.

πολλαπλᾱσίων, ον, gen ονος, = πολλαπλάσιος: Adv. -ιόνως.

πολλαπλήσιος, η, ον, Ion. for πολλαπλάσιος.

πολλᾰχῇ, Adv. (πολύς, πολλή) *many ways, many times, often*. II. *in various manners*.

πολλᾰχόθεν, Adv. (πολύς, πολλή) *from many places* or *sides*: *for many reasons*.

πολλᾰχόθι, Adv. (πολύς, πολλή) *in many places*.

πολλᾰχόσε, Adv. (πολύς, πολλή) *towards many sides, into many parts* or *quarters*.

πολλᾰχοῦ, Adv. = πολλαχῇ, *many times, often*. II. *in many places*.

πολλο-δεκάκις, Adv. (πολλός = πολύς, δεκάκις) *many tens of times*. [ᾰ]

πολλός, πολλόν, Ion. masc. and neut. for πολύς, πολύ, but used almost entirely in the oblique cases: v. πολύς.

πολλοστός, ή, όν, (πολλός, πολύς) *one out of many*, Lat. *multesimus*: *very little, slight, trivial*. II. of Time, πολλοστῷ ἔτει *in the last of many* years, i. e. after many years; πολλοστῷ χρόνῳ *after a very long time*. Adv. -τως, *in a very small degree*.

πόλος, ὁ, (πέλω, πολέω) *a pivot* or *axis* on which something turns, *the axis of the globe, the pole*. 2. *that which revolves on an axis, the vault of heaven, the sky* or *firmament*, Lat. *polus*. II. *land turned up with the plough*. III. *a basin-shaped sundial*.

πολύ-αγρος, ον, (πολύς, ἄγρα) *catching much game*.

πολῠ-ᾱθλός, όν, (πολύς, ἆθλον) *conquering in many contests*.

πολύ-αιγος, ον, (πολύς, αἴξ) *abounding in goats*.

πολῠ-αίμων, ον, gen. ονος, (πολύς, αἷμα) *very bloody*.

πολῠ-αίνετος, ον, and **πολύ-αινος**, ον, (πολύς, αἶνος) *much-praised*. 2. *full of wise discourse*.

πολῠ-ᾱΐξ, ῖκος [ῑ], (πολύς, ἀΐσσω) *with many shocks, impetuous*; κάματος πολυάϊξ weariness *caused by impetuous onsets*.

πολῠανδρέω, *to be full of men, to be populous*. From

πολύ-ανδρος, ον, (πολύς, ἀνήρ) of places, *with many men, full of men, thick-peopled*. II. of persons, *numerous*.

πολῠ-άνθεμος, ον, (πολύς, ἄνθεμον) *rich in flowers*.

πολῠ-ανθής, ές, (πολύς, ἀνθέω) *much-blossoming*.

πολῠανθρωπία, ἡ, *a large population, multitude of people*. From

πολῠ-άνθρωπος, ον, (πολύς, ἄνθρωπος) *full of people, populous*: *crowded*.

πολῠ-άνωρ [ᾱ], ορος, ὁ, ἡ, (πολύς, ἀνήρ) = πολύανδρος: *much frequented.* II. *of many husbands.*

πολῠ-άργῠρος, ον, (πολύς, ἄργυρος) *rich in silver.*

πολῠ-άρητος Att. -άρᾱτος, ον, (πολύς, ἀράομαι) *much prayed for, much desired.*

πολῠ-αρκής, ές, (πολύς, ἀρκέω) *much-sufficing, supplying many, abundant.*

πολυ-άρματος, ον, (πολύς, ἅρμα) *with many chariots.*

πολῠ-αρμόνιος, ον, (πολύς, ἁρμονία) *many-toned.*

πολύ-αρνος, ον, irreg. dat. πολύαρνι: (πολύς, ἀρνός): *with many lambs* or *sheep: with many flocks.*

πολῠαρχία, ἡ, (πολύς, ἄρχω) *the government of many.*

πολῠ-αστράγᾰλος, ον, (πολύς, ἀστράγαλος) *with many joints.*

πολύ-αστρος, ον, (πολύς, ἄστρον) *with many stars, starry.*

πολῠ-άσχολος, ον, (πολύς, ἄσχολος) *much-busied.*

πολῠ-αῦλαξ, ἄκος, ὁ, ἡ, (πολύς, αὖλαξ) *with many furrows: with broad acres, spacious.*

πολῠ-αύχενος, ον, (πολύς, αὐχήν) *with many necks.*

πολῠ-βᾰφής, ές, (πολύς, βαφῆναι) *deep-plunged, drowned.*

πολῠ-βενθής, ές, (πολύς, βένθος) *very deep.*

πολύ-βοσκος, ον, (πολύς, βόσκω) *much-nourishing.*

πολῠ-βότειρα Ep. πουλυβότειρα, ἡ, (πολύς, βόσκω) fem. Adj. *nourishing many, much-nourishing.*

πολύ-βοτος, ον, (πολύς, βόσκω) *much-nourishing.*

πολύ-βοτρυς, υος, ὁ, ἡ, (πολύς, βότρυς) *with many clusters, abounding in grapes.*

πολύ-βουλος, ον, (πολύς, βουλή) *much-counselling, exceeding wise.*

πολῠ-βούτης, ου, ὁ, (πολύς, βοῦς) *rich in oxen.*

πολύ-βροχος, ον, (πολύς, βρόχος) *with many nooses.*

πολῠ-γᾱθής, ές, Dor. for πολυγηθής.

πολῠ-γηθής, Dor. -γᾱθής, ές, (πολύς, γηθέω) *much-cheering, delightful, gladsome.*

πολυ-γήρως, ων, (πολύς, γῆρας) *exceeding old.*

πολύ-γλευκος, ον, (πολύς, γλεῦκος) *abounding in must* or *new wine.*

πολύ-γληνος, ον, (πολύς, γλήνη) *many-eyed.*

πολύ-γλωσσος Att. -ττος, ον, (πολύς, γλῶσσα) *many-tongued: harmonious.*

πολύ-γναμπτος, ον, (πολύς, γνάμπτω) *with many windings, curling.*

πολύ-γνωτος, ον, (πολύς, γιγνώσκω) *well-known.*

πολύ-γομφος, ον, (πολύς, γόμφος) *fastened with many nails, well-bolted.*

πολῠγονέομαι, Dep. (πολύγονος) *to multiply.*

πολύ-γονος, ον, (πολύς, γόνος) *producing many, prolific.*

πολῠ-δαίδᾰλος, ον, (πολυς, δαίδαλος) *much* or *highly wrought, richly dight.* II. act. *working with great art, very skilful.*

πολῠ-δάκρῠος, ον, and **πολύ-δακρῠς**, gen. υος, ὁ, ἡ, (πολύς, δάκρυ) *of* or *with many tears: hence much-wept, tearful.* II. act. *much-weeping.*

πολῠ-δάκρυτος, ον, (πολύς, δακρύω) *much wept, very lamentable, tearful.* II. act. *much-weeping.*

πολῠ-δάπᾰνος, ον, (πολύς, δαπάνη) *causing great expense:* of a person, *expensive, extravagant.*

πολῠ-δειράς, άδος, ὁ, ἡ, (πολύς, δειρή) *with many ridges* or *necks of land.*

πολῠ-δένδρεος and **πολύ-δενδρος**, ον, (πολύς, δένδρον) *with many trees, full of trees.*

πολυδένδρεσσι, poët. dat. pl. as if from πολυδένδρης.

πολῠ-δερκής, ές, (πολύς, δέρκομαι) *much-seeing.*

πολύ-δεσμος, ον, (πολύς, δεσμός) *with many bands, strong-bound.*

πολῠ-δευκής, ές, (πολύς, δεῦκος = γλεῦκος) *very sweet.* II. Πολυδεύκης, εως, ὁ, *Polydeuces,* Lat. *Pollux,* son of Leda, brother of Castor, one of the Dioscuri, celebrated as a boxer.

πολῠ-δίψιος, ον, (πολύς, δίψα) *very thirsty,* i. e. *ill-watered, afflicted with drought.*

πολύ-δονος, ον, (πολύς, δονέω) *much-driven.*

πολύ-δοξος, ον, (πολύς, δόξα) *very famous.*

πολύ-δρομος, ον, (πολύς, δραμεῖν) *much-running, much-wandering.*

πολύ-δροσος, ον, (πολύς, δρόσος) *very dewy.*

πολῠδωρία, ἡ, *liberality, munificence.* From

πολύ-δωρος, ον, (πολύς, δῶρον) *with rich gifts, well-dowered.*

πολῠ-ειδής, ές, (πολυς, εἶδος) *of many kinds, diverse, various.*

πολῠ-έλαιος, ον, (πολυς, ἔλαιον) *yielding much oil, abounding in oil.*

πολῠ-έλικτος, ον, (πολύς, ἑλίσσω) *many-folded, mazy, complicated.*

πολῠ-επαίνετος, ον, (πολύς, ἐπαινέω) *much-praised.*

πολῠ-επής, ές, (πολύς, ἔπος) *of many words, wordy.*

πολῠ-έραστος, ον, (πολύς, ἐράω) *much-loved.*

πολῠ-εργής, ές, and **πολύ-εργος**, ον, (πολύς, ἔργον) *much-working, hard-working.*

πολῠ-ετής, ές, (πολύς, ἔτος) *of many years, full of years.*

πολύ-ευκτος, and **πολῠ-εύχετος**, ον, (πολύς, εὔχομαι) *much wished for, much desired.*

πολύ-ζηλος, ον, (πολύς, ζῆλος) *much envied, much desired.* II. *full of envy.*

πολυ-ζήλωτος, ον, (πολύς, ζηλόω) *much envied* or *desired.*

πολύ-ζῠγος, ον, (πολύς, ζυγόν) *many-benched.*

πολυ-ήγορος, ον, (πολύς, ἀγορεύω) *speaking much, wordy.*

πολυ-ήρᾰτος, ον, (πολύς, ἐράω) *much-loved, very lovely.*

πολυ-ηχής, ές, (πολύς, ἦχος) *many-toned: much-resounding.*

πολυ-ήχητος Dor. **πολυάχ-**, ον, (πολύς, ἠχέω) *loud-* or *far-sounding.*

πολυ-θαρσής, ές, (πολύς, θάρσος) *very confident, over-courageous, bold.*

πολύ-θεος, ον, (πολύς, θεός) *of many gods, dedicated to many gods: consisting of many gods.*

πολύ-θηρος, ον, (πολύς, θήρ) *with much game, full of wild beasts.*

πολυ-θρέμμων, *ον*, gen. *ονος*, (*πολύς, θρέμμα*) of the Nile, *much-fertilising* or *abounding in monsters.*

πολύ-θρεπτος, *ον*, (*πολύς, τρέφω*) *much-nourishing.*

πολυ-θρήνητος, *ον*, (*πολύς, θρηνέω*) *much-bewailed.*

πολύ-θρηνος, *ον*, (*πολύς, θρῆνος*) *much-wailing*

πολύ-θριξ, *τρῐχος, ὁ, ἡ*, (*πολύς, θρίξ*) *with much hair*

πολύ-θροος, *ον*, contr. **-θρους**, *ουν*, (*πολύς, θρόος*) *with much noise, clamorous*

πολυ-θρύλητος, *ον*, (*πολύς, θρῡλέω*) *much talked of, notorious.*

πολύ-θῠρος, *ον*, (*πολύς, θύρα*) *with many doors* or *apertures* 2. metaph. *with many leaves.*

πολύ-θῠτος, *ον*, (*πολύς, θύω*) *celebrated with much sacrifice: abounding in sacrifices.*

πολυ-ίδμων, *ον*, gen. *ονος*, = *πολυΐδρις.*

πολυΐδρεια, *ἡ*, (*πολυΐδρις*) *much knowledge, sagacity, cunning.*

πολύ-ϊδρις, Ion. gen. *ιος* Att. *εως, ὁ, ἡ*, (*πολυς, ἴδρις*) *of much knowledge, very wise* or *learned.*

πολύ-ϊππος, *ον*, (*πολύς, ἵππος*) *having many horses, rich in horses.*

πολυ-ΐστωρ, *ορος, ὁ, ἡ*, (*πολύς, ἴσημι*) = *πολυΐδρις.*

πολῠ-ΐχθῠος, *ον*, (*πολύς, ἰχθύς*) *abounding in fish.*

πολῠ-καγκής, *ές*, (*πολύς*, **κάγκω* = *καίω*) *very dry* or *parched:* also *much-parching.*

πολῠ-κᾱής, *ές*, (*πολύς, καίω*) *much-burning.*

πολῠ-κάμμορος, *ον*, (*πολύς, κάμμορος*) *very ill-fated* or *miserable.*

πολῠ-καμπής, *ές*, (*πολύς, κάμπτω*) *with many twists and turns.*

πολῠ-κᾰνής, *ές*, (*πολύς, καίνω*) *much-slaughtering.*

πολύ-καπνος, *ον*, (*πολύς, καπνός*) *much-smoked: with smoky rafters.*

πολυ-κάρηνος, *ον*, (*πολύς, κάρηνον*) *many-headed.*

πολῠκαρπία, *ἡ*, *abundance of fruit.* From

πολύ-καρπος, *ον*, (*πολύς, καρπός*) *with much fruit, rich in fruit, fruitful.*

πολῠ-κέλᾰδος, *ον*, (*πολύς, κέλαδος*) *much-sounding.*

πολῠκέρδεια, *ἡ*, *great craft* or *cunning.* From

πολῠ-κερδής, *ές*, (*πολύς, κέρδος*) *very cunning* or *crafty.*

πολύ-κερως, *ωτος, ὁ, ἡ*, (*πολύς, κέρας*) *many-horned;* π. *φόνος* the slaughter *of much horned cattle.*

πολύ-κεστος, *ον*, (*πολύς, κεστός*) *much-wrought with the needle, well-stitched.*

πολῠ-κηδής, *ές*, (*πολύς, κῆδος*) *full of care, grievous.*

πολυ-κήριος, *ον*, (*πολύς, κήρ*) *very deadly.*

πολῠ-κήτης, *ες*, (*πολύς, κῆτος*) *full of monsters.*

πολύ-κλαυστος or **-κλαυτος**, *ον*, also *η, ον*, (*πολύς, κλαίω*) *much deplored* or *lamented.*

πολυ-κλεής, *ές*, (*πολύς, κλέος*) *far-famed.*

πολύ-κλειτος, *ον*, also *η, ον*, (*πολύς, κλειτός*) *far-famed, of great renown.*

πολυ-κλήεις, *εσσα, εν*, (*πολύς, κλέος*) = *πολύκλειτος.*

πολυ-κλήϊς, *ιδος* [ῑ], *ἡ*, (*πολύς, κλείς*) *with many benches* of rowers, *with many banks of oars.*

πολύ-κληρος, *ον*, (*πολύς, κλῆρος*) *with a large lot* or *portion, rich in land.*

πολύ-κλητος, *ον*, (*πολύς, καλέω*) *called from many a land.*

πολύ-κλυστος, *ον*, (*πολύς, κλύζω*) *much dashing* or *swelling.* II. pass. *washed by many a wave.*

πολύ-κμητος, *ον*, (*πολύς, κάμνω*) *much-wrought.* 2. later, *laborious*

πολύ-κνημος, *ον*, (*πολύς, κνημός*) *with many shoulders*, of mountains: *mountainous.*

πολύ-κοινος, *ον*, (*πολύς, κοινός*) *common to many.*

πολῠκοιρᾰνία Ion. **-ίη**, *ἡ*, *the rule of many.* From

πολῠ-κοίρᾰνος, *ον*, (*πολύς, κοίρανος*) *wide-ruling.*

πολυ-κόλυμβος, *ον*, (*πολύς, κολυμβάω*) *oft-diving.*

πολύ-κρᾱνος, *ον*, (*πολύς, κρᾶνον*) *many-headed.*

πολυ-κρᾰτής, *ές*, (*πολύς, κράτος*) *very mighty.*

πολύ-κροτος, *ον*, also *η, ον*, (*πολύς, κροτέω*) *ringing loud* or *clearly.*

πολύ-κρουνος, *ον*, (*πολύς, κρουνός*) *with many springs.*

πολυ-κτέᾰνος, *ον*, (*πολύς, κτέανον*) = *πολυκτήμων.*

πολυ-κτήμων, *ον*, gen. *ονος*, (*πολύς, κτῆμα*) *with many* or *great possessions, very wealthy.*

πολύ-κτητος, *ον*, (*πολύς, κτάομαι*) = *πολυκτημων.*

πολυ-κτόνος, *ον*, (*πολύς, κτείνω*) *much-slaying, murderous.*

πολῠ-κύδιστος, *ον*, also *η, ον*, (*πολύς, κύδιστος*) *held in highest honour, most glorious.*

πολῠ-κύμων, *ον*, gen. *ονος*, (*πολύς, κῦμα*) *swelling with many waves*

πολῠ-κώκῡτος, *ον*, (*πολύς, κωκύω*) *much-lamenting, very plaintive.*

πολύ-κωμος, *ον*, (*πολύς, κῶμος*) *much-revelling.*

πολύ-κωπος, *ον*, (*πολύς, κωπή*) *of many oars.*

πολῠ-κώτῑλος, *ον*, (*πολύς, κωτίλος*) *much-chattering, much-warbling.*

πολῠ-λήϊος, *ον*, (*πολύς, λήϊον*) *with many cornfields.*

πολύλ-λῐθος, *ον*, (*πολυς, λίθος*) *very stony.*

πολύλ-λιστος, *ον*, (*πολύς, λίσσομαι*) *much implored* or *entreated; νηὸς πολύλλιστος* a temple *where many prayers are offered.*

πολύλ-λῐτος, *ον*, (*πολύς, λιτομαι*) = *πολύλλιστος.*

πολῠλογία, *ἡ*, *much speaking, much talk.* From

πολύ-λογος, *ον*, (*πολύς, λόγος*) *much-talking, talkative.* 2. *much talked of.*

πολῠ-μᾰθής, *ές*, (*πολύς, μαθεῖν*) *having learnt much, knowing much.* Adv. *-θῶς*, *in a very learned way.*

πολυ-μανής, *ές*, (*πολύς, μανῆναι*) *very furious.*

πολῠ-μάχητος, *ον*, (*πολυς, μαχομαι*) *much* or *often fought for.* [ᾰ]

πολῠ-μεθής, *ές*, (*πολύς, μέθη*) *very drunk.*

πολῠ-μελής, *ές*, (*πολύς, μέλος*) *with many limbs* or *members.* II. *many-toned, musical.*

πολῠ-μερής, *ές*, (*πολύς, μέρος*) *consisting of many parts.* Adv. *-ρῶς*, *in many ways.*

πολύ-μετρος, *ον*, (*πολύς, μέτρον*) *holding many measures:* generally, *abundant.*

πολῠ-μηκάς, *άδος, ὁ*, (*πολύς, μηκάομαι*) *much-bleating,*

πολύ-μηλος Dor. **-μαλος**, ον, (πολύς, μῆλον) *with many sheep: rich in flocks.*

πολύ μηνις, ιος, ὁ, ἡ, (πολύς, μῆνις) *very wrathful.*

πολύ-μητις, ιος, ὁ, ἡ, (πολύς, μῆτις) *of many counsels* or *expedients, ever-ready.*

πολῦμηχᾰνία Ion. **-ίη**, ἡ, *fertility of resources, inventiveness, readiness.* From

πολῠ-μήχᾰνος, ον, (πολύς, μηχανή) *fertile in resources, inventive, ever-ready.*

πολῠ-μῐγής, ές, (πολύς, μιγῆναι) *mixed of many parts, motley.*

πολῠ-μῑσής, ες, (πολύς, μῖσος) *much-hated.*

πολύ-μισθος, ον, (πολύς, μισθός) *receiving much pay, hired at a high rate.*

πολύ-μῐτος, ον, (πολύς, μίτος) *consisting of many threads;* πέπλοι πολύμιτοι *pictured* or *brocaded* robes.

πολυ-μνήστη, ἡ, (πολύς, μνάομαι) as fem. adj. *much courted, wooed by many.*

πολύ-μνηστος, ον, (πολύς, μνάομαι) *much-remembering, mindful, grateful.* II. pass. *much-remembered, never to be forgotten.*

πολυ-μνήστωρ, ορος, ὁ, ἡ, (πολύς, μνᾰομαι) *remembering much, mindful.*

Πολ-ύμνια, ἡ, contr. from Πολυ-ύμνια, (πολύς, ὕμνος) *Polymnia*, i. e. *the Muse of many hymns*, one of the nine Muses, goddess of lyric poetry.

πολύ-μουσος, ον, (πολύς, Μοῦσα) *with many arts* or *accomplishments.*

πολύ-μοχθος, ον, (πολυς, μοχθος) *much-labouring, much-enduring.* II. pass. *won by much toil.*

πολύ-μῦθος, ον, πολύς, μῦθος) *of many words, wordy, talkative.* II. pass. *much-talked-of, famous in story, storied.*

πολύ-νᾱος, ον, (πολύς, ναος) *with many temples.*

πολῠ-ναύτης, ου, ὁ, (πολύς, ναύτης) *with many sailors.*

πολῠ-νείκης, ου, ο, (πολυς, νεῖκος) *much-wrangling:* often as a prop. n. *Polynices.*

πολῠ-νέφελος, ον, (πολύς, νεφέλη) *overcast with clouds, very cloudy:* there is also a Dor. form πολυνεφέλας, gen. α.

πολῠ-νίκης, ου, ὁ, (πολύς, νικάω) *a frequent conqueror.*

πολῠ-νῑφής, ές, (πολύς, νίφω) *deep with snow.*

πολύ-ξεινος, ον, Ion. for sq.

πολύ-ξενος Ion. **-ξεινος**, ον, also η, ον, (πολύς, ξένος, ξεῖνος):—of persons, *entertaining many guest very hospitable.* II. *visited by many guests.*

πολύ-ξεστος, ον, (πολύς, ξέω) *much-polished.*

πολῠοινέω, *to be rich, abound in wine.* From

πολύ-οινος, ον, (πολύς, οἶνος) *abounding in wine.*

πολύ-ολβος, ον, (πολύς, ὄλβος) *very wealthy: rich in blessings: abundant.*

πολύ-ομβρος, ον, (πολύς, ὄμβρος) *very rainy.*

πολῠ-όμμᾰτος, ον, (πολύς, ὄμμα) *many-eyed.*

πολῠ-όρνιθος, ον, (πολύς, ὄρνις) *abounding in birds.*

πολῠοψία, ἡ, *abundance of dainties: abundance of food.* From

πολύ-οψος, ον, (πολύς, ὄψον) *abounding in dainties: luxurious.*

πολυ-πᾰθής, ές, (πολύς, παθεῖν) *much-suffering.*

πολῠπαιδία, ἡ, (πολύπαις) *abundance of children.*

πολῠ-παίπᾰλος, ον, (πολύς, παιπάλη) *exceeding crafty.*

πολύ-παις, **-παιδος**, ο, ἡ, (πολυς, παῖς) *with many children.*

πολῠ-πάμ-φᾰος, ον, (πολύς, πᾶς, φάος) *very bright.*

πολῠ-πάμων, ον, gen. ονος, (πολύς, πέπᾶμαι) *with great possessions, very wealthy.*

πολῠπειρία, ἡ, *long experience.* 2. *frequent* or *daring enterprise.* From

πολύ-πειρος, ον, (πολύς, πεῖρα) *much-experienced.*

πολῠ-πείρων, ον, gen. ονος, (πολύς, πεῖρας) *with many boundaries: of* or *from many countries.*

πολῠ-πενθής, ές, (πολύς, πένθος) *much-mourning, very mournful.* II. pass. *much-mourned.*

πολῠ-πένθῐμος, ον, = πολυπενθής.

Πολυπημονίδης, ου, ὁ, *son of Polypemon*, in allusion to the meaning of the word; v. πολυπήμων.

πολύ-πήμων, ον, gen. ονος, (πολύς, πῆμα) *causing manifold woe, baneful.*

πολύ-πηνος, ον, (πολύς, πήνη) *close-woven.*

πολῠ-πῖδαξ, ᾰκος, ὁ, ἡ, (πολύς, πῖδαξ) *with many springs* or *fountains.*

πολύ-πῐκρος, ον, (πολύς, πικρός) *very keen* or *bitter;* neut. pl. πολύπικρα as Adv. *very bitterly.*

πολῠ-πῑνής, ές, (πολύς, πίνος) *very dirty.*

πολύ-πλαγκτος, ον, (πολύς, πλάζομαι) *much-wandering, roaming far a-field: much-erring.* II. act. (πολύς, πλάζω) *leading far astray:* metaph. *beguiling, delusive.*

πολυ-πλᾰνής, ές, (πολύς, πλᾰνάομαι) *roaming far* or *long;* πολυπλανὴς κισσός the *wandering ivy.* 2. *much-erring.*

πολυ-πλάνητος, ον, (πολύς, πλᾰνάομαι) *far-* or *oft-wandering:* of blows, *showered from all sides.*

πολύ-πλᾰνος, ον, = πολυπλανής.

πολυ-πλάσιος, α, ον, = πολλαπλάσιος.

πολύ-πλεθρος, ον, (πολύς, πλέθρον) *many* πλέθρα *in size:* generally *far-extending.*

πολύ-πλεκτος, ον, (πολύς, πλέκω) *closely-twined.*

πολυ-πλόκᾰμος, ον, (πολύς, πλόκαμος) *with many locks:* of the polypus, *with many feelers.*

πολυπλοκία, ἡ, *intricacy, cunning, craft.* From

πολύ-πλοκος, ον, (πολύς, πλέκω) *much-tangled, thick-wreathed.* 2. metaph. *tangled, intricate, complex.* II. act. *entangling intriguing.*

πολῠ-πόδης, ου, ὁ, poët. πουλῠπόδες, = πολύπους.

πολῠ-ποίκιλος, ον, (πολύς, ποικίλος) *much-variegated.*

πολύ-πονος, ον, (πολύς, πόνος) *much-labouring, much-suffering;* also *causing much pain, painful.*

πολύπος, ου, ὁ, see πολύπους.

πολῠ-πότᾰμος, *ον*, (πολύς, ποταμός) *with many* or *large rivers*

πολῠ-πότνια, ἡ, (πολύς, πότνια) *very venerable.*

πολύπους [ῠ], –ποδος, ὁ, ἡ, acc. πολύπουν, (πολύς, πούς) *many-footed* II. as Subst. πολύπους or more commonly (even in Att.) **πουλύ-πους**, *ου*, ὁ, *the many-footed one, the sea-polypus;* gen. πουλύποδος; acc. πουλύπουν or πολύποδα: plur. nom. πολύποδες, etc.: poët. nom. **πούλῠπος**, *ου*: Dor. **πώλῠπος**; Lat. *pōlypus*

πολυπραγμονέω Ion. **–πρηγμονέω**, f. ήσω, (πολυπράγμων) *to be busy about many things, to be very busy: to be meddlesome* or *officious: to meddle in public affairs, intrigue.*

πολυπραγμοσύνη, ἡ (πολυπράγμων) *officious interference, meddling: a meddling, active character.* From

πολυ-πράγμων, *ον*, gen. *ονος*, (πολύς, πράσσω) *busy after many things, officious, meddling, turbulent.*

πολύ-πρᾶος, *ον*, (πολύς, πρᾶος) *very mild.*

πολυ-πρηγμονέω, Ion. for πολυπραγμονέω.

πολυ-πρόβᾰτος, *ον*, (πολύς, πρόβατον) *rich in sheep* or *cattle:* Sup. πολυπροβατώτατος.

πολυ-πρώτιστος, *η*, *ον*, = πολὺ πρώτιστος.

πολυ-πτόητος Ion. **–πτοίητος**, *ον*, (πολύς, πτοέω) *much-scared, timorous.*

πολύ-πτῠχος, *ον*, (πολύς, πτυχή) *of* or *with many folds: with many glens* or *valleys.*

πολύ-πυργος, *ον*, (πολύς, πύργος) *with many towers.*

πολύ-πῡρος, *ον*, (πολύς, πυρός) *rich in corn.*

πολύρ-ραπτος, *ον*, = πολύρραφος.

πολύρ-ρᾰφος, *ον*, (πολύς, ῥάπτω) *much-worked, highly-wrought.*

***πολύρ-ρην**, *ηνος*, ὁ, ἡ, (πολύς, *ῥήν = ἀμνός) *rich in sheep* or *flocks:* only found in nom. pl. πολύρρηνες, never in nom. sing.

πολύρ-ρηνος, *ον*, = *πολύρρην.

πολύρ-ριζος, *ον*, (πολύς, ῥίζα) *with many roots.*

πολύρ-ροδος, *ον*, (πολύς, ῥόδον) *abounding in roses.*

πολύρ-ροθος, *ον*, (πολύς, ῥόθος) *much-dashing, loud-roaring: very clamorous.*

πολυρ-ροίβδητος, *ον*, (πολύς, ῥοιβδέω) *much-whizzing.*

πολύρ-ροος, *ον*, contr. **–ρους**, *ουν*, and **πολύρ-ρῠτος**, *ον*, (πολύς, ῥέω) *much-flowing;* of blood, *shed in streams.*

ΠΟΛΥ´Σ, πολλή, πολύ; gen. πολλοῦ, ῆς, οῦ; dat. πολλῷ, ῇ, ῷ; acc. πολύν, πολλήν, πολύ:—Ion. nom. πολλός, πολλή, πολλόν, acc. πολλόν, πολλήν, πολλόν: the Ion. declension is retained by the Att. in all cases, except nom. and acc. sing., masc. and neut. The following are Ep. forms: sing. gen. πολέος, pl. nom. πολέες contr. πολεῖς; gen. πολέων; dat. πολέσι, πολέσσι, πολέεσσι; acc. πολέας contr. πολεῖς; also gen. plur. fem. πολλέων and πολλάων [ᾱ]:—**πουλύς**, neut. πουλύ, are also Ep. forms.

I. Of Number, *many*, opp. to ὀλίγος few: also of anything often repeated; πολλὸν ἦν τοῦτο τὸ ἔπος this word was *often repeated.* 2. also of Size or Degree, as, πολὺς νιφετός *a heavy* storm of snow; πολὺς ὕπνος *deep* sleep; of a person, μέγας καὶ πολλός great and *large;* πολλὴ κέκλημαι I have been *much extolled;* πολλὸς λόγος *a far-spread* report; πολλὴ ἀνάγκη *strong* necessity. 3. of the Value of a thing; πολλοῦ ἄξιος worth *much;* πολλοῦ ποιεῖσθαί τι, Lat. *magni facere*, to reckon of *much* consequence. 4. c. gen., as πολλοὶ Τρώων for πολλοὶ Τρῶες; πολλὸν σαρκός for πολλὴ σάρξ. 5. πολύς is often joined to another Adj., πολέες τε καὶ ἐσθλοί *many* men and good. 6. in Att. with the article, οἱ πολλοί *the many, a majority;* so also, τὸ πολύ; ὡς ἐπὶ τὸ πολύ for *the most part* 7. πολύς is often joined with a Partic. and εἰμί, as, πολλὸς ἦν λισσόμενος he was *urgent* in his entreaties. II. of Space, *large, far, wide;* πολλὴ ὁδός a *long* way. III. of Time, *long.*

As Adv. in neut. sing. and pl., πολύ Ion. πολλόν, πολλά, *much, very:* also *many times, oft-times, often,* often strengthd. by μάλα: of Space, *a great way:* of Time, *long:* of Degree, *far, very much* 2. πολύ is joined with a Comp. Adj. to increase its force; πολὺ or πολλὸν ἀμείνων *much* better: with Comp Adv., πολὺ μᾶλλον *much* more: with Sup., as πολὺ πρῶτος *much* the first. 3. πολλά *many times, often:* τὰ πολλά *mostly, usually.* 4. with Preps.; ἐπὶ πολύ *for long;* ἐπὶ πολλὸν *far.*

Comp. **πλείων** Att. **πλέων**; Sup. **πλεῖστος.**

πολύ-σαθρος, *ον*, (πολύς, σαθρός) *very rotten.*

πολῠ-σαρκία, ἡ, (πολύς, σάρξ) *fleshiness, plumpness.*

πολῠ-σέβαστος, *ον*, (πολύς, σεβαστός) *most august.*

πολύ-σεμνος, *ον*, (πολύς, σεμνός) *very venerable.*

πολῠ-σημάντωρ, *ορος*, ὁ, (πολύς, σημαίνω) *a ruler over many.*

πολῠ-σῑνής, ής, (πολύς, σίνομαι) *very hurtful, baneful, mischievous.*

πολῠσῑτία, ἡ, *abundance of corn* or *food.* From

πολύ-σῖτος, *ον*, (πολύς, σῖτος) *abounding in corn* II. *high-fed, full of meat.*

πολύ-σκαλμος, *ον*, (πολύς, σκαλμός) *many-oared.*

πολύ-σκαρθμος, *ον*, (πολύς, σκαίρω) *far-springing, swift bounding.*

πολύ-σκηπτρος, *ον*, (πολύς, σκῆπτρον) *wide-ruling.*

πολύ-σκιος, *ον*, (πολύς, σκιά) *very shady.*

πολυ-σκόπελος, *ον*, (πολύς, σκόπελος) *very rocky.*

πολυ-σπᾰθής, ές, (πολύς, σπάθη) *thick-woven*

πολυ-σπερής, ές, (πολύς, σπείρω) *wide-spread, scattered abroad, numerous.*

πολύ-σπλαγχνος, *ον*, (πολύς, σπλάγχνον) *of great mercy* or *compassion.*

πολύ-σπορος, *ον*, (πολύς, σπείρω) *much-sown, fruitful.*

πολυ-στάφῠλος, *ον*, (πολύς, σταφυλή) *rich in grapes.*

πολύ-στᾰχυς, *υ*, gen. *υος*, (πολύς, στάχυς) *rich in ears of corn yielding rich crops.*

πολυ-στέλεχος, *ον*, *with many stems.*

πολυ-στένακτος, *ον*, (*πολύς, στενάζω*) *deep-sighing, miserable.*

πολυ-στέφανος, *ον*, *with many wreaths.*

πολυ-στεφής, *ές*, (*πολύς, στέφω*) *crowned with many a wreath; πολυστεφὴς δάφνης thick-crowned with* laurel.

πολύ-στικτος, *ον*, (*πολύς, στίζω*) *much-spotted, dappled.*

πολυστιχία, *ἡ*, *a number of lines.* From

πολύ-στιχος, *ον*, (*πολύς, στίχος*) *of* or *in many lines.*

πολύ-στοιχος, *ον*, (*πολύς, στοῖχος*) *with many rows.*

πολυστομέω, *to speak much.* From

πολύ-στομος, *ον*, (*πολύς, στόμα*) *many-mouthed.*

πολύ-στονος, *ον*, (*πολύς, στένω*) *much sighing, mournful, melancholy.*

πολυ-στροφία, *ἡ*, *a turning oneself to and fro.* From

πολύ-στροφος, *ον*, (*πολύς, στρέφω*) *much-twisted: pliant, versatile.*

πολῠ-σύλλᾰβος, *ον*, (*πολύς, συλλαβή*) *of many syllables.*

πολυ-σφόνδῠλος, *ον*, *many-jointed.*

πολύ-σχιστος, *ον*, (*πολύς, σχίζω*) *split into many parts, branching.*

πολύ-σχοινος, *ον*, (*πολύς, σχοῖνος*) *many-corded.*

πολύ-σωρος, *ον*, (*πολύς, σωρός*) *yielding large heaps of corn.*

πολῠ-τάλαντος, *ον*, (*πολύς, τάλαντον*) *weighing* or *worth many talents.*

πολυ-ταρβής, *ές*, (*πολύς, τάρβος*) *much-frightened.*

πολύ-τεκνος, *ον*, (*πολύς, τέκνον*) *bearing many children.*

πολῠτέλεια, *ἡ*, (*πολυτελής*) *great expense, costliness, expensiveness.*

πολῠ-τελής, *ές*, (*πολύς, τέλος*) *very expensive, costly*:—of persons, *sumptuous, extravagant*:—Comp. and Sup. *πολυτελέστερος, -έστατος.*

πολυτελῶς, Adv. of *πολυτελής*, *expensively*:—Sup. *πολυτελέστατα, in the costliest manner.*

πολῠ-τερπής, *ές*, (*πολύς, τέρπω*) *much-delighting.*

πολῠ-τέχνης, *ου*, *ὁ*, or **πολύ-τεχνος**, *ον*, (*πολύς, τέχνη*) *one skilled in many arts.*

πολῠ-τίμητος, *ον*, also *η, ον*, (*πολύς, τῑμάω*) *highly honoured* or *revered.* II. *of high value, costly.*

πολύ-τῑμος, *ον*, (*πολύς, τιμή*) *much revered.* II. *of high value, costl*

πολύ-τιτος, *ον*, (*πολυς, τίω*) *held in high honour*: also *worthy of high honour.* [ῐ metri grat.]

πολύ-τλας, *αντος, ὁ*, (*πολύς, τλῆναι*) *much-enduring.*

πολυ-τλήμων, *ονος, ὁ, ἡ*, (*πολύς, τλήμων*) *much-enduring, very patient.*

πολύ-τλητος, *ον*, (*πολύς, τλῆναι*) *having had much to endure*, hence *unfortunate.*

πολύ-τμητος, *ον*, (*πολυ., τέμνω*) *much-cut, much-lacerated.*

πολυ-τρήρων, *ωνος, ὁ, ἡ*, (*πολύς, τρήρων*) *abounding in doves.*

πολύ-τρητος, *ον*, (*πολύς, τρητός*) *much-pierced, perforated, full of holes, porous*

πολυ-τρίπους, *-ποδος, ὁ, ἡ*, (*πολύς, τρίπους*) *with many tripods.*

πολυτροπία Ion. *-ίη*, *ἡ*, *variety of resources, versatility, craft.* From

πολύ-τροπος, *ον*, (*πολύς, τρέπω*) *much-turned*, i.e. *much-travelled, wandering.* II. *turning many ways, versatile, ingenious: changeful.* 2. *manifold.* Hence

πολυτρόπως, Adv. *in divers manners.*

πολυ-τρόχᾰλος, *ον*, (*πολύς, τρέχω*) *running about much, bustling.*

πολῠ-ύμνητος, *ον*, (*πολύς, ὑμνέω*) *much-famed in song, much-renowned.*

πολύ-υμνος, *ον*, (*πολύς, ὕμνος*) *much sung of, famous: honoured with many hymns.*

πολῠ-φάρμᾰκος, *ον*, (*πολύς, φάρμακον*) *knowing many drugs* or *charms.*

πολύ-φᾰτος, *ον*, (*πολίς, φημί*) *much spoken of, very famous*: also *in a high strain.*

πολύ-φημος Dor. **-φαμος**, *ον*, (*πολύς, φήμη*) *with many tales* or *legends*: also *with loud cries.* II. *wordy, full of the din of voices: ἡ πολύφημος*, as Subst., = *ἀγορά, the many-voiced, the assembly; ἰς πολύφημον ἐκφέρειν* to bring before *the assembly.*

πολυ-φθόρος, *ον*, (*πολύς, φθείρω*) *destroying many, baneful, pernicious.* II. pass., *πολύφθορος, ον, utterly destroyed* or *ruined.*

πολύ-φῐλος, *ου*, (*πολύς, φιλέω*) *having many friends, much-beloved.*

πολύ-φιλτρος, *ον*, (*πολύς, φίλτρον*) *suffering from many love-charms: deeply enamoured, love-sick.*

πολύ-φλοισβος, *ον*, (*πολύς, φλοῖσβος*) *loud-roaring*, epith. of the sea.

πολυ-φόνος, *ον*, (*πολίς, *φένω*) *killing many, murderous.*

πολύ-φορβος, *ον*, also, *η, ον*, (*πολύς, φέρβομαι*) *feeding many, bountiful.*

πολῠφορία, *ἡ*, *productiveness.* From

πολῠ-φόρος, *ον*, (*πολίς, φέρω*) *bearing much; πολυφόρος οἶνος* wine *which will bear much water; πολυφόρος δαίμων* a fortune *that wants tempering.*

πολυ-φρᾰδής, *ές*, (*πολύς, φράζω*) *very eloquent, wise, sagacious.*

πολύ-φροντις, *ιδος, ὁ, ἡ*, (*πολύς, φροντίς*) *full of care.*

πολυ-φρόντιστος, *ον*, (*πολύς, φροντίζω*) *much-thinking, thoughtful.*

πολυφροσύνη, *ἡ*, *fullness of understanding, great wisdom* or *understanding.* From

πολύ-φρων, *ονος, ὁ, ἡ*, (*πολύς, φρήν*) *much-thoughtful, very sagacious*: also *ingenious, inventive.*

πολύ-χαλκος, *ον*, (*πολύς, χαλκός*) *abounding in copper* or *brass*: hence *rich in copper vessels* or *money.* II. *wrought of solid brass, all-brasen.*

πολυ-χανδής, *ές*, (*πολύς, χανδάνω*) *wide-yawning.*

πολύ-χαρμος, *ον*, (*πολύς, χάρμη*) *very warlike.*

πολύ-χειρ, *-χειρος, ὁ, ἡ*, (*πολύς, χείρ*) *many-handed, with many hands*: also *with many hands* or *men.* Hence

πολῠ-χειρία, ἡ, *a multitude of hands* or *workmen.*

πολύ-χορδος, ον, (πολύς, χορδή) *many-stringed:* hence *many-toned.*

πολυχρημᾰτία, ἡ, *possession of great wealth.* From

πολυ-χρήματος, ον, (πολύς, χρῆμα) *very wealthy.*

πολυ-χρόνιος, ον, (πολύς, χρόνος) *existing a long time, of the olden time, ancient.*

πολύ-χρῡσος, ον, (πολύς, χρυσός) *rich in gold, adorned with gold.*

πολύ-χωστος, ον, (πολύς, χώννυμι) *high-heaped.*

πολυ-ψάμᾰθος, ον, (πολύς, ψάμαθος), and

πολύ-ψαμμος, ον, (πολύς, ψάμμος) *very sandy.*

πολυψηφία, ἡ, *number* or *diversity of votes.* And

πολυ-ψήφῑς, ῖδος, ὁ, ἡ, *with many pebbles, pebbly,* of the beds of rivers. From

πολύ-ψηφος, ον, (πολύς, ψῆφος) *with many* or *various votes.*

πολύ-ψοφος, ον, (πολύς, ψοφέω) *loud-sounding.*

πολῠ-ώδῠνος, ον, (πολύς, ὀδύνη) *very painful.* II. pass. *suffering great pain.*

πολῠ-ώνῠμος, ον, (πολύς, ὄνυμα Aeol. for ὄνομα) *of many names, worshipped under many names* II. *of great name, famous, renowned.*

πολυ-ωπής, ές, and **πολῠ-ωπός**, όν, (πολύς, ὠπή) *with many holes* or *cells, close-meshed.*

πολῠ-ωρέω, (πολύς, ὥρα) *to pay much regard* or *attention to, to esteem highly.*

πολῠ-ωφελής, ές, (πολύς, ὄφελος) *very, highly useful, useful in many ways:* Sup. πολυωφελέστατος. Adv. -λῶς, *in a very serviceable manner.*

πολῠ-ώψ, ῶπος, ὁ, ἡ, = πολυωπός.

πόμα, ατος, τό, (πίνω, πέπομαι) *a drink, draught.*

πομπαῖος, α, ον, also ος, ον, (πομπή) *conducting, attending, escorting:* of a wind, *fair:* of Hermes, *conducting the souls of the dead* to the nether world.

πομπάν, **πομπᾶς**, Dor. for πομπήν, πομπῆς.

πομπεία, ἡ, (πομπεύω) *a leading in procession: any solemn* or *religious procession.* II. *jeering, ribaldry,* customary in the processions of Bacchus and Ceres.

πομπεῖον, τό, (πομπή) *any vessel employed in solemn processions.* II. at Athens, *the place where they were kept.*

πομπεύς, έως Ion. ῆος, ὁ, (πομπός) *one who attends* or *escorts, a guide, conductor.* 2. *one who goes in procession.*

πομπεύω, Ion. impf. πομπεύεσκον: f. σω: (πομπή):—*to attend, escort, guide, conduct.* II. *to lead a procession: to swagger* or *strut: to abuse with ribald jests,* as was customary in processions (see πομπεία).

πομπή, ἡ, (πέμπω) *a sending, despatching, escorting: guidance, conduct, escort.* 2. *a sending away, a sending home* to one's country. II. *a solemn procession,* Lat. *pompa.* III. *an intervention, suggestion, guidance.*

πομπῆες, **ῆας**, nom. and acc. pl. of πομπεύς.

πομπικός, ή, όν, (πομπή) *of* or *for a solemn procession: showy, stately.*

πόμπῐμος, ον, also η, ον, (πομπή) *conducting, escorting, guiding: homeward.* II. pass. *sent, brought.*

πομπός, ὁ, (πέμπω) *one who attends* or *escorts, an escort, guide:* plur. πομποί *attendants, guards.* 2. *a messenger.* II. as Adj. *conducting, leading;* πῦρ πομπόν the *signal* or *beacon fire.*

πομπο-στολέω, (πέμπω, στόλος) *to conduct a fleet* or *ship.*

πομφολῠγο-παφλασμα, τό, (πομφόλυξ, παφλάζω) *the noise made by bubbles rising.*

πομφολύζω, f. ξω, (πομφόλυξ) *to bubble* or *boil up: to gush forth.*

πομφόλυξ, ῠγος, ἡ, (πομφός) *a bubble.*

ΠΟΜΦΟ'Σ, οῦ, ὁ, *a bubble, blister.*

πονεύμενος, Aeol. for πονούμενος, part. pass. or med. of πονέω.

πονέω, (πόνος) used by Hom. mostly as Dep. πονέομαι, with fut. med. -ήσομαι; aor. 1 med. ἐπονησάμην and pass. ἐπονήθην; pf. pass. πεπόνημαι: I. absol. *to toil, work hard;* πονέεσθαι κατὰ ὑσμίνην *to toil* in the fight; hence *to be worn out, exhausted.* 2. metaph. *to be in distress* or *anxiety, feel pain of mind.* II. c. acc. *to work at, work hard at, to perform zealously.*

After Hom. the Act. **πονέω** is more freq., f. -πονήσω: aor. 1 ἐπόνησα: pf. πεπόνηκα:—Pass., aor. 1 ἐπονήθην: pass. πεπόνημαι I. c. acc. pers. *to cause toil* or *pain to* another. 2. c. acc. rei, *to gain by toil* or *labour, to work out:* Pass. *to be won by labour and pains.* II. intr. *to toil, suffer pain* or *hardship:* c. acc. cognato, πονεῖν πόνον, μόχθους *to undergo, endure* labour. Hence

πόνημα, ατος, τό, *that which is wrought out, work.*

πονήρευμα, ατος, τό, *a knavish trick.* From

πονηρεύομαι, Dep. (πονηρός) *to be evil* or *wicked, to deal wickedly.*

πονηρία, ἡ, (πονηρός) *badness, ill condition, wickedness, knavery,* Lat. *pravitas:* also *cowardice*

πονηρός, ά, όν, (πονέω) *causing pain* or *hardship:* hence, 1. *painful.* 2. *distressed, in sorry plight:* of things, *bad, sorry: useless, in bad state* or *condition;* πονηρὰ πράγματα *a bad* state of things. 3. in moral sense, *bad, worthless, villainous, knavish, wicked.* Hence

πονηρῶς, Adv. *ill, miserably;* πονηρῶς ἔχειν to be *ill* off, be in a *sorry* plight.

πονήσατο, Ep. 3 sing. aor. 1 med. of πονέω.

πόνος, ὁ, (πένω, πένομαι) *task-work, hard work, toil, drudgery,* Lat. *labor;* μάχης πόνος *the toil of* battle: hence πόνος, = μάχη, *a battle, action, the tug of war.* 2. *a task.* II. *pain* of body or mind, *suffering, grief:* in plur. *pains, distress.* III. *the fruit* or *result* of labour, *a work.*

ποντιάς, άδος, poët. fem. of πόντιος.

ποντίζω, f. ίσω, (πόντος) *to plunge* or *sink in the sea*, Lat. *mergo* :—Pass. *to be drowned*.

ποντικός, ή, όν, (πόντος) *of, from* or *in the sea*: esp. *of the* πόντος Εὔξεινος or *Black Sea*: cf. πόντος. II. *from Pontus, Pontic*; Ποντικὸν δένδρεον the tree *from Pontus, the hazel*.

πόντιος, α, ον, also ος, ον, (πόντος) *of, from* or *in the sea*: *ruling the sea*.

πόντισμα, ατος, τό, (ποντίζω) *that which is cast into the sea*.

ποντόθεν, Adv. (πόντος) *from* or *out of the sea*.

ποντο-θήρης, ου, ὁ, (πόντος, θηράω) *one who fishes in the sea*.

ποντο-μέδων, οντος, ὁ, (πόντος, μέδω) *lord of the sea*.

πόντονδε, Adv. (πόντος) *into the sea*.

Ποντοπόρεια, ἡ, (ποντοπόρος) a Nereïd, *the Sea-passer*.

ποντοπορεύω and –**πορέω**, *to pass over the sea*. From

ποντο-πόρος, ον, (πόντος, πόρος) *passing over the sea, sea-faring*.

Ποντο-ποσειδῶν, ῶνος, ὁ, (πόντος, Ποσειδῶν) *Sea-Poseidon, Neptune of the sea*.

ΠΟ'ΝΤΟΣ, οῦ, ὁ, *the sea*, esp. *the open sea, the high sea*. II. Πόντος *the Black Sea*; in full, Πόντος Εὔξεινος. 2. the country *Pontus* at the east end of the Black Sea.

ποντο-τίνακτος, ον, (πόντος, τινάσσω) *sea-shaken*.

ποντόφιν, Ep. gen. of πόντος.

ποπάνευμα, ατος, τό, = πόπᾰνον.

πόπᾰνον, τό, (πέπτω) *anything baked, a flat cake*, used at sacrifices.

πόπαξ, an exclamation of surprise, akin to πόποι.

ποπάς, άδος, ἡ, = πόπανον.

ποποί, *the cry of the hoopoe*.

ποποῖ, exclam. of surprise, anger, or pain, *oh! fie! shame!* akin to παπαί!—also ὢ ποποῖ.

ποποπό, *cry of the hoopoe*.

ποππύζω Dor. **ποππύσδω**: fut. ποππύσω: aor. 1 ἐπόπῡσα: Pass., aor. ἐποππύσθην :—*to whistle* with the lips compressed: *to cry hush!* also *to make a hissing sound* in playing the flute, *to play ill*. Hence

ποππῠλιάζω Dor. –άσδω, = ποππύζω.

ποππύσδω, Dor. for ποππύζω.

πόππυσμα, ατος, τό, and **ποππυσμός**, οῦ, ὁ, (ποππύζω) *a whistling*, esp. in applause.

πόρδᾰλις, ὁ, ἡ, older form of πάρδαλις.

πορδή, ἡ, (πέρδω) *crepitus ventris*.

πόρε, Ep. for ἔπορε; see *πόρω.

πορεία, ἡ, (πορεύω) *a walking, mode of walking, gait*, Lat. *incessus*. II. *a going, a journey, passage: a march*. 2. *a crossing beyond seas, crossing a river*.

πορευθείς, **πορευθῆναι**, aor. 1 part. and inf. of πορεύομαι.

πόρευμα, ατος, τό, (πορεύομαι) *a passage, way*; πόρευμα βροτῶν *a place where* men *resort*. 2. *a means of going, carriage, conveyance*.

πορεύσῐμος, ον, also η, ον, (πορεύω) *that may be crossed* or *traversed, passable*.

πορευτέος, α, ον, verb. Adj. of πορεύομαι, *to be traversed* or *travelled over*. II. neut. πορευτέον, *one must go*.

πορευτός, ή, όν, also ός, όν, (πορεύομαι) *travelling, journeying*.

πορεύω, f. –εύσω: (πόρος) :—*to bring, carry, convey*, esp. *to ferry* or *convey across* a river. 2. of things, *to bring, carry* : *to furnish, supply*. II. Pass. and Med. πορεύομαι, fut. med. –εύσομαι, aor. 1 pass. ἐπορεύθην: pf. πεπόρευμαι :—*to be carried* or *carry oneself, to go, walk, march, travel*. 2. c. acc. loci, *to pass over, traverse*.

πορθέω, f. ήσω: pf. pass. πεπόρθημαι :—collat. form of πέρθω, *to destroy, ravage, waste, plunder: to besiege* a town: of persons, *to slay, kill, destroy*:—Pass. *to be ruined, undone*. Hence

πόρθημα, ματος, τό, (πορθέω) *ravage, plunder*.

πόρθησις, εως, ἡ, (πορθέω) *the sack* of a town.

πορθητής, οῦ, ὁ, (πορθέω) *a ravager, plunderer*.

πορθήτωρ, ορος, ὁ, poët. for πορθητής, *a ravager*.

πορθμεῖον Ion. –ήιον, τό, (πορθμεύω) *a place for crossing, a passage over, ferry*. II. *a passage-boat, ferry-boat*. III. *the fare of a ferry*, Lat. *naulum*.

πόρθμευμα, ατος, τό, (πορθμεύω) *a crossing over, passage*.

πορθμεύς, έως Ion. ῆος, ὁ, (πορθμεύω) *a ferryman, boatman*, Lat. *portitor* : *a seaman*.

πορθμεύω, f. σω, (πορθμός) *to carry* or *ferry over* a strait, river, etc.: *to carry over, carry, convey*:—Pass. *to be carried* or *ferried over, to be transported from place to place*. II. intr. in Act., like Lat. *trajicere, to pass over, cross over*.

πορθμήιον, τό, Ion. for πορθμεῖον.

πορθμίς, ίδος, ἡ, (πορθμός) *a ferry; a strait*. II. *a ferry-boat, passage-boat*.

πορθμός, ὁ, (πείρω) *a ferry: a strait, frith*. II. *a crossing by ferry, a passage*.

πορίζω, f. ίσω Att. ιῶ: aor. 1 ἐπόρισα: Med., f. ποριοῦμαι: Pass., f. ποριςθήσομαι: aor. 1 ἐπορίσθην: pf. πεπόρισμαι: (πόρος) :—*to bring, conduct, fetch, convey*. II. *to furnish, provide, supply: to bring about, contrive, devise* :—Med. *to furnish for oneself, provide, procure, get* :—Pass. πορίζεται, impers. *it is in one's power* to do ...

πόρῐμος, ον, (πόρος) *able to provide* or *supply: wealthy, rich*. II. *full of resources, inventive*: c. acc., πόριμος ἄπορα *fertile of resource in* difficulties. III. of things, *practicable*.

πόρις, ιος, ἡ, poët. form of πόρτις.

πορισμός, ὁ, (πορίζω) *a procuring: a means of acquiring*: also *profit, gain*.

ποριστής, οῦ, ὁ, (πορίζω) *a provider, purveyor*: at Athens, the πορισταί were a financial board *to raise ways and means*. 3. *purveyors, conveyancers*, as pirates called themselves. Hence

ποριστικός, ή, όν, *fit for purveying: able to procure.*

ΠΟ'ΡΚΗΣ, ου, ὁ, *a ring* or *hoop*, which ran round the part where the iron head of a spear was fastened to the shaft.

πορνεία, ἡ, (πορνεύω) *fornication: prostitution.*

πορνεῖον, τό, (πορνεύω) *a brothel.*

πορνεύω, f. σω, (πόρνος) *to prostitute*:—Pass., of a woman, *to be* or *become a harlot.*

πόρνη, ἡ, (περνάω) *a harlot.*

πορνίδιον, τό, Dim. of πόρνη. [νῐ]

πορνικός, ή, όν, (πόρνη) *of* or *for harlots.*

πορνοβοσκέω, f. ήσω, (πορνοβοσκός) *to keep a brothel.* Hence

πορνοβοσκία, ἡ, *brothel-keeping.*

πορνο-βοσκός, ὁ, (πόρνη, βόσκω) *a brothel-keeper.*

πόρνος, ὁ, (πόρνη) *a fornicator.*

πόρος, ὁ, (περάω) *a means of passing* a river, *a ford* or *ferry: a strait, frith.* 2. πόροι ἁλός *the paths* of the sea. 3. *a way through* or *over, thoroughfare, passage: a way, track.* II. c. gen. rei, *a way* or *means of achieving;* πόρος ὁδοῦ *a means of performing* the journey; πόρος χρημάτων *a way of raising* money. 2. absol. *a contrivance, resource.* 3. in plur. '*ways and means,*' *resources, revenue.*

πορπακίζω, f. ίσω, (πόρπαξ) *to grasp by the handle, to hold a shield by the handle.*

πόρπᾱμα, ατος, τό, (πορπάω) *a garment fastened with a buckle* or *brooch.*

πόρπαξ, ᾱκος, ὁ, (πόρπη) *the handle* of a shield.

πορπάω: f. άσω [ᾱ] Ion. ήσω:—*to fasten with a buckle, to buckle* or *clasp down.* From

πόρπη, ἡ, (πείρω) like περόνη, *the pin* or *tongue* of the buckle, *a buckle* or *brooch.*

πόρπημα, ατος, τό, Ion. for πόρπαμα.

πόρρω, Adv., Lat. *porro*, Att. for πρόσω, *far, far off:* see πορρωτέρω, -ωτάτω. Hence

πόρρωθεν, Adv. *from afar;* and

πόρρωθι, Adv. *far.*

πορρώτατος, η, ον, Sup. Adj. (πόρρω) *furthest.*

πορρωτέρω, **-ωτάτω**, Adv., Comp. and Sup. of πόρρω, *further on* or *off, furthest off.*

πορσαίνω, = πορσύνω, *to offer, give:* hence *to attend to, cherish: to manage, arrange.*

πόρσιον, **πόρσιστα**, Adv., Comp. and Sup. of πόρσω or πρόσω, *further, furthest.*

πορσύνω [ῡ]: Ep. fut. πορσῠνέω contr. -ῠνῶ: (*πόρω):—*to proffer, offer, give, present, furnish:* fem. part. fut., κείνου πορσυνέουσα λέχος *to prepare* his bed. II. generally, *to make ready, provide:* —Med. *to provide for oneself, get ready.* 2. *to execute, order, arrange, adjust.* III. of persons, *to treat with care, to cherish, tend:* also *to esteem.*

πόρσω, Adv., = πόρρω, πρόσω: see πόρσιον, πόρσιστα.

πόρταξ, ᾰκος, ἡ, = πόρτις, *a calf.*

πόρτῐς, ῐος, ἡ, *a young heifer, calf: any young animal:* metaph. *a young maiden, girl,* Lat. *juvenca.*

πορτι-τρόφος, ον, (πόρτις, τρέφω) *breeding calves.*

πορφύρα Ion. -ύρη [ῠ], ἡ, (πορφύρω) *the purple-fish,* Lat. *murex.* II. *the purple dye obtained from it, purple.* III. in plur. *purple clothes* or *robes.*

πορφύρεος, η, ον, Att. contr. **πορφῠροῦς**, ᾶ, οῦν: (πορφύρα):—Lat. *purpureus, purple, dark,* first of the sea: πορφυρέη νεφέλη *a dark* cloud. 2. *dyed with murex* or *purple-fish, purple, red.* 3. *rosy, bright, beauteous,* like Lat. *purpureus.*

πορφῠρεύς, έως, ὁ, (πορφύρα) *a fisher for purple-fish, a purple-dyer,* Lat. *purpurarius.* Hence

πορφῠρευτικός, ή, όν, *of* or *for a purple-dyer.*

πορφῠρίς, ίδος, ἡ, (πορφύρα) *a purple garment* or *covering.* II. *a red-coloured bird.*

πορφῠρίων, ωνος, ὁ, (πορφύρα) *a red-coloured water-bird.*

πορφῠρο-ειδής, ές, (πορφύρα, εἶδος) *purpled, dark.*

πορφῠρο-πώλης, ου, ὁ, fem. -πῶλις, ιδος, (πορφύρα, πωλέω) *a dealer in purple, seller of purple.*

πορφῠρό-στρωτος, ον, (πορφύρα, στρώννυμι) *spread with purple cloth.*

πορφῠροῦς, ᾶ, οῦν, Att. contr. for πορφύρεος.

πορφύρω [ῡ], a redupl. form of φύρω, (as μορμύρω of μύρω), *to grow dark,* esp. of the sea; ὡς ὅτε πορφύρῃ πέλαγος μέγα κύματι κωφῷ as when the huge sea *grows dark* with its dumb swell (i. e. with waves that do not break, opp. to πολιὴ ἅλς): metaph. *to be troubled, disquieted,* πολλὰ δέ οἱ κραδίη πόρφυρε much was his heart *troubled.* II. *to grow purple.*

***ΠΟ'ΡΩ**, obsol. pres. of the aor. 2 ἔπορον, and pf. πέπρωμαι: I. aor. 2 ἔπορον Ep. πόρον, part. πορών:—*to bring to pass, contrive: to give, offer, bestow, grant;* εὖχος πορεῖν *to fulfil* a wish. II. pf. pass. πέπρωμαι, *to be given* or *assigned as one's portion* or *lot,* only used in 3 sing. pf. pass. πέπρωται, and 3 sing. plqpf. πέπρωτο, *it has, had been fated,* and part. πεπρωμένος, η, ον, *allotted* or *fated* to one: hence, ἡ πεπρωμένη, *an appointed lot, Fate, Destiny;* so also τὸ πεπρωμένον.

***ΠΟ'Σ**, assumed as the interrog. Pron., answering to the relat. ὅς, whence ποῦ, ποῖ, πῇ, πῶ, also, πόθεν, πόθι, πόσε, πότε, and the Adj. πότερος.

ποσάκις Ep. **ποσσάκι** [ᾰ], Adv. (πόσος) *how many times? how often?* Lat. *quoties?*

πόσε, Adv. (*πός) *whither?* Lat. *quo?*

Ποσειδᾶν and **Ποτειδᾶν**, ᾶνος, ὁ, Dor. for Ποσειδῶν.

Ποσειδάνιος and **-αόνιος**, α, ον, Dor. for Ποσειδώνιος.

Ποσείδειον, τό, *a temple of Neptune:* neut. from

Ποσείδειος, α, ον, = Ποσειδώνιος.

Ποσειδεών, ῶνος, *Poseideon*, ὁ, the sixth month of the Attic year, answering to the latter half of December and first half of January.

Ποσειδῶν, ῶνος, ὁ: acc. **Ποσειδῶ**: voc. **Πόσειδον**: Homeric form **Ποσειδάων** [ᾱ], άωνος, acc. άωνα, voc. Ποσείδαον: Dor. **Ποτειδᾶν** or **Ποτιδάν**, ᾶνος: Ion. **Ποσειδέων**, ωνος:—*Poseidon*, Lat. *Neptunus*, son of Cronos and Rhea, brother of Jupiter, god of the sea.

Ποσειδώνιος, α, ον, *sacred to Neptune*: τὰ Ποσειδώνια (sub. ἱερά), *the festival of Neptune*.

ΠΟ'ΣΘΗ, ἡ, *membrum virile*.

πόσθων, ωνος, ὁ, (πόσθη) *a little boy*.

ποσί, dat. pl. of πούς: but **πόσι**, vocat. of πόσις.

Ποσῑδήιον, τό, Ion. for Ποσείδειον.

Ποσῑδήιος, η, ον, Ion. for Ποσείδειος. *sacred to Poseidon* or *Neptune*.

ΠΟ'ΣΙΣ, ὁ, gen. πόσιος, dat. πόσει Ep. πόσεϊ, voc. πόσις or πόσι: pl., nom. πόσεις, Ep. acc. πόσιας:—*husband, spouse, mate*: when opp. to ἀνήρ, πόσις was *a lawful husband*, ἀνήρ *a paramour*.

πόσῐς, ιος Att. εως, ἡ, (πίνω) *a drinking, drink, beverage*: *a drinking-bout*; παρὰ τὴν πόσιν, Lat. *inter pocula, over their cups*.

πόσος Ion. **κόσος**, η, ον, interrog. Adj. of relat. ὅσος and demonstr. τόσος:—*how great? how much? of what value?* Lat. *quantus?* II. **ποσός**, ή, όν, indef. Adj., *of any size* or *number*, Lat. *aliquantus*: ἐπὶ ποσόν to *a certain degree*.

ποσσ-ῆμαρ, Adv. (πόσος, ἦμαρ) *in how many days? within how many days?*

ποσσί or -ίν, Ep. for ποσί, dat. pl. of πούς.

ποσσί-κροτος, ον, (πούς, κροτέω) *beaten by the foot* in dancing.

πόσσις, εως, ὁ, poët. for πόσις, *a husband*.

ποσταῖος, α, ον, (πόστος) *in how many days? on which day?*

πόστος, η, ον, (πόσος) *which of a number?* Lat. *quotus?* πόστον δὴ ἔτος ἐστὶν ὅτε..; *how many* years is it since..? II. *how small?* Lat. *quantulus*

πότ, shortd. Dor. for ποτί, πρός, only before the Article, as πὸτ τῶ, πὸτ τόν, πὸτ τό, etc.

πότα, Aeol. for πότε.

πότᾰγε, Dor. for πρόσαγε, imperat. of προσάγω.

ποτ-αείσομαι, Dor. fut. of προσαείδω.

ποτ-αίνιος, α, ον, also ος, ον, (ποτί = πρός, αἶνος) like πρόσφατος, *newly told of, fresh, new*, Lat. *recens*: metaph. *unwonted, unheard-of*.

ποτάμειος, α, ον, = ποταμίος. [ᾰ]

ποτᾰμείψατο, Dor. and poët. for προσημείψατο, 3 sing. aor. 1 med. of προσαμείβω.

ποτᾰμέλξομαι, Dor. fut. med. (in pass. sense) of προσαμέλγω.

ποτᾰμηδόν, Adv. (ποταμός) *like a river*.

ποτᾰμήιος, η, ον, Ion. and poët. for ποτάμειος.

ποτᾰμηίς, ίδος, poët. fem. of ποτάμειος.

ποτᾰμ-ήρῠτος, ον, (ποταμός, ἐρύτω) *drawn from a stream* or *in streams*.

ποτάμιος, α, ον, also ος, ον, (ποταμός) *of* or *from a river, on a river*.

ποτᾰμόνδε, Adv. *into, to, towards a river*. From

ποτᾰμός, οῦ, ὁ, (ΠΟ-, Root of πίνω) *a river, stream*. II. personified, Ποταμός, ὁ, *a river-god*.

ποτᾰμο-φόρητος, ον, (ποταμός, φορέω) *carried away by a river*.

ποτᾱνός, ά, όν, (ποτάομαι) Dor. for ποτηνός, *winged, flying, furnished with wings*.

ποτάομαι, poët. for πέτομαι, *to fly*: fut. med. ποτήσομαι: aor. 1 pass. ἐποτήθην Dor. -άθην: pf. πεπότημαι Dor. -αμαι (with pres. sense), Ep. 3 pl. πεποτήᾰται: 3 sing. plqpf. πεπότητο:—*to be upon the wing, hover, flit about*.

ποτᾰπός, ή, όν, = ποδαπός. Adv. -πῶς.

ποτ-αυλέω, Dor. for προσαυλέω.

ποτ-ᾱῷος, α, ον, Dor. for προσηῷος.

πότε Ion. **κότε**, (*πος) interrog. Particle, *when? at what time?* II. **ποτέ**, enclit. Particle, *at some time, at any time, once, erst*. In answering clauses, ποτὲ μέν.., ποτὲ δέ.., *at one time.., at another..; sometimes.. sometimes*; Lat. *modo.. modo..*:—in questions it strengthens the interrogation, τί ποτε; Ep. τίπτε; *how ever? how possibly?*

Ποτειδάν, ᾶνος, Dor. for Ποσειδῶν.

ποτεμάξατο, Dor. for προσεμάξατο, 3 sing. aor. 1 med. of προσμάσσω.

ποτέομαι, Ep. for ποτάομαι, *to fly*.

ποτέος, α, ον, verb. Adj. of πίνω, *to be drunk, drinkable*. II. ποτέον, neut. *one must drink*.

ποτ-ερίζω, Dor. for προσερίζω.

πότερος, α, ον Ion. **κότερος**, η, ον, (*πος, ἕτερος) *whether* or *which of the two?* Lat. *uter?* 2. the neut. πότερον or πότερα is freq. used as Adv. at the beginning of an interrog. sentence containing two contrary propositions, πότερον.., ἤ..; like Lat. *utrum.., an..? whether.., or..?* II. without interrog., like ὁπότερος, *either of the two*, Lat. *alteruter*.

ποτ-έρχομαι, Dor. for προσέρχομαι.

ποτέρωθι, Adv. (πότερος) *on whether of the two sides..? on which of two sides? at which of two places?*

ποτέρως, Adv. of πότερος, *in which of two ways?* Lat. *utro modo?*

ποτέρωσε, Adv. (πότερος) *to whether of two sides? to which of two places?*

ποτ-έχω, Dor. for προσέχω.

ποτή, ἡ, (ποτάομαι) *flight*.

ποτ-ῆμεν, Dor. for προσεῖναι, inf. of πρόσειμι.

πότημα, ατος, τό, (ποτάομαι) *flight*.

ποτήμενα, Dor. for ποτώμενα, part. of ποτάομαι.

ποτηνός, ή, όν, v. ποτᾱνός.

ποτήρ, ῆρος, ὁ, (ΠΟ- Root of πίνω) *a drinking-cup, wine-cup*.

ποτήριον, τό, (ΠΟ- Root of πίνω) *a drinking-cup, wine-cup*.

ποτής, ῆτος, ἡ, (ΠΟ- Root of πίνω) *drink*.

πότης, ου, ὁ, fem. **πότις**, ιδος, (ΠΟ- Root of πίνω) *a drinker, tippler*: with another Subst., πότης λύχνος *a tippling* lamp:—Comic Sup. fem., ποτιστάτη *a hard drinker*.

ποτητός, ή, όν, (ποτάομαι) *flying, winged*: ποτητά, τά, *fowls, birds*.

ποτί, Dor. for πρός.

ποτ-ῐάπτω, **ποτῐ-βάλλω**, Dor. for προσιάπτω, προσβάλλω.

ποτι-βλέπω, Dor. for προσβλέπω.

ποτιδέγμενος, Dor. for *προσδέγμενος*, part. Ep. aor. 2 of *προσδέχομαι*.

ποτ-ιδεῖν, Dor. for *προσιδεῖν*.

ποτῐ-δέρκομαι, -δεύομαι -δόρπιος, Dor. for *προσδ–*.

ποτῐ-ειλέω, Dor. for *προσειλέω*.

ποτίζω, f. *ίσω* Att. *ιῶ*, (*πότος*) *to give to drink: to water.*

ποτίθει, Dor. for *πρόσθες*, aor. 2 imperat. of *προστίθημι*.

ποτῐκέκλῐται, Dor. for *προσκέκλ–*, 3 sing. pf. pass. of *προσκλίνω*.

ποτιλέξατο, Dor. for *προσελέξατο*, 3 sing. aor. 1 med. of *προσλέγω*.

πότιμος, *ον*, (ΠΟ– Root of *πίνω*) of water, *fit to drink, fresh:* opp. to salt: metaph. *sweet, pleasant.*

ποτῐ-νίσσομαι, Dor. for *προσν–*.

ποτῐπεπτηυῖα, Ep. pf. part. fem. 1. of *προσπτήσσω*. 2. of *προσπίπτω*.

ποτι-πτύσσω, Dor. for *προσπτύσσω*.

ποτίσδω, Dor. for *ποτίζω*.

ποτι-στάζω, Dor. for *προ-στάζω*.

ποτίστατος, Comic Sup. of *πότης*.

ποτῐ-τέρπω, Dor. for *προστέρπω*.

ποτι-τρόπαιος, *ον*, Dor. for *προστρόπαιος*.

ποτι-φωνήεις, *εσσα*, *εν*, Dor. for *προσφωνήεις*.

πότμος, *ὁ*, (*πίπτω*) *that which befalls one, one's lot, destiny: one's evil destiny; death.*

πότνᾰ, *ἡ*, Ep. for *πότνια*.

πότνιᾰ, *ἡ*, a title used in addressing females:—as Subst. *lady, mistress, queen:* c. gen., *πότνια θηρῶν queen* of wild beasts:—as Adj. *revered, august, awful:*—only found in nom. and voc. *πότνια*, acc. *πότνιαν*, except that nom. pl. *πότνιαι* is used of Ceres and Proserpine.

ποτνιάδες, *αἱ*, (*πότνια*) *the shouting, screaming ones,* epith. of the Bacchanals. 2. also as pl. to *πότνια*, *awful*, used of the Erinyes.

ποτνιάομαι, Dep. *to call out πότνια, πότνια*, to a deity: *to invoke with loud cries, cry aloud, shriek.*

ποτ-όδδω, Lacon. for *προσόζω*.

ποτόν, *τό*, (ΠΟ– Root of *πίνω*) *that which one drinks, a drink, draught; σῖτα καὶ ποτά* meat and *drink.* 2. *a spring of fresh water, a well:* generally, *water.*

ποτ-οπτάζω, Dor. for *προσ-οπτάζω*.

ποτός, *ή*, *όν*, verb. Adj. from Root ΠΟ– (v. *πίνω*) *for drinking, drink.*

πότος, *ὁ*, (ΠΟ– Root of *πίνω*) *a drinking, a drinking-bout, carousal.*

ποτ-όσδω, Dor. for *προσόζω*.

ποττό, ποττόν, ποττῶ, ποττώς, ποττάν, etc., Dor. for *πρὸς τό, πρὸς τόν, πρὸς τοῦ, πρὸς τούς, πρὸς τήν*, etc.

ποτ-ῴκει, Dor. for *προσ-εῴκει*.

ποῦ; Ion. **κοῦ**; interrog. Adv.: (**πός*) *where?* Lat. *ubi?* c. gen., *ποῦ γῆς; ποῦ χθονός; where, in what part* of the world? Lat. *ubinam terrarum?* 2. *how? in what manner?* II. *πού* as enclit., *anywhere, somewhere.*

πουλυ-πόδης, Ion. for *πολυπόδης*.

πουλύ-πους, πουλύπος, Ion. for *πολύπους, πολύπος*.

πουλύς, neut. *πουλύ*, Ep. for *πολύς, πολύ*.

πουλῠ-βότειρα, *ἡ*, Ion. for *πολυβότειρα*.

πουλυ-πᾰθής, *ές*, Ion. for *πολυπαθής*.

πουλυ-πλάνητος, *ον*, Ion. for *πολυπλάνητος*.

ΠΟΥ´Σ, *ὁ*, gen. *ποδός*: dat. pl. *ποσί* Ep. *ποσσί, πόδεσσι*: Ep. gen. and dat. dual *ποδοῖιν*:—Lat. *PES, a foot:* in plur. also a bird's *talons* or *claws; the arms* or *feelers* of a polypus:—*ξύλινος πούς* a wooden, artificial *foot:* in plur. also *a foot-race, πὺξ .. ἠδὲ πόδεσσιν* in boxing and in *the foot-race; ποσὶν ἐρίζειν* to race *on foot:* but, *ἐς πόδας ἐκ κεφαλῆς* from head to *foot.* 2. of close proximity, *πρόσθεν πόδος* or *ποδῶν, προπάροιθε ποδῶν* just before one's *feet*, i.e. before *one;*—so also, *ἐν ποσί, παρὰ ποδός, πρὸ ποδός, παρὰ ποδί*, close before or beside one; *παρὰ ποδός straightway, at once:* hence, *τὰ ἐν ποσί* and *τὰ πρὸ ποδῶν* what *lies before one*, anything *obvious, common;* cp. *ἐμπόδων, ἐκπόδων*. 3. in various phrases: *ἐπὶ πόδα backwards, with one's face forwards; ἐπὶ πόδα ἀναχωρεῖν* to retreat without turning one's back, *at one's leisure:*—*κατὰ πόδας with all the power of one's feet, at full speed, on the track* or *trail*, Lat. *vestigio; ἡ κατὰ πόδας ἡμέρα* the *very next, following* day:—*ὡς ποδῶν ἔχει* as he is off *for feet*, i.e. as quick as he can:—*ἔξω τινὸς πόδα ἔχειν* to have one's *foot* out of a thing, be clear of it:—*ἐξ ἑνὸς ποδός*, i.e. *alone, singly; ἐξ ἡσύχου ποδός quietly.* II. metaph. of things, *the foot* or *lowest part, the foot of a hill*, Lat. *radix montis.* 2. in a ship, *πόδες* are *the two lower corners of the sail*, or rather *the ropes* by which the sails are tightened and slackened, *the sheets; παριέναι τοῦ ποδός* to slack *the sheet;* so *χαλᾶν πόδα*, opp. to *τείνειν πόδα* to haul *it* tight. III. *a foot*, as *a measure of length.* IV. *a foot in Prosody.*

πρᾶγμα Ion. **πρῆγμα**, *ατος*, *τό*: (*πράσσω*):—*that which has been done, a deed:*—generally, like Lat. *res, a thing done, a thing, fact, matter, affair:* esp. *a thing right* or *fit to be done, one's business: πρῆγμά ἐστί μοι*, c. inf. it is my *duty* or *business* to do: with a negat., *οὐδὲν πρᾶγμα* it is no *matter*, of no *consequence.* 2. *an object of consequence* or *consideration;* of a person, *ἦν μέγιστον πρῆγμα Δημοκήδης παρὰ βασιλέϊ* Democedes was treated with the greatest consideration by the king. 3. of a battle, *an action, affair.* 4. of something disgraceful, *the thing, the business, job.* II. in plur. *πράγματα affairs, circumstances.* 2. *state-affairs, public business, the power* of a state; *τὰ πράγματα τῶν Ἑλλήνων the affairs* or *interests* of the Greeks, *political power; οἱ ἐν τοῖς πράγμασι* men *in office, ministers.* 3. one's *private affairs; ἀγαθὰ πράγματα* a good *condition of affairs, success, good luck.* 4. *business*, esp. in bad sense, *troublesome business, trouble, annoyance; πράγματα ἔχειν to have trouble about* a thing: *πράγματα παρέχειν τινί* to cause one *trouble.*

πραγμᾰτεία, *ἡ*, (*πραγματεύομαι*) *the prosecution of a business, diligent study, diligence: the course* or *mode* *of treating* a thing. II. *an occupation, business; a trade, calling, way of life: law-business, a law-suit:* in plur. *troubles.*

πραγμᾰτεύομαι Ion. **πρηγμ-**: Dep. with fut. med. -εύσομαι, aor. 1 med. ἐπραγματευσάμην, pass. ἐπρηγματεύθην: pf. pass. πεπραγμάτευμαι: (πρᾶγμα):—*to be busy, take trouble:* c. acc. rei, *to make* a thing *one's business, take in hand, treat of, labour to bring* it *about;* esp. *to carry on a business,* Lat. *negotiari: to prosecute a lawsuit:* πραγματεύεσθαι τὴν νύκτα *to spend* the night *in business.* II. pf. πεπραγμάτευμαι also in pass. sense, *to be laboured at, worked out.*

πραγμάτιον, τό, Dim. of πρᾶγμα, *a petty lawsuit.*

πραγμᾰτο-δίφης, ου, ὁ (πράγματα, διφάω) *one who hunts up lawsuits, a pettifogger.*

πρᾶγος, εος, τό, poët. for πρᾶγμα: also = πράγματα, *state-affairs.*

πραέως, Adv. of πραΰς, *mildly, gently.*

πρᾰθέειν, Ep. for πρᾰθεῖν, aor. 2 inf. of πέρθω.

πρᾱθείς, aor. 1 pass. part. of πιπράσκω.

πρᾱθῆναι, aor. 1 pass. inf. of πιπράσκω.

πραιτώριον, τό, the Lat. *praetorium, the tent* or *hall of the praetor: a judgment-hall: the palace of the chief magistrate.*

πρακτέος, α, ον, verb. Adj. of πράσσω, *to be done.* II. neut. πρακτέον, *one must do.*

πρακτήρ Ion. **πρηκτήρ**, ῆρος, ὁ, (πράσσω) *one that does, a doer: a trader, merchant.* Hence

πρακτήριος, ον, *executing, accomplishing.*

πρακτικός, ή, όν, (πράσσω) *fit for doing, fit for action* or *business: active, busy, able, effective energetic.*

πρακτός, ή, όν, verb. Adj. of πράσσω, *done, to be done;* τὰ πρακτά *subjects of moral action,* opp. to τὰ ποιητά.

πράκτωρ, ορος, ὁ, poët. for πρακτήρ, *one who does* or *executes, a worker.* II. *one who exacts payment, a tax-gatherer.* 2. *one who exacts punishment, a punisher, avenger;* also as Adj., σὺν δορὶ καὶ χερὶ πράκτορι with *avenging* hand.

Πράμνειος or **Πράμνιος** οἶνος, ὁ, *Pramnian wine,* so called from Mount Pramné in the island of Icaria.

πράν, Doric Adv., = πρίν, *before: formerly, one time, lately;* πράν ποκα a short time ago. [ᾱ]

πρᾱνής, ές, Dor. and Att. for πρηνής.

πρᾶξις, εως Ion. **πρῆξις**, ιος, ἡ, (πράσσω) *a doing, transaction, business, affair;* κατὰ πρῆξιν on business, *for purposes of traffic.* 2. *the progress* or *result of a business;* οὔ τις πρῆξις πέλεται γόοιο no *good* comes of weeping; πρῆξις χρησμῶν *the issue* of the oracles. II. *a doing, acting, action,* opp. to πάθος, *suffering.* III. intr. *a doing* (*well* or *ill*), *a certain state, condition.* IV. *the exaction of money* or *of punishment: revenge.*

πρᾱόνως, Adv. of πρᾶος, formed from obsol. πραων, *temperately.*

ΠΡᾹΟΣ, neut. πρᾶον: the fem. in use is πραεῖα, from **πραΰς** (Ion. πρηΰς), which is also used in masc. and neut. of all the singul. cases: in plur. both πρᾶοι and πραεῖς in nom., πράοις and πραέσι in dat.: neut. nom. and acc. is πραέα, rarely πρᾶα:—*mild, soft:* of persons, *meek, gentle:* of animals, *tame:* of sound, *gentle, low, soft.* 2. *soothing, taming.*—Comp. πραότερος or πραΰτερος Ion. πρηΰτερος. Hence

πρᾱότης, ητος, ἡ, *mildness, meekness, gentleness.*

ΠΡᾸΠΙΊΣ, ίδος, ἡ, mostly used in pl. πραπίδες, αἱ, = φρένες, *the midriff, diaphragm:* — then, since this was thought to be the seat of the understanding, 2. like φρένες, *the understanding mind:* a *the heart.* [ῐ]

πρᾰσιά, ἡ, (πράσον) *a bed in a garden, garden-plot:* πρασιαὶ πρασιαί *by companies.*

πράσῐμος, ον, (πρᾶσις) *for sale, to be sold,* Lat. *venalis.*

πρᾶσις, εως Ion. **πρῆσις**, ιος, ἡ, (πιπράσκω) *a selling, sale.*

ΠΡΑ'ΣΟΝ, τό, *a leek,* Lat. *porrum.* [ᾰ]

πρᾰσό-κουρον, τό, (πράσον, κείρω) *a leek-slice.*

Πρασσοφάγος, ὁ, Ep. for Πρᾰσο-φάγος, (πράσον, φᾰγεῖν) *Leek-eater,* name of a frog.

Πρασσαῖος, ὁ, poët. for πρασαῖος, *Leek-green,* name of a frog.

πράσσομες, Dor. for πράσσομεν.

ΠΡΑ'ΣΣΩ Ion. **πρήσσω** Att. **πράττω**: fut. πράξω Ion. πρήξω: aor. 1 ἔπραξα Ion. ἔπρηξα: pf. πέπρᾱχα Ion. πέπρηχα, and in intr. sense pf. 2 πέπρᾱγα:—Pass., fut. πραχθήσομαι, paullo post f. πεπράξομαι: aor. 1 ἐπράχθην: pf. πέπραγμαι:—properly, *to pass through,* like περάω; ἅλα πρήσσειν *to pass through* the sea; ὅδον πρήσσειν *to pass through, finish* a journey:—hence, in common usage, *to achieve, bring about, effect, accomplish, to do, work;* πράσσειν κλέος, *to achieve, win* glory: *to take charge* of a thing. II. *to practise a business, trade, way of life;* πράττειν τὰ ἴδια *to attend to, mind* one's own affairs, opp. to πράττειν τὰ κοινά, τὰ τῆς πόλεως *to manage* state-affairs: also absol., ἱκανὸς πράττειν competent *to manage public affairs:* hence, generally, *to transact, manage;* πράττειν Θηβαίοις τὰ πράγματα to *manage* matters for the interest of the Thebans. III. *to do, practise,* Lat. *agere:* absol. *to act, be the doer* or *agent.* IV. intr. *to be in a certain state* or *condition, fare:* esp. εὖ or κακῶς πράττειν *to do* or *fare* well or ill; esp. in pf. 2 πέπρᾱγα. 2. εὖ and κακῶς πράττειν mean also *to deal well* or *ill, to behave well* or *ill towards.* V. c. dupl. acc. pers. et rei, πράττειν τινά τι *to do* something *to* one. VI. c. dupl. acc. in another sense, πράττειν τινὰ ἀργύριον *to exact* money from one: metaph., φόνον πράττειν *to exact punishment for* a murder: and so *to avenge:*—Pass., πεπραγμένος τὸν φόρον *having* the tribute *exacted:*—Med., πράξασθαι *to exact* or *extort for oneself.* VII. c. acc. pers., πράττειν τινά *to make an end of* him, Lat. *conficere;* pf. pass. part. πεπραγμένος *undone, utterly ruined,* Lat. *confectus.*

πράσω, fut. of πιπράσκω. [ᾱ]

πρᾱτήρ Ion. **πρητήρ**, ῆρος, ὁ, (πέ-πρᾱμαι) *a seller, dealer.*

πρᾱτήριον Ion. **πρητήριον**, τό, (πέ-πρᾱμαι) *a place for selling, a market, mart.*

πράτιστος, Dor. for πρώτιστος. [ᾰ]

πρᾱτός, ή, όν, verb. Adj. of πιπράσκω, *to be sold.*

πρᾶτος, α, ον, Dor. for πρῶτος.

πράττω, Att. for πράσσω.

πρᾱΰ-γελως Ion. **πρηΰγ-**, ωτος, ὁ, ἡ, (πραΰς, γέλως) *softly-smiling.*

πρᾱΰ-μητις, ιος, ὁ, ἡ, (πραΰς, μῆτις) *of gentle counsel.*

πρᾱΰνσις, εως, ἡ, *a softening, appeasing.* From

πρᾱΰνω Ion. **πρηΰνω** [ῡ]: fut. πραΰνῶ: aor. 1 ἐπράΰνα: Pass., aor. 1 ἐπραΰνθην: pf. πεπράΰσμαι: (πραΰς):—*to make soft, mild* or *gentle, to soften, soothe, calm, tame*:—Pass. *to become gentle, calm down*: of passion, *to abate.*

πρᾱΰ-πάθεια, ἡ, (πραΰς, πάθος) *gentleness.*

πρᾱΰς, πρᾱεῖα, πρᾱΰ, Ion. **πρηΰς**, = πρᾶος. Hence

πρᾱΰτης, ητος, ἡ, *mildness, gentleness.*

πράως, Adv. of πρᾶος, *mildly, gently.*

πρέμνοθεν, Adv. *from the stump, root and branch, utterly.* From

ΠΡΕ'ΜΝΟΝ, τό, *the lowest part of the trunk of a tree, the stump,* Lat. *caudex*: generally, *the stem, trunk.*

πρεπόντως, Adv. part. of πρέπω, *in fit manner, fitly, meetly, beseemingly, gracefully.*

πρεπτός, ή, όν, (πρέπω) *distinguished, eminent.*

ΠΡΕ'ΠΩ: fut. πρέψω: aor. 1 ἔπρεψα: no pf. is found;—*to be clearly seen* or *heard, be conspicuous*: *to be distinguished in* or *by* a thing: generally, *to be plain* or *manifest.* II. *to be like, resemble.* III. *to become, beseem, suit*; c. dat. pers., θνατὰ θνατοῖσι πρέπει mortal things *beseem* mortal men. 2. impers. πρέπει, Lat. *decet, it is fitting, it beseems, suits, becomes,* c. dat. pers. et inf.: when the acc. follows alone, this depends on an inf. omitted, as, τίσασθαι οὕτω, ὡς ἐκείνους [τίσασθαι] πρέπει to avenge ourselves, as *it is fit* [to avenge ourselves upon] them: rarely c. gen. pers., πρέπον ἦν δαίμονος τοῦ 'μοῦ τόδε this were *well worthy of* my evil genius. 3. part. neut. τὸ πρέπον, τοῦ πρέποντος, *that which is seemly, fitness, propriety,* Lat. *decorum.*

πρεπ-ώδης, ες, (πρέπω, εἶδος) *fitting, becoming, suitable, proper.*

πρέσβᾰ, ης, ἡ, old Ep. fem. of πρέσβυς, *the august, honoured.*

πρεσβεία, ἡ, (πρεσβεύω) *age, seniority*; κατὰ πρεσβείαν by *the right of the elder.* II. *rank, dignity.* III. as ambassadors were usually old men, *an embassy, embassage, the body of ambassadors.*

πρεσβεῖον, Ion. and Ep. -ήιον, τό, (πρεσβεύω) *a gift of honour,* such as was offered to *an elder*; mostly in pl. *privileges, prerogatives.*

πρεσβεῖος, α, ον Ion. -ήιος, η, ον, (πρέσβυς) *venerable.*

πρέσβειρα, ἡ, = πρέσβα, fem. of πρέσβυς, *the august, venerated.*

πρέσβευμα, ατος, τό, (πρεσβεύω) *one sent on an embassy, an ambassador.*

πρέσβευσις, ἡ, (πρεσβεύω) *a serving on an embassy, embassage.*

πρεσβευτής, οῦ, ὁ, (πρεσβεύω) *an ambassador.*

πρεσβεύω, f. εύσω: pf. πεπρέσβευκα: (πρέσβυς):—intr. *to be older* or *eldest.* 2. *to take place of others,* properly, *by right of seniority, to take precedence,* c. gen.: hence *to rule over, sway,* c. gen.: absol. *to be best.* II. trans. *to place as oldest, first, to put first in rank*: hence *to pay honour* or *worship to*:—Pass. *to be first* or *foremost, hold the first place*: also *to have the advantage, have the best of it,* Lat. *antiquior esse.* III. *to be an ambassador, treat* or *negotiate as one*:—Med. *to send ambassadors*: also *to go as ambassador*:—Pass., pf. part. τὰ πεπρεσβευμένα *the acts of an ambassador.*

πρέσβη, ἡ, Ion. for πρέσβα.

πρεσβήιον, τό, Ion. for πρεσβεῖον.

πρεσβήιος, η, ον, Ion. for πρεσβεῖος.

πρεσβηίς, ίδος, ἡ, = πρέσβα; πρεσβηὶς τιμή *the highest* or *most valued* honour.

πρέσβις, ἡ, poët. for πρεσβεία, *age.*

πρέσβιστος, η, ον, poët. Sup. of πρέσβυς.

πρέσβος, τό, (πρέσβυς) *an object of reverence.*

πρεσβῠγένεια, ἡ, *seniority of birth.* From

πρεσβῠ-γενής, ές, (πρέσβυς, γενέσθαι) *eldest-born.*

ΠΡΕ'ΣΒΥΣ, υος and εως, ὁ, *an old man,* poët. for πρεσβύτης:—hence, as from an Adj., come the Degrees of Comparison, see πρεσβύτερος, πρεσβύτατος, πρέσβιστος. II. *an elder*: then, since the elders were preferred to power and dignity, πρέσβεις, οἱ, dat. πρέσβεσιν, *elders, chiefs, princes.* 2. *an ambassador.*

πρεσβύτατος, η, ον, Sup. of πρέσβυς, *eldest*: hence *venerable, reverend, honoured.*

πρεσβῠτέριον, τό, *a council of elders* (πρεσβύτεροι). From

πρεσβύτερος, α, ον, Comp. of πρέσβυς, *elder*: hence *superior by birth,* and so generally, *greater, higher, more important*; τὰ τοῦ θεοῦ πρεσβύτερα ποιεῖσθαι ἢ τὰ τῶν ἀνδρῶν to reckon their duty to the gods *superior* to their duty to men. II. as Subst., πρεσβύτερος, ὁ, *an elder* of the Jewish Council: *an elder* of the Church, *a presbyter.*

πρεσβύτης [ῡ], ου, ὁ, (πρέσβυς) *an old man,* Lat. *senex*: fem. πρεσβῦτις, ιδος, *an old woman.* Hence

πρεσβῡτικός, ή, όν, *like an old man, elderly.*

πρεσβῡτο-δόκος, ον, (πρεσβύτης, δέχομαι) *receiving the aged.*

πρευμένεια, ἡ, *kindliness, graciousness.* From

πρευ-μενής, ές, (πρηΰς, μένος) *gentle of mood, kindly, gracious.* II. *propitiating.*

πρεών, όνος, ὁ, = πρών.

πρῆγμα, Ion. for πρᾶγμα.

πρηγμᾰτεύομαι, Ion. for πραγματεύομαι.

πρηγορεών or **πρηγορών**, ῶνος, ὁ, (πρό, ἀγείρω) *the crop* of a bird, so called because *the food is there collected before* it passes into the stomach.

πρηθῆναι, Ion. for πρᾱθῆναι, aor. 1 pass. inf. of πιπράσκω.

ΠΡΗ'ΘΩ, f. ήσω: aor. 1 ἔπρησα: no perf. in use: (see πίμπρημι):—*to blow up, swell out by blowing*; ἔπρησεν δ' ἄνεμος μέσον ἱστίον the wind *swelled out* the middle of the sail. 2. *to blow out, force* or *drive out by blowing*.

πρηκτήρ, ῆρος, ὁ, Ion. for πρακτήρ.

πρημαίνω, (πρήθω) *to blow, blow hard*.

ΠΡΗΝΗ'Σ Dor. πρᾱνής, ές, gen. έος contr. οῦς, Lat. *pronus, bent forward, head-foremost*, opp. to ὕπτιος. 2. *down-hill, downwards*, opp. to ὄρθιος (up-hill). Hence

πρηνίζω, f. σω: aor. 1 pass. ἐπρηνίχθην:—*to throw headlong*:—Pass. *to fall headlong*.

πρῆξαι, Ion. for πρᾶξαι, aor. 1 inf. of πράσσω.

πρῆξις, ιος, ἡ, Ep. and Ion. for πρᾶξις.

πρῆσεν, Ep. for ἔπρησεν, 3 sing. aor. 1 of πρήθω.

πρῆσις, ιος, ἡ, Ion. for πρᾶσις, *sale*.

πρήσσω, Ep. and Ion. for πράσσω.

πρηστήρ, ῆρος, ὁ, (πρήθω, πρήσω) *a flash of lightning, a thunderbolt*. II. *a hurricane*.

πρῆστις, εως, ἡ, see πρίστις.

πρήσω, fut. of πρήθω *to blow*. 2. fut. of πίμπρημι *to burn*.

πρητήριον, τό, Ion. for πρᾱτήριον, *a market*.

πρηΰ-νομος, ον, Ion. for πραΰνομος, (πρηΰς, νόμος) *of gentle manners, gentle, meek*. [ῠ]

πρηΰνω, Ion. for πραΰνω: [ῡ] From

πρηΰς, εῖα, ύ, Ion. for πρᾱΰς. [ῠ]

πρηΰ-τένων, οντος, ὁ, (πρηΰς, τένων) *with tamed neck*. [ῠ]

πρηών, ῶνος Ep. ονος, ὁ, = πρών, *a jutting rock, foreland, headland, promontory*.

πριάμενος, aor. 2 part. of ὠνέομαι.

πριαίμην, aor. 2 opt. of ὠνέομαι.

Πριᾰμικός, ή, όν, also fem. **Πριᾰμίς**, ίδος, *of* or *for Priam*.

Πρίᾰμος, ὁ, *Priam*, king of Troy: properly *the Chief, Leader* (from περί or πρίν).

Πριᾱπίζω Ion. **Πριηπίζω**, f. ισω, *to be like Priapus*. From

Πρίᾱπος Ion. **Πρίηπος**, ὁ, *Priāpus*, the god of gardens and vineyards, and generally, of agriculture, chiefly worshipped at Lampsacus.

πρίασθαι, aor. 2 inf. of ὠνέομαι.

πρίᾰσο, imperat. aor. 2 of ὠνέομαι.

πρίᾰτο, Ep. 3 sing. of ἐπριάμην, aor. 2 of ὠνέομαι.

πρίζω, f. πρίσω, = πρίω, *to saw*.

Πρίηπος, ὁ, Ion. for Πρίαπος. [ῐ]

ΠΡΙ'Ν Dor. πράν, Adv. of Time: I. in independent sentences, *before, formerly, erst*, Lat. *prius*: also with the Art., τὸ πρίν or τοπρίν, *formerly*. 2. *before that, first, sooner*; πρὶν δέ κεν οὔτι δεχοίμην *beforetime* I would not at all receive him; strengthd., πρίν ποτε *once on a time*; πολὺ πρίν long *ago*. 3. in Att. it is often inserted between the Art. and its Subst., ὁ πρὶν Αἰγεύς (sc. ὁ πρὶν ὤν), *ancient* Aegeus; ἡ πρὶν ἡμέρα (sc. ἡ πρὶν οὖσα), the day *before*. II. πρίν is often followed by ἤ, so that πρὶν ἤ is exactly like the Lat. *priusquam, before that..*, followed sometimes by the Infin., sometimes by Subj., etc.:—instead of ἤ, πρίν is often repeated in the relat. clause, as, τίς κεν ἀνὴρ πρὶν τλαίη, πρὶν λύσασθ' ἑτάρους:—πάρος and πρόσθε are often also put in the anteced. clause instead of the first πρίν:—but πρίν is also very often used alone for πρίν ἤ, so that it becomes a Conjunction, like *priusquam*.

πρῑνίδιον, τό, Dim. of πρῖνος.

πρίνῐνος, η, ον, (πρῖνος) *made from the holm* or *evergreen oak*, Lat. *ilignus*: metaph. *oaken, tough, sturdy*: ἄνδρες πρίνινοι *hearts of oak*.

ΠΡΙ'ΝΟΣ, ὁ, *the holm-oak, evergreen oak*, Lat. *ilex*. II. *the scarlet oak*.

πρῑν-ώδης, ες, (πρῖνος, εἶδος) *like holm-oak, tough as oak*.

πρῑον-ώδης, ες, (πρίων, εἶδος) *like a saw, jagged*.

πρισθείς, εῖσα, έν, aor. 1 part. pass. of πρίω.

πρῖσις, εως, ἡ, (πρίω) *a sawing*.

πριστήρ, ῆρος, ὁ, (πρίω) *a sawyer*: *a saw*: πριστῆρες ὀδόντες *the incisors* or *front teeth*.

πρίστις, εως, ἡ, a kind of *whale*: but the true name is **πρῆστις**, εως, ἡ, *the blower* (from πρήθω).

πριστός, ή, όν, verb. Adj. of πρίω, *cut with a saw, sawn*: *that may be sawn*.

πρίω, = πρίᾰσο, imperat. aor. 2 of ὠνέομαι.

πρίωμαι, aor. 2 subj. of ὠνέομαι.

ΠΡΙ'Ω, imperat. πρῖε: aor. 1 ἔπρῑσα: pf. πέπρῑκα. Pass., aor. 1 ἐπρίσθην: pf. πέπρισμαι:—*to saw, saw asunder*: *to sever, cut in twain*. II. *to grind* or *gnash the teeth*, Lat. *stridere* or *frendere dentibus*; esp. with rage: generally, *to bite*. III. *to seize as with the teeth, grip, hold fast*, Lat. *stringere*. [ῑ]

πρίων, ονος, ὁ, (πρίω) *a saw*. [ῑ]

πρίων, ωνος, ὁ, (πρίω) *a sawyer*. [ῑ]

ΠΡΟ', *before*, Lat. *PRO, PRAE*, Prep. with Genit., I. of Place, *before, in front of*; πρὸ οἴκου, πρὸ δόμων, *in front of* the house, hence *outside*. 2. of persons, going *before* another. 3. *in front of*, so as to defend; στῆναι πρὸ Τρώων to stand *in front of*, i.e. *in defence of* the Trojans: hence *in favour of, for*. 3. πρὸ ὁδοῦ *further on* the road, i.e. *forwards*. II. of Time, *before*, opp. to μετά c. acc. (*after*): often in phrase πρὸ τούτου and πρὸ τοῦ, *before this, ere this*: but πρὸ ὁ τοῦ, for ὁ πρὸ τοῦ, the one *before* the other. III. of Choice, *before, sooner* or *rather than*; αἱρεῖσθαί τι πρό τινος to choose one thing *before* another. IV. of Exchanging, *for, in lieu of, instead of*; ἓν πρὸ πολλῶν one thing *in lieu* of many. V. of Cause, Lat. *prae, for, because of*; πρὸ φόβοιο *for* fear; πρὸ τῶνδε therefore.

Position: some words may be put between πρό

and its Subst., but it is never put after its case, except after the Ep. gen. in -θι, as, Ἰλιόθι πρό, οὐρανόθι πρό.

πρό, absol. as Adv., I. of Place, *before: in front, forth.* II. of Time, *before, beforehand, sooner.*

IN COMPOS., of Place, *before, forth, forward: before the eyes, in one's presence;* as in προ-βαίνω, προ-βάλλω, προ-τίθημι: also *defence,* as in προ-κινδυνεύω. II. of Time, *before, beforehand, earlier,* as in προ-αγγέλλω. III. of Preference, *rather, sooner,* as in προ-αιρέομαι. IV. strengthening, as in πρό-πας, πρό-παλαι, πρό-κακος.

προ-αγγέλλω, f. -αγγελῶ, *to announce beforehand.*

προ-άγγελος, ον, (πρό, ἄγγελος) *announcing beforehand:* as Subst., προάγγελος, ὁ, *a herald, harbinger.*

προάγγελσις, ἡ, (προαγγέλλω) *a forewarning, early intimation.*

προ-ᾰγορεύω, f. σω: aor. 1 -ηγόρευσα pf. -ηγόρευκα: but the Att. fut., aor. and pf. are προερῶ, προεῖπον, προείρηκα:—*to tell beforehand:* c. inf. *to tell beforehand that ..: to forewarn.* 2. *to foretell, prophesy.* II. *to tell before others* or *publicly: to publish* or *proclaim publicly: to issue a public notice.*

προ-άγω, f. άξω: aor. 2 προήγαγον: pf. προῆχα: Pass., aor. 1 προήχθην: pf. προῆγμαι:—*to lead forward, lead on* or *onward:* also *to escort* or *conduct onward.* 2. δάκρυ προάγειν *to bring out* or *shed* a tear. 3. *to carry forward: to bring on:* metaph. *to lead on* to a thing, *induce, persuade.* 4. *to promote, advance:*—Pass. *to advance, increase.* II. intr. *to lead the way, go before, go onwards, proceed, advance.*

προᾰγωγεία, ἡ, *a leading on.* II. *a pandering, procuring.* From

προᾰγωγεύω, f. σω, (προαγωγός) *to lead on to prostitution,* of a procurer.

προ-ᾰγωγός, ὁ, (προάγω) *a pander, pimp, procurer.*

προ-ᾰγών, ῶνος, ὁ, (πρό, ἀγών) *a preliminary contest.*

προ-ᾰγωνίζομαι, f. ίσομαι, Dep. *to fight before.* 2. *to fight for* or *in defence of.*

προ-ᾰδῐκέω, f. ήσω, *to wrong* another *first: to commit the first wrong.*

προ-ᾴδω, *to sing before, make a prelude.*

προ-αιδέομαι, Dep. with fut. med. -έσομαι, aor. 1 pass. προῃδέσθην, pf. pass. προῄδημαι, Ion. 3 προῃδέατο for -ηντο:—*to owe* one *special respect, be under great obligations to* one.

προ-αιρέομαι, v. sub προαιρέω.

προαίρεσις, εως, ἡ, (προαιρέομαι) *a choosing one thing before another, deliberate choice, purpose;* ἐκ προαιρέσεως, Lat. *ex instituto, of set purpose, advisedly;* κατὰ προαίρεσιν, in same sense. 2. προαίρεσις βίου *a purpose* or *plan* of life. 3. προαίρεσις πολιτείας *a mode* of government, *a policy.*

προ-αιρετέον, verb. Adj. of προαιρέομαι, *one must choose* or *prefer.*

προαιρετικός, ή, όν, (προαιρέομαι) *disposed to prefer.*

προαιρετός, ή, όν, *chosen before, preferred.* From

προ-αιρέω, f. ήσω: aor. 2 προεῖλον: pf. προῄρηκα:—*to take away before* or *first.* 2. *to bring forward* or *forth, produce publicly.* II. Med. προαιρέομαι: f. -ήσομαι: aor. 2 προειλόμην: pf. pass. (in med. sense) προῄρημαι:—*to take* or *choose before* or *sooner than* another, *prefer* one thing to another. 2. absol. *to choose deliberately, prefer.* 3. *to purpose* or *intend* a thing: *to determine previously; to undertake.*

προ-αισθάνομαι, Dep. with fut. med. -αισθήσομαι, aor. 2 -ησθόμην, pf. pass. προῄσθημαι:—*to perceive, learn* or *observe beforehand.* 2. *to learn before.*

προ-αιτιάομαι, f. -άσομαι, Dep. *to accuse beforehand.*

προακήκοα, pf. of προακούω.

προ-ᾰκοντίζω, f. ίσω, *to throw a javelin beforehand:*—Pass. *to be darted before.*

προ-ᾰκούω, f. -ακούσομαι: pf. -ακήκοα:—*to hear beforehand.*

προ-ᾰλής, ές, (πρό, ἅλλομαι) *springing forward: overhanging, abrupt.*

προ-ᾰλίσκομαι, Pass., with fut. med. (in pass. sense) -αλώσομαι, and (in same sense) aor. 2 and pf. act. -εάλων, -εάλωκα:—*to be taken* or *convicted beforehand.*

προ-ᾰμαρτάνω, f. -αμαρτήσομαι: pf. -ημάρτηκα:—*to fail* or *sin before.*

προ-ᾰμύνομαι, f. -αμῠνοῦμαι, Med. *to ward off* or *repeal beforehand:* absol. *to defend oneself.*

προ-αναβαίνω, f. -βήσομαι, *to go up to* or *mount before,* so as to preoccupy.

προ-αναβάλλομαι, Med. *to sing* or *play by way of prelude* (ἀναβολή).

προ-ᾰνάγω, f. ξω, *to lead up before;* προανάγειν ναῦν *to put out into the high sea before:*—Pass. *to put to sea before.*

προ-αναιρέω, f. ήσω, *to remove before.*

προ-ᾰναισῑμόω, f. ώσω, *to use up, spend before:*—Pass., (Ion. part. pf. προαναισιμωμένος for προανησιμωμένος), *to be spent, consumed, used up before.*

προ-ανακῑνέω, f. ήσω, *to stir up before.*

προ-ανᾱλίσκω, fut. -ανᾱλώσω: aor. 1 -ανάλωσα:—*to use up, spend, consume before:*—Pass. *to throw away one's life before.*

προ-αναρπάζω, f. -άσομαι, *to arrest beforehand.*

προ-αναχωρέω, f. ήσω, *to go away before.* Hence

προαναχώρησις, ἡ, *a former departure.*

προ-ανέχω, f. ξω, *to hold up before.* 2. intr. *to jut out beyond.*

προ-ᾰνύτω [ῠ] and -ανύω: f. -ανύσω [ῠ]:—*to accomplish* or *complete first.*

προ-απᾰγορεύω, f. σω, *to give in* or *fail beforehand.*

προ-απαλλάσσω Att. -ττω, f. ξω, *to remove beforehand:*—Pass. *to depart* or *die before.*

προ-απαντάω, f. ήσω, *to go forth to meet, meet beforehand, be beforehand with.*

προ-άπειμι, *to go away first.*

προ-απεῖπον, aor. 2 with no pres. in use (cp. προαγορεύω): pf. προαπείρηκα: Med., aor. 1 προαπειπάμην: —*to renounce first.*

προαπελθεῖν, aor. 2 inf. of προαπέρχομαι.

προ-απέρχομαι, f. -ελεύσομαι: aor. 2 act. -ῆλθον: Dep.:—*to go away, depart first.*

προ-απεχθάνομαι. f. -απεχθήσομαι: Pass.:—*to be hated beforehand.*

προ-απηγέομαι, for προαφηγέομαι.

προ-απικνέομαι, Ion. for προαφικνέομαι.

προ-αποδείκνῡμι, f. -δείξω, *to prove* or *shew first.*

προ-αποθνήσκω, f. -θᾰνοῦμαι, *to die before* or *first*: of a coward, *to die beforehand.*

προ-αποθρηνέω, f. ήσω, *to bewail beforehand.*

προ-αποκληρόω, f. ώσω, *to assign away beforehand.*

προ-αποκτείνω, f. -κτενῶ, *to kill beforehand.*

προ-απολαύω, f. -σομαι, *to enjoy beforehand.*

προ-απολείπω, f. ψω, *to abandon beforehand.* II. intr. *to fail before* or *first.*

προ-απόλλῡμι, *to destroy first*:—Pass., with fut. med. -ολοῦμαι, pf. 2 act. -όλωλα, *to perish first.*

προ-αποπέμπω, f. ψω, *to send away, dismiss* or *disband first.*

προ-αποστᾰλῆναι, aor. 2 inf. pass. of ἀποστέλλω.

προ-αποστέλλω, f. -αποστελῶ, *to send away* or *despatch in advance*:—Pass. *to be sent in advance.*

προ-αποσφάζω, f. ξω, *to slay* or *butcher before.*

προ-αποτρέπω, f. ψω, *to turn away beforehand*:—Med. *to turn oneself away from, to leave off* doing.

προ-αποχωρέω, f. ήσω, *to go away before.*

προ-αρπάζω, f. άξω and άσομαι, *to snatch up first.*

προ-άστειον Ion. -ήιον, τό, (πρό, ἄστυ) *the space in front of a town, a suburb, the environs,* Lat. *pomoerium.*

προ-άστιον, τό, = προάστειον.

προ-αυδάω, inf. πρωυδᾶν, contr. for προαυδᾶν, f. ήσω, *to declare before* or *first.*

προ-αύλιον, τό, (πρό, αὐλή) *a place before a court, vestibule, porch.* II. (πρό, αὐλός) *a prelude on the flute.*

προ-αφηγέομαι Ion. **προαπηγ-**: f. -ήσομαι: Dep.:—*to relate, detail,* or *explain before.*

προ-αφικνέομαι, f. -ίξομαι: Dep.:—*to arrive* or *come to first.*

προ-αφίσταμαι, Pass., fut. med. -αποστήσομαι, aor. 2 and pf. act. -απέστην, -αφέστηκα:—*to revolt beforehand.* II. *to desist before.*

πρόβα, for πρόβηθι, aor. 2 imperat. of προβαίνω.

προβάδην [ᾰ], Adv. (προβαίνω) *as one goes along: going on, straight forward.*

προ-βαίνω, fut. -βήσομαι: pf. -βέβηκα: aor. 2 προέβην contr. προὔβην, inf. προβῆναι, part. προβάς: Ep. pres. part. προβῐβάς, ᾶσα, άν (as if from προβίβημι), and προβῐβῶν -ῶντος (as if from προβίβω):—*to step forward, go on, advance, make progress*; ἄστρα προβέβηκε the stars *are far gone*; προβῆναι πόρρω μοχθηρίας *to be* far *gone* in knavery: of Time, *to go on, wear away,* ἡ νὺξ προβαίνει the night *is wearing fast*; but also, *to be gone by, past.* 2. *to go before,* hence *to be before, be superior to* another. II. Causal, in fut. προβήσω, aor. 1 -έβησα, *to move* or *put forward, advance, promote.* III. the pres. and aor. 2 are sometimes used with an acc. of the instrument of motion, as, προβαίνειν πόδα, κῶλον *to advance* one's foot or leg.

προ-βακχήιος, ὁ, Ion. for προβάκχειος, (πρό, βάκχειος) *leader of the Bacchanals.*

προβάλεσκον, Ion. aor. 2 of προβάλλω.

προ-βάλλω, f. -βᾰλῶ: aor. 2 προὔβᾰλον: pf. -βέβληκα, pass. -βέβλημαι:—*to throw* or *cast before, throw to: to put forth beyond.* II. *to throw forward, throw away.* III. *to expose* or *give up to* a thing; προβάλλειν ἑαυτόν *to give* oneself *up for lost.* IV. *to put forward, put in the foreground: to propose:*—also *hazard, venture, stake, pledge.* 2. *to put forward an argument:* also *to allege, plead an excuse.*

Med. *to throw before one, throw away.* II. *to throw beyond, beat in throwing*: hence, *to surpass, excel.* III. *to set before oneself, propose to oneself.* IV. *to put forward, propose for election,* Lat. *designare:* also *to bring forward, cite, quote, produce on one's own side*: *to quote as an example*: *to use as an excuse* or *pretext.* V. *to hold before oneself, to put forth as a shield* or *defence*: absol. in Pass. *to stand on guard*:—hence also, προβάλλεσθαι συμμαχίαν *to put forward the plea of* an alliance: so in pf. pass. part., προβεβλημένος τινός *put before* another *as a cover* or *shield*; προβεβλημένος, η, ον, *defensive.* VI. *to denounce* or *accuse of* a thing:—Pass. *to be publicly impeached.*

προβάλοιμι [ᾰ], aor. 2 opt. of προβάλλω.

προβάς, ᾶσα, άν, aor. 2 part. of προβαίνω.

προ-βᾰσᾰνίζω, f. ίσω, *to try* or *torture before.*

πρόβᾰσις, ἡ, (προβαίνω) *a stepping forward.* II. as a Collective noun, *things that walk, cattle.*

προβᾰτεία, ἡ, (προβατεύω) *sheep-keeping, a shepherd's life.*

προβᾰτευτικός, ή, όν, *suited to the breeding of cattle*: ἡ -κή (sub. τέχνη), *the art of breeding* or *keeping cattle,* esp. *sheep,* Lat. *pecuaria.* From

προβᾰτεύω, f. σω, (πρόβατον) *to keep sheep, be a shepherd.*

προβᾰτικός, ή, όν, (πρόβατον) *of* or *for sheep*: ἡ προβατική (sub. πύλη), *the sheep-gate.*

προβάτιον, τό, Dim. of πρόβατον, *a little sheep*: προβατίου βίος the life *of a poor sheep,* i. e. a lazy, slothful life.

προβᾰτο-γνώμων, ον, gen. ονος, (πρόβατον, γνώμη) *a good judge of cattle*: metaph. *a good judge of character.*

πρόβᾰτον, τό, (προβαίνω) *anything that goes forward*: mostly used in plur. πρόβατα, *animals in general,* esp. *cattle, a drove* or *flock*: mostly of *small cattle,* esp. *sheep.*

προβᾰτο-πώλης, ου, ὁ, (πρόβατον, πωλέω) *a sheep-dealer.*

προβέβηκα, pf. of προβαίνω.

προβέβληκα, pf. of προβάλλω.

προβέβουλα, pf. 2 of προβούλομαι.

πρόβημα, ατος, τό, (προβαίνω) *a step forward.*

προβήσομαι, fut. of προβαίνω.

προ-βιάζομαι, f. -άσομαι: Dep.:—*to obtain by force, force through before.*

προ-βιβάζω: f. -βιβάσω Att. -βιβῶ:—Causal of προβαίνω, *to make to go forward, bring forward.* II. *to carry on further, to lead on, induce.*

προβιβάς, Ep. pres. part. of προβαίνω.

προβιβῶν, ῶντος, Ep. pres. part. of προβαίνω.

προ-βλέπω, f. ψω, *to foresee, to provide for* one.

πρόβλημα, ατος, τό, (προβάλλω) *anything that juts out* or *projects*; πρόβλημα πόντου *a headland that juts into* the sea. II. *anything held before one, a guard, a barrier, fence, armour*: c. gen., πρόβλημα πετρῶν *a defence against, a shelter from,* stones. III. *anything put forward as an excuse, a screen, cloak.* IV. *that which is proposed as a task, a task: a problem.*

προβλής, ῆτος, ὁ, ἡ, (προβάλλω) *thrown forward, jutting, projecting*:—προβλῆτες absol. as Subst., *forelands, headlands.*

πρόβλητος, ον, (προβάλλω) *thrown forth* or *away, cast out,* Lat. *projectus.*

προ-βλώσκω: aor. 2 προυμολον, inf. προμολεῖν: pf. προμέμβλωκα:—*to go* or *come forth, to go out of the house.*

προ-βοάω, f. -βοήσομαι, *to shout before, cry out.*

προβόλαιος, ον, ὁ, (προβάλλω) *a spear held out before* one. 2. as Adj. *outstretched, couched.*

προβολή, ἡ, (προβάλλω) *a putting forward,* esp. of a weapon for defence; τὰ δόρατα εἰς προβολὴν καθιέναι to bring the spears *to the rest,* couch them: of a boxer, *a lunging out with the fist.* II. *anything held out before one, a guard, defence*: c. gen. *a defence against.* III. *a jutting rock, foreland.* IV. as Att. law-term, προβολαί, αἱ, *a vote* of the Ecclesia *authorising a public prosecution, a vote for impeachment.*

προβόλιον, τό, Dim. of προβολή, *a weapon held out for attack* or *defence, a boar-spear.*

πρόβολος, ον, (προβάλλω) *anything that is held forward: a jutting rock, foreland.* II. *a weapon held out for defence, a hunting-spear.* 2. *a defence, bulwark*: of a person, *a protector, guardian.*

πρό-βοσκος, ὁ, (πρό, βόσκω) *one who drives the herd to pasture, a herdsman.*

προβούλευμα, ατος, τό, (προβουλεύω) *a preliminary decree* or *order* of the Senate.

προβουλευμάτιον, τό, Dim. of προβούλευμα.

προ-βουλεύω, f. σω, *to contrive before, concert measures before* or *first*: Med. *to debate* or *consider first.* 2. of the Senate (βουλή) at Athens, *to frame a decree.* 3. *to act as* πρόβουλος. II. *to have the chief voice in passing decrees.* III. προβουλεύειν τινός *to deliberate for* one, *provide for* his interest.

προ-βουλή, ἡ, (πρό, βουλή) *forethought: malice prepense.*

προ-βούλομαι, pf. 2 προβέβουλα in pres. sense: Dep.:—*to wish rather, to prefer* one *before* another.

προβουλό-παις, -παιδος, ἡ, (πρόβουλος, παῖς):—προβουλόπαις Ἄτης, = πρόβουλος παῖς Ἄτης, *the crafty child* of Até.

πρό-βουλος, ον, (πρό, βουλή) *debating beforehand* or *for others*:—as Subst., πρόβουλοι, οἱ, *preliminary counsellors, a committee to examine measures before* they were proposed to the people:—also, *deputies* or *representatives* elected by the people

προ-βύω, f. ύσω [ῡ], *to push forwards*; πρ. λύχνον *to push up* the wick of a lamp, *to trim* it.

προ-βωθέω, Ion. for προβοηθέω

προ-βώμιος, ον, (πρό, βωμός) *at* or *in front of the altar*: as Subst., προβώμια, τά, *the space in front of an altar.*

προ-γαστρίδιον, τό, (πρό, γαστήρ) *a piece of armour for the belly,* as προστέρνιον for the breast.

προ-γάστωρ, ορος, ὁ, (πρό, γαστήρ) *having a paunch in front, pot-bellied.*

προ-γένειος, ον, (πρό, γένειον) *with prominent chin.*

προ-γενής, (πρό, γένος) *of old time, ancient*:—Comp. προγενέστερος, α, ον, *earlier in birth, elder, older*:—Sup. προγενέστατος, η, ον, *earliest in birth, eldest, oldest.*

προ-γεννήτωρ, ορος, ὁ, *a forefather, ancestor.*

προ-γίγνομαι, Ion. and later -γίνομαι [ῑ]: f. -γενήσομαι: aor. 2 προυγενόμην: pf. 2 act. προγέγονα and pass. προγεγένημαι: Dep.:—*to come forwards: present oneself before.* II. of Time, *to be, happen, come to pass before* or *earlier*; οἱ προγεγονότες *men of former times*; τὰ προγεγενημένα *things that occurred of old.*

προ-γιγνώσκω, Ion. and later προγῑν-: f. -γνώσομαι: pf. act. προέγνωκα, pass. προέγνωσμαι:—*to know, perceive, learn* or *understand beforehand*: *to foreknow.* II. *to judge* or *decide beforehand.*

πρόγνωσις, ἡ, (προγιγνώσκω) *a perceiving beforehand, foreknowledge.*

πρό-γονος, ον, (πρό, γενέσθαι) *earlier born, elder, older*:—as Subst., πρόγονος, ὁ, *an ancestor*; οἱ πρόγονοι *forefathers, ancestors.* II. πρόγονοι are *early lambs,* cp. μέτασσαι.

πρό-γραμμα, ατος, τό, (προγράφω) *a public proclamation* or *notice, programme.*

προγραφή, ἡ, (προγράφω) *a public notice, advertisement.* 2. also used for the Lat. *proscriptio.*

προ-γράφω, f. ψω, *to write before* or *first.* II. *to write in public, give public notice of*:—also *to appoint by public notice.* 2. also used for the Lat. *proscribo*

προ-γυμνάζω, f. άσω, *to exercise beforehand.*

προδαείς, aor. 2 pass. part. from Root προδάω: see προδαῆναι.

προδαῆναι, aor. 2 pass. inf. of προυδάην with act. signf., from the root *δάω, *to know beforehand.*

προδέδωκα, pf. of προδίδωμι.

προ-δείδω, f. σω, *to fear* or *dread beforehand.*

προ-δείελος, ον, (πρό, δείελος) *happening* or *doing before evening.*

προ-δείκνῡμι and **-ύω**: f. -δείξω Ion. -δέξω:—*to shew beforehand, point out*, esp. *by way of example: to make known* or *publish beforehand: to foreshew.* II. *to point before* one; σκήπτρῳ προδεικνύναι *to feel one's way* with a staff: also c. acc. *to put out before* one. III. χερσὶ προδεικνύναι *to make a feint* with the hands, Lat. *praeludere:* also in war, *to make a demonstration.*

προ-δειμαίνω, *to fear* or *dread beforehand.*

προ-δέκτωρ, ορος, ὁ, Ion. for προδείκτωρ, (προδείκνυμι) *one who foreshews: a foreshewer.*

προ-δέρκομαι, f. -ξομαι, Dep. *to see beforehand.*

πρό-δηλος, ον, (πρό, δῆλος) *clear beforehand;* ἐκ προδήλου *manifestly.* Hence.

προ-δηλόω, f. ώσω, *to make clear beforehand.*

προ-διαβαίνω, f. -βήσομαι: pf. -βέβηκα:—*to go across before* others.

προ-διαβάλλω, f. -βᾰλῶ, *to raise prejudices against beforehand.*

προ-διαγιγνώσκω, f. -γνώσομαι, *to understand* or *know thoroughly beforehand.* II. *to resolve* or *decree beforehand.*

προ-διαιτάω, f. ήσω, *to prepare by diet.* Hence

προδιαίτησις, ἡ, *preparation by diet.*

προ-διαλέγομαι, f. -λέξομαι, Med. with aor. 1 pass. -διελέχθην:—*speak* or *converse beforehand.*

προ-διασύρω, *to jeer* or *ridicule beforehand.* [ῡ]

προ-διαφθείρω, f. -φθερῶ: aor. 1 -έφθειρα: pf. act. -έφθαρκα, pass. -έφθαρμαι:—*to ruin* or *destroy beforehand: to corrupt* or *seduce beforehand.*

προ-δῐδάσκω, f. άξω, *to teach beforehand: to teach thoroughly:*—Pass. *to learn beforehand.*

προ-δίδωμι, f. -δώσω: pf. act. -δέδωκα, pass. -δέδομαι: —*to give beforehand, pay in advanc* II. *to give up to the enemy, betray*, Lat. *prodo* 2. *to forsake, abandon:* absol. *to desert, turn traitor;* ἡ χάρις προδοῦσ' ἁλίσκεται gratitude is convicted *of proving traitor.* 3. of things, *to betray, fail* one:—intr. *to fail, give up*, like ἐνδιδόναι, Lat. *deficere.* 4. *to give up, surrender, lose.*

προ-διεξέρχομαι, f. -διεξελεύσομαι, Dep. *to go out through before, pass through first.*

προ-διερευνάω, f. ήσω, *to discover by searching beforehand.* Hence

προδιερευνητής, οῦ, ὁ, *one sent out to march beforehand.*

προ-διέρχομαι, f. -εξελεύσομαι, aor. 2 -ῆλθον: Dep.: —*to go through, detail, narrate before.*

προ-διηγέομαι, f. -ήσομαι, Dep. *to relate beforehand, premise.* Hence

προδιήγησις, ἡ, *a detailing beforehand.*

πρό-δῐκος, ὁ, (πρό, δίκη) *an advocate, defender; an avenger.* 2. at Sparta, a young king's *guardian, a regent.*

προ-διοικέω, f. ήσω, *to regulate, order, manage beforehand.*

προ-δῐώκω, f. ξω, *to pursue further* or *to a distance.*

προδοθείς, εῖσα, έν, aor. 1 pass. part. of προδίδωμι.

προ-δοκέω: pf. pass. προδέδογμαι, 3 sing. plqpf. προὐδέδοκτο:—*to think beforehand:*—only used in Pass., προὐδέδοκτο ταῦτά μοι *this was* my *former opinion;* τὰ προδεδογμένα *previous resolutions.*

προ-δοκή, ἡ, (πρό, δέχομαι) *a place where one lies in wait, a lair, ambush;* πέτρης ἐν προδοκῇσιν *in the lurking holes* of the rock.

πρό-δομος, ὁ, *the fore-house*, i. e. the room entered from the court (αὐλή), *the hall, vestibule.*

πρό-δομος, ον, *being before the house.*

προ-δοξάζω, f. άσω, *to form an opinion beforehand.*

προδοσία Ion. -ίη, ἡ, (προδίδωμι) *a giving up, betrayal, treachery, treason.*

πρόδοσις, ἡ, (προδίδωμι) *payment beforehand.* II. *a giving up, betrayal*

προδότης, ου, ὁ, (προδίδωμι) *a betrayer, traitor: one who abandons in danger.*—Fem. **προδότις**, ἴδος, *a traitress.* Hence

προδοτικός, ή, όν, *disposed to betray, traitorous.*

πρόδοτος, ον, (προδίδωμι) *betrayed, abandoned.*

πρό-δουλος, ον, *serving for a slave.*

προδοῦναι, **προδούς**, aor. 2 inf. and part. of προδίδωμι.

προδρᾰμεῖν, **προδρᾰμών**, aor. 2 inf. and part. of προτρέχω, formed from obsol. *δρέμω.

προδρομή, ἡ, (προδραμεῖν) *a running forward, a sally* or *sudden attack.*

πρόδρομος, ον, (προδραμεῖν) *running before, speeding forward.* II. as Subst., πρόδρομοι, οἱ, *men sent on before to reconnoitre, scouts.*

προ-δυστῠχέω, f. ήσω, *to be unhappy beforehand.*

προέδρᾰμον, aor. 2 of προτρέχω: cf. προδραμεῖν.

προεδρεύω, f. σω, (πρόεδρος) *to be president;* προεδρεύειν τῆς βουλῆς *to be president of* the council.

προεδρία Ion. -ίη, ἡ, (προεδρεύω) *the seat* or *dignity of president* (πρόεδρος), *the first seat, presidency.* 2. *the privilege of the front seats* at a theatre; at Athens a public honour. 3. *the front seat itself, chief place:* at Athens, *the seats of the* πρόεδροι in the Ecclesia

πρό-εδρος, ον, (πρό, ἕδρα) *sitting in front* or *in the first place.* II. as Subst., πρόεδρος, ὁ, *a president:* in the assembly (ἐκκλησία) at Athens, nine of the πρυτάνεις in office were so called;—see πρύτανις.

προ-έργω, Ep. for προείργω, *to stop by standing before, to obstruct.*

προέηκα, Ep. for προῆκα, aor. 1 of προΐημι.

προ-εθίζω, f. ίσω, *to accustom* or *inure beforehand.*

προ-εῖδον, aor. 2 with no pres. in use, προοράω being used instead, part. προϊδών, inf. προϊδεῖν:—*to look forward, keep a look out ahead: to see from afar: to foresee.* II. *to have a care for, provide against.*

προειλόμην, aor. 2 med. of προαιρέω.

πρό-ειμι, (πρό, εἶμι *ibo*) serving in Att. as fut. of

προ-έρχομαι, *to go forward, go on, advance*; προϊόντος τοῦ χρόνου as time *went on*: *to go first, go in advance.* 2. *to go forth.* 3. προϊέναι εἴς τι *to pass on to, proceed to* another thing. 4. also of a thing, *to go on well, succeed.*

προ-εῖπον, aor. 2 with no pres. in use (προαγορεύω being used instead), inf. προειπεῖν, part. προειπών:—*to foretell, say before: to premise.* II. *to order* or *bid beforehand, proclaim.* III. *to proclaim publicly, give notice* or *warning of* a thing.

προείρηκα, see προερέω.

προ-εισάγω Ion. προ-εσάγω: f. ξω:—*to bring in, introduce before*:—Med. *to bring in for one's own use before, import before.*

προεισενεγκεῖν, aor. 2 inf. of προεισφέρω.

προ-εισέρχομαι, Dep. *to come* or *go in before.*

προεισοίσω, fut. of προεισφέρω.

προ-εισπέμπω, f. ψω, *to send in before.*

προ-εισφέρω, *to bring in before.* 2. *to pay the property-tax* (εἰσφορά) *in advance for* others. Hence

προεισφορά, ἡ, *money advanced to pay the property-tax* (εἰσφορά) *for others.*

προ-εκθέω, f. -θεύσομαι, *to run out before, rush hastily on.*

προ-εκκομίζω, f. σω, *to carry out beforehand.*

προ-εκλέγω, f. -εκλέξω: pf. pass. -εξείλεγμαι:—*to collect money* or *taxes in advance*, τὰ προεξειλεγμένα *taxes collected in advance.*

προ-εκπέμπω, f. ψω, *to send out beforehand.*

προ-εκπλέω, f. -πλεύσομαι, *to sail out beforehand.*

προ-εκπλήσσω, f. ξω, *to terrify beforehand.*

προ-εκπονέω, f. ήσω, *to work out* or *finish before.*

προ-εκφοβέω, f. ήσω, *to terrify before.* Hence

προεκφόβησις, ἡ, *a previous panic.*

προέλᾰσις, ἡ, *a going* or *riding forward.* From

προ-ελαύνω, f. -ελάσω: pf. act. -ελήλακα, pass. -ελήλαμαι:—*to drive before* or *forward*:—intrans. (sub. ἵππον), *to ride on, ride forward*; c. gen. *to ride before* one: generally, *to advance*:—Pass., ὡς πρόσω τῆς νυκτὸς προελήλατο (3 sing. plqpf.) when the night *was far advanced.*

προελθεῖν, προελθών, aor. 2 inf. and part. of προέρχομαι.

προ-ελπίζω, f. ίσω, *to hope before.*

προελών, οῦσα, όν, aor. 2 part. of προαιρέω.

προ-εμβάλλω, *to project so as to strike in*: of ships, *to make the charge* (ἐμβολή) *first.*

προέμεν, Ep. for προεῖναι, aor. 2 inf. of προΐημι.

προέμενος, aor. 2 med. part. of προΐημι.

προ-εμπλήθω, *to be quite full.*

προ-ενάρχομαι, fut. -ξομαι, Dep. *to begin before*

προενεγκεῖν, aor. 2 inf. of προφέρω.

προ-εννέπω, contr. **προυννέπω**, *to announce before* or *publicly.*

προ-ενοικέω, f. ήσω, *to dwell in before.* Hence

προενοίκησις, ἡ, *a dwelling before in* a place.

προ-εξαγγέλλω, f. ελῶ, *to announce beforehand.*

προ-εξάγω, f. ξω, *to bring out beforehand* or *first*: *to lead out before*: intrans. *to move out before* or *in front*:—Pass. *to go out first.* [ᾰ]

προ-εξαΐσσω Att. -ᾴσσω, f. ξω,—*to dart out before.*

προ-εξᾰμαρτάνω, *to fail, do wrong before*

προ-εξανίστᾰμαι, Pass. with act. aor. 2 -ανέστην, pf. -ανέστηκα, plqpf. -ανεστήκειν:—*to rise and go out before*; προεξανίστασθαι ἐς τοὺς βαρβάρους *to rise before* others *and march* against the barbarians: in a race, *to start before* the signal is given, *start too soon.*

προ-εξέδρα Ion. -η, ἡ, *a raised seat, chair of state.*

προ-έξειμι, (πρό, ἐξ, εἶμι *ibo*) *to go out before, to sally forth before.*

προ-εξεπίστᾰμαι contr. **προὐξ-**: fut. med. -επιστήσομαι, aor. 1 pass. προὐξεπιστήθην: Dep.:—*to know exactly, thoroughly understand beforehand.*

προ-εξερευνάω contr. **προὐξ-**, *to investigate* or *search out before.* Hence

προεξερευνητής contr. **προὐξ-**, οῦ, *an explorer sent before.*

προ-εξέρχομαι: aor. 2 act. -εξῆλθον: pf. -εξελήλυθα: Dep.:—*to go out* or *forth before: to go forward.*

προ-εξετάζω, f. σω, *to examine* or *search out before.*

προ-εξίεμαι contr. **προὐξ-**, Dep. *to enjoin beforehand.*

προ-εξορμάω, f. ήσω, *to set out* or *start beforehand.*

προ-επαγγέλλω, f. ελῶ, *to announce before*:—Med. *to promise before.*

προ-επαινέω, f. έσω, *to praise beforehand*, or *in the presence of* others

προ-επανασείω, f. σω, *to raise the hand against before*: generally, *to set in motion before.*

προ-επαφίημι, *to send forward against.*

προεπεποίητο, 3 sing. plqpf. pass. of προποιέω.

προ-επιβουλεύω, f. σω, *to plot against beforehand.*

προ-επιξενόομαι, Pass. (πρό, ἐπιξενόω) *to be received as a guest before, abide in one's house first*

προ-επίστᾰμαι, fut. med. -επιστήσομαι, aor. 1 pass. προυπιστήθην: Dep.:—*to know* or *understand beforehand.*

προ-επιχειρέω, f. ήσω, *to undertake* or *attack before.*

προ-εργάζομαι, f. -άσομαι: pf. προείργασμαι: Dep.:—*to do* or *work at beforehand*: esp. of the ground, *to till, work first*:—the pf. is also used in pass. sense, τὰ προειργασμένα *former performances*; ἡ προειργασμένη δόξα glory *achieved before*

προ-ερέσσω, f. έσω, *to row forwards.*

προ-ερευνάω, f. ήσω, *to search out before*:—Med., οἱ προερευνώμενοι ἱππεῖς the horse *reconnoitring in advance.*

προ-ερέω Att. contr. **προερῶ**, serving as fut. to προεῖπον, (the pres. in use being προαγορεύω: from the same root come pf. προ-είρηκα, pass. -είρημαι; aor. 1 pass. προερρήθην contr. προὐρρήθην:—*to foretell.* II. *to order beforehand* or *publicly, give public notice*:—pf. pass. part. προειρημένος, *fore-ordained, appointed.*

προέρυσσα, Ep. aor. 1 from

προ-ερύω, f. *ύσω* [ῠ], *to draw on* or *forward; προερύσαι νῆα to move* a ship *forward.*

προ-έρχομαι, f. *-ελεύσομαι* (cp. *πρόειμι*): aor. 2 *-ῆλθον*: pf. *-ελήλυθα*: Dep.:—*to come* or *go forward, to go on, advance; τὰ Περσέων πρήγματα ἐς τοῦτο προελθόντα* the power of the Persians *having advanced* to this height; *προεληλυθὼς ἡλικίᾳ*, Lat. *provectus aetate, advanced* in age. 2. *to go before* or *first.*

πρόες, προέτω, aor. 2 imperat. of *προΐημι.*

προέσθαι, aor. 2 med. inf. of *προΐημι.*

προεστέᾶτε or **προέστᾰτε**, Ion. for *προεστήκατε*, 2 pl. pf. of *προΐστημι.*

προεστώς, contr. from *προεστηκώς*, pf. part. of *προΐστημι.*

προέσχον, aor. 2 of *προέχω.*

προετέον, verb. Adj. of *προΐημι, one must throw away, throw up.*

προετικός, *ή, όν*, (*προΐημι*) *disposed to throw away, lavish, prodigal.*

προ-ετοιμάζω, f. *άσω, to get ready before*:—Med. *to prepare for one's own use.*

προ-ευαγγελίζομαι, Dep. *to bring glad tidings beforehand*, esp. *to preach the gospel beforehand.*

προ-ευλᾰβέομαι, fut. med. *ήσομαι*, aor. 1 pass. *προευλᾰβήθην*: Dep.:—*to take heed, be cautious beforehand.*

προέφθᾰσα, aor. 1 of *προφθανω.*

προ-έχω contr. **προύχω**: f. *προέξω*:—*to hold before*, esp. so as to shield or protect:—Med. *προέχομαι* contr. *προὔχομαι*, impf. *προὐχόμην, to hold before oneself*: metaph. *to put forward* or *hold out as a pretext.* 2. *to hold forth, proffer, offer.* 3. *to have before* or *in preference to.* 4. *to have before* or *first*: hence *to know beforehand.* II. intr. *to be before, come forth, project, jut out*: *to be the first, have the start; ἡμέρης ὁδῷ προέχειν τινός to keep* a day's march *ahead of* him 2. of rank, c. gen. *to be chief* or *head of anything*: generally, *to be eminent* or *distinguished; οἱ προὔχοντες the chief men.* 3. *to surpass, exceed.* 4. impers., *οὔ τι προέχει it is* not at all *better, it* naught *avails.*

προεώρᾱκα, pf. of *προοράω.*

προ-ηγεμών, *όνος, ὁ, one who goes before as a guide.*

προ-ηγέομαι, f. *ήσομαι*, Dep. *to go first and lead the way*: generally, *to go before, guide, conduct*: *to be the leader.* Hence

προηγητήρ, *ῆρος.* and **προηγητής**, *οῦ, ὁ, one who goes before to shew the way.*

προηγορέω, f. *ήσω*, (*προήγορος*) *to speak for* others.

προ-ήγορος, *ὁ*, (*πρό, ἀγορεύω*) *one who speaks for others, a defender, advocate.*

προ-ηγουμένως, Adv. of pres. part. of *προηγέομαι, antecedently.*

προῆκα, aor. 1 of *προΐημι.*

προ-ήκης, *ες*, (*πρό, ἀκή*) *pointed in front.*

προ-ήκω, f. *ξω, to have gone before, to be the first*: *to have advanced.* II. *to jut forward, reach beyond.*

προῆχα, pf. of *προάγω.*

προ-θᾰλής, *ές*, (*πρό, θαλεῖν*) *growing, flourishing before the time, precocious.*

προθείς, *εῖσα, έν*, part. aor. 2 of *προτίθημι.*

προ-θέλυμνος, *ον*, (*πρό, θέλυμνον*) *by the roots; προθελύμνους ἕλκετο χαίτας* he tore his hair out *by the roots; προθέλυμνα χαμαὶ βάλε δένδρεα* he threw to earth trees *uprooted*; but, *σάκος σάκεϊ προθελύμνῳ φράξαντες* fencing shield upon shield *close-compact*;—*θέλυμνα* being *the several layers* or *coats of the shields*; and so *προθέλυμνος* means, *with layer upon layer.*

πρόθεσις, *ἡ*, (*προτίθημι*) *a placing before, setting forth; ἄρτοι τῆς προθέσεως* the bread *of the setting forth*, i. e. the *shew*-bread. II. *a purpose, resolve, design.*

προ-θέσμιος, *α, ον*, (*πρό, θεσμός*) *laid down before, appointed, fixed*: *ἡ προθεσμία* (sub. *ἡμέρα*), *a day fixed for* anything, *a limited* period, within which proceedings must be taken.

προ-θεσπίζω, f. *ίσω, to foretell.*

προ-θέω, Ion. impf. *προθέεσκον*: pf. *-θεύσομαι*:—*to run before.* 2. *to run forward* or *forth.* II. c. acc. *to outrun, outstrip.*

προ-θέω, old form of *προτίθημι, to put forward, permit; τοὔνεκά οἱ προθέουσιν ὀνείδεα μυθήσασθαι; do they* therefore *let* him speak reproachful words?

προ-θνήσκω, f. *-θᾰνοῦμαι, to die before.* II. *to die for* one.

προθορών, aor. 2 part. of *προθρώσκω.*

προθρῡλέω, f. *ήσω, to bruit abroad beforehand.*

προ-θρώσκω, f. *-θοροῦμαι*: aor. 2 *προὔθορον*, inf. *προθορεῖν*, part. *προθορών*:—*to spring before* or *forward, to dart in front.*

προ-θύελλα, *ἡ, a storm the harbinger of another.*

πρόθῡμα, *ατος, τό*, (*προθύω*) *a preparatory* or *preliminary sacrifice.*

προθῡμέομαι: Att. impf. *προὐθυμούμην*: fut. med. *προθυμήσομαι*, also pass. *προθυμηθήσομαι*: aor. 1 *προὐθυμήθην*: Dep.: (*πρόθυμος*):—*to be ready, willing, eager to do* a thing: c. acc. *to be earnest for* a person or thing, *desire eagerly*: absol. *to be earnest, zealous, shew zeal.* Hence

προθῡμητέον, verb. Adj. *one must desire eagerly.*

προθῡμία Ion. **-ίη**, *ἡ*, (*πρόθυμος*) *readiness, willingness, zeal, earnestness; πάσῃ προθυμίᾳ* with all *zeal.* II. *good will, ready kindness.*

πρό-θῡμος, *ον*, (*πρό, θυμός*) *ready, willing, eager, zealous, earnest*: c. gen. rei, *eager for.* II. *bearing good will, wishing well* to one, *well-disposed.* III. Adv. *προθύμως, readily, actively*: Comp. *-ότερον, more readily*: Sup. *-ότατα, most readily.*

προ-θύραιος [ῠ], *ον*, (*πρό, θύρα*) *before the door; τὰ προθύραια the space before a door.*

πρό-θῠρον, τό, (πρό, θύρα) *a front door.* 2. *the space before a door, a porch*, Lat. *vestibulum.*

προ-θύω, *to sacrifice before* or *first.* II. *to sacrifice in behalf of.*

προθῶμαι, aor. 2 med. subj. of προτίθημι.

προΐ, Adv. (πρό) = πρωΐ.

προ-ϊάλλω, *to send forth* or *away, dismiss.* II *to send before.*

προ-ϊάπτω, f. ψω: aor. 1 προΐαψα :—*to send forward, send before the time.*

προϊδών, οῦσα, ον, aor. 2 part. of προεῖδον.

προΐειν, εις, ει, Ion. and Att. impf. of προΐημι.

προϊείς, εῖσα, έν, pres. part. of προΐημι.

προΐζω, *to set* or *place before* :—Med. *to sit before, take the first seat.*

προ-ΐημι, 3 sing. προΐει and opt. προΐοι (as if from προ-ΐω): Att. impf. προΐειν, εις, ει: fut. προήσω: aor. 1 προῆκα Ep. προέηκα: aor. 2, 3 pl. πρόεσαν, imper. πρόες, προέτω, inf. προέμεν, Ep. for προεῖναι: —Med., aor. 2 προηκάμην: aor. 2 opt. προείμην or προοίμην :—Pass., pf. προεῖμαι: plqpf. προείμην :—*to send before, send on* or *forward;* generally, *to dismiss, let go:* also *to send on to* another. 2. *to let fall, let slip;* ἔπος προέηκε *he let drop* a word: an inf. is often added, αἰετὼ προέηκε πέτεσθαι he *sent* his eagles *forth* to fly; προέηκεν οὖρον ἀῆναι *he sent forth* the breeze to blow. 3. *to throw before, throw away:* of missiles, *to shoot forth, dart, hurl, discharge.* 4. *to give up, deliver over:* also *to devote oneself, exert oneself upon* a thing. II. Med. *to send forward from oneself, give up, betray:* also *to desert, forsake, throw overboard.* 2. of things, *to give freely:* in bad sense, *to throw away, squander, lavish;* λόγους προέσθαι *to throw* words *away* · also *to let go, let slip.* 3. *to give over* to one. 4. *to drive forward, force on.* 5. *to allow* or *suffer* a person to do a thing. III. Pass. *to be thrown away, be neglected.*

προΐητι, Dor. for προΐησι.

προῖκα, Adv. *freely, gratis:* properly acc. of προΐξ.

προΐκτης, ου, ὁ, (προΐξ) *one who asks for a free gift, a beggar.*

προΐξ Att. **προίξ**, ἡ, gen. προικός, dat. προικί, acc. προῖκα :—*a gift, present;* προικὸς γεύεσθαι to enjoy *a free gift* :—hence gen. προικός is used as Adv. *freely, without return.* Lat. *gratis:* also *with impunity;* so also acc. προῖκα. II. later *a marriage-portion, dowry*, Lat. *dos.* From

ΠΡΟΙ'ΣΣΟΜΑΙ: f. προΐξομαι Att. προίξομαι: Dep. :—*to ask a gift, to beg.*

προ-ΐστημι, f. προστήσω: aor. 1 προύστησα, inf. προστῆσαι, part. προστήσας: aor. 2 προύστην, inf. προστῆναι, part. προστάς: aor. 1 pass. προεστάθην, προὐστάθην, part. προσταθείς, εῖσα, έν: pf. προέστηκα, Ion. 2 pl. προεστέατε, part. προεστηκώς Ion. προεστεώς or προεστώς. I. Causal in pres., impf., fut. and aor. 1, *to set before* or *in front.* 2. so also in Med. προΐσταμαι, aor. 1 προεστησάμην, *to put before one, put in front.* 3. *to put before oneself, choose as one's leader.* 4. in Med. also *to put forward, put out: to put forward as an excuse* or *pretence.* II. intrans. in Pass., with aor. 2, pf. and plqpf. act. :—*to stand before* or *forward, come forward: to stand near.* 2. c. acc. pers. *to approach.* 3. c. gen. *to be set over, be at the head of, be the chief;* προστῆναι φόνου *to be the author* of slaughter: οἱ προεστῶτες Ion. -εῶτες, *the leading men, chiefs* :—hence *to manage, regulate, govern.* 4. *to stand before* so as *to protect* any one; hence *to protect, guard.*

προ-ΐσχω, = προέχω, *to hold before, hold out.* II. Med. προΐσχομαι, *to hold out before oneself, stretch forth.* 2. *to put forward, propose, offer.* 3. *to put forward, allege, plead.*

προϊών οὖσα, όν, aor. 2 part. of πρόειμι (εἶμι *ibo*).

προ-ΐωξις, ἡ, (πρό, ἰώκω = διώκω) *a driving before* or *onwards*, opp. to παλίωξις.

πρόκᾰ or **πρόκατε**, Ion. Adv. (πρό) *forthwith, straightway, suddenly.*

προ-καθεύδω, f. -καθευδήσω, *to sleep before* or *first.* II. *to sleep in front of.*

προ-κάθημαι Ion. **προ-κάτημαι**, properly perf. of προκαθέζομαι :—*to sit before* or *in front of;* τοσοῦτο πρὸ τῆς ἄλλης Ἑλλάδος προκάτησθαι *to be situated* so far *in front* of the rest of Greece: also *to protect, defend.*

προ-καθίζω Ion. **προ-κατίζω**, f. ίσω; also Med. **προκαθίζομαι** :—*to sit down before* or *in front.* II. *to sit in public, sit in state.*

προ-καθίημι, f. -καθήσω, *to let down beforehand:* metaph. *to involve in.* II. *to put forward.*

προ-καθίστημι, f. -καταστήσω, *to post before:* Med. *to post before oneself.* II. in Pass. and intr. tenses of Act., aor. 2 -κατέστην; pf. -καθέστηκα; plqpf. -εστήκειν :—*to be set* or *posted before.*

προ-καθοράω f. -κατόψομαι, *to view* or *examine beforehand.*

προ-καίω, f. -καύσω, *to burn before.*

προ-κᾰκοπᾰθέω, f. ήσω, *to suffer ills before.*

πρό-κᾰκος, ον, *very bad, exceeding bad.*

προ-κᾰλέω, f. έσω, *to call forth, call on* :—Med. *to call forth to one: to call out to fight, challenge, defy*, Lat. *provoco.* 2. *to invite beforehand.* II. c. acc. rei, *to offer* or *propose.* III. *to call up* or *forth, rouse.*

προ-κᾰλίζομαι, Dep. only used in pres. and impf., = προκαλέομαι, *to call forth, challenge, defy.*

προ-κᾰλινδέω, *to make roll forward* or *in front* :—Pass. *to fall prostrate before another.*

προκάλυμμα, ατος, τό, *anything hung in front to cover: a covering, curtain:* metaph. *a screen* or *blind.* From

προ-κᾰλύπτω, f. ψω, *to hang before as a covering:* —Med. *to put* something *over oneself, to veil* or *screen oneself;* of a woman, οὐ προκαλυπτομένα [τι] παρη-ἶδος *putting* no *veil over* her face. II. *to cover over, veil.*

προ-κάμνω, f. -κᾰμοῦμαι: aor. 2 προὔκαμον: pf. -κέκμηκα:—*to work* or *toil before.* II. *to work for* another. III. *to grow weary, faint too soon.* IV. *to have a previous illness: to be distressed beforehand.*

προκαμών, οῦσα, όν, aor. 2 part. of προκάμνω.

προ-κάρηνος, ον, (πρό, κάρηνον) *head-foremost.*

προκάς, άδος, ἡ, = πρόξ, *the roe-deer.*

προ-καταγγέλλω, *to announce* or *declare beforehand.*

προ-κατᾱγέτις, ιδος, ἡ, Ion. form, (πρό, καθηγέομαι) *a woman who goes before, a female leader.*

προ-καταγιγνώσκω, Ion. and in late Gr. -γῑνώσκω: f. -γνώσομαι: pf. -έγνωκα:—*to vote against beforehand, condemn by a prejudgement:* πρ. φόνον τινὸς *to give a verdict of* murder *against:* also c. inf. *to prejudge against* one that . . .

προ-κατάγω, f. ξω, *to bring to land before.*

προ-καταθέω, f. -θεύσομαι, *to run down beforehand.*

προ-κατακαίω, f. -καύσω, *to burn before:* of a country, *to ravage by fire all before* one.

προ-κατάκειμαι, Pass. *to lie down in front.*

προ-κατακλίνω, *to make to recline at table before.*

προ-καταλαμβάνω, f. -λήψομαι:—*to seize upon* or *occupy beforehand: to take possession of before* another: metaph. *to prevent, anticipate.*

προ-καταλέγω, *to detail* or *describe beforehand.*

προ-καταλύω, *to break up* or *annul beforehand:*—Med. *to adjust* or *compose beforehand:* προκαταλύεσθαι τὴν ἔχθρην *to end their mutual* enmity *before.*

προ-κατάρχομαι, Dep. *to begin first:* but mostly in technical sense, *to offer the first* of *the sacrifice.*

προ-κατασκευάζω, *to make ready beforehand.*

προ-καταφεύγω, *to escape to a place of refuge before;* προκαταφεύγειν ἐς τόπον *to escape before to* a place.

προ-καταχράομαι, Dep. *to use up beforehand.*

προ-κατεσθίω, f. -κατέδομαι, *to eat up beforehand.*

προ-κατέχω, aor. 2 -κατέσχον:—*to gain possession of* or *occupy beforehand, preoccupy:*—Med. *to hold before for oneself.*

προ-κατηγορέω, *to accuse beforehand.* Hence

προκατηγορία, ἡ, *previous accusation.*

προ-κάτημαι, Ion. for προκάθημαι.

προ-κατίζω, Ion. for προκαθίζω.

προκατόψομαι, fut. of προκαθοράω.

πρό-κειμαι, impf. προὐκείμην, Ion. inf. προκέεσθαι: fut. -κείσομαι:—used as Pass. of προτίθημι, *to be set before, lie before* or *in front of: to stretch forward, jut out.* II. *to be set before one:* metaph. *to be proposed* or *laid before one, mooted;* πρόκειται περὶ σωτηρίας *the question is* concerning safety; ἄεθλος προκείμενος a task *proposed;* τὸ προκείμενον πρῆγμα *the matter in debate.* III. *to lie before one, lie exposed; to lie dead,* ὁ προκείμενος *the corpse.* IV. *to be held out, set forth.*

προ-κέλευθος, ον, (πρό, κέλευθος) *forerunning.*

προ-κελευσματικός, ὁ, (πρό, κέλευσμα) *a proceleusmatic*, a foot consisting of four short syllables, e. g. κατέβαλε.

προ-κενόω, f. ώσω, *to empty beforehand.*

προ-κήδομαι, Dep. *to take care of, take thought for.*

προ-κηραίνω, (πρό, κήρ) *to be anxious for* one.

προ-κηρῡκεύομαι, f. εύσομαι, Med. *to have proclaimed by herald. to give public notice.*

προ-κηρύσσω Att. -ττω, f. ξω, *to proclaim by herald, proclaim publicly.*

προ-κινδῡνεύω, f. σω, *to run the first risk, bear the brunt of battle.*

προ-κῑνέω, f. ήσω, *to move forward: to urge on:*—Pass. with fut. med. -κινήσομαι, *to come on, advance.*

προ-κλαίω Att. -κλάω, fut. -κλαύσομαι, *to weep beforehand* or *openly.* II. trans. *to bewail beforehand.*

προκληθείς, aor. 1 pass. part. of προκαλέω.

πρόκλησις, gen. εως Ion. ιος, ἡ, (προκαλέω) *a calling forth:*—*a challenging to combat;* ἐκ προκλήσιος *in pursuance of a challenge.* II. *an invitation, proposal.* III. as law-term, *a formal challenge offered by either party* for the purpose of bringing disputed points to issue.

προ-κλίνω, f. -κλῐνῶ, *to lean forward.*

πρόκλῠτος, ον, *heard formerly: legendary.* From

προ-κλύω, *to hear* or *learn beforehand.*

προ-κόλπιον, τό, (πρό, κόλπος) *a robe falling over the breast.*

προ-κομίζω, f. ίσω, *to bring forward.* II. *to carry on before:*—Pass. *to be carried away.*

προ-κόμιον, τό, (πρό, κόμη) *the front hair: the forelock* of a horse.

προκοπή, ἡ, *progress on a journey.* II. metaph. *progress, advancement, improvement.* From

προ-κόπτω, impf. προὔκοπτον: f. ψω, *to cut away before one,* or *clear the way in front:* hence *to forward* or *promote* a work:—Pass. *to advance, thrive, prosper.* II. intr. in Act. *to make one's way forward, to make progress:* of time, *to be far gone, far advanced.*

πρόκρῐμα, ατος, τό, *preference, partiality.* From

προ-κρίνω [ῐ], f. -κρῐνῶ: *to choose before others, pick out, prefer before:*—Pass. *to be preferred before,* or *be superior to* others. II. *to judge beforehand, decide.*

πρόκρῐτος, ον, (προκρίνω) *preferred.*

πρό-κροσσος, η, ον or ος, ον, (πρό, κροσσαί) *with projecting battlements: ranged like battlements* or *in rows:* so of ships, νέες πρόκροσσαι ἐς πόντον ἐπὶ ὀκτώ, *ranged in rows* turned sea-wards eight deep: also of a cup, πέριξ αὐτοῦ γρυπῶν κεφαλαὶ πρόκροσσοι ἦσαν the heads of griffins were *set at regular distances* round it.

προ-κῠλινδέω, f. -κυλίσω [ῑ]:—*to roll forth, set rolling forward:*—Pass., προκυλινδεῖσθαί τινι *to grovel* or *prostrate oneself before* one.

προ-κύπτω, f. ψω, *to stoop forward and peep out.*

προ-κῡρόω, f. *ώσω*, *to confirm* or *ratify before*.

πρό-κύων, *-κυνός*, *ὁ*, *the star that rises before the Dog-star, Procyon*. II. *one who snarls like a dog, a snarling critic*.

προ-κώμιος, *ον*, (*πρό*, *κῶμος*) *before the festal revel*: *τὸ προκώμιον ὕμνου the prelude* of a hymn.

πρό-κωπος, *ον*, (*πρό*, *κώπη*) *grasping the hilt, sword-in-hand*. II. pass. *grasped by the hilt*.

προ-λαγχάνω, *to obtain by lot beforehand*.

προ-λάζῠμαι, Dep. *to receive beforehand*.

προ-λᾰλέω, f. *ήσω*, *to prate before*.

προ-λαμβάνω, f. *-λήψομαι*: aor. 2 *προὔλᾰβον*: pf. *-είληφα*, pass. *-είλημμαι*:—*to take beforehand*: *to receive as an earnest* or *deposit*. 2. *to take before* or *sooner* than another: *to take away before*. 3. *to obtain first, procure*. II. *to outstrip, get the start of*; *προλαμβάνειν τῆς ὁδοῦ to get a start* on the road. 2. *to be beforehand with, anticipate, claim* or *take before the time*: hence *to prejudge*. III. *to repeat from the beginning*.

προ-λέγω, f. *ξω*:—pf. pass. *προλέλεγμαι*:—*to pick out* or *choose before* others, *prefer*. II. *to say beforehand*: *to foretell, prophesy*, of an oracle. 2. *to tell publicly, proclaim*: *to warn*: *to profess, declare*: *to order*.

προ-λείπω, f. *ψω*: pf. *προλέλοιπα*:—*to leave by going forth, to leave behind, forsake*; *μῆτίς σε προλέλοιπε* prudence *forsook* thee: also *to quit beforehand*; *χώραν προλείπειν to abandon* one's post. 2. *to omit to do* a thing. II. intr. *to cease* or *fail beforehand*: absol. *to faint, fall into a swoon*.

προ-λεκτικός, *ή*, *όν*, (*προλέγω*) *foretelling, prophetic*.

προλέλοιπα, pf. of *προλείπω*.

προ-λεσχηνεύομαι, pf. pass. *προλελεσχήνευμαι*: Dep.:—*to converse with* one *before, arrange by word of mouth before*.

πρό-λεσχος, *ον*, (*πρό*, *λέσχη*) *prating, chattering*.

προ-λεύσσω, *to see before* or *in front*.

προλιπεῖν, aor. 2 inf. of *προλείπω*.

προλιπών, *οῦσα*, *όν*, aor. 2 part. of *προλείπω*.

πρόλογος, *ὁ*, (*προλέγω*) *a prefatory speech*: in Trag. and old Com., *the prologue* was *all of the piece that came before* the first chorus: after Euripides, it was *a narrative of facts introductory* to the main action, opp. to *ἐπίλογος*.

προ-λοχίζω, f. *ίσω*: pf. pass. *προλελόχισμαι*:—*to lay an ambush before*:—Pass., *αἱ προλελοχισμέναι ἐνέδραι* the ambush *that had before been laid*. II. *to beset with an ambuscade*.

προμᾰθεῖν, aor. 2 inf. of *προμανθάνω*.

προ-μᾰλάσσω Att. *-ττω*, f. *ξω*, *to soften beforehand*.

προ-μανθάνω, f. *-μᾰθήσω*: aor. 2 *προὔμᾰθον*:—*to ascertain* or *find out beforehand*.

προ-μαντεία Ion. *-ηίη*, *ἡ*, *the right of consulting the oracle first*. From

προ-μαντεύομαι, Dep. *to foretell, prophesy*.

προ-μαντηίη, *ἡ*, Ion. for *προμαντεία*.

πρό-μαντις, gen. *εως* Ion. *ιος*, *ὁ*, *ἡ*, *a prophet* or *prophetess*: *ἡ πρόμαντις* was the title of *the Pythia* or *Delphic priestess*. II. as Adj. *prophetic, presaging*.

προ-μαρτύρομαι, Dep. *to witness beforehand*. [ῡ]

προ-μάτωρ, *ορος*, *ἡ*, Dor. for *προμήτωρ*.

προ-μᾰχέω, = *προμαχίζω*.

προμᾰχεών, *ῶνος*, *ὁ*, (*προμάχομαι*) *a bulwark, rampart*, Lat. *propugnaculum*.

προμᾰχίζω, f. *σω*, (*πρόμαχος*) *to fight before* or *in front of*: also *to fight with* another *as champion*.

προ-μάχομαι: f. *-μᾰχήσομαι* Att. *-μᾰχοῦμαι*: Dep.:—*to fight before, fight in the front rank, fight in the van*. II. *to fight before* or *in defence of*.

πρό-μᾰχος, *ον*, (*πρό*, *μάχομαι*) *fighting before, fighting in front*: as Subst., mostly in plur., *the foremost fighters, champions*. II. *fighting for*, *τινός*.

προ-μελετάω, f. *ήσω*, *to practise beforehand*.

Προμένεια, *ἡ*, name of a prophetess of Dodona.

προ-μεριμνάω, f. *ήσω*, *to take earnest thought beforehand*.

προ-μετωπίδιος, *ον*, (*πρό*, *μέτωπον*) *worn* or *being on the forehead*. II. as Subst., *προμετωπίδιον*, *τό*, *the skin of the forehead*. 2. *a front-piece, frontlet* for horses.

προμήθεια Dor. **προμάθεια** [ᾱ], *ἡ*, (*προμηθής*) *foresight, forethought*: *consideration*.

Προμήθεια, *τά*, (*Προμηθεύς*) *the festival of Prometheus*.

Προμήθειος, *α*, *ον*, *of* or *from Prometheus*.

προμηθέομαι, fut. med. *-μηθήσομαι*: aor. 1 pass. *προὐμηθήθην*: Dep.: (*προμηθής*):—*to take care beforehand, to provide for*: *to shew forethought for*, Lat. *cavere*: c. acc. pers. *to shew regard* or *consideration for*.

Προμηθεύς, gen. *έως* Ion. *ῆος*, *ὁ*, (*προμηθής*) *Prometheus, Forethought*, son of the Titan Iapetus, brother of *Epimetheus* or *Afterthought*: inventor of many arts, esp. of working in metal and clay, whence he is said to have made man from clay, and to have furnished him with the *ἔντεχνον πῦρ*, stolen from Olympus. II. as appellat. *forethought, caution*.

προ-μηθής Dor. **προμᾱθής**, *ές*, (*πρό*, *μῆτις*) *forethinking, cautious, wary*: *caring about* a thing.

προμηθία Ion. *-ίη*, *ἡ*, = *προμήθεια*.

προμηθικός, *ή*, *όν*, (*προμηθής*) *inclined to forethought, wary*. Adv. *-κῶς*, *warily*.

προ-μηνύω, f. *ύσω* [ῡ], *to inform of* or *denounce beforehand*.

προ-μήτωρ Dor. **προμάτωρ**, *ορος*, *ἡ*, (*πρό*, *μήτηρ*) *the first mother, ancestress* of a race.

προμῐγῆναι, aor. 2 pass. inf. of *προμίγνυμι*.

προ-μίγνῡμι, f. *μίξω*, *to mingle beforehand*:—Pass., aor. 2 inf. *προμῐγῆναι*, *to have intercourse with beforehand*.

προ-μισθόω, f. *ώσω*, *to hire beforehand*.

προ-μνάομαι, Dep. *to woo for* another: generally, *to endeavour to obtain, solicit*: *to plead with*, c. dat. II. *to forebode, presage*.

προ-μνηστῖνοι, αι, α, *one by one, one after the other.* (Deriv. uncertain.)

προμνηστρία and **προμνηστρίς**, ίδος, ἡ, (προμνάομαι) *a woman who woos for another, a match-maker.*

πρό-μοιρος, ον, (πρό, μοῖρα) *before the destined term, untimely.*

προμολεῖν, aor. 2 inf. of προβλώσκω. Hence

προμολή, ἡ, *an approach, vestibule.* II. in plur. *the jutting foot of a mountain: the mouth of a river.*

προμολών, aor. 2 part. of προβλώσκω.

πρόμος, ὁ, (πρό) *the foremost man, a champion,* like πρόμαχος:—*a chief,* Lat. *princeps.*

προ-μοχθέω, f. ήσω, *to work beforehand.*

πρό-νᾱος or **προ-νάιος**, α, ον Ion. **προ-νήιος**, η, ον, (πρό, ναός) *before* or *in front of a temple:* as Subst., I. προνήιον, τό, *the court before a temple.* II. Προναία Ion. Προνηίη, ἡ, a name of Minerva at Delphi, because she had a chapel or statue there *before the great temple* of Apollo. III. πρόναος, ὁ, *the hall* or *vestibule* of a temple, through which was the way to the temple itself.

προ-ναυμαχέω, f. ήσω, *to fight at sea for* or *in defence of,* τινός.

προ-νέμω, f. -νεμῶ, *to assign beforehand: to hold forth, present.* II. Med. προνέμομαι, of cattle, *to go forward in grazing:* hence *to gain ground, spread.*

προ-νεύω, f. σω, *to nod* or *stoop forwards.*

προ-νήιος, η, ον, Ion. for πρόναιος.

προ-νηστεύω, f. σω, *to fast beforehand.*

προ-νῑκάω, f. ήσω, *to gain a victory beforehand.*

προ-νοέω, f. ήσω; also Med. **προ-νοέομαι**, f. ήσομαι, with aor. 1 med. and pass. προὐνοησάμην, προὐνοήθην:—*to perceive* or *observe beforehand.* II. *to plan* or *devise beforehand: to provide.* 2. c. gen. *to provide for, take thought for.* 3. absol. *to be provident, act warily.* Hence

προνοητέον, verb. Adj. *one must take care.*

προνοητικός, ή, όν, (προνοέω) *disposed to practise foresight, provident, cautious, wary.* II. of things, *shewing forethought* or *design.* Adv. -κῶς, *with forethought.*

πρόνοια Ion. **-νοίη**, ἡ, (πρόνοος) *a perceiving* or *knowing beforehand.* II. *foresight, forethought, forecast;* ἐκ προνοίας *with forethought, advisedly,* Lat. *ex consulto,* and of crimes, *with malice prepense.* 2. *the providence* of the gods.

προνομαία, ἡ, (προνέμομαι) *a proboscis.*

προνομεία, ἡ, *a foraging, plundering.* From

προ-νομεύω, f. σω, *to go out foraging, to forage.*

προνομή, ἡ, (προνέμομαι) *a foraging, foray, raid.*

πρόνομος, ον, (προνέμομαι) *going forward to feed, grazing forward.*

πρό-νοος, ον contr. **πρό-νους**, ουν, (πρό, νόος) *thinking beforehand, wary:*—Comp. προνοίστερος.

προ-νωπής, ές, (πρό, ὤψ) *bent* or *bending forwards: drooping, sinking.* 2. metaph. *inclined, ready.*

προ-νώπιος, ον, (πρό, ἐνώπια) *before* or *without the walls:* generally, *in front of, outside* a place. II. as Subst., προνώπιον, τό, *a hall* or *court.*

ΠΡΟ'Ξ, gen. προκός, ἡ, a kind of *deer: the gazelle* or perh. *the roe:* also προκάς.

πρό-ξεινος, ὁ, Ion. for πρόξενος.

προξενέω, impf. προὐξένουν: f. ήσω: aor. 1 προὐξένησα: (πρόξενος):—*to be* any one's πρόξενος, *to be* one's *protector* or *patron.* II. *to negotiate, manage, effect* anything for another: *to supply, furnish, present, grant.* 2. c. dat. et inf. *to contrive* for one that ..: also *to advise, give directions.* 3. *to introduce* one person to another.

προξενία, ἡ, *a treaty* or *compact of friendship between a state and a foreigner, public friendship,* Lat. *hospitium.* II. *the rights and privileges of a* πρόξενος or *public friend,* esp. of an ambassador. From

πρό-ξενος Ion. **πρό-ξεινος**, ὁ, (πρό, ξένος) *a public* ξένος, i.e. *a public guest* or *host:* the word expressed the same relation *between a state and an individual* of another state, that ξένος did *between two individuals* of different states: the πρόξενος possessed great privileges in the state to which he was allied; the relation usually passed on from father to son. II. *one who represented a foreign state,* a sort of *consul* or *agent.* III. generally, *a patron, assistant, defender, guardian.* 2. as Adj. *assisting relieving.*

προ-ξῠράω, f. ήσω, *to shave beforehand.*

προ-ογκάομαι, Dep. *to bray beforehand.*

προ-οδεύω, f. σω, *to travel before.*

προ-οδοποιέω, f. ήσω, *to prepare the way before, pave the way.* II. metaph. *to prepare beforehand.*

προ-οδοιπορέω, f. ήσω, *to travel before.*

πρό-οδος, ον, (πρό, ὁδός) *going before* or *in advance:* as Subst., πρόοδοι, οἱ, *a party of soldiers in advance.*

πρό-οδος, ἡ, (πρό, ὁδός) *a going on, advance.*

πρό-οιδα, inf. προειδέναι, part. προειδώς: plqpf. προῄδειν: fut. προείσομαι: (with no pres. in use):—*to know beforehand.* Cf. προεῖδον.

προ-οιμιάζομαι Att. contr. **φροιμιάζομαι**, f. -άσομαι: Dep.:—*to make a preamble* or *prelude:*—the pf. πεφροιμίασμαι is used in pass. sense, *to be stated by way of preamble.* From

προ-οίμιον Att. contr. **φροίμιον**, τό, (πρό, οἶμος) *an opening* or *introduction to* a thing: in Music, *a prelude, overture:* in speeches, *a preface, exordium* of laws, *a preamble:* metaph. *any beginning.* 2. *a hymn.*

προ-οίχομαι, fut. -οιχήσομαι: Dep.:—*to have gone on before.*

προ-όμνῡμι and -ύω, *to swear before* or *beforehand: to testify on oath before.*

προοπτέον, verb. Adj. of προοράω, *one must look beforehand, take care of:* cf. sq.

πρόοπτος Att. contr. **προὖπτος**, ον, verb. Adj. of προοράω (as if from *προόπτομαι), *foreseen: manifest.*

προορᾱτός, ή, όν, verb. Adj. of προοράω, *foreseen, to be foreseen.*

προ-οράω, f. προόψομαι: aor. 2 προεῖδον: pf. προεόρᾱκα:—*to foresee:* absol. *to look forward, be provident.* 2. *to look forward at, see before one:* also *to see from afar.* 3. c. gen. *to provide for* a person or thing. II. also in Med. προοράομαι, *to foresee.* 2. *to look before one.* 3. *to provide for, to provide,* Lat. *cavere.*

προ-ορίζω, f. σω, *to mark out beforehand, to predetermine.*

προ-ορμάω, f. ήσω, *to drive forward* or *onward:*—Pass. *to rush* or *start on.* II. intr. in Act. *to start forward.*

προ-ορμίζω, f. ισω, *to moor before* or *in front.*

προ-οφείλω Att. contr. **προὐφείλω**: f. -οφειλήσω:—*to owe beforehand:*—Pass. *to be due beforehand* or *before, to remain as a debt.*

πρό-οψις, εως, ή, (πρό, ὄψις) *a foreseeing.* II. *a seeing before* one.

προ-όψομαι, fut. of προοράω (as if from *προοπτομαι).

προ-πᾰγής, ές, (πρό, πάγηναι) *fixed in front, prominent.*

προπαθεῖν, aor. 2 inf. of προπάσχω.

προ-παιδεύω, f. σω, *to teach beforehand.*

πρό-πᾰλαι, Adv. *very long ago.*

πρό-πᾰρ, (πρό, παρά) Prep. with gen. *before.* II. Adv. *before, sooner.*

προ-παραβάλλω, *to put beside* or *along beforehand.*

προ-παρασκευάζω, f. άσω, *to prepare beforehand:*—Pass. *to be prepared beforehand.*

προ-παρέχω, *to supply beforehand: to offer before.*

προ-πάροιθε and before a vowel **-θεν**: Prep. with gen., *before, in front of;* προπάροιθε ποδῶν *before* one's feet, close at hand; προπάροιθε θυράων *before* the door. II. Adv., 1. of Place, *in front, forward, before.* 2. of Time, *before, formerly.*

πρό-πᾱς, -πᾶσα, -πᾶν, (πρό, πᾶς) strengthd. for πᾶς, πρόπαν ἦμαρ *all* day *long;* νῆας προπάσας *all* the ships *together:* neut. πρόπαν as Adv. *utterly.*

προ-πάσχω, f. -πείσομαι, *to suffer before* or *beforehand: to be ill-treated before.*

προ-πάτωρ, ορος, ὁ, (πρό, πάτηρ) *the first founder of a family, forefather:* in plur. προπάτορες, οἱ, *ancestors, forefathers.*

προ-πείθω, f. σω, *to persuade beforehand.*

πρό-πειρα, ή, *a previous trial* or *venture;* πρόπειραν ποιεῖσθαι, Lat. *experimentum facere,* to make *a trial.*

προ-πειράω, *to attempt beforehand:* also as Dep. **προ-πειράομαι**, with aor. 1 and pf. pass. προεπειράθην [ᾱ], προπεπείρᾱμαι.

προ-πέμπω, f. ψω: aor. 1 προὔπεμψα:—*to send before* or *beforehand: to send away, dismiss: to send on: to send forth;* προ-πέμπειν ἰοὺς *to shoot forth* arrows; also *to afford, furnish.* II. *to conduct, accompany;* esp. *to conduct in procession, to follow* a corpse *to the grave,* Lat. *efferre.* III. *to pursue.*

προπεσών, οῦσα, όν, aor. 2 part. of προπίπτω.

προ-πετάννυμι, f. -πετάσω [ᾰ], *to spread out before.*

προπέτεια, ή, *rashness, reckless haste.* From

προπετής, ές, (προπίπτω) *falling forwards, bending forward,* Lat. *prociduus, proclivis: drooping, at the point of death.* II. metaph. *being on the verge of, ready for, prone to* a thing. 2. *precipitate, sudden, rash, hasty, reckless.* Hence

προπετῶς, Adv. *forwards.* II. *in headlong haste.*

προπέφανται, 3 sing. pf. pass. of προφαίνω.

προπεφραδμένος, η, ον, pf. pass. part. of προφράζω.

προ-πηδάω, f. ήσομαι, *to spring out before: to spring forward from.*

προ-πηλακίζω, f. ίσω Att. ιῶ, (πρό, πηλός):—*to cover with mud: to treat with indignity, to abuse foully:*—also *to throw in one's teeth, reproach one with.* Hence

προπηλάκισις, εως, η, and **προπηλακισμός**, ὁ, *contumelious treatment.*

προ-πίνω [ῑ], impf. προὔπινον: f. προπίομαι: aor. 2 προὔπιον: pf. act. προπέπωκα, pass. προπέπομαι:—*to drink before* or *to* one, *to drink to* another's *health, pledge* him, Lat. *propinare,* because the Greek, as also the Roman, custom was to drink first oneself, and then pass the cup to the person pledged. as the cup was often given as a present, προπίνειν came to signify *to give away, make a present of, to compliment away:* προπίνειν τὴν ἐλευθερίαν Φιλίππῳ, *to pledge away* liberty to Philip: so, προπέποται τὰ τῆς πόλεως πράγματα the interests of the state *have been complimented away.*

προ-πίπτω, f. -πεσοῦμαι: aor. 2 προὔπεσον, inf. προπεσεῖν: pf. προπέπτωκα:—*to fall* or *throw oneself forward: to rush forward, rush headlong.*

προ-πιστεύω, f. σω, *to trust* or *believe beforehand.*

προ-πίτνω, poët. for προπίπτω (v. πίτνω):—*to fall down before, fall prostrate,* of suppliants.

προ-πλέω, f. -πλεύσομαι, *to sail before.* Hence

πρό-πλοος, ον contr. **-πλους**, ουν, *sailing before, in front* or *at the head.*

προ-πλώω, Ion. for προπλέω.

προ-ποδηγός, όν, *going before to shew the way, guiding.*

προ-ποδίζω, f. ίσω, (πρό, πούς) *to put the foot forward, stride forward.*

προ-ποιέω, f. ήσω, *to do beforehand, take the first step:*—Pass. *to be made* or *prepared beforehand.*

προ-πολεμέω, f. ήσω, *to fight before* or *in front of.*

προπόλευμα, ατος, τό, *service rendered.* From

προπολεύω, f. σω, (πρόπολος) *to serve as a priest.*

πρό-πολος, ὁ, ή, (πρό, πολέω) *a servant that goes before one*: *an attendant, minister: a rower.* 2. *one who serves a god, a priest* or *priestess: a temple-servant.* II. as Adj. *ministering to* a thing, *devoted* or *dedicated to* it.

προπομπή, ἡ, (*προπέμπω*) *a sending on before.* II. *an attending, escorting, conducting.*

προ-πομπία, ἡ, (*πρό, πομπή*) *the first place in a procession*, like *προεδρία*

προπομπός, *όν*, (*προπέμπω*) *escorting in a procession:* c. acc., *προπομπὸς χοάς carrying* drink-offerings *in procession.* II. as Subst. *a conductor, escort.*

προ-πονέω, f. *ήσω*, *to work* or *take pains beforehand.* II. *to labour for* or *instead of* another. III. c. gen. rei, *to work for* a thing, i. e. to obtain it. IV. c. acc. rei, *to obtain by previous labour:* hence in pf. pass. part., *τὰ προπεπονημένα things formerly pursued with zeal.* V. Med. *προπονέομαι*, *to grow weary* or *tire too soon.*

πρό-πονος, *ον*, *very toilsome, exceeding toilsome.*

Προ-ποντίς, *ίδος*, ἡ, (*πρό, πόντος*) the name of the Sea of Marmora, so called *because it leads into the Pontus* or Black Sea.

προ-πορεύω, f. *σω*, *to conduct forward:*—Pass. with fut. med. *-πορεύσομαι*, and pass. *-πορευθήσομαι*, *to go before* or *forward.*

προ-πορίζω, f. *ίσω*, *to provide beforehand:*—Pass. *to be provided beforehand.*

πρόποσις, *εως*, ἡ, (*προπίνω*) *a drinking before* or *to one: a pledging.* II. *a drink.*

προπότης, ὁ, (*προπίνω*) *one who drinks healths.*

πρό-πους, *-ποδος*, ὁ, *the projecting foot* of a mountain.

προ-πράσσω Att. *-ττω*, f. *ξω to do before.* II. *to exact beforehand.*

προ-πρεών, *ῶνος*, ὁ, *inclining forward:* metaph. *forward, ready, willing.*

προ-πρηνής, *ές*, *inclined* or *bent forwards: swaying forwards:*—neut. *προπρηνές* as Adv., *forward.*

προ-πρό, strengthened form of *πρό*, *right before.*

προπρο-κυλίνδομαι, Pass. strengthd. for *προκυλίνδομαι*, *to roll on and on, to keep rolling oneself before* another's feet: *to be driven about from place to place.*

πρό-πρυμνα, Adv. (*πρό, πρύμνα*) *stern-foremost*, properly of a ship on the point of sinking: hence *on the brink of ruin, utterly cast away.*

προ-πταίω, f. *σω*, *to stumble before*

προ-πύλαιος [ῠ], *ον*, (*πρό, πύλη*) *before the gate.* II. neut. pl. as Subst., *προπύλαια, τά, a gateway, entrance:* at Athens *the Propylaea*, the entrance to the Acropolis, built by Pericles.

πρό-πῠλον, *τό*, (*πρό, πύλη*) *a portico, vestibule.*

προ-πυνθάνομαι, f. *-πεύσομαι:* aor. 2 *προὐπῠθόμην:* Dep.:—*to learn by inquiry before, hear* or *ascertain beforehand.*

πρό-πυργος, *ον*, *before* or *for towers; θυσίαι πρόπυργοι* offerings *made for the city.*

προ-ρέω, f. *-ρεύσομαι*, *to flow forward, flow amain*, Lat. *profluere.*

πρόρ-ρησις, ἡ, (*πρό, ῥῆσις*) *a foretelling.* 2. *previous instructions* or *orders.* II. *a proclamation public notice.*

πρόρ-ρητος, *ον*, (*πρό, ῥητός*) *foretold.* II. *proclaimed, commanded.*

πρόρ-ριζος, *ον*, (*πρό, ῥίζα*) *by the roots, root and branch:* neut. *πρόρριζον* or *πρόρριζα* as Adv., *up by the roots*, Lat. *radicitus.*

ΠΡΟ'Σ, Prep. with gen., dat., and acc.: with gen. implying motion *from* or *from the side of* a place; with dat., abiding *at* a place; with acc., motion *to* a place:—Dor. **προτί** and **ποτί** [⏑⏑], contrd. **πότ.**

WITH GENIT., I. of Place, *from forth:* hence *from* or *on the side* or *quarter of; πρὸς Νότου on the side of* the South, i. e. in the direction of the South; *φυλακαὶ πρὸς Αἰθιόπων* garrisons *on the side of*, i. e. *against*, the Ethiopians; *Ἄβδηρα ἵδρυται πρὸς τοῦ Ἑλλησπόντου, μᾶλλον ἢ τοῦ Στρύμονος* Abdera is situated *on the side of* the Hellespont rather than of the Strymon, i. e. is nearer to it. 2. metaph., *πρὸς πατρός* on the father's *side:* also *on the part of, at the hand of, ἔχειν τιμὴν πρὸς Ζηνός* to have honour *at the hand of* Jove: so, *πρὸς Διός εἰσι ξεῖνοί τε πτωχοί τε* strangers and the poor are *sent by* Jove. 3. *in presence of, before*, whence its use in oaths and protestations: *μάρτυροι πρὸς θεῶν, πρὸς ἀνθρώπων* witnesses *before* gods and men: in which case the Att. insert *σέ* between the prep. and acc., *πρός σε θεῶν αἰτῶ* I beseech thee *by* the gods, Lat. *per te deos oro.* II. with a passive Verb = *ὑπό*, as, *διδάσκεσθαι πρός τινος* to be taught *by* one; *ἀτιμάζεσθαι πρός τινος* to be dishonoured *by* one. III. from the local sense *on* or *from the side of* comes the sense *suiting, becoming; οὐ πρὸς τοῦ ἅπαντος ἀνδρός* not *befitting* every man; *πρὸς δίκης agreeable to* justice; *πρὸς γυναικός ἐστι* it is *like* a woman.

WITH DAT., generally, *hard by, near, in the presence of, at, on; βάλλειν ποτὶ γαίῃ* to dash *upon* earth; *πρὸς ἀλλήλῃσιν ἔχεσθαι* to cling *close to* each other. II. *in addition to, besides; πρὸς τούτοις in addition to* this; *πρὸς τοῖς ἄλλοις κακοῖς in addition to* all other evils. III. of close engagement in a thing, *γίγνεσθαι πρὸς τῷ σκοπεῖν* to be *employed upon* considering.

WITH ACCUS., it expresses motion, I. of Place, *towards, to, upon; πρὸς ἠῶ towards* the East; *κλαίειν πρὸς οὐρανόν* to cry *to* heaven. 2. in hostile sense, *against:* in the titles of speeches, *πρός τινα in reference* or *reply to, in answer to*, Lat. *adversus;* not *in accusation of*, which is properly *κατά* with gen., Lat. *in.* 3. without hostile sense, *εἰπεῖν πρός τινα* to address oneself *towards* or *to* one. II. of Time, *towards, near, hard upon.* III. generally, of Relation, *with a view to, in regard* or *relation to; πρὸς ταῦτα in regard* to this, *therefore; τὰ πρὸς τὸν πόλεμον* things *relating to* war; *τὰ πρὸς τοὺς θεούς* our *relations to* the gods. 2. *according to, suitable to, at, upon; πρὸς τὴν φήμην at* the news; so, *πρὸς τί; to what end?* 3. *in proportion to, in comparison of; πρὸς τὸν πατέρα Κῦρον in comparison of* his father Cyrus; *πρὸς πάντας τοὺς ἄλλους in com-*

parison of all the rest, implying superiority, Lat. *prae aliis omnibus.* IV. in Att., πρός with acc. is often put for Adv., as, πρὸς βίαν, πρὸς ἀνάγκην *by* force, forcibly; πρὸς καιρόν in season; πρὸς χάριν τινί to please one; πρὸς τὸ βίαιον = βιαίως.

ABSOL. AS ADV., *besides, over and above.*

IN COMPOS. it implie I. motion *towards*, as in προσάγω. II. addition, *besides*, as in προσκτάομαι. III. a being *by* or *besides*: *a remaining beside*, as in πρόσ-ειμι (εἰμί *sum*).

προ-σάββᾰτος, ον, (πρό, σάββατα) *before the Sabbath*: as Subst., προσάββατον, τό, *the eve of the Sabbath.*

προσ-αγγέλλω, f. ελῶ, *to announce*: *to denounce.*

προσαγόρευσις, εως, ἡ, *an addressing.* From

προσαγορευτέος, α, ον, verb. Adj. *to be called* or *named*: From

προσ-ᾰγορεύω, f. σω: aor. -ηγόρευσα: pf. -ηγόρευκα: but the Att. fut., aor. and pf. are προσερῶ, προσεῖπον, προσείρηκα:—*to address, accost.* II. *to name, call by name.*

προσ-άγω, f. ξω: aor. 2 προσήγᾰγον, rarely aor 1. προσῆξα. fut. med. in pass. sense προσάξομαι:—*to bring to* or *upon*: *to supply, furnish* 2. *to put to, add.* 3. *to bring to, move towards, apply, employ.* 4. *to bring in, introduce.* 5. *to lead on, induce.* II. intr. *to draw near, approach*; πρόσαγε, *come on!* III. Med. *to attach to oneself, bring over to one's side.* 2. *to embrace, salute.* 3. *to induce* to do a thing. 4. *to get for oneself, procure, import*: hence in Pass., τὰ προσαχθέντα *imports.* Henc

προσᾰγωγεύς, έως, ὁ, *one who brings to an introducer.*

προσᾰγωγή, ἡ, (προσάγω) *a bringing to* or *towards*: *acquisition.* II. (from the intr. sense of προσάγω) *approach* or *access to, the privilege of entrance.*

προσαγωγός, όν, (προσάγω) *bringing to, attractive, persuasive*

προσ-ᾴδω, aor. f. ποτ-αείσομαι:—*to sing to*; τίν ποταείσομαι, Dor. for σοὶ προσᾴσομαι, to thee *will I sing.* 2. προσᾴδειν τραγῳδίαν *to sing the songs* in a Tragedy to music. II. *to harmonise* or *chime in with*, Lat. *concinere.*

προσαΐξας, aor. 1 part. of προσαΐσσω.

προσ-αιρέομαι, Med. *to choose to oneself, attach to oneself.* II. *to choose* or *elect in addition to.*

προσ-ᾱΐσσω Att. -ᾴσσω, f. ξω, *to spring* or *rush to*: *to come quickly upon* or *over.*

προσ-αιτέω, f. ήσω, *to ask besides*. *to demand in addition* II. *to continue asking, to beg of* one: absol. *to beg hard.* Hence

προσ-ακοντίζω, f. σω, *to shoot like a javelin.*

προσ-ακτέον, verb. Adj. of προσάγω, *one must bring to.*

προσαίτης, ου, ὁ, *a beggar.*

προσ-ᾰκούω, f. -ακούσομαι, *to hear besides.*

προσ-ᾰλείφω, f. ψω, *to rub* or *smear upon.*

προσ-ᾰλίσκομαι, Pass. *to be taken besides, to be cast* in a lawsuit *besides.*

προσ-άλλομαι, f. -αλοῦμαι: aor. 1 -ηλάμην: Dep.:—*to jump up, at* or *upon* one.

προσ-αμείβομαι, Dor. poët. aor. 1 ποταμειψάμην, *to answer.*

προσ-ᾰμέλγω, f. ξω, *to milk besides*: Dor. fut. med. (in pass. sense) ποταμέλξεται *will yield milk besides.*

προσ-αμπέχομαι, (πρός, ἀμπέχω), Pass *to be held fast in* a thing.

προσ-ᾰμύνω [ῡ], f. ῠνῶ, *to come to aid* one

προσ-αμφιέννυμι, Att. fut. -αμφιῶ, *to put on over.*

προσ-αναβαίνω, f. -βήσομαι, *to climb up to*: of riders, *to mount besides.* Hence

προσανάβᾰσις poët. προσάμβ-, ἡ, *a going up to, approach*, κλίμακος προσαμβάσεις *approach and ascent by means of a* ladder, i. e. a scaling-ladder.

προσανάβηθι, aor. 2 imperat. of προσαναβαίνω.

προσ-αναγιγνώσκω, *to read besides.*

προσ-ᾰναγκάζω, f. άσω, *to force* or *constrain besides.* 2. *to bring under command, discipline.* II. *to force* one *to do* a thing.

προσ-αναγορεύω, *to announce besides.*

προσ-αναγράφω, f. ψω, *to write* or *note down besides.*

προσ-αναιρέω, f. ήσω, *to lift up besides*: Med. *to take upon oneself* or *undertake besides.* II. of an oracle, *to give an answer besides.*

προσ-ᾰναισῑμόω, f. ώσω, *to spend* or *consume besides.*

προσανάκλῐμα, τό, *that on which one leans.* From

προσ-ανακλίνομαι, Pass. *to lean on.* [ῑ] Hence

προσανάκλῐσις, ἡ, *a leaning* or *lying on.*

προσ-αναλαμβάνω, f. -λήψομαι *to take up* or *receive besides.* 2. metaph. *to recruit* or *refresh besides.*

προσ-ᾰνᾱλίσκω, f. -ανᾱλώσω, *to spend* or *consume besides*:—aor. 1 part. προσανᾱλώσα

προσ-αναπληρόω, f. ώσω, *to fill up by pouring into fill up the measure of.*

προσ-αναρτάω, f. ήσω, *to hang up besides* or *upon.*

προσ-αναστέλλω, *to hold in check besides.*

προσ-ανατέλλω poët. προσαντ-, *to rise up towards.*

προσ-ανατίθημι, f. -θήσω:—*to offer* or *dedicate besides*:—Med. *to take something additional on oneself*: *to contribute besides*: also II. *to confer* or *consult with.*

προσ-ανδρᾰποδίζω, f. ίσω Att. ιῶ, *to enslave besides.*

προσ-άνειμι (ἀνά, εἶμι *ibo*), *to go up to*

προσ-ανεῖπον, aor. 2 without pres. in use (προσαναγορεύω being used instead) *to announce, publish* or *order besides.*

προσ-ᾱνής, ές, Dor. for προσηνής.

προσ-άντης, ες, gen. εος, (πρός, ἄντην) *rising up against* or so as *to meet* one, *up-hill*, Lat. *arduus.* II. metaph. *steep, arduous*: *irksome, displeasing painful.* III. of persons, *adverse, hostile*

προσ-απαγγέλλω, f. ελῶ, *to report besides.*

προσ-απαγορεύω, *to forbid besides.*

προσ-απαιτέω, f. ήσω, *to demand besides.*

προσ-ᾰπειλέω, f. ήσω, *to threaten besides.*

προσ-απεῖπον, aor. 2 without pres. in use (προσ-απαγορεύω being used instead), *to forbid, renounce besides.*

προσ-αποβάλλω, f. -βαλῶ, *to throw away* or *lose besides.*

προσ-απογράφω, f. ψω, *to enroll* or *register besides.*

προσ-αποδείκνυμι, f. -δείξω, *to prove besides.*

προσ-αποδίδωμι, *to pay as a debt besides.*

προσ-αποκρίνομαι, Med. *to answer besides.*

προσ-αποκτείνω, f. -κτενῶ, *to kill* or *slay besides.*

προσ-απολαύω, f. σω, *to enjoy besides.*

προσ-απόλλῦμι and -ύω: f. -ολέσω:—*to destroy, despatch, kill besides: to lose besides*:—Med., with pf. 2 act. προσαπόλωλα, *to perish besides* or *with others.*

προσ-αποπέμπω, f. ψω, *to send away* or *off besides.*

προσ-αποστέλλω, f. -στελῶ, *to send off besides.*

προσ-αποστερέω, f. ήσω, *to defraud besides*

προσ-αποτῑμάω, f. ήσω, *to value* or *estimate besides.*

προσ-αποφέρω, f. -αποίσω, *to carry off besides: to return* or *report in besides.*

προσ-άπτω Dor. **προτι-άπτω**, f. ψω, *to fasten to* or *upon, attach to, confer upon*: in bad sense, *to fix* or *impose upon, saddle with.* 2. *to apply to: to deliver, commit to.* II. intr. *to be added.* III. Med. προσάπτομαι, *to touch, lay hold on, meddle with.*

προσ-αραρίσκω, f. -άρσω: aor 2 -ήρᾰρον:—*to join, fit, fasten to*, c. dat. II. intrans. in pf. 2 προσ-ᾱρα Ion. -άρηρα: 3 sing. Ep. pf. pass. προσαρήρεται:—*to be fitted, attached* or *closely joined to.*

προσ-αράσσω Att. -ττω, f. ξω, *to dash against.*

προσ-άρηρα, Ion. pf. of προσαραρίσκω.

προσᾰρήρεται, 3 sing. Ep. pf. pass. of προσαραρίσκω.

προσ-αρκέω, f. έσω, *to lend sufficient aid, to succour, help, assist*, c. dat. II. *to afford, yield, present*, c. acc. rei.

προσ-αρμόζω later Att. -αρμόττω: f. όσω: pf. pass. -ήρμοσμαι:—*to fit to, put* or *attach closely to*: metaph. *to adapt.* II. intr. *to suit* or *agree with* a thing.

προσ-αρτάω, f. ήσω, *to fasten* or *attach to*:—Pass. *to be attached to, accrue* or *belong to: to be devoted to.*

προσ-ᾴσσω, Att. for προσ-αΐσσω.

προσ-ᾰτῑμόω, f. ώσω, *to dishonour* or *deprive of civil rights besides, to degrade besides.*

προσ-αυαίνομαι, Pass. (πρός, αὐαίνω) *to become dried up, waste* or *pine away upon.*

προσ-αυδάω, f. ήσω: impf. προσηύδων, 3 sing. -ηύδα, 3 dual -ηυδήτην:—*to speak to, address, accost.*

προσ-αύλειος, ον, (πρός, αὐλή) *near a farm-yard, rustic.*

προσ-αυλέω, f. ήσω, *to accompany on the flute.*

προσ-αυξάνω, f. -αυξήσω, *to increase besides*:—Pass. *to grow* or *wax larger.*

προσ-αύω, *to burn by touching.*

προσ-αφαιρέω, f. ήσω, *to take away besides*:—Med. *to take away for oneself besides*:—Pass. *to have* a thing *taken away besides.*

προσ-αφικνέομαι, f. -αφίξομαι, Dep. *to arrive at.*

προσ-αφίστημι, f. -στήσω, *to cause to revolt besides*:—Pass., with aor. 2 act. -απέστην, pf. -αφέστηκα, *to revolt besides.*

προσ-βαίνω, f. -βήσομαι: pf. -βέβηκα: aor. 2 -έβην, aor. 1 med. -εβησάμην:—*to go towards, step up on: to mount* or *ascend.* 2. *to come near: to come upon, attack.*

προσ-βάλλω, fut. -βαλῶ: aor. 2 -έβαλον: pf. -βέβληκα, pass. -βέβλημαι:—*to throw to* or *upon, to apply* or *affix.* 2. *to assign to, add* or *attach to*: of the Sun, ἀρούρας προσβάλλειν *to strike* the earth *with* his rays: *to strike* or *reach* the senses. 3. metaph., προσβάλλειν τί *to lay* a thing *to heart, attend to* it:—Med. *to throw oneself upon, attack.* II. intr. *to strike against, make an attack* or *assault upon, engage*: also *to attack, assail: to approach, come to.* 2. *to put in* with a ship, *come to* land or port.

προσβάς, ᾶσα, άν, aor. 2 part. of προσβαίνω.

πρόσβᾰσις, ἡ, (προσβαίνω) *a means of approach, access.*

προσβᾰτός, ή, όν, (προσβαίνω) *accessible.*

προσ-βῐάζομαι, f. -άσομαι, Dep. *to force, compel, constrain to a* thing. II. in aor. 1 pass. προσβιασθῆναι, *to be forced* or *hard pressed.*

προσ-βῐβάζω: f. -βιβάσω Att. -βιβῶ:—Causal of προσβαίνω, *to bring* or *convey to*: metaph. *to bring over, persuade.*

προσ-βλέπω, f. ψω, *to look at* or *upon.*

προσ-βλώσκω, f. -μολοῦμαι: aor. 2 -έμολον:—*to come* or *go to, to reach, arrive at: to approach.*

προσ-βοάω, f. -βοήσομαι, *to call to*:—Med., Ion. aor. 1 προσεβωσάμην, *to call to oneself, call in.*

προσ-βοηθέω Ion. -βωθέω, f. ήσω, *to come to aid, come up with succour: to bring succour* or *support to.*

προσβολή, ἡ, (προσβάλλω) *a putting to* or *upon; applying.* II. *a falling upon, an attack, assault*; προσβολὴ Ἀχαιῖς *an attack* of the Achaeans 2. generally, *a going towards, a means of approaching: an approach.* 3. of ships, *a place to touch at, harbour.*

πρόσ-γειος, ον, (πρός, γέα = γῆ) *near the earth: near land.*

πρόσ-βορρος, ον, (πρός, βορέας) *exposed to the north wind.*

προσ-γελάω, f. -άσομαι [ᾰ], *to look with a smile upon, to gladden*, Lat. *arridere.*

προσ-γίγνομαι, later **προσ-γίν-** [ῐ]: fut. -γενήσομαι: pf. -γεγένημαι: Dep.:—*to come* or *go to, attach oneself to.* 2. generally, *to be added, accrue*, Lat. *accedere.* 3. *to arrive*: of things, *to come to, happen to.*

προσ-γράφω, f. ψω: pf. -γέγρᾰφα, pass. -γέγραμμαι:—*to write besides, annex a clause* or *codicil*; τὰ προσγεγραμμένα *conditions added to a treaty.*

προσγυμνάζω, f. άσω, *to exercise at* or *with.*

προσ-δᾰνείζω, f. σω, *to lend in addition to*:—Med. with pf. pass. προσδεδάνεισμαι, *to have lent one, borrow in addition.*

προσ-δᾰπᾰνάω, f. ήσω, *to spend besides.*

πρόσδεγμα, ατος, τό, (προσδέχομαι) *reception.*

προσ-δεῖ, impers. *there is still wanting.* 2. c. gen. *there is still need of.*

προσ-δέκομαι, Ion. for προσδέχομαι.

προσ-δέομαι Dor. poët. **ποτι-δεύομαι**: f. -δεήσω: aor. 1 pass. -εδεήθην: Dep.:—*to be in want of, stand in need of besides*: absol. *to be in want.* II. *to beg* or *ask of* another: *to beg* one *to* do.

προσ-δέρκομαι Dor. **ποτι-δέρκομαι**: fut. med. -δέρξομαι: aor. 1 pass. -εδέρχθην; and in same sense aor. 2 act. -έδρᾰκον, pf. -δέδορκα: Dep.:—*to look at, behold.*

πρόσδετος, ον, (προσδέω) *tied to* a thing.

προσ-δεύομαι. poët. for προσδέομαι, Dor. **ποτιδ-**.

προσ-δέχομαι Ion. **προσ-δέκομαι**: fut. -δέξομαι: pf. -δέδεγμαι: Ep. aor. 2 προσεδέγμην, with Dor. part. ποτιδέγμενος:—*to accept* or *receive favourably*: *to admit into one's presence*: generally *to admit.* II. *to wait for* or *expect* a thing: absol. *to wait patiently, abide.*

προσ-δέω (A), f. -δήσω: pf. pass. προσδέδεμαι:—*to tie, bind,* or *fasten to* or *on.*

προσ-δέω (B), f. -δεήσω, *to need besides.*

προσ-δηλέομαι, f. -ήσομαι, Dep. *to injure* or *ruin besides.*

προσ-διαβάλλω, *to calumniate besides.* II. *to insinuate besides.*

προσ-διαιρέομαι, Dep. *to distinguish further.*

προσ-διαλέγομαι, aor. 1 pass. -διελέχθην, Dep. *to converse besides with.*

προσ-διαμαρτῠρέω, f. ήσω, *to testify in addition.*

προσ-διανέμω, *to distribute*:—Med. *to divide among themselves.*

προσ-διαπασσᾰλεύω, *to fasten to with nails.*

προσ-διαπράσσω, f. ξω, *to achieve* or *accomplish besides*:—Med. *to achieve for oneself besides.*

προσ-διαφθείρω, f. -φθερῶ: pf. -έφθαρκα, pass. έφθαρμαι: aor. 2 pass. -εφθάρην [ᾰ]:—*to destroy besides*:—Pass. *to perish besides.*

προσ-δίδωμι, f. δώσω, *to give besides* or *in addition.*

προσ-διηγέομαι, f. ήσομαι, Dep. *to narrate besides.*

προσ-δικάζω, f. άσω, *to award as a judge to* a person:—Med. *to be engaged in a lawsuit.*

προσ-διορθόω, f. ώσω, *to ordain besides*:—Med. *to correct oneself besides.*

προσ-διορίζω, f. σω, *to define* or *specify besides.*

προσ-δῐώκω, f. ξω, *to pursue besides.*

προσ-δοκάω Ion. -έω: fut. ήσω· aor. 1 -εδόκησα: *to expect, look for*: *to await.*

προσ-δοκέω, f. -δόξω: aor. 1 -έδοξα: *to seem* or *be thought besides.*

προσδόκητος, ον, (προσδοκάω) *expected.*

προσδοκία, ἡ, (προσδοκάω) *a looking for, expectation, anticipation,* whether of good or bad; πρὸς προσδοκίαν according to *expectation.*

προσδόκιμος, ον, (προσδοκάω) *expected, looked for,* or *to be expected*; ἐπὶ Μίλητον προσδόκιμος *expected to come against* Miletus.

προσ-δόρπιος Dor. **ποτιδόρπιος**, ον, (πρός, δόρπον) *belonging to* or *serving for supper.*

προσ-δρᾰκεῖν, aor. 2 inf. of προσδέρκομαι.

προσδρᾰμεῖν, aor. 2 inf. of προστρέχω: **προσδραμών**, part.: formed from obsol. δρέμω.

προσ-εάω, f. άσω [ᾱ], *to suffer to go further.*

προσέβην, aor. 2 of προσβαίνω.

προσεβήσετο, Ep. for -ατο, 3 sing. aor. 1 med. of προσβαίνω.

προσ-εγγίζω, f. σω, *to bring near.* II. intr. *to approach, draw near.*

προσ-εγγράφω, f. ψω, *to inscribe besides upon a pillar*: esp. *to add a limiting clause.*

προσ-εγγῠάομαι, f. -ήσομαι, Med. *to become surety besides.*

προσ-εγχρίω, f. ίσω [ῑ] *to smear on besides*: *to besmear* or *bedaub besides.*

προσ-εδᾰφίζω, f. σω, *to fasten to the ground*: generally *to make fast.*

προσεδρεία or -ία, ἡ, *a setting by* or *near*: esp. *a sitting down before* a place, *besieging, blockade,* Lat. *obsessio.* 2. *close attention to* a thing, Lat. *assiduitas*:—esp. *a sitting by a sick-bed.* From

προσεδρεύω, f. σω, (πρόσεδρος) *to sit beside* or *near, be near to,* Lat. *assidere.* 2. *to attend constantly.*

προσεδρία, ἡ, = προσεδρεία.

πρόσ-εδρος, ον, (πρός, ἕδρα) *sitting* or *abiding near;* πρόσεδρος λιγνὺς *the surrounding* smoke.

προσέειπε, Ep. for προσεῖπε: see προσεῖπον.

προσέθηκα, aor. 1 of προστίθημι.

προσ-εθίζω, f. σω, *to accustom* or *inure* one *to* a thing:—Pass. *to accustom* or *inure oneself to* a thing.

προσ-ειδέναι, -δώς, inf. and part. of πρόσοιδα.

προσ-εῖδον, inf. προσιδεῖν, part. προσιδών: aor. 2 without any pres. in use, προσοράω being used instead: inf. med. προσιδέσθαι:—*to look at* or *upon.* II. Pass. προσείδομαι, *to appear beside* or *near to, to be like.*

προσεῖκα, Att. for προσέοικα, q. v.

προσ-εικάζω, f. σω: aor. 1 -ήκᾰσα:—*to make like to, liken to, make to resemble*:—Pass. *to be like, resemble.* II. metaph. *to compare.*

προσ-είκελος, η, ον, also ος, ον, *somewhat like.*

προσ-ειλέω Dor. **ποτι-ειλέω**, *to press* or *force upon* or *against, compress.*

προσείληφα, -είλημμαι, pf. act. and pass. of προσλαμβάνω.

προσειλόμην, aor. 2 med. of προσαιρέω.

πρόσ-ειλος, ον, (πρός, εἵλη) *towards the sun, sunny, warm, light.*

πρόσ-ειμι, inf. προσιέναι: impf. προσ-ήειν Ion. -ήια Att. -ῇα: aor. 2 part. προσιών: (πρός, εἶμι *ibo*):—*to go to* or *towards*: *to approach* one. 2. in hostile sense, *to go* or *come against, attack.* 3. *to come forward* to speak. II. of Time, *to come on.* III. *to come in*; τὰ προσιόντα χρήματα or τὰ προσιόντα alone, *the public income, revenue*, Lat. *reditus*.

πρόσ-ειμι, inf. προσεῖναι: impf. προσῆν: (προς, εἰμί *sum*):—*to be at, near* or *by, to be against*. II. *to be added to, attached to: to belong to, be in:* absol. *to be there, be offered.*

προσ-εῖπον, inf. προσειπεῖν: aor. 2 without any pres. in use (προσαγορεύω being used instead):—*to speak to* one, *to address* or *accost: to salute.* 2. *to call* so and so: *to name*

προσ-εισπράσσω, f. ξω, *to exact payment of besides.*

προ-σείω, f. σω, *to hold out and shake;* προσείειν χεῖρα *to shake* one's hand *with a threatening gesture: to hold out as a bugbear, menace* one *with.*

προσ-εκβάλλω, *to cast out* or *expel besides.*

προσ-εκπέμπω, f. ψω, *to send away besides.*

προσ-εκπυρόω, f. ώσω, *to kindle, set on fire besides.*

προσ-εκτέον, verb. Adj. of προσέχω, *one must apply:* absol. *one must attend.*

προσεκτικός, ή, όν, (προσέχω) *attentive.*

προσ-εκτίλλω, *to pluck out besides.*

προσέκυρσα, aor. 1 of προσκυρέω.

προσ-εκχλευάζω, f. σω, *to ridicule besides.*

προσ-ελαύνω, f. -ελάσω [ᾰ], Att. -ελῶ: aor. 1 -ήλᾰσα:—*to drive towards* II. intr., 1. (sub. ἵππον or ἅρμα), *to ride towards, ride up to*, Lat. *adequitare.* 2. (sub. στρατόν), *to march up, proceed, arrive.*

προσέλεκτο, 3 sing. Ep. aor. 2 pass. of προσλέγω.

προσελέω, false form for **προυσελέω**.

προσελθεῖν, προσελθών, aor. 2 inf. and part. of προσέρχομαι.

προσ-έλκω, f. -έλξω or -ελκύσω [ῠ]: aor. 1 -είλκῡσα:—*to draw to* or *towards, draw on:*—Med. *to draw towards* oneself, *attract.*

προσ-ελλείπω, f. ψω, *to be still wanting.*

προσ-εμβαίνω, f. -εμβήσομαι: aor. 2 -ενέβην:—*to step upon: to trample upon*, Lat. *insultare.*

προσ-εμβλέπω, f. ψω, *to look into besides.*

προσ-εμπικραίνομαι, Pass., with fut. med. -ανοῦμαι, *to be angry with besides* or *further.*

προσ-εμφερής, ές, *resembling.*

προσ-ένᾱχε, Dor. for προσ-ένηχε, 3 sing. impf. of προσνήχω.

προσ-ενδείκνῡμι, f. -ενδείξω, *to declare besides:*—Med. *to shew oneself off to another.*

προσ-ενεχῠράζω, f. σω, *to seize as an additional pledge for payment.*

προσ-ενθῡμέομαι: fut. med. -ενθυμήσομαι and pass. -ενθυμηθήσομαι: Dep.:—*to think on* or *take into consideration besides.*

προσ-εννέπω, *to address, accost.* 2. *to intr* or *command* to do, c. inf. 3. *to call by name.*

προσ-εννοέω, f. ήσω, *to think on* or *observe besides.*

προσ-εντείνω, f. -τενῶ, *to inflict besides.*

προσ-εντέλλομαι, Dep. *to enjoin* or *command besides.*

προσ-εξαιρέομαι, Med. *to choose out for oneself* or *select besides.*

προσ-εξᾰμαρτάνω, f. -αμαρτήσομαι, *to fail still more.*

προσ-εξανδρᾰποδίζομαι, Att. fut. -ιοῦμαι: Dep.:—*to enslave utterly besides.*

προσ-εξανίστημι, f. -στήσω, *to make to stand forth* besides:—Pass., with aor. 2 act. *to rise up to.*

προσ-εξεργάζομαι, f. -άσομαι: Dep.:—*to work out* or *accomplish besides:* the pf. προσεξείργασμαι is used in the depon. sense, but also takes a pass. sense, *to have been achieved* or *effected besides:* cf. ἐργάζομαι.

προσ-εξετάζω, f. σω, *to examine, search into besides.*

προσ-εξευρίσκω, f. -ευρήσω, *to find out besides.*

προσ-έοικα, pf. with pres. sense, Att. **προσεῖκα**, inf. προσεικέναι: there is also a pass. form of pf., προσῄγμαι:—*to be like* or *resemble* in a thing. II. *to seem fit.* III. *to seem* to do.

προσ-επαινέω, f. έσω, *to praise besides.*

προσ-επαιτιάομαι, f. -άσομαι [ᾱ]:—*to accuse besides.*

προσ-επεμβαίνω, f. -βήσομαι, = προσεμβαίνω.

προσ-επεξευρίσκω, f. -ευρήσω, *to invent* or *devise for any purpose besides.*

προσέπεσον, aor. 2 of προσπίπτω.

προσ-επιβάλλω, f. -βᾰλῶ, *to throw upon besides, to add over and above*

προσ-επιγράφω [ᾰ], f. ψω, *to write upon besides.*

προσ-επίκειμαι, Pass. *to press* or *bear hard upon.*

προσ-επικτάομαι, f. -ήσομαι, Dep. *to gain* or *acquire besides: to make additions to.*

προσ-επιλαμβάνομαι, Med. *to help to take hold of* a thing: *to help* or *succour*, esp. in war

προσ-επιορκέω, f. ήσω, *to swear a false oath besides.*

προσ-επιπνέω, f. -πνεύσομαι, *to blow against still.*

προσ-επιπονέω, f. ήσω, *to trouble oneself still more.*

προσ-επισκώπτω, f. ψω, *to jest at besides.*

προσ-επίσταμαι, fut. med. -επιστήσομαι, aor. 1 pass. -ηπιστήθην: Dep.:—*to understand* or *know besides.*

προσ-επιστέλλω, f. -στελῶ: *to notify, enjoin, charge besides;* esp. *by letter.*

προσ-επισφρᾱγίζομαι, Att. fut. -ιοῦμαι:—Med.:—*to set one's seal to besides:* hence *to confirm* or *ratify besides*

προσ-επιτέρπομαι, Pass. *to enjoy oneself besides* or *still more.*

προσ-επιτροπεύω, f. σω, *to act as guardian to one further:*—Pass. *to be subject to as guardian, be the ward of* another.

προσ-επιφωνέω, f. ήσω, *to say by way of addition.*

προσ-επιχᾰρίζομαι, f. -ίσομαι, Dep. *to gratify besides.*

προσεπτάμην [ᾰ], aor. 2 of προσπέτομαι.

προσ-εργάζομαι, f. -άσομαι: pf. -είργασμαι: Dep.:—*to work* or *effect besides.*

πρόσ-εργος, ον, (πρός, ἔργον) *industrious.*

προσ-ερεύγομαι, Dep. *to vomit forth against:* metaph., κύματα προσερεύγεται πέτρην the waves *break foaming against* the rocks.

προσερέω Att. contr. **προσερῶ**, fut. to *προσεῖπον*:—*to speak to, to address.*

πρόσ-ερίζω, f. *σω*, *to strive, vie with* or *against.*

προσ-έρομαι, f. *-ερήσομαι*: aor. *-ηρόμην*, inf. *-ερέσθαι*: Dep.:—*to ask besides.*

προσ-έρπω Dor. **ποθέρπω**: f. *ψω*: aor. 1 *προσείρπυσα*:—*to creep* or *steal on, approach, draw nigh*; *ὁ προσέρπων χρόνος the coming* time; *τὸ πρόσερπον* the *coming event*, the *future.*

προσέρρηξα, aor. 1 of *προσρήγνυμι.*

προσ-ερυγγάνω, = *προσερεύγομαι.*

προσ-έρχομαι, impf. *-ηρχόμην*, f. *-ελεύσομαι* (but the Att. impf. and fut. are *προσῄειν, πρόσειμι*): Dep. with act. aor. 2 *-ῆλθον*, pf. *-ελήλυθα*:—*to come* or *go to*: *to come forward*: absol. *to approach, draw nigh*; also *to be nigh at hand.* 2. *to visit, associate with.* 3. in hostile sense, *to go* or *march against.* II. *to come in*, of revenue, Lat. *redire.*

προσ-ερωτάω, f. *ήσω*, *to ask* or *question besides.*

προσ-έσπερος Dor. **ποθ-έσπερος**, *ον*, *verging towards evening*: neut. pl. *τὰ ποθέσπερα* as Adv., *towards evening.*

προσ-εταιρίζομαι, Med. *to take to oneself as a friend, choose as one's comrade, attach to oneself.* Hence

προσεταιριστός, *όν*, *joined with as a comrade, attached to a party.*

προσ-έτι, Adv. *over and above, besides.*

πρόσευξαι, aor. 1 imperat. of *προσεύχομαι.*

προσ-ευπορέω, f. *ήσω*, *to procure* or *supply besides*: *be provided with.*

προσ-ευρίσκω, f. *-ευρήσω*, *to find besides.*

προσ-ευχή, *ἡ*, *prayer.* II. *a place of prayer.* From

προσ-εύχομαι, f. *-ξομαι*, Dep. *to offer prayers* or *vows*: absol. *to worship*: also c. acc. *to pray for* a thing.

προσέφην, *ης*, *η*, aor. 2 of *πρόσφημι.*

προσεχής, *ές*, (*προσέχω*) of place, *adjoining, bordering upon, close to, next.*

προσ-έχω, f. *ξω*: aor. 2 *προσέσχον*: pf. *προσέσχηκα*:—*to have besides* or *in addition.* II. *to hold to, bring to* or *near*; *προσέχειν ναῦν to bring* a ship *to port* or *to land*; and without *ναῦν*, *to put in* or *touch at* a place; *προσέχειν τῇ γῇ, τῇ νήσῳ* to *touch* at: *to land*: sometimes also *ναυσὶ προσέχειν.* III. *προσέχειν τὸν νοῦν, to turn one's mind, thoughts, attention to* a thing, Lat. *animum advertere*: also without *τὸν νοῦν*, *to attend*; *προσέχειν ἑαυτῷ to give heed to* oneself. 2. *to devote oneself to* a thing. 3. *to pay court to.* IV. Med. *to attach oneself to* a thing, *cling, cleave to* it: also *to devote oneself to the service of* any one. V. Pass. *to be held fast by* a thing: *to be implicated in.*

προσ-εῷος, *ον*, (*πρός, ἕως*) *towards dawn* or *morning.*

προσ-ζεύγνῡμι, f. *-ζεύξω*, *to yoke* or *fasten to*:—Pass. *to be bound* or *yoked to.*

πρόσ-ηβος, *ον*, (*πρός, ἥβη*) *near manhood.*

προσήγᾰγον, aor. 2 of *προσάγω.*

προσηγορέω, f. *ήσω*, (*προσήγορος*) *to address kindly*: *to console.* Hence

προσηγόρημα, *ατος*, *τό*, *the object of an address.*

προσηγορία, *ἡ*, (*προσηγορέω*) *an addressing kindly, friendly greeting.* II. *a naming, name.*

προσ-ήγορος, *ον*, (*πρός, ἀγορεύω*) *addressing, accosting*; *αἱ προσήγοροι δρύες the speaking* oaks: c. gen., *εὐγμάτων Παλλάδος προσήγορος addressing* prayers to Pallas: generally, *affable.* II. pass. *addressed, accosted*:—as Subst. *προσήγορος, ὁ, an acquaintance.*

προσηδάφισμαι, pf. pass. of *προσεδᾰφίζω.*

προσῄιξαι, 2 sing. pf. pass. of *προσέοικα.*

προσηκάμην, aor. 1 med. of *προσίημι.*

προσηκόντως, Adv. pres. part. of *προσήκω*, *suitably, fitly, becomingly.*

προσῆκον, part. neut. of *προσήκω* used absol., *it being fit* or *becoming*, Lat. *quum conveniat* or *conveniret.*

προσ-ήκω, *to have come to, to have arrived at* a place: *to be near, be at hand.* 2. metaph. *to belong to.* II. impers., *προσήκει πρός τινα it concerns, has reference to* one; c. dat., *προσήκει μοι it is* my *business.* 2. *it belongs to, beseems, befits*: see *προσῆκον.* III. the Partic. *προσήκων, ουσα, ον*, is very common, *belonging to, befitting, beseeming*: and of persons, *related, akin*: *οἱ προσήκοντες* (in full *οἱ προσήκοντες γένει*), *one's kinsmen, relatives*: *τὸ προσῆκον* or *τὰ προσήκοντα that which belongs to one*; *all that is proper to oneself*; *τὴν προσήκουσαν σωτηρίαν ἐκπορίζεσθαι* to devise means for *one's own* safety; *τὰ προσήκοντα what is fit* or *seemly, one's duties.*

προσ-ήλιος, *ον*, (*πρός, ἥλιος*) *towards the sun, exposed to the sun, sunny.*

προσ-ηλόω, f. *ώσω*, *to nail, pin*, or *affix to.* II. *to nail up, shut close up.*

προσήλῠθον, aor. 2 of *προσέρχομαι.*

προσ-ήλῠτος, *ον*, (*προσήλυθον*) *come to, arrived at*:—as Subst., *προσήλῠτος, ὁ, a new comer, stranger*, Lat. *advĕna*: hence, *one who has come over to Judaism, a convert, proselyte.*

πρόσ-ημαι, properly pf. of *προσέζομαι*: Pass.:—*to sit upon* or *close to*: *to remain close to.*

προ-σημαίνω, f. *ανῶ*: aor. 1 *προεσήμηνα*:—*to give previous* or *public intimation*: *to foretell, announce.* II. *to proclaim, publish.*

προσήνεγκα, used as aor. 1 of *προσφέρω.*

προσ-ήνεμος, *ον*, (*πρός, ἄνεμος*) *towards the wind, windward.*

προσηνέχθην, used as aor. 1 pass. of *προσφέρω.*

προσ-ηνής Dor. **προσ-ανής**, *ές*, (*πρός, ἐΰς*) *soft, gentle, kindly*: *well-disposed*: hence *inclined, suitable to.* Adv. *προσηνῶς.*

προσήρτημαι, pf. pass. of *προσαρτάω.*

προσηύδα, 3 sing. impf. of *προσαυδάω.*

προσ-ηῷος, *ον*, (*πρός, ἠώς*) Ion. for **προσεῷος**, *towards morn*: neut. as Adv. in Dor. form **τὸ ποτ-αῷον**, *towards morning.*

προσ-θᾶκέω, f. ήσω, *to sit beside, near* or *upon.*

πρόσθε, Ion. and poët. for *πρόσθεν.*

προσθεῖναι, προσθείς, aor. 2 inf. and part. of *προστίθημι.*

πρόσθεν Ion. and poët. **πρόσθε**: (*πρό*).
As Prep. with gen.: I. of Place, *before, in front of, in defence of.* II. of Time, *before.*
As Adv.: of Place, *before, in front, to the front, forwards:* with the Art., *εἰς τὸ πρόσθεν forward, further, to the front.* II. of Time, *before, formerly, of old:* also c. Art., *ἡ πρόσθεν ἡμέρα* the day *before:* also *τὸ πρόσθεν* as Adv., *formerly.* III. also *before,* in sense of *sooner,* Lat. *potius; πρόσθεν ἀποθανεῖν ἤ ..* to die *sooner than* ..

προσθέοντο, Ion. for *προσθεῖτο*, aor. 2 med. opt. of *προστίθημι.*

πρόσθες, aor. 2 imperat. of *προστίθημι.*

πρόσθεσις, ἡ, (*προστίθημι*) *a putting to, application.* II. *an adding, an addition*

προσθητέον, verb. Adj. of *προστίθημι*, *one must add:* also *one must teach.*

πρόσθετος, *ον*, or *η, ον*, verb. Adj. of *προστίθημι*, *added, fitted* or *adapted to: put on*, of false hair.

προσ-θέω, f. *-θεύσομαι*, *to run towards* or *to.*

προσθήκη, ἡ, (*προστίθημι*) *an addition, appendage, supplement.* 2. *something added, a mere accident.* II. *aid, help, assistance.*

πρόσθημα, *ατος, τό*, (*προστίθημι*) *an addition.*

προσ-θιγγάνω, f. *-θίξω*: aor. 2 *προσέθιγον*, inf. *προσθιγεῖν* :—*to touch.*

πρόσθιος, *α, ον*, (*πρόσθεν*) *the foremost; οἱ πρόσθιοι πόδες the fore* feet.

προσθό-δομος, ὁ, (*πρόσθε, δόμος*) *the chief of a house.*

προσθοῦ, aor. 2 med. imperat. of *προστίθημι*

προσ-θροέω, f. *ήσω*, *to call to, address*

προσ-θύμιος, *ον*, (*πρός, θυμός*) *according to one's mind, agreeable, welcome.*

προσιδεῖν, προσιδών, aor. 2 inf. and part. of *προσεῖδον.*

προσ-ιζάνω, *to sit by* or *near.* II. *to be always near, cleave to, follow close*, Lat. *instare*

προσ-ίζω, f. *-ιζήσω*, *to sit by* or *near*

προσ-ίημι: fut. *προσήσω*, med. *-ήσομαι*: aor. 1 *προσῆκα*, med. *-ηκάμην* :—*to send to* or *towards, let come to: to apply.* II. Med. *προσίεμαι*, *to let come to* or *near* one, *suffer to approach, admit.* 2. *to admit, allow, accede to, believe: to approve.* 3. *to accept, submit to, put up with.* 4. c. inf. *to undertake* to do, *venture:* c. acc. pers. *to please* one; *ἓν οὐ προσίεταί με* one thing *pleases* me not.

προσ-ικνέομαι, f. *-ίξομαι*, Dep. *to come to, arrive at, reach:* c. gen. *to reach so far as, come up to.* 2. *to come to as a suppliant.* Hence

προσίκτωρ, *ορος*, ὁ, *one that comes to the temples, a suppliant.* II. pass. *he to whom one comes as a suppliant, a protector, guardian.*

προσ-ιππεύω, f. *σω*, *to ride up to, charge.*

προσ-ίστημι, f. *-στήσω*: *to place near, bring near.* II. Pass. *προσίσταμαι*, with intr. tenses of Act., aor. 2 *-έστην*, pf. *-έστηκα* :—*to stand near to, beside* or *at:* also *to come to, arrive at.* 2. metaph., *προσίσταταί τί μοι* something *occurs* to me. 3. *to set oneself against:* hence *to offend, give offence to.*

προσ-ιστορέω, f. *ήσω*, *to narrate besides.*

προσ-ίσχω, = *προσέχω*, *to hold towards* or *against:* intr. *to put to land, put into port* :—Med. *to stick* or *cleave to.*

προσιτός, *ή, όν*, verb. Adj. of *πρόσειμι* (*εἶμι ibo*), *approachable.*

προσιών, *οῦσα, όν*, aor. 2 part. of *πρόσειμι* (*εἶμι ibo*).

προσ-καθέζομαι, f. *-καθεδοῦμαι*: aor. 2 *-καθεζόμην.* Dep. :—*to sit by, near, beside.* II. *to sit down before* a town, *besiege it*, Lat. *obsidere.*

προσ-κάθημαι Ion. **-κάτημαι**, properly pf. of *προσκαθέζομαι*: Pass. :—*to sit by* or *near, to sit beside* one, *to live with.* II. *to sit down before* a town, *besiege* it, Lat. *obsidere.*

προσ-καθέλκω, aor. 1 *-καθείλκυσα*, *to haul down besides.*

προσ-καθίζω, f. *σω*, *to sit down by* or *near:* also c. acc. cognato, *θᾶκον προσκαθίζειν*, *to sit on* a seat

προσ-καθίστημι, f. *στήσω*, *to appoint besides.*

προσ-καθοπλίζω, f. *σω*, *to arm* or *equip besides.*

πρόσ-καιρος, *ον*, *lasting but for a time, transitory*

προσ-καίω, f. *-καύσομαι*, *to set on fire besides* :—Pass., pf. *προσκέκαυμαι*, *to be burnt through; σκεύη προσκεκαυμένα* pots *burnt through:* also *to be inflamed with love, to be in love with.*

προσ-κᾰλέω, f. *έσω*, *to call to, call on, summon* :—Med. *to call to oneself, call to one's aid.* 2. in Att of a prosecutor, *to call into court, summon, accuse, lay an indictment against;* in full, *δίκην ἀσεβείας προσκαλεῖν πρὸς τὸν βασιλέα to bring an action* for impiety *against* .., but commonly without *δίκην προσκαλεῖν τινα ἀνανδρίας* (sub. *δίκην*) *to bring an action* for cowardice *against* :—Pass., *ὁ προσκληθείς the party summoned.*

προσ-κάρδιος Dor. **ποτι-κ-**, *ον*, (*πρός, καρδία*) *on* or *at the heart.*

προσ-καρτερέω, f. *ήσω*, *to persevere in* a thing. 2. *to adhere firmly to* a man. Hence

προσκαρτέρησις, ἡ, *perseverance.*

προσ-καταβαίνω, f. *-βήσομαι*, *to go down to besides*

προσ-καταβάλλω, f. *-βαλῶ*, *to pay so as to make up a deficiency.* Hence

προσκατάβλημα, *ατος, τό*, *that which is paid in addition, a sum paid to make up a deficiency* in the revenue.

προσ-καταγιγνώσκω, f. *-γνώσομαι*, *to condemn besides.* II. *to adjudge* or *award to.*

προσ-καταισχύνω, f. *ῠνῶ*, *to disgrace still further*

προσ-καταλέγω, f. *ξω*, *to enroll in addition to.*

προσ-καταλείπω, f. *ψω*, *to leave behind, bequeath besides:* also *to leave, lose besides.*

προσ-κατανέμω, f. *-νεμῶ*, *to allot* or *assign besides*

προσ-καταριθμέω, f. ήσω, *to count besides.*

προσ-κατασκευάζω, f. σω, *to furnish* or *prepare besides*:—Pass. *to be furnished* or *prepared besides.*

προσ-κατασύρω [ῡ], *to pull down besides.*

προσ-κατατίθημι, f. -καταθήσω, *to pay down besides, pay as a further deposit.*

προσ-κατηγορέω, f. ήσω, *to lay to one's charge besides*:—Pass. as logical term, *to be predicated besides.*

προσ-κάτημαι, Ion. for προσκάθημαι.

πρόσ-κειμαι Ion. **προσ-κέομαι**, f. -κείσομαι, serving as Pass. of προστίθημι, *to be placed* or *laid beside* or *upon, lie by, near,* or *upon*; τῇ θύρᾳ προσκεῖσθαι *to keep close to* the door. 2. *to lie with.* II. *to be joined with, involved in.* III. *to be attached* or *devoted to*; προσκεῖσθαι τῷ λεγομένῳ *to put faith in, subscribe to* a story: *to devote oneself to*: also in bad sense, *to be given* or *addicted to.* IV. *to press upon, solicit*: *to press close* or *hard.* V. of things, *to fall to* one, *belong to*: also *to be laid upon, imposed, inflicted*: also *to be added.*

προσκέκλημαι, pf. pass. of προσκαλέω.

προσ-κερδαίνω, f. δήσω, *to gain besides.*

προσ-κεφάλαιον, τό, *a cushion for the head, pillow*: also *a cushion for sitting on, a boat-cushion.*

προσ-κηδής, ές, (πρός, κῆδος) *attached to, affectionate.* II. *akin to, allied with.*

προσ-κηρῡκεύομαι, Dep. *to send a herald to* one.

προσ-κηρύσσω Att. **-ττω**, f. ξω, *to summon by herald.*

προσ-κιγκλίζω, (πρός, κίγκλος) *to move to and fro, wag the tail at*:—Pass., εὖ ποτεκιγκλίσδευ (2 sing. Dor. impf. for προσεκιγκλίζου) nimbly *didst thou twist* or *writhe about.*

προσ-κλάω, f. άσω [ᾰ], *to shatter* or *shiver against.*

προσ-κληρόω, f. ώσω, *to assign by lot*:—Pass. *to be associated with.*

πρόσκλησις, ἡ, (προσκαλέω) *a judicial summons.*

προσ-κλίνω, f. -κλῐνῶ: pf. pass. προσκέκλῐμαι, Dor. 3 sing. ποτικέκλιται:—*to make to lean against, to put to* or *against*:—Pass. *to lean against, to be turned towards.* Hence

πρόσκλῐσις, εως, ἡ, *inclination, bias, partiality.*

προσ-κλύζω, f. ύσω, *to wash with waves*: *to dash against,* of the waves.

προσ-κνάω, f. -κνήσω, *to rub against*:—Med. *to rub oneself against.*

προσ-κοιμίζομαι, Pass. *to go to sleep beside.*

προσ-κοινόω, f. ώσω, *to communicate to, give a share of* a thing to another.

προσ-κολλάω, f. ήσω, *to glue on* or *to*:—Pass. *to be fastened to, to cleave to.*

προσ-κομίζω, f. ίσω Att. ιῶ, *to carry* or *convey to* a place:—Med. *to bring with one, bring home*: *to import.*

πρόσκομμα, ατος, τό, (προσκόπτω) *a stumble*: *an occasion of stumbling, cause of offence* or *sin.*

προ-σκοπέω: fut. προσκέψομαι and aor. 1 προὐσκεψάμην (as if from προ-σκέπτομαι, which does not occur): pf. προὔσκεμμαι:—*to see beforehand, look out for*: *to provide against*:—Med. *to watch, take care of.* II. *to spy* or *reconnoitre beforehand.* Hence

προ-σκοπή, ἡ, *a spying* or *reconnoitring beforehand.*

προσ-κοπή, ἡ, (προσκόπτω) = πρόσκομμα.

πρό-σκοπος, ον, *seeing beforehand, foreseeing.* II. as Subst., πρόσκοποι, οἱ, *outposts, scouts.*

προσ-κόπτω, f. ψω, *to strike* or *dash against*; πρ. τὸν ποῦν *to strike* one's foot, i. e. *to stumble, against,* Lat. *offendere.* II. metaph. *to mistake, err.* 2. *to take offence, be angry at.*

προσ-κορής, ές, (πρός, κορέννυμι) *causing satiety, palling, disgusting.*

πρόσ-κρᾱνος, ον, (πρός, κρᾶνον) *on* or *for the head*:—as Subst., **πρόσκρᾱνον** Dor. **ποτικρ-**, τό, *a cushion for the head, pillow.*

προσ-κρούω, f. σω, *to strike against*: *to have a collision with, quarrel with.*

προσ-κτάομαι, f. -κτήσομαι: pf. -κέκτημαι: Dep.:—*to gain, get* or *win besides*: *to win over to one's side* or *party*: pf. part. also in pass. sense, τὰ προσκεκτημένα *things acquired besides.*

προσ-κῠλίω, f. -κυλίσω [ῑ]: aor. 1 -εκύλῑσα:—*to roll to* or *against.*

προσ-κῠνέω, f. ήσω: aor. 1 προσεκύνησα poët. προσέκῠσα:—*to prostrate* oneself *before* in token of respect, *to do obeisance to.* 2. of the gods, *to worship*: also *to deprecate* the wrath of the gods, *disarm* them *by worship.* Hence

προσκῠνητής, οῦ, ὁ, *a worshipper.*

προσ-κύπτω, f. ψω: pf. -κέκῡφα:—*to stoop to* or *over* one, *to stoop and whisper to* him.

προσ-κῠρέω, f. ήσω; with three irreg. tenses, impf. προσέκῠρον, f. προσκύρσω, aor. 1 προσέκυρσα:—*to reach, arrive at*, c. dat.: *to be at* or *near*: *to befall, betide*: c. acc. *to meet with.*

προσκύσαι, πρόσκῠσον, aor. 1 inf. and imper. of προσκυνέω.

πρόσ-κωπος, ον, (πρός, κώπη) *working at the oar*: as Subst., πρόσκωπος, ὁ, *a rower.*

προσλᾰβεῖν, aor. 2 inf. of προσλαμβάνω.

προσλᾰβών, προσλαβόμενος, aor. 2 part. act. and med. of προσλαμβάνω.

προσ-λαγχάνω, f. λήξομαι: aor. 2 -έλᾰχον: pf. -είληχα:—*to obtain by lot besides*; προσλαγχάνειν δίκην *to obtain the right of bringing* an action *besides.*

προσ-λάζῠμαι, Dep. = προσλαμβάνω.

προσ-λᾰλέω, f. ήσω, *to talk to* or *with.*

προσ-λαμβάνω, fut. -λήψομαι: aor. 2 -έλᾰβον: pf. -είληφα:—*to take* or *receive besides* or *in addition to*: *to get over and above, to gain* or *win besides*:—so also in Med. 2. *to take* another *to help one, take with one.* II. *to take hold of*: *to take part in*:—*to take hold of* a thing *besides*:—so also in Med., c. gen. rei, *to be accessory to, take part in* a work; and c. dat. pers. *to help, assist.*

προσ-λέγω, f. ξω, *to lay to* or *near*:—Pass. *to lie*

near or *by*; 3 sing. Ep. aor. 2 pass. προσέλεκτο. II. *to speak to, address, accost*:—Med. *to meditate*.

προσ-λεύσσω, *to look at* or *upon*.

πρόσληψις, ἡ, (προσλαμβάνω) *a taking* or *assuming besides*: *an assumption*.

προσ-λιπαρέω, f. ήσω, *to persist* or *persevere in*. II. *to importune*, c. dat. Hence

προσλιπάρησις, ἡ, *importunity*.

προσ-λογίζομαι, f. ίσομαι Att. ιοῦμαι, Dep. *to reckon* or *count in addition to*. II. *to impute to*. Hence

προσλογιστέον or plur. -έα, verb. Adj. *one must count besides, reckon in*.

προσμαθητέον, verb. Adj. *one must learn besides*. From

προσ-μανθάνω, f. -μαθήσομαι, *to learn besides*.

προσ-μαρτυρέω, f. ήσω, *to bear witness besides, bear additional witness*: *to confirm by additional evidence*.

προσ-μάσσω, f. ξω: aor. 1 -έμαξα:—Pass., aor. 1 προσεμάχθην: pf. -μέμαγμαι:—*to knead* or *plaster against, to attach closely to*; προσμάσσειν τὸν Πειραιᾶ τῇ πόλει *to knead* or *stick on* Peiræeus to the city:—Pass. *to be stuck fast to*; πλευραῖσι προσμαχθὲν *stuck close to* his sides: so aor. 1 med. with pass. sense, ποτιμαξάμενος, *stuck* or *sticking close to* (the hand).

προσ-μάχομαι [ᾰ]: f. μαχέσομαι Att. -μαχοῦμαι: Dep.:—*to fight against*: esp. *to assault* a town.

προσμεῖναι, προσμείνας, aor. 1 inf. and part. of

προσ-μένω, f. -μενῶ, *to abide* or *wait still longer*; προσμένειν τινί *to remain* or *wait for some* one. II. trans. *to await*, c. acc.: *to abide* one in battle, *stand one's ground against*.

προσ-μεταπέμπομαι, Med. *to send for besides*.

προσ-μηχανάομαι, f. ήσομαι, Med. *to contrive besides for oneself*. II. Pass. *to be cunningly fastened to*.

προσ-μίγνυμι and -ύω: fut. -μίξω:—*to mingle* or *join with, unite to, bring to*. II. intr. *to come into contact with, come* or *go to a place*: also *to land, arrive at*. 2. of persons, *to hold intercourse with, meet with*:—in hostile sense, *to go against, to meet in battle, engage with*.

πρόσμιξις, ἡ, (προσμίγνυμι) *a mixing* or *mingling with*. II. *a coming to, approaching*. 2. *an attacking, assault*.

προσ-μίσγω, Ion. form of προσμίγνυμι.

προσ-μισέω, f. ήσω, *to hate besides*.

προσ-μισθόω, f. ώσω, *to let out for hire* or *interest besides*:—Med. *to take into one's hire, hire*.

προσ-μολεῖν, aor. 2 inf. of προσβλώσκω.

πρόσ-μορος, ον, *doomed to woe, ill-fated*.

προσ-μυθέομαι, f. ήσομαι: Dor. ποτι-μ-: Dep.:—*to address, accost*.

προσ-μυθολογέω, f. ήσω, *to chatter in*.

προσ-μύρομαι, Dep. *to flow to* or *with*. [ῡ]

προσ-ναυπηγέω, f. ήσω, *to build ships in addition*.

προσ-νάχω [ᾱ], Dor. for προσνήχω.

προσ-νέμω, f. -νεμῶ: aor. 1 -ένειμα:—*to allot, assign, devote* or *dedicate to*: *to add*:—Pass. *to be assigned*:—Med. *to grant on one's own part, to devote, dedicate*. 2. προσνέμειν ποίμνας *to drive* flocks *to pasture*.

προσ-νέω, f. -νεύσομαι, *to swim to* or *towards*.

προσ-νήχω, also as Dep. **προσ-νήχομαι**, *to swim towards*. II. of water, *to dash upon*.

προσ-νίσσομαι Dor. ποτιν-, Dep. *to come* or *go to*. II. *to come against*.

προσ-νοέω, f. ήσω, *to perceive besides*.

προσ-νωμάω, f. ήσω, *to put to one's lips*.

προσ-ξυν-: for all words so beginning, see προσσυν-.

προσ-όδιος, ον, (πρός, ὅδιος) *belonging to a solemn procession, processional*: τὸ προσόδιον (sub. μέλος) *a solemn thanksgiving*, Lat. *supplicatio*.

πρόσ-οδος, ἡ, *a going* or *coming to, an approach, advance*: in pl. πρόσοδοι, *onsets, attacks*. 2. *a solemn procession* to a temple. 3. *a coming forward to speak, leave to speak*. II. *income, rent*, esp. *the public revenue*; mostly in plur. *revenues, returns, profits*, Lat. *reditus, proventus*.

πρόσ-οιδα, pf. without any pres. in use, (πρός, οἶδα) *to know besides*. 2. προσειδέναι χάριν *to owe* thanks *beside*.

προσ-οικειόω, f. ώσω, *to assign to* a person *as his own*.

προσ-οικέω, f. ήσω, *to dwell by* or *near*; of towns, *to lie near* or *next*. II. trans. *to dwell in* or *near* a place.

προσ-οικοδομέω, f. ήσω, *to build in addition* or *near*.

πρόσ-οικος, ον, (πρός, οἰκέω) *dwelling near to, bordering on, neighbouring*: as Subst., πρόσοικος, ὁ, *a neighbour*.

προσοιστέος, α, ον, verb. Adj. of προσφέρω, *to be added to*. 2. neut. προσοιστέον *one must add*.

προσ-οίσω, used as fut. of προσφέρω.

προσ-οίχομαι, Dep. *to go to* a place.

προσ-οκέλλω, aor. 1 -ώκειλα, *to run ashore*.

προσ-ολοφύρομαι, Dep. *to utter one's sorrows to*.

προσ-ομαρτέω, f. ήσω, *to go along with*.

προσ-ομιλέω, f. ήσω, *to hold intercourse* or *converse with, associate with*. II. c. dat. loci, *to remain at* or *cling to* a place. III. *to busy oneself with, be engaged with* a thing.

προσ-όμνυμι, *to swear besides* or *in addition*.

προσ-όμοιος, ον, *nearly like, resembling*. Hence

προσομοιόω, f. ώσω, *to make like to*.

προσ-ομολογέω, f. ήσω, *to concede* or *grant besides*: *to acknowledge* a *further* debt. 2. *to promise besides*. 3. *to give in, surrender, come to terms*. Hence

προσ-όμουρος, ον, *adjoining, adjacent*.

προσ-ονομάζω, *to call by a name*; προσονομάζειν θεοὺς *to give* them *the name* θεοί.

προσ-οπτάζω Dor. ποτ-, poët. for προσοράω.

προσ-οράω, f. -όψομαι: aor. 2 -εἶδον:—*to look at*:—so also in Med. προσοράομαι.

προσ-ορέγομαι, Med. *to reach out after*: c. dat. *to be urgent* or *pressing with*.

πρόσ-ορθρος, ον, (πρός, ὄρθρος) *towards morning*: neut. as Adv. in Dor. form τὸ ποτόρθρον, *at dawn*.

προσ-ορίζω, f. σω, *to mark out besides*:—Med. *to mark out for oneself besides*; προσορίζεσθαι οἰκίαν *to have* a house *marked* in proof of a mortgage.

προσ-ορμίζω, f. σω, *to bring to anchor at* or *near* a place:—Pass. and Med., f. -ορμιοῦμαι, aor. 1 -ωρμισάμην and -ωρμίσθην, *to come to anchor near* a place. Hence

προσόρμῐσις, ἡ, *a coming to anchor* or *to land*.

προσ-ουδίζω, f. σω, (πρός, οὖδας) *to dash to earth*.

προσ-ουρέω, f. ήσω, *to make water upon*.

πρόσ-ουρος, ον, Ion. for πρόσορος, (πρός, ὅρος) *adjoining, bordering on, adjacent*; τὰ πρόσορα *the adjacent parts*; ἵν' αὐτὸς ἦν πρόσουρος where he was *his own neighbour*, i. e. lived in solitude.

προσ-οφείλω, f. ήσω, *to owe yet more, be in debt besides*:—Pass. *to be still owing, be still due*.

προσ-οφλισκάνω, f. -οφλήσω: aor. 2 -ῶφλον, inf. -οφλεῖν:—*to owe besides, to incur as a further debt*: generally, *to incur* or *deserve besides*: as law-term, *to lose one's suit and incur a penalty besides*.

προσ-οχθίζω, f. σω, *to be wroth with*: *to be offended at*.

πρόσ-οψις, ἡ, *appearance, aspect, look*; σὴ πρόσοψις thy *presence*, i. e. thine own *self, thou*. II. *a seeing, beholding, sight*.

προσ-παίζω, f. -παίξομαι: aor. 1 -έπαισα:—*to play, sport* or *jest with*. 2. *to laugh at, banter, mock*.

πρόσ-παιος, ον, (πρός, παίω) *striking upon*: *sudden, new, fresh, recent*:—ἐκ προσπαίου as Adv., *suddenly, newly*

προσ-πᾰλαίω, f. σω, *to wrestle* or *struggle with* one.

προσ-παραγράφω, *to write beside* or *in addition*.

προσ-παρακαλέω, f. έσω, *to call in besides, invite*.

προσ-παραμένω, *to remain near besides*.

προσ-παρασκευάζω, f. σω, *to prepare besides*.

προσπαρδεῖν, aor. 2 inf. of προσπέρδω.

προσ-παρέχω, f. ξω, *to furnish* or *provide besides*.

προσ-πασσᾰλεύω Att. -παττᾰλεύω, f. σω, *to nail fast on* or *to*. II. *to nail up* or *hang upon a peg*.

προσ-πάσχω, f. -πείσομαι, *to be affected besides*. II. *to be passionately in love with*.

πρόσ-πεινος, ον, (πρός, πεῖνα) *hungry, a-hungered*.

προσ-πελάζω, f. άσω, *to bring near to, drive against*. II. intr. and Pass. *to approach, come nigh to*.

προσ-πέμπω, f. ψω, *to send to*: *conduct* or *convoy to*.

προσ-πέρδομαι, with aor. 2 act. -έπαρδον, *oppedere*.

προσ-περιβάλλω, *to throw* or *put around besides*:—Med. *to put round oneself*:—Pass. *to be put* or *drawn round*. II. Med. *to compass, seek to obtain*.

προσ-περιγίγνομαι, Dep. *to remain over and above*.

προσ-περιλαμβάνω, *to embrace besides*.

προσ-περιποιέω, *to lay by* or *preserve besides*.

προσ-περονάω, f. ήσω, *to fasten with a pin to* or *on*.

προσπεσών, οῦσα, όν, aor. 2 part. of προσπίπτω.

προσ-πέτομαι, f. -πτήσομαι: aor. 2 -επτάμην [ᾰ], for which an aor. 2 act. προσέπτην is often used: Dep.:—*to fly to* or *towards*: *to come* or *light upon* one *suddenly*.

προσ-πεύθομαι, poët. for προσπυνθάνομαι.

προσ-πήγνῡμι and -ύω, f. -πήξω, *to fix to* or *on*: *affix to* the cross.

προσ-πιέζω, f. έσω, *to press* or *oppress besides*.

προσ-πίλνᾰμαι, Dep. *to approach quickly*

προσ-πίπτω, f. -πεσοῦμαι: aor. 2 -έπεσον:—*to fall upon* or *against*: *strike against*. 2. *to fall upon, attack, assault*. 3. *to fall upon* a person, *embrace* him, *join* him. 4. *to run* or *rush up to*: *to embrace*: *to join* 5. *to fall in with, light upon, encounter*. II. of events, *to fall upon, befall* one: *to happen, occur*. 2. *to come suddenly to one's knowledge*. III. *to fall down to* or *before, to prostrate oneself*: c. acc. *to fall down to, supplicate*.

προσ-πίτνω, poët. for προσπίπτω, *to fall upon*: *to embrace*. II. *to fall down to* or *before, supplicate*.

προσ-πλάζω, shortd. for προσπελάζω, intr. *to come near, draw nigh, approach*.

προσ-πλάσσω Att. -ττω: f. -πλάσω [ᾰ]: pf. pass. -πέπλασμαι:—*to form* or *mould upon*.

πρόσ-πλᾱτος, ον, (προσπλάζω) *approachable*.

προσ-πλέω, f. -πλεύσομαι: Ion. pres. **προσπλώω**:—*to sail towards* or *against*.

προσ-πληρόω, f. ώσω, *to fill up* or *complete* a number: *to man* ships *besides, man more* ships; and in Med. *to get* them *manned*.

προσπλωτός, ή, όν, *to* or *on which one may sail, navigable*. From

προσ-πλώω, Ion. for προσπλέω.

προσ-πνέω Ep. -πνείω: f. -πνεύσομαι:—*to blow* or *breathe upon, inspire*: impers. with gen., προσπνεῖ μοι κρεῶν *there is a smell* of meat.

προσ-ποιέω, f. ήσω, *to make over to, attach* or *add to*. II. Med. προσποιέομαι, *to add* or *attach to oneself*: of persons, *to bring over to one's own side, win* or *gain over* 2. of things, *to take to oneself, pretend to, lay claim to*, Lat. *affectare*. 3. generally, *to pretend, feign, affect*; c. inf. *to pretend* to do: also *to use as a pretence, allege, adduce*: δεῖ μὴ προσποιεῖσθαι one must *make as if it were* not, *pretend it is* not so. Lat. *dissimulare*. Hence

προσποίησις, ἡ, *a gaining for oneself, an acquisition*. 2. *a taking to oneself, pretence* or *claim to* a thing.

προσποιητός, όν (προσποιέω) *taken to oneself, assumed, adopted*.

προσ-πολεμέω, f. ήσω, *to carry on war against, be at war with*: also *to attack* or *harass in war*.

προσ-πολεμόω, f. ώσω, *to make hostile besides*:—Med. *to go to war with besides*.

προσ-πολέω, f. ήσω, *to attend* or *wait upon*:—Pass. *to be attended, ministered to.* From

πρόσ-πολος, ον, (πρός, πολέω) *serving*:—as Subst., πρόσπολος, ὁ and ἡ, *a servant*, esp. *a ministering priest* or *priestess*; πρόσπολος φόνου *minister* of death.

προσ-πορεύομαι, f. εύσομαι, Dep. *to go to, approach.*

προσ-πορίζω, f. ίσω Att. ιῶ, *to procure besides.*

προσ-πορπᾱτός, ή, όν, (πρός, πορπάω) *fastened on* or *to with a pin, close-fastened.*

πρόσ-πράσσομαι, f. -πράξομαι: aor. 1 -επραξάμην: Med.: (πρός, πράσσω):—*to exact* or *demand besides.*

πρόσπταισμα, ατος, τό, *a stumble.* From

προσ-πταίω, f. σω, *to strike against*: esp. *to strike one's foot against*, and absol. *to stumble, to limp, halt.* II. metaph. *to fail: to suffer a disaster* or *defeat.*

προσπτῆναι, inf. of προσέπτην, aor. 2 act. of προσπέτομαι.

προσ-πτήσσω, f. ξω, *to crouch* or *cower towards*; ἀκταὶ λιμένος ποτιπεπτηυῖαι (Ep. and Dor. for προσπεπτηχυῖαι, pf. part. pl. fem.) headlands *verging towards* the harbour, i. e. closing it in.

πρόσπτυγμα, ατος, τό, *that which is embraced, the object of one's embrace* or *caress.* From

προσ-πτύσσω, f. ξω, aor. 1 -έπτυξα:—*to embrace.* II. as Dep., **προσ-πτύσσομαι** Dor. **ποτι-** or **προτι-πτύσσομαι**: f. -πτύξομαι: pf. -έπτυγμαι:—of a garment, *to fold itself close to, cling close round.* 2. of persons, *to fold to one's bosom, clasp, embrace*: hence *to greet warmly, welcome.* 3. of a festival, *to celebrate.*

προσ-πτύω, f. -πτύσω [ῠ]:—*to spit upon*: aor. 1 part. προσπτύσας, *spitting in sign of contempt.*

προσ-πυνθάνομαι, f. -πεύσομαι: aor. 2 -επῠθόμην:—*to enquire* or *learn besides.*

προσ-ραίνω, *to sprinkle besides* or *about.*

προσραπτέον, verb. Adj. *one must sew on.* From

προσ-ράπτω, f. ψω, *to sew on.*

προσ-ρέω, f. -ρεύσομαι: aor. 2 pass. (in act. sense) -ερρύην:—*to flow to* or *towards, flow in a stream to*, hence *to gather, assemble.*

προσ-ρήγνῡμι, f. -ρήξω: aor. 1 -έρρηξα:—*to dash* or *beat against.*

πρόσ-ρημα, ατος, τό, *an address, salutation*: *a name, designation.*

πρόσ-ρησις, ἡ, *an addressing, accosting*: *a name.*

προσ-ρήσσω, = προσρήγνυμι.

προσ-ρίπτω, f. ψω, *to throw to.*

προσ-σαίνω, *to fawn upon*, of dogs: metaph. *to wheedle, flatter*: of things, *to please*, Lat. *arrideo.*

προσ-σέβω, *to worship* or *honour besides.*

πρόσσοθεν, poët. for πρόσωθεν, *forwards, onwards.*

προσσοτέρω, Adv., poët. for προσωτέρω.

προσ-σπαίρω, *to pant for* a thing.

προσ-στάζω Dor. **ποτι-**, *to drop on, shed over.*

προσ-σταυρόω, f. ώσω, *to draw a stockade along* or *in front of* a place, c. acc.

προσ-στείχω, aor. 2 -έστῐχον:—*to go to* or *towards.*

προσ-στέλλω, f. -στελῶ, *to compress in small compass*: pf. pass. part. προσεσταλμένος, *tight-drawn, tucked up.* Lat. *adstrictus.* II. *to fit to*: Med. *to keep close to.*

προσ-σῡκοφαντέω, f. ήσω, *to slander besides.*

προσ-συμβάλλομαι, Med. *to contribute to besides* or *at the same time*, c. gen.

προσ-συνίστημι, f. -συστησω, *to recommend further.*

προσ-συνοικέω, f. ήσω, *to settle with* others *in* a place, *make a joint settlement with.*

πρόσσω, Adv., poët. for πρόσω.

προσ-σωρεύω, *to heap up besides.*

προστᾰκείς, **προστᾰκῆναι**, aor. 2 pass. part. and inf. of προστήκω.

προστᾰθείς, aor. 1 pass. part. of προΐστημι.

προσ-σφάζω or **-σφάττω**, f. ξω, *to slay at* or *near.*

πρόσταγμα, ατος, τό, (προστάσσω) *an order, command*; ἐκ προστάγματος *by command.*

προσ-τᾰθείς, aor. 1 pass. part. of προστείνω.

προστακτέον, verb. Adj. of προστάσσω, *one must order.*

προσ-τᾰλαιπωρέω, f. ήσω, *to persist* or *persevere still further.*

πρόσταξις, ἡ, (προστασσω) *an ordaining, ordinance*: πρόσταξιν ποιεῖσθαι to make *an assessment.*

προ-στᾰσία, ἡ, (προΐστημι) *a being at the head of, presidency, chieftainship, leadership*: *patron-ship.* 2. *partisanship, party, faction.* II. *a place before a building, a court, area.*

προσ-τάσσω Att. -ττω: fut. ξω: aor. 1 -έταξα: Pass., aor. 1 -ετάχθην: pf. -τέταγμαι:—*to place* or *post at* a place. 2. *to ascribe, assign, award* to a class or party; plqpf. pass., Ἰνδοὶ προσετετάχατο the Indians *had been assigned to* . . . 3. *to appoint* as commander. II. *to enjoin* or *give orders, to order* to do; τα προσταχθέντα *orders given.*

προστᾰτεία, ἡ, (προστάτης) = προστασία, *presidency, authority*: *patronage, protection.*

προ-στᾰτεύω, (προστάτης) *to be leader*: absol. *to exercise authority*: πρ. ὅπως . . , *to provide* or *take care that* . . .

προ-στᾰτέω, f. ησω, (προστατης) *to stand before* or *at the head of, be ruler over, be president* or *leader of*; ὁ προστατῶν *he that acts as chief*:—Pass. *to be ruled* or *led* by one. II. *to stand before, protect, guard*, c. gen.; in Att. *to be a patron* or *guardian.* III. ὁ προστατῶν χρόνος time *that is close at hand.* Hence

προστᾰτήριος, α, ον, *standing before, protecting, guarding.* II. *standing before* or *close to, hovering* or *flitting before* one.

προστάτης [ᾰ], ου, ὁ, (προΐσταμαι) *one who stands in front, a front-rank man.* II. *a chief, ruler, leader*: *the leader of a party.* III. *one who stands before and protects, a protector, patron, guardian*:—at Athens, a citizen, whom a μέτοικος chose as his *patron*, standing to him in much the same relation as the Roman *cliens* to his *patronus*; γράψασθαι προστάτου to *register* oneself *by one's patron's name*; in Pass., γεγράψομαι προστάτου I will be enrolled *under the name of a patron*. IV. *one who stands before a god, a suppliant.*

προ-στάτις, ιδος, fem. of προστάτης, *a protectress.*

προ-σταυρόω, f. ώσω, *to draw a stockade along.*

προσ-τεθήσομαι, fut. pass. of προστίθημι.

προσ-τειχίζω, f. σω, *to add to a wall, include within the walls.*

προ-στείχω, *to advance, go before.*

προσ-τεκταίνομαι, Med. *to add of one's own device.*

προσ-τελέω, f. έσω, *to pay* or *spend besides.*

προ-στέλλω, f. -στελῶ, *to guard* or *cover in front, shelter*:—Med., προστέλλεσθαί τινα *to send* one *forth equipped*:—Pass., aor. 2 προὐστάλην [ᾰ], *to equip oneself for a journey, go forth, start.*

προ-στενάζω, f. ξω, and **προ-στένω**, *to sigh* or *grieve beforehand.*

προ-στερνίδιος, ον, (πρό, στέρνον) *before the breast*: as Subst., προστερνίδιον, τό, *a covering* or *ornament for the breast* of horses.

πρό-στερνος, ον, (πρό, στέρνον) *before* or *on the breast.*

προσ-τέρπω Dor. **ποτι-τέρπω**, *to delight beside.*

προστεταγμένος, pf. pass. part. of προστάσσω.

προσ-τεχνάομαι, Dep. *to devise besides.*

προσ-τήκω, f. ξω, *to melt into besides.* II. intrans. in pf. act. προστέτηκα, aor. 2 pass. προσετάκην [ᾰ], *to stick fast to, to cleave to.*

προ-στήσας, aor. 1 part. of προΐστημι.

προσ-τίθημι, fut. -θήσω: aor. 1 -έθηκα: aor. 2 -έθην:—*to put to, apply, fit.* 2. *to put to, add.* 3. *to bestow* or *confer upon, to give*: in bad sense, *to impose, inflict.* 4. *to attribute* or *impute to.* 5. *to hand over, to deliver over, consign to.* II. Med. προστίθεμαι: aor. 2 -εθέμην, imperat. -θοῦ, subj. -θῶμαι:—*to add* or *associate oneself to, join*: *to agree with, consent to, to be well-inclined towards*: absol. *to come over, submit.* 2. *to take to oneself besides* or *to take as one's friend* or *ally*; προστίθεσθαι πολέμιον *to make one's* enemy *besides*; προστίθεσθαι δάμαρτα *to take* to wife. 3. *to apply to oneself, bring upon oneself.* 4. *to exhibit, declare.*

προσ-τῑλάω, f. ήσω, *to befoul with dung.*

προσ-τῑμάω, f. ήσω, *to award a further penalty*:—Med. *to propose an additional penalty*:—Pass. *to be imposed as an additional penalty.* Hence

προστίμημα, ατος, τό, *that which is awarded over and above the regular penalty, an additional penalty.*

προ-στόμιον, τό, *a mouth* of a river.

προσ-τρέπω, f. ψω, *to turn to* or *towards in prayer* or *supplication, to supplicate*:—so also in Med. *to turn oneself towards, supplicate.*

προσ-τρέφω, f. -θρέψω, *to bring up in.*

προσ-τρέχω, f. -δρᾰμοῦμαι: aor. 2 -έδρᾰμον:—*to run to, towards* or *against*: absol. *to run up.* 2. in hostile sense, *to run at, make a sally* or *sudden attack.*

προσ-τρίβω [ῑ]: f. ψω: Pass., aor. 2 -ετρίβην [ῐ]: pf. -τέτριμμαι:—*to rub on* or *against*:—Med. *to rub oneself against*: *to inflict* or *cause to be inflicted on* a person: *to attach the reputation of* a thing to him:—Pass. *to be inflicted.* II. in Pass. also *to have intercourse with.* Hence

πρόστριμμα, τό, *that which is rubbed on* or *inflicted upon* one: *a brand, disgrace, affliction.*

προσ-τρόπαιος Dor. **ποτι-τρ-**, ον, (προστροπή): I. act. *turning oneself towards* or *to* a god to obtain purification after being stained by crime, *a suppliant*: as Adj., προστρόπαιοι λιταί *suppliant* prayers. 2. also of one who has not yet been purified, *a polluted person*, Lat. *homo piacularis*: as Adj., προστρόπαιον αἷμα, *polluting* blood, blood-*guiltiness.* II. pass. *he to whom one turns*; θεὸς προστρόπαιος the god *to whom one turns for vengeance, the avenger*:—as Adj. *visiting with vengeance, implacable.*

προστροπή, ἡ, (προστρέπω) *a turning oneself towards in prayer* or *supplication*: in plur. *prayers, conjurings*; πόλεως προστροπὴν ἔχειν to address *a petition* to the city. 2. προστροπὴ γυναικῶν *a suppliant band* of women.

πρόστροπος, ον, (προστρέπω) *turning towards*: hence, like προστρόπαιος, *a suppliant.*

προσ-τυγχάνω, f. -τεύξομαι: aor. 2 -έτῠχον:—*to hit* or *light upon, meet* or *fall in with, obtain*, c. gen. 2. of events, *to befall one.* 3. ὁ προστυγχάνων, ὁ προστυχών *the first person one meets, anybody*; τὰ προστυχόντα ξένια the gifts *that come to one's share.*

προσ-υβρίζω, f. ίσω, *to insult* or *treat with indignity besides.*

προ-συγγίγνομαι Att. **προ-ξυγγ-**, Dep. *to be with beforehand, converse with beforehand.*

προ-συμμίσγω, *to intermix first.*

προ-συνοικέω, f. ήσω, *to live together before.*

προσ-υπάρχω, f. ξω, *to exist* or *happen besides.*

προσ-υπέχω, f. -υφέξω, *to be accountable also, stand surety for.*

προσ-υπισχνέομαι, Dep. *to promise besides*

πρόσ-φάγιον, τό, (πρός, φᾰγεῖν) *anything eaten with other food*: *something to eat.*

πρό-σφαγμα, ατος, τό, *that which is sacrificed to* or *before, a victim.* 2. *a sacrifice, slaughter.* From

προ-σφάζω later **-ττω**, *to sacrifice beforehand.* II. *to sacrifice for* or *in behalf of.*

προσ-φαίνομαι, Pass. *to appear besides.*

προσ-φάσθαι, inf. med. of πρόσφημι.

πρόσ-φᾰτος, ον, (πρός, πέφαται 3 sing. pf. pass. of *φένω) *lately slain, fresh-slaughtered*: generally, *fresh, new, late*, Lat. *recens*:—neut. πρόσφατον as Adv., *lately*: also regul. Adv. προσφάτως, *lately.*

προσφερής, ές, (προσφέρω) *brought to* or *near, approaching.* 2. *like, resembling.* II. = πρόσφορος, *serviceable, conducive.*

προσ-φέρω Dor. **ποτι-φέρω**: f. προσοίσω: aor. 1 pass. προσ-ενέγχθην Ion. -ενείχθην:—*to bring to, near* or *upon*: *to apply to, lay to* or *upon.* 2. *to* *present, offer:* also *to set before* one, *offer* meat or drink: and in Med. *to take meat or drink to oneself.* 3. *to give besides, to add.* 4. *to bring forward, produce* as authority. 5. *to contribute to, to bring in; yield.* II. Pass., with fut. med. προσοίσομαι. *to be borne* or *carried towards:* of ships, *to put in.* 2. *to rush against* or *upon, attack, make an onset:—to rush.* 3. *to approach, converse with, to have dealings with.* 4. absol. *to behave* or *bear oneself.* 5. *to come near, be like, resemble:* cp. προσφερής, ἐμφερής. 6. *to be put* or *imposed upon* one.

προσ-φεύγω, f. -φεύξομαι, *to flee for refuge to.* Hence

προσφευκτέον, verb. Adj. *one must be defendant in an action besides:* cf. φεύγω IV.

πρόσ-φημι, *to speak to, address:* impf. or aor. 2 προσέφην, ης, η; inf. med. προσφάσθαι.

προσ-φθέγγομαι Dor. **ποτι-φθέγγομαι:** f. -φθέγξομαι: Dep.:—*to call to, address, accost, salute.* II. *to call by name, call.* Hence

προσ-φθείρομαι, Pass. *to be ruined besides: to go to ruin, meet in an evil hour,* esp. in aor. 2 part. προσφθαρείς.

προσφθεγκτός, όν, *addressed, saluted.* II. act. *saluting.*

πρόσφθεγμα, ατος, τό, (προσφθέγγομαι) *an address, salutation;* in plur. *words, accents.*

πρόσφθογγος, ον, (προσφθέγγομαι) *addressing, saluting.*

προσ-φθονέω, f. ήσω, *to oppose through envy.*

προσφίλεια, ἡ, (προσφιλής) *kindness, good will.*

προσφιλέστερον, -έστατα, Comp. and Sup. of προσφιλῶς.

προσ-φιλής, ές, (πρός, φιλέω) *dear, beloved, friendly:* of things, *dear, pleasing, grateful,* Lat. *gratus.* II. of persons, *kindly affectioned, grateful.*

προσ-φιλοσοφέω, f. ήσω, *to study philosophy besides, to speculate further upon.*

προσφιλῶς, Adv. of προσφιλής, *kindly;* προσφιλῶς ἔχειν to be *kindly* affectioned.

προσ-φοιτάω, f. ήσω, *to go regularly to,* as to a school, to shops, and the like: see φοιτάω.

προσφορά, ἡ, (προσφέρω) *a bringing to, applying: a presenting, offering.* II. *that which is brought* to a person, *an addition, increase:* also *a kindness, benefit.*

προσ-φορέω, = προσφέρω *to put up, apply.* 2. *to present, offer.* Hence

προσφόρημα, ατος, τό, *that which is taken to one, food, victuals.*

πρόσφορος Dor. **ποτίφ-,** ον, (προσφέρω) *serviceable, useful, profitable.* 2. *convenient, suited to, fit* or *meet for:* c. inf. *fit* or *meet* to do:—τὰ πρόσφορα *what is fit* or *meet, fitting service;* τὰ πρόσφορα as Adv., *fitly.*

προσφυέως, Ion. Adv. of προσφυής: see προσφυῶς.

προσφυής, ές, (προσφύω) *growing upon, hanging to, attached to, devoted.* II. *naturally fitted, suitable.*

προσφύς, aor. 2 part. of προσφύω.

πρόσφυσις, ἡ, (προσφύομαι) *a growing to* or *upon, a clinging to.*

προσ-φύω, f. -φύσω: aor. 1 προσέφυσα:—*to make to grow to* or *upon, to hang upon, fasten to.* II. Pass., with intr. tenses of Act., viz. aor. 2 προσέφυν, part. προσφύς, ῦσα, ύν; pf. προσπέφυκα:—*to grow to* or *upon: to hang upon, cling to, be attached to*

προσφυῶς Ion. -έως, Adv. of προσφυής, *with natural fitness, suitably, ably.*

προσ-φωνέω, f. ήσω, *to call* or *speak to, address, accost.* 2. *to call by name, to name, speak of.* 3. *to address* or *dedicate* a thing to another.

προσφωνήεις Dor. ποτιφ-, εσσα, εν, (προσφωνέω) *addressing, capable of addressing.*

προσφώνημα, ατος τό, (προσφωνέω) *that which is addressed to* another, *an address.*

προσφώνησις, εως, ἡ, (προσφωνέω) *an addressing.* 2. *a dedication.*

προσ-χάσκω, f. -χᾰνοῦμαι: aor. 2 προσέχᾰνον: pf. (in pres. sense) προσκέχηνα:—*to gape* or *stare open-mouthed at* one, Lat. *inhiare.*

προ-σχεθεῖν, poët. for προσχεῖν, aor. 2 inf. of προέχω:—Med., προεσχεθόμην, *I warded off from myself.*

προσ-χέω, f. χεῶ, *to pour to* or *on.*

πρόσχημα, ατος, τό, (προέχω) *that which is held before,* hence, I. *a skreen, cloak, pretence, pretext;* πρόσχημα τοῦ πολέμου *the ostensible cause* for the war. II. *outward show, ornament;* so Miletus is called πρόσχημα τῆς Ἰωνίης *the chief ornament* of Ionia.

προσ-χόω, old form of προσχώννυμι, *to dam up.*

προσ-χρῄζω, f. ῄσω: Ion. **προσχρηΐζω,** f. ηΐσω:—*to require* or *desire besides;* προσχρηΐζω ὑμέων πείθεσθαι *I desire* you also to obey.

πρόσχυσις, ἡ, (προσχέω) *a pouring upon.*

προσ-χώννυμι and **-ύω:** f. -χώσω (from προσχόω): aor. 1 προσέχωσα:—*to heap up besides:* of water, *to deposit* mud, silt, etc.; προσχωννύναι χωρία *to form* new lands *by deposition.* 2. *to choke up with mud, silt up.* II. *to throw earth against:* Pass. *to have earth thrown against.*

προσ-χωρέω, f. ήσω or ήσομαι; *to go to, approach,* c. dat. II. *to come* or *go over to, join* another: *to surrender, give oneself up to.* 2. *to accede, assent* or *agree to: to concur in: to believe.* 3. *to approach, be near to, agree with, be like.* 4. *to put faith in, believe.*

πρόσ-χωρος, ον, (πρός, χώρα) *lying near, adjoining, adjacent:*—as Subst., **πρόσχωρος,** ὁ, *a neighbour.*

πρόσχωσις, ἡ, (προσχώννυμι) *a heaping up besides: deposition of* mud, etc. II. *a bank* or *mound raised against* a place.

προσ-ψαύω Dor. **ποτιψαύω,** *to touch upon, touch.*

προσ-ψηφίζομαι, f. -ίσομαι Att. -ιοῦμαι: Dep.:—*to vote besides: to grant by a majority of votes.*

προσ-ψιθυρίζω, f. σω, *to whisper, chirp* or *whistle to.*

όσω poët. **πρόσσω** Dor. and Att. **πόρσω** later ρω, like Lat. *porro*, Adv.: (πρό, πρός): I. dv., 1. of Space, *forwards, onward, further* opp. to ἐγγύς, *far off, afar:* also with the Art., πρόσω *forward.* 2. of Time, *forward, before.* c. gen. *far towards* or *to;* πρόσω τοῦ ποταμοῦ *into* the *river;* προβαίνειν πόρρω τῆς μοχθηρίας be *far gone* in wickedness: *far from*, οὐ πρόσω λησπόντου not *far from* the Hellespont. 2. of e, πρόσω τῆς νυκτός *far into* the night.—Comp. Sup. προσωτέρω, -άτω.

οσ-ῳδία, ἡ, (πρός, ᾠδή) *a song sung to* or *accom-ied by* music. II. *the tone* or *accent* of a lable.

ροσ-ῳδός, όν, (πρός, ᾠδή) *singing* or *sounding to, harmony with.*

ρόσωθεν Adv. Att. **πόρρωθεν** Ep. **πόρροθεν** (πρό-) *from afar.* II. *from long ago.*

ροσ-ωνέομαι. f. -ήσομαι, Dep. *to buy besides.*

ροσώπατα, τά, Ep. plur. of πρόσωπον.

ροσωπεῖον, τό, (πρόσωπον) *a mask.*

ροσωποληπτέω, *to be a respecter of persons.* From

ροσωπο-λήπτης, ου, ὁ, (πρόσωπον, λέληπται 3 g. pf. pass. of λαμβάνω) *a respecter of persons.*

ροσωποληψία, ἡ, (προσωποληπτέω) *respect of per-*:s.

ρόσ-ωπον, τό: pl. πρόσωπα Ep. προσώπατα, Ep. t. προσώπασι: (πρός, ὤψ):—*a face, visage, coun-nance;* κατὰ πρόσωπον *in front, face to face.* II. lso *one's look, countenance*, Lat. *vultus;* τὸ σὸν ρόσωπον, periphr. for σύ. III. = προσωπεῖον, *mask*, Lat. *persona:*—hence like πρόσχημα, *show, utward appearance.* IV. later, *a person.*

προ-σωρεύω, f. σω, *to pile* or *heap up before.*

προσώτατος, η, ον, Sup. Adj. formed from Adv. ρόσω, *furthest:*—hence Adv. προσωτάτω, or neut. lur. προσώτατα as Adv., *furthest.*

προσώτερος, α, ον, Comp. Adj. formed from Adv. ρόσω, *further off:* hence Adv., προσωτέρω or τὸ ροσωτέρω, *further.*

προσ-ωφελέω, f. ήσω, *to help* or *assist besides, con-ribute one's help to:* absol. *to be of use* or *assistance.* Ience

προσωφέλημα, ατος, τό, *assistance* in a thing: and

προσωφέλησις, ἡ, *a helping, aiding, advantage.*

προσωφελητέον, verb. Adj. of προσωφελέω, *one ıust assist.*

προτακτέον, verb. Adj. of προτάσσω, *one must lace* or *post in front.* 2. *one must prefer.*

προ-τᾰμιεύω, (πρό, ταμίας) *to lay in beforehand.*

προ-τάμνω, Ion. for προτέμνω.

προτᾰμοίμην, aor. 2 med. opt. of προτέμνω.

προτᾰμών, aor. 2 part. of προτέμνω.

προ-ταρβέω, f. ήσω, *to fear beforehand.* II. ɔ *fear* or *be anxious for one.*

προ-τᾰρῑχεύω, f. σω, *to salt* or *pickle beforehand:* ;enerally, *to preserve* or *prepare for keeping.*

πρότᾰσις, ἡ, (προτέτασαι, 2 sing. pf. pass. of τείνω) *a stretching forward.* II. *that which is put for-ward:* in Logic, *a proposition assumed, a premiss.* 2. in Gramm., *the antecedent clause* of a sentence, answered by the ἀπόδοσις.

προ-τάσσω Att. -ττω: f. ξω: aor. 1 -έταξα: pf. -τέτᾰχα: Pass., aor. 1 -ετάχθην: pf. -τέταγμαι:—*to place* or *post in front:* Med., προετάξατο τῆς φά-λαγγος τοὺς ἱππέας *he posted his* horse *in front* of the phalanx:—Pass. *to be stationed first, take the lead;* τὸ προταχθέν or οἱ προτεταγμένοι, *the front ranks, van.* II. generally, *to determine* or *arrange beforehand.*

προ-τείνω, f. -τενῶ: aor. 1 -έτεινα: pf. -τέτᾰκα: Pass., aor. 1 -ετάθην [ᾰ]: pf. -τέτᾰμαι:—*to stretch out, put forward: to expose to danger.* 2. metaph. *to hold out, put forward* as a pretext or excuse. II. *to stretch forwards* or *forth, hold out*, as a sup-pliant. 2. *to offer, tender, proffer:* also *to hold out, show at a distance*, Lat. *ostentare.* III. Med., μισθὸν προτείνεσθαι *to claim* or *demand* as a reward. IV. intr. *to stretch* or *project forward.*

προ-τειχίζω, f. σω, *to protect by a wall.* Hence

προτείχισμα, τό, *an advanced work, outwork.*

προ-τέλειος, ον, (πρό, τέλος) *before a solemnity* or *religious rite.* II. προτέλεια (sc. ἱερά), τά, *sacrifices* or *rites usual before any solemnity;* προτέ-λεια γάμων *the sacrifice before* the marriage-rite; θύειν τὰ προτέλεια to perform *an initiatory sacrifice in behalf of.* 2. προτέλεια, generally, *a beginning, outset.*

προ-τελέω, f. έσω, *to pay as toll* or *tribute, give, pay*, or *expend beforehand.*

προ-τελίζω, f. ίσω, (πρό, τέλος) *to present as a pre-vious sacrifice* or *offering*, esp. *before marriage.*

προ-τεμένισμα, ατος, τό, (πρό, τέμενος) *the pre-cincts* or *entrance of a* τέμενος or *sacred place.*

προ-τέμνω, f. -τεμῶ: aor. 2 προὔτᾰμον:—*to cut up beforehand.* II. *to cut off in front, cut short*, Lat. *praecidere.* III. *to cut forward* or *in front* of one: hence, in aor. 2 med. opt., εἰ ὦλκα διηνεκέα προταμοίμην if *I were to cut* a long furrow *in front of me.*

προτενθεύω, f. σω, *to pick out the dainty bits before-hand, to help oneself first to* anything. From.

προ-τένθης, ου, ὁ, *one who picks out dainty bits be-forehand, a gourmand, epicure.* (Deriv. uncertain.)

προτεραῖος, α, ον, (πρότερος) *on the day before*, like δευτεραῖος, τριταῖος, etc.: ἡ προτεραία (sub ἡμέρα), *the day before;* τῇ προτεραίᾳ, Lat. *pridie, on the day before;* c. gen., τῇ προτεραίᾳ τῆς καταστάσιος *on the day before* the audience.

προτεραίτερος, α, ον, Comp. of προτεραῖος, for πρότερος, *very long before, much earlier.*

προτερέω, f. ήσω, (πρότερος) *to be before, in front, at the head;* προτερεῖν τῆς ὁδοῦ *to be forward* on the way. 2. of Time, *to be beforehand, get the start.*

πρότερος, η, ον, Comp. without any Posit. in use (the Sup. being πρῶτος), answering to Lat. *prior:* of

Place, *before, in front, forward;* πόδες πρότεροι the *fore*-feet. II. of Time, *before, sooner, earlier, older;* in full, πρότερος γενεῇ *elder* in age; πρότεροι παῖδες children *by a former marriage;* τῇ προτέρῃ (sc. ἡμέρᾳ), *on the day before,* like προτεραίᾳ. 2. as Comp. c. gen., ἐμέο πρότερος *sooner, earlier than* I. 3. the neut. πρότερον was used as Adv., *before, sooner, earlier;* πρότερον ἤ or ἤπερ, Lat. *priusquam:* also with Artic., τὸ πρότερον: πρότερον is often put between Art. and Subst., e. g. ὁ πρότερον βασιλεύς the *former* king. III. of Rank or Precedence, *superior.*

προτέρω, Adv. of πρότερος, *further towards, further, forward.*

προτέρωσε, Adv. (προτέρω) *towards the front, forward.*

προ-τεύχω, f. ξω, *to make* or *do beforehand:* pf. pass. inf. προτετύχθαι, *to have been done beforehand, to be past.*

προτί, old Ep. form for πρός. [ῐ]

προτι-άπτω, Dor. for προσάπτω.

προτι-βάλλομαι, Dep. for προσβάλλομαι.

προτιδεγμένος, Dor. part. of Ep. aor. 2 pass. of προσδέχομαι.

προτιειλεῖν, Dor. of προσειλέω.

προτιείποι, Dor. for προσείποι, opt. of προσεῖπον.

προτίθεν, Ep. for προετίθεσαν, 3 pl. impf. of προτίθημι.

προ-τίθημι, f. -θήσω: aor. 1 προέθηκα Att. προὔθηκα: aor. 2 προέθην contr. προὔθην, inf. προθεῖναι:—*to place* or *set before, set out: to hand to, present to:*—Med. *to have* meat *set before one.* 2. *to put forth* or *expose* a child: *to expose to* danger. 3. *to set before, set up as a mark* or *prize, propose:* also *to set as a penalty:* generally, *to set, fix.* II. Med. *put forth on one's own part, to display:* also *to propose to one's mind, entertain.* III. *to set forth, put out publicly;* προθεῖναι νεκρόν *to lay out* a dead body, *let* it *lie in state:* also *to make a show of, expose for view.* IV. *to put forward: to hold forth, offer, tender.* 2. *to hold out* as a pretext. V. *to put before* or *over.* VI. *to put before, to prefer one to another.*

προτι-μάσσω, Dor. for προσμάσσω.

προ-τιμάω, f. ήσω, *to honour before* or *above* another, *to prefer to* another. 2. *to prefer in honour: to hold in esteem* or *regard:*—Pass. *to be preferred in honour;* προτιμᾶσθαι ἐς τὰ κοινά *to be preferred* to public honours. 3. c. gen. *to take heed of, care for.* 4. c. inf. *to wish rather, prefer:* also *to wish greatly, wish much.* Hence

προτίμησις, ἡ, *a preferring in honour, preference.*

προτιμητέος, α, ον, verb. Adj. of προτιμάω, *to be preferred.*

προ-τίμιον, τό, (πρό, τιμή) *money paid in advance, earnest-money.*

πρό-τιμος, ον, (πρό, τιμή) *honoured before, worth more than.*

προτι-μυθέομαι, Dor. for προσ-μυθέομαι.

προ-τιμωρέω, f. ήσω, *to help beforehand* or *first:*—Med. *to revenge oneself before.*

προτί-οπτος, ον, Dor. for πρόσ-οπτος.

προτι-όσσομαι, Ep. Dep., only used in pres. and impf.; (προτί Dor. for πρός, ὄσσομαι):—*to look at* or *upon, behold.* II. of the mind, *to foresee, forbode, presage.*

προ-τίω, f. -τίσω [ῑ], *to honour before* another, *prefer;* προτίειν τινὰ τάφου *to deem* one *more worthy of the honour* of burial than the other.

πρότμησις, ἡ, (προτέμνω) *the waist: the loins.*

προ-τολμάω, f. ήσω, *to venture before* or *more:*—Pass. *to be first ventured* or *risked.*

προτομή, ἡ, (προτέμνω) *the upper part of anything: a half-length figure, a bust.*

προτονίζω, f. σω, *to haul up with ropes.* From

πρότονος, ὁ (προτείνω) *a rope from the mast-head to the bow of a ship, the forestay of the mast.* 2. *a halyard.*

προ-τοῦ, for πρὸ τοῦ, = πρὸ τούτου, *formerly, before now, erst.*

προ-τρᾰπέσθαι, aor. 2 med. inf. of προτρέπω.

προτρεπτικός, ή, όν, *fitted for urging on, persuasive.* Adv. -κῶς, *persuasively.* From

προ-τρέπω, f. ψω, *to turn* or *urge forwards, urge on, exhort* or *persuade to* do a thing: so too in Med., *to persuade, exhort to:* also c. dupl. act., τὰ κατὰ τὸν Τέλλον προετρέψατο ὁ Σόλων τὸν Κροῖσον Solon *prompted* Croesus *to inquire* as to what concerned Tellus. III. Pass., with aor. 2 med. προὐτρᾰπόμην in pass. sense, *to turn forwards, turn in headlong flight:* metaph., ἄχεϊ προτραπέσθαι *to give oneself over to* grief.

προ-τρέχω, f. -δρᾰμοῦμαι: aor. 2 προὔδρᾰμον (formed from obsol. δρέμω):—*to run forward* or *forth.* II. *to outrun, run past, overtake.*

πρό-τρῑτα, Adv. (πρό, τρίτος) *three days before* or *for three successive days.*

προ-τροπάδην, Adv. (προτρέπω) *turned forwards head-foremost, headlong, with headlong speed.* [ᾰ]

προ-τυγχάνω, f. -τεύξομαι: aor. 2 -έτῠχον:—*to happen before* or *beforehand:* also *to meet with first;* τὸ προτῠχόν *the first thing that came to hand.*

προ-τύπτω, f. ψω, intr. *to strike forwards, break forth, burst out;* Τρῶες προὔτυψαν the Trojans *burst forward.* II. trans. *to drive, force on;* aor. 2 pass. part. προτῠπείς, *driven, urged on.*

προτῠχών, οῦσα, όν, aor. 2 part. of προτυγχάνω.

προὔβᾰλον, προὔβην, for προεβ-, aor. 2 of προβάλλω, προβαίνω.

προὔγρᾰφον, for προέγραφον, impf. of προγράφω.

προὐδῐδάξατο, προὔδωκα, προὔθετο, for προεδ-.

προὔθηκε, for προέθηκε, 3 sing. aor. 1 of προτίθημι.

προὐθῡμήθην, for προεθ-, aor. 1 of προθυμέομαι.

προὐθῡμούμην, impf. of προθυμέομαι.

προὔκᾰμον, for προέκαμον, aor. 2 of προκάμνω.

προὔλᾰβον, for προελ-, aor. 2 of προλαμβάνω.

προὔκειτο, προὐκινδύνευε, for προεκ-.

προὔμαθον, for προεμ-, aor. 2 of προμανθάνω.

προὐμηθήθην, for προεμ-, aor. 1 of προμηθέομαι.

προὔμολον, for προέμολον, aor. 2 of προβλώσκω.

προὐνοησάμην, for προεν-, aor. of προνοέομαι.

προὐννέπω, v. sub προενν-.

προὐξένησε, for προεξ-, aor. 1 of προξενέω.

προὐξ-επίσταμαι, προὐξ-ερευνάω, for προεξ-.

προὐξερευνάω, for προεξερευνάω.

προὐξεφίεμαι, for προεξεφίεμαι.

προ-ϋπάγω, f. ξω, *to lead on gradually*:—Med. *to reduce first under one's power*.

προ-ϋπάρχω, f. ξω: pf. pass. προϋπηργμαι: (πρό, ὑπάρχω) :—*to be beforehand in* a thing, *begin with*: c. gen. *to be the first to do* a thing. II. intr. *to exist before; προϋπάρξαντα things that happened before, past events*; τὰ προϋπηργμένα a man's *antecedents*.

προὔπεμψα, for προέπεμψα, aor. 1 of προπέμπω.

προ-ϋπεξ-ορμάω, f. ήσω, *to go out secretly before*.

προὔπεσον, for προέπ-, aor. 2 of προπίπτω.

προ-ϋπηργμένος, pf. pass. part. of προϋπάρχω.

προὔπινον, προὔπιον, for προεπ-, impf. and aor. 2 of προπίνω.

προὐπιστήθην, for προεπ-, aor. 1 of προεπίσταμαι.

προ-ϋπισχνέομαι, Dep. *to promise before*.

προ-ϋποβάλλω, *to put under as a foundation*.

προ-ϋπόκειμαι, f. -κείσομαι, Pass. *to exist before*.

προ-ϋπολαμβάνω, f. -λήψομαι, *to assume beforehand*.

προὔπτος, ον, contr. for πρόοπτος.

προὐπυθόμην, for προεπ-, aor. 2 of προπυνθάνομαι.

προὐργιαίτερος, α, ον, see προὔργου.

προὔργου, contr. for πρὸ ἔργου, *for a work* or *object*: hence *worth while, profitable, useful, good for anything*; προὔργου τι δρᾶν to do something *of use*: also as Adv. *serviceably, conveniently*.—Comp. προὐργιαίτερος, α, ον, *more serviceable, useful, important*; προυργιαίτερον ποιεῖσθαι to deem *of more consequence*:—Sup. προὐργιαίτατος, η, ον, *most serviceable*, etc.

προὐρρήθην, aor. 1 pass. of προερέω.

προυσελέω, *to maltreat, outrage*. (Deriv. uncertain.)

προὐστάλην, for προεστ-, aor. 2 pass. of προστέλλω.

προὔστησα, προὔστην, for προεστ-, aor. 1 and 2 of προΐστημι.

προὐτίθει, προὔτυψα, for προετ-.

προὔφαινε, for προέφαινε.

προ-υφαιρέω, f. ήσω, *to withdraw from one before*.

προὐφείλω, for προοφείλω.

προὔχω, προὔχουσι, προὔχοντο, for προέχ-.

προ-φαίνω, f. -φᾰνῶ: aor. 1 -έφηνα:—*to bring forth to light, shew forth, manifest, display*. 2. *to shew forth by word, to declare*:—Pass., aor. 2 προὐφάνην [ᾰ], part. προφανείς, εῖσα, έν, *to be shewn forth, come forth and appear, come into sight, come to light*; προὐφάνη κτύπος the sound was *clearly heard*. II. *to shew beforehand, foreshew*: metaph. *to hold out a prospect beforehand, promise*:—Pass. and Med. *to shew itself* or *appear before, be revealed before*. III. intr. *to shine forth*: *hold a light before*.

προφᾰνῆναι, aor. 2 pass. inf. of προφαίνω.

προφᾰνής, ές, (προφανῆναι) *shewing itself from afar*: *quite plain* or *clear*; ἀπό or ἐκ τοῦ προφανοῦς *openly*.

πρόφαντος, ον, (προφαίνω) *shewn* or *seen from afar, far-famed*. II. *foreshewn, disclosed beforehand*.

προφᾰσίζομαι, impf. προὐφασιζόμην: f. ίσομαι Att. ιοῦμαι: aor. 1 προὐφασισάμην: Dep.: (πρόφασις) —*to set up as a pretext, allege by way of excuse*, c. acc.: absol. *to make excuses*: the aor. 1 pass. προφασισθῆναι takes a pass. sense, *to be pretended, be made a pretence*.

πρόφᾰσις, gen. εως Ion. ιος, ἡ, (προφαίνω) *an apparent cause, reason, motive, pretext*: mostly in bad sense, *a mere pretext, a pretence, excuse, evasion*: absol. in acc. πρόφασιν, *as one pretends, ostensibly*: also in dat. προφάσει, absol. *for appearance, for a show* or *pretence*; ἐπὶ προφάσεως and ἐπὶ προφάσει by way of *excuse*; πρόφασιν προτείνειν or παρέχειν to put forward *an excuse*: elliptically, μή μοι πρόφασιν [make] me no *excuse*: προφάσιος ἔχεσθαι to lay hold of *a pretext*.

πρόφᾰτος, ον, (προφαίνομαι) *shewn forth, renowned*.

προ-φᾰτεύω, προ-φάτης [ᾰ], Dor. for προφητ-.

προφερής, ές, *placed before* or *in front, preferred, excellent*: Comp. and Sup. προφερέστερος, α, ον, προφερέστατος, η, ον, *more, most excellent*: the Sup. also signifies *most advanced in age, oldest*. There is also a contr. Comp. and Sup., προφέρτερος, προφέρτατος.

προφέρῃσι, Ep. for προφέρῃ, 3 sing. subj. of προφέρω.

προ-φέρω, f. προοίσω: aor. 1 προήνεγκα: aor. 2 προήνεγκον:—*to bring before* one, *bring to, present*. 2. of words, *to throw in one's teeth, bring forward, object to* one, Lat. *objicere, exprobrare*: also simply *to utter, assert, declare*: *to bring forward, quote, produce*. 3. of an oracle, *to propose, command*. II. *to bring forward, display*; πόλεμον προφέρειν *to declare* war. III. *to bear on* or *away, to carry* or *sweep away*. IV. metaph. *to put forward, further, assist*, Lat. *proferre, promovere*; προφέρειν τινὰ ὁδοῦ *to further* one on the road. V. intr. *to surpass, excel*.

προ-φεύγω, f. -φεύξομαι: aor. 2 προὔφῠγον:—*to flee forwards* or *away, flee*. II. c. acc. *to flee from, shun, avoid*.

πρό-φημι, *to say beforehand, foretell*.

προφητεία, ἡ, (προφητεύω) *the gift of interpreting the will of the gods*. 2. *the gift of expounding of scripture, public instruction, preaching*.

προφητεύω Dor. προφᾱτ-: f. σω: aor. 1 ἐπροφήτευσα: (προφήτης):—*to be an interpreter* of the gods, *interpret* or *expound* their word. II. *to expound publicly, preach*.

προφήτης, ου, ὁ, Dor. **προφάτης**: (πρόφημι): *one who speaks for* another: *an interpreter of the will of a god*, Διὸς προφήτης ἐστὶ Λοξίας πατρός Loxias is *the interpreter* of his father Jove: so Poets are called Μουσῶν προφῆται, *interpreters* of the Muses: generally, *an interpreter, proclaimer.* II. *an interpreter of scripture, inspired teacher, preacher.* III. *a foreteller, prophet.*

προφητικός, ή, όν, (προφήτης) *oracular.*

προ-φῆτις, ιδος, fem. of προφήτης, *a prophetess.*

προ-φθάνω, f. -φθάσω and -φθήσομαι: aor. 2 προὔφθην:—*to outrun, anticipate, be beforehand with*

προφθάς, aor. 2 part. of προφθάνω.

προ-φθίμενος, η, ον, *dead* or *killed before.* [ῐ]

προ-φοβέω, f. ήσω, *to frighten beforehand*:—Pass. with fut. med. -ήσομαι, *to fear beforehand*

προ-φορέω, *to bring forward*:—Med. προφορέομαι *to pass the weft to and fro*: metaph. *to run to and fro.*

προ-φράζω, f. σω: pf. pass. -πέφρασμαι: *to foretell.*

προόφρασσα, irreg. Ep. fem. of πρόφρων, *having forethought, thoughtful.*

προφρόνως Ep. -έως, *graciously, willingly, readily, gladly*: Adv. of πρόφρων.

πρό-φρων, ονος, ὁ, ἡ, (πρό, φρήν) *with forward mind*, i. e. *earnest, hearty, kindly, willing, ready* to do a thing.

προφῠγεῖν, aor. 2 inf. of προφεύγω,

προφύγοισθα, Ep. for προφύγοις, 2 sing. aor. 2 opt. of προφεύγω.

προφῠλᾰκή, (προφυλάσσω) *a guard in front, outpost, advanced guard*: αἱ προφυλακαί *outposts, picquets*: διὰ προφυλακῆς *on guard.*

προφῠλᾰκίς, ίδος, ἡ, fem. Adj. of sq.; ναῦς προφυλακίς *a look-out* ship.

προ-φύλαξ, ἄκος, ὁ, *an advanced guard.* [ῠ]

προ-φῠλάσσω Att. -ττω: f. ξω:—*to keep guard before* or *in front, to guard*, c. acc.: προφυλάσσειν ἐπί τινι *to keep guard over* a person or place: absol. *to be on guard, be on the look-out, keep watch*:—Med. *to guard oneself*: *to guard against, be on one's guard against*, Lat. *cavere*, c. acc.

προφύλαχθε, irreg. 2 plur. imperat. of προφυλάσσω.

προ-φῡράω, f. άσω [ᾱ]: pf. pass. προπεφύρᾱμαι:—*to knead beforehand.* II. metaph. *to concoct, brew.*

προ-φῠτεύω, f. σω, *to plant before*: metaph. *to produce, give birth to.*

προ-φύω, f. σω, *to generate before.* II. Pass., with aor. 2 act. προέφυν, pf. προπέφῡκα, *to be born before* another.

προ-φωνέω, f. ήσω, *to utter* or *declare beforehand.* II. *to command publicly.*

προ-χαίρω, *to rejoice beforehand*: 3 sing. imperat. προχαιρέτω, *far be it from me! away with it!* cf. χαῖρε, χαιρέτω, sub χαίρω.

προ-χαλκεύω, f. σω, *to forge beforehand.*

προ-χειρίζω, f. ίσω Att. ιῶ, *to put into the hand, deliver up*:—Pass., aor. 1 part. προχειρισθείς, and pf. προκεχειρισμένος, *to be taken in hand, undertaken*: also *to be arranged, made ready beforehand.* II. as Dep. προχειρίζομαι, Att. fut. -ιοῦμαι, *to take into one's hand, to make ready, make use of.* 2. *to choose, select, appoint.*

πρό-χειρος, ον, (πρό, χείρ) *at hand, close to, convenient*: *handy, ready* 2. *easy, common.* 3. of persons, *ready* or *inclined to* do.

προ-χειροτονέω, f. ήσω, *to elect before.*

προχείρως, Adv. of πρόχειρος, *offhand, readily*: Comp. -οτέρως.

προ-χέω, f. -χεῶ: aor. 1 προέχεα: pf. -κέχῠκα: Pass., aor. 1 προεχύθην [ῠ]: pf. -κέχῠμαι:—*to pour forth* or *forward*:—Pass., metaph. of a crowd of men; ἐς πεδίον προχέοντο *they poured* or *streamed on* to the plain.

πρόχνῠ, Adv. (πρό, γόνυ) *kneeling, on one's knees*; πρόχνυ ὀλέσθαι, to perish *in a kneeling state*, i. e. *in wretched plight.*

προχοή, ἡ, (προχέω) *a pouring out* or *forth*: in plur. προχοαί, *the mouth of a river.*

προχόη, ἡ, (προχέω) = πρόχοος.

προ-χοΐς, ΐδος, ἡ, Dim. of πρόχοος, *a pot.*

πρόχοος Att. contr. -χοῦς, ἡ: irreg. dat. pl. πρόχουσι: (προχέω):—*a vessel for pouring out, a jug, pitcher, vase, urn*: also *the flagon* or *wine-flask* from which the cup-bearer pours into the cups.

προ-χορεύω, f. σω, *to lead a chorus*; προχορεύειν κῶμον *to lead a* band of revellers.

πρό-χους, Att. for πρόχοος: **πρόχουσι**, irreg. dat. pl.

προ-χρίω, f. ίσω [ῑ], *to smear* or *anoint before.*

πρό-χρονος, ον, *previous, prior.*

πρόχῠσις, ἡ (προχέω), *a pouring* or *spreading out*; πρόχυσιν ποιεῖσθαι οὐλὰς κριθῶν = προχέειν οὐλὰς κριθῶν, to pour forth the sacrificial barley: also *a deposit, alluvial soil.*

προχύται (sub. κριθαί), αἱ, properly fem. pl. of προχυτός, *the barley cakes thrown forth* at the beginning of a sacrifice.

προχύτης, ου, ὁ, (προχέω) = πρόχοος; *a jug* or *pitcher*: *an urn, vase.* [ῠ]

προχῠτός, ή, όν, (προχέω) *poured forth.*

πρό-χωλος, ον, *very lame* or *halt.*

προ-χωρέω, f. ήσω, *to go* or *come forward, advance, go on.* II. metaph. of Power, *to advance, become greater*, προχωρεῖν ἐπὶ μέγα: of an enterprise, *to go on, succeed*; εὖ προχωρεῖν *to go on* well: impers., προχωρεῖ *it goes on well*; ὡς οἱ δόλῳ οὐ προεχώρεε when *it did* not *go on well* for him by craft, i. e. when he *did* not *succeed* by craft. III. *to come forward to speak.*

προ-ωθέω, f. -ωθήσω and -ώσω: aor. 1 προέωσα:—*to push forward, push* or *urge on*; προωθεῖν αὑτόν to *urge* oneself *on*, rush on. II. *to push off* or *away*, in wrestling.

προ-ώλης, ες, (πρό, ὄλλυμι) *ruined beforehand.*

προώρισα, aor. 1 of προορίζω.

πρό-ωρος, ον, (πρό, ὥρα) *before the time, untimely.*

προωφειλόμην, impf. pass. of προοφείλω.

πρυλέες, ων, οἱ, *soldiers, combatants on foot*: opp. to chiefs fighting from chariots. (Deriv. uncertain.)

πρύμνᾰ Ion. and poët. **πρύμνη**, ἡ, properly fem. of πρυμνός (sub. ναῦς), *the hindmost part of a ship, the stern, poop*, Lat. *puppis*: ἐπὶ πρύμνην ἀνακρούεσθαι (see ἀνακρούω); ἄνεμος ἐπείγει κατὰ πρύμνην the wind impels us *right astern*: ships were generally fastened to land by the stern, hence πρύμνας λῦσαι mean to loose the *cable*. II. metaph., πρύμνα πόλεος *the Acropolis*; πρύμνα Ὄσσας *the foot of* Mount Ossa.

πρυμναῖος, α, ον, (πρύμνα) *of a ship's stern.*

πρύμνη, ἡ, Ion. and poët. for πρύμνα.

πρύμνηθεν, Adv. of πρύμνη, *from the ship's stern*: generally, *from behind.*

πρυμνήσιος, α, ον, (πρύμνη) *of* or *from a ship's stern*:—as Subst., πρυμνήσια (sub. σχοινία), τά, *ropes from a ship's stern* to fasten her to the shore, *stern-cables*, Lat. *retinacula.*

πρυμνήτης, ου, ὁ, (πρύμνη) *the steersman, helmsman*: metaph. *the pilot* of the state. II. as masc. Adj. *attached* or *fastened to a ship's stern.*

πρυμνόθεν, Adv. (πρύμνη) *from the stern.* II. *from the lowest part*, Lat. *funditus*: *utterly, root and branch.*

πρυμνόν, τό, *the lower part, end*: properly neut. of πρυμνός.

πρυμνός, ή, όν, *the hindmost, undermost, endmost*: in Homer used of different limbs, where it means the end *next the body*, as, πρυμνὸς βραχίων *the end of* the arm (where it joins the shoulder): hence, πρυμνὴν ὕλην ἐκτάμνειν to cut off the wood *at the root.*—Sup. πρυμνότατος, *at the lowest end.*

πρυμν-οῦχος, ον, (πρύμνα, ἔχω) *holding the ship's stern.* II. *detaining the fleet.*

πρυμν-ώρεια, ἡ, (πρυμνός, ὄρος) *the bottom* or *foot of a mountain.*

πρῠτᾰνεία Ion. -ηΐη, ἡ, (πρυτανεύω) *the prytaneia* or *presidency*, at Athens a period of 35 or 36 days, during which *the prytanes* of each φυλή in turn presided in the βουλή or Council of 500, and in the ἐκκλησία or popular Assembly:—κατὰ πρυτανείαν *by presidencies*, i. e. every 35 or 36 days. II. *any public office held by rotation* for given periods: πρυτανεία τῆς ἡμέρης *the chief command* for the day.

πρῠτᾰνεῖον Ion. -ήιον, τό, (πρύτανις) *the presidents' hall, town-hall*, a public building in Greek cities, consecrated to Vesta, to whom a perpetual fire was kept burning in it, which in colonies was originally brought from the Prytaneion of the mother-city: the Prytanes for the time being had their meals there, and entertained foreign ambassadors; citizens also who had deserved well of the state, and the children of those who fell in battle, were rewarded with a seat at this public table. II. *a law-court* at Athens. III. pl. πρυτανεῖα, *a sum of money deposited by the parties to a lawsuit before the suit began*, Lat. *sacramentum*; τιθέναι πρυτανεῖά τινι to make *a deposit* against one, i. e. bring an action against him.

πρῠτᾰνεύω, f. σω, (πρύτανις) *to be πρύτανις* or *president, hold sway.* II. at Athens, *to hold office as Prytanis, to put to the vote as Prytanis, propose* or *lay before the assembly*: the φυλή or tribe, whose 50 βουλευταί were πρυτάνεις for the time being, was called φυλὴ πρυτανεύουσα, (see πρύτανις, πρυτανεία): ὁ πρυτανεύσας *he who put a question to the vote.* III. generally, *to manage, regulate, administer.*

πρυτᾰνηΐη, -ήιον, Ion. for πρυτανεία, -εῖον.

πρύτᾰνις, εως, ὁ, pl. πρυτάνεις, as if from πρυτανεύς: (πρό, πρότερος): *a prince, ruler, lord.* II. *a Prytanis* or *President*: at Athens the πρυτάνεις were a committee of 50, being the deputies of one of the ten φυλαί, and so forming $\frac{1}{10}$ part of the βουλή or Council of 500; out of these fifty πρυτάνεις one was chosen by lot as *chief-president* (ἐπιστάτης); he chose nine πρόεδροι: and these, with a secretary (γραμματεύς) not of their own body, formed *the Presidency* (πρυτανεία). The φυλή which first entered office every year was determined by lot, and their term of office was called πρυτανεία: during this time all public acts ran in their name, in this form; Ἀκαμαντὶς [φυλὴ] ἐπρυτάνευε, Φαίνιππος ἐγραμμάτευε, Νικιάδης ἐπεστάτει, 'the tribe of Acamas were πρυτάνεις, Phaenippus was secretary, Niciades was *chief-president.*' See πρυτανεία, πρυτανεῖον.

πρώ or **πρῴ**, Adv., Att. for πρωΐ.

πρώην Dor. **πρώαν**, (πρωΐ) *lately, just now, not long ago*, Lat. *nuper.* II. *the day before yesterday*; proverb., μέχρι οὗ πρώην τε καὶ χθές till *yesterday* or *the day before*, i. e. *till very lately.*

πρωθ-ήβης, ου, ὁ, (πρῶτος, ἥβη) *a youth in his first bloom.*

πρώθ-ηβος, ον, also η, ον, (πρῶτος, ἥβη) *in the bloom* or *flower of youth.*

πρωΐ [ῐ], Att. shortd. **πρῴ**: Adv.: (πρό):—*early, early in the day, at morn*, Lat. *mane*: c. gen., πρωὶ ἔτι τῆς ἡμέρης still *early* in the day; ἡμέρας τὸ πρωὶ *the early part* of the day; ἅμα πρωὶ at *early morn*; ἀπὸ πρωὶ *from morn.* 2. generally, *betimes, early, in good time*, Lat. *mature, tempestive.* II. Comp. πρωιαίτερον, *earlier*, Sup. πρωιαίτατα, *earliest*, formed from πρώιος.

πρωία (sub. ὥρα), ἡ, fem. of πρώιος, *morning.* [ῐ]

πρωιαίτερον, πρωιαίτατα, Comp. and Sup. of πρωί.

πρώιζος, ον, = πρώιος, *early, timely, in good time*: Adv. πρώιζα, like πρώην, *the day before yesterday*: but also *too early, before the time.*

πρώιμος, ον, (πρωί) *early.*

πρωινός, ή, όν, = πρώιος. [ῐ]

πρώιος Att. **πρῷος**, α, ον, (πρωί): *early, early in day, at morn*; δείλη πρωία *the early part of the afternoon*, opp. to δείλη ὀψία, the latter part; πρωίας, absol. as Adv., *early.* II. *early in the season*; πρῷα τῶν καρπίμων *early* fruits.

πρωκτο-πεντετηρίς, ίδος, ἡ, (πρωκτός, πεντετηρίς) *five years of debauchery.*

πρωκτός, ὁ, (προάγω) *the anus, the hinder parts, back, tail.*

πρών, πρῶνος, ὁ, contr. from πρηών, πρηόνος; nom. pl. πρώονες, as if from πρώων:—*anything that juts forward, a foreland, headland*, Lat. *promontorium*; ἅλιος πρὼν ἀμφοτέρας κοινὸς αἴας *the jutting ridge* of the sea (i. e. the bridge) which joined both lands.

πρῷος, α, ον, Att. for πρώιος.

πρῷρα, as Ion. ης, ἡ, (πρό) *the fore-part of a ship, a ship's head, prow, bows*, Lat *prora*: also (as if from an Adj. πρῷρος) νηῦς πρῴρη *the prow* of a ship, like νηῦς πρυμνή; πνεῦμα τοὐκ πρῴρας a *head*-wind, opp. to πνεῦμα κατὰ πρύμνην, a *stern*-wind. II. generally, *any front*: hence *a head, face*.

πρῴρᾱθεν, or before a consonant -θε, Adv. (πρῷρα) *from the ship's head, from the front*.

πρῳρᾱτεύω, f. σω, *to be a look-out man, look out ahead*. From

πρῳράτης [ᾱ], ου, ὁ, (πρῷρα) *a man who stood at the ship's head* to give signals to the steersman, *a look-out man*.

πρῳρεύς, έως, ὁ, (πρῷρα) = πρῳράτης.

πρῴρηθεν, Adv., Ion. for πρῴρᾱθεν.

πρῶσαι, **πρώσας**, **πρῶσον**, contr. for προ-ῶσαι, etc., aor. 1 inf., part., and imperat. of προωθέω.

πρῶτα, neut. pl. of πρῶτος, as Adv. *first of all, in the first place*.

πρωτ-ᾱγός, οῦ, ὁ, (πρῶτος, ἄγω) *leading in advance*; οἱ πρωταγοί, *the vanguard*.

πρωτ-άγρια, τά, (πρῶτος, ἄγρα) *the first-fruits of the chase*.

πρωτ-ᾱγωνιστής, οῦ, ὁ, (πρῶτος, ἀγωνιστής) *one who plays the first part, the chief actor*, Lat. *primarum partium actor*; the other two actors being called respectively δευτεραγωνιστής, τριταγωνιστής: generally, *the chief personage*.

πρώτ-αρχος, ον, (πρῶτος, ἄρχω) *first-beginning, primal, originating*.

πρωτεῖον, τό, (πρωτεύω) *the chief rank, first place*: esp. in pl., τὰ πρωτεῖα *the first prize* or *place*.

πρωτεύω, f. σω, (πρῶτος) *to be the first, to excel, be preëminent*. 2. *to be the first among, be superior to*, c. gen.

πρωτ-ηρότης, ου, ὑ, (πρῶτος, ἀρότης) *one who ploughs earliest* or *first*.

πρώτιστος, η, ον, also ος, ον, poët. Sup. of πρῶτος, *the first of the first, first of all, very first*; neut. πρώτιστον and -τα as Adv., *first of all*.

πρωτό-βολος, ον, (πρῶτος, βαλεῖν) *first thrown at* or *struck*. II. parox. **πρωτο-βόλος**, ον, act. *striking first*.

πρωτο-γλῠφής, ές, (πρῶτος, γλύπτω) *newly-carved*.

πρωτό-γονός, ον, (πρῶτος, γενέσθαι) *firstborn*. 2. of rank, *high-born, illustrious*. 3. *first-ordained*.

πρωτό-ζυξ, ῠγος, (πρῶτος, ζῠγῆναι) *newly married*.

πρωτό-θρονος, ον, *filling the first seat*: irreg. pl. πρωτόθρονες (as if from πρωτόθρων).

πρωτο-καθεδρία, ἡ, (πρῶτος, καθέδρα) *the first seat, chief place*.

πρωτο-κλῐσία, ἡ, (πρωτος, κλίνω) *the first place* or *seat at table*.

πρωτο-κτόνος, ον, (πρῶτος, κτείνω) *slaying first, committing the first murder*.

πρωτο-κύων, ὁ, (πρῶτος, κύων) *the first dog*, i. e. *the chief of the Cynics*.

πρωτό-λεια, τά, (πρῶτος, λεία) *the first spoils* in war, *the firstfruits*:—as Adv. *in the first place*.

πρωτολογία, ἡ, *the right of speaking first*. From

πρωτο-λόγος, ον, (πρῶτος, λέγω) *speaking first*.

πρωτό-μαντις, εως, ὁ, (πρῶτος, μάντις) *the first prophet* or *seer*.

πρωτό-μορος, ον, (πρῶτος, μόρος) *dying* or *dead first*.

πρωτο-πᾰγής, ές, (πρῶτος, παγῆναι) *first put together*, i. e. *newly made*.

πρωτο-πήμων, ονος, ὁ, ἡ, (πρῶτος, πῆμα) *hurling first*: *the first cause of ill*.

πρωτό-πλοος, ον, Att. contr. **-πλους**, ουν, (πρῶτος, πλόος) *making the first voyage, going to sea for the first time*. II. *sailing first* or *foremost*.

πρωτόρ-ριζος, ον, (πρῶτος, ῥίζα) *being the first root* or *origin*.

πρῶτος, η, ον, Sup. of πρό, as if contr. from πρότατος, πρόατος, Dor. **πρᾶτος** (the Comp. being πρότερος):—*first, foremost, front*, of Number or Place; of Time, *first, earliest*, Lat. *primus*; ἐνὶ πρώτοισι, μετὰ πρώτοισι among *the first fighters*, i. e. *in front*. 2. neut. pl. τὰ πρῶτα (sub. ἆθλα) *the first prize*; τὰ πρῶτα φέρεσθαι to carry off *the first prize*; ἐς τὰ πρῶτα to *the highest degree*: of persons, ἐὼν τὰ πρῶτα τῶν Ἐρετριέων being the *first* or *foremost man* among the Eretrians; τὰ πρῶτα τῆς ἐκεῖ μοχθηρίας *the chief* of the rascality there. 3. τὴν πρώτην, as Adv., *first, at present, just now*: so with εἶναι, τὴν πρώτην εἶναι, like ἑκὼν εἶναι, *at first*. 4. neut. sing. and plur. πρῶτον, πρῶτα as Adv., *first, in the first place*, Lat. *primum*: *first of all, above all*. 5. after a Relative, πρῶτον means *once, once for all*, as, ὅντινα πρῶτον λάβωσιν ἄελλαι whom storms may catch *for the first time*, i. e. *once for all*. 6. ἐν πρώτοις, Lat. *in primis, among the first, chiefly, especially*; ἐν τοῖς πρῶτοι, as if shortd. for ἐν τοῖς πρώτοις πρῶτοι, *first among the first*. II. πρῶτος is sometimes found as a Comp. c. gen., *before, sooner than*: also πρῶτον ἤ.., = πρὶν ἤ.., Lat. *priusquam*.

πρωτό-σπορος, ον, (πρῶτος, σπείρω) *first sown* or *begotten*.

πρωτο-στάτης, ου, ὁ, (πρῶτος, ἵσταμαι) *one who stands first, the first man on the right* of a line: but also, οἱ πρωτοστάται *the front-rank men*. II. *a chief, leader*. [ᾰ]

πρωτοτοκία, ἡ, *a bearing her firstborn*: and

πρωτοτόκια, ων, τά. *the privilege of the first-born, birthright*. From

πρωτο-τόκος, ον, (πρῶτος, τεκεῖν) *bearing her firstborn*. II. proparox. **πρωτότοκος**, ον, pass. *firstborn*.

πρωτό-τομος, ον, (πρῶτος, τεμεῖν) *first cut* or *cut off.*

πρωτό-φυτος, ον, (πρῶτος, φύω) *firstborn.*

πρωτό-χνοος, ον contr. **-χνους**, ουν, *with the first down.*

πρωτό-χῠτος, ον, (πρῶτος, χέω) *first-flowing.*

πρωὐδᾶν, contr. for προ-αυδᾶν, inf. of προαυδάω

πρώων, ονος, ὁ, Ep. lengthd. form for πρών.

πταίοισα, Dor. pres. part. fem. of πταίω.

ΠΤΑΙ´ΡΩ, f. πτᾰρῶ: aor. 1 ἔπτᾱρα: aor. 2 ἔπτᾰρον:—*to sneeze; μέγ᾽ ἔπτᾰρε be sneezed* aloud, which was taken for a good omen:—metaph. of a lamp, *to sputter.*

πταῖσμα, τό, (πταίω) *a stumble, false step:* metaph. *a mistake, blunder.* II. *a failure, misfortune.*

ΠΤΑΙ´Ω, f. πταίσω: aor. 1 ἔπταισα: Pass., aor. 1 ἐπταίσθην: pf. ἔπταισμαι:—*to make to stumble,* Lat. *offendere.* II. intrans. (sub. πόδα), *to strike the foot, stumble; πταίειν πρός τινι to stumble against;* also, περί τινι, as, μὴ περὶ Μαρδονίῳ πταίσῃ ἡ Ἑλλάς lest Hellas *should get a fall* over him. 2. metaph. *to make a false step* or *mistake, to fail.*

πτάμενος, η, ον, aor. 2 part. of πέταμαι. [ᾰ]

πτανός, Dor. for πτηνός.

πτάξ, gen. πτᾰκός, ὁ, ἡ, (πτήσσω) *the cowering animal,* i. e. *the hare.*

πταρμός, ὁ, (πταίρω) *a sneezing, sneeze.*

πτάρνῠμαι, Dep. = πταίρω, *to sneeze.*

πτάς, part. of ἔπτην, aor. 2 act. of πέτομαι.

πτάσθαι, aor. 2 inf. of πέταμαι.

πτάτο, Ep. for ἔπτᾰτο, 3 sing. aor. 2 of πέταμαι.

ΠΤΕΛΕ´Α Ion. -έη, ἡ, *the elm,* Lat. *ulmus.*

πτέρῐνος, η, ον, also ος, ον, (πτερόν) *made of feathers; πτέρινος κύκλος a* fan *of feathers.* II. *feathered, winged.*

πτέρῐς, ἴδος, ἡ, (πτερόν) a kind of *fern,* so called *from its leaves being like feathers.*

ΠΤΕ´ΡΝΑ Ion. **-νη**, ἡ, *the heel.* II. = πέρνα, *a ham.*

Πτερνο-γλύφος, ὁ, (πτέρνα, γλύφω) *Ham-scraper.* name for a mouse in the Batrachomyomachia.

Πτερνο-τρώκτης, ου, ὁ, (πτέρνα, τρώγω) *Ham-nibbler,* the name of a mouse in the Batrachomyomachia.

Πτερνο-φάγος, ὁ, (πτέρνα, φᾰγεῖν) *Ham-eater,* name of a mouse in the Batrachomyomachia.

πτερο-δόνητος, ον, (πτερόν, δονέω) *moved with flapping wings:* metaph. *high-soaring, high-flown.*

πτερόεις, εσσα, εν, contr. fem. πτεροῦσσα, gen. πτεροῦντος: (πτερόν):—*feathered, winged:* also *light as a feather:* used by Homer mostly in phrase ἔπεα πτερόεντα, *winged* words.

πτερόν, τό, (πέτομαι, πτέσθαι) *a feather,* mostly in plur. *feathers.* 2. *wings; ὑπὸ πτεροῖς εἶναι* to be under their mother's *wings.* II. *a winged creature.* 2. for οἰωνός, *an augury, omen.* III. of *anything like wings* or *feathers,* such as *oars,* ἐρετμά, τά τε πτερὰ νηυσὶ πέλονται which are *the wings* of ships. 2. ἀέθλων πτερά the prize *which wafts* the Poet as it were to heaven 3. *the leafage* of trees, like κόμη. 4. in Architecture. *the rows of columns along the sides* of Greek temples, whence the terms ἄπτερος, δίπτερος, περίπτερος.

πτερο-ποίκῐλος, ον, (πτερόν, ποικίλος) *motley-feathered, of pied plumage.*

πτερό-πους, -ποδος, (πτερόν, πούς) *wing-footed.*

πτερορ-ροέω and **-ρῠέω**, f. ήσω: (πτερόν, ῥέω):—*to shed the feathers, lose feather, moult:* metaph. *to be plucked, fleeced, pigeoned.*

πτερο-φόρος, ον, (πτερόν, φέρω) *feathered, winged; πτεροφόρα φῦλα* the *feathered* tribes.

πτερο-φυέω, (πτερόν, φύω) *to grow feathers* or *wings.*

πτερόω, f. ώσω, (πτερόν) *to furnish with feathers* or *wings, to feather; πτεροῦν βιβλίον* to tie a letter to a feathered arrow and shoot it off:—Pass. *to be feathered.* 2. of ships, *to furnish with oars.*

πτερύγεσσι, Ep. dat. pl. of πτέρυξ.

πτερῠγίζω, f. ίσω, (πτέρυξ) *to flutter* or *flap the wings.*

πτερύγιον [ῠ], τό, Dim. of πτέρυξ, *a little wing.* II. anything like a wing, as, *a turret* or *battlement;* or, *a pointed roof, a pinnacle.*

πτερῠγ-ωκής, ές, (πτέρυξ, ὠκύς) *swift of wing.*

πτερῠγωτός, ή, όν, (πτερυγόω) *fledged, winged, wing-shaped.*

πτέρυξ, ῠγος, ἡ, (πτερόν) *a wing.* II. *anything like a wing,* as 1. *a rudder.* 2. in plur. *the skirts* of a coat of mail. 2. *the wing* of a building. III. *anything that covers* or *protects* like wings, *a fold, flap* or *cape.* IV. metaph., πτέρυγες γόων *the wings,* i. e. *the flight* or *flow,* of grief.

πτερύσσομαι, f. ξομαι, Dep. = πτερυγίζω.

πτέρωμα, ατος, τό, (πτερόω) *that which is feathered, a feathered arrow.*

πτέρωσις, ἡ, (πτερόω) *a feathering, plumage.*

πτερωτός, ή, όν, also ός, όν, (πτερόω) *feathered: winged.*

πτέσθαι, aor. 2 inf. of πέτομαι.

πτῆναι, inf. of ἔπτην, aor. 2 act. of πέτομαι.

πτην-ολέτις, ιδος, ἡ, (πτηνός, ὄλλυμι) *bird-killing.*

πτηνός, ή, όν Dor. **πτανός**, ά, όν, (πτῆναι) *feathered, winged:* πτηνά, τά, *fowls, birds.* II. of young birds, *fledged.* III. metaph., πτηνοὶ μῦθοι, like ἔπεα πτερόεντα, *winged, passing* words; πτηναὶ ἐλπίδες *fleeting* hopes.

πτῆξαι, aor. 1 inf. of πτήσσω.

πτῆσις, ἡ, (πτῆναι) *a flying, flight.*

πτήσομαι, fut. of πέτομαι.

ΠΤΗ´ΣΣΩ, fut. πτήξω: aor. 1 ἔπτηξα Ep. πτῆξα: aor. 2 ἔπτᾰκον, only found in compd. καταπτᾰκών: pf. ἔπτηχα, Ep. part. πεπτηώς, ῶτος:—*to frighten, scare, alarm, terrify,* Lat. *terrere.* II. intr. *to crouch down* or *cower for fear; πτήσσειν βωμόν to flee cowering to* the altar. 2. c. acc. *to crouch for fear of* a thing.

πτῆται, Ion. for **πτᾶται**, 3 sing. aor. 2 subj. of πέτομαι.

ΠΤΙ´ΛΟΝ [ῐ], τό, *a feather: plumage:* esp. of *the under feathers, down.* II. *a wing.*

πτἴλό-νωτος, ον, (πτίλον, νῶτον) *with feathered back.*

πτἴσάνη [ᾰ], ἡ, (πτίσσω) *peeled barley.* II. *a drink made from it, barley-water, barley-gruel.*

ΠΤΙ'ΣΣΩ, fut. πτίσω: aor. 1 ἔπτἴσα: Pass., aor. 1 ἐπτίσθην: pf. ἔπτισμαι:—*to husk, peel* or *winnow grain:* also *to grind coarsely, to pound.*

πτόα Ion. **πτοίη**, ἡ, (πτοέω) *fear, terror.*

ΠΤΟΕ'Ω: f. ήσω: aor. 1 ἐπτόησα poët. ἐπτοίησα: —Pass., aor. 1 ἐπτοήθην poët. ἐπτοίηθην: pf. ἐπτόημαι poët. ἐπτοίημαι:—*to frighten, scare away:*—Pass. *to be scared* or *dismayed.* II. metaph. *to flutter, excite, agitate:*—Pass. *to be in a flutter, be agitated: to be wild, distracted;* τὸ πτοηθέν *distraction.* Hence

πτόησις or **πτοίησις**, εως, ἡ, *terror: any vehement passion, excitement.*

πτοιέω, πτοίησις, πτοιητός, v. sub πτοέω.

πτολεμίζω, πτολεμιστής, etc., Ep. for πολεμ–.

πτόλεμος, ὁ, Ep. for πόλεμος, *war.*

πτολί-αρχος, ον, Ep. for πολίαρχος.

πτολίεθρον, τό, Dim. of πτόλις, but used like πόλις, *a city.*

πτολί-πορθος and **πτολι-πόρθιος**, ον, (πτόλις, πέρθω) *sacking* or *wasting cities:* also **πτολι-πόρθης**, ου, ὁ.

πτόλις, Ep. for πόλις.

πτόλισμα, Ep. for πόλισμα.

πτόρθος, ὁ, *a young branch, shoot, sucker, sapling.* II. *a sprouting, shooting, budding.*

πτύγμα, ατος, τό, (πτύσσω) *anything folded, a fold.*

πτυκτός, ή, όν, (πτύσσω) *folded;* πτυκτὸς πίναξ, *folding tablets,* consisting of two thin plates of wood, one folding upon the other.

πτύξ, πτῠχός, ἡ, later **πτῠχή**, ῆς, ἡ, (πτύσσω):—*anything in folds, a fold, leaf, layer, plate,* πτύχες σάκεος *plates* forming a shield. II. of *the clefts* or *breaks* in the side of a hill, which at a distance look like *folds; a cleft, dell, coomb:* so also of the sky, *folds* or *clouds.* III. in form πτυχή, *a folding tablet.* IV. in Comedy, *wrinkle*

πτύον, τό, Ep. gen. πτῠόφιν, (πτύω) *a winnowing-shovel* or *fan,* Lat. *vannus.*

ΠΤΥ'ΡΩ [ῠ], f. πτῠρῶ:—*to frighten, scare, terrify:* —Pass. πτύρομαι, aor. 2 ἐπτύρην [ῠ]: *to be frightened.*

πτύσμα, ατος, τό, (πτύω) *spittle*

ΠΤΥ'ΣΣΩ, f. ξω: aor. 1 ἔπτυξα: Pass., aor. 1 ἐπτύχθην: pf. πέπτυγμαι:—*to fold* or *double up, fold and lay by.* II. Pass. *to be folded* or *doubled up:* of spear-points, *to be folded* or *bent back.* 2. *to fold* or *cling round* or *to.* III. Med. *to fold round oneself.* Hence

πτῠχή, ἡ, see πτύξ.

ΠΤΥ'Ω, f. πτύσω [ῠ]: aor. 1 ἔπτῦσα: pf. pass. ἔπτυσμαι:—*to spit out: to spit,* Lat. *spuo.* II. *to disgorge, cast out, throw up, vomit forth.* III. metaph., πτύσας *having spat, with an expression of disgust;* πτύσας προσώπῳ *with loathing* in his face.

πτωκάς, άδος, ἡ, (πτώξ, πτώσσω) *shy, timorous, fearful.*

πτῶμα, ατος, τό, (πίπτω, πέπτωκα) *a fall: a misfortune, calamity, disaster,* Lat. *casus.* II. *that which has fallen, a corpse, carcase*

πτώξ, ὁ, ἡ, gen. πτωκός, (πτώσσω) *the cowering animal,* i. e. *the hare.*

πτώσιμος, ον, (πίπτω, πέπτωκα) *fallen, slain.*

πτῶσις, εως, ἡ, (πίπτω, πέπτωκα) *a falling, fall.*

πτωσκάζω, poët. for πτώσσω, *to crouch for fear.*

ΠΤΩ'ΣΣΩ, like πτήσσω, intr. *to crouch* or *cower from fear:* also *to go cowering about,* like a beggar: *to visit like a beggar.* 2. *to flee affrighted:* c. acc. *to flee from.*

πτωχεία Ion. –ηίη, ἡ, (πτωχεύω) *begging, beggary.*

πτωχεύω, Ion. impf. πτωχεύεσκον: f. σω: (πτωχός):—*to be a beggar, beg.* II. trans., 1. c. acc. rei, *to get by begging.* 2. c. acc. pers. *to beg* or *ask an alms of.*

πτωχηίη, Ion. for πτωχεία.

πτωχικός, ή, όν, (πτωχός) *of* or *for a beggar, beggarly.*

πτωχίστερος, irreg. Comp. of πτωχός.

πτωχο-ποιός, όν, (πτωχός, ποιέω) *drawing beggarly characters,* of a poet.

πτωχός, ή, όν, also ός, όν, (πτώσσω) *one who crouches* or *cringes;* as Subst., πτωχός, ὁ, *a beggar:* also πτωχὸς ἀνήρ a *beggar*man. II. as Adj. *beggarly, mean, sorry:*—later also *poor.*—Comp. and Sup. πτωχότερος, –ότατος; irreg. Comp. πτωχίστερος.

Πῠᾰνέψια (sub. ἱερά), τά, (πύανος, ἕψω) *the Pyanepsia,* an Athenian festival in the month πυανεψιών, in honour of Apollo: said to be so called from *a dish of beans then eaten.* Hence

Πῠᾰνεψιών, ῶνος, ὁ, the fourth month of the Attic year, so named from the festival **Πυανέψια**: corresponding to the latter part of October and former of November.

ΠΥ'ΑΝΟΣ, ὁ, *a bean.*

πῡγαῖος, α, ον, (πυγή) *of* or *on the rump:* τὸ πυγαῖον ἄκρου the tip *of the rump*

πύγ-αργος, ον, (πῡγή, ἀργός) *white-rump,* name of a Libyan antelope; also of the sea-eagle.

ΠΥΓΗ', ῆς, ἡ, *the rump, buttocks.* Hence

πῡγίδιον, τό, Dim. *a thin, narrow rump.* [ῐ]

πυγμαῖος, α, ον, (πυγμή II) *about a foot long* or *tall.* II. Πυγμαῖοι, οἱ, *the Pigmies, a fabulous race of dwarfs* on the upper Nile, said to have been attacked and destroyed by Cranes.

πυγμᾰχέω, f. ήσω, *to practise boxing, be a boxer.* And

πυγμᾰχία, ἡ, *boxing,* Lat. *pugilatus.* From

πυγ-μάχος, ον, (πυγμή, μάχομαι) *fighting with the fist:* as Subst., πύγμαχος, ὁ, *a boxer,* Lat. *pugil.*

πυγμή, ἡ, (πύξ) *a fist,* Lat. *pugnus:* also *a battle with fists, boxing-match;* πυγμὴν νικᾶν to be conqueror *in the contest of boxing.* II. a measure of length, *the distance from the elbow to the knuckles,* =18 δάκτυλοι, about 1 ft. 1½ inches. III.

πυγμῇ, dat. used as Adv., either = πύκα, *often, frequently;* or *up to the elbow.*

πῡγο-στόλος, ον, (πυγή, στολή) *with sweeping train, with trailing robe.*

πῡγούσιος, α, ον, *about* 15 *inches long.* From

ΠΥΓΩ'Ν, όνος, ἡ, *the elbow.* II. as a measure of length, *the distance from the elbow to the first joint of the fingers,* = 20 δάκτυλοι or 5 παλασταί, about 15 inches.

πῡδᾰρίζω, f. ίσω, *to hop, jump, dance.*

ΠΥΈΛΟΣ, ἡ, *a tub, trough* or *vessel* for feeding animals: *a bathing-tub: a vat, boiler, copper.*

Πῡθᾰγόρας, ου Dor. α, ὁ, the philosopher *Pythagoras.* Hence

πῡθᾰγορίζω, f. ίσω, *to be a disciple of Pythagoras.*

Πῡθᾰγοριστής, οῦ, Dor. -ιστάς, ά, ὁ, (πυθαγορίζω) *a Pythagorean, follower of Pythagoras.*

πῠθέσθαι, aor. 2 inf. of πυνθάνομαι.

πύθευ, Dor. for πύθου, aor. 2 med. imperat. of πυνθάνομαι.

Πῡθία (sub. ἱέρεια), ἡ, fem. of Πύθιος, *the Pythia* or *priestess of Pythian Apollo* at Delphi, who uttered the responses of the oracle.

Πύθια (sub. ἱερά), τα, neut. pl. of Πύθιος, *the Pythian games,* celebrated every four years at *Pytho* (see Πυθώ) in honour of *Pythian Apollo.*

Πῡθιάς, άδος, pecul. fem. of Πύθιος; Πυθιὰς βοά a song *to Apollo.* II. (sub. περίοδος), *a Pythiad,* period of four years, after which the Pythian games were celebrated, like Ὀλυμπιάς. 2. *the celebration of the Pythian games.*

Πῡθικός, ή, όν, (Πυθώ) *of* or *for Pytho, Pythian, Delphic.*

Πύθιον, τό, *the temple of Pythian Apollo* at Delphi.

Πῡθιο-νίκης, ου, ὁ, (Πύθια, νικάω) *a conqueror in the Pythian games.*

Πῡθιό-νῑκος, ον, (Πύθια, νικάω) *of* or *belonging to a victory in the Pythian games.*

Πύθιος, α, ον, (Πυθώ) *Pythian, of* or *belonging to Pytho, Delphian.* II. Πύθιοι, οἱ, at Sparta, *four persons whose office it was to consult the Delphic oracle* on affairs of state.

πυθμήν, ένος, ὁ, (βυθός) *the hollow bottom* or *stand of a drinking-cup,* Lat. *fundus;* πυθμὴν θαλάσσης *the bottom* of the sea: metaph. *the base* or *foundation* of anything: in pl. *the depths, foundations.* II. *the bottom, root of a tree:* generally, *a root:* metaph. *the original stock* or *stem* of a family.

Πῡθοῖ, Adv., properly dat. of Πυθώ, *at Pytho* or *Delphi.*

πῡθοίατο, Ion. 3 pl. aor. 2 opt. of πυνθάνομαι.

Πῡθοῖδε, Adv., = Πυθώδε, *to Pytho* or *Delphi.*

Πῡθό-κραντος, ον, (Πυθώ, κραίνω) *confirmed by the Pythian god:* τὰ Πυθόκραντα *the Pythian oracles.*

Πῡθό-μαντις, εως, ὁ, ἡ, (Πυθώ, μάντις) *a Pythian prophet.* II. used as Adj., *of the Pythian prophet:* Πυθόμαντις ἑστία the *prophetic* hearth *of Pytho.*

Πῡθο-χρήστης, ου, Dor. -τας, α, ὁ, (Πυθώ, χράω) *a consulter of the Pythian god.*

Πῡθό-χρηστος, ον, (Πυθώ, χράω) *delivered by the Pythian god.* II. *consulting the Pythian god.*

ΠΥ'ΘΩ [ῡ]: fut. πύσω: aor. 1 ἔπῡσα Ep. πῦσα:—*to make rot, to rot, corrode:*—Pass. *to become rotten, to rot, decay, moulder.*

Πῡθώ, gen. οῦς, dat. οῖ, ἡ, *Pytho,* old name of that part of Phocis at the foot of Parnassus, in which lay the town of Delphi: also the oldest name of *Delphi* itself. Hence

Πῡθώδε, Adv. *to Pytho* or *Delphi;* and

Πῡθῶθεν, Adv. *from Pytho* or *Delphi.*

Πῡθών, ῶνος, ἡ, older form for Πυθώ.

Πῡθωνόθεν, Adv., = Πυθῶθεν, *from Pytho.*

ΠΥ'ΚΑ, poët. Adv. from same Root as πυκινός, πυκνός, *thickly, frequently.* 2. *wisely, prudently.*

πῠκάζω old Dor. -άσδω: f. άσω: aor. 1 ἐπύκασα Ep. πύκασα: Pass., aor. 1 ἐπυκάσθην: pf. πεπύκασμαι: (πύκα):—*to make thick* or *close, cover up closely, enwrap;* πυκάζειν στεφάνοις *to cover thick* with crowns: hence *to cover so as to protect, to shelter:* absol. *to crown:*—aor. 1 and pf. pass. part. πυκασθείς and πεπυκασμένος, *thickly covered, well clothed.* 2. metaph. *to overcloud, cast a shadow over:*—Med. *to prepare, fit, make ready for one.* II. *to close fast, shut up.*

πυκάσδω, Dor. for πυκάζω.

πῠκῐ-μηδής, ές, (πυκινός, μῆδος) *of close* or *cautious mind, discreet.*

πῠκῐνός, ή, όν, poët. lengthd. form for πυκνός: neut. πυκινόν and πυκινά as Adv. *closely, thickly: shrewdly.*

πῠκῐνό-φρων, ονος, (πυκινός, φρήν) *wise minded.*

πυκινῶς, Adv. of πυκινός; see πυκνός v.

πυκνά, neut. pl. used as Adv. of πυκνός; see πυκνός v.

πυκνίτης, ου, ὁ, = πυυκίτης, (Πνύξ) *assembling in the Pnyx.* [ῑ]

πυκνόν, neut. used as Adv. of πυκνός: see πυκνός v.

πυκνό-πτερος, ον, (πυκνός, πτερόν) *thick-feathered.*

πυκνόρ-ραξ, -ρᾶγος, (πυκνός, ῥάξ) or **πυκνό-ρωξ,** -ωγος, ὁ, ἡ, (πυκνός, ῥώξ) *thick with berries.*

πυκνός Ep. lengthd. **πῠκῐνός,** ή, όν, (πύξ):—*close, compact:* of substance, *close, solid: thick, close-packed, dense, crowded:* of foliage or plumage, *thick, close.* 2. *frequent, thick, rapid,* Lat. *creber, frequens;* πυκνὰ βέλεα *a thick shower of* darts. II. *well put together, well made, compact, fast, strong:* hence *well-concerted; well-guarded.* III. *great, excessive.* IV. metaph. of the mind, *close guarded, cautious;* hence *shrewd, discreet, wise.* V. besides the regular Adverbs πυκνῶς and πυκινῶς, Homer also uses neuters πυκνόν and πυκνά, πυκινόν and πυκινά as Adv., 1. *closely, firmly, fast.* 2. *much, often, excessively.* 3. *wisely, shrewdly.*

πυκνός, gen. of πνύξ.

πυκνό-στικτος, ον, (πυκνός, στίζω) *thick-spotted, dappled, brindled.*

πυκνότης, ητος, ἡ, (πυκνός) *closeness, thickness.*

denseness. II. *frequency.* III. metaph. *wisdom, shrewdness, discretion.*

πυκνόω, f. ώσω, (πυκνός) *to make close* or *solid: to pack close, roll into small compass, condense:*—Pass. *to be filled out with* a thing. Hence

πύκνωμα, ατος, τό, *a close covering, veil.*

πυκνῶς, Adv. of πυκνός: see πυκνός v.

πυκτᾰλίζω, f. σω, = πυκτεύω, *to box, spar.*

πύκτας, Dor. for πύκτης, *a boxer.*

πυκτεύω, f. σω, *to be a boxer, practise boxing, box, spar: to strike with the fist.* From

πύκτης, ου, ὁ, (πύξ, πυγμή) *a boxer*, Lat. *pugil.*

πυκτικός, ή, όν, (πύκτης) *skilled in boxing.*

πυκτίς, ίδος, ἡ, (πτύσσω) *a writing tablet.*

πυκτίς, ίδος, ἡ, an animal mentioned in Aristophanes, supposed to be *the beaver.*

Πῠλ-ᾰγόρας or **Πυλ-άγορος**, ου, ὁ, (Πύλαι, ἀγείρω) *one sent as an orator to the Amphictyonic Council at Pylae, the deputy of a Greek state at the Amphictyonic Council.* Hence

πῠλᾰγορέω, f. ήσω, *to be a* Πυλαγόρας, *to be sent as a deputy to the Amphictyonic Council.*

Πῠλ-ᾰγόρος, see Πυλαγόρας.

Πύλαι, αἱ, see πύλη II. 2.

Πῠλαία (sub. σύνοδος), ἡ, fem. of πυλαῖος, *the meeting of the Amphictyons at Pylae;* generally, *the Amphictyonic Council:* also *the right of sending deputies to the council.*

πυλαι-μάχος, ον, (πύλος or πύλη, μάχομαι) *fighting at the Gate*, or *fighting at Pylos.*

πυλαῖος, α, ον, (πύλη) *at* or *before the gate* 2. (Πύλαι) *at Pylae;* v. Πυλαία. [ῠ]

πῠλ-άρτης, ου, ὁ, (πύλη, ἀραρίσκω) *he that keeps the gate of hell:* Aeol. gen. πυλάρταο.

πῠλᾰ-ωρός, ὁ, (πύλη, ὥρα) Ep. for πυλωρός, *keeping the gate:* as Subst., πυλάωρος, ὁ, *a gate-keeper*, Lat. *janitor.*

ΠΥ'ΛΗ, η, *a gate:* in plur. *the gates* of a town, opp. to θύρα (*a house-door*): but also = θύρα, *the door of a house.* II. generally, *an entrance, inlet.* 2. *an entrance into a country* through a mountain-pass was called its *gate*, πύλαι, e. g. Πύλαι, αἱ, the shorter name for Θερμοπύλαι, *Pylae*, the pass under the mountains from Thessaly to Locris, considered *the Gates* of Greece; so too of the pass from Syria into Cilicia. 3. also of *narrow straits.* [ῠ]

Πῠλ-ηγόρης, ου, ὁ, Ion. for Πυλαγόρας.

πῠλη-δόκος, ὁ, (πύλη, δέχομαι) *watching at the gate.*

πῠλίς, ίδος, ἡ, Dim. of πύλη, *a little gate, postern.*

Πῠλόθεν, Adv. (Πύλος) *from Pylos.*

Πῠλοι-γενής, ές, (Πύλος, γενέσθαι) *born* or *sprung from Pylos.*

Πῠλόνδε, Adv. (Πύλος) *to* or *towards Pylos.*

πύλος, ὁ, = πύλη, *a gate.*

Πύλος, ὁ or ἡ, *Pylos*, a town and district of Triphylia in Peloponnesus, where Nestor ruled: there were two other towns of the same name in Elis and Messenia. [ῠ]

πῠλ-ουρός, ὁ, (πύλη, οὖρος) *a gate-keeper.*

πῠλόω, f. ώσω, (πύλη) *to furnish* or *enclose with gates:*—Pass. *to be furnished with gates.*

πύλωμα, ατος, τό, *a gate, gateway.*

πῠλών, ῶνος, ὁ, (πύλη) *a gateway, gate-house:* also *a porch* or *vestibule.*

πυλωρέω, *to be a gate-keeper.* From

πῠλ-ωρός, ὁ, (πύλη, ὥρα) *a gate-keeper, warder.*

πύμᾰτος, η, ον, (πυθμήν) *the hindmost, uttermost, last:* πύμᾰτον and πύματα as Adv. *at the last, for the last time.*

πύνδαξ, ακος, ὁ, (πυθμήν) *the bottom* of a vessel.

πυνθάνομαι, lengthd. from πεύθομαι: f. πεύσομαι Dor. πευσοῦμαι: aor. 2 ἐπῠθόμην, imperat. πυθοῦ Dor. πύθευ, inf. πῠθέσθαι, Ep. 3 sing. opt. πεπύθοιτο: pf. πέπυσμαι, 2 sing. πέπῠσαι Ep. πέπυσσαι: plqpf. ἐπεπύσμην, Ep. 3 sing. πέπυστο, Ep. 3 dual πεπύσθην:—*to ask, inquire*, hence *to learn, ascertain by asking* or *inquiry: to hear, learn, understand:* c. gen. *to hear of, hear news of:* also c. acc. *to inquire about:* c. inf. *to hear* or *learn that* ..

ΠΥ'Ξ, Adv. *with clenched fist;* πὺξ ἀγαθός good *at the fist*, i. e. *at boxing*

πυξίνεος, α, ον, and **πυξῖνος**, η, ον, (πύξος) *made of box-wood.*

ΠΥ'ΞΟΣ, ἡ, Lat. *BUXUS, the BOX-tree:* also *its wood.*

ΠΥΟ'Σ or **πῦος**, ὁ, *the first milk after the birth*, Lat *colostrum.*

πύππαξ, an exclamation of surprise, *bravo!*

ΠΥ~Ρ, πῠρός, τό, *fire;* πῦρ Διός *the fire* of Jove, i. e. *lightning.* II. metaph. *fever-heat*, also *feverish hope* III. to express things *terrible;* κρεῖσσον ἀμαιμακέτου πυρός stronger than invincible *fire;* διὰ πυρὸς ἰέναι to go through *fire and water.* Hence

πῠρά, ῶν, τά, *watch-fires*, only in pl.

πῠρά, ᾶs, Ion. **πῠρή**, ῆs, ἡ, *the place where fire is kindled: a funeral-pyre:* also *a burial-place.* 2. *an altar for burnt-sacrifice:* also *the fire burning upon the altar.*

πῠρ-άγρα, ἡ, (πῦρ, ἀγρέω) *a pair of fire-tongs*

πῠρ-αγρέτης, ου, ὁ, = πυράγρα

πῠρ-αίθω, (πυρά, αἴθω) *to light a watch-fire, keep it burning.*

πῠρ-ακτέω, f. ήσω, (πῦρ, ἄγω) *to turn in the fire, to harden in the fire, char.*

πῡράμῖνος, η, ον, (πυρός) = πυρινος, *of wheat, wheaten.*

πῡρᾰμίς, ίδος, ἡ, *a pyramid:*—an Egyptian word.

πῡρᾰμοῦς, οῦντος, ὁ, contr. for πυραμόεις, (πυρός) *a cake of roasted wheat and honey;* given as a prize to him who kept awake best during a night-watch: generally, *the meed* or *prize of victory.*

πῠρ-αυγής, ές, (πῦρ, αὐγή) *fiery bright.*

πυργηδόν, Adv. (πύργος) *like a tower.* II. of soldiers, *in masses* or *columns, in close array.*

πυργηρέω, f. ήσω, *to shut up in a tower:*—Pass. *to be beleaguered, besieged.* From

πυργ-ήρης, ες, (πύργος, ἀρᾰρεῖν) *shut up in a tower, beleaguered: besieged.*

πυργίδιον, τό, Dim. of πύργος, *a turret.*

πύργῐνος, η, ον, (πύργος) *strong as a tower.*

πυργίον, τό, Dim. of πύργος, *a turret.*

πυργο-δάϊκτος, ον, (πύργος, δαΐζω) *destroying towers.* [ᾰ]

πυργο-μᾰχέω, (πύργος, μάχομαι) *to assault* or *batter towers.*

ΠΥ'ΡΓΟΣ, ὁ, *a tower:* in plur. *walls and towers:* generally, *any fortification, a fortress, castle:* also *a moveable tower for* storming towns. 2. metaph. *a tower of defence, rampart, bulwark;* πύργος θανάτων *a bulwark against* death. 3. *the highest part of any building.* III. *a division of an army drawn up in close order, a column:* see πυργηδόν.

πυργο-φόρος, ον, (πύργος, φέρω) *tower-bearing.*

πυργο-φύλαξ, ἄκος, ὁ, (πύργος, φύλαξ) *a tower-guard, warder.* [ῠ]

πυργόω, f. ώσω, (πύργος) *to gird* or *fence with towers:*—Med. *to build towers:*—Pass. *to be furnished with a tower.* II. *to raise up to a towering height:* metaph., πυργῶσαι ῥήματα σεμνά 'to build the lofty rhyme:' hence *to exalt, extol, exaggerate:* — Pass. *to exalt oneself, be overbearing, haughty.*

πυργ-ώδης, ες, (πύργος, εἶδος) *like a tower.*

πύργωμα, ατος, τό, (πυργόω) *a place furnished with towers, a fenced city:* in plur. *towers and walls.*

πυργῶτις, ιδος, fem. Adj. (πυργόω) *towering.*

πυρ-δᾱής, ές, (πῦρ, δαίω) *burning with fire, incendiary.*

πῠρεῖον Ion. **πῠρήιον**, τό, (πῦρ) plur. πυρήια, *pieces of wood* rubbed one against another *till they caught fire:* generally, *any means of kindling fire.*

πῠρέσσω Att. **-ττω**: fut. πυρέξω: aor. 1 ἐπύρεξα: (πυρετός):—*to be feverish, be sick of a fever.*

πῠρετός, οῦ, ὁ, (πῦρ) *burning heat, fiery heat.* II. esp. *feverish heat, a fever;* πυρετὸς τριταῖος, τεταρταῖος *a* tertian, quartan *fever.*

πῠρεύς, έως, ὁ, (πῦρ) *a fire-proof vessel.*

πῠρή, ῆς, ἡ, Ion. and Ep. for πυρά.

πῠρήιον, τό, Ion. for πυρεῖον.

ΠΥ'ΡΗ'Ν, ῆνος, ὁ, *the stone* of stone-fruit, as olives, dates, pomegranates, etc.

πῡρ-ήνεμος, ον, (πῦρ, ἄνεμος) *fanning fire.*

πῡρη-τόκος, ον, (πυρός, τεκεῖν) *wheat-producing.*

πῡρη-φάτος, ον, (πυρός, πέφαται 3 sing. pf. pass. of *φένω) *wheat-slaying,* epith. of a millstone.

πῡρη-φόρος, ον, poët. for πυροφόρος, (πυρός, φέρω) *wheat-bearing.*

πῠρία, ἡ, (πῦρ) *a vapour-bath,* consisting of an air-tight covering, within which fragrant substances were thrown on hot embers to produce steam.

πῠριάτη [ᾱ], ἡ, (πύος) *a pudding made with beestings,* i. e. *the first milk after calving.*

πῠριᾱτήριον, τό, *a vapour-bath.* From

πῠριάω, (πυριά) *to put into a vapour-bath.*

πῠρί-βλητος, ον, (πῦρ, βάλλω) *striking with fire.*

πῠρῐ-γενέτης, ου, ὁ, = πυριγενής.

πῠρῐ-γενής, ές, (πῦρ, γενέσθαι) *born of fire: wrought* or *forged by fire.*

πῠρῐ-γόνος, ον, (πῦρ, γενέσθαι) *fire-producing.*

πῠρί-δαπτος, ον, (πῦρ, δάπτω) *devoured by fire.*

πῠρίδιον, τό, Dim. of πυρός.

πῠρῐ-ήκης, ες, (πῦρ, ἀκή) *pointed in the fire,* Lat. *praeustus.*

πῠρι-καής, ές, = πυρίκαυστος.

πῠρί-καυστος, ον, (πῦρ, καίω) *burnt in the fire.*

πῠρῐ-κοίτης, ες, (πῦρ, κοίτη) *wherein fire lies asleep.*

πῠρῐ-λαμπής, ές, (πῦρ, λάμπω) *bright with fire.*

πύρῐνος [ῠ], η, ον, (πῦρ) *of fire, fiery: sparkling.*

πύρῐνος [ῡ], η, ον, (πῡρός) *of wheat, wheaten.*

πῠρι-πνέων, ουσα, ον, (πῦρ, πνέων) *fire-breathing.*

πῠρί-πνοος, ον contr. **-πνους**, ουν, (πῦρ, πνέω) *fire-breathing: glowing, fiery.*

πῠρί-σπαρτος, ον, (πῦρ, σπείρω) *sowing fire, inflaming.*

πῠρι-σπείρητος, ον, (πῦρ, σπειράω) *swathed in fire.*

πῠρί-στακτος, ον, (πῦρ, στάζω) *streaming with fire.*

πῠρίτης [ῑ], ου, ὁ, fem. **πῠρῖτις**, ιδος, (πῦρ) *of* or *conversant with fire.*

πῠρι-τρόφος, ον, (πῦρ, τρέφω) *cherishing fire.*

πῠρί-φᾰτος, ον, (πῦρ, πέφαται) *slain by fire.*

Πῠρι-φλεγέθων, οντος, ὁ, (πῦρ, φλέγω) one of the rivers of hell, literally *Fireblazing.*

πυρι-φλεγής, ές, and **πῠρι-φλέγων**, οντος, ὁ, (πῦρ, φλέγω) *blazing with fire, flaming.*

πῠρί-φλεκτος, ον, (πῦρ, φλέγω) *burnt* or *blazing with fire: fiery.*

πυρίχη, ἡ, poët. for πυρρίχη.

πυρ-κᾰεύς, έως, ὁ, (πῦρ, καίω) *a fire-kindler.*

πυρκαϊά Ion. **-ιή**, ἡ, (πῦρ, καίω) *any place where fire is kindled, a funeral-pyre.* 2. *a fire, conflagration.* 3. metaph. *the flame* or *fire of love.* II. *an olive-tree which has been burnt down to the stump,* and grows up again *a wild-olive.*

πυρναῖος, α, ον, (πύρνον) *fit to eat, ripe.*

πύρνον, τό, shortd. for πύρινον (sub. σιτίον), neut. of πύρινος (πῡρός), *wheaten bread.* 2. *anything fit to eat, food generally.*

πῡρο-γενής, ές, (πυρός, γενέσθαι) *made from wheat.*

πῠρόεις, εσσα, εν, (πῦρ) *fiery.* II. ὁ πυρόεις *the planet Mars,* from his *fiery* colour.

πῠροκλοπία, ἡ, *the fire-theft.* From

πῠρο-κλόπος, ον, (πῦρ, κλέπτω) *fire-stealing.*

πῡρο-λόγος, ον, (πυρός, λέγω) *reaping wheat.*

πῡροπωλέω, f. ήσω, *to deal in wheat.* From

πῡρο-πώλης, ου, ὁ, (πυρός, πωλέω) *a wheat-merchant, corn-merchant.*

πῠρορ-ρᾰγής, ές, (πῦρ, ῥαγῆναι) *bursting* or *splitting in the fire:* as Adv. πυρορραγές, *cracked.*

πῡρός, ὁ, *wheat:* in plur. *grains of wheat.* (From πῦρ, because of its *flame colour* when ripe?)

πῠρο-φόρος, ον, (πῦρ, φέρω) *fire-bearing.*

πῡρο-φόρος, ον, (πῡρός, φέρω) *wheat-bearing.*

πῠρόω, f. ώσω, (πῦρ) *to set on fire, to burn: to burn*

as a burnt-sacrifice. 2. metaph. *to inflame.* II. *to fumigate.*

πυρ-πᾰλᾰμάω, f. ήσω, (πῦρ, παλαμάομαι) *to handle fire: to play tricks with fire, play mischievous pranks.*

πυρ-πάλᾰμος, η, ον, (πῦρ, παλάμη) *wrought of fire.*

πυρ-πνόος, ον, (πῦρ, πνέω) *fire-breathing.*

πυρπολέω, f. ήσω, (πυρπόλος) *to light* or *make a fire*, esp. *to keep up a fire, watch a fire;* πυρπολεῖν τοὺς ἄνθρακας *to stir up* or *fan* the fire. II. *to waste with fire, burn to the ground, burn down.* Hence

πυρπόλημα, ατος, τό, *a watch-fire, beacon.*

πυρ-πόλος, ον, (πῦρ, πολέω) *busied with fire: wasting with fire, scorching.*

πυρράζω, f. σω, (πυρρός) *to be fiery-red.*

πυρρίας, ου, ὁ, (πύρρος) name of a slave, used of the *red-haired slaves from Thrace.*

πυρρίχη (sub. ὄρχησις), ἡ, *the Pyrrhic dance, a* kind of *war-dance, a violent movement* or *contortion:* proverb., πυρρίχην βλέπειν 'to look daggers.' (Called from Πύρριχος, the inventor.) [ῐ]

πυρρῐχιᾰκός, ή, όν, (πυρρίχιος) *in the Pyrrhic metre.*

πυρρῐχίζω, f. ίσω, (πυρρίχη) *to dance the Pyrrhic dance.*

πυρρίχιος, ὁ, (πυρρίχη) *of* or *belonging to the Pyrrhic dance;* πυρρίχιον ὄρχημα *the Pyrrhic* dance. II. ποὺς πυρρίχιος *a pyrrhic*, i. e. a foot consisting of two short syll., as μετά, which was much used in the Pyrrhic song: also called παρίαμβος.

πυρρῐχιστής, οῦ, ὁ, (πυρριχίζω) *a dancer of the Pyrrhic dance.*

πύρρῐχος, η, ον, Dor. πυρρός, *red.*

πυρρο-γένειος, ον, (πυρρός, γένειον) *red-bearded.*

πυρρό-θριξ, τρῐχος, ὁ, ἡ, (πυρρός, θρίξ) *red-haired.*

πυρρ-οπίπης [ῐ], ου, ὁ, (πυρρός, ὀπιπτεύω) *one that ogles boys,* with an allusion to πῡρ-οπίπης *ogling wheat*, i. e. dinner in the Prytanēum.

πυρρός, ά, όν, Ion. ή, όν, old Att. **πυρσός**, ή, όν, (πῦρ) *flame-coloured, red,* Lat. *rufus*, darker than ξανθός: generally, *reddish, red, tawny.*

πυρρό-τρῐχος, ον, = πυρρόθριξ.

πυρσαίνω, (πυρσός) *to make red, tinge with red.*

πυρσεύω, (πυρσός) *to set on fire, light up with beacon-fires.* II. *to kindle torches* (πυρσοί), *make signals by torches* or *beacon-fires.*

πυρσο-βόλος, ον, (πυρσός, βαλεῖν) *fire-shooting.*

πυρσό-κομος, ον, (πυρσός, κόμη) *red-haired.*

πυρσό-νωτος, ον, (πυρσός, νῶτος) *red-backed.*

πυρσός, οῦ, ὁ: irreg. pl. πυρσά, τά: (πῦρ): *a firebrand, torch.* II. *a beacon* or *signal-fire.*

πυρσός, ή, όν, old Att. and Dor. for πυρρός.

πυρσο-τόκος, ον, (πυρσός, τεκεῖν) *fire-producing.*

πυρσ-ώδης, ες, (πυρσός, εἶδος) *like a firebrand, bright-burning.*

πυρσ-ώρος, ὁ, (πυρσός, ὥρα) *a watchman who makes signals by fire.*

πυρφορέω, f. ήσω, *to be a torch-bearer: to set on fire.* From

πυρ-φόρος, ον, (πῦρ, φέρω) *fire-bearing, charged with fire:* ὁ Πυρφόρος *the Fire-bringer,* name of Prometheus in a play of Aeschylus; πυρφόροι οἰστοί arrows with *combustibles tied to them.* II. θεὸς πυρφόρος *the fire-bearing* god, i. e. *who produces plague* or *fever.* III. πυρφόρος, in the Lacedaemonian army, was *a priest who kept the sacrificial fire:* hence proverb. of a total defeat, ἔδει μηδὲ πυρφόρον περιγενέσθαι it was fated that not even *a fire-guarding priest* should survive.

πῡρ-ωπός, οῦ, (πῦρ, ὤψ) *fiery-eyed.*

πύρωσις, εως, ἡ, (πυρόω) *a setting on fire, burning.*

πύστις, εως, ἡ, (πυνθάνομαι) *an asking, inquiring, ascertaining: a question.* II. *what is learnt by asking, news, tidings.*

πύσω, fut. of πύθω.

πῡτίζω, f. ίσω, (πτύω) *to spurt out* water from one's mouth.

πῡτῐναῖος, α, ον, *plaited with willows.* From

ΠΥΤΙ´ΝΗ, ἡ, *a flask covered with plaited willow twigs.* [ῐ]

πύτισμα, ατος, τό, (πυτίζω) *that which one spits out.*

πω Ion. **κω**, enclit. Particle, *up to this time, yet, ever yet, hitherto,* mostly with negat. II. πῶ; Sicilian for ποῦ; as interrog. *where?*

ΠΩΓΩΝ, ωνος, ὁ, *the beard;* πώγων πυρός *a beard* or *tail* of fire. Hence

πωγωνίας, ου, ὁ, *bearded;* ἀστὴρ πωγωνίας *a bearded* star, i. e. a comet.

πωγώνιον, τό, Dim. of πώγων, *a little beard.*

πωγωνο-φόρος, ον, (πώγων, φέρω) *wearing a beard.*

πώεα, τά, pl. nom. of πῶϋ.

πωλεία, ἡ, (πωλεύω) *a breeding of foals.*

πωλέομαι Ion. **πωλεῦμαι**, whence part. πωλεύμενος, impf. πωλεύμην; also Ion. 3 sing. impf. πωλέσκετο: fut. πωλήσομαι: Dep.:—Frequent. of πολέω, *to go up and down* in a place, *frequent, wander about,* Lat. *versari in loco: to go* or *come frequently to* a place: c. gen., ἀγγελίης πωλεῖσθαι *to go* on a message. II. *to pursue a walk* or *line of life.*

πωλεύμην, Ep. for ἐπωλούμην, impf. of πωλέομαι.

πώλευσις, ἡ, (πωλεύω) *horse-breaking.*

πωλεύω, (πῶλος) *to break in a young horse.*

πωλέω, Ion. impf. πωλέεσκον: f. ήσω; (*πολάω, which occurs in ἐμ-πολάομαι):—*to sell,* opp. to ὠνεῖσθαι πωλεῖν πρός τινα *to deal with* one:—πωλεῖν τέλη, *to let out* the taxes, Lat. *locare*:—Pass. *to be sold:* of persons, *to be bought and sold, betrayed;* cf πιπράσκω.

πώλης, ου, ὁ, (πωλέω) *a seller, dealer.*

πώλησις, ἡ, (πωλέω) *a selling, sale.*

πωλητήριον, τό, *a place where wares are sold, a mart, warehouse, shop.* II. *the place where the taxes were let to the highest bidder:* see πωλητής.

πωλητής, οῦ, ὁ, (πωλέω) *a seller, dealer.* II. at Athens the πωληταί were ten officers, *who used to let out* (ἐπώλουν, Lat. *locabant*) the taxes and other revenues to the highest bidders.

πωλικός, ή, όν, (πῶλος) *of foals* or *fillies:* generally, *of* or *for horses;* ἀπήνη πωλική a chariot *drawn by horses.* II. poët. *virgin, maidenly.*

πωλίον, τό, Dim. of πῶλος, *a pony.*

πωλοδαμνέω, f. ήσω, *to break young horses.* 2. metaph. *to train up, rear.* From

πωλο-δάμνης, ου, ὁ, (πῶλος, δαμάω) *a horse-breaker.*

πωλο-μάχος, ον, (πῶλος, μάχομαι) *fighting on horseback* or *in a chariot.* [ᾰ]

ΠΩ͂ΛΟΣ, ὁ and ἡ, *a foal,* whether *colt* or *filly:* generally, *a young animal.* II. poët. as fem. *a young girl, maiden,* like μόσχος, πόρτις, Lat. *juvenca:* more rarely as masc. *a young man, a son.*

πώλῠ-πος, ὁ, Aeol. and Dor. for πολύπους.

πῶμα, ατος, τό, *a lid, cover.* (Deriv. unknown.)

πῶμα, ατος, τό, (ΠΟ– Root of some tenses of πίνω) *a drink, a draught, potion.*

πώ-μᾰλᾰ, Adv. for πῶς μάλα; *how in the world?* hence in Att. without any question, = οὐδαμῶς, *not the least, by no means.*

πώ-ποτε, (πω, ποτέ) *ever yet,* mostly with a negat.

πώρῐνος, η, ον, (πῶρος) *made of tufa* or *tuff-stone.*

πῶρος, ὁ, *tuff-stone,* Lat. *tophus,* Ital. *tufa,* friable and porous.

πωρόω, f. ώσω, (πῶρος) *to petrify, turn into stone.* II. generally, *to harden, make callous.* III. metaph. in Pass. *to become hardened* or *callous,* of the heart.

πώρωσις, εως, ἡ, (πωρόω) *a turning into stone:* metaph. from Pass. πωρόομαι, *hardness of heart, callousness.*

πῶς Ion. **κῶς**, interrog. Adv. *how? in what way* or *manner?* Lat. *quomodo?* in Att. sometimes c. genit., πῶς ἀγῶνος ἥκομεν; *how* are we come off in the contest? II. at the beginning of a speech, *How now?* πῶς γάρ ..; as if something had gone before, *How should that be, for it cannot be that ..?* so also πῶς δή; πῶς γὰρ δή, III. πῶς ἄν with the opt. expresses a wish, *O how* might I ..? *would that* I could! πῶς ἂν ὀλοίμην; *would that* I could perish! V. καὶ πῶς; introducing an objection, *yet how* can that be? *but how?* V. πῶς οὔ; Lat. *quidni? why not? certainly.* VI. πῶς δοκεῖς; *how think you?* i. e. *you cannot think how.*

πως Ion. **κως**, enclit. Adv. *in any way, at all, by any means,* Lat. *aliquo modo.*

(Strictly speaking, πῶς is Adv. of *πός; *quis?* whence ποῦ, πω, ποῖ, etc.)

πωτάομαι, f. -ήσομαι, Ep. for πέτομαι, ποτάομαι, *to fly.* Hence

πώτημα, ατος, το, *flight.*

ΠΩ͂Υ, εος, τό, pl. πώεα, τά, *a flock of sheep,* with or without οἰῶν, opp. to βοῶν ἀγέλαι.

Ρ

Ρ, ρ, ῥῶ, τό, indecl., seventeenth letter of Greek Alphabet: as numeral ρʹ = 100, but ͵ρ = 100,000.

Dialectic changes of ρ: 1. Aeol. at the end of words σ passed into ρ, as, οὗτορ μάρτυρ for οὗτος μάρτυς: so in Lat. *arbor arbos, honor honos* II. in later Att., the Ion. and old Att. ρσ passed into ρρ, as ἄρρην θάρρος, for ἄρσην θάρσος. III. Att., ρ was often put for λ, as κρίβανος ναύκραρος σιγηρός, for κλίβανος ναύκληρος σιγηλός. IV. in Poets, ρ is transposed, as κάρτος Ep. for κράτος, θάρσος for θράσος. V. ρ is doubled after a Prep. or α privat., and commonly after the augment, as ἀπορ-ρίπτω, ἄρ-ρωστος, ἔρριψε. VI. ρ at the beginning of a word sometimes makes a short vowel at the end of foreg. word long by position, as, ψυχρὴ ὑπō ῥιπῆς, σπεύδειν ἄπō ῥυτῆρος. VII. ρ was called by the ancients *littera canina,—irritata canis quod 'rr' quam plurima dicat,* Lucil.

ῥά, enclit. Particle, Ep. for ἄρα, q. v. [ᾰ]

ῬΑ͂ or ῥᾶ, Adv. *easily:* see ῥέα, ῥεῖα.

ῥαββί, ὁ, indecl., Hebrew word, *Rabb-i,* i. e. *my master:*—so also ῥαββονί or ῥαββουνί, ὁ, *Rabb-oni, my master,* a term of higher honour than *Rabb-i.*

ῥαβδίζω, f. σω, (ῥάβδος) *to beat with a stick, cudgel: to thrash out* corn.

ῥαβδίον, τό, Dim. of ῥάβδος, *a small wand.*

ῥαβδονομέω, f. ήσω, *to sit as umpire.* From

ῥαβδο-νόμος, ον, (ῥάβδος, νέμω) *holding a rod* or *wand:* as Subst., ῥαβδονόμος, ὁ, = ῥαβδοῦχος, the Roman *Lictor.*

ῬΑ΄ΒΔΟΣ, ἡ, *a rod, wand, stick, switch.* 2. *a magic wand,* as that of Circé or Hermes. 3. *a fishing-rod.* 4. *a spear-staff* or *shaft.* 5. *a wand* or *staff of office: a sceptre.* 6. in pl. ῥάβδοι are *the fasces* of the Roman lictors

ῥαβδουχέω, f. ήσω, (ῥαβδοῦχος) *to carry a rod* or *wand of office.* 2. *to carry the fasces, to be a lictor:*—Pass. *to be attended by lictors.* Hence

ῥαβδουχία, ἡ, *the office of lictor.*

ῥαβδ-οῦχος, ον, (ῥάβδος, ἔχω) *carrying a rod:*—as Subst., ῥαβδοῦχος, ὁ, *one who bears a staff of office, a judge, umpire.* 2. *a magistrate's attendant,* a sort of *constable* or *beadle:*—at Rome, *a lictor.*

ῥαβδο-φόρος, ου, = ῥαβδοῦχ

ῥαβδωτός, ή, όν, (ῥάβδος) *striped, streaked,* Lat. *virgatus.*

ῥᾰγάς, άδος, ἡ, (ῥαγῆναι) *a rent, chink.*

ῥᾰγῆναι, aor. 2 pass. inf. of ῥήγνυμι.

ῥαγδαῖος, α, ον, (ῥάσσω) *tearing, furious.*

ῥᾱγίζω, f. ίσω, (ῥάξ) *to gather grapes.*

ῥᾱγο-λόγος, ον, (ῥάξ, λέγω) *gathering berries* or *grapes.*

ῥαδινάκη, ἡ, Persian name for *a black ill-smelling petroleum* found at Ardericca near Susa.

ῬΑ͂ΔΙΝΟ΄Σ, ή, όν, Aeol. **βραδινός**, ά, όν, *slender: taper, slim, delicate, tender.*

ῥάδιος, α, ον, Att. also ος, ον, Ion. **ῥηΐδιος**, η, ον [ῐ], or **ῥήδιος**, η, ον (ῥᾶ, ῥέα, ῥεῖα), *easy, easy to make* or *do;* οἶμος ῥηιδίη *an easy* road: c. inf., τάφρος ῥηιδίη περῆσαι a trench *easy* to cross:—also *light,* *simple, little-heeded.* II. of persons, *easy, ready, willing to oblige, complaisant, affable,* Lat. *facilis, commodus.* 2. in bad sense, *heedless, reckless.*—The degrees of Comparison are irreg., being formed from the Root ῥᾳ:—Comp. ῥᾴων, neut. ῥᾷον Ion. ῥηΐων, ῥήϊον Ep. ῥηΐτερος contr. ῥᾴτερος:—Sup. ῥᾷστος, η, ον Ion. ῥήϊστος Dor. ῥᾴϊστος Ep. ῥηΐτατος.

ῥᾳδιουργέω, f. ήσω, (ῥᾳδιουργός) *to do with ease.* II. in bad sense, *to act thoughtlessly, recklessly: to misbehave.* 2. *to lead an easy, lazy life.* Hence

ῥᾳδιούργημα, , ὁ, *a thoughtless, reckless action:* and

ῥᾳδιουργία, ἡ, *doing* or *acting easily, a ready way of doing* a thing, *facility.* II. in bad sense, *recklessness.* 2. *indolence, laziness.*

ῥᾳδι-ουργός, όν, (ῥᾴδιος, ἔργον) *doing* things *easily, ready.* II. in bad sense, *acting lightly* or *carelessly, thoughtless, reckles*

ῥᾳδίως Ep. and Ion. **ῥηϊδίως,** Adv. of **ῥᾴδιος,** *easily, lightly, readily:* ῥᾳδίως φέρειν to bear *lightly,* make *light* of a thing.

ῥᾰθάμιγξ, ιγγος, ἡ, (ῥαίνω) *a drop.* II. of solids, *a grain, bit.*

ῥᾰθᾰ-πῡγίζω, (ῥάσσω, πυγή) *to slap one on the back.*

ῥᾳθῡμέω, f. ήσω, (ῥᾴθυμος) *to be easy-tempered, thoughtless, careless.* II. *to slacken work, be idle.* Hence

ῥᾳθῡμία, ἡ, *easiness of temper: thoughtlessness, carelessness.* II. *a taking things easily, indifference, sluggishness, laziness.* III. *relaxation, amusement, pastime.*

ῥᾴ-θῡμος, ον, (ῥᾴδιος, θυμός) *easy-tempered, thoughtless, careless.* II. *sluggish, lazy, slothful.* Hence

ῥᾳθύμως, Adv. *with easy temper, carelessly;* ῥᾳθύμως φέρειν *to take easily, to shew indifference to* a thing.

ῥαιβό-κρᾱνος, ον, (ῥαιβός, κράνιον) *crook-headed.*

ῬΑΙΒΟ'Σ, ή, όν, *crooked, bent, bandy.*

ῥαιβο-σκελής, ές, (ῥαιβός, σκέλος) *crook-legged.*

ῥᾳΐζω Ion. **ῥηΐζω,** f. ίσω, (ῥᾴδιος) *to grow easy: to find relief, recover: to take one's rest.*

ῬΑΙ'ΝΩ, fut. ῥᾰνῶ: aor. 1 ἔρρᾱνα, Ep. 2 pl. imperat. ῥάσσατε (as if from *ῥάζω)): pf. pass. ἔρρασμαι (also from *ῥάζω), Ep. 3 pl. pf. and plqpf. ἐρράδαται, -ατο:—*to sprinkle, besprinkle,* of water: of solids, *to strew, bestrew, scatter:* metaph. *to bedew, besprinkle, bespatter.*

ῥαισέμεναι, Ep. for ῥαίσειν, fut. inf. of ῥαίω.

ῥαίσῃ, 3 sing. aor. 1 subj. of ῥαίω.

ῥαιστήρ, ῆρος, ὁ, (ῥαίω) *a breaker, crusher: a hammer.*

ῬΑΙ'Ω, f. σω: aor. 1 ἔρραισα:—*to break, smash, shiver, shatter:*—Pass. *to be shivered, shattered, crushed.* II. *to crush, destroy:*—Pass. *to be broken down, crushed.*

ῥακά, ὁ, *a worthless, wicked man.* (Hebrew word.)

ῥάκιον, τό, Dim. of ῥάκος, *a rag, shred, patch:* in plur., *rags.* [ᾰ]

ῥᾰκιο-συρραπτάδης, ου, ὁ, (ῥάκιον, συρράπτω) *a rag-stitcher, patcher of tatters,* of Euripides.

ῥᾰκό-δῡτος, ον, (ῥάκος, δύω) *clad in rags: ragged.*

ῥᾰκόεις, εσσα, εν, *ragged, tattered.* II. *wrinkled.* From

ῬΑ'ΚΟΣ [ᾰ], εος, τό, *a ragged, tattered garment:* in plur. ῥάκεα, ῥάκη, *rags, tatters:* generally, *a strip* or *shred of cloth.* 2. in plur. *wrinkles.* metaph., σώματος ῥάκος *a shred* of life, of an old man.

ῥακόω, f. ώσω, (ῥάκος) *to tear in strips.* Hence

ῥάκωμα, ατος, τό, = ῥάκος, *a rag:* in pl. *rags.* [ᾰ]

ῬΑ'ΜΝΟΣ, ἡ, *a thorn* or *prickly shrub.* Hence

Ῥαμνοῦς, οῦντος, ὁ, *Rhamnûs,* a demus or borough in Attica: properly contr. from ῥαμνόεις, εσσα, εν *thorny.* Hence

Ῥαμνούσιος, α, ον, *of Rhamnûs:* ἡ Ῥαμνουσία, *the Rhamnusian goddess,* name of Nemesis from her temple at Rhamnûs.

ῬΑ'ΜΦΟΣ, εος, τό, *the crooked beak* of birds, esp. of birds of prey: *a beak, bill*

ῥᾰνίς, ίδος, ἡ, (ῥαίνω) *anything sprinkled: a drop of rain,* etc.

ῥαντήριος, α, ον, (ῥαίνω) *sprinkled: reeking.*

ῥαντίζω, f. σω, (ῥαίνω) *to sprinkle, moisten:* hence *to cleanse by sprinkling.*

ῥαντισμός, ὁ, (ῥαντίζω) *a sprinkling, purification*

ῥάξ, gen. ῥᾶγός, ἡ, *a grape;* cp. Lat. *racemus.*

ῥᾷον, neut. of ῥᾴων, often used as comp. Adv., *more easily.*

ῥᾳόνως, Adv. of ῥᾴων, *more easily.*

ῥᾰπίζω, f. ίσω: pf. pass. ῥεράπισμαι: (ῥαπίς):—*to strike with a stick, to thrash, cudgel.* II. *to slap in the face, box on the ear, cuff.*

ῥᾰπίς, ίδος, ἡ, (ῥάβδος) *a rod, stick.*

ῥάπισμα, ατος, τό, (ῥᾰπίζω) *a blow with the palm of the hand, a slap on the face, cuff.*

ῥαπτός, ή, όν, (ῥάπτω) *sewn, stitched, patched:* generally, *strung together.* II. *worked with the needle, embroidered;* ῥαπτὴ σφαῖρα a ball *patched of divers colours.*

ῬΑ'ΠΤΩ, f. ῥάψω: aor. 1 ἔρραψα Ep. ῥάψα: Pass., aor. 2 ἐρράφην [ᾰ]: pf. ἔρραμμαι:—*to sew* or *stitch together:*—Med. *to stitch, sew, patch for oneself.* II. later, *to work with the needle, embroider.* III. metaph. *to devise, contrive, concert, plot:*—proverb., τοῦτο τὸ ὑπόδημα ἔρραψας μὲν σύ, ὑπεδήσατο δὲ Ἀρισταγόρης this shoe you indeed *stitched,* but Aristagoras put it on, i. e. you *planned* the plot, but he executed it. IV. *to link* or *string together.*

Ῥάριος, α, ον, *from Raros, Rarian:* Ῥάριον (sub. πεδίον), τό, *the Rarian plain* near Eleusis, sacred to Demeter: whence the goddess was herself called Ῥαριάς. From

Ῥᾶρος, ου, ὁ, *Raros,* father of Triptolemus.

ῥάσσατε, Ep. aor. 1 imperat. of ῥαίνω (as if from *ῥάζω).

ʽΡΑ'ΣΣΩ, f. ξω: aor. 1 ἔρραξα:—like ἀράσσω, *to strike, smite, dash down:* akin to Ion. ῥήσσω, ῥήγνυμι.

ῥᾷστα, neut. pl. of ῥᾷστος, as Adv., *most easily.*

ῥᾷστος, η, ον, irreg. Sup. of ῥᾴδιος, contr. of ῥάϊστος, *most easy.*

ῥᾳστωνεύω, = ῥᾳθυμέω, *to be idle, listless.* From

ῥᾳστώνη Ion. **ῥηστώνη**, ἡ, (ῥᾷστος) *easiness* of doing anything, *facility.* II. *easiness of temper, good nature,* Lat. *facilitas;* ἐκ ῥηστώνης τῆς Δημοκήδεος *from kindness to* Democedes. III. *relief, rest, cessation from* a thing: absol. *rest, leisure, ease: indolence.*

ῥᾴτερος, α, ον, irreg. Comp. of ῥᾴδιος, *more easy.*

ῥᾰφᾰνῑδόω, (ῥαφανίς) *to punish as an adulterer.*

ῥᾰφᾰνίς, ῖδος, ἡ, *the radish,* Lat. *raphanus.* From

ʽΡΑ'ΦΑ^ΝΟΣ, ἡ, *cabbage.* [ρᾰ]

ῥᾰφεύς, έως, ὁ, (ῥάπτω) *a stitcher, sewer.* II. metaph. *a plotter, contriver, planner.*

ῥᾰφή, ἡ, (ῥάπτω) *a seam;* ῥαφὴ κρανίου *the suture* of the skull.

ῥᾰφῆναι, aor. 2 inf. pass. of ῥάπτω.

ῥᾰφιδεύς, έως, ἡ, = ῥαφεύς.

ῥᾰφίς Dor. **ῥαπίς**, ίδος, ἡ, (ῥάπτω) *a needle, pin.*

ῥᾰχία Ion. **ῥηχίη**, ἡ, (ῥάσσω) like ῥηγμίν, *the breaking of the sea on the shore, breakers, surf: the flood-tide,* opp. to ἄμπωτις the ebb: generally, *a high tide, flood.* II. *an edge of the sea, the beach, on which the waves break.* 2. *a mountain-ridge.*

ῥᾰχίζω, f. ίσω, (ῥάχις) *to cut through the spine: to cleave in twain, hew in pieces.*

ῥάχις [ᾰ], gen. ιος Att. εως, ἡ, *the back* of men or animals, *the chine:* also *the backbone,* Lat. *spina dorsi;* ὑπὸ ῥάχιν παγῆναι to be impaled. II. *anything like the backbone, a mountain-ridge.*

ῥαχός Ion. **ῥηχός**, οῦ, ἡ, *a thorn-bush, briar.* 2. *a thorn-hedge.* 3. *a thorn-stick, a twig.*

ῥάψαι, aor. 1 inf. of ῥάπτω.

ῥαψῳδέω, f. ήσω: (ῥαψῳδός):—*to recite poems:*—Pass. of the poems, *to be recited.* 2. *to repeat by heart* or *rote, declaim: to reiterate, keep saying that* ... II. c. acc. pers., *to sing of* one. Hence

ῥαψῳδία, ἡ, *recital of Epic poetry: Epic composition,* opp. to Lyric.

ῥαψ-ῳδός, ὁ, (ῥάπτω ᾠδή) *one who stitches* or *strings songs together: one who recited Epic poems, a rhapsodist;* sometimes of *the bard who recited his own poem,* but mostly of *a class of persons who got their living by reciting the poems of Homer:* hence the poems of Homer came to be divided into certain lengths called *rhapsodies,* i. e. *lays* or *cantos,* which were recited at one time. II. the Sphinx is called ῥαψῳδὸς κύων, from proposing her riddle.

ῥᾴων, ον, irreg. Comp. of ῥᾴδιος, *more easy.*

ῥέᾰ, Ep. Adv. for ῥᾷ (whence ῥᾴδιος), *easily, lightly.* [υ υ, but also contr. as one long syll.]

ʽΡέᾱ, ἡ, Ep. and Ion. **ʽΡείη** or **ʽΡέη**, *Rhea,* wife of Saturn and mother of Jupiter. (Deriv. by transpos. from ἔρα, *Earth?*)

ʽΡΕΓΚΩ, f. ῥέγξω, *to snore:* of horses, *to snort.* (Formed from the sound.)

ʽΡΕΓΟΣ, εος, τό, = ῥῆγος, *a rug, coverlet.*

ῥέγχω, = ῥέγκω, q. v.

ῥέδη, ἡ, *a wagon,* from the Lat. *rheda.*

ῥέεθρον, τό, Ion. and poët. for ῥεῖθρον, *a stream.*

ʽΡΕ'ΖΩ, Ion. impf. ῥέζεσκον: fut. ῥέξω: aor. 1 ἔρεξα and ἔρρεξα: of Pass. only aor. 1 ῥεχθῆναι is used:—like ἔρδω, *to do, act:* absol., but mostly transit., *to do, accomplish, make, effect:* c. dupl. acc. *to do* something *to* one: also c. Adv., κακῶς ῥέζειν τινά *to maltreat* one. II. ἱερὰ ῥέζειν θεῷ *to fulfil* or *accomplish* a sacrifice to a god, Lat. *sacra facere:* hence *to sacrifice:* but also absol. *to do sacrifice,* like Lat. *operari, facere.*

ʽΡΕ'ΘΟΣ, εος, τό, *a limb.* II. *the face, countenance.*

ῥεῖα, another Ep. form of ῥέα, Adv. of ῥᾴδιος, *easily, lightly, carelessly.*

ʽΡείη, ἡ, Ep. and Ion. for ʽΡέα.

ῥεῖθρον, τό, Att. contr. from Ion. ῥέεθρον, (ῥέω) *a river, stream.* 2. later, *the bed of a river:* also *a channel, stream.*

ῥέκτειρα, ἡ, fem. of ῥεκτήρ.

ῥεκτήρ, ῆρος, ὁ, (ῥέζω) *a doer, agent.*

ῥέμβομαι, Dep. *to roam, rove, roll about: to act at random.*

ῥέξαι, ῥέξας, aor. 1 inf. and part. of ῥέζω.

ῥέος, τό, (ῥέω) *a stream.*

ʽΡΕ'ΠΩ, f. ψω, properly of the descending scale, *to incline downwards, to sink, fall, verge,* Lat. *vergere, inclinare:* hence simply *to fall* or *turn downwards.* 2. of one of two parties, *to preponderate, prevail, outweigh.* 3. of persons, *to incline* towards a thing. 4. of duties, *to fall* or *devolve upon one.* 5. of events, *to incline, fall, happen* in a certain way: *to incline, conduce towards* ... II. trans. *to make* the scale *incline* one way or the other: hence in Pass., ἴσως ῥέπεσθαι *to be* equally *balanced* or *poised.*

ῥερῠπωμένος, pf. pass. part. of ῥυπόω.

ῥεῦμα, ατος, τό, (ῥέω) *that which flows, a flow, stream, a river:* also *a stream of lava:* metaph. *a stream, flood* or *tide of men.* 2. *a flood.*

ῥεύσομαι, fut. of ῥέω, *to flow.*

ῥεχθείς, aor. 1 pass. part. of ῥέζω.

***ʽΡΕ'Ω**, *to say,* root of some tenses given under ἐρέω, εἶπον.

ʽΡΕ'Ω, f. ῥεύσομαι: Att. fut. ῥυήσομαι and aor. 2 ἐρρύην, in pass. form but with act. sense: pf. ἐρρύηκα:—*to flow, run, stream, gush;* ῥέεν αἵματι γαῖα the ground *streamed* with blood: also c. acc. cognato, ῥείτω χώρα γάλα, μέλι let the land *flow with* milk, honey; ῥέειν ἀπὸ χιόνος *to flow* from melted snow. 2. metaph. of a *flow* of words, *to stream, run glibly.* 3. *to fall, drop off.* 4. *to flow* or *melt away.* II. trans. *to let flow, make stream, pour.*

ῥῆγμα, ατος, τό, (ῥήγνυμι) *a fracture, breakage, crash, downfall.*

ῥηγμίν or -μίς, gen. ῖνος, ὁ, (ῥήγνυμι) *the sea breaking on the beach,* or *the edge of the shore on which the sea breaks: the breakers, surf.* 2. metaph. *the verge* or *edge* of a thing.

'ΡΗΓΝΥ'ΜΙ or -ύω: 3 sing. impf. ῥήγνυσκε, Ion. for ἐρρήγνυ: fut. ῥήξω: aor. 1 ἔρρηξα: pf. 2 ἔρρωγα (in the sense of the Pass.):—Med., f. ῥήξομαι: Ep. aor. 1 ῥηξάμην:—Pass.: fut. 2 ῥἄγήσομαι: aor. 1 ἐρρήχθην, more usu. aor. 2 ἐρράγην [ᾰ]: pf. ἔρρηγμαι:—*to break, burst, break asunder* or *in pieces, shiver, shatter:* of garments, *to tear, rend,* esp. in sign of grief. 2. as a term of war, *to break* a line of battle; τὸ μέσον ῥῆξαι *to break through* the centre:—also in Med., ῥήξασθαι στίχας *to break oneself a way through* the *ranks:*—also absol. both in Act. and Med., ῥῆξαι, ῥήξασθαι, *to break* or *force one's way through.* 3. *to let break loose, to unchain, let loose;* ῥῆξαι φωνήν *to let loose, give utterance to* the voice, properly of persons speaking for the first time; then *to speak freely, speak out,* like Virgil's *rumpere vocem:* so, ῥῆξαι βροντήν *to let loose* the thunder; ῥῆξαι δάκρυα *to burst* into tears. 4. in form ῥήσσω, absol. *to beat the ground, to dance.* 5. of boxers, *to fell, knock down.* II. Pass. *to break, burst: to break asunder: to break open, yawn,* as the earth in an earthquake. 2. *to burst forth,* like lightning. 3. of ships, *to be wrecked, shattered.* III. intr. chiefly in pf. ἔρρωγα, *to break* or *burst forth:* of a river, *to break its banks:*—metaph. *to burst* or *gush forth.*

ῥήγνυσκε, Ion. for ἐρρήγνυ, 3 sing. impf. of ῥήγνυμι.

'ΡΗ'ΓΟΣ, εος, τό, *a rug* or *blanket,* used as a *coverlet for a bed, for a seat,* or *as a garment.*

ῥῄδιος, η, ον, Ion. contr. from ῥηΐδιος, *easy.*

ῥηθείς, aor. 1 part. pass. of ἐρέω, ἐρῶ: ῥηθῆναι inf.

ῥηΐδιος, η, ον, Ion. for ῥᾴδιος, *easy.*

ῥήιστος, η, ον, Ion. for ῥᾷστος, Sup. of ῥᾴδιος.

ῥηΐτατος, η, ον, Ep. Sup. of ῥᾴδιος.

ῥηΐτερος, η, ον, Ep. Comp. of ῥᾴδιος.

ῥηκτός, ή, όν, (ῥήγνυμι) *broken, rent: to be broken* or *rent, vulnerable, made of penetrable stuff.*

ῥῆμα, ατος, τό, (*ῥέω = ἐρῶ) *that which is said* or *spoken, a word, saying, expression, phrase.* 2. also *the thing spoken of, a thing.* II. in Gramm. *a Verb,* opp. to ὄνομα (a noun).

ῥημάτιον, τό, Dim. of ῥῆμα, *a little word, a pet phrase.*

'ΡΗ'Ν, ἡ, gen. ῥηνός, acc. ῥῆνα, *a sheep, lamb.*

ῥηνο-φορεύς, ὁ, (ῥήν, φέρω) *wearing sheepskin.*

ῥῆξαι, ῥήξας, aor. 1 inf. and part. of ῥήγνυμι.

ῥηξηνορία, ἡ, *might to break through ranks of warriors.* From

ῥηξ-ήνωρ, ορος, ὁ, (ῥήγνυμι, ἀνήρ) *breaking through ranks of warriors.*

ῥηξί-κέλευθος, ον, (ῥήγνυμι, κέλευθος) *forcing a path, clearing the way.*

ῥηξί-νοος, ον, (ῥήγνυμι, νόος) *breaking the spirit.*

ῥῆξις, εως, ἡ, (ῥήγνυμι) *a breaking.* II. *a rent, cleft.* 2. *a bursting* or *breaking forth* of the entrails of victims.

ῥῆσις, gen. εως Ion. ιος, ἡ, (*ῥέω = ἐρῶ) *a saying, speaking; a word, speech;* καταπλέξαι τὴν ῥῆσιν to bring one's *speech* to an end. II. *a tale, legend.* III. *an expression* or *passage* in an author, *a speech in a play.*

ῥήσσω, rarer collat. form of ῥήγνυμι: ῥήσσειν τύμπανα *to beat* drums. 2. absol. *to strike the earth in dancing, to dance,* Lat. *tripudiare.*

ῥηστώνη, ἡ, Ion. for ῥᾳστώνη.

ῥητέον, verb. Adj. of *ῥέω, *one must say.*

ῥητήρ, ῆρος, ὁ, (*ῥέω = ἐρῶ) like ῥήτωρ, *a speaker.*

ῥητορεύω, f. σω, (ῥήτωρ) *to be a public speaker, practise oratory, speak in public:*—Pass., of a speech, *to be spoken.*

ῥητορικός, ή, όν, (ῥήτωρ) *fit for a public speaker* or *public speaking, oratorical, rhetorical:*—ἡ ῥητορική (sub. τέχνη), *rhetoric, the art of speaking.*

ῥητός, ή, όν, verb. Adj. of *ῥέω = ἐρῶ, *said, spoken: named, specified, settled,* Lat. *ratus;* ἐπὶ ῥητοῖς γέρασι with *specified* prerogatives; ἐπὶ ῥητοῖσι on *set terms.* 2. *spoken of, known, famous.*

ῥήτρα Ion. ῥήτρη, ἡ, (*ῥέω = ἐρῶ) *a word, saying, maxim.* 2. *an unwritten law,* whence the laws of Lycurgus were called ῥῆτραι. 3. *a verbal agreement, covenant.*

ῥήτωρ, ορος, ὁ, (*ῥέω = ἐρῶ) *a public speaker, pleader, orator,* Lat. *orator* II. *a rhetorician,* Lat. *rhetor.*

ῥητῶς, Adv. of ῥητός, *in express terms.*

ῥηχίη, ἡ, Ion. for ῥαχία.

ῥηχός, ἡ, Ion. for ῥάχος.

ῥῑγεδᾰνός, ή, όν, or ός, όν, *making one shudder, chilling;* ῥιγεδανὴ Ἑλένη Helen *at whose name one shudders.* From

ῥῑγέω, f. ήσω: aor. 1 ἐρρίγησα Ep. ῥίγησα: pf. ἔρρῑγα, Dor. 3 pl. ἐρρίγαντι (for -ᾱσι), Ep. 3 sing subj. ἐρρίγῃσι, Ep. dat. part. ἐρρίγοντι, in pres sense: (ῥῖγος):—*to shiver* or *shudder with cold:* metaph. *to shudder* with fear or horror: c. inf. *to shudder* or *fear to do* a thing. 2. *to grow cold, cool, slacken in zeal* II. trans. c. acc. *to shudder at* anything. Hence

ῥῑγηλός, ον, *making* one *shiver, chilling.*

ῥίγιον, Comp. Adv. formed from ῥῖγος, *more chilly.* II. metaph. *more horribly.*

ῥίγιστος, η, ον, Sup. formed (like Comp. Adv. ῥίγιον) from ῥῖγος, *most chilly.* II. metaph. *most horrible.*

ῥῑγο-μάχης, ου, ὁ, (ῥῖγος, μάχομαι) *fighting with frost* or *cold.* [ᾰ]

'ΡΙ~ΓΟΣ, εος, τό, Lat. *FRIGUS, frost, cold.* II. *shivering from cold, shuddering,* Lat. *horror*

ῥῑγόω, f. ώσω, (ῥῖγος) like ῥιγέω *to be cold, shiver from frost* or *cold, be chilled.*—This Verb sometimes contracts into ω instead of ου (as if it were ῥιγάω), as, part. ῥιγῶν, ῥιγῶσα, dat. ῥιγῶντι; also opt. ῥιγῴην.

ʽΡΙ΄ΖΑ, *a root:* in plur. *the roots:* metaph. *the roots of the eye; the roots* or *foundations* of the earth, of a mountain, etc. II. *that from which anything springs;* metaph. *a root, stem, stock* of a family, Lat. *stirps: a race, family.* 2. *the root* or *origin* of anything.

ῥίζιον, τό, Dim. of ῥίζα, *a little root.*

ῥιζόθεν, Adv. (ῥίζα) *from the root* or *roots.*

ῥιζο-τομός, όν, (ῥίζα, τεμεῖν) *cutting roots,* esp. for purposes of medicine or witchcraft.

ῥιζόω, f. ώσω: pf. pass. ἐρρίζωμαι: (ῥίζα):—*to make strike root, plant:* metaph. *to plant, fix firmly;* **τυραννὶς** ἐρριζωμένη a *firmly rooted* tyranny:—Pass., of trees and plants, *to take root:* also *to be rooted* or *made fast.* II. in Pass. also, of a place, *to be planted with trees.*

ῥίζωμα, ατος, τό, (ῥιζόω) *a root:* II. metaph. *a root, stem, stock, race, lineage.*

ῥιζ-ώρῠχος, ον, (ῥίζα, ὀρύσσω) *digging for roots.*

ῥικνός, ή, όν, (ῥῖγος) *stiff* or *stark with cold: withered, shrivelled.*

ῥικν-ώδης, ες, (ῥικνός, εἶδος) *shrivelled-looking.*

ῥίμφᾰ, Adv. (ῥίπτω) *lightly, swiftly, fleetly.*

ῥιμφ-άρμᾰτος, ον, (ῥίμφα, ἅρμα) *of a swift chariot;* ῥιμφάρματοι ἅμιλλαι *swift* racing *of chariots.*

ῥίν, ἡ, later form for ῥίς.

ῥινάω, f ήσω, *to file down* or *off:* Pass. *to be filed off: to be the result of filing.* From

ʽΡΙ΄ΝΗ, ἡ, *a file, rasp.* [ῑ]

ῥῑνηλᾰτέω, f. ήσω, *to track by the nose, follow by scent, hunt down.* From

ῥῑν-ηλάτης, ου, ὁ, (ῥίς, ἐλαύνω) *one who tracks by the nose* or *scent.*

ῥῑνό-βολος, ον, (ῥίς, βάλλω) *forced through the nostril, snorting.*

ῥῑνόν, τό, *a hide, skin.* 2. *an ox-hide, a shield.*

ʽΡΙΝΟ΄Σ, οῦ, ὁ and ἡ, *the skin* of a man. II. *the hide* of a beast, esp. *an ox-hide: a wolf's skin.* 2. *an oxhide shield.*

ῥῑνο-τόρος, ον, (ῥινός, τορέω) *piercing shields.*

ʽΡΙ΄ΟΝ, τό, *the peak* of a mountain. 2. *the end of a promontory, a headland, foreland.*

ῥίπεσσι, Ep. pl. dat. of ῥίψ.

ῥῑπή, ἡ, (ῥίπτω) *the force with which a thing is thrown, rushing motion, flight, sweep, swing,* Lat. *impetus;* ῥιπὴ πυρὸς *the rush* or *blast* of fire. 2. *a rushing sound, flapping, fluttering* of wings; *the buzzing* of a gnat; also *the quivering notes* of a lyre: of time, *a twinkling* of the eye. 3. *any quivering motion, a quivering* or *twinkling light,* as of stars:—also *the quick glancing* of feet.

ῥῑπίζω, f. ίσω, (ῥιπίς) *to blow up* or *fan* the flame, Lat. *conflare.*

ῥῑπίς, ῖδος, ἡ, (ῥιπή) *a fan for raising the fire,* used for *bellows.* 2. *a lady's fan.*

ῥίπισμα, ατος, τό, (ῥιπίζω) *the air* or *wind of a fan.*

ῥῖπος, (ῥίψ) *a mat* or *wicker hurdle.*

ῥιπτάζω, f. άσω, Frequentative of ῥίπτω, *to throw to and fro, throw* or *toss about,* Lat. *jactare:*—Pass. *to toss oneself about.*

ῥίπτασκον, Ion. impf. of ῥίπτω.

ῥιπτέω, a form of ῥίπτω, used only in pres. and impf. *to throw* or *toss about.*

ῥιπτός, ή, όν, verb. Adj. of ῥίπτω, *thrown, cast, hurled;* ῥιπτὸς μόρος death *by being thrown down* a precipice.

ʽΡΙ΄ΠΤΩ f. ῥίψω: aor. 1 ἔρριψα Ep. ῥῖψα: pf. ἔρρῖφα: Pass., fut. 1 ῥιφθήσομαι, fut. 2 ῥῖφήσομαι, paullo-p. fut. ἐρρίψομαι: aor. 1 ἐρρίφθην, and aor. 2 ἐρρίφην [ῐ]: pf. ἔρριμμαι: Ep. 3 sing. plqpf. ἐρέριπτο:—*to throw, cast, hurl;* ῥίπτειν χθονὶ *to throw* on the ground: *to cast* a net, ἔρριπται ὁ βόλος the cast *has been made.* 2. *to cast out.* 3. *to cast away: to throw away, waste.* 4. *to throw about.* 5. *to throw forth, let drop, utter,* of words; ῥίπτειν τί τινος *to throw* a thing *at* one. 6. *to cast down;* ῥ. ἑαυτόν. 7. ῥίπτειν κίνδυνον *to make a venture* or *hazard, run a risk.* II. intr. *to throw* or *cast oneself, to fall.*

ʽΡΙ΄Σ, ἡ, gen. ῥῑνός, acc. ῥῖνα: plur. ῥῖνες, Ion. gen. ῥινέων:—*the nose:*—in pl. *the nostrils,* Lat. *nares.*

ῥιφθείς, ῥῐφείς, aor. 1 and 2 pass. part. of ῥίπτω.

ʽΡΙ΄Ψ, ἡ, gen. ῥῖπός, *mat-work* of osiers or rushes, *wicker-work: a mat,* or *wicker hurdle,* Lat. *crates.*

ῥῖψα, Ep. for ἔρριψα, aor. 1 of ῥίπτω.

ῥίψ-ασπις, ιδος, ὁ, ἡ, (ῥίπτω, ἀσπίς) *throwing away a shield in battle, a dastard, recreant.*

ῥῖψις, εως, ἡ, (ῥίπτω) *a throwing: a casting.* II. *a being thrown, falling.*

ῥιψο-κίνδῡνος, ον, (ῥίπτω, κίνδυνος) *running needless risk, foolhardy;* see ῥίπτω 7.

ῥίψ-οπλος, ον, (ῥίπτω, ὅπλον) *throwing away one's arms, panic-struck.*

ῥόα, ἡ, see ῥοιά.

ῥοδάνη, ἡ, *the thread spun, woof, weft.* From

ῥοδᾰνός, ή, όν, (κραδάω) *waving, quivering.*

ῥοδέα contr. **ῥοδῆ,** ἡ, (ῥόδον) *a rose-bush, rose-tree.*

ῥόδεος, α, ον, (ῥόδον) *of roses,* Lat. *roseus.*

ῥοδῆ, ἡ, contr. for ῥοδέα.

ῥόδῐνος, η, ον, (ῥόδον) *made* or *twined of roses.*

ʽΡόδιος, α, ον, (ʽΡόδος) *Rhodian, of* or *from Rhodes.*

ῥοδο-δάκτῠλος, ον, (ῥόδον, δάκτυλος) *rosy-fingered.*

ῥοδο-ειδής, ές, (ῥόδον, εἶδον) *rosy-like, rosy.*

ῥοδόεις, εσσα, εν, (ῥόδος) *of roses.*

ῥοδό-κισσος, ὁ, (ῥόδον, κισσός) *rose-ivy.*

ῥοδό-μηλον Dor. **-μαλον,** τό, (ῥόδον, μῆλον) *a rose-apple:* metaph. *a rosy cheek.*

ʽΡΟ΄ΔΟΝ, τό, *the rose,* Lat. *rosa.*

ῥοδό-πηχυς Dor. **-παχυς,** υ, gen. υος, (ῥόδον, πῆχυς) *rosy-armed.*

ῥοδό-πνοος, ον contr. **-πνους,** ουν, (ῥόδον, πνέω) *breathing of roses.*

ʽΡόδος, ου, ἡ, the island of *Rhodes,* Lat. *Rhodus.*

ῥοδό-χρως, ωτος, ὁ, ἡ, (ῥόδον. χρώς) *rose-coloured, of rose complexion.*

ῥοδωνιά, ἡ, (ῥόδον) *a rose-bed, garden of roses, rosary*, Lat. *rosarium.*

ῥοή Dor. **ῥοά**, ἡ, (ῥέω) *a river, stream, current, flow:* ἀμπέλου ῥοή *the juice* of the grape;—metaph., ῥοαὶ *streams of events, the tide of affairs.*

ῥοθέω, f. ήσω, (ῥόθος) *to dash, plash*, esp. of the stroke of oars. 2. *to murmur, sound hoarse* or *loud.*

ῥοθιάζω, f. άσω, (ῥόθιος) *to dash with the oar.* 2. of pigs eating, *to make a guttling noise.*

ῥοθιάς, άδος, ἡ, poët. fem. of ῥόθιος, *roaring, dashing.*

ῥόθιον, τό, *a dashing wave, a breaker: surge, surf.* 2. *a loud roar* or *shout* of applause: generally, *a tumult, uproar.* Properly neut. from

ῥόθιος, ον, also α, ον, (ῥόθος) *rushing, roaring, dashing.*

ῬΟ'ΘΟΣ, ὁ, *a rushing noise, the roar* or *the dash of waves, the dash of oars;* ἐξ ἑνὸς ῥόθου with one *stroke*, all in time. 2. *a hoarse* or *tumultuous noise, din.* II. *a rushing motion.* (Formed from the sound.)

ῥοιά or **ῥόα** Ion. ῥοίη, ἡ, *a pomegranate-tree.* II. the fruit, *a pomegranate.*

ῥοιβδέω, f. ήσω, (ῥοῖβδος) *to swallow greedily down:* also *to make rustle.*

ῥοιβδήσειεν, 3 sing. Aeol. aor. 1 opt. of ῥοιβδέω.

ῥοίβδησις, ἡ, (ῥοιβδέω) *a whistling, piping.*

ῥοῖβδος, ὁ, *any rushing noise* or *motion, the whirring* or *flapping* of wings, *the rushing* of the wind.

ῥοίζασκε, 3 sing. Ion. impf. of ῥοιζέω.

ῥοιζέω, f. ήσω, (ῥοῖζος) *to make a whistling* or *rushing sound, whistle, hurtle, whiz*, Lat. *stridere.* Hence

ῥοιζηδόν, Adv. *with a rushing noise* or *motion.*

ῥοίζημα, ατος, τό, (ῥοιζέω) *a rushing noise* or *motion, the flapping* of wings.

ῬΟΙ͂ΖΟΣ, ὁ, Ion. ἡ, *any whistling* or *rushing sound, the whizzing* of an arrow, *the flapping* of wings, etc. (Formed from the sound.)

ῬΟΙΚΟ'Σ, ή, όν, *crooked.*

ῥομβητός, ή, όν, (ῥομβέω) *spun round like a top, whirled about.*

ῥόμβος, ὁ, (ῥέμβω) *anything that may be spun* or *whirled round: a top*, Lat. *turbo.* 2. *a magic wheel*, Lat. *rhombi rota.* II. *a spinning, whirling motion;* ῥόμβος αἰετοῦ the eagle's *wheeling flight.* III. *a rhombus*, i. e. a four-sided figure with *all* the sides, but only the *opposite* angles, equal.

ῥομβόω, f. ώσω, *to make into the shape of a rhombus.*

ῥομβωτός, ή, όν, (ῥομβόω) *panelled in lozenge.*

ῥομφαία, ἡ, *a large sword* or *scymitar*, used by the Thracians: generally, *a sword.* (Foreign word.)

ῥόος Att. contr. **ῥοῦς**, ου, ὁ, (ῥέω) *a stream, current;* κατὰ ῥόον, Ep. κὰρ ῥόον, down *stream*, with *stream;* ἀνὰ ῥόον up *stream*, against *stream.*

ῥόπαλον, τό, (ῥέπω) *a club, a stick* or *cudgel* which is thicker at one end: *a war-club* or *mace* of brass. II. *a knocker on a door.*

ῥοπή, ἡ, (ῥέπω) *inclination downwards, a sinking, falling, verging: the sinking of the scale, fall* or *turn of the scale.* 2. metaph. *the turn of the scale, the critical moment;* ἐπὶ ῥοπῆς μιᾶς ἐστι it is just *on the turning-point;* ῥοπὴ βίου *the turning-point, verge* of life. II. *the weight which makes the scale turn;* σμικρὰ παλαιὰ σώματ' εὐνάζει ῥοπή a slight *weight thrown in* puts aged frames to rest

ῥοπτρόν, τό, (ῥέμβω) *a club, mace, cudgel.* 2. *the wood in a trap* which strikes the mouse. 3. *the knocker on a house-door.* 4. *a kettle-drum* or *tambourine.*

ῥοῦς, ὁ, Att. contr. for ῥόος.

ῥοφέω, f. ήσομαι, (ῥόφος), *to sup greedily up, gulp* or *bolt down.*

ῬΟ'ΦΟΣ, ὁ, *a swallowing* or *gulping down.* 2. *that which is gulped down.*

ῥοχθέω, f. ήσω, *to roar*, of the waves. From

ῬΟ'ΧΘΟΣ, ὁ, *a roaring*, esp. of the sea.

ῥο-ώδης, ες, (ῥόος, εἶδος) *fluid, liquid:* also *surging, billowy, rough.*

ῥύαξ, ᾶκος, ὁ, (ῥέω) *a stream that bursts forth, a mountain-stream* or *torrent* swoln by rains: *a stream of lava.*

ῥύᾰτο, 3 pl. Ep. aor. 2 of ῥύομαι.

ῥυγχ-ελέφας, αντος, ὁ, (ῥύγχος, ἐλέφας) *with an elephant's trunk.*

ῥυγχίον, τό, Dim. of ῥύγχος, *a snout, muzzle.*

ῥύγχος, εος, τό, (ῥύζω) *a snout, muzzle*, of swine: of birds, *a beak, bill, neb.*

ῥύδην and **ῥυδόν**, Adv. (ῥέω) *flowingly, abundantly, copiously.*

ῥυείς, aor. 2 pass. part. of ῥέω.

ῥυήσομαι, Att. fut. of ῥέω.

ῬΥ'ΖΩ, *to growl, snarl.* (Formed from the sound.)

ῥύη, Ep. for ἐρρύη, 3 sing. aor. 2 pass. of ῥέω.

ῥυθμίζω, f. ίσω: pf. pass. ἐρρύθμισμαι: (ῥυθμός): —*to bring into measure* or *proportion, to set to time.* II. generally, *to order, arrange, control, train;* ὧδ' ἐρρύθμισμαι thus *have I been controlled.*

ῥυθμός Ion. ῥυσμός, οῦ, ὁ, (ῥέω) *measured motion, time*, Lat. *numerus, rhythm*, in Prose as well as Verse; ἐν ῥυθμῷ in *time*, Lat. *in numerum;* ῥυθμὸν ὑπάγειν to keep *time;* θάττονα ῥυθμὸν ἐπάγειν to introduce a quicker *time* (in playing). II. *proportion* or *symmetry* of parts: hence *form, shape.* III. generally, *proportion, arrangement, order, method.* 2. *the state* or *condition* of anything: of a man, *temper, disposition: the manner* or *fashion* of a thing.

ῬΥΚΑ'ΝΗ, ἡ, *a plane*, Lat. *runcina.* [ᾰ]

ῥῦμα, ατος, τό, (*ῥύω = ἐρύω) *that which is drawn, a drawing;* τόξου ῥῦμα *the drawing* of the bow, i. e. men that draw the bow (the Persians), opp. to λόγχης ἰσχύς the might of the spear (the Greeks); ἐκ τόξου ῥύματος within bow-*shot.* II. (ῥύομαι) *deliverance, protection.*

ῥύμβος, ου, ὁ, Att. for ῥόμβος.

ῥύμη [ῡ], ἡ, (*ῥύω = ἐρύω) *the force, swing, rush* of a body in motion, Lat. *impetus; πτερύγων ῥύμη the rush* of wings: absol. *an onset, charge, attack*: dat. *ῥύμῃ with a swing, with a run.* II. *a quarter of a city, street*, Lat. *vicus; also a lane, alley.*

ῥύμμα, ατος, τό, (ῥύπτω) *anything used for washing, soap.*

ῥῡμός, οῦ, ὁ, (*ῥύω = ἐρύω) *the pole of a car.*

ῬΥ΄ΟΜΑΙ: f. ῥύσομαι [ῡ]: aor. 1 ἐρρῡσάμην Ep. ῥῡσάμην: aor. 2, 3 sing. ἔρρῡτο Ep. ἔρῡτο, 3 pl. ἔρυντο Ep. ῥύατο; inf. ῥῦσθαι: Dep.:—*to draw to oneself, draw out of harm's way*: hence *to rescue, save*: c. inf., ῥύεσθαί τινα θανεῖν *to rescue* one from death:—absol. *to cure, heal.* II. *to free, redeem, deliver* III. *to shield, guard, protect, defend*: of armour, *to shield, cover*: also *to conceal.* IV. *to draw back, hold back, check.* V. *to draw down* the scale, *outweigh, counterbalance.*

ῥύπα, τά, irreg. plur. of ῥύπος.

ῥῠπαίνω, f. ανῶ: aor. 1 ἐρρύπᾱνα: (ῥύπος):—*to cover with dirt*:—Pass. *to be* or *become dirty.*

ῥῠπᾰρία, ἡ, *dirt, filth.* From

ῥῠπᾰρός, ά, όν, (ῥύπος) *foul, dirty*: metaph. *sordid, mean.* Adv. -ρῶς.

ῥῠπάω Ep. **ῥῠπόω**: impf. ἐρρύπων: (ῥύπος):—*to be foul* or *dirty.*

ῥῠπόεις, εσσα, εν, (ῥύπος) *foul, dirty.*

ῬΥ΄ΠΟΣ, ὁ, *dirt, filth, uncleanness*: irreg. pl. ῥύπα, τά, but also regul. ῥύποι, οἱ. II. Att. *sealing-wax.* [ῠ] Hence

ῥῠπόω, f. ώσω, pf. pass. ῥερύπωμαι:—*to make dirty*:—Pass. *to be dirty* or *filthy.*

ῥῠπόω, Ep. for ῥυπάω.

ῥυππᾰπαί, a cry of the Athenian rowers, *yoho!* τὸ ῥυππαπαί is put for *the rowers, the crew.*

ῥύπτω, f. ψω, (ῥύπος) *to remove dirt, to cleanse, wash*:—Pass. *to wash oneself.*

ῥυσαίνομαι, Pass. (ῥυσός) *to be wrinkled.*

ῥῦσθαι, Ep. aor. 2 pass. inf. of ῥύομαι.

ῥῡσιάζω, f. άσω, (ῥύσιον) *to seize as a pledge*: *to seize as one's own property*: hence *to drag away, carry off by force.*

ῥῡσί-βωμος, ον, (ῥύομαι, βωμός) *defending altars.*

ῥῡσί-διφρος, ον, (ῥύομαι, δίφρος) *preserving the chariot.*

ῥύσιον [ῡ], τό, (*ῥύω = ἐρύω) *that which is seized and dragged away*: *booty, plunder, prey*, mostly of cattle II. *that which is seized as a pledge* or *surety, a pledge, security*; ῥύσια, τά, *pledges entrusted to a god*, i. e. *suppliants.* III. *that which is seized by way of reprisals, reprisals.* 2. ῥύσια, τά, *claims to things alleged to have been seized*, Lat. *res repetundae.* 3. in plur., ῥύσια, τά, *deliverance.*

ῥύσιος, ον, (ῥύομαι) *delivering, rescuing.* [ῡ]

ῥῡσί-πολις, εως, ὁ, ἡ, (ῥύομαι, πόλις) *saving the city.*

ῥῡσί-πονος, ον, (ῥύομαι, πόνος) *setting free from toil and trouble.*

ῥύσις, ἡ, (ῥέω) *a flowing*: *a river, stream.* [ῠ]

ῥύσκομαι, collat form of ῥύομαι, Dep. *to save, rescue*: hence ῥύσκευ, Ep. 2 sing. impf.

ῥυσμός, ὁ, rarer form for ῥυθμός.

ῥῡσός, ἡ, όν, (*ῥύω = ἐρύω) *drawn, drawn up*: *wrinkled, shrivelled.*

ῥυστάζω, f. άσω, Frequentat. of *ῥύω = ἐρύω, *to drag along violently, drag to and fro*; πολλὰ ῥυστάζεσκε (3 sing. Ion. impf.) περὶ σῆμα *be dragged* it many times round the grave of Patroclus. Hence

ῥυστακτύς, ύος, ἡ, *a dragging violently*: generally, *violent treatment* or *behaviour.*

ῥῡσ-ώδης, ες, (ῥυσός, εἶδος) *wrinkled-looking.*

ῥῡτ-ᾰγωγεύς, έως, ὁ, (*ῥύω, ἀγωγεύς) *the rope of a horse's halter.*

ῥῡτήρ, ῆρος, ὁ, (*ῥύω = ἐρύω) *one who draws* or *stretches.* 2. *a rope to draw with, a trace*:—*the thong by which one holds a horse, a rein*; ἀπὸ ῥυτῆρος *with loose rein, at full speed.* II. (ῥύομαι) *a saver, defender, rescuer.*

ῥῡτῐδό-φλοιος, ον, (ῥυτίς, φλοιός) *with shrivelled rind.*

ῥῡτίς, ίδος, ἡ, (*ῥύω = ἐρύω) *a wrinkle*, Lat. *ruga.*

ῥῡτός, ἡ, όν, (*ῥύω = ἐρύω) *dragged along.* II. as neut. Subst., ῥῡτά, τά, poët. for ῥυτήρ, *a rein.*

ῥῠτός, ἡ, όν, also ός, όν, (ῥέω) *flowing, running, fluid, liquid.*

ῥύτωρ [ῡ], ορος, ὁ, (*ῥύω = ἐρύω) *one who draws*; ῥύτωρ τόξου *a bowman, archer.* II. (ῥύομαι) *a saver, deliverer, defender.*

ῥύψις, ἡ, (ῥύπτω) *a cleansing, purifying.*

***ῬΥ΄Ω**, = ἐρύω, *to draw*, not used in Act.; see ῥύομαι.

ῥωγᾰλέος, α, ον, (ῥώξ) *broken, rent, torn, ragged.*

ῥωγάς, άδος, ὁ, ἡ, (ῥώξ) fem. Adj. *rent, ragged*; ῥωγὰς πέτρα *a cloven* rock.

Ῥωμᾰϊκός, ή, όν and **Ῥωμαῖος**, α, ον, (Ῥώμη) *Roman*: as Subst., *a Roman.* Adv. -κῶς, *in Roman fashion.* Hence

Ῥωμᾰϊστί, Adv. *in the Roman* or *Latin language.*

ῥωμᾰλέος, α, ον, (ῥώμη) *strong of body*: generally, *powerful, mighty, strong.*

ῥώμη, ἡ, (ῥώομαι) *bodily strength, might*: generally, *strength, force.* II. *a force*, i. e. *army.* III. Ῥώμη, ἡ, *Roma, Rome.*

ῥώννῡμι or -ύω, f. ῥώσω: aor. 1 ἔρρωσα: (ῥώομαι):—*to strengthen, make strong*: *to confirm.* II. Pass. ῥώννῠμαι, but the pf. ἔρρωμαι is generally used as pres., and the plqpf. ἐρρώμην as impf.: aor. 1 ἐρρώσθην:—*to be strong* or *vigorous*: pf. imperat. ἔρρωσο, *fare-well*, Lat. *vale*, the usual way of ending a letter; also, φράζω τινὶ ἐρρῶσθαι, like Lat. *jubeo valere*:—see ἐρρωμένος.

ῥώξ, ἡ, gen. ῥωγός, (ῥήγνυμι) *a cleft, narrow passage*; ῥῶγες μεγάροιο *the narrow entrance* of a room.

ῬΩ΄ΟΜΑΙ, 3 pl. impf. ἐρρώοντο Ep. ῥώοντο: 3 pl. aor. 1 ἐρρώσαντο: Dep.:—*to move violently, to dart* or *rush on*; ῥώεσθαι περὶ πυρήν *to move rapidly* round the pyre; c. acc. cognato, χορὸν ἐρρώσαντο *they plied the lusty* dance; of hair, ἐρρώοντο μετὰ πνοιῆς ἀνέμοιο *it streamed* on the win*d*.

ῥωπήιον τό, (ῥώψ) Ep. and Ion. for ῥωπεῖον (which is not used), *a thicket, coppice:* in plur. *bushes, brushwood, underwood.*

ῥωπικός, ή, όν, (ῥῶπος) *of* or *like small-wares:* hence *cheap, worthless.*

ῬΩ͂ΠΟΣ, ὁ, *any small wares, frippery, trumpery.*

ῥωσθείς, εῖσα, έν, aor. 1 pass. part. of ῥώννυμι.

ῥωχμή, ή, = ῥωχμός.

ῥωχμός, οῦ, ὁ, (ῥώξ) like ῥῆγμα, *a cleft;* ῥωχμὸς γαίης *a gutter* or *channel* worked out in the earth.

ῬΩ͂Ψ, ή, gen. ῥωπός, *a low shrub, bush;* in plur. *underwood, brushwood.*

Σ

Σ, σ, σῖγμα, τό, indecl., eighteenth letter of the Gr. Alphabet: as numeral σ′ = 200, but ͵σ = 200,000.

The final σ was written ς. This ς must not be confounded with ϛ, *stau*, which was in fact the digamma, Ϝ, *vau*, and occupied the sixth place in the old Greek alphabet: hence ϛ′ = 6. There was another form, *san* or *sanpi*, ϡ, which was retained as a numeral, = 900.

Changes of σ in the dialects: I. Aeol., Dor. and Ion. into δ, as ὀδμῇ ἴδμεν for ὀσμῇ ἴσμεν. II. Dor. into θ, as σιὸς ἀγαθὸς παρσένος for θεὸς ἀγαθὸς παρθένος. III. Aeol. and Dor. into τ, as in τύ τέ φατί for σύ σέ φησί. 2. also in later Att., as μέτ-αυλος τήμερον τῦκον for μέσ-αυλος σήμερον σῦκον:—so σσ passed into ττ, as πράττω τάττω for πράσσω τάσσω; θάλαττα διττός for θάλασσα δισσός. IV. Aeol. and Ep., σ was often doubled, as ὅσσος μέσσος for ὅσος μέσος, and in the Ep. fut. and aor. forms ἄσω ἔσω ἴσω, as δαμάσσω ὀλέσσω κομίσσω for δαμάσω ὀλέσω κομίσω; so ὀπίσσω for ὀπίσω. V. σσ and ππ were sometimes interchanged, as, πέσσω πέπτω, ἐνίσσω ἐνίπτω. VI. Dor. σ becomes ξ in fut. and aor. 1 of Verbs, as θεσπιξῶ for θεσπίσω: so, διξός τριξός for δισσός τρισσός. 2. in old Att., the Prep. σύν was written ξύν. VII. σ took the place of the aspirate, esp. in Aeol., with which the Lat. agrees, ὗς, σῦς *sus*, ἅλς *sal*, ἕξ *sex*, ἑπτά *septem*, ἕρπω *serpo*. 2. σ was added to words beginning with a conson., esp. μ and τ, as μάραγδος σμάραγδος, μύραινα σμύραινα, μικρός σμικρός, τέγος στέγω Lat. *tego*. 3. σ was inserted by Poets in the 1 pers. pl. pass. and med., as, τυπτόμεσθα for τυπτόμεθα metri grat.: so too in the Adv. in -θεν, as, ὄπισθεν for ὄπιθεν. VIII. σ is changed into ρ when another ρ precedes, as, ἄρρην χερρός θάρρος for ἄρσην χερσός θάρσος. IX. σ is added to οὕτω ἄχρι μέχρι before a vowel.

σά μάν; Dor. for τί μήν;

Σᾰβάζιος, ὁ, (Σαβός) a Phrygian deity, afterwards taken as a name of *Bacchus* himself.

σᾰβάκτης, ου, ὁ, (σαβάζω) *a shatterer, destroyer,* name of *a mischievous goblin who broke pots.*

σᾰβαχθα-νί, Chaldaean form, *thou-hast-forsaken me,* or *hast-thou-forsaken me?*

σαβαώθ, Hebrew plur. noun, *hosts, armies.*

Σάββᾰσι, irreg. dat. pl. of Σάββατον.

Σαββᾰτίζω, f. ίσω, (Σάββατον) *to keep the Sabbath.*

Σαββατικός, ή, όν, (Σάββατον) *of* or *for the Sabbath.* 2. *for a Jew.*

Σαββᾰτισμός, ὁ, (Σαββατίζω) *a keeping of the Sabbath: rest on the Sabbath.*

Σάββᾰτον, τό, the Hebrew *Sabbath*, i.e. *Rest:* hence *the seventh day* or *day of Rest:*—also in plur., τὰ σάββατα; irreg. dat. pl. σάββασι, as if from a nom. σάββας. 2. *a week.*

σάγαρις, ιος, ή: pl. σαγάρεις, Ion. -ῑς:—a weapon used by the Scythian tribes; also by the Persians, Amazons, etc.: *a single-edged axe* or *bill.*

σάγη or **σαγή,** ή, (σάττω) *the housings, harness,* of a horse or mule; hence of a man, *furniture, equipment:* esp. *armour, harness.*

σᾰγηναῖος, α, ον, (σαγήνη) *belonging to a drag-net.*

σᾰγηνεύς, έως, ὁ, = σαγηνευτήρ.

σᾰγηνευτήρ, ῆρος, ὁ, *one who fishes with a drag-net:* hence *a comb* is called τριχῶν σαγηνευτήρ.

σᾰγηνεύω, f. σω, (σαγήνη) *to enclose fish in a drag-net:* metaph. of men, *to sweep as with a drag-net.*

ΣΑΓΗ͂ΝΗ, ή, *a large drag-net* for taking fish, *a seine.*

σᾰγηνο-βόλος, ον, (σαγήνη, βαλεῖν) *throwing the drag-net:* as Subst. *a fisherman.*

σᾰγηνό-δετος, ον, (σαγήνη, δέω) *attached to a net.*

σάγμα, ατος, τό, (σάττω) *the housings of a horse, a saddle, packsaddle.* II. of persons, *a covering, clothing, a large cloak.* III. *the covering* or *case of a shield.* IV. *a heap* or *pile.*

Σαδδουκαῖος, ου, ὁ, *a Sadducee, one of the Sadducees,* name of a Jewish sect who did not believe in a Resurrection, nor in the existence of Spirits.

σαθρός, ά, όν, = σαπρός, *rotten, decayed, unsound, cracked.* II. metaph. *unsound, decayed, rotten, perishable.*

ΣΑΙ΄ΝΩ, f. σᾰνῶ: aor. 1 ἔσηνα Dor. ἔσᾱνα:—*to wag the tail, fawn.* II. metaph. *to fawn upon, caress, wheedle;* σαίνειν μόρον *to deprecate, shrink from* death. 2. absol. *to be gentle, kind:* of a summer sea, *to smile.* III. *to cheer, please.*

ΣΑΙ΄ΡΩ, f. σᾰρῶ: pf. (with pres. sense) σέσηρα, part. σεσηρώς Dor. σεσᾱρώς, υῖα, ός, Ep. fem. σεσᾰρυῖα:—*to shew the teeth, grin* like a dog, Lat. *ringi;* esp. in scorn or malice: but also in good sense, *to smile.* II. *to sweep clean: to sweep away.*

σᾰκέσ-πᾰλος, ον, (σάκος, πάλλω) *wielding* or *brandishing a shield.*

σᾰκεσ-φόρος, ον, (σάκος, φέρω) *shield-bearing.*

σᾰκίον, = σακκίον.

σακίτας, α, Dor. for σηκίτης, ου.

σακκέω, (σάκκος) *to strain, filter.*

σακκίον Att **σᾰκίον**, τό, Dim. of σάκκος or σάκος, *a small bag.*

σακκο-γενειο-τρόφος, ον, (σάκκος, γένειον, τρέφω) *cherishing a large beard.*

ΣΑ'ΚΚΟΣ or **σάκος**, ὁ, *a coarse cloth of hair*, esp. of goats' hair. Lat. *cilicium: sackcloth.* II. *anything made of this cloth* 1. *a sack, bag.* 2. *a sieve, strainer.* III. *a shaggy beard.*

σάκος, ὁ, v. sub σακκος.

σᾱκός, ὁ, Dor. for σηκός.

σάκος [ᾰ], gen. σάκεος Ion. σακευς, τό, (σάττω) *a shield*, made of wickerwork or wood, covered with one or more ox-hides: it was concave, and was sometimes used as a vessel to hold liquid.

σάκτας, ου, ὁ, (σάττω) *a sack.*

σάκτωρ, ορος, ὁ, (σάττω) *one who crams* or *fills up;* Ἅιδου σάκτωρ one *who crowds* the nether world, i.e. a slayer of many.

σακχ-ῠφάντης, ου, ὁ, (σάκκος, ὑφαίνω) *a weaver of sackcloth* or *canvas, a sailmaker.*

σᾰλάκων [ᾰ], ωνος, ὁ, (σαλάσσω) *one who walks in a swaggering fashion, a swaggerer, roysterer.*

σᾰλᾰκωνεύω, f. σω, (σαλάκων) *to play the swaggerer, to swagger.*

σᾰλάμανδρα or **-μάνδρα**, *the salamander*, a kind of lizard, supposed to put out fire. (Deriv. uncertain.)

Σᾰλᾰμῑν-ᾰφέτης, ου, ὁ, (Σαλαμίς, ἀφίημι) *betrayer of Salamis.*

Σᾰλᾰμίνιος [μῑ], α, ον, also ος, ον, (*Salaminian, of* or *from Salamis.* II. ἡ Σαλαμινία (sub. ναῦς or τριήρης), *the Salaminia*, one of the two state galleys of the Athenians, used for special missions; cf. πάραλος. From

Σᾰλᾰμίς, gen. ῖνος, ἡ, *Salamis*, an island opposite Athens. II. a town of Cyprus founded by Teucer of Salamis.

σάλασσα, Dor. for θάλασσα.

σᾰλάσσω Att. **-ττω**: f. ξω: pf. pass. σεσάλαγμαι: (σάλος):—*to cram full, stuff.*

σᾰλεύω, f. σω: aor. 1 ἐσάλευσα: Pass., aor. 1 ἐσαλεύθην: pf. σεσάλευμαι: (σάλος):—*to shake much: to make to totter*:—Pass. *to be shaken, to totter, reel.* II. intr. *to move to and fro, to roll* or *toss like a ship* at sea: metaph. *to toss, be in sore distress.*

σάλος, ὁ, (ἅλλομαι) *the tossing* or *rolling swell of* the sea, *the surge*: hence *the open, exposed sea.* 2. *a roadstead, anchorage.* II. of ships, *a rolling about, tossing on the sea*: hence *sea-sickness*: metaph. *restlessness, disquiet.*

σαλπιγγο-λογχ-ῠπηναοαι, οἱ, (σάλπιγξ, λόγχη, ὑπήνη) *bearded-lance-trumpeters.*

σαλπιγκτής, οῦ, ὁ, (σαλπίζω) *a trumpeter.*

σάλπιγξ, ιγγος, ἡ, *a war-trumpet, trump*: the σαλπιγξ was called Tuscan, Τυρσηνική: ὑπὸ σάλπιγγος, by sound *of trumpet.* II. *a signal* by *trumpet, trumpet-call.* From

ΣΑΛΠΙ'ΖΩ, fut. -ίγξω, aor. 1 ἐσάλπιγξα: later fut. σαλπίσω, aor. 1 ἐσάλπισα:—*to sound the trumpet, give signal by trumpet: to peal like a trumpet-call*, of thunder:—impers., ἐπεὶ ἐσάλπιγξε (sc. ὁ σαλπιγκτής) when *the trumpet sounded*:—c. acc. *to proclaim, announce.* Hence

σαλπικτής, οῦ, ὁ, = σαλπιγκτής.

σάλπιξ, ῐγος, ἡ, poët. for σάλπιγξ.

σαλπιστής, οῦ, ὁ, = σαλπιγκτής.

σᾶμα, τό, Dor. for σῆμα.

σαμαίνω, Dor. for σημαίνω.

Σαμαρείτης, ου, ὁ, *a Samaritan, inhabitant of Samaria*, a district lying between Judea and Galilee formerly inhabited by part of the 12 Tribes: the Samaritans were bitter enemies of the Jews. Fem. **Σαμαρειτίς**, ίδος, ἡ, *a Samaritan woman.*

σάμβᾰλον, τό, Aeol. for σάνδαλον.

σάμερον, Dor. for σήμερον, *to-day.*

Σάμη, ἡ, *Samé*, the older name of Κεφαλληνία.

σαμῆον, τό, Dor. for σημεῖον.

Σάμιος, α, ον, (Σάμος 3) *of Samos, Samian.*

Σᾰμο-θρᾴκη Ion. **-θρηίκη**, ἡ, = Σάμος Θρᾳκία, *Samothrace*, an island near Thrace.

Σᾰμο-θρᾴκιος, α, ον Ion. **-θρηΐκιος** η, ον, *Samothracian.*

Σᾰμό-θρᾳξ Ion. **-θρήιξ**, ικος, ὁ, *a Samo-thracian*

Σάμος [ᾰ], ἡ, *Samos*, the name of several Greek islands: 1. an old name for Κεφαλληνία also called Σάμη. 2. Σάμος Θρηικίη, = Σαμοθρᾴκη 3 the large island over against Ephesus.

σαμπῖ, an old letter, see Σ, σ, σῖγμα.

σαμ-φόρας, ου, ὁ, (σάν, φέρω) *a horse branded with the letter* σάν (v. σῖγμα): cf. κοππατίας

σάν, Dor. for σῖγμα, q. v.

σανδάλιον, τό, Dim. of σάνδαλον, *a small sandal* or *slipper.*

σανδᾰλίσκος, ὁ, Dim. of σάνδαλον, = σανδάλιον.

σάνδᾰλον Aeol. **σάμβαλον**, τό, *a wooden sole*, bound on by straps round the instep and ankle, *a sandal.*

σανδᾰράκη, ἡ, *a bright-red mineral* hence *scarlet*, Lat. *sandaraca.* [ρᾰ] Hence

σανδᾰράκῐνος, η, ον, *of* or *like* σανδαράκη, *bright-red.*

σᾰνίδιον, τό, Dim. of σανίς, *a panel: a trencher.*

σᾰνίς, ίδος, ἡ, *a board, plank: anything made of board* or *plank: a door*, in plur. *folding doors.* 2. *a wooden scaffold* or *stage.* 3. *a wooden floor: a ship's deck.* 4. in plur. *wooden tablets* for writing on, *tablets covered with gypsum*, on which were written public notices. 5. *a plank to which offenders were bound* or *nailed as to a cross.*

σαοῖ, 3 sing. of σαόω.

ΣΑ'ΟΣ, as posit., found only in contr. form σῶς, *safe*: Comp. σαώτερος.

σᾰο-φρονέω, **σᾰο-φροσύνη**, **σᾰό-φρων** poët. for σωφρονέω, σωφροσύνη, σώφρων.

σᾰόω Ep. **σώω**, = σώζω, *to save*:—3 sing. pres. σαοι, 3 pl. σαοῦσι: 3 sing. impf. ἐσάω Ep. σάω: 2 sing. imperat. σάου or σάω: fut. σαώσω: aor 1 act. ἐσάωσα, pass. ἐσαώθην: fut. med. σαώσομαι.

σἄπείην, aor. 2 pass. opt. of *σήπω.*

σἄπείς, aor. 2 pass. part. of *σήπω.*

σἄπῇη, Ep. 3 sing. aor. 2 pass. subj. of *σήπω*

σἄπῆναι, aor. 2 pass. inf. of *σήπω.*

σἄπρός, *ά, όν*, (*σαπῆναι*) *rotten, putrid, diseased*, Lat. *tabidus: decayed unsound.* II. generally, *worthless, useless.* III. *old, obsolete, musty.*

σάπφειρος, *ἡ*, *the sapphire* or *the lapis lazuli*, a precious stone.

Σαπφώ, *οῦς*, vocat. *Σαπφοῖ*, *ἡ*, *Sappho.* Hence

Σαπφῷος, *α, ον*, *of Sappho, Sapphic.*

σἄπών, aor. 2 part. of *σήπω.*

σαργάνη, *ἡ*, like *ταργάνη*, *wickerwork, a basket: a plait, band.* [ᾰ]

σαρδάνιος, *α, ον*, (*σαίρω*) in phrase *σαρδάνιον* [sc. *γέλωτα*] **γελᾶν**, *to laugh a bitter laugh, laugh bitterly*, from anger or secret triumph; *μείδησε δὲ θυμῷ σαρδάνιον μάλα τοῖον* but he laughed in his soul a very *bitter* laugh. It was also written *σαρδόνιος, α, ον*, as if from *σαρδόνιον*, a plant of Sardinia (*Σαρδώ*), which was said to distort the face of the eater.

Σάρδεις, *εων*, Ion. **Σάρδιες**, *ίων, αἱ*, *Sardis*, the capital of Lydia:—hence Adj., **Σαρδιᾱνός** Ion. **-ίηνος**, and **Σαρδιᾱνικός**, *ή, όν*, *of* or *belonging to Sardis; βάμμα Σαρδιανικόν* a *Sardinian*, i e *scarlet*, dye, hence, of a sound thrashing.

σαρδίνη [ῑ], *ἡ*, or **σαρδῖνος**, *ὁ*, *the sardine.*

σάρδιον, *τό*, (*Σάρδεις*) *the Sardian stone.*

σαρδ-όνυξ, *ῠχος, ὁ*, (*σάρδιον, ὄνυξ*) *the sardonyx*, a kind of onyx, so called when the different colours were *disposed in layers*, or *intermingled.*

Σαρδώ, gen. *όος* contr. *οῦς*, *ἡ*, *Sardinia:* hence Adj., **Σαρδῷος**, *α, ον*, **Σαρδωνικός**, *ή, όν*, **Σαρδώνιος** and **Σαρδόνιος**, *α, ον*, *of* or *belonging to Sardinia, Sardinian.*

ΣΑΡΔΩ´Ν, *όνος, ἡ, the upper edge of a hunting-net.*

σάρισσα or rather **σάρῑσα**, *ἡ*, *the sarissa*, a long pike used in the Macedonian phalanx.

σαρκάζω, f. *σω*, (*σάρξ*) *to rend off flesh like dogs.*

σαρκασμο-πῐτῠο-κάμπτης, *ου, ὁ*. (*σαρκάζω, πίτυς, κάμπτω*) *sneering-pinebender.*

σαρκίζω, f. *σω*, (*σάρξ*) *to strip off the flesh*, *σαρκίζειν τὸ δέρμα to draw off the skin, to flay.*

σαρκικός, *ή, όν*, (*σάρξ*) *of flesh.* II. *fleshy, of the flesh, carnal, sensual*, opp. to *πνευματικός.*

σάρκῐνος, *η, ον*, (*σάρξ*) *of flesh.* II. *fleshy, fat.*

σαρκο-λῐπής, *ές*, (*σάρξ, λιπεῖν*) *forsaken by flesh, lean.*

σαρκο-πᾰγής, *ές*, (*σάρξ, παγῆναι*) *with compact flesh.*

σαρκοφᾰγέω, f. *ήσω*, *to eat flesh: devour.* From

σαρκο-φάγος, *ον*, (*σάρξ, φᾰγεῖν*) *eating flesh.* II. *λίθος σαρκοφάγος* a lime-stone *which* like slacked lime *consumed animal substances*, wherefore coffins were often made of it:—hence as Subst., *σαρκοφάγος, ὁ, a sarcophagus, coffin.*

σαρκόω, f. *ώσω*, (*σάρξ*) *to make fleshy, make into flesh.*

σαρκ-ώδης, (*σάρξ, εἶδος*) *like flesh, fleshy;* **θεοὶ ἐναιμοι** *καὶ σαρκώδεες* gods *of flesh* and blood.

ΣΑ´ΡΞ, *ἡ*, gen. *σαρκός, flesh:* in plur. *all the flesh* or *muscles* in the body: hence *the flesh, body.* 2. *flesh, human nature, human kind.*

σάρον, *τό*, (*σαίρω*) *a besom, broom.*

σᾰρόω, f. *ώσω*, (*σαίρω*) *to sweep with a besom, cleanse.*

Σαρπηδών, *όνος*, also *όντος, όντι, ὁ*; voc. **Σαρπηδόν**:—pr. n. *Sarpedon.*

σᾰρῶ, fut. of *σαίρω.*

Σᾰτᾰνᾶς, ᾶ and **Σᾰτᾶν**, *ὁ*, indecl. *Satan;* a Hebr. word meaning *the adversary, enemy.*

σατίνη, *ἡ*, *a war-chariot:* generally, *a chariot, car.*

σάτον, *τό*, *a Hebrew measure, about a modius and half.*

σατρᾰπεία Ion. **-ηίη**, *ἡ*, *a satrapy, the office* or *province of a satrap.* From

σατρᾰπεύω, f. *σω*, intr. *to be a satrap.* I. trans. *to rule as a satrap*, c. acc. or gen. From

σατράπης, *ου, ὁ*, a *satrap*, Lat. *satrăpa*, title of a Persian viceroy or governor of a province. (Persian word.)

ΣΑ´ΤΤΩ, fut. *σάξω:* aor. 1 *ἔσαξα:* Pass., aor. 1 *ἐσάχθην:* pf. *σέσαγμαι:* Ion. 3 pl. plqpf. pass. *ἐσεσάχατο:*—*to pack* or *load*, properly of beasts of burden:—hence of warriors, *to load with full armour, harness:* Pass. *to be armed* or *harnessed.* 2. *to load, furnish, equip, fit out.* II. *to load heavily:* in pf. pass., *πημάτων σεσαγμένος laden* with woes; *σεσαγμένος πλούτου overloaded with* riches. III. *to pack close, press down, stamp down.*

Σᾰτῠρικός, *ή, όν*, (*Σάτυρος*) *fit for* or *like a Satyr.*

Σᾰτῠρίσκος, *ὁ*, Dim. of *Σάτυρος, a little Satyr.*

ΣΑ´ΤΥΡΟΣ [ᾰ], *ὁ, a Satyr*, companion of Bacchus, represented with long pointed ears, and a goat's tail: later, goats' legs were added. The Satyr differed from Pan or the Faun in having no horns 2. *a lewd, goatish fellow.* II. *a* kind of *play, which the Chorus consisted of Satyrs, the Satyric drama.*

σαυλόομαι, Pass. (*σαῦλος*) *to be affected* or *effeminate* in one's gait.

σαυλο-πρωκτιάω, (*σαῦλος πρωκτός*) *to walk in a swaggering, affected way.*

ΣΑΥ´ΛΟΣ, *η, ον, conceited, affected, effeminate.*

ΣΑΥ´ΡΑ Ion. **σαύρη**, *ἡ*, *a lizard*, Lat. *lacerta.*

ΣΑΥ´ΡΟΣ, *ὁ*, = *σαύρα, a lizard*, Lat. *lacertus.*

σαυρωτήρ, *ῆρος, ὁ*, *a spike* at the butt-end of a spear, by which it was stuck into the ground, *the butt-end.*

σαυτοῦ, σαυτῆς contr. for *σεαυτοῦ, σεαυτῆς.*

σάφᾰ, poët. Adv. of *σαφής, clearly, plainly, assuredly; σάφα εἰδώς* knowing *of a surety:* also *truly*, **σάφα** *εἰπεῖν* to tell *plainly*, speak *truth.* [σᾰ]

σᾰφᾰνής, *ές*, Dor. for *σαφηνής.*

σᾰφέστερος, **-ατος**, Comp. and Sup. of **σαφής.**

σᾰφέως, Ion. for *σαφῶς.*

σαφ-ηγορίς, *ίδος*, fem. Adj. (*σάφα, ἀγορεύω*) *speaking truth.*

σᾰφήνεια, *ἡ*, (*σαφηνής*) *clearness, plainness: the truth.*

σᾰφηνέως, Ion. for *σαφηνῶς.*

σαφηνής Dor. **σᾰφανής**, ές, (σαφής) *clear, plain, open, manifest: true:* τὸ σαφανές *the whole truth.*

σᾰφηνίζω, f. ιῶ, (σαφηνής) *to make clear* or *plain, to explain, clear up.*

σαφηνῶς, Adv. of σαφηνής, *clearly, plainly.*

ΣΑ'ΦΗ'Σ, ές, gen. έος contr. οῦς, *clear, distinct, plain, sure, certain;* τὸ σαφές *the truth:* of seers, *sure, unerring.* Comp. and Sup. σαφέστερος, -έστατος.

σαφῶς Ion. **σαφέως**, like σάφα, *clearly, plainly, surely:* Comp. σαφέστερον: Sup. σαφέστατα.

σαχθείς, aor. 1 part. pass. of σάττω.

ΣΑ'Ω, Root. of σήθω, *to sift, bolt:* 3 pl. σῶσι.

σάω, Ep. pres. imperat., and 3 sing. impf. of σαόω.

σαωθείς, -θῆναι, aor. 1 pass. part. and inf. of σαόω.

σαωσέμεν, Ep. for σαώσειν, fut. inf. of σαόω.

σᾰώσω, fut. of σαόω.

σαώτερος, Comp. of σάος.

σᾰωτήρ, ῆρος, ὁ, poët. for σωτήρ, *a saviour, deliverer.*

σᾰώτης, ου, ὁ, (σαόω) poët. for σωτήρ, *a saviour.*

σβείην and **σβείς**, aor. 2 opt. and part. of σβέννυμι.

σβέννῡμι and **-ύω**, fut. σβέσω: aor. 1 ἔσβεσα Ep. σβέσα, Ep. inf. σβέσσαι:—*to quench, put out,* Lat. *extinguere.* 2. generally, *to quench, quell, put out, put down.* II. Pass. σβέννῠμαι: aor. 1 ἐσβέσθην: pf. ἔσβεσμαι: with intrans. tenses of Act., aor. 2 ἔσβην Dor. ἔσβᾱν, opt. σβείην, inf. σβῆναι: pf. ἔσβηκα:—*to be quenched, be put out, go out,* Lat. *extingui: to die.* 2. of liquids, *to become dry, be exhausted.* 3. generally, *to become still, lull, cease.*

σβέσσαι, Ep. for σβέσαι, aor. 1 inf. of σβέννυμι.

σβεστήριος, α, ον, (σβέννυμι) *serving to quench* or *put out.*

σβῆθι, aor. 2 imperat. of σβέννυμι.

-σε, adverbial termin., denoting *motion towards*, as, ἄλλο-σε *to some other place*, etc.

σεαυτοῦ Ion. **σεωυτοῦ**, -τῆς, -τοῦ, reflexive Pron. of 2nd pers., *of thyself*, only used in sing. gen., dat., acc., masc. and fem.: in plur. separated, ὑμῶν αὐτῶν, etc.: so also in sing. in Homer, who uses σοὶ αὐτῷ, σ' αὐτόν.

σεβάζομαι, f. -άσομαι: aor. 1 ἐσεβασάμην, Ep. 3 sing. σεβάσσατο: also aor. 1 pass. ἐσεβάσθην: Dep.: (σέβας):—*to feel awe of, to dread.*

σέβας, τό, (σέβομαι) *reverential awe, a feeling of awe;* generally *reverence, worship, honour, respect, awe.* II. *the object of reverential awe, majesty.* 2. *an object of wonder, a wonder.* III. *an honour conferred* on one.

σέβασμα, ατος, τό, (σεβάζομαι) *an object of awe* or *worship.*

Σεβαστιάς, άδος, ἡ, special fem. of Σεβαστός, *Augusta*, title of the Roman Empresses.

σεβαστός, ή, όν, (σεβάζομαι) *reverenced, awful, august.* II. the Lat. *Augustus*, as a title applied to the Roman Emperors, was rendered by Σεβαστός.

σεβίζω, f. ίσω: aor. 1 ἐσέβισα:—*to worship, honour.*

ΣΕ'ΒΟΜΑΙ: aor. 1 ἐσέφθην: Dep.:—*to feel awe* or *fear, to feel shame, be ashamed, be afraid.* 2. *to worship, pay high regard* or *respect to*

ΣΕ'ΒΩ, f. σέψω, = the earlier form σέβομαι, *to worship, honour:* absol. *to worship, be religious:*—hence σέβομαι also as Pass., *to be reverenced.*

σέθεν, old poët. form of σοῦ, gen. of σύ.

Σειληνός, ὁ, *Silenus*, a companion of Bacchus, the most famous of the Satyrs.

σεῖο, Ep. for σοῦ, gen. of σύ.

σεῖος, σεία, σεῖον, Lacon. for θεῖος, α, ον.

σειρά Ion. **σειρή**, ἡ, (εἴρω) *a cord, rope, string, thong:* also *a chain.* II. *a cord with a noose, a lasso*, used by the Sagartians to entangle and drag away their enemies.

σειραῖος, α, ον, (σειρά) *joined by a cord* or *band:* of a horse *fastened on by a rope outside, an outrigger;* see σειραφόρος.

σειρᾱ-φόρος Ion. **σειρη-φόρος**, ον, (σειρά, φέρω) *having a rope attached, led by a rope:* ὁ σειραφόρος (sub. ἵππος), the horse *which draws by the trace only, an outrigger*, whereas the ζύγιοι *drew by the yoke* or *collar:*—metaph. *a partner, coadjutor.* A quadriga (τέθριππος) had four horses abreast, two ζύγιοι in the middle, and two σειραφόροι—one on each side.

Σειρήν, ῆνος, ἡ, *a Siren:* in pl. Σειρῆνες, αἱ, *the Sirens*, nymphs who allured sailors by their sweet songs and then slew them. II. metaph. *a Siren, deceitful woman.*

σειριό-καυτος, ον, (σείριος, καίω) *scorched by the heat of the dog-star.*

σείριος, α, ον, (σειρός) *hot, scorching:* epith. of the heavenly bodies which cause this heat, σείριος ἀστήρ *the sun:* but, ὁ Σείριος (sub. ἀστήρ) *the dog-star*, Lat. *Sirius*, also called Κύων σείριος or Κύων.

ΣΕΙΡΟ'Σ, ά, όν, *hot, scorching*, of summer-heat.

σειρο-φόρος, ον, (σειρά, φέρω) = σειραφόρος.

σείσατο, Ep. 3 sing. aor. 1 med. of σείω.

σεισ-άχθεια, ἡ, (σείω, ἄχθος) *a shaking off of burdens*, the name given to *the disburdening ordinance* of Solon, by which all debts were lowered, answering to the Lat. *novae tabulae.*

σεισί-χθων, ονος, ὁ, (σείω, χθών) *earth-shaker.*

σεισμός ὁ, (σείω) *a shaking, shock: the shock of an earthquake, an earthquake.*

σειστός, ή, όν, (σείω) *shaken.*

-σείω, ending of Verbs expressing desire or intention, *Desideratives*, like Lat. *-urio.* They are formed from the fut. of the orig. Verb, as δράω, δράσω, δρασείω: γελάω, γελάσω, γελασείω.

ΣΕΙ'Ω, f. σείσω: aor. 1 ἔσεισα: Pass., aor. 1 ἐσείσθην: pf. σέσεισμαι:—*to shake, move to and fro, brandish.* .. absol., σείει *there is an earthquake* (see σεισμός), like ὕει *it rains*, etc 3. Pass. and Med. *to be shaken, shake, heave;* generally, *to move, sway to and fro:* of places, *to feel the shock of an earthquake.* II. in Att. *to harass, annoy with accusations*, so as to extort money.

σέλα, for σέλαϊ, dat. of σέλας.

σελᾰγέω, f. ήσω, (σέλας) *to enlighten*:—Pass. *to beam brightly, blaze, flash.* II. in Act. *to shine, to beam.*

σελᾱη-γενέτης, ου, ὁ, (σέλας, *γένω) *father of light.*

σελάνα, σελᾱναία, Dor. for σελήνη, σεληναία.

ΣΕ'ΛΑΣ, αος, τό: Ep. dat. σέλαϊ contr. σέλᾳ: *bright light, brightness, a bright flame, blaze, flash: a flash of lightning, lightning: a torch.*

σελασ-φόρος, ον, (σέλας, φέρω) *light-bringing.*

σέλᾰχος, τό, *a shark.*

Σεληναίη, ἡ, Ion. and Ep. for Σελήνη Att. **Σεληναία**:—*the Moon.*

σεληναῖος, α, ον, *lighted by the moon; σεληναία νύξ a moonlight* night. From

σελήνη, ἡ, (σέλας) *the moon; σελήνη πλήθουσα the full-moon; πρὸς τὴν σελήνην* by *the light of the moon.* II. *a moon, month; δεκάτῃ σελήνῃ* in the tenth *moon.*

σεληνιάζομαι, Dep. (σελήνη) *to be moon-struck* or *lunatic.*

σελῑδη-φάγος ον (σελίς, φᾰγεῖν) *devouring leaves of books.*

ΣΕ'ΛΙΝΟΝ, τό, *parsley*, Lat. *apium:* the victors at the Isthmian and Nemean games were crowned with chaplets made of its leaves.

ΣΕΛΙ'Σ, ίδος, ἡ, *the space between two rowing-benches (σέλματα).* II. *the space between two columns* in the page of a book: generally, *a page* or *column: a book.*

Σελλοί, οἱ, *the Selli*, original inhabitants of Dodona, among whom was the oracle of Jove.

σέλμα, ατος, τό, *the upper framing of a ship, the deck.* 2. pl. σέλματα, τά, *the rowing-benches*, Lat. *transtra.* 3. generally, *a seat, throne.* II. any *timberwork, a platform, scaffold.*

σεμίδᾱλις, ιος and εως, ἡ, *the finest wheat flour*, Lat. *simila, similāgo.*

σεμνό-θεσμος, ον, (σεμνός, θεσμός) *worshipped with solemn rites.*

σεμνολογέω, f ήσω, *to speak gravely and solemnly*:—Dep. σεμνολογέομαι, *to talk in solemn speech.* From

σεμνο-λόγος, ον, (σεμνός, λέγω) *speaking solemnly.*

σεμνό-μαντις, εως, ὁ, (σεμνός, μάντις) *a reverend seer.*

σεμνομῡθέω, f. ήσω, *to talk in solemn speech, assert gravely.* From

σεμνό-μυθος, ον, (σεμνός, μυθέομαι) *talking solemnly.*

σεμνοπροσωπέω, f. ήσω, *to assume a grave, solemn countenance.* From

σεμνο-πρόσωπος, ον, (σεμνός, πρόσωπον) *of a grave countenance.*

σεμνός, ή, όν, (σέβομαι) *august, holy, solemn, awful:* at Athens, esp. of the Furies or Erinyes, who were called σεμναὶ θεαί or Σεμναί. II. of men, *grave, solemn, stately, majestic:* in bad sense, *haughty, pompous, grand; σεμνὸν βλέπειν* to look *grave and solemn.* III. of things, *stately, solemn, august, grand.*

σεμνό-στομος, ον, (σεμνός, στόμα) *solemnly spoken.*

σεμνότης, ητος, ἡ, (σεμνός) *solemnity dignity, majesty:* in bad sense, *pomposity.*

σεμνό-τῑμος, ον, (σεμνός, τιμή) *reverenced with awe.*

σεμνόω, f. ώσω, (σεμνός) *to make grand* or *pompous, to dignify:* esp. in a tale, *to embellish, amplify.*

σεμνύνω [ῡ], f. ύνῶ, (σεμνός) *to make pompous* or *majestic, to dignify, magnify*:—Med. σεμνύνομαι, aor. 1 ἐσεμνυνάμην, *to be pompous* or *haughty: to affect a solemn air:* hence, *to vaunt oneself* or *be proud* of a thing.

σεμνῶς, Adv. of σεμνός, *solemnly, grandly.*

σέο, Ep. for σοῦ, gen. of σύ.

σεπτός, ή, όν, verb. Adj. of σέβομαι, *august, holy.*

ΣΕ'ΡΙΣ, εως or ἴδος, ἡ, *endive* or *succory.*

σέρφος, ὁ, a small winged insect, a *gnat* or *ant.*

σέσαγμαι, pf. pass. of σάττω.

σεσᾰρωμένος, pf. pass. part. of σαρόω.

σεσᾱρώς, υῖα, ός, Dor. for σεσηρώς, pf. part. of σαίρω:—**σεσᾰρυῖα**, Ep. fem.

σέσεισμαι, pf. pass. of σείω.

σέσηπα, pf. of σήπω.

σεσηρώς, pf. part. of σαίρω.

σεσοφισμένως, Adv. pf. pass. part. of σοφίζω, *cunningly, cleverly.*

σεσύλημαι, pf. pass. of σῡλάω.

σέσυρκα, σέσυρμαι, pf. act. and pass. of σύρω.

σέσωσμαι, pf. pass. of σώζω.

σεσωφρονισμένως, Adv. pf. pass. part. of σωφρονίζω, *temperately, soberly.*

σέτω, Lacon. for θέτω, 3 sing. aor. 2 imp. of τίθημι.

σεῦ enclit. σευ, Ion. and Dor. gen. of σύ.

σεῦα, Ep. for ἔσσευα, aor. 1 of σεύω: part. σεύας.

σεῦμαι, contr. for σεύομαι, pres. pass. of σεύω: 3 sing. σεῦται.

σεῦτλον, τό, Ion. for τεῦτλον.

ΣΕΥ'Ω, with σσ in augm. tenses, impf. ἔσσευον, pass. and med. ἐσσευόμην: aor. 1 ἔσσευα, med. ἐσσευάμην; also Ep. without augm. σεῦα, σεῦε, σεύατο: pf. pass. ἔσσῦμαι, part. ἐσσύμενος: plqpf. (in aor. sense) ἐσσύμην [ῠ], 2 sing. ἔσσῠο for ἔσσυσο, 3 sing. ἔσσῦτο Ep. σύτο; part. σύμενος: aor. 1 pass. ἐσσύθην [ῠ]. There is also 3 sing. σεῦται from a contr. pres. σεῦμαι: also σοῦμαι, 3 pl. σοῦνται: imperat. σοῦ, 3 sing. σούσθω, 2 pl. σοῦσθε: inf. σοῦσθαι. *To put in quick motion, drive, hunt, chase.* 2. *to set on, let loose at.* 3. *to drive* or *chase away.* 4. of things, *to throw, hurl:* also *to bring forth, cause to spring; αἷμα ἔσσευα I made* blood *spout forth*:—Med., αἷμα σύτο blood *spouted forth.* II. Pass. and Med. *to be in quick motion, to run, dart,* or *shoot along; συθείς having started, gone.* 2. c. inf. *to hasten, speed; ὅτε σεύαιτο διώκειν* when *he hasted* to pursue. 3. metaph. *to be eager, yearn after, long for.*

σεφθείς, aor. 1 pass. part. of σέβω.

σέω, Dor. for θέω, *to run.*

σεωυτοῦ, fem. σεωυτῆς, Ion. for σεαυτοῦ, σεαυτῆς.

σηκάζω, f. -άσω, (σηκός) *to drive into a pen, coop up, shut up.*

σήκασθεν, Ep. 3 pl. aor. 1 pass. of σηκάζω.

σηκίς, ίδος, ἡ, (σηκός) *a housekeeper, porteress.*

σηκίτης, ου, ὁ Dor. σακ-, (σηκός) *a stall-fed animal:* σακίταν ἄρνα *a house-fed* lamb.

σηκο-κόρος, ον, (σηκός, κορέω) *cleaning a stable* or *pen:* as Subst., σηκοκόρος, ὁ, *a herdsman.*

ΣΗΚΟ'Σ Dor. **σακός**, ὁ, *a pen* or *fold*, for sheep and goats. 2. *any dwelling.* II. *any enclosure: a sacred enclosure, a chapel, shrine:* also *a sepulchre* sacred to the dead. III. *the trunk of an olive-tree.* Hence.

σηκόω, f. ώσω, *to weigh, balance.* Hence

σήκωμα Dor. **σάκωμα**, ατος, τό, *a weight in the balance, a counterpoise.* II. like σηκός, *a chapel, sacred enclosure, shrine.*

ΣΗ͂ΜΑ Dor. **σᾶμα**, ατος, τό, *a sign, mark, token: the mark* or *star* on a horse's forehead. 2. *a sign from heaven, an omen, portent:* also, 3. *a battle-sign, signal.* 4. *a mound, barrow*, Lat. *tumulus, to mark a tomb by:* generally, *a grave, tomb.* 5. in plur. *written characters:* the σήματα λυγρά of Bellerophon in the Iliad were not *written letters*, but *pictorial tokens* or *devices.* 6. *the device* or *bearing on a shield:* also *the device on a seal, a seal.* 7. *a constellation:* in plur. *the heavenly bodies*, Lat. *signa.*

σημαίνοισα, Dor. pres. part. fem. from

σημαίνω: fut. -ᾰνῶ Ion. -ᾰνέω: aor. 1 ἐσήμηνα or ἐσήμᾱνα, inf. σημῆναι: Pass., aor. 1 ἐσημάνθην: pf. σεσήμασμαι, but 3 sing. σεσήμανται, inf. σεσημάνθαι: (σῆμα):—*to shew by a sign* or *token, point out:* absol. *to give a sign* or *token.* II. *to give a sign* or *signal to do* a thing: hence *to bear command over, rule:* absol., σημαίνων *a commander.* 2. in battle, *to give the signal* of attack: impers. σημαίνει (sc. ὁ σαλπιγκτής), like σαλπίζει, *signal is given;* τοῖς Ἕλλησι ὡς ἐσήμηνε *when the signal was given* for the Greeks to attack. III. *to signify, announce, intimate:* with a part., *to signify that* a thing is. IV. *to stamp with a sign* or *mark, to seal*, Lat. *obsignare:* pf. pass. σεσημασμένα, *things sealed*, opp. to ἀσήμαντα. V. Med. σημαίνομαι, *to infer* or *conclude for oneself from signs.* 2. *to mark for oneself, note down.*

σημαντήριον, τό, (σημαίνω) *a seal set upon a thing.*

σημαντρίς, ίδος, ἡ, (σημαίνω) fem. Adj. *suited for sealing;* σημαντρὶς γῆ clay *used for sealing.*

σήμαντρον, τό, (σημαίνω) *a seal.*

σήμαντωρ, ορος, ὁ, (σημαίνω) *one who gives a sign* or *signal: a leader, commander:* also of animals, *a driver, a herdsman.*

σημάτιον, τό, Dim. of σῆμα. [ᾰ]

σημᾰτόεις, εσσα, εν, (σῆμα) *full of tombs.*

σημᾰτ-ουργός, όν, (σῆμα, *ἔργω) *making devices for shields.*

σημειο-γράφος, ον, (σημεῖον, γράφω) *writing in cipher.* [ᾰ]

σημεῖον Ion. -ήιον, τό, (σῆμα) *a mark, sign* or *token by which something is known: a trace, track.* 2. *a sign from the gods, an omen.* 3. *a sign* or *signal to do anything: the signal for battle.* 4. *a flag* or *ensign* on the admiral's ship, or on the general's tent: generally, *a standard, ensign.* 5. *a device upon a shield;* also on a seal: *a seal* itself. II. in reasoning, *a sign* or *proof.*

σημειόω, f. ώσω, (σημεῖον) *to mark:*—Med. *to mark for oneself, remark:* also *to give notice of.*

σήμερον Dor. **σάμερον** Att. **τήμερον**, Adv. (ἡμέρα with σ prefixed) *to-day:* so also ἡ σήμερον (sub. ἡμέρα), and τὸ τήμερον.

σημήιον, τό, Ion. for σημεῖον.

σήμηνα, Ep. for ἐσήμηνα, aor. 1 of σημαίνω.

σημι-κίνθιον, τό, the Lat. *semi-cinctium, an apron.*

σημό-θετος, ον, (σῆμα, τίθημι) *made for ruling lines.*

σηπεδών, όνος, ἡ, (σήπω) *decay, putrefaction:* of quick flesh, *mortification.*

ΣΗΠΙ'Α, ἡ, *the sepia* or *cuttle-fish*, which when pursued troubles the water by ejecting a dark liquid.

ΣΗ'ΠΩ, f. σήψω: aor. 1 ἔσηψα:—*to make rotten* or *putrid: to make fester* or *mortify.* II. Pass. σήπομαι: aor. 2 ἐσάπην [ᾰ], Ep. 3 sing. subj. σαπήῃ, for σάπῃ: pf. act. (in pass. sense) σέσηπα:—*to be* or *become rotten, to moulder, putrefy:* of diseased flesh, *to mortify.*

Σήρ, Σηρός, ὁ, mostly in pl. Σῆρες, *the Seres*, an Indian people, from whom silk was first brought: hence, II. *the Seric worm, silkworm.*

σήρ, ὁ, Lacon. for θήρ.

σήραγξ, αγγος, ἡ, (σαίρω, σέσηρα) *a hollow rock, a cleft, cave hollowed out by the sea.*

σηρῐκός, ή, όν, (Σήρ) *Seric: silken.*

σηρο-κτόνος, ον, Lacon. for θηροκτ-.

ΣΗ'Σ, ὁ, gen. σεός, nom. pl. σέες, gen. σέων: later also gen. σητός:—*a moth*, Lat. *tinea: a book-worm.*

σῇς, Ion. for σαῖς, dat. pl. fem. of σός, σή, σόν.

σησᾰμαῖος, α, ον, *made of sesamé.* From

σησάμη, ἡ, *sesamé*, an eastern leguminous plant. [ᾰ]

σησᾰμῆ, ἡ, *a mixture of sesamé-seeds roasted and pounded with honey, a sesamé-cake.*

σησάμῐνος, η, ον, (σησάμη) *made of sesamé;* σησάμινον ἔλαιον *sesamé*-oil. [ᾰ]

σησᾰμόεις, εσσα, εν, (σησάμη) *of sesamé;* ὁ σησαμοῦς (sub. ἄρτος) *a sesamé-cake.*

σήσᾰμον, τό, (σησάμη) *the seed* or *fruit of the sesamé-tree* (σησάμη)

σησᾰμό-τῡρον, τό, (σησάμη, τυρός) *sesamé-cheese.*

σησᾰμοῦς, οῦντος, contr. from σησαμόεις.

Σηστός, ἡ, also ὁ, *Sestos*, a town on the European side of the Hellespont, over against Abydos.

σῆτες Att. **τῆτες**, (ἔτος) *this year:* see σήμερον.

σητό-βρωτος, ον, (σής, βιβρώσκω) *fretted by moths, moth-eaten.*

σητό-κοπος, ον, (σής, κοπῆναι) *fretted by moths.*

σθενᾰρός, ά, όν, (σθένος) *strong, mighty.*

ΣΘΕ'ΝΟΣ, εος, τό, *strength, might, prowess:* mostly of men, but also of things, as of a river; σθένος ἀελίου *the strength* of the sun; σθένει *by force;* παντὶ σθένει *with* all one's *might.* 2. *might, power, force.* II. *a force* of men. III. periphr., like βίη, ἴς, μένος with a gen., as, σθένος Ἕκτορος *Hector himself.*

σθενόω, f. ώσω, (σθένος) *to strengthen, make strong.*

σθένω, only used in pres. and impf.: (σθένος):—*to be strong* or *mighty, have power;* σθένειν χειρί, ποσί *to be strong* in hand, in foot; οἱ κάτω σθένοντες *they who rule* below. 2. c. inf. *to have strength* or *power* to do, *be able* or *competent* to do.

σιά, Lacon. for θεά.

ΣΙΑΓΩ'Ν Ion. σιηγών, όνος, ἡ, *the jaw-bone, jaw.*

ΣΙ'ΑΛΟΝ Ion. σίελον, τό, *spittle, foam* from the mouth, Lat. *saliva* (Engl. *slaver*).

ΣΙ'ΑΛΟΣ, ὁ, *a fat hog:* also with another Subst., σῦς σίαλος, like σῦς κάπριος, etc. II. *fat, grease.*

Σίβυλλα, ἡ, *a Sibyl, prophetess.* (Deriv. uncertain.) [ῐ] Hence

Σῐβύλλειος, α, ον, *Sibylline.*

Σῐβυλλιάω, (Σίβυλλα) *to play the Sibyl:* metaph. *to be like a Sibyl,* i. e. *credulous* or *silly.*

Σιβυλλιστής, οῦ, ὁ, *a believer in the Sibyl, diviner.*

ΣΙΒΥ'ΝΗ, ἡ, σῐβύνης, ου, ὁ, *a hunting-spear.* [ῠ]

σῖγᾰ, Adv. (σιγή) *silently, stilly, noiselessly:* as an exclam., σῖγα *hush! be still!*

σίγᾱ, imperat. of σιγάω, *hush! be still!*

σίγᾱ, Ep. for ἐσίγα, 3 sing. impf. of σιγάω.

σῑγᾷ, 3 sing. of σιγάω, or Dor. dat. of σιγή.

σῑγάζω, f. άσω, (σιγή) *to bid* one *be silent, force* or *constrain to silence.*

σῑγᾰλέος, α, ον, (σιγάω) *silent, still.*

σῐγᾰλόεις, εσσα, εν, (σίαλος) *smooth, glossy, shining, glittering,* esp. of horses' reins. 2. *rich, splendid, sumptuous.*

σῑγᾱλός, Dor. for σιγηλός.

σῑγάς, άδος, ἡ, (σιγή) *silent.*

σῑγάω, f. -ήσομαι, later -ήσω: pf. σεσίγηκα: Pass., aor. 1 ἐσιγήθην: pf. σεσίγημαι: (σιγή):—*to be silent* or *still, to keep silence:*—imper. σίγα, *hush! be still!* —Pass. *to be passed over in silence,* Lat. *taceri;* but the pf. σεσίγημαι is also used in act. sense, *to be silent.*

σῑγεῖν, Lacon. for θιγεῖν.

σῑγή Dor. **σιγά**, ἡ, (σίζω) *silence, a being silent;* σιγὴν ἔχειν to keep *silence,* to hold one's peace; σιγὴν ποιεῖσθαι to make *silence.* II. dat. σιγῇ as Adv., *in silence, silently:* also like σῖγα, as an exclam., σιγῇ νυν *silence now!* σιγῇ ποιεῖσθαι λόγον to carry on a conversation *in an under tone.* 2. *secretly:* also as a Prep., σιγῇ τινος, Lat. *clam aliquo,* like κρύφα τινός, *unknown to* him.

σῑγηθείς, εῖσα, έν, aor. 1 pass. part. of σιγάω.

σῑγηλός, ή, όν Dor. **σῑγαλός**, όν, (σιγή) *silent, still, mute hushed:*—τὰ σιγηλά *silence.*

σῑγηρός, ά, όν, = σιγηλός.

σῑγητέον, verb. Adj. of σιγάω, *one must be silent.*

σίγλος or **σίκλος**, ὁ, the Hebrew *shekel* = 2 drachmae: a Persian σίγλος is mentioned by Xenophon as worth 7½ or 8 oboli, about 1 shilling English.

σῖγμα, (σίζω) the letter *sigma,* see Σ, σ.

σῐγύνης, ου, ὁ, Cyprian word for δόρυ, *a spear.* II. among the Ligyes near Marseilles used for κάπηλος. III. the Σιγύναι were a people on the Danube, see Herodotus 5. 9.

σιγῶντι, Dor. 3 plur. of σιγάω: also dat. sing. pres. part.

σίδαρος, ὁ, Dor. for σίδηρος: for **σιδάρειος** and other Dor. forms, v. sub σιδηρ–.

ΣΙ'ΔΗ, ἡ, *a pomegranate tree:* also *the fruit.* [ῑ]

σῐδηρεία, ἡ, (σιδηρεύω) *a working in iron.*

σῐδήρεος, α Ion. η, ον, Att. contr. **σιδηροῦς**, ᾶ, οῦν, Ep. **σιδήρειος**, η, ον, Dor. **σιδάρεος** [ᾱ], α, ον: (σίδηρος):—*made of iron* or *steel, iron;* σιδήρεος οὐρανός the *iron* sky: metaph., σιδήρεος θυμός, a mind *of iron;* σιδήρειον ἦτορ an *iron* heart. II. σιδάρεοι, οἱ, *a Byzantine iron coin.*

σῐδηρεύς, έως, ὁ, (σίδηρος) *a worker in iron, a smith*

σῐδήριον, τό, (σίδηρος) *a tool of iron* or *steel, an iron: a sword* or *knife.*

σῐδηρίτης [ῑ], ου, ὁ, fem. **-ῖτις**, ιδος, Dor. **σιδᾱρίτας**, α, ὁ, (σίδηρος) *of iron.*

σῐδηρο-βρῑθής, ές, (σίδηρος, βρίθω) *iron-loaded.*

σῐδηρο-βρώς, ῶτος, ὁ, ἡ, (σίδηρος, βιβρώσκω) *iron-eating,* epith. of a whetstone

σῐδηρο-δάκτῠλος, ον, (σίδηρος, δάκτυλος) *iron fingered.*

σῐδηρό-δετος, ον, (σίδηρος, δέω) *iron-bound, shod with iron.*

σῐδηρο-κμής, ῆτος, ὁ, ἡ, (σίδηρος, κάμνω) *slain by iron, slain by the sword.*

σῐδηρο-μήτωρ, ορος, ὁ, ἡ, (σίδηρος, μήτηρ) *mother of iron,* epith. of the earth.

σῐδηρο-νόμος, ον, (σίδηρος, νέμω) *distributing by the sword,* or *swaying the sword.*

σῐδηρό-νωτος, ον, (σίδηρος, νῶτον) *iron-backed.*

σῐδηρό-πλακτος Dor. for **-πληκτος**, ον, (σίδηρος, πλήσσω) *smitten by iron* or *by the sword.*

σῐδηρό-πλαστος, ον, (σίδηρος, πλάσσω) *moulded of iron.*

ΣΙ'ΔΗΡΟΣ Dor. **σίδαρος**, ὁ, *iron:* it was of high value, in Homer's time, since pieces of it were given as prizes: it mostly came from the north and east of the Euxine. II. like Lat. *ferrum, anything made of iron, an iron tool* or *implement, a sword, spear, axe:* also *a knife, sickle.* III. *a place for selling iron, a cutler's shop.*

σῐδηρό-σπαρτος, ον, (σίδηρος, σπείρω) *sown* or *produced by iron.*

σῐδηρο-τέκτων, ονος, ὁ, (σίδηρος, τέκτων) *a worker in iron.*

σῐδηρο-τόκος, ον, (σίδηρος, τεκεῖν) *iron producing.*

σῐδηροτομέω, f. ήσω, *to cleave with iron.* From

σῐδηρο-τόμος, ον, (σίδηρος, τεμεῖν) *cutting with* on.

σῐδηροφορέω, f. ήσω, *to wear iron arms, wear arms:* also as Dep. -έομαι. From

σῐδηρο-φόρος, ον, (σίδηρος, φέρω) *wearing iron, aring arms.*

σῐδηρό-φρων, ον, gen ονος, (σίδηρος, φρήν) *of iron* 'art.

σῐδηρό-χαλκος, ον, (σίδηρος, χαλκός) *of iron and* pper.

σῐδηρο-χάρμης, ου, ὁ, (σίδηρος, χάρμη) *fighting in* on, epith. of mailed war-horses.

σῐδηρόω, f. ώσω, (σίδηρος) *to make of iron, overlay ith iron*:—impers. in plqpf. pass. ἐσεσιδήρωτο ἐπὶ έγα καὶ τοῦ ἄλλου ξύλου *iron had been laid* over a eat part also of the rest of the wood.

σίδιον, τό, (σίδη) *pomegranate-peel.* [σῐ]

Σῐδονίηθεν, Adv. *from Sidon.* From

Σῐδών, ῶνος, ἡ, *Sidon,* one of the oldest cities of hoenicia. Adj. Σῐδόνιος or Σῐδώνιος, α, ον, *of* or *elonging to Sidon;* fem. also Σιδωνιάς, άδος.

Σῐδών, όνος, ὁ, *a man of Sidon.*

ΣΙ'ΖΩ, impf. ἔσιζον Ep. σῖζον; no fut. in use:—*to ıss,* of hot iron plunged into water; σίζ' ὀφθαλμὸς λαϊνέῳ περὶ μοχλῷ the eye of the Cyclops *hissed* hen the burnt stake was thrust into it. II. *to t a dog on.*

Σῐθωνία, ἡ, *Sithonia,* a *part* of Thrace, generally for e whole country: Adj. Σῐθώνιος and Σῐθόνιος, α, ον, *Thracian:* Σῐθών, όνος, ὁ, *a Sithonian;* and Σῐθονίς, ίδος, ἡ, *a Sithonian woman.*

Σῐκᾱνία, ἡ, *Sicania,* properly a part of Sicily near Agrigentum, used generally for the *whole of Sicily.*

Σῐκᾱνός, οῦ, ὁ, *a Sicanian* (see Σικανία): Adj. Σικᾱνικός, ή, όν, *Sicania.*

σικάριος, ὁ, the Lat. *sicārius, assassin.* [ᾰ]

Σῐκελία, ἡ, (Σικελός) *Sicily:* Adj. Σικελικός, ή, όν, *Sicilian.* Hence

Σῐκελίζω, f. ίσω, *to do* or *speak like the Sicilians: to favour the Sicilians.*

Σῐκελικός, ή, όν, (Σικελος) *of* or *like a Sicilian.*

Σῐκελιώτης, ου, ὁ, *a Sicilian Greek, a Greek settler in Sicily,* as distinguished from the Σικελοί or *Siculi,* the more ancient inhabitants: cf. Ἰταλιώτης.

Σῐκελός, ή, όν, *Sicilian, of* or *from Sicily,* Lat. *Siculus:* the Σικελοί originally migrated from Italy to Sicily; the Σικελιῶται were the later Greek settlers.

σίκερα [ῐ], τό, gen. σίκερος, *a sweet fermented liquor, strong drink.* (Hebr. *shâkar, to be intoxicated.*)

σίκιννις or σίκῐνις, ιδος, ἡ, *the Sicinnis,* a dance of Satyrs used in the Satyrical drama, named from its inventor *Sicinnos.*

σίκλος, ὁ, = σίγλος.

σῐκύα Ion. σικύη, ἡ, a fruit like the *cucumber* or *gourd,* but eaten ripe. II. *a cupping glass,* from its shape, Lat. *cucurbĭta.* [ῠ]

σίκυος, ὁ, the common *gourd* or *cucumber.*

Σῐκυών, ῶνος, ἡ, *Sicyon,* a town and district on the north of the Peloponnesus: Adj. Σῐκυώνιος, α, ον, *Sicyonian:* Adv. Σῐκυώνοθε, *of* or *from Sicyon.*

σικχαίνω, *to loathe.* From

ΣΙΚΧΟ'Σ, ὁ, *a squeamish, fastidious person.*

Σιληνός, ὁ, see Σειληνός.

σίλι, τό, *the palma Christi,* called also σιλλικύπριον.

σιλλαίνω, (σίλλος) *to insult, mock, jeer.*

σιλλικύπριον, τό, = σίλι. (Deriv. uncertain.)

ΣΙ'ΛΛΟΣ, ὁ, *one who looks askance: a satirist.* II. *a satire, satirical poem.*

ΣΙ'ΛΟΥΡΟΣ, ὁ, a river-fish, prob. the *shad,* Lat. *silūrus.*

ΣΙ'ΛΦΗ, ἡ, a kind of *grub* or *beetle,* Lat. *blatta.* II. *a book-worm.*

ΣΙ'ΛΦΙΟΝ, τό, Lat. *laserpitium,* a plant, the juice of which was used in food and medicine, and was reckoned a valuable specific: according to Bentley, the *asa-foetida.* Hence

σιλφιωτός, ή, όν, *prepared with silphium.*

σιμβλεύω, f. σω, (σίμβλος) *to form* or *grow in the hive,* of honey.

ΣΙ'ΜΒΛΟΣ, ὁ, *a bee-hive:* metaph. *any store* or *hoard.*

σιμι-κίνθιον, less correct form of σημι-κίνθιον.

Σῐμόεις, -όεντος contr. Σῐμοῦς, -οῦντος, ὁ, *the Simoïs,* a river near Troy:—Adj. Σιμοέντιος contr. Σιμούντιος, α, ον, *of, near the Simoïs:* fem. also Σιμοεντίς, ίδος.

ΣΙΜΟ'Σ, ή, όν, *snub-nosed, flat-nosed*:—generally, *flat.* I. of other things, *steep, up-hill,* Lat. *acclivis;* πρὸς τὸ σιμὸν διώκειν to pursue *up hill.* 2. *bent in, hollow, concave.*

σῑμότης, ητος, ἡ, (σιμός) *the shape of a snub-nose; flatness.*

Σῐμοῦς, -οῦντος, ὁ, contr. form of Σιμόεις.

σῑμόω, f. ώσω, (σιμός) *to turn up the nose, bend upwards.* Hence

σίμωμα, ατος, τό, *anything bent upwards.* From

σῐνᾰμωρέω, f. ήσω, *to damage wantonly:* generally, *to handle roughly.* From

σῐνά-μωρος [ᾰ], ον, (σίνος, μῶρος) *mischievous, hurtful:* c. gen. rei, τῶν ἑωυτοῦ σινάμωρος *ruining* his own affairs: *wanton, lewd.*

σίνᾱπι, εως, and σίνᾱπυ, υος, τό, (νᾶπυ) *mustard,* Lat. *sinapi:* the better Att. form was νᾶπυ.

σινδώ, οῦς, ἡ, Att. for σινδών.

σινδών, όνος, ἡ, *sindon, a fine Indian cloth, muslin.* II. *a garment* or *napkin made of this cloth.*

σῑνέομαι, Ion. for σίνομαι.

σίνηπι, ιος, and σίνηπυ, υος, τό. Ion. for σίναπι, σίναπυ. [σῐ]

σινιάζω, f. σω, (σινίον) *to sift, fan, winnow.*

ΣΙΝΙ'ΟΝ, τό, *a sieve*

σίνις, ιδος, ὁ, acc. σίνιν, (σίνομαι) *a destroyer, ravager, robber:* as Adj. *destroying, ravening.* II. as prop. n., Σίνις, ὁ, *Sinnis, the Destroyer,* a famous robber of early Greece. [⏑ ⏑]

ΣΙ'ΝΟΜΑΙ [ῐ] Ion. σῑνέομαι: Ion. impf. σινεσκόμην: aor. 1 ἐσῖνάμην: Dep.:—*to plunder, spoil, pillage: to harry, ravage:* hence of wild beasts, *to tear in pieces, devour.* II. in more general sense, *to damage, distress.* ... also *to hurt, wound.* Hence

σίνος [ῐ], εος, τό, *hurt, harm, mischief, damage.* II. *anything hurtful, a mischief, plague.*

σίντης, ου, ὁ, (σίνομαι) *tearing, ravenous, devouring.*

σίντις, ιος, ὁ, = σίντης, only as plur. in prop. n., **Σίντιες**, *the Sintians*, the early inhabitants of Lemnos, who were *pirates.*

σίντωρ, ορος, ὁ, = σίντης.

Σινώπη, ἡ, *Sinopé, a town of Paphlagonia, on the Black Sea:*—**Σινωπίτης**, ου, ὁ, *an inhabitant of Sinopé:* Adj. **Σινωπικός**, ή, όν, *of* or *belonging to Sinopé.*

ΣΙ'ΟΝ, τό, *a marsh* or *meadow plant.*

σιός, Lacon. for θεός.

σιπύη, ἡ, *a flour-bin, meal-jar.*

ΣΙΡΑΙΟΝ, τό, *new wine boiled down*, Lat. *defrūtum.*

σιρός, ὁ, *a pit* or *hole sunk in the ground*, for keeping corn in: also *a pitfall.*

σισύμβριον, τό, = σίσυμβρον.

ΣΙ'ΣΥΜΒΡΟΝ, τό, a sweet-smelling plant, *mint* or *thyme.*

σισύρα [ῠ] or **σίσυρνα**, ἡ, *a shaggy goatskin worn as an outer garment: a rough outer garment*, with a coarse nap.

σισυρνο-φόρος, ον, (σίσυρνα, φερῶ) *wearing a σίσυρνα* or *cloak of goatskin.*

Σισύφειος, α, ον, *of Sisyphus, Corinthian:* fem. also **Σισυφίς**, ίδος. From

Σί-συφος [ῐ], ου, ὁ, an ancient king of Corinth, punished for bad faith in the shades below. (Redupl. from σοφός, *the Wise* or *Cunning.*)

σῖτα, τά, irreg. pl. of σῖτος.

σιτᾰγωγέω, f. ήσω, (σιταγωγός) *to transport corn to a place.* Hence

σιτᾰγωγία, ἡ, *conveyance of corn* to a place.

σιτ-ᾰγωγός, όν, (σῖτος, ἄγω) *transporting corn* to a place; σιταγωγὰ πλοῖα vessels *engaged in conveying corn, corn*-ships.

σιτάθην, Dor. for ἐσιτήθην, aor. 1 pass. of σιτέω.

σιτεύσιμος, η, ον, (σιτεύω) *well-fed, fatted.*

σιτευτός, ή, όν, *fatted, stalled*, Lat. *altĭlis.* From

σιτεύω, f. σω: Ion. impf. σιτεύεσκον: (σῖτος):—*to feed, fatten:*—Pass. *to be fed, to eat.*

σιτέω, f. ήσω, (σῖτος) *to feed:*—Pass. σιτέομαι, Ion. 3 pl. impf. σιτέσκοντο: fut. med. σιτήσομαι: aor. 1 pass. ἐσιτήθην:—*to be fed, to eat, take food: to feed on, eat* a thing, c. acc.

σιτηγέω, f. ήσω, (σιτηγός) *to convey* or *transport corn: to import corn.* Hence

σιτηγία, ἡ, *the conveyance* or *importation of corn.*

σιτ-ηγός, όν, (σῖτος, ἄγω) *conveying corn.*

σιτηρέσιον, τό, (σιτηρός) *provisions, victuals: forage-money*, of soldiers.

σιτηρός, ά, όν, (σῖτος) *of* or *belonging to corn.*

σίτησις, εως, ἡ, (σιτέω) *an eating, feeding:* also *food, provisions;* σίτησις ἐν Πρυτανείῳ *public maintenance* in the Prytanēum.

σιτίζω, f. ίσω, (σῖτος) *to feed, fatten:*—Pass. *to feed upon, eat.*

σιτίον, τό, (σῖτος) mostly in plur. σιτία, *food made of corn, bread;* generally, *food, victuals, provisions, diet;* σιτία τριῶν ἡμερῶν three days' *provision;* τὰ ἐν Πρυτανείῳ σιτίᾳ public *maintenance* in the Prytanēum, like σίτησις.

σιτιστός, ή, όν, verb. Adj. of σιτίζω, like σιτευτός, *fed, fatted:* as Subst *a fatling.*

σιτο-δεία Ion. -δηίη, ἡ, (σῖτος, δέομαι) *want* or *scarcity of corn: dearth, famine.*

σιτο-δόκος, ον, (σῖτος, δέχομαι) *holding food.*

σιτοδοτέω, f. ήσω, *to furnish with corn, victual:*—Pass. *to be provisioned* or *victualled.* From

σιτο-δότης, ου, ὁ, (σῖτος, δίδωμι) *a furnisher of corn.*

σιτο-μέτριον, (σῖτος, μετρέω) *a measured allowance of corn.*

σιτο-νόμος, ον, (σῖτος, νέμω) *dealing out corn* or *food;* σιτονόμος ἐλπίς the hope *of getting food.*

σιτοποιέω, f. ήσω, (σιτοποιός) *to prepare corn* or *food, to make bread: to prepare, purvey food* or *victuals:*—Med. *to prepare food for oneself: to take food.* Hence

σιτοποιία, ἡ, *bread-making, preparation of food.* Hence

σιτοποιικός, ή, όν, *of* or *for bread-making.*

σιτο-ποιός, όν, (σῖτος, ποιέω) *preparing corn for food:* as Subst., σιτοποιός (sub. γυνή), ἡ, *a woman that ground the corn in the hand-mill:* generally, *a maker of bread, baker.* 2. σιτοποιὸς ἀνάγκη the task *of grinding corn.*

σιτο-πομπία, ἡ, (σῖτος, πέμπω) *the conveyance of corn:* also *provision for its safe convoy, an escort, a convoy.*

σιτο-πώλης, ου, ὁ, (σῖτος, πωλέω) *a corn-merchant, corn-factor.*

ΣΙ'ΤΟΣ, ὁ, irreg. pl. σῖτα, τά, *wheat, corn, grain:* also *meal, flour, bread:* hence generally, *food, victuals, provisions;* but properly of bread, as opp. to meat: but also of anything eaten as opp. to drink; σῖτος ἠδὲ ποτῆς *meat* and drink.

σιτο-φάγος, ον, (σῖτος, φᾰγεῖν) *eating corn* or *bread.*

σιτο-φόρος, ον, (σῖτος, φέρω) *carrying corn.*

σιτο-φύλᾰκες, οἱ, (σῖτος, φύλαξ) *corn-watchers, corn-inspectors*, Athenian officers, originally three in number, but afterwards ten in the city and five in Peiræeus, who superintended the importation and sale of corn.

σίττᾰ and **σίττε**, a cry of drovers to their flocks, *st!* when ἀπό follows, to drive them *off;* when πρός follows, to call them *on.*

σιτ-ώνης, ου, ὁ, (σῖτος, ὠνέομαι) *a buyer of corn.*

σιτωνία, ἡ, (σιτώνης) *a buying of corn, purchase of corn.*

ΣΙΦΛΟ'Σ, ή, όν, *crippled, maimed:* also *lame, limping;* of the eyes, *blind.* Hence

σιφλόω, f. ώσω, *to maim, cripple: to hurt, confound, ruin:* σιφλώσειε, 3 sing. Aeol. aor. 1 opt.

Σίφνιος, α, ον, *of* or *from Siphnus, Siphnian.* From

Σίφνος, ἡ, *Siphnus*, one of the Cyclades.

σίφων, ωνος, ὁ, *a reed, straw, any tube*, esp. *the siphon*, used to draw wine out of the cask. 2. *a sucker*, as of a pump. Hence

σῑφωνίζω, f. σω, *to tap* a cask *with a siphon, to draw off wine.*

σῑωπάω, fut. -ήσομαι: aor. 1 ἐσιώπησα: pf. σεσιώπηκα:—*to be silent* or *still, to keep silence;* σιωπᾶν τινι *to keep silence towards* one: imperat., σιώπα *hush! be still!* II. transit. *to keep in silence, keep secret*, Lat. *tacere*:—Pass. *to be kept silent* or *secret*, Lat. *taceri.* From

ΣΙΩΠΗ', ἡ, *silence, a being silent:* dat. σιωπῇ, *in silence.* 2. *silence, stillness, a calm.*

σῑωπηλός, ή, όν, (σιωπάω) *silent, still.*

σῑωπηρός, ά, όν, collat. form of σιωπηλός.

σιωπήσειαν, 3 pl. Aeol. aor. 1 opt. of σιωπάω.

σιωπητέος, α, ον, verb. Adj. of σιωπάω, *to be passed over in silence.* II. **σιωπητέον**, *one must pass over in silence.*

ΣΚΑ'ΖΩ, f. άσω, *to limp, halt.* II. σκάζων, also χωλίαμβος (sub. πούς), ὁ, the iambic verse of Hipponax, which was a regular iambic senarius, except that a spondee or trochee was substituted for the iambus in the last place.

ΣΚΑΙΟ'Σ, ά, όν, Lat. *scaevus, left, on the left hand* or *side*, like ἀριστερός:—ἡ σκαιά (sub. χείρ), *the left hand.* II. *western, westward*, for the Greek *auspex* turned towards the north, and so had the *West* on his *left;* Σκαιαὶ πύλαι *the West*-gate (of Troy). 2. *unlucky, ill-omened*, because birds of ill-omen always appeared *on the left* of the Greek *auspex*, or *in the West;* birds of good omen on the right, or in the East; (cf. δεξιός). III. metaph. like French *gauche, left-handed, awkward, clumsy, uncouth.* Hence

σκαιοσύνη, ἡ, = σκαιότης.

σκαιότης, ητος, ἡ, (σκαιός) *lefthandedness, awkwardness, clumsiness, stupidity.*

σκαι-ουργέω, f. ήσω, (σκαιός, ἔργον) *to be left-handed in work, to behave rudely* or *indecorously.*

ΣΚΑΙ'ΡΩ, *to skip, dance, bound.*

σκαιῶς, Adv. of σκαιός, *in a left-handed manner, awkwardly.*

σκᾰλάθυρμα, ατος, τό, (σκαλαθύρω) *a subtle question:* generally, *trifling, nonsense.*

σκᾰλᾰθυρμάτιον, τό, Dim. of σκαλάθυρμα, *a trifling subtlety, petty quibble.*

σκᾰλᾰθύρω, = σκάλλω, *to dig:* metaph. *to explore over-subtly* or *cunningly.* [ῡ]

σκᾰλεύς, έως, ὁ, (σκάλλω) *one who hoes: a hoer* or *a hoe.*

σκᾰλεύω, = σκάλλω, *to stir, hoe;* σκαλεύειν, ἄνθρακας *to stir* or *poke a coal-fire.*

σκᾰληνός, ή, όν, or ός, όν, (σκάζω) *limping, halting.* II. *uneven;* ἀριθμὸς σκαληνὸς *an odd* number; τρίγωνον σκαληνόν a triangle *with unequal sides.*

ΣΚΑ'ΛΛΩ, *to stir up, hoe, harrow.*

σκαλμός, ὁ, (σκάλλω) *the pin* or *thole* to which the Greek oar was fastened by the τροπωτήρ, Lat. *scalmus, paxillus.*

σκάλοψ, οπος, ὁ, (σκάλλω) *the digger*, i. e. *the mole.*

Σκάμανδρος, ὁ, *the Scamander*, a river of Troy, ὃν Ξάνθον καλέουσι θεοὶ ἄνδρες δὲ Σκάμανδρον:—Adj.

Σκᾰμάνδριος, α, ον, *Scamandrian;* whence Hector called his son Σκαμάνδριος.

σκᾱνά, Dor. for σκηνή.

σκανδάληθρον, τό, *the stick* or *support in a trap* on which the bait is placed, and which, when touched, makes the trap shut, *the trap-spring:* metaph., σκανδάληθρ' ἱστὰς ἐπῶν setting word-*traps*, i. e. words which one's adversary will catch at, and be caught himself. (Deriv. uncertain.)

σκανδᾰλίζω, f. σω, *to make to stumble, give offence* or *scandal to* any one, *throw difficulties in his way.* From

σκάνδᾰλον, τό, = σκανδάληθρον, *a trap laid for an enemy:—a stumbling-block, offence, scandal.*

σκανδῐκο-πώλης, ου, ὁ, (σκάνδιξ, πωλέω) *a dealer in chervil.*

ΣΚΑ'ΝΔΙΞ, ῖκος, ἡ, *chervil*, Lat. *scandix.*

σκᾰπάνη, ἡ, (σκάπτω) *a spade* or *hoe.* [πᾰ]

σκάπετος, ὁ, (σκάπτω) = κάπετος.

σκάπτειρα, ἡ, fem. of σκαπτήρ, *a woman that digs.*

σκαπτήρ, ῆρος, ὁ, (σκάπτω) *a digger, delver.*

σκᾶπτον, τό, Dor. for σκῆπτρον.

σκαπτός, ή, όν, (σκάπτω) *dug: that may be dug.* II. Σκαπτὴ ὕλη a country in Thrace, named after *a forest in which mines had been worked.*

σκᾶπτρον, τό, Dor. for σκῆπτρον.

ΣΚΑ'ΠΤΩ, fut. σκάψω: Pass. aor. 2 ἐσκάφην [ᾰ]: pf. ἔσκαμμαι:—*to dig;* σκάπτειν τάφρον *to dig* a trench: also Med. σκάπτομαι, like Act.

σκαρδᾰ-μύσσω Att. -ττω, fut. ξω: (σκαίρω, μύω):—*to blink, wink.*

σκᾰρῑφισμός, ὁ, *a scratching* or *scraping up:* σκαριφισμοὶ λήρων *a raking up* of trifles. From

σκάρῑφος, ὁ, = κάρφος: also *a stile for drawing outlines: an outline, sketch.*

σκᾰτός, genit. of σκώρ.

σκᾰτο-φάγος, ον, (σκάτος, φαγεῖν) *dung-eating.*

σκᾰφεύς, έως, ὁ, (σκαφῆναι) *a digger, delver, ditcher*

σκάφη, ἡ, (σκᾰφῆναι) *anything dug* or *scooped out, a hollow vessel, a tub, trough, basin, bowl.* 2. *a light boat, skiff*, Lat. *scăpha.*

σκᾰφῆναι, aor. 2 pass. inf. of σκάπτω.

σκάφιον, Dim. of σκάφη or σκάφος, *a small tub, basin*, or *bowl: a small boat* or *skiff.* II. *a fashion of hair-cutting* (borrowed from the Scythians), *in which the hair was cut off all round the head*, leaving only the hair on the crown, which then looked like *a bowl.* 2. *the crown* of the head.

σκᾰφίς, ίδος, ἡ, like σκάφιον, Dim. of σκάφη or σκάφος, *a small tub, bowl, pail.* 2. *a small boat, skiff.* II. *a digging-tool, a spade, mattock.*

σκάφος, εος, τό, (σκαφῆναι) *a digging:* also *the time* or *season for digging.* II. *that which is dug* or *scooped out, any hollow vessel, a tub:* esp. *the hull of a ship,* Lat. *alveus,* and generally *a ship, boat.* III. *a digging-tool, spade.* [ᾰ]

σκεδάννῡμι and -ύω, lengthd. from obsol. *σκεδάω: fut. σκεδάσω [ᾰ] Att. σκεδῶ, ᾷς, ᾷ: aor. 1 ἐσκέδασα Ep. σκέδασα: Pass., aor. 1 ἐσκεδάσθην: pf. ἐσκέδασμαι:—*to scatter, disperse:* generally, *to scatter, spread abroad: to shiver, break* a thing. II. Pass. *to be scattered, to disperse:* of the rays of the sun, *to be shed abroad:* of a report, *to be spread about, bruited abroad.*

σκέδασα, Ep. aor. 1 of σκεδάννυμι.

σκέδᾰσις, ἡ, (σκεδάννυμι) *a scattering, dispersing.*

σκεδῶ, Att. fut. of σκεδάννυμι.

σκεθρός, ά, όν, *tight, exact, careful.* Adv. σκεθρῶς, *thoroughly, exactly.* (From σχεθεῖν, poët. aor. 2 of ἔχω.)

Σκείρων, ωνος, ὁ, *Sciron,* a robber who infested the coast between Attica and Megara: Σκείρωνος ἀκταί, i. e. the coast of Megara; also called Σκειρωνίδες πέτραι; Σκειρωνικὸν οἶδμα the sea off this coast.

σκελίς, ίδος, ἡ, = Att. σχελίς.

σκελίσκος, ου, ὁ, Dim. of σκέλος, *a small leg.*

ΣΚΕ'ΛΛΩ: fut. σκελῶ Ion. σκελέω: aor. 1 ἔσκηλα:—*to dry, dry up, parch, wither.* II. Pass. σκέλλομαι: fut. σκελοῦμαι: with intr. tenses of Act., aor. 2 ἔσκλην, inf. σκλῆναι (as if from *σκλῆμι): pf. ἔσκληκα with pres. signf.:—*to be parched, lean, withered.*

ΣΚΕ'ΛΟΣ, εος, τό, *the leg;* ἐπὶ σκέλος ἀνάγειν to retreat with the face towards the enemy, retire leisurely. II. τὰ σκέλη *the legs,* i. e. *the two long walls,* between Athens and the Peiræeus.

σκέμμα, ματος, τό, (ἔσκεμμαι, pf. pass. of σκέπτομαι) *a subject of reflexion, a question.*

σκένος, Aeol. for ξένος.

σκέπᾰ, poët. nom. and acc. pl. of σκέπας.

σκεπάζω, f. άσω, (σκέπας) like σκεπάω, *to cover, shelter, screen.* Hence

σκέπᾰνον, τό, (σκέπας) *a covering.*

σκεπᾰνός, ή, όν, (σκέπας) *covered, sheltered.*

ΣΚΕ'ΠΑΡΝΟΝ, τό, or **σκέπαρνος**, ὁ, *a carpenter's axe* or *adze.*

ΣΚΕ'ΠΑΣ, αος, τό, *a covering, shelter;* ἐπὶ σκέπας in or under *shelter;* σκέπας ἀνέμοιο *shelter from* the wind.

σκέπασμα, ατος, τό, (σκεπάζω) = σκέπας.

σκεπάω Ep. **σκεπόω**, *to cover, shelter.*

ΣΚΕ'ΠΗ, ἡ, like σκέπας, *a covering, shelter:* metaph., ἐν σκέπῃ τοῦ πολέμου *under shelter from* war; ἐν σκέπῃ τοῦ φόβου under *shelter from* fear.

σκεπόωσι, Ep. for σκεπῶσι, 3 pl. pres. from σκεπάω.

σκεπτέον, *one must look* or *consider:* verb. Adj. of **σκέπτομαι**, fut. σκέψομαι: aor. 1 ἐσκεψάμην: pf. ἔσκεμμαι: Dep.:—the pres. and impf. σκέπτομαι, ἐσκεπτόμην, are seldom found in Att., σκοπῶ or σκοποῦμαι being used instead: I. intr. *to look about, look carefully at, look after, watch.* II. of the mind, *to look to, view, examine, consider.*

ΣΚΕ'ΠΩ, rare radic. form of σκεπάζω.

σκερβολέω and **σκερβόλλω**, (σκέρβολος) *to scold, abuse, revile.* From

σκέρβολος, like κέρτομος, *scolding, abusive.* (Deriv. uncertain.)

σκευᾰγωγέω, f. ήσω, *to remove one's goods and chattels.* From

σκευ-ᾰγωγός, όν, (σκεῦος, ἄγω) *conveying* or *moving one's goods and chattels:*—as Subst., σκευαγωγός, ὁ, *the officer who looks to the baggage, baggage-master.*

σκευάζω, f. άσω: aor. 1 ἐσκεύασα: Pass., ἐσκεύασμαι, Ion. 3 pl. ἐσκευάδαται; Ion. 3 pl. plqpf. ἐσκευάδατο: (σκεῦος, σκευή):—*to prepare, make ready:* esp. *to prepare* or *dress food:* generally, *to provide:* —Med. *to prepare for oneself, to procure, devise.* II. of persons, *to furnish* or *supply with* a thing. 2. *to dress up, disguise:* pf. pass. part. ἐσκευασμένος, *dressed up.*

σκευάριον, τό, Dim. of σκεῦος or σκευή, *a trifling part of one's dress* or *equipment.* [ᾰ]

σκευαστέον, verb. Adj. of σκευάζω, *one must prepare.*

σκευαστός, ή, όν, (σκευάζω) *prepared, artificial.*

σκευή, ἡ, (σκεῦος) *equipment, attire, dress,* Lat. *apparatus: the properties* or *dress* of an actor, etc. 2. *a fashion in dress.* II. *an implement* of any kind, like σκεῦος: *the tackling* of a ship.

σκευο-θήκη, ἡ, (σκεῦος, θήκη) *a storehouse for all kinds of dress* or *equipments, an armoury, arsenal.*

σκευοποιέω, f. ήσω, (σκευοποιός) *to make arms* or *implements, to manufacture.* Hence

σκευοποίημα, ματος, τό, *the dress of an actor.*

σκευο-ποιός, όν, (σκεῦος, ποιέω) *making arms* or *implements: making masks and stage-dresses.*

ΣΚΕΥ'ΟΣ, εος, τό, *a vessel* or *implement of any kind.* 2. in plur. σκεύη, τά, *implements, tools: the baggage* of an army, Lat. *impedimenta. the trappings* of horses; *the tackling* of ships, *naval stores: the dresses of actors.* II. *the body,* as *the vessel* or *instrument* of the soul.

σκευοφορέω, f. ήσω, (σκευοφόρος) *to carry baggage:* —Pass. *to have one's baggage carried.*

σκευοφορικός, ή, όν, *of* or *for the carrying of baggage;* βάρος σκευοφορικόν the load *of a beast of burthen.* From

σκευο-φόρος, ον, (σκεῦος, φέρω) *carrying baggage:* οἱ σκευοφόροι *the sutlers, camp-followers:* σκευοφόροι κάμηλοι *the baggage*-camels; τὰ σκευοφόρα *the beasts of burden.*

σκευοφυλακέω, f. ήσω, *to watch the baggage.* From

σκευο-φύλαξ, ακος, ὁ, (σκεῦος, φύλαξ) *a storekeeper.*

σκευωρέομαι, Dep. with fut. med. -ήσομαι, pf. pass.

ἐσκευώρημαι; (σκευωρός):—*to watch* or *look after the baggage.* 2. *to examine thoroughly.* II. *to contrive cunningly:*—intr. *to act knavishly.* Hence

σκευώρημα, ατος, τό, *a cunning trick.*

σκευωρία, ἡ, (σκευωρέομαι) *care in looking after baggage: great care, diligence.* II. *cunning, knavery.*

σκευ-ωρός, όν, (σκεῦος, ὤρα) *looking after baggage.*

σκεψάμενος, aor. 1 part. of σκέπτομαι or σκοπέω.

σκέψις, εως, ἡ, (σκέπτομαι) *perception by the senses.* II. *examining: consideration, reflexion.*

σκῆλαι, aor. 1 inf. of σκέλλω: **σκήλειε**, 3 sing. opt.

σκηνάομαι, Dep., with pf. pass. ἐσκήνημαι, *to dwell, live.* II. also as Med. *to build for oneself.*

σκηνέω, f. ήσω, (σκηνή) *to be* or *dwell in a tent, to be encamped: to be quartered* or *billeted:* generally, *to dwell, stay, lodge* in a place.

ΣΚΗΝΗ', ἡ, *a tent, booth: a tabernacle:* in plur. *a camp*, Lat. *castra.* 2. *a dwelling-place, house: a temple.* II. *a wooden stage* or *scaffold* for actors to perform on:—hence *the stage, the part on which the actors performed*, opp. to the θυμέλη (where the Chorus danced and sang). III. *the tilted cover of a wagon* or *carriage:* also *a bed-tester.* IV. *an entertainment given in tents, a banquet.*

σκήνημα, ατος, τό, (σκηνέω) = σκηνή, *a dwelling-place, nest, abode.*

σκηνίδιον, τό, Dim. of σκηνή, *a little tent.* [νῐ]

σκηνίς, ίδος, ἡ, = σκηνή.

σκηνίτης, ου, ὁ, (σκηνή) *a dweller in tents: on a tent.* [ῑ]

σκηνοπηγέω, (σκηνόπηγος) *to put up a tent* or *booth.* Hence

σκηνοπηγία, ἡ, *a pitching of tents.* II. *the feast of tabernacles*, which lasted for eight days in the month Tisri, to commemorate *the dwelling in tents* in the wilderness: also **σκηνοπήγια**, τά.

σκηνό-πηγος, ον, (σκηνή, πήγνυμι) *fixing a tent.*

σκηνο-ποιός, όν, (σκηνή, ποιέω) *making tents:* as Subst., σκηνοποιός, ὁ, *a tent-maker.*

σκηνορ-ράφος, ον, (σκηνή, ῥαφῆναι) *stitching tents:* as Subst., σκηνορράφος, ὁ, *a tent-maker.*

σκῆνος Dor. **σκᾶνος**, εος, τό, like σκηνή. 2. *a body.*

σκηνο-φύλαξ, ἄκος, ὁ, ἡ, (σκηνή, φύλαξ) *a guard* or *watcher in a tent.*

σκηνόω, f. ώσω, (σκῆνος) *to pitch tents, encamp.* II. *to live* or *dwell in a tent:* generally, *to lodge, take up one's abode.*

σκηνύδριον, τό, Dim. of σκηνή.

σκήνωμα, ατος, τό, (σκηνόω) *a tent, tabernacle: a habitation:* in pl. *soldiers' cantonments.*

σκηπάνιον, τό, = σκῆπτρον, *a sceptre, staff.*

σκηπτο-βάμων [ᾰ], ον, gen. ονος, (σκῆπτον = σκῆπτρον, βαίνω) *sitting, perched on the sceptre.*

σκῆπτον, τό, = σκῆπτρον, only in Dor. form **σκᾶπτον**, and a few compds.

σκηπτός, ὁ, (σκήπτω) *a gust* or *squall of wind* that comes down suddenly: *a thunderbolt.* II. metaph. *a sudden visitation* or *calamity.*

σκηπτουχία, ἡ, *the bearing a staff* or *sceptre: chief command.* From

σκηπτ-οῦχος, ον, (σκῆπτον, ἔχω) *bearing a staff, baton* or *sceptre* as the badge of command. 2. as Subst., σκηπτοῦχος, ὁ, *the wand-bearer*, an officer in the Persian court.

σκηπτο-φόρος, ον, = σκηπτρο-φόρος.

σκῆπτρον Dor. **σκᾶπτον**, τό, (σκήπτω) *a staff* or *stick to lean upon: a walking-stick.* II. *a staff* or *baton*, as the badge of command, *a sceptre*, borne by kings, chiefs, and heralds: speakers on rising received a σκῆπτρον from the herald. 2. *the sceptre*, to express *royalty* or *kingly power.*

σκηπτροφορέω, f. ήσω, *to bear rule over.* From

σκηπτρο-φόρος, ον, (σκῆπτρον, φέρω) *bearing a sceptre, kingly, princely.*

ΣΚΗ'ΠΤΩ, f. ψω: aor. 1 ἔσκηψα: I. trans. *to prop, support, stay:* hence *to let fall upon, hurl, shoot:* also in Med. 2. intr. *to fall* or *dart down, light.* II. Pass. and Med., *to prop* or *support oneself by a staff, to lean upon:* metaph. *to depend* or *rely upon.* 2. σκήπτεσθαι c. acc. *to put before* oneself *as a prop* or *support, to pretend, allege by way of excuse:* c. inf. *to pretend to be.* 3. absol. *to excuse* or *defend oneself;* σκήπτεσθαι πρός τινα, *to excuse oneself* towards another.

σκήπων, ωνος, ὁ, (σκήπτω) like σκῆπτρον and σκίπων, *a staff.*

σκηρίπτω, like σκήπτω, *to prop, stay:*—Med. *to support oneself, to lean* or *press against.*

σκῆψις, εως, ἡ, (σκήπτω) *a pretext, excuse, pretence, reason alleged.*

ΣΚΙΑ', ᾶς Ion. **σκιή**, ῆς, ἡ, *a shadow, shade: the shade* or *ghost* of one that is dead, Lat. *umbra:* of things, *a mere shadow, phantom, spectre.* 2. *the shade* of trees; πετραίη σκιή *the shade* of a rock; ἐν σκιᾷ *indoors.* 3. *a shady place.*

σκιᾰγρᾰφέω, f. ήσω, (σκιαγράφος) *to paint in light and shade, to paint slightly, sketch out*, Lat. *adumbrare.*

σκιᾰγρᾰφία, ἡ, (σκιαγραφέω) *painting in light and shade, rough painting.*

σκιᾰ-γράφος, ον, (σκιά, γράφω) *painting in light and shade* (without colours). [γρᾰ]

σκιάδειον, τό, (σκιά) *anything that shades: an umbrella* or *parasol.*

σκιᾰδίσκη, ἡ, = σκιάδειον, *an umbrella, parasol.*

σκιάζω, f. σκιάσω Att. σκιῶ: aor. 1 ἐσκίασα: (σκιά):—*to shade, overshadow, darken: to throw a shadow on.* II. *to cover, veil.*

σκιᾰ-μᾰχέω, f. ήσω, (σκιά, μάχη) *to fight in the shade* (i. e. *in the school, not in real battle*), *to spar.* II. *to fight with a shadow:* hence *to fight in vain.*

Σκιά-ποδες [ᾰ], οἱ, (σκιά, πούς) *the Shadow-footed*, a fabulous people in Libya.

σκιᾰρό-κομος, ον, (σκιαρός, κόμη) *shady with leaves.*

σκιᾰρός, ά, όν, Dor. for σκιερός.

σκιάς, άδος, ἡ, (σκιά) *any shady covering, a canopy, pavilion.*

σκιάσμα, ματος, τό, (σκιάζω) *a shadow.*

σκιᾱ-τροφέω Ion. **σκιητρ-**, f. ήσω: (σκιά, τρέφω): —*to rear in the shade, to bring up tenderly*:—Pass. *to keep in the shade, shun heat and toil, live effeminately.* II. intr. *to wear a covering, keep one's head covered.*

σκιάω Ep. **σκιόω**, = σκιάζω: only in Pass. *to be shaded, become dark.*

σκίδναμαι, like κίδναμαι, Pass., only used in pres. and impf.:—*to be spread* or *scattered, scattered abroad, dispersed*; σκιδναμένης Δημήτερος ἢ συνιούσης when the corn *is scattered abroad* or gathered in, i. e. at seed-time or at harvest; ἅμα ἡλίῳ σκιδναμένῳ as the sun *begins to scatter his beams, spread his light.*

σκιερός Dor. **σκιαρός**, ά, όν, (σκιά) *shady, shaded.*

σκιή, ἡ, Ion. for σκιά.

ΣΚΙ'ΛΛΑ, ης, ἡ, *a sea-onion* or *squill*, Lat. *squilla.*

σκιμᾱλίζω, f. ίσω Att. ιῶ, *to give one a tap* or *fillip*, generally, *to insult.* (Deriv. unknown.)

σκίμπους, -ποδος, ὁ, (σκίμπτω) *a small couch, low bed, pallet*, Lat. *grabbătus.*

σκίμπτω, f. ψω, = σκήπτω.

σκινδάλᾰμος, ὁ, contr. **σκινδαλμός** Att. **σχινδάλαμος** contr. **σχινδαλμός**: (σχίζω): *a piece of cleft wood, a splinter*, Lat. *scindula*: metaph., λόγων ἀκριβῶν σχινδάλαμοι straw-splittings, quibbles.

σκινδᾰλᾰμο-φράστης, ου, ὁ, (σκινδάλαμος, φράζω) *a straw-splitter.*

σκινδαλμός, ὁ, contr. for σκινδάλαμος.

σκιο-ειδής, ές, (σκιά, εἶδος) *like a shadow, fleeting like a shadow, shadowy.*

σκιόεις, εσσα, εν, (σκιά) *shady, shadowy: gloomy, dark.*

σκιόωντο, Ep. 3 pl. impf. pass. of σκιάω.

σκίπων, ωνος, ὁ, (σκίμπτω) *a staff*, Lat *scipio.* [ῐ]

Σκῖρα, τά, (σκίρον) = Σκιροφόρια.

Σκῖράς, άδος, ἡ, epith. of Athena, see Σκιροφόρια.

σκῖράφειον, τό, *a gambling-house.* From

σκίρᾰφος [ῐ], ὁ, *a dice-box.* 2. metaph. *trickery, cheating.* (Deriv. uncertain.)

Σκῖρῖται, οἱ, *the Scirites*, a division of the Spartan army, consisting of 600 foot: they came from the Arcadian district Σκιρῖτις.

ΣΚΙ'ΡΟΝ [ῑ], τό, like σκιάδειον, *the parasol* borne, at Athens, by the priestesses in a festival of Athena Σκῖράς, thence called τὰ Σκῖρα or τὰ Σκῖροφόρια, giving name to the month Σκῖροφοριών.

σκῖρον, τό, *the hard rind* of cheese, *cheese-parings.*

ΣΚΙ'ΡΟΣ, ὁ, also **σκίρρος**, *gypsum, stucco.*

Σκῖρο-φόρια, τά, (σκίρον, φέρω) *the festival of* Athena Σκιράς, celebrated in the month Σκιροφοριών.

Σκῖρο-φοριών, ῶνος, ὁ, (Σκιροφόρια) *Scirophorion*, the 12th Attic month, answering to the latter part of June and former part of July.

ΣΚΙΡΤΑ'Ω, f. ήσω, *to spring, leap, bound.*

σκίρτημα, ατος, τό, *a bound, leap.*

σκιρτητής, οῦ, ὁ, (σκιρτάω) *a leaper, jumper.*

σκιρτο-πόδης, ου, ὁ, (σκιρτάω, πούς) *spring-footed, with bounding foot.*

σκιρτῷεν, 3 pl. pres. opt. of σκιρτάω.

Σκίτᾱλοι, οἱ, fellows invoked among the powers of Impudence by Aristophanes (Eq. 634).

σκῐφίζω, Dor. for ξιφίζω.

σκίφος, τό, Dor. for ξίφος, *a sword.* [ῐ]

σκι-ώδης, ες, = σκιοειδής, *shady: gloomy.*

σκλῆναι, inf. aor. 2 of σκέλλω.

σκληρ-ᾰγωγέω, (σκληρός, ἀγωγή) *to bring up hard*[illegible].

σκληρο-καρδία, ἡ, (σκληρός, καρδία) *hardness of heart.*

σκληρος, ά, όν, (σκλῆναι) *dry, hard*, Lat. *durus.* 2. of sound, *hoarse, harsh, rough.* 3. of taste and smell, *harsh, rough.* 4. *stiff, stark*, Lat. *rigidus: sturdy, tough.* II. metaph., I. of things, *hard, austere.* 2. of persons, *hard, harsh, stern*, also *stubborn.*

σκληρότης, ητος, ἡ, (σκληρός) *hardness, harshness, roughness.*

σκληρο-τράχηλος, ον, (σκληρός, τράχηλος) *stiff-necked.* [ᾰ]

σκληρύνω [ῡ], f. ὕνῶ: aor. I ἐσκλήρυνα: pf. pass. ἐσκλήρυμμαι: (σκληρός):—*to harden*, esp. *to harden the heart: to make thick, gross, stupid.*

σκληρῶς, Adv. of σκληρός, *in hard* or *rough fashion.*

σκνῑπαῖος, α, ον, (κνέφας) *of* or *in the twilight.*

σκολιό-θριξ, -τρῐχος, ὁ, ἡ, (σκολιός, θρίξ) *with curled, twining hair* or *leaves.*

σκόλιον, τό, neut. of σκολιός (sub. μέλος), *a song at banquets*, sung to the lyre; said to have been introduced by Terpander, and so called from the *irregular* way it was passed on: each guest who sung held a myrtle-branch (μυρρίνη) in his hand, which he passed on to any one he chose.

ΣΚΟΛΙΟ'Σ, ά, όν, *crooked, bent: twisting, winding.* II. metaph. *crooked, tortuous, unjust.*

σκολιῶς, Adv. *crookedly.*

σκολόπεσσι, Ep. dat. pl. of σκόλοψ.

σκολοπίζω, f. σω, (σκόλοψ) *to impale.*

ΣΚΟ'ΛΟΨ, οπος, ὁ, *a pale, stake*: in plur. σκόλοπες, οἱ, *pales, a palisade, stockade*: in Persia, used for impaling or fixing heads on, whence σκολοπίζω, ἀνασκολοπίζω. II. *a tree.*

ΣΚΟ'ΛΥΜΟΣ, ὁ, *an eatable* kind of *thistle: an artichoke*

ΣΚΟ'ΜΒΡΟΣ, ὁ, a kind of fish, of which the θύννος and πηλαμύς were varieties.

σκοπ-άρχης, ου, ὁ, (σκοπός, ἄρχω) *leader of the spies* or *of a party of videttes.*

σκοπελο-δρόμος, ὁ, (σκόπελος, δραμεῖν) *running over rocks.*

σκόπελος, ὁ, (σκοπέω) *a look-out place, a crag* or *headland*, Lat. *scopulus*: generally, *a high rock, peak.*

σκοπεύω, = σκοπέω.

σκοπέω, also **σκοπέομαι** as Dep.: only used in pres. and impf., the other tenses, fut. *σκέψομαι*, aor. 1 *ἐσκεψάμην*, pf. *ἔσκεμμαι*, being supplied by *σκέπτομαι*: (*σκοπός*):—*to look at* or *after* a thing: *to behold, contemplate, survey:* generally, *to look: to look out.* II. metaph. *to look to, consider, pay regard to;* σκοπεῖν τὰ ἑαυτοῦ *to look to* one's own affairs. III. *to inquire, ascertain.* Hence

σκοπή, ἡ, *a look-out place, watch-tower.*

σκοπιά Ion. **-ιή**, ἡ, (*σκοπός*) *a look-out place, mountain-peak.* 2. *a watch-tower*, Lat. *specula.* II. *a looking out, keeping watch;* σκοπιὴν ἔχειν to keep *watch.* Hence

σκοπιάζω, *to look about* or *spy from a watch-tower:* generally, *to spy, explore.* II. transit. *to spy out, search out, discover.*

σκοπιάω, later poët. form for *σκοπιάζω.*

σκοπιήτης, ου, ὁ, (*σκοπιάω*) *a spy, scout.* II. *a mountaineer*, epith. of Pan.

σκοπι-ωρέομαι, f. *ήσομαι*: Dep: (*σκοπιά, ὥρα*):—*to spy* or *observe from a look-out place*

σκοπός, ὁ and ἡ, (*σκέπ-τομαι*) *one that watches* or *looks out:* in bad sense, *one who lies in wait for* another. 2. of gods, *the guardian, protector, tutelary god* of a place. 3. *a look-out man* or *watcher* in war, Lat. *speculator;* also *one who marks* game: *a spy, scout: a messenger.* I. *the mark* or *object on which one fixes the eye, a mark*, Lat. *scopus;* ἀπὸ σκοποῦ away *from the mark*

σκορδῑνάομαι Ion. **-έομαι**: f. *ήσομαι*: Dep.:—*to stretch one's limbs, yawn, gape, feel tired* or *lazy.* (Deriv. uncertain.)

σκοροδ-άλμη, ἡ, (*σκόροδον, ἅλμη*) *a sauce* or *pickle composed of brine and garlic.*

σκοροδίζω, f. *ίσω*: pf. pass. *ἐσκορόδισμαι*: (*σκόροδον*):—*to feed with garlic: to train game-cocks on garlic* for fighting; *ἐσκοροδισμένος primed with garlic.*

σκορόδιον, τό, Dim. of *σκόροδον*: in pl. *sprouts* or *stalks of garlic.*

ΣΚΟ'ΡΟΔΟΝ contr. **σκόρδον**, τό, *garlic*, Lat. *allium;* often mentioned with the onion (*κρόμυον*), and leek (*πράσον*). Hence

σκοροδο-πανδοκευτρι-αρτόπωλις, ιδος, ἡ, (*σκόροδον, πανδοκευτ-*[illegible] *ἀρτόπωλις*) *a garlic-breadselling-hostess.*

ΣΚΟΡΠΙ'ΖΩ, f. *ίσω*, *to scatter, disperse, spread abroad: to be lavish:* cf. *σκεδάννυμι.*

ΣΚΟΡΠΙ'ΟΣ, ἡ, *a scorpion.*

σκοταῖος, α, ον, (*σκότος*) *dark, in the dark: before daybreak* or *after nightfall.*

σκοτεινός, ή, όν, (*σκότος*) *dark, dusky: in the dark, blind.* II. metaph. *dark, obscure*:—Adv. *-νῶς.*

σκοτία, ἡ, (*σκότος*) *darkness, gloom, dusk.*

σκοτίζω, f. *ίσω*, (*σκότος*) *to make dark*:—Pass. *to be dark, darkened.*

σκότιος, α, ον, also ος, ον, (*σκότος*) *dark, dusky: in the dark:* of love, *secret, stolen.*

σκοτο-δᾰσῠ-πυκνό-θριξ, *-τρῐχος*, ὁ, ἡ, (*σκότος, δασύς, πυκνός, θρίξ*) *with dark rough thick hair.*

σκοτο-δῑνέω, (*σκότος, δῖνος*) *to grow blind and dizzy, to have a dizziness* or *vertigo.* Hence

σκοτοδῑνία, ἡ, *dizziness, vertigo.*

σκοτοδῑνιάω, = *σκοτοδινέω.*

σκοτο-ειδής, ές, (*σκότος, εἶδος*) *dark-looking.*

σκοτόεις, εσσα, εν, poët. for *σκότιος*, (*σκότος*) *dark, gloomy.*

σκοτό-μαινα, ἡ, Att. for *σκοτομήνη.*

σκοτο-μήνη, ἡ, (*σκότος, μήνη*) *a moonless night.*

σκοτομήνιος, ον, (*σκοτομήνη*) *moonless, dark.*

ΣΚΟ'ΤΟΣ, ου, ὁ, *darkness, gloom:* in Homer often of *the darkness of death* in the phrase, τὸν δὲ σκότος ὄσσε κάλυψεν: of blindness, σκότον βλέπειν *to look on* darkness, i. e. to be blind: metaph., σκότῳ κρύπτειν to hide in *darkness.*—The neut. form *σκότος*, εος, τό, also occurs, but rarely in Attic Greek. Hence

σκοτόω, f. *ώσω*, *to make dark darken, to blind.*

σκοτώδης, ες, = *σκοτοειδής.*

σκύβᾰλον, τό, *dung, filth, refuse.* (Said to be derived from ἐς κύνας βαλεῖν.)

σκυδμαίνω, = *σκύζομαι*, *to be angry with* one.

ΣΚΥ'ΖΟΜΑΙ, Dep. *to be angry* or *wroth with* one.

Σκύθαινᾰ, ἡ, fem. of *Σκύθης.* [ῠ]

Σκύθης, ου, ὁ: voc. *Σκύθα*:—*a Scythian:* proverb., Σκυθῶν ἐρημία a *Scythian* wilderness. 2. as Adj. *Scythian.* II. at Athens, *one of the city-guard*, which was mostly composed of Scythian slaves. [ῠ] Hence

Σκῠθίζω, f. *ίσω*, *to be* or *behave like a Scythian: to side with the Scythians.* 2. *to drink like a Scythian.* 3. since the Scythians scalped their enemies, hence *to shave the head.*

Σκῠθιστί, Adv. (*Σκυθίζω*) *in the Scythian fashion, in the Scythian tongue.*

Σκῠθο-τοξότης, ου, ὁ, (*Σκύθος, τοξότης*) *a Scythian bowman.*

σκυθράζω, f. *άσω*, (*σκυθρός*) *to be angry* or *sullen.*

ΣΚΥΘΡΟ'Σ, ά, όν, *angry, sullen, gloomy.*

σκυθρωπάζω, f. *άσω*, (*σκυθρωπός*) *to look angry* or *sullen, be of a sad countenance.*

σκυθρ-ωπός, όν, also ή, όν, (*σκυθρός, ὤψ*) *sullen, angry-looking: of a sad countenance.* Adv. σκυθρωπῶς ἔχειν to be *of a sad countenance.*

σκῠλάκαινα, ἡ, fem. of *σκύλαξ*, *a she-whelp.*

σκυλάκευμα, ατος, τό, *a whelp, cub.* From

σκῠλᾰκεύω, f. *σω*, (*σκύλαξ*) *to pair dogs for breeding:* generally, *to breed dogs.*

σκῠλᾰκ-ώδης, ες, (*σκύλαξ, εἶδος*) *like a young dog:* neut. τὸ σκυλακῶδες as Subst., *the nature of puppies.*

σκύλαξ, ᾰκος, ὁ and ἡ, like *σκύμνος*, *any young animal*, esp. *a young dog, a whelp, puppy.*

σκύλευμα, ατος, τό, *plunder, booty, spoil.* From

σκῡλεύω, f. *σω*, (*σκῦλον*) *to strip* or *spoil a slain enemy* of his arms, Lat. *spoliare:* c. acc. pers. et rei, Κύκνον τεύχεα ἀπ' ὤμων σκυλεύσαντες *having stripped* the arms of Cygnus from off his shoulders.

σκῡλη-φόρος, ον, = *σκυλοφόρος.*

Y

Σκύλλᾰ or **Σκύλλη**, ἡ, *Scylla*, a female monster inhabiting a cavern in the Straits of Sicily, who *rended* her prey in pieces: (hence called Σκύλλα from σκύλλω.)

ΣΚΥ'ΛΛΩ, aor. 1 ἔσκῦλα:—properly *to flay*: generally, *to rend, mangle, tear*: metaph. *to trouble, annoy*, Lat. *vexare*. Hence

σκύλμα, ατος, τό, *a piece plucked out*.

σκυλμός, ὁ (σκύλλω) *a rending, mangling*: metaph. *trouble*.

σκῠλοδεψέω, f. ήσω, *to tan hides*. From

σκῠλο-δέψης or **-δέψος**, ου, ὁ, (σκῦλον, δέψω fut. of δέφω) *a tanner of hides*.

σκῦλον, τό, (σκύλλω) mostly in plur. σκῦλα, *the arms stript off a slain enemy, spoils*, Lat. *spolia*; σκῦλα γράφειν to write one's name on *arms gained as spoils*: rarely in sing. *booty, spoil, prey*.

σκύλος [ῠ], εος, τό, (σκύλλω) *the skin of an animal, a lion's hide*.

σκῠλο-φόρος, ον, (σκῦλον, φέρω) *receiving the spoil*.

σκῠλο-χᾰρής, ές, (σκῦλον, χαρῆναι) *delighting in spoils* or *booty*.

ΣΚΥ'ΜΝΟΣ, ὁ, like σκύλαξ, *any young animal*; but properly *a lion's whelp*. as σκύλαξ was a dog's whelp, puppy. Hence

σκυμνως, Dor. for σκύμνους, acc. pl. of σκυμνος.

Σκῦρος, ἡ, the isle of *Scyros*, one of the Sporades, not far from Euboea: **Σκῡρόθεν**, Adv. *from Scyros*.

σκῠτάλη [ᾰ], ἡ, (akin to ξύλον) *a stick, staff, cudgel*: at Sparta, *a staff*, used by way of a cipher for writing despatches: a strip of paper was rolled spirally round it, on which the despatches were written, so that when unrolled they were unintelligible: generals abroad had a similar staff, round which they rolled these papers, and so were able to read the despatches. Hence σκυτάλη meant *a Spartan despatch*, and metaph. *a message*.

σκῠτάλιον, τό, Dim. of σκύταλον, *a cane*. [ᾰ]

σκῠτᾰλίς, ίδος, ἡ, Dim. of σκυτάλη.

σκύτᾰλον, τό, = σκυτάλη, *a cudgel, club*. [ῠ]

σκῠτεύς, έως, ὁ, (σκῦτος) *a shoemaker, cobbler*.

σκῠτεύω, f. σω, (σκυτεύς) *to be a shoemaker*.

ΣΚΥ'ΤΗ Dor. **σκῡτά**, ἡ, *the neck*

σκύτῐνος, η, ον, (σκῦτος) *leathern, made of leather*; τὸ σκύτινον *a leathern ornament* or *appendage*.

σκῦτος, τό, (κύτος, whence Lat. *cutis*) *a skin, hide*, esp. *a dressed* or *tanned hide, leather*. II. *anything made of leather, a whip, thong*.

σκυτοτομεῖον, τό, *a shoemaker's shop*. From

σκῠτοτομέω, f. ήσω, (σκυτοτόμος) *to cut leather* for shoes, *to be a shoemaker*.

σκῠτοτομικός, ή, όν, *of* or *for a shoemaker*. From

σκῠτο-τόμος. ον, (σκῦτον, τεμεῖν) *cutting leather*: as Subst., σκυτοτόμος, ὁ, *a worker in leather, shoemaker*

σκῡτο-τρᾰγέω, (σκῦτον, τραγεῖν) *to consume leather*.

σκύφος, ου, ὁ, and **σκύφος**, έος, τό, (akin to κύπελλον, κύπη) *a cup, beaker, can, flagon*.

σκωληκό-βρωτος, ον, (σκώληξ, βιβρώσκω) *eaten of worms, worm-eaten*.

ΣΚΩ'ΛΗΞ, ηκος, ὁ, *a worm*, Lat. *lumbricus*.

ΣΚΩ'ΛΟΣ, ὁ, *a pointed stake*: *a thorn, prickle*.

σκῶμμα, ατος, τό, (σκώπτω) *a jest, joke, gibe, scoff*.

σκωμμάτιον, τό, Dim. of σκῶμμα, *a petty joke*.

σκωπτόλης, ου, ὁ, (σκώπτω) *a mocker, jester*.

ΣΚΩ'ΠΤΩ, fut. σκώψομαι: aor. 1 ἔσκωψα: aor. 1 pass. ἐσκώφθην:—*to mock, jeer, scoff at, jest at*:—absol. *to jest, joke, be in fun*.

ΣΚΩ'Ρ, τό, gen. σκᾰτός, *dung*.

σκώψ, ὁ, gen. σκωπός, nom. pl. σκῶπες: (from σκέπτομαι, as κλώψ from κλέπτω) a kind of *owl*.

σμᾶνος, Dor. for σμῆνος; dat. pl. σμάνεσσι.

σμᾰράγδῐνος, η, ον, *of emerald*. From

ΣΜΑ'ΡΑΓΔΟΣ or **μάραγδος**, ὁ and ἡ, Lat. *smaragdus, a precious stone of green colour*: prob. not *the emerald*.

ΣΜΑ'ΡΑΓΕ'Ω, f. ήσω, *to crash*: of the sea, *to roar*: of birds, *to scream*, etc. (Formed from the sound.)

Σμάρᾰγος, ὁ, (σμαραγέω) *a brawling goblin*.

σμάω, f. σμήσω Dor. σμάσω: aor. 1 ἔσμησα: in the pres., the Att. contr. is σμῶ, σμῇς, σμῇ, inf. σμῆν: (μάω):—*to smear, rub*: *to anoint*: Med., σμᾶσθαι τὴν κεφαλήν to anoint one's head. 2. *to rub, wipe, wash off, cleanse*. Cp. σμήχω.

σμερδᾰλέος, έα Ion. έη, έον, *terrible, fearful, awful*:—neut. σμερδαλέον as Adv. *terribly*.

σμερδνός, ή, όν, = σμερδαλέος.

σμέω, Ion for σμάω.

σμηνο-δόκος, ον, (σμῆνος, δέχομαι) *holding a swarm of bees*.

σμῆνος, εος, τό, (from ἑσμός) *a bee-hive*. II. *a swarm of bees*: generally, *a swarm, crowd, throng*.

σμήχω, f. ξω: aor. 1 pass. ἐσμήχθην:—collat. form of σμάω, *to rub, wipe off* or *away*. 2. *to wipe clean*. See σμάω.

σμῑκρο-, for words beginning thus, see μικρο-.

σμῑκρός, ά, όν, Ion. and old Attic for μικρός. [ῑ]

σμῑκρότης, **σμῑκρύνω**, v. sub μικρ-.

σμικρῶς, Adv. of σμικρός, *but little*.

σμῑλαξ, ᾰκος, ὁ, = Att. μῖλαξ, *the yew*, Lat. *taxus*.

σμίλευμα, ατος, τό, (σμῑλεύω) *carved work*: metaph., σμιλεύματα ἔργων finely carved works.

σμῑλευτός, ή, όν, verb. Adj. of σμιλεύω, *carved*.

σμῑλεύω, f. σω, *to cut out, carve finely*. From

ΣΜΙ'ΛΗ [ῑ], ἡ, *a knife for cutting* or *carving*, Lat. *scalprum*: *a graving tool, chisel*: generally, *a knife*.

Σμινθεύς, έως, ὁ, epith. of Apollo, from Σμίνθη a town in the Troad, *the Sminthian*.

σμῐνύη, ἡ, *a two-pronged hoe* or *mattock*, Lat. *bidens*.

σμῠγερός, Adv. -ρῶς, poët. for μογερός, -ρῶς.

σμῦξαι, aor. 1 inf. of σμύχω.

σμύρνα Ion. -νη, ἡ, (μύρρα) *myrrh*, the resinous gum of an Arabian tree, used for embalming the dead. Hence

σμυρναῖος, α, ον, *of myrrh*. II. Σμυρναῖος, α, ον, *of Smyrna, an inhabitant of Smyrna.*

σμυρνίζω, f. ίσω, (σμύρνα) *to flavour with myrrh.*

ΣΜΥ'ΧΩ [ῡ], f. ξω: aor. 1 ἔσμυξα: Pass., aor. 1 ἐσμύχθην: pf. ἔσμυγμαι:—*to burn in a smouldering fire, to make smoulder away:* Pass. *to smoulder away.*

ΣΜΩ'ΔΙΞ, σμώδιγγος, ἡ, *a weal* or *swollen bruise* caused by a blow, Lat. *vibex.*

σμώχω, f. ξω, = σμήχω, *to rub* · *to rub to pieces, grind down.*

σοβᾰρεύομαι, Dep. (σοβαρός) *to stalk about in a haughty way, to strut pompously.*

σοβᾰρο-βλέφᾰρος, ον, (σοβαρός, βλέφαρον) *with haughty eyebrows, in pompous fashion.*

σοβᾰρός, ά, όν, (σοβέω) *scaring people away:* hence *bustling, swaggering, pompous, haughty, insolent.* 2. of things, *stirring, bustling, violent.*

σοβέω, f. ήσω, *to make the noise* σοῦ, σοῦ (*shoo! shoo!*), *to scare away* birds: generally, *to drive away, knock off.* II. *to excite, agitate.* III. intr. in Act. *to walk in a pompous manner, to strut, swagger, bustle along.*

σοί, dat. of σύ.

σοῖο, Ion. gen. masc. and neut. of σός.

σολοικία, ἡ, = σολοικισμός.

σολοικίζω, f. ίσω Att. ιῶ, (σόλοικος) *to speak* or *write incorrectly, commit a solecism;* φωνῇ Σκυθικῇ σολοικίζειν to speak bad Scythian. Hence

σολοικισμός, ὁ, *incorrectness in the use of language, an ungrammatical mode of speaking, a solecism.*

σολοικιστής, οῦ, ὁ, (σολοικίζω) *one who speaks incorrectly, one who commits solecisms.*

σόλοικος, ον, *speaking incorrectly; using barbarisms* or *solecisms:*—hence *barbarous.* II. metaph. *awkward, clumsy, offensive.* (Derived from the corruption of the Attic dialect among the Athenian colonists of Σόλοι in Cilicia.)

ΣΟ'ΛΟΣ, ὁ, *a mass of iron used as a quoit,* spherical in shape, and so distinguished from the flat round δίσκος.

σόος, η, ον, Ep. form of σῶος, *safe and sound in* body, *whole, unhurt,* Lat. *integer.*

σορο-πηγός, ὁ, (σορός, πήγνυμι) *a coffin-maker.*

ΣΟΡΟ'Σ, ἡ, *a vessel* or *urn to hold the ashes of the dead: a coffin.*

σός, ή, όν, possessive Adj. of the 2nd pers. pron. σύ, *thy, thine, of thee,* Lat. *tuus, tua, tuum:* also objective, σὸς πόθος regret *for thee.* Earlier Ep. and Dor form τεός, τεή (Dor. τεά), τεόν.

σοῦ, gen. of σύ; also of σός.

σοῦ, σοῦ, *shoo! shoo!* a cry to scare away birds. Properly imperat. of σοῦμαι: see σοβέω.

σουδάριον, τό, the Lat. *sūdārium, a napkin* or *cloth to wipe off sweat with.*

σοῦμαι, contr. for σόομαι, = σεύω, σεύομαι.

σοὔνεκα, by crasis for σοῦ ἕνεκα, *on thy account.*

Σουνι-άρᾱτος, ον, (Σούνιον, ἀράομαι) *invoked* or *worshipped at Sunium.*

Σουνιάς, άδος, ἡ, *of Sunium,* epith. of Minerva, from her temple at Sunium.

Σουν-ιέρᾱκος, ὁ, (Σούνιον, ἱέραξ) *hawk of Sunium.*

Σούνιον, τό, *Sunium,* the southern promontory of Attica.

σοῦσθαι, inf. of σοῦμαι: **σοῦσθε, σούσθω**, imperat.

Σουσῑ-γενής, ές, (Σοῦσα, γενέσθαι) *born at Susa.*

σοῦσον, τό, *the lily,* Persian word:—hence **Σοῦσα**, τά, *Susa,* the royal city of the Persians, in the province of Susiana or Shushan: also **Σούσιος**, ὁ, *a man of Susa:* fem. **Σοῦσις**, ιδος (sub. γυνή) *a woman of Susa;* or (sub. χώρα), *the province of Susiana.*

σοὐστί, by crasis for σοι ἐστί.

σοφία Ion. -ίη, ἡ, (σοφός) *cleverness* or *skill* in art. 2. *cleverness, skill, wisdom in common things, prudence:* also *cunning, shrewdness, craft.* 3. *perfect scientific knowledge, wisdom, philosophy.*

σοφίζω, f. ίσω, (σοφός) *to make* σοφός, *to instruct, make wise* or *learned.* II. Pass. *to become* or *be wise: to be clever* or *skilled in* a thing. 2. *to play the sophist: to deal subtly* or *cunningly.* 3. aor. 1 inf. σοφισθῆναι in a strictly pass. sense, *to be cleverly devised* or *contrived.* II. σοφίζομαι, f. ίσομαι, pf. σεσόφισμαι, as Dep.: *to devise, contrive skilfully, shrewdly.* 2. *to deceive, beguile.* Hence

σόφισμα, ατος, τό, *any clever* or *cunning contrivance, a device, invention, trick: an artifice:* also *a stage-trick.* 2. *a captious argument, a quibble:* so a person is called σόφισμ' ὅλον, *a trick* all over.

σοφιστεύω, *to act as a sophist, give lectures.* From

σοφιστής, οῦ, ὁ, (σοφίζω) *a master of one's craft,* used of poets and musicians. 2. generally, *one who is clever* or *shrewd in matters of life, a prudent man;* so the seven Sages are called σοφισταί: hence *a wise man, philosopher.* II. at Athens, *one who professed to make men wise, a Professor of arts and sciences, a Sophist:* from their extravagant assumptions they fell into disrepute, esp. from being attacked by Socrates and Plato, as also by Aristophanes: hence, 2. *a sophist, quibbler, cheat.*

σοφιστικός, ή, όν, (σοφιστής) *of* or *for a sophist:* τὸ σοφιστικόν *the body of the sophists.*

Σοφοκλέης contr. -**κλῆς**; gen. -κλέους and -κλέος; acc. -κλέα: (σοφός, κλέος): *Sophocles,* the tragic Poet.

σοφό-νοος, ον, contr. -**νους**, ουν, (σοφός, νόος, νοῦς) *clever, wise of mind.*

ΣΟΦΟ'Σ, ή, όν, *clever* or *skilful in any art, cunning in* one's *craft:* esp. *one who has natural abilities for* anything: c. inf., σοφὸς λέγειν *clever* in speaking, etc. 2. *clever in common matters, prudent, shrewd, cunning.* 3. *skilled in the sciences, learned, wise:* hence ironically, *abstruse.* II. of things, *cleverly devised, prudent, wise.* Hence

σοφῶς, Adv. *cleverly, wisely:* Comp. -ώτερον Sup. -ώτατα. Hence

σοφ-ουργός, όν, (σοφός, *ἔργω) *working skilfully.*

σόω, Ep. for σώζω.

σπᾰδίζω, f. ίξω, (σπάω) *to draw off.*

σπάδιξ [ᾱ], ῖκος, ἡ, (σπάω) *a bough* or *branch torn off: a palm-branch, frond.* 2. as Adj. *of palm colour, bay,* Lat. *spādix.*

σπᾰδονίζω, f. σω, (σπάω) *to tear in pieces.* Hence

σπᾰδόνισμα, ατος, τό, *a tearing, rending.*

σπάδων [ᾰ], ωνος and οντος, ὁ, (σπάω) *an eunuch,* Lat. *spado.*

σπᾰθάω, f. ήσω, (σπάθη) *to strike down the woof with the σπάθη* (q. v); λίαν σπαθᾶν *to weave at a great rate, go fast,* a phrase for throwing away money. II. metaph. *to weave, contrive, devise,* Lat. *texere:* see ῥάπτω, ὑφαίνω.

ΣΠΑ'ΘΗ [ᾰ], ἡ, *any broad blade: a broad flat piece of wood used by weavers,* for striking the threads of the woof home, so as to make the web close. 2. *a spatula* for stirring or mixing anything. 3. *the stem of a palm-leaf.* 4. *a broadsword.*

σπάθιον, τό, Dim. of σπάθη, *a little spatula.* [ᾰ]

ΣΠΑΙ'ΡΩ, = ἀσπαίρω.

σπάκα, Persian for κύνα.

σπᾰλείς, Aeol. for σταλείς, aor. 2 pass. part. of στέλλω.

σπᾰνίζω, f. ίσω, (σπάνις) of things, *to be rare, scarce, few* or *scanty.* 2. of persons, *to lack* or *be in want of* a thing: so also pf. pass. ἐσπάνισμαι.

σπάνιος, α, ον, like σπανός, *rare, few, scarce, scanty:* —dat. fem. σπανίᾳ, as Adv. = σπανίως. II. of persons, *lacking, needy, in want.*—Comp. and Sup. σπανιώτερος, -ώτατος. Hence

σπᾰνιότης, ητος, ἡ, *want, lack, need.*

σπάνις, εως, ἡ, (σπᾰνός) of things, *scarceness, rareness;* οὐ σπάνις [ἐστί], c. inf., 'tis not *hard* to do a thing. II. of persons, *lack, want, need,* c. gen.

σπᾰνιστός, ή, όν, (σπανίζω) of things, *wanted, scarce, needed, lacking:* hence *poor, mean.*

σπανίως, Adv. of σπάνιος, *seldom:* Comp. -ώτερον, Sup. -ώτατα.

ΣΠΑ'ΝΟ'Σ, ή, όν, of things, *scarce, rare.* II. of persons, *in want of, lacking.* [ᾰ]

σπᾰνο-σῖτία, ἡ, (σπανός, σῖτος) *lack of corn* or *food.*

σπάραγμα, ατος, τό, (σπαράσσω) *a piece torn off, a torn body, a shred.* II. *a rending, tearing.*

σπᾰραγμός, ὁ, (σπαράσσω) *a rending, tearing, mangling.* II. *a convulsion, spasm.*

σπᾰράσσω Att. -ττω: f. ξω: aor. 1 ἐσπάραξα; (σπάω):—*to tear* or *rend in pieces, mangle,* Lat. *lacerare;* Med., σπαράσσεσθαι κόμας *to tear one's hair.* 2. generally, *to rend, cleave:* metaph. *to attack savagely.*

σπαργᾰνίζω, f. ίσω, (σπάργανον) *to swathe, wrap up.*

σπαργᾰνιώτης, ου, ὁ, *a child in swaddling-clothes.* From

σπάργᾰνον, τό, (σπάργω) *a swaddling* or *swathing band:* in pl. *swaddling-clothes;* and so, in Trag., *remembrances of one's childhood, tokens by which a person's extraction is discovered,* Lat. *monumenta, crepundia.* Hence

σπαργᾰνόω, f. ώσω, *to swathe in swaddling-clothes.*

ΣΠΑΡΓΑ'Ω, f. ήσω, *to be full to bursting, to teem, swell, be ripe,* Lat. *turgēre.*

ΣΠΑ'ΡΓΩ, f. ξω, *to swathe in swaddling-clothes.*

σπᾰρείς, σπᾰρῆναι, aor. 2 pass. part. and inf. of σπείρω.

σπαρνός, ή, όν, poët. for σπανός, σπανιος.

σπάρτη, ἡ, *a rope made from the shrub σπάρτος.*

Σπάρτη, ἡ, *Sparta* in Laconia:—Advs., **Σπάρτηθεν,** *from Sparta:* **Σπάρτηνδε** *to Sparta.* Hence

Σπαρτιάτης [ᾱ], ου, ὁ, *a Spartan:* fem. **Σπαρτιᾶτις,** ιδος, (sub. γυνή), *a Spartan woman;* or (sub. χώρα) *the Spartan land, Laconia.* Adj. **Σπαρτιατικός,** ή, όν, *Spartan.*

σπαρτίον, τό, Dim. of σπάρτον, *a small cord* or *rope.*

σπάρτον, τό, *a rope, cable;* properly *one made from the* shrub σπάρτος.

σπαρτός, ή, όν, (σπείρω) *sown, scattered:* metaph. *begotten.* II. at Thebes, **Σπαρτοί,** οἱ, *the Sown-men,* those who claimed descent from the dragon's teeth sown by Cadmus: hence Σπαρτοί generally = Θηβαῖοι.

ΣΠΑ'ΡΤΟΣ, ὁ and ἡ, *spartum, a kind of broom,* growing in Spain, used for making cords or ropes.

σπασθείς, εῖσα, έν, aor. 1 pass. part. of σπάω.

σπασσάμενος, Ep. for σπασ-, aor. 1 med. part. of σπάω.

σπασμός, ὁ, (σπάω) *a convulsion, spasm.* II. *tension.*

σπᾰτᾰλάω, f. ήσω, *to live riotously.* From

σπᾰτάλη, ἡ, (σπαθάω) *wantonness, riot.*

σπᾰτάλημα, ατος, τό, (σπαταλάω) = σπατάλη.

σπᾰτάλιον or **σπαθάλιον,** τό, a kind of *bracelet.*

σπᾰτᾰλός, όν, (σπατάλη) *wanton, riotous.*

σπᾰτίλη [ῑ], ἡ, *excrement, dung.* (From σκατός, gen. of σκώρ, and τιλάω.)

ΣΠΑ'Ω, f. σπάσω [ᾰ]: aor. 1 ἔσπᾰσα Ep. σπάσα: pf. ἔσπᾰκα: Med., aor. 1 ἐσπασάμην Ep. σπασάμην, Ep. part. σπασσάμενος: Pass., aor. 1 ἐσπάσθην: pf. ἔσπασμαι:—*to draw, draw out* or *forth,* of a sword, etc. II. *to pluck off* or *out.* 2. *to tear, rend.* 3. *to tear* or *drag away:* metaph. *to draw* or *drag aside, pervert.* III. *to draw in, suck in: to drain, quaff.* IV. *to draw tight, pull* the reins. 2. of angling, *to pull up, catch;* hence proverb., οὐκ ἔσπασε ταύτῃ γε '*he took* nothing by his motion.' V. in Pass. *to be wrenched, dislocated,* of a bone.

σπεῖν, aor. 2 inf. of ἕπω.

σπεῖο, Ep. for σπέο, aor. 2 imperat. of ἕπομαι.

σπεῖος, τό, Ep. for σπέος.

ΣΠΕΙ'ΡΑ, ἡ, Lat. *spira, anything wound* or *wrapped round* a thing. 2. in plur. *the twisted folds* or *coils* of a serpent (which Milton calls *spires*). 3. in pl. also, *the twists* or *coils of* a net. 4. σπεῖραι βόειαι *thongs* or *straps of ox-hide* to strengthen the blow of the fist, *the caestus.* II. *a body of soldiers,* the Roman *manipulus,* = two centuries: but also *a cohort.*

σπείρᾱμα, Dor. and Att. for *σπείρημα*.

σπείρεσκον, Ion. impf. of *σπείρω*.

σπειρηδόν, Adv. (*σπεῖρα*) *in coils* or *spires*.

σπείρημα, Dor. and Att. **-ᾱμα, ατος, τό**, (*σπεῖρα*) *a wreath folded round, a fold, coil, spire*.

σπειρίον, τό, *a light, thin garment:* Dim. of

σπεῖρον, τό, (*σπεῖρα*) *a cloth for wrapping about, a wrapper, cloth, garment.* 2. *sail-cloth, canvas.*

σπειρ-οῦχος, ὁ, (*σπεῖρα, ἔχω*) *containing a spiral figure* or *a circle, circular.*

ΣΠΕΙ´ΡΩ, f. *σπερῶ*: aor. 1 *ἔσπειρα*: Pass., aor. 2 *ἐσπάρην* [ᾰ]: pf. *ἔσπαρμαι*:—*to sow:* I. *to sow seed* or *grain.* 2. *to sow* or *plant a field; ἡ σπειρομένη* Αἴγυπτος *the arable part of* Egypt; *πόντον σπείρειν to sow* the sea, proverb. of lost labour, like Lat. *serere arenam.* II. metaph. *to engender* or *beget* children:—Pass. *to spring to light*, or *be born.* III. *to scatter like seed, fling, throw about: to spread* a report:—Pass. *to be scattered* or *dispersed.*

σπεῖσαι, σπείσας, aor. 1 inf. and part. of *σπένδω*.

σπείσασκε, Ion. 3 sing. aor. 1 of *σπένδω*.

σπείσω, fut. of *σπένδω*.

σπεκουλάτωρ, *opos*, ὁ, the Lat. *specŭlātor, a guard.*

ΣΠΕ´ΝΔΩ, f. *σπείσω*: aor. 1 *ἔσπεισα* Ep. *σπεῖσα*: Pass., aor. 1 *ἐσπείσθην*: pf. *ἔσπεισμαι*:—there are also Ion. forms of the impf. and aor. 1 *σπένδεσκε, σπείσασκε*, and an Ep. 2 sing. pres. subj. *σπένδῃσθα*:—*to pour out* or *offer a drink-offering* to a god before drinking wine, Lat. *libare*, mostly with dat. of the god to whom the libation was made, *σπένδειν θεοῖς, Διί*, etc.—The religious sense was not always retained, and sometimes it means simply *to pour: to sprinkle.* II. Med., f. *σπείσομαι*: pf. *ἔσπεισμαι* (which is also used in pass. sense):—*to pour libations one with another*, and since this was the custom in making treaties, *to make a treaty, make peace:* also absol. *to make a treaty:* c. acc., *σπείσασθαι εἰρήνην to conclude a formal* peace; *σπείσασθαι ἀναίρεσιν τῶν νεκρῶν to make* a truce so as to allow of taking up the dead.

ΣΠΕ´ΟΣ, τό; Ep. forms: nom. **σπεῖος**, gen. *σπείους*, dat. *σπῆϊ*, gen. pl. *σπείων*, dat. *σπέσσι* and *σπήεσσι*:—Lat. *SPECUS, a cave, cavern, grot.*

σπέρμα, ατος, τό, (*σπείρω*) *that which is sown, seed, the seed* or *germ* of anything; in plur. *seeds.* 2. also of animals, *seed*, Lat. *semen.* II. metaph. *seed, offspring, issue:* also *origin, descent, family.*

σπερμ-ᾰγοραιο-λεκῐθο-λᾰχᾰνο-πῶλις, *ιδος*, ἡ, (*σπέρμα, ἀγοραῖος, λέκιθος, λάχανον, πωλέομαι*) *a green-grocery market-woman.*

σπερμαίνω, (*σπέρμα*) *to sow:* metaph. *to beget.*

σπερμολογέω, f. *ήσω*, (*σπερμολόγος*) *to pick up seeds: to babble.* Hence

σπερμολογία, ἡ, *babbling, gossip.*

σπερμο-λόγος, ον, (*σπέρμα, λέγω*) *picking up seeds.* II. as Subst., *σπερμολόγος*, ὁ, *a crow that picks up seeds, rook.* 2. metaph. *one who picks up scraps of knowledge, an idle babbler.*

σπερμο-φόρος, *ον*, (*σπέρμα, φέρω*) *bearing seed.*

Σπερχεῖος, ὁ, *the Spercheios* or *Sperchēus*, a river of Thessaly, *the Rapid* (from *σπέρχω*).

σπερχνός, *ή, όν*, (*σπέρχω*) *hasty, rapid:* generally, *hasty, hot, violent.*

ΣΠΕ´ΡΧΩ, f. *ξω*: aor. 1 pass. *ἐσπέρχθην*:—*to drive, hasten, hurry on:*—Pass. *to move rapidly* or *hastily, to haste; σπέρχεσθαι ἐρετμοῖς to ply rapidly* with oars:—pres. pass. part. *σπερχόμενος* is used as Adj., *hasty, rapid;* of the mind, *eager, vehement:*—of temper, *to be hasty, hot; σπέρχεσθαί τινι to be angry with* one. II. intr. in Act. = Pass., *to rush* or *be driven rapidly.*

σπέσθαι, aor. 2 inf. of *ἕπομαι*, as *σχέσθαι* of *ἔχομαι*.

σπέσσι, Ep. dat. pl. of *σπέος*.

ΣΠΕΥ´ΔΩ, f. *σπεύσω*: aor. 1 *ἔσπευσα*, Ep. subj. 1 pl. *σπεύσομεν* (for *-ωμεν*): pf. pass. *ἔσπευσμαι*: I. trans. *to urge on, press on, hasten, quicken:* also *to seek eagerly, strive after: to promote* or *further zealously, to advance* or *forward* a thing. II. intr. *to press on, hasten: to exert oneself, strive eagerly: to be eager* or *anxious* to do a thing: also in Med. *to haste, hurry.*

σπεύδωμες, Dor. 1 plur. pres. subj. of *σπεύδω*.

σπευστέον, verb. Adj. of *σπεύδω*, *one must hasten.*

σπήεσσι, Ep. dat. pl. of *σπέος*.

σπῆι, Ep. dat. sing. of *σπέος*.

σπήλαιον, τό, (*σπέος*) *a grotto, cave, pit*, Lat. *spelaeum.*

σπῆλυγξ, *υγγος*, ἡ, (*σπέος*) = *σπήλαιον*, Lat. *spelunca.*

ΣΠΙ´ΔΗ´Σ, *ές* gen. *έος*, only in Il. 11. 754, *διὰ σπιδέος πεδίοιο* through the *far-stretched, broad* plain.

ΣΠΙ´ΖΩ, *to pipe, chirp*, of the shrill note of small *birds*, Lat. *pipio.*

ΣΠΙ˘ΘΑ˘ΜΗ´, ἡ, *the space one can span between the thumb and little finger, a span*, Lat. *dodrans:*—as a measure, *about* $7\frac{1}{2}$ *inches.*

ΣΠΙ˘ΛΑ´Σ, *άδος*, ἡ, *a rock* or *crag* against which the sea dashes:—generally, *a stone: a hollow rock, cave.*

ΣΠΙ˘ΛΟΣ, ὁ, *a stain, spot:* metaph. *a stain, blemish.* Hence

σπῖλόω, f. *ώσω*: pf. pass. *ἐσπίλωμαι*:—*to stain, spot, contaminate.*

σπινθάριγξ, *ιγγος*, ἡ, and **σπινθᾰρίς**, *ίδος*, ἡ, = *σπινθήρ, a spark.*

ΣΠΙΝΘΗ´Ρ, *ῆρος*, ὁ, *a spark*, Lat. *scintilla.*

σπίνος [ῐ], ὁ, (*σπίζω*) a small bird, *so called from its shrill piping note*, commonly eaten at Athens, a kind of *finch.*

σπλαγχνεύω, f. *σω*, (*σπλάγχνα*) *to eat the inwards* or *flesh of a victim* after a sacrifice.

σπλαγχνίζομαι, f. *-ισθήσομαι*: aor. 1 *ἐσπλαγχνίσθην*: Dep.: (*σπλάγχνον*):—*to feel bowels of pity, have pity, compassion* or *mercy.* Hence

σπλαγχνισμός, ὁ, *a feeding the inwards* of a victim, Dat. *visceratio.* II. *compassion.*

σπλάγχνον, τό:—mostly in plur. σπλάγχνα, τά, Lat. *viscera*, *the inward parts*, *inwards*, esp. the heart, lungs, and liver, and such inward parts as are fit for eating. 2. *a sacrificial feast*, Lat. *visceratio*. 3. *any of the inward parts*, *the bowels*, also *the womb*. 4. metaph. *the heart*, *the seat of the feelings*: as also in sing., ἀνδρὸς σπλάγχνον ἐκμαθεῖν to learn a man's *inward nature*.

ΣΠΛΗ'Ν, ὁ, gen. σπληνός, *the milt*, *spleen*.

σπογγιά, ἡ, = σπόγγος, *a sponge*, Lat. *spongia*.

σπογγίζω, f. ίσω, (σπόγγος) *to wipe with a sponge*.

σπογγίον, τό, Dim. of σπόγγος, *a small piece of sponge*.

ΣΠΟ'ΓΓΟΣ Att. σφόγγος, ὁ, *a sponge*.

σποδά, ἡ, Lacon. for σπουδή.

σποδ-ευνής, ές, (σποδός, εὐνή) *sleeping on ashes*.

σποδέω, f. ήσω, (σποδός) *to beat off a* or *dust*, *to dust*: hence *to knock*, *smite*, *beat*: Pass., ποδούμενος νιφάδι *pelted* by the storm; σποδούμενος πρὸς πέτρας *dashed* against the rocks; absol., στρατὸς κακῶς σποδούμενος an army *handled roughly*. II. *to eat greedily*, *devour*, *gulp down*.

σποδιά Ion. -ιή, ἡ, (σποδός) *a heap of ashes*: *ashes*.

σποδίζω, f. ίσω Att. ιῶ, (σποδός) *to roast* or *bake in the ashes*. II. *to burn to ashes*.

ΣΠΟ'ΔΟΣ, ἡ, *ashes*: *wood-ashes*, *embers*; *the ashes of the dead*. II. *dust*. III. metaph., σποδὸς κυλίκων *a soaker* of cups, i. e. a drunkard. Hence

σποδόω, f. ώσω, *to burn to ashes*:—Med. *to strew with ashes*.

σπολάς, άδος, ἡ, *a leathern garment*, *buff jerkin*. (For στολάς, from στέλλω.)

σπόμενος, aor. 2 part. med. of ἕπομαι

σπονδ-αρχία, ἡ, = σπονδῆς ἀρχή, *the beginning of the drink-offering* or *libation*, *the right of beginning it*.

σπονδεῖος, α, ον, (σπονδή) *of*, *belonging to a drink-offering* or *libation*. II. σπονδεῖος (sub. πούς), ὁ, in metre, *a spondee*, a foot consisting of two long syllables, as τῑμή, so called because at σπονδαί slow solemn melodies were used.

σπονδή, ἡ, (σπένδω) *a drink-offering*, *libation*, the wine which was poured out to the gods before drinking, Lat. *libatio*: *the libation made in concluding treaties* of peace, *covenants*, etc. 2. in plur. σπονδαί, αἱ, *a solemn treaty* or *truce*, because such treaties were made with libations; σπονδαὶ ἄκρητοι *a truce made by pouring* unmixed wine; σπονδὰς τέμνειν (like ὅρκια τέμνειν) to conclude *a treaty*.

σπονδο-φόρος, ον, (σπονδή, φέρω) *bringing drink-offerings*: as Subst., σπονδοφόρος, ὁ, *one who brings proposals for a truce* or *treaty of peace*. II. *a herald* or *officer who published the sacred truce* of the Olympic and other games.

σπονδύλη, ἡ, Att. σφονδύλη, q. v. [ῠ]

σπορά, ἡ, (σπείρω) *a sowing*: *a begetting of children*: *generation*, *birth*. 2. *seedtime*. II. *the seed sown*. 2. *that which is born*, *seed*, *offspring*, *issue*: in plur. *young ones*; θῆλυς σπορά the female *race*.

σποράδην, Adv. (σποράς, σπείρω) *spread* or *scattered about*, Lat. *passim*. [ᾰ]

σποράς, άδος, ἡ, (σπείρω) *scattered*, *spread about*: αἱ Σποράδες (sub. νῆσοι) the group of islands off the west coast of Asia Minor.

σπορεύς, έως, ὁ, (σπορά) *a sower*.

σπορητός, ὁ, (σπορά) *a sown field*, *corn-field*: *a crop*. 2. *a sowing*.—See ἀμητός.

σπόριμος, ον, (σπείρω) *sown*, *fit for sowing*: τὰ σπόριμα *the corn-fields*: μέτρον σπόριμον a measure of *seed-corn*.

σπόρος, ὁ, (σπείρω) *a sowing*. 2. *seed-time*. II. *seed*, *produce*, *a crop*.

σποῦ, in Scythian, *an eye*.

σπουδάζω, f. -άσομαι: aor. 1 ἐσπούδασα: pf. ἐσπούδακα: Pass., aor. 1 ἐσπουδάσθην: pf. ἐσπούδασμαι: (σπουδή): I. intr. *to make haste*, *to be busy*, *zealous* or *earnest*: absol. *to speak seriously*, *to be serious* or *earnest*. II. trans. *to do hastily* or *earnestly*: *to pursue* or *follow up zealously*:—Pass. *to be earnestly* or *zealously pursued*.

σπουδαιολογέω, f. ήσω, *to speak seriously*, *talk on serious subjects*:—Pass. *to be treated* or *discussed seriously*. From

σπουδαιο-λόγος, ον, (σπουδαῖος λέγω) *speaking seriously*.

σπουδαῖος, α, ον, (σπουδή): I. of persons, *busy*, *zealous*, *in earnest*, *serious*. 2. *good*, *excellent*. II. of things, *serious*, *grave*, *earnest*, *weighty*: generally, *excellent*; σπουδαῖος εἰς ὄψιν *goodly*, *comely* to look on.—Comp. and Sup. σπουδαιότερος, -ότατος:—also irreg. Comp. and Sup. σπουδαιέστερος, -έστατος. Hence

σπουδαίως, Adv. *seriously*, *earnestly*, *carefully*:—Comp. σπουδαιότερον, Sup. σπουδαιότατα.

σπουδ-άρχης, ου, ὁ, (σπουδή, ἀρχή) *one who canvasses eagerly for offices of state*, *a placeman*. Hence

σπουδ-αρχίδης, ου, ὁ, a comic Patronymic of σπουδάρχης, *Son of a Placeman*, a mock prop. n.

σπούδασμα, ατος, τό, (σπουδάζω) *a thing eagerly pursued*, *a study*.

σπουδαστέος, α, ον, verb. Adj. of σπουδάζω, *to be sought for zealously*. II. σπουδαστέον, *one must be anxious*, *be in earnest*.

σπουδαστής, οῦ, ὁ, (σπουδάζω) *a zealous supporter*.

σπουδή, ἡ, (σπεύδω) *haste*, *speed*, *eagerness*; σπουδῇ *in haste*, *hastily*; so also, διὰ σπουδῆς, κατὰ σπουδήν. II. *zeal*, *pains*, *earnestness*; σπουδῆς ἄξιος worth *pains*: dat. σπουδῇ as Adv. *with great trouble*, i. e. *scarcely*, *hardly*. 2. σπουδαί in plur. *heart-burnings*, *rivalries*. III. *earnestness*, *seriousness*; ἀπὸ σπουδῆς, μετὰ σπουδῆς, or σπουδῇ, *in earnest*, *seriously*. IV. *zeal*, *regard for* a person; κατὰ σπουδάς through *regard of persons*, through *party influence*.

σπυρίδιον, τό, Dim. of σπυρίς, *a hand-basket*. [ῐ]

σπυρίς, ίδος, ἡ, (σπεῖρα) *a round plaited basket: a fish-basket.*

στἄγῆναι, aor. 2 inf. pass. of στάζω.

στάγμα, ατος, τό, (στάζω) *a drop, a liquid; στάγμα τῆς ἀνθεμουργοῦ*, periphr. for honey.

στἄγών, όνος, ἡ, (στάζω) *a drop.*

στἄδαῖος, α, ον, (στάδην) *standing erect* or *upright; ἔγχη σταδαῖα* spears *for close fight.*

στάδην, Adv. (ἵστημι) *in a standing posture, upright.* [ᾰ]

στἄδιοδραμοῦμαι, irreg. fut. of

στἄδιοδρομέω, *to run in the stadium, run a race.* From

στἄδιο-δρόμος, ον, (στάδιον, δραμεῖν) *running in the stadium, running for a prize.*

στάδιον [ᾰ], τό: in plur. στάδιοι, οἱ, or στάδια, τά;—*a fixed standard of length, a stade*, = 100 ὀργυιαί, i.e. 600 Greek or 606¾ English feet, about ⅛ of a *Roman mile; ἑκατὸν σταδίοισιν ἄριστος*, 'a hundred miles best;' so, πλεῖν ἢ σταδίῳ λαλίστερος more talkative *by a mile* and more. II. *a race-course*, because that of Olympia was exactly a stade long: hence, ἀγωνίζεσθαι στάδιον to run *a race; στάδιον νικᾶν* to win *a race: ξύλινον στάδιον*, a kind of *chess-board.*

στάδιος [ᾰ], α, ον, (ἵστημι) *standing firm, standing fast: steady; σταδίη ὑσμίνη* a close fight, a battle fought *hand to hand*, Lat. *pugna stataria.*

ΣΤΑ'ΖΩ, fut. στάξω: aor. 1 ἔσταξα Ep. στάξα: I. trans. *to let drop, to fall drop by drop, distil.* II. intrans. *to drop, fall in drops, drip; στάζειν χεῖρας αἵματι to have* one's hands *dripping* or *reeking* with blood; *στάζειν κάρα ἱδρῶτι to have* one's head *dripping* with sweat. 2. *to fall off*, e.g. of ripe fruit.

στάθεν, Aeol. for ἐστάθησαν, 3 pl. aor. 1 pass. of ἵστημι:—but **σταθέν**, aor. 1 pass. part. neut. [ᾰ]

στᾰθερός, ά Ion. ή, όν, (ἵστημι) *standing fast, fixed, steady:* of liquids, *congealed:* also *calm, still*, of the sea; σταθερὰ μεσημβρία *high* noon, when the sun seems to *stand still* in the meridian:—ἡ σταθερά (sub. γῆ), *the solid earth.*

στᾰθευτός, ή, όν, *scorched, burnt, fried.* From

στᾰθεύω, f. σω, (σταθερός) *to scorch, burn, roast, fry.*

στᾰθήσομαι, fut. pass. of ἵστημι.

στᾶθι, Dor. for στῆθι, aor. 2 imperat. of ἵστημι.

σταθμάω, f. ήσω, (στάθμη):—*to measure by rule:* Pass., with fut. med. in pass. sense σταθμήσομαι, *to be measured.* II. σταθμάομαι, f. -ήσομαι: aor. 1 ἐσταθμησάμην: Dep.:—*to measure, prove by rule:* hence *to calculate, estimate.* 2. metaph. *to measure, estimate, judge of* a thing.

στάθμη, ἡ, (ἵστημι) *a carpenter's line* or *rule:*—proverb., παρὰ στάθμην *along the rule, by rule, straight*, Lat. *ad amussim;* also in bad sense, *beside the rule, wrongly:*—κατὰ στάθμην νοεῖν to guess *aright.* II. like γραμμή, *the line which bounds the race-course, the goal.* III. metaph. *order, law*, Lat. *norma.*

σταθμόνδε, Adv. *to the standing-place, to the stall: homewards.* From

σταθμός, ὁ, with irreg. pl. σταθμά, τά, but also σταθμοί, οἱ: (ἵσταμαι):—*a standing-place*, of farm-yard buildings, *a stable, stall, fold*, like Lat. *stabulum* from *stare:* generally, *a dwelling, abode.* 2. *quarters, lodgings* for travellers or soldiers, Lat. *statio:*—in Persia, σταθμοί were *stations* or *stages* on the royal road, where the king rested in travelling. 3. generally, *a day's journey, day's march*, mostly about 5 parasangs or 15 miles. II. *an upright standing-post, the bearing pillar* of the roof, *the roof-tree;* also *the door-posts.* III. *a balance, pair of scales:* also, *weight* by the balance; σταθμὸν ἔχειν τάλαντον to be a talent *in weight;* absol. σταθμὸν διτάλαντα two talents *in* or *by weight.*

σταθμόω, f. ώσω, (σταθμός) *to bring to the scale.* II. Med., esp. in aor. 1 ἐσταθμωσάμην, *to conjecture, conclude* or *infer by* or *from* a thing.

σταίην, ης, η, aor. 2 opt. of ἵστημι.

σταῖμεν, σταῖτε, σταῖεν, Att. for σταίημεν, σταίητε, σταίησαν, aor. 2 opt. plur. of ἵστημι.

ΣΤΑΙ'Σ or **σταίς**, τό, gen. σταιτός, *wheaten flour mixed and made into dough.* Hence

σταίτῐνος, η, ον, *of wheaten flour* or *dough.*

στακτός, ή, όν, (στάζω) oozing *out in drops, trickling, dropping.*

στάλα, ἡ, Dor. for στήλη.

στάλαγμα, ατος, τό, (σταλάζω) *that which drops, a drop.* [στᾰ]

στᾰλαγμός, ὁ, (σταλάζω) *a dropping, dripping:* also = στάλαγμα, *a drop.*

στᾰλάσσω, f. ξω, and **στᾰλάω**, *to fall in drops, drop, drip.* II. trans. *to let fall in drops, let drop, let fall.*

στᾰλῆναι, aor. 2 pass. inf. of στέλλω.

στᾰλίς, ίδος, ἡ, Dor. **στάλιξ**, (ἵστημι) *anything set up; a pole* or *stake to which nets were fastened.*

σταλ-ουργός, όν, Dor. for **στηλ-**, (στήλη, ἔργον) *marked, furnished with a gravestone.*

***στᾰμίν** or **στᾰμίς**, ῖνος, ἡ, only found in Ep. dat. pl. σταμίνεσσι: (ἵστημι): *anything set upright:* in plur. *the ribs of a ship standing up* from the keel, Lat. *statumina; ἴκρια ἀραρὼν θαμέσι σταμίνεσσι* having fitted planks to the close-set *ribs.*

σταμνίον, τό, Dim. of στάμνος, *a wine-stoup.*

στάμνος, ὁ, also ἡ, (ἵστημι) *an earthen jar* or *bottle for racking off wine, a jar, vase.*

στάν, Aeol. for ἔσταν, ἔστησαν, 3 pl. aor. 2 of ἵστημι. 2. aor. 2 part. neut. of ἵστημι.

σταξεῦμες, Dor. for στάξομεν, fut. of στάζω.

στάξις, εως, ἡ, (στάζω) *a dropping.*

στάς, στᾶσα, στάν, aor. 2 part. of ἵστημι.

στᾰσιάζω, f. άσω, (στάσις) intr. *to rebel, revolt, rise in rebellion, τινί against* one: generally, *to quarrel, dispute; στασιάζειν μετά τινος to side* with one *against* another: of states, *to be divided into factions, be distracted by party strife.*

στᾰσί-αρχος, ὁ, (στάσις, ἄρχω) *the chief of a band* or *company: the head of a faction, leader of a seditious party.*

στᾰσιασμός, ὁ, (στασιάζω) *a raising of sedition.*

στᾰσιασ.ικός, ή, όν, (στασιάζω) *seditious.*

στάσιμος, ον, (στάσις) *standing, stationary, stable, steady, fixed.* 2. στάσιμον, τό, in Tragedy, *a continuous song of the Chorus.*

στάσις [ᾰ], εως, ἡ, (ἵσταμαι) *a standing, the posture of standing.* 2. *a position, post, station: a point of the compass,* as, στάσις τοῦ νότου, τῆς μεσημβρίης. 3. *the state* or *condition in which a person is,* Lat. *status.* II. *a party, company:* esp. *a party formed for political purposes, a faction, party.* 2. *sedition, faction.*

στᾰσι-ώδης, ες, (στάσις, εἶδος) *seditious.*

στᾰσί-ωρον, τό, = στάσις ἐν ὄρει, *a mountain-fold;* but better **στασί-ωρος**, ὁ, (στάσις, ὤρα) *watcher of the station* or *fold.*

στᾰσιώτης, ου, ὁ, (στάσις II) *one of a party* or *faction, a partisan:* in plur. *the members of a party* or *faction in a state, partisans, conspirators.* Hence

στᾰσιωτικός, ή, όν, *inclined to faction, seditious.*

στάσκε, Ion. for ἔστη, 3 sing. aor. 2 of ἵστημι.

στασῶ, Dor. for στήσω, fut. of ἵστημι.

στᾰτήρ, ῆρος, ὁ, (ἵστημι) *any weight.* II. *a coin of a certain weight, a stater,* at Athens *of silver,* called also τετράδραχμος, worth about 3s. 3*d.* 2. later, *a gold stater* was current at Athens, worth 20 Att. drachmae, = 16s. 3*d.*: the oldest were struck by Croesus in Lydia: Darius Hystaspis struck them of very pure gold, called from him *Darics,* στατῆρες Δαρεικοί, worth about 1*l.* 1s. 10*d.*

στᾰτίζω, poët. for ἵστημι, *to place:* Pass. ἵσταμαι, *to stand.* II. intr. also in Act., *to stand.*

στᾰτικός, ή, όν, (ἵστημι) *causing to stand.* II. *skilled in weighing:* ἡ στατική (sub. τέχνη), *Statics,* the science which treats of the properties of bodies at rest, opp. to Dynamics.

στᾰτός, ή, όν, verb. Adj. of ἵστημι, *placed, standing;* στατὸς ἵππος *a stalled* or *stall-fed* horse; στατὸν ὕδωρ *standing* water.

σταῦ, see Σ, σ.

σταυρός, ὁ, (ἵστημι) *an upright pale, stake* or *pole;* in plur. *a palisade.* II. *the Cross.*

σταυρο-φᾰνής, ές, (σταυρός, φανῆναι) *appearing like a cross.* Adv. -νῶς.

σταυρο-φόρος, ον, (σταυρός, φέρω) *bearing the cross.*

σταυρόω, f. ώσω, (σταυρός) *to fence by driving in pales, to make a palisade round a place.* II. *to crucify.* Hence

σταύρωμα, ατος, τό, *a place fenced with a palisade: a palisade, stockade,* Lat. *vallum.*

σταύρωσις, ἡ (σταυρόω) *a palisading.* II. *crucifixion.*

στᾰφίς, ίδος, ἡ, *a dried grape, raisin,* also **ἀσταφίς.** (Akin to σταφυλή.)

ΣΤΑ'ΦΥ'ΛΗ', ἡ, *a bunch of grapes.* II. parox., σταφύλη, *the plummet of a carpenter's level, the level* itself; ἵπποι σταφύλῃ ἐπὶ νῶτον ἐΐσαι horses matched in height by *the level.*

στᾰφῠλίς, ίδος, ἡ, = σταφυλή, *a bunch of grapes.*

στᾰφῠλο-κλοπίδης, ου, ὁ, (σταφυλή, κλοπή) *a grape-stealer.*

στᾰχυη-τόμος, ον, (στάχυς, τεμεῖν) *cutting ears of corn, reaping.*

στᾰχυη-τρόφος ον, (στάχυς, τρέφω) *nourishing ears of corn.*

στᾰχυη-φόρος, ον, (στάχυς, φέρω) *bearing ears of corn.*

στᾰχῠ-μήτωρ, ορος, ἡ, (στάχυς, μήτηρ) *mother of ears of corn.*

στᾰχυό-θριξ, -τρῐχος, ὁ, ἡ, (στάχυς, θρίξ) *with leaves like ears of corn.*

στᾰχυο-στέφᾰνος, ον, (στάχυς, στέφανος) *crowned with ears of corn.*

ΣΤΑ'ΧΥ'Σ, υος, ὁ: pl. nom. and acc. **στάχυες**, -ας, contr. στάχῡς:—*an ear of corn,* Lat. *spica.* II. generally, *a plant:* metaph. *a scion, child.* [⏑–]

στέᾰρ, τό, gen. στέᾱτος [as trochee], contr. **στῆρ**, στητός: (ἵστημι):—*hard fat, tallow, suet,* Lat. *sevum, sebum;* opp. to πιμελή soft fat, Lat. *adeps.*

στεγάζω, f. άσω, = στέγω, *to cover, protect:*—Pass. *to be covered;* of a ship, *to be decked.*

στεγάνη, ἡ, (στεγανός) *a covering.* [ᾰ]

στεγᾰνός, ή, όν, (στέγω) *covered, sheathed: roofed over.* 2. *close-covered* or *close-covering, water-proof.* II. *covering: confining, enclosing.* Hence

στεγανῶς, Adv. *closely, through a covered* or *confined passage:* Comp. στεγανώτερον, *more closely.*

στέγ-αρχος, ὁ, (στέγη, ἄρχω) *master of the house*

στέγασμα, ατος, τό, (στεγάζω) *anything which covers* or *shelters, a covering, roof,* Lat. *tectum.*

στεγαστέον, verb. Adj. of στεγάζω, *one must cover.*

στεγαστρίς, ίδος, ἡ, (στεγάζω) fem Adj. *that covers* or *serves for covering.*

στέγαστρον, τό, (στεγάζω) *a cover, wrapper.*

στέγη, ἡ, (στέγω) *a roof,* Lat. *tectum.* II. *a covered place, a chamber, room: a tent.* 2. in plur., like Lat. *tecta, a house, dwelling, abode;* κατὰ στέγας *at home.*

στεγνός, ή, όν contr. from στεγανος, *covered, close, water-tight.*

στεγνο-φυής, ές, (στεγνός, φυή) *of a thick nature.*

στέγος, εος, τό, = στέγη, *a roof: a house.* 2. *an urn* for the dead.

ΣΤΕ'ΓΩ, f. ξω, *to cover closely,* so as *to keep out wet:* absol., νῆες οὐδὲν στέγουσαι ships not *water-tight.* 2. generally, *to keep off, fend off:*—Med., στέγεσθαι ὄμβρους *to keep off* rain *from oneself* II. *to cover, shelter, protect: to contain, hold.* 2. *to hide, to keep secret:*—Pass. *to be kept secret.* III. *to hold water;* τὸ μὴ στέγον *a leaky vessel.* IV. metaph. *to sustain, bear, endure.*

ΣΤΕΙ'ΒΩ, fut. στείψω: aor. 2 ἔστῐβον:—*to tread, tread on, tread under foot;* στεῖβον ἐν βόθροισιν εἵματα they *trod on* the clothes in pits, to wash them. 2. c. acc. cognato, *to tread, walk*; χορὸν στείβειν *to tread* a measure, dance: *to tread, walk on* a road, etc.:—Med. *to go upon* any one's track, *to trace* or *hunt out*.

στεῖλα, Ep. for ἔστειλα, aor. 1 of στέλλω.

στειλειά Ion. -ειή, ἡ, (στέλλω) *the hole for the handle of an axe*. Hence

στειλειόν, τό, *the handle* or *helve of an axe fitted into the* στειλειά.

στειν-αύχην, ενος, ὁ, ἡ, (στεινός Ion. for στενός, αὐχήν) *narrow-necked*.

στεινό-πορος, ον, Ion. for στενό-πορος.

στεινός, ή, όν, Ion. for στενός, *narrow*.

στεῖνος, εος, τό, (στείνω) *a narrow, close* or *confined space, a strait*: στεῖνος ὁδοῦ *a narrow part* of the way, *a pass*. II. metaph. *press, straits, distress*, Lat. *angustiae*.

στεινόω, (στεινός) Ion. for στενόω, = στείνω.

στείνω, (στεινός) *to make strait, narrow* or *close; to straiten*:—Pass. *to become strait, to be narrowed*: *to be straitened for room*. 2. *to be full, be thronged*. 3. metaph. *to be straitened, hard pressed, distressed*.

στειν-ωπός, Ion. for στενωπός.

στείομεν, Ep. for στῶμεν, 1 pl. aor. 2 subj. of ἵστημι.

στεῖρα Ion. -ρη, ἡ, (στεῖρος) *the stout beam of a ship's keel, the cutwater*, Lat. *carina*.

στεῖρα, ἡ, pecul. fem. of στεῖρος, *barren*.

στεῖρος, α, ον, also ος, ον, (στερρός, στερεός) *barren*, Lat. *sterilis*.

ΣΤΕΙ'ΧΩ, f. στείξω: aor. 1 ἔστειξα: aor. 2 ἔστῐχον: —*to walk, go* or *come*: *to approach*: *to go in line* or *order, to march*. 2. sometimes c. acc. cognato, στείχειν ὁδόν *to go* a journey; also, ἀνὴρ ὁπλίτης κλίμακος προσαμβάσεις στείχει an armed man *advances* scaling-ladders.

στείω, Ep. for στῶ, aor. 2 subj. of ἵστημι.

στελεά Ion. εή, ἡ, = στειλειή.

στελεόν, τό, = στειλειόν, *a handle*. Hence

στελεόω, f. ώσω, *to fit with a handle* or *haft*.

στελεχη-τόμος, ον, (στέλεχος, τεμεῖν) *cutting stems* or *trunks*.

ΣΤΕ'ΛΕΧΟΣ, τό, *the crown of the root* whence the trunk springs, *the stump*, Lat. *codex*: generally, *a trunk, log*, Lat. *fustis*. Hence

στελεχόω, f. ώσω, *to form a stem, to shoot out with*.

στελίδιον, τό, Dim. of στελεόν.

στέλλω: fut. στελῶ Ep. στελέω: aor. 1 ἔστειλα: pf. ἔσταλκα: Pass., aor. 2 ἐστάλην [ᾰ]: pf. ἔσταλμαι: plqpf. ἐστάλμην:—*to set in order, arrange, array*: *to furnish, equip, get ready*: of a ship, *to rig* or *fit out*; στόλον στεῖλαι *to fit out* an armament:—Med., στείλασθαι *to equip oneself, to put on clothes*: —Pass. *to fit oneself out, get ready, prepare*: also *to be dressed, decked*. II. *to despatch on an expedition, to despatch, send*: Pass. *to get ready for an expedition, start, set off*: hence *to go, depart, travel*. 2. intr. in Act. *to start, set forth*. III. *to fetch, bring, conduct* a person to a place:—so in Med. sometimes, στέλλεσθαί τινα *to send for* one. IV. as a nautical term, ἱστία στέλλειν *to take in* sail, *shorten* sail: generally, *to contract, draw in, withhold*: Med. *to avoid*.

στελμωνίαι, αἱ, (τελαμών) *broad belts* or *girths*, put round dogs when used to hunt wild beasts.

στέμμα, ατος, τό, (στέφω) *anything to crown with, a wreath, garland, chaplet*, from wool being chiefly used, it came to mean *the wool* itself: in plur. στέμματα, τά, *a shrine decked with chaplets*.

στεμμᾰτόω, f. ώσω, (στέμμα) *to furnish, adorn with a wreath* or *chaplet*.

στέμφῠλον, τό, mostly used in plur. στέμφυλα, (στέμβω = στείβω) *olives already pressed, the mass of pressed olives, oil-cake*.

στέναγμα, ατος, τό, (στενάζω) *a groan, moaning*.

στεναγμός, ὁ, (στενάζω) *a groaning, moaning*.

στενάζω, f. άξω, Frequentat. of στένω, *to sigh much* or *deeply, to groan, moan*. II. trans. *to bemoan, bewail*. Hence

στενακτέον, verb. Adj. *one must groan*.

στενακτός, ή, όν, (στενάζω) *to be sighed for, to be mourned*: *mournful*.

στεν-αύχην, ενος, ὁ, ἡ, (στενός, αὐχήν) *narrow-necked*.

στενᾰχίζω, f. ίσω, = στενάχω, *to sigh, groan, moan*. II. trans. *to bemoan, bewail, lament*.

στενάχω [ᾰ], lengthd. form for στένω, *to sigh, groan, moan*: metaph. of a torrent, etc., *to roar*; of horses galloping, *to breathe loudly*; στοὰ στενάχουσα the magazine *groaning from fulness*. II. trans. *to bemoan, bewail, lament*.

στενολεσχέω, *to talk subtly, raise nice points*. From

στενο-λέσχης, ου, ὁ, (στενός, λέσχη) *a quibbler*.

στενό-πορθμος, ον, (στενός, πορθμός) *at* or *on a strait*.

στενό-πορος Ion. στειν-, ον, (στενός, πόρος) *with a narrow pass* or *outlet*:—τὰ στενόπορα *narrow passes, defiles*; or in the sea, *straits, narrows*.

ΣΤΕΝΟ'Σ Ion. στεινός, ή, όν, *narrow, strait*, Lat. *angustus*: ἐν στενῷ *in a narrow compass*: τὸ στενόν *the strait* (i. e. the Hellespont); τὰ στενά *the straits, narrows*: στενή, ἡ, *a narrow strip* of land. II. metaph. *close, cribbed, confined, scanty*.—Comp. and Sup. στενότερος, -ότατος, Ion. στεινότερος, -ότατος: but the regular forms στενώτερος, -ώτατος, also occur. Hence

στένος Ion. στεῖνος, εος, τό, *a strait, difficulty, trouble*.

στενότερος, Comp. of στενός, ή, όν.

στενότης Ion. στειν-, ητος, ἡ, (στενός) *narrowness, straitness*.

στενο-χωρέω, f. ήσω, (στενός, χωρέω) *to crowd, straiten for room*. II. intr. *to be straitened* or *pressed for room*. Hence

στενοχωρία, ἡ, *narrowness of space, a confined space, want of room*. II. metaph. *straits, difficulty, distress*.

στενόω, f. ώσω, (στενός) *to make narrow.*

Στέντωρ, ορος, ὁ, *Stentor*, a Greek at Troy, famous for his loud voice: hence proverbially, *a Stentor.*

στενυγρός, ή, όν, Ion. for στενός, *narrow.*

στένω, only used in pres. and impf., (στενός) *to sigh, groan, moan.* 2. transit. *to bemoan, bewail, lament, deplore.*

στεν-ωπός Ion. **στειν-ωπός**, όν, (στένος, ὤψ) *made narrow, straitened, strait, confined*, Lat. *arctus.* 2. as Subst., στενωπός, ἡ, *a narrow way, by-way*, Lat. *angiportus.*

στεπτός, ή, όν, (στέφω) *crowned.*

στέργηθρον, τό, (στέργω) *a love-charm.* II. *love, affection, regard.*

στέργημα, ατος, τό, (στεργω) *a love-charm.*

στέργοισα, Dor. for στέργουσα, part. fem. of

ΣΤΕ'ΡΓΩ, f. ξω: aor. 1 ἔστερξα: pf. 2 ἔστοργα: Pass., aor. 1 ἐστέρχθην: pf. ἔστεργμαι:—*to love*, of the mutual love of parents and children: of any natural affection, as, between king and people. II. *to be fond of, like, be pleased with.* III. *to be content* or *satisfied, acquiesce*; c. acc., στέργειν τὰ παρόντα *to be content with, acquiesce in* the present state of things; στέργειν τὴν τυραννίδα *to bear with* tyranny; also c. dat., στέργειν τοῖς παροῦσι, etc. IV. *to pray, beg, entreat that* . . , c. acc. et inf.

ΣΤΕΡΕΟ'Σ, ά, όν, *stiff, stark, firm, solid*, Lat. *rigidus.* 2. metaph. *stiff, stubborn, unrelenting, cruel.* II. of bodies and quantities, *solid, cubic*; στερέος ἀριθμός *a cubic* number. Hence

στερεότης, ητος, ἡ, *stiffness, firmness.*

στερεό-φρων, ονος, ὁ, ἡ, (στερεός, φρήν) *hard* or *firm of soul, stubborn-hearted.*

στερεόω, f. ώσω, (στερεός) *to make firm* or *strong: to confirm.*

στερέσαι, aor. 1 inf. of στερέω.

ΣΤΕΡΕ'Ω, fut. στερήσω Att. στερῶ: aor. 1 ἐστέρησα, Ep. inf. στερέσαι:—Pass. στερέομαι, στεροῦμαι, with collat. form στέρομαι: fut. med. στερήσομαι: aor. 1 and pf. pass. ἐστερήθην, ἐστέρημαι:—*to deprive, bereave*, or *rob* a person *of* anything:—Pass. *to be deprived, bereaved*, or *robbed of* anything. II. *to take away* a thing: Pass. *to have* a thing *taken away.*

στερέωμα, ατος, τό, (στερεόω) *a solid body.* 2. *a foundation, basis:* metaph. *steadfastness.* 3. *the firmament* of heaven.

στερεῶς, Adv. of στερεός, *firmly, strongly, fast.*

στέρημα, ατος, τό, (στερέω) *that which is taken away, plunder, booty.*

στέρησις, ἡ, (στερέω) *privation, loss.*

στερήσομαι, fut. med. (with pass. sense) of στερέω.

στερίσκω, Att. collat. form of στερέω.

στέριφος, η, ον, = στερεός, στερρός, *firm, hard, solid.* II. *unfruitful:* of women, *barren.*

στερκτός, ή, όν, verb. Adj. of στέργω, *to be loved, lovely.*

ΣΤΕ'ΡΝΟΝ, τό, *the breast, chest.* 2. *the breast* as the seat of the affections, *the heart.*

στερνο-τυπής, ές, (στέρνον, τυπῆναι) *of a beaten breast, caused by beating the breast.* Hence

στερνοτυπία, ἡ, *a beating of the breast* for grief, Lat. *planctus.*

στερν-οῦχος, ον, (στέρνον, ἔχω) *with broad bosom, broad-swelling*, of the plain at Athens.

ΣΤΕ'ΡΟΜΑΙ, Pass., aor. 2 ἐστέρην:—collat. form of στερέομαι, *to be deprived of, to be without, to be wanting in, to lack, want*, Lat. *carere.*

στεροπή, ἡ, = ἀστεροπή, ἀστραπή, *a flash of lightning:* generally, *any flashing, dazzling light, glare.*

στεροπ-ηγερέτα, ὁ, (στεροπή, ἀγείρω) Aeol. for στεροπηγερέτης, *collector of lightning.*

Στερόπης, ου, ὁ, (στεροπή) *Lightner*, name of one of the three Cyclopes.

στέροψ, οπος, ὁ, ἡ, (στεροπή) *lightning, flashing, dazzling.*

στερρό-γυιος, ον, (στερρός, γυῖον) *strong-limbed.*

στερρός, ά, όν, also ός, όν, = στερεός, *stiff, firm, solid:* also *strong, stout:* of water, *frozen.* II. of countries, *hard, stony, barren*, Lat. *sterilis.* III. *stiff with age.* IV. metaph. *stiff, stubborn, obstinate, cruel.* Hence

ΣΤΕ'ΡΦΟΣ, τό, *a hide, skin.*

ΣΤΕ'ΡΩ, see στέρομαι.

στερρῶς, Adv. *stiffly, obstinately.*

στεῦμαι, Epic Dep., used only in 3 sing. pres. and impf. στεῦται, στεῦτο, and in 3 pl. pres. στεῦνται: (ἵστημι):—*to stand on the spot*:—c. inf. *to make gestures* or *a show of doing* something, *to promise, engage* or *threaten* to do.

στεφανεῦνται, Ion. for στεφανοῦνται.

στεφάνη [ᾰ], ἡ, (στέφω) *anything that encircles*, the head: *the brim of the helmet, a helmet.* II. part of a woman's head-dress, *a diadem, coronal:* generally, *a head-dress.* III. *the brim* or *border* of anything, *brow of a hill, edge, verge:* also *the parapet* or *battlement of a wall.*

στεφᾰνηπλοκέω, f. ήσω, (στεφανηπλόκος) *to plait wreaths* or *chaplets.*

στεφανηπλόκιον, τό, *the wreath-market.* From

στεφᾰνη-πλόκος, ον, (στεφάνη, πλέκω) *plaiting wreaths* or *chaplets.*

στεφᾰνηφορέω, f. ήσω, (στεφανηφόρος) *to wear a wreath* or *chaplet.* Hence

στεφᾰνηφορία, ἡ, *the wearing a wreath* of victory. II. *the right of wearing a crown.*

στεφᾰνη-φόρος, ον, (στεφάνη, φέρω) *wearing a crown* or *wreath, crowned, wreathed*; ἀγὼν στεφανηφόρος a contest *in which the prize was a crown.* II. στεφανηφόροι, οἱ, *certain magistrates in the Greek states who had the right of wearing crowns* when in office, as the Archons at Athens.

στεφᾰνίζω, f. σω: Dor. aor. 1 ἐστεφάνιξα: (στέφανος):—*to crown.*

στεφάνιον, τό, Dim. of στέφανος.

στεφᾰνίσκος, ὁ, Dim. of στέφανος.

στεφᾰνίτης [ῑ], ου, ὁ, fem. -ῖτις, ιδος, (στέφανος) *of* or *consisting of a crown* or *wreath*; στεφανίτης ἀγὼν a contest *in which the prize was a crown* or *wreath*.

στέφᾰνος, ὁ, (στέφω) *that which encircles*: στέφανος πολέμοιο *the circling crowd* of war. II. *a crown, wreath*: *the conqueror's wreath* at the public games, *crown of victory*: hence *the prize*, Lat. *palma*. These crowns were of *leaves*, viz., of *wild thyme* (κότινος) at the Olympic games, *laurel* (δάφνη) at the Pythian, *parsley* (σέλινον) at the Nemean, *ivy* (κίσσος) at the Isthmian. III. *a crown as a badge of office, public honours*: hence *a crown conferred* on a citizen in token of public services.—Cf. στεφάνη.

στεφᾰνόω, f. ώσω: pf. act. ἐστεφάνωκα, pass. ἐστεφάνωμαι: (στέφανος):—*to put round as a crown*: Pass. *to be so put round*; περὶ νῆσον πόντος ἐστεφάνωται the sea *lies round about* the island. II. *to wreath with a crown, to crown*: c. acc., στεφανοῦν εὐαγγέλια *to crown* one *for* good tidings:—Pass. *to be crowned* or *rewarded with a crown*:—Med. *to crown oneself, win a crown*. 2. *to crown, honour*. III. in Pass. also *to wear a crown*, as persons sacrificing, or magistrates in office.

στεφᾰν-ώδης, ες, (στεφανος, εἶδος) *like a crown* or *wreath, wreathing, twisted*.

στεφάνωμα, ατος, τό, (στεφανόω) *that which surrounds* or *encompasses, a circlet*. II. *a crown* or *wreath, as the prize* of victory. 2. generally, *a reward, honour, glory*.

στεφάνως, Dor. acc. pl. of στέφανος.

στέφος, εος, τό, (στέφω) poët. for στέφανος, *a crown, wreath*.

ΣΤΕ'ΦΩ, ψω: aor. 1 ἔστεψα: Pass., aor. 1 ἐστέφθην: pf. ἔστεμμαι:—*to put round as a crown*. II. *to surround, encompass, encircle, to crown, wreath*:—Med. *to crown oneself*:—Pass. *to be crowned, wreathed, garlanded*. 2. generally, *to crown, to honour*.

στέωμεν, Ion. for στῶμεν, 1 plur. aor. 2 subj. of ἵστημι.

στῇ, Ion. for ἔστη, 3 sing. aor. 2 of ἵστημι.

στήῃς, στήῃ, Ep. for στῇς, στῇ, 2 and 3 sing. aor. 2 subj. of ἵστημι.

στήθεσφι, Ep. dat. pl. of στῆθος.

στῆθι, aor. 2 imperat. of ἵστημι.

στηθο-μελής, ές, (στῆθος, μέλος) *singing with* or *from the breast*.

ΣΤΗ͂ΘΟΣ, εος, τό, *the breast, chest*, Lat. *pectus*. II. metaph. *the breast, the heart*, i. e. *the feelings, affections*: cf. στέρνον.

στήκω, formed from ἕστηκα, pf. of ἵστημι, used only in pres., *to stand*.

ΣΤΗ'ΛΗ Dor. **στάλα**, ἡ, *an upright stone, a post*: *a block* or *post*, Lat. *cippus*. II. *a post* or *slab bearing an inscription, a monument, a grave-stone*. 2. *a post* or *slab set up in a public place*, inscribed with treaties, decrees, etc.: hence, κατὰ τὴν στήλην according to *treaty*. III. *a boundary-post*; *the turning-post* at the end of the race-course, Lat. *meta*:—Στῆλαι Ἡρακλῆιαι *the pillars* of Hercules.

στηλίδιον, τό, Dim. of στήλη, *a small monument*. [ῐ]

στηλῑτεύω, f. σω, *to inscribe on a* στήλη, *to post* or *placard publicly*. From

στηλίτης [ῑ], ου, ὁ, fem. **-ῖτις**, ιδος, (στήλη) *of* or *like a block* or *pillar*. II. *inscribed on a pillar, placarded as infamous*.

στήμεναι, στῆμεν, Ep. aor. 2 inf. of ἵστημι.

στημορ-ρᾰγέω, f. ήσω, (στήμων, ῥαγῆναι) *to tear* or *undo the threads of a warp*. II. intr. *to be torn to shreds*.

στήμων, ονος, ὁ, (ἵστημι) *the warp* in the upright loom: the woof was called κρόκη. 2. *a thread spun*.

στῆναι, aor. 2 inf. of ἵστημι.

στῆρ, τό, gen. στητός, contr. for στέαρ, στέατος, as κῆρ for κέαρ: see στέαρ.

στήριγμα, ατος, τό, (στηρίζω) *a support, prop, stay*. 2. = Lat. *furca*.

στηριγμός, ὁ, (στηρίζω) *a setting firmly, propping, supporting*. II. pass. *a standing still, fixedness*: *steadfastness*.

στήριγξ, ιγγος, ἡ, (στηρίζω) *a support, prop, stay*.

ΣΤΗΡΙ'ΖΩ, f. ίσω: aor. 1 ἐστήριξα Ep. στήριξα: Pass., aor. 1 ἐστηρίχθην: pf. ἐστήριγμαι: 3 sing. plqpf. ἐστήρικτο:—*to set fast, make fast, prop, fix*: metaph. *to confirm, establish*. II. Pass. *to be firmly set* or *fixed, to stand fast, have a footing, be rooted to* a spot, *tarry, linger*. III. the Act. also is intrans. *to stand fast* or *firm*: *to be joined* or *fastened to*.

στῆσα, Ep. for ἔστησα, aor. 1 of ἵστημι.

στήσομαι, fut. med. of ἵστημι.

στήτη or **στήτα**, ἡ, Dor. for γυνή.

στήωσι, Ep. for στῶσι, 3 pl. aor. 2 subj. of ἵστημι.

στῐβᾰρός, ά, όν, (στείβω) *close pressed, compact*: *thick, stout, sturdy*: Comp. στιβαρώτερος. Adv. -ρῶς, *closely*.

στῐβάς, αδος, ἡ, (στείβω) *a bed of straw, rushes* or *leaves, a litter*: also *a mattress, pallet*.

στῐβεῖν, aor. 2 inf. of στείβω.

στῐβέω, f. ήσω: pf. pass. ἐστίβημαι: (στείβω):—*to tread, walk upon*; πᾶν ἐστίβηται πέδον all the plain *has been traversed, searched*.

στίβη [ῑ], ἡ, (στείβω) *frozen dew, rime, boar-frost*.

στίβος [ῑ], ὁ, (στείβω) *a trodden* or *beaten way, a track, foot-path*. II. *a track, footstep*; κατὰ στίβον on *the track* or *trail*. III. *a going, gait*.

στῐγεύς, έως, ὁ, (στίζω) *a brander*.

στίγμα, ατος, τό, (στίζω) *a prick* or *puncture of a pointed instrument, a brand-mark, a brand*: generally, *a mark, spot*.

στιγμᾰτηφορέω, *to bear brand-marks*. From

στιγματη-φόρος, ον, (στίγμα, φέρω) *bearing brand-marks*.

στιγμᾰτίας, ου, ὁ, (στίγμα) *one who has been branded*: *a runaway slave*.

στιγμή, ἡ, (στίζω) *a prick, mark, puncture*: *a ma-*

thematical point, Lat. *punctum*. II. metaph. *a jot, tittle*: of time, *a moment*.

ΣΤΙ'ΖΩ, f. στίξω: aor. 1 ἔστιξα: pf. pass. ἔστιγμαι, inf. ἐστίχθαι:—*to prick, puncture*, Lat. *pungere*: hence *to tattoo*: *to burn a mark in, to brand*, of runaway slaves: also *to brand* cattle *with a distinctive mark*; στίγματα στίζειν τινά *to brand* one *with a* mark. 2. *to make spotted*; βακτηρίᾳ στίζειν to beat black and blue:—Pass. *to be spotted*. 3. *to mark with a full stop*, Lat. *interpungere*.

στικτός, ή, όν, verb. Adj. of στίζω, *pricked, branded*: hence *marked, spotted, dappled*.

στικτό-χροος, ον, contr. **-χρους**, ουν, (στικτός, χρόος) *with spotted skin*.

ΣΤΙ'ΛΒΩ, f. ψω, *to shine, glitter, glisten*; στίλβειν ἀστραπάς *to flash* lightning. 2. metaph. *to shine, to be bright* or *brilliant*.

ΣΤΙ'ΛΗ [ῐ], ἡ, *a drop*, Lat. *stilla*: metaph. *a moment*.

στιλπνός, ή, όν, (στίλβω) *glittering, glistening*.

***στίξ**, ἡ, only used in gen. sing. στιχός, and in nom. and acc. plur. στίχες, στίχας: see στίχος.

στιπτός or **στειπτός**, ή, όν, (στείβω) *trodden down*: *close-pressed, close, firm, solid*, Lat. *stipatus*: hence *sturdy, tough, stout*.

στῖφος, εος, τό, (στείβω) *a close, compact body*: *a body of men in close array*; νεῶν στῖφος *the close array* of the ships; στῖφος ποιήσασθαι to form *a close column*.

στιφρός, ά, όν, (στείβω) *close-pressed*: *close, compact, solid, tough, stout*.

στῐχ-αοιδός, ὁ, (στίχος, ἀείδω) *a verse-maker, poet*.

στίχας, acc. pl. of *στίξ.

στῐχάω, (στίχος) *to set, range, place in ranks*:—Med. στιχάομαι, Ep. 3 sing. impf. ἐστιχόωντο, *to march in rows* or *ranks*.

στίχες, αἱ, pl. nom. of *στίξ.

στῐχο-γράφος, ον, (στίχος, γράφω) *writing verses*.

στίχος [ῐ], ὁ, there is also a gen. sing. στιχός, and a nom. and acc. pl. στίχες, στίχας, as if from an old nom. στίξ: (στείχω):—*a row, line, rank*: *a line of soldiers, a row* of trees. II. *a line of writing, a verse*.

στῐχός, τῆς, gen. from *στίξ.

ΣΤΛΕΓΓΙ'Σ, ίδος, ἡ, a sort of *scraper*, Lat. *strigil*, to remove the oil and dirt from the skin in the bath.

στοά or **στοιά**, ᾶς, ἡ, (ἵστημι) *a place enclosed by pillars, a colonnade, piazza, cloister*, Lat. *porticus*. II. at Athens this name belonged to various public buildings, *a storehouse, magazine, warehouse*, for corn. 2. ἡ βασίλειος στοά the court where the ἄρχων βασιλεύς sat. 3. *the Poecilé*, or *painted Stoa*:—since Zeno of Citium and his successors taught in this piazza, this school of philosophers was called οἱ ἐκ τῆς στοᾶς or Στωικοί, *Stoics*.

στοιά, ἡ, see στοά.

στοιβάζω, f. άσω, (στοιβή) *to pile* or *heap up*.

στοιβάς, άδος, ἡ, (στείβω) *anything trodden* or *pressed down, a bed of leaves*, etc.: hence *boughs* or *branches strewed on the ground*.

στοιβή, ἡ, (στείβω) *a stuffing, filling up*. II. metaph. *anything stuffed in, an expletive*.

Στοϊκός, ή, όν, = Στωικός.

στοιχεῖον, τό, Dim. of στοῖχος, *a small upright post*: *the gnomon* of the sun-dial, or *the shadow* thrown by it. II. *a first beginning, first principle* or *element*:—*a simple sound* of the voice, as the first element of language. 2. τὰ στοιχεῖα *the simplest component parts*: in physics, *the primary matter, elements*. 2. *the elements of knowledge, rudiments*.

στοιχέω, f. ήσω, (στοῖχος) *to stand in a line* or *rank, to stand in battle-order*. II. *to walk straight*.

στοιχ-ηγορέω, f. ήσω, (στοῖχος, ἀγορεύω) *to tell in regular order*.

στοιχίζω, f. ίσω, (στοῖχος) *to set a row of poles with nets* to drive the game into: *to set in order*.

στοῖχος, ὁ, (στείχω) *a row, line, rank*; ἐπὶ στοίχου or κατὰ στοῖχον *all in a row*: of soldiers, *a file*. II. *a line of poles with hunting-nets* into which the game was driven.

στολ-άρχης, ου, ὁ, (στόλος, ἄρχω) *a commander of a fleet, admiral*.

στολάς, άδος, ἡ, (στέλλω) *going in a body*. II. as Subst., στολάς, ἡ, *a horseman's cloak*.

στολή, ἡ, (στέλλω) *a fitting out, equipping*. II. *clothing, dress, equipment*: *a garment, robe*, Lat. *stola*.

στολῐδόω, f. ώσω, (στολίς) *to draw on, put on*:—Med. *to put on oneself, dress oneself in*.

στολίδωμα, ατος, τό, (στολιδόω) *a fold* of a robe.

στολῐδωτός, ή, όν, verb. Adj. of στολιδόω, *folded, hanging in folds*.

στολίζω, f. ίσω, (στολίς) *to make ready, trim, equip, deck*:—Pass. *to be equipped, armed*.

στόλιον, τό, Dim. of στολή, *a small* or *scanty garment*.

στολίς, ίδος, ἡ, (στολή) *a garment, robe*; νεβρῶν στολίδες *garments* of fawn-skin.

στόλισμα, ατος, τό, (στολίζω) *an equipment, dress*: *garment, mantle*.

στολμός, ὁ, (στέλλω) *a clothing, dressing*: in plur. στολμοί, *folds*.

στόλος, ὁ, (στέλλω) *an equipment* for warlike purposes, *an expedition* by land or sea, *a journey, voyage*; ἰδίῳ στόλῳ in *a journey* privately undertaken; opp. to κοινῷ στόλῳ in *a journey* on behalf of the state. 2. *the purpose* or *cause of a journey*. 3. *that which is sent on an expedition, an army, a fleet, band, troop, company*; πρόπας στόλος all the *people*. II. *a ship's beak*.

στόμα Aeol. **στύμα**, ατος, τό, *the mouth*, Lat. *os, oris*; also *the whole face*; sometimes used in pl. στόματα, like Lat. *ora*, of one person: ἐπὶ στόμα on *one's face*; κατὰ στόμα *face to face*: metaph., στόμα πτολέμοιο *the very jaws* of battle. 2. *the mouth, tongue*: *speech, words, language*: ἀπὸ στόματος εἰπεῖν to speak *by word of mouth*, i. e. by memory:

ἀνὰ στόμα or ἐν στόματι ἔχειν to have always in one's mouth; διὰ στόμα εἶναι to be in people's mouths; ἐξ ἑνὸς στόματος, with one voice, all at once. II. the mouth of a river, bay or sea, Lat. ostia, fauces: also a chasm or cleft in the earth: any outlet or entrance. III. the foremost part, front; of weapons, the point: the edge, point of a sword, Lat. acies: also the front ranks of the battle, the front; οἱ ἀπὸ στόματος the front ranks; ἄκρον στόμα πύργων the utmost verge of the towers.

στόμ-αργος Att. **στόμαλγος**, ον, (στόμα, ἀλγέω) grievous with the tongue, long-tongued, noisy, babbling, wearisome.

στομᾰτ-ουργός, όν, (στόμα, *ἔργω) making with the mouth, word-coining.

στόμᾰχος, ὁ, (στόμα) the throat, gullet.

στόμιον, τό, Dim. of στόμα, a small mouth. II. the mouth of a vessel; mouth of a cave, a cave, vault: the socket of a bolt. III. a bridle-bit, bit.

στομόω, f. ώσω, (στόμα) to stop the mouth, to muzzle, gag. II. to furnish with a mouth or opening. III. to furnish with a point or edge, to make into steel: metaph. to steel, harden.

στομφάζω, f. άσω, (στόμφος) to rant, mouth: metaph. to talk big, vaunt.

στόμφαξ, ᾱκος, ὁ, ἡ, (στόμφος) one who uses bombastic turgid words.

στόμφος, ὁ, (στόμα) lofty phrases, bombast, rant.

στόμωμα, ατος, τό, (στομόω) a mouth, inlet.

στόμωσις, εως, ἡ, (στομόω) a giving an edge to a thing, a hardening of iron into steel; στόμα πολλὴν στόμωσιν ἔχον a mouth that has much mouthing or sharpness of tongue.

στονᾰχέω, f. ήσω, (στοναχή) to groan, sigh, moan. II. trans. to sigh, groan over or for, lament.

στονᾰχή, ἡ, (στενάχω) a groaning, sighing, wailing: in plur. groans, sighs.

στονόεις, εσσα, εν, (στόνος) causing groans or sighs: generally, mournful, sad, wretched.

στόνος, ὁ, (στένω) a groaning, sighing, wailing.

στόνυξ, ῠχος, ὁ, like ὄνυξ, a sharp point: a sharp instrument, knife, scissors.

στοργή, ἡ, (στέργω) love, affection, the natural affection of parents and children.

ΣΤΟΡΕ'ΝΝΥ'ΜΙ shortd. **στόρνῡμι**, by metath. **στρώννῡμι** and **στρωννύω**: fut. στορέσω Att. στορῶ, also στρώσω: aor. 1 ἐστόρεσα, also ἔστρωσα: pf. pass. ἔστρωμαι:—to spread, spread out, stretch out, strew; λέχος στορέσαι, Lat. lectum sternere, to spread or make up a bed; to strew with a thing, ὁδὸν μυρσίνῃσι στορέσαι to strew the road with myrtle-boughs. 2. to spread smooth, level; ὁδὸν στορέσαι to make a level road, Lat. viam sternere:—metaph. to level, lay low; also to level, calm, assuage.

στορέσαι, aor. 1 inf. of στορέννυμι.

στορεσεῦντι, Dor. for στορέσουσι, 3 pl. fut. of στορέννυμι.

στορεστής, οῦ, ὁ, (στορέννυμι) one who lays low, a calmer.

στόρνῡμι, a later form of στορέννυμι.

στοχάζομαι, f. -άσομαι: aor. 1 med. ἐστοχασάμην: pf. pass. ἐστόχασμαι: Dep.: (στόχος):—to aim or shoot at, c. gen.: metaph. to aim at, seek after. 2. to guess, c. acc.: to surmise, conjecture.

στόχασμα, ατος, τό, (στοχάζομαι) a missile aimed at a mark, an arrow, javelin.

στοχαστικός, ή, όν, (στοχάζομαι) able to hit: able to guess, shrewd, sagacious. Adj. -κῶς.

ΣΤΟ'ΧΟΣ, ὁ, an aim, shot. 2. a guess, conjecture.

στραγγεύω, f. σω, (στράγγω) to twist, wind:—Med. στραγγεύομαι, to turn oneself about, waver, loiter.

στραγγ-ουρία, ἡ, (στράγξ, οὐρέω) retention of the urine, strangury. Hence

στραγγουριάω, to suffer from strangury or retention of the urine.

ΣΤΡΑΤΓΩ, fut. στράγξω, Lat. stringo, to draw tight, bind tight, squeeze, compress.

στράγξ, ἡ, gen. στραγγός, (στράγγω) that which oozes or is squeezed out, a drop.

στράπτω, f. ψω, for ἀστράπτω, to lighten.

στρᾰτ-άρχης, ου, ὁ, (στρατός, ἄρχω) the general of an army, a commander.

στράτ-αρχος, ὁ, = στρατάρχης.

στρατάω, (στρατός) to encamp:—Pass. to lie encamped; Ep. 3 pl. ἐστρατόωντο.

στρᾰτεία Ion. -ηίη, ἡ, (στρατεύω) an expedition, campaign; ἐπὶ στρατείας εἶναι to be on foreign service; οἴκοι καὶ ἐπὶ στρατείας, Lat. domi et militiae, at home and abroad: in pl. campaigns, military service, warfare.

στρᾰτεία, ἡ, fem. Adj. the Warlike, epith. of Minerva.

στράτευμα, ατος, τό, (στρατεύω) an expedition. II. an armament, army: a company.

στρᾰτεύσιμος, ον, (στρατεύω) belonging to or fit for military service, serviceable.

στράτευσις, ἡ, (στρατεύω) an expedition.

στρατευτέον, verb. Adj. one must march. From

στρᾰτεύω, f. σω, (στρατός) to serve in war, serve as a soldier: to take the field, march. II. Dep. **στρατεύομαι**, f. med. στρατεύσομαι: aor. 1 and pf. pass. ἐστρατεύθην, ἐστράτευμαι: to take the field, serve as a soldier; pf. pass. part. ἐστρατευμένος, having been a soldier.

στρᾰτηγεῖον, τό, incorrect form of στρατήγιον.

στρᾰτηγέω, f. ήσω, (στρατηγός) to be a general: c. gen. to be general of an army, command. II. c. acc. rei, to do a thing as general. Hence

στρᾰτήγημα, ατος, τό, the act of a general, esp. a stratagem, piece of generalship.

στρᾰτηγία Ion. -ίη, ἡ, (στρατηγός) the office, dignity, post of a general, command. 2. the qualifications of a general, generalship. 3. the time of a general's command.

στρᾰτηγιάω, Desiderat. of στρατηγέω, to wish to be general.

στρᾰτηγικός, ή, όν, (στρατηγός) *of* or *fit for a general: ἡ στρατηγική* (sub. τέχνη), or τὰ στρατηγικά, *generalship*, Lat. *scientia rei militaris.* II. *fitted for command, versed in generalship, skilled in military matters.* Adv. -κῶς, *like a general.*

στρᾰτήγιον, τό, (στρατηγός) *the general's tent*, Lat. *praetorium:* at Athens, *the place where the ten generals held their sittings.* II. = στρατόπεδον, *a camp.*

στρᾰτηγίς, ίδος, fem. Adj. (στρατηγός) *of a general; πύλαι στρατηγίδες* the door *of the general's tent; ναῦς στρατηγίς the admiral's* ship, the *flag*-ship; and so, ἡ στρατηγίς alone. II. as Subst. *a female commander* or *general.*

στρᾰτ-ηγός, ὁ, (στρατός, ἄγω) *the leader* or *commander of an army, a general:* also *the commander of a fleet, an admiral.* II. at Athens, οἱ στρατηγοί *were ten general officers elected by yearly vote to command the army and navy, and conduct the war-department.* III. στρατηγὸς ὕπατος *the* Roman *Consul;* στρατηγός alone, *the Praetor.*

στρατηΐη, ἡ, Ion. for στρατεία.

στρᾰτηλᾰσία Ion. -ίη, ἡ, *an expedition, campaign.* II. *the army itself.* From

στρᾰτηλᾰτέω, f. ήσω, *to lead an army into the field: to take the field.* II. trans. *to lead, command*, c. gen.; also c. dat. From

στρᾰτ-ηλάτης [ᾰ], ου, ὁ, (στρατός, ἐλαύνω) *a leader of an army, a general, commander.*

στρᾰτιά Ion. -ιή, ἡ, (στρατός) *an army, armament:* generally, *a company, band.* II. στρατεία, *an expedition.* Hence

στρᾰτί-αρχος, ὁ, = στρατάρχης, *a general.*

στράτιος, ον, (στρατός) *of, belonging to an army* or *expedition, warlike:* στράτιον as Adv., *valiantly.*

στρᾰτιώτης, ου, ὁ, (στρατιά) *a citizen on military service: a soldier.* Hence

στρᾰτιωτικός, ή, όν, *of* or *for soldiers:* τὸ στρατιωτικόν (sub. ἀργύριον), *the pay of the forces;* τὸ στρατιωτικόν (sub. πλῆθος) *the soldiery;* τὰ στρατιωτικά (sub. πράγματα) *military affairs.* II. *fit, suited for a soldier* or *military service.* Hence

στρατιωτικῶς, Adv. *in military style, like soldiers;* Comp., στρατιωτικώτερον παρεσκευάσθαι to be fitted out *more like transport-ships.*

στρᾰτιωτίς, ίδος, fem. of στρατιώτης, *a female soldier:* as fem. Adj. *martial.* 2. στρατιωτίς (sub. ναῦς), ἡ, *a troop-ship, transport.*

στρᾰτο-λογέω, f. ήσω, (στρατός, λέγω) *to levy an army, enlist soldiers.*

στρᾰτό-μαντις, εως, ὁ, (στρατός, μάντις) *a prophet to the army.*

στρᾰτοπεδ-άρχης, ου, ὁ, (στρατόπεδον, ἄρχω) *the commander of the praetorian guards* at Rome.

στρᾰτο-πεδεία, ἡ, and

στρᾰτο-πέδευσις, ἡ, *an encamping: an encampment:* also *the station of a fleet.* From

στρᾰτοπεδεύω, also as Dep. **στρατοπεδεύομαι**, (στρατόπεδον) *to encamp, take up a position.*

στρᾰτό-πεδον, τό, (στρατός, πέδον) *the ground on which soldiers are encamped:* Στρατόπεδα, τά, as pr. n. a part of Egypt *held on a military tenure.* 2. generally, *a camp, encampment, army encamped: an army.* 3. *a squadron* of ships, *fleet.*

ΣΤΡΑΤΟ΄Σ, ὁ, *a camp, encamped army:* generally, *an army, host, armament.* II. *the soldiers* as opp. to the chiefs, hence *the commons, people.*

στρατόφι, Ep. gen. of στρατός.

Στρᾰτ-ωνίδης, ου, ὁ, Comic patronymic as if from Στρατ-ώνης (στρατός, ὠνέομαι) *a dealer in armies.*

στρᾰφείς, στρᾰφῆναι, aor. 2 pass. part. and inf. of στρέφω.

στραφθείς, aor. 1 pass. part. of στρέφω.

στρέβλη, ἡ, (στρεβλός) *an instrument for winding, a windlass: a screw, press.* II. *an instrument of torture, rack.*

στρεβλός, ή, όν, (στρέφω) *twisted, bowed, distorted*

στρεβλόω, f. ώσω, (στρεβλός) *to strain with a windlass, to screw up, tighten, make tat* I. *to wrench, dislocate:* hence *to stretch on the rack, wrench, rack, torture:*—Pass. *to be racked, wrenched, tortured.*

στρέμμα, ατος, τό, (στρέφω) *that which is twisted* or *dislocated: a sprain.*

στρέπτ-αιγλος, η, ον, (στρέφω, αἴγλη) *whirling, bright.*

στρεπτήρ, ῆρος, ὁ, (στρέφω) *anything which turns, one of the vertebrae of the neck:* also *a socket.*

στρεπτός, ή, όν, also ός, όν, verb. Adj. of στρέφω. *easily bent* or *twisted, pliant;* στρεπτὸς χιτών a *flexible* coat, i.e. a shirt *of chain-armour* or *mail: pliant, supple.* 2. as Subst., στρεπτός (sub. κύκλος), ὁ, *a collar of twisted* or *linked metal*, Lat. *torques:* στρεπτά, τά, *necklaces.* II. metaph. *to be bent* or *turned, to be wrought u..;* στρεπτὴ γλῶσσα *a glib, pliant* tongue. III. *bent, curved.*

στρεπτο-φόρος, ον, (στρεπτός, φέρω) *wearing a collar* or *necklace*, Lat. *torquatus.*

στρεύγομαι, Pass. (στράγγω) *to be squeezed* or *pressed out: to be drained of strength, exhausted, grow weary, to be worn out.*

στρεφε-δινέω, f. ήσω, (στρέφω, δινέω) *to spin* or *whirl* a thing *round:*—Pass. *to be whirled, to spin round and round.*

στρεφθείς, aor. 1 pass. part. of στρέφω.

ΣΤΡΕ΄ΦΩ, f. ψω: aor. 1 ἔστρεψα Ep. στρέψα: pf. ἔστροφα:—Pass., aor. 1 ἐστρέφθην Dor. ἐστράφθην: aor. 2 ἐστράφην [ᾰ]: pf. ἔστραμμαι.

A. Act. *to twist, turn, bend;* ἵππους στρέφειν *to turn* or *guide* horses: *to wheel* soldiers *round.* II. *to turn about: to change, alter:* also *to pervert.* III. *to twist* a rope: *to twist, torture, torment:*—also of wrestlers, *to twist* the adversary *back.* IV. metaph. *to turn over* in one's mind, *revolve.* V. *to divert from the right course, embezzle, intercept.* VI. intrans., in same sense as Pass., *to turn* or *wheel about.*

B. Pass. and Med. *to twist* or *turn oneself, to turn round about, toss to and fro:* absol. *to turn back; to turn and flee:* of the heavenly bodies, *to revolve, circle.* 2. metaph., *στροφὰς στρέφεσθαι to twist about,* like a wrestler trying to elude the grasp of an adversary, *to shuffle, evade; πάσας στροφὰς στρέφεσθαι to twist* every way, practise every kind of evasion. 3. c. gen., *στρέφεσθαί τινος to turn oneself to, attend to.* II. *to attach oneself, stick close, adhere* III. of limbs, *to be twisted, dislocated.* IV. *to roam about:* of things, *to be rife.*

στρέψασκον, 3 pl. Ion. aor. 1 of *στρέφω.*

στρέψις, εως, ἡ, (*στρέφω*) *a turning, twisting.*

στρεψο-δῐκέω, f. ήσω, (*στρέφω, δίκη*) *to twist* or *pervert justice.*

στρεψοδῐκο-πᾰνουργία, ἡ, (*στρεψοδικέω, πανουργία*) *cunning villany in the perversion of justice.*

ΣΤΡΗΝΗ'Σ, ές, *rough, harsh, grating.*

στρηνιάω, f. άσω [ᾱ], (*στρῆνος*) *to riot, to wax wanton.*

στρῆνος, εος, τό, (*στρηνής*) *excess of strength: insolence, wantonness.*

στριφνολικίγξ, Comic word, *the very least fraction* or *particle.*

ΣΤΡΙ'ΖΩ, collat. form of *τρίζω, to cry in a shrill tone, to scream.*

στροβέω, f. ήσω, (*στρόβος*):—*to spin* or *whirl about like a top: to make giddy, dizzy:*—Pass., with fut. med. *στροβήσομαι, to spin round and round.* Hence

στροβητός, ή, όν, *whirled round* or *about.*

στροβῑλίζω, f. ίσω, (*στρόβιλος*) *to twist about.*

στρόβῑλος, ὁ, (*στροβέω*) *anything which whirls round* or *spins: a top:* hence, from likeness of shape, *a fir-cone, pine-cone.* 2. *a whirlwind.* 3. *a whirling dance, pirouette*

στροβῑλός, ή, όν, (*στροβέω*) *spinning, whirling.*

στροβῑλώδης, ες, (*στρόβιλος, εἶδος*) *like a pine-cone.*

στρόβος, ὁ, (*στρέφω*) *a whirling round.*

στρογγύλλω, (*στρογγύλος*) *to round off: to twirl.*

στρογγύλος [ῠ], η, ον, (*στράγγω*) *round, rounded; στρογγύλη ναῦς a merchant* ship, *from its round shape,* opp. to the long ship of war (*μακρὰ ναῦς*), Lat. *navis longa.* II. metaph. *well-rounded, neat, terse.*

στρομβέω, f. ήσω, (*στρόμβος*) = *στροβέω, to whirl.*

στρομβηδόν, Adv. (*στρομβέω*) *spinning like a ball.*

στρόμβος, ὁ, (*στρέφω*) *anything whirled round, a top.* 2. *a spiral shell.*

στρούθειος, α, ον, (*στρουθός*) *of* or *for small birds: στρούθειον μῆλον a quince*

στρουθίον, τό, Dim. of *στρουθός, a young sparrow.*

ΣΤΡΟΥΘΟ'Σ, ὁ, also ἡ, *any small bird,* esp. *a sparrow.* II. *any bird,* as *an eagle:*—*ὁ μέγας στρουθὸς the large bird, the ostrich,* called *στρουθὸς κατάγαιος* from its running along the ground: also simply *στρουθός* (ἡ).

στροφαῖος, α, ον, (*στροφή*) *cunning, versatile;* also (from *στροφεύς*) *standing at the door-post:*—name of Mercury, in both senses.

στροφάλιγξ, ιγγος, ἡ, (*στροφᾰλίζω*) *a whirl, eddy.* [ᾰ]

στροφᾰλίζω, a lengthd. form of *στρέφω, to turn quickly; ἠλάκατα στροφαλίζειν to whirl* the spindle.

στροφάς, άδος, ὁ, ἡ, (*στρέφω*) *whirling, circling; ἄρκτου στροφάδες κέλευθοι* the Bear's *circling* paths.

στροφεῖον, τό, (*στρέφω*) *a twisted noose, cord.* 2. *a wooden windlass.*

στροφεύς, έως, ὁ, (*στρέφω*) *one of the vertebrae.* II. *the socket* in which the pivot of a door moves; cf. *στρόφιγξ.*

στροφέω, = *στρέφω:* esp. *to have the colic.*

στροφή, ἡ, (*στρέφω*) *a turning: a turning round, circling, rolling.* 2. *a twist, a slippery trick* 3. in Music, *a twist* or *turn.* II. *the dancing* of the Chorus *towards one side of the ὀρχήστρα:* hence also *the song sung during this evolution, the strophé,* to which the *ἀντιστροφή* answers.

στρόφιγξ, ιγγος, ὁ, (*στρέφω*) *the pivot* or *axle on which a body turns* 2. *στρόφιγγες* were *pivots sunk in sockets,* which served as hinges; cf. *στροφεύς.* 3. *στρόφιγξ γλώττης,* of a *well-hung* tongue.

στρόφιον, τό, Dim. of *στρόφος, a band* or *girdle worn by women* round the head or round the breast.

στρόφις, ιος, ἡ, (*στρέφω*) *a twisting, slippery fellow, a shuffler.*

στροφίς, ῖδος, ἡ, = *στρόφιον, a band, girdle.*

στροφο-δῑνέομαι, Pass. (*στρόφος, δινέομαι*) *to wheel eddying round,* of birds.

στρόφος, ὁ, (*στρέφω*) *a twisted band, a belt: a cord, rope.* 2. *a swaddling-band.* II. *a twisting of the bowels, colic,* Lat. *tormina.*

Στρῡμονίας Ion. -ίης, ὁ, *a wind blowing from the Thracian river Strymon,* i. e. *a NNE. wind.*

Στρῡμόνιος, α, ον, *of the Strymon.* From

Στρῡμών, όνος, ὁ, *the Strymon,* a river in Thrace.

στρυφνός, όν, (*στρύφω*) *sour, harsh, rough* to the taste. II. metaph. *sour, harsh, austere, morose.*

στρῶμα, ατος, τό, (*στρώννυμι*) *anything spread out for lying* or *sitting upon:* in pl. *the bed and bed-clothes, mattress, bedding,* Lat. *vestis stragula.*

στρωμᾰτό-δεσμον, τό, (*στρῶμα, δεσμός*) *a sack in which slaves tied up the bed-clothes*

στρωματο-φύλαξ, ακος, ὁ, (*στρῶμα, φύλαξ*) *one who has the care of the bedding.*

στρωμνή, ἡ, *a bed spread out: a bed, mattress, bedding.* From

στρώννῡμι and **στρωννύω,** f. *στρώσω,* formed by metath. from *στόρνυμι, στορέννυμι:* v. *στορέννυμι.*

στρῶσον, aor. 1 imperat. of *στρώννυμι.*

στρωτός, ή, όν, (*στρώννυμι*) *spread, laid, covered,* Lat. *stratus,* of bed-furniture.

στρωφάω, Ion. Frequent. of *στρέφω,* as *τρωπάω* for *τρέπω:*—*to turn constantly, keep whirling* or *winding:* —Pass. *to turn oneself about,* like Lat. *versari, to stay* or *dwell* in a place.

στῠγ-άνωρ [ᾱ], ορος, ὁ, ἡ, (*στυγέω, ἀνήρ*) *hating the man* or *men in general.*

στῠγερός, ά, όν, (στυγέω) *hated, abominated, hateful, loathsome:* c. dat. *bearing malice* or *hatred* towards a man.

στῠγερ-ώπης, ες, and **στῠγερ-ωπός**, όν, (στυγερός, ὤψ) *with hateful look: hateful.*

στυγερῶς, Adv. of στυγερός, *to one's sorrow, miserably.*

στῠγέω, f. ήσω: aor. I ἐστύγησα: also (as if from στύγω), aor. I ἔστυξα, opt. στύξαιμι: aor. 2 ἔστῠγον: fut. 2 pass. στῠγήσομαι: (στύγος):—*to hate, abominate, abhor, loathe:* stronger than μισέω, *to express abhorrence.* II. *to make hateful* or *horrid.* Hence

στύγημα, ατος, τό, *a hated object, abomination.* [ῠ]

στῠγητός, όν, (στυγέω) *hated, abominated, loathed: hateful.*

Στύγιος, α, ον, also ος, ον, (Στύξ) *of the Styx* or *the nether world, Stygian.* II. = στυγητός. [ῠ]

στυγνάζω, f. άσω, (στύγνος) *to be sad* or *gloomy, to be of sad countenance.*

στυγνός, ή, όν, (στυγέω) *hated, abhorred, hateful, hostile.* II. *sad, gloomy,* Lat. *tristis:*—neut., στυγνόν as Adv., *gloomily.*

στυγνόω, f. ώσω, (στυγνός) *to make sad* or *gloomy:* —Pass. *to be* or *become gloomy*

στῠγό-δεμνος, ον, (στυγέω, δέμνιον) *hating the marriage-bed.*

στύγος, εος, τό, (στυγέω) *hatred, abhorrence: gloom, horror.* II. *an object of hatred, an abomination.* [ῠ]

ΣΤΥ΄ΛΟΣ, ὁ, *a pillar:* also, 2. *a post, pale, a beam* or *mast of a ship.*

στῡλόω, f. ώσω, (στῦλος) *to support with pillars.*

στύμα [ῠ], ἄτος, τό, Aeol. for στόμα.

ΣΤΥ΄Ξ, ἡ, gen. Στῠγός, *the Styx,* i. e. *the Hateful, Horrible,* a river of the nether world, by which the gods in Homer swore their most sacred oaths. II. *that which is hated, an abomination.*

στύξαιμι, aor. I opt. of στυγέω.

στῠπεῖον or **στυππεῖον**, τό, like στύπη, *tow, coarse flax* or *hemp: a rope* or *halter made of it.*

στῠπειο-πώλης or **στυππ-**, ου, ὁ, (στυπεῖον, πωλέω) *a hemp* or *rope-seller.*

ΣΤΥ΄ΠΗ, ἡ, *tow, the coarse part of flax* or *hemp.* [ῡ]

στύπος, εος, τό, (στύφω) *a stem, stump,* Lat. *stipes:* also *a stick.* [ῠ]

στυπτηρία Ion. **-ίη** (sub. γῆ), ἡ, *an astringent salt, alum:* strictly fem. of

στυπτήριος, α, ον, (στύφω) *binding, astringent.*

στῠράκιον, τό, Dim. of στύραξ. [ᾰ]

ΣΤΥ΄ΡΑΞ, ἄκος, ὁ, *the spike at the butt end* or *a spear-shaft.* [ῡ]

ΣΤΥ΄ΡΑΞ, ἄκος, ἡ, *the shrub* or *tree which yields the gum* called *storax.* [ῠ]

στῠφελιγμός, ὁ, *a striking, beating, pushing about;* generally, *ill-usage.* From

στῠφελίζω, f. ξω, (στυφελός) *to thrust* or *push rudely, shake, smite:* of the wind, *to scatter the clouds:* generally, *to treat roughly, maltreat.*

στῠφελός, ή, όν, also ός, όν, (στύφω) *close, solid, tough:* of flavour, *sour, acid.* 2. metaph. *harsh, crabbed, cruel.*

στυφλός, όν, also η, ον, snortd. from στυφελός, *hard, rugged.* 2. *rough*

στῠφο-κόπος, ον, (στύπος, κόπτω) *striking with a stick.*

στύφω, f. ψω, *to contract, draw together:* of an astringent taste, in Pass., **χείλεα στυφθείς** *having one's lips drawn in.* [ῡ]

στωά, ἡ, Dor. for στοά.

στωικός, ή, όν, (στοά) *of* or *like a colonnade* or *portico.* II. *Stoic, of* or *belonging to the Stoics* or *their system:* Στωικός, ὁ, *a Stoic.*

στωμῠλέω, = στωμύλλω. Hence

στωμῠλία, ἡ, *wordiness, chattering, gossip.*

στωμῠλιο-συλλεκτάδης, ου, ὁ, (στωμυλία, συλλέγω) *a gossip-monger.*

στωμύλλω or as Dep. **στωμύλλομαι**, (στωμύλος) *to be talkative, to chatter, prate:* in good sense. *to talk, converse.*

στώμυλμα, ατος, τό, = στωμυλία, *chattering:* of persons, *a gossip, chatterer.*

στωμύλος, ον, (στόμα) *mouthy, wordy, talkative, gossiping:* also *fluent.* [ῡ]

ΣΥ΄ Dor. **ΤΥ΄**, Lat. *TU, THOU;* subst. Pron. of 2nd pers.: Ep. nom. **τύνη**:—gen. σοῦ, dat. σοί, acc. σέ, enclit. σου, σοι, σε. There are also Ep. forms of gen. σεῦ, σέο, σεῖο, σέθεν, enclit. σευ, σεο: Dor. τεῦ, rarely τέο, lengthd. τεοῦ and τεοῖο: Aeol. and Dor. τεῦς, τεοῦς.—Ion. and Ep. dat. τοί; Dor. τεΐν and τίν.—Dor. acc. τέ, enclit. τυ.—Dual **σφῶι**, σφώ: gen. and dat. σφῶιν, σφῷν: pl. **ὑμεῖς**, ὑμῶν, ὑμῖν or ὕμιν, ὑμᾶς, Ep. ὔμεας.

συ-αγρεσία, ἡ, (σῦς, ἄγρα) *a boar-hunt.*

σύ-αγρος, ὁ, (σῦς, ἄγρα) *one who hunts wild boars.*

Σῠβᾰρίζω, f. ίσω, *to live like a Sybarite,* i. e. *luxuriously, effeminately.* From

Σύβᾰρις [ῠ], gen. εως, Ion. ιος, ἡ, *Sybaris,* a city of Magna Graecia, on a river of the same name noted for luxury.

Σῠβᾰρίτης [ῑ], ου, ὁ, (Σύβαρις) *a Sybarite: a luxurious liver, voluptuary.*

Σῠβᾰρῑτικός, ή, όν, (Σύβαρις) *of* or *like to Sybaris.*

Σῠβᾰρῖτις, ιδος, fem. of Συβαρίτης, *a woman of Sybaris.*

σῠβήνη, ἡ, *a flute-case.* (Deriv. uncertain.)

σῠ-βόσιον, or rather **σῠ-βοσεῖον**, τό, (σῦς, βόσκω) *a herd of swine.* II. *a pigsty.*

Σύ-βοτα [ῠ], τά, (σῦς, βόσκω) the name of some islets near Corcyra, and spots on the mainland opposite; originally, *swine-pastures.*

σῠ-βότης and **σῠ-βώτης**, ου, ὁ, (σῦς, βόσκω) *a swineherd.*

σύγ-γᾰμος, ον, (σύν, γαμέω) *united in marriage, married, wedded:* as Subst., σύγγαμος, ὁ, ἡ, *a hus-*

band or wife. 2. sharing the marriage-bed; in plur. of rival wives.

συγ-γείτων, ονος, ὁ, ἡ, (σύν, γείτων) bordering on.

συγ-γελάω, f. -άσομαι, (σύν, γελάω) to laugh with or together.

συγγένεια, ἡ, (συγγενής) connexion by descent or family, relationship, kin. 2. kinsfolk, kin, family.

συγγενέσθαι, aor. 2 inf. of συγγίγνομαι.

συγγενέτειρα, ἡ, a common mother: fem. of

συγ-γενέτης, ου, ὁ, (σύν, γενέσθαι) a common father.

συγ-γενής, ές, (σύν, γενέσθαι) born with, congenital, natural, inborn. II. of the same stock, descent or family, akin: οἱ συγγενεῖς kinsfolk, kinsmen; τὸ συγγενές = συγγένεια, kin, relationship. 2. metaph. of the same sort or kind, resembling: fitting, proper, natural.

συγγενικός, ή, όν, (συγγενής) becoming or like kinsmen. Adv. -κῶς, like kinsfolk.

συγ-γέρων, οντος, ὁ, (σύν, γέρων) a fellow in old age.

συγγεωργέω, f. ήσω, to be a fellow-labourer. From

συγ-γεωργός, ὁ, (σύν γεωργός) a fellow-labourer in the fields.

συγ-γηθέω, f. ήσω, to rejoice with.

συγ-γηράσκω, f -άσομαι [ᾱ], to grow old together with.

σύγ-γηρος, ον, (σύν, γῆρας) growing old together.

συγ-γίγνομαι later -γίνομαι [ῑ]: fut. -γενήσομαι:—to be with, hold communication or associate with, live with, hold intercourse with, converse with. 2. to come to assist. 3. absol. to come together, meet.

συγ-γιγνώσκω later -γῑνώσκω: f. συγγνώσομαι: aor. 2 συνέγνων: pf. συνέγνωκα:—to think with, agree with, hold the same sentiments with; absol. to consent, agree. II. to yield, concede, own, allow, acknowledge, confess:- also in Med. to grant, allow. III. συγγνῶναι ἑαυτῷ, to be conscious. IV. to have a fellow-feeling with another, to make allowance for another, excuse, pardon:—Pass. to obtain pardon or forgiveness.

σύγγνοια, ἡ, = συγγνώμ.

συγγνώμη, ἡ, (συγγνῶναι) fellow-feeling with another, allowance for him: pardon, forgiveness: also a claim to forgiveness, excuse.

συγγνωμονικός, ή, όν, (συγγνώμων) inclined to make allowance, indulgent II. of things, pardonable.

συγγνωμοσύνη, ἡ, fellow-feeling, forgiveness. From

συγγνώμων, ον, gen. ονος, (συγγνῶναι) disposed to pardon or forgive: indulgent. II. pass. pardoned, forgiven, deserving pardon, allowable.

συγγνῶναι, aor. 2 inf. of συγγιγνώσκω.

συγγνωστός, ή, όν, verb. Adj. of συγγιγνώσκω, to be pardoned, pardonable, allowable.

σύγ-γονος, ον, (σύν, γενέσθαι) born with, congenital, natural, inborn. 2. connected by blood, akin, Lat. cognatus: as Subst., **σύγγονος**, ὁ, ἡ, a brother, sister.

σύγγραμμα, ατος, τό, (συγγράφω) that which is noted or written down, a written paper or document: a writing, book: a prose work.

συγγρᾰφεύς, έως, ὁ, (συγγράφω) one who writes down, one who collects historical facts, an historian: generally, a prose-writer, author. II. συγγραφεῖς, οἱ, commissioners appointed at Athens in the Peloponnesian war to consider any suggested alterations of the Constitution.

συγγρᾰφή, ἡ, (συγγράφω) a writing or noting down. II. that which is written, a book, a history. 2. a written contract, a covenant, engagement. III. work done by contract.

συγγραφικός, ή, όν, given to writing history. From

συγ-γράφω, f. ψω, to write or note down, Lat. conscribere:—to describe. II. to compose or compile a work, Lat. componere: c. acc., πόλεμον ξυγγράφειν to write the history of the war: generally, to compose or write in prose. III. to draw a written contract: Med. to settle by written contract 2. to draw up a resolution. IV. to paint by contract.

συγ-γυμνάζω, f. άσω, to exercise with.

συγ-καθαιρέω Ion. **-καταιρέω**, f. ήσω: aor. 2 συγκαθεῖλον:—to pull down together, to join in pulling down or subduing: generally, to accomplish with any one.

συγ-καθαρμόζω, f. σω, to join in arranging or burying.

συγ-καθέζομαι, fut. -καθεδοῦμαι: Med.:—to sit with or together.

συγ-καθείργω Ion. **συγ-κατείργω**, to shut up or enclose with others.

συγ-καθέλκω, f. -ελκύσω [ῠ]: aor. 1 -είλκῠσα: fut. pass. -ελκυσθήσομαι: (see ἕλκω):—to drag down, destroy with.

συγ-καθεύδω, f. ήσω, to sleep with.

συγ-κάθημαι, properly pf. of συγκαθέζομαι, to be seated with or by the side of: to meet together in a council or assembly.

συγ-καθίζω, f. ήσω, to make to sit or place together: —Med. to sit together, meet for deliberation. II. intr. also in Act. to sit with.

συγ-καθίημι, f. -καθήσω, to let down with or together: —Pass. to let oneself down, stoop, condescend.

συγ-καθίστημι, f. -καταστήσω, to establish with or together, to join in establishing, settling, managing.

συγ-καίω Att. **-κάω** [ᾱ]: fut. -καύσω:—to set on fire with or at once, burn up, consume, Lat. comburo.

συγ-κᾰκοπᾰθέω, f. ήσω, to suffer with or together II. to feel with or for any one in suffering.

συγ-κᾰκουχέομαι, Pass. (σύν, κακουχέω) to endure trouble or suffering with.

συγ-κᾰλέω, f. έσω: pf. -κέκληκα pass. -κέκλημαι: —to call or summon together, call to council:—Med. to call to oneself 2. to call together, invite to a feast.

συγκᾰλυπτέος, α, ον, to be covered or veiled: and

συγκᾰλυπτός, ή, όν, covered, enwrapt. From

συγ-κἄλύπτω, f. ψω, *to cover* or *veil completely, shroud*:—Med. *to wrap oneself up, cover one's face.*

συγ-κάμνω, f. -κἄμουμαι: aor. 2 -έκἄμον:—*to labour* or *suffer with, sympathise with.* 2. *to labour* or *travail with.*

συγκαμπή, ἡ, (συγκάμπτω) *a joint.*

συγ-κάμπτω, f. ψω, *to bend together, bend* the knee:—Pass. *to bend oneself.*

συγ-κἄσιγνήτη, ἡ. *one's own sister.*

συγ-κἄσις, ιος, ὁ, and ἡ, (σύν, κάσις) *one's own brother* or *sister.*

συγ-καταβαίνω, f. -καταβήσομαι: aor. 2 -κατέβην: pf. -καταβέβηκα: *to go* or *come down with: to come to one's aid, come down to the contest with.* 2. *to condescend.*

συγ-καταβάλλω, f. -καταβἄλῶ: aor. 2 -κατέβἄλον:—*to pay down together.*

συγκατάβἄσις, ἡ, (συγκαταβαίνω) *a going down with.* 2. *condescension, submission, accommodation.*

συγ-καταγηράσκω, f. -γηράσομαι [ᾱ]:—*to grow old with* or *together.*

συγ-κατάγω, f. ξω, *to lead down with; to join in bringing back.*

συγ-καταδαρθάνω, aor. 2 -κατέδαρθον, *to sleep with.*

συγ-καταδιώκω, f. ξω, *to pursue with* or *in company.*

συγ-καταδουλόω, f. ώσω, *to join in enslaving.*

συγ-καταδύνω and **-δύω**: aor. 2 -κατέδυν:—*to sink* or *set together with.*

συγ-καταζεύγνῡμι, f. -ζεύξω, *to join together by the yoke, join in marriage, marry*: metaph., συγκαταζεῦξαί τινα ἄτῃ *to make* him *a yoke-fellow with* misery.

σύγ-καταθάπτω, f. ψω, *to bury along with.*

συγκατάθεσις, ἡ, (συγκατατίθημι) *agreement, approval, assent.* II. *submission.*

συγ-καταθέω, *to make an inroad with* another.

συγ-καταθνήσκω, *to die along with.*

συγ-καταίθω, *to burn all together.*

συγ-καταινέω, f. έσω or ήσω, *to agree with, favour, assent to*

συγ-κάταινος, ον, *agreeing, approving, assenting to.*

συγ-καταιρέω, Ion. for συγκαθαιρέω.

συγ-κατακαίω Att. **-κάω** [ᾱ]: f. -καύσω:—*to burn down along with*:—Pass. *to be burnt with.*

συγ-κατάκειμαι, Pass. *to lie down with, lie with.*

συγ-κατακλείω Ion. **-κληίω**, *to shut in* or *enclose with* or *together.*

συγ-κατακλίνω, *to make lie down with*:—Pass. *to recline on the same couch with* another *at table.*

συγ-κατακόπτω, *to cut up together.*

συγ-κατακτάομαι, f. ήσομαι: Dep. *to get* or *gain with, to join in acquiring.*

συγκατακτάς, ᾶσα, άν, aor. 2 part. of

συγ-κατακτείνω, f. -κτενῶ, *to slay with* or *together.*

συγ-καταλαμβάνω, f. -λήψομαι, *to seize* or *occupy with* or *together.*

συγ-καταλείπω, f. ψω, *to leave all together.*

συγ-καταλύω, f. σω, *to join in undoing* or *putting down: to help to depose.*

συγ-καταμίγνῡμι and **-ύω**, f. -μίξω, *to mix in with, mingle with*: metaph. *to absorb in* a thing.

συγ-καταμύω, f. σω, *to be shut close.*

συγ-καταναυμἄχέω, f. ήσω, *to assist in conquering.*

συγ-κατανέμω, *to allot jointly*:—Med. *to share among themselves.*

συγ-καταπίμπλημι, f. πλήσω, *to fill up with at the same time.*

συγ-καταπλέκω, f. ξω, *to intertwine with.*

συγ-καταπράσσω, f. ξω, *to join in effecting.*

συγ-καταρρίπτω, f. ψω, *to throw down together.*

συγ-κατασκάπτω, f. ψω, *to demolish with another* or *utterly.*

συγ-κατασκεδάννῡμι, f. -σκεδάσω [ᾰ], *to pour over at the same time*:—Med. *to pour over oneself at the same time.*

συγ-κατασκευάζω, f. σω, *to help in making* or *setting up.* 2. *to furnish completely.*

συγ-κατασκηνόω, f. ώσω, *to bring into one tent with.*

συγ-κατασκήπτω, f. ψω, *to dart down together.*

συγ-κατασπάω, f. -σπάσω [ᾰ], *to pull down together.* II. *to gulp down together.*

συγ-καταστρέφω, f. ψω, *to bring to an end together*:—*to make subject together* or *at the same time.*

συγ-κατατάσσω Att. **-ττω**, f. ξω, *to arrange* or *draw up with* or *together.*

συγκατατεθειμένος, pf. pass. part. of

συγ-κατατίθημι, f. -θήσω, *to lay down* or *deposit at the same time.* II. Pass. συγκατατίθεμαι, pf. συγκατατέθειμαι, *to agree with, assent to*

συγ-κατατρώγω, aor. 2 -έτρἄγον, *to eat up together.*

συγ-καταφαγεῖν, aor. 2 inf. of συγκατεσθίω.

συγ-καταψεύδομαι, f. σομαι, Dep. *to join in a lie against* another.

συγ-καταψηφίζομαι, f. ίσομαι, Dep. *to condemn with* or *together.* II. Pass. *to be reckoned along with.*

συγ-κάτειμι, (σύν, κατά, εἶμι ibo) *to go down with.*

συγ-κατείργω, Ion. for **συγκαθείργω**.

συγ-κατεργάζομαι, f. άσομαι: pf. -είργασμαι: Dep.:—*to help* or *join in accomplishing* a work: *to coöperate with* II. *to help in subduing.* III. *to kill with* or *together, help in slaying*

συγ-κατέρχομαι, f. -ελεύσομαι: aor. 2 act. -ῆλθον, pf. -ελήλυθα: Dep. *to come* or *go back together.*

συγ-κατεσθίω, f. -έδομαι: aor. 2 -έφἄγον:—*to eat up with* or *together.*

συγ-κατεύχομαι, f. -εύξομαι, Dep. *to pray for with* or *together.*

συγ-κατηγορέω, f. ήσω, *to accuse together.*

συγ-κάτημαι, Ion. for συγκάθημαι.

συγ-κατοικέω, f. ήσω, *to dwell with* or *together.*

συγ-κατοικίζω, f. ίσω, *to colonise jointly with* another, *join* or *assist in colonising.* II. *to settle* in a place *along with.* III. *to establish at the same time.*

συγ-κατοικτίζω, f. ίσω, *to pity with* or *together*:—Med. *to bewail with* or *together.*

συγ-κατορύσσω Att. -ττω, f. ξω, *to bury with.*

συγ-καττύω, *to patch up, cobble, furbish up.*

συγκέας, aor. 1 part. of συγκαίω.

σύγ-κειμαι, Pass. *to lie with* or *together.* II. *to have been put together, to be composed* or *compounded of.* III. *to be agreed on;* ὁ συγκείμενος χρόνος, or τὸ συγκείμενον χωρίον, the time or place *agreed upon;* κατὰ τὰ συγκείμενα according to *the terms of the agreement.* 2. impers. σύγκειται, *it is agreed on:* so absol. in neut. gen., συγκειμένου σφι *since it had been agreed to* by them.

συγκεκαλυμμένος, pf. pass. part. of συγκαλύπτω.

συγκέκλημαι, Att. pf. pass. of συγκλείω: Ion. **συγκεκλήιμαι.**

συγκεκομμένος, pf. pass. part. of συγκόπτω.

συγκέκρᾱμαι, pf. pass. of συγκεράννυμι.

συγκεκρᾱμένως, Adv. pf. pass. part. of συγκεράννυμι, *in a tempered manner.*

συγ-κεκροτημένως, Adv. pf. pass. part. of συγκροτέω, *as if welded together,* i. e. *firmly, closely.*

συγκεκύρηκα, pf. of συγκυρέω.

συγκέκῡφα, pf. of συγκύπτω.

συγ-κελεύω, f. σω, *to join in ordering* or *bidding.*

συγ-κεντέω, f. ήσω, *to pierce* or *stab together.*

συγ-κεράννῡμι or -ύω: f. -κεράσω [ᾰ]: pf. -κέκρᾱκα pass. -κέκρᾱμαι: aor. 1 pass. -εκράθην [ᾱ] Ion. -εκρήθην:—*to mix together, mingle: to blend together, temper by mixing:*—Med., συγκεράσασθαι φιλίαν *to form a close* friendship. II. Pass. *to be mixed with, become united, blend, coalesce.* 2. *to become deeply involved* or *implicated in.*

συγ-κεραυνόω, f. ώσω, *to strike with a thunderbolt, shiver in pieces:*—Pass. *to be thunder-stricken, astounded.*

συγ-κεφᾰλαιόω, f. ώσω, *to bring under one head* or *summary, to sum up, reckon up.*

συγκέχῠμαι, pf. pass. of συγχέω.

συγ-κέχωσμαι, pf. pass. of συγχώννυμι.

συγ-κινδῡνεύω, f. σω, *to incur danger along with* others: *to be partners in danger.*

συγ-κῑνέω, f. ήσω, *to move* or *put in commotion with.*

συγ-κλαίω Att. **-κλάω** [ᾱ]: f. -κλαύσομαι:—*to weep* or *lament with.*

συγ-κλάω, f. -κλάσω [ᾰ]: pf. pass. -κέκλασμαι:—*to break* or *shiver together, break in pieces, crush.*

σύγκλεισις Att. **σύγκλησις,** εως, ἡ, *a shutting up, closing up.* From

συγ-κλείω, f. κλείσω, Ion. **συγκληίω,** f. ηίσω, old Att. **ξυγκλῄω,** f. ῄσω: Pass., aor. 1 συνεκλείσθην old Att. ξυνεκλῄσθην: pf. -κέκλεισμαι or -ῃμαι Ion. -κεκλήισμαι or -ήιμαι:—*to shut up, to hem in, enclose.* 2. *to shut, close.* 3. *to close up;* συγκλείειν τὰς ἀσπίδας *to lock* their shields. II. Pass. *to be shut in, enclosed, surrounded* *to be closely united.*

συγ-κλέπτω, f. ψω, *to steal along with.*

συγ-κληίω, Ion. for συγκλείω.

συγ-κληρονόμος, ον, *a joint-heir.*

σύγ-κληρος, ον, *having one's lot together, having a neighbouring lot, neighbouring* II. *assigned by the same lot.* Hence

συγ-κληρόω, f. ώσω, *to embrace in one lot.* II. *to assign by the same lot.*

σύγ-κλησις, Att. for σύγκλεισις.

σύγ-κλητος, ον, (συγκαλέω) *called together, convened.* II. σύγκλητος (sub. ἐκκλησία), ἡ, *a specially convened assembly; a senate.*

συγκλῄω, Att. for συγκλείω.

συγκλινία, ἡ, *a meeting of slopes, a defile.* From

συγ-κλίνω [ῑ], f. ινῶ, *to lay together:*—Pass. *to lie with.*

συγ-κλονέω, f. ήσω, *to shake up together, confound.*

σύγ-κλῠς, ῠδος, ὁ, ἡ, (σύν, κλύζω) *washed together* by the waves: *thrown together, promiscuous.*

συγ-κοιμάομαι, Pass. with fut. med. -κοιμήσομαι, pf. pass. -κεκοίμημαι:—*to sleep with* another, *lie with.* Hence

συγκοίμημα, ατος, τό, *a sleeping together.* II. *the partner of one's bed, consort:* and

συγκοίμησις, ἡ, *a sleeping together.*

συγ-κοιμίζω, f. σω, *to put to bed together, join in wedlock.*

συγ-κοινόομαι, Dep. *to make common with, impart, give a share of.*

συγκοινωνέω, f. ήσω, *to have a joint share* of a thing, c. gen. rei. II. *to partake in* a thing, c. dat. rei. From

συγ-κοινωνός, ἡ, όν, *partaking jointly of* a thing.

σύγ-κοιτος, ον, (σύν, κοίτη) *sharing one's bed.* II. *of* or *belonging to the marriage-bed.*

συγ-κολλάω, f. ήσω, *to glue* or *stick together.* Hence

συγκολλητής, οῦ, ὁ, *one who glues* or *sticks together:* metaph. *a fabricator, concocter*

σύγ-κολλος, ον, (σύν, κόλλα) *glued together, closely joined:*—Adv. συγκόλλως, *in accordance with*

συγκομῐδή, ἡ, *a bringing together:* esp. of harvest *a gathering in, housing.* From

συγ-κομίζω, f. -ίσω Att. -ιῶ, *to carry* or *bring together:* of harvest, *to gather* it *in, house* it; in Pass., ὀργᾷ συγκομίζεσθαι it is ripe *for carrying:*—Med. *to get together* or *gather in for oneself, supply oneself with: to send for;* συγκομίζεσθαι πρὸς ἑαυτόν *to claim* as one's own. 2. in Pass. also *to be gained together.* II. *to help in burying.*

συγκοπή, ἡ, *a cutting into small pieces.* II. *a retrenching, cutting away:* in Gramm. *syncopé,* i. e. *a striking out one* or *more letters* in a word. III. *a fainting fit, swoon.* From

συγ-κόπτω, f. ψω, *to beat together.* 2. *to knock in pieces, cut up.* II. *to thrash soundly, maltreat.*

συγ-κοσμέω, f. ήσω, *to set in order together, arrange.* II. *to confer honour on.*

συγ-κουφίζω, f. ίσω, *to help to lighten.*

σύγκρᾱσις, εως, ἡ, (συγκεράννυμι) *a mixing together, blending, tempering.*

σύγκρᾶτος, ον, (συγκεράννυμι) *mixed together, blended: closely united.*

συγ-κρίνω [ῐ], f. -κρῐνῶ, *to compound, put together.* II. *to compare: to estimate.* Hence

σύγκρῐσις, ἡ, *a putting together, compounding.* II. *a comparing, comparison.*

συγ-κροτέω, f. ήσω: pf. pass. -κεκρότημαι:—*to strike together;* συγκροτεῖν τὼ χεῖρε *to clap* the hands: absol. *to clap, applaud.* II. *to beat, hammer,* or *weld together.* 2. metaph. *to weld into one;* of soldiers, *to drill, discipline:*—Pass. *to be well trained, in good discipline.* 3. metaph. also, *to concoct.*

σύγκρουσις, εως, ἡ, *a collision.* II. *a quarrel.* From

συγ-κρούω, f. σω, *to strike together;* συγκρούειν τὼ χεῖρε *to clap* the hands. II. *to bring into collision, to wear out by collision.* 2. *to confound, throw into confusion.*

συγ-κρύπτω, f. ψω, *to cover up completely, envelope: to conceal utterly, to hide.*

συγ-κτάομαι, f. -κτήσομαι Dep. *to gain along with, help to acquire.*

συγ-κτίζω, f. ισω, *to join in colonising.* Hence

συγκτίστης, ου, ὁ, *a joint founder* or *coloniser.*

συγκῠβευτής, οῦ, ὁ, *a person with whom one plays at dice, a fellow-gamester.* From

συγ-κῠβεύω, *to play at dice with.*

συγ-κῠκάω, f. ήσω, *to throw into an utter ferment.*

συγ-κῠλινδέομαι, Pass. *to roll about* or *wallow together.*

συγ-κῠνηγός Dor. and Att. **συγκῠνᾱγός**, ὁ, ἡ, *a fellow-hunter, fellow-huntress.*

συγ-κύπτω, f. ψω: pf. -κέκῡφα:—*to bend forwards* so as *to meet, to stoop and lay heads together, to conspire;* τοῦτο δ' ἐς ἕν ἐστι συγκεκυφός this *comes all to one* point. II. *to be bowed down, bent double.*

συγ-κῠρέω, f. -κυρήσω or -κύρσω: aor. 1 -εκύρησα or -έκυρσα: pf. -κεκύρηκα:—*to come together* or *encounter by chance: to meet with, light upon.* II. of events, *to happen at the same time:* also *to come to pass:* impers., συνεκύρησε γενέσθαι *it came to pass* that ... Hence

συγκῠρία, ἡ, *a coincidence.*

συγκύρσειαν, 3 pl. aor. 1 opt. of συγκυρέω.

σύγ-κωλος, ον, (σύν, κῶλον) *with limbs united: standing close together.*

συγ-κωμάζω, f. άσω Dor. άξω, *to march together in a κῶμος* or *band of revellers, to revel with.*

σύγ-κωμος, ον, (σύν, κῶμος) *a partner in a κῶμος, a fellow-reveller.*

συγ-κωμῳδέω, f. ησω, (σύν, κωμῳδέω) *to play with in a comedy.*

συγ-χαίρω, f. med. -χᾰρήσομαι: aor. 2 pass. -εχάρην [ᾰ]:—*to rejoice with, join in one's joy.* II. *to wish one joy, congratulate.*

συγχᾰρῆτε, 2 pl. aor. 2 pass. subj. of συγχαίρω.

συγχέας, aor. 1 part. of συγχέω.

συγ-χειμάζω, f. άσω, *to winter with* or *at the same time:*—Pass. *to weather the same storm.*

συγ-χειρουργέω, f. ήσω, *to bear a hand at the same time, to perform together.*

συγχεῦαι, Ep. aor. 1 inf. of

συγ-χέω, f. -χεῶ: aor. 1 συνέχεα Ep. συνέχευα, inf. συγχεῦαι: pf. -κέχῠκα: Pass., aor. 1 -εχύθην [ῠ], and 3 sing. Ep. aor. 2 pass. σύγχῠτο: pf. -κέχῠμαι: *to pour together, mix by pouring:* hence *to throw into disorder* or *confusion: to confound, disturb, trouble, disquiet:* of things, *to frustrate, make of none effect:* esp. of treaties, etc., *to confound, break through, violate.*

συγχορευτής, οῦ, ὁ, *a partner in a dance.* From

συγ-χορεύω, f. σω, *to dance with.*

συγχορηγέω, f. ήσω, *to assist in supplying.* From

συγ-χορηγός, όν, *acting as choregus with one:* generally, *helping to defray expenses.*

σύγ-χορτος, ον, (σύν, χόρτος) properly *with the grass joining; bordering upon, adjacent to.*

συγ-χόω, Ion. for συγχώννυμι.

συγ-χράομαι, f. -χρήσομαι, Dep. *to join with in using:* hence *to have dealings with.*

σύγ-χροος, ον contr. -**χρους**, ουν, (σύν, χρόα) *of like colour, of one colour.*

συγ-χύνω [ῡ], late form of συγχέω.

σύγχῠσις, εως, ἡ, (συγχέω) *a mixing together, blending: confounding: a breaking through, violating.*

σύγχῠτο, 3 sing. Ep. aor. 2 pass. of συγχέω.

συγ-χωνεύω, f. σω, *to melt together, to melt down.*

συγ-χώννῡμι and -ύω: Ion. pres. **συγχόω**, inf. συγχοῦν: f. συγχώσω: aor. 1 συνέχωσα: pf. pass. συγκέχωσμαι:—*to heap all together, to heap up with earth, bank up.* II. *to make into ruinous heaps, dismantle, demolish.* III. *to heap one thing on another, confound.*

συγ-χωρέω, f. ήσω and ήσομαι:—*to come together, unite.* II. *to give place, give way:* metaph. *to make concessions, compromise matters:* in bad sense, *to be in collusion with, connive at.* 2. c. acc. rei, *to concede, give up, yield.* 3. *to accede* or *agree to, assent, acquiesce in:* c. inf. *to agree* to do: absol. *to agree, acquiesce.* 4. impers. συγχωρεῖ, *it is agreed, it is possible.* Hence

συγχωρητέον or plur. -**έα**, verb. Adj. *one must agree to, concede.*

σύδην [ῡ], Adv. (σεύω) *with rushing motion, hurriedly.*

σύειος, α, ον, (σῦς) *of swine,* Lat. *suillus;* χρῖσμα σύειον *hog's*-lard.

συ-ζάω, inf. συζῆν: f. -ζήσω:—*to live with, live together.*

συ-ζεύγνῡμι and -ύω: f. -ζεύξω Pass., aor. 2 συνεζύγην [ῠ]:—*to yoke together, couple, unite,* esp. in marriage:—Pass. *to be yoked* or *coupled with:*—Med. *to yoke for oneself.*

συ-ζητέω, f. ήσω, *to seek* or *examine together with, to join in seeking out.* Hence

συζήτησις, ἡ, *joint inquiry: a disputation;* and

συζητητής, οῦ, ὁ, *a fellow-inquirer: a disputer.*

συ-ζοφόομαι, Pass. (σύν, ζόφος) *to grow dark together.*

συζῠγία, ἡ, (συζεύγνυμι) *union: a joint.* II. *a yoke* or *pair* of animals.

συζῠγῆναι, aor. 2 inf. pass. of συζεύγνυμι.

συζύγιος [ῠ], α, ον, poët. for σύζυγος, *yoked together, joined, united.*

σύζῠγος, ον, (συζυγῆναι) *yoked together, paired, united,* esp. *wedded*:—as Subst., σύζυγος, ἡ, *a wife*: but also, σύζυγος, ὁ, *a yoke-fellow, comrade, friend.*

σύζυξ, ῠγος, ὁ, ἡ, = σύζυγος.

σύζωμα, ατος, τό, *a girding together.* II. *a girdle.* From

συ-ζώννῡμι, f. -ζώσω, *to gird together, gird up*:—Med. *to gird oneself, gird up one's loins.*

συ-ζωοποιέω, f. ήσω, *to quicken at the same time.*

σῠθείς, aor. 1 pass. part. of σεύω.

σύθεν, Aeol. for ἐσύθησαν, 3 pl. aor. 1 pass. of σεύω.

σῡκάζω, f. άσω (συκῆ) *to gather ripe figs.*

σῡκάμῑνον, τό, *the fruit of the* συκάμινος, *a mulberry,* Lat. *morum.*

σῡκάμῑνος, ἡ, *the mulberry-tree,* Lat. *morus.*

σῡκέα, έας, Ion. and Ep. σῡκέη, έης contr σῡκῆ, ῆς, ἡ; Ion. gen. pl. συκέων: (σῦκον):—*the fig-tree,* Lat. *ficus.*

σῡκίδιον, τό, Dim. of σῦκον, *a small fig.*

σῡκίζω, f. ίσω, (σῦκον) *to fatten with figs.*

σύκῑνος, η, ον, (σῦκον) *of* or *belonging to the fig-tree* or *figs;* σύκινον ξύλον the wood *of the fig-tree.* II. metaph. from the spongy nature of this wood, σύκινοι ἄνδρες *weak, good-for-nothing fellows*: also with allusion to συκοφάντης, *false, treacherous.*

σῡκίς, ίδος, ἡ, (συκέη) *a slip* or *cutting from a fig-tree, a young fig-tree.*

σῡκολογέω, f. ήσω, *to gather figs.* From

σῡκο-λόγος, ον, (σῦκον, λέγω) *gathering figs.*

σῡκο-μορέα, ἡ, = συκόμορος.

σῡκό-μορος, ἡ, (σῦκον, μόρον) *the fig-mulberry,* an Egyptian kind, called also συκάμινος ἡ Αἰγυπτία.

ΣΥ͂ΚΟΝ, τό, *a fig,* Lat. *ficus.*

σῡκο-πέδῑλος, ὁ, (σῦκον, πέδιλον) *with sandals of fig,* a parody on Homer's χρυσοπέδιλος.

σῡκο-τρᾰγέω, f. ήσω, (σῦκον, τραγεῖν) *to eat figs.* Hence

συκοτρᾰγίδης, ου, ὁ, *a fig-nibbler.*

σῡκοφαντέω, f. ήσω, (συκοφάντης) *to be an informer*: c. acc. pers. *to inform against, accuse falsely, slander.* 2. c. acc. rei, *to lay information against a thing*: but, συκοφαντεῖν τριάκοντα μνᾶς *to extort* 30 minae *by laying informations;* συκοφαντεῖν τί τινος *to extort* money from another *by false informations.* Hence

σῡκοφάντημα, ατος, τό, *false accusation, slander, misrepresentation.*

σῡκο-φάντης, ου, ὁ, (σῦκον, φαίνω) properly *a fig-shewer,* i.e. *one who brings figs to light by shaking the tree;* or *a fig-informer,* i.e. *one who informed against persons exporting figs* from Attica: but used in the sense of *a common informer, a false accuser, slanderer.*

σῡκοφαντία, ἡ, (συκοφαντέω) *the behaviour of a sycophant, false accusation, slander.* Hence

συκοφαντίας, ου, ὁ, *the Sycophant-wind.*

σῡκοφαντικός, ή, όν, (συκοφάντης) *like a sycophant, slanderous.* Adv. -κῶς.

σῡκοφάντρια, ἡ, fem. of συκοφάντης, *a female informer.*

συκόφᾰσις, εως, ἡ, poët. for συκοφαντία.

συκοφορέω, f. ήσω, *to carry figs.* From

συκο-φόρος, ον, (σῦκον, φέρω) *carrying figs.*

συκόω, f. ώσω, *to feed with figs.*

σύλα, Ep. for ἐσύλα, 3 sing. impf. of σῡλάω.

σῡλ-ᾰγωγέω, f. ήσω, (σῦλον, ἄγω) *to carry off as booty* or *plunder.* II. *to rob, despoil.*

σύλασκε, Ion. for ἐσύλα, 3 sing. impf. of σῡλάω.

ΣΥ͂ΛΑ'Ω, f. ήσω: aor. 1 ἐσύλησα: Pass., aor. 1 ἐσυλήθην: pf. σεσύλημαι:—*to strip off* the arms of a slain enemy: c. acc. pers. et rei, *to strip off* arms *from* a person, or *to strip* him *of* his arms: so also c. acc. pers. et gen. rei:—Pass. c. acc. rei, *to be robbed* or *deprived of* a thing. 2. c. acc. pers. only, *to strip, despoil, pillage, plunder.* 3. c. acc. rei only, *to strip off*: hence *to take away, carry off*:—Pass. *to be taken away* or *carried off as spoil*: generally, *to be taken away.*

συλεύμενος, Dor. for συλούμενος, pres. pass. part. of συλέω.

σῡλεύω and **σῡλέω**, collat. forms of συλάω, *to despoil.* 2. *to rob secretly, defraud*: *to trick, cheat.*

σύλη, ἡ, or **σῦλον**, τό, only used in plur. σῦλαι, αἱ, or σῦλα, τά, (συλάω) *the right of seizing the ship or cargo* of a foreign merchant: *the right of seizure, right to make reprisals* in case of war, answering to modern *letters of marque.*

σῡληθείς, εῖσα, έν, aor. 1 pass. part. of συλάω.

σῡλητήρ, ῆρος, and **σῡλήτωρ**, ορος, ὁ, (συλάω) *a robber*:—fem. **σῡλήτειρα**.

συλλᾰβεῖν, aor. 2 inf. of συλλαμβάνω.

συλλᾰβέσθαι, aor. 2 med. inf. of συλλαμβάνω.

συλλᾰβή, ἡ, (συλλαβεῖν) *that which holds together.* II. (from pass.) *that which is held together,* esp. *several letters* forming one sound, *a syllable;* ἐν γραμμάτων ξυλλαβαῖς in written words.

συλλαβίζω, f. σω, (συλλαμβάνω) *to read in syllables.*

συλ-λᾰλέω, f. ήσω, *to talk* or *converse with.*

συλ-λαμβάνω, f. -λήψομαι: aor. 2 συνέλᾰβον, inf. συλλαβεῖν: pf. -είληφα, pass. -είλημμαι: cf. λαμβάνω:—*to bring together* or *collect into a body, to rally* troops. II. *to put together, close* the mouth and eyes (of a corpse). III. *to take together, lay hold of, seize, apprehend, arrest.* IV. *to comprehend, comprise*: of the mind, *to comprehend, understand.* V. *to receive all together, to enjoy.* VI. of a woman, *to conceive.* VII. c. dat. pers. *to take part with* another, *to assist* one *in* a thing: absol. *to assist*: so also in Med. συλλαμβάνομαι, *to help to take hold of* a thing, and so *to help, assist.*

συλ-λέγω, f. ξω: aor. 1 συνέλεξα: pf. συνείλοχα: Pass., fut. 2 συλλεγήσομαι: aor. 1 συνελέχθην, aor. 2 συνελέγην: pf. συνείλεγμαι and συλλέλεγμαι:—*to gather, collect, bring together:* of persons, *to call together*, also *to raise* or *levy an army*, Lat. *conscribere:*—Pass. *to come together, assemble* 2. of things, *to gather, collect:*—Pass., of things, *to become customary.*

σύλ-λεκτρος, ον, (σύν, λέκτρον) *sharing one's bed:* as Subst., **σύλλεκτρος, ὁ, ἡ,** *the partner of one's bed, husband* or *wife.*

συλλήβδην, Adv. (**συλλαμβάνω**) *taken together, collectively, in sum, in shor*

συλ-λήγω, f. ξω, *to cease* or *come to an end together.*

συλληπτέον, verb. Adj. of συλλαμβάνω, *one must lay hold of together.*

συλλήπτρια, ἡ, fem. of **συλλήπτωρ.**

συλλήπτωρ, ορος, ὁ, (συλλαμβάνω) *one that takes hold of with, a partner, sharer, assistant, coadjutor.*

συλληφθῆναι, aor. 1 pass. inf. of συλλαμβάνω.

σύλληψις, εως, ἡ, (συλλαμβάνω) *a taking* or *putting together.* II. *a seizing, laying hold of, apprehending.* III. *a grasping with the mind, comprehension.* IV. *conception* in the womb.

συλλήψομαι, fut. of **συλλαμβάνω.**

συλλογή, ἡ, (συλλέγω) *a gathering, collecting.* 2. *a raising, levying* of soldiers, Lat. *conscriptio.* II. *an assembling, an assembly, concourse, meeting.*

συλ-λογίζομαι, f. -ίσομαι, Dep. *to reckon all together, to sum up, reckon up.* II. *to collect* or *conclude from premises: to infer by way of syllogism.*

συλλογῐμαῖος, α, ον, (συλλέγω) *collected from different places*

συλλογισμός, ὁ, (συλλογίζομαι) *a reckoning all together, reckoning up.* II. *a collecting from premises, reasoning:—a syllogism, inference* or *conclusion drawn from premises.*

σύλλογος, ὁ, (συλλέγω) *a gathering together, an assembly* or *meeting* of persons; σύλλογον ποιήσασθαι to convene *an assembly.* II. metaph. *power of collecting oneself, presence of mind.*

συλ-λούομαι, Pass. *to bathe together*

συλ-λοχίτης [ῑ], ου, ὁ, (σύν, λόχος) *a soldier of the same* λόχος or *company.*

συλ-λῡπέω, f. ήσω, *to hurt together:*—Pass. with fut. -λυπηθήσομαι and med. -λυπήσομαι, *to sympathise* or *condole with.*

συλ-λυσσάομαι, Pass. *to be mad in company with.*

συλ-λύω, f. ύσω [ῡ], *to help in loosing* or *setting free.*

σῦλον, τό, see σύλη.

σῦλ-όνυξ, ῠχος, ὁ, ἡ, (συλάω, ὄνυξ) *paring the nails.*

συμβαίην, aor. 2 opt. of συμβαίνω.

συμ-βαίνω, f. -βήσομαι: aor. 2 συνέβην, inf. συμβῆναι: pf. -βέβηκα, syncop. 3 pl. -βεβᾶσι, Ion. inf. συμβεβάναι, part. -βεβώς: Pass., 3 sing. aor. 1 subj. συμβᾰθῇ: pf. inf. ξυμβεβάσθαι: (cf. -βαίνω):—*to stand with the feet together.* II. *to stand with* or *beside*, hence *to assist.* III. *to come together, meet:* hence, like συμμίσγω, *to reach to* or *be at a place*, c. dat.; συμβαίνειν κακοῖς *to fall in with* evils. 2. *to agree with*, Lat. *convenire; to come to an agreement, make an agreement;* generally, *to be* or *make friends with:* in perf. inf. συμβεβάναι, of the terms, *to be agreed on.* 3. *to suit, fit, be like: to coïncide* or *correspond with: to be fitting* IV. *to fall to one's lot.* V. of events, *to come to pass, fall out, happen*, Lat. *contingere:* impers. συμβαίνει, συνέβη *it happens* or *happened* that ..; so, συμβαίνει εἶναι or γίγνεσθαι:—τὸ συμβεβηκός, *a chance event, contingency;* κατὰ συμβεβηκός *by chance.* 2. *to turn out* in a certain way, whether *well* or *ill:* absol. *to turn out well, succeed,* ἢν ξυμβῇ ἡ πεῖρα if the attempt *succeed.* 3. of consequence, *to come out, result, ensue:* of conclusions, *to follow.*

συμ-βακχεύω, f. σω, *to join in the feast of Bacchus* or *Bacchic revelry.*

σύμ-βακχος, ὁ, ἡ, *joining in Bacchic revelry.*

συμ-βάλλω: f. -βᾰλῶ: aor. 2 συνέβᾰλον, inf. συμβᾰλεῖν: pf. -βέβληκα: Med., fut. -βλήσομαι: Pass., aor. 1 συνεβλήθην:—Homer uses Ep. aor. 2 pass. συνεβλήμην in forms ξύμβλητο, -βλήτην, -βληντο, subj. σύμβληται, inf. -βλήμεναι, part. -βλήμενος:—*to throw* or *dash together: to bring together*, esp. of rivers, *to unite* their streams: *to throw together, collect:*—συμβάλλειν ἀσπίδας, *to lock, join closely* their shields; συμβάλλειν βλέφαρα *to close* the eyes: generally, *to join, unite:* of contracts, *to conclude, to lend money on bond:*—Med. *to contribute of one's own property, to pay a share:* generally, *to contribute, bear a part in;* ξυμβάλλεται πολλὰ τοῦδε δείματος many things *contribute* [*their share*] *of* this fear, i. e. join in causing it; συμβάλλεσθαι ξενίαν *to contract* friendly relations; συμβάλλεσθαι λόγους, or absol. συμβάλλεσθαι, *to hold a conference with, converse, confer:* generally, *to do one's part, be useful.* II. *to bring* men *together, to set* them *together, match* them *to fight*, Lat. *committo;* so also, συμβάλλειν μάχην *to engage in, join* battle; ἔχθραν, ἔριν συμβάλλειν *to contract* enmity, etc. 2. Med. *to fall in with* one, *meet* him *by chance.* III. *to put together, to compare, reckon, compute:* Pass. *to correspond;* τὸ Βαβυλώνιον τάλαντον συμβαλλεόμενον πρὸς τὸ Εὐβοεικόν the Babylonian talent *being reduced to* the Euboïc. 2. *to conclude from a comparison of facts, to conclude, infer;* c. acc. *to guess* or *make out by conjecture, to interpret, understand.* IV. Med. *to agree upon.* V. intr. *to come together: to meet, join.* . *to engage, encounter.*

συμβάς, ᾶσα, άν, aor. 2 part. of συμβαινω.

συμ-βᾰσείω, Desiderat. of συμβαίνω, *to wish to make a league* or *covenant with.*

συμ-βᾰσῐλεύω, f. σω, *to rule conjointly with.*

σύμβᾰσις, εως, ἡ, (συμβαίνω) *an agreement, arrangement, convention, treaty.*

συμβᾰτήριος, *ον*, and **συμβᾰτικός**, *ή*, *όν*, (*συμβαίνω*) *tending to agreement, conciliatory.*

συμβεβάναι [ᾰ], Ion. for *συμβεβηκέναι*, perf. inf. of *συμβαίνω.*

συμβεβάσθαι, pf. inf. pass. of *συμβαίνω.*

συμβέβηκα, pf. of *συμβαίνω.*

συμβῆναι, aor. 2 inf. of *συμβαίνω.*

συμ-βιάζω, f. *άσω*, *to extort by force at the same time.*

συμ-βῐβάζω, f. *-βιβάσω*, Att. *-βιβῶ*:—Causal of *συμβαίνω*, *to bring together, put together*: metaph. *to bring to terms, reconcile*:—Pass. *to come to terms with* another. II. *to compare, contrast.* III. *to prove.* IV. *to teach, instruct.*

συμ-βιόω, f. *-βιώσομαι*: aor. 2 *συνεβίων*, inf. *συμβιῶναι*: pf. *συμβεβίωκα*:—*to live with.*

συμβιώτης, *ου*, *ὁ*, *one who lives with, a companion.*

συμβλήμενος, Ep. aor. 2 pass. part. of *συμβάλλω.*

συμβλήσεαι, Ep. 2 sing. fut. pass. of *συμβάλλω.*

συμβλητός, *ή*, *όν*, verb. Adj. of *συμβάλλω*, *comparable.*

συμ-βοάω, f. *-βοήσομαι*, *to cry aloud* or *shout together with*, *τινί*: c. acc. pers. *to shout to, call on at once.*

συμβοηθεία, *ἡ*, *joint aid* or *assistance.* From

συμ-βοηθέω, f. *ήσω*, *to render joint aid, join in giving aid.*

συμβόλαιον, *τό*, (*συμβάλλω*) *a mark* or *sign to conclude from, a token*: *a symptom.* II. plur. *συμβόλαια*, *τά*, *a contract, covenant* or *bond*: *acknowledgment for money lent.* 2. *intercourse.*

συμβόλαιος, *α*, *ον*, (*σύμβολον*) *of* or *referring to bargains* or *contracts*, esp. in trade.

συμβολέω, f. *ήσω*, (*συμβάλλω*) *to fall in with.*

συμβολή, *ἡ*, (*συμβάλλω*) *a bringing together.* II. (from Pass.) *a coming together, meeting, joining*: *the part that meets, the joining, end.* 2. *a meeting*, in hostile sense, *an engaging, encountering.* 3. *a contribution, subscription*:—plur. *συμβολαί*, *αἱ*, *contributions* to provide a common meal; *δειπνεῖν ἀπὸ συμβολῶν*, Lat. *de symbolis esse*; also *the meal* or *entertainment* itself. Hence

συμβολικός, *ή*, *όν*, *of* or *for a contribution* or *common meal.*

σύμβολον, *τό*, (*συμβάλλω*) *a sign* or *mark to infer a thing by, a signal, token*; *σύμβολα λαμπάδος a beacon-fire, signal.* 2. *σύμβολα* were also the two pieces of a coin, etc., which two contracting parties broke between them and each preserved one part, *tallies*, Lat. *tesserae hospitalitatis.* 3. at Athens, *σύμβολον* was *a ticket* or *cheque*, Lat. *tessera*, which the dicasts had given them on entering the court, and on presenting which they received their fee: also given on other occasions, as to persons who took part in a common meal: also *a permit* or *licence.* II. *σύμβολα*, *τά*, also denoted *a covenant* or *treaty between two states for mutual protection of commerce*; *σύμβολα ποιεῖσθαι πρὸς πόλιν* to make *a commercial treaty* with a state.

σύμβολος, *ον*, (*συμβάλλω*) *coming together*: *accidental.* II. *σύμβολος* (sub. *οἰωνός*), *ὁ*, *an augury, omen.*

συμβούλευμα, *ατος*, *τό*, (*συμβουλεύω*) *advice given.*

συμβουλευτέος, *α*, *ον*, (*συμβουλεύω*) *to be deliberated upon.* 2. *to be advised.*

συμβουλευτικός, *ή*, *όν*, (*συμβουλεύω*) *deliberative.*

συμ-βουλεύω, f. *σω*, *to advise, counsel*, c. dat. pers., as in Lat. *consulere alicui*; c. inf. *to advise* one to do: c. acc. rei, *to recommend* a thing. II. Med. *to take counsel with* a person, Lat. *consulere aliquem*: absol. *to consult together, deliberate.*

συμβουλή, *ἡ*, (*σύν, βουλή*) *advice* or *counsel given.* II. *a taking counsel, consultation.*

συμβουλία, *ἡ*, = *συμβουλή* I.

συμβούλιον, *τό*, (*σύν, βουλή*) *advice, counsel.* II. *a council.*

συμ-βούλομαι, fut. *-βουλήσομαι*, Dep. *to will* or *wish together with*: *to agree with.*

σύμ-βουλος, *ὁ*, (*σύν, βουλή*) *an adviser, counsellor.*

συμ-βύω, f. *ύσω* [ῡ], *to cram together.*

συμμᾰθεῖν, aor. 2 inf. of *συμμανθάνω.*

συμμᾰθητής, *οῦ*, *ὁ*, (*συμμανθάνω*) *a fellow-disciple, a school-fellow*, Lat. *condiscipulus.*

συμ-μαίνομαι: pf. 2 *συμμέμηνα*: aor. 2 pass. *συνεμάνην* [ᾰ]:—*to rave* or *be mad along with* or *together.*

συμ-μανθάνω, f. *-μᾰθήσομαι*: aor. 2 *συνέμαθον*:—*to learn along with* one:—*ὁ συμμαθών one who has learnt thoroughly*, i. e. *is used to* a thing.

συμ-μάρπτω, f. *ψω*, *to grasp together.*

συμμαρτῠρέω, f. *ήσω*, *to bear witness with* or *in accordance with, to testify to* a thing *with* another. And

συμμαρτύρομαι [ῡ], Dep. = *συμμαρτῠρέω.* From

συμμάρτῠς, *ῠρος*, *ὁ*, *ἡ*, *a fellow-witness.*

συμμᾰχέω, f. *ήσω*, (*σύμμαχος*) *to be an ally, be in alliance with*: and so generally, *to help, aid.* Hence

συμμᾰχία Ion. *-ίη*, *ἡ*, in war, *an alliance* offensive and defensive (whereas *ἐπιμαχία* is *a defensive alliance*):—generally, *aid, succour, help.* II. = *οἱ σύμμαχοι*, *the body of allies*: also *an auxiliary force.* Hence

συμμᾰχικός, *ή*, *όν*, *of* or *for alliance*; *θεοὶ ξυμμαχικοί* the gods *invoked at the making of an alliance.* II. *τὸ συμμαχικόν*, = *οἱ σύμμαχοι*, *the auxiliaries, allied forces.* 2. *a treaty of alliance.*

συμ-μᾰχίς, *ίδος*, pecul. fem. of *σύμμαχος*, *allied*: *ἡ ξυμμαχίς* (sub. *πόλις*), *an allied state.* II. *the body of allies.*

συμ-μάχομαι, f. *-μαχοῦμαι*, Dep. *to fight along with, to be an ally*: generally, *to take part with.*

σύμ-μᾰχος, *ον*, (*σύν, μάχη*) *fighting along with, allied with, auxiliary*:—as Subst., *σύμμαχος*, *ὁ*, *an ally, auxiliary* in war: *an assistant, helper, supporter.*

συμμέμιγμαι, pf. pass. of *συμμίγνυμι.*

συμ-μεθέπω, *to sway jointly with.*

συμ-μελετάω, f. *ήσω*, *to practise with* or *together.*

συμ-μένω, f. *-μενῶ*, *to stay together, keep together.* 2. *to hold together, abide, continue.*

συμ-μερίζω, f. σω, (σύν, μέρος) *to give a share of* a thing *with* others :—Med. *to receive a share of* a thing *jointly with* others, c. dat.

συμ-μεταβαίνω, f. -βήσομαι, *to go over* or *away along with*.

συμ-μεταβάλλω, f. -βᾰλῶ, *to join in changing* :—Pass. *to change sides and take part with*

συμ-μεταχειρίζομαι, f. -σομαι: Dep.: also Act. **συμμεταχειρίζω** :— *to manage* or *take charge of along with*.

συμ-μετέχω, f. -μεθέξω, (σύν, μετέχω) *to take part in* or *partake of along with*.

συμ-μετίσχω, = συμμετέχω.

συμμέτοχος, ον, (συμμετέχω) *partaking in jointly*.

συμ-μετρέω, f. ήσω, *to make commensurate with* or *proportional to* a thing:—Med. *to compute, ascertain: to make an estimate of* a thing :—Pass. *to be commensurate, measured out along with; ἦμαρ συμμετρούμενον χρόνῳ* this day *being measured with* the time of his absence. Hence

συμμέτρησις, ἡ, *a measuring by a standard, admeasurement*.

συμμετρία, ἡ, *symmetry, due proportion*. From

σύμ-μετρος, ον, (σύν, μέτρον) *measured* or *commensurate with* : *of like measure* or *size with*. II. *in due proportion, symmetrical, fitting, meet*. 2. *resembling, like : of like age with, keeping measure with*. II. Adv., συμμέτρως ἔχειν to be *in proportion* : Comp. -ότερον, *in a manner better fitted*.

συμ-μητιάομαι, f. -άσομαι [ᾱ], Dep. *to take counsel with* or *together*.

συμ-μηχᾰνάομαι, f. -ήσομαι, Dep. *to contrive together, to help to bring about*.

σύμμῐγα, Adv. *confusedly, all together with*. From

συμμῐγῆναι, aor. 2 inf. pass. of συμμίγνυμι.

συμμῐγής, ές, (συμμιγῆναι) *mixed up together, blended, mingled, promiscuous : common*.

συμ-μίγνῦμι or -ύω : fut. συμμίξω : Ep. and Ion. pres. **συμμίσγω** :—*to mix* or *mingle* one thing *with* another, *commingle, blend* : metaph. *to bring in connexi with, unite* : *to communicate* a thing to a person. II. Pass., with fut. med. συμμίξομαι, *to be commingled* or *blended* : *to be formed by combination* : of rivers, *to join, unite* : *to be brought in contact* or *collision with*. III. intrans. in Act., *to have dealings* or *intercourse with* : *to converse with* : *to treat* or *negotiate with* : also 2. *to engage, encounter, come to blows*. Hence

συμμικτός, όν, *commingled, promiscuous*. II. *mingled, confounded*.

συμ-μῑμέομαι, Dep. *to join in imitating*. Hence

συμμῑμητής, οῦ, ὁ, *a joint* or *fellow imitator*.

συμ-μιμνήσκομαι, pf. -μέμνημαι, Dep. (σύν, μιμνήσκω) *to remember, bear in mind along with*.

συμμῖξαι, aor. 1 inf. of συμμίγνυμι.

σύμμιξις, εως, ἡ, (συμμίγνυμι) *a mixing together, commixture*. II. *intercourse*.

συμ-μίσγω, Ep. and Ion. for συμμίγνυμι.

σύμ-μολπος, ον, (σύν, μολπή) *in harmony* or *unison with, harmonious*.

συμ-μορία, ἡ, (σύν, μέρος) *a joint division* : at Athens, the 1200 wealthiest citizens were divided into 20 συμμορίαι or *companies*, two in each tribe (φυλή), each company being in turn liable to discharge extraordinary expenses.

σύμ-μορος, ον, (σύν, μόρος) *contributing* or *rated along with* : οἱ ξύμμοροι *the confederate states* of Boeotia.

συμ-μορφίζω, = συμμορφόω. From

σύμ-μορφος, ον, (σύν, μορφή) *like-shaped, conformed to*. Hence

συμμορφόω, f. ώσω, *to form* or *fashion alike* :—Pass. *to be conformed to*.

συμ-μοχθέω, f. ήσω, *to share in toil with*.

συμ-μύω, f. ύσω [ῡ] : intrans. *to be shut up close, be closed*, of wounds; also of the eyelids and lips. II. trans. *to shut, close*.

συμπάθεια, ἡ, (συμπᾰθής) *fellow-feeling, sympathy*.

συμπᾰθέω, f. ήσω, *to feel with* or *together, to sympathise with* a person, *sympathise in* a thing. From

συμ-πᾰθής, ές, (σύν, παθεῖν) *of like feelings, sympathetic : sympathising with*.

συμπᾰθία, ἡ, poët. for συμπάθεια.

συμπᾰθῶς, Adv. of συμπαθής, *sympathetically*.

συμ-παιᾱνίζω, f. ίσω, *to raise the paean with* another : *to shout out together*.

συμ-παιδεύω, f. σω, *to teach together* :—Pass. *to be educated with* others.

συμ-παίζω, f. -παίξομαι, *to play* or *sport with* : absol. *to play together* : c. acc. cognato, συμπαίζειν ἑορτὴν μετά τινος *to keep* holiday *with*. Hence

συμπαίκτης, ου, ὁ, = συμπαιστής : fem. συμπαίκτρια.

συμ-παίκτωρ, ορος, ὁ, = συμπαιστής.

συμπαίσδεν, Dor. for συμπαίζειν.

συμ-παιστής, οῦ, ὁ, (συμπαίζω) *a playmate, playfellow* : fem. **συμπαίστρια**, ἡ.

συμ-παίστωρ, ορος, ὁ, = συμπαιστής.

συμ-παίω, f. -παιήσω : aor. 1 -έπαισα :—*to beat, strike, dash* one thing *against* another. II. intrans. *to dash* or *beat against*.

σύμπᾶν, τό, neut. of σύμπας, q. v.

συμ-παραβύω, f. ύσω [ῡ], *to cram in along with*.

συμ-παραγίγνομαι, Dep. *to come in* or *come to hand at the same time*. II. *to come in to assist*.

συμ-παραθέω, f. -θεύσομαι, *to run along with*.

συμ-παραινέω, f. έσω, *to exhort together* : *to join in recommending* or *approving*.

συμ-παρακαθίζω, f. ίσω, *to set beside with* another :—Med. *to set beside* or *with*.

συμ-παρακᾰλέω, f. έσω, *to call upon* or *exhort together* : *to invite at the same time*. II. *to ask for at the same time*.

συμ-παρακελεύομαι, Med. *to join in exciting*.

συμ-παρᾰκολουθέω, f. ήσω, *to follow along with* : *follow close, stick to*.

συμ-παρακομίζω, f. σω, *to conduct alongside together*; of ships, *to convoy along shore*.

συμ-παρακύπτω, f. ψω, *to bend oneself along with*.

συμ-παραλαμβάνω, f. -λήψομαι, *to take along with*.

συμ-παραμένω, *to stay along with* or *among*, c. dat.

συμ-παραμίγνυμι or -ύω, f. -μίξω, *to mix in together*.

συμ-παρανεύω, f. σω, *to nod assent, incline both ways*, of ambiguous oracles.

συμ-παρανήχομαι, f. -νήξομαι, Dep. *to swim beside together*.

συμ-παραπέμπω, f. ψω, *to escort along with* others.

συμ-παραπόλλυμι, f. -ολέσω, *to destroy along with*:—Pass. and Med., with pf. 2 -όλωλα, *to perish along with* or *besides*.

συμ-παρασκευάζω, f. σω, *to get ready* or *bring about along with* others: *to join in preparing* or *providing for*.

συμ-παραστᾰτέω, f. ήσω, *to stand by* one so *as to help* or *support*. From

συμπαραστάτης, ου, ὁ, (συμπαρίσταμαι) *one who stands by to aid, a joint helper* or *assistant*.

συμ-παρατάσσομαι Att. -ττομαι, Pass. *to be set in array with* others, *be drawn up in battle order along with*.

συμ-παρατηρέω, f. ήσω, *to watch alongside of* or *together*.

συμ-παρατρέφω, f. -θρέψω, *to feed* or *nurture along with*.

συμ-παραφέρω, f. -παροίσω, *to carry forth along with*:—Pass. *to rush forth* or *along with*.

συμ-παρεδρεύω, f. σω, *to sit beside* or *along with*.

συμ-πάρειμι, inf. παρεῖναι, (εἰμί *sum*) *to be present along with*: *to be present together* or *at the same time*.

συμ-πάρειμι, inf. παριέναι, (εἶμι *ibo*) *to go along at the same time*: *to go on together*.

συμ-παρεισέρχομαι, fut. -παρελεύσομαι: aor. 2 act. -παρῆλθον, pf. -παρελήλυθα: Dep.:—*to go* or *slip into along with*.

συμ-παρέπομαι, Dep. *to go along with, accompany*.

συμ-παρέχω, f. ξω, *to offer* or *present along with*.

συμ-παρίπταμαι, Dep. *to fly along with*.

συμ-παρίστημι, *to place together by the side of*:—Pass. and Med., with aor. 2 act. -παρέστην, pf. -παρέστηκα, *to stand beside so as to assist*.

συμ-παρομαρτέω, f. ήσω, *to follow together with, to accompany closely*.

συμ-παροξύνω, f. ὕνῶ, *to provoke together with*.

σύμ-πᾱς Ep. and Att. **ξύμ-πας**, -πᾶσα, -πᾶν: *all together, all at once, all in a body*: in sing. *the whole together*. II. τὸ σύμπαν *the whole together, the sum* of the matter:—τὸ σύμπαν also as Adv., *altogether, on the whole, in general*.

συμ-πάσχω, f. -πείσομαι, *to feel* or *be affected along with*: *to have a fellow-feeling, sympathise with*.

συμ-πᾰτάσσω, f. ξω, *to strike along with* or *together*.

συμ-πᾰτέω, f. ήσω, *to tread together, tread* clothes in washing. 2. *to trample under foot*.

συμ-πατριώτης, ου, ὁ, *a fellow-countryman*.

συμ-πεδάω, f. ήσω, *to bind together, bind hand and foot*; metaph. of frost, *to benumb, cramp*.

συμ-πείθω, f. σω, *to persuade along with* or *together*, *to join in persuading*:—Pass. *to be persuaded at the same time*.

σύμ-πειρος, ον, (σύν, πεῖρα) *acquainted with* a thing.

συμ-πέμπω, f. ψω, *to send* or *despatch along with* or *together*. 2. *to help in conducting*.

συμ-πενθέω, f. ήσω, trans. *to mourn for* or *bewail along with* others. II. intr. *to mourn together with*.

σύμ-πεντε, (σύν, πέντε) *five together, by fives*.

συμ-περαίνω, f. ᾰνῶ, *to finish along with* or *at the same time, to join in finishing*: *to secure* or *conclude firmly*:—in Logic, συμπεραίνεται *it is concluded, the conclusion is* so and so. II. Med. συμπεραίνομαι, *to join fully in* a thing *with*.

συμ-πέρθω, f. σω, *to destroy with, help to destroy*.

συμ-περιάγω, f. ξω, *to lead about along with* or *together*:—Med. *to lead about with oneself*.

συμ-περίειμι, inf. -ιέναι, (εἶμι *ibo*) *to go about along with*.

συμ-περιλαμβάνω, f. -λήψομαι, *to embrace* or *comprehend together with*: *to comprehend* in a treaty *with* others.

συμ-περινοστέω, f. ήσω, *to go to and fro, travel about with*.

συμ-περιφέρω, *to carry about with*. II. Pass. συμπεριφέρομαι, *to be carried round about with*: *to revolve with*. 2. *to have intercourse* or *associate with* one: *to accommodate* or *adapt oneself to*.

συμ-πέσσω Att. -ττω: fut. -πέψω:—*to help in cooking*: *to digest entirely*.

συμπέφρασμαι, pf. of συμφράζομαι.

συμπέφυρμαι, pf. pass. of συμφύρω.

συμ-πήγνυμι and -ύω: fut. -πήξω:—*to put together, frame, construct*. 2. *to make solid, congeal*. II. Pass., with pf. 2 act. συμπέπηγα, *to be compounded*. 2. *to congeal* or *become frozen together*. Hence

σύμ-πηκτος, ον, *joined together, framed, constructed*.

συμ-πιέζω, f. έσω, *to press* or *squeeze together, to grasp closely, squeeze hard*:—Pass. *to be squeezed up*.

συμ-πίνω [ῐ], f. -πίομαι: aor. 2 συνέπιον, inf. συμπιεῖν:—*to drink with* or *together, join in a drinking-bout with*.

συμ-πίπτω, f. -πεσοῦμαι: aor. 2 **συνέπεσον**: pf. συμπέπτωκα:—*to fall together, meet violently*, Lat. *concurrere*: *to meet in battle, to encounter, come to blows*. 2. generally, *to fall in with, meet with*. 3. of accidents, *to fall* or *light upon, happen to*. 4. absol. *to happen* or *fall out at the same time, concur*. 5. impers. συνέπιπτε, συνέπεσε *it happened, fell out, came to pass*. II. *to coincide, agree* or *be in accordance with*: absol. *to agree exactly*. III. *to fall together, fall in, collapse*, Lat. *concidere*; σῶμα συμπεσόν a frame *fallen away by sickness*.

συμ-πίτνω, poët. for συμπίπτω, *to fall together, dash together*. II. *to agree*.

συμπλἄκῆναι, aor. 2 pass. inf. of συμπλέκω.

σύμ-πλᾰνος, ον, (σύν, πλάνος) *wandering* or *roaming about together*.

συμπλάσας [ᾰ], aor. 1 part. of συμπλάσσω.

συμ-πλάσσω, f. -πλάσω [ᾰ]: aor. 1 συνέπλᾰσα:—*to mould* or *fashion together*, γαίης out of clay. II. metaph. *to fabricate together*.

συμ-πλᾰτᾰγέω, f. ήσω, *to clap together*.

σύμπλεκτος, ον, *twined together*, *interlaced*. From

συμ-πλέκω, f. ξω: aor. 1 συνέπλεξα: Pass., aor. 2 συνεπλάκην [ᾰ]: pf. συμπέπλεγμαι:—*to twine* or *plait together*: also *to twist*, *force together*. II. Pass. *to be twined together*, *plaited*: of persons wrestling, *to be locked together*, *to be engaged in a close struggle*: of a ship, *to be entangled* with her opponent: metaph. *to be entangled in*; ἴχνη συμπεπλεγμένα *a maze* of footsteps.

συμ-πλέω, f. -πλεύσομαι, *to sail*, *float*, *swim along with* or *together*.

συμ-πληγάς, άδος, fem. Adj. (συμπλήσσω) *striking* or *dashing together* II. Συμπληγάδες (sc. πέτραι), αἱ, *the clashing* or *jostling rocks*, the Κυάνεαι νῆσοι, *which were supposed to close* on all who sailed between them: also συνδρομάδες.

συμπλήγδην, Adv. (συμπλήσσω) *by beating* or *dashing together*

συμ-πληθύνω [ῡ], *to multiply together*.

συμ-πληθύω, *to help to fill*, *swell*, *increase*.

συμ-πληρόω, f. ώσω, *to help to fill*, *fill completely*: of ships, *to man with a full complement*.

συμπλοκή, ῆς, ἡ, (συμπλέκω) *an intertwining* II. *a close struggle*.

σύμπλοκος, ον, (συμπλέκω) *entwined*, *interwoven*.

σύμπλοος, ον contr. -πλους, ουν: (συμπλέω):—*sailing with* one *on board ship*:—as Subst., ξύμπλους, ὁ, *a shipmate*: metaph. *a partner* or *comrade in* a thing.

συμ-πλώω, Ep. and Ion. for συμπλέω.

συμ-πνέω, f. -πνεύσομαι, *to blow* or *breathe together*. II. metaph. *to agree with*, Lat. *conspirare*; συμπνεῖν ἐμπαίοις τύχαις *to blow with*, i.e. *be carried along with*, sudden blasts.

συμ-πνίγω [ῑ], f. -πνιξοῦμαι, *to throttle*: *to choke up*.

συμ-ποδίζω, f. ίσω Att. ιῶ, *to tie the feet together*, *bind hand and foot*: metaph. *to entangle*, *involve*.

συμ-ποιέω, f. ήσω, *to help in doing*.

συμ-ποιμαίνομαι, Pass. (σύν, ποιμαίνω) *to feed together*: *to herd together*.

συμ-πολεμέω, f. ήσω, *to take part in a war with*.

συμ-πολιορκέω, f. ήσω, *to join in besieging*, *besiege jointly*.

συμπολῑτεύω, f. σω, *to be a fellow-citizen*, *be a member of the same state*: so also in Med. συμπολιτεύομαι; οἱ συμπολιτευόμενοι *one's fellow-citizens*. From

συμ-πολίτης [ῑ], ου, ὁ, *a fellow-citizen*, Lat. *concivis*.

συμ-πομπεύω, f. σω, *to accompany in a procession*.

συμ-πονέω, f. ήσω, *to work with* or *together*, *to help*, or *relieve in work*.

συμ-πονηρεύομαι, Dep. *to join in villany*, *play the knave together*.

συμ-πορεύομαι, fut. med. -πορεύσομαι: aor 1 pass. συνεπορεύθην: Dep.:—*to go* or *journey together*.

συμ-πορθέω, f. ήσω, like συμπέρθω, *to help to demolish* or *lay waste*.

συμ-πορίζω. f. ίσω, *to help in procuring* or *providing*.

συμποσία, ἡ, (συμπίνω) *a drinking together*.

συμποσί-αρχος, ὁ, (συμπόσιον, ἄρχω) *the president of a drinking-party*, *toastmaster*, Lat. *magister bibendi*.

συμπόσιον, τό, (συμπίνω) *a drinking-party*, *entertainment*, Lat. *convivium*.

συμπότης, ου, ὁ, (συμπίνω) *a fellow-drinker*, *boon-companion*. Hence

συμποτικός, ή, όν, *of* or *suited for a* συμπόσιον or *drinking-party*, *convivial*:—as Subst., συμποτικός, ὁ, *a jolly fellow*.

συμ-πράκτωρ Ion. -πρήκτωρ, ορος, ὁ, *a helper*, *assistant*; συμπρακτὼρ ὁδοῦ *a fellow-wayfarer*. From

συμ-πράσσω Att. -ττω Ion. συμπρήσσω: fut. ξω: aor. 1 συνέπραξα:—*to do with* another, *to help in doing*: *to act with*, *assist*. 2. *to be in the interest of* another, *side with* another. II. Med. συμπράσσομαι, *to help in exacting a debt*.

συμ-πρεπής, ές, (σύν, πρέπω) *beseeming*, *befitting*.

συμπρεσβευτής, οῦ, ὁ, *a fellow-ambassador*. From

συμ-πρεσβεύω, *to be a fellow-ambassador*, *be associated with on an embassy*:—Med. *to join in sending an embassy*.

σύμ-πρεσβυς, εως, ὁ, *a joint-ambassador*.

συμ-πρεσβύτερος, ὁ, *a fellow-presbyter* or *elder*.

συμ-πρήκτωρ, ορος, ὁ, Ion. for συμπράκτωρ.

συμ-πρήσσω, Ion. for συμπράσσω.

συμ-πρίασθαι, aor. 2 inf. of συνωνέομαι (no pres. συμ-πρίαμαι in use), *to buy together*, *buy up*.

συμ-προθῡμέομαι: f. med. -ήσομαι: aor. 1 pass. -προὐθυμήθην: Dep.:—*to join zealously in promoting*, *to have equal zeal* for a thing: absol. *to share one's eagerness*.

συμ-προξενέω, f. ησω, *to help in furnishing with means*.

συμ-προπέμπω, f. ψω, *to escort together*, *join in escorting*.

σύμπτυκτος, ον, *folded together*, *fitted together*. From

συμ-πτύσσω, f. ξω, *to fold together*, *fold up and lay by*.

συμπτωθέν, aor. 1 pass. part. neut. of συμπίπτω.

σύμπτωμα, ατος, τό, (συμπίπτω) *anything that has befallen one*, *a chance*, *mischance*, *calamity*.

σύμ-πυκνος, ον, (σύν, πυκνός) *compressed*.

συμ-πυνθάνομαι, Dep. *to ascertain along with*.

συμ-πῡρόω, f. ώσω, *to burn up* or *consume along with* or *together*.

συμ-φᾰγεῖν, aor. 2 inf. of συν-εσθίω.

σύμφερον, τό, see συμφέρω II. 3. Hence

συμφερόντως, Adv. *profitably*, *with expediency*.

συμφερτός, ή, όν, (συμφέρω) *brought together, united, banded.*

συμ-**φέρω**, f. συνοίσω: aor. 1 συνήνεγκα Ion. -ήνεικα: aor. 2 συνήνεγκον: pf. συνενήνοχα: (cf. φέρω):—*to bring together, gather, collect: to contribute.* 2. *to match together.* 3. *to bear along with* or *jointly, help to bear; συμφέρειν κακά to bear* evils *with* others: hence *to bear with, excuse.* II. intr. *to be useful* or *profitable, conduce to one's advantage.* 2. impers. συμφέρει, *it is of use, profitable expedient.* 3. part. συμφέρων, ουσα, ον, *useful, expedient:* neut. συμφέρων, οντος, τό, *that which is useful, an advantage, expediency.* 4. *to agree with: to assist: to come to terms with, give way to.* 5. of events, *to happen, take place, turn out.* III. Pass. συμφέρομαι, fut. med. συνοίσομαι: aor. 1 pass. συνηνέχθην Ion. συνηνείχθην: pf. συνήνεγμαι:—*to come together, meet* in hostile sense, *to meet in battle, engage,* Lat. *congredi.* 2. *to agree together, agree with, allow, assent to: to bear with.* 3. generally, *to be acquainted, versed in.* 4. of events, *to happen, turn out:* also impers., *it happens, falls out;* οὐδὲν σφι χρηστὸν συνεφέρετο no good *came of it* to them.

συμ-**φεύγω**, f. -φεύξομαι, *to flee along with: to be banished* or *be in exile along with.*

σύμ-**φημι**, *to assent, say yes to, approve fully: to agree with,* τινί: c. inf. *to agree* that ...

συμ-**φθέγγομαι**, f. -ξομαι, Dep. *to accord with.*

συμ-**φθείρω**, *to destroy along with* or *entirely.*

συμ-**φθίνω** [ῐ], *to perish along with:* so in aor. 2 pass. συνεφθῐτο.

σύμ-**φθογγος**, ον, *sounding together.*

συμ-**φῐλέω**, f. ήσω, *to love mutually, join in loving.*

συμ-**φῐλονεικέω**, f. ήσω, *to be emulous along with: to take zealous interest in.*

συμ-**φλέγω**, f. ξω, *to set on fire together, burn to ashes.*

συμ-**φιλοσοφέω**, f. ήσω, *to join in philosophic study.*

συμ-**φιλοτῑμέομαι**, f. -ήσομαι, Dep. *to join in emulous efforts.*

συμ-**φοβέω**, f. ήσω, *to frighten along with:*—Pass. *to be afraid at the same time.*

συμ-**φοιτάω** Ion. -έω: fut. ήσω:—*to go regularly* to a place *together: to go to school together.* Hence

συμφοίτησις, ή, *a going to school together.* And

συμφοιτητής, οῦ, ὁ, *a schoolfellow.*

συμ-**φονεύω**, f. σω, *to kill along with* or *together.*

συμφορά Ion. -ρή, ή, (συμφέρω) *a bringing together.* II. *an event, circumstance, chance,* either in good or bad sense, but commonly the latter, *a mishap, mischance, misfortune, disaster, calamity:* but also *good luck, a piece of good fortune.*

συμφορεύς, ὁ, (συμφέρω) a Lacedaemonian officer, *a kind of aide-de-camp.*

συμ-**φορέω**, f. ήσω, *to bring together, gather, heap up.*

συμφόρησις, εως, ή, (συμφορέω) *a bringing together.*

συμφορητός, ή, όν, (συμφορέω) *brought together, promiscuous.*

σύμφορος, ον, (συμφέρω) *happening with, accompanying.* II. *useful, profitable, expedient: suitable, proper, convenient.* Hence

συμφόρως, Adv. *profitably:* συμφόρως ἔχειν to be *expedient:* Comp. συμφορώτερον; Sup. -ώτατα.

συμφράδμων, ονος, ὁ, ή, *giving good counsel:* as Subst. *a counsellor.* From

συμ-**φράζομαι**, f. -άσομαι: aor. 1 συνεφρᾰσάμην, Ep. 3 sing. συμφράσσατο: pf. pass. συμπέφρασμαι: Dep.:—*to take counsel with: to debate, consider, contrive together.*

συμ-**φράσσω** Att. -ττω: f. ξω: aor. 1 συνέφραξα: *to press* or *pack closely together.* II. *to force into an enclosed space.*

συμ-**φροντίζω**, f. ίσω, *to have a joint care for.*

σύμ-**φρουρος**, ον, (σύν, φρουρά) *keeping ward together;* μέλαθρον ξύμφρουρον ἐμοί the chamber *that keeps watch with me,* i.e. *in which I lie without sleeping.*

σύμ-**φρων**, ονος, ὁ, ή, (σύν, φρήν) *of one mind, agreeing, brotherly: favouring, propitious.*

συμ-**φῠγάς**, άδος, ὁ, ή, (σύν, φυγή) *a fellow-exile.*

συμφυείς, aor. 2 pass. part. of συμφύω.

συμ-**φυής**, ές, (συμ-φύομαι) *growing together, attached to, congenital.*

συμ-**φύλαξ**, ᾰκος, ὁ, *a fellow-watchman, warder,* or *guard.* [ῠ]

συμ-**φῠλάσσω**, f. ξω, *to keep guard along with* or *together.* 2. c. acc. *to guard together.*

συμ-**φῠλέτης**, ου, ὁ, *of* or *from the same tribe,* Lat. *contribŭlis:* generally, *a countryman.*

σύμ-**φῡλος**, ον, (σύν, φυλή) *of the same tribe* or *race:* οἱ σύμφυλοι *his congeners.*

σύμφυρτος, ον, *kneaded* or *mixed together:* metaph. *confounded, confused.* From

συμ-**φύρω** [ῡ]: pf. pass. συμπέφυρμαι:—*to knead* or *mix together, to blend, combine:* metaph. *to confound, confuse.*

συμ-**φῡσάω**, f. ησω, *to blow together, make up,* Lat. *conflare.* II. metaph. *to agree exactly, harmonise.*

συμ-**φῠτεύω**, f. σω, *to plant in together:* metaph. *to contrive* or *concoct with.*

σύμφῠτος, ον, (συμφύω) *planted together with, congenital, innate, inborn;* σύμφυτος αἰών one's *natural* age; ἐς τὸ σύμφυτον according to *one's nature.*

συμ-**φύω**, f. ύσω: aor. 1 συνέφῡσα:—*to make to grow together.* II. Pass., with act. pf. συμπέφῡκα, aor. 2 συνέφῡν, aor. 2 pass. part. συμφυείς:—*to grow together, to grow into one.*

συμ-**φωνέω**, f. ήσω, *to agree in sound, be in harmony* or *unison.* II. generally, *to agree with, to make an agreement* or *engagement with.* Hence

συμφώνησις, ή, *an agreeing in sound, agreement.*

συμφωνία, ή, (σύμφωνος) *an agreeing in sound, harmony.* II. *symphony* or *unison of voices* or *instruments in concord.*

σύμ-**φωνος**, ον, (σύν, φωνή) *agreeing in sound, harmonious:* as Subst. *a musician.* II. metaph. *in unison* or *concert with, friendly.*

συμ-**ψαύω**, f. σω, *to touch one another.*

συμ-ψάω, inf. -ψῆν: f. -ψήσω: aor. 1 συνέψησα:—*to scrape together, to wipe out, sweep away*, as a torrent.

συμ-ψηφίζω, f. ίσω Att. ιῶ, *to reckon together, count up, compute.* II. Med. *to vote with.*

σύμ-ψηφος, ον, *voting with* another.

σύμ-ψῡχος, ον, (σύν, ψυχή) *of one mind, unanimous.*

ΣΥ'Ν old Att. ξύν, Prep. with dat., Lat. *cum:*—*along with, in company with, together with.* 2. with collat. notion of help, σὺν θεῷ *with* God's *help*, (the God being conceived *as standing with* or *by* one); σύν τινι εἶναι to be *with* another, *on* his *side.* 3. *furnished with, endued with;* σὺν ὅπλοις *with* arms. 4. *in connexion, conjunction with;* σὺν τῷ σῷ ἀγαθῷ *with* advantage to you; σὺν τοῖς νόμοις *in accordance with* the laws. 5. more rarely of the instrument or means *with* or *by* which a thing is done, *with, by means of;* σὺν νεφέεσσι κάλυψεν γαῖαν καὶ πόντον he covered earth and sea *with* clouds.

σύν as Adv., *together, at once, jointly.* 2. *besides, moreover, furthermore, too.*

συν- in Compos., *with, along with, together, at the same time.* With a transit. Verb it may mean two things, e. g. σύν in συγ-κτείνειν may mean *to kill one person as well as others*, or *to join with others in killing.* 2. of the completion of an action, *quite, thoroughly, completely.* 3. with numerals it has a separate force, σύνδυο two and two *together, by twos.* II. συν-, before β, μ, π, φ, ψ, changes into συμ-; before γ, κ, ξ, χ, into συγ-; before λ, into συλ-; before σ into συσ-

σῦν, acc. of σῦς.

συνᾰγᾰγεῖν, aor. 2 act. inf. of συνάγω.

συνάγᾰγον, Dor. for συνήγαγον, aor. 2 of συνάγω.

συν-άγγελος, ὁ, *a fellow-messenger.*

συν-ᾰγείρω: f. -αγερῶ: aor. 1 συνήγειρα Ep. ξυνάγειρα: Pass., aor. 1 συνηγέρθην, Ep. 3 pl. συνάγερθεν: *to gather* persons *together, assemble* or *collect* them: Med. and Pass. *to gather themselves together* or *be gathered together, to come together, assemble;* συναγρόμενοι, Ep. aor. 2 pass part., *those assembled.* II. *to collect* things: and in Med. *to collect for oneself.* III. συναγείρειν ἑαυτόν *to collect oneself:* Pass. *to recover one's strength, rally.*

συν-αγῑνέω, f. ήσω, *to bring together, to collect.*

συν-αγκεία, ἡ, (σύν, ἄγκος) = μισγαγκεία.

συν-άγνῡμι, f. -άξω: aor. 1 συνέαξα:—*to break together, break in pieces, shiver.*

συν-ᾰγορεύω, f. σω, *to speak with* another, *join in advising* or *recommending: to agree to, concur in.* II. *to speak with* or *in behalf of* a person, *support, advocate* his *cause.*

συν-αγρεύω, (σύν, ἄγρα) *to join in the chace.*

συναγρόμενος, Ep. aor. 2 pass. part. of συναγείρω.

συν-άγω, f. -άξω: aor. 1 σύνηξα: aor. 2 συνήγᾰγον: Att. pf. συνῆχα, later συναγήοχα: pf. pass. σύνηγμαι:—*to lead* or *bring together, to gather together, assemble;* συνάγειν Ἄρηα, πόλεμον *to join* battle: also *to set to fight, match one against the other:* also intr. *to engage.* II. *to bring together, unite, combine;* συνάγειν γάμους *to contract* a marriage. 2. metaph. *to bring together, reconcile.* III. *to draw together, straiten, narrow, contract.* IV. *to gather* from premises, *collect, infer.* Hence

συνᾰγωγεύς, έως, ὁ, *one who brings together, a uniter.*

συνᾰγωγή, ἡ, (συνάγω) *a bringing together, a gathering, uniting, collecting;* συναγωγὴ πολέμου *a levying war.* 2. *a place of meeting* or *assembling:* among the Jews after the captivity, *a synagogue.* II. *a drawing together, contracting.*

συν-ᾰγωνίζομαι, f. -ίσομαι Att. -ιοῦμαι: Dep.:—*to contend along with, to share* or *take part in a contest: to help in a contest.* Hence

συνᾰγωνιστής, οῦ, ὁ, *one who contends along with, a fellow-combatant:* generally, *an assistant.*

συν-άδελφος, ον, *one that has a brother* or *sister.*

συν-ᾰδῐκέω, f. ήσω, *to join in doing wrong* or *injury.*

συν-ᾴδω Ion. **συν-αείδω**: f. -ᾴσομαι:—*to sing with* or *together, to accompany in a song.* 2. generally, *to accord with, agree with.* II. c. acc. *to sing of* or *celebrate together.*

συν-αείρω, aor. 1 -ήειρα, poët. form of συναίρω. II. *to yoke together:* Med. *to yoke together for oneself.*

συν-αέξω, poët. for συναύξω.

συν-αθλέω, f. ήσω, *to contend along with, share* or *take part in a contest.*

συν-ᾰθροίζω, f. σω, *to gather together, assemble.*

συν-ᾱΐγδην, Adv. (σύν, ἀΐσσω) *pressing violently together.*

σύν-αιμος, ον, (σύν, αἷμα) *of common blood, kindred;* νεῖκος ξύναιμον *strife between kinsmen;* Ζεὺς ξύναιμος Jove *the protector of kin:*—as Subst., σύναιμος, ὁ, ἡ, *a kinsman* or *kinswoman, a brother* or *sister.*

συναίμων, ονος, ὁ, ἡ, = σύναιμος.

συν-αινέω, f. έσω, *to join in praising* or *approving: to agree* or *come to terms with* a person. II. *to agree to* a thing, *grant* it *at once.*

συν-αίνῠμαι, defect. Dep. *to take hold of together, to gather up:* Ep. 3 sing. impf. συναίνῠτο.

συν-αιρέω, fut. ήσω: fut. 2 συνελῶ: aor. 2 συνεῖλον Ep. σύνελον, part. συνελών: (cf. αἱρέω):—*to grasp* or *seize together, seize at once* 2. *to bring into small compass, comprise, comprehend;* hence, ξυνελὼν λέγω I say *briefly.* II. *to help to conquer* or *subdue:* metaph. *to cut short, make an end of, destroy.*

συν-αίρω poët. **συναείρω** (q. v.), *to raise, lift,* or *take up together;* συναίρειν λόγον *to cast up* accounts. II. Med. *to take part in* a thing, c. gen. rei: *to help bear* or *support, undertake jointly.* III. Pass. *to be joined, knitted together.*

συν-αισθάνομαι, f. -αισθήσομαι, *to perceive* or *feel together.*

συν-αίτιος, ον, also α, ον, (σύν, αἰτία) *being the joint cause of* a thing, *helping towards: sharing in the guilt, accessory to:*—as Subst., συναίτιος, ὁ, ἡ, *an accomplice,* τινός *in* a thing.

συν-αιχμάζω, f. άσω, *to fight along with.*

συν-αιχμάλωτος, ον, *a fellow-prisoner.*

συν-αιωρέομαι, Pass. *to be held in suspense with.*

συν-ακμάζω, f. σω, *to blossom* or *flourish together.*

συν-ακολασταίνω, *to live dissolutely together.*

συν-ἄκολουθέω, f. ήσω, *to follow along with* or *closely: to follow an argument, understand.*

συν-ἄκοντίζω, f. ίσω, *to throw a javelin together* or *at the same time.*

συν-ἄκούω, f. -ακούσομαι, *to hear along with* or *at the same time.* 2. *to hear one another.*

συνακτέον, verb. Adj. of συνάγω, *one must bring together.*

συνακτικός, ή, όν, (συνάγω) *able to bring together: τὸ συνακτικόν power of accumulation* in oratory.

συν-ἄλἄλάζω, f. άσω, *to cry aloud with.*

συν-αλγέω, f. ήσω, *to share in suffering* or *grieving for.* II. *to feel with, sympathise in:* absol. *to share in sorrow.*

συν-αλγηδών, όνος, ἡ, *joint pain* or *grief:*—in plur. = αἱ συναλγοῦσαι, *partners in grief.*

συν-αλείφω, f. ψω, *to smear together, daub over: to help to anoint.*

συν-ᾱλιάζω, f. ξω, (σύν, ἁλία) = συναλίζω.

συν-ᾱλίζω, f. ίσω: aor. 1 Ion. συνάλισα: *to gather together, collect, assemble:*—Pass. *to come together, meet.*

συναλλἄγή, ἡ, (συναλλάσσω) *an interchange; λόγων ξυναλλαγαί interchange* of words: absol. *a making up of strife, reconciliation;* pl. ξυναλλαγαί, *a treaty of peace.* 2. *commerce, intercourse.* II. *intervention, interference, interposition; νόσου ξυναλλαγῇ by the intervention* of disease. 2. *a contingency, result.*

συνάλλαγμα, ατος, τό, (συναλλάσσω) *a mutual agreement, covenant, contract.*

συν-αλλάσσω Att. -ττω: f. ξω: aor. 1 συνήλλαξα: —Pass., aor. 1 συνηλλάχθην: pf. συνήλλαγμαι:—*to interchange with: to exchange.* 2. intr. *to deal, associate, have intercourse with.* II. *to bring into association* or *union with: to reconcile:*—Pass. and Med. *to be reconciled with, come to terms: make a league* or *alliance with: make peace.*

συν-ᾰλοάω poët. -ᾰλοιάω: f. ήσω: aor. 1 συνηλοίησα:—*to thresh with* or *together: to dash to pieces, smash.*

συν-ᾰμᾰ, Adv. for σὺν ἅμα, *together.*

συν-ᾰμιλλάομαι, f. med, ήσομαι: aor. 1 pass. -ημιλλήθην: Dep.:—*to race* or *contend together.*

συν-αμπέχω: fut. -αμφέξω: aor. 2 -ήμπεσχον, inf. -αμπισχεῖν:—*to cover up entirely, wrap closely:* metaph. *to shroud.*

συν-αμπίσχω, = συναμπέχω.

συν-αμφότερος, α, ον, *both together:* used both in sing. and plur.

συν-αναβαίνω: f. -αναβήσομαι: aor. 2 -ανέβην:—*to go up along with* or *together,* esp. of *going up* into central Asia from the coast.

συν-αναβοάω, f. -βοήσομαι, *to cry out together.*

συν-ᾰναγκάζω, f. άσω, *to compel* or *constrain at the same time,* c. inf.:—Pass. *to be compelled at the same time.* II. *to extort by force.*

συν-ανάγω, f. ξω, *to carry up along with:*—Pass. *to go to sea together.*

συν-αναδίδωμι, *to give up along with* or *together.*

συν-αναιρέω, f. ήσω, *to take away* or *destroy along with* or *together.* II. *to give the same answer.*

συν-ανακεῖμαι, Pass. *to recline together at table.*

συν-ανακλίνομαι, Pass. *to lie down along with, to recline along with at table.* [ῑ]

συν-ᾰνᾱλίσκω, f. -ανᾱλώσω, *to spend* or *waste along with.* II. *to help by furnishing money.*

συν-αναμίγνῡμι, f. -αναμίξω, *to mix up with at the same time:*—Med. and Pass. *to associate with.*

συν-αναπαύομαι, Pass. *to take rest together, to refresh oneself* or *receive comfort together with.*

συν-αναπείθω, f. σω, *to join in persuading.*

συν-αναπέμπω, f. ψω, *to send up together.*

συν-αναπλέκω, f. ξω, *to entwine together.*

συν-αναπράσσω Att. -ττω, f. ξω, *to join in exacting payment.*

συν-αναρριπτέω, f. ήσω, *to throw up together.*

συν-ανάσσω, *to rule as king with* another.

συν-αναστρέφω, f. ψω, *to turn back together:*—Pass. *to live along with* or *among.*

συν-ανατήκω, f. ξω, *to melt with* or *together.*

συν-ανατρέχω, f. -θρέξω, *to run up along with.*

συν-ανατίθημι, f. -θήσω, *to set up along with.*

συν-αναφθέγγομαι, Dep. *to cry out together.*

συν-αναφύρω [φῡ], *to knead* or *mix up together:*—Pass. and Med. *to have constant intercourse with, to associate constantly with.*

συν-αναχρέμπτομαι, Dep. *to cough up together.*

συν-ανίστημι, *to make to stand up* or *rise together.* II. Pass., with act. aor. 2 -ανέστην, pf. -ανέστηκα, *to rise at once* or *together.* 2. *to help in setting up again* or *restoring.*

συν-αντάω Ion. -έω: f. ήσω: aor. 1 -ήντησα:—*to meet face to face:* generally, *to meet together, assemble.* II. *to meet with.* III. of things, *to happen to one.* Hence

συν-άντησις, ἡ, *a meeting.*

συναντήτην, 3 dual Ep. impf. of συναντάω.

συν-αντιάζω, f. άσω, = συναντάω, *to encounter.*

συναντιλάβηται [ᾰ], 3 sing. aor. 2 subj. of

συν-αντιλαμβάνομαι, Dep. *to lay hold of along with: to take part with, help.*

συν-αντλέω, f. ήσω, *to drain along with* or *together;* συναντλεῖν πόνους τινί *to join* him *in bearing all* his sufferings, Lat. *una exhaurire labores.*

συν-άντομαι, Dep., used only in pres. and impf., = συναντάω, *to come to meet, fall in with:* also *to engage in battle.*

συν-ᾰνύτω [ῠ], *to come to an end together with.*

συν-αξιόω, f. ώσω, *to join in thinking fit:* generally, *to approve, allow.*

συν-ᾰοιδός, όν, = συνῳδός.

συν-άορος, ον, Dor. for συνήορος.

συν-απάγω, f. ξω, *to lead away with* :—Pass. *to be led away together with* or *besides*.

συν-άπᾱς, ᾱσα, ᾰν, like σύμπας, *all together, the whole together*.

συν-άπειμι, inf. -απιέναι, (εἶμι *ibo*) *to go away together*.

συν-απεργάζομαι, f. άσομαι, Dep. *to help in finishing*.

συν-απίσταμαι, Ion. for συναφίσταμαι.

συν-αποβαίνω, f. -βήσομαι, *to go away along with* or *together: to disembark along with*.

συν-αποδιδράσκω, f. -δράσομαι [ᾱ]: aor. 2 -απέδραν :—*to run away* or *escape along with*.

συν-αποδοκῐμάζω, f. σω, *to join in reprobating* or *disapproving*.

συναποθᾰνεῖν, aor. 2 inf. of συναποθνήσκω.

συν-αποθνήσκω, f. -αποθᾰνοῦμαι: aor. 2 -απέθᾰνον :—*to die together with*.

συν-αποικίζω, f. ίσω, *to go as colonists together*.

συν-αποκάμνω, *to be tired* or *worn out together*.

συν-αποκτείνω, *to kill along with* or *together*.

συν-απολαμβάνω, f. -λήψομαι :—*to receive from* another *with* or *together: to take* or *receive in common*.

συν-απολάμπω, f. ψω, *to shine forth together*.

συν-απόλλῡμι, fut. -απολῶ :—*to destroy with* or *together*; συναπολλύναι τοὺς φίλους *to involve* one's friends *in one's own ruin* :—Pass., with pf. 2 -απόλωλα, *to perish along with* or *together*.

συν-απολογέομαι, f. ήσομαι, Dep. *to join* or *help in defending*.

συν-απομᾰραίνω, *to make to wither away together* :—Pass. *to fade away* or *wither together*.

συν-απονεύω, f. σω, *to swerve away from a blow together*.

συν-αποπέμπω, f. ψω, *to send away together*.

συν-αποῤῥήγνυμι, f. -ρήξω, *to break off together*.

συν-αποστέλλω, *to send off* or *despatch together with*.

συν-αποστερέω, f. ήσω, *to help to strip* or *cheat, join in robbing*.

συν-αποφαίνομαι, Med. *to declare together*.

συν-αποφέρω, *to carry off along with* or *together*.

συναπτός, ή, όν, also ός, όν, verb. Adj. *joined together, fastened, tied: continuous*. From

συν-άπτω, f. -άψω: aor. 1 συνῆψα: Pass., pf. συνῆμμαι :—*to tie* or *join together, unite*; συνάπτειν πόδα to meet; συνάπτειν βλέφαρα *to close* the eyes; συνάπτειν στόμα *to join* lips, to kiss; συνάπτειν μηχανήν *to frame, concert* a plan; ξυνάπτειν τινὶ κακά *to fasten* evil *upon* him. II. *to make* persons *engage* or *encounter, bring into action*; συνάπτειν μάχην *to join* battle. 2. in friendly sense, *to join, attach oneself to* a person; συνάπτειν ἑαυτὸν ἐς λόγους τινί to enter into conversation with a person; so συνάπτειν μῦθον, etc.; also συνάπτειν λόγοισι or εἰς λόγους τινί (sub. ἑαυτόν); συνάπτειν γάμους *to form an alliance by* marriage. III. intrans., of lands, *to border on, lie next to: to be joined to*. 2. of Time, *to be nigh at hand*. IV. Med. *to reach, attain to: to take part with, contribute towards*.

συνᾶραι, aor. 1 inf. of συναίρω.

συν-ᾰρᾰρίσκω, *to join together*. II. intr. in pf. συνάρηρα Att. συνάρᾱρα, *to be well fitted, suit well together*.

συν-ᾰράσσω Att. -ττω, f. ξω, *to dash together: to dash in pieces, crush, destroy* :—Pass. *to be dashed in pieces*; but, συναράσσεσθαι κεφαλάς *to get their* heads *broken*.

συν-ᾰρέσκω, f. -ᾰρέσω :—*to please* or *satisfy together*. II. impers., like Lat. *placet*, συναρέσκει μοι I *am content also*, c. inf.

συνάρηρε, 3 sing. pf. 2 of συναραρίσκω.

σύν-αρθρος, ον, (σύν, ἄρθρον) *linked together: in accordance with*.

συναριθμέω, f. ήσω, *to count along with*.

συν-άριθμος [ᾰ], ον, (σύν, ἀριθμός) *included in a number*. II. *of like* or *equal number*.

συν-ᾱριστάω, f. ήσω, (σύν, ἄριστον) *to take breakfast* or *luncheon with*.

συν-ᾰριστεύω, f. σω, *to do feats of bravery together*.

συν-άριστος, ον, (σύν, ἄριστον) *breakfasting with*. [ᾱ]

συν-αρμόζω Att. -ττω: f. όσω Dor. όξω: Pass., aor. 1 συν-ηρμόσθην: pf. -ήρμοσμαι :—*to fit together, close, join exactly*; συναρμόζειν βλέφαρα *to close* the eyelids; εὐχερείᾳ συναρμόσαι βροτούς *to adapt* mortals to recklessness. 2. *to join together, unite*, 3. *to put together, compact, construct*. II. intr. *to agree together, fit, suit*.

συν-αρμολογέω, f. ήσω, *to frame accurately together*.

συναρμοστής, οῦ, ὁ, (συναρμόζω) *one who joins together*; συναρμοστὴς πολιτείας *a remodeller of* a state.

συν-αρμόττω, Att. for συναρμόζω.

συν-αρπάζω, fut. άσω or άσομαι: aor. 1 συνήρπασα :—*to carry off* or *away with* one :—Pass. *to be seized and carried off*. 2. *to hold fast together* :—Med. aor. 1 ξυναρπάσασθαι, of a wrestler, *to seize and hold one fast*. 3. metaph. *to seize* with the mind, *catch at*.

συν-αρτάω, f. ήσω: aor. 1 συνήρτησα :—*to hang up with: to fasten on along with, knit together* :—Pass. *to be closely engaged* or *entangled with*.

συν-άρχω, f. ξω, *to rule jointly with: to be a colleague in office*; ὁ συνάρχων *a colleague*.

συν-ᾰρωγός, όν, *a joint-helper*.

συν-ᾰσεβέω, f. ήσω, *to join in impiety*.

συν-ασκέω, f. ήσω, *to practise together, join in practising*.

συν-ᾰσοφέω, f. ήσω, (σύν, ἄσοφος) *to be unwise* or *foolish along with*.

συν-ασπῐδόω, f. ώσω, (σύν, ἀσπίς) *to keep the shields locked close together*.

συν-ασπίζω: fut. ίσω Att. ιῶ: (σύν, ἀσπίς) :—*to hold the shields together*: generally, *to fight together, be comrades*; συνασπίζειν τινί *to be* his *messmate*.

συν-ασπιστής, οῦ, ὁ, *a fellow-soldier, comrade*.

συν-ασχᾰλάω, *to feel joint indignation at* a thing.

συν-ατυχέω, f. ήσω, *to be unlucky with* or *together, to share* a person's *ill luck.*

συν-αυαίνω, f. ἀνῶ, *to dry quite up:* Pass. *to wither away.*

συν-αυδάω, f. ήσω, *to speak together: to agree, confess, allow.*

συν-αυλέω, f. ήσω, *to accompany on the flute.* Hence **συναυλία**, ἡ, *a playing on the flute together, a concert;* ξυναυλίαν κλάειν Οὐλύμπου νόμον to sob one of Olympus' pieces *in concert.* 2. *any concert, agreement, fellowship.*

συν-αυλίζομαι, f. med. ίσομαι: aor. 1 pass. συνηυλίσθην: Dep.:—*to lodge, dwell together, take up one's abode with.*

σύν-αυλος, ον, (σύν, αὐλός) *playing the flute together: in concord* or *union with, harmonious:* metaph. *agreeing with, in harmony with.*

σύν-αυλος, ον, (σύν, αὐλή) *dwelling together* or *with;* σ. μανίᾳ *associated with* madness, i. e. mad.

συν-αυξάνω and **συν-αύξω**, f. -αυξήσω, *to increase, enlarge, augment with* or *together:*—Pass. *to increase* or *grow with, grow larger together.*

συν-αφαιρέω, f. ήσω, *to take away together:*—Med. *to assist in rescuing.*

συν-αφίστημι, *to make to revolt together, draw into a revolt.* II. Pass., with act. aor. 2 -έστην pf. -έστηκα, *to fall off* or *revolt along with.*

συναχθῆναι, aor. 1 inf. of συνάγω.

συν-άχθομαι: fut. med. -αχθέσομαι Att. -αχθήσομαι: aor. 1 pass. -ηχθέσθην: Dep.:—*to be troubled* or *grieved along with* or *together, to mourn with.*

συν-δαΐζω, f. ξω, *to kill together with another.*

συν-δαίνυμι, f. -δαίσω, *to feast along with* or *together;* συνδαῖσαι γάμους τινί *to share* a marriage *feast with* one. Hence

συνδαίτωρ, ορος, ὁ, *a companion at table, messmate.*

συν-δάκνω, f. -δήξομαι, *to bite* or *champ together, hold fast between the teeth.*

συν-δακρύω, f. ύσω [ῡ], *to weep with* or *together.*

συν-δειπνέω, f. ήσω, *to dine* or *sup with: to dine* or *eat together.*

σύν-δειπνον, τό, *a common meal* or *banquet.*

σύν-δειπνος, ον, (σύν, δεῖπνον) *dining together:* as Subst., σύνδειπνος, ὁ, *a companion at table,* Lat. *conviva.*

συν-δεκάζω, f. άσω, *to bribe in a lump, to bribe all together.*

συν-δέομαι, fut. med. -δεήσομαι: aor. 1 pass. -εδεήθην: Dep.:—*to beg along with, to join in begging.*

σύν-δεσμος, ὁ, irreg. plur. σύνδεσμα, τά:—*that which binds together, a band, bond: a cramp.* 2. in Surgery, *a ligament.* 3. in Grammar, *a conjunction: a particle.*

συν-δεσμώτης, ου, ὁ, *a fellow-prisoner.*

συν-δετός, όν, (συνδέω) *bound together, bound hand and foot,* Lat. *constrictus.* II. as Subst., σύνδετον, τό, *a band, bond.*

συν-δέω, f. -δήσω, *to bind together;* συνδῆσαί τινα *to bind* him *hand and foot: to bind up* a wound.

συν-διαβαίνω, *to go through* or *cross over together.*

συν-διαβάλλω, *to convey over together:* and intrans. *to cross over together,* Lat. *trajicio.* II. *to accuse along with* or *together:* Pass. *to be so accused.*

συν-διαγιγνώσκω, f. -διαγνώσομαι, *to decide along with, join in decreeing.*

συν-διαιτάομαι, f. -διαιτήσομαι: Dep.: (σύν, διαιτάω):—*to live with* or *together.*

συν-διαιτητής, οῦ, ὁ, *a joint arbitrator.*

συν-διακινδῡνεύω, f. σω *to meet danger along with, incur danger jointly.*

συν-διακοσμέω, f. ήσω, *to set in order together.*

συν-διάκτορος, ὁ, *a co-mate of Mercury.*

συν-διαλύω, f. -λύσω [ῡ], *to help to reconcile:*—Med. *to help to pay.*

συν-διαμένω, f. -μενῶ, *to continue with throughout.*

συν-διαμνημονεύω, f. σω, *to bring to remembrance along with.*

συν-διαπολεμέω, f. ήσω, *to join in carrying on a war to the end* or *throughout.*

συν-διαπράσσω Att. **-ττω**, f. ξω, *to carry through* or *effect together:* Med. *to negotiate with.*

συν-διασκοπέω, f. -διασκέψομαι, *to examine along with.*

συν-διασώζω, f. σω, *to help in preserving.*

συν-διαταλαιπωρέω, f. ήσω, *to endure hardship with* or *together.*

συν-διατελέω, f. -τελέσω, *to continue with throughout* or *to the end.*

συν-διατίθημι, f. -διαθήσω, *to help in arranging.*

συν-διατρίβω [ῑ], f. ψω, *to pass one's time with* or *together;* esp. with a master, οἱ τῷ Σωκράτει συνδιατρίβοντες the disciples of Socrates. II. of things, *to occupy oneself with.*

συν-διαφέρω, f. -διοίσω, *to carry through* or *over with.* II. *to bear throughout along with* or *together, to help in sustaining.*

συν-διαφθείρω, f. -φθερῶ, *to destroy with* or *together:*—Pass. *to perish along with.*

συν-διαφῠλάσσω, f. ξω, *to guard along with* or *together.*

συν-διαχειρίζω, f. ίσω, *to take in hand together, assist in managing.*

συν-διέξειμι, inf. -διεξιέναι (εἶμι *ibo*) *to go through in detail along with.*

συν-διημερεύω, f. σω, *to spend the day with.*

συνδιήνεικα, Ion. for -ήνεγκα, aor. 1 of συνδιαφέρω.

συν-δῐκάζω, f. άσω, *to help to judge: act as assessor to a judge.*

συν-δικαστής, οῦ, ὁ, *a fellow-dicast* or *juryman.*

συνδῐκέω, f. ήσω, (σύνδικος) *to defend one accused, to be the defendant's advocate:* generally, *to speak for* or *in support of* anything.

σύν-δῐκος, ον, (σύν, δίκη) *helping one in a trial* or *lawsuit:* as Subst., σύνδικος, ὁ, *an advocate,* esp. at Athens, *the defendant's advocate,* opp. to συνήγορος the prosecutor's: generally, *an advocate, supporter, backer.* 2. at Athens after the thirty Tyrants, σύνδικοι were *the syndics* or *judges appointed to determine on confiscations*. II. *belonging to, befitting in common*: Adv. συνδίκως, *jointly*.

συν-διοικέω, f. ήσω, *to administer or arrange together*.

συν-διοραω. f. –διόψομαι, *to see through* or *examine together*.

συν-δισκεύω, *to play at quoits with*.

συν-διώκω, f. –διώξω or –ώξομαι, *to chase away along with*. II. as law-term, *to join in a prosecution*.

συν-δοκέω, f. –δόξω and –δοκήσω, *to seem alike to several*: *to seem good* to another *also*: συνδοκεῖ, impers. like Lat. *placet*, συνδοκεῖ ἡμῖν we *are all agreed*: —the neut. part. is also used absol., συνδοκοῦν ἅπασιν ὑμῖν *since it seems good* to all of you, *since* you all *agree*; σύνδοξαν πατρί *since it seemed good* to the father *also*.

συν-δοκιμάζω, f. άσω, *to test* or *examine along with*.

συν-δοξάζω, f. άσω, *to agree in opinion*. II. *to glorify* or *extol jointly*.

συνδόξαν, aor. 1 part. neut. of συνδοκέω.

σύν-δουλος, ὁ, ἡ, *serving with*: as Subst., σύνδουλος, ὁ, *a fellow-slave*.

συν-δράω, f. άσω [ᾱ], *to do along with* or *together*, *help* or *concur in doing*; αἷμα συνδρᾶν *to assist in shedding* blood.

συν-δρομάς, άδος, fem. of σύνδρομος: αἱ συνδρομάδες πέτραι, = συμπληγάδες.

συν-δρομή, ἡ, (σύν, δρόμος) *a running together*: *a concourse* of people.

σύν-δρομος, ον, (σύν, δραμεῖν) *running together*, *meeting*; σύνδρομοι πέτραι = συμπληγάδες. II. *running along with, following close*. Hence

συνδρόμως, Adv. *close upon the track*.

συν-δυάζω, f. άσω, (σύν, δύο) *to join two together*, *to couple*, *pair*, *unite in wedlock*.

συν-δυάς, άδος, ἡ, (σύνδυο) *two together*, *paired*, *wedded*.

σύν-δυο, οἱ, αἱ, τά, (σύν, δύω) *two together*, *two and two*, *by pairs*, Lat. *bini*.

συν-δυστυχέω, f. ήσω, *to be unlucky along with* or *together*, *to be in like misfortune*.

συν-δώδεκα, οἱ, αἱ, τά, *every twelve*, *by twelves* or *dozens*.

συνέβαλον, aor. 2 of συμβάλλω.

συνέβαν, Dor. for συνέβην, aor. 2 of συμβαίνω.

συνέβην, aor. 2 of συμβαίνω.

σύν-εγγυς, Adv. *quite near*, *close to*, *hard upon*.

συν-εγείρω, f. –εγερῶ, *to awaken together*: esp. *to raise from the dead with* another:—Pass. *to rise together*.

συνέδραμον, aor. 2 of συντρέχω.

συνεδρεύω, f. σω, (σύνεδρος) *to sit together in council*, *sit in consultation*: οἱ συνεδρεύοντες *the members of a council*.

συνεδρία, ἡ, (σύνεδρος) *a sitting together*, of gregarious birds. II. *a sitting in council*, *a council*.

συνέδριον, τό, (σύνεδρος) *a number of persons assembled in council*, *a council-board*, *council*:—in N. T. *the Sanhedrim*. 2. *a council-chamber*, *senate-house*, Lat. *curia*.

σύν-εδρος, ον, (σύν, ἕδρα) *sitting together* or *with*, *assembled in council*. II. as Subst., σύνεδρος, ὁ, *one who sits with others in council*, *a councillor*, *senator*.

συν-εείκοσι, Ep. for συνείκοσι

συν-εέργαθον, Ep. lengthd. impf. of συνείργω.

συν-εέργω, Ep. for συνείργω.

συνέζευξα, aor. 1 of συζεύγνυμι.

συνέηκα, Ion. for συνῆκα, aor. 1 of συνίημι.

συν-εθέλω poët. **συν-θέλω**, *to wish with* or *together to concur in a wish*.

συνέθεντο, 3 pl. aor. 2 med. of συντίθημι.

συνεθηκάμην, aor. 1 med. of συντίθημι.

συν-εθίζω, f. ίσω, *to accustom*, *inure*, *make habitual*: —Pass. *to become used* or *inured to*.

συνειδέναι, inf. of σύνοιδα; v. *συνείδω. Hence

συνείδησις, ἡ, *a joint knowledge*, *consciousness*. 2. *conscience*.

***συν-είδω**, in aor. 2 συν-εῖδον, inf. –ιδεῖν:—*to see together*, *see in one view*, *see plainly*: *understand*: in this sense, the pres. in use is συν-οράω, fut. συν-όψομαι, pf. συν-εόρᾱκα. II. pf. σύνοιδα in pres. sense, inf. συνειδέναι: plqpt. with impf. sense συνῄδειν Att. συνῄδη, Ion. 2 plur. συνῃδέατε: also fut. συνείσομαι: —*to share in the knowledge*, *be cognisant of* a thing, *privy to* it: part. συνειδὼς *an accomplice*: τὸ συνειδὸς = συνείδησις. 2. c. dat. pers. *to know the same as* another; συνειδέναι ἑαυτῷ οὐδ᾽ ὁτιοῦν σοφὸς ὤν *I am conscious* to myself of not being in the least wise; or in the dat., σύνοιδα ἐμαυτῷ οὐδὲν ἐπισταμένῳ *I am conscious* to myself of knowing naught: also *to be in a person's confidence*, *be privy to his plans* or *opinions*.

συν-είκοσι Ep. **συνεείκοσι**, *twenty together*, *by twenties*, Lat. *viceni*.

συνειλεγμένος, pf. part. of συλλέγω.

συν-ειλέω, f. ήσω, *to crowd* or *throng together*:—of persons, *to bind firmly together*:—Pass. *to be crowded* or *pressed together*.

συνείληφα, pf. of συλλαμβάνω.

συνείληχα, pf. of συλλαγχάνω.

συνείλκυσα, aor. 1 of συνέλκω.

συνείλοχα, pf. of συλλέγω.

σύν-ειμι, f. –έσομαι, (σύν, εἰμί *sum*) *to be with*, *be joined* or *united with*, *be conversant with*; συνεῖναι νόσῳ = νοσεῖν; συνεῖναι μερίμναις *to be acquainted* with cares; συνεῖναι πράγμασι *to be engaged in business*. 2. of persons, *to have intercourse*, *associate*, *live with*: of a woman, *to live with* her husband: generally, *to associate with*, *have to do with*, *take part with*, *follow*; οἱ συνόντες *partisans*, *disciples*

σύν-ειμι, (σύν, εἶμι *ibo*) *to go* or *come together*, hence *to assemble*, *meet* 2. in hostile sense, *to meet in battle*, *engage with*: of states, *to engage in war*. 3. in peaceable sense, *to come together*, *meet* *to deliberate.* 4. of revenue, *to come together, to come in.*

συν-εῖπον, inf. –ειπεῖν, aor. 2 of συναγορεύω or σύμφημι, there being no pres. in use:—*to speak with* any one, *agree with, confirm: to advocate* a person's cause: generally, *to help, further.* 2. *to tell along with* one, *help one to tell.*

συν-είργνῦμι, = συνείργω.

συν-είργω Ep. –εέργω old form –έργω: Ep. impf. συνέεργον: Ep. aor. 2 συνεέργᾰθον: f. συνείρξω:—*to shut in* or *enclose together: to bind together:* generally, *to join together, fasten together, unite.*

συνείρηκα, used as pf. of σύμφημι.

συν-είρω, *to string together, join one after another, add on without stopping.* II. intr. *to string words together, to speak on and on, go on continuously.*

συνείς, εῖσα, έν, part. aor. 2 of συνίημι.

συν-εισάγω, f. ξω, *to bring in with* or *together.*

συν-εισβαίνω, f. βήσομαι, *to embark together with.*

συν-εισβάλλω, intr. *to make an inroad* into a country *together, join in an incursion* or *invasion.*

συν-εισέρχομαι, aor. 2 act. –εισῆλθον, pf. –εισελήλυθα: Dep.:—*to enter along with* or *together.*

συνείσομαι, fut. without any pres. in use; v. *συνείδω II.

συν-εισπίπτω, f. –πεσοῦμαι: aor. 2 –έπεσον:—*to fall* or *be thrown into along with* II. *to rush in along with* or *together, to burst* or *break in together.*

συν-εισπλέω, f. –πλεύσομαι, *to sail into together.*

συν-εισπράσσω Att. –ττω, f. ξω, *to help in exacting* money *from others.*

συν-εισφέρω, *to join in paying the war-tax* (εἰσφορά).

συν-εκβαίνω, f. –βήσομαι, *to go out together.*

συν-εκβάλλω, f. –βᾰλω, *to cast out along with: to assist in casting out.*

συν-εκβιβάζω, f. –εκβιβάσω Att. –εκβιβῶ, Causal of συνεκβαίνω, *to help in bringing out.*

συν-έκδημος, ον, *travelling with:* as Subst. *a fellow-traveller.*

συν-εκδίδωμι, f. –εκδώσω, *to give out together: to help* a poor man *in portioning out* his daughter.

συν-εκδύω, f. –εκδύσω [ῡ], *to strip off together:*—Med. *to strip oneself of* or *put off together.*

συν-εκθνήσκω, f. –εκθᾰνοῦμαι, *to die along with* or *together:* metaph. *to fail* or *be exhausted together.*

συν-εκκαίδεκα, *sixteen together, by sixteens.*

συν-εκκλέπτω, f. ψω, *to help to steal away;* συνεκκλέπτειν γάμους *to help in frustrating* a marriage.

συν-εκκομίζω, f. σω, *to help in carrying out.* II. *to help in bearing* or *supporting.*

συν-εκκόπτω, f. ψω, *to help to cut out* or *away.*

συνέκλεισα, aor. 1 of συγκλείω.

συν-εκλεκτός, ή, όν, *chosen along with* or *together.*

συν-εκλύω, f. –λύσω [ῡ], *to dissolve with* or *together.*

συν-εκμᾰχέω, f. ήσω, (σύν, ἐκ, μάχομαι) *to march out to fight together.*

συν-εκμοχλεύω, f. σω, *to join in forcing with a lever.*

συν-εκπέμπω, f. ψω, *to send out together.*

συν-εκπεράω, f. άσω [ᾱ], *to pass out together.*

συν-εκπίνω [ῑ], f. –πίομαι, *to drink off together.*

συν-εκπίπτω, f. –πεσοῦμαι, *to rush out along with.* II. of the votes taken out of the voting urn, *to fall out in agreement with each other, to concur:* c. dat. *to come out equal* to another, *run a dead heat with.* III. *to fall out, be thrown out, fail together.*

συν-εκπλέω Ion. –πλώω, f. –πλεύσομαι, *to sail out along with.*

συν-εκπνέω, f. –πνεύσομαι, *to breathe out one's breath along with* another.

συν-εκπονέω, f. ήσω, *to help in working out* or *achieving: to coöperate with.*

συν-εκπορίζω, f. σω, *to help in supplying* or *providing.*

συν-εκποτέον or –έα, verb. Adj. of συνεκπίνω, *one must drink out* or *off together.*

συν-εκπράσσω Att. –ττω Ion. –πρήσσω, f. ξω, *to exact* money *with* or *together:*—Med. *to help* a person *in taking vengeance for* a thing.

συν-εκσώζω, f. σω, *to help in preserving* or *delivering.*

συν-εκτάσσω Att. –ττω, f. ξω, *to arrange in line* or *battle order along with* others.

συν-εκτέον, verb. Adj. of συνέχω, *one must keep with one* or *together.*

συν-εκτίνω [ῐ], f. –τίσω [ῑ], *to pay along with, to help in paying.*

συν-εκτρέφω, f. –θρέψω, *to rear up along with:*—Pass. *to grow up with.*

συν-εκτρέχω, f. –εκδραμοῦμαι: aor. 2 –εξέδρᾰμον:—*to run out along with, to sally out together.*

συνεκύρησα and **συνέκυρσα**, aor. 1 of συγκυρέω.

συνέκυψα, aor. 1 of συγκύπτω.

συν-εκφέρω, f. –εξοίσω, *to carry out together to burial: to attend a funeral.*

συνέλᾰβον, aor. 2 of συλλαμβάνω.

συνελάλουν, impf. of συλλᾰλέω.

συν-ελαύνω: f. –ελάσω [ᾰ]: aor. 1 –ήλασα Ep. –έλασσα: pf. –ελήλακα:—*to drive, force* or *bring together;* συνελαύνειν ὀδόντας *to gnash* the teeth *together, to set together, match in combat, set to fight.* 2. intr., ἔριδι ξυνελαύνειν *to meet* in quarrel.

συνελεῖν, **σύνελεν**, Ep. inf. and 3 sing. aor. 2 of συναιρέω.

συν-ελευθερόω, f. ώσω, *to join in freeing from:* absol. *to join in freeing* or *delivering.*

συνελεύσομαι, fut. of συνέρχομαι.

συνελήλυθα, pf. of συνέρχομαι.

συνελήφθην, aor. 1 pass. of συλλαμβάνω.

συνελθεῖν, aor. 2 inf. of συνέρχομαι.

συν-ελκυστέον, verb. Adj. of aor. 1 of συνέλκω, *one must draw together.*

συν-έλκω, f. ξω: aor. 1 συνείλκῠσα (as if from συνελκύω):—*to draw together* or *to a point.* 2. *to draw up, contract.* II. *to help to draw out.*

συνελών, aor. 2 part. of *συναιρέω*.

συν-εμβάλλω, f. -βᾰλῶ, *to put in along with, help in putting in*. II. intr. *to fall in* or *upon together, join in attacking: to make a joint inroad*. Hence

συνεμβολή, ἡ, *a throwing in together; συνεμβολὴ κώπης the regular dip* of all the oars *together*.

συνέμεν, poët. for *συνεῖναι*, aor. 2 inf. of *συνίημι*.

συνέμιξα, aor. 1 of *συμμίγνυμι*.

συνέμιχθεν, Ep. 3 pl. aor. 1 pass. of *συμμίγνυμι*.

συν-εμπίπρημι, fut. -εμπρήσω: aor. 1 -ενέπρησα: —*to burn along with* or *together*.

συν-έμπορος, ον, *travelling with*: as Subst., συνέμπορος, ὁ, *a fellow-wayfarer, fellow-traveller, companion, attendant; συνέμπορος χορείας a partner* in dancing.

συνεμπρῆσαι, aor. 1 inf. of *συνεμπίπρημι*.

συνενέγκαντες, aor. 1 part. pl. of *συμφέρω*.

συν-ενείκομαι, Ep. for *συμφέρομαι*, Pass. *to be carried so as to meet, to strike* or *dash against*.

συν-ενθουσιάω, *to be inspired together with*.

συν-εξάγω, f. ξω, *to lead out together*: Pass. *to be carried away with*.

συν-εξαιρέω, f. ήσω, *to take out together, to help in removing: to help in taking* or *capturing*:—Med. *to take away forcibly from* one.

συν-εξᾰκούω, f. -ακούσομαι, *to hear* of a thing *all together*.

συν-εξᾰμαρτανω, .. -αμαρτησομαι *to err along with, to commit a joint error, have part in a fault*.

συν-εξανίστημι, f. -στήσω, *to make to stand up together*. II. Pass., with aor. 2 act. -εξανέστην, pf. -εξανέστηκα:—*to rise and come forth together*.

συν-εξᾰπᾰτάω, f. ήσω, *to cheat along with* or *together*.

συν-έξειμι, (εἶμι *ibo*) *to go out along with* or *together*.

συν-εξελαύνω, f. -εξελάσω, *to drive out along with* or *together*. II. (sub. στράτον, ἵππον) *to march* or *ride out together*.

συν-εξερύω, f. σω, *to draw out with* or *together*.

συν-εξέρχομαι, Dep., with aor. 2 act. -εξῆλθον, pf. -εξελήλυθα: (cf. ἔρχομαι):—*to go* or *come out with*.

συν-εξετάζω, f. άσω, *to search out* or *examine along with* or *together*:—Pass. *to be reckoned with* or *among*.

συν-εξευρίσκω, f. -εξευρήσω, *to find out together*.

συν-εξορμάω, f. ήσω, *to help to urge on*. II. intr. *to sally forth together: to shoot up along with*.

συν-εοχμός, ὁ, poët. for *συνοχμός*.

συν-επάγω, f. ξω, *to join in bringing against* another, *join in inviting*.

συν-επᾴδω poët. -αείδω, *to join in celebrating*.

συν-επαινέω, f. έσω Ep. ήσω, *to approve* or *advise together: to join in advising* or *recommending: to approve, agree to*. II. *to join in praising*.

συν-έπαινος, ον, *joining in, consenting to* a thing, *being a consenting party to* it.

συν-επαίρω, f. -επᾰρῶ, *to raise* or *lift at the same time* II. *to urge on together* or *also*:—Pass. *to rise together with*.

συνέπαισα, aor. 1 of *συμπαίζω*.

συν-επαιτιάομαι, f. -άσομαι [ᾱ], Dep. *to accuse together, involve in a common charge with*.

συν-επᾰκολουθέω, f. ήσω, *to follow together, follow close*.

συν-επᾰμύνω, f. -αμῠνῶ, *to join in repelling*.

συν-επανίστημι, f. -στήσω, *to make to rise* or *rebel along with* or *together*. II. Pass., with aor. 2 act. -έστην, pf. -έστηκα:—*to join in a revolt* or *rebellion*.

συν-επανορθόω, f. ώσω, *to join in re-establishing*.

συνέπᾶξα, Dor. aor. 1 of *συμπήγνυμι*.

συν-επάπτομαι, Ion. for *συνεφάπτομαι*.

συνεπέδησα, aor. 1 of *συμπεδάω*.

συν-έπειμι, (σύν, ἐπί, εἶμι *ibo*) *to go to.. against, join in attacking*.

συν-επεισφέρομαι, Med. *to join in bringing in*.

συν-επεκπίνω [ῐ], f. -πίομαι, *to drink off quickly*.

συν-επελαφρύνω [ῡ], *to help to make light, to help to bear* or *sustain*.

συν-επερίζω, f. ίσω, *to contend with*.

συνέπεσον, aor. 2 of *συμπίπτω*.

συνεπεσπόμην, aor. 2 of *συνεφέπομαι*.

συνεπέστην, aor. 2 of *συνεφίστημι*.

συν-επεύχομαι, f. -εύξομαι, Dep. *to join in a prayer to vow at the same time*.

συν-επηχέω, f. ήσω, *to join in singing, join in a chant* or *chorus*.

συν-επιβαίνω, f. -βήσομαι, *to mount together upon*. II. *to enter upon along with*.

συν-επιβουλεύω, f. σω, *to join in plotting against*.

συν-επιγρᾰφεύς, ὁ, *a fellow-registrar, fellow-clerk*.

συν-επιθῡμέω, f. ήσω, *to desire along with*.

συν-επίκειμαι, f. -κείσομαι, Pass. *to press upon together, to join in attacking*.

συν-επικοσμέω, f. ήσω, *to help to array* or *adorn*.

συν-επικουρέω, f. ήσω, *to join as an ally, help to support* or *relieve*.

συν-επικουφίζω, f. ίσω, *to lighten at the same time*.

συν-επικρᾰδαίνω, *to move backwards and forwards together with*.

συν-επιλαμβάνομαι, f. -επιλήψομαι, Dep. *to take part in* a thing *together, have a share in: to take part with* a person, *support him*

συν-επιμαρτῠρέω, f. ήσω, *to join in attesting* or *ratifying: to confirm*.

συν-επιμελέομαι, Dep., with fut. med. -ήσομαι, aor. 1 pass. -επεμελήθην:—*to join in taking care of: to have joint charge of: to join in providing*.

συν-επιμελητής, οῦ, ὁ, *one who joins in taking care of, an associate, coadjutor*.

συνέπιον, aor. 2 of *συμπίνω*.

συν-επιπλέκω, f. ξω, *to help to twine* or *plait*.

συν-επιπλέω, f. -πλεύσομαι, *to join in sailing against together, to make a naval expedition in concert*.

συν-επιρρώννῡμι, f. -επιρρώσω, *to help to strengthen*.

συν-επισκοπέω, f. -επισκέψομαι: pf. -επέσκεμμαι: —*to examine along with* or *together*.

συν-επισπάω, f. άσω [ᾰ], *to draw on together*:—

Mea. *to draw along with* or *together: to draw to oneself, draw over to one's own views.*

συνεπισπέσθαι, συνεπισπόμενος, aor. 2 inf. and part. of *συνεφέπομαι.*

συν-επισπεύδω, f. *σω, to join in urging forward.*

συν-επίσταμαι, Dep. *to know along with, be privy to.*

συν-επιστέλλω, f. *-στελῶ, to send with* or *together.*

συν-επιστρᾰτεύω, f. *σω, to make war together with.*

συν-επιστρέφω, f. *ψω, to assist in turning* a person *to* a thing.

συν-επισχύω, f. *ύσω* [ῡ], *to help to strengthen* or *support.*

συν-επιτελέω, f. *έσω, to join in performing* or *accomplishing.*

συν-επιτίθημι, f. *-επιθήσω, to throw upon together:* —Med. *to set on* or *attack jointly: to apply oneself to* a thing *together.*

συν-επιτρίβω [ῑ], f. *ψω, to wear away* or *destroy utterly.*

συν-επίτροπος, ὁ, *a joint-guardian.*

συνέπλᾰσα, aor. 1 of *συμπλάσσω.*

συνέπλεξα, aor. 1 of *συμπλέκω.*

συν-έπομαι, aor. 2 *-εσπόμην,* Dep. *to follow close upon, to keep up with; ποίμναις συνέπεσθαι to follow* the flocks. II. *to follow with the mind, understand.*

συν-επόμνῡμι, *to swear to in addition* or *besides.*

συνέπνιξα, aor. 1 of *συμπνίγω.*

συνέπρηξα, Ion. aor. 1 of *συμπράσσω.*

συν-εραστής, οῦ, ὁ, *a fellow-lover, joint-lover.* From

συν-εράω, *to love jointly* or *in concert:*—Med., *συνερᾶσθαί τινι to return love for love.*

συν-εργάζομαι, f. *-άσομαι,* pf. *-είργασμαι* (used both in act. and pass. sense): Dep.:—*to work* or *labour together with* another, *to help, assist* or *contribute to* a thing: pf. part. in pass. sense, *λίθοι ξυνειργασμένοι* stones *wrought for building.*

συν-εργάτης [ᾰ], ου, ὁ, *a fellow-worker, partner, colleague, coadjutor.*

συν-εργᾰτίνης [ῑ], ου, ὁ, poët. for *συνεργάτης.*

συν-εργάτις [ᾰ], ιδος, ἡ, fem. of *συνεργάτης.*

συνεργέω, impf. *συνήργουν,* (*συνεργός*) *to work together with, to join* or *help in work: to coöperate with, assist, do service to* one.

συν-εργήτης, ου, ὁ, poët. for *συνεργάτης.*

συνεργία, ἡ, (*συνεργός*) *a joint-work, assistance, coöperation;* in bad sense, *conspiracy, collusion.*

συν-εργός, όν, (*σύν, ἔργον*) *working together with* another, *joining* or *helping in work: taking part in* a thing, *contributing towards* it:—as Subst., *συνεργός,* ὁ or ἡ, *an associate* or *partner in a work, a fellow-workman, a coöperator, coadjutor.*

συνέργω, old form of *συνείργω.*

συν-έρδω, f. *ξω, to join in a work, coöperate with.*

συν-ερείδω, f. *σω:* aor. 1. *συνήρεισα*:—*to set firmly together: to bind* or *fasten close together, to clench* : —Pass., aor. 1 *συνηρείσθην*: pf. *συνήρεισμαι* or *-ερήρισμαι*:—*to be fast bound* or *set firmly together.*

συν-ερέω Att. **συν-ερῶ,** fut. without any pres. in use (*συναγορεύω* or *σύμφημι* being used instead): —*I shall speak with* or *in support of, advocate, support.*

συν-έρῑθος, ὁ, also ἡ, *a fellow-worker, helpmate.*

συνερκτικός, ή, όν, (*συνέργω*) of a speaker, *driving* his opponent *into a corner, cogent, forcible.*

συν-έρπω, f. *ψω, to creep together.*

συνέρραξα, aor. 1 of *συρράσσω.*

συνέρρηγμαι, pf. pass. of *συρρήγνυμι.*

συνέρρηξα, aor. 1 of *συρρήγνυμι.*

συνέρρωγα, pf. 2 intr. of *συρρήγνυμι.*

συν-έρχομαι, f. *-ελεύσομαι*: aor. 2 act. *-ῆλθον,* pf. *-ελήλυθα*: Dep.:—*to go along with* or *together.* II. *to come together, meet: to have dealings* or *intercourse with.* 2. in hostile sense, *to meet in battle, encounter,* Lat. *concurrere:* of a battle, *to be engaged in.* 3. c. acc. cognato, *στρατείαν συνελθεῖν to join in* an expedition; *συνελθεῖν λέχος σύν τῳ share* thy bed. III. of things, *to be joined in one, be united.* IV. of events, *to concur, coincide, happen together.*

συν-ερωτάω, f. *ήσω, to ask questions with* or *at the same time.* II. *to establish a point by questioning:* —Pass. *to be established by questioning.*

σύνες, aor. 2 imperat. of *συνίημι, mind! mark!*

συν-εσθίω, f. *-έδομαι*: aor. 2 *-έφᾰγον*:—*to eat together with.*

σύνεσις Att. **ξύνεσις,** εως, ἡ, (*συνίημι*) *a joining, meeting together.* II. *the faculty of apprehension, judgment, understanding, intelligence.* 2. *conscience,* = *συνείδησις.*

συνεσπάραξα, aor. 1 of *συσπᾰράσσω.*

συνεσπόμην, aor. 2 of *συνέπομαι.*

συνέσταλμαι, pf. pass. of *συστέλλω.*

συνεσταότες, Ep. pf. part. pl. of *συνίστημι.*

συνεσταυρωμένος, pf. pass. part. of *συσταυρόω.*

συνεστάλην [ᾰ], aor. 2 pass. of *συστέλλω.*

συνέστειλα, aor. 1 of *συστέλλω.*

συνέστην, aor. 2 of *συνίστημι.*

συν-εστιάω, f. *άσω* [ᾱ], *to entertain in one's house:* —Pass. *to feast along with* or *together.*

συν-εστίη, ἡ, (*σύν, ἑστία*) *a common feast.*

συν-έστιος, ον, (*σύν, ἑστία*) *sharing one's hearth* or *home, living* or *dwelling together:* as Subst., *συνέστιος,* ὁ, ἡ, *an inmate, guest.* 2. of Jupiter, *the guardian of the hearth.*

συνεστώς, pf. part. of *συνίστημι.*

συνέσχον, aor. 2 of *συνέχω.*

συν-έταιρος, ὁ, (*σύν, ἑταῖρος*) *a companion, partner, comrade.*

συνετᾰράχθην, aor. 1 pass. of *συνταράσσω.*

συνετάφην [ᾰ], aor. 2 pass. of *συνθάπτω.*

συνετάχθην, aor. 1 pass. of *συνταράσσω.*

συνετέθειντο, 3 pl. plqpf. pass of *συντίθημι.*

συνέτλᾱν, Dor. aor. 2 of *συντλάω.*

σύνετο Ep. **ξύνετο,** 3 sing. aor. 2 med. of *ξυνίημι.*

συνετός, ή, όν, (*συνίημι*) *quick at apprehending, understanding, intelligent, sagacious.* II. pass. *easy* to be comprehended intelligible: neut. pl. συνετά as Adv. intelligibly.

συνετρίβην [ῐ], aor. 2 pass. of συντρίβω.

συνετῶς, Adv. of συνετός, intelligently.

συν-ευδαιμονέω, f. ήσω, to share in happiness with.

συν-ευδοκέω, f. ήσω, to approve of, be well pleased with or together, to consent.

συν-εύδω, f. -ευδήσω, to sleep or lie with; ὁ ξυνεύδων χρόνος the time which sleeps with one, i. e. which passes while one is asleep.

συν-ευνάζω, f. σω, to make to sleep together, to marry to each other:—Pass. to lie with.

συν-ευνέτης, ου, ὁ, a bedfellow, husband, consort: fem. **συνευνέτις**, ιδος, a wife, mate.

σύν-ευνος, ον, (σύν, εὐνή) sharing one bed: as Subst., σύνευνος ὁ, ἡ, a bedfellow, consort, husband or wife.

συν-ευπάσχω, f. -πείσομαι, to be well treated with, to receive favours along with.

συν-ευπορέω, f. ήσω, to help to provide, contribute, c. acc. rei: c. gen. rei, to provide a part of, contribute towards:—c. dat. pers. to assist, help.

συν-ευτῠχέω, to be fortunate along with or together.

συν-εύχομαι, f. -ξομαι, Dep. to pray with or together, to join in making a prayer.

συν-ευωχέομαι, to feast with or together.

συνέφᾰγον, used as aor. 2 of συνεσθίω.

συν-εφάπτομαι Ion. -επάπτομαι: f. -εφάψομαι: Dep.:—to lay hold of, put hand to along with or together, c. gen. rei. 2. c. gen. pers. to join in attacking.

συν-εφέλκω, f. ξω, aor. 1 -εφείλκῠσα:—to draw after or towards along with.

συν-εφέπομαι, aor. 2 -εφεσπόμην Ion. -επεσπόμην: Dep.:—to follow along with or together

συν-έφηβος, ον, at the age of youth together.

συν-εφίστημι, to place over together: metaph. to make attentive: also (sub. τὸν νοῦν) to attend to. II. Pass., with aor. 2 act. -επέστην, pf. -εφέστηκα:—to be placed over, superintend along with or together. 2 to rise up against, attack jointly.

συνέφραξα, aor. 1 of συμφράσσω

συνεχάρην [ᾰ], aor 2 pass. of συγχαίρω.

συνέχεα, aor. 1 of συγχέω.

συνέχεια, ἡ, (συνεχής) a continuous series of things, continuity. II. continued attention, perseverance.

συνέχευα, Ep. aor. 1 of συγχέω.

συνεχέως, Ion for συνεχῶς.

συνεχής, ές, (συνέχω) keeping or holding together: continuous, in an unbroken line: c. dat. continuous with, next to, adjacent. II. of Time, continuous, continued, unceasing, unintermitting: the neut. συνεχές is used as Adv., = συνεχῶς.

συν-εχθαίρω, to hate along with, join in hating

συν-έχθω, poët. for συνεχθαίρω.

συνεχύθην [ῠ], aor. 1 pass. of συγχέω.

συν-έχω Att. ξυν-: f. ἕξω: aor. 2 συνέσχον:—to hold or keep together: —συνέχειν τὴν εἰρεσίαν to keep the rowers together. 2. to contain, comprise. 3. to constrain, oppress · Pass. to be constrained, distressed, affected by. 4. in Pass., συνέχεσθαι αἰχμῇσι to engage with spears.

συνεχῶς Ion. -έως, Adv. of συνεχής, continually, unceasingly.

συν-εψιάω, (σύν, ἐψιάομαι) to play together.

συνεώνημαι, pf. of συνωνέομαι.

συν-ηβάω, f. ήσω, to pass their youth together: to be young together.

συν-ηβολέω, to fall in with.

σύν-ηβος, ον, (σύν, ἥβη) young at the same time: as Subst., σύνηβος, ὁ, ἡ, a young friend or comrade.

συνήγᾰγον, aor. 2 of συνάγω.

συνηγμένος, pf. pass. part. of συνάγω.

συνηγορέω, f. ήσω, (συνήγορος) to plead another's cause, to be an advocate for, esp. for the prosecution, opp. to σύνδικος; συνηγορεῖν τῷ κατηγόρῳ to second the accuser. Hence

συνηγορία, ἡ, advocacy of another's cause, pleading for another, esp. for the prosecutor.

συνηγορικός, ή, όν, of or for a συνήγορος or advocate; τὸ συνηγορικόν, the advocate's fee, being a drachma per diem paid to the public συνήγοροι while the court sat.

συν-ήγορος, ον, (σύν, ἀγορεύω) speaking with, agreeing with. 2. supporting, on one's side, esp in a court of justice: as Subst., συνήγορος, ὁ, an advocate, counsel for the prosecution, opp. to σύνδικος.

συνῄδειν Att. ξυνῄδη, plqpf. of σύνοιδα.

συνῃδέατε, Ion. 2 pl. plqpf. of *συνείδω.

συν-ήδομαι: fut. -ησθήσομαι. aor. 1 -ήσθην: Dep.: —to rejoice together; συνήδεσθαί τινι to rejoice with one, to congratulate: also c. dat. rei to rejoice at a thing, to be pleased or gratified, to sympathise with one's good fortune.

συνήθεια, ἡ, a dwelling or living together, intercourse, intimacy, Lat. consuetudo. II. use, custom, habit, usage. From

συν-ήθης, ες, gen. εος contr. ους: gen. pl. συνηθέων contr συνηθῶν: (σύν, ἦθος):—dwelling or living together, of like habits or customs, akin, well suited to; συνήθης τινί well-acquainted or intimate with him; χειρὶ συνήθης = χειροήθης, tame. II. habitual, customary: familiar.

συνηθροισμένος, pf. pass. part. of συναθροίζω.

συνήθως, Adv. of συνήθης, customarily.

συνῆκα, aor. 1 of συνίημι.

συν-ήκω, to have come together, to be assembled.

συνήλᾰσα, aor. 1 of συνελαύνω.

συνῆλθον, aor. 2 of συνέρχομαι.

συν-ηλῐκιώτης, ου, ὁ, = συνῆλιξ.

συν-ῆλιξ, ῐκος, ὁ, ἡ, (σύν, ἧλιξ) of like or equal age, Lat. aequalis: as Subst., συνῆλιξ, ὁ, ἡ, an associate of one's own age, a comrade.

συνηλῠσίη and **συνήλυσις**, ἡ, (συνέρχομαι, συνελεύσομαι) a meeting, assembly.

συν-ημερεύω, f. σω, (σύν, ἡμέρα) to pass the day with or together, to live with.

συνημοσύνη, ἡ, *union, connexion:* in plur. *covenants, solemn promises.* From

συνήμων, ον, gen. ονος, (συνίημι) *joined together, united: a companion.*

συν-ήορος Dor. and Att. **συν-άορος**, ον, (σύν, αἰωρέω) *hanging together, linked with, wedded to:* as Subst., συνήορος, ὁ, ἡ, *a consort, a husband* or *a wife.*

συν-ηπεροπεύω, f. σω, *to join in cheating* or *tricking.*

συν-ηρετέω, f. ήσω, (σύν, ἐρετής) = συνηρετμέω.

συν-ηρετμέω, f. ήσω, *to row with:* generally, *to work* or *ply with, be friends with.*

συνηρεφέω, f. ήσω, *to throw a shade over.* From

συν-ηρεφής, ές, (σύν, ἐρέφω) *thickly shaded, covered over.*

συν-ήριθμος, ον, poët. for συνάριθμος.

συνήρπᾰκα, pf. of συναρπάζω.

συνήρπασα, aor. 1 of συναρπάζω.

συνήρτημαι, pf. pass. of συναρτάω.

συνηυλίσθην, aor. 1 of συναυλίζομαι.

συνήρων, impf. of συνεράω.

συν-ησσάομαι Att. **-ττάομαι**, Pass. *to be conquered* or *overcome together.*

συν-ηχέω, f. ήσω, *to sound* or *ring together.*

συνήχθην, aor. 1 pass. of συνάγω.

συνῆψα, aor. 1 of συνάπτω.

συνθᾰκέω, f. ήσω, *to sit with* or *together, to sit in council with, take counsel with.* From

σύν-θᾰκος, ον, *sitting with* or *together.* 2. *sharing in, partaking of.*

συν-θαμβέω, *to be astounded along with.*

συν-θάλπω, f. ψω, *to warm with* or *together:* metaph. *to soothe by flattery.*

συν-θάπτω, f. ψω, *to bury with* or *together:*—Pass. *to be buried with* or *together.*

συν-θεάομαι, f. -άσομαι [ᾱ], Dep. *to view together, to see a spectacle together.* 2. *to examine together, examine carefully.* Hence

συνθεᾱτής, οῦ, ὁ, *a fellow-spectator* or *looker on.*

συν-θεάτρια, ἡ, fem. of συνθεατής.

συνθείς, aor. 2 part. of συντίθημι.

συν-θέλω, poet. for συνεθέλω.

σύνθεμα, ατος, τό, poët. for σύνθημα.

συνθέμενος, aor. 2 med. part. of συντίθημι.

σύνθεο, Ep. for σύνθου, aor. 2 med. imperat. of συντίθημι.

συνθεσία, ἡ, (συντίθημι) *a placing together, an arrangement, covenant, treaty:* in plur. *injunctions, instructions.*

σύνθεσις, ἡ, (συντίθημι) *a putting together, compounding, composition;* σύνθεσις γραμμάτων *a combination* of letters. II. metaph. *an agreement, treaty, covenant:* cf. συνθήκη.

συνθετικός, ή, όν, (συντίθημι) *skilled in putting together.*

σύνθετο, Ep. for συνέθετο, 3 sing. aor. 2 med. of συντίθημι.

σύνθετος, ον, also η, ον, (συντίθημι) *put together, compounded of parts, compound: complex.* II. *put together, feigned, forged.* III. metaph. *agreed upon, covenanted;* ἐκ συνθέτου *by agreement,* Lat. *ex compacto.*

συν-θέω, f. -θεύσομαι, *to run along with, to run together:* of things, *to go along with, to go smoothly with, concur with one's wishes: to run together, meet.*

συν-θεωρέω, f. ήσω, *to contemplate together: to go to a spectacle together.*

συνθήκη, ἡ, (συντίθημι) *a putting together.* II. *an agreement, arrangement:* in plur. *articles of agreement, a covenant, contract, treaty.*

σύνθημα ατος, τό, (συντίθημι) *that which is put together.* II. *anything agreed upon, a preconcerted signal:* generally, *a token, sign.* 2. *a watchword,* Lat. *tessera.* 3. *an agreement, covenant, engagement.* Hence

συνθημᾰτιαῖος, α, ον, *agreed upon: bargained for.*

συνθηρᾱτής, οῦ, ὁ, *a fellow-hunter.* From

συν-θηράω, f. άσω [ᾱ], *to hunt with* or *together:*—Med. *to catch together:*—Pass. *to be caught and bound together.*

συνθηρευτής, οῦ, ὁ, = συνθηρατής. From

συν-θηρεύω, = συνθηρά*·* *to hunt together:*—Pass. *to be found out to be.*

σύν-θηρος, ον, (σύν, θήρα) *hunting with* or *in company: joining in chase* or *pursuit of.*

συν-θιᾰσώτης, ου, ὁ, *a partner in the* θίασος or *sacred company:* generally, *a fellow, comrade.*

συν-θλάω, f. άσω [ᾰ], *to crush along with* or *together.*

συν-θλίβω [ῑ], f. ψω, *to press together, compress.*

συν-θνήσκω: f. -θᾰνοῦμαι: aor. 2 -έθᾰνον, inf. -θανεῖν:—*to die with* or *together.*

συν-θοινάτωρ [ᾱ], ορος, ὁ, (σύν, θοινάω) *a partaker of the same feast, a fellow-banqueter.*

συν-θρᾰνόω, f. ώσω, *to break in pieces, shiver.*

συν-θραύω, f. σω, *to break in pieces, crush, shiver.*

σύν-θρηνος, ον, *mourning with* or *together.*

σύν-θρονος, ον, *sitting on the same seat* or *throne with: ruling jointly.*

σύν-θροος, ον, *sounding with, in harmony with.*

συν-θρύπτω, f. ψω, *to break in pieces, crush:* metaph. *to enervate, weaken.*

συν-θύω, f. -θύσω [ῡ], *to offer sacrifice along with.*

συνῐδεῖν, aor. 2 inf. of *συνείδω.

συνίει [ῑ], imperat. and 3 sing. impf. of συνίημι.

συνῑέμεν, Ep. for συνιέναι, inf. pres. of συνίημι.

σύνῑεν, Ep. 3 pl. impf. of συνίημι.

συν-ιεροποιέω, f. ήσω, *to join in sacrifice with.*

συν-ιζάνω, *to settle down, collapse, shrink.* 2. *to sink, fall,* of the wind.

συν-ίζω, f. -ιζήσω, intr. *to sit together, to hold a sitting.*

συν-ίημι Att. **ξυνίημι** [for the quantity, see ἵημι]: impf. συνίην or συνίειν: f. συνήσω or συνήσομαι: aor. 1 συνῆκα: pf. συνεῖκα —also (as if from συνιέω) 3 pl. pres. συνιοῦσι, inf. συνιεῖν, imperat. ξυνίει, inf. συνιέμεν; 3 sing. impf. συνίει, 3 pl. ξυνίεσαν Ep. ξυνίεν; also (as if from συνίω) impf. 3 pl. ξύνιον; aor. 1 ξυνέηκα: aor. 2

imperat. ξύνες; aor. 2 med. 3 sing. ξύνετο, 3 pl. subj. συνώμεθα:—*to send, bring* or *set together*, Lat. *committere*. II. metaph. *to perceive, bear: to take notice of, observe, understand, know.* III. Med. *to come to an understanding about* a thing.

συνίμεν, Ep. for συνιέναι, inf. of σύνειμι (εἶμι *ibo*). [ῐ]

συνιοῦσι, 3 pl. pres. of συνίημι, as if from συνιέω.

συν-ίππαρχος, ὁ, *a joint commander of horse.*

συν-ιππεύς, έως, ὁ, *a fellow-rider* or *horseman, a fellow-knight.*

σύνῐσαν, Ep. 3 pl. impf. of σύνειμι (εἶμι *ibo*), *they went together.* II. Ep. 3 pl. plqpf. of σύνοιδα, *they shared in the knowledge.*

συνίσᾱσι, 3 pl. of σύνοιδα.

σύνισθι, imperat. of σύνοιδα.

σύνισμεν, 1 pl. of σύνοιδα.

συν-ίστημι, impf. συνίστην: f. συστήσω: aor. 1 συνέστησα:—*to place* or *set together, to combine, unite: to associate, band together*; also *to annex, attach to.* 2. *to put together, organise, compose, create, frame*: hence *to arrange, contrive, concert together.* 3. *to bring together as friends, introduce, recommend: to advise* one to do. 4. *to produce, exhibit, represent* to one. 5. *to make firm* or *solid, harden.* II. Pass., with aor. 2 act. συνέστην; pf. συνέστηκα, part. συνεστηκώς contr. συνεστώς, ῶσα, ώς, Ion. συνεστεώς, εῶσα, εώς:—*to stand together, stand in close order*: also *to stand one's ground.* 2. *to meet* or *come together*; in hostile sense, *to join battle, to engage, encounter*, and of the battle, *to be joined, to begin*: absol., συνεστηκότων τῶν στρατηγῶν when the generals *were in dispute.* 3. of friends, *to form a league* or *association, to club, league together*; τὸ ξυνιστάμενον or τὸ συνεστηκός, *a conspiracy*: then generally, *to be connected* or *allied.* 4. *to be engaged, involved, implicated* in a thing. 5. *to be put together, to be composed, framed: to hold together, endure, continue.* 6. *to be contracted, condensed: to be gloomy, sullen.*

συν-ίστωρ, ορος, ὁ, ἡ, *knowing also* or *along with, conscious of* a thing; θεοὶ συνίστορες the gods are *witnesses.*

συν-ισχναίνω, *to help dry up*: metaph. *to join with in diminishing* or *reducing.*

συν-ισχῡρίζω, f. ίσω Att. ιῶ, *to help to strengthen.*

συνιῶν, Ion. for συνιείς, pres. part. of συνίημι.

συν-ναίω, *to dwell along with* or *together.*

συν-νάσσω, f. ξω, *to pack tight together.*

συν-ναυβάτης, ου, ὁ, *a shipmate.* [ᾰ]

συν-ναύκληρος, ον, *a joint owner of* a vessel.

συν-ναυμᾰχέω, *to engage in a sea-fight along with.*

συν-ναυστολέω, f. ήσω, *to be shipmate with* another.

συν-ναύτης, ου, ὁ, *a shipmate.*

συν-νεάζω, f. σω, *to spend one's youth* or *be young with.*

συννενέᾰται, 3 pl. pf. pass. of συννέω.

συν-νεύω, f. σω, *to bend together*: also, 2. intr. *to incline to the same point, converge.* II. *to assent to* or *approve by a nod, consent.*

συν-νέφελος, ον, (σύν, νεφέλη) *cloudy, overcast.*

συννεφέω, f. ήσω, *to collect clouds.* II. intr. *to be clouded over*: impers. συννεφεῖ, *it is cloudy.* III. metaph. *to be under a cloud, in adversity.* From

συν-νεφής, ές, (σύν, νέφος) *overcast with clouds, clouded.*

συν-νέω, f. -νήσω: pf. pass. συννένημαι, Ion. 3 pl. συννενέᾰται:—*to pile* or *heap together, heap up.*

σὺν-νέω, f. -νεύσομαι, *to swim together.*

συν-νήχομαι, f. -ξομαι, Dep. *to swim together with.*

συν-νῑκάω, f. ήσω, *to have part in a victory with.* II. transit. *to help in conquering.*

συν-νοέω, f. ήσω, *to think upon together, to think over, meditate* or *reflect on*: also in Med. Hence

σύννοια Ion. -οίη, ἡ, *meditation, thought: anxious thought, trouble.* 2. *consciousness.*

συν-νομοθετέω, f. ήσω, *to be a joint-lawgiver.*

σύν-νομος, ον, (σύν, νέμω) *feeding* or *herding together, consorting*:—metaph. *consorting with.* 2. *partaking* or *sharing in* a thing: hence, 3. as Subst., σύννομος, ὁ, ἡ, *one who lives with, a consort*; of birds, *a mate*; generally, *a partner, fellow, companion, congener.*

σύν-νοος, ον Att. contr. -νους, ουν, *thinking deeply, thoughtful, anxious.*

συν-νοσέω, f. ήσω, *to be ill together* or *along with.*

σύν-νους, ουν, contr. for σύννοος.

συν-νυμφοκόμος, ον, *helping to deck a bride.*

συν-οδεύω, f. σω, *to journey along with.* Hence

συνοδία, ἡ, *a journey in company.* II. *a party of travellers, a caravan.*

συν-οδίτης, ου, ὁ, *a fellow-traveller.*

συνοδοιπορέω, f. ήσω, *to travel together.* And

συνοδοιπορία, ἡ, *a travelling together.* From

συν-οδοιπόρος, ὁ, *a fellow-traveller.*

σύν-οδος, ὁ, ἡ, = συνοδοιπόρος.

σύν-οδος, ἡ, *a coming together, assembly, meeting*; also *an association.* 2. in hostile sense, *a meeting* of two armies, *engagement*, Lat. *concursus.* 3. of things, *a coming together*; χρημάτων σύνοδοι *a coming in* of money, *income*, like πρόσοδοι. 4. *a meeting, joining, junction.*

σύν-οιδα, pf., with pres. sense, of *συνείδω, q. v.

συν-οικειόω, f. ώσω, *to bind* one to another *by ties of friendship.*

συν-οικέω, f. ήσω: pf. -ῴκηκα:—*to dwell* or *live together*: of the scattered inhabitants of a country, *to dwell together, form a community*: of persons, *to live together* as man and wife: absol. *to marry, wed*: metaph. *to be wedded* or *yoked* to misery. II *to make to dwell in together*: in Pass., of a country, *to be thickly peopled.* Hence

συνοίκημα, ατος, τό, *that with which one lives*; σ. ἀχαριτώτατον *a* most unpleasant *house-mate.*

συνοίκησις, ἡ, (συνοικέω) *a dwelling* or *living together*: *wedded life, marriage.*

συνοικήτωρ, ορος, ὁ, ἡ, (συνοικέω) *one that lives with.*

συνοικία Att. ξυνοικία, ἡ, (συνοικέω) *a living to-*

gether. 2. a body of people living together, a community. II. a place where people live together: a house in which several families live, a house divided into chambers or flats, opp. to οἰκία, as Lat. insula to domus (a house occupied by one family). 2. a room built on to a house, an out-house.

συνοίκια (sub. ἱερά), τά, (συνοικέω) an annual feast at Athens to commemorate Theseus uniting all the towns of Attica under the government of Athens, celebrated on the 17th of Boëdromion.

συν-οικίζω, f. ίσω Att. ιῶ, to make to live with: to give in marriage. 2. to make to live together, to join in one city; ξυνοικίσαι τὴν Λέσβον ἐς τὴν Μυτιλήνην to concentrate all the people of Lesbos at Mytilené. II. to join in peopling or colonising a country. Hence

συνοίκισις, ἡ, a making to live together, joining under one city as a capital.

συνοικιστήρ, ῆρος, ὁ, (συνοικίζω) one who joins in peopling, a fellow-colonist.

συν-οικοδομέω, f. ήσω, to build with or together:—Pass. to be built up with other materials.

σύν-οικος, ον, (σύν, οἰκέω) living with or together, inhabiting jointly: as Subst. a joint inhabitant, a denizen:—metaph., ξύνοικος ἀλλαγᾷ βίου associated with change of life.

συν-οικουρός, όν, keeping house together: metaph., συνοικουρὸς κακῶν a partner in mischief.

συν-οικτίζω, f. ίσω Att. ιῶ, to pity along with or together.

συνοίσω, fut. of συμφέρω, med. συνοίσομαι.

συν-ολισθάνω, to slip and fall together with.

συν-όλλυμι: f. -ολέσω Att. -ολῶ: to destroy along with or together:—Med., with pf. 2 -όλωλα, to perish along with or together.

συν-ολολύζω, f. ξω, to raise a loud cry together, properly of women, and usually to raise a shout of joy.

σύν-ολος, ον, also η, ον, all together: τὸ σύνολον the whole together. Hence

συνόλως, Adv. on the whole, at once.

συν-ομαίμων, ον, gen. ονος, (σύν, ὅμαιμος) of the same blood, kindred: as Subst., συνομαίμων, ὁ, ἡ, a brother, sister.

συν-ομᾶλιξ, Dor. for συν-ομῆλιξ.

συν-ομαρτέω, f. ήσω, to follow along with, attend upon.

συν-ομῆλιξ Dor. -ομᾶλιξ, ῐκος, ὁ, ἡ, a friend of the same age, a fellow, comrade.

συν-ομῑλέω, f. ήσω, to converse or associate with.

συν-όμνῡμι or -ύω: f. -ομόσω: aor. 1 -ώμοσα:—to swear along with or together, to join in a league or confederacy, to form league or conspiracy. II. to swear to one, promise by oath; συνομόσαι θάνατόν τινι to join in swearing death against a man.

συν-ομολογέω, f. ήσω, to say the same thing with, agree with: to agree mutually. II. to agree to do, promise, make a covenant with.

συν-ομορέω, f. ήσω, (σύν, ὅμορος) to border or abut on

συν-οπᾱδός, όν, following along with, attending on.

σύν-οπλος, ον, (σύν, ὅπλον) armed together, allied.

συν-οράω, f. συνόψομαι (as if from συνόπτομαι): aor. 2 συνεῖδον, inf. συνῐδεῖν (as if from συν-είδω):—to see together or at the same time. II. to see all at once, take in all at a glance: to take a view of a thing.

συν-οργίζομαι, fut. med. -ίσομαι: aor. 1 pass. συνωργίσθην: Dep.:—to be angry along with or together.

σύν-ορθρος, ον, dawning together with.

συν-ορίνω [ῑ], to stir up together or violently:—Pass. to be moved or urged on together.

σύν-ορκος, ον, (σύν, ὅρκος) bound by oath.

συν-ορμάς, άδος, ἡ, (σύν, ὁρμή) clashing together.

συνόρμενος, Ep. aor. 2 pass. part. of συνόρνυμι.

συν-ορμίζω, f. ίσω, to bring to anchor together.

συν-όρνῡμι, = συνορίνω: Ep. aor. 2 pass. part. συνόρμενος, having started or set forth together.

σύν-ορος Ion. **σύνουρος**, ον, bordering on; κόνις πηλοῦ κάσις ξύνουρος dust twin-brother of mud.

συν-οροφόω, f. ώσω, (σύν, ὀροφή) to roof all over, cover completely.

σύν-ουρος, ον, Ion. for σύνορος.

συν-ουσία Ion. -ίη, ἡ, (from συνών, συνοῦσα, part. of σύνειμι) a being with or together: a living together, social intercourse, association, society. II. a society, meeting of friends, party.

συνουσιαστής, οῦ, ὁ, (συνουσία) one who lives with, a companion: a disciple. Hence

συνουσιαστικός, ή, όν, suited for society, sociable.

συν-οφρυόομαι, f. med. ώσομαι: pf. pass. -ωφρύωμαι: Dep.: (σύν, ὀφρύς):—to knit the brow, frown.

συν-οχή Att. **ξυνοχή**, ἡ, (συνέχω) a holding or being held together, a meeting, joining. 2. metaph. straitness, distress, anguish. Hence

συνοχηδόν, Adv. holding together.

συν-οχμός, ὁ, Ep. συνεοχμός, = συνοχή, junction.

σύνοχος, ον, (συνέχω) held together: metaph. agreeing with, suiting.

συνόχωκα, for συνόκωχα, Ep. intr. pf. of συνέχω, to be held together, come together; ὤμω ἐπὶ στῆθος συνοχωκότε shoulders contracted over the chest.

συνόψομαι, fut. of συνοράω.

σύνταγμα, ατος, τό, (συντάσσω) that which is put together in order: a body of troops drawn up in order, a squadron, corps, contingent. 2. the constitution of a state.

συντᾰκῆναι, aor. 2 pass. inf. of συντήκω.

συντακτέον, verb. Adj. of συντάσσω, one must arrange.

συν-τᾰλαιπωρέω, f. ήσω, to endure hardships together, to share in misery.

συν-τάμνω, Ion. for συντέμνω.

συν-τᾰνύω, = συντείνω, to bring together into one.

σύνταξις, εως, ἡ, (συντάσσω) a putting together in order: of soldiers, a drawing up in order, a complete array: hence 2. order, arrangement: organisation, system. 3. a body of troops 4. in Gramm.

the combination of words and sentences, syntax. II. *a covenant, contract.* 2. *a contribution, quota.* 3. = σύνταγμα, *a contingent* of soldiers. 4. *a settled rate of remuneration.*

συν-τᾰράσσω Att. -ττω: f. ξω: aor. 1 -ετάραξα: Pass., aor. 1 -εταράχθην: pf. -τετάραγμαι:—*to throw into utter confusion, to disturb,* Lat. *conturbare: to trouble, confound, perplex, disquiet:*—Pass. *to be thrown into utter confusion: to be much disturbed, troubled, disquieted, vexed.*

συν-τάσσω Att. -ττω: f. ξω: aor. 1 -έταξα: Pass., aor. 1 -ετάχθην: pf. -τέταγμαι:—*to put together in order, to draw up in order of battle, put in array:* also *to draw up* or *bring into line along with* others. 2. *to arrange, organise,* Lat. *constituere: to regulate, ordain: to command.* II. Pass. *to be drawn up in order of battle.* 2. *to be joined to, drawn up with.* 3. metaph. *to be collected* or *firm.* 4. *to be assessed for taxation.* III. Med. *to put themselves in order of battle, form in line.* 2. *to arrange for oneself.* 3. *to agree together, bargain.* 4. *to take leave of, bid farewell.*

συν-τᾰχύνω [ῡ], *to help to urge on, hurry.* II. intr. *to hasten, hasten to an end.*

συντεθραμμένος, pf. pass. part. of συντρέφω.

συν-τείνω, pf. -τέτᾰκα, pass. -τέτᾰμαι:—*to stretch together, strain, draw tight:* metaph. *to exert, strain:* Pass. *to exert oneself, use all one's endeavours* II. intr. *to exert oneself, strive,* Lat. *contendere.* 2. *to direct one's powers to* one object, *tend towards,* Lat. *tendere ad.*

συν-τειχίζω, f. ίσω Att. ιῶ, *to help to build a fortification.*

συν-τεκμαίρομαι, aor. 1 -ετεκμηράμην: Dep. *to conjecture, guess, calculate.*

συν-τεκνοποιέω, f. ήσω, *to breed children with* another.

συν-τεκνόω, f. ώσω, *to help in breeding:* also *to breed.*

συν-τελέθω, = συντελέω intr., *to belong to.*

συντέλεια, ἡ, (συντελής) *a joint payment, a contribution to the public burdens, subscription.* II. at Athens, *a party* of 5, 6, 10, or more citizens, who equipped a ship *at their joint expense,* and were called συντελεῖς. III. *an union* or *partnership* formed for bearing public burdens, *a club* or *company.* IV. *an accomplishment, completion, end, consummation.*

συν-τελέω, f. έσω: pf. pass. συντετέλεσμαι:—*to bring to an end together, bring quite to an end, complete, finish off.* II. *to pay joint taxes, contribute equally;* **συντελεῖν εἰς τὸν πόλεμον** *to pay all alike* towards the war. 2. συντελεῖν εἰς τοὺς ἱππεῖς *to be rated* or *assessed* as belonging to the knights; hence *to belong to* or *be counted* in a class or body: esp. of a number of small states *tributary* or *confederate with* a larger.

συν-τελής, ές, (σύν, τέλος) *paying joint taxes, contributing one's share;* **συντελὴς πόλις** the city *which had to pay its share* of the penalty. 2. *belonging to the same* συντέλεια or *company.* 3. *tributary to another's state.*

συν-τέμνω Ion. -ταμνω: fut. -τεμῶ: aor. 2 -έτεμον:—*to cut in pieces, to chop up.* II. *to cut down, cut short,* Lat. *concidere:* metaph. *to cut short, abridge, curtail.* III. intr. (sub. ὁδόν), *to make a short cut:* (sub. λόγον), *to cut the matter short, speak briefly, concisely:* **τοῦ χρόνου συντάμνοντος** as the time *became short.*

συν-τερετίζω, *to whistle an accompaniment.*

συν-τέρμων, ον gen. ονος, (σύν, τέρμα) *bordering on.*

συντεταγμένως, Adv. pf. pass. part. of συντάσσω, *in an orderly manner, in set terms.*

συντετᾰμένως, Adv. pf. pass. part. of συντείνω, *earnestly, eagerly, vigorously.*

συντετάραγμαι, pf. pass. of συντᾰράσσω.

συντετέλεσμαι, pf. pass. of συντελέω.

συντέτηκα, pf. with intrans. sense of συντήκω.

συν-τετραίνω: f. -τρήσω: aor. 1 -έτρησα: pf. pass. -τέτρημαι:—*to bore through so as to meet, to perforate:*—Pass. *to be connected by openings* or *channels* II. metaph., συντετραίνειν μῦθον δι' ὤτων *to let* words *pierce* through the ears, *sink deeply.*

συντετριμμένος, pf. pass. part. of συντρίβω.

συντετρίφθαι, pf. pass. inf. of συντρίβω.

σύν-τεχνος, ὁ, ἡ, (σύν, τέχνη) *practising the same art:* as Subst., σύντεχνος, ὁ, *a fellow-workman.*

συν-τήκω, f. ξω: aor. 1 -έτηξα:—*to melt together, melt* or *fuse into one mass.* II. *to melt down, dissolve by melting, make to waste away.* 2. Pass. συντήκομαι, aor. 1 συνετήχθην: aor. 2 συνετάκην [ᾰ]: with pf. act. intrans. συντέτηκα:—*to melt away, dissolve, disappear.*

συν-τηρέω, f. ήσω, *to watch closely; to preserve, keep safe: keep in mind.* 2. *to watch one's opportunity.*

συν-τίθημι, f. -θήσω:—*to place* or *put together, to add together.* 2. *to put together* so as *to form a whole, frame, construct: to compose.* 3. *to compose* a book. 4. *to contrive, devise.* 5. *to put together in one, unite, comprehend.* II. Med. συντίθεμαι: aor. 1 συνεθηκάμην: aor. 2 συνεθέμην:—*to put together for oneself, perceive, observe, take heed to;* σὺ δὲ σύνθεο do thou *take heed,* 2. *to set in order, organise.* 3. *to agree on, conclude: to covenant* or *contract* to do a thing.

συν-τῑμάω, f. ήσω, *to value together:*—Med. *to fix an estimate:*—Pass. *to increase in value, rise in price.*

συν-τῑνάσσω, f. ξω, *to shake together, shake to the foundations, shake violently,* Lat. *concutere: to confuse, confound.*

συν-τιτρώσκω, f. -τρώσω, *to wound in many places.*

***συν-τλάω**, aor. 2 συνέτλην, *to venture together.*

σύντομος, ον, (συντεμεῖν) *cut off, cut short:* metaph. *abridged, shortened,* esp. of a road, σύντομος ὁδός a *short* cut; **συντομώτατον** or **τὰ συντομώτατα**, *by the shortest cut.* 2. *concise, brief, short.* Hence

συντόμως, Adv. *concisely, shortly*: Comp. -ώτερον and -ωτέρως: Sup. -ώτατα and -ωτάτως.

σύντονος, ον, (συντείνω) *on the stretch, strained tight.* 2. metaph. *intense, excessive*: of persons, *earnest, serious, vehement*: neut. pl. σύντονα as Adv. *earnestly, vehemently.* II. (σύν, τόνος) *in harmony* or *unison with.*

συν-τρᾰγῳδέω, f. ήσω, *to act tragedy together.*

συν-τράπεζος, ον, (σύν, τράπεζα) *eating at the same table*: as Subst., συντράπεζος, ὁ, ἡ, *a messmate.*

σύν-τρεις, οἱ, αἱ, σύν-τρια, τά, (σύν, τρεῖς) *three together, three and three.*

συν-τρέφω, f. -θρέψω, *to feed besides, help to feed*: —Pass. *to grow up together, live together.* II. of liquids, *to congeal*:—Pass. *to be congealed, freeze.*

συν-τρέχω, f. -θρέξομαι, or more commonly -δρᾰμοῦμαι: aor. 2 -έδρᾰμον:—*to run together, gather together*: *to commingle.* 2. of enemies, *to rush together, meet in battle, encounter*, Lat. *concurrere.* 3. as friends, *to come together, agree*· generally, *to concur, coincide.* 4. *to meet with.* 5. *to run* or *shrivel up.*

συντρῆσαι, aor. 1 inf. of συντετραίνω.

συν-τριαινόω, f. ώσω, (σύν, τρίαινα) *to overthrow with a trident*: generally, *to overwhelm in ruin.*

συντρῐβήσομαι, fut. pass. of συντρίβω.

συν-τρίβω [ῑ]: f. ψω: aor. 1 -έτριψα: Pass., aor. 2 -ετρίβην [ῐ]: pf. -τέτριμμαι:—*to rub together* II. *to crush, grind down, shiver to atoms*, Lat. *conterere*; συντρίβειν τὰς ναῦς *to stave* the ships *in*: Pass., συντριβῆναι τῆς κεφαλῆς *to have* one's head *broken.* III. metaph. in Pass. *to run against, clash with.*

συντριηραρχέω, f. ήσω, *to be a* συντριήραρχος. From

συν-τριήραρχος, ὁ, *a partner in fitting out a trireme.*

σύντριμμα, ατος, τό, (συντρίβω) *a fracture, destruction.* II. *a stumbling-block, offence.*

σύντριψ, ῐβος, ὁ, ἡ, (συντρίβω) *shattering, smashing*; of a lubber-fiend that breaks the pots in the kitchen.

συντροφία, ἡ, *a being reared together*: *a brood.* From

σύντροφος, ον, (συντρέφω) *brought up together with*: *of the same origin as.* 2. generally, *living with*: *familiar, ordinary, common*: of animals, *brought up together.* 3. *natural, usual, common.* II. act., σύντροφος ζωῆς *helping to preserve lif*

συν-τροχάζω, = συντρέχω.

συν-τυγχάνω, fut. -τεύξομαι: aor. 2 -έτῠχον:—*to meet with, fall in with*: *to converse, speak with*: ὁ συντυχών, like ὁ τυχών, *the first that meets one, any one*: τὸ συντυχόν *the first thing that comes to hand, anything common* or *mean.* II. of accidents, *to happen to, befal*: absol. *to happen, fall out, chance*; εὖ ξυντυχόντων if things *should go well*: impers., συνετύγχανε, συνέτυχε *it happened that* ..

συν-τυμβωρῠχέω, f. ήσω, *to help in robbing graves.*

συν-τῠραννοκτονέω, f. ήσω, *to join in slaying tyrants.*

συν-τῡρόω, f. ώσω, (σύν, τυρός) *to make into cheese together*, hence *to concoct*, Lat. *concoquer*

συντῠχεῖν, aor. 2 inf. of συντυγχάνω

συντῠχία Ion. -ίη, ἡ, (συντυχεῖν) *an occurrence, incident*: *a conjuncture, happy chance, happy event*· also *a mischance, accident.*

συν-υποκρίνομαι, Dep. *to play a part along with*: *to help in maintaining* a character.

συν-υποτίθημι, f. -θήσω, *to help in putting under*: Med. *to help in composing.*

συν-υπουργέω, f. ήσω, *to join in serving* or *assisting.*

συν-ῠφαίνω, aor. 1 -ύφηνα [ῡ]: aor. 1 pass. -ῠφάνθην:—*to weave together*: metaph. *to combine as in one web, frame cunningly.*

συν-ωδίνω [ῑ], *to be in travail together*: *to share in any agony.*

συν-ῳδός, όν, (σύν, ᾠδή) *singing* or *sounding in unison*: *echoing* or *responsive to*: metaph. *according with, in unison with.*

συνῴκησα, aor. 1 of συνοικέω.

συνώμεθα, 1 pl. aor. 2 med. subj. of συνίημι.

συνωμοσία, ἡ, (συνόμνυμι) *a being leagued by oath, a conspiracy*: *confederacy.*

συνωμότης, ου, ὁ, (συνόμνυμι) *one who is leagued by oath, a fellow-conspirator, confederate.*

συνώμοτος, ον, (συνόμνυμι) *leagued* or *banded by oath*: *confederate.*

συν-ωνέομαι, f. ήσομαι: pf. pass. -εώνημαι: Dep.: —*to buy together*: *to collect by offering pay, take into one's pay.* II. *to buy up*, Lat. *coëmere*: pf. also in pass. sense, ὁ συνεωνημένος σῖτος corn *bought up.*

συν-ώνῠμος, ον, (σύν, ὄνυμα Aeol. for ὄνομα) *of like name* or *meaning*

συνωριαστής, οῦ, ὁ, (συνωρίς) *one who drives a pair-horsed chariot*

συνωρίζω, f. σω, (συνωρίς) *to yoke together*:—Med. *to link with oneself.*

συνωρῐκεύομαι, Dep. *to drive a* συνωρίς. From

συνωρίς, ίδος, ἡ, (συνάορος) *a pair of horses* or *mules, a two-horse chariot.* II. generally, *a pair* or *couple of* anything, Lat. *biga.* III. *that which binds together, a pair of fetters.*

συν-ωφελέω, f. ήσω, *to join in helping*: absol. *to be of use, assist together*:—Pass. *to derive profit together.*

συνωφρυωμένος, pf. part. of συνοφρυόομαι.

συν-ωχᾰδόν, Adv. (συνέχω) of Time, *perpetually, continually*: *continuously.*

σῠο-κτᾰσία, ἡ, (σῦς, κτείνω) *a slaying of swine.*

σῠο-φόντης, ου, ὁ, (σῦς, *φένω) *a slayer of swine.*

συο-φόντις, ιδος, ἡ, fem. of συοφόντης.

Σύρα, ἡ, fem. of Σύρος, *a Syrian woman.*

Σῠράκουσαι [ᾱ], αἱ, Ion. **Συρήκουσαι** Dor. **Συράκοσαι**, *Syracuse.* Hence

Σῠρᾱκούσιος, α, ον, Ion. **Σῠρηκ-**, Dor. and Att. **Σῠρᾱκόσιος**, *Syracusan.*

σύρ-γαστρος, ὁ, (σύρομαι, γαστήρ) *trailing the belly,* of a worm or snake.

Z

σύρδην, Adv. (σύρω) *rushing furiously.* 2. *in a long line.*

Συρία, ἡ, (Σύρος) *the land of the Syrians, Syria.*

σύριγμα, ατος, τό, (σύριττω) *the sound of a pipe, a piping* or *whistling sound.*

συριγμός, ὁ, (συρίττω) *the sounding of a pipe, a piping, whistling.*

σύριγξ, ιγγος, ἡ, *a shepherd's pipe, Pan's-pipe.* II. *anything in shape like a pipe,* as, 1. *a spear-case.* 2. *the box* or *hole in the nave of a wheel.* 3. metaph. of *the nostrils* or *wind-pipe.* From

ΣΥΡΙ'ΖΩ Att. **συρίττω** Dor. **συρίσδω**: fut. -ίξω Att. -ίξομαι: aor. 1 ἐσύριξα later ἐσύρισα, inf. συρίσαι:—*to play on the Pan's pipe* (σῦριγξ). II. *to make a piping, whistling sound:* hence *to hiss* an actor, Lat. *explodere.*

Συρι-γενής, ές, (Συρία, γένος) *Syrian-born.*

συρικτάς, ά, ὁ, Dor. for συριστής, οῦ.

Σύριος, α, ον, (Σύρος) *Syrian.*

συρίσδω, **σύρισδες**, Dor. for συρίζω, συρίζεις.

σύρισμα, ατος, τό, = σύριγμα.

συριστήρ, ῆρος, ὁ, = συριστής.

συριστής, οῦ, ὁ, (συρίζω) *a player on the Pan's pipe* (σῦριγξ), *a piper.*

Συριστί, Adv. (Σύρος) *in the Syrian language.*

συρίττω, f. ίξω, = συρίζω, q. v.

σύρμα, ατος, τό, (σύρω) *anything which is drawn* or *trailed along: a robe with a long train.*

συρμαία Ion. -αίη, ἡ, (συρμός) *an emetic* or *purgative draught,* used by the Egyptians, chiefly consisting of the juice of the radish and salt water. whence *the radish* itself is called συρμαίη. Hence

συρμαΐζω, f. σω, *to take an emetic* or *purge.*

συρμάς, άδος, ἡ, (σύρω) *anything swept together, refuse, rubbish.*

συρμός, ὁ, (σύρω) *any sweeping* or *trailing motion,* Lat. *tractus, the track* of meteors, etc. II. *that which is dragged along, a trail.* III. *a vomiting, purging.*

σύροισα, Dor. for σύρουσα, part. fem. of σύρω.

Σῦρος, ὁ, *Syros,* one of the Cyclades: also called **Σύρα**, ἡ, and in the Odyssey **Συρίη**.

Σύρος, ὁ, *a Syrian.* [ῠ]

Σῠρο-φοίνιξ, ῖκος, ὁ, (Σύρος, Φοινίκη) *a Syrophoenician:* fem. **Σῠροφοίνισσα**, *a Syrophoenician woman.*

συρ-ράπτω, f. ψω, *to sew* or *stitch together, sew up.*

συρ-ράσσω Att. -ττω, f. ξω, = συρρήγνυμι in intr. sense, *to dash together, clash together, fight with,* Lat. *confligere.*

συρ-ρέζω, f. ξω, *to sacrifice together.*

συρ-ρέω, f. -ρεύσομαι: pf. -ερρύηκα: aor. 2 in pass. form -ερρύην:—*to flow together* or *in one stream:* metaph. of men, *to flow* or *stream in together.*

συρ-ρήγνῡμι or -ύω: f. -ρήξω: aor. 1 συνέρρηξα: Pass. aor. 2 συνερράγην [ᾰ]: pf. συνέρρηγμαι, but also pf. 2 intr. συνέρρωγα:—*to break to pieces:* συρρῆξαι εἰς ἕν *to break up and make into one:* metaph. in Pass. *to be broken down* by sufferings. II. Pass. and intr. in Act. (esp. in pf. 2 συνέρρωγα): *to break* or *fall to pieces, to be broken up and run together:* of rivers, *to run into one another:* of war, *to break out.*

συρ-ριζόομαι, Pass. (σύν, ῥιζόω) *to have the root, united: to take root together with.*

Σύρτις, ιδος, ἡ, (σύρω) *a sand-bank in the sea:* of the sand-banks on the coast of Africa, of which there were two, the Syrtis Major and Minor.

σύρφαξ, ᾱκος, ὁ, (σύρω) = συρφετός. II. as Adj. *swept together like refuse, vulgar, promiscuous.*

συρφετός, ὁ, (σύρω) *anything swept together, refuse, litter, rubbish,* Lat. *quisquiliae.* II. metaph. *a mixed crowd, mob, rabble.*

ΣΥ'ΡΩ [ῡ]: f. συρῶ: aor. 1 ἔσῡρα: pf. σέσυρκα: Pass., aor. 2 ἐσύρην [ῠ]: pf. σέσυρμαι:—*to draw, drag, trail along: to drag by force, force away, hale:* generally, *to sweep away.*

ΣΥ'Σ, ὁ and ἡ, gen. συός, acc. σῦν: nom. pl. σύες, acc. σύας contr. σῦς, dat. συσί Ep. σύεσσι:—Lat. *SUS,* = ὗς, *a swine, pig,* whether *hog* or *boar,* or *sow;* σῦς κάπριος a wild boar.

συ-σκεδάννῡμι, f. -σκηδάσω, *to toss all about.*

συ-σκευάζω, f. άσω, *to put baggage* or *furniture together, to pack up:* generally, *to make ready, prepare; to contrive, concert.* II. Med. *to pack up one's own baggage,* and generally *to pack up:* part. pf. pass. συνεσκευασμένος or συσκευασάμενος *all packed up, in marching order.* 2. *to prepare, make ready, provide.* 3. *to contrive, concert.* 4. generally, *to bring together, scrape together for one's own use: to band together.* Hence

συσκευᾰσία, ἡ, *a packing up, getting ready,* for a journey or march.

συ-σκευοφορέω, f. ήσω, *to carry baggage together.*

συ-σκευωρέομαι, f. ήσομαι, Dep. *to contrive, devise, concert.*

συ-σκηνέω, f. ήσω, *to live in the same tent* or *house with* another, *to lodge together: to mess with* any one. Hence

συσκηνητήρ, ῆρος, ὁ, *one who lives in the same tent, a messmate,* Lat. *contubernalis.*

συσκηνήτρια, ἡ, fem. of συσκηνητήρ.

συσκηνία, ἡ, (σύσκηνος) *a dwelling in one tent:* of soldiers, *a messing together.*

συσκήνιον, τό, *a common meal,* of the Lacedaemonians. From

σύ-σκηνος, ον, (σύν, σκηνή) *living in one tent:* as Subst., σύσκηνος, ὁ, *a messmate, comrade,* Lat. *contubernalis.* Hence

συ-σκηνόω, f. ώσω, = συσκηνέω.

συ-σκιάζω, f. άσω, *to throw a shade quite over, to cover entirely.*

σύ-σκιος, ον, (σύν, σκιά) *shaded over, shaded.*

συ-σκοπέω, *to contemplate along with* or *together.*

συ-σκοτάζω, f. άσω, *to grow* or *become dark:* impers., συσκοτάζει *it grows dark.*

συ-σκυθρωπάζω, f. σω, *to look sad* or *gloomy together.*

συ-σπᾰράσσω Att. **-ττω**, f. ξω, *to rend in pieces.*

συ-σπάω, f. άσω [ᾰ], *to draw* or *squeeze together:* of skins, *to sew together.*

συ-σπειράομαι, Pass. (σύν, σπεῖρα) *to be coiled up together:* of soldiers, *to be formed in close order: to march in close order.*

συ-σπείρω, *to sow* or *sprinkle together.*

συ-σπένδω, f. -σπείσω, *to join in making a libation:*—Med. *to join in making a peace, treaty,* etc.

συ-σπεύδω, f. σω, *to join in hastening* or *promoting, to lend a helping hand.*

συ-σπλαγχνεύω, f. σω, (σύν, σπλάγχνα) *to help to the flesh of the victim at a sacrifice.*

σύ-σπονδος, ον, (σύν, σπονδή) *making a libation with: joining in the same treaty.*

συ-σπουδάζω, f. άσω, *to make haste along with* or *together, to be in earnest about* a thing. II. trans. *to pursue* or *manage zealously together.*

συσ-σείω, f. σω, *to shake together: to make to quiver* or *tremble.*

συσ-σημαίνομαι, Dep. (σύν, σημαίνω) *to join in sealing and signing.*

σύσ-σημος, ον, (σύν, σῆμα) *marked in common:* as Subst., σύσσημον, τό, *a fixed sign* or *signal.*

συσσῑτέω, f. ήσω, (σύσσιτος) *to eat* or *mess with: to eat* or *mess together.* Hence

συσσίτησις, εως, ἡ, = συσσιτία: and

συσσῑτία, ἡ, *a messing together* or *in common.* II. *a club* or *mess.*

συσσίτιον, τό, (συσσιτέω): I. in pl. *a common meal,* esp. at Sparta where all dined together according to the institution of Lycurgus. II. *a dining-room, hall.*

σύσ-σῑτος, ον, (σύν, σιτέω) *eating together with* or *in common:* as Subst. σύσσιτος, ὁ, *a messmate.*

συσ-σώζω, f. σω, *to help to save* or *deliver.*

σύσ-σωμος, ον, (σύν, σῶμα) *united in one body.*

συσ-σωφρονέω, f. ήσω, *to be a partner in temperance.*

συστᾰδόν, Adv. (συνίσταμαι) *standing close together:* of fighting, *at close quarters,* Lat. *cominus.*

συστᾰθείς, aor. 1 pass. part. of συνίστημι.

συστᾰλείς, aor. 2 pass. part. of συστέλλω.

συ-στᾰσιάζω, f. άσω, *to join in sedition, be factious with.* Hence

συστᾰσιαστής, οῦ, ὁ, *one who takes part in a sedition, a fellow-rioter.*

σύστᾰσις, ἡ, (συνίσταμαι) *a standing together, meeting:* in hostile sense, *close combat, conflict, battle:* σύστασις γνώμης *a conflict* of mind. 2. *an union, association, club.* 3. metaph. *sternness, harshness, rigour.*

συ-στᾰσιώτης, ου, ὁ, (σύν, στασιώτης) *a member of the same party, a partisan.*

συστᾰτικός, ή, όν, (συνίστημι) *of* or *for bringing together, introductory, commendatory;* ἡ συστατικὴ ἐπιστολή a letter *of introduction.*

συ-σταυρόω, f. ώσω, *to crucify along with.*

συ-στεγάζω, f. άσω, *to cover together* or *entirely.*

συ-στέλλω, f. -στελῶ: aor. 1 -έστειλα: pf. act. -έσταλκα, pass. -έσταλμαι:—*to draw together, draw in:* hence *to shorten sail.* 2. *to draw in, contract, compress, condense:*—Pass. *to be contracted, get smaller;* συστέλλεσθαι εἰς εὐτέλειαν *to be drawn in* towards economy, i. e. to retrench: so also in pf. pass. part. συνεσταλμένος, *drawn in, brought into narrow compass, moderate.* 3. metaph. *to lower, humble, abase:*—Pass. *to be lowered* or *cast down.* II. *to wrap closely up, shroud, veil:*—Med., συστέλλεσθαι θοιμάτιον *to wrap one's* cloak *close round one;* συστέλλεσθαι ἑαυτόν *to gird up one's* loins; so aor. 2 pass. part. συσταλείς *ready for action.* III. in Gramm. *to use a syllable short.*

συ-στενάζω, f. ξω, *to sigh* or *groan with.*

συ-στεφανόω, f. ώσω, *to crown along with* or *together.*

σύστημα, ατος, τό, (συνίστημι) *that which is put together, a composite whole: a composition: a college, assembly.*

συ-στοιχέω, f. ήσω, (σύν, στοῖχος) *to stand in the same row* or *line with: to be coördinate* or *in conformity with, to correspond to.*

συ-στολίζω, f. ίσω, = συστέλλω, *to put together, fabricate.* II. *to unite.*

συστρᾰτεία, ἡ, *a common campaign* or *expedition.* From

συ-στρᾰτεύω, f. -εύσω; also as Dep. **συστρατεύομαι**, f. -εύσομαι:—*to make a campaign, serve along with* or *together, to join* or *share in an expedition.*

συστρᾰτηγέω, f. ήσω, *to be the fellow-general of.* From

συ-στράτηγος, *a fellow-general, joint commander.*

συ-στρᾰτιώτης, ου, ὁ, *a fellow-soldier.*

συ-στρᾰτοπεδεύομαι, Dep. *to encamp along with.*

συ-στρέφω, f. ψω: Pass., aor. 2 συνεστράφην [ᾰ]: pf. συνέστραμμαι:—*to twist* or *coil up together, roll into a mass,* Lat. *conglobare;* generally, *to collect in one, combine:* of soldiers, *to rally, form into a solid body;* συστρέφειν ἑαυτόν *to rally* or *collect* oneself:—Pass. *to be united in one body, combine: to club together, conspire.* 2. of sentences, *to compress, condense, make terse* or *concise;* συνεστραμμένη λέξις *a rounded, periodic* style. II. *to twist* or *whirl round, whirl away, carry off.* III. *to turn all together, to make wheel round.* Hence

συστροφή, ἡ, *a rolling up together, winding into a ball.* II. *any dense* or *compact mass: a body of men, a crowd,* Lat. *globus: a coming together, gathering.*

συ-σφάζω, f. ξω: aor. 2 pass. συνεσφάγην [ᾰ], inf. συσφαγῆναι:—*to slay along with* or *together.*

συ-σφίγγω, f. γξω, *to lace* or *bind close together.*

συ-σχημᾰτίζω, f. σω, *to conform* one thing *to* another:—Pass. *to be conformed* to another's example.

συ-σχολάζω, f. σω, *to pass one's leisure with* or *together.*

σύτο [ῦ], Ep. for ἐσσῦτο, 3 sing. plqpf. pass. (with aor. sense) of σεύω.

σῡφειός, ὁ, lengthd. form for συφεός.

σῠφεός, ὁ, (σῦς) *a hog-sty*; συφεόνδε = εἰς or πρὸς συφεόν, *to the sty*.

σῠ-φόρβιον, τό, (σῦς, φέρβω) *a herd of swine*.

σῠ-φορβός, ὁ, (σῦς, φέρβω) = ὑφορβός, *a swineherd*.

σύφος, α, ον, Aeol. for σοφός

ΣΥΧΝΟ'Σ, ή, όν, of Time, *long*; with plur. nouns, *many together*. 2. of Number and Quantity, *many*, *much, frequent, great*: with singular nouns, *much*, *numerous, frequent*. 3. the dat. συχνῷ is often joined with a Comp. Adj., like πολλῷ, as, συχνῷ βελτίων *far* better. 4. neut. συχνόν and συχνά as Adv. *often*, *much*.

σφᾰγεῖον, τό, (σφαγῆναι) *a bowl for catching the blood of the victim* in sacrifices. II. like σφάγιον, *the victim* itself

σφᾰγείς, aor. 2 pass. part. of σφάζω.

σφᾰγεύς, έως, ὁ, (σφάζω) *a slayer, butcher*: *a murderer*: ὁ σφαγεὺς ἕστηκε *the slayer* is set, of the sword on which Ajax is about to throw himself: *a sacrificial knife*.

σφᾰγή, ἡ, (σφαγῆναι) *slaughter, butchery, sacrifice*: *the victim itself*: σφαγαὶ πυρὸς *the sacrificial fire*. 2. *a wound*. II. *the throat*, Lat. *jugulum*, mostly in plur.

σφαγιάζομαι, f. άσομαι, Dep. (σφάγιον) *to slay a victim, to sacrifice*. II. more rarely an Act. σφαγιάζω occurs in the same sense, whence aor. 1 part. σφαγιασθείς as Pass., *having been sacrificed*. Hence

σφᾰγιασμός, ὁ, *a slaying, sacrificing*.

σφάγιον, τό, mostly in plur., σφάγια, τά, *a victim*: δοῦλα σφάγια *the sacrifice* of a slave. Properly neut. from sq. [ᾰ]

σφάγιος, ον, also α, ον, (σφάζω) *slaying, sacrificing*: *killing, deadly*.

σφᾰγίς, ίδος, ἡ, (σφάζω) *a sacrificial knife*: generally, *a knife*.

ΣΦᾸΔΑ'ΖΩ, f. σω, *to struggle, plunge*, like a restive horse: *to writhe* or *struggle convulsively*. Hence

σφᾰδασμός, ὁ, *a spasm, convulsion*.

ΣΦΑ'ΖΩ Att. σφάττω: f. σφάξω: aor. 1 ἔσφαξα: Pass., aor. 1 ἐσφάχθην: aor. 2 ἐσφάγην [ᾰ]: fut. σφᾰγήσομαι: pf. ἔσφαγμαι:—*to slay by cutting the throat*, Lat. *jugulare*: *to slay, slaughter, sacrifice, immolate*.

ΣΦΑΙ͂ΡΑ, ας, ἡ, *a ball*, esp. *a ball to play with*; σφαίρῃ παίζειν to play *at ball*; σφαῖραν ῥίπτειν to toss *the ball* about. 2. *a sphere, globe*.

σφαιρηδόν, Adv. (σφαῖρα) *like a globe* or *ball*.

σφαιρίζω, f. ίσω, (σφαῖρα) *to play at ball*.

σφαιρικός, ή, όν, (σφαῖρα) *like a ball, spherical*: τὰ σφαιρικά *the science of the spheres, astronomy*.

σφαιρίον, τό, Dim. of σφαῖρα, *a small ball*.

σφαιριστής, οῦ, ὁ, (σφαιρίζω) *a ball-player*.

σφαιρο-ειδής, ές, (σφαῖρα, εἶδος) *ball-like, globular, spherical*: *rounded, blunted*.

σφαιρόω, f. ώσω: pass. pf. ἐσφαίρωμαι, plqpf. ἐσφαιρώμην: (σφαῖρα):—*to make globular* or *spherical*: —Pass., στήθεα δ' ἐσφαίρωτο his chest *was round and arched*. II. *to tip with a ball* or *button*; ἀκόντια ἐσφαιρωμένα spears *tipped with buttons*.

σφαιρωτός, ή, όν, (σφαιρόω) *rounded, made globular*. II. *tipped with a ball* or *button*.

σφᾰκελίζω, f. σω, *to be gangrened, mortify*; ἐσφακέλισέ τε τὸ ὀστέον καὶ ὁ μηρὸς ἐσάπη the bone *became gangrened* and the thigh mortified. From

σφάκελος, ὁ, *gangrene, mortification*. 2. *a spasm, convulsion*: *convulsive fury*. [ᾰ]

ΣΦΑ'ΚΟΣ, ὁ, the plant *sage*, Lat. *salvia*. [ᾰ]

σφακτός, ή, όν, (σφάζω) *slaughtered, sacrificed*.

σφᾰλείς, aor. 2 part. pass. of σφάλλω.

σφᾰλερός, ά, όν, (σφάλλω) *making to fall, totter* or *stagger*: metaph. *slippery, perilous, precarious*, Lat. *lubricus*. II. intr. *ready to fall, tottering, staggering*. Adv. -ρῶς.

σφᾰλῆναι, aor. inf. pass. of σφάλλω.

σφαλλόντι, Dor. 3 pl. pres. of σφάλλω.

ΣΦΑ'ΛΛΩ: f. σφᾰλῶ: aor. 1 ἔσφηλα, inf. σφῆλαι. Pass., with fut. med. σφᾰλήσομαι, σφᾰλοῦμαι: aor. 2 ἐσφάλην [ᾰ]: pf. ἔσφαλμαι: 3 sing. plqpf. ἔσφαλτο:—*to make to fall*; properly, *to trip up in wrestling*: *make to stumble, throw down, overthrow*: *to make to totter* or *reel*. 2. metaph. *to baffle, foil, balk, disconcert, disappoint*. II. Pass. *to be tripped up*, *to stumble, stagger, reel*: *to fall*, esp. by disasters. 2. *to be baffled, foiled, disappointed*: *to be defeated, to fail, be unsuccessful*; οὔ τι μὴ σφαλῶ γ' ἐν σοί ποτε *I shall never be disappointed* in thee:—c. gen. rei, *to be balked* or *disappointed of* a thing. 3. *to fail, err, be deceived, blunder*. Hence

σφάλμα, ατος, τό, *a stumble, false step*. II. metaph. *a failure, defeat, disaster*. 2. *a fault, failing, trespass*.

σφάξ, Dor. for σφήξ, *a wasp*.

σφάξας, aor. 1 part. of σφάζω.

σφᾰρᾰγέομαι, Dep. (σφάραγος) *to burst with a noise, to crack, crackle, hiss*. 2. *to groan with fulness, be full to bursting*.

σφᾰρᾰγίζω, f. σω, *to stir up with a loud noise*. From

ΣΦΑ'ΡΑΓΟΣ, ὁ, *a bursting with a noise, cracking, crackling*. (Formed from the sound.) [σφᾰρᾰ]

σφᾶς, enclit. acc. of σφεῖς.

σφάς [ᾱ], acc. pl. fem. of σφός.

σφάττω, Att. for σφάζω.

σφε, Ep. and Ion. enclit. acc. pl. masc. and fem. of σφεῖς, *them*. II. in Attic and later Poets, also acc. sing. *him, her*.

σφέᾰ, nom. and acc. pl. neut. of σφεῖς.

σφέᾱς, Ep. and Ion. acc. pl. for σφᾶς.

σφεδᾰνός, ή, όν, collat. form of σφοδρός, *eager, vehement, earnest*: neut. σφεδανόν as Adv. *eagerly, vehemently*.

ΣΦΕΙ'Σ, nom. pl. masc. and fem. of the personal Pron. of 3rd person, *they*, neut. σφέα: gen. σφῶν: dat. σφίσι: acc. σφᾶς, neut. σφέα. The Ep. and Ion. forms are,—nom. σφεῖς: genit. σφέων Ep. also σφείων: dat. σφῐ and σφῐν, very rarely used also for dat. sing.: accus. σφέας Ep. also σφείας, also σφε (both sing. and pl.). There are also some Aeol. and Dor. forms, —nom. σφές, dat. φῐν and ψῐν, acc. ψε. In Homer this Pron. is always personal, and therefore he uses no neut., which first occurs in Herodotus. The notion is often strengthened by αὐτός, as in σφῶν αὐτῶν, σφέας αὐτούς. II. there is a rare usage of σφεῖς for 2nd pers. pl., μετὰ σφίσιν for μεθ' ὑμῖν.

ΣΦΕ'ΛΑΣ, ατος, τό, *a footstool*: Ep. contr. plur. σφέλᾱ, for σφέλατα, σφέλαα.

σφενδάμνῐνος, η, ον, *of maple wood*, Lat. *acernus*: metaph., ἄνδρες σφενδάμνινοι '*hearts of maple*.' From

ΣΦΕ'ΝΔΑΜΝΟΣ, ἡ, *the maple*, Lat. *acer*.

σφενδονάω, f. ήσω, *to sling, to use the sling*. II. *to throw as from a sling, hurl violently*. 2. *to move like a sling, to swing, brandish*. 3. *to smite with a sling*. From

σφενδόνη, ἡ, *a sling*, Lat. *funda*, being a strip of leather broad in the middle and narrow at each end. II. *anything like a sling in shape; the hoop* of a ring *in which the stone was set as in a sling, the outer* or *broader part round the stone*, Lat. *funda* or *pala annuli*. III. *the act of slinging, a throw, cast*. IV. *that which is slung, the stone* or *bullet of the sling*.

σφενδονήτης, ου, ὁ, (σφενδονάω) *a slinger*.

σφές, Aeol. and Dor. for σφεῖς.

σφετερίζω, f. ίσω Dor. ίξω, (σφέτερος) *to make one's own, appropriate, usurp*: also as Dep. **σφετερίζομαι**, whence Dor. aor. 1 part. σφετεριξάμενος.

σφέτερος, α, ον, possessive Adj. of the 3rd pers. Pron. σφεῖς, *their own, their, belonging to them*:—also of the 3rd pers. sing., *his, hers*. II. sometimes also used of others than the 3rd pers., as: 1. of the 2nd pers. pl., = ὑμέτερος, *your own*: and of the 2nd pers. sing., = σός, *thy, thine own*. 2. of the 1st pers. pl., = ἡμέτερος, *our own*; and of the 1st pers. sing., = ἐμός, *my own, mine*.

σφέων, Ep. and Ion. for σφῶν, gen. of σφεῖς.

σφῇ, dat. fem. of σφός.

σφηκιά, ἡ, (σφήξ) *a wasps' nest*.

σφηκίσκος, ὁ, (σφήξ) *a piece of wood pointed like a wasp's sting, a pointed stick* or *stake*.

σφηκο-ειδής, ές, (σφήξ, εἶδος) = σφηκώδης.

σφηκόω, f. ώσω, (σφήξ) *to make like a wasp, to pinch in at the waist*: generally, *to pinch in, bind tightly*:—Pass., πλοχμοὶ χρυσῷ τε καὶ ἀργύρῳ ἐσφήκωντο (3 pl. plqpf.) the braids of hair *were tight bound* with gold and silver.

σφηκ-ώδης, ες, contr. for σφηκοειδής, (σφήξ, εἶδος) *wasp-like, pinched in at the waist like a wasp*.

σφήκωμα, ατος, τό, (σφηκόω) *the point of a helmet* in which the plume is fixed.

σφῆλαι, aor. 1 inf. of σφάλλω.

σφῆλα, Ep. for ἔσφηλα, aor. 1 of σφάλλω.

ΣΦΗ'Ν, σφηνός, ὁ, *a wedge*, Lat. *cuneus*.

σφηνο-πώγων, ωνος, ὁ, (σφήν, πώγων) *with a wedge-shaped* or *peaked beard*, as Mercury is represented: in Comedy old men were thus brought on the stage.

σφηνόω, f. ώσω, (σφήν) *to wedge up, close*.

ΣΦΗ'Ξ, ηκός, ὁ, *a wasp*, Lat. *vespa*.

Σφηττός, ὁ, an Attic deme: Adv. **Σφηττοῖ** *at Sphettus*: Adj. **Σφήττιος**, α, ον, *a Sphettian*.

σφῐ, σφῐν, Ep. and Ion. dat. pl. of σφεῖς: also, but very rarely, as dat. sing.

σφιγγίον, τό, (σφίγγω) *a band, a bracelet* or *necklace*.

ΣΦΙ'ΓΓΩ, f. σφίγξω: aor. 1 ἔσφιγξα: Pass., aor. 1 ἐσφίγχθην: pf. ἔσφιγμαι:—*to bind tight, bind in* or *together*: *to squeeze, throttle*, hence *to torture*: *to shut close*: also *to straiten, compress*. Hence

σφιγκτήρ, ῆρος, ὁ, *a tight binder, a lace, band*.

σφιγκτός, ή, όν, verb. Adj. of σφίγγω, *tight-bound*: θάνατος σφιγκτός death *by strangling*.

σφίγκτωρ, ορος, ὁ, poët. for σφιγκτήρ.

Σφίγξ, ἡ, gen. Σφιγγός, *the Sphinx*, a she-monster, who proposed a riddle to the Thebans and murdered all who failed to guess it; Oedipus guessed it, and thereupon she killed herself: in works of art she is represented with a woman's bust on the body of a lioness. (From σφίγγω, so the *Sphinx* properly means *the Throttler*.)

σφῐν, v. σφι.

σφῐσί, σφῐσῐν, dat. of σφεῖς.

σφογγιά, σφόγγιον, σφόγγος, Att. for σπογγ-.

σφόδρᾰ, Adv., properly neut. pl. of σφοδρός, *very, very much, exceedingly, with vehemence*.

ΣΦΟΔΡΟ'Σ, ά, όν, also ός, όν, *vehement, violent, excessive*. II. of men, *violent, impetuous*: also *active, zealous*.

σφοδρύνω, (σφοδρός) *to make vehement*:—Pass. σφοδρύνομαι, *to be violent* or *overbearing*: σφοδρύνεσθαί τινι *to put overweening trust in* a thing. [ῠ]

σφοδρῶς, Adv. of σφοδρός, *violently*; Sup. σφοδρότατον.

σφονδύλη, ἡ, Att. for σπονδύλη, *an insect which lives on the roots of plants*, a kind of *beetle*.

σφονδύλιος, ὁ, like σφόνδυλος, *a vertebre*.

σφονδῠλο-δίνητος, ον, (σφόνδυλος, δῑνέω) *twirled on a spindle*.

σφόνδῠλος, ὁ, Att. for σπόνδυλος, *a vertebre*, Lat. *vertebra*. II. *any round body; the round weight* which twirls a spindle.

σφός, σφή, σφόν, (σφέ) sing. masc., *his, his own*; fem., *her, her own*. II. (σφεῖς) plur. masc. and fem., *their, their own*, like σφέτερος.

σφρᾱγίδιον, τό, Dim. of σφραγίς.

σφρᾱγῑδ-ονῠξ-αργο-κομήτης, ου, ὁ, (σφραγίς, ὄνυξ, ἀργός, κομέω) Comic name for a coxcomb, *a lazy long-haired fellow that wears an onyx signet-ring*.

σφρᾱγίζω Ion. **σφρηγ-**: f. ίσω: pf. pass. **ἐσφρά-**

γισμαι: (σφραγίς):—*to seal: to seal up, shut up.* II. generally, *to mark as with a seal, stamp.* III. metaph. *to seal* or *stamp with approval, limit, define, determine.*

ΣΦΡΑΓΙ'Σ Ion. σφρηγίς, ῖδος, ἡ, *a seal to mark* anything *with: a seal, signet-ring:* generally, *a ring:* also *the gem* or *stone for a ring.* II. *the impression of a signet-ring, a seal.* III. *anything sealed* or *marked with a seal, a token, ticket, passport, permit.*

σφράγισμα, ατος, τό, (σφρᾶγίζω) *an impression of a signet-ring, a seal.*

σφρηγίζω, σφρηγίς, Ion. for σφραγ-.

σφρῑγάω, f. ήσω, *to be full to bursting, to be plump and full,* Lat. *turgere, turgescere:* esp. of horses, *to be in full health and strength,* Lat. *vigere.* II. metaph. *to swell with pride; σφριγῶν μῦθος an overweening* speech.

σφυγμός, ὁ, (σφύζω) *the throbbing pulse in inflamed parts:* also *the beating of the heart, the pulse.*

σφύζω, f. ξω, *to throb, beat violently:* of the pulse, *to beat; τὰ σφύζοντα, the veins* or *arteries.*

ΣΦΥ'ΡΑ, ἡ, *a hammer.* II. *an implement of husbandry, a beetle, mallet,* for breaking clods of earth.

σφῠράς, άδος, ἡ, Att. for σπυράς, σπύραθος, *the dung* of goats and sheep.

σφῠρ-ήλᾰτος, ον, (σφῦρα, ἐλαύνω) *wrought* or *beaten out with the hammer.* II. metaph. *wrought as out of iron, rigid.*

ΣΦΥΡΟ'Ν, τό, *the ankle:* metaph., ὀρθῷ στῆσαι ἐπὶ σφυρῷ to set upon upright *ankle,* i. e. to set upright. II. metaph. *the lowest part* or *base.*

σφύσδω, Dor. for σφύζω.

σφώ, apocopate Att. nom. and acc. for σφῶι: gen. and dat. σφῷν for σφῶιν.

ΣΦΩΕ', dual masc. and fem. nom. and acc. of person Pron. of 3rd pers.; gen. and dat. σφωίν:—*they two, both of them.*

ΣΦΩΊ, nom. and acc. dual masc. and fem. of person. Pron. of 2nd pers.; gen. and dat. σφῶιν;—*you two, both of you.*

σφωίτερος, α, ον, possess. Adj. of 2nd person dual σφῶι, *of* or *belonging to you two* . as possess. Adj. of 3rd pers. dual σφωέ, *of* or *belonging to them two* or *both of them* II. also used as possess. Adj. of 2nd pers. sing., *thy, thine.* 2. of 3rd pers. sing., *his, her.*

σφῷν, contr. Att. for σφῶιν, gen. and dat. of σφῶι.

ΣΧΑ'ΔΩ'Ν, όνος, ἡ, *the larva of the bee* or *wasp.* II. *the cell of a honeycomb, the honeycomb.* Lat. *favus.*

ΣΧΑ'ΖΩ, f. άσω: aor. I ἔσχασα:—*to slit, cut open; σχάζειν φλέβα to lance* or *open* a vein. II. *to let fall, let drop, let down:* metaph., σχάζεσθαι τὴν ἱππικὴν *to give up* one's love for horses, *to cut* the turf. 2. *to check, stop, master.* 3. *to let go; σχάζειν τὴν φροντίδα to let* the mind *go free.*

ΣΧΑ'ΛΙ'Σ, ίδος, ἡ, *a forked stick, used as a ladder,* Lat. *scala:*—*a forked stick, used as a prop for* nets.

σχάω, impf. ἔσχων, rare Att. form of σχάζω.

σχέ, aor. 2 imperat. of ἔχω, for σχές.

σχεδία Ion. -ίη, ἡ, *a light boat* or *craft, raft, float;* σχεδία διφθερίνη *a raft* of hides: poët. *a boat, ship.* 2. *a light bridge, a bridge of rafts* or *pontoons.*

σχεδιάζω, f. άσω, (σχέδιος) *to make* or *do a thing off-hand: to speak* or *write off-hand.*

σχεδίην, Ep. Adv. formed from the fem. of σχέδιος, *near, nigh,* Lat. *cominus.* II. *at once.*

σχέδιος, α, ον, (σχεδόν) *near, at close quarters;* σχεδία μάχη *a close* fight, *hand to hand.*

σχεδόθεν, Adv. (σχεδόν) *from near, from nigh at hand:* also *nigh at hand, near.*

σχεδόν, Adv. (σχεῖν) of Place, *near, nigh, close,* Lat. *cominus:* also used as Prep., c. dat. and c. gen. 2. of Motion, *into the neighbourhood of, towards.* 3. of Degree, *nearly, hard upon all but;* σχεδὸν πάντες *nearly all*, σχεδὸν ἐπίσταμαι I am *pretty well* assured.

σχέθον, Ep. for ἔσχεθον, poët. aor. 2 of ἔχω.

σχεθεῖν Ep. σχεθέειν, poët. aor. 2 inf. of ἔχω: see ἔσχεθον.

σχεῖν, aor. 2 inf. of ἔχω.

σχελίς, ίδος, ἡ, Att for σκελίς, mostly in plur. σχελίδες, *ribs of beef.*

σχέμεν, σχέμεναι, Ep. for σχεῖν, aor. 2 inf. of ἔχω.

σχένδῠλα or **σχενδύλη**, ἡ, (σχεῖν) *a carpenter's tool, a pair of pincers* or *tongs.*

σχέο, Ep. for σχοῦ, aor. 2 med. imperat. of ἔχω.

Σχερία, ἡ, *Scheria,* the island of the Phaeacians: later Κέρκυρα, Lat. *Corcyra,* now *Corfu.*

σχερός, ὁ, used only in the phrase ἐν σχερῷ, *in a row* or *line, one after another, successively.* Compare ἐπισχερώ.

σχές, aor. 2 imperat. of ἔχω.

σχέσθαι, aor. 2 med. inf. of ἔχω.

σχέσις, εως, ἡ, (σχεῖν) *state, condition, habit of body: the nature* or *fashion* of a thing; βίου σχέσις *a way* of life.

σχετήριον, τό, (σχεῖν) *a check, a remedy.*

σχετλιάζω, f. άσω, (σχέτλιος) *to complain of hardship, to inveigh bitterly.* Hence

σχετλιασμός, ὁ, *angry complaining, invective.*

σχέτλιος, α, ον, also ος, ον: (σχεῖν):—properly, *able to bear:* I. of Persons, *hardhearted, merciless, cruel, savage* 2. *much-suffering, unflinching, hardy.* 3. *miserable, unhappy.* II of Things, *cruel, shocking, horrid, abominable.* Hence

σχετλίως, Adv. *cruelly, abominably:* Sup. σχετλιώτατα.

σχέτο, Ep. for ἔσχετο, 3 sing. aor. 2 med. of ἔχω.

σχῆμα, ατος, τό, (σχεῖν) *form, shape, outward appearance, the figure, person.* 2. *the form, outside,* opp. to the reality: *a mere show, pretence.* 3. *the bearing, look, mien; stateliness, dignity:* in plur.

gestures. 4. *the fashion, manner, way* of a thing; σχῆμα στολῆς *fashion* of dress. 5. *the state, nature, constitution* of a thing. 6. *a figure* in dancing; in plur. *steps.* Hence

σχημᾰτίζω, f. ίσω Att. ιῶ, *to form, fashion, shape, arrange:* so in Med., σχηματίζεσθαι κόμην *to dress her* hair, Lat. *fingere.* 2. intr. *to assume a certain form* or *position: to make steps* or *figures, to dance.* II. Pass. σχηματίζομαι, *to be fashioned, dressed out, adorned* in a certain way. 2. *to demean oneself* in a certain way, hence *to pretend;* σχηματίζονται ἀμαθεῖς εἶναι *they pretend* to be unlearned. 3. *to gesticulate.*

σχημάτιον, τό, Dim. of σχῆμα: in plur. *the figures of a dance;* σχημάτια Λακωνικά Laconian *figures.*

σχημᾰτο-ποιέω, f. ήσω, (σχῆμα, ποιέω) *to form, shape* or *fashion* a thing:—Pass. *to adopt a certain shape* or *appearance, to gesticulate.*

σχήσω, fut. of ἔχω.

σχίδαξ, ἄκος, ὁ, (σχίζω) = σχίζα.

σχίζα Ion. **σχίζη**, ἡ, (σχίζω) *a cleft piece of wood, splinter, lath, splint,* Lat. *scindula:* in plur. *wood cleft small, firewood.* II. *an arrow, spear.*

ΣΧΙ'ΖΩ, f. ίσω: aor. 1 ἔσχισα: Pass., aor. 1 ἐσχίσθην: pf. ἔσχισμαι:— *to split, cleave,* Lat. *scindo: to rend asunder:* generally, *to part asunder, separate, divide:*—so in Pass., Νεῖλος σχίζεται τριφασίας ὁδοὺς the Nile *branches* into three channels; ἐσχίζοντό σφεων αἱ γνῶμαι their opinions *were divided.* Hence

σχινδάλᾰμος, Att. for σκινδάλαμος.

ΣΧΙ'ΝΟΣ, ἡ *the mastich tree,* Lat. *lentiscus.* II. *a squill.*

σχῖνο-τρώκτης, ου, ὁ, (σχῖνος, τρώγω) *one who chews mastich-wood.*

σχισθῆναι, aor. 1 pass. inf. of σχίζω.

σχίσις, εως, ἡ, (σχίζω) *a cleaving, parting, division.*

σχίσμα, ατος, τό, (σχίζω) *that which is cloven* or *parted: a rent, cleft, division.* II. generally, *division, schism.*

σχισμός, ὁ, (σχίζω) *a cleaving, splitting, rending.*

σχίσσα, poët. for ἔσχισα, aor. 1 of σχίζω.

σχιστός, ή, όν, (σχίζω) *split, cloven, parted, divided;* σχιστὴ ὁδός a road that *branches off.*

σχοίᾰτο, poët. 3 pl. aor. 2 med. opt. of ἔχω.

σχοίην, aor. 2 opt. of ἔχω.

σχοίνῐνος, η, ον, (σχοῖνος) *of rushes, made of rushes.*

σχοινίον, τό, (σχοῖνος) *a rope twisted of rushes:* generally, *a rope, cord, line.*

σχοινίς, ῐδος, ἡ, (σχοῖνος) = σχοινίον.

σχοινίτης [ῑ], ου, ὁ, (σχοῖνος) *made of rushes:* fem. **σχοινῖτις**, ιδος.

σχοινο-βάτης [ᾰ], ου, ὁ, (σχοῖνος, βαίνω) *a rope-dancer,* Lat. *schoenobătes.*

ΣΧΟΙ͂ΝΟΣ, ὁ, also ἡ, *a rush,* Lat. *juncus.* 2. *a sharp, tough rush* or *reed,* used *as an arrow;* also *as a spit.* 3. *a place where rushes grow, a rush-bed.* II. *anything twisted* or *plaited of rushes, a rope, cord;* πλεκτὴ σχοῖνος *a wicker basket.* III. in Greece, the σχοῖνος was *a land measure,* = 2 Persian parasangs, or 60 stades.

σχοινο-τενής, ές, (σχοῖνος, τείνω) *stretched out like a measuring-line: in a straight line, straight.* II. *twisted or plaited of rushes.*

σχολάζω, f. άσω, (σχολή) *to have leisure* or *spare time, be at leisure:* also *to have rest* or *respite* from a thing: c. inf. *to have leisure* or *time to do a* thing. 2. *to act leisurely, linger, delay, loiter.* II. σχολάζειν τινί, Lat. *vacare rei, to have leisure, time* or *opportunity for* anything, *to devote one's time to* anything: also c. dat. pers. *to devote oneself* to one.

σχολαῖος, α, ον, (σχολή) *at one's leisure* or *ease, leisurely, slow:*—Comp. σχολαίτερος. Hence

σχολαιότης, ητος, ἡ, *slowness, laziness.*

σχολαίως, Adv. of σχολαῖος, *leisurely:*—Comp. σχολαίτερον or -αίτερα: Sup. σχολαίτατα:—formed like παλαίτερος.

σχολαστικός, ή, όν, (σχολάζω) *being at leisure, leisurely, at ease,* Lat. *otiosus.* II. *devoting all one's leisure to learning, learned:* hence *pedantic.*

ΣΧΟΛΗ', ἡ, *leisure, spare time, ease,* Lat. *otium;* σχολὴν ἄγειν to be at *leisure;* σχολῆς ἔργον a work for *leisure;* ἐπὶ σχολῇ *at leisure;* so, ἐπὶ or μετὰ σχολῆς, κατὰ σχολήν. II. dat. σχολῇ absol. as Adv., (1) *leisurely, slowly:* (2) *at one's leisure, by leisure, hardly, scarcely, scarcely at all.* III. c. gen. *leisure, rest from* a thing. IV. *idleness.* V. *a work of leisure,* esp. *a learned discussion, disputation,* Lat. *schola.* VI. *the place where such lectures were given, a school.*

σχολῇ, dat. of σχολή, used as Adv.: *in a leisurely way, slowly, late.* 2. *scarcely, hardly, not at all.*

σχόλιον, τό, (σχολή) *a scholium, note, comment.*

σχόμενος, aor. 2 med. part. of ἔχω.

σχοῦ, aor. 2 med. imperat. of ἔχω.

σχῶ, aor. 2 subj. of ἔχω: 1 plur. **σχῶμεν.**

σχών, aor. 2 part. of ἔχω.

σῷ, Att. nom. pl. contr. for σῷοι.

σώεσκον, Ion. impf. of σώω.

σώζω, lengthd. from ΣΑ'Ω, ΣΑΟ'Ω, ΣΩ'Ω: f. σώσω: aor. 1 ἔσωσα: pf. σέσωκα: Pass., aor. 1 ἐσώθην: pf. σέσωσμαι Att. σέσωμαι. From the obsol. σαόω are formed fut. σᾰώσω, aor. 1 act. ἐσάωσα [ᾰ]: fut. med. σᾰώσομαι: aor. 1 pass. ἐσᾰώθην. 2. from contr. pres. **σώω** we have part. σώοντες, Ion. impf. σώεσκον. 3. from **σόω**, subj. σόῃ, σόῃς, σόωσι:—*to save, keep:* esp. *to keep alive, preserve:*—Pass. *to be saved, preserved;* σώζεο, Lat. *salvus sis! vale! God be with you!* 2. of things, *to keep safe, preserve.* 3. of the laws, *to keep, observe.* 4. *to keep in mind, remember,* opp. to διολλύναι to forget; mostly in Med. II. σώζω is often used with the additional sense of motion to a place, *to bring one safe to:*—Pass. *to get safe* or *escape to* a place; ἐς οἶκον σωθῆναι *to be brought* or *get safe* home. 2. σώζειν ἐκ πολέμου, *to carry off safe, rescue from* war;

ἐχθρῶν σῶσαι χθόνα *to rescue* a country *from* the enemy.

σωθῆναι, aor. 1 inf. of σώζω.

σωκέω, f. ήσω, like ἰσχύω, *to have power* or *bodily strength: to be able to* do, c. inf. From

ΣΩ'ΚΟΣ, ὁ, *stout, strong.*

Σωκρᾰτέω, f. ήσω, *to do like Socrates, to imitate his dress, gait, speech,* etc. From

Σωκράτης, gen. εος contr. ους: acc. Σωκράτη or Σωκράτην: vocat. Σώκρατες:—*Socrates, the philosopher.* Hence

Σωκρᾰτίδιον, τό, Dim. *dear little Socrates.* [τῐ]

Σωκρᾰτικός, ή, όν, Adj. of Σωκράτης, *of* or *befitting Socrates, Socratic;* οἱ Σωκρατικοὶ *the philosophers of his school, Socratics.*

ΣΩΛΗ'Ν, ῆνος, ὁ, *a channel, gutter, pipe.*

σῶμα, ατος, τό, *the body:* in Homer *the dead body* of man or beast, *a corpse, carcase,* whereas *the living body* is δέμας: but later either of the *living* or *dead body.* 2. *body,* as opp. to *soul* (ψυχή); τὰ τοῦ σώματος ἔργα *bodily* labours; αἱ τοῦ σώματος ἡδοναί pleasures *of the body, sensual* pleasures. 3. *one's bodily existence, life.* II. *any material body.* III. *a person, human being:* esp. of slaves, as opp. to other goods.

σωμ-ασκέω, f. ήσω, (σῶμα, ἀσκέω) *to exercise the body, train, to practise wrestling.* Hence

σωμασκία, ἡ, *bodily exercise, training.*

σωμᾰτικός, ή, όν, (σῶμα) *of* or *for the body, bodily,* Lat. *corporeus.* Hence

σωμᾰτικῶς, Adv. *in bodily form.*

σωμάτιον, τό, Dim. of σῶμα, *a small body.* [ᾰ]

σωμᾰτο-ειδής, ές, (σῶμα, εἶδος) *of the nature of a body, coporeal.*

σωμᾰτο-φθορέω, f. ήσω, (σῶμα, φθείρω) *to corrupt* or *enervate the body*

σωμᾰτο-φῠλάκιον, τό, (σῶμα, φυλακή) *a place where a body is kept, a grave, sepulchre.* [ᾰ]

σῶος, α, ον, contr. σῶς, acc. σῶν; v. σῶς.

σωπάω, Dor. for σιωπάω, *to be silent.*

σώρευμα, ατος, τό, (σωρεύω) *that which is heaped up: a heap, pile.*

σωρεύω, f. σω, (σωρός) *to pile* or *heap* one thing *on* another. II. *to heap with, cover over with.*

ΣΩΡΟ'Σ, ὁ, *a heap,* Lat. *cumulus: a heap of corn:* generally, *a heap, quantity, store: a heap* or *mound of earth.*

ΣΩ'Σ, ὁ, σῶν, τό, acc. sing. σῶν, acc. pl. masc. and fem. σῶς: defect. Adj. σῶος = σόος, qq. v.: (the radic. form ΣΑΟΣ was found only in the Homeric comp. σαώτερος):—*safe and sound, in good case, healthy,* Lat. *salvus:* of things, *sound, whole, entire,* Lat. *integer.* 2. metaph. *safe, sure, certain.*

σωσί-πολις, εως, ὁ, ἡ, (σώζω, πόλις) *saving the city* or *state.* [ῐ]

σωστέον, verb. Adj. of σώζω, *one must save.*

σῶστρον, τό, mostly in plur. **σῶστρα**, τά, (σώζω) like ζωάγρια, *a reward for saving one's life, a thank-offering for deliverance* from a danger; σῶστρα τοῦ παιδὸς θύειν θεοῖς to offer *a sacrifice in thanksgiving* for his son's *deliverance.* II. *the reward for bringing back a runaway slave.*

σώτειρα, ἡ, fem. of σωτήρ, *she that saves.* II. epith. of protecting goddesses, as of Τύχα.

σωτήρ, ῆρος, ὁ, vocat. σῶτερ, (σώζω) *a saviour, deliverer, preserver;* c. gen. subjecti, σωτὴρ Ἑλλάδος *a saviour* of Greece; also c. gen. objecti, σωτὴρ νόσου *a preserver from* disease. 2. as epith. of protecting gods, esp. of Jupiter, to whom, under the name of Ζεὺς Σωτήρ, *the third cup* of wine was dedicated: generally, *a guardian* or *tutelary god:* also instead of σώτειρα, as epith. of Τύχη. II. poët. as Adj. *saving, preserving;* even with a fem. noun, σωτῆρες τιμαί the office *of saving.* Hence

σωτηρία Ion. –ίη, ἡ, *a saving, deliverance, means of safety, safety,* Lat. *salus.* 2. *a safe return,* ἡ οἴκαδε σωτηρία *a safe return* home. 3. *a keeping safe;* ἐπὶ σωτηρίᾳ for *safeguard.*

σωτήριος, ον, (σωτήρ) *saving, delivering:* neut. pl., σωτήρια, τά, like σωτηρία, ἡ, *deliverance, safety.* 2. σωτήρια (sc. ἱερά), τά, *an offering in return for safety.* II. pass. *saved, delivered, preserved.*

σῶτρον, τό, (σώζω) *the wooden circumference of the wheel, the felloe:* the iron hoop or *tire* being ἐπίσωτρον.

σωφρονέστερον, –έστατα, Comp. and Sup. of σωφρόνως.

σωφρονέω, f. ήσω: poët. **σαοφρονέω**: (σώφρων):—*to be of sound mind, be in one's sound senses: to practise self-control, to be discreet, temperate, moderate.* 2. *to learn moderation, to recover one's senses.* Hence

σωφρόνημα, ατος, τό, *an act of self-control, an instance of temperance, act of moderation:* and

σωφρονητέον, verb. Adj. *one must be temperate.*

σωφρονητικός, ή, όν, (σωφρονέω) *disposed to temperance, moderate, under self-control*

σωφρονίζω, f. ίσω Att. ιῶ, (σώφρων) *to moderate, control, chasten.* 2. *to chastise, correct.*

σωφρονικός, ή, όν, (σώφρων) *disposed to temperance, moderate, sober.* Adv. –κῶς

σωφρονισμός, ὁ, (σωφρονίζω) *a making temperate, chastening.*

σωφρονιστής, οῦ, ὁ, (σωφρονίζω) *one that makes temperate, a chastener, chastiser, censor.*

σωφρόνως, Adv. of σώφρων, *temperately, moderately, soberly:* Comp. σωφρονέστερον: Sup. σωφρονέστατα.

σωφροσύνη Ep. **σαοφροσύνη**, ἡ, *the character* or *conduct of the* σώφρων, *moderation, discretion: self-control, temperance, chastity, sobriety,* Lat. *temperantia.* From

σώ-φρων Ep. **σαοφρων**, ονος, ὁ, ἡ: neut. **σῶφρον**: (σῶς, φρήν):—*of sound mind, discreet, prudent, moderate:* esp. *self-controlling, temperate, chaste, sober.* Comp. and Sup., **σωφρονέστερος**, **–έστατος.**

σώχω, Ion. form for *ψώχω*, *to rub to pieces*.

σώω, Ep. for *σώζω*.

T

T, τ, ταῦ, *τό*, indecl., nineteenth letter of the Greek alphabet: as numeral, *τ′* = 300, but *,τ* = 300,000.

Changes of *τ*: in Aeol. and Dor., *τ* into *σ*, as *τύ* (Lat. *tu*), *τοί τέ*, *τῦκον*, *φατί*, etc. for *σύ*, *σοί*, *σέ*, *σῦκον*, *φησί*, etc. 2. in new Att., *ττ* for *σσ*, as *πράττω*, *τάττω*, for *πράσσω*, *τάσσω* 3. in Ion., *τ* for *θ*, as *αὖτις* for *αὖθις*: in the substantive termin. *-τρον* for *-θρον*, as in *κόσμητρον*, *φόβητρον*, for *κόσμηθρον*, *φόβηθρον*. 4. *τ* is inserted in some words metri grat., as *πτόλις*, *πτόλεμος*, for *πόλις*, *πόλεμος* 5. in Dor. and Ion., *τ* is omitted in the oblique cases of some neut. nouns of 3rd decl., as *κέραος*, *τέραος*, for *κέρᾰτος*, *τέρᾰτος*.

τ', apostroph. for *τε*, *ana*. 2. the particle *τοι* is joined by crasis with other particles beginning with a vowel, as *τἄν*, *τἆρα*, *μεντἄν*, for *τοι ἄν*, *τοι ἆρα*, *μέντοι ἄν*. 3. the Artic. *τό*, *τά*, is never elided, though joined with another word by crasis, as *τἀγαθόν* for *τὸ ἀγαθόν*.

τά, neut. pl. of *ὁ*, *ὅ*, and *ὅς*.

ταβέρνη, *ης*, *ἡ*, the Lat. *taberna*, *a tavern*, *inn*: *τρεῖς ταβέρναι the Three Taverns*, a place on the Appian Road.

τἀγαθά, Att. contr. for *τὰ ἀγαθά*.

τᾱγεία, *ἡ*, (*ταγεύω*) *the office* or *rank of Tagus*: generally, *command*, *rule*.

τᾰγείς, *εῖσα*, *έν*, aor. 2 pass. part. of *τάσσω*.

τᾱγεύω, f. *σω*, (*ταγός*) *to be Tagus*: generally, *to command*, *rule*:—Pass. *to be united under one ταγός*.

τᾱγέω, f. *ήσω*, (*ταγός*) *to be commander* or *ruler*.

τᾰγή, *ἡ*, = *τάξις*, *an ordering*, *arraying*.

τᾱγή, *ἡ*, (*τᾱγός*) *authority*: as Collective Noun. *the commanders*.

τάγηνον, *τό*, like *τήγανον*, *a frying-pan*.

τἄγκλημα, *ατος*, Att. crasis for *τὸ ἔγκλημα*.

τάγμα, *ατος*, *τό*, (*τάσσω*) *an ordinance*, *command*. 2. *a regular body of soldiers*, *a corps*, *division*.

τᾱγός, *ὁ*, (*τάσσω*) *an orderer*, *commander*, *ruler*: esp. as title of *the Chief of Thessaly*.

τᾱγ-οῦχος, *ὁ*, (*ταγή*, *ἔχω*) *he that has the command* or *rule*, *a commander*, *ruler*.

τἀδελφοῦ, Att. crasis for *τοῦ ἀδελφοῦ*

τἄδικον, Att. crasis for *τὸ ἄδικον*

τᾰθείς, *εῖσα*, *έν*, aor. 1 pass. part. of *τείνω*.

τάθην, Ep. aor. 1 pass. of *τείνω*. [ᾰ]

ταί, Ep. and Ion. for *αἱ*, nom. pl. fem. of the Art. *ὁ*.

Ταίνᾰρος, *ὁ*, *ἡ*, also **Ταίνᾰρον**, *τό*, *Taenarus*, a promontory and town at the southern extremity of Laconia.

ταινία, *ἡ*, (*τείνω*) *a band*, *riband*, *fillet*, Lat. *taenia*: esp. *a riband* or *headband* worn in token of victory.

ταινιό-πωλις, *ἡ*, (*ταινία*, *πωλέω*) *a dealer in ribands*.

ταινιόω, f. *ώσω*, (*ταινία*) *to bind with a ταινία* or *head-band*, esp. as conqueror:—Med. *ταινιόομαι*, *to wear a head-band* or *fillet*.

ταἴτιον, crasis for *τὸ αἴτιον*.

τἀκεῖ, **τἀκείνων**, crasis for *τὰ ἐκεῖ*, *τὰ ἐκείνων*.

τᾰκερός, *ά*, *όν*, (*τακῆναι*) *fluid*, *melting*, *soft*, *tender*: metaph. *melting*, *languishing*.

τᾰκῆναι, aor. 2 pass. inf. of *τήκω*.

τακτικός, *ή*, *όν*, (*τάσσω*) *fit for ordering* or *arranging*, *of* or *fit for military tactics*; *τὰ τακτικά military tactics*.

τακτός, *ή*, *όν*, verb. Adj. of *τάσσω*, *ordered*, *arranged*, *fixed*, *stated*; *τακτὸν ἀργύριον a stated sum*.

τάκω, Dor. for *τήκω*.

τᾰλᾰ-εργός, *όν*, (*τλάω*, *ἔργον*) *enduring labour*, *painful*, *drudging*: generally, *much-enduring*.

τάλαινα, fem. of *τάλας*.

τᾰλαιπωρέω, f. *ήσω*: pf. *τεταλαιπώρηκα*: also as Dep. **ταλαιπωρέομαι**, with f. med. *-ήσομαι*, aor. pass. *ἐταλαιπωρήθην*: (*ταλαίπωρος*):—*to endure hardship*, *do hard work*: *suffer hardship* or *distress*. II. trans. *to weary*, *wear out*, *annoy grievously*. Hence

τᾰλαιπωρία Ion. *-ίη*, *ἡ*, *hard work*, *severe labour*: in pl. *bodily hardships* or *exertions* 2. *bodily pain*, *suffering*: *affliction*, *misery*.

τᾰλαίπωρος, *ον*, (*τάλας*) *enduring toil*, *laborious*. II. *suffering hardship*, *miserable*. Adv. *-ρως*.

τᾰλαί-φρων, *ονος*, *ὁ*, *ἡ*, (*τλάω*, *φρήν*) *patient of mind*, *wretched*: also *stout-hearted*, *daring*.

τᾰλᾰ-κάρδιος, *ον*, (*τλάω*, *καρδία*) *patient of heart*, *stout-hearted*. 2. *much-enduring*, *miserable*.

τᾰλάντερος, *α*, *ον*, **τᾰλάντατος**, *η*, *ον*, Comp. and Sup. of *τάλας*.

τᾰλαντεύω, f. *σω*, (*τάλαντον*) *to balance*: Pass. *to sway to and fro*, *oscillate*. 2. *to weigh out*, *measure out by weight*.

τᾰλαντιαῖος, *α*, *ον*, (*τάλαντον*) *worth a talent*. 2. *weighing a talent*.

ταλαντίζω, = *ταλαντεύω*, q. v.

ΤΑ΄ΛΑΝΤΟΝ [*τᾰ-*], *τό*, *a balance*: in plur. *a pair of scales*. II. *anything weighed*: but mostly used of *a fixed weight*, *a talent*: in the post-Homeric times it had a double sense: 1. *the talent of weight*: *the Euboïc* or *old Attic talent* weighed about 57lb. avoird., and *the Aeginetan* 95. 2. *the talent of money*, i. e. *a talent's weight of silver*, or *a sum of money equivalent to this*, which would make the *Euboïc* or *old Attic talent* worth in our money 243*l*. 15*s*. The talent contained 60 minae, and each mina 100 drachmae. 3. *that which is weighed out* or *apportioned to* one.

τᾰλαντ-οῦχος, *ον*, (*τάλαντον*, *ἔχω*) *holding the scale* or *balance*: metaph. *turning the scale* of battle.

τᾰλᾰός, *ή*, *όν*, (*τλάω*) = *τάλας*, *patient*, *enduring*: hence *hard-fated*, *wretched*.

τᾰλᾰ-πείριος, *ον*, (*τλάω*, *πεῖρα*) *one who has suffered much*, epith. of Ulysses: hence later *rambling*, *vagabond*.

τᾰλᾰ-πενθής, ές, (*τλάω, πένθος) *enduring woe, patient in woe.* 2. of things, *toilsome.*

ΤΑ´ΛΑ῍ΡΟΣ [τᾰ-], ὁ, *a basket*, Lat. *qualus: a cheese-basket*, through which the whey ran off.

ταλάρως, Dor. acc. pl. of ταλάρος.

τάλᾱς, τάλαινᾰ (sometimes τάλας), τάλᾰν: gen. ᾰνος, αίνης, ᾰνος: voc. τάλᾱν or τάλας: (*τλάω):—*suffering, wretched*, Lat. *miser: enduring, patient:* also *fool-hardy, headstrong; τάλαν O wretch!* Comp. τᾰλάντερος, α, ον: Sup. τᾰλάντατος, η, ον. [τᾰλᾱς: Dor. also τᾰλᾰς.]

τᾰλάσειος, α, ον, Ion. and Ep. **τᾰλᾰσήϊος**, η, ον, (ταλασία) *of wool-spinning.*

τᾰλᾰσία, ἡ, (τλάω) *wool-spinning.*

τᾰλᾰσιουργέω, f. ήσω, (ταλασιουργός) *to spin wool:* generally, *to spin.*

τᾰλᾰσιουργικός, ή, όν, *of* or *for wool-spinning.* From

τᾰλᾰσι-ουργός, όν, (ταλασία, *ἔργω) *spinning wool:* as Subst., ταλασιουργός, ὁ, ἡ, *a wool-spinner.*

τᾰλᾰσί-φρων, ονος, ὁ, ἡ, (*τλάω, φρήν) *patient of mind, stout-hearted, of enduring spirit.*

ταλάσσῃς, -σσῃ, Ep. 2 and 3 sing. aor. 1 subj. of *τλάω.

τᾰλαύ-ρῑνος, ον, (*τλάω, ῥινός) *with shield of tough bull's-hide:* neut. as Adv., ταλαύρινον πολεμίζειν to fight on *toughly, stoutly.*

τᾰλά-φρων, ονος, ὁ, ἡ, shortd. for ταλασίφρων.

τἀληθές, Att. crasis for τὸ ἀληθές.

ταλιθά, Syrian word, *a damsel, maiden.*

ΤΑ῍ΛΙΣ, ιδος, ἡ, *a marriageable maiden, bride.*

τᾶλλα or **τἄλλα**, crasis for τὰ ἄλλα.

τἀμά, Att. crasis for τὰ ἐμά.

τάμε [ᾰ], Ion. 3 sing. aor. 2 of τέμνω.

τᾰμεῖν Ep. **τᾰμέειν**, aor. 2 inf. of τέμνω.

τᾰμεῖον, τό, = ταμιεῖον, *a chamber, closet.*

τᾰμέσθαι, aor. 2 med. inf. of τέμνω.

τᾰμεσί-χρως, οος, ὁ, ἡ, (τάμνω, χρώς) *cutting* or *penetrating the skin, wounding.*

τᾰμία, Ep. -ίη, ἡ, fem. of ταμίας, *a housekeeper, housewife;* also γυνὴ ταμίη.

τᾰμίας Ep. ταμίης, ου, ὁ, (τάμνω) *one who cuts up and distributes, a distributer, dispenser: a manager, overseer.* II. *a steward, receiver, treasurer; ταμίης τοῦ ἱροῦ the comptroller* of the sacred treasure in the citadel of Athens. 2. = Lat. *quaestor.*

τᾰμιεία, ἡ, (ταμιεύω) *the office of steward, housekeeping, management.* II. = Lat. *quaestura, the quaestorship.*

τᾰμιεῖον, τό, (ταμιεύω) *a magazine, storehouse, treasury.*

τᾰμίευμα, ατος, τό, (ταμιεύω) *management, housekeeping.*

ταμιευτικός, ή, όν, *of* or *for housekeeping.* II. = Lat. *quaestorius, of the quaestor* or *the quaestorship.* From

τᾰμιεύω, f. σω, and Dep. **τᾰμιεύομαι**, f. σομαι: (ταμίας):—*to be a housekeeper, manager* or *steward;* οὐκέτι ταμιεύσεις μοι *thou shalt* no longer *be* my *steward.* 2. *to be quaestor.* II. trans. *to serve out stores, dispense.* III. *to regulate, manage.* 2. *to husband save, store up:* metaph. *to turn to good account.*

τᾰμίη, ἡ, Ep. and Ion. for ταμία.

τᾰμίης, ου, ὁ, Ep. and Ion. for ταμίας.

τάμνω, Ion. for τέμνω.

τᾶμος, Dor. for τῆμος.

τᾱμπαλιν, Att. crasis for τὰ ἔμπαλιν

τᾰμών, Ion. aor. 2 part. of τέμνω.

τάν or **τᾶν**, indecl., only used in the Att. phrase ὦ τάν or ὦ τᾶν, as a form of address, *sir, my good friend.*

τἄν, Att. crasis for τοι ἄν.

τἀν, Att. crasis for τὰ ἐν.

Τάναγρα, ἡ, *Tanagra*, a town of Boeotia. Hence

Ταναγραῖος, α, ον, *of* or *from Tanagra.*

τᾰνᾰ-ηκής, ές, (ταναός, ἀκή) *with long point* or *edge, cutting far* or *deep.*

τᾰναί-μῡκος, ον, (ταναός, μυκάομαι) *bellowing so as to be heard far off, loud-bellowing.*

τἀναντία, crasis for τὰ ἐναντία.

τᾰνᾰό-δειρος, ον, (ταναός, δειρή) *long-necked.*

τᾰνᾰός, ή, όν, also ός, όν, (τανύω, τείνω) *stretched, outstretched, tall, taper, long.*

τᾰναύ-πους, -ποδος, ὁ, ἡ, Ep. for τανύπους.

τἀνδον or **τἄνδον**, Att. crasis for τὰ ἔνδον.

τἀνδρί, **τἀνδρός**, Att. crasis for τῷ ἀνδρί, τοῦ ἀνδρός.

τᾰνη-λεγής, ές, (ταναός, λέγω) *stretching one at length,* epith. of death.

τἀνθένδε, Att. crasis for τὰ ἐνθένδε.

τᾱνίκα, Dor. for τηνίκα.

Ταντάλειος or **Ταντάλεος**, α, ον, *of* or *for Tantalus:* and

Τανταλίς, ίδος, ἡ, *daughter of Tantalus.* From

Τάντᾰλος, ου, ὁ, *Tantalus* king of Phrygia, ancestor of the Pelopidae.

ταντᾰλόω, f. ώσω, (τάλαντον) quasi ταλαντόω, *to swing:*—aor. 1 pass. part. ταντταλωθείς, *swung, hurled, dashed down.*

τᾰνύ-γλωσσος, ον, (τανύω, γλῶσσα) *long-tongued, chattering, noisy.*

τᾰνυ-γλώχῑς, ῖνος, ὁ, ἡ, (τανύω, γλωχίς) *with long point* or *head.*

τᾰνύ-δρομος, ον, (τανύω, δρόμος) *running at full stretch.*

τᾰνῠ-έθειρος, ον, (τανύω, ἔθειρα) *long-haired, with flowing hair:* fem. also τανυέθειρα.

τανῠ-ήκης, ες, like ταναήκης, (τανύω, ἀκή) *with a long point* or *long edge.* II. *far-stretching.*

τᾰνῠ-ῆλιξ, ῐκος, ὁ, ἡ, (τανύω, ἧλιξ) *of extended age.*

τᾰνύ-θριξ, -τρῐχος, ὁ, ἡ, (τανύω, θρίξ) *long-haired, shaggy.*

τᾰνύ-κραιρος, ον, (τανύω, κραῖρα) *long-horned.*

τάνῠμαι, Pass. = τανύομαι, *to be stretched, extend.*

τᾰνῠ-μήκης, ες, (τανύω, μῆκος) *long-stretched, long drawn out, tall and tapering.*

ταυῦν, Adv., = τὰ νῦν, *now at present.*

τᾰνύ-πεπλος, ον, (τανύω, πέπλος) *with flowing robe.*

τᾰνύ-πλεκτος, ον, (τανύω, πλέκω) *in long plaits.*

τᾰνύ-πλευρος, ον, (τανύω, πλευρά) *long-sided, enormous.*

τᾰνύ-πους Ep. **τανaύ-πους**, –ποδος, ὁ, ἡ, (τανύω, πούς) *stretching the feet, long-striding, long-shanked.*

τᾰνύ-πτερος, ον, (τανύω, πτερόν) shorter form for τανυσίπτερος.

τᾰνῠ-πτέρῠγος, ον and **τᾰνυ-πτέρυξ**, ῠγος, ὁ, ἡ, (τανύω, πτέρυξ) = τανύπτερος, τανυσίπτερος.

τᾰνύρ-ριζος, ον, (τανύω, ῥίζα) *with speading roots.*

τᾰνύσειεν [ῠ], 3 sing. Aeol. aor. 1 opt. of τανύω.

τᾰνυσθείς, aor. 1 pass. part. of τανύω.

τᾰνύσθην, Ep. aor. 1 pass. of τανύω: Ep. 3 pl. τανυσθεν.

τᾰνῠσί-πτερος, ον, (τανύω, πτερόν) *with extended wings, long-winged.*

τάνυσσα, Ep. aor. 1 of τανύω.

τᾰνυστύς, ύος, ἡ, (τανύω) *a stretching, straining:* τανυστὺς τόξου *a stringing* of the bow.

τᾰνύ-σφῠρος, ον, (τανύω, σφυρόν) *with taper ankles.*

τᾰνύ-φλοιος, ον, (τανύω, φλοιός) *with extended bark:* of trees, *of tall* or *slender growth.*

τᾰνύ-φυλλος, ον, (τανύω, φύλλον) *with long-pointed leaves,* of the olive. II. *with thick foliage, leafy.*

τᾰνύω [ῠ]: fut. ύσω, Ep. also –ύω: aor. 1 ἐτάνῠσα Ep. ἐτάνυσσα or τάνυσσα: Pass., aor. 1 ἐτανύσθην: pf. τετάνυσμαι:—Ep. form of τείνω, *to stretch, strain, stretch out;* τανύειν τόξον *to draw* a bow: in Med., τόξον τανύσασθαι *to stretch one's* bow, i. e. *to string it;* ἱμᾶσι τανύειν *to pull* or *guide* with the reins. 2. *to stretch out, to lay along, lay out, stretch at full length* 3. metaph. *to strain, make more intense.* II. Pass. *to be on the stretch, to expand, be filled out.* 2. *to lie stretched out, to extend;* aor. 1 pass. part. τανυσθείς, *stretched* on the ground. 3. metaph. *to strain* or *exert oneself, to run at full stretch.*

ταξιαρχέω, f. ήσω, *to be a taxiarch* or *commander of a division.* From

ταξι-άρχης, ου, ὁ, = ταξίαρχος.

ταξί-αρχος, ὁ, (τάξις, ἄρχω) *a taxiarch, the commander of a brigade* or *division, a brigadier.* II. at Athens, *the commander of the* τάξις or *quota of infantry* furnished by each of the ten φυλαί.

ταξι-λόχος, ον, (τάξις, λόχος) *commanding a division* of an army.

ταξιόω, f. ώσω, (τάξις) *to arrange, set in order.*

τάξις, εως Ion. ιος, ἡ, (τάσσω) *an arranging:* of soldiers, *a drawing up in order, the disposition* of an army. 2. *battle-array, order of battle,* Lat. *acies.* 3. *a single rank* or *line* of soldiers, Lat. *ordo.* 4. *a post* or *place in the line* of battle, Lat. *statio;* ἐκλείπειν τὴν τάξιν to desert *one's post.* 5. like τάγμα, *a division* of an army, *a brigade:* at Athens, *the quota of infantry furnished by each* φυλή: also of smaller bodies, *a company, cohort:* generally, *a band, company.* II. *an arranging, arrangement.* 2. *an assessment of tribute.* III. *order;* ὕστερον τῇ τάξει later *in order.* IV. *the post, rank* or *position* one holds; ἐν ἐχθροῦ τάξει in *the light* or *position* of an enemy. 2. *one's duty towards* another; ἡ εὐνοίας τάξις *the duty* of good-will. V. *an order, class* of men.

ΤΑ'ΞΟΣ, ὁ, *the yew tree,* Lat. *taxus.*

ΤΑΠΕΙΝΟ'Σ, ή, όν, *low,* Lat. *humilis:* of Place, *lying low:* of stature, *low.* 2. of Condition, Rank, etc, *brought down, humbled, lowly.* 3. *humbled, humiliated:* in bad sense, *mean, abject;* in good sense, *lowly, humble.* Hence

τᾰπεινότης, ητος, ἡ, *lowness* of stature. 2. of condition, *lowliness, low estate, abasement.* 3. *lowness of spirits, dejection, baseness, vileness.* in good sense, *lowliness, humility*

τᾰπεινοφροσύνη, ἡ, *lowliness of mind.* From

τᾰπεινό-φρων, ονος, ὁ, ἡ, (ταπεινός, φρήν) *low-minded, base.* 2. *lowly in mind, humble.*

τᾰπεινόω, f. ώσω, (ταπεινός) *to make low, lower, humble, abase:* also *to make light of* a thing. 2. *to cast down, discourage* 3. *to make lowly* or *humble.*

ταπεινῶς, Adv. of ταπεινός, *humbly, poorly.*

τᾰπείνωσις, ἡ, (ταπεινόω) *a lowering, humbling.* 2. *lowliness, humility.*

ΤΑΠΗΣ, ητος, ὁ, Lat. *TAPES, a carpet, rug,* made of wool. [ᾰ]

τἀπί, Att. crasis for τὰ ἐπί.

τἀπιεικῆ, Att. crasis for τὰ ἐπιεικῆ.

ταπίς, ίδος, ἡ, later form of τάπης.

τἀπό, Att. crasis for τὰ ἀπό.

τα-πρῶτα, Adv. for τὰ πρῶτα, *at first.*

τἆρα, Att. crasis for τοι ἄρα.

τάραγμα, ατος, τό, (ταράσσω) *disquietude, trouble.*

τᾰραγμός, ὁ, (ταράσσω) = τάραξις.

τάρακτρον, τό, (ταράσσω) *a thing to stir with: a ladle.*

τᾰράκτωρ, ορος, ὁ, (ταράσσω) *a disturber, disquieter, agitator.*

Τᾰραντῑνίδιον, τό, (Τάρας) *a fine Tarentine garment.*

Ταράντῑνος, η, ον, (Τάρας) *Tarentine.*

τᾰραξί-κάρδιος, ον, (ταράσσω, καρδία) *heart-troubling, vexing the heart.*

τᾰραξ-ιππό-στρᾰτος, ον, (ταράσσω, ἵππος, στρατός) *troubling troops of horse.*

τάραξις, ἡ, (ταράσσω) *disturbance, confusion, disquietude, tumult.*

Τάρας, αντος, ὁ, also ἡ, *Tarentum,* a town of Magna Graecia.

ΤΑΡΑ'ΣΣΩ Att. –ττω, Att. also contr. **θράσσω**: fut. ταράξω contr. θράξω: aor. 1 ἐτάραξα: Pass., fut. ταραχθήσομαι, but also fut. med. ταράξομαι in pass. sense: aor. 1 ἐταράχθην: pf. τετάραγμαι:—*to stir, stir up, disturb, trouble, disquiet;* ταράσσειν τὸν θῖνα *to stir up* the sand: metaph. *to stir up, rouse, provoke.* 2. *to trouble* the mind, *to confound, alarm, frighten:* generally, *to disturb, throw into disorder:*—Pass. *to be in disorder.* 3. of political matters, *to* *agitate, distract*:—Pass. *to be in a state of disorder* or *anarchy*. II. to this Verb belongs the intrans. pf. τέτρηχα, *to be in disorder* or *confusion, be in an uproar*: plqpf. Ep. 3 sing. τετρήχει: part. τετρηχώς, υῖα, *troublous, disturbed, confused*. Hence

τᾰρᾰχή, ἡ, *trouble, disorder, confusion: commotion, tumult.*

τάρᾰχος, ὁ, (ταράσσω) = τᾰραχή.

τᾰρᾰχ-ώδης, ες, (ταραχή, εἶδος) *troublous, fond of troubling* or *perplexing*. II. *troubled, disordered: confused*:—Adv. -δως. *in confusion.*

ταρβᾰλέος, α, ον, (τάρβος) *frighted, fearful.*

ταρβέω, f. ήσω, (τάρβος) *to be frightened* or *alarmed, to fear*: τὸ ταρβεῖν *the being frightened, a state of fear*: also *to feel awe*. 2. c. acc. *to stand in awe of, fear, dread.*

ΤΑ'ΡΒΟΣ, εος, τό, *fright, alarm, terror*: also *awe, reverence*. II. *an object of alarm, a cause of dread.*

ταρβοσύνη, ἡ, poët. for τάρβος.

ταρβόσυνος, η, ον, (τάρβος) *affrighted.*

τᾶργα or **τἄργα**, Att. crasis for τὰ ἔργα.

τἀργύριον, Att. crasis for τὸ ἀργύριον.

τᾰρῖχεία Ion. -ηίη, ἡ, (ταριχεύω) *a preserving, pickling, salting*: ταριχηίαι were places in Egypt *where fish was salted.*

τᾰρίχευσις, ἡ, (ταρῖχεύω) = ταριχεία, *an embalming.*

τᾰρῖχευτής, οῦ, ὁ, (ταριχεύω) *a salter, pickler, embalmer.*

τᾰρῖχευτός, ή, όν, verb. Adj. *salted, pickled.* From

τᾰρῖχεύω, f. -εύσω, (τάριχος) *to preserve the body by artificial means, to embalm* as in the case of the Egyptian mummies. II. *to preserve meat, fish,* etc. *by smoking, salting, pickling*; τεμάχη τεταριχευμένα *preserved, pickled* meat. III. metaph. in Pass. *to waste away, wither, pine.*

τᾰρίχιον, τό, Dim. of τάριχος. [ρῐ]

τᾰρῖχοπωλεῖον, τό, *the salt-fish market.* From

τᾰρῖχο-πωλέω, f. ήσω, (τάριχος, πωλέω) *to sell dried* or *salt fish*. II. *to be engaged in the embalming of corpses.*

τάρῖχος, ου, ὁ, or **τάρῖχος**, εος, τό, *anything preserved* or *pickled by artificial means*: *a dead body preserved by embalming, a mummy*. II. generally, *meat preserved by smoking, salting* or *pickling, dried* or *smoked fish.*

ταρπῆναι Ep. -ήμεναι, aor. 2 pass. inf. of τέρπω.

ταρρός, ὁ, Att. for ταρσός.

Ταρσεύς, έως, ὁ, *a native of Tarsus* in Cilicia.

ταρσός Att. **ταρρός**, ὁ, (τέρσομαι) *a stand* or *frame of wicker-work, a crate, flat-basket*, Lat. *crates*, for drying cheeses on: also *a mat of reeds*, such as were built into brickwork to bind it together: also, *a wicker-basket*, like τάλαρος. II. *any broad, flat surface*; ταρσὸς ποδός *the flat* of the foot, *the part between the toes and the heel*. 2. ταρσὸς κωπέως *the flat end, blade* of an oar, Lat. *palmula*: generally, *an oar*. 3. ταρσὸς πτέρυγος *the flat of the wing*, when stretched out, then generally, *a wing*:—from the fabled fall of *the wing of Pegasus* there, the city of *Tarsus* was so called.

Ταρτάρειος, α, ον, *of* or *like Tartarus, Tartarean.* From

Τάρτᾰρος, ὁ, also ἡ: irreg. pl. Τάρταρα (as in Lat., *Tartarus, Tartara*):—*Tartarus*, a dark abyss, as deep below Hades, as earth below heaven, the prison of the Titans, etc. Later, Tartarus was either *the nether-world* generally, or *a place of torment and punishment*, as opp. to the Elysian fields.

Ταρτᾰρόω, f. ώσω, *to hurl into Tartarus.*

ταρφέες, οἱ, ταρφέα, τά, pl. of ταρφύς.

ταρφειός, ά, όν, = ταρφύς, *thick, close, frequent.*

τάρφθεν, Ep. 3 pl. aor. 1 pass. of τέρπω.

τάρφθη, Ep. 3 sing. aor. 1 pass. of τέρπω.

τάρφος, εος, τό, *a thicket.* From

ΤΑΡΦΥ'Σ, εῖα or ύς, ύ, *thick, close, frequent, dense*: neut. pl. ταρφέα as Adv., *ofttimes, often*. The Ep. fem. ταρφειαί belongs to ταρφειός: if referred to ταρφύς, it must be written ταρφεῖαι

ταρχύω, f. ύσω, shortened form of ταριχεύω, *to bury solemnly, inter.*

τάσις, εως, ἡ, (τείνω) *a stretching, straining*. [ᾰ]

ΤΑ'ΣΣΩ Att. -ττω: fut. τάξω: aor. 1 ἔταξα: pf. τέτᾰχα: Pass., fut. ταχθήσομαι, and paullo-p. fut. τετάξομαι: aor. 1 ἐτάχθην: aor. 2 ἐτάγην [ᾰ]: pf. τέταγμαι:—*to arrange* or *put in order*, esp. in military sense, *to draw up in line, array*; so in Med., ἐπὶ τεσσάρων ταξάμενοι τὰς ναῦς *having drawn up their* ships in four lines; and absol., τάξασθαι *to draw up, form in order of battle*:—Pass. *to be drawn up in order of battle*. 2. *to post, station*. 3. *to appoint*: *to appoint one to do* a thing:—Pass. *to be appointed* to do, τοῦτο τετάγμεθα this *we have been charged* to do. 4. *to order, command, give instructions*. 5. *to assign to* a class. 6. *to fix* or *assess payments* to be made:—Med. *to agree to pay* a sum, χρήματα ἀποδοῦναι ταξάμενοι *having covenanted* to return the money: absol. in part. ταξάμενος, *paying at intervals* or *by instalments*. 7. *to assign* or *impose* punishments. 8. generally, *to fix, settle*, ὁ τεταγμένος χρονός the *appointed* time.

τατάω, Dor. for τητάω.

τἄτιον, Att. crasis for τὸ αἴτιον.

τάττω, Att. for τάσσω.

ταύρειος, α, ον, also ος, ον, (ταῦρος) *of bulls, oxen* or *cows*, Lat. *taurinus*: in Homer, *of bull's-hide.*

ταυρ-ελάτης, ου, ὁ, (ταῦρος, ἐλαύνω) *a bull-driver, a bull-fighter.*

ταύρεος, α, ον, (ταῦρος) = ταύρειος.

ταυρηδόν, Adv. (ταῦρος) *like a bull: savagely*, Lat. *torvo vultu.*

ταυρο-βόλος, ον, (ταῦρος, βαλεῖν) *striking* or *slaughtering bulls.*

ταυρο-βόρος, ον, (ταῦρος, βορά) *devouring bulls.*

ταυρο-γάστωρ, ορος, ὁ, (ταῦρος, γαστήρ) *with the paunch* or *body of a bull*: *enormous.*

ταυρο-δέτης, ου, ὁ, (ταῦρος, δέω) *binding bulls:* fem. **ταυρο-δέτις**, ιδος.

ταυρό-κερως, ωτος, ὁ, ἡ, (ταῦρος, κέρας) *with bull's horns.*

ταυρό-κρᾶνος, ον, (ταῦρος, κρᾶνον) *bull-headed.*

ταυροκτονέω, f. ήσω, *to slaughter* or *sacrifice bulls;* with cognate acc., ταυροκτονεῖν βοῦς. From.

ταυρο-κτόνος, ον, (ταῦρος, κτείνω) *bull-slaying.* II. proparox. **ταυρόκτονος**, *slain by a bull.*

ταυρό-μορφος, ον, (ταῦρος, μορφή) *bull-formed.*

ταυρο-πάτωρ, ορος, ὁ, ἡ, (ταῦρος, πᾰτήρ) *sprung from a bull.*

ταυρο-πόλος or **ταυρο-πόλη**, ἡ, (ταῦρος, πολέω) *hunting bulls*, epith. of Diana.

ταυρό-πους, -ποδος, ὁ, ἡ, -πουν, τό, (ταῦρος, πούς) *bull-footed.*

ΤΑΥ῀ΡΟΣ, ὁ, *a bull:* joined with another Subst., ταῦρος βοῦς, like σῦς κάπρο

ταυροσφᾰγέω, f. ήσω, *to cut a bull's throat; ταυροσφαγεῖν ἐς σάκὸς to cut its throat* (so that the blood runs) *into* a hollow shield. From

ταυρο-σφάγος, ον, (ταῦρος, σφάττω) *bull-slaughtering: sacrificial.* [ᾰ]

ταυρο-φάγος, ον, (ταῦρος, φᾰγεῖν) *bull-eating: a beef-eater.*

ταυρο-φόνος, ον, (ταῦρος, *φένω) *bull-slaughtering: sacrificial.*

ταυρόω, f. ώσω, (ταῦρος) *to change into a bull:*— Pass., ταυρόομαι, *to be* or *become savage as a bull, to look savagely at, eye savagely.*

ταῦτα, neut. pl. of οὗτος.

ταὐτά, Att. crasis for τὰ αὐτά, *the same.*

ταύτῃ, also **ταυτῃί** dat. fem. of οὗτος, freq. as Adv. *in this way* or *manner.*

ταυτί [ῑ], strengthd. Att. for ταῦτα.

ταὐτό Ion. **ταὐτό**, Att. also **ταὐτόν**, Att. crasis for τὸ αὐτό, τὸ αὐτόν, *the same.*

ταὐτόγε, Att. crasis for τὸ αὐτό γε.

ταὐτο-λόγος, ον, (τὸ αὐτό, λέγω) *repeating the same that has been said, tautologous.*

ταὐτόμᾰτον, Att. crasis for τὸ αὐτόματον, *what falls out by accident, a hap, chance;* ἀπὸ ταὐτομάτου, for ἀπὸ τοῦ αὐτομάτου *of itself, by chance:* cf. αὐτόματος.

τάφε, in Pindar for ἔτᾰφε, 3 sing. aor. 2 with no pres. in use: see τέθηπα.

τᾰφεῖος, α, ον, see ταφήιος.

τᾰφεύς, έως, ὁ, (θάπτω) *one who buries the dead, a burier.*

ΤΑ῀ΦΗ', ἡ, (θάπτω) *burial*, Lat. *sepultura: a mode of burial:* in plur. *a burial-place.*

τᾰφήιος, η, ον, Ep. and Ion. for ταφεῖος, (ταφή) *of a burial* or *a grave;* φᾶρος ταφήιον) a *burial*-cloth, winding-sheet, shroud.

τᾰφῆναι, aor. 2 pass. of θάπτω.

τάφιος [ᾰ], α, ον, (τάφος) *of a grave;* **τάφιος λίθος** a *gravestone.*

τᾰφόδια, Att. crasis for τὰ ἐφόδια.

ΤΑ'ΦΟΣ [ᾰ], ὁ, (θάπτω) *a burial*, Lat. *funus:* also *a funeral-feast, wake;* τάφου τυχεῖν to obtain *the rites of burial.* II. *the grave, tomb:* in plur. *a burial-place.*

ΤΑ'ΦΟΣ [ᾰ], τό, (τέθηπα) *astonishment, amazement.*

Τάφος, ἡ, old name of one of the small islands between Acarnania and Leucadia: the Taphians were famous as seamen and pirates

ταφρεύω, f. σω, (τάφρος) *to make a ditch.*

τάφρη, ἡ, Ion. for τάφρος.

ΤΑ'ΦΡΟΣ, ἡ, *a ditch, trench;* **τάφρον ἐλαύνειν** to draw *a trench.*

τᾰφών, part. of aor. 2 ἔταφον: see **τέθηπα**.

τάχα, Adv. (τᾰχύς) *quickly. soon*, Lat. *statim.* II. in prose and Att., τάχα is often joined with ἄν, when it means, *probably, perhaps*, like ἴσως:—Sup. τάχιστα; see **τάχος**, ταχύς.

τᾰχέως, Adv. of ταχύς, *quickly.*

τᾰχῑνός, ἡ, όν, poët. for ταχύς, *swift, speedy.*

τάχῑον, ονος, neut. of ταχίων, Comp. of τᾰχύς, often as comp. Adv. of τάχα.

τάχιστα, sup. Adv.: see τᾰχύς.

τάχιστος, η, ον, Sup. of τᾰχύς, *quickest, swiftest.*

τᾰχίων, ονος, neut. τάχιον, Comp. of ταχύς. [ῑ]

ΤΑ'ΧΟΣ, εος, τό, (ταχύς) *swiftness, speed, quickness, fleetness;* τάχος ψυχῆς *quickness* of mind. II. τάχος is often used as Adv. for ταχέως, *quickly, with speed;* so also with a Prep., ἀπὸ τάχους, διὰ τάχους, ἐν τάχει, κατὰ τάχος, σὺν τάχει: also ὡς or ὅ τι τάχος, like ὡς or ὅ τι τάχιστα, *with all speed;* ὡς εἶχον τάχους as they were *for speed*, i. e. as quickly as they could.

ταχυ-άλωτος, ον, (ταχυς, ἁλίσκομαι) *conquered* or *captured quickly*

τᾰχύ-βουλος, ον, (ταχύς, βουλή) *quick* or *hasty of counsel.*

τᾰχύ-δακρυς, υ, gen. υος, (ταχύς, δάκρυ) *soon moved to tears.*

ταχυ-δρόμος, ον, (ταχύς, δραμεῖν) *fast-running.*

τᾰχῠ-εργία, ἡ, (ταχύς, ἔργον) *quickness in working.*

τᾰχῠ-ήρης, ες, (ταχύς, ἐρέσσω) *fast-rowing.*

τᾰχύ-μηνις, εως, ὁ, ἡ, (ταχύς, μῆνις) *quick to anger.*

τᾰχῠ-μήτωρ, ορος, ἡ, (ταχύς, μήτηρ) *being quickly a mother.*

τᾰχύ-μορος, ον, (ταχύς, μόρος) *quick-dying, short-lived.*

τᾰχῠ-ναυτέω, (ταχύς, ναύτης) *to sail fast.*

τᾰχύνω [ῡ], f. ῠνῶ, (ταχύς):—*to make quick, to hasten, to urge on.* II. intr. *to make haste, speed.*

τᾰχῠ-πειθής, ές, (ταχύς, πείθω) *soon persuaded, credulous.*

τᾰχύ-πομπος, ον, (ταχύς, πέμπω) *quickly-sending, quick-sailing.*

τᾰχύ-πορος, ον, (ταχύς, πόρος) *quick-passing, quick of motion.*

τᾰχύ-ποτμος, ον, (ταχύς, πότμος) *quick-fated, short-lived.* [ῠ]

τᾰχύ-πους, -ποδος, ὁ, ἡ, (ταχύς, πούς) *swift-footed.*

τᾰχύ-πτερνος, ον, (ταχύς, πτέρνα) *with swift heels, swift-footed.*

τᾰχύ-πτερος, ον, (ταχύς, πτερόν) *swift-winged.*

τᾰχύ-πωλος, ον, (ταχύς, πῶλος) *with swift, fleet horses.* [ῠ]

τᾰχύρ-ροθος, ον, (ταχύς, ῥοθέω) *rushing rapidly.*

τᾰχύρ-ρωστος, ον, (ταχύς, ῥώομαι) *borne quickly along, quick-rushing.*

ΤΑΧΥ΄Σ, εῖα, ύ, *quick, swift, fast, fleet.* 2. of events, *quick, speedy.* II. Comparison: 1. regul. Comp. ταχύτερος, α, ον only in Ion. 2. irreg. Comp. θάσσων Att. -ττων, neut. θᾶσσον, gen. ονος; neut. θᾶττον, also used as Adv. *more quickly.* 3. another Comp. is ταχίων [ῑ], neut. ιον: Sup., τάχιστος, η, ον; neut. pl. τάχιστα as Adv., *most quickly, most speedily;* ὅττι τάχιστα *as soon as may be, as soon as possible;* also in Prose, τὴν ταχίστην (sub. ὁδόν), as Adv. *by the quickest way,* i. e. *most quickly.*

ταχύ-σκαρθμος, ον, (ταχύς, σκαίρω) *quick-springing.*

τᾰχυτής, ῆτος, ἡ, (ταχύς) *quickness, swiftness, speed.*

τᾰχύ-χειλής, ές, (ταχύς, χεῖλος) *over which the lips run quickly,* of a flute.

τάων, Dor., and Aeol. gen. pl. fem. of the Article.

ΤΑΩ΄Σ, ὁ, gen. ταῶ, acc. ταῶν: nom. pl. ταῷ: another form of the nom. is **ταών**, gen. ταῶνος; pl. ταῶνες, dat. ταῶσι:—Lat. *PAVO, a peacock:* metaph. of *coxcombs.*

ΤΕ, enclitic Particle, *and,* answering to Lat. *que,* as καί answers to *et.* When it stands before another τε or before καί, it takes the sense of *both;* εἶδός τε μέγεθός τε, *both* in form *and* in size; αὐτοί τε καὶ ἵπποι, *both* themselves *and* their horses. II. in Ep. and Ion., τε is attached to Relatives, without altering their sense, as, ὅστε, ὅσος τε, etc., which is to be explained from the fact that the Relative Pronouns were originally Demonstratives, and required to be joined by a Conjunction: afterwards when they gained a relative force the Conjunction was retained as a mere affix, as in ὥστε, οἷός τε, ἐφ' ᾧτε. It is also joined in like manner with many relat. Advs. as ἔνθα τε, ὅτε τε, ὡσεί τε, ἵνα τε, ἀλλά τε, etc.

τέ, Dor. for σέ, acc. sing. of σύ.

τέ', apostroph. for τεά, neut. pl. of τεός.

ΤΕ΄ΓΓΩ, fut. τέγξω: aor. 1 ἔτεγξα: aor. 1 pass. ἐτέγχθην:—*to wet, moisten,* esp. *with tears: to bedew with tears.* 2. with cognate acc., τέγγειν δάκρυα *to shed* tears: Pass., ὄμβρος ἐτέγγετο a shower *was poured, fell.* II. *to soften, melt:* metaph. *to soften, move to compassion, make to relent.* III. *to dye, stain,* Lat. *tingere:* metaph. *to stain* or *mix with* anything else.

Τεγέα Ion. -έη, ἡ, *Tegea,* in Arcadia. Hence

Τεγεάτης [ᾱ] Ion. -ήτης, ὁ, *a man of Tegea, a Tegeate:* fem. Τεγεᾶτις, ιδος, (sub. γῆ) *the land of Tegea.* Hence

Τεγεᾱτικός Ion. -ητικός, ή, όν, *of* or *for a Tegeate.*

τέγεος, ον, (τέγος) *with a roof, roofed,* or *near the roof.*

ΤΕ΄ΓΟΣ, εος, τό, like στέγος, *a roof, covering of a house* or *room,* Lat. *tectum* II. *a room, chamber, garret: a brothel.*

τέθᾰλα, **τεθᾱλώς**, ότος, Dor. for τέθηλα, etc.

τεθᾰλυῖα, Ep. for τεθηλυῖα, pf. part. fem. of θάλλω.

τεθάλφθαι, pf. pass. inf. of θάλπω.

τέθαμμαι, -ψαι, -πται, pf. pass. of θάπτω.

τεθάφᾰται, Ion. 3 pl. pf. pass. of θάπτω.

τεθάψομαι, paullo-p. fut. pass. of θάπτω.

τεθέᾱται, for τέθεινται, 3 pl. pf. pass. of τίθημι.

τέθεικα, **τέθειμαι**, pf. act. and pass. of τίθημι.

τεθεμελίωτο, 3 sing pass. plqpf. of θεμελιόω.

τέθηγμαι, pf. pass. of θήγω.

τέθηλα, pf. of θάλλω: 3 sing. plqpf. Ep. τεθήλει.

τεθῆναι, aor. 1 pass. inf. of τίθημι.

τέθηπα, pf. with pres. sense, without a pres. in use:—intr. *to be astonished, astounded* or *amazed,* chiefly used in part. τεθηπώς: also in Ep. plqpf. as impf. ἐτεθήπεα. II. from same root comes aor. 2 ἔτᾰφον, with part. ταφών, *astonished* or *amazed.*

τεθήσομαι, fut. pass. of τίθημι.

τεθλασμένος, pf. pass. part. of θλάω.

τεθλιμμένος, pf. pass. part. of θλίβω.

τέθμιος, α, ον, Dor. for θέσμιος, *fixed, settled, stated, regular,* Lat. *solennis:* generally, *due, fitting.*

τεθμός, ὁ, (τίθημι) Dor. for θεσμός, *that which is fixed, a law, custom, ordinance.*

τέθνᾰθι, pf. imperat. of θνήσκω.

τεθναίην, pf. opt. of θνήσκω.

τεθνάκαμες, Dor. for τεθνήκαμεν, 1 pl. pf. of θνήσκω.

τεθνάμεν, **τεθνάμεναι** [ᾰ], Ep. pf. inf. of θνήσκω.

τέθνᾰμεν, Att. for τεθνήκαμεν, 1 pl. pf. of θνήσκω.

τεθνάναι [ᾰ], rarely **τεθνᾶναι**, pf. inf. of θνήσκω.

τεθνᾶσι, for τεθνήκασι, 3 pl. pf. of θνήσκω.

τεθνειώς, Dor. and Ep. for τεθνεώς.

τεθνεώς, -ῶτος, ὁ, Att. part. pf. of θνήσκω; fem. τεθνεῶσα; neut. τεθνεώς and τεθνεός.

τέθνηκα, pf. of θνήσκω.

τεθνήξομαι, Att. fut. of θνήσκω.

τεθνηώς, -ῶτος, Ep. for τεθνεώς, masc. and neut. part. pf. of θνήσκω: Ep. gen. τεθνηότος, acc. -ότα: but the fem. is τεθνηκυῖα formed from the orig. τεθνηκώς.

τεθνώς, poët. for τεθνεώς.

τεθορεῖν, redupl. for θορεῖν, aor. 2 inf. of θρώσκω.

τέθραμμαι and **τέθρεμμαι**, pf. pass. of τρέφω

τεθρ-ήμερον, τό, (τέτταρα, ἡμέρα) *a time of four days.*

τεθριππο-βάμων [ᾱ], ονος, ὁ, (τέθριππος, βαίνω) *driving a four-horsed chariot: a driver of four horses.*

τεθριππο-βάτης, ου, ὁ, (τέθριππος, βαίνω) *driver of a four-horsed chariot.* [βᾰ]

τέθρ-ιππος, ον, (τέτταρα, ἵππος) *with four horses yoked abreast:* as Subst., τέθριππον (sub. ἅρμα), τό, *a four-horsed chariot;* τέθριππον ἵππων *a team of four abreast.*

τεθριπποτροφέω, f. ήσω, *to keep a four-horsed chariot.* From

τεθριππο-τρόφος, ον, (τέθριππον, τρέφω) *keeping*

a four-horsed chariot; τεθριπποτρόφος οἰκία a family *that could furnish such a chariot* in the games.

τεθυμένος, pf. pass. part. of θύω.

τεθυωμένος, pf. pass. part. of θυόω.

τεί, poët. for τέ, which is Dor. for σέ, acc. sing. of σύ.

τεΐν, Dor. for σοι, dat. of σύ. [ῐ]

τεῖδε, Dor. for τῇδε, *this way, here.*

τεῖνα, Ep. for ἔτεινα, aor. 1 of τείνω.

ΤΕΙ'ΝΩ: f. τενῶ: aor. 1 ἔτεινα: pf. τέτᾰκα: Pass., aor. 1 ἐτάθην [ᾰ]: pf. τέτᾰμαι: Ep. 3 sing. plqpf. τέτᾰτο, 3 dual τετάσθην, 3 pl. τέτανται:—*to stretch, strain, extend, to draw tight; τόξον τείνειν to stretch* the bow *to its full compass*:—Pass. *to be stretched to the full; ἱστία τέτατο* the sails *were stretched taught; ναὸς πόδα τείνειν to keep* the sheet *taught; νύξ τέταται βροτοῖσιν* night *is spread* over mankind. II. *to lay along, stretch out, stretch on the earth, lay prostrate; ταθεὶς ἐπὶ γαίῃ stretched* upon the ground. III. metaph. *to strain to the utmost, make earnest* or *intense*:—Pass. *to be strained to the utmost, to be intense:* also, *to be stretched* on *the rack:* also *to exert oneself, be anxious.* IV. *to extend, lengthen,* of Time. 2. *to aim at, direct towards* a point; hence *to design.*

B. intr. *to stretch out* or *extend towards* .. : absol. *to stretch, extend.* II. *to aim at, strive to reach* a thing: generally, *to reach.* III. *to tend, refer, belong to,* Lat. *spectare, pertinere ad* .. ; *τείνει ἐς σέ it has reference to* you.

τεῖος, Adv., Ep. for τείως, τέως.

τείρεα, Ep. pl. of τέρας, *the heavenly bodies, signs.*

ΤΕΙ'ΡΩ, impf. ἔτειρον; only found in pres. and impf.:—*to rub, rub away:* metaph. *to wear away, wear out:*—Pass. *to be worn away, worn out, distressed.* II. intr. *to suffer greatly.*

τειχεσι-πλήτης, ου, ὁ, (τεῖχος, πελάζω) *approacher, assailer, stormer of walls.*

τειχέω, f. ήσω, (τεῖχος) *to build walls: to build.* II. *to wall, fortify,* c. acc.

τειχ-ήρης, ες, (τεῖχος, ἀραρεῖν) *enclosed by walls, beleaguered, besieged.*

τειχίζω, f. ίσω Att. ιῶ: aor. 1 ἐτείχισα: pf. τετείχικα: Pass., pf. τετείχισμαι: 3 sing. Ion. plqpf. τετείχιστο: (τεῖχος):—*to build a wall,* generally, *to build; τεῖχος τειχίσασθαι to build oneself* a wall: 3 sing. plqpf. pass. τετείχιστο, impers., *there were buildings.* II. *to wall* or *fortify*:—Pass. *to be walled, fenced* or *fortified with walls.*

τειχιόεις, εσσα, εν, (τεῖχος) *walled.*

τειχίον, τό, Dim. of τεῖχος, *a wall,* mostly of the walls of private buildings, as opp. to those of a town (τεῖχος, τείχη).

τείχισις, ἡ, (τειχίζω) *the work of walling, building a wall.*

τείχισμα, ατος, τό, (τειχίζω) *a wall* or *fort, a raised fortification.*

τειχισμός, ὁ, (τειχίζω) = τείχισις.

τειχοδομέω, f. ήσω, *to build a wall* or *fort.* From

τειχο-δόμος, ον, (τεῖχος, δέμω) *building a wall.*

τειχομᾰχέω, f. ήσω, *to attack the walls, to assault* or *besiege a fortified place; τειχομαχεῖν δυνατοί* skilled in *conducting sieges.* From

τειχο-μάχης, ου, ὁ, (τεῖχος, μάχομαι) *assaulting walls* or *fortified places: an engineer.* [ᾰ]

τειχομᾰχία Ion. -ίη, ἡ, (τειχομαχέω) *an assault of walls, a siege:* this was the name of Il. 12.

τειχο-μελής, ές, (τεῖχος, μέλος) *raising walls by music,* of Amphion's lyre.

τειχο-ποιός, όν, (τεῖχος, ποιέω) *building walls* or *forts: οἱ τειχοποιοί,* at Athens, *officers charged with repairing the city walls.*

ΤΕΙ'ΧΟΣ, εος, τό, *a wall,* esp. *a wall round a city, city-wall; τειχέων κιθῶνες coats* of wall, i. e. walls one within the other; *τείχεα ῥήξασθαι to make a breach in* the wall.—It differs from τοῖχος, τείχιον, as Lat. *murus, moenia* from *paries,* or *city-walls* from *a house-wall.* II. *any fortification, a castle, fort: a walled town* or *city: a fortified post.*

τειχο-φύλαξ, ᾰκος, ὁ, (τεῖχος, φύλαξ) *one that guards the walls, a sentinel, warder.*

τειχύδριον, τό, Dim. of τεῖχος, *a small wall* or *fortified place.*

τείως, Adv. Ep. and Ion. for τέως.

τέκε, Ep. 3 sing. aor. 2 of τίκτω.

τεκεῖν, τεκέσθαι, aor. 2 act. and med. inf. of τίκτω.

τεκμαίρομαι: fut. τεκμᾰροῦμαι: aor. 1 ἐτεκμηράμην: Dep.: (τέκμαρ):—*to fix by a mark* or *boundary, to ordain, decree:* generally, *to enjoin, appoint: to mark out.* II. *to perceive from certain signs and tokens, to infer, conclude, judge; τεκμαίρεσθαι τὰ καινὰ τοῖς πάλαι to judge* of new by old events: *to conjecture.* III. the Act. τεκμαίρω is rare, *to shew by a sign* or *token.*

ΤΕ'ΚΜΑΡ Ep. τέκμωρ, τό, *a fixed mark* or *boundary, a goal, end; Ἰλίου τέκμωρ the end* of Troy: generally, *a finishing, accomplishment:* metaph. *an end, purpose.* II. *a fixed sign, sure sign* or *token, a solemn pledge.*

τέκμαρσις, ἡ, (τεκμαίρομαι) *a concluding from signs* or *tokens:* generally, *a proving, shewing, a way* or *mode of shewing.*

τεκμηράμην, Ep. aor. 1 of τεκμαίρομαι.

τεκμήριον, τό, (τεκμαίρομαι) *a sure sign* or *token, a positive proof; τεκμήριον δέ* is sometimes put in an independent clause, *here is the proof.* II. in Logic, *a demonstrative* or *certain proof,* opp. to the fallible σημεῖον. Hence

τεκμηριόω, f. ώσω, *to give a token* or *proof, to shew* or *prove by evidence*:—Med. *to conclude from a sure sign* or *token.*

τεκνίδιον, τό, = τεκνίον.

τεκνίον, τό, Dim. of τέκνον, *a little child.*

τεκνογονέω, (τεκνογόνος) *to bear children.* Hence

τεκνογονία, ἡ, *child-bearing.*

τεκνο-γόνος, ον, (τέκνον, *γένω) *begetting* or *bearing children.*

τεκνο-κτόνος, ον, (τέκνον, κτείνω) *child-murdering.*

τεκνολετηρ, ῆρος, ὁ, (*τέκνον, ὄλλυμι*) *losing* or *having lost one's children:* fem. *τεκνολέτειρα*, of the nightingale, *having lost her young.*

τέκνον, ου, τό, (*τεκεῖν*) *that which is borne* or *born, a bairn, child*, whether son or daughter: but often used in addresses from elder to younger persons, *τέκνον ἐμόν*, my *son:* sometimes with masc. Adj., *φίλε τέκνον.* 2. of animals, *the young.*

τεκνοποιέω, f. *ήσω*, (*τεκνοποιός*) *to bear children*, of the mother;—Med. *to beget children*, of the father; but Med. also of both parents, *to breed children.* Hence

τεκνοποιΐα, ἡ, *a bearing* or *begetting of children.*

τεκνό-ποινος, ον, (*τέκνον, ποινή*) *child-avenging.*

τεκνο-ποιός, όν, (*τέκνον, ποιέω*) *bearing* or *begetting children.*

τεκνο-σπορία, ἡ, (*τέκνον, σπείρω*) *a begetting of children.*

τεκνο-τροφέω, f. *ήσω*, (*τεκνον, τρέφω*) *to bring up* or *rear children.*

τεκνοῦς, οῦσσα, οῦν, (*τέκνον*) contr. from *τεκνόεις, οεσσα, οεν, having children.*

τεκνο-φάγος, ον, (*τέκνον, φᾰγεῖν*) *eating children.*

τεκνοφονέω, *to murder children.* From

τεκνο-φόνος, ον, (*τέκνον*, **φένω*) *child-murdering*,

τεκνόω, f. *ώσω* (*τέκνον*), *to furnish with children.* II. *to beget children*, of the father:—Med. of the mother, *to bear children;* metaph., *χθὼν ἐτεκνώσατο τέκνα* the earth *gave birth to* her children: also of wealth, etc.:—Pass. *to be born.*

τέκνωσις, εως, ἡ, (*τεκνόω*) *a begetting* or *bearing of children.*

τέκοιεν, 3 pl. aor. 2 opt. of *τίκτω.*

τέκον, Ep. aor. 2 of *τίκτω.*

τέκος, εος, τό, Ep. dat. pl. *τεκεσσι, τεκέεσσι:* (*τεκεῖν*):—poët. for *τέκνον, a child.*

τεκταίνομαι, Dep. (*τέκτων*) *to make, build, frame:*—metaph. *to devise, plan, contrive.* II. later also in Act.: whence in Pass. *to be built, contrived.*

τεκτήναιτο, 3 sing. aor. 1 opt. of *τεκταίνομαι.*

τεκτήνατο, Ep. 3 sing. aor. 1 of *τεκταίνομαι.*

τεκτονεῖον, τό, (*τέκτων*) *a carpenter's shop.*

τεκτονικός, ή, όν, (*τέκτων*) *of* or *for a carpenter* or *builder, skilled in building:* as Subst., *τεκτονικός, ὁ, a good carpenter; ἡ τεκτονική* (sub. *τέχνη*) *carpentry.*

τεκτοσυνη, ἡ, *the art of a carpenter* or *builder: carpentry, building.* From

τέκτων, ονος, ὁ, *a worker in wood, a carpenter, joiner, builder; νηῶν τέκτων* a ship-*carpenter*, ship-*builder.* 2. *any craftsman* or *workman, a master* of any art; hence of the art of poetry, *τέκτονες ὕμνων makers* of songs. II. a *planner, contriver, plotter:* generally, *an author.*

τεκών, aor. 2 part. of *τίκτω.*

ΤΕΛΑ΄ΜΩ΄Ν, ῶνος, ὁ, *a broad band* or *strap for bearing* or *supporting* anything, *a leathern strap* or *belt* for carrying either the shield or sword. 2. *a broad linen bandage* or *roller* for wounds; also for swathing mummies.

τελέεις, εσσα, εν, shortened form of *τελήεις.*

ΤΕΛΕ΄ΘΩ: 3 sing. Ion. impf. *τελέθεσκε:*—*to come forth, come into being, arise:* hence *to be, become.*

τέλειον, τό, *a complete feast, a royal feast.* From

τέλειος or **τέλεος**, α, ον, in Att. also ος, ον: (*τέλος*):—*complete, perfect, entire;* of victims, *without spot* or *blemish:* but, *ἱερὰ τέλεια* are *perfect* sacrifices, *performed with full* rites. 2. of animals, *full-grown; τέλειος ἀνήρ a full-grown man*, Lat. *adultus:* hence *perfect in his* or *its kind.* 3. of numbers. etc., *full, complete.* 4. of actions, *ended, finished:* of vows, etc., *fulfilled, accomplished:* also *fixed, resolved upon.* II. act. *bringing to pass, accomplishing; ἀρὰ τελεία* a curse *working its own fulfilment* 2. *able to do* or *bring about; τέλειος ἀνήρ* a man *who has full rule* or *authority.*

τελειότης, ητος, ἡ, (*τέλειος*) *completeness, perfection.*

τελειόω or **τελεόω**, f. *ώσω*, (*τέλειος*):—*to make perfect: to inaugurate, consecrate.* II. *to complete, bring to accomplishment: to make successful.* 2. generally, *to fulfil, accomplish, effect.*

τελεῖται, 3 sing. pres. pass. and fut. med. of **τελέω.**

τελείω, Ep. for *τελέω.*

τελείως, doubtful form for **τελέως.**

τελείωσις, ἡ, (*τελειόω*) *a becoming perfect, completion, accomplishment, consummation.*

τελειωτής, οῦ, ὁ, (*τελειόω*) *a perfecter, finisher.*

τελεό-μηνος, ον, (*τέλεος, μήν*) *revolving with full completion of months; ἄροτος τελεόμηνος*, i. e. *a full twelvemonth.*

τέλεον, Ep. impf. of *τελέω.*

Τελέοντες, οἱ, one of the four original Attic tribes, (*τελέω* II) *Payers, Farmers;* or (*τελέω* III), *Priests.*

τέλεος, α, ον, (*τέλος*) = *τέλειος.*

τελέσεια, Aeol. aor. 1 opt. of *τελέω.*

τελεσθείς, aor. 1 pass. part. of *τελέω.*

τέλεσμα, ατος, τό, (*τελέω*) *a payment, outlay.*

τέλεσσα, Ep. aor. 1 of *τελέω.*

τελεσσι-δότειρα, ἡ, poët. for *τελεσιδ-*, (*τέλος, δίδωμι*) *she that gives completeness* or *accomplishment.*

τελεσσί-φρων, ονος, ὁ, ἡ, Ep. for *τελεσίφρων*, (*τελέω, φρήν*) *working its complete will.*

τελεστήριον, τό, (*τελέω*) *a place of initiation.* plur. *τελεστήρια, τά, a thank-offering for success.*

τελέστωρ, ορος, ὁ, poët. for *τελεστής*, (*τελέω*) *a magistrate.*

τελεσφορέω, f. *ήσω*, *to bring fruit to perfection:* generally, *to bring to perfection.* II. *to pay toll* or *custom.* From

τελεσ-φόρος, ον, (*τέλος, φέρω*) *brought to an end, coming to an end; τελεσφόρον εἰς ἐνιαυτόν* for the space of a *complete* year. 2. *brought to an end* or *fulfilment, accomplished.* II. act. *bringing to an end, accomplishing; πεσεῖν ἐς τὸ μὴ τελεσφόρον* to fall *with fruitless result*, i. e. *powerless, idle.* 2.

bearing fruit in due season. 3. *bearing rule, having the control* or *management of.*

τελετή, ἡ, (τελέω) *a making perfect: initiation in* the mysteries, *the celebration of mysteries.* II. in plur. *mystic rites, any religious rites, a festival.*

τελεύμενος, Ion. part. fut. med. (in pass. sense) of τελέω.

τελεῦντι, Dor. for τελοῦσι, 3 pl. of τελέω.

τελευταῖος, α, ον, (τελευτή) *at the end, last,* Lat. *ultimus, extremus.* 2. *the last, worst, extreme.* II. neut. τὸ τελευταῖον, as Adv. *the last time, last of all.* 2. *last, in the last place.*

τελευτάω, f. ήσω: pf. τετελεύτηκα: fut. med. τελευτήσομαι in pass. sense: Pass., aor. 1 ἐτελευτήθην: pf. τετελεύτημαι: (τελευτή):—*to bring to an end, complete, accomplish,* Lat. *perficere: to fulfil, ratify:*—Pass. *to be fulfilled, to come to pass, happen.* II. τελευτᾶν τὸν βίον, τὸν αἰῶνα *to bring* one's life *to an end,* i. e. *to die:* absol. τελευτᾶν, *to die, be deceased;* τελευτᾶν ὑπό τινος *to die by* another's hand: c. gen., τελευτᾶν βίου *to make an end of* life. 2. intrans. *to come to an end, finish;* αἱ εὐτυχίαι ἐς τοῦτο ἐτελεύτησαν his good fortune *came to* this *end.* 3. the part. pres. τελευτῶν, ῶσα, ῶν, was used with Verbs like an Adv., *at the end, lastly, at last;* as, κἂν ἐγίγνετο πληγὴ τελευτῶσα there would have been blows *at the last.*

τελευτέω, Ion. for τελευτάω: part. τελευτέοντες.

τελευτή, ἡ, (τελέω, τέλος) *a bringing to an end, fulfilment, accomplishment.* II. *a finish, end:* βίου τελευτή *the end, finish* of life: absol. *the end of life, death;* so, θανάτοιο τελευτή *the end* that death brings, Lat. *mortis exitus:* ἐς τελευτὴν *at the end, at last:* in plur. *the boundaries* or *extremities,* esp. of countries: metaph. *the issues* or *events* of things.

τελευτήσεια, Aeol. aor. 1 opt. of τελευτάω.

τελέω, Ep. also **τελείω**: f. τελέσω Ep. τελέσσω, Ion. τελέω contr. τελῶ: aor. 1 ἐτέλεσα Ep. ἐτέλεσσα: pf. τετέλεκα:—Pass. τελέομαι Ep. -είομαι: fut. med. in pass. sense τελέσομαι Ep. τελέομαι contr. τελοῦμαι: aor. 1 ἐτελέσθην: pf. τετέλεσμαι:—(τέλος):—*to complete, fulfil, accomplish:* generally, *to perform, execute,* Lat. *perficere; to fulfil* or *keep* one's word: with dat. pers. *to fulfil for* one, *grant* one *the accomplishment of* anything: generally, *to work out, accomplish one's end:*—Pass. *to be completed, fulfilled, accomplished: to come to pass, happen:* part. pf., τὸ καὶ τετελεσμένον ἔσται which *shall also be accomplished.* 2. *to make perfect, bring to maturity.* 3. *to bring to an end, finish, end:* in Pass. *to come to one's end.* 4. sometimes intr. like τελευτάω, *to come to an end, be fulfilled, turn out:* also, τελεῖν εἰς τόπον *to finish (one's course)* to a place, i. e. *arrive at* it. II. *to pay* one's dues or taxes, *to pay as tax, duty, due:* generally, *to lay out, spend:*—Pass. of money, *to be paid, spent:* of persons, *to be liable to pay tax.* 2. since at Athens the citizens were distributed into classes and rated according to their property, τελεῖν meant *to be rated* or *assessed* in a certain class, *to belong to, be classed among,* as, τελεῖν εἰς ἱππέας *to be rated among* the knights; so of states, τελεῖν ἐς Ἕλληνας, ἐς Βοιωτούς *to belong to, be rated among the* Greeks, the Boeotians; εἰς ἀστοὺς τελεῖν *to be rated among* the citizens. III. *to consecrate, initiate,* esp. in the mysteries:—Pass. *to have oneself initiated,* Lat. *initiari;* Διωνύσῳ τελεσθῆναι *to be initiated in* the mysteries of Bacchus; c. acc., τελεσθῆναι Βακχεῖα *to be initiated in the rites* of Bacchus. 2. τελεῖν ἱερά *to perform* sacred rites.

τελέως, Adv. of τέλεος or τέλειος, *at last.* II. *completely, perfectly.* Comp. τελεώτερον, Sup. -ώτατα.

τελήεις, εσσα, εν, (τελέω) *perfect, complete, of full tale* or *number;* ῥέζειν τεληέσσας ἑκατόμβας to offer hecatombs *of full number* or *without blemish;* τελήεντες οἰωνοί birds *of sure augury;* ἔπεα τελέεντα *sure* predictions (from shortened form τελέεις). II. τελήεις ποταμός, of Ocean, the *last* river, *in which all others end.*

ΤΕ'ΛΛΩ: f. τελῶ: aor. 1 ἔτειλα: pf. τέταλμαι: plqpf. ἐτετάλμην:—Med. τέλλομαι, aor. 1 ἐτειλάμην:—*to make to arise:* generally, *to accomplish:*—Pass. *to come forth, arise.* 2. intr. *to arise;* ἡλίου τέλλοντος at sun-*rise.*

τέλμα, ατος, τό, (τέλλω) *water which has accumulated, standing water, a pool, pond.* II. *the mud of a pool: mud* or *clay* to build with, *mortar.*

ΤΕ'ΛΟΣ, εος, τό, *an end accomplished: the completion* or *fulfilment* of anything, Lat. *effectus:* τέλος ἔχειν to have reached *the end, to be finished* or *ready;* also of wishes, prayers, etc., to have their *accomplishment, be fulfilled;* also in Att. *to have full powers,* of ambassadors. 2. *a complete state, full condition,* as, τέλος γάμοιο; τέλος ἥβης *manhood:*—generally, *an end, issue,* Lat. *eventus, exitus;* τέλος βίου *the end* of life, then like τελευτή, without βίου, *the end of life, death:* but also, τέλος θανάτου *the end* or *completion* of death, i. e. *death* itself: so, νόστοιο τέλος *the end* or *accomplishment* of return, i. e. *a safe return.* 3. τέλος is often used adverbially; τέλος for κατὰ τὸ τέλος, *at the end, at last:* so also, ἐς τὸ τέλος, εἰς τέλος:—in dat. τέλει, *at all, Lat. omnino:*—διὰ τέλους, *throughout, for ever, in perpetuity.* II. *the end proposed, chief matter.* III. *a body of soldiers,* κατὰ τέλεα *in regular bodies, in divisions* or *troops,* Lat. *turmatim;* τέλη νεῶν *squadrons* of ships; ὀρνίθων τέλεα *flocks* of birds. IV. *the highest station, the possession of full power, a magistracy, office;* οἱ ἐν τέλει *men in authority;* so, οἱ τὰ τέλη ἔχοντες; in Att., τὸ τέλος *the government,* τὰ τέλη *the magistrates.* V. *that which is paid to the state* (cf. τελέω II), *a tax, duty, toll, due;* τέλος πρίασθαι to farm *a tax;* λύειν τέλη to pay *dues* or *tolls,* hence *to be profitable, advantageous,* like λυσιτελέω. 2. at Athens, *the property at which a citizen was as-*

sessea: hence *a class* or *order* of citizens. VI. *consummation by being admitted to mysteries, initiation,* esp. into the Eleusinian mysteries: in pl. also, *the mysteries themselves.* 2. generally, *any religious ceremony, a solemnity,* esp. *of marriage.*

τέλοσδε, as Adv. *towards the end* or *term.*

τέλσον, τό, collat. form of τέλος, *a boundary, limit,* τέλσον ἀρούρης *a piece* of corn land *marked off.*

Τελχίν, ῖνος, ὁ, (θέλγω) *one of the Telchīnes,* the first workers in metal: also *a mischievous elf:*—as Adj., τελχῖνες σῆτες *mischievous* moths.

τελωνέω, f. ήσω, *to be a farmer of tolls, be a tax-gatherer, to farm the taxes.* From

τελ-ώνης, ου, ὁ, (τέλος, ὠνέομαι) *one who farms the tolls, customs* or *taxes* of a state, *a tax-gatherer,* Lat. *publicanus.*

τελωνία, ἡ, (τελωνέω) *the office of a farmer of the customs, the farming of the taxes.*

τελωνιάς, άδος, ἡ, (τελώνης) *of tax-gatherers.*

τελωνικός, ή, όν, (τελώνης) *of* or *for tax-gathering.*

τελώνιον, τό, (τελωνέω) *a toll-house, custom-house.*

τέμαχος, εος, τό, (τέμνω) *a slice cut off, a slice of salt-fish.*

τεμεῖν, aor. 2 inf. of τέμνω.

τεμένιος, α, ον, (τέμενος) *of* or *in the sacred precincts;* φυλλὰς τεμενία the grove *in the sacred precincts.*

τεμενίτης [ῑ], ου, ὁ, (τέμενος) *the God of the sacred precincts,* epith. of Apollo at Syracuse, whence a quarter of the city was called Τεμενίτης: fem., ἡ ἄκρα ἡ Τεμενῖτις the height *on which stood the temple of Apollo Temenītes.*

τέμενος, εος, τό, (τέμνω) *a piece of land cut off and allotted* for any purpose: *a portion of land,* esp. *of corn-land.* II. *a piece of land sacred to a god: the precincts of a temple:* hence, from the worship offered to the Nile, the valley of the Nile is called τέμενος Νείλοιο.

ΤΕ'ΜΝΩ Ion. **τάμνω**: fut. τεμῶ: aor. 2 ἔτεμον Ep. and Ion. ἔτᾰμον, Ep. inf. ταμέειν: pf. τέτμηκα: Med., fut. τεμοῦμαι: aor. 2 ἐταμόμην, inf. ταμέσθαι: Pass., aor. 1 ἐτμήθην: pf. τέτμημαι:—*to cut* or *hew* in battle, *to wound, maim.* 2. of the surgeon, *to cut, use the knife,* as opp. to cautery II. of animals, *to cut up, cut in pieces: to slaughter, sacrifice:*—since truces, covenants, and the like were solemnised *with sacrifices,* ὅρκια τάμνειν came to mean *to conclude, ratify* oaths, as in Lat. *foedus ferire, foedus ictum.* III. of timber, *to cut, cut down, fell, hew, lop:* in Med. c. acc., δοῦρα τάμνεσθαι *to fell oneself* timber; λίθους τάμνεσθαι *to have* stone *wrought* or *hewn.* 2. φάρμακον τέμνειν *to cut* or *chop up* a plant for medicinal purposes: metaph., πόρον τέμνειν *to contrive* a means. 3. τέμνειν γῆν, πεδίον, *to lay waste* a country *by felling fruit trees, cutting the corn,* etc. IV. *to cut off, sever: to part off, mark off: to divide.* V. *to cut* or *draw a line,* τέμνειν ἄρουραν *to plough* corn land; τέμνειν ὀχέτους *to cut* trenches: also, τεμνειν ὁδοὺς *to cut* or *make* roads: τέμνειν ὁδὸν *to cut* or *cleave* one's way, *go on, advance* (cf. προκόπτω); μέσον τέμνειν *to hold* a middle *course.* 2. of ships, *to cut through* or *cleave* the waves, Lat. *secare mare:* so too of birds, *to plough* or *cleave* the air: absol., τέμνειν *to go.* VI. *to cut short, bring to a crisis.*

Τέμπεα contr. **Τέμπη**, τά, *Tempé,* the valley between mounts Olympus and Ossa, through which the river Peneius flows into the sea.

τεμῶ, fut. of τέμνω.

τενᾰγίτης [ῑ], ου, ὁ, fem. **-ῖτις**, ιδος, used as Adj., *shallow.* From

ΤΕ'ΝΑΓΟΣ, εος, τό, *a shoal, shallow,* Lat. *vadum.*

ΤΕ'ΝΔΩ Att. **τένθω**, *to gnaw, nibble at.* Hence

τενθεία, ἡ, *a nibbling: epicurism, gluttony.*

τένων, οντος, ὁ, (τείνω) *a sinew, tendon:* usually, *a tendon of the foot:* hence *the foot itself.*

τέξω, **τέξομαι**, fut. act. and med. of τίκτω.

τέο, Ion. and Dor. for τίνος, gen. of interrog. τίς. II. **τεο**, enclit., Ion. and Dor. for τινός, gen, of enclit. τὶς.

τέο, Dor. for σου, gen. of συ.

τεοῖο, Ep. for σοῦ, gen. of σύ.

τέοισι, Ion. for τισί, dat. pl. of τίς.

τεός, ή, όν, Ep. and Ion. for σός, Lat. *tuus.*

τεοῦς, Dor. and Aeol. for σοῦ, gen. of σύ.

τεράζω, f. άσω, (τέρας) *to interpret portents* or *prodigies, to bode.*

τέραμνον or **τέρεμνον**, τό, *anything closely shut, a room, chamber;* only used in plur.

ΤΕ'ΡΑΣ, gen. ατος Ep. αος Ion. εος, τό: plur., nom. τέρᾰτᾰ Ep. τέρᾰᾱ contr. τέρᾱ; Ep. gen. τεράων; dat. τέρᾰσι Ep. τεράεσσι:—*a sign, wonder, marvel, portent.* II. *anything that serves as an omen: a monster, strange creature,* Lat. *monstrum.* 2. like Lat. *signum, a sign in the heavens, a constellation, meteor;* cf. τείρεα.

τερα-σκόπος, ον, poët. for τερατο-σκόπος (τέρας, σκοπέω) *boding, prophetic.*

τεράστιος, α, ον, (τέρας) *of portents, portentous.*

τερᾰτεία, ἡ, (τερατεύομαι) *a dealing in the marvellous, imposture, quackery.*

τεράτευμα, ατος, τό, *a juggling trick, quackery.* From

τερᾰτεύομαι, Dep. (τέρας) *to talk marvels,* Lat. *portenta loqui: to deal in the marvellous, be an impostor.*

τερατολογέω, f. ήσω, (τερατολόγος) *to tell of marvels.*

τερᾰτολογία, ἡ, (τερατολογέω) *a telling of marvels.*

τερᾰτο-λόγος, ον, (τέρας, λέγω) *telling of marvellous sights* or *portents.* II. pass. *of which marvellous things are told, marvellous.*

τερᾰτο-σκόπος, ον, (τέρας, σκοπέω) *observing portents:* as Subst., τερατοσκόπος, ὁ, *a soothsayer.*

τερᾰτουργία, ἡ, *a working of wonders.* From

τερᾰτ-ουργός, όν, (τέρας, ἔργω) *wonder-working.*

τερᾰτ-ώδης, ες, (τέρας, εἶδος) *like a prodigy, marvellous, wondrous.*

τερᾰτ-ωπός, όν, (τέρας, ὤψ) *with a marvellous face;* τερατωπὸς ἰδέσθαι *marvellous* to behold.

τερεβίνθῐνος, η, ον, *made* or *taken from the turpentine-tree, made from turpentine.* From

ΤΕΡΕ΄ΒΙΝΘΟΣ, ἡ, *the terebinth* or *turpentine-tree:* also *the resin that flows from it, turpentine.*

τερεβινθ-ώδης, ες, (τερέβινθος, εἶδος) *like turpentine: full of turpentine-trees.*

ΤΕ΄ΡΕΙΝΑ, fem. of **τέρην**.

τέρεμνον, τό, = **τέραμνον**.

τέρενος, η, ον, collat. form of **τέρην**.

τερετίζω, f. σω, *to whistle.* (Formed from the sound.) Hence

τερέτισμα, ατος, τό, *a whistling, trilling.*

τέρετρον, τό, *a borer, gimlet*, Lat. *terebra.* From

τερέω, f. ήσω and έσω, (τείρω) *to bore, pierce, perforate.* Hence

τερηδών, όνος, ἡ, *the wood-worm*, Lat. *terēdo.*

τέρην, εινᾰ, εν, gen. τέρενος, είνης, ενος, etc.: (τείρω): —*worn smooth, smooth, soft, delicate,* Lat. *tener:*— Comp. τερενώτερος.

τερθρεύομαι, Dep. = τερατεύομαι, *to practise juggling tricks, use rhetorical artifices.*

τέρθριος, ὁ, (τέρθρον) *the rope from the end of a sail-yard* (τέρθρον), *the brace.*

ΤΕ΄ΡΘΡΟΝ, τό, *an end, extremity:* properly, *the end of a sail-yard.*

τέρμα, ατος, τό, *an end, boundary*, Lat. *terminus: the goal round which horses and chariots had to turn* at races, Lat. *meta.* 2. *a mark for throwing* or *shooting at.* II. *an end, limit:* in plur. *the boundaries.* 2. metaph. *the finishing point: the acmé, height, summit.*

τερμίνθῐνος, η, ον, = τερεβίνθινος.

τέρμινθος, ἡ, = τερέβινθος.

τερμιόεις, εσσα, εν, (τέρμα) *reaching to the end;* ἀσπὶς τερμιόεσσα a shield *that covers one from top to toe;* χιτὼν τερμιόεις a tunic *reaching to the ground.*

τέρμιος, α, ον, (τέρμα) *at* or *coming to the end, last, final:* of Time, τερμία ἡμέρα the day *of death.*

τερμόνιος, α, ον, (τέρμων) *at the far-end.*

τέρμων, ονος, ὁ, = τέρμα, *a boundary.* II. *an end.*

τερπῐ-κέραυνος, ον, (τέρπω, κεραυνός) *delighting in thunder.*

τερπνός, ή, όν, (τέρπω) *delightful, pleasant, agreeable, cheering.* II. pass. *delighted, pleased.*— Comp. and Sup. τερπνότερος, -ότατος. Hence

τερπνῶς, Adv. *agreeably, pleasantly.*

ΤΕ΄ΡΠΩ, f. ψω: aor. 1 ἔτερψα:—Pass., aor. 1 ἐτέρφθην or ἐτάρφθην: aor. 2 ἐτάρπην, inf. ταρπῆναι Ep. ταρπήμεναι, Ep. 1 sing. and pl. subj. τρᾰπείω, τρᾰπείομεν:—Med. aor. 1 ἐτερψάμην: aor. 2 ἐταρπόμην, Ep. redupl. τεταρπόμην, τετάρπετο, 1 pl. subj. τεταρπώμεσθα, part. τεταρπόμενος:—*to delight, please.* II. in Pass. and Med. *to be cheered, enjoy oneself, make merry:*—absol., πῖνε καὶ τέρπου drink and *be merry.* 2. c. gen. rei, *to have enough of, have one's full enjoyment of, be content with.* 3. rarely c. acc., τέρπεσθαι ὄνησιν, *to enjoy* profit. Hence

τερπωλή, ἡ, poët. for τέρψις, *delight.*

τερσαίνω: aor. 1 ἐτέρσηνα Ep. τέρσηνα: (τέρσομαι):—*to dry, dry up, wipe up;* αἷμα μέλαν τέρσηνε *he dried up* the black blood. Cp. τέρσομαι.

τερσιά, ἡ, like ταρσιά, τρασιά, *a frame for drying anything on, a frame of wickerwork.* From

ΤΕ΄ΡΣΟΜΑΙ: aor. 2 inf. τερσῆναι Ep. τερσήμεναι (but no indic. ἐτέρσην occurs):—*to be* or *become dry, to dry, dry up, be staunched:* also *to be parched* or *dried up:* c. gen., ὄσσε δακρυόφιν τέρσοντο his eyes *became dry* from tears. II. the Act. τέρσω occurs in Alexandr. poets, = τερσαίνω.

τερφθείη, 3 sing. aor. 1 pass. opt. of τέρπομαι.

τερψίμ-βροτος, ον, (τέρπω, βροτός) *gladdening the heart of man.*

τερψί-νοος, ον, (τέρπω, νόος) *gladdening the heart.*

τέρψις, εως, ἡ, (τέρπω) *enjoyment: gladness, delight.*

Τερψι-χόρη Att. -χόρᾱ, η, (τέρπω, χορός) *she that delights in the dance, Terpsichoré*, one of the nine Muses.

τερψί-χοος, ον, (τέρπω, χόος) *delighting in the dance.*

τέσσᾰρα, neut. of τέσσαρες.

τεσσᾰρά-βοιος, ον, (τέσσαρα, βοῦς) *worth four steers.*

τεσσᾰρᾰ-καί-δεκα, τά, see τεσσαρεσ-καί-δεκα.

τεσσᾰρᾰκαιδεκά-δωρος, ον, (τεσσερακαίδεκα, δῶρον) *fourteen handbreadths long, broad* or *high.*

τεσσᾰρᾰκαιδεκ-έτης, ου, ὁ, (τεσσερακαίδεκα, ἔτος) *fourteen years old:* fem. **-έτις**.

τεσσᾰράκοντα Att. **τεττᾰράκοντα**, οἱ, αἱ, τά, indecl. (τέσσαρες) *forty*, Lat. *quadraginta.* [ρᾰ]

τεσσᾰρᾰκοντᾰ-έτης, ου, ὁ, and **-ετής**, ές, (τεσσαράκοντα, ἔτος) *forty years old.*

τεσσᾰρᾰκοντ-όργυιος, ον, (τεσσαρακοντα, ὄργυια) *forty fathoms high, deep*, etc.

τεσσᾰρᾰκοντ-ούτης, ου, ὁ, contr. for τεσσαρακονταέτης.

τεσσᾰρᾰκοστός, ή, όν, (τεσσεράκοντα) *fortieth*, Lat. *quadragesimus.* II. ἡ τεσσαρακοστή (sub. μοῖρα): 1. *a tax of one fortieth*, i. e. $2\frac{1}{2}$ *per cent.* 2. *a fortieth*, a coin of Chios.

ΤΕ΄ΣΣΑ΄ΡΕΣ, οἱ, αἱ, τέσσαρα, τά; gen. τεσσάρων; dat. τέσσαρσι poët. τέτρασι:—Att. τέττᾰρες, τέττᾰρα: in Ion. prose τέσσερες, τέσσερα, dat. pl. τέσσερσι: Dor. τέττορες or τέτορες: Aeol. πίσυρες:—*four*, Lat. *quatuor.*

τεσσᾰρεσ-καί-δεκα Ion. **τεσσερεσ-**, οἱ, αἱ, τά, indecl. = τέσσαρες καὶ δέκα, *fourteen:* the neut. form τέσσαρα-καί-δεκα is very rare. Hence

τεσσᾰρεσκαιδέκᾰτος, η, ον, Ion. **τεσσερεσκ-**, *the fourteenth.*

τεσσεράκοντα, Ion. for τεσσαράκοντα.

τέσσερες, τέσσερα, Ion. for τέσσαρες, τέσσαρα.

τεσσερήκοντα, f. l. for *τεσσεράκοντα*.

τεταγμένος, pf. pass. part. of *τάσσω*: hence Adv. *τεταγμένως*, *in set order, regularly.*

τετᾰγών, *όντος*, ὁ, Ep. redupl. aor. 2 part. with no pres. in use; *ῥῖψε ποδὸς τεταγών* he threw him *taking* him *by* the foot.

τέτᾰκα, pf. of *τείνω*.

τέταλμαι, pf. pass. of *τέλλω*.

τέταλτο, Ep. 3 sing. plqpf. of *τέλλω*

τέτᾰμαι, pf. pass. of *τείνω*.

τετᾰνός, *όν*, (*τείνω*) *stretched, strained, smooth.*

τέτᾰνος, ὁ, (*τείνω*) *a stretching, straining: tension.*

τετάνυστο, Ep. 3 sing. plqpf. pass. of *τᾰνύω*.

τετάξομαι, paullo-p. fut. of *τάσσω*.

τεταραγμένος, pf. pass. part. of *ταράσσω*:—hence Adv. *τεταραγμένως*, *confusedly.*

τετάρπετο, -πώμεσθα, -πόμενος, Ep. redupl. aor. 2 3 sing., 1 pl. subj., and part. med. of *τέρπω*.

τεταρταῖος, *α, ον*, (*τέταρτος*) *of* or *for four days: on the fourth day.*

τεταρτη-μόριον, *τό*, (*τεταρτος*, *μόριον*) *the fourth part; a quarter-obolus*, Lat. *quadrans.*

τέταρτος Ep. **τέτρατος**, *η, ον*, (*τέσσαρες*) *the fourth*, Lat. *quartus*:—neut. *τὸ τέταρτον* as Adv., *the fourth time.* II. *ἡ τετάρτη* (sub. *ἡμέρα*), *the fourth day.* 2. (sub. *μοῖρα*), *a liquid measure, a quart.*

τετάσθην, Ep. 3 dual plqpf. pass. of *τείνω*.

τέτᾰτο, Ep. 3 sing. plqpf. pass. of *τείνω*.

τετάχᾰται, Ion. 3 pl. pf. pass. of *τάσσω*.

τετελεσμένος, pf. pass. part. of *τελέω*.

τετέλεστο, Ep. 3 sing. plqpf. pass. of *τελέω*.

τετεύξομαι, paullo-p. fut. of *τεύχω*.

τέτευχα, pf. of *τυγχάνω*.

τετεύχᾰται, τετεύχᾰτο, Ion. 3 pl. pf. and plqpf. pass. of *τεύχω*.

τετεύχετον, 3 dual pf. of *τεύχω*.

τετεύχημαι, inf. *τετευχῆσθαι*, Ep. pf. pass. with pres. sense, formed from the Subst. *τεύχεα*, without any pres. *τευχέω* in use:—*to be armed.*

τέτηκα, intr. pf. of *τήκω*.

τετίημαι, Ep. pf. pass. without any pres. *τιέω* in use, *to be sorrowful, be grieved, to sorrow, mourn*:—used in 2 dual *τετιήσθον*; but more commonly in part. *τετιημένος, τετιημένη*, *grieved, sorrow-stricken*, esp. in phrase *τετιημένος ἦτορ grieved at* heart.

τετιηώς, Ep. pf. act. part. without any pret. *τιέω* in use, = *τετιημένος*, *grieved, sorrowing.*

τέτῑμαι, pf. pass. of *τίω*.

τετῑμῆσθαι, pf. inf. pass. of *τιμάω*.

τέτισμαι, pf. pass. of *τίνω*.

τέτλᾰ, shortd. for *τέτλαθι*.

τέτλᾰθι, Ep. pf. imperat. of **τλάω*.

τετλαίην, Ep. pf. opt. of **τλάω*.

τετλάμεν, τετλάμεναι [ᾰ], Ep. pf. inf. of **τλάω*; but **τέτλᾰμεν**, 1 pl. pf. for *τετλήκαμεν*.

τετλάτω [ᾰ], 3 sing. aor. 2 imperat. of *τλάω*.

τέτληκα, pf. of *τλῆμι*.

τετληώς, *υῖα*, gen. *ότος*, Ep. pf. part. of **τλάω*.

τέτμηκα, pf. of *τέμνω*.

τετμημένος, pf. pass. part. of *τέμνω*.

τετμηώς, Ep. pf. part. of *τέμνω*.

τέτμοιμεν, 1 pl. opt. of *τέτμον*.

τέτμον, Ep. for *ἔτετμον*, an aor. 2 without pres. in use, *to overtake, come upon.* 2. c. gen. *to partake of.*

τετοκώς, τετοκυῖα, pf. part. of *τίκτω*.

τέτορες, *οἱ, αἱ, τέτορα, τά*, Dor. for *τέσσαρες*

τετορήσω, irreg. fut. of *τορέω*.

τετρᾰ-, shortd. for *τέτορα* = *τέσσαρα*, only found in compd. words.

τετρᾰ-βάμων, *ον*, gen. *ονος*, (*τετρα-*, *βαίνω*) *four-footed, quadruped.* [βᾰ]

τετρα-γλώχῑς, *ῖνος, ὁ, ἡ*, (*τετρα-*, *γλωχίς*) *with four points* or *angles, square.*

τετρά-γῠος, *ον*, (*τέτρα-*, *γύα*) *as large as four acres* (*γύαι*) *of land.* II. *τετράγυον*, *τό*, as Subst., *a measure of land, as much as a man can plough in a day.*

τετρᾰγωνέω, (*τετράγωνος*) an astrological term, *to stand in square with*, c. acc.

τετρᾰγωνο-πρόσωπος, *ον*, (*τετράγωνος*, *πρόσωπον*) *square-faced*, like otters and beavers.

τετρά-γωνος, *ον*, (*τετρα-*, *γωνία*) *with four equal angles, square*:—as Subst., *τετράγωνον, τό*, *a square, a body of men drawn up in square*, Lat. *agmen quadratum* II. *perfect as a square, complete, perfect.* III. *τετράγωνος ἀριθμός a square* number, i. e. a number *multiplied into itself.*

τετράδιον, *τό*, (*τετράς*) *the number of four, four persons* or *things, a quaternion.* [ᾰ]

τετρᾰ-έλικτος, *ον*, (*τετρα-*, *ἑλίσσω*) *four times wound* or *coiled.*

τετρᾰ-ένης, *ες*, (*τετρα-*, *ἔνος*) = *τετραετής.* [ᾰ]

τετρᾰ-ετής, *ές*, (*τετρα-*; *ἔτος*) *four years old.* II. *of four years.*

τετρά-ζῠγος, *ον*, (*τετρα-*, *ζυγόν*) *four-yoked, with four horses*: as Subst., *τὸ τετράζυγον* (sc. *ἅρμα*) *a four-horsed chariot.*

τετρᾰ-θέλυμνος, *ον*, (*τετρα-*, *θέλυμνον*) *of four layers*; *τετραθέλυμνος σάκος* a shield *of four ox-hides.*

ΤΕΤΡΑΙ'ΝΩ, fut. *τετρᾰνῶ*: aor. 1 *ἐτέτρηνα* Ep. *τέτρηνα*: aor. 1 pass. *ἐτετράνθην*: also (from the root ΤΡΑ'Ω), fut. *τρήσω*: aor. *ἔτρησα*: pf. pass. *τέτρημαι*:—*to bore through, pierce, perforate.*

τετρᾰ-και-δεκ-έτης, fem. *-ετις, ιδος*, (*τετρα-*, *καί*, *δέκα*, *ἔτος*) *fourteen years old.*

τετρά-κερως, *ων*, (*τετρα-*, *κέρας*) *four-horned.* [ᾰ]

τετρᾰ-κέφαλος, *ον*, (*τετρα-*, *κεφαλή*) *four-headed.*

τετράκις, Adv. (*τετρα-*) *four times.* [ᾰ]

τετρᾰκισ-μύριοι, *αι, α*, (*τετράκις*, *μύριοι*) *four times ten thousand, forty thousand.* [ῡ]

τετρᾰκισ-χίλιοι, *αι, α*, (*τετράκις*, *χίλιοι*) *four thousand.* [χῑ]

τετρά-κλῑνος, *ον*, (*τετρα-*, *κλίνη*) *with four beds* or *couches to recline on at table.*

τετρά-κνᾱμος, *ον*, Dor. for *τετράκνημος*, (*τετρα-*, *κνήμη*) *with four spokes, fastened to a four-spoked wheel.*

τετρᾰ-κόρυμβος, ον, (τετρα-, κόρυμβος) *with four bunches* or *clusters*; generally, *thick-clustering*.

τετρᾰ-κόρωνος, ον, (τετρα-, κορώνη) *four times a crow's age*.

τετρᾰκόσιοι, αι, α, (τετρα-) *four-hundred*. Hence

τετρᾰκοσιοστός, ή, όν, *the four-hundredth*.

τετρακτύς, ύος, ἡ, (τετράς) *the number four*.

τετρά-κυκλος, ον, (τετρα-, κύκλος) *four-wheeled*.

τετρᾰ-λογία, ἡ, (τετρα-, λόγος) *a tetralogy*, i. e. *series of four dramas*, viz. three Tragedies and one Satyric play, which were exhibited together on the Attic stage for the prize at the festivals of Bacchus:—without the Satyric play, the three Tragedies were called *a trilogy*, τριλογία, such as the Agamemnon, Choëphoroe, and Eumenides of Aeschylus.

τετρά-μετρος, ον, (τετρα-, μέτρον) *consisting of four metres*, i. e. in iambic, trochaic and anapaestic verse, *consisting of four double feet*, cp. Lat. *versus octonarius*; in dactylic, choriambic, dochmiac verse, *consisting of four feet*:—as Subst., τετράμετρος (sub. στίχος), ὁ, *a tetrameter* or *verse of four feet*.

τετρᾰ-μηνιαῖος, α, ον, and **τετράμηνος**, ον, (τετρα-, μήν) *of four months, lasting four months*.

τέτραμμαι, pf. pass. of τρέ

τετρᾰμοιρία, ἡ, *a fourfold portion*. From

τετρά-μοιρος, ον, (τετρᾰ-, μοῖρα) *consisting of four parts, fourfold*.

τετρανθείς, aor. 1 pass. part. of τετραίνω.

ΤΕ'ΤΡΑΞ, ἄγος, and ἄκος, ὁ, prob. *the pheasant*, Lat. *avis Phasianus*.

τετρᾱορία, ἡ, *a four-horsed chariot*. From

τετρά-ορος contr. **τέτρωρος**, ον, (τετρα-, ἀείρω) *yoked four together*; τετράορον ὅρμα a *four-horsed* chariot. II. *four-legged*. [ᾱ]

τετρᾰ-πάλαι, Adv. *four times long ago, long long ago*.

τετρᾰ-πάλαιστος, ον, (τετρα-, παλαιστή) *of four spans, four spans long* or *broad*.

τετρά-πηχυς, υ, gen. εος, (τετρᾰ-, πῆχυς) *four cubits* (i. e. six feet) *long, broad*, etc.: of men, *six feet high*.

τετρᾰπλάσιος, α, ον, (τετρα-) *fourfold, four times as much*, Lat. *quadruplus*. [πλᾰ]

τετρά-πλευρος, ον, (τετρᾰ-, πλευρά) *four-sided*.

τετρᾰπλῆ, Adv. (τετρα-) *in a fourfold manner, fourfold*.

τετρᾰπλόος, η, ον contr. **-πλοῦς**, ῆ, οῦν, (τετρα-) *fourfold*, Lat. *quadruplus*: as Subst., τὸ τετραπλοῦν = τετραμοιρία, *a fourfold portion*.

τετρᾰ-ποδηδόν, Adv. (τετρα-, πούς) *on four feet*.

τετρᾰ-ποδιστί, Adv. (τετρα-, πούς) *on all fours*.

τετρά-πολις poët. **τετράπτολις**, εως, ἡ, (τετρᾰ-, πόλις) *of, with four cities*

τετρά-πολος, ον, (τετρᾰ-, πολέω) *turned up* or *ploughed four times*.

τετρά-πους, ὁ, ἡ, -πουν, τό, (τετρᾰ-, πούς) *four-footed*:—as Subst., τετράποδα, τά, *quadrupeds*. II. *of four feet in length*.

τετρά-πτερος, ον, (τετρά-, πτερόν) *four-winged*. Hence

τετρα-πτερυλλίς, ίδος, ἡ, (τετρα-, πτερόν) *a four-winged creature, grasshopper, locust*.

τετρά-πτῐλος, ον, (τετρα-, πτίλον) *four-winged*.

τέτραπτο, Ep. 3 sing. plqpf. pass. of τρέπω.

τετρά-πτολις, ἡ, poët. for τετράπολις.

τετράρ-ρῡμος or **τετρά-ρυμος**, ον, (τετρα-, ῥυμός) *with four poles*, i. e. *drawn by eight horses*.

τετραρχέω, *to be a tetrarch*. From

τετρ-άρχης, ου, ὁ, (τετρα-, ἄρχω) *a tetrarch, one of four chiefs* or *princes* in a tribe or country. Hence

τετραρχία, ἡ, *a tetrarchy, the power* or *dominions of a tetrarch*:—Thessaly was anciently divided into four tetrarchies. and so Palestine under the Romans.

τετράς, άδος, ἡ, (τέτταρες) *the number four*. 2. *the fourth da*

τετρα-σκελής, ές, (τετρα-, σκέλος) *four-legged, four-footed*.

τετρα-στάτηρος, ον, (τέτρα-, στᾰτήρ) *worth four staters*, i. e. about 13 shillings.

τετρα-σύλλᾰβος, ον, (τετρα-, συλλαβή) *of four syllables*.

τετρᾰ-σώματος, ον, (τετρα-, σῶμα) *with four bodies*.

τέτρᾰτος, η, ον, poët. for τέταρτος, *fourth*:—neut. τὸ τέτρατον as Adv., *for the fourth time*.

τετρά-τρῠφος, ον, (τετρα-, θρύπτω) *broken* or *that may be broken into four pieces*.

τέτρᾰφα, pf. of τρέπω.

τετρᾰ-φάληρος, ον, of a helmet, = τετράφαλος. [φᾰ]

τετρά-φᾰλος, ον, (τετρα-, φάλος) of a helmet, *with four* φάλοι; see φάλος.

τετράφᾰται, -φᾰτο, Ion. 3 pl. pf. and plqpf. pass. of τρέπω.

τετράφθω, 3 sing. pf. pass. imperat. of τρέπω.

τετρά-φῡλος, ον, (τετρα-, φυλή) *divided into four tribes*.

τέτρᾰχᾰ, Adv. (τέτταρες) *fourfold, in four parts*.

τετρᾰχῆ, Adv. = τέτραχα.

τετραχθά, Adv. poët. for τέτραχα.

τετρά-χοος, ον contr. **-χους**, ουν, (τετρα-, χοεύς) *holding four* χόες

τετρά-χορδος, ον, (τετρα-, χορδή) *four-stringed*:—as Subst., τὸ τετράχορδον, *the tetrachord*, a scale comprising two tones and a half.

τετρά-χυτρος, ον, (τετρα-, χύτρος) *made of four pots*.

τετρεμαίνω, redupl. form of τρέμω, *to tremble*.

τέτρημαι, pf. pass. of τετραίνω.

τέτρηνα, Ep. for ἐτέτρηναι, aor. 1 of τετραίνω.

τέτρηχα, intr. pf. with pres. signf. of ταράσσω; part. fem. τετρηχυῖα; 3 sing. plqpf. τετρήχει.

τετρίγει, Ep. 3 sing. plqpf. of τρίζω. [ῐ]

τετρῑγώς, **τετριγυῖα**, pf. part. of τρίζω.

τετρῑγῶτος, Ep. for τετριγότας, acc. pl. pf. part. of τρίζω.

τέτριμμαι, pf. pass. of τρίβω.

τετρ-όργυιος, ον, (τετρα-, ὄργυια) *four fathoms long* or *broad*.

τέτροφα, pf. of τρέπω; also intr. pf. of τρέφω.

τετρῦσθαι, pf. pass. inf. of τρύω.

τετρ-ώβολος, ον, (τετρα–, ὀβολός) *weighing* or *worth four obols*:—as Subst., τετρώβολον, τό, *a four-obol piece.*

τετρώκοστος, η, Dor. for τεσσαρακοστός, *fortieth.*

τέτρωμαι, pf. pass. of τετρώσκω.

τετρ-ώρος, ον, contr. for τετράορο

τετρ-ώροφος, ον, (τετρα–, ὀροφή) *of four stories.*

τετρ-ώρυγος, ον, more correct form of τετρόργυιος.

τέττα, an address of youths to their elders, *Father*, like ἄττα, πάππα.

τεττᾰράκοντα, τέτταρες, etc., Att. for τεσσαρ–.

τεττῖγο-φόρος, ον, (τέττιξ, φέρω) *wearing a τέττιξ* or *cicada*: epith. of the Athenians, because in early times they wore golden grasshoppers in their hair as an emblem of their being αὐτόχθονε

τεττῖγ-ώδης, ες, (τέττιξ, εἶδος) *like a τέττιξ* or *cicada.*

ΤΕ'ΤΤΙΞ, ῖγος, ὁ, *a* kind of *grasshopper, the cicala*, Lat. *cicāda*, a winged insect fond of basking on single trees or bushes, when it made a chirping noise:—see τεττιγοφόρος.

τετύγμαι, pf. pass. of τεύχω.

τετύγμην, Ep. plqpf. pass. of τεύχω.

τετῠκεῖν, Ep. redupl. aor. 2 inf. of τεύχω.

τετῠκέσθαι, Ep. redupl. aor. 2 med. of τεύχω.

τετυμμένος, pf. pass. part. of τύπτω.

τέτυγμαι, ξαι, κται, pf. pass. of τεύχω.

τέτυγμην, ξο, κτο, plqpf. pass. of τεύχω.

τετῡφωμένως, Adv. pf. pass. part. of τυφόω, *stupidly.*

τετύχηκα [ῠ], pf. of τυγχάνω.

τετύχθαι, pf. pass. inf. of τεύχω.

τετύχθω, 3 sing. pf. pass. imperat. of τεύχω.

τεῦ, Dor. for σοῦ, gen. of τύ, σύ.

τεῦ, Ion. and Dor. for τίνος, gen. of τίς (interrog.) II. **τεῦ** enclit. gen. for τινός, from τὶς (enclit.)

τεῦγμα, ατος, τό, (τεύχω) *that which is made, a work.*

τευθίς, ίδος, ἡ, *a cuttle-fish*, Lat. *sepia, loligo.*

τευκτός, ή, όν, verb. Adj. of τεύχω, *made, prepared, wrought.*

τεῦξα, Ep. aor. 1 opt. of τεύχω: opt. τεύξεια.

τεύξομαι, fut. of τυγχάνω. 2. fut. med. of τεύχω.

τεύτλιον, = τεῦτλον, *beet.*

ΤΕΥ'ΤΛΟΝ, τό, Att. for σεῦτλον, a kitchen-herb, *beet*, Lat. *beta.*

τεύχεα, τά, see τεῦχος.

τευχεσ-φόρος, ον, (τεύχεα, φέρω) *bearing arms, wearing armour.*

τευχηστήρ, ῆρος, ὁ, or **τευχηστής**, οῦ, ὁ, (τεύχεα) *an armed man, warrior.*

τεύχοισα, Dor. pres. part. fem. of τεύχω.

τεῦχος, εος, τό, (τεύχω) like ὅπλον, *a tool, implement, utensil*: mostly in plur. τεύχεα *implements of war, armour, arms, harness.* 2. in plur. also *the tackle* or *rigging* of a ship. 3. *a vessel* of any kind, as *a bathing-tub, a balloting* or *funereal urn.* 4. *a book*, whence the term *Pentateuch* or *Five-books.*

ΤΕΥ'ΧΩ; f. ξω: aor. 1 ἔτευξα: Ep. aor. 2 τέτῠκον: pf. τέτευχα: Med., fut. τεύξομαι: Ep. aor. 2 τετῠκόμην: Pass., fut. 3 τετεύξομαι: aor. 1 ἐτύχθην: pf. τέτυγμαι: Ep. 3 pl. pf. and plqpf. τετεύχᾰται, τετεύχᾰτο:—*to make, construct*, of works in wood or metal, *to build, forge*: *to weave*: also metaph. *to work, bring about, cause*: *to form, create*:—Pass., c. gen. rei, τεύχεσθαι χρυσοῖο *to be wrought of* gold. II. c. dupl. acc. *to make* a person so and so: and pf. pass. τέτυγμαι is often used = εἰμί or γίγνομαι, *to have been made*, i. e. *to be*, so and so; γυναικὸς ἀντὶ τέτυξο, *thou hadst been made*, i. e. *thou wert*, like a woman. 2. the pf. pass. part. τετυγμένος commonly means *well* or *fitly made, well-wrought, compact, lasting*; metaph. of a field, *well-tilled*, also of the mind, *active, vigorous.*

τέφρα Ion. **τέφρη**, ἡ, (τύφω) *ashes*, sprinkled over the head and clothes in token of grief: *the ashes of the funeral pile.*

τεφρόω, f. ώσω, (τέφρα) *to reduce to ashes, consume.*

τεχθείς, aor. 1 pass. part. of τίκτω.

τεχνάζω, f. άσω, (τέχνη) *to use art* or *cunning, deal subtly, contrive cunningly.*

τεχνάεις, εσσα, εν, Dor. for τεχνήεις.

τέχνασμα, ατος, τό, (τεχνάζω) *anything made by art, a piece of handiwork.* II. *an artifice, trick.*

τεχνάομαι, f. ήσομαι: aor. 1 ἐτεχνησάμην: Dep.: (τέχνη):—*to make, contrive, devise by art, execute skilfully*: also followed by a relat., *to contrive* that ... I. τεχνάομαι also occurs as a Pass., with pf. τετέχνημαι, *to be made by art.*

τέχνη, ἡ, (τεκεῖν) *art, skill, regular method of making* a thing; τέχνῃ *by rules of art.* 2. *art, craft, cunning, sleight*: in plur. *cunning devices, arts, wiles.* 3. generally, *a way, manner, means whereby a thing is gained*; μηδεμιῇ τέχνῃ in *no wise*; πάσῃ τέχνῃ by all *means*; παντοίῃ τέχνῃ by all manner of *means.* II. *an art, craft, trade.* III. *a work of art.*

τεχνήεις, εσσα, εν, (τέχνη) *cunningly wrought, ingenious.* Adv. τεχνηέντως, *artfully, with art.*

τέχνημα, ατος, τό, (τεχνάω) *that which is wrought by art, a work of art, a handiwork.* II. *an artful device, trick, artifice*: of a man, *all trick and cunning.*

τεχνήμων, ον, gen, ονος, = τεχνήεις.

τεχνῆσσα, contr. for τεχνήεσσα, fem. of τεχνήεις.

τεχνικός, ή, όν, (τέχνη) *artistic, skilful.* Adv. -κῶς, *artistically.*

τεχνίτης [ῑ], ου, ὁ, (τέχνη) *an artificer, artist, craftsman, workman*: *one who works by rules of art.*

τεχνῖτις, ιδος, fem. of τεχνίτης.

τεχνοσύνη, ἡ, poët. for τέχνη, *art, skilfulness.*

τέῳ, Ion. for τίνι, dat. of τίς (interrog.). 2. τεῳ Ion. for τινί, dat. from τὶς (enclit.)

τέων, Ion. for τίνων, gen. pl. of τίς (interrog.) 2. for τινῶν, gen. pl. of τὶς (enclit.).

τέως Ep. **τείως**, Adv. of Time, *so long, meanwhile, the while*; also *before, ere this*:—antecedent to the relat. ἕως. II. absol. *a while, for a time.* [τέως: but it also occurs as one long syllable.]

τῆ, Ep, 2 sing. imperat., with no other form in use, like λάβε, ἔχε, φέρε, *there! take!* always followed by a second imperat., as τῆ, σπεῖσον Διί .. *take* and pour a libation to Jove ..: τῆ, πίε οἶνον.. *take* and drink wine.

τῇ, dat. fem. of the Art. ὁ. 2. in the Poets, dat. fem. of the Relat. ὅς. II. as Adv., like ταύτῃ, *here, this way.*

τῇδε, dat. fem. of ὅδε, used as Adv., *in this direction, in this way.*

τηδί, dat. fem. of ὁδί, used as Adv. = τῇδε.

ΤΗ'ΘΗ or **τηθή**, ἡ, *a grandmother.*

τηθίς, ίδος, ἡ, (τήθη) *a father's* or *mother's sister, aunt.*

ΤΗ῀ΘΟΣ, εος, τό, *an oyster.*

Τηθύς, ύος, ἡ, (τήθη) *Tethys*, wife of Oceanos, daughter of Uranos and Gaia a Sea Deity. II. later, put for *the sea itself.*

τηκεδών, όνος, ἡ, (τήκω) *a melting away, wasting away:* hence *consumption, decline, phthisis.*

τηκτός, ή, όν, verb. Adj. of τήκω, *melted, melted down so as to be poured in: soluble.*

ΤΗ'ΚΩ Dor. **τάκω**: fut. τήξω: aor. 1 ἔτηξα: I. transit. *to melt, melt down, make to melt away; to smelt* metals: metaph. *to make pine* or *melt away.* II. Med. and Pass., f. med. τήξομαι, pass. τᾰκήσομαι: aor. 2 pass. ἐτάκην [ᾰ]:—*to melt, melt away: to pine, waste away: to ooze away, vanish, fall away.* III. the pf. act. τέτηκα is used intr. = pres. pass., and plqpf. ἐτετήκειν = impf. pass., *to pine, melt away;* κρέα τετηκότα *sodden* flesh.

τηλ-αυγής, ές, (τῆλε, αὐγή) *far-shining, glittering from afar:* hence *far-seen, conspicuous.* Comp. and Sup. τηλαυγεστέρος, -έστατος. Adv. τηλαυγῶς, *clearly, distinctly.*

ΤΗ῀ΛΕ, Adv., like τηλοῦ, *far off, far away, far: abroad:* c. gen. *far from.*

τηλε-βόας, ου, ὁ, (τῆλε, βοάω) *shouting afar* or *loud.*

τηλε-βόλος, ον, (τῆλε, βαλεῖν) *striking from afar.*

τηλέ-γονος, ον, (τῆλε, γενέσθαι) *born far from one's father* or *one's fatherland.*

τηλεδᾰπός, ή, όν, (τῆλε) *from a far country, foreign:* also *afar off, distant.*

τηλεθάω, lengthd. for θάλλω (cp. pf. τέθηλα), used only in Ep. part. pres. τηλεθάων, Ep. -όων, όωσα, *luxuriant, blooming, flourishing*, of trees and plants, as, ὕλη, ἐλαῖαι, δένδρεα, etc.: metaph., παῖδες τηλεθάοντες *blooming* children; χαίτη τηλεθόωσα *luxuriant* hair.

τηλε-κλειτός, όν, (τῆλε, κλέος) *far-famed.*

τηλέ-κλητος, ον, (τῆλε, κλητός from καλέω) *called from afar, summoned from afar.*

τηλε-κλῠτός, όν, (τῆλε, κλυτός from κλύω) = τηλεκλειτός.

τηλε-μάχος, ον, (τῆλε, μάχομαι) *fighting from afar:* as pr. name, Τηλέμαχος, ὁ, a son of Ulysses.

τηλέ-πλᾰνος, ον, (τῆλε, πλανάομαι) *far-wandering, devious.*

τηλέ-πομπος, ον, (τῆλε, πέμπω) *sent from afar, far-journeying.*

τηλέ-πορος, ον, (τῆλε, πόρος) *far-reaching.*

τηλέ-πῠλος, ον, (τῆλε, πύλη) *with gates far apart.*

τηλε-σκόπος, ον, (τῆλε, σκοπέω) *far-seeing.* II. proparox. τηλέσκοπος, ον, pass., *far-seen, conspicuous.*

τηλε-φᾰνής, ές, (τῆλε, φανῆναι) *appearing afar, seen from far:* of sound, *heard from afar.*

τηλέ-φῐλον, τό, (τῆλε, φίλος) *far-love, love-in-absence*, poetic name of a plant used as a charm by lovers to see whether their love was returned: if the leaf, when placed on one hand and struck by the other, burst with a loud crack, it was a good omen.

ΤΗΛΙ'Α, ἡ, *any flat board with a raised rim*, as, 1. *a sieve, the hoop of a sieve.* 2. *a stand* or *platform* on which flour, etc., was set out for sale. 3. *a gambling-table.* 4. *a chimney-top*, i. e. *a lid* which covered the aperture in the roof.

ΤΗΛΙ'ΚΟΣ, η, ον, Dor. **τᾱλίκος**, α, ον [ῐ]:—*of such an age*, so *old* or so *young*. generally, *so great*, Lat. *tantus:* anteced. to the Relative ἡλίκος, Interrog. πηλίκος. Hence

τηλῐκόσδε, -ήδε, -όνδε, and **τηλῐκοῦτος**, -αύτη or -οῦτος, -οῦτο, Att. for πηλίκος, *so very, so much.*

τηλόθεν or -θε, Adv. (τηλοῦ) *from afar, from a foreign land:* c. gen. *far from.*

τηλόθῐ, Adv. (τηλοῦ) = τῆλε, τηλοῦ, *far, afar, at a distance:* also c. gen., τηλόθι πάτρης *far from* fatherland.

τηλο-πέτης, ες, (τῆλε, πέτομαι) *far-flying.*

τηλ-ορός, όν, collat. form of τηλουρός.

τηλόσε, Adv. (τηλοῦ) *to a distance, far away.*

τηλοτάτω, Adv., Sup. of τηλοῦ, *furthest away.*

τηλοτέρω, Adv., Comp. of τηλοῦ, *further away.*

τηλοῦ, Adv., like τῆλε, *afar, far off* or *away, in a far country:* also c. gen. *far from.*

τηλ-ουρός, όν, (τῆλε, ὅρος) *with distant boundaries* or *confines:* generally, *far, distant, remote.*

τηλῠγετος, η, ον, also ος, ον, an epith. of sons, *who have no brother*, or of daughters *who have no sister, a darling;* hence in bad sense, τηλύγετος ὥς like *a spoilt child* or *pet.* II. *born afar off.* (The latter sense points to the deriv. τῆλε, *γένω. But Homer always uses the word in the first sense; and its derivation, as he used it, remains doubtful.)

τηλ-ωπός, όν, (τῆλε, ὤψ) *looking afar, seeing to a distance.* II. pass. *perceived* or *heard from afar.*

τημελέω, f. ήσω, *to take care of*, c. gen. 2. *to heed, look after, see to*, c. acc. From

τη-μελής, ές, *careful, heedful.* (From μέλω, with the inseparable prefix τη- added.)

τήμερα, τήμερον, Att. for σήμερον.

τἠμῇ, Att. crasis for τῇ ἐμῇ.

τῆμος, Adv. *then, thereupon;* ἐς τῆμος till *then.*

τημόσδε Dor. **ταμόσδε**, Adv. = τῆμος.

τημοῦτος, Adv. = τῆμος.

τηνεῖ, Adv., Dor. for ἐκεῖ, *there:* also for ὧδε *here.*

τήνελλα, a word formed by Archilochus to imitate

the twang of a guitar-string at the beginning of a triumphal hymn to Hercules, *τήνελλα ὦ καλλίνικε, χαῖρε*; hence *τήνελλα καλλίνικε* became a common mode of saluting conquerors in the games. Hence

τήνελλος ὁ, Comic word, *a conqueror who is received with a cry of τήνελλα, a victor in the games.*

τηνίκᾰ, Adv. (*τῆνος*) *at this* or *that time* of day, *then.* [ῐ]

τηνῐκάδε, Adv. (*τηνίκα*) *at this time of day, so early; αὔριον τηνικάδε* to-morrow *at this time of day.* [ᾰ]

τηνῐκαῦτα, commoner form for *τηνίκα, at this particular time:* c. gen., *τηνικαῦτα τοῦ θέρους at this time* of the summer. II. *in this case, then.*

τηνόθι, Adv. (*τῆνος*) Dor. for *ἐκεῖ, there.*

τῆνος, *τήνα, τῆνο*, Dor. for *κῆνος, = κεῖνος, ἐκεῖνος, that.* Hence

τηνῶ, Adv., Dor. for *ἐκεῖ, there.*

τηνῶθε and **–θεν**, Adv., Dor. for *ἐκεῖθεν, thence.*

τηξῐ-μελής, *ές*, (*τήκω, μέλος*) *melting* or *wasting away of the limbs.*

τῆπερ, Ep. and Ion. for *ᾗπερ*, dat. fem. of *ὅσπερ*, used as Adv., *in which direction* or *way.*

τηρέω, f. *ήσω*, (*τηρός*) *to give heed to, watch narrowly; to take care of, keep, guard; τηρεῖν εἰρήνην to keep, observe* peace. 2. metaph. *to observe, watch for* a person or thing; *τηρήσας νύκτα ἀσέληνον having watched for* a moonless night. II. Med., f. *ήσομαι*, like *φυλάσσομαι, to be on one's guard against, take care* or *heed:* fut. med. *τηρήσομαι* is also used in pass. sense. Hence

τήρησις, *εως, ἡ, a watching, guarding: vigilance.* II. *a means of keeping secure, a ward, prison.*

ΤΗΡΟ'Σ, *ου, a watch, guard.*

τῇς, τῇσι, Ep. and Ion. dat. fem. pl. of *ὁ* and *ὅς.*

τητάω, f. *ήσω, to bereave, deprive:*—Pass. *to be in want:* c. gen. *to be bereft* or *deprived of* a thing.

τῆτες, Adv., Att. for Ion. *σῆτες, this year, of* or *in this year.* (From *ἔτος*, as *τήμερον* from *ἡμέρα.*)

τητῐνός, *η, ον*, (*τῆτες*) *of this year*, Lat. *hornus.*

τηΰσιος, *α, ον, empty, idle, vain.* Adv. *–ίως, in vain.*

τί and **τὶ**, neut. of *τίς* (interrog.) and *τὶς* (enclit.).

τιάρᾱ [ᾱ], *ἡ*, or **τιάρας** Ion. **τιήρης**, *ου, ὁ, a tiāra*, the Persian head-dress worn *upright* by the king. (Persian word.)

τιᾱρο-ειδής, *ές*, (*τιάρα, εἶδος*) *shaped like a tiara, like* or *resembling a tiara.*

τιέμεν, τιέμεναι, Ep. inf. for *τίειν.*

τίεσκεν, τιέσκετο, 3 sing. Ion. impf. act. and med. of *τίω.*

τίη, strengthd. for *τί*; *why? wherefore?*

τιήρης, *ου, ὁ*, Ion. for *τιάρας.*

τῐθαιβώσσω, *to build, make a nest:* of bees, *to make honeycombs.* (Akin to *τιθήνη, τιθασός.*)

τῐθάς, *άδος, ἡ*, (*τιθασός*) *a barn-door fowl.*

τῐθᾰσευτής, *οῦ, ὁ, one who tames, domesticates.* From

τῐθᾰσεύω, *to tame, break in, domesticate.* From

τῐθᾰσός, *όν*, (*τίτθη, τιθήνη*) *tamed, domesticated*, of animals, *tame:* of plants, *cultivated:* of men, *moderate, mild:* metaph., *τιθασὸς Ἄρης domestic* strife.

τιθέᾰμεν, for *τίθεμεν*, like *διδόᾰμεν* for *δίδομεν*, 1 pl. pres. of *τίθημι:* so *τιθέᾱσι*, 3 pl. for *τιθεῖσι.*

τιθείς, *εῖσα, έν*, pres. part. of *τίθημι.*

τίθεις, τίθει, Ep. 2 and 3 sing. impf. of *τιθέω = τίθημι.*

τιθεῖς, τιθεῖ, 2 and 3 sing. of *τιθέω = τίθημι.*

τιθέμεν, Ep. for *τιθέναι*, inf. of *τίθημι:* but **τίθεμεν**, 1 pl.

τίθεν, Aeol. and Dor. for *ἐτίθεσαν* Ep. *τίθεσαν*, 3 pl. impf. of *τίθημι.*

τίθεσκε, 3 sing. Ion. impf. of *τίθημι.*

τίθεσο Ep. **τίθεσσο**, pres. med. imperat. of *τίθημι.*

τῐθέω, poët. form of *τίθημι*, whence 2 and 3 sing. *τιθεῖς, τιθεῖ*, and impf. *ἐτίθεις, ἐτίθει* Ep. *τίθει.*

τιθήμεναι, Ep. for *τιθέμεναι, τιθέναι*, inf. of *τίθημι.*

τιθήμενος, Ep. for *τιθέμενος*, pres. med. part. of *τίθημι.*

τίθημι, *τίθης, τίθησι*, also Ep. 2 sing. *τίθησθα*; 3 pl. *τιθεῖσι* Ion. *τιθέᾱσι*; inf. *τιθέναι* Ep. *τιθήμεναι, τιθέμεν*; Impf. *ἐτίθην*, Ep. 3 pl. *τίθεσαν*; Ion. *τίθεσκον*: (there are also some forms from the pres. *τιθέω*, q. v.): Fut. *θήσω*, Ep. inf. *θησέμεναι* or *θησέμεν*: Aor. 1 *ἔθηκα* Ep. *θῆκα*: Pf. *τέθεικα*, plqpf. *ἐτεθείκειν*: Aor. 2 *ἔθην* only used in pl. *ἔθεμεν, ἔθετε, ἔθεσαν* Ep. *θέσαν*; imperat. *θές*; subj. *θῶ* Ion. *θέω*, 1 pl. *θέωμεν*; lengthd. Ep. *θείω*, 2 sing. *θήῃς*, pl. *θείομεν* for *θείωμεν, θῶμεν*: opt. *θείην*, pl. *θείημεν* or *θεῖμεν, θεῖτε, θεῖσαν*: inf. *θεῖναι* Ep. *θέμεναι, θέμεν*; part. *θείς.*—Med. *τίθεμαι, τίθεσαι, τίθεται*; imperat. *τίθεσο, τιθοῦ*, Ep. part. *τιθήμενος*: impf. *ἐτιθέμην*: Fut. *θήσομαι*: Aor. 1 *ἐθηκάμην*, Ep. 3 sing. *θήκατο*: part. *θηκάμενος*: Aor. 2 med. *ἐθέμην*; imperat. *θέο* contr. *θοῦ*; opt. *θείμην*, 3 sing. *θεῖτο.*—Pass. *τίθεμαι*: fut. *τεθήσομαι*: aor. 1 *ἐτέθην*: pf. *τέθειμαι*: plqpf. *ἐτεθείμην.* *To place, put, set*, Lat. *ponere; θεῖναί τινί τι ἐν χερσί to place* a thing in a person's hands: metaph., *θεῖναί τινι ἔπος ἐν φρεσί* or *βουλὴν ἐν στήθεσσι, to plant* a word, warning, etc., in his mind; but, *τιθέμεν νόῳ to lay* a thing to one's own heart, *bear* in mind.—Med., *θέσθαι θυμὸν ἐν στήθεσσι to lay up* or *treasure* anger in one's heart. II. *to fix, settle, determine; τιθέναι ἀγῶνα to appoint, hold* games: of the prizes, *θεῖναι ἐς μέσσον to set them* in the middle, *propose* them for competition; also of sovereign power, *ὑμῖν ἐς μέσον ἀρχὴν τιθείς throwing it open* to you publicly. 2. *to assign, award; θεῖναι νόμον to lay down, fix* the law, of a king or legislator; *θέσθαι νόμον to give oneself* a law, of the people. 3. *to ordain, establish, order, institute.* 4. in Med. *to fix in common with others, agree upon, settle.* III. *to set up*, in a temple, *to devote, dedicate.* 2. of Artists, *to represent, portray, depict.* IV. *to assign to a place* or *class, to hold, reckon, esteem: to believe, consider.* V. in Med., *τίθεσθαι ψῆφον to put down one's* ballot, *to give* one's vote: hence *τίθεσθαι τὴν γνώμην to determine, decide: τίθεσθαί τινι* (sc.

τὴν ψῆφον) *to decide in a* person's *favour:* τίθεσθαι τῇ γνώμῃ *to agree* or *subscribe to* an opinion. 2. *to lay to one's account:* but also *to pay down, pay, discharge.* VI. *to deposit,* as in a bank. VII. in military language, τίθεσθαι τὰ ὅπλα has three senses: 1. *to stack* or *pile arms, to bivouack, take up one's quarters:* generally, *to take up a position.* 2. *to get* soldiers *under arms, to draw* them *up in order of battle.* 3. *to lay down one's arms, surrender.* VIII. τίθημι is often used of persons and things, *to make* or *render* so and so, *bring into a certain state, effect;* ναῦν λᾶαν ἔθηκε he *made* the ship a stone: of persons, *to make* so and so, *appoint.* 2. with an Adj., θεῖναί τινα ἀθάνατον καὶ ἀγήραον *to make* him undying and undecaying. 3. παῖδα τίθεσθαί τινα *to make* him *one's* child, *adopt* him, like θετὸν παῖδα ποιεῖσθαι. IX. of things, *to make, cause, bring to pass:*—Med. *to make* or *prepare for oneself;* θέσθαι δῶμα *to build oneself* a house; θέσθαι κέλευθον *to make oneself* a road. 2. εὖ or καλῶς θέσθαι τί *to manage* or *arrange* a thing well *for oneself, to make* good *use of* it. X. τίθημι, with acc., often stands for a simple Verb, as σκέδασιν θεῖναι *to make* a scattering, for σκεδάσαι; θεῖναι κρύφον, θεῖναι αἶνον, for κρύπτειν, αἰνεῖν, etc.

τῑθηνέω, f. ήσω, *to take care of, tend, nurse;* and so generally, *to cherish, foster:* mostly used in Med. From

τῑθήνη, ἡ, (τιθηνός) *a nurse.*

τῑθηνητήρ, ῆρος, ὁ, (τιθηνέω) = τιθηνός. Hence

τῑθηνητήριος, α, ον, *nursing, tending.*

τῑθηνός, όν, (τίτθη) *nursing:* as Subst., τιθηνός, ὁ, *a foster-father.*

τίθησθα [ῐ], Ep. for τίθης, 2 sing. of τίθημι.

τίθητι [ῐ], Dor. for τίθησι, 3 sing. of τίθημι.

τιθύμαλος, ὁ, irreg. pl. τὰ τιθύμαλα:—*spurge,* Lat. *euphorbia.* (Deriv. uncertain.)

Τῑθωνός, ὁ, *Tithonus,* brother of Priam, husband of Aurora, and father of Memnon: metaph. of a decrepit old man, because he had immortal life without the continuance of youth.

τίκτω, for τιτέκω, which is formed by redupl. from Root *ΤΕ'ΚΩ: fut. τέξω or τέξομαι, poët. τεκοῦμαι, inf. τεκεῖσθαι: aor. 2 ἔτεκον Ep. τέκον: pf. τέτοκα, part. τετοκώς, υῖα, ός:—Med. τίκτομαι occurs in the same sense:—*to bring into the world,* 1. of the mother, *to bring forth, bear,* Lat. *parĕre.* 2. of the father, *to beget,* Lat. *gignere:* hence, 3. οἱ τεκόντες *the parents;* ὁ τεκών *the father;* ἡ τεκοῦσα *the mother:* and even as Subst. c. gen., ὁ κείνου τεκών his *father.* II. of beasts, *to bear young, breed;* of birds, *to hatch;* ᾠὰ τίκτειν *to lay* eggs. III. of trees, *to bear, produce.* IV. metaph. *to produce, bring about, give birth to.*

τίλλοισα, Dor. for τίλλουσα, fem. part. of τίλλω.

ΤΙ'ΛΛΩ, f. τῐλῶ: aor. 1 ἔτῖλα: pf. pass. τέτιλμαι:—*to pluck, pull, tear,* esp. the hair in token of lamentation;—Med., χαίτας τίλλεσθαι *to pluck out one's* hair. 2. from *tearing the hair in token of sorrow,* it came to mean absol. *to mourn bitterly for* any one. 3. *to pluck at, vex, annoy.*

τίλων, ὁ, *a* kind of *fish,* found in the Thracian lake Prasias.

τιλμός, ὁ, (τίλλω) *a plucking, tearing.*

τίλφη, ἡ, = σίλφη.

τῑμαλφέω, f. ήσω, *to do bonour* or *observance to, worship, exalt, celebrate.* From

τῑμ-αλφής, ές, (τιμή, ἀλφεῖν) *fetching a price:* hence, *costly, precious.*

τιμάν, Dor. for τιμήν.

τῑμᾶντα, Dor. for τιμῆντα, acc. of τιμῆς.

τῑμ-άορος, ον, Dor. for τιμωρός·

τῑμά-οχος, ον, poët. for τιμοῦχος, *held in honour, honoured, esteemed.*

τῑμᾱσεῦντι, Dor. 3 pl. fut. of τιμάω.

τῑμάω, f. ήσω: aor. 1 ἐτίμησα: pf. τετίμηκα: Med., fut. τιμήσομαι (but always in pass. sense): aor. 1 ἐτιμησάμην: Pass., fut. τιμηθήσομαι, also paullo-p. fut. τετιμήσομαι: aor. 1 ἐτιμήθην: pf. τετίμημαι: (τιμή):—*to deem* or *hold worthy, to honour, respect, revere, hold in reverence;* in Pass. c. gen. rei, τετιμῆσθαι τιμῆς *to be deemed worthy* of honour: also *to value, cherish, love.* 2. of things, *to value, prize:* c. gen. *to estimate* or *value at a* certain price; πλοῖα τετιμημένα χρημάτων vessels *valued at* a certain sum: Med., πολλοῦ τιμᾶσθαι, like πολλοῦ ποιεῖσθαί τι, *to hold* in much *account.* II. c. dat. rei, *to honour with* a thing, τιμᾶν τινα τάφῳ, στεφάνοις, etc., *to honour with* burial, garlands, etc.: hence *to reward.* III. as Att. law-term: 1. Act., of the judge, *to estimate the amount of punishment due* to the prisoner, Lat. *litem aestimare;* τ. τὴν δίκην *to award* the sentence; τιμᾶν μακράν τινι *to award* the long line, i.e. sentence of death; hence, τιμᾶν τινι θανάτου (sc. δίκην) *to give sentence* of death *against* a man. 2. Med., of the accuser, τιμᾶσθαί τινι [δίκην] δεσμῶν, φυγῆς, θανάτου, etc., *to lay* or *assess the punishment at* death, exile, bonds, etc.: in answer the accused could, if found guilty, lay the punishment at a less rate, which was called ἀντιτιμᾶσθαι or ὑποτιμᾶσθαι.

τῑμή, ἡ, (τίω) *the price, cost, worth* of a thing. II. metaph. *the honour in which one is held, worship, esteem, respect.* 2. *a place* or *post of honour, rank, dignity.* 3. generally, *distinction, privilege* hence *a dignity, office, magistracy.* 4. *an offering* to the gods, Lat. *honor: a reward, present.* III. *a prizing, valuing.* 2. *an estimate, valuation* or *assessment* of damages; then *compensation, satisfaction,* esp. in money: *a penalty,* as *the price* or *payment* for wrong, and so *punishment, damages.* Hence

τῑμήεις, εσσα, εν; contr. **τιμῆς**, acc. τιμῆντα; Dor. **τιμάεις**:—*valued, honoured, esteemed,* of men. 2. of things, *prized, costly, precious.* Comp. τιμηέστερος: Sup. -έστατος.

τίμημα, ατος, τό, (τιμάω) *that which is estimated or valued, the worth, price, value* of a thing, τίμημα *τύμβου the honour* of a tomb. II. *an estimate, valuation;* esp. *the estimate of damages:* hence *a penalty, punishment: a fine.* 2. *the value at which an Athenian citizen's property was rated, rate of assessment,* Lat. *census;* ἡ ἀπὸ τιμημάτων πολιτεία a government where the magistrates were chosen *according to property* or *assessment.* [ῐ]

τῑμῆντα, poët. for τιμήεντα, contr. acc. of τιμήεις.

τῑμή-ορος, ον, Ion. for τιμάορος, τιμωρός

τῑμῆς, poët. contr. for τιμήεις.

τίμησις, εως, ἡ, (τιμάω) *an estimating, valuing the worth* or *price* of a thing: *an assessment of* damages. [ῐ]

τῑμῆσσα, contr. poët. for τιμήεσσα, fem. of τιμήεις.

τῑμητεία or **τιμητία,** ἡ, (τιμητής) *the censorship* at Rome, Lat. *censura.*

τιμητέος, α, ον, verb. Adj. of τιμάω, *to be honoured.* II. τιμητέον, *one must honour.*

τῑμητής, οῦ, ὁ, (τιμάω) *a valuer,* assessor. II. at Rome, *a censor.*

τῑμητικός, ή, όν, (τιμητής) *estimating, valuing: for the purpose of estimating, for determining the amount of punishment.* II. [illegible] Rome, *of censorial rank.*

τῑμητός, ή, όν, verb. Adj. of τιμάω, *estimated, valued, assessed:* as Att. law-term, δίκη τιμητή a suit *in which the damages are to be assessed by the judges;* opp. to δίκη ἀτίμητος, where the penalty is fixed by law.

τίμιος, α, ον, also ος, ον, (τιμή) *valued:* of persons, *esteemed, held in honour:* of things, *prized, precious, honourable.* 2. *of high price, dear,* Lat. *carus.* Hence

τῑμιότης, ητος, ἡ, *worth, value, preciousness.*

τῖμος, ὁ, poët. form for τιμή.

τῑμωρέω, f. ήσω, (τιμωρός) *to help, aid, succour:* esp. *by way of redressinσ injuries, to avenge:*—in full, τιμωρεῖν τινι τοῦ παιδὸς τὸν φονέα *to avenge* a man *on* the murderer *for* (the murder of) his son:—Pass., τετιμωρῆσθαί τινι *to have vengeance taken for* any one. II. Med., f. -ήσομαι, with pf. pass. (in med. sense) τετιμώρημαι:—*to exact vengeance from* any one, *avenge oneself upon* him, *punish, chastise* him, c. acc. pers.: also c. gen. rei, τιμωρεῖσθαί τινά τινος *to take vengeance on* one, *punish* him *for* a thing: absol. *to avenge, right oneself, seek vengeance.* Hence

τῑμώρημα, ατος, το, *help, aid, succour.* II. *an act of vengeance.*

τῑμωρητέον, verb. Adj. of τιμωρέω, *one must assist: one must avenge, punish.*

τῑμωρητήρ, ῆρος, ὁ, (τιμωρέω) *a helper, aider.* 2. *an avenger.*

τῑμωρία Ion. -ίη, ἡ, (τιμωρέω) *help, aid, succour.* II. *vengeance, retribution:* also *punishment, torture.*

τῑμ-ωρός, όν, (τιμή, αἴρω) contr. from τιμάορος: *helping, aiding, succouring:* as Subst., τιμωρός, ὁ, *a helper, aider.* II. *avenging, punishing for* wrong.

τίν, like **τείν** or σοί, dat. of σύ. II. Dor. for σέ.

τίναγμα, ατος, τό, (τῐνάσσω) *a shake, quaking.*

τῐνακτήρ, ῆρος, and **τινάκτωρ,** ορος, ὁ, (τινάσσω) *one who shakes, a shaker:* fem. τῐνάκτειρα.

τιναξάσθην, Ep. 3 dual aor. 1 of τινάσσω.

τῐνάσσω, f. ξω, (τείνω) *to swing, shake, branaιsɒ: disturb, upset:* of a harp, *to make* the strings *quivɜr:*—Pass. *to be shaken* or *moved violently:* also *to quake with fear.*

τῐναχθείς, aor. 1 pass. part. of τινάσσω.

τῐνάχθεν, Ep. 3 pl. aor. 1 pass. of τινάσσω.

τίνῠμαι, Med., poët. for τίνομαι, *to take vengeance upon, punish, chastise,* c. acc. pers.: absol. *to avenge oneself.* 2. *to avenge, take vengeance for.*

τίνω [ῑ Ep., ῐ Att]: f. τίσω [ῑ]: aor. 1 ἔτῑσα: pf. act. τέτῑκα, pass. τέτισμαι: I. Act. *to pay a price,* mostly *to pay a penalty,* Lat. *dare poenas:* also *to pay a debt, quit oneself of a debt:* **τίνειν χάριν τινί** *to pay* or *render* thanks: *the thing for which one pays* is put in gen., τίνειν ἀμοιβὴν βοῶν *to pay* compensation *for* the oxen: but, the price being omitted, in acc., *to pay* or *atone for* a thing, τῖσαι ὕβριν *to atone* for one's insolence: also c. acc. pers. *to make atonement, pay the price for* a person slain: absol. *to make return* or *recompence, repay.* II. Med. *to have a price paid one, make another pay for* a thing, *avenge oneself on* him, *to punish, take retribution on* one, Lat. *poenas sumere de aliquo:*—mostly c. acc. pers. et c. gen. rei, τίσεσθαι Ἀλέξανδρον κακότητος *to punish* Alexander *for* his wickedness: c. acc. rei only, *to take vengeance for* a thing: but also c. dupl. acc. pers. et rei, τίσασθαί τινι δίκην *to exact* retribution *from* a person: but also with the means of punishment in the dat., τίνεσθαί τινι φυγῇ *to requite, punish* with exile: absol. *to repay oneself, take vengeance.*

τιό, τιό, imitation of a bird's note.

τῖον, Ep. for ἔτιον, impf. of τίω.

τί-ποτε; contr. **τίπτε;** Adv. (τί, πότε) *what* or *why then? why ever? why? wherefore?* Lat. *quid tandem?*

ΤΙΣ, neut. τι; gen. τινός Ep. τευ Att. του; dat. τινί Ep. τῳ or τεῳ; acc. τινά, τι; plur. τινές, τινά; gen. τινῶν: dat. τισί; acc. τινάς, τινά:—indef. Pronoun, enclit. through all cases: masc. and fem., *one, any one, some one,* freq. answering to our indef. Article, *a, an:* of places and things, νῆσός τις *an* island, etc.; neut. *anything, something:* εἴ τις, εἴ τι, Lat. *si quis, si quid,* if *any one* or *anything, whoever, whatever.* II. τις is often used indef. of a number of persons, as ὧδε δέ τις εἴπεσκεν but thus *some one* said, i. e. thus *men* said. 2. like ἕκαστος or πᾶς, *each, each one, every one;* εὖ μέν τις δόρυ θηξάσθω let *each man* look to sharpening his spear; ἀλλά τις αὐτὸς ἴτω let *each* come of himself. 3. so in Att., φοβεῖταί τις *some one* fears, fear is among them; πείσεταί τις *some one* will suffer. III. τις, τι, of a person or thing, *some great person, some great thiɲg,* ηὔχεις τις εἶναι you boasted that you were *somebody:* opp. to οὐδείς, μηδείς; λέγειν τι to speak sense, hit the truth, opp. to οὐδὲν λέγειν. 2. emphatically *a man*, opp. to *a brute;* τις ἢ κύων *a man* or a dog; but also in sign of contempt, *somebody or other*, Θερσίτης τις ἦν there was *one* Thersites: hence τις is used for *a slave.* IV. joined with Adjs., τις makes them less precise; μαινόμενος *a madman*, μαινόμενός τις *a crazy sort* of fellow: so with an Adj. of *number* or *size*, οἷός τις *such a kind of person* as..; πᾶς τις every *one;* εἷς τις some *one;* ὀλίγοι τινὲς *some* few; τρεῖς τινες *some* three *or so.* 2. joined with Adjectives, *somewhat, in a certain way;* ἧττόν τι *somewhat* less. V. in long sentences τις is often repeated, else it generally is found in the second clause: and when ὅστις follows in the relative clause, τις must often be supplied from it in the antecedent.

ΤΙ'Σ, neut. τί; gen. τίνος, Hom. τέο contr. τεῦ, Att. τοῦ; dat. τινί Att. τῷ; acc. τίνα, neut. τί; Plur. τίνες, τίνα; gen. τίνων Hom. τέων; dat. τίσι; acc. τίνας, τίνα;—interrog. Pronoun masc. and fem. *who? which?* neut. *what? which?* Lat. *quis, quae, quid?* strengthd. τίς γάρ; τί γάρ; like Lat. *quisnam? quidnam?* ἐς τί; *until when? how long?* with another Pronoun it must be rendered by two clauses; τίς δ' οὗτος ἔρχεαι; *who art* thou *that* comest? II. the question is modified by ἄν or κεν and a change of mood; τίς ἄν or κεν with the opt. expresses strong doubt, *who could, who would* do so? when there is no doubt the ἄν or κεν is omitted, τίς ἐργάσαιτο *who* could do it? i. e. no one. III. τίς is also used in indirect questions; ἠρώτα δὴ ἔπειτα, τίς εἴη καὶ πόθεν ἔλθοι he asked thereupon *who* he was, and *whence* he came. IV. sometimes two questions are asked in one clause; ἐκ τίνος τίς ἐγένετο; *who* is he, *and from whom* descended? V. τίς is also used for ποῖος; *of what sort?* as Lat. *quis* for *qualis?* so also for πότερος; as Lat. *quis* for *uter?* VI. τί; alone, *what?*—it takes the Article, τὸ τί; when the question refers to something going before. VII. τί; often stands absol. as Adv., *how? for why? wherefore?* 2. τί δέ; *but how?* 3. τί δή; τί δή ποτε; *why ever? τί δῆτα; how pray?* expressing surprise. 4. τί μήν; *why not? how else?* i. e. *yes surely!* Lat. *quidni?*

[τί was never elided, and sometimes stands before a vowel even in Trag., as τί οὖν; τί εἶπας;]

τισαίατο, Ion. 3 pl. aor. 1 med. opt. of τίω.

τίσις [ῐ], εως, ἡ, (τίνω) *payment made by way of recompence, a penalty, punishment;* τίσιν δοῦναι to suffer *punishment*, Lat. *poenas dare.* II. *a requital* in good sense, *reward.* III. in plur. *retributive justice, retribution.*

τῖσον, aor. 1 imperat. of τίνω: inf. τῖσαι.

τίσω [ῑ], fut. of τίνω: also aor. 1 subj.

τῐταίνω, aor. 1 ἐτίτηνα, Ep. for τείνω, τανύω, *to stretch:* Med., τόξα τιταίνεσθαι *to stretch one's* bow. 2. *to spread out* or *along, spread, extend:*—Med. or Pass. *to stretch oneself, to extend, spread.* 3. *to draw along:*—in Med. *to strain* or *exert oneself;* τιταινόμενος πεδίοιο *stretching on* over the plain; ἂψ ὤσασκε τιταινόμενος he thrust it back *exerting himself, with all his strength.*

τῖταίνων, part. from Τιτάν, only in passage, φάσκε δὲ τιταίνοντας ἀτασθαλίῃ μέγα ῥέξαι ἔργον he said that, *being Titans*, they had done violence in their pride.

Τῑτάν [ῑ], ᾶνος, ὁ, mostly in plur. Τῑτᾶνες, Ep. and Ion. Τῑτῆνες, οἱ, *the Titans*, a race of gods placed beneath Tartarus; acc. to Hesiod six sons and six daughters of Uranos and Gaia. Later any descendants of Uranos and Gaia are so called, and in Latin Poets *Titan* is a name for the Sun.

Τῑτᾱνίς Ion. **Τιτηνίς**, ίδος, fem. of Τιτάν, *a Titaness.*

ΤΙΤΑ'ΝΟΣ, ἡ, *a white earth, chalk* or *gypsum.*

Τῑτᾱν-ώδης, ες, (Τιτάν, εἶδος) *like Titans;* Τιτανῶδες βλέπειν to look *Titanic.*

τίτας, ου, ὁ, (τίω) Dor. for τίτης, = τιμωρός, *an avenger.* [ῐ]

Τῑτῆνες, οἱ, Ep. and Ion. for Τιτᾶνες

τιτθεία, ἡ, *a suckling by a nurse, fostering.* From

τιτθεύω, f. σω, *to suckle, nurse, foster.* From

ΤΙ'ΤΘΗ, ἡ, *the teat* of a woman's breast: *a nurse.*

τιτθίον, τό, Dim. of τίτθος, *a nipple, teat.*

ΤΙΤΘΟ'Σ, ὁ, *the teat* or *nipple* of a woman's breast.

τίτλος, ου, ὁ, formed from Lat. *titulus, a title, superscription.*

τιτρώσκω, f. τρώσω: aor. 1 ἔτρωσα: Pass., fut. τρωθήσομαι, but also fut. med. τρώσομαι in pass. sense: aor. 1 ἐτρώθην: pf. τέτρωμαι: (formed from Root *ΤΡΩ'Ω):—*to wound, hurt;* τετρῶσθαι τὸν μηρὸν *to have been wounded in* the thigh:—of ships, *to damage, cripple, scatter:* of wine, *to overpower.*

τιττῠβίζω, properly of the cry of partridges; but also of swallows and other small birds, *to twitter, chirrup* (Formed from the sound.)

Τιτυο-κτόνος, ὁ, (Τιτυός, κτείνω) *slayer of Tityos.*

Τῐτῠός, ὁ, *Tityos*, son of Gaia, a giant.

τιτύσκομαι, only used in pres. and impf., akin both to τεύχω and τυγχάνω: I. like τεύχω, *to make, make ready, prepare.* II. like τυγχάνω, *to aim;* ἄντα τιτύσκεσθαι *to aim* straight before one; c. gen. *to aim at* an object. 2. metaph., φρεσὶ τιτύσκεσθαι *to aim at* a thing in one's mind, i. e. *to purpose* or *design* to do, c. inf.

ΤΙ'ΦΗ, a kind of *beetle* or *water-spider*, that runs on the top of smooth water. [ῐ]

τίφθ', for τίπτε, before an aspirate.

τῖφος, εος, τό, *a pool.*

ΤΙ'Ω [ῑ], Ep. inf. τιέμεν: impf. ἔτιον: Pass., pres. τίομαι: pf. τέτῑμαι, part. τετῑμένος:—Ion. impf. act. and pass. τίεσκον, τιεσκόμην, 3 sing. τιέσκετο:—*to pay honour to* a person, *to esteem, honour, respect, regard:* also of things, θεοὶ δίκην τίουσιν the gods *honour* right. 2. *to value* or *rate at a certain worth.* II. fut. and aor. 1 act. τίσω, ἔτῑσα, and fut. and aor. 1 med. τίσομαι, ἐτισάμεν, are only used in the sense of τίνω, τίνομαι:—in Act. *to pay a price, make return:* in Med. *to have a price paid*, or *return made* one: see τίνω.

τλά-θῦμος, ον, Dor. for τλήθυμος.

τλαίην, aor. 2 opt. of *τλάω.

τλάμων, Dor. for τλήμων.

τλάς, τλᾶσα, τλάν, aor. 2 part. of *τλάω.

***ΤΛΑ'Ω**, a radic. form never found in pres.: fut. τλήσομαι: aor. 2 ἔτλην (formed as if from τλημί), imperat. τλῆθι, opt. τλαίην, Ep. 3 pl. τλαῖεν (for τλαίησαν), inf. τλῆναι, part. τλάς, τλᾶσα, τλάν: pf. τέτληκα, also used in pres. sense; from this pf. is formed imperat. τέτλᾰθι, τετλάτω [ᾰ]; opt. τετλαίην; inf. τετλάναι [ᾰ] Ep. τετλάμεν, τετλάμεναι, Ep. part. τετληώς, τετληυῖα, gen. τετληότος:—there is also a poët. aor. 1 ἐτάλᾰσα (as if from a pres. ταλάω), Ep. ἐτάλασσα, subj. ταλάσσω, ῃς, ῃ:—*to take upon oneself, to bear, suffer, undergo, endure* hardship: sometimes absol., esp. in imperat. τλῆθι, *bear up, endure:* so in pf. part., τετληότι θυμῷ with *enduring, patient* heart. II. *to bear steadfastly, hold out:* c. inf. *to dare to do* something, whether good or bad: also c. acc. *to dare* a thing, i. e. *dare to do* it.

τλῆ, Ep. 3 sing. aor. 2 of *τλάω.

τλή-θῦμος Dor. **τλά-**, ον (*τλάω, θυμός) *of enduring soul, stout-hearted.*

τλήμεναι, Ep. aor. 2 inf. of *τλάω.

τλημόνως, Adv. of τλήμων, *patiently.*

τλημοσύνη, ἡ, *that which is to be endured, misery, distress.* II. *endurance, patience.* From

τλήμων, ονος, ὁ, ἡ, vocat. τλῆμον, (*τλάω) *suffering, enduring:* hence, I. *patient, steadfast, stout-hearted:* also *bold, daring:* in bad sense, *reckless, rash*, Lat. *audax.* II. *full of suffering, wretched, miserable.*

τλῆναι, aor. 2 inf. of τλάω.

τλησῐ-κάρδιος, ον, (*τλάω, καρδία) *of patient heart, much-enduring, miserable.* II. *hard-hearted.*

τλήσομαι, fut. of *τλάω.

τλῆτε, 2 pl. aor. 2 imperat. of *τλάω.

τλητός, ή, όν, verb. Adj. of *τλάω: I. act. *suffering, patient, constant in suffering* or *labour.* II. pass. *suffered, endured: to be suffered, endurable.*

τμάγεν, Ep. 3 pl. aor. 2 pass. of τμήγω. [ᾰ]

τμάγον, Ep. for ἔτμᾰγον, aor. 2 of τμήγω.

τμήγω, f. τμήξω: aor. 1 ἔτμηξα: aor. 2 ἔτμᾰγον: aor. 1 med. ἐτμηξάμην: aor. 2 pass. ἐτμάγην [ᾰ] and ἐτμήγην:—Ep. collat. form of τέμνω, *to cut, cleave:*—Pass. *to be divided, be parted asunder.* Hence

τμήδην, Adv. *by cutting, scratching, grazing.*

τμηθῆναι, aor. 1 pass. inf. of τέμνω.

τμήξας, aor. 1 part. of τμήγω.

τμητός, ή, όν, (τέμνω) *cut, hewn, cut into shape.* 2. *cut lengthwise, furrowed.*

τμητο-σίδηρος, ον, (τμητός, σίδηρος) *cut down with iron.*

τοδί, neut. of ὁδί.

τόθεν, demonstr. Adv., answering to relat. ὅθεν and interrog. πόθεν, (properly an old form of the gen. τοῦ) *hence, thence.* II. *hence, therefore, thereupon.*

τόθῐ, demonstr. Adv. *there, in that place.* II. also for relat. ὅθι, *where.*

τοι, enclit. Particle of inference, *therefore, accordingly;* also strengthening an assertion, *in truth, in sooth, verily:* it is often joined with other Particles: with ἄρα it coalesces by crasis into τἄρα, with ἄν into τἄν, with μέντοι ἄν into μεντἄν.

τοι, Dor., Ion., and Ep. for σοί, dat. sing. of σύ: always enclitic.

τοί, **ταί**, Ep. and Ion. nom. plur. masc. and fem. of the Art. ὁ and the Relat. ὅς.

τοι-γάρ, strengthd. form of the enclit. Particle τοι, *so then, wherefore, therefore, accordingly.*

τοι-γαρ-οῦν Ion. **τοι-γαρ-ῶν**, strengthd. form of τοιγάρ, *therefore indeed, therefore assuredly.*

τοι-γάρ-τοι, strengthd. form of τοιγάρ, used at the beginning of a speech or narrative.

τοῖιν, Ep. for τοῖν, gen. and dat. dual of ὁ.

τοί-νῦν, (τοί, νυν) strengthd. form of the Particle τοι, *so then, therefore.* 2. in Att. often used to continue a speech, *further, moreover.*

τοῖο, Ion. and Ep. for τοῦ, gen. sing. of Art. ὁ.

τοῖος, τοία Ion. τοίη, τοῖον: (from τοῖο, old gen. of ὁ, ἡ, τό):—*of such kind, nature* or *quality, such, such-like*, Lat. *talis*, demonstr. Pron., to which the relat. οἷος, interrog. ποῖος, and indefin. ποιός correspond: τοῖος in Homer commonly refers to something gone before: in later authors it points to something to come, *the following.* 2. τοῖος c. inf., *such as* to do, i. e. *fit* or *able* to do; τοῖοι ἀμυνέμεν *able to* assist; cf. οἷος. II. with an Adj. it makes the sense of the Adj. more prominent, *so very, just;* ἐπιεικὴς τοῖος *just of* moderate size; κερδαλέος τοῖος *so very* crafty. III. Homer uses neut. τοῖον as Adv., *so, thus, so very, so much.*

τοιόσδε, τοιάδε Ion. τοιῆδε, τοιόνδε: Att. also **τοιοσδί**, etc., like τοῖος, with stronger demonstr. sense, *of such kind, nature* or *quality;* more commonly of what follows than what has gone before, to which τοιοῦτος properly refers; ἕτερος τοιόσδε *just such* another.

τοιοῦτος, τοιαύτη, τοιοῦτο, Att. also τοιοῦτον: and in strengthd. form Att. **τοιουτοσί**, like τοῖος and τοιόσδε, *of such kind, nature* or *quality:* more commonly of what has gone before than what follows, *such as the foregoing:* absol., ἐν τῷ τοιούτῳ, ἐν τοῖς τοιούτοις in *such a state* of things: strengthd., τοιοῦτος ἕτερος: also in neut. ἕτερον τοιοῦτον, ἕτερα τοιαῦτα.

τοιουτό-τροπος, ον, (τοιοῦτος, τρόπος) *of such fashion* or *kind, such like.* Adv. -τρόπως, *after such a fashion.*

τοιουτ-ώδης, ες, (τοιοῦτος, εἶδος) *of such kind* or *form.*

τοῖσδεσι and **τοῖσδεσσι**, **τοῖσδεσσιν**, Ep. forms for τοῖσδε, dat. pl. of ὅδε.

τοίχ-αρχος, ὁ, (τοῖχος, ἄρχω) *captain of the rowers on each side of the ship.*

τοῖχος, ὁ, (τεῖχος) *the wall of a house* or *court*, opp. to τεῖχος, as Lat. *paries* to *moenia*: proverb., ὁ εὖ πράττων τοῖχος, = 'the right side of the hedge.' II. in plur. *the sides of a ship.*

τοιχωρῠχέω, f. ήσω, (τοιχωρύχος) *to be a housebreaker, burglar: to play rogue's tricks.* Hence

τοιχωρῠχία, ἡ, *housebreaking, burglary.*

τοιχ-ωρύχος [ῠ], ὁ, (τοῖχος, ὀρύσσω) *one who breaks through the wall, a housebreaker, burglar:* generally, *a thief, knave.*

τοίως, τοιῶσδε, Advs. of **τοῖος, τοιόσδε.**

τόκᾰ, Dor. for τότε.

τοκάς, άδος, ἡ, (τεκεῖν) *one who has* just *brought forth*, Lat. *foeta:* as Adj., τοκὰς λέαινα a lioness *with cubs;* ἐκ τοκάδων from *one's birth.*

τοκετός, ὁ, = τόκος.

τοκεύς, έως, ὁ, (τεκεῖν) *one who begets, a father:* plur. τοκεῖς Ion. τοκῆες, *parents.*

τοκίζω, (τόκος) *to lend on interest;* **τοκίζειν** τόκον *to practise* usury. Hence

τοκισμός, ὁ, *the practice of usury.*

τόκος, ὁ, (τεκεῖν) *a bringing forth, birth, the time of delivery.* 2. *offspring, young child, son.* II. metaph. *the produce* or *usance of money* lent out, *interest*, Lat. *usura:* also in pl., τόκοι τόκων *interest of interest*, i. e. *compound interest.*

τοκο-φορέω, (τόκος, φέρω) *to bring in interest.*

ΤΟ΄ΛΜΑ˘ Ion. **τόλμη** Dor. **τόλμᾱ**, ἡ, *courage to venture on* a thing, *boldness, daring.* 2. in bad sense, *over-boldness, recklessness* Lat. *audacia: a bold* or *daring deed.*

τολμᾶσεῖς, Dor. 2 fut. of τολμάω.

τολμάω Ion. **τολμέω**, 2 pl. τολμῆτε Dor. for τολμᾶτε: f. ήσω: (τόλμα):—*to undertake, take heart to do* or *bear* anything, *to endure, to go.* 2. *to take courage, have the heart* or *resolution to do* a thing: c. acc., τολμᾶν πόλεμον *to venture on* war; πάντα τολμᾶν *to dare* all things.

τολμήεις, εσσα, εν, Dor. **-άεις**, Ep. contr. **τολμῆς**, ῆσσα, ῆν (whence Sup. τολμήστατος) *enduring, steadfast, stout-hearted: daring, bold, adventurous.*

τόλμημα, ατος, τό, (τολμάω) *a daring deed, adventure, enterprise.*

τολμηρός, ά, όν, (τολμάω) *daring, bold:*—Comp. τολμηρότερος. Adv. *-ρῶς, boldly;* Comp. *-ρότερον;* Sup. *-ρότατα.*

τολμῆς, ῆσσα, ῆν, Ep. contr. for τολμήεις, q. v.

τολμητέον, verb. Adj. of τολμάω, *one must venture.*

τολμητής, οῦ, ὁ, (τολμάω) *a bold, venturous man.*

τολμητός, ή, όν, verb. Adj. from τολμάω, *ventured, to be ventured* or *hazarded.*

τολμίστατος, η, ον, irreg. Sup. of τολμήεις.

το-λοιπόν or divisim **τὸ λοιπόν**, (λοιπός) as Adv., *henceforward, for the future.* 2. *for the rest, accordingly.*

τολῠπεύω, f. σω, (τολύπη) *to wind off* carded wool *into a clew* for spinning. II. metaph. *to contrive, devise, invent.* 2. *to wind up, achieve, accomplish a hard task.*

ΤΟΛΥ΄ΠΗ, ἡ, *a clew* or *ball wound up, wool carded and made into a ball for spinning*, Lat. *glomus.* [ῠ]

τομαῖος, α, ον, also ος, ον, (τομή) *cut, cut off;* ἄκος τομαῖον a remedy *cut ready for use.*

τομάω, (τομή) *to need cutting;* πῆμα τομῶν a disease *that needs the knife.*

τομή, ἡ, (τέμνω) *the place from which a* thing *has been cut: the end left after cutting, a stump* of a tree: *the end of a beam*, where it had been cut off; λίθοι ἐν τομῇ ἐγγώνιοι stones squared at the *end.* II. *a cut, stroke, wound.* III. *a cutting, cutting off;* καῦσις καὶ τομή cautery and *the knife.*

τόμιος, ον, (τομή) *cut up:* in pl., τὰ τόμια (sc. ἱερά), *parts of a sacrifice* used on taking solemn oaths: cf. τέμνω.

τομός, ή, όν, verb. Adj. of τέμνω, *cutting, sharp:* Comp. τομώτερος, *cutting sharper:* Sup. τομώτατος.

τόμος, ὁ, (τέμνω) *a cut, a piece cut off, a slice.* II. *a part of a book rolled up by itself, a tome, volume.*

τονθορύζω or **-ίζω**, *to speak inarticulately, mutter:* also of inarticulate cries of animals. (Formed from the sound.)

τόνος, ὁ, (τείνω) *that which strains and tightens* a thing, or *that which can itself be stretched, a rope, cord, brace, band;* οἱ τόνοι τῶν κλινέων *the cords* of beds: also *the strand* of a rope. 2. in animals, *the sinews* or *tendons*, Lat. *nervi.* II. *a stretching, tightening, bracing, straining, strain.* 2. of sounds, *a straining* or *pitching* of the voice: hence, *a tone, note:* also *the tone* or *stress* falling on a syllable in a verse; τόνος ἑξάμετρος hexameter *measure.* 3. in Music, τόνοι were *measures* or *modes*, Lat. *modi:* of which in the earliest Greek music there were three, *the Dorian, Lydian and Phrygian.* III. *exertion of force, force, intensity:* also *direction, tenour.*

το-νῦν, = τὸ νῦν, *for the present.*

τοξάζομαι, f. -άσομαι, Dep. (τόξον) *to shoot with a bow:* c. gen. *to shoot at, take aim at.*

τοξ-αλκέτης, ου, ὁ, (τόξον, ἀλκή) *a strong archer.*

τόξ-αρχος, ὁ, (τόξον, ἄρχω) *master of the bow, a bowman, archer.* II. *the captain of the* τοξόται at Athens.

τόξευμα, ατος, τό, (τοξεύω) *that which is shot, an arrow, bolt;* ὅσον τόξευμα ἐξικνέεται as far as *an arrow* reaches, i. e. a bowshot. II. collective in plur. for οἱ τοξόται, *the archers.*

τοξευτής, οῦ, ὁ, (τοξεύω) *a bowman, archer.*

τοξευτός, ή, όν verb Adj. of τοξεύω, *struck by an arrow, shot.*

τοξεύω, f. σω, (τόξον) *to shoot with the bow, use the bow:* c. gen., τοξεύειν τινός *to shoot at* a mark. 2. metaph. *to shoot* or *wound with an arrow.* II. *to shoot as from a bow, discharge, launch forth.*

τοξ-ήρης, ες, (τόξον, ἀραρεῖν) *furnished with the bow.* 2. *of* or *for the bow.*

τοξικος, ή, όν, (τόξον) *of* or *for the bow: skilled in the use of the bow.* 2. ἡ τοξική (sub. τέχνη), *bowmanship, archery.*

τοξο-δάμᾱς, *αντος, ο*, and **τοξό-δαμνος**, *ον*, (τόξον, δᾰμάω) *subduing with the bow;* τοξόδαμνος Ἄρης the war *of archers*, i. e. of the Persians, see τόξον.

ΤΟ'ΞΟΝ, *τό, a bow*, its arrows being ὀϊστοί or ἰοί, the string νευρά or νεῦρον: often in pl. τόξα, because the bow consisted of two pieces of horn joined by the πῆχυς in the middle; τόξα τιταίνειν to draw *the bow.* As *the bow* was the Oriental weapon, τόξου ῥῦμα, i. e. the Persians, is opp. to λόγχης ἰσχύς, i. e. the Greeks, whose chief weapon was the spear; see τοξοδάμος. II. in plur. also, *bow and arrows*, or even *the arrows* only.

τοξοποιέω, f. ήσω, *to make like a bow, to arch.* From

τοξο-ποιός, *όν*, (τόξον, ποιέω) *making bows.*

τοξοσύνη, ἡ, (τόξον) *bowmanship, archery.*

τοξο-τευχής, *ές*, (τόξον, τεύχεα) *armed with the bow.*

τοξότης, *ου*, ὁ, (τόξον) *a bowman, archer.* II. at Athens, οἱ τοξόται were *the police*, also called Σκύθαι, because they were public slaves bought from the parts north of Greece.

τόξοτις, *ιδος*, fem. of τοξότης, *an archeress;* as Adj., τόξοτις χείρ an *archer* hand.

τοξ-ουλκός, *όν*, (τόξον, ἕλκω) *drawing the bow;* τοξουλκὸν λῆμα the spirit *of archers*, i. e. of the Persians; see τόξον.

τοξο-φόρος, *ον*, (τόξον, φέρω) *bearing a bow:* as Subst., τοξοφόρος, ὁ, = τοξότης, *an archer, bowman.*

τοπάζιον, *τό*, = τόπαζος.

ΤΟ'ΠΑΖΟΣ, ὁ, *the topaz*, a precious stone.

τοπάζω, f. άσω, (τόπος) *to guess, divine.*

το-πάν, Adv., = τὸ πᾶν, *altogether, quite, wholly:* ἐς τοπάν *in general, for the mass.*

το-πᾰραυτίκα, Adv., = αὐτίκα, *immediately, on the instant.*

το-πάροιθε, –θεν, Adv., = πάροιθε.

το-πάρος, Adv., = πάρος. [ᾰ]

τόπ-αρχος, ὁ, also ἡ, (τόπος, ἄρχω) *ruling over a place:* as Subst., τόπαρχος, ὁ, ἡ, *a master* or *mistress.*

ΤΟ'ΠΟΣ, ὁ, *a place, spot*, Lat. *locus;* χθονὸς πᾶς τόπος *the* whole *space* of earth. 2. *place, position.* 3. *a place* or *passage in* an author, Lat. *locus.* III. metaph. *a place, occasion, opportunity.*

το-πρίν, Adv., = τὸ πρίν.

το-πρόσθεν, Adv., = τὸ πρόσθεν.

το-πρῶτον, Adv., = τὸ πρῶτον, *first, at first, in the first place.*

τόρευμα, *τό*, *embossed work, work in relief.* II. = τόρνευμα, *a circling* or *wheeling round.*

τορεύς, *έως*, ὁ, (τορεύω) *the graver of a sculptor* II. *a borer, auger.*

τορευτός, ή, όν, verb. Adj. of τορεύω, *worked in relief* or *chased:* metaph. *elaborate.*

τορεύω, properly, = τορέω, *to bore through:* metaph *to sing in a piercing tone.* II. *to work in relief.* 2. *to chase*, Lat. *caelare.*

*ΤΟΡΕ'Ω, obsol. pres., whence aor. 2 ἔτορον, also aor. 1 ἐτόρησα, part. τορήσας, and redupl. fut. τετορήσω:—*to bore, pierce.* II. metaph. *to utter in a loud and piercing tone.* Hence

τόρμος, ὁ, *a hole, socket: the nave* of a wheel.

τορνευτο-λῠρ-ασπῐδο-πηγός, ὁ, (τορνεύω, λύρα, ἀσπίς, πήγνυμι) *lyre-turner and shield-maker.*

τορνεύω, f. σω, *to turn, work with a lathe and chisel*, Lat. *tornare:* metaph. of verses, *to turn neatly, round off:* and generally, *to twist round.* From

τόρνος, ὁ, (τορέω) *a carpenter's tool to draw a circle with, compasses*, Lat. *tornus.* II. *a turner's chisel, a lathe-chisel.* Hence

τορνόομαι, f. –ώσομαι, Dep. *to make round, mark off with compasses;* τορνώσαντο σῆμα *they rounded off* the barrow; ἔδαφος νηὸς τορνώσεται ἀνήρ *he will round him off* the ship's bottom.

τορός, ά, όν, (τείρω) *piercing;* of the voice, *piercing, thrilling.* 2. metaph. *clear, distinct, plain.* II. of persons, *sharp, quick, smart.*

τοροτίγξ or **τοροτίξ**, imitation of *a bird's note.*

τορύνη, ἡ, (τείρω) *a stirrer, ladle* to stir things boiling, Lat. *tudicula.* [ῡ]

τορύνω, (τορύνη) *to stir, stir up* or *about.* [ῡ]

τοσάκῐς Ep. **τοσσάκι** [ᾰ], Adv. (τόσος) *so many times, so often.*

τόσος Ep. **τόσσος**, η, ον, Lat. *tantus*, of Size, *so great;* of Space, *so wide;* of Time, *so long;* of Number, *so many;* of Sound, *so loud;* generally, *so much, so very:* answered by the Relat. ὅσος; but τόσος often stands alone in Homer, as τρὶς τόσοι thrice *as many.* In Homer τόσον and τόσσον are often Adv., so *much*, so *far*, so *very*, Lat. *tantum;* λίην τόσον so *much* too much. 2. ἐκ τόσου, *so long since.*

τοσόσ-δε Ep. **τοσσόσ-δε**, –ήδε, –όνδε, = τόσος, with stronger demonstr. force, so *great, large, wide*, etc.:—c. inf. so *strong*, so *able* to do a thing. II. τοσόνδε Ep. τοσσόνδε, as Adv., so *very*, so *much, to such a degree.*

τοσουτ-άριθμος, *ον*, (τοσουτος, ἀριθμός) *of so large a number.* [ᾰ]

τοσοῦτος Ep. **τοσσοῦτος**, –αύτη, –οῦτο Att. –οῦτον; = τόσος, with a stronger demonstr. force, so *great*, so *large*, etc.: also to designate a very small degree, hence τοσοῦτον, *only* so *much*, so *much* and no more; ἐς τοσοῦτο, Lat. *eatenus*, so *far;* ἕτερον τοσοῦτο *as great, as much* or *many* again. II. τοσοῦτο or –ον, Ep. τοσσοῦτο or –ον, as Adv., so *much*, so *far.*

τοσουτοσί, τοσαυτηι, τοσουτονι, Att. for τοσουτος.

τοσσάκῐ and **τοσσάκις**, Adv. Ep. for τοσάκις. [ᾰ]

τόσσας, in Dor. form τόσσαις, = τυχών, aor. 1 part. of an obsol. pres., = τυγχάνω, *to hit, hit upon.*

τοσσῆνος, Dor. for τοσοῦτος.

τόσσος, η, ον, Ep. for τόσος.

τοσσόσ-δε -ή-δε, -όν-δε, Ep. for τοσόσδε.

τοσσοῦτος, -αύτη, -οῦτο and -οῦτον, Ep. for τοσοῦτος.

τόσως, Adv. of τόσος, *so much, as much.*

τότε, Adv. *at that time, then:* often in Att., *aforetime, formerly:* sometimes emphatic, *at that famous time.* 2. joined with other Particles, τότε δή, τότ' ἔπειτα, δὴ τότε γε 3. with the Article, οἱ τότε people *then* living; ἐν τῷ τότε in the *then* time. It answers to the Relat. ὅτε and interrog. πότε.

τοτέ, Adv. *at times, now and then,* mostly in answering clauses, τοτὲ μέν .., τοτὲ δέ .., *at one time* .., *at another;* τότ' ἢ τότ', *at one time* or *other.*

το-τέταρτον, Adv. = τὸ τέταρτον, *for the fourth time,* like τόπρωτον, etc.

το-τηνίκα, or divisim το τηνίκα, Adv., = τηνικα. [ῐ]

τοτοβρίξ, imitation of *a bird's note.*

το-τρίτον, Adv., = τὸ τρίτον, *for the third time;* cf. τοτέταρτον. [ῐ]

τοῦ, gen. of Art. ὁ, and interrog. Pron. τίς.

του, enclit., gen. of enclit. Pron. τις.

τοὐβολοῦ, Att. crasis for τοῦ ὀβολοῦ.

τοὐκ, Att. crasis for τοῦ ἐκ.

τοὔλασσον, Att. crasis for τὸ ἔλασσον.

τοὐλάχιστον, Att. crasis for τὸ ἐλάχιστον.

τοὐλεύθερον, Att. crasis for τὸ ἐλεύθερον.

τοὐμόν, Att. crasis for τὸ ἐμόν.

τοὔμπαλιν, Att. crasis for τὸ ἔμπαλιν.

τοὐμπόδων, Att. crasis for τὸ ἐμπόδων.

τοὔμπροσθεν, Att. crasis for τὸ ἔμπροσθεν.

τοὐμφᾰνές, Att. crasis for τὸ ἐμφανές.

τοὔμφῡλον, Att. crasis for τὸ ἔμφυλον.

τοὐναντίον, Att. crasis for τὸ ἐναντίον.

τοὔνεκα, Att. crasis for τοῦ ἕνεκα, *for that reason, therefore.*

τοὐνθένδε, Att. crasis for τὸ ἐνθένδε.

τοὔνομα, Att. crasis for τὸ ὄνομα.

τοὐντεῦθεν, Att. crasis for τὸ ἐντεῦθεν, *henceforth.*

τοὐπέκεινα, Att. crasis for τὸ ἐπέκεινα.

τοὖπος or **τοὔπος,** Att. crasis for τὸ ἔπος.

τοὖργον or **τοὔργον,** Att. crasis for τὸ ἔργον.

τοὐρανοῦ, Att. crasis for τοῦ οὐρανοῦ.

τοντάκῐς or **τοντάκι,** Adv. poët. for τότε, *then.* II. *so many times, so often.* [ᾰ]

τουτεί, Adv., Dor. for ταύτῃ, *in that direction, there, yonder.*

τοὔτερον, Ion. crasis for τὸ ἕτερον.

τουτόθε Adv. (οὗτος) *hence, thence.*

τουτῶθεν, Dor. Adv. (οὗτος) *thence.*

τόφρᾰ, Adv. of Time, *up to that time, so long;* answering to the Relat. ὄφρα. II. τόφρα sometimes stands absol., *meantime, meanwhile.*

τρᾰγᾰλίζω, = τρώγω

Τρᾰγᾰσαῖος, α, ον, *of* or *from the city* Τραγασαί in Epirus: but of swine, ὡς τραγασαῖα φαίνεται, with allusion to τραγεῖν, *to eat:* and again τραγασαίου πατρός, with play upon τράγος, *a goat.*

τρᾰγεῖν, aor. 2 inf. of τρώγω.

τράγειος, α, ον, poët. for τραγεος: τραγείη (sub δορά), ἡ, *a goat's skin.* [ᾰ]

τρᾰγ-έλᾰφος, ὁ, (τράγος, ἔλαφος) *the goat-stag,* a fabulous creature mentioned in Aristophanes.

τράγεος, α, ον, (τράγος) *of* or *from a he-goat; τραγῆ* (sub. δορά), ἡ, *a goat's skin.* [ᾰ]

τράγημα, ατος, τό, (τρᾰγεῖν) mostly in plur. *sweetmeats, dessert,* Lat. *bellaria.*

τρᾰγηματίζω, f. σω, *to eat sweetmeats:* so also in Med. τραγηματίζομαι.

τρᾰγῐκός, ή, όν, (τράγος) *of* or *for a goat.* II. *of* or *for a tragedy, tragic* (cf. τραγῳδία): τραγικὸς λῆρος the tawdry decorations *of tragedy:*—hence generally, *stately, majestic;* in bad sense, *pompous:* Adv. -κῶς, *in tragic style.*

τράγῑνος, η, ον, (τράγος) like τράγειος, *of a he-goat.*

τρᾰγίσκος, ὁ, Dim. of τράγος, *a young he-goat.*

τρᾰγο-κουρικός, ή, όν, (τράγος, κουρά) *of* or *for shearing he-goats.*

τρᾰγό-κτονος, ον, (τράγος, κτείνω) *of slaughtered goats.*

τρᾰγο-μάσχᾰλος, ον, (τράγος, μασχάλη) *with armpits smelling like a he-goat.*

τρᾰγό-πους, ποδος, ὁ, ἡ, (τράγος, πούς) *goat-footed.*

τράγος, ὁ, (τρᾰγεῖν) *a he-goat,* Lat. *hircus, caper.* II. *the smell of the arm-pits,* Lat. *hircus alarum.*

τρᾰγο-σκελής, ές, (τράγος, σκέλος) *goat-shanked,* of Pan.

τράγω, Dor. for τρώγω, like πρᾶτος for πρῶτος. [ᾱ]

τρᾰγῳδέω, f. ήσω, (τραγῳδός) *to act a tragedy:* generally, *to represent* or *exhibit in tragedy:*—Pass. *to be made the subject of a tragedy.* II. metaph. *to tell in tragic phrase, to declaim, speak theatrically.* Hence

τρᾰγῳδία, ἡ, *a tragedy* or *heroic play,* invented by the Dorians, and with them of *lyric* character (τραγικοὶ χοροί); then transplanted to Athens, where it assumed its *dramatic* character. See τραγῳδός.

τρᾰγῳδικός, ή, όν, (τραγῳδός) *befitting a tragic poet* or *tragedy.*

τρᾰγῳδο-δῐδάσκᾰλος, ὁ, (τραγῳδός, διδάσκω) *a tragic poet, who himself trained* the chorus and actors.

τρᾰγῳδο-ποιός, όν, (τραγῳδός, ποιέω) *making tragedies:* as Subst., τραγῳδοποιός, ὁ, *a tragic poet.*

τρᾰγ-ῳδός, ὁ, (τράγος, ἀοιδός contr. ᾠδός) *a tragic poet and singer,* as the poet took part in the performance of his play: later, the term τραγῳδός was confined to *the tragic actor.* Properly, *the goat-singer,* either because a goat was the prize, or because the actors were clothed in goat-skins.

ΤΡΑ'ΝΗ'Σ, ές, *piercing:* metaph. *clear, plain, distinct.*

τρᾱνός, ή, όν, collat. form of τρανής.

τρᾱνόω, (τρανός) *to make clear, plain, distinct.*

τρᾱνῶς, Adv. of τρανής, *clearly, distinctly.*

τράπε, for ἔτραπε, Ep. 3 sing. aor. 2 of τρέπω. [ᾰ]

τρά-πεζα [τρᾰ], ης, ἡ, *a table,* esp. *a dining-table;* ξενίη τράπεζα the *hospitable* board; τραπέζῃ καὶ κοίτῃ δέχεσθαι to entertain at bed and *board*. 2 *a table, dinner, meal*. II. *a money-changer's table* or *counter, a bank*, Lat. *mensa argentaria*. III. *any table* or *flat surface, a tablet*, Lat. *tabula*. (Acc. to some from **τετρα-**, πέζα; acc. to others from **τρι-**, πέζα: Horace speaks of *mensa tripes*.) Hence

τρᾰπεζεύς, έως, ὁ, *at* or *of a table*; κύνες τραπεζῆες dogs *that were fed at mealtime*.

τρᾰπεζῑτεύω, *to be a money-changer* or *banker*. From

τρᾰπεζίτης [ῑ], ου, ὁ, (τράπεζα) *one who keeps an exchange-table, a money-changer, banker*, Lat. *mensarius, argentarius*. Hence

τρᾰπεζῑτικός, ή, όν, *concerning a banker* or *banking*.

τρᾰπείομεν, Ep. for τραπέωμεν, τραπῶμεν, 1 pl. aor. 2 pass., both of τέρπω and τρέπω.

τράπεσδα, ἡ, Dor. for τράπεζα.

τρᾰπέσθαι, aor. 2 med. inf. of τρέπω.

τράπεσκε, Ion. 3 sing. impf. of τράπω = τρέπω. [ᾰ]

ΤΡΑ˘ΠΕ´Ω, *to tread grapes*: hence Lat. *trapētes, trapētum*, an oil-press.

τρᾰπῆναι, aor. 2 pass. inf. of τρέπω.

τρᾰπητέον, verb. Adj. of τρέπω, in pass. sense, *one must turn*.

τράπω, Ion. for τρέπω. [ᾰ]

τρᾰσιά, ἡ, (from ταρσός, as if ταρσιά) *a crate to dry* figs *on*.

τραυλίζω, f. ίσω, *to lisp, mispronounce a letter*, Lat. *balbutire*; so of children. From

ΤΡΑΥΛΟ´Σ, ή, όν, *lisping*, Lat. *balbus*: of the swallow, *twittering*.

τραῦμα Ion. **τρῶμα**, ατος, τό, (τιτρώσκω) *a wound, hurt*; ἀπὸ τοῦ τρώματος ἀποθνήσκειν to die of *the wound*. II. *a hurt, damage*, as of ships. III. metaph. *a blow, disaster, defeat*. Hence

τραυμᾰτίας, ου, ὁ, Ion. τρωμ-, *a wounded man*.

τραυμᾰτίζω Ion. **τρωμ-**, f. ίσω, (τραῦμα) *to wound*.

τρᾰφέμεν, Ion. for τραφεῖν, aor. 2 inf. of τρέφω: see τρέφω II. 4.

τράφεν, Ep. and Aeol. for ἐτράφησαν 3 pl. aor. 2 pass. of τρέφω. [ᾰ]

τρᾰφερός, ά, όν, (τρέφω) like τρόφις, *well-fed, fat, solid, substantial*: τραφερή (sub. γῆ), as opp. to ὑγρή, *dry land*, ἐπὶ τραφερήν τε καὶ ὑγρήν over *dry land* and sea: as Subst. οἱ τραφεροί or τὰ τραφερά, *the fishes*.

τράφη [ᾰ], Ep. 3 sing. aor. 2 pass. of τρέφω.

τρᾰφῆναι, aor. 2 inf. pass. of τρέφω.

τράφω, Aeol. and Dor. for τρέφω. [ᾰ]

τρᾱχέως Ion. **τρηχέως**, Adv. *roughly, harshly*; τρηχέως περιεφθῆναι to be *roughly* handled.

τρᾰχήλια, τά, (τράχηλος) *scraps of meat from about the neck thrown away, gristle, offal*.

τρᾰχηλιάω, (τράχηλος) *to arch the neck*, as a pampered horse: metaph. *to be haughty, headstrong*.

τρᾰχηλίζω, f. ίσω, (τράχηλος) *to take by the throat*: *to bend back* the victim's *neck*, hence *to expose to view, lay bare*.

τρᾰχηλο-δεσμότης, ου, ὁ, (τράχηλος, δεσμός) as masc. Adj., *chaining the neck*.

ΤΡΑ´ΧΗΛΟΣ, ὁ, *the throat, neck*. [ᾰ]

Τρᾱχίς Ion. **Τρηχίς**, ῖνος, ἡ, *Trāchis*, a city and district in Thessaly, named from its *mountainous* surface (τραχύς). Hence

Τρᾱχίνιος, α, ον Ion. **Τρηχίνιος**, η, ον, *of* or *from Trachis, Trachinian*; αἱ Τραχίνιαι *the Trachinian women*, title of a tragedy by Sophocles.

τρᾱχύνω Ion. **τρηχύνω** [ῡ]: f. ῠνῶ: pf. τετράχυκα: Pass., aor. 1 ἐτραχύνθην: pf. τετράχυσμαι and τετράχῠμαι: (τραχύς):—*to make rough, rugged*: in Aesch. Theb. 1045, τράχυνε refers to τραχὺς ὁ δῆμος just before, *call them, make them rough*.

ΤΡΑ¯ΧΥ´Σ Ion. **τρηχύς**, εῖα, ύ, *rough, rugged*; metaph. *rough, harsh, savage*.

τρᾱχύτης, ητος, ἡ, (τραχύς) *roughness, ruggedness*; *the sharpness of a bit*:—metaph. *roughness, harshness*.

τράχω, Dor. for τρέχω. [ᾰ]

τρᾱχών, ῶνος, ὁ, *a rugged, stony district*: hence as fem. Subst. **Τραχωνῖτις**, ιδος, *Trachonitis*, i. e. *the rugged country*.

ΤΡΕΙ˜Σ, οἱ, αἱ, **τρία**, **τά**; gen. τριῶν; dat. **τρισί**: acc. τρεῖς, τρία:—*THREE*, Lat. *TRES, tria*.

τρεισ-καί-δεκα, οἱ, αἱ, τρια-καί-δεκα, τά, *thirteen*, Lat. *tredecim*.

τρείω, poët. for τρέω.

τρέμω, only used in pres. and impf., (τρέω) Lat. *tremo, to tremble, quake, quiver*. II. c. inf. *to tremble* or *fear to* do: also c. acc. *to tremble at, fear*.

τρεπτέον, verb. Adj. of τρέπω, *one must turn*.

ΤΡΕ´ΠΩ Ion. **τράπω**: f. τρέψω: aor. 1 ἔτρεψα: aor. 2 ἔτρᾰπον: pf. τέτροφα or τέτραφα: Med., aor. 2 ἐτρᾰπόμην: Pass., aor. 1 ἐτρέφθην Ion. ἐτράφθην: aor. 2 ἐτράπην, whence Ep. 1 plur. τραπείομεν (for τραπέωμεν, τραπῶμεν): pf. τέτραμμαι, 3 plur. τετράφαται; imperat. τέτραφθι, τετράφθω: plqpf. ἐτετράμμην, Ep. 3 sing. τέτραπτο; 3 plur. τετράφατο:—*to turn*, Lat. *vertere*; τρέπειν τινὰ εἴς τι *to turn, lead, guide* to a thing:—Pass. and Med. *to turn, betake oneself*, Lat. *converti*; ἐπὶ ἔργα τρέπεσθαι *to turn* or *go* to work; also of place, ἀντ' ἠελίοιο τετραμμένος *turned* towards the sun; τρέπεσθαι ὁδόν *to turn oneself to* (i.e. *take*) a course; ποῖ τράπωμαι; which way *must I turn me?* II. *to turn*, i. e. *turn round, put about*; also, πάλιν τρέπειν *to turn* back: *to turn away, divert*: τρέπειν τὴν ὀργὴν εἴς τινα *to divert* anger *on* any one: Pass. and Med. *to turn round*. 2. *to turn another way, alter, change*: Pass. and Med. *to be changed, change*: absol., τράπομαι *I am changed, change my opinion*: also, οἶνος τρέπεται the wine *is turned, become sour*. III. *to turn* or *put to flight, rout, defeat*: later, τρέπειν εἰς φυγήν, Lat. *convertere in fugam, to put to flight*:—Pass. *to be put to flight, turn and flee*:—Med. *to turn oneself to flight, flee* IV. *to turn away* or *off, keep off*: *to hinder, prevent*. V. *to overturn, upset*. VI. *to turn, apply* to a purpose.

τρέσσαι, Ep. for τρέσαι, aor. 1 inf. of τρέω.

τρεφθῆναι, aor. 1 pass. inf. of τρέπω.

ΤΡΕ'ΦΩ Aeol. and Dor. **τράφω** [ᾰ]: fut. *θρέψω*: aor. 1 *ἔθρεψα*: Ep. aor. 2 *ἔτρᾰφον*: pf. *τέτροφα*: Pass., aor. 1 *ἐθρέφθην*: aor. 2 *ἐτράφην* [ᾰ]: pf. *τέθραμμαι* and *τέθρεμμαι*, inf. *τεθράφθαι*:—*to make firm* or *solid, to thicken* or *congeal*; *γάλα θρέψαι to curdle* milk; *τυρὸν τρέφειν to make* cheese:—Pass., with intr. pf. act. *τέτροφα, to become firm, curdle, congeal.* II. commonly, *to nourish, feed, make to grow* or *increase, nurse, bring up, rear*: Med. *to rear for oneself*:—Pass. *to grow, grow up, wax, thrive, increase*: hence *to be born*: and simply, *to live, be.* 2. of slaves, *to keep, maintain*: of plants, *to rear, tend*: *τρέφειν κόμην to cherish* one's hair, *wear* it *long*, Lat. *comam alere*: of the earth, sea, etc., *to feed, rear, nourish, produce*, Lat. *nutrire, alere*: hence poët. *to contain, have.* III. Homer uses aor. 2 act. *ἔτραφον* in intrans. or pass. sense, as, *ἔτραφε* for *ἐτράφη, ἐτραφέτην* for *ἐτραφήτην*, inf. *τραφέμεν* (Att. *τραφεῖν*) = *τραφῆναι*.

ΤΡΕ'ΧΩ Dor. **τράχω** [ᾰ]: fut. *θρέξομαι*: aor. 1 *ἔθρεξα*: but more commonly (from Root *ΔΡΕ'ΜΩ), fut. *δρᾰμοῦμαι* Ion. *δραμέομαι* poët. *δράμομαι*: aor. 2 *ἔδρᾰμον*: pf. *δεδράμηκα* [ᾰ] poët. *δέδρομα*:—*to run*, Lat. *currere*: of things, *to move quickly.* 2. c. acc. loci, *to run over.* 3. c. acc. cognato, *τρέχειν δρόμον to run* a course; metaph., *ἀγῶνας δραμεῖν περὶ ἑαυτοῦ to run* a race for one's life or safety; hence without *δρόμον* or *ἀγῶνα, to run a risk* or *chance*, as *τρέχειν περὶ τῆς ψυχῆς to run a race* for one's life; also, *παρ' ἓν πάλαισμα ἔδραμε νικᾶν* he was within one bout of carrying off the victory

τρέψειαν, 3 pl. Ep. aor. 1 opt. of *τρέπω*.

ΤΡΕ'Ω poët. **τρείω**, inf. *τρεῖν*: f. *τρέσω*: aor. 1 *ἔτρεσα* Ep. *τρέσσα*:—*to tremble, quake*, esp. for fear: hence *to run away, flee, fly*: *ὁ τρέσας the coward.* II. trans. *to fear, dread, be afraid of*, c. acc.

τρῆμα, *ατος, τό*, (*τιτράω*) *that which is pierced* or *bored through*: *a hole, aperture.*

τρημᾰτόεις, *εσσα, εν*, (*τρῆμα*) *with many holes, porous.*

τρήρων, *ωνος, ὁ, ἡ*, (*τρέω*) *fearful, timorous, shy*: epith. of doves (*πέλειαι* or *πελειάδες*): hence later as Subst., *τρήρων, ἡ*, = *πέλεια, a dove.*

τρήσω, fut. of *τιτράω*.

τρητός, *ή, όν*, verb. Adj. of *τιτράω, bored* or *pierced through*; *τρῆτα λέχεα* bedsteads *perforated* for inlaid work.

τρηχᾰλέος, *η, ον*, poët. for *τρηχύς· τραχύς*.

τρηχύς, *εῖα, ύ*, Ion. for *τραχύς*: Adv. *τρηχέως*, Sup. *τρηχύτατα*.

τρῐ-, in compds. *three times, thrice*, Lat. *ter.*

τρίᾰ, neut. from *τρεῖς*.

τριάζω, f. *άσω*, (*τρία*) *to conquer, vanquish*; metaph. from a wrestler, who did not win until *he had thrice thrown* his adversary, or conquered him *in three bouts*: hence, *διὰ τριῶν ἀπόλλυσθαι* to be *utterly* undone.

τρίαινα, *ἡ*, (*τρία*) Lat. *tridens, a trident*, the attribute of Neptune: generally, *a three-pronged spear.* Hence

τριαινόω, f. *ώσω*, *to move* or *heave with the trident*: hence *to heave* or *prise up, overthrow*; *τριαινοῦν τὴν γῆν δικέλλῃ to break up* the ground with a mattock.

τριᾱκάς Ep. and Ion. **τριηκάς**, *άδος, ἡ*, (*τρεῖς, τρία*), *the number thirty.* II. *the thirtieth day of the month*, also in pl. *τριακάδες.* III. also *any division of thirty.*

τριᾱκονθ-άμμᾰτος, *ον*, (*τριάκοντα, ἅμμα*) *with* or *of thirty knots.*

τριᾱκονθ-ήμερος Ion. **τριηκοντήμερος** Dor. **τριακοντάμερος**, *ον*, (*τριάκοντα, ἡμέρα*) *of thirty days.*

τριάκοντα Ep. and Ion. **τριήκοντα**, *οἱ, αἱ, τά*, indecl.: (*τρεῖς, τρία*), Lat. *TRIGINTA, thirty.* II. as Subst. *οἱ τριάκοντα* 1. at Sparta, *the council of thirty*, assigned to the kings. 2. at Athens, *the thirty tyrants*, appointed on the taking of Athens by Lysander (B. C. 404).

τριᾱκοντᾰ-ετής Ion. **τριηκ-**, *ές*, (*τριάκοντα, ἔτος*):—*thirty years old.* II. *of* or *lasting thirty years*: also fem. *-έτις, ιδος*:—Att. contr. **τριακοντούτης**, *ες*: fem. *τριακόντουτις, ιδος*, whence *τριακοντουτίδες σπονδαί* a *thirty years'* truce.

τριᾱκοντά-ζῠγος, *ον*, (*τριάκοντα, ζυγόν*) *with* or *of thirty benches of oars.*

τριᾱκοντ-αρχία, *ἡ*, (*τριάκοντα, ἄρχω*) *the rule of the thirty tyrants* at Athens: cf. *τριάκοντα* II. 2.

τριᾱκοντ-όργυιος, *ον*, (*τριάκοντα, ὄργυια*) *of thirty fathoms.*

τριᾱκόντορος Ion. **τριηκόντερος**, *ον*, *with thirty oars*:—as Subst. *τριακόντορος* (sub. *ναῦς*), *ἡ, a vessel of thirty oars.*

τριᾱκοντ-ούτης, *ες*, see *τριακονταετής*.

τριᾱκοντ-ώρῠγος, *ον*, more correct form of *τριακοντόργυιος*.

τριᾱκόσιοι Ion. **τριηκόσιοι**, *αι, α*, (*τρεῖς, τρία*) *three hundred*, Lat. *triceni.*

τριᾱκοσιο-μέδιμνος, *ον*, (*τριακόσιοι, μέδιμνος*) *of three hundred medimni*: *οἱ τριακοσιομέδιμνοι those whose property produced three hundred medimni*, which was the qualification for admission into the Athenian Ἱππεῖς.

τριᾱκοστός Ion. **τριηκ-**, *ή, όν*, (*τριάκοντα*) *the thirtieth*: *ἡ τριακοστή* (sub. *μοῖρα*), *a duty of one thirtieth.*

τριακτήρ, *ῆρος, ὁ*, (*τριάζω*) *a conqueror*: see *τριάζω*.

τρι-άρμενος, *ον*, (*τρία, ἄρμενον*) *with three sails.*

τριάς, *άδος, ἡ*, (*τρεῖς*) *the number three, a triad.*

τριάσσω, *άξω*, = *τριάζω*

τρῐβᾰκός, *ή, όν*, (*τρίβω*) *rubbed, worn*, Lat. *tritus*: *ἡ τριβακή a threadbare coat*: cf. *τρίβων*.

Τρῐβαλλοί, *the Triballi*, a people on the borders of Thrace: hence as a name for *barbarian gods.*

τρῐ-βελής, *ές*, (*τρι-, βέλος*) *three-pointed.*

τρῐβή, *ἡ*, (*τριβῆναι*) *a rubbing* II. metaph. *a rubbing* or *grinding away, wearing away*: also of time, *the spending*; *βίος οὐκ ἄχαρις ἐς τὴν τριβήν* a pleasant life in *the spending.* 2. *a busying oneself* about a thing, *practising* it, *practice:* also *mere practice, routine.* 3. *that about which one is busied, the object of one's care.* 4. *delay, putting off, evasion;* ἐς τριβὰς ἑλᾶν to seek *delays;* and without a Verb, μὴ τριβὰς ἔτι no more *delays.*

τρῐβῆναι, aor. 2 pass. inf. of τρίβω.

τρῐβολ-εκτράπελος, ον, (τρίβολος, ἐκτραπελός) neut. plur. as Subst., τριβολεκτράπελα *unmannerly, coarse jests.* [ᾰ]

τρί-βολος, ον, (τρῐ-, βαλεῖν) *three-pointed, three-pronged.* II. as Subst., τρίβολος, ὁ. 1. *a prickly plant, burr.* 2. in plur. *smart sayings, gibes.* 2. in plur. also, *a threshing-machine.*

τρίβος, ἡ, also ὁ, (τριβῆναι) *a worn* or *beaten track, a road, path: the high road, highway.* 2. metaph. *a path of life, course, career.* II. *a rubbing*, like τρῖψις. III. metaph. *practice.* 2. *delay.*

ΤΡΙ´ΒΩ [ῑ]: f. τρίψω: aor. 1 ἔτριψα, inf. τρῖψαι: pf. τέτρῐφα: Pass., fut. 1 τριφθήσομαι, fut. 2 τρῐβήσομαι, paullo-p. fut. τετρίψομαι, also fut. med. τρίψομαι in pass. sense: aor. 1 ἐτρίφθην: aor. 2 ἐτρίβην [ῐ]: pf. τέτριμμαι:—*to rub:* esp. *to rub* corn, *thresh* it *out*, because the Greeks threshed corn by rubbing it: also *to grind, pound, bruise: to rub* a thing *in* or *on* another; μόχλον τρίψαι ἐν ὀφθαλμῷ *to grind* the stake in his eye; χρυσὸν βασάνῳ τρίβειν *to rub* gold on a touchstone, so as to test its purity: Med. *to rub upon another*, hence *to infect, defile with.* II. *to rub away, grind down, wear out, damage, bruise;* of a road, *to wear* or *tread it smooth.* 2. of Time, *to wear away, spend;* τρίβειν βίον *to pass away* life, Lat. *terere vitam:* absol. *to waste time, tarry.* 3. metaph. of persons, *to wear out, oppress:* of a country, *to ravage:* of money, *to waste, squander.* 4. *to wear* or *use:*—Pass. *to be much busied* or *engrossed* with a thing.

τρίβωμες [ῐ], Dor. for τρίβωμεν, 1 pl. subj. of τρίβω.

τρίβων [ῐ], ωνος, ὁ, (τριβῆναι) *a worn garment, threadbare cloak.* II. as Adj. ὁ, ἡ, *practised, well versed* or *skilled in* a thing, c. gen.; also c. acc. 2. absol. as Subst. *a hackneyed rogue, crafty knave.*

τρῐβωνικῶς, Adv. (τρίβων) *in the fashion of a* τρίβων, *cloak-wise.*

τρῐβώνιον, τό, Dim. of τρίβων, *a small cloak, a cape.*

τρῐ-γέρων, οντος, ὁ, ἡ, (τρι-, γέρων) *triply old, very very old.*

ΤΡΙΓΛΑ˘, ἡ, *a mullet*, Lat. *triglia.*

τρί-γληνος, ον, (τρι-, γλῆνος) epith. of ear-rings or drops, *with three bright drops* or *brilliants.*

τριγλο-φόρος, ον, (τρίγλα, φέρω) *catching mullets.*

τρί-γλῠφος, ον, (τρῐ-, γλύφω) *thrice-cloven:* as Subst., τρίγλυφος, ἡ, in Doric architecture, *the triglyph, a three-grooved tablet* placed at equal distances along the frieze.

τρῐ-γλώχῑς, ῖνος, ὁ, ἡ, (τρι-, γλωχίς) *three-barbed, three-forked.*

τριγμός, ὁ, = τρισμός.

τρῐγονία, ἡ, *the third generation.* From

τρί-γονος, ον, (τρῐ-, γενέσθαι) *produced at three births*, of children; τρίγονοι κόραι *three* daughters.

τρί-γωνος, ον, (τρῐ-, γωνία) *three-cornered, triangular.* Hence

τρίγωνον, τό, *a triangle.* II. *a musical instrument of triangular form.* [ῐ]

τρί-δουλος, ον, (τρῐ-, δοῦλος) *a slave through three generations, thrice* or *trebly a slave*

τρί-δραχμος, ον (τρι-, δραχμή) *worth* or *weighing three drachms.*

τρῐ-δύστηνος, ον, *thrice wretched.*

τρι-έλικτος, ον, (τρι-, ἑλίσσω) *thrice wound* or *coiled:* of a rope, *consisting of three strands* or *cords.*

τρι-έμβολος, ον, (τρι-, ἔμβολον) *with* or *like three ships' beaks.*

τρι-έσπερος, ον, (τρι-, ἑσπέρα) *in three successive nights*

τρι-ετηρίς, ίδος, (τρι-, ἔτος) fem. Adj. *triennial:* as Subst. (sub. ἑορτή) *a triennial festival.*

τρι-έτης, ου, ὁ, (τρι-, ἔτος) *of three years, three years old.* Adv. τριέτες, *three years long.*

τριετία, ἡ, (τριέτης) *a space of three years*, Lat. *triennium.*

τρι-ζῠγής, ές, and **τρί-ζῠγος**, ον, and **τρι-ζυξ**, ῠγος, ὁ, ἡ, (τρι-, ζυγῆναι) *three-yoked: three-fold, triple:* also simply *three.*

ΤΡΙ´ΖΩ, f. τρίξω; pf. τετρῖγα with pres. sense; part. τετριγώς, Ep. pl. τετριγῶτες for τετριγότες; plqpf. ἐτετρίγειν Ep. τετρίγειν, with sense of impf.:—of animals and birds, *to make a shrill, piercing cry, to squeak:* of ghosts, *to squeak, gibber:* also of joints, νῶτα τετρίγει their backs *cracked:* of things, *to creak, grate, jar*, Lat. *stridere.* (Formed from the sound.)

τριηκάς, άδος, ἡ, Ep. and Ion. for τριακάς.

τριήκοντα, τριηκόσιοι, Ep. and Ion. for τριακ–.

τρι-ημι-πόδιον, τό, (τρι-, ἡμι-, πούς) *three half feet*, i. e. *a foot and half.*

τριηραρχέω, f. ήσω, *to be a* τριήραρχος, *command a trireme, to be captain of a trireme;* c. gen. τριηραρχεῖν νηός *to be captain of* a ship. II. at Athens, *to be trierarch, fit out a trireme for the public service.* Hence

τριηραρχία, ἡ, (τριηραρχέω) *the command of a trireme.* II. at Athens, *the fitting out of a trireme for the public service: the office of trierarch.* Hence

τριηραρχικός, ή, όν, *fitted for a trierarch* or *his office.*

τριήρ-αρχος, ὁ, (τριήρης, ἄρχω) *the captain of a trireme.* II. at Athens, *a trierarch, one who had to fit out a trireme for the public service.*

τριηρ-αύλης, ου, ὁ, (τριήρης, αὐλέω) *the flute-player who gave the time to the rowers in a trireme.*

τρι-ήρης, gen. εος Ion. ευς; acc. εα, η: plur., nom. εες, εις; gen. τριηρέων contr. τριηρῶν: (τρίς, ἀρᾰρεῖν or ἐρέσσω): properly an Adj. *thrice-fitted* or *thrice-rowed:*—but only used as Subst. τριήρης (sub. ναῦς), ἡ, Lat. *triremis, a galley with three banks of oars*, first built by the Corinthians: the lowest **rowers**

being called θαλάμιοι, the middle ζυγῖται, and the topmost θρανῖται; one man managed each oar. This was the usual size of ships of war; but in later times *quadriremes* (τετρήρεις), *quinqueremes* (πεντήρεις), etc., came into use.

τρι-ηρίτης [ῑ], ου, ὁ, (τριήρης) *one who serves on board a trireme.*

τριηρο-ποιός, όν, (τριήρης, ποιέω) *building triremes.*

τρῐ-κάρηνος, ον, (τρῐ-, κάρηνον) *three-headed.* [κᾰ]

τρῐ-κέφᾰλος, ον, (τρῐ-, κεφαλή) *three-headed.*

τρί-κλῑνος, ον, (τρι-, κλίνη) *with three beds* or *couches*, for sleeping or reclining on at meals:—as Subst., τρίκλινος (sc. οἶκος), ὁ, like the Roman *triclinium*, *a diningroom with three couches;* also τρίκλινον, τό.

τρί-κλωστος, ον, (τρι-, κλώθω) *thrice spun.*

τρῐ-κόρῠθος, ον, and **τρί-κορυς**, ῠθος, ὁ, (τρι-, κόρυς) *with triple plume.*

τρῐ-κόρωνος, ον, (τρῐ-, κορώνη) *thrice a crow's age.*

τρί-κρᾱνος, ον, (τρι-, κρᾶνον) *three-headed, with triple crest.*

τρῐ-κύᾰθος, ον, (τρῐ-, κύαθος) *holding three κύαθοι.*

τρῐ-κῡμία, ἡ, (τρῐ-, κῦμα) *the third wave, a huge, overwhelming wave*, since every third wave (as also every tenth, cf. δεκακυμία) was supposed to be larger than the rest: metaph., τρικυμία κακῶν *a flood* of evils.

τρίλ-λιστος, ον, poët. for τρίλιστος, (τρι-, λίσσομαι) *thrice prayed for*, i. e. *often* or *earnestly prayed for.*

τρῐλογία, ἡ, (τρῐ-, λόγος) *a trilogy;* see τετραλογία.

τρῐλοφία, ἡ, *a triple crest.* From

τρί-λοφος, ον, (τρῐ-, λόφος) *with three crests.*

τρί-μᾰκαρ, -μακαίρα, (τρῐ-, μάκαρ) *thrice-blessed.*

τρί-μετρος, ον, (τρῐ-, μέτρον) of verses, *consisting of three metres;* the metre consisting either of one foot as in dactylic, or of two feet as in iambic verse; τόνος τρίμετρος *trimeter* iambic verse.

τρί-μηνος, ον, (τρῐ-, μήν) *of three months, three months old:* ἡ τρίμηνος *a period of three months.*

τρίμμα, ατος, τό, (τρίβω) *that which is rubbed:* metaph., like τρίβων, *a practised, backneyed knave.*

τριμμός, ὁ, (τρίβω) *a beaten road*, like τρίβος.

τρῐμοιρία, ἡ, *triple pay.* From

τρί-μοιρος, ον, (τρῐ-, μοῖρα) *threefold, triple.*

τρί-μορφος, ον, (τρῐ-, μορφή) *three-formed, triple:* Μοῖραι τρίμορφοι *the three* fates.

Τρῖν-ακρία, ἡ, (τρι-, ἄκρα) epith. of Sicily, from its *three promontories* (ἄκραι): also written **Τρινακία** Ion. -ίη (from τρίναξ).

Τρῖνάκριος, α, ον, *of Trinacria* or *Sicily, Sicilian.*

τρῖν-αξ, ἄκος, ἡ, (τρίς, ἀκή) *a trident.*

τριξός, ή, όν, Ion. for τρισσός, *threefold, triple;* so διξός for δισσός.

τρί-οδος, ἡ, (τρι-, ὁδός) *a meeting of three roads, three cross-roads*, Lat. *trivium.*

τρι-όδους, -όδοντος, ὁ, ἡ, (τρι-, ὀδούς) *with three teeth:* as Subst., τριόδους, ὁ, *a trident.*

τρι-όργυιος, ον, (τρι-, ὄργυια) *three fathoms long.*

τρι-όροφος, ον, = τριώροφος.

τρι-όρχης, ου, ο, and **τρί-ορχος**, ον, (τρι-, ὄρχις) a kind of *falcon* or *kite.*

τριοτό, a sound imitative of a bird's voice.

τρί-πᾰλαι, Adv. (τρῐ-, πάλαι) *thrice long since*, i. e. *very long ago.*

τρῐ-πάλαιστος, ον, (τρι-, παλαιστή) *three hands broad, long*, etc.

τρί-παλτος, ον, (τρῐ-, πάλλω) *thrice-brandished;* metaph. *furious, fierce.*

τρῐ-πάνουργος, ον, (τρι-, πᾰνοῦργος) *trebly a rogue.*

τρῐπάχυιος, ον, Dor. for τριπήχυς, q. v.

τρῐ-πέτηλος, ον, (τρι-, πέτηλον) *three-leafed.*

τρί-πηχυς, υ, gen. εος, (τρι-, πῆχυς) *three cubits long.*

τρῐ-πῑθήκῑνος, η, ον, (τρι-, πίθηκος) *thrice apish.*

τρίπλαξ, ἄκος, ὁ, ἡ, (τρίς) *triple, threefold*, Lat. *triplex.* [ῐ]

τρῐπλάσιος, α, ον, (τρι-) *thrice as many, thrice as much, thrice as great as*, c. gen.; neut. τριπλάσιον as Adv., τριπλάσιον σοῦ *thrice as much as* you

τρί-πλεθρος, ον, (τρι-, πλέθρον) *three plethra long.*

τρῐπλῆ, v. τριπλόος.

τριπλοιστός, όν, (τριπλός) *made threefold, tripled, trebled.*

τρῐπλόος, η, ον contr. **τριπλοῦς**, ῆ, οῦν, (τρεῖς) *triple, threefold.* Adv. -πλῶς, but dat. fem. τριπλῇ is also used as Adv., *triply, trebly.*

τρῐπόδεσσι, Ep. dat. pl. of τρίπους.

τρῐ-πόδης, ου, ὁ, (τρῐ-, πούς) *three feet long.*

τρῐ-πόθητος, ον, (τρῐ-, ποθέω) *thrice longed for, much* or *earnestly desired.*

τρί-πολις, εως Ion. ιος, ὁ, ἡ, (τρῐ-, πόλις) *with three cities;* cf. δεκάπολις.

τρῐ-πόλιστος, ον, (τρι-, πολίζω) *thrice-built, triply* or *firmly founded.*

τρί-πολος, ον, (τρῐ-, πολέω) *thrice turned up* or *ploughed, bearing three crops in a year*, of corn land.

τρῐ-πόνητος, ον, (τρῐ-, πονέω) *thrice-worked:* ἔρις τριπόνητος a dispute *between three labourers.*

τρί-πορθος, ον, (τρῐ-, πορθέω) *thrice wasted.*

τρί-πος, ου, ὁ, poët. for τρίπους. [ῐ]

τρί-πους, -ποδος, ὁ, ἡ, -πουν, τό, (τρῐ-, πούς) *three footed, three-legged* or *with three feet: measuring three feet.* II. *going on three feet;* proverb. of an old man who leans on a staff, τρίποδας ὁδοὺς στείχει. 2. as Subst., τρίπους, ὁ, *a tripod, a three-footed brass kettle* or *caldron;* tripods were often made of exquisite material and workmanship, and dedicated in temples. 3. *the stool* or *throne of the Delphic priestess.*

τρί-πρᾱτος, ον, (τρῐ-, πιπράσκω) *thrice sold.*

τριπτήρ, ῆρος, ὁ, (τρίβω) *a rubber* or *tool for rubbing with, a pestle.*

τρίπτης, ου, ὁ, (τρίβω) *a rubber, shampooer.*

Τρι-πτόλεμος, ὁ, *Triptolemus*, an Eleusinian, who established the worship of Demeter.

τρί-πτῠχος, ον, (τρι-, πτύσσω) *consisting of three layers* or *plates, threefold, triple;* also simply *three.*

τρί-πωλος, ον, (τρῐ-, πῶλος) *of* or *with three horses.*

τρίρ-ρυμος, ον, (τρι–, ῥυμός) *with three poles*, i. e. *with four horses abreast.*

τρίς, Adv. of τρεῖς, *thrice, three times*, Lat. *ter*; τρὶς τόσος *thrice* as much; ἐς τρίς up to *three times*: often used indefinitely in compds., to strengthen the force of the simple word, like Lat. *ter*, and our *thrice*. Proverb., τρὶς ἓξ βάλλειν to throw *thrice* six, i. e. the highest throw (there being three dice), hence *to have the best luck*. [ῐ]

τρῐσ-άθλιος, α, ον, *thrice-unhappy.*

τρῐσ-άλαστος, ον, *thrice-tormented.*

τρῐσ-άριθμος, ον, *thrice-numbered.*

τρῐσ-άσμενος, η, ον, *thrice-pleased*, i. e. *well-contented.*

τρῐσ-άωρος, ον, *very untimely.*

τρισ-δείλαιος, ον, = τρισάθλιος.

τρισ-δύστηνος, ον, *trebly*, i. e. *very, miserable.*

τρῐσ-εινάς, άδος, ἡ, (τρίς, ἐννεάς) sub. ἡμέρα, *the third ninth day* in a month; i. e. *the ninth day of the third decad*, the 29th.

τρῐ-σέληνος, ον, (τρι–, σελήνη) *of three moons* or *nights.*

τρῐσ-έπαρχος, ὁ, (τρίς, ἔπαρχος) *thrice an overseer.*

τρισ-θᾰνής, ές, (τρίς, θανεῖν) *thrice worthy of death.*

τρισ-καί-δεκα, οἱ, αἱ, τά, = τρεισκαίδεκα.

τρισκαιδεκά-πηχυς, υ, gen. εος, *thirteen cubits, high, long*, etc.

τρισκαιδεκα-στάσιος, ον, (τρισκαίδεκα, ἵστημι) *of thirteen times the weight* or *value*. [στᾰ]

τρισκαιδέκᾰτος, η, ον, (τρισκαίδεκα) *the thirteenth.*

τρισκαιδεκ-έτης, ου, ὁ, fem. τρισκαιδεκέτις, ιδος, (τρισκαίδεκα, ἔτος) *of thirteen years, thirteen years old.*

τρισ-κᾰκοδαίμων, ον, gen. ονος, *thrice-unlucky, trebly ill-fated.*

τρί-σκαλμος, ον, (τρῐ–, σκαλμός) *with three benches of rowers*; νῆες τρίσκαλμοι = τριήρεις.

τρισ-κᾰτάρᾱτος, ον, (τρίς, καταράομαι) *thrice accursed.*

τρισ-κοπάνιστος, ον, (τρίς, κοπανίζω) *thrice struck*; ἄρτος τρισκοπάνιστος *thrice-kneaded* bread.

τρίσ-μᾰκαρ, fem. –μακαρα, gen. –μάκᾰρος, ὁ, ἡ, (τρίς, μάκαρ) *thrice blest*; τρισμάκαρες καὶ τετράκις, Virgil's *terque quaterque beati.*

τρισ-μᾰκάριος, α, ον, = τρίσμακαρ.

τρισμός, ὁ, (τρίζω) *a squeaking*: *a squeak.*

τρισ-μύριοι, αι, α, (τρίς, μύριοι) *thrice ten thousand*, 30,000: also in sing. with a collective Subst., as, τρισμυρία ἵππος *thirty thousand* horse. [ῡ]

τρισμῡριό-πᾰλαι, (τρισμύριοι, πάλαι) Adv. *thirty thousand times long ago, immensely long ago.*

τρῐσ-ολυμπιο-νίκης, ου, ὁ, (τρίς, Ὀλυμπιονίκης) *thrice victorious at Olympia*. [νῑ]

τρι-σπίθᾰμος, ον, (τρι–, σπιθαμή) *three spans long.*

τρί-σπονδος, ον, (τρι–, σπονδή) *thrice-poured, forming a triple libation* or *drink-offering.*

τρισσάκις, Adv. (τρίς) *thrice, three times.* [ᾰ]

τρισσάτιος, η, ον, poët. for τρισσός. [ᾰ]

τρισσόθεν, Adv. (τρισσός) *from three sides.*

τρισσός Att. **τριττός** Ion. **τριξός**, ή, όν, like δισσός, διξός, (τρίς) *threefold*, Lat. *triplex*: in plur. = τρεῖς. Adv. –σῶς, *three times.*

τρισσο-φαής, ές, and **τρισσο-φωτος**, ον, (τρίς, φάος, φῶς) *in a threefold light.*

τρί-στεγος, ον, (τρι–, στέγη) *of* or *with three stories*; τὸ τρίστεγον (sub. οἴκημα), *the third story.*

τρι-στοιχεί or **–χί** [ῑ], Adv. of τρίστοιχος, *in three rows.*

τρί-στοῐχος, ον, (τρι–, στοῖχος) *in three rows.*

τρί-στομος, ον, (τρι–, στόμα) *three-mouthed.* II. *three-edged* or *three-pointed.*

τρισ-χίλιοι, αι, α, (τρίς, χίλιοι) *three thousand*: also in sing. with a collective Subst., τρισχιλία ἵππος 3000 horse. [χῑ]

τρῐ-σώμᾰτος, ον, (τρι–, σῶμα) *with three bodies*, Lat. *tricorpor.*

τρῐτᾰγωνιστέω, f. ήσω, *to be a τριταγωνιστής, to play third-rate characters.* From

τρῐτ-ᾰγωνιστής, οῦ, ὁ, (τρίτος, ἀγωνιστής) *the player who takes the third part, a third-rate performer.*

τρῐταῖος, α, ον, (τρίτος) of time, *in three days, on the third day*; τριταῖοι ἐγένοντο they arrived *on the third day*. 2. *three days old*; τριταῖος γενόμενος after being *three days* dead. 3. *three days ago.* 4. generally for τρίτος, *third.*

τρῐ-τάλαντος, ον, (τρι–, τάλαντον) *of three talents weight* or *worth*. [τᾰ]

τρῐ-τάλᾱς, τάλαινα, τάλᾰν, (τρι–, τάλας) *thrice-wretched*. [τᾰ]

τρῐ-τάνυστος, ον, (τρι–, τανύω) *triply stretched* or *drawn out*, i. e. *very long.*

τρίτᾰτος, η, ον, poët. lengthd. for τρίτος, like μέσσατος for μέσος. [ῐ]

τρῐτη-μόριος, α, ον, (τρίτος, μόρος) *equal to a third part, forming a third part*: as Subst., **τριτη-μόριον** (sub. μόριον), τό, *a third part.*

τρῐτη-μορίς, ίδος, ἡ, like τριτημόριον, *a third part.*

τρῐτο-βάμων [ᾱ], ον, gen. ονος, (τρίτος, βαίνω) *going as third, forming a third foot.*

Τρῐτο-γένεια, ἡ, *the Trito-born*, epith. of Minerva; derived from the lake Τρῑτωνίς in Libya, near which the goddess was born.

Τρῑτο-γενής, έος, ἡ, = Τριτογένεια.

τρῐτοκέω, *to bring forth thrice, have three at a birth.* From

τρι-τόκος, ον, (τρι–, τεκεῖν) *bearing thrice* or *three at a birth.*

τρίτος, η, ον, (τρίς, τρεῖς) *the third*, Lat. *tertius*; τρίτος ἐλθεῖν to come *as third*, i. e. with two others; τρίτος γενέσθαι to be *third* in a race; ἐς τρίτην ἡμέραν on *the third* day, i. e. the day after to-morrow. II. τρίτον as Adv. *thirdly*, also τὸ τρίτον: also ἐκ τρίτου or ἐκ τρίτων, *in the third place*. III. τὰ τρίτα λέγειν τινί to play *the third part* to any one, like τριταγωνιστεῖν τινι. [ῐ]

τρῐτό-σπονδος, ον, (τρίτος, σπονδή) = τρίσπονδος, *crowned with triple libation*; τριτόσπονδος αἰών a life in which one pours the third libation (to Ζεὺς Σωτήρ), i. e. a life without drawback.

τρῐτό-σπορος, ον, (τρίτος, σπείρω) *sown for the third time; τριτόσπορος γονή the third* generation.

τριττός, ή, όν, Att. for τρισσός.

τριττύς, ύος, ἡ, also **τριτύς**, (τρεῖς) *the number three*, Lat. *ternio*. II. *a sacrifice of three animals*, a bull, he-goat and boar, or of a bull, he-goat and ram, (like the Roman *su-ove-taurilia*). III. at Athens, *a third of the φυλή* or *tribe*.

Τρίτων, ωνος, ὁ, *Triton*, a sea-god, son of Poseidon and Amphitrité. 2. the god of the Libyan lake Tritonis. II. a river in Libya, joining the lake Tritonis with the sea. [ῑ] Hence

Τρῑτωνιάς, άδος, ἡ, like Τριτωνίς, epith. of Minerva: λίμνη Τριτωνιάς the Libyan lake *Tritonis*.

Τρῑτωνίς, ίδος, ἡ, the lake *Tritonis* in Libya famous for the birth of Athena. 2. epith. of Minerva.

τρῐφάσιος, α, ον, (τρεῖς) *threefold*, Lat. *triplex:* also simply *three*. [ᾰ]

τρῐ-φίλητος Dor. **-ᾱτος**, ον, (τρι-, φῐλέω) *thrice-beloved*.

τρί-φυλλον, τό, (τρι-, φύλλον) a plant, *trefoil, clover*.

τρί-φῡλος, ον, (τρι-, φυλή) *of three tribes; τριφύλους ποιεῖν* to divide them *into three tribes*.

τρίχα or **τριχῆ**, Adv. (τρίς) *threefold, in three parts*, Lat. *trifariam:* c. gen., *τρίχα νυκτὸς in the third watch* of the night; *τρίχα σχίζειν* to divide *in three*. [ῐ]

τρῐ-χάϊκες [ῐ], οἱ, *the threefold people*, i. e. the Dorians, so called from their three tribes. (Deriv. uncertain.)

τρῐ-χάλεπτος, ον, (τρι-, χαλέπτω) *very angry*.

τρί-χᾱλος, ον, Dor. for τρί-χηλος, (τρῐ-, χηλή) *cloven in three*.

τρίχες, αἱ, nom. pl. of θρίξ. [ῐ]

τρῐχῇ, Adv. (τρίχα) *in threefold manner*.

τριχθά, Adv. poët. for τρίχα, *triply, into three parts*. [ᾰ] Hence

τριχθάδιος, α, ον, *threefold*. [ᾰ]

τρίχῐνος, η, ον, (θρίξ) *of* or *from hair*. [τρῐ]

τρῐχίς, ίδος, ἡ, (θρίξ) a kind of *anchovy full of small bones like hair*, whence its name.

τρῐχό-βρως, ωτος, (θρίξ, βιβρώσκω)) *eating hair:* as Subst., *τριχόβρωτες, hair-eaters*, i. e. *moths*.

τρῐ-χοίνῐκος, ον, (τρί-, χοῖνιξ) *holding three χοίνικες: τριχοίνικον ἔπος a most capacious* word.

τρῐ-χόλωτος, ον, (τρι-, χολόω) *thrice-detested*.

τρῐχό-μαλλος, ον, (θρίξ, μαλλός) *with fleece-like hair*.

τρῐχορρυέω, f. ήσω, *to shed* or *lose the hair*. From

τρῐχορ-ρῠής, ές, (θρίξ, ῥέω) *shedding* or *losing the hair*.

τριχός, gen. of θρίξ.

τρῐχοῦ, Adv. (τρίχα) *in three places*.

τρί-χρωμος, ον, (τρῐ-, χρῶμα) *three-coloured*.

τρίχωμα, ατος, τό, (τρῐχόω) *a growth of hair, shock of hair*

τρῐχῶς, Adv. (τρίχα) *in threefold manner*.

τρῖψαι, aor. 1 inf. of τρίβω.

τριψ-ημερέω, f. ήσω, (τρίβω, ἡμέρα) *to idle away the day, waste time in delays*, Lat. *terere tempus*.

τρῖψις, εως, ἡ, (τρίβω) *a rubbing, friction*. II. *firmness, resistance to the touch when rubbed*. III. *τρίψεις, αἱ, potted meat*.

τρι-ώβολον, τό, (τρι-, ὀβολός) *a three-oboi piece*, i. e. *a half-drachma*, about $4\frac{1}{2}d.$, from the time of Pericles, the pay of the Athenian jurymen for a day's sitting in court.

τρῐ-ώροφος, ον, (τρι-, ὀροφή) *of three stories* or *floors:*—as Subst., *τριώροφον, τό, the third story*.

τριώρυγος, ον, more correct Att. form of τριόργυιος.

Τροίᾱθεν Ion. –ηθεν or –θε, (Τροία) Adv. *from Troy*.

Τροίανδε Ion. –ηνδε, (Τροία) Adv. *to Troy*.

Τροία Ion. Τροίη, ἡ, either the city or the country, *Troy* or *the Troad:* also Τροΐα as trisyll.

τρομεοίατο, Ion. for τρομέοιντο, 3 pl. med. opt. of τρομέω.

τρομέοντι, Dor. and Ep. for τρομέουσι, 3 pl. of τρομέω. 2. dat. pres. part. of τρομέω.

τρομερός, ά, όν, (τρομέω) *trembling: quaking, quivering*.

τρομεύμενος, Ion. part. med. of τρομέω.

τρομέω, f. ήσω, (τρόμος) *to tremble, quake, quiver:* hence *to be afraid*. II. c. acc. *to tremble before* or *at, to fear, dread, shudder at*.

τρόμος, ὁ, (τρέμω) *a trembling, quaking, quivering*, esp. from fear.

τροπαία (sub πνοή), ἡ, (τροπαῖος) *a returning wind, alternating wind: one which blows back from the sea to land:* metaph., *λήματος τροπαία a change in* one's spirit. 2. *a change from, release from*.

τρόπαιον Ion. **τροπαῖον**, τό, properly neut. of τροπαῖος; *a trophy*, Lat. *tropaeum*, in token of the enemy's rout (τροπή): consisting of shields, helmets, etc., taken from the enemy, hung on trees, or fixed on upright posts:—στῆσαι or στήσασθαι τρόπαια to set up *trophies*.

τροπαῖος, α, ον, (τρέπω) *of a turning* or *change*. II. *of defeat* or *rout* (τροπή); *θεοὶ τροπαῖοι* the gods *who caused the defeat; Ἕκτορος ὄμμασι τροπαῖοι terrible* to the eyes of Hector. III. *turning away, averting*, Lat. *averruncus*.

τροπαιο-φόρος, ον, (τρόπαιον, φέρω) *bearing trophies*.

τροπᾰλίζω, poët. for τρέπω.

τροπᾰλίς, ίδος, ἡ, *a bundle, bunch*. (Deriv. uncertain.)

τροπέω, poët. form of τρέπω, *to turn*.

τροπή, ἡ, (τρέπω) *a turn, turning round* or *about; τροπαὶ ἠελίοιο the solstices* or *tropics*, i. e. *the points of midsummer and midwinter*, when the sun appears to turn his course, called *τροπαὶ θεριναί* and *χειμεριναί*, Lat. *solstitium* and *bruma*. II. *the turning about of the enemy, putting* him *to flight; τροπήν τινος ποιεῖν* or *ποιεῖσθαι* to put one to *flight; ἐν τροπῇ δορὸς in the rout of* the spear. 2. (from Pass. τρεπομαι) *a flying, fleeing, flight*, Lat. *conversio in fugam.* 2. *a turn, turning, change.*

τροπίας, ου, ὁ, (τρέπω) of wine, *turned*, i. e. *sour.*

τροπικός, ή, όν, (τρόπος) *of* or *like a turn* or *turning*: ὁ τροπικός (sc. κύκλος) *the tropic circle* on the globe: cp. τροπή. II. in Rhetoric, *tropical, figurative.*

τρόπις, ἡ, Ep. gen. τρόπιος or -ιδος; acc. τρόπιν: (τρέπω):—*a ship's keel:* metaph., ἡ τρόπις τοῦ πράγματος *the keel*, i. e. *foundation*, of the matter.

τρόπος, ὁ, (τρέπω) *a turn, direction, way.* II. metaph. *a way, manner, fashion, mode:* in adverbial usages; dat., τρόπῳ τοιῷδε in such *wise;* οὐδενὶ τρόπῳ in no *wise;* παντὶ τρόπῳ by all *means;* ἑκουσίῳ τρόπῳ willingly; τρόπῳ φρενός *according to one's way* or *humour;* ἐν τρόποις Ἰξίονος after *the fashion* of Ixion. 2. absol. in acc., πάντα τρόπον *in every way* or *manner;* βάρβαρον τρόπον in barbarous *fashion.* 3. ἐκ παντὸς τρόπου by all *means.* III. of persons, *a way of life, habit, custom:* a man's *habits, character, temper;* οὐ τοὐμοῦ τρόπου not *after my taste;* πρὸς τοῦ Κύρου τρόπον suitably to his *temper* or *taste.* IV. in Music, a particular *mode.*

τροπός, ὁ, (τρέπω) *a twisted leathern thong*, with which the oar was fastened to the thole, used instead of a rowlock.

τροπο-φορέω, f. ήσω, (τρόπος, φέρω) *to bear with* another man's *manners.*

τροπόω, f. ώσω, *to furnish the oar with its thong* (τροπός): Med., τροποῦτο κώπην *fastened his own* oar *by its thong:*—Pass. of the oar, *to be furnished with a thong.*

τροπωτήρ, ῆρος, ὁ, = τροπός, *the thong that fastens the oar to the thole.*

τροφᾱλίς, ίδος, ἡ, (τρέφω) *fresh cheese.*

τροφεῖα, τά, (τροφεύω) *pay* or *recompence for rearing, the wages of a nurse* or *foster-mother.* II. *living, food, subsistence.*

τροφεύς, έως, ὁ, (τροφή) *one who rears* or *brings up, a rearer, foster-father:* metaph. of inanimate objects, ὦ τροφῆς ἐμοί *ye who have fed me.*

τροφέω, = τρέφω, as φορέω for φέρω.

τροφή, ἡ, (τρέφω) *nourishment, food, victuals, maintenance;* βίου τροφή *a livelihood, living: one's means of living.* II. *a rearing* or *nursing, bringing up: a tending* or *keeping of animals.* III. *that which is reared, a nursling, brood.*

τρόφῐμος, η, ον, also ος, ον, (τροφή) *nourishing, nutritious, fruitful:* c. gen., γῆ τρόφιμος τέκνων earth *prolific in* children. II. pass. *nourished, reared up:* as Subst. *a nursling, foster-child.*

τρόφις, ὁ, ἡ, τρόφι, τό, gen. ιος, (τρέφω) *well-fed, stout, large, big;* τρόφι κῦμα *a huge, swollen* wave.

τροφόεις, εσσα, εν, (τρέφω) *well-fed, stout, large, huge.*

τροφός, ὁ and ἡ, (τρέφω) *a feeder, rearer, nurse.*

τροφο-φορέω, f. ήσω, (τροφή, φέρω) *to bring nourishment to, maintain, support.*

Τροφώνιος, ὁ, the builder of the first temple of Apollo at Delphi; to whom afterwards a cave and oracle were dedicated.

τροχάδην, Adv. (τρέχω) *running in the course, running along.* [ᾰ]

τροχάζω, f. άσω, (τρόχος) *to run along, run quickly, trip along.*

τροχαῖος, α, ον, (τρόχος) *running, tripping:* in prosody, ὁ τροχαῖος (sc. πούς) *a trochee, foot consisting of a long and short syllable*, used esp. in quick time, as more lively than the iambic.

τροχᾰλός, ή, όν, (τρέχω) *running: swift: round.*

τροχηλᾰτέω, f. ήσω, *to drive a chariot.* II. metaph. *to drive about, drive round and round, chase.* From

τροχ-ηλάτης [ᾰ], ου, ὁ, (τροχός, ἐλαύνω) *a driver of a wheeled carriage, a charioteer.*

τροχ-ήλᾰτος, ον, (τροχός, ἐλαύνω) *moved on wheels, wheel-drawn.* 2. *dragged by* or *at the wheels.* 3. *turned* or *fashioned on the potter's wheel.* 4. metaph. *driven round and round, driven about.*

τροχιά, ἡ, (τροχός) *the track of wheels.* 2. *the round of a wheel.*

τροχίζω, f. ίσω, (τροχός) *to turn upon the wheel, torture.*

τροχῐλία, ἡ, (τροχός) *a pulley*, Lat. *trochlea.*

τροχίλος, ὁ, (τρέχω) *a small bird of the wagtail kind* found in Egypt, said by Herodotus to pick βδέλλαι out of the crocodile's throat. 2. a small land-bird, *the wren.* [Ĭ]

τροχιός, ά, όν, (τροχός) *running round* or *quickly.*

τρόχις, ιος and εως, ὁ, (τρέχω) *a runner, messenger.*

τροχο-δῑνέω, f. ήσω, (τροχός, δινέω) *to turn round and round, whirl* or *roll round.*

τροχο-ειδής, ές, (τροχός, εἶδος) *like a wheel, round, circular.*

τροχόεις, εσσα, εν, (τροχός) *round, circular.*

τροχοποιέω, f. ήσω, *to make wheels.* From

τροχο-ποιός, όν, (τροχός, ποιέω) *making wheels:* as Subst., τροχοποιός, ὁ, *a wheelwright.*

τροχός, οῦ, ὁ, (τρέχω) *anything that runs round: anything round* or *circular, a round ball* or *cake; the sun's disc:* esp., II. *a wheel: a potter's wheel.* III. a boy's *hoop*, Lat. *Graecus trochus.* IV. *the wheel of torture*, cf. τροχίζω; ἐπὶ τροχοῦ στρεβλοῦσθαι to be tortured on *the wheel.*

τρόχος, ου, ὁ, (τρέχω) *a running, course, a circular course, revolution.* 2. *a place for running.*

ΤΡΥ'ΒΛΙΟΝ, τό, *a cup, bowl.*

τρῠγάω, f. ήσω, (τρύγη) *to gather in ripe fruits, gather in the vintage* or *harvest*, with acc. of the fruit gathered: also in Med. II. with acc. of the field or trees, *to reap the crop off* a field: metaph., τρυγᾶν τινα *to reap advantage from* some one. 2. proverb., ἐρήμας τρυγᾶν (sc. ἀμπέλους) *to strip unwatched vines*, of one that is bold where there is nothing to fear.

τρύγη [ῠ], ἡ, (τρύγω) *ripe fruit gathered in, a crop*

of corn, fruit, grapes, etc. II. a gathering of such fruits; ἀμπέλων τρύγη the vintage

τρῠγητήρ, ῆρος, ὁ, (τρυγάω) one who gathers ripe fruits, esp. grapes.

τρύγητος, ὁ, (τρῠγάω) a gathering of fruits, harvest, esp. the vintage. 2. the time of gathering in the crops or vintage.

τρῠγήτρια, ἡ, fem. of τρυγητήρ, a woman that gathers in the crops, esp. the vines.

τρῠγη-φόρος, ον, (τρύγη, φέρω) wine-bearing.

τρῠγικός, ή, όν, (τρύξ) made of lees. II. = τρυγῳδικός, of or for comedy.

τρῠγο-δαίμων, ονος, ὁ, (τρύξ, δαίμων) for τρυγῳδός, with allusion to κακοδαίμων, a luckless wight of a poet.

τρύγ-οιπος, ὁ, (τρύξ, ἶπος) a straining-cloth, strainer, esp. for wine. [ῠ]

τρῠγόῳεν, Ep. for τρυγῷεν, 3 pl. opt. of τρυγάω.

ΤΡΥ'ΓΩ, to dry. [ῠ]

τρῠγ-ῳδία, ἡ, (τρυγῳδός) = κωμῳδία, comedy. Hence

τρῠγ-ῳδικός, ή, όν, = κωμῳδικός, of or for comedy or the comic art.

τρῠγ-ῳδός, ὁ, (τρύξ, ᾠδή) a must-singer or lees-singer; because, according to Horace, the singers smeared their faces with lees as a ludicrous disguise: afterwards called κωμῳδός when their performance assumed a more regular character.

τρῡγών, όνος, ἡ, (τρύζω) the turtle-dove, named from its cooing.

ΤΡΥ'ΖΩ, only used in pres. and impf. to make a murmuring sound; of doves, to coo: of men, to mutter, murmur. (Formed from the sound.)

τρῡμᾰλία, ἡ, (τρύω) = τρύμη: the eye of a needle.

τρύμη, ἡ, (τρύω) a hole. II. metaph. a sharp fellow, a sly knave. [ῡ]

τρύξ, ἡ, gen. τρῠγός, (τρύγω) new wine not yet fermented, must, Lat. mustum. II. the lees of wine, dregs, Lat. faex: generally, refuse, dross, as of metal, Lat. scoria: metaph. of an old man or woman.

τρύπᾰνον, τό, (τρυπάω) a carpenter's tool, a borer, auger, gimlet. [ῡ]

τρῡπάω, f. ήσω: pf. pass. τετρυπημαι: (τρῡ́πη):—to bore, pierce through, perforate; ὦτα τετρυπημένα ears pierced for earrings; ψῆφος τετρυπημένη the pebble of condemnation (which had a hole through it).

τρύπη, ἡ, (τρύω) a hole.

τρύπημα, ατος, τό, (τρῡπάω) that which is bored, a hole: in a ship, a port-hole.

τρῡπῷ, contr. for τρυπάοι, 3 sing. opt. of τρυπάω.

τρῡσ-άνωρ, ορος, ὁ, ἡ, (τρύω, ἀνήρ) boring, i.e. wearing out, men, harassing. [ᾱ]

τρῡσί-βιος, ον, (τρύω, βίος) wearing out life. [σῐ]

ΤΡΥΤΑ'ΝΗ, ἡ, the tongue of a balance: generally, a balance, pair of scales, Lat. trutina. [ᾰ]

τρυ-φάλεια, ἡ, a helmet. (Prob. from τρύω and φάλος, strictly a helmet with a crest fixed in the φάλος.)

τρῠφάω, f. ήσω, (τρυφή) to live softly or delicately, fare sumptuously, live in luxury:—part. τρυφῶν, ῶσα, delicate, effeminate; neut. τὸ τρυφῶν as Subst., effeminacy. 2. to be licentious, to revel. 3. to carry oneself high, give oneself airs, be insolent.

τρῠφεραίνομαι, Pass. (τρυφερός) to be fastidious or delicate: aor. 1 part. τρυφεοανθείς, with a fastidious air.

τρῠφερός, ά, όν, (τρυφή) soft, delicate, dainty, effeminate, luxurious, fastidious: neut. τὸ τρυφερόν as Subst., effeminacy. Adv. -ρῶς, voluptuously.

τρῠφερότης, ητος, ἡ, (τρυφερός) delicacy, luxury.

τρῠφή, ἡ, (θρύπτω) softness, delicacy, daintiness, luxury, fastidiousness: in plur. luxuries, daintinesses, Lat. deliciae. 2. conceit, insolence.

τρῠφηλός, ή, όν, poët. for τρυφερός.

τρύφημα, ατος, τό, (τρῠφάω) the object in which one takes pleasure: in plur. luxuries, Lat. deliciae.

τρῠφῆναι, aor. 2 pass. inf. of θρύπτω.

τρύφος, εος, τό, (τρυφῆναι) that which is broken off, a piece, morsel, lump, fragment. [ῠ]

τρῡχηρός, ά, όν, (τρῦχος) ragged, tattered in rags and tatters.

τρύχνος, ὁ, = στρύχνος, rough, rugged.

τρῦχος, εος, τό, (τρύχω) a worn out, tattered garment, a rag, shred: in plur. rags tatters. Hence

τρῡχόω, rare form of τρύχω.

τρύχω, f. ξω, (τρύω) to wear out, consume, waste: metaph. to eat one out of house and home. 2. generally, to distress, afflict, harass, vex:—Pass. to be worn out; λιμῷ τρύχεσθαι to be worn away with hunger: also c. gen., τρύχεσθαί τινος to waste or pine away for some one. [ῡ]

ΤΡΥ'Ω, chiefly in pf. pass. τετρῡμαι, part. τετρῡμένος, inf. τετρῦσθαι:—to wear out: to distress, harass, afflict, vex; τετρῦσθαι ἐς τὸ ἔσχατον κακοῦ to have been ground down to the extreme of misery. [ῡ]

Τρῳάς, άδος, ἡ, fem. of Τρώς, a Trojan woman. II. the region of Troy, the Troad.

τρωγάλια, τά, (τρώγω) fruits eaten at dessert, figs, almonds, sweetmeats, etc. [γᾰ]

τρώγλη, ἡ, (τρώγω) a hole.

τρωγλο-δύτης, ου, ὁ, (τρώγλη, δύω) one who creeps into holes; οἱ Τρωγλοδύται, Troglodytes, as name of an Aethiopian tribe who dwelt in holes or caves. [ῡ]

τρωγλο-δύω, (τρώγλη, δύω) to creep into holes.

τρωγοίσας, Dor. for τρωγούσας, fem. part. acc. pl. of τρώγω.

τρώγοντι, Dor. for τρωγουσι, 3 pl. pres. of τρώγω.

ΤΡΩ'ΓΩ, f. τρώξομαι: aor. 1 ἔτρωξα: aor. 2 ἔτρᾰγον: Pass., aor. 2 ἐτράγην [ᾰ]: pf. τέτρωγμαι:—to gnaw, chew: of men, to eat raw vegetables, fruit, etc.; opp. to eating dressed food: esp. of dessert, to eat fruits, cp. τρωγάλια

Τρωικός, ή, όν, (Τρώς) of Troy, Trojan.

Τρώιος, η, ον, Ep. for Τρῳός, Trojan: fem. Τρωιάς, άδος, a Trojan woman.

τρωκτά, τά, see τρωκτός.

τρώκτης, ου, ὁ, (τρώγω) a gnawer, nibbler, lover of dainties: in the Odyssey the Phoenician traffickers are called *τρῶκται, greedy knaves;* so as Adj., *τρῶκται χεῖρες greedy, grasping* hands.

τρωκτός, ή, όν, verb. Adj. of *τρώγω, gnawed, nibbled at;* of vegetables, fruit, etc., *eaten raw, eatable:* neut. *τρωκτά, τά,* as Subst., = *τρωγάλια.*

τρῶμα, τρωματίζω, τρωματίης, Ion. for *τραυμ-.*

τρώμη Dor. *τρώμᾱ, ἡ,* = *τρῶμα,* Ion. for *τραῦμα.*

τρῶξις, εως, ή, (τρώγω) *a gnawing.*

Τρῳός, ά, όν, contr. for Τρώιος, (Τρώς) *Trojan.*

Τρωο-φθόρος, ον, (Τρώς, φθείρω) *destructive to the Trojans* or *to Troy.*

τρωπάω, Ep. for *τρέπω, to turn, to change, alter;*—Med. *to turn oneself, turn about* or *back;* 3 sing. Ep. and Ion. impf. *τρωπάσκετο φεύγειν be turned himself to flight.*

Τρώς, ὁ, gen. **Τρωός,** *Tros,* the founder of Troy: plur. Τρῶες, οἱ, gen. Τρώων, dat. Τρωσί, *Trojans.*

τρώσεσθαι, fut. med. inf. of *τιτρώσκω.*

τρώσω, fut. of *τιτρώσκω.*

τρωτός, ή, όν, verb. Adj. of *τρώω, τιτρώσκω, wounded, that can be wounded, vulnerable.*

τρωῦμα, false reading for *τρῶμα,* Ion. for *τραῦμα.*

τρωχάω, Ep. for *τρέχω, to run.*

ΤΡΩ'Ω, radic. form of *τιτρώσκω, to wound: to hurt, harm, damage, do* one *a mischief.*

τύ, Dor. for *σύ:* also acc. for *σέ.* [ῠ]

τῦβι, τό, an Egyptian winter month.

τυγχάνω, fut. *τεύξομαι:* aor. 2 *ἔτῠχον,* Ep. subj. *τύχωμι:* Ep. aor. 1 *ἐτύχησα* [ῠ]: pf. *τετύχηκα* [ῠ], Ion. also *τέτευχα:* plqpf. *ἐτετεύχειν:*—*to hit,* esp. *to hit* with an arrow, commonly joined with acc., when the object hit is alive, with gen. when it is lifeless. II. generally, *to hit, hit upon, light upon:* so of persons, *to meet by chance, fall in with,* c. gen. 2. of things, *to meet with, hit, reach, gain, get, obtain* a thing, also c. gen. 3. in aor. 2 part., ὁ *τυχών one who meets one by chance, the first one meets, any one whatever,* Lat. *quivis;* οἱ *τυχόντες every-day men, the ordinary run of men;* τὸ *τυχόν any chance thing.* 4. in bad sense, *βίας τυχεῖν to meet with, suffer* violence. III. absol. *to hit the mark, gain one's end* or *purpose;* *καλῶς τυχεῖν to fare* well, *succeed,* in speaking, *to hit the mark,* i. e. *to be right.* 2. generally, *to have the lot* or *fate.*

Intr. *to happen, to be* at a place 2. of things, *come to pass, fall out, occur by chance;* often impers., ὅπως *ἐτύγχανεν, ὥσπερ ἔτυχεν,* etc., *as it chanced, by mere accident.* 3. of events or undertakings, *to happen to, befal* one, *come to* one's *lot* or *share,* c. dat. pers.: esp. *to fall out well, come to a good end, succeed.* II. in Att. *τυγχάνω* was used almost as an auxiliary Verb, and was esp. joined with the participles of other Verbs, *τυγχάνω ἔχων* I *happen* to have, i. e. I have in possession; *παρὼν ἐτύγχανον* I *chanced* to be by; *ἔτυχε κατὰ τοῦτο καιροῦ ἐλθών* he *happened* to come at that nick of time; but, *τυγχάνω ὤν* = *εἰμί,* I am; so also without any part., *εἴ σοι χαρτὰ τυγχάνει τάδε* if these things *are* pleasant to thee. 2. in such phrases as *ὅτι ἂν τύχωσι, τοῦτο λέγουσι,* we must supply a part. from the other Verb, *ὅτι ἂν τύχωσι λέγοντες, τοῦτο λέγουσιν,* etc.

Τῡδεύς, έως, Ep. έος, ὁ, *Tydeus.*

τυῖδε, Adv. Dor. for *τῇδε, here.*

τῠκίζω, f. ίσω, (τύκος) *to work stones with a chisel* or *pick, to dress stones.* Hence

ΤΥ'ΚΗ, ή, (τέτυγμαι) *mason's work.* [τῠ]

τύκισμα, ατος, τό, *a working* or *dressing of stones:* in plur., *κανόνων τυκίσματα walls of stone worked square* by rule. [ῠ]

τύκος, ὁ, (τέτυγμαι) *a tool to dress stones with, a mason's hammer* or *pick.* II. *a battle-axe, pole-axe.* [τῠ]

τυκτά, a Persian word, which Herodotus explains by *τέλειον δεῖπνον βασιλήιον.*

τυκτός, ά, όν, verb. Adj. of *τεύχω* (τέτυγμαι), *made, made ready:* esp. *made by art, artificial,* as opp. to natural: *τυκτὴ κρήνη* a fountain *made by man's hand:* esp. *well-made, well-wrought, finished carefully.*

ΤΥ'ΛΗ, ή, like *τύλος, any swelling* or *lump:* esp., I. *a place worn hard by rubbing,* Lat. *callus: the shoulder.* II. *a pad for carrying burdens on, a porter's knot.* III. *a cushion.* [ῠ in Att., ῡ later.]

τύλος, ὁ, = *τύλη, a knot* or *callus;* esp. on the hands, as from rowing, etc. II. *anything rising like a lump, a knob, knot;* esp. *a wooden nail* or *bolt* used in ship-building. [ῠ]

τῠλόω, freq. used in pf. part. *τετυλωμένος:* (τύλος):—*to make hard* or *callous:*—Pass. *to grow hard* or *callous from rubbing,* as the hand from rowing or digging; *ῥόπαλα σιδήρῳ τετυλωμένα* clubs *knobbed* or *knotted with iron:* cf. *τυλωτός.*

τῠλωτός, ή, όν, verb. Adj. of *τυλόω;* *ῥόπαλα τυλωτά* clubs *knobbed* with iron, like *τετυλωμένα.*

τύμβευμα, ατος, τό, (τυμβεύω) *a burial, grave.* II. *the corpse to be burnt* or *buried.*

τυμβεύω, f. σω, (τύμβος) *to bury, burn* or *entomb* a corpse. 2. *χοὰς τυμβεῦσαί τινι* to pour libations *as an offering on one's grave.* II. intr. *to be entombed.*

τυμβ-ήρης, ες, (τύμβος, ἀρᾰρεῖν) *buried, entombed, interred, sepulchred.* II. *like a grave* or *tomb.*

τυμβίτης [ῑ], ου, ὁ, fem. *τυμβῖτις,* ιδος, (τύμβος) *in* or *at the grave.*

τυμβο-γέρων, οντος, ὁ, (τύμβος, γέρων) *an old man on the verge of the grave.*

τυμβ-ολέτης, ου, ὁ, (τύμβος, ὄλλυμι) *a destroyer of tombs:* fem. *τυμβόλετις,* ιδος.

ΤΥ'ΜΒΟΣ, ὁ, *the place where a dead body is burnt,* Lat. *bustum:* commonly, *a mound of earth heaped over the ashes, a cairn, barrow,* Lat. *tumulus:* generally, *a tomb, grave.* II. metaph., *γέρων τύμβος,* = *τυμβογέρων, a decrepit old man:* so also *τύμβος,* absol.

τυμβ-οῦχος, ον, (τύμβος, ἔχω) *dwelling in a tomb, sepulchral.*

τυμβο-φόνος, ον, (τύμβος, *φένω) *tomb-destroying.*

τυμβοχοέω, f. ήσω, (τυμβοχόος) *to throw up a cairn* or *barrow: to raise a mound over a grave.* Hence

τυμβοχοή, *a throwing up a cairn* or *barrow.*

τυμβο-χόος, ον, (τύμβος, χέω) *throwing up a cairn* or *barrow.* II. pass. *thrown* or *poured upon the tomb.*

τυμβό-χωστος, ον, (τύμβος, χώννυμι) *heaped up into a cairn* or *barrow.*

τυμβωρυχέω, f. ήσω, *to break open graves.* From

τυμβ-ωρύχος, ον, (τύμβος, ὀρύσσω) *digging up, breaking open graves:* as Subst., τυμβώρυχος, ὁ, *a grave-robber.* [ρῡ]

τύμμα, ατος, τό, (τύπτω) *a blow, stroke, wound.*

τυμπᾰνίζω, f. ίσω, (τύμπανον) *to beat a drum.* II. generally, *to beat with a stick, bastinado.*

τυμπᾰνισμός, ὁ, (τυμπανίζω) *a beating of drums,* as the Galli did in the worship of Cybelé.

τυμπᾰνιστής, οῦ, ὁ, (τυμπανίζω) *one who beats the τύμπανον, a drummer:* fem. *τυμπανίστρια*, of a priestess of Cybelé.

τύμπᾰνον, τό, (properly for *τύπανον*, from *τυπεῖν*) *a kettle-drum,* such as was used in the worship of Cybelé. II. *a drum-stick:* generally, *a staff, cudgel.* III. in Lat., *tympana* were *wagon-wheels made of a solid piece of wood, rollers.*

Τυνδάρειος, α, ον, or ος, ον, *of Tyndarus.* From

Τυνδάρεος Att. **Τυνδάρεως**, εω, ὁ, *Tyndarĕus, Tyndarus,* husband of Leda.

Τυνδαρίδης [ῐ], ου, ὁ, (formed as if from Τύνδαρος) *son of Tyndarus:* Τυνδαρίδαι, οἱ, *Castor and Pollux:* fem. **Τυνδαρίς**, ίδος, *daughter of Tyndarus.*

τύνη, Ep. and Dor. for τύ, σύ, as ἐγώνη for ἐγώ.

τυννός, ή, όν, akin to *τυτθός*, *so small, so little.* Hence

τυννοῦτος, ον, Att. **τυννουτοσί**, -*ονί*, *so small, so little,* Lat. *tantillus.*

τυντλάζω, *to dabble in the mud* or *mire:* esp. *to grub round the roots* of a vine. From

ΤΥ'ΝΤΛΟΣ, ὁ, *mud, mire, dirt.*

τύπᾰνον, τό, (τύπτω) orig. form of *τύμπανον*, preserved also in Latin *typanum.*

τῠπείην, ης, η, aor. 2 pass. opt. of *τύπτω.*

τῠπεῖν, aor. 2 inf. of *τύπτω.*

τῠπείς, εῖσα, έν, aor. 2 part. pass. of *τύπ*

τῠπή, ή, (τύπτω) *a blow, wound.*

τῠπῆναι, aor. 2 inf. pass. of *τύπτω.*

ΤΥ'ΠΟΣ, ὁ, *a blow.* II. *the mark of a blow, the impress* of a seal, *the stamp* of a coin, *a print, mark* of any kind; *τύποι στίβου the prints* or *tracks of* footsteps 2. *figures* or *impressions wrought in metal* or *stone:* simply, *a figure, image, statue* of a man. 3. *an outline, sketch, draught; τύπῳ λέγειν* to describe in *outline* 4. *the original pattern, model, mould, type:* metaph. *a type, figure.* 5. *a system, form of doctrine.* III. *the effect produced on the ear by a blow,* as *the beat* of horses' feet. Hence

τῠπόω, f. ώσω, *to impress, stamp.* II. *to form, mould, model.*

τυπτήσω, Att. fut. of *τύπτω.*

τύπτοντι, Dor. for *τύπτουσι.*

ΤΥ'ΠΤΩ, fut. *τύψω* or *τυπτήσω*: aor. 1 *ἔτυψα*: aor. 2 *ἔτῠπον*: Pass., fut. *τῠπήσομαι*: aor. 1 *ἐτύφθην*: aor. 2 *ἐτύπην* [ῠ]: pf. *τέτυμμαι*:—*to beat, strike, smite, knock:* metaph. *to strike* or *smite at heart; ἄχος ὀξὺ κατὰ φρένα τύψε* sharp grief *smote* him to the heart; *ἡ ἀληθηίη ἔτυψε Καμβύσεα* the truth of it *struck* Cambyses: later of bees, etc., *to sting.* In Homer *τύπτω* is chiefly used of *a blow struck hand to hand,* as opp. to *βάλλω*, which implies *a blow from a missile.* 2. *ἅλα τύπτειν ἐρετμοῖς to beat* the sea with oars, i. e. to row: absol., *Ζέφυρος λαίλαπι τύπτων* the west wind *beating, lashing* with fury. II. Med. *to beat* or *strike oneself;* esp. like *κόπτομαι*, Lat. *plangor, to beat one's breast* for grief:—c. acc. pers., *τύπτεσθαί τινα to mourn for* a person. III. Pass. *to be beaten, struck* or *wounded;* c. acc. cognato, *τύπτομαι πολλάς* (sc. *πληγάς*) *I get* many blows.

τύπωμα, ατος, τό, (τῠπόω) *that which is formed, fashioned, modelled: a vessel wrought; τύπωμα χαλκόπλευρον a* brazen *urn: a figure, outline.*

τῠραννεύω, f. εύσω and **τυραννέω**, f. ήσω: fut. med. *τυραννήσομαι* in pass. sense: (τύραννος):—*to be a τύραννος* or *absolute sovereign: to rule absolutely:* c. gen. *to be ruler of* a people or place; *τυραννεύειν Ἀθηνῶν to be tyrant* of Athens:—the aor. 1 *τυραννεῦσαι* means *to have acquired a tyranny, to have made oneself tyrant.* II. Pass. *τυραννεύομαι* or -*έομαι*, *to be ruled by τύραννοι, to be governed with absolute power.*

τῠραννικός, ή, όν, (τύραννος) *of* or *fit for an absolute prince, royal, imperial: befitting a tyrant, lordly, imperious.* Sup. *τυραννικώτατος.*

τῠραννίς, ίδος, ή, vocat. *τυραννί*: (τύραννος):—*the rule of an absolute prince, absolute power* or *sway, sovereignty, royalty.*

τύραννος [ῠ], ὁ also ή, properly Dor. for *κοίρανος* (from *κῦρος, κύριος*) *a lord* and *master;* hence *an absolute sovereign,* unlimited by law or constitution: it was applied to *anyone who had made himself king by force;* not to hereditary monarchs, as (for instance) not to the kings of Sparta, nor to the king of Persia; and it did not necessarily imply cruel or overbearing conduct: later however the term was used as our *tyrant* or *despot;* and in poets it was taken loosely for *a king.* 2. in a wider sense, *the whole family of a τύραννος*:—hence also, *ἡ τύραννος* was *the queen, princess;* as *ὁ τύραννος* was *the king's son, prince.* II. *τύραννος, ον,* as Adj., like *τυραννικός, princely, lordly: imperious, despotic; τύραννον δῶμα the king's* palace.

τῠραννο-φόνος, ον, (τύραννος, *φένω) *slaying tyrants.*

τυρβάζω f. άσω, *to trouble, confuse, stir up,* Lat. *turbare*:—Pass. *to be in disorder, be jumbled* or *crowded together.* From

ΤΥ'ΡΒΗ, ή, *disorder, throng, bustle,* Lat. *turba.*

τύρευμα, ατος, τό, (τυρεύω) *that which is curdled, cheese.* [ῡ]

τῡρευτήρ, ῆρος, ὁ, and **τῡρευτής** οῦ, ὁ, (τυρεύω) *one who makes cheese;* said of Hermes as god of goat-herds and goats-milk cheese.

τῡρεύω, f. εύσω, and **τῡρέω**, f. ήσω: (τυρός):—*to make cheese.* II. metaph. *to stir up, jumble, confound.* 2. *to concoct, brew* a thing *cunningly.*

Τύριος, α, ον, *of* or *from Tyre: a Tyrian.* [ῠ]

τῡρίσδω Dor. for συρίζω.

τῡρόεις, εσσα, εν contr. **τῡροῦς**, οῦσσα, οῦν, (τυρός) *like cheese:* as Subst., τυροῦς Dor. τυρῶς, ὁ, *cheese-bread, a cheese-cake* or *cheese.*

τῡρό-κνηστις, ἡ, (τυρός, κνάω) *a cheese-grater.*

τῡρό-νωτος, ον, (τυρός, νῶτος) *with a layer of cheese, spread with cheese.*

τῡροπωλέω, f. ήσω, *to sell cheese, sell like cheese.* From

τῡρο-πώλης, ου, ὁ, (τυρός, πωλέω) *a cheesemonger.*

ΤΥ'ΡΟ'Σ, οῦ, ὁ, *cheese.* II. *the cheese-market.*

Τύρος, ὁ, *Tyre*, an ancient city of Phoenicia. [ῠ]

τυροῦς, contr. for τυρόεις.

τῡρο-φόρος, ον, (τυρός, φέρω) *bearing cheese, spread with cheese.*

Τυρρην-ολέτης, ου, ὁ, (Τυρρηνός, ὄλλυμι) *destroyer of Tyrrhenians.*

Τυρρηνός Ion. and old Att. **Τυρσηνός**, ή, όν, *Tyrrhenian, Etruscan:* Τυρσηνοί or Τυρρηνοί *the Etruscans:*—Adj. **Τυρσηνικός**, ή, όν, *Etruscan.*

ΤΥ'ΡΣΙΣ, ἡ, gen. ιος: acc. τύρσιν: nom. pl. τύρσεις, gen. έων, dat. εσι, Lat. *TURRIS:—a tower: a tower on a wall, a bastion.*

τυρῶς, ῶντος, Dor. for τυροῦς.

ΤΥΤΘΟ'Σ, όν, also ή, όν, *little, small, young*, of children. II. neut. τυτθόν as Adv., *a little, a wee bit:* hence *scarcely, hardly:* of the voice, *low, softly, gently.* 2. also in pl., τυτθὰ διατμῆξαι to cut into *small pieces.*

Τῠφάων, ονος, ὁ, poët. Ep. lengthd. form for Τυφῶν: hence, Τυφαόνιος, α, ον, poët. for Τυφώνιος.

τῡφεδᾰνός, ὁ, (τύφω) *one with clouded wits. a stupid fellow, a dullard.*

τυφ-ήρης, ες, (τῦφος, ἀρᾰρεῖν) *set on fire, burning.*

τυφλό-πους, -ποδος, ὁ, ἡ, (τυφλός, πούς) *with blind foot, stepping in blindness.*

τυφλός, ή, όν, *blind*, Lat. *caecus:* c. gen., τυφλός τινος *blind to* a thing. 2. metaph., τυφλὸς τά τ' ὦτα τόν τε νοῦν τά τ' ὄμματα *blind* in ears and mind and eyes. 3. of things, *dark, unseen, dim, obscure;* τυφλαὶ σπιλάδες *blind*, i. e. sunken, rocks.

τυφλόω, (τυφλός) *to blind, make blind:*—Pass. *to be blinded* or *blind.* II. metaph. *to blind, dull, baffle, dim.* Hence

τυφλῶς, Adv. of τυφλός, *blindly.*

τύφλωσις, ἡ, *a making blind, blinding.*

τυφλώττω, (τυφλός) *to be blind.*

τῡφο-γέρων, οντος, ὁ, (τύφω, γέρων) *a silly old man, a dotard;* cf. τυμβογέρων.

τῦφος, ὁ, (τύφω) *smoke, mist, cloud.* II. metaph. *conceit, vanity*, Lat. *fucus.*

τῡφόω, f. ώσω, (τῦφος) *to wrap in smoke* or *mist:* metaph. *to make dull* or *senseless, dim, obscure:* pf. pass. τετύφωμαι, *to be shrouded in conceit and folly, to be silly, stupid, absurd.*

ΤΥ'ΦΩ [ῡ], f. θύψω: aor. 1 ἔθυψα: Pass., aor. 2 ἐτύφην [ῠ]: pf. τέθυμμαι:—*to raise a smoke;* c. acc. cognato, καπνὸν τύφειν *to make a cloud* of smoke. II. *to smoke;* καπνῷ τύφειν μελίσσας *to smoke* bees, and metaph., καπνῷ τύφειν πόλιν *to fill* the town *with smoke.* III. *to consume in smoke, burn with fire and smoke:*—Pass. *to smoke, smoulder.*

Τῡφωεύς, έως, Ep. έος, ὁ: contr. **Τῡφώς**, ῶ:—*Typhöeus, Typhos*, a giant buried by Jove in Cilicia: cf. τυφώς.

Τῡφῶν, ῶνος, Ep. **Τῡφάων**, αονος, ὁ, *Typhon, Typhaon*, the same giant who is more freq. called Τυφώς, Τυφωεύς. II. as storms were ascribed to the agency of giants, the name came to mean *a furious storm, hurricane, typhoon.* Hence

Τῡφωνικός, ή, όν, *of* or *from Typhon.* II. *stormy, tempestuous.*

Τῡφώς, ὁ, contr. for Τῡφωεύς. II. as appellat., τυφώς, gen. τυφῶ, dat. τυφῷ, acc. τυφῶ:—like τυφών II, *a furious storm, hurricane.*

τύχε, Ep. for ἔτῠχε, 3 sing. aor. 2 of τυγχάνω.

τῠχεῖν, aor. 2 inf. of τυγχάνω.

ΤΥ'ΧΗ [ῠ], ἡ, *what man obtains* (τυγχάνει) *from the gods, good fortune, luck*, Lat. *fortuna;* κοινὸν τύχη *luck* is a thing common to all; τύχᾳ θεῶν, σὺν θεοῦ τύχᾳ *by luck* from the gods; esp. in phrase, θείᾳ τύχῃ by divine *providence;* later, Τύχη was deified, like Lat. *Fortuna*, by the name of Τύχη Σώτειρα or Σωτήρ. 2. generally, *chance, fortune, good* or *bad, good luck* or *ill luck;* often with an Adj. to shew which; e. g. τύχῃ ἀγαθῇ was often used in public acts, by crasis τὐχἀγαθῇ, also ἐπ' ἀγαθῇ τύχῃ and μετ' ἀγαθῆς τύχης, like Lat. *quod felix faustumque sit.* 3. Adverbial usages, τύχῃ *by chance*, Lat. *forte, forte, fortuna:*—so also ἀπό or ἐκ τύχης, κατὰ τύχην. II. *a chance, hap, lot, accident:* in plur., τύχαι ὑμέτεραι your *fortunes.* Hence

τῠχηρός, ά, όν, *fortunate, lucky.* 2. *by chance, accidental.* Hence

τῠχηρῶς, Adv. *luckily.*

τῠχήσας, aor. 1 part. of τυγχάνω.

τυχθείς, aor. 1 pass. part. of τεύχω.

τύχοιμι [ῠ], aor. 2 opt. of τυγχάνω.

τῠχόν, Adv., *by chance, perhaps;* properly acc. neut. of the aor. 2 part. of τυγχάνω.

τῠχών, οῦσα, όν, aor. 2 part. of τυγχάνω.

τύψασκον, Ion. aor. 1 of τύπτω.

τῷ, dat. sing. of neut. τό, used absol., *therefore, so, in this wise.* II. for τίνι, dat. sing. of τίς; *quis?*

τῳ, enclit. for τινί, dat. sing. of τὶς, *aliquis.*

τὤγαλμα, ατος, Ion. crasis for τὸ ἄγαλμα.

τῷδε, dat. of ὅδε, used as Adv., = οὕτως, *in this manner, thus.*

ΤΩΘΑ'ΖΩ Dor. **τωθάσδω**: fut. -άσομαι: aor. 1

ἐτώθασα, subj. τωθάσω:—*to mock* or *scoff at, jeer, flout.*

τωθάσδοισαι, Dor. pres. part. fem. of τωθάζω.

τὠληθές, Ion. crasis for τὸ ἀληθές

τὠποβαῖνον, Ion. crasis for τὸ ἀποβαῖνον.

τὠρχαῖον, Ion. crasis for τὸ ἀρχαῖον.

τώς, demonstr. Adv., answering to Interrog. πῶς; and to the Relat. ὥς, = ὥς, οὕτως. so, *in this wis* II. Dor. = οὗ, *where.*

τὠτρεκές, crasis for τὸ ἀτρεκές.

τωὐτό, gen. τωὐτοῦ, dat. τωὐτῷ, Ion. for **τὸ αὐτό, τοῦ αὐτοῦ, τῷ αὐτῷ.**

Υ

Υ, υ, ὖ ψιλόν, τό, indecl., twentieth letter of the Greek Alphabet: as a numeral υ′ = 400, but ͵υ = 400,000. The written character Υ is supposed to have also stood for the digamma, which was a consonant; hence *as a vowel* it was distinguished by the name of Υ ψιλόν.

The use of υ was most freq. with the Aeolians, being put by them for ο, as in ὄνυμα ὔμοιος μύγις for ὄνομα ὅμοιος μόγις. They often inserted υ after α and ε, as, θεύω χεύω for θέω χέω. The Aeol. sometimes changed the diphthong ου into οι, as Μοῖσα for Μοῦσα, λέγοισα for λέγουσα.

Ὑάδες, ων, αἱ, (ὕω) *the Hyades, the Rainers,* Lat. *Pluviae,* seven stars in the head of the bull, which threatened rain when they rose with the sun. [ῠ in Hom., ῡ in Eur.]

ὕαινᾰ, ἡ, (ὗς) a Libyan wild beast, *the hyena,* an animal of the dog kind, with a bristly *hog's* mane (whence the name).

Ὑᾰκίνθια (sub. ἱερά), τά, *the Hyacinthia,* a Lacedaemonian festival in honour of *Hyacinthus.*

ὑᾰκινθῐνο-βᾰφής, ές, (ὑακίνθινος, βαφῆναι) *dyed hyacinth colour.* [ῠ]

ὑᾰκίνθῐνος, η, ον, (ὑάκινθος) *hyacinthine, hyacinth-coloured.*

Ὑάκινθος, ὁ, *Hyacinthus,* a Laconian youth, beloved by Apollo, but killed by him by a cast of the discus. Hence

ὑάκινθος, ὁ or ἡ, *the hyacinth,* a flower said to have sprung from the blood of Hyacinthus, or acc. to others from that of Telamonian Ajax:, some pretended to decipher on the petals the initial letters of these names, ΥΑ or ΑΙ, or the interjection αἲ αἴ; hence it is called γραπτὰ ὑάκινθος, cf. Virg. Ecl. 3. 106. The older poets describe it as very dark, later authors make it lighter; so that several flowers seem to have been included under the name. II. ὑάκινθος, ἡ, *the jacinth* or perhaps *the sapphire,* a precious stone of blue colour.

ὑᾰλέος, α, ον, contr. **ὑαλοῦς,** ᾶ, οῦν, (ὕαλος) *of glass, like glass, glassy, transparent.*

ὑάλῐνος later **ὑέλινος,** η ον (ὕαλος) *of* or *made of glass, glass.*

ὑᾰλόεις, εσσα, εν, (ὕαλος) *of glass: like glass, glassy.*

ὕᾰλος or **ὕελος,** ἡ, *a clear, transparent stone,* of which the Egyptians made cases to enclose their mummies: *oriental alabaster:* also *crystal, amber,* etc. 2. *a convex lens of crystal,* used as a burning-glass, explained by Aristophanes as λίθος διαφανὴς ἀφ' ἧς τὸ πῦρ ἅπτουσι a transparent stone from which they light fire. II. *glass,* Lat. *vitrum;* glass itself seems to have existed in the time of Herodotus, but was not called ὕαλος till the time of Plato. (Egyptian word.)

ὑᾰλοῦς, ᾶ, οῦν, contr. for ὑαλέος.

ὑᾰλό-χροος, ον, contr. **-χρους,** ουν, (ὕαλος, χρόα) *glass-coloured.*

ὑᾰλο-χρώδης, ες, = ὑαλόχροος.

ὑβ-βάλλω, Ep. contr. for ὑποβάλλω.

ὙΒΟ'Σ, ή, όν, *bent outwards, bump-backed.*

ὑβρίζω: f. ὑβρίσω Att. -ιῶ: aor. 1 ὕβρισα: pf. ὕβρικα: plqpf. ὑβρίκειν. Med., fut. ὑβριοῦμαι: Pass., fut. ὑβρισθήσομαι: aor. 1 ὑβρίσθην: pf. ὕβρισμαι:—*to wax wanton, run riot,* Lat. *lascivire,* opp. to σωφρονεῖν to practise moderation; of over-fed horses, *to neigh, snort, prance,* etc.; of plants, *to run riot, grow over-rank.* II. with regard to others, *to treat despitefully, do despite to, to outrage, insult, affront, ill-treat;* in Att. more commonly, ὑβρίζειν εἴς τινα *to deal wantonly, commit outrages* towards one; ὑβρίζειν ἐπί τινα *to exult* over one: c. acc. cognato, ὑβρίζειν ὕβρεις *to commit* outrages; so, ὑβρίζειν ἀδικήματα *to do wanton* wrongs. 2. at Athens *to do* one *a personal outrage, to beat and insult, assault.* [υ naturally short, but long in the augmented tenses.]

ὝΒΡΙΣ [ῠ], εως Ep. ιος, ἡ, *wanton violence,* arising from the pride of strength, passion, etc., *riotousness, insolence, lewdness, licentiousness.* 2. of acts towards others, *a piece of wanton violence, despiteful treatment, an outrage, gross insult, assault and battery:*—at Athens, in law proceedings, ὕβρις meant *an aggravated personal assault,* the slighter kind being αἰκία [ῑ]; hence in the former case the injured person proceeded by γραφή or *prosecution;* in the latter by δίκη or *private suit* 3. *harm, detriment, damage, loss.* II. as mascul. Adj., ὕβρις ἀνήρ, = ὑβριστής.

ὑβρίσδω, Dor. for ὑβρίζω, 3 sing. ὑβρίσδει for ὑβρίζει.

ὕβρισμα, ατος, τό, (ὑβρίζω) *a wanton act, outrage, insult,* Lat. *contumelia.* II. *the object of insult.*

ὑβριστήρ, ῆρος, ὁ, poët. for ὑβριστής.

ὑβριστής, οῦ, ὁ, (ὑβρίζω) *one who is violent and overbearing, a wanton insolent man, a licentious ungovernable man.* II. as masc. Adj. *unbridled, ungovernable:* of beasts, *tameless, savage.* Hence

ὑβριστικός, ή, όν, *given to wantonness* or *insolence, outrageous:* τὸ ὑβριστικόν *an insolent disposition.* Adv. -κῶς, *insolently.*

ὕβριστος, η, ον, (ὕβρις) *insulting, insolent:* Comp. and Sup., ὑβριστότερος, -τατος.

ὑγιάζω, f. σω: aor. 1 ὑγίασα (ὑγιής) *to make sound* or *healthy, to heal.*

ὑγιαίνω, f. ᾰνῶ: aor. 1 ὑγίᾱνα: (ὑγιής):—*to be sound, healthy*, Lat. *bene valere: to be in a certain state of health*, Lat. *valere.* 2. metaph. *to be sound of mind:* also *to be staunch, true, trustworthy;* τὸ ὑγιαῖνον τῆς Ἑλλάδος *the sound part* of Greece. 3. ὑγίαινε, like χαῖρε, a common form of taking leave, *farewell*, Lat. *vale.* [ῠ, but ῡ in augmented tenses.]

ὑγίειᾰ Ion. -είη, ἡ, and sometimes in Att. ὑγιείᾱ: (ὑγιής):—*health, soundness* of body, Lat. *salus;* ὑγίεια φρενῶν *soundness* of mind. [ῠ]

ὑγιεινός, ή, όν, (ὑγιής) *wholesome, sound, healthy, healthful:* of food, *wholesome.* II. of persons, *sound, healthy, stout*, Lat. *sanus.* [ῠ] Hence

ὑγιεινῶς, Adv. *healthily:*—Comp. ὑγιεινοτέρως and -ρον; Sup. -ότατα.

ὑγίεις, εσσα, εν, Boeot. for ὑγιής: acc. masc. ὑγίεντα. [ῠ]

ὑγιηρός, ά, όν, (ὑγιής) *good for the health, wholesome, hearty, strong*, Lat. *sanus:*—Sup. ὑγιηρότατος.

ὑγιής, ές, gen. έος: acc. ὑγιᾶ or -ιῆ Ion. -έα: plur. nom. neut. ὑγιᾶ or -ιῆ:—*sound, healthy, hearty, stout*, Lat. *sanus;* σῶς καὶ ὑγιής *safe* and *sound.* II. *sound in mind, sound-minded:* metaph. of advice, *sound, wholesome, wise;* οὐδὲν ὑγιὲς προφέρειν to make no one *sound* proposal:—Comp. and Sup. ὑγιέστερος, -έστατος. [ῠ]

ὑγραίνω, f. ᾰνῶ, (ὑγρός) *to wet, moisten:* of a river, *to water* a country.

ὑγρο-βόλος, ον, (ὑγρὸς, βαλεῖν) *wetting, moistening.*

ὑγρο-μελής, ές, (ὑγρός, μέλος) *with pliant limbs.*

ὑγροπορέω, f. ήσω, *to traverse water.* From

ὑγρο-πόρος, ον, (ὑγρός, πόρος) *traversing water.*

ὑγρός, ά, όν, (ὕω, ὕδωρ) *wet, moist, liquid*, Lat. *liquidus*, opp. to ξηρός (*siccus*); ὑγρὸν ἔλαιον *liquid* oil, as opp. to fat; ἄνεμοι ὑγρὸν-ἀέντες winds blowing *moist* or *rainy:* ἡ ὑγρά Ion. ὑγρή, *the moist, the sea*, opp. to χέρσος the dry land; so, ὑγρὰ κέλευθα, or ὑγρά alone, *the watery* ways: τὸ ὑγρόν and τὰ ὑγρά, *wet, wetness, moisture, water, liquor:* θῆρες ὑγροί *water* animals. II. *soft, pliant, supple, lithe, waving*, Lat. *mollis;* κέρας ὑγρόν a *pliant* bow: metaph. of the mind, *pliant, facile, easy.* 2. *slack, languid, faint.* III. of the eyes, *swimming, melting, languishing;* ὑγρὸς πόθος *languishing* desire; neut. pl. as Adv., ὑγρὰ δεδορκώς with *languishing glances.* Hence

ὑγρότης, ητος, ἡ, (ὑγρός) *wetness, moisture.* II. generally, *softness, pliancy, suppleness:* metaph. *pliancy of mind, softness* or *easiness* of temper. 2. *feebleness.*

ὑγρό-φθογγος, ον, (ὑγρός, φθόγγος) of liquid poured from a bottle, *making a gurgling sound.*

ὑγρῶς, Adv. of ὑγρός, *in liquid fashion: softly, pliably.*

ὑγρώσσω, poët. for ὑγραίνω, *to be wet* or *moist.*

ὑδᾰρής, ές, gen. έος, (ὕδωρ) *watery, washy:* metaph. *unstable as water, unstable, wavering.*

ὑδάτῐνος, η, ον also ος, ον, (ὕδωρ) *of water, watery: wet, moist.* II. *transparent as water*, of thin garments II. like ὑγρός, *pliant, supple, flexible.*

ὑδάτιον, τό, Dim. of ὕδωρ, *a small stream, rivulet.*

ὑδᾰτόεις, εσσα, εν, (ὕδωρ) *watery, like water.*

ὑδᾰτοποσία, ἡ, *water-drinking.* And

ὑδᾰτοποτέω, f. ήσω, *to drink water.* From

ὑδᾰτο-πότης, ου, ὁ, (ὕδωρ, πίνω) *a water-drinker*, Lat. *aquae potor.*

ὕδᾰτος, gen. of ὕδωρ.

ὑδᾰτο-τρεφής, ές, (ὕδωρ, τρέφω) *bred in water, growing in* or *by the water.*

ὑδᾰτ-ώδης, ες, (ὕδωρ, εἶδος) *like water: watery, wet, sloppy.*

ὕδερος, ὁ, (ὕδωρ) *the dropsy.*

ὕδνης, ου, ὁ, ἡ, (ὕω) *watered, nourished.*

ὕδρα, ἡ, (ὕδωρ) like ὕδρος, *a water-serpent*, Lat. *hydra.*

ὑδραίνω, (ὕδωρ) *to water, to sprinkle* or *bedew with water:*—Med. *to wash oneself, to bathe;* λουτρὰ ὑδράνασθαι χροΐ *to pour* water *over one's body.*

ὑδρεία, ἡ, (ὑδρεύω) *a drawing water, fetching water.* II. *a watering place.*

ὑδρεῖον Ion. -ήιον, τό, (ὑδρεύω) *a water-bucket, well-bucket.*

ὑδρεύω, f. σω, (ὕδωρ) *to draw, fetch* or *carry water:*—Med. *to draw water for oneself, get water.*

ὑδρήιον, τό, Ion. for ὑδρεῖον.

ὑδρηλός, ή, όν, (ὕδωρ) *watery, moist, wet, damp.*

ὑδρηναμένη, aor. 1 med. part. fem. of ὑδραίνω.

ὑδρία, ἡ, (ὕδωρ) *a water-pot, bucket, pitcher.* II. *a vessel* of any kind, *a balloting urn, a funereal urn.*

ὑδριάς, άδος, ἡ, (ὕδωρ) *of* or *from the water.*

ὑδριᾱ-φόρος, ον, (ὑδρία, φέρω) *carrying a water-vessel.*

ὑδρο-ειδής, ές, (ὕδωρ, εἶδος) *like water, watery.*

ὑδρόεις, εσσα, εν, (ὕδωρ) *watery.*

ὑδροποσία, ἡ, *water-drinking;* and

ὑδροποτέω, f. ήσω, *to drink water.* From

ὑδρο-πότης, ου, ὁ, (ὕδωρ, πίνω) *a water-drinker, a drinker of thin potations;* hence, in Comic phrase, for *a thin-blooded fellow*, Horace's *aquae potor.*

ὑδρορ-ρόα or -ρόη, ἡ, (ὕδωρ, ῥοή) *a water-course, a conduit, canal, sluice, gutter.*

ὕδρος, ὁ, (ὕδωρ) like ὕδρα, *a water-serpent.*

ὑδροφορέω, *to carry water.* From

ὑδρο-φόρος, ον, (ὕδωρ, φέρω) *carrying water:*—as Subst., ὑδροφόρος, ὁ or ἡ, *a water-carrier.*

ὑδρο-χόος, ὁ, (ὕδωρ, χέω) *the water-pourer*, the constellation *Aquarius:* Ep. dat. ὑδροχοῆι, as if from ὑδροχοεύς.

ὑδρό-χῠτος, ον, (ὕδωρ, χέω) *gushing with water.*

ὑδρωπικός, ή, όν, (ὕδρωψ) *dropsical.*

ὕδρωψ, ωπος, also οπος, ὁ, (ὕδωρ) *dropsy.* II. *a dropsical person.*

ὕδωρ, τό, gen. ὕδατος: Ep. dat. ὕδει:—*water* of any kind; of *rivers*, ὕδατα Καφίσια *the waters* of

Cephisus; ὕδωρ πότιμον *fresh* water; ὕδωρ πλατύ *salt* water:—Proverb., γράφειν τι εἰς ὕδωρ to write *in water*. . *rain-water*, and then *rain*, also called ὕδωρ ἐξ οὐρανοῦ. 3. in Attic law-phrase, τὸ ὕδωρ was *the water of the water-clock* (κλεψύδρα), and also *the time it took in running out*; ἐπιλαβεῖν τὸ ὕδωρ to stop *the water* (which was done while the speech was interrupted by the calling of evidence, as only a certain time was allowed for the speech of the plaintiff or defendant). [ῠ]

ὑεικός, ή, όν, and **ὕειος**, α, ον, (ὗς) *of* or *belonging to a swine*. [ῠ]

ὑέλινος, ὑελίτης, Ion. forms of ὑαλ-.

ὕελος, v. sub ὕαλος.

ὕεσσι, dat. pl. of ὗς.

ὑέτιος, α, ον, and **ὑετόεις**, εσσα, εν, (ὑετός) *rainy, bringing* or *causing rain*.

ὑετός, ὁ, (ὕω) *rain*, Lat. *pluvia: a heavy shower, a storm of rain*, Lat. *nimbus*; whereas ὄμβρος, Lat. *imber*, is a lasting rain, and ψεκάς or ψακάς, a drizzling rain. II. as Adj. in Sup., ἄνεμοι ὑετώτατοι the *rainiest* winds.

ὑηνία, ή, *swinishness, hoggishness*. From

ὑηνός, ή, όν, (ὗς) *swinish, hoggish*.

ὑθλέω, f. ήσω, (ὕθλος) *to talk nonsense, drivel, trifle*, Lat. *nugari*.

ὝΘΛΟΣ, ὁ, *idle talk, nonsense*, Lat. *nugae*.

υἷα, υἷας, Ep. acc. sing. and pl. of υἱός, as if from υἶς.

υἱάσι, poët. dat. pl. of υἱός. [ᾰ]

υἱδεύς, έως, ὁ, (υἱός) *a son's son, grandson*: fem. **υἱδῆ**, *a son's daughter, granddaughter*.

υἱδιον, τό, Dim. of υἱός, *a little son*. II. Dim. of ὗς, *a little pig*.

υἱδοῦς, οῦ, ὁ, (υἱός) *a son's son, grandson*.

υἱϊ, Ep. dat. of υἱός.

ὑϊκός, ή, όν, (ὗς) *of* or *fit for swine, like a swine, swinish, hoggish*.

υἱο-θεσία, ή, (υἱος, τίθημι) *adoption as a son*.

υἷος, Ep. gen. of υἱός, as if from υἷς

ΥἹΌΣ, ὁ, declined regul. υἱοῦ, υἱῷ, υἱόν, etc.: but it is also declined as if from nom. *υἱεύς,—gen. υἱέος, dat. υἱέϊ, υἱεῖ, acc. υἱέα; Dual. υἱέε, υἱέοιν; Plur. υἱέες or υἱεῖς, gen. υἱέων, υἱῶν, dat. υἱέσιν, acc. υἱέας, υἱεῖς:—there is also an Ep. declension, as if from nom. υἶς,—gen. υἷος, dat. υἱϊ, acc. υἷα; Dual. υἷε; Plur. υἷες, dat. υἱάσι, acc. υἷας:—Lat. *FILIUS, a son*; υἱὸν ποιεῖσθαί or τίθεσθαί τινι to adopt as *son*. 2. later, the plur. was often periphr., ἰατρῶν υἱεῖς, ῥητόρων υἱεῖς *sons* of physicians, *sons* of orators, i. e. physicians, orators themselves; so in Homer, υἷες Ἀχαιῶν for Ἀχαιοί.

υἷος, Ep. gen. of υἱός, as if from *υἷς.

υἱωνός, οῦ, ὁ, (υἱός) *a child's child, a grandson*.

ὕλαγμα, ατος, τό, (ὑλάω) *the bark of a dog, a bark, howl, yelp*: metaph. in plur. *snarling words*. [ῠ]

ὑλαγμός, ὁ, (ὑλάω) *a barking, baying*. [ῠ]

ὑλᾰγωγέω [ῡ], f. ήσω, *to carry wood*. From

ὑλ-ᾰγωγός, όν, (ὕλη, ἄγω) *carrying wood*. [ῡ]

ὑλάεις, Dor. for ὑλήεις.

ὑλαῖος, α, ον, (ὕλη) *woody, belonging to wood* or *to a wood, of the wood* or *forest*. [ῡ]

ὑλᾰκή, ή, (ὑλάω) *a barking, howling*. [ῠ]

ὑλᾰκό-μωρος, ον, (ὑλακή) *ever barking, howling* or *yelling*. Ep. word, formed like ἐγχεσίμωρος, ἰόμωρος.

ὑλακτέω, f. ήσω, (ὑλάω) *to bark, bay, howl*, Lat. *latrare*; metaph. of a hungry stomach, *to cry out, yelp, bark*: also, ἄμουσα ὑλακτεῖ he *howls* his uncouth songs. II. transit. *to bark* or *yelp at*, Lat. *allatrare*. Hence

ὑλακτητής, οῦ, ὁ, *a barker, bawler*. [ῠ]

ὑλακτικός, ή, όν, (ὑλακτέω) *yelping*.

ὑλᾶς, gen. ᾶντος, contr. for ὑλάεις, –ήεις.

ὑλάσκω, = ὑλακτέω.

ὙΛΑ'Ω [ῠ], radic. form of ὑλακτέω, only used in pres. and impf., *to bark, bay*:—3 pl. impf. med. ὑλάοντο in same sense. II. transit. *to bark* or *bay at*.

ὝΛΗ [ῡ], ή, Lat. *SYLVA, wood, a wood, forest, woodland*, as opp. to δένδρα (fruit-trees): also of *copse, brushwood, underwood*, as opp. to timber-trees. II. *wood cut down, timber, firewood, fuel, logs of wood*. III. generally, like Lat. *materia, the stuff* of which a thing is made; *the raw material of any kind*: hence metaph. *the matter treated of, subject-matter*, Lat. *sylva*. 2. *matter*, as opp. to mind, Lat. *sylva*.

ὑλήεις, εσσα or –εις, εν, (ὕλη) *woody, wooded*.

ὑλη-κοίτης, ου, ὁ, (ὕλη, κοίτη) *one who lodges* or *makes his lair in the wood*. [ῡ]

ὑλη-τόμος Dor. ὑλᾱτ–, ον, = ὑλοτόμος.

ὑλη-φόρος, ον, = ὑλοφόρος.

ὑλη-ωρός, όν, (ὕλη, οὖρος) *watching the wood, forest-ranging*. [ῡ]

ὑλο-δρόμος, ον, (ὕλη, δραμεῖν) *wood-ranging*.

ὑλό-κομος, ον, (ὕλη, κόμη) *overgrown with wood*.

ὑλο-νόμος, ον, (ὕλη, νέμομαι) *haunting the woods*.

ὑλοτομέω, f. ήσω, *to cut* or *fell wood*. From

ὑλο-τόμος, ον, (ὕλη, τεμεῖν) *cutting* or *felling wood*:—as Subst., ὑλοτόμος, ὁ, *a woodcutter, woodman*. II. proparox. ὑλότομος, ον, pass. *cut in the wood*:—as Subst., ὑλότομον, τό, *a plant cut in the wood*, used as a charm. [ῡ]

ὑλ-ουργός, όν, (ὕλη, *ἔργω) *working wood*:—as Subs., ὑλουργός, ὁ, *a carpenter* or *woodman*. [ῡ]

ὑλο-φάγος, ον, (ὕλη, φᾰγεῖν) *feeding in the woods*.

ὑλο-φορβός, όν, (ὕλη, φέρβω) *feeding in the woods*.

ὑλο-φόρος, ον, (ὕλη, φέρω) *carrying wood*.

ὑλ-ώδης, ες, (ὕλη, εἶδος) *woody, wooded, bushy*.

ὑμεῖς [ῡ], old Aeol., Dor., and Ep. **ὕμμες** Ion. **ὑμέες** Dor. **ὑμές**: gen. ὑμῶν Ion. ὑμέων, Ep. also ὑμείων: dat. ὑμῖν, old Aeol. ὔμμι, ὔμμιν: but ὑμὶν [–◡] or ὕμιν, only in Trag.: also ὑμᾶς Ion. ὑμέας: Aeol. ὔμμε Dor. ὑμέ, in Trag. also ὑμάς [–◡] or ὕμας. —Pron. of 2nd pers. plur. of σύ *ye, you*.

ὑμέναιος [ῡ], ὁ, (Ὑμήν) *hymenaeus, a wedding-song*, sung by the bride's attendants as they led her to the bridegroom's house. II. later, = Ὑμήν, *Hymen*, the god of marriage, addressed in the wedding-songs as Ὑμὴν ὦ Ὑμέναιε Dor. Ὑμὰν ὦ Ὑμέναιε, Lat. *Hymen o Hymenaee.* Hence

ὑμεναιόω, f. ώσω, *to sing the wedding-song.* II. *to take to wife.* [ῠ]

ὑμένιος, ὁ, (Ὑμήν) epith. of Bacchus as god of joy.

ὑμενό-πτερος, ον, (ὑμήν, πτέρον) *with wings of skin, membrane-winged*, of the bat. [ῡ]

ὑμεν-όστρᾰκος, ον, (ὑμήν, ὄστρακον) *made of earthenware as thin as a membrane.* [ῡ]

ὑμές, Dor. for ὑμεῖς.

ὑμέτερος, α, ον, (ὑμεῖς) *your, yours*, Lat. *vester;* also with gen. of the personal pron. added, as ὑμέτερος αὐτῶν θυμός *your* own mind; ὑμετερόνδε *to your house;* τὸ ὑμέτερον (sc. μέρος) *what in you lies*, for your part. [ῠ]

ὙΜΗ'Ν [ῡ], ένος, ὁ, *a skin, membrane.*

Ὑ'ΜΗ'Ν [ῡ], ένος, ὁ, *Hymen*, the god of marriages, cf. Ὑμέναιος. II. like ὑμέναιος, *a wedding-song.*

ὔμμε, Aeol., Dor. and Ep. acc. of ὑμεῖς.

ὔμμες, Aeol., Dor. and Ep. for ὑμεῖς.

ὔμμι, ὔμμιν, Aeol., Dor. and Ep. dat. of ὑμεῖς.

ὔμμος, α, ον, Aeol. for ὑμός, ὑμέτερος.

ὑμν-ᾱγόρας, ου, ὁ, (ὕμνος, ἀγορεύω) *a singer of hymns.*

ὑμνέαται [ᾰ], Ion. for ὕμνηνται, 3 pl. pf. pass. of ὑμνέω.

ὑμνείω, Ep. for ὑμνέω.

ὑμνέομες, Dor. for ὑμνέομεν, 1 pl. of ὑμνέω.

ὑμνέω, Dor. 3 pl. ὑμνεῦσι, part. fem. ὑμνεῦσα: fut. ήσω: aor. 1 ὕμνησα: pf. ὕμνηκα: (ὕμνος):—*to sing, praise, sing of, tell of, descant upon*, Lat. *canere*, c. acc.: part. pass. ὑμνούμενος, *renowned, famous.* 2. in bad sense, *to tell of, reproach, chide*, Lat. *increpare.* 3. *to tell over and over again, to be always telling of, keep harping upon*, Lat. *decantare: to recite*, as, τὸν νόμον ὑμνεῖν *to recite the form* of the law. II. intr. *to sing, chant.*

ὑμνητήρ, ῆρος, ὁ, and **ὑμνητής**, οῦ, ὁ, (ὑμνέω) *a singer of hymns, a minstrel, bard.*

ὑμνητός, ή, όν, verb. Adj. of ὑμνέω, *sung, praised, lauded, famous.*

ὑμνίω, Dor. for ὑμνέω.

ὑμνο-θέτης, ου, ὁ, (ὕμνος, τίθημι) *a composer of hymns, a lyric poet:*—as Adj., ὑμνοθέτης στέφανος a garland *of minstrelsy.*

ὑμνο-ποιός, όν, (ὕμνος, ποιέω) *making hymns:* as Subst. ὑμνοποιός, ὁ, *a minstrel.*

ὑμνο-πόλος, ον, (ὕμνος, πολέω) *busied with hymns:* as Subst., ὑμνοπόλος, ὁ, *a lyric poet, minstrel.*

ὝΜΝΟΣ, *a song: a hymn, festive song* or *ode*, commonly in honour of gods or heroes.

ὑμνῳδέω, f. ήσω, (ὑμνῳδός) *to sing a hymn* or *song of praise:* c. acc. cognato, *to sing, chant.* II. *to give a prophetic response.* Hence

ὑμνῳδία, ἡ, *the singing* or *chanting of a hymn.* II. *a prophetic strain.*

ὑμν-ῳδός, όν, (ὕμνος, ᾠδή) *singing hymns* or *odes;* ὑμνῳδοί κόραι the *minstrel* maids.

ὑμός, ά and ή, όν, Dor. and Ep. for ὑμέτερος, *your.*

ὗν, acc. of ὗς.

ὑο-μουσία, ἡ, (ὗς, Μοῦσα) *swine's music, swinish taste in music.*

ὑός, gen. of ὗς.

ὑοσ-κύᾰμος, ὁ, (ὗς, κύαμος) *hog-bean*, answering to our *hen-bane*, which causes giddiness and madness.

ὑπ-άγγελος, ον, (ὑπό, ἄγγελος) *summoned by a messenger.*

ὑπ-αγκᾰλίζω, f. ιῶ, (ὑπό, ἀγκαλίζομαι) *to take in the arms, embrace, clasp in the arms:* so in pf. part. pass, γένος ὑπηγκαλισμένη *having clasped* the children *in her arms.* Hence

ὑπαγκάλισμα, ατος, τό, *that which is taken into the arms, a wife, mistress.*

ὑπ-ᾰγορεύω, f σω, *to dictate*, Lat. *praeire verbis.*

ὑπ-άγω [ᾰ]: impf. ὑπῆγον: f. ὑπάξω: aor. 2 ὑπήγᾰγον: —*to lead* or *bring under;* ὑπάγειν ἵππους ζύγον *to bring* the horses *under the yoke, yoke* them; also simply ὑπάγειν ἵππους. 2. *to bring under one's power:*—Med. *to bring under one's own power, reduce.* 3. *to draw from under*, Lat. *subducere:*— Pass., ὑπαγομένου τοῦ χώματος as the mound of earth *was drawn away from under.* II. *to bring* a person *before the judge;* ὑπάγειν τινὰ ὑπὸ τὸ δικαστήριον *to bring* one *before* the court or *under the cognisance of* the court, i. e. *to accuse, impeach* him: ὑπάγειν τινὰ θανάτου ὑπὸ τὸν δῆμον *to impeach* him before the commons on a capital charge; so ὑπάγειν τινά alone. III. *to lead slowly on*, Lat. *inducere; to lead* one *by degrees* or *secretly, to draw on* an enemy by stratagem: *to lead, draw* one *on, induce* one (to do a thing):—Med. *to suggest, throw out* so *as to lead* a person *on:* so in Pass., *to be led, drawn on, induced*, mostly in bad sense. IV. *to lead* or *take secretly away, draw off, withdraw.* V. intrans. *to take oneself away secretly, withdraw, retire:* of an army, *to draw off* or *retire slowly.* 2. *to go after, go slowly on:* ὕπαγε, like ἄγε, *come! cheer up!*

ὑπᾰγωγεύς, έως, ὁ, (ὑπάγω) *a trowel* or *tool for shaping bricks.*

ὑπᾰγωγή, ἡ, (ὑπάγω) *a leading on gradually* or *secretly.* II. intr. *a withdrawing, a retreat.*

ὑπ-ᾴδω, f. -ᾴσομαι, (ὑπό, ᾄδω) *to sing, to accompany with the voice.* II. *to sing by way of prelude.*

ὑπαί, poët. for ὑπό.

ὑπαιδείδοικα, Ep. for ὑποδέδοικα, pf. of ὑποδείδω.

ὑπ-αιδέομαι, f. -έσομαι, Dep. *to shew some respect to* another, c. acc.

ὕπαιθᾰ, Adv. (ὑπαί poët. for ὑπό) *out under, slipping under and away: escaping to one side.* II. as Prep. with gen., *under, near, at one's side.*

ὑπ-αίθριος, ον, also α, ον, (ὑπό, αἰθήρ) *under the sky, in the open air.*

ὕπ-αιθρος, ον, = ὑπαίθριος, mostly in phrase, ἐν ὑπαίθρῳ, Lat. *sub Dio, in the open air.*

ὑπ-αίθω, = ὑποκαίω, *to set on fire from beneath* or *secretly.*

ὑπ-αινίσσομαι Att. -ττομαι: f. -ξομαι: Dep.:—

to intimate darkly give a slight hint of, make a covert allusion to.

ὑπ-αιρέω, Ion. for ὑφαιρέω.

ὑπ-ᾱΐσσω, f. ξω, *to dart beneath*, c. acc. II. *to dart from under*, c. gen.

ὑπ-αισχύνομαι, Pass. (ὑπό, αἰσχύνω) *to be somewhat ashamed* of a thing before a person, c. dupl. acc.

ὑπ-αίτιος, ον (ὑπό, (αἰτία) *under accusation, called to account for* a thing; ὑπαίτιός τινι *responsible* or *accountable to* one.

ὑπᾰκοή, ἡ, (ὑπακούω) *hearkening to, obedience.*

ὑπάκουσιν Dor. for ὑπάκουσον, aor. 1 imperat. of ὑπακούω.

ὑπ-ᾰκούω, f. -ακούσομαι: pf. -ακήκοα:—*to listen, hearken give ear to · to listen to and answer.* II. *to hearken to, give ear to*, with gen. or dat.: often used of porters, *to answer* a knock at the door. 2. *to obey, submit to*, c. gen. pers.: *to yield to, comply with*, c. dat. pers.: absol. *to submit, comply.*

ὑπ-ᾰλείφω, f. ψω, *to spread thinly on, spread like salve.* II. *to anoint:*—Med. *to anoint oneself;* ὑπαλείφεσθαι τοὺς ὀφθαλμοὺς *to anoint one's* eyes.

ὑπ-ᾰλεύομαι, imperat. -αλεύεο: Dep.: (ὑπό, ἀλεύω): —*to avoid, shun, flee from, escape, elude*, c acc.; mostly used in aor. 1 part. ὑπαλευάμενος

ὑπαλλᾰγή, ἡ, (ὑπαλλάσσω) *an interchange, exchange.* II. *hypallagé*, a figure of speech, by which the parts of a proposition seem to be interchanged.

ὑπ-αλλάσσω Att. ττω, f. ξω, *to interchange, exchange, barter*

ὑπᾰλύξας, aor. 1 part. of ὑπαλύσκω

ὑπάλυξις, εως, ἡ, *an avoiding, shunning escaping, eluding.* From

ὑπ-ᾰλύσκω, f. ξω. aor. 1 part. ὑπαλύξας·—like ὑπαλεύομαι, *to avoid, shun, flee from, escape, evade*, c. acc.; χρεῖος ὑπαλύξας *having got quit* of a debt.

ὑπ-αναγιγνώσκω, later -γῑνώσκω: f. -γνώσομαι: —*to read by way of preface.*

ὑπ-ανακῑνέω, f. ήσω, intr. *to rise up and go away.*

ὑπ-ανᾱλίσκω, f. -ανᾱλώσω: aor. 1 -ανάλωσα:—*to spend, waste, consume gradually.*

ὑπ-αναχωρέω, f. ήσω, *to retire slowly.*

ὑπαναστᾰτέον, verb. Adj. of ὑπανίσταμαι, *one must rise up, to make room for another.*

ὑπ-ανδρος, ον, (ὑπό, ἀνήρ) *under* or *subject to a man, married.*

ὑπανηλώθην, aor. 1 pass. of ὑπαναλίσκω.

ὑπ-ανῑάω, f. άσω Ion. ήσω:—*to trouble* or *vex a little:*—Pass. *to be somewhat distressed.*

ὑπ-ανίστημι, f. -αναστήσω: aor. 1 -ανέστησα:—*to make to rise up, raise up gradually.* II. Pass., with aor. 2 act. -ανέστην; pf. -ανέστηκα:—*to rise, stand up:* of game, *to start up, to be sprung* or *roused;* ὑπαναστῆναι τῆς ἕδρας *to rise up from* one's seat to shew respect to another, Lat. *assurgere alicui;* ὑπαναστῆναι τοῖς πρεσβυτέροις *to rise up* so as *to make room* for one's elders.

ὑπ-ανοίγω, f. ξω, *to open underhand* or *furtively;* ὑπανοίγειν γράμματα *to intercept and open* letters.

ὑπ-αντάω Ion. -έω: f. ήσω:—*to come* or *go to meet*, either as friend or foe. II. *to meet, reply to.* Hence

ὑπάντησις, εως, ἡ, *a coming to meet.*

ὑπ-αντιάζω, f. άσω, *to come* or *go to meet, step forth to meet*, c. dat.; also c. acc.

ὑπ-ᾰπειλέω, f. ήσω, *to threaten underhand.*

ὑπ-άπειμι, (ὑπό, ἀπό, εἶμι *ibo*) *to depart underhand* or *slowly, to retreat, retire.*

ὑπ-αποκῑνέω, f. ήσω, intr. *to move off secretly, slink away*, c. gen.:—verb. Adj. ὑπαποκῑνητέον, *one must make off, slink away.*

ὑπ-αποτρέχω, f. -θρέξομαι and -δρᾰμοῦμαι, *to run away secretly, slip away.*

ὑπ-άπτω, Ion. for ὑφάπτω.

ὝΠΑ'Ρ, τό, indecl. *a real appearance when one is awake, a waking vision*, opp. to ὄναρ a mere dream: οὐκ ὄναρ, ἀλλ' ὕπαρ, i.e. no illusion but *a reality.* II. the acc. is used absol. as Adv., *in a waking state, awake:* hence *really, actually.* [ῠ]

ὕπαργμαι, Ion. for ὕπηργμαι, pf. pass. of ὑπάρχω.

ὑπ-άργῠρος, ον, (ὑπό, ἄργυρος) *having silver underneath:* of rocks, *containing silver, veined with silver:* of metallic substances, *containing a proportion of silver.* II. *turned into silver, sold for silver.* III. *of silver-gilt.* IV. *hired for silver, venal.*

ὑπ-αρνος, ον, (ὑπό, ἀρνός gen. of ἀμνός) *with a lamb under, suckling a lamb:* metaph. *suckling an infant.*

ὕπαρξις, εως, ἡ, (ὑπάρχω) *subsistence:* one's *substance, possessions, goods.*

ὑπ-αρπάζω, Ion. for ὑφαρπάζω.

ὑπ-αρχή, ἡ, (ὑπό, ἀρχή) *the beginning;* ἐξ ὑπαρχῆς from *the beginning, over again, afresh.*

ὕπ-αρχος, ὁ, (ὑπό, ἄρχω) *commanding under* another: *a lieutenant-governor, viceroy.*

ὑπ-άρχω, f. ξω: aor. 1 ὑπῆρξα: Pass., pf. ὕπηργμαι: 3 sing. plqpf. ὑπῆρκτο: (ὑπό, ἄρχω):—*to begin:* c. gen.: 1. *to make a beginning of.* 2. c. part. *to begin* doing; ὑπάρχει εὖ ποιῶν τινα *he begins* doing good to one. 3. c. acc., ὑπάρχειν εὐεργεσίας εἴς τινα *to begin* [doing] kindnesses to one: Pass., τὰ ἔκ τινος ὑπαργμένα (Ion. for ὑπηργμένα) *the beginnings made* by one; τὰ παρὰ τῶν θεῶν ὑπηργμένα *what has been given* by the gods. 4. absol. *to begin* II. *to come into being, arise, spring up.* 2. *to be at hand, be ready.* 3. *to be:* ὑπάρχει impers., *the case is ..;* ἡ ὑπάρχουσα τιμή the price *being what it may.* III. *to lie under*, hence like ὑπόκειμαι, *to be taken for granted;* τούτου ὑπάρχοντος, Lat. *his positis, this being granted, this being the case.* IV. *to belong to, fall to:* of persons, *to be devoted to.* 2. often in part., τὰ ὑπάρχοντα one's *property*, or *present circumstances* or *advantages;* ἐκ τῶν ὑπαρχόντων according to *one's means.* 3. impers., ὑπάρχει μοι *it belongs* to me I have. IV. *to be sufficient:* ὑπάρχει impers., *it is possible*, c. inf.; so absol. in part. neut. ὕπαρχον, *since it is possible.*

ὑπ-ασπίδιος, *ον*, (ὑπό, ἀσπίς) *under cover of the shield*; ὑπασπίδιος κόσμος *the body*-armour. [ῐ]

ὑπ-ασπίζω, f. ίσω, *to carry the shield* for one, *serve as a shield-bearer.* Hence

ὑπασπιστήρ, ῆρος, ὁ, and **ὑπασπιστής**, οῦ, ὁ, *a shield-bearer, esquire*, generally, *an armour-bearer.*

ὕπ-αστρος, *ον*, (ὑπό, ἄστρον) *under the stars: guided by the stars.*

ὑπᾰτικός, *ή*, *όν*, (ὕπατος II) *of consular rank*, Lat. *consularis.*

ὕπᾰτος [ῠ], *η*, *ον*, contr. for ὑπέρτατος, like Lat. *summus* for *supremus*, *the highest, uppermost, first*, epith. of Jove; οἱ ὕπατοι, Lat. *superi*, *the gods above*, opp. to those beneath the earth (χθόνιοι, ἐνεροί, Lat. *inferi*). 2. of Place, *highest, topmost*; ἐν πυρῇ ὑπάτῃ *on the very top* of the funeral pile, c. gen. (as if it were a superlative Preposition), ὕπατοι λεχέων *high above* their nest. 3. of Quality, *highest, best.* 4. of Time, *last*, Lat. *supremus.* II. ὕπατος, ὁ, as Subst., was used to render the Roman *Consul.*

ὑπ-αυγάζω, f. άσω, *to begin to shine, dawn*, of daybreak.

ὑπ-αυλέω, f. ήσω, *to play the flute in accompaniment.*

ὕπ-αυλος, *ον*, (ὑπό, αὐλή) *under the tent*; σκηνῆς ὕπαυλος *under cover of* the tent.

ὑπ-αυχένιος, *α*, *ον*, (ὑπό, αὐχήν) *under the neck*: as Subst., ὑπαυχένιον, τό, *a cushion* or *pillow for the neck.*

ὑπ-αφίσταμαι, with aor. 2 act. ὑπαπέστην, pf. -αφέστηκα:—*to step back slowly, retire.*

ὕπ-αφρος, *ον*, (ὑπό, ἀφρός) *somewhat frothy, moist.*

ὑπ-άφρων, *ονος*, ὁ, ἡ, (ὑπό, ἄφρων) *somewhat silly* or *senseless*: Comp. ἀφρονέστερος.

ὑπέᾱσι, Ion. for ὕπεισι, 3 pl. of ὕπειμι (εἰμί *sum*).

ὑπέβᾰλον, aor. 2 of ὑποβάλλω.

ὑπ-έγγῠος, *ον*, (ὑπό, ἐγγύη) *under surety*: of persons, *having given surety, responsible, liable to be called to account*; ὑπέγγυος πλὴν θανάτου *subject to any punishment* except death.

ὑπεδάμνα, 3 sing. impf. of ὑποδάμνημι.

ὑπέδδεισαν, Ep. for ὑπέδεισαν, 3 pl. aor. 1 of ὑποδείδω.

ὑπ-εδείδῐσαν, 3 pl. plqpf. of ὑποδείδω.

ὑπέδειξα, aor. 1 of ὑποδείκνυμι.

ὑπέδεκτο, 3 sing. Ep. aor. 2 pass. of ὑποδέχομαι.

ὑπέδρᾰμον, aor. 2 of ὑποτρέχω.

ὑπέδῡν, aor. 2 of ὑποδύω.

ὑπεδύσετο [ῡ], Ep. 3 sing. aor. 1 med. of ὑποδύω.

ὑπεθερμάνθην, aor. 1 pass. of ὑποθερμαίνω.

ὑπ-ειδόμην, (ὑπό, *εἴδω), aor. 2 med. with no pres. in use, *to look at, view from below*: metaph. *to mistrust, suspect*, Lat. *suspicari.*

ὑπ-είκᾰθον, inf. ὑπεικαθεῖν, poët. aor. 2 of ὑπείκω.

ὑπ-εικτέον, verb. Adj. *one must give way.* From

ὑπ-είκω Ep. **ὑποείκω**: fut. -είξω or -είξομαι: aor. ὑπεῖξα Ep. ὑπόειξα: poët. aor. 2 ὑπεικᾰθον:—*to retire, withdraw*; ὑπείκειν τινὶ ἕδρης *to retire from* one's seat *for* another, make room for him; ὑπείκειν τινὶ λόγων *to give* him the first word. 2. c. acc. *to escape, shun, elude*; χεῖρας ἐμὰς ὑπόειξε *he scaped* my hands. II. *to yield, give way*: generally, *to submit to, to obey.*

ὕπ-ειμι, (ὑπό, εἰμί *sum*), *to be under*, Lat. *subesse*; φίλτατοι ἄνδρες ἐμῷ ὑπέασι μελάθρῳ my best friends *are under* my roof: of horses, *to be under* the yoke, *to be yoked in* the chariot. II. *to be* or *lie underneath*: *to be at the bottom.* 2. *to be laid down, granted, assumed.* 3. of things, *to be left remaining*: *to remain behind, after* everything else. III. generally, *to be at* or *near, be at hand, at command.* IV. *to be subjected* or *subject.*

ὕπ-ειμι, (ὑπό, εἶμι *ibo*) *to come* or *go under, to steal in secretly*, Lat. *subire*; ὑπιέναι τινά *to insinuate oneself into* a person's *favour.* II. *to depart gradually* or *secretly.*

ὑπείξομαι, fut. med. of ὑπείκω: Ep. 2 sing. ὑπείξεαι.

ὑπεῖπον, (ὑπό, εἶπον) aor. 2 with no pres. in use, *to say* or *repeat before* another, Lat. *praeire verba*: also *to premise, say by way of introduction*: *to suggest.* 2. *to explain, interpret.*

ὑπείρ, poët. for ὑπέρ, used when a long syll. is needed before a vowel, e. g. ὑπεὶρ ἅλα. [ῠ]

ὑπειρέβᾰλον, Ep. aor. 2 of ὑπερβάλλω.

ὑπείρ-εχον, Ep. for ὑπέρειχον, impf. of ὑπερέχω.

ὑπείρηκα, **ὑπείρημαι**, see ὑπερέω.

ὑπείρ-οχος, *ον*, poët. and Ion. for ὑπέροχος.

ὑπείσας, Ion. for ὑφείσας, aor. 1 part. of ὑφεῖσα *having set on, suborned.*

ὑπ-εισδύομαι, Dep., with aor. 2 act. -εισέδῡν, pf. -εισδέδῡκα:—*to slip* or *steal in, enter secretly.*

ὑπ-είσειμι, (εἶμι *ibo*) *to go in covertly.*

ὑπ-έκ, before a vowel **ὑπέξ**, (ὑπό, ἐξ) Prep. with gen., *out from under, from beneath*: also written divisim ὑπ' ἐκ.

ὑπεκ-βάλλω, *to cast out secretly.*

ὑπεκδρᾰμεῖν, aor. 2 inf. of ὑπεκτρέχω.

ὑπ-εκδύομαι, Dep., with aor. 2 act. -εξέδῡν, pf. -εκδέδῡκα:—*to get secretly out of, slip out of, shun, escape*, c. acc.: absol. *to slip out, steal out.*

ὑπ-εκέχῠτο, 3 sing. plqpf. pass. of ὑποχέω.

ὑπ-εκκαίω, f. -καύσω, *to set on fire from below* or *by degrees*: metaph. *to set on fire secretly.*

ὑπ-εκκᾰλύπτω, f. ψω, *to uncover from below* or *a little.*

ὑπέκκαυμα, *ατος*, *τό*, (ὑπεκκαίω) *fuel put under to light a fire, combustible matter.* 2. metaph. *a provocative, incentive.*

ὑπ-έκκειμαι, Pass. *to be carried out and away, to be put safe away, to be stored up* or *stowed in a safe place.*

ὑπ-εκκλίνω, *to bend aside, escape, delude.*

ὑπ-εκκομίζω, f. ίσω Att. ιῶ, *to carry out* or *away secretly*:—Med., ὑπεκκομίσασθαι πάντα *to get* all one's goods *carried secretly out.*

ὑπ-εκλαμβάνω, f. -λήψομαι, *to carry off underhand.*

ὑπεκλίνθην, aor. 1 pass. of ὑποκλίνω.

ὑπ-εκπέμπω, f. ψω, *to send away underhand; ὑπεκπέμπειν χθονός to send secretly out of* the land.

ὑπ-εκπροθέω, f. -θεύσομαι, *to run forth from under, start out before:* c. acc. *to outrun, outstrip.*

ὑπ-εκπρολύω, f. σω, *to loose from under:* of horses, *to unloose from under the yoke.*

ὑπ-εκπρορέω, f.-ρῠήσομαι, *to flow forth from under.*

ὑπ-εκπροφεύγω, f. -φεύξομαι, *to flee away secretly, escape and flee:* c. acc. *to flee away secretly from.*

ὑπεκπροφυγεῖν, aor. 2 inf. of ὑπεκπροφεύγω.

ὑπεκρύφθην, aor. 1 pass. of ὑποκρύπτω.

ὑπ-εκσώζω, *to save from under, rescue* or *deliver from.*

ὑπ-εκτᾰνύω, *to stretch out under.*

ὑπ-εκτίθημι, f. -θήσω, *to put out secretly:*—Med. *to remove one's effects from a place of danger, carry safely away:*—Pass. *to be carried safe away.*

ὑπ-εκτρέπω, f. ψω, *to turn gradually* or *secretly from* a thing:—Med. *to turn aside from,* c. acc.

ὑπ-εκτρέχω, f. -θρέξομαι and -δρᾰμοῦμαι: aor. 2 -εξέδρᾰμον (cf. τρέχω):—*to run out from under, run beyond: to escape from,* c. acc.

ὑπέκυψα, aor. 1 of ὑποκύπτω.

ὑπ-εκφέρω, *to lift up a little.* II. *to carry out from under,* esp. from danger: *to carry away.* III. intr., ὑπεκφέρειν ἡμέρης ὁδῷ *to get on before, to get the start* of another by a day's journey.

ὑπ-εκφεύγω, f. -φεύξομαι, *to fly out* or *escape secretly: to escape secretly from,* c. acc.

ὑπέκφυγε, Ep. 3 sing. aor. 2 of ὑπεκφεύγω.

ὑπεκ-χαλάω, f. άσω [ᾰ], *to slacken from below* or *slightly.*

ὑπ-εκχωρέω, f. ήσω, *to retire secretly: withdraw quietly from* a place: c. dat. pers. *to retire and give place to* one.

ὑπέλᾰβον, aor. 2 of ὑπολαμβάνω.

ὑπ-ελαύνω: f. -ελάσω [ᾰ] Att. -ελῶ:—*to drive under:* intr. (sub. ἵππον) *to ride up to.*

ὑπελείφθην, aor. 1 pass. of ὑπολείπω.

ὑπέλθοι, 3 sing. aor. 2 opt. of ὑπέρχομαι.

ὑπέλοντο, Ep. for ὑφείλοντο, 3 pl. aor. 2 med. of ὑφαιρέω.

ὑπέλυντο, 3 pl. Ep. aor. 2 pass. of ὑπολύω.

ὑπελύσαο [ῡ], Ep. 2 sing. aor. 1 med. of ὑπολύω.

ὑπέμεινα, aor. 1 of ὑπομένω.

ὑπεμνάασθε, Ep. 2 pl. impf. of ὑπομνάομαι.

ὑπεμνήμῡκε, Ep. for ὑπήμυκε, 3 sing. pf. of **ὑπημύω**, *to hang down the head.* This is the only form of the Verb in use, and this only in one place, of an orphan boy,—πάντα δ' ὑπεμνήμυκε *he stands with head* utterly *hung down:* see ἡμύω.

ὑπ-εναντιόομαι, Dep. *to oppose covertly.*

ὑπ-εναντίος, α, ον, (ὑπό, ἐναντίος) *set over against, opposite.* II. *set against, hostile:* as Subst., οἱ ὑπενάντιοι *the enemy:*—neut. as Adv., τὸ ὑπεναντίον τούτου *in opposition* thereto.

ὑπεναντίωσις, εως, ἡ, (ὑπεναντιόομαι) *a being opposed to: contrariety.*

ὑπ-ενδίδωμι, *to give way a little, give in a little.*

ὑπ-ένδῡμα, ατος, τό, (ὑπό, ἐνδύω) *an under-garment.*

ὑπ-ένερθε and -θεν, Adv. (ὑπό, ἔνερθε) *under, underneath, beneath: under the earth, in the world below:* c. gen. *under, beneath.*

ὑπ-εξ, form assumed by ὑπ-εκ before a vowel.

ὑπεξᾰγάγοι [γᾰ], 3 sing. aor. 2 opt. of ὑπεξάγω.

ὑπ-εξάγω, f. ξω, *to carry out from under* or *secretly,* esp. *out of* danger *into* safety. II. intr. *to retire* or *withdraw gradually.*

ὑπ-εξαιρέω, f. ήσω: pf. pass. -εξῄρημαι Ion. -εξαραίρημαι: aor. 2 -εξεῖλον:—*to take away privily, destroy, remove secretly* or *gradually;* τοὐπίκλημ' ὑπεξελὼν *having done away* with the offence: generally, *to set aside, put out of the question,* hence in pf. pass. part., τουτέων ὑπεξαραιρημένων these things *having been put out of the question:*—Med. *to take out* or *away privily for oneself: to steal* or *purloin.*

ὑπ-εξαίρω, *to raise, lift up from below.*

ὑπ-εξακρίζω, *to go up to the mountain-top.*

ὑπεξᾰλέασθαι, aor. 1 inf. of ὑπεξᾰλέομαι (a Dep. pres. not in use, see ἀλεύομαι), *to flee out away and escape,* c. acc.

ὑπ-εξᾰλύσκω, f. ύξω, *to flee away* or *escape from secretly,* c. acc.

ὑπ-εξαναβαίνω, f. -βήσομαι, *to rise out from under secretly* or *gradually.*

ὑπ-εξανάγομαι, Pass. with aor. 2 med. -εξηγαγόμην, *to sail out and away secretly.* [ᾰγ]

ὑπεξαναδύομαι, Med., with aor. 2 act. -εξανέδῡν, pf. -εξαναδέδῡκα:—*to come up from under gradually,* esp. *to rise from out* the sea.

ὑπεξαναδύς, ῦσα, ύν, aor. 2 part. of foreg.

ὑπ-εξανίσταμαι, Pass. *to rise up and give place to.*

ὑπ-εξαντλέω, f. ήσω, *to drain out from below, exhaust.*

ὑπεξαραίρημαι, Ion. for ὑπεξῄρημαι, pf. pass. of ὑπεξαιρέω.

ὑπ-έξειμι, (ὑπό, ἐξ, εἶμι *ibo*) *to go away under* or *secretly, withdraw gradually;* ὑπεξιέναι τινί *to make way for* one. II. *to go out to meet* or *against* one.

ὑπ-εξειρύω, Ion. for ὑπεξερύω.

ὑπ-εξελαύνω: fut. -εξελάσω [ᾰ] Att. -εξελῶ:—*to drive out from under, drive off secretly.* II. intr. *to march away secretly* or *slowly.*

ὑπεξελεῖν, -ών, aor. 2 inf. and part. of ὑπεξαιρέω.

ὑπ-εξερύω Io... -εξειρύω, *to draw out from under, draw away underhand.*

ὑπ-εξέρχομαι, Dep., with aor. 2 act. -εξῆλθον, pf. -εξελήλυθα:—*to go out from under: to go out secretly, withdraw, retire:* also c. acc. *to retire, withdraw from* or *before.* 2. *to rise up and quit one's settlements, to emigrate.* II. *to go out to meet.*

ὑπεξεσάωσεν, 3 sing. aor. 1 of an Ep. pres. ὑπεκσαόω, = ὑπεκσώζω.

ὑπεξέφυγε, 3 sing. aor. 2 of ὑπεκφεύγω.

ὑπ-εξέχω, intr. *to withdraw secretly from* a place.

ὑπ-εξίστᾰμαι, Pass., with aor. 2 act. -εξέστην, pf. -εξέστηκα:—*to go out from under, come out suddenly.* II. *to go out of the way of, shun, avoid;*

c. dat. *to give place to, rise up and make way for.* III. c. gen. rei, *to withdraw one's claims to* a thing, *retire from competition.*

ὑπέπλευσα, aor. 1 of ὑποπλέω.

ὑπέπτᾰτο, 3 sing. aor. 2 of ὑποπέταμαι.

ὙΠΕ´Ρ Ep. **ὑπείρ**, in phrases ὑπεὶρ ἁλός and ὑπεὶρ ἅλα: Prep. governing gen. and acc., Lat. *SUPER.* Hence are formed the Comp. and Sup. ὑπέρτερος, -τατος. [ῠ]

With Genit., expressing that *over* which something is: 1. of Place, *over:* of rest, *over, above;* ὑπὲρ κεφαλῆς στῆναι to stand *over* a person's head: 2. of motion, *over, across;* or *over, beyond.* II. (from the notion of *standing over* to protect) *for, in defence of, in behalf of;* ὑπὲρ τῆς πατρίδος ἀμύνειν to fight *in defence of* one's country. 2. *for, because of, by reason of: for the purpose of, for the sake of;* ὑπὲρ τοῦ μὴ ἀποθανεῖν *for the sake of* not dying. 3. *for, instead of, in the name of, acting for;* ὑπερ ἑαυτοῦ *in* his *stead.* III. like περί, *on, of, concerning, respecting,* Lat. *de.*

With Accus., expressing that *over* and *beyond* which a thing goes: I. of Place, *over, beyond, past.* II. of Measure, *over, above, exceeding, beyond;* ὑπὲρ τὴν ἡλικίαν *above* his years. 2. *beyond what is right, against, contrary to;* ὑπὲρ αἶσαν *contrary to* right; ὑπὲρ θεόν *contrary to the will* of the god. III. of Number, *above, upwards of, beyond, up to and over;* ὑπὲρ τὸ ἥμισυ *above* half.

Position: ὑπέρ may follow its Subst. in all cases, when it is written ὕπερ.

In Compos., ὑπέρ signifies *over, above,* of Place, as in ὑπερ-βαίνω. 2. *in defence of, in behalf of,* as in ὑπερ-αλγέω, mostly c. gen. 3. of excess, as in ὑπερ-ήφανος.

ὑπέρα, ἡ, (ὑπέρ) *the uppermost rope, the brace* attached to each end of the sailyards (ἐπίκρια), by means of which the sails are shifted. [ῠ]

ὑπερ-ᾰβέλτερος, ον, also α, ον *above measure simple* or *silly.*

ὑπερ-άγᾰμαι, Dep. *to admire above measure.* [ᾰγ]

ὑπερ-ᾰγᾰνακτέω, f. ήσω, *to be exceedingly angry* or *indignant at* a thing.

ὑπερ-ᾰγᾰπάω, f. ήσω, *to love exceedingly.*

ὑπερ-ᾰγωνιάω, *to be in great distress of mind.*

ὑπερ-ᾱής, ές, gen. έος, (ὑπέρ, ἄημι) *blowing down from above* or *blowing very hard.*

ὑπερ-αιμόω, (ὑπέρ, αἷμα) *to have overmuch blood.*

ὑπερ-αίρω, *to lift up over:* Med. and Pass. *to rise above, be lifted up.* II. *to rise up over, to climb over, scale,* Lat. *transcendere,* c. acc. 2. *to transcend, excel, outdo: to conquer.* 3. *to overshoot, go beyond, exceed* c. acc. 4. absol. of a river, *to overflow.*

ὑπέρ-αισχος, ον, *exceeding base* or *ugly.*

ὑπερ-αισχύνομαι, Pass. *to feel much ashamed.*

ὑπερ-αιωρέω, f. ήσω, *to hang up over* or *above.* II. Pass. *to be suspended over, project over* a thing:—of ships, c. gen. loci, *to lie off* a place.

ὑπέρ-ακμος, ον, (ὑπέρ, ἀκμή) *beyond the bloom of youth.*

ὑπερ-ᾰκοντίζω, f. ίσω, *to overshoot,* hence *to outdo, surpass:* c. part., ὑπερακοντίζειν τινὰ κλέπτων *to outdo* one in stealing.

ὑπερ-ᾰκρῑβής, ές, *exceedingly accurate* or *careful.*

ὑπερ-ᾰκρίζω, f. σω, *to mount and climb over.* II. *to project* or *beetle over,* c. gen.

ὑπερ-άκριος, ον, (ὑπέρ, ἄκρα) *over* or *upon the heights:* τὰ ὑπεράκρια *the heights above* the plain; οἱ ὑπεράκριοι, at Athens, *the inhabitants of the Attic uplands.*

ὑπέρ-ακρος, ον, (ὑπερ, ακρος) *over the top:* metaph. *going to extremes;* Adv. ὑπεράκρως, *to excess.*

ὑπερ-αλγέω, f. ήσω, *to be afflicted* or *feel pain for* a thing: *to grieve exceedingly at* a thing: absol. *to feel great pain of mind.*

ὑπερ-αλγής, ές, gen. έος, (ὑπέρ, ἄλγος) *exceeding grievous* or *painful.*

ὑπερ-άλλομαι, f. -αλοῦμαι: aor. 1 -ηλάμην: Ep. aor. 2 ὑπερᾶλτο, part. ὑπεράλμενος: Dep.:—*to spring* or *leap over,* c. gen.; also c. acc.

ὑπέρ-αλλος, ον, *over* or *above others.*

ὑπεράλμενος, Ep. aor. 2 part. of ὑπεράλλομαι.

ὑπερᾶλτο, 3 sing. aor. of ὑπεράλλομαι.

ὑπερ-αναιδεύομαι, Pass. *to be surpassed in impudence.*

ὑπερ-αναίσχυντος, ον, *exceeding impudent.*

ὑπερ-ανατείνω, f. -ανατενῶ, *to stretch excessively.*

ὑπερ-ανίσταμαι, Pass. with aor. 2 act. -ανέστην, pf. -ανέστηκα, *to stand up* or *project above.*

ὑπερ-αντλέομαι, Pass. (ὑπέρ, ἀντλέω) *to be very leaky, to be waterlogged.*

ὑπέρ-αντλος, ον, *quite full of water, waterlogged:* metaph. *overwhelmed, borne down.* II. act. *overflowing, overwhelming.*

ὑπερ-άνω, Adv. *over, above:* ὑπεράνω γίγνεσθαι to get *the upper hand of.* [ᾰ]

ὑπερ-άνωρ, ορος, ὁ, Dor. for ὑπερήνωρ.

ὑπερ-ᾰπᾰτάω, f. ήσω, *to deceive* or *cheat excessively.*

ὑπερ-αποθνήσκω, f. -αποθᾰνοῦμαι, *to die for.*

ὑπερ-αποκρίνομαι, Med. *to answer for* any one, *vindicate.* [ῑ]

ὑπερ-απολογέομαι, fut. med. ήσομαι: Dep. *to speak for* or *in behalf of* any one, *defend.*

ὑπερ-αρρωδέω, f. ήσω, Ion. for ὑπερορρωδέω, *to be exceedingly afraid,* τῇ Ἑλλάδι for Hellas.

ὑπέρ-ασθμος, ον, (ὑπέρ, ἆσθμα) *gasping* or *panting exceedingly.*

ὑπερ-ασπάζομαι, f. άσομαι Dep. *to be exceeding fond of, greet very kindly.*

ὑπερ-άτοπος, ον, *beyond measure absurd.*

ὑπερ-αττῐκός, ή, όν, *excessively Attic, carrying the Attic dialect to excess.* Adv. -κῶς.

ὑπερ-αυγής, ές, (ὑπέρ, αὐγή) *exceedingly bright.*

ὑπερ-αυξάνω, f. -αυξήσω, *to increase* or *enlarge*

above measure. II. intr. to abound beyond measure.

ὑπερ-αύξω, rarer form of ὑπεραυξάνω.

ὑπεραυχέω, f. ήσω, to be over-proud. From

ὑπέρ-αυχος, ον, (ὑπέρ, αὐχή) exceeding boastful, overproud.

ὑπερ-άφανος, ον, Dor. for ὑπερήφανος.

ὑπερ-αχθής, ές, gen. έος, (ὑπέρ, ἄχθος) overburdened.

ὑπερ-άχθομαι, Pass. with fut. med. -αχθέσομαι, to be exceedingly vexed or grieved at a thing, c. dat.

ὑπερ-βαίνω, fut. -βήσομαι: aor. 2 ὑπερέβην Ep. ὑπέρβην: pf. -βέβηκα:— to step over, climb over, scale, c. acc.: of rivers, to overflow, run over their banks. 2. to overstep or transgress a law: absol. to transgress, trespass, offend. 3. to pass over, pass by, take no notice of, Lat. praetermitto: hence to omit. 4. to go beyond: to surpass, outdo in a thing: also absol. to exceed. II. Causal, in aor. 1 ὑπερέβησα, to put over, lift or raise over.

ὑπέρβᾰλον, Ep. aor. 2 of ὑπερβάλλω.

ὑπερ-βαλλόντως, Adv. pres. act. part. of ὑπερβάλλω, above measure, exceedingly.

ὑπερ-βάλλω, f. -βᾰλῶ: Ep. aor. 2 ὑπειρ-έβᾰλον: pf. -βέβληκα, pass. -βέβλημαι:—to throw over or beyond a mark, to overshoot: to beat at throwing, to throw further. 2. to outstrip in racing. II. to overshoot, outdo, excel, surpass, exceed; ὑπερβάλλειν τὸν χρόνον to exceed the time; ὑπερβάλλειν τὸν καιρόν to go beyond the right time: absol. to exceed all bounds, to go too far. 2. to go on further and further, bid more and more; προέβαινε τοῖς χρήμασι ὑπερβάλλων he went on bidding more and more. 3. to be at its height, at the zenith, of the sun. 4. to be over and above. 5. part. ὑπερβάλλων, ουσα, ον, exceeding great, excessive, beyond measure; τὰ ὑπερβάλλοντα an exceeding high estate. III. to pass over, cross, or traverse mountains, rivers, etc., Lat. trajicere; of ships, to double a headland. 2. of rivers, to overflow; of a kettle, to boil over.

Med. to outdo, surpass, excel, exceed, c. acc. 2. to exceed all bounds: so in pf. pass. part., ὑπερβεβλημένη γυνή an excellent woman. II. to put off, delay, c. acc.: c. part., to put off doing: absol. to delay, linger.

ὑπερ-βᾰρής, ές, gen. έος, (ὑπέρ, βάρος) overloaded, overweighed, exceedingly heavy.

ὑπέρβᾰσαν, Ep. 3 pl. aor. 2 of ὑπερβαίνω.

ὑπερβᾰσία, ἡ, (ὑπερβαίνω) an overstepping or transgression of law, trespass: wanton violence.

ὑπερβᾰτός, ή, όν, verb. Adj. of ὑπερβαίνω, stepped over: to be passed or crossed: of a wall, to be scaled. II. act. overstepping: in bad sense, beyond bounds, excessive, outrageous.

ὑπέρβη, Ep. 3 sing. aor. 2 of ὑπερβαίνω.

ὑπερβήῃ, Ep. 3 sing. aor. 2 subj. of ὑπερβαίνω.

ὑπερ-βιάζομαι, f. ήσομαι: Dep.: (ὑπέρ, βιάζω):— to press with great violence, of the plague.

ὑπερ-βῐβάζω, f. -βιβάσω Att. -βιβῶ, Causal of ὑπερβαίνω, to carry over, transport.

ὑπέρ-βῐος, ον, (ὑπέρ, βία) of overwhelming strength or might: overweening, outrageous, wanton: neut. ὑπέρβιον as Adv. wantonly, arrogantly.

ὑπερβολάδην, Adv. (ὑπερβολή) immoderately, excessively. [ᾰ]

ὑπερβολή, ἡ, (ὑπερβάλλω) a throwing beyond: an overshooting, superiority, excess in anything; οὐκ ἔχει ὑπερβολήν it can go no further; εἰς or καθ' ὑπερβολήν as Adv., excessively. 2. excessive praise, hyperbolé. II. a passing over or crossing mountains, rivers, etc. 2. a place of passage, a mountain-pass. III. (from Med.) delay, putting off.

ὑπερ-βόρεος, ον, (ὑπέρ, Βορέας) beyond Boreas, i. e. in the extreme north: οἱ Ὑπερβόρεοι the Hyperboreans, a supposed people in the extreme north distinguished for piety and happiness; τύχη ὑπερβόρεος more than mortal fortune.

ὑπερ-βράζω, f. σω, to boil or foam over.

ὑπερ-βρῑθής, ές, gen. έος, (ὑπέρ, βρῖθος) overloaded, exceedingly heavy.

ὑπερ-βρύω, to be overfull, overflow.

ὑπ-εργάζομαι, f. άσομαι: pf. pass. ὑπείργασμαι (in act. and pass. sense): Dep.:—to work under, plough up, prepare for sowing, Lat. subigere. II. to subdue, reduce, bring under one: pf. in pass. sense, to be subdued, ὑπείργασμαι ψυχὴν ἔρωτι I have been subdued in my soul by love. III. = ὑπηρετέω, to do a service: here also pf. in pass. sense, πόλλ' ὑπείργασται φίλα many kind services have been done.

ὑπερ-γέλοιος, ον, (ὑπέρ, γέλοιος) above measure ridiculous or laughable.

ὑπερ-γεμίζω, f. ίσω, to overfill, overload.

ὑπερ-γήρειος, and **ὑπέρ-γηρος**, ον, = ὑπέργηρως.

ὑπέρ-γηρως, ων, (ὑπέρ, γῆρας) exceeding old, of extreme age: as Subst., τὸ ὑπέργηρων extreme old age.

ὑπέρ-δᾰσυς, υ, gen. έως, very hairy.

ὑπερ-δεής, ές, gen. έος, Ep. acc. ὑπερδέα, for ὑπερδεέα, -ᾶ: (ὑπέρ, δέος): above or beyond fear, undaunted.

ὑπερ-δείδω, f. -δείσω, to fear for or on account of one: absol. to be in exceeding fear.

ὑπερ-δειμαίνω, to be much afraid of, c. acc.

ὑπέρ-δεινος, ον, exceeding dangerous or formidable.

ὑπερ-δέξιος, ον, placed high above one on the right hand. 2. placed above or over; ὑπερδέξιον χωρίον higher ground; ἐξ ὑπερδεξίου from vantage-ground. II. superior.

ὑπερ-δέω, f. -δήσω, to bind upon.

ὑπερ-διατείνομαι, Pass. to strain or exert oneself above measure.

ὑπερ-δίδωμι, f. -δώσω, to give up in behalf of.

ὑπερδῐκέω, f. ήσω, to plead or act as advocate for one, advocate his cause. From

ὑπέρ-δῐκος, ον, (ὑπέρ, δίκη) exceeding righteous or just. II. pleading for.

ὑπ-ερεθίζω, to stimulate a little.

ὑπερ-εῖδον, inf. ὑπεριδεῖν, aor. 2 without any pres. in use, ὑπεροράω being used instead:—*to overlook, neglect, slight, despise*, c. acc.; also c. gen.: cf. *εἴδω.

ὑπ-ερείδω, f. σω, *to put under as a prop.* 2. *to prop* or *support from beneath.*

ὑπ-ερείπω, f. ψω, *to undermine, subvert.* II. intr. in aor. 2 ὑπήρῖπον, *to tumble, fall down.*

ὑπερ-έκεινα, Adv. (ὑπέρ, ἐκεῖνος) *on yon side, on the further part, beyond.*

ὑπερ-εκθεράπεύω, f. σω, *to seek to win over by excessive attention.*

ὑπερ-εκκρεμάννῡμι, f. -κρεμάσω [ᾰ], *to hang out over.*

ὑπερ-εκ-περισσοῦ, Adv. for ὑπὲρ ἐκ περισσοῦ, *more than superabundantly:* also **ὑπερεκπερισσῶς**.

ὑπερ-εκπίπτω, f. -εκπεσοῦμαι, *to fall out over* or *beyond.* II. absol. *to go beyond all bounds.*

ὑπερ-εκπλήσσω, f. ξω: pf. pass. ὑπερεκπέπληγμαι:—*to frighten* or *astonish beyond measure*:—Pass. *to be astonished excessively*: c. acc. *to be frightened beyond measure at.*

ὑπερ-εκτείνω, f. -τενῶ, *to stretch beyond measure:* ὑπερεκτείνειν ἑαυτόν *to stretch oneself beyond one's measure.*

ὑπερ-εκτίνω [ῑ], f. ίσω [ῑ], *to pay for* any one.

ὑπερ-εκχέω, f. -χεῶ, also **ὑπερ-εκχύνω** [ῡ], *to pour out over*:—Pass. *to run over, overflow.*

ὑπερ-έλαφρος, ον, *exceedingly light* or *active.*

ὑπερ-εμπίπλημι, f. -εμπλήσω, *to fill overfull* of a thing:—Pass. *to be overfull, be overloaded.*

ὑπερ-εμφορέομαι, Pass. *to be filled quite full of.*

ὑπερ-εντυγχάνω, f. τεύξομαι, *to intercede for* another.

ὑπερ-εξηκοντα-έτης, ες, gen. εος, (ὑπέρ, ἑξήκοντα, ἔτος) *above sixty years old.*

ὑπερ-επαινέω, f. έσω and ήσω, *to praise above measure.*

ὑπερ-επιθῡμέω, f. ήσω, *to desire exceedingly.*

ὑπερέπτα, Dor. 3 sing. aor. 2 act. of ὑπερπέτομαι.

ὑπ-ερέπτω, f. ψω, (ὑπό, ἐρέπτω) *to cut away from below, undermine.*

ὑπερ-έρχομαι, f. -ελευσομαι: Dep. with aor. 2 act -ῆλθον, pf. -ελήλυθα:—*to come* or *go out over, pass over*, c. acc.: absol. *to exceed, excel.*

ὑπερ-εσθίω, f. -έδομαι: aor. 2 -έφαγον:—*to eat immoderately.*

ὑπερέσσῡμαι, pf. pass. of ὑπερσεύω.

ὑπερέσχεθον, poët. aor. 2 of ὑπερέχω.

ὑπερ-έσχον, aor. 2 of ὑπερέχω.

ὑπέρ-ευ, Adv. *exceeding well.*

ὑπέρ-ευγε, Adv., strengthd. for εὖγε, *bravo, capital.*

ὑπερ-ευτῠχία, ἡ, *exceeding good luck.*

ὑπερ-ευφραίνομαι, Pass. *to rejoice exceedingly.*

ὑπερ-εχθαίρω, *to hate exceedingly*, c. acc

ὑπερ-έχω Ep. ὑπειρέχω: Ep. impf. ὑπείρεχον: f. ὑπερέξω: aor. 2 ὑπερέσχον poët. -έσχεθον:—*to hold over*, esp. *to hold over so as to protect*; ὑπερέχειν χεῖράς τινος *to hold* one's arms *over* one *to shield him.* II. intr. *to be above, stand out above*, as out of water: *to rise above, overtop: to rise up over* a thing, c. gen., e. g. γαίης: of a star, *to rise above* the horizon. 2. metaph. *to be above, be superior, to excel, surpass, be the better*; οἱ ὑπερέχοντες *the more powerful*; ἐὰν ἡ θάλαττα ὑπερσχῇ if the sea *be too powerful*:—Pass. *to be outdone.* 3. c. gen. rei, *to rise above, rise superior to, be able to bear.* 4. *to outflank, overlap.* 5. *to get over, cross.*

ὑπ-ερέω Att. -ερῶ, fut. of ὑπεῖπον, in same senses: from same root come pf. act. ὑπ-είρηκα, pass. ὑπ-είρημαι.

ὑπερ-ζέω, f. -ζέσω, *to boil over.*

ὑπερηδέως, Adv. of ὑπέρηδυς, *very pleasantly:* Sup. ὑπερήδιστα.

ὑπερ-ήδομαι, Pass. *to rejoice beyond measure:* c. part., ὑπερήδετο ἀκούων *he rejoiced much* at hearing.

ὑπέρ-ηδυς, υ, *exceeding sweet* or *pleasant:* Sup. -ήδιστος.

ὑπερηκόντισα, aor. 1 of ὑπερακοντίζω.

ὑπερ-ῆλιξ, ῐκος, ὁ, ἡ, *above a certain age.*

ὑπέρ-ημαι, properly pf. of ὑπερέζομαι, *to sit above.*

ὑπερ-ημερία, ἡ, (ὑπέρ, ἡμέρα) *a being beyond the day:* as law-term, *a not meeting one's engagements at the proper day.* 2. *forfeiture of recognisances, a distraining of goods, execution.*

ὑπερ-ήμερος, ον, (ὑπέρ, ἡμέρα) *waiting over the day, not observing the appointed day:* hence, *suffering a distress, having an execution levied:* metaph., c. gen., ὑπερήμερος γάμων *over-due for* marriage.

ὑπερ-ήμῐσυς, υ, (ὑπέρ, ἥμισυς) *above half more than half.*

ὑπ-έρημος, ον, *somewhat desolate.*

ὑπερ-ηνορέων, οντος, ὁ, (ὑπέρ, ἠνορέη) *exceeding manly:* in bad sense, *overbearing, overweening.* II. *excelling men, thinking oneself more than man.*

ὑπερ-ήνωρ, ορος, ὁ, ἡ, (ὑπέρ, ἀνήρ) *overbearing.*

ὑπερήσω, fut. of ὑπερίημι.

ὑπερηφᾰνέω, f. ήσω, (ὑπερήφανος) *to be conspicuous above* others: in bad sense, esp. in part., like ὑπερηνορέων, *overweening, arrogant.* II. transit. *to treat disdainfully.*

ὑπερηφᾰνία, ἡ, (ὑπερηφανέω) *arrogance, haughtiness: contempt for* a person or thing, c. gen.

ὑπερή-φᾰνος, ον, = ὑπερ-φανής with η inserted, *conspicuous above* others: in good sense, *magnificent, splendid, nobl* 2. in bad sense, *extravagant, overweening, arrogant.* Hence

ὑπερηφάνως, Adv. *magnificently: arrogantly.*

ὑπερ-θᾰλασσίδιος, ον, (ὑπέρ, θάλασσα) *some way above the sea.* [σῐ]

ὑπερ-θαυμάζω Ion. **υπερθωμ**–, f. άσομαι, *to wonder exceedingly.* 2. c. acc. *to admire above measure.*

ὑπερ-θαύμαστος, ον, *exceedingly admirable.*

ὕπερθε and **-θεν**, Adv. (ὑπέρ) *from above: above:* c. gen. *above, over*; ὕπερθεν εἶναι ἤ.. to be *above* or *beyond*, i. e. worse than.

ὑπερ-θέω, f. -θεύσομαι, *to run over* or *beyond*. 2. *to outstrip, to surpass, excel.*

ὑπερ-θνήσκω, fut. -θᾰνοῦμαι, *to die for* or *instead of.*

ὑπερθοροῦμαι Ion. -έομαι, fut. of ὑπερθρώσκω.

ὑπερθορεῖν Ion. -έειν, aor. 2 inf. of ὑπερθρώσκω.

ὑπερ-θρώσκω: fut. -θοροῦμαι Ep. -θορέομαι: aor. 2 ὑπερέθορον Ep. ὑπέρθορον, inf. -θορέειν contr. -εῖν:—*to overleap, leap, spring, vault* or *bound over*, c. acc.

ὑπέρ-θῡμος, ον, *high-spirited, daring.* II. in bad sense, *over-spirited, overweening:* of a horse, *too high-couraged, restive.* Henc

ὑπερθύμως, Adv. *in excessive wrath.*

ὑπερ-θύριον, τό, (ὑπέρ, θύρα) *the lintel of a door.* [ῠ]

ὑπέρ-θῠρος, ον, (ὑπέρ, θύρα) *above the door:* as Subst., ὑπέρθυρον, τό, = ὑπερθύριον

ὑπερ-ιάχω, *to shout above, outdo in shouting*, c. gen. [ᾰ]

ὑπερῐδεῖν, inf. of aor. 2 ὑπερεῖδ

ὑπερ-ίημι, f. -ήσω, *to send* or *throw further hurl beyond the mark.*

ὑπερ-ικταίνομαι, Pass. *to move exceeding swiftly:* the simple Verb is nowhere found, and its derivation is uncertain.

Ὑπερῑονίδης, ου, ὁ, patronym. from Ὑπερίων [ῑ], *son of Hyperion*, i. e. *the Sun.*

ὑπερ-ίστᾰμαι, Pass., with aor. 2 act. -έστην, pf. -έστηκα: (ὑπέρ, ἵστημι):—*to stand over*, c. gen.: *to stand over so as to protect one, to shield, guard.*

ὑπερ-ίστωρ, ορος, ὁ, ἡ, *knowing but too well*, c. gen.

ὑπερ-ίσχῡρος, ον, (ὑπέρ, ἰσχυρός) *exceeding strong.*

ὑπερ-ίσχω, = ὑπερέχω, *to hold above.* II. intr. *to be above: to prevail over*, c. gen. 2. *to protect*, c. gen.

Ὑπερ-ίων [ῑ], ονος, ὁ, *Hyperion, the sun-god*, commonly joined with Ἥλιος in Homer, as Ὑπερίων Ἠέλιος, or Ἠέλιος Ὑπερίων. (Said to be derived from ὑπέρ, ἰών, *he that walks on high.*)

ὑπερ-κάθημαι, properly pf. pass. of ὑπερκαθέζομαι, *to sit over, above* or *upon.* II. metaph. *to sit over and watch, keep an eye upon.*

ὑπερ-καλλής, ές, gen. έος, (ὑπέρ, κάλλος) *exceeding beautiful* or *fine.*

ὑπερ-κάμνω, f. -κᾰμοῦμαι, *to suffer* or *labour for* any one, c. gen

ὑπερ-καταβαίνω, f. -καταβήσομαι, *to get down over.*

ὑπερ-καταγέλαστος, ον, *exceedingly absurd.*

ὑπερκατέβησαν, 3 pl. aor. 2 of ὑπερκαταβαίνω

ὑπερ-καχλάζω, f. σω, *to laugh outright.*

ὑπέρ-κειμαι, Pass. *to be situated over* or *above.*

ὑπερ-κηλέω, f. ήσω, *to charm beyond measure.*

ὑπερ-κολᾰκεύω, f. σω, *to flatter immoderately.*

ὑπέρ-κομπος, ον, (ὑπέρ, κόμπος) *over-confident, overweening, boastful, arrogant:* generally, *excessive;* c. dat., νῆες ὑπερκόμποι τάχει ships *surpassing* in swiftness.

ὑπέρ-κοπος, ον, (ὑπέρ, κόπτω) like ὑπέρκομπος, *overweening, overbearing, boastful.* Hence

ὑπερκόπως, Adv. *exceedingly.*

ὑπερ-κορέω, f. ήσω, *to overfill* or *glut.*

ὑπέρ-κοτος, ον, *exceedingly angry* or *furious: exceedingly savage.* Adv. -τως, *overmuch, exceedingly.*

ὑπερ-κρεμάννῡμι: f. -κρεμάσω [ᾰ] Att. -κρεμῶ:—*to hang up over* or *out of the way.*

ὑπερ-κτάομαι, f. -κτήσομαι: aor. 1 -εκτησάμην:—*to acquire over and above.*

ὑπερκύδαντας, acc. pl. of

ὑπερ-κύδας, αντος, ὁ, (ὑπέρ, κῦδος) *exceeding famous* or *renowned, very glorious.*

ὑπερ-κύπτω, f. ψω, *to bend, stretch over, peep over.* 2. c. acc. *to overstep.*

ὑπέρ-λαμπρος, ον, *exceeding bright* or *glistening.* II. of sound, *exceeding clear* or *loud.*

ὑπερ-λαμπρύνομαι, Pass. *to make a very splendid show:* also *to shew great eagerness.* [ῡ]

ὑπερ-λίαν, Adv. (ὑπέρ, λίαν) *beyond all measure* or *doubt, undeniably.* [ῑ]

ὑπερ-λῡπέω, f. ήσω, *to pain exceedingly, cause one great distress:*—Pass. *to be distressed beyond measure.*

ὑπερ-μαίνομαι, Pass., with f. med. -μᾰνοῦμαι: aor 2 pass. ὑπερεμάνην [ᾰ]:—*to be struck mad.*

ὑπερ-μάκης, ες, Dor. for ὑπερμήκης.

ὑπερ-μᾰχέω, f. ήσω, (ὑπέρ, μάχη) *to fight for* or *in defence of* one: also *to fight with* one *for another.*

ὑπερμᾰχητικός, ή, όν, *inclined to fight for* another.

ὑπερ-μάχομαι [μᾰ], fut. -μαχοῦμαι, Dep., like ὑπερμαχέω, *to fight for* any one; ὑπερμαχοῦμαι τάδε πατρός *I will fight out* this *for* my father.

ὑπέρ-μᾰχος, ον, (ὑπέρ, μάχομαι) *fighting for:* as Subst., ὑπέρμαχος, ὁ, *a champion.*

ὑπερ-μεγάθης, Ion. for ὑπερμεγέθης. [ᾰ]

ὑπερ-μέγας, μεγάλη, μεγα, *enormously great.*

ὑπερ-μεγέθης Ion. **ὑπερμεγάθης** [ᾰ], ες, gen. εος, (ὑπέρ, μέγεθος) *excessively large, enormous.* II. *exceedingly difficult.*

ὑπερ-μεθύσκομαι, aor. 1 -μεθύσθην: Pass.:—*to be excessively drunk.*

ὑπερ-μενέτης, ου, ὁ, poët. for ὑπερμενης.

ὑπερμενέων, οντος, ὁ, *excessively mighty.* From

ὑπερ-μενής, ές, (ὑπέρ, μένος) *exceeding strong:* also in bad sense, *overweening, insolent.*

ὑπέρ-μετρος, ον, (ὑπέρ, μέτρον) *beyond all measure, excessive.* Adv. -τρω

ὑπερ-μήκης, ες, gen. εος, (ὑπέρ, μῆκος) *exceeding long, high, broad*, etc.: of sound, *exceeding loud.*

ὑπερ-μῑσέω, f. ήσω, *to hate exceedingly.*

ὑπέρ-μορον, Adv. = ὑπὲρ μόρον, *beyond fate* or *destiny.*

ὑπερ-νέφελος, ον, (ὑπέρ, νεφέλη) *above the clouds.*

ὑπερ-νῑκάω, f. ήσω, *to be more than conqueror*

ὑπερ-νοέω, f. ήσω, *to think* or *reflect upon*, c. acc.

ὑπερ-νότιος, ον, (ὑπέρ, νότος) *beyond the south wind, at the extreme south*, opp. to ὑπερβόρεος.

ὑπέρ-ογκος, ον, (ὑπέρ, ὄγκος) *of excessive size* or *bulk, overgrown, immensely great.*

ὑπερ-οιδαίνω or -άνω, *to swell, be much swollen.*

ὑπερ-οιδάω Ion. -έω, f. ήσω, *to swell excessively.*

ὑπερ-οικέω, f. ήσω, *to dwell above* or *beyond*.

ὑπέρ-οικος, ον, (ὑπέρ, οἰκέω) *dwelling above, beyond*.

ὑπεροπλία, ἡ, (ὑπέροπλος) *proud confidence, defiance, presumption: high courage*. [ῑ Ep.]

ὑπερ-οπλίζομαι, f. ίσομαι, Dep. (ὑπέρ, ὁπλίζω) *to vanquish by force of arms*.

ὑπέρ-οπλος, ον, (ὑπέρ, ὅπλον) *confident in arms*, hence *overweening, arrogant*; neut. as Adv., ὑπέροπλον εἰπεῖν to speak *haughtily, arrogantly*. II. generally, *excessive, immense*.

ὑπερόπτης, ου, ὁ, (ὑπερόψομαι) *a contemner, disdainer*: absol. *disdainful, haughty*.

ὑπεροπτικός, ή, όν, *contemptuous, disdainful, scornful*. Adv. -κῶς, *disdainfully*. From

ὑπέρ-οπτος, ον, (ὑπερόψομαι) *overlooking*: hence *disdainful, haughty*: neut. pl. as Adv. *haughtily*.

ὑπερ-οράω, fut. -όψομαι: aor. 2 -εῖδον inf. -ῐδεῖν: aor. 1 pass. -ώφθην: (cf. ὁράω):—*to look over, survey*. II. *to overlook, pay no heed to, disregard: to slight, despise, disdain*, both with acc. and gen.

ὑπερ-όριος poët. **-ούριος**, ον, (ὑπέρ, ὅρος) *over* or *beyond the boundaries: foreign, outlandish*. 2. ἡ ὑπερορία (sc. γῆ) *the country beyond one's own frontiers, a foreign land* or *country*.

ὑπερ-όρνῡμαι, Pass. (ὑπέρ, ὄρνυμι) *to rise up over* a thing.

ὑπερ-ορρωδέω Ion. **-αρρωδέω**: f. ήσω:—*to be much afraid, be in great terror on account of*.

ὝΠΕΡΟΣ, ὁ, or **ὕπερον**, τό, *a pestle to bray and pound with*.

ὑπερ-ουράνιος, ον, (ὑπέρ, οὐρανός) *above the heavens*.

ὑπεροχή, ἡ, (ὑπερέχω) *a projection, prominence, summit*. II. metaph. *preëminence, superiority, supremacy: excellence*. 2. *excess, superabundance*.

ὑπέροχος Ep. **ὑπείροχος**, ον, (ὑπερέχω) *prominent, eminent, distinguished above others*; c. gen., ὑπείροχον ἔμμεναι ἄλλων to be *distinguished above* others: in bad sense, *overbearing*. Sup. -ώτατος.

ὑπεροψία, ἡ, *contempt, disdain: arrogance*. From

ὑπερ-όψομαι, used as fut. of ὑπεροράω, from obsol. ὑπερόπτομαι.

ὑπερ-πᾰγής, ές, (ὑπέρ, πάγος) *excessively frosty*: as Subst., τὸ ὑπερπαγές *extremely hard frost*.

ὑπερ-πᾰθέω, f. ήσω, (ὑπέρ, παθεῖν) *to suffer excessively, be grievously afflicted*.

ὑπερ-παίω, f. -παιήσω: pf. -πέπαικα:—*to strike beyond*: hence *to overstep, surpass, excel*.

ὑπερ-παλύνω, *to strew* or *scatter over*. [ῡ]

ὑπερ-περισσεύω, also Dep. **-εύομαι**:—*to abound overmuch, to superabound*.

ὑπερ-πέρισσος, η, ον, *excessive*:—Adv. -σως, *beyond measure*.

ὑπερ-πέτᾰμαι, Dep., = ὑπερπέτομαι.

ὑπερ-πετάννυμι, f. -πετάσω [ᾰ], *to stretch over*.

ὑπερ-πέτομαι or **-πέτᾰμαι**: fut. -πτήσομαι: aor. 2 -επτάμην [ᾰ], whence Ep. 3 sing. ὑπέρπτατο: we also find Dor. 3 sing. aor. 2 act. ὑπερέπτᾱ, from ὑπερέπτην: Dep.:—*to fly over, above* or *beyond*.

ὑπερ-πέττω, Att. for ὑπερπέσσω.

ὑπερ-πηδάω, f. -ήσομαι, *to leap over* or *beyond*, and so *to escape from*. II. metaph. *to overleap, transgress: to overleap, escape from*.

ὑπέρ-πῐκρος, ον, *exceeding sharp* or *bitter*.

ὑπερ-πίμπλημι, f. -πλήσω, *to overfill*:—Pass. *to be overfull of* a thing.

ὑπερ-πίνω, f. -πίομαι, *to drink overmuch*. [ῐ]

ὑπερ-πίπτω, f. -πεσοῦμαι, *to fall over* or *beyond*. II. of time, *to be past, gone by, be spent*.

ὑπερ-πλεονάζω, f. άσω, *to abound exceedingly*.

ὑπερ-πλήθης, ες, (ὑπέρ, πλῆθος) *superabundant*.

ὑπερ-πληρόω, *to fill overfull*:—Pass. *to be overfull*.

ὑπερπλουτέω, f. ήσω, *to be exceeding rich*. From

ὑπέρ-πλουτος, ον, (ὑπέρ, πλοῦτος) *exceeding rich*.

ὑπέρ-πολυς, πόλλη, πολυ, (ὑπέρ, πολύς) *overmuch, very much* or *many*.

ὑπερ-πονέω, f. ήσω, *to toil* or *labour beyond measure: to suffer very greatly*. II. *to bear* or *endure for* another:—Med., ὑπερπονεῖσθαί τινος *to take trouble on oneself for* another.

ὑπερ-πόντιος, ον, also α, ον, (ὑπέρ, πόντος) *over* or *beyond the sea, far away* II. *over* or *across the sea*.

ὑπέρπτᾰτο, Ep. 3 sing. aor. 2 of ὑπερπέτομαι.

ὑπερ-πυππάζω, (ὑπέρ, πύππαξ) *to make very much of* one, *to caress fondly*.

ὑπερ-πυρριάω, f. άσω [ᾱ] (ὑπέρ, πυρρός) *to redden* or *blush for* another.

ὑπερ-πωτάομαι, Ep. for ὑπερπέτομαι.

ὑπερράγην, aor. 2 pass. of ὑπορρήγνυμι. [ᾰ]

ὑπερ-σεμνύνομαι, Pass. (ὑπέρ, σεμνύνω) *to be exceeding solemn* or *pompous*.

ὑπέρ-σοφος, ον, *extremely wise* or *cleve*.

ὑπερ-σπουδάζω, f. σω, *to take excessive pains, be very anxious*.

ὑπερ-στᾰτέω, = ὑπερίσταμαι, *to stand over and protect*, c. gen.

ὑπέρσχῃ, ὑπέρσχοι, 3 sing. aor. 2 subj. and opt. of ὑπερέχω.

ὑπέρτᾰτος, η, ον, Sup. Adj. of ὑπέρ, *uppermost, highest: eldest*: more used in shortened form **ὕπατος**: there is also a form ὑπερώτατος. [ῠ]

ὑπερτείλας, aor. 1 part. of ὑπερτέλλω.

ὑπερ-τείνω, f. -τενῶ: pf. -τέτᾰκα:—*to stretch over* or *above: to hold out over*; ὑπερτείνειν σκιὰν σειρίου κυνός *to spread* a shade from the dog-star *over* the house; ὑπερτείνειν πόδα ἀκτῆς *to stretch* one's foot *over* the beach, i. e. pass over it. II. intr. *to stretch, stand out* or *project beyond*: c. acc., ὑπερτείνειν τὸ κέρας *to outflank* the enemy's wing. 2. metaph. *to surpass, excel*.

ὑπερτελέω, *to pass quite over, overleap*. From

ὑπερ-τελής, ές, gen. έος, (ὑπέρ, τέλος) *going over* or *beyond the mark*: generally, *going over, overleaping*: c. gen., ἄθλων ὑπερτελής *one who has reached the end* of his labours. II. = ὑπερτέλλων, *rising over* or *above*.

ὑπερ-τέλλω, f. -τελῶ; aor. 1 -έτειλα:—*to rise or*

appear over or *above*; ὑπερτείλας ὁ ἥλιος the sun *having risen above the horizon*: ὑπερτέλλειν ἐκ γαίας *to start* from the ground: c. gen. *to hang* or *project over*.

ὑπερτερία Ion. **-ίη**, **ἡ**, *the upper part*, esp. *the upper frame of a carriage*. From

ὑπέρτερος, *α*, *ον*, Comp. Adj of ὑπέρ, *over* or *above*, *upper*, *higher*: hence *better*, *more excellent*; γενεῇ ὑπέρτερος *higher* by birth, *nobler*; ὑπέρτερα νέρτερα θεῖναι to turn topsy-turvy. II. *stronger*, *mightier*; *victorious over*, c. gen.: neut. as Adv., μαντέων ὑπέρτερον *better than* soothsayers. III. *further*, *more*.

ὑπερ-τίθημι, f. -θήσω: aor. 1 -έθηκα: aor. 2 -έθην: —*to put* or *set over*:—Med., ὑπερτιθέσθαί τινί τι *to make over*, *commit* or *intrust* a thing to any one, *to disclose* a thing, *refer* it to another *for advice*.

ὑπερ-τῑμάω, f. ήσω, *to prize* or *honour above measure*.

ὑπέρ-τολμος, *ον*, (ὑπέρ, τόλμα) *overbold*.

ὑπέρτονος, *ον*, (ὑπερτείνω) *overstrained*, *strained to the utmost*, *at full pitch* or *stretch*.

ὑπερτοξεύσιμος, *ον*, *to be overshot*: metaph. *to be surpassed* or *outdone*. From

ὑπερ-τοξεύω, f. σω, *to overshoot*.

ὑπερ-τρέχω: f. -δρᾰμοῦμαι: aor. 2 ὑπερέδρᾰμον:— *to run over* or *beyond*, *outrun*, *escape from*. 2. *to excel*, *surpass*. 3. *to overstep*, *transgress a law*.

ὑπερ-τρῠφάω, f. ήσω, *to revel extravagantly*.

ὑπ-ερυθριάω, f. άσω [ᾱ], *to grow rather red*, *to blush* or *colour a little*.

ὑπ-έρυθρος, *ον*, (ὑπό, ἐρυθρός) *somewhat red*.

ὑπερ-ύψηλος, *ον*, (ὑπέρ, ὑψηλός) *exceedingly high*.

ὑπερ-υψόω, f. ώσω, *to exalt* or *extol exceedingly*.

ὑπερ-φαίνομαι, aor. 2 ὑπερεφάνην [ᾰ]: Pass. *to appear over* or *above*.

ὑπερ-φᾰλαγγέω, f. ήσω, (ὑπέρ, φάλαγξ) *to extend one's phalanx so as to outflank*

ὑπερφᾰνῆναι, aor. 2 pass. inf. of ὑπερφαίνομαι. Hence

ὑπερφᾰνής, *ές*, gen. *έος*, *appearing over* or *above*.

ὑπέρ-φᾰτος, *ον*, *beyond expression*, *ineffable*

ὑπερ-φέρω, f. -οίσω: aor. 1 act. -ήνεγκα, pass. -ηνέχθην:—*to carry over* or *across*. II. intr. *to have the advantage over*, *to surpass*, *excel*: *to excel in* a thing.

ὑπέρ-φευ, Adv. like ὑπερφυῶς, *excessively*, *overmuch*: t., *highly*.

ὑπερ-φθίνομαι, poët. 3 sing. aor. 2 -έφθιτο: Pass. *to perish for* or *in behalf of* o

ὑπερφίᾰλος, *ον*, properly *exceeding in power*, *exceeding puissant*: but mostly in bad sense, *overbearing*, *overweening*, *arrogant*; θυμὸς ὑπερφίαλος *an overbearing* spirit. Adv. ὑπερφιάλως, *exceedingly*, *excessively*: also *haughtily*, *arrogantly*. (Deriv. uncertain: perhaps another form of ὑπέρβιος.)

ὑπερ-φῐλέω, f. ήσω, *to love beyond measure*.

ὑπερ-φοβέομαι, Pass. with fut. med. -ήσομαι, *to be excessively afraid*.

ὑπέρ-φοβος, *ον*. *exceeding timid*, *very fearful*.

ὑπερ-φορέω, *to carry over*

ὑπερ-φρίσσω Att. **-ττω** f. ξω:—*to shudder at* one *beyond measure*, *to be terribly afraid of*

ὑπερφρονέω, f. ήσω, *to have high thoughts*, *to be overproud*. 2. *to look down upon*, *disdain* From

ὑπέρ-φρων, *ονος*, *ὁ*, *ἡ*, (ὑπέρ, φρήν) *highminded*, *highspirited*: *haughty*, *disdainful*, *arrogant*: ἐκ τοῦ ὑπέρφρονος from *a confidence in one's superiority*.

ὑπερ-φυής, *ές*, (ὑπέρ, φυή) *beyond natural size*, *over grown*, *enormous*, *immense*. II. of things, *extraordinary*, *singular*: *beyond the natural course* of things, *marvellous*, *strange*, *absurd*: also joined with a relat., ὑπερφυής ὅσος, like Lat. *mirum quantum wonderful* how great, i. e. excessively great

ὑπερ-φύομαι, Pass., with aor. 2 act ἔφῡν pf. πέφῡκα:—*to spring* or *shoot up over* or *above*: hence *to outshoot*, *surpass*, *excel*

ὑπερφυῶς, Adv. of ὑπερφυής, *excessively*, *marvellously*: ὑπερφυῶς ὡς *wonderfully how*, i. e. *most wonderfully*.

ὑπερφύς, *ῦσα*, *ύν*, aor 2 part. of ὑπερφύομαι

ὑπερ-χαίρω, f. -χᾰρήσω:—*to rejoice exceedingly at* a thing, c. dat II. c. part. *to delight in* doing.

ὑπερ-χᾰλάω, f. άσω [ᾰ], *to let down over*

ὑπερ-χθόνιος, *ον*, (ὑπέρ, χθών) *above the earth*.

ὑπερ-χλῐδάω, f. ήσω, strengthd. for χλιδάω, like ὑπερτρυφάω, *to be over wanton* or *arrogant*

ὑπ-έρχομαι, f. -ελεύσομαι: aor. 2 act. -ήλῠθον or -ῆλθον pf. -ελήλῠθα: (cf. ἔρχομαι): Dep.:—*to go* or *come under*, *get under*, *enter*, Lat. *subire*, c. acc. II. *to go into secretly*, *to steal* or *creep into*: metaph. *to come upon* or *over* one; ὑπέρχεταί με φρίκη a shuddering *steals over* me. III. *to creep into* another's *good graces*, *to fawn on*: hence *to undermine*, *deceive* IV. *to advance slowly*

ὑπέρ-χρεως, *ων*, (ὑπέρ, χρέος) *excessively in debt*

ὑπ-ερωέω, f. ήσω, (ὑπό, ἐρωέω) *to shrink back*, *recoil*.

ὑπερῴη Att. ὑπερῴᾱ, *ἡ*, *the upper part of the mouth*, *the palate*: properly fem. of ὑπερῷος.

ὑπερωιόθεν, Adv. *from the upper story*. From

ὑπερῷον, Ep. and Ion. **ὑπερώιον**, *τό*, *the upper part of the house*, *the upper story* or *upper rooms*, where the women resided: properly neut. of ὑπερῷος (sub. οἴκημα).

ὑπερῷος, *α*, *ον*, Ion. and Ep. **ὑπερώιος** (from ὑπέρ, as πατρῷος from πατήρ), *being above* or *over*, *overhead*

ὑπερώτατος, *η*, *ον*, poët. Sup. for ὑπέρτατος.

ὑπεσσεῖται, Dor. 3 sing. fut. of ὕπειμι (εἰμί *sum*).

ὑπέσταν, Ep. 3 pl. aor. 2 of ὑφίστημι, also 2 Dor. for ὑπέστην, 1 sing. of same.

ὑπέστειλα, aor. 1 of ὑποστέλλω.

ὑπέστρεψα, aor. 1 of ὑποστρέφω.

ὑπέσχεθον, poët. aor. 2 of ὑπέχω.

ὑπέσχετο, 3 sing. aor. 2 of ὑπισχνέομαι

ὑπέσχημαι, pf. of ὑπισχνέομαι.

ὑπέτρεσας, 2 sing. aor. 1 of ὑποτρέω.

ὑπέτυψα, aor 1 of ὑποτύπτω.

ὑπ-εύθῡνος, *ον*, (ὑπό, εὐθύνη) *liable to give account*, *accountable, responsible; ὑπεύθυνος ἀρχή* an office *at the expiration of which the magistrate has to give an account of his conduct.* 2. c. genit. *liable to, amenable to, liable to make amends for* a thing: *guilty of* a thing. 3. also c. dat. *subject, liable, exposed to.*

ὑπ-ευνάομαι, Pass. (ὑπό, εὐνάω) *to lie under.*

ὑπέφηνα, aor. 1 of ὑποφαίνω.

ὑπέφραδε, 3 sing. aor. 2 of ὑποφράζω.

ὑπέχευα, aor. 1 of ὑποχέω.

ὑπέχρῖσα, aor. 1 of ὑποχρίω.

ὑπ-έχω, f. ὑφέξω: aor. 2 ὑπέσχον poët. ὑπεσχεθον: (cf. ἔχω):—*to hold under* or *underneath.* 2. *to put under* or *place under.* 3. *to hold out* the hand as a pledge: ὑπέχειν οὖας, Lat. *praebere aurem, to lend* an ear: hence *to hold out, suggest:* also *to allege, make a pretence of.* 4. *to supply, afford, place at one's disposal.* II. *to hold from underneath, uphold,* c. acc.: hence *to bear up against, undergo, submit to, suffer.* 2. in law-phrase, ὑπέχειν δίκην τινός *to have to give* an account of a thing; ὑπέχειν λόγον *to have to give* account.

ὕπηγμαι, pf. pass. of ὑπάγω.

ὑπῆγον, ὑπήγἄγον, impf. and aor. 2 of ὑπάγω.

ὑπήκοος, ον, (ὑπακούω) *giving ear, hearkening, listening to.* II. *obeying, obedient, subject,* c. gen.: as Subst., ὑπήκοοι, οἱ, *subjects.*

ὑπῆλθον, aor. 2 of ὑπέρχομαι.

ὑπ-ημύω, *to hang down:* see ὑπεμνήμῡκε.

ὑπήνεικαν, 3 pl. Ion. aor. 1 of ὑποφέρω.

ὑπ-ηνέμιος, ον, (ὑπό, ἄνεμος) *full of wind; ὑπηνέμιον ᾠόν* a *wind*-egg which produces no chicken.

ὑπ-ήνεμος, ον, (ὑπό, ἄνεμος) *under the wind, under shelter from it; ἐκ τοῦ ὑπηνέμου* on *the lee side.*

ὑπήνη, ἡ, (ὑπό) *the under part of the face, on which the beard grows: the beard* itself. Hence

ὑπηνήτης, ου, ὁ, *a bearded man; πρῶτον ὑπηνήτης a youth with his* first *beard.*

ὑπ-ηοῖος, η, ον, (ὑπό, ἠώς) *about dawn, towards morning, early.*

ὕπηργμαι, pf. pass. of ὑπάρχω.

ὑπηρεσία, ἡ, (ὑπηρετέω) *the service* or *duty of rowers* 2. Collective for οἱ ὑπηρέται, *the complement* of *rowers and sailors, a ship's crew.* II. generally, *hard service, hard work:* also *service rendered* to another, *assistance.*

ὑπηρέσιον, τό, (ὑπηρετέω) *the cushion on a rower's bench, a rowing mat.*

ὑπηρετέω, f. ήσω: pf. act. ὑπηρέτηκα, pass. ὑπηρέτημαι: (ὑπηρέτης):—*to row, serve on board ship.* II. generally, *to do hard service, to work for, aid and abet: to serve, comply with, obey, act under instructions: to comply with, gratify; ὑπηρετεῖν τι to do a service:*—Pass. *to be done as service; τὰ ἀπ' ἡμέων ἐς ὑμέας ὑπηρετέεται the services* which are *rendered* to you from us. 2. *to suit oneself to, gratify, humour.* 3. absol. *to be a servant.* Hence

ὑπηρέτημα, ατος, τό, *service rendered, service, help,* Lat. *officium.*

ὑπ-ηρέτης, ου, ὁ, (ὑπό, ἐρέτης) *a rower:* generally, *a seaman, sailor.* II. *any labourer: an assistant, servant, inferior officer,* Lat. *apparĭtor; ὑπηρέτης ἔργου a helper in* a work. 2. *the servant who attended each heavy-armed soldier.*

ὑπηρετικός, ή, όν, (ὑπηρέτης) *of* or *fit for rowing.* II. generally, *belonging to, suited for serving: of* or *for an ὑπηρέτης* or *inferior officer* or *soldier; ὅπλα ὑπηρετικά* the arms *of the common men; κέλης ὑπηρετικός* a boat *attending on* a larger vessel, *a tender.*

ὑπ-ηρέτις, ιδος, fem. of ὑπηρέτης, *a helpmate, assistant.*

ὑπήρῖπε, 3 sing. aor. 2 of ὑπηρείπω.

ὑπήσω, Ion. for ὑφήσω, fut. of ὑφίημι.

ὑπ-ηχέω, f. ήσω, *to sound under, answer with a sound from below.*

ὑπ-ίημι, Ion. for ὑφίημι.

ὑπ-ίλλω: aor. 1 ὑπῖλα: (ὑπό, ἴλλω = εἴλω):—*to force* or *draw in underneath:* metaph. *to keep under, check, restrain; ὑπίλλειν στόμα to check* one's tongue.

ὑπιοῦσα, part. fem. of ὕπειμι (εἶμι *ibo*).

ὑπ-ίστημι, Ion. for ὑφίστημι.

ὑπ-ισχνέομαι, contr. -οῦμαι Ion. **ὑπίσχομαι:** fut. ὑποσχήσομαι: aor. 2 ὑπεσχόμην, imperat. ὑπόσχου: pf. ὑπέσχημαι: (ὑπό, ἴσχω = ἔχω):—*to hold oneself under,* i. e. *to take upon oneself, undertake, promise, engage:* of a father, *to promise* his daughter *in marriage, betroth:* of the bride, *to plight her troth:* also *to promise* or *vow* to the gods: generally, *to assure, assert, profess.*

ὑπ-ίσχομαι, Ion. for ὑπισχνέομαι.

ὑπνᾰλέος, α, ον, (ὕπνος) *sleep-bringing, drowsy.*

ὑπν-ᾰπάτης, ου, ὁ, (ὕπνος, ἀπᾰτάω) *cheating of sleep.*

ὑπνίδιος, α, ον, (ὕπνος) *sleepy, drowsy.* [νῐ]

ὑπνο-δοτήρ, ῆρος, ὁ, and **ὑπνο-δότης,** ου, ὁ, (ὕπνος, δίδωμι) *giver of sleep; νόμος ὑπνοδότης a lulling* strain: fem. **ὑπνοδότειρα.**

ὑπνο-μᾰχέω, f. ήσω, (ὕπνος, μάχομαι) *to resist* or *strive against sleep.*

ὝΠΝΟΣ, ὁ, *sleep, slumber:* metaph. *the sleep of death.* II. *Sleep,* as a god, twin-brother of Death.

ὑπνο-φόβης, ου, ὁ, (ὕπνος, φοβέω) *frightening in sleep.*

ὑπνόω, f. ώσω: pf. act. ὕπνωκα, pass. ὕπνωμαι: (ὕπνος):—*to lull to sleep:*—Pass. *to fall asleep, go to sleep, sleep, slumber.* II. intr. in Act. *to fall asleep.*

ὕπνω, Dor. gen. of ὕπνος.

ὑπν-ώδης, ες, (ὕπνος, εἶδος) *of a sleepy nature, drowsy.*

ὑπνῶν, Lacon. for ὑπνοῦν, inf. of ὑπνόω.

ὑπνώσσω Att. -ττω, = ὑπνόω, *to be sleepy* or *drowsy; οὐκ ὑπνώσσει κέαρ* my heart *slumbers* not.

ὑπνώω, Ep. for ὑπνόω, *to sleep, fall asleep.*

ὙΠΟ', Prep., governing gen., dat., et acc.: *under:* poët. ὑπαί, metri grat.

WITH GENIT., I. of Place, *from under;* μέ…

κρήνη ὑπὸ σπείους a fountain flows *from under* a cavern; ἵππους ὑπὸ ζυγοῦ λύειν to unharness horses *from under* the yoke; ὑπ' ἀρνειοῦ λυόμην I loosed myself *from under* the ram. 2. of that *under* which a thing is, *under, beneath*; ὑπὸ στέρνοιο τυχήσας having hit him *under* the chest. II. of the Agent, with pass. Verbs, and with neuters in pass. sense, *by, through*, Lat. *a* or *ab*; κτείνεσθαι ὑπό τινος to be slain *by* a man; θανεῖν ὑπ' αὐτοῦ to fall *by* his hand; ὑφ' ἑαυτοῦ *by* one's own free action; ἀκούειν ὑπό τινος to hear, i. e. be told *by*, one. 2. where it is not the immediate act of the agent; φεύγειν ὑπό τινος to flee *by reason of* one; ὑπὸ κήρυκος προηγόρευε he proclaimed *by voice of* herald. 3. ὑπό is often extended to feelings, passions, etc.; ὑπὸ δέους, χαρᾶς, etc., *by* or *from* fear, joy, etc.: hence with active Verbs also, as πράττειν τι ὑπ' ἀρετῆς to do somewhat *by reason of* courage; ὑπὸ δέους *by reason of* fear, etc.; ὀρύσσειν ὑπὸ μαστίγων to dig *by constraint of* the lash 4. to express subjection, ἀρετῶσιν ὑπ' αὐτοῦ they are virtuous *under* his sway. 5. ὑπό is often used of attendant circumstances; ὑπὸ Ζεφύροιο ἰωῆς *at* the blast of Zephyr; of music, κωμάζειν ὑπ' αὐλοῦ to revel *to the sound of* the flute; πίνειν ὑπὸ σάλπιγγος to drink *to the sound of* the trumpet; so, ὑπ' εὐφήμου βοῆς θῦσαι to offer a sacrifice *accompanied by* a cheerful cry.

WITH DAT. of the object, *under* which a thing is: I. of Place; ὑπὸ ποσσί *under* one's feet; ὑπὸ τῇ ἀκροπόλει *under* the acropolis; ὑφ' ἅρμασι *under, yoked to* the chariot; ὑπὸ χερσὶ δαμῆναι to be subdued *under*, i. e. *by force* of, one's arm; so φοβεῖσθαι ὑπό τινι to fear *under*, i. e. *by reason of*, one; ὑπὸ πομπῇ τινος βῆναι to proceed *under* one's guidance. II. expressing *subjection* or *dependence*; hence ὑπό τινι *under* one's *power*; εἶναι ὑπό τινι to be *subordinate, subject to* a person; ἔχειν ὑφ' ἑαυτῷ to have *under* one, *at* one's *command*.

WITH ACCUS., I. of Place, to express motion *towards and under* an object, as, ὑπὸ σπέος ἤλασε μῆλα he drove the sheep *under cover of* the cave; ὑπὸ Τροίην ἰέναι to go *under the walls of* Troy; so, ὑπὸ δικαστήριον ἄγειν to bring *under* the judgment-seat. 2. *under* an object, *without* signf. of motion, ὑπ' ἠῶ τ' ἠέλιόν τε *under* morning and the su II. of Time, like Lat. *sub, about, near upon*, ὑπὸ νύκτα *towards* night; ὑπὸ τὴν ἕω *about* morning; ὑπὸ τὸν σεισμόν *about the time of* the earthquake; also c. part., ὑπὸ τὸν νηὸν κατακαέντα *about the time of* the burning of the temple.

POSITION: ὑπό sometimes follows its Subst., when it is written ὕπο.

Ὑπό stands absol. AS ADV., *under, below, beneath* 2. *behind*. II. *secretly, unnoticed*.

IN COMPOS.: 1. *under*, either of rest, as in ὕπ-ειμι *to be under*; or of motion, as in ὑπο-βαίνω *to go under*. 2. of the mixing of one thing with another, as in ὑπ-άργυρος, ὑπό-χρυσος. 3. to express subjection, as in ὑπο-δαμάω, ὑπο-δμώς. II. denoting what is gradual, secret, etc., *somewhat, a little, by degrees*, like Lat. *sub*, as in ὑπο-θωπεύω.

ὑπό-βαθρον, τό, *anything set under, a prop, stay, base, pedestal*. 2. *a carpet spread under foot*.

ὑπο-βαίνω, f. -βήσομαι: aor. 2 -έβην: pf. -βέβηκα:—*to go under, step* or *stand under*, esp. *as a prop* or *base* II. metaph. *to be below, be less in height*; τεσσαρακοντα πόδας ὑποβὰς τῆς ἑτέρης [πυραμίδος] τωὐτὸ μέγαθος *going* forty feet *below* the like size of the other pyramid, i. e. building it forty feet lower.

ὑπο-βάλλω Ep. **ὑββάλλω**: f. -βᾰλῶ: pf. act. -βέβληκα, pass. -βέβλημαι:—*to throw, put* or *lay under*, Lat. *substernere* II. Med. *to substitute* another's child *for one's own, palm a supposititious child upon one*. 2. metaph. *to palm* or *pass off false charges*. III. *to throw in* a word *after* another, *to rejoin, reply, retort*. IV. *to suggest, submit to* one.

ὑπόβᾰσις, εως, ἡ, (ὑποβαίνω) *a stooping* or *crouching down*, as of a camel to take up a burden.

ὑπο-βένθιος, ον, (ὑπό, βένθος) *in the depths below*.

ὑπο-βήσσω Att. **-βήττω**: f. -βήξω:—*to cough a little, have a slight cough*.

ὑπο-βῐβάζω, f. -βιβάσω Att. -βιβῶ, Causal of ὑποβαίνω, *to draw* or *bring down*:—Med. *to let oneself down, stoop* or *crouch down*

ὑπο-βλέπω, f. -βλέψομαι *to look up from underneath at, glance at* or *look askance at, eye scornfully, suspiciously* or *angrily*.

ὑποβλήδην, Adv. (ὑποβάλλω) *throwing in underhand* or *covertly*: *suggesting a word, by way of suggestion, by way of caution* or *reproof*. II. *looking sidelong*.

ὑποβλητέος, α, ον, verb. Adj. of ὑποβάλλω, *to be laid* or *put under*.

ὑπόβλητος, ον, (ὑποβάλλω) *put instead of* another, *spurious, counterfeit, false*.

ὑποβολή, ἡ, (ὑποβάλλω) *a putting* or *laying under*. 2. *a suggesting, reminding*. II. pass. *that which is put under, a foundation, groundwork*: metaph. *the subject, subject-matter*.

ὑποβολιμαῖος, α, ον, (ὑποβάλλομαι) *substituted by stealth, supposititious, spurious, counterfeit*; τὰ ὑποβολιμαῖα (sub. τέκνα) *supposititious children*.

ὑπο-βρέμω, *to roar under* or *in answer to*.

ὑπο-βρέχω, f. ξω: pf. pass. -βέβρεγμαι:—*to wet* or *moisten a little*: metaph. *to drink moderately*:—pf pass. part. ὑποβεβρεγμένος, *somewhat drunk*.

ὑπο-βρύχιος, ον, also α, ον, *under water*: generally, *beneath the surface, under ground*. (Deriv. uncertain.) [ῠ]

ὑπόβρῠχος, ον, = ὑποβρύχιος, but only used in neut. plur. ὑπόβρυχα as Adv. *under water*; γενέσθαι ὑπόβρυχα to be *covered with water*.

ὑπό-γαιος or **ὑπόγειος**, ον, (ὑπό, γαῖα) *under ground, under the earth, subterraneous*.

ὑπο-γάστριον, τό, (ὑπό, γαστήρ) *the lower part of*

the belly, the paunch. II. *the lower part of a sea-fish*, considered a delicacy at Athens.

ὑπό-γειος, *ον*, = ὑπόγαιος.

ὑπο-γελάω, f. *-άσομαι* [ᾰ] :—*to laugh at.* II. *to laugh quietly, smile*, Lat. *subridere.*

ὑπο-γενειάζω, f. *σω*, (ὑπό, γένειον) *to intreat by touching the chin.*

ὑπο-γίγνομαι, later and Ion. **-γίνομαι**: aor. 2 *-εγενόμην*: Dep. :—*to grow up by degrees* or *in succession*, Lat. *subnasci.*

ὑπό-γλαυκος, *ον*, *somewhat gray.*

ὑπο-γλαύσσω, (ὑπό, γλαύξ) *to glance from under, to eye askance* or *suspiciously.*

ὑπο-γλῠκαίνω, (ὑπό, γλυκύς) *to sweeten a little:* metaph. *to coax and smooth down.*

ὑπο-γνάμπτω, f. *ψω*, *to bend under* or *gradually.*

ὑπογνώσῃς, 2 sing. aor. 1 subj. of ὑπογιγνώσκω.

ὑπόγραμμα, *ατος*, *τό*, (ὑπογράφω) *that which is written under: a signature.* 2. *an inscription.*

ὑπο-γραμμᾰτεύς, *έως*, *ὁ*, *an under clerk, under secretary.* Hence

ὑπογραμμᾰτεύω, f. *σω*, *to be a* ὑπογραμματεύς, *act as under clerk.*

ὑπογραμμός, *ὁ*, (ὑπογράφω) *a writing-copy, pattern, model.*

ὑπογρᾰφεύς, *έως*, *ὁ*, (ὑπογράφω) *one who writes under another's orders, a secretary, amanuensis:* at Athens, *the clerk of the Popular Assembly* (ἐκκλησία).

ὑπογραφή, *ἡ*, *a subscription, signature: an indictment.* 2. *an impression, mark, print.* II. *a sketch, design, outline*, Lat. *adumbratio.* III. *a painting under* of the eyelids. From

ὑπο-γράφω [ᾰ], f. *ψω*: pf. *γέγραφα*, pass. *γέγραμμαι*: —*to write under, subjoin: to subscribe, sign: to write the name* or *title upon* a thing. II. Med. *to set one's name to a bill of indictment, to join in bringing a charge against* any one, Lat. *subscribere accusationem in aliquem.* 2. in drawing, *to sketch, draw in outline* or *make a rough draught*, Lat. *adumbrare:* metaph. *to sketch out, delineate.* III. *to paint under* the eyelids.

ὑπό-γυιος or **-γυος**, *ον*, (ὑπό, γυῖον) *under the hand, close at hand: fresh, new;* hence *late, recent.* II. *sudden, unexpected;* ἐξ ὑπογύου *off hand, on the spur of the moment.* Hence

ὑπογυίως or **-γύως**, Adv. *newly, lately:* Comp. ὑπογυιότερον *more recently;* Sup. ὑπογυιότατα *very lately.*

ὑπό-γυος, *ον*, = ὑπόγυιος.

ὑπο-δακρύω, f. *ύσω* [ῡ], *to weep a little* or *in secret.*

ὑπο-δᾰμάω, f. *άσω* [ᾰ]: pf. *δέδμηκα*: Pass., aor. 1 *ὑπεδμήθην*: pf. *-δέδμημαι* :—*to subdue under* one, *to overpower, overcome:* aor. 1 pass. part. fem. ὑποδμηθεῖσα, *having yielded to.*

ὑπο-δάμνημι, = ὑποδαμάω; so also in Med. :—Pass. ὑποδάμνᾰμαι, *to be overcome, let oneself be overcome.*

ὑποδδείσας, Ep. aor. 1 part. of ὑποδείδω.

ὑποδέγμενος, Ep. aor. 2 part. of ὑποδέχομαι.

ὑποδέδηγμαι, pf. of ὑποδέχομαι.

ὑποδεδεμένος, pf. pass. of ὑποδέω.

ὑποδεδιώς, pf. part. of ὑποδείδω.

ὑποδεδίως, *ὁ*, (ὑπό, δεδιώς) literally, *crouching for fear*, name of a bird in Aristophanes.

ὑποδέδρομα, poët. pf. of ὑποτρέχω.

ὑπο-δεής, *ές*, gen. *έος*, (ὑπό, δέος) *somewhat deficient, slighter, less*, generally, *below another, inferior to* him; esp. in Comp., ὑποδεέστερος *inferior;* ἐκ πολλῷ ὑποδεεστέρων *with means* much inferior.—Comp. Adv. ὑποδεεστέρως, *in inferior numbers.*

ὑπόδειγμα, *ατος*, *τό*, (ὑποδείκνυμι) *a sign, token, mark.* II. *a pattern, copy, example.*

ὑπο-δείδω, f. *σω*: aor. 1 ὑπέδεισα Ep. ὑπέδδεισα: Ep. pf. ὑποδείδια: 3 pl. Ep. plqpf. ὑποδείδισαν: poët. pf. ὑπαιδείδοικα, for ὑποδέδοικα :—*to fear a little* or *slightly, be somewhat afraid of*, c. acc. 2. *to shrink in fear from, cower before.* II. absol. *to be somewhat afraid.*

ὑπο-δείκνῡμι and **-ύω**: fut. *-δείξω* Ion. *-δέξω*: aor. 1 ὑπέδειξα Ion. *-έδεξα* :—*to shew underhand* or *secretly: to give a mere glimpse of.* 2. *to intimate, give to understand.* II. *to mark out: to shew, teach by example.* III. *to shew forth, make a display of, pretend to:* also simply, *to shew.*

ὑπο-δειλιάω, f. *άσω* [ᾱ], *to be somewhat cowardly.*

ὑπο-δειμαίνω, *to stand in secret awe of.*

ὑπο-δειπνέω, f. *ήσω*, *to dine instead of another.*

ὑποδείσας, aor. 1 part. of ὑποδείδω.

ὑπο-δέκομαι, Ion. for ὑποδέχομαι.

ὑπο-δέμω, *to build under, lay as a foundation.*

ὑποδεξίη, *ἡ*, (ὑποδέχομαι) *reception of a guest, means of entertainment.* [ῑ in Ep., metri grat.]

ὑποδέξιος, *α*, *ον*, (ὑποδέχομαι) *able to receive, capacious, ample.*

ὑπο-δερίς, *ίδος*, *ἡ*, (ὑπό, δέρη) *a neck-ornament, necklace.*

ὑπόδεσις, *εως*, *ἡ*, (ὑποδέω) = ὑποδήματα, *one's shoes.*

ὑποδέχθαι, Ep. aor. 2 pass. inf. of ὑποδέχομαι.

ὑπο-δέχομαι Ion. **-δέκομαι**: f. *-δέξομαι*: aor. 1 *-εδεξάμην*: pf. *-δέδεγμαι*: also aor. 1 pass. *-εδέχθην* (in pass. sense): Dep :—*to receive beneath the surface of the sea.* 2. *to receive under one's roof, welcome, entertain;* ὁ ὑποδεξάμενος one's *entertainer* or *host.* 3. *to give ear to, hearken to.* II. *to undertake, engage, promise*, Lat. *in se recipere:* also *to undertake* a work or task. 2. *to admit* or *allow the justice* of a thing; with a negat., οὐχ ὑποδέχεσθαι *to refuse to admit, deny.* III. *to endure, bear.* IV. *to wait for, abide the attack of*, Lat. *excipere.* 2. *to follow in rank* or *order: to come next to, border upon.* V. of a woman, *to conceive, become pregnant.*

ὑπο-δέω, f. *-δήσω*: pf. pass. ὑποδέδεμαι :—*to bind* or *tie under* :—Med. *to bind under one's feet, put on* shoes, etc., κοθόρνους ὑποδέεσθαι *to put on one's* buskins: absol., ὑποδέεσθαι *to put on one's shoes:* pf. pass. part., ὑποδεδεμένος, *with one's shoes on;* ὑποδεδεμένοι τὸν ἀριστερὸν πόδα with the left foot shod.

ὑπο-δηλόω, f. ώσω, *to shew secretly, indicate.*

ὑπόδημα, ατος, τό, (ὑποδέω) *that which is bound under, a sandal,* Lat. *solea:* also, *a shoe, boot,* Lat. *calceus.*

ὑπόδησαι, aor. 1 med. imperat. of ὑποδέω.

ὑποδῆσαι, aor. 1 act. inf. of ὑποδέω.

ὑπο-δἴδάσκἄλος, ὁ, *the under-teacher* of a chorus.

ὑπό-δἴκος, ον, (ὑπό, δίκη) *subject to trial, brought to trial;* c. gen., ὑπόδικος γενέσθαι χερῶν to be *brought to trial* on a charge of violence.

ὑπο-δἰφθερας, ον, (ὑπό, διφθέρα) *clothed in skins.*

ὑποδμηθείς, aor. 1 pass. part. of ὑποδαμάω.

ὑπο-δμώς, -ῶος, ὁ, *an under-servant, assistant.*

ὑποδοχή, ἡ, (ὑποδέχομαι) *a reception, a hospitable reception, entertainment:* also *a harbouring,* as of slaves. II. *acceptance, approval:* hence *support, aid, succour.* III. *a supposition, assumption.* IV. *a receptacle: a place of refuge, quarters.*

ὑπόδρᾰ, (ὑποδρακεῖν) poët. Adv., used by Homer only in phrase ὑπόδρα, ἰδών, looking *askance,* i. e. *fiercely, sternly.*

ὑποδρᾰκεῖν, aor. 2 inf. of ὑποδέρκομαι.

ὑποδρᾰμεῖν, aor. 2 inf. of ὑποτρέχω.

ὑπο-δράω poët. **ὑποδρώω**: f. -δράσω:—*to act under, be serviceable* or *useful to* one, c. dat.

ὑποδρηστήρ, ῆρος, ὁ, (ὑποδράω) *an under-servant, attendant, assistant.*

ὑποδρομή, ἡ, (ὑποδραμεῖν) *a running under* or *into the way of* a thing.

ὑπόδρομος, ον, (ὑποδραμεῖν) *running under;* πέτρος ὑπόδρομος ἴχνους a stone *that got under, got in the way of,* his foot.

ὑπό-δροσος, ον, *somewhat dewy* or *damp.*

ὑποδρώωσι, poët. for ὑποδρῶσι, 3 pl. of ὑποδράω.

ὑπο-δύνω, = ὑποδύω. [ῡ]

ὑποδύς, ῦσα, ύν, aor. 2 part. of ὑποδύω.

ὑπόδῠσις, εως, ἡ, *a diving* or *plunging under.* II. *refuge, escape from* a thing. From

ὑπο-δύω or **-δύνω** [ῡ]: f. -δύσω [ῡ]: aor. 1 ὑπέδῡσα: —*to put on under.* 2. intr. *to slip in under, to slip* or *slide into, insinuate oneself into:* but also *to slip from under,* c. acc. II. mostly in Med. ὑποδύομαι, aor. 1 ὑπεδῡσάμην: also with aor. 2 act. ὑπέδυν, pf. ὑποδέδῠκα:—*to dive under, slip into, steal* or *slink into: to put on, slip one's feet into* shoes. 2. c. gen. *to creep* or *come forth, emerge from.* 3. *to go under, take on one's shoulders:* then, *to undergo, take on oneself,* c. acc. 4. of feelings, *to steal into* or *over, come on gradually.* 5. ὀφθαλμοὶ ὑποδεδυκότες *sunken* eyes.

ὑπο-είκω, f. ὑπο-είξομαι, Ep. for ὑπείκω, ὑπείξομαι.

ὑπο-εργός, όν, contr. ὑπουργός, q. v.

ὑπο-ζάκορος, ὁ, also ἡ, *an under-priest* or *priestess.*

ὑπο-ζεύγνῡμι and -ύω, f. -ζεύξω: aor. 1. ὑπέζευξα: Pass., aor. 2 ὑπεζύγην [ῠ]: pf. ὑπέζευγμαι:—*to yoke under, put under the yoke: to bring under:*—Pass. *to be yoked under, be subjected to.*

ὑπο-ζύγιον, τό, (ὑπό, ζῠγόν) *a beast under the yoke, a beast of draught* or *burden.*

ὑπο-ζῠγόω, f. ώσω, = ὑποζεύγνυμι.

ὑπόζωμα, ατος, τό, (ὑποζώννυμι) *a flat rope* or *strap for undergirding* a ship; cf. ὑποζώννυμι.

ὑπο-ζώννῡμι and -ύω: f. -ζώσω: pf. act. ὑπέζωκα, pass. ὑπέζωσμαι:—*to undergird, gird together:* esp. *to undergird* a ship, i. e. to fasten ropes round her so as to prevent her going to pieces.

ὑπο-θάλπω, f. ψω, *to heat underneath* or *inwardly:* —Pass. *to glow beneath.*

ὑποθείς, εῖσα, έν, aor. 2 part. of ὑποτίθημι.

ὑπο-θερμαίνω, *to heat gently:*—Pass. *to grow somewhat hot, to glow.*

ὑπό-θερμος, ον, *somewhat hot* or *passionate:*—Comp. -ότερος, *too hasty* or *passionate.*

ὑποθέσθαι, aor. 2 med. inf. of ὑποτίθημι.

ὑπόθεσις, εως, ἡ, (ὑποτίθημι) *a placing under,* or *that which is placed under, a groundwork, foundation.* II. *that which is laid down* or *assumed, a hypothesis, supposition,* Lat. *assumtio.* 2. *a question for discussion, the subject under discussion,* Lat. *argumentum.* III. *that which is laid down as a rule of action, a principle.* 2. generally, *a purpose, plan, design: a proposal.*

ὑπο-θέω, f. -θεύσομαι, *to run in under, trip up.* II. *to run in before, slip in before* in running a race. III. *to run in too hastily.*

ὑποθήκη, ἡ, (ὑποτίθημι) *a suggestion, hint, piece of advice.* II. *a pledging, mortgage.*

ὑποθημοσύνη, ἡ, (ὑποτίθημι) *ready suggestion, a piece of advice.*

ὑποθήσομαι, fut. med. of ὑποτίθημι.

ὑπο-θλίβω [ῑ], f. ψω, *to press under* or *gently.*

ὑπο-θορῠβέω, f. ήσω, *to make a little noise: to begin to make a noise.*

ὑπο-θράσσω Att. **-ττω**, fut. -θράξω, Att. contr. from ὑποταράσσω.

ὑπο-θρύπτομαι, fut. -θρύψομαι: aor. 1 ὑπεθρύφθην: Dep.:—*to be affected* or *effeminate:* also *to play the wanton.*

ὑπο-θῡμιάω, f άσω [ᾱ]:—*to burn scents so as to fumigate,* Lat. *suffire.*

ὑπο-θῡμίς, ίδος, ἡ, (ὑπό, θυμός) *a garland worn on the neck.* II. a kind of bird.

ὑπο-θωπεύω, *to flatter a little, win by flattery.*

ὑπο-θωρήσσω, f. ξω, *to arm underhand:*—Med. *to arm oneself secretly* or *unobserved.*

ὑπο-ιάχω [ᾰ], *to sound forth a little* or *below.*

ὑπ-οίγνῡμι and **ὑπ-οίγω**, f. ὑποίξω, *to open a little* or *secretly.*

ὑπ-οικέω, f. ήσω, *to dwell* or *lie under.*

ὑπ-οικίζομαι, Pass. (ὑπό, οἰκίζω) = ὑποικέω

ὑπ-οικοδομέω, f. ήσω, *to build under* or *beneath.*

ὑπ-οικουρέω, f. ήσω, *to keep house, stay at home.* II. c. acc. rei, *keep secretly at home, to contrive underhand.* 2. c. acc. pers. *to intrigue with.*

ὑπ-οιμώζω, fut. -ώξομαι, *to moan a little* or *softly.*

ὑπο-καθέζομαι, fut. *-εδοῦμαι*, Dep. *to sit down under.*

ὑπο-κάθημαι Ion. **-κατημαι**, (properly perf. or ὑποκαθέζομαι):—*to sit down under* or *in* a place, *take one's station under.* II. *to sit down under cover, lie in ambush* 2. c. acc. pers., *to lie in wait for.*

ὑπο-καθίζω, fut. Att. *ιῶ*, *to set down under: to place in ambush:* Med. *to lie in ambush,* Lat. *subsidēre.*

ὑπο-καίω, f. *-καύσω*, *to set on fire from below.*

ὑπο-κάμπτω, f. *ψω*, transit. *to bend under, bend short back.* 2. intr. *to turn short back, double,* as a hare. II. metaph. *to fall short of,* c. acc.

ὑπο-κάρδιος, *ον*, (ὑπό, καρδία) *under* or *in the heart.*

ὑπο-καταβαίνω, fut. *-βήσομαι*: aor. 2 *-έβην*: pf. *-βέβηκα*:—*to go down* or *descend by degrees: to go down by stealth.*

ὑπο-κατακλίνω, f. *-κλῐνῶ*, *to lay down under:*—Pass. *to lie down below:* metaph. *to give way, submit, yield.*

ὑπο-κάτημαι, Ion. for ὑποκάθημαι.

ὑπο-κάτω, Adv. *below, under: beneath, underneath.* [ᾰ]

ὑπό-κειμαι, f. *-κείσομαι*, used as Pass. of ὑποτίθημι, *to lie under* or *below;* πεδίον ἱερῷ ὑπόκειται the plain *lies below* the temple: *to lie bidden under.* II. metaph. *to be put under the eyes, to be set* or *proposed before* one; δυοῖν ὑποκειμένων two things *being proposed.* 2. *to be laid down, assumed, taken for granted:* ὑπόκειται absol. *a rule is laid down.* 3. *to be suggested.* 4. *to be left at bottom, left remaining, reserved.* 5. *to be subject to, submit:* also *to form the subject* or *matter* of an inquiry; ὕλη ὑποκειμένη *subject* matter. 6. *to be subject to a mortgage, to be pledged* or *mortgaged;* τὰ ὑποκείμενα *the articles pledged.*

ὑπο-κελεύω, f. *σω*, *to act as* κελευστής: *to give the time in rowing.*

ὑπο-κηρύσσω Att. **-ττω**, f. *ξω*, *to proclaim by voice of herald:*—Med. *to have a thing proclaimed* or *cried.*

ὑπο-κῑνέω, f. *ήσω*: aor. 1 *-εκίνησα*:—*to move below* or *a little, move gently:* metaph. *to urge gently on.* II. intr. *to move a little* or *gently;* οὐδεμία πόλις ἂν ὑπεκίνησε no city *would ever have moved so gently.*

ὑπ-οκλάζω, f. *σω*, *to bend the knees under one, sink slowly down:* of an expiring lamp, *to flicker.*

ὑπο-κλαίω, *to weep in secret.*

ὑπο-κλάω, f. *άσω* [ᾰ], *to break underneath* or *by degrees.*

ὑπο-κλέπτω, f. *ψω*, *to steal underhand:*—Pass. *to be defrauded in* a matter.

ὑπο-κλίνω, *to lay under:*—Pass., aor. 1 ὑπεκλίνθην, *to be laid* or *lie under.*

ὑπο-κλονέω, f. *ήσω*, *to rout under* one or *by one's prowess:*—Pass. *to be routed, scattered before* one.

ὑπο-κλοπέω, f. *ήσω*, like ὑποκλέπτω, *to conceal under:*—Pass. *to be hidden under.*

ὑπο-κλύζω, f. *ύσω*, *to wash* or *cleanse from below:*—Pass. *to be flooded,* as with mischief.

ὑπο-κνίζω, f. *ίσω*, *to irritate* or *excite secretly:*—Pass. *to be provoked.*

ὑπο-κόλπιος, *ον*, (ὑπό, κόλπος) *lying on the bosom:* as Subst. *a darling.* 2. *worn under the girdle.*

ὑπό-κοπος, *ον*, (ὑπό, κόπος) *somewhat tired.*

ὑπο-κορίζομαι, f. *-ίσομαι*, Dep. *to play the child, to speak like a child:* hence, I. *to call by endearing names.* 2. *to call by a soft* or *fair name, gloss over, extenuate, palliate.* 3. also *to call* something good *by a bad name, to disparage.* Hence

ὑποκόρισμα, *ατος*, *τό*, *a coaxing* or *endearing word: a fair name* for something base.

ὑποκορισμός, *ὁ*, = ὑποκόρισμα.

ὑπο-κουρίζομαι, Ion. for ὑποκορίζομαι: *to console with songs.*

ὑπο-κρέκω, f. *ξω*, of stringed instruments, *to sound under one's hand: to sound in harmony with,* c. dat. 2. c. acc. *to play an accompaniment.*

ὑπο-κρητηρίδιον, *τό*, *a small stand* or *saucer to put under the bowl* (κρητήρ). [ῐ]

ὑποκρίναιτο, 3 sing. aor. 1 opt. of ὑποκρίνομαι. [ῑ]

ὑποκρίνασθαι, aor. 1 inf. of ὑποκρίνομαι. [ῑ]

ὑπο-κρίνομαι [ῑ], f. *-κρῐνοῦμαι*: aor. 1 med. ὑπεκρινάμην, pass. ὑπεκρίθην [ῐ]: Med.:—*to reply, make answer, answer,* of an oracle, *to make a response: to expound, interpret* II. in Att., of the actors, *to speak dialogue; play a part* on the stage, the part played being put in acc.; ὑποκρίνεσθαι Προμηθέα *to play* Prometheus. 2. of a theatrical style, *to exaggerate, rant.* 3. metaph. *to play a part, dissemble, play the hypocrite.*

ὑποκρῐσία, *ἡ*, = ὑπόκρισις.

ὑπόκρῐσις, *εως*, *ἡ*, (ὑποκρίνομαι) *a reply, answer.* II. *the playing a part* on the stage, *playing* or *acting, the player's art, declamation:* also an orator's *delivery, elocution.* 2. metaph. *the playing a part, feigning, hypocrisy.*

ὑποκρῐτής, *οῦ*, *ὁ*, (ὑποκρίνομαι) *one who answers. an interpreter* or *expounder* II. *one who plays a part* on the stage, *a player, actor.* 2. *a dissembler, pretender, hypocrite.* Hence

ὑποκρῐτικός, *ή*, *όν*, *befitting an actor: skilled in elocution: suited for speaking* or *delivery:* ἡ ὑποκριτική (sub. τέχνη), *the art of delivery, elocution.*

ὑπο-κρούω, f. *σω*, *to strike gently,* of a harper striking the strings: *to beat time.* II. metaph. *to take up the word, to break in upon, interrupt, attack.*

ὑπο-κρύπτω, f. *ψω*: aor. 1 pass. ὑπεκρύφθην:—*to hide under* or *beneath:*—Med., c. acc. pers. *to keep* something *secret from one.*

ὑπο-κρώζω, f. *ξω*, *to croak against.*

ὑπό-κυκλος, *ον*, *running upon wheels.*

ὑπο-κύπτω, f. *ψω*: aor. 1 ὑπέκυψα:—*to bend* or *stoop under,* esp. under a yoke; οἱ Μῆδοι ὑπέκυψαν Πέρσῃσι the Medes *submitted to* the Persians: *to bow down, prostrate oneself: to stoop down to drink,* also *to stoop so as to peep into* a place. II. c. acc. ὑποκύπτειν τὰν τύλαν *to stoop* the shoulder so as to let a load be put on.

ὑπο-κυομαι, Med. (ὑπό, κυέω) of the woman, *to conceive, to become pregnant;* aor. 1 part. ὑποκῡσαμένη.

ὑπο-κώλιον τό (ὑπό, κῶλον) *the hip-bone,* or *the thigh.*

ὑπο-κωμῳδέω, f. ήσω, *to ridicule a little* or *underhand.*

ὑπό-κωφος, ον, *somewhat deaf, rather deaf.*

ὑπολᾰβεῖν, aor. 2 inf. of ὑπολαμβάνω.

ὑπο-λαμβάνω, f. -λήψομαι: aor. 2 ὑπέλᾰβον: pf. ὑπείληφα, pass. ὑπείλημμαι: (cf. λαμβάνω):—*to take up from below, take on one's back,* Lat. *suscipere.* 2. *to catch up, come suddenly upon, overtake:* of events, *to follow next, come next.* 3. *to take up* a word and *answer, to reply, rejoin, retort;* often in aor. 2 part., ἔφη ὑπολαβών he said *in answer.* 4. *to take up* the conqueror, *fight with* him, Lat. *excipere.* II. = ὑποδέχομαι, *to take* or *receive under one's protection.* 2. *to accept* or *entertain* a proposal. III. *to take up* a notion, *assume, understand:*—Pass. *to be supposed;* ἡ ὑπειλημμένη χάρις the *supposed* favour. 2. *to suspect.* IV. *to seize underhand: to draw away, entice.* V. ὑπολαμβάνειν ἵππον *to hold up* or *check* a horse.

ὑπολαμπής, ές, gen. έος, *shining with inferior light, gleaming.* From

ὑπο-λάμπω, f. ψω, *to shine in under, to gleam beneath* II. *to shine a little, begin to shine* or *dawn.*

ὑπο-λείβω, f. ψω, *to pour a libation therewith* or *to.*

ὑπο-λείπω, f. ψω, *to leave remaining, leave behind.* 2. of things, *to fail* one, *fail.* II. Pass., with fut. med. ὑπολείψομαι, *to be left behind, stay behind* or *at home;* ὑπολείπεσθαι τοῦ στόλου *to stay behind* the expedition: generally, *to remain behind, to be left over and above.* 2. *to be left behind* or *distanced by* any one, properly in a race: of stragglers, *to lag behind:* metaph. *to be inferior to* one. 3. absol. *to fail, come to an end:* also *to fall short* of what one expects. III. Med. *to leave* a thing *behind one,* c. acc.: *to leave remaining, keep in reserve;* ὑπολείπεσθαι αἰτίαν *to leave* cause for reproach *against oneself.*

ὑπό-λεπτος, ον, *somewhat fine* or *delicate.*

ὑπο-λεπτύνω, *to make rather fine* or *delicate.*

ὑπο-λευκαίνω, *to make white underneath:*—Pass., *to become white underneath* or *somewhat white.*

ὑπο-λήγω, f. ξω, *to desist gradually.*

ὑπο-λήνιον, τό, (ὑπό, ληνός) *the vessel under a press* to receive the wine or oil, *a vat,* Lat. *lacus.*

ὑπο-ληπτέον, verb. Adj. of ὑπολαμβάνω, *one must suppose* or *understand.*

ὑπόληψις, εως, ἡ, (ὑπολαμβάνω) *a taking* or *catching up a word;* ἐξ ὑπολήψεως, *in turn, alternately.* 2. *a rejoinder, reply* II. *a taking in a certain sense, an understanding, opinion.*

ὑπ-ολίζων, ον, gen. ονος. (ὑπό, ὀλίζων) *somewhat less, slighter* or *smaller.*

ὑπό-λῐθος, ον, *somewhat stony.*

ὑπο-λιμπάνω, collateral form of ὑπολείπω.

ὑπό-λισπος Att. -λισφος, ον, *somewhat smooth, worn smooth.*

ὑπό-λιχνος, ον, *somewhat dainty.*

ὑπο-λογίζομαι, f. -ίσομαι Att. -ιοῦμαι: Dep.:—*to take into account* or *consideration.*

ὑπό-λογος, ὁ, *a taking into account, a reckoning, account;* ὑπόλογον ποιεῖσθαί τινος, to take *account* of a thing, Lat. *rationem habere rei.*

ὑπο-λόγος, ον Adj. *taken into account, held accountable, responsible.*

ὑπό-λοιπος, ον, *left behind, staying behind: surviving,* Lat. *superstes.*

ὑπο-λόχᾱγος, ὁ, *a lieutenant.*

ὑπο-λύριος, ον, (ὑπό, λύρα) *under the lyre;* δόναξ ὑπολύριος a bridge of reed *on which the strings rest.* [ῠ]

ὑπο-λύω, f. -λύσω [ῡ]: aor. 1 -έλῡσα: pf. -λέλῠκα: Pass., pf. -λέλῠμαι: plqpf. -ελελύμην: Ep. 3 sing. aor. 2 pass. ὑπέλῠτο, 3 pl. ὑπέλυντο:—*to loosen, untie* or *unbind from below, loosen* or *slacken gradually;* ὑπέλυσε γυῖα he *loosened* his limbs *under* him, i. e. gave him his death-blow: so in Pass., γυῖα ὑπέλυντο his limbs *were relaxed under* him. II. *to loose from under the yoke: to loose from* bonds, *set free by stealth.* 2. *to untie* a person's sandals *from under* his feet, *take off* his *shoes, unshoe* him:—Med., *to take off one's own sandals* or *shoes,* opp. to ὑποδεῖσθαι.

ὑπό-μακρος, ον, *rather long, longish.*

ὑπο-μᾰλᾰκίζομαι, Pass. (ὑπό, μαλακίζω) *to grow soft* or *cowardly by degrees.*

ὑπο-μᾰλάσσω Att. -ττω, f. ξω, *to soften a little* or *by degrees:*—Pass. *to be softened gradually.*

ὑπό-μαργος, ον, *somewhat mad, crazy:* Comp. -ότερος.

ὑπο-μάσσω Att. -ττω, f. ξω, *to knead underneath: to smear* or *rub underneath.*

ὑπο-μειδιάω, f. άσω [ᾱ], *to smile a little* or *gently.*

ὑπομεῖναι, aor. 1 inf. of ὑπομένω.

ὑπο-μείων, ον, gen. ονος, *somewhat less* or *inferior:* as Subst., ὑπομείονες, οἱ, among the Spartans, *subordinate citizens,* opp. to ὅμοιοι (peers).

ὑπο-μενετέον or -ητέον, verb. Adj. *one must abide, endure.* From

ὑπο-μένω, fut. -μενῶ: aor. 1 -έμεινα:—*to stay behind: to stay at home.* 2. *to survive, remain alive.* II. trans. *to abide* or *await* another, *to bide* his attack. 2. c. acc. rei, *to be patient under, to abide patiently, submit to, endure:* absol. *to stand one's ground, stand firm:* c. inf. *to undertake* to do a thing. 2. *to wait for* an event: *to abide the issue* of a thing. 3. *to uphold, support, maintain.*

ὑπο-μίγνῡμι, f. -μίξω: pf. pass. -μέμιγμαι:—*to mix among* or *up with.* II. intr. *to come near secretly,* c. dat.; ὑπομῖξαι τῇ γῇ *to run close under* land.

ὑπο-μιμνήσκω, f. -μνήσω: aor. 1 ὑπέμνησα:—I. c. acc. pers. *to put* one *in mind* or *remind* one *of* a thing. 2. c. acc. rei, *to bring back to one's mind, mention, suggest.* II. Pass. and Med., f. -μνήσομαι: aor. 1 -εμνησάμην: pf. -μέμνημαι:—*to call to mind, remember: to make mention of.*

ὑπό-μισθος, ον, *serving for pay, hired, retained.*

ὑπο-μνάομαι contr. -μνῶμαι: Dep.:—*to court a woman underhand* or *behind her husband's back.*

ὑπο-μνάομαι, Ion. pass. of ὑπομιμνήσκω; Ep. 2 pl. impf. ὑπεμνάασθε. Hence

ὑπόμνημα, ατος, *a remembrance, memorial, memorandum, reminder: mention.* 2. in plur. *notes, memoranda*, Lat. *commentarii.*

ὑπομνῆσαι, aor. 1 inf. of ὑπομιμνήσκω.

ὑπόμνησις, εως, ἡ, (ὑπομιμνήσκω) *a reminding, calling to mind.* II. *remembrance.*

ὑπο-μνηστεύομαι, Med. *to betroth underhand.*

ὑπ-όμνυμι, *to interpose by oath.* II. Med. ὑπόμνυμαι, f. ὑπομοῦμαι: aor. 1 ὑπωμοσάμην:—*to swear in bar of further proceedings.* 2. *to stay proceedings by making an oath, apply for a longer term on affidavit: to plead in excuse of non-appearance.*

ὑπομονή, ἡ, (ὑπομένω) *a remaining behind.* II. *a holding out, endurance, patience:* c. gen. *patience under, endurance of* a thing.

ὑπό-μωρος, ον, (ὑπό, μωρός) *rather stupid* or *silly.*

ὑπο-ναίω, *to dwell under.*

ὑπο-νείφω, incorrect form of ὑπονίφω.

ὑπο-νέμομαι, aor. 1 -ενειμάμην: Med.:—*to eat away from beneath*: metaph. *to consume secretly, undermine.*

ὑπο-νέφελος, ον, (ὑπό, νεφέλη) *under the clouds.*

ὑπο-νήιος, ον, (ὑπό, Νήιον) *under the promontory Neïum, lying at its base.*

ὑπο-νήχομαι, f. -ήξομαι, Dep. *to swim under, dive.*

ὑπο-νίφω [ῐ], *to snow a little*:—impers. ὑπένιφε, *there was a little snow*:—Pass., νὺξ ὑπονιφομένη *a snowy* night.

ὑπο-νοέω, f. ήσω, *to think covertly, suspect: to conjecture, guess, guess at;* ὑπονοεῖν τι εἴς τινα *to entertain a suspicion* of one. Hence

ὑπόνοια, ἡ, *a hidden meaning* or *sense:* I. *a suspicion, conjecture, guess, supposition, fancy.* 2. *the true meaning which lies at the bottom of* a thing.

ὑπονομηδόν, Adv. *underground, by pipes.* From

ὑπόνομος, ον, (ὑπονέμω) *going underground, underground.* II. as Subst. ὑπόνομος, ὁ, *an underground passage, mine*, Lat. *cuniculus: a water-pipe.*

ὑπο-νοσέω, f. ήσω, *to be somewhat sickly.*

ὑπο-νοστέω, f. ήσω, *to go down, sink, settle down*, Lat. *subsidĕre:* of a river, *to abate, retire, fall.*

ὑπο-νύσσω, f. ξω, *to prick underneath: to sting.*

ὑπο-ξενίζω, f. ίσω, *to tell in a foreign accent.*

ὑπό-ξυλος, ον, (ὑπό, ξύλον) *wooden underneath, made of wood plated over.*

ὑπο-ξυράω or έω, f. ήσω, (ὑπό, ξυράω) *to shave* or *cut off some of the hair*: ὑπεξυρημένος, *half-shaven.*

ὑπο-ξύριος, α, ον, (ὑπό, ξυρόν) *under the razor.*

ὑπο-ξύω, f. ύσω, [ῡ], *to scrape a little: to graze slightly*, Lat. *stringo.*

ὑπο-παρωθέω, f. -ωθήσω and -ώσω, *to thrust aside by degrees* or *underhand.*

ὑπο-πάσσω, f. -πάσω [ᾰ], *to strew under.*

ὑπο-πεινάω, f. ήσω, *to be rather hungry, begin to be hungry.*

ὑποπεμπτός, όν, *despatched underhand, sent covertly*, Lat. *submissus.* From

ὑπο-πέμπω, f. ψω, *to send under* or *into*, c. acc. II. *to send secretly: to send as a scout* or *spy*, Lat. *submittere.*

ὑποπεπτηῶτες, Ep. pf. part. nom. pl. of ὑποπτήσσω.

ὑποπέπτωκα, pf. of ὑποπίπτω.

ὑποπέπωκα, pf. of ὑποπίνω.

ὑπο-πέρδομαι, aor. 2 act. ὑπέπαρδον: Dep.:—*to break wind a little*, Lat. *suppedere.*

ὑπο-περκάζω, f. άσω, *to become dark-coloured by degrees*, esp. of grapes, *to begin to ripen.*

ὑποπεσεῖν, aor. 2 inf. of ὑποπίπτω.

ὑπο-πετάννυμι, f. -πετάσω [ᾰ]: pf. pass. -πέπτᾰμαι:—*to spread out under, lay under.*

ὑπό-πετρος, ον, (ὑπό, πέτρα) *somewhat rocky.*

ὑπο-πιθηκίζω, f. σω, *to play the ape a little.*

ὑπο-πίμπλημι, f. -πλήσω: aor. 1 ὑπέπλησα, pass. -επλήσθην:—*to fill a little, fill by degrees*:—Pass., τέκνων ὑποπλησθῆναι *to abound with* children.

ὑπο-πίμπρημι, f. -πρήσω, *to set on fire, burn from below* or *gradually.*

ὑπο-πίνω [ῐ]: f. -πίομαι: pf. -πέπωκα:—*to drink gradually* or *slowly, to keep on drinking* or *tippling:* ὑποπεπωκώς *rather tipsy.*

ὑπο-πίπτω, f. -πεσοῦμαι: pf. -πέπτωκα: aor. 2 ὑπέπεσον:—*to fall under* or *down, sink.* . *to fall down before* anyone: of a flatterer, *to cringe to, fawn on.* 3. *to fall behind, fall in the rear.* 4. *to get in under* or *among.* III. of things, *to fall out, happen to, befall.*

ὑπο-πισσόω Att. -ττόω, f. ώσω, *to smear with pitch* or *tar.*

ὑπο-πλάκιος, α, ον, (ὑπό, Πλάκος) *under mount Placos* near Troy: cf. ὑπονήιος. [ᾰ]

ὑπό-πλᾰτυς, υ, *somewhat flat* or *extended.* II. *somewhat salt:* cf. πλατύς.

ὑπό-πλεος, ον Att. -πλεως, ων, (ὑπό, πλέως) *pretty full of*, c. gen.

ὑπο-πλέω, f. -πλεύσομαι, *to sail close under.*

ὑπό-πλεως, ων, gen. ω, Att. for ὑπόπλεος.

ὑπο-πλήσσω Att. -ττω, f. ξω, *to strike beneath.*

ὑπο-πλώω, Ion. for ὑποπλέω.

ὑπο-πνέω, f. -πνεύσομαι, *to blow underneath, blow gently.*

ὑπο-πόδιον, τό, (ὑπό, πούς) *a footstool.*

ὑπο-ποιέω, f. ήσω, *to bring under*:—Med. *to make subject to oneself, bring into one's power, win by secret art* II. in Med. also *to assume, put on.*

ὑπο-πόλιος, ον, (ὑπό, πολιός) *somewhat gray.*

ὑπο-πορεύομαι, Dep. *to go under: go secretly.*

ὑπό-πορτις, ιος, ἡ, *with a calf under it:* of a mother, *with a child at the breast.*

ὑπο-πραΰνω Ep. and Ion. -πρηΰνω, *to appease a little* or *by degrees.* [ῡ]

ὑπο-πρίαμαι, Dep. *to buy under the price.*
ὑπο-πρίω, *to gnash* (the teeth) *secretly.* [ῐ]
ὑπό-πτερος, *ον*, (*ὑπό*, *πτερόν*) *feathered, winged: swift-winged, fleet:* also *soaring, flighty.*
ὑποπτεύω, f. *σω*, *to be suspicious, have suspicion of, suspect that*, c. inf.: also *to suspect, surmise:*—Pass. *to be suspected, mistrusted.* From
ὑπ-όπτης, *ου*, *ὁ*, (*ὑπόψομαι*, f. of *ὑφοράω*) as masc. Adj., *suspicious, jealous:* of a horse, *shy.*
ὑπο-πτήσσω, f. *ξω*: pf. *-πέπτηχα*, Ep. part. *-πεπτηώς*, pl. *-πεπτηῶτες*:—*to crouch* or *cower down from fear; πετάλοις ὑποπεπτηῶτες crouching under* the leaves. II. metaph. *to crouch* or *cower before* another: absol. *to be modest, abashed.*
ὕποπτος, *ον*, (*ὑπόψομαι*, f. of *ὑφοράω*) *looked at from under: looked askance at, viewed with suspicion* or *jealousy, suspected.* II. act. *suspecting, fearing*, Lat. *suspicax:* as Subst., *τὸ ὕποπτον*, *suspicion, jealousy.*
ὑπόπτως, Adv. *with suspicion, jealously.*
ὑπ-όρθριος, *ον*, also, *α*, *ον*, (*ὑπό*, *ὄρθρος*) *towards morning, about dawn, at break of day.*
ὑπο-ρῑπίζω, f. *σω*, (*ὑπό*, *ῥιπίς*) *to fan from below* or *gently.*
ὑπ-όρνῡμι, f. *-όρσω*: aor. 1 *-ῶρσα*:—*to stir up from under, rouse gently* or *gradually:*—Pass. *ὑπόρνυμαι*, Ep. 3 sing. aor. 2 *ὑπῶρτο*: pf. 2 *-ώρορα*:—*to arise from under* or *gradually.*
ὑπ-όροφος, *ον*, = *ὑπώροφος*. II. *sounding softly from a reed; ὑπόροφος βοά the soft* note *of the pipe.*
ὑπορ-ράπτω, f. *ψω*, *to sew underneath, to patch up:* metaph. *to devise, make up.*
ὑπορ-ρέω: f. pass. *-ρυήσομαι* and aor. 2 *ὑπερρύην* (in act. sense): pf. *-ερρύηκα*:—*to flow away under: to glide into unperceived*, Lat. *subrepere; to flow* or *fall in gradually.* 2. *to slip away:* of the hair, *to fall off:* of Time, *to run on*
ὑπορ-ρήγνῡμι and *-ύω*, f. *-ρήξω*, *to make to break underneath:*—Pass. *to be rent from beneath, break gradually open.*
ὑπόρ-ρηνος, *ον*, (*ὑπό*, *ῥήν*) poët. for *ὕπαρνος*, *with a lamb under it.*
ὑπορ-ρῑπίζω, f. *ίσω* Att. *ιῶ*, = *ὑποριπίζω.*
ὑπ-ορύσσω Att. *-ττω*, f. *ξω*, *to dig under, undermine.*
ὑπ-ορχέομαι, f. *-ήσομαι*, Dep. *to dance with* or *to music.*
ὑπό-σαθρος, *ον*, *somewhat rotten, tainted.*
ὑπο-σαλπίζω, f. *ίγξω*, *to sound the trumpet slightly.*
ὑπο-σείω Ep. **ὑποσσείω**: f. *-σείσω*:—*to shake from below* or *gently, set in motion a little*
ὑπο-σημαίνω, f. *ἀνῶ*, *to give a hint of, intimate, indicate quietly:* c. dat., *σάλπιγγι ὑποσημαίνειν to make signal* by sound of trumpet.
ὑπο-σῑγάω, f. *-ήσομαι*, *to be silent to* or *during.*
ὑπο-σιωπάω, f. *-ήσομαι*, *to pass over in silence.*
ὑπο-σκάζω, f. *άσω*, *to halt a little.*
ὑπο-σκᾰλεύω, f. *σω*, *to stir from underneath*, of fire.
ὑπο-σκάπτω, f. *ψω*, *to dig under, trench.*
ὑπο-σκελίζω, f. *σω*, (*ὑπό*, *σκέλος*) *to trip up one's heels, to upset, throw down*, Lat. *supplantare.*
ὑπό-σκιος, *ον*, (*ὑπό σκιά*) *under the shade, overshadowed:* of suppliants, *shaded by their olive-branches.*
ὑπο-σμύχω, *to burn by a slow* or *smouldering fire:*—Pass. *to smoulder away.* [ῡ]
ὑπο-σπᾰνίζομαι, pf. *ὑπεσπάνισμαι*: Pass.:—*to suffer want a little*, c. gen. rei, *βορᾶς ὑπεσπανισμένος stinted* or *in want* of food.
ὑπο-σπάω, f. *άσω* [ᾰ], *to draw away from under, to withdraw secretly:*—Med., *ὑποσπάσασθαι τὸν ἵππον to give a slight pull at one's* horse's *rein.*
ὑπό-σπονδος, (*ὑπό*, *σπονδή*) *under a truce* or *treaty, secured by treaty: subject to the conditions of a truce* or *treaty: τοὺς νεκροὺς ὑποσπόνδους ἀποδιδόναι* or *ἀναιρεῖσθαι*, to grant or ask for a truce to take up the bodies of the slain.
ὑποστάθμη, *ἡ*, (*ὑφίσταμαι*) *that which settles at the bottom, sediment.*
ὑποσταίην, aor. 2 opt. of *ὑφίστημι.*
ὑποστάς, *ᾶσα*, *άν*, aor. 2 part. of *ὑφίστημι.*
ὑπόστᾰσις, *εως*, *ἡ*, (*ὑφίσταμαι*) *that which settles at the bottom, sediment.* II. *anything set under, a support:* metaph. *the groundwork* or *subject-matter* of a thing. 2. metaph. *the foundation* or *ground of hope* or *confidence, confidence, resolution.* III. *subsistence, reality: substance, nature, essence.*
ὑποστᾰτός, *όν*, verb. Adj. of *ὑφίσταμαι*, *set under.* II. *borne, endured, to be borne* or *endured.*
ὑπο-στᾰχύομαι, Pass. (*ὑπό*, *στάχυς*) *to grow up gradually like ears of corn*
ὑπό-στεγος, *ον*, (*ὑπό*, *στέγη*) *under the roof, under cover of a house.* 2. *covered over.*
ὑπο-στέγω, f. *ξω*, *to cover, stow, hide under.*
ὑπο-στέλλω, f. *-στελῶ*: aor. 1 *ὑπέστειλα*: pf. *ὑπέσταλκα*, pass. *-έσταλμαι*:—*to let down, lower, take in: to furl, strike sail*, etc. II. Med. *to draw* or *shrink back from, shrink from the presence of.* 2. *to cloak, conceal, suppress through fear:* absol. *to dissemble; οὐδὲν ὑποστειλάμενος with* no *dissimulation.*
ὑπο-στενάζω, f. *ξω*, = *ὑποστένω*, *to sigh* or *moan in an under tone.* II. c. acc., *οὐράνιον πόλον νώτοις ὑποστενάζει he groans under* the weight of heaven on his back.
ὑπο-στενᾰχίζω, f. *ίσω* = *ὑποστενάζω.*
ὑπο-στένω, *to sigh* or *groan in a low tone, begin to sigh* or *groan.*
ὑποστῆναι, aor. 2 inf. of *ὑφίστημι.*
ὑπο-στηρίζω, f. *ξω*, *to underprop.*
ὑποστήτω, 3 sing. aor. 2 imperat. of *ὑφίστημι.*
ὑπο-στίλβω, f. *ψω*, *to shine a little, shine softly.*
ὑποστολή, *ἡ*, (*ὑποστέλλω*) *a letting down* or *lowering* of sails: *a shrinking back.* II. *submission.*
ὑπο-στονᾰχίζω, = *ὑποστεναχίζω.*
ὑπο-στορέννῡμι also **-στόρνυμι** and **-στρώννυμι**:

fut. -στορέσω and -στρώσω: aor. 1 ὑπεστόρεσα and -έστρωσα: pf. ὑπέστρωκα, pass. ὑπέστρωμαι:—*to spread, lay* or *strew under*:—Med., *to strew* or *lay under for oneself*: 3 sing. pf. pass., ᾧ χαλκὸς ὑπέστρωται which *has* copper *laid under* it.

ὑποστορέσαι, aor. 1 inf. of ὑποστορέννυμι.

ὑποστρᾰτηγέω, f. ήσω, *to serve under as lieutenant*. From

ὑπο-στράτηγος, ὁ, *a lieutenant-general*.

ὑποστρεφθείς, εῖσα, έν, aor. 1 pass. part. from

ὑπο-στρέφω, f. ψω: Pass., aor. 1 -εστρέφθην: pf. -έστραμμαι:—*to turn round about, guide back*. II. intr. *to turn short round, wheel round, turn and flee*: *to return*: so in fut. med. ὑποστρέψομαι and aor. 1 pass. 3. *to turn away, elude* a person. Hence

ὑποστρεψείω, Ep. aor. 1 opt. of ὑποστρέφω.

ὑποστροφή, ἡ, (ὑποστρέφω) *a turning round*: *a turning about*, either to flee or to rally; ἐξ ὑποστροφῆς, Lat. *denuo, again, anew*: also *on the contrary*.

ὑπόστρωμα, ατος, τό, (ὑποστρώννυμι) *that which is spread* or *strewed under, a bed, litter*.

ὑπο-στρώννῡμι, = ὑποστορέννυμι.

ὑπο-σῡρίζω or -ίττω, f. ξω, *to whistle gently, rustle*.

ὑπο-σύρω, *to drag down*: *to trip up*. [ῡ]

ὑπο-σφίγγω, f. γξω, *to bind tight below*.

ὑπόσχεο, 2 sing. aor. 2 imperat. of ὑπισχνέομαι.

ὑποσχές, έτω, aor. 2 imperat. of ὑπέχω.

ὑποσχέσθαι, aor. 2 med. inf. of ὑπισχνέομαι.

ὑποσχεσίη, ἡ, Ep. for ὑπόσχεσις, *a promising*.

ὑποσχέσιον, τό, = ὑπόσχεσις.

ὑπόσχεσις, εως, ἡ, (ὑπισχνέομαι) *a promising, promise, engagement*; ὑπόσχεσιν ἐκπληρῶσαι to fulfil *a promise*; ὑπόσχεσιν ἀπολαβεῖν to receive the fulfilment of *a promise*.

ὑποσχόμενος, aor. 2 part. of ὑπισχνέομαι.

ὑπόσχωμαι, aor. 2 subj. of ὑπισχνέομαι.

ὑποσχών, aor. 2 part. of ὑπέχω.

ὑποτᾰγή, ἡ, (ὑποτάσσω) *subordination, subjection*.

ὑπο-ταμνόν, τό, *a plant cut off at the root* for magic purposes. From

ὑπο-τάμνω, Ion. for ὑποτέμνω.

ὑπο-τᾰράσσω Att. -ττω, contr. -θράσσω: f. ξω: pf. pass. τετάραγμαι:—*to stir up, trouble from below* or *a little*:—Pass. *to be somewhat troubled*.

ὑπο-ταρβέω, f. ήσω, *to be somewhat afraid*: c. acc. *to be somewhat afraid of* a thing, *to fear a little*.

ὑπο-ταρτάριος, ον, (ὑπό, Τάρταρος) *under Tartarus, dwelling below Tartarus*.

ὑπότᾰσις, εως, ἡ, (ὑποτείνω) *a stretching* or *spreading out from under*; πεδίων ὑποτάσεις the plains that *stretch below*.

ὑπο-τάσσω Att. -ττω: f. ξω: pf. pass. τέταγμαι:—*to place* or *arrange under, subject*.

ὑπο-τείνω, f. -τενῶ: aor. 1 -έτεινα:—*to stretch under, put under as a prop* or *stay*. . *to hold out before* or *towards, to hold out, suggest hopes, to promise, offer*:—Med. *to propose by way of question, submit*. 3. *to strain to the utmost, make intense*.

ὑπο-τειχίζω, f. ίσω Att. ιῶ, *to build a w*... *under* or *across*: *to build a cross-wall*. Hence

ὑποτείχῐσις, εως, ἡ, *the building of a cross-wall*; and

ὑπο-τείχισμα, ατος, τό, *a cross-wall*.

ὑπο-τελέω, f. έσω, *to pay off, discharge, liquidate*: absob *to pay tribute, be tributary*.

ὑπο-τελής, ές, gen. έος, (ὑπό, τέλος) *subject to taxes* or *tribute, tributary*, Lat. *vectīgalis, tributarius*. II. act. *receiving payment*, c. gen.

ὑπο-τέμνω Ion. -τάμνω: f. -τεμῶ and -τᾰμοῦμαι: aor. 2 ὑπέτᾰμον: Pass., aor. 1 -ετμήθην: pf. -τέτμημαι:—*to cut away* or *under*: *to cut unfairly*. II. *to cut off*, Lat. *intercipere*; ὑποτέμνειν τὴν ἐλπίδα *to cut off all ground* for hope; so also in Med., ὑποτέμνεσθαι τὸν πλοῦν *to cut off* one's passage:—Pass., ὑποτάμνεσθαι τὸ ἀπὸ τῶν νεῶν *to be cut off* from the ships.

ὑπο-τίθημι, f. -θήσω: aor. 1 ὑπέθηκα: aor. 2 ὑπέθην:—*to place under*: *to put under, make subject*. 2. *place under as a foundation, to lay down*: esp. in Med. *to lay down as a principle* or *rule for oneself, presuppose, premise*. 3. *to propose to oneself for discussion* or *argument*: *to propose* to do. II. *to suggest*, mostly in Med.: c. dat. pers. *to advise, counsel, admonish*: c. inf. *to advise* one *to do* a thing. III. *to put down as a deposit* or *stake, pawn, pledge, mortgage*: hence, 2. *to stake, hazard, venture*. 3. *to lay in store, store up, keep*.

ὑπο-τῑμάομαι, f. -ήσομαι, Med.: as Att. law-term, *to propose a less penalty for onesel*f *to lay the damages at a lower rate*.

ὑπο-τῑτράω, *to bore through below*.

***ὑπο-τλάω,** obsol. pres., whence are formed fut. ὑποτλήσομαι, aor. 2 ὑπέτλην, pf. ὑποτέτληκα:—*to bear, endure, submit to*.

ὑπο-τονθορίζω or -ύζω, *to murmur* or *hum softly*.

ὑποτοπεύω, = ὑποτοπέω.

ὑποτοπέω, f. ήσω: aor. 1 ὑπετόπησα: also as Dep. **ὑποτοπέομαι**: aor. 1 ὑπετοπήθην: (ὕποπτος):—*to suspect* or *surmise* that: also c. acc., *to suspect* a person or thing.

ὑπο-τραυλίζω, f. σω, *to lisp a little*.

ὑπο-τρείω, Ep. for ὑποτρέω.

ὑπο-τρέφω, f. -θρέψω, *to bring up secretly* or *in succession*: Med. *to foster* or *cherish secretly*.

ὑπο-τρέχω, fut. -θρέξομαι and -δρᾰμοῦμαι: aor. 2 ὑπέδρᾰμον: pf. ὑποδέδρομα:—*to run in under*; ὁ κύων ὑπέδραμε ὑπὸ τοὺς πόδας τοῦ ἵππου the dog *ran under* the horse's legs. II. *to run under* or *below*. III. *to run in between, intercept*. IV. *to insinuate oneself into anyone's good graces, flatter, deceive*.

ὑπο-τρέω, f. -τρέσω, *to tremble a little*: *to shrink back, give ground*. II. c. acc. *to tremble at* anyone, *be afraid of* him.

ὑπο-τρίβω, f. ψω, *to rub beneath, rub* or *wear away gradually*. II. *to grate* or *pound ingredients* for a dish; cf. ὑπότριμμα. [ῑ] ὑπο-τρίζω, *to chirp* or *whistle softly.*

ὑπότριμμα, ατος, τό, (ὑποτρίβω) *an acid dish of various ingredients grated and pounded up together* · ὑπότριμμα βλέπειν to look *sharp and sour.*

ὑπο-τρομέω, f. ήσω, *to tremble under* or *a little.* II. c. acc. *to tremble before* anyone.

ὑπότρομος, ον, (ὑποτρέμω) *trembling a little, somewhat fearful.*

ὑποτροπή, ἡ, (ὑποτρέπω) *a turning back, repulse.* II. *a return, recurrence.*

ὑπότροπος, ον, (ὑποτρέπω) *turning back, returning* or *returned home.*

ὑπο-τροχάω, poët. for ὑποτρέχω, *to run under.*

ὑπο-τρύζω, *to hum in an undertone.*

ὑπο-τρώγω, f. -τρώξομαι: aor. 2 -έτρᾰγον:—*to eat underhand* or *secretly.*

ὑπο-τῡπόω, f. ώσω, (ὑπό τύπος) *to sketch out,* Lat. *adumbrare.*

ὑπο-τύπτω, f. ψω, *to strike* or *push down, to strike under the surface* of a thing; ὑποτύψας κηλωνηΐῳ ἀντλέει he draws it up *dipping* with the bucket *under the surface;* ὑποτύπτουσα φιάλῃ τοῦ χρυσοῦ ἐδαφέετο *dipping down* with a cup she gave him of the gold.

ὑποτύπωσις, εως, ἡ, (ὑποτῡπόω) *a general representation, outline,* Lat. *adumbratio: a copy, pattern.*

ὑπ-ουθάτιος, α, ον, (ὑπό, οὖθαρ) *under the udder,* hence *sucking.* [ᾰ]

ὕπ-ουλος, ον, (ὑπό, οὐλή) of wounds, *festering under the scar, only skinned over:* hence *unsound* or *rotten underneath, hollow, unreal;* κάλλος κακῶν ὕπουλον a fair outside *that skins over* evils *below.*

ὑπ-ουράνιος, ον, (ὑπό, οὐρᾰνός) *under heaven* or *the heavens: reaching up to heaven.*

ὑπουργέω, f. ήσω: pf. act. ὑπούργηκα, pass. ὑπούργημαι: (ὑπουργός):—*to render service, to serve, succour: to be of service:* c. neut. acc., χρηστὰ Ἀθηναίοισι ὑπουργεῖν *to do* the Athenians good *service;* τὰ ὑπουργημένα *services that have been rendered.* Hence

ὑπούργημα, ατος, τό, *a service rendered.*

ὑπουργητέον, verb. Adj. of ὑπουργέω, *one must serve* or *be kind to.*

ὑπουργία, ἡ, (ὑπουργέω) *service, duty rendered,* Lat. *officium:* in bad sense, *obsequiousness, complaisance.*

ὑπ-ουργός, όν, contr. for ὑποεργός, (ὑπό, *ἔργω) *rendering service, serviceable, conducive to.*

ὑπο-φαίνω, f. -φᾰνῶ: aor. 1 -έφηνα:—*to shew* or *bring to light from under;* θρῆνυν ὑπέφηνε τραπέζης *he drew* the stool *from under* the table. 2. *to shew a little, give a glimpse of.* II. Pass. *to shew oneself* or *to be seen under;* ὑπὸ τὰς πύλας πόδες ὑποφαίνονται feet *are seen under* the gates. III. intr. *to shine forth a little:* of morning, *to dawn, break, glimmer:* so also of the first appearance of spring; cf. ὑπολάμπω.

ὑπο-φᾶτις, ιος, ἡ, Dor. for ὑποφῆτις, fem. of ὑποφήτης, *the priestess of an oracle.*

ὑπόφαυσις, ἡ, *a small light glimmering* through a hole: generally, *a narrow opening.* From

ὑπο-φαύσκω, (ὑπό, φάος) *to begin to shine.*

ὑπό-φαυτις, ιος, ἡ, Aeol. for ὑπόφασις, (ὑπό, φάσις) *a secret whispering.*

ὑπο-φείδομαι, f. σομαι, Dep. *to spare* or *forbear.*

ὑπο-φέρω, f. ὑποίσω: aor. 1 ὑπήνεγκα Ion. ὑπήνεικα: aor. 2 ὑπήνεγκον: (cf. φέρω):—*to bear* or *carry away under, to bear out of danger, to rescue.* II. *to bear* or *carry by being under, to bear* or *support a burden:* generally, *to bear, endure, suffer.* III. *to hold out under* or *before: to hold out, suggest, proffer.* 2. *to pretend, allege.*

ὑπο-φεύγω, f. -φεύξομαι, *to flee from under, evade: to retire a little, shrink back.*

ὑποφητεύω, *to hold the office of ὑποφήτης.* From

ὑπο-φήτης, ου, ὁ, (ὑπό, φημί) *an announcer* or *interpreter* of the divine will, *a priest who declares an oracle.*

ὑπο-φθάνω [ᾰ]: f. ὑποφθήσομαι later also -φθάσω [ᾰ]: aor. 1 ὑπέφθᾰσα: aor. 2 ὑπέφθην, inf. ὑποφθῆναι, part. ὑποφθάς: pf. ὑπέφθᾰκα:—*to haste before, be* or *get beforehand;* ὑποφθὰς δουρὶ μέσον περόνησεν *getting beforehand* he pierced him through the middle with a spear; so in aor. 2 med. part., ὑποφθάμενος κτεῖνεν he killed him *beforehand.*

ὑπο-φθονέω, f. ήσω, *to feel secret envy at.*

ὑπό-φθονος, ον, *a little envious* or *jealous:* Adv. -νως, *somewhat jealously.*

ὑπο-φλέγω, f. ξω, *to set on fire* or *heat from below.*

ὑπο-φόνιος, ον, (ὑπό, φόνος) *in return for murder, avenging murder.*

ὑπο-φραδμοσύνη, ἡ, *suggestion:* in plur. *counsels.* From

ὑπο-φράζομαι, Med. *to conjecture.*

ὑπο-φρίσσω Att. -ττω: f. ξω: pf. -πέφρῑκα:—*to shudder a little.*

ὑποφῠγών, οῦσα, όν, aor. 2 part. of **ὑποφεύγω.**

ὑπο-φωλεύω, *to lie hidden under.*

ὑπο-φωνέω, f. ήσω, *to call gently to.*

ὑπο-χάζομαι, aor. 2 -κεκᾰδόμην: Dep.:—*to give way gradually* or *a little, retire slightly.*

ὑπο-χᾰλῑνίδιος [νῐ], α, ον, (ὑπό, χαλινός) *under the bridle;* ὑποχαλινιδία (sc. ἡνία), ἡ, *a* kind of *snaffle-bridle.*

ὑπο-χᾰροπός, όν, (ὑπό, χαροπός) *of a somewhat fiery* or *fierce look.*

ὑπο-χάσκω, *to gape* or *yawn open a little.*

ὑπο-χείριος, ον, also α, ον, (ὑπό, χείρ) *under one's hands, in the hand: under anyone's power* or *control, subject to;* ὑποχειρίους ποιεῖσθαι to make *subject.*

ὑπο-χέω, f. -χεῶ: aor. 1 ὑπέχεα Ep. **ὑπέχευα:** pf. pass. -κέχῠμαι: 3 sing. plqpf. ὑπεκέχῠτο:—*to pour under, pour out for* another: of dry things, *to strew* or *spread under;* φύλλα ὑποκεχυμένα ὑπὸ τοῖς ποσί the leaves *strewn under* their feet: metaph. in Pass., *to be spread* or *steal over* one *gradually;* ἀπιστίη **ὑπεκέχυτο αὐτῷ** distrust *stole over* him.

ὑπο-χθόνιος, ον, (ὑπό, χθών) *under the earth, subterraneous.*

ὑπό-χθων, ονος, ὁ, ἡ, = ὑποχθόνιος.

ὑποχος, ον, (ὑπέχω) *subject, under control,* τινί to one: also c. gen., ὑποχοί τινος a king's *subjects.*

ὑπό-χρεως, ων, gen. ω, (ὑπό, χρέος) *subject to debt, in debt:* of property, *involved, embarrassed,* Lat. *obaeratus.*

ὑπο-χρίω, f. -χρίσω [ῑ]: aor. 1 act. ὑπέχρῑσα, pass. ὑπεχρίσθην:—*to smear under* or *on: to besmear* or *anoint a little,* Lat. *sublinere: to paint* or *colour the face under the eyes.*

ὑπό-χρῡσος, ον, *containing a mixture of gold.*

ὑπο-χωρέω, f. ήσομαι, *to go back, recoil;* ὑποχωρεῖν τοῦ πεδίου *to retire from* the plain; ὑποχωρεῖν τινι τοῦ θρόνου *to withdraw from one's seat* in honour of one, give it up to him. 2. c. acc. pers. *to retire before, avoid meeting.* II. *to go on in succession.*

ὑπό-ψαμμος, ον, *having sand under* or *in it, mixed with sand, sandy*: Comp. -ότερος, *somewhat sandy.*

ὑποψία Ion. -ίη, ἡ, (ὑπόψομαι) *suspicion, jealousy;* ὑποψίαν λαμβάνειν κατά τινος to entertain *suspicion* of a person; of things, ἔχειν ὑποψίαν to admit of *suspicion* II. *a jealous watchfulness, censoriousness.*

ὑπόψιος, ον, (ὑπόψομαι) *viewed from below,* Lat. *suspectus;* hence *viewed with suspicion.*

ὑπόψομαι, serving as fut. of ὑφοράω.

ὑπ-οψωνέω, f. ήσω, (ὑπό, ὀψωνέω) *to underbid* or *cheat in the purchase of provisions.*

ὑπτιάζω, f. άσω, (ὕπτιος) *to bend oneself back: to carry one's head high.* II. transit. *to bend* or *throw back:* Pass., ὑπτιάζεται κάρα his head *is stretched back.*

ὑπτίασμα, ατος, τό, (ὑπτιάζω) *that which is stretched out with the under side uppermost;* ὑπτιάσματα χερῶν hands *stretched up in supplication,* cp. Lat. *supinis manibus.* II. *a backward fall.*

ὑπτιαστέον, verb. Adj. of ὑπτιάζω, *one must throw back.*

ὕπτιος, α, ον, (ὑπό) *with the under side uppermost, bent back, laid back, on one's back,* Lat. *supīnus, resupinus;* of one falling, πέσεν ὕπτιος he fell *on his back;* ὑπτίοις σέλμασιν ναυτίλλεται he sails with planks *turned bottom upwards;* γαστὴρ ὑπτία belly *uppermost.* 2. generally, anything *turned up, inverted;* κρᾶνος ὕπτιον a helmet *with the hollow uppermost;* so, ἀσπὶς ὑπτία; but, κύλιξ ὑπτία a cup *with the bottom uppermost;* ἀψὶς ὑπτία a half-wheel *with the concave side uppermost.* 3. of Place, *sloping away* from one, *sloping evenly and gradually.* Hence

ὑπτιόω, f. ώσω, *to turn over, upset.*

ὑπ-ωθέω, (ὑπό, ὠθέω) *to push* or *thrust away.*

ὑπ-ωλένιος, ον, also α, ον, (ὑπό, ὠλένη) *under the arm* or *elbow.*

ὑπωμοσάμην, aor. 1 med. of ὑπόμνυμι.

ὑπωμοσία, ἡ, (ὑπόμνυμι) *an oath taken to bar proceedings at law, an application for delay upon affidavit:* it was resisted by an ἀνθυπωμοσία.

ὑπωπιάζω, f. άσω, (ὑπώπιον) *to strike* one *under the eye:* generally, *to beat black and blue:* metaph. *to mortify, afflict, vex* or *annoy greatly.* Hence

ὑπωπιασμός, ὁ, *a striking under the eye: affliction.*

ὑπ-ώπιον, τό, (ὑπό, ὤψ) *the part under the eyes, the face.* II. generally, like ὑπωπιασμός, *a blow under the eye, a black eye.*

ὑπ-ωρεία or **ὑπ-ωρέα**, ἡ, (ὑπό, ὄρος) *the foot of a mountainous track:* plur. ὑπωρέαι, *the roots of a mountain,* Lat. *radices montis.*

ὑπώροφε, 3 sing. pf. intrans. of ὑπόρνυμι.

ὑπ-ωρόφιος, ον, also α, ον, (ὑπό, ὄροφος) *under the roof, under cover of a house, in a house:* generally, *under shelte.*

ὑπ-ώροφος, ον, = ὑπωρόφιος.

ὙΡΧΑ, ἡ, *an earthen vessel for pickled fish, a pickle-jar,* Lat. *orca.* (Aeol. word.)

ὟΣ, ὁ and ἡ, gen. ὑός [ῠ]: acc. ὗν:—like σῦς, *a swine, pig, boar* or *sow, a tame pig;* but ὗς ἄγριος, a wild *boar.*

ὝΣΓΗ, ἡ, *a shrub* from which comes the dye ὕσγινον.

ὑσγῑνο-βᾰφής, ές, (ὕσγινον, βαφῆναι) *dipped* or *dyed in* ὕσγινον, *scarlet.*

ὕσγῑνον, τό, (ὕσγη) a vegetable dye *of scarlet colour.*

ὕσδος, for ὄσδος, Aeol. for ὄζος.

ὕσθην, aor. 1 pass. of ὕω.

ὙΣΜΙ'ΝΗ [ῑ], ἡ, irreg. dat. ὑσμῖνι, *a fight, battle, combat;* πρώτῃ ὑσμίνῃ the front *of the fight*: ὑσμίνηνδε to *the fight.* Ep. word.

ὑσπλαγίς, ίδος, ἡ, Dor. for ὑσπληγίς, = ὕσπληγξ.

ὕσπλαγξ, αγγος, ἡ, Dor. for ὕσπληγξ.

ὕσπληγξ, ηγγος, or -πληξ, ηγος, ἡ, *a rope which was drawn across a race-course and was let down when the racers were to start.* II. *the snare of the fowler.* (Deriv. uncertain.)

ὕσσωπος, ἡ, the aromatic plant *hyssop.* (Orientai word.)

ὑστάτιος, α, ον, = ὕστατος, (cp. μεσσάτιος = μέσσος, τοσσάτιος = τόσσος,) *last, hindmost:* neut. ὑστάτιον as Adv., *last, at last.* [ᾰ]

ὕστᾰτος, η, ον, (Comp. ὕστερος, q. v.) *last, utmost, hindmost,* of space: also of time, ἡ ὑστάτη (sc. ἡμέρα) the *last* day:—neut. ὕστατον and ὕστατα, as Adv., *last, at last.*

ὑστέρα Ion. -έρη, ἡ, (ὕστερος) *the womb,* mostly in plur. ὑστέραι, αἱ, Ion. gen. -έων.

ὑστεραῖος, α, ον, (ὕστερος) properly *on the day after;* ἡ ὑστεραία (sub. ἡμέρα) *the day after, following day;* τῇ ὑστεραίᾳ Ion. -αίῃ, *on the following day, next day,* Lat. *postridie:* generally, = ὕστερος, *later, next.*

ὑστερέω, f. ήσω: aor. 1 ὑστέρησα: pf. ὑστέρηκα: Pass., aor. 1 ὑστερήθην: (ὕστερος):—*to be behind, come later:* of Place, *to come after* or *afterwards.* II. of Time, c. gen. rei, *to come later than, come too late for;* ὑστερεῖν τῆς μάχης πέντε ἡμέρας they *were* five days *too late for* the battle: c. dat. pers. *to be too late for* him: absol. *to come late* or *too late.* III. metaph. *to come short of, be inferior to:* also *to be robbed of* a thing. 2. *to be in want of:*—in Pass. *to be in want.* IV. of things, *to fail, lack, be wanting.* Hence

ὑστέρημα, ατος, τό, *a coming short, deficiency.*

ὑστέρησις, εως, ἡ, (ὑστερέω) *a coming short: want, need.*

ὑστερίζω, f. ίσω Att. ιῶ: aor. 1 ὑστέρισᾰ: (ὕστερος):—*to come after, come later* or *too late.* II. c. gen. rei, *to come later than;* ἡμέρῃ μιῇ τῆς συγκειμένης ὑστερίζειν *to be* one day *behind* the day appointed. III. metaph. *to come short of, be inferior to,* c. gen. IV. *to be in want of, to lack*

ὑστερό-ποινος, ον, (ὕστερος, ποινή) *late-avenging.*

ὑστερό-πους, -ποδος, ὁ, ἡ, *with late foot, late-coming.*

ὕστερος, α, ον, (Sup. ὕστατος, q. v.):—*the latter, coming after, following,* opp. to πρότερος. II. of Time, *after, later, too late;* c. gen., ὕστερός τινος *later* than a person. c. gen. rei, *too late for* a thing; with Preps., ἐς ὕστερον *afterwards;* so, ἐν ὑστέρῳ, ἐξ ὑστέρου and ἐξ ὑστέρης. III. *standing after, inferior, weaker;* γυναικὸς ὕστερος *under* a woman's *power.* IV. the neut. ὕστερον is used as Adv. of Time, *after, afterwards, hereafter, in future, for the future;* also ὕστερα; c. gen., ὕστερον τουτέων *later than* these events.

ὑστερο-φθόρος, ον, (ὕστερος, φθείρω) *destroying after, late-destroying.*

ὑστερό-φωνος, ον, (ὕστερος, φωνή) *sounding after, echoing.*

ὝΣΤΡΙΞ, ἴχος, ὁ and ἡ, *a hedgehog, porcupine.* Hence

ὑστρῐχίς, ίδος, ἡ, *a whip for punishing slaves.*

ὑφᾱγεῦ, Dor. for ὑφηγοῦ, 2 sing. pres. imperat. of ὑφηγέομαι.

ὕφ-αιμος, ον, (ὑπό, αἷμα) *suffused with blood, bloodshot.* II. *hot-blooded.*

ὑφαίνεσκον, Ion. impf. of ὑφαίνω.

ὙΦΑΙ΄ΝΩ, f. ὑφᾰνῶ: aor. 1 ὕφηνα later ὕφᾱνα: Pass., aor. 1 ὑφάνθην: pf. ὕφασμαι:—*to weave;* ἱστὸν ὑφαίνειν *to weave* a web. II. absol. *to weave, ply the loom.* III. metaph. *to spin, contrive, plot, plan, devise,* Lat. *texere,* as, μῆτιν or δόλον ὑφαίνειν. 2. *to make, construct, fabricate.*

ὑφαίρεσις, εως, ἡ, (ὑφαιρέω) *a taking away under* or *underhand, a purloining, pilfering.*

ὑφ-αιρέω Ion. ὑπ-αιρέω: f. αιρήσω: aor. 2 ὑφεῖλον: pf. ὑφῄρηκα: Pass., aor. 1 ὑφῃρέθην: pf. ὑφῄρημαι, part. ὑφῃρημένος Ion. ὑπαραιρημένος:—*to seize underneath* or *inwardly, to seize secretly.* II. *to draw from under.* 2. *to take away something of,* c. gen. 3. *to draw away, seduce.* III. Med. *to take away from underhand, filch away, purloin:* ὑφαιρεῖσθαί τινά τι or τινος *to deprive* one *secretly of* a thing. . *to make away with underhand, keep out of the way.*

ὕφ-ᾰλος, ον, (ὑπό, ἅλς) *under the sea;* ὕφαλον Ἔρεβος the darkness *of the deep.*

ὑφάντης, ου, ὁ, (ὑφαίνω) *a weaver.* Hence

ὑφαντικός, ή, όν, *of* or *for weaving: skilled in weaving.*

ὑφαντο-δόνητος, ον, (ὑφαντός, δονέω) *swung in the weaving, woven.*

ὑφαντός, ή, όν, verb. Adj. of ὑφαίνω, *woven:* τὰ ὑφαντά *cloth inwoven with figures.*

ὑφ-άπτω Ion. ὑπ-άπτω: f. ψω: aor. 1 ὕψηψα Ion. ὑπῆψα: pf. pass. ὕφημμαι:—*to set on fire from underneath:* metaph. *to inflame secretly, excite.* 2. absol. *to light underneath: to light a fire under* or *in* a place.

ὑφ-αρπάζω Ion. ὑπ-αρπάζω: f. -άσομαι later -άσω: aor. 1 ὑφήρπασα:—*to snatch away from under, take away underhand, filch away,* Lat. *surripere: to take the* word *out of* one's *mouth, interrupt.*

ὑφαρπάμενος, poët. for ὑφαρπασάμενος, aor. 1 med. part. of ὑφαρπάζω.

ὕφασμα, ατος, τό, (ὑφαίνω) *a thing woven, web, woven garment.* [ῠ]

ὑφάω, poët. for ὑφαίνω: Ep. 3 pl. ὑφόωσι.

ὑφειμένος, pf. pass. part. of ὑφίημι: Adv. ὑφειμένως, *slackly, less violently* or *insolently, quietly,* Lat. *submissé.*

ὑφ-εῖσα, (ὑπό, εἷσα) Causal aor. 1 of ὑφίζω, *I placed under* or *secretly;* Ion. part., ὑπείσας ἄνδρας *having set* men *in ambush.*

ὑφ-εκτέον, verb. Adj. of ὑπέχω, *one must support.*

ὑφ-ελκτέον, verb. Adj. of ὑφέλκω, *one must draw away under* or *underhand.*

ὑφ-έλκω, f. -έλξω or -ελκύσω [ῠ]: aor. 1 ὑφείλκῠσα: (cf. ἕλκω):—*to draw away under, underhand* or *gently;* ὑφέλκειν τινὰ ποδοῖιν *to draw* one *away* by the two legs:—*to draw away by undermining, diminish by drawing from under:*—Med. *to draw along under one, trail along,* as a pair of slippers.

ὑφελοίατο, Ion. 3 pl. aor. 2 med. opt. of ὑφαιρέω.

ὑφέντας, acc. pl. of ὑφείς, aor. 2 part. of ὑφίημι.

ὑφ-έρπω, f. -έρψω or -ερπύσω [ῠ]: aor. 1 ὑφείρπῠσα: (cf. ἕρπω):—*to creep under* or *secretly;* ὑφεῖρπε πολὺ *it crept* far on *secretly, spread abroad.* II. c. acc. *to steal upon, come over.*

ὑφ-έσπερος, ον, (ὑπό, ἑσπέρα) *towards evening:* neut. pl. ὑφέσπερα as Adv., *about evening.*

ὑφή, ἡ, (ὑφαίνω) *a weaving, web;* πέπλων ὑφαί *woven* garments.

ὑφ-ηγεμών, όνος, ὁ, = ἡγεμών.

ὑφ-ηγέομαι, f. ήσομαι: pf. ὑφήγημαι: Dep.:—*to go just before, to guide, lead the way.* 2. *to shew the way to do, instruct in* a thing. 3. hence also *to lead to, prove* a thing. Hence

ὑφήγησις, εως, ἡ, *a leading, guiding;* and

ὑφηγητήρ, ῆρος, ὁ, and **ὑφ-ηγητής,** οῦ, ὁ, *one who leads the way, a conductor:* metaph. *a leader, adviser.*

ὕφηνα, aor. 1 of ὑφαίνω.

ὑφηνιοχέω, f. ήσω, *to be a charioteer:*—Pass. *to drive after* or *behind.* From

ὑφ-ηνίοχος, ὁ, (ὑπό, ἡνίοχος) *the charioteer,* as *subordinate to the warrior* in his chariot.

ὑφ-ήσσων, *ον*, gen. *ονος*, (ὑπό, ἥσσων) *somewhat less* or *younger*.

ὑφ-ιζάνω, f. ζήσω, = ὑφίζω.

ὑφ-ίζω, f. ζήσω, (ὑπό, ἵζω) *to sit* or *crouch down: to sink* or *fall in*.

ὑφ-ίημι Ion. **ὑπίημι**: f. ὑφήσω: aor. 1 ὕφηκα: pf. ὕφεικα, pass. ὕφειμαι: (see ἵημι):—*to send down, let down, to lower*; ὑφιέναι ἱστόν *to lower* the mast; ὑφιέναι ἱστία *to let down* the sails. 2. *to put under, to put* a young one *under its dam, put* it *to suck*: in Med., of a woman, ὑφίεσθαι μαστοῖς *to put* a child *to her own* breasts, *to suckle* it. 3. *to engage secretly*, Lat. *submittere*: hence pf. pass. part. ὑφειμένος, *secretly lurking*. II. intr. *to slacken, relax* or *abate from* a thing; c. gen. rei, ὑφιέναι τῆς ὀργῆς *to cease* from anger; so in Med., ὑφίεσθαι ὀργῆς; τὸ ὕδωρ ὑπίεται τοῦ ψυχροῦ the water *abates* its coldness. 2. absol. *to submit, give in, slacken, abate*. III. in Pass. absol., *to submit, surrender*: c. inf., *to submit* to do a thing: so in pf. pass. part., πλεῖν ὑφειμένῃ to sail *with lowered sails*.

ὑφίησι, Dor. for ὑφίησι, 3 sing. of ὑφίημι.

ὑφ-ίστημι: (cf. ἵστημι): I. Causal in pres. and impf., in f. ὑποστήσω and aor. 1 ὑπέστησα:—*to place* or *set under*. 2. *to post secretly*. 3. *to submit, propose, suggest*: so also in fut. and aor. 1 med. *to lay down, suggest*; εἰ μή τι πιστὸν ὑποστήσει unless *thou shalt give* some *ground* for confidence. II. Pass., with aor. 2 act. ὑπέστην, pf. ὑφέστηκα:—*to stand under, be under* or *beneath*; τὸ ὑφιστάμενον *that which is underneath*, of milk, as opp. to τὸ ἐφιστάμενον that which comes to the top, the cream. 2. *to place oneself under an engagement, engage* or *promise* to do: c. acc. cognato, ὑποστῆναι ὑπόσχεσιν *to make* a promise: absol. *to promise*. 3. *to submit, yield to* one: also c. inf. *to submit* to do. 4. c. acc. rei, *to submit to*. 5. ὑποστῆναι ἀρχήν *to undertake* an office. 6. *to put oneself under, hide oneself, lie concealed*. 7. *to support an attack, to resist, withstand*: absol. *to stand one's ground, face the enemy*, Lat. *subsistere*.

ὑφ-οράω, or as Dep. **ὑφοράομαι**: fut. ὑπόψομαι: (ὑπό, ὁράω):—*to look at from below, to look askance at, to view with suspicion*, Lat. *suspicĕre, suspicari*. II. *to keep in view*.

ὑ-φορβός, ὁ, (ὗς, φέρβω) *a swineherd*.

ὑφ-ορμίζω, f. ίσω Att. ιῶ, *to bring into harbour secretly*:—Pass. *to come to anchor secretly*, or generally, *to come to anchor*. Hence

ὑφόρμῐσις, ἡ, *a place for ships to run into, harbour*.

ὕφος, εος, τό, = ὑφή.

ὑφόωσι, Ep. for ὑφῶσι, 3 pl. of ὑφάω.

ὕφ-υδρος, *ον*, (ὑπό, ὕδωρ) *under water*.

ὑψ-ᾰγόρας, *ου*, ὁ, Ion. **-αγόρης**, (ὕψι, ἀγορεύω) *a big talker, a boaster, braggart*.

ὑψαυχενέω, f. ήσω, and **ὑψαυχενίζω**, f. ίσω, *to carry the neck high, strut proudly*. From

ὑψ-αύχην, *ενος*, ὁ, ἡ, (ὕψι, αὐχήν) *carrying the neck high*: hence *stately, towering: haughty*.

ὑψ-ερεφής, *ές*, (ὕψι, ἐρέφω) *high-roofed, high-vaulted*.

ὑψ-ηγόρας, Ion. for ὑψαγ—.

ὑψ-ήγορος, *ον*, (ὕψι, ἀγορεύω) *talking loftily, vaunting*.

ὑψήεις, *εσσα*, *εν*, poët. for ὑψηλός.

ὑψηλᾶς, Dor. for ὑψηλῆς, fem. gen. of ὑψηλός.

ὑψηλ-αυχενία, ἡ, (ὑψηλός, αὐχήν) *a carrying the neck high*.

ὑψηλό-κρημνος, *ον*, (ὑψηλός, κρημνός) *with high crags*.

ὑψηλός, ή, όν, (ὕψι, ὕψος) *high, lofty, towering*; χώρα ὑψηλή a *highland* country:—metaph. *high, lofty, stately, proud*.

ὑψηλοφρονέω, f. ήσω, *to be highminded, bearing oneself haughtily*. From

ὑψηλό-φρων, *ονος*, ὁ, ἡ, (ὕψηλος, φρήν) *highminded, high-spirited, haughty*.

ὑψ-ηρεφής, *ές*, gen. *έος*, = ὑψερεφής.

ὑψ-ηχής, *ές*, gen. *έος*, (ὕψι, ἦχος) *sounding on high*.

ὝΨΙ, Adv. *high, aloft, on high: on the high sea*: hence are formed Comp. ὑψίων, Sup. ὕψιστος.

ὑψί-βᾰτος, *ον*, (ὕψῐ, βαίνω) *set on high, standing high, high-placed*.

ὑψῐ-βρεμέτης, *ου*, ὁ, (ὕψι, βρέμω) *high-thundering*.

ὑψῐ-γέννητος, *ον*, (ὕψι, γεννάω) *high-grown, topmost*.

ὑψί-γυιος, *ον*, (ὕψῐ, γυῖον) *with high limbs* or *branches, high-stemmed*. [ῐ]

ὑψί-ζῠγος, *ον*, (ὕψῐ, ζυγόν) of the benches in ships, *sitting high* or *aloft on the bench*: metaph. of Jove, *high-enthroned*.

ὑψί-θρονος, *ον*, (ὕψῐ, θρόνος) *high-throned*.

ὑψῐ-κάρηνος, *ον*, (ὕψι, κάρηνον) *with high head, high-topped*. [ᾰ]

ὑψῐ-κέλευθος, *ον*, (ὕψι, κέλευθος) *with a path on high, moving on high* or *aloft*.

ὑψικέρᾱτα, irreg. acc. of ὑψίκερως.

ὑψί-κερως, *ων*, gen. *ω*, (ὕψῐ, κέρας) *with high* or *lofty horns*; there is also an irreg. acc. in phrase, ὑψικέρατα πέτραν a *high-peaked* rock.

ὑψί-κομος, *ον*, (ὕψῐ, κόμη) *with lofty foliage*, of the oak.

ὑψῐ-κόμπως, Adv. (ὕψι, κόμπος) *with high boasts, arrogantly*.

ὑψί-κρημνος, *ον*, (ὕψῐ, κρημνός) *with high steeps* or *cliffs, high-beetling, built on a cliff*.

ὑψί-λοφος, *ον*, (ὕψῐ, λόφος) *high-crested*. [ῐ]

ὑψῐ-μέδων, *οντος*, ὁ, (ὕψι, μέδω) *high-ruling, ruling on high: lofty*.

ὑψῐ-μέλαθρος, *ον*, (ὕψι, μέλαθρον) *high-built*.

ὑψῐ-νεφής, *ές*, (ὕψι, νέφος) *dwelling high in the clouds*.

ὑψῐ-πᾰγής, *ές*, (ὕψι, παγῆναι) *built on high*.

ὑψί-πεδος, *ον*, (ὕψῐ, πέδον) *with high ground, high-placed*.

ὑψῐ-πετήεις, *εσσα*, *εν*, poët. for ὑψιπέτης.

ὑψῐ-πέτηλος, *ον*, (ὕψι, πέτηλον) *with high leaves* or *foliage*.

ὑψῐ-πέτης, *ου, ὁ,* (ὕψι, πέτομαι) *flying on high, soaring.*

ὑψί-πολις, ὁ, ἡ, (ὕψῐ, πόλις) *highest in one's city.* [ῐ]

ὑψί-πους, ὁ, ἡ, neut. -πουν, gen. -ποδος, (ὕψῐ, πούς) *high-footed: on high, sublime.*

ὑψί-πῠλος, *ον,* (ὕψῐ, πύλη) *with high gates.*

ὑψί-πυργος, *ον,* (ὕψῐ, πύργος) *high-towering.*

ὕψιστος, *η, ον,* Sup. from Adv. ὕψι, *highest, loftiest;* τὰ ὕψιστα *the highest heavens.* 2. of persons, *most high, dwelling on high.*

ὑψίτερος, *α, ον,* Comp. from Adv. ὕψι, *higher, loftier.*

ὑψῐ-φαής, *ές,* (ὕψι, φάος) *beaming on high.*

ὑψῐ-φᾰνής, *ές,* (ὕψι, φανῆναι) *seen on high.*

ὑψῐ-φόρητος, *ον,* (ὕψι, φορέω) *high-borne, soaring on high.*

ὑψί-φρων [ῐ], *ονος, ὁ, ἡ,* (ὕψῐ, φρήν) *high-minded, haughty.*

ὑψῐ-χαίτης, *ου, ὁ,* (ὕψι, χαίτη) *long-haired.*

ὑψίων, *ον,* gen. *ονος,* poët. Comp. from ὕψι, *higher, loftier.*

ὑψόθεν, Adv. (ὕψος) *from on high, from aloft, from above,* Lat. *desuper.* II. *high, aloft, on high, above, over.*

ὑψόθι, Adv. (ὕψος) *high, aloft, on high.*

ὑψ-όροφος, *ον,* (ὕψι, ὀροφή) *high-roofed, high-vaulted.*

ὕψος, *εος, τό,* (ὕψι) *height: the top, summit, crown:* absol. in acc. ὕψος, *in height.*

ὑψόσε, Adv. (ὕψος) *on high, upwards, aloft, up.*

ὑψοῦ, Adv. (ὕψος) *high, aloft, on high, up.*

ὑψόω, f. ώσω: aor. 1 ὕψωσα: Pass., fut. ὑψωθήσομαι: aor. 1 ὑψώθην: (ὕψος):—*to heighten, raise, elevate, exalt.* Hence

ὕψωμα, *ατος, τό, height, elevation.*

ὝΩ, f. ὕσω [ῡ]: aor. 1 ὗσα: Pass., fut. med. ὕσομαι in pass. sense: aor. 1 ὕσθην: pf. ὕσμαι:—*to wet, water: to rain,* Ζεὺς ὗε Jove *sent rain;* so, ὁ θεὸς ὕει the god *sends rain;* but the nom. was soon omitted, and ὕει used impers., like Lat. *pluit, it rains;* εἰ ὗε *if it rained;* part. neut. used absol., ὕοντος πολλῷ as *it was raining heavily:* c. acc. loci, ἑπτὰ ἐτέων οὐκ ὗε τὴν Θήρην for seven years *it did* not *rain on* Thera: c. acc. cognato, ὗσε χρυσὸν *it rained* gold. II. Pass., of places, *to be rained on, to be wetted;* λέων ὑόμενος a lion *drenched with rain;* ὕσθησαν αἱ Θῆβαι Thebes *was rained upon;* ἡ γῆ ὕεται the country *is rained upon,* it rains in the country.

Φ

Φ, φ, φῖ, *τό,* indecl., twenty-first letter of the Greek alphabet: as a numeral φ′ = 500, but ͵φ = 500,000.

The Consonant Φ arose from the labial Π followed by the aspirate; and was anciently written ΠΗ, and was expressed in Lat. by *ph,* though φ was used to express the Lat. *f.*

Changes of Φ. I. in Aeol., Dor. and Ion. the aspirate was often dropped, and φ became π, as λίσπος σπόγγος σπονδύλη for λίσφος σφόγγος σφονδύλη: the Att. sometimes used it for π, as φανός φάτρα for πανός πάτρα. II. in Aeol., Dor. and Ion., φ is put for θ, as φήρ φλάω for θήρ θλάω.

Φ was sometimes considered as a double consonant, so that a short vowel before it became long by position, as in ὄφις, quasi ὄπφις.

φᾶ, Dor. and poët. for ἔφα, ἔφη. 3 sing. aor. 2 of φημί.

φάανθεν, lengthd. for φάνθεν, Ep. for ἐφάνθησαν, 3 pl. aor. 1 pass. of φαίνω.

φαάντατος, *η, ον,* Ep. Sup. of φαεινός, *most brilliant, brightest.*

φαάντερος, *α, ον,* Ep. Comp. of φαεινός, *more brilliant, brighter.*

ΦΑΓΕΙ͂Ν Ion. **φαγέειν** Ep. **φαγέμεν,** inf. of ἔφᾰγον, with no pres. in use, used as aor. 2 of ἐσθίω, *to eat, devour,* c. acc.: c. gen. *to eat of* a thing: generally, *to eat up, devour, consume, waste.*

φάγες, Ep. for ἔφᾰγες, 2 sing. aor. 2: see φαγεῖν.

φάγῃσι, Ep. for φάγῃ, 3 sing. aor. 2 subj.: see φαγεῖν.

φάγος, *ὁ,* (φαγεῖν) *a glutton.* [ᾰ]

φάγωντι, Dor. for φάγωσι, 3 pl. aor. 2 subj.: see φαγεῖν. [ᾰ]

φάε, 3 sing. impf. of φάω.

φαεθοντίς, *ίδος,* poët. for φαέθουσα, fem. of φαέθων, *shining.*

φαέθω, (φάος) *to shine;* only found in part. φαέθων, *beaming, radiant:* hence φαέθων as Subst., *the beaming one, the Sun;* neut. pl., πάννυχα καὶ φαέθοντα whole nights and *days.*

Φαέθων, *ὁ,* (properly part. of φαέθω) *Shining,* one of the steeds of Morning. 2. son of Apollo, famous for upsetting the chariot of the sun.

φαεινός, *ή, όν* poët. **φαεννός,** (φάος) *shining, beaming, radiant:*—Comp. φαεινότερος. 2. also like λαμπρός, of the voice, *clear, distinct.* 3. generally, *splendid, brilliant.*

φαείνω, poët. form of φαίνω, *to shine, give light.*

φαεννός, *ή, όν,* poët. form of φαεινός.

φαεσί-μ-βροτος, *ον,* (φάος, βροτός) *bringing light to mortals, shining on mortals.*

φαεσ-φορός contr. **φωσφόρος,** *ον,* (φάος, φέρω) *light-bringing.*

φάη, contr. for φάεα, pl. of φάος.

φᾰθί, imperat. pres. and aor. 2 of φημί.

Φαίαξ, *ᾱκος,* Ep. and Ion. **Φαίηξ,** *ηκος, ὁ, a Phaeacian: the Phaeacians* are in Homer inhabitants of the island of Scheria (afterwards Corcyra, now Corfu), and were famous as sailors.

φαιδῐμόεις, *εσσα, εν,* poët. form of φαίδιμο

φαίδῐμος, *ον,* also *η, ον,* (φαίνω) *shining, brilliant;* metaph. *famous, glorious,* Lat. *clarus*

φαιδρό-νους, *ουν,* (φαιδρός, νοῦς) *of cheerful, joyous mind.*

φαιδρός, *ά, όν,* (φάω, φαίνω) *beaming, radiant:*

metaph. *beaming* or *radiant with joy, jocund, gay.* Adv. -δρῶς, *joyously, cheerily:* also neut. pl. φαιδρά as Adv. Hence

φαιδρότης, ητος, η, *brightness, lustre.* I. metaph. *joyousness.*

φαιδρόω, f. ώσω, (φαιδρός) *to make bright.* II. metaph. in Pass. *to be cheerful* or *joyous.*

φαιδρύντρια, ἡ, *a washer, cleanser.* From

φαιδρύνω [ῠ]: f. ὕνῶ: aor. 1 ἐφαίδρῡνα: (φαιδρός): —*to make bright, clean, cleanse.* II. metaph. *to cheer, please*:—Pass. *to brighten up* with joy.

φαιδρ-ωπός, όν, (φαιδρός, ὤψ) *with a bright, joyous look.*

φαίην, pres. or aor. 2 opt. of φημί.

φαικάς, άδος, ἡ, (φάος) a kind of *white shoe.*

φαῖμεν, for φαίημεν, 1 pl. pres. or aor. 2 opt. of φημί.

φαινέμεν, Ep. for φαίνειν, inf. of φαίνω.

φαινέσκετο, 3 sing. Ion. impf. med. of φαίνω.

φαινόλης, ου, ὁ, formed from the Lat. *paenula, a thick upper garment* or *cloak.*

φαινολίς, ίδος, ἡ, (φαίνω) *light-bringing.*

φαινομένηφι, Ep. part. dat. fem. of φαίνομαι.

φαίνω, f. φᾰνῶ: Att. also φᾱνῶ: aor. 1 ἔφηνα, inf. φῆναι Dor. ἔφᾱνα: 3 sing. Ion. aor. 2 φάνεσκε: pf. πέφαγκα: pf. 2 (intr.) πέφηνα: Pass. and Med. φαίνομαι: fut. φᾰνοῦμαι Ion. φανέομαι; also φᾰνήσομαι: also poët. paullo-p. fut. πεφήσομαι: aor. 1 ἐφάνθην, Ep. 3 sing. φαάνθη, 3 pl. φάανθεν: aor. 2 ἐφάνην, Ep. inf. φᾰνήμεναι: pf. pass. πέφασμαι, 3 sing. πέφανται, inf. πεφάνθαι, part. πεφασμένος: (φάω). I. *to bring to light, make to appear: to shew, to make clear* or *known,* hence *to lay bare, uncover, disclose:* hence almost *to grant,* as, γόνον Ἑλένῃ φαίνειν *to grant* Helen a child:—at Sparta, φρουρὰν φαίνειν *to proclaim* a levy, call out the array. 2. of sound, *to make distinct, make ring clear.* 3. *to bring to light, display, exhibit:* also *to explain, expound.* 4. in Att. *to inform against, indict, impeach: to inform of a thing as contraband*: τὰ φανθέντα articles *informed against* as contraband. 5. aor. 1 med. φήνασθαι *to shew* or *display as one's own.* II. intr. *to give light, shine forth.* 2. *to appear,* like the Pass., only in Ion. aor. 2 φάνεσκε, pf. 2 πέφηνα. III. Pass. *to come to light, be seen, appear, to be clear* or *manifest.* 2. of the rising of heavenly bodies, *to appear:* ἅμα ἠοῖ φαινομένηφιν at break of day. 3. generally, *to appear to be,* c. part. or c. inf., which are used in different senses, φαίνεται c. inf. denoting *what appears* or *is likely;* φαίνεται c. part. *what is apparent* or *manifest;* as, φαίνεται εἶναι *he appears* or *seems to be* (like δοκεῖ), φαίνεται ἰὼν *he manifestly is.* 4. often in dialogue, φαίνεταί σοι ταῦτα; *does this appear so?* is not this so? Answ., φαίνεται *it does appear so, yes.* 5. the phrase φανῆναι ὁδόν, *to appear* on the road, is shortd. for ἰέναι ὁδὸν ὥστε φανῆναι: so also, κέλευθον φανείς. 6. in Att., esp. in aor. 1 ἐφάνθην, *to be denounced, informed against;* see φαίνω I. 4.

ΦΑΙΟ´Σ, ά, όν, *dusky, dun, gray,* Lat. *fuscus.* II. also like Lat. *fuscus,* of the voice, *deep, hollow.*

φαιο-χίτων, ωνος, ὁ, ἡ, (φαιός, χιτών) *dark-robed.*

ΦΑ´ΚΕΛΟΣ, ὁ, *a bundle,* Lat. *fasciculus.*

φᾰκῆ, ῆς, ἡ, (φάκος) *a dish of lentils* or *pulse, pease-porridge.*

ΦΑ´ΚΟΣ, ὁ, the plant *lentil;* also *its fruit,* which was eaten at funerals.

φᾰλαγγηδόν, Adv. (φάλαγξ) *in phalanxes.*

φᾰλάγγιον, τό, (φάλαγξ) *a venomous kind of spider.*

φᾰλαγγομᾰχέω, f. ήσω, *to fight with* or *in a phalanx: to fight in the ranks.* From

φᾰλαγγο-μάχης, ου, ὁ, (φάλαγξ, μάχομαι) *one that fights in the phalanx: fighting in the ranks.*

ΦΑ´ΛΑΓΞ, αγγος, ἡ, in Homer, *a line* or *order of battle, battle-array:* mostly in plur. *the ranks of an army in battle.* 2. later, *the Greek mode of drawing up infantry, the phalanx, a compact mass* of infantry usu. of 8 deep, but also as much as 25 deep: the phalanx was brought to great excellence under Epaminondas, though it reached perfection under Philip of Macedon; ἐπὶ φάλαγγος ἄγειν to lead *in phalanx,* Lat. *quadrato agmine.* 3. generally, *the main body, centre,* as opp. to the wings (κέρᾱτα). 4. also *a camp.* II. *a round piece of wood, a trunk* or *log;* φάλαγγες ἐβένου logs of ebony. III. *a spider:* see φαλάγγιον.

φάλαγξι, dat. pl. of φάλαγξ.

ΦΑ´ΛΑΙΝΑ, ἡ, *a whale,* Lat. *balaena:* hence of *a devouring monster.* [φᾰ]

φᾰλάκρα, ἡ, (φαλακρός) *baldness, a bald head.*

φᾰλᾰκρός, ά, όν, (φάλος) *bald-headed, bald-pated.*

φᾰλᾰκρόω, f. ώσω, (φαλακρός) *to make bald:* Pass. *to become bald.*

φᾰλανθίας, ου, ὁ, *a bald man.* From

φάλανθος, ον, (φάλος) = φαλακρός. [φᾰ]

φάλᾰρα, τά, (φάλος) *the cheek-pieces of the helmet.* II. *the cheek-pieces of horses:* generally, *trappings.* [φᾰ]

φᾰλᾱρίς Ion. **φαληρίς,** ίδος, ἡ, (φαλᾱρός) *a coot,* Lat. *fulica,* so called from its *bald white head.*

φᾰλᾱρός, ά, όν, Dor. for Ion. φαληρός, (φάλος) *having a patch of white, white-crested.*

Φᾰληρεύς, έως, ὁ, *a man of Phalerum, a Phalerian.*

φᾰληριάω, (φαληρός) *to be* or *become white:* Ep. part., κύματα φαληριόωντα waves *crested with white foam.*

Φάληρον, τό, *Phalērum,* the western harbour of Athens: Φαληρόθεν *from Phalerum;* Φαληρόνδε *to Phalerum.* [ᾰ]

φᾰληρός, ά, όν, Ion. for φαλαρός.

φᾰλῆς or **φάλης,** ητος, ὁ, = φάλλος.

φάλλαινα, ἡ, = φάλαινα.

ΦΑΛΛΟ´Σ, ὁ, *membrum virile, a figure thereof,* which was borne in solemn procession in the Bacchic orgies, as an emblem of the generative power in nature.

ΦΑ´ΛΟΣ, ὁ, *a part of the helmet* worn by the

Homeric heroes: either *the peak* or *fore-piece*, or perh. *a metal ridge on the crown in which the plume* (λόφος) *was fixed.* [ᾰ]

φάμα, ἡ, Dor. for φήμη.

φάμεν, Ep. for ἔφαμεν, 1 pl. aor. 2 of φημί. 2. poët. for φάναι, inf. of φημί. [ᾰ]

φᾰμέν (enclit.), 1 pl. pres. of φημί.

φᾰμένα, Dor. fem. of φάμενος.

φάμενος, pres. and aor. 2 med. part. of φημί. [ᾰ]

φαμί, Dor. for φημί.

φάν, poët. for ἔφησαν, 3 pl. aor. 2 of φημί. [ᾰ]

φάναι, pres. or aor. 2 inf. of φημί. [ᾰ]

φᾶναι, aor. 1 inf. of φαίνω.

φᾰνείης, 2 sing. aor. 2 pass. opt. of φαίνω.

φᾰνεῖμεν, Att. for φανείημεν, 1 pl. aor. 2 pass. opt. of φαίνω.

φᾰνείς, εῖσα, έν, aor. 2 pass. part. of φαίνω.

φάνεν, Aeol. and poët. for ἐφάνησαν, 3 pl. aor. 2 pass. of φαίνω: but **φανέν**, aor. 2 part. neut. [ᾰ]

φᾰνερός, ά, όν, also ός, όν, (φαίνω) *open to sight, visible: manifest, evident:* freq. joined with part., ἐπισπεύδων φανερὸς ἦν he was *conspicuous* urging the matter forward: ἐκ τοῦ φανεροῦ = Adv., φανερῶς, *plainly, clearly:* so, ἐν φανερῷ, ἐν τῷ φανερῷ, κατὰ τὸ φανερόν. 2. of persons, *known, famous, conspicuous.* 3. of property, *tangible, real,* opp. to money.

φᾰνερόω, f. ώσω, (φανερός) *to make visible* or *manifest.* II. *to make known* or *famous:*—Pass. with aor. 1 -ώθην:—*to become known* or *famous.* Hence

φᾰνερῶς, Adv. of φανερός, *openly, manifestly:* Comp. φανερώτερον: Sup. φανερώτατα.

φᾰνέρωσις, ἡ, *a making visible: a manifestation.*

φάνεσκε, 3 sing. Ion. aor. 2 pass. of φαίνω. [ᾰ]

φᾰνή, ἡ, (φαίνω) *a torch:* in plur. φαναί, *torch-processions.*

φᾰνήῃ, Ep. 3 sing. aor. 2 pass. subj. of φαίνω.

φάνηθι, aor. 2 pass. imperat. of φαίνω. [ᾰ]

φᾰνήμεναι, for φανῆναι, aor. 2 pass. inf. of φαίνω.

φᾰνήσομαι, fut. pass. of φαίνω.

φᾰνίον, τό, Dim. of φανός, (Subst.), *a small torch, taper.*

φᾰνοίην, for φανοῖμι, aor. 2 opt. of φαίνω.

φᾰνός, ή, όν, (φαίνω) *light, bright;* τὸ φανόν *brightness:* —of garments, *washed clean.* 2. *bright, joyous,* like φαιδρός. Comp. and Sup. φανότερος, -ότατος. [ᾱ]

φᾱνός, also **πᾱνός**, ὁ, (φαίνω) *a lamp, lantern, torch.*

φᾰνοῦμαι, fut. med. of φαίνω.

φαντάζω, f. άσω, (φαίνω) *to make visible, clear* or *manifest.* II. Pass., fut. φαντασθήσομαι: aor. 1 ἐφαντάσθην:—*to become visible, appear, shew oneself.* 2. *to make a show* or *parade,* Lat. *se ostentare.* 3. φαντάζεσθαί τινι *to be like, assume a likeness to* some one. 4. used for φαίνεσθαι or συκοφαντεῖσθαι, *to be informed against.* Hence

φαντᾰσία, ἡ, *a making visible, displaying.* 2. *display, parade,* Lat. *ostentatio.* II. as a term of philosophy, *the power of the mind,* by which it *places* objects *before* itself, *presentative power.*

φάντασμα, ατος, τό, (φαντάζω) *an appearance, image, phantom,* like φάσμα: also *a vision, dream.* 2. *an image presented to the mind by an object,* Lat. *visum: a mere image, unreal appearance.*

φάντες, aor. 2 part. nom. pl. of φημί.

φαντί, Dor. for φασί, 3 pl. of φημί.

φάο, Ep. pres. or aor. 2 med. imperat. of φημί.

φάος, φάεος, εος contr. **φάους**, τό contr. **φῶς**, φωτός: Ep. also **φόως**: (φάω):—*light, daylight:* ἐν φάει by *daylight;* ἔτι φάους ὄντος while there was still *daylight;* often in phrases ὁρᾶν φάος ἠελίοιο, or φάος βλέπειν, to see *the light* of the sun, i. e. to be alive; so also, φάος λείπειν ἠελίοιο, i. e. to be dead; εἰς φῶς ἰέναι to come into *the light,* i. e. *into public.* 2. *the light* of a fire or torch, *fire-light* or *torch-light.* II. metaph. *light,* i. e. joy, deliverance, happiness, and the like; ὦ μέγιστον Ἕλλησιν φάος O greatest *light of safety* to the Greeks. III. plur. φάεα, *the eyes,* Lat. *lumina:* so in sing. of the Cyclops' *eye.*

ΦΑ'ΡΑΓΞ [φᾰ], αγγος, ἡ, *a mountain cleft, a deep chasm, ravine, gully.* (Akin to φάρυγξ.)

φᾰράω, *to plough.*

φᾰρέτρα Ion. -τρη, ἡ, (φέρω) *a quiver* for *carrying* arrows, Lat. *pharetra.* Hence

φᾰρετρεών, ῶνος, ὁ, = φαρέτρα.

φᾰρέτριον, τό, Dim. of φαρέτρα, *a small quiver.*

φᾰρετρο-φόρος, ον, (φαρέτρα, φέρω) *quiver-bearing.*

Φαρισαῖος, ου, ὁ, *a Pharisee:* pl. οἱ Φαρισαῖοι, *the Pharisees* or *Separatists,* a sect of the Jews, who affected superior holiness of life and manners, and a rigid adherence to the law of Moses. They believed in the Resurrection, and in the existence of angels and spirits, which the Sadducees denied.

φαρμᾰκάω, (φάρμακον) *to suffer from poison, be mad from the effects of poison.* II. *to require medicine,* as τομάω to require cutting.

φαρμᾰκεία, ἡ, (φαρμακεύω) *the use of any kind of drugs, potions* or *spells: poisoning, witchcraft, sorcery.*

φαρμᾰκία, ἡ, poët. for φαρμακεία.

φαρμᾰκεύς, έως, ὁ, (φάρμακον) *one who deals in drugs* or *poisons, a sorcerer, poisoner:* fem. **φαρμᾰκεύτρια.**

φαρμᾰκεύω, f. σω, (φάρμακον) *to administer a drug: to use enchantments, practise sorcery;* φαρμακεύειν τι ἐς τὸν ποταμόν *to use* a thing *as a charm to calm* the river. 2. c. acc. pers. *to drug, purge.*

φαρμᾰκίς, ίδος, fem. of φαρμακεύς, *a sorceress, witch.*

φαρμᾰκόεις, εσσα, εν, (φάρμακον) *drugged, poisonous.*

ΦΑ'ΡΜΑ'ΚΟΝ, τό, *a medicine, drug, remedy;* φάρμακον νόσου *a medicine for* disease; metaph., φάρμακον λύπης, *a remedy against* grief. The φάρμακα *applied outwardly* were χριστά *ointments* or *salves,* and παστά, ἐπίπαστα or καταπλαστά *plasters; those taken inwardly* were βρώσιμα, such as *pills*, and πότιμα, ποτά, πιστά, *draughts* or *potions*. II. *a poisonous drug, drug, poison*. III. *an enchanted potion, philtre*: also *a charm, spell, enchantment*: *any secret means of effecting* a thing. IV. also *a means of producing* something, as, φάρμακον σωτηρίας *an expedient to procure* safety. V. *a means for colouring, a dye, colour*.

φαρμᾰκο-ποσία, ἡ, (φάρμακον, ΠΟ- Root of πίνω) *a drinking of medicine* or *poison*.

φαρμᾰκο-πώλης, ου, ὁ, (φάρμακον, πωλέω) *one who sells drugs* or *poisons, a druggist, apothecary*.

φαρμᾰκός, ὁ, ἡ, (φάρμακον) = φαρμακεύς. II. *one who is sacrificed as a purification* for others, *a scape-goat*: then since worthless fellows were reserved for this fate, *an arrant rascal, polluted wretch*, Lat. *homo piacularis*.

φαρμᾰκο-τρίβης [ῐ], ὁ, (φάρμακον, τριβῆναι) *one who grinds and prepares drugs* or *colours*.

φαρμᾰκόω, f. ώσω, (φάρμακον) *to endue with healing power*.

φαρμάσσω Att. -ττω: f. ξω: pf. pass. πεφάρμαγμαι: (φάρμακον):—*to medicate, practise upon by drugs* or *philtres*; φαρμάσσειν χαλκόν *to temper* metal by plunging it in cold water. II. *to enchant* or *bewitch by the use of potions, to poison*. III. *to alloy, adulterate*: *season, spice*.

ΦΑ῀ΡΟΣ [ᾱ] or **φάρος** [ᾰ], εος, τό, *a cloth, sheet, web*: *sail-cloth*. II. *a wide, loose cloak* or *mantle*, worn as an outer garment, also used as a shroud; πύματον φάρος my last *rag*.

Φάρος, ἡ, *Pharos*, an island in the bay of Alexandria, afterwards famous for its lighthouse. II. as appellat. φάρος, ὁ, *a lighthouse*.

φᾰρόωσι, Ep. 3 pl. of φαράω.

φάρσος, εος, τό, (φάρω) *a piece torn off* or *severed, a part, portion, division*, Lat. *pars*; φάρσεα πόλιος *the quarters* of a city.

φάρυγξ, ἡ or ὁ, gen. ῠγος, (φάρω) *the throat*. II. *a gulf, cleft, chasm* in the earth: cf. φάραγξ. [ᾰ]

ΦΑ'ΡΩ, f. φάρσω: pf. πέφαρκα :—*to cleave, part*.

φάς, φᾶσα, φάν, part. pres. and aor. 2 of φημί.

φασγᾰνίς, ίδος, ἡ, Dim of φάσγανον, *a knife*.

φάσγᾰνον, τό, (σφάζω, for σφάγανον) *a thing to cut with, a sword*.

φασγᾰν-ουργός, όν, (φάσγανον, *ἔργω) *forging swords*.

φᾶσε, Dor. and poët. for ἔφησε, 3 sing. aor. 1 of φημί.

φάσηλος [ᾰ], ὁ, a sort of *bean*, Lat. *phasēlus*. II. *a light boat, canoe, skiff*, from its likeness to the pod of the φάσηλος. (Egyptian word.)

φάσθαι, Ep. med. inf. of φημί.

φάσθε, φάσθω, 2 pl. and 3 sing. imperat. med. of φημί.

φᾱσί, 3 pl. of φημί.

Φᾱσιᾱνῑκός, ή, όν, *from the river Phasis*, but with a play on συκο-φαντικός, *informing-like*.

Φᾱσιᾱνός, όν, (Φᾶσις) *from the river Phasis*: hence ὁ φασίανος (sub. ὄρνις) *the Phasian bird, pheasant*, Lat. *phasianus*: but Φασίανος ἀνήρ with a play on συκο-φάντης, *an informer*: cf. Φασιανικός.

φάσις, εως, ἡ, for φάνσις, (φαίνω) *an accusation, information*. [ᾰ]

φάσις, εως, ἡ, (φημί) *a saying, speech, sentence*. II. *affirmation, assertion*. [ᾰ]

Φᾶσις, ιος, ὁ, *the river Phasis* in Colchis or Pontos.

φάσκω, impf. ἔφασκον Ep. φάσκον, (which is used as impf. of φημί): = φημί, *to say*, but often with a collat. notion of *saying what you do not believe, to allege, to pretend*, Lat. *prae se ferre*: also *to think, suppose*: *to promise* to do.

φάσμα, ατος, τό, (φαίνω) *an apparition, phantom*; φάσμα ἀνδρός *the phantom* of a man. 2. *a sign from heaven, a portent, omen*. 3. *a monster, prodigy, portent*; φάσμα ταύρου *a monster* of a bull.

ΦΑ'ΣΣΑ Att. **φάττα**, ἡ, *the wood-pigeon, ring-dove* or *cushat*, Lat. *palumbes*.

φασσο-φόνος, ον, (φάσσα, *φένω) *dove-killing*, of the hawk; as Subst., φασσοφόνος, ὁ, name of a kind of hawk.

φᾰσῶ, φᾰσεῖς, Dor. for φήσω, φήσεις, fut. of φημί.

φᾰτέ, 2 plur. of φημί.

φᾰτειός, ά, όν, (φημί) poët. for φατός, *to be spoken of, pronounced*.

φᾰτέον, verb. Adj. of φημί, *one must say*.

φᾱτί, Dor. for φησί, 3 sing. pres. of φημί.

φᾰτίζω, f. ίσω Dor. ίξω: aor. 1 ἐφάτισα: Pass., aor. 1 ἐφατίσθην: pf. πεφάτισμαι: (φάτις):—*to say, speak, report*; τὸ φατιζόμενον used absol., *as the saying is*. II. *to promise, plight, betroth*. III. *to call, name*.

φάτις, εως Ion. ιος, ἡ, (φημί) *a saying, speech, report*; κατὰ φάτιν as the report goes; ἡ φάτις ἔχει μιν *the report* goes of him. II. *one's* (good or bad) *report, reputation, fame, report*, Lat. *fama*. III. *the saying, answer of an oracle*. [ᾰ]

φάτνη, ἡ, (πατέομαι) *a manger, crib*.

φάτο, Ep. for ἔφᾰτο, 3 sing. aor. 2 of φημί.

φᾰτός, ή, όν, verb. Adj. of φημί, *said, spoken*; *that may be spoken, uttered* or *pronounced*: with a negat., οὐ φατός, *unspeakable, unutterable*. II. *famous*.

φάττα, ἡ, Att. for φάσσα.

φαυλ-επί-φαυλος, (φαῦλος, ἐπί, φαῦλος) *bad upon bad, bad as bad can be*.

φαυλίζω, f. ίσω Att. ιῶ, (φαῦλος) *to hold cheap, to depreciate, disparage*.

ΦΑΥ῀ΛΟΣ, η, ον, also ος, ον, like φλαῦρος, *light, easy, slight, trifling*. 2. *trivial, paltry, petty, sorry, bad*. II. of persons, *low in rank, mean, common*: *worthless, poor, common, of no account*; οἱ φαῦλοι *the vulgar, the common sort*, also *the weak* or *uneducated*, as opp. to οἱ σοφοί. 2. of outward appearance, *ugly, mean-looking*. 3. *careless, thoughtless*.

φαυλότης, ητος, ἡ, *meanness, paltriness*. 2. *want of accomplishments*; ἡ ἐμὴ φαυλότης my *lack of judgment*.

φαύλως, Adv. of φαῦλος, *easily, lightly*; φαύλως

φέρειν τι to bear a thing *lightly*, take it *easily*. 2. *at a rough guess*; φαύλως λογίσασθαι to estimate *roughly*; φαύλως εἰπεῖν to speak *loosely*.

φαυσίμ-βροτος, ον, = φαεσίμβροτος.

ΦΑ'Ω, Root of φαίνω, *to give light, shine, beam*, esp. of the heavenly bodies.

ΦΕ'ΒΟΜΑΙ, poët. Dep., used only in pres. and impf., = φοβέομαι, *to be put to flight, flee affrighted*: c. acc. *to flee from*.

ΦΕΓΓΟΣ, εος, τό, *light, splendour, lustre*: *sunlight, daylight*; δεκάτῳ φέγγει ἔτους, periphr. for *in the tenth year*. II. poët. *light, gladness, joy*. Hence

φέγγω, *to make bright*:—Pass. *to shine, gleam, be bright*.

φειδέομαι, Ion. for φείδομαι.

φείδεο, Dor. pres. imperat. of φείδομαι.

φειδίτιον, τό, (φείδομαι) mostly in plur. φειδίτια, τά, *spare thrifty meals*, being the Spartan name for the public tables (συσσίτια), at which all citizens ate together the same *frugal meal*. 2. also *the common hall*, in which these meals were taken.

ΦΕΙ'ΔΟΜΑΙ: fut. φείσομαι Ep. paullo-p. fut. πεφἴδήσομαι: aor. 1 ἐφεισάμην Ep. φεισάμην: Ep. redupl. aor. 2 πεφἴδόμην, opt. πεφιδοίμην, πεφίδοιτο, inf. πεφιδέσθαι: Dep.:—*to spare, to be sparing* or *chary of* a thing, Lat. *parcere*, c. gen.: of provisions, *to use sparingly* or *thriftily*: also *to draw back* or *from, turn away from*: c. inf. *to spare* or *forbear* to do. Hence

φειδομένως, Adv. pres. part. of φείδομαι, *sparingly, thriftily, charily*.

φειδώ, όος contr. οῦς, ἡ, (φείδομαι) *a sparing, refraining*. II. *thrift, stinginess*.

φειδωλή and **φειδωλία**, ἡ, = φειδώ. From

φειδωλός, ή, όν, (φειδώ) *sparing, thrifty, chary* of a thing: c. gen., φειδωλὸς χρημάτων *sparing of* money. Adv. -λῶς, *sparingly, thriftily*.

φείσασθαι, aor. 1 inf. of φείδομαι.

φείσατο, Ep. 3 sing. aor. 1 of φείδομαι.

φειστέον, verb. Adj. of φείδομαι, *one must spare*.

φελλεύς, έως, ὁ, *stony ground* or *soil*: hence as the name of a rocky district of Attica.

φέλλἴνος, η, ον, (φελλός) *made of cork*.

φέλλιον, τό, mostly in plur. *stony ground*: cf. φελλεύς.

φελλό-πους, -ποδος, ὁ, ἡ, neut. -πουν, (φελλός, πούς) *cork-footed*.

ΦΕΛΛΟ'Σ, ὁ, *the cork-tree*, Lat. *quercus suber*. 2. *the bark of the cork-tree, a cork*, Lat. *cortex*.

φενᾰκίζω, f. ίσω, (φέναξ) *to play the impostor, cheat, lie*. 2. trans. *to cheat, trick*:—Pass. *to be cheated*. Hence

φενᾰκισμός, ὁ, *quackery, imposture, trickery*.

ΦΕ'ΝΑΞ, ᾶκος, ὁ, *a cheat, quack, impostor*.

***ΦΕ'ΝΩ**, *to slay*, obsol. Root, to which belong Ep. aor. 2 πέφνον, shortd. from the redupl. form πέφενον, also with augm. ἔπεφνον, infin. πεφνέμεν, part. πέφνων (not πεφνών) as if it were part. pres.:—Pass., pf. πέφᾰμαι, 3 sing. πέφᾰται, 3 pl. πέφανται, inf. πεφάσθαι: paullo-p. fut. πεφήσομαι Ep. 2 sing. πεφήσεαι.

φερ-ανθής, ές, (φέρω, ἄνθος) *bringing flowers*.

φέρ-ασπις, ιδος, ὁ, ἡ, (φέρω, ἀσπίς) *shield-bearing*.

φερ-αυγής, ές, (φέρω, αὐγή) *bringing light, shining*.

ΦΕ'ΡΒΩ, plqpf. ἐπεφόρβειν:—*to feed, nourish*: *to preserve*. II. Pass. *to be fed* or *feed upon* a thing: hence *to eat, consume*, Lat. *depasci*: metaph. *to feed on*. III. Med. c. acc. *to feed oneself on* a thing; φέρβεσθαι νόον *to feed one's* mind.

φερ-έγγῠος, ον, (φέρω, ἐγγύη) *giving surety* or *bail, able to give security, trusty, responsible*: generally, *capable, competent*: c. inf., λιμὴν φερέγγυος διασῶσαι τὰς νέας a harbour *capable* of preserving the ships: c. gen. *able to answer sufficiently for* a thing, *trusty*:—cf. ἐχέγγυος.

φερέμεν, Ep. inf. of φέρω.

φερεμ-μελίης, poët. for φερεμελίης, ου, ὁ, (φέρω, μελία) *a warrior bearing an ashen spear*, generally, *a spear-bearer*.

φερέ-νῑκος, ον, (φέρω, νίκη) *carrying off victory, victorious*.

φερέ-οικος, ον, (φέρω, οἶκος) *carrying one's house with one*, of the nomad Scythians:—as Subst., φερέοικος, ὁ, *the house-carrier*, i. e. *snail*; cf. πουλύπους, ἀνόστεος.

φερέ-πονος, ον, (φέρω, πόνος) *bringing trouble* or *sorrow*.

φερέσ-βιος, ον, (φέρω, βίος) *bearing life* or *food, life-giving, food-giving*.

φέρεσκε, 3 sing. Ion. impf. of φέρω.

φερεσ-σᾰκής, ές, gen. έος, (φέρω, σάκος) *shield-bearing, heavy-armed*.

φερε-στάφῠλος, ον, (φέρω, σταφυλή) *bearing bunches of grapes*.

φέρετρον contr. **φέρτρον**, τό, (φέρω) *a bier, litter*, Lat. *feretrum*.

φέρην, Aeol. for φέρειν, inf. of φέρω.

φέρῃσι, Ep. for φέρῃ, 3 sing. subj. of φέρω.

φέριστος, η, ον, like φέρτατος, *stoutest, bravest, best*; mostly in addresses, ὦ φέριστε.

φέρμα, ατος, τό, (φέρω) *that which is borne, a load, burden*: *the burden* or *fruit of the womb*.

φερνή, ἡ, (φέρω) *that which is brought by the wife, a dowry, portion*, Lat. *dos*; φερναὶ πολέμου *the dowry* of war, i. e. a wife won in battle.

φέροισα, Dor. part. fem. of φέρω.

φέροντι, Dor. 3 pl. of φέρω: but also part. dat.

Φερσεφάττιον Att. **Φερρεφάττιον**, τό, *a temple* or *sanctuary of Persephonè*. From

Φερσέφασσα Att. -ττα, and **Φερρέφαττα**, ἡ, = Περσέφασσα, -ττα, Περσεφόνη, *Proserpine*.

Φερσεφόνη, ἡ, = Περσεφόνη.

φέρτατος, η, ον, Sup. Adj. = φέριστος, *stoutest, bravest, best, mightiest, most powerful*. (From φέρω, as Lat. *fortis* from *fero*.)

φέρτε, Ep. for φέρετε, 2 pl. of φέρω.

φέρτερος, α, ον, Comp. Adj. *stouter, braver, better, mightier, more powerful*. See φέρτατος.

φερτός, ή, όν, verb. Adj. of φέρω, *to be borne, endurable.*

φέρτρον, contr. for φέρετρον.

ΦΕ'ΡΩ, a Root only used in pres. and impf.: Ep. forms, 2 pl. imperat. φέρτε for φέρετε; 3 sing. subj. φέρησι, Ep. for φέρῃ; Ion. impf. φέρεσκον, φέρεσκε. From the Root *ΟΙ'Ω comes the fut. οἴσω, med. οἴσομαι; Ep. imperat. οἶσε, inf. οἰσέμεν, οἰσέμεναι; also fut. pass. οἰσθήσομαι. From the Root *'ΕΝΕΓΚΩ come aor. 1 ἤνεγκα, Ion. ἤνεικα Ep. ἔνεικα, subj. ἐνείκω, inf. ἐνεῖκαι: aor. 2 ἤνεγκον Ion. ἤνεικον, Ep. inf. ἐνεικέμεν: Ion. aor. 1 pass. ἠνείχθην: 3 pl. aor. 1 med. ἠνείκαντο. From the same Root come pf. act. ἐνήνοχα, pass. ἐνήνεγμαι, fut. pass. ἐνεχθήσομαι, aor. 1 pass. ἠνέχθην. I. like Lat. *FERO, to bear* or *carry* a load. II. *to bear along*, with an idea of *motion* added, as of horses, ἅρμα φέρειν, etc. III. *to bear, endure, suffer*, esp. with an Adv., βαρέως, χαλεπῶς φέρειν τι, Lat. *aegré, graviter ferre, to bear* a thing impatiently, *take* it ill or amiss, be disconcerted at it; opp. to κούφως φέρειν τι, Lat. *leviter ferre*, to bear a thing cheerfully, *take* it easily. IV. *to fetch: to bring, present, give;* δῶρα φέρειν *to bring* presents; and Med. *bring with one* or *for one's own use*:—χάριν τινὶ φέρειν *to grant* any one a favour, do him a kindness; but later, *to shew* gratitude to one. 2. *to occasion, cause, work;* as, κακόν or πῆμα φέρειν. 3. *to bring in, pay, discharge;* φόρον or δασμὸν φέρειν *to pay* tribute; τιμὴν φέρειν *to pay* a fine. 4. ψῆφον φέρειν *to give* one's vote, Lat. *ferre suffragium.* V. *to bear, bring forth, produce:* absol. of the earth or of trees, *to bear fruit, be fruitful:* metaph. *to bring in, yield, produce;* ἀγὼν ὁ τὸ πᾶν φέρων the contest *that bestows* everything. VI. *to bear off, carry off* or *away: to carry away as booty* or *plunder*, mostly in phrase φέρειν καὶ ἄγειν, Lat. *agere et ferre*, where φέρειν refers to the moveables which are carried off, and ἄγειν to the cattle which are driven away: also simply φέρειν *to rob.* 2. *to carry off, gain: to win, achieve, gain:* also *to receive one's due*, e. g. *to receive* pay:—Med., esp. in phrases ἄεθλον φέρεσθαι *to carry off* a prize; τὰ πρῶτα, τὰ δεύτερα φέρεσθαι *to win and hold* the first, the second rank: the Med. φέρεσθαι is used generally of everything *which one gets for oneself* or *for one's own use* and *behoof*, so as to *take* and *carry away to one's home.* VII. absol. of roads, *to lead to* a place; ἡ ὁδὸς φέρει, like Lat. *via fert* or *ducit.* 2. of a tract of country, *to stretch, extend, verge to* or *towards:* metaph. *to lead* or *tend to* an end or object; τὰ πρὸς τὸ ὑγιαίνειν φέροντα that which *is conducive* to health; and so generally, *to contribute* or *conduce to* or *towards.* 3. *to aim at, hint* or *point at, refer to* a thing; ἐς ἀρηίους ἀγῶνας φέρον τὸ μαντήιον the oracle *referring* to martial contests; τῶν ἡ γνώμη ἔφερε συμβάλλειν their opinion *inclined to* giving battle: also c. dat. pers., πλέον ἔφερέ οἱ ἡ γνώμη, c. inf., his opinion *inclined* rather to do so and so:—φέρει is also used like συμφέρει, *it tends* [to one's interest], *is expedient.* VIII. *to carry about by word of mouth, in the mouth, to speak much of;* εὖ or πονηρῶς φέρεσθαι to be well or ill *spoken of.* 2. *to be carried about, to be in circulation.* IX. φέρε is used in Homer as imperat., *bear, carry, bring:* but, like ἄγε, it was afterwards used as an Adv., *come, now, well*, before the 1 sing. or plur. subj., φέρε ἀκούσω, *come* let me hear; φέρε στήσωμεν *come* let us set.

Pass. *to be borne* or *carried from* a place, esp. involuntarily: *to be borne, carried on* or *along* by waves, *to be hurried, swept away, rush, fly along*, Lat. *ferri;* ἰθὺς φέρεσθαι *to rush* right upon; φερόμενοι ἐσέπιπτον ἐς τοὺς Αἰγινήτας *bearing down* they fell upon the Aeginetans: so also part. act. used intrans., φέρουσα ἐνέβαλε νηὶ φιλίῃ *bearing down* she ran into a friendly ship. 2. also of bodies moved by their own power, *to hasten, run, fly, speed.* 3. metaph., εὖ or κακῶς φέρεσθαι, of schemes, etc., *to turn out, prosper well* or *ill;* τὰ πράγματα κακῶς φέρεται our affairs *are in a bad state.*

ΦΕΥ῀, Exclamation of grief or anger, *ah! alas! woe!* like Lat. *vah, vae*, our *fye!*: c. gen., φεῦ τῆς Ἑλλάδος *woe* for Hellas! II. of astonishment or admiration, *ah! oh!*

φευγέμεν, -έμεναι, Ep. for φεύγειν, inf. of φεύγω.

φεύγεσκεν, 3 sing. Ion. impf. of φεύγω.

φευγόντων, Ep. for φευγέτωσαν, 3 pl. imperat., *let them flee:* also part. gen. pl. of φεύγω.

ΦΕΥ'ΓΩ: Ion. impf. φεύγεσκον: f. φεύξομαι Dor. φευξοῦμαι: aor. 2 ἔφῠγον: pf. act. πέφευγα, pass. (in act. sense) πέφυγμαι: there is also Ep. pf. part. πεφυζότες, as if from φύζω:—*to flee, take flight:* c. acc. cognato, φεύγειν φυγὴν *to flee* in flight: also, φεύγειν τὴν παρὰ θάλασσαν [sc. τὴν ὁδόν] *to flee* [the way] by the sea. 2. the pres. part. φεύγων often expresses only *the purpose* or *endeavour to flee*, the compds. ἀποφεύγω, ἐκφεύγω, προφεύγω being added to denote *the escape;* as, βέλτερον, ὡς φεύγων προφύγῃ κακὸν ἠὲ ἁλώῃ it is better that *running off* one should escape than be caught; so, φεύγων ἐκφεύγειν, φεύγων ἀποφεύγειν. 3. φεύγειν ὑπό τινος *to flee before* any one. 4. c. inf. *to shun* or *shrink from doing:* absol. *to fear, flinch.* II. c. acc. *to flee, shun, avoid:* as, φεύγειν θάνατον, πόλεμον, etc.: metaph. of any rapid movement, ἡνίοχον φύγον ἡνία the reins *escaped from* the hands of the charioteer. 2. pf. pass. part. retains the acc. in Homer, πεφυγμένος μοῖραν, ὄλεθρον *having escaped, being quit of* fate, destruction: but also c. gen., πεφυγμένος ἀέθλων *escaped from* toils. III. *to flee one's country* for a crime; φεύγειν ὑπό τινος *to be banished* by one: hence *to go into exile, live in banishment, be banished*, Lat. *exulare.* IV. as Att. law-term, *to be accused* or *prosecuted at law*, opp. to διώκω: hence, ὁ φεύγων *the accused, defend-*

ent, Lat. *reus*, ὁ διώκων *the accuser, prosecutor;* c. acc., φεύγειν γραφήν or δίκην, *to be put on one's trial* on a public or private indictment: the crime being added in gen., as φεύγειν φόνου (sc. δίκην) *to be defendant* on a charge of murder, i.e. *to be charged with* murder.'

φεύζω, f. ξω: aor. 1 ἔφευξα:—*to cry* φεῦ, *cry woe, wail.* (From φεῦ, as οἰμώζω from οἴμοι, αἰάζω from αἶ αἴ.)

φευκτέον, verb. Adj. of φεύγω, *one must flee.*

φευκτός, ή, όν, verb. Adj. of φεύγω, *to be avoided: that can be shunned* or *avoided.*

φευξείω, Desiderat. of φεύγω, *to wish* or *desire to flee.*

φεῦξις, εως, ἡ, (φεύγω) = φύξις.

φεύξομαι Dor. **φευξοῦμαι**, fut. of φεύγω.

φεύξω, fut. of φεύζω (not of φεύγω).

ΦΕ'ΨΑ˘ΛΟΣ, ου, ὁ, and **φεψάλυξ**, ῠγος, ὁ, *a spark, brand, piece of the embers* or *hot ashes.* Hence

φεψᾰλόω, f. ώσω, *to reduce to ashes, to burn up.*

φεψάλυξ, υγος, ὁ, = φέψαλος. [ᾰ]

φῆ, Ion. for ἔφη, 3 sing. aor. 2 of φημί.

φῇ, 3 sing. aor. 2 subj. of φημί.

φηγῐνέος, α, ον, and **φήγῐνος**, η, ον, (φηγός) *oaken, of oak,* Lat. *fagĭnus.*

φηγῐνοῦς, ῆ, οῦν, contr. for φηγινέος.

ΦΗΓΟ'Σ, ἡ, a kind of *oak,* bearing an esculent acorn, not the Lat. *fagus* (beech). II. *the esculent fruit of the same tree.*

φήῃ, Ep. for φῇ, 3 sing. pres. subj. of φημί

φήληξ, ηκος, ὁ, (φηλός) *deceiver,* name of a wild-fig, which *seems ripe when it is not really* so.

φηλητεύω f. σω, *to cheat, deceive, trick.* From

φηλήτης, ου, or **φηλητής**, οῦ, ὁ, (φηλός) *a deceiver, cheat, knave, thief.*

ΦΗΛΟ'Σ, ή, όν, *deceitful, knavish.* Hence

φηλόω, f. ώσω, *to deceive, cheat, trick.* Hence

φήλωμα, ατος, τό, *a deceit, deception, cheat.*

φήμη Dor. **φάμα**, ἡ, Lat. *fama,* (φημί) *a voice from heaven, a prophetic voice: an oracle, an augury.* II. *any voice* or *words, a speech, saying:* also *a song.* 2. *a common saying,* an old *tradition, legend, adage.* 3. like Lat. *fama, a rumour, report:* hence a man's *good* or *bad report,* his *fame, reputation, character.* 4. *a message.*

ΦΗΜΙ', φῄς, φησί: aor. 2 ἔφην (the impf. being ἔφασκον, see φάσκω), ἔφησθα Ep. φῆσθα, ἔφη; imperat. φάθι; inf. φάναι; part. φάς, φᾶσα, φάν: fut. φήσω: aor. 1 ἔφησα. Med., aor. 2 ἐφάμην [ᾰ], inf. φάσθαι, part. φάμενος: impf. or aor. 2 ἐφάμην: also pf. pass. πέφασμαι; 3 sing. imperat. πεφάσθω. Ep. forms 1 pl. pres. opt. φαῖμεν for φαίημεν; 3 sing. subj. φήῃ for φῇ; aor. 2 φῆν, φῆς, φῆ, for ἔφην, ἔφης, ἔφη; and 3 pl. ἔφαν, φάν for ἔφασαν; med. imperat. φάο for φάσο:—'Ημί is a shortd. form of φημί: φάσκω is also a collat. form. The pres. indic. φημί is enclitic, except in 2 pers. φῄς. *To say, speak, tell: to express one's opinion* or *thoughts:* hence *to be of opinion, believe, think, imagine,* esp. in Med.; ἶσον ἐμοὶ φάσθαι *to fancy* himself equal to me; in familiar language φημί is often put before its pronoun, as, ἔφην ἐγώ *said I;* ἔφη ὁ Σωκράτης *said Socrates:* φημί is sometimes joined with a synon. Verb, as, ἔφη λέγων, ἔλεγε φάς, etc. II. φημί often means, *to say yes, affirm, assert:* opp. to οὔ φημι or φημὶ οὐχί, *to say no, deny, refuse.*

φημίζω: f. ίσω Att. ιῶ Dor. ίξω: aor. 1 ἐφήμισα: (φήμη):—*to speak, utter, name:*—Med. *to express in words.*

φῆμις, ιος, ἡ, poët. for φήμη, *speech, talk: report, rumour, one's* good or bad *report, reputation;* δήμοιο φῆμις *the voice* or *judgment* of the people.

φῆν, Ep. for ἔφην, aor. 2 of φημί.

φῆναι, aor. 1 inf. of φαίνω.

φήνειε, 3 sing. aor. 1 opt. of φαίνω.

ΦΗ'ΝΗ, ἡ, a kind of *vulture.*

φήρ, ὁ, gen. φηρός, Aeol. for θήρ, esp. in plur. Φῆρες, *the Centaurs.*

φηρο-μᾰνής, ές, gen. έος, (φήρ, μανῆναι) *madly fond of wild animals* or *hunting.*

φῄς, 2 sing. of φημί: but 2. **φῆς**, Ep. for ἔφης, 2 sing. aor. 2 of φημί.

φῆσθα, Ep. 2 sing. aor. 2 of φημί.

φήτρη, ἡ, Ion. for φάτρα.

φθαίη, 3 sing. aor. 2 opt. of φθάνω.

φθαίρω, Dor. for φθείρω.

φθάμενος, aor. 2 med. part. of φθάνω. [ᾰ]

φθάν, Ep. for ἔφθασαν, 3 pl. aor. 2 of φθάνω.

ΦΘΑ'ΝΩ: fut. φθήσομαι, later also φθάσω [ᾰ]: aor. 1 ἔφθᾰσα: aor. 2 ἔφθην, 3 pl. φθάν for ἔφθασαν, subj. φθῶ, Ep. 3 sing. φθήῃ and φθῇσιν, Ep. 1 pl. φθέωμεν, 3 pl. φθέωσιν, opt. φθαίην, inf. φθῆναι, part. φθάς: pf. ἔφθᾰκα: Ep. aor. 2 med. part. φθάμενος [ᾰ]: Dor. fut. φθαξῶ, aor. 1 ἔφθαξα. *To come before, do, reach before;* ὁ φθάσας *the first comer;* φθάνειν εἰς τὴν πόλιν *to come first* into the city:—c. acc. pers. *to be beforehand with, overtake, outstrip, anticipate,* Lat. *praevenire;* and sometimes simply *to arrive;* ἔφθησαν τὸν χειμῶνα *they anticipated* the storm; it is often joined with a part. act. agreeing with the agent, ἔφθη βαλὼν αὐτόν *he was beforehand* in striking him; ἦ κε πολὺ φθαίη πόλις ἁλοῦσα the city *would be beforehand* in being taken, i.e. it would be taken *first.* II. in these constructions, φθάνειν is best rendered in English by an Adv. *before, sooner, first;* ἔφθην ἀφικόμενος I came *sooner* or *first:* we also find the part. of φθάνω joined with another Verb, οὐκ ἄλλος φθὰς ἐμεῦ κατήγορος ἔσται no other shall be an accuser *before* me; φθάσας προσπεσοῦμαι I will *first* fall upon you; so part. φθάσας with imperat., λέγε φθάσας speak *quickly.* III. φθάνειν with οὐ and part., followed by καί, etc., like Lat. *simul ac,* denotes two actions following close on each other, οὐ φθάνει ἐξαγόμενος καὶ εὐθὺς ὅμοιός ἐστι *no sooner* is he brought out than he is like; οὐκ ἔφθη μοι συμβᾶσα ἡ ἀτυχία καὶ εὐθὺς ἐπεχείρησαν *scarcely* or *no sooner* had misfortune befallen me *than* they attempted. IV. in questions with οὐ, φθάνω denotes impatience to have the thing done; ἀποτρέχων οὐκ ἂν φθάνοις; *will you* not *be quick* and run off? i. e. make haste and run off. V. in answers with οὐ and opt. c. ἄν, οὐκ ἂν φθάνοιμι I could not *be too quick*, i. e. I will begin directly.

φθἄρῆναι, aor. 2 pass. inf. of *φθείρω*.

φθαρτός, ή, όν, verb. Adj. of *φθείρω*, *corruptible, destructible, mortal, transitory*.

φθάς, φθᾶσα, φθάν, aor. 2 part. of *φθάνω*.

ΦΘΕΓΓΟΜΑΙ, f. *φθέγξομαι*: aor. 1 *ἐφθεγξάμην*: pf. *ἔφθεγμαι*: Dep.:—*to utter a sound* or *voice, to speak loud and clear, articulate; τὸ φθεγγόμενον, that which uttered the sound, the voice.* 2. of animals, as of a horse *to neigh, snort;* of a fawn, *to cry;* of a door, *to creak.* II. c. acc. cognato, *φθέγγεσθαι ἔπος to utter* or *say* a word III. *to extol, praise, sing, celebrate.*

φθέγμα, ατος, τό, (*φθέγγομαι*) *a voice: language, speech: a saying, word:* in plur. *accents, words.* 2. generally, *a cry, roar, sound.*

φθέγξομαι, fut. of *φθέγγομαι*.

φθείομεν, Ep. for *φθέωμεν, φθῶμεν*, 1 pl. aor. 2 subj. of *φθάνω*.

ΦΘΕΙ'Ρ, ὁ, gen. *φθειρός*, *a louse*, Lat. *pediculus.* II. *the small fruit* or *cone of a kind of pine.*

φθειριάω, f. *άσω*, (*φθείρ*) *to be lousy, suffer from morbus pedicularis.*

φθειρο-τρᾰγέω, f. *ήσω*, (*φθείρ, τραγεῖν*) *to eat lice*, or rather *to eat fir-cones;* cf. *φθείρ*

φθείρω: fut. *φθερῶ* Ep. *φθέρσω*: aor. 1 *ἔφθειρα*: pf. *ἔφθαρκα*, pf. 2 *ἔφθορα*: Pass., pf. *ἔφθαρμαι*, 3 pl. *ἐφθάραται*: aor. 2 *ἐφθάρην* [ᾰ]: (*φθίω*):—*to corrupt, spoil, ruin, waste, destroy*, Lat. *perdere, pessumdare:*—Pass. *to go to ruin, perish;* in Att., *φθείρου* was a common imprecation, *go and be banged!* Lat. *abi in malam rem!* hence, *εἰ μὴ φθερεῖ* unless *thou depart;* but, *φθείρεσθαι εἰς* or *πρός τι to run headlong* into a thing 2. in Pass., of shipwrecked persons, *to be cast away.* II. of men, *to kill, slay, destroy:* also of wom *to seduce:*—Pass. *to perish, pine away.*

φθερσῐ-γενής, ές, (*φθείρω, γένος*) *destroying the race* or *family*

φθέωμεν, φθέωσιν, Ep. for *φθῶμεν, φθῶσιν*, 1 and 3 pl. aor. 2 subj. of *φθάνω*.

φθῆ, Ep. for *ἔφθη*, 3 sing aor. 2 of *φθάνω*.

φθήῃ, Ep. for *φθῇ*, 3 sing. aor. 2 subj. of *φθάνω*.

φθῆναι, aor. 2 inf. of *φθάνω*.

φθῆσιν, Ep. for *φθῇ*, 3 sing aor. 2 subj. of *φθάνω*.

φθήσομαι, fut. of *φθάνω*

Φθία, *ας*, Ep. and Ion. **Φθίη**, *ης*, ἡ, *Phthia*, a district in Thessaly, the home of Achilles. [ῑ]

Φθιάς, ἄδος, ἡ, fem. of *Φθῖος*, *a Phthian woman.*

φθίεται, Ep. for *φθίηται*, aor. 2 pass. subj. of *φθίω*.

Φθίηνδε, Adv. *to Phthia.* [ῑ]

Φθίηφι, Ep. dat. sing. of *Φθίη*, *at Phthia.* [ῑ]

φθίμενος, part. Ep. aor. 2 pass. of *φθίνω*. [ῐ]

φθινάς, άδος, ἡ, (*φθίνω*) intr. *perishing, wasting, waning.* II. act. *causing to decline, wasting:* νόσοι φθινάδης *wasting* diseases.

φθίνασμα, ατος, τό, (*φθίνω*) *a declining, wasting, pining, waning.* [ῐ]

φθῐνάω and **φθινέω**, (*φθίνω*) *to waste* or *pine.*

φθῐνό-καρπος, ον, (*φθίνω, καρπός*) *with blighted fruit*

φθῐνοπωρῐνός, ή, όν, (*φθινόπωρον*) *autumnal.*

φθῐνοπωρίς, ίδος, fem. of *φθινοπωρινό*

φθῐν-όπωρον, τό, (*φθίνω, ὀπώρα*) *the last part of ὀπώρα* or *the time after ὀπώρα, late autumn, the fall of the year*

φθῐνύθεσκε, 3 sing. Ion. impf. of *φθινύθω*. [ῠ]

φθῐνύθω, poët. for *φθίνω*, used only in pres. and impf.: I. intr. *to waste away, decay.* II. trans. *to consume, waste.* [ῠ]

ΦΘΙ'ΝΩ, common form of *φθίω*. [ῐ]

φθίομαι, Ep. for *φθιῶμαι*, aor. 2 pass. subj

Φθῖος, α, ον, (*Φθία*) *Phthian; οἱ Φθῖοι, the Phthians.*

φθίσεσθαι [ῑ], fut. med. inf. of *φθίνω*.

φθῑσ-ήνωρ, ορος, ὁ, ἡ, (*φθίνω, ἀνήρ*) *man-destroying, destructive, deadly, fatal.*

φθίσθαι, Ep. aor. 2 pass. of *φθίω*. *φθίνω*.

φθῑσίμ-βροτος, ον, (*φθίνω, βροτός*) *man-destroying.*

φθίσις, εως, ἡ, (*φθίνω*) of persons, *consumption, decline, decay*, Lat. *tabes.* 2. generally, *a dwindling* or *wasting away, decay, waning.* [ῐ]

φθῖτο, 3 sing. Ep. aor. 2 pass. opt. of *φθίω*: but, 2. **φθίτο** [ῐ], Ep. 3 sing. Ep. aor. 2 pass. indic.

φθῑτός, ή, όν, verb. Adj. of *φθίω*, *wasted, decayed, dead; οἱ φθιτοί the dead.*

ΦΘΙ'Ω, impf. *ἔφθῐον*, more common in form ΦΘΙ'ΝΩ [ῑ Hom., ῐ Att.]: fut. *φθίσομαι* [ῑ]: pf. pass. (in same sense as act.) *ἔφθῐμαι*: plqpf. *ἐφθίμην* [ῐ]: —but *ἐφθίμην* is more commonly Ep. aor. 2 pass., 3 pl. *ἐφθίατο*; subj. *φθίωμαι* Ep. *φθίομαι*, 3 sing. *φθίεται* (for *φθίηται*), 1 pl. *φθιόμεσθαι* (for *φθιώμεθα*); opt. *φθίμην, φθῖο, φθῖτο*; inf. *φθίσθαι*; part. *φθίμενος* [ῐ]:—*to decline, decay, wane, pine* or *waste away, perish, die; οἱ φθίμενοι the dead:* of Time, *πρίν κεν νὺξ φθῖτο* first would the night *come to an end; φθίνουσιν νύκτες* the nights *wane; μηνῶν φθινόντων* in the moon's *wane*, i. e. towards the month's end: in Homer's time, the month was divided into two parts, *μὴν ἱστάμενος* and *μὴν φθίνων*, as in phrase, *τοῦ μὲν φθίνοντος μηνὸς τοῦ δ' ἱσταμένοιο* both at the *waning* of the month, and at its beginning; at Athens the month was divided into 3 decads, *μὴν ἱστάμενος, μὴν μεσῶν, μὴν φθίνων*; in the two first of which the days were reckoned forwards, in the last backwards. 2. of plants, *to fade, wither, die.* II. Causal in fut. *φθίσω* [ῑ], aor. 1 act. *ἔφθῑσα* (like *βήσω, ἔβησα*):—*to make to decline, decay* or *pine away, to consume:* also of money, etc., *to waste, squander.*

Φθῑώτης, ου, ὁ, (*Φθία*) *a man of Phthia:*—fem. **Φθιῶτις**, ιδος (sub. *γῆ*), *the land of Phthia.*

φθογγή, ἡ, (*φθέγγομαι*) like *φθόγγος, the voice of* men: also *the cry* of animals.

φθογγός, ὁ, (φθέγγομαι) *the voice* of men: also *the cry* of animals: generally, *a sound*.

ΦΘΟΙ͂Σ, ῖος, ὁ, nom. pl. φθοῖς, *a* kind of *cake*.

φθονερός, ά, όν, (φθόνος) *envious, jealous; τὸ θεῖον πᾶν ἐστι φθονερόν* the gods are altogether *jealous*. Adv. φθονερῶς ἔχειν to be *enviously* disposed.

φθονέω, f. ήσω: aor. 1 ἐφθόνησα, in late Poets ἐφθόνεσα: Pass., aor. 1 ἐφθονήθην: (φθόνος):—*to be envious* or *jealous, to envy, bear a grudge* or *ill-will;* c. dat. pers., φθονεῖν τινι εὖ πρήσσοντι *to envy* a man in a state of prosperity: absol., μὴ φθονήσῃς *bear* no *malice*, Lat. *ne graveris:* also c. gen. rei, οὔ τοι ἡμιόνων φθονέω I *bear* thee no *grudge for* the mules. 2. c. acc. rei, *to grudge, refuse* or *withhold through envy* or *jealousy*. 3. c. inf., οὐκ ἂν φθονέοιμι ἀγορεῦσαι I will not *grudge* to tell; ἐφθόνησαν ἄνδρα ἕνα τῆς τε Ἀσίης καὶ τῆς Εὐρώπης βασιλεῦσαι they *were jealous* that one man should be king both of Asia and Europe. 4. Pass. φθονοῦμαι, *to be envied* or *begrudged*, Lat. *invideor* (in Horace). Hence

φθόνησις, εως, ἡ, *an envying, a being jealous* or *grudging: envy*.

ΦΘΟ´ΝΟΣ, ὁ, *ill-will, envy, jealousy*, at the good fortune of another: also *an envying, a grudge, malice*, Lat. *invidia; οὐδεὶς φθόνος* there is no *grudging*, i. e. I am willing: c. gen. rei, *envy for* or *because of* a thing—φθόνος *jealousy* at the great prosperity of men was ascribed to the gods, whence the phrase τὸν φθόνον πρόσκυσον, intreat, i. e. disarm, their *envy*.

φθορά Ion. **φθορή**, ἡ, (ἔφθορα) *corruption, decay: destruction, ruin:* also *a mortality, perdition, death*. 2. *seduction* of a woman. II. *moral corruption, depravity, wickedness*.

φθόρος, ὁ, = φθορά, *destruction, ruin, perdition:* hence, οὐκ ἐς φθόρον [sc. ἄπει]; as a curse, like Lat. *abi in malam rem*, wilt thou not go to *ruin?* i.e. go *hang*. II. like ὄλεθρος, *a pestilent fellow*.

-φι, -φιν, in Ep. poetry a termin. of the dat. and of genit., both in sing. and plur.: hence as an adverbial termin., mostly *of place*.

ΦΙΑ´ΛΗ [ᾰ], ἡ, *a flat shallow cup* or *bowl*, esp. *a drinking-bowl* or *bowl for libations*, Lat. *patera:* also *a funereal vase* or *urn:*—from its broad flat shape, Ἄρεος φιάλη *the bowl* of Mars, was a comic metaph. for ἀσπὶς *a shield*.

φιάλλω, f. φιᾰλῶ, *to take in hand, undertake, set about* a thing. (Deriv. uncertain.)

φιᾰρός, ά, όν Ion. **φιερός**, ή, όν (πῖαρ) *sleek, plump*.

φιβάλεοι Att. **φιβαλέῳ**, αἱ, with or without ἰσχάδες, a kind of *early figs*, so called from Φίβαλις, a district of Attica or Megaris.

φιδίτιον, see φειδίτιον.

φῐλ-άβουλος, ον, (φίλος, ἄβουλος) *wilfully thoughtless, wayward*.

φῐλ-άγᾰθος, ον, (φίλος, ἀγαθός) *loving goodness*.

φῐλ-άγλᾰος, ον, (φίλος, ἄγλαος) *loving splendour*.

φῐλ-άγραυλος, ον, (φίλος, ἄγραυλος) *fond of a country life*. [ᾰγρ]

φῐλ-ᾰγρέτης, ου, ὁ, (φίλος, ἄγρα) *a lover of the chase:* fem. **φιλαγρέτις**, ιδος, *a huntress*.

φίλ-ᾰγρος, ον, (φίλος, ἀγρός) *fond of the country* or *of a country life*.

φῐλ-άγρυπνος, ον, (φίλος, ἄγρυπνος) *fond of waking* or *watching, wakeful*. [ᾰγρ]

φῐλ-άγων, ωνος, ὁ, ἡ, (φίλος, ἀγών) *fond of contests: used in contests*. [ᾰ]

φῐλᾰδελφία, ἡ, *brotherly* or *sisterly love*. From

φῐλ-άδελφος, ον, (φίλος, ἀδελφός) *fond of one's brother* or *sister, brotherly, sisterly*. [ᾰ]

φῐλ-άεθλος, ον, (φίλος, ἄεθλον) *fond of the games*.

φῐλ-ᾰθήναιος, ον (φίλος, Ἀθηναῖος) *fond of the Athenians*.

φῖλαι, Ep. 2 sing. aor. 1 med. imperat. of φιλέω.

φῐλ-αίακτος, ον, (φίλος, αἰάζω) *fond of wailing: lamentable*.

φῐλ-αιδήμων, ον, gen. ονος, (φίλος, αἰδώς) *loving modesty*.

φῐλ-αίμᾰτος, ον, (φίλος, αἷμα) *fond of blood, blood-thirsty*.

φῐλαίτερος, α, ον and **φῐλαίτατος**, η, ον, irreg. Comp. and Sup. of φίλος, *dearer, dearest*.

φῐλ-αίτιος, ον, (φίλος, αἰτία) *fond of bringing charges, fault-finding, censorious*. II. *liable to blame*.

φῐλ-ᾰκόλουθος, ον, (φίλος, ἀκόλουθος) *readily following*.

φῐλ-άκρᾱτος Ion **-ακρητος**, ον, (φίλος, ἄκρατος) *fond of sheer wine: given to wine*. [ᾰκρ]

φίλᾱμα, Dor. for φίλημα.

φῐλάμενος, poët. aor. 1 med. part. of φιλεω, in pass. sense.

φῐλ-άμπελος, ον, (φίλος, ἄμπελος) *friend of the vine*.

φῐλανδρία, ἡ, *love for a husband: love for men*. From

φίλ-ανδρος, ον, (φίλος, ἀνήρ) *loving one's husband, conjugal*. II. *loving men*. [ῐ]

φιλ-ανθής, ές, (φίλος, ἄνθος) *fond of flowers*.

φῐλ-ανθρᾰκεύς, έως, ὁ, (φίλος, ἀνθρακεύς) *friend of colliers*.

φῐλανθρωπεύω, (φιλάνθρωπος) *to be a friend to mankind:* in Med. φιλανθρωπεύομαι, *to act humanely* or *kindly*.

φῐλανθρωπία, ἡ, (φιλάνθρωπος) *love for mankind, humanity, benevolence, kindliness, clemency:* in plur. *acts of humanity* or *kindness*.

φῐλ-άνθρωπος, ον, (φίλος, ἄνθρωπος) *loving mankind, humane, benevolent, kind*. Hence

φιλανθρώπως, Adv. *humanely, kindly:* Sup. -ότατα, *most humanely*.

φῐλ-άνωρ [ᾱ], ορος, ὁ, ἡ, Dor. for φιλήνωρ, (φίλος, ἀνήρ) *loving one's husband, affectionate*.

φῐλ-αοιδός, όν, (φίλος, ἀοιδός) *fond of singing* or *singers*.

φιλαοιδῶ, Dor. gen. of φιλαοιδός.

φῐλ-ᾰπεχθημοσύνη, ἡ, *fondness for making enemies, readiness at picking quarrels:* in pl. *quarrelsome attempts*. From

φῐλ-απεχθήμων, ον, gen. ονος, (φίλος, ἀπεχθάνομαι) *fond of making enemies, quarrelsome, wrangling.* Adv. -μόνως

φῐλ-απλοϊκός, ή, όν, (φίλος, ἁπλόος) *fond of simplicity* or *frankness*

φῐλ-απόδημος, ον, (φίλος, ἀπόδημος) *fond of going abroad* or *travelling*

φῐλαργυρία, ἡ, *love of money, covetousness.* From

φῐλ-άργῠρος, ον, (φίλος, ἄργυρος) *fond of money, covetous, avaricious.*

φῐλ-αριστείδης, ου, ὁ, (φίλος, Ἀριστείδης) *a friend of Aristides.*

φῐλ-άρμᾰτος, ον, (φίλος, ἅρμα) *fond of chariots* or *the chariot-race.*

φῐλαρχία, ἡ, *love of rule, lust of power.* From

φίλ-αρχος, ον, (φίλος, ἀρχή) *fond of rule, ambitious.* [φῐ]

φῐλᾶσε, -ᾶσας, Dor. for ἐφίλησε, φιλήσας.

φῐλᾱσεῖ, Dor. for φιλήσει, 3 sing. fut. of φιλέω.

φῐλ-αστράγᾰλος, ον, (φίλος, ἀστράγαλος) *fond of playing at dice.* [τρᾰ]

φιλ-άσωτος, ον, (φίλος, ἄσωτος) *fond of profligacy.*

φίλᾰτο, 3 sing. Ep. aor. 1 med. of φιλέω. [ῐ]

φίλ-αυλος, ον, (φίλος, αὐλός) *fond of the flute.* [ῐ]

φίλ-αυτος, ον, (φίλος, αὑτοῦ) *fond of oneself, self-loving, selfish.* Adv. -τως. [ῐ]

φῐλέεσκε, 3 sing. Ion. impf. of φιλέω

φῐλ-έθειρος, ον, (φίλος, ἔθειρα) *loving the hair*, i.e. *worn in the hair.*

φῐλ-έλλην, ηνος, ὁ, ἡ, (φίλος, Ἕλλην) *fond of the Hellenes* or *Greeks.*

φῐλ-έννῠχος, ον, (φίλος, ἔννυχος) *loving night.*

φῐλέοισαι, Dor. pres. part. fem. pl. of φιλέω.

φῐλέοντι, Dor. 3 pl. pres. of φιλέω: but also pres. part. dat. sing.

φῐλ-έορτος, ον, (φίλος, ἑορτή) *fond of feasts* or *holidays.*

φῐλ-επιτῑμητής, οῦ, ὁ, (φίλος, ἐπιτιμάω) *fond of fault-finding: a censorious person.*

φῐλ-εραστής, οῦ, ὁ, (φίλος, ἐραστής) *dear to lovers.*

φῐλεργία, ἡ, *love of labour, industry.* From

φῐλ-εργός, όν, (φίλος, ἔργον) *loving work, working willingly, industrious.*

φῐλ-έρῑθος ον, (φίλος, ἔριθος) *fond of wool-spinning.*

φίλ-ερως, ωτος, ὁ, ἡ, (φίλος, ἔρως) *prone to love, full of love.* [ῐ]

φῐλ-έσπερος, ον, (φίλος, ἑσπέρα) *fond of evening.*

φῐλεταιρία, ἡ, *love of comrades, friendship.* From

φῐλ-έταιρος, ον, (φίλος, ἑταῖρος) *fond of one's comrades* or *friends, true to them.* Adv. -ρως.

φῐλ-εύϊος, ον, (φίλος, εὐοῖ) *loving the cry of εὐοῖ*, epith. of Bacchus.

φῐλ-εύ-λειχος, ον, (φιλόs, εὖ, λείχω) *fond of dainties.*

φίλ-ευνος, ον, (φίλος, εὐνή) *fond of the bed.* esp. *the marriage-bed.* [ῐ]

φιλεῦντα, φιλεῦντι, φιλεῦσα, Dor. for φιλοῦντα, φιλοῦντι, φιλοῦσα, forms of the pres. part. of φιλέω.

φιλ-εύτακτος, ον, (φίλος, εὔτακτος) *fond of order.*

φῐλ-έφηβος, ον, (φίλος, ἔφηβος) *fond of youth.*

φῐλ-εχθής, ές, gen. έος, (φίλος, ἔχθος) *fond of making enemies, quarrelsome.*

φῐλέω, f. ήσω: aor. 1 ἐφίλησα: pf. πεφίληκα: Med, Ep. aor. 1 ἐφῑλάμην in 3 sing. ἐφίλατο, φίλατο; imperat. φῖλαι; 3 plur. subj. φίλωνται. part. φιλάμενος in pass. sense, *beloved;* also fut. φιλήσομαι in pass. sense: Pass., paullo.-p. fut. πεφιλήσομαι; aor. 1 ἐφιλήθην: pf. πεφίλημαι: (φίλος):—*to love.* Pass. *to be beloved* by one. From the general sense of *loving* came various special meanings, as, *to treat affectionately* or *kindly, to welcome, to befriend;* παρ' ἄμμι φιλήσεαι *thou shalt be welcome* with us. 2. *to shew signs of love*, esp. *to kiss;* φιλεῖν τῷ στόματι *to kiss on* the mouth:—Med. *to kiss one another.* 3. *to like, be fond of, practise.* II. c. inf., like Lat. *amo, to be fond of doing, be wont, use to do:* impers, φιλεῖ γίγνεσθαι it *is wont* to happen, *usually*, happens: absol., οἷα δὴ φιλεῖ as *is wont*, Lat. *ut solet* [ῐ, except in Ep. aor. ἐφῖλάμην.]

φίλη, ἡ, fem. of φίλος, *a mistress* [ῐ]

φῐληδέω, *to love pleasure, find delight in* a thing, c dat. From

φῐλ-ηδής, ές, (φίλος, ἧδος) *loving pleasure.* Hence

φῐληδία, ἡ, (φιληδέω) *fondness for pleasure, delight.*

φῐλ-ήδονος, ον, (φίλος, ἡδονή) *fond of pleasure.* 2. *causing pleasu*

φῐληκοΐα, ἡ, *fondness for listening, attentiveness.* From

φῐλ-ήκοος, ον, (φίλος, ἀκοή) *fond of listening: fond of hearing discussions.*

φῐλ-ηλάκατος, ον, (φίλος, ἠλακάτη) *fond of the spindle.* [ᾰ]

φῐλ-ηλιαστής, οῦ, ὁ, (φίλος, ἡλιαστής) *one who delights in trials*, esp. as a juryman in the court Heliaea.

φίλημα, ατος, τό, (φιλέω) *a kiss.* [ῐ]

φῐλημάτιον, τό, Dim. of φίλημα, *a little kis*

φῐλήμεναι, Ep. pres. inf. of φιλέω.

φίλημι, Aeol. for φιλέω. [ῐ]

φῐλημοσύνη, ἡ, (φιλέω) *friendliness.*

φῐλ-ήνιος, ον, (φίλος, ἡνία) *obeying the rein, tractable.*

φῐλ-ήρετμος, ον, (φίλος, ἐρετμός) *loving the oar, fond of the sea.*

φίλησα, Ep. for ἐφίλησα, aor. 1 of φιλέω. [ῐ]

φῐλησέμεν, Ep. fut. inf. of φιλέω.

φῐλησί-μολπος, ον, (φίλος, μολπή) = φιλόμολπος.

φῐλητέον, verb. Adj. of φιλέω, *one must love.*

φῐλήτωρ, ορος, ὁ, = φιλητής, *a lover.*

φῐλία Ion. φιλίη, ἡ, (φιλέω) *love, affection, friendship*, Lat. *amicitia;* φιλία ἡ ἐμή, ἡ σή, *friendship* for me, for thee.

φῐλικός, ή, όν, (φίλος) *of* or *for a friend, friendly, affectionate;* φιλικά *proofs* or *marks of friendship.* Adv. -κῶς, *in a kind, friendly way:* Comp. φιλικώτερον; Sup. -ώτατα.

φίλιος, α, ον, also ος, ον, (φίλος) *of* or *from a friend, friendly, kindly:* opp. to πολέμιος, *friendly, in alliance with* one: ἡ φιλία (sc. χώρα) *a friendly* country, opp. to ἡ πολεμία. 2. Ζεὺς φίλιος, Jove as god of friendship. II. beloved, dear. Adv. φιλίως, in a friendly way. [φῐ]

Φῐλίππειος, α, ον, of Philip.

Φῐλιππήσιος, ον, (Φίλιπποι) of or from Philippi: as Subst. a Philippian.

Φῐλιππίζω, f. ίσω Att. ιῶ, (Φίλιππος) to be on Philip's side or party, to Philippize.

Φίλιπποι, αἱ, a town in Thrace.

φίλ-ιππος, ον, (φίλος, ἵππος) fond of horses: Sup. φιλιππότατος. II. as masc. pr. n., Philip. [φῐ]

φιλίτιον, τό, (φίλος) = φειδίτιον.

φῐλίων, ον, gen. ονος, poët. Comp. of φίλος, dearer.

φῐλίως, Adv. of φίλιος, in a friendly manner.

φῐλό-βακχος, ον, (φίλος, Βάκχος) loving Bacchus or wine.

φῐλο-γᾱθής, ές, Dor. for φιλογηθής.

φῐλό-γαιος, ον, (φίλος, γαῖα) loving the earth.

φῐλό-γᾰμος, ον, (φίλος, γάμος) longing for marriage.

φιλο-γαστορίδας, ου, ὁ, (φίλος, γαστήρ) fond of one's belly.

φῐλο-γέλοιος, ον, (φίλος, γέλοιος) fond of the ludicrous, loving a joke.

φιλό-γελως, ωτος, ὁ, ἡ, (φίλος, γέλως) laughter-loving.

φῐλογεωργία, ἡ, fondness for farming or for a country life. From

φῐλο-γεωργός, όν, (φίλος, γεωργός) fond of farming or of a country life.

φῐλο-γηθής Dor. **-γᾱθής**, ές, gen. έος, (φίλος, γῆθος) loving mirth, mirthful, cheerful.

φῐλό-δαφνος, ον, (φίλος, δάφνη) loving the laurel.

φῐλό-δενδρος, ον, (φίλος, δένδρον) fond of trees.

φῐλο-δέσποτος, ον, (φίλος, δεσπότης) loving one's lord or master: of slaves, attached, submissive.

φῐλό-δημος, ον, (φίλος, δῆμος) befriending the commons or people, the commons' friend.

φῐλοδῐκέω, f. ήσω, to be fond of law, litigious. From

φῐλό-δῐκος, ον, (φίλος, δίκη) fond of lawsuits: litigious.

φῐλ-οδίτης, ου, ὁ, (φίλος, ὁδίτης) a friend of travellers. [ῑ]

φῐλό-δοξος, ον, (φίλος, δόξα) loving honour or glory.

φῐλό-δουπος, (φίλος, δοῦπος) loving noise.

φῐλ-όδυρτος, ον, (φίλος, ὀδύρομαι) fond of lamenting, indulging sorrow, melancholy.

φῐλό-δωρος, ον, (φίλος, δῶρον) fond of giving, bountiful. Adv. -ρως.

φῐλο-εργός, όν, (φίλος, ἔργον) fond of work, industrious.

φῐλο-ζέφῠρος, ον, (φίλος, Ζέφυρος) loving the west-wind.

φῐλό-ζωος, ον, (φίλος, ζωή) fond of one's life, cowardly. II. (φίλος, ζῷον) fond of animals.

φιλο-θεάμων [ᾰ], ον, (φίλος, θεάομαι) fond of seeing, fond of spectacles or shows.

φῐλό-θεος, ον, (φίλος, θεός) loving God, pious, devout.

φῐλοθηρία, ἡ, love of hunting, love of the chase. From

φῐλό-θηρος, ον, (φίλος, θήρα) fond of hunting.

φῐλο-θουκυδίδης, ου, ὁ, (φίλος, Θουκυδίδης) fond of Thucydides.

φῐλο-θρηνής, ές, (φίλος, θρῆνος) fond of wailing or lamentation.

φῐλο-θύτης, ου, ὁ, (φίλος, θύω) one fond of sacrificing, a zealous worshipper. [ῠ]

φῐλό-θῠτος, ον, (φίλος, θύω) fond of sacrificing; φιλόθυτα ἔργα sacrifices offered with zeal.

φιλ-οικόδομος, ον, (φίλος, οἰκοδομέω) fond of building.

φῐλ-οικτίρμων, ον, gen. ονος, (φίλος, οἰκτείρω) prone to pity, compassionate. Adv. -μόνως.

φῐλ-οίκτιστος, ον, (φίλος, οἰκτίζω) = φίλοικτος.

φίλ-οικτος, ον, (φίλος, οἶκτος) fond of compassionating, fond of lamentation: piteous. [ῐ]

φῐλοινία, ἡ, love, fondness of wine. From

φίλ-οινος, ον, (φίλος, οἶνος) fond of wine.

φῐλ-οίφης, ου, ὁ, (φίλος, οἰφάω) a lewd fellow.

φῐλοκᾰλέω, f. ήσω, to be a lover of the beautiful, to indulge a taste for refinement. From

φῐλό-κᾰλος, ον, (φίλος, καλός) loving the beautiful, loving beauty and goodness: fond of refinement and elegance. II. also fond of honour, seeking honour.

φῐλο-καμπής, ές, gen. έος, (φίλος, καμπή) easily bent, pliant, lithe.

φῐλο-καρποφόρος, ον, (φίλος, καρποφόρος) bearing fruit abundantly.

φῐλοκέρδεια, ἡ, (φιλοκερδής) love of gain.

φῐλοκερδέω, f. ήσω, to be greedy of gain. From

φῐλο-κερδής, ές, gen. έος, (φίλος, κέρδος) loving gain, greedy of gain.

φῐλο-κέρτομος, ον, (φίλος, κέρτομος) fond of jeering or mocking.

φῐλο-κηδεμών, όνος, ὁ, ἡ, (φίλος, κηδεμών) fond of one's relatives or connections.

φῐλο-κίνδῡνος, ον, (φίλος, κίνδυνος) fond of danger, venturous, enterprising, bold. Adv. -νως, venturously, in an enterprising way.

φῐλο-κισσοφόρος, ον, (φίλος, κισσοφόρος) fond of wearing ivy.

φῐλό-κνῖσος, ον, (φίλος, κνίζω) fond of pinching.

φῐλό-κοινος, ον, (φίλος, κοινός) fond of what is common

φῐλό-κρημνος, ον, (φιλος, κρημνός) loving steep rocks, crag-loving.

φῐλο-κρινέω, f. ήσω, (φίλος, κρίνω) to pick and choose as friends.

φῐλο-κρότᾰλος, ον, (φίλος, κρόταλον) loving a rattle or din.

φῐλό-κροτος, ον, (φίλος, κρότος) loving noise or din.

φῐλο-κτέᾰνος, ον, (φίλος, κτέανον) = φιλοκτήμων, loving possessions, greedy of gain, covetous: Sup. φιλοκτεανώτατος, most covetous, most grasping.

φῐλο-κτήμων, ον, gen. ονος, (φίλος, κτῆμα) = φιλοκτέανος.

φῐλό-κῠβος, ον, (φίλος, κύβος) fond of dice or gambling.

φῐλο-κῡδής, ές, gen. έος, (φίλος, κῦδος) *loving splendour, joyous, brilliant.*

φῐλο-κῠνηγέτης, ου, ὁ, (φίλος, κυνηγέτης) *a lover of hunting* or *the chase.*

φῐλό-κωμος, ον, (φίλος, κῶμος) *fond of feasting and dancing, fond of revelry.*

φῐλο-λάκων, ωνος, ὁ, (φίλος, Λάκων) *fond of the Lacedaemonians.* [ᾰ]

φῐλο-λήιος, ον, poët. for φιλόλειος, (φίλος, ληίη, λεία) *loving booty.*

φῐλό-λιχνος, ον, (φιλος, λίχνος) *loving dainties.*

φῐλολογία, ἡ, *love of discussion, love of learning and literature: the study of language and history.* From

φῐλό-λογος, ον, (φίλος, λέγω) *fond of words, wordy.* II. *fond of dissertation; fond of learning and literature,* Lat. *studiosus*:—as Subst., φιλόλογος, ὁ, *a student of language and history, a learned man.*

φῐλο-λοίδορος, ον, (φίλος, λοίδορος) *fond of reviling, abusive.*

φῐλομάθεια, ἡ, *love of knowledge.* [μᾰ] From

φῐλο-μᾰθής, ές, gen. έος, (φίλος, μαθεῖν) *fond of learning, loving knowledge.* Adv. -θῶς.

φῐλό-μαντις, εως, ὁ, (φίλος, μάντις) *loving soothsayers* or *soothsaying.*

φῐλό-μαστος, ον, (φίλος, μαστός) *loving the breast.*

φῐλομᾰχέω, f. ήσω, *to be fond of fighting, eager to fight.* From

φῐλό-μᾰχος, ον, (φίλος, μάχη) *loving fighting, warlike.*

φῐλ-όμβριος and φῐλ-ομβρος, ον, (φίλος, ὄμβρος) *rain-loving.*

φῐλομήλᾱ Ion. -λη, ἡ, *the nightingale,* so called, because, acc. to the legend, Philomela was changed into this bird. Hence

φῐλομήλειος, α, ον, *of, belonging to the nightingale.*

φῐλο-μήτωρ, ορος, ὁ, ἡ, (φίλος, μήτηρ) *loving one's mother.*

φῐλομ-μειδής, ές, poët. for φιλομειδής, (φίλος, μειδάω) *laughter-loving,* epith. of Venus.

φῐλό-μολπος, ον, (φίλος, μολπή) *loving the dance and song.*

φῐλομουσέω, f. ήσω, (φιλόμουσος) *to love the Muses.*

φῐλομουσία, ἡ, (φιλομουσέω) *love of the Muses.*

φῐλό-μουσος, ον, (φίλος, Μοῦσα) *loving the Muses, loving music and the arts: refined, learned.*

φιλό-μῡθος, ον, (φίλος, μῦθος) *fond of fables.*

φῐλό-μωμος, ον, (φίλος, μῶμος) *given to find fault, censorious.*

φιλό-μωσος, Dor. for φιλόμουσος.

φῐλο-ναύτης, ου, ὁ, (φίλος, ναύτης) *loving sailors.*

φῐλονεικέω, f. ήσω, (φιλόνεικος) *to be fond of dispute, to act in a contentious spirit, contend eagerly* or *obstinately;* c. dat. *to strive* or *contend eagerly with one;* τὰ χείρω φιλονεικεῖν *to choose* the worse part *out of obstinacy.* Hence

φῐλονεικία, ἡ, *love of strive, contentiousness, rivalry, party-spirit, pertinacity, obstinacy.*

φῐλό-νεικος, ον, (φίλος, νεῖκος) *fond of strife, contentious, pertinacious, obstinate.*

φῐλονῑκέω, f. ήσω, (φιλόνικος) *to strive for victory.* Hence

φιλονικητέον, verb. Adj. *one must strive for victory.*

φῐλό-νῑκος, ον, (φίλος, νίκη) *striving for victory.*

φῐλο-νύμφιος, ον, (φίλος, νύμφιος) *loving the bridegroom* or *bride.*

φῐλό-ξεινος, ον, poët. for φιλόξενος.

φῐλό-ξενος poët. -ξεινος, ον, (φίλος, ξένος) *loving strangers, hospitable.* Adv. -νως, *hospitably.*

φῐλό-οινος, ον, poët. for φίλοινος.

φῐλο-παίγμων, ον, gen. ονος, (φίλος, παῖγμα) *fond of play* or *sport, playful, sportive.*

φῐλό-παις, -παιδος, ὁ, ἡ, (φίλος, παις) *loving one's children, loving boys.*

φῐλο-πᾰτρία, (φίλος, πάτρις) *love of one's country.* 2. (φίλος, πατήρ) *love of one's father.*

φιλό-πᾰτρις, ιδος, ἡ, acc. -πάτριν, (φίλος, πατρίς) *loving one's country.*

φῐλο-πάτωρ, ορος, ὁ, ἡ, (φίλος, πᾰτήρ) *loving one's father.*

φῐλό-πλεκτος, ον, (φίλος, πλέκω) *constantly braided.*

φῐλό-πλοος, ον contr. -πλους, ουν, (φίλος, πλόος) *fond of sailing.*

φῐλ-όπλος, ον, (φίλος, ὅπλον) *loving arms* or *war.*

φῐλοπλουτία, ἡ, *love of riches.* From

φῐλό-πλουτος, ον, (φίλος, πλοῦτος) *loving* or *seeking riches;* φιλόπλουτος ἅμιλλα the race *for wealth.*

φῐλο-ποίμνιος, ον, (φίλος, ποίμνη) *loving the flock.*

φῐλο-πόλεμος poët. φῐλοπτόλεμος, ον, (φίλος, πόλεμος) *fond of war, warlike.* Adv. -μως.

φῐλό-πολις, εως and ιδος, Ion. ιος, ὁ, ἡ: acc. -ιν: poët. also φιλόπτολις: (φίλος, πόλις):—*loving one's city, state* or *country:* as Subst., φιλόπολις, ὁ, *a patriot:* φιλόπολις ἀρετή or τὸ φιλόπολι *patriotism:*—at Athens, φιλόπατρις was used of one who loved Greece in general, φιλόπολις of *one who was devoted to his own state.*

φῐλοπονέω, f. ήσω, (φιλόπονος) *to love labour, work hard, be diligent;* τὸ φιλοπονεῖν, = φιλοπονία *love of labour, industry.*

φιλοπονηρία, ἡ, *love of bad men* From

φιλο-πόνηρος, ον, (φίλος, πονηρός) *fond of bad men.*

φῐλοπονία, ἡ, (φιλοπονέω) *love of labour, patient industry.*

φῐλό-πονος, ον, (φίλος, πόνος) *loving labour, diligent, industrious.* II. of things, *toilsome, laborious.* Adv. -νως, *laboriously:* Comp. -νώτερον; Sup. -νώτατα.

φῐλοποσία, ἡ, *love of drinking, drunkenness,* Lat. *vinolentia.* From

φῐλο-πότης, ου, ὁ, (φίλος, ΠΟ- Root of some tenses of πίνω) *a lover of drinking, a toper,* Lat. *vinolentus.*

φῐλοπραγμοσύνη, ἡ, *a restless, meddling disposition, officious interference, meddlesomeness.* From

φῐλο-πράγμων, ον, gen. ονος, (φίλος, πρᾶγμα) *fond*

of business, meddlesome, officious: as Subst., φιλοπράγμων, ὁ, *a busybody, meddling fellow.* Adv. -μόνως.

φῐλοπροσηγορία, ἡ, *easiness of address, affability, courtesy.* From

φῐλο-προσήγορος, ον, (φίλος, προσήγορος) *easy of address, affable.*

φῐλο-πρωτεύω, f. σω, (φίλος, πρωτεύω) *to strive to be first* or *in the front rank.*

φῐλο-πτόλεμος, ον, poët. for φιλοπόλεμος.

φῐλό-πτολις, ὁ, ἡ, poët. for φιλόπολις.

φῐλό-πῡρος, ον, (φίλος, πυρός) *loving wheat.*

φῐλ-οπωριστής, οῦ, ὁ, (φίλος, ὀπώρα) *a lover of autumn fruits.*

φῐλ-όργιος, ον, (φίλος, ὄργια) *fond of orgies.*

φῐλ-όρθιος, ον, (φίλος, ὄρθιος) *loving what is right.*

φῐλ-ορμίστειρα, ἡ, (φίλος, ὁρμίζω) *she who loves the harbour.*

φῐλ-ορνῑθία, ἡ, *fondness of birds.* From

φῐλορνις, ῑθος, ὁ, ἡ, (φίλος, ὄρνις) *fond of birds: sheltering, harbouring birds.*

φῐλορ-ρώξ, ῶγος, ὁ, ἡ, (φίλος, ῥώξ) *loving* or *bearing grapes.*

φῐλ-όρτυξ, ῠγος, ὁ, ἡ, (φίλος, ὄρτυξ) *fond of quails.*

ΦΙ'ΛΟΣ, η, ον; vocat. φίλε, sometimes even with neut. nouns, as φίλε τέκνον:—*loved, beloved, dear,* Lat. *amicus, carus.* 2. as Subst., φίλος, ὁ, φίλη, ἡ, Lat. *amicus, amica, a friend;* ὁ Διὸς φίλος *the friend* of Jove: in addressing others, ὦ φίλος, ὦ φίλε, ὦ φίλοι, *O friend, O friends:* οἱ φίλοι *friends, kinsmen, one's kith and kin;* κοινὰ τὰ τῶν φίλων *friends* have all in common. 3. of things, *dear, pleasing;* φίλον ἐστί μοι it is *dear* to me, *pleases* me, Lat. *cordi est.* 4. Homer and other Poets use φίλος for the possessive Pronoun, *my, thy, his,* esp. of the heart, limbs, etc., as, φίλον ἦτορ, φίλα γυῖα, γούνατα, φίλος θυμός, ἄλοχος, τέκνα etc.; even when no affection is implied in it, as, μητρὶ φίλῃ Ἀλθαίῃ χωόμενος κῆρ enraged in heart with *his* mother Althaea: also to denote possession or custom, φίλα εἵματα *their own* garments; φίλος πόνος *their wonted* labour. II. in Poets also, with an act. sense, like φίλιος, *loving, friendly, fond: kindly, kind;* φίλα φρονεῖν to feel *kindly;* φίλα ποιεῖσθαί τινα to do one *a kindness.*

φίλος has several forms of Comparison: 1. Comp. φιλίων, ον: Sup. φίλιστος, η, ον, 2. Comp. φίλτερος: Sup. φίλτατος. 3. Comp. φιλαίτερος, Sup. φιλαίτατος.

φῐλό-σῑτος, ον, (φίλος, σῖτος) *fond of corn, agricultural.* II. generally, *fond of food* or *eating.*

φῐλό-σκηπτρος, ον, (φίλος, σκῆπτρον) *sceptered.*

φῐλο-σκήπων, ωνος, ὁ, ἡ, (φίλος, σκήπων) *loving* or *carrying a staff.*

φῐλο-σκόπελος, ον, (φίλος, σκόπελος) *loving* or *haunting the rocks.*

φῐλο-σκώμμων, ον, gen. ονος, (φίλος, σκῶμμα) *loving a jest.*

φῐλοσοφέω, f. ήσω: pf. πεφιλοσόφηκα: (φιλόσοφος):—*to be a lover of knowledge, seek to become wise, to seek after knowledge, study hard,* Lat. *philosophari.* II. c. acc. rei, *to discuss* or *examine* a subject *by method, to inquire into, treat scientifically,* Lat. *meditari;* φιλοσοφίαν φιλοσοφεῖν *to seek out* a philosophic system. 2. generally, *to study, work at* a thing. Hence

φιλοσοφητέον, verb. Adj. *one must pursue wisdom.*

φῐλοσοφία, ἡ, (φιλοσοφέω) *love of knowledge and wisdom, fondness for studious pursuits.* 2. *the systematic treatment of* a subject, *scientific investigation,* Lat. *meditatio.* 3. *philosophy,* Lat. *philosophia* or *sapientia.*

φῐλό-σοφος, ον, (φίλος, σοφία) *loving wisdom* or *knowledge,* first used by Pythagoras, who called himself φιλόσοφος, *a lover of wisdom,* not σοφός *a sage:* hence *learned, literary, scientific,* as opp. to the vulgar (οἱ πολλοί) 2. as Subst., φιλόσοφος, ὁ, *one who professes an art* or *science;* later, *a philosopher, one who discusses subjects scientifically.* II. *philosophic, loving knowledge.* Hence

φιλοσόφως, Adv. *philosophically.*

φῐλο-σπῆλυγξ, υγγος, ὁ, ἡ, (φίλος σπῆλυγξ) *fond of dwelling in grottoes.*

φῐλό-σπονδος, ον, (φίλος, σπονδή) *loving drink-offerings* or *libations, employed in libations.*

φῐλό-σπουδος, ον, (φίλος, σπουδή) *loving zeal, zealous.*

φῐλο-στέφᾰνος, ον, (φίλος, στέφανος) *loving crowns, wreathed, garlanded.*

φῐλό-στονος, ον, (φίλος, στόνος) *loving sighs* or *groaning, fond of lamentation.* Adv. -νως.

φῐλοστοργία, ἡ, *tender love, warm affection.* From

φῐλό-στοργος, ον, (φίλος, στοργή) *loving tenderly, affectionate,* esp. of natural affection. Adv. -γως.

φῐλο-στρᾰτιώτης, ου, ὁ, (φίλος, στρατιώτης) *the soldier's friend.*

φῐλο-σώμᾰτος, ον, (φιλος, σῶμα) *loving, indulging the body; sensual.*

φῐλοτάσιος [ᾱ], α, ον, Dor. for φιλοτήσιος.

φῐλό-τεκνος, ον, (φίλος, τέκνον) *loving one's children* or *offspring.*

φῐλοτεχνέω, f. ήσω, *to love art, practise an art.* From

φῐλό-τεχνος, ον, (φίλος, τέχνη) *fond of art, ingenious:* of things, *curious.*

φῐλότης, ητος, ἡ, (φίλος) *friendship, love, affection:* also of *friendship between nations.*

φῐλοτήσιος, α, ον, also ος, ον, (φιλότης) *of friendship* or *love, tending to* or *promoting it;* φιλοτήσια ἔργα works *of love.* II. ἡ φιλοτησία κύλιξ, or absol. ἡ φιλοτησία (sub. κύλιξ), the cup *sacred to friendship, the loving-*cup; φιλοτησίαν λαβεῖν to have *one's health drunk;* φιλοτησίαν προπίνειν *to drink* a health.

φῐλοτῑμέομαι: fut. med. ήσομαι: aor. 1 med. ἐφιλοτιμησάμην, and pass. ἐφιλοτιμήθην: pf. πεφιλοτίμημαι: Dep.: (φιλότιμος):—*to love honour* or *distinction; to be ambitious* or *emulous.* 2. *to place one's fame* or *glory* in a thing, *pride oneself* on it, c. dat.;

φιλοτιμεῖσθαί τι or πρός τι *to be eager for* a thing, *pursue* it *eagerly*, hence *to contribute liberally* towards an object; φιλοτιμεῖσθαι πρός τινα *to vie eagerly* with another, *rival* him. 3. c. inf. *to strive emulously, endeavour earnestly, aspire* to do a thing; οἳ πάνυ ἂν φιλοτιμηθεῖεν φίλῳ σοι χρῆσθαι who *would prize* it *above measure* to have you for a friend.

φῐλοτῑμία Ion. -ίη, ἡ, (φιλοτιμέομαι) *love of honour* or *distinction, ambition; emulation, rivalry:* hence *the placing one's pride* or *distinction in* a thing: in bad sense, *pertinacity, obstinacy.* 2. *ostentatiousness:* in good sense, *liberality.* II. *a coveted object, honour, distinction.*

φῐλό-τῑμος, ον, (φίλος, τιμή) *loving honour, ambitious: zealous, emulous.* Adv. –μως. *emulously.* II. pass. *much-honoured.*

φῐλοττάριον, τό, poët. for φιλοτάριον. Dim. of φιλότης, *a little pet, darling.*

φῐλό-φθογγος, ον, (φίλος, φθογγή) *noise-loving.*

φιλό-φιλος, ον, *loving one's friends.*

φῐλο-φόρμιγξ, ιγγος, ὁ, ἡ, (φίλος, φόρμιγξ) *loving the lyre, accompanying it.*

φῐλο-φρονέομαι: f. med. ήσομαι: aor. 1 med. ἐφιλοφρονησάμην, and pass. ἐφιλοφρονήθην: (φιλόφρων):—*to treat* or *deal with affectionately, to shew kindness to:* metaph. *to foster, indulge, gratify:* in aor. 1 pass. φιλοφρονηθῆναι, *to shew kindness to one another, to greet* or *embrace one another*, = φιλοφρονήσασθαι ἀλλήλους. II. absol. *to be of a kindly, cheerful disposition.*

φῐλοφρονέστερος, α, ον, Comp. of φιλόφρων.

φῐλοφροσύνη, ἡ, (φιλόφρων) *friendly treatment* or *behaviour, friendliness, kindliness: friendly greeting, welcome.* II. *cheerfulness, gaiety.*

φιλοφρόσυνος, η, ον, = φιλόφρων.

φῐλό-φρων, ονος, ὁ, ἡ, (φίλος, φρήν) *kindly minded* or *affectioned, friendly, kindly.* Adv. –φρόνως, *kindly, affectionately, cheerfully.*

φῐλο-χορευτής, οῦ, ὁ. (φίλος, χορεύω) *friend of the choral dance.*

φῐλό-χορος, ον, (φιλος, χορος) *loving the choir* or *choral dance*, epith. of Pan.

φῐλοχρημᾰτέω, f. ήσω, (φιλοχρήματος) *to love money, be covetous.* Hence

φῐλοχρημᾰτία, ἡ, *love of money, covetousness.*

φῐλο-χρήμᾰτος, ον, (φίλος, χρήματα) *loving money, fond of money, covetous.* Adv. –τως.

φῐλό-χρηστος, ον, (φίλος, χρηστός) *loving goodness, fairness* or *honesty.*

φῐλό-χριστος, ον, (φίλος, Χριστός) *loving Christ.*

φῐλό-χρῡσος, ον, (φίλος, χρυσός) *greedy of gold.*

φῐλοχωρέω, f. ήσω, (φιλόχωρος) *to be fond of a place* or *country, to haunt a particular spot.* Hence

φῐλοχωρία, ἡ, *fondness for a place, attachment to a particular spot* or *haunt.*

φιλό-χωρος, ον, (φίλος, χώρα) *fond of a place.*

φῐλο-ψευδής, ές, gen. έος, (φίλος, ψεῦδος) *fond of lies* or *lying.*

φῐλό-ψογος, ον, (φίλος, ψόγος) *fond of blaming, censorious.*

φῐλοψῡχέω, (φιλόψυχος) *to be fond of one's life, to be cowardly, dastardly* or *fainthearted.* Hence

φῐλοψῡχία Ion. -ίη, ἡ, *excessive love of life, cowardice, faintheartedness*

φῐλό-ψῡχος, ον, (φίλος, ψυχή) *loving one's life too well;* hence *cowardly, dastardly, fainthearted.* Adv. –χως.

φίλτατος, η, ον, irreg. Sup. of **φίλος**, *dearest, most loved, best beloved.*

φίλτερος, α, ον, irreg. Comp. of **φίλος**, *dearer, more* or *better loved.*

φίλτρον, τό, (φιλέω) *a love-charm, spell to produce love*, Shakespere's '*medicine to make me love him*': generally, *a charm, spell*:—so also, Apollo's oracles are called φίλτρα τόλμης *spells to produce* boldness: cf. φάρμακον. II. in plur. *charms, loveliness.*

φῐλ-υβριστής, οῦ, ὁ, (φίλος, ὑβριστής) *one given to wanton violence.*

φῐλ-ύδρηλος, ον, (φιλος, ὑδρηλός) *abounding in moisture.*

φίλ-υμνος, ον, (φίλος, ὕμνος) *loving song.* [ῐ]

φίλ-υπνος, ον, (φίλος, ὕπνος) *loving sleep.* [ῐ]

ΦΙΛΥΡΑ Ion. **φιλύρη**, ἡ, *the lime* or *linden tree*, Lat. *tilia.* II. *the bass underneath its bark*, Lat. *philyra*, used to tie up flowers, etc. [ῠ]

φῐλύρῐνος, η, ον, (φιλύρα) *of the lime* or *linden tree, light as linden wood.* [ῠ]

φῐλ-ῳδός, όν, (φίλος, ᾠδή) *fond of singing* or *song.*

φῐλ-ωρείτης, ου, ὁ, (φίλος, ὄρος) *a lover of mountains.*

φίλως, Adv. of φίλος, *in friendly manner, in a pleasing way, kindly.* [ῐ]

ΦΙΜΟΣ, ὁ, with irreg. neut. pl. φῑμά, τά, *any instrument for keeping the mouth closed, a muzzle* for dogs, calves, etc., Lat. *capitrum, fiscella* II. *the nose-band* of a horse's bridle, to which pipes and bells were sometimes attached. III. a kind of *cup*, used as *a dice-box*, Lat. *fritillus.* Hence

φῑμόω, f. ώσω: aor. 1 pass. ἐφιμώθην: pf. πεφίμωμαι:—*to muzzle, gag, shut up as with a muzzle;* φιμοῦν τῷ ξύλῳ τὸν αὐχένα *to make fast* his neck in the pillory: metaph. *to muzzle, gag, put to silence;* Pass., φιμώθητι *be thou silent;* πεφίμωσο *be still.*

ΦΙΤΡΟΣ, ὁ, *the stem of a tree, a trunk, block, log;* generally, *a piece of wood.*

φῖτυ, τό, poët. contr. for φίτυμα, as δῶ for δῶμα.

φίτῡμα, ατος, τό, (φιτύω) *a shoot, scion:* metaph. *a son, scion.*

φῑτῠ-ποιμήν, ένος, ὁ, (φῖτυ, ποιμήν) *a tender of plants, gardener.*

φῑτύσεαι, Ep. 2 sing. fut. med. of φιτύω.

φῑτύω, f. ύσω [ῑ]: aor. 1 ἐφίτυσα: (φῖτυ):= φυτεύω, *to sow, plant, raise:* also *to beget:* in Med. of the woman, *to bear, give birth to.*

*__φλάζω__, aor. 2 ἔφλαδον, (φλάω) *to be broken or rent asunder with a noise.*

φλασῶ, Dor. for φλάσω, fut. of **φλάω**.

φλαττόθρατ and **φλαττοθραττοφλαττόθρατ**, Comic words in Aristophanes, meant to ridicule *sound without sense.*

φλαυρίζω, f. ίσω, Att. for φαυλίζω. From

φλαῦρος, α, ον, collat. form of φαῦλος, preferred by Ion. writers.

φλαυρότης, ητος, ἡ, = φαυλότης.

φλαυρ-οῦργος, ον, (φλαῦρος, ἔργον) *working badly:* φλαυροῦργος, ὁ, *a sorry workman.*

φλαύρως, Adv. of φλαῦρος, *badly, meanly;* φλαύρως ἔχειν τὴν τέχνην to know an art *indifferently well;* φλαύρως ἀκούειν, Lat. *male audire*, to be *ill* spoken of.

ΦΛΑ'Ω, 3 sing. impf. ἔφλα: f. φλάσω [ᾰ] Dor. φλᾰσῶ: aor. 1 ἔφλᾰσα: Pass., aor. 1 ἐφλάσθην: pf. πέφλασμαι:—collat. form of θλάω, *to crush, bruise, pound:* hence *to hurt, wound.* II. in Att. Comedy, *to bruise* or *grind with the teeth, swallow greedily.*

φλεγέθω, collat. form of φλέγω, used only in pres.:—transit. *to burn, scorch, burn up:*—Pass. *to be burnt* II. intr. *to blaze, blaze up, be in flames.*

φλέγμα, ατος, τό, (φλέγω) *a flame, fire, heat.* II. as Medic. term, *inflammation, heat.* 2. *phlegm*, Lat. *pituita*

φλεγμαίνω, f. ᾰνῶ: aor. 1 ἐφλέγμᾱνα and ἐφλέγμηνα: (φλέγμα):—*to be heated, inflamed, to fester.*

Φλέγρα, ας, ἡ, *Phlegra;* Φλέγρας πεδίον a plain in Thrace famous for underground fire; here the giants are said to have been conquered by the gods: also in plur. Φλέγραι, as name of any place exposed to volcanic agency.

Φλεγραῖος, α, ον, (Φλέγρα) *of Phlegra, Phlegraean.*

φλεγῦρός, ά, όν, (φλέγω) like φλογερός, *burning, scorching:* metaph. *hot, ardent.*

φλεγύας, ου, ὁ, (φλέγω) a kind of *vulture* or *eagle*, so called from being *flame-coloured.*

ΦΛΕ'ΓΩ, fut. φλέξω: aor. 1 ἔφλεξα:—trans. *to burn, scorch:* Pass. *to become hot, blaze up.* 2. metaph. *to kindle, inflame*, Lat. *urere:* Pass., like Lat. *uri*, *to be inflamed, burn, glow.* 3. metaph., also c. acc. rei, *to make to blaze up, rouse up, excite.* 4. Causal, *to make to flash;* φλέγειν βέλος *to hurl a flaming* bolt:—metaph. *to make illustrious* or *famous*, Lat. *illustrare:*—Pass. *to be* or *become renowned* or *famous.* II. intrans. *to flame, blaze, flash.* 2. metaph. *to burst* or *break forth.* 3. *to shine forth, become famous.*

φλέδων, ονος, and **φλεδών**, ῶνος, ὁ, (φλέω) *an idle talker, babbler.*

ΦΛΕ'ΞΙΣ, εως, ἡ, name of an unknown *bird.*

φλέψ, ἡ, gen. φλεβός, (φλέω) *a vein:* metaph. *any vein* or *channel: a vein* of metal: *a spring* of water.

ΦΛΕ'Ω, *to gush, teem, overflow.*

φλέως, ω, ὁ, Att. for the Ion. φλοῦς, *a* kind of *rush* or *reed.*

φληνᾰφάω, f. ήσω, *to chatter, babble, drivel.* From

φλήνᾰφος, ὁ, (φλέω) *idle talk, babble, chatter.*

ΦΛΙΓΑ', ἡ, in plur. φλιαί, *the doorposts, jambs.*

φλίβω, f. ψω, Aeol. and Ion. for θλίβω. [ῑ]

φλόγεος, α, ον, (φλόξ) *flaming, blazing, flashing.*

φλογυρός, ά, όν, (φλόξ) *flaming, blazing, gleaming.*

φλογίζω, f. ίσω, (φλόξ) *to set on fire, burn up, kindle, scorch:* metaph. *to inflame:*—Pass. *to flame, blaze.*

φλόγῐνος, η, ον, (φλόξ) *flaming, fiery, burning.*

φλογιστός, ή, όν, verb. Adj. of φλογίζω, *burnt, set on fire.*

φλογμός, ὁ, (φλέγω) *a blazing, blaze: inflammation.*

φλογόεις, εσσα, εν, (φλόξ) *flaming, fiery, blazing.*

φλογ-ώδης, ες, (φλόξ, εἶδος) *like flame, fiery hot.*

φλογ-ωπός, όν, (φλόξ, ὤψ) *fiery-looking, flaming.*

φλόγωσις, εως, ἡ, (φλογόω) *burning heat.*

φλογ-ώψ, ῶπος, ὁ, ἡ, = φλογωπός.

φλόϊνος, η, ον, (φλοῦς, φλέως) *of* or *from the water-plant* φλοῦς or φλέως; ἐσθῆτες φλόϊναι garments made of φλοῦς, *mat*-garmen..

φλοιός, ὁ, (φλέω) *the inner-bark of trees, smooth bark, bass.*

φλοῖσβος, ὁ, *any roaring noise, the hum* or *din of a large mass of men, the battle-din: the roaring of the sea.* (Formed from the sound.)

φλόξ, ἡ, gen. φλογός, (φλέγω) *a flame, blaze;* φλόγα ἐγείρειν to raise *a flame:* metaph., φλὸξ οἴνου *the fiery heat*-of wine: pl. φλόγες, *flames, fire.*

φλοῦς, ὁ, Ion. for φλέως.

φλυᾱρέω Ion. φλυηρ-: f. ήσω: (φλύᾱρος):—*to talk folly* or *nonsense, speak idly:* also *to play the fool, trifle*, Lat. *nugari.* Hence

φλυᾱρία, ἡ, *silly talk, nonsense, foolery.*

φλύᾱρος, ὁ, (φλύω) *silly talk, foolery.* II. *a silly talker, prater.*

φλύκταινα, ἡ, (φλύω) *a rising on the skin: a blister: a pustule.*

φλύος, τό, = φλυαρία, *idle talk, foolery.*

φλύω, f. φλύσω [ῡ]: aor. 1 ἔφλυσα: (φλέω):—*to boil over, rise up.* II. metaph. *to overflow with words, talk idly, babble;* γράμματ' ἐπ' ἀσπίδος φλύοντα devices *idly threatening* on his shield.

φνεῖ, Comic word to imitate a nasal sound.

φοβᾱθῇς, Dor. for φοβηθῇς, 2 sing. aor. 1 pass. subj. of φοβέω.

φοβέεσκε, 3 sing. Ion. impf. of **φοβέω.**

φοβεόντων, 3 pl. imperat. of φοβέω.

φοβερός, ά, όν, (φοβέω) *fearful:* either, I. act. *causing fear, frightful, awful, formidable;* πλήθει φοβερός *formidable* only from numbers. 2. *fearful, giving cause for fear;* οὐδὲ ὅρκος φοβερός nor was an oath *a matter of dread;* φοβερόν [ἐστι] μή there is *reason to dread* that ... II. pass. *feeling fear, frightened, affrighted, afraid.* 2. *caused by fear, panic: anxious.*

φοβερῶς, Adv. of φοβερός, *fearfully*, both in act. and pass. sense.

φοβεσι-στράτη, ἡ, (φοβέω, στρατός) *scarer of hosts*, epith. of Minerva.

φοβέ-στρᾰτος, ἡ, (φοβέω, στρατός) *striking fear* or *panic into armies.*

φοβεύμενος, Ep. and Dor. for φοβούμενος, pres. pass. part. of φοβέω.

φοβέω, f. ήσω: aor. 1 ἐφόβησα: (φόβος):—*to strike with fear, to frighten, terrify, dismay: to put to flight.* II. Pass. φοβέομαι: fut. med. φοβήσομαι, and pass. φοβηθήσομαι: aor. 1 med. ἐφοβησάμην, and pass. ἐφοβήθην: pf. pass. πεφόβημαι:—*to be put in fear, take fright, be affrighted, to fear, dread:* in Hom. usually, *to be put to flight, to flee;* ὑπό τινος φοβέεσθαι *to flee* before him: c. acc., φοβεῖσθαί τινα *to flee from, fear, dread* anyone; φοβεῖσθαι εἴς or πρός τι *to be alarmed* at a thing: but, φοβεῖσθαι ἀμφί τινι, περί τινος or τινι, *to fear* or *be anxious* about a thing; c. acc. cognato, φόβον φοβεῖσθαι *to fear:* c. inf. *to fear to* do, *be afraid of* doing.

ΦΟΒΗ, ἡ, *a lock, curl* or *tuft of hair, hair; the mane* of a horse: δρακόντων φόβαι, the Gorgon's snaky *locks.* II. metaph. like κόμη, Lat. *coma, the leaves, foliage* of trees; ἴων φόβαι *tufts* of violets.

φοβηθείς, aor. 1 pass. part. of φοβέω.

φόβηθεν, Ep. and Dor. for ἐφοβήθησαν, 3 pl. aor. 1 pass. of φοβέω.

φόβημα, ατος, το, (φοβέω) *an object of fear, a terror.*

φοβητικός, ή, όν, (φοβέω) *liable to fear, timid.*

φόβητρον, τό, (φοβέω) *an object of terror, a terror.*

φόβος, ὁ, (φέβομαι) *fear, terror, fright, dismay:* in Homer *flight*, properly *the outward show* (as opp. to δέος *the sensation*) *of fear:* c. gen., φόβος ἀνδρῶν *the flight* of men; but also c. gen. objecti, *fear* or *dread* of another:—φόβονδε ἵππους ἔχειν, τρωπᾶσθαι, ἀΐσσειν to turn the horses, turn, start *to flight*, like φύγαδε; φόβονδε ἀγορεύειν to advise *to flight:* also in plur., *causes of fear.* ἣν φόβους λέγῃ. 2. *an object of terror, a terror.* II. Φόβος, personified, son of Mars, coupled with his brother Δεῖμος.

φοιβάζω, f. άσω, (φοῖβος) *to cleanse, purify.* II. (Φοῖβος) *to utter prophetic words.*

φοιβάς, άδος, ἡ, (Φοῖβος) *the priestess of Phoebus:* generally, *one inspired by Phoebus, a prophetess.*

φοιβάω, f. ήσω, (φοῖβος) poët. for φοιβάζω, *to cleanse, wash.*

Φοίβειος, α, ον, also ος, ον, Ion. **Φοιβήιος**, η, ον: (Φοῖβος): *of Phoebus, belonging* or *sacred to Phoebus;* hence *prophetic, inspired.*

Φοίβη, ἡ, *Phoibé*, Lat. *Phoebé*, a frequent name of Diana, as is Phoebus of Apollo.

Φοιβηΐς, ΐδος, poët. fem. of Φοιβεῖος.

Φοιβό-λαμπτος, ον, Ion. for Φοιβόληπτος, (Φοῖβος, λαμβάνω) *rapt* or *inspired by Phoebus.*

φοῖβος, η, ον, (φάος) *pure, bright, radiant, beaming.* II. as prop. n., **Φοῖβος**, ὁ, *Phoebus, the Bright One*, epith. of Apollo: often joined Φοῖβος Ἀπόλλων.

φοινήεις, εσσα, εν, (φοινός) *blood-red, deep-red;* δράκων φοινήεις *a blood-red* dragon.

φοινῑκ-άνθεμος, ον, (φοῖνιξ, ἄνθεμον) *with purple flowers;* φοινικάνθεμον ἔαρ, Lat. *purpureum ver.*

φοινίκεος, α, ον, contr. -οῦς, ῆ, οῦν, (φοῖνιξ) *of a purple dye, purple* or *crimson*, Lat. *puniceus.* [ῐ]

Φοινίκη [νῑ], ἡ, (Φοῖνιξ) *Phoenicia.*

φοινῑκήιος, η, ον, Ion. for φοινίκειος, = φοινικινος, *of the date* or *palm-tree;* ἐσθὴς φοινικηίη a garment *of palm-leaves;* φοινικήιος οἶνος *palm*-wine. II. = Φοινικικός, *Phoenician.*

Φοινῑκικός, ή, όν, (Φοῖνιξ) *Phoenician:* later, *Punic, Carthaginian:*—Adv. -κῶς, *in Phoenician fashion.* II. φοινίκεος, *red.*

φοινίκῐνος, η, ον, (φοῖνιξ) = φοινικήιος, *of, from the palm-tree;* φοινίκινον μύρον *palm*-unguent. [νῑ]

φοινῑκιοῦς, ῆ, οῦν, = φοινίκεος, *purple, crimson.*

φοινῑκίς, ίδος, ἡ, (φοῖνιξ) *a red* or *purple cloth, a red cloak*, Lat. *punicea vestis:* esp. *a dark-red military cloak* worn by the Lacedaemonians. 2. *a red curtain.* 3. at sea, *a red flag* hung out by the admiral as the signal for action: generally, *a red standard* or *banner.*

φοινῑκιστής, οῦ, ὁ, (φοῖνιξ) among the Persians, *a wearer of purple*, i. e. *one of the highest rank*, Lat. *purpuratus.*

φοινῑκό-βαπτος, ον, (φοῖνιξ, βαπτω) *purple-dyed, crimson.*

φοινῑκο-βᾰτέω, f. ήσω, (φοῖνιξ, βαίνω) *to climb palms.*

φοινῑκο-γενής, ές, (Φοῖνιξ, *γένω) *Phoenician-born.*

φοινῑκο-δάκτυλος, ον, (φοῖνιξ, δάκτυλον) *crimson-fingered.*

φοινῑκόεις, εσσα, εν, poët. for φοινίκεος, *dark-red, purple* or *crimson:* *of a blood-red.*

φοινῑκό-κροκος, ον, (φοῖνιξ, κροκός) *of purple woof.*

φοινῑκο-λόφος, ον, (φοῖνιξ, λόφος) *purple-crested.*

φοινῑκο-πάρειος Ion. -**πάρῃος**, ον, (φοῖνιξ, παρειά) *purple-cheeked, red-cheeked*, of ships having red bows.

φοινῑκό-πεδος, ον, (φοῖνιξ, πέδον) *with a red bottom* or *ground*, of the Red Sea.

φοινῑκό-πεζα, ἡ, (φοῖνιξ, πέζα) *the ruddy-footed goddess*, Virgil's *rubicunda Ceres.*

φοινῑκό-πτερος, ον, (φοῖνιξ, πτερόν) *with purple* or *crimson wings:* as Subst., φοινικόπτερος, ὁ, a red water-bird, *the flamingo.*

φοινῑκό-ροδος, ον, (φοῖνιξ, ῥόδον) *red with roses.*

φοινῑκο-σκελής, ές, (φοῖνιξ, σκέλος) *red-legged, red-shanked.*

φοινῑκο-στερόπης, ου, Dor. -**ας**, α, ὁ, (φοῖνιξ, στεροπή) *hurling red lightnings.*

Φοινῑκό-στολος, ον, (Φοῖνιξ, στέλλω) *sent by Phoenicians.*

φοινῑκοῦς, ῆ, οῦν, contr. for φοινίκεος.

φοινῑκο-φᾰής, ές, (φοῖνιξ, φαός) *red-shining.*

Φοῖνιξ, ῖκος, ὁ, *a Phoenician*, first mentioned in Homer; Φοῖνιξ ἀνὴρ ἀπατήλια εἰδώς *a Phoenician* skilled in trickery, so mentioned as being the first commercial nation: fem. Φοίνισσα, ἡ, *a Phoenician woman.* 2. *a Carthaginian*, Lat. *Poenus.*

φοῖνιξ, ῖκος, ὁ, Subst. *a purple-red, deep purple* or *crimson*, because the discovery of this colour was ascribed to the Phoenicians. II. *the palm, date-palm:* the male palm is called by Herodotus ὁ φοῖνιξ ἔρσην, to distinguish it from ἡ φοῖνιξ βαλανηφόρος the female or fruit-bearing palm. 2. *the fruit of the palm, date.* 3. *a musical instrument*, like a guitar, invented by the Phoenicians. III. the fabulous Egyptian bird *phoenix*, described by Herodotus 2. 73.

φοῖνιξ, ῑκος, ὁ, ἡ, also fem. φοίνισσα, Adj. *purple-red*, *purple* or *crimson*, *red*; hence of a *bay* horse, of *red* cattle: also like Lat. *fulvus*, of the colour of fire. The words φοῖνιξ, φοινίκεος, etc., included all *dark reds*, from crimson to purple, while the *brighter shades* were denoted by πορφύρα, πορφύρεος, etc., *scarlet* being κόκκινος, κοκκοβαφής.

φοίνιος, α, ον, also ος, ον, (φοινός) *blood-red*: hence *blood-stained*, *bloody*, Lat. *cruentus*: also *warlike*.

Φοίνισσα, fem. of Φοῖνιξ (Subst.), *a Phoenician woman*. II. φοίνισσα, fem. of φοῖνιξ (Adj.)

φοινίσσω, f. ξω: aor. 1 pass. ἐφοινίχθην: (φοινός):—*to redden*, *to make red*: *to tinge*, *dye red*:—Pass. *to become red*, *to colour*, *blush*.

φοινός, ή, όν, (φόνος) *blood-red*: *blood-stained*, *bloody*.

φοιτᾰλέος, α, ον, also ος, ον, (φοιτάω) *straying*, *ranging*, *roaming about*: metaph. *distraught*, *raving*, *frenzied*. II. act. *driving madly about*, *maddening*.

φοιτᾰλιώτης, ου, ὁ, (φοιτάω) epith. of Bacchus, *a roamer*, *ranger*.

φοιτάς, άδος, ἡ, (φοιτάω) poët. fem. of φοιταλέος, *a strolling woman*: metaph. *a frenzied woman*, esp. of the Bacchantés. II. as Adj. *mad* or *maddening*; φοιτὰς νόσος *madness*, *frenzy*. 2. also with a neut. Subst., φοιτάσι πτεροῖς on *roaming*, *wandering* wings.

φοιτάω Ion. έω: f. ήσω: (φοῖτος):—*to go to and fro*, *go up and down*, *to roam* or *range about*, of irregular or hasty motion; διὰ νηὸς φοιτᾶν *to range up and down* the ship; ἐφοίτων ἄλλοθεν ἄλλος *they roamed* one one way, one another. 2. *to roam wildly about*: hence *to go mad*, *rave*; cf. φοιταλέος, φοιτάς. 3. of pain, *to come in fits*, *to come on at regular times*. II. *of constant*, *regular motion*, esp. of objects of commerce, *to come in constantly*, *be imported regularly*; κέρεα τὰ ἐς Ἕλληνας φοιτέοντα horns *which are imported* into Greece; σῖτός σφισι πολλὸς ἐφοίτα corn *was imported* for them in abundance: also of tribute or taxes, *to come in*, like Lat. *redire*; τάλαντον ἀργυρίου Ἀλεξάνδρῳ ἡμέρης ἑκάστης ἐφοίτα a talent of silver *came in* to Alexander every day. 2. φοιτᾶν παρά τινα *to go to visit* a person; φοιτᾶν ἐπὶ τὰς θύρας τινός *to be a regular visitor* at a great man's door; so of a dream, *to recur again and again*. 3. *to go constantly* or *resort* to a person, esp. of attending lectures or lessons; φοιτᾶν εἰς διδασκάλου [οἶκον] *to go* to school; absol. *to go to school*: whence συμφοιτάω, *to go to school* with another. Hence

φοίτησις, εως, ἡ, *a constant going* or *coming*, *a visiting*. 2. *a going to school*.

φοιτήτην, Ep. for ἐφοιτάτην, 3 dual impf. of φοιτάω.

φοιτητήρ, ῆρος, ὁ, and **φοιτητής**, οῦ, ὁ, (φοιτάω) *one who goes* or *comes regularly*: *one who goes to school*, *a disciple*, *pupil*.

φοιτίζω, poët. for φοιτάω.

ΦΟΙΤΟΣ, ὁ, *a going to and fro*. II. *madness*, *frenzy*.

φολκός, ὁ, found only in the description of Thersites, either (from φάεα ἕλκειν) *squint-eyed*; or more probably (akin to ἕλκω, ὁλκός) *bandy-legged*, Lat. *valgus*.

φόλλις, εως, ἡ, also ὁ, *a single piece of money*, formed from Lat. *follis*.

φονάω, f. ήσω, (φόνος) *to be athirst for blood*, *have murderous desires*.

φόνευμα, ατος, τό, (φονεύω) *that which is to be slaughtered*, *a victim*.

φονεύς, έως Ion. ῆος, ὁ; acc. φονέᾱ or φονέᾰ: nom. pl. φονέες, φονεῖς, acc. φονέας: (φονεύω):—*a murderer*, *slayer*, *homicide*.

φονεύω, (φόνος) *to murder*, *kill*, *slay*.

φονή, ἡ, (*φένω) *murder*, *homicide*, *slaughter*; ἐν φοναῖς, *in the midst of slaughter*; σπᾶν φοναῖς to rend *in murder*, i. e. *murderously*.

φονικός, ή, όν, (φόνος) *inclined to slay*, *murderous*, *bloody*. II. *of*, *relating to blood* or *murder*; φονικαὶ δίκαι trials *for homicide*.

φόνιος, α, ον, also ος, ον, (φόνος) *of blood*, *bloody*. II. *bloody*, *blood-stained*: *murderous*.

φονο-λῐβής, ές, (φόνος, λείβω) *blood-dripping*.

φονόρ-ρῡτος, ον, (φόνος, ῥέω) *blood-streaming*.

φόνος, ὁ, (*φένω) *murder*, *homicide*, *slaughter*, Lat. *caedes*; φόνος Ἑλληνικός *a slaughter* of Greeks: in plur. *murders*. 2. *blood shed in murder*, *gore*, *blood*, Lat. *cruor*. 3. *a murdered body*, *corpse*.

φοξί-χειλος, ὁ, (φοξός χεῖλος) *narrowing towards the lips*; of a cup, *narrower at the brim*.

φοξός, ή, όν, (ὀξύς) *pointed*, *tapering to a point*: in the description of Thersites, φοξὸς ἔην κεφαλήν he was *pointed* or *peaked* in the head.

φορά, ἡ, (φέρω) *a carrying*, *bringing*; ψήφου φορά *the giving* one's vote. 2. *a bringing in*, *paying* of money, *payment*. 3. *a bearing*, *producing*. II. (from Pass. φέρομαι) *a being borne* or *carried*, *motion*: *the course*, *career*, *orbit* in which a body moves; ἡ φορὰ ἀκοντίου *the* javelin's *range*. 2. *rapid motion*, *a rush*, *onset*, Lat. *impetus*. III. (also) from Pass. *that which is borne* or *carried*, *a load*, *freight*, *burden*. 2. *that which is paid as rent* or *tribute*, Lat. *vectigal*. 3. *that which is brought forth*, *fruit*, *produce*, *a crop*, Lat. *proventus*: metaph. *a large crop*, *harvest*.

φοράδην [ᾰ], Adv. (φέρομαι) *with a rushing* or *violent motion*. II. *borne* or *carried in a litter*.

φορβάς, άδος, ὁ, ἡ, (φέρβω) *giving pasture* or *food*, *feeding*. II. *grazing in the pasture*.

φορβεία, ἡ, (φέρβω) *the halter by which a horse is tied to the manger*, Lat. *capistrum*. 2. *a mouth-band* of leather put round the lips and cheeks of fifers to assist them in blowing.

φορβή, ἡ, (φέρβω) *pasture*, *food*, *fodder*, *forage*: of men, *food*, *meat*, *victuals*: metaph. *fuel*.

φορέεσκε, 3 sing. Ion. impf. of φορέω.

φορέησι, Ep. 3 sing. subj. of φορέω.

φορεῖον, τό, (φορά, φέρω) *a handbarrow, litter, sedan-chair*, Lat. *sella, lectica*.

φορέοισα, Dor. part. fem. of φορέω.

φορεῦντος, Dor. part. gen. of φορέω.

φορεύς, έως Ion. ῆος, ὁ, (φέρω) *a bearer, carrier.*

φορέω, f. ήσω: aor. 1 ἐφόρησα Ep. φόρησα :—Frequentat. of φέρω, *to bear* or *carry constantly*: hence *to wear*: and so, *to have, possess*: as differing from φέρειν, ἀγγελίην φέρειν meant *to convey* a message; but, ἀγγελίας φορέειν *to be in the habit of conveying* messages, serve as a messenger :—Pass. *to be borne violently along, be hurried along*: *to be tossed about at sea* :—Med. *to fetch for oneself, fetch regularly.*

φορηδόν, Adv. (φορέω) *like a bundle.*

φόρημα, ατος, τό, (φορέω) *that which is carried*: *a load, freight*: *a burden.*

φορήμεναι, Ep. for φορεῖν, inf. of φορέω.

φορῆναι, Ep. for φορεῖν, inf. of φορέω.

φορητός, ή, όν, also ός, όν, verb. Adj. of φορέω, *borne, carried*: *to be borne* or *endured, bearable.*

φόρῐμος, ον, (φέρω) *bearing, fruitful.*

Φορκίδες [ῐ], ίδων, αἱ, *the daughters of Phorcys*, i. e. the three Gorgons, Stheino, Euryalé, Medusa.

Φόρκος, ὁ, = Φόρκυς.

Φόρκῡς, ῡνος and ῠος, ὁ, *Phorcys*, an old sea-god, son of Pontos and Gaia, father of the Gorgons.

φορμηδόν, Adv. (φορμός) *like mat-work* or *watling*: *crosswise, athwart.*

φόρμιγξ, ιγγος, ἡ, *the phorminx*, a kind of lyre, the oldest stringed instrument of the Greek minstrels, esp. the instrument of Apollo: it was richly inwrought, and had seven strings. (From φέρω, because it was carried on the shoulder by a strap.) Hence

φορμίζω, f. ίσω Dor. ίξω, *to play the* φόρμιγξ or *lyre.* Hence

φορμικτής, οῦ, ὁ, Dor. -τάς, *a lyre-player, harper.*

φορμίς, ίδος, ἡ, Dim. of φορμός, *a small basket.*

φορμο-ρᾰφέω or **φορμορ-ραφέω**, f. ήσω, (φορμος, ῥάπτω) *to stitch mats* :—Pass. *to be stitched up like a mat, straitened, hampered.*

φορμός, ὁ, (φόρω) *anything made of wicker-work* 1. *a wicker basket to carry* corn, sand, etc. 2. *a mat*, Lat. *storea*: also *a seaman's cloak made of coarse plaited stuff.* II. *a measure of corn.*

φόρον, ου, τό, the Lat. *forum*; Φόρον Ἀππίου *Appii Forum*, a small town on the Appian Way.

φόρος, ὁ, (φέρω) *that which is brought in, tribute*, paid by foreigners to a ruling state, as that paid to Athens by her subject states; φόρον ὑποτελεῖν to pay *tribute*; φόρον τάξασθαι to agree to pay *tribute*; φόρον τάξαι to impose *tribute*; φόρου ὑποτελής subject to pay *tribute.*

φορτᾰγωγέω, f. ήσω, *to carry loads* or *burdens*: of a merchant-ship, *to carry a freight* or *cargo.* From

φορτ-ᾰγωγός, όν, (φόρτος, ἄγω) *carrying freights*; ναῦς φορταγωγός a ship *of burden*, merchantman.

φορτηγέω, f. ήσω, (φορτηγός) = φορταγωγέω.

φορτηγικός, ή, όν, *belonging to the freight of a ship*; πλοῖον φορτηγικόν a ship *of burden*, merchantman. From

φορτ-ηγός, όν, (φόρτος, ἄγω) like φορταγωγός, *carrying burdens*: of a ship, *freighted* :—as Subst. φορτηγός, ὁ, *a carrier, porter*: *a trafficker, merchant.*

φορτίζω, f. ίσω, (φόρτος) *to load*; φορτία φορτίζειν τινάς *to load* men *with* loads:—Med., τὰ μείω φορτίζεσθαι *to ship* the smaller part *of one's wealth* :—Pass., pf. part. πεφορτισμένος *heavy laden.*

φορτῐκός, ή, όν, (φόρτος) of persons, *burdensome, tiresome, common, vulgar* :—so of things, φορτικὴ κωμῳδία *a vulgar, commonplace* comedy. Hence

φορτικῶς, Adv., *vulgarly.*

φορτίον, τό, (φόρτος) *a burden, load*. *a ship's freight* or *lading*: in plur. *wares, merchandise.* II. *the burden of the womb, a child unborn.*

φορτίς, ίδος, ἡ, (φόρτος) *a ship of burden, merchantman.*

φόρτος, ὁ, (φέρω) *a ship's freight* or *cargo.* II. in Att. *something coarse* or *vulgar, tiresome stuff.*

φορύνω, = φύρω, of dough, *to knead*: generally, *to mix up, spoil, defile.* [ῡ]

φορύσσω, f. ξω, = φορύνω, *to stain, defile.*

φορῠτός, ὁ, (φέρω) *whatever is swept along by the wind, rubbish, refuse*, Lat. *quisquiliae*: also *chaff, sawdust*, etc., used for packing earthenware

φόως, τό, Ep. lengthd. from φῶς, *light.* Hence

φόωσδε, Adv. *to the light, to the light of day.*

φραγέλλιον, τό, the Lat. *flagellum, a scourge.* Hence

φραγελλόω, f. ώσω, the Lat. *flagello, to scourge.*

φρᾰγῆναι, aor. 2 pass. inf. of φράσσω.

φρᾰγήσομαι, fut. pass. of φράσσω.

φράγμα, ατος, τό, (φράσσω) *a fence, protection, palisade, defence.*

φραγμός, ὁ, (φράσσω) *a shutting up, blocking up*: *fencing, partition.* II. like φράγμα, *a hedge, fence, paling.*

φράγνῡμι, = φράσσω.

φρᾰδάζω: f. άσω: aor. 1 ἐφράδασα poët. φράδασσα: (φραδή) :—*to tell of, make known.*

φρᾰδή, ἡ, (φράζω) *understanding, knowledge.* II. *advice, a hint, warning, intimation.* Hence

φρᾰδής, ές, gen. έος, *understanding, shrewd, cunning.*

φραδμοσύνη, ἡ, *understanding, shrewdness, cunning.* From

φράδμων, ον, gen. ονος, (φράζω) = φραδής. From

ΦΡΑ'ΖΩ, f. φράσω: aor. 1 ἔφρᾰσα Ep. φράσα and φράσσα: pf. πέφρᾰκα: Ep. aor. 2 πέφρᾰδον or ἐπέφρᾰδον, inf. πεφραδέειν or πεφραδέμεν :—*to tell, declare, pronounce*, stronger than λέγω :—c. dat. pers. et inf., *to counsel, advise, bid, order*: also absol. *to advise, counsel* :—c. acc. rei, σήματα πέφραδε *he gave indications* by signs :—φράζειν χειρί *to make signs, signal* with the hand. Med. and Pass. φράζομαι:

3 sing. Ion. impf. *φραζέσκετο*: fut. *φράσομαι*: aor. 1 med. *ἐφρᾰσάμην*, pass. *ἐφράσθην*: pf. pass. *πέφραδμαι* and *πέφρασμαι*: *to speak with oneself, to think* or *muse upon, consider, ponder;* foll. by *εἰ* with indicat. fut., *to consider* whether; *ἀμφὶς φράζεσθαι to think* differently. 2. *to devise* or *plan for* a person, *purpose, design* or *intend* something *for* him. 3. c. acc. et inf. *to think, suppose, believe, imagine* that. 4. *to remark, perceive, notice: to come to know, see, understand:* also 5. *to mind, heed, take care* or *heed of*, c. acc.

φράν, ἡ, gen. *φρᾰνός*, Dor. for *φρήν*.

φράξαντο, Ep. 3 pl. aor. 1 med. of *φράσσω*.

φράξας, *ασα, αν*, aor. 1 part. of *φράσσω*.

φράσδω, Dor. for *φράζω*.

φράσσαντο, Ep. 3 pl. aor. 1 med. of *φράζω*.

φρασθείς, *εῖσα, έν*, aor. 1 pass. part. of *φράζω*.

ΦΡΑ'ΣΣΩ Att. -ττω: f. *ξω*: aor. 1 *ἔφραξα*: Pass., fut. *φρᾰγήσομαι*: aor. 1 *ἐφράχθην*: aor. 2 *ἐφράγην* [ᾰ]: pf. *πέφραγμαι*:—in Att. the letters are sometimes transposed, as *φάρξασθαι* for *φράξασθαι*, *πέφαργμαι* for *πέφραγμαι*, *φαρκτός* for *φρακτός*:—*to fence in, hedge round*, for defence; *to fence, defend, fortify; φράξαι δέμας ὅπλοις to fence in* one's body with arms, *to arm* oneself:—so in Med., *ἐφράξαντο τὸ τεῖχος they strengthened* the wall: in Med. also, *to fence oneself, strengthen one's fortifications.*—Pass. *to be fenced in, fortified; φραχθέντες σάκεσιν fenced* with shields: absol. *πεφραγμένος, fenced, secured.* II. *to put up as a fence; φράξαντες δόρυ δουρί, σάκος σάκεϊ locking* spear *fast* to spear, shield to shield (so as to make a fence); *φράξαντες τὰ γέρρα having put up* the shields *as a fence.* III. *to block up: make close, fill quite full.*

φραστήρ, *ῆρος, ὁ*, (*φράζω*) *a teller, informer, of* or *about* a thing; *φραστὴρ ὁδῶν a man who tells one* the way, *a guide:*—*φραστῆρες ὀδόντες* the teeth *that tell* the age.

φράστωρ, *opos, ὁ*, (*φράζω*) = *φραστήρ*.

φράτηρ, *ερος*, or **φράτωρ**, *opos, ὁ*, (*φράτρα*) *a member of a φράτρα:* pl. *φράτερες* or *φράτορες those of the same φράτρα* or *ward*, Lat. *curiales; εἰσάγειν τὸν υἱὸν εἰς τοὺς φράτερας* to introduce one's son to his *clansmen*, which was done when the boy came of age; *οὐκ ἔφυσε φράτερας* he has not yet got his *φράτερες*, i. e. he has been entered in no *φρατρία*, is no true citizen, with allusion to *φραστῆρες ὀδόντες* (see *φραστήρ*). [ᾱ]

φρᾱτορικός, *ή, όν*, (*φράτωρ*) *of, belonging to a clan* or *clansmen.*

φράτρα or **φράτρη** Ion. **φρήτρη** Dor. **πάτρα**, ἡ:—*a tribe of kindred race, a sept* or *clan; κρῖν' ἄνδρας κατὰ φρήτρας, ὡς φρήτρη φρήτρηφιν ἀρήγῃ* choose men by *clans*, that *clan* may stand by *clan:* originally derived from ties of blood: but, II. at Athens, *the subdivision of the φυλή*, as at Rome the *curia* was the subdivision of the *tribus;* every *φυλή* consisted of three *φράτραι* or *φρατρίαι*, whose members were called *φράτερες* or *φράτορες*, as those of a *φυλή* were called *φυλέται*, and at Rome the members of a *tribus, tribules*, those of a *curia, curiales.* (The word is derived from the same Root as Lat. *frater*, and properly meant *a brotherhood.*)

φρᾱτρία, ἡ, = *φράτρα*.

φρᾱτριάζω, f. *άσω*, *to be in the same φρατρια.*

φρᾱτρι-άρχης, *ου, ὁ* and **φρᾱτρί-αρχος**, *ὁ*, (*φρατρία, ἄρχω*) *president of a φρατρία*, Lat. *magister curiae.*

φράτριος, *α, ον*, (*φράτρα*) *of* or *concerning a φράτρα:* at Athens, epith. of Jupiter and Minerva, as *tutelary deities of the phratriae.* [ᾱ]

φράττω, Att. for *φράσσω*.

φράτωρ, *opos, ὁ*, see *φράτηρ*.

ΦΡΕ'Α˘Ρ, *τό*, gen. *φρέᾰτος*: Ion. **φρεῖαρ**, gen. *φρείᾰτος*:—*a well; or more commonly a water-tank, cistern, reservoir*, Lat. *puteus: an oil-jar.* Hence

φρεᾰτία, ἡ, *a tank* or *reservoir.*

φρεᾰτίας, *ου, ὁ*, (*φρέαρ*) *of a tank* or *reservoir.*

φρεῖαρ, *ᾰτος, τό*, Ion. and poët. for *φρέαρ*.

φρεν-ᾰπᾰτάω, f. *ήσω*, (*φρήν, ἀπατάω*) *to deceive the mind, deceive.* Hence

φρενᾰπάτης, *ου, ὁ*, *one who deceives the mind, a seducer.*

φρεν-ήρης, *ες*, gen. *εος*, (*φρήν, ἀρᾰρεῖν*) *master of his mind, sound of mind*, Lat. *compos mentis.*

φρενοβλάβεια, ἡ, *damage of the understanding.* From

φρενο-βλᾰβής, *ές*, (*φρήν, βλαβῆναι*) *damaged in understanding, crazy.*

φρενο-γηθής, *ές*, (*φρήν, γῆθος*) *of glad heart, delighting the heart.*

φρενο-δᾰλής, *ές*, (*φρήν, δηλέομαι*) *impairing the mind, maddening.*

φρενόθεν, Adv. (*φρήν*) = *ἐκ φρενός, from the heart, heartily, of one's own will* or *accord.*

φρενο-κλόπος, *ον*, (*φρήν, κλέπτω*) *stealing away the brains, deceiving.*

φρενο-ληστής, *οῦ, ὁ*, (*φρήν, ληστής*) *a robber of the understanding, a deceiver.*

φρενο-μᾰνής, *ές*, (*φρήν, μανῆναι*) *frenzied in mind.*

φρενο-μόρως, Adv. (*φρήν, μόρος*) only found in phrase *φρενομόρως νοσεῖν* to be diseased *in mind.*

φρενο-πληγής, *ές*, (*φρήν, πληγῆναι*) *giving a stroke to the mind, maddening.*

φρενό-πληκτος, *ον*, (*φρήν, πλήσσω*) *stricken in mind, smitten with madness, frenzied.*

φρενο-πλήξ, *ῆγος, ὁ, ἡ*, = *φρενόπληκτος*.

φρενο-τέκτων, *ον*, gen. *ονος*, (*φρήν, τέκτων*) *making with the mind, ingenious.*

φρενόω, f. *ώσω*, (*φρήν*) *to make wise, make understanding, instruct, inform, teach; φρενοῦν οὐκέτ' ἐξ αἰνιγμάτων to teach* no longer by riddles; *κλαίων φρενώσεις thou shalt teach me* to thy sorrow.

φρεν-ώλης, *ες*, (*φρήν, ὄλλυμι*) *destroyed in mind, frenzied.*

ΦΡΕ'Ω, f. *φρήσω*, a root, which is found only in the compds. *ἐκ-φρέω, εἰσ-φρέω, δια-φρέω.*

φρε-ωρυχέω, f. ήσω, (φρέαρ, ὀρύσσω) *to dig tanks*: metaph. of a gnat, *to make a hole in one's skin*.

ΦΡΗΝ, ἡ, gen. φρενός, plur. φρένες, gen. φρενῶν, etc.: Dor. **φράν**, gen. φρανός, dat. plur. φρασί, φρασίν:—in plur. *the midriff* or *the muscle which parts* the heart and lungs from the lower viscera; also called διάφραγμα. 2. in Homer both in sing. and plur., *the heart and parts near the heart, the breast*, Lat. *praecordia*; the seat of the passions and affections: hence *the heart, mind, understanding, reason*: often joined with θυμός, as, κατὰ φρένα καὶ κατὰ θυμόν, as in Lat. *mens animusque*; φρενῶν ἐκστῆναι to be out of *one's wits*; φρενῶν ἐπήβολος possessed *of sense*, in one's right mind; ἐκ φρενός from one's *very heart*; ἐξ ἄκρας φρενός from the surface of *one's mind*, i. e. *superficially, carelessly*. 3. of beasts, *sense, instinct*. 4. φρένες is also used in Homer in the sense of *the seat of life* or *life* itself, as opp. to ψυχή (the *departed* soul).

φρήτρη, ἡ, Ion. for φράτρα, *a clan*.

φρήτρηφιν, Ep. dat. of φρήτρη.

φρήτριος, η, ον, Ion. for φράτριος.

φρίκη [ῑ], ἡ, = φρίξ, *the ruffling* or *ripple* on a smooth sea. II. *a shuddering, shivering, chill*. 2. *shivering fear, shuddering*, esp. from religious awe, Lat. *horror*: then *any fear*.

φρῑκ-ώδης, ες, (φρίξ, εἶδος) *that causes shuddering* or *horror, awful, horrible*: neut. φρικῶδες as Adv., *horribly*.

ΦΡΙ͞ΜΑ'ΣΣΟΜΑΙ Att. **-ττομαι**: f. -ξομαι: Dep.:—*to snort, neigh*, of horses, *to shew their mettle*: *to move briskly* or *wantonly*.

φρίξ, ἡ, gen. φρῑκός, (φρίσσω) *the ruffling* of a smooth surface, *the ruffling* or *ripple* caused by a gust of wind sweeping over the smooth sea, Lat. *horror*; μέλαινα φρίξ the *dark ripple*. II. *a bristling up*, of the hair: a *shivering fit*.

φρῖξαι, aor. 1 inf. of φρίσσω.

φριξο-κόμης, ου, ὁ, (φρίσσω, κόμη) *with bristling hair*.

φρῖξος, ὁ, *a shivering, shuddering*. From

ΦΡΙ'ΣΣΩ Att. **-ττω**: f. φρίξω: aor. 1 ἔφριξα: pf. πέφρῑκα: poet. part. πεφρίκοντες formed as if from a redupl. pres. πεφρίκω:—*to be rough* or *ruffled, to bristle*, Lat. *horrere*, as of corn fields, or spears; of hair or mane, *to bristle up, stand on end*: c. acc., φρίσσειν λοφιήν *to bristle with* the mane; πτεροῖσι νῶτα πεφρίκοντες *bristling on* their backs with feathers: of smooth water, *to be ruffled, to ripple*, Lat. *horrescere*. II. often of a feeling *of chill*, which causes what we call *goose-skin* and makes the hair bristle; *to have a chill* or *shiver come* over one, *to shiver with cold*. 2. *to shudder* with fear: also c. acc. *to shudder before* anyone, *to dread* him. 3. also *to thrill* or *quiver* with delight; ἔφριξ' ἔρωτι *I thrilled* with love.

φροιμιάζομαι, f. -άσομαι, Dep. (φροίμιον) contr. for προοιμιάζομαι, *to make a prelude* or *beginning, to begin*: c. acc., φροιμιάζεσθαι θεοὺς *to begin with invoking* the god.

φροίμιον, τό, contr. for προοίμιον (cp. φροῦδος) *a prelude*.

φρονέῃσι, Ep. for φρονέῃ, 3 sing. subj. of φρονέω.

φρονέω, Ep. impf. φρόνεον: f. ήσω: (φρήν):—*to think, to have understanding*; ἄριστοι μάχεσθαί τε φρονέειν τε best both in battle and *counsel*; οἱ φρονοῦντες *the wise*; τὸ φρονεῖν, like φρόνησις, *understanding*. 2. *to be in one's sound senses*; ἔξω ἐλαύνειν τινὰ τοῦ φρονεῖν to drive one out of his *understanding* or *senses*; ἐξίστασθαι τοῦ φρονεῖν to lose *one's wits*. 3. c. acc. rei, *to have in mind, purpose*. II. *to be minded* or *disposed* in a certain way, *to mean, intend, purpose*; φρονῶν ἔπρασσον I did it *designedly*, Lat. *prudens faciebam*; c. inf. *to mean* to do a thing; ἰθὺς φρονεῖν *to purpose to go* straight, *make* straight *for* a place; τοῦτο φρονεῖ ἡ ἀγωγὴ ἡμῶν this *is what* your bringing us *means*. 2. often with a neut. Adj., ἀγαθὰ or φίλα φρονεῖν τινι *to be* well or kindly *minded towards* him; κακὰ φρονεῖν τινι *to be* evil *minded* towards him; τὰ ἀμείνω φρονέειν *to be of* the better *mind, hold* the better *opinion*: and without a dat. pers., *to be minded* or *inclined* in a certain way; πυκνὰ φρονεῖν *to have* wise *thoughts*; μέγα φρονεῖν, *to have high thoughts*, either in good sense *to be high-minded*, or in bad sense *to be presumptuous and conceited*, of animals, *to be high-spirited*; σμικρὸν φρονεῖν to be low-*minded*, poor-*spirited*; οὐ κατ' ἄνθρωπον φρονεῖν *to think* beyond what becomes a man:—also, τά τινος φρονεῖν *to hold* a person's *opinions, be on* his *side* or *of* his *party*; τὸ αὐτὸ φρονεῖν *to be like-minded*; ἄλλῃ φρονεῖν *to think* in another way. III. *to think of, mind, heed*, hence *to take heed of, guard against* a thing. IV. *to have one's senses*: *to be alive, have life*. Hence

φρόνημα, ατος, τό, *the mind, will, spirit*, Lat. *animus*: in plur. *thoughts, purposes*. II. *high feeling, high spirit*: and in bad sense, *pride, presumption, arrogance, insolence*. Hence

φρονημᾰτίας, ου, ὁ, *one who is high-spirited*, or in bad sense, *one who is proud, presumptuous*.

φρόνησις, εως, ἡ, (φρονέω) *a being minded* to do so and so, *purpose, intention*. 2. *high-mindedness*: and in bad sense, *pride, presumption*. II. *thoughtfulness, good sense, practical wisdom, prudence*.

φρονητέον, verb. Adj. of φρονέω, *one must pride oneself*.

φρόνῐμος, ον, (φρονέω) *understanding, in one's right mind* or *senses*. II. *discreet, sensible, steady*. III. *thoughtful, practically wise, prudent*, Lat. *prudens*; τὸ φρόνιμον *practical wisdom, good sense*; ἄπορος ἐπὶ φρόνιμα without resource in *matters of thought*.

φρονίμως, Adv. *sensibly, discreetly, prudently, skilfully*.

φρόνις, εως, ἡ, (φρονέω) *wise thoughts, wisdom*.

φρονούντως, Adv. pres. act. part. of φρονέω, *wisely, prudently*.

φροντίζω: f. ίσω Att. ιῶ: aor. 1 ἐφρόντισα: (φροντίς):—*to think, consider, reflect, to take thought, give heed;* φροντίζειν ὅπως τι γενήσεται *to take thought* how a thing may be done. II. c. acc. rei, *to think of, consider: to devise, contrive, invent.* III. c. gen. *to take thought for, give heed to* a thing, *care about, reck of, regard* it; μηδὲν φροντίζειν τῶν θεῶν *to take* no *thought* of the gods; φροντίζειν περί τινος *to be concerned* or *anxious* about a thing; μὴ φροντίσῃς *heed* not. IV. absol. *to be thoughtful* or *anxious;* πεφροντικὸς βλέπειν to have a *careworn* look.

φροντίς, ίδος, ἡ, (φρονέω) *thought, care, heed* to a thing, c. gen. II. absol. *thought, reflection, meditation:* in plur. *thoughts.* 2. *deep thought, anxiety, concern.* 3. *power of thought, mind.*

φρόντισμα, ατος, τό, (φροντίζω) *that which is thought out, a contrivance, invention.*

φροντιστέον, verb. Adj. of φροντίζω, *one must take care.*

φροντιστήριον, τό, (φροντίζω) *a place for hard thinking, a thinking-shop,* as the school of Socrates is called by Aristophanes.

φροντιστής, οῦ, ὁ, (φροντίζω) *a deep, hard thinker;* φροντιστὴς τῶν μετεώρων or φροντιστὴς τὰ μετέωρα, *a thinker on* supra-terrestrial things. Hence

φροντιστικός, ή, όν, *of* or *for thinking, thoughtful, speculative.* Adv. -κῶς, *thoughtfully, carefully.*

φροῦδος, η, ον, also ος, ον: (contr. from πρὸ ὁδοῦ, as φροίμιον from προοίμιον):—*gone away:* 1. of persons, *gone, departed;* c. part., φροῦδοί [εἰσι] διώκοντές σε they are *gone* in pursuit of thee; of the dead, φροῦδος εἶ θανών thou art *departed* by death, art dead *and gone:* metaph. *undone, ruined.* 2. of things, *gone, vanished.*

φρουρά Ion. **φρουρή**, ἡ, (φροῦρος) *a looking out, watch and ward, guard;* φρουρὰν ὀχεῖν to keep *watch;* φρουρᾶς ᾄδειν (sub. ἑνεκά) to sing *on guard.* 2. *a watch of the night.* 3. *ward, prison, imprisonment.* II. of men, *a watch* or *guard, a garrison.* 2. at Sparta, *a body of men destined for service, a levy, conscription;* for φρουρὰν φαίνειν, see φαίνω.

φρουραρχία, ἡ, *the post of commandant.* From

φρούρ-αρχος, ὁ, (φρουρά, ἄρχω) *a commander of a watch, an officer* or *guard: the commandant of a garrison* or *fortress.*

φρουρέω, f. ήσω: aor. 1 ἐφρούρησα: Pass., f. med. -ήσομαι in pass. sense: aor. 1 ἐφρουρήθην: (φρουρός) —*to keep watch* or *guard;* οἱ φροροῦντες *those on guard, the watch* or *guard.* II. trans. *to watch, guard, keep: to garrison* a place. 2. *to watch for, observe.* 3. Med., like φυλάσσομαι, *to be on one's guard against, beware of,* c. acc. Hence

φρούρημα, ατος, τό, *that which is watched* or *guarded;* λείας βουκόλων φρουρήματα the herdsmen's *charge* of cattle. II. *a guard, garrison:* also of a single man. III. *watch, ward, guard;* φρούρημα ἔχειν to keep *watch.*

φρουρητός, ή, όν, verb. Adj. of φρουρέω, *watched, guarded.*

φρουρήτωρ, ορος, ὁ, (φρουρέω) *a watcher, guard.*

φρουρικός, ή, όν, (φρουρά) *of, belonging to a watch, guard,* or *garrison.*

φρούριον, τό, (φρουρός) *a watch-post, garrisoned fort, citadel: a castle, tower, isolated fort.* II. *the guard* or *garrison* of a place.

φρουρίς, ίδος, ἡ, (φρουρός) *a guard-ship.*

φρουρο-δόμος, ον, (φρουρός, δόμος) *watching* or *guarding the house.*

φρουρός, ὁ, (contr. for προορός from προοράω, as φροῦδος from πρὸ ὁδοῦ): *a watcher, guard;* οἱ φρουροί *the guards* or *garrison* of a fort or city.

φρουρῶμες, Dor. 1 pl. subj. of φρουρέω.

φρύαγμα, ατος, τό, (φρυάσσομαι) *a violent snorting, the neighing* of a spirited horse. II. metaph. *insolence, arrogance.*

φρυαγμο-σέμνᾰκος, ον, (φρύαγμα, σεμνός) *wanton and haughty.*

φρυάσσομαι Att. **-ττομαι**, f. ξομαι, Dep. *to snort and neigh,* of a spirited horse. II. metaph. *to be wanton, insolent.*

φρῡγᾰνίζομαι, f. ίσομαι Att. ἰοῦμαι, Dep. (φρύγανον) *to gather sticks for fuel.*

φρῡγᾰνισμός, ὁ, (φρυγανίζομαι) *a gathering of dry sticks for fuel, a collecting of firewood.*

φρύγᾰνον [ῡ], τό, (φρύγω) *a dry stick:* mostly in plur. *dry sticks for fuel, firewood,* Lat. *sarmenta, virgulta.*

φρῠγῆναι, aor. 2 pass. inf. of φρύγω.

ΦΡΥ͂ΓΙ΄ΛΟΣ, ὁ, *a finch,* Lat. *fringilla.* [ῐ]

Φρύγιος, α, ον, (Φρύξ) *Phrygian;* Φρύγιοι νόμοι, Φρύγια μέλη *Phrygian* music, i. e. music played on the flute, said to be invented by Marsyas, wilder than the music for the lyre. [ῠ] Hence

Φρῠγιστί, Adv. *in Phrygian fashion;* of music, *in the Phrygian mode.*

ΦΡΥ΄ΓΩ [ῡ], also **ΦΡΥ΄ΣΣΩ** Att. **-ττω**: f. φρύξω Dor. ξῶ: aor. 1 ἔφρυξα: Pass., aor. 1 ἐφρύχθην: aor. 2 ἐφρύγην [ῠ]: pf. πέφρυγμαι:—*to roast, toast, broil:* of the sun, *to parch,* Lat. *torrere.* Hence

φρυκτός, ή, όν, verb. Adj. *roasted, toasted, parched.* II. as Subst., φρυκτός, ὁ, *a firebrand, torch:* in plur. *a signal-fire, alarm-fire, beacon;* φρυκτοὶ πολέμιοι αἴρονται ἐς τόπον *fire-signals* of an enemy's approach are made to a place.

φρυκτωρέω, f. ήσω, (φρυκτωρός) *to give signals by fire:*—Pass., ἐφρυκτωρήθησαν νῆες προσπλέουσαι the approach of ships *was signalled* or *telegraphed by alarm-fires.* Hence

φρυκτωρία, ἡ, *a giving signals by beacon* or *alarm-fires.* II. *a night-watch to make fire-signals.*

φρυκτ-ωρός, ὁ, (φρυκτός, οὖρος) *one who watches to give signals by beacons* or *alarm-fires.*

ΦΡΥ΄ΝΗ, ἡ, *a toad.* [ῡ]

ΦΡΥ΄Ξ, ὁ, gen. Φρῠγός, *a Phrygian.*

φρύξω Dor. **-ξῶ**, fut. of φρύγω.

φρύσσω Att. **-ττω**, = φρύγω.

φρυχθῆναι, aor. 1 pass. inf. of φρύγω.

φῦ, *faugh!* an exclamation of disgust.

φῦ, Ep. for ἔφυ, 3 sing. aor. 2 of φύω.

φυά, Dor. for φυή.

φύγᾰδε, Adv. (φῠγή) like φόβονδε, *to flight*; φυγαδ' ἔτραπεν ἵππους he turned his horse *to flight*.

φῠγᾰδεύω, f. σω, (φυγάς) *to make* one *an exile, drive from a country, banish*. II. intr. *to be an exile, live in banishment*.

φῠγᾰδικός, ή, όν, (φυγάς) *fit for an exile* or *refugee*; φυγαδικὴ προθυμία the zeal *of an exile*.

φῠγ-αίχμης, ου, ὁ, (φυγεῖν, αἰχμή) *fleeing from the spear, unwarlike, cowardly*.

φῠγάς, άδος, ὁ, ἡ, (φυγεῖν) *a fugitive*, esp. *a banished man, exile, refugee*, Lat. *exul, profugus*; κατάγειν φυγάδας to recal *the exiles*; κατιέναι or κατελθεῖν was said of their returning themselves. 2. *a deserter*.

†**φυγγάνω**, collat. form of φευγω.

φύγδᾰ, Adv., contr. for φύγαδε, *to flight*.

φύγε, Ep. for ἔφῠγε, 3 sing. aor. 2 of φεύγω.

φῠγεῖν Ion. **φυγέειν**, aor. 2 inf. of φεύγω.

φῠγή, ἡ, (φυγεῖν) *flight* in battle, Lat. *fuga*: dat. φυγῇ, *in hasty flight, hastily*. 2. *flight* or *escape* from a thing, c. gen.; νόσων ἀμηχάνων φυγὰς ξυμπέφρασται he has devised *means of escape* from incurable diseases. II. *banishment*, Lat. *exilium*; φυγὴν φεύγειν to live in *banishment*. 2. as a collective Noun φυγή, = φυγάδες, *a body of exiles* or *refugees*.

φύγῃσι, Ep. for φύγῃ, 3 sing. aor. 2 of φεύγω.

φῠγο-δέμνιος, ον, (φυγεῖν, δέμνιον) *shunning the marriage-bed*.

φῠγο-δῐκέω, f. ήσω, (φυγεῖν, δίκη) *to shun a lawsuit*: *to dislike litigation*.

φῠγό-ξενος, ον, (φυγεῖν, ξένος) *shunning strangers* or *guests*, hence *inhospitable*.

φῠγο-πτόλεμος, ον, poët. for φυγοπόλεμος, (φυγεῖν, πόλεμος, πτόλεμος) *shunning war, cowardly*.

φῠγών, οῦσα, όν, aor. 2 part. of φυγεῖν.

φυείς, εῖσα, έν, aor. 2 pass. part. of φύω.

φύζα, (φεύγω) poët. for φυγή, *flight, rout*. Hence

φυζᾰκῐνός, ή, όν, *flying, shy, scared*.

φυζᾰλέος, α, ον, = φυζακινός.

φυή Dor. **φυά**, ἡ, (φύω) *growth, stature, fine growth, noble stature* II. *one's natural powers* or *parts, talents, genius*: *nature*. III. *the flower* or *prime of age*.

φύη, for φυίη, 3 sing. aor. 2 opt. of φύω

φυῆναι, aor. 2 pass. inf. of φύω.

φυίην, aor. 2 opt. of φύω.

φῡκιόεις, εσσα, εν, (φῦκος) *full of sea-weed, weedy*.

φῡκίον or **φύκιον**, τό, (φῦκος) *sea-weed*.

φῡκο-γείτων, ονος, ὁ, ἡ, (φῦκος, γείτων) *near the sea-weed, dwelling by the sea*

ΦΥ'ΚΟΣ, εος, τό, Lat. *FUCUS, sea-weed, sea-wrack, tangle*. II. *a red paint* or *dye* formed from φῦκος, Lat. *fucus*.

φυκτός, ή, όν, = φευκτος, V[illegible] Adj. of φευγω, *to be shunned* or *escaped, that can be escaped*. II. *shunned, avoided*.

φυλάκεσσι, Ep. dat. pl. of φύλαξ.

φῠλᾰκή, ἡ, (φυλάσσω) *a watching* or *guarding, keeping watch* or *guard, watch* or *guard*: in plur. *a night-watch*, Lat. *excubiae*; φυλακὰς ἔχειν to mount *the night-guard*; φυλακὰς φυλάττειν to keep *guard* or *watch*; τὰς φυλακὰς καταστήσασθαι to set *the watches*. 2. *a watch* or *guard*, Lat. *custodia*: also *a guard* or *garrison* of a place. 3. *a watch-tower*: *a fortified post* or *station*. 4. of time, *a watch*, esp. *a watch* of the night. 5. *a ward, prison, place of security*. II. *a watching, guarding, keeping in ward*; ἔχειν τινὰ ἐν φυλακῇ to keep in *custody*:—also φυλακὴν ἔχειν, = φυλάττεσθαι to take *heed* or *care, be cautious*; δεινῶς ἔχειν ἐν φυλακῇσι to be straitly *on one's guard*.

φῠλᾰκίζω, f. ίσω Att. ιῶ, (φυλακή) *to throw into prison*.

φύλᾰκος, ὁ, poët. for φύλαξ.

φυλακτέος, α, ον, verb. Adj. of φυλάσσω, *to be watched* or *kept*. II. φυλακτέον (from Med. φυλάσσομαι) *one must guard against*

φῠλακτήρ, ῆρος, ὁ, = φύλαξ, *a guard*. Hence

φῠλακτήριον, τό, *a post for a garrison, a fort* or *castle*: *an outpost*, Lat. *statio*. 2. *a safeguard, preservative, amulet*: amongst the Jews, φυλακτήρια were *strips of parchment* with a portion of the Law written upon them, believed to be *of efficacy against evil spirits*.

φῠλακτικός, ή, όν, (φῠλάσσω) *fit for preserving, preservative*, c. gen. II. *cautious*:—Adv. -κῶς.

φύλαξ, ᾰκος, ὁ, also ἡ, (φυλάσσω) *a watcher, guard*: *a sentinel*, Lat. *excubitor*; οἱ φύλακες *the garrison*; also *body-guards*. II. *a guardian, keeper, protector, governor*; φύλαξ παιδὸς *a protector* of the lad.

φῠλαξεῖς, Dor. for φυλάξεις, 2 sing. fut. of φυλάσσω.

φύλαξις, εως, ἡ. (φῠλασσω) *a watching, guarding*. II. (from Med.) *occasion for guarding against, caution*

φῡλαρχέω, f. ήσω, *to command the contingent of a tribe* (φυλή). II. *to command the cavalry*. From

φύλ-αρχος, ὁ, (φῡλή, ἄρχω) *the chief of a tribe* (φυλή). II. *a commander of cavalry*.

φῠλασσέμεναι, Ep. inf. of φυλάσσω.

ΦΥ'ΛΑ'ΣΣΩ Att. -ττω: fut. φυλάξω: aor. 1 ἐφύλαξα Ep. φύλαξα: pf. πεφύλακα: Pass., f. φυλαχθήσομαι, also f. med. φυλάξομαι: aor. 1 ἐφυλάχθην: pf. πεφύλαγμαι: I. absol. *to watch, be sleepless*: esp. *to keep watch and ward, be on guard*; νύκτα φυλάσσειν *to watch* the night through. II. trans. *to watch, guard, keep, secure*; φυλάττειν τινὰ ἀπό τινος *to guard* one from a person or thing. 2. *to watch for, lie in wait* or *ambush for*; *to watch, wait for* or *observe the right* time. 3. metaph. *to preserve, keep, maintain*; φυλάσσειν ὅρκια *to keep, respect* oaths; φυλάσσειν ἔπος *to observe* a command. III. Med. *to heed, take heed* or *care, be on one's guard*; used by Homer only in pf. pass.,

πεφυλαγμένος εἶναι to be *cautious, prudent.* 2. *to keep* a thing, *bear it in mind* or *memory:* c. inf. *to take care* to do; φυλάσσεσθαι μὴ ποιεῖν *to take care* not to do, *to guard against* doing. 3. c. acc. *to take heed, beware of, be on one's guard against, shun, avoid;* φυλάσσεσθαι τοὺς πολεμίους *to be on one's guard against* the enemy.—The Act. is sometimes used in the sense of the Med.

φῡλέτης, ου, ὁ, (φυλή) *one of the same tribe, a tribesman,* Lat. *tribūlis.*

φῡλή, ἡ, (φύω) *a union among the citizens* of a state, *a class* or *tribe* formed according to blood, *a clan* or *caste.* 2. later, *a union according to local habitation, a tribe,* Lat. *tribus,* independent of connexion by blood. II. *a division in an army, the soldiers of one* φυλή: also *a certain number, a brigade,* esp. of cavalry.

ΦΥ˜ΛΙ΄Α, ἡ, *a wild olive-tree.*

φυλλάς, άδος, ἡ, (φύλλον) *a heap of leaves, a bed* or *litter of leaves.* II. *the leaves, leafage, foliage* of a tree: metaph. of man, φυλλάδος ἤδη κατακαρφομένης when *his leaf* now becoming sere and withered. 2. *a tree* or *plant itself: a branch* or *bough.*

φυλλεῖον, τό, (φύλλον) in plur. *green stuff, herbs,* such as mint, parsley, etc., *that were given into the bargain;* ῥαφανίδων φυλλεῖα, radish-*tops.*

φύλλινος, η, ον, (φύλλον) *of leaves, made of leaves.*

φυλλοβολέω, f. ήσω, *to shed the leaves.* From

φυλλο-βόλος, ον, (φύλλον, βαλεῖν) *shedding leaves.*

φυλλό-κομος, ον, (φύλλον, κόμη) *covered with leaves, thick-leaved, leafy.*

ΦΥ΄ΛΛΟΝ, τό, *a leaf;* in plur. *leaves, foliage;* οἵηπερ φύλλων γενεή, τοιήδε καὶ ἀνδρῶν as is the generation *of leaves,* so is also that of men; πλεκτὰ φύλλα wreathed *leaves.* 2. in pl. also *flowers.*

φυλλόρ-ροος, ον, (φύλλον, ῥέω) *leaf-shedding.* Hence

φυλλορροέω, f. ήσω, *to shed the leaves:* hence the Comic phrase, φυλλορροεῖν ἀσπίδα *to shed* or *let drop* one's shield.

φυλλό-στρωτος, ον, and **φυλλο-στρώς**, gen. ῶτος, ὁ, ἡ, (φύλλον, στρώννυμι) *strewed* or *covered with leaves.*

φυλλο-φόρος, ον, (φύλλον, φέρω) *bearing leaves;* φυλλοφόρος ἀγών a contest in which the prize is *a crown of leaves.*

φυλλο-χοέω, f. ήσω, (φύλλον, χέω) *to shed like leaves.*

φῡλο-κρῐνέω, f. ήσω, (φῦλον, κρίνω) *to distinguish races, choose by races.*

φῦλον, τό, (φύω) *a stock, race, kind;* φῦλον θεῶν, γυναικῶν. 2. in plur. to denote *a number of one kind, a troop, host, crowd,* as, φῦλα θεῶν, φῦλα γυναικῶν, etc.: *a swarm of gnats:* φῦλον ὀρνίθων *the race* of birds. 3. *sex,* τὸ γυναικεῖον φῦλον *the female sex.* II. *a race, people, nation.* III. in a more restricted sense, *a clan, tribe;* κατὰ φῦλα by *races* or *clans.*

φύλ-οπις, ιδος, ἡ: acc. φύλοπιν or φυλόπιδα:—(φῦλον, ὄψ) *the battle-cry, din of battle, battle.*

φῦμα, (φύω) *a thing that grows upon the body, a tumour, boil, cancer,* Lat. *tuber, vomĭca.*

φῦναι, aor. 2 inf. of φύω.

φυξ-άνωρ, ορος, ὁ, ἡ, (φεύγω, ἀνήρ) *fleeing men.* [ā]

φύξηλις, ιος and ιδος, ὁ, ἡ, (φεύγω) *fugitive, shy, cowardly.*

φύξῐμος, ον, (φεύγω) of places, *whither one can flee, where one can take refuge;* as Subst., φύξιμον, τό, *a place of refuge.* II. c. acc., φύξιμός τινα *able to flee from* or *escape* one.

φύξις, εως, ἡ, (φεύγω) = φυγή, *flight.*

φύρᾱμα, ατος, τό, (φῡράω) *that which is mixed* or *kneaded, paste, dough.*

φῡράω: f. άσω [ā]: aor. 1 ἐφύρᾱσα Ion. -ησα: Pass., aor. 1 ἐφυράθην [ā] Ion. -ήθην: pf. πεφύρημαι:—lengthd. form of φύρω, *to mix up, mingle, knead:* metaph. in Med., μαλακὴν φωνὴν πρὸς τοὺς ἐραστὰς φυράσασθαι *to make up* a soft voice towards one's lovers.

φύρδην, Adv. (φύρω) *mixedly, in utter confusion.*

φῠρῆναι, aor. 2 inf. pass. of φύρω.

ΦΥ΄ΡΩ, f. φύρσω: aor. 1 ἔφυρσα: Pass., paullo-p. fut. πεφύρσομαι: aor. 1 ἐφύρθην: aor. 2 ἐφύρην [ῠ]: pf. πέφυρμαι:—*to mix, mix up, mingle together,* esp. *with* something *wet:* hence *to wet, soil, defile.* 2. *to mix and knead* dough; ὁ φύρων *one who kneads bread, a baker.* II. metaph. *to mingle* or *jumble together, confound, confuse:*—Pass. *to be in confusion* or *disorder.* [ῡ]

φύς [ῡ], aor. 2 part. of φύω: ὁ φύς *a son.*

φῦσα, ης, ἡ, (φύω) *a pair of bellows, bellows.* II. *a breath, blast:* of fire, *a stream* or *jet.*

φῡσαθείς, εῖσα, έν, Dor. for φυσηθείς, aor. 1 pass. part. of φυσάω.

φῡσᾰλίς and **φῡσᾰλλίς**, ίδος, ἡ, (φυσάω) *a bladder, bubble,* Lat. *pustŭla.* II. *a wind-instrument, a pipe, bagpipe.*

φύσᾰλος, ὁ, (φυσάω) *a toad* from its *puffing itself up.* [ῠ]

φύσας, aor. 1 part. of φύω; ὁ φύσας one's *father.* [ῡ]

φῡσᾱτήριον, τό, Dor. for φυσητήριον.

φῡσάω Ion. -έω: f. ήσω: (φῦσα):—*to blow, puff,* either with the breath or with bellows: *to snort, snuff, breathe;* δεινὰ φυσᾶν *to snort* furiously. II. trans. *to puff* or *blow up,* Lat. *inflare;* φυσᾶν κύστιν *to blow up* a bladder: Pass., plqpf. ἐπεφύσητο ἡ γαστήρ my belly *was blown out;* pf. part. πεφυσημένος, *blown out, swoln.* 2. metaph. *to cheat;* φυσᾶν τινα *to puff* one *up, make* him *vain:*—Pass. *to be puffed up, elated.* 3. *to blow out, spurt out, discharge.* 4. *to blow out* a lamp. 5. *to blow* a wind-instrument.

φυσέω, Ion. for φυσάω: **φυσεώμενος**, Ion. for φυσώμενος, pres. pass. part.

φύση, ἡ, Ion. for φῦσα.

φύσημα, ατος, τό, (φῡσάω) *that which is blown* or *blown out: a breath: any sound made by blowing* or *snorting: a roaring, raging*: of a horse, *a snorting, snuffing*: **αἵματος** φύσημα *a blowing forth* blood.

φῡσητέον, verb. Adj. of φυσάω, *one must blow up.*

φῡσητήρ, ῆρος, ὁ, (φυσάω) *an instrument for blowing, a blow-pipe* or *tube.* 2. *a pair of bellows, a fan for blowing* fire.

φῡσητήριον Dor. **φυσατήριον**, τό, (φυσάω) *a pair of bellows.* II. *a wind-instrument.*

φῡσίᾱμα, ατος, τό, *a blowing, snorting.* From

φῡσιάω, Ep. part. φῡσιόων, (φυσάω) *to blow, puff, snort, breathe hard, pant.* II. transit. *to blow* or *puff up*:—metaph. *to elate, make vain.*

φῡσιγγόομαι, Pass. (φῦσιγξ) *to be excited by eating garlic*, properly of fighting cocks: of the Megarians, ὀδύναις πεφυσιγγωμένοι *inflamed to fury* with their woes, in allusion to the garlic grown in Megara: cf. φῦσιγξ.

φῡσι-γνώμων, ον, gen. ονος, = φυσιογνώμων.

φῦσιγξ, ιγγος, ἡ, (φυσάω) *the hollow stalk* or *clove of garlic: garlic* itself.

φῡσί-ζοος, ον, (φύω, ζωή) *producing* or *sustaining life, life-giving.*

φῠσικός, ή, όν, (φύσις) *natural, produced* or *implanted by nature, inborn, native.* II. *of* or *belonging to external nature, physical*, as opp. to moral, metaphysical, etc.

φῠσιογνωμονέω, f. ήσω, (φυσιογνώμων) *to judge of a man by his features, know* or *detect him by his looks.*

φῠσιογνωμονία, ἡ, *the art of judging a man by his features, physiognomy*

φῠσιο-γνώμων, ον, gen. ονος, (φύσις, γνώμη) *judging of a man's character by his outward look.*

φῡσιόω, f. ώσω, (φυσάω) *to puff up, make proud.*

φῡσιόων, Ep. pres. part. of φυσιάω.

φύσις [ῠ], εως, ἡ, (φύω) *the nature, inborn quality, property* or *constitution* of a person or thing; φύσις ἀριθμῶν *the nature, natural power* of numbers, Lat. *vis*; φύσεως ἀποστῆναι χαλεπόν it is hard to part from *one's nature.* 2. of the mind, *one's nature; natural powers, parts, temper, disposition*, etc. 3. *the outward form, stature, look*, Lat. *species*, like φυή. 4. *natural order, nature*; φύσει or κατὰ φύσιν *by nature, naturally*, opp. to νόμῳ or κατὰ νόμον (by custom, conventionally); ἅπας ὁ ἀνθρώπων βίος φύσει καὶ νόμοις διοικεῖται the whole life of man is regulated by *the constitution of nature* and by laws; ὁ κατὰ φύσιν θάνατος *a natural* death, opp. to παρὰ φύσιν, contrary to *nature*; so, προδότης ἐκ φύσεως a traitor *by nature.* II. *natural origin, birth*; φύσει *by birth.* III. *a creature*; θνητὴ φύσις mankind; πόντου εἰναλία φύσις *the creatures* of the sea; θηλεῖα φύσις woman-*kind.*

φῡσίωσις, εως, ἡ, (φυσιόω) *a being puffed up, vanity.*

φύσκη, ἡ, (φυσάω) *the large intestine: a sausage* or *black pudding.*

φυστή or **φύστη**, ἡ, (φύρω) a kind of *barley-cake*, not kneaded firmly.

φύτλη…

φύσις, εως, ἡ, (φύω) *a progeny, race.*

φῠτᾰλιά, ἡ, (φυτόν) *a planted place, an orchard* or *vineyard*, as opp. to corn-land (ἄρουρα). II. *a plant*, esp. of the vine.

φῠτάλμιος, ον, (φυτός) *producing, nourishing, fostering; fatherly* II. *by nature, from one's birth*: ἆρα καὶ ἦσθα φυτάλμιος δυσαίων; wast thou thus miserable *from thy birth?*

φῠτεία, ἡ, (φυτεύω) *a planting.* II. *a plantation*; or simply *a plant.*

φύτευθεν, Aeol. and Ep. for ἐφῠτεύθησαν, 3 pl. aor. 1 pass. of φυτεύω: but **φυτευθέν**, aor. 1 pass. part neut. of φυτεύω.

φύτευμα, ατος, τό, (φῠτεύω) *that which is planted, a plant.*

φῠτευτήριον, τό, *a plant grown as a sucker, a seedling*, Lat. *planta, stolo.* From

φῠτεύω, f. σω: aor. 1 ἐφύτευσα: Pass., aor. 1 ἐφῠτεύθην: pf. πεφύτευμαι: (φυτόν):—*to plant* trees or plants: mostly as opp. to ἀρόω (to sow). 2. metaph. *to beget*; ὁ φυτεύσας πατήρ or ὁ φυτεύσας alone, *the father*; οἱ φυτεύσαντες *the parents*:—Pass. *to be begotten, to spring* from parents. 3. generally, *to produce, bring about, cause.* II. *to plant* ground *with trees*; φυτεύειν χωρίον *to plant* a spot *with trees*:—Pass., γῆ πεφυτευμένη land *planted with trees.*

φύτλη, ἡ, (φύω) poët. for φύσις, *a stock, generation, race, tribe*

φῠτο-εργός, όν, poët. for φυτουργός.

φῠτόν, τό, (φύω) *that which has grown, a plant, tree, fruit-tree* II. *a creature*: of men, *a descendant, child.* Properly neut. of φυτός.

φῠτός, ή, όν, verb. Adj. of φύω, *grown, growing.* 2. metaph. of a statue, *made of the natural wood, native.*

φῠτο-σκάφος, ον, (φυτόν, σκάπτω) *digging* or *delving round plants*; φυτοσκάφος ἀνήρ *a gardener.*

φῠτο-σπόρος, ον, (φυτόν, σπείρω) *planting trees*: —metaph. *begetting*, φυτοσπόρος, ὁ, *a father.*

φῠτ-ουργός poët. **φυτο-εργός**, όν, (φυτόν, *ἔργω) *cultivating plants* or *trees*: as Subst., φυτουργός, ὁ, *a gardener, vine-dresser.* II. metaph. *begetting*: as Subst., φυτουργός, ὁ, *a father.*

ΦΥ'Ω, fut. φύσω [ῡ]: aor. 1 ἔφῡσα: in these tenses Causal, *to bring forth, produce, make to grow*; τρίχας φύειν *to make* hair *grow*; φύειν πτερά *to put forth, grow* wings; of a country, φύειν καρπόν τε θαυμαστὸν καὶ ἄνδρας ἀγαθοὺς *to produce* excellent fruits and brave men:—also *to beget, generate*: ὁ φύσας, *the begetter, father* 2. metaph., φρένας φύειν *to get* understanding; δόξας φύειν *to get* or *gain* reputation. II. Pass. and Med. φύομαι: f. φύσομαι: the sense of Pass. and Med. also belongs to intr. tenses of Act., aor. 2 ἔφῡν, inf. φῦναι, part. φύς, φῦσα, φύν; later in pass. form ἐφύην, φυῆναι, φυείς: perf. πέφῡκα, plqpf. ἐπεφύκειν:—Ep. 3 pl. pf. πεφύᾱσι for πεφύκᾱσι, part. πεφυώς, πεφυυῖα, πεφυκῶτος, for πεφῡκώς, -κυῖα, -κότος: there is also an Ep. redupl. impf. ἐπέφῡκον, as if from a pres. πεφύκω; Ep. 3 plur. aor. 2

ἔφυν for ἔφυσαν: aor. 2 opt. φύην for φυίην:—*to grow, spring up* or *forth, come into being, be produced*; δένδρα πεφυκότα trees *growing there*. 2. of men, *to be begotten* or *born*, μὴ φῦναι νικᾷ not *to have been born* were best:—φῦναι or πεφυκέναι τινός *to be born* or *descended from* any one; ὁ φύς *the son*, opp. to ὁ φύσας *the father*. 3. *to be* so and so *by nature, be formed* so and so: hence simply *to be*; the pf. πέφῡκα being often used as a pres., *I have been born, I am*; plqpf. ἐπεφύκειν as impf., I *had been born, I was*; so also aor. 2 ἔφῡν *I am*; often expressed by an Adv., as, τὰ δεύτερα πέφυκε κρατεῖν *it is the nature* of second things to prevail, i. e. they *naturally* prevail. 4. c. dat. *to fall* to one *by nature, be* one's *natural lot*; ἄνθρωπος πεφυκώς man *according to his nature, as he is*.

φωίς, ίδος, ἡ, contr. **φῴς**, φῳδός: pl. φωΐδες, φῷδες: (φῶς):—*a blister* or *weal*, caused by a burn *a burn, blister*.

Φώκαια Ion. **-αίη**, ἡ, a city in Ionia. Hence

Φωκαιεύς Att. **-ᾱεύς**, έως, and **Φωκαΐτης**, ὁ, *a Phocaean*: fem. **Φωκαΐς**, ίδος, *a Phocaean woman*.

Φωκεύς, έως, ὁ, (Φωκίς) *a Phocian*.

ΦΩ'ΚΗ, ἡ, *a seal, sea-calf*, Lat. *phoca*.

Φωκικός, ή, όν, (Φωκίς) *of Phocis, Phocian*.

Φωκίς (sub. γῆ), ίδος, ἡ, *Phocis*, a country on the Corinthian gulf, west of Boeotia.

φωλάς, άδος, ἡ, fem. Adj. (φωλεός) *lurking in a hole: lying torpid in its den*, epith. of the bear.

φωλειός, ὁ, Ep. for φωλεός.

ΦΩΛΕΟ'Σ, ὁ, with irreg. plur. φωλεά, τά, *a den, lair, hole*, as of bears, foxes, mice.

φωλεύω, f. εύσω, or **φωλέω**, f. ήσω, (φωλεός) *to lie in a hole* or *den*: *to lie torpid in a hole*.

φωνάεις, Aeol. and Dor. for φωνήεις.

φωνᾶσαι, Dor. for φωνῆσαι, aor. 1 inf. of φωνέω.

φωνασκέω, f. ήσω, (φωνασκός) *to practise* or *cultivate one's voice, learn to sing* or *declaim*. Hence

φωνασκία, ἡ, *practice of the voice*.

φων-ασκός, όν, (φωνή, ἀσκέω) *practising the voice*.

φωνεῦντες, **φωνεῦντα**, Dor. for φωνοῦντες, φωνοῦντα, pres. part. from

φωνέω, f. ήσω, (φωνή) *to produce an articulate sound* or *tone*: of men, *to speak loud* or *clearly, to call out, cry, pronounce*; with a neut. Adj., μέγιστα φωνέειν *to have the* loudest *voice*. 2. of animals, *to cry*. 3. *to sound*: of a musical instrument, *to sound sweetly*. 4. τὰ φωνοῦντα *the vowels*, like τὰ φωνήεντα. II. c. acc. pers. *to speak to, accost, address*: *to call by name, call to, cry to, call upon*: c. acc. pers. et inf. *to bid, command* one to do. III. c. acc. rei, *to speak of*.

ΦΩΝΗ', ἡ, *a sound, tone*: mostly of men, *the voice*, Lat. *vox*: *a loud clear voice, a cry*; φωνὴν ῥηγνύναι to utter *a clear, articulate sound*. 2. *the voice* or *cry* of animals. 3. *sound*: *the sound* of musical instruments. 4. *any articulate sound*, as opp. to inarticulate (ψόφος); *a vowel-sound*, as opp. to that of consonants. II. *the faculty of speech, discourse*, Lat. *sermo*. 2. *language*, Lat. *lingua*. 3. *a kind of language, dialect*. Hence

φωνήεις Dor. **φωνάεις**, εσσα, εν; contr. in neut. plur. φωνᾶντα:—*sounding, speaking, gifted with speech*: of wise sayings, φωνᾶντα συνετοῖσι *that have speech* to the wise: *uttering a sound, tone* or *speech*: —τὰ φωνήεντα *vowels* opp. to ἄφωνα (consonants). See φωνή.

φώνημα, ατος, τό, (φωνέω) *a sound made* or *uttered, voice*. 2. *a thing spoken, word, speech*.

φωνῆσα, Ep. for ἐφώνησα, aor. 1 of φωνέω.

ΦΩ'Ρ, ὁ, gen. φωρός, dat. pl. φωρσί, Lat. *FUR*, *a thief*; φωρῶν λιμήν, a harbour at Athens, *used by smugglers*. Hence

φωρά, ᾶς, Ion. **φωρή**, ῆς, ἡ, (φώρ) *a theft*. II. *detection*.

φωράω, f. άσω [ᾱ]: Pass., aor. 1 ἐφωράθην [ᾱ]: pf. πεφώρᾱμαι: (φωρά):—*to search after a thief, search* a house *to discover a theft*: generally, *to trace, detect, discover*:—Pass. *to be caught, detected*; c. part., φωρᾶσθαι κλέπτης ὤν *to be convicted* of being a thief; of things, ἀργύριον ἐφωράθη ἐξαγόμενον specie *was discovered* to be in course of exportation.

φώρη, Ion. for **φώρα**.

φωριαμός, ὁ, *a chest, trunk, coffer*, esp. for clothes and linen. (Deriv. uncertain.)

φωρίδιος, α, ον, poët. for φώριος, *stolen*.

φώριος, ον, (φώρ) *stolen*: *secret, clandestine, illicit*.

φώς, ὁ, gen. φωτός; dual φῶτε, φωτοῖν; pl. φῶτες, φωτῶν: (*φάω, the Root of φημί):—poët. for ἀνήρ, *a man*: *a mortal*, as opp. to a god.

φῶς, τό, contr. for φάος.

φωστήρ, ῆρος, ὁ, (φῶς) *a light-giver, luminary*. II. metaph. *an opening for light, a door* or *window*.

φωσ-φόρος, ον, (φῶς, φέρω) *bringing light*; as Subst., φωσφόρος, ὁ, with or without ἀστήρ, *the light-bringer*, Lat. *Lucifer*, i. e. *the morning-star*. 2. φωσφόροι κόραι, the eyeball *that gives him light*, of the Cyclops' eye. II. *torch-bearing*.

φωτ-ᾱγωγός, όν, (φῶς, ἄγω) *guiding with a light*: —φωταγωγὸς (sub. θύρα), ἡ, *an opening for light, a window*.

φωτεινός, ή, όν, (φῶς) *shining bright, giving light*.

φωτίζω, f. ίσω Att. ιῶ, (φῶς) intr. *to shine, give light, beam*. II. transit. *to bring to light, make known*. 2. metaph. *to enlighten, instruct, teach*: —Pass. *to be enlightened* or *instructed*.

φωτισμός, ὁ, (φωτίζω) *an enlightening*. *that which enlightens, illumination, light*.

X

X, χ, χῖ, τό, indecl., twenty-second letter of the Greek alphabet: as numeral χ′ = 600, but ͵χ =

600,000: also in Inscr. χ stands as first letter of χίλιοι, 1000.

Changes of χ, esp. in the dialects: I. Dor. for θ, as ὄρνιχος for ὄρνιθος. II. Ion. very freq. into κ, as δέκομαι κιθών κύθρα for δέχομαι χιτών χύτρα. III. put before λ, as χλαῖνα for λαῖνα, χλιαρός for λιαρός.

Like φ, χ was sometimes considered as a double consonant, so as to make a short syllable before it long by position, as in *φαιŏχίτων*.

χάδε, Ep. for ἔχᾰδε, 3 sing. aor. 2 of χανδάνω.

χᾰδεῖν Ep. **χᾰδέειν**, aor. 2 inf. of χανδάνω.

ΧΑ'ΖΩ, Ep. fut. κεκᾰδήσω: Ep. aor. 2 κέκᾰδον, for κέχαδον:—*to force to retire from, bereave of* a thing, c. gen. II. Med. **χάζομαι**: f. χάσομαι Ep. χάσσομαι: aor. 1 ἐχασάμην, Ep. 3 sing. χάσσατο, Ep. part. χασσάμενος: there is also Ep. 3 pl. κεκάδοντο for κεχάδοντο, from a redupl. aor. 2 κεκαδόμην:—*to give way, give ground, draw* or *shrink back, recoil, retire*: absol., ὀπίσω χάζεσθαι *to retire* or *retreat* back. 2. c. gen. *to draw back* or *retire from*; πυλάων χάζεσθαι *to retire from* the gates; χάζεσθαι ἑτάρων εἰς ἔθνος *to retire* into the troop of his companions. 3. in Att. c. inf. *to doubt, scruple, hesitate, fear* to do.

ΧΑΙ'ΝΩ, seldom used in pres. and impf., **ΧΑ'ΣΚΩ**, ἔχασκον being used instead: fut. χᾰνοῦμαι: aor. 2 ἔχᾰνον: pf. κέχηνα, with pres. sense:—*to yawn, gape, open wide*; τότε μοι χάνοι εὐρεῖα χθών then may earth *yawn* wide for me: *to open* the mouth: of a wound, *to gape, yawn*. II. in Comic Poets, *to gape* or *yawn* from weariness or in eager expectation; ἄνω κεχηνέναι *to look gaping* up; οἱ κεχηνότες *gapers, starers*: χάσκειν πρός τι *to gape* or *look greedily* after a thing; χάσκειν πρός τινα *to gape* in wonder or admiration at a person: also *to gape about, stare about*. III. *to open the mouth to speak, to utter, pronounce*, Lat. *hiscere*, c. acc.; δεινὰ ῥήματα κατά τινος χανεῖν *to speak* foul words against any one.

ΧΑΤ'ΟΣ, α, ον, *genuine, true, good, staunch*.

χαίρεσκε, 3 sing. Ion. impf. of χαίρω.

χαιρετίζω, f. σω, (χαῖρε) *to greet*. Hence

χαιρετισμός, οῦ, ὁ, *a greeting*.

χαιρηδών, όνος, ἡ, (χαίρω) *joy, delight*. formed like ἀλγηδών.

χαίρην, Dor. for χαίρειν, inf. of χαίρω.

χαίροισα, Dor. for χαίρουσα, pres. part. fem. of χαίρω.

χαιρόντων, 3 pl. imperat. of χαίρω.

ΧΑΙ'ΡΩ: f. χαιρήσω Ep. κεχᾰρήσω: pf. κεχάρηκα, Ep. part. κεχᾰρηώς:—Med., fut. χᾰροῦμαι: Ep. aor. 1 ἐχηράμην, 3 sing. χήρατο: and from a redupl. aor. 2 κεχᾰρόμην the 3 pl. ind. κεχάροντο, 3 sing. and pl. opt. κεχάροιτο, κεχαροίατο: Pass., in same sense as Act., fut. χᾰρήσομαι; Ep. paullo-p. fut. κεχᾰρήσομαι: aor. 2 ἐχάρην [ᾰ], Ep. 3 sing. χάρη, opt. χαρείην, inf. χαρῆναι, part. χαρείς: pf. κεχάρημαι, later κέχαρμαι: Ep. 3 pl. plqpf. κεχάρηντο:—*to rejoice, be glad, be delighted* or *pleased*; χαίρειν νόῳ *to rejoice* in one's mind. 2. c. dat. *to rejoice at, be delighted with, take pleasure in* a thing; also, χαίρειν γέλωτι *to express one's joy* by laughter; more rarely c. acc. pers. as, χαίρω δέ σ' εὐτυχοῦντα *I rejoice* at your prosperity. 3. c. part., χαίρω ἀκούσας *I rejoice at* having heard, *am glad to* hear; χαίρεις ὁρῶν φῶς *thou rejoicest* at seeing the light. 4. with the pres. part., χαίρω is used also in sense of φιλέω, *to delight* in doing, *to be wont* to do. II. often with a negat., οὐ χαιρήσεις *thou wilt* or *shalt not rejoice*, i.e. *thou shalt pay dearly* for it, *shalt repent*; so also part. χαίρων *with impunity*; οὐ χαίροντες ἀπαλλάξετε ye shall not get off *with impunity*. III. the imperat. χαῖρε is a common form of greeting, either at meeting, *hail, welcome*, Lat. *salve*; or at parting, *farewell*, Lat. *vale*; so in part., χαίρων ἴθι *fare-thee-well*. V. inf. χαίρειν, in phrase χαίρειν λέγω σοι, is used as a greeting like χαῖρε; προσειπών τινα χαίρειν having bid one *welcome* or *farewell*; so at the beginning of letters the inf. usually stood alone, as, Κῦρος Κυαξάρῃ χαίρειν [sc. λέγει], Lat. *salvere jubet, salutem dicit*. 2. in bad sense, χαίρειν ἐᾶν or κελεύειν to say *farewell* to a person or thing, *to renounce, set at naught*; πολλὰ χαίρειν εἰπεῖν τινι *to bid* a long *farewell* to one; also in 3 sing. imperat. χαιρέτω, like ἐρρέτω, *let it go, away with it, a murrain with it*.

ΧΑΙ'ΤΗ, ἡ, *long flowing hair*, both in sing. and plur.: also *a horse's mane*; later also a lion's *mane*, Lat. *juba*. II. of trees, like Lat. *coma, leaves, foliage*. Hence

χαιτήεις Dor. **-άεις**, εσσα, εν, *with long flowing hair*: also *with a long mane*.

χαίτωμα, = χαίτη, *hair, the plume* of a helmet.

χαλά, ἡ, Dor. for χηλή.

ΧΑ'ΛΑΖΑ˘, ης, ἡ, *hail*: *a hail-shower, hail-storm*: metaph. *any shower, sleet, a pelting storm, a shower of stones* or *arrows*. II. *a small pimple* or *tubercle*. Hence

χᾰλαζάω, *to hail*. II. *to have pimples* or *tubercles*.

χαλαζ-επής, ές, (χάλαζα, ἔπος) *hurling abuse as thick as hail*.

χᾰλαζήεις Dor. **-άεις**, εσσα, εν, (χάλαζα) *like hail, thick as hail, pelting, pitiless*.

χᾰλαζο-βολέω, f. ήσω, (χάλαζα, βαλεῖν), *to strike with hail*.

χᾰλαίνω, poët. for χαλάω.

χᾰλᾰρός, ά, όν, (χαλάω) *slackened, loosened, slack*; χαλαρὰ κοτυληδών *a loose, supple* joint: of music, *languid, effeminate*. Hence

χᾰλᾰρότης, ητος, ἡ, *slackness, looseness*.

ΧΑ˘ΛΑ'Ω: f. άσω [ᾰ]: aor. 1 ἐχάλᾰσα Ep. χάλασσα, Dor. part. χαλάξαις; pf. κεχάλᾰκα: Pass., aor. 1 ἐχαλάσθην: pf. κεχάλασμαι: I. transit. *to make slack* or *loose, slacken, loosen*; χαλᾶν τόξα *to unstring* the bow; ἡνίας χαλᾶν *to slack* the reins; χαλᾶν πόδα *to slack* the sheet of the sail. 2. *to let down, let fall* or *droop*; μέτωπον χαλᾶν *to smooth* the brow. 3. *to let loose, loose, release;* κλῆθρα or κλῇδας χαλᾶν *to loose* the bar or bolts. 4. metaph. *to relax, let go, give up.* II. intr. *to become slack* or *loose: to gape, stand wide open.* 2. metaph. c. gen. *to relax* or *leave off from* a thing, *to cease from.* 3. c. dat. *to give way* or *yield to* any one: *to be indulgent to* any one, *pardon* him. 4. absol., like εἴκειν, *to give in, yield:*—Pass., like the intr. usage, *to be loosened* or *slackened.*

Χαλδαῖος, ὁ, *a Chaldaean.* II. *an astrologer, caster of nativities,* since the Chaldaeans were much given to such pursuits. Hence

Χαλδαϊστί, Adv. *in the Chaldee tongue.*

χᾰλ-ειμάς, άδος, ἡ, (χαλάω, εἷμα) Lat. *laxivestis, loose-robed, ungirt.*

χᾰλεπαίνω, f. ἀνῶ: aor. 1 ἐχαλέπηνα, pass. ἐχαλεπάνθην: (χαλεπός):—*to be hard, sore, grievous, severe,* of violent storms, Lat. *ingravescere:* metaph. of men, *to deal severely* or *harshly, to be harsh, ill-tempered;* χαλεπαίνειν τινί *to be embittered* or *shew harshness* towards one; χαλεπαίνειν ἐπί τινι *to be angry* at a thing: Med., χαλεπαίνεσθαι πρὸς ἀλλήλους *to be angry* or *grow embittered* towards one another.

χαλεπῆναι, aor. 1 inf. of χαλεπαίνω.

χᾰλεπηρής, ές, poët. for χαλεπός.

ΧΑΛΕΠΟ΄Σ [ᾰ], ἡ, όν, *hard to bear, sore, severe, grievous;* τὸ χαλεπὸν τοῦ πνεύματος *the severity of* the wind; τὰ χαλεπά *hardships, sufferings.* 2. *hard to do* or *deal with, difficult, troublesome.* 3. *difficult, dangerous.* 4. of approaches, *difficult, rough, rugged, steep.* II. of persons, *hard to deal with, bitter, hostile, angry:* οἱ χαλεπώτεροι *bitterer enemies: mischievous, dangerous, troublesome.* 2. *harsh, cruel:* of judges, *severe, rigid, strict.* 3. *ill-tempered, angry, testy, morose.* Hence

χᾰλεπότης, ητος, ἡ, *difficulty, roughness, ruggedness.* II. of persons, *harshness, severity, rigour.*

χᾰλέπτω, f. ψω: Pass., aor. 1 ἐχαλέφθην:—poët. for χαλεπαίνω, *to deal harshly with, oppress, distress, harass:* also *to bring low, humble.* 2. *to provoke, enrage, irritate.* II. intr. *to be angry, irritated.*

χαλεπῶ, Dor. for χαλεποῦ, gen. of χαλεπός.

χαλεπῶς, Adv. of χαλεπός, *hardly, with difficulty;* χαλεπῶς ἦν, c. inf., it was *difficult* to do. 2. *scarcely,* Lat. *aegre.* II. of persons, *severely, cruelly, harshly.* 2. *angrily, bitterly;* χαλεπῶς φέρειν τι, Lat. *aegre, graviter ferre,* to bear a thing *ill.*

χαλεπώτερον, -ώτατα, Comp. and Sup. of χαλεπῶς.

χᾰλί-κρᾱτος Ion. **χᾰλί-κρητος**, ον, (χάλις, κεράννυμι) *unmixed,* of wine, Lat. *merus.*

χᾰλῑν-ᾰγωγέω, f. ήσω, (χαλινός, ἄγω) *to guide with* or *as with a bridle:* hence *to curb, restrain.*

χᾰλῑνός, ὁ, irreg. pl. χαλινά, τά, (χαλάω) *a bridle,* esp. *the bit of a bridle;* χαλινὸν ἐνδακεῖν *to champ* the bit; χαλινοὺς διδόναι *to give* a horse *the rein* 2. metaph. *of anything which curbs* or *compels;* Διὸς χαλινός *the curb* imposed by Jove.

χᾰλῑνόω, f. ώσω, *to bridle* or *bit* a horse:—Pass. *to be bridled* or *curbed.* Hence

χᾰλίνωσις, εως, ἡ, *a bridling.* [ῑ]

χᾰλῑνωτήρια, τά, (χαλινόω) *cables* or *ropes to moor* ships *to the shore.*

ΧΑ΄ΛΙΞ, ῐκος, ὁ and ἡ, *a small stone, pebble:* as a collection, *gravel, rubbish for filling up, rubble,* Lat. *caementum.* [ᾰ]

χάλις, ιος, ὁ, (χαλάω) *sheer wine,* Lat. *merum.*

χᾰλιφρονέω, f. ήσω, (χαλίφρων) *to be light-minded, flighty, silly.* Hence

χᾰλιφροσύνη, ἡ, *levity, thoughtlessness, rashness.*

χᾰλί-φρων, ονος, ὁ, ἡ, (χαλάω, φρήν) *light-minded, flighty, thoughtless.*

χαλκ-αρμᾰτος, ον, (χαλκός, ἅρμα) *with brasen chariot,* epith. of Mars.

χάλκ-ασπις, ιδος, ὁ, ἡ, (χαλκός, ἀσπίς) *with brasen shield.*

χαλκ-έγχης, ες, gen. εος, (χαλκός, ἔγχος) *with brasen lance.*

χαλκεῖον Ion. **-ήιον**, τό, (χαλκεύω) *a smith's shop, forge, smithy,* Lat. *officina.* II. *anything made of copper:* 1. *a copper vessel, caldron.* 2. *a concave copper reflector* in a lamp. 3. *a copper badge.* Strictly neut. from

χάλκειος, α, ον Ion. **χαλκήιος**, η, ον, poët. for χάλκεος, (χαλκός) *of brass, brasen.*

χαλκ-έλᾰτος, ον, (χαλκός, ἐλαύνω) poët. for χαλκήλατος.

χαλκ-εμβολάς, poët. fem. of χαλκέμβολος.

χαλκ-έμβολος, ον, (χαλκός, ἔμβολον) *with brasen beak* or *prow,* of a ship.

χαλκ-εντής, ές, (χαλκός, ἔντεα) *armed with brass.*

χαλκεό-γομφος, ον, (χάλκεος, γόμφος) *fastened with brasen nails.*

χαλκεο-θώραξ, ᾱκος, Ep. **-θώρηξ**, ηκος, ὁ, ἡ: (χάλκεος, θώραξ) *with brasen breastplate.*

χαλκεο-κάρδιος, ον, (χάλκεος, καρδία) *with heart of brass.*

χαλκεό-πεζος, ον, (χάλκεος, πέζα) *brass-footed.*

χαλκεό-οπλος, ον, (χάλκεος, ὅπλον) *with arms* or *armour of brass.*

χάλκεος, έα Ion. έη, εον, also εος, εον: contr. **χαλκοῦς**, ῆ, οῦν: poët. **χάλκειος** Ion. **-ήιος**, η, ον: (χαλκός):—*of copper* or *bronze, brasen,* Lat. *aeneus;* χάλκεος Ζεύς *a brasen statue* of Jove; χάλκεόν τινα ἱστάναι to raise *a brasen statue* to one. 2. metaph., *like brass, hard, stout;* χάλκεον ἦτορ, a heart *of brass;* χάλκεος ὕπνος a *brasen* sleep, i. e. sleep of death.

χαλκεο-τευχής, ές, (χάλκεος, τεῦχος) *in arms of brass.*

χαλκεό-φωνος, ον, (χάλκεος, φωνή) *with voice of brass,* i. e. *ringing strong and clear.*

χάλκευμα, ατος, τό, (χαλκεύω) *anything made of brass, a brasen instrument* or *implement: a weapon,* etc.: in plur. *brasen bonds.*

χαλκεύς, έως, ὁ, (χαλκεύω) *a worker in copper, a*

coppersmith, brasier. 2. more generally, *a worker in metal, smith*, even of a *goldsmith; esp. a blacksmith.*

χαλκευτής, οῦ, ὁ, (χαλκεύω) = χαλκεύς: metaph. *a forger.*

χαλκευτικός, ή, όν, *of* or *for the brasier* or *his art: skilled in metal-working:* ἡ χαλκευτική (sub. τέχνη), *the smith's art* or *trade.*

χαλκευτός, ή, όν, verb. Adj. of χαλκεύω, *wrought of copper* or *metal.*

χαλκεύω, f. σω, (χαλκός) *to make of copper* or *of metal, to forge:*—Pass. *to be wrought* or *forged.* II. intr. *to be a smith, work as a smith, ply the hammer* or *forge;* τὸ χαλκεύειν *the smith's art.*

χαλκεών, ῶνος, ὁ, = χαλκεῖον, *a forge, smithy.*

χαλκηδών, όνος, ὁ, (χαλκός) *chalcedony*, name of a gem like an onyx.

χαλκήιον, τό, Ion. for χαλκεῖον.

χαλκήιος, η, ον, Ion. for χάλκειος.

χαλκ-ήλᾰτος also **χαλκ-έλατος**, ον, (χαλκός, ἐλαύνω) *forged out of brass, of beaten brass.*

χαλκήρης, ες, gen. εος, (χαλκός, ἀρᾰρεῖν) *furnished with brass:* of spears and arrows, *tipped with brass.*

χαλκί-οικος, ον, (χαλκός, οἶκος) *dwelling in a brasen house* or *shrine.*

χαλκίον, τό, (χαλκός) *a copper utensil, vessel, implement.* 2. *copper money, copper coin.*

χαλκίς, ίδος, ἡ, *a bird of prey.*

Χαλκίς, ίδος, ἡ, *Chalcis*, a city in Euboea, said to have its name *from neighbouring copper-mines.*

χαλκοάρης, ες, gen. εος, poët. lengthd. form for χαλκήρης. [ᾰ]

χαλκο-βᾰρής, ές, gen. έος, (χαλκός, βάρος) *heavy* or *loaded with brass.*

χαλκοβάρεια, used as fem. of χαλκοβαρής.

χαλκο-βᾰτής, ές, gen. έος, (χαλκός, βαίνω) *standing on brass, with foundation of brass, with brasen base.*

χαλκο-βόας, ου, ὁ, (χαλκός, βοή) *with voice of brass.*

χαλκο-γένειος, ον, (χαλκός, γένειον), and **χαλκόγενυς**, υ, gen. υος, (χαλκός, γένυς) *with teeth of brass.*

χαλκο-γλώχῑν, ῖνος, ὁ, ἡ, (χαλκός, γλωχίς) *with point* or *barbs of brass.*

χαλκο-δαίδᾰλος, ον, (χαλκός, δαιδάλλω) *inlaid with brass.* II. act. *working in brass.*

χαλκο-δάμᾱς, αντος, ὁ, ἡ, (χαλκός, δαμάω) *subduing*, i. e. *sharpening brass.*

χαλκό-δετος, ον, (χαλκός, δέω) *brass-bound.*

χαλκο-θώραξ, ᾶκος, ὁ, ἡ, (χαλκός, θώραξ) = χαλκεοθώραξ, *with brasen breastplate.*

χαλκο-κνήμῑς, ῖδος, ὁ, ἡ, (χαλκός, κνημίς) *with greaves of brass.*

χαλκο-κορυστής, οῦ, ὁ, (χαλκός, κορύσσω) as masc. Adj., *with* or *in brasen armour.*

χαλκό-κροτος, ον, (χαλκός, κροτέω) *sounding* or *rattling with brass:* of horses, *brasen-hoofed.* II. *beaten* or *forged of brass.*

χαλκο-λῐβᾰνον, τό, *fine* or *glowing brass.* (Deriv. uncertain.)

χαλκο-μίτρας, ου, ὁ, (χαλκός, μίτρα) *with girdle of brass.*

χαλκό-νωτος, ον, (χαλκός, νῶτος) *brass-backed.*

χαλκο-πᾰγής, ές, (χαλκός, παγῆναι) *compacted of brass.*

χαλκο-πάρῃος Dor. **-πάρᾱος**, ον, (χαλκός, παρειά) *with cheeks* or *sides of brass*, epith. of helmets.

χαλκό-πεδος, ον, (χαλκός, πέδον) *with floor of brass.*

χαλκό-πλευρος, ον, (χαλκός, πλευρά) *with sides of brass*, of an urn.

χαλκο-πληθής, ές, gen. έος, (χαλκός, πλῆθος) *filled with brass, armed all in brass.*

χαλκό-πληκτος Dor. **-πλακτος**, ον, (χαλκός, πλήσσω) *forged* or *welded of brass.*

χαλκό-πους, ὁ, ἡ, -πουν, τό; gen. -ποδος (χαλκός, πούς):—*brasen-footed, with brasen tramp.* II. *with steps of brass, brasen.*

χαλκό-πῠλος, ον, (χαλκός, πύλη) *with gates of brass* or *bronze.*

ΧΑΛΚΟ'Σ, οῦ, ὁ, *brass*, or rather *copper*, Lat. *aes*, called from its colour ἐρυθρός and αἶθοψ. Copper was the first metal that was wrought, and hence χαλκός was used as a name for *metal* in general; and afterwards, when *iron* began to be worked, the word χαλκός was used for σίδηρος. Later, χαλκός was applied to *bronze, a mixture of copper with tin*, which was the chief metal used by the ancients in the arts. II. in the Poets, *anything made of brass* or *metal*, esp. of *brasen arms:* also *a brasen vessel, urn.*

χαλκο-σκελής, ές, (χαλκός, σκέλος) *with legs of brass.*

χαλκο-στέφᾰνος, ον, (χαλκός, στέφανος) *crowned* or *compassed with brass.*

χαλκό-στομος, ον, (χαλκός, στόμα) *with brasen mouth.* II. *with edge* or *point of brass.*

χαλκό-τευκτος, ον, (χαλκός, τεύχω) *made of brass.*

χαλκο-τευχής, ές, (χαλκός, τεῦχος) *in brasen armour.*

χαλκό-τοξος, ον, (χαλκός, τόξον) *with brasen bow.*

χαλκοτορέω, f. ήσω, *to form* or *mould of brass.* From

χαλκό-τορος, ον, (χαλκός, τείρω) *wrought of brass.*

χαλκο-τύπος, ον, (χαλκός, τύπτω) *beating* or *working copper:*—as Subst., χαλκοτύπος, ὁ, *a worker in copper, coppersmith:* generally, *a smith.* 2. *striking brass together, beating the cymbals*, of the priests of Cybelé. II. χαλκότῠπος, ον, pass., *struck with brass, inflicted with brasen arms.*

χαλκ-οῦργος, ὁ, (χαλκός, *ἔργω) *a coppersmith.*

χαλκοῦς, ῆ, οῦν, Att. contr. from χάλκεος. II. as Subst., χαλκοῦς, ὁ, *a copper coin*, somewhat less than a farthing.

χαλκο-φάλᾰρος, ον, (χαλκός, φάλαρα) *adorned* or *ornamented with brass* or *copper.* [φᾰ]

χαλκόφῐ, Ep. for χαλκοῦ, gen. of χαλκός.

χαλκο-χάρμης, ου, ὁ, (χαλκός, χάρμη) *fighting in brasen armour.*

χαλκο-χίτων, ωνος, ὁ, ἡ, (χαλκός, χιτών) *brasen-coated, brass-clad.*

χαλκό-χῠτος, ον, (χαλκός, χέω) *cast in copper* or *brass*.

χαλκόω, f. ώσω, (χαλκός) *to cover with brass*:—aor. 1 pass. part. χαλκωθείς, *clad in brass*. II. *to make in brass* or *bronze*

χάλκωμα, ατος, τό, (χαλκόω) *anything made of bronze* or *copper*, *a brasen vessel* or *instrument*.

χᾰλυβδικός, ή, όν, (χάλυψ) *of steel*; τὸ χαλυβδικόν *steel*.

χάλῠβος, ὁ, poët. for χάλυψ, *steel*.

Χάλυψ, ῠβος, ὁ, *one of the nation of the Chalybes* in Pontus, famous for the working of steel. II. as appellat., χάλυψ, ῠβος, ὁ, *hardened iron*, *steel*.

χᾰμάδῑς [μᾰ], Adv. (χαμαί) poët. for χαμᾶζε, *on the ground*, *to the ground*.

χᾰμᾶζε, Adv. (χαμαί) *to the ground*, *on the ground*, Lat. *humi*.

χᾰμᾶθεν, Adv. (χαμαί) *from the ground*.

ΧΑ-ΜΑΙ', Adv. *on the earth*, *on the ground*. 2. like χαμᾶζε, Lat. *humi*, *to the ground*, *to earth*.

χᾰμαι-γενής, ές, gen. έος, (χαμαί, γενέσθαι) *earth-born*, *sprung from the soil*.

χᾰμαι-εύνας, άδος, poët. fem. of sq. [αῐ metri grat.]

χᾰμαι-εύνης, ου, ὁ, (χαμαί, εὐνή) *making one's bed* or *lair on the ground*. [αῐ metri grat.]

χᾰμαίζηλος, ον, (χαμαί) *growing low* or *near the ground*: generally, *low*: ὁ χαμαίζηλος (sub. δίφρος), *a low stool*. II. metaph. *fond of mean things*, *humble*; τὸ χαμαίζηλον *humility*.

χᾰμαικοιτέω, f. ήσω, *to lie*, *make one's bed on the ground*. From

χᾰμαι-κοίτης, ου, ὁ, (χαμαί, κοίτη) *lying* or *making one's bed on the ground*.

χᾰμαιλεχής, ές, gen. έος, (χαμαι, λέχος) = χαμαικοίτης.

χᾰμαι-λέων, οντος, ὁ, (χαμαί, λέων) *the chameleon*, a kind of lizard known for changing its colour.

χᾰμαιπετέω, f. ήσω, *to fall to the ground*; γνώμα χαμαιπετοῖσα a thought *that falls to the ground*. From

χᾰμαι-πετής, ές, (χαμαί, ΠΕΤ- Root of πίπτω) *falling to* or *on the earth*; χαμαιπετὴς πίπτειν to fall *to earth*: *fallen*, *prostrate in the dust*. 2. *lying* or *sleeping on the ground*. 3. *on the ground*. II. metaph. *falling to the ground*, *coming to naught*, *fruitless*.

χαμαιπετοῖσα, Dor. for χαμαιπετοῦσα, part. fem. of χαμαιπετέω.

χᾰμαι-τῠπεῖον, τό, (χαμαί, τυπεῖν) *a brothel*.

χᾰμ-ερπής, ές, (χαμαί, ἕρπω) *creeping on the ground*, *grovelling*.

χᾰμ-εύνη, ή, for χαμαιεύνη, (χαμαί, εὐνή) *a bed on the ground*, *pallet-bed*, *truckle-bed*. II. *a bedstead*.

χᾰμ-ευνίς, ίδος, ή, (χαμαί, εὐνή) *a low bed*, *a pallet-bed*.

χᾰμηλός, ή, όν, (χαμαί) *on the ground*. 2. *diminutive*, *trifling*: metaph. *low*, *mean*.

χᾰμόθεν, Adv. (χαμαί) later form for χαμᾶθεν, *from the ground*.

χάμψαι, οἱ, the Egyptian name for *crocodiles*.

χάν, ή, Dor. for χήν, *a goose*.

Χαναναῖος, α, ον, *Canaanitish*, *of Canaan*:—as Subst., Χαναναῖος, ὁ, *a Canaanite*; Χαναναία, ἡ, *a Canaanitish woman*. See Κανανίτης.

χανδάνω, fut. χείσομαι: aor. 2 ἔχᾰδον Ep. χάδον: pf. with pres. sense κέχανδα: Ep. 3 sing. plqpf. with impf. sense κεχάνδει:—*to hold*, *take in*, *comprise*, *contain*, ἓξ μέτρα χάνδανε κρητήρ the bowl *held* six measures: οὐκ ἐδυνήσατο πάσας αἰγιαλὸς νῆας χαδέειν the beach could not *hold* all the ships.

χανδόν, Adv., (χαίνω) *gaping*, *with mouth wide open*: metaph. *greedily*, *eagerly*.

χᾰνεῖν, aor. 2 inf. of χαίνω.

χάνοι [ᾰ], 3 sing. aor. 2 opt. of χαίνω.

ΧΑ'ΟΣ [ᾰ], εος, τό, *Chaos*, *Space*, personified by Hesiod, who represents Chaos as the first state of existence, *the rude unformed mass*. 2. *infinite space*, *the atmosphere*: later *any wide*, *empty space*, *a gulf*, *chasm*.

χᾱός, όν, like χάϊος, *genuine*, *true*, *good*.

χᾰρά, ή, (χαρῆναι) *joy*, *delight*, *pleasure*; χαρᾷ with *joy*: c. gen. *joy in* or *at* a thing.

χάραγμα, ατος, τό, (χᾰράσσω) *any mark imprinted*: χ. ἐχίδνης the serpent's *bite*. 2. *a graven mark* or *line*, *character*, *inscription*.

χᾰράδρα Ion. **χαράδρη**, ή, (χαράσσω) like χείμαρρος, *a mountain-stream*, *torrent*, which cuts itself (χαράσσει) a way down the mountain-side, Lat. *torrens*. II. *the bed of such a stream*, *a deep gully*, *rift*, *ravine*. Hence

χᾰραδραῖος, α, ον, *of* or *from a mountain-torrent*.

χᾰραδριός, ὁ, (χαράδρα) a bird *dwelling in clefts* (χαράδραι) whence its name, *the curlew*.

χᾰραδρόω, f. ώσω: Pass., aor. 1 ἐχαραδρώθην: pf. κεχαράδρωμαι: (χαράδρα):—*to tear up into clefts*:—Pass. *to be broken into clefts by mountain-streams*, *to be full of ravines and gullies*; χώρη κεχαραδρωμένη a country *intersected with ravines*.

χᾰρᾰκόω, f. ώσω, (χάραξ) *to pale round*, *palisade*. *fortify*. II. *to prop with a pole* or *stake*.

χᾰρακτήρ, ῆρος, ὁ, (χαράσσω) *that which is cut in* or *marked*, *the impress* or *stamp* on coins, seals, etc.; χαρακτῆρα ἐπεμβάλλειν τινί to set *a stamp* upon a thing. 2. metaph. *the mark* or *token impressed on* a person or thing, *a characteristic*, *distinctive mark*, *character*; ἀνδρῶν οὐδεὶς χαρακτὴρ ἐμπέφυκε σώματι no *outward mark* has been impressed by nature on the person of men. 3. *a likeness*, *image*, *exact representation*.

χᾰρακτός, ή, όν, verb. Adj. of χαράσσω, *cut in*. *notched*, like a saw.

χᾰράκωμα, ατος, τό, (χαρᾰκόω) *a place paled round* or *palisaded*, *a fortified camp*. II. *a paling*, *palisade*, Lat. *vallum*.

χᾰράκωσις, εως, ή, (χαρᾰκόω) *a fencing with pales*, *a palisading*, *fortifying*.

χάραξ, ᾰκος, ὁ, also ἡ, (χᾰράσσω) *a pointed stake*: *a vine-prop*, *vine-pole*. II. *a pale* used in fortifying the rampart of a camp, Lat. *vallus*: hence 2.

collectively, *a place paled in, a fortified camp*, Lat. *vallum.*

ΧΑ'ΡΑ'ΣΣΩ Att. -ττω: f. ξω: aor. 1 ἐχάραξα: Pass., aor. 1 ἐχαράχθην: pf. κεχάραγμαι:—*to make sharp* or *pointed, sharpen*: Pass. *to be notched* or *jagged*: of eyes, *to sparkle*. 2. metaph. *to exasperate, irritate, provoke*:—Pass. *to be irritated, exasperated.* II. *to cut by furrows, furrow, plough.* III. *to engrave, inscribe.*

χᾰρῆναι, aor. 1 inf. pass. of χαίρω.

χᾰρήσομαι, later fut of χαίρω.

χᾰρῐ-δώτης, ου, ὁ, (χάρις, δίδωμι) *he that gives joy* or *grace.*

χᾰρίεις, χαρίεσσα, χαρίεν, gen. εντος: (χάρις):—*graceful, pleasing, agreeable, lovely, pretty, elegant.* II. in Att., χαρίεις was often used of persons, *graceful, elegant, accomplished, refined*; οἱ χαρίεντες *men of taste and refinement, men of education.* III. the neut. was used in Att. as Adv., when it was written χάριεν. Hence

χᾰριεντίζομαι, f. -ίσομαι Att. -ιοῦμαι: Dep.:—*to act* or *speak with grace* or *elegance*: *to be witty, to jest*; σπουδῇ χαριεντίζεσθαι *to jest* in earnest.

χᾰριέντως, Adv. of χαρίεις, *gracefully, elegantly*: *neatly, cleverly.* 2. *kindly, courteously.*

χᾰρι-εργός, όν, (χαίρω, ἔργον) *delighting in the arts*, epith. of Minerva.

χᾰρίζομαι: fut. med. -ίσομαι Att. -ιοῦμαι, also f. pass. -ισθήσομαι: aor. 1 ἐχαρισάμην and ἐχαρίσθην: pf. κεχάρισμαι both in act. and pass. sense: Dep.: (χάρις):—*to shew favour* or *kindness, to oblige* or *gratify* a person, c. dat.: absol. *to be pleasing* or *agreeable, court favour.* 2. in Att. *to gratify* or *indulge* a passion, like Lat. *indulgere*; χαρίζεσθαι τῷ σώματι *to indulge one's* body. II. c. acc. rei, *to offer willingly, offer as a free gift, give freely*: c. gen. *to give freely of* a thing; χαρίζεσθαι ἀλλοτρίων *to give freely of* what does not belong to one; ταμίη χαριζομένη παρεόντων the housekeeper *giving freely of* the stores in hand. III. in pass. sense, *to be pleasing, agreeable, to be granted as a favour*; τοῖσι Εὐβοέεσσι ἐκεχάριστο *it was done to please* the Euboeans. 2. pf. part. κεχαρισμένος, *pleasing, acceptable, welcome*; ἐμῷ κεχαρισμένε θυμῷ *most welcome* to my heart; κεχαρισμένος ἦλθεν he came *wished for*, was *welcome.*

χαριξῆ, Dor. for χαρίσει, 2 sing. fut. of χαρίζομαι.

χάρις [ᾰ], ἡ, gen. χάριτος: acc. χάριν or χάριτα: plur. χάριτες, dat. pl. χάρισι Ep. χαρίτεσσι poët. also χάρισσι: (χαίρω):—*favour, grace*, Lat. *gratia*: I. *outward grace, grace, loveliness*; χάριν καταχεύαί τινι to shed *grace* over one. 2. of things, *a grace, a charm.* II. *grace* or *favour felt*, either, 1. by the Doer, *kindness, good-will*: or, 2. by the Receiver, *the sense of favour received, thanks, gratitude*, esp. in phrases χάριν εἰδέναι to feel *gratitude*; χάριν ὀφείλειν to owe *a debt of gratitude*, be beholden; χάριν or χάριτα καταθέσθαι τινί to lay up a store of *gratitude* with a person, i. e. earn his *thanks*; χάριν λαμβάνειν to receive *thanks.* 3. *influence*, as opp. to force, Lat. *gratia*; χάριτι πλεῖον ἢ φόβῳ more *by favour* than fear. III. *a favour done, a grace, kindness, boon*; χάριν φέρειν τινί to confer *a favour* on one: hence in phrases, χάριν θέσθαι, νέμειν, δρᾶσαι to confer *a grace, favour, kindness.* IV. *a gratification, delight*; φόρμιγγος from the harp. 2. δαιμόνων χάρις *homage* or *worship due* to the gods: *an offering, gift*; εὐκταία χάρις *a gift* in consequence of a vow. V. special usages: acc. sing. absol. χάριν, c. gen., *in* anyone's *favour, for* his *pleasure, for* his *sake*, χάριν Ἕκτορος *for the sake of* Hector: also with the Artic., τὴν Ἀθηναίων χάριν *for the sake of* the Athenians:—it soon became used as a Prep., c. gen., = ἕνεκα, Lat. *gratia, causa, for the sake, in behalf of, on account of*: so too, ἐμὴν χάριν, σὴν χάριν for my, thy *pleasure* or *sake*, Lat. *mea, tua gratia.* 2. εἰς χάριν τινός *to do* one *a pleasure*; πρὸς χάριν λέγειν τινί to speak to one *for the sake of pleasing* him; but, πρὸς χάριν ἐμᾶς σαρκός *for the sake* of my flesh, i. e. *of* devouring it. 3. ἐν χάριτι κρίνειν τινά to decide *from partiality to* one. 4. διὰ χαρίτων εἶναι or γίγνεσθαί τινα to be *on terms of friendship* or *mutual favour* with one. VI. in Mythology, αἱ Χάριτες *the Charités* or *Graces*, were *the goddesses who confer all grace*, even the favour of Victory in the games: three in number, *Aglaïa, Euphrosyne, Thalia.*

χάρισμα, ατος, τό, (χᾰρίζομαι) *a grace, favour*: *a free gift, grace.*

χᾰρίσσασθαι, Ep. aor. 1 med. inf. of χαρίζομαι.

χᾰριστήριος, ον, (χαρίζομαι) *in token of thanksgiving.* II. as Subst., χαριστήριον, τό, *a grace, gift.* 2. τὰ χαριστήρια (sub. ἱερά), *thank-offerings.*

χᾰρῖτία, ἡ, (χάρις) *a jest, joke.*

χᾰρῐτο-βλέφαρος, ον, (Χάρις, βλέφαρον) *with eyelids like the Graces.*

χᾰρῐτο-γλωσσέω Att. -ττέω, f. ήσω, (χάρις, γλῶσσα) *to speak to please, gloze with the tongue.*

χᾰρῐτόω, f. ώσω, (χάρις) *to shew favour* or *grace to* anyone:—Pass. *to be highly favoured.*

χᾰρῐτ-ώπης, ες, (χάρις, ὤψ) *graceful of aspect*: fem. χαριτῶπις, ιδος.

χάρμα, ατος, τό, (χαίρω) *a source of joy, a joy*: *joy, delight.*

χάρμη, ἡ, (χαίρω) = χάρμα, *joy*: *the joy of battle, battle.*

χαρμονή, ἡ, (χάρμα) *joy, delight*: in pl. *joys, delights.*

χαρμόσῠνος, η, ον, (χάρμη) *joyful, glad*; χαρμόσυνα ποιεῖν to make *rejoicings.*

χαρμό-φρων, ονος, ὁ, ἡ, (χάρμα, φρήν) *gladdening the heart* or *of joyous heart.*

χᾰρο-ποιός, όν, (χαρά, ποιέω) *causing joy, gladdening.*

χᾰρ-οπός, ή, όν, also ός, όν, (χαρά, ὤψ) *glad-eyed, bright-eyed*: properly it only implied *brightness* and *fierceness*: later, it came to mean *light blue* or *gray*, such like γλαυκός.

χαρτάριον, *τό*, Dim. of *χάρτης*.

χάρτης, *ου*, *ὁ*, (*χαράσσω*) Lat. *charta*, *a leaf of paper*, made from the separated layers of the papyrus.

χαρτός, *ή*, *όν*, verb. Adj. of *χαίρω*, *delightful*, *gladdening*, *cheerful*.

Χάρυβδις, *εως* Ion. *ιος*, *ἡ*, *Charybdis*, a dangerous whirlpool on the coast of Sicily, opposite the Italian rock Scylla: then generally *a whirlpool*, *gulf*: metaph. of *a greedy rapacious person*, like Lat. *barathrum*.

Χάρων [ᾰ], *ωνος*, *ὁ*, *Charon*, the ferryman of the Styx, so called from his *bright fierce eyes*. Cp. *χάροπο*

χασκάζω, f. *άσω*, Frequentat. of *χάσκω*, c. acc., *to keep yawning* or *gaping at* or *for* a thing.

χάσκω, *ἔχασκον*, *to gape*, *yawn*, used as pres. and impf. of *χαίνω*: see *χαίνω*.

χάσμα, *ατος*, *τό*, (*χαίνω*) *a yawning hollow*, *a chasm*, *gulf*. II. *the open mouth*, like Lat. *rictus*. III. *any wide space* or *expanse*.

χασμάομαι, f. *-ήσομαι*, Dep. (*χαίνω*) *to yawn*, *gape wide*, of the mouth.

χασμέομαι, Ion. for *χασμάομαι*.

χασμεύμενος, Dor. pres. part. of *χασμάομαι*.

χάσμημα, *ατος*, *τό*, (*χασμάομαι*) *a wide yawn*, *gape*, Lat. *rictus*.

χασσάμενος, Ep. aor. 1 med. part. of *χάζομαι*.

χάσσατο, Ep. 3 sing. aor. 1 med. of *χάζομαι*.

ΧΑ˘ΤΕ´Ω, f. *ήσω*, *to long*, *desire*, *wish much* to do a thing, c. inf.: absol. *to wish*, *desire*. II. c. gen. *to crave*, *want*, *have need of* a thing.

χᾰτίζω, f. *ίσω*, like *χατέω*, *to long for*, *desire*, *crave*: *to want*, *have need of*; *χατίζειν ἔργοιο to want* or *be without* work: absol. in part., *one who is in want*, *a needy*, *poor person*.

χᾰτίς, *ἡ*, and **χάτος**, *εος*, *τό*, *want*, *need*, = *χητίς*, *χῆτος*.

χαυλι-όδους, *-όδοντος*, *ὁ*, *ἡ*, (*χαύλιος*, *ὀδούς*) *with outstanding* or *projecting teeth*. II. *χαυλιόδοντες ὀδόντες* of the crocodile's teeth, *outstanding*, *tusky*: absol., *χαυλιόδοντες sharp*, *jagged teeth*.

χαυνο-πολίτης, *ου*, *ὁ*, (*χαῦνος*, *πολίτης*) *an open-mouthed citizen*, *a gaping cit*. [ῑ]

χαυνό-πρωκτος, *ον*, (*χαῦνος*, *πρωκτός*) *wide-breeched*.

χαῦνος, *η*, *ον*, and *ος*, *ον*, (*χαίνω*) *gaping*: *flaccid*, *loose*, *porous*. II. metaph. *loose*, *foolish*, *silly*, *vain*. Hence

χαυνότης, *ητος*, *ἡ*, *looseness*, *porousness*. II. metaph. *folly*, *vanity*.

χαύνωσις, *εως*, *ἡ*, (*χαυνόω*) *a making loose* or *slack*. II. metaph. *making a thing light*, *weakening its force*.

χέε, **χέεν**, Ep. 3 sing. impf. or aor. 1 of *χέω*.

χεζητιάω, like *χεσείω*, Desiderat. of *χέζω*, *to wish to ease oneself*.

ΧΕ´ΖΩ: f. *χεσοῦμαι*: pf. *κέχοδα*: aor. 1 *ἔχεσα*: aor. 2 *ἔχεσον*: pf. pass. *κέχεσμαι*:—*to ease oneself*:—Pass., *σπέλεθος ἀρτίως κεχεσμένος* dung just *dropt*.

ΧΕΙΑ´ Ion. **χειή**, *ἡ*, *a hole*, esp. of serpents.

χείλευς, Dor. for *χείλεος*, gen. of *χεῖλος*.

χειλο-ποτέω, f. *ήσω*, (*χεῖλος*, *πίνω*) *to drink with the lips only*, *to sip*.

ΧΕΙ˜ΛΟΣ, *εος*, *τό*: plur., gen. *χειλέων* contr. *ῶν*; dat. *χείλεσι* Ep. *-εσσι*:—*a lip*: proverb., *χείλεσι γελᾶν* to laugh *with the lips* (only); *χείλεα μέν τ' ἐδίην'*, *ὑπερῴην δ' οὐκ ἐδίηνεν it* wetted *the lips*, but the palate it wetted not 2. of beasts, *the snout*, *muzzle*: of birds, *a bill*, *beak*. II. metaph. of things, *the edge*, *brink*, *brim*, *rim*, esp. of a river or a cup.

χεῖμα, *ατος*, *τό*, *winter-weather*, *cold*, *frost*, Lat. *hiems*: *winter*, as a season of the year, opp. to *θέρος*: *χεῖμα* absol. in acc., *in winter*. II. *a storm*: metaph. *a storm of passion*.

χειμάδιον [ᾰ], *τό*, *a winter-dwelling*, *winter-quarters*; *χειμαδίῳ χρῆσθαι Λήμνῳ* to fix upon Lemnos as *winter quarters*. From

χειμάζω, f. *άσω*: (*χεῖμα*): I. transit. *to expose to the winter*, *set in the frost* or *cold*: Pass. *to be exposed to the frost* or *cold*: *live through the winter*. II. intr. *to pass the winter*: *to go into winter quarters*, *to winter*, Lat. *hiemare*. III. *to raise a storm* or *tempest*: metaph. *to trouble*, *afflict*. 2. absol. *χειμάζει* (sc. *ὁ θεός*), *there is a storm*, like *ὕει*, *νίφει*, etc.; *ἐχείμαζε ἡμέρας τρεῖς the storm lasted* three days. 3. Pass. *to be driven by a storm*, *suffer from it*: metaph. *to be tempest-tost*, *distressed*, esp. of the state: *to be distracted*, *overwhelmed by suffering*.

χειμαίνω, f. *ᾰνῶ*, (*χεῖμα*) *distress by a storm* or *tempest*:—Pass. *to be driven by a storm*, *be tempest-tost*. II. intr. *to be stormy*.

χείμᾰρος, *ὁ*, (*χεῖμα*) *a plug in a ship's bottom*, drawn out when the ship was brought on land, to let out the bilge-water.

χειμάρ-ροος, *ον*, Att. contr. **-ρους**, *ουν*: (*χεῖμα*, *ῥέω*):—*winter-flowing*, *swoln in winter*; *χειμάρροος ποταμός a mountain-stream* or *torrent swoln by rain and melted snow*. 2. as Subst., *χειμάρρους*, *ὁ*, *a water-drain*, *conduit*. II. *wintry*, *stormy*.

χείμαρρος or **χειμάρρος**, *ον*, poët. for *χειμάρροος*.

χειμᾰσία Ion. *-ίη*, *ἡ*, (*χειμάζω*) *a passing the winter*, *wintering*: *winter-quarters*.

χειμερίζω, f. *ίσω* Att. *ιῶ*, (*χεῖμα*) *to pass the winter*, *winter*.

χειμερῑνός, *ή*, *όν*, (*χεῖμα*) *of* or *in winter*, *in winter-time*, *wintry*, *stormy*; *χειμερινὸν χωρίον a wintry*, *bleak* place. See *χειμέριος*.

χειμέριος, *α*, *ον*, Att. also *ος*, *ον*: (*χεῖμα*):—*in*, *of*, *belonging to winter*, *wintry*; *ὥρη χειμερίη the winter-*season; *μῆνες χειμεριώτατοι the most wintry*, i.e. *most stormy*, months; *ἀκτὰ χειμερία κυματοπλήξ* a shore lashed by the waves *of winter*: metaph., *χειμερία λύπη raging* pain.—Generally, *χειμέριος* and *χειμερινός* are distinguished thus:—*χειμέριος wintry*, *like winter*, *stormy*; *χειμερινός wintry*, *in winter-time*.

χειμο-θνής, *ῆτος*, *ὁ*, *ἡ*, (*χεῖμα*, *θνήσκω*) *frozen to death*.

χειμών, *ῶνος*, *ὁ*, (*χεῖμα*) *winter*, *the season of winter*; *τὸν χειμῶνα during winter*; *χειμῶνος in winter*.

time. II. wintry weather: a st^ m, tempest; χειμὼν νοτερός a storm of rain. 2. m taph. storm, fury: also great distress or suffering.

χειμωνο-τύπος, ον, (χειμών, τύπτω) b ing tempestuously.

ΧΕΙΡ, ἡ, gen. χειρός: plur. χεῖρες, χειρῶν, χερσί: Ion. decl., χείρ, χερός, χερί, χέρα, χέρες, etc.: but gen. and dat. dual are χεροῖν (rarely χειροῖν) even in Att.: Ep. dat. pl. χείρεσι and χείρεσσι:—the hand, or rather the hand and arm, the arm; ἄκρα χείρ the hand; χεὶρ σιδηρᾶ an iron hand, i. e. a grappling-iron, grapnel. 2. χείρ is often joined with δεξιός and ἀριστερός, to mark the side on which a thing is; see ἀριστερός, δεξιός. 3. to denote act or deed, as opp. to mere words; ἔπεσιν καὶ χερσὶν ἀρήξειν to assist with word and deed; προσφέρειν χεῖρας to apply force; of deeds of violence, χειρῶν αρχειν to begin the fray. 4. like Lat. ..anus, a number or body of men, a band: the hand, skill of an artist or workman: also his handywork. II. special usages: χειρὸς ἔχειν τινά to have, hold one by the hand; χεῖρας ἀνασχεῖν θεοῖς to raise one's hands to the gods in prayer; χεῖρας ὀρέξαι to stretch or spread the arms in token of entreaty. 2. ἄγεσθαί τι ἐς χεῖρας to take a thing in hand; ἐν χερσί, μετὰ or διὰ χεῖρας ἔχειν τι to have a thing in hand, be engaged in it. 3. ἐν χερί, ἐν χερσί, in one's hand or hands, and so in one's power: but also in warlike sense, ἐν χερσί in the fray, in close fight. Lat. cominus. 4. εἰς χεῖρας ἐλθεῖν to fall into anyone's hands or power, but also to come to blows. 5. ἐκ χειρός, out of hand, off hand; ἀπὸ χειρὸς λογίσασθαι to reckon off hand, roughly. 6. πρὸ χειρῶν at hand, in readiness. 7. ὑπὸ χειρός or χειρῶν, under the hands, under the power; cp. ὑποχείριος.

χειρ-άγρα, ἡ, (χείρ, ἄγρα) gout in the hand; as ποδάγρα in the feet.

χειρᾰγωγέω, f. ήσω, to lead by the hand. From

χειρ-ᾰγωγός, όν, (χείρ, ἄγω) leading by the hand: as Subst., χειραγωγός, ὁ, one that leads by the hand

χειρ-απτάζω, f. άσω, (χείρ, ἅπτω) to touch with the hand, take in hand, handle.

χείρεσι, χείρεσσι, Ep. dat. pl. of χείρ.

χειρῐδωτός, όν, (χείρ) having sleeves, sleeved, of the χιτών or tunic: the χιτών without sleeves was called ἐξωμίς.

χείριος, α, ον, (χείρ) in the hands, in the power of, subject, captive.

χειρίς, ίδος, ἡ, (χείρ) a covering for the hand, a glove: also a covering for the arm, a sleeve.

χείριστος, η, ον, irreg. Sup. of χείρων, worst, Lat. pessimus: οἱ χείριστοι men of lowest degree.

χειρο-βολέω, f. ήσω, (χείρ, βαλεῖν) to throw with the hand.

χειρό-γρᾰφος, ον, (χειρ, γράφω) written with the hand, in handwriting:—as Subst., χειρόγραφον, τό, a handwriting, written decree.

χειρο-δάϊκτος, ον, (χείρ, δαΐζω) slain by the hand.

χειρό-δεικτος, ον, (δείκνυμι) pointed out by the hand, Lat. digito monstratus: manifest, confessed.

χειρο-δίκης, ου, ὁ, (χείρ, δίκη) one who asserts his right by force of hands, who uses the right of might. [ῐ]

χειρο-δράκων, οντος, ὁ, (χείρ, δράκων) with serpent-hands or arms. [ᾰ]

χειρο-ήθης, ες, (χείρ, ἦθος) accustomed to the hand manageable, esp. of animals, tame, Lat. mansuetus: used or habituated to a thing: submissive, obedient.

χειρό-μακτρον, τό, (χείρ, μάσσω) a cloth for wiping the hands, a towel, napkin, Lat. mantile: the Scythians used scalps as χειρόμακτρα.

χειρομᾰχέω, f. ήσω, to fight with the hands. From

χειρο-μάχος, ον, (χείρ, μάχομαι) fighting with the hand.

χειρο-μύλη, ἡ, (χείρ, μύλη) a hand-mill. [ῠ]

χειρονομέω, f. ήσω, (χειρονόμος) to move the hands to a certain time or order; σκέλεσι χειρονομεῖν to gesticulate with one's legs as though with one's arms. Hence

χειρονομία, ἡ, measured motion of the hands, gesticulation.

χειρο-νόμος, ον, (νέμω) moving the hands regularly, gesticulating: as Subst., χειρονόμος, ὁ, Lat. pantomimus, a pantomimic performer.

χειρόνως, Adv. of χείρων, worse.

χειρο-πληθής, ές, (χείρ, πίμπλημι) filling the hand, as large as can be held in the hand.

χειρο-ποιέομαι, f. ήσομαι, Dep. to make or do by hand. Hence

χειροποίητος, ον, made by hand, artificial: made on purpose.

χειρό-σοφος, ον, (χείρ, σοφός) skilled with the hands: hence = χειρονόμος.

χειρο-τένων, οντος, ὁ, ἡ, (χείρ, τείνω) with outstretched arms, of the crab.

χειρότερος, α, ον, poët. for χείρων, worse.

χειρο-τέχνης, ου, ὁ, (χείρ, τέχνη) a handicraftsman, artisan, mechanic; χειροτέχνης ἰατορίας a chirurgeon, surgeon. Hence

χειροτεχνία, ἡ, handicraft, art.

χειροτεχνικός, ή, όν, (χειροτέχνης) of or for handicraft or a handicraftsman, skilful, mechanical. Adv. -κῶς.

χειροτονέω, f. ήσω, (χειροτόνος) to stretch out the hand, esp. to give one's vote in the Athenian ἐκκλησία. II. c. acc. to vote for, elect:—Pass. to be chosen by vote, opp. to λαγχάνειν κλήρου to be chosen by lot: c. acc. rei, to vote for a thing. 2. to choose, appoint, ordain. Hence

χειροτονητέον, verb. Adj. one must vote.

χειροτονητός, ή, όν, verb. Adj. of χειροτονέω, elected by show of hands; ἀρχὴ χειροτονητή an elective magistracy.

χειροτονία, ἡ, (χειροτονέω) a stretching out of hands, at Athens, a voting or electing by show of hands; χειροτονία τοῦ δήμου election by the people. II. a vote, Lat. suffragium: also collectively, the votes.

χειρο-τόνος, ον, (χείρ, τείνω) *stretching out the hands; of prayers, offered with outstretched hands.*

χειρο-τύπης, ές, (χείρ, τυπεῖν) *striking with the hands.*

χειρουργέω, f. ήσω, (χειρουργός) *to do with the hands, execute; to commit acts of violence.* Hence

χειρουργία, ἡ, *a working by hand, practice of a handicraft* or *art.* II. *a trade, business.*

χειρ-ουργός, όν, (χείρ, *ἔργω) *working* or *doing by hand, practising a handicraft* or *art.* 2. as Subst., χειρουργός, ὁ, *a chirurgeon, surgeon.*

χειρόω, f. ώσω: Med., f. χειρώσομαι: aor. 1 ἐχειρωσάμην: Pass., fut. χειρωθήσομαι: aor. 1 ἐχειρώθην: pf. κεχείρωμαι: (χείρ):—*to take in hand, handle: to get into one's hands, to master, subdue, take possession of: to take prisoner*:—Pass. χειροῦμαι, *to be mastered, subdued, led captive, taken prisoner.* Hence

χείρωμα, ατος, τό, *that which is done by hand; τυμβοχόα χειρώματα offerings* to the dead poured *by one's own hand.* II. *that which is brought into one's hands* or *under one's power, a conquest.* 2. *a deed of violence.*

χείρων, ὁ, ἡ, neut. ον; gen. ονος: plur., nom. and acc., χείρονες, χείρονας contr. χείρους, neut. χείρονα contr. χείρω; dat. χείροσι poët. χειρόνεσσι: Ep. χερείων, ον: Dor. χερήων: poët. also χειρότερος, χερειότερος: irreg. Comp. of κακός (formed from *χέρης):—*worse, meaner, inferior:* the comparative force sometimes almost disappears, esp. with a negat., as, οὔ τι χέρειον ἐν ὥρῃ δεῖπνον ἑλέσθαι, 'tis not *ill* to take one's meal in season; so, οὐ χεῖρόν [ἐστι] it is *well:* of persons, ὁ χείρων *one of lower degree;* οἱ χείρονες *men of lower degree:*—ἐπὶ τὸ χεῖρον τρέπεσθαι to fall off. II. χεῖρον, as Adv., *worse.*—See χείριστος.

Χείρων, ωνος, ὁ, *Cheiron,* one of the Centaurs, teacher of Aesculapius, Achilles, Jason, etc.; famous for his skill in *surgery* (whence his name, cf. χειρουργός).

χειρ-ῶναξ, ακτος, ὁ, (χείρ, ἄναξ) *one who is master of his hand, a handicraftsman, artisan, mechanic,* like κώπης ἄναξ: also as Adj., πᾶς ὁ χειρῶναξ λεώς all the *mechanic* sort. Hence

χειρ-ωναξία Ion. -ίη, ἡ, *skill in workmanship, handicraft, trade.*

Χειρωνίς, ίδος, fem. Adj. *of Cheiron:* as Subst. (sub. βίβλος) *a book on surgery.*

χειρωτός, ή, όν, verb. Adj. of χειρόω, *subdued: to be subdued.*

χείσομαι, fut. of χανδάνω.

χείω, Ep. for χέω, *to pour.*

χελῖδοῖ, irreg. voc. of χελιδών, as if from χελιδώ.

χελῖδονίζω, f. ίσω Att. ιῶ, (χελιδών) *to twitter like a swallow: to speak unintelligibly, to speak a foreign language.*

χελῖδόνιον, τό, (χελιδών) *swallow-wort, celandine,* of which there were two kinds, χελιδόνιον κυάνεον (or γλαυκόν) and χλωρόν. Properly neut. of

χελῖδόνιος, α, ον, (χελιδών) *of the swallow, like the swallow: coloured like the swallow's throat, russet brown.*

χελῖδόνισμα, ατος, τό, (χελιδονίζω) *the swallow-song,* an old popular song at the return of the swallows.

χελῖδών, όνος, ἡ: irreg. vocat. χελιδοῖ (as if from χελιδώ):—*the swallow,* Lat. *hirundo.* The twittering of the swallow was a proverbial expression for foreign or barbarous speech; for χελιδόνων μουσεῖα, see μουσεῖον: proverb., μία χελιδὼν ἔαρ οὐ ποιεῖ one *swallow* does not make a summer. II. *the frog in the hollow of a horse's foot.*

χελύνη [ῡ], ἡ, (χεῖλος) *the lip;* χελύνην ἐσθίειν ὑπ' ὀργῆς to bite *the lip* from passion. II. Aeol. for χελώνη.

ΧΕ'ΛΥ˘Σ, ῠος, ἡ, *a tortoise,* Lat. *testūdo:* Mercury made the first lyre by stretching strings on its shell: hence 2. *the shell* or *lyre* itself, Lat. *testudo.* II. *the arched breast, the chest.*

χελώνη, ἡ, (χέλυς) *a tortoise:* proverb., ἰὼ χελῶναι μακάριαι τοῦ δέρματος oh *tortoises,* happy in your thick hides! 2. *the shell of the tortoise.* II. *the lyre:* see χέλυς. III. as a military term, *a pent-house formed of shields overlapping each other as in a tortoise's back,* the Roman *testudo,* used by storming parties in approaching a city's walls: hence *a shed* or *moveable roof* for protecting besiegers.

χένας, poët. for χῆνας, acc. pl. of χήν.

χέννιον, τό, a kind of *quail.*

χερ-άγρα, ἡ, = χειράγρα.

ΧΕ'ΡΑ˘ΔΟΣ, τό, *the gravel* and *silt* brought down by rivers, *shingle.*

ΧΕΡΑ'Σ, άδος, ἡ, doubtful form of χέραδος.

χέρεια, see χέρης.

χερειότερος, α, ον, Ep. Comp. for χερείων.

χερείων, ὁ, ἡ, neut. χέρειον, poët. for χείρων, *worse.*

χέρεσσι, poët. for χερσί, dat. pl. of χείρ.

ΧΕ'ΡΗΣ, an obsol. Adj. from which the irreg. Comparatives χείρων and χερείων are formed, used in dat. χέρηι; acc. χέρηα; nom. pl. χέρηες; acc. neut. χέρηα or χέρεια:—χέρης itself has a comparative sense, *weaker, worse, inferior.*

χερήων, ον, gen. ονος, Dor. for χερείων.

χερῐ-άρης, ου, ὁ, (χείρ, ἀρᾰρεῖν) *fitting with the hand.*

χερῐ-φῡρής, ές, gen. έος, (χείρ, φύρω) *mixed* or *kneaded by hand.*

χερμάδιον, τό, = χερμάς, properly neut. of χερμάδιος.

χερμάδιος, ον, *of the size of a large stone, fit for throwing.* [ᾰ] From

χερμάς, άδος, ἡ, *a stone* or *large pebble,* for throwing or slinging, *a sling-stone.* (Deriv. doubtful: either from χέραδος; or from χείρ, *a stone that can be grasped in the hand.*)

χερμαστήρ, ῆρος, ὁ, (χερμας) *a slinger:* as masc. Adj., χειμαστὴρ ῥινός the leather *of a sling.*

χέρνης, ητος, ὁ, (χείρ) *one who lives by the work of his hands, a day-labourer: a poor, needy man.* as Adj., *poor, needy*

χερνήτης, ου, ὁ, = χέρνης.

χερνῆτις, ιδος, fem. of χερνήτης, *a workwoman, a woman that works for her daily bread.*

χερ-νῐβεῖον and **χέρ-νῐβον**, τό, (χείρ, νίζω) *a vessel for water to wash the hands, a hand-basin.*

χερνίπτομαι, f. ψομαι, Med. *to wash one's hands with holy water: to sprinkle* or *purify with holy water*, Lat. *lustrare.* From

χέρ-νιψ, ῐβος, ἡ, (χείρ, νίζω) *holy water to wash* or *sprinkle the hands* before a sacrifice. II. plur. χέρνιβες, *purifications with holy water; εἴργεσθαι χερνίβων* to be excluded from *such purifications*, as was done with those who were defiled by bloodshed; χερνίβων κοινωνός a partaker *in the purifications by lustral water*, i. e. an inmate of the same house.

χερνίψαντο, Ep. 3 pl. aor. 1 of χερνίπτομαι.

χερο-μῠσής, ές, (χείρ, μύσος) *hand-defiling.*

χερό-πληκτος, ον, (χείρ, πλήσσω) *stricken by* or *with the hand.*

χερός, Ion. and poët. gen. of χείρ.

χερρό-νησος, ἡ, Att. for χερσόνησος. For all words formed from it, see under χερσ–.

χέρρος, Att. for χέρσος.

χερσαῖος, α, ον, also ος, ον, (χέρσος) *from* or *of dry land, living* or *found on dry land; ὄρνιθες χερσαῖοι land*-fowl, opp. to λιμναῖοι *sea*-fowl: also of landsmen as opp. to seamen; metaph., χερσαῖον κῦμα στρατοῦ the *land* wave of an army.

χερσεύω, f. σω, (χέρσος) *to lie waste* or *barren.*

χερσόθεν, Adv. (χέρσος) *from dry land: from the earth* or *ground.*

χερσόθῐ, Adv. (χέρσος) *on dry land.*

χέρσονδε, Adv. (χέρσος) *to* or *on dry land.*

χερσονησίτης Att. χερρον–, ου, ὁ, (Χερσόνησος) *a dweller in the Chersonese.*

χερσονησο-ειδής Att. χερρον–, ές, (χερσόνησος, εἶδος) *like a peninsula, peninsular.*

χερσό-νησος Att. χερρόν–, ἡ, (χέρσος, νῆσος) *a land-island*, i. e. *a peninsula:* the long slip of Thrace that runs along the Hellespont was specially called *The Chersonese* or *Peninsula:* the Crimea was also called *the Tauric Chersonese.*

χερσονησ-ώδης Att. χερρον–, ες, contr. for χερσονησοειδής.

ΧΕ'ΡΣΟΣ Att. χέρρος, ἡ, *dry land, land*, as opp. to water, esp. as opp. to the sea; χέρσον ἱκέσθαι to reach *the land.* II. as Adj., χέρσος, ον, *dry, firm*, of land; χέρσος Εὐρώπα *the mainland* of Europe. 2. *dry, barren, waste, hardened:* χέρσα *waste places.* 3. c. gen. *barren* or *destitute of.*

χερύδριον, τό, Dim. of χείρ, *a little hand* or *arm.*

χεσείω, Desiderat. of χέσω, *to want to ease oneself.*

χεῦαι, χεῦαν, χεῦε, Ep. inf., 3 plur., and 3 sing. aor. 1 of χέω.

χεῦμα, ατος, τό, (χέω) *that which is poured: a stream.* II. *that into which water is poured, a basin, bowl.*

χεύομεν, Ep. for χέωμεν, 1 pl. aor. 1 subj. of χέω.

χεύω, Ep. fut. and aor. 1 subj. of χέω.

ΧΕ'Ω, fut. χεῶ Ep. χεύω: aor. 1 ἔχεα Ep. ἔχευα or χεῦα; imperat. χέον Ep. χεῦον; subj. χέω Ep. χεύω, Ep. 1 pl. χεύομεν; inf. χέαι Ep. χεῦαι, part. χέας Ep. χεύας: Ep. aor. 1 med. ἐχευάμην: Pass., f. χῠθήσομαι: aor. 1 ἐχύθην [ῠ]: pf. κεχύμαι [ῠ]: 3 sing. Ep. plqpf. κέχῠτο: also Ep. aor. 2 ἐχύμην [ῠ], used in 3 sing. ἔχυτο, χύτο, 3 pl. ἔχυντο, χύντο, part. χύμενος:—*to pour:* of liquids, *to pour out, shed, spill:*—Pass. *to be poured forth, flow, stream, gush forth.* 2. *to become liquid, melt, dissolve:* so of the ground after rain, *to be softened, relaxed:*—Med. *to pour for oneself*, esp. of drink-offerings to the dead: c. acc. cognato, χοὴν χεῖσθαι νεκύεσσι *to pour forth* a libation to the dead. II. of solids, *to pour or shoot out, shed, scatter:* also, like χόω, *to throw up* earth, so as to form a mound; τύμβον χέειν *to raise* a mound. 2. χέειν δοῦρα *to pour* or *shower* spears. 3. *to let fall* or *drop:*—Pass. *to be thrown* or *heaped up together:* of men, *to pour or stream in a dense mass.* III. metaph. of sounds, *to pour, let stream* or *flow.* 2. ἀχλὺν κατ' ὀφθαλμῶν χέαι *to shed* darkness over the eyes; so, χέειν ἠέρα *to shed* a mist *abroad:*—Pass. *to be spread* or *flung around; ἀμφὶ δέ οἱ θάνατος χύτο* death *was shed* or *spread* around him; πάλιν χύτο ἀήρ the mist *dissolved* or *vanished.* 3. ἀμφ' αὐτῷ χυμένη *throwing herself* around him; in pf. pass. part., κεχυμένος εἴς τι *given up* to a thing.

χηλ-αργός Dor. **χᾱλ–**, ον, (χηλή, ἀργός) *with fleet hoofs;* χηλαργοὶ ἅμιλλαι the racing *of fleet horses.*

χηλευτός, ή, όν, verb. Adj. *netted, plaited.* From

χηλεύω, f. σω, (χηλή) *to net, plait.*

ΧΗΛΗ', ἡ, *a horse's hoof:* also *a cloven hoof*, as of an ox: pl. χηλαί also of *bird's talons*, of *a wolf's claws*, of *a crab's claws.* II. *a sea-bank, sea-wall* or *breakwater*, Lat. *moles*, so called from its stretching out *like a claw:* also *a projecting ridge of rocks* forming a natural mole.

χηλῑνός, ή, όν, = χηλευτός.

ΧΗΛΟ'Σ, οῦ, ὁ, *a large chest, coffer* or *strong box.*

ΧΗ'Ν, ὁ and ἡ, gen. χηνός: irreg. acc. plur. χένας: Dor. χάν: (χαίνω, κέχηνα):—*a gander, goose*, named *from its wide bill*, Lat. *anser.*

χην-ᾰλώπηξ, εκος, ὁ, (χήν, ἀλώπηξ) *the fox-goose*, an Egyptian species, living in holes, like our sheldrake,

χήνειος, α, ον, (χήν) *of* or *belonging to a goose, like a goose*, Lat. *anserinus.*

χήνεος, η, ον, Ion. for χήνειος.

χηνίσκος, ὁ, (χήν) *the end of a ship's stern which turned up like a goose's neck.*

χήρα Ion. **χήρη**, ἡ, see χῆρος.

ΧΗΡΑ'ΜΒΗ, ἡ, a kind of *muscle.*

χηρᾰμο-δύτης, ου, ὁ, (χηραμός, δύω) *one who creeps into holes.* [ῡ metri grat.]

ΧΗΡΑ'ΜΟ'Σ, ὁ, *a hole, cleft, gap, hollow.*

χήρατο, Ep. 3 sing. aor. 1 med. of χαίρω.

χηρεία, ἡ, (χηρεύω) *widowhood, widowed estate.*

χήρειος, α, ον, (χῆρος) *widowed.*

χηρεύω, f. σω, (χῆρος) intr. *to be bereaved, be destitute*: c. gen., νῆσος ἀνδρῶν χηρεύει the island is *destitute* of men: *to be bereaved of a husband* or *wife, to be widowed, be a widower* or *widow*: hence *to live in solitude.* II. transit. *to keep in widowhood, keep aloof* or *apart.*

χηρήιος, η, ον, Ion. for χήρειος.

χῆρος, α, ον, *bereaved, bereft of*, c. gen.: absol. *bereft of a husband* or *wife, widowed.* II. as Subst., χήρα Ion. χήρη, ἡ, *a widow*, Lat. *vidua.* Hence

χηρόω, f. ώσω: aor. 1 ἐχήρωσα Ep. χήρωσα, pass. ἐχηρώθην:—*to bereave, make desolate* or *deserted.* 2. c. gen. *to bereave of* . ; Ἄργος ἀνδρῶν ἐχηρώθη *was left destitute* of men: *to bereave of* a husband or wife, *to make widowed.* II. intr., like χηρεύω, *to be bereaved* or *destitute of.* Hence

χηρωστής, οῦ, ὁ, *a collateral relation, heir-at-law.*

χήσεῖτε, Dor. crasis for καὶ ἥσετε, fut. of ἵημι.

χῆτις, ιος Att. εως, ἡ, = χῆτος.

χῆτος, εος, τό, (χατέω) *want, need, destitution*; mostly in dat., χήτεϊ τοιοῦ δ' ἀνδρὸς *from want* or *loss* of such a man; χήτι (Ion. dat. of χῆτις) συμμάχων *from need* of allies. Hence

χητοσύνη, ἡ, *want, need, destitution.*

χῆφθᾱ, Dor. for καὶ ἥφθη, 3 sing. aor. 1 pass. of ἅπτω.

χθᾰμᾰλός, ή, όν, (χαμαί) *near the ground, on the ground, low, sunken, flat.*

ΧΘΕ΄Σ, Adv., lengthd. **ἐχθές**, *yesterday*; πρώην τε καὶ χθές or χθὲς καὶ πρώην *yesterday* and the day before, i. e. *the other day.* Hence

χθεσῖνός, ή, όν, = χθιζός, *of yesterday*; τὸ σκόροδον τὸ χθεσινόν *yesterday*'s onion.

χθιζά, Adv.: see χθιζός.

χθιζῖνός, ή, όν, = χθεσινός.

χθιζός, ή, όν, (χθές) = χθεσινός, *of yesterday*, ὁ χθιζὸς πόνος *yesterday*'s labour: mostly used with Verbs, as, χθιζὸς ἔβη he went *yesterday*: the neut. χθιζόν and χθιζά are used as Adv., = χθές, *of yesterday*; χθιζά τε καὶ πρώιζα *yesterday* and the day before, *lately*, like χθὲς καὶ πρώην.

χθόνιος, α, ον, also ος, ον, (χθών) *in* or *under the earth*: esp. of the gods below; θεοὶ χθόνιοι the gods *of the nether world*, Lat. *Inferi*; χθόνιος Ἑρμῆς Hermes *conducting below the earth.* II. *of* or *from the earth.*

χθονο-στῐβής, ές, (χθών, στιβεῖν) *treading the earth, on* or *of the earth.*

χθονο-τρεφής, ές, gen. έος, (χθών, τρέφω) *nourished by* or *growing on earth.*

ΧΘΩ΄Ν, ἡ, gen. χθονός, *the earth, ground*; χθόνα δῦναι to go beneath *the earth*, i. e. to die; ὑπὸ χθονὸς κεκευθέναι to be hidden under *the earth*, i. e. to be buried. 2. οἱ ὑπὸ χθονὸς those beneath *the earth*, i. e. those in the shades below, Lat. *inferi.* II. *Earth*, personified as a goddess. III. *a particular land* or *country.*

ΧΙ῀ΔΡΟΝ, τό, pl. χῖδρα, τά, *a dish of unripe wheaten groats toasted*:—as ἄλφιτα is a dish of *barley groats.*

χῑλιάκις, Adv., (χίλιοι) *a thousand times.* [ᾰ]

χῑλί-ανδρος, ον, (χίλιοι, ἀνήρ) *containing a thousand men.*

χῑλι-άρχης or **χῑλί-αρχος**, ου, ὁ, (χίλιοι, ἄρχω) *the commander of a thousand men.* II. used to translate the Roman *tribunus militum, a legionary tribune.* Hence

χῑλιαρχία, ἡ, *the office* or *post of* χιλίαρχος, *command of* 1000 *men.*

χῑλιάς, άδος, ἡ, (χίλιοι) *the number one thousand, a thousand.*

χῑλι-έτης, ου, ὁ, or **χιλι-ετής**, έος, ὁ, ἡ, (χίλιοι, ἔτος) *lasting a thousand years.*

ΧΙ΄ΛΙΟΙ, αι, α, *a thousand*, Lat. *mille*: the sing. is used with collective nouns, as, χιλία ἵππος *a thousand* horse, like μυρία ἵππος, etc.

χῑλιό-ναυς, εως, ὁ, ἡ, (χίλιοι, ναῦς) *of* or *consisting of a thousand ships.*

χῑλιο-ναύτης, ου, ὁ, Dor. **-τάς**, (χίλιοι, ναύτης) *with* or *of a thousand sailors*: with fem. Subst., χιλιοναύτης ἀρωγή the help of *a thousand ships.*

χῑλιό-πᾰλαι, Adv. (χίλιοι, πάλαι) *long ago a thousand times over, very long ago.*

χῑλιοστός, ή, όν, (χίλιοι) *the thousandth.*

χῑλιοστύς, ύος, ἡ, (χίλιοι) *the body of a thousand.*

ΧΙ῀ΛΟ΄Σ, οῦ, ὁ, *green fodder for cattle*, esp. for horses, *forage, provender, grass*; προέρχεσθαι ἐπὶ χιλόν to go on *to forage*; χιλὸς ξηρὸς *hay.* Hence

χῑλόω, f. ώσω, *to turn out to graze.*

χίμαιρα [ῐ], ἡ, *a she-goat*, Lat. *capra*, fem. of χίμαρος. II. as prop. n., Χίμαιρα, ἡ, *Chimaera*, a monster breathing fire, with a lion's head, serpent's tail, and goat's middle, killed by Bellerophon.

χῐμαιρο-βάτης [ᾰ], ου, ὁ, (χίμαιρα, βαίνω) epith. of Pan, *he who mounts goats*, or *goat-footed.*

χῐμαιρο-θύτης, ου, ὁ, (χίμαιρα, θύω) *one who sacrifices goats.*

χῐμαιρο-φόνος, ον, (χίμαιρα, *φένω) *slaying goats.*

χῐμάρ-αρχος, ὁ, (χίμαρος, ἄρχω) *leading goats*; τράγος χιμάραρχος the he-goat *that leads the flock.*

ΧΙ΄ΜΑ῾ΡΟΣ [ῐ], ὁ, *a he-goat*, Lat. *caper*, = τράγος.

χῐμᾰρο-σφάκτης, ου, ὁ, (χίμαρος, σφάζω) *a goat-slayer.*

χιμάρως, Dor. for χιμάρους, acc. pl. of χίμαρος.

χίμετλον [ῐ], τό, (χεῖμα) *a chilblain, kibe.*

Χῑο-γενής, ές, (Χῖος, γενέσθαι) *of Chian birth* or *growth*, of wine.

χῖον, τό, (χῖος) *a wine-vessel, holding about* 1½ χοῦς, i. e. about a gallon.

χιόνεος, α, ον, (χιών) *of snow, snowy.*

χιονίζω, f. ίσω, (χιών) *to snow upon, cover with snow*: impers., εἰ ἐχιόνιζε τὴν χώρην if *snow fell upon* the country; absol., ἐχιόνιζε *it was snowing.*

χιονο-βλέφᾰρος, ον, (χιών, βλέφαρον) *with eye of dazzling white.*

χιονό-βλητος, ον, (χιών, βάλλω) *beaten* or *covered with snow.*

χιονο-βοσκός, *ον*, (χιών, βόσκω) *fostering snow, snow-clad.*

χιονο-θρέμμων, *ον*, gen. *ονος*, (χιών, θρέμμα) *feeding snow, snow-clad.*

χιονό-κτῠπος, *ον*, (χιών, κτυπέω) *snow-beaten.*

χιονο-τρόφος, *ον*, (χιών, τρέφω) *nursing snow, snow-clad.*

χιονό-χρως, *ωτος* and *οος*, ὁ, ἡ, (χιών, χρώς) *with snow-white* skin: generally, *snow-white.*

χιον-ώδης, *ες*, (χιών, εἶδος) *like snow, snow-white.*

Χίος, ἡ, *Chios*, an island in the Aegean sea, now *Scio.* Hence

Χῖος, *α, ον, Chian, of* or *from Chios:* οἱ Χῖοι *the Chians.* II. ὁ χῖος (sub. βόλος), an unlucky throw with the dice: the side with the ace-dot was χῖος ἀστράγαλος, the opp. side with the size-dot was called Κῷος, Lat. *unio;* cp. Κῷος. The proverb οὐ Χῖος ἀλλὰ Κεῖος referred to the contrast between the dishonest Ch ıns and the honest Ceians.

ΧΙΤΩ'Ν, ῶνος, ὁ, in Ion. Prose **κιθών**, *an under-garment, frock, kirtle*, Lat. *tunica*, both of men and women: it was *a woollen shirt* worn next the body: on going out they threw a wide cloak over it, called φᾶρος, χλαῖνα, or ἱμάτιον: the χιτών sometimes reached to the feet, and was then called χιτὼν ποδήρης: with sleeves it was called χιτὼν χειριδωτός. II. of soldiers, *a coat of mail, cuirass;* χιτῶνες λεπίδος σιδηρέης *coats* of iron scales. III. in plur. *the pieces of a shoe.* IV. metaph. *any coat, case* or *covering;* λάινος χιτών *a coat* or *covering* of stones, i. e. a tomb; τειχέων κιθῶνες *coats, lines* of walls: also in plur. *the coats of an onion.*

χῑτώνιον, τό, Dim. of χίτων, *a little tunic, short coat.*

χῑτωνίσκος, ὁ, = χιτώνιον.

ΧΙΏΝ, όνος, ἡ, *snow;* properly *fallen snow*, opp. to νιφάς or νιφετός, *falling* snow; χιὼν τηκομένη melting *snow.* II. *snow-water.*

ΧΛΑ'ΖΩ, only found in pf. κέχλᾱδα part. κεχλᾰδώς, and plur. κεχλᾱδόντες (for κεχλαδότες):—*to sound, ring, shout:* hence redupl. καχλάζω.

ΧΛΑΙ'ΝΑ Ion. χλαίνη, ης, ἡ, Lat. *laena, a large square upper garment, a cloak, mantle*, worn loose over the χιτών: it was made of wool, was thrown over the shoulders, and fastened with a clasp; it served also as a covering in sleep. It was nearly the same as the φᾶρος and ἱμάτιον.

χλαινίον, τό, Dim. of χλαῖνα, *a small cloak.*

χλαινόω, f. ώσω, (χλαῖνα) *to clothe* or *cover with a cloak:* generally, *to clothe.* Hence

χλαίνωμα, *ατος*, τό, *a clothing, covering.*

χλᾰμῠδη-φόρος, *ον*, (χλαμύς, φέρω) *wearing a χλαμύς* or *horseman's cloak:* as Subst., χλαμυδηφόρος, ὁ, *a horseman, cavalier.*

χλᾰμῠδ-ουργία, ἡ, (χλαμύς, *ἔργω) *the making of cloaks, the art* or *trade of a cloak-maker.*

χλᾰμύς, ύδος [ῠ], ἡ, *a short cloak* or *mantle*, worn by horsemen: generally, *a military cloak, the general's cloak*, Lat. *paludamentum.* It was fastened by a brooch on the right shoulder so as to hang over the left. (Akin to χλαῖνα.)

χλᾰνίδιον, τό, Dim. of χλανίς, *a small cloak* or *coverlet.* [νῐ]

χλᾰνῐδο-ποιία, ἡ, (χλανίς, ποιέω) *the art* or *trade of cloak-making.*

χλᾰνίς, ίδος, ἡ, (χλαῖνα) *an upper garment of wool*, like the χλαῖνα, but of finer make: worn by women as well as men: hence χλανίδα φορεῖν, to wear *the* χλανίς, was a mark of effeminacy.

χλᾰνισκίδιον [κῐ], or **χλᾰνίσκιον**, τό, and **χλᾰνίσκος**, ὁ, Dim. of χλανίς, *a small cloak.*

χλευάζω, f. άσω, (χλεύη) *to joke, jest, scoff.* II. trans. *to mock, scoff at, jeer, treat scornfully.* Hence

χλεῠασία, ἡ, and **χλευασμός**, ὁ, *mockery, scoffing.*

ΧΛΕΥ'Η, ἡ, *a joke, jest;* χλεύην ποιεῖν or ποιεῖσθαί τινα to make one *a jest.*

ΧΛΗ'ΔΟΣ, ὁ, *slime, mud: the dirt and rubbish carried down by a flood;* also *rubbish swept out of a house*, Lat. *quisquiliae.*

χλιαίνω, f. ᾰνῶ: aor. 1 ἐχλίηνα: (χλίω):—*to make warm:*—Pass. *to warm oneself: to grow warm.* II. *to soften by warmth, melt.*

χλιᾰρός, ά, όν Ion. **χλιερός**, ή, όν, (χλίω) *warm, lukewarm*, Lat. *tepidus.*

χλῐδαίνω, (χλιδή) *to make soft* or *delicate:*—Pass. *to be luxurious* or *delicate, revel in luxury.*

χλῐδᾰνός, ή, όν, (χλιδάω) *delicate, voluptuous, luxurious.*

χλῐδάω, f. ήσω, (χλιδή) *to be soft* or *delicate:* in bad sense, *to live delicately* or *luxuriously, to revel, luxuriate;* χλιδᾶν ἐπί τινι *to pride oneself* upon a thing: hence *to be insolent* or *arrogant.*

χλῐδή, ἡ, (χλίω) *delicacy, luxury, voluptuousness.* 2. *wantonness, insolence, arrogance.* *any sign* or *accessory of luxury:* in plur. *fine raiment, costly ornaments*, Lat. *deliciae:* also *charms, beauty.*

χλίδημα, *ατος*, τό, (χλιδάω) = χλιδή. [ῐ]

χλιερός, ή, όν, Ion. for χλιαρός.

χλιόω, Ep. for χλιάω.

ΧΛΙ'Ω, only used in pres. and impf., *to become warm* or *soft, melt:* metaph. *to be luxurious, to revel, luxuriate.* [ῑ]

χλόα, see χλόη.

χλο-αυγής, ές, (χλόη, αὐγή) *with a greenish lustre.*

χλοερός, ά, όν, poët. lengthd. for χλωρός.

χλοερο-τρόφος, *ον*, (χλοερός, τρέφω) *producing green herbs, grass-growing.*

χλοερ-ῶπις, ιδος, ἡ, (χλοερός, ὤψ) *greenish looking.*

ΧΛΟ'Η, ης, and **χλόα**, *ας*, also Ion. **χλοίη**, ἡ, *the tender shoot of plants* in spring, *the blade of young corn* or *grass:* poët. *the young verdure* of trees, *foliage, leaves.*

χλοη-κομέω, f. ήσω, (χλόη, κόμη) *to be green as a young leaf.*

χλο-ήρης, ες, (χλόη, ἀρᾰρεῖν) = χλοερός, χλωρός.

χλοη-τόκος, *ον*, (χλόη, τεκεῖν) *producing young shoots.*

χλοη-φόρος, *ον*, (χλόη, φέρω) *putting out young shoots*, *bearing grass* or *leaves*.

χλοιάω, (χλοίη) Ion. for χλοάω.

χλοίη, ἡ, Ion. for χλόη.

χλούνης, *ου*, ἡ, Epic epith. of the wild boar, taken to mean *feeding* or *living alone*: later as Subst. = κάπρος, *the wild boar itself*. (Deriv. uncertain.)

χλοῦνις, ἡ, a doubtful word in Aesch. Eum. 189, commonly derived from χλόη, and taken to mean *green age*, i. e. *youth*, *freshness*.

χλωρ-αύχην, *ενος*, ὁ, ἡ, (χλωρός, αὐχήν) *with pale green* or *olive neck*, of the nightingale: see χλωρηίς.

χλωρηίς, ίδος, poët. fem. of χλωρός, for χλωρά, *pale green*, *olive-green*, epith. of the nightingale.

χλωρό-κομος, *ον*, (χλωρός, κόμη) *green-leafed*.

χλωρός poët. **χλοερός**, ά, όν, (χλόη) *pale green*, *light-green*, *bright green*, *green*, of the colour of young grass: also of the colour of honey and sand, *yellow*. II. generally, *pale*, *pallid*. III. without regard to colour, *green*, *fresh*, as opp. to dry; τυρὸς χλωρὸς *fresh* cheese: metaph. *fresh*, *blooming*, *youthful*: *tender*, *delicate*.

χναύω, = κνάω, *to scrape*, *to gnaw*, *gnaw off*, *nibble*.

χνοάζω, f. άσω, (χνόος) properly of youths, *to get the first down* on their chin: also of the first growth of gray hair, χνοάζων ἄρτι λευκανθὲς κάρα *having* his head *just sprinkled* with white.

χνοάω, = χνοάζω.

ΧΝΟΗ Ion. **χνοίη**, ἡ, *the iron box of a wheel* in which the axle turns, *the nave*, also *the axle* itself. 2. metaph., χνόαι ποδῶν *the joints on* which the feet are set.

χνόϊος, α, ον, (χνόος) *downy*.

ΧΝΟ'ΟΣ Att. contr. **χνοῦς**, gen. χνοῦ, ὁ, *any light*, *porous substance*, *the foam* of the sea: *the fine down* or *bloom* on the peach: *the first down on the chin*, like ἀχνή.

χόα, acc. of χόος, χοῦς.

χοᾰνεύω contr. **χωνεύω**, *to cast metal*. From

χοάνη contr. **χώνη**, ἡ, *a funnel*. II. = χόανος. [ᾰ]

χόᾰνος, ὁ, (χέω) *the hollow in which metal was placed for melting*, *a melting-pot*: also *the mould for casting metal in*.

χόες, οἱ, nom. pl. of χόος, χοῦς.

χοή, ἡ, (χέω) *a pouring*, esp. *a drink-offering*, Lat. *libatio*, made to the dead (λοιβή or σπονδή being that made to the gods); mixed of honey, wine and water.

χο-ήρης, *ες*, gen. *εος*, (χοή, ἀρᾰρεῖν) *furnished with drink-offerings to the dead*; ἄγγος χοῆρες a vessel *filled with them*.

χοη-φόρος, *ον*, (χοή, φέρω) *bearing drink-offerings*.

χοϊκός, ή, όν, (χοῦς) *of rubbish*, *of earth* or *clay*.

χοινῑκίς, ίδος, ἡ, (χοῖνιξ) *an iron ring*.

χοῖνιξ, ῑκος, ἡ, *a choenix*, *a dry* measure, containing three κοτύλαι (about $1\frac{1}{2}$ pint Engl.) or four κοτύλαι (about a quart): the *choenix* of corn was a slave's daily allowance; ὅς κεν ἐμῆς γε χοίνικος ἅπτηται whoever tastes of my *rations*. II. from the shape, *the box* or *nave of a wheel*. 2. a kind of *shackle* or *stocks* for fastening the legs in.

χοιράς, άδος, ἡ, (χοῖρος) *a low rock* rising above the sea, *like a hog's back*, Virgil's *dorsum immane mari summo*; χοιρὰς ἀμυδρά *a* sunken *rock*; χοιρὰς Δηλία the Delian *rock*, i. e. *the rocky isle* of Delos. II. χοιράδες, αἱ, *glandular swellings*.

χοίρειος, α, ον, (χοῖρος) *of a swine* or *hog*.

χοίρεος, α, ον, poët. for χοίρειος: χοίρεα (sub. κρέατα), τά, *hog's*-flesh.

χοιρίδιον, τό, Dim. of χοῖρος, *a little pig*. [ρῐ]

ΧΟΙΡΙ'ΝΗ, ἡ, *a small sea-muscle*, used by the Athenian dicasts in voting. [ῑ]

χοιρίον, τό, Dim. of χοῖρος, *a little pig*, *porker*.

χοιρίσκος, ὁ, Dim. of χοῖρος, = χοιρίον.

χοιρο-κομεῖον, τό, (χοῖρος, κομέω) *a fence for keeping swine in*, *a pig-sty*.

χοιρο-κτόνος, *ον*, (χοῖρος, κτείνω) *slaying swine*. II. χοιρόκτονος, pass. *of* or *belonging to a slain swine*; αἷμα χοιρόκτονον blood *of a slain swine*.

χοιρο-πώλης, *ου*, ὁ, Dor. **-πώλας**: (χοῖρος, πωλέω):—*a dealer in swine*.

ΧΟΙ῀ΡΟΣ, ὁ, *a young pig*, *porker*, Lat. *porcus*: generally, *a pig*.

χολάς, άδος, ἡ, (χολή) in plur. χολάδες, *the bowels*, *intestines*.

χολάω, (χολή) like μελαγχολάω, *to be full of black bile*, *to be melancholy mad*. II. = χολόομαι, *to be angry*, *rage*.

ΧΟΛΗ', ἡ, = χόλος, *gall*, *bile*, Lat. *fel*, *bilis*; χολὴ μέλαινα black, i. e. diseased *bile*: pl. χολαί, *the gall-bladder*. II. metaph. like Lat. *bilis*, *anger*, *wrath*, *bitterness*: *anything which causes disgust* or *aversion*.

ΧΟ'ΛΙΞ, ῐκος, ἡ, mostly in plur. χόλῐκες, like χολάδες, *the entrails* or *bowels* of oxen, *tripe*.

χόλιος, α, ον, also ος, ον, (χόλος) *enraged*, *angry*.

ΧΟ'ΛΟΣ, ὁ, like χολή, in physical sense, *gall*, *bile*, though this sense was mostly confined to χολή. II. *bitter anger*, *wrath*, Lat. *bilis*; χόλον σβέσαι, παῦσαι, to smother, get rid of *wrath*: c. gen., χόλος τινός either *rage towards* another or another's *rage towards* oneself. Hence

χολόω, f. ώσω, *to stir one's gall* or *bile*: hence *to make angry*, *embitter*. II. Med. and Pass., f. χολώσομαι, paullo-post fut. κεχολώσομαι: aor. 1 med. ἐχολωσάμην, pass. ἐχολώθην: pf. pass. κεχόλωμαι:—*to have one's bile stirred*, *be angered* or *embittered*; κεχολωμένος τινί *angry at* or *with* a person.

χολωθείς, εῖσα, έν, aor. 1 pass. part. of χολόω.

χολώθην, Ep. aor. 1 pass. of χολόω.

χολωσέμεν, Ep. fut. inf. of χολόω.

χολωτός, ή, όν, verb. Adj. of χολόω, *angry*, *wrathful*, *passionate*.

χόνδρος, ὁ, *a corn*, *grain*, *groat*, Lat. *granum*, *mica*; ἁλὸς χόνδροι *lumps* of salt. 2. *wheat-groats*. 3.

a drink made from groats, a kind of gruel: proverbial of an old man, χόνδρον λείχειν to sip *gruel.*

χονδρός, ά, όν, (χόνδρος) *like groats;* χονδροὶ ἅλες *coarse-grained* salt, opp. to λεπτοὶ ἅλες, fine salt.

χόος, see χοῦς.

χορ-άγιον, χορ-ᾱγός, Dor. and Att. for χορηγ—.

χόρδευμα, ατος, τό, *a sausage* or *black-pudding.* From

χορδεύω, f. σω, (χορδή) *to make into sausages:* metaph., χορδεύειν τὰ πράγματα *to make mincemeat of* state affairs.

χορδή, ἡ, *a string of gut: the string* or *chord* of a lyre. II. *a sausage.*

χορεία, ἡ, (χορεύω) *a dancing: the choral dance.*

χόρευμα, ατος, τό, (χορεύω) *a choral dance.*

χορευτέον, verb. Adj. of χορεύω, *one must lead the choral dances, one must dance.*

χορευτής, οῦ, ὁ, (χορεύω) *a choral dancer;* θεοῦ χορευτής *the votary* of a god.

χορεύω; fut. -εύσω: aor. 1 ἐχόρευσα: Med., fut. -εύσομαι: aor. 1 ἐχορευσάμην: Pass., aor. 1 ἐχορεύθην: pf. κεχόρευμαι: (χορός):—*to join in the dance, to dance: to form a chorus, perform the part of chorus,* esp. at a festival in honour of the gods: *to be one of a chorus.* 2. metaph. *to practise for the chorus;* hence *to practise a thing, be versed* in it: c. acc. cognato, χορείας χορεύειν *to ply* the dance; φροίμιον χορεύσομαι *I will begin festivities with a dance:* pass., κεχόρευται ἡμῖν our *dance has been danced.* II. trans. *to celebrate with choral dances.* III. Causal, *to set dancing, to rouse* or *call to the dance.*

χορηγέω Dor. **χορᾱγέω:** f. ήσω: (χορηγός):—*to lead a chorus.* II. in Att. of the χορηγός, *to defray the cost of bringing out a chorus;* χορηγεῖν ταῖς αὑτοῦ ἡδοναῖς *to find money* for one's own pleasures, *to pay the piper:*—Pass. *to have choregi found* or *supplied* one; χορηγοῦσιν μὲν οἱ πλούσιοι, χορηγεῖται δὲ ὁ δῆμος the rich men *act as choregi,* but the people *is supplied with them.* III. generally, *to supply: to equip* or *furnish abundantly with* a thing. Hence

χορηγία, ἡ, *the office of* χορηγός: at Athens, *the defraying of the cost of the solemn public choruses,* being the chief of the Athenian λειτουργίαι. II. *means and fortunes sufficient for the cost of a chorus: abundance of means, wealth, plenty.*

χορηγικός, ή, όν, (χορηγός) *of* or *for a* χορηγός; χορηγικοὶ ἀγῶνες rivalry *in bringing out choruses.*

χορήγιον Dor. and Att. **χοράγιον,** τό, *a place of rehearsal for the chorus, the place where a chorus was trained.* From

χορ-ηγός Dor. and Att. **χορᾱγός,** ὁ, (χορός, ἡγέομαι) *one who leads the chorus,* = κορυφαῖος: generally, *the leader of a train* or *band.* 2. at Athens, *one who defrays the cost for bringing out a chorus.* II. generally, *one who supplies the costs* for any purpose.

χορ-ίαμβος, ὁ, (χόριος, ἴαμβος) in metre, *a choriambus,* i. e. a foot of four syllables, consisting of a *chorius* (or trochee) and *iambus,* as ἱππŏμĕδŏν.

χορικός, ή, όν, (χορός) *of* or *for a choral dance;* τὸ χορικόν *the choral song.*

ΧΟ'ΡΙΟΝ, τό, *skin, leather,* Lat. *corium:* Doric proverb., χαλεπὸν χορίῳ κύνα γεῦσαι 'tis bad to let the dog taste *leather,* Horace's *canis a corio nunquam absterrebitur uncto.*

χόριος, ὁ, (χορός) a metrical foot, = τροχαῖος or *trochee,* e. g. ἵππŏς.

χορο-δῐδάσκᾰλος, ὁ, (χορός, διδάσκαλος) *one who teaches and trains the chorus, the chorus-master* who was commonly the poet himself. 2. = χοραγός or κορυφαῖος, *the leader of the chorus,* because the older Tragic Poets not only *taught,* but *led* their own choruses.

χορο-ήθης, ες, gen. εος, (χορός, ἦθος) *accustomed to the dance.*

χοροι-θᾰλής, ές, gen. έος, (χορός, θαλεῖν) *rejoicing in the dance.*

χορο-μᾰνία, ἡ, (χορός, μανία) *a rage for dancing.*

χοροιτῠπία, ἡ, *a beating the ground in the dance, dancing:* also in plur. From

χοροι-τύπος, όν, (χορός, τυπεῖν) *beating the ground in the dance: dancing.* II. χοροίτυπος, ον, pass. *played to the choral dance.*

χορο-μᾰνής, ές, gen. έος, (χορός, μανῆναι) *mad after dancing.*

χορόνδε, Adv. (χορός) *to the festive dance.*

χορο-παίγμων, ον, gen. ονος, and **χορο-παίκτης,** ου, ὁ, (χορός, παίζω) *sporting in the choral dance, dancing merrily.*

χορο-ποιός, όν, (χορός, ποιέω) *forming* or *arranging a chorus: leading the dance.*

ΧΟΡΟ'Σ, οῦ, ὁ, properly *a dance in a ring, a circling dance:* generally, *a festive* or *choral dance,* such as were danced on public festivals in honour of the gods. 2. *a chorus, choir,* i. e. *a band of dancers and singers,* who performed such dances. 3. generally, *a troop, band, company* of persons; also of things, as, χορὸς ἄστρων *the company* of the stars; χορὸς καλάμων *a row* of reeds. II. *a place for dancing.*

The ancient Choral Dance of Greece, which originated among the Dorians, reached its perfection in the χορὸς κυκλικός performed at the Athenian Dionysia. This Chorus consisted of fifty persons. Hence arose the Attic Drama, which consisted at first of mere tales in the intervals of the Dance, told by a single *Actor.* The Chorus was then distinguished into three principal kinds, the χόρος τραγικός consisting of twelve or fifteen persons, the κωμικός of twenty-four, and the σατυρικός. When a Poet wished to bring out a piece, the Archon granted him a Chorus (χορὸν ἔδωκε) the expenses of which were defrayed by some rich citizen, hence called χορηγός: the Chorus was regularly trained by the Poet himself, who was hence called χοροδιδάσκαλος.

χορτάζω, f. άσω, (χόρτος) *to feed* or *fatten in a stall:* generally, *to feed* or *fatten with* a thing. Hence

χορτᾰσία, ἡ, *a feeding at the stall:* generally, *a feeding, fattening.*

χόρτασμα, ατος, τό, (χορτάζω) *fodder* for cattle: rarely, *food* or *provisions* for men.

ΧΟ'ΡΤΟΣ, ὁ, *a feeding-place; αὐλῆς ἐν χόρτῳ in the feeding-place* of the court-yard: plur. *feeding-grounds; χόρτοι λέοντος the haunt* of the lion. II. *fodder, provender,* esp. for cattle, *grass, hay,* opp. to σῖτος (food for man); but in Poets used for *food* generally.

χορ-ωφελήτης, ου, ὁ, (χορός, ὠφελέω) *helping* or *cheering the chorus.*

χοῦν, inf. of χόω: see χώννυμι.

χοῦσι, 3 pl. of χόω: see χώννυμι.

χοῦς, ὁ and ἡ, gen. χοός; dat. χοΐ; acc. χόᾱ: plur. χόες, χοῶν, χουσί, χόας: but also, gen. χοῶς, acc. χόα [ᾰ] (χέω):—*a liquid measure,* Lat. *congius,* = 12 κοτύλαι or 6 *sextarii,* about 3 quarts. 2. οἱ Χόες *the feast of Pitchers,* the second day of the Athenian Anthesteria, on the twelfth day of the month Anthesterion.

χοῦς, ὁ, gen. χοῦ, acc. χοῦν, (χέω) *a bank, mound, heap of earth, earth thrown up so as to form a mound.*

χόω, see χώννυμι.

χραίνω, f. χρᾰνῶ: aor. 1 ἔχρᾱνα: = χράω, *to touch slightly,* Lat. *stringo:* hence *to smear, paint.* 2. metaph. *to stain, soil, defile, pollute.*

χραισμέω, (χράομαι) a Verb hardly used in pres., whence the following Ep. forms, fut. χραισμήσω, inf. χραισμησέμεν: aor. 1 χραίσμησα: aor. 2 χραῖσμον, 3 sing. subj. χραίσμῃ and -ῃσι, inf. χραισμεῖν:—like ἀμύνω, *to ward off* something *from* one, Lat. *defendo;* ὄλεθρόν τινι χραισμεῖν or χραισμῆσαι *to ward off* destruction *from* one. 2. c. dat. pers. only, *to defend any one, help, aid, succour* with a neut. Adj., χραισμεῖν τι *to assist* or *avail* at all. Hence

χραισμήιον, τό, *a means of help, remedy.*

χραισμησέμεν, Ep. fut. inf. of χραισμέω.

χραίσμησι, Ep. 3 sing. aor. 2 of χραισμέω.

χράομαι, see χράω C.

ΧΡΑ'Ω (A), Aeol. **χραύω**, f. σω, *to touch lightly, wound slightly,* Lat. *radere, stringere.*

ΧΡΑ'Ω (B), only used in impf. *to fall upon, attack, annoy;* στυγερὸς οἱ ἔχραε δαίμων a hateful god *vexed* him. II. *to be eager to* do a thing; 2 sing. χρῄς, χρῄσθα = χρῄζεις.

ΧΡΑ'Ω (C), Ion. **χρέω** Ep. **χρείω**: fut. χρήσω: aor. 1 ἔχρησα: Med., fut. χρήσομαι: aor. 1 ἐχρησάμην: Pass., paullo-p. fut. κεχρήσομαι, aor. 1 ἐχρήσθην: pf. κέχρησμαι and κέχρημαι. — χράω contracts αε into η, as χρῄς, χρῇ, inf. χρῆν, etc., but Ion. into ᾱ, as χρᾷς, χρᾷ, χρᾶν, etc.: there are also special Ion. forms of Med., χρέομαι, χρέεσθαι, χρεόμενος, ἐχρέοντο. Radic. sense, *to give what is needful:* I. Act., of the gods and their oracles, *to give the needful answer, to proclaim, declare, pronounce;* χρήσω βουλὴν Διὸς ἀνθρώποισιν *I will proclaim* the counsel of Jove to mankind. 2. Pass. of the response, *to be uttered, delivered;* τὸ χρησθέν *the divine response.* 3. Med. of the votaries, *to consult a god* or *oracle:* also in pf. pass. part., κεχρημένος *one who has consulted* or *has received an answer from a god* or *oracle;* χρῆσθαι περί τινος *to consult* an oracle about a thing: more commonly c. dat. *to inquire of* or *consult* a god or oracle; ψυχῇ χρησόμενος Θηβαίου Τειρεσίαο *to consult* the shade of the Theban Tiresias: hence, χρῆσθαι μαντηΐῳ, χρηστηρίῳ, Lat. *uti oraculo,* whence comes the common sense of χράομαι *to use;* see below. II. in aor. 1 ἔχρησα, pf. κέχρηκα, with the pres. κίχρημι, this word has a different sense, *to supply,* hence *to lend:* in Med. κίχραμαι, aor. 2 ἐχρησάμην, *to have furnished one,* hence *to borrow;* πόδας χρήσας, ὄμματα χρησάμενος having *lent* feet and *borrowed* eyes. III. the Med. **χράομαι** Ion. **χρέομαι**, is also used as a Dep., with pf. pass. κέχρημαι in same sense, (see above χράω 3), *to use,* Lat. *uti,* c. dat. 2. metaph. in various relations, *to be possessed of, shew, express* a feeling or state of mind, *to experience* anything; φρεσὶ γὰρ κέχρητ' ἀγαθῇσιν for *he was endowed* with a kind disposition; ὀργῇ or θυμῷ χρῆσθαι *to indulge one's* anger; συντυχίᾳ, εὐτυχίᾳ χρῆσθαι, Lat. *uti fortuna mala, prospera,* to be ill or well off; ὁμολογίᾳ χρῆσθαι *to come to* an agreement: ὠνῇ καὶ πράσει χρῆσθαι to buy and sell: often periphr. with a Subst. for the simple Verb; as, μόρῳ χρῆσθαι *to meet* one's death, i. e. to die: also *to practise, pursue* a trade, etc.; χρῆσθαι τέχνῃ *to follow* a trade; χρῆσθαι ἀνομίᾳ *to practise* lawlessness. 3. χρῆσθαί τινι εἴς τι *to use* a thing for an end or purpose: also with a neut. Adj. as Adv., τί χρήσομαι τουτῳ; what *use shall I make* of him? χρῆσθαί τινι ὅτι βούλεταί τις *to make* what *use* one likes *of* him; ἀπορέων ὅ τι χρήσεται not knowing what *to make of* it. 4. of persons, *to have intercourse* or *dealings with* any one, *have to do with* him, *treat, behave, conduct oneself to;* χρῆσθαί τινι ὡς φίλῳ, ὡς πολεμίῳ *to treat* one as a friend or enemy:—also, χρῆσθαί τινι, like Lat. *uti aliquo* or *uti aliquo familiariter, to be intimate with* a man, to make use of his good offices; παρέχειν ἑαυτόν τινι χρῆσθαι to place oneself at the disposal of another: absol., οἱ χρώμενοι *friends.* 5. absol., or with an Adv., οὕτω χρῶνται οἱ Πέρσαι such *is the practice of* the Persians. 6. c. acc. rei, χρέεσθαι πάντα δι' ἀγγέλων *to manage, transact* everything by messengers. 7. the perf. κέχρημαι with pres. sense, *to be in need* or *want of* a thing, c. gen.; τοῦ κεχρημένοι; *in want* of what? absol. as an Adj. *needy, poor;* but κεχρημένος occurs in the regular sense of χράομαι, as συμφορῇ κεχρημένος *having experienced* a misfortune. 8. the aor. 1 pass. ἐχρήσθην has a pass. sense, αἱ νῆες οὐκ ἐχρήσθησαν the ships *were not used.*

χρέᾰ, Ep. shortened for χρέεα, acc. pl. of χρέος.

χρέεσθαι, Ion. for χρῆσθαι, inf. of χράομαι.

χρεία, ἡ, (χράομαι) *use*, Lat. *usus: advantage, service:* τὰ οὐδὲν εἰς χρείαν things of no *use* or *service:* in plur. *services.* 2. *using, usance, use;* κτῆσις καὶ χρῆσις having and *using.* 3. of persons, *acquaintance, intimacy* II. like Lat. *opus, need, necessity;* ἐν χρείᾳ εἶναι or γίγνεσθαί τινος to be *in need, want* of a thing. 2. *want, poverty, lack:* c. gen. *want, lack of* a thing. 3. *need of a person's help*, hence *a request on the score of necessity:* generally, *a request.* 4. *a needful matter, business;* ἐν πάσαις ταῖς τοῦ σώματος νοσείαις in all *functions* of the body.

χρείη, 3 sing. pres. opt. of χρή.

χρεῖος, τό, Ep. for χρέος.

χρεῖος, ον, (χρή) *useful: needful, fitting.* II. act. *needing, being in want of*, c. gen.: absol. *needy.*

χρείω, Ep. for χρέω, χράω, *to deliver an oracle.*

χρειώ, όος contr. οῦς, ἡ, Ep. for χρεώ.

χρεμετίζω, f. ίσω, *to neigh, snort*, Lat. *hinnire*, of a horse. · (Formed from the sound.) Hence

χρεμέτισμα, τό, and **χρεμετισμός**, ὁ, *a neighing.*

χρέμισαν, shortd. poët. for ἐχρεμέτισαν, 3 pl. aor. 1 of χρεμετίζω.

ΧΡΕ΄ΜΠΤΟΜΑΙ, f. -ψομαι, Dep. *to hawk and spit, expectorate.*

χρέομαι, Ion. for χράομαι: part. χρεομενος.

χρεόν, Ion. for χρεών.

χρέος, τό, gen. χρέεος contr. χρέους: Ep. nom. and acc. pl. χρέᾰ Att. χρέᾱ: Ep. nom. sing. χρεῖος Att. χρέως: (χράομαι, χρή): I. like χρεία, *want, need.* II. *a needful matter, business, affair;* κατὰ χρέος τινὸς ἐλθεῖν to come for *need of* a person or thing; ἐφ' ὅ τι χρέος ἐμόλετε; for what *need* came ye?—also, like χρῆμα, *a thing.* III. *a debt;* χρεῖος ὀφείλεταί μοι *a debt* is due to me; χρέος ἀποδιδόναι and ἀπολαμβάνειν to pay and recover *debts;* τὴν οὐσίαν ἅπασαν χρέα κατέλιπε he left all property *in outstanding debts* 2. metaph. *a debt, trespass, sin.* 3. *a debt, due, duty;* κατὰ χρέος according *to what is due:* hence *a promise due*, ἀρᾶς τίνειν χρέος to pay the *debt*, i. e. do the *work*, of a curse.

χρέω, Ion. for χράω, *to deliver an oracle.*

χρεώ Ep. **χρειώ**, gen. όος contr. οῦς, ἡ: (χρέος, χρεία):—*want, need*, hence *desire, longing, urgent wish*, c. gen., χρειὼ ἐμεῖο *want, need of* me; ἵν' οὐ χρεὼ πείσματός ἐστιν where there is no *need of* a cable. 2. in phrase, χρειὼ ἱκάνεται *want* or *necessity* arises, c. acc. pers.; τίνα χρειὼ τόσον ἵκει; to whom doth *necessity* come so much? so also with γίγνομαι and εἰμί, ἐμὲ δὲ χρεὼ γίγνεται νηός *need* of a ship comes upon me; οὐδέ τι μιν χρεὼ ἔσται τυμβοχοῆς nor will *need* of a grave come upon him. 3. hence χρεώ is often used without a verb expressed c. acc. pers., τίπτε δέ σε χρεώ [sc. ἱκάνει] wherefore *does need* [come to] thee, i. e. why *must* thou do so? so also c. gen., οὔτι με ταύτης χρεὼ τιμῆς no *need of* this honour [touches] me; an inf. is also used, οὐδέ τί μιν χρεὼ νηῶν ἐπιβαινέμεν nor *does need* at all [reach] him to embark on board this ship. [χρέω in Homer is used as a monosyllable, χρεω.]

χρεώμενος, Ion. for χρώμενος, part. of χράομαι.

χρεών, τό, Ion. **χρεόν**, indecl., but seldom used except in nom. and acc.: properly a part. neut. from χρέω (Ion. for χράω), = τὸ χρεὸν γίγνεσθαι, *that which an oracle declares, that which must be, fate, necessity;* χρεών or χρεόν ἐστι it is *fated* or *necessary*, it *must be:*—absol. χρεών, *it being necessary, since it was necessary.* 2. *that which is expedient* or *right:* absol. as Adv., οὐ χρεὼν ἄρχετε ye rule *not rightfully.* [⏑ –, but sometimes poët. χρεων as one long syllable.]

χρέωνται, Ion. for χρῶνται, 3 pl. of χράομαι

χρέως, τό, Att. for χρέος, *a debt.*

χρεώστης, ου, ὁ, (χρέως) *a debtor.*

χρε-ωφειλέτης, ου, ὁ, (χρέως, ὀφείλω) *a debtor.*

χρῆ or **χρή**, ἡ, = χρεία II, *need, necessity.*

χρή, impers.: subjunct. χρῇ: optat. χρείη: inf. χρῆναι, poët. also χρῆν: impf. ἐχρῆν and χρῆν: fut. χρήσει: (for part., see χρέων):—*it is fated, necessary:* c. inf. *it must, must needs* be, *it is good, fit, meet* 2. like δεῖ, Lat. *oportet, decet*, c. acc. pers. et inf.; *one must needs* do a thing, *it behoves* or *befits, it is right and proper* that one should do.—Sometimes the inf. must be supplied from the context, as in the phrase οὐδέ τί σε χρή, as τίπτε μάχης ἀποπαύεαι; οὐδέ τί σε χρή why restest thou from the battle? *it behoves* thee not (sc. ἀποπαύεσθαι μάχης). 3. c. acc. pers. et gen. rei, οὐδέ τί σε χρὴ ἀφροσύνης thou *hast* no *need of* impudence, i. e. it does not *befit* thee; οὔ σε χρὴ ἔτ' αἰδοῦς thou *hast* no longer *need of* shame. II. in a less strong sense, *one may, one can;* πῶς χρὴ τοῦτο περᾶσαι; how *is one to* get through this? III. τὸ χρῆν *fate, destiny.*

χρῇ, shortened for χρῄζει.

χρῄζω, used only in pres. and impf.: Ep. and Ion. **χρηΐζω**: Dor. **χρῄσδω** and **χρῄδδω**: (χρεία):—*to need, want, lack, have need of:* absol. in part. χρηΐζων, *needy, poor.* 2. *to desire, long for: to ask, crave, desire*, Lat. *solicitare:*—c. gen. rei, *to ask* or *demand* a thing. 3. μὴ ἔχρῃζες θανεῖν, like μὴ ὤφελες, thou *oughtest* not to have died, oh that thou hadst not ..! 4. the part. χρῄζων is used absol. for εἰ χρῄζει, *if one will, if one chooses:* hence wishing *well, well-inclined.*

χρήζω, like χράω I, *to deliver an oracle, foretell.* V.

χρηΐα, ἡ, Ion. for χρεία, *use, need.*

χρηΐζω, Ep. and Ion. for χρῄζω.

χρηΐσκομαι, Ion. collat. form of χράομαι, *to use, make use of.*

χρῆμα, ατος, τό, (χράομαι) *a thing that one uses* or *needs:* mostly used in plur. *goods, money:* proverb., κρείσσων χρημάτων superior to *money*, i.e. inaccessible *to bribes.* II. *a thing, matter, business, affair, event;* κινεῖν πᾶν χρῆμα to set every*thing* in motion, 'to leave no stone unturned:' *a dealing, business,* *transaction*, like Lat. *res*. 2. χρῆμα is often expressed to strengthen a phrase, as, τί χρῆμα; for τί; *what?* 3. χρῆμα is also used to express something strange or unusual, μέγα συὸς χρῆμα a huge *monster* of a boar; τοῦ χειμῶνος χρῆμα ἀφόρητον the intolerable *violence* of the storm:—also to express a great number or mass, χρῆμα πολλῶν ἀρδίων, νεῶν, etc., *a vast amount* of javelins, ships, etc.; ὅσον τὸ χρῆμα παρνόπων what *a lot* of locusts! μέγα χρῆμα Λακαινᾶν a great *host* of Laconian women.

χρημᾰτίζω, f. ίσω Att. ιῶ: pf. κεχρημάτικα: (χρῆμα):—*to do* or *carry on business, have dealings: to negotiate, transact business.* 2. *to consult, debate, advise* about a matter. 3. *to give an answer after due deliberation: to warn solemnly:* Pass. *to be solemnly warned.* II. Med. χρηματίζομαι, f. -ιοῦμαι, *to transact business for one's own profit, to make money, enrich oneself: to transact business, have dealings* with another. III. in late Greek, the Act. χρηματίζω means *to bear a title* or *name;* χρηματίζει βασιλεύς *he takes the title* of king; οἱ μαθηταὶ Χριστιανοὶ ἐχρημάτισαν πρῶτον ἐν τῇ Ἀντιοχείᾳ the disciples *bore the name of* Christians first in Antioch.

χρημᾰτικός, ή, όν, (χρῆμα) *of* or *for money.*

χρημάτῐσις, εως, ἡ, and **χρημᾰτισμός**, ὁ, (χρηματίζω) *transaction of business.* 2. of an oracle, *a response:* also *a divine warning.* II. (from Med.) *a doing business for one's own gain: money-making, gain, profit.*

χρημᾰτιστέον, verb. Adj. of χρηματίζω, *one must make money.*

χρημᾰτιστής, οῦ, ὁ, (χρηματίζω) *one who carries on business*, so as to make money, *a moneyed man, a man of business, tradesman.* Hence

χρημᾰτιστικός, ή, όν, *fitted for money-making;* χρηματιστικὸς οἰωνός an omen *portending gain.*

χρημᾰτο-δαίτης, ου, ὁ, (χρῆμα, δατέομαι) *a divider of money* or *of possessions.*

χρημᾰτο-ποιός, όν, (χρήματα, ποιέω) *money-making, money-getting.*

χρημοσύνη, ἡ, (χράομαι) = χρεία, *need, want, lack.*

χρῆναι, inf. of χρή.

χρῄσδω, Dor. for χρῄζω.

χρῇς, **χρῆσθα**, shortd. for χρῄζεις, see χράω (B) II.

χρήσῐμος, η, ον, also ος, ον: (χράομαι):—*useful, serviceable, apt, fit, useful* of its kind: τὸ χρήσιμον *use, advantage.* 2. of men, *serviceable, useful, serviceable to the state.* 3. *used, made use of.* Hence

χρησίμως, Adv. *usefully, serviceably.*

χρησίμως, Dor. for χρησίμους, acc. pl. of χρήσιμος.

χρῆσις, εως, ἡ, (χράομαι) *a using, employment, use made* of a thing: in plur. *uses.* 2. *power* or *means of using.* 3. *intimacy, acquaintance*, Lat. *usus.* II. (χράω C) *an oracle.*

χρησμολογέω, f. ήσω, *to utter oracles, divine.* From

χρησμο-λόγος, ον, (χρησμός, λέγω) *uttering oracles, divining;* χρησμολόγος ἀνήρ *a soothsayer, diviner.* II. *an expounder* or *interpreter of oracles.*

χρησμο-ποιός, όν, (χρησμός, ποιέω) *making oracles in verse.*

χρησμός, ὁ, (χράω C) *the answer of an oracle, an oracular response, oracle.*

χρησμοσύνη, ἡ, (χράομαι) like χρημοσύνη, *need, want, poverty: an eager request, importunity.*

χρησμο-φύλαξ, ακος, ὁ, (χρησμός, φύλαξ) *a keeper of oracular responses.*

χρησμῳδέω, f. ήσω, (χρησμῳδός) *to recite oracles in verse, to give oracles, prophesy.* Hence

χρησμῳδία, ἡ, *the answer of an oracle*, given in verse, *a prophecy.*

χρησμῳδικός, ή, όν, *of* or *fit for a soothsayer* or *diviner, oracular.* Adv. -κῶς. From

χρησμ-ῳδός, όν, (χρησμός, ᾠδή) *reciting oracles in verse: prophesying, prophetic:*—as Subst., χρησμῳδός, ὁ, *a soothsayer, prophet.*

χρῆσον, 2 sing. aor. 1 imperat. of κίχρημι, *to lend.*

χρηστέον, verb. Adj. of χράομαι, *one must us*

χρηστεύομαι, Dep. (χρηστός) *to behave kindly, be kind* or *merciful.*

χρηστηριάζω, f. άσω, like χράω, *to give oracles, prophesy:*—in Med., like χράομαι, *to have an oracle given one, consult an oracle;* χρηστηριάζεσθαι θεῷ *to consult* a god; ἱροῖσι χρηστηριάζεσθαι *to consult* victims. From

χρηστήριον, τό, *the seat of an oracle*, such as Delphi. 2. *the answer of an oracle, oracular response.* II. *an offering made at the time of consulting an oracle, a sacrificial victim:* metaph. *a victim, sacrifice.* Properly neut. of χρηστήριος.

χρηστήριος, α, ον, also ος, ον, (χράω) *of* or *belonging to an oracle, oracular, foreboding, presaging.* 2. *of, belonging to a prophet, prophetic.*

χρήστης, ου, ὁ: gen. pl. χρήστων (to distinguish it from χρηστῶν, gen. pl. of χρηστός): (χράω):—*one who gives* or *expounds oracles, a prophet, soothsayer.* II. *a creditor, usurer.* 2. (χράομαι) *a debtor.*

χρηστολογέω, f. ήσω, (χρηστολόγος) *to use fair words.* Hence

χρηστολογία, ἡ, *fair-speaking: a kind address.*

χρηστο-λόγος, ον, (χρηστός, λέγω) *speaking fairly.*

χρηστός, ή, όν, verb. Adj. of χράομαι, like χρήσιμος, *useful, serviceable:* χρηστά, τά, as Subst. *good services, benefits, kindnesses.* 2. *good, favourable;* τελευτὴ χρηστή a *happy* end or issue: of victims and omens, *boding good, auspicious, lucky.* II. of men, *good, stout, brave* in war; of citizens, *upright, deserving:* ironically, χρηστὸς εἶ you are *a nice fellow.* 2. of the gods, *kind, propitious:* and so of men, *good-natured, kind.* Hence

χρηστότης, ητος, ἡ, of persons, *goodness, honesty, uprightness.* 2. *kindness, good-nature*, like εὐήθεια.

χρῖμα, ατος, τό, = χρῖσμα.

χρίμπτω, f. ψω: also as Dep. **χρίμπτομαι**, f. χρίμψομαι; aor. 1 med. ἐχριμψάμην, pass. ἐχρίμφθην, part. χριμφθείς:—poët. for χραύω *to touch the surface* of a body, *to **graze**, scratch, wound*, Lat. *radere, stringere*; χριμφθεὶς πέλας *grazing* close:—more generally, *to come nigh, draw near, approach*, c. dat.; δόμοις χρίμπτεσθαι *to draw near* the house. 2. also intr. in Act., *to come* or *keep near*: also with πόδα added, πόδας χρίμπτουσα ῥαχίαισι *keeping* her feet *close* to the shore; so, ὑπ' ἐσχάτην στήλην ἔχριμπτ' ἀεὶ σύριγγα he *kept* the axle *close* upon the post.

χρῖσαν, Ep. for ἔχρῖσαν, 3 pl. aor. 1 of χρίω.

χρῖσμα, ατος, τό, (χρίω) *anything smeared on, a scented unguent*, of thicker consistency than μύρον.

Χριστιανός, ὁ, (Χριστός) *a Christian*.

χριστός, ή, όν, verb. Adj. of χρίω, *to be rubbed on, used as ointment* or *salve*; φάρμακα χριστά *salves*. II. *anointed*; τὸ χριστόν *anointing* oil. 2. Χριστός, ὁ, *the Anointed One, the CHRIST*, as a transl. of the Hebrew *Messiah*.

ΧΡΙ'Ω, f. χρίσω [ῑ]: aor. 1 ἔχρῖσα Ep. χρῖσα: Pass., aor. 1 ἐχρίσθην: pf. κέχρῖμαι:—*to touch the surface of a body: to anoint with scented unguents* or *oil*, esp. after bathing:—Med. χρίομαι, aor. 1 ἐχρισάμην, *to anoint oneself*; χρίεσθαι ἰούς *to anoint*, i.e. *poison, one's* arrows. 2. *to rub over with colour, to colour, dye, stain*; χρίεσθαι τὰ σώματα μίλτῳ *to dye their* bodies with vermilion. 3. *to puncture the skin slightly, prick, sting*.

χρόα, χροΐ, irreg. acc. and dat. of χρώς.

χροιά, ἡ, Ep. and Ion. **χροιή**, Att. also **χρόα**: (χρώς):—*the surface of a body, the skin*; hence *the body* itself. II. *the colour of the skin, the complexion*; χροιὰν ἀλλάσσειν to change *colour*: also *the colour* of a thing.

χροΐζω, f. ίσω: contr. **χρώζω**, f. σω: (χρόα):—*to touch* or *graze the surface*, also generally, *to touch*:—Med. χροΐζομαι, *to touch another person, to lie with*.

χρόμᾰδος, ὁ, *a grating* or *creaking noise, jarring, gnashing, crushing*. (Formed from the sound.)

χρονίζω, f. ίσω Att. ιῶ, (χρόνος) intr. *to spend time, tarry: to continue* or *last long, hold out*: c. part. *to persevere* in doing; c. inf. *to delay* to do: absol. *to linger, delay, be slow*. II. *to prolong, put off*:—Pass. *to be prolonged* or *protracted*: absol. *to grow up*.

χρόνιος, α, ον, and Att. ος, ον: (χρόνος):—*after a long time* or *interval, late*. 2. *for a long time*; χρόνιός εἰμι ἀπὸ βορᾶς I have been *for a long time* apart from food. 3. *long, lasting long*; χρόνιοι πόλεμοι *lasting* wars: *lingering, delaying*:—neut. pl. χρόνια as Adv., *after a long time*.

ΧΡΟ'ΝΟΣ, ὁ, *time*, indefinitely: also *a certain time, a period, season, space of time*: absol. in acc. χρόνον *for a while*; πολὺν χρόνον for a long *time*; τὸν ἀεὶ χρόνον for ever; ὀλίγου χρόνου in a short *time*: πόσου χρόνου; *for* how *long*? χρόνῳ in *time*, at last. 2. with Prepositions:—ἀνὰ χρόνον in course of *time*: διὰ χρόνου after *an interval*; ἐκ πολλοῦ χρόνου long ago; ἐν χρόνῳ in *time, at length*; ἐντὸς χρόνου within *a certain time*; ἐπὶ χρόνον for *a time*: ἐς χρόνον till *aftertime*. II. *time of life*; χρόνῳ βραδύς slow *from his time of life*.

χρονο-τρῑβέω, (χρόνος, τρίβω) *to waste time, loiter*.

χρόος, gen. of χρώς.

χρυσ-ᾱλάκατος, ον, Dor. for χρυσηλ—.

χρῡσ-ᾰμοιβός, ὁ, (χρυσός, ἀμείβω) *changing gold* or *gold money*: metaph., Ἄρης σωμάτων χρυσαμοιβός Mars *who buys* men's bodies *with gold*.

χρῡσ-άμπυξ, ῠκος, ὁ, ἡ, (χρυσός, ἄμπυξ) *with fillet* or *frontlet of gold*, epith. of horses: also of goddesses.

χρῡσ-ανθής, ές, gen. έος, (χρυσός ἄνθος) *with flower of gold*.

χρυσ-άνιος, Dor. for χρυσήνιος.

χρυσ-ανταυγής, ές, (χρυσός, ἀνταυγής) *reflecting a golden light*.

χρῡσ-άορος, ον, (χρυσός, αορ) *with sword of gold*, epith. of the gods.

χρῡσ-άρμᾰτος, ον, (χρυσός, ἅρμα) *with* or *in car of gold*, epith. of the moon.

χρύσ-ασπις, ιδος, ὁ, ἡ, (χρυσός, ἀσπίς) *with shield of gold*. [ῡ]

χρῡσ-αυγής, ές, gen. έος, (χρυσός, αὐγή) *gold-gleaming*.

χρῡσ-άωρ, ορος, ὁ, ἡ, (χρυσός, ἄορ) = χρυσάορος.

χρῡσεῖον, τό, (χρυσός) mostly in plur., χρυσεῖα, τά, *gold mines*, in full χρύσεια μέταλλα.

χρύσειος, η, ον, poët. for χρύσεος.

χρῡσ-ελεφαντ-ήλεκτρος, ον, (χρυσός, ἐλέφας, ἤλεκτρον) *of* or *overlaid with gold, ivory, and electrum*.

χρῡσεο-βόστρῠχος, ον, (χρύσεος, βόστρυχος) *with locks* or *ringlets of gold*.

χρῡσεό-δμητος, ον, (χρύσεος, δέμω) *built* or *formed of gold*.

χρῡσεό-κμητος, ον, (χρύσεος, κάμνω) *wrought of gold*.

χρῡσεό-κυκλος, ον, (χρύσεος, κύκλος) *with disk of gold*.

χρῡσεό-μαλλος, ον, = χρυσόμαλλος.

χρῡσεο-μίτρης, ου, ὁ, = χρυσομίτρης.

χρυσεό-νωτος, ον, = χρυσόνωτος.

χρῡσεο-πήληξ, ηκος, ὁ, ἡ, (χρύσεος, πήληξ) *with helm* or *casque of gold*.

χρῡσεο-πήνητος, ον, (χρυσεος, πήνη) *with woof of gold, inwrought with gold*.

χρύσεος, η, ον, and ος, ον; Att. contr. **χρυσοῦς**, ῆ, οῦν; Ep. **χρύσειος**, η, ον, (χρυσός):—*golden, of gold, inlaid with gold*: also *gilded, gilt*; χρυσοῦν τινα ἱστάναι to raise a statue *of gold* to one. 2. χρύσεια μέταλλα *gold* mines; see χρυσεῖον. II. *gold-coloured, of golden hue*. III. metaph. *golden, happy, blessed*: hence the first Age of Man was *the golden*. [In Homer, χρῡσέη, χρῡσέην, χρῡσέου, χρῡσέῳ, etc. must be pronounced as spondees.]

χρῡσεο-σάνδᾰλος, ον, (χρύσεος, σάνδαλον) *with sandals of gold*; ἴχνος χρυσεοσάνδαλον the step *of golden sandals*.

χρῡσεο-στέφᾰνος, ον, = χρυσοστέφανος.

χρῡσεό-στολμος, ον, or **χρῡσεό-στολος**, ον, (χρύσεος, στέλλω) *decked* or *dight with gold*.

χρῡσεό-τευκτος, ον, = χρυσότευκτος.

χρῡσεο-φάλᾰρος, ον, (χρύσεος, φάλαρα) *with trappings of gold.*

Χρῡσηΐς, ίδος, ἡ, patronym. of Χρύσης, ου, ὁ, *daughter of Chryses.*

χρῡσ-ηλάκᾰτος, ον. (χρυσός, ἠλακάτη) *with spindle* or *arrow of gold.*

χρῡσ-ήλᾰτος, ον, (χρυσός, ἐλαύνω) *beaten out of gold, of beaten gold.*

χρῡσ-ήνιος, ον, (χρυσός, ἡνία) *with reins of gold.*

χρῡσ-ήρης, ες, gen. εος, (χρυσός ἀρᾰρεῖν) *furnished or decked with gold, golden.*

χρῡσίδιον, τό, Dim. of χρύσιον, *a small piece of gold.*

χρῡσίον, τό, Dim. of χρυσός, *a piece of gold, gold* in general: *anything made of gold, gold coin, money;* ἀργύριον καὶ χρυσίον silver and *gold money:* but the generic term for money was ἀργύριον, as in Lat. *argentum.* II. as a term of endearment, *my little treasure!*

χρῡσίς, ίδος, ἡ, (χρυσός) *a vessel of gold.* 2. *a golden dress.*

χρῡσίτης [ῑ], ου, ὁ, fem. **χρυσῖτις**, ιδος, (χρυσός) *like gold, containing a proportion of gold.*

χρῡσο-βᾰφής, ές, (χρυσός, βαφῆναι) *gilded, gold-embroidered.*

χρῡσό-βωλος, ον, (χρυσός, βῶλος) *with soil containing gold.*

χρῡσό-γονος, ον, (χρυσός, γενέσθαι) *born* or *descended of gold,* of the Persians, because they were descended from Perseus, the son of Danaë.

χρῡσο-δαίδαλτος, ον, (χρυσός, δαιδάλλω) *richly wrought with gold.*

χρῡσο-δακτύλιος, ον, (χρυσός, δακτυλιον) *with a gold ring.* [κτῠ]

χρῡσό-δετος, ον, also η, ον, (χρυσός, δέω) *bound with gold, set in gold: overlaid with gold.*

χρῡσο-έθειρ, ειρος, ὁ, ἡ, (χρυσός, ἔθειρα) *with golden hair.*

χρῡσο-ειδής, ές, (χρυσός, εἶδος) *like gold.*

χρῡσό-ζῠγος, ον, (χρυσός, ζυγόν) *with yoke of gold.*

χρῡσό-θριξ, -τρῐχος, ὁ, ἡ, (χρυσός, θρίξ) *golden-haired.*

χρῡσό-θρονος, ον, (χρυσός, θρόνος) *on throne of gold, gold-enthroned.*

χρῡσο-κάρηνος Dor. -ᾱνος, ον, (χρυσός, κάρηνον) *with head of gold.* [κᾰ]

χρῡσό-κερως, ωτος, ὁ, ἡ, and **χρῡσό-κερως**, ων, gen. ω: (χρυσός, κέρας):—*with horns of gold.* II. *with gilded horns,* like a victim for the sacrifice.

χρῡσο-κόλλητος, ον, (χρυσός, κολλάω) *welded* or *wrought of gold:* generally, *of gold, golden.*

χρῡσό-κολλος, ον, (χρυσός, κολλάω) *welded* or *inlaid with gold.*

χρῡσο-κόμης, ὁ, Dor. -μας, α, ὁ, (χρυσός, κόμη) *he of the golden hair:* ὁ Χρυσοκόμης *the golden-haired,* for Apollo.

χρῡσό-κομος, ον, (χρυσός, κόμη) *golden-haired: with golden plumage.*

χρῡσο-κρότᾰλος, ον, (χρυσός, κρόταλον) *rattling* or *ringing with gold.*

χρῡσό-λῐθος, ἡ, (χρυσός, λίθος) *the chrysolith* or *gold-stone,* a bright yellow stone, perhaps *the topaz.*

χρῡσολογέω, f. ήσω, *to talk of gold.* II. *to collect gold,* i. e. *money.* From

χρῡσο-λόγος, ον, (χρυσός, λέγω) *speaking of gold.*

χρῡσό-λογχος, ον, (χρυσός, λόγχη) *with golden spear.*

χρῡσό-λοφος, α, ον, (χρυσός, λόφος) *with golden crest.*

χρῡσο-λύρης, ου, ὁ, Dor. -λύρας, (χρυσός, λύρα) *with golden lyre.* [λῠ]

χρῡσό-μαλλος, ον, (χρυσός, μαλλός) *with golden fleece.*

χρῡσο-μανής, ές, (χρυσός, μανῆναι) *mad after gold.*

χρῡσο-μηλολόνθη, ἡ, (χρυσός, μηλολόνθη) *the gold-beetle* or *cockchafer.* Hence

χρῡσο-μηλολόνθιον or -όντιον, τό, Dim. of χρυσομηλολόνθη, *a little cockchafer:* used as a term of endearment.

χρῡσο-μίτρης, ου, ὁ, (χρυσός, μίτρα) *with girdle* or *head-band of gold.* [μῐ]

χρῡσό-μορφος, ον, (χρυσός, μορφή) *in the shape* or *likeness of gold.*

χρῡσό-νωτος, ον, (χρυσός, νῶτος) *with golden back: covered with gold;* χρυσόνωτος ἡνία a rein *studded with gold.*

χρῡσό-παστος, ον, (χρυσός, πάσσω) *sprinkled* or *shot with gold;* χρυσόπαστος τιήρης a turban *of gold tissue;* τὰ χρυσόπαστα *gilded splendours.*

χρῡσο-πέδῑλος, ον, (χρυσός, πέδιλον) *with sandals of gold.*

χρῡσό-πεπλος, ον, (χρυσός, πέπλον) *with robe of gold.*

χρῡσο-πήληξ, ηκος, ὁ, ἡ, (χρυσός, πήληξ) *with helm* or *casque of gold.*

χρῡσο-πλόκᾰμος, ον, (χρυσός, πλόκαμος) *with tresses of gold.*

χρῡσο-ποιός, όν, (χρυσός, ποιέω) *working in gold:* as Subst., χρυσοποιός, ὁ, *a goldsmith.*

χρῡσό-πρᾰσος, ὁ, (χρυσός, πράσον) *the chrysoprase,* a precious stone *of a yellow-green colour.*

χρῡσό-πτερος, ον, (χρυσός, πτερόν) *with wings of gold.*

χρῡσό-ρᾰπις, ὁ, poët. for χρυσόρραπις.

χρῡσό-ροος, ον, (χρυσός, ῥέω) *streaming with gold.*

χρῡσ-όροφος, ον, (χρυσός, ὀροφή) *with golden roof* or *ceiling.*

χρῡσόρ-ρᾰπις, ιδος, ὁ, ἡ, (χρυσός, ῥαπίς) *with wand of gold.*

χρῡσόρ-ρῡτος, ον, (χρυσός, ῥέω) *flowing with gold, in a stream of gold.*

ΧΡΥ͂ΣΟ´Σ, οῦ, ὁ, *gold,* Lat. *aurum;* χρυσὸς κοῖλος *gold wrought into vessels, gold plate;* χρυσὸς ἄπεφθος refined *gold;* λευκὸς χρυσός white *gold,* i. e. alloyed with silver.

χρῡσο-στέφᾰνος, ον, (χρυσός στέφανος) *gold-crowned.*

χρῦσό-στομος, *ον*, (χρυσός. στόμα) *of golden mouth, dropping words of gold.*

χρῦσό-στροφος, *ον*, (χρυσός, στρέφω) *twisted with gold*: of a bow, *strung with twisted gold.*

χρῦσο-τέκτων, *ονος*, ὁ, *a worker in gold, goldsmith.*

χρῦσότερος, *α*, *ον*, Comp. Adj. formed from χρυσός, *more golden.*

χρῦσό-τευκτος, *ον*, (χρυσός, τεύχω) *wrought of gold.*

χρῦσο-τευχής, *ές*, (χρυσός, τεῦχος) *with golden armour.*

χρῦσό-τοξος, *ον*, (χρυσός, τόξον) *with bow of gold.*

χρῦσο-τρίαινος, *ον*, (χρυσός, τρίαινα) *with trident of gold.* [ῐ]

χρῦσ-ούᾰτος, *ον*, (χρυσός, οὖας) *with ears* or *handles of gold.*

χρῦσοῦς, ῆ, οῦν, Att. contr. for χρυσεος.

χρῦσο-φάεννος, *ον*, (χρυσός, φαίνομαι) = χρυσοφαής.

χρῦσο-φαής, *ές*, (χρυσός, φάος) *with golden light.*

χρῦσο-φεγγής, *ές*, (χρυσός, φέγγος) *with golden beam.*

χρῦσό-φῐλος, *ον*, (χρυσός, φίλος) *gold-loving.*

χρῦσοφοοέω, f. ήσω, *to wear gold* or *golden apparel.* From

χρῦσο-φόρος, *ον*, (χρυσός, φέρω) *wearing gold* or *golden apparel.*

χρῦσο-φύλαξ, ᾰκος, ο, η, (χρυσος, φύλαξ) *a guarder* or *keeper of gold: a treasurer.* [φῠ]

χρῦσο-χαίτης, *ου*, ὁ, (χρυσός, χαίτη) *with golden hair*: fem. **χρυσόχαιτις**, *ιδος.*

χρῦσο-χάλῖνος, *ον*, (χρυσός, χαλινός) *with gold-studded bridle.* [ᾰ]

χρῦσό-χειρ, –χειρος, ὁ, ἡ, (χρυσός, χείρ) *with gold on one's fingers.*

χρῦσο-χίτων ωνος, ὁ, ἡ, (χρυσός, χιτων) *with coat of gold.* [χῐ]

χρῦσοχοεῖον, τό, *the shop of a goldsmith.* From

χρῦσοχοέω, f. ήσω, (χρυσοχόος) *to be a goldsmith* or *gold-refiner: to work in gold.*

χρῦσοχοϊκός, ή, όν, *belonging to a goldsmith* or *gold-refiner*; χρυσοχοϊκὴν τέχνην ἐργάζεσθαι *to follow* the trade *of a goldsmith.* From

χρῦσο-χόος, *ον*, (χρυσός, χέω) *melting* or *casting gold*:—as Subst., χρυσοχόος, ὁ, *one who gilds the horns* of a victim; *a goldsmith.*

χρῦσό-χροος, *ον* contr. **–χρους**, *ουν*, (χρυσός, χρόα) *gold-coloured.*

χρῦσόω, f. ώσω, (χρυσός) *to make golden, gild.*

χρυσῶ, Dor. for χρυσοῦ, gen. of χρυσός.

χρύσωμα, *ατος*, τό, (χρυσόω) *that which is made of gold, wrought gold, gold-plate.* [ῡ]

χρῦσ-ωνέω, (χρυσός, ὠνέομαι) *to buy* or *change gold.*

χρῦσ-ώπης, *ου*, ὁ, fem. –ῶπις, ιδος, = χρυσωπός.

χρῦσ-ωπός, *όν*, (χρυσός, ὤψ) *with golden eyes* or *face, beaming like gold.*

χρύσωσις, *εως*, ἡ, (χρυσόω) *a gilding.* [ῡ]

χρῦσ-ώψ, ῶπος, ὁ, ἡ, (χρυσός, ὤψ) *gold-coloured, shining like gold.*

χρᾶ, contr. from χραου, pres. imperat. of χράομαι.

χρῷ, irreg. dat. of χρώς.

χρώζω, f. χρώσω: aor. 1 ἔχρωσα: Pass., aor. 1 ἐχρώσθην: pf. κέχρωσμαι: (χρώς):—like χροΐζω, *to touch the surface of a body*: generally, *to touch, clasp.* 2. *to tinge, stain*: generally, *to taint, defile.*

χρῶμα, *ατος*, τό, (χρώννυμι) *the surface of the body, the skin.* II. *the colour of the skin, the complexion*; μεθιστάναι τοῦ χρώματος to change *colour.* III. metaph. in pl. *ornaments, embellishments.* IV. as a technical term in Greek Music, *a modification of the diatonic music.* Hence

χρωματικός, ή, όν, *suited for colour.* II. ἡ χρωματικὴ (sc. μουσική) *the chromatic music* of the ancients, differing from the diatonic in having the tetrachord divided into less simple intervals.

χρωμάτιον, τό, (χρῶμα) *a colour, paint, dye.* [ᾰ]

χρώννῦμι, = χρώζω.

χρώς, ὁ, χρωτός, χρωτί, χρῶτα: Ion. χροός, χροΐ, χρόα: Att. dat. χρῷ:—like χροιά and χρῶμα, *the surface of the body, the skin*, also *the body itself: the flesh*, as opp. to the bone: generally, *one's body, frame.* 2. ἐν χροΐ, Att. ἐν χρῷ, *close to the skin*: ἐν χροῒ κείρειν to shave *close*: metaph., ξυρεῖ ἐν χρῷ it shaves *close*, i. e. it touches one *nearly*, comes *home*; ἐν χρῷ παραπλέειν to sail past *so as to shave* or *graze*, Virgil's *radere littus.* II. *the colour of the skin, complexion*; χρὼς τρέπεται *his colour* changes.

χρωστήρ, ῆρος, ὁ, (χρώζω) *one who colours* or *dyes*: χρωστὴρ μόλυβος *a* lead-*pencil.*

χρωτίζω, f. ίσω, (χρώς) like χρώζω, *to colour, dye, tint*:—Med., χρωτίζεσθαι τὴν φύσιν τινί *to tinge one's* nature with something.

χύδην [ῠ], Adv. (χέω) *in a stream* or *flood, without order, confusedly.* II. *in flowing language*, i. e. *in prose*, opp. to poetry. III. *abundantly, utterly.*

χῠθείην, aor. 1 pass. opt. of χέω.

χῡλός, οῦ, ὁ, (χέω) *juice, moisture: a decoction.* 2. *juice drawn out by digestion, chyle.* II. *the flavour, taste* of a thing.

χύμενος, Ep. aor. 2 pass. of χέω. [ῠ]

χῡμίζω, f. ίσω Att. ιῶ, (χυμός) *to make savory, season*: metaph. *to tone down, temper.*

χυμός, οῦ, ὁ, (χέω) *juice.* II. *taste, flavour.*

χύντο, 3 pl. Ep. aor. 2 pass. of χέω

χύσις, *εως*, ἡ, (χέω) *a pouring, shedding.* II. *a flood, stream, gush.* 2. of dry things, *a heap: a quantity.* [ῠ]

χῠτλάζω, f. ασω, *to pour out*: metaph. *to throw carelessly down.* From

χύτλον, τό, (χέω) *anything that can be poured, a liquid, fluid*: esp., 1. in plur. χύτλα, τά, *water for washing* or *bathing.* 2. *a mixture of water and oil* rubbed in after bathing. [ῠ] Hence

χῠτλόω, f. ώσω, *to wash, bathe, anoint*:—Med. *to anoint oneself after bathing.*

χῠτλώσαιτο, 3 sing. aor. 1 med. of χυτλόω.

χύτο, 3 sing. Ep. aor. 2 pass. of χέω. [ῠ]

χῠτός, ή, όν, verb. Adj. of χέω, *poured, shed.* 2. of dry things, *heaped up; χυτὴ γαῖα a mound of* earth. 2. as Subst., χυτοί, οἱ, *mounds, dykes, dams.* II. *made liquid, cast, melted; ἀρτήματα λίθινα χυτά* pendants of *melted* stone, i. e. of glass. III. *liquid, fluid, flowing.*

χύτρα, ἡ, (χέω) *an earthen pot*:—pl. χύτραι, αἱ, *the pottery-market*:—χύτραι were also *pots of pulse,* used to consecrate altars and statues of inferior gods; hence of a statue, ταύτην χύτραις ἱδρυτέον this must be erected *with pots of pulse.* [ῠ]

χύτρειος, α, ον, = χυτρεοῦς, *of earthenware: τὰ χύτρεια earthenware, pottery.* [ῠ]

χῠτρεοῦς, ῆ, οῦν, (χύτρα) *of earthenware.*

χῠτρεύς, έως, ὁ, (χύτρα) *a potter.*

χῠτρίδιον, τό, Dim. of χυτρίς, *a small pot.* [ῐ]

χῠτρίζω, f. ίσω Att. ιῶ, (χύτρα) *to put in a pot: to expose a child in a pot.*

χύτρῖνος, η, ον, (χύτρα) *of* or *like a pot, earthen,* Lat. *testaceus.* [ῠ]

χῠτρίς, ίδος, ἡ, Dim. of χύτρα or χύτρος, *a pot.*

χῠτρό-πους, -ποδος, ὁ, (χύτρος, πούς) *a pot* or *caldron with feet:* also a kind of *chafing-dish.*

χύτρος, ὁ, (χέω) *an earthen pot,* esp. *for boiling:* οἱ χύτροι was the name given to *the hot-baths* at Thermopylae. II. οἱ χύτροι, also, *the feast of pots,* the third day of the Anthesteria, and thirteenth of the month Anthesterion. [ῠ]

χῶ, contr. for καὶ ὁ.

χώεο, 2 Ep. sing. imperat. of χώομαι.

χωλαίνω, f. ᾰνῶ, (χωλός) *to be* or *go lame.*

χωλεύω, (χωλός) *to be* or *become lame, to halt, limp.*

χωλ-ίαμβος, ὁ, (χωλός, ἴαμβος) *a lame* or *halting iambic,* i. e. one that has a spondee for an iambus in the last place, said to have been invented by Hipponax; also called σκάζων.

χωλο-ποιός, όν, (χωλός, ποιέω) *making lame men,* of Euripides, who was fond of *introducing lame men* upon the stage.

ΧΩΛΟ'Σ, ή, όν, *lame, halting, limping:* also of the hand, *maimed.* II. metaph. *maimed, imperfect, defective,* Lat. *mancus.*

χῶμα, ατος, τό, (χώννυμι) *earth thrown up, a bank, mound,* thrown up by besiegers against the walls of cities: *a dam, mound, mole* or *pier,* thrown into the sea, Lat. *moles:* also like Lat. *tumulus, a sepulchral mound.*

χῶν, part. of χόω: see χώννυμι.

χώνη, ἡ, contr. from χοάνη, (χέω) *a melting-pit, a mould to cast in.* 2. *a funnel.*

χώννῦμι: f. χώσω: aor. 1 ἔχωσα: Pass., fut. χωσθήσομαι: aor. 1 ἐχώσθην: pf. κέχωσμαι: there is also the regul. pres. χόω, inf. χοῦν, part. χῶν: (χέω): —*to throw* or *heap up; χώματα χοῦν to heap up* a mound: *to raise a sepulchral mound.* 2. *to block up by throwing in earth, to dam up*:—Pass. *to be filled with earth, be silted up with deposit* from rivers. 3. in Pass. of cities, *to be raised on mounds* or *moles.* 4. *to cover with a mound of earth, bury; χῶσαί τινα λίθοις to cover* any one over with stones: —Pass. *to be heaped up with earth, have a sepulchral mound raised over* one.

ΧΩ'ΟΜΑΙ, f. χώσομαι: aor. 1 ἐχωσάμην:—Pass. *to be angry, be wroth, be enraged:* c. acc., χωόμενος κῆρ *enraged* at heart; also c. dat., χώεσθαι φρέσιν ᾗσιν:—c. dat. pers. *to be angry at* one: also c. gen. pers. vel rei, *to be angry about* a person or thing: and c. neut. acc., μή μοι τόδε χώεο *be not angry with me for* this.

χώρα Ion. **χώρη**, ἡ, = χῶρος, *the space* or *room in which a thing is, a place, spot,* Lat. *locus: the place assigned, the proper place;* κατὰ χώραν εἶναι to be in *one's place;* κατὰ χώραν μένειν to stay *in one's place, to stand one's ground;* ἐᾶν κατὰ χώραν to leave in *its place,* leave as it *was;* χώραν λαβεῖν to take *a position,* find *one's place;* ἕως ἂν χώραν λάβῃ τὰ πράγματα till the affairs find *their proper place.* 2. metaph. *the place assigned to any one, one's post, station, office, position;* ἐν ἀνδραπόδων χώρᾳ εἶναι to be ranked *in the place* of slaves; ἐν οὐδεμιᾷ χώρᾳ εἶναι to be of no *account,* Lat. *nullo in numero haberi.* II. *a land, country, tract,* Lat. *regio;* ἡ χώρα *one's country.* 2. *landed property, land, an estate, farm,* Lat. *ager.* 3. *the country,* opp. to the town, Lat. *rus.*

χωρέω, f. ήσω Att. ήσομαι: aor. 1 ἐχώρησα: pf. κεχώρηκα: (χῶρος):—*to make room for another give way: to draw back, retire, withdraw;* νεκροῦ χωρήσουσι *they will retire* from the dead body; ἀπὸ νηῶν ἐχώρησαν προτὶ Ἴλιον *they retired* from the ships to Ilium. 2. c. dat. pers. *to give way to* one, *make way for* him. II. *to make room;* and so, *go forward, advance, to go on, come on;* χωρεῖν πρὸς ἔργον *to come to* action; χωρεῖν πρὸς ἧπαρ *to go* to one's heart. 2. *to advance, make way, proceed:* οὐ χωρεῖ τοὔργον the work *advances* not. 3. *to come to an issue, turn out* in a certain manner: absol. *to go on well, succeed;* παρὰ σμικρὰ χωρεῖν *to come* to little. 4. *to spread abroad, become current,* of reports. III. transit. *to have space* or *room for* a thing, *to hold, contain,* like χανδάνω; ὁ κρητὴρ χωρεῖ ἀμφορέας ἑξακοσίους the bowl *holds* 600 amphorae; ἡ πόλις αὐτὸν οὐ χωρεῖ the city *cannot contain* him.

χωρίδιον, τό, Dim. of χωρίον, *a little spot.* [ρῐ]

χωρίζω, f. ίσω Att. ιῶ: pf. pass. κεχώρισμαι, Ion. 3 pl. κεχωρίδαται: (χωρίς):—*to separate, part, sever, divide*:—οἱ χωρίζοντες *Separatists,* a name given to those Grammarians who ascribed the Iliad and Odyssey to different authors:—Pass. *to be separated, severed* or *divided,* hence *to differ, be at variance;* νόμοι κεχωρισμένοι *different* laws.

χωρίον, τό, Dim. of χῶρος and χώρα, *a particular place, a place, spot, country;* ἐκ τοῦ αὐτοῦ χωρίου from the same *spot.* 2. also *a place* or *passage in a book,* Lat. *locus.* II. *a strong place, outpost,* *a fortified post* or *town*, esp. *a detached fort.* III. *landed property*, *an estate.*

χωρίς, Adv. *separately, asunder, apart by oneself; κεῖται χωρὶς ὁ νεκρός* the corpse lies *apart.* 2. *separately, one by one.* 3. *χωρὶς μέν .., χωρὶς δέ .., on one side .., on the other, by themselves .., by themselves ..* 4. *χωρὶς ἢ ὁπόσοι except* so many as .. ; *χωρὶς ἤ except; χωρὶς ἢ ὅτι except* that. II. *of different* or *distinct kind; χωρὶς τό τ' εἰπεῖν πολλὰ καὶ τὰ καίρια* it is *a different thing* to say many things and to the purpose.

χωρίς, Prep. with gen., *without: without the help* or *will of; χωρὶς θεοῦ*, Lat. *sine diis, without the favour of* the gods. 2. *separate from, apart from; χωρὶς ὀμμάτων ἐμῶν far from* my eyes. 3. *independent of, without reckoning, besides.*

χωρισμός, ὁ, (χωρίζω) *a separating, separation.*

χωρίτης [ῑ], ου, ὁ, fem. **χωρῖτις**, ιδος, (χώρα, χῶρος) *a countryman, rustic, boor:* fem. *χωρῖτις, ιδος, a country girl.* Hence

χωρῖτικός, ή, όν, *beseeming a countryman, rustic, rural.* Adv. -κῶς, *in rustic fashion.*

χῶρος, ὁ, *space to hold a thing, room, a place, spot.* II. *a place, a land, country*, Lat. *regio:* c. gen. *the district* or *tract belonging to* or *about a place*; *χῶρος τῆς Ἀραβίης the tract* of Arabia. 2. *landed property, an estate.* (Akin to χανδάνω, χάζομαι.)

Χῶρος, ου, ὁ, *Corus* or *Caurus, the north-west wind: the NW. quarter.*

χωρο-φιλέω, f. ήσω, (χῶρος, φιλέω) *to love a place* or *spot, haunt, frequent it.*

χὡς, contr. for καὶ ὡς.

χῶσαι, aor. 1 inf. of χώννυμι.

χωσάμενος, aor. 1 part. of χώομαι.

χωσθῆναι, aor. 1 pass. inf. of χώννυμι.

χῶσις, εως, ἡ, (χῶσαι) *a heaping up* of earth, *raising a mound* or *bank*, esp. by besiegers against a city: *a filling in, blocking up by earth thrown in; ἡ χῶσις τῶν λιμένων the blocking up* of harbours.

χὤσους, crasis for καὶ ὅσους.

χωστός, ή, όν, verb. Adj. of χώννυμι, *heaped up made of earth thrown up.*

Ψ

Ψ, ψ, ψῖ, τό, indecl., twenty-third letter of the Greek alphabet: as a numeral ψʹ = 700, but ͵ψ = 700,000.—The letter ψ is a double Consonant, compounded of σ and a labial, = πσ, βσ, or φσ. The *character* ψ was at first only Ion., and was adopted at Athens at the same time with η, ω and ξ: see H, η.

Changes of ψ, esp. in the dialects: I. in Aeol. the older πσ was retained, esp. in prop. names, as Πέλοπς for Πέλοψ. II. ψ was resolved into σπ, as, ἀσπίνθιον for ἀψίνθιον, ψίν Dor. for σφίν, ψέ for σφέ. III. ψ was sometimes put for σ or σσ, as, ψιττακός for σιττακός, κόψιχος for κόσσυφος. IV. ψ was omitted or added as in ἄμμος ἄμαθος, ψάμμος ψάμαθος.

ψᾰθῠρός, όν, (ψάω) *friable, crumbling, falling to pieces, loose*

ψαίρω, (ψάω) *to graze* or *touch gently; ψαίρειν πτεροῖς οἶμον αἰθέρος to skim* with wings the path of ether, as in Virgil *radere iter liquidum.* II. intrans. *to move lightly, to quiver, flutter.*

ψαιστίον, τό, Dim. of ψαιστόν, *a small cake.*

ψαιστός, ή, όν, verb. Adj. of ψαίω, *ground;* **τὰ** *ψαιστά* (sub. πέμματα) *cakes of ground barley.*

ψαίστωρ, ορος, ὁ, masc. Adj. *that which wipes off.*

ψαίω, f. σω, (ψάω) *to rub away, grind down, pound.*

ψᾰκάζω later **ψεκάζω**, f. άσω, (ψακάς) *to rain in small drops, drizzle, drip:* impers., like ὕει, etc., *ψακάζει it drizzles.*

ψᾰκάς later **ψεκάς**, άδος, ἡ, (ψάω) *any small piece rubbed* or *broken off, a grain, crumb, morsel, bit; ἀργυρίου μηδὲ ψακάς* not even *a farthing* of money: as collective Subst., *ψάμμου ψακάς grains* of sand. 2. *a small drop, a quantity of small drops, a small drizzling rain*, opp. to ὄμβρος; *ὕσθησαν αἱ Θῆβαι ψακάδι* Thebes was rained on *by a drizzling rain:* metaph., *φοίνισσα ψεκάς a shower* of blood.

ψᾰλῐδό-στομος, ον, (ψαλίς, στόμα) *having a mouth* or *head like a pair of shears*, epith. of a crab.

ψᾰλίζω: fut. ίσω and ίξω Att. ιῶ: (ψαλίς):—*to clip with shears* or *scissors.*

ΨΑ΄ΛΙΟΝ, *a ring on the curb-chain* of a bridle, to which the leading-rein was fastened: plur. *ψάλια, τά, the curb-chain* itself: hence more generally, *a chain*, and metaph. *a curb, constraint.*

ψᾰλίς, ῖδος, ἡ, (ψάω) *a pair of shears* or *scissors*, Lat. *forfex.*

ΨΑ΄ΛΛΩ, strengthd. from ψάω: f. ψᾰλῶ: aor. 1 ἔψηλα: pf. ἔψαλκα:—*to touch, stir* or *move by touching, to pull, pluck.* 2. *to pull and let go again, to pull, twang with the fingers; τόξου νευρὰν ψάλλειν to twang* the bow-string: *to play* a stringed instrument *with the fingers*, instead of with the plectrum: absol. *to play*, and later, *to sing to a harp.* 3. Pass., of the instrument, *to be struck* or *played.* Hence

ψάλμα, ατος, τό, *a tune played on a stringed instrument.*

ψαλμός, ὁ, (ψάλλω) *a pulling* or *twanging* musical strings with the fingers. 2. *a strain* or *burst of music:* later, *a song sung to a stringed instrument: a psalm.* Hence

ψαλμο-χᾰρής, ές, (ψαλμός, χαρῆναι) *delighting in harp-playing.*

ψαλτήρ, ῆρος, also τῆς, του, ὁ, (ψάλλω) *a harper.*

ψάλτρια, ἡ, fem. of ψαλτήρ.

ψάμᾰθος, ἡ, (ψάω) *sea-sand, the sandy shore, the sands:* proverb. of a countless multitude, *ὅσα ψάμαθός τε κόνις τε* as many as *the sand* and *dust.* See ψάμμος. [ψᾰ]

ψᾰμᾰθ-ώδης, ες, (ψάμαθος, εἶδος) *sandy.*

ψᾰμᾰθών, ῶνος, ὁ, (ψάμαθος) *a sandy place, sand-pits*, Lat. *sabuletum.*

ψαμμᾱκοσιο-γάργᾱροι, αι, α, (ψαμμακόσιοι, Γάργαρα) Comic word in Aristophanes, *numberless as heaps of sand:* cf. sq.

ψαμμ-ᾱκόσιοι, αι, α, *sand-hundred, numberless as the sand*, a Comic word formed from ψάμμος ἕκατον, as the cardinal numbers διακόσιοι, τριακόσιοι from δὶς ἑκατόν, τρὶς ἑκατόν, to denote a countless multitude.

ψάμμη Dor. **ψάμμα**, ἡ, = ψάμμος, *sand.*

ψάμμῐνος, η, ον, (ψάμμος) *of sand, in the sand, sandy.*

ψάμμιος, α, ον, = ψάμμινος, *on the sand.*

ψαμμίτης [ῑ], ου, ὁ, fem. **ψαμμῖτις**, ιδος, (ψάμμος) *of sand, sandy.*

ψάμμος, ἡ, (ψάω) *sand*, so called from its loose crumbling nature: proverb., ἐκ ψάμμου σχοινίον πλέκειν to weave a rope *of sand*, of labour in vain. II. *a tract of sand, the sand.*—Both ψάμμος and its poët. form ψάμαθος sometimes drop the ψ, and become ἄμμος ἄμαθος.

ψαμμ-ώδης, ες, (ψάμμος, εἶδος) *sandy.*

ψᾱνός, Dor. for ψηνός.

ψάρ, ψᾱρός, Ion. **ψήρ**, ψηρός, ὁ, *a starling*, Lat. *sturnus.*

ψᾱρός, ά, όν, (ψάρ) *like a starling, ashen-gray* or *speckled;* ψαρὸς ἵππος *a dapple-gray* horse.

ψαύω, f. ψαύσω: aor. 1 ἔψαυσα: pf. act. ἔψαυκα, pass. ἔψαυσμαι: (ψάω):—*to touch*, c. gen.: c. dat. instrumenti, ψαῦον κόρυθες φάλοισιν the helmets *touched with* their plumes; it is also used c. acc. in two passages of Sophocles, (1) ἔψαυσας ἀλγεινοτάτας ἐμοὶ μερίμνας, πατρὸς τριπόλιστον οἶτον *thou hast touched upon* themes of grief most painful to me, the thrice-told fate of my father; (2) κεῖνος ἐπέγνω ψαύων τὸν θεὸν ἐν κερτομίοις γλώσσαις he knew too late *that he had attacked* the god with abusive speech. II. *to touch as an enemy, lay hands upon.* III. *to touch, reach, affect:* also *to reach, gain.*

ψᾰφᾰρίτης, ου, ὁ, fem. –ῖτις, ιδος, = ψαφαρός.

ψᾰφᾰρός, ά, όν Ion. **ψαφερός**, ή, όν, (ψάω) *friable, loose, crumbling, without consistency.* II. *dry, dusty, sandy:*—as Subst., ἡ ψαφαρά *the shore*, opp. to ἅλς.

ψᾰφᾰρό-τρῐχος, ον, (ψαφαρός, θρίξ) *with rough shaggy hair* or *coat.*

ψᾰφᾰρό-χροος, ον contr. –**χρους**, ουν, (ψαφαρός, χρόα) *rough on the surface.*

ψᾶφιγξ, **ψᾶφος**, Dor. for ψῆφιγξ, ψῆφος.

ΨΑ'Ω [ᾱ], ψῇς, ψῇ, inf. ψῆν (for the regular forms ψᾷς, ψᾷ, ψᾶν are incorrect): f. ψήσω: Pass., aor. 1 ἐψήθην: pf. ἔψημαι:—*to touch on the surface, to rub: to rub away:* intr. *to crumble away, trickle away, disappear.*

ψέ, Dor. for σφέ, as ψίν for σφίν: always enclit.

ΨΕ'ΓΩ, f. ψέξω: aor. 1 ἔψεξα:—*to blame, disparage, find fault with*, c. acc.; ψέγειν τινὰ περί τινος *to blame* one for a thing: also, with a neut. Adj., ἅ με ψέγεις the things wherein *thou blamest me.*

ψεδνός, ή, όν, (ψέω) *rubbed off, thin, spare, scanty*, of hair; of a person. *bald-headed.*

ψεδῡρός or **ψεθυρός**, ά, όν, = ψιθυρός.

ψείω, Ep. for ψέω, which is Ion. for ψάω.

ψεκάζω, **ψεκάς**. see ψακάζω, ψακάς.

ψέκτης, ου, ὁ, (ψέγω) *a blamer, censurer, disparager.*

ψεκτός, ή, όν, verb. Adj. of ψέγω, *blamed, to be blamed, blameable.* Adv. –τῶς.

ΨΕ'ΛΙΟΝ, τό, *an armlet, bracelet*, Lat. *armilla:* in pl. ψέλια, τά, *bracelets, armlets*, a favourite ornament of the Persians.

ψελιο-φόρος, ον, (ψέλιον, φέρω) *wearing bracelets.*

ψελιόω, f. ώσω, (ψέλιον) *to twine, wreath.*

ψέλλιον, incorrect form of ψέλιον.

ΨΕΛΛΟ'Σ, ή, όν, *unable to pronounce certain letters* or *syllables*, like a child. II. of words, *indistinctly uttered, unintelligible, obscure.*

ψευδ-αγγελής, ές, gen. έος, = ψευδάγγελος. Hence

ψευδαγγελία, ἡ, *a false message* or *report.*

ψευδ-άγγελος, ον, (ψευδής, ἀγγέλλω) *bringing a false message* or *report:*—as Subst., ψευδάγγελος, ὁ, *a false* or *lying messenger.*

ψευδ-άδελφος, ὁ, (ψευδής, ἀδελφός) *a false brother: a pretended Christian.* [ᾰ]

ψευδ-ᾰμάμαξῠς, υος, ὁ, (ψευδής, ἀμάμαξυς) *a false, barren vine.* [μᾰμ]

ψευδ-ᾰπόστολος, ὁ, (ψευδής, ἀπόστολος) *a false apostle.*

Ψευδ-αρτάβας, (ψευδής, ἀρτάβη) Comic name of a mock-Persian in Aristophanes, literally, *False-measure:* see ἀρτάβη.

ψευδ-ατράφαξυς, υος, ἡ, (ψευδής, ἀτράφαξυς) *false orach*, Comic name of a plant in Aristophanes.

ψευδ-αττικός, ή, όν, (ψευδής, Ἀττικός) *false Attic sham Attic.*

ψευδ-αυτόμολος, ὁ, ἡ, (ψευδής, αὐτόμολος) *a sham deserter.*

ψευδ-ενέδρα, ἡ, (ψευδής, ἐνέδρα) *a sham ambuscade.*

ψεύδεο, Ep. imperat. of ψεύδομαι.

ψευδηγορέω, f. ήσω, *to speak falsely* or *untruly, to lie.* From

ψευδ-ηγόρος, ον, (ψευδής, ἀγορεύω) *false-speaking.*

ψευδη-λογέω, f. ήσω, = ψευδολογέω.

ψευδής, ές, gen. έος, (ψεύδομαι) *lying, false, untrue*, Lat. *mendax, falsus*, opp. to ἀληθής; ψευδὴς φαίνεσθαι to be detected *in falsehood:*—as Subst. ψευδής, ὁ, *a liar:* ψευδῆ, τά, *falsehoods:*—ψευδεῖς λόγοι *fallacies.* II. pass. *belied, deceived.* III. Att. irreg. Sup. ψευδίστατος, η, ον, *most lying:* as Subst., ψευδίστατος, ὁ, *an arch-liar.*

ψεῦδις, ιος, ὁ, ἡ, poët. for ψευδής.

ψευδο-βοήθεια, ἡ, (ψευδής, βοήθεια) *pretended help.*

ψευδο-δῐδάσκᾰλος, ὁ, (ψευδής, διδάσκαλος) *a false teacher.*

ψευδο-κήρυξ, ῡκος, ὁ, (ψευδής, κῆρυξ) *a false* or *lying herald.*

ψευδο-κλητεία or **-κλητία**, ἡ, (ψευδής, κλητεύω) *a false citation* or *summons, false indorsement of a summons*, as if the indorser had witnessed the service of it; γραφὴ ψευδοκλητείας a prosecution *for such false indorsement.*

ψευδό-λιτρος, ον, (ψευδής, λίτρον) Att. for ψευδόνιτρος, *made from adulterated soda.*

ψευδολογέω, f. ήσω, (ψευδολόγος) *to speak falsely, spread false reports.* Hence

ψευδολογία, ἡ, *a false speech, falsehood, false report.*

ψευδο-λόγος, ον, (ψευδής, λέγω) *speaking falsely.*

ψευδό-μαντις, εως, ὁ, ἡ, (ψευδής, μάντις) *a false, lying prophet.*

ψευδομαρτῠρέω, f. ήσω, *to be a false witness, bear false witness.* Hence

ψευδομαρτῠρία, ἡ, *false witness, a bearing false witness, perjury:* mostly in plur., ψευδομαρτυριῶν ἁλῶναι to be convicted of *perjury.*

ψευδομαρτυρίου δίκη, (ψευδής, μαρτύριον) an action *for false witness* or *perjury*, only used in gen.

ψευδο-μάρτυς, ῠρος, ὁ, (ψευδής, μάρτυς) *a false witness.*

ψευδό-νιτρος ον, (ψευδής, νίτρον) see ψευδόλιτρος.

ψευδο-νύμφευτος, ον, (ψευδής, νυμφεύω) *falsely wedded;* ψευδονύμφευτος γάμος *a pretended* marriage.

ψευδο-πάρθενος, ἡ, (ψευδής, παρθένος) *a pretended maid* or *virgin.*

ψευδο-ποιός, όν, (ψεῦδος, ποιέω) *framing lies.*

ψευδο-προφήτης, ου, ὁ, (ψευδής, προφήτης) *a false* or *lying prophet.*

ψευδορκέω, f. ήσω, (ψεύδορκος) *to swear falsely, be forsworn.*

ψευδ-όρκιος, ον, (ψευδής, ὅρκιον) *perjured, forsworn.*

ψεύδ-ορκος, ον, (ψευδής, ὅρκος) = ψευδόρκιος.

ψεῦδος, εος, τό, Ep. dat. pl. ψεύδεσσι, (ψεύδω) *a lie, falsehood, untruth: a fraud, deceit.* II. *a pimple on the nose.*

ψευδοστομέω, f. ήσω, *to speak falsely, lie.* From

ψευδό-στομος, ον, (ψευδής, στόμα) *speaking falsely.*

ψευδό-φημος, ον, (ψευδής, φήμη) *of false augury* or *divination,*

Ψευδό-χριστος, ὁ, (ψευδής, Χριστόν) *a false Christ.*

ΨΕΥ'ΔΩ, f. ψεύσω: aor. I ἔψευσα: Pass., aor. I ἐψεύσθην: pf. ἔψευσμαι:—*to cheat* or *impose upon by lies, to beguile, defraud:* c. gen. *to cheat of* a thing; ἔψευσάς **με ἐλπίδος** *thou hast defrauded* me of my hope:—Pass. ψεύδομαι, *to be cheated, to be disappointed* or *deceived;* ψευσθῆναι δείπνου *to be cheated of* a supper; ἐψευσμένοι τῆς τῶν Ἀθηναίων δυνάμεως *deceived in their notions of* the Athenian power: absol. *to be mistaken, be false;* ἡ τρίτη τῶν ὁδῶν μάλιστα ἔψευσται the third mode of explanation *is* most *untrue.* II. c. acc. rei, *to represent* a thing *as a lie* or *deception.* 2. *to falsify:* Pass., ἡ ψευσθεῖσα ὑπόσχεσις the promise *broken.*

Dep. **ψεύδομαι**, f. ψεύσομαι: aor. I ἐψευσάμην: pf. pass. ἔψευσμαι in act. sense:—absol. *to lie, speak false, play false.* 2. generally, *to be false* or *faithless, to be perjured* or *forsworn.* II. *to belie, falsify;* ὅρκια ψεύσασθαι *to falsify* or *break* the oaths; οὐκ ἐψεύσαντο τὰς ἀπειλάς *they did* not *belie,* i. e. they made good, their threats; τὰ χρήματα ἐψευσμένοι ἦσαν *they had broken their word about* the money. III. *to belie* or *deceive by lies, cheat, impose upon.*

ψευδ-ώνῠμος, ον, (ψευδής, ὄνυμα Aeol. for ὄνομα) *under a false name, falsely called.* Adv. **-μως.**

ψευδῶς, Adv. of ψευδής, *falsely, untruly.*

ψευσί-στυξ, ῠγος, ὁ, ἡ, (ψεῦσις, στυγέω) *hating falsehood and fraud.*

ψεῦσμα, τό, (ψεύδω) *a lie, untruth, fraud.*

ψευστέω, f. ήσω, *to be a liar: to lie, cheat, play false.* From

ψεύστης, ου, ὁ, (ψεύδω) *a liar, cheat.* 2. also as Adj., like ψευδής, *lying, false.*

ψεφηνός, ή, όν, (ψέφος) *dark, obscure:* metaph. *obscure, base, mean.*

ΨΕ'ΦΟΣ, εος, τό, *darkness, smoke, mist.*

ψέω, Ion. form for ψάω.

ψῇ, 3 sing. pres. of ψάω; but **ψῆ**, Ep. for ἔψη, 3 sing. impf.

ψῆγμα, ατος, τό, (ψήχω) *that which is rubbed* or *scraped off, shavings,* Lat. *ramentum;* **ψῆγμα** χρυσοῦ gold-*dust;* and so absol. ψῆγμα, *gold-dust.*

ψηκτήρ, ῆρος, ὁ, and **ψήκτρα**, ἡ, (ψήχω) *an instrument for scraping off, a scraper, strigil.*

ψηλᾰφάω, f. ήσω, (ψάω) *to feel, grope one's way,* like a blind man; χερσὶ ψηλαφόων (Ep. for -άων) *feeling one's way* with one's hands: c. acc. *to feel for, grope after.* II. *to feel, stroke,* Lat. *palpare, mulcere.* Hence

ψηλάφημα, ατος, τό, *a touch: a caress.* [λᾰ]

ψηλᾰφόων, Ep. part. of ψηλαφάω.

ΨΗ'Ν, ψηνός, ὁ, *the gall-insect,* which lives in the fruit of the wild-fig (ὄλυνθος) and male palm. Hence

ψηνίζω, f. ίσω, *to hang wild figs* (ὄλυνθοι) on the cultivated tree, *in order that the gall-insects* (ψῆνες) passing from the former may puncture the fruit of the latter. II. *to write a play called the* Ψῆνες, as the Comic poet Magnes had done.

ψηνός Dor. **ψανός**, ὁ, like ψευδός or ψιλός, = φαλακρός, *a bald-head.*

ψῆξις, εως, ἡ, (ψήχω) *a rubbing* or *scraping: the currying of a horse.*

ψήρ, gen. ψηρός, ὁ, Ion. for ψάρ (q. v.), *a starling.*

ψῆσσα Att. **ψῆττα**, ἡ, a kind of *flat-fish,* such as *a plaice, sole,* or *turbot,* Lat. *rhombus.*

ψηφῑδο-φόρος, ον, (ψηφίς, φέρω) *giving one's vote, entitled to vote.*

ψηφίζω, f. ίσω Att. ιῶ, *to count* or *reckon.* II. Med. **ψηφίζομαι**, f. -ίσομαι Att. -ιοῦμαι: aor. I ἐψηφισάμην: pf. pass. ἐψήφισμαι: (ψῆφος):—*to give one's vote with a pebble,* which was thrown into the voting-urn; ψηφίζεσθαι ἐς ὑδρίαν *to throw one's ballot* into the urn: generally, *to vote,* Lat. *suffragari,* ψηφίζεσθαί τινι *to vote for* any one. 2. c. acc. *to vote for, adjudge* a thing *by vote*, ψηφίζεσθαί τινι τὸν πλοῦν *to vote* him the voyage: also, *to decide by vote, to vote:* κλῆρόν τινι ψηφίζεσθαι *to adjudge* the inheritance to one. 3. c. inf. *to vote* or *resolve to do* something: the aor. 1 ἐψηφίσθην, and sometimes pf. ἐψήφισμαι, are used in pass. sense, *to be voted, adjudged* or *decided by vote;* τοῖς στρατηγοῖς εἴ του προσδέοιντο ψηφισθῆναι that anything which they wanted *should be voted* to the generals.

ψηφίς, ῖδος, ἡ, (ψῆφος) *a small stone: a pebble for counting*, Lat. *calculus.*

ψήφισμα, ατος, τό, (ψηφίζομαι) *a proposition carried by vote:* at Athens, *a measure passed in the popular assembly* (ἐκκλησία), *a vote, decree;* ψήφισμα γράφειν to move *such a measure* in the ἐκκλησία, propose *a vote;* ψήφισμα καθαιρεῖν to rescind *a vote.*

ψηφισμᾰτο-πώλης, ου, ὁ, (ψήφισμα, πωλέω) *one who drives a traffic in acts* or *statutes.*

ψηφο-ποιός, ὁ, (ψῆφος, ποιέω) *a making* or *tampering with votes.*

ψῆφος Dor. **ψᾶφος**, ἡ, (ψάω, ψέω) *a small stone, a small round stone*, found in river beds, *a pebble.* II. *a pebble used for reckoning, a counter*, Lat. *calculus:* —in plur. *accounts*, καθαραὶ ψῆφοι an exact balance. 2. in Att. *a pebble used in voting*, which was thrown into the voting-urn (ὑδρία), *the vote* itself; ψῆφον φέρειν to give *one's vote* Lat. *suffragium ferre;* ψήφῳ κρίνειν, διακρίνειν to determine *by vote;* also *that which is carried by vote, a vote* of the Assembly; ψῆφος καταγνώσεως *a vote* of condemnation: hence *any resolution* or *decree.* The ψῆφος Ἀθηνᾶς, *calculus Minervae*, was a proverbial phrase to express *acquittal* when the votes were even; because Minerva interfered to procure the acquittal of Orestes, when the judges were equally divided. The voting by ψῆφος, *ballot*, was different from that by κύαμος, *lot;* the former being used in *trials*, the latter in the *election* of various officers. The ψῆφοι of condemnation or acquittal were sometimes distinguished by the former being bored (τετρυπημέναι), the latter whole (πλήρεις). 3. *the place of voting* (as πεσσοί is used for the place of play).

ψήχω, f. ξω, from ψάω, (as νήχω from νέω), *to rub down, curry* a horse. II. *to rub down, wear away.*

ΨΙΑ΄ΖΩ Dor. **ψιάσδω**, fut. άσω, *to play, sport, dance, be merry.*

ψίᾰθος Ion. **ψίεθος**, ἡ, *a covering of rushes* or *reeds, a rush mat.*

ψιάθως, Dor. acc. pl. of ψίαθος.

ψῐάς, άδος, ἡ, (ψίω) like ψακάς or ψεκάς, *a drop:* in plur. *a shower of drops, small rain.*

ΨΙ΄ΖΩ f. ψίσω: pf. pass. ἔψισμαι:—*to feed on pap.*

ψῐθῠρίζω Dor. **ψιθυρίσδω**: fut. ίσω Att. ιῶ: (ψιθυρός):—*to whisper, speak in a* low tone: also *to mutter, mumble.* 2. of any *whispering noise* as of trees, *to rustle.*

ψῐθύρισμα, ατος, τό, (ψιθυρίζω) *a whispering, rustling.*

ψῐθῠρισμός, ὁ, (ψιθυρίζω) *a whispering.* 2. *a whispering of slander, slander.*

ψῐθῠριστής, οῦ, ὁ, (ψιθυρίζω) *a whisperer.* 2. *a tale-bearer, slanderer.*

ψῐθῠρός, όν, *whispering.* 2. *whispering, slanderous.* (Formed from the sound.)

ψῑλο-μετρία, ἡ, (ψιλός, μέτρον) *heroic poetry as not being accompanied by music*, opp. to *lyric.*

ΨΙΛΟ΄Σ, ή, όν, *bare, naked:* c. gen. *stript bare of* a thing: of land, *without trees*, ψιλὴ ἄροσις a *bare* corn-field (without trees); πεδίον μέγα τε καὶ ψιλόν a champaign country of large extent and *without trees;* full, γῆ ψιλὴ δενδρέων land *bare of* trees. II. of animals, *stript of hair, feathers*, etc., *bald*, Lat. *calvus;* ἶβις ψιλὴ κεφαλήν the ibis *without feathers* on the head. 2. generally, *unclad, uncovered, bare:* c. gen., ψιλὴ σώματος οὖσα ἡ ψυχή the soul being *divested* of the body; ψιλὴ τρόπις the *bare* keel with the planks torn from it; ψιλὴ θρῖδαξ a lettuce *with the side leaves pulled off.* III. in Att. Prose, as a military term, οἱ ψιλοί (sc. τῶν ὅπλων) *soldiers without heavy armour, light troops*, such as archers, slingers, etc., opp. to ὁπλῖται; ψιλὸς ἵππος a horse *without housings:* generally, *unarmed, defenceless.* IV. ψιλὸς λόγος language *without accompaniments* or *accessories, prose*, as opp. to poetry: also of a speech, *unsupported by evidence.* 2. ψιλὴ ποίησις *mere* poetry *without singing* or *music, Epic* poetry, as opp. to *Lyric;* cf. ψιλομετρία.

ψῑλόω, f. ώσω: pf. pass. ἐψίλωμαι: (ψιλός):—*to strip bare, to make bald:*—Pass. *to become bald.* II. c. gen. *to strip bare of* a thing; ψιλοῦν τινα τὰ πλεῖστα τῆς δυνάμιος *to strip* one *of* the chief part of his power: generally, *to leave naked* or *defenceless.* 2. *to strip* one thing *off* another: pf. pass. part., κρέα ἐψιλωμένα τῶν ὀστέων the flesh *stript from* the bones.

ψῑλῶς, Adv. of ψιλός, *simply, merely, only.*

ψιμίθιον, **ψίμῐθος**, etc., later forms for ψιμύθιον, etc.

ψιμύθιον or **ψιμμύθιον**, later also **ψιμίθιον**, τό: (ψίμυθος):—*white lead*, Lat. *cerussa*, used as a pigment, esp. to whiten the skin of the face. Hence

ψιμῡθιόω, f. ώσω, *to paint with white lead:* Med., ψιμυθιοῦσθαι τὸ πρόσωπον *to apply a pigment of white lead* to one's face.

ΨΙ΄ΜΥ΄ΘΟΣ, ὁ, radic. form of ψιμύθιον, *white lead.*

ψίν, Dor. for σφίν, as ψέ for σφέ.

ΨΙ΄Ξ, ὁ and ἡ, gen. ψῖχός: nom. pl. ψῖχες: *a crumb, morsel, bit.*

ψίττᾰ, = σίττα, a drover's or shepherd's cry, '*st.*'

ψίττᾰκος, ὁ, or **ψιττάκη** ἡ, *a parrot.* (Foreign word.)

ψῑχίον, τό, Dim. of ψίξ, *a crumb of bread.*

ψίω, aor. 1 ἔψῑσα, = ψίζω.

ψογερός, ά, όν, (ψόγος) *fond of blaming, censorious.*

ψόγιος, α, ον, *blaming, fond of blaming.* From

ψόγος, ὁ, (ψέγω) *blame, censure.*

ψολόεις, εσσα, εν, (ψολός) *sooty, smoky:* of the thunderbolt, *smouldering.*

ψολο-κομπία, ἡ, (ψολός, κομπέω) *talk that ends in smoke: empty noise and fury.*

ΨΟ'ΛΟΣ, ὁ, *soot, smoke.*

ψοφέω, f. ήσω: pf. ἐψόφηκα: (ψόφος):—*to make a noise* or *din,* Lat. *strepere,* of the creaking or sound made in opening a door; εἰ αἱ θύραι νύκτωρ ψοφοῖεν if the doors *were heard to open* at night, Lat. *si crepuissent fores.*

ψοφο-δεής, ές, gen. έος, (ψόφος, δέος) *frightened at every noise.* Adv. –εῶς, *timidly.*

ψοφο-μήδης, ες, gen. εος, (ψόφος, μῆδος) *caring for noise, noisy, uproarious.*

ΨΟ'ΦΟΣ, ὁ, *any inarticulate sound,* as opp. to φωνή: *a noise, sound,* Lat. *strepitus: the sound of a door opening.* 2. *a mere sound, empty sound* or *noise;* τοῦ σοῦ ψόφου οὐκ ἂν στραφείην I would not heed your *noise;* ψόφοι *mere sounds* without sense.

ψοφ-ώδης, ες, (ψόφος, εἶδος) *noisy, ranting.*

ψῠγῆναι, aor. 2 pass. of ψύχω.

ψῠγήσομαι, fut. pass. of ψύχω.

ψυδνός, ή, όν, = ψυδρός.

ψυδρός, ά, όν, (ψύθος, ψεύδομαι) with collat. form ψυδνός. *lying untrue.*

ψῠθής, ές, (ψύθος) = ψευδής, *lying, false.*

ψύθος, εος, τό, collat. form for ψεῦδος, *a lie.* [ῠ]

ψυκτήρ, ῆρος, ὁ, (ψύχω) *a wine-cooler.* II. in plur. οἱ ψυκτῆρες *cool shady places.*

ψυκτήριον, τό, (ψυκτήρ) *a cool shady place.*

ψυκτήριος, α, ον, (ψυκτήρ) *cooling, shady.*

ΨΥ'ΛΛᾸ, ης, ἡ, *a flea,* Lat. *pulex.*

ψύλλιον, τό, (ψύλλα) *flea-wort.*

ψυλλο-τοξότης, ου, ὁ, (ψύλλα, τοξότης) *a flea-archer, flea-knight,* formed like ἱπποτοξότης, Comic word in Lucian.

ψύξασα, aor. 1 part. fem. of ψύχω.

ψῦξις, εως, ἡ, (ψύχω) *a cooling: a becoming cold.*

ψύττᾰ, = ψίττα, σίττα.

ψῡχ-αγωγέω, f. ήσω, (ψυχαγωγός) *to be a conductor of the dead, to lead departed souls to the nether world,* esp. of Hermes. II. *to evoke* or *conjure up the dead* by sacrifice. 2. metaph. *to win* or *attract the souls of the living, to win over, persuade:* mostly in bad sense, *to lead away, seduce, delude.* Hence

ψῡχᾰγωγία, ἡ, *an evoking of souls from the nether world.* 2. metaph. *a winning of men's souls, persuasion.*

ψυχ-ᾰγωγός, όν, (ψυχή, ἄγω) *leading departed souls to the nether world,* as epith. of Mercury, like ψυχοπομπός. II. *conjuring up the dead, evoking the dead:* as Subst., ψυχαγωγός, ὁ, *a necromancer.*

ψῡχ-ᾰπάτης, ου, ὁ, (ψυχή, ἀπᾰτάω) *deluding the soul:* in good sense, *beguiling the weary soul, gladdening.*

ψῡχεινός, ή, όν, (ψῦχος) *cooling, cool, fresh.*

ψῡχή, ἡ, (ψύχω) *breath,* Lat. *anima,* esp. as the sign of life, *life, spirit;* ψυχή τε μένος τε *life* and strength; ψυχή τε καὶ αἰών *spirit* and life, etc.; ποινὴν τῆς Αἰσώπου ψυχῆς ἀνελέσθαι to take revenge for *the life* of Aesop; ψυχὴν παρθέμενος staking or risking one's *life;* so, μάχεσθαι, θέειν περὶ ψυχῆς to fight, run for *one's life.* II. *the soul of man,* as opp. to the body: 1. in Homer, only *a departed soul, spirit, ghost,* which still retained the shape of its living owner. 2. generally, *the soul* or *spirit of man,* Lat. *animus;* ἀνθρώπου ψυχὴ ἀθάνατός ἐστι *the soul* of man is immortal; hence ψυχή τινος is used for the man himself, e.g. ψυχὴ Ὀρέστου = Ὀρέστης: ψυχαί absol. = ἄνθρωποι, ψυχαὶ πολλαὶ ἔθανον many *souls* perished: so in addressing persons, ὦ μελέα ψυχή O wretched *being.* 3. also as the seat of the will, desires, and passions, *the soul, heart;* ἐκ τῆς ψυχῆς from the inmost *soul,* with all the *heart: desire, appetite.* III. *the soul, mind, reason, understanding.* Hence

ψῡχήιος, η, ον, *having breath, alive, living.*

ψῡχίδιον, τό, Dim. of ψυχή, Lat. *animula.* [χῐ]

ψῡχικός, ή, όν, (ψυχή) *of the soul* or *life.* II. *mental,* opp. to bodily. 2. *concerned with this life only, animal, natural,* opp. to spiritual.

ψῡχο-δαΐκτης, ου, ὁ, (ψυχή, δαΐζω) *destroying* or *killing the soul.*

ψῡχο-δοτήρ, ῆρος, ὁ, (ψυχή, δίδωμι) *giver of the soul* or *life.*

ψῡχο-λῐπής, ές, (ψυχή, λιπεῖν) *left by the soul, lifeless.*

ψῡχό-μαντις, εως, ὁ, (ψυχή, μάντις) *one who conjures up the souls of the dead* to divine by them, *a necromancer.*

ψῡχο-μᾰχέω, f. ήσω, (ψυχή, μάχομαι) *to fight to the last gasp, fight desperately.*

ψῡχο-πλᾰνής, ές, (ψυχή, πλανάω) *perplexing* or *misleading the soul.*

ψῡχο-πομπός, όν, (ψυχή, πέμπω) *conducting souls to the nether world,* epith. of Charon, also of Mercury: cf. ψυχαγωγός.

ψῡχορρᾰγέω, f. ήσω, *to let the soul break loose, to lie at the last gasp, be at the point of death,* Lat. *animam agere.* From

ψῡχορ-ρᾰγής, ές, gen. έος, (ψυχή, ῥαγῆναι) *letting the soul break loose, lying at the last gasp.*

ψῦχος, εος, τό, (ψύχω) *coolness, cold, chill: cold, frost,* in pl. ψύχεα, *extreme colds:* also *winter-time,* ἐν ψύχει in *winter.*

ψυχοσ-σόος, ον, (ψυχή, σώζω) *saving the soul.*

ψῡχο-τᾰκής, ές, (ψυχή, τακῆναι) *melting the soul.*

ψῡχόω, f. ώσω, (ψυχή) *to give soul* or *life, to animate.*

ψῡχρο-βᾱφής, ές, (ψυχρός, βαφῆναι) *dipt in cold water,* like red-hot iron.

ψῡχρο-δόχος, ον, (ψυχρός, δέχομαι) *receiving what is cold;* οἶκος ψυχροδόχος *the cold-bath* room.

ψῡχρο-λογία, ἡ, (ψυχρός, λέγω) *the use of frigid phrases, exaggeration.*

ψῡχρο-πότης, ου, ὁ, (ψυχρός, ΠΟ- Root of some tenses of πίνω) *a cold-water drinker.*

ψῡχρός, ά, όν, (ψύχω) *cold, chill,* Lat. *frigidus:* τὸ ψυχρόν (sc. ὕδωρ) *cold water,* Lat. *gelida* (sc. *aqua*); ψυχρῷ λοῦνται they bathe *in cold water:*—τὸ ψυχρόν also = ψῦχος, *cold.* II. metaph. *cold, vain, fruitless, unreal;* ψυχρὰ νίκη a *delusive* victory: also *chilling, horrible.* 2. of persons, *cold-hearted, heartless, spiritless, indifferent.* 3. of exaggerated phrases, *cold, frigid.* Hence

ψῡχρότης, ητος, ἡ, *coldness, chill.* II. metaph. of persons, *coldness of heart, indifference.* 2. of phrases, *frigidity.*

ψῡχρόω, f. ώσω, (ψυχρός) *to make cold:*—Pass. *to grow cold* or *cool.*

ψῡχρῶς, Adv. of ψυχρός, *coldly, frigidly.*

ΨΥ'ΧΩ [ῡ], f. ψύξω: aor. 1 ἔψυξα: Pass., aor. 1 ἐψύχθην: aor. 2 ἐψύχην and ἐψύγην [ῠ]:—*to breathe, blow;* ἦκα μάλα ψύξασα *breathing* very faintly. II. *to make cool* or *cold:* hence *to refresh, recruit.* 2. Pass. *to grow cool* or *cold.*

ψωλός, (ψάω) ὁ, *one circumcised.* 2. *a lewd fellow.*

ψωμίζω, f. ίσω Att. ιῶ: (ψωμός):—*to feed by putting little bits into the mouth,* as nurses do children: hence *to pamper, feed, fatten.*

ψωμίον, τό, Dim. of ψωμός, *a morsel, crumb.*

ψωμός, οῦ, ὁ, (ψώω) *a bit, morsel, scrap,* esp. of meat or bread; ψωμοὶ ἀνδρόμεοι *gobbets* of man's flesh.

ψώρα Ion. **ψώρη**, ἡ, (ψώω) *a cutaneous disease, the itch, scab* or *mange,* Lat. *scabies.*

ψωρᾰλέος, α, ον, (ψώρα) *scabby, mangy.*

ψώχω Ion. σώχω, (ψώω) *to rub in pieces, rub.*

* **ψώω**, collat. form of ψάω, *to rub, rub in pieces.*

Ω

Ω, ω, ὦ μέγα, twenty-fourth letter of the Greek Alphabet: as a numeral ω′ = 800, but ͵ω = 800,000. The name of ὦ μέγα, *great* or *long o,* was given to distinguish it from the ὂ μικρόν *little* or *short o.* It was not introduced as a written character at Athens till the Archonship of Euclides, see Η, η.

Changes of ω in the dialects: I. Ion. sometimes for α, as ὤνθρωπος ὥριστος for ἄνθρωπος ἄριστος. II. Ion. also for αυ, as θῶμα τρῶμα for θαῦμα τραῦμα. III. Aeol. and Dor., ω is often put for ου, as ὠρανός Μῶσα κῶρος λιπῶσα for οὐρανός Μοῦσα κοῦρος λιποῦσα; also in genit. sing. and acc. pl. of 2nd decl., as, βροτῶ βροτώς for βροτοῦ βροτούς. IV. Dor. ω into ᾱ, as πρῶτος πρώτιστος θεωρός into πρᾶτος πράτιστος θεᾱρός; and so the gen. plur. of first decl. ων becomes ᾶν, as Μουσᾶν for Μουσῶν.

ὦ and **ὢ**, an exclamation, expressing surprise, joy or pain, like our *O! oh!* 2. with the vocative it is a mere address, less emphatic than the Engl. *O!* As an exclamation it is written ὤ, as an address ὦ.

ᾠα or **ὠά** ἡ, (ὄϊς) *a sheepskin with the wool on, a garment made of it.* 2. *the edge* or *skirt* of a garment.

Ὠᾰρίων [ῐ], ωνος, ὁ, poët. for Ὠρίων. Hence

Ὠᾰρῑώνειος, α, ον, *of Orion.*

ὦας, ατος, τό, Dor. for οὖας, οὖς, *the ear.*

ὠγαθέ, with apostr. ὠγάθ', contr. for ὦ ἀγαθέ.

ὠγμός, οῦ, ὁ, (ὤζω) *a crying oh!*

Ὠγῠγία, ἡ, *Ogygia,* a fabulous island in the Mediterranean, the abode of Calypso. II. the oldest name of *Egypt.*

Ὠγύγιος, α, ον, Att. also ος, ον, *Ogygian, of* or *from Ogyges,* an Attic king of the earliest times: hence *primeval, primal.* [ῠ]

ᾠδᾶς, Dor. for ᾠδῆς, gen. of ᾠδή.

ὧδε Att. **ὡδί**, from ὅδε, demonstr. Adv., I. of Manner, *in this wise, so, thus,* also *so very, so exceedingly:* as opp. to οὕτω it refers to what follows, *in the following way, as follows;* ὧδ' ἠμείψατο he answered *in the following terms.* 2. c. gen., ὧδε γένους *thus off* for family. II. of Place, *hither, here.*

ᾤδεε, 3 sing. impf. of οἰδέω.

ᾠδεῖον, τό, (ᾠδή) *the Odēum,* a public building at Athens built by Pericles for musical performances, but commonly used as a law-court.

ᾠδή, ἡ, contr. for ἀοιδή, (ἀείδω, ᾄδω) *a song, lay, ode, strain:* in plur. *lyric poetry.*

ᾠδήκαντι, Dor. for ᾠδήκασι, 3 pl. pf. of οἰδέω.

ὡδί, Att. strengthd. form of ὧδε. [ῑ]

ᾠδικός, ή, όν, (ᾠδή) *fond of singing, musical.* Adv. -κῶς, *musically, in good time* or *harmony.*

ὠδῖνας, acc. pl. of ὠδίς.

ὠδίνω [ῑ], f. ινῶ: aor. 1 ὤδῖνα: (ὠδίς):—*to have the pains* or *throes of childbirth, to be in travail* or *labour:* c. acc. *to be in travail* of a child: metaph. of a bee, κηρίον ὠδίνειν *to be in labour with* honey. 2. of any great pain, *to be in travail, be in pangs* or *pains.* 3. *to work painfully* or *hard, to travail, labour with,* c. acc. 4. metaph. of the mind, *to be in the throes* or *agonies of thought.*

ὨΔΙ'Σ, ῖνος, ἡ, *the pain of childbirth, travail-pain;* mostly in plur. *the pangs* or *throes of labour.* 2. in sing. also *the fruit of travail* or *labour, a birth, child.* II. generally, *travail, pain, distress.* (Akin to ὀδύνη.)

ᾠδο-ποιός, όν, (ᾠδή, ποιέω) *making songs* or *odes.*

ᾠδός, ὁ, contr. for ἀοιδός, *a singer, minstrel.*

ὠδώδει, poët. for ὀδώδει, 3 sing. plqpf. of ὄζω.

ὤεον, τό, = ᾠόν, *an egg.*

ὤζησα, aor. 1 of ὄζω.

ὤζω, *to cry oh!* hence ὠγμός. (From ὦ or ὤ, as οἴζω from οἴ, οἰμώζω from οἴμοι.)

ὠή, a call to another, *ho! holla!* Lat. *ohe! heus!*

ᾠήθην, aor. 1 pass. of *οἴομαι*.

ὤθεσκε, 3 sing. Ion. impf. of *ὠθέω*.

ὠθεῦντο, Dor. for *ὠθοῦντο*, 3 pl. impf. med. of

'ΩΘΕ'Ω, impf. *ἐώθουν*: fut. *ὠθήσω* and *ὤσω*: aor. 1 *ἔωσα* Ion. and Ep. *ὦσα*: pf. *ἔωκα*: Pass., aor. 1 *ἐώσθην*: pf. *ἔωσμαι* Ion. *ὦσμαι*:—Ion. 3 sing. impf. *ὤθεσκε*, 3 sing. aor. 1 *ὤσασκε*:—*to thrust, push, shove, force away* or *from* a place; *ἐκ μηροῦ δόρυ ὦσε he forced* the spear from the thigh; *ξίφος ἂψ ἐς κουλεὸν ὦσε he thrust back* the sword into its sheath: *to push* or *force back* in battle; *ὦσαι ἑαυτὸν ἐς τὸ πῦρ* to rush into the fire; *ὦσαι τὴν θύραν to force* the door: also *to break open, force a passage*: metaph. *to hurry, push on; ὠθεῖν τὰ πρήγματα to push* matters *on*:—absol. *to push off* from land:—Pass. *to be thrust* or *pushed away*: also *to force one's way*:—Med. *to thrust* or *push from oneself, push* or *force back*.

ὠθίζω, f. *ίσω*, = *ὠθέω*, *to thrust* or *push on*:—Pass. and Med. *to push against one another, struggle*; metaph. *to be in hot dispute*, Lat. *altercari*. Hence

ὠθισμός, ὁ, *a thrusting, pushing; a struggling, wrestling*: metaph., *ὠθισμὸς λόγων a struggle* of words, a hot debate.

ὠίγνυντο, Ep. for *ᾠγνυντο*, 3 pl. impf. pass. of *οἴγνυμι*.

ὠίετο, Ep. for *ᾤετο*, 3 sing. impf. of *οἴομαι*. [ῑ]

ὤιξαι, Ep. for *οἶξαι*, inf. of *οἴγνυμι*.

ὤιξε, ὤιξαν, Ep. for *ᾦξε, ᾦξαν*, 3 sing. and 3 pl. aor. 1 act. of *οἴγνυμι*.

ὠίσθην, Ep. aor. 1 of *οἴομαι*.

ὦκα, poët. Adv. of *ὠκύς*, *quickly, swiftly, fast*.

ὠκῠλέος, *η, ον*, later Ep. form for *ὠκύς*.

ὠκέα, Ep. and Ion. for *ὠκεῖα*, fem. from *ὠκύς*.

'Ωκεᾰνίνη, ἡ, (*'Ωκεανός*) *daughter of Ocean, an Ocean-nymph*. [ῑ]

'Ωκεᾰνίς, *ίδος*, ἡ, (*'Ωκεανός*) *daughter of Ocean*

'Ωκεᾰνόνδε, Adv. *to the ocean* or *sea*. From

'Ωκεᾰνός, *οῦ*, ὁ, *Oceanos*, acc. to Hesiod, son of Uranos and Gaia, the source of all smaller waters: according to Homer, Ocean was a river which encompassed the whole earth, hence often called *ὠκεανὸς ποταμός*. In later times, *Ocean* remained as the name of the great Outward Sea, opp. to the Inward or Mediterranean, which was called *θάλασσα*. (From *ὠκύς* and *νάω*.)

ὠκειάων, Ep. gen. pl. fem. of *ὠκύς*.

ὠκέως, Adv. of *ὠκύς*, *quickly, swiftly*.

ὠκήεις, *εσσα, εν*, poët. for *ὠκύς*, swift.

ὤκιστα, neut. plur. of *ὠκύς* used as Adv., *most swiftly, very swiftly*.

ὤκιστος, *η, ον*, irreg. Sup. of *ὠκυς*.

ὠκίων, *ον*, gen. *ονος*, irreg. Comp. of *ὠκύς*.

ὤκνεον, impf. of *ὀκνέω*.

ᾤκτειρα, aor. 1 of *οἰκτείρω*.

ὠκύ-ἄλος, *ον*, (*ὠκύς, ἅλς*) *sea-swift, speeding over the sea*, epith. of a ship. [ῠ]

ὠκῠ-βόλος, *ον*, (*ὠκύς, βαλεῖν*) *quick-hitting* or *quick-shot: quick-darting*.

ὠκῠ-δήκτωρ, *ορος*, ὁ, (*ὠκύς, δάκνω*) *biting sharply*.

ὠκῠ-δίδακτος, *ον*, (*ὠκύς, διδάσκω*) *quickly taught*.

ὠκῠ-δίνητος Dor. **-δίνᾱτος**, *ον*, (*ὠκύς, δινέω*) *quick-whirling*. [ῑ]

ὠκυ-δρόμας, *ου*, ὁ, = *ὠκυδρόμος*.

ὠκυ-δρόμος, *ον*, (*ὠκύς, δραμεῖν*) *swift-running*.

ὠκυ-επής, *ές*, gen. *έος*, (*ὠκύς, ἔπος*) *quick-speaking*.

ὠκύ-θοος, *ον*, also *η, ον*, (*ὠκύς, θέω*) *swift-running*.

ὠκῠ-μάχος [ᾰ], *ον*, (*ὠκύς, μάχομαι*) *quick to fight*.

ὠκύ-μορος, *ον*, (*ὠκύς, μόρος*) *short-lived, dying early*: Sup., *ὠκυμορώτατος*. II. act. *bringing a quick* or *early death*.

ὠκῠ-πέτης, *ου*, ὁ, (*ὠκύς*, **ΠΕΤ-** Root of *πίπτω*) *quick-flying*.

ὠκύ-πλᾰνος, *ον*, (*ὠκύς, πλάνη*) *quick-wandering*.

ὠκύ-πλοος, *ον*, (*ὠκύς, πλέω*) *fast-sailing*.

ὠκῠ-πόδης, *ου*, ὁ, poët. for *ὠκύπους*, *swift-footed*.

ὠκύ-ποινος, *ον*, (*ὠκύς, ποινή*) *quickly-avenged*.

ὠκύ-πομπος, *ον*, (*ὠκύς, πέμπω*) *swift-conveying*.

ὠκύ-πορος, *ον*, (*ὠκύς, πόρος*) *swift-passing*.

ὠκύ-πος, *ον*, collat. form of *ὠκύπους*. [ῠ]

ὠκύ-πους, ὁ, ἡ, *-πουν*, τό, gen. *-ποδος* (*ὠκύς, πούς*), *swift-footed, fleet of foot*.

ὠκύ-πτερος, *ον*, (*ὠκύς, πτερόν*) *swift-winged, swift-flying*: *τὰ ὠκύπτερα the long quill-feathers in a wing*.

ὠκῠ-ρόης, *ου*, ὁ Dor. **-ρόας**, = *ὠκύροος*.

ὠκύ-ροος, *ον*, (*ὠκύς, ῥέω*) *swift-flowing*.

ὠκύς [ῠ], *ὠκεῖα, ὠκύ*, gen. *ὠκέος, είας, έος*, Ep. fem. *ὠκέᾰ*:—*quick, swift, fleet, speedy*. Adv. *ὠκέως*, but more commonly *ὦκα*, *swiftly, fleetly*.—Comp. and Sup. *ὠκύτερος, ὠκύτατος*: irreg. *ὠκίων, ον*, gen. *ονος* (like Lat. *ocyor, ocyus*), *ὤκιστος*. (Akin to *ὀξύς*.)

ὠκύ-σκοπος, *ον*, (*ὠκύς, σκοπέω*) *quick-aiming*.

ὠκύτης, *ητος*, ἡ, (*ὠκύς*) *quickness, swiftness, fleetness, speed*. [ῠ]

ὠκῠτόκειος or **-τόκιος**, *ον*, *belonging to* or *promoting a quick and easy birth*: *τὸ ὠκυτόκιον* (sc. *φάρμακον*) *a medicine to cause easy delivery*. From

ὠκῠ-τόκος, *ον*, (*ὠκύς, τεκεῖν*) *causing quick and easy birth*; of a river, *fertilising*: *τὸ ὠκυτόκον a quick and easy birth*.

ὦλαξ, *ακος*, ἡ, Dor. for *αὖλαξ*.

ὠλάφιον, contr. for *ὦ ἐλάφιον*.

ὠλέ-κρᾱνον, τό, properly *ὠλενό-κρανον*, = *ὠλένης κρᾶνον*, *the point of the elbow*: also *ὀλέκρανον*.

'ΩΛΕ'ΝΗ, ἡ, *the elbow*, or rather *the arm from the elbow to the wrist, the lower arm*, Lat. *ulna*: generally, *an arm*; *περὶ ὠλένας δέρᾳ βάλλειν* to throw one's *arms* round a person's neck.

ὤλεσα, aor. 1 of *ὄλλυμι*.

ὠλεσί-βωλος, *ον*, (*ὄλλυμι, βῶλος*) *crushing clods of earth*.

ὠλεσί-καρπος, *ον*, (*ὄλλυμι, καρπός*) of a tree, *losing its fruit*, i. e. *shedding its fruit before it is ripe*.

ὠλεσί-οικος, *ον*, (*ὄλλυμι, οἶκος*) *destroying* or *ruining the house*.

ὤλετο, 3 sing. aor. 2 med. of *ὄλλυμι*.

ὤλισθον, aor. 2 of *ὀλισθάνω*.

ὠλίσθηκα, pf. of *ὀλισθάνω*.

ὦλλος, ὦλλοι, Ion. for *ὁ ἄλλος, οἱ ἄλλοι*.

ὦλξ, *ἡ*, poet. contr. for **ὦλαξ, αὖλαξ**, *a furrow*: mostly used in acc. *ὦλκα*.

ὠλόμην, aor. 2 med. of *ὄλλυμι*.

ὠμ-αχθής, *ές*, (*ὦμος, ἄχθος*) *heavy to the shoulders*.

ὦμες, Dor. for *ὦμεν*, 1 pl. pres. subj. of *εἰμί sum*.

ὠμ-ηστής, *οῦ*, *ὁ*, (*ὠμός, ἐσθίω*) as masc. Adj. *eating raw flesh*: also with a fem. Subst., *Ἔχιδνα ὠμηστής*. II. generally, *savage, brutal*.

ὦμμαι, pf. pass. of *ὁράω*, formed from **ὄπτομαι*.

ὠμο-βοέος or **-βόειος**, *α, ον*, (*ὠμός, βοῦς*) *of raw, untanned ox-hide*:—as Subst., *ὠμοβοέη* (sc. *δορά*), *ἡ*, *a raw ox-hide*, like **λεοντέη**, etc.: but, *ὠμοβόειον* (sc. *κρέας*), *τό*, *raw ox-flesh*.

ὠμο-βοεύς, *έως*, *ὁ*, (*ὠμός, βοῦς*) as masc. Adj. *of raw ox-hide*: acc. pl. *ὠμοβοεῖς*.

ὠμο-βόϊνος, *η, ον*, like *ὠμοβοέος*, *of raw ox-hide*.

ὠμο-βρώς, *ῶτος*, *ὁ, ἡ*, (*ὠμός, βιβρώσκω*) *eating raw flesh*.

ὠμό-βρωτος, *ον*, (*ὠμός, βιβρώσκω*) *eaten raw*.

ὠμο-γέρων, *οντος*, *ὁ, ἡ*, (*ὠμός, γέρων*) *a fresh, active old man, a man in a green old age*; cp. Virgil's *cruda viridisque senectus*.

ὠμο-δᾰκής, *ές*, (*ὠμός*, **δακεῖν**) *fiercely stung* or *fiercely stinging*.

ὠμό-δροπος, *ον*, (*ὠμός, δρέπω*) *plucked unripe*; *νόμιμα ὠμόδροπα* the rights *of the marriage-bed*.

ὠμο-θετέω, f. *ήσω*, (*ὠμός, τίθημι*):—in sacrificing, *to place the raw pieces* cut from a victim on the thigh-bones (*μηρία*) wrapped in the fat (*δημός*): also in Med.

ὠμό-θῡμος, *ον*, (*ὠμός, θυμός*) *savage-hearted*.

ὤμοι, not **ὦμοι**,—*ὦ μοι*, *ah me, woe's me*, Lat. *hei mihi*.

ὠμο-κρᾰτής, *ές*, gen. *έος*, (*ὦμος, κράτος*) *strong-shouldered*, or (*ὠμός, κράτος*) *of savage strength*.

ὡμολογημένως, Adv. pf. pass. part. of *ὁμολογέω*, *confessedly, without contradiction*.

ὠμο-πλάτη, *ἡ*, (*ὦμος, πλάτη*) *the shoulder-blade*, mostly in plur. *ὠμοπλάται, αἱ*, Lat. *scapulae*. [ᾰ

ὯΜΟΣ, *ὁ*, *the shoulder with the upper part of the arm, the shoulder*, Lat. *humerus*; *φέρειν ὤμοις* to bear on *one's shoulders*; *ὤμοισι τοῖς ἐμοῖσι by the strength of* mine *arms*: also of animals, as of a lion: of a horse, like Lat. *armus*.

ὨΜΟΣ, *ή, όν* *raw, undressed*, Lat. *crudus*, esp. of flesh; *ὠμὸν καταφαγεῖν τινα* to eat one *raw*: of food, *undigested*. 2. *unripe, unseasonable*, properly of fruits: also of a man, *ὠμὸν γῆρας an untimely* old age. II. metaph. *savage, rude, cruel*. 2. *rough, hardy*.

ὤμοσα, aor. 1 of *ὄμνυμι*.

ὠμό-σῑτος, *ον*, (*ὠμός, σιτέομαι*) *eating* men *raw*: hence *savage, ferocious*.

ὠμο-σπάρακτος, *ον*, (*ὠμός, σπᾰράσσω*) *torn in pieces raw*.

ὠμότης, *ητος*, *ἡ*, (*ὠμός*) *rawness, unripeness*. II. metaph. *savageness, cruelty*.

ὠμο-φάγος, *ον*, (*ὠμός, φᾰγεῖν*) *eating raw flesh*. II. *ὠμόφαγος*, *ον*, pass., *eaten raw, raw*.

ὠμό-φρων, *ονος ὁ ἡ*, (*ὠμός, φρήν*) *savage-minded*. Adv. *-φρόνως*.

ᾤμωξα, aor. 1 of *οἰμώζω*

ὠμῶς, Adv. of *ὠμός*, *savagely*.

ὦν, Ion. for *οὖν*, *now, therefore*.—Herodotus often places this particle between a verb and its preposition as, *ἀπ' ὦν ἔδοντο* for *ἀπέδοντο ὦν*.

ὦνα, ὦναξ, poët. contr. for *ὦ ἄνα, ὦ ἄναξ*.

ὠνάθην, Dor. for *ὠνήθην*, aor. 1 pass. of *ὀνίνημι*.

ὠνάμην, *ὤνᾰτο*, 1 and 3 sing. aor. 2 med. of *ὀνίνημι*.

ὤνᾱσα, Dor. aor. 1 of *ὀνίνημι*.

ὤνεμος, Dor. contr. for *ὁ ἄνεμος*.

ὠνέομαι contr. **ὠνοῦμαι**: fut. *ὠνήσομαι*: impf. *ἐωνούμην* Ion. *ὠνεόμην*: aor. 1 *ἐωνησάμην*, pf. *ἐώνημαι*; (but pf. part. *ἐωνημένος*, and 3 sing. plqpf. are also used in a pass. sense):—*ἐπριάμην* [ᾰ] is used as aor. 2, Ep. 3 sing. *πρίᾰτο*; imperat. *πρίᾰσο, πρίω*; subj. *πρίωμαι*; opt. *πριαίμην*; inf. *πρίασθαι*; part. *πριάμενος*: (*ὦνος*): Dep.:—*to buy, purchase*, opp. to *πωλέω, πιπράσκω*, as Lat. *emere* to *vendere*; *ὠνεῖσθαί τι παρά τινος to buy* a thing from a person: c. gen. pretii, *for* so much, *ὠνεῖσθαι δραχμῆς to buy for* a drachma. 2. *to farm public taxes* or *tolls*. 3. in pres. and impf. *to wish* or *offer to buy*, hence *to bargain, bid for* a thing, Lat. *liceri*: hence *to buy off, effect a compromise by money*: hence *to bribe*. II. as Pass. *to be bought*. Hence

ὠνή, *ἡ*, (*ὦνος*) *a buying*, Lat. *emptio*, *ὠνὴ καὶ πρᾶσις buying* and selling. 2. *purchase, a bargain*: esp. *a contract for the farming of taxes*.

ὠνήμην, Ep. aor. 2 med. of *ὀνίνημι*.

ὤνησα, aor. 1 of *ὀνίνημι*.

ὠνητής, *οῦ*, *ὁ*, (*ὠνέομαι*) *a buyer*.

ὠνητός, *ή, όν*, also *ός, όν*, verb. Adj. of *ὠνέομαι*, *bought*. II. *to be bought, that may be bought*.

ὤνθρωπε, crasis for *ὦ ἄνθρωπε*.

ὤνθρωποι, Ion. crasis for *οἱ ἄνθρωποι*.

ὤνιος, *α, ον*, (*ὦνος*) *to be bought, for sale*, Lat. *venalis*; *πῶς ὁ σῖτος ὤνιος*; how is corn *selling*? what is the market price? *τὰ ὤνια goods for sale, market-wares*.

ὤνομα, *ατος, τό*, Aeol. for *ὄνομα*.

ὠνομάδαται, Ion for *ὠνομασμένοι εἰσίν*, 3 pl. pf. pass. of *ὀνομάζω*.

ὯΝΟΣ, *ὁ*, *a price, value, payment* for a thing. *a buying*, like *ὠνή*. (Hence Lat. *venum*, as *vinum* from *οἶνος*, *vicus* from *οἶκος*.)

ὠνοσάμην, aor. 1 med. of *ὄνομαι*.

ᾠνοχόει, 3 sing. impf. of *οἰνοχοέω*.

ᾤνωμαι, pf. pass. of *οἰνόω*.

ὦξ, Dor. contr. for *ὁ ἐξ*.

ᾦξε, 3 sing. aor. 1 of *οἴγνυμι*.

ὨΟΝ, *τό*, *an egg*, Lat. *OVUM*.

ὠόπ, a cry of the *κελευστής* to make the rowers stop pulling, *avast!*

ωπᾶσα, aor. 1 of *ὀπάζω*.

ὦπερ, Dor. for *οὗπερ*, Adv. *where*.

ὤπολλον, poët. crasis for *ὦ Ἄπολλον*.

ὡπόλλων, by crasis for *ὁ Ἀπόλλων*.

ὡπόλοι, Dor. crasis for *οἱ αἰπόλοι*.

ὦπται, 3 sing. pf. pass. of *ὁράω*.

ὤπτησα, **ὤπτων**, aor. 1 and impf. of *ὀπτάω*.

ὄπωπα, pf. 2 of *ὁράω*.

ὭΡΑ Ion. **ὥρη**, ἡ, Lat. *CURA*, *care*, *concern*, *heed*, *regard for* a person or thing; *ὥραν τινὸς ἔχειν* or *ποιεῖσθαι* to pay *heed* or *regard* to a thing.

ὭΡΑ Ion. **ὥρη**, ἡ, Lat. *HORA*, *any limited time* or *period* fixed by natural laws, *a season*: in plur. *the seasons*; hence also in plur. *the climate* of a country as dependent on its seasons. 2. *the blooming season of the year*, *the spring-time*, in full *ἔαρος ὥρη* or *ὥρη εἰαρίνη*; but it was also used of summer and winter: the fourth season, *ὀπώρα* or *autumn*, was not distinguished in Homer's time. 3. later, *the whole year*, *ἐν τῇ πέρυσιν ὥρᾳ* last *year*, (as we say) last *season*. II. *the time of day*: also, *ὥρα νυκτός* night-*time*. III. generally, *the right*, *fitting time* or *hour*, *the time* or *season* for a thing: *the time of corn ripening*; *ἐν ὥρῃ in good time*, *early*: c. gen. rei, *ὥρη ὕπνου the time for* sleep, bed-*time*. IV. in plur. also as connected with the seasons, *the four quarters of the heavens*. V. in Att. *the spring* or *prime of life*, *youth*: also *manhood*. VI. in Att. also sometimes for *τὰ ὡραῖα*, *the fruits* or *produce of the year*. VII. as pr. n., *Ὧραι*, *αἱ*, *the Hours*, keepers of Heaven-gate: generally, ministers of the gods; often joined with the *Χάριτες* or Graces

ὡραῖος, *α*, *ον*, (*ὥρα*) *produced* or *ripened at the fit season*: hence *in due season*, *ripe*, *mature*; *ὡραῖοι καρποί* or *τὰ ὡραῖαι*, the fruits *of the season*. 2. as Subst., *ὡραία*, *ἡ*, *the season of corn* or *fruit ripening*: generally, *the good season*, *season fit for military operations*. II. *happening in due season*, *suitable to the season*, *seasonable*. III. of persons, *seasonable*, *ripe* for a thing; *παρθένος γάμου ὡραία* a maid *ripe for* marriage: of old persons, *ripe* or *ready for death*. IV. of the age of man, *at the freshest*, *fairest age*, *in the spring* or *prime of life*, *youthful*, *blooming*: hence of things, *beautiful*. Hence

ὡραιότης, *ητος*, *ἡ*, *the bloom of youth*, *beauty*.

ὡρᾱκιάω, f. *άσω* [ᾱ], *to faint*, *swoon away*. (Deriv. uncertain.)

ὡρᾰνός, *ὁ*, Dor. for *οὐρανός*.

ὥρᾱσι, **ὥρᾱσιν**, Adv. (*ὥρα*) *in season*, *in good time*.

ὡρεί-τροφος, *ον* poët. for *ὀρείτροφος*, (*ὄρος*, *τρέφω*) *mountain-bred*.

ὠρέξατο, 3 sing. aor. 1 med. of *ὀρέγω*.

ὡρεσί-δουπος, *ον*, (*ὄρος*, *δουπέω*) *making a din on the mountains*.

ὡρεσῐ-δώτης, *ου*, *ὁ*, (*ὥρα*, *δίδωμι*) *one who gives the fruits in their due season*.

ὤρεσσιν, Ep. for *ὄρεσσιν*, dat. of *ὄαρ*.

ὤρετο, 3 sing. aor. 2 med. from *ὄρνυμι*.

ὡρεύω, (*ὥρα*) *to take care of*, *attend to*, c. acc.

ὤρη, ἡ, Ion. for *ὥρα*.

ὥρη, ἡ, Ion. for *ὥρα*.

ὡρη-φόρος, *ον*, (*ὥρα*, *φέρω*) *leading on the season* or *bringing on the fruits in their season*.

ὦρθαι, pf. pass. inf. of *ὄρνυμι*.

ὠρίζεσκον, Ion. impf. of *ὀαρίζω*.

ὡρῐκός, *ή*, *όν*, (*ὥρα*) *ripe*, *in one's prime* or *bloom*. II *in season*, *seasonable*: Adv. *-κῶς*, *ὡρικῶς πυνθάνει* you ask *seasonably*.

ὥρῐμος, *ον*, (*ὥρα*) *ripe*, *timely*, *in season*.

ὠρίνθην, aor. 1 pass. of *ὀρίνω*.

ὥριος, *ον*, (*ὥρα*) *happening or returning in due season*; *ὥρια πάντα* all *the fruits of the seasons*. II. *timely*, *seasonable*, *ripe*. III. *at the right time*, *in season*, *seasonable*.

ὡρισμένος, pf. pass. part. of *ὁρίζω*.

ὤριστος, Ion. crasis for *ὁ ἄριστος*.

Ὠρίων, *ωνος*, *ὁ*, *Orion*, a hunter beloved by Aurora, slain by Artemis. II. *a bright constellation* named after him, which rose just after the summer solstice, and was usually followed by rains. [ῑ Ep., ĭ Att.]

ὡρμάθη [ᾱ], Dor. for *ὡρμήθη*, 3 sing. aor. 1 pass. of *ὁρμάω*.

ὡρμᾶτο, **ὡρμήθη**, 3 sing. impf. and aor. 1 pass *ὁρμάω*.

ὡρμέᾰται, **-ᾰτο**, Ion. for *ὥρμηνται*, *ὥρμηντο*, 3 pl pf. and plqpf. pass. of *ὁρμάω*.

ὥρμηναν, 3 pl. aor. 1 of *ὁρμαίνω*.

ὤρνῠτο, 3 sing. impf. med. of *ὄρνυμι*.

ὡρο-θετέω, f. *ήσω*, (*ὥρα*, *τίθημι*) *to take note of a* thing *in casting a nativity* or *observing the natal hour*. II. *to be in the ascendant at that hour*, of one's ruling planet.

ὤρορε, 3 sing. redupl. aor. 2 of *ὄρνυμι*.

ὦρος, *εος*, *τό*, Dor. for *ὄρος* Ion. *οὖρος*, *a mountain*.

ὦρσα, aor. 1 of *ὄρνυμι*.

ὦρτο, 3 sing. Ep. aor. 2 med. of *ὄρνυμι*.

ὠρυθμός, *ὁ*, *a howling*, *bellowing*, *roaring*.

ὤρυξα, aor. 1 of *ὀρύσσω*.

ὠρύομαι, fut. *ύσομαι* [ῡ]: aor. 1 *ὠρῡσαμην*: Dep.:—*to howl*, *bellow*, *roar*, Lat. *rugire*: mostly of animals, but sometimes of men, esp. of savages, either in mourning or joy: also of the sea, *to roar*. II. transit. *to howl over*, *bewail*.

ὡρχαῖος, Ion. crasis for *ὁ ἀρχαῖος*.

ὠρχείσθην, 3 dual impf. of *ὀρχέομαι*.

ὠρχεῦντο, Dor. 3 plur. impf. of *ὀρχέομαι*.

ὠρώρει, 3 sing. plqpf. of *ὄρνυμι*.

ὠρωρέχᾰται, Ion. for *ὀρωρεγμένοι εἰσίν*, 3 pl. pf. pass. of *ὀρέγω*.

ὠρώρυκτο, 3 sing. plqpf. pass. of *ὀρύσσω*.

ὯΣ, I. as Adv. of Manner, and that either, 1. Demonstr. Adv. *so*, *thus*, when it takes an accent, *ὥς*. 2. Relat. Adj. *as*, when it is without accent, *ὡς*. II. as Conj. *that*, when it is also without accent, *ὡς*.

I. **ὧς**, **Demonstr. Adv. of Manner**, *so, thus*, Lat. *sic*. 2. **καὶ ὧς**, *even so, nevertheless:* with a negat., οὐδ' ὧς, μηδ' ὧς, *not even so, in no way soever.* 3. in Comparisons, ὧς is answered by ὡς, *so as*, Lat. *sic ut:* also, ὥστε .. ὧς, *as .. thus.* II. ὡς, Relat. Adv. of Manner, *as*, Lat. *ut*, properly coming after a demonstrat. Adv., which however is very often omitted.—Ὡς in this usage is never accentuated, except at the end of a sentence, or when it follows the word dependent on it, as, θεὸς ὥς for ὡς θεός. 2. with Elliptical Phrases, ὡς ἐμοί or ὥς γ' ἐμοί (sc. δοκεῖ); ὡς ἀπ' ὀμμάτων (sc. εἰκάσαι) to judge by eyesight; ὡς Λακεδαιμόνιος (sc. εἶναι) *for* a Lacedaemonian; συμπέμψας αὐτὸν ὡς φύλακα (sc. εἶναι) having sent him with them *as* a guard. 3. so with Participles, to give the reason of the principal Verb; ἀγανακτοῦσιν ὡς ἀδικούμενοι they are indignant *as* being injured, i. e. *by reason of* being injured; so with questions, ὡς τί δὴ θέλων; *as* wishing what? i. e. for the sake of what? so in the case of the object; εἴργουσιν αὐτὸν ὡς ἀδικοῦντα they restrain him *as* acting wrongfully, i. e. *by reason of:* so also with Participles used absol., ὡς οὕτως ἐχόντων, Lat. *res cum ita sint*, since things are so, i. e. *by reason of* their being so. 4. so also with Prepositions; ὡς ἐπὶ ναυμαχίαν *as* for a sea-fight, i. e. as if about to fight; ὡς ἐπὶ φρυγανισμόν *as* though to collect fuel: usu. with the Preps. ἐπί, εἰς, πρός, but also with others; ὡς ἐκ κακῶν ἐχάρη he rejoiced *as in* an evil plight, i. e. considering his evil plight: hence 5. sometimes the Prep. is omitted, and ὡς itself is used like a Prep., = εἰς, c. acc., as Lat. *usque* for *usque ad*, only with the names of persons, as, ὡς τὸν Φίλιππον *to* Philip: first in Homer, ὡς αἰεὶ τὸν ὁμοῖον ἄγει θεὸς ὡς τὸν ὁμοῖον how God does ever bring like *to* like. 6. with Adverbs:—with the Positive, ὡς ἀληθῶς, ὡς ἑτέρως *how* truly! *how* differently! Lat. *quam veré, quam aliter:* so too ὡς follows Adverbs expressing anything extraordinary, θαυμαστῶς ὡς, ὑπερφυῶς ὡς, etc. 7. ὡς strengthens the Superlative, like ὅτι and ὅπως, Lat. *quam*, ὡς μάλιστα, Lat. *quam maxime, as* much *as* possible; ὡς ῥᾷστα, Lat. *quam facillime, as* easily *as* possible; ὡς τάχιστα, Lat. *quam celerrime, as* quickly *as* possible, etc.; so also the phrases ὡς τὸ πολύ, ὡς ἐπὶ τὸ πολύ, ὡς ἐπὶ τὸ πλεῖστον for the most part, commonly, Lat. *plerumque, ut plurimum.* 8. so also with Superlative Adjectives, ὡς ἄριστος, ὡς βέλτιστος the best *possible*, etc.

III. ὡς as Conjunction 1. expressing a fact, *that*, like ὅτι, Lat. *quod.* 2. = ὥστε, *so that*, Lat. *adeo ut.* 3. ὡς, *that*, Lat. *quod*, where, as in Latin, the acc. c. inf. may be put instead; εἶπον ὡς τοῦτο εἴη, or εἶπον τοῦτο εἶναι. 4. ὡς, marking an end, like ἵνα or ὅπως, *that, in order that*, Lat. *ut.* 5. in Inferences, like ὥστε, c. inf., *so that*, Lat. *adeo ut, ita ut;* εὖρος ὡς δύο τριήρεας πλέειν ὁμοῦ in breadth *such that* two triremes could sail abreast. 6. ὡς is also used like ὅτι and ἐπεί, *as, since*, Lat. *quippe, quandoquidem:* also for ὅτε, *when*, Lat. *ut:* sometimes also = ὅπως, Lat. *quomodo, quemadmodum.*

IV. ὡς is sometimes used in independent sentences, as in phrase ὡς αἰεὶ τὸν ὁμοῖον ἄγει θεὸς ὡς τὸν ὁμοῖον *how* God ever brings like to like: also with Adjs. and Advs., ὡς ἠλίθιος εἶ *how* silly thou art; ὡς σεμνὸς ὁ καταράτος *how* pompous the rascal is; ὡς ὀξέα κλάζει *how* shrilly it screams. 2. at the beginning of several clauses, it denotes a quick succession of events, ὡς ἴδεν, ὥς μιν Ἔρως πυκινὰς φρένας ἀμφεκάλυψεν *how* he saw, *how* did Love encompass his soul; so, ὡς ἴδον, ὡς ἐμάνην, ὥς μευ περὶ θυμὸς ἰάφθη, as in Virgil, *ut vidi, ut perii, ut me malus abstulit error.* 3. ὡς to express a wish, *oh that!* like εἴθε, Lat. *utinam*, with the optat., ὡς ἀπόλοιτο καὶ ἄλλος *oh that* another also might perish: also negatively, ὡς μὴ θάνοι *oh that* he might not die!

V. ὡς with Numerals marks that they are to be taken as round numbers, *about, nearly;* ἀπέθανον ὡς πεντακόσιοι about 500 fell

VI. ὡς in some Elliptical Phrases: 1. ὡς τί (sc. γένηται); *in order that what may happen? for what end? wherefore?* 2. ὡς ἕκαστοι ἦσαν or ἔτυχον ὄντες, each separately, Lat. *pro se quisque.*

(Ὡς is an old pl. acc. of ὅς, as τώς pl. acc. of ὁ: οὕτως from οὗτος, etc.: so ἅτε is used Adv.)

ὧς or **ὥς**, Dor. for οὗ, *where.*

ὦς, τό, gen. ὠτός, Dor. for οὖς, *the ear.*

ὦσα, Ion. and Ep. for ἔωσα, aor. 1 of ὠθέω.

ὤσαιμεν, 1 pl. aor. 1 opt. of ὠθέω.

ὡς ἄν, Ep. ὥς κε or ὥς κεν, = ὡς with a conditional force added.

ὡσ-αν-εί or **ὡς ἂν εἰ**, *like as if, as if.*

ὡσαννά, Hebr. word meaning *save now! save we pray!*

ὤσασκε, 3 sing. Ion. aor. 1 of ὠθέω.

ὡσ-αύτως, Adv. of ὁ αὐτός (*the same*), strengthd. for ὥς, *in like manner, just so;* ὡσαύτως καί .. in like manner as..

ὦσδε, Dor. for ὦζε, 3 sing. impf. of ὄζω.

ὡσ-εί or **ὡς εἰ**, Adv. *as if, as though:* in Comparisons, *as if, like, just as:* so also **ὡσ-εί-τε.** II. with Numerals, *about.*

ὠσθήσομαι, fut. pass. of ὠθέω.

ὡσίν, dat. plur. of οὖ.

ὦσμαι, pf. pass. of ὠθέω: part. ὠσμένος.

ὥσ-περ, Adv. (ὡς, περ) *even as, just as;* in Homer there is often a word interposed between ὡς and περ, as, ὡς τοπάρος περ, ὡς ἔσεταί περ, etc. 2. of Time, *as soon as*, Lat. *simul ac.* 3. to limit or modify an assertion, *as if, as it were:* and so with Participles used absolutely, ὥσπερ ἐξόν *as if* it were in our power.

ὡσ-περ-εί or **ὡσπερεί**, *just as if, even as*, Lat. *tanquam.*

ὡσ-περ-οῦν, Adv. *even as, just as: as really*, εἰ δ' ἔστιν ὥσπερουν ἔστι θεός but if he is, *as* he *really* is a god.

ὥσ-τε, as Adv. (ὡς, τε) being to ὡς, as ὅστε to ὅς,

used to introduce a comparison, *as, like as, just as.* 2. to mark the power by which one does a thing, *as, as being*, like ἅτε, Lat. *utpote*; τὸν δ' ἐξήρπαξ' Ἀφροδίτη ῥεῖα μάλ', ὥστε θεός but Aphrodité bore him very easily away, *as being* a goddess.

II. as Conjunction, to express *a result* or *effect*; εἰ δέ σοι θυμὸς ἐπέσσυται, ὥστε νέεσθαι if thy heart is eagerly bent, *so as to* return.—This Construct. is very freq. in Att. 2. ὥστε is sometimes used like ὡς with a Part.; ὥστε φυλασσομένων τῶν ὁδῶν *as* or *since* the ways were guarded. 3. ὥστε is used after Comparatives with ἤ; μέζω κακὰ ἢ ὥστε ἀνακλαίειν greater woes than *that one could* weep for: but ὥστε is sometimes left out, as, μεῖζον ἢ φέρειν too great to bear:—the Posit. is sometimes used, ψυχρὸν ὥστε λούσασθαι cold to bathe in, implying, too cold to bathe in. III. ὥστε is also joined with the Indic., with the Opt., and even with the Imperat. when it is emphatic, e. g. ὥστε θάρρει *so that*, or *therefore*, be of good cheer.

ὠστίζω, f. ίσω, Frequentat. of ὠθέω, *to push to and fro*, Lat. *trudo*. II. in Med., Att. fut. ὠστιοῦμαι, c. dat. *jostle with another*: so absol., ὠστίζεσθαι εἰς τὴν προεδρίαν *to jostle* for the first seat.

ὤστοργος, crasis for ὁ ἄστοργος.

ὠσφρόμην Ion. **ὀσφράμην**, aor. 2 med. of ὀσφραίνομαι.

ὤσω, fut. of ὠθέω.

ὠτ-ἄκουστέω, f. ήσω, (οὖς, ἀκούω) *to hearken* or *listen covertly* or *anxiously*.

ὦ τᾶν or **ὦ τάν**, see τᾶν.

ὠτάριον, τό, Dim. of οὖς, *a little ear.* [ᾰ]

ὦτε, Dor. for ὥστε.

ὠτειλή, ἡ, (οὐτάω) *a wound*: later also *a scar*, Lat. *cicatrix*.

ὠτίον, τό, Dim. of οὖς, *a little ear.*

ὠτίς, ίδος, ἡ, (οὖς) *a bustard with long ear-feathers.*

Ὦτος, ὁ, *Otos*, son of Aloëus, brother of Ephialtes.

ὤτρῦνα, aor. 1 of ὀτρύνω.

ὠτώεις, εσσα, εν, (οὖς) *with ears* or *handles*.

ὡὐτός, Ion. and Dor. for ὁ αὐτός: also **ὠυτός** or **ὡὐτός**.

ὤφειλα, aor. 1 of ὀφέλλω.

ὠφέλεια Ion. **ὠφελίη** also in Att. **ὠφελία**, ἡ, (ὠφελέω) *help, aid, assistance, succour*, esp. in war. 2. *profit, advantage, gain*: in plur. *gains, profits*.

ὤφελον, aor. 2 of ὀφείλω.

ὠφελέω, f. ήσω: (ὄφελος):—*to help, aid, assist, succour, benefit*: *to be of use* or *service* to any one: absol. *to be of use* or *service*; οὐδὲν ὠφελεῖ *it does* no *good*: also with a neuter Adj., οὐδέν τινα ὠφελεῖν *to do* one *no service*: sometimes c. dat. pers., like Lat. *prodesse*:—in phrase οὐδεὶς ἔρωτος τοῦδ' ἐφαίνετ' ὠφελῶν, the part. is taken as a Subst. *a helper*. II. Pass. ὠφελοῦμαι, with fut. med. ὠφελήσομαι, pass. ὠφεληθήσομαι:—*to be helped, to receive help, aid* or *succour, to derive profit, benefit* or *advantage*; πρός τινος *from* a person or thing: so, ἔκ or ἀπό τινος; and c. dat., ὠφελεῖσθαί τινι *to be profited by* a thing: c. part., ὠφελεῖσθαι ἰδών *to be benefited by* the sight of a thing. Hence

ὠφέλημα, ατος, τό, *that which is of use, a useful* or *serviceable thing.* II. generally = ὠφελία, *use, advantage, benefit.*

ὠφελήσῐμος, ον, (ὠφελέω) *useful, serviceable.*

ὠφέλησις, εως, ἡ, (ὠφελέω) *a helping, aiding*: generally, *service, advantage.*

ὠφελητέος, α, ον, verb. Adj. of ὠφελέω, *necessary* or *proper to be assisted.* II. ὠφελητέον, *one must assist.*

ὠφελία, Att. for ὠφέλεια.

ὠφέλῐμος, ον, sometimes also η, ον, (ὠφελέω) *helping, aiding*: *useful, serviceable, profitable, advantageous.* Adv. -μως: Sup. ὠφελιμώτατα.

ὤφελλον, Ep. for ὤφελον.

ὤφελον, aor. 2 of ὀφείλω.

ὤφθην, aor. 1 of ὁράω, in pass. sense.

ὤφληκα, pf. of ὀφλισκάνω: **ὦφλον**, aor. 2.

ὠφρόντιστος, crasis for ὁ ἀφρόντιστος.

ᾦχα, pf. of οἴγνυμι.

ᾠχᾰτο, Ion. for ᾠγμένοι ἦσαν, 3 plur. plqpf. pass. of οἴγνυμι.

ᾤχετο, **ᾤχοντο**, 3 sing. and pl. impf. of οἴχομαι.

ᾤχηκα, Ep. for ᾤχωκα, pl. of οἴχομαι.

ὤχθησαν, 3 pl. aor. 1 of ὀχθέω.

ὠχράω, f. ήσω, (ὠχρός) *to turn pale, be pale, wan*, etc.

ὠχριάω, f. άσω [ᾱ], (ὠχρός) *to be* or *turn pale.*

ὨΧΡΟ΄Σ, ά, όν, *pale, wan, sallow.* Hence

ὦχρος, ου, ὁ, or εος, τό, like ὠχρότης, *paleness, wanness*, esp. *the paleness of fear.*

ᾤχωκα, Ion. pf. of οἴχομαι.

ὤψ, ἡ, gen. ὠπός acc. ὦπα, (ὄψομαι, fut. of ὁράω) *the eye, face, countenance*; εἰς ὦπα ἰδέσθαι τινί to look one full in *the face*: so absol., εἰς ὦπα ἰδέσθαι: but, θεῇς εἰς ὦπα ἔοικεν as to *the face*, i. e. in *face* she is like the goddesses.

FINIS.

APPENDIX

OF

PROPER AND GEOGRAPHICAL NAMES

PREPARED BY

GEORGE RICKER BERRY, Ph.D.

PROFESSOR OF SEMITIC LANGUAGES IN COLGATE UNIVERSITY

EDITOR OF

THE NEW GREEK-ENGLISH LEXICON TO THE NEW TESTAMENT

HINDS & NOBLE, Publishers

4-5-6-12-13-14 Cooper Institute New York City

INTRODUCTORY NOTE.

THIS APPENDIX is designed especially for use in the study of the Greek language in preparation for college. It aims, therefore, to contain all the proper and geographical names found in those Greek works usually read in such preparatory study, which are Xenophon's Anabasis, the first two Books of Xenophon's Hellenica, the first six Books of the Iliad, and the first two Books of the Odyssey. A brief treatment has been necessary, in order to keep within reasonable limits; it has been the intention, however, to omit no really necessary item of information, but to give the most important facts in a condensed form. No attempt has been made to give a complete account of the various views on points where there is difference of opinion. The purpose has been, rather, to present the view which seemed to be preferable, and, where there exists reasonable doubt concerning any statement made, to indicate the fact.

JANUARY, 1901.

TYPOGRAPHY AND ELECTROTYPING BY
THE UNIVERSITY PRESS, CAMBRIDGE, U. S. A.

APPENDIX.

A

Ἄβαντες, *ων*, *οἱ*, *the Abantes*, the ancient inhabitants of Eubœa, probably of Thracian origin.

Ἀβαρβαρέη, *ης*, *ἡ*, *Abarbarea*, a Naiad.

Ἀβαρνίς, *ιδος*, *ἡ*, *Abarnis*, a town, district, and promontory near Lampsacus in Mysia.

Ἄβας, *αντος*, *ὁ*, *Abas*, a Trojan.

Ἀβδηρίτης, *ου*, *ὁ*, *an Abderite*, an inhabitant of Abdera, a city of Thrace, at the mouth of the Nestus; used proverbially, meaning a simpleton.

Ἄβληρος, *ου*, *ὁ*, *Ablerus*, a Trojan.

Ἀβροζέλμης, *ου*, *ὁ*, *Abrozelmes*, a Thracian.

Ἀβροκόμας, *α*, *ὁ*, *Abrocomas*, a Persian satrap, opposed to Cyrus the younger.

Ἀβροκόμης, *ου*, Ion. *εω*, *ὁ*, (another form of the preceding word), *Abrocomes*, a son of Darius I. and half-brother of Xerxes I., slain at Thermopylæ.

Ἀβρώνιχος and **Ἀβρώνυχος**, *ου*, *ὁ*, *Abronichus* or *Abronychus*, an Athenian, ambassador to Sparta.

Ἀβῡδηνός, *ή*, *όν*, *belonging to Abydus;* **οἱ Ἀβῡδηνοί**, *the inhabitants of Abydus.*

Ἀβῡδόθεν, *from Abydus.*

Ἄβῡδος, *ου*, *ἡ*, *Abydus*, a city of Troas, on the Hellespont, at the narrowest part.

Ἀγαμεμνονίδης, *ου*, *ὁ*, *son of Agamemnon*, i. e. Orestes.

Ἀγαμέμνων, *ονος*, *ὁ*, *Agamemnon*, king of Mycenæ, and commander-in-chief of the Greek forces before Troy.

Ἀγαπήνωρ, *ορος*, *ὁ*, *Agapenor*, son of Ancæus, leader of the Arcadians before Troy.

Ἀγασθένης, *εος* contr. *ους*, *ὁ*, *Agasthenes*, son of Augeas king of Elis.

Ἀγασίας, *ου*, *ὁ*, *Agasias*, of Arcadia, a captain in the army of the ten thousand.

Ἀγγενίδας, *ου* and *α*, *ὁ*, *Angenidas*, a Spartan ephor.

Ἀγήνωρ, *ορος*, *ὁ*, *Agenor*, a Trojan leader.

Ἀγησίλᾱος, *ου*, Ion. forms **Ἡγησίλᾱος**, *ου*, and **Ἡγησίλεως**, *ω*, *ὁ*, *Agesilaus*, the name of several kings of Sparta, especially: (1) the son of Doryssus; (2) the son of Archidamus, a celebrated general.

Ἀγησίστρατος, *ου*, *ὁ*, *Agesistratus*, a Spartan ephor.

Ἀγίας, *ου*, *ὁ*, *Agias*, an Arcadian commander in the army of Cyrus the younger.

Ἆγις, Ion. **Ἧγις**, *ιδος*, *ὁ*, *Agis*, the name of several kings of Sparta, the first of whom was son of Eurysthenes and founder of the line of the Agidæ.

Ἀγκαῖος, *ου*, *ὁ*, *Ancæus*, an Arcadian, son of Lycurgus.

Ἀγλαΐη, *ης*, *ἡ*, *Aglaïa*, wife of Charopus and mother of Nireus.

Ἄγλαυρος, *ου*, *ἡ*, *Aglaurus*, a daughter of Cecrops, worshipped on the Acropolis at Athens.

Ἅγνων, or **Ἄγ-**, *ωνος*, *ὁ*, *Hagnon* or *Agnon*, an Athenian, father of Theramenes.

Ἀγχίαλος, *ου*, *ὁ*, *Anchialus:* (1) father of Mentes, king of the Taphians; (2) a Greek warrior at Troy.

Ἀγχίσης, *ου*, *ὁ*, *Anchises*, a Trojan prince, father of Æneas.

Ἀδείμαντος, *ου*, *ὁ*, *Adimantus:* (1) a commander of the Corinthian fleet; (2) an Athenian commander.

Ἄδμητος, *ου*, *ὁ*, *Admetus*, son of Pheres, king of Pheræ in Thessaly, one of the Argonauts.

Ἀδρήστεια (Ion. for **-δρά-**), *ας*, *ἡ*, *Adrastea*, a city of Asia Minor on the Propontis, in a district of the same name.

Ἀδρηστίνη (Ion. for **-δρα-**), *ης*, *ἡ*, *daughter of Adrastus.*

Ἄδρηστος (Ion. for **-δρα-**), *ου*, *ὁ*, *Adrastus:* (1) a king of Argos and of Sicyon; (2) a son of Merops, who fought on the side of the Trojans.

Ἀζείδης, *ου*, *ὁ*, *son of Azeus*, i. e. Actor.

'Αθηνᾶ, ᾶς, ἡ, *Athena*, the Roman *Minerva*, the tutelary goddess of Athens.

'Αθηνάδης (Ion. for **-δας**), ου, ὁ, *Athenades*, an inhabitant of Trachis.

'Αθῆναι, ῶν, αἱ, *Athens*, the famous city.

'Αθηναῖος, ου, ὁ, *an inhabitant of Athens, an Athenian.*

Αἶα, ης, ἡ, *Æa*, (lit. *land*), an ancient name for the country of Colchis, or some part of it.

Αἰακίδης, ου, ὁ, *son of Æacus*, a patronymic of the descendants of Æacus, including Peleus the son, Achilles the grandson, etc.

Αἰακός, οῦ, ὁ, *Æacus*, son of Zeus and Ægina, and king of Ægina, said to have been one of the three judges in the lower world.

Αἴας, αντος, ὁ, *Ajax*, the name of two Grecian leaders in the Trojan war: (1) the greater, son of Telamon king of Salamis, a hero next in bravery to Achilles; (2) the less, son of Oileus king of the Locrians.

Αἰγαίων, ωνος, ὁ, *Ægæon*, one of the three hundred-armed giants, so called by men, but *Briareus* by the gods.

Αἰγάλεως, ω, ὁ, *Ægaleos*, a mountain in Attica, opposite Salamis.

Αἰγείδης, ου, ὁ, *son of Ægeus*, i. e. Theseus.

Αἰγιάλεια (poetic for **-λη**), ας, ἡ, *Ægialea*, daughter of Adrastus and wife of Diomedes.

Αἰγιαλός, οῦ, ὁ, *Ægialus:* (1) an ancient name of Achaia; (2) a city in Paphlagonia.

Αἰγίλεια, ας, ἡ, *Ægilea*, a small island west of Eubœa.

Αἰγίλιψ, ιπος, ἡ, *Ægilips*, probably an island near Epirus.

Αἴγῑνα, ης, ἡ, *Ægina*, a rocky island in the Saronic gulf, near Argolis.

Αἰγῑναῖος, α, ον, *belonging to Ægina.*

Αἰγῑνήτης, ου, ὁ, *an inhabitant of Ægina.*

Αἴγιον, ου, τό, *Ægium*, a city of Achaia, the capital after the destruction of Helice.

Αἴγισθος, ου, ὁ, *Ægisthus*, son of Thyestes, murderer of Agamemnon.

Αἰγὸς ποταμοί, and **ποταμός**, (lit. *goat's river*), *Ægos-potami*, a small river, and a city at its mouth, in the Thracian Chersonese.

Αἰγύπτιος, α, ον, *Egyptian.*

Αἰγύπτιος, ου, ὁ, *Ægyptius*, an inhabitant of Ithaca.

Αἰήτης, ου, ὁ, *Æëtes*, the name of several kings of Colchis; the first was brother of Circe and father of Medea.

Αἴθῑκες, ων, οἱ, *the Æthices*, an ancient Thessalian tribe, dwelling on and near Mount Pindus.

Αἴθρη, ης, ἡ, *Æthra*, mother of Theseus.

Αἱμονίδης, ου, ὁ, *son of Hæmon*, i. e. Mæon.

Αἵμων, ονος, ὁ, *Hæmon*, son of Creon, of Thebes.

Αἰνησίας, ου, ὁ, *Ænesias*, a Spartan ephor.

Αἰνιᾶνες, or **Αἰνιῆνες**, Ion. **'Ενιῆνες**, ων, οἱ, *the Ænianes*, an ancient Grecian tribe, in the Homeric period inhabiting northern Thessaly around Mt. Ossa, subsequently dwelling in southern Thessaly.

Αἰνόθεν, *from Ænus.*

Αἶνος, ου, ἡ, *Ænus*, an ancient city of Thrace, at the mouth of the Hebrus.

Αἰξωνεύς, έως, ὁ, *a resident of Æxone*, an Attic deme; they were notorious as slanderers.

Αἰολίδης, ου, ὁ, *a son* or *descendant of Æolus*, applied to Sisyphus, Cretheus, etc.; **οἱ Αἰολίδαι**, *the descendants of Æolus, the Æolidæ.*

Αἰολίς, ίδος, adj., peculiar fem. of **Αἰολικός**, *Æolian;* **γῆν τὴν Αἰολίδα**, *the Æolian land*, an early name of Thessaly. As subst. (χώρα understood), **Αἰολίς**, ίδος, ἡ, *Æolis*, a district of Mysia on the west coast of Asia Minor.

Αἶπυ, εος, τό, *Æpy*, a city in Elis, situated on a height.

Αἰπύτιος, η, ον, *of Æpytus*, an ancient Arcadian chief; commonly used with τύμβος.

Αἴσηπος, ου, ὁ, *Æsepus:* (1) a river of northern Mysia, flowing into the Propontis near Cyzicus; (2) a son of Bucolion.

Αἰσῡήτης, ου, ὁ, *Æsyetes*, a Trojan prince.

Αἰσχίνης, ου, ὁ, *Æschines:* (1) a commander of Greek light-armed troops; (2) a pupil and friend of Socrates.

Αἰσχραίας, also **Αἰσχρέας**, ου, ὁ, *Æschræas*, an Athenian.

Αἴσωπος, ου, ὁ, *Æsopus* (*Æsop*), the celebrated writer of fables.

Αἰτωλός, οῦ, ὁ, and **Αἰτώλιος**, ου, ὁ, *an Ætolian, an inhabitant of Ætolia;* also as adj., *Ætolian.*

'Ακαδήμεια, ας, ἡ, *The Academy*, a gymnasium in the suburbs of Athens (so named from the hero Academus), where Plato taught.

'Ακάμας, αντος, ὁ, *Acamas:* (1) a son of Antenor; (2) a Thracian leader in the Trojan war.

'Ακάνθιος, α, ον, *Acanthian, belonging to Acanthus;* in pl., **οἱ 'Ακάνθιοι**, *the Acanthians.*

"Ακανθος, ου, ἡ, *Acanthus*, a city near Mt. Athos, on the Strymonian Gulf.

'Ακαρνάν, ᾶνος, (in Herodotus **-νήν**, ῆνος), ὁ, *an Acarnanian, an inhabitant of Acarnania.*

'Ακαρνᾱνία, ας, ἡ, *Acarnania*, the most westerly province of Greece, west of Ætolia.

'Ακήρατος, ου, ὁ, *Aceratus*, a priest at Delphi.

'Ακράγας, αντος, ὁ, *Agrigentum*, the name of a city, and also of a river, in Sicily.

Ἀκτορίων, ωνος, ὁ, *son of Actor*, i. e. Eurytus.

Ἄκτωρ, ορος, ὁ, *Actor*, son of Azeus, of Orchomenus.

Ἁλαί, ῶν, αἱ, *Halæ*: (1) a deme of the tribe Ægeis on the east coast of Attica; (2) a deme of the tribe Cecropis on the west coast.

Ἀλαλκομενηΐς, ΐδος, fem. adj., *Alalcomenean*, epithet of Athene, from Alalcomenæ, a city in Bœotia, where was a temple to her.

Ἀλάστωρ, ορος, ὁ, *Alastor*: (1) a Greek warrior, son of Neleus; (2) a Lycian, slain by Ulysses.

Ἀλείσιον, ου, τό, *Alisium*, a city in Elis.

Ἀλεξίας, ου, ὁ, *Alexias*, an Athenian archon.

Ἀλεξιππίδας, α, ὁ, *Alexippidas*, a Spartan ephor.

Ἀλήϊον πεδίον, τό, *the Aleian plain, land of wandering* (ἄλη, *wandering*), located by Homer in Lycia, by Herodotus in Cilicia.

Ἁλίαρτος, ου, ὁ and ἡ, *Haliartus*, an ancient city of Bœotia, on the lake Copais.

Ἁλιζῶνες and **Ἁλίζωνοι**, ων, οἱ, *the Halizones* or *Halizoni*, a tribe of Bithynia.

Ἁλιθέρσης, ου, ὁ, *Halitherses*, an inhabitant of Ithaca.

Ἅλιος, ου, ὁ, *Halius*, a Lycian.

Ἁλίπεδον, ου, τό, (lit. *a plain near the sea*), *Halipedon*, the name of the plain lying between Athens and Piræus and bordering on the coast.

Ἁλίσαρνα, ης, ἡ, *Halisarna*, a city of Mysia.

Ἀλκαμένης, ους, ὁ, *Alcamenes*, son of Teleclus, ninth king of Sparta.

Ἄλκανδρος, ου, ὁ, *Alcander*, a Lycian.

Ἀλκή, ῆς, ἡ, *Alce, Might* personified.

Ἄλκηστις, ιδος and ιος, ἡ, *Alcestis*, daughter of Pelias, and wife of Admetus, in whose stead she died.

Ἀλκιβιάδης, ου, ὁ, *Alcibiades*: (1) a celebrated Athenian leader; (2) a cousin of the former.

Ἀλκμαιωνίδαι, ῶν, οἱ, *the descendants of Alcmæon, the Alcmæonidæ*, a noble family at Athens.

Ἀλκμήνη, ης, ἡ, *Alcmene*, daughter of Electryon king of Mycenæ, mother of Hercules.

Ἀλόπη, ης, ἡ, *Alope*, a town in Phthiotis, in southern Thessaly, near the Malian Gulf.

Ἄλος (also Ἄλ-), ου, ὁ and ἡ, *Alus*, a town of Phthiotis, in southern Thessaly, at the extremity of Mt. Othrys.

Ἀλπηνός, οῦ, ἡ, (and **Ἀλπηνοί**), *Alpenus* (or *Alpeni*), a city at the entrance of the pass of Thermopylæ.

Ἀλυάττης, ου, ὁ, *Alyattes*, one of the most important kings of Lydia, father of Crœsus.

Ἀλύβη, ης, ἡ, *Alybe*, a city in Bithynia on the coast of the Euxine.

Ἅλυς, υος, ὁ, *Halys*, the chief river of Asia Minor, flowing north into the Euxine.

Ἀλφειός, οῦ, ὁ, *Alpheus*, the chief river of the Peloponnesus.

Ἀλφεός, οῦ, ὁ, (Doric for **Ἀλφειός**), *Alpheus*, a brave Lacedæmonian warrior at Thermopylæ.

Ἀλωεύς, έως, ὁ, *Aloeus*, son of Poseidon.

Ἀμαρυγκείδης, ου, ὁ, *son of Amarynceus*, i. e. Diores.

Ἀμβρακιώτης, ου, ὁ, *an Ambraciot*, inhabitant of Ambracia, the capital of Epirus.

Ἀμεινίας, ου and α, ὁ, *Aminias*, an Athenian naval captain.

Ἀμεινοκλῆς, έους, ὁ, *Aminocles*, an inhabitant of Magnesia in Thessaly.

Ἀμυδών, ῶνος, ἡ, *Amydon*, a city of the Pæonians, on the Axius, in Macedonia.

Ἀμύκλαι, ῶν, αἱ, *Amyclæ*, an ancient city of Laconia, on the Eurotas, famous for the worship of Apollo.

Ἀμφιγένεια, ας, ἡ, *Amphigenia*, a city of Triphylia, in southern Elis.

Ἀμφίδημος, ου, ὁ, *Amphidemus*, father of Amphicrates.

Ἀμφικράτης, ους, ὁ, *Amphicrates*, an Athenian captain.

Ἀμφίμαχος, ου, ὁ, *Amphimachus*: (1) son of Cteatus, one of the leaders of the Epeï before Troy; (2) son of Nomion, a leader of the Carians in assisting the Trojans.

Ἄμφῖος, ου, ὁ, *Amphius*: (1) son of Merops; (2) son of Selagus.

Ἀμφιπολίτης, ου, ὁ, *an Amphipolite*, an inhabitant of Amphipolis in southern Macedonia, on the Strymon.

Ἄμφισσα, ης, ἡ, *Amphissa*, one of the chief cities of the Locri Ozolæ, on the borders of Phocis.

Ἀμφιτρύων, ωνος, ὁ, *Amphitryon*, son of Alcæus, king of Tiryns, and subsequently of Thebes; husband of Alcmene the mother of Hercules.

Ἀναγυράσιος, ου, ὁ, *a resident of Anagyrus*, an Attic deme.

Ἀναίτιος, ου, ὁ, *Anætius*, one of the thirty tyrants at Athens.

Ἀναξανδρίδης, ου, ὁ, *Anaxandrides*, a king of Sparta, father of the famous Leonidas.

Ἀνάξανδρος, ου, ὁ, *Anaxander*, a king of Sparta.

Ἀναξίβιος, ου, ὁ, *Anaxibius*, a Spartan admiral.

Ἀναξικράτης, ους, ὁ, *Anaxicrates*, a Byzantine.

Ἀναξίλᾱος, ου, ὁ, *Anaxilaus*, a Byzantine.

Ἀνδραίμων, ονος, ὁ, *Andræmon*, king of Calydon in Ætolia, father of Thoas.

Ἄνδριος, α, ον, *belonging to Andrus*; as noun, **Ἄνδριος**, ου, ὁ, *an inhabitant of Andrus.*

Ἀνδρόβουλος, ου, ὁ, *Androbulus*, a Delphian, the father of Timon.

Ἀνδροδάμας, αντος, ὁ, *Androdamas*, a Samian, father of Theomestor.

Ἀνδρομάχη, ης, ἡ, *Andromache*, daughter of Eëtion, wife of Hector.

Ἄνδρος, ου, ἡ, *Andrus*, the most northerly and one of the most important of the Cyclades islands, with a city of the same name.

Ἀνεμώρεια, ας, ἡ, later called **Ἀνεμώλεια**, *Anemoria*, a town in Phocis, located on a hill.

Ἀνθεμίδης (for **Ἀνθεμιωνιάδης**), ου, ὁ, *son of Anthemion*, i. e. Simoisius.

Ἀνθεμίων, ωνος, ὁ, *Anthemion*, a Trojan.

Ἀνθηδών, όνος, ἡ, *Anthedon*, a city with a harbor on the east coast of Bœotia.

Ἀνθήλη, ης, ἡ, *Anthele*, a town in Phocis, in the immediate vicinity of Thermopylæ, one of the two places where the Amphictyonic council met.

Ἀννίβας, α, ὁ, *Hannibal*, the famous Carthaginian general.

Ἀνόπαια, ας, ἡ, *Anopæa*, a mountain, part of the chain of Œta; the name is also given to a pass in the mountain.

Ἀντάνδριος, ου, ὁ, *an inhabitant of Antandrus.*

Ἄντανδρος, ου, ἡ, *Antandrus*, a city of Troas, at the foot of Mt. Ida, an Æolian colony.

Ἄντεια, ας, ἡ, *Antea*, daughter of the Lycian king Iobates, wife of Prœtus king of Tiryns.

Ἀντηνορίδης, ου, ὁ, *son* or *descendant of Antenor.*

Ἀντήνωρ, ορος, ὁ, *Antenor*, a Trojan prince related to Priam.

Ἀντιγένης, ους, ὁ, *Antigenes*, an Athenian archon.

Ἀντίδωρος, ου, ὁ, *Antidorus*, a Lemnian shipcaptain.

Ἀντίκυρα, ας, ἡ, (earlier **-κιρρα**), *Anticyra*, a town of Thessaly near the mouth of the Sperchēus.

Ἀντικυρεύς, έως, ὁ, *an inhabitant of Anticyra.*

Ἀντιλέων, οντος, ὁ, *Antileon*, of Thurii in southern Italy.

Ἀντίλοχος, ου, ὁ, *Antilochus*, son of Nestor, a warrior against Troy.

Ἀντίνοος, contr. **Ἀντίνους**, ου, ὁ, *Antinoüs*, a native of Ithaca, a suitor of Penelope.

Ἀντίοχος, ου, ὁ, *Antiochus*, an Athenian pilot.

Ἀντίπατρος, ου, ὁ, *Antipater*, a Thasian, son of Orges.

Ἀντισθένης, ους, ὁ, *Antisthenes*, an Athenian philosopher, a pupil and friend of Socrates, founder of the school of Cynics.

Ἄντιφος, ου, ὁ, *Antiphus*: (1) a son of Ægyptius of Ithaca; (2) a leader of the Greeks from Nisyrus; (3) a leader of the Mæonians allied with the Trojans; (4) a son of Priam and Hecuba.

Ἀντιφῶν, ῶντος, ὁ, *Antiphon*, an Athenian.

Ἀντρών, ῶνος, ὁ and ἡ, *Antron*, a city of Phthiotis in Thessaly, at the entrance of the Malian Gulf.

Ἄνυτος, ου, ὁ, *Anytus*, an Athenian, son of Anthemion, the leading accuser of Socrates.

Ἀξιός, οῦ, ὁ, (also **Ἄξιος**), *Axius*, the largest river in Macedonia, flowing into the Thermaic Gulf.

Ἄξῦλος, ου, ὁ, *Axylus*, a Thracian prince.

Ἀπαισός, οῦ, ἡ, (same as **Παισός**), *Apæsus*, a city in Mysia, at the entrance of the Propontis.

Ἀπατούρια, ων, τά, *the Apaturia*, a family festival at Athens in the month Pyanepsion, lasting three days.

Ἀπιδανός, Ion. **Ἠπι-**, οῦ, ὁ, *Apidanus*, a river of Thessaly, flowing into the Peneus.

Ἀπολλόδωρος, ου, ὁ, *Apollodorus*, a common Grecian name; especially, an intimate friend of Socrates.

Ἀπολλωνία, ας, ἡ, *Apollonia*, a city of Mysia, near Lydia; also the name of several other cities.

Ἀπολλωνίδης, ου, ὁ, *Apollonides*, a Lydian.

Ἀραβία, ας, ἡ, *Arabia*; often used as including a part of Mesopotamia.

Ἀραιθυρέα, ας, ἡ, *Aræthyrea*, an ancient city in the Peloponnesus, near the site of the later Phlius.

Ἄρακος, ου, ὁ, *Aracus*, a Lacedæmonian.

Ἀράξης, ου, ὁ, *Araxes*, a tributary of the Euphrates on the east; more commonly called Chaboras.

Ἀρβάκης, ου, ὁ, *Arbaces*, a satrap of Media.

Ἀργεῖος, α, ον, *of* or *belonging to Argos, Argive*; **Ἀργεῖοι**, ων, οἱ, *Argives*, often used by Homer for all the Greeks, as is also Ἀχαιοί.

Ἀργινοῦσαι, ῶν, αἱ, *Arginusæ*, three small islands between Lesbos and Æolis.

Ἄργισσα, ης, ἡ, *Argissa*, the Homeric name for Argura, a town of Thessaly on the Peneus near Larissa.

Ἄργοσδε, *to Argos.*

Ἀρεσίας, ου, ὁ, *Aresias*, one of the thirty tyrants at Athens.

Ἀρετάων, ονος, ὁ, *Aretaon*, a Trojan warrior.

Ἀρήνη, ης, ἡ, *Arene*, a city in southern Elis, the residence of Alphareus.

Ἀρηξίων, ονος, ὁ, *Arexion*, an Arcadian soothsayer.

Ἀριαβίγνης, ου, ὁ, *Ariabignes*, a Persian naval commander, son of Darius I. and half-brother of Xerxes I., slain in the battle of Salamis.

Ἀριαῖος, ου, ὁ, *Ariæus*, a Persian general in the service of Cyrus the younger, commander of the Asiatics.

Ἀριαράμνης, ου, ὁ, *Ariaramnes*, a Persian.

Ἄριμα, ων, τά, *Arima*, a mythical mountain district in Asia Minor, under which the giant Typhon lay.

Ἀριοβαρζάνης, ους, ὁ, *Ariobarzanes*, a Persian satrap.

Ἀρίσβη, ης, ἡ, *Arisbe*, a city of Troas, south-east of Abydus.

Ἀρίσβηθεν, *from Arisbe.*

Ἀρίσταρχος, ου, ὁ, *Aristarchus:* (1) a Lacedæmonian, governor of Byzantium; (2) an Athenian commander.

Ἀριστέας, ου, ὁ, *Aristeas*, a Chian, a leader in the army of Cyrus the younger.

Ἀριστείδης, ου, ὁ, *Aristides*, son of Lysimachus, a distinguished Athenian leader, archon, and general.

Ἀρίστιππος, ου, ὁ, *Aristippus:* (1) a Thessalian, of Larissa; (2) a native of Cyrene, disciple of Socrates, and founder of the Cyrenaic school of philosophy.

Ἀριστογείτων, ονος, ὁ, *Aristogiton*, an Athenian, who, with Harmodius, murdered Hipparchus.

Ἀριστογένης, ους, ὁ, *Aristogenes:* (1) an Athenian commander; (2) a Syracusan, father of Heraclides.

Ἀριστόδημος, ου, ὁ, *Aristodemus*, a Spartan warrior.

Ἀριστοκράτης, ους, ὁ, *Aristocrates*, a general of the Athenians.

Ἀριστόμαχος, ου, ὁ, *Aristomachus*, a king of Sparta.

Ἀριστονίκη, ης, ἡ, *Aristonice*, priestess at Delphi.

Ἀριστοτέλης, ους, ὁ, *Aristotle*, one of the thirty tyrants at Athens, who was not the famous philosopher of Stagira.

Ἀρίστων, ωνος, ὁ, *Ariston:* (1) an Athenian in the service of Cyrus the younger; (2) a king of Sparta, one of the Proclidæ; (3) a Byzantine.

Ἀριστώνυμος, ου, ὁ, *Aristonymus*, an Arcadian.

Ἀρκαδία, ας, ἡ, *Arcadia*, the central country of the Peloponnesus, and next to the largest.

Ἀρκαδικός, ή, όν, *Arcadian.*

Ἀρκάς, άδος, ὁ, *an Arcadian.*

Ἀρκεσίλᾱος, ου, ὁ, *Arcesilaus*, son of Lycus, a leader of the Bœotians at Troy.

Ἅρμα, ατος, τό, *Harma*, a small town in eastern Bœotia.

Ἁρματίδης, ου, ὁ, *Harmatides*, a Thespian, father of Dithyrambus.

Ἀρμενία, ας, ἡ, *Armenia*, a country of Asia, lying between Asia Minor and the Caspian sea, divided into Armenia Major and Armenia Minor, the latter being the portion east of the Euphrates.

Ἀρμένιος, α, ον, *Armenian*; **οἱ Ἀρμένιοι**, *the Armenians.*

Ἁρμήνη (also **Ἀρμένη**), ης, ἡ, *Harmene*, a town on the coast of Paphlagonia, near Sinope.

Ἁρμόδιος, ου, ὁ, *Harmodius*, an Athenian, who, with Aristogiton, murdered Hipparchus.

Ἁρμονίδης, ου, ὁ, (prop. *son of Harmon*), *Harmonides*, a Trojan artificer.

Ἀρνάπης, ου, ὁ, *Arnapes*, a Persian.

Ἄρνη, ης, ἡ, *Arne*, an ancient town in Bœotia, mentioned by Homer.

Ἅρπασος, ου, ὁ, *Harpasus*, a river of Armenia Major, flowing south into the Araxes.

Ἀρσάμης, ου, ὁ, *Arsames*, grandfather of Darius I.

Ἀρτάβᾱνος, ου, ὁ, *Artabanus*, brother of Darius I. and uncle to Xerxes I.

Ἀρταγέρσης, ους, ὁ, *Artagerses*, a cavalry officer of Artaxerxes II.

Ἀρτακάμας, α, ὁ, *Artacamas*, a Persian satrap.

Ἀρτάνης, ου, ὁ, *Artanes*, a brother of Darius I.

Ἀρταξέρξης, ου, ὁ, *Artaxerxes*, the name of three Persian kings. The second, surnamed Mnemon, was brother of Cyrus the younger.

Ἀρτάοζος, ου, ὁ, *Artaozus*, a friend of Cyrus the younger.

Ἀρταπάτας, α, or **Ἀρταπάτης**, ου, ὁ, *Artapatas*, a friend of Cyrus the younger.

Ἀρταφέρνης, ου, ὁ, *Artaphernes:* (1) brother of Darius I.; (2) son of the foregoing, commander in the Persian army.

Ἄρτεμις, ιδος, ἡ, *Artemis*, the Roman *Diana*, goddess of the chase.

Ἀρτεμισία, ας, ἡ, *Artemisia*, queen of a few Carian cities, and ally of Xerxes I.

Ἀρτεμίσιον, ου, τό, *Artemisium*, the name of a region on the northern coast of Eubœa.

Ἀρτίμας, α, ὁ, *Artimas*, a Persian satrap of Lydia.

Ἀρτούχης, ου, or **Ἀρτούχας**, α, ὁ, *Artuchas*, a Persian satrap.

'Αρύστας, α, ὁ, *Arystas*, an Arcadian.
'Αρχαγόρας, α, ὁ, *Archagoras*, an Argive.
'Αρχέδημος, ου, ὁ, *Archedemus*, an Athenian.
'Αρχέλαος, ου, Ion. **'Αρχέλεως**, εω, ὁ, *Archelaus*, son of Agesilaus, a king of Sparta, one of the Agidæ.
'Αρχέλοχος, ου, ὁ, *Archelochus*, a Trojan, son of Antenor.
'Αρχέστρατος, ου, ὁ, *Archestratus*, an Athenian commander.
'Αρχίδαμος, Ion. **-δημος**, ου, ὁ, *Archidamus*, the name of five kings of Sparta.
'Αρχύτας, α and ου, ὁ, *Archytas*, a Spartan ephor.
'Ασία, ας, ἡ, *Asia*, at first used by the Greeks as the name of a district in Lydia, near the river Caÿster, and later used sometimes to designate what is known now as Asia Minor, and sometimes as a general name for the country east of Greece.
'Ασιδάτης, ου, ὁ, *Asidates*, a Persian.
'Ασιναῖος, α, ον, *of Asine, Asinæan.*
'Ασίνη, ης, ἡ, *Asine:* (1) a city on the south coast of Argolis, west of Hermione; (2) a city on the south coast of Messenia.
"Ασιος, α, ον, *Asian, belonging to Asia*, in the phrase **"Ασιος λειμών**, *the Asian meadow.*
"Ασιος, ου, ὁ, *Asius*, from Arisbe, an ally of the Trojans.
'Ασκάλαφος, ου, ὁ, *Ascalaphus*, son of Ares and Astyoche, leader of the Minyæ against Troy.
'Ασκανία, ας, ἡ, *Ascania*, a district in the west of Bithynia.
'Ασκάνιος, ου, ὁ, *Ascanius*, a Phrygian ally of the Trojans.
'Ασκληπιάδης, ου, ὁ, *son of Æsculapius.*
'Ασπένδιος, ου, ὁ, *an Aspendian*, an inhabitant of Aspendus, a city of Pamphylia.
'Ασπληδών, όνος, ἡ, *Aspledon*, an ancient city in Bœotia, near Orchomenus.
'Ασσυρία, ας, ἡ, *Assyria*, as used by the Greeks in the narrowest sense, designated the country bounded on the north by Mt. Niphates, on the east by Mt. Zagros, on the south by Susiana, and on the west by the Tigris. It was often used loosely in a wider sense, and frequently of the whole Assyrian empire.
'Ασσύριος, α, ον, *Assyrian;* **οἱ 'Ασσύριοι**, *the Assyrians.*
'Αστέριον, ου, τό, *Asterium*, a town of Magnesia in Thessaly.
'Αστύαλος, ου, ὁ, *Astyalus*, a Trojan.
'Αστυάναξ, ακτος, ὁ, (*lord of the city*), *Astyanax*, son of Hector, so named by the Trojans as a compliment to his father, his name being originally Scamandrius.
'Αστύνοος, ου, ὁ, *Astynoüs*, a Trojan.
'Αστυόχη, also **-χεια**, ης, ἡ, *Astyoche:* (1) daughter of Actor; (2) daughter of Phylas.
'Αστύοχος, ου, ὁ, *Astyochus*, a Spartan naval commander.
'Ασωπός, οῦ, ὁ, *Asopus:* (1) a river flowing through the southern part of Bœotia, and emptying into the Eubœan sea in the north of Attica; (2) a river of Thessaly flowing into the Malian Gulf near Thermopylæ.
'Αταρνεύς, έως, ὁ, *Atarneus*, a city of Mysia, opposite Lesbos.
'Ατραμύττιον, or **-ειον**, more commonly **'Αδραμύττιον** or **-ειον**, ου, τό, *Atramyttium*, a coast city in Mysia, on the Caicus.
'Ατρείδης, ου, ὁ, *son* or *descendant of Atreus;* **οἱ 'Ατρεῖδαι**, or **τὼ 'Ατρείδα**, *the Atridæ*, Agamemnon and Menelaus, grandsons of Atreus.
'Ατρείων, ωνος, ὁ, same as **'Ατρείδης.**
'Ατρεύς, έως, ὁ, *Atreus*, son of Pelops, king of Mycenæ.
'Αττική, ῆς, ἡ, *Attica*, a country of Greece.
'Αττικός, ή, όν, *Attic, Athenian.*
'Ατυμνιάδης, ου, ὁ, *son of Atymnius*, i. e. Mydon.
Αὐγειαί, ῶν, αἱ, *Augeæ:* (1) a Locrian city, near the southern coast of the Malian Gulf; (2) a city in southern Laconia.
Αὐγηϊάδης, ου, ὁ, *son of Augeas* king of Elis, i. e. Agasthenes.
Αὐλίς, ίδος, ἡ, *Aulis*, a city and harbor in Bœotia where the Greek fleet assembled before sailing for Troy.
Αὐτοβοισάκης, ου, ὁ, *Autobœsaces*, a Persian.
Αὐτόνοος, ου, ὁ, *Autonoüs*, a Delphian hero.
Αὐτόφονος, ου, ὁ, *Autophonus*, a Theban.
'Αφεταί, ῶν, αἱ, (and **'Αφέται**), *Aphetæ*, a city and promontory of Thessaly, not far from Artemisium, with a port from which the Argonauts sailed.
'Αφιδναῖος, ου, ὁ, *a resident of Aphidna* an Attic deme.
'Αχαιοί, ῶν, οἱ, *the Achaians, inhabitants of Achaia.*
'Αχερουσιάς, άδος, ἡ, fem. adj., *Acherusian;* **'Αχερουσιὰς Χερρόνησος**, *the Acherusian peninsula*, near Heraclea in Bithynia, where Hercules was said to have descended through a cavern to the lower world.

B

Βαβυλών, ῶνος, ἡ, *Babylon*, on the Euphrates, the capital of the Babylonian empire, and later a prominent city in the Persian empire.

Βαβυλωνία, ας, ἡ, *Babylonia,* a country extending northwest from the Persian Gulf considerably beyond Babylon.

Βάκις, ιδος, ὁ, *Bacis,* a soothsayer of Bœotia.

Βάκτριος, α, ον, *Bactrian ;* **οἱ Βάκτριοι,** *the Bactrians,* inhabitants of the Persian province of Bactria or Bactriana, now southeastern Turkestan and northeastern Afghanistan.

Βασίας, ου, ὁ, *Basias :* (1) an Arcadian ; (2) a soothsayer of Elis.

Βατίεια, ας, ἡ, *Batiea,* a hill near Troy.

Βελβῑνίτης, ου, ὁ, *a Belbinite,* an inhabitant of Belbina, a small island in the Ægæan sea.

Βέλεσυς, υος, ὁ, *Belesys,* a satrap of Syria.

Βελλεροφόντης, ου, ὁ, (lit., *slayer of Bellerus*), *Bellerophontes* (*Bellerophon*), son of Glaucus, so called from having killed Bellerus, his original name being Hipponoüs.

Βενδίδειον, ου, τό, *Bendideum, the temple of Bendis* the Thracian Diana.

Βῆσσα, or **Βῆσα,** ης, ἡ, *Bessa,* a Locrian city near Augeæ.

Βίας, αντος, ὁ, *Bias,* a warrior from Pylus.

Βῑθῡνοί, ῶν, οἱ, *the Bithynians,* inhabitants of Bithynia, a country of Asia Minor on the Propontis and Euxine.

Βισάνθη, ης, ἡ, *Bisanthe,* a city in Thrace, on the Propontis.

Βίων, ωνος, ὁ, *Bion,* a Spartan officer.

Βοάγριος, ου, ὁ, *Boagrius,* a river in Locris, flowing into the Malian Gulf, also called *Manes.*

Βοίβη, ης, ἡ, *Bœbe,* a city in Thessaly near the Bœbean Lake.

Βοιβηΐς, ίδος, ἡ, fem. adj., *Bœbean ;* **ἡ Βοιβηῒς λίμνη,** *the Bœbean Lake.*

Βοίσκος, ου, ὁ, *Boiscus,* a Thessalian.

Βοιώτιος, ου, ὁ, *Bœotius,* a Lacedæmonian.

Βοιώτιος, α, ον, *Bœotian, belonging to Bœotia.*

Βοιωτός, οῦ, ὁ, *a Bœotian.*

Βουκολίων, ωνος, ὁ, *Bucolion,* son of Laomedon.

Βουπράσιον, ου, τό, *Buprasium,* an ancient city in Elis, one of the chief cities of the Epeï.

Βρασίδας, α and ου, ὁ, *Brasidas,* a Spartan general in the Peloponnesian war.

Βρῑσηΐς, ίδος, ἡ, *daughter of Briseus,* i. e. Hippodamia, the captive belonging to Achilles, seized by Agamemnon.

Βρῡσειαί, ῶν, αἱ, *Bryseæ,* an ancient town of Laconia, near Sparta.

Βυζάντιον, ου, τό, *Byzantium,* a city of Thrace, on the Bosporus, the modern Constantinople.

Βυζάντιος, α, ον, *of Byzantium ;* **οἱ Βυζάντιοι,** *the Byzantians.*

Βῶρος, ου, ὁ, *Borus,* a Mæonian.

Γ

Γαῖα, ης, ἡ, see **Γῆ**.

Γάνος, ου, ἡ, *Ganus,* a fortress in Thrace, on the Propontis.

Γαυλίτης, ου, ὁ, *Gaulites,* a Samian.

Γαύριον, ου, τό, *Gaurium,* a haven and fortress in the island of Andros.

Γέλα, ης, ἡ, *Gela,* a city on the southern coast of Sicily.

Γέλων, ωνος, ὁ, *Gelon,* a tyrant of Gela and afterward of Syracuse.

Γεραιστός, οῦ, ὁ and ἡ, *Geræstus,* a promontory and harbor at the southwestern extremity of Eubœa.

Γερήνιος, ου, ὁ, *Gerenian,* applied to Nestor, from his birthplace, Gerenia in Messenia.

Γῆ, ῆς, ἡ, poetic **Γαῖα,** *Ge,* or *Gæa, Earth* personified as a goddess, wife of Uranus, mother of the Titans, Cyclops, and other monsters.

Γλαῦκος, ου, ὁ, *Glaucus :* (1) son of Sisyphus, father of Bellerophon ; (2) son of Hippolochus, grandson of Bellerophon, and leader of the Lycians in aid of Troy.

Γλαύκων, ωνος, ὁ, *Glaucon,* an Athenian, grandfather of Plato.

Γλαφυραί, ῶν, αἱ, *Glaphyræ,* a city in southeastern Thessaly.

Γλῖσας, αντος, ἡ, *Glisas,* an ancient city of Bœotia, on Mt. Hypaton.

Γλοῦς, οῦ, ὁ, *Glus,* an Egyptian, son of Tamos.

Γνήσιππος, ου, ὁ, *Gnesippus,* an Athenian.

Γνωσίας, ου, ὁ, *Gnosias,* a Syracusan.

Γογγύλος, ου, ὁ, *Gongylus,* an Eretrian.

Γονόεσσα, ης, ἡ, *Gonoëssa,* a promontory on the Corinthian Gulf, near Pallene, in Achaia.

Γόργειος, α, ον, *belonging to the Gorgon* (Γοργώ).

Γοργίας, ου, ὁ, *Gorgias,* a statesman and orator of Leontini in Sicily.

Γοργίων, ωνος, ὁ, *Gorgion,* son of Hellas.

Γόργος, ου, ὁ, *Gorgus,* king of Salamis in Cyprus.

Γόρδιον, ου, τό, *Gordium,* a city of Greater Phrygia, on the Sangarius.

Γόρτῡν, υνος, also **Γόρτῡνα,** ης, ἡ, *Gortyn* or *Gortyna,* the second city of Crete, on the Lethæus.

Γουνεύς, έως, ὁ, *Guneus,* leader of the Ænianes before Troy.

Γραῖα, ας, ἡ, *Græa,* a city in Bœotia.

Γῡγαίη, ης, ἡ : (1) with **λίμνη,** *the Gygæan Lake,* near Sardis, in Lydia ; (2) *Gygæa,* the nymph of this lake.

Γύθειον, ου, τό, *Gythium,* a city near the head of the Laconian bay, which served as the harbor for Sparta.

Γυμνίας, ου, ἡ, *Gymnias,* a city in northeastern Armenia.

Γυρτώνη, ης, also **Γυρτών,** ῶνος, ἡ, *Gyrtone* or *Gyrton,* a town in the central part of Thessaly, on the Peneus.

Γωβρύας, ου, ὁ, *Gobryas,* a Persian general.

Δ

Δαμασίθῡμος, ου, ὁ, *Damasithymus,* son of Candaules, king of Calynda.

Δάνα, ης, ἡ, *Dana,* a large and wealthy city of Cappadocia.

Δαράδαξ, ακος, ὁ, *Daradax,* a river of upper Syria, flowing into the Euphrates.

Δαρδανεύς, έως, ὁ, *a Dardanian,* an inhabitant of Dardanus, a city of Troas on the Hellespont.

Δᾱρεῖος, ου, ὁ, also spelled occasionally **Δαρειαῖος,** *Darius,* the name of three kings of Persia. The second, called Ὦχος and Νόθος, was an illegitimate son of Artaxerxes I.

Δάρης, ητος, ὁ, *Dares,* a Trojan, priest of Hephæstus.

Δᾶτις, ιδος, ὁ, *Datis,* a Mede, associate commander of the Persian army at the battle of Marathon.

Δαύλιοι, ων, οἱ, *the Daulians,* inhabitants of Daulis.

Δαυλίς, ίδος, ἡ, *Daulis,* a city of Phocis, near Delphi.

Δαφναγόρας, α, ὁ, *Daphnagoras,* a Mysian.

Δεῖμος, ου, ὁ, *Dimos, Fear* personified.

Δεινομένης, ους, ὁ, *Dinomenes,* father of Hiero and Gelon.

Δεκέλεια, ας, ἡ, *Decelea,* an Attic deme, seized and fortified by the Spartans in the Peloponnesian war.

Δέλτα, τό, *the Delta,* a region of Thrace, near Byzantium.

Δελφίνιον, ου, τό, *Delphinium,* a city in the island of Chios.

Δέξιππος, ου, ὁ, *Dexippus,* a Laconian.

Δερκυλίδας, also **-κυλλί-,** α and ου, ὁ, *Dercylidas,* a Spartan general.

Δέρνης, ου, ὁ, *Dernes,* a Persian satrap of Arabia.

Δηϊκόων, ωντος, ὁ, *Deïcoön,* a Trojan.

Δηΐπυλος, ου, ὁ, *Deïpylus,* a Greek, comrade of Sthenelus.

Δημάρᾱτος, Dor. **Δᾱμάρᾱτος,** Ion. **Δημάρητος,** ου, ὁ, *Demaratus,* an exiled king of Sparta, who accompanied Xerxes in his invasion of Greece.

Δήμαρχος, ου, ὁ, *Demarchus,* a Syracusan commander.

Δημοκόων, ωντος, ὁ, *Democoön,* a son of Priam.

Δημοκράτης, ους, ὁ, *Democrates,* of Temenium in Argolis.

Δημοσθένης, ους, ὁ, *Demosthenes,* a celebrated Athenian general in the Peloponnesian war.

Δημόφιλος, ου, ὁ, *Demophilus,* a leader of the Thespians at Thermopylæ.

Διαγόρας, ου and α, ὁ, *Diagoras,* an inhabitant of Rhodes, father of Dorieus.

Διαδρόμης, ου, ὁ, *Diadromes,* a Thespian, father of Demophilus.

Διηνέκης, ους, ὁ, *Dieneces,* a courageous Spartan.

Διθύραμβος, ου, ὁ, *Dithyrambus,* a Thespian who distinguished himself at Thermopylæ.

Δίκαιος, ου, ὁ, *Dicæus,* an Athenian.

Διοκλῆς, έους, ὁ, *Diocles*: (1) king of Pheræ in Messenia; (2) one of the thirty tyrants at Athens.

Διομέδων, οντος, ὁ, *Diomedon,* an Athenian commander in the Peloponnesian war.

Διομήδης, εος, ὁ, *Diomedes,* son of Tydeus, king of Argos, one of the bravest of the Greeks before Troy.

Δῖον, ου, τό, *Dium,* a town in northwestern Eubœa, near Histiæa.

Διονῦσιος, ου, ὁ, *Dionysius,* a tyrant of Syracuse, son of Hermocrates.

Διότῑμος, ου, ὁ, *Diotimus,* an Athenian commander.

Διώρης, ους, ὁ, *Diores,* son of Amaryncеus, a chief of the Epeï before Troy.

Δόλοπες, ων, οἱ, *the Dolopes,* a Thessalian tribe, dwelling about Mt. Pindus in Epirus.

Δολοπίων, ονος, ὁ, *Dolopion,* a Trojan, priest of the river-god Scamander.

Δορίσκος, ου, ὁ, *Doriscus,* a plain in Thrace at the mouth of the Hebrus, containing a city of the same name, ἡ Δορίσκος.

Δόρυσσος, ου, ὁ, *Doryssus,* son of Leobotes.

Δουλίχιον, ου, τό, *Dulichium,* the largest island in the group of the Echinades, near the coast of Acarnania.

Δουλιχιόνδε, *to Dulichium.*

Δρακοντίδης, ου, ὁ, *Dracontides,* one of the thirty tyrants at Athens.

Δρακόντιος, ου, ὁ, *Dracontius,* a Spartan.

Δρῆσος, ου, ὁ, *Dresus,* a Trojan.

Δρῖλαι, ῶν, οἱ, *the Drilæ,* a brave people in Pontus, on the borders of Colchis, near Trapezus.

Δρύας, αντος, ὁ, *Dryas:* (1) one of the Thessalian Lapithæ; (2) a Thracian prince, father of Lycurgus.

Δρυοπίς, ίδος, ἡ, *Dryopis,* the territory of the Dryopes, which was, originally, Mt. Œta and the surrounding region.

Δύρας, ου, ὁ, *Dyras,* a river in Thessaly flowing into the Malian Gulf.

Δωριεύς, έως, ὁ, *Dorieus:* (1) son of Anaxandrides king of Sparta; (2) son of Diagoras, a Rhodian naval commander, who aided the Spartans.

Δωρόθεος, ου, ὁ, *Dorotheus,* an Athenian.

E

Ἕβρος, ου, ὁ, *Hebrus,* the chief river in Thrace, flowing into the Ægean sea.

Εἰλέσιον, ου, τό, *Ilesium,* a city in Bœotia.

Εἰρέτρια, see **Ἐρέτρια.**

Ἑκάβη, ης, ἡ, *Hecuba,* wife of Priam.

Ἑκατώνυμος, ου, ὁ, *Hecatonymus,* an inhabitant of Sinope.

Ἐκβάτανα, ων, τά, *Ecbatana,* the capital of the Median empire, and afterward the favorite summer residence of the Persian kings.

Ἑκτορίδης, ου, ὁ, *son of Hector,* i. e. Astyanax.

Ἕκτωρ, ορος, ὁ, *Hector,* eldest son of Priam and Hecuba, chief hero of the Trojans, slain by Achilles.

Ἐλαιοῦς, οῦντος, ὁ, *Elæus,* a town at the southeastern point of the Thracian Chersonese.

Ἔλατος, ου, ὁ, *Elatus,* an ally of the Trojans, from Pedasus.

Ἑλένη, ης, ἡ, *Helene (Helen),* daughter of Zeus and Leda, and wife of Menelaus, the cause of the Trojan war.

Ἕλενος, ου, ὁ, *Helenus,* son of Priam, a warrior and prophet.

Ἐλευσίν or **Ἐλευσίς,** ῖνος, ἡ, *Eleusis,* an ancient city of Attica, sacred to Demeter (Ceres) and Cora (Proserpina), containing a famous temple of Ceres; in it were celebrated the Eleusinian mysteries.

Ἐλευσίνιος, ου, ὁ, *an Eleusinian, an inhabitant of Eleusis.*

Ἐλεφήνωρ, ορος, ὁ, *Elephenor,* leader of the Eubœan Abantes against Troy.

Ἐλεών, ῶνος, ἡ, *Eleon,* a town in Bœotia, near Tanagra.

Ἑλικάων, ονος, ὁ, *Helicaon,* a Trojan noble, son of Antenor.

Ἑλίκη, ης, ἡ, *Helice,* the ancient capital of Achaia, on the Corinthian Gulf, destroyed by an earthquake in B. C. 373.

Ἕλιξος, ου, ὁ, *Helixus,* an inhabitant of Megara.

Ἑλλησποντιακός, ή, όν, equivalent to the following.

Ἑλλησπόντιος, α, ον, *on* or *of the Hellespont, Hellespontic.*

Ἑλλήσποντος, ου, ὁ, *Hellespont,* the strait connecting the Propontis with the Ægean sea.

Ἕλος, ους, τό, *Helos:* (1) a town in Laconia near the mouth of the Eurotas; (2) a town or district of Elis, on the Alpheus.

Ἔνδιος, less correctly **Εὔδιος,** ου, ὁ, *Endius* or *Eudius,* a Spartan ephor.

Ἐνετοί, ῶν, οἱ, *the Eneti,* a people of Paphlagonia.

Ἐνιῆνες, see **Αἰνιᾶνες.**

Ἐνίσπη, ης, ἡ, *Enispe,* an Arcadian town.

Ἔννομος, ου, ὁ, *Ennomus,* an ally of the Trojans, from Mysia.

Ἐνυάλιος, ου, ὁ, *(the Warlike), Enyalius,* an epithet of Ares (Mars).

Ἐξάδιος, ου, ὁ, *Exadius,* one of the Thessalian Lapithæ.

Ἔξαρχος, ου, ὁ, *Exarchus,* a Spartan ephor.

Ἐπαμεινώνδας, ου, ὁ, *Epaminondas,* the leading general and statesman of Thebes.

Ἐπειοί, ῶν, οἱ, *the Epeï,* one of the tribes inhabiting Elis from ancient times.

Ἐπήρατος, ου, ὁ, *Eperatus,* a Spartan ephor.

Ἐπιάλτης, see **Ἐφιάλτης.**

Ἐπιγένης, ους, ὁ, *Epigenes,* son of Antiphon, a friend of Socrates.

Ἐπιδαύριος, α, ον, *of Epidaurus;* **οἱ Ἐπιδαύριοι,** *the Epidaurians.*

Ἐπίδαυρος, ου, ἡ, *Epidaurus,* an important town in Argolis, on the Saronic Gulf.

Ἐπίζηλος, ου, ὁ, *Epizelus,* an Athenian.

Ἐπικύδης, ους, ὁ, *Epicydes,* a Syracusan, father of Demarchus.

Ἐπισθένης, ους, ὁ, *Episthenes:* (1) of Amphipolis, commander of the light-armed Greek troops, peltastæ, in the expedition of Cyrus the younger; (2) an Olynthian, serving in the same expedition.

Ἐπίστροφος, ου, ὁ, *Epistrophus:* (1) son of Iphitus, a leader of the Phocians before Troy; (2) an ally of the Trojans from Alybe; (3) son of Euenus, king of Lyrnessus.

Ἐπιτάδας, α and ου, ὁ, *Epitadas,* a Spartan commander at Sphacteria.

Ἐπύαξα, ης, ἡ, *Epyaxa,* wife of Syennesis a king of Cilicia.

Ἐρασινίδης, *ου, ὁ, Erasinides,* one of the Athenian commanders in the naval battle at Arginusæ.

Ἐρασίστρατος, *ου, ὁ, Erasistratus,* one of the thirty tyrants at Athens.

Ἐρατοσθένης, *ους, ὁ, Eratosthenes,* one of the thirty tyrants at Athens.

Ἐρέτρια, poetic **Εἰρ-,** *ας, ἡ, Eretria,* an ancient and important city on the west coast of Eubœa.

Ἐρετριεύς, *έως, ὁ, an Eretrian ;* **οἱ Ἐρετριεῖς,** or Ion. **Ἐρετριέες,** *the Eretrians.*

Ἐρευθαλίων, *ωνος, ὁ, Ereuthalion,* a leader of the Arcadians against Pylos.

Ἐρεχθεύς, *έως, ὁ, Erechtheus,* an ancient hero and king of Athens.

Ἑρμιόνη, *ης, ἡ, Hermione,* a city on the southern coast of Argolis, opposite the island Hydrea.

Ἑρμογένης, *ους, ὁ, Hermogenes,* an Athenian, a friend of Socrates.

Ἑρμοκράτης, *ους, ὁ, Hermocrates,* a leader of the Syracusans in the Peloponnesian war, father of Dionysius.

Ἕρμων, *ωνος, ὁ, Hermon,* an inhabitant of Megara.

Ἐρυθῖνοι, *ων, οἱ, Erythini,* a city and range of cliffs on the coast of Paphlagonia.

Ἐρυθραί, *ῶν, αἱ, Erythræ,* an ancient city in southern Bœotia, on the Asopus, at the foot of Mt. Cithæron.

Ἑσπερῖται, *ῶν, οἱ, the Hesperitæ,* a tribe in western Armenia.

Ἐτεοκλήειος (poet. for **Ἐτεόκλειος**), *α, ον, of* or *belonging to Eteocles* a king of Thebes.

Ἐτεόνικος, *ου, ὁ, Eteonicus,* a Spartan.

Ἐτεωνός, *οῦ, ὁ, Eteonus,* a town in southern Bœotia, on the Asopus, later called Scarphe.

Εὐαγόρας, *ου, ὁ, Euagoras :* (1) a king of Salamis in Cyprus, a contemporary of Conon ; (2) an inhabitant of Elis.

Εὐαίμων, *ονος, ὁ, Euæmon,* a Thessalian prince.

Εὐαιμονίδης, *ου, ὁ, son of Euæmon,* i. e. Eurypylus.

Εὐάρχιππος, *ου, ὁ, Euarchippus,* a Spartan ephor.

Εὔβοια, *ας, ἡ, Eubœa,* a large and celebrated island, lying along the coast of Locris, Bœotia, and Attica, now Negropont.

Εὐβοιεύς, *έως, ὁ, a Eubœan ;* **οἱ Εὐβοιεῖς,** or Ion. **Εὐβοιέες,** *the Eubœans.*

Εὐβοϊκός, *ή, όν, of Eubœa, Eubœan.*

Εὐβώτας, and **-βό-,** *ου, ὁ, Eubotas,* a Cyrenean.

Εὔδιος, see **Ἔνδιος.**

Εὐηνορίδης, *ου, ὁ, son of Euenor,* i. e. Liocritus.

Εὐηνός, *οῦ, ὁ, Euenus :* (1) the name of two Elegiac poets of Paros, one of whom is said to have instructed Socrates in poetry ; (2) son of Selapius, a king of Lyrnessus.

Εὐκλείδης, *ου, ὁ, Euclides (Euclid) :* (1) a soothsayer of Phlius ; (2) an officer of the Spartan general Thibron ; (3) one of the thirty tyrants at Athens ; (4) of Megara, a pupil of Socrates, founder of the Megarian school of philosophy.

Εὐκλῆς, *έους, ὁ, Eucles,* son of Hippon, a Syracusan commander.

Εὐκτήμων, *ονος, ὁ, Euctemon,* an Athenian archon.

Εὐμάθης, *ους, ὁ, Eumathes,* one of the thirty tyrants at Athens.

Εὔμαχος, *ου, ὁ, Eumachus,* an Athenian general.

Εὐμένης, *ους, ὁ, Eumenes,* a brave Athenian at Salamis.

Εὔμηλος, *ου, ὁ, Eumelus,* son of Admetus, a Thessalian leader against Troy.

Εὐοδεύς, *έως, ὁ,* another reading is **Ἐνοδίας,** *ου, ὁ,* a designation in Xen. Anab. 7, 4, 18 of Hieronymus of Elis. Probably a geographical term of uncertain reference.

Εὐπείθης, *ους, ὁ, Eupithes,* an Ithacan noble.

Εὐρύαλος, *ου, ὁ, Euryalus,* a commander of the Myceneans before Troy.

Εὐρυβάτης, *ου, ὁ, Eurybates :* (1) a herald of Agamemnon ; (2) a herald of Ulysses.

Εὐρυβιάδης, *ου, ὁ, Eurybiades,* a Spartan, commander of the Grecian fleet at Artemisium and Salamis.

Εὐρυδάμας, *αντος, ὁ, Eurydamas,* a Trojan prince, skilful in interpreting dreams.

Εὐρύδημος, *ου, ὁ, Eurydemus,* father of the traitor Ephialtes.

Εὐρύκλεια, *ας, ἡ, Euryclia,* daughter of Ops, nurse of Ulysses.

Εὐρυκλείδης, *ου, ὁ, Euryclides,* a Spartan.

Εὐρυκράτης, *ους, ὁ, Eurycrates,* a king of Sparta.

Εὐρυκρατίδης, *ου, ὁ, Eurycratides,* a king of Sparta.

Εὐρύλοχος, *ου, ὁ, Eurylochus,* an Arcadian from Lusi.

Εὐρύμαχος, *ου, ὁ, Eurymachus :* (1) son of Polybus, a suitor of Penelope ; (2) a Dardanian ; (3) a Theban, father of Leontiades ; (4) a grandson of the preceding.

Εὐρυμέδων, *οντος, ὁ, Eurymedon,* charioteer of Agamemnon.

Εὐρύνομος, ου, ὁ, *Eurynomus*, son of Ægyptius of Ithaca, a suitor of Penelope.

Εὐρυπτόλεμος, ου, ὁ, *Euryptolemus*, an Athenian, son of Pisianax.

Εὐρύπυλος, ου, ὁ, *Eurypylus*: (1) a Thessalian chief before Troy; (2) a king of Cos.

Εὐρυσθένης, ους, ὁ, *Eurysthenes*, son of Aristodemus, king of Sparta. From him and his twin brother Procles were descended the two royal families of Sparta, the Eurysthenidæ (called also Agidæ), and the Proclidæ.

Εὔρυτος, ου, ὁ, *Eurytus*: (1) a leader of the Epeï; (2) a brave Spartan at Thermopylæ.

Εὔσσωρος (poet. for **Εὔσωρος**), ου, ὁ, *Eusorus*, a Thracian.

Εὔτρησις, ιος, ἡ, *Eutresis*, a Bœotian village, near Thespiæ.

Εὔφημος, ου, ὁ, *Euphemus*, leader of the Cicones, an ally of the Trojans.

Εὐφορίων, ωνος, ὁ, *Euphorion*, an Athenian, father of the poet Æschylus.

Εὐφράτης, ου, ὁ, *Euphrates*, a celebrated river of western Asia, rising in Armenia, and flowing into the Persian Gulf.

Ἐφέσιος, α, ον, *Ephesian*; **οἱ Ἐφέσιοι**, *the Ephesians.*

Ἔφεσος, ου, ἡ, *Ephesus*, the chief city of Ionia, on the coast, at the mouth of the Caÿster, containing a celebrated temple of Diana.

Ἐφιάλτης, ου, Ion. **Ἐπιάλτης**, εω, ὁ, *Ephialtes*: (1) a giant, the son of Poseidon, one of the Aloïdæ; (2) a Trachinian, who betrayed the Greeks at Thermopylæ.

Ἐφύρα, ας, ἡ, *Ephyra*: (1) a Pelasgian city of Elis; (2) a town of Thesprotia in Epirus; (3) the ancient name of Corinth.

Ἐχεκράτης, ους, ὁ, *Echecrates*, of Phlius, a friend of Socrates.

Ἐχέμων, poet. **Ἐχέμμων**, ονος, ὁ, *Echemon* or *Echemmon*, a son of Priam.

Ἐχέπωλος, ου, ὁ, *Echepolus*, a Trojan, son of Thalysius.

Ἐχέστρατος, ου, ὁ, *Echestratus*, son of Agis I., king of Sparta.

Z

Ζάκυνθος, ου, ἡ, *Zacynthus*, an island in the Ionian sea, off the coast of Elis, containing a city of the same name.

Ζαπάτας, α, more commonly **Ζάβατος**, ου, ὁ, *Zapatas* or *Zabatus*, a river of Assyria, flowing into the Tigris.

Ζέλεια, ας, ἡ, *Zelia*, an ancient city of Troas, at the foot of Mt. Ida.

Ζεύξιππος, ου, ὁ, *Zeuxippus*, a Spartan ephor.

Ζήλαρχος, ου, ὁ, *Zelarchus*, a market official.

Ζωστήρ, ῆρος, ὁ, *Zoster*, a promontory, consisting of several slender points, on the west coast of Attica, between Phalerum and Sunium.

H

Ἡγήσανδρος, ου, ὁ, *Hegesander*, an officer in the army of the ten thousand Greeks.

Ἡγησίλᾱος and **Ἡγησίλεως**, see **Ἀγησίλᾱος**.

Ἧγις, see **Ἆγις**.

Ἠερίβοια, ας, ἡ, poetic for **Ἐρ-**, *Eribœa*, the second wife of Aloeus.

Ἠετίων, ωνος, ὁ, *Eëtion*, king of Thebe in Mysia, and father of Andromache.

Ἠϊόνες, ων, αἱ, *Eïones*, a town in Argolis, near the promontory Scyllæum.

Ἠϊών, όνος, ἡ, *Eïon*, a city in Macedonia, at the mouth of the Strymon, the port of Amphipolis.

Ἠλεῖος, α, ον, *of Elis, Elean*; **οἱ Ἠλεῖοι**, *the Eleans.*

Ἦλις, ιδος, ἡ, *Elis*, a country on the west coast of the Peloponnesus.

Ἠλώνη, ης, ἡ, *Elone*, an ancient town in Thessaly, at the foot of Mt. Olympus.

Ἠπιδανός, see **Ἀπιδανός**.

Ἡράκλεια, ας, ἡ, *Heraclea*: (1) **Ἡράκλεια ἡ Ποντική**, *the Pontic Heraclea*, a city of Bithynia, on the coast of the Euxine; (2) **Ἡράκλεια ἡ Τρᾱχῑνία**, *the Trachinian Heraclea*, a city of Thessaly in the territory of Trachis, built by the Lacedæmonians and Trachinians together.

Ἡρακλείδης, ου, ὁ, *son* or *descendant of Hercules;* as a proper name, *Heraclides*: (1) of Maronea in Thrace; (2) a Syracusan commander, son of Aristogenes.

Ἡράκλειον, ου, τό, *the Heracleum, temple of Hercules.*

Ἡρακλεώτης, ου, ὁ, *a Heraclean.*

Ἡρακλεῶτις, ιδος, ἡ, fem. adj., (χώρα understood), *the Heraclean (territory).*

Ἡσίοδος, ου, ὁ, *Hesiodus (Hesiod)*, a celebrated Grecian poet, born at Ascra in Bœotia.

Θ

Θάλπιος, ου, ὁ, *Thalpius*, a leader of the Epeï before Troy.

Θαλυσιάδης, ου, ὁ, *son of Thalysius*, i. e. Echepolus.

Θαμνήρια, ων, τά, *Thamneria*, a town of Media, near the Cadusii.

Θάμυρις, *ιδος* and *ιος*, ὁ, *Thamyris*, an ancient Thracian bard.

Θαρύπας, *ου*, ὁ, *Tharypas*, a favorite of the Thessalian commander Menon.

Θάσιος, *α*, *ον*, *Thasian*, *belonging to Thasus.*

Θάσος, *ου*, ἡ, *Thasus*, an island of the Ægean off the coast of Thrace, having a city of the same name.

Θαυμακία, *ας*, ἡ, *Thaumacia*, a city of Magnesia in Thessaly.

Θαψακηνοί, *ῶν*, *οἱ*, *the Thapsacenes*, inhabitants of Thapsacus.

Θάψακος, *ου*, ἡ, *Thapsacus*, a city of Syria on the west bank of the Euphrates, where was an important ford.

Θεᾱνώ, *οῦς*, ἡ, *Theano*, sister of Hecuba, priestess of Athena, and wife of Antenor.

Θεμιστοκλῆς, *έους*, ὁ, *Themistocles*, the great statesman and leader of the Athenians, conqueror of the Persians at Salamis.

Θεογένης, *ους*, ὁ, *Theogenes:* (1) one of the thirty tyrants at Athens ; (2) a Locrian captain.

Θέογνις, *ιος* and *ιδος*, ὁ, *Theognis*, one of the thirty tyrants at Athens.

Θεοκῡδης, *ους*, ὁ, *Theocydes*, an Athenian.

Θεομήστωρ, *ορος*, ὁ, *Theomestor*, a tyrant of Samos.

Θεόπομπος, *ου*, ὁ, *Theopompus:* (1) an Athenian in the army of the ten thousand Greeks ; (2) a Milesian pirate.

Θερμαῖος, *ου*, ὁ, with **κόλπος**, *the Thermaic Gulf*, the northwestern arm of the Ægean sea, between Pieria and Chalcidice.

Θέρμη, *ης*, ἡ, *Therme*, a city in Macedonia, at the head of the Thermaic Gulf, later called Thessalonica.

Θερμώδων, *οντος*, ὁ, *Thermodon*, a river of Pontus, flowing into the Euxine.

Θερσίτης, *ου*, ὁ, *Thersites*, the most ugly and abusive of the Greeks before Troy.

Θέσπια, and **-πεια,** *ας*, ἡ, usually in pl. **Θεσπιαί,** *ῶν*, *αἱ*, *Thespiæ*, an ancient city in Bœotia, at the foot of Mt. Helicon.

Θεσπιεύς, *έως*, ὁ, *a Thespian ;* **οἱ Θεσπιεῖς,** or Ion. **Θεσπιέες,** *the Thespians.*

Θεσπρωτοί, *ῶν*, *οἱ*, *the Thesproti*, the most ancient inhabitants of Epirus, of Pelasgic origin, dwelling on the coast.

Θεσσαλία, *ας*, ἡ, *Thessaly*, the largest country of Greece, in the north, mostly a plain.

Θεσσαλός, ἡ, *όι*, *Thessalian.*

Θεσσαλός, *οῦ*, ὁ, *Thessalus*, a son of Hercules.

Θεστορίδης, *ου*, ὁ, *son of Thestor*, i. e. Calchas.

Θετταλία, Θετταλός, Att. for **Θεσσαλία,** &c., which see.

Θῆβαι, *ῶν*, *αἱ*, *Thebes*, the chief city of Bœotia.

Θηβαῖος, *ου*, ὁ, *an inhabitant of Thebes.*

Θηρᾱμένης, *ους*, ὁ, *Theramenes*, one of the thirty tyrants at Athens, a distinguished general, noted for his frequent changes in politics.

Θήχης, ὁ, *Theches*, a mountain in Pontus, from which the ten thousand Greeks caught sight of the sea (the Euxine).

Θίβραχος, *ου*, ὁ, *Thibrachus*, an Athenian polemarch.

Θίβρων, *ωνος*, ὁ, *Thibron*, a Spartan general.

Θίσβη, *ης*, ἡ, *Thisbe*, a city of Bœotia, near Mt. Helicon.

Θόας, *αντος*, ὁ, *Thoas*, a leader of the Ætolians before Troy.

Θορικός, *οῦ*, ὁ, *Thoricus*, one of the twelve ancient cities of Attica.

Θούριος, *α*, *ον*, *Thurian*, *of Thurii*, a city on the southern coast of Italy, an Athenian colony.

Θόων, *ωνος*, ὁ, *Thoön*, a Trojan.

Θόωσα, *ης*, ἡ, *Thoösa*, a nymph, mother of Polyphemus.

Θρᾴκη, *ης*, ἡ, *Thrace*, a district extending from Macedonia to the Euxine along the Ægean and Propontis.

Θρᾴκιον, *ου*, *τό*, *the Thracian square*, a place in Byzantium near the Thracian gate.

Θρᾷξ, *ᾳκός*, ὁ, *a Thracian*, used chiefly of the residents in Thrace, but also of those who had migrated from Thrace into Bithynia.

Θρασύβουλος, *ου*, ὁ, *Thrasybulus*, an Athenian, son of Lycus, the leader in the overthrow of the thirty tyrants at Athens.

Θρασύλεως, *ω*, (Ion. for **Θρασύλᾱος,** *ου*), ὁ, *Thrasylaus*, an Athenian.

Θράσυλλος, *ου*, ὁ, *Thrasyllus*, one of the ten victorious Athenian generals at Arginusæ.

Θρασυμηλίδας, *α*, ὁ, *Thrasymelidas*, a Spartan naval commander.

Θριάσιος, *α*, *ον*, *of Thria* an Attic deme ; **τὸ Θριάσιον πεδίον,** *the Thriasian plain*, a fertile plain between Thria and Eleusis.

Θρόνιον, *ου*, *τό*, *Thronium*, the chief town of the Locri Epicnemidii, near the Boagrius, a short distance from the Malian Gulf.

Θρύον, *ου*, *τό*, *Thryum*, a city of Elis, on the Alpheus, in the territory of Nestor.

Θυέστης, *ου*, ὁ, *Thyestes*, son of Pelops, brother of Atreus, and father of Ægisthus.

Θύμβριον, *ου*, *τό*, *Thymbrium*, a city in eastern Phrygia, containing the fountain of Midas.

Θυμοίτης, *ου*, ὁ, *Thymœtes*, one of the elders of Troy.

Θῡμοχάρης, *ους*, ὁ, *Thymochares*, a leader of the Athenians in the Peloponnesian war.

Θυνοί, ῶν, οἱ, *the Thyni,* a branch of the Thracians, dwelling at first near Salmydessus, who afterwards crossed into Asia and settled on the coast of Bithynia.

Θώραξ, ακος, ὁ, *Thorax,* a Spartan commander.

I

Ἰάλμενος, ου, ὁ, *Ialmenus,* son of Ares and Astyoche, a chief of the Minyæ.

Ἰασόνιος, α, ον, *belonging to Jason ;* **ἡ Ἰασονία ἀκτή,** *the Jasonian promontory,* on the coast of Pontus, between Cotyore and the Iris, where Jason is said to have landed with the Argonauts.

Ἰαωλκός (poetic for Ἰωλ-), οῦ, ἡ, *Iolcus,* a city of Magnesia in Thessaly, the birthplace of Jason and gathering-place of the Argonauts.

Ἴδα, ης, ἡ, *Ida,* a mountain in Mysia near Troy.

Ἰδαῖος, ου, ὁ, *Idæus :* (1) a Trojan herald ; (2) a Trojan, son of Dares.

Ἴδηθεν, *from Ida.*

Ἰδομενεύς, έως, ὁ, *Idomeneus,* son of Deucalion, and grandson of Minos, king of Crete and leader of the Cretans before Troy.

Ἱεραμένης, ους, ὁ, *Hieramenes,* a Persian.

Ἱέρων, ωνος, ὁ, *Hieron,* one of the thirty tyrants at Athens.

Ἱερώνυμος, ου, ὁ, *Hieronymus,* a captain, from Elis.

Ἰηλυσός (Ion. for Ἰαλ-), οῦ, ἡ, *Ialysus,* an ancient Dorian city in the island of Rhodes.

Ἰήσων (Ion. for **Ἰάσων**), ονος, ὁ, *Jason,* son of Æson, leader of the expedition of the Argonauts to obtain the golden fleece.

Ἰθώμη, ης, ἡ, *Ithome,* a fortress in Thessaly, near Metropolis.

Ἰκάριος, ου, ὁ, *Icarius,* father of Penelope.

Ἱκετάων, ονος, ὁ, *Hicetaon,* a Trojan, son of Laomedon.

Ἰκόνιον, ου, τό, *Iconium,* an ancient city of Asia Minor, during the Persian dominion the easternmost city of Phrygia, but later the capital of Lycaonia.

Ἴλαρχος, ου, ὁ, *Ilarchus,* a Spartan ephor.

Ἰλιάς, άδος, ἡ, fem. adj., *Trojan ;* used of the goddess Athene.

Ἴλιος, ου, ἡ, *Ilium, Troy,* the famous city.

Ἰλισσός, οῦ, ὁ, *Ilissus,* a small river flowing through the southeastern part of Athens.

Ἶλος, ου, ὁ, *Ilus,* son of Mermerus, dwelling in Ephyra.

Ἰμβρασίδης, ου, ὁ, *son of Imbrasus,* i. e. Piroüs.

Ἴμβριος, α, ον, *of Imbrus ;* **οἱ Ἴμβριοι,** *the Imbrians.*

Ἴμβρος, ου, ἡ, *Imbrus,* an island in the northern Ægean, near the Thracian Chersonese, with a city of the same name.

Ἱμέρα, ας, ἡ, *Himera,* a city of Sicily on the Himeras, a colony of the Zancleans.

Ἰνδοί, ῶν, οἱ, *the Indians, inhabitants of India.*

Ἶπνοι, ων, οἱ, (lit. *ovens*), *Ipni,* a rugged place in Magnesia in Thessaly, at the foot of Mt. Pelium.

Ἱππαγρέτας, α and ου, ὁ, *Hippagretas,* a Spartan commander at Sphacteria.

Ἱππεύς, έως, ὁ, *Hippeus,* a commander of the Samians.

Ἱππίας, ου, Ion. **Ἱππίης,** εω, ὁ, *Hippias,* a tyrant of Athens, who finally joined the Persians.

Ἱπποδάμεια, ας, ἡ, *Hippodamia,* daughter of Adrastus, wife of Pirithoüs.

Ἱπποδάμειος, ον, *of Hippodamus ;* in the phrase **ἡ Ἱπποδάμειος ἀγορά,** *the Hippodamian market-place,* the great square of Piræus, so named from the architect Hippodamus of Miletus.

Ἱππόθοος, ου, ὁ, *Hippothoüs,* son of Lethus, of Larissa in Troas.

Ἱπποκράτης, ους, ὁ, *Hippocrates,* an Athenian, father of Pisistratus.

Ἱππόλοχος, ου, ὁ, *Hippolochus :* (1) a son of Bellerophon, and father of Glaucus ; (2) one of the thirty tyrants at Athens.

Ἱππόμαχος, ου, ὁ, *Hippomachus,* one of the thirty tyrants at Athens.

Ἵππων, ωνος, ὁ, *Hippon,* a Syracusan, father of Eucles.

Ἶρις, ιος and ιδος, ὁ, *Iris,* a river of Pontus, flowing into the Euxine near Amisus.

Ἴσανδρος, ου, ὁ, *Isandrus,* a son of Bellerophon.

Ἰσάνωρ, ορος, ὁ, *Isanor,* a Spartan ephor.

Ἰσίας, ου, ὁ, *Isias,* a Spartan ephor.

Ἰσσοί, ῶν, οἱ, also written **Ἰσσός,** οῦ, ἡ, *Issi* or *Issus,* a city in the southeastern extremity of Cilicia.

Ἱστίαια, ας, ἡ, (this and its derivatives are Ion. for **Ἑστίαια,** etc.), *Histiæa,* an ancient and important city at the northeastern extremity of Eubœa, later called Oreus.

Ἱστιαιεύς, έως, ὁ, *a Histiæan.*

Ἱστιαιῆτις, ιδος, ἡ, fem. adj., *Histiæan ;* **γῆ ἡ Ἱστιαιῆτις,** *the Histiæan territory.*

Ἱστιαῖος, ου, ὁ, *Histiæus,* a Samian.

Ἰσχένοος, ου, ὁ, *Ischenoüs,* an inhabitant of Ægina.

Ἰταβέλιος, ου, ὁ, *Itabelius,* a Persian commander in Comania.

Ἴτων, ωνος, ἡ, *Iton,* a city of Phthiotis in Thessaly.

Ἴφικλος, ου, ὁ, *Iphiclus,* of Thessaly, son of Phylacus, an Argonaut.

Ἴφιτος, ου, ὁ, *Iphitus,* of Phocis, son of Naubolus, an Argonaut.

Ἰωκή, ῆς, ἡ, *Ioce, the Battle-Din* personified.

Ἰωνία, ας, ἡ, *Ionia,* a strip of the western coast of Asia Minor extending from Phocæa in the north to Miletus in the south, containing twelve important cities; so named because inhabited chiefly by Ionian Greeks.

K

Καδούσιοι, ων, οἱ, *the Cadusii,* a Scythian tribe dwelling on the southwest of the Caspian, between the Araxes and the Amardus.

Κάϊκος, ου, ὁ, *Caïcus,* a river of Mysia, flowing into the Cumæan Gulf.

Καιναί, ῶν, αἱ, *Cænæ,* a city of Mesopotamia, on the west bank of the Tigris.

Καινείδης, ου, ὁ, *son of Cæneus,* i. e. Coronus.

Καινεύς, έως, ὁ, *Cæneus,* son of Elatus, king of the Thessalian Lapithæ.

Καλήσιος, ου, ὁ, *Calesius,* charioteer of Axylus.

Καλλιάδης, ου, ὁ, *Calliades,* an Athenian archon.

Καλλίαρος, ου, ἡ, *Calliarus,* a city in Locris.

Καλλίας, ου, ὁ, *Callias,* an Athenian archon.

Καλλίβιος, ου, ὁ, *Callibius,* the Spartan harmost of Athens under the thirty tyrants.

Καλλικρατίδας, ου, ὁ, *Callicratidas,* a Spartan naval commander.

Καλλίμαχος, ου, ὁ, *Callimachus:* (1) an Athenian polemarch at Marathon; (2) an Arcadian captain in the army of the ten thousand.

Καλλίξενος, ου, ὁ, *Callixenus,* an Athenian demagogue.

Καλλίστρατος, ου, ὁ, *Callistratus,* an Athenian of the tribe Leontis.

Κάλπη, ης, ἡ, *Calpe,* a promontory and town on the northern coast of Bithynia.

Κάλυδναι (νῆσοι), αἱ, *the Calydnæ* (*Islands*), a group of islands off the coast of Caria, near Cos, belonging to the Sporades.

Καλυδών, ῶνος, ἡ, *Calydon,* an ancient city in southern Ætolia, on the Evenus.

Καλυνδεύς, έως, ὁ, *an inhabitant of Calynda,* a city in southeastern Caria; **οἱ Καλυνδεῖς,** *the Calyndians.*

Καλυνδικός, ἡ, όν, *Calyndian.*

Καλχηδών, όνος, ἡ, *Calchedon,* a Greek city on the coast of Bithynia, nearly opposite Byzantium.

Καλχηδονία, ας, ἡ, (χώρα understood), *the territory of Calchedon.*

Καλχηδόνιος, ου, ὁ, *an inhabitant of Calchedon, a Calchedonian.*

Καμάρινα, ας, ἡ, *Camarina,* a city on the southern coast of Sicily, a colony of Syracuse.

Καμβύσης, ου, ὁ, *Cambyses,* the name of two Persian kings; the second was the son and successor of Cyrus the Great.

Κάμειρος, ου, ὁ, *Camirus,* a city on the west coast of the island of Rhodes.

Κάννωνος, ου, ὁ, *Cannonus,* an Athenian statesman.

Καπανεύς, έως, ὁ, *Capaneus,* son of Hipponoüs, and father of Sthenelus.

Καπανηϊάδης, ου, ὁ, *son of Capaneus,* i. e. Sthenelus.

Καπανήϊος, α, ον, *of* or *belonging to Capaneus.*

Καππαδοκία, ας, ἡ, *Cappadocia,* a country of eastern Asia Minor, between Pontus and Cilicia. In early times its boundaries were more extended.

Καρδία, ας, ἡ, *Cardia,* a city in the Thracian Chersonese.

Καρδούχειος, α, ον, *of the Carduchi, Carduchian.*

Καρδοῦχοι, ων, οἱ, *the Carduchi,* a warlike nation dwelling between the upper waters of the Tigris and Lake Arissa.

Κᾱρία, ας, ἡ, *Caria,* a country on the southwest coast of Asia Minor, south of Lydia.

Κάρσος, ου, ὁ, *Carsus,* a river of Cilicia.

Καρύστιος, α, ον, *of Carystus, Carystian.*

Κάρυστος, ου, ἡ, *Carystus,* a town at the southern extremity of Eubœa, at the foot of Mt. Oche.

Καρχηδόνιοι, ων, οἱ, *the Carthaginians, inhabitants of Carthage.*

Κασθαναία (and **Καστ-**), ας, ἡ, *Casthanæa,* a city of Magnesia in Thessaly, near Mt. Pelium.

Κάσος, ου, ἡ, *Casus,* an island, one of the Cyclades.

Κασταλία, ας, ἡ, *Castalia,* a fountain on Mt. Parnassus, sacred to Apollo and the Muses.

Καστωλός, οῦ, ὁ, *Castolus,* a city of Lydia.

Κατάνη, ης, ἡ, *Catane,* a city on the east coast of Sicily, at the foot of Mt. Ætna.

Καΰστριος (and **Κάϋστρος**), ου, ὁ, *the Caÿstrius* or *Caÿster,* a river of Lydia and Ionia, flowing into the Ægean sea near Ephesus.

Καΰστρου πεδίον, τό, (lit. *plain of Caÿster*), *Caÿstrupedium,* a city of Asia Minor, probably in Pamphylia.

Καφηρεύς, έως, ὁ, *Caphereus*, the southeast promontory of Eubœa, where the Greek fleet was wrecked on its return from Troy.

Κεάδης, ου, ὁ, *son of Ceas*, i. e. Trœzenus.

Κέβης, ητος, ὁ, *Cebes*, a Theban, a friend of Socrates.

Κεδρεῖαι, ῶν, αἱ, *Cedreæ*, a city of Caria on the Ceramic Gulf.

Κεῖοι, ων, οἱ, *the Ceans*, inhabiting the island Ceos.

Κελαιναί, ῶν, αἱ, *Celænæ*, a city in southern Phrygia, on the Mæander.

Κεντρίτης, ου, ὁ, *Centrites*, a small tributary of the Tigris, the boundary between the Carduchi and Armenia.

Κεραμεικός, οῦ, ὁ, *Ceramicus*, a place outside of the walls of Athens, probably northwest, where those who fell in battle were often buried. The name is also applied to an adjoining part of the city within the walls.

Κεράμειος, α, ον, same as **Κεραμικός**.

Κεραμικός, ή, όν, *belonging to Ceramus*, a city in Caria; **ὁ κόλπος Κεραμικός**, *the Ceramic gulf.*

Κεραμῶν ἀγορά, ἡ, (lit. *market-place of the Ceramians*), *Ceramon-agora*, a town in western Phrygia.

Κερασούντιοι, ων, οἱ, *the Cerasuntians*, inhabitants of Cerasus.

Κερασοῦς, οῦντος, ὁ, *Cerasus*, a Greek city on the coast of Pontus, a colony of Sinope.

Κέρκωπες, ων, οἱ, *the Cercopes*, a fabled race of dwarfs, located at the pass of Thermopylæ, and in other places.

Κερτόνιον, ου, τό, *Certonium*, a city on the coast of Mysia.

Κέως, ω, (Ion. **Κέος**, ου), ἡ, *Ceos*, an island, one of the Cyclades, opposite the promontory Sunium in Attica.

Κήρινθος, ου, ἡ, *Cerinthus*, a small coast town in northeastern Eubœa, on the Budorus.

Κηφισόδοτος, ου, ὁ, *Cephisodotus*, an Athenian commander.

Κηφισόδωρος, ου, ὁ, *Cephisodorus*, an Athenian captain.

Κηφισός, οῦ, ὁ, *Cephisus*, a small stream which crosses the roads between Athens and Piræus, and empties into the bay of Phalerum.

Κηφισοφῶν, ῶντος, ὁ, *Cephisophon*, a common Athenian name. Especially the name of an envoy to Sparta.

Κιθαιρών, ῶνος, ὁ, *Cithæron*, a lofty range of mountains separating Bœotia from Megaris and Attica.

Κίκονες, ων, οἱ, *the Cicones*, inhabiting the western part of the coast of Thrace.

Κιλικία, ας, ἡ, *Cilicia*, a country on the southeast coast of Asia Minor, next to Syria.

Κίλλα, ης, ἡ, *Cilla*, a city of Troas, on the Cilleus, containing a celebrated temple of Apollo.

Κίμων, ωνος, ὁ, *Cimon*, a common Athenian name: (1) the father of Miltiades; (2) the son of Miltiades, a distinguished general and statesman.

Κίος, ου, ἡ, *Cius*, a city of Bithynia on the Propontis.

Κισσηΐς, ίδος, ἡ, *daughter of Cisseus* or *Cisses* king of Thrace.

Κίσσιοι, ων, οἱ, *the Cissians*, inhabitants of Cissia, the district in which the city of Susa was located, a part of Susiana.

Κλαζομεναί, ῶν, αἱ, *Clazomenæ*, a city in Ionia, on the Gulf of Smyrna.

Κλεαγόρας, ου, ὁ, *Cleagoras*, a painter, of Phlius.

Κλεαίνετος, ου, ὁ, *Cleænetus*, a captain in the army of the ten thousand.

Κλέανδρος, ου, ὁ, *Cleandrus*, a Spartan harmost at Byzantium.

Κλεάνωρ, ορος, ὁ, *Cleanor*, an inhabitant of Orchomenus in Arcadia, a general in the army of the ten thousand.

Κλεάρετος, ου, ὁ, *Clearetus*, a captain in the army of the ten thousand.

Κλέαρχος, ου, ὁ, *Clearchus*, a Lacedæmonian, a commander in the army of the ten thousand, especially esteemed by Cyrus.

Κλεινόμαχος, ου, ὁ, *Clinomachus*, a Spartan ephor.

Κλεόδαιος, ου, ὁ, *Cleodæus*, son of Hyllus, grandson of Hercules.

Κλεόκριτος, ου, ὁ, *Cleocritus*, a herald at the Eleusinian mysteries.

Κλεόμβροτος, ου, ὁ, *Cleombrotus*: (1) a Spartan, brother of Leonidas; (2) a pupil of Socrates.

Κλεομένης, ους, ὁ, *Cleomenes*, a Spartan king, half-brother of Leonidas.

Κλεομήδης, ους, ὁ, *Cleomedēs*, one of the thirty tyrants at Athens.

Κλεοσθένης, ους, ὁ, *Cleosthenes*, a Spartan.

Κλεόστρατος, ου, ὁ, *Cleostratus*, an Argive ambassador.

Κλεοφῶν, ῶντος, ὁ, *Cleophon*, a commander of the Athenians.

Κλέων, ωνος, ὁ, *Cleon*, an Athenian demagogue and commander in the Peloponnesian war.

Κλεωναί, ῶν, αἱ, *Cleonæ*: (1) an ancient town in Argolis, near Corinth, in whose territory the Nemean games were celebrated; (2) a town of Macedonia, on the peninsula of Athos.

Κλεώνυμος, *ου*, *ὁ*, *Cleonymus*, a brave Spartan.

Κλονίος, *ου*, *ὁ*, *Clonius*, son of Alector, a leader of the Bœotians before Troy.

Κλυμένη, *ης*, *ἡ*, *Clymene*, an attendant of Helen.

Κλυταιμνήστρα, *ας*, *ἡ*, *Clytæmnestra*, the wife of Agamemnon.

Κλυτίος, *ου*, *ὁ*, *Clytius*, a Trojan, elder son of Laomedon.

Κνωσός, *οῦ*, *ἡ*, *Cnosus*, an ancient capital of Crete, near the north coast.

Κοῖλα, *ων*, *τά*, (lit. *the Hollows*), *Cœla*, a name given to a very dangerous part of the coast of Eubœa, between the promontories Caphareus and Chersonesus.

Κοίρανος, *ου*, *ὁ*, *Cœranus*, a Lycian.

Κοιρατάδης, and **-δας**, *ου*, *ὁ*, *Cœratades* or *Cœratadas*, a Theban.

Κοῖτοι, *ων*, *οἱ*, *the Cœtœ*, a people of Pontus whom the ten thousand Greeks passed on their retreat.

Κολοσσαί, *ῶν*, *αἱ*, *Colossæ*, an important city in southwestern Phrygia, on the Lycus.

Κολοφών, *ῶνος*, *ἡ*, *Colophon*, one of the twelve Ionian cities on the coast of Asia Minor.

Κολοφώνιος, *ου*, *ὁ*, *a Colophonian*, an inhabitant of Colophon.

Κομανία, *ας*, *ἡ*, *Comania*, a fortress near Pergamus in Mysia.

Κόνων, *ωνος*, *ὁ*, *Conon*, an Athenian general, son of Timotheus.

Κορησσός, *οῦ*, *ὁ*, *Coressus*, a mountain near Ephesus.

Κορίνθιοι, *ων*, *οἱ*, *the Corinthians*.

Κορίνθιος, *α*, *ον*, *Corinthian*, *belonging to Corinth*, the well known city on the Isthmus of Corinth.

Κορσωτή, *ῆς*, *ἡ*, *Corsote*, a city on the Euphrates, near the Mascas, found deserted in the time of Xenophon.

Κορύδαλλος, and **-αλος**, *ου*, *ὁ*, *Corydallus*, of Anticyra.

Κορύλας, *α* and *ου*, *ὁ*, *Corylas*, a satrap of Paphlagonia.

Κορυφάσιον, *ου*, *τό*, *Coryphasium*, a promontory on the west coast of Messenia, near Pylus.

Κορώνεια, *ας*, *ἡ*, *Coronea*, an important city in western Bœotia, near lake Copaïs.

Κόρωνος, *ου*, *ὁ*, *Coronus*, son of Cæneus, an Argonaut.

Κοτύωρα, *ων*, *τά*, *Cotyora*, a Greek city on the coast of Pontus, a colony of Sinope.

Κοτυωρῖται, *ῶν*, *οἱ*, *the Cotyorites*, inhabitants of Cotyora.

Κουφαγόρας, *ου*, *ὁ*, *Cuphagorus*, an Athenian.

Κρανάη, *ης*, *ἡ*, *Cranaë*, a small island, probably in the Laconian gulf, near Gythium.

Κράπαθος, *ου*, *ἡ*, (poetic for **Κάρπαθος**), *Carpathus*, an island between Crete and Rhodes.

Κρατησικλῆς, *έους*, *ὁ*, *Cratesicles*, a Spartan.

Κρατησιππίδας, *α*, *ὁ*, *Cratesippidas*, a Spartan naval commander.

Κρήθων, *ωνος*, *ὁ*, *Crethon*, son of Diocles, of Pheræ in Messenia.

Κρητίνης, *ου*, *ὁ*, *Cretines*, father of Aminocles the Thessalian.

Κρῖος, *ου*, *ὁ*, *Crius*, son of Polycritus, one of the chief men of Ægina.

Κρίταλλα, *ων*, *τά*, *Critalla*, a city of Cappadocia, on the Halys.

Κριτίας, *ου*, *ὁ*, *Critias*, an uncle of Plato, and one of the thirty tyrants at Athens.

Κριτόβουλος, *ου*, *ὁ*, *Critobulus*, an Athenian, a pupil of Socrates.

Κρίτων, *ωνος*, *ὁ*, *Criton* (*Crito*), an Athenian, an intimate friend of Socrates.

Κροῖσος *ου*, *ὁ*, *Crœsus*, the last king of Lydia, son of Alyattes.

Κροκίνας, *ου*, *ὁ*, *Crocinas*, a Thessalian, a victor in the Olympic games.

Κροκύλεια, *ων*, *τά*, *Crocylea*, a place in Ithaca.

Κρῶμνα, *ης*, *ἡ*, *Cromna*, a fortress of Paphlagonia, near Amastris.

Κτέατος, *ου*, *ὁ*, *Cteatus*, a son of Poseidon and Molione, a chief of the Epeï.

Κτησίας, *ου*, *ὁ*, *Ctesias*, of Cnidus, a distinguished physician and historian.

Κτήσιππος, *ου*, *ὁ*, *Ctesippus*, an Athenian, a friend of Socrates.

Κύδνος, *ου*, *ὁ*, *Cydnus*, a river of Cilicia, flowing through Tarsus.

Κυδοιμός, *οῦ*, *ὁ*, *Cydœmus*, *Uproar* personified.

Κύδων, *ωνος*, *ὁ*, *Cydon*, a Byzantine.

Κυζικηνός, *ή*, *όν*, *of Cyzicus*.

Κυζικηνός, *οῦ*, *ὁ*, *an inhabitant of Cyzicus*; (*στατήρ* understood) *a Cyzicene*, a gold coin of Cyzicus, worth about $4.93.

Κύζικος, *ου*, *ἡ*, *Cyzicus*, an important city on an island of the same name in the Propontis, close to Mysia.

Κύμη, *ης*, *ἡ*, *Cyme*, the principal city of Æolis in Asia Minor, on the coast, near Phocæa.

Κυναίγειρος, or **Κυνέγειρος**, *ου*, *ὁ*, *Cynægirus*, a brave Athenian warrior, brother of the poet Æschylus.

Κυνίσκος, *ου*, *ὁ*, *Cyniscus*, a Spartan.

Κῦνος, *ου*, *ἡ*, *Cynus*, a port of Locris, on the Malian Gulf.

Κυνόσουρα, ας, ἡ, (lit. *dog's tail*), *Cynosura:* (1) a promontory on the east coast of Attica, sheltering the bay of Marathon; (2) a promontory on or near the island of Salamis.

Κυπαρισσήεις, εντος, ἡ, *Cyparisseïs,* a city on the west coast of Messenia, near the river Cyparissus, later called Cyparissia (Κυπαρισσία).

Κυπάρισσος, ου, ἡ, *Cyparissus,* a small city in Phocis, on Mt. Parnassus, near Delphi.

Κυρεῖος, α, ον, *of Cyrus, Cyreian.*

Κῦρος, ου, ὁ, *Cyrus,* the name of two Persian kings. The second, called "the Great," or "the Elder," was son and successor of Cambyses I. and conqueror of Media. It was also the name of a son of Darius II., called "the Younger," who perished in an expedition to dethrone his brother Artaxerxes II.

Κύτωρος, ου, ἡ, *Cytorus,* a coast city of Paphlagonia, near Amastris.

Κύφος, ου, ἡ, *Cyphus,* a city in northern Thessaly.

Κῶπαι, ῶν, αἱ, *Copæ,* an old town of Bœotia on the northern shore of the lake Copais.

Κωρύκιος, α, ον, *of Corycia* the name of a nymph; especially in the phrase **τὸ Κωρύκιον ἄντρον,** *the Corycian cave,* in Mt. Parnassus, above Delphi, sacred to Pan and the Corycian nymphs.

Κῶς, ῶ, ἡ, *Cos,* an island in the Ægean sea, opposite Caria, with a city of the same name.

Λ

Λάας (poet. for **Λᾶς),** Λάος, ἡ, *Las,* an ancient city of Laconia, on the west side of the Laconian gulf, near the coast.

Λαβώτας, α, ὁ, *Labotas,* a Spartan governor.

Λᾱέρτης, ου, ὁ, *Laërtes,* king of Ithaca and father of Ulysses.

Λᾱερτιάδης, ου, ὁ, *son of Laërtes,* i. e. Ulysses.

Λακεδαιμόνιος, α, ον, *Lacedæmonian:* **οἱ Λακεδαιμόνιοι,** *the Lacedæmonians;* often used as equivalent to Laconians.

Λακεδαίμων, ονος, ἡ, *Lacedæmon,* the capital of Laconia; also called Σπάρτη.

Λᾱκράτης, ους, ὁ, *Lacrates,* a Spartan, an Olympic victor.

Λάκων, ωνος, ὁ, *a Laconian, an inhabitant of Laconia;* often used as equivalent to Lacedæmonian.

Λακωνική, ῆς, ἡ, *Laconia,* the southeastern country of the Peloponnesus.

Λάμπος, ου, ὁ, *Lampus,* a son of Laomedon.

Λαμψακηνός, ή, όν, *of Lampsacus, Lampsacenc.*

Λάμψακος, ου, ἡ, *Lampsacus,* a flourishing city of Mysia, on the Hellespont, earlier Pityusa.

Λᾱοδάμεια, ας, ἡ, *Laodamia,* daughter of Bellerophon and mother of Sarpedon.

Λᾱοδίκη, ης, ἡ, *Laodice,* a daughter of Priam.

Λαόδοκος, ου, ὁ, *Laodocus,* a Trojan, son of Antenor.

Λᾱομεδοντιάδης, ου, ὁ, *son of Laomedon,* i. e. Priam.

Λᾱομέδων, οντος, ὁ, *Laomedon,* king of Troy, son of Ilus, and father of Priam.

Λᾱρισαῖος, ου, ὁ, *a Larissæan, an inhabitant of Larissa* a city of Thessaly.

Λαύρειον, ου, τό, *Laurium,* a range of hills in southern Attica, near the promontory Sunium, celebrated for silver mines.

Λειώκριτος, ου, ὁ, *Liocritus,* son of Euenor, a suitor of Penelope.

Λεοντεύς, έως, ὁ, *Leonteus,* son of Coronus.

Λεοντιάδης, ου, ὁ, *Leontiades,* son of Eurymachus, leader of the Thebans at Thermopylæ.

Λεοντῖνος, η, ον, *of Leontini* in eastern Sicily; **οἱ Λεοντῖνοι,** *the inhabitants of Leontini.*

Λεοντίς, ίδος, ἡ, *Leontis,* an Attic tribe, named from the old hero Leos.

Λέσβος, ου, ἡ, *Lesbos,* an island of the Ægean sea, off the coast of Mysia.

Λευκάδιοι, ων, οἱ, *the Leucadians,* inhabitants of Leucas, an island off the coast of Acarnania, originally a peninsula, having a city of the same name.

Λευκολοφίδης, ου, ὁ, *Leucolophides,* an Athenian, father of Adimantus.

Λεῦκος, ου, ὁ, *Leucus,* a comrade of Ulysses before Troy.

Λεωβώτης, εω, (Ion. for **Λαβώτας,** α), ὁ, *Labotas,* a ruler of Sparta.

Λέων, οντος, ὁ, *Leon:* (1) a king of Sparta, grandfather of Leonidas; (2) an Athenian, native of Salamis; (3) a Spartan ephor.

Λεωνίδας, α and ου, Ion. **-δης,** ὁ, *Leonidas,* king of Sparta, the leader in the celebrated defence of Thermopylæ.

Λεωπρέπης, ους, ὁ, *Leoprepes,* father of Simonides the poet of Ceos.

Λῆθος, ου, ὁ, *Lethus,* a prince of the Pelasgi in Larissa, allied with Troy.

Λήϊτος, ου, ὁ, *Leitus,* a leader of the Bœotians before Troy.

Λίβυς, υος, ὁ, *Libys,* a Spartan naval commander.

Λικύμνιος ου, ὁ, *Licymnius,* son of Electryon and Midea, half-brother of Alcmene.

Λίλαια, ας, ἡ, *Lilæa,* an ancient town in Phocis, near the sources of the Cephisus.

Λίνδος, *ου*, *ἡ*, *Lindus*, a city on the east coast of Rhodes, the ancient capital.

Λουσιάτης, *ου*, *ὁ*, and **Λουσιεύς**, *έως*, *ὁ*, *a Lusian*, an inhabitant of Lusi in northern Arcadia.

Λυδία, *ας*, *ἡ*, *Lydia*, a country of Asia Minor, on the Ægean sea.

Λυκαονία, *ας*, *ἡ*, *Lycaonia*, a country of Asia Minor, west of Cappadocia and north of Cilicia.

Λυκάριος, *ου*, *ὁ*, *Lycarius*, a Spartan ephor.

Λύκαστος, *ου*, *ἡ*, *Lycastus*, an ancient city in Crete.

Λυκάων, *ονος*, *ὁ*, *Lycaon*: (1) father of Pandarus, of Zelea; (2) a son of Priam.

Λύκειον, *ου*, *τό*, *Lyceum*, a gymnasium in the southeastern part of Athens, outside of the walls, where Aristotle taught.

Λύκιοι, *ων*, *οἱ*, *the Lycians*, inhabiting Lycia, a country of southwestern Asia Minor.

Λύκιος, *ου*, *ὁ*, *Lycius*: (1) a Syracusan; (2) an Athenian cavalry commander.

Λυκίσκος, *ου*, *ὁ*, *Lyciscus*, an Athenian archon.

Λυκομήδης, *ους*, *ὁ*, *Lycomedes*, an Athenian ship-captain.

Λύκος, *ου*, *ὁ*, *Lycus*, a river of Bithynia, flowing into the Euxine near Heraclea.

Λυκοῦργος (poet. **-κόοργ-**), *ου*, *ὁ*, *Lycurgus*: (1) a king of the Edones, in Thrace, punished by the gods for insulting Bacchus; (2) a Byzantine.

Λυκόφρων, *ονος*, *ὁ*, *Lycophron*, a tyrant of Pheræ in Thessaly.

Λύκτος, *ου*, *ἡ*, *Lyctus*, an ancient city of Crete, near Cnosus.

Λύκων, *ωνος*, *ὁ*, *Lycon*, an Achaian.

Λυρνησσός, *οῦ*, *ὁ*, *Lyrnessus*, a city of Troas.

Λύσανδρος, *ου*, *ὁ*, *Lysander*, the celebrated Spartan commander, conqueror of Athens.

Λυσίας, *ου*, *ὁ*, *Lysias*, an Athenian commander.

Λυσικλῆς, *έους*, *ὁ*, *Lysicles*, an Athenian, father of Abronichus.

Λυσίμαχος, *ου*, *ὁ*, *Lysimachus*: (1) an Athenian, father of the celebrated Aristides; (2) a commander of cavalry under the thirty tyrants at Athens.

Λυσίστρατος, *ου*, *ὁ*, *Lysistratus*, an Athenian soothsayer.

M

Μαγνησία, *ας*, *ἡ*, *Magnesia*, a long and narrow strip on the eastern coast of Thessaly.

Μάδυτος, *ου*, *ἡ*, *Madytus*, a port-town in the Thracian Chersonese.

Μαίανδρος, *ου*, *ὁ*, *Mæander*, a river of Caria, flowing into the Icarian sea near Miletus, noted for its windings.

Μαιονία, *ας*, *ἡ*, poet. **Μῃονίη**, *Mæonia*, an early name of Lydia, afterwards used of the eastern portion.

Μαιονίς, *ίδος*, *ἡ*, poet. **Μῃονίς**, fem. adj., *Mæonian*.

Μαισάδης, *ου*, *ὁ*, *Mæsades*, father of the Thracian prince Seuthes.

Μαίων, *ονος*, *ὁ*, poet. **Μῄων**, *a Mæonian*; **οἱ Μῄονες**, *the Mæonians*.

Μαίων, *ονος*, *ὁ*, *Mæon*, son of Hæmon of Thebes.

Μακεδονία, *ας*, *ἡ*, *Macedonia*, a country extending along the coast of the Ægean sea from Thessaly to Thrace.

Μακέστιος and **Μακίστιος**, *α*, *ον*, *of Macestus* or *Macistus*, a city in southern Elis.

Μάκρωνες, *ων*, *οἱ*, *the Macrones*, a people dwelling on the southeast shore of the Euxine.

Μαλέα, *ας*, *ἡ*, *Malea*: (1) a promontory on the southeast of Laconia; (2) a promontory at the south of the island of Lesbos.

Μαντίθεος, *ου*, *ὁ*, *Mantitheus*, an Athenian.

Μαντίνεια, *ας*, Ion. **Μαντινέη**, *ἡ*, *Mantinea*, an ancient and celebrated city in eastern Arcadia.

Μαντινεύς, *έως*, *ὁ*, *a Mantinean*.

Μάρδοι, *ων*, *οἱ*, *the Mardi*, a powerful and warlike tribe dwelling on the south shore of the Caspian sea.

Μαρδόνιος, *ου*, *ὁ*, *Mardonius*, son of Gobryas and son-in-law of Darius I., a commander under Darius I. and Xerxes I.

Μαριανδῦνοί, *ῶν*, *οἱ*, *the Mariandyni*, an ancient people on the coast of Bithynia, east of the Sangarius.

Μαρσύας, *ου*, *ὁ*, *Marsyas*: (1) a mythological flute-player in Phrygia; (2) a Phrygian river, a tributary of the Mæander.

Μάρων, *ωνος*, *ὁ*, *Maron*, a Spartan who fought at Thermopylæ.

Μαρωνείτης, *ου*, *ὁ*, *a Maronite*, belonging to Maronea, an important town on the south coast of Thrace, west of the Hebrus.

Μάσης, *ητος*, *ὁ*, *Mases*, an ancient city on the south coast of Argolis, the port of Hermione.

Μασκᾶς, *ᾶ*, (and **Μάσκας**), *ὁ*, *Mascas*, an eastern tributary of the Euphrates in Mesopotamia.

Μαστορίδης, *ου*, *ὁ*, *son of Mastor*, i. e. Halitherses.

Μεγάβυζος, *ου*, *ὁ*, *Megabyzus*, a common Persian name, also the name of a high priest of Diana at Ephesus.

Μεγακρέων, *οντος*, *ὁ*, *Megacreon*, an inhabitant of Abdera.

Μέγαρα, ων, τά, *Megara*, the chief city of Megaris.

Μεγαρεύς, έως, ὁ, *a Megarian, an inhabitant of Megara.*

Μεγαφέρνης, ου, ὁ, *Megaphernes*, a Persian noble.

Μέγης, ητος, ὁ, *Meges*, son of Phyleus, a leader of the Dulichians before Troy.

Μεγιστίας, ου, ὁ, *Megistias*, a soothsayer of Acarnania.

Μεδεών, ῶνος, ὁ, *Medeon*, an ancient city of Bœotia, near Lake Copais.

Μέδων, οντος, ὁ, *Medon*, son of Oileus, half-brother of the lesser Ajax, and commander of the Phthians before Troy.

Μεθυδριεύς, έως, ὁ, *a Methydrian*, an inhabitant of Methydrium, a city in central Arcadia.

Μεθώνη, poet. **Μη-**, ης, ἡ, *Methone*, a city of Magnesia in Thessaly.

Μελάμπους, οδος, ὁ, *Melampus*, son of Amythaon, said to have been the first soothsayer and physician.

Μελάμπῡγος, ου, ὁ, (with λίθος), *Melampygus*, a rock or cliff on Mt. Anopæa, near Thermopylæ.

Μελανδῖται, ῶν, οἱ, *the Melanditæ*, inhabitants of Melandia, a region of Thrace.

Μελάνθιος, ου, ὁ, *Melanthius*, an Athenian commander.

Μέλας, ανος, ὁ, *Melas*, a river of Malis in Thessaly, flowing into the Malian Gulf near Thermopylæ.

Μελέαγρος, ου, ὁ, *Meleager*, of Calydon, an Ætolian hero and hunter, an Argonaut.

Μέλητος, ου, ὁ, *Meletus*, an adherent of the thirty tyrants at Athens.

Μελίβοια, ας, ἡ, *Melibœa*, a city on the coast of Magnesia in Thessaly, near Mt. Ossa.

Μένανδρος, ου, ὁ, *Menander*, an Athenian commander.

Μενεκλῆς, έους, ὁ, *Menecles*, an Athenian orator.

Μενεκράτης, ους, ὁ, *Menecrates*, a Syracusan, father of Myscon.

Μενέξενος, ου, ὁ, *Menexenus*, an Athenian, a pupil of Socrates.

Μενέσθης, ους, ὁ, *Menesthes*, a Greek, slain by Hector.

Μενοιτιάδης, ου, ὁ, *son of Menœtius*, i. e. Patroclus.

Μέντης, ου, ὁ, *Mentes*, king of the Taphians, a friend of Ulysses.

Μέντωρ, ορος, ὁ, *Mentor*, son of Alcimus, a faithful friend of Ulysses in Ithaca.

Μένων, ωνος, ὁ, *Menon*, a Thessalian of Pharsalus, a commander in the army of Cyrus the younger.

Μερμερίδης, ου, ὁ, *son of Mermerus*, i. e. Ilus.

Μέροψ, οπος, ὁ, *Merops*, a prince of Percote on the Hellespont, and a celebrated soothsayer.

Μέσθλης, ου, ὁ, *Mesthles*, son of Pylæmenes, a leader of the Mæonians before Troy.

Μέσπιλα, ης, ἡ, *Mespila*, a city of Assyria on the Tigris, near Nineveh, in ruins in the time of Xenophon.

Μέσση, ης, ἡ, *Messa*, a city and harbor in Laconia, near the promontory of Tænarum.

Μεσσηΐς, ίδος, ἡ, *Messeïs*, a fountain at Pheræ in Thessaly.

Μεσσηνία, ας, ἡ, *Messenia*, the southwest country of the Peloponnesus.

Μεσσήνιοι, ων, οἱ, *the Messenians.*

Μήδεια, ας, ἡ, *Medea*, a queen of Media (Xen. *Anab.* 3, 4, 11).

Μηδία, ας, ἡ, *Media*, a large and important country of Asia, lying southwest of the Caspian Sea. **Τὸ Μηδίας τεῖχος**, *the wall of Media*, extending from the Tigris to the Euphrates, built near the northern boundary of Babylonia as a defence against the Medes.

Μήδοκος, ου, ὁ, *Medocus*, a king of the Odrysæ in Thrace.

Μῆδος, ου, ὁ, *a Mede.*

Μηδοσάδης, ου, ὁ, *Medosades*, an ambassador of Seuthes a Thracian prince.

Μήθυμνα, ης, ἡ, *Methymna*, a city in the north of Lesbos.

Μηθυμναῖος, ου, ὁ, *an inhabitant of Methymna.*

Μηθώνη, see **Μεθώνη**.

Μηκιστεύς, έως, ὁ, *Mecisteus*, son of Talaus, and father of Euryalus.

Μηκιστιάδης, ου, ὁ, *son of Mecisteus*, i. e. Euryalus.

Μήλιος, ου, ὁ, *an inhabitant of Melos*, an island in the Ægean sea, one of the Cyclades.

Μηλόβιος, ου, ὁ, *Melobius*, one of the thirty tyrants at Athens.

Μηονίη, **Μηονίς**, &c., see **Μαιονία**, &c.

Μηριόνης, ου, ὁ, *Meriones*, son of Molus, a Cretan hero, and friend of Idomeneus.

Μίδας, ου, ὁ, *Midas*, an ancient king of Phrygia, noted for his wealth and covetousness.

Μίδεια (poet. for **Μίδεα**), ας, ἡ, *Midea*, an ancient city of Bœotia, near Lake Copaïs.

Μιθριδάτης (and **-ρα-**), ου, ὁ, *Mithridates*, a Persian satrap, friend of Cyrus the younger.

Μῑλήσιος, α, ον, *Milesian, of Miletus;* **Μῑλήσιος**, ου, ὁ, *an inhabitant of Miletus.*

Μίλητος, ου, ἡ, *Miletus:* (1) a great city, the southernmost in Ionia; (2) an ancient city in Crete.

Μιλτιάδης, *ου*, *ὁ*, *Miltiades*, an Athenian, son of Cimon, the victorious commander at Marathon.

Μιλτοκύθης, *ου*, *ὁ*, *Miltocythes*, a Thracian.

Μίνδαρος, *ου*, *ὁ*, *Mindarus*, a Spartan admiral.

Μισγολαΐδας, *α*, *ὁ*, *Misgolaïdas*, a Spartan ephor.

Μιτραῖος, *ου*, *ὁ*, *Mitræus*, a Persian.

Μιτροβάτης, *ου*, *ὁ*, *Mitrobates*, a governor in Dascylium in Asia Minor.

Μιτυλήνη, *ης*, *ἡ*, more correctly **Μυτιλήνη**, which see.

Μνησιθείδης, *ου*, *ὁ*, *Mnesithides*, one of the thirty tyrants at Athens.

Μνησίλοχος, *ου*, *ὁ*, *Mnesilochus*, one of the thirty tyrants at Athens.

Μνησίφιλος, *ου*, *ὁ*, *Mnesiphilus*, an Athenian.

Μοσσύνοικοι, *ων*, *οἱ*, *the Mossynœci*, a barbarian people on the coast of Pontus, east of the city of Cerasus, living in conical wooden houses (*μόσσυν, a wooden tower*, and *οἰκέω, to dwell*).

Μουνιχία and **-νυ-**, *ας*, *ἡ*, *Munichia* or *Munychia*, a hill and harbor in the peninsula of Piræus.

Μουσαῖος, *ου*, *ὁ*, *Musæus*, a famous semi-mythical Greek poet.

Μύγδων, *ονος*, *ὁ*, *Mygdon*, a king of Phrygia.

Μύδων, *ωνος*, *ὁ*, *Mydon*, a Trojan, charioteer of Pylæmenes.

Μυκάλη, *ης*, *ἡ*, *Mycale*, a celebrated mountain and promontory on the Ionian coast, opposite Samos.

Μυκαλησσός, *οῦ*, *ἡ*, *Mycalessus*, a city in northeastern Bœotia, opposite Chalcis.

Μυκήνη, *ης*, *ἡ*, *Mycene*, daughter of Inachus and wife of Arestor.

Μύνης, *ητος*, *ὁ*, *Mynes*, husband of Briseïs.

Μυρίανδος, *ου*, *ἡ*, (later **Μυρίανδρος**), *Myriandus*, a coast city of Syria, on the east side of the gulf of Issus.

Μυρίνη, *ης*, *ἡ*, (poet. for **Μυρίνα** or **Μύρῑνα**), *Myrina*, daughter of Teucer, and wife of Dardanus.

Μύρσινος, *ου*, *ἡ*, *Myrsinus*, a city in northwestern Elis, later Myrtuntium.

Μῡσία, *ας*, *ἡ*, *Mysia*, the northwestern district of Asia Minor.

Μύσιος, *α*, *ον*, *Mysian* ; **οἱ Μύσιοι**, *the Mysians*, inhabitants of Mysia.

Μύσκων, *ωνος*, *ὁ*. *Myscon*, son of Menecrates, a general of the Syracusans.

Μυτιληναῖος, *ου*, *ὁ*, *an inhabitant of Mytilene.*

Μυτιλήνη, *ης*, *ἡ*, *Mytilene*, the chief city of the island of Lesbos, on the eastern side.

N

Νάστης, *ου*, *ὁ*, *Nastes*, son of Nomion, leader of the Carians before Troy.

Ναυβολίδης, *ου*, *ὁ*, *son of Naubolus*, i. e. Iphitus.

Ναυκλείδας, *α*, *ὁ*, *Nauclidas*, a Spartan ephor.

Ναύπακτος, *ου*, *ὁ*, *Naupactus*, a city of the Locri Ozolæ, near the entrance of the Corinthian Gulf, with a celebrated harbor.

Νεοκλῆς, *έους*, *ὁ*, *Neocles*, an Athenian, father of Themistocles.

Νέον τεῖχος, *τό*, (*new wall*), *Neontichus*, a fortress on the coast of Thrace, near the Chersonese.

Νεστορίδης, *ου*, *ὁ*, *son of Nestor*, i. e. Antilochus.

Νέστωρ, *ορος*, *ὁ*, *Nestor*, king of Pylus in Messenia, one of the leaders against Troy, distinguished for bravery, wisdom, and eloquence.

Νέων, *ωνος*, *ἡ*, also **τὰ Νέωνα**, *Neon*, an ancient city in Phocis, on the slope of Mt. Parnassus, later Tithorea.

Νέων, *ωνος*, *ὁ*, *Neon*, a Spartan commander in the return of the ten thousand.

Νήϊον, *ου*, *τό*, *Neïum*, a mountain in the south of Ithaca.

Νηλήϊος, *ον*, *of Neleus* ; **ὁ Νηλήϊος υἱός**, *the son of Neleus*, i. e. Nestor.

Νήριτον, *ου*, *τό*, *Neritum*, the highest mountain in Ithaca, in the north.

Νίκανδρος, *ου*, *ὁ*, *Nicander*, a Spartan.

Νίκαρχος, *ου*, *ὁ*, *Nicarchus*, an Arcadian in the army of the ten thousand.

Νῑκήρατος, *ου*, *ὁ*, *Niceratus*, an Athenian, son of the noted general Nicias.

Νικίας, *ου*, *ὁ*, *Nicias*, an Athenian, son of Niceratus, distinguished as a general in the Peloponnesian war.

Νῑκόμαχος, *ου*, *ὁ*, *Nicomachus*, an Œtæan.

Νῑκόστρατος, *ου*, *ὁ*, *Nicostratus*, an Athenian in the cavalry force of the thirty tyrants.

Νῑρεύς, *έως*, *ὁ*, *Nireus*, from the island of Syme, next to Achilles the handsomest of the Greeks at Troy.

Νῖσα, *ης*, *ἡ*, *Nisa*, a city of Bœotia mentioned by Homer.

Νίσαια, *ας*, *ἡ*, *Nisæa*, the port of Megara, on the Saronic gulf.

Νισαῖος, *ον*, *Nisæan* ; used especially of fine horses bred on the Nisæan plain, a district in the North of Media, near Rhagæ.

Νίσῡρος, *ου*, *ἡ*, *Nisyrus*, a small island between Cos and Telos, one of the Sporades.

Νοήμων, *ονος*, *ὁ*, *Noëmon* : (1) a Lycian ; (2) an Ithacan.

Νομίων, *ονος, ὁ, Nomion*, a Carian chief.

Νότιον, *ου, τό, Notium*, an Æolian city on the coast of Ionia near Colophon.

Νυσήϊον (poet. for **Νυσαῖον**), *ου, τό,* (*ὄρος* understood), *Nysæum*, a mountain in Thrace, where Bacchus was worshipped.

Ξ

Ξανθικλῆς, *έους, ὁ, Xanthicles*, an Achaian, a commander in the return of the ten thousand.

Ξανθίππη, *ης, ἡ, Xanthippe*, the wife of Socrates.

Ξάνθος, *ου, ὁ, Xanthus:* (1) a Trojan; (2) the chief river of Lycia; (3) a river of Troas, also called Scamander.

Ξενίας, *ου, ὁ, Xenias*, an Arcadian commander in the army of Cyrus the younger.

Ξενοφῶν, *ῶντος, ὁ, Xenophon*, son of Gryllus, distinguished as an author, philosopher, and commander.

Ξέρξης, *ου, ὁ, Xerxes*, the name of two kings of Persia. The first was son and successor of Darius I.

O

Ὀγχηστός, *οῦ, ὁ, Onchestus*, an ancient city of Bœotia, near Lake Copaïs, on the southern side.

Ὀδίος, *ου, ὁ, Odius*, a leader of the Halizones, and ally of Priam.

Ὀδρύσης, *ου, ὁ, an Odrysian ;* **οἱ Ὀδρύσαι,** *the Odrysians*, a people of Thrace, around the Hebrus.

Ὀϊλεύς, *έως, ὁ, Oïleus*, a king of the Locrians, father of Ajax the less, an Argonaut.

Οἰνείδης, *ου, ὁ, son of Œneus*, i. e. Tydeus.

Οἰνεύς, *έως, ὁ, Œneus*, a king of Calydon in Ætolia.

Οἰνόη, *ης, ἡ, Œnoë*, an Athenian fortress on the borders of Bœotia.

Οἰνόμαος, *ου, ὁ, Œnomaus*, a Greek, slain at Troy.

Οἰνοπίδης, *ου, ὁ, son of Œnopion*, i. e. Helenus.

Οἰταῖος, *α, ον, Œtæan ;* **οἱ Οἰταῖοι,** *the Œtæans*, inhabiting Œtæa, a district in the south of Thessaly containing the mountain range of Œta.

Οἴτυλος, *ου, ὁ, Œtylus*, an ancient town of Laconia, on the Messenian Gulf.

Οἰχαλιεύς, *έως, ὁ, an Œchalian.*

Οἰχαλίηθεν, *from Œchalia*, a city of Histiæotis in Thessaly, on the Peneus.

Ὀλιζών, *ῶνος, ἡ, Olizon*, a city in the southern part of Magnesia in Thessaly, on the coast.

Ὀλοοσσών, *όνος, ἡ, Oloösson*, a city of the Perrhæbi in Histiæotis in Thessaly.

Ὀλύνθιος, *α, ον, of Olynthus*, the most important Greek city on the coast of Macedonia, at the head of the Toronaic Gulf; **οἱ Ὀλύνθιοι,** *the Olynthians.*

Ὅμηρος, *ου, ὁ, Homer*, the great epic poet of Greece.

Ὀνήτης, *ου, ὁ, Onetes*, a Carystian.

Ὀνομακλῆς, *έους, ὁ, Onomacles:* (1) one of the thirty tyrants at Athens; (2) a Spartan ephor.

Ὀνομάντιος, *ου, ὁ, Onomantius*, a Spartan ephor.

Ὀνόχωνος, *ου, ὁ, Onochonus*, a river of Thessaly.

Ὀπόεις, *εντος,* contr. **Ὀποῦς,** *οῦντος, ἡ, Opus*, the capital city of the Opuntian Locrians.

Ὀπούντιος, *α, ον, of Opus, Opuntian.*

Ὄργης, *εος, ὁ, Orges*, a Thasian.

Ὀρέσβιος, *ου, ὁ, Oresbius*, a Bœotian, of Hyle.

Ὀρέστης, *ου, ὁ, Orestes:* (1) son of Agamemnon, the slayer of his mother Clytæmnestra; (2) a Greek, slain at Troy.

Ὄρθη, *ης, ἡ, Orthe*, a city of the Perrhæbi in northern Thessaly.

Ὀρμένιον, *ου, τό, Ormenium*, an ancient city in southern Magnesia in Thessaly.

Ὀρνειαί, *ῶν, αἱ.* (poet. for **Ὀρνεαί**), *Orneæ*, an ancient city in the western part of Argolis.

Ὀρόντας, *α* and *ου*, and **Ὀρόντης,** *ου, ὁ, Orontas* or *Orontes:* (1) a satrap of Armenia; (2) a Persian noble, executed by Cyrus the younger.

Ὀρσίλοχος, *ου, ὁ, Orsilochus:* (1) the father of Diocles king of Pheræ in Messenia; (2) grandson of preceding, son of Diocles.

Ὀρσίφαντος, *ου, ὁ, Orsiphantus*, a Spartan.

Ὀρχομένιος, *α, ον, of Orchomenus ;* **οἱ Ὀρχομένιοι,** *the Orchomenians.*

Ὀρχομενός, *οῦ, ἡ,* sometimes *ὁ, Orchomenus:* (1) an important city of the Minyæ in Bœotia, northwest of Lake Copaïs, near the Cephissus; (2) a city in eastern Arcadia.

Ὄσσα, *ης, ἡ, Ossa*, a celebrated mountain range in the north of Magnesia in Thessaly.

Ὀτάνης, *ου, ὁ, Otanes*, a Persian.

Ὀτρεύς, *έως, ὁ, Otreus*, a Phrygian prince.

Οὐκαλέγων, *οντος, ὁ, Ucalegon*, one of the elders of Troy.

Ὀφέλτιος, *ου, ὁ, Opheltius*, a Trojan.

Ὀφρύνιον (and **-νειον**), *ου, τό, Ophrynium*, a small town in Troas, near Dardanus.

Ὀχήσιος, *ου, ὁ, Ochesius*, an Ætolian.

Π

Παγασαί, ῶν, αἱ, *Pagasæ*, a port in Thessaly, at the head of the Pagasæan Gulf, where Jason built the Argo.

Παιάνιεύς, έως, ὁ, *a Pæanian*, a resident of the Attic deme Pæania.

Παίονες, ων, οἱ, *the Pæonians*, inhabitants of Pæonia.

Παιονία, ας, ἡ, *Pæonia*, the northern part of Macedonia, but in very early times including most of Macedonia and Thrace.

Παισός, see **Ἀπαισός.**

Παλαμήδης, ους, ὁ, *Palamedes*, of Eubœa, said to have made many inventions.

Παλληνεύς, έως, ὁ, *a Pallenian*, a resident of Pallene, an Attic deme.

Πάμμων, ονος, ὁ, *Pammon*, a Scyrian.

Παναίτιος, ου, ὁ, *Panætius*, a Tenian ship-captain.

Πάνδαρος, ου, ὁ, *Pandarus*, son of Lycaon, commander of the Zeleans in the Trojan army.

Πάνθοος, ου, ὁ, *Panthoüs*, one of the elders of Troy, a priest of Apollo.

Πανοπεῖς, έων, οἱ, *the Panopeans*, inhabitants of Panopeus.

Πανοπεύς, έως, ὁ, *Panopeus*, a city of Phocis near the border of Bœotia.

Παντακλῆς, έους, ὁ, *Pantacles*, a Spartan ephor.

Παντίτης, ου, ὁ, *Pantites*, a Spartan, the only survivor at Thermopylæ.

Πάραλος, ου, ἡ, *Paralus*, the name of one of the two state triremes of Athens, the name of the other being *Σαλαμινία*.

Παρθένιον, ου, τό, *Parthenium:* (1) a range of mountains between Arcadia and Argolis; (2) a city in Mysia, south of Pergamum.

Παρθένιος, ου, ὁ, *Parthenius*, the chief river of Paphlagonia, in the west.

Παριᾶνοί, ῶν, οἱ, *the inhabitants of Parium.*

Πάριον, ου, τό, *Parium*, a city in the north of Troas, on the coast of the Propontis.

Πάρις, ιδος, Ion. ιος, ὁ, *Paris*, son of Priam, whose seduction of Helen led to the Trojan war.

Πάρος, ου, ἡ, *Paros*, an island, one of the Cyclades, famous for its white marble.

Παρρασία, ας, ἡ, *Parrhasia*, a city and district in southwestern Arcadia.

Παρράσιος, α, ον, *Parrhasian.*

Παρύσατις, ιδος, ἡ, *Parysatis*, daughter of Artaxerxes I., wife of Darius II., and mother of Artaxerxes II. and Cyrus the younger.

Πασιππίδας, ου, ὁ, *Pasippidas*, a Spartan admiral.

Πασίων, ωνος, ὁ, *Pasion*, a Megarean, a general in the expedition of Cyrus the younger.

Πατηγύας, ου, ὁ, *Pategyas*, a Persian, connected with Cyrus the younger.

Πατησιάδας and **-δης**, ου, ὁ, *Patesiadas*, a Spartan ephor.

Πατιράμφης, ου, ὁ, *Patiramphes*, a Persian, charioteer of Xerxes.

Παυσανίας, ου, ὁ, *Pausanias*, a king of Sparta.

Παφλαγονία, ας, ἡ, *Paphlagonia*, a country of Asia Minor, on the Euxine, between Pontus and Bithynia.

Παφλαγονικός, ή, όν, *Paphlagonian.*

Πειραΐδης, ου, ὁ, *son of Piræus*, i. e. Ptolemæus, and sometimes his son, Eurymedon.

Πειραιεύς, έως and ῶς, ὁ, *Piræeus*, the most important harbor of Athens.

Πειρίθοος, ου, ὁ, *Pirithoüs*, of Larissa in Thessaly, a king of the Lapithæ.

Πείροος, ου, ὁ, *Piroüs*, a leader of the Thracians in alliance with Troy.

Πεισηνορίδης, ου, ὁ, *son of Pisenor*, i. e. Ops.

Πεισήνωρ, ορος, ὁ, *Pisenor*, a herald, of Ithaca.

Πεισιάναξ, ακτος, ὁ, *Pisianax*, an Athenian, father of Euryptolemus.

Πεισιστρατίδης, ου, ὁ, *son of Pisistratus;* **οἱ Πεισιστρατίδαι**, *the Pisistratidæ*, used of Hippias and Hipparchus, and also of Hippias and his party.

Πεισίστρατος, ου, ὁ, *Pisistratus*, son of Hippocrates, a tyrant of Athens.

Πείσων, ωνος, ὁ, *Pison*, one of the thirty tyrants at Athens.

Πελάγων, οντος, ὁ, *Pelagon:* (1) a Pylian, follower of Nestor; (2) a Lycian, friend of Sarpedon.

Πελίας, ου, ὁ, *Pelias*, son of Poseidon, a half-uncle of Jason.

Πελληνεύς, έως, ὁ, *a Pellenian.*

Πελλήνη, ης, ἡ, *Pellene*, a city in eastern Achaia, near the Corinthian gulf.

Πελοποννήσιος, ου, ὁ, *an inhabitant of the Peloponnesus*, the southern part of Greece.

Πέλται, ῶν, αἱ, *Peltæ*, a city in Phrygia.

Περαιβοί, see **Περραιβοί.**

Πέργαμον, ου, τό, *Pergamum:* (1) the acropolis of Troy, on a hill to the southeast of the city, a branch of Mt. Ida; (2) (also called **Πέργαμος** ου, ἡ), a city in southwestern Mysia.

Περγασίδης, ου, ὁ, *son of Pergasus*, i. e. Deïcoon.

Περικλῆς, έους, ὁ, *Pericles*, an Athenian general, son of Pericles the famous statesman.

Περίνθιοι, ων, οἱ, *the Perinthians.*

Πέρινθος, ου, ἡ, *Perinthus*, a flourishing town of Thrace, on the Propontis, later called Heraclea.

Περίφας, αντος, ὁ, *Periphas*, an Ætolian.

Περκώσιος, α, ον, *of Percote, Percosian.*

Περκώτη, ης, ἡ, *Percote*, an ancient city of Mysia, near the Hellespont.

Περραιβοί, poet. **Περαι-**, ῶν, οἱ, *the Perrhæbians*, inhabitants of Perrhæbia, a region in Thessaly north of the Peneus.

Περσείδης, ου, ὁ, *son of Perseus.* Perses, son of Perseus, was said to have been the founder of the Persian nation, so the epithet Περσεῖδαι was applied to the Achæmenidean kings of Persia.

Πέρσης, ου, ὁ, *a Persian.*

Πετεών, ῶνος, ὁ, *Peteon*, a small town in Bœotia.

Πετεώς, ῶ and ῶο, ὁ, *Peteos*, father of Menestheus.

Πηγαί, ῶν, αἱ, (lit. *the Springs*), *Pegæ*, a town of Megaris on the Alcyonian sea.

Πηδαῖος, ου, ὁ, *Pedæus*, son of Antenor.

Πήδασος, ου, ἡ, *Pedasus*, a city of the Leleges in Troas.

Πήδασος, ου, ὁ, *Pedasus*, son of Bucolion.

Πηνειός, οῦ, ὁ, *Peneus*, the chief river of Thessaly, rising in Mt. Pindus and flowing into the Thermaic Gulf through the vale of Tempe.

Πηνέλεως, ω, ὁ, *Penelcos*, a leader of the Bœotians before Troy.

Πήρεια, ας, ἡ, *Perea*, a region of Thessaly.

Πίγρης, ητος, ὁ, *Pigres*, an interpreter of Cyrus the younger, from Caria.

Πιδύτης, ου, ὁ, *Pidutes*, of Percote.

Πιερία, ας, ἡ, *Pieria:* (1) a district in Macedonia, on the coast of the Thermaic Gulf, north of Mt. Olympus, celebrated as the first seat of the Muses; (2) a district in Macedonia east of the Strymon, near Mt. Pangæum, settled by the inhabitants driven out of the former region.

Πισίδης, ου, ὁ, *a Pisidian*, an inhabitant of Pisidia in Asia Minor.

Πιτθεύς, έως, ὁ, *Pittheus*, king of Trœzen in Argolis, grandfather of Theseus.

Πιτύας, α, ὁ, *Pityas*, a Spartan ephor.

Πιτύεια, ας, ἡ, *Pityea*, a city of Mysia on the Propontis.

Πλάκος, ου, ἡ, *Placus*, a mountain of Mysia, above Thebe.

Πλάτων, ωνος, ὁ, *Plato*, son of Ariston, the celebrated Athenian philosopher, pupil of Socrates.

Πλειστόλᾱς, α, ὁ, *Plistolas*, a Spartan ephor.

Πλευρών, ῶνος, ἡ, *Pleuron*, an ancient city in southern Ætolia, on the south slope of Mt. Aracynthus.

Πλυντήρια, ων, τά, (lit. *pertaining to washing*), *Plynteria*, a festival at Athens in which the clothing of the statue of Athena Polias was washed.

Ποδαλείριος, ου, ὁ, *Podalirius*, a Thessalian chief, son of Æsculapius, and a physician of the Greeks before Troy.

Ποδάρκης, ους, ὁ, *Podarces*, a leader of the Thessalians of Phylace before Troy.

Πολίτης, ου, ὁ, *Polites*, a son of Priam.

Πολυάρχης, ου, ὁ, *Polyarches*, one of the thirty tyrants at Athens.

Πολύας, ου, ὁ, *Polyas*, a Greek scout at Artemisium.

Πόλυβος, ου, ὁ, *Polybus*, an Ithacan.

Πολύδωρος, ου, ὁ, *Polydorus*, a king of Sparta.

Πολύειδος, and **Πολυΐδος**, ου, ὁ, *Polyidus*, a Trojan.

Πολυκράτης, ους, ὁ, *Polycrates*, an Athenian captain in the army of the ten thousand.

Πολύκριτος, ου, ὁ, *Polycritus*, of Ægina, a brave ship-captain.

Πολυνείκης, ους, ὁ, *Polynices*, a son of Œdipus king of Thebes.

Πολύνικος, ου, ὁ, *Polynicus*, a Lacedæmonian.

Πολύξεινος (Ion. for **-ξεν-**), ου, ὁ, *Polyxenus*, leader of the Epeï before Troy.

Πολυποίτης, ου, ὁ, *Polypœtes*, one of the Thessalian leaders against Troy.

Πολύστρατος, ου, ὁ, *Polystratus*, an Athenian.

Πολύφημος, ου, ὁ, *Polyphemus:* (1) one of the Lapithæ, of Larissa in Thessaly, an Argonaut; (2) a Cyclops, son of Neptune, dwelling in Sicily.

Πολυφόντης, ου, ὁ, *Polyphontes*, a Theban chief.

Πολυχάρης, ους, ὁ, *Polychares*, one of the thirty tyrants at Athens.

Ποντικός, ή, όν, (lit. *belonging to the sea*), *belonging to the Pontus Euxinus.*

Πόντος, ου, ὁ, (lit. *the sea*), *the Pontus Euxinus*, or *Black Sea.*

Ποταμίς, ίδος, ὁ, *Potamis*, a commander of the Syracusans.

Πράκτιος, ου, ὁ, *Practius*, a small river of Troas flowing into the Hellespont, north of Abydus.

Πριαμίδης, ου, ὁ, *son of Priam.*

Προθοήνωρ, ορος, ὁ, *Prothoenor*, a leader of the Bœotians before Troy.

Πρόθοος, ου, ὁ, *Prothoüs*, leader of the Magnesians before Troy.

Προῖτος, ου, ὁ, *Prœtus*, king of Tiryns in Argolis.

Προκλέης, cont. **Προκλῆς**, έους, ὁ, *Procles*, a Spartan, ruler of Teuthrania in Mysia.

Προκόννησος, ου, ἡ, *Proconnesus*, an island in the Propontis celebrated for its marble.

Προμηθεύς, έως, ὁ, *Prometheus*, a popular leader in Thessaly.

Πρόξενος, ου, ὁ, *Proxenus:* (1) a Bœotian, one of the generals in the expedition of Cyrus the younger ; (2) a Syracusan.

Πρύτανις, ιος and ιδος, ὁ, *Prytanis*, a Lycian.

Πρωτεσίλᾱος, ου, ὁ, *Protesilaus*, a Thessalian chief, the first of the Greeks slain at Troy.

Πρώτη, ης, ἡ, *Prote*, a small island near the coast of Messenia.

Πρωτόμαχος, ου, ὁ, *Protomachus*, an Athenian commander.

Πτελεόν, οῦ, τό, *Pteleum :* (1) a city on the coast of Phthiotis in Thessaly ; (2) a place in Triphylia in Elis.

Πτολεμαῖος, ου, ὁ, *Ptolemæus*, father of Eurymedon the charioteer of Agamemnon.

Πύγελα, ων, τά, *Pygela*, a small town of Ionia.

Πυγελεύς, έως, ὁ, *an inhabitant of Pygela.*

Πῡθαγόρας, ου, ὁ, *Pythagoras*, a Lacedæmonian with a naval command under Cyrus the younger.

Πυθέας, ου, ὁ, *Pytheas*, of Ægina, a brave ship-captain.

Πυθόδωρος, ου, ὁ, *Pythodorus*, an Athenian archon.

Πυλαιμένης, ους, ὁ, *Pylæmenes*, a king of the Paphlagonians, allied with Troy.

Πύλαιος, ου, ὁ, *Pylæus*, from Larissa in Æolis, a leader of the Pelasgians in alliance with Troy.

Πυλήνη, ης, ἡ, *Pylene*, a town of southwestern Ætolia.

Πύλιοι, ων, οἱ, *the Pylians*, inhabitants of Pylos.

Πυραίχμης, ου, ὁ, *Pyræchmes*, a leader of the Pæonians in alliance with Troy.

Πύραμος, ου, ὁ, *Pyramus*, one of the largest rivers of Asia Minor, flowing through Cilicia, and emptying into the Mediterranean.

Πύρασος, and **Πύρρ-**, ου, ὁ, *Pyrasus*, a city on the coast of Phthiotis in Thessaly.

Πυρρίας, ου, ὁ, *Pyrrhias*, an Arcadian captain.

Πυρρόλοχος, ου, ὁ, *Pyrrholochus*, an Argive.

Πώγων, ωνος, ὁ, *Pogon*, the harbor of Trœzen in Argolis.

Πῶλος, ου, ὁ, *Polus*, a Lacedæmonian naval commander.

Ρ

Ῥαδάμανθυς, υος, ὁ, *Rhadamanthys*, son of Zeus, and brother of Minos king of Crete, said to have been, on account of his justice, one of the judges in the lower world.

Ῥαθίνης, ου, ὁ, *Rhathines*, a Persian, general under Pharnabazus.

Ῥαμφίας, ου, ὁ, *Rhamphias*, a Lacedæmonian, father of Clearchus.

Ῥεῖθρον, ου, τό, *Rhithrum*, a harbor on the east coast of Ithaca.

Ῥήνη, ης, ἡ, *Rhene*, a nymph, wife of Oïleus.

Ῥίπη, ης, ἡ, *Rhipe*, a city in Arcadia, near Stratia.

Ῥόδιος, ου, ὁ, *an inhabitant of Rhodes.*

Ῥόδος, ου, ἡ, *Rhodes*, an island off the south coast of Caria.

Ῥοίτειον, ου, τό, *Rhœteum*, a city and promontory of Mysia on the Hellespont.

Ῥύτιον, ου, τό, *Rhytium*, a city of Crete.

Ῥωπάρας, ου, ὁ, *Rhoparas*, a Persian satrap in Babylon.

Σ

Σαγγάριος, ου, ὁ, *Sangarius*, one of the largest rivers of Asia Minor, flowing through Bithynia into the Euxine.

Σάκαι, ῶν, οἱ, *the Sacæ*, a Scythian nomadic race inhabiting the steppes of central Asia, east of Sogdiana ; sometimes used as equivalent to Scythians.

Σαλαμίς, ῖνος, ἡ, *Salamis*, an island and town of the same name, over against Athens.

Σαλμυδησσός οῦ, ὁ, *Salmydessus*, a city of Thrace, on the Euxine.

Σάμιος, α, ον, *Samian, belonging to Samos ;* **Σάμιος**, ου, ὁ, *an inhabitant of Samos.*

Σαμόλας, ου, ὁ, *Samolas*, an Achaian in the army of the ten thousand.

Σάμος, ου, ἡ, *Samos*, a large island over against Ephesus.

Σάνη, ης, ἡ, *Sane*, a city on the peninsula Athos, a colony of Andros.

Σάρδεις, έων, αἱ, *Sardis*, the capital of Lydia.

Σάρος, see **Ψάρος**.

Σατνιόεις, εντος, ὁ, *Satnioïs*, a small river of southern Troas, flowing into the Ægean sea, north of the promontory Lectum.

Σάτυρος, ου, ὁ, *Satyrus*, chief of the eleven sheriffs at Athens.

Σέλαγος, ου, ὁ, *Selagus*, of Pæsus, father of Amphius.

Σεληπιάδης, ου, ὁ, *son of Selepius*, i. e. Euenus.

Σελῖνοῦς, οῦντος, ὁ and ἡ, *Selinus:* (1) a river of Triphylia in Elis; (2) a river flowing by Ephesus; (3) a coast city of Sicily, on a river of the same name, a colony of the Megarians.

Σελῖνούσιος, α, ον, *of Selinus.*

Σελλασία, ας, ἡ, *Sellasia*, a city of Laconia, north of Sparta.

Σελλήεις, εντος, ὁ, *Selleïs:* (1) a river of Elis, south of the Peneus; (2) a river of Troas, near Arisbe.

Σεύθης, ου, ὁ, *Seuthes*, the name of several kings of the Odrysæ in Thrace.

Σηλυμβρία, also **Σηλυβρία,** ας, ἡ, *Selymbria*, a Thracian city on the Propontis, east of Perinthus.

Σηλυμβριανός, οῦ, ὁ, *an inhabitant of Selymbria.*

Σηπιάς, άδος, ἡ, *Sepias*, a promontory at the southeastern point of Magnesia in Thessaly.

Σήσαμος, ου, ὁ, *Sesamus:* (1) a small river in the western part of Paphlagonia, flowing into the Euxine; (2) a coast city on this river.

Σηστός, οῦ, ἡ and ὁ, *Sestus*, a town on the European side of the Hellespont, over against Abydus.

Σθενέλᾱος, ου, ὁ, *Sthenelaüs*, a Lacedæmonian.

Σθένελος, ου, ὁ, *Sthenelus*, of Argos, a commander of the Argives under Diomedes before Troy.

Σικελία, ας, ἡ, *Sicily*, the well known island.

Σικελιώτης, ου, ὁ, *a Sicilian Greek.*

Σίκιννος, ου, ὁ, *Sicinnus*, a slave of Themistocles.

Σῑλᾱνός, οῦ, ὁ, *Silanus:* (1) an Ambraciot soothsayer in the army of the ten thousand; (2) a soldier in the same army from Macistus in Elis.

Σιμμίας, ου, ὁ, *Simmias*, of Thebes, a disciple and friend of Socrates.

Σιμοείσιος, ου, ὁ, *Simoïsius*, a Trojan.

Σιμωνίδης, ου, ὁ, *Simonides*, a celebrated lyric poet, of Ceos.

Σινωπεύς, έως, ὁ, *a Sinopean*, an inhabitant of Sinope, in eastern Paphlagonia, an important coast city, a Greek colony.

Σίρις, ιος, ἡ, *Siris*, a city of Pæonia in Thrace, east of the Strymon.

Σιτάλκας, ου, ὁ, *Sitalcas*, the name of several Thracian kings.

Σιττάκη, ης, ἡ, *Sittace*, a city of Babylonia, near the west bank of the Tigris, a little south of the Median wall.

Σκαμάνδριος, ου, ὁ, *Scamandrius:* (1) a Trojan; (2) the son of Hector.

Σκάρφη, ης, ἡ, *Scarphe*, a small town of the Epicnemidii Locri near Thermopylæ.

Σκίαθος, ου, ἡ, *Sciathus*, a small island near the coast of southern Magnesia in Thessaly.

Σκιλλοῦς, οῦντος, ἡ, *Scillus*, a town of Triphylia in Elis, where Xenophon lived during his banishment.

Σκιρωνίς, ίδος, fem. adj., *Scironian*, *of Sciron* a noted robber; **ἡ Σκιρωνὶς ὁδός,** *the Scironian road*, a narrow and dangerous pass on the coast of Megaris, near Megara.

Σκιωναῖος, α, ον, *Scionean*, *of Scione* the chief city on the peninsula Pallene in Macedonia; **Σκιωναῖος,** ου, ὁ, *an inhabitant of Scione.*

Σκυθῑνοί, ῶν, οἱ, *the Scythini*, a people on the west border of Armenia.

Σκυλλίας, ου, ὁ, *Scyllias*, a diver of Scione.

Σκύριος, α, ον, *Scyrian*, *of Scyros* an island, one of the Sporades.

Σκῶλος, ου, ὁ, *Scolus*, a town in Bœotia, near Thebes.

Σμίκρης, ητος, ὁ, *Smicres*, an Arcadian commander.

Σόλοι, ων, οἱ, *Soli*, an important city on the coast of Cilicia.

Σόλυμοι, ων, οἱ, *the Solymi*, ancient inhabitants of Lycia.

Σοφαίνετος, ου, ὁ, *Sophænetus*, an Arcadian, one of the Greek generals of Cyrus the younger.

Σοφοκλῆς, έους, ὁ, *Sophocles*, one of the thirty tyrants at Athens.

Σπάρτη, ης, ἡ, *Sparta*, see **Λακεδαίμων.**

Σπιθριδάτης, ου, ὁ, *Spithridates*, a Persian, general under Pharnabazus.

Στάγης, ὁ, *Stages*, a Persian.

Στησαγόρας, ου, ὁ, *Stesagoras*, an Athenian, grandfather of Miltiades.

Στησίλαος, ου, ὁ, Ion. **Στησίλεως,** *Stesilaus*, son of Thrasylus, a commander of the Athenians at Marathon.

Στρατίη (Ion. for **Στρατία**), ης, ἡ, *Stratia*, an ancient city of Arcadia.

Στρατοκλῆς, έους, ὁ, *Stratocles*, commander of the corps of slingers in the army of the ten thousand.

Στρόφιος, ου, ὁ, *Strophius*, a Trojan.

Στυμφάλιος, α, ον, *of Stymphalus.*

Στύμφᾱλος, Ion. **-φηλος,** ου, ὁ and ἡ, *Stymphalus*, the name of a city, district, mountain, and river in the northeast of Arcadia.

Στύρα, ων, τά, *Styra*, a city on the southwest coast of Eubœa, northwest of Carystus.

Στυρεύς, έως, ὁ, *a Styrian*, inhabiting Styra.

Στύφων, ωνος, ὁ, *Styphon*, a Spartan commander.

Συέννεσις, εως and ιος, ὁ, *Syennesis,* the name of several kings of Cilicia.

Σύμηθεν, *from Syme,* a small island between Rhodes and the coast of Caria.

Συρᾱκόσιος, ου, ὁ, *an inhabitant of Syracuse.*

Συρᾱ́κουσαι, ῶν, αἱ, *Syracuse,* the chief city of Sicily.

Σφακτηρία, ας, ἡ, *Sphacteria,* a long narrow island on the west coast of Messenia, near Pylus.

Σχεδίος, ου, ὁ, *Schedius,* a chief of the Phocians before Troy.

Σχοῖνος, ου, ἡ, *Schœnus,* a city in Bœotia, near Thebes.

Σωκράτης, εος contr. ους, ὁ, *Socrates,* son of Sophroniscus, the famous Athenian philosopher.

Σωσίας, ου, ὁ, *Sosias,* of Syracuse, an officer in the Greek army of Cyrus the younger.

Σωσιμένης, ους, ὁ, *Sosimenes,* a Tenian.

Σωστρατίδας, ου and α, ὁ, *Sostratidas,* a Spartan ephor.

Σωτηρίδης (and **-ας**), ου, ὁ, *Soteridas,* of Sicyon, a soldier in the army of the ten thousand.

Σωφρονίσκος, ου, ὁ, *Sophroniscus,* an Athenian, father of Socrates.

T

Ταλαιμένης, ους, ὁ, *Talæmenes,* a Mæonian prince.

Ταλαϊονίδης, ου, ὁ, an irregular patronymic for **Ταλαΐδης,** *son of Talaus,* i. e. Mecisteus.

Ταλθύβιος, ου, ὁ, *Talthybius,* the herald of Agamemnon.

Ταμώς, ώ, ὁ, *Tamos,* of Memphis in Egypt, lieutenant-governor of Ionia, and subsequently commander of the fleet of Cyrus the younger.

Τάοχοι, ων, οἱ, *the Taochi,* a people on the borders of Pontus and Armenia.

Τάρνη, ης, ἡ, *Tarne,* a city of Lydia, on Mt. Tmolus.

Ταρσός, οῦ, ἡ, sometimes **Ταρσοί,** ῶν, αἱ, *Tarsus,* the capital and chief city of Cilicia, on the Cydnus, a commercial and educational centre, the birthplace of the apostle Paul.

Τάρφη, ης, ἡ, *Tarphe,* an ancient city in the west of Locris, near Thermopylæ.

Τάφιοι, ων, οἱ, *the Taphians,* a race of pirates inhabiting the Taphian islands, west of Acarnania.

Τελαμών, ῶνος, ὁ, *Telamon,* son of Æacus, father of Ajax, and king of Salamis.

Τελαμώνιος, α, ον, *Telamonian.*

Τεμενίτης, in Xen. Anab. 4, 4, 15, probably for **Τημενίτης,** which see.

Τεμέση, ης, ἡ, *Temese,* a town in Cyprus, whither the Taphians went for copper.

Τένεδος, ου, ἡ, *Tenedus,* an island near the coast of Troas.

Τενθρηδών, όνος, ὁ, *Tenthredon,* leader of the Magnesians from Thessaly before Troy.

Τερψίων, ωνος, ὁ, *Terpsion,* of Megara, a pupil of Socrates.

Τευθρανία, ας, ἡ, *Teuthrania,* a district of the south of Mysia, on the coast, with a city of the same name.

Τευθρανίδης, ου, ὁ, *son of Teuthras,* i. e. Axylus.

Τεύθρᾱς, αντος, ὁ, *Teuthras,* a Greek from Magnesia in Thessaly, slain before Troy.

Τευταμίδης, ου, ὁ, *son of Teutamus,* i. e. Lethus.

Τηλεβόας, ου, ὁ, *Teleboas,* a river of Armenia, tributary to the Euphrates.

Τήλεκλος, ου, ὁ, *Teleclus,* son of Archelaus, a king of Sparta.

Τημενίτης, ου, ὁ, *a Temenite,* an inhabitant of Temenium, in Argolis, at the upper end of the Argolic Gulf.

Τήνιος, α, ον, *of Tenus,* an island, one of the Cyclades, near Andrus ; **οἱ Τήνιοι,** *the Tenians.*

Τήρεια, ας, ἡ, *Terea,* a high mountain in Mysia near Zelea.

Τήρης, ους and έω, ὁ, *Teres,* king of the Odrysæ in Thrace, founder of the Odrysian monarchy.

Τιβαρηνοί, ῶν, οἱ, *the Tibareni,* a people on the coast of Pontus, east of the Iris.

Τίγρης, ητος, and **Τίγρις,** ιδος, ὁ, *Tigris,* a famous river rising in Armenia, and, after uniting with the Euphrates, flowing into the Persian Gulf.

Τιθορέα, ας, ἡ, *Tithorea :* (1) the northwestern summit of Mt. Parnassus ; (2) a fortress on the slope of this mountain.

Τῑμᾱσίων, ωνος, ὁ, *Timasion,* a Dardanian, one of the generals who directed the retreat of the ten thousand.

Τῑμησίθεος, ου, ὁ, *Timesitheus,* an inhabitant of Trapezus.

Τῑμόδημος, ου, ὁ, *Timodemus,* of Athens, an opponent of Themistocles.

Τῑμοκράτης, ους, ὁ, *Timocrates,* an Athenian.

Τίμων, ωνος, ὁ, *Timon,* an inhabitant of Delphi.

Τιρίβαζος, ου, ὁ, *Tiribazus,* a Persian satrap.

Τίρυνς, υνθος, ἡ, *Tiryns,* a very ancient city in Argolis, near the head of the Argolic Gulf, now celebrated for its massive ruins.

Τισσαφέρνης, ους, ὁ, *Tissaphernes,* a distinguished Persian, satrap of Lydia.

Τίτανος, *ου, ὁ, Titanus,* a mountain in central Thessaly.

Τιταρήσιος, *ου, ὁ, Titaresius,* a river of northern Thessaly, flowing into the Peneus.

Τληπόλεμος, *ου, ὁ, Tlepolemus,* a son of Hercules, a leader of the Rhodians before Troy.

Τμῶλος, *ου, ὁ, Tmolus,* a mountain range of Lydia, south of Sardis.

Τολμίδης, *ου, ὁ, Tolmides,* a herald of Cyrus the younger.

Τορωναῖος, *η, ον, of Torone;* **Τορωναῖος,** *ου, ὁ, an inhabitant of Torone.*

Τορώνη, *ης, ἡ, Torone,* a city in the peninsula of Sithonia, in Macedonia.

Τράλλεις, *εων, αἱ, Tralles,* a wealthy city in Caria, near Mt. Messogis.

Τράνιψαι, *ῶν, οἱ, the Tranipsæ,* a Thracian people near Byzantium.

Τραπεζούντιος, *α, ον, of Trapezus;* **οἱ Τραπεζούντιοι,** *the Trapezuntians.*

Τραπεζοῦς, *οῦντος, ὁ* and *ἡ, Trapezus,* an important city on the eastern part of the coast of Pontus.

Τρᾱχίνιος, *α, ον, Trachinian, belonging to Trachis,* see **Ἡράκλεια.**

Τρῆχος, *ου, ὁ, Trechus,* a Greek slain at Troy.

Τρίκκη, *ης, ἡ, Tricca,* an ancient city in western Thessaly.

Τροιζήν, *ῆνος, ἡ, Trœzen,* an ancient city in the southeast of Argolis, near the Saronic Gulf.

Τροιζήνιος, *α, ον, Trœzenian.*

Τῡδείδης, *ου, ὁ, son of Tydeus,* i. e. Diomedes.

Τῡδεύς, *έως, ὁ, Tydeus,* an Athenian general.

Τυριαῖον, *ου, τό, Tyriæum,* a city of western Lycaonia, near Phrygia.

Τυρώ, *οῦς, ἡ, Tyro,* daughter of Salmoneus, and wife of Cretheus.

Υ

Ὑάμπεια, *ας, ἡ, Hyampea,* a lofty cliff near Delphi.

Ὑάμπολις, *εως, ἡ, Hyampolis,* a city in the north of Phocis, near Cleonæ.

Ὑδάρνης, *ους, ὁ, Hydarnes,* a Persian, the commander of the division of the army of Xerxes I. called "the immortals."

Ὕλη, *ης, ἡ, Hyle,* a small town of Bœotia, on lake Hylice.

Ὕλλος, *ου, ὁ, Hyllus,* a son of Hercules, from whom the Spartan kings traced their descent.

Ὑπείρων, *ονος, ὁ, Hypiron,* a Trojan chief.

Ὑπεράνθης, *ους, ὁ, Hyperanthes,* a son of Darius I.

Ὑπέρεια, *ας, ἡ, Hyperea,* a fountain in Thessaly.

Ὑπερησίη, *ης, ἡ, Hypercsia,* a city in the east of Achaia, near the coast, the later Ægira.

Ὑποθῆβαι, *ῶν, αἱ, Hypothebæ,* a city of Bœotia, probably the later Potniæ, south of Thebes.

Ὑρία, *ας, ἡ, Hyria,* a small city of Bœotia, near Aulis.

Ὑρκάνιος, *α, ον, of Hyrcania,* a country bordering the Caspian Sea on the southeast; **οἱ Ὑρκανιοι,** *the Hyrcanians.*

Ὑρμίνη, *ης, ἡ, Hyrmine,* a city off the coast of Elis, near the promontory Hyrmina.

Ὑρτακίδης, *ου, ὁ, son of Hyrtacus,* i. e. Asius.

Ὑσιαί, *ῶν, αἱ, Hysiæ,* a town of Bœotia, near the northern base of Mt. Cithæron.

Ὑστάσπης, *εος* and *ου, ὁ, Hystaspes,* father of Darius I.

Ὑψήνωρ, *ορος, ὁ, Hypsenor,* a Trojan.

Φ

Φαιδρίας, *ου, ὁ, Phædrias,* one of the thirty tyrants at Athens.

Φαίδων, *ωνος, ὁ, Phædon,* of Elis, a disciple of Socrates, the founder of a school of philosophy.

Φαιδωνίδης and **Φαιδώνδας,** *ου, ὁ, Phædonides* or *Phædondas,* a pupil and friend of Socrates.

Φαῖνοψ, *οπος, ὁ, Phænops,* son of Asius of Abydus, a friend of Hector.

Φαιστος, *ου, ἡ, Phæstus,* a city of Crete, near Gortyna.

Φαῖστος, *ου, ὁ, Phæstus,* of Tarne, an ally of the Trojans.

Φαλῖνος, *ου, ὁ, Phalinus,* a Greek of Zacynthus in the service of Tissaphernes.

Φαναγόρας, *ου, ὁ, Phanagoras,* of Carystus.

Φανοσθένης, *ους, ὁ, Phanosthenes,* a general of the Athenians from Andrus.

Φάραξ, *ακος, ὁ, Pharax,* a Spartan commander.

Φᾶρις, *ιος, ἡ, Pharis,* an old city in Laconia, south of Sparta.

Φαρνάβαζος, *ου, ὁ, Pharnabazus,* a Persian satrap of Lesser Phrygia and Bithynia.

Φασιᾱνοί, *ῶν, οἱ, the Phasiani,* a people of western Armenia, around the Phasis.

Φειδιππίδης, *ου, ὁ, Phidippides,* an Athenian courier.

Φείδιππος, ου, ὁ, *Phidippus*, a grandson of Hercules, a leader in the Trojan war of Greeks from the Sporades islands.

Φείδων, ωνος, ὁ, *Phidon*, one of the thirty tyrants at Athens.

Φένεος, ου, ὁ and ἡ, *Pheneüs*, a town in northern Arcadia, at the foot of Mt. Cyllene.

Φεραί, ῶν, αἱ, *Pheræ*, an important city of Pelasgiotis in Thessaly, near Pagasæ.

Φεραῖος, ου, ὁ, *an inhabitant of Pheræ*.

Φέρεκλος, ου, ὁ, *Phereclus*, builder of the ship in which Paris carried off Helen.

Φηγεύς, έως, ὁ, *Phegeus*, a Trojan warrior.

Φήμιος, ου, ὁ, *Phemius*, a famous minstrel in Ithaca.

Φηρή, ῆς, ἡ, also **Φηραί**, **Φαραί**, and **Φεραί**, *Phere*, a city of Messenia, near Laconia, on the Messenian Gulf.

Φηρητιάδης (for **Φερητιάδης**), ου, ὁ, *son* or *descendant of Pheres*.

Φθειρῶν Ὄρος, τό, *Mountain of Pines*, a mountain in Caria, near Miletus.

Φθῖῶται, and **-ῖῆ-**, ῶν, οἱ, *the* (Achaian) *inhabitants of Phthiotis*, a district in south Thessaly, bordering on the Pagasean Gulf; used with **Ἀχαιοί**, *the Achaians of Phthiotis*, so called in distinction from the Achaians of the Peloponnesus.

Φιλάων, ωνος, or **Φιλέων**, ωνος, ὁ, *Philaon* or *Phileon*, brother of king Gorgus of Salamis in Cyprus.

Φιλήσιος, ου, ὁ, *Philesius*, an Achaian, a general in the army of the ten thousand.

Φιλοκλῆς, έους, ὁ, *Philocles*, an Athenian naval commander at Ægospotami.

Φιλοκτήτης, ου, ὁ, *Philoctetes*, a Thessalian chief, a friend of Hercules, and a renowned archer.

Φιλοκύδης, εος, ὁ, *Philocydes*, an Athenian.

Φιλόλᾱος, ου, ὁ, *Philolaus*, a native of Italy, a distinguished Pythagorean philosopher.

Φλῑάσιος, α, ον, *of Phlius, Phliasian.*

Φλῑοῦς, οῦντος, ὁ, *Phlius*, an independent city, whose territory lay between Sicyonia and Argolis.

Φοῖνιξ, ῑκος, ὁ, *Phœnix*, a small river of Thessaly flowing into the Asopus near Thermopylæ.

Φρασίας, ου, ὁ, *Phrasias*, an Athenian.

Φραταγούνη, ης, ἡ, *Phratagune*, wife of Darius I.

Φρόνιος, ου, ὁ, *Phronius*, an Ithacan, father of Noemon.

Φρυγία, ας, ἡ, *Phrygia*, a country in Asia Minor of varying extent. In general Phrygia Major, usually called Phrygia, occupied the western part of the great central table-land of Asia Minor. Phrygia Minor included the region about Troas.

Φρῡνίσκος, ου, ὁ, *Phryniscus*, an Achaian with a command in the army of the ten thousand.

Φυλάκη, ης, ἡ, *Phylace*, a city of Phthiotis in Thessaly, on the north slope of Mt. Othrys.

Φυλακίδης, ου, ὁ, *son of Phylacus*, i. e. Iphiclus.

Φύλακος, ου, ὁ, *Phylacus:* (1) the supposed founder of Phylace in Thessaly; (2) a Trojan warrior; (3) a Delphian hero.

Φυλείδης, ου, ὁ, *son of Phyleus*, i. e. Meges.

Φυλεύς, έως, ὁ, *Phyleus*, son of Augeas a king of Elis.

Φῡλή, ῆς, ἡ, *Phyle*, a strong fortress in Attica, near Bœotia, on the southwest slope of Mt. Parnes; also the name of the surrounding deme.

Φύσκος, ου, ὁ, *Physcus*, an eastern tributary of the Tigris in lower Assyria.

Φώκαια, ας, ἡ, *Phocæa*, the most northern city of Ionia.

X

Χαιρέλεως, ω, ὁ, *Chærelaus*, one of the thirty tyrants at Athens.

Χαιρίλας, ου, ὁ, *Chærilas*, a Spartan ephor.

Χαίρων, ωνος, ὁ, *Chæron*, an Athenian polemarch.

Χαλκιδεύς, έως, ὁ, *a Chalcidian*, an inhabitant of Chalcis in Eubœa.

Χαλκίς, ίδος, ἡ. *Chalcis:* (1) the chief city of Eubœa, separated from Bœotia by the strait of Euripus; (2) a city on the coast of Ætolia, near the mouth of the Evenus.

Χαλκωδοντιάδης, ου, ὁ, *son of Chalcodon*, i. e. Elephenor.

Χάλος, ου, ὁ, *Chalus*, a river of northern Syria, near Chalcis.

Χαρικλῆς, έους, ὁ, *Charicles*, one of the thirty tyrants at Athens.

Χαρμάνδη, ης, ἡ, *Charmande*, a large city of Mesopotamia, on the Euphrates.

Χαρμίδης, ου, ὁ, *Charmides*, an Athenian, an uncle of Plato.

Χαρμῖνος, ου, ὁ, *Charminus*, a Spartan officer under Thibron.

Χάροπος, ου, ὁ, *Charopus*, king of the island of Syme.

Χειρίσοφος, ου, ὁ, *Chirisophus*, a Spartan, successor to Clearchus in command of the army of the ten thousand.

Χερρονησίτης, ου, ὁ, *a dweller in the Chersonese.*

Χερρόνησος, ου, ἡ, *Chersonese.* The word means *land-island*, i. e. *peninsula*, and has various applications. Without special limitation it commonly designated the long strip of Thrace that runs along the Hellespont.

Χέρσις, ιος, ὁ, *Chersis*, of Salamis in Cyprus.

Χῖοι, ων, οἱ, *the Chians, inhabitants of Chios.*

Χίος, ου, ἡ, *Chios*, an island in the Ægean on the coast of Asia Minor, now Scio. Also a city, the capital of the island.

Χρέμων, ωνος, ὁ, *Chremon*, one of the thirty tyrants at Athens.

Χρομίος, ου, ὁ, *Chromius:* (1) a son of Priam; (2) a son of Neleus; (3) a Lycian warrior.

Χρόμις, ιος, ὁ, *Chromis*, a leader of the Mysians in alliance with Troy.

Χρῦσα, poet. **-ση**, ης, ἡ, *Chrysa*, a city on the coast of Troas, near Hamaxitus.

Χρυσηΐς, ΐδος, ἡ, *daughter of Chryses*, i. e. Astynome.

Χρύσης, ου, ὁ, *Chryses*, priest of Apollo at Chrysa, father of Astynome.

Χρυσόπολις, εως, ἡ, *Chrysopolis*, a city of Bithynia on the Bosporus, opposite Byzantium, modern Scutari.

Ψ

Ψάρος, more commonly **Σάρος**, ου, ὁ, *Psarus* or *Sarus*, a large river of Cilicia, flowing not far from Tarsus.

Ψυττάλεια, ας, ἡ, *Psyttalea*, a small island between Salamis and the mainland of Attica.

Ω

Ὠιδεῖον, ου, τό, *the Odeüm*, a public building at Athens built by Pericles, used as a law-court.

Ὠκαλέα, ας, ἡ, *Ocalea*, an ancient town of Bœotia just south of lake Copaïs.

Ὤκυτος, ου, ὁ, *Ocytus*, a Corinthian.

Ὠλενία, ας, ἡ, poet. **-ίη**, with **πέτρα**, *the Olenian rock*, probably the summit of Mt. Scollis, between Elis and Achaia.

Ὤλενος, ου. ἡ and ὁ, *Olenus*, an ancient town in southern Ætolia at the foot of Mt. Aracynthus.

Ὦπις, ιδος, ἡ, *Opis*, an important commercial city of Assyria, at the junction of the Physcus and the Tigris.

Ὠρείθυια, ας, ἡ, *Orithyia*, a daughter of Erechtheus king of Athens, carried off by Boreas.

Ὦψ, Ὠπός, ὁ, *Ops*, father of Euryclia the nurse of Ulysses.

Handy Literal Translations. Cloth, *pocket*. **50 cents** per vol.
Eighty-eight volumes, viz.: (*See also "Tutorial Translations."*)

Cæsar's Gallic War. *The Seven Books.*
Cæsar's *Civil* War.
Catullus.
Cicero's Brutus.
Cicero's Defence of Roscius.
Cicero De Officiis.
Cicero On Old Age and Friendship.
Cicero On Oratory.
Cicero On The Nature of the Gods.
Cicero's Orations. *Four vs. Catiline; and others. Enlarged edition.*
Cicero's Select Letters.
Cicero's Tusculan Disputations.
Cornelius Nepos, *complete.*
Eutropius.
Horace, *complete.*
Juvenal's Satires, *complete.*
Livy, Books I and II.
Livy, Books XXI and XXII.
Lucretius, *in preparation.*
Martial's Epigrams (*paper*).
Ovid's Metamorphoses, *complete in 2 volumes.*
Phædrus' Fables.
Plautus' Captivi, and Mostellaria.
Plautus' Pseudolus, and Miles Gloriosus.
Plautus' Trinummus, and Menæchmi.
Pliny's Select Letters, *complete in 2 volumes.*
Quintilian, Books X and XII.
Roman Life in Latin Prose and Verse.
Sallust's Catiline, and The Jugurthine War.
Seneca On Benefits.
Tacitus' Annals. *The 1st Six Books.*
Tacitus' Germany and Agricola.
Tacitus On Oratory.
Terence: Andria, Adelphi, and Phormio
Terence: Heautontimorumenos.
Virgil's Æneid, *the 1st Six Books.*
Virgil's Eclogues and Georgics.
Viri Romæ.

Æschines Against Ctesiphon.
Æschylus' Prometheus Bound; Seven Against Thebes.
Æschylus' Agamemnon.
Aristophanes' Clouds.
Aristophanes' Birds, and Frogs.
Demosthenes On The Crown.
Demosthenes' Olynthiacs and Philippics.
Euripides' Alcestis, and Electra.
Euripides' Bacchantes, and Hercules Furens.
Euripides' Hecuba, and Andromache.
Euripides' Iphigenia In Aulis, In Tauris.
Euripides' Medea.
Herodotus, Books VI and VII.
Herodotus, Book VIII.
Homer's Iliad, *the 1st Six Books.*
Homer's Odyssey, *the 1st Twelve Books.*
Isocrates' Panegyric, *in preparation*
Lucian's Select Dialogues, *2 volumes.*
Lysias' Orations. *The only Translation extant*

Handy Literal Translations, continued next page.

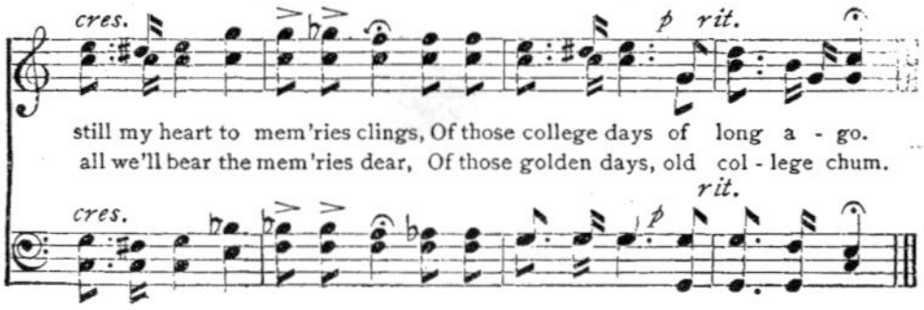